The Chancellor ILLUSTRATED FAMILY ENCYCLOPEDIC DICTIONARY A-K

CHANCELLOR PRESS

Originally published in 1986 in ten volumes by
The Leisure Circle Ltd
by arrangement with Oxford University Press
under the title The Mini Oxford Encyclopedic Dictionary

This edition published in Great Britain in 1989 by
Chancellor Press
Michelin House
81 Fulham Road
London SW3 6RB

Line drawings by M.G. Croft
ISBN 1 85152 094 5 (A-K)

Printed in Czechoslovakia

50331

PREFACE

ACCORDING to the distinction used by H. W. Fowler in the preface to the *Concise Oxford Dictionary*, a dictionary normally takes the uses of words and phrases as such for its subject-matter and is concerned with giving information about the things for which these words and phrases stand only so far as correct use of the words depends upon knowledge of the things. In an encyclopaedia, on the other hand, the emphasis will be much more on the nature of the things for which the words and phrases stand.

This book attempts to combine in a form that can be handled conveniently the essential features of dictionary and encyclopaedia. Where things are more easily explained by pictures or diagrams than by words, illustration has been used to help out definition.

VOCABULARY

The general reader for whom the book is intended may not always have another dictionary or encyclopaedia at his ready disposal and so the vocabulary has been chosen with an eye to the needs of one who may require either type of information. Information about words, however, is more often sought by the average user of a reference book than information about things and the vocabulary has therefore been based on that of the *Concise Oxford Dictionary* and the definitions retain its historical ordering. Familiar words are less fully treated, however, and the phrases illustrating such words have been more sparingly used so as to obtain a wider scope for the treatment of things.

The vocabulary should thus be adequate for the reader who consults the book for ordinary dictionary purposes. But it also contains terms in everyday use which would be excluded from an ordinary dictionary because of their technical and scientific character or which would be very briefly dealt with; familiar words in semi-technical use (e.g. *vertical trust*, *combine*, etc.); the names of famous people (e.g. statesmen, explorers, inventors, artists, and writers), historical, contemporary, or fictitious; and the names of important places and events.

Special pains have been taken to ensure that scientific and technical terms are accurate in definition and at the same time intelligible to the user, but the present pace of development in science and technology is so swift that no reference book which deals with them in even the most general way can ever be completely up to date: between the time the book is compiled and its publication new words and senses will have acquired fresh shades of meaning or become obsolescent.

In order to keep the book within reasonable compass obsolete words and phrases have been omitted except for a few which some special interest has made it desirable to retain.

ABBREVIATIONS

Abbreviations in current use appear in their alphabetical place in the body of the text to save a separate alphabet. But there is a separate list of those abbreviations used in the dictionary itself.

ETYMOLOGY

For the sake of space derivations have been omitted with a few exceptions. These occur where the etymology is especially interesting or unexpected (e.g. *penicillin*, *derrick*), or when a thing has been named after its inventor or place of origin (e.g. *Fortin barometer*, *Borstal*). In these cases the etymology is given in square brackets at the end of the entry.

CROSS-REFERENCES

Where a word is given in small capitals in a definition, this indicates that reference to the word in its alphabetical place will provide further information (e.g. INSULIN in the entry for *pancreas*) or discuss the term which is given in comparison or contradistinction (e.g. NOBLE OR PRECIOUS metals as opposed to *base* metals).

PRONUNCIATION

The pronunciation indicated represents the standard speech of southern England.

1. **Accent.** The accentuation mark ′ is placed after the vowel or vowel sound in the stressed syllable.

2. **Phonetic system.** Where the pronunciation of a word or part of a word cannot be shown by the ordinary spelling and markings, a phonetic spelling is given in round brackets immediately after the black-type word. The phonetic scheme is as follows:

CONSONANTS: b; ch (ch*in*); d; dh (dh*e* = the); f; g (g*o*); h; j; k; l; m; n; ng (*s*i*ng*); ngg (*f*i*nger*); p; r; s (s*ip*); sh (sh*ip*); t; th (th*in*); v; w; y; z; zh (*vi*zh*on* = vision).

ṅ indicates French nasalization of preceding vowel.

The symbol χ represents the ch in *Ba*ch, *lo*ch, pronounced as a guttural sound or as k.

VOWEL COMBINATIONS:

ā ē ī ō ū o͞o (mate mete mite mote mute moot)
ă ĕ ĭ ŏ ŭ o͝o (rack reck rick rock ruck rook)
ār ēr īr ūr (mare mere mire mure)
ar er or (part pert port)
ah aw oi oor ow (bah bawl boil boor brow)

Vowels and combinations (as *er*) printed in italic within the brackets indicate vague sounds frequently indistinguishable from each other.

Vowels marked ˘̄ may be pronounced either way, e.g. **pā̆′trĭot** (pā- or pă-).

3. **Pronunciation without respelling.** As far as possible pronunciation is shown without respelling by placing symbols over the words (e.g. **ā, ĕ, a͞r, e͞r, o͝o,** etc.) in the black type. Unmarked vowels in the black-type words indicate vague sounds.

(*a*) The ordinary spelling often coincides with the phonetic system described in paragraph 2.

(*b*) The following additional symbols are used in the black type:

ė = ĭ (nā′kėd, rėlȳ′, cŏ′llėge, prī′vėt)
i͡r, u͡r = **e͡r** (bi͡rth, bu͡rn)
ȳ, y̆ = ī, ĭ (ĭmplȳ′, sŭ′nny̆)
y͞r=i͞r (ly͞re)

(*c*) Final *e* when unmarked is mute, i.e. not to be pronounced. Thus **āpe** is to be pronounced āp. Where final *e* is pronounced, it is marked as in **rĕ′cĭpė.** Where *e* is mute in the headword it is mute also (unless marked) in derivatives placed in the same entry, e.g. **ba͞re, ba͞r′elȳ, ba͞r′enėss.**

(*d*) A doubled consonant is pronounced as single (**sĭ′llȳ, mă′nnĭsh**) unless indicated as in **plai′nnėss** (-n-n-).

(*e*) The following letters and combinations have the usual values in English spelling which are shown alongside them:

Vowel Combinations

ae = ē (aegis)
ai = ā (pain)
air = a͞r (fair)
au = aw (maul)
ay = ā (say)
ea, ee = ē (mean, meet)
ear, eer = e͞r (fear, beer)
ei = ē (ceiling)
eu, ew = ū (feud, few)
ey = ĭ (donkey)
ie = ē (thief)
ier = e͞r (pier)
oa = ō (boat)
ou = ow (bound)
our = ow*er* (flour)
oy = oi (boy)

Consonants

c is hard and = k (cob, cry, talc) *but*
c before **e, i, y,** is soft and = s (ice, icy, city)
dg before **e, i, y,** = j (judgement)
g before **e, i, y,** is soft and = j (age, gin, orgy), except when doubled (digger, haggis, baggy)
n before **k,** hard **c, q, x** = ng (zinc uncle, tank, banquet, minx)
ph = f (photo)
qu = kw (quit)
tch = ch (batch)
wh = w or hw (when)
x = ks (fox)

Thus in **gĕm** the pronunciation of *g* is not marked because it comes under the rule above for soft *g*, but **gĕt** is followed by (g-) to show that here exceptionally **g** before **e** is hard as in *go*.

The following combinations have the values shown:

-age = -ĭj (garbage)

-al, -el preceded by *d, n, t* = -l (Handel, mental)

-en, -ent preceded by *d, t,* = -n, -nt (madden, fatten, student)

-sion after vowels = -zh*o*n (division)

-sm = -zm (atheism, spasm)

-tion = -sh*o*n (salvation)

-nch when final = -nsh or -nch (trench)

-ous = -*us* (furious)

-sion after consonants = -sh*o*n (passion, tension)

-tual, -tue, -ture = -cho͞o*a*l, -cho͞o, -ch*er* as well as -tū*a*l, -tū, -tūr, esp. in common words

SWUNG DASH (~)

The 'swung dash' or 'tilde' is frequently used to save space in the body of the entry. It represents the headword (or a derivative of the headword printed in black type in the same entry) when this is repeated as a different part of speech or when it is used in combination with another word, either hyphenated or detached (but not when it has become part of a complete new word). For example, in the article **pitch**[1] *n.* we have ~ *v.t.* when the headword becomes a new part of speech, and ~*black* and ~*-pine* when it is in combination (but *pitchblende* as a whole word). The addition of an initial letter to the swung dash indicates a change from a small letter in the headword to a capital or vice versa (e.g. *F*~ in the article **flood** represents the Flood recorded in Genesis).

ABBREVIATIONS USED IN THE DICTIONARY

(Abbreviations in general use have entries in the main text)

abbrev./iation, -iated
abl./ative
abs./olute(ly)
acc./ording
accus./ative
act./ive
adj(s)., adjective(s)
adv(s)., adverb(s)
aeron./autics
AF, Anglo-French
Afr./ican
alg./ebra
allus./ive(ly)
Amer./ican
anal./ogy
anat./omy
Anglo-Ind./ian
anon./ymous
antiq./uities
anthrop./ology
app./arently
Arab./ic
Aram./aic
arbitr./ary
archaeol./ogy
archit./ecture
arith./metic
assim./ilated
assoc./iated
astrol./ogy
astron./omy
at. wt, atomic weight
attrib./utive(ly)
augment./ative
Austral./ian
av./oirdupois

b./orn
back form./ation
bibl./ical
bibliog./raphy
biochem./istry
biol./ogy
Boh./emian
bot./any
Br./itish
Braz./ilian
Bulg./arian
Burm./ese
Byz./antine

c./entury
Camb./ridge
c/irca
cap./ital
Celt./ic
cf., compare
Ch./urch
chem./istry
Chin./ese
chronol./ogy
cinemat./ography
cogn./ate
collect./ive(ly)
colloq./uial(ly)
com./mon
comb./ination
commerc./ial
comp., compar./ative
compl./ement
conch./ology
confus./ion
conj., conjunction, conjugation
conn./ected
constr./uction
contempt./uous(ly)
contr./action
cop./ulative
correl./ative
corresp./onding
corrupt./ion
cryst./allography
cu./bic

d./ied
Dan./ish
dat./ive
demonstr./ative
deriv./ative
derog./atory
dial./ect
dict./ionary
diff./erent
dim./inutive
diplom./acy
dist./inct, -inguished
distrib./utive
Du./tch
dub./ious

E., east(ern)
eccles./iastical

ecol./ogy
econ./omics
Egyptol./ogy
E. Ind., East Indian (i.e. of the East Indies)
elect./ricity
ellipt./ical
embryol./ogy
emphat./ic(ally)
eng., engin./eering
Engl., England, English
entom./ology
erron./eous(ly)
esp./ecial(ly)
ethnol./ogy
etym./ology
euphem./ism
Eur./ope(an)
exagg./eration
exc./ept
exch./ange
excl., exclamation, exclusive
expr./essing etc.

f./rom
facet./ious etc.
fam./iliar etc.
fem./inine etc.
fig./urative etc.
Fl./emish
foll./owing (word)
footb./all
fort./ification
Fr./ench
freq./uent(ly)
frequent./ative(ly)
fut./ure (tense)

Gael./ic
gen., general(ly), genitive
geog./raphy
geol./ogy
geom./etry
Ger./man
Gk, Greek
govt., government
gram./mar

Heb./rew
her./aldry
Hind./ustani
hist./orical, history
hort./iculture

i., intransitive
Icel./andic
illit./erate
imit./ative
imp., imper./ative
imperf./ect
impers./onal
improp./er(ly)
incl./uding, inclusive
Ind./ian (i.e. of the Indian sub-continent)
ind., indicative, indirect
indecl./inable
indef./inite
inf./initive
infl./uence(d)
instr./umental (case)
int./erjection
interrog./ative(ly)
intrans./itive
Ir./ish
iron./ically
irreg./ular(ly)
It., Ital./ian

Jap./anese
Jew./ish
joc./ular(ly)

L, Latin
lang./uage
l.c., lower case
LG, Low German
lit./eral(ly)
Lith./uanian
LL, late Latin

magn./etism
manuf./acture
masc./uline
math./ematics
MDu., Middle Dutch
ME, Middle English
mech./anics
med./icine
med.L, medieval Latin
metall./urgy
metaph./or(ically)
metaphys./ics
meteor./ology
Mex./ican
MG, Middle German
MHG, Middle High German
mil./itary
min./eralogy
MLG, Middle Low German
mod./ern
morphol./ogy
mus./ic
myth./ology

N., north(ern)
n./oun
N. Amer., North America(n)
nat. hist., natural history
naut./ical
nav./al
nec./essary, -essarily

neg./ative(ly)
neut./er
nom./inative
Norm./an
north./ern
Norw./egian
ns., nouns
N.T., New Testament
num./eral

obj./ect
obl./ique
obs./olete
obsolesc./ent
occas./ional(ly)
OE, Old English
OF, Old French
OHG, Old High German
OIr., Old Irish
OLG, Old Low German
ON, Old Norse
onomat./opoeic
ophthalm./ology
opp., (as) opposed (to), opposite
ord./inary, -inarily
orig./inal(ly)
ornith./ology
O.T., Old Testament

p./age
paint./ing
palaeog./raphy
palaeont./ology
parenth./etic(ally)
parl./iament(ary)
part./iciple, -icipial
pass./ive(ly)
past t./ense
path./ology
pedant./ic(ally)
perf./ect (tense)
perh./aps
Pers./ian
pers./on(al)
Peruv./ian
pharm./acy, -acology
philol./ogy
philos./ophy
phon., phonet./ics
phot., photog./raphy
phr./ase
phrr., phrases
phys./ics
phys. chem., physical chemistry
physiol./ogy
pl./ural
pluperf./ect
poet./ical
Pol./ish
pol./itics etc.
pol. econ., political economy

pop./ular(ly)
Port./uguese
poss./essive
pp., pages
pr./onounced
prec., (the) preceding (word)
pred./icate, -icative
pref./ix
prep./osition(al)
pres./ent (tense)
pret./erite
print./ing
prob./able, -ably
pron., pronoun,
pronounced, pronunciation
prop./er(ly)
pros./ody
psych., psychol./ogy
psychoanal./ysis

railw./ay
R.C., Roman Catholic
ref./erence
refl./exive(ly)
rel./ative
repr./esent
rhet./oric
Rom./an
Russ./ian

S., south(ern)
S. Afr., South African
Sansk./rit
Sax./on
Sc./ottish
Scand./inavian
sculp./ture
sent./ence
Serb./ian
sing./ular
Slav./onic
sociol./ogy
sp./elling
Span./ish
spec./ial(ly)
specif./ic(ally)
sport./ing
Stock Exch., Stock Exchange
subj., subject, subjunctive
superl./ative
surg./ery
surv./eying
Swed./ish
syn./onym

tech./nical(ly)
teleg./raphy
term./ination
Teut./onic
theatr./ical

theol./ogy
trans./itive
transf., in transferred sense
transl./ation
trig./onometry
Turk./ish
typ./ography

U.K., United Kingdom
ult./imate(ly)
unexpl./ained
Univ./ersity
Univv., Universities
U.S., United States
usu./al(ly)

v./erb
var., variant, various
varr., variants
v. aux., verb auxiliary

vbl, verbal
vbs., verbs
v.i., verb intransitive
voc./ative
v.r., verb reflexive
v.t., verb transitive
vulg./ar(ly)

W., west(ern)
w./ith
W. Afr., West African
wd, word
wds, words
W. Ind., West Indian (i.e. of the West Indies)

yr(s), year(s)

zool./ogy

A

A, a (ā). 1. 1st letter of modern English and ancient Roman alphabet, descended, through Greek and Latin, from first letter, *aleph* (א), of Hebrew and Phoenician alphabets, in English representing orig. a low-back-wide vowel sound and now a number of vowel sounds. 2. 1st in series, order, or class, esp. (alg. etc.) first known quantity. 3. *A*, (mus.) 6th note of natural scale (C major); scale or key with this note for tonic. 4. *A.1*, applied in Lloyd's Register to ships in first-class condition in respect of both hull (designated by A) and equipment (1); hence, first-class, prime, perfect.

A *abbrev.* Adult (i.e. that may contain material unsuitable for children, of cinema film); alto; ampere(s); Australian (in $A, Australian dollars).

a, an (*a, an*; emphat., ā, ăn) *adj.* (the indefinite article) One; some, any; (in, to, for) each.

Å *abbrev.* Ångström(s).

a- *prefix.* 1. On, in, at. 2. (also *an-*) Without, not.

A.A. *abbrev.* Anti-aircraft; Automobile Association; *AA*, (of cinema film) for exhibition only to persons over 14 years.

A.A.A. *abbrev.* (U.S.) Agricultural Adjustment Administration; Amateur Athletic Association; Automobile Association of America.

Aa'chen (ahχ-). (Fr. *Aix-la-Chapelle*) Ancient city of Germany near Belgian and Dutch borders, scene of coronation of German kings until 16th c.

A. and M., A. & M. *abbrev.* (Hymns) Ancient and Modern.

aar'dvârk (âr-) *n.* S. Afr. ant-eating quadruped (*Orycteropus*

afer) with long extensile tongue. [Du., = 'earth-pig']

aardwolf (âr'dwŏŏlf) *n.* (pl. *-ves*). Carnivorous mammal (*Proteles cristatus*) resembling the hyena.

Aaron (âr'*on*). Brother of Moses and traditional founder of Jewish priesthood; *~'s beard*, (see Ps. 133: 2) any of various plants, esp. a St. John's wort (*Hypericum calycinum*); *~'s rod*, (see Numbers 17: 8) plant with tall flowering stem, esp. a mullein (*Verbascum thapsus*).

aasvogel (ah'sfōgl) *n.* Any of several large S. Afr. vultures. [Du., = 'carrion-bird']

ab-, abs- *prefix.* Off, away, from.

A.B. *abbrev.* Able seaman.

ă'ba, ă'bba, abay'a *ns.* Sack-like outer garment worn by Arabs.

abă'ck *adv.* Backwards; *taken ~*, (of ship) with square sails pressed back against the mast by the wind; (fig.) surprised, disconcerted.

ă'bacus *n.* (pl. *-cuses* or *-cī*). 1. Frame for arithmetical calculation

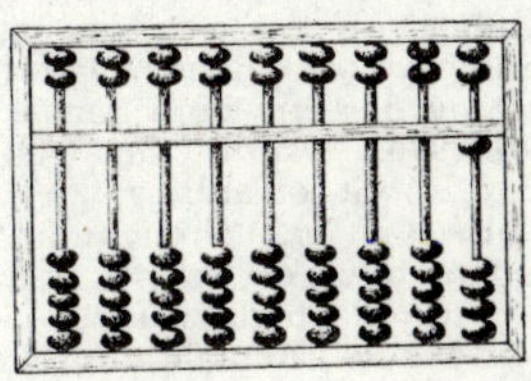

with balls sliding on wires, used before the adoption of the nine figures and zero, and still in China etc. and in elementary teaching. 2. (archit.) Upper member, often a square flat slab, of capital, supporting architrave.

Abă'ddon. Hebrew name of APOLLYON.

aba'ft (-bah-) *adv.* On or towards stern of ship. ~ *prep.* Aft of, behind.

ăbalō'nė *n.* (U.S.) Haliotis.

abă'ndon *v.t.* Give up, surrender, forsake. ~ *n.* Careless freedom. **abă'ndonment** *n.* **abă'ndoned** (-nd) *adj.* (esp.) Profligate.

abăndonee' *n.* Underwriter to whom salvage of wreck is abandoned.

abā'se *v.t.* Humiliate, lower, make base. **abā'sement** *n.*

abă'sh *v.t.* Embarrass, confound.

abā'te *v.* Diminish, make or become less; lower; deduct (part of price); (law) quash (action), end (nuisance). **abā'tement** *n.*

ă'batĭs, abă'ttĭs *n.* (mil.) Obstacle of felled trees with branches pointing outwards.

ă'battoir (-twar) *n.* Slaughterhouse.

abaya: see ABA.

A'bba[1] (ă-). Used (in '~, *Father*') in invocations to God; title of bishops in Syriac and Coptic Churches. [Aram. = 'father']

abba[2]: see ABA.

ă'bbacy̆ *n.* Office, jurisdiction, or tenure of abbot or abbess.

A'bbas[1] (ă-; *or* abah's) (566–652). Uncle of Muhammad.

A'bbas[2] (ă-; *or* abah's), 'the Great'. Shah of Persia; reigned 1587–1628.

A'bbasĭd (ă-; *or* abah'-) *n.* Member of dynasty of caliphs ruling in Baghdad 750–1258, claiming descent from ABBAS[1].

abbā'tial (-shal) *adj.* Of an abbey, abbot, or abbess.

ă'bbé (-ā) *n.* Frenchman entitled to wear ecclesiastical dress, esp. without official duties.

ă'bbėss *n.* Female superior of community of nuns, in those orders in which monks are governed by abbots.

Abbevĭ'llĭan (ăbv-) *adj.* & *n.* (Culture) of the earliest palaeolithic period in Europe, represented by the remains found at Abbeville, N. France (formerly called CHELLEAN).

ă'bbey *n.* Body of monks or nuns governed by an abbot or abbess; monastic buildings; church or house once an abbey or part of it.

A'bbey Thē'atre (ă-, *-er*). Irish national theatre, located since 1904 in Abbey St., Dublin.

ă'bbot *n.* Superior of community of monks (now chiefly in Benedictine and Augustinian orders), usu. elected by the monks for life or period of years, and freq. holding certain episcopal rights; ~ *of misrule*: see MISRULE. [Aram. *abba* father]

abbrē'vĭāte *v.t.* Shorten, contract (esp. word, by writing part for the whole). **abbrēvĭā'tion** *n.*

A B C *n.* Alphabet; rudiments of subject; alphabetical railway timetable.

ă'bdĭcāte *v.* Renounce, relinquish, (esp. crown) formally or by default. **ăbdĭcā'tion** *n.*

ă'bdomėn (*or* ăbdō'-) *n.* 1. (anat.) Part of body between diaphragm and floor of pelvis, containing digestive and other organs. 2. (zool.) Hinder part, not bearing walking limbs, of insects, spiders, etc. **ăbdŏ'mĭnal** *adj.* **ăbdŏ'mĭnally̆** *adv.*

ăbdū'cent *adj.* (anat., of muscles) Drawing back.

abdŭ'ct *v.t.* Take away (esp. woman) by force or fraud; (of muscle etc.) draw limb from normal position. **abdŭ'ction, abdŭ'ctor** *ns.*

abea'm *adv.* On a line at right angles to ship's or aircraft's length; opposite the middle of ship's or aircraft's side.

ābėcėdār'ian *adj.* 1. Arranged alphabetically, as the 119th Psalm. 2. Elementary, ignorant. ~ *n.* (U.S.) Pupil learning the alphabet.

à Becket, Thomas: see BECKET[2].

abĕ'd *adv.* (archaic, poet.) In bed.

Abĕdnē'gō (ă-; *or* abĕ'dnĭgō). One of three Jewish youths who came unharmed from a furnace into which they were thrown by Nebuchadnezzar (Dan. 3).

A'bel (ā-). 2nd son of Adam, killed by his brother Cain (Gen. 4: 1–16).

Abélard (ăbā-), Pierre (1079–1142). French philosopher; lecturer in the schools of Paris; advocate of rational theological inquiry and founder of scholastic theology. (See also HÉLOÏSE.)

abē'le (*or* ā'bl) *n.* White poplar, *Populus alba.*

Aberdee'n (ă-). City on E. coast of N. Scotland, former county town of Aberdeenshire, since May 1975 part of the region of Grampian; known as the 'granite city' and humorously credited with extremely parsimonious population; university, 1494; ~ *Angus*, (one of) a breed of polled black beef cattle; ~ *terrier*, Scotch terrier. **Aberdō'nian** *adj.* & *n.*

aberglaube (ah'berglowbe) *n.* Superstition, irrational belief. [Ger.]

ăbĕ'rrant *adj.* 1. Wandering, straying from moral standard. 2. (biol.) Diverging from normal type. **ăbĕ'rrance** *n.*

ăberrā'tion *n.* 1. Mental or moral slip or error; deviation from type. 2. (optics) Non-convergence of rays to one focus. 3. (astron.; also ~ *of light*) Displacement of true position of heavenly body to observer on earth, due to earth's motion and non-instantaneous transmission of light; *planetary* ~, aberration due to motion of the planet itself.

abĕ't *v.t.* Help or encourage, esp. in wrongdoing. **abĕ'tter, abĕ'ttor** *ns.*

ăb ĕ'xtra. From outside. [L]

abey'ance (-bā-) *n.* State of suspension, dormant condition (of rights etc.).

ABERDEEN

abhor' *v.t.* Regard with disgust and hatred. **abhŏ'rrent** *adj.* Inspiring disgust, repugnant, detestable. **abhŏ'rrentlў** *adv.* **abhŏ'rrence** *n.*

abī'de *v.* (past t. and past part. *abōde*, occas. *abided*). Remain; continue; dwell (archaic); wait for (archaic); (with neg.) tolerate; ~ *by*, remain faithful to.

A'bigail (ă-). 1. Wife of Nabal

and subsequently of David (1 Sam. 25). 2. In Beaumont and Fletcher's 'Scornful Lady', the 'waiting gentlewoman' (cf. 1 Sam. 25: 24–31); hence (*a*~), waiting-woman, lady's-maid.

abi'litȳ *n.* Sufficient power, capacity (*to* do); legal competency (to act); cleverness, talent, mental power.

Abī'mėlĕch (-k). 1. Son of Gideon, one of the judges of Israel: see Judges 8, 9. 2. King of Gerar, southern Palestine: see Gen. 20, 26.

ăb ĭnĭ'tio (-shīō) From the beginning (abbrev. *ab init.*). [L]

ābīōgĕ'nėsis *n.* T. H. Huxley's term for spontaneous generation (opp. BIOGENESIS).

ă'bjĕct *adj.* Brought low, miserable, craven, degraded. **ă'bjĕctlȳ** *adv.*

abjur'e (-oor) *v.t.* Renounce on oath. **ăbjurā'tion** *n.*

abl. *abbrev.* Ablative.

ăblā'tion *n.* 1. Removal (esp. in surgery, of part of body). 2. (geol.) Wastage of a glacier by evaporation and melting.

ă'blative *adj.* (gram.) Of the case denoting direction from a place, also time and source, agent, or instrument. ~ *n.* (Word in) ablative case; ~ *absolute*, Latin construction of noun and participle (both in ablative case), expressing time, occasion, or circumstances.

ă'blaut (-owt) *n.* (philol.) Systematic vowel permutation (not due to influence of contiguous sounds) in root of word in derivation, as in s*i*ng, s*a*ng, s*u*ng.

ablā'ze *adv.* Blazing; on fire.

ā'ble *adj.* Having the power or ability; talented, clever; ~*-bodied*, physically fit, robust; ~ *seaman*, (abbrev. A.B.) rating in Royal Navy above *ordinary seaman*.

ablū'tion (*or* -ōō-) *n.* Ceremonial washing; water or wine used in this; (pl.) process of washing oneself.

ă'bnėgāte *v.t.* Deny oneself (thing), renounce (right, belief). **ăbnėgā'tion** *n.*

abnôr'mal *adj.* Deviating from type, exceptional, irregular. **ăbnôr'mallȳ** *adv.* **ăbnôrmă'litȳ** *n.*

abnôr'mitȳ *n.* Irregularity; monstrosity.

A'bō (ă-), **ă'bō** *n.* (Austral. slang) Aboriginal.

Åbo (aw'bōō). Swedish name of TURKU, Finland.

aboar'd (-ôrd) *adv.* & *prep.* On board (ship, railway train, etc.)

abō'de *n.* Dwelling-place.

abŏ'lish *v.t.* Put an end to.

ăboli'tion *n.* Action or fact of abolishing; in 18th and 19th centuries esp. movement against slavery. **ăboli'tionism** *n.* **ăboli'tionist** *n.* One advocating abolition, esp. of slavery or capital punishment.

ăbomā'sum *n.* Fourth stomach of ruminant.

A-bŏmb (-m) *abbrev.* Atom(ic) bomb.

abŏ'minable *adj.* Morally or physically loathsome, detestable, odious, revolting; *A*~ *Snowman*, YETI. **abŏ'minablȳ** *adv.*

abŏ'mināte *v.t.* Loathe, dislike strongly.

abŏminā'tion. *n.* Loathing; object or practice deserving of aversion or disgust; ~ *of desolation*, desecration of the Temple at Jerusalem: see Dan. 9: 27, Matt. 24: 15.

ăbori'ginal *adj.* Indigenous, existing or present at dawn of history or before arrival of colonists or invaders. ~ *n.* Aboriginal inhabitant. **ăbori'ginēs** (-z) *n.pl.* (also sing. *-ine*) Aboriginal inhabitants, plants, etc.

abôr't *v.* 1. (Cause to) miscarry; (biol.) become sterile, remain undeveloped. 2. Fail, cease prematurely. 3. (aeronaut., U.S.) Terminate (space-flight) prematurely. ~ *n.* (aeronaut., U.S.) Premature termination of space-flight.

abôrtifā'cient (-shent) *adj.* & *n.* (Drug etc.) causing abortion.

abôr'tion *n.* 1. Expulsion of foetus from uterus before 28th week of pregnancy, either spontaneous or induced (in law, expulsion at any time before the full term); (pop.) operation etc. inducing this. 2. Foetus expelled in abortion. 3. Misshapen creature. **abŏr'tionist** *n*. One who performs abortion.

abŏr'tive *adj*. Premature; fruitless; rudimentary. **abŏr'tivelȳ** *adv*. **abŏr'tiveness** *n*.

Aboukir Bay (*abōō'kēr*): see NILE.

abou'lia, abū'lia *n*. (psychol.) Loss of will-power.

abou'nd *v.i*. Be plentiful; be rich *in*, teem or be infested *with*.

abou't *adv*. On every side; near; somewhere round; here and there; astir; almost; (naut.) on or to the opposite tack (so *come*, *put*, ~, = TACK *v*.²); *be* ~ *to* (do), be on the point of doing; *come* ~, happen; *put* ~, distracted, annoyed; ~ *turn!* (mil. etc.) turn so as to face in opposite direction. ~ *prep*. 1. On every side of; near; with. 2. Concerning. 3. Occupied with. 4. Here and there in, on, etc.

abo've (-ŭv) *adv*. Higher up, overhead; upstream; earlier in a book etc. ~ *prep*. Over, higher than, of higher rank, etc., than; in addition to; ~*-board*, without concealment; fair, open, honest.

ăb ō'vō. From the (very) beginning. [L]

Abp *abbrev*. Archbishop.

ăbracadă'bra *n*. Cabbalistic word formerly used as charm, orig. by Gnostics, and believed to have power of curing agues etc. when written in triangular arrangement and worn as amulet; (now) spell, mysterious formula, gibberish.

abrā'de *v.t*. Scrape off, wear away, injure, by rubbing.

A'brahăm (ā-). Hebrew patriarch, from whom all Jews trace their descent (Gen. 11: 27–25: 10); ~*'s bosom*, heavenly abode of the blessed dead (Luke 16: 22); *Plains of* ~, plateau near Quebec, scaled from St. Lawrence River by English army under WOLFE (1759) and scene of subsequent battle with French under Montcalm which decided fate of Canada.

ăbrā'sion *n*. Rubbing or scraping off; rough or sore place on skin caused by this; (geol.) wearing away of earth's surface by windborne particles of rock or sand- (cf. EROSION).

abrā'sive *adj*. Tending to produce abrasion. ~ *n*. Any substance, as emery, carborundum, etc., used for grinding or polishing.

ăbrēă'ction *n*. (psychiatry) Removal, by revival and expression, of the emotion associated with an event which has undergone repression in memory.

abrea'st (-ĕst) *adv*. Side by side and facing the same way; ~ *of*, keeping up with, not behind (times etc.).

abrĭ'dge *v.t*. Condense, shorten, curtail. **abrĭ'dgement, -gment** *n*. Curtailment; epitome, abstract.

abroa'd (-awd) *adv*. In or to foreign lands; broadly, in different directions; (of rumour etc.) current; *from* ~, from foreign countries.

ă'brogāte *v.t*. Repeal, cancel. **ăbrogā'tion** *n*.

abrŭ'pt *adj*. Sudden, hasty; brusque; disconnected; steep; (bot.) truncated. **abrŭ'ptlȳ** *adv*. **abrŭ'ptness** *n*.

abs-: see AB-.

A'bsalom (ă-). 3rd and favourite son of DAVID, killed while leading rebellion against his father (2 Sam. 13–19).

ă'bscess *n*. Local inflammation of body tissues with deep suppuration caused by bacteria which destroy the cells in the centre of the area and leave a cavity filled with pus.

absci'ssa *n*. (pl. *-s* or *-ae*). (geom.) Part of line between fixed point on it and ordinate to it from any other point.

abscĭ'ssion *n*. Cutting off; (bot.) separation.

abscŏ'nd *v.i*. Go away secretly, fly from the law.

ă'bseil (-sāl) *n*. (mountaineering) Descent using a rope doubled over a projection. ~ *v.i*. Use abseil.

ă'bsence *n*. Being away or

absent; non-existence, want (*of*); abstracted state.

ă'bsent *adj.* Not present; not existing; abstracted in mind: *~-minded*, abstracted, preoccupied, whence *~-mindedly*, *~-mindedness*. **absĕ'nt** *v.t.* Keep (oneself) away, withdraw (oneself).

ăbsentee' *n.* Person not present, one who absents himself from his duties etc.; person (esp. landlord) habitually living away from property. **ăbsentee'ism** *n.*

ă'bsinth, -the *n.* Wormwood, the plant or its essence; strong greenish-grey liqueur flavoured with wormwood and aniseed.

ă'bsĭt ō'mĕn. May no ominous significance attach to the words. [L]

ă'bsolute (-ūt *or* -o͞ot) *adj.* Complete, perfect, pure; unrestricted, independent; despotic, ruling arbitrarily; not in (the usual) grammatical relation with other words; real, not relative or comparative; unqualified; self-existent and conceivable without relation to other things; *~ alcohol*, containing at least 99% pure alcohol by weight; ~ DROUGHT, ~ HUMIDITY: see these words; *~ magnitude*, magnitude of a star as it would appear at a distance of 10 parsecs; *~ music*, self-dependent instrumental music without literary or other extraneous suggestions (opp. PROGRAMME music); *~ pitch*, ability to recognize or reproduce pitch of notes, (also) pitch of a note defined scientifically in terms of vibrations per second; *~ temperature*, temperature measured on a Centigrade (Celsius) scale which has its zero at absolute zero; *~ zero*: see ZERO. **ă'bsolutelȳ** *adv.* Completely, independently; (colloq., *absolu'tely*) yes, quite so.

ăbsolu'tion (-ū- *or* -o͞o-) *n.* Formal forgiveness, esp. ecclesiastical declaration of forgiveness of sins; remission of penance.

ă'bsolutism (-ū- *or* -o͞o-) *n.* 1. (theol.) Dogma that God acts absolutely in matter of salvation. 2. (pol.) Principle of absolute government, despotism. **ă'bsolutist** *n.* Supporter of absolute government; (metaphys.) one who maintains absolute identity of subject and object.

absŏ'lve (*or* -z-) *v.t.* Set or pronounce free from blame etc.; acquit.

absor'b (*or* -z-) *v.t.* Swallow up, incorporate; engross the attention of; suck in (liquid); take in (heat, light, etc.). **absor'bable** *adj.* That can be absorbed.

absor'bent (*or* -z-) *adj.* Having a tendency to absorb; *~ cotton*, (U.S.) = COTTON[1] wool. *~ n.* Absorbent substance.

absor'ption (*or* -z-) *n.* Action of absorbing, fact of being absorbed; natural or medicinal removal of tissues or deposits.

abstai'n *v.i.* Keep oneself *from* doing something, esp. from drinking alcohol. **abstai'ner** *n.*

abstē'mious *adj.* Sparing or moderate in food, drink, etc. **abstē'miouslȳ** *adv.* **abstē'miousnėss** *n.*

abstĕ'ntion *n.* Refraining or holding back; (parl. etc.) not using one's vote.

ă'bstinence *n.* Abstaining from food, pleasure, etc.: *total ~*, abstaining from alcohol. **ă'bstinent** *adj.* Practising abstinence.

ă'bstrăct *adj.* Not concrete; theoretical, not practical; (of art etc.) concerned with pure form and pattern, free from representational qualities. *~ n.* 1. *the ~*, ideal or theoretical way of regarding things. 2. Epitome, summary. 3. Abstraction, abstract term. **abstră'ct** *v.t.* Deduct, remove; steal; disengage (attention etc.); summarize; *abstra'cted*, withdrawn in thought, not attending.

abstră'ction *n.* Withdrawal, removal; abstract idea; absent-mindedness; abstract art.

abstru'se (-o͞os) *adj.* Hard to understand, profound. **abstru'selȳ** *adv.* **abstru'senėss** *n.*

absur'd *adj.* Incongruous, unreasonable, ridiculous. **absur'dlȳ** *adv.* **absur'ditȳ** *n.*

abŭ'ndance *n.* Plenty, more than enough; affluence; call in solo whist (see SOLO); (phys.) amount present. **abŭ'ndant** *adj.* Plentiful, rich, in abundance. **abŭ'ndantlÿ** *adv.*

abū'se (-z) *v.t.* Make bad use of, misuse; speak insultingly to or about. ~ (-s) *n.* Misuse, perversion; unjust or corrupt practice; insulting speech. **abū'sĭve** *adj.* **abū'sĭvelÿ** *adv.* **abū'sĭvenėss** *n.*

abŭ't *v.* Have common boundary with; border (*on*); end *on*, lean *against*. **abŭ'tment** *n.* (archit.) Support from which arch, vault, etc., springs, and which receives the lateral thrust. **abŭ'tter** *n.* (law) Owner of adjoining property.

Abȳ'dŏs. 1. Ancient city on the Hellespont, home of LEANDER. 2. Ancient ruined city of Upper Egypt.

abȳ'sm *n.* (poet.) Abyss.

abȳ'smal (-z-) *adj.* Bottomless (esp. fig.). **abȳ'smallȳ** *adv.*

abȳ'ss *n.* Primal chaos; bottomless chasm; deep gorge.

abȳ'ssal *adj.* Of lowest depths of ocean.

Abȳssĭ'nĭa (ă-) *n.* Former name of Ethiopia. **Abȳssĭ'nĭan** *adj.* & *n.*

A.C. *abbrev.* Aircraftman (also A/C); Alpine Club; alternating current (also a.c.); *ante Christum* (L, = 'before Christ').

a/c *abbrev.* Account.

A.C.A. *abbrev.* Associate of the Institute of Chartered Accountants.

acā'cia (-sha) *n.* 1. Leguminous shrub or tree of genus *A*~ (subfamily Mimoseae), found in warmer regions of Old World and Australia, some species of which yield gum arabic, catechu, etc. 2. N.-Amer. locust-tree (*Robinia pseud-Acacia*, false ~), with sweet-scented pea-like flowers, freq. grown as ornamental tree in England etc.

ă'cadēme *n.* (properly) = ACADEMUS; (used by mistake in poet. style for) the Greek ACADEMY, hence, college, university. [Gk; mistake perh. caused by Milton's 'grove of Academe', i.e. Academus]

ăcadĕ'mĭc *adj.* 1. Of an academy or academician; of a university or college. 2. Of the philosophic school of Plato, sceptical. 3. Scholarly; abstract, cold, merely logical; unpractical; theoretical, conventional. ~ *n.* Member of university; (pl.) academic arguments.

ăcadĕ'mĭcal *adj.* Of a college or university. **ăcadĕ'mĭcallȳ** *adv.*

ăcadĕ'mĭcals (-z) *n.pl.* Academical robes, college or university costume.

acădemĭ'cian (-shan) *n.* Member of academy, esp. of Académie française or Royal Academy of Arts.

Académie française (ăkădāmē frahṅsāz). French literary academy, founded by Richelieu (1635); membership, limited to 40, is considered the highest distinction for men of letters; among its functions are the compilation and periodical revision of a dictionary of the French language (1st ed. 1694), and of a grammar (1st ed. 1932).

Acadē'mus (ă-). (Gk legend) Hero who revealed hiding-place of their sister Helen to the Dioscuri when they invaded Attica.

acă'demȳ *n.* 1. *A*~, pleasure-garden near Athens (said to have belonged to ACADEMUS) in which Plato taught; Plato's followers, the philosophical school founded by him. 2. A secondary or high school (esp. private). 3. Place of training in a special art. 4. Society for cultivating literature, art, etc.; *the A*~, (esp.) the Royal Academy of Arts; one of its annual exhibitions.

Acā'dĭa. Name given by French to district in what is now known as Nova Scotia, first settled by them at end of 16th c. **Acā'dĭan** *adj.* & *n.* (Native, inhabitant) of Acadia; (descendant) of Acadians.

acănthŏpterȳ'gĭan *adj.* & *n.* (Fish) of group Acanthopterygii, usu. with hard spiny rays in dorsal and anal fins.

acă'nthus *n.* 1. Herbaceous plant of genus *A*~ with large, deeply-cut, hairy, shining leaves, native of southern Europe, Asia, and Africa. 2. (archit.) Conventionalized leaf of *A. mollis* or *A. spinosus* (with narrower spiny-toothed leaves) used as ornament, esp. on the Corinthian and Composite capitals.

ă'carĭd *n.* Arachnid of family Acaridae, a mite or tick.

acătalĕ'ctĭc *n.* & *adj.* (pros.) (Line) that is not catalectic.

acc. *abbrev.* Account; accusative.

Accad, Accadian: see AKKAD.

accē'de (*a*ks-) *v.i.* Consent, agree (*to*); (also ~ *to*) enter upon office or dignity, join party.

accĕleră'ndō (*a*ks- *or a*ch-) *adv.*, *adj.*, & *n.* (pl. *-os*). (mus.) (Passage performed) with gradual increase of speed. [It.]

accĕ'lerāte (*a*ks-) *v.* Make, become, quicker; cause to happen earlier; put on pace; *accelerated particle*, (phys.) one subjected to acceleration, esp. by electrical or magnetic means.

accĕlerā'tion (*a*ks-) *n.* Accelerating; vehicle's power to accelerate; (phys.) rate of increase in velocity of moving body (written, e.g., 10 ft per sec./sec. if body moves 10 ft per second faster in every second).

accĕ'lerative (*a*ks-) *adj.* Tending to increase speed.

accĕ'lerātor (*a*ks-) *n.* Thing that increases anything's speed; pedal which operates throttle of internal combustion engine; substance added to mixture to reduce time taken by chemical reaction; electrical or magnetic apparatus giving high velocities to free electrons or other atomic particles; ~ *nerve*, any of the cardiac sympathetic nerves, discharges from which quicken and strengthen the heart-beats.

ă'ccent (ăks-) *n.* Prominence given to syllable by stress or pitch; mark used to indicate syllabic pitch, vowel quality, etc. (see ACUTE, CIRCUMFLEX, GRAVE², ~); individual, local, or national mode of pronunciation; (pl.) speech; (pros.) rhythmical stress; (mus.) stress recurring at intervals; (fig.) distinctive character; emphasis *on*.

accĕ'nt *v.t.* Pronounce with accent or stress, emphasize; mark with (written) accents; intensify, make conspicuous.

accĕ'ntor (*a*ks-) *n.* Bird of family Prunellidae, including the DUNNOCK (*hedge* ~).

accĕ'ntūal (*a*ks-) *adj.* Of accent; (esp. of verse) in which metre or rhythm results from alternation of strong and weak (not long and short) syllables. **accĕ'ntuallў** *adv.*

accĕ'ntūāte (*a*ks-) *v.t.* Accent (esp. in fig. senses). **accĕntūā'tion** *n.*

accĕ'pt (*a*ks-) *v.t.* Consent to receive; answer (invitation etc.) affirmatively; receive as adequate or true; tolerate; agree to meet (bill of exchange); undertake (office). **accĕ'ptance, accĕ'ptor** *ns.*

accĕ'ptable (*a*ks-) *adj.* Worth accepting, welcome, pleasing. **accĕ'ptablў** *adv.* **accĕptabĭ'lĭtў** *n.*

acceptā'tion (ăks-) *n.* Particular sense given to word or phrase; generally recognized meaning.

accĕ'ptėd (*a*ks-) *adj.* Generally recognized or believed in.

ă'ccĕss (ăks-) *n.* 1. Approach; addition; right or means of approach; being approached. 2. Attack or outburst.

accessary: see ACCESSORY *n.*

accĕ'ssĭble (*a*ks-) *adj.* Able to be reached or entered; open to influence (of). **accĕ'ssĭblў** *adv.* **accĕssĭbĭ'lĭtў** *n.*

accĕ'ssion (*a*ks-) *n.* Acceding or attaining (esp. to throne or manhood); joining, addition; (law) addition to property by natural growth or artificial improvement.

accĕ'ssorў (*a*ks-) *adj.* Additional, subordinately contributive, adventitious. ~ *n.* 1. (correctly spelt *accessary* but *-ory* is now more usual) Person who is privy *to* an (esp. criminal) act or helps in it but is not the chief actor. 2. Accompaniment, adjunct; (pl., commerc.) smaller articles of (esp. woman's) dress, as shoes, gloves, etc.; minor fittings for motor-car, camera, etc.

acciaccatura (*a*chahk*a*toor'*a*) *n.*

(mus.) Grace-note performed quickly before an essential note of a melody.

ă'ccidence (ăks-) *n.* Part of grammar dealing with inflexions, i.e. with the accidents or non-essentials of words; book, or part of one, on this subject.

ă'ccident (ăks-) *n.* 1. Event without apparent cause, the unexpected; unintentional act, chance misfortune, mishap. 2. Property or quality not essential to our conception of a substance, attribute; mere accessory. **ăccidě'ntal** *adj.* **ăccidě'ntallȳ** *adv.* **ăccidě'ntal** *n.* (mus.) Sharp ♯, flat ♭, or natural ♮ sign occurring not in key signature but before particular note.

accidie (ă'ksĭdĭ) *n.* Sloth; laziness or indifference.

acclai'm *v.t.* Welcome or applaud loudly, hail. ~ *n.* Shout of applause or welcome.

ăcclamā'tion *n.* Loud and eager assent; (pl.) shouting in person's honour.

acclī'mate (*or* ă'klīmāt) *v.* (U.S.) = ACCLIMATIZE. **ăcclĭmā'tion** *n.*

acclī'matīze *v.t.* Habituate to new climate or surroundings. **acclīmatīzā'tion** *n.* Fact, process, of acclimatizing, esp. (biol.) in ref. to transference of plants or animals to a new environment.

acclĭ'vitȳ *n.* Upward slope.

ăccolā'de (*or* -ahd) *n.* 1. Ceremony of conferring knighthood, usu. by stroke on shoulder with flat of sword. 2. Expression of approval. 3. (mus.) Vertical line or brace coupling staves.

accŏ'mmodāte *v.t.* 1. Adapt (*to*); harmonize; reconcile, settle differences between; compose (quarrel). 2. Equip, supply (*with*); oblige, confer favour on; find lodging for. **accŏ'mmodāting** *adj.* Obliging.

accommodā'tion *n.* 1. Adaptation, adjustment; (of eye) adjustment of shape of lens to bring light rays from various distances to focus upon retina; (of sense organs) property which causes the nervous discharges initiated by a stimulus of constant activity to diminish or die out. 2. Settlement, compromise. 3. Serviceable thing, convenience. 4. Lodgings. 5. Money loan. 6. ~ *address*, address where letters are sent for person who has no permanent address or wishes to conceal it; ~ *bill*, bill of exchange given not for value received but for purpose of raising money on credit; ~ *ladder*, ladder up ship's side for entering or leaving small boat.

acco'mpanĭment (-ŭm-) *n.* Accompanying thing; appendage; (mus.) subsidiary part, gen. instrumental, supporting a solo instrument or voice, choir, etc.

acco'mpanist, -ȳist (-ŭm-) *n.* Performer of accompaniment.

acco'mpanȳ (-ŭm-) *v.t.* Go with, escort, attend; coexist with; (mus.) support (player, singer, chorus, etc.) by performing subsidiary part.

accŏ'mplice (*or* -ŭm-) *n.* Associate, usu. subordinate, in guilt or crime.

accŏ'mplish (*or* -ŭm-) *v.t.* Perform, carry out, succeed in doing. **acco'mplished** (-sht) *adj.* Having accomplishments. **acco'mplishment** *n.* Achievement, fulfilment; social attainment.

accōr'd *v.* 1. Agree, be consistent (*with*). 2. Grant (indulgence, request, etc.). ~ *n.* Consent; mutual agreement; harmonious correspondence in colour, tone, etc.; volition (as *of one's own* ~).

accōr'dance *n.* Conformity, agreement. **accōr'dant** *adj.*

accōr'ding *adv.* ~ *as*, in proportion as, in a manner depending on which of certain alternatives is true; ~ *to*, in a manner consistent with; on the authority of. **accōr'dinglȳ** *adv.* Correspondingly; in accordance with what might be expected; in due course; therefore.

accōr'dion *n.* Small portable musical instrument with bellows and keyboard admitting wind to metal reeds when keys are depressed; ~ *door*, ~ *pleat*(*ing*), door, pleat(ing), having a series of folds like the bellows of an accordion.

accŏ'st *v.t.* Approach and address (esp. boldly); (of prostitute) solicit.

accouchement (ăkōōshmahṅ) *n.* Lying-in, delivery. ***accoucheur*** (ăkōōshẽr) *n.* Man-midwife. ***accoucheuse*** (-ẽrz) *n.* Midwife. [Fr.]

accou'nt *n.* 1. Counting, reckoning; *money of* ~, denominations of money used in reckoning. 2. Amount of money deposited with a bank; credit facilities allowed by shop etc. to customer; statement of money received and expended, with balance; statement of discharge of responsibilities generally, answering for conduct; final account at judgement-seat of God (esp. in *sent, gone, to one's* ~); *balance, square* ~*s* (*with*), settle account by payment of money due (freq. fig.); *for* ~ *of*, to be sold on behalf of; *give* (*good*) ~ *of oneself*, be successful, give favourable impression; *keep* ~*s*, keep statement of expenditure and receipts; *on* ~, as interim payment; *on* ~ *of*, in consideration of, because of; *on no* ~, not for any reason, certainly not; *on one's own* ~, for one's own purposes and at one's own risk. 3. Reckoning in one's favour, profit, advantage; *turn to* ~, make useful. 4. Estimation; *make* ~ *of*, value, esteem; *take into, leave out of*, ~, (fail to) take into consideration. 5. Narration, report, description (*of*). ~ *v.* 1. Consider, regard as. 2. ~ *for*, give reckoning for; answer for; explain cause of, serve as explanation of.

accou'ntable *adj.* 1. Bound to give account, responsible, liable. 2. Explicable. **accountabĭ'lĭtȳ** *n.*

accou'ntancȳ *n.* Profession or duties of accountant.

accou'ntant *n.* Professional keeper or inspector of accounts; *chartered* ~: see CHARTER *v.t.*

accou'tre (-ōōter) *v.t.* Attire, equip, esp. with special costume (chiefly in past part. *accoutred*). **accou'trement** (-ōōtre-) *n.* (usu. in pl.) Equipment, trappings.

Accra (*a*krah'). W.-Afr. seaport on Gulf of Guinea, capital of Ghana.

accrĕ'dĭt *v.t.* Gain credit for, dispose one to believe; send out with credentials; attribute *to*. **accrĕ'dĭtėd** *adj.* Officially recognized; generally accepted.

accrē'te *v.* Grow together or into one; form round or on *to*; attract (such additions). **accrē'tion** *n.* Growth by organic enlargement; increase by external additions; adhesion of extraneous matter; matter so added, extraneous addition.

accru'e (-ōō) *v.i.* Fall (*to* one) as a natural growth, advantage or result (esp. of interest on invested money).

accū'mūlāte *v.* Heap up, amass, make money; grow numerous, form increasing mass or heap. **accūmūlā'tion** *n.* **accū'mūlatĭve** *adj.*

accū'mūlātor *n.* 1. One who collects. 2. Electric cell (or group of these connected in series) in which the chemical action which produces the current can be reversed by passing an electric current through it in the opposite direction, and which thus constitutes a means of storing electric energy in the form of chemical energy; storage battery. 3. Bet in which the amount won on one event is staked on a subsequent event.

ă'ccūrate *adj.* Precise, exact, correct. **ă'ccūratelȳ** *adv.* **ă'ccūracȳ** *n.*

accūr'sėd, accūr'st *adj.* Lying under a curse; execrable, detestable.

ăccūsā'tion (-z-) *n.* Accusing, being accused; indictment.

accū'satĭve (-z-) *adj.* (gram.) Of the case chiefly denoting the direct object of a verb or used following certain prepositions. ~ *n.* (Word in) accusative case. **accū'satĭvelȳ** *adv.*

accūsatōr'ial (-z-) *adj.* ~ *procedure* etc., that in which prosecutor and judge are not the same (opp. *inquisitorial*).

accū'satorȳ (-z-) *adj.* Conveying or implying accusation.

accū'se (-z) *v.t.* Charge with

fault, indict; blame, lay fault on.

accŭ′stom *v.t.* Familiarize by habit or custom. **accŭ′stomed** (-md) *adj.* Customary, usual; wonted, used.

āce *n.* 1. Card, die-face, etc., with one pip; one point at rackets etc. 2. Distinguished airman (orig., one who has brought down ten enemy aircraft); person excelling in any sport or skill; (tennis etc.) unreturnable stroke, esp. a service; point thus scored.

acē′dĭa *n.* = ACCIDIE.

Acĕ′ldama (*or* ak-). Field near Jerusalem purchased for cemetery with blood-money received by Judas Iscariot (see Matt. 27: 8; Acts 1: 19); scene of slaughter or bloodshed. [Aram. = 'field of blood']

acĕ′phalous *adj.* Headless; (zool.) having no part of body specially organized as head; (bot.) with head aborted or cut off; (pros.) lacking the regular first syllable.

acĕr′bĭty̆ *n.* Astringent sourness; bitterness of speech, manner, or temper.

ă′cėtal *n.* Colourless pleasant-smelling liquid formed by slow oxidation of alcohol; class of complex ethers, derivatives of aldehyde, of which this is the type.

ăcetă′ldėhȳde *n.* Aldehyde.

ăcėtă′nĭlīde *n.* White crystalline solid made by action of acetic acid on aniline and used as febrifuge and analgesic.

ă′cėtāte *n.* Salt of acetic acid; synthetic material in the manufacture of which acetic acid is used; ~ *fibre*, textile fibre made from cellulose acetate.

acē′tĭc *adj.* Of, producing, vinegar; ~ *acid*, colourless pungent biting organic acid (CH_3COOH) which gives vinegar its characteristic taste.

acĕ′tifȳ *v.* Turn into vinegar, make or become sour. **acĕtĭfĭcā′tion** *n.*

aceto-, acet- *prefix.* (chem.) Derived from, connected with, acetic acid or acetyl.

ă′cėtōne *n.* Colourless fragrant inflammable liquid ketone (CH_3COCH_3) widely used as an organic solvent and in making chloroform etc.

ă′cėtous (*or* asē′-) *adj.* Of, producing, vinegar; sour, acid.

ă′cėty̆l *n.* Monovalent radical (CH_3CO) of acetic acid. **acĕty̆lā′tion** *n.* Introduction of acetyl group(s) into (a compound) by means of a chemical reaction. **acĕ′ty̆lāte** *v.* **acĕ′ty̆lātėd, acĕ′ty̆lating** *adjs.*

acĕ′ty̆lēne *n.* Colourless, nearly odourless (when pure), highly inflammable gaseous hydrocarbon, usu. prepared by adding water to calcium carbide (impurities in which produce the characteristic unpleasant smell), and used for lighting, for welding and cutting metals, etc.

A.C.F. *abbrev.* Army Cadet Force.

Achaea (*akē′a*). 1. District of ancient Greece along S. shore of Gulf of Corinth. 2. Roman province comprising all the southern part of Greece. **Achae′an** *adj.* & *n.* 1. In Homer, apparently = Greek; hence, (one) of the early Greeks; of the early Greek civilization. 2. In classical times, (inhabitant) of Achaea.

Achates (*akā′tēz*). (Gk & Rom. legend) Friend of Aeneas, usu. called *fidus* (faithful) ~; hence, *fidus* ~, faithful friend.

ache (āk) *v.i.* & *n.* (Suffer, be a source of) continuous dull pain.

ă′chēne (-k-; *or* -kē′n) *n.* (bot.) Small dry one-seeded fruit which does not open to liberate seed.

A′cheron (ăk-). (Gk myth.) One of the rivers of Hades, over which the dead were carried by Charon's ferry.

A′chėson (ăch-), Edward Goodrich (1856–1931). American inventor of carborundum and artificially prepared graphite.

Acheu′lĭan (*ashōō*-) *adj.* & *n.* (Of) the palaeolithic period succeeding the Abbevillian. [*St. Acheul*, Amiens, France]

achie′ve *v.t.* Accomplish;

acquire; reach (an end). **achie'vement** *n.* 1. Completion, accomplishment; thing accomplished. 2. (her.) Escutcheon or ensign armorial commemorating distinguished feat, hatchment.

Achilles (*a*kĭ'lēz). (Gk legend) Hero of the Trojan war, son of Peleus and Thetis; was killed by Paris with a poisoned arrow that pierced his heel where his mother had held him in infancy when she plunged him into the Styx to make him invulnerable; hence, *Achilles' heel*, vulnerable part; ~ *tendon*, tendon in heel by which calf-muscles extend foot.

ăchromă'tic (-k-) *adj.* Colourless; transmitting light without dispersing it into its constituent colours; ~ *lens*, pair of lenses, e.g. one of crown glass and the other of flint glass, the dispersion of one correcting the dispersion of the other. **achrōmatism** *n.* Achromatic quality. **achrō'matize** *v.t.*

acĭ'cūlar *adj.* Like a small needle or bristle.

ă'cid *adj.* 1. Sour, sharp to taste; (fig.) biting, severe. 2. Having properties of an acid. ~ *n.* One of a class of chemical compounds in which hydrogen may be replaced by metals to form salts, neutralizing alkalis, usu. corroding or dissolving metals, and having sour taste; ~ *drop*, sweet made of sugar strongly flavoured with tartaric acid; ~ *salt*, a salt derived from an acid having more than one replaceable hydrogen atom, one at least of which has not been replaced by a metal; ~ *test*, testing for gold by means of aqua fortis; (fig.) crucial test. **acĭ'dĭfȳ** *v.*

acĭ'dĭc *adj.* Acid; acid-forming.

ăcĭ'dĭtȳ *n.* Acid property.

ăcidō'sis *n.* (path.) Acid condition of blood and body tissues.

acĭ'dūlātėd, acĭ'dūlous *adjs.* Made slightly acid.

ACHILLES

A'cĭs (ā-). (Gk myth.) Lover of GALATEA[2].

ăck-ăck *adj.* & *n.* Anti-aircraft (gun etc.). [from letter A in signallers' former phonetic alphabet]

ăck ĕ'mma. 1. *Ante meridiem.* 2. Air mechanic. [names in signallers' former phonetic alphabet of letters A, M]

acknow'lĕdge (-nŏl-) *v.t.* Admit the truth of, admit, own; announce receipt of; express appreciation of. **acknow'ledg(e)ment** *n.* Acknowledging; thing given or done in return for service etc.

aclĭ'nĭc *adj.* ~ *line*, magnetic equator, line on which magnetic needle has no dip.

ă'cmė *n.* Highest point or pitch, culmination; (fig.) point of perfection.

ă'cnė *n.* Skin eruption due to inflammation of sebaceous glands, common in adolescence, and characterized by red pimples esp. on face.

ă'colўte *n.* Officer of one of the two 'ministries' which replaced minor orders in R.C. Church in 1973, attending priests and deacons, lighting and carrying candles, etc.; attendant, esp. at altar; assistant.

Aconcagua (ăkŏnkah'gwa). Extinct volcano and highest peak (7035 m.; 23,080 ft) in Andes, near boundary between Argentina and Chile.

ă'conīte *n.* Plant of poisonous ranunculaceous genus *Aconitum*, with five blue or yellow sepals, of which one is helmet-shaped; esp. the common European *A. napellus*, monkshood, or *A. lycoctonum*, wolfsbane; dried root of this plant used in pharmacy and as poison.

acŏ'nĭtine (*or* -ēn) *n.* Bitter white crystalline highly poisonous alkaloid, essential principle of aconite.

ā'cōrn *n.* Fruit of oak, oval nut growing in shallow woody cup; ~ *barnacle*, sessile barnacle, of many genera.

acŏtўlē'don *n.* (bot.) Plant with no distinct cotyledons or seed-leaves, as fern, moss, etc. **acŏtўlē'donous** *adj.*

acou'stĭc (-ōō- *or* -ow-) *adj.* Of the sense of hearing; of sound, of acoustics; (of building material) sound-absorbent; ~ *mine*, underwater mine designed to be detonated by sound-waves proceeding from ship's propellers. **acou'stĭcs** *n.* Science of sound; properties of building, room, etc., in respect of audibility of sounds. **acou'stĭcal** *adj.* **acou'stĭcallў** *adv.*

acquai'nt *v.t.* Make aware or familiar, inform; *be acquainted with*, have personal knowledge of. **acquai'ntance** *n.* Personal knowledge; person with whom one is acquainted but not intimate. **acquai'ntanceshĭp** *n.*

ăcquiĕ'sce *v.i.* Agree, esp. tacitly; not object. **ăcquiĕ'scence** *n.* **ăcquiĕ'scent** *adj.*

acquīr'e *v.t.* Gain, get, come to have; *acquired characteristic*, characteristic gained through influence of environment, and not inherited from parents; *acquired taste*, (object of) liking gained by experience. **acquīr'ement** *n.* Acquiring; (pl.) mental attainments.

ăcquĭsĭ'tion (-z-) *n.* Acquiring; thing acquired, useful or pleasant addition.

acquĭ'sĭtive (-z-) *adj.* Desirous of, given to, acquiring and retaining. **acquĭ'sĭtivelў** *adv.* **acquĭ'sĭtivenĕss** *n.*

acquĭ't *v.t.* Pay (debt); declare not guilty, free from blame; ~ *oneself* (*well, ill*, etc.), perform one's part or duty.

acquĭ'ttal *n.* Discharge from debt; performance (of duty); deliverance from a charge by verdict etc.

acquĭ'ttance *n.* Payment of or release from debt; receipt in full.

acre[1] (ā'ker) *n.* Land-measure, legally 4840 sq. yds (4047 sq. m), but varying in some districts, (pl.) lands, fields; *county* (*land*) *of broad* ~*s*, Yorkshire. **acreage** (ā'kerĭj) *n.* Amount of acres, acres collectively.

Acre[2] (ā'ker). (also *St. Jean d'Acre*; Arab. *'Akkā*) Seaport of Israel; captured by Christians in 3rd Crusade, 1191; recaptured, the last Christian stronghold in the Holy Land, 1291.

ă'crĭd *adj.* Bitterly pungent, irritating; of bitter temper or manner. **ă'crĭdlȳ** *adv.* **acrĭ'dĭtȳ** *n.*

ăcrĭflā'vĭne (*or* -ēn) *n.* Orange-red powder used as antiseptic for wounds etc.

ăcrĭmō'nĭous *adj.* Marked by acrimony. **ăcrĭmō'nĭouslȳ** *adv.* **ăcrĭmō'nĭousnėss** *n.*

ă'crĭmonȳ *n.* Bitterness of temper or manner.

ă'crobăt *n.* Performer of daring and spectacular gymnastic feats, rope-dancer. **ăcrobă'tĭc** *adj.* **ăcrobă'tĭcallȳ** *adv.* **ăcrobă'tĭcs** *n.*

ăcromĕ'galȳ *n.* Disease due to over-activity of pituitary gland, resulting in overgrowth of bones esp. of extremities and skull.

ă'cronȳm *n.* Word formed from initial letters of other words (e.g. *Ernie*, *Nato*).

ăcrophō'bĭa *n.* (psych.) Dread of high places.

acrŏ'polĭs *n.* Citadel or upper fortified part of ancient Greek city, esp. (*A~*) that of Athens, situated on a hill about 250 ft high and richly adorned, esp. in 5th c. B.C., with architecture and sculpture.

acrŏ'ss *prep.* & *adv.* From side to side (of), to or on the other side (of), forming a cross with.

acrŏ'stĭc *n.* Poem etc. in which first or first and last letters of lines form word(s), the alphabet, etc.; puzzle so made.

ăcrotēr'ĭon *n.* (pl. *-ĭa*). (archit.) Pedestal for statue or ornament on angle of classical pediment.

acrȳ'lĭc *adj.* ~ *acid*, monobasic acid (CH_2:CH.COOH); ~ *fibre*, *resin*, synthetic substance prepared from acrylic acid or its derivatives. ~ *n.* Acrylic fibre, resin, etc.

ăct *n.* 1. Thing done, deed; process of doing something. 2. Decree passed by legislative body, court of justice, etc.; statute; (law) instrument in writing to verify facts. 3. Each of main divisions of dramatic work, in which definite part of whole action is completed. 4. Variety or circus turn. 5. *Acts* (*of the Apostles*), book of N.T. immediately following Gospels, relating early history of Christian Church and dealing largely with the lives and work of the Apostles Peter and Paul; traditionally ascribed to St. Luke. ~ *v.* 1. Represent in mimic action, perform (play); personate, play part of (on stage or fig. in real life); perform on stage. 2. Perform actions, do things; perform special functions; (of things) work, fulfil functions; ~ *as*, perform in character of, serve as; ~ *on*, influence, affect; regulate one's conduct by, put into practice.

A.C.T. *abbrev.* Australian Capital Territory.

Actae'on (ă-). (Gk myth.) Hunter who, because he accidentally saw Artemis bathing, was changed into a stag and killed by his own hounds.

ă'ctĭng *adj.* (esp., prefixed to title) Temporarily doing duties of; doing alone duties nominally shared with others.

ăctĭ'nĭc *adj.* Of actinism; ~ *rays*, rays possessing actinism, as the green, blue, violet, and ultra-violet rays of sunlight, which have a marked photochemical effect.

ă'ctĭnīde *n.* Element with atomic number between 89 (actinium) and 103.

ă'ctĭnĭsm *n.* That property of radiant energy, found esp. in the shorter wavelengths of the spectrum, by which chemical changes are produced, as in photography.

ăctĭ'nĭum *n.* (chem.) Radioactive element, found in pitchblende; symbol Ac, at. no. 89, principal isotope at. wt 227.

ăctĭnŏ'mėter *n.* Instrument for measuring heat radiation.

ăctĭnomŏr'phĭc *adj.* (biol.) Radially symmetrical. **ăctĭnomŏr'phĭsm** *n.*

ăctĭnomȳcē'tēs (-z) *n.pl.* Group of minute organisms of the order Actinomycetales, commonly held to be filamentous bacteria.

ăctĭnozō'an *adj.* & *n.* = ANTHOZOAN.

ă'ction *n.* 1. Process of acting, exertion of energy or influence; *out of* ~, not functioning; ~ *committee*, one chosen to take active steps; ~ *painting*, form of abstract art in which paint is applied by spontaneous or random action of artist. 2. Thing done. 3. Series of events represented (in drama). 4. Mode of acting; mechanism of instruments etc. 5. Legal process; *take* ~, institute legal proceedings; take steps in regard to any matter. 6. Battle, engagement between opposing forces. ~ *v.t.* Bring legal action against. **ă'ctionable** *adj.* Affording ground for action at law.

A'ctium (ă-). Promontory of W. coast of Greece (opposite modern Preveza on Gulf of Amurakia), near which, in 31 B.C., the fleets of Mark Antony and Cleopatra were decisively defeated by Octavian (Augustus).

ă'ctivāte *v.t.* Make active, esp. (phys.) radioactive; render (molecules) capable of reacting chemically. **ăctivā'tion** *n.*

ă'ctive *adj.* 1. Working, acting, operative; consisting in or marked by action; energetic, diligent; (of volcano) liable to erupt; ~ *list*, list of officers who are on active service or available for it; ~ *service*, full-time service in one of the armed forces. 2. (gram.) Applied to a voice of the verb comprising all forms of intransitive verbs, and those forms of transitive verbs that attribute the verbal action to the person or thing whence it proceeds; (loosely, of verb) in which the subject acts on or affects something else. 3. Radioactive. ~ *n.* Active voice or form of verb. **ă'ctivelў** *adv.*

ă'ctivist *n.* One who advocates taking action.

ăcti'vitў *n.* Exertion of energy; state or quality of being active, energy, diligence, liveliness; active force or operation; (phys.) radioactivity.

ă'ctor *n.* (fem. *a'ctrėss*) Dramatic performer; ~-*manager*, actor who is also manager of theatre or company.

ă'ctūal *adj.* Existing, real, present, current. **ă'ctūallў** *adv.* In actual fact, really; even, as a matter of fact.

ăctūă'litў *n.* Reality, realism.

ă'ctūalīze *v.t.* Realize in action, treat realistically.

ă'ctūarў *n.* Expert on insurance who calculates risks and premiums. **ăctūār'ial** *adj.*

ă'ctūāte *v.t.* Serve as motive to; communicate motion to. **ăctūā'tion** *n.*

acū'itў *n.* Sharpness, acuteness.

acū'lėate *adj.* 1. (zool.) Having a sting. 2. (bot.) Prickly, pointed.

acū'mĕn (*or* ă-) *n.* Keen discernment, penetration.

acū'mināte *adj.* (biol.) Tapering to a point.

ăcūpŭ'ncture *n.* 1. Chinese practice of pricking areas of skin with needles for therapeutic purposes. 2. (med.) Pricking of tissue with a needle for drainage etc.

acu'shla (-ōō-) *n.* Darling. [Ir. *ā cuisle* O pulse (of my heart)!]

acū'te *adj.* 1. Sharp, keen, penetrating; clever. 2. (of disease) Coming sharply to a crisis, not chronic. 3. (of sound) Sharp, shrill; having acute accent. 4. (fig.) Severe, crucial. 5. ~ *accent*, accent ´, originally indicating a high or rising pitch on the vowel so marked; ~ *angle*: see ANGLE[1]. **acū'telў** *adv.* **acū'tenėss** *n.*

A.C.W. *abbrev.* Aircraftwoman.

ă'cўl *n.* (chem.) Acid radical.

ăd *n.* (colloq.) Advertisement; advertising.

ad- *prefix.* To, with sense of motion or direction to, reduction or change into, addition, adherence, increase, or intensification.

A.D. *abbrev.* Anno Domini.

ă'dage *n.* Traditional maxim, proverb.

adagio (*a*dahj'yō) *adv.*, *adj.*, *n.* (pl. *-os*). (mus. & dancing) Leisurely (passage or movement). [It.]

A'dalbĕrt (ă-), St. (*c* 955–97). Missionary in N. Germany and Poland, called 'apostle of the

ADAM AND EVE

Prussians'; martyred in Bremen, commemorated 23 April.

A'dam[1] (ă-). (in Hebrew tradition) The first man (see Gen. 2: 4, 3: 24), who lived with his wife Eve in the Garden of Eden, but was driven from it for eating the fruit (traditionally an apple) of 'the tree of the knowledge of good and evil'; *the old* ~, person's innate sinful nature; ~*'s ale*, water; ~*'s apple*, projection formed by the THYROID cartilage, particularly prominent in males; ~*'s Peak*, mountain in Ceylon with a hollow on the summit which is said by Muslims to be Adam's footprint and by Buddhists to be Buddha's. [Heb., = 'man']

A'dam[2] (ă-), Robert (1728–92). The best known of a family of Scottish architects; introduced into Britain a neo-Classical style of decoration, furniture, etc., based on ancient Roman and Italian Renaissance designs; *James* ~ (1730–94), architect, his brother.

ă'damant *n.* Thing impenetrably hard; stubborn or unyielding person; fabulous mineral with properties of hardness and attraction. **ădamă'ntīne** *adj.* **ă'damant** *adj.* Unshakeable, inflexible. **ă'damantlў** *adv.*

A'damīte (ă-) *n.* 1. Child of Adam, human being; unclothed man. 2. Member of heretical sect in N. Africa (2nd and 3rd centuries), who believed that they enjoyed Adam's original state of innocency, and wore no clothes.

A'dams[1] (ă-, -z), John (1735–1826). 2nd president of U.S. 1797–1801; member of committee formed to draft Declaration of Independence.

A'dams[2] (ă-, -z), John (*c* 1760–1829) alias Alexander Smith. English seaman, one of the *Bounty*[2] mutineers; founded settlement on Pitcairn Island.

A'dams[3] (ă-, -z), John Couch (1819–92). English astronomer, discoverer of the planet Neptune.

A'dams[4] (ă-, -z), John Quincy (1767–1848). Son of John ADAMS[1]; 6th president of U.S. 1825–9.

Adanson (ădahńsawń), Michel (1727–1806). French botanist; first exponent of classification of plants into natural orders.

adă'pt *v.* Suit, make suitable, fit (*to*, *for*); alter, modify, so as to make suitable for new surroundings, purpose, etc. **adăptabĭ'lĭtў** *n.* **adă'ptable** *adj.*

ădaptā'tion *n.* (esp. biol.) Process, characteristic of living matter by which organism or species becomes adjusted to its environment; that which is so adapted.

A.D.C. *abbrev.* Aide-de-camp.

ădd *v.* Join by way of increase or supplement; perform arithmetical process of addition; ~ *up*, find sum of; make desired total (also fig.); *adding machine*, machine that performs arithmetical processes.

ă'ddăx *n.* Large light-coloured antelope (*Addax nasomaculatus*) of N.-Afr. deserts, with spiral horns.

addĕ'ndum *n.* (pl. *-da*). Something to be added, addition, appendix.

ă'dder *n.* Small venomous snake, viper (*Vipera berus*), only poisonous snake found in England; *death* ~, *horned* ~, *puff* ~, highly poisonous African and Australian species of Viperidae; ~*'s tongue*,

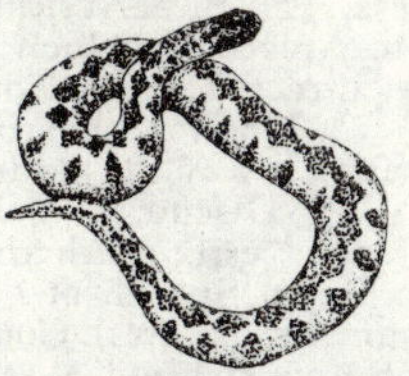

fern (*Ophioglossum vulgatum*); Amer. white- or yellow-flowered dog-tooth violet.

ă'ddĭct *n.* One addicted to drug etc.; devotee of pastime etc. **addĭ'ctėd** *adj.* Devoted *to* or enslaved by drug, pastime, etc. **addĭ'ction** *n.* **addĭ'ctĭve** *adj.* Causing addiction.

A'ddĭson[1] (ă-), Joseph (1672–1719). English essayist and poet; contributor to 'Tatler' and joint-author (with Steele) of 'Spectator'.

A'ddĭson[2] (ă-), Thomas (1793–1860). English physician; first to recognize *~'s disease*, disease connected with defective functioning of suprarenal glands and freq. characterized by bronzy pigmentation of skin.

addĭ'tion *n.* Adding; arithmetical process of putting together two or more numbers or amounts to form a total; thing added; *in ~*, as an added thing etc. (*to*); *~ reaction*, (chem.) one in which two univalent atoms or radicals are taken up by an unsaturated molecule, the double bond being converted into a single bond. **addĭ'tional** *adj.* **addĭ'tionallȳ** *adv.*

ă'ddĭtĭve *adj.* Of addition; to be added; *~ process*, process of colour reproduction in which the primary colours are superimposed one upon another. *~ n.* Substance added to mixture or alloy in order to impart specific qualities to the resulting product.

ă'ddle *v.* Make or become addled. *~ adj. ~-headed, ~-pated*, confused in mind. **ă'ddled** (-ld) *adj.* (of egg) Rotten, producing no chicken; muddled, crazy; *A~ Parliament*, that summoned in April 1614 and dissolved in June, without having passed a Bill.

addrĕ'ss *n.* 1. Readiness, skill, adroitness. 2. Superscription of letter etc.; place to which letters etc. are directed; place of residence. 3. Manner, bearing, in conversation; way of addressing person. 4. Discourse delivered to audience; esp., parliamentary reply to Royal Speech at opening of Parliament. 5. (pl.) Courteous approach, courtship. *~ v.t.* 1. Direct in speech or writing; speak to; send as written message (*to*); write address on outside of (letter etc.). 2. Apply *oneself*, direct one's skill or energies (*to*). 3. (golf) *~ the ball*, take aim, prepare to make stroke.

ăddrĕssee' *n.* Person to whom letter etc. is addressed.

addrĕ'ssogrăph (*or* -ahf) *n.* Machine for addressing letters. [trade-name]

addū'ce *v.t.* Cite as proof or instance.

addū'cent *adj.* (anat., of muscles) Drawing together certain parts of the body.

addŭ'ct *v.t.* Draw to a common centre or towards median line or long axis of body. **addŭ'ction, addŭ'ctor** *ns.*

A'dėlaide (ă-). Seaport and capital of South Australia.

Adélie Lănd (*a*dā'lē). French territory in coastal region of Antarctica, south of Australia.

A'den (ā-). Seaport and coaling-station in SW. Arabia near entrance to Red Sea; capital city of the People's Democratic Republic of Yemen; until 1967 part of a British protectorate.

ă'dėnoids (-z) *n.pl.* Pathological enlargement of lymphoid tissue between back of nose and throat, occurring usu. in children and often obstructing breathing. **ădėnoi'dal** *adj.* **ădėnoi'dallȳ** *adv.*

ădėnō'ma *n.* (pl. *-ata, -as*) (med.) Benign tumour in or resembling glandular tissue.

ă'dĕpt (*or* adĕ'pt) *adj.* Thoroughly proficient (*in*). **ă'dept** *n.* Adept person.

ă'dėquate *adj.* Proportionate *to* what is necessary; sufficient. **ă'dėquatelȳ** *adv.* **ă'dėquacȳ** *n.*

ăd fīnĕm (*or* fē-). Towards the end (abbrev. *ad fin.*). [L]

adhēr'e *v.i.* Stick fast, cleave (*to*).

adhēr'ent *adj.* Sticking; connected with (*to*). *~ n.* Supporter (*of* party etc.). **adhēr'ence** *n.*

adhē'sion *n.* Adhering; (chem.) molecular force of attraction between different kinds of molecules (opp. COHESION); (med.) abnormal union of tissue as a result of inflammation.

adhē'sĭve (*or* -z-) *adj.* & *n.* Adhering, sticky (substance). **adhē'sĭvelȳ** *adv.*

ăd hŏc. Arranged for this purpose; special(ly). [L]

ădiabă'tĭc *adj.* (of physical change) Involving neither loss nor gain of heat.

adieu (*a*dū') *int.* & *n.* (pl. *-s, -x*, pr. -z) Goodbye; *make, take, one's ~*, say good-bye. [Fr. *à Dieu* to God]

ăd ĭnfĭnī'tum. Without limit, for ever. [L]

ăd ĭnĭ'tium (-shium). At the beginning (abbrev. *ad init.*). [L]

ăd ĭ'nterĭm. For the meantime. [L]

ă'dĭpocēre *n.* Greyish fatty or saponaceous substance, chiefly fatty acids with minor qualities of mineral salts, etc., formed in dead animal bodies by decomposition of body fats when exposed to moisture.

ă'dĭpōse *adj.* Of fat, fatty; ~ *tissue*, connective tissue cells in animal body containing large globules of fat. **ădĭpŏ'sĭtȳ** *n.*

Adĭrŏ'ndăck Mou'ntains (ă-, -tĭnz). (also *Adirondacks*) Group of mountains in New York State, U.S., a holiday resort.

ă'dĭt *n.* Horizontal entrance to, or passage in, mine.

A'dĭtĭ (ah-). (in Veda) Personification of infinity or of all-embracing nature; (Hinduism) mother of the gods.

Adj. *abbrev.* Adjutant.

adjā'cent (*a*j-) *adj.* Lying near *to*, contiguous. **adjā'cencȳ** *n.*

ă'djėctĭve (ăj-) *adj.* Additional, not standing by itself, dependent; ~ *law*, subsidiary part of law, procedure. ~ *n.* (gram.) Name of attribute added to name of thing to describe thing more fully or definitely. **ădjėctī'val** *adj.* **ădjėctī'vallȳ** *adv.*

adjoi'n (*a*j-) *v.t.* Be contiguous with.

adjourn (*a*jẽr'n) *v.* Put off, postpone; break off; (of persons met together) suspend proceedings and separate; move *to* another place. **adjour'nment** *n.*(esp.) *move the* ~ (in House of Commons), bring motion that the House shall adjourn, esp. in order to discuss a specified matter (which, if the motion is carried, is discussed the same evening).

Adjt *abbrev.* Adjutant.

adjŭ'dge (*a*j-) *v.t.* Adjudicate upon; pronounce or award judicially; condemn.

adju'dĭcāte (*a*jōō-) *v.* Decide upon; pronounce; sit in judgement and pronounce sentence; award prizes etc. in competition. **adjudĭcā'tion, adju'dĭcātor** *ns.*

ă'djŭnct (ăj-) *n.* Subordinate or incidental thing, accompaniment; (gram.) amplification of the predicate, subject, etc.; (logic) non-essential attribute. **adjŭ'nctĭve** *adj.* **adjŭ'nctĭvelȳ** *adv.*

adjure (*a*joor') *v.t.* Charge under oath or penalty of curse *to* do; request earnestly. **ădjurā'tion** *n.*

adjŭ'st (*a*j-) *v.* Arrange, put in order; harmonize; adapt (*to*). **adjŭ'stment** *n.* **adjŭ'stable** *adj.*

ă'djutant (ăjōō-) *n.* 1. (army etc.) Officer assisting commanding officer by communicating orders, conducting correspondence, etc.; *A~-General*, second executive officer of British General Staff of Army, whose duties are concerned with recruiting, training, etc. 2. (also ~ *bird*) Large stork of genus *Leptoptilus*, esp. Indian *L. dubius*, walking with stiff-legged gait.

A'dler (ă-), Alfred (1870–1937). Austrian psychologist; put forward theory of inferiority complex.

ad lib. *abbrev.* *Ad libitum.*

ă'dlĭ'b *v.* (colloq., orig. U.S.) Improvise (words, music, etc.) in acting etc.

ăd lĭ'bĭtum. To the extent etc. desired. [L]

Adm. *abbrev.* Admiral.

Admē'tus (ă-). (Gk legend) Husband of ALCESTIS.

admĭ'nĭster *v.* 1. Manage (affairs, estate, etc.); dispense (justice, sacraments, etc.); act as administrator. 2. Formally present (oath to be sworn) *to*. 3. Furnish, give; apply (remedies). 4. Contribute *to* (one's comfort etc.)

admĭnĭstrā'tion *n.* 1. Administering; management; management of public affairs, government; (law) management of deceased person's estate; *letters of* ~, authority to administer intestate estate. 2. Body of administrators; ministry, Government. **admĭ'nĭstrāte** *v.* Administer. **admĭ'nĭstratĭve** *adj.* Of administration; executive. **admĭ'nĭstrātor** *n.* **admĭ'nĭstrātrĭx** *n.* (pl. *-trīcēs*).

Female administrator (in legal sense).

ă'dmirable *adj.* Worthy of admiration; estimable, excellent. **ă'dmirablў** *adv.*

ă'dmiral *n.* 1. Naval officer commanding fleet or subdivision of fleet; (hist.) commander-in-chief of navy; *A~ of the Fleet*, highest rank of British naval officers. 2. Privileged commander of fishing or merchant fleet. 3. (hist.) Ship that carries the admiral, flagship. 4. *red ~*, *white ~*, two European species of butterfly (*Vanessa atalanta*, *Limenitis sibylla*). [Arab. *'amīr* commander]

ă'dmiraltў *n.* 1. Office, rank, of admiral; (rhet.) command of the seas. 2. *A~ Board*, department of Ministry of Defence superintending Royal Navy; (*High*) *Court of A~*, part of High Court of Justice concerned with maritime questions and offences.

A'dmiraltў I'slands (ă-, īlandz). Group of small islands of Bismarck Archipelago, under Australian administration.

admīr'e *v.t.* Regard with pleased surprise or approval; (colloq.) express admiration of. **ădmirā'tion** *n.* **admīr'er** *n.* One who admires; (archaic) lover.

admĭ'ssion *n.* Admitting, being admitted, fee for this; acknowledgement that something is true.

admĭ't *v.* 1. Allow entrance or access (*to*). 2. Allow, permit; accept as valid or true; acknowledge; *~ of*, be capable of or compatible with; leave room for. **admĭ'ttance** *n.* **admĭ'ttėdlў** *adv.*

admĭ'x *n.* Add as an ingredient, mingle *with*. **admĭ'xture** *n.*

admŏ'nish *v.t.* Urge; give advice; warn; remind, inform. **admŏ'nĭshment** *n.*

ădmonĭ'tion *n.* Admonishing; warning, reproof. **admŏn'itorў** *adj.*

ăd nau'sėăm (*or* -z-). To a disgusting extent. [L]

ado' (-ōō) *n.* Fuss; difficulty.

adō'bė (*or* -ō'b) *n.* Sun-dried clay used for building by Indians in Mexico etc.; house made of such clay bricks. [Span., f. *adobar* daub, plaster]

ădolĕ'scent *adj.* & *n.* (Person) between childhood and maturity; between the ages (roughly) of 14 and 20. **ădolĕ'scence** *n.*

Adōnā'ī (*or* -ah'ī). 1. Hebrew title of reverence for God, pronounced as substitute for the tetragrammaton. 2. (liturgy) Appellation of Christ. [Heb., = 'my lord(s)']

Adō'nĭs. (Gk myth.) Beautiful youth loved by Aphrodite; he was killed by a boar but restored to life by Persephone; Zeus decreed that he should spend part of each year with her and the rest on earth with Aphrodite; hence, handsome young man; *~ blue*, kind of butterfly, *Lysandra bellargus*.

adŏ'pt *v.t.* Take into relationship not previously occupied, esp. take as one's own child, assume rights and duties of parent towards; take (idea etc.) from another and use as one's own; take up, choose; assume responsibility for (road etc.); approve (accounts, report). **adŏ'ption** *n.* *~ society*, organization which arranges adoption of orphaned or unwanted infants. **adŏ'ptive** *adj.*

adôr'e *v.t.* Regard with very deep respect and affection; worship as a deity; like very much; (R.C. Ch.) offer form of reverence to. **adôr'able** *adj.* **adôr'ablў** *adv.* **ădorā'tion** *n.*

adôr'er *n.* Worshipper; ardent admirer, lover.

adôr'n *v.t.* Add beauty or lustre to; furnish with ornament(s). **adôr'nment** *n.*

Adră'stus. (Gk myth.) King of Argos and leader of expeditions against Thebes.

ăd rĕm. To the point; to the purpose. [L]

adrē'nal *adj.* At or near kidney; *~ gland*, suprarenal gland, one of two yellowish-brown ductless glands lying on upper anterior surface of kidneys. *~ n.* Adrenal gland.

adrĕ'nalin *n.* Hormone secreted by adrenal glands and affecting circulation and muscular action;

this obtained from these glands in animals or prepared synthetically, used in medicine as a stimulant.

A'drian (ā-). Name of six popes: *Adrian I*, pope 772–95; *Adrian II*, pope 867–72; *Adrian III*, pope 884–5; *Adrian IV* (Nicholas Breakspear), pope 1154–9, only English pope; *Adrian V*, pope in 1276; *Adrian VI*, pope 1522–3, most recent non-Italian pope, born at Utrecht.

Adrianō'ple (ā-). Former name of Edirne; scene of a battle (A.D. 378) in which Romans were defeated by Visigoths. [f. the emperor HADRIAN]

Adriă'tic (ā-) *adj.* ~ *Sea*, arm of Mediterranean lying between Italy and Balkan peninsula. ~ *n.* Adriatic Sea; *Marriage of the* ~, (hist.) annual Ascension-Day ceremony symbolizing the sea-power of Venice, during which the Doge dropped a ring into the water from his state barge.

adrĭ'ft *adj.* Drifting; at mercy of wind and tide or of circumstances; (colloq.) not at one's post; deficient in knowledge, training, etc.

adroi't *adj.* Dextrous, deft. **adroi'tlў** *adv.* **adroi'tnėss** *n.*

ădscĭtĭ'tious (-shus) *adj.* Adopted from without; supplemental.

adsŏr'b *v.t.* Act as adsorbent of. **adsŏr'bent** *adj.* & *n.* (Substance) producing adsorption.

adsŏr'ption *n.* Process by which specific gases, vapours, or substances in solution adhere to exposed surfaces of certain, usu. solid, materials. **adsŏr'ptĭve** *adj.*

ă'dsŭm (*or* -sōōm) *int.* I am here, as answer in roll-call etc. [L]

ă'dūlāte *v.t.* Flatter basely. **ădūlā'tion** *n.* **ă'dūlātorў** *adj.*

Adŭ'llam. Cave where all who were distressed, in debt, or discontented came to join David when he fled from Saul (see 1 Sam. 22: 1–2); applied by John Bright to Liberal M.P.s who voted with Conservatives against Reform Bill of 1866. **Adŭ'llamīte** *n.* Member of any dissident political group.

ă'dult (*or* adŭ'lt) *adj.* Fully grown, mature. ~ *n.* Adult person, animal, plant, etc.; ~ *education*, courses etc. provided by local authorities for persons over school age.

adŭ'lterant *adj.* & *n.* (Thing) employed in adulterating.

adŭ'lterāte[1] *v.t.* Falsify, corrupt, debase, esp. by admixture of baser ingredients. **adŭlterā'tion** *n.*

adŭ'lterate[2] *adj.* Defiled by adultery; spurious, counterfeit.

adŭ'lterer *n.* (fem. *adŭ'lterėss*) Person guilty of adultery.

adŭ'lterīne *adj.* Of, born of, adultery; adulterated, counterfeit; illegal, unlicensed.

adŭ'lterў *n.* Voluntary sexual intercourse of married person with one who is not his or her spouse. **adŭ'lterous** *adj.* **adŭ'lterouslў** *adv.*

ă'dumbrāte (*or* adŭ'm-) *v.t.* Represent in outline; faintly indicate; typify, foreshadow; overshadow. **ădumbrā'tion** *n.*

ăd valŏr'ĕm. (of taxes or duties) In proportion to (estimated) value of goods. [L]

adva'nce (-vah-) *n.* 1. Going forward, progress. 2. Personal approach, overture; (pl.) amorous approaches. 3. Rise in price. 4. Payment beforehand; loan. 5. *in* ~, in front, ahead; beforehand; ~ *copy*, copy of book etc., supplied before publication; ~ *guard*, guard before main body of army. ~ *v.* Move or put forward; bring forward (claims etc.); accelerate (events); pay (money) before it is due; lend; help on, promote; make progress; raise (price), rise (in price). **adva'nced** (-st) *adj.* Far on in progress; ahead of times, others, etc. **adva'ncement** *n.* (esp.) Promotion, preferment; furtherance, improvement.

adva'ntage (-vah-) *n.* Better position, precedence, superiority; favourable circumstance; (lawn tennis) next point won after deuce (~ *in*, ~ *out*, advantage to server, striker); *mechanical* ~: see MECHANICAL; *take* ~ *of*, use (circumstance) profitably; exploit (person) unfairly. ~ *v.t.* Be beneficial to;

be an advantage to; further, promote. **ădvantā'geous** (-j*us*) *adj.* **ădvantā'geouslў** *adv.*

ă'dvent *n.* 1. Arrival, esp. important one. 2. *A~*, season before Christmas, beginning on 4th Sunday before it; coming of Christ; (also *Second A~*) second coming of Christ.

A'dventist (ă-) *n.* (also *Second ~*) Member of one of various sects believing in imminence of second coming of Christ.

ădventi'tious (-sh*us*) *adj.* Coming from without, accidental, casual; (bot.) in an unusual position, sporadic (*~ root*); (law, of inheritance) coming from a stranger or by collateral succession. **ădventi'tiouslў** *adv.*

advĕ'nture *n.* Unexpected or exciting experience; daring enterprise, hazardous activity. *~ v.* 1. (rhet.) Hazard, imperil; incur risk. 2. Dare to go or come *into*, dare to enter *on*.

advĕ'nturer (-ch*er*-) *n.* (fem. *advĕ'nturĕss*) One who seeks adventure; speculator; one who lives by his wits.

advĕ'nturous (-ch*er*-) *adj.* Venturesome, enterprising. **advĕ'nturouslў** *adv.*

ă'dvêrb *n.* (gram.) Word expressing any relation of place, time, circumstance, causality, manner, or degree, or modifying or limiting attribute or predicate. **ădvêr'bial** *adj.* **advêr'biallў** *adv.*

ă'dversarў *n.* Opponent, enemy; *the A~*, the Devil.

advêr'sative *adj.* (of words etc.) Expressing opposition or antithesis. **advêr'sativelў** *adv.*

ă'dvêrse *adj.* Contrary, hostile *to*; hurtful, injurious. **ă'dverselў** *adv.*

advêr'sitў *n.* Condition of adverse fortune; misfortune.

advêr't[1] *v.i.* Refer *to*.

ă'dvert[2] *n.* (colloq.) Advertisement.

ă'dvertīse (-z) *v.* Notify, warn, inform; make generally or publicly known; proclaim merits of; esp., try to encourage sales of (product) by public announcement; *~ for*, ask for by public notice. **ă'dvertīser** *n.*

advêr'tisement (-sm-) *n.* Advertising; public announcement (in newspaper, by posters, etc.).

advī'ce *n.* Opinion given or offered as to action; information given, news; (pl.) communications from a distance; (commerc.) formal notice of transactions.

advī'sable (-z-) *adj.* To be recommended; expedient. **advīsabĭ'litў** *n.*

advī'se (-z) *v.* Offer advice (to); recommend; (commerc.) announce. **advī'sed** (-zd) *adj.* Deliberate, considered; judicious. **advī'sĕdlў** *adv.*

advī'ser (-z-) *n.* Counsellor, esp. person habitually consulted; *legal ~*, solicitor.

advī'sorў (-z-) *adj.* Giving advice; consisting in giving advice.

ă'dvocacў *n.* Function of advocate; pleading in support *of*.

ă'dvocate *n.* Professional pleader in court of justice, counsel (technical title in Roman law courts and in countries retaining Roman law, as Scotland, France, etc.); one who pleads for another; one who speaks for cause etc.; *Faculty of Advocates*, Scottish bar; *Lord A~*, principal law-officer of Crown in Scotland; *Advocates' Library*, library in Edinburgh opened 1689 and presented to nation by Faculty of Advocates, 1924; since 1925 the National Library of Scotland. **ă'dvocāte** *v.t.* Plead for, support (policy etc.).

ădvocā'tus dĭă'bolī (*or* -aht-, -lē). Devil's advocate (see DEVIL). [L]

advow'son (-z-) *n.* (law) Right of presentation to benefice.

advt. *abbrev.* Advertisement.

ă'dўtum *n.* (pl. *-ta*). Innermost part of temple; private chamber, sanctum. [Gk *aduton* not to be entered (*duō* enter)]

ădze *n.* Carpenter's tool for cutting away surface of wood, like axe with arched blade at right angles to handle. *~ v.t.* Dress or cut with adze.

A.E. Pseudonym of G. W. RUSSELL[2].

ae'dīle *n.* (Rom. hist.) Magistrate who superintended public buildings, games, shows, etc.

Aegē'an (ĭj-) *adj.* ~ *Sea*, arm of Mediterranean between Greece and Asia Minor; ~ *Civilization*, Bronze Age civilization of the coasts and islands of the Aegean Sea, the MINOAN and MYCENAEAN civilizations. ~ *n.* Aegean Sea.

Aegir (ē'jēr). (Scand. myth.) Chief of the sea-giants, representing the peaceful ocean.

ae'gis *n.* (Gk myth.) Shield of Zeus or Athene; *under the* ~ *of*, under the protection or sponsorship of.

Aegi'sthus (ĭg- *or* ĭj-). (Gk legend) Nephew of Atreus, whom he murdered, and lover of CLYTEMNESTRA, who helped him murder her husband Agamemnon.

ae'grotăt *n.* (Degree awarded on) certificate that candidate is ill. [L, = 'he is sick']

Æ'lfric (ăl-) (*c* 955–1020). English monk and writer, chiefly of homilies and lives of saints.

Aenē'as (ĭn-) (Gk & Rom. legend) Trojan hero; son of Anchises and Aphrodite; escaped after fall of Troy and after long wandering reached the Tiber; regarded by Romans as founder of their State.

Aenē'id (ĭn-; *or* ē'nĭĭd). Epic poem by Virgil in twelve books of Latin hexameters relating story of Aeneas after fall of Troy.

Aeō'lian *adj.* 1. Of Aeolis. 2. Of Aeolus; caused by, relating to, wind; ~ *deposit*, substance deposited on earth by wind, as desert sand; ~ *harp*, musical instrument consisting of rectangular box on or in which are stretched strings or wires producing musical sounds as the wind passes across them; ~ *Islands*, ancient name of Lipari Islands; ~ *mode*, (mus.) ancient Greek mode; 9th of ecclesiastical modes, with A as final and E as dominant.

Ae'olis. Coastal district of NW. Asia Minor colonized by Greeks at very early date.

Ae'olus. (Gk myth.) God of the winds.

ae'on, ē'on *n.* An age of the universe; immeasurable period; eternity.

aepyŏr'nis *n.* Gigantic flightless extinct bird of genus *A* ~, resembling moa and known from remains found in Madagascar.

ā'erāte (*or* ār-) *v.t.* Expose to mechanical or chemical action of air; charge with carbon dioxide; *aerated waters*, sweetened flavoured beverages charged with carbon dioxide. **aerā'tion, aer'ātor** *ns.*

aer'ial (ār-) *adj.* Of air, gaseous; ethereal; immaterial, imaginary; atmospheric; existing, moving, happening, in the air; conducted by aircraft. ~ *n.* Radiating or receiving wire(s) or rod used in radio communication. **aer'ialist** *n.* Performer on high wire or trapeze.

aer'ie, aer'y̆ (*or* ārĭ) *n.* Varr. of EYRIE.

aer'ifŏrm (ār-) *adj.* Of the form of air, gaseous; unsubstantial.

aero-, aer- (ār-) *prefix.* Air-; of aircraft.

aerobă'tics (ār-) *n.pl.* Feats of expert and often spectacular aviation. **aerobă'tic** *adj.*

ā'erōbe (*or* ār'-) *n.* Micro-organism capable of living only in the presence of atmospheric oxygen; opp. ANAEROBE. **āerō'bic** *adj.*

aerobiŏ'logy̆ (ār-) *n.* Study of airborne micro-organisms esp. as agents of infection.

aer'odrōme *n.* Airfield.

aerody̆nă'mics (ār-) *n.* Branch of dynamics dealing with the effects produced in air by the motion of solid bodies through it and the effects produced on such bodies by the air through which they pass. **aerody̆nă'mic, -ical** *adjs.* **aerody̆nă'micallly̆** *adv.* **aerody̆nă'micist** *n.*

aer'ody̆ne (ār-) *n.* Heavier-than-air aircraft.

aer'ofoil (ār-) *n.* Any or all of the lift-producing surfaces of an aircraft, as wings, ailerons, tailplane, fins, etc.

aer'olīte, -lith (ār-) *n.* Meteorite.

aer'onaut (ār-) *n.* (obs.) Navigator or pilot of airship or aeroplane. **aeronaut'ic, -ical** *adjs.* Of, pertaining to, aeronautics.

aeronau'tĭcs *n.pl.* Science or practice of flight; aerial navigation.

aer'oplāne (ār-) *n.* Heavier-than-air powered flying machine with wings. (*Illustration, p. 12.*)

aer'osŏl (ār-) *n.* System of colloidal particles dispersed in a gas, as mist, fog, etc.; (container

holding) substance packed under pressure with spraying device.

aer'ospāce (ār-) *n.* Earth's atmosphere and outer space; (*attrib.*) of (industry concerned with) aircraft etc. for operation in aerospace.

aerostă'tĭcs (ār-) *n.* Physics of gases in equilibrium; science of air navigation. **aerostăt'ĭc, -ĭcal** *adjs.*

Ae'schȳlus (ēsk-) (525–456 B.C.). Athenian poet regarded as founder of Greek tragic drama; of his many tragedies only seven are extant: 'The Persians', 'The Seven against Thebes', 'Prometheus Bound', 'The Suppliants', and the Orestes trilogy, 'Agamemnon', 'Choephori', and 'Eumenides'.

Aescūlā'pĭus. (Rom. myth.) = ASCLEPIUS.

Æ'sir (ă-). (Scand. myth.) Collective name of the gods.

Ae'sŏp (6th c. B.C.). Semi-legendary Phrygian teller of fables about animals, said to have been a slave in Samos; the fables attributed to him are prob. compiled from various sources.

ae'sthēte *n.* Professed lover of beauty.

aesthĕ'tĭc *adj.* Of appreciation of the beautiful; having such appreciation; in accordance with principles of good taste; *A~ Movement*, movement in late 19th-c. England advocating 'art for art's sake'. **aesthĕ'tĭcallȳ** *adv.* **aesthĕ'tĭcism** *n.* **aesthĕ'tĭc, -ĭcs** *ns.* Philosophy of the beautiful; philosophy of art.

ae'stĭval *adj.* Of summer. **ae'stĭvāte** *v.i.* Spend the summer, esp. (zool.) in state of torpor. **aestĭvā'tion** *n.* (zool.) Aestivating; (bot.) arrangement of petals in flower-bud before expansion.

aeta'tĭs (ītah-). Of or at the age of (abbrev. *aet.*, *ae'tăt.*). [L]

Æthelred: see ETHELRED.

Æthelstan: see ATHELSTAN.

aetĭŏ'logȳ *n.* Assignment of a cause; philosophy of causation; (med.) science of causes of disease. **aetĭolŏ'gĭcal** *adj.* **aetĭolŏ'gĭcallȳ** *adv.*

Aëtius (āĕ'tĭŭs) (d. 454). Roman general who, with Theodoric, defeated Attila at Châlons, 451.

A.F. *abbrev.* Admiral of the Fleet; audio FREQUENCY.

A.F.A. *abbrev.* Amateur Football Alliance.

afar' *adv.* At, to, a distance; *from ~*, from a distance.

A'fars and I'ssas (ăfarz, ĭ-), Territory of the. Small French territory on NE. coast of Africa; formerly Somaliland, independent since 1977; capital, Jibouti.

A.F.A.S. *abbrev.* Associate of the Faculty of Architects and Surveyors.

A.F.C. *abbrev.* Air Force Cross.

ă'ffable *adj.* Easy of address, courteous, complaisant. **ă'ffablȳ** *adv.* **affabĭ'lĭtȳ** *n.*

affair' *n.* Business, concern; (colloq.) thing; love affair; (pl.) ordinary pursuits of life; (pl.) public, commercial or professional business or transactions.

ăffaire *n.* Love affair. [Fr.]

affĕ'ct[1] *v.t.* Practise, use; assume (character); pretend to have or feel; pretend (*to* do). **affĕ'ctĕd**

adj. Artificially assumed or displayed; full of affectation. **affĕ'ctėdlў** *adv.*

affĕ'ct² *v.t.* Attack (as disease); move, touch; produce (material effect on). **affĕ'cting** *adj.* Emotionally moving. **affĕ'ctinglў** *adv.*

ă'ffĕct³ *n.* (psychol.) Emotion, feeling, as antecedent of action.

ăffėctā'tion *n.* Studied display *of*; artificiality of manner; pretence.

affĕ'ction *n.* 1. Affecting, being affected. 2. Mental state, emotion; kindly feeling, love. 3. Bodily state due to any influence; (esp.) malady, disease. 4. Temporary or non-essential state, relation, etc.; property, attribute. **affĕ'ctionate** *adj.* Loving, fond; showing love or tenderness. **affĕ'ctionatelў** *adv.*

affĕ'ctive *adj.* Of the affections, emotional.

ă'fferent *adj.* (of blood- and lymph-vessels, nerves, etc.) Bringing, conducting, inwards or towards.

affī'ance *v.t.* Promise solemnly in marriage.

ăffĭdā'vĭt *n.* Written statement, confirmed by oath, to be used as judicial proof. [L, = 'has stated on oath']

affĭ'liāte *v.t.* 1. (of institution) Adopt (persons as members, societies as branches); attach *to*, connect *with* (a society). 2. (law) Fix paternity of (illegitimate child) for purpose of maintenance; father (thing) *upon*, trace *to*. **affĭliā'tion** *n.* ~ *order*, (law) magistrate's order requiring payment of maintenance by man for his illegitimate child.

affĭ'nĭtў *n.* Relationship, relations, by marriage or in general; structural resemblance; similarity of character suggesting relationship; liking, attraction; (chem.) tendency of substances to combine with others.

affir'm *v.* Assert strongly; make formal declaration or affirmation; state in the affirmative; ratify (judgement). **ăffirmā'tion** *n.* Affirming, esp. (law) solemn declaration by person who conscientiously declines taking oath.

affir'matĭve *adj.* Affirming, expressing assent; (logic) expressing agreement of the two terms of a proposition. ~ *n.* Affirmative answer. **affir'matĭvelў** *adv.*

affĭ'x *v.t.* Fasten, append, attach. **ă'ffĭx** *n.* Appendage, addition; (gram.) prefix or suffix.

afflā'tus *n.* Divine impulse; inspiration.

afflĭ'ct *v.t.* Distress with bodily or mental suffering. **afflĭ'ction** *n.* Misery, distress; pain, calamity.

ă'ffluent (-lōō-) *adj.* Flowing freely; abounding; wealthy. ~ *n.* Tributary stream. **ă'ffluence** *n.* Wealth, abundance.

ă'fflŭx *n.* Flow towards a point; accession.

affor'd *v.t.* (with *can*) Have the means, be rich enough, manage to spare (time etc.); furnish; bestow; yield supply of.

affŏ'rėst *v.t.* Convert into a forest; plant with trees. **affŏrėstā'tion** *n.*

affră'nchīse (-z) *v.t.* Free from servitude or obligation.

affray' *n.* Breach of peace caused by fighting or rioting in public place.

affri'ght (-īt) *v.t.* (archaic) Frighten. ~ *n.* Alarm, terror.

affro'nt (-ŭnt) *v.t.* Insult openly; face defiantly. **affro'ntėd** *adj.* (her.) Guardant; also face to face. **affro'nt** *n.* Open insult.

affū'sion *n.* Pouring on, esp. of water in baptism.

Afghan (ă'fgăn) *adj.* Of Afghanistan or its people; (strictly) of the Duranni tribe of Pathans who inhabit E. Afghanistan and speak Pashtu; of the Pashtu language; ~ *hound*, hunting dog of ancient breed with long silky hair and tuft on head; ~ *Wars*, three campaigns (1839–42, 1879–80, 1919) fought by the British in Afghanistan in order to secure the NW. frontier of India. ~ *n.* 1. Afghan person or language. 2. (*a*~) knitted or crocheted woollen coverlet.

ăfghă'nĭ (ăfg-) *n.* Principal monetary unit of Afghanistan, = 100 puls.

Afghă'nĭstăn (ăfg-). Inland republic of SW. Asia bounded on

W. by Iran, on S. and E. by Pakistan and on N. by U.S.S.R.; founded in 18th c. by Durrani tribe of Pathans who broke away from Mogul Empire; later under British protection but declared a sovereign state in 1921; inhabited by various chiefly Muslim peoples, including Afghans and Tajiks, speaking several languages of which the principal are Pashtu and Persian (the official language); capital, Kabul.

afĭciona'do (-syonahdō) *n.* Devotee of bullfighting (or other sport or pastime). [Sp.]

afie'ld *adv.* On, in, or to the field; away, at a distance.

afīr'e *adv.* & *pred. adj.* On fire.

A.F.L. *abbrev.* American Federation of Labor.

aflā'me *adv.* & *pred. adj.* In flames; in a glow of light.

afloa't *adv.* & *pred. adj.* Floating; at sea, on board ship; full of water; out of debt, paying one's way.

A.F.M. *abbrev.* Air Force Medal.

afo͝o't *adv.* & *pred. adj.* On one's feet; astir; in operation or employment.

afōr'e *adv.* & *prep.* (naut.) In front (of); (archaic, dial.) before, previously.

afōre- *prefix.* Before, previously.

ā fōrtĭōr'ī. With stronger reason. [L]

afrai'd *pred. adj.* Alarmed, frightened; sorry to say or suspect.

ă'freet, -rit, rite (-rēt) *n.* (Muslim myth.) Evil demon.

afrĕ'sh *adv.* Anew, with fresh beginning.

A'frĭca (ă-). Continent, largest southward projection of the landmass which constitutes the Old World, surrounded by sea except where Isthmus of Suez joins it to Asia, and extending nearly as far southward of equator as northward; its indigenous inhabitants are dark-skinned peoples varying in colour from light copper in N. to black in equatorial and southern parts; it was visited by Portuguese from 15th c. onwards but remained largely unknown, except for limited colonization by the Dutch and British in the Cape region and by the French in Algeria, until mid-19th c.; in the 'scramble for Africa' of the 1880s the leading European nations competed for colonies and the continent was divided between them, Liberia and Ethiopia alone remaining under native rule; since 1946 many former colonies have secured political independence.

A'frĭcan (ă-) *adj.* Of Africa or its people. ~ *n.* African person, esp. dark-skinned person as dist. from European or Asiatic settlers or their descendants. **A'frĭcanĭsm** *n.* (esp.) African nationalism. **A'frĭcanĭst** *adj.* & *n.* **A'frĭcanīze** *v.t.* Subject to rule of African Negroes. **Afrĭcanizā'tion** *n.*

Afri'dĭ (-rē-) *n.* (Member of) a Pathan people of the mountainous region between Afghanistan and Pakistan.

Afrĭkaa'ns (ă-, -ahns) *n.* Language, derived from Dutch, used in the Republic of South Africa as one of its two official languages, the other being English. ~ *adj.* Of Afrikaans or its speakers.

Afrĭkă'nder (ă-) *n.* 1. (hist.) Afrikaner. 2. (One of) a breed of red beef cattle.

Afrĭka'ner (ă-, -kah-) *n.* Person born in South Africa of European stock (now usu. one descended from Dutch, not British, settlers).

Afro- (ă-) *prefix.* African; African and —.

ăfrōrmō'sia *n.* N. and W. African tree of genus *A*~; its timber.

A.F.S. *abbrev.* Army Fire Service; Auxiliary Fire Service.

aft (ah-) *adv.* In, to, or towards stern of ship or tail of aircraft.

a'fter (ah-) *adv.* Behind; later. ~ *prep.* Behind; in pursuit of; following in point of time; in view of; next in importance to; according to; in imitation of; ~ *all*, in spite of everything that has happened, been said, done, etc. ~ *conj.* In or at a time subsequent to that when. ~ *adj.* Later, following; nearer stern of ship or tail of aircraft; *a'fterbirth*, placenta and membrane enveloping foetus in womb, extruded after the child; *~-care*, attention bestowed on person(s) after period of treatment or training, e.g. after discharge from hospital or prison; *a'fterdamp*, mixture of gases containing lethal amount of carbon monoxide, found in coal-mine after explosion of fire-damp; *~-effect*, delayed effect; effect following after an interval; *a'fterglow*, glow in west after sunset; (phys.) glow persisting after cessation of electric current; *~-grass*, grass that grows after the first crop has been mown for hay, or among stubble after harvest; *~-image*, image retained by retina and producing visual sensation after the eyes are turned away or closed; *~-life*, life after death; later period of person's life; *a'ftermath*, after-grass; (fig.) results, consequences; *~-pains*, pains caused by uterine contraction after childbirth; *~-taste*, taste remaining or recurring after eating or drinking (freq. fig.); *a'fterthought*, reflection after the act; later expedient or explanation.

a'ftermōst (ah-) *adj.* (naut.) Farthest aft.

afternōō'n (ah-) *n.* Time between noon and evening.

a'fters (ah-, -z) *n.pl.* (colloq.) Course which follows main course of meal.

a'fterwards (ah-, -z) *adv.* Later, subsequently.

A.F.V. *abbrev.* Armoured fighting vehicle.

A.G. *abbrev.* Adjutant-General; air gunner.

a'ga (ah-) *n.* Commander or chief officer in Ottoman Empire; *Aga Khan*, title given to Hasan Ali Shah (1800–81), when he fled from Persia and settled in Bombay under British protection, and subsequently held by his successors; as direct descendant of Muhammad's son-in-law Ali, the Aga Khan is spiritual leader (Imam) of the Ismaili sect of Muslims. [Turk. *aghā* master, *khan* ruler, king]

A'găg (ā-). King of Amalekites, spared by Saul but killed by Samuel: see 1 Sam. 15: 7–33.

agai'n (*or* -ĕn) *adv.* Another time, once more; further, besides; on the other hand; in return, in response; *~ and ~*, repeatedly; *as much ~*, twice as much; *half as much ~*, one-and-a-half times as much.

agai'nst (*or* -ĕnst) *prep.* In opposition to; in contrast to; in anticipation of; into collision with; opposite to (usu. *over ~*). *~ conj.* (archaic) By the time that.

aga'l (-ahl) *n.* Cord wound round keffiyeh, keeping it in position. [Arab. *'iqāl* rope]

Agamĕ'mnon (ă-). (Gk legend) King of Argos, brother of Menelaus, and commander of the Greek host which besieged Troy; murdered on his return from Troy by his wife Clytemnestra and her lover Aegisthus.

Aganĭ'ppė (ă-). (Gk antiq.) Fountain on Mt. Helicon sacred to the Muses.

ăgapă'nthus *n.* African LILY.

agā'pe[1] *adv.* & *pred. adj.* Gaping.

ă'gapē[2] *n.* 1. Love-feast held by early Christians in connection with Lord's Supper. 2. Spiritual love (opp. EROS[1]). [Gk, = 'brotherly love']

Agapĕ'monė (ă-) *n.* (= 'abode of love') Institution founded in Somerset (1845) by Henry James Prince (1811–99), where he and his followers lived with property in common, professed certain religious doctrines, and were believed to practise free love. **Agapĕ'monīte** *adj.* & *n.* (Member) of the Agapemone.

ā'gar-ā'gar *n.* Gelatinous substance obtained from various seaweeds and used as laxative, as solidifying agent in culture media for bacteria etc., and in East as food. [Malay]

ă'garĭc *n.* Fungus of family Agaricaceae, including common mushroom, with central stalk and umbrella-like cap with radiating gills on lower side.

ă'gate *n.* 1. Any of various semi-precious stones, semi-pellucid and variegated, usu. having a banded appearance and consisting largely of silica. 2. (U.S., print.) = RUBY *n.* 3.

agā'vė *n.* Plant of genus *A*~ (family Agavaceae), including American aloe, with large rosette of spiny leaves and, after a number of years, a gigantic terminal inflorescence bearing numerous flowers once in the plant's life.

āge *n.* 1. Length of life or of existence; a generation; (colloq., esp. in pl.) long time. 2. Particular length of life qualifying one for a purpose; *come of* ~, (Engl. law) attain age of 18 (formerly 21) years, assume rights and responsibilities of adult; *under* ~, not of full age; of less than age required. 3. Latter part of life (also *old* ~). 4. Great period, as *Ice A*~, *Patriarchal A*~. ~ *v.* 1. (Cause to) grow old. 2. Become mature. 3. Fix colours and mordants in (printed cloth etc.) by exposing to steam or to warm moist atmosphere. **ā'g(e)ing** *n.* (esp.) Change of properties occurring in some metals after heat treatment or cold working. **aged** *adj.* 1. (ājd) Of the age of; (of horses) more than 6 years old. 2. (ā'jĭd) Old. **ā'gelėss** *adj.* Never becoming old or outmoded. **ā'gelėssnėss** *n.*

ā'gencў *n.* Active operation, action; instrumentality; action personified; office of agent; agent's business establishment.

agĕ'nda *n.pl.* (freq. as sing.) Things to be done, items of business to be considered at a meeting.

ā'gent *n.* One who, thing that, exerts power or produces effect; one acting for another in business, law, politics, etc.; natural force acting on matter.

agent prŏvŏcateur (ahzhahṅ, -têr). Person employed to detect suspected offenders by tempting them to overt action. [Fr.]

Agēsĭlā'us (444–360 B.C.). King of Sparta, leader of successful campaign against Persians; killed in war against Thebes.

agglŏ'merāte[1] *v.* Collect into a mass. **agglŏmerā'tion** *n.* **agglŏ'merative** *adj.*

agglŏ'merate[2] *adj.* Collected into a mass. ~ *n.* Mass; (geol.) aggregate of angular fragments of rock (of any or of several kinds) that has been shattered by volcanic action and subsequently consolidated into a mass.

agglu'tĭnāte (-lōō-) *v.* 1. Unite as with glue; combine simple words to express compound ideas without important change of form or loss of meaning. 2. Turn into glue. **agglutinā'tion** *n.* **agglu'tĭnatĭve** *adj.* (of languages) Characterized by the joining of simple roots to express compound ideas without material change of form or loss of meaning.

ă'ggrandīze *v.t.* Increase the power, rank, wealth, etc., of; exaggerate. **aggră'ndĭzement** *n.*

ă'ggravāte *v.t.* Increase the gravity of; (colloq.) exasperate. **ăggravā'tion** *n.*

ă'ggrėgāte[1] *v.* Collect together; unite; amount to. **ăggrėgā'tion** *n.*

ă'ggrėgate[2] *adj.* Collected into one body; collective, total; (law) composed of associated individuals; (bot., of fruit) formed from carpels of one flower (as raspberry). ~ *n.* Total; assemblage, collection; (phys.) mass formed by union of homogeneous particles; (geol.) mass of minerals formed into one rock; (building) material mixed with lime, cement, bitumen, etc., to make concrete.

aggrĕ'ssion *n.* Beginning of quarrel; unprovoked attack. **aggrĕ'ssor** *n.*

aggrĕ'ssĭve *adj.* Of attack, offensive; disposed to attack; self-assertive. **aggrĕ'ssĭvelў** *adv.* **aggrĕ'ssĭvenėss** *n.*

aggrie'ved (-vd) *pred. adj.* Distressed, oppressed; injured, having a grievance.

agha'st (*a*gah-) *adj.* Terrified; struck with amazement.

ă'gīle *adj.* Quick-moving; nimble, active. **ă'gīlelў** (-l-lĭ) *adv.* **agĭ'lĭtў** *n.*

A'gĭncourt (ăj-, -kôrt). Village of NW. France, scene of victory (1415) of Henry V of England over French.

BATTLE OF AGINCOURT

ă'giō *n.* Percentage charged for changing paper money into cash, or one currency into another more valuable; excess value of one currency over another. **ă'giotage** *n.* Exchange business; speculation in stocks; stock-jobbing.

agĭ'stment *n.* (law) Contract for feeding cattle etc. on pasture-land for money payment; profit from this.

ă'gĭtāte *v.* 1. Shake, move; disturb, excite. 2. Revolve mentally, discuss, debate; keep up an agitation (*for*).

ăgĭtā'tion *n.* 1. Shaking. 2. Commotion, disturbance. 3. Debate, discussion; keeping of matter constantly before public; public excitement.

ăgĭta'tō (-tah-) *adv.* (mus.) In an agitated manner. [It.]

ă'gĭtātor *n.* 1. Person who creates excitement or disturbance, esp. for political ends. 2. Mechanical device for keeping liquid etc. in motion.

Aglā'ia (-y*a*). (Gk myth.) One of the three Graces (see GRACE *n.* 3).

ă'glėt *n.* Metal tag of a lace; tag or spangle as dress-ornament, esp. (now written *aiguillette*) tagged braid or cord hanging from shoulder in some military or naval uniforms; catkin of hazel, birch, etc.

A.G.M. *abbrev.* Annual general meeting.

ă'gnail *n.* Torn skin at root of finger-nail; resulting soreness.

ă'gnāte *adj.* Descended from the same male ancestor; of same clan or nation. ~ *n.* Agnate person or animal.

A'gnės (ă-), St. (4th c.). Patron saint of virgins, martyred in the persecution of Diocletian and commemorated 21 Jan.

A'gnĭ (ă-). (Vedic myth.) God of fire.

ăgnō'mĕn *n.* Additional name, esp. (Rom. antiq.) fourth name occas. assumed by Romans.

ăgnŏ'stĭc *n.* One who holds that nothing is known, or likely to be known, of the existence of God or gods or of anything beyond material phenomena. ~ *adj.* Pertaining to agnostics or agnosticism. **ăgnŏ'stĭcism** *n.* [Gk *agnōstos* (*theos*) unknown (god); taken by T. H. Huxley f. Acts 17: 23]

Agnus Dei (ăg'nŏŏs dā'ē). Part of the Mass beginning with these words; figure of lamb as emblem of Christ bearing cross or banner; small disc of wax stamped with this figure and blessed by pope. [L, = 'lamb of God']

agō' *adv.* Past, gone by; since.

agŏ'g *adv.* & *pred. adj.* Eager(ly), expectant(ly).

agŏ'nĭc *adj.* Making no angle; ~ *line*, line joining places where magnetic compass points to true north.

ă'gonize *v.* Torture; suffer agony, writhe in anguish; wrestle; make desperate efforts for effect.

ă'gonȳ *n.* Extreme bodily or mental suffering, esp. the last sufferings of Jesus Christ before the Crucifixion; *death* ~, *last* ~, death pangs; ~ *column*, in newspaper, column of personal advertisements (for missing friends etc.).

ăgora' (-ah) *n.* (pl. *-rōt*) $\frac{1}{100}$ of an Israeli pound.

ăgoraphō'bĭa *n.* Morbid dread of open spaces.

ăgou'ti (-ōō-) *n.* Rodent (several species in genus *Dasyprocta*) of Central America and W. Indies, related to guinea-pig, nocturnal in habit and destructive to sugar-plantations etc.

Agra (ah'-). City on river Jumna in Uttar Pradesh, capital of Mogul emperors from early 16th c. to mid-17th c.; site of the TAJ MAHAL.

agrār'ĭan *adj.* Of landed property or cultivated land. **agrār'ĭanism** *n.*

agree' *v.* Consent (*to*); be in accord, harmonize in opinion etc. (*with*); (gram.) have same number, gender, case, or person.

agree'able (-rĭa-) *adj.* Pleasing (*to*); (colloq.) well-disposed (*to, to* do); **agree'ablȳ** *adv.*

agree'ment *n.* Mutual understanding, covenant; (law) contract legally binding on parties; accordance in opinion; (gram.) concord in number, case, gender, person.

agrĕ'stĭc *adj.* Rural, rustic.

Agrĭ'cola, Gnaeus Julius (A.D. 40–93). Roman general; governor of Britain for several years from 78.

ă'grĭcŭlture *n.* Cultivation of the soil. **ăgrĭcŭ'ltural** *adj.* (-cher-) **ăgrĭcŭ'lturĭst, -turalĭst** *ns.*

ă'grĭmonȳ *n.* Perennial plant of the rose family, esp. *Agrimonia eupatoria*, which has yellow flowers and hooked clinging fruit; *hemp* ~, see HEMP.

Agrĭ'ppa, Marcus Vipsanius (*c* 63–12 B.C.). Roman general, son-in-law of the Emperor Augustus.

agrŏ'nomȳ *n.* Rural economy, husbandry. **ăgronŏ'mĭc, -ĭcal** *adjs.* **ăgronŏ'mĭcs, agrŏ'nomĭst** *ns.*

agrou'nd *adv.* & *pred. adj.* On the bottom of shallow water.

ā'gūe *n.* Malarial fever; cold shivering stage of this; shivering fit.

ah *int.* Exclamation of joy, sorrow, surprise, entreaty, etc.

A.H. *abbrev.* *Anno Hegirae* (L, = in the year of the HEGIRA).

aha (ah-hah') *int.* Exclamation of surprise, triumph, mockery.

A'hăb (ā-). King of Israel (see 1 Kings 16–22).

Ahasūēr'us (ahăz-). Persian king (see Esther *passim*, Ezra 4: 6, Dan. 9: 1); generally supposed to be XERXES.

A'hăz (ā-). King of Judah (see 2 Kings 16).

ahead (ahĕ'd) *adv.* & *pred. adj.* In advance *of*, in a direct line forward.

ahoy' *int.* (naut.) Call used in hailing.

Ah'rĭman. Principle of evil in the Zoroastrian system.

Ahura-Mă'zda (*ahoor'a*). = ORMAZD.

ai (ah'-ī) *n.* Three-toed sloth (*Bradypus tridactylus*) of S. America. [f. its cry]

A.I. *abbrev.* Artificial insemination (*A.I.D.* by donor, *A.I.H.* by husband).

aid *v.t.* Help, assist, promote. ~ *n.* Help, assistance; (hist.) grant of subsidy or tax to king, exchequer loan; helper; material source of help.

Ai'dan, St. (d. 651). Monk of Iona, apostle to Northumbria and first bishop of Lindisfarne.

aide n. Aide-de-camp; assistant.

aide-de-camp (ā'dekahṅ) *n.* (pl. *aides-de-camp*). (orig. mil.) Officer acting as confidential assistant to senior officer. [Fr.]

aide-mémoire (ādmāmwar̂) *n.* Manual of formulae etc. to serve as aid to the memory; in diplomatic use, memorandum. [Fr.]

ai'grĕtte *n.* = EGRET; long white plume grown by this in breeding-season; tuft of feathers or hair; spray of gems etc.

aiguille (ā'gwēl) *n.* Sharp peak of rock.

aiguillette (āgwĭlĕ't): see AGLET.

ail *v.* Trouble, afflict; be ill. **ai'lment** *n.* Illness, esp. slight one.

ai'leron *n.* Hinged flap on trailing edge of aircraft wing, near the tip, providing variation of lift on either side and used to execute the movement known as 'banking'. [Fr. 'little wing, fin', dim. of *aile* wing]

ailūrophō'bia (īl-) *n.* Morbid fear of cats. **ailūr'ophōbe** *n.*

aim *v.* Direct *at*; point (gun etc.); deliver blow, discharge missile (*at*); take aim; form designs. ~ *n.* Direction of or act of directing a missile or weapon towards an object; design, purpose, object. **ai'mlėss** *adj.* **ai'mlėsslў** *adv.* **ai'mlėssnėss** *n.*

Ai'nū (īn-) *n.* (Member of) a Caucasoid people in Japan and U.S.S.R. with hairy bodies; their language.

air *n.* 1. Invisible, odourless, and tasteless mixture of gases enveloping the Earth, consisting chiefly of oxygen and nitrogen, with some carbon dioxide and traces of other gases, and breathed by all land animals; atmosphere; unconfined space; breeze; *on the* ~, broadcast(ing) by radio transmission. 2. Appearance; mien; affected manner. 3. (mus.) Melody, tune, aria. 4. (attrib.) Of aircraft or flying. 5. ~ *ball*, *-balloon*, *-bladder*, *-jacket*, etc., containing air or inflated by air; *air'borne*, transported by air or aircraft; (of aircraft) having left the ground; in flight; *~-brake*, brake operated by piston driven by compressed air; also, brake consisting of flaps or other movable surfaces, normally lying parallel to air-flow, turned through 90° to retard progress of aircraft or car; ~ *brick*, ventilating brick; *air'brush*, fine spray for paint used in commercial art and for retouching photographs; *Air Chief Marshal*, title, rank, of officer in R.A.F., ranking next below a Marshal and above an Air Marshal; *Air Commodore*, title, rank, of officer in R.A.F. immediately above Group Captain; ~ *-conditioning*, process of cleaning air and controlling its temperature and humidity before it enters a room, building, etc., and in certain manufacturing processes; *~-cooled* (*adj.*) cooled by exposure to stream of air; *air'craft*, (pl. same) any kind of flying machine, including aeroplanes, airships, helicopters, etc.; these collectively; *aircraft carrier*, ship designed to carry aeroplanes, with special deck for taking-off and landing; *air'craftman*, *air'craftwoman*, lowest rank in R.A.F., W.R.A.F.; *~-cushion*, cushion inflated by air; body of air serving to provide support, esp. in *~-cushion vehicle*, hovercraft; *air'field*, area of land where aircraft are accommodated and maintained and may take off or land; ~ *force*, branch of armed forces using aircraft in fighting (in U.K., Royal Air Force) *air'graph*, photographic reproduction of letter etc. conveyed by air mail in form of microfilm to save weight; ~*-gun*, gun from which missile is discharged by compressed air; ~ *hostess*, stewardess in passenger aircraft; ~ *letter*, folding form for air mail letters; ~*-lift*, transportation of supplies by air to area cut off from normal communications; (*v.t.*) transport thus; *air'line*, line of aircraft for public service; *air'liner*, large passenger aeroplane; ~ *-lock*, stoppage of flow of liquid in pump or pipe by bubble of air; also, see LOCK[2] *n.* 2; ~ *mail*, mail carried by aircraft; *air'man*, member of crew of aircraft; member of air force; *Air Marshal*, title, rank, of officer in R.A.F., equivalent to Lieutenant-General in the army; ~*-minded* (*adj.*) interested in, or enthusiastic for, use and development of aircraft; *air'plane*, (orig. U.S.) aeroplane; ~ *pocket*, local condition of atmosphere, as a down current or sudden change of wind velocity, which causes aircraft to lose height suddenly; *air'port*, aerodrome for transport of passengers and goods by air; ~*-power*, power of offensive and defensive action dependent upon a supply of aircraft; ~*-pump*, pump for exhausting vessel etc. of its air; (also) compressor; ~ *raid*, attack by aircraft; *air'screw*, aircraft propeller; ~*-sea rescue*, applied to the branch of the R.A.F. whose task is to rescue airmen and passengers from the sea, and to such operations; ~ *-shaft*, passage for ventilating mine or tunnel; *air'ship*, flying machine lighter than air; dirigible balloon; ~*-sickness*, kind of nausea sometimes affecting persons in an aircraft; ~*-space*, space containing air; air lying over a particular territory and considered subject to its jurisdiction; ~ *speed*, speed of aircraft in relation to the air, as dist. from *ground speed*; *air'strip*, strip of land prepared for the taking off and landing of aircraft, often for temporary use; ~ *terminal*, town office of airline equipped for reception of passengers; *air'tight*, impermeable to air; *A~ Training Corps*, organization for the training of cadets for the R.A.F.; *air'way*, ventilating passage in mine; route regularly followed by aircraft; (device to secure) passage for air into lungs; *air'worthy*, (of aircraft) in fit condition to be flown. ~ *v.* Expose to open air, ventilate; finish drying (clothes etc.) by warmth; parade (grievances, opinions, etc.).

Air'edāle (ārd-) *n.* One of a breed of large terriers with rough reddish-brown coats. [Valley of river Aire, West Yorkshire]

air'lėss *adj.* Stuffy; breezeless, still. **air'lėssnėss** *n.*

air'ȳ *adj.* Breezy; light, thin; immaterial; sprightly, graceful, delicate; superficial, flippant. **air'ĭlȳ** *adv.*

aisle (īl) *n.* Division of church,

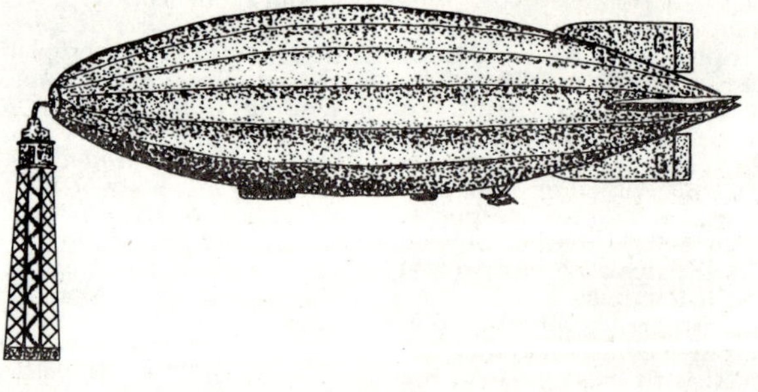

AIRSHIP

esp. parallel to nave, choir, or transept, and divided from it by pillars; passage between rows of seats, in church, theatre, etc. [L *ala* wing]

ait *n.* Small isle, esp. one in a river.

aitch *n.* Letter H, h.

ai'tchbōne *n.* Rump bone, cut of beef over this bone.

Aix-la-Chăpĕlle (-lah-sh-). French name of AACHEN.

Aja'nta (*a*jŭ-). Village in S. central India with caves containing Buddhist frescoes and sculptures.

ajar' *adv.* (of a door) Slightly open.

A'jăx (ā-). (Gk legend) 1. Greek hero of the Trojan war, son of Telamon king of Salamis. 2. Another Greek, son of Oileus king of Locris, who was killed after a shipwreck on his homeward journey after the fall of Troy.

A'kbar (ă-). Jalaludin Muhammad (1542–1605), Mogul emperor; enlarged the Mogul Empire in India to its greatest extent.

à Kempis, Thomas: see THOMAS À KEMPIS.

Akhna'ten (ăknah-). Name (lit. 'glory of the sun') taken by Amenhotep IV, king of Egypt of 18th dynasty (14th c. B.C.), who tried to replace the worship of Ammon by that of Ra, and built a new capital at Tell el Amarna, away from Thebes where the old priesthood was established.

aki'mbō *adv.* & *adj.* (of arms) With hands on hips and elbows out.

aki'n *pred. adj.* Related by blood; (fig.) of similar character.

A'kkăd, A'cc- (ă-). Northern part of ancient Babylonia; also, the city (Agade) founded by Sargon *c* 2300 B.C. **Akkā'dian, Acc-** *adj.* & *n.* (Native or inhabitant) of Akkad; (of) the language of this people, the oldest known Semitic language.

a.l. *abbrev.* Autograph letter.

à la (*ah lah*). After the manner of. [Fr]

Ala. *abbrev.* Alabama.

A.L.A. *abbrev.* American Library Association.

Alabama (ăl*a*bah'm*a*, U.S. -ă'm*a*). State in south-eastern U.S., admitted to the Union in 1819; capital, Montgomery.

ă'labaster (-bah-) *n.* Translucent granular gypsum rock of white, pink, or yellowish colour, used for statues etc. ~ *adj.* Of alabaster; resembling it in whiteness or smoothness.

à la carte (ah lah kart). (of meal) Ordered by separate items from the bill of fare (opp. *table d'hôte*). [Fr.]

ală'crity̆ *n.* Briskness, cheerful readiness.

Ală'ddĭn. Hero of a story in 'Arabian Nights', who acquired a lamp the rubbing of which brought a genie to do the will of the owner.

A'lamein (ă-, -ăn), El. Place near the NE. coast of Egypt, where German forces advancing on Egypt were checked and defeated in 1942.

à la mode (ah lah mōd). In the fashion, fashionable; *beef* ~, a kind of beef stew. [Fr.]

Å'land I'slands (aw-, īlandz). Group of islands in the Gulf of Bothnia constituting a department of Finland.

ā'lar *adj.* Pertaining to wings; wing-shaped, wing-like; axillary.

Alarcón (ălârkō'n), Pedro Antonio de (1833–91). Spanish poet, dramatist, and prose writer.

Alarcón y Mendoza (ălârkō'n ĭ mĕndō'tha), Juan Ruiz de (*c* 1581–1639). Mexican-Spanish dramatist.

A'laric (ă-) (*c* 370–410). A Visigoth, the first Germanic conqueror of Rome (A.D. 410).

alâr'm *n.* Call to arms; warning sound giving notice of danger; warning; frightened anticipation of danger; sudden uneasiness; mechanism that sounds alarm; ~ *clock*, clock with apparatus that can be set to ring at predetermined time; ~*s and excursions*, (joc.) noise and bustle. ~ *v.t.* Arouse to sense of danger; disturb, agitate. **alâr'ming** *adj.* **alâr'mingly** *adv.* [It. *all' arme* to arms]

alâr'mist *n.* One who raises alarm on slight grounds; panic-monger.

alâr'um *n.* (archaic) Alarm.

ală's (*or* -ahs) *int.* Exclamation of grief, pity, concern.

Ală'ska. State of the U.S. in the extreme NW. of N. America, with coasts in Arctic Ocean, Bering Sea, and North Pacific; discovered by Russian explorers (under Vitus Bering) in 1741, and further explored by Cook, Vancouver, and others during the last quarter of 18th c.; the territory was purchased from Russia in 1867 and admitted to the Union in 1959; capital, Juneau. **Ală'skan** *adj.* & *n.*

ălb *n.* Vestment reaching to feet, worn by celebrant at Eucharist over the cassock and by some consecrated kings.

Alba, Duke of: see ALVA.

ă'lbacōre *n.* Large species of fish of N. Amer. E. and W. coasts (*Thunnus alalunga*) allied to tunny; other fish of the same genus. [Arab. *al* the, *bakr* young camel]

A'lban (awl-), St. (d. *c* 304). First British martyr, commemorated on 22 June; martyred at Verulamium, which was afterwards named St. Albans.

Alban. *abbrev.* (Bishop) of St. Albans (replacing surname in his signature).

Albā'nia (ă-). Balkan State between Greece and Yugoslavia; under Turkish rule from 16th c. until 1912, when disputes arising from the demand for Albanian autonomy nearly caused a European war; in Jan. 1925 the country was proclaimed a republic, which continued until 1928 when it was changed into a monarchy; again proclaimed a republic in 1946; capital, Tirana. **Albā'nian** *adj.* & *n.* (Native, inhabitant, language) of Albania.

A'lbany[1] (awl-). Ancient poetic name, of Gaelic origin, for the N. part of Britain.

A'lbany[2] (awl-). House near Piccadilly, London, formerly belonging to Frederick, Duke of York and Albany, converted *c* 1803 into sets of chambers where many famous men of letters have resided.

ă'lbatrŏss *n.* Very long-winged oceanic bird (genus *Diomedea*), allied to petrel, found chiefly in the S. hemisphere; *wandering* ~, one of the largest sea-birds (*D. exùlans*), white when adult, with dark wings and hooked beak. [f. obs. *alcatras* frigate-bird, f. Span. and Port., f. Arab. *al-qadus* the bucket (name for the pelican, from its supposed water-carrying habit)]

albē'it (awl-) *conj.* Though.

Albéniz (ălbānē'th), Isaac (1860–1909). Spanish pianist and composer, famous chiefly for works based on the rhythm of Spanish popular music.

A'lberich (ă-, -ĭχ). (Scand. myth.) King of the elves, guardian of the treasure of the Nibelungs, stolen from him by Siegfried.

A'lbert[1] (ă-), Prince (1819–1861). Prince of Saxe-Coburg-Gotha; cousin and consort (1840) of Queen Victoria; *Lake* ~, large shallow lake in Uganda, discovered in 1864, re-named *Lake Mobutu Sese Seko*,

1973; *Royal* ~ *Hall*, large concert and exhibition hall erected (1867–71) in Kensington, London; ~ *Medal*, (abbrev. A.M.) awarded since 1866 for 'gallantry in saving life at sea or on land'; ~ *Memorial*, an elaborate monument, designed by Sir Gilbert Scott, erected (1872–6) in Hyde Park, London.

A′lbert[2] (ă-) (1875–1934). King of the Belgians (1909–34), commander-in-chief of the Belgian army during the war of 1914–18.

ă′lbert[3] *n.* (archaic) Watch-chain, with cross-bar for insertion in button-hole of waistcoat, named after Prince ALBERT[1].

Alber̄′ta (ă-). Western prairie province of Canada, bounded on the south by the U.S.A., and on the west by the Rocky Mountains; capital, Edmonton.

Alberti (ălbar̄′tĭ), Leon Battista degli (1404–72). Italian architect, painter, writer on art, poet, and musician.

Alber̄′tus Mă′gnus (ă-) (1193 or 1206–1280). Swabian Dominican monk, one of the great scholastic philosophers; known as 'Doctor Universalis'.

ălbĕ′scent *adj.* Growing white, fading into white.

Albigĕ′nsēs (ă-, -z) *n.pl.* Members of a heretical sect preaching a form of Manichaean dualism in S. France, 11th–13th c. **Albĭgĕ′nsĭan** *adj.* & *n.* [L, f. town of *Albi*]

ălbi′nō (-bē-) *n.* Animal or human being marked by congenital absence of pigment in skin and hair, which is white, and eyes, which are pink or very pale blue and unduly sensitive to light; plant lacking normal colouring. **ălbĭnŏ′tĭc** *adj.* **ă′lbĭnism** *n.*

Albī′nus (ă-). = ALCUIN.

A′lbĭon (ă-). Ancient poetical name for Britain.

Alboin (ălbwăṅ) (d. 573). King of the Lombards, conqueror and settler of northern Italy (568).

Albuera (ălbwar̄′*a*). Small village in Spain, scene (1811) of a combined English, Portuguese, and Spanish victory over the French under Marshal Soult.

ă′lbum *n.* Blank book for insertion of autographs, photographs, etc.; long-playing record or set of records.

ă′lbūmėn (*or* -bū′-) *n.* White of egg; a constituent of animal cells, milk, etc., found nearly pure in white of egg; (bot.) substance found between skin and embryo of many seeds, usu. the edible part. **ălbū′mėnīze** *v.t.* Coat (paper) with an albuminous solution. **ălbū′mĭnōse, ălbū′mĭnous** *adjs.*

ălbū′mĭn *n.* Any of a class of water-soluble proteins.

ălbū′mĭnoid *n.* Any of a class of organic compounds forming chief parts of organs and tissues of animals and plants; protein. **ălbūmĭnoi′dal** *adj.*

ălbūminūr̄′ĭa *n.* (med.) Condition in which the urine contains proteins, sometimes a symptom of kidney disease.

A′lbūquerque (ă-, -ker̄k), Afonso d' (1453–1515). Portuguese navigator, founder of Portuguese power in India.

ălbur̄′num *n.* Recently formed wood in trees, sap-wood.

Alcae′us (ălsē-) (b. *c* 620 B.C.). Greek lyric poet of Mitylene in Lesbos. **ălcā′ĭc** *adj.* (esp.) Of a metre invented by Alcaeus, a stanza of four lines:

— — ∪ — — | — ∪ ∪ — ∪ ⏓
— — ∪ — — | — ∪ ∪ — ∪ ⏓
— — ∪ — — — ∪ — —
— ∪ ∪ — ∪ ∪ — ∪ — ∪

A′lcatrăz (ă-). Island in San Francisco Bay, California; former site of U.S. federal prison.

Alcĕ′stis (ă-). (Gk legend) Wife of Admetus, whose life she saved by giving her own; she was brought back from Hades by Hercules.

ă′lchėmy (-k-) *n.* Medieval forerunner of chemistry, primarily the attempt to transmute base metals into gold or silver. **ălchĕ′mĭc, -ĭcal** *adjs.* **ă′lchėmĭst** *n.* [Arab. *al-kimia*; f. *al* the, Gk *khēmeia* transmutation of metals]

Alcĭbī′adēs (ă-, -z) (*c* 450–404

B.C.). Athenian general and politician to whose irresponsibility the defeat of Athens in the Peloponnesian War was partly due.

Alcĭ'nōus (ă-). (Gk legend) King of Phaeacia and father of Nausicaa; entertained Ulysses during his journey home from Troy.

A'lcman (ă-). (7th c. B.C.). Principal lyric poet of Sparta, a native of Lydia, brought to Sparta as a slave.

Alcmē'nė (ă-). (Gk myth.) Wife of Amphitryon and mother of Hercules by Zeus.

A'lcŏck (awl-), Sir John William (1892–1919). English aviator; with A. W. BROWN[2] made first non-stop flight across the Atlantic, 1919 (Newfoundland to Ireland, 16 hrs 12 m.).

ă'lcohŏl *n.* 1. Colourless volatile inflammable liquid, also called *ethyl* ~ (C_2H_5OH), formed by fermentation of sugars and contained in wine ('spirit of wine'), beer, whisky, etc., of which it is the intoxicating principle, also used in medicine and industry as a solvent for fats, oils, etc., and as a fuel. 2. Any liquor containing alcohol. 3. (chem.) Any of a class of compounds analogous to alcohol in constitution and derived from hydrocarbons by the replacement of hydrogen atoms by hydroxyl groups. [Arab. *al* the, *koh'l* powder (for staining eyelids)]

ălcohŏ'lic *adj.* Pertaining to, containing, alcohol. ~ *n.* Person suffering from alcoholism.

ă'lcoholism *n.* Diseased condition caused by excessive consumption of alcoholic liquors.

ălcoholŏ'mėter *n.* Instrument for measuring alcoholic content of liquids.

A'lcŏtt (awl-), Louisa May (1832–88). Amer. author of 'Little Women' and other books for girls.

ă'lcōve *n.* Vaulted recess in room-wall; recess in garden-wall or hedge; summer-house. [Arab. *al-qobbah* the vault]

Alcuin (ă'lkwĭn) (735–804). English theologian and man of letters, Charlemagne's coadjutor in educational reforms, and finally abbot of Tours.

Alcȳ'onė (ă-). (Gk legend) Wife of Ceyx; threw herself into the sea after finding the body of her shipwrecked husband on the shore; the gods changed both into kingfishers, and the sea is said to be calm while they are nesting; hence the expression 'halcyon days'.

Ald. *abbrev.* Alderman.

Aldĕ'baran (ă-). Bright, reddish star in the constellation Taurus. [Arab., = 'the following' (because it follows the Pleiades)]

ă'ldėhȳde *n.* Any of a class of organic compounds containing the group CHO— in their structures, esp. acetaldehyde, CH_3CHO. [abbrev. of L. *al*cohol *dehyd*rogenatum (deprived of hydrogen)]

a'lder (awl-) *n.* Tree (genus *Alnus*) of birch family, esp. *A. glutinosa*, growing by lakes and streams and in marshy ground; ~ *buckthorn*, shrub (*Rhamnus frangula*) of buckthorn family growing in damp peaty soils.

a'lderman (awl-) *n.* (hist.) Co-opted member of an English county or borough council, next in dignity to mayor; as an Anglo-Saxon title, a noble or person of high rank. **aldermă'nic** *adj.* **a'ldermanship** *n.* **a'ldermanrȳ** *n.* (hist.) Ward, district of a borough having its own alderman; rank of alderman.

A'lderney (awl-). One of the four larger Channel Islands. ~ *n.* One of the dairy cattle bred in the Channel Islands, now including Jersey and Guernsey breeds.

A'ldershŏt (awl-). Town in Hampshire having a permanent military camp and training centre.

A'ldhĕlm (ă-), St. (*c* 640–709). English churchman and scholar, 1st bishop of Sherborne; author of Latin works in verse and prose.

A'ldīne (awl-) *adj.* & *n.* (Edition) printed by Aldus Manutius.

A'ldĭs lămp (awl-). Signalling lamp, used esp. in navy and air force, in which Morse signs are transmitted by rotating a mirror at whose focus the light is located. [inventor, A. C. W. *Aldis*]

A'ldus Manū'tius (awl-, -shĭ*us*) (1450–1515). Aldo Manuzio, Italian printer whose press at Venice

issued the first printed editions of many Greek authors, and introduced italics into typography.

āle *n.* Liquor made from an infusion of malt by fermentation, flavoured with hops etc.; beer; ~-*house*, (hist.) house selling ale.

Alĕ'ctō. (Gk myth.) One of the Furies (see FURY).

alee' *adv.* & *pred. adj.* On the lee side of a ship, to leeward.

Aleman (ălĭmah'n), Mateo (*c* 1550–1614). Spanish picaresque novelist.

Alembert (ălahṅbār), Jean le Rond d' (1717–83). French encyclopaedist, philosopher, and mathematician.

alĕ'mbic *n.* (hist.) Apparatus used by alchemists for distilling. [Arab. *alanbig* still, f. Gk *ambix -ikos* cup, cap of a still]

Alençon (ălahṅsawṅ). Town in NW. France, famous for the manufacture of needlepoint lace (*point d'Alençon*), orig. copied from Venetian lace.

Alĕ'ppō. Ancient city in Syria, twice besieged (though not taken) during the Crusades.

alẽr't *adj.* Watchful, vigilant; lively, nimble. ~ *n.* Warning-call, alarm; warning of air-raid etc., period of warning; *on the* ~, on the look-out. **alẽr'tlȳ** *adv.* **alẽr'tnėss** *n.* **alẽr't** *v.t.* Make alert, warn. [It. *all' erta* to the watch-tower]

Aleu'tian I'slands (-sh*a*n īl*a*ndz). (also *Aleutians*) Group of islands in U.S. possession extending SW. from Alaska.

Alexa'nder[1] (ălĭgzah-) (356–323 B.C.), 'the Great'. King of Macedon; son of Philip II of Macedon; educated by Aristotle;

became king 336 B.C.; was nominated by the Greek states to conduct the war against Persia, in which he was victorious; he extended his conquests to Egypt (where he founded Alexandria) and India.

Alexa'nder[2] (ălĭgzah-). Name of three kings of Scotland: *Alexander I* (*c* 1078–1124), reigned 1107–24; *Alexander II* (1198–1249), reigned 1214–49; *Alexander III* (1241–85), reigned 1249–85.

Alexa'nder[3] (ălĭgzah-). Name of eight popes: *Alexander VI*, see BORGIA, Rodrigo.

Alexa'nder[4] (ălĭgzah-). Name of three emperors of Russia: *Alexander I* (1777–1825), emperor 1801–25 during the Napoleonic Wars; sponsor of the Holy Alliance; *Alexander II* (1818–81), emperor 1855–81, assassinated in St. Petersburg; *Alexander III* (1845–94), emperor 1881–94.

Alexa'nder Nĕ'vskĭ (ălĭgzah-; nĕf-) (1220–63). Russian saint and national hero, called 'Nevski' from the river Neva, on the banks of which he defeated the Swedes.

Alexa′ndra (ălĭgzah-) (1844–1925). Wife of Edward VII and queen of Gt Britain, daughter of Christian IX of Denmark.

Alexa′ndrĭa (ălĭgzah-). City and seaport of Egypt, founded by Alexander the Great 332 B.C.; capital of Egypt under the Ptolemies; until the Roman conquest of Egypt it was a centre of Greek culture, and possessed a famous library, part of which was accidentally burnt when Julius Caesar was besieged in the city.

Alexa′ndrĭan *adj.* Of Alexandria; ~ *period*, period of Hellenistic literature with Alexandria as its chief centre from end of the time of Alexander the Great to the Roman conquest of Greece, 300–146 B.C.

ălexă′ndrīne (-igz-) *adj.* & *n.* (pros.) (Line) of six iambic feet, or twelve syllables, the French heroic verse. [so called because it was used in early poems on the subject of Alexander the Great]

ălfă′lfa *n.* = LUCERNE[1].

Alfieri (ălfyār′ĭ), Vittorio, Count (1749–1803). Italian dramatist; author of tragedies on classical and other subjects, satirical comedies, and political works.

Alfŏ′nsō (ă-). Name of several kings of Spain, the last of whom, *Alfonso XIII* (1886–1941), was deposed in 1931 when Spain became a republic.

A′lfrėd (ă-) (849–899), 'the Great'. King of the West Saxons 871; drove the Danes from his territories; built a navy; composed

a code of laws; encouraged the revival of letters in the W. of England, himself translating Latin works into English.

ălfrĕ′scō *adv.* In the open air. ~ *adj.* Open-air.

ă′lga *n.* (pl. *-gae*). One of the Algae, a division of primitive

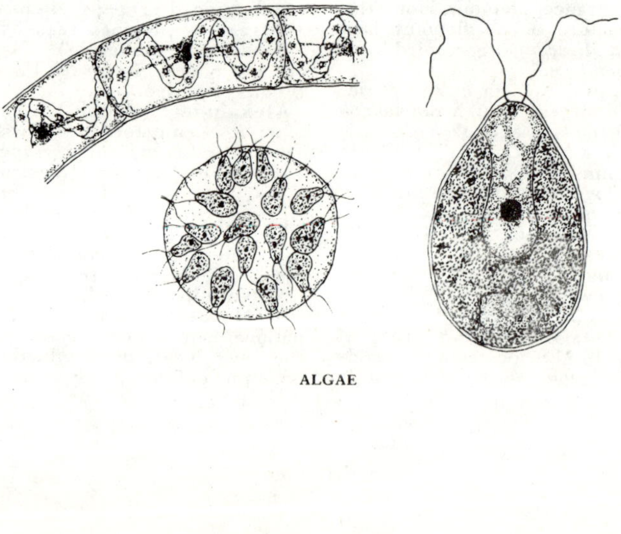

ALGAE

cryptogamic plants including green, brown, and red seaweeds, pond-scums, and many microscopic water-plants showing immense diversity of structure.

ă'lgėbra *n.* Branch of mathematics dealing with relations and properties of numbers by means of letters and other general symbols. **ălgėbrā'ĭc, -ĭcal** *adjs.* **ălgėbrā'ĭcallȳ** *adv.* **ă'lgėbrāist** *n.* [Arab. *al-jebr* the reunion of fragments]

Algēr'ia (ă-). Republic in N. Africa; under French rule until 1962; capital, Algiers. **Algēr'ian** *adj.* & *n.*

ălgĭ'nĭc *adj.* ~ *acid*, colloidal acid ($C_6H_8O_6$) obtained from certain algae.

A'lgŏl[1] (ă-). Eclipsing binary star in the constellation Perseus. [Arab. *al-gul* the destruction]

A'lgŏl[2], **ALGOL** (ă-) *n.* International algebraic language for use in programming computers. [*algo*rithmic *l*anguage]

Algŏ'nquĭan (ă-) *n.* & *adj.* (One) of a widely-spread group of N.-Amer. Indian languages; Algonquin.

Algŏ'nquĭn, -kĭn (ă-) *n.* & *adj.* (Member) of a group of N.-Amer. Indian tribes formerly living near the Ottawa River in Canada; (of) their language; Algonquian.

ă'lgorĭsm *n.* Arabic system of notation. [med. L *algorismus*, f. Arab. *al-Khowarazmi* the man of Khiva, surname of a 9th-c. Muslim mathematician]

ă'lgorĭthm *n.* 1. = ALGORISM. 2. Process or rules, usu. expressed algebraically, for (esp. machine) calculation etc. **ălgorĭ'thmĭc** *adj.*

Alhă'mbra (ă-). Palace of the Moorish kings at Granada, built in 13th c. [Arab. *al* the *ḥamrā'* red: thought to refer to the colour of the bricks or the name of the founder]

A'lĭ (ă-). Cousin and son-in-law of Muhammad; regarded by some Muslims as the first caliph, his three predecessors being considered interlopers.

ā'lĭas *adv.* & *n.* (Name by which one is or has been called) on other occasions.

A'lĭ Ba'ba (ă-, bah-). Hero of a story supposed to be from the 'Arabian Nights'; discovered the magic formula ('Open Sesame!') which opened the cave in which forty robbers kept the treasures they had accumulated.

ă'lĭbī *n.* Plea that when an alleged act took place one was elsewhere; (colloq., orig. U.S.) excuse. ~ *v.t.* (colloq.) Provide with an alibi.

Alĭcă'ntė (ă-) *n.* Red wine made in Alicante, a province of SE. Spain.

A'lĭce (ă-). Heroine of 'Alice's Adventures in Wonderland' and 'Through the Looking-Glass' by Lewis Carroll; ~ *band*, type of hair-band worn by Alice in Tenniel's illustrations to the latter.

ă'lĭdāde *n.* Movable arm of quadrant etc. carrying the sights and indicating degrees cut off on the arc. [Arab *al'idadah* the revolving radius (upper arm)]

ā'lĭen *adj.* Not one's own; foreign; differing in nature (*from*); repugnant (*to*). ~ *n.* Stranger, foreigner. ~ *v.t.* (law) Transfer ownership of. **ā'lĭenable** *adj.* **ālĭenabĭ'lĭtȳ** *n.*

ā'lĭenāte *v.t.* Estrange, transfer ownership of; divert (*from*). **ālĭenā'tion** *n.* Estrangement; transference of ownership; diversion to different purpose.

ā'lĭenist *n.* (formerly) Psychiatrist.

Alighieri: see DANTE.

ali'ght[1] (-īt) *v.i.* Dismount, descend (*from*); settle, come to earth (from the air).

ali'ght[2] (-īt) *pred. adj.* Kindled, on fire, lighted up.

ali'gn (-īn) *v.* Place, lay, in a line; bring into line; form a line. **ali'gnment** *n.* Act of aligning; formation in a straight line, esp. of soldiers.

alī'ke *pred. adj.* Similar, like. ~ *adv.* In like manner.

ă'lĭment *n.* Food; mental sustenance. **ălĭmĕ'ntal** *adj.* **ălĭmĕ'ntallȳ** *adv.*

ălimĕ'ntarȳ *adj.* Nourishing; performing functions of nutrition; providing maintenance; ~ *canal,*

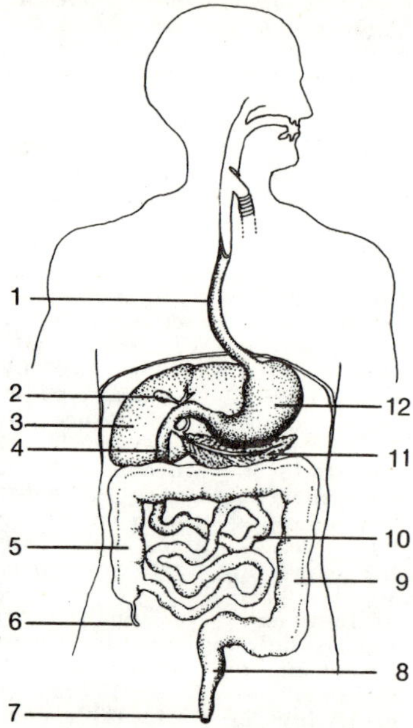

1. Oesophagus 2. Gall bladder 3. Liver 4. Duodenum 5. Caecum 6. Appendix 7. Anus 8. Rectum 9. Colon 10. Small intestine 11. Pancreas 12. Stomach

ALIMENTARY CANAL

channel in animal body through which food passes, including whole length from mouth, through the intestines to the anus.

ălĭmentā'tion *n.* Nourishment; maintenance.

ă'lĭmonȳ *n.* Maintenance allowance made to woman from (former) husband after legal separation or divorce.

ălĭphă'tic *adj.* (chem.) Fatty; belonging to the group of organic compounds in which the carbon atoms are linked in open chains as opposed to rings.

ă'liquŏt *adj.* & *n.* (Part) contained by the whole an integral number of times, thus, 6 is an aliquot part of 18.

alī've *pred. adj.* Living; active, brisk; fully susceptible *to*; swarming *with*.

alĭ'zarĭn *n.* Red colouring matter of madder. [prob. f. Arab. *al* the, *'uṣāra* juice, extract]

ă'lkalī *n.* (pl. *-is*). (chem.) Any of a number of substances having strongly basic properties and including the carbonates and hydroxides of the alkali metals of ammonium and the hydroxides of some other reactive metals; ~ *metal,* any of a group of highly reactive metallic elements including lithium, sodium and potassium. **ă'lkalīne** *adj.* **ălkalĭ'nĭtȳ** *n.* [Arab. *al* the, *qily* cinders, lye]

ă'lkaloid *n.* Any of a large group of nitrogenous organic substances of vegetable origin having basic or alkaline properties, many, as morphine, strychnine, cocaine, etc., being used as drugs.

ă'lkāne *n.* Any member of the paraffin series of hydrocarbons.

ă'lkēne *n.* Any member of the ethylene series of hydrocarbons; olefine.

ă'lkȳl *adj.* Derived from, or related to, the paraffin series of hydrocarbons; ~ *radical,* any of the series of radicals derived from paraffin hydrocarbons by removal of a hydrogen atom, e.g. methyl (CH_3), ethyl (C_2H_5).

all (awl) *adj.* The entire; the greatest possible; the entire number of; ~ *clear,* signal giving information that there is no danger; esp., signal that hostile aircraft have left the neighbourhood; *A~ Fools' Day,* 1 April (the celebration of which is probably a survival of ancient festivities held at spring equinox) when the unsuspecting are made victims of practical jokes or sent on fools' errands; *A~ Hallows,* (archaic) All Saints' Day; *~-Hallows Eve,* Hallowe'en, 31 Oct., the last day of the year in the old Celtic calendar, and the night of all the witches; *A~ Saints' Day,* 1 Nov., day on which there is a general celebration of all Christian saints; *A~ Souls' Day,* 2 Nov., day on which prayers are offered for the souls of all the faithful deceased. ~ *n.* All men; the whole, every one, everything; *at* ~, in any way; in any degree; of any kind; *~-in*, inclusive; (of wrestling) with no restrictions; ~ *one*, just the same. ~ *adv.* Wholly, quite; ~ *in*, (colloq.) quite exhausted; ~ *out*, using or involving all resources; fully extended; at top speed; ~ *over*, (colloq.) displaying great affection towards; in characteristic behaviour; ~ *right*, safe and sound, in good state; satisfactorily; (as sentence) I consent; all is well; *~-round*, having ability and skill of all kinds, esp. in a game; *~-rounder* (*n.*); ~ *there*, (colloq.) having all one's wits about one; ~ *the same*, in spite of this, notwithstanding.

Allah (ă'la). Muslim name of God. [Arab., f. *al* the, *ilah* god, cf. Heb. *eloah*]

Allăhăbă'd (ă-). Indian city at the confluence of the Jumna with the Ganges; capital of Uttar Pradesh; a place of Hindu pilgrimage.

ă'lla prī'ma (*or* -ē-) *adv.* & *n. phr.* (Using) the direct method of painting without underpainting.

allay' *v.t.* Put down, repress; alleviate; diminish.

ăllėgā'tion *n.* Alleging; assertion (esp. one not proved).

allĕ'ge *v.t.* Affirm, advance as argument or excuse.

Allėghe'nȳ Mou'ntains (ă-, -gā-; -tinz). (also *Alleghenies*) Ranges of the Appalachian system in eastern U.S.

allē'giance (-jans) *n.* Duty of subject to sovereign or government; loyalty.

ă'llėgorīze *v.* Treat as an allegory, make allegories.

ă'llėgorȳ *n.* Narrative description of subject under guise of another suggestively similar; figurative story. **ăllėgŏ'rĭc, -ical** *adjs.* **ăllėgŏ'ricallȳ** *adv.*

ăllėgrĕ'ttō *adv.*, *adj.*, & *n.* (pl. *-os*). (mus.) (Passage or movement played) somewhat briskly. [It.]

alle'grō (-lā-) *adj.*, *adv.*, & *n.* (pl. *-os*). (mus.) Lively, gay (passage or movement), in brisk time. [It.]

allē'le, allē'lomorph *ns.* Gene which occupies the same relative position on homologous chromosomes.

ăllėlu'ia (-lōōya) *n.* Song of praise to God. [Heb. *hallĕlū-yāh* praise ye the Lord]

allemande (ă'lmahnd) *n.* (Music for) dance in quadruple time and moderately quick. [Fr., = 'German (dance)']

A'llenbȳ (ă-), Edmund Henry Hynman, Viscount (1861–1936). Commander of British forces in Egypt and Palestine, 1917–18; High Commissioner for Egypt and Sudan, 1919–25.

ăllergĕ'nic *adj.* Causing allergic reaction.

ă'llergȳ *n.* Hypersensitivity of body tissues esp. to the action of some particular foreign material, as certain foods, pollens, micro-organisms, etc.; (fig.) antipathy. **aller'gic** *adj.* Of, possessing, allergy; susceptible *to* (also fig.).

allē'viāte *v.t.* Make less burdensome or severe. **allēviā'tion** *n.* **allē'viative, allē'viatorȳ** *adjs.*

ă'lley *n.* Narrow street; walk, passage; (U.S.) back street; enclosure for skittles etc.

Alleyn (alā'n), Edward (1566–1626). English actor; built with Henslowe the Fortune Theatre in Cripplegate, London; built and endowed Dulwich College. **Alley'nian** *n.* Member of Dulwich College.

allī'ance *n.* Act, state, of allying or being allied; union by marriage; relationship; confederation, league (esp. between States); *Holy A~*: see HOLY; *Triple ~*: see TRIPLE.

ă'llied (-īd) *adj.* Combined, united (*to*, *with*); *the A~ Powers*, the Allies.

ă'llĭgātor *n.* Crocodilian (genera *Alligator* and *Cayman*) of New World and China, having certain teeth in lower jaw which fit into pits, not into notches as in crocodiles proper; *~-pear*, AVOCADO. [Span. *el lagarto*, f. L *lacerta* lizard]

allĭterā'tion *n.* Commencement of two or more words in close connection with the same letter or sound, esp. as a device in verse. **allĭ'terāte** *v.i.* (Contain words that) begin with the same sound. **allĭ'terătive** *adj.* **allĭ'teratively̆** *adv.*

ă'llocāte *v.t.* Assign (*to*); locate. **ăllocā'tion** *n.* Apportionment.

allō'dium *n.* (hist.) Estate held absolutely, without acknowledgement to an overlord. **allō'dial** *adj.* **allō'dially̆** *adv.*

allŏ'pathy̆ *n.* Traditional medical practice which aims at curing disease by remedies having opposite effect to that caused by the disease (opp. HOMOEOPATHY). **ăllopă'thic** *adj.* **ăllopă'thically̆** *adv.* **allŏ'pathist** *n.*

allŏ't *v.t.* Give as due share.

allŏ'tment *n.* Apportioning; lot in life; share allotted to one; portion of land let out for cultivation, esp. small plot where occupier produces vegetables and fruit crops for home consumption.

ă'llotrōpe *n.* One form of an element, differing from another or others in crystal form, or in chemical properties, or in molecular complexity, or in all three (as oxygen and ozone; yellow and red phosphorus; graphite and diamond). **ăllotrŏ'pic** *adj.* **ă'llotropy̆** (*or* alŏ'-) *n.* Existence of elements in allotropic form.

allow' *v.* Admit; (U.S.) form the opinion (*that*); permit; admit *of*; give (limited periodical sum); add, deduct, in consideration of something; ~ *for*, take into consideration. **allow'able** *adj.*

allow'ance *n.* 1. Permission; tolerance. 2. Limited portion, esp. yearly income; addition to salary to cover special expenses, as *entertainment* ~, *foreign service* ~; *family* ~, allowance paid by State or employer to parent of family. 3. Deduction, discount; *make* ~(*s*) *for*, allow for. ~ *v.t.* Make allowance to (person).

allow'ĕdly̆ *adv.* Admittedly.

ă'lloy (*or* aloi') *n.* 1. Metal consisting of a metallic element with admixture of another metal or non-metals, usu. having more useful properties than its constituents (e.g. brass is an alloy of copper and zinc, type-metal an alloy of lead and tin and antimony). 2. (archaic) Base metal mixed esp. with gold or silver. **alloy'** *v.t.* 1. Form an alloy (of). 2. Debase.

a'llspīce (awl-) *n.* Pimento, supposed to combine flavour of cinnamon, nutmeg, and cloves.

A'llston (awl-), Washington (1779–1843). American Romantic painter.

allū'de (*or* -ōōd) *v.i.* Make indirect or passing reference *to*.

allūr'e *v.t.* Tempt, entice; fascinate, charm. ~ *n.* Personal charm. **allūr'ement** *n.*

allū'sion (*or* -ōō-) *n.* Indirect or passing reference.

allū'sĭve (*or* -ōō-) *adj.* Containing an allusion, full of allusions. **allū'sĭvely̆** *adv.* **allū'sĭvenĕss** *n.*

allū'vion (*or* -ōō-) *n.* Wash of sea against shore or of river against banks; flood; (esp.) alluvium; (law) formation of new land by action of water.

allū'vium (*or* -ōō-) *n.* (pl. *-via*, *-viums*). Deposit of earth, sand, etc., left by flood esp. in river valleys and deltas. **allū'vial** *adj.* ~ *cone*, *fan*, deposit left by swift stream entering a valley or plain. **allū'vially̆** *adv.*

ally̆'[1] *v.t.* Combine, unite, for special object. **ă'lly̆** (*or* ălī') *n.* Person, State, etc., allied with another; *the Allies*, members of the Triple Entente and those who joined them in the 1914–18 war; nations opposed to the Axis Powers in the 1939–45 war.

ă'lly̆[2] *n.* Choice playing-marble of marble, alabaster, or glass.

A'lma (ă-). River in the Crimea, scene of first battle in the Crimean War, 1854, in which the French and British defeated the Russians.

almacantar: see ALMUCANTAR.

A'lmăck (awl- *or* ŏl-), William (d. 1781). Founder of ~*'s Assembly Rooms* in St. James's, London, celebrated in the 18th and early 19th centuries as the scene of social functions, and of a gaming-club.

A'lmagĕst (ă-). 1. Arabic version of Ptolemy's astronomical treatise. 2. (in the Middle Ages; also *a*~) Any of various other celebrated textbooks of astrology and alchemy. [Arab. *al* the, Gk *megistē* (*suntaxis*) great (system)]

A'lma Mā'ter (ă-; *or* mah-). Title used in reference to one's university or school. [L, = 'fostering mother']

a'lmanăc, -ck (awl- *or* ŏl-) *n.* Annual calendar of months and days with astronomical and other data.

A'lmanăch de Gō'tha (awl- *or* ŏl-; -k, -t*a*). Annual publication giving information about European royalty, nobility, and diplomats.

Alma-Tă'dėma (ăl-), Sir Lawrence (1836–1912). Painter of classical subjects; born in Holland, naturalized as an Englishman.

almighty (awlmī'tĭ) *adj.* All-powerful; *the A*~, God.

a'lmond (ahm-) *n.* Kernel of stone-fruit of two varieties of *Prunus amygdalus* (*sweet, bitter* ~), allied to plum and peach; the tree; anything almond-shaped.

ă'lmoner (*or* ahm-) *n.* 1. Official distributor of alms. 2. Medical social worker, usu. woman at hospital or clinic, with duty of helping patients to carry out doctor's advice esp. after discharge from hospital (formerly also responsible for collecting fees).

ă'lmonrȳ (*or* ahm-), *n.* (hist.) Place where alms were distributed; almoner's residence.

a'lmōst (awl-) *adv.* Very nearly.

alms (ahmz) *n.* Charitable relief of the poor; donation; *a'lmshouse*, one founded by charity for reception of poor, usu. old, people; *a'lmsman*, one supported by alms.

ălmūcă'ntar, -mac- *n.* Line of constant altitude above the horizon. [Arab. *al-mukanṭar*, f. *ḳanṭara* to bridge]

ă'lōe *n.* Liliaceous plant of genus *A*~, with erect spikes of flowers, rosettes of fleshy leaves (often spiny), and bitter juice; (pl.) purgative drug procured from juice of aloes; *American* ~, kind of agave. **ălōē'tĭc** *adj.* (med.) Containing aloes.

alŏ'ft *adv.* & *pred. adj.* High up; upward; esp. in(to) the upper parts of a ship's rigging.

alō'ne *pred. adj.* Not with others, solitary. ~ *adv.* Only, exclusively.

alŏ'ng *prep.* From end to end of, through any part of the length of; *alo'ngside*, close to side of ship; *alongside of*, side by side with. ~ *adv.* In company or conjunction *with*; *all* ~, all the time.

aloo͞'f *adv.* & *pred. adj.* Away, apart.

ălōpē'cĭa *n.* (med.) Baldness; (pop. used for) ~ *areata*, affection of scalp causing temporary bald patches. [Gk *alopekia* fox-mange f. *alopex* fox]

alou'd *adv.* Audibly, not in a whisper; (archaic) loudly.

ălp *n.* Mountain-peak; green pasture-land on (Swiss) mountain-side.

ălpă'ca *n.* S. Amer. domesticated camel-like hoofed mammal, bred in Andes for its long woolly hair; its fleece; fabric of alpaca hair mixed with cotton; any of various silk, cotton or rayon fabrics more or less resembling this. [Arab *al* the, Peruvian name *paco*]

ă'lpėnstŏck *n.* Staff with iron point used in mountain climbing.

ă'lpha *n.* 1st letter of Greek alphabet (Α, α), corresponding to *a*, used in enumerations etc.; examiner's first-class mark; (astron.) chief star of constellation; ~ *and omega*, first and last letters of Greek alphabet; hence, beginning and end (see Rev. 1: 8); ~ *particles, rays*, first of three types of radiation emitted by radioactive substances, consisting of positively charged particles; ~ *plus*, superlatively good.

ă'lphabĕt *n.* Set of letters (in customary order) used in a language; first rudiments; symbols representing speech sounds (*phonetic* ~); *deaf-and-dumb* ~: see DEAF. **ălphabĕ'tĭcal** *adj.* Of the alphabet; esp. in ~ *order*. **ălpha-**

bĕ'ticallў̆ *adv.* [Gk *alpha, beta,* first two letters of alphabet]

ă'lpīne *adj.* Of the Alps or other lofty mountains; (geol.) of a European episode of mountain formation during the Tertiary era. *~climate,* (geog.) that of regions above coniferous forests and below line of permanent snow; ~ *plant,* plant native to these regions, or (loosely) to mountain districts, or suited to similar conditions. **ă'lpinist** *n.* Alpine climber.

Alps (ă-). Mountain range extending from Ligurian Sea and Rhône valley through Switzerland to the western Hungarian plain.

already (awlrĕ'dĭ) *adv.* Beforehand; by this time, thus early.

a.l.s. *abbrev.* Autograph letter signed.

A'lsăce (ă-; *or* -săs'). French province W. of the Rhine; inhabited by mixed German and Latin stocks; annexed with part of Lorraine (the annexed territory was known as Alsace-Lorraine) by Germany after the Franco-Prussian war of 1870; restored to France after the 1914–18 war.

Alsā'tia (ă-, -sha). 1. Old name of Alsace. 2. Former cant name of precinct of Whitefriars, London, which, until its privileges (orig. those enjoyed by the Carmelites) were abolished in 1697, was a sanctuary for debtors and lawbreakers. **Alsā'tian** *adj.* & *n.* (Native, inhabitant) of Alsace; (also ~ *wolf-dog*) German shepherd dog.

a'lsō (awl- *or* ŏl-) *adv.* In addition; *~-ran,* horse not among first three in a race; (fig.) person etc. not distinguished in contest.

ălt *n.* (mus.) High note; *in* ~, in the octave (beginning with G) above the treble stave.

Altā'ic (ă-) *adj.* & *n.* (Of) a family of languages comprising Turkish, Mongol, and Tungus.

a'ltar (awl- *or* ŏl-) *n.* Flat-topped block for offerings to deity; Communion table; *lead to the* ~, marry (a woman); *~-cloth,* linen cloth used at Communion or Mass; silk frontal and super-frontal; *a'ltarpiece,* painting or sculpture above back of altar.

a'lter (awl- *or* ŏl-) *v.* Change in character, position, etc.; *altered rock,* (geol.) rock which has been metamorphosed by pressure or heat. **alterā'tion** *n.*

a'lterative (awl- *or* ŏl-) *adj.* Tending to alter. ~ *n.* Treatment, medicine, that alters processes of nutrition.

a'ltercāte (awl- *or* ŏl-) *v.i.* Dispute hotly, wrangle. **altercā'tion** *n.*

ă'lter ĕ'gō. One's other self, intimate friend. [L]

altêr'nate (awl- *or* ŏl-) *adj.* (of things of two kinds) Coming each after one of the other kind; placed on alternate sides (of line, stem, etc.). **altêr'natelў̆** *adv.* **a'lternāte** *v.* Arrange, perform, alternately; interchange (one thing) alternately *with,* by another; succeed each other by turns; consist of alternate things; *alternating current,* (abbrev. A.C. or a.c.) electric current whose direction is regularly reversed; *alternating generations,* (biol.) reproductive cycle in which the offspring differ in structure and habits from their parents but resemble their grandparents; (also, erron.) cycle in which sexual reproduction is preceded and followed by asexual. **alternā'tion** *n.*

altêr'native (awl- *or* ŏl-) *adj.* Available in place of another (thing); (of two things) mutually exclusive. ~ *n.* Permission to choose between two things; either of two possible courses; one of more than two possibilities. **altêr'nativelў̆** *adv.*

a'lternātor (awl- *or* ŏl-) *n.* Dynamo producing alternating current.

ă'lthôrn (-t-h-) *n.* Alto saxhorn.

although (awl-dhō') *conj.* Though.

ă'ltimēter *n.* Aneroid barometer indicating altitude reached, as in aviation.

ă'ltitūde *n.* 1. Height. 2. (geom.) Length of perpendicular from vertex to base. 3. (geog.) Height above mean sea-level. 4.

(astron., of heavenly body) Angular distance above horizon. 5. High place, (fig.) eminence.

ă'ltō *n.* (pl. *-os*). Highest adult male voice; female voice of similar range, contralto; singer with alto voice; musical part for this. ~ *adj.* (of instrument) Tenor; ~ *clef*: see CLEF.

ăltocū'mūlus *n.* (meteor.) Type of cloud, of medium height, in form of thin patches often very close together or almost joined.

altogĕ'ther (awl-, -dh-) *adv.* Totally; on the whole. ~ *n. in the* ~, completely naked.

ă'lto-rėlie'vo (-lē-) *n.* (Sculpture in) high relief. [It. *alto-rilievo*]

ăltostrā'tus *n.* (meteor.) Continuous veil of cloud, thin or thick, of medium height.

ă'ltruism (-rōō-) *n.* Regard for others as a principle of action. **ăltrui'stic** *adj.* **ăltrui'stically** *adv.*

ă'lum *n.* One of series of double sulphates, esp. that of potassium and aluminium, used industrially, esp. in paper-making and leather tanning.

alū'mina *n.* Aluminium oxide (Al_2O_3), which occurs as ruby, sapphire, etc., and as bauxite from which aluminium is obtained. **alū'mināte** *n.* Compound of alumina with one of the stronger bases.

ălūmi'nium *n.* (chem.) Light silvery white metallic element (symbol Al, at. no. 13, at. wt. 26·9815), not found naturally but widely distributed in the form of compounds, obtained by electrolysis and widely used esp. in alloys for construction of aircraft etc.

ălū'minīze *v.t.* Coat with aluminium. **ălūminīzā'tion** *n.*

ălū'minous *adj.* Of the nature of alum or alumina; containing aluminium.

ălū'minum *n.* (U.S.) = ALUMINIUM.

alŭ'mnus *n.* (pl. *-nī*). (Former) pupil of a school or university. [L, = 'foster-child']

A'lva, A'lba (ă-), Fernando Alvarez de Toledo, Duke of (1508–82). Spanish general, Stadholder of the Netherlands, 1567–73.

ălvē'olar (*or* -vĭō'-) *adj.* Of an alveolus; ~ *consonant*, one formed with point of tongue behind the upper teeth. ~ *n.* Alveolar sound or consonant.

ă'lvėolate *adj.* Honey-combed, pitted with small cavities.

alvē'olus (*or* -vĭō'-) *n.* (pl. *-lī*). Small cavity, socket of a tooth; terminal air-sac of lung in which exchange of gases between lung and blood takes place; cell of honeycomb; conical chamber of belemnite.

always (aw'lwāz) *adv.* At all times, on all occasions, in all circumstances.

ăm. 1st pers. sing. pres. of BE.

a.m. *abbrev. Anno mundi* (L, = in the year of the world); *ante meridiem.*

A.M. *abbrev.* Albert Medal.

A'madis of Gaul (ăm-). Hero of a Spanish (or Portuguese) 15th-c. romance of chivalry.

amai'n *adv.* (archaic) Vehemently; in all haste.

Amă'lėkīte *adj.* & *n.* (Member) of a nomadic people descended from Esau (Gen. 36: 12), proverbial for treachery.

amă'lgam *n.* Alloy of a metal or metals, with mercury, freq. plastic and used, e.g., in dentistry.

amă'lgamāte *v.* Combine, unite (esp. of business firms); mix; (of metals) alloy with mercury. **amălgamā'tion** *n.*

amănūĕ'nsis *n.* (pl. *-ses*). One who writes from dictation, or copies; literary assistant.

ă'marănth *n.* Imaginary unfading flower; plant of genus *Amaranthus*, including love-lies-bleeding; purple colour. **ămară'nthīne** *adj.* (poet.) Unfading; purple.

Amar'na, Tell el. Site of Akhetaten, city of ancient Egypt built by AKHNATEN; ~ *letters, tablets*, cuneiform tablets of 14th c. B.C. found there, containing letters from neighbouring governors etc.

ămarȳ'llis *n.* Autumn-flowering bulbous plant of genus *A*~ comprising only one species, *A. belladonna* from Cape of Good Hope, also called belladonna lily. [Gk *Amarullis* name of a country girl in Theocritus and Virgil]

amă'ss *v.t.* Heap together; accumulate.

ă'mateur (-têr *or* -tūr) n. One who is fond *of*; one who practises a thing, esp. an art or game, as a pastime (freq. opp. *professional*). **ămateu'rish** (*or* ă'-) *adj.* Like an amateur; imperfect in execution, unskilful. **ămateu'rishlȳ** *adv.* **ămateu'rishnėss, ămateu'rism** *ns.*

Ama'ti (-ah-). Name of a family of violin-makers of Cremona, flourishing *c* 1550–*c* 1700: *Nicola* ~ (1596–1684) taught Antonio Stradivari.

ă'mative *adj.* Disposed to loving. **ă'mativenėss** *n.*

ă'matŏl *n.* High explosive, a mixture of ammonium nitrate and trinitrotoluene. [irreg. f. *am*(monia) + (trinitro)*tol*(uol)]

ă'matorȳ *adj.* Pertaining to a lover or sexual love.

amā'ze *v.t.* Overwhelm with wonder. ~ *n.* (poet.) Amazement. **amā'zėdlȳ, amā'zinglȳ** *advs.* **amā'zement** *n.*

A'mazon[1] (ă-). (Gk myth.) One of a race of female warriors alleged by Herodotus to exist in Scythia; hence, female warrior; tall strong or athletic woman.

A'mazon[2] (ă-). Great river of S. America, flowing into the southern Atlantic on N. coast of Brazil; it bore various names after its discovery in 1500 and was finally named because of a legend that a tribe of female warriors lived somewhere on its banks.

Amazō'nian (ă-) *adj.* Of the Amazons; of the Amazon river.

ămbă'ssador *n.* Minister sent by one sovereign or State on mission to another; minister permanently representing sovereign or State at foreign court or government; official messenger. **ămbăssadŏr'ial** *adj.* **ămbă'ssadrėss** *n.* Female ambassador; ambassador's wife.

ă'mber *n.* & *adj.* (Made of, coloured like) yellow translucent fossil resin found chiefly on S. shore of Baltic and valued as ornament; (of) cautionary traffic light between red (= stop) and green (= go). [Fr. *ambre*, f. Arab. *ʿanbar* ambergris, to which the name originally belonged]

ă'mbergris (-ēs) *n.* Wax-like grey or blackish substance found floating in tropical seas, and in intestines of sperm-whale, odoriferous and used in perfumery. [Fr. *ambre gris* grey amber]

ămbidĕ'xtrous *adj.* Able to use left hand as readily as right; double-dealing. **ămbidĕ'xtrouslȳ** *adv.* **ămbidĕ'xtrousnėss** *n.*

ă'mbient *adj.* Surrounding. **ă'mbience** *n.* Environment, surroundings; atmosphere.

ămbi'gūous *adj.* Obscure; of double meaning; of doubtful classification; of uncertain issue. **ămbi'gūouslȳ** *adv.* **ămbi'gūousnėss** *n.* **ămbigū'itȳ** *n.* Double meaning; expression capable of more than one meaning.

ă'mbit *n.* Precincts; bounds; compass, extent.

ămbi'tion *n.* Ardent desire for distinction; aspiration *to* (be or do); object of such desire.

ămbi'tious (sh*us*) *adj.* Full of or showing ambition; strongly desirous. **ămbi'tiouslȳ** *adv.* **ămbi'tiousnėss** *n.* [L *ambitio* canvassing for votes, f. *ambire* go round]

ămbi'valence *n.* State of having either or both of two contrary values or qualities; co-existence in one person of contradictory emotions (as love and hatred) towards the same person or thing. **ămbi'valent** *adj.*

ă'mble *v.i.* (of horse etc.) Move by lifting two feet on one side together; ride, move, at an easy pace. ~ *n.* Pace of an ambling horse; easy pace.

ămblȳō'pia *n.* Dimness of vision without discernible change in the eye. **ămblȳŏ′pĭc** *adj.* **ămblȳŏ′pĭcallȳ** *adv.*

ă′mbō *n.* (pl. *-bōs, -bō′nēs*) Pulpit in early Christian churches.

Amboi′na (ă-), **ăm-** *n.* Very hard ornamental wood (*Pterocarpus indicus*) exported from the Moluccas. [town and island of the Moluccas]

A′mbrōse (ă-, -z), St. (*c* 340–97). Bishop of Milan; Doctor of the Church; commemorated 7 Dec. (in B.C.P. calendar 4 April). **Ambrō′sĭan** *adj.* Of St. Ambrose; ~ *chant*, mode of chanting reputedly developed by St. Ambrose.

ămbrō′sĭa (-z-) *n.* (myth.) Food of the gods; anything delightful to taste or smell; bee-bread. **ămbrō′sĭal** *adj.* **ămbrō′sĭallȳ** *adv.* [L, f. Gk, f. *ambrotos* immortal].

ă′mbrȳ *n.* Var. of AUMBRY.

ă′mbūlance *n.* Vehicle for conveyance of sick or injured persons.

ă′mbūlant *adj.* (med.) Walking, not confined to bed.

ă′mbūlatorȳ *adj.* Pertaining to, adapted for, walking, movable; not permanent. ~ *n.* Place for walking; arcade, cloister; esp., aisle round apse at east end of church.

ămbuscā′de *n.* Ambush. ~ *v.* Lie, conceal, in ambush.

ă′mbush (-ŏŏ-) *n.* Concealment of troops, troops concealed, in a wood, etc.; lying in wait. ~ *v.* Lie in wait (for); *ambushed*, (of troops) concealed.

A.M.D.G. *abbrev.* *Ad majorem Dei gloriam* (L, = 'to the greater glory of God').

âme damnée (ahm dahnā). Devoted adherent, tool. [Fr., = 'damned soul']

ameer′ *n.* Var. of EMIR.

amē′lĭorāte *v.* (Cause to) become better. **amēlĭorā′tion** *n.* **amē′lĭoratĭve** *adj.* **amē′lĭoratĭvelȳ** *adv.*

āmĕ′n[1] (*or* ah-) *int.* So be it (used at end of prayer etc.). ~ *n.* Utterance of 'amen'; expression of assent. [Heb. *'āmēn* certainly, truly]

Amen[2]: see AMMON.

amē′nable. *adj.* Responsible; liable *to*; capable of being tested by (*to*); responsive, tractable. **amē′nableness, amēnabĭ′lĭtȳ** *ns.* **amē′nablȳ** *adv.*

amĕ′nd *v.* Abandon evil ways; correct an error in (document), make professed improvements in (measure before Parliament, proposal, etc.); make better. **amĕ′ndment** *n.*

amende honorable (ămahnd ŏnŏrahbl). Public apology and reparation. [Fr.]

amĕ′nds (-z) *n.* Reparation, restitution, compensation.

Amĕnhō′tĕp (ah-). Name of four pharaohs of the 18th dynasty in Egypt; ~ *IV*: see AKHNATEN.

amĕ′nĭtȳ *n.* Quality of being pleasant, agreeable; (characteristic of) situation, climate, disposition, etc., that is agreeable or pleasant (often pl.); ~ *bed*, accommodation for which a charge is made in a National Health Service hospital, for patient desiring privacy.

Amĕnō′phĭs (ah-). = AMENHOTEP.

āmĕnorrhoe′a (-rēa) *n.* (physiol.) Absence of menstruation.

amĕ′ntum *n.* (pl. *-ta*). Catkin. **ămĕntā′ceous** (-sh*u*s), **ămentĭ′ferous** *adjs.*

amer′ce *v.t.* Fine; punish. **amer′cĭable** *adj.* **amer′cement, amer′cĭament** *ns.*

Amĕ′rĭca. Continent of the New World or western hemisphere, consisting of two great land-masses, *North* ~ and *South* ~, joined by the narrow isthmus of *Central* ~; N. America comprises Canada, the United States, and Mexico; Central and S. America are divided into a number of independent States. N. America was prob. visited by Norse seamen in 8th or 9th c., but for the modern world the continent was discovered by Christopher Columbus, who reached the W. Indies in 1492 and the S. American mainland in 1498. [named after *Amerigo* VESPUCCI]

Amĕ′rĭcan *adj.* Of America or its people; of the United States of

America; ~ *Civil War*, war (1861–5) between eleven Southern (Confederate) States and the rest of the Union, arising from the secession of the Southern States who disagreed esp. with the Northern (Federal) States' policy of freeing the Negro slaves imported from Africa to work in the plantations, and ending in their defeat; ~ *cloth*, flexible cotton cloth treated with cellulose nitrates to make it resemble shiny leather; ~ *English*: see ENGLISH; (*North-*) ~ *Indian*, one of the aboriginal inhabitants of N. America, chiefly nomadic tribes of hunters and warriors with red skins and black smooth hair; ~ *organ*, instrument resembling harmonium but sucking wind inward through reeds instead of expelling it; ~ *Revolution*, ~ *War of Independence*, revolt (1775–83) of the English colonies in N. America which subsequently formed the United States. ~ *n.* 1. American person. 2. Citizen of the U.S. 3. American English.

Amĕ'rĭcanĭsm *n.* 1. Word or phrase peculiar to or borrowed from U.S. 2. Attachment to, sympathy with, U.S.

Amĕ'rĭcanīze *v.* Naturalize as an American; make, become, American in character. **Amĕ'rĭcanīzātion** *n.*

Amĕ'rĭca's Cŭp (-z). Yachting trophy orig. presented by the R.Y.S. for a race round the Isle of Wight (1851), and won by the American schooner *America*; offered as a challenge trophy for a race between English and American yachts, but in spite of many attempts not subsequently regained by an English yacht.

ămerĭ'cium (*or* -shĭ-) *n.* (chem.) Metallic radioactive transuranic element; symbol Am, at. no. 95, principal isotope at. wt 241. [f. *America* (first made at Berkeley, California)]

ă'mĕthy̆st *n.* Purple or violet precious stone, a variety of quartz coloured by manganese. **ămĕthy̆'stīne** *adj.* [Gk *amethustos* not drunken (*methu* wine), because the stone was supposed to have the power of preventing intoxication]

Amhă'ric (ă-) *adj.* & *n.* (Of) the official and court language of Ethiopia, a Semitic language related to ancient Ethiopic.

ā'mĭable *adj.* Feeling and inspiring friendship; lovable. **āmĭabĭ'lĭty̆** *n.* **ā'mĭably̆** *adv.*

ă'mĭcable *adj.* Friendly. **ămĭcabĭ'lĭty̆** *n.* **ă'mĭcably̆** *adv.*

ă'mĭce[1] *n.* Square of white linen worn by celebrant priest about the neck and shoulders (formerly on head).

ă'mĭce[2] *n.* Cap, hood, cape, of religious orders; badge worn by French canons on left arm.

A.M.I.C.E. *abbrev.* Associate Member of the Institution of Civil Engineers.

amī'cus cūr'iae. Disinterested adviser. [L, = 'friend of the court']

amĭ'd *prep.* In the middle of; in the course of.

ā'mĭde *n.* Compound formed from ammonia by replacement of one or more hydrogen atoms by a metal or acid radical.

amĭ'dshĭps *adv.* In the middle of ship.

amĭ'dst *prep.* (poet.) Amid.

A.M.I.E.E. *abbrev.* Associate Member of the Institution of Electrical Engineers.

A.M.I.Mech.E. *abbrev.* Associate Member of the Institution of Mechanical Engineers.

Amĭndi'vĭ I'slands (ŭm-, -dē-, īlandz): see LACCADIVE ISLANDS.

ă'mīne *n.* (chem.) Compound derived from ammonia by replacing one or more of the hydrogen atoms by certain aliphatic or aromatic radicals.

amīno- *prefix* (chem.) Pertaining to, or containing the group NH_2, as ~*-acid*.

amir' (-ēr) *n.* Var. of EMIR.

amĭ'ss *adv.* & *pred. adj.* Out of order; wrong(ly); untoward(ly).

ămĭtō'sĭs *n.* (pl. *-sēs*). (biol.) Direct division of a nucleus or cell without mitosis. **ămĭtŏ'tĭc** *adj.*

ă'mĭty̆ *n.* Friendship, friendly relations.

ă'mmĕter *n.* Instrument for

measuring electric currents. [AM(PERE) + METER]

ă'mmō *n.* (colloq.) Ammunition.

A'mmon[1], **A'men**[2] (ă-). Supreme god of the ancient Egyptians in the Theban religion; his worship spread to Greece, where he was identified with Zeus, and to Rome, where he was known as Jupiter Ammon.

A'mmon[2] (ă-). Ancient country of the Ammonites, in S. Transjordan. **A'mmonīte**[2] *adj.* & *n.* (Member) of a Semitic people traditionally descended from Lot (Gen. 19: 38), living in Ammon.

ammō'nia *n.* Colourless gas (NH_3) with pungent smell, very soluble in water, giving alkaline solution; aqueous solution of this gas. [f. Jupiter AMMON[1], near whose temple sal ammoniac is said to have been prepared]

ammō'niăc *adj.* Of the nature of ammonia; *sal* ~, ammonium chloride (NH_4Cl), a hard white crystalline salt used in pharmacy, electric batteries, etc. **ămmonī'acal** *adj.* Of or resembling ammonia.

ammō'niātėd *adj.* Combined with ammonia.

ă'mmonīte[1] *n.* Member of an extinct group of cephalopods with chambered shell coiled in a flat

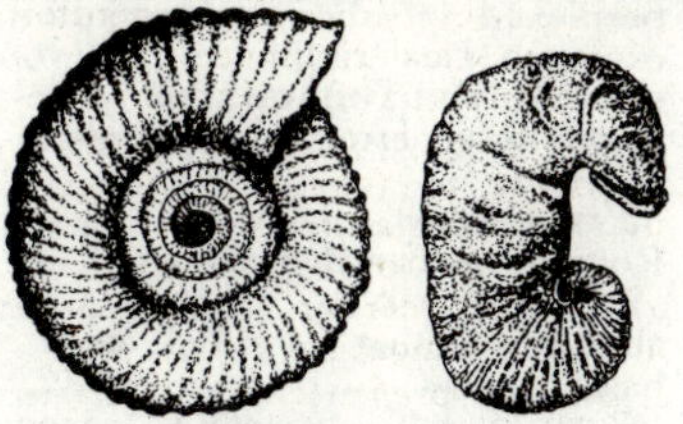

AMMONITE

spiral, freq. found fossilized in some Mesozoic rocks. [L *cornu Ammonis* horn of AMMON]

Ammonite[2]: see AMMON[2].

ammō'nium *n.* (chem.) Radical (NH_4), which has not been isolated, whose compounds resemble those of the alkali metals.

ămmūnī'tion *n.* Military stores (now only of projectiles with their necessary propellants, detonators, fuses, etc.); also fig.

ămnē'sia (-z- *or* -zh*a*) *n.* Loss of memory.

ă'mnėstў *n.* Pardon granted by sovereign or State for an offence, esp. one of a political character. ~ *v.t.* Give amnesty to.

ă'mnīŏn *n.* (zool., physiol.) Membrane enclosing embryo or foetus. **ămnīŏ'tic** *adj.* Of the amnion; ~ *fluid*, fluid filling amniotic sac; ~ *sac*, cavity enclosed by amnion.

amoe'ba (*amēba*) *n.* Primitive single-celled animalcule perpetually changing shape by pro-

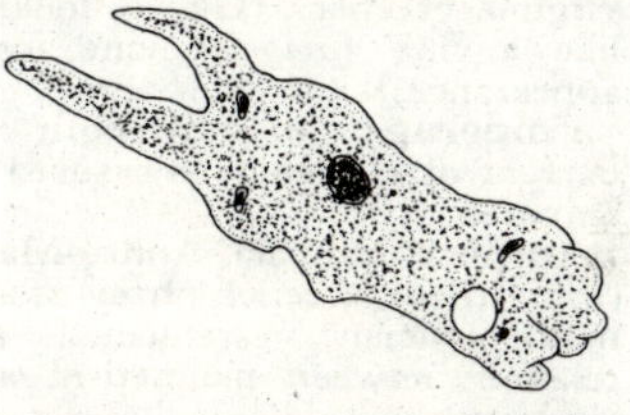

truding portions of its body (pseudopods) and reproducing by fission. **amoe'bĭc, amoe'boid** *adjs.*

amŏ'k, amŭ'ck *adv.* *run* ~, run about in murderous frenzy; get out of control. [Malay *amok* rushing in frenzy]

amo'ng, amo'ngst (-mŭ-) *prep.* In the assemblage or number of; surrounded by, within the limits of; by joint action of; between; ~ *themselves*, with one another.

Amŏntĭlla'dō, a- (-ah-) *n.* One of the principal types of dry sherry, with nutty flavour. [Span., = 'made like (the wine of) *Montilla*' (place in Cordova)]

āmŏ'ral *adj.* Non-moral; outside the sphere of morals.

A'morīte (ă-) *adj.* & *n.* (Member) of an ancient Semitic people of the Middle East.

ă'morous *adj.* Inclined to love; in love; of or pertaining to love. **ă'morouslў** *adv.* **ă'morousnėss** *n.*

amŏr'phous *adj.* Shapeless; (chem., min.) not crystalline. **amŏr'phĭsm** *n.* **amŏr'phouslў** *adv.* **amŏr'phousnėss** *n.*

amŏr'tīze *v.t.* Alienate in mortmain; extinguish (debt, usu. by sinking-fund); gradually write off initial cost of (asset). **amŏrtīzā'tion** *n.*

A'mŏs (ā-) (*c* 760 B.C.). Hebrew minor prophet; book of O.T. containing his prophecies.

amou'nt *v.i.* Be equivalent *to*; add up *to*. ~ *n.* Total, quantity.

amour' (-oor). Love affair, intrigue.

amour prŏpre (ămoor prŏpr). Self-esteem. [Fr.]

ămp *n.* = AMPERE.

ămpėlŏ'psĭs *n.* (pl. *-sēs*). Climbing plant allied to vine, esp. virginia creeper. [Gk, = 'looking like a vine' (*ampelos* vine, *opsis* appearance)]

ă'mperage *n.* Strength of current of electricity measured in amperes.

Ampère (ahṅpār), Andre-Marie (1775–1836). French physicist and mathematician; established the relation between magnetism and electricity.

ă'mpēre (*or* -ār) *n.* Fundamental unit of electric current, that which if maintained in two straight parallel conductors 1 metre apart would produce between these a force equal to 2×10^{-7} newton per metre of length (abbrev. A); ~ *turn*, magnetomotive force produced by one ampere passing through one complete turn of a conducting coil. [f. AMPÈRE]

ă'mpersănd *n.* The sign '&' (= *and*). [f. phrase 'and *per se* (= by itself) and']

ămphĕ'tamĭne *n.* Powerful synthetic drug which stimulates the heart and respiration, constricts blood-vessels, and induces sleeplessness.

ămphĭ-, ămph- *prefix.* Both, of both kinds, on both sides, around.

ămphĭ'bĭan *adj.* & *n.* 1. (Animal) living both on land and in water; (animal) of the Amphibia, a class of vertebrates intermediate between reptiles and fishes and including anurans, caecilians, and urodeles. 2. (Aeroplane, tank, etc.) able to operate both on land and water. [Gk *amphibios* leading a double life]

ămphĭ'bĭous *adj.* Living both on land and in water, connected with both; (mil.) amphibian; involving both land and sea forces.

ă'mphĭbrach (-ăk) *n.* Metrical foot of three syllables, one long between two short, or one accented between two unaccented (◡ – ◡).

ămphĭŏ'xus *n.* Lancelet of genus *Branchiostoma*.

ămphĭ'prostȳle *adj.* & *n.* (Building) with portico at both ends.

ămphĭsbae'na *n.* 1. Fabulous serpent with head at each end. 2. (zool.) Worm-like lizard of genus *A*~. [Gk *amphis* both ways, *baino* go]

ă'mphĭtheatre (-ĭater) *n.* Oval or circular building or arena with seats rising in tiers round a central open space; natural formation resembling this; semicircular gallery in theatre; (fig.) scene of a contest.

Amphĭtrī'tė (ă-). (Gk myth.) Sea-goddess, the wife of Poseidon.

Amphĭ'trȳon (ă-). (Gk myth.) Husband of Alcmene; while he was absent Zeus impersonated him and became the father of Hercules by Alcmene. In Moliere's comedy 'Amphitryon' (iii. 5) a servant, perplexed by the impersonation, exclaims 'Le véritable Amphitryon est l'Amphitryon où l'on dine'; hence, a generous host or a gastronome.

ă'mphora *n.* (pl. *-rae*). Greek or Roman two-handled vase.

ămphotĕ'rĭc *adj.* (chem.) Capable of reacting as either acid or base.

ă'mple *adj.* Spacious, extensive; abundant; quite enough. **ă'mplȳ** *adv.*

ă'mplĭfȳ *v.* Enlarge; increase strength of (electric current, signal, etc.); add details. **ămplĭficā'tion** *n.* **ă'mplĭfīer** *n.* (esp.) Appliance for increasing strength of electrical signals.

ă'mplĭtūde *n.* 1. Breadth; abundance; wide range. 2. (astron.) Distance from due east or

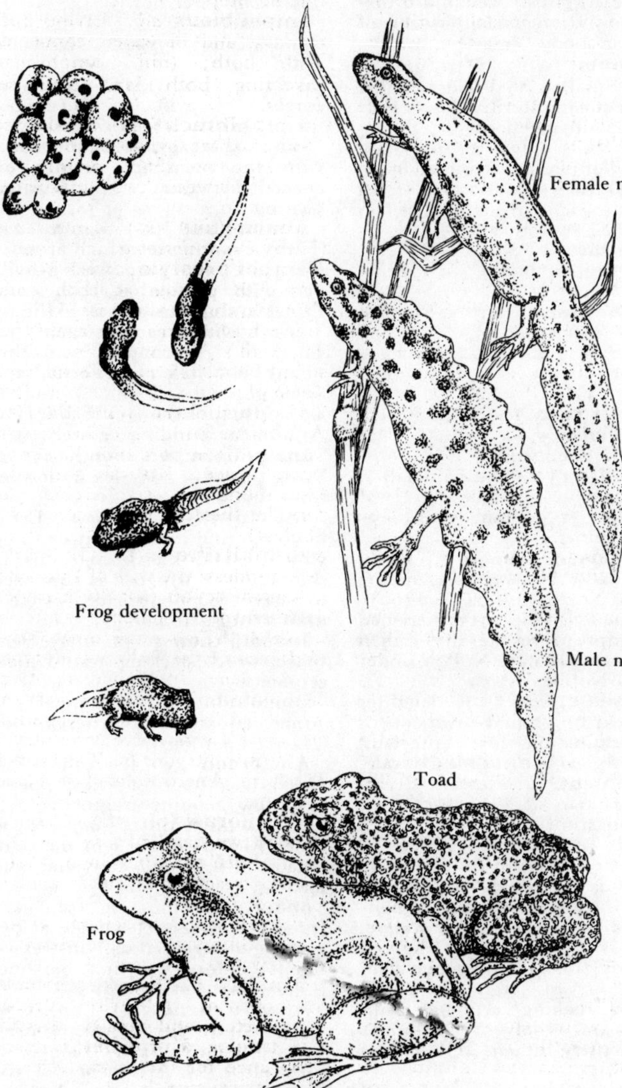

AMPHIBIANS

west at which celestial body rises or sets. 3. (phys.) Maximum displacement from mean position of vibrating body etc.

ă'mpoule (-ōōl), **ă'mpūle** *n.* (med.) Small sealed glass vessel used for storing sterilized materials prepared for injection.

ămpu'lla (-ŏŏl*a*) *n.* (pl. *-ae*). Roman globular two-handled flask; medieval pilgrim's bottle; vessel for holding chrism or oil used in ceremonial anointing.

ă'mpūtāte *v.t.* Cut off (esp. part of animal body). **ămpūtā'tion** *n.*

A.M.S. *abbrev.* Army Medical Staff (*or* Service).

A.M.S.E. *abbrev.* Associate Member of the Society of Engineers.

Am'sterdă'm (ă-). Capital of the Netherlands.

amuck: see AMOK.

Amu Da'rȳa (ahmōō' dah-): see OXUS.

ă'mūlėt *n.* Thing worn as charm against evil.

A'mundsen (ămŏŏ-), Roald (1872–1928). Norwegian explorer; explored North-west Passage 1903–6; reached S. Pole 1911; perished in attempt to rescue the Italian airship expedition to N. Pole under General Nobile.

amū'se (-z) *v.t.* Cause laughter or smiles; be or find diversion or light occupation for; entertain. **amū'sing** *adj.* **amū'singly̆** *adv.* **amū'sement** *n.* Pleasant diversion; excitement of laughter or smiles; pastime.

ă'my̆l *n.* (chem.) Radical (C_5H_{11}) occurring in the structure of various isomeric alcohols (~ *alcohols*), some of which are constituents of fusel-oil; ~ *acetate*, colourless volatile liquid derived from amyl alcohol and acetic acid, with odour of jargonelle pears, used in making artificial fruit essences and as solvent of cellulose acetate. **amy̆'lic** *adj.* [Gk *amulon* fine meal]

ămy̆lā'ceous (-sh*u*s) *adj.* Of starch, starchy.

ă'my̆loid *adj.* & *n.* Starchy (food).

an[1] *adj.*: see A.

ăn[2] *conj.* (archaic) If.

an-[1]: see A-, 2.

ăna-, an-[2] *prefix.* Up, back, again, anew.

ā'na *n.* (pl. *-s*). Collection of person's sayings; anecdotes, literary gossip, about a person.

-āna *suffix.* Appended to a name with the meaning: sayings of, anecdotes about, publications bearing on, persons or places.

Anabă'ptist (ă-) *n.* & *adj.* (Member) of a sect which arose in Germany in 1521, was heavily persecuted by both Catholics and Protestants, and suppressed (lit. = 'one who baptizes over again' because the Anabaptists held that infant baptism was ineffectual and some of them rebaptized adults); also (opprobriously) = BAPTIST. **Anabă'ptism** *n.*

ănă'bolism *n.* Synthesis by living things of complex molecules from simpler ones.

ană'chronism (-kr-) *n.* Error in computing time; event or thing which would be incongruous in the period in which it is supposed to have happened or existed. **anăchroni'stic** *adj.*

ănacolū'thon *n.* (pl. *-tha*). Sentence, words, lacking grammatical sequence.

ănacŏ'nda *n.* Tropical S. Amer. aquatic and arboreal boa (*Eunectes murinus*).

Ană'crėon (*c* 563–478 B.C.). Greek lyric poet, of whose poems very few genuine fragments survive. **anăcrėŏ'ntic** *adj.* & *n.* (Poem) in the manner or metre of Anacreon's lyrics; convivial and amatory.

ănacru'sis (-ōō-) *n.* (pl. *-sēs*). (pros.) Unstressed syllable at beginning of verse; (mus.) unstressed note(s) before the first bar-line. [Gk *anakrouō* strike up]

Anady̆ŏ'menė (ă-) Epithet of Venus (Aphrodite) as sprung from the sea-foam. [Gk, = 'rising']

anae'mia *n.* Deficiency of red blood-corpuscles or their haemoglobin, often causing paleness. **anae'mic** *adj.* (freq. fig.).

anā'erōbe (*or* anār-) *n.* Micro-organism which can live and reproduce in the absence of atmospheric oxygen. **anaerō'bĭc** *adj.*

ănaesthē'sia (ănĭs-, -zĭa) *n.* Loss of sensation; insensibility, esp. to pain, induced by certain drugs; *general* ~, anaesthesia of the whole body; *local* ~, anaesthesia induced in a limited area of the body.

ănaesthĕ'tĭc (ănĭs-) *adj.* & *n.* (Drug) inducing local or general anaesthesia, used esp. in surgical operations.

anae'sthėtĭst *n.* One who administers anaesthetics during surgical operation.

anae'sthėtīze *v.t.* Render insensible; administer anaesthetics to.

ă'naglȳph *n.* Embossed ornament in low relief; (photog.) composite stereoscopic picture printed in superimposed complementary colours.

ă'nagrăm *n.* Word or phrase formed by transposing letters of another.

ā'nal *adj.* Of the anus.

ă'nalĕcts, analĕ'cta *ns.pl.* Literary gleanings.

ănălgē'sĭa (-z-) *n.* Absence of pain; relief of pain. **ănălgē'tĭc, ănălgĕ'sĭc** *adjs.* & *ns.* (Drug) giving analgesia.

ănalŏ'ġĭc *adj.* Of analogy. **ănalŏ'ġĭcal** *adj.* According to analogy; expressing an analogy. **ănalŏ'ġĭcallȳ** *adv.*

ană'logous *adj.* Similar, parallel (to); (biol., of limb or organ) similar in function but not necessarily in structure or position (cf. HOMOLOGOUS). **ană'logouslȳ** *adv.*

ă'nalogue (-ŏg) *n.* Analogous word or thing; ~ *computer*: see COMPUTER.

ană'logȳ *n.* Agreement, similarity; analogue; (math.) proportion; (logic) process of reasoning from parallel cases; (gram.) process whereby words and grammatical forms are built up on the model of others.

ă'nalȳse (-z) *v.t.* Examine minutely the constitution of; PSYCHOANALYSE; (chem.) ascertain the elements present in a compound or the constituents of a mixture, sample of food, etc.: (gram.) resolve into grammatical elements.

ană'lȳsĭs *n.* (pl. *-sēs*). Resolution into simple elements; PSYCHOANALYSIS; (math.) branch of mathematics using algebraic and calculus methods; (philos.) clarification of concepts and knowledge; (cricket, also *bowling*, *bowler's* ~) statement of number of balls bowled, wickets taken, runs made, etc.; *chemical* ~, determination of composition of substances; *qualitative* ~, identification of elements or compounds present; *quantitative* ~, determination of precise amounts of elements etc. present. **ă'nalȳst** *n.* One skilled in (chemical) analysis; PSYCHOANALYST. **ănalȳ'tĭc** *adj.* Pertaining to analysis; **ănalȳ'tĭcal** *adj.* Employing the method of analysis; (of language) using separate words instead of inflexions; ~ *psychology*: see PSYCHOLOGY. **ănalȳ'tĭcallȳ** *adv.*

anā'nas (*or* *a*nahn-) *n.* Pineapple.

Ananī'as (ă-). 1. Jewish high priest before whom Paul was brought (Acts 23). 2. Husband of Sapphira, struck dead because he 'lied unto God' (Acts 5).

ă'napaest *n.* Metrical foot of three syllables, the first two short and the last long (◡◡—). **ănapae'stĭc** *adj.*

ană'phora *n.* 1. (also *A*~) Part of Eucharistic service in the Greek Orthodox Church; (R.C. Ch.) Canon of the Mass. 2. Repetition of words or phrases at beginning of a succession of clauses.

ănaphȳlă'xĭs *n.* (med.) Extreme sensitivity of tissues to the re-introduction of an antigen. **ănaphȳlă'ctĭc** *adj.*

ă'narchĭst (-k-) *n.* Advocate of **ă'narchĭsm,** system or theory which conceives of society without government.

ă'narchȳ (-k-) *n.* Absence of government; disorder, political and social confusion. **anar'chĭc, -ĭcal** *adjs.* Lawless. **anar'chĭcallȳ** *adv.*

anăstigmă'tic *adj.* Free from astigmatism (used esp. of photographic lenses in which this error is corrected).

anăstomō'sis *n.* (pl. *-ōsēs*). Cross-connection of arteries, rivers, etc.

ană'thėma *n.* Accursed thing; curse of God; curse of the Church, excommunication; imprecation. **ană'thėmatīze** *v.* Curse. [Gk *anathema* thing devoted, (later) accursed thing]

Anatō'lia (ă-). Asiatic part of Turkey; (in ancient usage) Asia Minor. **Anatŏ'lic** *adj.* **Anatō'lian** *adj.* & *n.*

ănatŏ'mical *adj.* Belonging to anatomy; structural. **ănatŏ'mically** *adv.*

ană'tomist *n.* Dissecter of bodies; one skilled in anatomy. **ană'tomīze** *v.* Dissect; (fig.) analyse.

ană'tomy *n.* (Science of) bodily structure; dissection; analysis.

Anăxă'gorăs (ă-) (5th c. B.C.). Greek philosopher and scientist; acc. to his explanation of the universe, the permanent elements of which it is constituted are unlimited in number, and are combined in bodies in changing proportions, as the result of a system of circulation directed by Spirit or Intelligence, a supreme independent force; he also explained solar eclipses.

ă'ncėstor *n.* (fem. *ă'ncėstrėss*) Any of those from whom one's father or mother is descended, progenitor.

ăncĕ'stral *adj.* Belonging to, inherited from, ancestors.

ă'ncėstry *n.* Ancestral lineage; ancient descent; ancestors.

Anchises (ăngkī'sēz). (Rom. myth.) Father of Aeneas by Venus.

ă'nchor (-k-) *n.* Heavy implement consisting usu. of long shank and two (curved) barbed arms, used for mooring ship to bottom of sea etc.; anchor-plate; (also ~ *man*) last man of relay team; (fig.) source of confidence; BOWER[2]-~, KEDGE-~, SHEET-ANCHOR: see these words; ~*-plate*, heavy piece of metal or timber as point of support, e.g. for cables of suspension-bridge. ~ *v.* Secure (ship) with anchor; (fig.) fix firmly; cast anchor, come to anchor.

ă'nchorage (-k-) *n.* Anchoring; lying at anchor; anchoring-ground; (fig.) thing to depend upon.

ă'nchorīte (-k-) *n.* (fem. *ă'nchorėss*) Hermit, recluse. **ănchorĕ'tic** *adj.*

ă'nchovy (*or* ănchō'-) *n.* Small fish of herring family, esp. the Mediterranean *Engraulis encrasicholus*, esteemed for its rich pungent flavour and used in sauces.

ănchu'sa (-chōō- *or* -kū-) *n.* Plant of borage family of genus *A~*, with blue or purple trumpet-shaped flowers.

ancien régime (ahṅsyăṅ rāzhēm). System of government in France before the Revolution; (transf.) former regime. [Fr., = 'old rule']

ā'ncient[1] (-shent) *adj.* Belonging to times long past; having existed, lived, long; ~ *history*; see HISTORY; so ~ *historian*; ~ *lights*: see LIGHT[1] 6; ~ *monument*, structure scheduled by the Department of the Environment as being of historical or architectural interest. ~ *n. the A~ of Days*, God (Dan. 7: 9); *the ~s*, civilized people of antiquity. **ā'nciently** *adv.* **ā'ncientnėss** *n.*

ā'ncient[2] (-shent) *n.* (obs.) = ENSIGN.

ănci'llary (*or* ă'-) *adj.* Subservient, subordinate.

ă'ncon *n.* 1. (physiol.) Elbow; *A~ sheep*, breed of sheep with long bodies and short legs, the forelegs crooked. 2. (archit.) Console usu. consisting of two reversed volutes.

and (*a*nd; emphat., ănd) *conj.* Particle connecting words, clauses, and sentences.

Andalusia (ănd*a*lōō'zĭa). Ancient province of S. Spain. **Andalu'sĭan** *adj.* & *n.*

A'ndaman I'slands (ă-, īl*a*ndz). Large group of islands in Bay of Bengal; administered (with Nicobar Islands) by the Republic of India; chief city, Port Blair.

ăndă'ntė *adv.* & *n.* (mus.) (Movement) in moderately slow time. ***ăndănti'nō*** (-tē-) *adv.* & *n.* (pl. *-os*). (Movement) slightly quicker (orig. slower) than *andante*. [It.]

A'ndersen (ă-), Hans Christian (1805–75). Danish poet and dramatist, best known for his fairy-tales.

A'nderson (ă-), Mrs Elizabeth Garrett (1836–1917). English physician, a pioneer of the professional education of women.

A'ndēs (ă-, -z). Mountain range running from N. to S. along the whole of the Pacific coast of S. America.

Andhra Prade'sh (ah'ndr*a*, -dāsh). State of SE. India; chief city, Hyderabad.

ă'ndiron (-īrn) *n.* Stand for supporting logs on hearth, fire-dog.

Andŏ'rra (ă-). Semi-independent State (generally regarded as an autonomous republic) in the Pyrenees, on the border between France and Spain; under the joint suzerainty of France and the Spanish bishop of Urgel; capital, Andorra la Vella. **Andŏ'rran** *adj.* & *n.*

A'ndrėa dĕl Sar'tō (ă-) (1486–1531). Florentine painter.

Andrea Ferrara: see FERRARA.

Andreev (ăndrā'ĕf), Leonid Nikolaevich (1871–1919). Russian novelist and playwright.

A'ndrew (ă-, -rōō), St. Apostle and patron saint of Scotland, commemorated 30 Nov.; *St. ~'s Ambulance Association*, organization, founded 1882, responsible for Red Cross work in Scotland; *St. ~'s cross*, cross shaped like the letter X, saltire; (her.) white saltire on blue ground, used as national cross of Scotland.

A'ndrewes (ă-, -rōōz), Lancelot (1555–1626). English bishop, one of the translators of the Authorized Version of the Bible.

A'ndroclēs (ă-, -z). Runaway slave in story by Aulus Gellius (2nd c. A.D.) who extracted a thorn from the paw of a lion which later recognized and refrained from attacking him in the arena.

ăndroe'cium (-rēs-) *n.* (bot.) Stamens collectively.

ă'ndrogėn *n.* Any organic compound which promotes development of masculine characteristics. **ăndrogĕ'nic** *adj.*

ăndrŏ'gy̆nous (*or* -g-) *adj.* Hermaphrodite; (bot.) with both staminate and pistillate flowers in a cluster. **ăndrŏ'gy̆ny̆** *n.*

Andrŏ'machė (ă-, -k-). (Gk legend) Wife of HECTOR[1].

Andrŏ'mėda (ă-). 1. (Gk legend) Daughter of Cassiopeia; was rescued by Perseus from a sea-monster for whom she was fastened to a rock. 2. (astron.) Constellation, conspicuous for its great spiral nebula. **Andrŏ'mėdēs, Andrŏ'mėdĭds** (-z) *ns. pl.* (astron.) System of meteors appearing to radiate from a point in Andromeda and usu. seen in November.

ă'nėcdōte *n.* Narrative of detached incident. **ă'nėcdōtage** *n.* Anecdotes; (joc.) garrulous old age. **ă'nėcdōtist** *n.* **ănėcdō'tal, ănėcdŏ'tĭc, -ĭcal** *adjs.*

anē'le *v.t.* Anoint; give extreme unction to.

anĕ'mogrăph (*or* -ahf) *n.* Anemometer equipped with recording apparatus (usu. pen and rotating drum). **anĕ'mogrăm** *n.* Record traced by this.

ănėmŏ'mėter *n.* Instrument for measuring speed (sometimes also direction) of wind. **ănėmomĕ'trĭc** *adj.* **ănėmŏ'mėtry̆** *n.*

anĕ'monė *n.* Plant of the buttercup family of genus *A~*, with flowers of various colours. [Gk, = 'wind-flower']

ănėmŏ'phĭlous *adj.* (bot.) Pollinated by wind.

anĕ'nt *prep.* (archaic) Concerning.

ă'neroid *adj.* & *n.* (Barometer) that measures air-pressure by its action on the flexible lid of a metal box nearly exhausted of air, not by height of fluid column.

ă'neurўsm, -ĭsm (-ūr-) *n.* (path.) Localized dilatation of an artery caused by a weakening in its wall.

anew' *adv.* Again; in a different way.

ă'ngarў (ăngg-) *n.* (law) Belligerent's right (subject to compensation) of seizing or destroying neutral property under stress of military necessity.

ā'ngel (-j-) *n.* 1. Divine messenger; *orders of ~s*, three hierarchies, each consisting of three orders, to which angels were held to belong by Dionysius the Pseudo-Areopagite, namely: seraphim, cherubim, thrones; dominations, virtues, powers; principalities, archangels, angels. 2. Lovely or innocent being; loving or obliging person. 3. (also *~-noble*) Old English gold coin showing the archangel Michael piercing a dragon. 4. (U.S.) Financial backer, esp. of theatrical production. 5. (pl., colloq.) Height (of aircraft from ground), specif. 1,000 ft. 6. *~ cake*, very light sponge-cake; *~-fish*, (esp.) S. Amer. freshwater fish (various species of *Pterophyllum*), laterally flattened, with bars of black and silver; *~s on horseback*, savoury dish of oysters wrapped in slices of bacon. [Gk *aggelos* messenger]

ănġĕ'lĭc (-j-) *adj.* Like an angel; *A~ Doctor*, St. Thomas Aquinas.

ănġĕ'lĭca (-j-) *n.* Aromatic umbelliferous plant used in cooking and medicine; candied stalk of this.

Angĕ'lĭco (ănj-), Fra. Name given after his death to a Dominican friar, Fra Giovanni da Fiesole (1387–1455), painter of religious subjects, active in Florence and Rome.

ānġėlŏ'logў (-j-) *n.* Doctrine concerning angels.

ă'ngėlus (-j-) *n.* (R.C. Ch.) Devotional exercise (beginning *Angelus domini*; L, = 'the angel of the Lord') commemorating the Incarnation, said at morning, noon, and evening, at sound of bell; bell for this.

ă'nger (-ngg-) *n.* Hot displeasure, rage. *~ v.t.* Make angry, enrage. [ON *angr* affliction]

ANGELICO Annunciation

A'ngėvin (ănj-) *adj.* Of Anjou or its ruling house; ~ *kings*, PLANTAGENET kings of England. ~ *n.* Native or inhabitant of Anjou; member of its ruling house.

ăngī'na (-j-) *n.* Constrictive sensation or pain; (in full ~ *pectoris*) intense pain in chest, accompanied by sense of suffocation, caused by insufficient blood-supply to heart during sudden exertion.

ă'ngĭosperm (-j-) *n.* Flowering plant, i.e. one which has ovules enclosed in an ovary (opp. GYMNOSPERM).

angle[1] (ă'nggl) *n.* Space between two meeting lines or planes; inclination of two lines to each other (*acute* ~, angle smaller than 90°; *obtuse* ~, greater than 90°; *reflex* ~, greater than 180°; *right* ~, angle of 90°); corner, sharp projection; (colloq.) point of view; ~*-iron*, metal plate of L-shaped section. **ă'ngled** (-ld) *adj.* ~ *deck*, flight deck on aircraft-carrier with landing path inclined to ship's fore-and-aft axis.

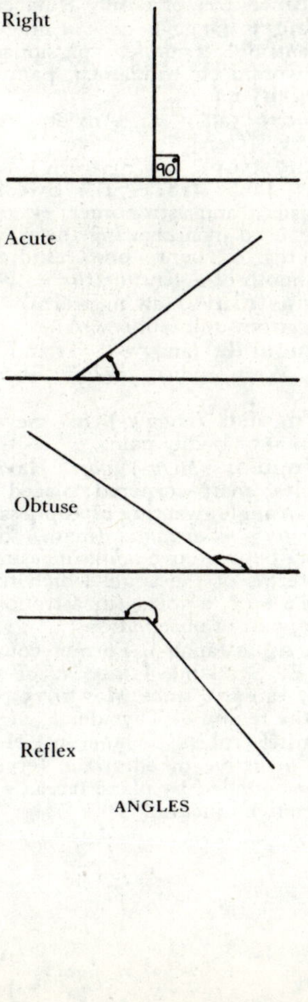

ANGLES

angle[2] (ă'nggl) *v.i.* Fish with hook and bait; (fig.) use artifice, hints, etc., to obtain something. **ă'ngler** *n.* 1. Fisherman. 2. (zool.) Fish (esp. *Lophius piscatorius*) that preys on smaller fish, attracting them by filaments attached to its head and mouth.

Angles, A'nglī (ă'ngglz, ăngg-) *ns.pl.* People of Angul (Angel), a district of Holstein; one of the Germanic tribes that settled in Britain, where they formed the kingdoms of Northumbria, Mercia, and East Anglia, and finally gave their name to England and the English.

Anglesey (ă'ngglsĭ). Island of NW. Wales across the Menai Strait; former county of Wales, since April 1974 part of Gwynedd.

A'nglĭcan (ăngg-) *adj.* Of the reformed Church of England or any Church in the Anglican Communion; ~ *chant*, short harmonized melody in two or more phrases each beginning with a reciting note, for singing to unmetrical words, as psalms, canticles; ~ *Communion*, Churches in communion with, and recognizing the leadership of, the see of Canterbury. ~ *n.* Member of Anglican Church. **A'nglĭcanism** *n.*

ă'nglĭcė (ăngg-) *adv.* In English. [L]

ă'nglĭcīze (ăngg-) *v.* Make, become, English in form or character. **ă'nglĭcism** *n.* English idiom; preference for what is English.

Anglo- (ăngg-) *prefix.* English; English and —, as ~*-German.*

A'nglo-Că'tholĭc (ăngg-) *adj.* & *n.* (Adherent) of the section of the Church of England which emphasizes both the continuity of the Reformed Church with the medieval Church and its status as the national branch of the Catholic Church.

A'nglo-I'ndĭan (ăngg-, ĭ-) *adj.* & *n.* 1. (Person) of British birth having lived long in India. 2. (in Eurasian use) = EURASIAN. 3. (English vocabulary) adopted from Indian language.

A'nglo-Nôr'man (ăngg-) *adj.* & *n.* (Of) the variety of the Norman dialect of Old French spoken in England after the Norman Conquest.

A'nglophīle, -phĭl, A'nglophōbe (ăngg-) *ns.* One who loves, hates, the English. **Anglophō'bĭa** *n.*

A'nglo-Să'xon (ăngg-) *adj.* & *n.* English Saxon (as dist. from Old Saxon); Old English (person, language) before the Norman Conquest; (person) of English descent; (U.S.) (plain, forthright) English language.

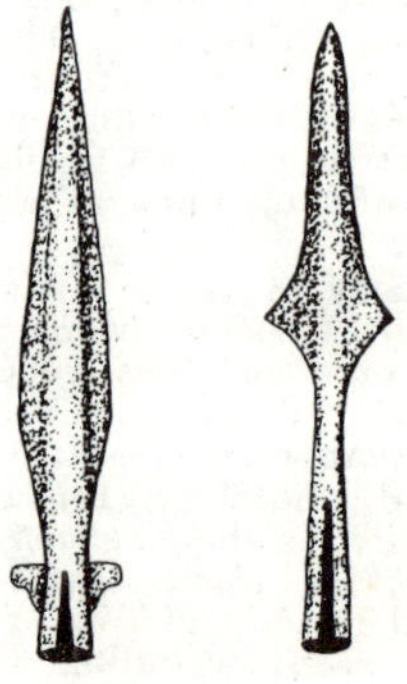

Spearheads

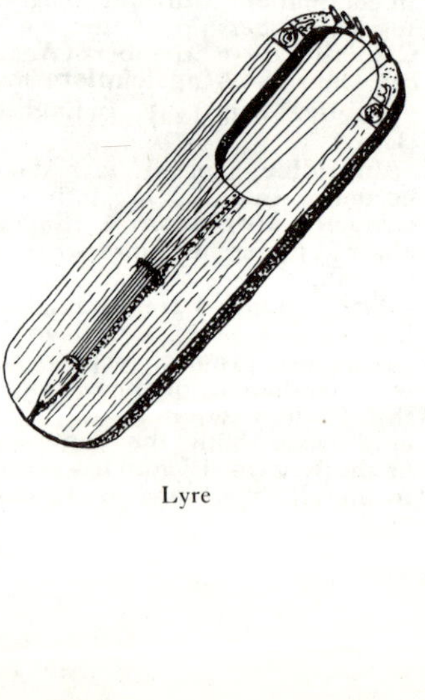

Lyre

Angō'la (ăngg-). Former Portuguese province of W. Africa, N. of SW. Africa; independent 1975.

Angôr'a (ăngg-). Former name of ANKARA; fabric made from fleece of Angora goat, mohair; (also ~ *wool*) sheep's wool mixed with hair of Angora rabbit; ~ *cat, goat, rabbit*, varieties of these animals with long silky hair.

Angostūr'a (ăngg-). Former name of Ciudad Bolivar, town in Venezuela on Orinoco; *a*~ (*bark*), aromatic bark formerly used as tonic and febrifuge, obtained from S. Amer. tree of family Rutaceae.

ă'ngrȳ (ăngg-) *adj.* Enraged, resentful; irritable, passionate; (of wound etc.) inflamed, painful. **ă'ngrĭlȳ** *adv.*

angst (ah-) *n.* Anxiety; remorse. [Ger.]

Ångström[1] (aw'ngstrẽrm), Anders Jonas (1814–74). Swedish physicist and astronomer; ~ *unit*, unit used in measuring the wavelengths of light, one hundred-millionth of a centimetre.

ångström[2] (aw'ngstrẽrm) *n.* Ångström unit (abbrev. Å).

Anguĭ'lla (ănggw-). Island in the West Indies, under British rule.

ă'nguish (ănggw-) *n.* Severe mental or bodily pain.

ă'ngūlar (ăngg-) *adj.* Having angles; sharp-cornered; placed in, at, an angle; wanting plumpness or suavity; ~ *distance*, (math.) distance between two points measured in terms of the angle which they make with a third (in astronomy the point of observation).

A ngus (ăngg-). Former county of E. Scotland, lying N. of the Tay estuary, since May 1975 part of the region of Tayside.

ănhē'dral *adj.* 1. (aeron.) Having negative dihedral. 2. (cryst.) Not bounded by plane faces. ~ *n.* Negative dihedral.

Anhwei (ah′nhwā′). Province of China on the Yangtze Kiang.

ănhȳ′drīde *n.* Substance formed by removal of water from a compound; substance which combines with water to form an acid or base.

ănhȳ′drous *adj.* (chem.) Having no water; deprived of water of crystallization.

ănīcŏ′nĭc *adj.* (Gk antiq.; of idols and symbols) Not shaped in human or animal form.

ă′nĭlīne *n.* Phenylamine ($C_6H_5NH_2$), an oily liquid with characteristic smell, made by reduction of nitro-benzene and used in the manufacture of many chemicals, dye-stuffs, drugs, etc. ~ *adj.* Derived from aniline; ~ *dye*, (pop.) any synthetic dye-stuff. [formerly got from *anil*, the shrub indigo]

ă′nĭma *n.* (psychol.) Inner aspect of personality, esp. its unconscious facets. [L, = 'breath', 'soul']

ănĭmadvẽr′sion *n.* Criticism, censure. **ănĭmadvẽr′t** *v.i.* Pass criticism or censure *on*.

ă′nĭmal *n.* Organized being endowed with life, sensation, and voluntary motion; animal other than man; quadruped; brutish man. ~ *adj.* Pertaining to the functions of animals; pertaining to animals as opp. to vegetables; carnal; ~ *magnetism*, (formerly) mesmerism; ~ *spirits*, natural buoyancy. [L *anima* breath]

ănĭmă′lcūle *n.* Microscopic animal.

ă′nĭmalism *n.* Animal activity; sensuality; doctrine that men are mere animals.

ă′nĭmalīze *v.t.* Convert into animal substance, sensualize.

ă′nĭmate *adj.* Living, lively. **ă′nĭmāte** *v.t.* Give life to; make lively; encourage; *animated cartoon*: see CARTOON, 3. **ănĭmā′tion** *n.* **ă′nĭmātėdlȳ** *adv.*

ă′nĭmĭsm *n.* Attribution of living soul to inanimate objects and natural phenomena. **ă′nĭmĭst** *n.* **ănĭmĭ′stĭc** *adj.*

ănĭmŏ′sĭtȳ *n.* Active enmity.

ă′nĭmus *n.* Animating spirit; animosity.

ă′nīŏn *n.*: see ION. **ănīŏ′nĭc** *adj.* Of anions; having an active anion. (Gk *ana* up, + ION]

ă′nĭse *n.* Umbelliferous plant (*Pimpinella anisum*) with aromatic fruits.

ă′nĭseed *n.* Fruits of anise, used as carminative and for flavouring.

ănĭsĕ′tte (-z-) *n.* Colourless sweet liqueur flavoured with aniseed.

Anjou (ahṅzhōō). Old French province on the Loire, W. of Touraine; Henry II of England, as a Plantagenet, was count of Anjou, but it was lost to the English Crown by King John (1204).

A′nkara (ă-). Capital city of Turkey since 1923.

ă′nkle *n.* Joint connecting foot with leg; slender part between this and calf. **ă′nklėt** *n.* Fetter or ornamental band round ankle.

ănkylō′sĭs *n.* (pl. *-osēs*). Formation of stiff joint by consolidation of articulating surfaces. **ă′nkȳlōse** (-z) *v.* (of joints, bones) Stiffen, unite.

ă′nna *n.* Former coin of India and Pakistan, $\frac{1}{16}$ of rupee.

ă′nnals (-z) *n.pl.* Narrative of events year by year; historical records. **ă′nnalĭst** *n.* Writer of annals.

A′nnăm (ă-). Formerly, eastern coastal portion of Indo-China, since 1946 part of Vietnam. **Annamē′se** (-z) *adj.* & *n.*

Annă′polĭs (*a*-). Capital of Maryland, U.S., site of the U.S. Naval Academy.

ă′nnātes (-ts) *n.pl.* (R.C. Ch.) First year's revenue of see or benefice, formerly paid to pope.

Anne[1] (ăn) (1665–1714). Queen of Gt. Britain 1702–14; 2nd daughter of James II; succeeded William, husband of her sister Mary, in 1702, and died with no surviving issue; *Queen* ~, (archit.) applied to a style of red-brick and stone houses of *c* 1660–*c* 1720; *Queen ~'s Bounty*, Crown revenues from tithes and first-fruits (formerly paid to the pope, and appropriated by the Crown in

1534), granted by her to the Church of England.

Anne[2] (ăn), St. Mother of the Virgin Mary; commemorated 26 July.

annea'l *v.t.* Toughen (glass or metals) by heating and then cooling; temper.

Anne Boleyn: see BOLEYN.

ă'nnėlĭd *n.* One of the phylum Annelida, segmented worms (including earth-worms, leeches, etc.)

Anne of Cleves (ăn, ŏv, klēvz) (1515–57). Daughter of John, Duke of Cleves, and 4th wife of Henry VIII of England; the marriage (1540) was annulled after a few months.

annĕ'x *v.t.* Add as subordinate (part); append; take possession of (territory); attach as an attribute, addition, or consequence. **ănnėxā'tion** *n.* **ă'nnĕxe, -ĕx** *n.* Addition to document; building added to larger one, esp. to provide extra accommodation.

annī'hĭlāte (-nīĭ-) *v.t.* Demolish, destroy utterly. **annīhĭlā'tion** *n.* Utter destruction; (theol.) destruction of soul as well as body.

ănnivĕr'sarȳ *n.* Yearly return of a date, celebration of this.

ă'nnō aeta'tĭs su'ae (ītah-, sōōī). In the (specified) year of his or her age. [L]

A'nnō Dŏ'mĭnī (ă-). In the year of our Lord, of the Christian era (abbrev. A.D.); (as *n.*, colloq.) advancing age. [L]

ă'nnotāte *v.t.* Furnish with notes. **ănnotā'tion, ă'nnotātor** *ns.*

annou'nce *v.t.* Declare, make publicly known; intimate the approach of. **annou'ncement** *n.* **annou'ncer** *n.* (esp.) Broadcasting official who announces programme, reads news items, etc.

annoy' *v.t.* Irritate; molest, harass. **annoy'ance** *n.* Molestation; vexation; disgust.

ă'nnūal *adj.* Reckoned by the year; recurring yearly; lasting for one year; that lives only for a year; published in yearly numbers. ~ *n.* Plant that lives for one year; book etc. published in yearly numbers. **ă'nnūallȳ** *adv.*

annū'ĭtȳ *n.* Sum payable in respect of a particular year; yearly grant; investment of money entitling investor to series of equal annual sums. **annū'ĭtant** *n.* One who holds an annuity.

annŭ'l *v.t.* Abolish, cancel; declare invalid. **annŭ'lment** *n.*

ă'nnūlar *adj.* Ring-like; ~ *eclipse*, partial eclipse of sun, during which a ring of the sun's surface can be seen outside the moon's disc, occurring when the distance of the moon from the earth in relation to the distance of the sun from the earth is too great for the eclipse to be total.

ă'nnūlate, -ātėd *adjs.* Furnished, marked, with rings; formed of rings.

ă'nnūlėt *n.* Little ring; (her.) small circle; (archit.) fillet or moulded band encircling a column.

ă'nnūlus *n.* (pl. *-lī*). Ring, ring-like body, esp. (bot.) ring of cells round sporangia in ferns.

annŭ'nciāte (*or* -shĭ-) *v.t.* Announce.

ănnŭnciā'tion *n.* Announcement; *the A~*, the announcement of the Incarnation made by the angel Gabriel to the Virgin Mary (Luke 1: 26–38); festival commemorating this, Lady Day, 25 March.

Annunzio (*a*nōō'ntsĭō), Gabriele d' (1863–1938). Italian poet, airman, and politician.

ă'nōde *n.* (elect.) Positive pole or terminal. **ă'nodal, ănŏ'dĭc** *adjs.* **ă'nodīze** *v.t.* Cover (metal) with a protective film by electrolysis in which the metal acts as the anode. [Gk *anodos* way up]

ă'nodȳne *adj.* & *n.* (Medicine, drug) able to assuage pain; (anything) mentally soothing.

anoi'nt *v.t.* Apply ointment, oil, to, esp. as religious ceremony at baptism or on consecration as priest or king; *the Lord's Anointed*, Christ; king by divine right.

anŏ'malous *adj.* Irregular, abnormal. **anŏ'malouslȳ** *adv.* **anŏ'malousnėss** *n.*

anŏ'malȳ *n.* Irregularity; (astron.) angular distance of planet or satellite from its last perihelion or perigee. **anŏmalĭ'stic** *adj.* (astron.) ~ *year*, time (365 days, 6 hrs, 13 m., 53·1 sec.) earth takes to pass from perihelion to perihelion; ~ *month*, time (27 days, 13 hrs, 18 m., 33·1 sec.) moon takes to pass from perigee to perigee.

anŏ'n *adv.* (archaic) Soon, presently.

anon. *abbrev.* Anonymous.

ă'nŏnȳm *n.* Person whose name is not revealed; pseudonym. **ănonȳ'mĭtȳ** *n.*

anŏ'nȳmous *adj.* Not named; not bearing author's, painter's, etc., name. **anŏ'nȳmouslȳ** *adv.*

anŏ'phelēs (-z) *n.* Mosquito of genus *A*~, comprising numerous species, many of which are carriers of malaria. [Gk, = 'hurtful']

ă'norăk *n.* Long hooded jacket of skin or cloth worn esp. in Arctic regions; weather-proof jacket of similar style for sports wear etc. [Eskimo *anoraq*]

ănorĕ'xĭa *n.* (path.) Loss of appetite.

anŏ'smĭa (-z-) *n.* Lack of the sense of smell.

ano'ther (-ŭdh-) *adj.* Additional, different; a similar (one). ~ *pron.* Additional one; unnamed additional party to legal action; different one.

anŏ'xĭa *n.* (med.) Lack of oxygen, caused by asphyxiation or high altitude (*direct* ~), or by various diseases which render the blood incapable of conveying enough oxygen to the tissues (*indirect* ~).

Anschluss (ă'nshlo͞os) *n.* Annexation, esp. of Austria to Germany. [Ger. = 'union']

A'nsĕlm (ă-), St. (1033–1109). Italian monk, a pupil of Lanfranc; became abbot of Bec in Normandy and later (1093) archbishop of Canterbury; commemorated 21 April.

ă'nserīne *adj.* Of, like, a goose; silly.

answer (ah'ns*er*) *v.* Give answer; reply to (charge); be responsible *for*; fulfil (purpose); suffice; correspond *to* (description etc.); act or operate in response (*to*); ~ *back*, reply (esp. to rebuke) impertinently. ~ *n.* Something said or done in response to a question, accusation, etc.; defence; solution; (mus.) repetition of theme by another voice or instrument, esp. in fugue. **a'nswerable** *adj.* Responsible.

ănt *n.* Small hymenopterous insect of superfamily Formicoidea, with complex instincts and social system, proverbial for industry; ~*-eater*, any of various mammals

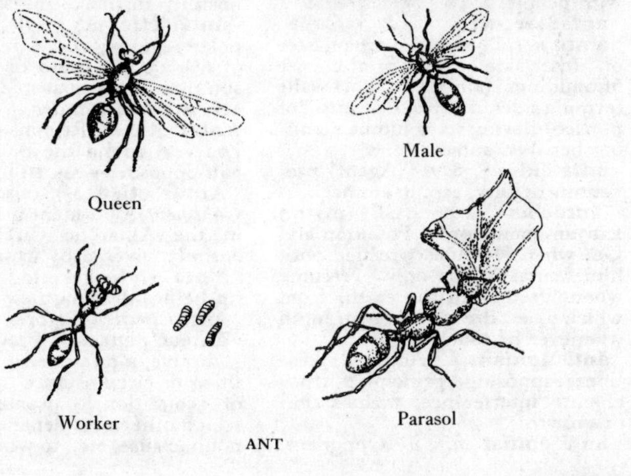

ANT

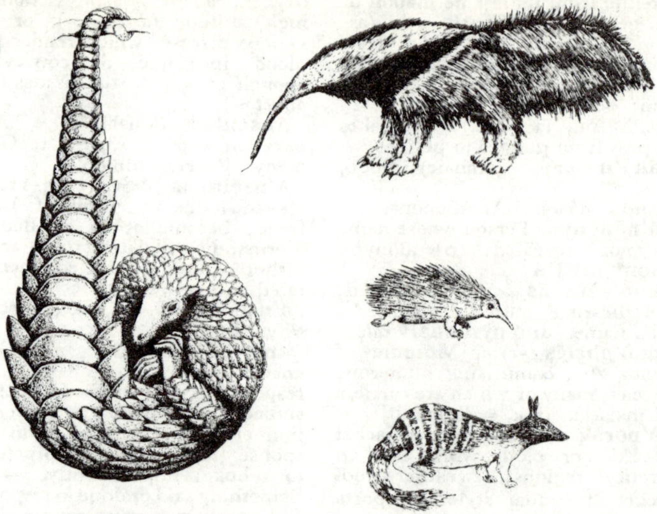

ANT-EATERS

living on ants; *~-heap*, *~-hill*, mound over ants' nest; (loosely) conical nest of termites; (fig.) crowded dwelling(s) swarming with people.

ant-: see ANTI-

ă'nta *n.* (pl. *-tae*). Square pilaster on either side of door or at corner of buildings; one of two short walls forming sides of portico; *in antis*, (of portico) having its columns standing between antae.

ăntă'cĭd *adj.* & *n.* (Agent) preventing acidity, esp. in stomach.

Antae'us (ă-). (Gk myth.) Libyan giant, son of Poseidon and Ge; when Hercules wrestled with him, Antaeus was only overcome when lifted from the earth, from which he drew new strength whenever he touched it.

ăntă'gonĭsm *n.* Active opposition; opposing principle; (biochem.) interference with action or growth.

ăntă'gonĭst *n.* 1. Opponent. 2. (physiol.) Counteracting muscle.

ăntăgonĭ'stĭc *adj.*

ăntă'gonīze *v.* Counteract, tend to neutralize (force etc.); evoke hostility in, make into an enemy.

ăntar'ctĭc *adj.* Of the south polar regions; *A~ Circle*, parallel of 66° 33′ S., south of which the sun does not rise at mid-winter or set at midsummer.

Antar'ctĭc *n.* Regions (both land and sea) round the S. Pole. [Gk *anti* opposite + ARCTIC]

Antar'ctĭca (ă-). (also *Antarctic Continent*) Continent mainly within the Antarctic Circle, almost entirely covered by ice-sheet.

ă'ntė *n.* (poker etc.) Stake put up before drawing new cards.

ăntė- *prefix.* Before.

ăntėcē'dent *adj.* Previous; presumptive, *a priori*. *~ n.* Preceding thing or circumstance; (logic) part of conditional proposition on which other part depends; (gram.) noun, clause, etc., to which following (relative) pronoun or adverb refers; (math.) first term of ratio; (geog., of river) one which has maintained its course in spite of changes in land formation; (pl.) past history.

ă'ntėchāmber *n.* Room leading to chief apartment.

ă'ntėchăpel *n.* Outer part at west end of chapel.

ăntėdā'te *v.t.* Affix, assign, an earlier than the true date to; precede; anticipate.

ăntėdilū'vian (*or* -ōō-) *adj.* Belonging, referring, appropriate, to the time before the Flood; very old, old-fashioned. ~ *n.* Antediluvian person.

ă'ntėfix *n.* Ornament above cornice of classical building concealing joint between tiles.

ăntėfi'xal *adj.*

ă'ntėlōpe *n.* Any of several cloven-hoofed ruminants (related to deer, goats, and cattle) including the chamois, gazelle, and gnu.

ă'ntė merĭ'dĭĕm. (abbrev. a.m.) Between midnight and noon.

ă'ntė-merĭ'dĭan *adj.* [L]

ăntėnā'tal *adj.* Previous to birth or childbirth; relating to the care of pregnant women.

ăntĕ'nna *n.* (pl. *-nae*). 1. Sensory organ found in pairs on heads of insects and crustacea, usually long slender projections like horns, sometimes knobbed. 2. Aerial. [L, = 'sail-yard']

ăntĕ'nnūle *n.* (zool.) Minute organ resembling antenna.

ăntėpĕ'ndium *n.* (pl. *-dia*). Veil, hanging, for front of altar; frontal.

ăntėpėnŭ'lt, ăntėpėnŭ'ltimate *adjs.* & *ns.* (Syllable) last but two.

ăntēr'ior *adj.* More to the front; prior *to*.

ă'ntėrōōm *n.* Room leading to another, antechamber.

ănthē'lĭon *n.* Luminous ring

ANTELOPES

projected on cloud or fog-bank opposite the sun.

ă'nthĕm *n.* Composition for church use sung antiphonally; any non-metrical setting of sacred words as non-essential item in service; song of praise.

ănthē'mĭon *n.* (pl. *-ia*). (archit.) Ancient Greek ornament of radiating plant forms.

ă'nther *n.* Terminal part of stamen containing pollen in pollen sacs.

ănthŏ'logy̆ *n.* Collection of small choice poems; literary collection; collection of paintings, songs, etc.; *Greek A~*, large collection of epigrams and short poems from Greek writers of 5th c. B.C.–6th c. A.D. **ănthŏ'logize** *v.* Make an anthology *from*. [Gk *anthologia*, f. *anthos* flower, *-logia* collection (*legō* gather)]

A'nthony̆[1], **A'ntony̆**[2] (ănto-), St. (*c* 251–356). Born in Egypt, the first Christian monk; ~ *pig*, smallest pig of litter, named after St. Anthony as patron saint of swine-herds; *St. ~'s cross*, T-shaped cross; *St. ~'s fire*, any of various inflammatory or gangrenous skin diseases, as erysipelas, ergotism, popularly supposed in the Middle Ages to be cured by the intercession of St. Anthony.

A'nthony̆[2], **A'ntony̆**[3] (ănto-) of Padua, St. (1195–1231). Portuguese Franciscan monk, patron saint of Portugal.

ănthozō'an *adj.* & *n.* (Aquatic animal) of the class Anthozoa, including corals, sea-anemones, etc. [Gk *anthos* flower, *zōon* animal]

ă'nthracēne *n.* (chem.) Aromatic hydrocarbon ($C_{14}H_{10}$) obtained by distillation of coal-tar and used in manufacture of alizarin and other dyes.

ă'nthracīte *n.* Glossy variety of coal containing much carbon and low percentage of volatile matter, burning with hot smokeless flame and leaving little ash. **ănthracĭ'tic** *adj.*

ă'nthrăx *n.* Disease of sheep and cattle, transmitted to man by infected wool, bristles, etc., and characterized by inflammatory skin lesions, caused by a bacillus (*B. anthracis*).

ă'nthropoid *adj.* Resembling man; ~ *ape*, one of the primates most nearly related to man, i.e. chimpanzees, gibbons, orang-utans, and gorillas. ~ *n.* Anthropoid ape.

ănthropŏ'logy̆ *n.* Science of man; study of man as an animal (*physical* ~) and of human, esp. primitive, societies (*social* ~). **ănthropolŏ'gical** *adj.* **ănthropolŏ'gically̆** *adv.* **ănthropŏ'logist** *n.*

ănthropŏ'mĕtry̆ *n.* Measurement of human body. **ănthropomĕ'tric** *adj.*

ănthropomŏr'phism *n.* Ascription of human form and attributes to God, or of human attributes to something irrational or impersonal. **ănthropomŏr'phic** *adj.*

ănthropomŏr'phous *adj.* Having human form. **ănthropomŏr'phize** *v.* Regard as anthropomorphous.

ănti-, ănt- *prefix.* Opposite, against; (in the arts, literature, etc.) unlike the conventional form.

ănti-air'craft (-ahft) *adj.* & *n.* (Force) for shooting down, or for defence against, hostile aircraft (abbrev. A.A.).

ă'ntiar *n.* Upas tree of Java; poison obtained from it.

ăntibīō'sis *n.* Condition of antagonism between organisms, esp. micro-organisms (opp. SYMBIOSIS).

ăntibīŏ'tic *adj.* & *n.* (Substance, drug, as penicillin, streptomycin) obtained from a mould, fungus, or other micro-organism, or prepared synthetically, and having the power to inhibit the growth of other micro-organisms, e.g. bacteria.

ă'ntibŏdy̆ *n.* (physiol.) Protein formed within the body to inactivate other compounds (esp. bacterial toxins and viruses) which are foreign to it, and found in blood-plasma.

ă'ntĭc *n.* (often pl.) Grotesque posture or trick.

A'ntĭchrīst (ă-, -k-). Great personal opponent of Christ expected by early Christians to appear before the end of the world; person hostile to Christ and his teaching.

ăntĭchrĭ'stian (-k-) *adj.* Opposed to Christianity.

ănti'cĭpāte *v.t.* Look forward to, expect; perform action before (another person or event), (of event) happen before (another event); satisfy (wish), obey (command), before it is expressed; use in advance. **ănti'cĭpative, ănti'cĭpātorў** *adjs.* **ănti'cĭpatively** *adv.* **ănticĭpā'tion** *n.* (esp., mus.) Sounding of single note of chord before chord itself.

ănticlĕ'rical *adj.* & *n.* (Person) opposed to undue influence of clergy, esp. in politics, or to existence of organized clerical hierarchy. **ănticlĕ'rĭcalism** *n.*

ănticlī'măx *n.* Lame end to anything promising a climax.

ă'nticlīne *n.* (geol.) Arch-like fold in bed(s) of rock (opp. SYNCLINE). **ănticlī'nal** *adj.*

ănti-clŏ'ckwīse (-z) *adj.* & *adv.* (Moving) in opposite direction to hands of a clock, in curve from right to left as seen from centre.

ănticȳ'clōne *n.* Atmospheric system in which barometric pressure is high, and from centre of which air tends to flow spirally outward (clockwise in N. hemisphere, anti-clockwise in S. hemisphere).

ă'ntidōte *n.* Medicine etc. used to counteract disease or poison.

ă'nti-free'ze *n.* Chemical agent (usu. ethylene glycol) added to water to lower its freezing-point.

ă'ntigėn *n.* Substance that stimulates production of an antibody when introduced into a living organism.

Anti'gonė (ă-). (Gk legend) Daughter of Oedipus; she buried the body of her brother Polynices by night, against the order of King Creon; he condemned her to death but she took her own life.

Anti'gūa (ă-; *or* -tē'gw*a*). One of the Leeward Islands, in the West Indies, discovered in 1493 by Columbus and settled by English in 1632; independent since 1967; capital, St. John's.

ă'nti-hēr'ō *n.* Hero of unconventional type in novel etc.

ăntihĭ'stamine (-ēn) *adj.* & *n.* (Drug) that counteracts the effect of histamine, used esp. in treatment of allergic conditions.

Anti-Jă'cobĭn (ă-) *adj.* & *n.* (Person) opposed to the Jacobins, or to the French Revolution; see JACOBIN[2], 2.

ă'nti-knŏck (-ĭ-n-) *n.* Substance added to fuel to reduce pinking in engines (see PINK[5]).

Anti'llēs (ă-, -z). Group of West Indian islands; *Greater* ~, Cuba, Jamaica, Hispaniola (Haiti and the Dominican Republic), and Puerto Rico; *Lesser* ~, group of smaller islands to the SE.

ă'ntĭlŏg, ăntĭlŏ'garĭthm (-dhm) *ns.* Number to which a logarithm belongs (100 is the ~ of 2 to the base 10).

ăntĭmacă'ssar *n.* Covering on chair-back to protect it from hair-grease or as ornament. [f. *Macassar oil*, pop. as hair-oil in 19th c.]

ă'ntimonў *n.* (chem.) Brittle metallic element, bluish-white, of flaky crystalline texture, used in alloys esp. with lead, and in medicine; symbol Sb, at. no. 51, at. wt 121·75.

ă'nting *n.* Rubbing or placing of ants in their plumage by birds, apparently to kill parasites.

ăntinō'mian *adj.* & *n.* (Person) holding that the moral law is not binding on Christians on the ground that faith alone is sufficient to salvation. **ăntinō'mianism** *n.*

ănti'nomў *n.* Contradiction in a law, or between laws, principles, etc.

Anti'nōus (ă-). Bithynian youth, favourite of the Emperor Hadrian, represented in art as the ideal type of youthful beauty.

A'ntiŏch (ă-, -k). Name of several ancient cities of the Near East, esp. (1) the capital of Syria under the Seleucid kings (now Antakya in Turkey near the Syrian border); (2) 'Antioch towards Pisidia' in the Roman province of Galatia (near the present Yalvac in SW. Anatolia, Turkey).

ă'ntĭpa͡rtĭcle *n.* (phys.) One of a pair of particles of equal mass but with opposite electrical charge (e.g. electron and positron) or direction of magnetic moment.

Antĭ'pater (ă-) (*c* 398–319 B.C.). Macedonian general; succeeded Alexander as ruler of Macedonia.

ăntĭ'pathȳ *n.* Constitutional or settled aversion (*to, against, between*). **ăntĭpathĕ'tĭc, ăntĭpă'thĭc** *adjs.*

ăntĭ-pe͡rsonnĕ'l *adj.* (of bombs) Designed to kill or injure persons.

ăntĭpe͡r'spĭrant *n.* Substance applied to the skin to reduce perspiration.

ă'ntĭphon *n.* Verse of psalm or other traditional scriptural passage sung during divine service, freq. one sung responsively by alternating choirs.

ăntĭ'phonal *adj.* Sung alternately. ~ *n.* Collection of antiphons.

ăntĭ'phonarȳ *n.* Antiphonal.

ăntĭ'phonȳ *n.* Antiphon; antiphonal singing.

Antĭ'podēs (ă-, -z) *n.pl.* Places on opposite sides of the earth; esp. Australasia as region diametrically opposite to Europe. **ăntĭ'podal** *adj.* **ăntĭpodē'an** *adj.* & *n.* [Gk, 'having the feet opposite']

ă'ntĭpōpe *n.* Pope in opposition to one (held to be) canonically chosen.

ăntĭpȳrĕ'tĭc *adj.* & *n.* (Drug) allaying or preventing fever.

ă'ntĭquarȳ *n.* Student or collector of antiques or antiquities. **ăntĭquār'ĭan** *adj.* & *n.* **ăntĭquār'ĭanĭsm** *n.*

ă'ntĭquātėd *adj.* Out of date; antique.

ănti'que (-ēk) *adj.* Of or existing from old times; old-fashioned; of the ancients. ~ *n.* Relic of ancient art or of old times; piece of old furniture, work of art, etc., regarded as valuable esp. by collectors.

ăntĭ'quĭtȳ *n.* Ancientness; ancient times, esp. (*classical* ~) the period of the ancient Greek and Roman civilizations; (pl.) customs, practices, etc., of ancient times, objects surviving from them.

ăntĭrrhī'num (-rī-) *n.* Plant of genus *A~*, with pouched flowers that can be made to gape; snapdragon. [Gk *anti* counterfeiting + *rhinos* nose]

ăntĭsco͡rbū'tĭc *adj.* & *n.* (Medicine etc.) preventing or curing scurvy.

ăntĭ-Sĕ'mīte *adj.* & *n.* (Person) hostile to Jews. **ăntĭ-Sėmĭ'tĭc** *adj.* **ăntĭ-Sĕ'mĭtĭsm** *n.*

ăntĭsĕ'psĭs *n.* (med.) Antiseptic treatment or condition.

ăntĭsĕ'ptĭc *adj.* & *n.* (Agent) counteracting sepsis. **ăntĭsĕ'ptĭcallȳ** *adv.*

ă'ntĭse͡rum *n.* (pl. *-a*) Antitoxic serum; serum containing antibodies, esp. one used therapeutically.

ăntĭsō'cial (-shl) *adj.* Opposed to principles on which society is based. **ăntĭsō'ciallȳ** *adv.*

ăntĭstă'tĭc *adj.* Counteracting the effect of static electricity.

Antĭ'sthenēs (ă-, -z) (5th c. B.C.). Athenian philosopher, pupil of Socrates and founder of the Cynic school of philosophy.

ăntĭ'strophė *n.* (Lines recited during) returning movement from left to right in ancient Greek choruses. **ăntĭstrŏ'phĭc** *adj.* [Gk, = 'turning about']

ăntĭ'thėsĭs *n.* (pl. *-esēs*). Contrast of ideas marked by parallelism of strongly contrasted words; direct opposite. **ăntĭthĕ'tĭc, -ĭcal** *adj.*

ăntĭtŏx'ĭn *n.* Serum or principle serving to neutralize a toxin. **ăntĭtŏ'xĭc** *adj.*

ă'ntĭ-trāde *adj.* & *n.* 1. (Wind) blowing in opposite direction to trade wind in the upper air of the same region. 2. (Wind) blowing in opposite direction to trade wind, but in different region, and on the surface.

ă'ntĭtȳpe *n.* That which a type or symbol represents; see TYPE *n.* 4. **ăntĭtȳ'pĭcal** *adj.*

ă'ntler *n.* Whole or any branch of either horn of deer.

A'ntonīne (ă-) *adj.* Of Antoninus Pius or Marcus Aurelius Antoninus; ~ *Wall*, wall built during the reign of the former from Forth to Clyde.

Antonī'nus Pī'us (ă-) (A.D. 86–161). Roman emperor 138–161.

ăntŏnomā'sia (-z-) *n.* Substitution of epithet etc. for proper name; use of proper name to express general idea (e.g. *a Solomon*).

A'ntonȳ[1] (ă-), Mark. Marcus Antonius (*c* 83–30 B.C.), Roman general and consul; member of 2nd triumvirate; became enthralled by Cleopatra; was deprived of his powers (32 B.C.) by the senate and defeated at battle of Actium.

Antony[2, 3], St.: see ANTHONY[1, 2].

ă'ntonȳm *n.* Word of contrary meaning to another.

A'ntrĭm (ă-). Town and county of Northern Ireland.

ă'ntrum *n.* (pl. *-tra*). Cavity in the body, esp. one in the upper jaw-bone.

A'ntwẽrp (ă-). (Fl. *Antwerpen*, Fr. *Anvers*) Belgian city-port.

Anū'bĭs. (Egyptian myth.) Jackal-headed deity, ruler of the dead, whom he conducts to the shades.

anūr'an *adj.* & *n.* (Member) of the Anura, an order of the Amphibia comprising frogs and toads, the adult forms of which have no tails or gills but have strong hind legs for leaping and swimming.

ā'nus *n.* Opening, at end of alimentary canal, through which solid matter is excreted.

ă'nvĭl *n.* Block (usu. of iron) on which metal is worked by smith; thing resembling this, esp. the INCUS.

anxī'ėtȳ (ăngz-) *n.* Uneasiness, concern; solicitous desire; neurotic fear. **ă'nxious** (-kshus) *adj.* Troubled, uneasy; earnestly desirous; causing anxiety. **ă'nxiouslȳ** *adv.*

a'nȳ (ĕ-) *adj.* & *pron.* One or some but no matter which; whichever is chosen; ~ *amount of*, a great deal of. ~ *adv.* At all, in some degree.

a'nȳbŏdȳ (ĕ-) *n.* & *pron.* Any person; important person.

a'nȳhow (ĕ-) *adv.* Anyway; in any case.

a'nȳone (ĕ-, -wŭn) *n.* & *pron.* Anybody.

a'nȳthĭng (ĕ-) *n.* & *pron.* Whatever thing; a thing, no matter which.

a'nȳway (ĕ-) *adv.* In any way whatever; anyhow.

a'nȳwhere (ĕ-, -ār) *adv.* & *pron.* (In to) any place.

A'nzăc (ă-) *n.* Member of the Australian and New Zealand Army Corps; Australian or New Zealand serviceman. [initials of name]

A.O.C.(-in-C.) *abbrev.* Air Officer Commanding(-in-Chief).

ā'orĭst *adj.* (Gk & Sansk. gram., of tense) Denoting in the indicative mood a simple past tense, in other moods occurrence, without limitations as to continuance etc. ~ *n.* Aorist tense or form.

āōr'ta *n.* Great artery issuing from left ventricle of heart, carrying blood through its branches to all other parts of body.

à outrance (ah o͞otrahṅs). To the death. [Fr.]

A.P. *abbrev.* Associated Press.

apā'ce *adv.* Swiftly.

Apache *n.* & *adj.* 1. (*a*pă'chĭ) (Member) of tribe of N. Amer.

Indians fierce and skilful in raiding. 2. (*a*pă'sh) Violent street ruffian in Paris.

ă'panage, ăpp- *n.* Provision for younger children of kings etc.; dependency; perquisite.

apar̂'t *adv.* Aside, separately; into pieces; to or at a distance.

apar̂'theid (-hāt) *n.* Policy of racial segregation in S. Africa; similar policy elsewhere. [Afrikaans]

apar̂'tment *n.* Single room of a house; (pl. *or* sing.) set of rooms; (sing., chiefly U.S.) flat.

ă'pathy̆ *n.* Insensibility to suffering; indifference; mental indolence. **ăpathĕ'tic** *adj.* **ăpathĕ'tically̆** *adv.*

ă'patite *n.* Crystallized phosphate of lime.

āpe *n.* Anthropoid ape (see ANTHROPOID); (pop.) monkey; *great*

Orang-utan

Chimpanzee

APE

~s, gorilla, chimpanzee, orang-utan; *~-man*, pithecanthrope. ~ *v.t.* Imitate, mimic.

Apĕ'llēs (-z) (4th c. B.C.). Greek painter.

A'pĕnnīnes (ă-, -nz). Mountain range running down the length of Italy.

aperçu (ahpar̄sōō) *n.* Summary exposition, conspectus; an insight. [Fr.]

apēr'ient *adj.* & *n.* Laxative.

apĕ'ritif, apéritif (-ĕrĭtēf) *n.* Alcoholic drink taken before meal to stimulate appetite; appetizer.

apĕ'rĭtive *adj.* & *n.* Laxative.

ă'perture *n.* Opening, gap; space through which light passes in camera or other optical instrument.

āpĕ'talous *adj.* Without petals.

ā'pĕx *n.* (pl. *ā'pĭcēs*, *ā'pĕxes*). Tip, top; vertex (of cone, triangle).

aphā'sĭa (-z-) *n.* Loss of speech, partial or total, or loss of power to understand written or spoken language as result of damage to the brain.

aphē'lĭon *n.* (pl. *-lĭa*). Point of planet's or comet's orbit farthest from sun.

ă'phĭd *n.* Aphis. **aphĭ'dĭan** *adj.*

ā'phĭs *n.* (pl. *-idēs*). Small soft-bodied insect of family Aphididae, infesting leaves and stems of plants.

aphō'nĭa *n.* Absence or loss of the power of speech, due to congenital defect or organic disease or functional disturbance.

ă'phorĭsm *n.* Short pithy statement or maxim. **ăphorĭ'stic** *adj.*

ăphrodĭ'sĭăc (-z-) *adj.* & *n.* (Drug, food, etc.) provoking sexual desire. [f. APHRODITE]

Aphrodī'tė (ă-). (Gk myth.) Goddess of love (esp. sensual), beauty, and fertility, born of the sea-foam; identified by the Romans with Venus; her cult was of eastern origin, and she was identified with Astarte, Ishtar, etc.

ā'pĭary̆ *n.* Place where bees are kept. **ā'pĭarist** *n.* Bee-keeper.

ă'pĭcal *adj.* Belonging to an apex; placed at the tip; (phon., of sound) articulated with tip of tongue.

ā'pĭcŭlture *n.* Bee-keeping.

apie'ce *adv.* Severally, each.

A'pĭs (ah- *or* ā-). (Egyptian myth.) God, the incarnation as a bull of the sun-god Ptah, represented as a bull with the disc of the sun between his horns.

ā'pish *adj.* Like an ape.

aplŏ'mb (-m) *n.* Self-possession.

Apŏ'calÿpse *n.* Revelation, esp. that made to St. John in the island of Patmos; book of N.T. ('Revelation of St. John the Divine') recording this. **apŏcalÿ'ptic** *adj.* & *n.* (Teaching, literature) involving revelation. **apŏcalÿ'ptical** *adj.* **apŏcalÿ'ptically** *adv.*

ăpocar'pous *adj.* (bot.) Having the carpels distinct.

apŏ'copė *n.* Cutting off of last sound or syllable of word.

Apocr. *abbrev.* Apocrypha.

apŏ'crÿpha *n.pl.* 1. *the A~*, set of books which were included in the Septuagint but excluded from the Jewish canon, accepted as canonical by the early Church, since the Reformation not so regarded by Protestant churches but freq. included in Bibles between O.T. and N.T. 2. Other writings of doubtful authenticity. **apŏ'crÿphal** *adj.* 1. Of the Apocrypha; also applied to a number of early Christian writings in similar form to the canonical books of N.T. 2. Of doubtful authenticity, spurious. [Gk *apokrupha* hidden or secret (writings), i.e. those reserved for the initiated and often falsely ascribed]

ă'podal *adj.* & *n.* (zool.) Limbless (creature); (member) of the Apoda, an order of the Amphibia containing tropical legless wormlike animals some of which have scales; (fish) with no ventral fin.

apŏ'dosis *n.* (pl. *-sēs*). Concluding clause of sentence; consequent clause in a conditional sentence.

ă'pogee *n.* Point in orbit of moon, planet, or artificial satellite farthest from earth; (fig.) highest point. **ăpogē'an** *adj.*

Apŏllinar'ius, -ar'is (*c* 310–*c* 390). Bishop of Laodicea *c* 360; asserted that in Christ were to be found human body and soul but not human spirit, which was rereplaced by the divine Logos. **Apŏllinar'ian** *adj.* & *n.* (Supporter) of Apollinarius or his heresy.

Apŏ'llō. (Gk & Rom. myth.) God sometimes identified with the sun and called *Phoebus* (*Apollo*); son of Zeus and Leto and brother of Artemis; represented ideal type of manly beauty; associated esp. with music, poetry, and prophecy.

Apŏ'llyon. 'The destroyer', the angel of the bottomless pit (Rev. 9: 11).

apŏlogĕ'tic *adj.* Regretfully

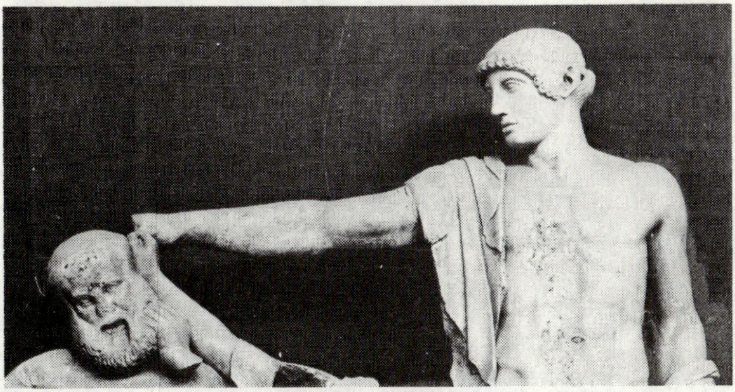

APOLLO

acknowledging, excusing, fault or failure; of the nature of an apology. **apologĕ'tically** *adv.* **apologĕ'tics** *n.pl.* Reasoned defence, esp. of Christianity. **apŏ'logist** *n.* One who defends by argument. **apŏ'logize** *v.i.* Make an apology.

ăpolō'gia *n.* Defence or justification of conduct or opinions.

ă'pologue (-ŏg) *n.* Moral fable.

apŏ'logy̆ *n.* Regretful acknowledgement of offence; statement of regret; apologia; ~ *for*, poor or scanty specimen of.

ă'pophthegm (-*o*fthĕm; -*o*thĕm) *n.* Terse or pithy saying. **ăpophthegmă'tic** (-*o*fthĕg-, -*o*thĕg-) *adj.*

ă'pophy̆ge *n.* (archit.) Outward curve at top or bottom of a column.

ăpoplĕ'ctic *adj.* Pertaining to, causing, apoplexy; liable to, suffering from, apoplexy. **ăpoplĕ'ctically̆** *adv.*

ă'poplĕxy̆ *n.* Seizure caused by blockage or rupture of an artery in the brain.

ăposiopē'sis *n.* (pl. *-pēsēs*). (rhet.) Breaking off short for effect.

apŏ'stasy̆ *n.* Renunciation of religious vows, faith, party, etc. **apŏ'state** *n.* & *adj.* (One) guilty of apostasy. **apŏ'statize** *v.i.* Become an apostate.

ā pŏstĕrĭor'ī. (Reasoning) from effects to causes. [L, = 'from what comes after']

apŏ'stle (-sl) *n.* Messenger, esp. (*A~*) any of the twelve sent forth by Christ to preach Gospel (Matt. 10: 2); first successful Christian missionary in a country; leader of reform; ~ *spoon*, one with figure of one of the Apostles on the handle; *Apostles' Creed*, simplest and prob. oldest of the Christian creeds, ascribed by tradition to the Apostles. **apostŏ'lic** *adj.* Of the Apostles; of the character of an Apostle; of the pope, esp. as successor of St. Peter.

apŏ'strophė *n.* Exclamatory address, esp. to absent person or to inanimate object; sign (') of omission of letter(s) or of possessive case. **apŏ'strophize** *v.t.*

apŏ'thėcary̆ *n.* (archaic) Druggist, pharmaceutical chemist. [Gk *apothēkē* store-house]

ăpothē'cium *n.* (pl. *-cĭa*). (bot.) Cup-shaped fruit body containing asci, freq. brightly coloured, produced by some fungi.

apŏthėō'sis *n.* (pl. *-ōsēs*). Deification; transformation; deified ideal. **apŏ'thėosize** *v.t.*

ăpotropā'ic *adj.* Having or reputed to have the power of averting evil influence or ill luck. **ăpotropā'ically̆** *adv.*

app. *abbrev.* Appendix; apparent(ly).

appa'l (-awl) *v.t.* Dismay, terrify. **appa'lling** *adj.* Horrifying; (colloq.) very bad.

Appalā'chian Mou'ntains (ă-, -tĭnz). (also *Appalachians*) Mountain system of eastern N. America, which in early days of settlement in America confined English settlers to the eastern coastal belt.

appanage: see APANAGE.

ăpparā'tus *n.* Mechanical requisites, an appliance, for doing something, esp. for scientific experiment; ~ *crĭ'tĭcus*, materials for critical study of document; variant readings of manuscripts or early editions, usu. printed below text.

appă'rel *v.t.* Dress, attire. ~ *n.* 1. Dress, clothing. 2. (eccles.) Embroidered panel on dalmatic or tunicle.

appă'rent (*or* -ār-) *adj.* Manifest; seeming; *heir* ~, one who cannot be superseded by birth of nearer heir (cf. PRESUMPTIVE). **appă'rently̆** *adv.*

ăppari'tion *n.* Appearance, esp. of startling kind; thing thought to be seen but having no material existence.

appea'l *v.i.* Call *to* higher tribunal for alteration of decision of lower; call (*to* witness) for corroboration, (*to* person) for assistance etc.; make earnest request; call upon umpire for decision; ~ *to*, be, prove, attractive to. ~ *n.* Act or right of appealing; quality that appeals; *Court of A~*, one hearing cases previously tried in inferior court.

appear' *v.i.* Become visible;

present oneself; act as counsel; be published; seem; be manifest. **appear'ance** *n.* Appearing; look, aspect; (pl.) outward show (of prosperity etc.); apparition.

appea'se (-z) *v.t.* Pacify, soothe; satisfy. **appea'sement** *n.* (esp.) Policy (orig. that of Neville Chamberlain in 1938–9) of making concessions to an aggressor.

appĕ'llant *adj.* Appealing; concerned with appeals. ~ *n.* One who appeals to higher court. **appĕ'llate** *adj.* Taking cognizance of appeals.

ăppellā'tion *n.* Name, title.

appĕ'llative *adj.* (of words) Designating a class (not an individual). ~ *n.* Common noun.

appĕ'nd *v.t.* Attach as an accessory; add, esp. in writing. **appĕ'ndage** *n.*

appĕndicĕ'ctomy̆ *n.* (surg.) Excision of appendix.

appĕndici'tis *n.* Inflammation of vermiform appendix.

appĕ'ndix *n.* (pl. *-icēs, -ixes*). 1. Subsidiary addition (*to* book etc.) 2. Small process developed from organ, esp. vermiform appendix of the intestine.

ăppertai'n *v.i.* Belong, be appropriate, relate, *to*.

ă'ppėtite *n.* Desire, inclination (*for* food, pleasure, etc.); relish. **ă'ppėtizer** *n.* Anything taken to give appetite for a meal. **ă'ppėtizing** *adj.* Rousing appetite.

A'ppian Way (ă-). Roman highway running SE. from Rome to Brundisium (Brindisi), begun by the censor Appius Claudius Caecus, 312 B.C.

applau'd *v.* Express approval (of), esp. by hand-clapping; praise.

applau'se (-z) *n.* Approbation loudly expressed.

ă'pple *n.* Firm fleshy edible fruit of a rosaceous tree of genus *Malus; upset person's ~-cart*, spoil plans; *a'pplejack*, (U.S.) spirit distilled from cider; apple brandy; *~ of the eye*, pupil, treasured object; *~-pie bed*, one with sheets folded (as a joke) so as to prevent a person from stretching at full length between them; *~-pie order*, extreme neatness; *~ of discord*, (Gk myth.) golden apple, inscribed 'For the fairest', contended for by Hera, Athene, and Aphrodite; hence, cause, subject, of dispute; *~ of Sodom*, fruit which, acc. to ancient writers, dissolved into smoke and ashes when plucked, Dead Sea apple.

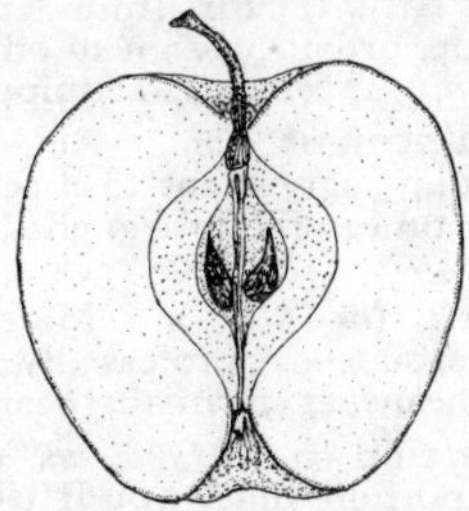

A'ppleton (ăplt-), Sir Edward Victor (1892–1965). British physicist; Nobel Prize for physics 1947; *~ layer*, F^2-layer of the ionosphere.

appli'ance *n.* Applying; device, piece of equipment.

ă'pplicable *adj.* Capable of being applied. **ăpplicabi'lity̆** *n.*

ă'pplicant *n.* One who applies.

ăpplicā'tion *n.* Applying; thing applied; request; relevancy, diligence.

ă'pplicātor *n.* Device for applying substance.

appliqué (-ē'kā) *n.* & *adj.* (Needlework) consisting of pieces of material cut out and sewn to the surface of other material of different colour or texture; material so applied. ~ *v.t.* Sew (material) to another as appliqué.

apply̆' *v.* Put close *to*, put in

contact; administer (remedy); devote (*to*); refer (*to*); address oneself (*for* help etc.) *to*; make application (*for*); make use of; *applied*, put to practical use.

appoggiatura (-ŏjatoor′a) *n.* (mus.) Grace-note consisting of momentary delay of melodic note into following chord of which it does not properly form a part, eventually moving one degree to the note it has displaced. [It.]

appoi′nt *v.t.* Fix (time etc.); prescribe, ordain; assign *to* office; *well, badly, appointed*, so equipped.

appoi′ntment *n.* Act of appointing; agreement to meet at specific time; office assigned; (pl.) fitments.

appor′t (*or* ă′-) *n.* Material thing produced, professedly by occult means, at spiritualist séance.

appor′tion *v.t.* Give as due share; portion out. **appor′tionment** *n.*

ă′pposite (-z-) *adj.* Well put; appropriate. **ăpposi′tion** *n.* Placing side by side; *in* ~, (gram.) syntactically parallel; in same case etc.

apprai′se (-z) *v.t.* Fix price for; estimate. **apprai′sal, apprai′sement** *ns.*

apprē′ciable (-sha-) *adj.* Capable of being estimated; perceptible. **apprē′ciablў** *adv.*

apprē′ciāte (*or* -shi-) *v.* Estimate rightly; recognize, understand; be sensitive to; esteem highly; raise, rise, in value. **apprēciā′tion** *n.* **apprē′ciative** *adj.*

ăpprėhĕ′nd *v.t.* Seize, arrest; understand; anticipate with fear.

ăpprėhĕ′nsible *adj.* Perceptible to senses.

ăpprėhĕ′nsion *n.* 1. Arrest. 2. Understanding. 3. Uneasiness.

ăpprėhĕ′nsive *adj.* Relating to sensuous perception, or intellectual understanding; uneasy in mind. **ăpprėhĕ′nsivelў** *adv.* **ăpprėhĕ′nsivenėss** *n.*

apprĕ′ntice *n.* Learner of a craft, bound to serve, and entitled to instruction from, his employer for a specified term. ~ *v.t.* Bind as apprentice (*to*). **apprĕ′nticeship** *n.*

apprī′se (-z) *v.t.* Give notice *of*, inform.

ă′pprō *n.* (colloq.) Approval (*on* ~).

approa′ch *v.* Come near or nearer (to); set about (task); make overtures to. ~ *n.* Approaching; access, passage; (golf) shot which is intended to reach green. **approa′chable** *adj.* Easy of access; welcoming, friendly to advances.

ă′pprobāte *v.t.* (U.S.) Approve formally, sanction.

ăpprobā′tion *n.* Sanction, approval. **ă′pprobātive, ă′pprobātorў** *adjs.*

apprō′priate *adj.* Suitable, proper. **apprō′priatelў** *adv.* **apprō′priāte** *v.t.* Take possession of; devote to special purposes. **apprōpriā′tion** *n.*

appro′ve (-oov) *v.* Confirm, sanction, commend; ~ *of*, pronounce or consider good; *approved school*: see COMMUNITY home. **appro′val** *n.* Approving; *on* ~, (of goods supplied) to be returned if not satisfactory.

apprŏ′ximate *adj.* Very near; fairly correct. **apprŏ′ximatelў** *adv.* **apprŏ′ximāte** *v.* Bring or come near (*to*). **apprŏximā′tion** *n.*

appur′tėnance *n.* Appendage; accessory; belonging. **appur′tėnant** *adj.* Belonging, appertaining.

Apr. *abbrev.* April.

après-ski (ă′prĕ skĭ *or* shĭ) *n.* & *adj.* (Of, suitable for) time after a day's skiing.

ā′pricŏt *n.* Succulent orange-pink fruit, with smooth stone, of the rosaceous tree *Prunus armeniaca*; this tree; colour of the fruit.

A′prĭl (ā-). 4th month of Gregorian (2nd of Julian) calendar, with 30 days; ~ *Fool*, one hoaxed on ~ *Fool's Day*, All Fools' Day. [L *Aprīlis*]

ā priōr'ī *adv.* & *adj. phr.* (Reasoning) from cause to effect; deductive(ly). [L, = 'from what is before']

ā'pron *n.* 1. Garment worn in front of body to protect clothes; *tied to ~-strings of* (mother, wife, etc.), unduly dependent on. 2. Part of ceremonial dress (of bishops, freemasons, etc.). 3. (theatr.) Advanced strip of stage for playing scenes before proscenium arch; ~ *stage*, stage equipped with this. 4. Part of lathe carrying gears and controls. 5. Area near hangars of airfield for accommodation of aircraft manœuvring on ground. 6. Broad strip on inner side of boat's bow strengthening the stem.

ăpropo's (-pō) *adv.* To the purpose; in respect *of.* ~ *adj.* Pertinent.

ăpse *n.* Semicircular or polygonal recess, usu. with vaulted roof, in church or other building.

ă'psidal *adj.* 1. Of the form of an apse. 2. Of the apsides (see foll.)

ă'psis *n.* (pl. *ă'psidēs, apsī'dēs*). Aphelion or perihelion of planet; apogee or perigee of moon.

ăpt *adj.* Suitable, appropriate: quick, ready; inclined (*to*). **ă'ptlȳ** *adv.* **ă'ptnėss** *n.*

ă'pterous *adj.* Wingless.

ă'pterȳx *n.* = KIWI, 1. [Gk *a-* not, *pterux* wing]

ă'ptitūde *n.* Fitness; natural propensity; ability; (psychol.) capacity to acquire skill in a particular field of bodily or mental performance.

Apuleius (ăpūlē'*us*), Lucius (b. *c* A.D. 123). Platonic philosopher, of Madaura in N. Africa; author of the satire known as 'The Golden Ass'.

Apū'lia. Ancient country and modern region (It. *Puglia*) forming the 'heel' of SE. Italy. **Apū'lian** *adj.* & *n.*

ă'qua fōr'tis. (obs.) Nitric acid; *aqua forti* or *a.f.* (on prints), etched by (so-and-so). [L, = 'strong water']

ă'qualŭng *n.* & *v.i.* (Use) diver's portable breathing apparatus, consisting of cylinders of compressed air with valve and mouthpiece.

ăquamari'ne (-ēn) *n.* Bluish-green transparent beryl; colour of this. [L *aqua marina* sea-water]

ă'quaplāne *n.* Board towed behind speed-boat, carrying a rider. ~ *v.i.* 1. Ride on aquaplane. 2. (of vehicle travelling on wet surface) Lose contact with surface through build-up of water beneath tyres.

ă'qua rē'gia. Mixture of concentrated nitric and hydrochloric acids, able to dissolve gold and platinum, which are not attacked by the unmixed acids. [L, = 'royal water']

ăquarĕ'lle *n.* (Painting in) transparent water-colour.

aquār'ium *n.* (pl. *-s, -ia*). Artificial pond or tank for keeping live aquatic plants, fishes, or animals; place containing such tanks.

Aquār'ius. The Water-carrier, a constellation; 11th sign (♒) of the zodiac, which the sun enters about 21 Jan. **Aquār'ian** *adj.* & *n.*

aquă'tic (*or* -ŏt-) *adj.* Living in or frequenting water; (of sports) conducted in or on water. ~ *n.* Aquatic plant or animal; (pl.) aquatic sports.

ă'quatint *n.* (Colour-)print with finely grained transparent effect, produced by coating a copper plate (or plates) with a porous resin ground, painting the design on it with varnish, immersing it in nitric acid, and inking it, when the protected parts, being less corroded by the acid, will take up less ink; this process. ~ *v.* Work in aquatint; reproduce by this means.

ăquavi't (-vēt) *n.* Colourless or yellowish alcoholic spirit distilled from potatoes or other starch-containing plant; schnapps.

ă'qua vi'tae (vētī). (obs.) Brandy or other alcoholic spirit. [L, = 'water of life']

AQUEDUCT

ă'quėdŭct *n.* Artificial channel, esp. elevated structure of masonry across valley etc. for conveyance of water.

ā'quėous *adj.* Of water, watery; (geol.) produced by the action of water; ~ *humour*: see HUMOUR *n.* 3.

ăquilē'gia *n.* Plant of genus *A*~; columbine.

ă'quilīne *adj.* Of an eagle; eagle-like; curved like eagle's beak.

Aquī'nas, St. Thomas (*c* 1225–

74). Italian philosopher, a Dominican friar, whose writings, notably his 'Summa Totius Theologiae', represent the culmination of scholastic philosophy.

Aquitai'ne (ă-). Ancient province of SW. France, comprising at some periods the whole country from the Loire to the Pyrenees; by the marriage of Eleanor of Aquitaine to Henry II it became one of the English possessions in France.

A.R.A. *abbrev.* Associate of the Royal Academy.

A'rab (ă-) *n.* 1. One of an orig. Semitic people inhabiting Saudi Arabia and neighbouring countries. 2. Arab horse of a breed noted for its graceful build and speed. 3. *street a*~, homeless child. ~ *adj.*

ărabĕ'sque (-sk) *adj.* Arabian; Moorish, esp. in design; fantastic. ~ *n.* 1. Decoration of fancifully twisted scroll-work, leaves, etc., orig. devised by Muslim artists owing to ban on images. 2. Musical composition suggestive of this decoration. 3. (ballet) Pose in which dancer stands on one foot with one arm extended in front and the other arm and leg extended behind.

Arā bia. Peninsula of SW. Asia, largely desert, lying between the Red Sea and the Persian Gulf and bounded on the north by Jordan and Iraq; SAUDI ~: see entry; ~ *Deserta*, ancient name for the Syrian desert and parts of the Arabian peninsula; ~ *Felix*, ancient name for the more fertile SW. mountainous coastal regions of Arabia (see YEMEN); ~ *Petraea*, ancient name for the Sinai peninsula, including PETRA.

Arā'bian *adj.* Of Arabia or the Arabs; ~ *camel*, one-humped camel (*Camelus dromedarius*); ~ *Nights'* (*Entertainments*), also called the 'Thousand and One Nights', a collection of fairy-stories and fantastic romances written in Arabic, linked together by a framework of Persian origin, though the tales themselves, which were probably collected in Egypt at some time in the 14th–16th centuries, are for the most part not Persian but Arabian in character; ~ *Sea*, NW. part of Indian Ocean, between Arabia and India. ~ *n.* Arab.

A'rabĭc (ă-) *adj.* Arabian; *gum a~*, gum exuded from various kinds of acacia and used in the manufacture of adhesives, confectionery, and in textile printing, pharmacy, etc.; ~ *numerals*, those (1, 2, 3, etc.) now in common use in all western countries, most of which were first used in India and were introduced into the west by the Arabs. ~ *n.* Semitic language, orig. that of the Arabs, but now spoken in a large part of N. Africa, Syria, and neighbouring countries.

Ara'bĭ Pă'sha (-ah-) (*c* 1839–1911). Egyptian soldier and politician of anti-European sympathies.

A'rabĭst (ă-) *n.* Student of Arabic or of Arab civilization etc.

ă'rable *adj.* & *n.* Ploughed or ploughable land.

A'rabȳ (ă-). (poet.) Arabia.

arā'ceous (-sh*u*s) *adj.* Of the Araceae or arum family of plants.

Ară'chnė (-k-). (Gk legend) Skilful weaver who challenged Athene to a contest; Athene tore the work up and when Arachne hanged herself changed her into a spider.

ară'chnĭd (-k-) *n.* (zool.) Member of the Arachnida, a class of wingless arthropods including spiders, scorpions, mites, king crabs, and others, and distinguished from insects esp. by having eight or more legs and no antennae.

ară'chnoid (-k-) *adj.* 1. Of the arachnids. 2. (anat.) Of the three membranes surrounding the brain and supporting the blood-vessels. ~ *n.* Arachnoid membrane.

A'ragon (ă-). Region of Spain, bounded on N. by the Pyrenees and on E. by Catalonia and Valencia.

A'ral Sea (ă-). Inland sea of U.S.S.R., E. of Caspian Sea.

A'răm (ă-). Biblical name of Syria. **Aramae'an** *adj.* & *n.*

A.R.A.M. *abbrev.* Associate of the Royal Academy of Music.

Aramā'ic (ă-) *adj.* & *n.* (Of) the NW. Semitic language, closely related to Hebrew, spoken in SW. Asia in the later Babylonian Empire and until *c* 7th c. A.D.

A'ran I'slands (ă-, īl*a*ndz). Group of three islands off W. coast of Ireland, lying across mouth of Galway Bay. **A'ran** *adj.* Of a type of patterned knitwear.

A'ranȳ (ah-), János (1817–82). Hungarian national epic poet.

A'rarăt (ă-). Either of two peaks of the Armenian plateau, in which region Noah's ark is said (Gen. 8: 4) to have rested after the Flood (*Great* ~, 5165 m, 16,945 ft).

ăraucâr'ia *n.* Coniferous tree of genus *A~* including monkey puzzle. [*Arauco* district in Chile]

âr'balĕst *n.* Crossbow with special mechanism for drawing it.

âr'bĭter *n.* Judge; one appointed by two parties to settle dispute, umpire; one with entire control *of*; *elegantiae* ~: see PETRONIUS ARBITER.

ârbĭ'trament *n.* Decision of dispute by arbiter; authoritative decision.

âr'bĭtrarȳ *adj.* Derived from mere opinion, capricious; despotic; (law) discretionary. **âr'bĭtrarĭlȳ** *adv.*

âr'bĭtrāte *v.* Decide by arbitration. **ârbĭtrā'tion** *n.* Settlement of dispute by an arbiter.

âr'bĭtrātor *n.* One appointed to settle dispute.

âr'bor *n.* Main support of machine; axle or spindle on which wheel revolves.

ârborā'ceous (-sh*u*s) *adj.* Tree-like; wooded.

Ar'bor Day (âr-). Day set apart annually in U.S., S. Australia, and elsewhere for public tree-planting.

ârbôr'ėal *adj.* Of, living in, trees.

ârbôr'ėous *adj.* Wooded; arboreal; arborescent.

ârborĕ'scent *adj.* Tree-like; branching. **ârborĕ'scence** *n.*

ârborē'tŭm *n.* (pl. -*ta*). Tree-garden.

ar'borĭcŭlture *n.* Cultivation of trees and shrubs. **arborĭcŭ'ltural** (-cher-) *adj.* **arborĭcŭ'lturĭst** *n.*

ar'bor vi'tae (vētī). Coniferous evergreen shrub of genus *Thuja.*

ar'bour (-*er*) *n.* Shady retreat with sides and roof of trees or climbing plants.

Ar'buthnot (ar-), John (1667–1735). Scottish physician and writer of political pamphlets and medical works.

arbū'tus *n.* Evergreen plant of genus *A*~ of the heather family including strawberry tree.

arc *n.* 1. Part of circumference of circle or other curve. 2. (elect.) Intense electrical discharge in gas or vapour, a luminous bridge of conducting gas formed between two separate electrical poles; ~ *lamp*, ~ *light*, lamp using this; ~ *welding*: see WELD².

A.R.C.A. *abbrev.* Associate of the Royal College of Art.

arcā'de *n.* 1. Passage arched over; any covered walk, esp. one with shops etc. at side(s). 2. (archit.) Series of arches supporting, or attached to, a wall.

Arcā'dia (ar-). Mountainous district in the Peloponnese, taken as an ideal region of rustic contentment (in this sense also *Ar'cady̆*). **Arcā'dian** *adj.* & *n.* (Native, inhabitant) of Arcadia; ideal(ly) rustic.

arcā'ne *adj.* Mysterious, secret.

arcā'num *n.* (usu. in pl. *-na*). Mystery, secret.

arch¹ *n.* Structure, usu. curved, consisting of wedge-shaped pieces so arranged as to support one another by mutual pressure, and used to carry weight of roof, wall, etc., or as ornament; any curved structure resembling this in form and function; curve; vault; (anat.) curve on inner side of foot; *Court of Arches*, ecclesiastical court of the province of Canterbury, orig. held in church of St. Mary-le-Bow (or 'of the Arches'); ~ *bridge*, bridge supported on arches; *ar'chway*, arched passage or entrance. **ar'chwise** (-z)

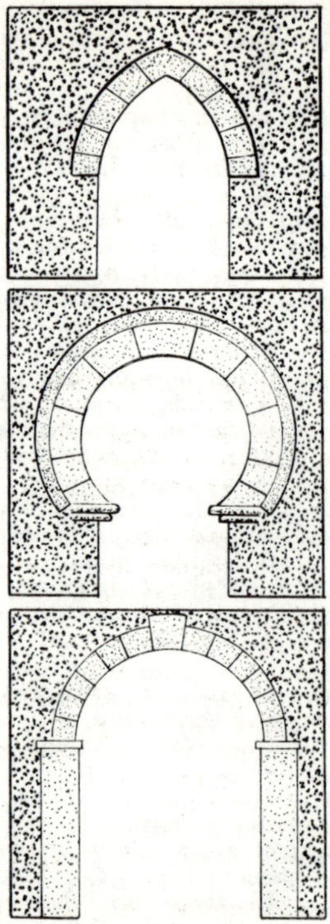

adv. **arch** *v.* Furnish with, form into, form, an arch; span.

arch² *adj.* Making hints or allusions in a jocose affected manner. **ar'chly̆** *adv.* **ar'chnĕss** *n.*

arch- *prefix.* Chief, superior; leading; extreme; first.

archaeŏ'logy̆ (-kĭ-) *n.* Study of ancient cultures through their material remains; *industrial* ~, study of machinery etc. formerly used in industry. **archaeolŏ'gĭcal** *adj.* **archaeolŏ'gĭcally̆** *adv.* **archaeŏ'logĭst** *n.*

archā'ic (-k-) *adj.* Primitive, antiquated; no longer in common use. **archā'ĭcally̆** *adv.*

ar'chāĭsm (-k-) *n.* Obsolete word or phrase; retention or imitation of the old or obsolete (esp.

in language and art). **ar'chaize** *v.*

ar'changel[1] (-k-, -j-) *n.* Angel of highest rank (see ANGEL). **archangĕ'lic** *adj.*

Ar'changel[2] (ark-, -j-). (Russ. *Ar'khange'lsk*) Port of northern U.S.S.R., on White Sea.

archbi'shop *n.* Chief bishop. **archbi'shopric** *n.*

archdea'con *n.* Ecclesiastical dignitary next below bishop, superintending rural deans and holding ecclesiastical court. **archdea'conrў** *n.*

archdi'ocese *n.* Archbishop's see.

ar'chdūke *n.* Prince of former imperial house of Austria. **archdū'cal** *adj.* **archdŭ'chess, archdŭ'chў** *ns.*

archegō'nium (-k-) *n.* Female organ in cryptogams, corresponding to pistil in flowering plants.

arch-ĕ'nemў *n.* Chief enemy; *the* ~, Satan.

ar'cher *n.* One who shoots with bow and arrows. **ar'cherў** *n.*

ar'chetўpe (-k-) *n.* 1. Original model, prototype. 2. (Jungian psychol.) Universal symbol; mental image given by inheritance.

ar'chfie'nd *n.* Satan.

archidiă'conal (-ki-) *adj.* Of an archdeacon.

archiepi'scopal (-ki-) *adj.* Of an archbishop.

Archi'lochus (-kil'*okus*) (*fl.* 648 B.C.). Greek poet of Paros, celebrated for satirical iambic verse.

archimă'ndrīte (-k-) *n.* Superior of monastery of Orthodox Church, equivalent to abbot in Western Churches.

Archimē'dēs (ark-, -z) (*c* 287–212 B.C.). Greek mathematician of Syracuse; said to have made many mechanical inventions, including the screw (named after him) for raising water; *principle of* ~, (phys.) principle that when a body is partly or completely immersed in a fluid the apparent loss of weight is equal to the weight of the fluid displaced. **Archimē'dean** *adj.*

archipĕ'lagō (-k-) *n.* (pl. *-os*). Sea with many islands; group of islands; *the A*~, the Aegean Sea.

ar'chitĕct (-k-) *n.* 1. Designer of buildings who prepares plans and superintends execution. 2. Designer of ship. 3. (fig.) Designer.

architĕctŏ'nic (-k-) *adj.* 1. Of architecture. 2. Of the systematization of knowledge.

ar'chitĕcture (-k-) *n.* Science of building; thing built; style of building; construction. **architĕ'ctural** (-kcher-) *adj.* **architĕ'cturallў** *adv.*

ar'chitrāve (-k-) *n.* 1. Main beam resting immediately on two or more columns; lowest part of entablature. 2. Moulded frame round doorway, window, or arch.

ar'chīve (-k-) *n.* (usu. pl.). Public records; place in which these are kept. **ar'chivist** *n.* Keeper of archives.

ar'chivōlt (-k-) *n.* Under-curve of arch; mouldings decorating this.

ar'chon (-k-) *n.* One of 9 chief magistrates in ancient Athens; chief magistrate of other ancient Greek cities; ruler, president. **ar'chonship** *n.*

A.R.C.M., A.R.C.O., A.R.C.S. *abbrevs.* Associate of the Royal College of Music, of Organists, of Science.

ar'ctic *adj.* Of the North Pole; northern; intensely cold; *A*~ *Circle*, parallel of 66° 32′ N., north of which the sun does not rise at midwinter or set at midsummer; *A* ~ *Ocean*, ocean N. of the Arctic Circle. **Ar'ctic** *n.* Regions (both land and sea) round the North Pole. [Gk *arktos* bear, Ursa Major]

Arctūr'us (ar-). (astron.) Brightest star in the constellation Boötes. [Gk *arktos* bear, *ouros* guardian, because of its position in a line with the tail of Ursa Major]

Ar'den (ar-). Woodland district of N. Warwickshire, part of an ancient forest formerly covering a great part of the Midlands and W. England.

Ardennes (ardĕ'n *or* -ĕ'nz). Ancient forest district including parts of Belgium, Luxemburg, and N. France.

ar'dent *adj.* Eager, zealous, fervent; burning. **ar'dently** *adv.*

ar'dour (-*er*) *n.* Zeal; warmth,

ar'dūous *adj.* Hard, laborious; strenuous. **ar'dūously** *adv.* **ar'dūousness** *n.*

are[1] *n.* Unit of square measure, = 100 square metres.

are[2]. 1st, 2nd, and 3rd pers. pl. pres. of BE.

ar'ea *n.* Extent of surface; region; space intended for specific use, as *dining*, *parking*, ~; scope, range; sunk court or yard before basement of house.

ă'rēca (*or* arē'ka) *n.* Tropical Asiatic palm of genus *A*~, bearing pungent astringent fruit; ~ *nut*, astringent seed of a species of areca; betel.

arē'na *n.* Central part of amphitheatre, in which combats took place; central part of stadium; scene of conflict or action.

ărėnā'ceous (-sh*us*) *adj.* Sandy; sand-like.

Arėŏ'pagus (ă-). Hill at Athens where (in antiquity) highest judicial court met; hence, this court. **Arėŏ'pagīte** (-g-) *n.* Member of court of Areopagus. [Gk *Areios pagus* hill of Ares]

Ares (ar'ēz). (Gk myth.) God of war, son of Zeus and Hera; identified with the Roman MARS. **Ar'ian**[1] *adj.* & *n.*

arête (-ā't) *n.* Sharp ridge of mountain. [Fr.]

Arėthū'sa (ă-, -z*a*). (Gk legend) Water-nymph who fled from Greece to Ortygia in Sicily, pursued by the river-god Alpheus; the waters of the river Alpheus (in the Peloponnese) were believed to flow unmixed through the sea and emerge mingled with the fountain of Arethusa at Ortygia.

Arėti'nō (ă-, -ēnō), Pietro (1492–1556). Italian author of comedies, satires, and licentious poems.

ar'gali *n.* Large Asiatic wild sheep, *Ovis ammon.*

Argand (argahn), Aimé (*c* 1750–1803). Swiss inventor of the ~ *lamp* (ar'gand), with a tubular wick, which allows air to reach both inner and outer surfaces of the flame; ~ *burner*, gas-burner constructed on the same principle.

ar'gent *n.* & *adj.* Silver (colour, esp. in heraldry).

argenti'ferous *adj.* Yielding silver.

Ar'gentīne[1] (ar-). Republic occupying most of S. part of S. America E. of the Andes; first settled by Spaniards (1526 onwards); remained a Spanish colony until a revolt, beginning in 1810, led to the declaration in 1816 of the independence of the *Provincias Unidas del Rio de la Plata* ('United Provinces of the Silver River'); capital, Buenos Aires. **Argenti'nian** *adj.* & *n.* [L *argentum* silver, because the Rio de la Plata district exported it]

ar'gentīne[2] *adj.* Of silver; silvery.

ar'gil *n.* (Potter's) clay. **argillā'ceous** (-sh*us*) *adj.*

Ar'gīve (arg-) *adj.* & *n.* (Native, inhabitant) of ARGOS or Argolis; Greek.

Ar'gō (ar-): see ARGONAUTS.

ar'gŏl *n.* Crude tartar; grey or red substance deposited from fermented wines.

Ar'golis (ar-): see ARGOS.

ar'gŏn *n.* (chem.) Inert gaseous element, present to extent of about 1 % in the air, discovered *c* 1894 by Lord Rayleigh and Sir William Ramsay, used in gas-filled electric light bulbs etc.; symbol Ar, at. no. 18, at. wt 39·948.

Ar'gonauts (ar-) *n.pl.* (Gk legend) Heroes who accompanied Jason on board the ship *Argo* on the quest for the Golden Fleece.

Ar'gŏs (ar-). Ancient Greek town of the E. Peloponnese, from which the peninsula of Argolis derived its name.

ar'gosy̆ *n.* (hist., poet.) Large vessel (orig. of Ragusa or Venice) carrying rich merchandise; (poet.) ship. [prob. from It. *Ragusea* (*nave*) (ship) of Ragusa]

ar'got (-ō) *n.* Jargon, slang, of a class or group, formerly esp. of thieves.

ar'gue *n.* Maintain by reasoning; reason; prove, indicate; raise objections, dispute. **ar'guable** *adj.*

ar'gufy *v.i.* (colloq.) Dispute excessively.

ar'gument *n.* Reason advanced; debate; summary of subject-matter of book etc. **argumentā'tion** *n.* Methodical reasoning; debate.

argume'ntative *adj.* Logical; fond of arguing. **argume'ntatively** *adv.* **argume'ntativeness** *n.*

Ar'gus[1] (ar-). 1. (Gk myth.) Fabulous person with 100 eyes, slain by Hermes; after his death Hera transferred his eyes to the tail of the peacock. 2. (Gk legend) Dog of Ulysses, who recognized his master on his return from Troy after an absence of 20 years.

ar'gus[2] *n.* Pheasant of genus *Argusianus*, natives of Asia. [f. ARGUS[1]]

Argy'llshire (arg-). Former county on W. coast of Scotland, since May 1975 part of the region of Strathclyde.

ar'ia *n.* Long accompanied song for one voice in opera and oratorio; song-like movement in instrumental composition. [It.]

Aria'dne (ă-). (Gk myth.) Daughter of Minos, king of Crete; helped Theseus to escape from the labyrinth of the Minotaur by providing him with a clue of thread; then became his wife, but he deserted her in the island of Naxos, where she was found and married by Dionysus.

Arian[1]**:** see ARES.

Arian[2]**, Arianism:** see ARIUS.

A.R.I.B.A. *abbrev.* Associate of the Royal Institute of British Architects.

ă'rid *adj.* Dry, parched; (geog., of climate or region) having insufficient water to support vegetation. **ari'dity** *n.*

Ar'iel (ar-). In Shakespeare's **'The Tempest', a spirit released by the magician Prospero from imprisonment by a witch, Sycorax.**

Aries (ar'ēz). The Ram, a constellation; 1st sign (♈) of the zodiac, which the sun enters at the vernal equinox.

ari'ght (-it) *adv.* Rightly.

ă'ril *n.* (bot.) Extra seed-covering, freq. brightly coloured (e.g. yew, spindle).

Arimathē'a (ă-): see JOSEPH[1], 3.

Arī'on (7th c. B.C.). Greek poet and musician of Lesbos; said to have perfected the dithyramb; acc. to legend, sailors on a ship resolved to murder him, but he begged first to play a tune, did so, and leapt overboard; dolphins were attracted by the music, and one bore him on its back to land.

Ario'stō (ă-), Lodovico (1474–1533). Italian poet, author of the romantic epic 'Orlando Furioso'.

arī'se (-z) *v.i.* (past t. *arō'se*, past part. *arisen* pr. -ĭzn). Appear, spring up, occur, get up, rise.

arī'sings (-z) *n.pl.* Secondary or waste products; remains.

Aristar'chus[1] (ă-, -k-) of Samos (3rd c. B.C.). Astronomer and mathematician; maintained that the earth revolved round the sun, though he thought that its orbit was a circle (not an ellipse).

Aristar'chus[2] (ă-, -k-) of Samothrace (*c* 217–*c* 145 B.C.). Librarian at Alexandria; edited the Greek classics; regarded as the originator of scientific scholarship.

Aristī'dēs (ă-, -z) (d. *c* 466 B.C.). Athenian general and statesman, called 'the Just'; commanded his tribe at the battle of Marathon; was archon in 489, but was later ostracized and died in poverty.

Aristi'ppus (ă-). Name of two Greek philosophers: the elder (late 5th c. B.C.), a native of Cyrene and friend of Socrates, is freq. called the founder of the Cyrenaic school, prob. by confusion with the younger, his grandson (fl. *c* 400–365), who taught that immediate pleasure is the only end of action.

ăristo'cracy *n.* The nobility; supremacy of privileged order; government by nobles.

ă'ristocrăt *n.* Member of aristocracy. **ăristocră'tic** *adj.* Belonging to the aristocracy; having distinguished bearing and manners. **ăristocră'tically** *adv.*

Aristŏ′phanēs (ă-, -z) (*c* 445–*c* 385 B.C.) Athenian comic dramatist; author of comedies (the 'Birds', 'Frogs', 'Wasps', etc.) caricaturing his contemporaries and their attitude to public affairs.

A′ristŏtle (ă-) (384–322 B.C.). Greek philosopher; pupil of Plato at Athens; became tutor to the young Alexander of Macedon; returned to Athens in 335; there conducted the PERIPATETIC school; wrote the 'Ethics', 'Politics', and 'Poetics', and works of zoology, physics, metaphysics, logic (which he invented), and rhetoric. **Aristotē′lian** *adj.* & *n.*

ari′thmĕtic *n.* Science of numbers; computation. **ărithmĕ′tical** *adj.* **ărithmĕ′ticallў** *adv.* **ărithmĕti′cian** (-sh*a*n) *n.*

Ar′ius (ar̄-) (*c* 250–*c* 336). Priest of Alexandria; denied the true Divinity of Christ. **Ar′ian**[2] *adj.* & *n.* (Supporter) of Arius or his heresy. **Ar′ianism** *n.*

Ariz. *abbrev.* Arizona.

Arizō′na (ă-). State in south-western U.S., admitted to the Union in 1912; capital, Phoenix.

ark *n.* 1. Chest, box; *A~ of the Covenant*, *of Testimony*, wooden coffer containing tables of Jewish law, the most sacred religious symbol of early Israel; *~ of the Law*; chest or cupboard in Jewish synagogue containing scrolls of the Law. 2. Covered floating vessel in which NOAH was saved at the Deluge.

Ark. *abbrev.* Arkansas.

Arkansas (ar̄′k*a*nsaw). State in south-central U.S., admitted to the Union in 1836; capital, Little Rock.

Arkwright (ar̄′krīt), Sir Richard

(1732–92). English engineer, inventor of the spinning-frame.

Arles (ar̄l). Town of S. France, on the river Rhône, on the site of a Roman city (*Arelate*), the chief residence of Constantine.

arm[1] *n.* Upper limb of human body; sleeve; branch; arm-like thing; *armchair*, chair with supports for arms; (fig.) applied to persons who theorize without actively participating; *ar′mpit*, hollow under arm at shoulder. **ar′mful** *n.* **ar′mlėss** *adj.*

arm[2] *n.* 1. Particular kind of weapon; (pl.) weapons. 2. Each

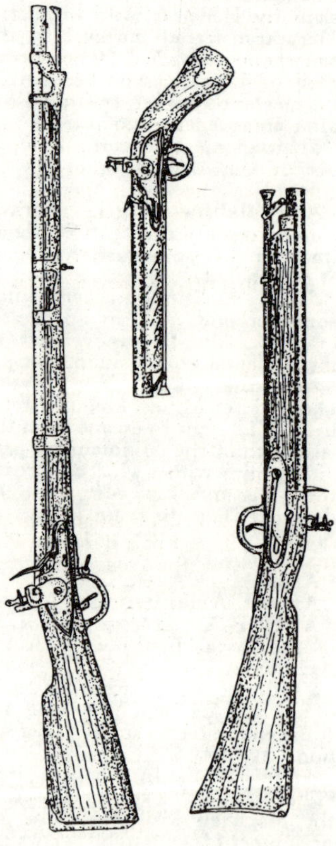

FIREARMS

kind of force, as *air* ~, *infantry* ~. 3. (pl.) Heraldic devices; *coat of* ~S: see COAT; *King of Arms:* see KING. ~ *v.* Furnish with arms; take up arms; provide, furnish, *with.*

Armada (armah'da). (also *Spanish* ~) Fleet sent by Philip II of Spain against England in 1588; it was defeated in the Channel and dispersed by the English fleet under Lord Howard of Effingham and such captains as Drake, Frobisher, and Hawkins; many of the ships were lost in attempting to return round the N. of Scotland.

armadi'llō *n.* (pl. *-os*). Burrowing, usu. nocturnal, S.-Amer. mammal, protected by bony plates resembling armour. [Span. dim. of *armado* armed creature]

Armagĕ'ddon (ar-, -g-). Place where the kings of the earth are to be gathered together for 'the battle of that great day of God Almighty' (Rev. 16: 14–16).

Armagh (armah'). County and county town of Northern Ireland.

ar'mament *n.* Force equipped for war; military weapons and munitions; process of equipping for war.

ar'mature *n.* 1. Arms, armour, defensive covering of animals or plants. 2. Piece of soft iron placed in contact with poles of a magnet to preserve the intensity of magnetization or to support a load; core of laminated iron wound round by coils of insulated copper-wire, that part of a dynamo which rotates in the magnetic field. 3. Framework of wire, wood, etc., round which sculptor builds clay or plaster model.

Armē'nia (ar-). Constituent republic of U.S.S.R., lying S. of the Caucasus, part of the former kingdom of Armenia, most of which was under Turkish rule from the 16th c.; capital, Erivan.

Armē'nian *adj.* Of Armenia or its people or language. ~ *n.* Armenian person or language.

ar'miger *n.* One entitled to bear heraldic arms.

armi'llarȳ *adj.* Pertaining to bracelets; ~ *sphere*, skeleton celestial globe consisting of metal rings representing the equator, ecliptic, tropics, etc., revolving on an axis.

Armi'nius[1] (ar-) (18 B.C.–A.D. 19). Latinized form of Hermann, chief of the German tribe of the Cherusci, leader of the insurrection against the Romans under Varus, who were defeated at the battle of the Teutoburg forest (A.D. 8).

Armi'nius[2] (ar-), Jacobus (d. 1609). Latinized form of Harmensen, a Dutch Protestant theologian, with views opposed to those of CALVIN esp. on predestination. **Armi'nian** *adj.* & *n.* **Armi'nianism** *n.*

ar'mistice *n.* Cessation of hostilities by agreement between belligerents; short truce; *A~ Day*, 11 Nov., formerly kept as anniversary of the armistice that ended hostilities in the war of 1914–18 (since war of 1939–45 celebrated on Remembrance Sunday). [L *arma* arms + *-stitium* stopping]

ar'mlėt *n.* Band worn round arm.

armor'ial *adj.* Of heraldic arms.

ar'morȳ *n.* Heraldry.

Armŏ'rican (ar-) *adj.* = HERCYNIAN.

ar'mour (-mer) *n.* 1. (hist.) Defensive covering for body worn in fighting. 2. (also ~ *plate*) Steel plates etc. protecting ship, tank, car, etc., from projectiles etc. (so ~*-plated*); tanks and other fighting vehicles equipped with such armour. ~ *v.t.* Furnish with such protective covering; *armoured car, train*, one supplied with protective armour and (usu.) guns; *armoured column, division*, etc., one equipped with armoured cars, tanks, etc.

ar'mourer (-mer-) *n.* Manufacturer of arms; one in charge of ship's or regiment's small arms.

ar'mourȳ (-mer-) *n.* Place where small arms are kept; armourer's workshop.

ar'mȳ *n.* Organized body of persons armed for fighting on land; vast host; ~ *corps*, main subdivision of an army in the field

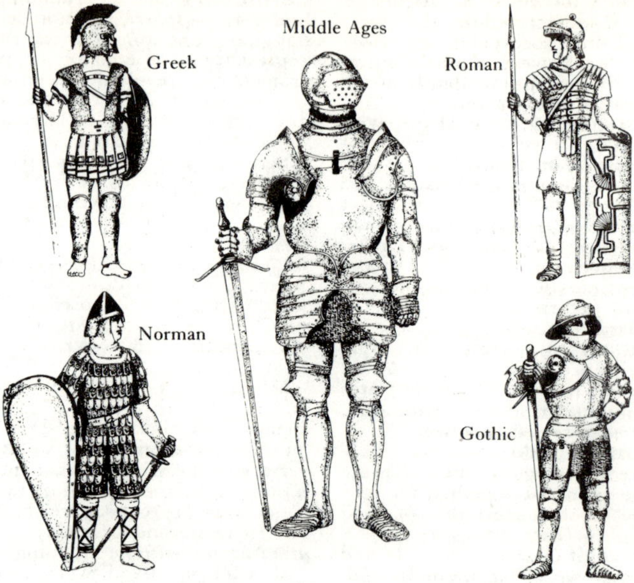

ARMOUR

consisting of two or more divisions and certain technical and administrative units; ~ *list*, official list of commissioned officers.

Arne (ar̂n), Thomas (1710–78). English composer of operas, masques (including 'Alfred' which contains 'Rule, Britannia!'), and songs.

ar̂'nica *n.* Composite plant of genus *A~*, largely American, including mountain tobacco; tincture, prepared from root and rhizome of mountain tobacco and used for bruises, sprains, etc.

Ar'nō (ar̂-). River of N. Italy, flowing through Florence and Pisa.

Ar'nold[1] (ar̂-) of Brescia (d. 1155). Italian Augustinian, an ascetic who vigorously condemned the temporal power and abuses of the clergy and the papacy; executed by Adrian IV.

Ar'nold[2] (ar̂-), Matthew (1822–88). English poet and critic; son of Thomas ARNOLD[3].

Ar'nold[3] (ar̂-), Thomas (1795–1842). Headmaster of Rugby (1828–42) which he raised to the rank of a great public school.

ar̂'oid *adj.* & *n.* Araceous (plant).

arō'ma *n.* Fragrance; subtle pervasive quality.

ăromă'tic *adj.* 1. Fragrant, spicy. 2. (chem.) Of the group of organic compounds in which the carbon atoms are arranged in 6-membered rings (as in benzene).

arou'nd *adv.* On every side; round; here and there. ~ *prep.* All round; about; enveloping; approximately.

arou'se (-z) *v.t.* Awaken; stir up into activity.

A.R.P. *abbrev.* Air-raid precautions.

ar̂pĕ'ggĭō (-ĕjiō) *n.* (pl. *-os*). Chord of which notes are not played simultaneously but 'harpwise', i.e. in succession. [It. *arpa* harp]

arquebus: see HARQUEBUS.

arr. *abbrev.* Arrives, arriving, etc.

ă'rrack (*or* ară'k) *n.* Alcoholic spirit manufactured in the East, esp. from coco-palm or rice. [Arab. *ʿaraḳ* sweat, alcoholic spirit made from grapes or dates]

arrai'gn (-ān) *v.t.* Indict, accuse; call in question. **arrai'gnment** *n.*

A'rran (ă-). Scottish island at mouth of Firth of Clyde.

arrā'nge (-j) *v.* Put in order; settle; settle beforehand order etc. of; form plans, take steps; adapt. **arrā'ngement** *n.*

ă'rrant *adj.* Downright, notorious.

ă'rras[1] *n.* Rich tapestry; hangings of this round walls of room. [f. ARRAS[2]]

Arras[2] (ărah). Town in NE. France famous in 13th–16th centuries for tapestry weaving.

array' *v.t.* Dress, esp. with display; marshal (forces). ~ *n.* Dress; imposing series; martial order; (math.) arrangement of numbers etc. in rows or columns; (radio) assembly of aerials.

arrear' *n.* That which is behind; (pl.) outstanding debts; work etc. in which one is behindhand; *in* ~(*s*), behindhand. **arrear'age** *n.* Arrear.

arrĕ'st *v.t.* Stop; (law) ~ *judgement*, stay proceedings after verdict; seize (person) esp. by legal authority; catch (attention); catch attention of. ~ *n.* Legal apprehension; stoppage; seizure. **arrĕ'stable** *adj.* (esp.) ~ *disease*, one that can be prevented from getting worse; ~ *offence*, (law) offence for which person can be arrested without a warrant.

arrĕ'ster *n.* (mech.) Attachment for bringing an object to a stop.

Arrhe'nius (ărān-), Svante August (1859–1927). Swedish physical chemist, awarded Nobel Prize in 1903 for his work on the physical chemistry of electrolytes.

arrière-pensée (ăriār pahṅsā) *n.* Ulterior motive; mental reservation. [Fr.]

ă'rris *n.* 1. (archit.) Sharp edge where two planes or curved surfaces meet; ~ *gutter*, V-shapped gutter; ~ *rail*, rail made by cutting a square section of timber across its diagonal. 2. (eng.) Raised circle of material left on surface of metal plate when hole is drilled through it.

arrī've *v.i.* Come to destination or end of journey; be brought; come; establish one's reputation or position. **arrī'val** *n.*

arriviste (ărēvēst) *n.* Person determined to 'arrive' or succeed. [Fr.]

ă'rrogant *adj.* Overbearing, presumptuous. **ă'rrogantly̆** *adv.* **ă'rrogance** *n.*

ă'rrogāte *v.t.* Claim unduly. **ărrogā'tion** *n.*

arrondissement (arawṅdēsmahṅ) *n.* Administrative subdivision of French department. [Fr.]

ă'rrow (-ō) *n.* Missile shot from bow, usu. consisting of straight slender wooden shaft with sharp point or head of stone or metal, and feathers fastened to the butt; mark like an arrow or arrowhead, often used as indication of direction etc.; *a'rrowhead*, water-plant, *Sagittaria sagittifolia*, with arrow-shaped leaves, growing in ponds and slow streams; *a'rrowroot*, tropical plant *Maranta arundinacea*; starch obtained from its rhizomes, used as food esp. for invalids.

ar̂se *n.* (vulg.) Buttocks, rump.

ar̂'senal *n.* State establishment where weapons and ammunition are made and stored. [Arab. *dār aṣ-ṣināʿa* factory, place where fighting ships are equipped]

ar̂'senic *n.* (chem.) Brittle steel-grey semi-metallic element, symbol As, at. no. 33, at. wt 74·9216; (pop.) white mineral substance (~ *trioxide*), a violent poison. **ar̂'senic** (*or* -sĕ'n-) *adj.* Of arsenic; (chem.) applied to compounds in which arsenic is pentavalent. **ar̂sĕ'nical** *adj.* [Gk *arsenikon*, f. Arab. *az-zirnīḵ* orpiment, arsenic]

ar̂sē'nious *adj.* Containing arsenic in trivalent form.

ar̂'sine (-ēn) *n.* Colourless inflammable poisonous gas (AsH_3)

having an odour like garlic; any of a group of poisonous gases derived from this.

ar'sis *n.* (pl. *-sēs*). (pros.) Accented syllable in a metrical foot (opp. THESIS).

ar'son *n.* Wilful setting on fire of houses or other property.

art *n.* Skill, esp. applied to design, representation, or imaginative creation; human skill as opp. to nature; cunning, stratagem; subject in which skill may be exercised; (pl.) certain branches of learning (*liberal ~s*) traditionally serving as preparation for more advanced studies or for life (*Bachelor, Master, of Arts*, one who has obtained a standard of proficiency in these at a university); *applied, decorative ~s*, those concerned with the design and decoration of objects in practical use, handicrafts; *fine ~s*, (usu.) painting, architecture, sculpture, music, poetry; *Arts Council of Great Britain*, organization (incorporated 1946) for promotion of the fine arts.

Artaxer'xes (artazerksēz). Name of two kings of ancient Persia: *Artaxerxes I*, son of Xerxes, reigned 464–424 B.C.; *Artaxerxes* II, son of Darius II, reigned 404–358 B.C.

ar'tėfăct, ar'tĭ- *n.* 1. (archaeol.) Object, as palaeolithic flint, made by human workmanship. 2. (biol.) Something not present in the natural state of an organism but produced while it is being prepared for examination.

Ar'tėmĭs (ar-). (Gk myth.) Goddess of chastity and of hunting; daughter of Leto; twin sister of Apollo, identified with Selene and DIANA.

arter'ial *adj.* Belonging to, of the nature of, an artery; *~ road*, important main road.

arter'ialize *v.t.* Convert (venous blood) into arterial blood by impregnating it with oxygen in lungs; furnish with arterial system. **arterializā'tion** *n.*

arter'iōle *n.* Small artery.

arteriōsclerō'sis *n.* Hardening of the walls of arteries.

ar'tery̆ *n.* Muscular-walled blood-vessel conveying the blood impelled by the heart to the small vessels which supply the tissues; something serving as channel of supplies, e.g. main road.

artē'sian (-zhan) *adj.* *~ well*, perpendicular bore into a curved or slanting water-saturated stratum, penetrating it at a level lower than the source of the water, which rises spontaneously to the surface in a continuous flow. [f. *Artois*, Fr. province]

ar'tful *adj.* Cunning, crafty.

arthrī'tĭs *n.* Inflammation of joint. **arthrĭ'tĭc** *adj.*

ar'thrŏpŏd *n.* One of the Arthropoda, the largest animal phylum, comprising insects, arachnids, myriapods, crustaceans, and trilobites, and characterized by jointed limbs and a hard jointed external skeleton.

Ar'thur[1] (ar-). King of Britain; historically perh. a 5th- or 6th-c. chieftain or general; acc. to legend he was the son of Uther Pendragon and Igerne, wife of Gorlois of Cornwall; became king of Britain at age of 15; married Guinevere; held court at Caerleon-on-Usk and established there a company of knights whose seats were at a Round Table so that none had precedence; was mortally wounded at Camelford in battle against his usurping nephew Modred; was then borne off in a magic boat to Avalon whence he will one day return; *~'s Seat*, saddle-backed hill on E. side of Edinburgh, dominating the city. **Arthur'ian** *adj.*

Ar'thur[2] (ar-), Prince, Duke of Brittany (1187–1203). Grandson of Henry II of England; declared by his uncle, Richard I, to be heir to the throne, to which his other uncle, John, also laid claim; but during the war between France and Britain he was captured and, prob. by John's orders, murdered at Rouen.

Ar'thur[3] (ar-), Chester Alan (1830–86). American politician, lawyer, and soldier (in Civil War); 21st president of U.S., 1881–5.

ar̄′tĭc *n.* (colloq.) Articulated vehicle.

ar̄′tĭchōke *n.* 1. Plant, *Cynara scolymus* (of which bottom of flower and bases of its scales are edible), allied to thistle. 2. *Jerusalem* ~, species of sunflower with edible tuberous roots. [It. *articiocco*, f. Arab. *alkaršūfa*; Jerusalem, corrupt. of It. *girasole* sunflower]

ar̄′tĭcle *n.* Separate portion of anything written; separate clause, literary composition forming part of magazine etc.; particular; particular thing; (gram.) either of the adjectives 'a, an' (*indefinite* ~) and 'the' (*definite* ~), or their equivalents in other languages. ~ *v.t.* Bind by articles of apprenticeship; set forth in articles.

ar̄tĭ′cūlar *adj.* Of the joints.

ar̄tĭ′cūlate *adj.* Having joints; distinctly jointed, distinguishable; able to express oneself well; (of speech) clearly defined. **ar̄tĭ′cūlāte** *v.* Connect by joints; divide into words, pronounce distinctly; speak distinctly; *articulated vehicle*, one with flexibly connected sections. **ar̄tĭ′cūlatorў** *adj.*

ar̄tĭcūlā′tion *n.* Articulate utterance, speech; jointing.

artifact: see ARTEFACT.

ar̄′tĭfĭce *n.* Device; cunning; skill. **ar̄tĭ′fĭcer** *n.* Craftsman; (in Royal Navy) mechanic.

ar̄tĭfĭ′cial (-shal) *adj.* Produced by art; not natural; not real; ~ *horizon*, (i) level reflector used in determining altitudes of stars etc.; (ii) instrument in aircraft indicating attitude of the aircraft to the horizon; ~ *insemination*, injection of semen into uterus by artificial means; ~ *language*, invented language, esp. one designed for international use; ~ *rain*, rain made by dispersal of solid carbon dioxide or other chemical material in suitable cloud, causing the cloud to cool and condense; ~ *respiration*: see RESPIRATION; ~ *silk*: see RAYON. **ar̄tĭfĭ′ciallў** *adv.* **ar̄tĭfĭcĭă′lĭtў** *n.*

ar̄tĭ′llerў *n.* Large mounted firearms of calibre greater than small arms; cannon; ordnance; branch of army that uses these; *art′illeryman*, one belonging to the artillery, gunner. **ar̄tĭ′llerĭst** *n.* Artilleryman.

ar̄tĭsă′n (-z-) *n.* Mechanic; handicraftsman.

ar̄′tĭst *n.* One who practises one of the fine arts, esp. painting; one who makes his craft a fine art; artiste. **ar̄tĭ′stĭc** *adj.* **ar̄′tĭstrў** *n.*

ar̄tĭ′ste (-ēst) *n.* Professional singer, dancer, etc.

ar̄′tlėss *adj.* Guileless, simple; lacking art, crude. **ar̄′tlėsslў** *adv.* **ar̄′tlėssnėss** *n.*

art nouveau (ar̄ nōōvō). Decorative style (*c* 1880–*c* 1910) using flowing curves and naturalistic motifs. [Fr., = 'new art']

Artois (ar̄′twah). Ancient province of NE. France.

ar̄′tў *adj.* Having artistic pretensions.

ār′um *n.* Plant of genus *A*~ including cuckoo-pint (lords and ladies); ~ *lily*, inflorescence of

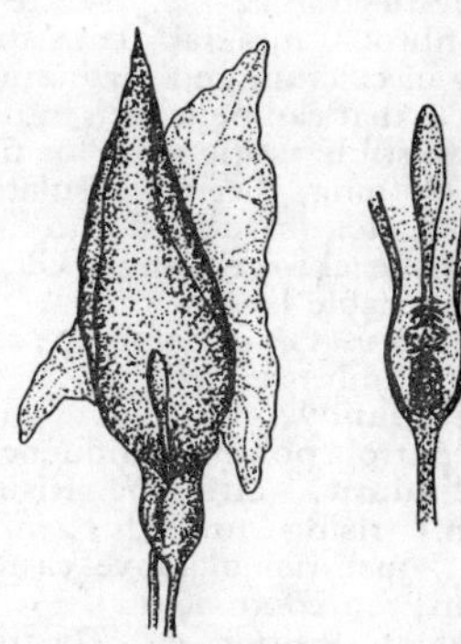

plant *Zantedeschia aethiopica*, used for decoration, esp. on altar.

A.R.W.S. *abbrev.* Associate of the Royal Society of Painters in Water-colours.

Ar′ўan (ār-) *adj.* & *n.* 1. (archaic) Indo-European; (esp.) Indo-Iranian. 2. (loosely) (Member) of a people speaking an Indo-European language; in Nazi Germany esp. contrasted with SEMITE.

[Sansk. *ārya* noble (in earlier use a national name comprising worshippers of the gods of the Brahmans); the earlier *Arian* is f. L *Arianus*, = 'of Aria' (f. Gk *Areia* eastern Persia)]

ărўbă'llos (pl. *-oi*) *n.* (Gk antiq.) Globular oil-flask with narrow neck.

as[1] (ăz, unemphat. *az*) *adv.* In the same degree; similarly. ~ *conj.* While, when; since, seeing that. ~ *prep.* In the capacity or role of.

ăs[2] *n.* (pl. *ă'ssēs*). Roman copper coin, orig. weighing 12 oz. but finally reduced to ½ oz.

A.S. *abbrev.* Anglo-Saxon.

ăsafoe'tĭda (-fēt-) *n.* Concreted resinous gum of various Persian plants of genus *Ferula* with strong smell of garlic and bitter taste, used in medicine. [Pers. *aza* mastic, L *foetida* stinking]

A'saph (ā- *or* ă-), St. (d. *c* 596). Welsh saint, prior of Llanelwy, and first bishop of St. Asaph; commemorated 1 May.

ăsbĕ'stos (*or* ăz-) *n.* White or grey fibrous mineral (consisting largely of calcium and magnesium silicates) that can be woven into an incombustible fabric used for fireproof clothing, thermal insulation of pipes, etc., or formed into light sheet material for roofing. [Gk, = 'unquenchable']

ascĕ'nd *v.* Go or come up; rise, mount, climb.

ascĕ'ndancў, -encў *n.* Dominant control, powerful influence.

ascĕ'ndant, -ent *adj.* Rising; (astron.) rising towards zenith; (astrol.) just rising above eastern horizon; predominant. ~ *n.* Ascendant position etc.; (astrol.) ascendant point of ecliptic or degree of zodiac.

ascĕ'nder *n.* (esp. printing) Limb of letter above x-height.

ascĕ'nsion *n.* Ascent; ascent of Christ into Heaven on fortieth day after resurrection; rising of a celestial body; *A~ Day*, day commemorating Christ's ascension, sixth Thursday after Easter.

Ascĕ'nsion I'sland (īl-). Small island in S. Atlantic, discovered by Portuguese on Ascension Day 1501, but uninhabited until a British garrison was placed there in 1815.

ascĕ'nt *n.* Ascending, rising; upward path or slope.

ăscertai'n *v.t.* Find out. **ăscertai'nable** *adj.* **ăscertai'nment** *n.*

ascĕ'tic *adj.* Severely abstinent, austere. ~ *n.* One who practises severe self-discipline, esp. (eccles. hist.) one who retired into solitude for this purpose. **ascĕ'tĭcal** *adj.* **ascĕ'tĭcallў** *adv.* **ascĕ'tĭcism** *n.*

Ascham (ă'sk*a*m), Roger (1515–68). English scholar and prose-writer, author of 'The Scholemaster', a treatise on the (private) education of boys.

ascĭ'dĭan *n.* Tunicate, esp. of the order Ascidiacea. [Gk *askidion* dim. of *askos* wine-skin]

asclē'pĭăd *n.* Verse of a spondee, two or three choriambs, and an iambus (said to have been invented by Asclepiades).

Asclē'pĭadēs (-z) (*c* 290 B.C.). Greek epigrammatic poet.

Asclē'pius. (Gk myth.) Hero and god of healing, freq. represented bearing staff with serpent coiled round it.

ăscomў'cēte *n.* Fungus producing ascospores, e.g. cup fungus

ascŏr'bĭc *adj.* ~ *acid*, Vitamin C, which occurs in fresh foods, esp. fruits and vegetables, and is necessary to obviate scurvy.

ă'scospōre *n.* Spore developed in an ascus.

A'scot (ă-). (Used for) ~ *Heath*, race-course in Berkshire; ~ *Week*, annual race-meeting there in June, instituted by Queen Anne, 1711.

ascrī'be *v.t.* Attribute, impute; consider as belonging *to*. **ascrĭ'ption** *n.* Ascribing; formula ascribing praise to God at end of sermon.

ă'scus *n.* (pl. *-cī*). (bot.) Round or elongated sac-like body containing spores, in certain fungi.

ă'sdĭc (ăz-) *n.* Echo-sounding device for detecting under-water objects. [initials of *A*nti-*S*ubmarine *D*etection *I*nvestigation *C*ommittee]

A.S.E. *abbrev.* Associated Society (*or* Associate of the Society) of Engineers.

āsĕ'psis *n.* Absence of putrefactive matter or harmful bacteria; aseptic method in surgery.

āsĕ'ptĭc *adj.* Free from putrefaction or blood-poisoning; sterilized; seeking the absence, rather than counteraction, of septic matter.

āsĕ'xūal *adj.* Not sexual, without sex; ~ *generation*, (biol.) any form of reproduction not brought about by the union of gametes.

A'sgârd (ăz-). (Scand. myth.) Region in the centre of the universe, inhabited by the gods.

ăsh[1] *n.* Forest-tree of genus *Fraxinus* with silver-grey bark, pinnate leaves, and close-grained wood; wood of this; *mountain* ~, rowan tree; *~-plant*, sapling of ash-tree used as walking-stick etc.

ăsh[2] *n.* (freq. pl.) Powdery residue left after combustion of any substance; (pl.) remains of human body after cremation; *the Ashes*, imaginary trophy claimed by winner of each series of cricket matches (Test Matches) between England and Australia (from epitaph in 'Sporting Times' on occasion of first match won by Australia, 1882, lamenting death of English cricket and stating that the ashes would be taken to Australia); ~ *blond*(*e*) (*adj.*) light blond; (*n.*) person with ash-blond hair; *A~ Wednesday*, first day of Lent (from early custom of sprinkling ashes on penitents' heads); *a'shtray*, receptacle for tobacco ash etc.

ashā'med (-md) *adj.* Abashed, upset, by consciousness of guilt.

Ashă'ntĭ *n.* (pl. *-s* or as sing.). Native of Ashanti, a division of Ghana.

ă'shen *adj.* Pertaining to an ash-tree; made of ash-wood; pale.

A'sher (ă-). Hebrew patriarch, son of Jacob (Gen. 30: 12, 13); tribe of Israel, traditionally descended from him.

Ashkėna'zĭm (ă-, -ah-) *n.pl.* Polish-German Jews (as dist. from SEPHARDIM). [mod. Heb., f. *Ashkenaz* (Gen. 10: 3), typifying race identified in medieval times with Germans]

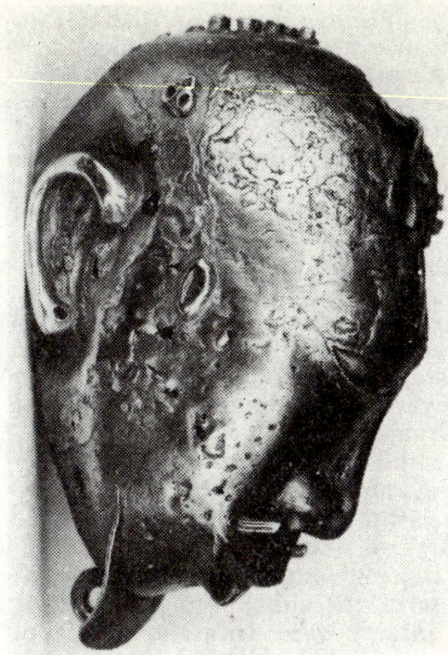

ASHANTI HEAD

ă'shlar *n.* Squared hewn stone(s); masonry of this.

ă'shlarĭng *n.* Short upright wall in garrets, cutting off acute angle formed by rafters with floor.

A'shmōle (ă-), Elias (1617–92). English antiquary, founder of the Ashmolean Museum at Oxford.

ashôr'e *adv.* To or on shore.

A'shtorĕth, -arōth (ă-). = ASTARTE. [Heb.]

ă'shȳ *adj.* Of ashes; ash-coloured; pale.

Asia (ā'sh*a*). Continent of N. hemisphere, E. part of the great land-mass formed by the Old World; separated from Europe by the Ural Mountains and the Caspian Sea; home of the oldest known civilizations; ~ *Minor*, westernmost part of Asia, a peninsula bounded by the Black Sea, the Aegean, and the Mediterranean, and comprising most of Turkey; Anatolia. **A'sian, Asiă'tĭc** (*or* -shĭ-) *adjs.* & *ns.*

asī'de *adv.* To or on one side; away, apart. ~ *n.* Words spoken by an actor and supposed not to be heard by other performers.

ă'sĭnīne *adj.* Of asses; stupid.

Asir (*azēr'*). Region of SW. Arabia, forming with Hejaz and Nejd the Kingdom of Saudi Arabia.

ask (ah-) *v.* Call for an answer (to); make a request (for); invite; demand, require.

A'skalon (ă-). Ancient Philistine city of the E. Mediterranean coast (near Majdal in modern Israel), destroyed *c* 1270 after several times changing hands in the Crusades.

askă'nce (*or* -ahns) *adv.* Sideways; *look ~ at,* view suspiciously.

ăskar'i *n.* European-trained African native soldier. [Arab.]

askew' *adv.* Obliquely, awry.

asla'nt (-ahnt) *adv.* Obliquely.

aslee'p *adv.* In a state of sleep. *~ pred. adj.* (of limbs) Benumbed; (of top) spinning without apparent motion.

A.S.L.E.F., A'slĕf (ăz-) *abbrev.* Associated Society of Locomotive Engineers and Firemen.

A.S.L.I.B., A'slĭb (ăz-) *abbrev.* Association of Special Libraries and Information Bureaux.

aslō'pe *adv.* & *pred. adj.* Sloping, crosswise.

Asmodē'us, -daeus (ăz-). (Jewish legend) Evil spirit (Tobit 3: 8).

āsō'cial (-sh*a*l) *adj.* Antagonistic to society or social order.

Asō'ka (*or a*sh-) (d. *c* 232 B.C.). Emperor of India from *c* 269 B.C.; ruled over the greater part of the peninsula; was converted to Buddhism, did much to propagate it, and is revered by Buddhists.

ăsp *n.* 1. Small viper of S. Europe (*Vipera aspis*). 2. Viper of N. Africa and Arabia (species of *Cerastes*).

aspă'ragus *n.* Liliaceous plant of genus *A~* with many-branched fine stems, and leaves reduced to scales; species of this (*A. officinalis*) whose vernal shoots are a table delicacy; *~ fern,* the species *A. plumosus* used as decoration.

Aspā'sia (-zĭ*a or* -zhĭ*a*) (5th c. B.C.). Greek courtesan, mistress of Pericles.

ă'spĕct *n.* Way a thing presents itself to eye or mind; side (of building etc.) looking, fronting, in a given direction; appearance; (philol.) form of the verb expressing duration, completion, etc., of an action.

ă'spen *n.* Kind of poplar (*Populus tremula*) with leaves tremulous on account of long thin leaf-stalks.

Aspĕr'gēs (-z) *n.* (R.C. Ch.) Anthem beginning with this word (L, = 'Thou shalt sprinkle') sung before High Mass while altar, clergy, and people are sprinkled with holy water; the rite itself.

ăspĕ'rĭtỹ *n.* Roughness; severity; harshness.

aspĕr'se *v.t.* Attack the reputation of, calumniate. **aspĕr'sion** *n.*

ă'sphălt *n.* 1. Solid or plastic pitch derived from petroleum either naturally (as in asphalt lakes of Trinidad and Venezuela) or by distillation. 2. Mixture of this with sand etc. used for surfacing roads etc. *~ v.t.* Lay (road) with asphalt.

ă'sphodĕl *n.* Any of various hardy liliaceous plants from Mediterranean and India, including classical *Asphodeline lutea* in Greece; (poet.) immortal flower in Elysium.

asphỹ'xĭa *n.* Defective aeration of blood, caused by blockage of air-passages or paralysis of respiratory muscles or collapse of the lungs, and resulting in death if air-flow fails completely. **asphỹ'xĭāte** *v.* Kill by asphyxia, suffocate. **asphỹxĭā'tion** *n.* [Gk *a-* not, *sphuxis* pulse]

ă'spic *n.* Savoury jelly, used as a garnish or for making moulds of cooked meat, fish, eggs, etc.

ăspidĭ'stra *n.* Plant of the lily family, with broad tapering leaves, freq. grown as a pot-plant, and often regarded as a symbol of dull middle-class respectability. [Gk *aspis* shield]

ă'spirant (*or a*spīr'-) *n.* One who aspires.

ă'spirate *adj.* Aspirated. ~ *n.* Aspirated consonant; the sound of *h.* **ă'spirāte** *v.t.* 1. Pronounce with a breathing, blended with sound of *h.* 2. Draw out (gas) from vessel.

ăspirā'tion *n.* Drawing of breath; desire; action, use of, aspirator.

ă'spirātor *n.* Apparatus for drawing gas through tube or through a liquid.

aspīr'e *v.i.* Feel earnest desire or ambition; (fig.) reach high.

ă'spirin (*or* -pr-) *n.* Compound of acetylsalicylic acid, used as an analgesic and febrifuge; tablet of this.

asquĭ'nt *adv.* & *pred. adj.* With a squint.

A'squith (ă-), Herbert Henry, first Earl of Oxford and Asquith (1852–1928). British Liberal statesman; prime minister 1908–16.

ăss (*or* ahs) *n.* 1. Quadruped (*Equus onager*, *E. hemippus*, *E. hemionus*, etc.) related to the horse but smaller, with tuft at end of tail and long ears, domesticated for draft and riding and descended from the *wild* ~ (*Equus asinus* or *E. taeniopus*) of Ethiopia; donkey. 2. (slang) Ignorant or stupid person.

ăssa'i (-ah-ē) *adv.* (mus.) Very. [It.]

assai'l *v.t.* Attack, assault. **assai'lant** *n.* One who assails.

Assă'm (*or* ă'-). State of NE. India; capital, Shillong. **Assamē'se** (-z) *adj.* & *n.*

assă'ssin *n.* One who undertakes to kill treacherously; *Assassins*, (hist.) fanatical sect of the Ismaili Muslims in time of Crusades, founded in the 11th c. by the 'Old Man of the Mountains' (Hasan-ben-Sabbah), and notorious for secret murders carried out at the order of their chief. [Arab. *ḥashshāshīn*, oblique pl. of *ḥashshāsh* hashish addict]

assă'ssināte *v.t.* Kill (person) for political or sectarian reasons. **assăssinā'tion** *n.*

assau'lt (*or* -ŏlt) *n.* Hostile attack; rush against walls of fortress etc.; (law) unlawful personal attack, menacing words. ~ *v.t.* Make attack upon.

assay' *n.* Testing of an alloy or ore to determine the proportion of a given metal; determination of strength of substance by testing on an organism; ~ *mark* (on gold and silver), hallmark indicating standard of fineness. ~ *v.* Try the purity or strength of; attempt.

ă'ssėgai (-gī) *n.* Slender spear of hard wood tipped with iron, used as missile by S. Afr. tribes. [Fr. *azagaye*, f. Arab.]

assĕ'mblage *n.* Collection, concourse.

assĕ'mble *v.* Bring or come together; collect; fit together parts of (machine etc.).

assĕ'mblȳ *n.* 1. Gathering of persons, esp. of deliberative body; *~-room*, large room for social gatherings. 2. (eng.) Assembling of those parts of a machine etc. that form a unit; parts so assembled; *~-line*, sequence of machines and workers for assembly of product.

assĕ'nt *v.i.* Agree (*to*), defer (*to*); express agreement; say yes. ~ *n.* Concurrence; sanction.

assẽr't *v.t.* Vindicate a claim to (rights); declare; ~ *oneself*, insist upon one's rights.

assẽr'tion *n.* Insistence upon a right; affirmation, positive statement.

assẽr'tive *adj.* Given to assertion; positive, dogmatic. **assẽr'tivelȳ** *adv.* **assẽr'tiveness** *n.*

assĕ'ss *v.t.* Fix amount of (taxes, fine); fine, tax; estimate value of (esp. for taxation). **assĕ'ssment** *n.*

assĕ'ssor *n.* One who assesses taxes or estimates value of property for purpose of taxation; adviser to judge or magistrate.

ă'ssĕt *n.* 1. (pl., law) Enough goods to enable heir to discharge debts and legacies of testator; property liable to be so applied; effects of insolvent debtor; property that may be made liable for debts; (sing.) item of this in balance-sheet. 2. (loosely) Any possession; any useful quality. [med. L *ad satis* sufficiently]

assĕ′verāte *v.t.* Solemnly declare. **assĕverā′tion** *n.*

ăssidū′ĭtў *n.* Close attention, persistent application.

assĭ′dūous *adj.* Persevering, diligent. **assĭ′dūouslў** *adv.* **assĭ′dūousnėss** *n.*

assi′gn (-īn) *v.t.* Make over formally; allot; appoint; ascribe. ~ *n.* One to whom a property, right, etc., is legally transferred.

ăssĭgnā′tion *n.* Assigning; appointment (of time and place).

ăssignee′ (-īnė) *n.* One appointed to act for another; assign.

assi′gnment (-īn-) *n.* Allotment; legal transference; document effecting this, attribution; task, commission.

assĭ′milāte *v.* Make or become like; absorb, be absorbed into the system. **assĭmĭlā′tion** *n.* **assĭ′mĭlatĭve, assĭ′mĭlatorў** *adjs.*

Assi′sĭ (-ēzĭ). Town of Umbria, central Italy; birth-place of St. Francis.

assĭ′st *v.* Help; be present at meeting etc. **assĭ′stance** *n.*

assĭ′stant *adj.* Helping. ~ *n.* Helper, subordinate worker.

assī′ze *n.* (usu. pl.) Periodical sessions in counties of England and Wales held (until 1971) by judges on circuit for administration of civil and criminal judgement; (hist.) statutory price (of bread and ale).

assoc. *abbrev.* Association.

assō′ciāte (*or* -shĭ-) *v.* Join; connect in idea; combine; have frequent dealings (*with*); *Associated State*, any of various States of the E. Caribbean regarded as forming part of the Commonwealth through their relationship with member States. **assō′ciate** (*or* -shĭat) *adj.* Joined, allied. ~ *n.* Partner, companion; subordinate member of an association; thing connected with another. **assō′ciatĭve, assō′ciatorў** *adjs.*

assōcĭā′tion *n.* Associating; organized body of persons; connection of ideas; intercourse; *free* ~: see FREE; ~ *football*, kind of football played by two teams of eleven players, with spherical ball, which must not be handled when in play except by the goalkeeper.

assoi′l *v.t.* (archaic) Absolve from sin, pardon.

ă′ssonance *n.* Resemblance of sound between two syllables; rhyming of one word with another in the accented vowel but not in the following consonants (e.g. *sonnet, porridge*). **ă′ssonant** *adj.*

assôr′t *v.* 1. (archaic) Arrange in sorts. 2. Suit, harmonize (*with*). **assôr′tėd** *adj.* Of various sorts.

assôr′tment *n.* Assorting; mixture of various sorts.

A.S.S.R. *abbrev.* Autonomous Soviet Socialist Republic.

Asst *abbrev.* Assistant.

assuā′ge (-sw-) *v.t.* Calm, soothe; appease. **assuā′gement** *n.*

assū′me *v.t.* Take upon oneself; undertake; simulate; take to be true for purpose of argument or action. **assū′ming** *adj.* Taking much upon oneself, arrogant.

assŭ′mption *n.* Assuming; thing assumed; arrogance; *the A*~, the reception of the Virgin Mary into heaven; feast in honour of this, 15 Aug.

A′ssur, A′shur (ă-). Local god of the city of that name, the ancient capital of Assyria (on the Tigris at modern Sharqat in N. Iraq); he became the supreme god of the Assyrians, the god of war, and the protector of the people.

assur′ance (*a*shoor-) *n.* Positive assertion; self-confidence; impudence; (life) insurance.

assur′e (*a*shoor) *v.t.* Make safe; make certain, ensure; insure (life); make (person) sure (*of*); tell (person) confidently. **assur′ėdlў** *adv.*

Assў′rĭa. More northerly of the two ancient empires of Mesopotamia; capital, Assur; supremacy ended soon after the death of Assur-bani-pal (7th c. B.C.), who subdued rebellious Egypt and Elam but left the empire too exhausted to repel the Medes; these finally destroyed Nineveh, the last Assyrian stronghold, in 612 B.C.

Assў′rĭan *adj.* & *n.* 1. (Member)

ASSYRIAN

of the Assyrian people, a mixed Semitic race; (of) the Assyrian language, a dialect of Akkadian. 2. (Member) of the NESTORIAN community. [f. ASSUR]

Assўrĭŏ'lo̤gў *n.* Study of the civilization, language, etc., of Assyria. **Assўrĭŏ'logist** *n.*

Astar'tė (ă-). Goddess of love and fertility; Phoenician equivalent of Aphrodite.

ă'statine *n.* (chem.) Radioactive element of short life (symbol At, at. no. 85, principal isotope at. wt 211), which does not occur in nature but can be made artificially; the heaviest element of the halogen group. [Gk *astatos* unstable]

ă'ster *n.* Herbaceous plant of

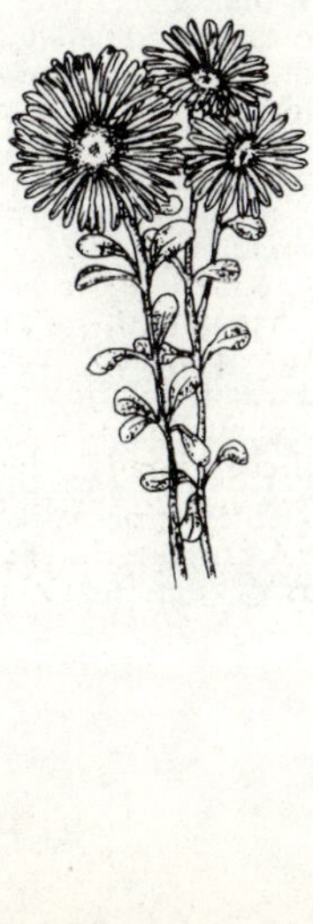

genus *A*~ including Michaelmas daisies, with showy radiated flowers of various colours. [Gk *aster* star]

ă'sterisk *n.* Star * used to mark words for reference or distinction, to indicate a hypothetical form or fill up space in a line where something is omitted. ~ *v.t.* Mark with asterisk.

ă'sterism *n.* Cluster of stars; three asterisks ⁂ calling special attention to word or passage.

aster'n *adv.* In, at, the stern; behind.

aster'nal *adj.* ~ *rib*: see RIB.

ă'steroid *n.* 1. (astron.) Any of the small planets revolving round sun mainly between orbits of Mars and Jupiter. 2. (zool.) One of the class of Asteroidea or starfishes. **ăsteroi'dal** *adj.* [Gk *asteroeidēs* starlike]

ă'sthma (-sm-) *n.* Disorder, freq. of allergic origin, characterized by paroxysms of difficult breathing. **ăsthmă'tic** *adj.* & *n.* (Person) suffering from asthma. **ăsthmă'tically** *adv.*

A'stĭ (ă-). Town in Piedmont producing wines, sparkling (~ *spumante*) and still.

asti'gmatism *n.* Structural defect in eye or lens, preventing rays of light from being brought to a common focus, arising from unequal refraction at different points. **ăstĭgmă'tĭc** *adj.* **ăstĭgmă'tĭcallȳ** *adv.*

astīr' *adv.* In motion; out of bed.

Aston: see BIRMINGHAM.

astŏ'nĭsh *v.t.* Amaze, surprise. **astŏ'nĭshment** *n.*

astou'nd *v.t.* Shock with alarm or surprise; amaze.

ă'stragal *n.* 1. (archit.) Small moulding round top or bottom of column. 2. Ring round cannon near mouth.

astră'galus *n.* 1. Ball of ankle-joint. 2. Leguminous plant of genus *A~* which includes milk-vetch (*A. glycyophyllos*).

Astrakha'n[1] (ă-, -kăn). Province of R.S.F.S.R. on the lower Volga; town on Caspian Sea at head of Volga delta.

ăstrakhă'n[2] (-kăn) *n.* Caracul fur; cloth imitating this.

ă'stral *adj.* Connected with, consisting of, stars; ~ *body*, (theosophy) ethereal counterpart of the human body accompanying it in life and surviving its death.

astray' *adv.* Out of the right way.

astrī'de *adv.* & *prep.* With legs apart or on either side (*of*); extending across.

astrĭ'ngent (-j-) *adj.* Causing to contract, styptic; severe; austere. ~ *n.* Astringent substance.

ă'strodōme *n.* Dome-shaped window in aircraft used for aeronautical observations.

ă'strolābe *n.* Instrument used to take altitudes and solve other problems of practical astronomy, especially of stars; *prismatic* ~, surveying instrument for determining position by observations to stars at a fixed altitude (45° or 60°).

astrŏ'logȳ *n.* Art of understanding the reputed occult influence of the stars on human affairs. **astrŏ'loger** *n.* **ăstrolŏ'gĭcal** *adj.* **ăstrolŏ'gĭcallȳ** *adv.*

ă'stronaut *n.* One who travels in space.

ăstronau'tĭcs *n.* Science of navigation in space. **ăstronau'tĭc, -ĭcal** *adjs.*

astrŏ'nomer *n.* One who studies astronomy; *A~ Royal*, astronomer appointed by the

ASTRONAUT

Crown, the first holder being appointed by Charles II in 1675 when the Royal Observatory at Greenwich was founded.

ăstronŏ'mĭcal *adj.* Relating to, concerned with, astronomy; (of numbers, distances, etc.) very big, immense; ~ *unit*, (abbrev. a.u.) mean distance of the earth from the sun as unit of measurement, approx. 150 million kilometres (93 million miles). **ăstronŏ'mĭcallȳ** *adj.*

astrŏ'nomȳ *n.* Science of the heavenly bodies.

ă'strophȳ'sĭcs (-z-) *n.* That branch of physics which deals with the physical or chemical properties of heavenly bodies. **ăstrophȳ'sĭcal** *adj.* **ăstrophȳ'sĭcĭst** *n.*

Astūr'ĭas (ă-). Region of NW. Spain; *Prince of the* ~, former title of eldest son of the king of Spain. **Astūr'ĭan** *adj.* & *n.*

astū'te *adj.* Shrewd; crafty. **astū'telȳ** *adv.* **astū'tenėss** *n.*

Asunción (*a*sōōnsĭŏ'n *or* -thĭŏ'n). Capital city of Paraguay.

asŭ'nder *adv.* Apart; to pieces.

Asūr'a. (Hinduism) Evil demon, enemy of the gods; (in Veda) freq. a god.

Aswan Dăm (ă'swahn). Dam (1⅓ m. long) built on the Nile at Aswan in SE. Egypt for irrigation 1902, enlarged 1933; *Aswan High Dam*, larger dam, *c* 4 m. upstream, for hydro-electric power as well as irrigation, completed 1969.

asȳ'lum *n.* Sanctuary, place of

refuge; (formerly) institution for the care of the afflicted or destitute, esp. the insane; (also *political* ~) protection from arrest or extradition given by one nation to refugee from another.

asy̆'mmėtry (*or* ā-) *n.* Absence of symmetry. **ăsy̆mmĕ'trĭc, -ĭcal** *adjs.* **ăsy̆mmĕ'trĭcally̆** *adv.*

ă'symptōte *n.* Line which continually approaches a given curve, but does not meet it within a finite distance.

at[1] (ăt, unemphat. *at*), *prep.* Particle expressing exact, approximate, or vague position (*at York, at school, at dinner*) or time of day (*at one o'clock*); ~ *that*, at that estimate, moreover.

ăt[2] (*or* aht) *n.* Small coin of Laos, $\frac{1}{100}$ of a kip.

A.T.A.(S.) *abbrev.* Air Transport Auxiliary (Service).

Atală'nta (ă-). (Gk legend) Huntress and athlete; she required all her suitors to run a race with her and killed them if they lost; but Milanion (or Hippomenes) won the race by throwing down three golden apples given to him by Aphrodite, which were so beautiful that Atalanta stopped to pick them up.

Atatürk (ă'tatêrk), Kemal (*c* 1880–1938). Turkish nationalist leader; first president of the republic 1923–38; known first as Mustapha Kemal, then as Kemal Pasha; took surname Atatürk in 1934. [Turk., = 'father-Turk']

ă'tavĭsm *n.* Resemblance to remote ancestors, reversion to earlier type. **ătavĭ'stĭc** *adj.* **ătavĭ'stĭcally̆** *adv.* [L *atavus* great-grandfather's grandfather]

ată'xĭa *n.* Irregularity of animal functions; *locomotor* ~, disease (*tabes dorsalis*) causing loss of control of co-ordinated movement by destruction of the sensory nerves concerned. **ată'xĭc** *adj.*

A.T.C. *abbrev.* Air Training Corps.

A'tė (ā- *or* ah-). (Gk myth.) Goddess of evil, who incites men to wickedness and strife.

ătĕ'lier (-yā) *n.* Workshop, studio.

a tĕ'mpō (ah). (mus.) In the previous tempo. [It., = 'in time']

A'ten, A'ton (ah-). Name by which the sun was worshipped in ancient Egypt, esp. in reign of AKHNATEN.

Athanā'sĭus (ă-), St. (*c* 296–373). Bishop of Alexandria. Doctor of the Church. **Athanā'sian** (-shan) *adj.* Of Athanasius; ~ *Creed*, that beginning 'Quicunque vult' (L, = 'Whosoever will'), prob. composed not by Athanasius but by Caesarius, bishop of Arles in 6th c.

ā'thėĭsm *n.* Disbelief in the existence of God or gods; godlessness. **ā'thėĭst** *n.* **āthėĭ'stĭc** *adj.*

A'thelstan (ă-) (*c* 894–939). King of the West Saxons 925–39; grandson of Alfred the Great.

Athėnae'um (ă-). 1. (Rom. antiq.) College of rhetoric and poetry, founded at Rome *c* A.D. 133 by the Emperor Hadrian. 2. (also ~ *Club*) London club, founded 1824 as an association of men of distinction in literature, art, and learning. [L, f. Gk *Athēnaion* temple of ATHENE]

Athē'nė. (Gk myth.) Goddess of wisdom, industry, and war, identified with the Roman Minerva; she sprang fully grown and armed from the brain of her father, Zeus; her emblem was an owl.

A'thėns (ă-, -z). (Gk *Athenai*) Leading city of ancient Greece; capital of modern Greece. **Athē'nĭan** *adj.* & *n.*

athîr'st *pred. adj.* Thirsty; eager (*for*).

ă'thlēte *n.* One who competes or excels in physical exercises; ~*'s foot*, tinea of the foot, esp. attacking skin between toes.

ăthlĕ'tĭc *adj.* Pertaining to athletes; physically powerful. **ăthlĕ'tĭcs** *n.pl.* Physical exercises; athletic sports (comprising, in organized sport, running, jumping, throwing, walking, hurdling, and steeplechasing). **athlĕ'tĭcism** *n.*

A'thŏs (ă-), Mount. Peninsula projecting into the Aegean Sea from Macedonia, occupied since the Middle Ages by various com-

munities of monks. **Athō'an** *adj.* **A'thonīte** (ă-) *adj.* & *n.*

athwar't (-ôrt) *adv.* Across from side to side (usu. obliquely). ~ *prep.* Across; ~-*hawse*, (of ship) across stem of another ship at anchor.

Atlă'ntic *adj.* Of, adjoining the Atlantic Ocean; ~ *Ocean*, great ocean lying between Europe and Africa on E. and America on W.; (orig.) sea near the NW. coast of Africa. ~ *n.* Atlantic Ocean; *Battle of the* ~, German offensive against Allied Atlantic shipping during the war of 1939–45; ~ *Charter*, declaration of eight common principles in international relations, drawn up at a conference in mid-Atlantic in Aug. 1941 by Winston Churchill and President Franklin D. Roosevelt on behalf of U.K. and U.S. and endorsed by other nations at war with Germany, Italy, and Japan; ~ *Pact*, agreement (1949) to ensure defence of countries with sea-boards on N. Atlantic: [f. ATLAS[2]]

Atlă'ntĭs. (Gk legend) Fabled island in the ocean W. of the Pillars of Hercules; it was beautiful and prosperous, the seat of an empire which dominated part of Europe and Africa, but was overwhelmed by the sea because of the impiety of its inhabitants.

A'tlas[1] (ă-). (Gk legend) One of the Titans, who was punished for revolting against Zeus by being made to support the heavens with his head and hands; acc. to another legend Perseus, with the aid of Medusa's head, turned him into a mountain (the ~ *Mountains* of N. Africa).

ă'tlas[2] (ă-) *n.* 1. Collection of maps in a volume, so called from the use of a figure of ATLAS[1] supporting the heavens as a frontispiece. 2. Size of drawing-paper (26 × 33 in. (660 × 838 mm)). 3. Uppermost vertebra of backbone, supporting the skull.

ă'tmosphēre *n.* Gaseous envelope surrounding a heavenly body, esp. the envelope of air surrounding the earth, which consists of gases (nitrogen, oxygen, argon, carbon dioxide, helium, and others) and water vapour, and is rarer as distance from the earth increases; air (of a place); mental or moral environment. **ătmosphĕ'rĭc** *adj.* ~ *pressure*, pressure of the column of air above a given point, equivalent on the earth's surface to about 760 mm of mercury, but decreasing with increasing height above the earth. **ătmosphĕ'rĭcs** *n.pl.* Atmospheric disturbances of electrical origin causing interference in telecommunications; crackling or other interference so caused.

at. no. *abbrev.* Atomic number.

ă'toll (*or* *a*tŏ'l) *n.* Ring-shaped coral reef enclosing lagoon. [Malay]

ă'tom *n.* 1. Body too small to be divided; minute portion, small thing. 2. (chem.) Smallest particle of an element that cannot be further subdivided without destroying its identity, regarded as consisting of a minute central positively charged nucleus in which almost all the mass is concentrated, and a number of negative electrons arranged round the nucleus; ~ *bomb*, = ATOMIC bomb.

atŏ'mĭc *adj.* Of atoms; of, using, concerned with, atomic energy or weapons; ~ *bomb*, bomb deriving its destructive power from ~ *energy*, energy

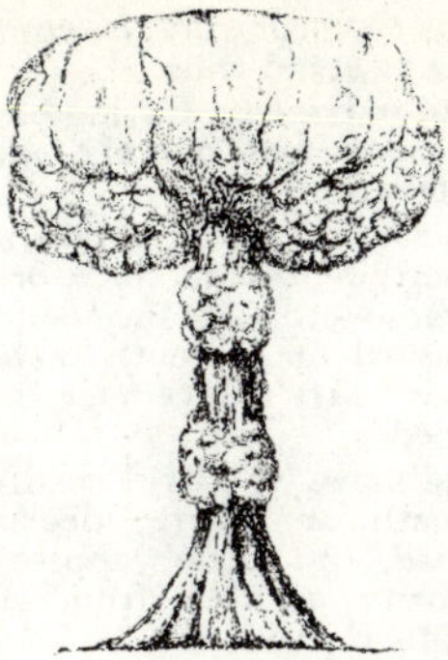

ATOM BOMB

released by fission of atomic nuclei of certain heavy elements such as uranium 235 or plutonium or by the fusion of light nuclei; ~ *mass*, mass of an atom measured in units based (since 1960) on one-twelfth of the mass of the carbon-12 atom; ~ *number*, (abbrev. at. no.) number of unit positive charges carried by the nucleus of an atom of an element, number determining the position of the element in the periodic table; ~ *theory*, theory that elements consist of atoms of definite relative weight and that atoms of different elements unite with one another in fixed proportions; (philos.) atomism; (*international*) ~ *time*, standard of time based on scale obtained by using continuously-running quartz clocks calibrated in terms of the caesium frequency standard; ~ *weight*, (abbrev. at. wt) = atomic mass (see above). **atŏ'mically** *adv.*

ă'tomism *n.* (philos.) Theory that all matter consists of minute indivisible particles. **ă'tomist** *n.* **ătomĭ'stic** *adj.*

ă'tomize *v.t.* Reduce to atoms. **ă'tomizer** *n.* Instrument for reducing liquids to a fine spray.

ă'tomy̆ *n.* (archaic) Atom, tiny being.

Aton: see ATEN.

atō'nal *adj.* (mus.) Not conforming to any system of key or mode. **ătonă'lity̆** *n.*

atō'ne *v.i.* Make amends; ~ *for*, expiate. **atō'nement** *n.* *the A~*, expiation of man's sin by Christ; *Day of A~*: see YOM KIPPUR.

atŏ'nic *adj.* Unaccented; (path.) wanting tone. ~ *n.* Unaccented word (esp. in Gk gram.).

ătrabi'lious *adj.* Affected by black bile; melancholy; acrimonious. [L *atra bilis* black bile, transl. of Gk *melagkholia* MELANCHOLY]

A'treūs (ā-). (Gk legend) King of Argos, who set the flesh of his brother Thyestes' children before their father at a banquet in revenge because Thyestes had seduced his wife; he was himself murdered by Aegisthus.

ā'trium *n.* (pl. *-ia*, *-iums*). 1. Central court of Roman house. 2. Covered portico, esp. before church door. 3. Either of the two upper cavities (*left* and *right* ~) of the heart into which the veins pour the blood.

atrō'cious (-shus) *adj.* Extremely wicked; very bad. **atrō'ciously̆** *adv.*

atrŏ'city̆ *n.* Atrocious deed; bad blunder; (colloq.) hideous object.

ă'trophy̆ *n.* Wasting away through imperfect nourishment or lack of use. ~ *v.* Waste away.

ă'tropine (-ēn) *n.* White crystal-like alkaloid prepared from *Atropa belladonna* (deadly nightshade) and used to dilate the pupil of the eye or to relieve pain. [f. ATROPOS]

A'tropŏs (ă-). (Gk myth.) Eldest of the three Fates, who cut the thread of human life with her shears. [Gk, = 'inflexible']

A.T.S. *abbrev.* Auxiliary Territorial Service (now W.R.A.C.).

ă'tta *n.* Common wheaten flour or meal of India.

ă'ttaboy *int.* (orig. U.S.) Exclamation expressing encouragement or admiration.

attă'ch *v.* Fasten, join; attribute (importance etc. *to*); adhere, be incident *to*; seize by legal authority; bind in friendship, make devoted. **attă'chment** *n.* (esp.) ~ *of earnings*, court order by which employer is required to make deductions from employee's wages for the payment of certain debts etc.

attaché (-ă'shā) *n.* Junior official attached to ambassador's suite; military or naval officer connected with embassy in a foreign country in order to report on military or naval affairs; ~ *case*, small rectangular valise for carrying documents etc.

attă'ck *v.* Take the initiative in fighting; act destructively on; criticize adversely; (mus.) perform with precision and clarity. ~ *n.* Act of attacking; bout of illness etc.

attai'n *v.* Reach, gain, accomplish; ~ *to*, arrive at. **attai'nment** *n.* Attaining; thing attained; (pl.) personal accomplishments.

attai'nder *n.* (hist.) Consequences of sentence of death or outlawry (loss of civil rights, forfeiture of estate, etc.); *bill of* ~, legislative act inflicting attainder without judicial trial

attai'nt *v.t.* Subject to attainder (hist.); affect; infect; sully.

ă'ttar *n.* Fragrant essential oil distilled from flowers, esp. roses. [ult. f. Arab. *'iṭr* perfume]

attĕ'mper *v.t.* Qualify by admixture; modify; temper.

attĕ'mpt *v.t.* Try; try to master. ~ *n.* Attempting; endeavour.

attĕ'nd *v.* 1. Turn the mind, apply oneself (*to*). 2. Be present (at); go regularly to (school, church, etc.). 3. Wait upon; serve; escort; accompany.

attĕ'ndance *n.* Attending (ATTEND *v.* 2, 3); number of persons present; ~ *centre*, centre at which boys under 17 are required to attend when found guilty of offences for which older persons could be sent to prison.

attĕ'ndant *adj.* & *n.* (Person) attending (another).

attĕ'ntion *n.* Act or faculty of attending (ATTEND *v.* 1); consideration, care; (pl.) ceremonious politeness; courtship, addresses; *at* ~, (mil.) formal attitude of troops standing on parade as dist. from *at* EASE or EASY; (as command) order to stand thus.

attĕ'ntĭve *adj.* Giving or paying attention. **attĕ'ntĭvelȳ** *adv.* **attĕ'ntĭvenėss** *n.*

attĕ'nūāte *v.t.* 1. Make slender or thin; reduce in force or value. 2. (radio etc.) Reduce amplitude of (signal or current). **attĕnūā'tion** *n.* **attĕ'nūate** *adj.* Slender; rarefied.

attĕ'st *v.* Testify, certify; put on oath or solemn declaration; *attested*, (of cattle) approved by authority as free from disease. **ăttėstā'tion** *n.*

A'ttĭc[1] (ă-) *adj.* Of Attica; ~ *dialect*, Greek spoken by ancient Athenians; ~ *order*, square column of any of the five orders (*see* ORDER); ~ *salt*, *wit*, refined wit. ~ *n.* Attic dialect.

ă'ttĭc[2] *n.* 1. (archit.) Structure consisting of small order placed above another of greater height. 2. (Room in) highest storey of building, usu. immediately under the roof and not having a flat ceiling. [Fr. *attique* upper part of house, so called from Attic order of architecture]

A'ttĭca (ă-). District of ancient Greece of which Athens was the capital.

ă'ttĭcism *n.* Style, idiom of Athens; extreme elegance of speech; attachment to Athens.

A'ttila (ă-) (d. A.D. 453). King of the Huns, known as the 'scourge of God'; ravaged the Eastern Roman Empire (445–50); after making peace with Theodosius invaded the Western Empire and was defeated at Châlons by Aëtius in 451.

attīr'e *v.t.* & *n.* Dress, array.

A'ttĭs, A'tȳs (ă-). (myth.) Youthful consort of CYBELE; his death was mourned for two days in the spring, and his recovery (when his spirit passed into a pine-tree and violets sprang up from his blood) then celebrated.

ă'ttĭtūde *n.* 1. Posture of body; settled behaviour, as indicating opinion; ~ *of mind*, settled mode of thinking. 2. Angular relation between aircraft's or spacecraft's axis and the wind, course, etc.

ăttitū'dĭnīze *v.i.* Practise attitudes; act, speak, etc., affectedly.

A'ttlee (ă-), Clement Richard, 1st Earl Attlee (1883–1967). British statesman; Labour prime minister 1945–51.

attor'ney (-tėr-) *n.* One appointed to act for another in business in legal matters; *power of* ~, formal instrument of such appointment; *A~-General*, chief legal officer empowered to act in all cases in which the State is a party (in U.K. usu. a member of the House of Commons, appointed on advice of Government and resigning with it; in U.S. appointed by president).

attră'ct *v.t.* Draw to itself or oneself; excite pleasurable emotions of; draw forth and fix on oneself (attention etc.) **attră'ction** *n.* Attracting; thing that attracts. **attră'ctive** *adj.* **attră'ctĭvelў** *adv.* **attră'ctĭvenėss** *n.*

attrĭ'būte *v.t.* ~ *to*, consider as caused by, resulting or originating from, made or composed by; consider as belonging or appropriate *to*. **ăttrĭbū'tion** *n.* **ă'ttribūte** *n.* Quality ascribed to anything; material object regarded as appropriate to person or office; characteristic quality; (gram.) attributive word.

attrĭ'bụtĭve *adj.* Assigning an attribute to a subject; (gram.) expressing an attribute, qualifying. ~ *n.* Word denoting an attribute. **attrĭ'būtĭvelў** *adv.*

attrĭ'tion *n.* Friction; abrasion; wearing out; weakening by harassment.

attū'ne *v.t.* Bring into musical accord; adapt; tune.

A'twŏŏd's machi'ne (ă-, -z, -shēn). Apparatus, consisting essentially of a nearly frictionless wheel which carries a cord with equal weights suspended from its ends, designed to demonstrate the mechanical law that a body which is not disturbed by force continues to move with uniform speed in a straight line. [named after George *Atwood* (1745–1807), English mathematician]

at. wt *abbrev.* Atomic weight.

ātў'pĭcal *adj.* Not typical.

aubade (ōbahd) *n.* Music for singing or playing at dawn; morning concert. [Fr.]

Auber (ōbār), Daniel François Esprit (1782–1871). French musician, composer of operas.

aubergine (ō'berzhēn) *n.* Elongated, usu. purple, fruit of the egg-plant (*Solanum melongena*), used as a vegetable.

aubrietia, erron. **-retia** (-rē'sha) *n.* Spring-flowering dwarf perennial plant of genus *Aubrieta* of mustard family, with flowers of colours ranging through purple, red, and blue. [after Claude *Aubriet* (d. 1743) French painter of flowers and animals]

au'burn *adj.* Reddish brown (usu. of hair).

Aubusson (ōbūsawṅ). Town in central France, famous since the 16th c., and esp. in the 18th, for the manufacture of tapestries and carpets.

A.U.C. *abbrev. Ab urbe condita* or *anno urbis conditae* (L, = from, in the year of, the founding of the city, i.e. Rome).

Au'ckland. Largest city and chief seaport of New Zealand; also, the province comprising the northern part of North Island.

au courant (ō kōōrahṅ). Acquainted *with* what is going on, well informed. [Fr.]

au'ction *n.* Public sale at which articles are sold to person making the highest bid; *Dutch* ~, sale at which price is reduced until a buyer is found; ~ *bridge*: see BRIDGE[2]. ~ *v.t.* Sell (*off*) by auction.

auctioneer' *n.* One who conducts auctions. ~ *v.i.* Conduct auctions.

audā'cious (-shus) *adj.* Daring, bold; impudent. **audā'ciouslў** *adv.* **audā'ciousnėss, audă'cĭtў** *ns.*

Au'den, Wystan Hugh (1907–73).

English-born poet and dramatist.

au'dĭble *adj.* That can be heard. **au'dĭblÿ** *adv.* **audibĭ'litÿ** *n.*

au'dĭence *n.* Hearing; formal interview; persons within hearing; group of listeners or spectators.

au'dĭō *adj.* Of (the reproduction of) sound; ~ *frequency*, (abbrev. A.F.) FREQUENCY perceived aurally; ~ *typing, typist*, (one) typing direct from tape or other recording; ~*-visual*, of, involving, both hearing and sight. ~ *n.* Reproduction of sound.

audiŏ'logÿ *n.* Science of hearing. **audiŏ'logist** *n.*

audiŏ'meter *n.* Instrument for measuring the sensitivity of the ear to sounds.

au'dit *n.* Official examination of accounts; periodical settlement of accounts between landlord and tenant; ~ *ale*, strong ale brewed in some colleges of Oxford and Cambridge, orig. for use on day of audit. ~ *v.t.* Examine (accounts) officially.

audi'tion *n.* Hearing; trial hearing of actor, singer, etc., seeking employment. ~ *v.* Test, be tested, by an audition.

au'dĭtor *n.* One who audits accounts.

audĭtŏr'ium *n.* Part of building occupied by audience.

au'dĭtorÿ *adj.* Of hearing. ~ *n.* Hearers, audience; auditorium.

Au'drey, St. (630?–679). Etheldreda, first abbess of Ely.

Au'dūbon, John James (1785–1851). Amer. naturalist and painter; author of 'Birds of America', engraved in aquatint (1827–38).

A.U.E.W. *abbrev.* Amalgamated Union of Engineering Workers.

au fait (ō fā). Conversant, instructed. [Fr.]

au fond (ō fawṅ). At bottom; basically. [Fr.]

Aug. *abbrev.* August.

Augē'an *adj.* Abominably filthy; resembling the stables of Augeas, legendary king of Elis, which were uncleansed for many years until Hercules, as one of his labours, accomplished the cleansing by diverting the river Alpheus through them.

au'ger (-g-) *n.* Tool for boring holes in wood, having a long shank with cutting edge and screw point, and handle at right angles.

aught (awt) *n.* Anything.

au'gment *n.* (gram.) Vowel prefixed to past tenses in the older Indo-European languages. **augmĕ'nt** *v.* Increase; prefix augment to. **augmĕ'ntėd** *adj.* (esp., mus., of an interval) Widened by a semitone. **augmentā'tion** *n.* Enlargment; addition; (mus.) repetition of a passage in notes longer than those of the original

augmĕ'ntative *adj.* & *n.* Increasing; (gram.) (word or affix) increasing in force the idea of the original word; (mus.) lengthening of phrase by increasing the values of the notes.

au grand sérieux (ō grahṅ sĕrēēr). Quite seriously. [Fr.]

Au'gsbŭrg (ow-). City of Bavaria; ~ *Confession*, statement of the Protestant position drawn up by Melanchthon for the Diet of 1530.

au'gur *n.* 1. (Rom. antiq.) Religious official who foretold future events by observing flight or notes of birds etc. 2. Soothsayer. ~ *v.* Forebode, anticipate; ~ *well, ill*, have good (bad) implications or

AUGSBURG

expectations *of*, *for*. **au'gūrў** *n.* Divination; omen; promise.

augŭ'st[1] *adj.* Majestic, venerable. **augŭ'stlў** *adv.* **augŭ'stnėss** *n.* [L *augustus* consecrated, venerable]

Au'gust[2]. 8th month of Gregorian (5th of Julian) calendar, with 31 days. [named after Rom. emperor AUGUSTUS]

Augŭ'stan *adj.* Of AUGUSTUS; ~ *Age*, period of literary eminence in the life of a nation, so called because Virgil, Horace, Ovid, etc., all flourished during Augustus' reign; in English literary history, the period of Pope and Addison.

Augŭ'stīne[1], St. (354–430). Doctor of the Church; son of a pagan father and Christian mother (St. Monica); was for a time attracted by Manichaeism, but baptized as a Christian 387; became bishop of Hippo in N. Africa, 391; defended Christianity in numerous writings, of which the best known are the 'City of God' ('Civitas Dei') and the autobiographical 'Confessions'; commemorated 28 Aug.

Augŭ'stīne[2], St. (d. 604). First archbishop of Canterbury; led mission to England from Rome and founded a monastery at Canterbury; commemorated in England 26 May, elsewhere 28 May.

Augustĭ'nĭan *adj.* Of St. AUGUSTINE[1] of Hippo; ~ *Canons*, order of R.C. canons regular, who adopted the 'rule of St. Augustine' (based largely on Augustine's writings but not formulated by him) in the 11th c.; ~ (or *Austin*) *Friars*, mendicant order founded *c* 1250 and observing the Augustinian rule.

Augŭ'stus (63 B.C.–A.D. 14). Gaius Octavius ('Octavian'), named Gaius Julius Caesar Octavianus after his adoption by Julius Caesar, his great-uncle; member of the 2nd triumvirate and first Roman emperor; the title of Augustus was conferred on him by senate and people in 27 B.C. and was borne by all subsequent Roman emperors.

auk *n.* Any of the Alcidae, a family of sea-birds which includes the guillemot, puffin, razor-bill, little auk (*Plautus alle*), and the great auk (*Pinguinus impennis*),

AUKS

formerly inhabiting N. Atlantic but extinct since mid-19th c.

auld *adj*. & *n*. (Sc.) Old.

au′lĭc *adj*. Pertaining to a court; *A~ Council*, official council of the emperor in the Holy Roman Empire, established by Maximilian I in 1499.

Au′lĭs. Ancient Greek town on Boeotian coast, where (in legend) the Greek fleet was detained by contrary winds before the Trojan War, and where Iphigenia was offered for sacrifice.

au′mbrȳ̆ *n*. Closed recess in wall of church; (hist.) small cupboard.

au naturel (ō nătūrĕl). (Cooked) in the simplest way; uncooked. [Fr.]

aunt (ahnt) *n*. Father's or mother's sister; uncle's wife; (children's colloq.) unrelated woman who is a family friend; *A~ Sally*, game in which sticks or balls are thrown at wooden dummy (orig. at pipe in mouth of wooden woman's head); (fig.) any person or institution which becomes a mark of popular attack.

au′ntie, -tȳ̆ (ahn-) *n*. (colloq.) Aunt.

au pair (ō pār). (Person, esp. young girl) performing domestic duties in foreign country in return for hospitality etc. ~ *adv. phr.* [Fr.]

au pied de la lettre (ō pyā de lah lĕtr). Literally. [Fr.]

au′ra *n*. 1. Subtle emanation; atmosphere diffused by or attending a person etc. (esp. in mystical use as definite envelope of body or spirit). 2. (path.) Sensation as of cold air rising from part of body to head, premonitory symptom in epilepsy and hysterics. **au′ral**[1] *adj*.

au′ral[2] *adj*, Of, received by, the ear. **au′rallȳ̆** *adv*.

Au′rangzēb (1618–1707). Mogul emperor of India, 1658–1707, a period of great wealth and splendour for the empire.

aurar: see EYRIR.

Aurē′lĭan. Lucius Domitius Aurelianus (*c* A.D. 212–75). Roman emperor, 270–5.

aurē′ola, au′rėōle *ns*. Celestial crown worn by martyrs, saints, virgins, etc.; pictorial representation of this in form of golden ring or disc painted behind and round head of wearer; halo, esp. that of the sun seen in eclipses. [L *aureola* (*corona*) golden crown]

aurėomȳ′cĭn *n*. Yellow crystalline antibiotic substance produced by the micro-organism *Streptomyces aureofaciens*.

au revoir (ō revwār). (Goodbye) till we meet again. [Fr.]

au′rĭcle *n*. 1. External ear of animals; process shaped like lobe of ear. 2. Small appendage of the ATRIUM, sense 3.

aurĭ′cūla *n*. Species of Alpine primula, with ear-shaped leaf. [L *auris* ear]

aurĭ'cūlar *adj.* Pertaining to the ear; pertaining to auricle of the heart; ~ *confession*, confession made privately (in the ear of the priest).

aurĭ'ferous *adj.* Yielding gold.

Aurī'ga. The Wagoner or Charioteer, a northern constellation between Perseus and Gemini. [L]

Aurĭgnā'cian (-shan) *adj.* & *n.* (Of) a palaeolithic culture believed to have existed in France *c* 11,500–10,000 B.C. [f. *Aurignac* in Haute-Garonne, SW. France, where flint implements were found]

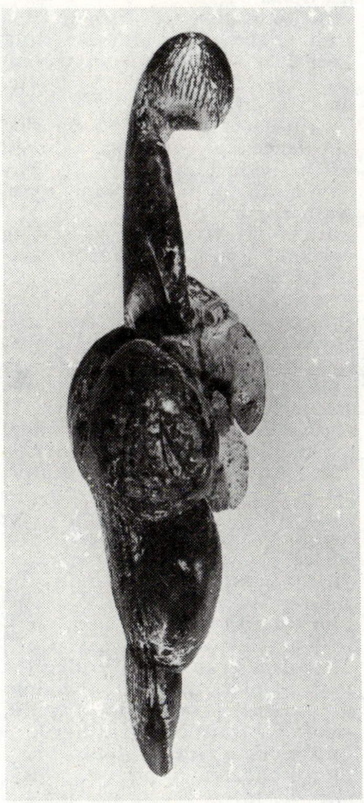

au'rĭst *n.* Ear specialist.

au'rŏchs (-ŏks) *n.* Extinct European wild ox; (improperly) European bison.

Aurōr'a¹. (Rom. myth.) Goddess of the dawn, corresponding to the Greek Eos.

aurōr'a² *n.* (poet.) Dawn; ~ *australis*, phenomenon similar to aurora borealis, seen in southern latitudes; ~ *borealis*, luminous phenomenon, popularly called the *northern lights*, seen in northern latitudes esp. at night, usu. appearing as streamers of many colours ascending from above the northern horizon and supposed to be of electrical origin.

auscultā'tion *n.* Act of listening, esp. (med.) to movement of heart, lungs, etc. **auscŭ'ltatorȳ** *adj.*

au'spĭce *n.* Observation of birds for purpose of taking omens; (pl.) patronage. **auspĭ'cious** (-shus) *adj.* Of good omen; favourable; prosperous. **auspĭ'ciouslȳ** *adv.* **auspĭ'ciousnėss** *n.*

Au'ssie (*or* ŏ'zĭ) *n.* Australian, orig. of Australian troops in the war of 1914–18.

Au'stėn, Jane (1775–1817). English author of six novels: 'Pride and Prejudice', 'Northanger Abbey', 'Sense and Sensibility', 'Mansfield Park', 'Emma', and 'Persuasion'.

austēr'e *adj.* Harsh; stern; stringently moral; severely simple. **austēr'elȳ** *adv.* **austēr'enėss** *n.* **austĕ'rĭtȳ** *n.* Quality of being austere; severity, austere or ascetic practice; applied esp. during the war of 1939–45 to clothes etc. in which non-essentials were reduced to a minimum as a wartime measure of economy.

Au'sterlitz (ow-). (Czech *Slavkov*) town in Moravia, scene in 1805 of Napoleon's defeat of the Austrians and Russians.

Au'stĭn (*or* ŏ-), Alfred (1835–1913). English minor poet, poet laureate from 1896.

Au'stĭn Frī'ars (-z; *or* ŏ-): see AUGUSTINIAN Friars.

au'stral *adj.* Southern; of Australia or Australasia. [L *Auster*, the south wind]

Australā'sia (-zha; *or* ŏ-). Term used loosely to include Australia and the islands scattered over the

SW. Pacific. **Australā'sian** *adj.* & *n.*

Austrā'lia (*or* ŏ-). Continent of S. hemisphere in the SW. Pacific; federal commonwealth, member State of the British Commonwealth. The existence of a *Terra Australis* ('southern land') was known in Europe in the 16th c.; from 1606 onwards its W. coast was explored by the Dutch and in 1642 Tasman proved that it was an island; it was visited by an Englishman, William Dampier, in 1699; in 1770 Capt. James Cook, on the first of his three voyages, landed at Botany Bay on the E. side and formally took possession of New South Wales; British colonization began in 1788 (also the settling of convicts at Port Jackson, discontinued in 1840); in 1901 the six colonies (New South Wales, Victoria, Queensland, South Australia, Western Australia, and Tasmania) federated as sovereign states of the *Commonwealth of* ~, which also administers Northern Territory, Capital Territory (site of the federal capital, Canberra), and certain areas outside the continent.

Austrā'lian (*or* ŏ-) *adj.* Of Australia; ~ *Capital Territory*, federal territory in New South Wales consisting of two enclaves ceded by New South Wales, one in 1911 to contain Canberra, the other in 1915 containing Jervis Bay. ~ *n.* Australian person.

Au'strĭa (*or* ŏ-). German-speaking country of central Europe, which became a republic in 1918; formerly it was the nucleus of the Austro-Hungarian Empire; for much of its earlier history it was a mark (the Ostmark or eastern mark) of the German Empire, an outpost of defence against Slavs and Magyars; it became a duchy in 1156 and later the seat of the Habsburg emperors; in 1918 the empire was divided between Hungary, Poland, Czechoslovakia, Italy, Rumania, Yugoslavia, and Austria itself; in March 1938 Austria was forcibly annexed to the Third Reich; it was liberated from Nazi rule in 1945; capital, Vienna. **Au'strĭan** *adj.* & *n.* (Native) of Austria.

au'tarchy̆[1] (-k-) *n.* Absolute sovereignty, despotism. [Gk *autarkhia* (*arkho* rule)]

au'tarchy̆[2] (-k-), **au'tarky̆** *ns.* Economic self-sufficiency of a political unit. [Gk *autarkeia* (*arkeō* suffice)]

authĕ'ntĭc *adj.* Reliable, trustworthy; of undisputed origin; ~ *mode*, (mus., of eccles. modes) having their sounds comprised within an octave from the final. **authĕ'ntĭcally̆** *adv.* **authĕntĭ'cĭty̆** *n.*

authĕ'ntĭcāte *v.t.* Establish the truth or authorship of: make valid.

au'thor *n.* (fem. *au'thoress*) Originator; writer of book etc. **au'thorshĭp** *n.*

authorĭtār'ĭan *adj.* Favouring obedience to authority as opp. to individual liberty; of, pertaining to, a dictatorship. ~ *n.* Authoritarian person.

authŏ'rĭtatĭve *adj.* Possessing or claiming authority. **authŏ'rĭtatĭvely̆** *adv.*

authŏ'rĭty̆ *n.* Power or right to enforce obedience; delegated power; person etc. having authority; personal influence; expert.

au'thorīze *v.t.* Sanction; give ground for; give authority to; *Authorized Version*, (of the Bible) the English translation of 1611.

au'tĭsm *n.* Morbid absorption in fantasy; condition, esp. in children, preventing proper response to environment. **autĭ'stĭc** *adj.*

auto-, aut- *prefix.* Self-, by one's or its own agency.

au'tobahn *n.* (pl. *-nen*, *-ns*). In Germany, a motorway. [Ger.]

autobīŏ'graphy̆ *n.* Writing the story of one's own life; the story so written. **autobīogră'phĭc, -ĭcal** *adjs.* **autobīŏ'grapher** *n.*

au'tocar *n.* (rare) Motor-car.

autŏ'chthon (-k-) *n.* (usu. pl.; *-ones*, *-ons*) Original inhabitants. **autŏ'chthonous** *adj.*

au'toclāve *n.* Vessel in which chemical reactions take place at high temperatures under pressure;

apparatus for sterilizing by steam at high pressure. ~ *v.*

autŏ'cracy̆ *n.* Absolute government.

au'tocrăt *n.* Absolute ruler; dictatorial overbearing person; *A~ of all the Russias*, (hist.) title of the Tsar. **autocră'tic** *adj.* **autocră'tically̆** *adv.*

au'tocrŏss *n.* Cross-country racing in motor vehicles.

au'to-da-fé' (-dah-fā) *n.* Sentence of the Inquisition; execution of this, esp. burning of a heretic. [Port., = 'act of faith']

autogīr'ō *n.* Type of aeroplane, or gyroplane, deriving its lift mainly from a system of freely rotating horizontal wings and capable of landing in a very small space. [trade-name]

au'togrăph (*or* -ahf) *n.* Author's own manuscript; person's own handwriting, esp. signature; document signed by its author, as dist. from HOLOGRAPH, one wholly written in his hand (freq. attrib., as ~ *letter*). ~ *v.t.* Write one's signature on or in; sign. **autogră'phic, -ical** *adjs.* **autogră'phically̆** *adv.*

auto-immū'nity̆ *n.* (med.) Allergy of the body to its own secretions of antibodies or lymphoid cells. **auto-immū'ne** *adj.*

au'tomāte *v.* Apply automation (to).

automă'tic *adj.* Working of itself, without direct human actuation; mechanical; unconscious; necessary, inevitable; ~ *control*, device enabling machine to maintain a predetermined temperature, pressure, speed, etc., without intervention of operator; ~ *pilot*, similar device in aircraft for maintaining a set course or height; ~ *pistol, rifle*, firearm which, after each shot is exploded, by gas pressure or force of recoil automatically ejects the empty case, loads another into the chamber, and fires, repeating this movement until the ammunition in the mechanism is exhausted or pressure on the trigger is released; ~ *transmission*, system in motor vehicle in which gears engage automatically according to the speed of the vehicle or by means of a torque converter. ~ *n.* Automatic pistol; machine, tool, etc., operated automatically. **automă'tically̆** *adv.*

automā'tion *n.* (eng., orig. U.S.) Completely automatic control of a manufactured product through a number of successive stages; use of automatic mechanical or electronic devices.

autŏ'matism *n.* 1. Involuntary action; (psychol.) action performed unconsciously or subconsciously. 2. Doctrine that movements or actions of organic beings are mechanical, not resulting from volition.

autŏ'maton *n.* Mechanical device with concealed motive power; person whose actions are mechanical, following a customary routine.

au'tomobile (-ēl; *or* -ē'l) *n.* (chiefly U.S.) Motor-car.

autonŏ'mic *adj.* (physiol.) Of that part of the nervous system (~ or *involuntary nervous system*) which functions more or less independently of the will, comprising the sympathetic and parasympathetic nervous systems.

autŏ'nomous *adj.* 1. Self-governing. 2. (physiol., path.) Independent of the usual processes which regulate the growth of an organism. **autŏ'nomously̆** *adv.*

autŏ'nomy̆ *n.* Right of self-government; freedom of the will; self-governing community.

au'topista *n.* In Spain and Spanish-speaking countries, a motorway. [Span.]

autŏ'psy̆ (*or* aw'-) *n.* Personal inspection; post-mortem examination. **autŏ'ptic, -ical** *adjs.*

au'toroute (-rōōt) *n.* In France, a motorway. [Fr.]

autostra'da (-ah-) *n.* (pl. *-dė, -das*). In Italy, a motorway. [It.]

auto-suggĕ'stion *n.* Hypnotic suggestion proceeding from the subject himself.

au'toty̆pe *n.* Photographic printing process for reproducing in monochrome. ~ *v.t.* Reproduce by autotype.

au'tumn (-m) *n.* Season of year between summer and winter, popularly reckoned in N. hemisphere as comprising the months September, October, and November, but astronomically as lasting from autumnal equinox (22 or 23 Sept.) to winter solstice (21 or 22 Dec.); (fig.) season of incipient decay. **autŭ'mnal** (-m-n-) *adj.* Of autumn.

Auvergne (ōvārn). Ancient province of S. central France.

auxi'liarў (awgzīly*a*-) *adj.* Helpful; subsidiary; (gram., of verbs) serving to form tenses, moods, voices, of other verbs. ~ *n.* Assistant; (esp. pl.) foreign troops serving with another country in war; (naval) vessel auxiliary to fighting vessels, as tanker, supply ship, etc.

A.V. *abbrev.* Authorized Version (of the Bible).

avai'l *v.* Be of use or assistance (to); help, benefit. ~ *n.* Use, profit.

avai'lable *adj.* At one's disposal, at hand; capable of being used. **availabi'litў** *n.*

ă'valanche (-ahnsh) *n.* Mass of snow, rock, and ice, falling down mountain (also fig.); ~ *cone*, pile of material deposited by an avalanche; ~ *wind*, wind produced by avalanche, freq. causing further destruction.

A'valon (ă-). In the Arthurian legend, the place to which ARTHUR[1] was conveyed after death; (Welsh myth.) kingdom of the dead.

avant-garde (ăvahṅ-) *n.* Pioneers or innovators, esp. in any art in a particular period (freq. attrib.) [Fr.]

A'var (ah- *or* ā-) *n.* Member of a Turkic people prominent in SE. Europe in 6th–9th centuries; in the 7th c. their kingdom extended from the Black Sea to the Adriatic; finally subdued by Charlemagne. ~ *adj.*

ă'varice *n.* Greed for gain, cupidity. **ăvari'cious** (-sh*u*s) *adj.* **ăvari'ciouslў** *adv.*

ava'st (-ahst) *int.* (naut.) Stop, cease. [Du. *houd vast* hold fast]

ă'vatar *n.* (Hinduism) Descent to earth and incarnation of a deity.

avau'nt *int.* (archaic, joc.) Begone.

avdp. *abbrev.* Avoirdupois.

a'vē (ah-; *or* -vā) *int.* Hail, welcome; *A~ Maria, A~ Mary* (= Hail, Mary!), the angelic salutation to the Virgin (Luke 1: 28), combined with that of Elizabeth (1: 42), used as a devotional recitation, together with a prayer to the Virgin. ~ *n.* Utterance of 'ave'. [L]

A'veburў (āvb-). Village in Wiltshire, site of a very large prehistoric stone circle.

avĕ'nge (-j) *v.t.* Inflict retribution on behalf of; exact retribution for.

A'ventīne (ă-). Most southerly of the seven hills of Rome.

avĕ'ntūrine *n.* Brownish glass with copper crystals, first manufactured near Venice; quartz, spangled with mica or haematite, resembling this. [It. *avventura* chance (from its accidental discovery)]

ă'vēnūe *n.* Way of approach; approach to house bordered by trees; roadway with trees etc. at regular intervals; wide street.

aver' *v.t.* Assert, affirm.

ă'verage *n.* 1. Arithmetical mean; ordinary standard; generally prevailing degree etc.; (cricket) mean number of runs per completed innings of batsman; mean cost in runs per wicket of bowler. 2. Damage to or loss of insured ship or cargo; ~ *adjustment*, apportionment of liability resulting from this. ~ *adj.* Estimated by average; of usual standard. ~ *v.t.* Estimate average or general standard of; amount on an average to. [Arab. *'awārīya* damaged goods]

Aver'nus. Lake in Campania, Italy, filling crater of an extinct volcano, and regarded by the ancients as the entrance to the infernal regions.

Avĕ'rroës (-rōĕz). Abul Walid Muhammad ben Ahmed ibn Rushd (1126–98), Muslim doctor born at Cordova, philosopher, and author of a famous commentary on Aristotle.

avĕr'se *adj.* Opposed, disinclined (*to*, *from*); unwilling.

avĕr'sion *n.* Dislike, unwillingness; object of dislike.

avĕr't *v.t.* Turn away; ward off.

Avĕ'sta *n.* Collection of sacred Zoroastrian writings. **Avĕ'stan, Avĕ'stic** *adjs.* & *ns.* (Of) the ancient E. Iranian language in which the Avesta is written.

ā'vĭarȳ *n.* Large cage or building for keeping birds.

āvĭā'tion *n.* Operation of heavier-than-air aircraft. **ā'vĭātor** *n.*

Avĭcĕ'nna (ă-). Abu ibn Sina (980–1037), Persian physician, philosopher, and commentator on Aristotle.

ă'vĭd *adj.* Eager, greedy. **ă'vĭdlȳ** *adv.* **avĭ'dĭtȳ** *n.*

Avignon (ăvēnyawṅ). City on river Rhône, in S. France, to which Clement V removed the papal seat in 1308; it remained there until 1377, and after the papal schism in 1378 two anti-popes, Clement VII and Benedict XIII, resided there; the latter was expelled in 1408, but the city remained in papal possession until 1791.

avo (ah'vōō) *n.* $\frac{1}{100}$ of a pataca.

ăvoca'dō (-kah-) *n.* (also ~ *pear*) Succulent pear-shaped fruit, a drupe with soft-coated seed, borne by the tropical Amer. and W. Indian tree *Persea gratissima*. [Span. *avocado* advocate, corrupt. of Mex. name]

ăvocā'tion *n.* Minor occupation; vocation, calling.

ă'vocėt *n.* Wading bird with long upturned beak (*Recurvirostra avosetta*).

Avoga'drō (ă-, -gah-), Amadeo (1776–1856). Italian physicist; *~'s law*, hypothesis that equal volumes of all gases at the same temperature and pressure contain equal numbers of molecules; *~'s number*, number of molecules in the gramme-molecular weight of any gas; value, $6{\cdot}02 \times 10^{23}$.

avoi'd *v.t.* Shun, refrain from; evade, escape; (law) quash. **avoi'dable** *adj.* **avoi'dablȳ** *adv.* **avoi'dance** *n.*

avoirdupois (ăverdūpoi'z), *n.* System of weights used for all goods except precious metals and stones, and medicine; weight, heaviness. [corrupt. of Fr. *avoir de pois* goods of weight]

A'von[1] (ā-). River, flowing through Warwickshire, a tributary of the Severn (*Swan of ~*, Ben Jonson's sobriquet for Shakespeare, who was born at Stratford-upon-Avon); also, one of several other English rivers.

A'von[2] (ā-). County of SW. England (since April 1974), comprising Bath and Bristol and parts

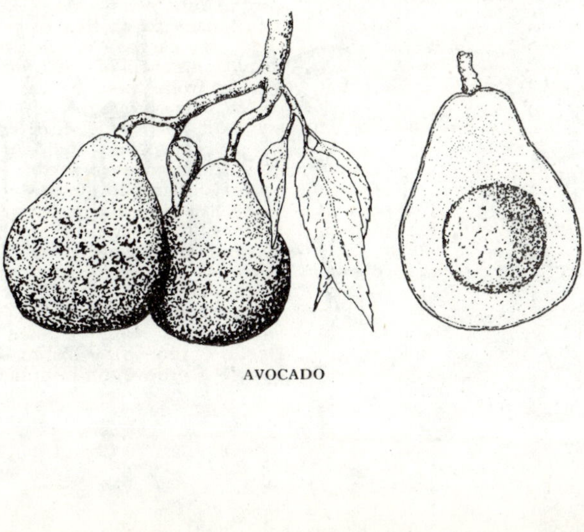

AVOCADO

of the former counties of Gloucester and Somerset.

avou'ch *v.* Guarantee; affirm; confess.

avow' *v.t.* Admit, confess. **avow'al** *n.* **avow'ėdlў** *adv.*

avŭ'ncūlar *adj.* Of, resembling, an uncle.

awai't (*a-*) *v.t.* Wait for.

awā'ke (*a-*) *v.* (past t. *awōke*; past part. *awōke, awāked*). Cease to sleep; rouse from sleep. ~ *pred. adj.* Not asleep; vigilant. **awā'ken** *v.* Awake.

awar'd (*awŏrd*) *v.t.* Order to be given as payment, prize, etc.; grant, assign. ~ *n.* Judicial decision; payment, penalty, assigned by this; prize; grant.

awār'e (*a-*) *pred. adj.* Conscious, not ignorant (*of, that*). **awār'enėss** *n.*

awa'sh (*awŏ-*) *pred. adj.* Flush with or washed by the waves.

away' (*a-*) *adv.* To or at a distance; on opponent's ground; constantly, continuously. ~ *adj.* (of game) Played on opponent's ground. ~ *n.* (football pools) Win in an away match.

awe *n.* Reverential fear. ~ *v.t.* Inspire with awe. **aw'esome** *adj.* **aw'estrĭcken, aw'estrŭck** *adjs.* Struck with awe.

aweigh (*awā'*) *adv.* (of anchor) Just raised from bottom in weighing.

aw'ful *adj.* Inspiring awe; solemnly impressive; (colloq.) notable in its kind (usu. of thing or person disliked). **aw'fullў** *adv.* (esp. colloq.) Extremely. **aw'fulnėss** *n.*

awhee'l (*a-*) *adv.* On wheels, riding (esp. cycle).

awhī'le (*a-*) *adv.* For a short time.

aw'kward *adj.* Ill-adapted for use; hard to deal with; clumsy. **aw'kwardlў** *adv.* **aw'kwardnėss** *n.*

awl *n.* Small pointed tool for piercing holes in leather, wood, etc., esp. that used by shoemakers.

awn *n.* Stiff bristle-like process terminating grain-sheath of barley, oats, etc. **awned** (-nd) *adj.*

aw'nĭng *n.* Sheet of canvas etc. stretched on framework as protection from sun etc.

A.W.O.L. *abbrev.* Absent without leave.

awry (*arī'*) *adv.* & *pred. adj.* Crookedly; amiss.

ăxe *n.* Metal tool for chopping, cleaving, etc., with wooden handle; drastic reduction of public expenditure. ~ *v.t.* Cut down (personnel, expenses, etc.); put an end to (project).

ă'xĭal *adj.* Forming, belonging to, an axis. **ă'xĭallў** *adv.*

ă'xĭl *n.* Upper angle between leaf and stem it springs from, or between branch and trunk.

ăxĭ'llarў *adj.* 1. Of the armpit. 2. (bot.) In, growing from, the axil (~ *bud*).

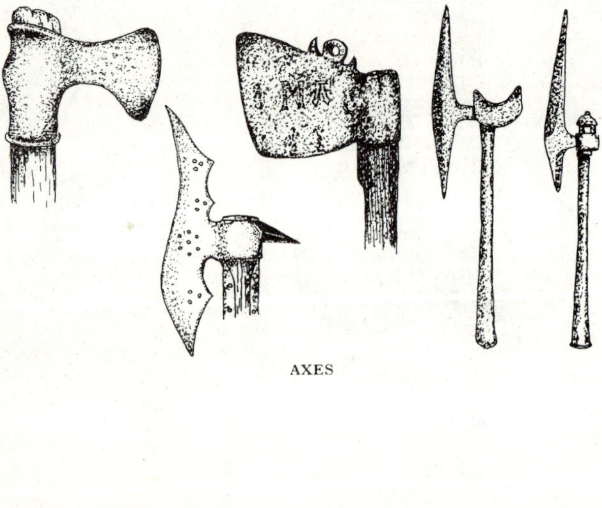

AXES

ă'xĭom *n.* Self-evident truth; established principle; maxim; (geom.) self-evident theorem. **ăxĭomă'tĭc** *adj.* **ăxĭomă'tĭcallȳ** *adv.*

ă'xĭs *n.* (pl. *axēs*). 1. Line about which a body rotates (~ *of equator*, that between N. and S. Poles, round which the earth turns daily); straight line from end to end of a body. 2. (math.) Line dividing a regular figure symmetrically; line by revolution about which a plane figure is conceived as generating a solid. 3. (bot.) Stem or shoot; *floral* ~, that part of a shoot which bears the floral organs, receptacle 4. (anat.) Second cervical vertebra, on which the head turns 5. (optics) Ray passing through centre of eye or lens or falling perpendicularly on it. 6. *Rome–Berlin A*~, alliance between Germany and Italy, May 1939, later joined by Japan (*Rome–Berlin–Tokyo–A*~); *A*~ *Powers*, these nations.

a'xle *n.* Spindle on or with which wheel revolves. end of axle-tree; axle-tree; ~*-box,* box closed by detachable cap, in nave of wheel, through which the ends of axle-tree pass; ~*-tree*, bar connecting wheels of carriage etc.

A'xmĭnster (ă-). Small town in Devon; ~ *carpet*, carpet of cut pile made by various methods, first made at Axminster, orig. in imitation of hand-knotted oriental carpets.

ă'xolŏtl *n.* Salamander of genus *Amblystoma* of mountain lakes of Mexico and south-western U.S., usu. retaining larval form throughout life. [Aztec]

ă'xon *n.* That part of the nerve which is its conducting element or nerve fibre.

ay (ī) *adv.* = AYE[1].

ayah (ī'*a*) *n.* Hindu nurse. [Port. *aia* fem. of *aio* tutor]

aye[1] (ī) *adv.* (esp. Sc. & dial.) Yes. ~ *n.* Affirmative answer or vote.

aye[2] (ā) *adv.* Always; *for* ~, for ever.

aye-aye (ī'ī) *n.* Small tree-climbing animal (genus *Daubentonia*) found in Madagascar, a primate related to the lemurs.

Aylesburȳ (ā'lz-). County town of Buckinghamshire; ~ *duck*, duck of white domestic breed.

Ayrshire (ār'-). Former county of SW. Scotland, since May 1975 part of the region of Strathclyde; hence, breed of dairy cattle, mostly white with reddish or black markings, orig. raised there; kind of bacon cured in Ayrshire.

azā'lėa *n.* Flowering shrubby plant of the genus *Rhododendron*, chiefly native of N. America and China. [mod. L, f. Gk *azaleos* parched, because Linnaeus believed them to grow in dry situations]

Azerbaijan (ăzerbījah'n). 1. One of the constituent republics of the U.S.S.R., lying between the Black and Caspian Seas; capital, Baku. 2. Province of NW. Iran. **Azerbaija'n, -a'nĭ** *adjs.* & *ns.* (Native, inhabitant, language) of Azerbaijan.

Azĭ'lĭan *adj.* & *n.* (Of) a mesolithic culture of S. France. [f. Mas d'*Azil* in Fr. Pyrenees, where remains were found]

ă'zĭmuth *n.* Arc of the heavens extending from the zenith to the horizon, which it cuts at right angles; (in full, *true* ~ of a heavenly body) arc of horizon intercepted between north (in S. hemisphere, south) point of horizon and the point where the vertical circle passing through the body cuts the horizon; *magnetic* ~, arc intercepted between this circle and the magnetic meridian; ~ *circle*, circle of which this is a quadrant, passing through zenith and nadir. **ăzĭmū'thal** *adj.* ~*projection:* see ZENITHAL projection. **ăzĭmū'thallȳ** *adv.* [Arab. *al samt* the way, road, used in astron. for azimuth]

ă'zō *adj.* (chem.) Containing the *azo group*, —N = N—, where both bonds are attached to carbon atoms; ~ *dye*, dye containing this.

Azores (-ōr'z). Group of islands in N. Atlantic, some 800 miles

W. of Portugal; in Portuguese possession.

Azov (ā'zŏf), Sea of. Inland sea of southern U.S.S.R., separated from the Black Sea by the Crimea and communicating with it by a narrow strait.

A'zrāel (ă-). (Jewish & Muslim myth.) Angel who at death severs the soul from the body.

A'ztĕc (ă-) *n.* Member of a native Amer. people first known (*c* A.D. 1100) as inhabitants of the valley of Mexico; they built their capital (on the same site as modern Mexico City) in 1324 and extended their conquests in the 15th c., their most successful leader being Montezuma I (reigned 1440–69); they were conquered by the invading Spaniards under Cortez, early in the 16th c. ~ *adj.*

ă'zure (-zh*er*, -zhy*er*) *adj.* & *n.* Sky-blue; blue of unclouded sky; lapis lazuli; (heraldry) blue [Arab *al lāzuward* lapis lazuli, cerulean blue, f. Pers. *lazhward*]

AZTEC

B

B, b (bē). 1. 2nd letter of modern English and ancient Roman alphabet, representing a voiced bilabial stop, and derived from the Greek *beta* (β) and Phoenician and Hebrew *beth* (𐤁, ב). 2. 2nd in series, order, or class. 3. *B*, (mus.) 7th note in the natural scale (C major); scale or key with this note for tonic.

b. *abbrev.* Born; (in cricket) bowled, bye.

B. *abbrev.* *Beatus*, *-a* (L, = 'blessed'); *B*, black (of pencil-lead); (phot.) bulb-release.

B.A. *abbrev.* Bachelor of Arts; British Academy.

baa (bah) *n.* & *v.* (of sheep) Bleat.

Bā'al (pl. *-ĭm*). God of the ancient Phoenicians and Canaanites; false god. **Bā'alĭsm** *n.* Worship of Baal, idolatry. [Heb. *ba'al* lord, master]

Baalbĕ'k (bahl-). Site in Lebanon of the Roman colony of Heliopolis (1st–3rd centuries A.D.), a centre of worship of the sun-god Helios, identified with BAAL.

baas (bahs) *n.* Boss, master; S. Afr. form of address, esp. of non-European to white man. [Du., = 'master', 'uncle']

baba (bah'bah) *n.* (also ~ *au rhum*, pr. ō ro͞om) Small rich sponge-cake soaked in rum syrup.

bă'bbĭtt *n.* Soft alloy of tin, copper, and antimony, used for machine bearings (also *Babbitt's metal*); bearing made of this. ~ *v.* Line with babbitt. [I. *Babbitt* (1799–1862), Amer. inventor]

Bă'bbĭtt. Hero of a novel (1922) by Sinclair Lewis; hence, typical business man of U.S. Middle West. **Bă'bbĭttĭsm, Bă'bbĭttrў** *ns.*

bă'bble *v.* Talk half-articulately, incoherently, foolishly or excessively; murmur (of stream etc.). ~ *n.* Foolish or childish talk. **bă'bbler** *n.* Chatterer; teller of secrets; any of a group of Old World passerines with loud babbling cry, related to warblers.

bābe *n.* Baby.

Bā'bel[1]. (Heb. myth.) = BABYLON; its people (Gen. 11) tried to build a tower which would reach heaven, but God prevented them by 'confounding' their language (so that they could not understand one another) and scattering them abroad; hence, *tower of* ~, visionary scheme.

bā'bel[2] *n.* Scene of confusion and uproar; noisy assembly. [f. BABEL[1]]

Ba'bī (bah-) *n.* (Member of) sect whose doctrines combined Muslim, Christian, Jewish, and Zoroastrian elements, founded in 1844 by a Persian, Mirza Ali Muhammad, who became known as the *Bab* (pr. bahb; Arab. *bāb ad-dīn* gate of the faith). **Ba'bĭsm, Ba'bīte, Ba'bĭst** *ns.*

Bă'bĭngton, Anthony (1561–86). Page to Mary Queen of Scots; executed for conspiring to murder Elizabeth and release Mary from imprisonment.

băbĭru'sa, -r(o)ussa (-ro͞o-) *n.* Wild hog (*Babirusa babyrussa*), male of which has long upper canine teeth which pierce the lip and grow upward like horns; found only in islands of Celebes and Buru. [Malagasy, = 'hog deer']

babo͞o'n *n.* Medium-sized monkey (several species in genus *Papio*) of Arabia and Africa S. and E. of Sahara, living in bands in open rocky country, occas. tree-climbing, characterized by dog-like snout, cheek-prominences, and coloured bare patches on the buttocks; *sacred* ~, species living on Red Sea coasts and formerly in Egypt (*P. hamadryas*).

TOWER OF BABEL

babu (bah'bo͞o) *n.* Hindu gentleman; Indian clerk or official who writes English; (contempt.) Hindu, esp. Bengali, with superficial English education.

Babur (bah'boor) (1483–1530). First Mogul emperor, descended from Tamburlaine; he invaded India *c* 1525 and conquered the territory from the Oxus to Patna.

bā'bȳ *n.* Infant, very young child; childish person; very young animal; thing small of its kind; (fig.) one's responsibility; one's particular interest; *~-farmer*, person who keeps babies for payment; *~ grand*: see GRAND; *~-sitter*, (colloq.) person who looks after young child when parents go out. **bā'bȳhood** *n.* **bā'bȳish** *adj.*

Bă'bȳlon. Capital city, on the Euphrates, of the ancient Chaldean Empire; the Jews were brought there in captivity by Nebuchadnezzar (597 and 586 B.C.); its *hanging* (i.e. terraced) *gardens* were one of the Seven Wonders of the ancient world; it was sacked by Cyrus of Persia in 538 B.C.; *Whore of ~*: see WHORE. **Băbȳlō'nĭa.** Empire of Babylon. **Băbȳlō'nĭan** *adj.* & *n.*

băccalau'rėate *n.* University degree of bachelor.

bă'ccarat (-ah) *n.* Gambling card-game, played against banker by punters staking that their hand will total nine.

bă'ccāte *adj.* (bot.) 1. Bearing berries. 2. Berry-shaped.

bă'cchanal (-k-) *adj.* Of Bacchus or his rites. *~ n.* Priest or votary of Bacchus; reveller.

Băcchanā'lia (-k-) *n.pl.* Festival held in honour of Bacchus; drunken revelry, orgy.

Bă'cchant (-k-), **Bacchă'ntė** (*or* -kă'nt) *ns.* Priest or priestess of Bacchus, often represented with loose hair garlanded with ivy, and dressed in a leopard-skin; (drunken or noisy) reveller.

bă'cchĭc (-k-) *adj.* Of Bacchus or his worship; riotous, drunken.

Bă'cchus (-k-). (Gk & Rom. myth.) God of wine: see DIONYSUS.

băcci'ferous, bă'cciform, bacci'vorous (băks-) *adjs.* Berry-bearing, -shaped, -eating.

bă'ccy (-k-) *n.* (colloq.) Tobacco.

Bach (bahχ), Johann Sebastian (1685–1750). German musical composer, the great master of contrapuntal music; author of many fugues and other works for organ and other keyboard instruments, a

great Mass, and much other choral church-music. Of his eleven sons, several distinguished in music, two of the better-known are *Carl Philipp Emanuel* ~ (1714–88), who contributed much to the development of the sonata form, and *Johann Christian* ~ (the 'English Bach', 1735–82), who spent some time in England.

bă'chelor *n.* Unmarried man; (hist.) knight serving under another's banner; *B~ of Arts* (B.A.), *of Science* (B.Sc.), etc., holder of university degree below master; *~'s button*, any of various flowers of round or button-like form, orig. the double variety of *Ranunculus acris*; *~ girl*, young unmarried woman living independently.

baci'llary *adj.* Consisting of little rods; connected with bacilli.

baci'lliform *adj.* Rod-shaped.

baci'llus *n.* (pl. *-llī*). Any straight rod-shaped bacterium; (loosely and usu. pl.) disease-producing bacteria. [L dim. of *baculus* stick]

băck *n.* Hinder surface of human body, part of this between shoulders and hips; corresponding part of animal's body; side or part normally more remote or away from spectator or direction of motion; side of hand opposite palm; edge of book, opposite openings of pages, where sections are joined together; (footb. etc.) player positioned behind forwards; *Backs,* gardens behind colleges bordering on the river Cam at Cambridge. *~ adj.* Situated behind or at rear; remote; inferior; belonging to past period. *~ adv.* To the rear; in (to) an earlier position; to or in remote or retired position. *~ v.* Put, or be, a back, lining, support, or background to; support with money, argument, etc. (also *~ up*); bet on; endorse (cheque etc.); ride (horse); (cause to) move back; lay (sail) against the wind; (of wind) change anti-clockwise (cf. VEER); *~ out of*, withdraw from. **bă'cker** *n.* One who backs or supports. **bă'cking** *n.* Support, assistance.

băck- in comb.: *~-bench, ~-bencher*: see BENCH *n.* 3; *ba'ckbite* (*v.*) slander; *ba'ckbiter* (*n.*); *ba'ckblocks*, (Austral.) the remotest fringe of settlement; *ba'ckboard*, (esp.) board worn to support or straighten the back; (basket ball) board or surface behind the basket ; *ba'ckbone*, spine; main support; firmness of character; *~-chat*, (slang) impudent retort(s); *~-cloth*, painted cloth hung at the back of scene or stage; *~-comb* (*v.*) comb underlying hairs of a strand towards scalp; *~-date* (*v.t.*) affix earlier date to (document etc.); make (agreement etc.) valid retroactively; *~-door* (*adj.*) using underhand or secret approach; *backfire*, (of internal combustion engine) premature ignition in the cylinder during suction stroke; explosion in hot exhaust-pipe of gases escaping when a cylinder has misfired; (*v.i.*) ignite, explode, thus; (fig. of plan etc.) go wrong; have adverse effect on instigator; ~ *formation*, making from a supposed derivative (as *burglar*) of the non-existent word (*burgle*) from which it might have come; word so formed; *ba'ckground* (*n.*) back part of scene or picture; social surroundings, environment; obscurity, retirement; (*adj.*) in, providing, a background; *ba'ckhand*(*ed*) (*adjs.*) delivered with the back of the hand, or with the back of hand turned in the direction of the stroke; (fig.) ambiguous, equivocal; *backha'nder* (*n.*) backhand blow; indirect attack: *backlash*(*ing*), irregular recoil of wheels in machinery due to defect or sudden pressure (also fig.); *ba'cklog*, arrears of uncompleted work etc.; ~ *number*, out-of-date issue of magazine etc., (slang) out-of-date person or thing; ~*-pedal* (*v.i.*) check movement of wheel when bicycling by pressing rising pedal down; also fig. (*v.*); ~*-projection*, (cinemat.) projection of a film on to a translucent screen from behind, as background for action taking place in front of the screen; ~*-scattering*, (phys.) scattering of radiation in a reverse direction from an irradiated substance; ~ *seat*, humble or obscure position; ~*-seat driver*, one who gives unsolicited advice while taking no responsibility; *ba'ckside*, buttocks; *ba'cksight*, (of gun) that nearer the stock; (surveying) sight taken backwards; ~ *slang*, slang in which words are pronounced backwards; *backsli'de*, relapse into sin, error, etc.; ~ *spacer*, typewriter key that moves the carriage one space backward; ~ *stage*, (part of theatre) behind the scenes; also fig.; ~*-stairs* (*adj.*) underhand, secret; *ba'ckstays*, ropes from the upper mast-heads to the sides of a ship, supporting the masts under sail; *ba'ckstitch*, sew by inserting the needle each time behind the place where it has just been brought out; (*n.*) stitch made thus; *ba'ckstroke*, stroke made whilst swimmer is lying on his back; *ba'ckwash*, motion of receding wave; motion of water caused by passage of vessel; *ba'ckwater*, stretch of still water parallel with a stream and fed from it at the lower end; (fig.) place or condition of intellectual stagnation; *ba'ckwoods*, remote, only partially cleared forest-land; *ba'ckwoodsman*, settler in backwoods, uncivilized person; peer who rarely attends House of Lords.

băckgă'mmon *n.* Game for two persons, played by moving pieces like draughtsmen, according to the

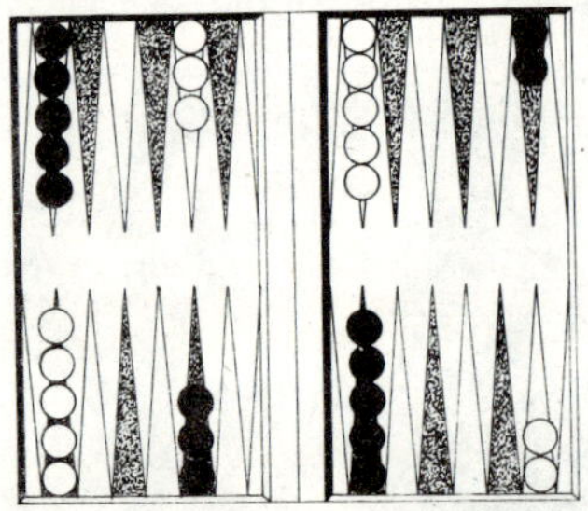

throw of dice, on a board of two tables, each marked off into twelve spaces of alternating colours.

bă'cklėss *adj.* Having no back; (of dress etc.) cut low at the back.

bă'ckward *adv.* Back foremost; back towards the starting-point; the reverse way; ~ *and forward*, to and fro. ~ *adj.* Directed to rear or starting-point; reversed; slow in learning or developing. **bă'ckwardnėss** *n.* **bă'ckwards** (-z) *adv.* Backward.

băckwardā'tion *n.* (Stock Exch.) Percentage paid by seller of stock for right of delaying delivery (cf. CONTANGO).

bā'con[1] *n.* Cured back and sides of a pig; piece of this.

Bā'con[2], Francis, Baron Verulam and Viscount St. Albans (1561–1626). Lord Chancellor of England (1618–20), philosopher who introduced the inductive method into science, and author of 'Essays'.

Bācō'nĭan *adj.* & *n.* (Advocate)

of the theory that Bacon wrote the plays of Shakespeare.

Bă'con[3], Roger (1214?–94). English Franciscan, philosopher and student of experimental science (esp. optics) at Paris and Oxford; credited, then and later, with magical powers.

băctēr'ĭcīde *n.* Substance that destroys bacteria. **băctērĭcī'dal** *adj.*

băctērĭŏ'logy̆ *n.* Study of bacteria, esp. as a branch of medicine. **băctērĭolŏ'gĭcal** *adj.* ~ *warfare*, use of bacteria to spread disease in the enemy. **băctērĭŏ'logĭst** *n.*

băctēr'ĭophāge (*or* -fahzh) *n.* Virus capable of destroying bacteria. **băctērĭophā'gal, -phā'gĭc** *adjs.*

băctēr'ĭum *n.* (pl. *-rĭa*) Any of several types of microscopic or ultra-microscopic single-celled organisms occurring in enormous numbers everywhere in nature, not only in land, sea, and air, but also on or in many parts of the tissues

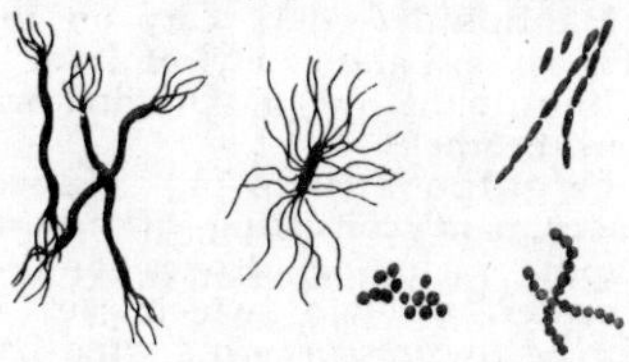

of plants and animals, and forming one of the main biologically interdependent groups of organisms in virtue of the chemical changes which many of them bring about, e.g. many forms of decay, certain diseases, and the building up of nitrogen compounds in the soil. **băctēr'ĭal** *adj.* Of or caused by bacteria. [Gk, dim. of *baktron* stick]

Bă'ctrĭa. Ancient country of central Asia (now *Balkh* in N. Afghanistan), lying between the Hindu Kush and the Oxus.

Bă'ctrĭan *adj.* Of Bactria or its people; ~ *camel*, two-humped camel of central Asia, *Camelus bactrianus*. ~ *n.* Native or inhabitant of Bactria.

băd *adj.* (comp. *worse*, superl. *worst*). 1. Worthless, inferior, defective, inefficient; not valid; unpleasant; (of coinage) counterfeit; (of weather) unpleasant; *go* ~, decay; *not* ~, (colloq.) rather good; ~ *debt*, one not recoverable; *B~ Lands*, arid rocky regions (esp. those in S. Dakota, U.S.), seamed with deep vertical gullies by occasional heavy rain and thus uncultivable. 2. Wicked, vicious. 3. Painful; harmful; ~ *blood*, ill feeling. 4. Ill, in pain. ~ *n.* Ill fortune, ruin; *go to the* ~, go to ruin, degenerate. **bă'ddĭsh** *adj.* **bă'dly̆** *adv.* **bă'dnėss** *n.*

Badar'ĭan *adj.* & *n.* (Member) of a predynastic culture of Upper Egypt using stone tools and pottery. [f. *Badari*, village in Upper Egypt]

Bă'ddėley (*or* -dlĭ), Robert (1732?–94). English actor, who left money to provide wine and cake (the ~ *cake*) on Twelfth Night in the green-room of Drury Lane Theatre, London.

Ba'den (bah-). Former State of SW. Germany; now part of the Federal Republic.

Ba'den-Ba'den (bah-). Health resort, with mineral springs, in Baden, Germany.

Bă'den-Powell (pō'el), Robert Stephenson Smyth, 1st Baron Baden-Powell of Gilwell (1857–1941). English soldier; defended Mafeking, 1900; founded the Boy SCOUT organization, 1908.

bădge *n.* Distinctive emblem or mark as a sign of office, membership, etc.

bă'dger *n.* Nocturnal plantigrade quadruped (*Meles vulgaris*), intermediate between weasel and bear, with coarse dark-coloured fur and a white blaze on the forehead, which digs a burrow, hibernates, and defends itself fiercely against attack; *honey* ~, ratel; ~ *game*, extortion scheme in which a man is lured into a compromising situation and then surprised and blackmailed. ~ *v.* Pester as dogs worry a badger; tease, torment.

bă'dĭnage (-ahzh) *n.* Banter.

bă'dmĭnton *n.* Game like lawn tennis played with shuttlecocks

SHUTTLECOCK

and rackets over a net 1·5 m high. [name of Gloucestershire seat of Duke of Beaufort]

Bae'dėker (bād-) *n.* Any of the guide-books issued by Karl ~ (1801–59), German publisher, and his successors; ~ *raids*, reprisal raids undertaken by German air force in April and May 1942 on places of cultural and historical importance in Britain.

Baer (bār), Karl Ernst von (1792–1876). Estonian biologist; discovered human ovum and made important contributions to embryology.

Baeyer (bī'y*er*), Johann Friedrich Wilhelm Adolf, Ritter von (1835–1917). German chemist; discovered synthetic indigo; exerted profound influence on development of organic chemistry.

Bă'ffin, William (1584?–1622). English navigator and explorer; discovered ~ *Land*, large island off the NE. coast of Canada, and ~ *Bay*, sea between it and Greenland.

bă'ffle *v.t.* Foil, frustrate, perplex. **bă'ffling** *adj.* Bewildering.
bă'ffle *n.* Shielding device or structure; esp. (also ~*-board*) one checking or deflecting sound-waves, improving tone of loud-speaker by hindering return of sound-waves to back of speaker; (also ~*-plate*) one hindering or regulating passage of gases or fluids; one in exhaust-pipe of an internal combustion engine to reduce noise; (photog.) one that screens light; ~*-wall*, wall parallel with doorway to stop draughts, blast from air-raids, etc.

bă'ffy̆ *n.* Short wooden golf-club for lofting the ball.

baft (-ah-) *adv.* & *prep.* Abaft.

băg *n.* Receptacle of flexible material with an opening usu. at the top; sac in animal body for storing honey, poison, etc.; all a sportsman has shot in one expedition; (esp. pl.) folds of loose skin beneath the eyes; (pl.) (slang) trousers; large number or amount; ~*-wig*, wig with the back hair tied in a bag. ~ *v.* Put in a bag; secure (game); (colloq.) take possession of, steal; bulge, hang loosely.

Bagă'nda *n.* (Member of) a Negroid Bantu-speaking people inhabiting Buganda.

băgatĕ'lle *n.* 1. Mere trifle; short unpretentious piece of music. 2. Game played on a table with a semicircular end, the object being to strike balls into numbered holes with a cue.

bă'ggage *n.* Portable equipment of an army; luggage; (joc.) saucy girl.

bă'ggy̆ (-gĭ) *adj.* That bags or hangs loosely.

Băghdă'd (-gd-). City on the Tigris, now the capital of Iraq.

bagnio (bă'nyō) *n.* Oriental prison; brothel.

bă'gpīpe *n.* (freq. pl.) Musical instrument consisting of several pipes, including drones and a chanter through which air is forced by pressure on a wind-bag held under the arm; now associated chiefly with Scotland and Ireland, but once popular in England and

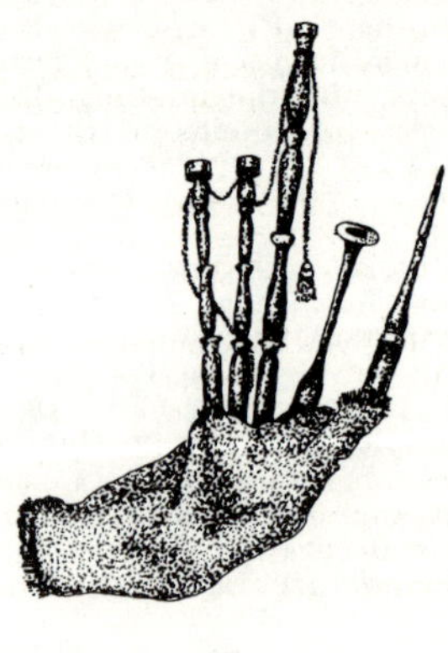

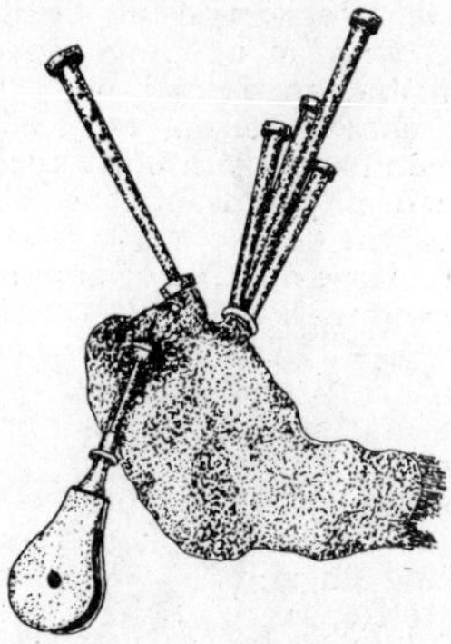

still played in some places on the Continent, notably Brittany.

B.Agr., B.Agric. *abbrevs.* Bachelor of Agriculture.

Baha'dur (b*a*hah-). Title of respect appended in India to person's name.

Baha'ism (b*a*hah-) *n.* Religion, based on Babism, founded by the Babist leader Mirza Hosain Ali (1817–92), known as *Baha-ullah* (Pers. *bahā'u-'l-lāh* 'splendour of God'). **Baha'i, Baha'ist** *ns.* & *adjs.*

Baha'mas (b*a*hahm*a*z). (also *Bahama Islands*) Archipelago of British W. Indies, the first land touched by Columbus in 1492; first colonized by Spaniards and later (in 17th c.) by the English; British colony 1783–1973; independent 1973; capital, Nassau. **Bahā'mian** *adj.* & *n.*

Bahrai'n, -ei'n (-ān *or* -īn). Independent sheikdom consisting of a group of islands, the largest being Bahrain Island, in the Persian Gulf; capital, Manama.

Bahram V (b*a*rah'm) (d. 439). Sassanid king and national hero of Persia, known as *Bahrām Gūr*, 'the Wild Ass'.

baht *n.* Principal monetary unit of Thailand, = 100 stangs.

Baikal (bīkah'l), Lake. Large lake in S. Siberia.

bail[1] *n.* 1. Security for a prisoner's appearance for trial. 2. Person who becomes surety. ~ *v.t.* 1. Become bail for, secure the liberation of on bail. 2. Deliver (goods) in trust.

bail[2] *n.* 1. Bar separating horses in an open stable. 2. (cricket) Either of the crosspieces resting on top of the stumps. 3. (also ~ *bar*) Hinged bar holding paper against platen of typewriter. **bai'ler**[1] *n.* Ball that hits the bails.

bail[3], **bāle** *v.t.* Scoop water out of (boat etc.). **bai'ler**[2] *n.* Utensil for bailing.

bailee' *n.* Person to whom goods are entrusted.

bai'ley *n.* Open space enclosed by a fortification; *Old B~*: see OLD.

Bai'ley bridge. Bridge of lattice steel designed for rapid assembly from standard parts. [f. Sir Donald *Bailey* (1901–) designer]

bai'lie *n.* Senior burgh councillor in Scotland (corresp. to former English alderman) serving also as magistrate.

bai'liff *n.* 1. King's representative in district (now chiefly hist.), esp. chief officer of a hundred. 2. Sheriff's officer who executes writs and processes, distrains, and arrests. 3. Lord of the manor's agent; steward.

bai'liwick *n.* District, jurisdiction, of bailie or bailiff.

bai'lment *n.* Delivery of goods in trust; bailing of prisoner.

bai'lor *n.* One who entrusts goods to another.

Bain, Alexander (1818–1903). Scottish philosopher: exponent of a system of psychology which traces psychological phenomena to the nerves and brain.

bain-marie (băṅ-mărē') *n.* Vessel of hot water in which pans of food are placed for slow cooking; double boiler.

Bairam (bīrah'm). Each of the two principal festivals of the Muslim year, *Lesser* ~ (lasting 3 days) following the fast of Ramadan, and *Greater* ~ (lasting 4 days) 70 days later.

bairn *n.* (Sc.) Child.

bait *v.* 1. Worry (animal) by setting dogs at it; worry (person) by jeers. 2. Give (horse etc.) food, esp. on a journey; (of horse) take food thus. 3. Put bait on or in (fish-hook, trap, etc.). ~ *n.* 1. Food etc. used to entice prey; allurement. 2. (obs.) Halt for refreshment.

bai'za (bī-) *n.* One thousandth of a rial saidi.

baize *n.* Coarse woollen usu. green stuff used chiefly for coverings, linings, etc.

bāke *v.* Cook by dry heat, as in an oven; harden by heat; be or become baked; *baked beans*, haricot beans so cooked (esp. as a tinned food, in tomato sauce); *baked meats*, (obs.) pastry; *ba'kehouse*, place for baking bread etc.; *ba'king-powder*, powder consisting of bicarbonate of soda and cream of tartar with a filling of starch or flour, used instead of yeast to make cakes etc. rise.

bā'kelīte *n.* Synthetic plastic material used for insulating, to make moulded articles etc. [trade-name, f. L. H. *Baekeland* (1863–1944), Belgian-American inventor]

bā'ker *n.* One who bakes and sells bread; ~*'s dozen*, 13 objects of any kind. **bā'kerȳ** *n.* Bakehouse; trade of baking.

Bā'kewĕll (-kw-). Town in Derbyshire; ~ *tart*, pastry case, lined with a layer of jam, with rich almond paste filling.

bă'kshēēsh *n.* Small gift of money. [Pers. *bakhshish* gift, munificence]

Băkst, Leon (1866–1924). Russian stage-designer who worked in Paris for Diaghilev's Russian ballet company.

bă'kū[1] *n.* Fine kind of straw grown in the Philippines and woven in China, and used for hats; hat woven of this.

Băku'[2] (-ōō). Capital of Azerbaijan, on the shore of the Caspian Sea; a centre of the petroleum industry.

Bakunin (-kōō'nĭn), Mikhail Alexandrovich (1814–76). Russian anarchist, revolutionary leader, and founder of NIHILISM.

BAL *abbrev.* British Anti-Lewisite, drug (*dimercaprol*) used to neutralize metallic poisons, e.g. arsenic.

BAKST

Bā'laam (-l*a*m). Gentile prophet (see Num. 22–4).

Bălacla'va (-klah-). Crimean village near Sebastopol, scene of battle (1854) of the Crimean War during which occurred the Charge of the Light Brigade; ~ *helmet*, knitted woollen cap covering the whole head and neck, with an opening for the face, worn esp. by soldiers on active service.

bălalai'ka (-līk*a*) *n.* Russian stringed instrument played by plucking, resembling guitar but with triangular body and 2, 3, or 4 strings.

bă'lance *n.* 1. Weighing apparatus consisting of a beam moving freely on a central pivot with a scale-pan at either end; spring or lever substitute for this. 2. Regulating gear of a clock, watch, etc. 3. (State of) even distribution of weight or amount. 4. Preponderating weight or amount. 5. Excess of assets over liabilities or vice versa. 6. Remainder. 7. ~ *of payments*,

difference of value between payments into and out of a country, including invisible exports and imports; ~ *of power*, equilibrium of military and political power between several States; ~ *of trade*, difference between total exports and total imports of a country, *favourable* if exports exceed imports, and *adverse* if there is an excess of imports; ~*-sheet*, statement of assets and liabilities, esp. of public company. ~ *v.* 1. Weigh. 2. Equalize, match; bring or come into equilibrium. 3. Find the balance of assets and liabilities in (an account-book). **bă'lanced** (-st) *adj.* (esp., of diet) Containing essential nutriments in suitable proportions.

bă'las *n.* Rose-red kind of spinel ruby. [med. L *balascus*, f. Pers. *Badakshān*, district of origin, near Samarkand]

bă'lata (*or* balah'-) *n.* Dried milky juice of tropical Amer. tree, used as substitute for gutta-percha.

Bălbō'a[1], Vasco Nuñez de (1475–1517). Spanish explorer, esp. of Central America; first sighted the Pacific Ocean in 1513.

bălbō'a[2] *n.* Principal monetary unit of Panama = U.S. dollar.

bă'lconȳ *n.* 1. Balustraded or railed platform on the outside of a building with access from an upper-floor window. 2. In a theatre, the seats above the dress or upper circle usu. = GALLERY in other public buildings, (seats in) a gallery above ground-floor seats.

bald (bawld) *adj.* 1. Having the scalp wholly or partly hairless; (of animal, bird) without fur, feathers, etc. 2. Bare; meagre; dull. **ba'ldlȳ** *adv.* **ba'ldnėss** *n.*

baldachin, -quin (baw'ldakĭn) *n.* Canopy over an altar, throne, etc., dependent from a ceiling or projecting from a wall. [It. *baldacchino* silk material exported by *Baldacco* Baghdad]

ba'ld-coot, ba'ldĭcoot (bawl-) *n.* = COOT.

Ba'lder, -dur (bawl-). (Scand. myth.) God of the summer sun, invulnerable to all things except mistletoe, with which Loki by a trick induced the blind god Hödur to kill him.

ba'lderdăsh (bawl-) *n.* Jumble of words; nonsense, rubbish.

ba'lding (bawl-) *adj.* Becoming bald.

ba'ldrĭc (bawl-) *n.* Belt for supporting a sword, bugle, etc., worn over shoulder and across body to opposite hip.

Ba'ldwĭn[1] (bawl-) (1058–1118). First Christian king of Jerusalem, a leader in the 1st Crusade, and brother and successor of Godfrey of Bouillon.

Ba'ldwĭn[2] (bawl-), Stanley (1867–1947), 1st Earl Baldwin of Bewdley. British Conservative statesman; prime minister 1923–4, 1924–9, 1935–7.

bāle[1] *n.* (archaic) Evil, destruction, woe.

bāle[2] *n.* Large bundle or package, esp. of merchandise, usu. wrapped and corded or looped. ~ *v.t.* Make up into bales.

bāle[3] *v.* Erroneous but more usual spelling of BAIL[3] *v.*; ~ *out*, make emergency descent by parachute from aircraft.

Bāle[4], John (1495–1563). English priest, author of the first English historical play, 'King John'.

Bălėă'rĭc I'slands (īlandz). Group of islands, including Majorca and Minorca, off E. coast of Spain; a province of Spain.

balē'n *n.* Whalebone.

bā'lefīre (-lf-) *n.* (archaic) Great fire in the open, beacon fire.

bā'leful (-lf-) *adj.* Pernicious, destructive, malignant. **bā'lefullȳ** *adv.* **bā'lefulnėss** *n.*

Bă'lfour (-foor), Arthur James, 1st Earl of Balfour (1848–1930). British Conservative statesman and philosopher; prime minister 1902–5; author of 'A Defence of Philosophic Doubt' (1879).

bălĭbŭ'ntal *n.* Fine straw of very close weave, used for hats.

Balīnē'se (bah-, -z) *adj.* & *n.* (Native, language, people) of the island of Bali in Indonesia.

Bā'lĭol. Surname of several kings of Scotland: John de Baliol (1249–1315) was that claimant to the Scottish throne in 1290 in whose favour Edward I of England decided.

balk, baulk (bawk; *or* -lk) *n.* 1. Roughly squared beam of timber; tie-beam. 2. Stumbling-block. 3. (usu. *baulk*) Area on billiard table where ball may be exempt from direct hit by another ball. 4. Ridge left unploughed between two furrows. *v.* 1. Thwart, hinder; discourage. 2. Jib, shy.

Ba'lkan (bawl- *or* bŏl-) *adj.* Of the Balkan Peninsula or States; ~ *Peninsula*, peninsula of Europe south of the Danube and Sava rivers; home of various peoples (Albanians, Vlachs, Greeks, Serbs, Bulgars, and Turks) with differing cultures. From the 3rd to the 7th centuries the peninsula, nominally ruled by the Byzantine emperors, was invaded by successive migrations of Slavs; later, parts of it were conquered by Venice and other States; in 1356 began the Ottoman invasion; Constantinople fell to the Turks in 1453, and by 1478 most of the peninsula was in their power; the subject nations, though largely retaining their languages and religions, did not recover independence until the 19th c.; in 1912–13 Turkey was attacked and defeated by other Balkan peoples in alliance; during the war of 1914–18 (the immediate cause of which was the assassination of the Austrian Archduke Franz Ferdinand in Serbia) Turkey and Bulgaria sided with Austria and Germany and the other Balkan States with the Allies; after the war the peninsula was divided between Greece, Bulgaria, Albania, and Yugoslavia, with Turkey retaining only Constantinople and the surrounding land; ~ *States*, countries of the Balkan Peninsula. **Ba'lkans** (-z) *n.pl.* Balkan States.

Ba'lkĭs (bawl- *or* bŏl-). Name of the Queen of Sheba in Arabic literature.

ball[1] (bawl) *n.* 1. Solid or hollow sphere, esp. one used in a game; rounded mass (as of snow, string, etc.); ~ *of foot*, *thumb*, rounded

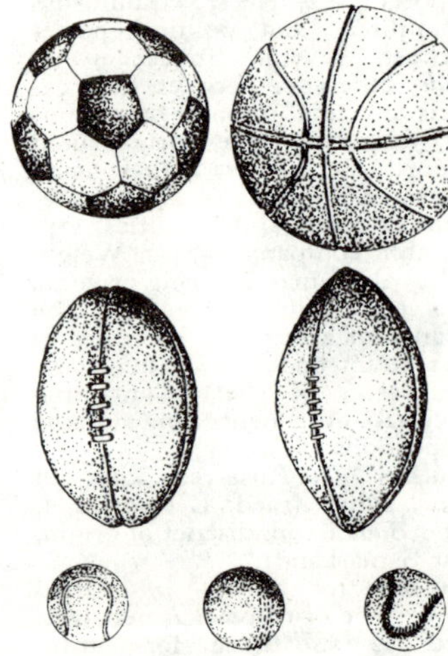

base of great toe, thumb. 2. (cricket) Single delivery of the ball by a bowler. 3. Missile for cannon, rifles, etc. 4. ~ *bearing*, bearing in which revolving parts of a machine turn upon a number of hard balls running in grooves, which diminish friction; one of these balls; ~ *cartidge*, cartridge containing bullet; ~-*cock* device for regulating inflow of water, esp. in cisterns, consisting of a floating ball which rises or falls with the height of the water, thereby shutting or opening a valve through which the water flows in; ~-*flower*, ornament resembling a round bud, carved in hollow of moulding in Gothic architecture; ~-*point* (*pen*), writing instrument having for point a small ball-bearing moistened from a reservoir of semi-liquid ink; ~-*turret*, turret protecting underside of a bomber. ~ *v*. (of snow etc.) Form lumps.

ball[2] (bawl) *n*. Social assembly for dancing; *ba'llroom*, large room suitable for this.

Ball[3] (bawl), John (d. 1381). English priest, one of the leaders of Wat TYLER's rebellion, for his share in which he was executed.

bă'llad *n*. 1. Narrative poem (esp. traditional) designed to be sung, with the same melody for each verse. 2. Any poem in similar style. 3. ~ *metre*: see COMMON metre; ~-*monger*, (contempt.) dealer in ballads. **bă'lladrӯ** *n*. Ballad poetry. [Provençal *ballada* dancing-song]

bălla'de (-ahd) *n*. 1. Poem of one or more triplets of 7- or 8-lined stanzas, each ending with the same line as refrain, followed by an envoy freq. of 4 lines. 2. Piece of esp. lyrical or romantic instrumental music.

bă'llast *n*. 1. Heavy material, as sand or water, placed in a ship's hold or carried in a balloon or airship for stability. 2. Coarse stone, clinker, etc., forming bed of railway or substratum of road. 3. (elect.) Device for stabilizing current. 4. (fig.) Elements of character which give stability. ~ *v.t.* Furnish with ballast.

bălleri'na (-ēn*a*) *n*. Female ballet-dancer (strictly, dancer who takes one or more of certain classical roles).

bă'llet (-lā) *n*. Stage entertainment in which a story is enacted or a dramatic idea expressed by means of dancing to music with the aid of costume and scenery, dating from the late 16th c. and developed principally in France, Italy, and Russia; members of company performing this.

bàllėtomā'nĭa *n*. Enthusiasm for ballet. **bă'llėtomāne** *n*.

ballĭ'sta *n*. (pl. -*ae*). Ancient military engine for hurling stones etc.

ballĭ'stĭc *adj*. Of projectiles; ~ *missile*, *rocket*, one that is powered and sometimes guided in the initial stage of its flight but falls freely. **ballĭ'stĭcs** *n*. Science of projectiles.

ballon d'essai (bălawṅ dĕsā). Experiment to see how a policy etc. will be received. [Fr., = 'trial balloon']

bă'llonĕt *n*. Secondary envelope in a balloon designed to be inflated with air as the buoyant gas is released from the envelope proper.

ballōō'n *n*. Large air-tight envelope of silk or other light material inflated with gas lighter than air so as to rise in the air, sometimes provided with a basket or car slung beneath from a net enclosing the envelope, used for making observations and as an anti-aircraft

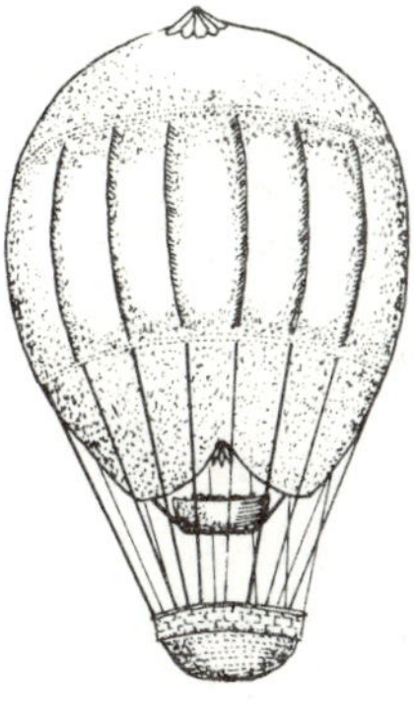

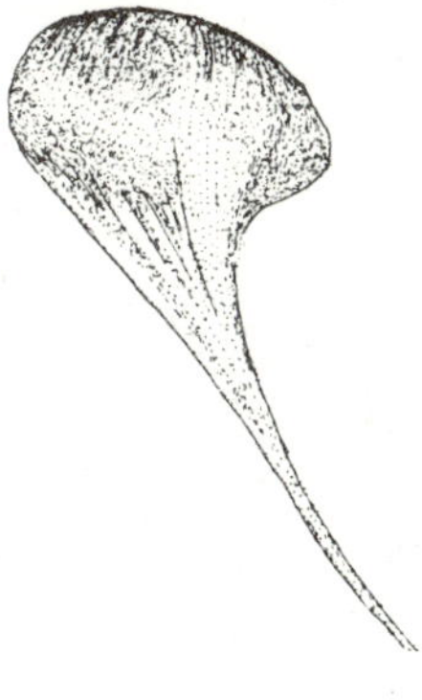

defence; small usu. rubber envelope inflated with air as toy; (colloq.) balloon-shaped outline enclosing speech or thought of character in strip cartoon etc. or added matter for printing etc.; ~ *tyre*, low-pressure motor tyre of large section. ~ *v.t.* Swell out like a balloon (of sails, tyres, etc.).

bă'llot *n.* 1. Secret voting (usu. by placing a voting-paper etc. in a closed ~*-box*). 2. Ball, ticket, or paper used in this. 3. Drawing of lots. ~ *v.i.* Vote by ballot (*for*); draw lots. [It. *ballotta* little ball]

bă'llȳ *adj.* & *adv.* (slang) Euphemism for *bloody*, used as a vague intensive.

băllȳhoo͞' *n.* (orig. U.S.) Advance publicity of vulgar or misleading kind; vulgar advertisement; 'eyewash'.

bă'llȳrăg *v.* Play practical jokes on; indulge in horse-play.

balm (bahm) *n.* 1. Aromatic substance consisting of resin mixed with volatile oils, exuding naturally from various trees; tree yielding this; ~ *of Gilead*, plant or tree of genus *Commiphora* yielding fragrant resinous substance; this substance. 2. Aromatic herb *Melissa officinalis*. 3. Aromatic oil or ointment. 4. Healing or soothing influence.

Bălmŏ'ral[1]. Scottish residence in upper Deeside, Grampian, of the British sovereign.

bălmŏ'ral[2] *n.* 1. Kind of round cap worn by some Scottish regiments. 2. (obs.) Laced walking shoe or boot. 3. (obs.) Kind of striped woollen petticoat.

ba'lmȳ (bahmĭ) *adj.* 1. Of or like balm; fragrant, mild, soothing. 2. (slang) Crazy, silly. **ba'lmĭlȳ** *adj.* **ba'lmĭnėss** *n.*

bă'lnėarȳ *adj.* Of baths or bathing.

ba'lsa (bawl- *or* bŏl-) *n.* Tropical American tree, *Ochroma lagopus*; its wood (~ *wood*, *corkwood*), used for life-belts, model aeroplanes, etc., because of its extreme lightness.

ba'lsam (bawl- *or* bŏl-) *n.* 1. = BALM 1; balm of Gilead; *Canada* ~: see CANADA. 2. Aromatic ointment, of various substances dissolved in oil or turpentine. 3. Tree yielding balm. 4. Flowering plant of genus *Impatiens*, with hooded and spurred coloured sepals and thick succulent stem.

Balt (bawlt *or* bŏlt) *n.* Native or inhabitant of one of the Baltic States of Lithuania, Latvia, and Estonia, esp. a German inhabitant. ~ *adj.*

Bălthă'zar[1]. 1. = BELSHAZZAR[1]. 2. Traditional name of one of the three MAGI, represented as king of Chaldea.

Bălthă'zar[2] *n.* = BELSHAZZAR[2].

Ba'ltic (bawl- *or* bŏl-) *adj.* Of the Baltic Sea, States, or languages; ~ *Exchange*, world market, in

BALMORAL CASTLE

London, for the chartering of cargo ships; ~ *languages*, branch of Indo-European languages containing Lithuanian, Lettish, and Old Prussian; ~ *Sea*, almost land-locked sea in N. Europe, bordered by Sweden, U.S.S.R., Germany, Denmark, etc.; ~ *States*, former independent republics of Estonia, Latvia, and Lithuania. ~ *n.* Baltic Sea.

Ba'ltimōre (bawl- *or* bŏl-). Seaport in N. Maryland; ~ *oriole*, bird of the starling family (*Icterus galbula*) found throughout N. America whose colours, black and orange, are like the coat of arms of Lord Baltimore. [Lord *Baltimore* (d. 1632), English proprietor of territory which later became Maryland]

Balto-Slă'vic, -Slavŏ'nic (bawl- *or* bŏl-) *adjs.* & *ns.* (Of) the group of languages including the Baltic and Slavonic branches.

Balu'chi (-ōō-) *n.* Native or inhabitant of, the Iranian language of, Baluchistan. **Baluchista'n** (-ahn). Mountainous region of southern Asia, forming part of Iran and Pakistan.

bă'luster *n.* Short pillar of circular section and curving outline. [Gk *balaustion* wild-pomegranate flower]

bălustrā'de *n.* Row of balusters with a rail or coping as the parapet of a balcony etc.

Bălzăc, Honoré de (1799–1850). French realistic novelist, whose

'Comédie Humaine' is a long series of novels intended to depict the whole of contemporary French society.

bămbōō' *n.* Tropical giant grass of genus *Bambusa*, with hollow

jointed stem; stem of this as a stick, as material etc.

bămbōō'zle *v.t.* Hoax, mystify.

băn[1] *v.t.* Prohibit, interdict. ~ *n.* Curse, formal prohibition.

ban[2] (bahn) *n.* (pl. -*i* pr. -ē). $\frac{1}{100}$ of a leu.

bana'l (-ahl; *or* bă-; *or* bā'nal) *adj.* Commonplace, trite. **bană'lity** *n.*

bana'na (-ahna) *n.* Tropical fruit-tree, *Musa sapientum*; finger-shaped yellow pulpy fruit of this, growing in clusters or bunches; ~ *republic*, (esp. derog.) any small country whose economy depends on export of fruit. [Port. or Span., f. native name in Guinea]

Banaras: see BENARES.

Bă'nburў. Town in Oxfordshire, formerly noted for the number and zeal of its Puritan inhabitants; ~ *cake*, pastry filled with a currant mixture, orig. made at Banbury.

bănd *n.* 1. Thing that binds, bond (archaic). 2. Strip or hoop of material for supporting or holding things together or for decoration etc.; belt connecting wheels, pulleys, etc.; strip forming part of garment, esp. binding the neck or waist; (pl.) pair of white linen strips worn at neck as part of legal, ecclesiastical, or academic dress. 3. Body of musicians playing together, esp. wind-instrument performers (*brass*, *dance*, *military* ~); organized company or group of persons; *B~ of Hope*, association of people pledged to total abstinence from alcoholic drinks. 4. (elect.) Range of frequencies or wavelengths falling between two limits (also *wave-~*). 5. (phys.) Group of closely spaced lines in a molecular spectrum. 6. (sound-recording) One of several separately recorded sections of a record. 7. *ba'ndbox*, box for hats (orig. for neck-bands); (*adj.*) conspicuously neat and clean; *ba'ndmaster*, conductor of a band of musicians; *~-saw*, endless saw running over wheels *ba'ndsman* member of a military or brass band; *ba'ndstand*, (covered, open-air) platform for musicians; *ba'ndwagon*, (orig. U.S.) wagon carrying the band at the head of a procession; *climb*, *jump*, *on the bandwagon*, join an enterprise that is likely to be successful. ~ *v.* Form into band or league; put a band on; *ba'ndėd*, (bot., zool.) marked with coloured bands or bars.

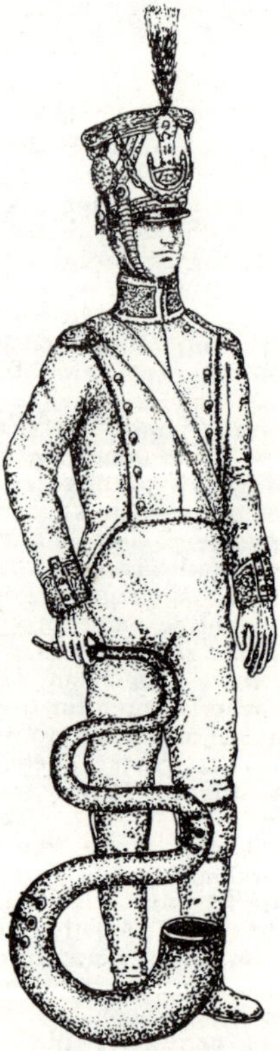

BANDSMAN

bă'ndage *n.* Strip or band of textile material used to bind a wound, sore, etc., or for blindfolding the eyes. ~ *v.t.* Bind up with a bandage.

bändă'nna *n.* Coloured handkerchief with yellow or white spots. [prob. from Hind. *bāndhnū*, a method of dyeing in different colours]

bă'ndeau (-ō) *n.* Band of ribbon etc. round the head; band inside a woman's hat.

Băndĕ'llō, Matteo (1480–1562). Italian writer of short stories.

bă'nderōle *n.* Long narrow flag with cleft end flying from a ship, lance, etc.; ribbon-like scroll; (archit.) feature resembling this and bearing inscription.

Bă'ndersnătch *n.* Fleet furious creature of dangerous propensities in Lewis Carroll's 'Through the Looking-Glass' and 'Hunting of the Snark'.

bă'ndicōōt *n.* 1. Insectivorous and herbivorous Australian marsupial of genus *Perameles*, somewhat rat-like in appearance. 2. (also ~ *rat*) Large rat (*Nesocia bandicota*), up to 1 m in length, found in India. [Telugu]

bă'ndit *n.* (pl. *-s*, *banditti*). Outlaw, brigand; lawless and violent robber, esp. member of an organized gang.

băndoleer', -lier' *n.* Shoulder-belt with loops or pockets for cartridges.

băndolēr'ō *n.* Highwayman, robber.

bă'ndy̆ *v.t.* Throw or pass to and fro; discuss; exchange. ~ *n.*

(obs.) Hockey; hockey-stick. ~ *adj.* (of legs) Curving outwards at the knees; so ~-*legged*.

bāne *n*, Ruin; poison. **bā'neful** *adj.* Poisonous; pernicious; injurious. **bā'nefullÿ** *adv.* **bā'nefulnĕss** *n.*

Bă'nffshire. Former county of NE. Scotland, since May 1975 part of the region of Grampian.

băng[1] *v.* Strike or shut noisily; make sound as of a blow or explosion; thrash. ~ *n.* Sharp blow; loud noise. ~ *adv.* (colloq.) Right, exactly.

bang[2]: see BHANG.

băng[3] *n.* & *v.t.* (Cut *hair* in) a fringe.

bă'nger *n.* (esp., slang) Sausage; noisy old car.

Băngkŏ'k. Capital city of Thailand.

Banglade'sh (bŭ- *or* bŭngg-). Muslim country in SE. Asia, formerly East Pakistan; member State of the Commonwealth, independent since 1971; capital, Dacca. [Bengali, = 'land of Bengal']

bă'ngle (-nggl) *n.* Ring bracelet or anklet.

bani: see BAN[2].

bă'nian, bă'nyan *n.* 1. Hindu trader; (Bengal) native broker to European business house. 2. Indian flannel jacket. 3. (also ~ *tree*) E. Indian fig tree, *Ficus bengalensis*, whose branches root themselves like new trees over a large area (first applied to a particular tree under which banians had built a pagoda).

bă'nish *v.t.* Compel (person) to leave his country; dismiss from one's presence or mind. **bă'nishment** *n.*

bă'nister, bă'nn- *n.* Post supporting hand-rail of a staircase; (pl.) posts and handrail together. [corrupt. of BALUSTER]

bă'njō *n.* (pl. *-os* or *-oes*). Musical instrument having 4, 5, 6, or 7 strings, head and neck like guitar, and body like tambourine, played with fingers or with plectrum; introduced into Europe by Amer. Negroes. **bă'njōist** *n.* [Gk *pandoura* 3-stringed mus. instrument]

bănjule'le (-lālĭ) *n.* Musical instrument combining features of banjo and ukulele.

bănk[1] *n.* 1. Raised shelf of ground; artificial slope. 2. Ground at edge of river. 3. (Flat-topped) mass of cloud. ~ *v.* 1. Contain or confine as or with bank(s). 2. Make (road, track) higher at outer edge of a bend to facilitate cornering at high speeds; (aeronaut.) incline (aircraft) laterally in turning so as to avoid a side-slip; ~ *up*, heap or rise into banks; pack tightly (fire, for slow burning).

bănk[2] *n.* 1. Establishment for custody of money, which it pays out on customer's order; building housing this; *central* ~: see CENTRAL; *savings* ~: see SAVING; ~-*bill*, bill drawn by one bank on another; (U.S.) bank-note; ~-*book*, book showing the state of a customer's account at a bank; ~ *holiday*, day on which banks (and therefore most places of business) are closed by statute; *B~ of England*, London corporation nationalized in 1946, the central bank of England and Wales; ~ *manager*, superintendent of local branch of bank; ~-*note*, banker's promissory note payable to the bearer on demand, used as currency as a substitue for coinage; ~ *rate*, rate at which the Bank of England would discount for its customers approved bills of exchange, regarded as an important indicator of money conditions and used as a basis for fixing certain interest rates in other banks (abolished Oct. 1972). 2. Money-box; *piggy-*~: see PIGGY. 3. Money before keeper of a gaming-table. 4. Store, reserve supply (of blood, tissue, etc.). ~ *v.* Keep a bank; deposit money at a bank; ~ *on*, count or rely on.

bank[3] *n.* Galley-rowers' bench; tier (of oars) in galley; row of organ keys; group of similar objects connected in line.

bă'nker *n.* 1. Proprietor or director of a BANK[2]; keeper of money. 2. Keeper of money staked at gaming-table. 3. Card-game in which punters bet that the bottom card of their pile will have a higher value than the bottom card of the banker's pile.

bănkĕ't *n.* Conglomerate rock containing gold, found in Witwatersrand area of S. Africa. [Du., = kind of hardbake (BANQUET)]

bă'nking *n.* Business of a banker or commercial BANK[2].

bă'nkrŭpt *n.* (law) Insolvent person whose effects, on his own or his creditors' petition to the Bankruptcy Court, are administered and distributed for the benefit of all his creditors; (pop.) any insolvent person; *~'s certificate*, one stating that he has satisfied legal requirements and may re-commence business. ~ *v.t.* Make bankrupt. ~ *adj.* That is a bankrupt; insolvent. **bă'nkruptcy̆** *n.* [It. *banca rotta* broken bank]

Bănks, Sir Joseph (1743–1820). English explorer and natural historian who accompanied James Cook in his voyage round the world in the *Endeavour*, 1768–71.

bă'nksia *n.* Australian shrub of genus *B~* with spicate flowers; ~ (or *banksian*) *rose*, Chinese species of climbing rose bearing small white or yellow flowers in clusters. [f. BANKS]

bă'nner *n.* Rectangular flag of a king, country, army, etc.; strip or piece of fabric bearing emblem or slogan etc.; (also ~ *headline*) newspaper headline in large type, esp. running across whole page.

bă'nneret *n.* Knight with vassals under his banner; one knighted on the field for valour.

bannister: see BANISTER.

bă'nnock *n.* (Sc. & north.) Round flattish loaf usu. of unleavened bread.

Bă'nnockbûrn. Town in Stirlingshire where the Scots under Robert Bruce defeated Edward II and the English coming to the relief of Stirling in 1314.

bănns (-z) *n.pl.* Notice of intended marriage, read three times in church, in order that any objections may be lodged.

bă'nquet *n.* Sumptuous feast; dinner with speeches. ~ *v.* Regale with, take part in, banquet. [Fr., f. It. *banchetto*, dim. of *banco* bench]

bănquĕ'tte (-kĕt) *n.* Firing-step in trenches.

bă'nshee *n.* Spirit supposed by Irish and Highland superstition to wail under the windows of a house in which one of the inmates is about to die. [Ir., = 'fairy woman']

bă'ntam *n.* 1. Small variety of domestic fowl, of which the cock is a spirited fighter. 2. Small but spirited person. 3. *ba'ntamweight*, boxer of weight between flyweight and featherweight (see BOXING). [f. *Bantam*, seaport in W. Java]

bă'nter *n.* Humorous ridicule. ~ *v.* Make good-humoured fun of, rally; jest.

Bă'nting[1], William (1797–1878). English undertaker who advocated a method of reducing weight by dieting.

Bă'nting[2], Sir Frederick Grant (1891–1941). Canadian physiologist, co-discoverer of insulin 1922; Nobel Prize for medicine 1923.

bă'ntling *n.* Brat, young child.

Bă'ntu (-ōō) *n.* (Member of) an extensive group of Negroid peoples inhabiting the equatorial and southern region of Africa; language(s) spoken by them.

Băntusta'n (-ōōstahn) *n.* Any of several reservations for Bantus in S. Africa.

Banville (bahṅvēl), Theodore Faullain de (1823–91). French poet of the Parnassian school.

banyan: see BANIAN (used esp. for the tree).

bā'obăb *n.* African tree, *Adansonia digitata*, naturalized also in Australia, India and Ceylon, having extremely thick stem and large woody fruit with edible pulp, known as 'monkey-bread'.

B.A.O.R. *abbrev.* British Army of the Rhine.

bă'ptism *n.* Religious rite of immersing in or sprinkling with water in sign of moral or spiritual purification or regeneration, and initiation into the (Christian) church; ~ *of fire*, soldier's first experience of battle. **băpti'smal** (-z-) *adj.*

bă'ptist *n.* One who baptizes; *the B~, St. John the B~*: see JOHN[2]; *B~*, member of a Protestant Christian sect, founded early in the 17th c., which holds that baptism should be administered only to believers, not to infants, and by immersion.

bă'ptistery̆, -try̆ *n.* Part of church (or in early times separate building) used for baptism.

băptī'ze *v.t.* Administer baptism to; christen; name.

bâr[1] *n.* 1. Long piece of rigid material; straight strip; heating element of electric fire; *~ tracery*: see TRACERY. 2. Rectangular piece (of soap, chocolate, etc.). 3. Strip of silver below clasp of medal as additional distinction. 4. (mus.) Vertical line across stave dividing composition into sections of equal time-value (also *~ line*); such a section. 5. (her.) Stripe across shield, narrower than fesse; *~ sinister*, erron. for BEND[1] sinister. 6. Rod or pole used to confine or obstruct; bolt or beam for fastening door etc.; = BARRE. 7. Barrier of any shape; bank of sand across mouth of harbour. 8. Barrier limiting access etc.; place in law-court where prisoner stands; (parl.) rail dividing off space to which non-members may be admitted on business; *the B~*, the profession of advocate, barristers in general (from bar in Inns of Court seperating benchers' seats from rest of hall); *be called to the ~*, be admitted a barrister; *be called within the ~* (i.e. that in courts within which Q.C.s plead), be appointed Queen's Counsel. 9. Plea arresting action or claim at law; obstacle; restriction. 10. Counter in inn etc. across which alcoholic drinks or other refreshments are served directly to customers; space behind this or room containing it; place serving refreshments across a counter; *bar'maid, bar'man, bar'tender*, attendant at bar of inn etc. *~ v.t.* 1. Fasten with bars, keep in or out thus; obstruct, prevent; stay (process or party) by legal objection; exclude from consideration; object to, dislike (person etc.). 2. Mark with stripes.

bâr[2] *n.* Unit of barometric pressure, = 10^5 newtons per square metre.

bâr[3] *prep.* Except, excluding.

Bară'bbas. Robber released instead of Jesus Christ (Matt. 27: 16–26).

bărathē'a *n.* Fine cloth of wool or wool and silk or cotton.

bârb[1] *n.* Beard-like feelers of barbel etc.; chin-piece of nun's head-dress; lateral filament branching from shaft of feather; subordinate recurved point of arrow, fish-hook, etc. *~ v.t.* Furnish with barb; *barbed wire*, wire used in fencing and as an obstruction in war, with short

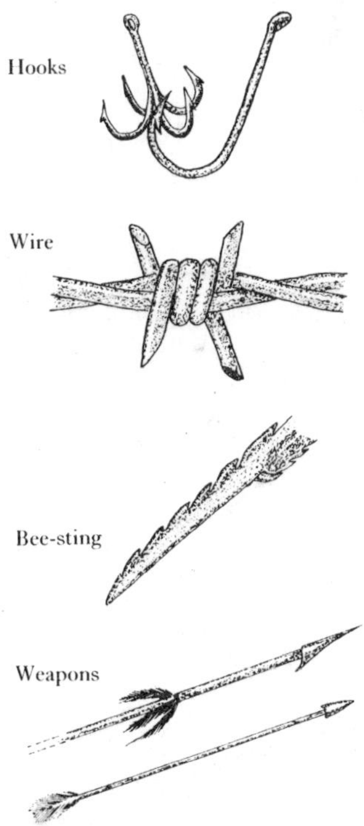

BARB

pointed pieces of wire twisted in at intervals. [L *barba* beard]

bărb² *n.* 1. Horse of the breed imported from Barbary, noted for speed and endurance. 2. Fancy black or dun-coloured pigeon, orig. introduced from Barbary.

Bărbā'dos (-ōz). Island in W. Indies settled by the British 1627, crown colony 1652; member State of the Commonwealth 1966; capital, Bridgetown. **Bărbā'dĭan** *adj.* & *n.*

băr'bara *n.* (logic) First word of the scholastic mnemonic lines for figures and moods of the syllogism.

bărbār'ĭan *n.* 1. Rough, wild, uncultured or uncivilized person (orig. foreigner, one differing in language and customs). 2. (hist.) Non-Greek; person outside the Roman Empire; person outside the civilization of Christendom. ~ *adj.* Of or like a barbarian.

bărbă'rĭc *adj.* Rough, uncultured; of barbarians. **bărbă'rĭcallȳ** *adv.*

băr'barĭsm *n.* Absence of culture; ignorance; (use of) word or expression not in accordance with the classical standard of a language.

bărbă'rĭtȳ *n.* Savage or barbarous cruelty.

băr'barīze *v.* Make, become, barbarous.

Barbarossa: see FREDERICK[1].

băr'barous *adj.* Uncivilized, uncultured, savage. **băr'barouslȳ** *adv.* **băr'barousnėss** *n.*

Băr'barȳ. Old name for the part of N. Africa comprising Morocco, Algeria, Tunisia, and Tripoli; ~ *ape*, large tailless ape of N. Africa and Gibraltar; ~ *sheep*, wild N. Afr. sheep with large horns.

băr'bėcūe *n.* 1. Framework for cooking meat above an open fire; (freq. portable) fireplace with such a framework. 2. Barbecued meat or fish; animal roasted whole; ~ *sauce*, highly seasoned sauce of vinegar, spices, etc. 3. (Open-air) social gathering where barbecue is served. 4. Open floor for spreading out and drying coffee-beans etc. ~ *v.t.* Cook on barbecue or with barbecue sauce. [Haitian *barbacòa* crate on posts]

băr'bel *n.* Large European freshwater fish of genus *Barbus* with fleshy filaments hanging from mouth; such a filament.

băr'ber *n.* Men's hairdresser; ~'*s itch*, skin disease affecting face and neck caused by a fungoid organism and communicated by (unsterilized) shaving apparatus; ~'*s pole*, pole painted spirally with red and white stripes, used as barber's sign.

băr'berrȳ *n.* European shrub of genus *Berberis* with spiny shoots and small yellow flowers; oblong, red, sharply acid fruit of this.

bărbĕ'tte *n.* Platform or mound for mounting guns in a fortification; circular armoured platform with hood protecting heavy guns in warship.

băr'bĭcan *n.* Outer defence to city or castle, esp. double tower over gate or bridge.

bărbĭ'tūrate *n.* (chem.) Salt of barbituric acid; (pharmac.) any of various hypnotic substances derived from barbituric acid. **bărbĭtūr'ĭc** *adj.* ~ *acid*, white crystalline substance ($C_4H_4O_3N_2$) from which barbiturates are derived.

Băr'bĭzon (-zawṅ). Village near Fontainebleau, near Paris, frequented in mid-19th c. by the ~ *School*, a colony of painters (T. Rousseau, Millet, Daubigny, and others) who produced naturalistic pictures of landscapes and peasant life.

bărbō'la *n.* Decorative work of flowers etc. modelled in a plastic paste and coloured.

Băr'bour (-*ber*), John (1316–95). Author of 'The Bruce' (*c* 1375), a long historical poem; regarded as father of Scottish poetry.

băr'carōle, -ŏlle *n.* Gondolier's song; imitation of this.

Bărcėlō'na. City and province of Catalonia, NE. Spain; ~ *nuts*, hazel-nuts imported from France and Portugal.

Băr'chėster: see TROLLOPE.

bârd[1] *n.* Celtic minstrel, (in Wales) poet recognized at the Eisteddfod; poet. **bâr'dic** *adj.*

bârd[2] *v.t.* Cover (meat) with slices of bacon before cooking.

bāre *adj.* Unclothed, uncovered; exposed; unadorned; scanty; mere; unarmed; *bar'eback* (*adj.* & *adv.*) on unsaddled horse; *ba'refaced*, shameless, impudent; *ba'refoot* (*adj.* & *adv.*) with bare feet; *bare-ha'nded* (*adj.* & *adv.*) unarmed. **bār'elỹ** *adv.* Scarcely; only just. **bār'enėss** *n.* **bāre** *v.t.* Make bare, strip, expose.

Barebones Pâr'liament (bār'-bōnz, -lam-). Nickname of Cromwell's 'Little' Parliament (1653), from one of its members, Praise-God Barbon, an Anabaptist leather-seller in Fleet Street.

Bār'ėnts, Willem (d. 1597). Dutch Arctic explorer, after whom is named the ~ *Sea*, the extreme NE. part of the Atlantic Ocean.

bâr'gain (-gĭn) *n.* Agreement on terms of transaction between two parties, compact; thing acquired by bargaining; advantageous purchase; *into the* ~, moreover; *strike a* ~, come to terms. ~ *v.i.* Haggle over terms of transaction; stipulate; ~ *for*, be prepared for, expect.

bârge *n.* Flat-bottomed freight-boat for canals and rivers; large oared vessel for State occasions; house-boat; ~*-pole*, pole with which a barge is propelled. ~ *v.i.* (colloq.) Lurch or rush heavily *into, against*.

bârge- *prefix.* (archit.) Gable: ~*-board*, board or ornamental screen under edge of gable; ~*- couple*, two beams which meet at the point of a gable; ~*-course*, that part of the roof which projects beyond them; ~*-stones*, those forming the sloping or stepped line of a gable. [med. L *bargus* gallows]

bârgee' *n.* Man in charge of barge; *swear like a* ~, swear fluently and forcibly.

barite : see BARYTES.

bă'ritōne *n.* Male voice between tenor and bass; singer with this voice. ~ *adj.*

bār'ium *n.* (chem.) White metallic element, first separated by Sir Humphry Davy in 1808, occurring as the basis of baryta; symbol Ba, at. no. 56, at. wt 137·34; ~ *sulphate*, white, very insoluble heavy powder ($BaSO_4$), opaque to X-rays, used in a mixture (~ *meal* etc.) in radiological examination of the alimentary tract.

bârk[1] *n.* Rind or outer sheath of the trunk and branches of trees; bark used in tanning. ~*v.t.* Strip bark from (tree); abrade (shins etc.).

bârk[2], **bârque** (-k) *n.* Three-masted vessel with fore- and main-masts square-rigged, and mizen fore-and-aft rigged; (poet.) ship, boat.

bârk[3] *v.* (of dogs etc.) Utter sharp explosive cry; make sound like this; speak sharply or petu-

BARK

lantly; (slang) cough; *barking deer*, Indian muntjak, *Cervulus muntjak*, so named from its call. ~ *n.* Sharp explosive cry of dogs, foxes, squirrels, etc.; sound of gunfire; cough.

bar'ker[1] *n.* (esp.) 1. Pistol, gun. 2. Auction-room or side-show tout.

Bar'ker[2], Harley Granville (1877–1946). English dramatic critic, producer, and playwright, author of 'Waste', 'The Madras House', etc.

bar'ley *n.* Awned cereal (*Hordeum distichon* and *H. vulgare*), used as food and in the preparation of malt; grain of this; *bar'ley-corn*, grain of barley; *John Barleycorn*, personification of barley, esp. as the grain from which malt liquor is made; ~*-sugar*, sweet of boiled sugar, freq. shaped in twisted sticks, formerly made by boiling in decoction of barley; ~*-water*, soothing drink made by the decoction of pearl barley.

barm *n.* Froth from fermenting malt liquor, used as leaven; yeast.

Bar'mecide. Patronymic of a noble Persian family who held high offices at Baghdad under Abbasid caliphs; acc. to the 'Arabian Nights', one of them set a number of empty dishes before a beggar, pretending that they contained a sumptuous banquet; hence, ~*'s feast*, imaginary or illusory benefits.

bar'my *adj.* (slang) = BALMY, 2.

barn *n.* Covered building for storing grain (or hay, straw, etc.); ~*-door*, large door of this; target too big to be easily missed; ~*-door fowls*, domestic poultry; ~*-owl*, screech-owl, *Strix flammea*; *bar'nstormer*, strolling player; ~*-yard*, farmyard.

Bar'nabas, St. Joseph, surnamed Barnabas, an early leader of the Christian Church and companion of St. Paul on his missionary journeys (see Acts 4, 9, 11, etc.).

Bar'naby. ~ *bright*, *long* ~, St. Barnabas's Day, 11 June, in the Old Style reckoned the longest day of the year.

bar'nacle[1] *n.* (usu. pl.) Pincers put on a horse's nose to keep him still for shoeing etc.

bar'nacle[2] *n.* 1. Arctic wild goose, *Anas leucopsis*, visiting the British coasts in winter. 2. Crustacean of the sub-class Cirripedia, either with a footstalk (*goose* ~), found attached to ships' bottoms etc., or without a footstalk (*acorn*

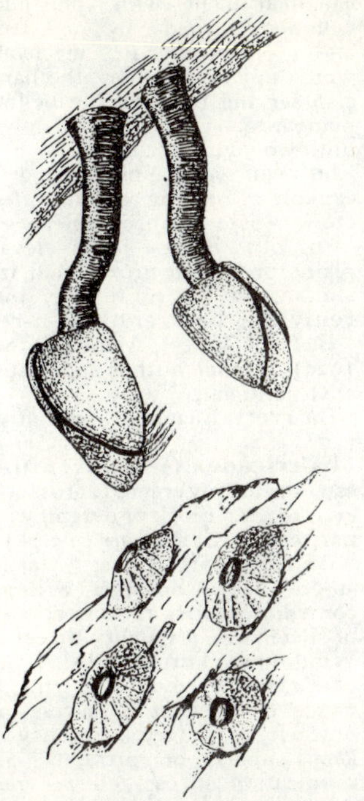

or *rock* ~), found attached to rocks.

Barnar'dō, Thomas John (1845–1905). British philanthropist, founder of homes (named after him) for destitute children.

Barnes (-nz), William (1801–86). Dorsetshire dialect poet.

bă'rogrăm *n.* Record of variations in atmospheric pressure.

bă'rogrăph (*or* -ahf) *n.* Barometer with apparatus (usu. paper roll on drum rotated by clockwork) for making a barogram.

barŏ'mėter *n.* Instrument for measuring atmospheric pressure (and hence for predicting changes in the weather) by means of a tube containing a column of mercury (which rises and falls according to the weight of the atmosphere) or of a vacuum box (see ANEROID ~). **bărométric, -ical** *adjs.* **bărométrically** *adv.*

bă'ron *n.* 1. (hist.) Great noble, noble holding directly from the king by military service; *Barons' War*, revolt (1263–5) of English barons under Simon de Montfort against Henry III. 2. Member of lowest order of nobility in British peerage; holder of foreign title; (orig. U.S.) important financier or merchant (as *beef* ~). 3. ~ *of beef*, joint consisting of two sirloins left uncut at backbone. **bă'ronėss** *n.* Wife, widow, of baron; woman with baronial title in her own right.

bă'ronage *n.* Barons collectively; book with list of barons etc.

bă'ronėt *n.* Member of the lowest hereditary titled order, ranking as a commoner.

bă'ronėtage *n.* List of baronets.

bă'ronėtcy̆ *n.* Baronet's rank or patent.

barō'nĭal *adj.* 1. Of, belonging to, befitting, a baron. 2. *Scotch* or *Scottish B*~, applied to a style of architecture in Scotland in which the upper stories are decorated with corbelled turrets etc.

bă'rony̆ *n.* Baron's rank, domain, or tenure; division of Irish county; large manor in Scotland.

barŏ'que (-k) *adj.* 1. Irregularly shaped (of jewels, esp. pearls); grotesque, odd. 2. Of the style of art which, evolved in Italy *c* 1600 out of that of the Renaissance, prevailed in Europe (chiefly in Catholic countries) until *c* 1720, being characterized by massive and complex design in which architecture was combined with painting, sculpture, etc., and esp. by vigorous, restless or violent movement; of the music or literature of this period. 3. Applied loosely to any style which is held to have similar characteristics. ~ *n.* Baroque style. [Fr., f. Span. *barrueco* rough pearl]

Barŏ'tsė *n.* Negroid people of Zambia; their language. **Barŏ'tsėlănd.** Region of W. Zambia.

bărou'che (-ōōsh) *n.* Four-wheeled horse-drawn carriage with a seat in front for the driver, and seats inside for two couples facing each other.

barque: see BARK², *n.*

barquentine (bar̂′kentēn) *n.* Three-masted vessel with foremast square-rigged and main and mizen fore-and-aft rigged.

bă′rrack *n.* (usu. pl.) Building(s) for lodging soldiers; large building of severely plain, dull, or dreary appearance. ~ *v.* Jeer (at), cheer ironically.

bărracou′ta (-ōōt*a*) *n.* Long narrow edible fish, *Thyrsites atun*, found in waters of S. Australia, New Zealand, and S. Africa (where it is called *snoek*).

bărracu′da (-ōōd*a*) *n.* Voracious fish of family Sphyraenidae, 2–3 m long, found in warm seas.

bă′rrage (-ahzh) *n.* 1. Artificial bar in river or watercourse. 2. (mil.) Obstacle to offensive or defensive action on part of an enemy, usu. in form of a line, area, or volume into which high-explosive shells are fired from a large number of guns either continuously or for pre-arranged periods; ~ *balloon*, large balloon supporting steel cable in an almost vertical position, esp. as one of a series forming anti-aircraft defence; *creeping* ~, one laid down in front of an advance of one's own troops and moving with them.

bă′rrator *n.* One who vexatiously incites to litigation or raises discord.

bă′rratrў *n.* 1. Purchase or sale of ecclesiastical preferments or offices of State. 2. Vexatious persistence in or incitement to litigation. 3. Fraud or gross and criminal negligence of ship's master or crew to the prejudice of the owners and without their consent. **bă′rratrous** *adj.*

bar̂re *n.* Hand-rail at waist level used by dancers to maintain balance while exercising.

bă′rrel *n.* 1. Wooden vessel of curved staves bound by hoops, with flat ends; contents or capacity of such a vessel. 2. Revolving cylinder in capstan, watch, etc. 3. Cylindrical body of object; belly and loins of horse. 4. Metal tube of firearm, through which the missile is projected. 5. ~-*organ*, musical instrument with pinstudded cylinder turned by a handle and operating a mechanism which opens the pipes, the handle also serving to work the bellows; piano organ; ~ *vault*, vault with uniform concave roof.

bă′rren *adj.* Not bearing, incapable of bearing (children, fruit, etc.); waste; unprofitable. ~ *n.* (usu. pl.) Barren land; elevated plains on which grow small trees and shrubs, but no timber. **bă′rrenlў** *adv.* **bă′rrennėss** (-n-n-) *n.*

Barrès (bărĕz), Maurice (1862–1923). French author and Nationalist politician.

Bă′rrett, Elizabeth: see BROWNING[1].

bă′rricāde *n.* (Defensive) barrier, esp. one hastily erected across street etc. ~ *v.t.* Block or defend with a barricade. [Span. *barrica* cask]

Bă′rrie, Sir James Matthew (1860–1937). Scottish writer of comedies and short stories, author of 'Peter Pan', 'Quality Street', 'A Window in Thrums', etc.

bă′rrier *n.* Fence barring advance or preventing access; any obstacle, boundary, or agency that keeps apart, or prevents communication, success, etc.; ~ *cream*, cream that protects the skin against dirt, corrosive substances, etc.; ~ *reef*, high wall of coral rock separated from land by a broad deep channel and with a precipitous face on the seaward side, esp. the *Great B~ Reef*, off E. coast of Australia, some 1,100 miles long and 30 broad.

bă′rrister *n.* Student of law, who, having been called to the Bar (see BAR[1] *n.* 8), has the privilege of practising as advocate in the superior courts of law.

bă′rrow[1] (-ō) *n.* Prehistoric grave-mound, tumulus.

bă′rrow[2] (-ō) *n.* Rectangular frame with short shafts for carrying loads; shallow box with two shafts and one wheel, small two-wheeled handcart; ~ *boy*, costermonger.

bar̂′rў[1] *adj.* (her.) Divided horizontally by bars.

Bă′rrў[2], Sir Charles (1795–1860).

Architect (with A. W. Pugin) of the English Houses of Parliament.

Bar'săc *n.* White wine, less sweet than most Sauternes, produced at Barsac, adjoining the district of Sauternes, in the Gironde.

Bar'sėt, Bar'sėtshire. Imaginary county in novels of Anthony Trollope, containing Barchester.

Bart *abbrev.* Baronet (commonly written after the name of one who holds that rank, to distinguish him from a knight).

bar'ter *v.* Exchange (goods, rights, etc.) *for* things of like kind. ~ *n.* Traffic by exchange.

Barth (-t), Karl (1886–1968). Swiss Protestant theologian.

Barthŏ'lomew, St. One of the 12 Apostles, commemorated on 24 Aug.; *Massacre of St.* ~, massacre of Huguenots throughout France ordered by Charles IX at the instigation of his mother Catherine de Médicis and begun without warning on the feast of St. Bartholomew, 1572; *St.* ~*'s Hospital*, (colloq. *Bart's*) London hospital founded 1123 by the English monk Rahere, prebendary of St. Paul's.

bartiză'n *n.* Battlemented parapet, or overhanging battlemented corner turret, at top of castle or church tower. [Coined by Sir W. Scott from misunderstanding of an illiterate Sc. spelling of *bratticing* parapet]

Bar'tŏk, Béla (1881–1945). Hungarian composer and collector of Hungarian folk-music.

Bartolommeo (-mā'ō) di Pagholo, Fra (1475–1517). Florentine painter.

Bartolŏ'zzi (-tsĭ), Francesco (1727–1815). Italian engraver (after Holbein etc.), active chiefly in England.

bar'ton *n.* (archaic) Farmyard.

Bart's. (colloq.) St. Bartholomew's Hospital, London.

Bar'uch (-ōōk). Book of the Apocrypha, attributed in the text to Baruch, the scribe of Jeremiah (Jer. 36).

bă'ryon *n.* (phys.) Elementary particle whose mass is equal to or greater than that of a proton.

bă'rўsphēre *n.* Core of the earth, consisting of a very heavy substance, prob. nickel iron.

barȳ'ta *n.* Barium monoxide, an alkaline earth distinguished by its great density.

barȳ'tēs (-z) *n.* (also *bar'ite*) Barium sulphate, heavy spar, used as a white paint.

bă'rȳtōne *n.* 1. = BARITONE. 2. Brass wind instrument of saxhorn family, used in military bands. 3. (hist.) Stringed instrument resembling viola da gamba. 4. (Gk gram.) Barytone word. ~ *adj.* 1. = BARITONE. 2. (Gk gram.) With no or grave accent on last syllable.

bā'sal *adj.* Of or at the base. **bā'sallȳ** *adv.*

bă'salt (-awlt *or* basaw'lt) *n.* Dark-coloured fine-grained rock occurring as a lava or as an intrusion, often showing columnar structure, as at the Giant's Causeway in N. Ireland. **basa'ltic** *adj.*

bă'sanīte *n.* Smooth fine-grained black variety of quartz; touchstone.

bă'scūle *n.* Lever apparatus used in ~ *bridge*, kind of drawbridge balanced by a counterpoise which rises or falls as the bridge is lowered or raised, as the Tower Bridge, London.

bāse[1] *adj.* Morally low, mean, ignoble, debased; menial; ~*-born*, of low birth; illegitimate; ~ *metals*, those which quickly corrode or tarnish (opp. NOBLE OR PRECIOUS *metals*). **bā'selȳ** *adv.* **bā'senėss** *n.*

bāse[2] *n.* 1. That on which anything stands or depends; support, foundation, principle, groundwork, starting-point, principal element; substance used as first layer (of paint, make-up, etc.). 2. (biol.) End at which an organ is attached to trunk. 3. (geom.) Line or surface on which a plane or solid figure is held to stand. 4. (surv., also ~*-line*) Known line used as geometrical base for trigonometry. 5. (math.) Starting-number for system of numeration or logarithms (as 10 in decimal counting). 6. (chem.) Antithesis of ACID, substance capable of combining with an acid to form a salt (including, but wider than, ALKALI). 7. (archit.) Part of column between shaft or pedestal and pavement. 8. (mil.) Town or other area in rear of any army where drafts, stores, hospital, etc., are concentrated. 9. (gram.) Form of a word to which suffixes are attached. 10. One of the four corners of the diamond in baseball. 11. ~-*line*, (surv.) see sense 4; line at end of court in lawn tennis; *ba'seman*, fielder at base in baseball. ~ *v.t.* Found or establish *on*.

bā'seball (-sbawl) *n.* National field-game of U.S., played between two teams of nine players on a diamond-shaped field with four bases round which the batter runs in order to score; ball used in this game.

bā'selėss (-sl-) *adj.* Groundless, unfounded.

bā'sement (-sm-) *n.* Lowest part of a structure; inhabited storey partly or wholly below ground-level.

basĕ'nji *n.* Small hunting dog of African breed which rarely barks.

băsh *v.t.* Strike heavily so as to smash *in*. ~ *n.* Heavy blow; *have a* ~ (*at*), (slang) attempt.

Bā'shan. Ancient kingdom beyond Jordan, conquered by Israelites under Moses (Num. 21: 33), and famous for its cattle (Ps. 22: 12, Amos 4: 1).

bă'shful *adj.* Shy, sheepish. **bă'shfullў** *adv.* **bă'shfulnėss** *n.*

băshi-bazou'k (-o͞ok) *n.* (hist.) Mercenary soldier of Turkish irregular troops, notorious for lawlessness, plundering, and brutality. [Turk. *başıbozuk* irregular soldier, not in uniform]

bā'sic *adj.* 1. Of, forming, or serving as a base or basis, fundamental; ellipt. (as *n.*) basic allowance, pay, etc. 2. (chem.) Having the chemical properties of a base. 3. (min., of igneous rocks) Having little silica in proportion to the amount of lime, potash, etc. 4. Applied to processes of steel manufacture from phosphoric pig-irons and to the steel thus produced; ~ *slag*, slag from this process, used finely ground as a fertilizer because of its phosphorus and manganese content. 5. *B~ English*, system of English comprising a select vocabulary of 850 words, devised by C. K. Ogden of Cambridge as a medium of international communication. **bā'sicallў** *adv.*

bāsi'citў *n.* (chem.) Number of equivalents of a base with which one molecule of an acid can react.

basidiomў'cēte *n.* Fungus producing basidiospores, e.g. mushroom and toadstool.

basi'diospōre *n.* (bot.) Spore borne at the extremity of a basidium.

basi'dium *n.* (pl. -*dia*). Spore-bearing structure in some fungi.

bă'sil[1] (-z-) *n.* Aromatic herb of the genus *Ocimum*, esp. *sweet* ~ (*O. basilicum*) and the dwarf *bush* ~ (*O. minimum*), the leaves of which are used for flavouring soups, salads, etc. [L *basilisca* the plant (supposed antidote to basilisk's bite)]

Bă'sil[2] (-z-), St. (*c* 330–79). Doctor of the Church, founder of a monastic rule which is still the basis of monasticism in the Orthodox Church.

basi'lic (-z-) *adj.* ~ *vein*, large vein of the upper arm.

basi'lica (-z-) *n.* 1. (in ancient Rome) Large oblong building used as exchange or law-court, having an apse at one or each end and freq. side-aisles; colonnaded hall, resembling this, in Roman house. 2. Church of similar shape, having a wide nave with aisles, and an apse at one (orig. western) end. **basi'lican** *adj.* [Gk *basilika* (*oikia*) royal (house), f. *basileus* king]

bă'silisk (băz-) *n.* 1. Cockatrice, fabulous reptile hatched by a serpent from a cock's egg, said to kill by its breath or glance. 2. Small Amer. lizard of the family Iguanidae, with a hollow crest that can be inflated at will. [L *basilicus* kind of lizard, f. Gk *basiliskos* little king]

bā'sin (-sn) *n.* 1. Circular or oval vessel of greater width than depth and with sloping or curving sides, for holding water etc.; contents of a basin. 2. Hollow depression; circular or oval valley; tract of country drained by river and its tributaries. 3. = DOCK[3] 1, 2; land-locked harbour. **bā'sinful** *n.*

bā'sĭs *n.* (pl. *basēs*). Base; foundation, beginning, determining principle; main ingredient; common ground for negotiation etc.

bask (-ah-) *v.i.* Revel in warmth and light (*in* the sun, firelight, etc.); *basking shark*, one of the largest species of shark, *Cetorhinus maximus*, found in northern seas, so called from its habit of lying near surface of water.

ba'skėt (bah-) *n.* Receptacle of plaited or interwoven canes, osiers, etc.; contents of this; ~ *ball*, ball game played with inflated ball which is tossed into baskets suspended from posts; ~ *chair*, chair made from wickerwork; *B~ Maker*, member of an ancient Amer. Indian culture of south-western U.S., preceding the Pueblo; *ba'sketwork*, interlaced osiers, twigs, etc.

Basle (bahl). (Ger. *Basel*, Fr. *Bâle*) Town and canton of Switzerland.

basque[1] (bahsk) *n.* Short continuation of bodice below waist; bodice having this.

Basque[2] (bahsk) *adj.* & *n.* (Member) of a people inhabiting both slopes of the W. Pyrenees and speaking a non-Indo-European language; (of) this language.

băs-rėlie'f (-lēf; *or* bah-) *n.* Low relief, carving or modelling in which figures project less than one half of their true proportions from the background.

băss[1] *n.* (pl. *bass* or *-es*). Any of a large group of perch-like fishes in sea or fresh water including *sea-~* (family Serranidae), *white ~* (*Roccus chrysops*), *yellow ~* (*Morone interrupta*), etc.

bāss[2] *adj.* Deep-sounding; of, suited to, lowest part in harmonized music; having a voice extending 1½ octaves or more below middle C; ~ CLARINET, DRUM, FLUTE, see these words; ~ *clef*: see CLEF; ~ *viol*, viola da gamba. ~ *n.* Bass part; music for, singer with, bass voice.

bass[3]: see BAST.

bă'ssėt *n.* (also *~-hound*) Short-legged dog of breed originating in France, used in hunting hares or badgers, followed on foot.

bă'ssėt-hôrn *n.* Tenor clarinet, of somewhat greater compass than the ordinary clarinet.

băssinĕ't *n.* Hooded wicker cradle or perambulator.

bă'ssō *adj.* & *n.* (mus.) Bass; ~ *profundo*, (singer having) deep bass voice.

bassōō'n *n.* Double-reed musical instrument, the bass of the wood-wind family, having an 8-ft pipe turned back so that the whole instrument measures only 4 ft; organ or harmonium stop of similar quality.

Băss Rŏck. Rock 350 ft (106 m) high, off coast of E. Lothian; in 17th c. the site of a prison; now a bird sanctuary.

băst, băss[3] *ns.* Inner bark of lime or linden-tree, which, cut into strips and coarsely plaited, is used for matting etc.; similar fibre obtained from leaf-bases or leaf-stalks of certain palms and used for ropes, brooms, etc.; any flexible or fibrous bark.

bă'stard (*or* bah-) *n.* Person born out of wedlock; hybrid, counterfeit thing; used as term of abuse, or sometimes merely = fellow. ~ *adj.* **bă'stardy̆** *n.*

bă'stardīze (*or* bah-) *v.t.* Declare or render bastard.

bāste[1] *v.t.* Sew together loosely, sew with long loose stitches, tack.

bāste[2] *v.t.* 1. Moisten (roasting meat etc.) by pouring over it melted fat, gravy, etc. 2. (colloq.) Thrash, cudgel.

Băsti'lle (-tēl). (hist.) 14th-c. prison-fortress in Paris, used for political and other prisoners, stormed and destroyed by the mob on 14 July 1789; the anniversary

of its fall, as marking the end of absolute monarchy in France and the beginning of the French Revolution, is the national holiday of republican France.

băstĭnā'dō *n.* & *v.t.* (Punish with) caning or cudgelling on the soles of the feet.

bă'stĭon *n.* Mass of masonry or brick- or stone-faced earthwork projecting from fortification in the form of an irregular pentagon; (fig.) stronghold.

Basu'to (-ōō-) *n.* (Member of) a S. African people of Bantu stock.

băt[1] *n.* Small nocturnal mammal of the order Chiroptera, resembling a mouse, with leather-like wings consisting of a membrane stretched from neck over forearms and elongated fingers, and along sides of body to hind-limbs and (usu.) tail; *have ~s in the belfry,* (slang) be insane; hence *bats,* (slang) insane.

băt[2] *n.* Wooden implement with handle and striking surface, esp. that used in cricket; long, round stick with handle at one end used in baseball and other games; signalling object resembling table-tennis bat used for guiding landing aircraft; (slang) blow, knock; *ba'tsman,* player with bat in cricket etc.; man who signals with bats held in the hands. ~ *v.* Use bat, have innings (in cricket etc.).

băt[3] *v.t.* (colloq.) Blink; *not to ~ an eye(lid),* (fig.) be unperturbed.

băt[4] *n.* (slang) Pace.

batā'ta (*or* -aht*a*) *n.* Sweet potato.

Batā'vĭa. 1. Former name of DJAKARTA. 2. (hist.) Region between Rhine and Waal, inhabited in Roman times by a Celtic tribe, the Batavi. 3. (literary, poet.) The Netherlands. **Batā'vĭan** *adj.* & *n.*

bătch *n.* Quantity of loaves etc. baked at one time; quantity, number, or set of people or things associated together, esp. in time.

bāte[1] *v.* Let down; restrain (breath); deduct; fall off in force.

bāte[2] *n.* (school slang) Rage.

bă'teau (-tō) *n.* (pl. *bateaux* pr. -ōz). Light river-boat, esp. the long, tapering, flat-bottomed boat used by French Canadians.

bath[1] (-ah-) *n.* 1. Immersion in liquid for cleansing or therapy; exposure to air etc. for therapy; water etc., for bathing. 2. Vessel, room (also *ba'throom*), or (usu. pl.) building for bathing in; (usu. pl.) swimming-bath. 3. Spa re-

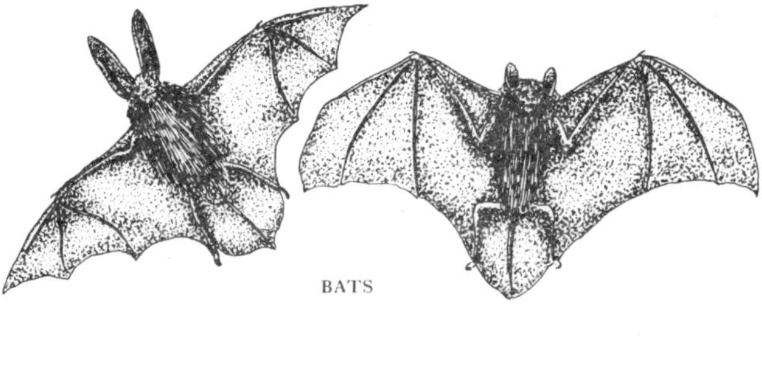

BATS

sorted to for medical treatment by bathing etc. 4. *Order of the B~*, high order of British knighthood, founded 1725 as revival of the 'Knights of the Bath' first created 1399 at coronation of Henry IV and so named from the ceremonial bath which preceded installation. ~ *v.* Wash in bath.

Bath[2] (-ah-). City in county of Avon (since 1974), noted for its hot springs; site of a Roman city (Aquae Sulis) and baths; a medicinal spa since 17th c., in 18th c. a fashionable resort; university, 1966; *~-brick*, calcareous earth moulded into a brick, used for cleaning metal; ~ *bun*, round, spiced currant-bun with sugar-icing; ~ *chair*, wheeled chair for invalids; ~ *chap*, pickled lower half of pig's cheek; ~ *Oliver*, unsweetened biscuit said to have been invented by William Oliver (1695–1764) a physician of Bath; ~ *stone*, oolite building-stone.

Bath: et Well: *abbrev.* (Bishop) of Bath and Wells (replacing surname in his signature).

bāthe (-dh) *v.* Immerse (in liquid, air, etc.); moisten all over; envelop; go swimming; *ba'thing-costume*, *-dress*, etc., garment for bathing or swimming in; *ba'thing-machine*, small hut on wheels, formerly used by sea-bathers for undressing and dressing. ~ *n.* Taking of bath, esp. in sea, river, or swimming-bath. **bā'ther** *n.*

bă'tholith *n.* Large body of intrusive rock (e.g. granite) such as is found esp. along Pacific coast of America.

bā'thŏs *n.* Fall from sublime to ridiculous; anticlimax. **bathĕ'tĭc** *adj.*

Băthshē'ba. Wife of Uriah the Hittite (2 Sam. 11); she became one of the wives of David and the mother of Solomon.

bă'thÿscăphe, -scăph *n.* Vessel for deep-sea diving and exploration. [Fr., f. Gk *bathus* deep+

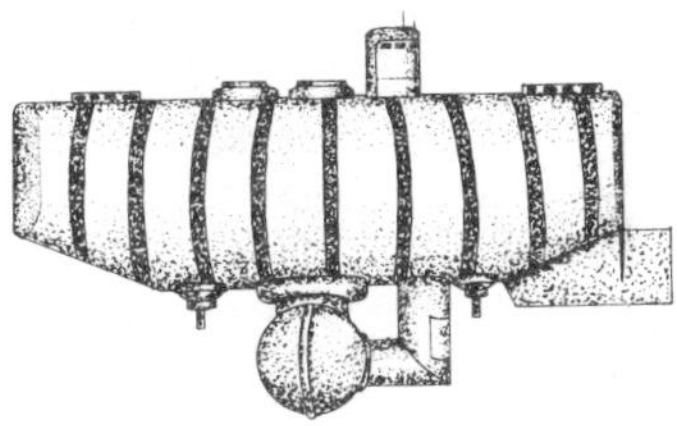

skaphos ship; coined by A. Piccard (1884–1962), Swiss physicist]

bă'thÿsphēre *n.* Spherical diving apparatus for deep-sea observation.

bă'tĭk *n.* Javanese method, practised also in the West, of executing designs on textiles by

BATH

painting parts of the pattern in wax, dyeing the parts left exposed, and then removing the wax; material dyed thus. [Javanese = 'drawing']

bati'ste (-ēst) *n.* Fine light cotton fabric of same texture as cambric, but differently finished; fine smooth woollen fabric. [Fr., f. *Baptiste* of Cambrai, first maker]

bă'tman *n.* (fem. *bă'twoman*). Member of army or air force acting as officer's servant. [orig. man who carried officer's baggage (Fr. *bât* pack-saddle)]

bă'ton *n.* 1. Staff of office, esp. *Marshal's* ~; constable's truncheon. 2. (her.) Ordinary like a narrow bend broken off at the extremities, in English heraldry only as ~ *sinister*, = BEND[1] sinister. 3. (mus.) Conductor's wand for beating time. 4. Short rod passed from one runner to another in a relay race. 5. Stroke replacing figure on face of clock or watch. ~ *v.t.* Strike with baton or truncheon.

batrā'chĭan (-k-) *adj.* & *n.* = ANURAN.

battă'lĭon *n.* Large body of men in battle array; unit of infantry, consisting of four companies and an H.Q. company and forming part of a brigade.

bă'ttels (-z) *n.pl.* College account at Oxford for board and provisions supplied, or for all college expenses.

bă'tten[1] *n.* 1. Long thin piece of squared timber used for flooring, hanging roof-tiles, etc. 2. (naut.) Strip of wood, esp. used to fasten down edges of hatchway tarpaulin in bad weather. ~ *v.t.* Strengthen, fasten *down*, with battens.

bă'tten[2] *v.i.* Feed gluttonously *on*; grow fat, (fig.) thrive at another's expense.

bă'tter[1] *v.* Strike repeatedly so as to bruise or break; beat out of shape; handle severely; *battered baby*, young child with injuries which appear to have been inflicted by a parent; *battering-ram*, heavy beam anciently used for breaching walls, sometimes with ram's-head end. ~ *n.* 1. Mixture of flour and eggs beaten up with liquid for cooking. 2. Defect in printing type or stereotype plate.

bă'tter[2] *v.i.* (of walls etc.) Incline from perpendicular so as to have a receding slope. ~ *n.* Slope of wall etc. from the perpendicular.

bă'tter[3] *n.* Batsman, esp. in baseball.

bă'ttery̆ *n.* 1. (law) Infliction of blows or the least menacing touch to clothes or person. 2. (mil.) Set of guns with their men, horses, and vehicles; group of guns on a warship; unit of artillery consisting of two troops and forming part of an artillery regiment. 3. Set of similar or connected instruments, utensils, etc.; cell or set of cells supplying electricity; series of individual cages in which laying hens, cattle, etc., are confined.

bă'ttle *n.* Combat, esp. between large organized forces; *line of* ~, troops or ships drawn up to fight; *line-of-~ ship*, (obs.) battleship of 74 or more guns; *~-axe*, kind of long-handled axe used as a medieval weapon; prehistoric stone weapon; (fig.) formidable or domineering woman; *~-cruiser*, large, fast, and heavily armed cruiser; *~-cry*, war-cry; slogan; *ba'ttledress*, (formerly) soldier's etc. everyday uniform of blouse and trousers; *ba'ttlefield*, scene of battle; *ba'ttleship*, warship of the largest and most powerfully armed class. ~ *v.i.* Struggle *with* or *against*.

Bă'ttle A'bbey (ă-) Abbey founded by William the Conqueror (1069) on site of battle of Hastings; ~ *Roll*, document, prob. compiled in 14th c., which purports to show the names of families which came over to England with William; extant versions date from the 16th c.

bă'ttledōre *n.* Wooden, stringed, or parchment bat like a small racket for striking shuttlecock; ~ (*and shuttlecock*), game played with this by two persons who strike the shuttlecock to and fro between them. [prob. f. Span. *batallador* champion]

bă'ttlement (-lm-) *n.* Indented parapet at top of wall etc., orig. for purposes of defence against assailants.

băttū'e (*or* -ōō) *n.* Driving of game from cover towards point where sportsmen are stationed to shoot them; wholesale slaughter, esp. of unresisting crowds.

bă'ttȳ *adj.* (slang.) Crazy.

bau'ble *n.* 1. Showy trinket. 2. Baton surmounted by fantastic head with asses' ears carried by Court fool or jester.

Baudelaire (bōdlār), Charles Pierre (1821–67). French lyric poet, author of 'Les Fleurs du Mal' (1857).

Bauhaus (bow'hows). School of design founded by Walter Gropius (1883–1969) in Weimar in 1919; closed in 1933.

baulk: see BALK.

Baumé (bōmā), Antoine (1728–1804). French chemist; inventor of a hydrometer and two scales for use in measuring the specific gravity of liquids.

bau'xīte (bŏks-) *n.* Hydroxide of alumina, one of the chief sources of aluminium. [originally found at *Les Baux* near Arles, France]

Bavār'ia. Former State of S. Germany, now a province of the Federal Republic; capital, Munich.

Bavār'ian *adj.* & *n.*

baw'bee *n.* (Sc.) Halfpenny.

bawd *n.* (archaic) Procuress.

baw'dȳ *adj.* Humorously vulgar or indecent; ~*-house*, brothel. ~ *n.* Bawdy language; bawdiness.

baw'dĭlȳ *adv.* **baw'dĭnėss** *n.*

bawl *v.* Shout at the top of one's voice; ~ *out*, (slang) reprimand severely.

Băx, Sir Arnold Edward Trevor (1883–1953). English composer.

bay¹ *n.* 1. Kind of laurel, esp. the sweet bay or bay laurel, *Laurus nobilis*, with deep-green leaves (used to flavour soups etc.) and many dark-purple berries. 2. (usu. pl.) Wreath of bay leaves as a garland for a conqueror or poet. 3. (also *bay'berry*) West-Indian tree, *Pimenta acris*; ~ *-rum*, aromatic liquid made from its leaves, used as an astringent.

bay² *n.* Part of sea filling wide-mouthed opening of land; ~ *salt*, salt obtained from sea-water by evaporation.

bay³ *n.* 1. Division of wall between columns or buttresses. 2. Recess; compartment; *sick-*~, part of main deck used as hospital; part of building similary used. 3. Space added to room by advancing window from wall line; ~ *window*, window in a bay. 4. Railway platform having a cul-de-sac and serving as terminus for a sideline; the cul-de-sac itself; ~ *-line*, side-line starting from this.

bay⁴ *n.* Bark of large dog or of hounds in pursuit, esp. as they draw near the quarry; *at* ~, in great straits; *stand, be, at* ~, show fight, turn against pursuers. ~ *v.* (of large dog) Bark, bark at.

bay⁵ *adj.* (of horse) Having body of light to dark brown, with black mane and tail. ~ *n.* Bay horse; *the Bays*, the 2nd Dragoon Guards, who were mounted on bay horses *c* 1767.

bayadère (-ār') *n.* Hindu dancing-girl.

Bay'ârd, Pierre du Terrail, Seigneur de (1473–1524). French soldier of great valour and generosity, known as the knight 'sans peur et sans reproche'; hence (also *b*~), gentleman of high courage and honour.

Bayeux tă'pėstrȳ (bāyẽr). Long strip of embroidered linen at Bayeux Cathedral, containing scenes representing the Norman Conquest of England, with which it is usu. held to be nearly contemporary.

Bayle, Pierre (1647–1706). French philosopher and sceptic, author of a 'Dictionnaire historique et critique' (1695–7), which had great influence on Voltaire and other 18th-c. French sceptics.

bay'onėt *n.* 1. Stabbing blade which may be attached to rifle muzzle. 2. Cap on base of electric lamp etc. which engages with a

BAYEUX TAPESTRY

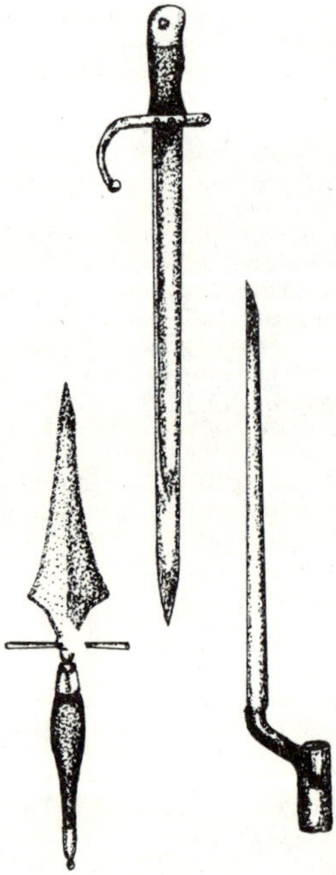

BAYONETS

shaped slot in a corresponding socket. ~ *v.t.* Stab with bayonet.

bayou (bī′o͞o) *n.* (U.S.) Marshy inlet or creek of river or sea in southern states of U.S.

Bayreuth (bī′roit *or* bīroi′t). Bavarian town in which Wagner festivals are held in a theatre specially built for the production of his operas.

bazaar′ (-zâr) *n.* Oriental market-place or permanent market; fancy shop; fancy fair, esp. sale of goods for charities. [Pers. *bāzār* street of shops]

bazo͞o′ka *n.* (U.S.) 1. Crude, pipe-shaped musical instrument. 2. Amer. infantry light tubular projector for armour-piercing (esp. anti-tank) rockets.

BB, BBB *abbrevs.* Double-, treble-, black (of pencil-lead).

B.B. *abbrev.* Boys' Brigade.

B.B.C. *abbrev.* British Broadcasting Corporation.

B.C. *abbrev.* Battery Commander; before Christ; British Columbia.

B.C.E. *abbrev.* Before the Common Era.

B.Ch. *abbrev.*: see CH.B.

B.C.L. *abbrev.* Bachelor of Civil Law.

B.Com. *abbrev.* Bachelor of Commerce.

B.D. *abbrev.* Bachelor of Divinity.

bdĕ'llium (d-) *n.* Any of several trees or shrubs, chiefly of the genus *Commiphora*, yielding a gum-resin resembling impure myrrh, of bitter or acrid taste and more or less agreeable smell; the resin itself.

Bdr *abbrev.* Bombardier.

bds *abbrev.* Boards (in bookbinding).

bē (*unstressed* bĭ) *v.i.* (past t. *was, were*, past part. *bēen*). Exist, occur; remain, continue; have a certain state or quality (specified by following noun, adj., etc.); *~-all* (*n.*) whole being, essence; esp. in *be-all and end-all*, absolutely everything, the whole *of*; *~ off*, go away.

B.E.A. *abbrev.* British Epilepsy Association.

beach *n.* Sandy or pebbly shore of the sea (or lake or large river); *~-comber*, (orig. U.S.) long wave rolling up from the sea; white man in Pacific Islands who lives by pearl-fishing, collecting jetsam, etc.; *~-head*, fortified position of troops landed on a beach. *~ v.t.* Run (ship etc.) ashore, haul up.

beach-la-mar̄ *n.* Jargon English used in the W. Pacific. [Port. *bicho do mar* sea-worm]

bea'con *n.* 1. Signal, signal-fire on hill or on pole raised above building. 2. Conspicuous hill suitable for the lighting of beacons. 3. Lighthouse; conspicuous object; (also *Belisha ~*) one of a pair of amber-coloured globes on poles marking certain crossing-places on highways. 4. Radio station enabling ship or aircraft to fix position.

Bea'consfield (bĕkonz-). Town in Buckinghamshire, England; *Earl of ~* (bēk-): see DISRAELI.

bead *n.* 1. Small perforated ball etc. for threading with others on a string or for sewing on to fabric; small bubble or drop of liquid; (pl.) rosary. 2. Small metal knob forming front sight of gun (*draw a ~ on*, take aim at). 3. (archit., also *beading*) Narrow cylindrical moulding sometimes carved to resemble a row of beads; so *~-and-reel*. 4. *~-roll* list or string of names, catalogue. *~ v.* Furnish or adorn with beads or a beading. [OE, 'prayer' from the use of strings of beads for keeping count of the number of prayers said]

bea'dĭng *n.* see BEAD *n.* 3.

bea'dle *n.* 1. (hist.) Inferior parish officer appointed to keep order in church, punish petty offences, and carry messages, etc. 2. Apparitor or precursor who walks officially in front of dignitaries, mace-bearer (in the Engl. universities usu. spelt *bedel(l)*).

bea'dledom *n.* Stupid officiousness.

bea'dsman (-z-) *n.* (hist.) One who prays for the soul or spiritual welfare of another, one paid to do this; hence, pensioner or almsman, inmate of alms-house. [see BEAD etym.]

bea'dȳ *adj.* (of eyes) Small and bright like beads.

bea'gle *n.* Small hound for hunting hares, followed on foot.

bea'glĭng *n.* Hunting with beagles.

beak[1] *n.* Horny projecting mandibles of bird; extremities, often horny in structure, of mandibles of other animals; hooked nose; projection at prow of ancient ships, esp. war-galleys; spout; *bea'khead*, one of a series of grotesque beaked heads carved as ornament on moulding in Romanesque architecture.

beak[2] *n.* (slang) Magistrate; master at public school.

bea'ker *n.* 1. Large drinking-cup. 2. (archaeol.) Wide-mouthed vessel found in graves of a neolithic people (*~ folk, ~ people*) who came to Britain from Europe in the second millennium B.C. 3. Straight-sided lipped glass for scientific experiments.

beam *n.* 1. Long piece of squared timber such as is used in house- or ship-building; horizontal support in building. 2. Great timber of plough, to which all other parts of plough-tail are fixed. 3. Wooden cylinder in loom on which the warp is wound 4. Transverse bar of balance; *~ compass*, compasses with transverse bar. 5. Transverse horizontal timber of a ship; hence, the greatest breadth of a ship; *on the* ~, at right angle to direction of ship. *on her* ~*-ends*, (of ship) lying on its side and in danger of capsizing; *on one's* ~*-ends*, (fig.) extremely hard-up. 6. Ray or pencil of light, or of electric radiation, etc.; (also *radio, wireless* ~) radio waves sent as a beam (i.e. not dispersed or broadcast) by a special aerial system, part of which acts as a reflector; (aeron.) directional radio signal used to guide aircraft or missiles; course indicated by this; (phys.) directional flow of radiation or particles. 7. Radiance, bright look, smile. ~ *v.* Emit (light, affection, etc.); direct, aim (radio signals etc.); shine, smile radiantly.

bean *n.* 1. Kidney-shaped non-endospermic seed borne in pods of the family Leguminosae. 2. Similar seed of other plants, as coffee. 3. (slang) *not a* ~, no money; *old* ~, familiar form of address; *full of* ~*s*. in high spirits; *give a person* ~*s*, deal severely with him; *spill the* ~*s*, give away information. 4. ~*-feast*, annual dinner given by employers to their workpeople; fête, merry time; *bea'nstalk*, stem of the bean-plant. ~ *v.t.* (U.S. slang) Hit on the head.

bea'nō *n.* (slang) Bean-feast.

bear[1] (bār) *n.* 1. Heavily-built, thick-furred plantigrade quadruped of family Ursidae; child's toy in shape of this, Teddy bear. 2. Rough, unmannerly or uncouth person. 3. (Stock Exch.) Speculator for a fall, one who sells stock for future delivery hoping to buy it cheaper in the interval; ~ *market*, one with falling prices. 4. *Great, Little B*~: see URSA. 5. ~ *animalcule*: see TARDIGRADE; ~*-garden*, orig. place for baiting bears; scene of strife and tumult; *bear'skin*, Guards'tall furry cap; ~ *leader*, travelling tutor to a rich young man. **bear'ish** *adj.* Rough-mannered, surly; (of stock market or prices) tending to fall. **bear** *v.* (Stock Exch.) Speculate for, cause, a fall in price of stocks etc.

bear[2] (bār) *v.* (past t. *bōre*, past part. *bōrne* exc. as below). 1. Carry, support; ~ *out*, confirm. 2. Endure, tolerate; ~ *up*, keep up one's courage; ~ *with*, be patient with. 3. (past part. usu. *born* in passive) Give birth to. 4. Produce, yield. 5. Apply weight; tend, incline; *bring to* ~, apply; ~ *down*, press downwards; (naut.) sail to leeward; ~ *down on*, move towards; ~ *hard on*, oppress, ~ *on*, relate to.

beard *n.* Hair upon lower part of man's face (now usu. excluding moustache and whiskers); chin tuft of animals; gills of oyster; awn of grasses; (print.) part of type above and below face which allows for ascending and descending letters. **bear'dless** *adj.* Youthful, immature. **beard** *v.t.* Oppose openly, defy.

Bear'dsley (-dzlĭ), Aubrey Vincent (1872–98). English artist and illustrator, chiefly in black and white; art editor of the 'Yellow Book'.

bear'er (bār-) *n.* 1. Bringer of letter etc., presenter of cheque; one who helps to carry coffin; ~ *bond, security*, etc., one not registered, the title to which is vested in its possessor. 2. (eng.) Plate or beam supporting load.

bear'ing (bār-) *n.* (esp.) 1. Behaviour. 2. Heraldic charge or device. 3. Relation, reference, aspect; tendency to exert influence *on*. 4. Part of machine that bears the movement. 5. Situation or direction of one point, object, etc., with respect to another; determination of this; (pl.) relative position (also fig.). 6. ~*-rein*, fixed rein from bit to saddle forcing horse to arch its neck.

beast *n.* 1. Animal; quadruped as dist. from birds, man, insects, etc.; bovine animal; animal used for riding, driving, etc. 2. Human being acting like an animal; brutal, savage man; person one dislikes.

bea'stly̆ *adj.* Like a beast or its

ways; unfit for human use, dirty; (colloq.) undesirable, unpleasant, annoying. **bea'stliness** *n.*

beat *v.* (past. t. *beat*, past part. *beaten* and occas. *beat*). 1. Strike repeatedly; (of sun etc.) strike *upon.* 2. Overcome, surpass; be too hard for, perplex; *dead* ~, (slang) utterly exhausted. 3. (of wings etc.) Move up and down; (of heart etc.) pulsate, throb; ~ *it*, (slang) go away; ~ *time*, mark the time of music by the beat of a wand, tapping with the foot, etc. 4. Shift, drive, alter, deform, or shape by blows; (also ~ *up*) mix to a froth or paste by turning (mixture etc.) over and over with a circular motion. 5. Strike bushes etc. to rouse game. 6. ~ *up*, (naut.) strive or tack against the wind; ~ (person) *up*, (colloq.) attack and injure him by blows and kicks. ~ *n.* 1. Stroke on drum; signal so given; movement of conductor's baton; measured sequence of strokes or sounds; throbbing. 2. Sentinel's or constable's appointed course; habitual round. 3. Idle worthless fellow (U.S.); (colloq.) = BEATNIK.

bea'ten *adj.*: see BEAT; (esp.) ~*gold* etc., gold etc. hammered into foil, shaped by the hammer; ~ *track, way*, well-trodden way (also fig.).

bea'ter *n.* (esp.) Man employed to rouse game; man who beats gold etc.; implement which beats, as *carpet-*~, *egg-*~, etc.

beat gĕnerā'tion. Young people (esp. after 1939–45 war) adopting unconventional dress, manners, habits, etc., as a means of self-expression and social protest. [Prob. f. *beat* = 'exhausted'; perh. infl. by *beat* = 'rhythm'; but coined by J. Kerouac (b. 1922), U.S. novelist, connecting *beat* with *beatitude*]

bēati'fic *adj.* Making blessed, imparting supreme happiness; blissful.

bėă'tifȳ *v.t.* Make supremely happy or blessed; (R.C. Ch.) declare to be in enjoyment of heavenly bliss (as the first step towards canonization). **bėătificā'tion** *n.*

bėă'titūde *n.* 1. Supreme blessedness; declaration of blessedness, esp. (pl.) those pronounced by Jesus Christ in the Sermon on the Mount (Matt. 5: 3–11). 2. (*B*~) Title of clergy of Orthodox Church of patriarchal rank.

bea'tnik *n.* Member of the beat generation.

Bē'atrice. Dante's name for a lady whom he loved, although he never spoke to her; he tells of his few meetings with her in the 'Vita Nuova', and in the 'Divina Commedia' she is his guide through Paradise; she represents for him the type of ideal love.

Bea'ttȳ, David, Earl (1871–1936). Naval officer, commander of the British battle-cruiser fleet at the battle of Jutland, 1916.

beau (bō) *n.* Fop; lady's-man, woman's male escort; *B*~ *Brummell, B*~ *Nash*: see these names.

Beau'fort scāle (bōf-). Series of numbers used by meteorologists to indicate force of wind (measured at 10 m above level ground), thus:

Force	*m.p.h.*		*knots*
0	less than 1	calm	less than 1
1	1–3	light air	1–3
2	4–7	light breeze	4–6
3	8–12	gentle breeze	7–10
4	13–18	moderate breeze	11–16
5	19–24	fresh breeze	17–21
6	25–31	strong breeze	22–27
7	32–38	near gale	28–33
8	39–46	gale	34–40
9	47–54	strong gale	41–47
10	55–63	storm	48–55
11	64–72	violent storm	56–63
12	73 or more	hurricane	64 or more

[devised by Admiral Sir F. *Beaufort* (1774–1857)]

beau geste (bō zhĕst). Display of magnanimity. [Fr., = 'beautiful (or splendid) gesture']

beau idė'al (bō; *or* -ē'al). One's highest type of excellence or beauty. [Fr. (*idéal*), = 'the ideal Beautiful', often misconceived in English as a beautiful ideal]

Beaujolais (bō'zholā *or* -ŏlā) *n.* Red or white Burgundy from the Beaujolais district in the Rhône department of France.

Beaumarchais (bōmărshā), Pierre Auguste Caron de (1732–90). French dramatist, author of two famous comedies, 'Le Barbier de Séville' (1775), 'Le Mariage de Figaro' (1778).

beau monde (bō mawṅd). Fashionable society.

Beau'mont (bōm-), Francis (1584–1616). English playwright, collaborator with John FLETCHER from *c* 1606 to 1616.

Beaune (bōn) *n.* Red wine produced near Beaune in the Côte d'Or district of France.

beau'tėous (būt-) *adj.* (archaic & poet.) Endowed with beauty.

beautician (būtĭ'shan) *n.* (U.S.) One who runs a beauty parlour; specialist in beauty treatment.

beau'tĭful (būt-) *adj.* Having beauty; capital, excellent. **beau'tĭfullȳ** *adv.* **beau'tĭful** *n.* *the* ~, beauty in the abstract.

beau'tĭfȳ (būt-) *v.t.* Make beautiful.

beauty (bū'tĭ) *n.* Combination of qualities (as form, colour, etc.) that delights the eye; combined qualities delighting the other senses, the moral sense, or the mind; beautiful trait or feature; person or thing possessing beauty; ~ *parlour*, place where the business of applying cosmetics, face-massage, and other beauty treatment is carried on; ~ *sleep*, sleep obtained before midnight; ~-*spot*, small patch placed on woman's face as foil to a beautiful complexion; beautiful scene; ~ *treatment*, use of massage, cosmetics, exercise, etc., in order to improve personal beauty.

bea'ver[1] *n.* 1. Amphibious rodent of genus *Castor* with broad, oval, horizontally flattened tail, webbed hind feet, soft fur, and hard incisor teeth with which it cuts down trees, remarkable for its industry esp. in constructing dams of wood and mud; *eager* ~, (colloq.) zealous person. 2. Soft, short, rather woolly light-brown fur of this animal; hat made from this.

Bea'verbrŏŏk, William Max-

BEAUNE

well Aitken, 1st Baron (1879–1964). British newspaper proprietor and Conservative politician.

bē'bŏp *n.* Kind of jazz music.

bėca'lm (-kahm) *v.t.* Make calm; deprive (ship) of wind.

bėcau'se (-ŏz) *adv.* By reason *of* ~ *conj.* For the reason that.

Béchamel sauce (bā'shamĕl). Rich white sauce. [f. its inventor, Marquis de *Béchamel*, steward of Louis XIV]

bêche-de-mer (bĕsh, mār) *n.* = TREPANG.

Bĕchūa'na (-k-, -ahna; *or* -ch-). *n.* = TSWANA.

bĕck[1] *n.* (north.) Brook, mountain stream.

bĕck[2] *n.* Significant gesture, nod, etc.; *at the* ~ *and call of*, entirely dominated by, completely at the service of. ~ *v.* (poet.) Make beck (to).

bĕ'ckėt[1] *n.* (naut.) Loop of rope or other simple contrivance for securing loose ropes, tackle, or spars, and for holding or securing the tacks or sheets of sails etc.

Bĕ'ckėt[2], St. Thomas à (1117–70). Archbishop of Canterbury (1162) and Chancellor of England (1158) under Henry II; he successfully opposed Henry's policy in taxation and other matters, and was murdered by Henry's orders, in Canterbury Cathedral; he was canonized in 1173, and his shrine became the most famous in Christendom; it was destroyed in 1538.

Bĕ'ckėtt, Samuel (1906–). Irish novelist and dramatist, many of whose works are written in French; author of the play 'En attendant Godot' (1952, transl. 'Waiting for Godot', 1954); Nobel Prize for literature 1969.

Bĕ'ckford, William (1759–1844). English eccentric; author of 'Vathek', an Oriental novel in French (1787).

bĕ'ckon *v.* Summon, call attention of, by gesture; make mute signal *to*.

bėclou'd *v.t.* Cover with clouds, obscure.

bėco'me (-ŭm) *v.* (past t. *became*, past part. *become*). 1. Come into being; begin to be; ~ *of*, (past t. & fut.) happen to (as in *what has, will, become of him?*). 2. Suit, befit, look well on. **bėco'ming** *adj.* Suitable; (of clothes etc.) giving pleasing appearance. **bėco'minglȳ** *adv.*

Becquerel (bĕkerĕl), Antoine Henri (1852–1908). French physicist; discoverer of radioactivity; Nobel Prize for physics 1903; ~ *rays*, rays emitted by a radioactive substance.

bĕd *n.* 1. Thing to sleep or rest on; mattress; framework with mattress and coverings; animal's resting-place, litter; *go to* ~ *with*, (esp.) have sexual intercourse with. 2. Flat base on which anything rests; foundation of road or railway; garden-plot for plants; bottom of sea, river etc.; stratum. 3. ~*-bug*: see BUG; *be'dchamber*, (archaic) bedroom; *be'dclothes*, sheets, pillows, blankets, etc., of bed; *be'dfellow*, sharer of bed; (fig.) associate; *be'dgoer*, (formerly) one who accompanied monarch to his bedchamber as protection against assassins, (now) title of an official; *be'dlinen*, sheets and pillowcases; *be'dpan*, shallow pan for containing excreta, used by persons confined to bed; ~*-plate*, metal plate forming base of machine. *be'dpost*, upright support of bedstead; ~*-ridden* (*adj.*) confined to bed by infirmity; ~*-rock*, solid rock underlying alluvial deposits etc.; also fig.; *be'droom*, room for sleeping in; *be'dside*, side esp. of invalid's bed; ~*-si'tting-room*, (colloq. ~*-si'tter*) combined bedroom and sitting-room; *be'dsore*, sore developed by long lying in bed; *be'dspread*, coverlet; *be'dstead*, framework of bed; *be'dstraw*, plant of genus *Galium* with slender stem and small clustered flowers; *be'dtime*, hour for going to bed. ~ *v.* 1. Put or go to bed; provide bedding for horses etc. 2. Plant *out* in a garden bed. 3. Cover up or fix firmly in something; (eng.) fit accurately. 4. Arrange as, be or form, a layer.

B.Ed. *abbrev.* Bachelor of Education.

bėdă'bble *v.t.* Splash with liquid.

bėdau'b *v.t.* Smear or daub with paint, mud, etc.

bĕ'ddĭng *n.* (esp.) 1. Mattress and bedclothes; litter for horses etc. to sleep on. 2. (geol). Layered structure visible in some rocks resulting from their deposition in water in layers or beds.

Bēde, St. (*c* 673–735). English historian and scholar, a monk of Jarrow; author of a Latin history of the English Church and many other works in Latin; known since 9th c. as 'the Venerable ~'.

bėdĕ'ck *v.t.* Adorn.

bĕ'dėguar (-gâr) *n.* Kind of gall caused by the puncture of an insect, *Cynips rosae*, and forming a moss-like excrescence on rose-bushes. [Pers. *badawar* brought by the wind]

bedel(l): see BEADLE.

bėdĕ'vil *v.t.* Torment diabolically, bewitch. **bėdĕ'vilment** *n.* Possession by devil; maddening trouble, confusion.

bėdew' *v.t.* Cover with drops of or like dew.

Bĕ'dfordshire. E. midland county of England.

bėdĭ'm *v.t.* Make dim, obscure.

bėdī'zen *v.t.* Deck out gaudily.

Bĕ'dlam[1]. (hist.) Popular name for the hospital of St. Mary of Bethlehem, founded as a priory in 1247 in Bishopsgate, and used as a hospital for lunatics; it was removed to Moorfields, then to Lambeth, and finally to Beckenham.

bĕ'dlam[2] *n.* 1. (hist.) Lunatic asylum. 2. Scene of uproar. **bĕ'dlamīte** *n.* (hist.) Lunatic.

Bĕ'dlĭngton *n.* (also ~ *terrier*) Curly-haired, grey terrier with narnow head, short body, and longish legs. [*Bedlington* in Northumberland]

Bĕ'douĭn, bĕ'douĭn (-ōō-) *n.* (pl. same). Arab of the desert. [Arab. *badawiyyūn*, oblique case *badawiyyīn* desert-dwellers]

bėdră'ggle *v.t.* Wet (dress etc.) by trailing it, or so that it trails or hangs limp.

Beds. *abbrev.* Bedfordshire.

bee *n.* 1. Hymenopterous four-winged stinging insect living in societies composed of one queen, a small number of drones, and a number of workers, who produce wax and collect honey, which they store up in wax cells for winter food. 2. Any of a large group of allied insects. 3. (chiefly U.S.) Meeting of neighbours to unite their labours for the benefit of one of them; gathering or meeting for some object, esp. for a competition in spelling (*spelling-* ~). 4. ~ *in one's bonnet*, eccentric whim, craze on some point; ~*-bread*, honey and pollen eaten by nurse-bees; *bee'hive*, HIVE; domed structure resembling one type of hive; ~*-line*, straight line between two points, such as a bee is supposed to make returning to the hive; *bee'swax* (*n.* & *v.t.*) (polish with) wax secreted by bees (see WAX[1], 1); *bee'swing*, crust of shiny filmy scales of tartar formed on port and some other wines after long keeping.

beech *n.* Forest-tree of Europe and W. Asia (genus *Fagus*) with fine thin smooth bark, glossy oval leaves, boughs and foliage which form a dense canopy, and three-sided nuts borne in pairs in a rough or prickly involucre; its wood; any of various other trees more or less resembling this; ~*-marten*, marten (*Martes foina*) of Europe and Asia, with white patch on breast and throat, stone-marten; ~*-mast*, beech nuts collectively. **bee'chen** *adj.* Of beech or beechwood.

beef *n.* Flesh of ox, bull, or cow used as food; ox, any animal of the ox kind; (slang) complaint, ground for this; *bee'featers*, (f. obs. sense of 'dependants') pop. name of Yeomen of the Guard and of warders of the Tower of London, who wear the same uniform; ~*-steak*, slice of beef cut from hind-quarters and suitable for grilling, frying, etc. ~ *tea* ,stewed beef juice for invalids.

bee'fў *adj.* Solid, muscular;

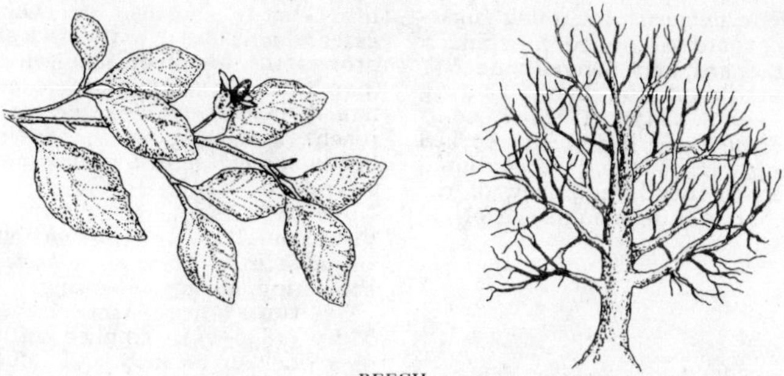

BEECH

stolid. **beef** *v.i.* (slang) Complain, grumble.

Bēē'lzėbŭb. Canaanite god, mentioned in 2 Kings 1 : 2 as the 'god of Ekron', and in the N.T. as 'prince of demons'; the Devil. [Heb. *ba'al-z^{e}b̲ûb̲* fly-lord]

been: see BE.

beer *n.* Alcoholic liquor made from fermented malt flavoured with hops, ale; (in trade usage) any of the liquors brewed from malt, as ale, stout, porter, lager; (pop.) ale as distinct from the others; *small* ~, weak beer; (fig.) trifling matter or person; *~-engine,* apparatus for drawing beer from the barrel in the cellar to the tap in the bar of a public house.

Beer'bohm (-bōm), Sir Max (1872–1956). English author and caricaturist.

beer'y̆ *adj.* Of or like beer; betraying its influence.

bee'stings (-z) *n.pl.* First milk drawn from a cow after parturition.

beet *n.* (pl. same). Any of several plants with edible roots (varieties

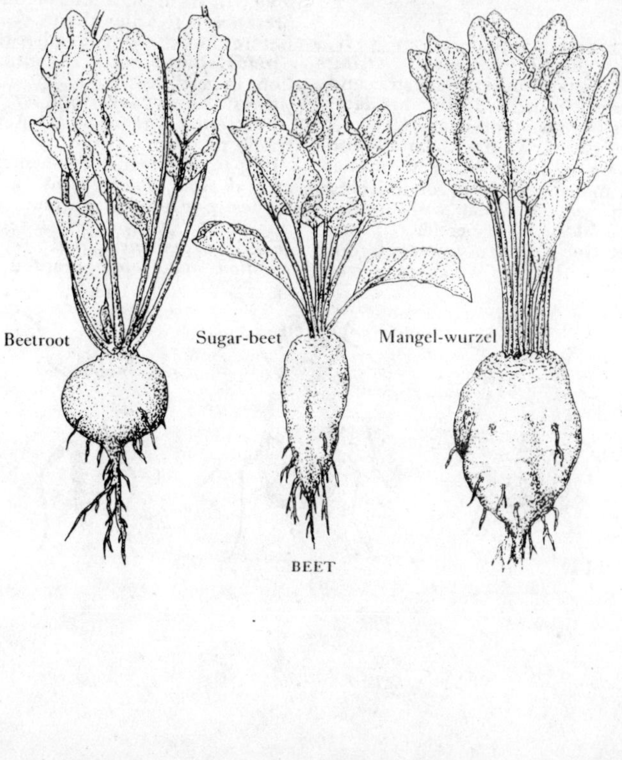

BEET

of *Beta vulgaris*), including sugar-beet, garden beetroot, spinach beet, chard, and mangel-wurzel.

Beethoven (bā′tōvn), Ludwig van (1770–1827). German composer of Flemish descent; worked mainly in Vienna; contributed much to the development of the symphony and other musical forms;

wrote nine symphonies, an opera, many pianoforte sonatas, string quartets, and other orchestral and chamber music; during his later years he was stone-deaf.

bee′tle[1] *n.* Tool with handle and heavy head for crushing, ramming, etc., mallet; machine for finishing cloth. ~ *v.t.* Beat with beetle; finish (cloth) with beetle.

bee′tle[2] *n.* 1. Any coleopterous insect with front wings converted into hard sheaths or wing-cases which close over the back and protect the lower or true wings; (pop.) insect resembling these, esp. largish black one; *black-~*, cockroach. 2. Dice-game in which a beetle-shaped figure is drawn or assembled.

bee′tle[3] *v.i.* 1. Overhang threateningly. 2. Go *off* etc. ~ *adj.* (in ~ *brows*, *~-browed*) Projecting, shaggy, scowling.

Bee′ton (-tn), Mrs. Isabella Mary (1836–65). English author of a book of cookery and household management, first published serially 1859–61.

bee′troot *n.* **(pl. same). Crimson root of garden beet, used in salads etc.**

B.E.F. *abbrev.* British Expeditionary Force.

bėfa′ll (-awl) *v.* Happen, happen to.

bėfĭ′t *v.t.* Be suited to, become.

bėfŏ′g *v.t.* Envelop in fog; confuse, obscure.

bėfōō′l *v.t.* Make a fool of, dupe.

bėfôr′e *adv.* Ahead; in front; at an earlier time, already. ~ *prep.* In front of, ahead of; in the presence of; earlier than. ~ *conj.* Before the time when; rather than.

bėfôr′ehănd *adv.* In anticipation, in readiness.

bėfou′l *v.t.* Make foul.

bėfrie′nd (-rĕnd) *v.t.* Act as friend to, help.

bĕg *v.* 1. Ask for (food, money, etc.) as alms; live by alms. 2. Ask earnestly or humbly, entreat. 3. (of dog etc.) Sit up with forepaws raised expectantly. 4. ~ ***the question***, take for granted the

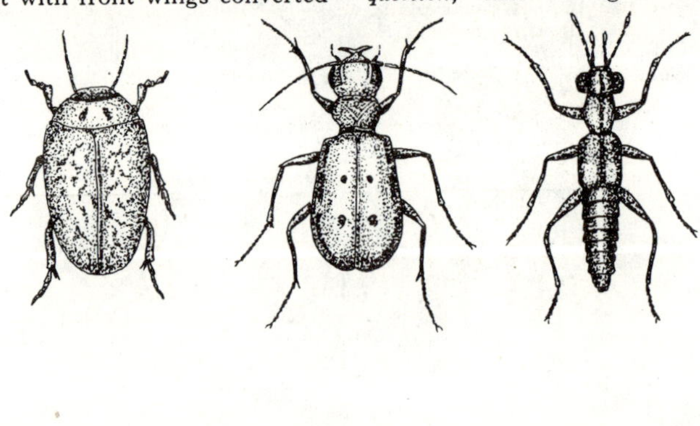

matter in dispute, assume by implication what one is trying to prove.

bėgĕ'́t *v.t.* (past t. *begŏ't*, past part. *begŏ'tten*). Procreate (usu. of father); give rise to, occasion. **bėgĕ'tter** *n.*

bĕ'ggar *n.* One who begs, esp. one who lives by begging; poor person; (colloq.) fellow. ~ *v.t.* Reduce to poverty; exhaust resources of; *~-my-neighbour*, simple card-game in which the object of each player is to acquire all the cards.

bĕ'ggarlȳ *adj.* Needy, poverty-stricken; mean, sordid, intellectually poor.

bĕ'ggarȳ *n.* Extreme poverty.

Bĕ'ghard (-gerd) *n.* Member of lay brotherhoods which arose (in imitation of the BÉGUINES) in the Low Countries in 13th c.; the name was soon adopted by many who were simply idle mendicants, and from the 14th c. the brotherhoods were denounced by Popes and Councils and persecuted by the Inquisition; in the 17th c. those which survived were absorbed in the Tertiarii of the Franciscans.

bėgi'n *v.* (past t. *begă'n*, past part. *begŭ'n*). Start, perform first part of, set about; be the first; originate; come into being, arise. **bėgĭ'nner** *n.* (esp.) Tiro, learner. **bėgĭ'nnĭng** *n.* (esp.) Time at which anything begins; source, origin; first part.

bėgĭr'd *v.t.* (past part. *begirt*) Gird, encircle.

bėgŏ'ne *v.imp.* Be off, away with you (also occas. as infin.).

bėgō'nĭa *n.* Tropical plant of genus *B~*, having flowers with brightly coloured perianths (but no petals) and often richly coloured foliage; often cultivated as an ornamental plant. [Michel *Bégon*, Fr. patron of science (1638–1710)]

begotten: see BEGET.

bėgrī'me *v.t.* Make grimy.

bėgrŭ'dge *v.t.* Grudge.

bėgui'le (-gīl) *v.t.* Delude; cheat; charm, amuse; divert attention from (passage of time etc.). **bėgui'lement, bėgui'ler** *ns.*

Béguine[1] (bāgē'n) *n.* Member of certain lay sisterhoods, small communities of which still exist esp. in Belgium, first founded in the Netherlands in the 12th c., who devoted themselves to a religious life but did not bind themselves by strict vows. [f. Lambert *Bègue* (or *le bègue* the stammerer), the founder]

bėgui'ne[2] (-gēn) *n.* S. Amer. dance; kind of syncopated dance rhythm.

bē'gum *n.* Indian Muslim woman of high rank. [Turk. *bīgam*, fem. of *beg* lord]

begun: see BEGIN.

bėha'lf (-ahf) *n.* Part, account, or interest *of*.

bėhā've *v.i.* & *refl.* Act in a particular way (~ *well*, *badly*, etc.); show good manners.

bėhā'viour (-yer) *n.* Manners, conduct, way of behaving. **bėhā'vioural** *adj.*

bėhā'viourĭsm (-yer-) *n.* Psychological doctrine, based on the objective study of behaviour, that all human actions admit of analysis into stimulus and response. **bėhā'viourĭst** *n.*

bėhea'd (-hĕd) *v.t.* Cut off the head of.

beheld: see BEHOLD.

bėhē'moth *n.* Enormous creature; in Job 40: 15, prob. the hippopotamus.

bėhĕ'st *n.* Command.

bėhī'nd *adv.* In or to the rear; past, too late; in concealment; in arrear. ~ *prep.* In or to the rear of; hidden by; supporting. ~ *n.* The buttocks.

bėhī'ndhănd *adv.* & *pred. adj.* Late; backward, out of date.

Behn (bān), Mrs Aphra (1640–89). English dramatist and novelist, author of 'Oroonoko'.

bėhō'ld *v.t.* (past t. & past part. *behĕ'ld*). (archaic & rhet.) See; take notice, attend. **bėhō'lder** *n.*

bėhō'lden *pred. adj.* Under obligation *to*.

bėhōō'f *n.* (archaic) Benefit, advantage.

bėhō've, bėhōō've *v.t. impers.* Be incumbent on; befit.

Behring: see BERING.

beige (bāzh) *n.* Yellowish-grey colour of unbleached wool. ~ *adj.* Of colour of beige.

bē'ing *n.* (esp.) Existence; constitution, nature, essence; anything that exists; person.

bĕl[1] *n.* Unit, = 10 decibels. [A. G. BELL[2]]

Bĕl[2]. (Babylonian & Assyrian myth.) = BAAL; ~ *and the Dragon*, book of the Apocrypha, included as part of Daniel in the Vulgate.

bėlā'bour (-ber) *v.t.* Thrash.

Bela Kun: see KUN.

bėlā'tėd *adj.* Coming late. **bėlā'tėdlў** *adv.*

bėlau'd *v.t.* Load with praise.

bėlay' *v.t.* Coil (running rope) round cleat etc., to secure it; *imp.* (naut.) stop!; *belaying pin*, fixed wooden or iron pin for belaying on.

bĕl că'ntō. Singing in the Italian manner, characterized by full rich tone and accomplished technique. [It.]

bĕlch *v.* Emit wind noisily from stomach through mouth; utter noisily or drunkenly; (of gun or volcano) emit (fire, smoke, etc.). ~ *n.* Belching.

bĕ'lcher *n.* Neckerchief with blue ground and large white spots having a dark-blue spot in the centre. [James *Belcher* (1781–1811), English prize-fighter]

bĕ'ldam, -dame *n.* Old woman, hag; virago.

bėlea'guer (-ger) *v.t.* Besiege.

bĕ'lemnīte *n.* Common fossil, occurring in Mesozoic rocks, consisting of the hard part of an extinct marine animal similar to the squid, freq. torpedo-shaped and up to 304 mm long. [Gk *belemnon* dart]

Bĕlfa'st (-ahst). Seaport in Ulster, capital city of N. Ireland; centre of the Irish linen industry; university, 1908.

bĕ'lfrў *n.* Bell tower; room or storey in which the bells are hung

Bĕ'lgian (-jan) *adj.* & *n.* (Native or inhabitant) of Belgium.

Bĕ'lgic *adj.* Of the Belgae, an ancient people of N. Gaul.

Bĕ'lgium (-jum). Small kingdom of N. Europe, the S. part of the Low Countries (see NETHERLANDS, 2), inhabited by people of French and Flemish stock speaking both languages; established in 1831, its independence and neutrality were guaranteed by the European powers and Russia in 1839 and violated by the German invasion in 1914; capital, Brussels. [L, territory occupied by the *Belgae*]

Bĕlgrā'de. (Serbo-Croatian *Beograd*) City on the Danube, capital of Yugoslavia and formerly of Serbia.

Bĕlgrā'via. Fashionable residential district of London, S. of Knightsbridge. [f. *Belgrave* Square, named after Belgrave in Leicestershire]

Bē'lĭal. 1. (O.T.) Spirit of evil personified (as *sons of* ~); (2 Cor. 6: 15) the Devil. 2. (in Milton) Fallen angel representing impurity. [Heb. *b[e]līyya'al* without use, without avail]

bėlī'e *v.t.* Fail to justify or act up to; give false notion of.

bėlie'f *n.* Trust, confidence (*in*); acceptance of any received theology; acceptance as true or existing; thing believed.

bėlie've *v.* Have faith (*in*), trust word of; accept as true; suppose, think; be of opinion *that*. **bėlie'vable** *adj.* **bėlie'ver** *n.*

bėlī'ke *adv.* (archaic) Probably; perhaps.

Bĕlisār'ĭus (?505–65). General under JUSTINIAN I.

Beli'sha bea'con (-lē-): see BEACON 3. [Leslie Hore-*Belisha*, Minister of Transport 1931–7]

bėlĭ'ttle *v.t.* Disparage, dwarf.

Bĕlī'ze (-ēz): see HONDURAS 2.

bĕll[1] *n.* 1. Hollow object of cast metal esp. in deep cup shape

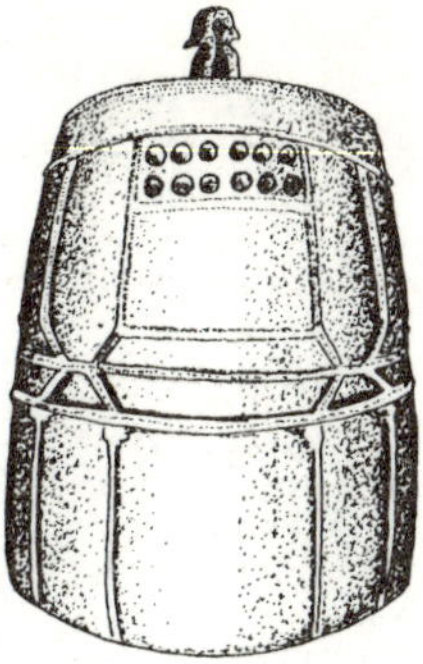

Japanese Temple

Christian Church

BELL

widening at lip, made to emit clear musical sound when struck by a tongue or clapper suspended inside it or by a hammer impelled by a spring or by electricity etc. 2. Sound of this, esp. as signal; (naut.) *one* to *eight* ~*s*, half-hours of watch, indicated by strokes of bell. 3. Bell-shaped object or part. 4. ~*-bottomed*, (of trousers) widening from below knee to bottom of leg; ~*-boy*, (U.S.) hotel page-boy; ~*-buoy*, buoy with a bell rung by the motion of the sea; ~*-founder*, caster of bells; ~*-foundry*, place where bells are cast; ~*-glass*, bell-jar; ~*-hop*, (U.S. slang) bell-boy; ~*-jar*, bell-shaped glass used to protect instruments or contain gases etc. in a laboratory; ~*-man*, crier, town-crier (who attracted attention to his announcements by ringing a bell); ~*-metal*, alloy of copper and tin, with more tin than in ordinary bronze, used for bells; ~*-ringer*, one who rings church-bells, campanologist; ~*-ringing*, art of ringing church-bells, campanology; ~*-tent*, conical tent; ~*-wether*, leading sheep of flock, with bell on neck (also fig.).

Bĕll[2]**,** Alexander Graham (1847–1922). Scottish-American inventor of the telephone.

Bĕll[3]**,** Currer, Ellis, and Acton. Pen-names of Charlotte, Emily, and Anne BRONTË.

bĕlladŏ'nna *n.* Specific name of the deadly nightshade, *Atropa belladonna*, with dark purple flowers and poisonous black berries; dried parts of this, containing atropine and related alkaloids, used as a drug which causes marked dilatation of the pupils; ~*-lily*, amaryllis. [It., = 'fair lady']

Bĕ'llay, Joachim du (*c* 1524–60). French poet and critic, a member of the PLEIAD and author of its

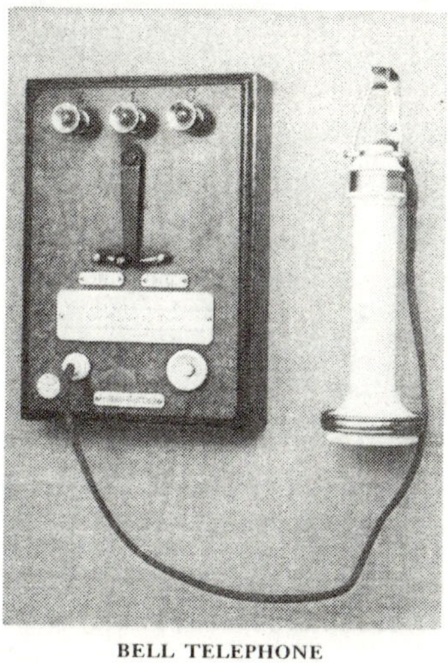

BELL TELEPHONE

manifesto, 'Deffence et Illustration de la Langue Françoyse' (1549).

bĕlle *n.* Handsome woman; reigning beauty.

Bėllĕ'rophon. (Gk legend) Hero who slew the Chimaera with the help of Pegasus.

belles-lettres (bĕl lĕtr) *n.pl.* Studies, writings, of a purely literary kind; essays, literary criticism, etc., as a division of literature. **bĕllėtrĭ'stĭc** *adj.*

bĕ'llĭcōse *adj.* Inclined to war or fighting. **bĕllĭcŏ'sitў̆** *n.*

bėllĭ'gerent *adj.* Waging war, bellicose. ~ *n.* Belligerent State, party, or person. **bėllĭ'gerencў̆** *n.*

Bĕlli'nĭ[1] (-lē-), Giovanni (*c* 1435–1516). Italian painter of the Venetian School; his father Jacopo (*c* 1400–70) and brother Gentile (1429?–1507) were also painters.

Bĕlli'nĭ[2] (-lē-), Vincenzo (1801–35). Italian composer of operas.

Bĕ'llŏc, Joseph Hilaire Pierre (1870–1953). English essayist, novelist, and poet, born in France.

Bĕllō'na. (Rom. myth.) Goddess of war.

bĕ'llow (-ō) *v.* Roar as a bull; shout, roar with pain; shout loudly and angrily; reverberate, roar. ~ *n.* Bellowing sound.

bĕ'llows (-ōz) *n.pl.* 1. Instrument or machine for driving strong blast of air into fire, organ, etc., in its simplest form consisting of a pair of boards joined by flexible leather sides, with a valve through

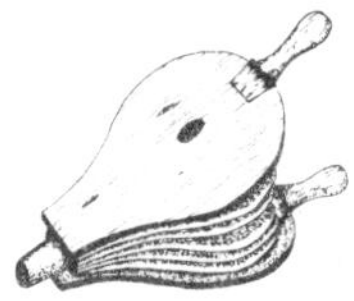

which air enters when the boards are moved apart, and a nozzle or tube through which air is forced as they are brought together. 2. Expansible portion of folding camera.

bĕ'llў̆ *n.* Abdomen; stomach; underpart of animal as cut of meat; cavity or bulging part of anything; *be'llyache* (*v.i.*, slang) complain; ~ *dance*, erotic oriental dance involving movements of the abdominal muscles; so ~ *dancer*; *be'llyflop* (*n.*, slang) dive in which abdomen hits the water (also *be'llyflopper*); (of aircraft) belly landing; (*v.i.*) dive, land, thus; *be'llyful*, (colloq.) surfeit; ~ *landing*, (of aircraft) crash-landing on underside of fuselage; ***~-laugh,***

BELLINI

(colloq.) deep unrestrained laugh. ~ *v.* Swell out.

bėlŏ'ng *v.i.* Have a rightful or appropriate place or position; fit an environment etc.; ~ *to*, (esp.) be a member or adherent etc. of; be a possession of. **bėlŏ'ngings** (-z) *n.pl.* Person's movable property etc.

Bĕlōrŭ'ssia (-sh*a*). White Russia, one of the constituent republics of the U.S.S.R., including the former provinces of Minsk, Vitebsk, and Mogilov; capital, Minsk. **Bĕlorŭ'ssian** *adj.* & *n.* (Native, language) of Belorussia; White Russian.

bėlo'vėd (-lŭ-; *or* -vd) *adj.* Dearly loved; ~ *disciple*, St. John the Apostle. ~ *n.* Beloved person.

bėlow' (-ō) *adv.* At or to a lower level; in a lower position or rank. ~ *prep.* Lower in position, amount, degree, rank, etc., than; unworthy of, beneath.

Bĕlshă'zzar[1]. (also *Balthazar*) Acc. to O.T. (Dan. 5), son of Nebuchadnezzar and last king of Babylon, who was killed in the sack of the city by Cyrus (538 B.C.); his doom was foretold by writing which appeared on the walls of his palace at a great banquet; but in inscriptions and documents from Ur, Belshazzar was the son of the last king of Babylon, Nabonidos, and did not himself reign.

Bĕlshă'zzar[2] *n.* (also *Balthazar*) Very large wine-bottle. [f. BELSHAZZAR[1]]

bĕlt *n.* 1. Broadish flat strip of leather etc., used to gird or encircle the person, confine some part of the dress, or support various articles; such an article awarded to boxing champion or worn as a mark of rank by knight or earl. 2. Strip of colour etc., line of trees, round or on anything; zone or district; endless strap connecting pulleys in machinery; flexible strip holding machine-gun cartridges and carrying them to firing chamber. ~ *v.* Put belt round, fasten with belt; thrash with belt; (slang) rush.

Bĕ'ltāne. Celtic name for 1 May (Old Style), formerly a quarter-day in Scotland, and of the ancient Celtic May Day celebrations, in which bonfires were kindled on the hills.

bĕ'lvėdēre *n.* Raised turret or lantern, summer-house, to view scenery from. [It., = 'fine view']

B.E.M. *abbrev.* British Empire Medal.

bėmea'n *v.t.* Render mean or base.

bėmīr'e *v.t.* Besmirch, befoul.

bėmoa'n *v.t.* Lament.

bėmū'se (-z) *v.t.* Make confused or muddled; stupefy.

bĕn[1] *n.* (Sc.) Inner room (usu. of two-roomed cottage); *but and* ~, outer and inner room, i.e. the whole house.

bĕn[2] *n.* (Sc.) Mountain peak.

Bėnar'ės (-z). = VARANASI.

bĕnch *n.* 1. Long seat of wood or stone; thwart of boat. 2. Judge's or magistrate's seat; office of judge, law-court (*King's*, *Queen's*, *B*~, a division of the High Court of Justice); judges, magistrates; *on the* ~, serving as judge or magistrate. 3. (parl.) Seats in Houses of Parliament traditionally appropriated to certain groups, as *back benches*, for members who have never held office (*back benchers*), *front benches*, for members of Government and leaders of Opposition, *Treasury* ~, front bench on Government side, i.e. on Speaker's right, occupied by First Lord of the TREASURY, Chancellor of the Exchequer, and other members of the Government. 4. Working-table in carpenter's shop, laboratory, etc. 5. Level ledge or terrace in masonry, earthwork, hillside, etc.; ~*-mark*, surveyor's mark, consisting of a broad arrow with a horizontal line through its apex, cut in stone etc. to indicate a point in a line of levels. ~ *v.t.* Exhibit (dog) at show.

bĕ'ncher *n.* (esp.) One of the senior members of the Inns of Court, who form for each Inn a self-elective body managing its affairs; *back* ~: see BENCH *n.* 3.

bĕnd[1] *n.* 1. (naut.) Knot. 2.

(her.) Diagonal band from dexter chief to sinister base of shield; ~ *sinister*, bend in the opposite direction, a mark of bastardy. 3. Shape in which hides are tanned.

bĕnd[2] *v.* (past t. & past part. *bent*). 1. Force into, receive, curved or angular shape. 2. Tighten up; bring to bear; (pass.) be determined. 3. Attach (sail etc.) with bend or knot. 4. Turn in new direction. 5. Incline from perpendicular; bow, stoop, submit, force to submit. 6. Direct, apply (oneself) *to*. 7. Modify (law, rule, etc.) for one's own purposes. ~ *n.* 1. Bending, curve; bent part. 2. (pl.) Caisson disease. 3. *round the* ~, (slang) insane.

bĕ'ndėd *adj.* (of knee) Bent.

bĕ'nder *n.* (slang) Drinking spree.

bĕ'ndў *adj.* 1. (colloq.) That bends. 2. (her.) Divided diagonally into equal fields.

bėnea'th *adv.* & *prep.* Below, under, underneath.

bĕnėdĭ'cĭtė *n.* 1. Blessing invoked; grace at table. 2. *B*~, One of the canticles, from the opening words, *Benedicite omnia opera* (L, = 'O all ye works (of the Lord), bless ye (the Lord)'). [L, = 'bless ye']

Bĕ'nėdĭck. Character in Shakespeare's 'Much Ado about Nothing'; hence, a newly married man.

Bĕ'nėdict, St. (*c* 480–543). Italian monk, founder (529) of the first of the monastic orders of the Western Church, for which he built the abbey of Monte Cassino.

Bĕnėdĭ'ctine *adj.* Of the order of St. Benedict; ~ *Rule*, rule written for it by St. Benedict, later adopted by other monastic communities. ~ *n.* 1. Benedictine monk. 2. (-ēn) Liqueur of brandy flavoured with herbs etc., made at Fécamp in Normandy, orig. by the monks of the Benedictine abbey there.

bĕnėdĭ'ction *n.* Utterance of blessing, at end of church service, or at table; *B*~, R.C. service; a blessing, blessedness. **bĕnėdĭ'ctorў** *adj.*

Bĕnėdĭ'ctus. 1. Fifth movement in the service of Mass, beginning *Benedictus qui venit* (L, = 'blessed is he that cometh'). 2. Hymn of Zacharias (Luke 1: 68) used as a canticle in the Church of England. [L, = 'blessed']

bĕnėfă'ction (*or* bĕ'-) *n.* Doing good; charitable gift.

bĕ'nėfăctor *n.* (fem. *bĕ'nėfăctrėss*) Person who has given friendly aid; patron of, or donor to, cause or charity.

bĕ'nėfĭce *n.* (C. of E.) Material livelihood of incumbent of a parish; rectory, vicarage, or perpetual curacy. **bĕ'nėficed** (-ĭst) *adj.*

bėnĕ'fĭcent *adj.* Doing good, showing active kindness. **bėnĕ'fĭcence** *n.*

bĕnėfĭ'cial (-sh*a*l) *adj.* 1. Advantageous. 2. (law) Of, having, the usufruct of property. **bĕnėfĭ'ciallў** *adv.*

bĕnėfĭ'ciarў (-sh*a*-) *adj.* Holding or held by feudal tenure. ~ *n.* Holder by feudal tenure; holder of living; receiver of benefits.

bĕ'nėfĭt *n.* 1. Advantage. 2. Allowance, pension, etc. to which person is entitled; *sickness, unemployment*, etc. ~, allowance payable under National Insurance Acts to person who is sick, unemployed, etc. 3. ~ *of clergy*, (hist.) exemption from ordinary courts by the privilege of one's order. 4. Theatre performance, game, etc., of which proceeds go to particular players or charity. ~ *v.* Do good to; receive benefit.

Bĕ'nėlŭx. Collective name for *Be*lgium, the *Ne*therlands, and *Lux*emburg, esp. with reference to their economic collaboration.

Beneš (bĕ'nĕsh), Eduard (1884–1948). President of Czechoslovakia 1935–8 and 1946–8.

bėnĕ'volent *adj.* Desirous of doing good; charitable. **bėnĕ'volentlў** *adv.* **bėnĕ'volence** *n.*

B.Eng. *abbrev.* Bachelor of Engineering.

Bĕnga'l (-nggawl). District of the Ganges delta, formerly a province of British India, divided into *West* ~, a state of India (capital,

Calcutta), and BANGLADESH; *Bay of* ~, part of Indian Ocean lying between Indian peninsula and Burma; ~ *light*, firework with steady vivid light, used as a signal; ~ *tiger*, the tiger proper, so called from its abundance in lower Bengal.

Bĕnga'lī (-nggaw-) *adj.* & *n.* (Of) the Indo-European language spoken in Bengal; (native) of Bengal.

bėnī'ghtėd (-nīt-) *adj.* Overtaken by night; involved in moral or intellectual darkness; ignorant.

bėnī'gn (-īn) *adj.* Gracious, gentle; fortunate, salutary; (path., of disease) mild, not malignant; (of tumour) not cancerous, displacing but not destroying surrounding tissue (opp. MALIGNANT).

benĭ'gnant *adj.* Kind, kindly, to inferiors; gracious; salutary. **benĭ'gnancȳ, benĭ'gnitȳ** *ns.*

Benin. See DAHOMEY.

bĕ'nĭson (-zn) *n.* (archaic) Blessing.

Bĕ'njamĭn. Hebrew patriarch, youngest and favourite son of Jacob (Gen. 35: 8, 42, etc.); smallest tribe of Israel, traditionally descended from him.

Bĕ'nnėtt, Enoch Arnold (1867–1931). English novelist; author of novels of life in the Potteries, including 'The Old Wives' Tale' (1908), 'Clayhanger' (1910), 'Riceyman Steps' (1923), etc.

Bĕn Nĕ'vĭs. Mountain in Highland region, Scotland, the highest peak (4,406 ft, 1343 m.) in the British Isles.

bĕnt[1] *n.* Reedy or rush-like stiff-stemmed grass of various kinds; grass of genus *Agrostis*; stiff flower-stalk, old stalk, of grasses; heath, unenclosed pasture.

bĕnt[2] *n.* Inclination, bias.

bĕnt[3] *adj.*: see BEND[2] *v.*; (esp.) curved, crooked; (slang) dishonest, perverted, homosexual.

Bĕ'ntham (-*tam*), Jeremy (1748–1832). English Utilitarian philosopher, and writer on ethics, jurisprudence, and political economy; prison and poor-law reformer; he believed that the end of life is happiness (which he identified with pleasure) and that the highest morality is the pursuit of the greatest happiness of the greatest number. **Bĕ'nthamĭsm, Bĕ'nthamīte** *ns.*

bĕn trova'tō (-ah-). Well invented, characteristic if not true. [It.]

bėnŭ'mb (-m) *v.t.* Make torpid; paralyse.

bĕ'nzėdrine (-ēn) *n.* Preparation of amphetamine. [tradename]

bĕ'nzēne *n.* (chem.) Aromatic hydrocarbon (C_6H_6), a colourless, volatile, and highly inflammable liquid obtained from coal-tar etc., used as a solvent and in the chemical industry; ~ *ring*, ring-like arrangement of the six carbon atoms in the benzene molecule.

bĕ'nzine (-ēn) *n.* Mixture of

BEN NEVIS

hydrocarbons obtained from petroleum and used as a solvent, for removing grease stains etc.

bĕ'nzōin *n.* 1. (also *gum-~*) Fragrant aromatic resin obtained from various trees of the genus *Styrax* from Sumatra and Thailand, and used in perfumery, medicine, etc. 2. (chem.) Constituent of gum-benzoin. **bĕnzō'ic** *adj.* (chem.) Of or derived from benzoin; ~ *acid*, benzene carboxylic acid (C_6H_5COOH). [Fr. *benjoin* f. Arab. *lubān jāwī* Java frankincense]

bĕ'nzŏl *n.* 1. (obs.) Benzene. 2. (in trade use) Unrefined benzene, used as a motor spirit.

Be'owulf (bā'owōō-). Legendary Swedish hero celebrated in the Old English epic poem 'Beowulf'.

bėquea'th (-dh), *v.t.* Leave by will.

bėquĕ'st *n.* Bequeathing; thing bequeathed.

Béranger (bārahṅzhā), Pierre Jean de (1780–1857). French poet, author of many satirical and political songs of great contemporary influence.

bėrā'te *v.t.* (now chiefly U.S.) Scold.

Bêr'ber *adj.* & *n.* (Member) of a fair-skinned aboriginal people of N. Africa.

berceuse (bārsêr'z) *n.* Cradle-song; composition in style of this.

bėrea've *v.t.* 1. (past t. & past part. *bereaved* or *berĕft*) Rob, dispossess *of*. 2. Leave desolate; deprive of relation, wife, etc. **bėrea'vement** *n.*

Bĕrėnī'cė[1] (3rd c. B.C.). Egyptian queen, wife of Ptolemy III Euergetes; during his absence on a warlike expedition in Syria, she dedicated her hair as votive offering for his safe return; the hair was stolen, and legend said that it was carried to the heavens, where it became the constellation *Coma Berenices*.

Bĕrėnī'cė[2] (b. *c* A.D. 28). Jewish princess, called Bernice in Acts 25; daughter of Agrippa I and wife of her uncle Herod, king of Chalcis; after his death she lived with her brother Agrippa II.

beret (bĕ'rā) *n.* Round flat woollen cap, worn by Basque peasantry; similar cap worn esp. as part of sports or holiday costume or as a military cap.

bêrg *n.* = ICEBERG.

bêr'gamŏt[1] *n.* 1. Tree of the lemon kind, *Citrus bergamia*; fragrant oil extracted from its fruit. 2. Any of various plants of the family Labiatae, esp. *Monarda* species. [f. *Bergamo* in Italy]

bêr'gamŏt[2] *n.* Fine kind of pear. [Turk. *beg* prince, *armūdī* pear]

Bergerăc (bārzh-), Cyrano de (1619–55). French soldier and author of comedies.

bergschrund (bār'kshrōōnt) *n.* Crevasse or gap at junction of steep upper slope with glacier or nevé.

Bergson (bārgsawṅ), Henri (1859–1941). French philosopher who regarded reality as change and movement, 'becoming' rather than 'being'. **Bêrgsō'nian** *adj.* & *n.*

bĕ'rĭbĕrĭ *n.* Disease, with symptoms including polyneuritis, oedema, heart failure, etc., caused by deficiency of vitamin B_1 in diet and affecting chiefly tropical and sub-tropical populations whose staple food is rice from which the outer layer of the grain (containing the vitamin) has been polished away. [Sinhalese *beri* weakness]

Bĕ'rĭng, Behr'- (bār-), Vitus Jonassen (1680–1741). Danish navigator and explorer of Arctic Asia; sailed along coast of Siberia from Kamchatka and reached America from the E.; died on an island near Kamchatka subsequently called ~ *Island*; ~ *Sea*, northernmost part of Pacific; ~ *Strait*, strait between Asia and America, connecting Bering Sea with Arctic Ocean.

Berkeley (bâr'klĭ), George (1685–1753). Irish bishop and idealist philosopher. **Berkelei'an** (-lēan) *adj.* & *n.*

bêrkē'lium *n.* (chem.) Metallic radioactive transuranic element; symbol Bk, at. no. 97, principal isotope at. wt 243. [*Berkeley*, Calif., where first made]

Berks. *abbrev.* Berkshire.

Ber'kshire (bârk-). Southern inland county of England, on right bank of Thames; hence, one of a breed of black pigs with occas. white markings.

Berli'n[1]. Chief city of Germany, on river Spree; formerly capital of Prussia; capital of Germany from 1871; since 1945 divided into *East* ~, capital of East Germany, and *West* ~, an isolated part of West Germany; ~ *wall*, wall dividing Berlin; ~ *wool*, fine wool used for knitting or tapestry. **Berli'ner** *n.* Native, inhabitant, of Berlin.

berli'n[2] *n.* Four-wheeled covered carriage with hooded seat behind, invented in Berlin in 17th c., popular in France and England in the 18th c.

Berlioz (bār-), Hector (1803–69). French composer of operas, symphonic works, etc.

berm *n.* Narrow space or ledge; (esp., fort.) space between ditch and parapet.

Bermū'da. (also ~ *Islands*, *Bermudas*) Group of islands, a British colony, in W. Atlantic, discovered early in 16th c. by Juan Bermudez, a Spaniard; ~ *rig*, rig for yacht, carrying a very high tapering sail (*Bermudian mainsail*); ~ *shorts*, (also *Bermudas*) knee-length shorts. **Bermū'dian** *adj.* & *n.*

Bernadotte (bār-), Jean Baptiste (1763–1844). French soldier; one of Napoleon's marshals; was adopted by Charles XIII of Sweden in 1810 and himself became king (as Charles XIV) in 1818, thus founding the present royal house.

Ber'nard[1], St. (923–1008). Priest of Menthon; founder of the Alpine hospices of the Great and Little St. Bernard; *St.* ~ (*dog*), dog of large and very intelligent breed, of the mastiff type, usu. light brown and white, orig. bred by the monks of the St. Bernard hospices and trained to search for travellers lost in the snowdrifts of the Alpine passes.

Ber'nard[2], St. (1090–1153). French churchman, first abbot of Clairvaux; he reformed the Cistercian Order and preached the 2nd Crusade.

Bernard[3] (bārnār), Claude (1813–78). French physiologist; famous for his research on the pancreas and the glycogenic function of the liver, and his discovery of the vaso-motor system.

Bernardin de Saint-Pierre (bārnārdăn, săn pyār), Jacques Henri (1737–1814). French naturalist; author of the novel 'Paul et Virginie'.

Berne (*or* bārn). Canton and capital city of Switzerland. **Bernē'se** (-z) *adj.* & *n.*

Ber'nhardt (bārnhârt), Sarah. Name adopted by the French romantic and tragic actress Rosine Bernard (1845–1923).

Bernini (bārnē'nī), Giovanni Lorenzo (1598–1680). Italian baroque architect and sculptor; designer of the colonnade of St. Peter's in Rome.

Bernou'lli (-ōō-). Surname of Swiss family including several eminent mathematicians and scientists, including Jacob or James (1654–1705) and Daniel (1700–82).

bĕ'rry̆ *n.* 1. Any small round or oval juicy fruit without a stone; grain (of wheat etc.). 2. (bot.) Fruit of any size with seed(s) enclosed in pulp. 3. Egg of lobster, crayfish, etc.

ber'serk *n.* (also *ber'serker*) Wild Norse warrior fighting with mad frenzy; *go* ~ (b*erzer'*k), behave thus. [Icel., prob. = 'bear-coat']

berth *n.* 1. Convenient sea-room; room for ship to swing at anchor; ship's place at wharf; *give a wide* ~ *to*, avoid. 2. Sleeping-place in ship, railway-carriage, etc. 3. Situation, appointment. ~ *v.* Moor (ship); reach moorings.

ber'tha[1], **berthe** *n.* Deep falling collar or small cape on dress.

Ber'tha[2]. In the war of 1914–18, a German gun of large bore, esp. (*Big* ~) a long-range gun used to bombard Paris in 1918. [Frau *Berta* Krupp von Bohlen und Halbach, head of the Krupp steel works in Germany]

Bertillon (bārtēyawṅ), Alphonse (1853–1914). French inventor and general anthropologist; advocate of a system of anthropometric measurements for the identification of criminals, and esp. of the use of finger-prints for this purpose.

Berwickshire (bĕ'rĭk-). Former county of SE. Scotland, since May 1975 part of the region of Borders.

bĕ'rȳl *n.* Transparent precious stone of pale-green colour or of light-blue, yellow, or white, chemically a beryllium aluminium silicate; mineral species including also the emerald, which differs from the beryl only in its rich green colour, due to traces of chromium.

bėrȳ'llĭum *n.* (chem.) Very light metallic element obtained from beryl; symbol Be, at. no. 4, at. wt 9·01218.

Berzē'lĭus, Jons Jakob (1779–1848). Swedish chemist; discovered selenium and other elements, and invented the present system of representing chemical elements by symbols.

Bĕ'sant (-z-), Mrs Annie (1847–1933). English writer and ardent supporter of socialism and agnosticism; became a theosophist in 1887 and President of the Theosophical Society in 1907; was active in the cause of Indian self-government and in 1917 was President of the Indian National Congress.

bėsee'ch *v.t.* (past t. & past part. *besought*, pr. -awt). Ask earnestly for; entreat.

bėsee'm *v.t.* Suit, be fitting or suitable to.

bėsĕ't *v.t.* Hem in; assail, encompass.

bėshrew' (-ōō) *v.t.* (archaic, only in imprecations) Plague take.

bėsī'de *prep.* At the side of, close to; compared with; wide of; ~ *oneself*, strongly moved by emotion.

bėsī'des (-dz) *adv.* In addition; otherwise, else. ~ *prep.* In addition to; except.

bėsie'ge *v.t.* Lay siege to; assail, crowd round.

bėslă'ver *v.t.* Slaver upon or over; flatter fulsomely.

bėsmear' *v.t.* Smear, bedaub.

bėsmĭr'ch *v.t.* Soil, discolour; sully.

bĕ'som (-z-; *or* bĭ-) *n.* Bundle of twigs tied round stick for sweeping; (colloq., derog.) woman.

bėsŏ'ttėd *adj.* Stupefied (esp. with drink); infatuated; foolish.

besought: see BESEECH.

bėspă'tter *v.t.* Spatter; asperse.

bėspea'k *v.t.* (past t. *bespō'ke*, past part. *bespō'ken*). Engage beforehand; order; speak to (poet.); indicate, be evidence of. **bėspō'ke** *adj.* Ordered (now only in ~ *tailoring*, *footwear*, etc., opp. ready-made, or of tradesman making goods to order).

bėsprĭ'nkle *v.t.* Sprinkle.

Bĕ'ssėmer, Sir Henry (1813–98). English engineer; inventor of ~ *process*, process for making steel, in which iron is decarbonized by blowing a blast of air through the molten metal.

bĕst *adj.* (superl. of *good*) Of the most excellent kind; most advantageous, desirable, or serviceable; ~ *man*, bridegroom's supporter at wedding; *the* ~ *part*, most; ~ *seller*, (orig. U.S.) book wth large sale. ~ *adv.* (superl. of *well*) In the most excellent way etc.; *had* ~, would find it wisest. ~ *n.* That which is best; *for the* ~, with good intentions or outcome; (collect.) most excellent persons.

bĕ'stĭal *adj.* Of, like, a beast; brutish, barbarous; depraved, obscene. **bĕstĭă'lĭtȳ** *n.* (esp., law) Crime of person having sexual intercourse with animal. **bĕ'stĭalīze** *v.t.*

bĕ'stĭarȳ *n.* Medieval moralizing treatise on beasts.

bėstĭr' *v.refl.* Exert, rouse.

bėstow' (-ō) *v.t.* Confer as gift; deposit, lodge. **bėstow'al** *n.*

bėstrew' (-ōō) *v.t.* (past part. *bestrewed* or *bestrewn*). Strew.

bėstrī'de *v.t.* (past t. *bestrōde*, past part. *bestridden*). Get or sit upon with legs astride; stand astride over.

bĕt *v.* (past t. & past part. *bet*). Risk one's money etc. against another's on result of doubtful event; (loosely) think, reckon (something to be true etc.); *betting shop*, bookmaker's shop or office. ~ *n.* Act of betting; money etc. so risked.

bē'ta *n.* 2nd letter of Gk alphabet (Β, β), corresponding to *b*, used of the 2nd star in a constellation, and in other classifications; examiner's second-class mark; ~ *brass*, compound of zinc and copper with special metallurgical properties; ~ *particles, rays*, fast-moving electrons emitted by radioactive substances, orig. regarded as rays, and having greater penetrating power than alpha particles and less than gamma rays.

bėtā'ke *v.refl.* (past t. *betook*, past part. *betaken*). Commit (oneself) *to* some cause or means; turn one's course, go.

bē'tatron *n.* (phys.) Apparatus for accelerating electrons.

bē'tel *n.* Leaf of a shrubby evergreen plant, *Piper betle*, which is wrapped round a few parings of areca nut and chewed by people of India etc.; hence (erron.) ~ *nut*, areca nut. [Malayalam *veṭṭila*]

Bĕ'telgeuse (-zhẽrz *or* -jōōz). Yellowish-red variable star, the brightest in the constellation of Orion.

bête noire (bāt nwar). Person or thing one particularly dislikes. [Fr.]

bĕ'thel *n.* Hallowed spot; Nonconformist, esp. Methodist or Baptist, chapel; seamen's church (ashore or floating). [Heb., = 'house of God'; see Gen. 28: 17–19]

bėthi'nk *v.refl.* (past t. & past part. *bethou'ght*, pr. -awt). Reflect, stop to think; remind oneself.

Bĕ'thlėhĕm. Town near Jerusalem; birthplace of Jesus Christ.

bėtī'de *v.* Happen, befall.

bėtī'mes (-mz) *adv.* Early; in good time.

bêtise (bātēz) *n.* Foolish remark; folly. [Fr.]

Bĕ'tjeman (-tch-), Sir John (1906–84). English poet, admirer of Victorian architecture; poet laureate 1972.

bėtō'ken *v.t.* Be token of; presage; indicate.

bĕ'tony̆ *n.* Labiate plant, *Stachys officinalis*, with spike of reddish-purple flowers; *water* ~, plant, *Scrophularia aquatica*, common beside streams.

bėtray' *v.t.* Give up or reveal treacherously; be disloyal to; lead astray; reveal involuntarily; be evidence or symptom of. **bėtray'al, bėtray'er** *ns.*

bėtrō'th (-dh) *v.t.* Bind with a promise to marry. **betrō'thal** *n.* **betrō'thed** (-dhd) *adj.* & *n.*

bĕ'tter *adj.* (comp. of *good*) Of a more excellent kind; ~ *half*, (joc.) wife; ~ *part*, greater part; ~ *world*: see WORLD. ~ *adv.* (comp. of *well*) In a more excellent way; (of person) (partially) recovered from illness; *had* ~, would find it wiser; *think* ~ *of it*, reconsider, decide more wisely. ~ *n.* Person of higher rank (usu. pl.); *get the* ~ *of*, defeat, outwit. ~ *v.* Improve; surpass. **bĕ'tterment** *n.* Improvement.

bė'tween *prep.* In, into, along, or across, a space or interval bounded by (*lies* ~ *Paris and Rouen*; *happened* ~ *Monday and Friday*); separating; connecting; intermediately in time, place or order (*to*); shared by, confined to; to and from; reciprocally on the part of; ~*-maid*, servant helping two others, as cook and housemaid; ~ *whiles*, in the intervals. ~ *adv.* Between two points.

bėtwi'xt *prep.* & *adv.* 1. (archaic) Between. 2. ~ *and between*, in position intermediate between; neither one thing nor the other.

BeV *abbrev.* (U.S.) Billion (= 1,000 million) electron volts.

bĕ'vel *n.* 1. Joiner's and mason's tool, a flat rule with movable

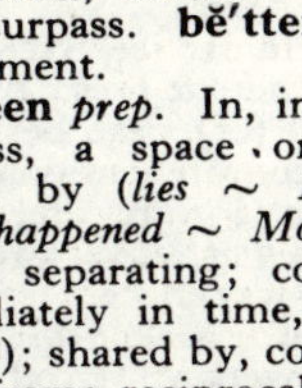

tongue or arm stiffly jointed to one end for setting off angles. 2. Slope from right angle, or from horizontal or vertical, surface so sloped; ~ *gear*, gear with toothed surface oblique with the axis usu. meshing with another set at right angles. ~ *v.* Impart bevel to, slant.

bĕ'verage *n.* Drink.

bĕ'vy̆ *n.* Flock (of birds, esp. larks or quails); group (of women or girls); group (of roebucks).

bėwai'l *v.t.* Wail over, mourn for.

bėwār'e *v.* (used without inflexions). Be cautious (of), take heed (*of, lest, how*).

bėwĭ'lder *v.t.* Lead astray, confuse, perplex. **bėwĭ'lderment** *n.*

bėwĭ'tch *v.t.* Affect by magic; charm, enchant.

bey (bā) *n.* Turkish governor of province or district. **bey'lic** *n.* District or jurisdiction of bey. [Turk., = 'lord']

Beyle, Henri: see STENDHAL.

bėyŏ'nd *adv.* & *prep.* At, to, the further side (of), past, besides; out of reach, comprehension or range (of). ~ *n.* Future life, the unknown; *back of* ~, very remote or out-of-the-way place.

Bĕ'zaleel. Maker of the Ark of the Covenant (Exod. 31: 2, 35: 30, etc.).

bĕ'zant (*or* bĭză'nt) *n.* 1. (hist.) Gold coin current in England in 9th and 10th centuries; later, silver coin. 2. (her.) Roundel or [f. *Byzantium*, where orig. struck]

bĕ'zel *n.* Sloped edge or face of chisel etc; oblique side or face of cut gem; groove holding gem or watch-glass in setting.

bezi'que (-ēk) *n.* Card-game for two players who score chiefly by holding various sequences and combinations of cards; combination of queen of spades and knave of diamonds in this game.

b.f. *abbrev.* Bloody fool; bold face (type); brought forward.

B.F.B.S. *abbrev.* British and Foreign Bible Society.

bhăng (bă-), **băng**[2] *n.* Leaves of Indian hemp mixed with resin used as intoxicant and narcotic.

b.h.p. *abbrev.* Brake horsepower.

Bhutan (bōōtăh'n). Independent kingdom, a protectorate of the Republic of India, lying on the SE. of the Himalayas; capital, Punakha.

bi- *prefix.* Twice-, doubly, having two.

bī'as *n.* 1. (in bowls) Curving course in which bowl runs, shape of bowl causing it to do this. 2. Inclination, predisposition, prejudice, influence; (statistics) systematic distortion; (elect.) steady voltage or current applied to electronic device. 3. (dressmaking) Diagonal across material, direction in which material stretches; ~ *binding*, bias-cut binding; ~*-cut*, cut on the bias. ~ *v.t.* Give bias to, influence, prejudice.

bĭb[1] *v.i.* (archaic) Drink much or often, tipple. **bĭ'bber** *n.*

bĭb[2] *n.* Cloth etc. placed under child's chin to keep dress-front clean; apron-top.

bĭb[3] *n.* Sea-fish (*Trisopterus luscus*) which can inflate a membrane covering the eyes and other parts of the head.

bĭb-cŏck *n.* Cock or tap with turned-down nozzle (dist. from *stopcock*).

Bī'ble *n.* Sacred book of Christianity; edition or copy of this; sacred book, authoritative text-book; ~ *Belt*, those parts of the (Southern and Middle Western) U.S. reputed to be fanatically puritan or fundamentalist; ~ *Christians*, Protestant sect, existing chiefly in SW. England, founded 1816 by a Wesleyan preacher, William O'Bryan; ~ *oath*, solemn oath taken on the Bible.

bĭ'blĭcal *adj.* Of, in, concerning, the Bible; (of language) of the Authorized Version.

bĭblĭŏ'graphy̆ *n.* History of books, their authorship, editions, etc.; book containing such details; list of books of any author, subject, printer, etc. **bĭblĭŏ'grapher** *n.* **bĭblĭogră'phĭcal** *adj.*

bĭbliŏ'later *n.* Worshipper of books. **bĭbliŏ'latrȳ** *n.* **bĭbliŏ'latrous** *adj.*

bĭbliomā'nia *n.* Mania for collecting books. **bĭbliomā'niăc** *n.* & *adj.*

bĭ'bliophile *n.* Book-lover.

bĭ'būlous *adj.* Addicted to drinking.

bīcă'meral *adj.* With two (legislative) chambers.

bīcar'bonate *n.* 1. Salt of carbonic acid in which only one hydrogen atom is replaced by a metal. 2. (pop.) Sodium bicarbonate ($NaHCO_3$) used in medicine and as constituent of baking-powder etc.

bīce *n.* Dullish blue pigment obtained from smalt; *green* ~, dull green pigment made by adding yellow orpiment to smalt; colour of either of these.

bīcĕntē'narȳ (*or* -sĕ'ntĭn-) *n.* 200th anniversary.

bīcĕntĕ'nnial *adj.* Occurring every, lasting for, 200 years. ~ *n.* (U.S.) Bicentenary.

bīcĕ'phalous *adj.* Two-headed.

bī'cĕps *n.* & *adj.* (Muscle) with 2 heads or attachments, esp. that on front of upper arm, which bends forearm.

bĭ'cker *v.i.* & *n.* Quarrel, wrangle.

bīcŭ'spĭd *adj.* & *n.* (Tooth) with two cusps.

bī'cȳcle *n.* Vehicle having two wheels and a seat on which the rider sits astride, driven either by two pedals operating a crank or by a motor. ~ *v.i.* Ride bicycle. **bī'cȳclist** *n.*

bĭd *v.* (past t. *băde, bid,* past part. *bi'dden, bid*). Command to; invite; salute with (greeting etc.); (past t. & past part. *bid*) offer (price) for a thing; (at bridge) made a bid. **bĭ'dder** *n.* **bĭd** *n.* Offer of price, esp. at an auction; (at bridge) announcement of the number of tricks that a player will undertake to win at no trumps or with a specified suit as trumps; attempt.

bĭ'ddable *adj.* Obedient; (of a suit in a hand at bridge) on which a bid can reasonably be made.

bīde *v.* Abide (archaic except in ~ *one's time*).

bidet (bē'dā) *n.* Shallow oval basin fitted in bathroom, for washing the genital region.

bīĕ'nnial *adj.* Lasting, recurring every, two years. **bīĕ'nniallȳ** *adv.* **bīĕ'nnial** *n.* Plant which springs from seed one year and flowers, fructifies, and dies the next.

bier *n.* Movable frame on which corpse or coffin is taken to grave.

B.I.F. *abbrev.* British Industries Fair.

biff *n.* (slang) Blow, whack. ~ *v.t.* Strike, hit.

bĭ'ffin *n.* Deep-red variety of cooking-apple. [= *beefing,* f. *beef* (with ref. to the colour)]

bī'fĭd *adj.* Divided by a deep cleft into two lobes.

bīfō'cal *adj.* (of spectacle lenses) Having two segments of different focal lengths, the upper for dis-

EARLY BICYCLE

tant, the lower for near, vision. **bīfō'cals** (-z) *n.pl.* Bifocal spectacles.

bīfō'liate *adj.* Of two leaves.

bī'furcāte (-fer-) *v.* Divide into two branches, fork. ~ *adj.* Forked. **bīfurcā'tion** *n.*

big *adj.* Large; grown-up; important; boastful; (colloq., orig. U.S.) magnanimous; ~ *with child*, advanced in pregnancy (also fig. *with news* etc.); *B~ Ben*, great bell which strikes the hours in Houses of Parliament; *B~ Brother*, head of State in George Orwell's novel '1984'; hence, head of authoritarian organization exercising dictatorial pseudo-benevolent power; ~ *business*, commerce on **grand scale**; ~ *end*: see END *n.* 5; ~*-headed*, (colloq.) conceited; ~ *gun*, *noise*, (fig.) important person; ~ *money*, large amount of money; ~ *three*, *four*, etc., predominant few; ~ *toe*, innermost, largest toe; ~ *top*, circus marquee; *bi'gwig*, important person. ~ *adv.* **bi'gness** *n.*

BIG BEN

bi'gamy̆ *n.* Crime of going through a form of marriage while first marriage is still valid. **bi'gamous** *adj.* **bi'gamously̆** *adv.* **bi'gamist** *n.*

bigarade (-ahd) *n.* Spanish bitter orange. [Fr.]

bight (bīt) *n.* Loop of a rope; curve, recess, of coast, river, etc., bay.

bi'got *n.* Person obstinately and unreasonably holding some creed or view and intolerant towards others. **bi'goted** *adj.* **bi'gotry̆** *n.*

Bihar'. State of NE. India; capital, Patna. **Bihar'i** *n.*

bijou (bē'zhōō) *n.* Jewel, trinket. ~ *adj.* Small and elegant.

bīke *n.* & *v.i.* (colloq.) Bicycle, motor-cycle.

biki'ni (-kē-) *n.* Scanty two-piece beach-garment worn by women. [f. name of island in the Pacific]

bīlā'bial *adj.* & *n.* (phon.) (Consonant) produced by the junction or apposition of both lips. **bīlā'bially̆** *adv.*

bīlă'teral *adj.* Of, on, with, two sides; affecting, between, two parties; ~ *symmetry*, symmetry about a plane, such that one half is a mirror-image of the other (as left and right in general outward appearance of human body and in all other vertebrate and many invertebrate animals). **bīlă'terally̆** *adv.*

bi'lberry̆ *n.* Small blue-black edible berry of *Vaccinium myrtillus*, a dwarf hardy shrub of N. Europe abundant on heaths and stony moors and in mountain woods (also *blaeberry*, *whortleberry*, U.S. *blueberry*).

bi'lbō *n.* (hist.) Sword noted for its temper and elasticity. [*Bilbao* in Spain]

bi'lboes (-ōz) *n.* Iron bar with sliding shackles for prisoner's ankles, and a lock to fix one end of the bar to the floor or ground.

bīle *n.* Bitter, brownish-yellow fluid secreted by the liver and poured into the duodenum in the process of digestion; (hist.) one of the four humours; (fig.) anger, peevishness.

bilge *n.* Nearly horizontal part of ship's bottom; foulness that collects in bilge; (slang) nonsense, rot belly of a cask; *~-water*, foul water that collects in ship's bilge. *v.* Stave in the bilge of, spring a leak in the bilge; bulge, swell.

bilhar'zia *n.* Disease produced by trematode worm of genus *B~*, parasitic in veins of human pelvic region and urinary organs, esp. in Africa. [f. Theodor *Bilharz* (1825–62), German physician]

bi'liary *adj.* Of the bile.

bili'ngual (-nggw-) *adj.* Having, written in, speaking, etc., two languages. **bili'ngualism, bili'ngualist** *n.*

bi'lious *adj.* Arising from derangement of the bile; liable to, affected by, this. **bi'liously** *adv.* **bi'liousness** *n.*

bilk *v.t.* 1. (cribbage) Balk or spoil person's score in his crib. 2. Evade payment of (creditor, esp. taxi-driver, or bill); cheat, give the slip to. **bi'lker** *n.*

bill[1] *n.* 1. Obsolete weapon, varying from simple concave blade with long wooden handle, to kind of concave axe with spike at the back of shaft terminating in a spear-head; 2. (also *bi'llhook*) Implement used for pruning etc., having long blade with concave edge, often ending in a sharp hook, and a wooden handle in line with blade.

bill[2] *n.* 1. Bird's beak, esp. when slender or flattened; horny beak of platypus. 2. Narrow promontory. 3. (naut.) Point of anchor-fluke. ~ *v.i.* Stroke bill with bill (as doves); (also ~ *and coo*) exchange caresses.

bill[3] *n.* 1. Draft of proposed Act of Parliament. 2. (obs., law) Written statement of (plaintiff's) case, proposed indictment submitted to grand jury. 3. Note of charges for goods delivered or services rendered. 4. Poster, placard; programme of entertainment; *fill the* ~, (orig. U.S.) suffice. 5. (also ~ *of exchange*) Written order to pay sum on given date to drawer or named payee. 6. (U.S.) Bank-note. 7. ~ *of fare*, list of dishes to be served; ~ *of health*, certificate regarding infectious disease on ship or in port at time of sailing; ~ *of lading*, ship-master's receipt for goods to consignor, undertaking to deliver them to a specified port; ~ *of sale*, document transferring personal property or authorizing its seizure by lender of money if payment is delayed; *~s of mortality*, (hist.) weekly return of deaths in London and district, which began to be published in 1592; *within the ~s of mortality*, within the district covered by these bills; *B~ of Rights*: see RIGHT *n.* 2; *~-broker*, dealer in bills of exchange; *~-poster*, man who pastes up placards. ~ *v.t.* Announce, put in the programme; plaster with placards; send a bill to.

bi'llabong *n.* (Austral.) Branch or effluent of river forming back-water or stagnant pool.

bi'llet[1] *n.* Order requiring householder to board and lodge soldier etc. bearing it; place where such a person is lodged; appointment, situation. ~ *v.t.* Quarter (soldiers etc.) *on* town, householder, etc., *in*, *at*, place. **billetee'** *n.* Person billeted.

bi'llet[2] *n.* 1. Thick piece of fire-wood. 2. Small bar of metal. 3. (archit.) Short roll inserted at intervals in hollow moulding.

billet-doux (bilidōō') *n.* (pl. *billets-doux*). Love-letter (joc.).

bi'lliards (-lyardz) *n.pl.* Game played with three small solid balls, one red, one plain white, and one spot white, driven about by cues on a horizontal rectangular table covered with smooth green cloth, surrounded by a cushioned ledge, and provided with six pockets at the corners and in the middle of the long sides; *billiard ball, cue, table*, etc., one used in billiards; *billiard marker*, one (esp. attendant) who marks the score at billiards.

Bi'llingsgate (-z-; *or* -āt). Fish-market established at one of the old gates of London on the river-side; hence (also *b*~), foul language (for which the market was famous in 17th c.).

bĭ'llion (-yon) *n.* One million millions; (U.S.) one thousand millions. **bĭllionair'e** *n.* One whose wealth is a billion (dollars, pounds, etc.) or more.

bĭ'llon *n.* Alloy of gold or silver with a predominating amount of some base metal, used for coinage.

bĭ'llow (-ō) *n.* Great wave; anything that sweeps along, as sound etc. ~ *v.i.* Rise, move, in billows. **bĭ'llowy̆** *adj.*

bĭ'lly̆[1] *n.* (also *bi'llycan*; orig. Austral.) Tin can for boiling water etc. in camping.

bĭ'lly̆[2] *n.* = BILLY-GOAT.

bĭ'llycŏck *n.* Man's round, low-crowned, hard felt hat; bowler.

bĭ'lly̆-goat *n.* Male goat.

bīlō'bed (-bd) *adj.* Having, or divided into, two lobes.

bĭ'ltŏng *n.* Strips of sun-dried lean meat (antelope, buffalo, etc.).

bīmĕtă'llic *adj.* 1. Of two metals; ~ *strip*, sensitive element in some thermostats, made of two bands of different metals, one of which expands more than the other when temperature rises, and so causes the strip to bend. 2. Using both gold and silver as currency, at fixed ratio to each other. **bīmĕ'tallism, bīmĕ'tallist** *ns.*

bī-mo'nthly̆ (-mŭ-) *adj.* & *n.* (Periodical) produced or occurring every two months.

bĭn *n.* Receptacle for corn, coal, bottled wine, etc.; receptacle for household rubbish; canvas receptacle used in hop-picking.

bī'nary̆ *adj.* Dual, of or involving pairs; ~ *compound*, (chem.) one consisting of two elements; ~ *form*, (mus.) applied to a melody or composition having two sections, the 2nd of which is balanced against the 1st and seems to answer it; ~ *measure*, (mus.) having two beats to a bar; ~ *scale*, (math.) system of numbers etc. using only two elements, 0 and 1.

bīnd *v.* (past t. & past part. *bound*). 1. Tie, fasten; put in bonds, restrain; fasten or hold together; (cookery) cause to cohere. 2. Be obligatory, impose constraint or duty upŏn; (pass.) be required by duty; subject to legal obligation; indenture as apprentice; ~ *over*, (esp.) make person give recognizance not to commit a breach of the peace. 3. Make costive. 4. Bandage; wreath *with*; edge *with* braid, iron, etc.; fasten (sheets, book) into cover. 5. (slang) Complain. ~ *n.* 1. (mus.) = TIE *n.* 4. 2. (slang) Bore, nuisance.

bī'nder *n.* (esp.) 1. Book-binder. 2. Long broad band of material to bind round body. 3. Long stone extending through a wall 4. Reaping-and-binding machine.

bī'nding *adj.* Obligatory (*on*). ~ *n.* (esp.) Book-cover; braid etc. for binding raw edges of textiles.

bī'ndweed *n.* Convolvulus.

bīne *n.* Flexible shoot; stem of climbing plant, esp. the hop.

Binet (bēnā), Alfred (1857–1911). French psychologist; experimented in the measurement of intelligence and was the first to devise intelligence-tests.

bĭnge (-j) *n.* (slang) Heavy drinking-bout; spree.

bĭ'ngō (-ngg-) *n.* Form of lotto in which the player who first covers all numbers on his card wins the money staked.

bĭ'nnacle *n.* Box for compass on a ship.

bĭnŏ′cūlar *adj.* Adapted for both eyes; ~ *vision*, type of vision, peculiar to man and some other primates, in which both eyes co-operate in observing the same object and receive a stereoscopic impression. **bĭnŏ′cūlars** (-z) *n.pl.* Binocular field- or opera-glasses.

bīnō′mĭal *adj.* Consisting of two terms; ~ *theorem*, general algebraic formula, discovered by Newton, by which any power of a binomial quantity may be found without performing the progressive multiplications. ~ *n.* Algebraic expression consisting of two terms joined by + or −.

bīnŏ′mĭnal *adj.* Of two names; ~ *system*, (biol.) system of nomenclature by genus and species.

bĭnt *n.* (colloq., usu. derog.) Girl, woman. [Arab., = 'daughter', girl]

bĭntur′ŏng (-oor-) *n.* Prehensile-tailed civet, *Arctictis binturong*, of S. Asia.

bīo- *prefix.* (Course of) life of, concerning, organic life; biological.

bīochĕ′mĭstrỹ (-k-) *n.* Science dealing with the chemical properties of the parts of living organisms. **bīochĕ′mĭcal** *adj.* **bīochĕ′mĭst** *n.*

bīoclīmatŏ′logỹ *n.* Study of climate in relation to life and esp. to human health.

bīogĕ′nėsis *n.* 1. (usu. hist.) T. H. Huxley's term for descent of living matter from living matter (opp. ABIOGENESIS). 2. Hypothetical development of living matter from complex but inanimate substances.

bīogėŏ′graphỹ *n.* Study of the distribution of animals and plants.

bīŏ′graphỹ *n.* Written life of a person, branch of literature dealing with such lives. **bīŏ′grapher** *n.* **bīogră′phical** *adj.* **bīogră′phĭcallỹ** *adv.*

bīŏ′logỹ *n.* Science of life, dealing with the morphology, physiology, behaviour, origin, and distribution of animals and plants. **bīolŏ′gĭcal** *adj.* Of biology; ~ *control*, control of pests by the use of other organisms which devour or destroy them; ~ *warfare*, use of toxins to spread disease in the enemy. **bīolŏ′gĭcallỹ** *adv.* **bīŏ′logĭst** *n.*

bīolūmĭnĕ′scence (*or* -lōō-) *n.* Emission of light by living organisms. **bīolūmĭnĕ′scent** *adj.*

bī′ōme *n.* (ecol.) Biotic community of plants and animals.

bīŏ′mėtrỹ *n.* Application of mathematics to biology, esp. the study of resemblances between living things by statistical methods. **bīomĕ′trĭcal** *adj.* **bīomėtrĭ′cian** (-shan) *n.*

bīophỹ′sĭcs (-z-) *n.* Science dealing with the mechanical and electrical properties of the parts of living organisms. **bīophỹ′sĭcal** *adj.* **bīophỹ′sĭcĭst** *n.*

bī′opsỹ *n.* (med.) Examination of tissue removed from the living body.

bī′oscōpe *n.* Early form of cinematograph; (S. Afr.) cinema.

bī′osphēre *n.* Regions of earth's crust and atmosphere occupied by living organisms.

bīŏ′tĭc *adj.* (biol.) Relating to life; peculiar to living organisms.

bīpartĭsă′n (-z-) *adj.* Of or involving two (political) parties.

bīpar′tīte *adj.* Divided into or consisting of two parts; (law, of agreement etc.) drawn up in two corresponding parts, each party delivering a counterpart to the other.

bī′pĕd *n.* & *adj.* Two-footed (animal).

bīpĭ′nnate *adj.* (bot.) Having leaflets arranged in two rows on either side of leaf-stalk, the leaflets being themselves subdivided.

bī′plāne *n.* Aeroplane with two planes or main supporting surfaces, one above the other.

bīquadră′tĭc (-kwŏd-) *adj.* Of, raised to, the square of a square (or 4th power) of a number; ~ *equation*, one in which the unknown quantity is biquadratic. ~ *n.* Biquadratic equation; 4th power of a number.

bīrch *n.* 1. Hardy northern forest-tree of genus *Betula* with smooth tough bark and slender graceful branches; wood of this;

~*-bark canoe*, one made of the bark of *B. papyrifera*. 2. Bundle of birch-twigs used for flogging. ~ *v.t.* Flog with birch. **bîr'chen** *adj.* Made of birch.

bîrd *n.* 1. Any feathered vertebrate animal, member of a class nearly allied to reptiles but distinguished by warm blood, feathers, and adaptation of the fore-limbs as wings. 2. Game bird. 3. (slang) Young woman; (joc.) person, esp. *old* ~. 4. (slang) Prison (sentence). 5. *get the* ~, (slang, esp. theatr.) be hissed, booed, etc.; be dismissed; so *give the* ~; ~*-bath*, dish of water set in garden for birds' use; ~*-brain(ed)*, (person) with small brain; *bir'dcage*, wire cage for bird(s), object of similar design; ~*-call*, note of bird; instrument imitating this; ~*-cherry*, species of cherry tree (*Prunus padus*); ~*-lime*: see LIME[1]; ~ *of paradise*, bird of family Paradiseidae native to New Guinea and notable for its brilliant colours and elegant plumes; ~ *of passage*, migratory bird (also fig. of sojourner); ~*-sanctuary*, island or enclosed piece of land where birds are protected by law; ~*-seed*, any of various kinds of seed used esp. for feeding caged birds; ~*'s-eye*, any of several plants, esp. the speedwell, with small round bright flowers; ~*'s-eye maple*, wood of the sugar maple when full of little knots; ~*'s-eye view*, view of landscape from above; résumé of a subject; ~*'s nest*, (esp.) edible nest of certain swallows found in the China Sea; ~*'s nesting*, search for birds' nests usu. in order to collect eggs; ~*-table*, raised platform on which food for birds is placed; ~*-watching*, study of birds in their natural surroundings.

bī'rēme *n.* Ancient galley with two banks of oars.

birĕ'tta *n.* Square cap worn by R.C. and some Anglican clerics.

Birgitta, Birgittine: see BRIDGET[2].

Bîr'mingham (-ng-*a*m). Midland city in West Midlands, 2nd largest in England, noted for its metal manufactures; university, 1900; university of Aston, 1966.

bîr'ō. Ball-point pen. [tradename]

bîrth *n.* 1. Emergence of child or animal from body of female parent; process of producing young; *give* ~ *to*, (of female parent) produce (young) from body (also fig.). 2. Origin, beginning. 3. Parentage, descent; noble lineage. 4. ~ *certificate*, form showing date and place etc. of birth; ~ *control*, regulation of birth by means of contraceptive methods or devices; *bir'thday*, (anniversary of) day of one's birth; *birthday honours*, titles of honour annually conferred by the British sovereign, announced on his or her official birthday; *birthday suit*, (slang) state of nakedness; *bir'thmark*, congenital mark on the body; ~*-place*, place at which one was born; *bir'thrate*, number of births per 1,000 of population per annum; *bir'thright*, rights, privilege, or position to which one is entitled by birth, esp. by being the eldest son.

bĭs *adv.* Twice; (mus.) repeat. [Fr. & It.]

Bi'scay, Bay of. Part of N. Atlantic between N. coast of Spain and W. coast of France, notorious for storms.

bĭ'scuit (-kĭt) *n.* 1. Kind of crisp, dry bread or cake more or less hard, variously flavoured, and usu. unleavened, prepared usu. in small flat thin pieces; (U.S.) kind of small leavened cakes resembling scones. 2. Porcelain and other pottery-ware after first firing and before being glazed or painted. 3. Characteristic light-brown colour of biscuit. 4. Small square army mattress, three of which form full-size mattress. ~ *adj.* Of the colour of biscuit.

bīsĕ'ct *v.t.* Cut or divide into two (usu. equal) parts. **bīsĕ'ction** *n.* **bīsĕ'ctor** *n.* Bisecting line.

bīsĕ'xūal (*or* -kshōō-) *adj.* Of two sexes; having both sexes in one individual, hermaphrodite. **bīsĕxūă'lĭtỹ** *n.*

bĭ'shop *n.* 1. Clergyman consecrated as ecclesiastical governor of a diocese; *Bishops' Bible*, English translation prepared by the bishops and printed 1568; ~ *sleeves*, very full sleeves like those worn by bishop. 2. Mitre-shaped chessman moved diagonally. 3. Mulled spiced wine. **bĭ'shopric** *n.* Diocese or office of a bishop.

Bĭ'sley (-z-). Village in Surrey where annual meeting of National Rifle Association is held.

Bĭ'smârck (-z-), Otto Eduard Leopold, Prince von (1815–98). German statesman; Prussian prime minister 1862; chancellor of N. German Federation 1867; after the

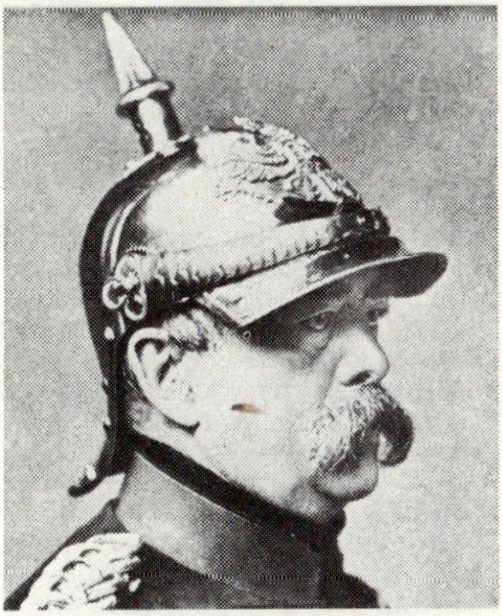

war with France, in which the S. German States co-operated, became first chancellor of the German Empire 1871; resigned, having displeased William II, 1890.

Bĭ'smârck Archĭpĕ'lagō (-z-, ârk-). Group of small islands in the Pacific, NE. of New Guinea, under Australian administration.

bĭ'smuth (-z-) *n.* (chem.) Reddish-white brittle metallic element melting at low temperatures; symbol Bi, at. no. 83, at. wt 208·9806; (pop.) salt of this, used to relieve digestive disorders.

bī'son *n.* 1. Species of wild ox (*Bison europaeus*) of heavy build with humped shoulders, formerly

prevalent in Europe and still existing in the Caucasus. 2. N. Amer. wild ox (*B. americanus*) formerly roaming in vast herds over the continent, now almost extinct except in protected areas.

bĭsque[1] (-k) *n.* Point given to opponent in certain games, which he may take at any stage, esp. in tennis and golf; (croquet) right of playing extra turn.

bĭsque[2] (-k) *n.* (pottery) Unglazed white porcelain used for statuettes etc., biscuit.

bĭsque[3] (-k) *n.* Soup made with shellfish etc.

bĭssĕ'xtĭle *adj.* & *n.* Leap (-year). [L *bis sextilis* (*annus*) (year) containing the doubled sixth day (because in the Julian calendar the day repeated, 24 Feb., was acc. to the inclusive Roman method of reckoning the sixth before the Calends of March)]

bĭ'stôrt *n.* Plant (*Polygonum bistorta*) with large twisted rhizome and cylindrical spike of small flesh-coloured flowers, yielding an astringent medicinal drug.

bĭ'stoury (-orĭ) *n.* Surgeon's scalpel.

bĭ'stre (-*ter*) *n.* Brown pigment prepared from soot; colour of this.

bĭt[1] *n.* 1. Biting or cutting end or part of tool, as boring-piece of drill, cutting-iron of plane, etc.; part of key which engages with levers of lock. 2. Mouthpiece of horse's bridle. ~ *v.t.* Furnished (horse) with bit; restrain, curb.

bĭt[2] *n.* 1. Morsel of food; something to eat. 2. Small piece of anything; small portion or quantity; small coin; *do one's* ~, play one's part; ~ *part, player*, (theatr.) (player of) very small part.

bĭtch *n.* 1. Female of dog, fox,

wolf. 2. (colloq.) Malicious or ill-tempered woman; difficult or unpleasant thing. **bĭ′tchȳ** *adj.* **bĭ′tchĭlȳ** *adv.* **bĭ′tchĭnėss** *n.*

bīte *v.* (past t. *bĭt*, past part. *bĭ′tten*). 1. Cut into or off, nip, with teeth; (of insects etc.) sting, suck; ~ *back*, restrain (speech) by biting lips. 2. (of fishes) Accept bait. 3. Cause glowing, smarting pain to. 4. Corrode. 5. (of wheels, screw, etc.) Grip. ~ *n.* Act of, wound made by, piece detached by, biting; occlusion; taking of bait by fish; snack; grip, hold.

Bĭthȳ′nĭa. Ancient region of NW. Asia Minor. **Bĭthȳ′nĭan** *adj.* & *n.*

bī′tĭng *adj.* (esp.) Pungent, stinging, sarcastic.

bĭ′tter *adj.* Tasting like wormwood, quinine, aloes, etc., obnoxious, irritating, or unfavourably stimulating to the gustatory nerve; unpalatable to the mind, full of affliction; virulent, relentless; biting, harsh; piercingly cold; *~-apple*, colocynth; *~-sweet*, sweet(ness) with bitter after-taste or element; woody nightshade. **bĭ′tterlȳ** *adv.* **bĭ′tternėss** *n.*

bĭ′tter *n.* 1. Bitterness. 2. Bitter beer; (pl.) liquors impregnated with wormwood etc. taken as stomachics.

bĭ′ttern *n.* Bird of genus *Botaurus*, allied to herons, but smaller; esp. *B. stellaris*, a European marsh-bird noted for its booming cry.

bĭ′ttȳ *adj.* Scrappy. **bĭ′ttĭnėss** *n.*

bĭ′tūmėn (*or* -tū′-) *n.* Mineral pitch, asphalt; any of various kinds of native oxygenated hydrocarbon, as naphtha, petroleum. **bĭtū′mĭnous** *adj.*

bĭ′tūmĭnīze *v.t.* Impregnate, cover, with bitumen.

bīvā′lent *adj.* (chem.) = DIVALENT.

bī′vălve *adj.* Having two valves, having two hinged shells. ~ *n.* Mollusc with shell consisting of two halves hinged together by elastic ligament.

bĭ′vouăc (-ōō-) *n.* Temporary encampment without tents, etc.; improvised shelter, small tent. ~ *v.i.* Remain, esp. during the night, in open air without tents.

bĭ′vvȳ *n.* (army slang) Bivouac.

bĭzârre (-âr′) *adj.* Eccentric, fantastic, grotesque, mixed in style, half barbaric. **bĭzarr′elȳ** *adv.* **bĭzarr′enėss** *n.* [Span. *bizarro* brave, handsome]

Bizet (bēzā), Georges (1838–75). French composer of 'Carmen' and other operas.

bīzō′nal *adj.* Of or concerning both of two zones.

Björnsen (byėr′-), Björnstjerne (1832–1910). Norwegian playwright, novelist, and poet.

B.L. *abbrev.* Bachelor of Law.

blăb *v.* Talk or tell foolishly or indiscreetly, reveal, let out; hence, **blă′bber** *n.* **blăb** *n.* Blabbing.

blăck *adj.* 1. Opposite to white, colourless from the absence or complete absorption of all light; so near this as to have no distinguishable colour; very dark-coloured. 2. Dark-skinned; dark-clothed; dusky, gloomy; dirty. 3. Deadly, sinister, wicked; dismal; angry, lowering; implying disgrace or condemnation (as ~ *mark* etc.); performed by blackleg labour; boycotted by trade unions during a dispute; existing, bought, sold, in contravention of economic regulations. 4. ~ *and blue*, discoloured with bruise(s); ~ *and tan*, (dog) of these two colours; *B~ and Tans* (from their black and khaki uniform, a mixture of con-

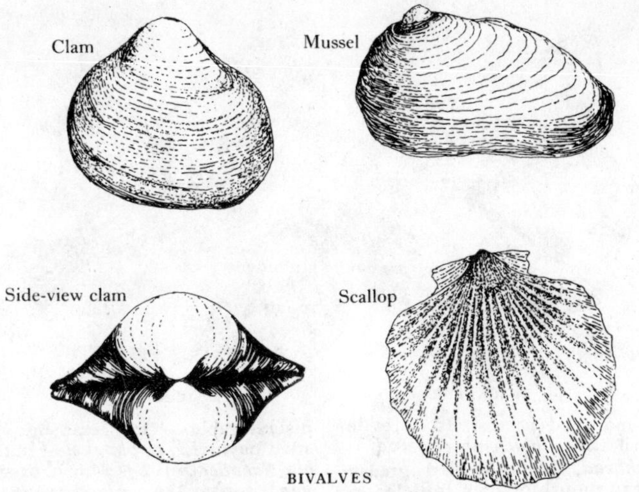

BIVALVES

stabulary and military uniforms), armed force specially recruited in 1921 to combat Sinn Fein in Ireland; ~ *art*, magic; ***bla'ckball*** (*v.t.*) exclude from club, society, etc. (orig. by putting black ball into urn or ballot box to express adverse vote); *~-**beetle***, domestic cockroach (*Blatta orientalis*); (slang) cleric, parson; ~ ***belt***, (belt worn by) person who has attained a certain degree of proficiency in judo; ***bla'ckberry***, bramble (*Rubus fruticosus*) or its fruit; ***bla'ckberrying***, gathering blackberries; ***bla'ckbird***, European song-bird (*Turdus merula*, one of the thrushes), the male being black with yellow bill, the female dark brown; (hist.) captive Negro on slave- or pirate-ship; ***bla'ckboard***, large black board, panel, etc., used in schools and lecture-rooms for writing or drawing on in chalk; ~ *body*, (phys.) body or surface that absorbs all radiation falling upon it; ~ *box*, (esp.) device in aircraft recording details of flight; ~ *cap*, cap worn by English judges in full dress, formerly put on when passing sentence of death; ***bla'ckcap***, bird, the warbler *Sylvia atricapilla*, which has the top of the head black; *~-cock*, male of black grouse; ~ *coffee*, coffee without milk; *B~ Country*, parts of Staffordshire and Warwickshire grimed and blackened by the fumes and refuse of coal and iron-works; ~ *currant*, shrub *Ribes nigrum*; its small black fruit; ~ *damp*, choke-damp of coal-mines; *B~ Death*, outbreak of plague, mostly in bubonic form, which spread into Europe from Asia in the 14th c., its most lethal year in England being 1348–9, so called from the symptom of internal haemorrhages which blackened the skin of sufferers; ~ *earth*, dark soil rich in humus; *~-earth zone*, belt of this in U.S.S.R. from Ukraine to S. Siberia; ~ *eye*, eye with black or very dark iris; (also) discoloration round eye due to bruise; *~-eyed Susan*, flower with light usu. yellow petals and dark centre, esp. *Thunbergia alata* and *Rudbeckia hirta*; *~-fellow*, Australian aboriginal; ~ *flag*, black flag used by pirates as ensign, as signal of execution etc.; *bla'ckfly*, kind of aphis; also collect.; *B~ Friar*, Dominican; ~ *frost*, hard frost without snow or rime; ***blackguard*** (blă'gârd) (*adj.* & *n.*) scoundrel(ly),

BLACKBERRY BLACKBIRD

foul-mouthed (person); (*v.t.*) revile scurrilously; *blackguardly* (*adj.*); **bla'ckhead, black-headed greasy plug in mouth of hair follicle**; ~ *hole*, any dark hole or deep cell, esp. (hist.) punishment-cell or guard-room in barracks; *B~ Hole of Calcutta*, punishment-cell of the barracks in Fort William, Calcutta, in which 146 Europeans were confined for a night (1756) by order of Suraj ud Daula and only 23 survived until the morning; *~-house*, (Sc.) turf house; house built of unmortared stone, esp. in NW. Scotland and the Hebrides; ~ *jack*, pirate's black flag; ~ *jack*: see JACK[2]; *~-lead*, (pencil containing) graphite; (*v.t.*) colour or rub with (preparation of) graphite; *bla'ckleg*, swindler (esp. on turf); workman who breaks rules of a particular trade or group, works for employer whose men are on strike, etc.; (*v.*) act as blackleg; ~ *letter*, Gothic type, style of type used by early printers and still occas., esp. in Germany, as dist. from roman; ~ *list*, list of persons against whom charges are made, convictions recorded, etc.; *bla'cklist* (*v.t.*); *bla'ckmail*, (hist.) tribute exacted on Scottish and Highland borders by freebooters in return for protection and immunity; hence, payment extorted by threats or pressure, esp. by threatening to reveal discreditable secret; extortion of such payment; so *bla'ckmail* (*v.t.*); *bla'ckmailer* (*n.*); *B~ Maria*, prison van; during the war of 1914–18, large shell which on bursting emitted masses of black smoke; ~ *mark*: see sense 3; ~ *market*, illegitimate traffic in controlled goods or currencies or commodities in short supply; hence *blackmarketeer* (*n.* & *v.i.*); ~ *mass*, mass for the dead, at which vestments and drapings are black; travesty of this, used in the cult of Satanism; ~ *monk*, Benedictine (from the colour of his habit); *B~ Museum*, collection of objects connected with crime, at Scotland Yard; *B~ Prince*, 16th-c. name given, for unknown reasons, to Edward (1330–76), the eldest son of Edward III; ~ *pudding*, kind of sausage made of blood and suet; *B~ Rod*, gentleman usher to Lord Chamberlain's department, the House of Lords, and the Chapter of the Garter, so called from his ebony rod of office; *B~ Sea*, tideless sea between U.S.S.R. and Turkey; ~ *sheep*, scoundrel, unsatisfactory or disreputable member *of* (family etc.); *Bla'ckshirt*, Fascist (from black shirt in uniform of Fascist militia); *bla'cksmith*, smith working in iron (dist. from whitesmith, who works in tin etc.); ~ *spot*, place notorious for accidents, esp. on highway;

~ *tea*: see TEA; *bla'ckthorn*, sloe (*Prunus spinosa*), a thorny shrub bearing white flowers before the leaves and small dark-purple fruits; *blackthorn winter*, time when this thorn blossoms, usu. with cold weather and NE. winds; ~ *velvet*, mixture of stout and champagne; ~ *vomit*, (blackish matter vomited in severe cases of) yellow fever; *B~ Watch*: see WATCH; *bla'ckwater fever*, tropical fever, originating in malarial infection, characterized by brown or blue-black urine; ~ *widow*, female of venomous black spider *Latrodectus mactans*. **blă'ckish** *adj.* **blă'cklў** *adv.* **blă'cknėss** *n.*

blăck *n.* 1. Black colour, paint, etc.; *in the* ~, (book-keeping) showing a credit balance. 2. Black substance, as soot etc.; fungus, smut, in wheat etc. 3. Black variety of anything; black cloth or clothing. 4. Negro. 5. (Player using) dark pieces in chess etc. 6. (slang) Blackmail (*put the* ~ *on*). ~ *v.t.* Make black, polish with blacking; declare to be 'black' (see *adj.*, 3); ~ *out*, obliterate (printed matter) with printer's ink; obscure (window, street, etc.) so that no light is visible from outside or from the air; extinguish lights during stage performance; become unconscious; *bla'ckout* (*n.*) (1) (period of) obscuration of artificial lights, esp. in war-time; material with which this is done; (2) failure or stoppage of electrical power, radio signal, etc.; (3) temporary loss of vision and consciousness, esp. in aviators when changing direction at high speeds, caused by blood being drawn away from the head; (4) temporary loss of memory.

blă'ckamoor *n.* (joc. or derog.) Negro; dark-skinned person.

blă'cken *v.* Make, grow, black or dark; speak evil of.

blă'cking *n.* (esp.) Paste or liquid for blacking or polishing boots.

Blă'ckmôre, Richard Doddridge (1825–1900). English novelist, author of 'Lorna Doone'.

Blă'ckstone, Sir William (1723–80). English jurist, author of 'Commentaries on the Laws of England' (1765–9).

Blă'ckwŏŏd, William (1776–1834). Scottish publisher; founded 'Blackwood's Magazine' (1817).

blă'dder *n.* 1. Membranous bag in human and other animal bodies esp, urinary bladder; animal's bladder or part of it prepared for various uses, inflated, etc. 2. Anything inflated and hollow, wordy man, windbag; inflated pericarp or vesicle in plants and seaweeds; *bla'dderwrack*, species of seaweed (*Fucus vesiculosus*) with air-bladders in substance of fronds

blāde *n.* 1. Flat lanceolate leaf of grass and cereals; (bot.) broad thin expanded part of leaf as opp. to petiole or leaf-stalk. 2. Broad flattened leaf-like part of instrument, as oar, paddle, spade, aircraft propeller, etc.; front flat part of tongue; broad flattened bone, esp. shoulder-blade; *~-bone*, scapula; this part of animal as cut of meat. 3. Thin cutting part of edged tool or weapon; detachable usu. two-edged cutting part of safety razor. 4. Gallant, free-and-easy fellow.

blae'berrў (blāb-) *n.* = BILBERRY.

blague (-ahg) *n.* Humbug, claptrap.

blain *n.* Inflamed swelling or sore on skin.

Blair[1], Eric Arthur (1903–50). English novelist and essayist, born in Bengal; author, under his pseudonym George Orwell, of the political satires 'Animal Farm' (1945) and '1984' (1949), and writings on social themes.

Blair[2], Robert (1699–1746). Scottish poet, author of a melancholy and (in his own time) highly successful blank-verse poem, 'The Grave' (1743).

Blāke[1], Robert (1599–1657). English admiral; fought with distinction against the Dutch and Spanish fleets.

Blāke[2], William (1757–1827). English poet, painter, and mystic; engraved, and sometimes coloured by hand, many of his own works,

BLAKE: GOD CREATING THE UNIVERSE

which included the lyrical 'Songs of Innocence' (1789) and 'Songs of Experience' (1794), and the 'Prophetic Books' (1793–1804).

blāme *n.* Censure; responsibility for bad result. ~ *v.t.* Find fault with; fix responsibility on. **blā'melėss** *adj.* Innocent. **blā'melėsslў** *adv.* **blā'melėssnėss** *n.* **blā'meworthy** (-mwêrdhĭ) *adj.*

Blanc (blahṅ), Jean Joseph Charles Louis (1811–82). French socialist and historian; was given by the revolution of 1848 an opportunity to put into practice his theories of the organization of labour; his experiment lasted less than two months and he was forced to flee to England, not returning to France until 1871.

blanch (-ah-) *v.* Make white by withdrawing colour, peeling (almonds), immersing in boiling water (raw meat), or depriving of light (plants); make or grow pale with fear, cold, etc.

blancmange (bl*a*mŏ′nzh) *n.* Opaque jelly of cornflour etc. and milk, usu. sweetened and flavoured.

blă′ncō *n.* White preparation for whitening accoutrements; similar preparation of khaki colour. ~ *v.t.* Treat with blanco. [tradename]

blănd *adj.* Smooth and suave in manner, gentle; balmy, mild. **blă′ndlỹ** *adv.* **blă′ndnėss** *n.*

blă′ndĭsh *v.* Flatter, coax. **blă′ndĭshment** *n.*

blănk *adj.* 1. Not written or printed on; with spaces left for signature or details. 2. Empty, not filled. 3. Void of interest, incident, result, or expression; unrelieved, sheer. 4. ~ *cartridge*, one without a ball; ~ *cheque*, cheque signed by drawer, with amount left for payee to fill in; hence, full discretionary power; ~ *verse*, (esp.) English unrhymed verse of five-foot iambics; ~ *wall*, wall without opening; (fig.) impassable obstacle. **blă′nklỹ** *adv.* **blănk** *n.* 1. Void; space left to be filled up in document; dash (—) written in place of omitted letter or word(s); (parl.) provisional words printed in italics in bill. 2. Blank ticket in sweepstake (i.e. one not inscribed with the name of a runner); hence, *draw* ~, elicit no response, fail. 3. Piece of metal ready for stamping as coin, medal, etc.

blă′nkėt *n.* Rectangular piece of woollen etc. material used for warmth esp. as bed-covering, horse-cloth, etc.; (as *adj.*) covering or including all contingencies etc.; *born on the wrong side of the* ~, illegitimate; *wet* ~, (fig.) discouraging person; ~*-bath*, washing of sick person by stages while keeping him warm between coverings; ~ *stitch*, stitch for finishing raw edge, used on blankets. ~ *v.t.* Cover with blanket; stifle, keep quiet (scandal, question, etc.); toss in a blanket; take wind from sails of (yacht) by passing to windward of her.

Blănkėteer′s (-z) *n.pl.* (hist.) Body of workmen who met at the so-called Blanket Meeting in St. Peter's Field, Manchester, in March 1817, provided with blankets or rugs in order to march to London and put their grievances before the Government.

blă′nkėting *n.* (esp.) Material for blankets.

blanquette (blahṅkĕ′t) *n.* Dish of meat etc. in white sauce.

blāre *v.* & *n.* (Make) sound of trumpet; utter loudly.

Blâr′ney[1]. Village near Cork in S. Ireland; ~ *stone*, inscribed stone, very difficult to reach, in the Castle of Blarney, supposed to confer upon anyone who kisses it a cajoling tongue and the art of flattery or of telling lies with unblushing effrontery.

blâr′ney[2] *n.* & *v.* (Use, assail with) cajoling talk or nonsense.

blasé (blah′zā) *adj.* Cloyed, exhausted, with pleasure.

blăsphē′me *v.* Talk impiously; utter profanity about, revile. **blăsphē′mer, blă′sphėmỹ** *ns.* **blă′sphėmous** *adj.* **blă′sphėmouslỹ** *adv.*

blast (-ah-) *n.* Strong gust of wind; violent gust of air caused by explosion of bomb etc.; blowing or sound of trumpet or other wind-instruments; strong current of air used in smelting etc.; quantity of explosive used in blasting; (colloq.) violent reprimand; (*at*) *full* ~, (colloq.) at maximum speed, capacity, etc.; ~*-furnace*, smelting-furnace into which a blast of compressed heated air is driven by a blowing-engine. ~ *v.t.* 1. Blow up, break, dislodge, with explosives. 2. Wither, shrivel, blight. 3. (of rocket or spacecraft, usu. ~ *off*) Take off, be launched into space; use power in flight; ~*-off*, (thrust used in) launching of rocket etc. ~ *int.* Exclamation of annoyance. **bla′stėd** *adj.* (esp., colloq.) Damnable.

blă'stoderm *n.* External layer of cells formed as a result of cleavage of a yolked egg, characteristic of eggs of reptiles, birds, and, in a different form, insects.

blă'stūla *n.* (pl. *-lae*). (biol.) Early embryonic stage, usu. a hollow ball of cells, produced by cleavage of an egg (cf. GASTRULA).

blā'tant *adj.* Noisy, vulgarly clamorous; palpably obvious. **blā'tantlў** *adv.* **blā'tancў** *n.*

blather: see BLETHER.

Blavă'tskў, Helena Petrovna (1831–91). Russian spiritualist, founder (in New York) of the Theosophical Society.

blāze[1] *v.i.* Burn with bright flame; be brilliantly lighted; burn with excitement etc.; show bright colours; emit light. ~ *n.* Bright flame or fire; glow of colour, bright display; *go to ~s*, (slang) go to hell.

blāze[2] *n.* White mark on face of horse or ox; white mark made on tree by chipping off bark, to indicate path, boundary, etc. ~ *v.t.* Mark (tree, path) with blaze; (fig.) ~ *a trail*, show a new way by pioneering activity.

blāze[3] *v.t.* Proclaim as with trumpet.

blā'zer *n.* (esp.) Unlined (orig. brightly coloured) jacket, usu. with badge on pocket, worn with

sports clothes or as part of school uniform.

blā'zon *n.* Heraldic shield, coat of arms, bearings, or banner; correct description of these; record, description, esp. of virtues etc. ~ *v.t.* Describe or paint (arms) heraldically; inscribe with arms etc. in colours; give lustre to; set forth in fitting words; proclaim. **blā'zonrў** *n.* (Art of describing or painting) heraldic devices, armorial bearings; brightly coloured display.

bleach *v.* Whiten by exposure to sunlight or chemical process; *bleaching powder*, chemical, such as chloride of lime, used for bleaching. ~ *n.* Bleaching process or substance.

bleak[1] *n.* Small European river-fish, *Alburnus lucidus*.

bleak[2] *adj.* Bare of vegetation; exposed, wind-swept; cold, chilly, dreary; (of person) depressed, lifeless. **blea'klў** *adv.* **blea'kness** *n.*

blear *adj.* Dim, filmy, rheumy; misty, indistinct; ~*-eyed* (*adj.*). ~ *v.t.* Dim (eyes) with tears, rheum, etc.; blur. **blear'ў** *adj.*

bleat *v.* (of sheep, goat, etc.) Utter characteristic tremulous cry; make sound resembling this, speak feebly or foolishly. ~ *n.* Cry of sheep, goat, etc.; any similar sound.

blĕb *n.* Small blister or bubble.

bleed *v.* (past t. & past part. *blĕd*). 1. Emit blood; suffer wounds or violent death; (of plants) emit sap; (of dyes) come out in water. 2. Draw blood surgically from; allow (liquid or gas) to escape from (a container). 3. Part with money, suffer extortion; extort money from. 4. (print.) Cut into print when trimming margin.

blee'der *n.* (esp.) Person suffering from haemophilia.

blee'dĭng *adj.* (esp., slang) Euphemism for 'bloody'.

bleep *n.* & *v.i.* (Emit) high-pitched intermittent sound.

blĕ'mish *v.t.* Mar, spoil beauty or perfection of, sully. ~ *n.* Physical or moral defect, stain, flaw.

blĕnch *v.i.* Start aside, flinch, quail.

blĕnd *v.* (past part. occas. *blent*). Mix, mingle (esp. sorts of tea, tobacco, spirits, etc., to produce a certain quality); mingle intimately *with*; mix so as to be inseparable

BLENHEIM PALACE

and indistinguishable; pass imperceptibly into each other. ~ *n.* Blending; mixture made by blending.

blĕnde *n.* Zinc sulphide. [Ger. *blenden* deceive, because although it often resembled galena, it did not yield lead]

Blĕ'nheim (-nĭm). Village in Bavaria, scene of the victory (1704) of MARLBOROUGH and Prince Eugene over the French and Bavarians; ~ *Palace*, mansion near Woodstock, Oxfordshire, built by the nation for Marlborough after the battle, and designed by Sir John Vanbrugh; ~ *Orange*, variety of golden-coloured late-ripening eating apple, first grown at Blenheim Palace.

blĕ'nnȳ *n.* Small spiny-finned fish of genus *Blennius* of family Blenniidae, mostly shore-fishes found in shallow pools.

blent: see BLEND.

blĕphari'tĭs *n.* Inflammation of the eyelids.

Blériot (blārĭō), Louis (1872–1936). French airman, first man to cross the English Channel in an aeroplane (1909).

blĕss *v.t.* (past part. *blessed*, sometimes *blest*). 1. Consecrate (esp. food); sanctify by making sign of cross. 2. Call holy, adore; glorify for benefits received. 3. Pronounce words (held) to confer supernatural favour and well-being upon; make happy or successful; make happy *with* some gift; *bless me!*, *bless you!*, (*God*) *bless my soul!*, *I'm blest!*, etc., exclamations of surprise or indignation.

blĕ'ssėd (*or* -st) *adj.* 1. Consecrated; revered; fortunate; in paradise. 2. Blissful, bringing happiness. 3. (euphem.) Cursed etc. **blĕ'ssėdlȳ** *adv.* **blĕ'ssėdnėss** *n.*

blĕ'ssĭng *n.* Declaration, invocation, or bestowal, of divine favour; grace before or after food; gift of God, nature, etc., that one is glad of; ~ *in disguise*, misfortune that works for eventual good.

blest: see BLESS.

blĕ'ther, blă'ther (-dh-) *n.* & *v.i.* (Talk) loquacious nonsense.

Bligh (blī), William (1754–1817). English vice-admiral, who as a lieutenant commanded the BOUNTY[2].

blight (-īt) *n.* 1. Disease of plants caused by fungoid parasites; kind of aphis destructive to fruit-trees. 2. Any obscure or mysterious malignant withering influence. ~ *v.t.* Affect with blight; exert baleful influence on; nip in the bud, mar, frustrate.

blī'ghter (-īt-) *n.* (esp., slang) Contemptible or annoying person or thing; fellow, thing.

Blī'ghtȳ (-ītĭ) *n.* (army slang) England, home, after foreign service. [Hind. *bilāyatī* foreign, European]

blī'mey *int.* (slang) Exclamation of surprise or contempt. [f. *Gorblimey* = God blind me!]

blĭmp[1] *n.* Small non-rigid type of airship.

Blĭmp[2], Colonel. Character invented by the cartoonist David Low (1891–1963) representing a muddle-headed, obese, elderly gentleman, pop. interpreted as type of diehard or reactionary. **blĭm'perȳ** *n.* **blĭ'mpĭsh** *adj.*

blīnd *adj.* 1. Without sight; (aeronaut.) without direct observation of objects etc., relying on instruments. 2. Without foresight, discernment, or moral or intellectual light; reckless; not ruled by purpose. 3. Secret, obscure, concealed; without windows or openings; walled up; closed at one end; (of plant) failing to flower; (cookery, of pastry case) baked without filling. 4. (slang) Very drunk. 5. ~ *alley*, one closed at one end, not leading anywhere (also fig.); ~ *arcade*, series of arches attached to wall; ~ *corner*, corner of road round which a motorist etc. cannot see; ~ *date*, social engagement arranged between two persons of opposite sex who have not met; either of these persons; ~ *man's buff*, game in which blindfolded player tries to catch others; ~ *spot*, point in the retina not sensitive to light, where the optic nerve passes through the inner coat of the eyeball (also fig.); ~ *stamping*, *tooling*, (bookbinding), stamping, tooling, without the use of ink or gold-leaf; *bli'ndworm*, slow-worm. ~ *adv*. **blī'ndlў** *adv*. **blī'ndnėss** *n*.

blind *v*. Deprive of sight permanently or temporarily; take away power of judgement, deceive; (slang) go blindly or heedlessly; drive very fast. ~ *n*. Obstruction to sight or light; screen for windows etc., esp. on roller; pretext; legitimate business concealing an illegitimate one; stalking-horse; heavy drinking-bout.

blī'ndfōld *adj*. With eyes covered with cloth; without circumspection. ~ *v.t.* Deprive of sight by covering eyes with cloth.

blĭnk *v*. 1. Shut one's eyelids momentarily, esp. involuntarily; (of eyes) shut thus. 2. (fig.) Shut one's eyes to, evade. 3. Send (tears etc.) away by blinking. 4. Shine suddenly or momentarily. ~ *n*. Blinking; momentary gleam or glimpse; shining whiteness on horizon produced by reflection from distant masses of ice; *on the* ~, (slang) failing.

blĭ'nker *n*. Either of two leather screens on horse's bridle preventing him from seeing sideways; ~ *plate*, smoke deflector. ~*v.t.* Obscure with blinkers (freq. fig.).

blĭ'nkĭng *adj*. & *adv*. (slang) Damnable, damnably.

blĭp *v*. Strike with brisk rap; make quick popping sound. ~ *n*. Act, sound, of blipping; (radar) image of object as projected on to a screen.

blĭss[1] *n*. Gladness, enjoyment; perfect joy, blessedness; being in heaven. **blĭ'ssful** *adj*. **blĭ'ssfullў** *adv*. **blĭ'ssfulnėss** *n*.

Blĭss[2], Sir Arthur (1891–). British composer; Master of the Queen's Music 1953– .

blĭ'ster *n*. Thin vesicle on skin filled with serum, caused by friction, a burn, etc.; similar swelling on plant, metal, painted surface, etc.; rounded compartment protruding from body of aeroplane; anything applied to raise a blister; ~-*gas*, poison for causing blisters or intense irritation of the skin. ~ *v*. Raise blister on, be or become covered with blisters; (fig.) criticize scathingly.

B.Lit. *abbrev*. Bachelor of Literature.

blīthe (-dh) *adj*. (poet.) Gay, joyous. **blī'thelў** *adv*. **blī'thesome** *adj*.

blĭ'ther *v.i.* (-dh-) = BLETHER. **blĭ'therĭng** *adj*. (esp.) Consummate; contemptible.

B.Litt. *abbrev*. *Baccalaureus Literarum* (L, = Bachelor of Letters).

blĭtz *n*. Quick, violent campaign intended to bring speedy victory, intensive air-attack; (fig.) sudden violent attack. ~ *v.t.* Damage, destroy, by air-attack. [Ger. *Blitzkrieg* lightning war]

blĭ'zzard *n*. (orig. U.S.) Dense snow-storm, esp. one in which powdery snow is swept up from the ground by a high wind.

bloat[1] *v.t.* Cure (herring) by salting and smoking. **bloa'ter** *n*. Herring cured by bloating.

bloat[2] *v*. Inflate, swell. **bloa'tėd** *adj*. Inflated, swollen; (fig.) swollen with pride, excessive wealth, etc.

blŏb *n*. Drop of liquid; small

roundish mass; spot of colour; (cricket) score of nought.

blŏc *n.* Combination of political parties, or of governments, groups, etc., formed to forward some interest.

Blŏch (-χ), Ernest (1880–1959). Swiss-American composer.

blŏck *n.* 1. Log of wood; large piece of wood for chopping or hammering on, mounting horse from, etc., (hist.) on which condemned persons were beheaded. 2. Compact usu. solid piece of any substance; unhewn lump of rock; prepared piece of building-stone; mould or form on which something is shaped or displayed; piece of wood or metal engraved for printing; mech.) pulley, system of pulley mounted in case; (slang) head. 3. Section, compact set or group; large single building containing a number of flats, offices, etc.; group of buildings surrounded by (usu. four) streets; number of sheets of paper fastened together at edge; (Austral.) each large plot into which land for settlement is divided. 4. Obstruction; line of vehicles unable to proceed; (parl.) notice that bill will be opposed, which prevents its being taken at certain times; (psychol.) mental obstruction preventing a particular thought or expression; (path.) obstruction of a nervous or muscular impulse. 5. (cricket) Spot on which batsman blocks ball and rests bat before playing. 6. ~-*buster*, (slang) large high-explosive bomb; *blo'ckhead*, stupid person; *blo'ckhouse*, detached fort (orig. one blocking passage), occas. one of connected chain of posts; one-storeyed timber building with loopholes; reinforced concrete shelter; ~ *letters*, *writing*, (writing with) detached letters, as in printing, usu. capitals; ~ *printing*, hand-printing of fabrics with wooden blocks on which design is carved. ~ *v.t.* Obstruct (passage etc.); put obstacles in way of; restrict use or conversion of currency etc.; announce opposition to (bill); (cricket) stop (ball) with bat; shape on block; emboss (book cover); ~ *in*, *out*, sketch roughly, plan; *blocked*, (of ballet shoes) with stiffened toes.

blŏckā'de *n.* Surrounding of place, blocking of harbour, etc., by hostile forces to prevent goods etc. from reaching or leaving it; *raise*, *run the* ~, remove, evade, the blockading force. ~ *v.t.* Subject to blockade.

blŏ'ckage *n.* Obstruction.

Blŏk, Alexander (1880–1921). Russian poet, famous for his poem 'The Twelve', an apologia for the Russian Revolution.

blōke *n.* (slang) Man, fellow.

blŏnde *adj.* (also, esp. U.S., *blŏnd*; of hair) Light coloured, flaxen; (of complexion) fair. ~ *n.* Woman with blonde hair.

Blŏ'ndel de Nesle (nāl) (12th c.). Minstrel who, acc. to legend, discovered the place of captivity of his master Richard Cœur-de-Lion by singing under the window a song they had jointly composed.

blood (-ŭd) *n.* 1. Liquid circulating in the veins and arteries of vertebrates, carrying nourishment and oxygen to all parts of the body and bringing away waste products to be excreted, consisting of a serum or plasma in which corpuscles are suspended and usu. red because of their haemoglobin content; (hist.) one of the four humours (see HUMOUR, 4). 2. Analogous liquid in invertebrates performing (some of) the same functions. 3. (fig.) Sap, grape-juice, etc. 4. Taking of life, guilt of bloodshed; passion, temperament, mettle. 5. Race, relationship, kin, descent, parentage. 6. Dandy, man of fashion. 7. ~-*ally*, ally (marble) with red veins; ~-*bath*, massacre; ~-*brother*, brother by birth; one bound to another in solemn friendship by ceremonial mingling of blood; ~ *count*, (determination of) number of blood cells in a given volume of blood; ~-*donor*: see DONOR; ~-*feud*, feud between families of which one has spilt the other's blood; ~ *group*, one of several types into which human blood may

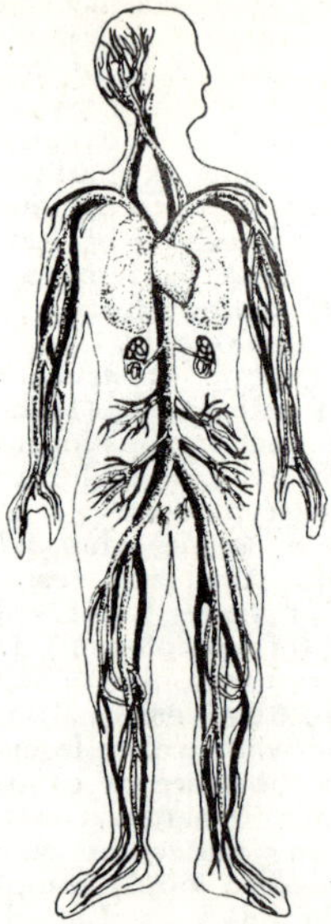

VENOUS and ARTERIAL SYSTEM

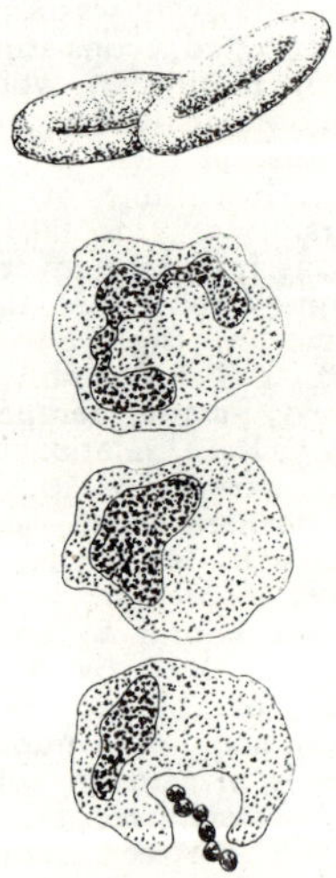

BLOOD CELLS

be divided on basis of its compatibility with that of other persons; *~-heat*, normal heat of the blood, 37 °C (98·4 °F) in man; *bloo'dhound*, large keen-scented dog formerly used for tracking cattle, criminals, etc.; *~-letting*, surgical removal of some of patient's blood; *~-money*, reward to witness for securing capital sentence; compensation for slaughter of relative; *~ orange*, orange with red-streaked pulp; *~ poisoning*, condition caused by presence of pathogenic bacteria in the blood; *~-pressure*, pressure of blood against walls of arteries as it is impelled along them, freq. measured in diagnosis because in certain conditions it may be higher (hypertension) or lower (hypotension) than normal; *~ relation*, one related by virtue of common descent, not by marriage; *bloo'dshed*, spilling of blood, slaughter; *bloo'dshot*, (of eye) suffused, tinged, with blood; *~ sport*, sport involving killing of animals, esp. hunting; *bloo'dstock*, thoroughbred horses collectively; *bloo'dstone*, green chalcedony with spots or veins of red jasper; helioptrope; *bloo'dstream*, circulating blood in human or animal system; *~-sucker*, leech; extortioner; *bloo'dthirsty*, eager for bloodshed; *~-vessel*, vein, artery, or capillary conveying blood; *bloo'dworm*, bright red larva of a midge, used as bait in fishing. *~ v.t.* Remove surgically some of the blood of; allow first taste of blood to (hound); smear face of (novice at hunting) with blood of fox after kill. **bloo'dlėss** *adj.* Without blood; unfeeling; pale; without bloodshed.

bloo'dy̆ (-ŭdĭ) *adj.* 1. Of, like, running or smeared with, blood. 2. Involving, loving, resulting from, bloodshed; cruel. 3. (slang) Damned. 4. *B~ Assizes*, those held in 1685 by Judge JEFFREYS; *~-minded*, cruel; stubbornly intransigent or obstructive. *~ adv.* (slang) Confoundedly, very. *~ v.t.* Make bloody; stain with blood.

blōōm[1] *n.* Flower, esp. of plants grown or admired chiefly for the flower, florescence. 2.

Prime, perfection; flush, glow; delicate powdery deposit on grapes, plums, etc.; cloudiness on a shiny surface; freshness. ~ *v.* Bear flowers, be in flower; come into, be in, full beauty; flourish; (photog.) coat (lens) with metallic fluoride to reduce surface reflection. **blōō'ming** *adj.* (esp., slang) = BLOODY, 3.

blōōm[2] *n.* Mass of puddled iron hammered or squeezed into thick bar. ~ *v.t.* Make (puddled iron) into a bloom.

blōō'mer[1] *n.* (slang) Blunder.

Blōō'mer[2], Mrs. Amelia Jenks (1818–94). American advocate of 'rational dress' for women, invented by Mrs. E. S. Miller and consisting of a small jacket, a full skirt descending a little below the knee, and trousers down to the ankle.

blōō'mers (-z) *n.pl.* 1. (hist.) Costume advocated by Mrs. BLOOMER[2]; loose trousers reaching to the knee, knickerbockers, formerly worn by women for gymnastics, cycling, etc. 2. Undergarment of this shape, (colloq.) knickers.

Blōō'msbury̆ (-z-). District of west-central London containing British Museum and many buildings of London University, formerly a fashionable and later a literary quarter; (attrib.) intellectual, highbrow.

blŏ'ssom *v.i.* Open into flower (lit. & fig.). ~ *n.* Flower, mass of flowers on fruit-tree etc.; early stage of growth, promise. **blŏ'ssomy̆** *adj.*

blŏt[1] *n.* Spot or stain of ink etc., dark patch; disfigurement, blemish, defect; disgraceful act or quality in good character. ~ *v.* 1. Spot or stain with ink, etc.; make blots; smudge; sully, detract from; obliterate (writing etc.) with blot, destroy. 2. Dry with *blotting-paper*, absorbent paper for soaking up wet ink-marks.

blŏt[2] *n.* Exposed piece in backgammon.

blŏtch *n.* Discoloured or inflamed patch on skin; irregular patch of ink, colour, etc. **blŏ'tched** (-cht), **blŏ'tchy̆** *adjs.*

blŏ'tter *n.* Pad of blotting-paper.

blŏ'ttō *adj.* (slang) Very drunk.

blouse (-z) *n.* 1. (French) workman's or peasant's loose linen or cotton garment, usu. belted at waist. 2. Woman's or child's loose garment for upper part of body, usu. worn tucked into skirt or trousers. 3. Upper part of battledress, fitting closely at waist. ~ *v.* Arrange (material, bodice), be arranged, in loose light folds like a blouse.

blow[1] (-ō) *v.* (past t. *blew* pr. blōō, past part. *blown*). 1. Move as wind does, act as current of air; send current of air from mouth; pant, puff; (of whales etc.) eject water and air; cause to pant, put out of breath. 2. Drive, be driven, by blowing; sound (wind instrument, or note *on* or *with* this); direct air-current at; clear, empty, by air-current; break *in* or send flying *off*, *out*, *up*, by explosion; (of instrument) sound; ~ *in*, (colloq.) come in unexpectedly, drop in; ~ *up*, inflate, shatter or be shattered by explosion; reprove violently; (photog., colloq.) enlarge. 3. (of flies) Deposit eggs in. 4. (of electric fuse or lamp filament) Melt when overloaded; (of tin of food) swell or burst from internal pressure. 5. (slang) Curse, confound; squander. 6. *blow'fly*, bluebottle, flesh-fly; *blow'hole*, each of two holes (containing the nostrils) at top of head in whales etc. through which they blow; hole in ice through which seals etc. can breathe; *blow'lamp*, portable apparatus for directing intensely hot flame on a limited area; *blow'out*, bursting (of motor-tyre etc.); (slang) large meal, feast; *blow'pipe*, tube for heating flame by blowing air or other gas into it; tube through which arrows or darts are propelled by blowing; ~*-up*, explosion; (colloq.) enlargement. ~ *n.* Blowing, taste of fresh air; blowing of flute, one's nose, etc.

blow[2] (-ō) *v.i.* (past t. *blew* pr. blōō, past part. *blown*). (archaic

& poet.) Burst into, be in, flower. ~ *n.* Blossoming.

blow[3] (-ō) *n.* Hard stroke with fist, hammer, etc.; disaster, shock; *~-by-~*, (of narrative) giving all details in sequence.

blow'er (-ō*er*) *n.* (esp.) 1. Apparatus for increasing draught of fire, esp. sheet of iron held or fixed before grate. 2. (slang) Speaking-tube, telephone.

blown: see BLOW[1,2].

blow'y (-ōĭ) *adj.* Windy, windswept.

blowzed (-zd), **blow'zy̆** *adjs.* (of woman) Red-faced, coarse-looking; slatternly.

blŭb *v.i.* (colloq.) Cry, weep.

blŭ'bber *n.* 1. Fatty tissue of aquatic mammals, which keeps them warm, esp. *whale-~*, used as source of oil. 2. Weeping. ~ *adj.* (of lips) Swollen, protruding. ~ *v.* Utter with sobs, weep noisily.

Blü'cher (-ūχ-), Gebhard Lebe-recht von (1742–1819). Prussian soldier; led the Prussian army at the battle of WATERLOO.

blu'chers (-ōō*kerz*) *n.pl.* (19th-c.) Strong leather half-boots or high shoes. [f. BLÜCHER]

blŭ'dgeon (-jon) *n.* Short heavy-headed stick. ~ *v.t.* Strike heavily or repeatedly with or as with bludgeon.

blue (-ōō) *adj.* 1. Coloured like the cloudless sky, or with darker or paler shades of this colour; livid, leaden-coloured. 2. Affected with fear, discomfort, anxiety, low spirits, etc. 3. Dressed in blue; belonging to a political party (in Britain usu. Conservative) whose badge is blue; (of talk etc.) indecent, obscene. 4. ~ *baby*, infant suffering from congenital cyanosis; *blue'bell*, wild hyacinth, *Endymion non-scriptus*; (Sc. & north.) harebell; ~ *blood*, high birth; ~ *bonnet*, round flat blue woollen cap formerly generally worn in Scotland; (hist.) Scottish soldier wearing this; ~ *book*, parliamentary or Privy Council report, issued in blue paper cover; *blue'-bottle*, dipterous insect with blue body of genus *Calliphora* (esp. *C. vomitoria* and *C. erythroce-*

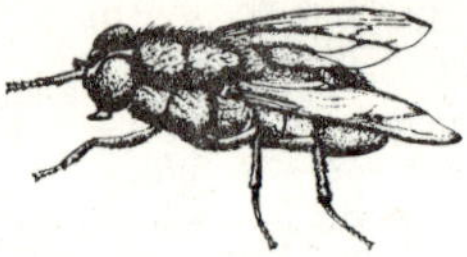

phala), which deposits eggs on meat, carrion, etc.; blue cornflower; (slang) policeman; ~ *cheese*, cheese with veins of blue mould; ~ *chip*, (Stock Exch.) share that is a fairly reliable investment, though less secure than gilt-edged (also attrib.); *~-coat boy, school*, (pupil of) charity school, esp. of Christ's Hospital, whose uniform is a long dark-blue belted gown and yellow stockings; *~-eyed boy*, (colloq.) favourite; ~ *grass*, species of *Poa*, esp. *P. pratensis* as found in Kentucky and Virginia; ~ *gum*, Australian variety of eucalyptus, *Eucalyptus globulus*, with bluish bark; *blue'-jacket*, seaman in Royal Navy; *B~ John*, blue fluorspar found in Derbyshire; ~ *law*, (U.S.) severely Puritanical law; ~ *mould*, fungus of genus *Penicillium* forming on food; *B~ Nile*: see NILE; ~ *pencil*, pencil making blue mark, used chiefly in making corrections, obliterations, etc.; *~-pencil* (*v.t.*) make marks, cuts, or alterations in; censor; *B~ Peter*, blue flag with white square in centre, hoisted by ship before sailing; *~-point*, (U.S.) small well-flavoured oyster from south shore of Long Island [f. name of headland]; *~-print*, photographic print of white lines on blue ground or blue lines on white ground, used in copying plans, machine-drawings, etc.; (fig.) detailed plan, scheme; ~ *ribbon*, ribbon of the Garter; greatest honour or distinction in any sphere; badge of teetotalism; *blue'stocking*, woman having or affecting literary tastes and learning [f. *B~ Stocking Society*, name given in 18th c. to meetings for literary conversation etc. at the houses of Mrs Elizabeth Montagu (1720–1800) and her circle, from the fact that the men attending might wear the blue worsted stockings of ordinary day-time dress instead of the black silk of evening]; ~ *tit*: see TIT[1]; ~ *vitriol*, copper sulphate; ~ *water*, deep water, the open sea. **blū'ish** *adj.* **blue'nėss** *n.* **blue** *n.* 1. Blue colour or pigment; blue powder used in laundering; blue cloth etc. 2. Sky, sea (*the* ~); *out of the* ~, unexpectedly. 3. (Place in team etc. given to) one chosen to represent Oxford University (*dark* ~) or Cambridge (*light* ~) in athletic or sporting contests. 4. (pl.) Melancholy; (type of) melancholy song of Amer. Negro origin; *the Blues*, the Royal HORSE Guards. ~ *v.t.* (pres. part. *blueing* or *bluing*) Make blue; treat with laundering blue; (slang) squander (money).

Blue'beard (blo͞ob-). Hero of a popular tale, who killed several wives in turn because they showed undue curiosity about a locked room; *~'s chamber*, repository of mysterious or horrible secrets.

blŭff[1] *adj.* Having prependicular broad front; abrupt, blunt, frank, hearty. **blŭ'fflÿ** *adv.* **blŭ'ffnėss** *n.* **blŭff** *n.* Headland with perpendicular broad face.

blŭff[2] *v.* Make pretence of strength to gain advantage etc. (orig. in poker); mislead thus. ~ *n.* Bluffing; *call person's* ~, challenge his attempted bluff.

blŭ'nder *v.* Move blindly, stumble; make gross mistake. ~ *n.* Stupid or careless mistake. **blŭ'nderer** *n.*

blŭ'nderbŭss *n.* Short flintlock gun with large bore, firing many balls or slugs, used esp. in 17th and 18th centuries. [Corupt of Du. *donderbus* lit. thundergun]

blŭnge (-j) *v.t.* (pottery) Mix (clay, powdered flint, etc.) with water.

blŭnt *adj.* Dull, not sensitive; without sharp edge or point; outspoken. **blŭ'ntlÿ** *adv.* **blŭ'ntnėss** *n.* **blŭnt** *v.t.* Make less sharp or sensitive.

blûr *n.* Smear of ink etc.; dimness, confused effect. ~ *v.* Smear with ink etc.; sully, disfigure; make indistinct; efface; dim.

blûrb *n.* (orig. U.S. slang) Publisher's eulogy or description of book printed on jacket etc.; descriptive or commendatory paragraph.

blûrt *v.t.* Burst *out* with, utter abruptly.

blŭsh *v.i.* Become red with shame or other emotion; be ashamed; be red or pink. ~ *n.* Glance, glimpse; reddening of face in shame etc.; rosy glow, flush of light.

blŭ'ster *v.* Storm boisterously; utter overbearingly. **blŭ'sterer** *n.* **blŭ'ster** *n.* Boisterous blowing, noisy self-assertive talk, threats. **blŭ'sterous, blŭ'sterÿ** *adjs.*

B.M. *abbrev.* Bachelor of Medicine; British Museum.

B.M.A. *abbrev.* British Medical Association.

B.Mus. *abbrev.* Bachelor of Music.

B.N.C. *abbrev.* Brasenose College, Oxford.

bō, boh (bō) *int.* Exclamation used to startle; *he cannot say bo to a goose*, he behaves meekly or timidly.

B.O. *abbrev.* Body odour.

bō'a *n.* 1. S. Amer. tropical non-poisonous snake of genus *B~* that kills its prey by constriction or compression (pop. extended to pythons); ~ *constrictor*, large Brazilian species of boa; any great crushing snake. 2. Long round fur or feather wrap formerly worn round throat by women.

B.O.A.C. *abbrev.* British Overseas Airways Corporation.

Bōadicē'a: see BOUDICCA.

boar (bôr) *n.* Uncastrated male swine (wild or tame); flesh of this; *wild* ~, European wild swine, *Sus scrofa*.

board (bôrd) *n.* 1. Thin piece of timber, usu. rectangular, and of greater length than breadth; one or more pieces of this or similar substance, used in games, for posting notices, etc.; (pl.) the stage; thick stiff paper used in bookbinding etc.; *across the* ~, embracing all categories. 2. Table spread for meals; food served, daily meals provided at contract price or in return for services; council-table, councillors, committee. 3. Ship's side (only in certain phrases); (naut.) tack; *on* ~, aboard, in or into ship, train, etc. 4. ~ *school*, (hist.): see SCHOOL board; *B~ of Trade*, former British government department dealing with problems of trade; (U.S.) association of businessmen etc. to promote trade; *B~ of Trade unit*, (abbrev. B.T.U.) = KILOWATT-hour; ~ *wages*, wages paid to servants while their masters are away from home, including cost of food etc.; ~-*walk*, (U.S.) footway of boards or planks. ~ *v.* 1. Cover with boards. 2. Provide with, receive, stated meals at fixed rate; ~ *out*, place (children) in families where they are treated as members. 3. Go on board, enter (ship, train, etc.); (naut.) come alongside and force one's way on board (ship). 4. (naut.) Tack.

boar'der (bôr-) *n.* One who boards with someone; boy or girl at boarding-school; one who boards a ship to capture it.

boar'dĭng (bôr-) *n.* (esp.) ~-*house*, house in which persons are boarded and lodged for payment; ~-*school*, school in which pupils live during term-time, as dist. from day-school.

boast *n.* Exceedingly proud statement; cause of pride. ~ *v.* Praise oneself, make boast(s) (*of, about*); possess as thing to be proud of. **boa'ster** *n.* **boa'stful** *adj.* **boa'stfullȳ** *adv.* **boa'stfulnėss** *n.*

boat *n.* 1. Small open oared or sailing vessel; fishing-vessel, mail packet, small steamer; occas. large sea-going vessel; *in the same* ~, in the same predicament or circumstances. 2. Boat-shaped table-utensil for sauce etc. 3. ~-*axe*, boat-shaped battle-axe of the neolithic period in Scandinavia; ~-*hook*, long pole with hook and spike; ~-*house*, shed at water's edge for keeping boat; *boa'tman*, hirer, or rower or sailer of boat for hire; *B~ Race*, (esp.) race between crews of Oxford and Cambridge Universities, rowed annually on the Thames from Putney to Mortlake; *boatswain* (bō'sn), *bo'sun*, ship's officer in charge of sails, rigging, etc., and summoning men to duty with whistle; ~ *train*, train having connection with a steamer at a port. ~ *v.i.* Go in boat, esp. for pleasure.

boa'ter *n.* Straw hat with flat crown and brim.

Bō'ăz: see RUTH[2].

bŏb[1] *n.* 1. Weight on pendulum, plum-line , or kite tail. 2. Knot of hair, tassel-shaped curl; horse's docked tail bobbed hair. ~ *v.t.* Cut (hair) to hang short of the shoulders.

bŏb[2] *n.* 1. Jerk, bouncing movement; curtsy. 2. (bell-ringing) Kinds of change in long peals; *treble* ~, one in which the bells, esp. the treble, dodge; ~ *minor, triple, major, royal, maximus*, bobs on 6, 7, 8, 10, and 12 bells. ~ *v.i.* Move up and down, dance, rebound; curtsy; ~ *for*, try to catch (cherries, apples, etc., floating or hanging) with the mouth.

bŏb[3] *n.* (at Eton) *dry-~*, one who plays cricket, opp. *wet-~*, one who rows. [prob. pet-form of *Robert*]

bŏb[4] *n.* (slang) Shilling.

bŏb[5] *n.* & *v.i.* (Ride on) a bob-sled or -sleigh.

bŏ'bbĭn *n.* 1. Cylinder on which thread, wire, etc., may be wound, reel, spool; ~ *lace*: see LACE. 2. Rounded piece of wood attached to a string, for raising door-latch.

bŏ'bbĭnėt *n.* Machine-made net imitating bobbin lace.

bŏ'bbish *adj.* (slang) Brisk, well.

bŏ'bble *n.* Small woolly ball used as ornament or trimming.

bŏ'bbȳ *n.* (slang) Policeman. [Pet-form of *Robert*, in allusion to Sir Robert Peel, who was Home Secretary when the Metropolitan Police Act was passed in 1828]

bŏ'bbȳ sŏcks. Socks reaching just above the ankle, worn esp. by teenage girls. **bŏ'bbȳ-sŏ'xer** *n.* (freq. derog.) Girl wearing bobby socks.

bŏ'bolĭnk *n.* A N. Amer. songbird, the rice-bunting (*Dolichonyx oryzivorus*). [orig. *Bob* (*o'*) *Lincoln*; imit. of its call]

bŏb-slĕd, bob-sleigh (-slā) *ns.* Sledge made of two short sledges coupled together.

bŏ'bstay *n.* (naut.) Rope holding bowsprit down.

bŏ'btail *n.* (Horse or dog with) docked tail; *tag, rag, and* ~, rabble.

boca'ge (-ahzh) *n.* Representation of sylvan scenery in ceramics.

Boccă'ccio (-chĭō), Giovanni (1313–75). Italian novelist, poet, and humanist, author of the 'Decameron'.

Bŏccheri'nĭ (-kerē-) Luigi (1740–1805). Italian composer, important chiefly for his works for violoncello.

Bŏche (-sh) *n.* & *adj.* (slang, esp. in 1914–18 war) German.

bŏck *n.* Strong dark-coloured German beer. [Ger., f. *Einbockbier*, beer from *Einbeck*, in Hanover]

bōde[1] *v.* Foresee, foretell (evil); portend, foreshow; promise *well, ill.* **bō'deful** *adj.* Ominous.

Bode[2] (bō'de), Johann Elert (1747–1826). German astronomer; gave currency to an empirical rule, previously formulated by J. D. Titius, but known as ~'*s law*, for determining the approximate distances of the planets from the sun.

bodē'ga *n.* Cellar or shop selling wine. [Sp., f. L, f. Gk *apothēkē* store]

Bŏdhĭsa'ttva (-dĭsah-) *n.* (Buddhism) Person who is entitled by his good deeds to enter Nirvana, but who delays doing so out of compassion for human suffering.

bŏ'dice *n.* Upper part of woman's dress, down to waist; undergarment for same part of body. [orig. (pair of) *bodies*, stays, corset]

bŏ'dĭlėss *adj.* Incorporeal, separated from the body.

bŏ'dĭlў *adj.* Of, affecting, the human body or physical nature (opp. *spiritual*). ~ *adv.* With the whole bulk, as a whole.

bŏ'dkĭn *n.* 1. Thick, blunt needle with large eye for threading tape etc. through hem. 2. Dagger (obs.); small pointed instrument for piercing holes in cloth etc.

Bŏ'dleian Lī'brarў (-lēan).

BODLEIAN LIBRARY

(also *the Bodlei'an*; colloq. *Bo'dley*) Library of Oxford University; founded by Humphrey, duke of Gloucester (1391–1447), and re-founded, 1603, by Sir Thomas Bodley (1545–1613), diplomat and scholar, one of the COPYRIGHT libraries.

bŏ'dȳ *n.* 1. Material frame of man or animal; corpse. 2. Trunk apart from head and limbs; main portion of anything; part of vehicle etc. fitted to receive the load; shank of piece of type. 3. Bulk, majority. 4. Person. 5. Aggregate of persons or things; collection; *in a ~*, in a group. 6. Piece of matter (*heavenly ~*); mass of tissue forming a structure; solidity, substance; (of wine) rich full flavour. 7. (pottery) Main substance. 8. *~ carpet(ing)*, carpet(ing) manufactured in strips that are joined to form required size; *bo'dyguard*, guard for the person (esp. of sovereign or dignitary), retinue, escort; *~-image*, (psychol.) mental image of one's own body; *~-line bowling*, (cricket) fast bowling on the leg side directed or alleged to be directed at the person of the batsman; *the ~ politic*, the State; *~-snatcher*, (hist.) one who secretly disinters corpses to sell them for dissection; *~ stocking*, woman's undergarment covering trunk and legs; *bo'dywork*, (esp.) body of a vehicle. *~ v.t.* (usu. with *forth*) Give mental shape to; exhibit in outward shape; typify.

Boehme (bẽr'me), Jakob (1575–1624). German mystic; held that will is the original force, that every manifestation involves opposition, and that existence is a process of conflict between pairs of contrasted principles, which are ultimately resolved into a new unity.

Boeotia (bēō'sha). Ancient country of central Greece, whose inhabitants were proverbial for slow-wittedness. **Boeo'tian** *adj.* & *n.*

Bō'er (*or* boor) *n.* S. Afr. farmer of Dutch origin; *~ War*, each of two wars fought by Gt Britain: the 1st (1880–1) against Transvaal, which, annexed by Britain in 1877, had proclaimed its independence; the 2nd (1899–1902) against the Transvaal and Orange Free State, resulting in the annexation of these States by Gt Britain.

Bōē'thĭus, Anicius Manlius Severinus (*c* 475–525). Roman philosopher; consul under Theodoric the Ostrogoth; was suspected of treason and confined to prison, where he wrote 'De Consolatione Philosophiae'; the Neoplatonic and stoic ideas of this work had great influence throughout the Middle Ages.

bŏ'ffĭn *n.* (slang) One engaged in scientific esp. technical research.

Bō'fors (-z) *n.* (also *~ gun*) Clip-fed, rapid-firing light anti-aircraft gun. [name of a munition works in Örebro Län, Sweden]

bŏg *n.* (Piece of) wet spongy ground, consisting chiefly of decayed or decaying moss or other vegetable matter; *~-myrtle*, sweet gale, *Myrica gale*; *~ oak*, oakwood preserved in a black state in peat-bogs etc. **bŏ'ggȳ** *adj.* **bŏ'gginess** *n.* **bŏg** *v.t.* Submerge in bog; *~ down* (fig.).

bō'gey (-gĭ) *n.* 1. Bogy. 2. (golf) Number of strokes a good player is reckoned to need for the course or for a hole, freq. personified as *Colonel B~*. [app. jocular application of *bogy*, 'something to be afraid of']

bŏ'ggle *v.i.* Start with fright, shy; hesitate, demur. *at.*

bō'gie (-gĭ) *n.* Under-carriage with two or more pairs of wheels, pivoted below front part of railway-engine or ends of long railway-carriage, tram-car, etc., to facilitate travelling round curves.

bō'gus *adj.* (orig. U.S.) Sham, fictitious, spurious.

bō'gȳ (-gĭ) *n.* (also *bo'gey*) 1. (esp. *Old B~*) The Devil. 2. Goblin. 3. Bugbear.

bohea' (-hē) *n.* Black tea of lowest quality, the last crop of the season (in 18th c., the finest kinds of black tea). [Chin. *Wu-i* district]

Bohē′mia. Slavonic kingdom of central Europe; came under Austrian rule, 1526; by the treaty of Versailles (1919) became a province of Czechoslovakia. **Bohē′mĭan** *adj.* & *n.* 1. (Native, inhabitant) of Bohemia. 2. (Person, esp. artist or writer) of free-and-easy habits, manners, and sometimes morals (from mistaken belief that gipsies came orig. from Bohemia).

Bohr (bôr), Niels Henrik David (1885–1962). Danish physicist; applied the quantum theory to the problem of atomic structure; Nobel Prize for physics 1922.

Boiar′dō, Matteo Maria (1434–94). Italian poet, author of 'Orlando Innamorato' and other poems taking their subject from the Arthur and Charlemagne cycles.

boil[1] *n.* Hard inflamed suppurating tumour.

boil[2] *v.* (of a liquid) Reach or be at that temperature (*boiling-point*) where the vapour pressure is equal to the pressure of the atmosphere above its surface and vapour is consequently evolved in bubbles from all parts of the liquid (also used of containing vessel); be agitated by the evolution, rising, and bursting of such bubbles; bring a liquid by the application of heat to this temperature; subject to heat of boiling water, cook, be cooked thus; (fig.) be agitated with anger etc.; ~ *down*, reduce by boiling; ~ *down to*, (fig.) mean basically; ~ *over*, bubble up so as to run over sides of vessel; said also of the vessel; *boiled shirt*, (orig. U.S.) dress shirt; *boiled sweets*, sweets made of boiled sugar. ~ *n.* Boiling, boiling-point.

Boileau (bwălō), Nicolas (1637–1711). French poet and critic, whose 'Art Poétique' greatly influenced French poetic theory and practice.

boi′ler *n.* 1. Vessel for boiling, esp. for making steam under pressure; tank for heating water for domestic use; metal tub in which laundry is boiled; ~ *suit*, man's sleeved overalls; ~*-tube*, (in older type of boiler) tube by which heat is diffused through water in boiler; tube (in a water-tube boiler) by which water is carried through heat of a furnace or through hot gases. 2. (colloq.) Fowl suitable for boiling.

boi′lĭng *n.* (esp.) *the whole* ~, (slang) the whole lot; ~*-point*: see BOIL[2]. ~ *adj.* (esp.) ~ *hot*, (colloq.) very hot.

boi′sterous *adj.* Violent, rough; noisily cheerful. **boi′sterouslў** *adv.* **boi′sterousnĕss** *n.*

bōld *adj.* Courageous, enterprising, confident; forward, immodest; vigorous, free, well-marked, clear; ~*-face(d)*, (type) having a thick face; ~*-faced*, impudent. **bō′ldlў** *adv.* **bō′ldnĕss** *n.*

bōle[1] *n.* Stem or trunk of tree.

bōle[2] *n.* Fine compact earthy or unctuous clay, usu. yellow, red, or brown with iron oxide.

bolĕ′ction *adj.* & *n.* (Moulding) placed round a panel, which it holds in a groove.

boler′ō (-ārō) *n.* (pl. *-os*). 1. Lively Spanish dance, music for this. 2. (bŏ′lerō) Short jacket coming barely to the waist.

Boleyn (bŏŏ′lĭn *or* -ĭ′n), Anne (*c* 1507–36). Daughter of Sir

Thomas Boleyn; became 2nd wife of Henry VIII and mother of Queen Elizabeth; she was beheaded on a charge of unfaithfulness.

Bŏ'lĭngbroke (-ōōk), Henry St. John, Viscount (1678–1751). English Tory statesman and writer on politics and philosophy.

Bŏlĭvâr'[1], Simon (1783–1830). Venezuelan patriot and statesman, called 'the Liberator'; founded (1819) the republic of Colombia,

uniting Venezuela, New Granada (Colombia), and Ecuador; became dictator of Peru; formed the republic of Bolivia.

bŏlĭvâr'[2] *n.* (pl. *-ares*). Monetary unit of Venezuela.

Boli'vĭa. S. Amer. inland republic, formerly part of the Incan Empire, and subsequently of the Spanish possession of Peru; capital, La Paz. **Boli'vian** *adj.* & *n.*

bōll *n.* Rounded seed-vessel, as in flax or cotton; *~-weevil*, weevil, *Anthonomus grandis*, destructive to the cotton-plant in America.

Bŏ'lland, John (1596–1665). Flemish Jesuit; began the publication of the 'Acta Sanctorum' (1643), legends of saints arranged according to the days of the calendar.

Bŏ'llandĭst *n.* Any of the Jesuit compilers of 'Acta Sanctorum', succeeding John Bolland until after the dispersal of the Jesuits in 1773 and re-established in Brussels in 1837.

bŏ'llard *n.* Post on ship or quay for securing ropes to; short post on traffic island, marking traffic lane, etc.

bolŏ'mėter *n.* Electrical instrument for measuring radiant heat. **bŏlomĕ'trĭc** *adj.*

Bŏ'lshėvĭk *n.* & *adj.* 1. (Member) of the Revolutionary party led by Lenin, which seized power in Russia in 1917 in the name of the proletariat and based its rule on the ideas of Karl Marx. 2. (loosely) (Of) a socialist or person suspected of subversive ideas. **Bŏ'lshėvĭst** *adj.* & *n.* **Bŏlshėvĭ'stĭc** *adj.* **Bŏ'lshėvĭsm** *n.* [Russ. *Bol'shevik* majority man (i.e. member of majority group in the Social-Democratic party) f. *bol'shiy* more]

Bŏ'lshĭe *adj.* & *n.* (derog.) = BOLSHEVIK, 2.

bō'lster *n.* Long, stuffed (under-) pillow for bed, sofa, etc.; pad or support in many machines and instruments. ~ *v.t.* (usu. with *up*) Support with bolster, prop; aid and abet, countenance; give fictitious support to (something unable to stand of itself); pad.

Bōlt[1] *n.* 1. Short heavy arrow of crossbow. 2. Discharge of lightning. 3. Door-fastening of sliding bar and staple; sliding part of mortise lock. 4. Sliding part of rifle which contains striker and mainspring and which locks the breech. 5. Metal pin with head, for holding things together, usu. secured by riveting or by a nut. 6. Length of fabric woven on a loom in one operation. 7. Bundle of osiers or reeds of certain size. ~ *adv.* ~ *upright*, upright as a bolt.

bōlt[2] *v.* 1. Dart off or away; (of horse) break from control, make violent dash; (cause fox, rabbit etc., to) escape from hole or burrow; *~-hole*, hole or burrow into which animal bolts for safety (also fig.). 2. Gulp down (food) hastily or unchewed. 3. Fasten (door etc.) with bolt; fasten together with bolts. ~ *n.* Sudden start; running away.

bōlt[3], **boult** (bō-) *v.t.* Sift; investigate. **bō′lter, bou′-** (bō-) *n.* Sieve, bolting-machine.

bō′ltĕl *n.* Var. of BOWTEL.

bō′lus *n.* Large pill, esp. one administered to an animal; lump of food at moment of swallowing.

bŏmb (-m) *n.* Case filled with explosive, inflammable material, gas, etc., fired from a gun, dropped from aircraft, or thrown or deposited by hand; *the B~*, (esp.) nuclear bomb; *~-bay*, compartment in aircraft for holding bombs; *~-proof*, strong enough to resist explosion of a bomb; *bo′mbshell*, artillery bomb; shell; (fig.) cause of great surprise. ~ *v.* Assail with bombs, throw bombs.

bŏ′mbard *n.* Earliest kind of cannon, throwing stone ball or very large shot. **bŏmbar′d** *v.t.* Batter with shot and shell; assail persistently with abuse, argument, etc.; (phys.) subject to a stream of (charged) atoms or sub-atomic particles. **bŏmbar′dment** *n.*

bŏmbardier′ *n.* Second lowest rank of non-commissioned officer in Royal Artillery (*lance-~*, lowest rank); (U.S.) airman who releases bombs from aircraft.

bŏ′mbardon *n.* (mus.) Low-pitched brass instrument; organ stop imitating this.

bŏ′mbasine, -zin(e) (-zēn) *n.* Twilled dress-material of worsted, or of silk or cotton with worsted weft, formerly much used for mourning.

bŏ′mbăst *n.* Pompous language, tall talk. **bŏmbă′stic** *adj.* **bŏmbă′stically** *adv.* [orig. = cotton wool, used in 16th c. as padding for clothes; f. Gk *bombux* silk, silk-worm]

Bŏmbay′. Capital city of Maharashtra, on W. coast of India; ~ *duck*, bummalo, esp. as relish.

bombe (bŏṅb) *n.* Conical or cup-shaped confection, freq. frozen.

bŏ′mber (-m*er*) *n.* 1. Soldier who throws hand-grenades or bombs. 2. Aircraft designed to carry bombs.

bō′na fī′dė *adj.* & *adv. phr.* Genuine(ly), sincere(ly). **bō′na fī′dēs** (-z). Honest intention, sincerity. [L]

bonă′nza *n.* Prosperity, large output (esp. of mines); run of luck, fine weather, good crops, etc. ~ *adj.* Yielding great wealth or a large output. [Sp., = 'fair weather']

Bō′naparte. Name of Corsican family including NAPOLEON I; *Joseph* ~, (1775–1844), brother of Napoleon I; king of Naples 1806; king of Spain 1808.

Bŏnavėntūr′a, St. (1221–74). John of Fidanza, Italian Franciscan, scholastic theologian, and mystic; known as the 'seraphic doctor'; commemorated 14 July.

bŏ′nbŏn *n.* Piece of confectionery, sweet.

bond[1] *n.* 1. Thing restraining bodily freedom, shackle (archaic, chiefly pl.); restraining or uniting force; connection; adhesion between two surfaces etc.; (chem.) = VALENCY bond. 2. Binding agreement; document by which person binds himself and his heirs etc. to pay a sum to another and his heirs etc.; government's or public company's document undertaking to repay borrowed money, usu. with fixed rate of interest; any of various kinds of investment; *in* ~, (of goods) stored under charge of Customs in bonded warehouse until importer pays duty (which he pledges himself by bond to do); *~-holder*, person holding bond(s) of another person or of company or government; *~-paper*, paper of superior quality as used for bonds. 3. Bond paper. 4. Any of various methods (as *English*, *Flemish*, ~) of holding wall together by making bricks etc. overlap so that vertical joints do not exceed the thickness of one brick; *in* ~, arranged thus ~ *v.t.* Bind together (bricks etc.) in bond; connect with a bond; put (goods) into bond; *bonded warehouse*, customs warehouse in which goods in bond are stored.

bŏnd[2] *adj.* (archaic) In serfdom or slavery; not free; so *bo′ndmaid*, *bo′ndman*, *bo′ndservant*, *bo′ndslave*, *bo′ndsman*.

bŏ′ndage *n.* Serfdom, slavery;

subjection to some bond, influence, or obligation.

Bŏnd Street. London street noted for its fashionable shops. [named after Sir Thomas *Bond*, who began its construction *c* 1688]

bōne *n.* One of the parts making up the skeleton of a human being or other vertebrate; substance (mainly calcium phosphate and fibrous protein) of which these consist; article made of this substance; strip of stiff substance in corset etc.; (pl.) skeleton, bodily frame, body, mortal remains; ~ *to pick*, ~ *of contention*, subject of dispute; *make no ~s of* or *about*, make no objections; ~ *china*, china-ware made of clay mixed with bone-dust or phosphate of lime; *~-dry*, quite dry; *bo'nehead*, (orig. U.S.) blockhead; ~ *idle*, *lazy*, downright idle, lazy; ~ *lace*, see LACE; *bo'nemeal*, animal food, fertilizer, made from finely crushed bone; *~-shaker*, (colloq.) old shaky vehicle; (formerly) bicycle without rubber tyres; *~-spavin*, bony swelling on inside of horse's hock. ~ *v.t.* 1. Take out bones from; stiffen with bone. 2. (slang) Steal. **bō'nelėss** *adj.*

bŏ'nfīre. Large fire in the open air; *B~ Night*, evening of 5 Nov. (see Guy FAWKES).

bŏ'ngō[1] (-nggō) *n.* Large striped African antelope, *Boocercus eurycerus*, related to bushbuck, living in dense forests.

bŏ'ngō[2] (-nggō) *n.* (also ~ *drum*) One of a pair of small drums played with the fingers.

bŏ'nhomie (-nomĭ) *n.* Good nature; geniality. **bŏ'nhomous** *adj.*

Bŏ'nĭfāce[1], St. (680–755). Winfrith, English Benedictine, apostle to the Germans under Pope Gregory II; commemorated 5 June.

Bŏ'nĭfāce[2] *n.* Jovial innkeeper. [Name of the jovial innkeeper in Farquhar's 'Beaux' Stratagem' (1707)]

bon mot (bawṅ mō). Witty saying. [Fr.]

bŏ'nnėt *n.* 1. Woman's outdoor head-dress with strings. 2. (Sc.) Man's cap. 3. Protective cap or cover in various machines etc.; hinged cover over engine etc. or luggage compartment at front of motor vehicle.

bŏ'nnȳ *adj.* 1. (chiefly Sc.) Comely. 2. Healthy-looking. **bŏ'nnĭlȳ** *adv.*

bŏ'nsai. *n.* Potted plant or shrub artificially dwarfed as ornament; method of cultivating this. [Jap.]

bŏ'nspiel *n.* Curling-match.

bō'nus *n.* Something to the good, into the bargain; (esp.) extra dividend to company's shareholders, distribution of profits to holders of insurance policies, gratuity to employees beyond their wages.

bon vivant (bawṅ vēvahṅ) Gourmand. [Fr.]

bon voyage (bawṅ vwăyahzh). Pleasant journey (used as expression of farewell to a traveller). [Fr.]

bō'nȳ *adj.* Of, like, bone; big-boned; with little flesh; ~ *fishes*, those (including most of the common species) which have bones as opp. to cartilage.

bŏnze *n.* (European name for) Japanese or Chinese Buddhist priest.

bōō *int.*, *n.*, & *v.* (Make) sound of disapproval or contempt (at); jeer (at).

bōō'bȳ *n.* Stupid or babyish person; kind of gannet; ~ *prize*, prize given in derision or fun to player with worst score; *~-trap*, collection of objects balanced on top of door left ajar, so as to fall on head of first person passing through; (mil.) harmless-looking object concealing an explosive charge, designed to go off when disturbed; hence, *~-trap* (*v.t.*).

bōō'gie-wōō'gie (-gĭ, -gĭ) *n.* (also *boogie*) Style of playing blues usu. on the piano, marked by persistent bass rhythm.

bŏŏk *n.* 1. Treatise written or printed on a number of sheets which are folded, fastened together hingewise at the folded edges, and protected by a binding or cover; in antiquity, set of written sheets pasted together to form a roll; literary composition that would fill a book; main division of literary composition or of the Bible; libretto; anything from which one may learn; (colloq.) magazine. 2. Blank sheets of paper for keeping accounts, taking notes etc., fastened together in the shape of a book; anything bound together in this shape, as cheques, stamps, tickets, pieces of flannel for holding needles, etc. 3. Betting-book, record of bets made; (pl.) merchants' accounts. 4. *boo'kbinder*, *boo'kbinding*, binder, binding, of books; *~-case*, case containing bookshelves; *~-club*, society which produces books for its members; *~-ends*, pair of (ornamental) props used to keep row of books upright; *~-hand*, kind of handwriting used in books before the invention of printing; *~-keeper*, *~-keeping*, one who keeps, art of keeping, accounts of merchant, etc.; *~-learned*, *~-learning*, (having) knowledge gained from books not life; *~-maker*, (esp.) professional betting man; *~-muslin*, (19th c.) fine muslin folded like a book when sold; *~-plate*, label with owner's name, crest, or other device, for pasting into books; *~ value*, value of a commodity as entered in a firm's books (opp. *market value*); *boo'kshelf*, shelf for standing books on; *boo'kwork*, study involving reading, opp. practical experiment etc.; paperwork; *boo'kworm*, larva of various moths or beetles, which burrows into or destroys pages of books; (fig.) one who is always poring over books. ~ *v.* Enter in book or list; secure (seat etc.) in advance; issue, obtain, ticket for journey etc.; enter (name) in police register etc. for alleged offence; *~ in*, register one's name at hotel etc.; register (guest) thus.

bŏŏ'kie *n.* (slang) Book-maker.

bŏŏ'kish *adj.* Literary; addicted to reading books. **bŏŏ'kishlў** *adv.* **bŏŏ'kishnėss** *n.*

bŏŏ'klėt *n.* Small usu. paper-covered book, pamphlet.

Bōōle, George (1815–64). English mathematician and logician.

bōōm[1] *n.* Long spar used to keep the bottom sail extended; floating timber barrier across mouth of a river, entrance to a harbour etc.; beam of derrick supporting weights; extendible arm carrying microphone or camera.

bōōm[2] *n.* & *v.i.* (Make, speak, etc., with) deep resonant sound.

bōōm[3] *v.* & *n.* (orig. U.S.) (Show) sudden increase or development (esp. of prices, commercial ventures, etc.: opp. SLUMP); (win) sudden popularity.

bōō'merăng *n.* Australian missile of thin curved wood that can be thrown so as to return to the

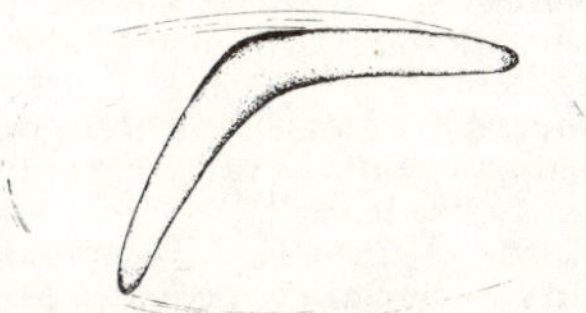

thrower; (fig.) scheme etc. that recoils on its originator. ~ *v.i.* Recoil on originator.

bōōn[1] *n.* Request; favour, gift; blessing, advantage.

bōōn[2] *adj.* ~ *companion*, congenial companion.

Bōōne, Daniel (1735–1820). American pioneer; played a notable part in the opening up and settlement of Kentucky and Missouri.

boor *n.* Ill-mannered fellow. **boor'ĭsh** *adj.* **boor'ĭshlў** *adv.* **boor'ĭshnėss** *n.*

bōōst *v.t.* 1. (orig. U.S. slang) Push from below; advance the progress of; praise. 2. Raise power of electromotive force in (engine, circuit, etc.). ~ *n.* Boosting. **bōō'ster** *n.* (esp.) Auxiliary rocket giving acceleration; (med.) dose increasing or renewing effect of earlier one.

bōōt[1] *n.* Advantage (now only in *to ~*, as well). ~ *v.t.* (archaic; usu. impers. & abs.) Do good (*to*), avail. **bōō'tlėss** *adj.* Unavailing.

bōōt[2] *n.* 1. Outer foot-covering of leather etc., reaching above the ankle; covering for lower part of horse's leg; *give* (*person*) *the* ~, dismiss; ~-*jack*, contrivance for pulling off boots; *boo'tlace*, lace fastening boots; *boo'tleg*, (orig. U.S.) smuggled, sold illicitly; *boo'tlegger*, *boo't-legging*, smuggler, smuggling, of liquor (esp. in U.S., during prohibition); ~-*licker*, (slang) toady; ~-*tree*, shaped block for keeping boot in shape. 2. (hist.) Instrument of torture encasing the foot. 3. Luggage compartment in motor-car (orig., in coach, under guard's and coachman's seat). ~ *v.t.* Kick; (slang) kick (person) *out* (of the house, of employment, etc.). **boo'tĕd** *adj.* Wearing boots.

bōōtee' *n.* Infant's knitted or crocheted boot; woman's short lined boot.

Boötes (bōō'tēz). Northern constellation containing ARCTURUS. [Gk, = 'ox-driver']

bōōth[1] (-dh) *n.* Temporary shelter of canvas etc., covered stall in market, tent at fair, etc.; compartment, as *telephone* ~, one containing a telephone; *polling* ~, place where one votes at parliamentary or other election.

Bōōth[2] (-dh), William (1829–1912). English revivalist preacher, founder and first General of the Salvation Army.

bōōts *n.* Hotel servant who cleans boots, carries luggage, etc.

bōō'tȳ *n.* Plunder or profit acquired in common and to be divided; spoil, prize, plunder.

bōōze *n.* Drink; a drinking-bout. ~ *v.i.* Drink deeply, go on drinking. **bōō'zer** *n.* Drinker; (slang) public house. **bōō'zȳ** *adj.* Addicted to drink; fuddled.

bō'pee'p *n.* Game, played with young child, of hiding and suddenly appearing again, saying 'Bo'.

bora'cic *adj.* = BORIC.

bŏ'rage (*or* bŭ-) *n.* Blue-flowered hairy-leaved plant, *Borago officinalis*, used in salads etc.

bor'āte *n.* Salt of boric acid.

bor'ăx *n.* Sodium borate ($Na_2B_4O_7.IOH_2O$), a white crystalline substance giving a slightly alkaline solution, used in manufacture of glass and ceramics and as a cleansing agent.

bor'azon *n.* Crystalline compound of boron nitride, extremely hard and resistant to oxidation at high temperatures.

Bordeau'x (-dō). City and port of SW. France; any of the wines of the district round Bordeaux, including Graves, Sauternes, and Médoc; ~ *mixture*, mixture of copper sulphate, lime, and water, used for the destruction of fungi.

bor'der *n.* Side, edge, boundary or part near it; frontier of country (*the B*~, the boundary between England and Scotland, and the adjoining districts; (U.S.) that between U.S. and Mexico); continuous bed round garden or part of it, or along path, etc.; distinct edging for strength or ornament or definition round or along anything; *bor'derland*, land or district on or near a border (also fig.); *bor'derline*, strip of land along border; (*adj.*) near the margin of anything. ~ *v.* Put or be a border to; (also ~ *on*) adjoin; come close to being. **bor'derer** *n.* Dweller on or near border, esp. that between England and Scotland.

Bor'ders. Region of SE. Scotland (since May 1975), comprising the former counties of Berwickshire, Peeblesshire, Roxburghshire, Selkirkshire, and the S. tip of Midlothian.

Bordō'nė. Paris (1500–71). Venetian painter, pupil of Titian.

bor'dure (-yer) *n.* (her.) Bearing round the edge of a shield, a fifth part of the field in breadth.

bore[1] *v.* 1. Make hole in, usu. with revolving tool; hollow out evenly; make by boring, persistent pushing or excavation. 2. (of horse) Thrust head out; (racing) push (another) out of the course. ~ *n.* 1. Hollow of gun-barrel; diameter of this, calibre; inside diameter of tube, esp. in musical instrument 2. Deep hole made in earth to find water, oil, etc.

bore[2] *n.* Nuisance; tiresome, esp. talkative, person. ~ *v.t.*

Weary by tedious talk or dullness. **bŏr′edom** *n.* Being bored, ennui.

bōre[3] *n.* Tidal wave with precipitous front moving up some estuaries; also called eagre.

bŏr′ėal *adj.* Of the north wind; of the North.

Bŏr′ėas. (Gk myth.) North wind, son of the Titan Astraeus and of Eos the goddess of dawn.

bŏr′ecōle (-ŏrk-) *n.* Kale. [prob. f. Du. *boerenkool* peasant's cabbage]

Bŏr′gia. (Span. *Bor′ja*, pr. -hа) Name of Italian noble family of Spanish origin: *Alfonso de* ~, bishop of Valencia, became Pope Calixtus III and gave preferment to his nephew *Rodrigo de* ~ (1431–1503), who became Pope Alexander VI in 1492; *Cesare* ~ (1475-1507), one of Rodrigo's many illegitimate children, was notorious for his violence and crimes, but an able soldier and an early believer in the unity of Italy; *Lucrezia* ~ (1480–1519), sister of Cesare, was associated by rumour with his crimes and her 2nd husband, Alfonso of Aragon, was murdered by his direction; she afterwards married Alfonso d'Este, heir of the Duke of Ferrara, and her court became a centre for artists, poets, and scholars.

bŏr′ĭc *adj.* ~ *acid*, acid (H_3BO_3) occurring in hot springs in some volcanic areas, a mild antiseptic, widely used in the form of an ointment as a dressing for wounds and sores.

Bŏ′rĭs Gŏ′dunov (-ŏŏnŏf) (1552–1605). Tsar of Russia from 1598; an able ruler, but regarded as a usurper and suspected of having contrived the death of the heir, Dmitri; died suddenly during a revolt headed by a pretender, the 'false Dmitri'.

bŏrn *adj.*: see BEAR[2]; (esp.) ~ *of*, owing origin to; ~ *fool*, *idiot*, etc., utter, hopeless, fool, etc.

borne: see BEAR[2].

Bŏr′nėō. Large island of Malay archipelago, comprising (1) Kalimantan, a region of Indonesia; (2) Sabah and Sarawak, formerly British colonies, now parts of Malaysia; (3) Brunei, a British protected State. **Bŏr′nėan** *adj.*

Bŏr′nholm dĭsea′se (-hōm, -zēz). Epidemic pleurodynia, a virus disease characterized by acute pain and a short febrile period. [*Bornholm*, Dan. island in Baltic]

Bŏ′rodĭn, Alexander Porfiryevich (1834–87). Russian composer and chemist.

Bŏrodi′nō (-dē-). Village, some 120 miles W. of Moscow, scene of a battle (1812) in which Napoleon defeated the Russians.

bŏr′on *n.* (chem.) Dark-brown or greenish-brown non-metallic solid element; symbol B, at. no. 5, at. wt 10·81.

borough (bŭ′rо) *n.* (hist.) Town with corporation and privileges conferred by royal charter or defined by statute; ~ *status*, (since April 1974) name, style, and privileges of a borough, granted to a district by royal charter; (U.S.) incorporated town or village; *county* ~, (hist.) borough, usu. with population of 50,000 or more, administered independently of the county authority; *London* ~, (since April 1974) administrative area of Greater London; *pocket* ~, (hist.) borough in which election of member of Parliament was controlled by a private person; *rotten* ~, (hist.) before the Reform Act of 1832, a borough which had so decayed as to have no longer any real constituency.

Bŏrromi′nĭ (-mē-), Francesco (1599–1667). Italian baroque architect.

bŏ′rrow[1] (-ō) *v.t.* Obtain or take temporary use of (something to be returned); adopt, use without being the true or original owner or inventor, import from an alien source; *borrowed time*, unexpected extension of time, esp. of life. **bŏ′rrower** *n.*

Bŏ′rrow[2] (-ō), George (1803–81). English traveller and linguist; author of 'The Romany Rye' and other books which combine fiction with autobiography and reflect his interest in gipsies.

bŏrsch, bŏrtsch (-sh *or* -tsh) *n.*

Soup of beetroot etc., made esp. in Russia and Poland.

Bôr'stal *n.* One of a number of institutions in Gt Britain to which young offenders may be sent for reformative training. [f. *Borstal*, village in Kent where first experimental training was carried out]

bôrt *n.* Coarse diamonds; diamond fragments made in cutting.

bôr'zoi *n.* Dog of large high-standing breed, called also Russian or Siberian wolf-hound, of greyhound type, but with thick silky coat, usu. white with yellow markings. [Russ. *bórziy* swift]

bŏ'scage *n.* Mass of growing trees or shrubs; wooded scenery.

bŏsh *n.* (slang) Contemptible nonsense. [Turk., = 'empty', 'worthless' (popularized by Morier's novel 'Ayesha', 1834)]

bŏ'skў *adj.* Wooded, bushy.

Bŏ'snia (-z-). Federal unit of Yugoslavia, formerly a province of the Austro-Hungarian Empire. **Bŏ'snian** *adj.* & *n.*

bo'som (bŏŏz-) *n.* Breast; enclosure formed by breast and arms; breast of dress, space between dress and breast; surface of sea, ground, etc.; heart, thoughts, desires, etc.; ~ *friend*, specially intimate or beloved friend.

Bŏ'sporus, Bŏ'sph-. Strait connecting the Black Sea and the Sea of Marmara.

bŏss[1] *n.* Protuberance; round metal knob or stud on centre of shield or ornamental work; (archit.) projection; freq. carved, at intersecting point of vault-ribs; enlarged part of shaft etc. **bŏ'ssў**[1] *adj.*

bŏss[2] *n.* (colloq.) Master, person in authority; (U.S.) manager of political organization. ~ *v.t.* Be master or manager of. **bŏ'ssў**[2] *adj.* Domineering. [orig. U.S., f. Du, *baas* master]

bŏss[3] *adj.* (slang) ~*-eyed*, squint-eyed; having only one good eye; crooked; ~ *shot*, bad shot or aim; unsuccessful attempt.

Bossuet (-swā), Jacques Bénigne (1627–1704). French divine and theologian, famous for his eloquence, especially in funeral orations.

Bŏ'ston[1]**.** Capital city and seaport of Massachusetts, U.S., founded *c* 1630 and named after Boston, town in Lincolnshire; ~ *tea-party*, throwing of a cargo of tea into Boston harbour by colonists, 1773, as a protest against tea duties imposed by the English Parliament; it occasioned the general revolt of the American colonies and the War of Independence. **Bŏstō'nian** *adj.* & *n.*

bŏ'ston[2] *n.* Card-game resembling whist, named after the siege of Boston in the American War of Independence, to which the technical terms of the game refer.

bo'sun (bō'sn) *n.* Boatswain (see BOAT).

Bŏ'swell (-z-), James (1740–94). Scotsman, by profession a lawyer, who became a friend of Samuel Johnson and recorded his conversation in a biography published 1791. **Bŏswĕ'llian** *adj.* **Bŏ'swellīze** *v.i.*

Bŏ'sworth Field (-werth, -z-). Scene, near Market Bosworth in Leicestershire, of the last battle of the Wars of the Roses (1485), in which Richard III was defeated and killed.

bot: see BOTT.

bŏ'tanīze *v.i.* Study plants, esp. by seeking them as they grow.

bŏ'tanў[1] *n.* Science of plants. **botă'nic** *adj.* **botă'nical** *adj.* (esp.) ~ *garden*, garden for the display and study of plants. **botă'nicallў** *adv.* **bŏ'tanist** *n.*

Bŏ'tanў[2]**, bŏ't-** *adj.* ~ *wool*, fine wool from merino sheep, esp. from Australia. ~ *n.* Botany wool. [f. BOTANY BAY]

Bŏ'tanў Bay. Bay on E. coast of New South Wales (5 miles S. of modern Sydney) where Capt. Cook first landed in 1770, so named because of the variety of its plant life; an English penal settlement was established near there at Port Jackson in 1788.

bōtâr'gō *n.* Relish of mullet- or tunny-roe.

bŏtch *n.* Clumsy patch, bungled work. ~ *v.* Patch or mend clumsily or badly; spoil by unskilful work, bungle.

bōth *adj.* & *pron.* The two (and not merely one of them); the pair (of). ~ *adv.* ~ . . . *and*, not only . . . but also.

Bō'tha (-t*a*), Louis (1862–1919). S. Afr. soldier and statesman, Boer general in the Boer War; conquered German SW. Africa in war of 1914–18.

bŏ'ther (-dh-) *v.* Pester, worry; be troublesome; worry oneself, take trouble. ~ *n.* Minor trouble, worry; fuss; worried state. ~ *int.* Exclamation of impatience.

bŏtherā'tion (-dh-) *n.* & *int.* Bother.

bŏ'thersome (-dh-) *adj.* Annoying, troublesome.

Bŏ'thwell, James Hepburn, 4th Earl of (*c* 1536–78). 3rd husband of Mary Queen of Scots; implicated in the murder of DARNLEY.

Bŏ'tŏlph, St. (d. 680). English Benedictine monk; commemorated 17 June.

Bŏtswa'na (-ahn*a*). Republic of South-central Africa; member State of the Commonwealth, independent 1966; capital, Gaborone.

bŏtt, bŏt *n.* Parasitic larva of the ~-*fly*, an insect of genus *Oestrus*; *botts*, disease of horses, cattle, etc., caused by this.

Bŏttĭcĕ'llĭ (-ch-), Sandro (1447–1510). Alessandro Filipepi, Florentine painter of the Renaissance.

bŏ'ttle[1] *n.* Narrow-necked vessel of glass or plastic (orig. of leather) for storing liquid; amount of liquid in it; HOT-water bottle; feeding-bottle; ~-*fed*, (of infant or young animal) fed on milk etc. from a feeding-bottle, not from breast; ~-*glass*, coarse dark-green glass; ~-*green*, dark green; ~-*neck*, narrow stretch of road, narrow outlet, esp. one causing congestion of traffic (freq. fig.); ~-*nose*, swollen nose; ~-*nosed dolphin, whale*, dolphin of genus *Tursiops*, whale of genus *Hyperoödon*, with bottle-shaped snout; ~-*party*, party to which guests contribute drinks; drinking-party; ~-*washer*, factotum, underling. ~ *v.t.* Store in bottles; preserve (fruit etc.) in glass jars; ~ *up*, conceal, restrain for a time.

bŏ'ttle[2] *n.* Bundle (of hay or straw).

bŏ'ttom *n.* 1. Lowest part, part on which thing rests; buttocks; seat (of chair). 2. Ground under water of lake etc.; river-basin etc., low-lying land; farthest or inmost point. 3. Less honourable end of table, class, etc., person occupying this. 4. Keel, horizontal part near keel, hull; ship, esp. as cargo-carrier. 5. Basis, origin; essential character, reality; *at the* ~ *of*, causing, responsible for. ~ *adj.* Lowest; last; ~ *drawer*, woman's collection of linen etc. in preparation for marriage. ~ *v.* Put bottom to; base *on*; touch bottom (of); sound.

bŏ'ttomlėss *adj.* Unfathomable.

bŏ'ttomrȳ *n.* System of lending money to shipowner for purposes of voyage on security of ship itself. ~ *v.t.* Pledge (ship).

bŏ'tūlism *n.* Poisoning caused by eating food that contains *botulinus toxin*, an exceptionally powerful toxin poisonous to nerve tissue, produced by the bacillus *Clostridium botulinum* usu. in preserved foods that have been imperfectly sterilized.

Boucher (bōōshā), François (1703–70). French painter of elegantly artificial pastorals.

Early wine bottles

Early beer bottles

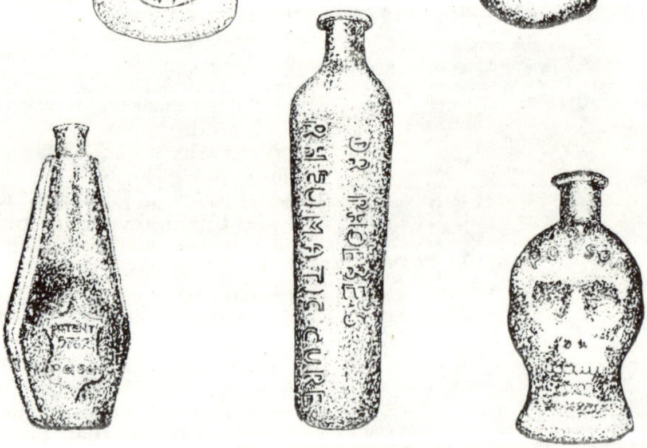

Early poison bottles

BOTTLES

bouclé (bo͞o'klā) *n.* Yarn of looped or curled ply; fabric of this.

Boudi'cca (bŏd-) (d. A.D. 62). (pop. *Boadicea*) British queen of the Iceni; headed a revolt against the Romans and destroyed Camulodunum and Londinium; took poison when finally defeated by Suetonius Paulinus.

boudoir (bo͞o'dwar) *n.* Woman's small private room. [Fr., = 'sulking-place' (*bouder* sulk)]

bouffant (bo͞o'fahn) *adj.* Puffed out.

bougainvi'llaea (bo͞og*a*n-, -ĭa) *n.* Tropical climbing plant of genus *B~*, with large bright-coloured bracts. [named after BOUGAINVILLE]

Bougainville (bo͞ogănvīl), Louis Antoine de (1729–1811). French navigator.

bouget (bo͞o'zhā) *n.* (her.) Representation of an ancient water-vessel.

bough (bow) *n.* Tree-branch.

bought: see BUY.

bougie (bo͞o'zhē) *n.* Wax candle; thin flexible surgical instrument for exploring, dilating, etc., passages of the body. [*Bougie*, Algerian town with wax trade]

bouillabai'sse (bo͞oy*a*-) *n.* Provençal dish of various kinds of Mediterranean fish stewed in water or spiced white wine.

bouillon[1] (bo͞o'yawn) *n.* Broth.

Bouillon[2] (bo͞oyawn), Godfrey of, Duke of Lorraine (d. 1100). Leader of the 1st Crusade.

Boulanger (bo͞olahnzhā), Georges Ernest Jean Marie (1831–91). French general; advocated (*c* 1886–9) policy of militarism and revenge against Germany. **Boulă'ngism** (-j-), **Boulă'ngist** *ns.*

bou'lder (bōl-) *n.* Large irregular water-worn or weather-worn stone; (geol.) rounded rock fragment about the size of a football or larger; ~ *clay*, mixture of boulders in clay, resulting from a melting glacier.

boulevard (bo͞o'lvar *or* -levard) *n.* Wide tree-lined street, esp. in Paris; (U.S.) wide, well-laid-out main street or road.

Boulle[1] (bo͞ol). Name of a French family of cabinet-makers (esp. André Charles ~, 1642–1732), noted for ebony furniture inlaid with brass, tortoiseshell, etc., and mounted with gilt bronze.

boulle[2], **buhl** (bo͞ol) *adj.* & *n.* (Furniture, ornament) of the type made by the Boulle family.

boult, boulter[1]: see BOLT[3].

bou'lter[2] (bōl-) *n.* Long fishing-line with many hooks. ~ *v.i.* Fish with boulter.

bounce *n.* Rebound; boast, exaggeration, swagger. ~ *v.* Rebound, bound like a ball; throw oneself about; burst *into*, *out of*, etc.; swagger, talk big; (of cheque) be returned to drawer when there are insufficient funds to meet it. **bou'ncing** *adj.* Big and lively; boisterous. **bou'ncy̆** *adj.* That bounces; springy.

bound[1] *n.* Limit of territory or estate; (pl.) limitation, restriction, limit beyond which schoolchildren, students, soldiers, etc., may not pass. ~ *v.t.* Set bounds to, limit; be boundary of. **bou'ndlėss** *adj.*

bound[2] *n.* Springy movement upward or forward; recoil (of ball etc.). ~ *v.i.* (of ball etc.) Recoil from wall or ground, bounce; spring, leap, advance lightly.

bound[3] *adj.* Ready to start, having started (*for*).

bound[4]: see BIND.

bou'ndary̆ *n.* That which serves to indicate bounds or limits of anything; bounds; (cricket) bounds or limit line of cricket field, hit to boundary, runs allowed for this.

bou'nden *adj.* Obliged, beholden, indebted; esp. ~ *duty*.

bou'nder *n.* (esp., slang) Cad; (in milder use) person.

bou'ntėous *adj.* Beneficent, liberal; freely bestowed. **bou'ntėously̆** *adv.* **bou'ntėousnėss** *n.*

bou'ntĭful *adj.* Bounteous; *lady* ~, beneficent lady of a neighbourhood [f. *Lady Bountiful* in Farquhar's 'Beaux' Stratagem'] **bou'ntĭfully̆** *adv.* **bou'ntĭfulnėss** *n.*

bou'nty̆[1] *n.* Munificence, liberality in giving; gift, gratuity; subsidy (~*-fed*, subsidized); *Queen Anne's B~*: see ANNE[1].

Bou'nty[2], Mutiny of the. Mutiny (28 April 1789) of the crew of H.M.S. *Bounty*, bound from Tahiti to the Cape of Good Hope and the W. Indies, against their commander, Lieut. BLIGH. He and eighteen companions, set adrift in an open boat, succeeded in reaching Timor in the E. Indies, nearly 4,000 miles away. The mutineers returned to Tahiti whence some of them went on to Pitcairn Island, founding a settlement there which was not discovered until 1808; this was eventually adopted by the British Government as a colony.

bouquet (bōōkā' *or* bō-) *n.* Bunch of flowers, esp. one presented as a compliment (also fig.); characteristic perfume of wine; ~ *gārnī*, bunch of herbs for flavouring.

bour'bon[1] (bẽr- *or* boor-) *n.* (also ~ *whisky*; chiefly U.S.) Whisky distilled from Indian corn and rye, orig. made in Bourbon County, Kentucky.

Bour'bon[2] (boor-). Surname of branch of royal family of France; they became the ruling monarchs when Henry IV succeeded to the throne in 1589; members of this family became kings of Spain (1700–1931) and of Naples.

bour'don (boor-) *n.* Low-pitched (usu. 16-ft) stop in organ; similar stop in harmonium; lowest bell in peal of bells; drone pipe of bagpipe. [Fr., = 'drone bee, bass stop in organ']

bourgeois[1] (boor'zhwah) *n.* & *adj.* 1. (orig.) (Of) a French citizen or freeman of a burgh. 2. (Member) of shop-keeping or mercantile middle class; (person) of humdrum middle-class ideas (now freq. a rather vague term of abuse). **bourgeoisie'** (-zhwahzē) *n.* Middle class.

bourgeois[2] (b*er*joi's) *n.* Size of type (approx. 9 point) between long primer and brevier. [Perh. f. a French printer's name]

Bourget (boorzhā), Paul Charles Joseph (1852–1935). French novelist, whose works are notable for their psychological analysis.

bourne, bourn (boorn) *n.* (archaic) Limit, terminus, boundary, goal.

bourrée (boor'ā) *n.* Lively dance, in duple time, of French or Spanish origin; music suitable for or derived from this, esp. as a movement in a suite.

bourse (boors) *n.* Money market, esp. (*B*~) the equivalent in Paris of the Stock Exchange.

bout *n.* 1. Spell or turn of work, illness, exercise, etc.; fit of drinking. 2. Round at fighting, contest, trial of strength. 3. Curve of rib forming waist of violin etc.

boutique (bōōtē'k) *n.* Small shop or department selling clothes or accessories.

bō'vīne *adj.* Of, like, an ox; inert, dull.

bow[1] (bō) *n.* 1. Curve; rainbow. 2. Weapon for shooting arrows, a strip of flexible wood or other

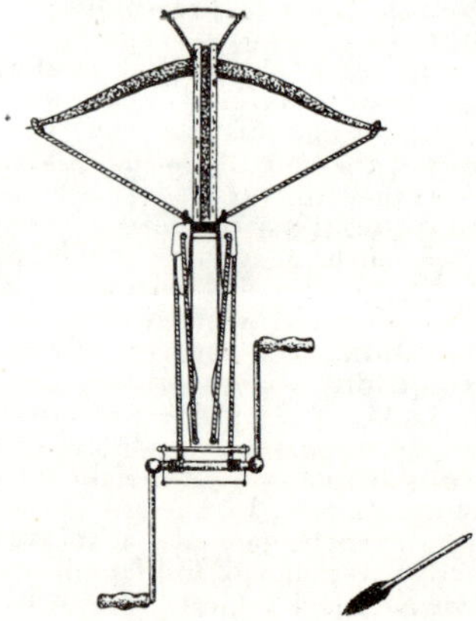

CROSSBOW AND BOLT

material held in bent position, when in use, by a string stretched between its two ends. 3. Appliance for playing instruments of violin class, rod with a number of horsehairs stretched from end to end, for drawing across the strings. 4. Slip-knot with double or single loop, ribbon etc. so tied. 5. ~ *compass*(*es*), compass with jointed legs;

~ *-head*, Greenland whale; ~*-legged*, bandy; *bow'man*, archer; ~*-saw*, saw stretched between ends of bow-shaped handle; *bow'shot*, distance to which arrow can be shot from bow; ~*-tie*, necktie tied in a bow; ~ *window*, curved bay window. ~ *v.* Play with bow (on violin etc.), use bow.

bow[2] *v.* Submit *to*; bend or kneel in sign of submission or reverence, incline head in greeting or assent; express by bowing, usher *in*, *out*, by bowing; cause to bend. ~ *n.* Bending of head or body in salutation, respect, content, etc.

bow[3] *n.* Fore-end of boat or ship from where it begins to arch inwards (often pl.); *on the* ~, (of objects) within 45° of the point right ahead; (also ~ *oar*) oarsman nearest the bow.

Bow běllš (bō, -z). Peal of bells of St. Mary-le-Bow, a church in Cheapside near the centre of the City of London; hence, *within the sound of* ~, within the City of London.

Bow chī'na (bō). Porcelain from the factory at Stratford-le-Bow near London (founded *c* 1745 and active for 20–30 years).

Bow'dler, Thomas (1754–1825). M.D. of Edinburgh, editor of the 'Family Shakespeare' (1818), an edition 'in which those words and expressions are omitted which cannot with propriety be read aloud in a family'. **bow'dlerīze** *v.t.* Expurgate.

bow'el *n.* Division of alimentary canal below stomach, intestine; (pl.) entrails, inside of body; pity, tender feeling; inside of anything, esp. in ~*s of the earth.*

bow'er[1] *n.* 1. (poet.) Dwelling, abode; inner room, boudoir. 2. Place closed in with foliage, arbour, summer-house; ~*-bird*, Australian bird related to bird of paradise, remarkable for building bowers or runs adorned with feathers, flowers, shells, etc., in courtship. **bow'erў**[1] *adj.*

bow'er[2] *n.* Either of two anchors, or their cables, carried at ship's bow.

bow'er[3] *n.* Each of the two highest cards at euchre, the knave of trumps (*right* ~) and the knave of the other suit of the same colour (*left* ~). [Ger. *Bauer* peasant]

Bow'erў[2], The. Street in S. part of New York, formerly notorious as a haunt of criminals. [Du. *bouwerij* husbandry, farm]

bow'ie (bō'ĭ) *n.* (also ~ *knife*) Large knife with long hollow-ground blade, curved and double-edged near the point. [*Bowie*, name of Amer. inventor]

bowl[1] (bōl) *n.* Basin for holding liquid or food; drinking-vessel; contents of a bowl; bowl-shaped part of tobacco-pipe, spoon, etc.; tract of country noted for abundance of a particular product, as *wheat-*~.

bowl[2] (bōl) *n.* 1. Wooden ball made slightly out of spherical shape (formerly spherical and weighted on one side) to make it run in a curved course (see BIAS); (pl.) game played on a bowling-green with bowls, the object being to lay the bowls near the jack. 2. Flattened or spherical wooden ball at skittles. ~ *v.* 1. Play bowls; roll (bowl, hoop, etc.); roll like bowl or hoop, move on wheels. 2. (cricket) Deliver (ball); dismiss (batsman) by knocking off the bails with the ball; ~ *over*, knock down; disconcert, render helpless.

bow'ler[1] (bōl-) *n.* One who bowls at cricket.

bow'ler[2] (bōl-) *n.* (also ~ *hat*) Hard round felt hat.

bow'līne (bōl-) *n.* Rope in ship's rigging from weather side of square sail to bow; (also ~ *knot*) simple but very secure knot used in fastening bowline to sail.

bow'līng (bōl-) *n.* Playing bowls; playing skittles; delivery of ball in cricket; ~-*alley*, skittle-alley; ~-*crease*: see CREASE; ~-*green*, lawn for playing bowls.

bow'sprĭt (bōs-) *n.* Spar running out from ship's stem, to which forestays are fastened.

Bow Street (bō). Street in London near Covent Garden, in which the principal Metropolitan police court is situated; ~ *Runners*, name in early 19th c. for police officers or detectives, attached to this court before the formation of the London police force.

bow'tĕl (bōt-). *n.* (archit.) Projecting moulding of more or less cylindrical form.

bow'yer (bōy*er*) *n.* Maker, seller, of bows.

bŏx[1] *n.* Evergreen shrub or small tree of genus *Buxus*, esp. *B. sempervirens*, with small dark-green leathery leaves, much used in garden borders and hedges; (also *bo'xwood*), wood of this.

bŏx[2] *n.* 1. Receptacle (usu. with lid, rectangular or cylindrical, and for solids) of wood, cardboard, etc.; quantity contained in this; receptacle at newspaper office for replies to advertisement; (colloq.) gramophone, radio, or television set; *post-office* ~: see POST[2]. 2. Coachman's seat. 3. Small separate compartment in theatre etc., or for horse in stable or railway truck (*loose* ~, in which it can move about); jury-box; witness-box; hut for sentry etc.; small country house for temporary residence; box junction. 4. Protective case for piece of mechanism etc.; (typ.) space enclosed by rules etc. 5. *Christmas* ~: see CHRISTMAS; ~ *barrage*: see BARRAGE; ~-*bed*, bed shut in like large wooden box with hinged shutters or sliding panels in front; ~ *camera*, box-shaped camera; ~-*key*, = box-spanner; ~ *junction*, road junction with grid of yellow lines on which vehicles must not be stationary; ~-*kite*, kite with light rectangular frame at each end; ~-*office*, office for booking theatre or cinema seats; (fig.) quality of entertainment etc. likely to attract audiences; ~-*pleat*: see PLEAT; ~-*room*, room for storing boxes, trunks, etc.: ~-*spanner*, -*wrench*, one with a socket-head fitting over nut etc. to be turned; ~ *spring*, one of a set of pocketed springs in a mattress etc. ~ *v.t.* Provide with, put into, confine as in, box; partition *off* from other compartments; ~ -*haul*, veer ship round on her keel (for want of room); ~ *in*, block the movement of (a vehicle) so that it cannot manœuvre; ~ *the compass*, (naut.) repeat compass-points in correct order; (fig.) make complete revolution and end where one began (in argument etc.); *Boxing Day*, first week-day after Christmas, traditional day for giving of Christmas boxes.

bŏx[3] *v.* 1. Slap person's *ears*. 2. Fight with fists, usu. in padded gloves. **bŏ'xĭng** *n.* (esp.) Act or sport of fighting with fists, usu. in padded leather gloves (~-*gloves*); ~ *match*, match between pugilists fighting in boxing-gloves; ~ *weight*, weight at which boxers are matched against each other. **bŏx** *n.* Slap with hand *on the ear*.

TABLE OF BOXING WEIGHTS

amateur

light fly	not more than	48 kg (7 st. 8 lb.)
fly	,,	51 kg (8 st.)
bantam	,,	54 kg (8 st. 6 lb.)
feather	,,	57 kg (9 st.)
light		60 kg (9 st. 7 lb.)
light welter	not more than	63·5 kg (10 st.)
welter	,,	67 kg (10 st. 8 lb.)
light middle	,,	71 kg (11 st. 2 lb.)
middle	,,	75 kg (11 st. 11 lb.)
light heavy	,,	81 kg (12 st. 10 lb.)
heavy		81 kg (12 st. 10 lb.) and over

professional

fly	not more than	8 st.
bantam	,,	8 st. 8 lb.

feather	,,	9 st.
light	,,	9 st. 9 lb.
welter	,,	10 st. 7 lb.
middle	,,	11 st. 6 lb.
light heavy	,,	12 st. 7 lb.
heavy		12 st. 7 lb. and over

Bŏx and Cŏx. Characters in a farce (1847) by J. M. Morton, a printer and a hatter to whom a landlady lets the same room without their knowing it, the one being out at work all night and the other all day; hence, two persons who take turns in sustaining a part.

bŏx-calf (-kahf) *n.* Chrome-tanned calfskin, having a grain of rectangularly crossed lines. [Named after a London bootmaker]

bŏ'xer[1] *n.* Person who fights in boxing match(es), pugilist.

bŏ'xer[2] *n.* Dog of smooth-

coated brown breed of the bulldog type.

Bŏ'xer[3] *n.* Member of a Chinese secret society which organized an anti-foreign rising in China (1900) during which the legations at Peking were besieged. [transl. of Chinese word meaning 'fist of harmony']

bŏ'xȳ *adj.* Resembling a box (BOX[2]) in shape.

boy *n.* Male child or youth, son; man retaining boy's character, tastes, etc.; male native servant or labourer; familiarly as term of address; *~-friend*, woman's usual or preferred male companion; *B~ Scout*: see SCOUT; *Boys' Brigade*, organization, connected with church or mission, founded in Glasgow 1883, to promote boys' activities on Christian principles. *~ int.* (colloq., orig. U.S.; also *oh ~*) Exclamation of surprise, approval, etc.

boy'cott *v.t.* Combine to punish or coerce by systematic refusal of social or commercial relations; abstain from (goods etc.) with this aim. *~ n.* Boycotting. [f. Captain *Boycott*, an Irish landlord, original victim of this treatment]

boy'hŏŏd *n.* Boyish age; boys.

boy'ish *adj.* Of or like boys; **boy'ishlȳ** *adv.* **boy'ishnėss** *n.*

Boyle, Hon. Robert (1627–91). English natural philosopher and chemist, one of the founders of the Royal Society; *~'s law*, law, formulated by him, that the volume of a given quantity of gas varies inversely with the pressure when the temperature is constant.

Boyne, Battle of the. Battle fought across the river Boyne in E. Ireland, 1690; William III and a Protestant (largely English) army defeated the Catholic (Irish and French) army of the exiled James II, who fled to France.

Bŏz. Pseudonym used by Charles DICKENS.

Bp *abbrev.* Bishop.

B.P. *abbrev.* British Pharmacopoeia; British Public.

B.P.C. *abbrev.* British Pharmaceutical Codex.

B.Phil. *abbrev.* Bachelor of Philosophy.

B.R. *abbrev.* British Rail.

bra (-ah) *n.* (colloq.) Brassière.

Brabă'nt. Former duchy in W. Europe, now divided into 2 provinces: ~ in Belgium and *N.* ~ in the Netherlands.

brāce *v.t.* Strengthen or tighten; make taut; give firmness to, invigorate. *~ n.* 1. Thing that braces or connects; connecting mark in printing or writing ({); strengthening piece of iron or timber in buildings; (dentistry) wire device for straightening teeth; (naut.) rope attached to yard for trimming sail; (pl.) straps worn over shoulders for supporting trousers; *~ and bit*, tool for boring in which the bit is made to revolve by turning the brace etc. 2. Couple, pair esp. of dogs or game.

brā'celėt (-sl-) *n.* Ornamental band, chain, etc., for wrist or arm; (pl., slang) handcuffs.

brā'cer *n.* Wrist-guard in archery and fencing.

brā'chĭal (-k-) *adj.* Of the arm; like an arm.

brăchȳcėphă'lĭc (-ăk-) *adj.* Short-headed; with breadth of skull at least ⅘ of length.

bră'cken *n.* Kind of large fern, *Pteridium aquilinum*, abundant on heaths etc.; mass of this.

bră'ckėt *n.* 1. Flat-topped projection from wall serving as support; shelf with slanting under-prop for hanging against wall; wooden or metal angular support. 2. (freq. pl.) Pair of marks ( ), [ ], { }, used for enclosing words, figures, etc., so as to separate them from the context. 3. (artillery) Specified distance between pair of shots fired beyond target and short of it, in finding range. 4. Group bracketed together as of equal standing or falling between certain limits (as *income* ~). ~ *v.t.* Enclose in brackets; couple with brace, imply connection or equality between; (artillery) fire shots beyond and short of target (see above).

bră'ckĭsh *adj.* (of water) Rather salty.

brăct *n.* (bot.) Modified usu. small leaf or scale below flower.

bră'ctėate *adj.* Bearing bracts.

bră'ctėōle *n.* (bot.) Small bract on flower-stalk.

brăd *n.* Thin flattish nail of same thickness throughout.

bră'dawl *n.* Small tool consisting of slender stem of steel with chisel edge for making holes for screws, nails, etc.

Bră'dford. City in West Yorkshire; university, 1966.

Bră'dlaugh (-law), Charles (1833–91). English free-thinker, journalist and politician; was elected M.P. for Northampton in 1880, but unseated, having refused to swear on the Bible.

Bră'dley, James (1693–1762). English astronomer, discoverer of the aberration of light.

Bră'dshaw *n.* Copy of 'Bradshaw's Railway Guide', a time-table (issued until 1961) of all railway trains running in Gt Britain, the earliest form of which was first issued at Manchester in 1839 by George Bradshaw (1801–53), engraver and printer.

brae (-ā) *n.* (Sc.) Steep bank, hillside.

brăg *v.* Talk boastfully. ~ *n.* 1. Boastful talk. 2. Card-game like poker.

Brăgg, Sir William Henry (1862–1942). English physicist, famous for his researches on crystal structure; awarded Nobel Prize for physics in 1915 with his son Sir William Laurence Bragg (1890–1971).

brăggadō'cĭō (-sh-) *n.* Empty boasting. [formed by Spenser from *brag* as proper name of personification of vainglory]

bră'ggart *n.* & *adj.* (Person) given to bragging.

Brah'e (-*e* or -ah-h*e*), Tycho (1546–1601). Danish astronomer; his observations of the sun prepared the way for the discoveries of Kepler (who worked under him) but he did not accept the Copernican system.

brah'ma[1], **brahmapōō'tra** *n.* Kind of domestic fowl.

Brah'ma[2]. (Hinduism) Supreme God, the divine reality, of which the entire universe is only a manifestation.

Brah'mi (-mē) *n.* One of the oldest alphabets of India, prob. of Semitic origin.

Brah'mĭn, -man *n.* Member of the highest or priestly caste among Hindus. **Brahmĭ'nĭc, -ĭcal, -mă'n-** *adjs.* **Brah'mĭnĭsm, -man-** *ns.*

Brahms (-z), Johannes (1833–97). German composer of symphonies, chamber music, songs, etc.

braid *n.* 1. Entwined hair, plait; band, etc., entwined with the hair. 2. Woven fabric of silk, linen, etc., in the form of a band. ~ *v.t.* Plait, interweave, arrange in braids; trim, edge, with braid.

brail *n.* Small rope on sail-edge for trussing sails before furling. ~ *v.t.* Haul up by brails.

Braille *n.* System of printing for the blind consisting of embossed characters recognizable by

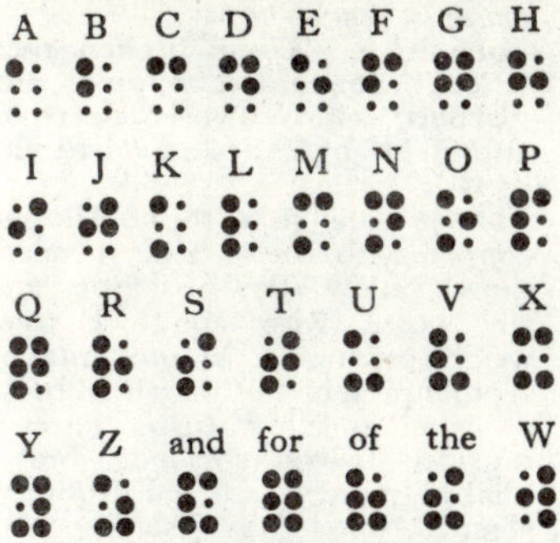

BRAILLE CHARACTERS

touch, invented by a blind French teacher, Louis Braille (1809–52). ~ *v.t.* Print in Braille.

brain *n.* 1. Convoluted mass of nervous tissue, contained in the skull, which controls the processes of sensation, learning, and memory in vertebrates and is regarded as the centre of thought and intellectual power in man; *fŏr'ebrain, mi'dbrain, hi'ndbrain*, parts which develop from the foremost, middle, hindmost of the three main dilatations of the primitive brain; *great* ~, cerebrum; *lesser* ~, cerebellum; *~-stem*, medulla oblongata. 2. In many invertebrates, that part of the nervous system which corresponds to the vertebrate brain in function and position. 3. (colloq.) Clever person; *the* ~*s*, cleverest person (in group etc.). 4. *brai'nchild*, invention, scheme; ~ *drain*, (colloq.) emigration of highly qualified persons esp. to U.S.; *~-fag*, mental exhaustion; *~-fever*, inflammation of the brain; *~-pan*, skull; *brai'nstorm*, paroxysm of cerebral disturbance; ~ *trust*, (hist.) group of advisers called in by President Franklin Roosevelt; *~s trust*, group of experts assembled to answer questions impromptu; *brai'nwashing*, systematic elimination from person's mind of (esp. political) established ideas, esp. coercive conversion of dissidents in totalitarian State; so *brai'nwash* (*v.t.*); *brai'nwave*, sudden inspiration, bright thought. **brai'nlėss** *adj.* **brain** *v.t.* Dash out brains of.

brai'nў *adj.* (colloq.) Clever.

braise (-z) *v.t.* Steam (meat) slowly with vegetables, herbs, etc., in tightly closed pan (prop. with fire above and below).

brāke[1] *n.* Bracken.

brāke[2] *n.* Thicket, brushwood.

brāke[3] *n.* Toothed instrument for braking flax and hemp; (also ~ *harrow*), heavy harrow. ~ *v.t.* Crush (flax, hemp) by beating.

brāke[4] *n.* Frictional apparatus for checking motion of vehicle or machine by pressure, usu. applied to circumference of wheel or to special drum or hub on axle; (also ~ *pedal*) pedal operating this; ~ *horsepower*, (abbrev.

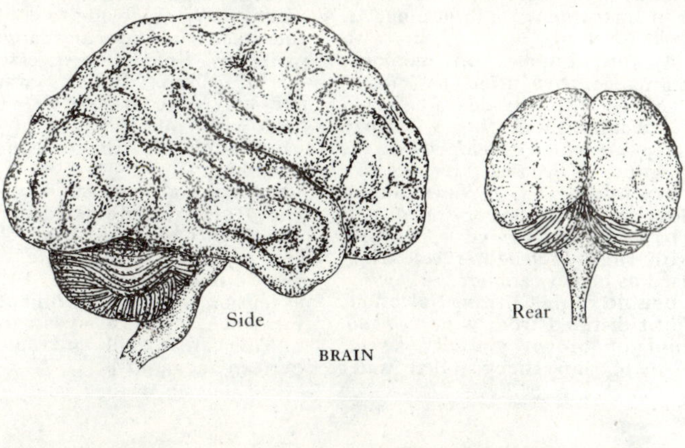

BRAIN

b.h.p.) horsepower of an engine measured by an absorption dynamometer (orig. by resistance of an applied brake); *bra'ke(s)man*, man in charge of brake, (U.S.) guard of train; *~-van*, railway-carriage containing brake, guard's van. ~ *v.* Apply brake; check with brake.

brāke[5] *n.* Large wagonette; estate car.

Brămă'ntė, Donato (*c* 1444–1514). Italian High Renaissance architect.

bră'mble *n.* Rough prickly rambling shrub, esp. the blackberry.

bră'mbling *n.* Mountain finch, *Fringilla montifringilla.*

brăn *n.* Husks of grain separated from flour after grinding; *~-tub*, tub of bran into which children dip for toys etc.

branch (-ah-) *n.* Limb of tree etc. growing from stem or bough; lateral extension or subdivision of river, road, family, business, etc.; nozzle of fireman's hose; (U.S.) small stream. **branched** (-sht), **bra'nchȳ** *adjs.* **branch** *v.i.* Put branches *out*, *forth*, spring *out*; spread *forth*, tend *away*, *off*, diverge *into.*

bră'nchiae (-kĭē) *n.pl.* Gills. **bră'nchial, bră'nchiate** *adjs.*

brănd *n.* 1. Burning or charred piece of wood from hearth. 2. Mark made by burning with hot iron; stigma; trade-mark, goods of particular make or trade-mark; *bran(d)-new*, perfectly new. 3. Iron instrument for branding. 4. (poet.) Sword. ~ *v.t.* Burn with hot iron; impress on memory; stigmatize. **bră'ndėd** *adj.* (esp.) Labelled with a trade-name.

Bră'ndenbûrg. (hist.) German electorate which developed into the kingdom of Prussia.

bră'ndish *v.t.* Wave about, flourish, in display or threat.

bră'ndling *n.* Red earthworm with rings of brighter colouring, used as bait by anglers.

bră'ndȳ *n.* Strong alcoholic spirit distilled from wine; ~ *ball*, kind of brown globular sweet; *~-snap*, thin sticky rolled wafer flavoured with ginger. [Du. *brandewijn*, burnt, distilled wine]

brănt *n.* (esp. U.S.; also *~-goose*) = BRENT-GOOSE.

brăsh[1] *n.* Loose broken rock or ice; hedge refuse, clippings, etc.

brăsh[2] *adj.* Vulgarly assertive, impudent. **bră'shlȳ** *adv.* **bră'shnėss** *n.*

brass (-ahs) *n.* 1. (hist.) Alloy of copper with tin or zinc, bronze; (now) yellow alloy of copper and zinc, usu. with about $\frac{1}{3}$ total weight of zinc. 2. Monumental or sepulchral tablet of inscribed brass or similar alloy (usu. latten); musical instruments of brass; (dial.) money. 3. Effrontery, shamelessness. 4. (slang; also *top* ~) Brass hats; senior officials. ~ *adj.* Made of brass; ~ *band*, band of musicians with brass instruments; ~ *hat*, (slang) officer of high rank; ~ *tacks*, (slang) actual details, real business.

bră'ssârd *n.* Badge worn on arm.

bră'sserie *n.* Restaurant providing beer and food.

bra'ssie (-ah-) *n.* Wooden-headed golf-club with brass plate under the head.

bră'ssière (-ĭār) *n.* Woman's undergarment supporting breasts.

bra'ssȳ (-ah-) *adj.* Yellow like brass; sounding or tasting like brass; impudent, shameless. ~ *n.* Brassie.

brăt *n.* (contempt.) Child.

brava'dō (-vah-) *n.* Show of courage, bold front.

brāve *adj.* 1. Ready to confront and steady in enduring danger or pain. 2. Splendid, spectacular. ~ *n.* Red Indian warrior. **brā'velȳ** *adv.* **brāve** *v.t.* Defy, meet with courage.

brā'verȳ *n.* Brave conduct; splendour.

bra'vō[1] (-ah-) *n.* (pl. *-oes*, *-os*). Hired assassin; desperado.

bra'vō[2] (-ah-) *int.* & *n.* Cry of approval, esp. to actors etc.

bravur'a (-oor*a*) *n.* Brilliant execution, attempt at brilliant performance; musical passage requiring great skill and spirit in performance. [It.]

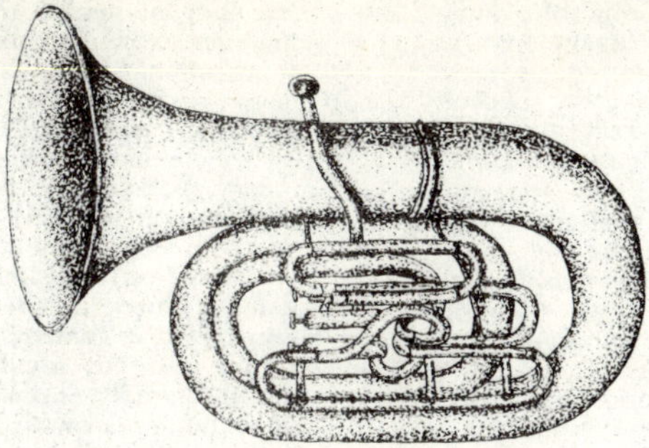

Tuba

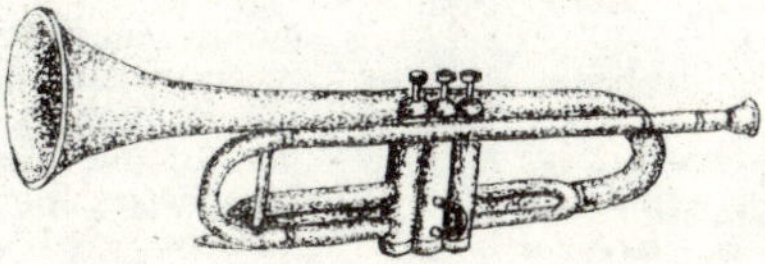

Trumpet

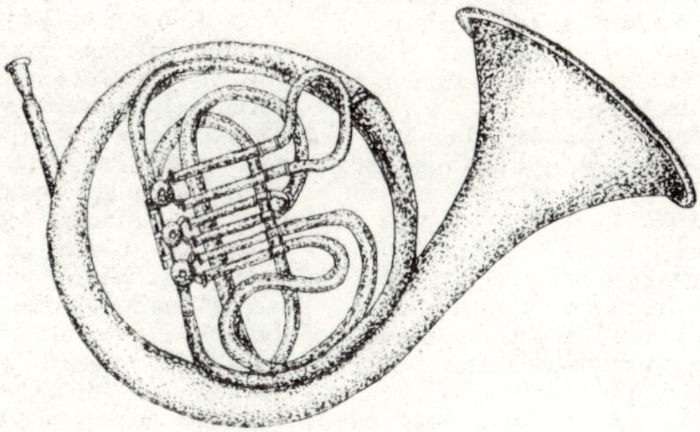

Horn

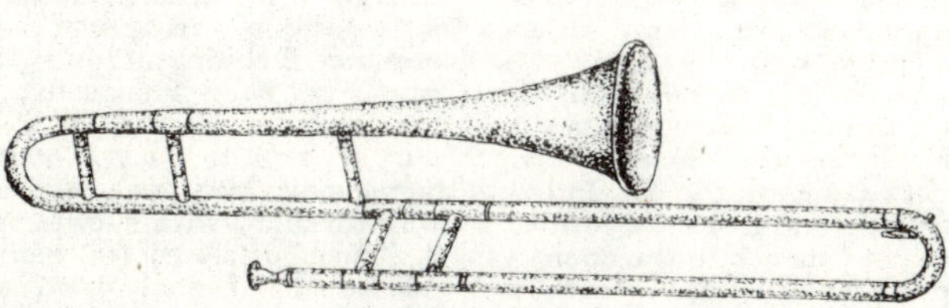

Trombone

BRASS INSTRUMENTS

brawl *n.* Squabble, noisy quarrel. ~ *v.i.* Engage in brawl; (of stream) run noisily.

brawn *n.* 1. Muscle. 2. Chopped cooked meat from pig's head, pressed into a mould.

braw'ný *adj.* Strong, muscular.

bray[1] *n.* Peculiar cry of some animals, esp. the ass; loud harsh jarring sound resembling this. ~ *v.* Make bray; utter harshly.

bray[2] *v.t.* Pound, usu. in mortar.

Bray[3]**,** Vicar of. Parson who in an 18th-c. song boasts of having kept his benefice from Charles II's reign to George I's by changing his beliefs to suit the times; the song is apparently based on an anecdote of an unidentified vicar of Bray, Berks., in T. Fuller, 'Worthies of England' (1662).

brāze *v.t.* Solder with alloy of brass and zinc.

brā'zen *adj.* Of brass; strong, yellow, or harsh-sounding, as brass; shameless. **brā'zenlý** *adv.* **brā'zenness** *n.* **brā'zen** *v.t.* Face shamelessly or defiantly under charge or suspicion, esp. ~ *it out.*

brā'zier[1] (-zĭ- *or* -zher), *n.* Worker in brass.

brā'zier[2] (-zĭ- *or* -zher) *n.* Large flat pan for holding burning charcoal etc.; iron cage or basket for charcoal fire.

Brazi'l[1]**.** Large S. Amer. Portuguese-speaking State; colonized by Portugal in the early 16th c.; proclaimed a republic, 1889; capital, Brasilia. **Brazi'lian** *adj.* & *n.* [see BRAZIL[2]]

brazi'l[2] *n.* 1. (usu. ~-*wood*) Sappan-wood; similar wood of a S. Amer. species, *Caesalpina echinata*. 2. ~-*nut*, large three-sided edible nut, the seed of a lofty tree, *Bertholletia excelsa*, which forms large forests in Brazil. [orig. the Span., Port., and Fr. name of the E. Indian wood; transferred to the S. Amer. species, and thence to the country where this was found]

B.R.C.S. *abbrev.* British Red Cross Society.

breach *n.* 1. (archaic, also ~ *of the sea*) Breaking of waves. 2. Breaking or neglect (of rule, duty, promise, etc.); breaking of relations, alienation, quarrel; ~ ***of the peace***, disturbance of public peace by affray, riot, etc.; ~ ***of promise***, (esp.) breaking of promise to marry. 3. Injury, broken place, gap, esp. in wall or fortification; ~ ***v.t.*** Break through, make gap in.

bread (-ĕd) *n.* Flour moistened, usu. leavened, kneaded into dough, and baked in loaves; this as staple article of food; livelihood, means of subsistence; ~ ***and butter***, slices of bread spread with butter; livelihood; ~***-and-butter letter***, letter of thanks for hospitality; ***brea'd-crumb***, crumb of bread; (esp., pl.) bread crumbled for use in cooking; ~***-fruit***, farinaceous fruit, about the size of a melon, and with whitish pulp like new bread, of *Artocarpus incisa*, the ~***-fruit tree*** of the South Sea islands etc.; ~***-winner***, person supporting a family.

breadth (-ĕd-) *n.* 1. Broadness, measure from side to side; piece (of cloth etc.) of full breadth. 2. Extent, distance, room; largeness, liberality, catholicity. **brea'dthways** (-z), **brea'dthwīse** (-z) *advs.*

break (brāk) *v.* (past t. *brōke*, past part. *brō'ken*). 1. Divide, disperse, split, separate, otherwise than by cutting; tame, subdue, crush; fall to pieces; burst, issue, *forth*; solve (cipher etc.); (of voice) crack, change tone (at puberty); (boxing) come out of clinch; ~ *down*, (intrans.) collapse; lose control, become tearful; (of machine etc.) cease to function; (trans.) itemize, analyse; ~ ***even***, emerge with neither loss nor gain; ~ ***in***, tame, discipline; ~ ***up***, become feeble; disband; break small. 2. Ruin financially, make bankrupt. 3. Interrupt, change; put an end to; act contrary to (agreement, law, etc.). 4. Make a way through, with suddenness or violence; disclose; (of news) be disclosed; (of day) dawn; (of a storm) begin violently. 5. (of cricket-ball) Deviate from original direction after pitching. 6. *brea'kaway* (*adj.*, esp.) seceding;

brea'kdown, collapse, stoppage; failure of health or (esp. mental) power(s); act of disintegrating or analysing a substance; analysis of statistical figures etc.; *brea'kneck*, endangering the neck, headlong; *brea'kthrough*, (esp.) significant advance in knowledge, achievement, etc.; *~-up*, disintegration, collapse, dispersal; *brea'kwater*, mole etc. built to break force of waves. **brea'kable** *adj.* **brea'kage** *n.* **break** *n.* Breaking; breach, gap, broken place; pause in work etc.; escape; deviation of cricket-ball after pitching; (billiards) points scored continuously; (slang) stroke of luck.

brea'ker[1] (brāk-) *n.* (esp.) Heavy ocean-wave breaking on coast or over reefs.

brea'ker[2] (brāk-) *n.* (naut.) Small keg.

brea'kfast (brĕk-) *n.* First meal of the day. *~ v.i.* Take breakfast.

bream *n.* 1. Yellowish fresh-water fish of genus *Abramis* with high-arched back. 2. Sea-fish of the family Sparidae, including many different genera.

breast (-ĕst) *n.* 1. Each of two soft protuberances on woman's thorax, secreting milk for feeding young; corresponding rudimentary organ of man. 2. Upper front part of human body; corresponding part in animals, this as cut of meat; part of dress, coat, etc., covering this. 3. Heart, emotions, thoughts. 4. *~ -bone*, sternum; *~ -fed*, (of infant) fed at mother's breast; *~-hook*, strengthening piece athwart bows; *brea'stplate*, leather strap worn at base of horse's neck, attached to saddle to prevent its slipping back; piece of embroidered fabric worn on breast of Jewish high priest; (hist.) piece of armour covering breast; *~ -stroke*, stroke in swimming in which breast is squarely opposed to water; *~ -wheel*, water wheel turned by water flowing in level with the axle; *brea'stwork*, temporary defence or parapet a few feet high. *~ v.t.* Oppose breast to, face, contend with.

brea'stsŭmmer (-ĕst-), **brĕ'ssŭmmer** *n.* Beam across broad opening, sustaining superstructure.

breath (-ĕth) *n.* 1. Exhalation as perceptible to sight or smell; slight movement of air; whiff. 2. Air taken into and expelled from lungs; respiration; power of breathing; whisper, murmur; *take person's ~ away*, dumbfound him. 3. (phon.) Voiceless expiration of air.

brea'thalȳser (brĕ-, -*zer*) *n.* Device for measuring the percentage of alcohol in the blood by means of a breath sample. **brea'thalȳse** *v.t.* Test with breathalyser.

breathe (-dh) *v.* Take air into and expel it from lungs or other respiratory organs; live; take breath, pause; sound, speak, blow, softly; take in (air etc.); utter softly or passionately, exhibit.

brea'ther (-dh-) *n.* (esp.) Short spell of exercise; spell of rest to recover one's breath after exertion.

brea'thing (-dh-) *n.* (esp. Gk gram.) *rough, smooth, ~*, sign indicating that initial vowel is or is not aspirated; *~-space*, time to breathe; pause.

brea'thlėss (-ĕth-) *adj.* Panting; holding the breath; unstirred by wind. **brea'thlėsslȳ** *adv.* **brea'thlėssnėss** *n.*

brea'thȳ (brĕ-) *adj.* (of voice) With sound of emission of breath. **brea'thinėss** *n.*

brĕ'ccia (-ch-; *or* -cha) *n.* (geol.) Composite rock of angular fragments of stone etc. cemented together by some matrix.

Brĕcht (-χt), Bertolt (1898–1956). German playwright.

Brĕ'cknockshire, Brĕ'conshire. Former county of Wales, since April 1974 part of Powys.

bred : see BREED.

breech *n.* 1. Buttocks (archaic exc. physiol.); *~ birth, delivery*, birth, delivery, of infant with breech presenting. 2. Part of cannon behind bore; back part of rifle or gun barrel; *~ -loader, -loading*, (gun) loaded at breach, not through muzzle (hist.); (of guns) in which obturation is effected by a specially designed breech and not by a metal cartridge-case. 3. (pl., pr. brĭ′chĭz) Short trousers fastened above or (esp.) below knee, now used only for riding or in court costume etc.; (loosely) trousers, knickerbockers; *Breeches Bible*, Geneva Bible of 1560 with *breeches* for *aprons* in Gen. 3: 7; *breeches-buoy*, lifebuoy, slung on a rope, with canvas supports like breeches for the legs. ~ *v.t.* (archaic) Put (boy) into breeches instead of petticoats.

bree′chĭng (-ĭch-) *n.* Leather strap round shaft-horse's hindquarters for pushing backwards.

breed *v.* (past t. & past part. *brĕd*). 1. Bear, generate; (make) propagate; yield, produce, result in; arise, spread. 2. Train up; fit for being, adapt *to*, bring up. 3. (phys.) Create fissile material from non-fissile by nuclear reaction. ~ *n.* 1. Strain of animals etc. visibly resembling each other, esp. developed under control of man; similar group of plants. 2. Stock, lineage. 3. Sort, kind.

bree′der *n.* One who breeds cattle etc.; animal that breeds; (phys., also ~ *reactor*) reactor that can create more fissile material than it consumes in the chain reaction.

bree′dĭng *n.* (esp.) Result of training, (good) behaviour or manners.

breeze[1] *n.* 1. Gentle wind; wind blowing in from sea during day (*sea-~*), or from land to sea during night (*land-~*); (meteor.): see BEAUFORT scale. 2. (slang) Quarrel. ~ *v.i.* (colloq.) Move *along* briskly; come *in*.

breeze[2] *n.* Small cinders, coke, coke-dust, etc., used in burning bricks, and to make *~-blocks*, flat slabs used for the interior walls of buildings.

bree′zȳ *adj.* Wind-swept; pleasantly windy; lively, jovial. **bree′zĭlȳ** *adv.* **bree′zĭnėss** *n.*

Bre′men (brā-). Province of W. Germany; its capital, a seaport on river Weser.

Brĕn *n.* (also ~ *gun*) Lightweight machine-gun used in the British Army in the war of 1939–45, noted for its steadiness in action and ease with which barrel can be changed when over-hot. [*Brno*, town in Czechoslovakia where it was orig. made, and first syllable of *Enfield*, Greater London, site of British Royal Small Arms Factory].

Brĕ′ndan, St. (484–577). Irish saint reputed in legend to have made a voyage in search of the earthly paradise, touching at many fabulous islands on the way; commemorated 16 May.

brĕ′nt-gōōse *n.* Smallest species of wild goose, *Bernicla brenta*, of Arctic origin, visiting Britain in winter.

brer (brār; U.S. -ēr) *n.* (colloq., orig. U.S.; as title prefixed to name) Brother. [repr. Amer. Negro pronunc. of *brother*]

bressummer: see BREASTSUMMER.

Brĕst-Litŏ′vsk (-fsk). Polish town on Russian frontier (now in U.S.S.R.), in which was signed the treaty of peace between Germany and Russia in March 1918.

brĕ′thrėn (-dh-) *n.pl.* 1. (archaic) Brothers. 2. Members of religious order etc. (see BROTHER, 3); *Elder B~*, senior members of Trinity House.

Brĕ′ton *n.* & *adj.* (Native, inhabitant, language) of Brittany.

Breughel: see BRUEGHEL.

brev. *abbrev.* Brevet.

brēve *n.* 1. (mus.) Note equal to two semibreves, now rarely used (||𝅜||). 2. Mark ˘ placed over vowel to show that it is short. 3. (hist.) Letter of authority from sovereign or pope.

brĕ′vėt *n.* Document conferring privilege from sovereign or government, esp. rank without corresponding pay in army. ~ *v.t.* Confer brevet rank on.

brĕv′ĭarȳ *n.* Book containing R.C. office for each day, to be recited by those in orders.

brėvier′ (-vēr) *n.* (print.) Size of type (approx. 8 point) between bourgeois and minion.

BREEDS OF CATTLE

brĕ′vitў *n.* Shortness, briefness.

brew (-o͞o) *v.* 1. Make (beer etc.) by infusion, boiling, and fermentation, or (tea, punch) by infusion or mixture. 2. Concoct, set in train; fester, gather force. ~ *n.* Brewing; amount brewed; beverage etc. brewed.

brew′er (-o͞o*er*) *n.* (esp.) One who brews malt liquors. **brew′erў** *n.* Establishment where brewing is carried out.

brew′ster[1] (-o͞o-) *n.* (archaic) Brewer; *B~ Sessions*, magistrates' sessions for issuing licences to trade in alcoholic liquors.

Brew′ster[2] (-o͞o-), Sir David (1781–1868). Scottish physicist; made discoveries relating to polarization of light.

Brī′an Boru′ (-o͞o) (926–1014). King of Munster; defeated the Danes and in 1002 became high king of Ireland; was killed after a great victory over the Danes at Clontarf.

briar: see BRIER.

Brīār′ėus. (Gk myth.) Giant with 100 hands and 50 heads, confined under Mt Etna for fighting, with the other giants, against the gods.

bribe *n.* Money or other inducement offered to procure (often illegal or dishonest) action in favour of the giver. ~ *v.t.* Persuade by bribe. **brī′berў** *n.*

brĭ′c-a-brăc *n.* Antiquarian or artistic odds and ends.

brĭck *n.* 1. Clay kneaded, moulded, and baked by fire or sun, used as a building material; rectangular block of this, usu. about 225×112·5×75 mm.; *drop a ~*, (slang) say something indiscreet. 2. Brick-shaped block, e.g. of tea; child's toy building-block. 3. (slang) Generous or loyal person. 4. *bri′ckbat*, piece of brick, esp. as missile (also fig.); *~-field*, piece of ground where bricks are made; *bri′cklayer*, workman who lays bricks in building; *~-red*, colour of red brick; *bri′ckwork*, brick construction. ~ *v.t.* Block *up* with brickwork.

brī′dal *adj.* Of bride or wedding. ~ *n.* (archaic) Wedding-feast.

brīde[1] *n.* Woman on her wedding day and shortly before or after it; *bri′decake*, wedding-cake.

brīde[2] *n.* Small band or tie-bar connecting motifs of lace.

Bride[3], St.: see BRIDGET[1].

brī′degro͞om (-dg-) *n.* Man on his wedding day and shortly before or after it.

brī′desmaid (-dz-) *n.* Unmarried woman or girl attending bride at wedding.

Brī′dewell (-dw-). Orig. a royal palace in London near the old well of St. Bride at the mouth of the Fleet river; it was rebuilt by Henry VIII and later became a hospital and then a house of correction.

brĭdge[1] *n.* 1. Structure carrying road, path, etc., across stream, ravine, road, etc.; *B~ of Sighs*, 16th-c. bridge in Venice between the doges' palace and the State prison, crossed by prisoners on way to execution. 2. (naut.) Platform amidships for officer in command. 3. Upper bony part of nose. 4. Movable piece over which strings of violin etc. are stretched. 5. (billiards) Support for cue formed with hand; contrivance consisting of a long stick with device at end to support cue. 6. (dentistry; also *bri′dgework*) Partial denture supported by teeth on each side. 7. *bri′dgehead*, (mil.) fortification, post, at end of bridge or on side of a river nearest enemy; any position established in face of enemy, e.g. by landing force; *~ passage*, passage connecting principal subjects in musical composition. ~ *v.t.* Form bridge; span as if with a bridge.

brĭdge[2] *n.* (orig.) Card-game, app. of Near-Eastern origin, based on whist, (now esp.) contract bridge; *auction ~*, variety of bridge in which the right to name trumps and play with the dummy goes, with each deal, to the player who undertakes to make the highest score; *contract ~* (the most usual form of bridge), form of auction bridge in which only the tricks which the declarer has undertaken to make count towards the game.

Brĭ'dgės (-z), Robert (1844–1930). English poet, poet laureate from 1913.

Brĭ'dgėt[1], **Brĭ'gĭt, Brīde,** St. (453–523). Second patron saint of Ireland, traditionally held to have been born in Louth in the time of St. Patrick; commemorated 1 Feb.

Brĭ'dgėt[2], **Brĭ'gĭd, Bĭrgĭ'tta** (-g-), St. (1304–73). Founder of an order of nuns (Order of the Most Holy Saviour) at Vadstena, Sweden, 1344. **Brĭ'dgėttīne, Brĭ'gittīne, Bĭrgĭ'ttīne** *adjs.* & *ns.* (Nun) of this order.

brī'dle *n.* 1. Head-gear of harness, including headstall, bit, and rein; restraint, curb; ~ *-path*, path fit for horses but not for vehicles. 2. (naut.) Mooring-cable. 3. (physiol.) Ligament or membrane checking motion of a part, or binding one part to another. ~ *v.* Put bridle on, curb, control; express resentment, vanity, etc., by throwing up head and drawing in chin.

Brie *n.* Soft cheese produced in Brie, a district of N. France.

brief[1] *n.* 1. Pope's letter on matter of discipline (less formal than BULL[1]). 2. (law) Summary of facts and points of law of a case drawn up (usu. by solicitors) for counsel; piece of employment for barrister; *dock* ~: see DOCK[4]; *watching-*~, brief of barrister who watches case for a client not directly concerned; *brie'fcase*, rectangular case for carrying documents etc. ~ *v.t.* Instruct (counsel) by brief; give instructions, necessary information, etc., to.

brief[2] *adj.* Short, concise. **brie'flў** *adv.* **brie'fnėss** *n.*

brie'flėss *adj.* (of barrister) Without briefs, unemployed.

briefs *n.pl.* Very short knickers or pants.

brī'er[1], **brī'ar**[1] *n.* Prickly bush, esp. wild rose; ~*-rose*, wild rose, dog-rose.

brī'er[2], **brī'ar**[2] *n.* White heath, *Erica arborea*, a native of S. France, Corsica, etc.; ~ *pipe*, tobacco-pipe made from its root.

Brieux (brēē̆r), Eugène (1858–1932). French playwright, author of plays dealing with social problems.

brĭg[1] *n.* Two-masted square-rigged vessel having additional lower fore-and-aft sail with a gaff and boom on the mainmast.

brĭg[2] *n.* (Sc.) Bridge.

Brig. *abbrev.* Brigadier.

brĭgā'de *n.* Major sub-unit of an army division, commanded by a brigadier, normally consisting, in British Army, of 3 battalions; organized or uniformed band of workers; *Boys' B*~: see BOY.

brĭgadier' *n.* (formerly ~*-general*) Army officer ranking immediately above colonel and below major-general.

brĭ'gand *n.* Bandit, robber. **brĭ'gandage** *n.*

brĭ'gantine (-ēn) *n.* Two-masted vessel with square-rigged foremast and fore-and-aft rigged mainmast.

bright[1] (-īt) *adj.* Emitting or reflecting much light, shining; lit up with joy etc.; vivid; illustrious; vivacious; quick-witted; ***bri'ght-work***, polished metalwork on ships etc. **bri'ghtlў** *adv.* **bri'ghtnėss** *n.* **bri'ghten** *v.* **bright** *adv.* Brightly.

Bright[2] (-īt), John (1811–89). English Liberal politician, famous as a leading agitator against the Corn Laws and as an orator.

Bright's dĭsea'se (-īts, -zēz). Granular degeneration of the kidneys. [Dr Richard *Bright*, English physician (1789–1858)]

Brigid, Brigittine: see BRIDGET[2].

brĭll *n.* European flatfish, *Scophthalmus rhombus*, resembling turbot in shape and the quality of its flesh.

brĭ'lliant (-lya-) *adj.* Bright, sparkling; illustrious; highly talented; showy. **brĭ'lliantlў** *adv.* **brĭ'lliance, brĭ'lliancў** *ns.* **brĭ'lliant** *n.* 1. Diamond or other gem of faceted cut; ~*-cut*, faceted (in diamond) cut; *cut* designed to give maximum brilliance, consisting of 58 facets, except when culet is omitted 2. (print)

Very small size of type, approx. 3½ point.

brĭ'lliantine (-lyantēn) *n.* Cosmetic for keeping hair smooth and glossy.

brĭm *n.* Edge or lip of cup, bowl, or hollow; projecting edge of hat; *brimful*, *~-full*, full to the brim. ~ *v.* Fill, be full, to the brim.

brĭ'mstone *n.* Sulphur (obs.); fuel of hell-fire; ~ *and treacle*, old-fashioned medical concoction; ~ *moth*, sulphur-coloured species, *Opisthograptis luteolata*.

brĭ'ndle, -dled (-dld) *adjs.* Brownish or tawny with streaks of other colour.

brīne *n.* Water saturated, or strongly impregnated, with salt; the sea. ~ *v.t.* Steep or pickle in, wet with, brine.

brĭng *v.* (past t. & past part. *brought* pr. -awt). Cause to come, come with or convey in any fashion: cause, result in; prefer (charge), adduce (argument); cause to become; persuade; ~ *about*, cause to happen; ~ *down*, kill or wound, cause to fall, cause (penalty) to alight *on*, abase, lower, continue (record) *to* a point; ~ *down the house*, (colloq.) receive loud applause; ~ *forth*, bear, produce; cause; ~ *in*, produce, introduce; pronounce (*guilty*, *not guilty*, etc.); ~ *off*, rescue from wreck etc., conduct with success; ~ *out*, (esp.) introduce (girl) to society; ~ *to*, restore to consciousness; (cause to) come to a stop; ~ *to book*, exact account from; ~ *to mind*, cause (oneself) to remember; ~ *to pass*, cause to happen; ~ *up*, rear, educate, anchor, come to a stop, call attention (*again*) to, continue (accounts etc.) to a further point.

brĭnk *n.* Edge of steep place; border of water, esp. when steep; verge (also fig.). **brĭ'nkmanship** *n.* Art of advancing to the very brink of war but not engaging in it.

brī'nȳ *adj.* Very salt. ~ *n.* (joc.) Sea.

brĭ'o (-ēō) *n.* Vivacity, dash. [It.]

brĭque'tte (-kĕt), **brĭ'quet** (-kĭt) *n.* Block of compressed coal-dust, usu. with addition of binding substance such as pitch.

Brĭ'sbane (-z-). Capital of Queensland, Australia.

Brīse'ĭs (-sā-). (Gk legend) Slave-concubine of Achilles, taken from him by Agamemnon; this resulted in the temporary refusal of Achilles to take part in the Trojan War.

brĭsk *adj.* Active, lively; enlivening, keen. **brĭ'sklȳ** *adv.* **brĭ'skness** *n.* **brĭsk** *v.* Make, become, brisk.

brĭ'skėt *n.* Breast of animals, esp. as joint of meat.

brĭ'sling *n.* Young herring or sprat.

brĭ'stle (-sl) *n.* Stiff hair (esp. of hog's back and sides), used for brushes; anything resembling this. **brĭ'stlȳ** *adj.* **brĭ'stle** *v.* (Cause to) stand on end, raise, rise, like bristles; show temper, prepare for fight; be thickly set (*with* difficulties etc.).

Brĭ'stol. City and port on river Avon, in the county of Avon; university, 1909; ~ *board*, fine paste-board for drawing; ~ *Channel*, arm of the Atlantic between Wales and SW. England; ~ *Cream*, ~ *Milk*, trade-name of kinds of sherry first imported at Bristol; *~-fashion*, in good order.

Brit. *abbrev.* Britain; British.

Brĭ'tain (-*a*n). (also *Great* ~) Island containing England, Wales, and Scotland, with their dependencies; *Battle of* ~, series of air battles (Aug.–Sept. 1940) over London and SE. England between R.A.F. and German air force in which British victory ended the threat of German invasion.

Brĭtă'nnĭa. 1. (poet.) Britain. 2. Britain personified, usu. represented (e.g. on coins) as a woman with shield, helmet, and trident. 3. ~ *metal*, an alloy of tin and regulus of antimony, used for tableware etc. [L]

Brĭtă'nnĭc *adj.* (now chiefly in *His, Her ~ Majesty*) Of Britain.

Brĭ'tish *adj.* 1. Of Britain, esp. of ancient (or Roman) Britain. 2. Of Gt Britain; ~ *Academy*, institution founded in 1901 for the promotion of historical, philosophical, and philological studies; ~ *Association* (*for the Advancement of Science*), association of scientists, founded in 1831; ~ *Broadcasting Corporation*, (abbrev. B.B.C.) public corporation responsible for all sound radio and for non-commercial television broadcasting in U.K., established 1927 by royal charter to carry on work previously performed by the British Broadcasting Company; ~ *Commonwealth of Nations*: see COMMONWEALTH; ~ *Council*, organization established in 1934 to make the culture of the British peoples more widely known abroad; ~ *Empire*, (formerly) territories under leadership or control of Gt Britain; *Order of the ~ Empire*, military and civil award (instituted 1917) for services rendered to the British Empire; ~ *Israel*, theory that the Anglo-Saxon peoples are descended from the lost tribes of Israel; supporters of this view, who regard John Wilson (d. 1870), a Scotsman, as their founder; so ~ *Israelite*, supporter of this theory; ~ *Legion*: see LEGION; ~ *Museum*, British national museum of antiquities etc. in Bloomsbury, London, occupying the site of Montagu House, which was acquired in 1753 to house the library and collections of Sir Hans Sloane; one of the COPYRIGHT libraries; ~ *thermal unit*: see THERMAL. 3. (U.S., freq.) = ENGLISH. ~ *n.* People of Britain.

Brĭ'tĭsh Colŭ'mbĭa. Province on W. coast of Canada; capital, Victoria.

Brĭ'tĭsher *n.* (orig. U.S.) Native, inhabitant, of Gt Britain.

Brĭ'tĭsh Isles (īlz). Britain and Ireland, with the islands near their coasts.

brĭ'tĭshism *n.* Idiom used in Gt Britain but not in U.S.

Brĭ'ton *n.* 1. Inhabitant of Gt Britain. 2. (also *ancient* ~) Inhabitant of the S. part of the island at the Roman invasion.

Britt. *abbrev. Brit(t)an(n)iarum* (on coins). [L, = 'of the Britains']

Brĭ'ttanȳ. (Fr. *Bretagne*) NW. district of France, an ancient province and duchy, largely inhabited by a Celtic stock related to that of Britain.

Brĭ'tten, (Edward) Benjamin, 1st Baron (1913–76). British composer of operas ('Peter Grimes' etc.) and other music.

brĭ'ttle *adj.* Apt to break, fragile. ~ *n.* Brittle sweet made from melted sugar, usu. containing nuts. **brĭ'ttlenėss** *n.*

broach[1] *n.* 1. Spit for roasting. 2. (also ~ *spire*) Octagonal church-spire with sloping triangular faces of masonry built up against it from each angle of the tower. 3. Boring-bit. ~ *v.t.* Pierce (cask) to draw liquor, begin drawing (liquor), open (bale, box, etc.); begin discussion of (subject).

broach[2] *v.* (usu. ~ *to*) Veer, cause (ship) to veer and present side to wind and waves.

broad (-awd) *adj.* 1. Large across, wide, not narrow; in breadth (as *20 ft* ~); extensive; *county, land, of ~ acres*, Yorkshire. 2. Full, clear, main, explicit; general; tolerant; bold in effect or style; (of humour) coarse; (of speech) strongly dialectal. 3. ~ *arrow*, mark like upward-pointing arrow-head distinguishing British Government stores (formerly prison dress etc.); similar sign used as bench-mark (see BENCH *n.*); ~ *bean*, (seed of) a variety of edible bean, *Vicia faba*; *B~ Church*, in the Anglican Church, that section favouring comprehension and not pressing doctrines; *broa'dcloth*, fine twilled woollen cloth, (also) plainly woven cotton cloth (the name refers rather to quality than width); *broa'dloom*, (carpet) woven in width greater than 54 in.; loom weaving this; *broa'dsheet*, large sheet of paper printed on one side only; *broa'dside*, ship's side above water between bow and quarter; (discharge of) all guns on one side of ship; (fig.) direct attack; *broa'dsword*, broad-bladed cutting-sword; *broa'dtail* [transl. Ger. *breitschwanz*], caracul fur.

BRITTEN with Sir Peter Pears

~ *n.* Broad part; *the Broads*, large stretches of fresh water in East Anglia, formed by widening of rivers. **broa'dlў** *adv.* **broa'dnėss** *n.* (esp. of indelicacy of speech). **broad** *adv.* Broadly.

broa'dcast (-awdkah-) *adj.* 1. (of seed) Scattered freely, not in drills or rows. 2. (of information, news, music, etc.) Sent or received by broadcasting. ~ *adv.* (Sown, disseminated) in this manner. ~ *n.* Action of broadcasting; broadcast programme etc. ~ *v.* (past t. *-cast* or *-casted*, past part. *-cast*). 1. Sow (seed) broadcast. 2. Disseminate (news, musical performances, etc.) from a radio or television transmitting station; said also of performer etc. **broa'dcaster** *n.* **broa'dcasting** *n.* & *adj.*

broa'den (-awdn) *v.* Make, grow, broader.

Broa'dmoor (-awd-). Institution at Crowthorne, Berks., for mental patients requiring treatment under conditions of special security (formerly, for insane criminals).

Broa'dway (-awd-). Street in New York, famous for its theatres.

Brŏ'bdĭngnăg. In Swift's 'Gulliver's Travels', a country inhabited by giants. **Brŏbdĭngnă'gian** (-g-) *adj.* & *n.*

brocā'de *n.* 1. Fabric, of any weave or yarn, enriched by a design which is formed by additional weft threads, often of metal, running back and forth across each motif only (not from selvage to selvage). 2. Fabric superficially resembling this, produced by Jacquard loom. ~ *v.t.* Enrich (fabric) with design by these means.

brŏ'ccolĭ *n.* Hardy variety of cauliflower; (also *sprouting* ~) form of this bearing numerous small white or purple heads.

brŏch (-χ) *n.* Prehistoric round stone tower found on mainland and islands of N. Scotland.

brō'chure (-shoor; *or* brŏshoor') *n.* Stitched booklet, pamphlet.

brŏck *n.* Badger.

Brŏck'en. Highest of the Harz Mountains in Saxony, reputed to be the scene of witches' Walpurgis-night revels; ~ *spectre*, magnified shadow of the spectator thrown on a bank of cloud in high mountains when the sun is low (first observed on the Brocken).

brŏ'ckėt *n.* Stag in its 2nd year, with straight horns like small daggers.

brōderie anglaise (ahṅglāz). Open embroidery on fabric of fine cotton etc. [Fr.]

brogue[1] (-ōg) *n.* Rough Irish and Scottish Highland shoe of untanned leather; strong outdoor shoe with bands of ornamental perforations.

brogue[2] (-ōg) *n.* Dialectal, esp. Irish, accent.

broil[1] *n.* Quarrel, tumult.

broil[2] *v.* Cook (meat), be cooked, on fire or gridiron; scorch, make or be very hot.

broi'ler *n.* (esp.) Chicken suitable for broiling; ~*-house*, building in which chickens are reared in close confinement.

brōke *adj.* (colloq.) Ruined, penniless.

brō'ken *adj.*: see BREAK; (esp., in painting, of colour) mixed with another; (of pediment) with space at apex; ~ *English* etc. imperfect English etc.; ~*ground*, uneven ground; ~ *-hearted*, crushed by grief; ~*-winded*, (of horse) disabled by ruptured air-cells in lungs. **brō'kenlȳ** *adv.* Spasmodically, by jerks, with breaks.

brō'ker *n.* Middleman, agent; pawnbroker; stockbroker; person licensed to sell or value distrained goods. **brō'kerage** *n.* Broker's fees or commission, esp. on Stock Exchange transactions. [OF *brocheor* 'broacher', retailer of wine]

brō'kiṅg *n.* Broker's trade, acting as broker.

brŏ'llȳ *n.* (colloq.) Umbrella.

brō'mīde *n.* 1. Compound of bromine with an element or organic radical; ~ *paper*, (phot.) printing-paper coated with an emulsion containing silver bromide. 2. Potassium bromide, KBr, taken as a sedative; (fig., colloq.) conventional and commonplace person or remark.

brō'mine (-ēn) *n.* (chem.) Nonmetallic element, closely resembling chlorine in its properties and compounds; dark reddish-black heavy liquid with a strong irritating smell; symbol Br, at. no. 35, at. wt 79·904. [Gk *brōmos* stink]

brō'moil *n.* (phot.) Reproduction produced by the ~ *process*, a process of bleaching a bromide print and restoring the image by applying oily pigment with a brush.

brŏ'nchia (-ngk-) *n.pl.* Ramifications of bronchi in lungs.

brŏ'nchial (-ngk-) *adj.* Of the bronchi or bronchia.

brŏnchī'tis (-ngk-) *n.* Inflammation of bronchial mucous membrane.

brŏ'nchocele (-ngkosēl) *n.* Swelling of thyroid gland, goitre.

brŏ'nchoscōpe (-ngk-) *n.* Instrument for inspecting interior of bronchi. **brŏnchŏ'scopȳ** *n.* Examination of bronchi with bronchoscope.

brŏ'nchus (-ngk-) *n.* (pl. -ī). Either of the two main divisions of the windpipe.

brŏ'ncō *n.* (pl. -*os*). Wild or half-tamed horse of California or New Mexico; ~*-buster*, (U.S.) one who breaks in broncos.

Brŏ'ntë (-ĭ), Charlotte (1816–55), Emily (1818–48), and Anne (1820–49). Novelists, daughters of a Yorkshire clergyman of Irish descent; wrote under pseudonyms of Currer, Ellis, and Acton Bell; Charlotte is famous esp. for 'Jane Eyre' (1847) and 'Villette' (1853), Emily for 'Wuthering Heights' (1848) and her poems.

brŏ'ntosaur *n.* Herbivorous dinosaur of genus *Brontosaurus* from the Jurassic and Cretaceous periods, one of the largest terrestrial vertebrates. [Gk *brontē* thunder, *sauros* lizard]

brŏnze *n.* Brown alloy chiefly of copper and tin (as used for British 'copper' coins approx. 95½% cop-

BRONTË SISTERS

per, 3% tin, and 1½% zinc); work of art made of bronze; colour of bronze; *B~ Age*, that stage of a people's culture during which its weapons etc. were made of bronze. ~ *adj*. Made of, coloured, like, bronze. ~ *v*. Give bronze-like surface to; make or become brown, tan. [L (*aes*) *Brundisinum* (brass) from Brundisium (Brindisi)]

brooch (-ō-) *n*. Ornamental clasp worn on dress etc., secured by hinged pin and catch.

brōōd *n*. Young birds etc. produced at one hatch; (usu. contempt.) human family, children. ~ *adj*. For breeding. ~ *v.i.* 1. (of bird) Sit on eggs to be hatched. 2. Hang close *over*, *on*; meditate, often sullenly or with resentment (*on*, *over*, etc.).

brōō'dȳ *adj*. (of hen) Wanting to remain on nest to hatch eggs.

brŏŏk[1] *n*. Small stream.

brŏŏk[2] *v.t.* Put up with, tolerate.

Brŏŏke, Sir James (1803–68). First English rajah of Sarawak (1841–63); travelling there privately, he found it in revolt against its ruler, the Malay sultan of Brunei; he restored order and was made rajah by the Sultan and acclaimed by the people.

brōōm *n*. 1. Yellow-flowered shrub, *Sarothamnus scoparius*, growing on sandy banks, heaths, etc.; shrub of related genus *Genista*; *broo'mrape*, brown leafless fleshy-stemmed parasitic plant of genus *Orobranche*, growing on roots of brooms and other plants. 2. Implement for sweeping, orig. of broom twigs fixed to long stick or handle, now of any material; *broo'mstick*, handle of broom (on which witches were reputed to fly through the air, and over which parties to a mock-marriage used to jump).

Bros *abbrev*. Brothers.

brŏth *n*. Uncleared meat or fish stock used for making soup or as medium for culture of bacteria.

brŏ'thel *n.* House where prostitutes are available.

bro'ther (-ŭdh-) *n.* 1. Male with the same parents as another person. 2. Fellow, companion, equal. 3. (with pl. *brethren*) Member of religious order, fellow member of church, guild, order, etc. 4. *~-in-law*, brother of one's husband or wife, husband of one's sister. **bro'therlȳ** *adj.* Of, like, a brother('s), fraternal. **bro'therlĭnėss** *n.*

bro'therhŏŏd (-ŭdh-) *n.* Fraternal tie; companionship; (members of) association for mutual help etc.

Brougham[1] (brōōm), Henry Peter, Baron Brougham and Vaux (1778–1868). English lawyer, Whig politician, and Lord Chancellor of England.

brougham[2] (brōōm) *n.* One-horse four-wheeled closed carriage; closed electrically-driven shrub, *Sarothamnus scoparius*, carriage for four or five passengers; limousine with open seat for driver. [f. Lord BROUGHAM[1]]

brought: see BRING.

brow *n.* Arch of hair over eye (usu. in pl.); forehead; edge, projection, of cliff, etc., top of hill in road; *~ band*, (esp.) strap of bridle passing over horse's brow.

brow'beat *v.t.* Bully, bear down, with looks and words.

brown[1] *adj.* 1. Of the colour produced by a mixture of orange and black pigments, or by partial charring of starch or woody fibre, as in toasted bread etc. 2. Dark, dark-skinned; tanned. 3. *~ bread*, bread of unbolted flour; *~ coal*, lignite; *~ paper*, unbleached paper used for packing etc.; *brow'n-shirt*, Nazi storm-trooper; *brow'n-stone*, dark-brown sandstone used in building; *~ study*, reverie; *~ sugar*, unrefined or partially refined sugar. *~ n.* Brown colour or pigment; (ellipt.) brown butterfly, fishing-fly, clothes, etc. *~ v.* Make or become brown by roasting, sun-burn, or chemical process; *browned off*, (orig. R.A.F. slang) having had too much of something tedious, bored.

Brown[2], Arthur Whitten (1886–1948). British aviator: see ALCOCK.

Brown[3], John (1800–59). Amer. anti-slavery leader, hanged at Charlestown, Virginia, for a successful armed attack, with only eighteen men, on the Federal arsenal at Harper's Ferry, Virginia; hero of the popular marching-song 'John Brown's body lies a-mouldering in the grave, But his soul goes marching on'.

Brown[4], Lancelot (1716–83). 'Capability Brown', English architect and reviver of the natural style of landscape gardening; laid out gardens at Kew.

Browne, Sir Thomas (1605–82). English physician, author of 'Religio Medici' (1642).

Brow'nian mo'vement (mōōvm-). Irregular oscillatory movement of microscopic particles in fluids, due to molecular bombardment. [discovered by Robert *Brown* (1773–1858), Scottish botanist]

brow'nĭe *n.* 1. Benevolent shaggy goblin said to haunt house and do household work secretly. 2. (*B~*, *B~ Guide*) Member of junior branch of Girl Guides Association.

Brow'nĭng[1], Elizabeth Barrett (1806–61). English poet, wife of Robert Browning.

Brow'nĭng,[2] Robert (1812–89), English poet, author of numerous philosophical and dramatic lyrics and of several dramas.

Brow'nĭng[3] *n.* (also *~ pistol*) Small automatic pistol *~ gun*,

automatic rifle. [J. M. *Browning* (1885–1926), Amer. inventor]

Brow'nĭst *adj.* & *n.* (Member) of an English Puritan sect, followers of Robert Browne (1550–1633), who denounced the parochial system and ordination and is regarded as the founder of Congregationalism.

browse (-z) *v.* Feed *on*, crop (leaves, twigs, scanty vegetation); feed thus; (fig.) read desultorily for enjoyment. ~ *n.* Browsing.

Bruce (-ōōs), Robert de (1274–1329). Robert I, king of Scotland 1306–29; liberated his country from the English, whom he defeated at the Battle of BANNOCKBURN.

brucellō'sĭs (brōō-) *n.* Disease caused by bacteria of genus *Brucella*, causing abortion in cattle; (in man) undulant fever.

bru'cine (-ōōsēn) *n.* Highly poisonous vegetable alkaloid found in false Angostura bark and in nux vomica.

Bru'ckner (-ŏŏk-), Anton (1824–96). Austrian composer of church music and symphonies.

Brueghel, -gel, Breughel (brêr'gl *or* brōō'-). Surname of a large family of Flemish painters, the most famous of whom is Pieter Bruegel the Elder (*c* 1520–69), painter of lively peasant scenes.

Bruges (brōōzh). (Fl. *Brugge*) City in Belgium, famous for its bells and its many canals.

Bru'in (-ōō-). Personifying name for a bear. [Name of bear in fable of Reynard the Fox]

bruise (-ōōz) *n.* Injury by blow to body, fruit, etc., discolouring skin. ~ *v.* Injure by blow that discolours skin without breaking it, contuse; dint, batter; pound, bray, grind small; show effects of blow. **brui'ser** *n.* (esp.) Prizefighter.

bruit (-ōōt) *v.t.* (archaic) Spread *abroad*, *about*, make famous, celebrate.

Brumaire (-ōōmār). 2nd month in French Revolutionary calendar, 22 Oct.–20 Nov.; *18* ~, 9 Nov. 1799, day on which Napoleon Bonaparte became First Consul. [Fr. *brume* mist]

Brŭ'mmagem *adj.* Applied contemptuously to an article of Birmingham manufacture, esp. cheap jewellery etc. [dial. form of *Birmingham*, orig. used of counterfeit coin made there in 17th c.]

Brŭ'mmell, George Bryan (1778–1840). 'Beau Brummell', English dandy, a leader of fashion and favourite of the Prince Regent.

Bru'nei (-ōōnī). British protected State on NW. coast of Borneo.

Brunĕ'l (-ōō-), Sir Marc Isambard (1769–1849). French-born engineer; built the Thames tunnel with his son Isambard Kingdom Brunel (1806–59), who

BRUNEL

also built bridges, railways, ships, etc.; ~ *University*, university (at Uxbridge, 1966) named after I. K. Brunel.

Brunĕllĕ'schĭ (brōō-, -kĭ), Filippo (1377–1446). Italian architect, reviver of the Roman style.

brunĕ'tte (-ōō-) *n.* & *adj.* Dark-skinned and brown-haired (woman).

Bru'nhĭld (-ōō-, -lt). In the Nibelungenlied, wife of Gunther,

BRUNELLESCHI: Florence

who instigated the murder of Siegfried; in Norse versions, a Valkyrie whom Sigurd wins by penetrating the wall of fire behind which she lies in an enchanted sleep.

Bru'nō[1] (-ōō-), St. (*c* 1035–1101). Founder of the Carthusian order.

Bru'nō[2] (-ōō-), Giordano (*c* 1548–*c* 1599). Italian philosopher; regarded God as the unity reconciling spirit and matter; was condemned to death by the Inquisition.

Brŭ'nswick (-z-). (Ger. *Braunschweig*) City and ancient duchy of N. Germany; ~ *black*, black varnish made of turpentine and asphalt or lamp-black; ~ *green*, green pigment, oxychloride of copper.

brŭnt *n.* Chief stress of shock or attack etc.

brŭsh *n.* 1. (U.S., Canadian, & Austral.) Thicket, brushwood, growing or (in U.S.) cut in faggots; land covered with thicket; backwoods. 2. Implement of bristles, hair, wire, etc., set in wood etc. for sweeping or scrubbing dust and dirt from a surface, usu. named acc. to its use, as *clothes*-~, *hair*-~; bunch of hairs etc. in straight handle for painting etc.; application of brush, brushing; (mus.) one of a pair of devices with wire bristles for striking drums etc. 3. Tail, esp. of fox; brush-like tuft. 4. (elect.) Brush-like discharge of sparks; strip of conducting material (usu. hardened carbon) for making or breaking contact; fixed contact which bears on slip ring of dynamo. 5. Short sharp encounter skirmish. 6. *bru'shwood*, cut or broken twigs etc.; undergrowth, thicket; *bru'shwork*, painter's (style of) manipulation. ~ *v.* Move briskly; sweep or scrub, put in order, remove, with brush; graze or touch in passing; ~ *aside, away*, (fig.) ignore, pass over; ~ *off*, dismiss, rebuff; ~ *up*, furbish, renew one's memory of; ~-*up* (*n.*). **brŭshed** (-sht) *adj.* (esp., of fabric) With nap raised by brushing.

brusque (-ŏŏsk *or* -ŭsk) *adj.* Blunt, off-hand, abrupt.

Brŭ'ssels (-z). (Fr. *Bruxelles*) Capital city of Belgium; ~ *carpet*, carpet with back of stout linen thread and pile of wool; ~ *lace*, rich pillow-lace of the type first made in Brussels in 18th c.; (also) needlepoint lace made there in same period; ~ *sprout*, bud-bearing cabbage, *Brassica oleracea gemmifera*, producing buds like small cabbages in the axils of its leaves; one of its buds.

Brut (-ōōt) *n.* Chronicle of British history from BRUTUS[1].

bru'tal (-ōō-) *adj.* Savagely cruel, coarse, sensual. **bru'tallȳ** *adv.* **brută'litȳ** *n.* **bru'talīze** *v.t.*

brute (-ōōt) *adj.* 1. (of beast) Not possessing the capacity to reason. 2. Stupid, sensual, beast-like, cruel, or passionate; ~ *force*, unreasoning force. ~ *n.* Brute beast, lower animal; lower nature in man. **bru'tish** *adj.* **bru'tĭshlȳ** *adv.* **bru'tĭshnėss** *n.*

Bru'tus[1] (-ōōt-). Legendary founder of the British people, great-grandson of AENEAS; brought a group of the Trojans to England and founded Troynovant or New Troy (later called London); progenitor of a line of kings.

Bru'tus[2] (-ōōt-), Lucius Junius (d. 508 B.C.). Legendary First Consul of Rome, and leader in the expulsion of the Tarquins.

Bru'tus[3] (-ōōt-), Marcus Junius (85–42 B.C.). Roman soldier; joined the conspirators who assassinated Julius Caesar in hope of restoring republican government.

Brȳn Mawr. College for women students and for men and women postgraduates in Philadelphia, Penn.

brȳ'onȳ *n.* Either of two unrelated climbing plants found esp. in hedgerows; *black* ~, *Tamus communis*, dark shining green, without tendrils; *white* ~, *Bryonia dioica*, rough textured and light coloured, with conspicuous coiled tendrils.

brȳ'ophȳte *n.* Member of the Bryophyta, a group of plants comprising the liverworts and mosses. **brȳophȳ'tic** *adj.*

brȳozō'an *adj.* & *n.* (Member) of the Bryozoa, a phylum of aquatic animals that form colonies of small polyps.

B.S.A. *abbrev.* Birmingham Small Arms (Co.).

B.Sc. *abbrev.* Bachelor of Science.

b.s.g.d.g. *abbrev.* *Breveté sans garantie du gouvernement* (Fr., = patented without government guarantee).

B.S.I. *abbrev.* British Standards Institution.

B.S.T. *abbrev.* British Summer Time.

Bt *abbrev.* Baronet.

Btu *abbrev.* British thermal unit(s).

B.U.A. *abbrev.* British United Airways.

bŭ'bble *n.* 1. Spherical or hemispherical envelope of liquid (or solidified liquid, as glass) enclosing air etc. 2. Unsubstantial or visionary project, enterprise, etc. 3. Sound or appearance of boiling; ~*-and-squeak*, cooked vegetables fried together with or without meat; ~ *car*, miniature motor-car with transparent domed cover; ~ *chamber*, (phys.) container of superheated liquid for detection of ionizing particles; ~*-gum*, chewing-gum which can be blown into large bubbles. ~ *v.i.* Send up, rise in, make the sound of, bubbles.

bŭ'bblȳ *adj.* Full of bubbles. ~ *n.* (slang) Champagne.

bū'bō *n.* (pl. *-oes*). Inflamed swelling in glandular part esp. groin or armpit.

būbŏ'nic *adj.* Characterized by buboes; ~ *plague*, disease characterized by these and by fever and prostration, carried by rats and transmitted to man by fleas.

bŭccaneer' *n.* Sea-rover, pirate, esp. of Spanish-American coasts in 17th c.; unscrupulous adventurer. ~ *v.i.* Act as buccaneer. [Fr. *boucanier* f. *boucaner* to cure meat on a *boucan* (i.e. barbecue), a Brazilian wd]

bŭ'ccĭnātor (-ks-) *n.* Flat thin

muscle forming wall of cheek. [L, = 'trumpeter']

Būcĕ'ntaur *n.* (hist.) Italian state barge, esp. that used in Venice in the ceremony called the Marriage of the ADRIATIC.

Būcĕ'phalus. Favourite horse of Alexander the Great.

Bŭ'chan[1] (-χ-), Alexander (1829–1907). Scottish meteorologist; ~'*s cold spells*, certain specified periods of cold weather stated by him to occur annually.

Bŭ'chan[2] (-χ-), John, 1st Baron Tweedsmuir (1875–1940). Author of novels of adventure (e.g. 'The Thirty-nine Steps', 1915) and historical works.

Būchă'nan (-k-), James (1791–1868). 15th president of U.S., 1857–61.

Būcharĕ'st (-k-). (Rumanian *București*) Capital city of Rumania.

Bu'chmanism (bo͝ok-) *n.* Name for the Oxford Group movement. **Bu'chmanīte** *adj.* & *n.* [Dr Frank N. D. *Buchman* (1878–1961) Amer. founder]

bŭck[1] *n.* Male of fallow-deer, reindeer, chamois, hare, rabbit; dandy; ~*-bean*, water plant, *Menyanthes trifoliata*, with pinkish-white flowers; ~*-hound*, small stag-hound; ~*-shot*, coarse shot; *bu'ckskin*, (leather made of) buck's skin; (pl.) breeches of this; *bu'ckthorn*, thorny shrub esp. of genus *Rhamnus*; ~*-tooth*(*ed*), (having) projecting tooth. ~ *adj.* (slang) Male; of, for, males.

bŭck[2] *v.* (of horse) Jump vertically with back arched and feet drawn together (also ~*-jump*); *bu'ckjumper*, horse given to bucking.

bŭck[3] *v.* (slang) ~ *up*, make haste, hurry; become or make vigorous or cheerful. **bŭcked** (-kt) *adj.* (slang) Elated.

bŭck[4] *n.* Body of cart; chiefly in combination, as (U.S.) *bu'ckboard*, plank slung upon wheels, light vehicle with body consisting of this.

bŭck[5] *n.* (U.S. slang) Dollar.

bŭck[6] *n.* Saw-buck (U.S.); padded block in gymnasium, used esp. for vaulting.

bŭck[7] *n.* Article placed as a reminder before a person whose turn it is to deal at poker; *pass the* ~, (slang, orig. U.S.) shift responsibility (*to*).

bŭck[8] *n.* (slang; esp. *old* ~) Boastful talk.

bŭ'ckėt *n.* 1. Vessel for collecting, holding, or carrying water etc.; amount contained in this (also *bu'cketful*). 2. Anything resembling this; (esp.) compartment of

water-wheel; scoop of dredger or grain-elevator. 3. ~*-seat*, seat with high rounded back; car-seat which tips forward; ~*-shop*, (orig. U.S.) office for gambling in stocks, speculating on markets, etc. ~ *v.* Ride hard; (rowing) hurry the forward swing, row hurried stroke; drive or (of vehicle) move jerkily or bumpily; (of rain) pour down heavily.

Bŭ'ckingham (-ng-*a*m), George Villiers, 1st Duke of (1592–1628). Favourite of James I of England; assassinated by John Felton; his son, George Villiers, the 2nd Duke (1628–87), was a statesman under Charles II and author of satirical verses.

Bŭ'ckingham Pă'lace (-ng-*a*m). Royal residence in London, on site of house of John Sheffield, 1st Duke of Buckingham and Normanby (1648–1721), sold in 1762 to George III, rebuilt 1825 by the architect John Nash.

Bŭ'ckinghamshire (-ng-*a*m-). Southern English county lying N. of the Thames.

bŭ'ckle[1] *n.* Clasp usu. with hinged tongue for securing strap, belt, etc.; ornament for shoe etc. resembling this. ~ *v.* Fasten with buckle; (cause to) give way, crumple up, under pressure; ~ (*down*) *to*, prepare for, set about; ~ *to*, get to work, start vigorously.

Bŭ'ckle[2], Henry Thomas (1821–62). English historian, author of two volumes (1857, 1861) of a 'History of Civilization in England'.

bŭ'ckler *n.* Small round shield; protection, protector. ~ *v.t.* Shield, protect.

bŭ'ckram *n.* Coarse linen or cotton fabric stiffened with gum or paste, used in linings and for binding books.

Bucks. *abbrev.* Buckinghamshire.

bŭ'ckshee *n.* (army slang) Allowance above the usual amount. ~ *adj.* & *adv.* Gratuitous(ly). [altered f. *baksheesh*]

bŭ'ckwheat *n.* Cereal plant, *Polygonum fagopyrum*, with seed used for horse and poultry food, and in U.S. for breakfast cakes. [= *beech wheat*, from its three-cornered seeds like beechmast]

būcŏ'lic *adj.* Of shepherds, pastoral, rustic. **būcŏ'lics** *n.pl.* Pastoral poems.

bŭd[1] *n.* 1. Projection at end of shoot or axil of leaf, protected by scales which are altered leaves, forming rudiment of shoot, foliage, or flower; leaf or flower not fully; open ~ *scale*, altered leaf protecting a bud. 2. (zool.) Asexual reproductive growth attached to parent and developing into new individual esp. in coelenterates. 3. *nip in the* ~, (fig.) stop (something) before it is fully developed. *v.* 1. Put forth buds; begin to grow or develop. 2. Graft a bud on to another plant.

bŭd[2] *n.* (U.S. colloq.) = BUDDY.

Būdapĕ'st. Capital city of Hungary, orig. consisting of two towns, Buda on right bank of river Danube and Pest(h) on left.

Buddha (bo͞o'da). 'Enlightened one', name applied esp. to Siddartha Gautama (*c* 560–*c* 480 B.C.), son of the rajah of the Sakya tribe (hence also called *Sakyamuni*, 'sage of the Sakyas'); as a young man he abandoned his home in Nepal and renounced the world; practised an extreme asceticism, preached, and became the founder of one of the great Asian religions.

BUDDHA

Bu'ddhism (bo͞odĭ-) *n.* Religion founded by the Buddha, orig. practised chiefly in India; it was in decline there by the 4th c. A.D. but was diffused over China (which it reached in the 1st c.), Japan, and central and SE. Asia; there are two principal schools, MAHAYANA and THERAVADA or Hinayana; the principal doctrines are: that suffering is inseparable from existence, which is an evil; that the principal cause of suffering is desire; and that the suppression of desire, and consequently of suffering, can be obtained by discipline and ultimately rewarded by NIRVANA.

Bu'ddhist *adj.* & *n.*

bŭ'ddleia (*or* -lē'*a*) *n.* Shrub or tree of genus *B*~ of America, Asia, and S. Africa, much grown in gardens, and often having honey-scented flowers. [Adam *Buddle* (d. 1715), Engl. botanist]

bŭ'ddy̆ *n.* (U.S.) Brother; companion, friend (freq. as form of address). [Childish or Negro pronunciation of *brother*]

bŭdge *v.* Move in the slightest degree, stir.

bŭ'dgerigar *n.* Grass or zebra parakeet (*Melopsittacus undulatus*), native to Australia, freq. kept as pet.

bŭ'dgėt *n.* 1. (archaic) Contents of a bag or bundle (chiefly fig. of news etc.). 2. Annual estimate of revenue and expenditure, esp. by Chancellor of Exchequer in House of Commons, or by finance minister of other countries; private person's similar estimate. 3. Amount of money required or available. 4. *attrib.* Inexpensive. **bŭ'dgėtarў** *adj.* **bŭ'dgėt** *v.i.* ~ *for*, allow or arrange for in budget.

Buĕ'nos Air'ės (bwĕ-, -z; *or* bwā-; *or* īr-). Capital city and chief port of Argentina.

bŭff *n.* 1. Stout velvety dull-yellow leather of buffalo or ox-hide; *in* (*the*) ~, naked. 2. Dull-yellow colour of buff; *the Buffs*, the former East Kent Regiment, orig. so called from the buff-coloured facings on their scarlet uniforms. 3. (path.) Coagulated coating on blood drawn from fever patients. ~ *adj.* Made of, coloured like, buff. ~ *v.t.* Polish (metal) with buff, make (leather) velvety like buff.

bŭ'ffalō *n.* (pl. -*oe*s). Any of several kinds of ox, esp. (*a*) *Bos primigenius*, orig. a native of India (where it is tamed), inhabiting most of Asia, parts of S. Europe, and N. Africa; (*b*) *Bos caffer*, Cape buffalo of S. Africa; (*c*) (pop.) Amer. BISON; ~ *grass*, prairie grass, *Sesleria dactyloides*; ~ *gnat*, two-winged fly of family *Simuliidae* with humped back and blood-sucking proboscis.

Bŭ'ffalō Bill. Popular nickname of William Cody (1846–1917), Amer. cattle-herder and scout, credited with legendary exploits against Indians and bandits.

bŭ'ffer[1] *n.* 1. Apparatus for deadening by springs or padding, or sustaining by strength of beams etc., a concussion, esp. of railway carriages, engines, etc. 2. Shield or device preventing contact or interaction (also fig.); ~ *state*, small State lying between two larger possible belligerents. 3. (chem.) Substance or mixture which in solution resists change in acidity on addition of a small amount of acid or alkali. ~ *v.t.* Protect with a buffer; cushion; (chem.) treat with a buffer.

bŭ'ffer[2] *n.* (slang; usu. *old* ~) Fellow.

bŭ'ffėt[1] *n.* Blow with the hand; blow of fate etc. ~ *v.* Strike with the hand; knock, hunt, plague; contend (*with* waves etc.).

buffet[2] (bo͝o'fā) *n.* 1. Sideboard, recessed cupboard, for china, glass, etc. 2. Refreshment bar; service of food from this or from sideboard where guests help themselves.

bŭ'fflehead (-flhĕd) *n.* (also ~ *duck*) Small N. Amer. duck, *Bucephala albeola.*

Buffon (bo͞ofawn), George Louis Leclerc, comte de (1707–88). French naturalist, author of 'Histoire Naturelle'.

BUFFON: American skunk

buffōō'n *n.* (usu. contempt.) Wag, clumsy jester, mocker. **buffōō'nerў** *n.*

bŭg *n.* 1. Hemipterous insect; (also *bed-*~) flat ill-smelling blood-sucking insect, *Cimex lectularius*, infesting wooden beds, furniture, etc.; (U.S.) small insect; ~-*hunter*, (slang) entomologist. 2. (colloq.) Micro-organism, (esp.) virus; (fig.) craze. 3. *big* ~, (slang) important person. 4. (slang) Defect in machine etc. 5. (slang) Concealed microphone. ~ *v.t.*

(slang) Equip with alarm or concealed microphone.

bŭ'gabo͞o *n.* = BUGBEAR.

Bugă'nda (bo͞o-). Kingdom of the Baganda, forming a district of Uganda.

bŭ'gbear (-bār) *n.* Fancied object of fear; imaginary terror.

bŭ'gger *n.* (law) Sodomite; (vulg.) term of abuse, or sometimes merely = fellow. ~ *v.* 1. Commit buggery with. 2. (slang) ~ *about*, interfere with; (intrans.) move or act aimlessly or ineffectively; ~ *off*, go away; ~ *up*, spoil. **bŭ'ggerȳ** *n.* (law) Sodomy, bestiality.

bŭ'ggȳ *n.* Light two-wheeled vehicle; (U.S.) four-wheeled vehicle, often hooded, drawn by one or two horses.

bū'gle[1] *n.* Brass instument like small trumpet used for military signals. ~ *v.* Sound bugle, sound (call) on a bugle.
bū'gler *n.*

bū'gle[2] *n.* Tube-shaped glass bead, usu. black, sewn on dress as ornament.

bū'gle[3] *n.* Plant of genus *Ajuga*, esp. *A. repetans*, perennial with blue flowers.

bū'glŏss *n.* Any of several plants allied to borage, esp. species of *Echium*, as *viper's* ~, *E. vulgare*. [Gk *bouglōssos* ox-tongued]

bu'gsha (bo͞o-) *n.* $\frac{1}{40}$ of a Yemen riyal.

buhl: see BOULLE[2].

build (bĭ-) *v.* (past t. & past part. *built* pr. bĭ-). Construct by putting parts or material rightly together; be busy making one's house or nest; lay *into* (wall etc.) in building; make gradually; base *on*, rely *on*; ~ *up*, establish, make or accumulate gradually; strengthen; praise; surround or cover with houses etc.; ~*-up* (*n.*). ~ *n.* Style of construction, make; proportions of human body.

bui'lder (bĭ-) *n.* (esp.) Master-builder, contractor for building houses.

bui'ldĭng (bĭ-) *n.* (esp.) House, edifice; ~ *blocks*, small solid shapes, as child's toy for building; ~ *society*, limited liability company making mortgage advances to members for building or purchasing a house.

built (bĭ-) *adj.*: see BUILD; (esp.) ~*-in*, forming integral part of structure; ~*-up*, increased in height, thickness, etc., by addition of parts; (of area) covered with houses etc.

bŭlb *n.* 1. Globular base of the stem of certain plants, such as lily, onion, etc., consisting of thick fleshy scales and sending roots downwards and leaves etc. upwards; leaf-bud detaching itself

from stem and becoming separate plant; (anat.) roundish swelling of any cylindrical organ, as of hair-root. 2. Dilated part of glass tube; (glass vessel of) electric lamp; bulb-shaped swelling of rubber tube; ~ *release*, (phot.) regulation of exposure by pressure and release of a lever (formerly, of a rubber bulb). ~ *v.i.* Swell into bulb(s).

bŭ'lbous *adj.* Of, having, like, springing from, a bulb.

bu'lbul (bo͝olbo͝ol) *n.* Eastern song-thrush of numerous genera; singer, poet.

Bŭ'lgar *adj.* & *n.* (Native, inhabitant) of Bulgaria.

Bŭlgār'ia. Balkan republic (until 1946 a kingdom), with a population largely descended from a people related to the Huns and Avars and speaking a Slavonic language; capital, Sofia.

Bŭlgār'ian *adj.* Of Bulgaria or its people or language; ~ *atrocities*, massacre in S. Bulgaria by Turks and Muslim Bulgars (1876) on occasion of rising in Bosnia against Turkey. ~ *n.* Bulgarian person or language.

bŭlge *n.* Convex part, irregular swelling, tendency to swell out, on surface; (esp.) outward swell on ship's side below waterline constructed as defence against torpedoes; salient; (fig.) temporary increase in volume or numbers. ~ *v.* Swell outwards irregularly; extend (bag etc.) by stuffing it. **bŭ'lgȳ** *adj.* **bŭ'lgĭnėss** *n.* [L *bulga* knapsack]

bŭlk *n.* 1. Cargo; *in* ~, loose, not in packages; in large quantities (so *~-buying* etc.). 2. Large shape, body, person. 3. Size, magnitude; great size; mass, large mass; greater part or number *of*. ~ *v.i.* Seem in respect of size or importance.

bŭ'lkhead (-hĕd) *n.* Upright partition dividing watertight compartments of ship; such compartment in ship, aircraft, or train; partition dividing engine from body in motor vehicle.

bŭ'lkȳ *adj.* Large, voluminous. **bŭ'lkĭnėss** *n.*

bull[1] (bŏŏl) *n.* Papal edict. [L *bulla* seal]

bull[2] (bŏŏl) *n.* 1. Uncastrated male of ox or other bovine animal; male of elephant, whale, seal, and other large animals. 2. (astron.) *the B~*: see TAURUS. 3. (Stock Exch.) Speculator for a rise, who buys low in expectation of a rise in prices or in order to effect such a rise; ~ *market*, one with rising prices. 4. Bull's-eye of target. 5. *~-calf*; male calf; *bu'lldog*, dog of powerful and courageous large-headed smooth-haired breed formerly used for bull-baiting; university proctor's attendant whose duty it is to chase and apprehend undergraduates suspected of any offence; *bu'lldoze*, clear (ground etc.) with bulldozer; make *way* forcibly (also fig.); intimidate, coerce (orig. used in elections in Southern States of U.S. of intimidating voters, esp. Negroes); *bu'lldozer*, powerful tractor with broad vertical blade in front for clearing ground etc.; *bu'llfight*, Spanish spectacle of baiting a bull with horsemen (picadors), footmen (banderilleros), and a swordsman (matador) who finally kills him; similar sport in S. France in which bull is not killed; *bu'llfinch*, strong-beaked, handsome-plumaged song-bird (*Pyrrhula pyrrhula*); [perh. = 'bull-fence'] high quickset hedge with ditch; *bu'llfrog*, large frog esp. of genus *Rana* with loud bellowing note; *bu'llhead*, small fish with large head, esp. the miller's thumb; *~-puncher*, (U.S.) cowboy; *bu'llring*, arena for bull-fight; *~-roarer*, flat piece of wood with string passed through a hole, which when swung round the head gives a booming sound, used in religious ceremonies by Australian aborigines; similarly made toy; *~'s-eye*, boss of glass formed at centre of sheet of blown glass; hemispherical piece or thick disc of glass; hemispherical lens; lantern with such a lens; small circular window; central area of target; hit on this part; large globular sweet usu. flavoured with peppermint; *~-terrier*, dog of heavily-built smooth-haired usu. white breed. **bu'llĭsh** *adj.* Like a bull; (of stock market or prices) tending to rise. **bull** *v.* (Stock Exch.) Speculate for, cause, a rise in price of stocks etc.

bull[3] (bŏŏl) *n.* (freq. *Irish* ~) Expression containing contradiction in terms or implying ludicrous inconsistency, as *the hot water is cold and there is none of it.*

Bull[4], John: see JOHN[1] Bull.

bullace (bŏŏ'lĭs) *n.* Wild or semi-wild plum, *Prunus insititia*, larger than the sloe.

Bu'ller (bŏŏ-), Sir Redvers Henry (1839–1908). Irish soldier; commanded the Natal force during the Boer War; relieved LADYSMITH after three unsuccessful attempts; was criticized for his conduct of the campaign and was retired on half-pay for making a public speech in answer to his critics.

bu'llėt (bŏŏ-) *n.* Missile of lead etc., spherical or conical, used in small arms; *~-head* (*ed*), (with) round head.

bu'llėtĭn (bŏŏ-) *n.* Short official statement of news or of invalid's condition; broadcast report of news, weather, etc.

bullion (bo͞o′lyon) *n.* 1. Gold and silver before (or as valued apart from) coining or manufacturing. 2. Fringe of gold or silver thread.

bu′llock (bo͞o-) *n.* Castrated bull, ox.

Bull Rŭn (bo͞ol). Small river in E. Virginia, U.S., scene of two important battles (1861 and 1862) in which the Federal side was defeated in the Amer. Civil War.

bu′llȳ[1] (bo͞o-) *n.* One who oppresses or dominates by (threat of) superior force; hired ruffian. ~ *v.t.* Persecute, oppress, tease, physically or morally; frighten *into* or *out of*; play the bully. ~ *adj.* & *int.* (slang, esp. U.S.) Capital, first-rate.

bu′llȳ[2] (bo͞o-) *n.* Scrummage in Eton football; bullying in hockey. ~ *v.i.* (also ~ *off*; in hockey, of centre-forwards) Attempt to secure ball at beginning of game etc. after each player has hit ground and then opponent's stick three times.

bu′llȳ[3] (bo͞o-) *n.* (also ~-*beef*) Tinned beef.

Bülow (bū′lō), Prince Bernhard von (1849–1929). German statesman and diplomat; imperial Chancellor 1900–9.

bu′lrŭsh (bo͞o-) *n.* Kind of tall rush, *Scirpus lacustris*; reed-mace; (in the Bible) papyrus of Egypt.

Bu′ltmann (bo͞o-, -ahn), Rudolf (1884–). German theologian; advocated demythologizing of N.T.

bu′lwark (bo͞o-) *n.* 1. Rampart, earthwork, etc.; mole, breakwater; person, principle, etc., that acts as a defence. 2. Ship's side above deck.

Bulwer-Lytton: see LYTTON.

bŭm[1] *n.* (slang) Buttocks; ~-*bailiff*, bailiff employed for making arrests; ~-*boat*, boat, plying to ships in port or off shore with fresh provisions.

bŭm[2] *n.* (U.S. colloq.) Lazy and dissolute person; loafer, tramp. ~ *adj.* Worthless, poor, wretched. ~ *v.* Loaf or wander (*around*); lead life of a bum; cadge.

bŭ′mble[1] *v.i.* Make buzzing or humming sound, as a bee; ~-*bee*, humble-bee.

Bŭ′mble[2]. Name of beadle in Dickens's 'Oliver Twist', a type of the self-important petty official.

Bŭ′mbledom *n.* Petty officialdom.

bŭ′mble-pŭppȳ *n.* 1. (obs.) Outdoor game resembling bagatelle. 2. Game of striking tennis-ball slung to post so as to wind the string round the post. 3. Whist played unscientifically.

bŭ′mmalō *n.* (pl. -*os*). Small fish, *Harpodon nehereus*, found off coasts of S. Asia; when dried and salted as relish known as 'Bombay duck'.

bŭmmaree′ *n.* Middleman at Billingsgate fish-market; (also) independent porter at Smithfield meat-market.

bŭmp *v.* 1. Push, throw down, impinge violently, strike solidly (*against*, *into*, *on*). 2. (in boat-racing when boats start at fixed intervals) Overtake and touch (boat ahead). 3. (of cricket-ball) Rise abruptly on pitching, (of bowler) cause (ball) to bump. 4. ~ *off*, (slang) remove by violence, murder. ~ *n.* 1. Dull-sounding blow, knock, collision; swelling caused by this. 2. Protuberance; (phrenol.) prominence on skull, faculty supposed to be indicated by it. 3. (boat-racing) Bumping; ~- *supper*, supper in celebration of this. 4. Irregularity in aircraft's motion; rising current of air causing this. **bŭ′mpȳ** *adj.*

bŭ′mper *n.* 1. Brim-full glass of wine etc. 2. (slang) Anything (as harvest, theatre audience) unusually large or abundant. 3. Fender on front or back of a motor-car etc. to take the first shock of collision.

bŭ′mpkĭn *n.* Country lout, awkward or bashful fellow.

bŭ′mptious (-shus) *adj.* Self-assertive, offensively conceited.

bŭn *n.* 1. Small soft round sweet cake usu. with currants etc.; (in Scotland) very rich fruit cake; rich currant bread; (in parts of Ireland) round loaf of bread; *hot cross* ~, spiced bun marked with cross and eaten (esp. hot) on Good Friday. 2. Hair coiled at back of head in bun-shape.

bŭ'na *n.* German synthetic rubber made by the polymerization of BUTADIENE. [orig. Ger. tradename]

Bŭ'nburÿ. In Oscar Wilde's play 'The Importance of Being Earnest', mythical friend whose misfortunes provide the hero with pretexts for absence.

bŭnch *n.* Cluster of things growing or fastened together; lot, collection; (U.S.) company, band. **bŭ'nchÿ** *adj.* **bŭnch** *v.* Make into bunch(es), gather (fabric) thickly into folds; come, cling, crowd, together.

bŭnd *n.* (Ind.) Embankment, causeway, quay.

bŭ'ndle *n.* Collection of things fastened together; sets of sticks, rods, etc., bound up; set of parallel fibres, nerves, etc. (*vascular* ~,). ~ *v.* Tie in, make *up* into, bundle; throw confusedly *in* any receptacle; go, put, or send hurriedly or unceremoniously *out*, *off*, etc.

bŭng *n.* Stopper, esp. large cork stopping hole in cask; ~*-hole*, hole in cask closed with bung. ~ *v.t.* Stop (cask with bung); stop, close, shut up (esp. the eyes); (slang) throw.

bŭ'ngalow (-ngg*a*lō) *n.* One-storeyed house. **bŭ'ngaloid** *adj.* Of or resembling bungalow(s). [Hind. *bangla* of Bengal]

bŭ'ngle (-nggl) *n.* Clumsy work, confusion, blunder. ~ *v.* Make bungle; blunder over, fail to accomplish.

Bu'nĭn (bōō-), Ivan Alexeyevich (1870–1953). Russian novelist and poet; Nobel Prize for literature 1933.

bŭ'nion (-yon) *n.* Inflamed swelling on foot, esp. at joint of great toe.

bŭnk[1] *n.* Sleeping-berth, platform bed, freq. one of two or more in tiers; ~*-house*, (U.S.) house in which miners, lumbermen, etc., are lodged. ~ *v.i.* Sleep in bunk.

bŭnk[2] *v.i.* (Slang) Make off. ~ *n.* *do a* ~, (slang) run away.

bŭnk[3] *n.* (orig. U.S.) Humbug, nonsense. [abbrev. of BUNKUM]

bŭ'nker *n.* 1. Large compartment in a ship for storing coal or oil; bin for storing domestic fuel. 2. Pit or hollow in which the natural soil, sometimes top-dressed with sand, is exposed, any natural obstruction, forming hazard on golf-course. 3. Underground shelter, esp. of reinforced concrete. ~ *v.* 1. Fill bunkers of (ship etc.), fuel. 2. (pass., golf) Be hit into bunker, have one's ball in bunker.

Bŭ'nker Hĭll. Hill near Boston, Massachusetts; scene of the first battle (1775) of the American War of Independence, in which an English force, after severe fighting and with much loss, compelled the insurgents to withdraw.

bŭ'nkum *n.* Humbug, claptrap. [*Buncombe* county in N. Carolina; the member for this county is said to have insisted on causing an obstruction to business in Congress by 'making a speech for Buncombe']

bŭ'nnÿ *n.* Childish or pet name for rabbit.

Bŭ'nsen (*or* bōō-), Robert Wilhelm von (1811–99). German chemist, credited with the invention of the ~ (*gas*) *burner*,

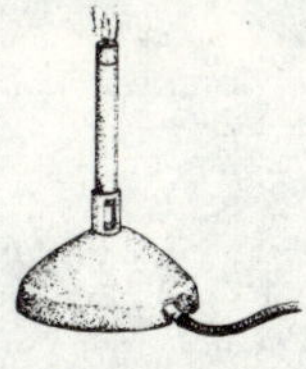

which produces a very hot, non-luminous flame by the mixture of air with the stream of gas before it is lighted.

bŭnt[1] *n.* Cavity, baggy part, of fishing-net, sail, etc.

bunt[2] *n.* Reverse loop in aerobatics.

Bŭ'nter, Billy. Name of schoolboy, noted for fatness and gluttony, in stories by Frank Richards (pseudonym of Charles Hamilton, 1875–1961).

bŭ'ntĭng[1] *n.* Bird of sub-family Emberizinae, allied to finches.

bŭ'ntĭng[2] *n.* Worsted or cotton material of open weave used for flags; flags (esp. of ship) collectively; streamers etc. used as festive decorations.

Bŭ'nyan, John (1628–88). English Nonconformist preacher; author of the allegory 'Pilgrim's

Progress' (which he is said to have written while imprisoned for unlicensed preaching), and of other pious works.

buoy (boi) *n.* 1. Anchored float marking a channel or indicating position of something, e.g. wreck, reefs. 2. (also *lifebuoy*) Contrivance for keeping person afloat in water, consisting of belt of cork or one inflated with air. ~ *v.t.* 1. (usu. with *up*) Keep afloat; bring to surface of water; sustain, uplift. 2. Mark with buoy(s).

buoy'age (boi-). System, provision of, buoys.

buoy'ancy̆ (boi-). Capacity for floating, tendency to float in water or air; (fig.) elasticity, recuperative power.

buoy'ant (boi-) *adj.* Apt to float, rise, keep up, or recover; able to keep things up; light-hearted.

B.U.P. *abbrev.* British United Press.

bûr, bûrr[1] *n.* 1. Clinging hooked fruit or flower-head; hence, person hard to shake off. 2. Female catkin of hop before fertilization. 3. Knob or knot in wood; ~-*walnut*, walnut wood containing many knots used for veneering. 4. See BURR[2], 4.

Bûr'bage, Richard (*c* 1567–1619). English actor; part-owner of the Blackfriars and Globe Theatres; acted principal parts in plays by Shakespeare, Jonson, and Beaumont and Fletcher.

bûr'ble *n.* Murmurous noise. ~ *v.* Speak or say murmurously.

bûr'bot *n.* Eel-like flat-headed bearded freshwater fish, *Lota lota*.

bûr'den[1] *n.* 1. Load; obligation; bearing of loads; obligatory expense. 2. (freq. *bur'then*) Ship's carrying capacity, tonnage. ~ *v.t.* Load; encumber; oppress.

bûr'den[2] *n.* Refrain, chorus of song; chief theme or gist of poem, complaint, etc. [var. of BOURDON]

bûr'densome *adj.* Oppressive, wearying.

bûr'dock *n.* Coarse weedy plant, *Arctium lappa*, with prickly flower-heads and dock-like leaves.

bûr'eau (-rō *or* -ō') *n.* (pl. *-eaux*, pr. ōz). 1. Writing-desk with drawers; (U.S.) chest of drawers. 2. Office, esp. of Government department.

bûreau'cracy̆ (-ŏkr-) *n.* Government by bureaux, centralization; body of officials. **bûr'eaucrăt** *n.* **bûreaucră'tĭc** *adj.*

bûrĕ'tte *n.* Graduated glass tube with tap at lower end for delivering measured small quantities of liquid in chemical analysis.

bûrg *n.* (U.S. colloq.) Town.

bŭrgee′ *n.* Small swallow-tailed pendant used by yachts etc., usu. as distinguishing flag.

bŭr′geon (-jon) *v.i.* Put forth, spring forth as, young shoots, bud, begin to grow.

Bür′ger (bŭrg-), Gottfried August (1747–94). German writer of lyrics and ballads.

bŭr′gėss *n.* Inhabitant of borough with full municipal rights, citizen; (hist.) member of Parliament for borough, corporate town, or university.

burgh (bŭ′ru) *n.* (Sc.) Borough.

bŭr′gher (-ger) *n.* 1. (archaic) Citizen (chiefly of foreign towns). 2. (hist.) Citizen of one of the Boer republics.

Burghley (bŭr′lĭ), William Cecil, 1st Baron (1521–98). English statesman, Lord Treasurer, and Queen Elizabeth's most trusted councillor and minister.

bŭr′glar *n.* One who enters building as trespasser and commits or intends to commit a felony (e.g. theft). **bŭrglār′ious** *adj.* **bŭrglār′iouslȳ** *adv.* **bŭr′glarȳ** *n.*

bŭr′gle *v.* (colloq.) Commit burglary; rob by burglary.

bŭr′gomaster (-mah-) *n.* Mayor of Dutch or Flemish town.

Bŭr′goyne, John (1722–92). 'Gentleman Johnny', English general and playwright; capitulated to the Americans at Saratoga (1777) in the American War of Independence.

Bŭr′gundȳ. (Fr. *Bourgogne*) Ancient kingdom of SE. France, later an independent duchy, united to France as a province in 1477; any of the wines produced there of high quality and considerable potency, including Beaune, Chambertin, Pommard (red), and Chablis and Montrachet (white); similar wine made elsewhere.

bu′rial (bĕ-) *n.* Burying, esp. of dead body.

Bŭridan (-ahṅ), Jean (*c* 1300–58). French scholastic philosopher and logician, chiefly remembered for the sophism attributed to him (but not found in his works) of the ass dying of hunger between two equally attractive bundles of hay.

bŭr′in *n.* 1. Tool for engraving on copper, graver. 2. Prehistoric pointed flint tool.

Bŭrke¹, Edmund (1729–97). English Whig statesman, political and philosophical writer, and orator.

Bŭrke², John (1787–1848). Irish-born genealogical and heraldic writer, first compiler of a 'Peerage and Baronetage' (1826), issued annually since 1847.

Bŭrke³, William (1792–1829). Irishman who was executed in Edinburgh for smothering friendless people in order to sell their bodies for dissection to the Edinburgh School of Anatomy; his accomplice, William Hare, turned King's evidence and was set free.

bŭrke⁴ *v.t.* Smother (lit. & fig.); hush up, suppress quietly. [BURKE³]

bŭrl *n.* Knot in wool or cloth, or (U.S.) in wood; overgrown knot in walnut etc., used in veneering.

bŭr′lap *n.* Coarse canvas of jute, used for sacks.

bŭrlĕ′sque (-sk) *adj.* Imitating derisively; bombastic, mock-serious; caricaturing, parodying (esp. literary or dramatic work). ~ *n.* Burlesque work or performance; bombast, mock-seriousness; derisive imitation. ~ *v.* Make or perform burlesque (of); caricature, travesty.

Bŭr′lington House. Large

building in Piccadilly, London; begun by the 1st earl of Burlington *c* 1664, and bought by the government in 1854; it houses the Royal Academy and various learned societies.

bur′ly̆ *adj.* Large and sturdy. **bur′linėss** *n.*

Bur′ma. Republic, established in 1948, occupying the NW. portion of the peninsula projecting southwards from Asia between India and China; formerly a province of British India; capital, Rangoon. **Burmēse** (-z) *adj.* & *n.*

burn[1] *n.* (Sc.) Small stream.

burn[2] *v.* (past t. & past part. *burnt* or *burned*). Consume, be consumed, waste, by fire; blaze or smoulder; injure by burning; brand; utilize the nuclear energy of (uranium etc.); feel intense heat or emotion; *burning-glass*, lens by which sun's rays may be concentated on an object so as to burn it. ~ *n.* Sore, mark, made by burning; (U.S.) burnt area in forest etc.; (aeron.) provision of thrust by engine of spacecraft.

Burne-Jōnes (-nz), Sir Edward Coley, Bt (1833–98). English painter and designer of tapestries and stained glass.

bur′ner *n.* (esp.) That part of lamp etc. from which the flame comes.

bur′nėt[1] *n.* 1. Brown-flowered plant of genus *Sanguisorba* or genus *Poterium*. 2. ~*-moth*, greenish-black moth of family Zygaenidae, with crimson-spotted wings.

Bur′nėt[2], Gilbert (1643–1715). Scottish bishop of Salisbury; author of a 'History of the Reformation in England' and 'History of My Own Times'.

Bur′ney, Frances (Madame d'Arblay) (1752–1840). English novelist, originator of the simple novel of home life.

Bur′nham (-n*a*m). Name of Viscount Burnham (1862–1933), chairman of committee which recommended a scale of salaries etc. for teachers in State-aided schools in England and Wales, adopted in 1924 and periodically revised.

bur′ning *adj.* That burns; flagrant; hotly discussed, exciting; ~ *bush*, 'the bush that burned and was not consumed' (Exod. 3: 2); any of various shrubs or plants with scarlet berries or foliage turning red in autumn etc.

bur′nish *v.* Polish by friction; take a polish.

burnou′s (-ōōs) *n.* Arab or Moorish hooded cloak.

Burns (-z), Robert (1759–96). Scottish poet, many of whose poems are written in Lowland

Scots; ~ *night*, evening of 25 Jan. (his birthday), celebrated by many Scots with feasting and drinking.

bur′nsīdes (-dz) *n.pl.* (U.S.) Sideburns. [f. A. E. *Burnside* (1824–81), U.S. general]

burnt *adj.*: see BURN[2]; (esp., of pigment) calcined to a deeper colour; (of colour) of a deeper shade; ~ *offering*, sacrifice offered by burning.

burp *n.* & *v.* (slang) (Cause to) belch.

burr[1]: see BUR.

burr[2] *n.* 1. Rough edge left on cut metal etc. 2. Small drill for cutting into tooth or bone. 3. Silicious rock used for millstones; whetstone; any of several kinds of limestone. 4. (also *bur*) Rough sounding of letter *r*, esp. rough uvular trill. ~ *v.* 1. Pronounce with burr; speak with rough or indistinct articulation. 2. Make burring sound.

bûrr[3] *n.* (Nebulous) circle of light round moon or star.

bŭ'rrō (*or* bo͞o-) *n.* Small donkey used as pack animal.

bŭ'rrow (-ō) *n.* Hole or excavation in ground in which rabbits, foxes, etc., live. ~ *v.* Make, live in, burrow; make by excavating; hide oneself, move, *into, under.*

bûr'sa *n.* (pl. *-ae*). (physiol.) Synovial sac between muscles, skin, etc., and bones, for lessening friction. **bûr'sal** *adj.*

bûr'sar *n.* 1. Treasurer, esp. of a college. 2. Student holding bursary in school or university. **bûrsār'ĭal** *adj.*

bûr'sarȳ *n.* 1. Treasury (hist.); bursar's room in college etc. 2. Endowment given to student.

bûrsī'tĭs *n.* Inflammation of a bursa.

bûrst *v.* (past t. & past part. *burst*). Fly violently asunder, give way suddenly; explode; rush, move, appear, violently or suddenly; speak, utter, be uttered, explosively. ~ *n.* Bursting, split; explosion, outbreak; spurt; continuous gallop. **bûr'stĭng** *adj.* (esp.) Full to overflowing.

burthen: see BURDEN[1], 2.

Bûr'ton[1] (-tn), Sir Richard Francis (1821–90). Traveller, the first Englishman to reach Mecca; Arabic scholar, and translator of the 'Arabian Nights'.

Bûr'ton[2] (-tn), Robert (1577–1640). English divine, author of the 'Anatomy of Melancholy', a storehouse of curious learning.

Buru'ndĭ (bo͝oro͞o-). Republic on E. side of Lake Tanganyika, formerly a Belgian trusteeship under the U.N.; independent 1962; capital, Bujumbura.

bu'rȳ (bĕ-) *v.t.* 1. Deposit in, commit to, earth, tomb, or sea; perform burial rites over; put under ground. 2. Put away, forget; consign to obscurity; hide in earth, cover up, submerge; plunge (head *in* hands, hands *in* pockets, etc.).

bŭs *n.* (pl. *-es*). Large passenger-carrying vehicle plying on fixed route or transporting employees etc. to and from works etc.; (slang) motor-car, aeroplane; *miss the* ~, (fig.) lose an opportunity, fail; *~-bar, ~ conductor*, (elect.) system of conductors in a generating station on which all the power of generators is collected for distribution, or, in a receiving station, on which the power from the generating station is recieved for distribution; *bu'sman,* bus driver or conductor; *busman's holiday,* leisure time spent in same occupation as working hours; ~-*stop*, place at which bus makes regular halt.

bŭ'sbȳ (-z-) *n.* Tall fur cap of hussars etc.

bush[1] (bo͞o-) *n.* Woody plant with numerous stems of moderate length; clump of shrubs; woodland, untilled district (esp. in Australia, N.Z., and S. Africa); luxuriant growth of hair etc.; bunch of ivy formerly used as vintner's sign (chiefly in phr. *good wine needs no* ~); *~-baby*, galago; *bu'shbuck,*

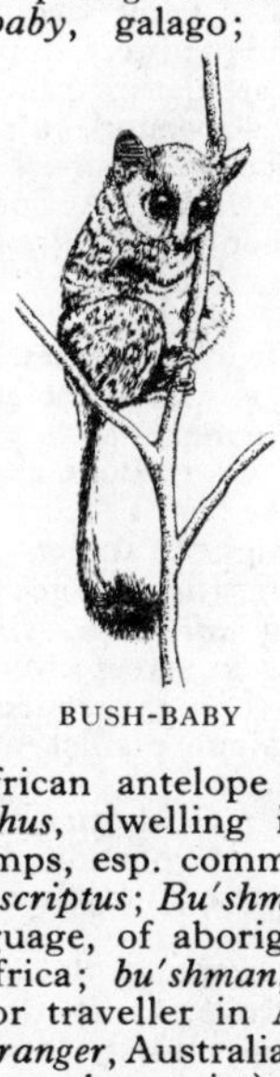

BUSH-BABY

small African antelope of genus *Tragelaphus*, dwelling in forests and swamps, esp. common bushbuck, *T. scriptus*; *Bu'shman,* member, language, of aboriginal tribe of S. Africa; *bu'shman*, dweller, farmer, or traveller in Australian bush; *~-ranger*, Australian brigand (orig. escaped convict) living in bush; ~ *telegraph*, rapid spreading of information, rumour, etc.;

~-*veld*(*t*), veld consisting largely of bush; low country of the Transvaal; ~-*whacker*, backwoodsman. ~ *v.t.* Preserve (trees, land from poachers etc.) by surrounding or strewing with bushes. **bushed** (-sht) *adj.* (colloq., esp. Austral.) Lost, as in the bush; (U.S.) exhausted.

bush[2] (bŏŏ-) *n.* Metal lining of axle-hole etc.; box or bearing in which shaft revolves; perforated plug. ~ *v.t.* Furnish with bush.

bu'shel (bŏŏ-) *n.* Measure of capacity (8 gallons) for dry goods.

Bushi'dō (bŏŏshē-) *n.* Code of honour and morals evolved by the samurai of Japan. [Jap., = 'military knight way']

bu'shȳ (bŏŏ-) *adj.* Abounding in bushes; growing thickly.

business (bĭ'znĭs) *n.* 1. Task, duty, province; errand; agenda. 2. Serious occupation, work; habitual occupation, profession; trade, commercial transactions; commercial house, firm; ~ *end*, (colloq.) working end of object, opp. handle; ~-*like*, systematic, practical; ~ *man*, (fem. ~ *woman*), *bu'sinessman*, one engaged in business or commerce. 3. (theatr.) Action, dumbshow. 4. (contempt.) Process, concern, affair, thing.

bŭsk *n.* Rigid strip formerly stiffening front of corset.

bŭ'sker *n.* Itinerant actor etc.; street performer.

bŭ'skin *n.* 1. Boot reaching to calf or knee. 2. Thick-soled boot lending height to ancient Athenian tragic actor; (fig.) tragedy.

bŭ'sking *adj.* & *n.* Singing or performing in street etc.

Busō'nĭ (bŏŏ-), Ferruccio (1866–1924). Italian pianist and composer.

bŭst[1] *n.* 1. Sculpture of person's head and upper portion of body. 2. Upper front of body, bosom, esp. of woman.

bŭst[2] *v.* (slang) Burst. ~ *adj.* (slang) Broke, without money. ~ *n.* (slang) Burst, (esp.) spree; ~-*up*, quarrel.

bŭ'stard *n.* Large swift-running bird of genus *Otis*.

bŭ'stle[1] (-sl) *v.* Bestir oneself, make show of activity, hurry *about*; make (others) hurry or work hard. ~ *n.* Excited activity, fuss.

bŭ'stle[2] (-sl) *n.* Pad or framework puffing out top of woman's skirt at the back.

bu'sy (bĭzĭ) *adj.* Occupied, working, engaged, with intention concentrated; unresting, always employed, stirring; fussy, meddlesome, prying; (excessively) full of detail; ~-*body*, meddlesome person, mischief-maker. ~ *Lizzie*, house-plant of genus *Impatiens*. **bu'silȳ** *adv.* **bu'sy** *v.t.* Occupy, keep busy. ~ *n.* (slang) Police detective.

bŭt[1] *prep.* Without, apart from. ~ *adv.* Merely. ~ *conj.* On the other hand; except; unless; yet.

bŭt[2] *n.* (Sc.) Outer room of house; ~ *and ben*: see BEN[2].

bū'tadiene *n.* Highly unsaturated carbon (C_4H_6), gaseous at ordinary temperatures, readily polymerized to rubber-like solid.

bū'tāne *n.* Colourless hydrocarbon gas (C_4H_{10}), used compressed in cylinders as an illuminant.

butch (bŏŏch) *n.* (slang, orig. U.S.) Tough youth or man; mannish woman.

bu'tcher (bŏŏ-) *n.* One who slaughters animals for food, dealer in meat; person who causes or delights in bloodshed; ~-*bird*, kind of shrike; ~'*s broom*, low-growing spiny evergreen, *Ruscus aculeatus*, with stiff stems and spiny leaf-like branches bearing the flower and fruit; ~'*s meat*, meat sold by butchers, as dist. from poultry, bacon, etc. ~ *v.t.* Slaughter in the manner of a butcher (lit. & fig.). **bu'tcherlȳ** *adj.* & *adv.*

bu'tcherȳ (bŏŏ-) *n.* Butcher's trade; needless or cruel slaughter.

Bū'teshire (-tsh-). Former Scottish island county, in the Firth of Clyde, since May 1975 part of the region of Strathclyde.

bŭ'tler[1] *n.* Male servant in charge of wine-cellar, plate, etc., head servant.

Bŭ'tler[2], Samuel (1612–80).

English poet and satirist; author of 'Hudibras'.

Bŭt'ler[3], Samuel (1835–1902). English critic and novelist; author of a Utopian novel, 'Erewhon' (1872) and an autobiographical novel, 'The Way of All Flesh', published posthumously in 1903.

bŭtt[1] *n.* Wine or ale cask (holding 108–40 gallons) ; any barrel.

bŭtt[2] *n.* 1. Thicker end, esp. of tool or weapon. 2. Trunk of tree just above ground . 3. Hide of back and flanks of ox etc. reduced to a rough rectangle; leather made from this, sole-leather. 4. Square end of plank meeting a similar end. 5. Stub of cigar or cigarette.

bŭtt[3] *n.* 1. Mound behind target; grouse-shooter's stand screened by low turf or stone wall; (pl.) shooting-range; target. 2. End, aim, object *of* (ridicule etc.); object of teasing and ridicule.

bŭtt[4] *v.* Push with the head; ~ *in*, intervene, meddle; meet end to end. ~ *n.* Butting, push with the head.

būtte *n.* Isolated abrupt flat-topped hill in western U.S.

bŭ'tter *n.* Fatty pale-yellow substance made from cream by churning, used for spreading on bread and in cookery; substance of similar consistency or look (as *peanut* ~); fulsome flattery; ~ *bean*, dried seed of white varieties of Lima bean, used as culinary vegetable; *bu'ttercup*, any of various kinds of ranunculus with yellow cup-shaped flowers, flowering esp. in spring meadows; *~-fingers, -fingered*, (person) inclined to drop things; *~-fish*, GUNNEL; *bu'ttermilk*, acidulous milk remaining after butter has been churned out; *~-muslin*, thin, loosely woven fine-meshed fabric orig. used for wrapping butter, carcasses of meat, etc.; *~-nut*, (large oily fruit of) N. Amer. white walnut-tree, *Juglans cinerea*; *bu'tterscotch*, kind of toffee made chiefly of sugar and butter; *bu'tterwort*, violet-flowered fleshy-leaved bog-plant, *Pinguicula vulgaris*. ~ *v.t.* Spread, cook, sauce, with butter; flatter.

bu'tterflȳ *n.* 1. Diurnal lepidopterous insect (cf. MOTH) with knobbed antennae, carrying the wings erect when at rest. 2. Vain or frivolous person; trifler. 3.

(swimming) Stroke in which the arms are lifted out of the water simultaneously.

bŭ'tterȳ[1] *adj.* Of, resembling, covered in, butter.

bŭ'tterȳ[2] *n.* Place in colleges etc. where provisions are kept. [AF *boterie* butt-store, i.e. place for casks]

bŭ'ttock *n.* One of the two protuberances of the rump; (usu. pl.) rump; manœuvre in wrestling in which buttock or hip is used.

bŭ'tton (-tn) *n.* Knob or disc attached to garment etc. to serve as fastening when passed through loop or buttonhole, or for ornament; bud; unopened mushroom; small rounded body; terminal knob (on foil etc.), knob, handle, catch, as in electric bell; *bu'ttonhole*, slit through which button passes; flower(s) for wearing in buttonhole in lapel of coat; (*v.t.*) sew with buttonhole stitch; seize, detain (reluctant listener); *bu'ttonhole stitch*, looped stitch used for edging buttonholes; *Bu'ttonhook*, small hook for pulling button through buttonhole. ~ *v.* Furnish with button(s); fasten (often *up*) with button(s); enclose (person thing) within buttoned garment or covering.

bŭ'ttons (-tnz) *n.* Page-boy in livery. [from rows of buttons on front of jacket]

bŭ'ttrėss *n.* Support built against wall etc., prop; buttress-like projection of hill. ~ *v.* Support with buttress, by argument etc.

butut (bōōtōō't) *n.* $\frac{1}{100}$ of a dalasi.

būtȳʹric *adj.* ~ *acid*, colourless syrupy liquid (C_3H_7COOH) in rancid butter.

būʹtȳrin *n.* Oily liquid obtained by action of butyric acid on glycerine.

bŭʹxom *adj.* (of woman) Plump and comely. **bŭʹxomnėss** *n.*

buy (bī) *v.t.* (past t. & past part. *bought* pr. bawt). Obtain in exchange for money or other consideration; gain over by bribery; ~ *in*, buy a stock of; withdraw at auction by naming higher price than the highest offered; ~ *it*, (slang) suffer some reverse; be killed. ~ *n.* Purchase; *good* ~, bargain; useful purchase. **buyʹer** *n.* (esp.) One who buys stock for a shop etc.

bŭzz *n.* Hum of bee etc., confused low sound like this; ~-*saw*, circular saw. ~ *v.* Make buzz; move *about* busily; (colloq.) throw hard; (of aircraft) warn, annoy, etc., by flying fast and close to; ~ *off*, (slang) go away.

bŭʹzzard *n.* 1. Name of various kinds of hawk of genus *Buteo*. 2. (U.S.) Turkey-buzzard.

bŭʹzzer *n.* (esp.) Steam-whistle; electric buzzing machine for sending signals; (army slang) signaller.

B.V.M. *abbrev.* Blessed Virgin Mary.

B.W.I. *abbrev.* British West Indies.

bȳ *prep.* 1. Near to, beside; (of compass-point) slightly inclining to (as *N.* ~ *E.*, between N. and NNE.); ~ *oneself*, alone. 2. Along, via, past. 3. During 4. Through the agency, means, etc., of; (of animals) having as sire. 5. As soon as, not later than. 6. According to. 7. After succeeding. 8. To the extent of. 9. In respect of. 10. (in oaths etc.) In the belief of. ~ *adj.* (occas. *bȳe*) 1. Side, out-of-the-way, devious, as *byʹpath*, ~-*road*, ~-*street*, *byʹway* (also fig.). 2. Collateral, side; *byʹplay*, action, usu. dumb show, carried on aside, esp. on stage; ~-*product*, substance etc. produced incidentally in making something else. 3. Additional, subsidiary; *byʹname*, secondary name, nickname; ~-*election*: see ELECTION; *byʹword*, proverb; person, place, etc., taken as type of some (usu. bad) quality. ~ *adv.* Near; aside, in reverse; past; ~ *and* ~, before long; ~ *and large*, on the whole; *byʹstander*, spectator.

bȳʹ-blow (-ō) *n.* Side blow; bastard.

bye[1]: see BY *adj.*

bȳe[2] *n.* (cricket) Run scored from ball that passes batsman and wicket-keeper, *leg* ~, one that touches the batsman; (in games when competitors are paired off) odd man, position of odd man; (golf) hole(s) remaining unplayed when match is finished; *by the* ~, incidentally.

bȳeʹ-bȳe[1], **bȳe-bȳes** (-bīz) *n.* (nursery colloq.) Sleep.

bȳe-bȳeʹ[2] *int.* (colloq. and nursery var. of) GOOD-BYE.

Byĕlōrŭʹssia (-sh*a*). = BELORUSSIA. **Byĕlōrŭʹssian** *adj.* & *n.*

bȳʹgŏne *adj.* Past, departed; antiquated. **bȳʹgones** (-gŏnz) *n.pl.* Past, past offences; (in museums etc.) domestic objects of former times.

bȳʹ-law, bȳʹe-law (bīl-) *n.* Regulation made by local authority or corporation.

Bȳng, John (1704–57). English admiral; he was shot for neglect of duty after trying unsuccessfully to relieve Fort St. Philip, Minorca, which was threatened by the French fleet; the incident occasioned Voltaire's observation, in 'Candide', that it is a good thing to kill an admiral now and then 'pour encourager les autres'.

bȳʹpass (-ahs) *n.* 1. Secondary pipe or channel conveying gas or liquid round fixture etc.; alternative passage for blood during surgical operation on heart; (elect.) shunt. 2. Road designed to relieve congestion by providing an alternative route for through traffic, esp. round town. ~ *v.t.* Furnish with a bypass; make detour round (town etc.) (also fig.).

Byrd[1] (bẽrd), Richard Evelyn (1888–1957). Amer. polar explorer; made first flight over N. Pole (1926) and over S. Pole (1929).

Byrd[2] (bẽrd), William (1543?–1623). Composer; the first English madrigalist and the greatest English master of polyphonic music.

bȳre *n.* Cow-shed.

Bȳr'on, George Gordon, 6th Baron (1788–1824). English Romantic poet, whose poetry, though much criticized on moral grounds, exerted great influence on the European Romantic movement; he joined the Greek insurgents in 1823, and died of fever at Missolonghi. **Bȳrŏ'nic** *adj.* **Bȳr'onism** *n.*

bȳssinō'sis *n.* Chronic lung disease caused by inhaling dust from cotton or linen fibre.

Bȳză'ntīne *adj.* Of Byzantium or the Byzantine Empire; of the style of art and architecture typical of this, characterized esp. by use of the round arch, circle, dome, and cross, and by rich mosaic ornament; ~ *Empire*, Eastern part of Roman Empire, esp. after collapse of Western Empire in 476, with its capital at Constantinople until this city was captured by the Turks in 1453. ~ *n.* Native, inhabitant, of Byzantium or the Byzantine Empire.

Bȳză'ntium. Original name of CONSTANTINOPLE.

C

C, c (sē). 1. 3rd letter of modern English and ancient Roman alphabet, deriving its form from Gk *gamma* (Γ); in English representing three or more sounds: (*a*) the hard sound (k) usu. before *a*, *o*, *u*, before consonants except *h*, and when final; (*b*) the soft sound (s) usu. before *i*, *e*, *y*; (*c*) *ci-* and some times *ce-* before another vowel has the sound (-sh-). 2. 3rd in series, order, or class. 3. *C*, (mus.) name of the key-note in the natural major scale and the corresponding minor scales; name of these scales. 4. Roman numeral symbol for 100. 5. *C 3*, lowest medical grade in British system of man-power classification in the war of 1914–18; hence, unfit, worthless.

c. *abbrev.* Caught; cent(s); century; chapter; *circa*, *circiter* (also *c.*, *c*); colt; cubic.

C *abbrev.* Celsius; centigrade; command paper; coulomb(s).

© Symbol for 'Copyright'.

C.A. *abbrev.* Chartered accountant (Sc.).

Ca'aba, K- (kah'*a*-). Muslim sacred building at Mecca, the 'holy of holies', containing the 'black stone' which is supposed to have fallen from Paradise with Adam and been given by the angel Gabriel to Abraham when he was building the Caaba. [Arab. *ka'ba* cubic structure; sacred building in Mecca]

căb *n.* 1. Hackney carriage, esp. of brougham or hansom shape, or taxi; *ca'bman*, driver of cab; *~-rank*, row of cabs on *ca'bstand*, where cabs are authorized to wait for hire. 2. Driver's shelter on locomotive, motor-lorry, etc.

C.A.B. *abbrev.* Citizens' Advice Bureau.

cabă'l *n.* 1. Secret intrigue; clique, faction. 2. (also *C~*; hist.) Under Charles II, the 'Committee for Foreign Affairs', precursor of the modern cabinet: esp. the 5 ministers who signed the treaty of alliance with France for war against Holland in 1672; Clifford, Arlington, Buckingham, Ashley (Earl of Shaftesbury), and Lauderdale. ~ *v.i.* Combine in cabal, intrigue privately. [f. CABBALA, not f. the ministers' initials]

cabala: see CABBALA.

că'baret (-rā) *n.* 1. French tavern. 2. Entertainment provided in restaurant etc. while guests are at table.

că'bbage *n.* Any of various kinds of green culinary vegetable, esp. of *Brassica oleracea*, with compact globular heart or head of unexpanded leaves; ~ *lettuce*, variety of lettuce with cabbage-like head; ~ *palm*, *tree*, any of various trees with edible cabbage-like terminal bud, esp. the W. Ind. *Areca* (*Oreodoxa*) *oleracea*; ~ *rose*, double rose with large round compact flowers, esp. *Rosa centifolia*; *C~ White*, butterfly which feeds on cabbage leaves (*Pieris brassicae*, large white; *P. rapae*, small white).

că'bbala, că'bala *n.* 1. Jewish oral tradition handed down from Moses to the rabbis of the Mishna and Talmud, or the pretended tradition of the mystical interpretation of the O.T. 2. Mystery; esoteric doctrine. **că'bbalism, că'bbalist** *ns.* **căbbali'stic** *adj.* **căbbali'sticallў** *adv.* [Heb. *ḳabbālāh* traditional law]

că'bbў *n.* (colloq.) Cab-driver.

că'ber *n.* Roughly trimmed young pine-trunk used in Sc. Highland sport of *tossing the ~*. [Gael. *cabar* pole]

că'bin *n.* 1. Small rude dwelling. 2. Room or compartment in ship for sleeping or eating in; officer's or passenger's room; compartment in aircraft; *~-boy*, boy waiting on officers or passengers; *~ cruiser*, cruiser with cabin for living in. **că'bĭned** (-nd) *adj.* Confined in small space, cramped.

că'bĭnėt *n.* 1. (archaic) small private room, closet. 2. Case with drawers, shelves, etc., for keeping valuables or displaying curiosities. 3. Private room in which confidential advisers of a sovereign or chief ministers of a State meet; (*C~*) these advisers or ministers collectively. 4. *~-maker*, one whose business is the making of cabinets and the finer kind of joiner's work; *~-making*; *~ photograph*, one of a size larger than a *carte-de-visite*; *~ pudding*, pudding made of bread or cake, dried fruit, eggs, and milk.

cā'ble *n.* 1. Strong thick rope of hemp or wire; (naut.) studded link chain attached to an anchor; measurement of distance at sea, = 200 yards. 2. Any insulated conductor of electricity, orig. the conductor of a submarine telegraph. 3. = CABLEGRAM. 4. (archit., also *~ moulding*) Moulding with twisted rope-like ornament; cabled moulding (see CABLE *v.*, 2). 5. (also *~-stitch*) Any of various twisted rope-like stitches in knitting and embroidery. 6. *~-laid*, (of rope) made of three hawser-laid ropes laid up left-handed; *~ railway*, railway worked by cable and stationary engine. *~ v.* 1. Furnish, fasten with cable. 2. (archit.) Fill lower part of flutings of (column) with convex mouldings. 3. Transmit (message), communicate, by cable.

cā'blegrăm (-lg-) *n.* Telegraph message transmitted by submarine cable.

cabŏ'b *n.* = KEBAB.

căbocho'n (-shawn) *n.* Gem, polished, not cut into facets, circular or elliptical in shape, with domed top and base which is flat or of other form.

cabōō'dle *n.* (slang, orig. U.S.) *the whole ~*, the whole lot.

cabōō'se *n.* 1. Cook-room or kitchen on ship's deck. 2. (U.S.) Workmen's or railmen's van on freight-train.

Că'bot, John (*c* 1450–98). Venetian navigator in the service of England; discovered Labrador in 1497 with his son Sebastian (1477–1557).

că'brĭōle *n.* Kind of curved leg in 17th- and 18th-c. furniture, esp. that of Chippendale type. [orig. = a kind of small armchair; see CABRIOLET]

căbriolet (-lā') *n.* Light two-wheeled hooded one-horse chaise. [Fr., f. *cabriole* goat's leap]

ca'că'nnȳ (kah-) *n.* Go-slow (see GO *v.*, 25). [Sc. pron. of *call+canny*, lit. 'drive warily']

cacā'ō *n.* Seed of a tropical Amer. tree, *Theobroma cacao*, from which cocoa and chocolate are prepared; the tree itself (also *~-tree*).

că'chalŏt (-sh-) *n.* Sperm whale.

căche (-sh) *n.* Hiding-place for treasures, ammunition, provisions, etc., esp. as used by explorers; the stores hidden. *~ v.t.* Place in cache.

că'chet (-shā) *n.* Stamp (fig.), distinguishing mark; prestige.

că'chĭnnāte (-k-) *v.i.* Laugh loudly. **căchĭnnā'tion** *n.* **că'chĭnnatorȳ** *adj.*

că'chou (-shōō) *n.* Lozenge used for sweetening the breath. [Malay *kachu*; cf. CATECHU]

caci'que (-sēk) *n.* W. Ind. and Amer. Ind. native chief.

că'ckle *n.* Clucking of hen after laying; glib, noisy, inconsequent talk; loud silly laughter. *~ v.i.* Make cackle; talk glibly and noisily.

căcodē'mon *n.* Evil spirit; malignant person.

că'codȳl *n.* (chem.) The radical dimethyl arsenic ($As(CH_3)_2$). [Gk *kakōdēs* stinking]

căcoē'thēs (-z) *n.* Itch for doing something unadvisable; *~ scribĕ'ndi*, scribbling-mania. [L, f. Gk *kakos* bad *ēthos* disposition]

cacŏ'graphȳ *n.* Bad handwriting or spelling.

cacŏ'phonȳ *n.* Ugly sound, discord. **cacŏ'phonous** *adj.*

că'ctŭs *n.* (pl. *-tī*, *-tuses*). Plant of the family Cactaceae, flourish-

ing in arid districts of the New World, having a thick fleshy stem adapted for retaining moisture (usu. with spines, rarely with leaves) and bearing brilliantly coloured flowers; ~ *dahlia*, dahlia with ray florets recurved at the edges, orig. from Mexico. **căctā'ceous** (-sh*us*) *adj.*

căd *n.* Vulgar ill-bred person; person guilty of ungentlemanly conduct; (in milder use) person. **că'ddish** *adj.*

cadă'stral *adj.* Of, showing, the extent, value, and ownership of land for taxation.

cadā'ver *n.* Corpse. **cadă'veric, cadă'verous** *adjs.* [L]

că'ddie, că'ddy[1] *n.* Golf-player's attendant who carries his clubs etc.; *~-cart*, small two-wheeled trolley for the same purpose. **că'ddy** *v.i.* Act as caddie. [f. CADET[1]]

că'ddis *n.* *~-fly*, feebly flying freq. nocturnal insect of order Trichoptera, with membranous or hairy wings, living near water; *~-worm*, larva of caddis-fly etc., living in water and making cylindrical case of sticks, stone, shells, etc., used as bait for fishing.

că'ddy[2] *n.* Small box for holding tea; *~-spoon*, short-handled spoon for measuring tea from caddy. [Malay *kati*, weight of 1⅓ lb.]

cā'dence *n.* Rhythm; measured movement, esp. of sound; falling tone, esp. of voice at end of period; intonation; (mus.) close of musical movement or phrase.

cadĕ'nza *n.* (mus.) Flourish for solo instrument (or, less freq., voice) at close of movement or between two parts of movement, sometimes improvised by performer.

cadĕ't[1] *n.* 1. Younger son or brother. 2. Student in military, naval, or air force college; member of cadet force receiving training for service in armed forces or police force.

cadĕ't[2] *n.* (hist.) Member of Russian Constitutional Democratic (or Liberal) Party, formed 1905. [Russ., f. *ka*, *de*, names of initial letters of *K*onstitutsionniy *D*emokrat; *t* added for sake of pun on *kadet* CADET[1]]

cădge *v.* Get by begging; *~ for*, try to get by begging or 'sponging'.

cā'di (*or* kah-) *n.* Civil judge, usu. of towns, etc., in Muslim country.

că'dmium *n.* (chem.) Soft bluish-white metallic element resembling tin, used in a number of alloys and as a protective coating on iron and steel; symbol Cd, at. no. 48, at. wt 112·40; ~ *yellow*, cadmium sulphide, an intense yellow pigment.

Că'dmus. (Gk legend) Founder of Thebes in Boeotia, reputed to have introduced the alphabet into Greece; slew a dragon and sowed its teeth in the earth, from which armed men sprang up and slew one another. **Cădmē'an** *adj.* Of Cadmus; ~ *victory*, victory involving one's own ruin.

Cadō'mian *adj.* (geol.) Of an episode of mountain formation during the pre-Cambrian era.

cadre (kahdr *or* kah'd*er*) *n.* Framework, scheme; (mil.) permanent establishment of regiment forming nucleus for enlargement at need; in Communist countries, = CELL, 6.

cadū'cĕus *n.* (pl. -*cĕī*). Ancient Greek or Roman herald's wand; esp. that of Mercury, usu. represented with two serpents twined round it.

cadū'cous *adj.* Fleeting, perishable; (biol., of organs and parts) shed when their work is done. **cadū'citȳ** *n.*

caecĭ'lian (sĭs-) *adj.* & *n.* (zool.) (Member) of the Apoda (see APODAL).

cae'cum (sē-) *n.* (pl. *-ca*). Any blindly ending tube in the structure of an animal, esp. that arising from the colon and ending at the vermiform appendix in mammals.

Cæ'dmon (kăd-) (7th c.). English monk; said by Bede to have received in a vision the power of song and put into English verse passages from the Scriptures, but the only authentic fragment of his work is the first Hymn, which Bede quotes.

Caenozō'ic (sē-) *adj.* & *n.* = CAINOZOIC.

Caernar'vonshire (k*er*-). Former county of N. Wales, since April 1974 part of Gwynedd.

Caerns. *abbrev.* Caernarvonshire.

Caerphĭ'llȳ (kar-) *n.* Creamy-white mild cheese made esp. in West of England, orig. made at Caerphilly, West Glamorgan.

Cae'sar (sēz-). Cognomen of the Roman dictator Caius JULIUS CAESAR, used as title by the Roman emperors from Augustus to Hadrian, and subsequently by the emperor's heir-presumptive.

Caesar'ėan, -ĭan (*or* sĭz-) *adj.* Of Caesar or the Caesars; ~ *operation, section,* delivery of a child by cutting through walls of abdomen, as was done, acc. to Pliny, in the case of Julius Caesar.

cae'sĭum (sēz-) *n.* (chem.) Rare alkali-metal element discovered spectroscopically by Bunsen in 1861; symbol Cs, at. no. 55, at. wt 132·9054. [L *caesius* bluish-grey, f. the distinctive lines in its spectrum]

caesur'a (sĭz-) *n.* (Gk & Rom. pros.) Break between words within a metrical foot; (modern pros.) pause about the middle of metrical line.

café (kă'fā) *n.* Coffee-house, tea-shop, restaurant; ~ *au lait* (ō lā), coffee taken with about an equal quantity of hot milk; the brownish-cream colour of this; ~ *noir* (nwahr), black coffee.

căfėter'ĭa *n.* (orig. U.S.) Restaurant in which the customer fetches food from the counter.

că'ffeine *n.* Vegetable alkaloid crystallizing in white silky needles, found in leaves and seeds of coffee and tea plants etc. (and hence in these beverages); used in medicine as a cardiac stimulant.

Caffre: see KAFFIR.

că'ftan, k- *n.* Long girdled under-tunic worn in eastern countries; woman's long loose dress.

cāge *n.* 1. Fixed or portable prison, of wire or with bars, esp. for birds or beasts; prison. 2. (mining) Frame for hoisting and lowering wagons etc.; open framework of various kinds. ~ *v.t.* Place or keep in cage.

cā'gey *adj.* (slang) Wary, non-committal.

Căgliŏ'strō (kălyŏ-), Count Alessandro (1743–95). Name assumed by Giuseppe Balsamo, a notorious charlatan born at Palermo; he was implicated in the 'Affair of the DIAMOND Necklace'.

caiman: see CAYMAN.

Cain. Eldest son of Adam, and the first murderer (see Gen. 4); murderer, fratricide.

Cainozō'ic (kī-), **Cēn-** *adj.* & *n.* (geol.) (Of) the era or group of systems following the Mesozoic and including the present era, characterized by the first appearance of birds and mammals; sometimes = TERTIARY.

caique (k*a*ē'k) *n.* Light rowing-boat used on the Bosporus; Levantine sailing-vessel.

cairn *n.* 1. Pyramid of rough stones as memorial, landmark, etc. 2. (also ~ *terrier*) Small terrier (named from being used to hunt among cairns) with longish body, short legs, and shaggy coat.

cair'ngôrm (-n-g-) *n.* Yellow or wine-coloured semi-precious stone, consisting of quartz coloured by iron oxide or titanic acid, named after the mountain in Scotland where it is chiefly found. [Gael. *carn gorm* blue cairn]

Cairo (kīr'ō). Capital city of Egypt, situated on the Nile about 100 miles from its mouths. **Cair'ēne** *adj.* & *n.* [Arab. *al-kāhira* the victorious (conjuncture)]

cai'sson (*or* kasōō'n) *n.* 1. Ammunition chest or wagon. 2. Large watertight chamber used in laying foundations under water; buoyant chamber attached to side of ship engaged in raising wreck; boat-shaped vessel used as dock gate; ~ *disease*, disease, caused by working under high atmospheric pressure, in which bubbles of nitrogen released from body fluids if pressure is reduced too rapidly collect in joints and blood-vessels; bends.

Caithnĕ'ss. Former county in extreme NE. of Scotland, since May 1975 part of the region of Highland.

cai'tiff *n.* & *adj.* (archaic) Base, despicable (person); coward(ly).

cajaput: see CAJUPUT.

cajō'le *v.t.* Persuade or soothe by flattery, deceit, etc. **cajō'lement, cajō'lerȳ** *ns.*

că'jupŭt, -apŭt *n.* E. Ind. tree of genus *Melaleuca*; (also ~ *oil*) aromatic oil obtained from this, used as stimulant, anti-spasmodic, and sudorific. [Malay *kayu* wood, *puteh* white]

cāke *n.* 1. (archaic) Small flattish loaf of bread; (Sc. & north.) thin oaten bread; *land of ~s*, Scotland. 2. Baked sweetened mixture of flour and other ingredients, as butter, eggs, spices, currants, raisins, etc. 3. Flattish compact mass of other food (as fish etc.) or of any compressed substance, as soap, wax, tobacco. 4. *ca'kewalk*, (orig.) form of entertainment among Amer. Negroes in which a prize of a cake was given for the most graceful steps and figures in walking; popular stage dance developed from these steps. ~ *v.* Form into compact flattish mass.

Călabar' bean *n.* Highly poisonous seed of tropical African vine (*Physostigma venenosum*), an extract of which is used to contract the pupil of the eye, and medicinally. [*Calabar* in Nigeria]

că'labăsh *n.* Any of various gourds or pumpkins, the shell of which is used for holding liquids etc.; the vessel made from such a shell; ~ *tree*, tropical Amer. and W. Ind. tree *Crescentia*, bearing a large oval or globular fruit with a hard shell.

călabōō'se *n.* (U.S. colloq.) Prison.

călamă'ncō *n.* Glossy Flemish woollen stuff, chequered on one side, much used in 18th c.

călamă'nder *n.* Beautiful, extremely hard, cabinet wood of Ceylon and India, from the tree (related to ebony) *Diospyros quaesita*.

că'lamarȳ *n.* Any of various cuttle-fish (genus *Loligo*) with pen-shaped internal shell, long narrow body and two triangular fins.

că'lamīne *n.* 1. Carbonate of zinc ($ZnCO_3$). 2. Pink powder containing zinc carbonate and ferric oxide, used in skin lotions and ointments.

cală'mitȳ *n.* Adversity, deep distress; grievous disaster; *C~ Jane*, nickname of Martha Jane Burke (*née* Canary; ? 1852–1903), Amer. horse-rider and markswoman, applied to a prophet of disaster. **cală'mitous** *adj.* **cală'mitouslȳ** *adv.*

cală'sh *n.* (hist.) 1. Light carriage with low wheels and folding hood; Canadian two-wheeled one-seated vehicle with driver's seat on splash-board. 2. Woman's silk hood hooped with cane or whalebone.

calcār'ėous, ious *adj.* Of, containing, calcium carbonate or limestone.

călcėolār'ia *n.* S. Amer. plant of genus *C~*, with flowers somewhat resembling a broad-toed slipper.

că'lcėolate *adj.* (bot.) Slipper-shaped.

că'lcicōle *n.* Plant or animal inhabiting a soil with free calcium carbonate (or, in wider sense, soils rich in calcium). **călcĭ'colous** *adj.* **călcĭ'ferous** *adj.* Yielding or containing chalk or calcium carbonate.

că'lcify̆ *v.* Convert, be converted, into chalk or calcium carbonate; harden by deposit of calcium salts; petrify. **călcificā'tion** *n.*

că'lcine *v.* Reduce to quicklime or friable substance by heating strongly; desiccate; refine by consuming grosser part; burn to ashes; be calcined. **călcinā'tion** *n.* Process of calcining. **călci'ner** *n.* Machine for calcining.

că'lcīte *n.* (min.) Crystalline calcium carbonate, widely distributed in nature as marble, limestone, etc.

că'lcium *n.* (chem.) Silver-white malleable light metal, an element in the alkaline earth group (symbol Ca, at. no. 20, at. wt 40·08), widely distributed in nature as limestone or chalk (~ *carbonate*, $CaCO_3$); ~ *car'bide*, compound of calcium and carbon (CaC_2), produced by intense heating of limestone and coke in an electric furnace and giving acetylene gas on treatment with water; ~ *hypochlorite*, chloride of lime or bleaching powder ($CaOCl_2$), used as disinfectant; ~ *oxide*, (CaO) quicklime.

călc-spar *n.* (min.) Crystalline form of calcium carbonate (limestone).

că'lcūlable *adj.* That may be reckoned, measured, computed, or relied upon. **călcūlabi'lity̆** *n.*

că'lcūlāte *v.* Compute by figures; ascertain beforehand by exact reckoning; plan deliberately; rely upon; suppose, believe (U.S.); (usu. pass.) arrange, adapt, *for*, *to*; *calculating machine*, machine that performs arithmetical processes. **că'lcūlātėd** *adj.* (esp.) Fit, suitable *to* do.

călcūlā'tion *n.* (Result got by) calculating; forecast.

că'lcūlātor *n.* (esp.) Set of tables for use in calculating; calculating machine.

că'lcūlus *n.* 1. (med., pl. *-lī*) Stone, concretion in some part of the body. 2. (math.) Particular method of calculation, esp. DIFFERENTIAL and INTEGRAL calculus. **că'lcūlous** *adj.* Of, suffering from, stone or calculus. [L, = small stone used in reckoning on abacus]

Călcŭ'tta. City and port in India, capital of W. Bengal; *Black Hole of* ~: see BLACK *adj.*

Ca'lderón de la Bâr'ca (kawl- *or* kŏl-), Pedro (1600–81). Spanish dramatist and poet, author of some 120 plays.

ca'ldron (kawl- *or* kŏl-) *n.* = CAULDRON.

Călėdō'nia. 1. Roman name of part of northern Britain. 2. (poet. & rhet.) Scotland, the Scottish Highlands.

Călėdō'nian *adj.* Of Caledonia; of Scotland; (geol.) of a European episode of mountain formation during the Palaeozoic era; ~ *Canal*, canal from Inverness on the E. coast of Scotland to Fort William on the W. coast. ~ *n.* Native, inhabitant, of Caledonia or of Scotland.

că'lėndar *n.* 1. System by which the beginning, length, and subdivision of civil year is fixed, esp. the GREGORIAN ~, used in England since 1752; ~ *month*, one of the 12 months into which year is divided by calendar, as opp. to LUNAR month of 4 weeks; *Jewish* ~: see JEWISH. 2. Table(s) showing months, weeks, and festivals, etc., of a given year or years. 3. Register, list, esp. of canonized saints, prisoners for trial, or documents chronologically arranged with summaries. ~ *v.t.* Register, enter in list; arrange, analyse, and index (documents).

că'lėnder[1] *n.* Machine in which cloth, paper, etc., is pressed under rollers to glaze or smooth it. ~ *v.t.* Press in calender.

că'lėnder[2] *n.* Mendicant dervish.

că'lėnds, k- (-z) *n.pl.* 1st day of month in Roman calendar; *Greek* ~, date or occasion which never comes (because the Greeks had no calends).

că'lėnture *n.* Tropical fever or

delirium in which, it is said, sailors etc. fancy the sea to be green fields and desire to leap into it.

calf[1] (kahf) *n.* (pl. *-ves*). 1. Young of bovine animal, esp. domestic cow, for first year; young of elephant, whale, etc.; *golden* ~: see Exod. 32; wealth as an object of worship; *~-love,* romantic affection between boy and girl; *~'s foot,* dish made of calves' feet boiled and seasoned. 2. Leather made from skin of domestic calf. 3. (naut.) Floating piece of ice detached from glacier, iceberg, or floe.

calf[2] (kahf) *n.* (pl. *-ves*). Fleshy hinder part of shank of leg; part of stocking covering this.

Că'lĭbăn. Character in Shakespeare's 'Tempest', a 'savage and deformed slave'.

că'lĭbrāte *v.t.* Find calibre of; calculate irregularities of (tube, gauge) before graduating; graduate (a gauge) making allowance for irregularities.

că'lĭbre (-ber; *or* kalē'ber) *n.* 1. Internal diameter of gun or any tube; diameter of bullet or shell. 2. Degree of personal capacity or ability, or of merit or importance. [Arab. *qalib* mould]

că'lĭcō *n.* Plain white unprinted bleached or unbleached cotton cloth; (U.S.) printed cotton cloth. ~ *adj.* Of calico; (U.S.) like printed calico; variegated, piebald. [*Calicut,* town on Malabar coast]

Calif. *abbrev.* California.

Călĭfôr'nia. State on Pacific coast of U.S., admitted to the Union in 1850; capital, Sacramento.

Călĭfôr'nian *adj.* Of California; ~ *poppy*: see ESCHSCHOLTZIA. ~ *n.*

călĭfôr'nium *n.* (chem.) Transuranic element; symbol Cf, at. no. 98, principal isotope at. wt 244.

Calĭ'gūla, Gaius Caesar. Roman emperor A.D. 37–41; notorious for his cruelty and vices.

că'lĭpăsh *n.* Part of turtle next upper shell, containing a dull green gelatinous substance.

că'lĭpee *n.* Part of turtle next lower shell, containing light yellow gelatinous substance.

că'lĭph *n.* (in certain Muslim countries) Chief civil and religious ruler, as successor of Muhammad.

că'lĭphate *n.* [Arab. *kalīfa* successor]

calisthenic(s): see CALLISTHENIC.

calk (kawk) *n.* Sharp iron to prevent horseshoe or boot from slipping. ~ *v.t.* Provide with calk.

că'lkĭn (*or* kawk-) *n.* Turned-down heels of horseshoe, also turned edge in front, esp. when sharpened in frost; iron pieces nailed on soles of boots or clogs.

call (kawl) *v.* 1. Cry, shout, speak loudly; utter characteristic note; cry *out, to*; read *over* (names of those present); name (suit as trumps, at cards); pay brief visit (*at* house, *on* person) in order to speak, deal, etc.; communicate by radio or telephone. 2. Summon; summon or nominate by divine authority *into* the Church; *be called to the bar*: see BAR[1]. 3. Name, describe as; consider, regard as. 4. ~ *for,* order; demand; need; go and fetch; ~ *forth,* elicit; ~ *off* (a project), cancel it; ~ *on,* invoke, appeal to; ~ *out,* elicit; challenge to duel; summon (troops) esp. to aid civil authorities; summon (workers) to strike; shout or utter loudly; ~ *up,* imagine; ring up (on telephone); summon to serve in army etc.; rouse from sleep. ~ *n.* 1. Shout, cry; special cry of bird etc., imitation of, instrument for imitating, this; signal on bugle etc.; roll-call (also *~-over*). 2. Looking-in on business; short formal visit. 3. Invitation, summons; duty, need, occasion; demand, claim. 4. Telephone conversation. 5. Demand for money, esp. for unpaid capital from company shareholders; (Stock Exch.) option of claiming stock at given date. 6. *~-box,* small enclosed erection containing public telephone; *~-boy,* prompter's attendant summoning actors; *~-girl,* (orig. U.S.) prostitute accepting appointments by telephone.

că'lla *n.* 1. Aquatic plant (genus *C~*) of N. Europe and eastern N.

America. 2. Plant of genus *Zantedeschia* (esp. *Z. aethiopica*) or genus *Arum*.

ca'ller[1] (kaw-) *n.* (esp.) Person paying a call or visit; person who initiates telephone call.

că'ller[2] *adj.* (Sc.) Fresh (of herrings etc.); fresh, cool (of wind, weather, etc.).

calli'graphy̆ *n.* (Art of) beautiful handwriting. **calli'grapher** *n.* **călligră'phic** *adj.*

ca'lling (kaw-) *n.* (esp.) Occupation, profession, trade; persons following a particular occupation.

Calli'opė[1]. (Gk & Rom. myth.) Muse of eloquence and heroic poetry. [Gk *kalliope* beautiful-voiced]

calli'opė[2] *n.* (U.S.) Set of steam whistles producing musical notes, played by a keyboard like that of an organ.

că'lliper *n.* 1. (pl., also ~ *compasses*) Compasses with bowed legs for measuring diameter of convex bodies, or with out-turned points for measuring cavities; *~-square*, rule with movable cross-heads for taking internal or external diameters. 2. (also ~ *brake*) Brake, esp. on bicycle, consisting of two brake blocks operated through central pivot to grip rim of wheel; brake on similar principle on motor vehicle, by which two brake pads grip a revolving disc. 3. Metal support for weak or injured leg. ~ *v.t.* Measure with callipers. [var. of CALIBRE]

călliсthĕ'nic, căli- *adj.* Suitable for producing strength and grace. **călliсthĕ'nics, căli-** *n.* Art and practice of bodily exercises calculated to produce strength and grace.

Calli'stō. 1. (Gk myth.) Daughter of Lycaon, loved by Zeus and punished for her unchastity by being turned into a she-bear; she and her son were transformed into constellations. 2. (astron.) Constellation URSA Major.

callŏ'sity̆ *n.* Abnormal hardness and thickness of skin; hardened insensible part, lump.

că'llous *adj.* 1. Hardened, hard (of parts of skin). 2. Unfeeling, insensible. ~ *n.* Callus. **că'llously̆** *adv.* **că'llousnėss** *n.*

că'llow (-ō) *adj.* 1. Unfledged; downy like young birds. 2. Raw, inexperienced.

că'llus *n.* Thickened part of skin or soft tissue; bony material formed while bone-fracture heals; (bot.) new tissue, usu. more or less corky, covering a wound.

calm (kahm) *n.* Stillness, serenity; windless period. ~ *adj.* Tranquil, quiet; windless; undisturbed; unabashed, impudent. **ca'lmly̆** *adv.* **ca'lmnėss** *n.* **calm** *v.* Make calm; pacify; ~ *down*, become calm.

că'lomĕl *n.* Mercurous chloride (HgCl), a heavy white powder used as a purgative.

că'lorie *n.* 1. (also *great* or *large* ~) Standard unit of heat, amount required to raise the temperature of 1 kilogramme (1 litre) of water 1 degree centigrade; unit for measuring the heat and other energy produced by the metabolism of food. 2. (also *lesser* ~) Amount of heat required to raise 1 gramme (1 cu. cm) of water 1 degree centigrade.

călori'fic *adj.* Producing heat; ~ *value*, amount of heat, usu. expressed in form of kilogramme calories, given out on the complete combustion of a substance.

călori'mėter *n.* Apparatus for measuring heat. **călorimĕ'tric** *adj.* **călorimĕ'trically̆** *adv.* **călori'mėtry̆** *n.*

că'ltrop *n.* 1. (hist.) 4-spiked iron ball thrown on ground to impede cavalry horses. 2. (also *ca'ltrap*) Representation of this as heraldic charge. 3. (usu. pl.) Any of various plants that catch or entangle the feet.

că'lūmėt *n.* Amer. Ind. tobacco-pipe with reed stem and clay bowl; used as symbol of peace or friendship (the *pipe of peace*).

calŭ'mniāte *v.t.* Slander. **calŭmniā'tion** *n.*

că'lumny̆ *n.* Malicious misrepresentation; false report; slander.

Că'lvary̆. 1. Hill near Jerusalem on which Jesus Christ was crucified. 2. Representation of the crucifixion, esp. in the open air. [L *calvaria* skull, transl. of GOLGOTHA in Matt. 27: 33]

calve (kahv) *v.i.* Give birth to calf; (of iceberg etc.) throw off masses of ice.

Că'lvĭn, John (1509–64). French theological writer and reformer; settled in Geneva, 1536; wrote

'Institutes of the Christian Religion' (1535), in which he expounded his doctrine of original sin, of predestination and election; his dogma is held by the continental Reformed Churches and forms the basis of Scottish Presbyterianism.

Că'lvĭnism *n.* Tenets and doctrines of CALVIN and his followers and of the Calvinistic Churches, whose distinguishing doctrines, usu. called *the five points of* ~, are election or predestination, limited atonement, total depravity, irresistibility of grace, and the perseverance of the saints. **Că'lvĭnist** *n.* Follower of Calvin, adherent of Calvinism. **Călvĭnĭ'stic** *adj.* Pertaining to, characteristic of, Calvinism; ~ *Methodists*, section of the Methodists who followed the Calvinistic opinions of WHITEFIELD as opposed to the Arminian opinions of John WESLEY.

călx *n.* (pl. *că'lcēs*). (archaic) Powder or friable substance left after heating metal or mineral.

Calȳ'psō[1]. (Gk legend) In the 'Odyssey', a nymph who kept ODYSSEUS 7 years on her island, Ogygia.

calȳ'psō[2] *n.* W. Ind. free-verse narrative chant, freq. topical, with accompaniment on guitar or similar instrument.

calȳ'ptra *n.* (bot.) Hood or cover, esp. hood of spore-case in mosses. [Gk *kaluptra* veil]

că'lȳx *n.* (pl. *-ycēs, -yxes*). (bot.) Whorl of members, often leaf-like, forming outer protective envelope of flower.

căm *n.* Portion of revolving shaft or wheel bearing against, and shaped so as to impart a particular type of motion to, a lever or other movable part of a machine; *ca'm-shaft*, shaft bearing cam(s).

cămara'derie (-ahderē) *n.* Intimacy, mutual trust, and sociability, of comrades. [Fr.]

că'mber *n.* Slight convexity of upper surface, arched form (of road, ship's deck, aeroplane wing, etc.); sideways inclination of wheel of vehicle. ~ *v.* Have, construct with, camber.

Că'mberwĕll Beau'tȳ (bū-). Species of butterfly, *Nymphalis antiopa.* [*Camberwell,* borough of London]

că'mbium *n.* (bot.) Layer of cells from which annual growth of woody tissue and bark takes place

Cămbō'dĭa. Former name of KHMER. **Cămbō'dĭan** *adj.* & *n.*

Cambrensis. (Archbishop) of Wales (replacing surname in his signature).

Că'mbrĭa. Ancient or poetic name for Wales. **Că'mbrĭan** *adj.* & *n.* 1. Welsh(man). 2. (geol.) (Of) the earliest period or system of the Palaeozoic era. [Latinized f. *Cymry* Welshman]

că'mbrĭc *n.* Fine white linen or cotton fabric of plain weave. [*Kamerijk*, Fl. name of *Cambrai*, where linen cambric was made]

Cā'mbrĭdge[1]. City in Cambridgeshire on River Cam, seat of university organized as a *studium generale* in 1209, recognized in a royal writ to the chancellor in 1230, recognized by the pope in 1233; ~ *blue*, light blue.

Că'mbrĭdge[2]. Town in Massachusetts (U.S.), the seat of Harvard University.

Că'mbrĭdgeshire. E. midland county of England; *the* ~ (*Handicap*), a horse-race run annually at Newmarket since 1839.

Cambs. *abbrev.* Cambridgeshire.

că'mel *n.* 1. Large ruminant quadruped of genus *Camelus* with long neck, cushioned feet, and either two humps (*Bactrian* ~) or one (*Arabian* ~) which store food, closely related to the llama and alpaca, used as chief beast of burden in arid regions; *~'s hair*, *ca'melhair*, hair of this animal, woven into a thick, warm, lightweight, usu. long-piled textile material; imitation of this fabric; *~'s hair*, *ca'melhair*, *brush*, artist's paint-brush usu. made of squirrel-hair. 2. Buoyant apparatus for attaching to ship's sides and raising her in the water. 3. Shade of fawn.

camĕ'llia *n.* Flowering evergreen shrub of genus *C~* of the tea family, chiefly native of China and Japan. [Joseph *Kamel* (1661–1706), Moravian Jesuit who described botany of island of Luzon in the Philippines]

că'melopârd (*or* kamĕ'-) n. Giraffe.

Că'mėlŏt. In Arthurian legend, the place where King Arthur held his court, stated by Malory to be Winchester.

Că'membert (-bār) *n.* Small rich soft cheese made near the village of Camembert in Normandy; cheese of similar type.

că'mėō *n.* (pl. *-os*). 1. Small piece of relief-carving in stone (onyx, agate, etc.), freq. with two layers of different colours, the lower of which serves as background. 2. (fig.) Short literary sketch etc., small well-defined acting part.

că'mera *n.* Apparatus for taking photographs, consisting essentially of a box holding at one end a plate or film which is sensitized so as to retain the image projected through a lens at the other; (television) apparatus which forms the image and converts it into electrical impulses; ~ *lū'cida*, prism which when placed in front of a draughtsman's eye appears to him to project an image upon his paper and thus assists him in copying, so named to distinguish it from the ~ *obscura*, a much older device for tracing images, consisting of a large box, or a room, with a lens at one end and at the other a reflector which throws the image upon a screen or table [L, *lucida* light, *obscura*

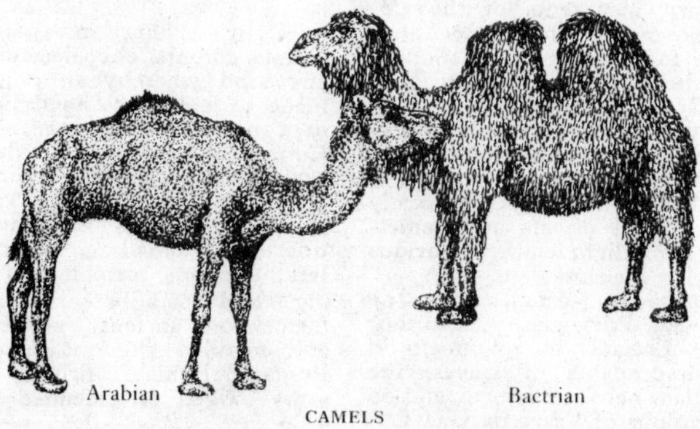

Arabian Bactrian

CAMELS

dark]; *ca'meraman*, (esp.) one who operates a cinema camera. [L, = 'vaulted room']

cămerlĭ'ngō (-ngg-) *n.* 1. Pope's chamberlain and financial secretary, highest officer in the papal household. 2. Cardinals' chamberlain, treasurer of the Sacred College.

Că'meron, Richard (d. 1680). Scottish Covenanter and field preacher who rejected the indulgence granted to non-conforming ministers and formally renounced allegiance to Charles II; his followers afterwards constituted the 'Reformed Presbyterian Church of Scotland'. **Cămerō'nĭan** *adj.* & *n.* (Follower) of Richard Cameron; *the ~s*, the old 26th Regiment of Foot in the British Army, orig. formed of Cameronians and other Presbyterians who fought at the battle of Killiecrankie.

Cămeroo'n. Republic on W. coast of Africa between Nigeria and Congo; from 1884 to 1916 a German protectorate; after war of 1914–18 administered under League of Nations (later U.N.) trusteeship by France (*East ~*) and Great Britain (*Southern ~s*); became a Federal Republic in 1960–1, and a United Republic in 1972; capital, Yaoundé.

că'mĭknĭckers (-ĭnĭ-, -z) *n.* Woman's undergarment combining camisole and knickers.

că'mĭon *n.* Large dray; lorry.

Că'misard *n.* One of the Calvinist insurgents of the Cévennes during the persecutions which followed the revocation of the Edict of Nantes by Louis XIV in 1685. [Provençal *camisa* shirt]

că'mĭsōle *n.* Woman's underbodice, often embroidered or trimmed with lace.

că'mlėt *n.* (archaic) Orig., costly eastern stuff of silk and camel-hair; later, light cloth of various materials for cloaks etc.

Că'moëns (-ōenz), Luis de (1524–80). Portuguese poet, author of the 'Lusiads', an epic poem on the descendants of Lusus, the legendary hero of Portugal, and on the exploits of Vasco da GAMA.

că'momīle, chă'm- (k-) *n.* Aromatic creeping herb, *Anthemis nobilis*, with downy leaves and yellow or white daisy-like flowers of which an infusion is used as a tonic, hair-wash, etc.; *~ tea*, infusion of camomile flowers.

Camŏ'rra. In the 19th c., a secret society of lawless malcontents in Naples and Neapolitan cities. **Camŏ'rrĭst** *n.*

că'mouflage (-*e*flahzh) *n.* Disguising, disguise, of objects used in war, as guns, ships, camps, factories, etc., by means of smoke-screens, boughs, obscuring out-

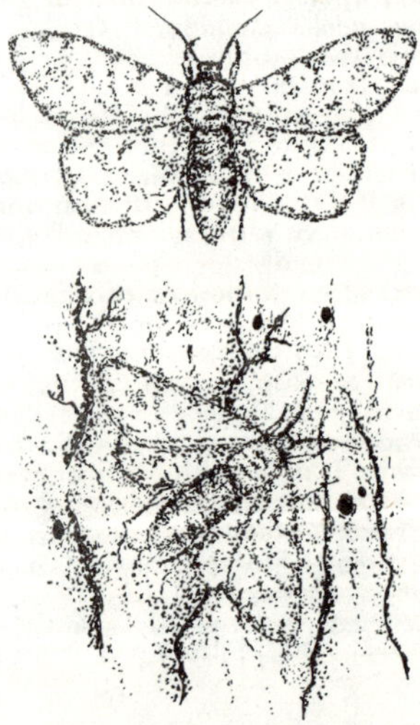

lines by netting and paint of various colours, etc.; deception of any kind whereby an object is made to look like something else or concealed altogether. *~ v.t.* Conceal by or as by camouflage.

cămp[1] *n.* 1. Place where troops are lodged in tents etc. or received for training. 2. Temporary quarters of nomads, gipsies, travellers; (persons) camping out. 3. (fig.) Body of adherents. 4. (Remains of ancient) entrenched and fortified site within which Roman, Danish, British, etc., army lodged or defended itself. 5. *~-bed, -chair, -stool*, portable folding bed etc.; *~-fire*, fire in camp or encampment, open-air fire; *~-follower*, non-military follower or hanger-on of camp or army; *~-meeting*, religious meeting, esp. in U.S., held in open air or in a tent and usu. lasting several days. ~ *v.* Encamp, lodge in camp; (also ~ *out*) lodge in tent or in the open, take up quarters; station (troops) in camp.

cămp² *adj.* (slang) 1. Extravagant, bizarre. 2. Homosexual, perverted. ~ *v.* Behave, do, in a camp way.

Cămpa'gna (-ahnya). Rich level district of Italy SE. of river Tiber, extending from the sea on the W. to the Sabine Hills.

cămpai'gn (-pān) *n.* 1. Series of military operations in a definite theatre or with one objective or constituting the whole or a distinct part of a war. 2. Organized course of action, esp. in politics, as before an election etc. ~ *v.i.* Serve on a campaign. **cămpai'gner** *n.*

Cămpā'nia. SW. region of Italy. **Cămpā'nian** *adj.* & *n.*

cămpani'lė (-nē-) *n.* Bell-tower, esp. one detached from main building.

cămpanŏ'logy̆ *n.* The subject of bells (founding, ringing, etc.). **cămpanŏ'logist** *n.* **cămpanolŏ'gical** *adj.*

cămpă'nūla *n.* Herbaceous plant of genus *C~*, with bell-shaped, usu. blue or white, flowers, including the harebell and Canterbury bells.

Că'mpbell (-mbl), Thomas (1777–1844). Scottish poet chiefly remembered for his war-songs 'Hohenlinden', 'Ye Mariners of England', etc.

Că'mpbell - Bă'nnerman (-mbl-), Sir Henry (1836–1908). British Liberal statesman; supporter of home rule for Ireland and women's suffrage; prime minister 1905–8.

Cămpea'chy̆ wŏŏd. Logwood, orig. exported from Campeche, city and State of SE. Mexico. [alteration of *Campeche*]

Că'mperdown. (Du. *Kamperduin*) Village on coast of Netherlands, off which in 1797 the British fleet defeated the Dutch.

că'mphor *n.* Translucent waxy crystalline substance with strong characteristic smell and bitter taste, obtained from a species of laurel growing in Japan, China, etc., also made synthetically from turpentine; used in pharmacy and in manufacture of celluloid etc. **cămphŏ'ric** *adj.*

că'mphorate *n.* Salt of camphoric acid. **că'mphorāte** *v.t.* Impregnate or treat with camphor.

că'mpion *n.* Any of various plants of genus *Lychnis*, with red or white flowers.

că'mpus *n.* (orig. U.S., first used at Princeton) Grounds of a college or university, open space between or around the buildings; (transf.) college or university life or people. [L, = 'field']

Cămus (-ū), Albert (1913–60). French novelist and playwright.

că'mwŏŏd *n.* Hard red wood of W. Afr. tree *Baphia nitida*, used in dyeing, cabinet-making, etc.

căn¹ *n.* 1. Vessel for liquids, usu. of tinned metal, and with handle over top. 2. (orig. U.S.) Tinplate vessel in which meat, fruits, etc., are sterilized and sealed for preservation. ~ *v.t.* Preserve in a can. **cănned** (-nd) *adj.* Preserved in a can; (slang, of music etc.) recorded; (slang) drunk.

căn² *v. auxil.* (neg. *că'nnot*, colloq. *can't*, pr. kahnt; past t. & conditional *could*, pr. kŏŏd; defective parts supplied from *be able to*). Be able to; have the right to; be permitted to.

Can. *abbrev.* Canada.

Cā'naan (-nan *or* -nyan). Biblical name of esp. western part of region later called Palestine, promised by God to Abraham (Gen. 12: 5–10). **Cā'naanīte** *adj.* & *n.* (Non-Jewish native or inhabitant) of Canaan. **Cā'naanītish** *adj.*

Că'nada. Member State of the Commonwealth, occupying the N. part of the N. Amer. continent (with the exception of Alaska) from 49° N. to the N. Pole and from the Pacific to the Atlantic

Ocean; discovered by Cabot in 1497, occupied by the French in 1534, and ceded to Gt Britain by the Treaty of Paris in 1763; the Provinces of Canada were united under the title of the Dominion of Canada in 1867; capital, Ottawa; ~ *balsam*, oleo-resin obtained from the pine *Abies balsamea*, used for mounting microscope slides; ~ *goose*, wild goose (*Branta canadensis*) of N. America. **Canā'dian** *adj.* & *n.*

canaille (kanahē) *n.* Rabble. [Fr.]

cană'l *n.* 1. Duct in plant or animal body for food, liquid, air, etc. 2. Artificial watercourse for inland navigation or for irrigation. 3. (zool.) Prolongation of shell of certain molluscs for protection of respiratory tube. 4. One of the faint seasonal markings formerly thought to be visible on the planet Mars.

Cănalĕ'ttō. Giovanni Antonio Canal (1697–1768). Venetian painter; known esp. for his topographical works.

că'nalize *v.t.* 1. Furnish with canals; convert (river) into canal by embanking, straightening course, making locks, etc. 2. Direct (energies, wealth, etc.) into a particular course or channel. **cănalīzā'tion** *n.*

că'napé (-pĭ) *n.* Small biscuit, piece of pastry, or fried bread, on which savoury food is served. [Fr.]

cănar'd (*or* -ar') *n.* Absurd extravagant rumour or report; hoax. [Fr., = 'duck', 'false report']

Canarese: see KANARESE.

Canār'ȳ[1]. Island (*Grand* ~, *Gran Canaria*) off NW. coast of Africa; ~ *Islands*, *Canaries*, the group to which it belongs, in Spanish possession. [L *canaria* (*insula*) (isle) of dogs]

canār'ȳ[2] *n.* 1. (also ~ *sack*) Light sweet wine from the Canary Islands, resembling sherry. 2. Singing-bird (*Serinus canarius*), orig. brought from the Canary Islands and commonly kept in captivity; the wild canary, or serin, is greenish above and yellow below, but the cage-breed is mainly yellow (~ *yellow*); ~ *creeper*, yellow flowered creeper (*Tropaeolum peregrinum*); ~ *grass*, grass from the Canary Islands (*Phalaris canariensis*) seed of which (~ *seed*) is used for feeding cage-birds.

cană'sta *n.* Card-game, orig. from Uruguay, for 2–6 persons, played with 108 cards (2 standard 52-card packs and 4 jokers), combining features of rummy and pinochle; meld of 7 cards. [prob. as CANASTER]

cană'ster *n.* Tobacco prepared from dried leaves, coarsely broken. [orig. the rush basket container, f.

CANALETTO

Span. *canastra*, ult. f. Gk *kanastron*]

Că'nberra. Capital of the Commonwealth of Australia, built on land acquired in 1911 from New South Wales.

că'ncăn (-n-k-) *n.* High-kicking dance. [Fr.]

că'ncel *v.* Obliterate, annul, make void, countermand; neutralize, balance, make up for; (print.) suppress and reprint (sheet etc.); (mus., chiefly U.S.) resume natural pitch of note after sharpening or flattening; (arith. etc.) strike out (same factor) from numerator and denominator, from two sides of equation, etc.; (of items) neutralize or balance each other (also ~ *out*). **cancellā'tion** *n.* **că'ncel** *n.* (print.) Suppression and reprinting of page or leaf; the suppressed or substituted page or leaf; (mus., chiefly U.S.) sign (♮), = NATURAL *n.* 2.

că'ncer[1] *n.* Malignant tumour. **că'ncerous** *adj.* [L, = 'crab', f. resemblance of swollen veins round tumour to crab's limbs]

Că'ncer[2]. The Crab, a constellation; 4th sign (♋) of the zodiac, which the sun enters at the summer solstice; *Tropic of* ~, northern tropic, forming a tangent to the ecliptic at the first point of Cancer about 23° 28′ from the equator. **Căncēr'ian** *adj.* & *n.*

că'ncroid *adj.* Crab-like; like cancer. ~ *n.* Crustacean of crab family; disease like cancer.

c. and b. *abbrev.* Caught and bowled.

căndē'la *n.* (abbrev. cd) Unit of luminous intensity, the light emitted by $\frac{1}{600,000}$ of a square metre of a black body at the temperature (1773·5 °C) at which molten platinum solidifies, under a pressure of 101,325 newtons per square metre.

căndėla'brum (-lah-) *n.* (pl. *-bra*). Large, usu. branched, candlestick.

căndĕ'scence *n.* Bright glow, as of white-hot metal. **căndĕ'scent** *adj.* Glowing (as) with white heat.

că'ndĭd *adj.* Unbiased; not censorious; frank. **că'ndidlȳ** *adv.* **că'ndĭdnėss** *n.* [L *candidus* white]

că'ndĭdacȳ *n.* (U.S.) Candidature.

că'ndĭdate *n.* One who puts himself or is put forward for appointment to an office or honour; one who undergoes a test or examination; one thought likely to gain any position. [L *candidatus* one aspiring to an office (who was clothed in white toga)]

că'ndĭdature *n.* Standing for election, being a candidate.

că'ndied (-dĭd) *adj.*: see CANDY; (esp.) preserved by impregnating and coating with sugar.

că'ndle *n.* Cylinder of wax, tallow, etc., enclosing wick, for giving light; candle power; *ca'ndlelight*, light of candles; any artificial light; *ca'ndlepower*, illuminating power of electric lamp etc., formerly measured in terms of the light of a standard candle; *ca'ndlestick*, support for candle(s); *ca'ndlewick*, (material with raised usu. tufted pattern in) thick soft yarn.

Că'ndlemas (-lm-). Feast of the Purification of the Virgin Mary, 2 Feb.; a quarter-day in Scotland. [Mass celebrated with a great display of candles]

că'ndour (-d*er*) n. Fairness, impartiality; openness, frankness.

că'ndȳ *n*, 1. (also *sugar-*~) Crystallized sugar made by repeated boiling and slow evaporation. 2. (U.S.) Sweet; chocolate, toffee, etc. 3. *~-floss*, fluffy mass of spun sugar usu. on stick; ~ *stripe*, *-striped*, pattern(ed) in alternate stripes of white and colour. ~ *v.* Preserve by coating with candy; form into crystals. [Fr. *sucre candi*, f. Arab.-Pers. *qand* crystallized sugar-cane juice, ult. f. Sansk. *khand* broken crystallized sugar]

că'ndȳtŭft *n.* Herbaceous cruciferous plant of genus *Iberis*, with white, pink, or purple flowers in flat corymbs or 'tufts'. [*Candia* the island of Crete]

cāne *n.* Hollow jointed stem of giant reeds and grasses, or solid stem of slender palms, used as walking-stick or instrument of

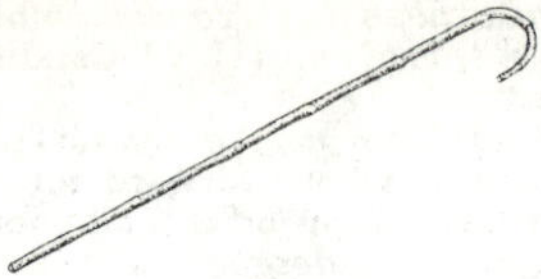

punishment etc.; stem of raspberry and similar plants; any slender walking-stick; ~*-brake*, (U.S.) tract of land thickly overgrown with canes; ~*-sugar*, sugar obtained from the sugar-cane as contrasted with beet-sugar. ~ *v.t.* Beat with cane; fit (seat of chair) with (plaited) cane. **că'nĭng** *n.*

căngue (-ng), **căng**, *n.* Heavy wooden frame or board formerly worn round neck as punishment in China. [Port. *canga* yoke]

că'nīne *adj.* Of, as of, a dog or dogs; ~ *tooth*, one of the four strong pointed teeth between incisors and molars, eye-tooth. ~ *n.* Canine tooth.

că'nion (-nyon) *n.* (pl., hist.) Close-fitting extensions of short stuffed breeches, covering thighs.

că'nĭster *n.* Small case or box, usu. of metal, for tea, shot, etc.; ~*-shot*, case-shot. [Gk *kanastron* wicker basket]

că'nker *n.* 1. Ulcerous disease of animals; disease of fruit-trees; (also ~*-worm*) caterpillar of a moth destroying leaves or buds. 2. Corrupting influence, rotten tendency. **că'nkerous** *adj.* **că'nker** *v.t.* Consume with canker; infect, corrupt. **că'nkered** (-kerd) *adj.* (esp.) Soured, malignant, crabbed. [as CANCER]

că'nna *n.* Monocotyledonous plant of genus *C*~ with bright yellow, red, or orange flowers and ornamental foliage, native of warm climates.

că'nnabĭs *n.* Hemp, esp. *C*~ *sativa* or *C. indica*; preparation of hemp-plant as drug; ~ *resin*, sticky resin produced by hemp-plant, containing the active principles.

Că'nnae. (It. *Canne*) Ancient town in Apulia (near mouth of modern river Ofanto), scene of a great defeat of the Romans by Hannibal in 216 B.C.

că'nnel *n.* (also ~ *coal*) Coal with high gas content which burns with smoky flame and can be lit by a match, formerly an important source of paraffin oil.

că'nnĭbal *n.* Person who eats human flesh; animal that eats its own species. ~ *adj.* Of, having, these habits, **că'nnĭbalism** *n.* **cănnĭbalĭ'stic** *adj.* [Span. *Canibales*, variant form of *Caribs*]

că'nnĭbalize *v.t.* Take parts from (machine) as spares for others.

că'nnĭkin *n.* Small can.

Că'nnĭng, George (1770–1827). British statesman and author; foreign secretary under Duke of Portland and prime minister in 1827.

că'nnon *n.* 1. (pl. usu. same) Piece of ordnance (hist.); gun of the kind that needs mounting; automatic shell-firing gun in aircraft. 2. (mech.) Hollow cylinder moving independently on shaft; watch-key barrel. 3. Smooth round bit (~*-bit*) for horse. 4. (billiards) Hitting of two balls successively by player's ball. 5. = CANON[1], 7. 6. ~*-ball*, projectile fired by cannon; ~*-bone*, large metacarpal or metatarsal bone in leg of horse etc. ~*-fodder*, (fig.) men regarded merely as material to be consumed in war; ~*-shell*, shell from aircraft's cannon. ~ *v.i.* Make cannon at billiards; come into collision, run or strike (obliquely) *against*, *into*, *with*.

cănnonā'de *n.* Continuous gunfire. ~ *v.* Fire continuously; bombard.

cannot: see CAN[2].

că'nnȳ *adj.* Shrewd; worldly-wise; thrifty; gentle, circumspect; sly, pawky. **că'nnĭlȳ** *adv.*

canoe' (-ōō) *n.* Small light keelless boat propelled by paddle(s). ~ *v.i.* Paddle or propel canoe; travel by canoe.

că'non[1] *n.* 1. Church decree; ~ *law*, ecclesiastical law as laid down in decrees of the pope and statutes of councils. 2. General rule, fundamental principle, axiom;

CANNON

standard of judgement or authority, test, criterion. 3. Collection or list of books of the Bible accepted by the Christian Churches as genuine and inspired; any set of books or works accepted as belonging to a particular author etc. 4. Portion of the Mass between Preface and Pater, containing the words of consecration. 5. (mus.) Composition in which the different parts take up the same subject one after another, in strict imitation. 6. (print.) Large size of type (48 point), equal to 4-line pica. 7. (also *cannon*) Metal loop or ear by which a bell is hung.

că′non[2] *n.* 1. (hist.; fem. *ca′nonėss*) Clerk living according to rule with others in clergy-house or in a house within the precinct or close of a cathedral or collegiate church. 2. (in Church of England) Member of cathedral chapter.

cañon: see CANYON.

canŏ′nĭcal *adj.* 1. Appointed by canon law; ~ *dress*, dress of clergy; ~ *hours*, hours appointed for prayer, for the solemnization of marriage, etc. 2. Included in the canon of Scripture. 3. Authoritative, standard, accepted. 4. (mus.) In canon form. 5. Of a cathedral chapter or a member of it. **canŏ′nĭcallў** *adj.* **canŏ′nĭcals** (-z) *n.pl.* Canonical dress.

că′nonĭst *n.* Canon lawyer.

că′nonīze *v.t.* Admit formally to calendar of saints; regard as a saint; sanction by authority of Church. **cănonīzā′tion** *n.*

că′nonrў *n.* Benefice, status, etc., of a canon.

canōō′dle *v.* (slang, orig. U.S.) Fondle, cuddle.

Canō′pĭc *adj.* Of the town of Çanopus; ~ *vase*, Egyptian vase with a lid in the form of a human head, used for holding the entrails of embalmed bodies.

Canō′pus. 1. (Gk myth.) Helmsman of Menelaus who died in Egypt on the return from Troy. 2. Town in ancient Egypt named after him. 3. (astron.) Bright star Alpha in the southern constellation Argo.

că′nopў *n.* Covering suspended or held throne, bed person, etc.; part of parachute which fills with air when released from its packing; (fig.) any overhanging shelter; the sky etc. ~ *v.t.* Supply, be, a canopy to. [Gk *kōnōpeion* mosquito net (*kōnōps* gnat)]

canōr'ous *adj.* Melodious, resonant.

Canŏ'ssa. Castle in Tuscany where in 1077 the Emperor Henry IV submitted to the penance and humiliation imposed on him by Pope Gregory VII; hence, *go to* ~, make a humiliating submission.

cănt[1] *n.* Bevel, oblique face, of crystal, bank, etc.; sloping or tilted position. ~ *v.* 1. Bevel; slope, slant, tilt. 2. Throw, jerk. 3. (naut.) Swing round.

cănt[2] *n.* Jargon of class, profession, sect, etc.; temporary catchwords; words used for fashion without being meant; unreal use of words implying piety; hypocrisy. ~ *v.i.* Use cant; (her.) *canting arms, coat*, etc., arms etc. containing allusion to name of bearer.

can't: see CAN[2].

Cant. *abbrev.* Canticles.

Cantab. *abbrev.* Cantabrigian; *Cantabrigiensis* (L, = of Cambridge (University)).

căntabĭ'lė (-tah-) *adj.* & *n.* (Music) in a smooth flowing style, song-like, melodious. [It.]

Căntabrĭ'gian *adj.* & *n.* (Member) of Cambridge University.

că'ntaloup, -oupe (-ōōp) *n.* Small, round, ribbed, delicate-flavoured variety of musk-melon with reddish-orange flesh. [*Cantalupo*, castle near Rome]

căntă'nkerous *adj.* Cross-grained, quarrelsome. **căntă'nkeroușlў** *adv.* **căntă'nkerousnėss** *n.*

cănta'ta (-ah-) *n.* Choral work, either a short oratorio or a short lyric drama set to music but not intended for acting.

căntee'n *n.* 1. Provision and liquor shop in barracks, camp, etc., refreshment room in factory or office building. 2. Box of cooking and table utensils for camp or expedition; box or case with compartments holding table cutlery. 3. Soldier's water-vessel or mess-tin.

că'nter *n.* Easy gallop. ~ *v.* Go, make (horse) go, at this pace. [shortened f. CANTERBURY[1] gallop]

Că'nterburў[1]**.** City in Kent,

CANTERBURY CATHEDRAL

on river Stour, see of the archbishop and primate of all England; the shrine of Thomas à Becket (St. Thomas of Canterbury), who was murdered in the cathedral, was in pre-Reformation times a favourite object of pilgrimage; ~ *bell*, kind of campanula (f. bells of pilgrims' horses); ~ *gallop*, *pace*, *trot*, etc., the easy pace of the mounted pilgrims to Canterbury.

că'nterburў[2] *n.* Stand with light partitions to hold music etc. [f. CANTERBURY[1]]

Că'nterburў[3]. Province of South Island, New Zealand; ~ *lamb*, lamb or mutton imported from New Zealand; (N.Z.) grade of lamb or mutton.

cănthă'rĭdēs (-z) *n.pl.* Dried Spanish flies, *Lytta* (*Cantharis*) *vesicatoria*, formerly used in medicine.

că'ntĭcle *n.* Hymn; one of the hymns, mostly taken from the Scriptures, used in church services, as the *Benedicite*, *Nunc Dimittis*, *Te Deum*; *Canticles*, Song of Solomon.

că'ntĭlēver *n.* (archit., eng.) Beam or girder fixed at one end to a pier or wall and free at the other; long bracket; ~ *bridge*, bridge composed of girders projecting from piers and meeting midway between them or carrying intermediate sections. **că'ntĭlēvered** (-verd) *adj.* Projecting like, supported by, a cantilever.

că'ntle *n.* Piece, slice, cut off; hind-bow of saddle.

că'ntō *n.* (pl. *-ōs*). Division of long poem.

că'nton[1] (*or* -tŏ'n) *n.* 1. Subdivision of country; one of the sovereign States of the Swiss federation. 2. (her.) Square division less than a quarter in upper (usu. dexter) corner of shield, flag, etc. **că'ntonal** *adj.* **cănton** *v.t.* 1. (-tŏ'n) Divide into cantons. 2. (-tōō'n) Quarter (troops).

Căntŏ'n[2]. City of S. China. **Căntonē'se** (-z) *adj.* & *n.* (Native, inhabitant, dialect) of Canton.

cănto'nment (-ōōn-) *n.* Lodging assigned to troops; military station.

că'ntŏr *n.* Precentor. **căntŏr'ĭal** *adj.* Of the precentor; of his side of the choir (see foll.).

căntŏr'ĭs *adj.* (mus.) To be sung by the precentor's side of the choir (usu. the N.; opp. DECANI, dean's side). [L]

Cantuar. *abbrev.* (Archbishop) of Canterbury (replacing surname in his signature).

Canŭ'ck *n.* (U.S. slang) Canadian, esp. French Canadian; Canadian horse or pony.

Canū'te, Cnut (-ōōt). Danish king of England, 1016–35.

că'nvas *n.* 1. Strong unbleached plain-woven cloth of hemp, flax, or other coarse yarn, for sails, tents, etc.; open kind of this, usu. flax or cotton, for tapestry, embroidery, etc. 2. (also *artists'* ~) Canvas prepared for painting on by coating with size, white lead, etc.; hence, a painting, a picture (lit. and fig.). 3. Canvas covering over ends of racing-boat. 4. *ca'nvas-back*, N. Amer. duck, *Aythya valisineria*, (from the colour of its grey-and-white mottled back feathers).

că'nvass *v.* 1. Discuss thoroughly. 2. Solicit votes, solicit votes from; ascertain sentiments or opinion of; ask custom of. **că'nvasser** *n.* **că'nvass** *n.* Canvassing for votes; (U.S.) scrutiny of votes. [f. CANVAS, the original sense being 'toss in a sheet etc.', and hence 'shake up, agitate', etc.]

că'nyon, cañon (kă'nyon) *n.* Deep gorge or ravine with steep sides formed by river cutting through soft rock, characteristic of Rocky Mountains, Sierra Nevada, and western plateaux of N. America. [Span. *cañon* tube, f. L *canna* reed]

Caodaʹĭsm (kah-ōdī-) *n.* Religion combining elements of Buddhism, Taoism, Confucianism, and Christianity, founded in Cochin-China in 1926. **Caoda'ĭst** *n.* [Vietnamese *Cao Dai* great house]

caoutchouc (kow'chŏŏk) *n.* Indiarubber (see RUBBER[1] *n.* 3). [Fr., f. Carib]

căp[1] *n.* 1. Covering for the head, esp. close-fitting and usu. soft and brimless; ~ *in hand*, (fig.) humbly, in supplication. 2. Special head-dress denoting rank, occupation, etc.; one worn as sign of inclusion in sports team; hence, one who obtains such a cap; ~ *and bells*, jester's insignia; ~ *of liberty*, conical cap given to Roman slave on emancipation, later (esp. French) Republican symbol. 3. Mortar-board. 4. Cap-like covering, as of mushroom, toe of shoe, etc. 5. (also *percussion* ~), Cap-shaped piece of copper lined with fulminating composition, for igniting explosive in firearms etc.; paper percussion cap of toy pistol. 6. (naut.) Pierced block of wood for joining two masts etc., end to end. 7. (also ~*-money*) Money collected at a hunt from those present who are not hunt-subscribers. **că'pful** *n.* **căp** *v.t.* 1. Put cap upon; confer cap on as symbol of inclusion in team; (Sc. universities) confer degree on. 2. Form or serve as cap of; overlie. 3. Surpass; follow with another (story etc.).

cap² *abbrev.* (pl. *caps*). Capital letter.

cap. *abbrev.* *Caput* (L, = chapter).

cāpăbĭ'lĭtў *n.* Power *of*, *for*, *to*; undeveloped faculty.

cā'pable *adj.* 1. Susceptible. 2. ~ *of*, having the power or fitness for; wicked enough for. 3. Able, gifted, competent. **cā'pablў** *adv.*

capā'cious (-sh*us*) *adj.* Roomy. **capā'ciouslў** *adv.* **capā'ciousnėss** *n.*

capă'cĭtance *n.* (elect.) Ratio of change in electric charge to corresp. change in potential; ability to store an electric charge.

capă'cĭtāte *v.t.* Render capable; make legally competent.

capă'cĭtor *n.* Device which stores electricity during part of an operation; condenser.

capă'cĭtў *n.* 1. Ability to contain or receive; cubic content, volume; *measure of* ~, measure used for liquids, grain, etc. 2. (elect.) = CAPACITANCE. 3. (fig.) Mental power; faculty, talent; capability, opportunity, *to*, *of*, etc.; relative character (as *in his* ~ *as critic*); legal competency. 4. Maximum number or amount that can be contained, produced, etc.; *to* ~, to the limit.

căp-à-pie (-pē), *adv.* (in arming) From head to foot.

capă'rĭson *n.* Horses' trappings; equipment, outfit. ~ *v.t.* Put caparison upon.

cāpe¹ *n.* Short sleeveless cloak, either as separate garment or as fixed or detachable part of cloak or coat. **cāped** (-pt) *adj.*

cāpe² *n.* Promontory.

Cāpe³, The. The Cape of Good Hope; ~*-cart*, two-wheeled horse-drawn vehicle of S. Africa; ~ *Coloured*, S. African(s) of mixed black and white descent; ~ *Dutch*, early form of Afrikaans; ~ *gooseberry*, species of *Physalis* with edible fruits; ~ *of Good Hope*, promontory near southern extremity of Africa; ~ *Province*, province of the Republic of S. Africa (capital, Cape Town); *ca'peskin*, soft leather made from S. Afr. sheepskin.

Čă'pěk (ch-), Karel (1890–1938). Czech writer; author of 'R.U.R.' and other plays etc.

Capě'lla. Star of first magnitude in the constellation Auriga.

cā'per¹ *n.* Bramble-like S. European shrub, *Capparis spinosa*; (pl.) its flower-buds, pickled for use in sauces; *English* ~*s*, pickled seed-vessels of garden nasturtium.

cā'per² *n.* Capering movement. *cut a* ~, caper. ~ *v.i.* Dance or leap merrily or fantastically; prance as a horse.

căpercai'llie (-lyĭ) **-kai'lzie** *n.* Wood-grouse, *Tetrao urogallus*, the largest European gallinaceous bird, formerly native to the Scottish Highlands, where it was reintroduced from Scandinavia after becoming extinct. [Gael. *capull coille* horse of the wood]

Capér'nāum. City of ancient Israel by the Sea of Galilee.

Căpet (-ā). French dynasty founded by Hugo Capet in 987, which ruled until 1328, when it was succeeded by the House of Valois; *Louis* ~, name given to

Louis XVI when he was tried before the Convention in 1793.

Cāpe Town. Capital city of Cape Province and legislative capital of the Republic of S. Africa.

Cāpe Verde I'slands (vār'dā, ilandz). Two groups of islands, Windward and Leeward, off the W. coast of Africa, formerly in Portuguese possession; independent 1975.

capi'llarȳ *adj.* 1. Of, or resembling, hair. 2. Having very minute or hair-like internal diameter. 3. Of capillaries. 4. ~ *attraction*, effect of surface tension of liquid that wets material of fine tube in raising liquid inside tube to a level higher than that outside; ~ *repulsion*, corresponding effect of surface tension of liquid that does not wet tube in depressing level inside tube. ~ *n.* One of the hair-like vessels joining arteries and veins in which the blood is brought into effective contact with the tissues.

că'pĭtal[1] *n.* Head of pillar or pilaster, wider than the shaft and usu. ornamented.

că'pĭtal[2] *adj.* 1. Involving loss of life; punishable by death; ~ *punishment*, punishment by death for a crime. 2. Standing at the head; ~ *letter*, one of the form and size used at beginning of name, sentence, etc., majuscule. 3. Chief; important, leading, first-class; ~ *ship*, battleship or battle cruiser. 4. (colloq.) Excellent, first-rate. 5. Original, principal, of money capital. ~ *n.* 1. Chief town of county, country, etc., usu. the seat of government or administrative centre. 2. Stock of company etc. with which they enter business and on which dividends are paid; (econ.) accumulated wealth of individual, community, etc., used as fund for starting fresh production; wealth of any kind used in producing more wealth; *make ~ (out) of*, (fig.) turn to account or advantage, esp. in argument; ~ *gain*, profit from sale of investments or property; hence ~ *gains tax*; ~ *goods*, goods for use in producing commodities, opp. *consumer goods*; ~ *sum*, amount payable by insurance company in specified contingency. 3. Capitalists or employers of labour collectively. 4. Capital letter.

că'pĭtalism (*or* kapĭ'-) *n.* Economic system by which ownership of capital or wealth, the production and distribution of goods, and the reward of labour are entrusted to, and effected by, private enterprise. **că'pĭtalist** *n.* Private owner or holder of capital, esp. in large amounts; one who has capital available for employment in finance or industry. **căpĭtalĭ'stĭc** *adj.* **că'pĭtalīze** *v.t.* Convert into, use as, capital; compute or realize present value of (income); *capitalized value*, value of asset calculated by estimating future income and offsetting this against cost measured by prevailing rate of interest. **căpĭtalīzā'tion** *n.*

că'pĭtāte *adj.* Head-shaped; ~ *bone*, largest and central bone of the carpus.

căpĭtā'tion *n.* (Levying of) tax or fee of so much a head; (attrib.) of so much a head.

Că'pĭtol. 1. Great national temple of ancient Rome, dedicated to Jupiter Optimus Maximus, on the Saturnian or Tarpeian (afterwards called Capitoline) Hill; the hill itself. 2. Building in Washing-

CAPITOL, Washington

ton occupied by the Congress of the United States; in many States, the state-house, building in which State legislature meets.

Că'pĭtolīne *adj.* Of the CAPITOL (sense 1). ~ *n.* Capitoline Hill.

capĭ'tūlar *adj.* 1. Of a cathedral chapter. 2. (physiol.) Of a terminal protuberance of bone.

capĭ'tūlarȳ *n.* Collection of ordinances, esp. those made on their own authority by the Frankish kings.

capĭ'tūlāte *v.i.* Surrender on terms.

capĭtūlā'tion *n.* 1. Statement of heads of subject, summary. 2. Agreement, conditions. 3. Surrender on terms, agreement containing such terms.

capĭ'tūlum *n.* 1. (physiol.) Protuberance of bone received into a hollow portion of another bone. 2. (bot.) Close head of sessile flowers 3. (zool.) Part of a barnacle born by and forming a head to the peduncle.

cā'pon *n.* Castrated cock. **cā'ponīze** *v.t.*

că'poral *n.* Kind of French tobacco.

capŏ't *n.* (piquet) Winning of all tricks by one player. ~ *v.t.* Score a capot against.

Căppadō'cia (-sh*a*). Ancient region of eastern Asia Minor. **Căppadō'cian** *adj.* & *n.*

caprĭ'ccĭō (-ch-) *n.* Lively, usu. short, musical composition. [see CAPRICE]

caprĭ'ce (-ēs) *n.* Unaccountable change of mind or conduct; fancy, freak; inclination to these; (mus.) capriccio. [It. *capriccio* sudden start, app. f. *capra* goat]

caprĭ'cious (-sh*u*s) *adj.* Guided by whim; inconstant, irregular, incalculable. **caprĭ'ciouslȳ** *adv.* **caprĭ'ciousnėss** *n.*

Că'pricorn. The Goat, a constellation; 10th sign (♑) of the zodiac, which the sun enters at the winter solstice; *Tropic of* ~, southern tropic, forming a tangent to the ecliptic at the first point of Capricorn, about 23° 28′ from the equator. [L *caper* goat, *cornu* horn]

că'priōle *n.* 1. Leap or caper. 2. (in manège) Horse's high leap and kick without advancing. ~ *v.i.* Make capriole.

caps. *abbrev.* Capital letters.

Că'psĭan *adj.* & *n.* (Of) a Stone Age culture of N. Africa. [f. *Capsa* (Gafsa), Tunisia]

că'psĭcum *n.* Tropical plant of genus *C*~ with very pungent capsule and seeds; fruit of these, used as condiment and as a digestive stimulant and carminative.

căpsī'ze *v.* Upset, overturn, esp. on water.

că'pstan *n.* Revolving barrel, worked by men walking round and pushing horizontal levers, or by steam etc., for winding-in cable, hoisting sails, etc.

că'psūle *n.* 1. (physiol.) Membranous envelope. 2. (bot.) Dry seed-case opening when ripe by parting of valves. 3. (med.) Gelatine envelope enclosing drug or other medicinal substance. 4. (chem.) Shallow saucer formerly used for evaporating etc. 5. Metallic cap for bottle etc. 6. Detachable nose-cone of rocket or cabin of spacecraft for carrying instruments or astronauts. ~ *adj.* Compact, concise; summary. **că'psular** *adj.* **că'psulīze** *v.t.* Condense (information etc.) into compact form.

Capt. *abbrev.* Captain.

că'ptain (-ĭn) *n.* 1. Chief, leader; great soldier, strategist, experienced commander. 2. (mil.) Army officer, of rank next below major and above lieutenant, normally commanding company or troop; (nav.) officer of rank between commander and commodore or rear-admiral, officer commanding warship; master of merchant ship; pilot of civil aircraft. 3. Leader of team in game or sport. **că'ptaincȳ** *n.* **că'ptain** *v.t.* Be captain of; lead.

că'ption *n.* 1. Legal arrest. 2. (law) Certificate attached to or written on document. 3. (orig. U.S.) Heading of chapter, section, newspaper article, etc.; wording under illustration; title, descriptive passage, dialogue, etc., inserted in (silent) cinema picture. ~ *v.t.* Provide with caption.

că'ptious (-sh*u*s) *adj.* 1. Fallacious, sophistical. 2. Fond of taking exception; trying to catch people in their words. **că'ptiouslў** *adv.* **că'ptiousnėss** *n.*

că'ptĭvāte *v.t.* Fascinate, charm. **căptĭvā'tion** *n.*

că'ptĭve *adj.* & *n.* (Person, animal) taken prisoner, kept in confinement, unable to escape; (of, like) prisoner; ~ *balloon*, one moored to the ground. **căptĭ'vĭtў** *n.* (esp.) *the C~*, that of the Jews in Babylon in 6th c. B.C.

că'ptor *n.* (fem. *că'ptrėss*) One who takes a captive or prize.

că'pture *n.* Capturing; thing or person captured. ~ *v.t.* Take prisoner; seize as prize; (geog.) divert (stream) into another by headwater erosion; (phys., of atomic particle, atom, or nucleus) acquire an additional particle; (astron., of star or planet) bring (object) within its gravitational field.

capu'che (-o͞osh) *n.* Hood of cloak, esp. sharp-pointed one worn by Capuchins.

Că'pūchĭn *n.* 1. Franciscan friar of the new rule of 1528, so called from the capuche first adopted in 1525. 2. Woman's garment of cloak and hood. 3. ~ *monkey*, Amer. monkey of genus *Cebus*, with black hair like a cowl at back of head; ~ *pigeon*, variety of jacobin pigeon with inverted feathers like a hood or cowl at back of head.

căpўbar'a *n.* Large tailless rodent (*Hydrochoerus capybara*), allied to guinea-pig, living about the rivers of tropical S. America.

car *n.* Wheeled vehicle, (poet.) chariot; (in U.K. now usu. word for) motor-car; (U.S.) any railway carriage or van (so in U.K. but with specification, as *dining-~*, *sleeping-~*); part of airship or balloon holding passengers; (U.S.) lift-cage; *car'man*, driver of van, carrier. ~ *port*, roofed open shelter for motor-car; *~-sick*, sick from motion of motor-car; *~-sickness* (*n.*).

cărabĭneer', **-ier'** *n.* Soldier who carries a carbine; *the Carabiniers*, a regiment of the Royal Scots Dragoon Guards.

că'racal *n.* Kind of lynx, *Felis caracal*, of N. Africa and SW. Asia, with reddish fur and black-tipped ears and tail; pelt of this animal. [Turk. *kara* black *kulak* ear]

Cărăcă'lla. Marcus Aurelius Antoninus Bassianus (188–217), Roman emperor 211–17.

că'racōle *n.* Horseman's half-wheel to right or left, succession of such turns to right and left alternately. ~ *v.i.* Execute caracole(s); caper.

că'racul, k- (-ko͝ol) *n.* Asian sheep whose young have dark curled fleece; fur made from or resembling this.

cara'fe (-ahf) *n.* Glass bottle for water or wine at table. [Fr.,

ult. f. Arab. *ġarrāfa* drinking vessel]

că'ramĕl (*or* -ml) *n.* Brown substance obtained by heating sugar or syrup and used for colouring spirits etc.; brown colour of this; soft toffee made with caramel.

că'ramėlīze *v.* Make (sugar) into caramel; (of sugar) turn brown when heated.

că'rapāce *n.* Upper body-shell of tortoises and crustaceans.

că'rat *n.* 1. Measure of weight, about $3\frac{1}{5}$ grains, for precious stones. 2. Measure of $\frac{1}{24}$ in. stating the fineness of gold; if e.g. the mass contains 22 parts of gold and two of alloy it is 22 carats fine, or 22-carat gold. [Fr., f. It. *carato*, f. Gk *keration* fruit of carob]

căravă'n (*or* kă'-) *n.* 1. Company of merchants, pilgrims, etc., in the East or in N. Africa, travelling together for security, esp. through desert. 2. Covered cart or carriage; house on wheels of gipsy, travelling showman, camping-party, etc. ~ *v.i.* Travel, live, in a caravan. [Pers. *kārwān*]

cărav̆ă'nserai (-ī *or* -ĭ) *n.* Eastern inn with large courtyard where caravans put up.

că'ravel *n.* (hist., also *carvel*) Small light fast ship, chiefly Spanish or Portuguese of 15th–17th centuries.

că'raway *n.* Umbelliferous plant, *Carum carvi*, with small aromatic carminative fruits, ~ *seeds*, used in cakes, etc.

car'bīde *n.* Compound of carbon with a metal; esp. *calcium* ~: see CALCIUM, and *iron* ~, (Fe_3C) an important constituent of steel.

car'bīne *n.* Kind of short rifle orig. introduced for cavalry use.

carbohȳ'drate *n.* One of a group of compounds of carbon, hydrogen, and oxygen in which the last two elements are present in the same proportions as in water; including sugars, starches, and cellulose and forming an important part of the structure of plant material and of the food of man and other animals; any of various other compounds of a different formula but closely related to the above substances, e.g. *rhamnose* ($C_6H_{12}O_5$).

carbŏ'lic *adj.* ~ *acid*: see PHENOL.

car'bon *n.* 1. (chem.) Element occurring in two crystalline forms (diamond and graphite) and an amorphous form (charcoal), and in combination in all organic compounds; symbol C, at. no. 6, at. wt 12·011. 2. (elect.) Rod of carbon used in arc-lamps. 3. Carbon paper; carbon copy. 4. ~ *copy*, copy made with carbon paper; (fig.) exact copy; ~ *cycle*, (biol.) cycle in which carbon dioxide is absorbed from the atmosphere by plants and replaced mainly by respiration of plants and animals and by decay of organic matter; (astron.) cycle of thermonuclear reactions in which carbon acts as a catalyst in the conversion of hydrogen into helium, the energy released being held to be the source of that radiated by sun and stars; ~ *dioxide*, compound (CO_2) of carbon with oxygen, a colourless odourless gas formed by combustion of carbon, breathed out by animals, formed during fermentation, etc.; ~ *14*, long-living radioactive isotope of mass-number 14, the regular decay-rate of which makes RADIOCARBON dating possible; ~ *lamp*, electric lamp with a carbon filament; ~ *monoxide*, highly poisonous inflammable colourless odourless gas (CO), formed by the incomplete combustion of carbon or carbon compounds, as in charcoal stoves, petrol engines, etc.; ~ *paper*, thin paper, coated on one side with a coloured wax preparation, which when it is inserted between two sheets of paper causes anything written on the upper sheet to appear also on the lower one.

carbonā'ceous (-shus) *adj.* Of, like, coal or charcoal; consisting of or containing carbon.

carbonā'dō *n.* Dark opaque variety of diamond found in Brazil, used as an abrasive etc.

Carbonar'ī *n.pl.* Secret republican association formed in the kingdom of Naples during the French occupation under Murat in the early 19th c. [It., = 'charcoal-burners', name of the society]

car'bonate *n.* Salt of carbonic acid. **car'bonāte** *v.t.* Form into a carbonate; aerate.

carbŏ'nic *adj.* Of carbon; ~ *acid*, compound (H_2CO_3) of carbon dioxide and water; ~ *acid gas*, old name for carbon dioxide.

carboni'ferous *adj.* Producing coal; *C*~, (geol.) of the period or system of the Upper Palaeozoic between Devonian and Permian, containing workable coal in at least three continents. **Carboni'ferous** *n.* Carboniferous period or system.

car'bonīze *v.t.* Reduce to charcoal or coke by burning off superfluous material. **carbonīzā'tion** *n.*

cârborŭ'ndum *n.* SILICON carbide. [trade-name]

câr'boy *n.* Large globular wicker-covered glass bottle for holding acids or other corrosive liquids. [Pers. *ḳarāba* large flagon]

câr'buncle *n.* 1. Red semiprecious stone (formerly, any of several kinds; now, cabochon garnet, an iron-aluminium-silicate, usu. hollowed to allow colour to be seen). 2. (med.) Infective gangrene of subcutaneous tissues caused by invasion of staphylococci; (pop.) red spot or pimple on face. **carbŭ'ncūlar, câr'bŭncled** (-ld) *adjs.*

cârbūrā'tion *n.* Process of charging air with hydrocarbon fuel in finely divided liquid form.

câr'būrėt *v.t.* Combine chemically with carbon.

cârbūrĕ'ttor, -er *n.* (in petrol engines) Apparatus for impregnating air with fine particles of fuel and thus preparing the explosive mixture for the cylinders.

câr'būrīze *v.t.* Cause carbon to penetrate (surface of solid steel) in order to harden it.

câr'cass, câr'case *n.* 1. Dead body (of human body now only in contempt or ridicule); (butchering, cookery) dead body of beast or bird without head, limbs, or offal. 2. Mere body, dead or alive. 3. Worthless remains; skeleton, framework (of house, ship, pneumatic tyre, etc.).

cârcĭ'nogėn *n.* Cancer-producing substance or agent. **cârcinogĕ'nĭc** *adj.*

cârcinō'ma *n.* (pl. *-ata*). (path.) Cancer, esp. of epithelial origin.

Card. *abbrev.* Cardinal.

card[1] *n.* Toothed instrument, wire brush, or wire-set rubber or vulcanite strip, for combing wool, flax, cotton, hemp, etc., raising nap on cloth etc. ~ *v.t.* Prepare (wool, tow, etc.) for spinning by combing out impurities and straightening the fibres with cards.

card[2] *n.* 1. Thin pasteboard; small, usu. oblong, piece of this, or of thick paper, used for various purposes, as for greetings or invitation or programme or race-meeting etc. 2. (also *playing-~*) One of a

PLAYING CARDS

pack of small oblong pieces of pasteboard used in playing games, consisting (except in some special games) of 52 cards divided into 4 suits; (pl.) card-playing; game(s) with cards; *on the ~s*, (fig.) likely, possible. 3. Document, esp. that held by delegate of trade union meeting etc., representing number of his constituents (so ~ *vote*: see below); (pl.) set of documents of insurance etc. for employee, held by employer; *ask for, be given*, etc. *one's ~s*, ask, be told, to leave one's employment. 4. Odd, original, or eccentric person. 5. *car'dboard*, pasteboard for cutting cards from, making boxes, etc.; ~ *case*, case for carrying visiting-cards; ~ *catalogue*, catalogue with items entered on separate cards; ~ *index*, index recorded on separate cards; (*v.t.*) make card index of; *~-sharper*, one who makes a trade of cheating at cards; ~ *tray*, tray for holding visitors' cards; ~ *vote*, system by which vote of each delegate to a meeting (e.g. of trade unions) counts for the number of his constituents.

câr'damom *n.* Spice consisting of seed-capsules of various species of the E. Ind. and Chinese genera *Amomum* and *Elettaria*, used as a stomachic and in curries etc.

câr'dan *adj.* ~ *joint*, (eng.) joint between two shafts enabling one to be driven by the other at varying angles, universal joint; ~ *shaft*, shaft with cardan joint at one or both ends. [Geronimo *Cardano* (1501–76), Italian mathematician]

cār'dĭăc *adj*. 1. Of the heart; ~ *murmur*, abnormal heart-sound heard in auscultation. 2. (anat.) Of, adjoining, the upper orifice of the stomach. ~ *n*. Heart-stimulant, cordial.

Cār'dĭff. Seaport in South Glamorgan, and capital city of Wales.

cār'dĭgan[1] *n*. Knitted woollen etc. jacket with or without sleeves. [f. 7th Earl of *Cardigan*, distinguished in the Crimean War]

Cār'dĭgan[2] *n*. Variety of Welsh corgi with long tail. [town in SW. Wales]

Cār'dĭganshire. Former county on W. seaboard of Wales, since April 1974 part of Dyfed.

cār'dĭnal *adj*. 1. On which something hinges; fundamental, important; ~ *number*, number which answers the question 'how many' (*one*, *two*, *three*, etc.); ~ *point*, any of the four chief points of the compass; *half-~ point*, point half-way between two of these; ~ *virtue*, in scholastic philosphy, one of the four 'natural' virtues, justice, prudence, temperance, and fortitude, as distinct from the 'theological' virtues, faith, hope, and charity; sometimes, the natural and the theological virtues. 2. Of the colour of a cardinal's robes, scarlet. **cār'dĭnallў** *adv*. **cārdĭnal** *n*. 1. (*C~*) One of the ecclesiastical princes of the R.C. Church who constitute the Sacred College, and whose duty it is to elect the Pope. 2. (hist.) Woman's cloak, orig. of scarlet cloth with hood. 3. (also ~ *grosbeak*) N. Amer. crested grosbeak, *Richmondena cardinalis*, with scarlet plumage. 4. ~ *flower*, N. Amer. flower, the scarlet lobelia; ~ *red*, bright scarlet-red colour, from the colour of a cardinal's robes; ~*'s hat*: see HAT. **cār'dĭnalate, cār'dĭnalship** *ns*.

cārdio- *prefix*. Of the heart.

cārdōō'n *n*. Composite culinary vegetable, *Cynara cardunculus*, allied to the globe artichoke.

cāre *n*. (Occasion for) solicitude, anxiety; serious attention; heed, caution, pains; charge, protection; thing to be done or seen to; (also *child ~*) esp., care by local authority of children temporarily deprived of normal home life; *car'efree*, free from anxiety; *car'etaker*, person hired to take charge, as of house during owner's absence, of school or factory buildings, of empty shop, etc.; *caretaker government*, temporary government; *car'eworn*, worn by anxiety and trouble. ~ *v.i.* Feel concern or interest *for*, *about*; feel regard, deference, affection *for*, be concerned *whether*, etc.; be willing or wishful *to*; ~ *for*, look after.

caree'n *v*. Turn (ship) on one side for cleaning, caulking, etc.; (cause to) heel over. **caree'nage** *n*.

career' *n*. 1. Swift course; impetus. 2. Course or progress through life, esp. when publicly conspicuous or successful; development and success of party, principle, etc.; course of professional life or employment, way of making livelihood. ~ *v.i.* Go swiftly or wildly.

career'ĭst *n*. Person (esp. holder of public or responsible office) who is mainly intent on personal advancement.

cār'eful (-ārf-) *adj*. Painstaking, watchful, cautious; done with, showing, care. **cār'efullў** *adv*. **cār'efulnėss** *n*.

cār'elėss (-ārl-) *adj*. Unconcerned, light-hearted; inattentive, negligent, thoughtless; inaccurate. **cār'elėsslў** *adv*. **cār'elėssnėss** *n*.

carĕ'ss *n*. Fondling touch, kiss; blandishment. ~ *v.t.* Bestow caress(es) on; pet, make much of.

că'rėt *n*. Mark (‸) placed below line in writing to indicate place of omission. [L, = 'is wanting']

cār'gō *n*. Ship's freight.

Cār'ĭa. Ancient province of Asia Minor. **Cār'ĭan** *adj*. & *n*.

Că'rĭb *n*. One of the native people who occupied the southern islands of the W. Indies at their discovery; their language.

Cărĭbbē'an *adj*. ~ *Sea*, sea lying between the Antilles and the mainland of Central and S. America. ~ *n*. Caribbean Sea.

că'ribou (-o͞o) *n.* N. Amer. reindeer.

că'ricatūre *n.* Grotesque or ludicrous representation of person or thing by over-emphasis on characteristic or striking features. ~ *v.t.* Represent in caricature. **că'ricatūrist** *n.*

câr'ies (-z; *or* -ĭēz) *n.* Decay (of teeth or bones). **câr'ious** *adj.* Decayed.

că'rillon (-lyon) *n.* Set of bells sounded either from keyboard or mechanically; air played on these; instrument or part of organ imitating bells.

cari'na (-rē-) *n.* (bot., zool.) Structure in form of keel or ridge. **că'rĭnātėd** *adj.* Having a keel-like part. **cărinā'tion** *n.*

câr'king *adj.* Burdensome, oppressive.

câr1, câr1e *n.* (Sc.) Man, fellow.

câr'line *n.* (Sc.) Old woman.

Carliol. *abbrev.* (Bishop) of Carlisle (replacing surname in his signature).

Câr'lism *n.* Support of Don Carlos, 2nd son of Charles IV of Spain, and his heirs, as the legitimate successors of Ferdinand VII (d. 1833), to the exclusion of Ferdinand's daughter and her heirs. **Câr'list** *n.*

Carlovingian: see CAROLINGIAN.

Câr'low (-ō). County of Leinster.

Câr'lton Clŭb. London club in St. James's St., the chief conservative club in England, founded 1831 by the Duke of Wellington and his political associates.

Cârlȳ'le, Thomas (1795–1881). Scottish literary critic, historian, and writer on social and political problems. **Cârlȳ'lism** *n.*

Carmâr'thenshire (-dh-). Former county in S. Wales, since April 1974 part of Dyfed.

Câr'mel. Mountain in Israel projecting into sea SW. of Haifa; scene of Elijah's contest with the priests of Baal (1 Kings 18: 19–40), whence its Arabic name Jebel Mar Elias.

Câr'mėlite *adj.* & *n.* (Member) of order of mendicant friars (White Friars) originating in a colony founded in the 12th c. on Mount Carmel by Berthold, a Calabrian; (member) of an order of nuns organized on similar lines.

câr'minative *adj.* & *n.* (Drug) curing flatulence.

câr'mīne *n.* & *adj.* (Coloured like, colour of) a crimson-red pigment obtained from cochineal.

Carms. *abbrev.* Carmarthenshire.

câr'nage *n.* Great slaughter.

câr'nal *adj.* Sensual; sexual; worldly. **câr'nalism, cârnăl'ity** *ns.* **câr'nallȳ** *adv.*

cârnā'tion[1] *n.* 1. Light rosy pink or bright red colour. 2. Flesh tints in a painting; the representation of naked flesh. ~*adj.* Rose-pink.

cârnā'tion[2] *n.* Any of the cultivated kinds of clove-pink derived from *Dianthus caryophyllus.*

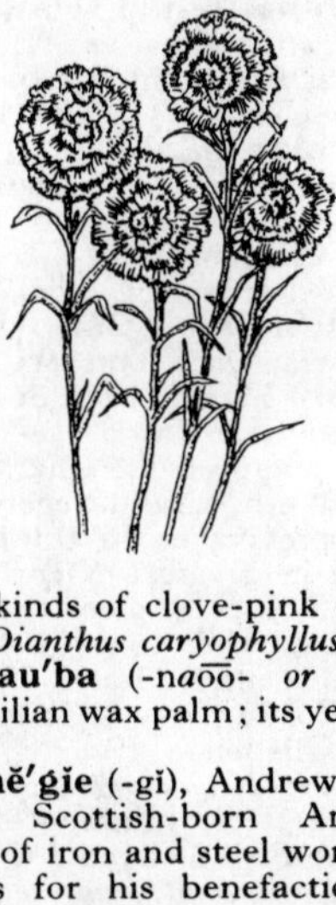

cârnau'ba (-nao͞o- *or* -now-) *n.* Brazilian wax palm; its yellowish wax.

Cârnĕ'gie (-gĭ), Andrew (1835–1919). Scottish-born American owner of iron and steel works etc., famous for his benefactions for libraries, educational work, etc.

cârnē'lian *n.* = CORNELIAN.

cârnet (-nā) *n.* Permit, esp. one allowing motor vehicle etc. to be taken across a frontier. [Fr., = 'note-book']

câr'nival *n.* 1. Last three days or last week before Lent, Shrovetide; festivities usual during this in R.C. countries. 2. Riotous revelry, feasting, merrymaking; public festivity, esp. with procession, sideshows, etc. [Fr., f. It. *carnevale* Shrovetide, f. L *caro carn-* flesh and *levare* put away]

car'nivore *n.* Member of the Carnivora, a large order of mammals including many (cats, dogs, seals, etc.) that feed on other animals, having usu. sharp teeth and well-developed canines; animal that feeds on other animals. **carni'vorous** *adj.*

că'rob *n.* Evergreen Mediterranean tree (*Ceratonia siliqua*) bearing edible seed-pods whose seeds are said to have been the original carat weight used by goldsmiths.

că'rol *n.* Joyous song, esp. Christmas hymn. ~ *v.* Sing joyfully, sing carols.

Cărolē'an *adj.* = CAROLINE.

Cărolī'na. (hist.) English colony, named after Charles II, in N. America, from which NORTH and SOUTH CAROLINA were formed. **Cărolĭ'nian** *adj.* & *n.*

Că'rolīne *adj.* Of, pertaining to, Charles (usu. Charles I or Charles II of England); ~ *script*: = CAROLINGIAN script.

Căroli'ngian, Carlovi'ngian (-j-) *adjs.* Of CHARLEMAGNE; of the line of French kings descended from him (usu. *Carlo-*); ~ *Empire*, empire acquired by Charlemagne early in 9th c. and regarded by him as a revival of the Roman Empire; at its greatest extent it comprised France (except Brittany), Germany, the Low Countries, N. and central Italy, Bohemia, and Croatia, its capitals being Aix-la-Chapelle (Aachen) and Rome; ~ *Renaissance*, revival of art and letters, imitation of classical antiquity, fostered by Charlemagne; ~ *script*, rounded script adopted in Carolingian period.

că'rotēne, -tĭn *n.* (chem.) Red crystalline hydrocarbon ($C_{40}H_{56}$) contained in carrots, tomatoes, and many other vegetables, important source of vitamin A. **cărŏ'tėnoid** *adj.* & *n.* (Of) a pigment, resembling carotene, found in plants and animals.

carŏ'tĭd *adj.* & *n.* (Of, near to) one of the two main pairs of arteries in the neck, that which in mammals carries blood to the face and cerebral hemispheres.

carou'se (-z) *n.* Drinking-bout. ~ *v.i.* Engage in carouse, drink deep. **carou'sal** (-zl) *n.* [Ger. *gar aus* (*trinken*) drink to the bottom]

cărousĕ'l (-roo-; *or* -z-) *n.* (U.S.) Merry-go-round.

carp[1] *n.* Freshwater fish, *Cyprinus carpio*, commonly bred in ponds; other fish of this genus, which includes goldfish, silverfish, etc.

carp[2] *v.i.* Talk querulously, find fault. **car'ping** *adj.* (esp.) Captious.

Carpā'thian Mou'ntains (-tĭnz). (also *Carpathians*) Mountain system between Poland and Czechoslovakia.

car'pel *n.* (bot.) One of the units of which a compound ovary is composed. **car'pellarў** *adj.*

car'penter *n.* Artificer in woodwork, esp. of rough solid kinds as in ship- or house-building. ~ *v.* Do, make by, carpenter's work. **car'pentrў** *n.*

car'pėt *n.* Thick fabric for spreading on floor or stair, commonly of wool, freq. patterned in colours, and made by knotting short lengths of yarn on to the warp threads of a fabric during weaving, or by same means as tapestry, or by various mechanical weaving processes; covering or expanse of grass, flowers, etc., resembling a carpet; *~-bag*, travelling bag, orig. one made of carpet; *~-bagger*, after the Amer. Civil War, an immigrant from Northern to Southern States whose property qualification was the contents of a carpet-bag; any person interfering with the politics of a locality with which he has no permanent or genuine connection; ~ *slipper*, slipper the uppers of which were orig. made of carpet-like material; *~-snake*, large Austral. snake with variegated skin, *Morelia variegata*; ~ *sweeper*, household implement with revolving brush for sweeping carpets.

car̂'pėting *n.* **car̂'pėtlėss** *adj.* **car̂'pėt** *v.t.* Cover (as) with carpet.

car̂'pus *n.* (anat.) Set of bones (eight in a man) connecting forearm or foreleg to metacarpus; wrist; corresponding joint in other animals. **car̂'pal** *adj.* & *n.* (Bone) of the carpus.

car̂r *n.* Association of trees and shrubs developing at edges of fens and swamps, as *willow* ~, *alder* ~.

că'rrageen (-g-) *n.* (also ~ *moss*) Seaweed, *Chondrus crispus*, common on British coasts, yielding when dried and boiled a jelly used for food and in medicine. [*Carragheen* near Waterford in Ireland]

Că'rrantuohil (-tōō'ĭl). Highest mountain (1,401 m, 3,414 ft) of Ireland, in the MacGillycuddy's Reeks range, Co. Kerry.

că'rrel *n.* Apartment in library for use of one reader.

că'rriage (-rĭj) *n.* 1. Conveying, transport; cost of conveying. 2. Passing, carrying (of motion in committee etc.). 3. Manner of carrying; bearing, deportment. 4. Wheeled vehicle for persons; esp. four-wheeled private vehicle with two or more horses. 5. Wheeled support of gun; wheeled framework of vehicle apart from body; (mech.) sliding etc part of machinery for shifting position of other parts. 6. Railway passenger-coach. 7. *ca'rriageway*, (part of) road intended for vehicular traffic.

că'rrĭer *n.* 1. One who or that which carries; person plying for hire with cart, van, etc., for conveyance of parcels; paper or plastic bag with handles, for carrying parcels etc. (also ~*-bag*). 2. Attachment to bicycle etc. for carrying luggage. 3. Person or animal carrying disease-germs. 4. Aircraft carrier. 5. ~ *pigeon*: see PIGEON[1]; ~ *wave*, radio wave whose modulations carry telecommunication signals.

că'rrĭon *n.* Dead putrefying flesh; anything vile, garbage, filth; ~ *crow*, species of crow, *Corvus corone*, smaller than raven and larger than rook, feeding on carrion, small animals, poultry, etc.

Că'rroll, Lewis: see DODGSON.

cărronā'de *n.* Short large-calibre ship's gun. [*Carron* near Falkirk, Central, where orig. cast]

că'rron oil. Mixture of linseed oil and lime-water, formerly used for treating burns. [said to have been first used at *Carron* ironworks near Falkirk, Central]

că'rrot *n.* 1. Umbelliferous plant, *Daucus carota*, with large tapering root; orange-red, fleshy, sweet root of cultivated varieties of this, used as culinary vegetable. 2. (pl., slang), (Person with) red hair. **că'rrotў** *adj.*

că'rrў *v.* 1. Convey, transport, bear; conduct; be the bearer of; push (process, principle, etc.) to specified point. 2. Support, hold up; hold (oneself etc.) in specified way; have about the person ready for use. 3. Have specified range; (of sound) penetrate, travel; (golf, etc.) cross, pass over; (make) pitch beyond. 4. Keep (audience) in agreement *with* one; succeed in establishing, passing, electing, etc. 5. Capture, take by storm. 6. (arith.) Transfer (figure) to column of higher notation. 7. Have as result or corollary, involve. 8. ~ *away*, inspire, transport, deprive of self-control; (naut.) lose (mast etc.) by breakage; ~ *forward*, (arith.) transfer (figure) to top of new page or column; ~ *off*, remove from life; win; make passable; make brave show of (event etc.); ~ *on*, advance (process) a stage; continue; manage; go on with what one is doing; (colloq.) behave strangely, flirt, have amorous intrigue; ~ *out*, put in practice; ~ *through*, bring safely out of difficulties; complete. ~ *n.* 1. (mil.) Position of carrying sword. 2. (golf) Ball's flight before pitching. 3. Portage between rivers etc. 4. Range (of gun, sound, etc.).

car̂se *n.* (Sc.) Alluvial land along river bank(s).

car̂t *n.* Strong two- or four-wheeled vehicle used in farming and for carrying heavy goods; light two-wheeled one-horse vehicle for driving in; ~*-horse*, large thickset horse used for heavy work; *car't-load*, amount that a cart can carry; very large quantity; *car'troad, car'tway*, rough track unsuitable for light or spring-vehicles; *car't-wheel*, wheel of a cart; large coin (as crown or silver dollar); *turn cartwheels*, execute lateral somersaults, with arms and legs extended like spokes of a wheel. ~ *v.* Carry in a cart; work with a cart. ***car'ter*** *n.* ***car'tful*** *n.*

carte *n.* = QUART[2].

carte blanche (blahñsh) *n.* Full discretionary power. [Fr., = 'blank card']

carte-de-visite (-zēt) *n.* (archaic) Photograph $3\frac{1}{2} \times 2\frac{1}{4}$ in. (approx. 89×57 mm) [Fr., = 'visiting-card']

car'tel *n.* 1. (Written agreement for) exchange or ransom of prisoners. 2. (-tĕ'l) Manufacturers' union to control production, marketing, and prices; political combination between parties.

car'telīze *v.i.* Combine to form a business cartel.

Cartē'sian (-zhan) *adj.* & *n.* (Follower) of DESCARTES or his philosophy or mathematical methods.

Car'thage. Ancient city near Tunis on N. coast of Africa, founded by the Phoenicians; destroyed during the PUNIC Wars, and rebuilt by Augustus.

Carthagi'nian *adj.* Of Carthage; ~ *peace*, treaty of peace so severe that it means the virtual destruction of the defeated contestant. ~ *n.* Native, inhabitant, of Carthage.

Carthū'sian (-z-) *adj.* & *n.* 1. (Member) of order of monks founded in Dauphiné in 1086 by St. Bruno, and remarkable for the severity of their rule. 2. (Member) of CHARTERHOUSE school. [*Chatrousse*, place of the first monastery]

Cartier (-tyā), Jacques (1491–1557). French explorer of Canada.

car'tilage *n.* Elastic flexible tissue which forms the skeleton of young vertebrates and (except for some parts near the joints) changes later into bone; structure composed of this; gristle.

cartilă'ginous *adj.* Of, like, cartilage; ~ *fish*, one having a cartilaginous skeleton.

cartŏ'graphy̆ *n.* Map-drawing. **cartŏ'grapher** *n.* **cartogră'phic, -ical** *adjs.*

car'tomancy̆ *n.* Fortune-telling by playing-cards.

car'ton *n.* 1. (Shot striking) white disc in bull's-eye of target. 2. Light box or case for holding goods.

cartōō'n *n.* 1. Drawing on stout paper as design for painting of same size or for tapestry, mosaic, etc. 2. Humorous or topical drawing in newspaper etc.; *strip* ~, series of small drawings depicting events usu. concerning some central character, freq. serial. 3. (cinemat., also *animated* ~) Drawings photographed in series to give illusion of movement.

cartou'che (-ōōsh) *n.* (archit.) Scroll ornament, e.g. volute of Ionic capital; tablet imitating, drawing of, scroll with rolled-up ends, usu. bearing inscription; (archaeol.) oval containing hieroglyphic names and titles of Egyptian kings etc.

car'tridge *n.* 1. Case containing explosive charge and (for small arms) bullet or shot; ~ *belt*, belt with pockets for cartridges; ~ *clip*, device for holding cartridge conveniently for use in magazine-rifle etc.; ~ *paper*, thick rough paper

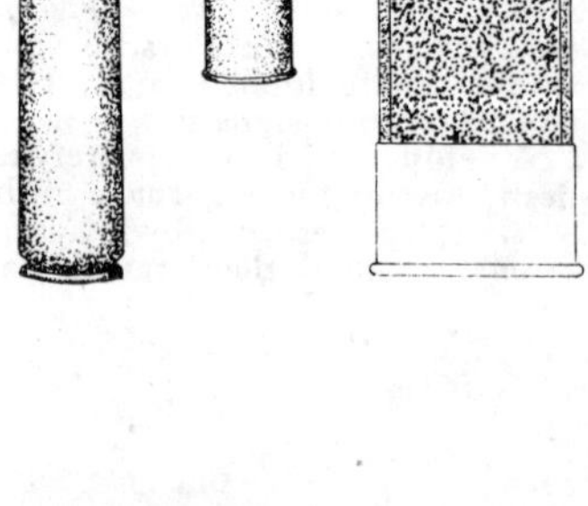

used for making cartridges, and also for drawings and envelopes. 2. Small cylindrical container.

câr'tūlarў̆ *n.* Collection or list of charters and records; place where these are kept.

că'rŭncle *n.* 1. Fleshy excrescence, as turkeycock's wattles. 2. Small hard outgrowth formed on seeds of certain plants, e.g. castor-oil plant.

Caru'sō (-rōō-), Enrico (1873–1921). Italian operatic tenor.

cârve *v.* Cut; produce by cutting; change by cutting *into*; cover or adorn *with* cut figures, designs, etc.; cut up meat at or for table; subdivide; *carving*, carved work, carved figure or design; *carving knife*, long knife for carving meat.

câr'vel *n.* 1. (hist.) = CARAVEL. 2. ~*-built*, (of boat) with planks flush with the side (opp. *clinker-built*).

câr'ver[1] *n.* (esp.) Knife (pl., knife and fork) for carving meat.

Câr'ver[2], John (1576–1621). First governor of Plymouth Colony in America; ~ *chair*, one of a type first owned by him, with rush seat, arms, and back consisting of three horizontal and three vertical spindles.

câr'ver[3] *n.* (colloq.) Armchair of a set of dining-room chairs. [f. CARVER[2]]

cărў̆ă'tĭd *n.* Female figure used as column to support entablature. [Gk *Caryatis*, a priestess of Artemis at Caryae in Laconia]

cărў̆ŏ'psĭs *n.* (pl. *-sēs*). (bot.) One-seeded indehiscent fruit with pericarp fused to seed-coat, as in wheat and barley.

Căsanō'va. Giovanni Jacopo Casanova de Seingalt (1725–98), Italian adventurer, author of memoirs, in French, describing his escapades and amours in most countries of Europe.

căscā'de *n.* Waterfall, one section of large broken waterfall; wavy fall of lace etc. ~ *v.i.* Fall in or like cascade.

căscâr'a *n.* (also ~ *sagra'da*, pr. -rah-) (Extract of) bark of a Californian buckthorn, *Rhamnus purshiana*, used as a laxative or cathartic. [Span., = 'sacred bark']

cāse[1] *n.* 1. Instance of thing's occurring; state of affairs; circumstances; *in* ~, if (something should happen); *in any* ~, no matter what happens. 2. (med.) Condition of disease in a person; instance of disease. 3. (law) Cause, suit, for trial; statement of facts in cause drawn up for consideration of higher court; cause that has been decided; (fig.) ~ *of conscience*, practical question concerning which conscience may be in doubt. 4. (gram.) In inflected languages, form of substantive, pronoun, or adjective expressing its relation to other words in sentence; in uninflected languages, this relation apart from form. 5. ~ *history*, (record of) information about patient etc.; ~*-law*, law as settled by decided cases; *ca'sework*, social work done by personal study of cases (individuals or families), whence *ca'seworker*.

cāse[2] *n.* Thing to contain or hold something else; box, chest, bag, sheath, etc.; outer protection and covering part of anything; box or chest with its contents; (print.) shallow wooden tray for holding type, divided into compartments to take the various letters of the alphabet; *lower* ~ , case usu, holding letters other than capitals; hence (in) small letters; *upper* ~ , case holding large or capital letters etc., hence, (in) capital letters; ~*-bottle*, (square) bottle fitting into case with others; ~*-harden*, harden surface of, esp. give steel surface to (iron etc.) by carbonizing; (fig.) make callous; ~*-knife*, knife worn in sheath; ~*-shot*, bullets in sheet-iron case fired from cannon; shrapnel. ~ *v.t.* 1. Enclose in case; surround (*with*). 2. (U.S. slang) Examine (house etc.) in planning a crime.

cā'sein *n.* Protein, one of the constituents of milk, coagulated by acids, and forming the basis of cheese.

cā'semāte (-sm-) *n.* Vaulted chamber in thickness of fortress-wall, with embrasures for defence;

(in warships) armoured enclosure in which guns are mounted, with embrasures through which they are fired.

cā'sement (-sm-) *n.* Metal or wooden hinged frame with glass, forming window or part of one; (poet) window; ~ *cloth,* plain-woven fabric used for curtains etc.

cā'sėous *adj.* Of or like cheese.

căsh[1] *n.* Ready money; specie and bank-notes; ~ *crop*, crop grown for sale; ~ *register*, till for recording and adding amounts put into it. ~ *v.t.* Give or obtain cash for (cheque, money-order, etc.); ~ *in* (*one's checks*), (U.S.) settle accounts in game of poker; (fig.) realize one's assets; (U.S. slang) die.

căsh[2] *n.* (pl. same) Any of several coins of very small value used in China, E. Indies, etc.

că'shew (-ōō) *n.* Large tree, *Anacardium occidentale*, of W. Indies etc., cultivated for its kidney-shaped edible nut (~ *nut*). [Port. *caju*, f. Tupi (*a*)*caju*]

căshier'[1] *n.* One in charge of cash of bank or other business firm, paying and receiving money etc.; one in shop etc. who receives customers' payments.

cashier'[2] *v.t.* Dismiss from service, depose; discard.

că'shmēre *n.* Material woven from fine soft wool found beneath the hair of goats of Kashmir and Tibet; woollen fabric imitating this.

cā'sĭng *n.* (esp.) = CASE[2]; framework; external fabric of tyre.

casi'nō (-ē-) *n.* (pl. *-os*). 1. Public music or dancing-room; (esp.) building in which gambling takes place, as well as dancing, public entertainments, and other social activities. 2. Card-game in which each player tries to win cards by matching those exposed on the table, points being scored for winning the greatest number of cards, one for the greatest number of spades, two for ten of diamonds (*great* ~) and one for two of spades (*little* ~). [It., = 'little house']

cask (-ah-) *n.* Barrel used esp. for beer, wine, and cider; contents or capacity of cask.

ca'skėt (kah-) *n.* 1. Small, often ornamental, box for holding jewels, letters, etc.; *C~ letters*, letters supposed to have passed between Mary Queen of Scots and Bothwell and to have established her complicity in the murder of Darnley. 2. (U.S.) Coffin.

Că'slon (-z-), William 1692–1766). English typographer; established a type foundry, continued by his son William (1720–78); hence, applied to old-face type cut there, or imitation of this.

Că'spĭan Sea. Inland sea between Europe and Asia.

căsque (-k) *n.* (hist., poet.) Helmet.

Cassă'ndra. (Gk myth.) Daughter of Priam king of Troy; she was loved by Apollo, who gave her the gift of prophecy and when she deceived him ordained that her prophecies, though true, should not be believed.

cassa'va (-sah-) *n.* 1. Plant of genus *Manihot*, widely cultivated in W. Indies, tropical America, and Africa for its fleshy tuberous roots. 2. Nutritious starch obtained from manioc roots, bread made from this.

că'sserōle *n.* Heatproof vessel in which food is cooked and served; food cooked in this. ~ *v.t.* Cook (food) in casserole. [Fr., = 'stew-pan']

cassĕ'tte *n.* Light-proof container for spool of film, X-ray plate or film; closed container of magnetic tape for tape-recorder.

că'ssĭa *n.* 1. Inferior coarse kind of cinnamon, esp. the bark of *Cinnamonum cassia*; this tree. 2. Plant of genus *C~* of warm climates, yielding senna-leaves; any medicinal preparation from these.

Cässĭopei'a. 1. (Gk myth.) Wife of Cepheus king of Ethiopia, and mother of Andromeda; she boasted herself more beautiful than the Nereids, thus incurring the wrath of Poseidon. 2. (astron.) Northern constellation.

căssĭ′terīte *n.* Stannic dioxide, TIN-stone.

că′ssock *n.* Long close-fitting tunic, usu. black, buttoning up to the neck and reaching to the feet, worn by clergy.

că′ssowarў (-*o*-w-) *n.* Large flightless running bird of genus *Casuarius*, related to ostrich, found in Australia, New Guinea, etc. [Malay *kasuari*]

cast (kah-) *v.* (past t. & past part. *cast*). 1. Throw, cause to fall or drop; ~ *anchor*, let it down; ~ *an eye*, glance. 2. Throw off, shed, esp. in process of growth; (of horse) lose (a shoe). 3. Form (metal etc.) into desired shape by melting and pouring into a mould; found; ~ *iron*: see IRON; ~-*iron* (*adj.*) made of cast iron; hard, very strong, unadaptable. 4. Arrange (facts *into* a shape, actors *for* parts in play). 5. ~ *about*, look about, search here and there, *for*; ~ *adrift*, leave to drift; ~ *ashore*, leave behind on sea-shore; ~ *away*, reject; (pass., of ship, sailor, etc.) be wrecked; *ca′staway*, person shipwrecked or cast adrift or rejected; reprobate; ~ *down*, depress; ~ *off*, abandon, throw away; finish off (knitting) by taking stitches off needle and passing each one over the next; (print.) estimate printed length or size of (MS.); ~-*off* (*n.*) thing discarded; (print.) estimated length; ~ *up*, add up. **ca′ster**[1] *n.* **cast** *n.* 1. Throw of missile, fishing-line, sounding-lead, etc.; throw of dice, number thrown. 2. Model, shape, made by running molten metal or pressing soft substance into a mould; the mould itself; plaster copy of sculpture made thus. 3. Earth excreted by earth- or lug-worm (*worm*-~); undigested food thrown up by bird. 4. Set of actors taking the parts in a play, distribution of parts among them. 5. Twist, inclination; slight squint. 6. Tinge, hue. 7. Type, quality.

Căstā′lĭa. (Gk myth.) Spring on Mount Parnassus, sacred to Apollo and the Muses. **Căstā′lĭan** *adj.*

căstanĕ′t *n.* Small concave shell of ivory or hard wood used by Spaniards, Moors, etc., to make rattling sound as accompaniment to dancing, a pair being held in the palm of the hand and struck with the middle finger.

caste (kah-) *n.* 1. Indian hereditary class, with members socially equal, united in religion, and usu. following same trade, having no social intercourse with persons of other castes; exclusive class elsewhere; this system, the position it confers; *lose* ~, descend in social scale. 2. (zool.) One of the groups into which social Hymenoptera and termites are divided (usu. queens and different types of worker). **ca′stelėss** *adj.*

că′stellan *n.* Governor or constable of castle.

că′stėllātėd *adj.* Built like a castle, having battlements; castle-like. **căstėllā′tion** *n.*

caster[2]**:** see CASTOR[2].

că′stĭgāte *v.t.* Chastise, punish. **căstĭgā′tion, că′stĭgātor** *ns.*

Căsti′le (-ēl). Central part of Spain, an ancient kingdom; ~ *soap*, fine hard white or mottled soap made with olive oil and soda. **Căstĭ′lĭan** *adj.* & *n.* (Native, inhabitant) of Castile; (of) the language of Castile, literary Spanish.

ca′stĭng (kah-) *adj.* ~ *vote*, (f. obs. sense of cast = 'turn the scale') vote that decides between two equal parties. ~ *n.* (esp.) Piece of metal or other substance shaped by melting and pouring into a mould; this process of manufacture; DIE-[1], SAND-, PRESSURE-~: see these words.

ca′stle (kahsl) *n.* 1. Large fortified building or set of buildings; dwelling that was once fortified. 2. *the C*~, (hist.) in Ireland, Dublin Castle as the seat of the viceregal court and administration; the officials who administered the government of Ireland under the viceroy. 3. (hist.) Small wooden tower used in war etc. and borne on elephant's back or ship's deck. 4. (chess) = ROOK[2]. 5. ~ *in the air*, *in Spain*, day-dream, vision-

BEAUMARIS CASTLE

ary project or scheme; ~ *pudding*, sponge pudding made in small mould. ~ *v.i.* (chess) Move king two squares towards one of the rooks and (in the same move) this rook to the square next past the king.

Castlereagh (kah'slrā), Robert Stewart, 2nd Marquis of Londonderry (1769–1822). Chief secretary for Ireland 1799–1801; secured the passing of the Act of Union by the Irish Parliament; foreign secretary 1812–22; took a leading part in the Congress of Vienna.

ca'stor[1] (kah-) *n.* 1. Reddish-brown unctuous bitter substance obtained from anal glands of beaver and used in perfumery and formerly in medicine. 2. (archaic, slang) Hat (orig. one of beaver or imitation beaver).

ca'stor[2], **-er**[2] (kah-) *n.* 1. Small vessel with perforated top for sprinkling pepper, sugar, flour, etc.; ~ *sugar*, finely powdered sugar suitable for use in castor. 2. Small solid wheel and swivel on leg of piece of furniture for moving it without lifting.

Ca'stor[3] (kah-). 1. (Gk myth.) One of the twin sons (~ *and Pollux*) of Tyndareus and Leda, and half-brother of Helen. 2. (astron.) More northerly of the two bright stars in the constellation Gemini.

ca'stor oil (kah-). Pale yellow nauseous acrid oil obtained from seeds of *Ricinus communis* (castor-oil plant), used as purgative and lubricant.

căstrā'te *v.t.* Remove testicles of, geld; deprive of vigour; expurgate (book). **căstrā'tion** *n.*

căstra'tō (-rah-) *n.* (pl. *-ti*, pr. -tē). Adult male singer retaining boy's voice as a result of castration. [It.]

Că'strō Ruz (ro͞os), Fidel (1927–). Cuban statesman; prime minister 1959– .

că'sūal (-z-; *or* -zho͞o-) *adj.* Accidental; irregular; undesigned, coming by chance or accident; unmethodical, careless; unconcerned, uninterested; (of clothes) informal; ~ *labourer*, one without fixed employment, who does casual or occasional jobs; ~ *pauper, poor*, (one of) those not receiving regular or systematic relief, esp. one admitted to the ~ *ward* of a workhouse, in which were received tramps and others not permanent inmates. **că'sūallȳ** *adv.* **că'sūalnėss** *n.* **că'sūal** *n.* Casual labourer, casual pauper.

că'sūaltȳ (-z-; *or* -zhŏŏ-) *n.* Accident, mishap, disaster; killed, wounded, or injured person; (pl.) list or number of such persons; ~ *ward*, hospital ward where accidental injuries are treated.

căsūarī'na (*also* -ēn*a*) *n.* Quickly growing tree of genus *C~*, with jointed leafless branches, like great horse-tails. [f. fancied resemblance to the CASSOWARY]

că'sūist (-z-; *or* -zhŏŏ-) *n.* Person, esp. theologian, who studies and resolves cases of conscience or doubtful questions of duty and conduct; sophist, quibbler. **căsūi'stic, -ical** *adjs.* **căsūi'sticallȳ** *adv.*

că'sūistrȳ (-z-; *or* -zhŏŏ-) *n.* That part of ethics which applies general rules of morality and religion to particular cases, esp. those in which there appears to be a conflict of duties; sophistry, quibbling.

ca'sus bĕ'llī (kah-; *or* -z-). Occasion of war, act justifying or regarded as reason for war.

căt *n.* 1. Small domesticated furry carnivorous quadruped, *Felis domesticus*, kept to destroy mice, and as pet; *wild* ~: see WILD. 2. Any member of the genus *Felis*, which includes lions, tigers, panthers, etc. 3. Cat-like animal of other species, as *civet-cat*, *polecat*, etc. 4. (colloq.) Spiteful or backbiting woman. 5. (naut.) Cathead, beam projecting from bows of ship, for raising the anchor, or carrying it suspended, so called because in early times the ring to which the anchor was drawn commonly hung from an ornament often an animal mask 6. Cat-o'-nine-tails (see below). 7. Piece of wood used in game of tip-cat. 8. *~-and-dog*, very quarrelsome (life etc.); *C~-and-mouse Act*, the Prisoners (Temporary Discharge for Ill-health) Act of 1913, enabling hunger-strikers to be released temporarily; *ca'tbird*, any of several birds with mewing cry (N. Amer. mocking-bird, Austral. bower-bird, etc.); ~ *burglar*, one who enters house by climbing to upper storey; *ca'tcall*, shrill whistle expressing disapproval; (*v.*) make catcalls, receive with catcalls; *ca'tfish*, any fish of the group Siluridae, most of which live in fresh water and have barbels round the mouth; also, the largest of the Blenniidae, a fierce carnivorous fish also called *wolf-fish*; *ca'thead*: see sense 5 above; *~-ice*, thin ice in shallow places from underneath which water has receded; *~-lap*, (slang) slops, weak tea, etc.; *ca'tmint*, aromatic labiate plant with pale-blue flowers; *Nepeta cataria*; *~-nap*, short light sleep taken sitting in chair etc.; *ca'tnip*, (U.S.) catmint; *~-o'-nine-tails*, whip of nine knotted cords formerly used in military and naval punishments and still for certain criminal offences; *~'s-cradle*, child's game with two players lifting intertwined string from each other's fingers in such a way as to form new patterns; *~'s eye*, precious stone resembling cat's eye with contracted pupil, a hard chalcedonic quartz from Ceylon, Malabar, etc.; one of the chain of light-reflecting studs used to demarcate traffic lanes on roads at night; *~'s-meat*, horseflesh sold as cat's food; *~'s-paw*, person used as tool by another; slight breeze rippling water in some places; *~('s) whisker*, fine adjustable usu. copper wire placed in contact with sensitive spot in crystal wireless receiver; *ca'twalk*, narrow bridge or footway giving access to machinery etc. ~ *v.* 1. (slang) Vomit. 2. (naut.) Raise (anchor) to cathead.

C.A.T. *abbrev.* College of Advanced Technology.

cata-, cat-, cath- *pref.* Down from, down to, against, in opposition to, mis-.

cată'bolism *n.* Phase of metabolism which consists in breaking

Leopard

Tiger

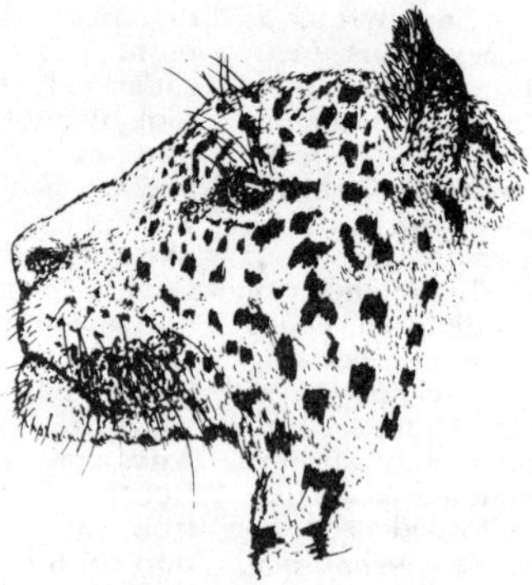

Jaguar

WILD CATS

down complex compounds into simpler ones. **cătabŏ'lĭc** *adj.*

cătachrē'sis (-k-) *n.* Perversion, improper use, of words.

că'taclăsm *n.* Violent break, disruption.

că'taclȳsm *n.* Deluge, esp. the Flood; sudden convulsion or alteration of conditions, political, social, etc., upheaval. **cataclȳ'smal, cataclȳ'smĭc** *adjs.*

că'tacōmb (-m; *or* -ōōm) *n.* Subterranean cemetery (orig. that under the basilica of St. Sebastian near Rome, supposed burying-place of Peter and Paul); (pl.) subterranean galleries made by Jews and early Christians in and near Rome, with recesses in the sides for tombs; similar works elsewhere (in Paris, worked-out stone quarries with bones from emptied churchyards); wine-cellar. [LL *catacumbas,* name given to the catacomb under St. Sebastian; origin unknown]

cătadiŏ'ptrĭc *adj.* Of refraction and reflection (e.g. lens-mirror combination). **cătadiŏ'ptrĭcs** *n.* Study of this.

cată'dromous *adj.* (of fish) Descending to lower reaches of river, or to sea, to spawn.

că'tafălque (-k) *n.* Decorated stage for coffin or effigy of distinguished person at funeral; open hearse.

Catalan: see CATALONIAN.

că'talāse *n.* (chem.) Any of various enzymes capable of decomposing hydrogen peroxide.

cătalĕ'ctĭc *adj.* & *n.* (pros.) (Line) wanting a syllable in last foot.

că'talĕpsȳ *n.* Disease characterized by seizure or trance lasting for hours or days, with suspension of sensation and consciousness.

cătalĕ'ptĭc *adj.* & *n.* Of, (person) subject to, catalepsy.

că'talŏgue (-g) *n.* Complete list, usu. alphabetical or arranged under headings, and often with descriptive or other particulars; ~ *raisonné* (-nā), (Fr.) descriptive catalogue arranged according to subject etc. ~ *v.* Enumerate, enter, in a catalogue.

Cătalō'nĭa. (Span. *Catalunya*) NE. part of Spain, formerly a province. **Că'talan, Cătalō'nĭan** *adjs.* & *ns.* (Native, inhabitant) of Catalonia; (of) the dialect of Provençal (or Langue d'Oc) spoken in Catalonia.

cată'lpa *n.* Tree of genus *C*~ with large simple leaves and trumpet-shaped flowers, native of N. America, W. Indies, Japan, and China.

cată'lȳsis *n.* (pl. *-sēs*). Facilitation of a chemical reaction by the presence of an added substance which is itself not consumed in the reaction. **că'talȳse** (-z) *v.t.* **cătalȳ'tĭc** *adj.*

că'talȳst *n.* Substance causing catalysis.

cătamară'n *n.* 1. E. Ind. raft or float of logs tied together, with longer one in middle; similar W. Ind. craft; raft of two boats side by side used on St. Lawrence etc.; sailing boat with twin hulls. 2. (colloq.) Quarrelsome woman. [Tamil *kaṭṭa-maram* tied tree]

că'tamīte *n.* Boy kept for homosexual practices. [L *Catamitus,* corrupt form of *Ganymēdes* Ganymede]

că'tamount *n.* (U.S.) Puma or other tiger-cat.

că'taplăsm *n.* Poultice.

că'taplĕxȳ *n.* Sudden temporary paralysis. **cătaplĕ'ctĭc** *adj.*

că'tapŭlt *n.* 1. Ancient military engine worked with lever and ropes for discharging stones etc. 2. Forked stick with elastic band fastened to two prongs, for shooting small stones etc. 3. Mechanical device for launching aircraft from deck of ship, starting gliders, etc. ~ *v.* Shoot with catapult; hurl as from catapult; launch with catapult.

că'tarăct *n.* 1. Waterfall, esp. large precipitous fall or series of falls; downpour, rush of water. 2. Progressive opacity of lens of eye, resulting, unless treated, in impairment of vision and eventual blindness.

catarrh (-âr') *n.* Inflammation of mucous membrane, esp. of nose, throat, and bronchial tubes, causing increased flow of mucus. **catar'rhal** (-ral) *adj.*

că'tarrhīne (-arī-) *adj.* & *n.* (Animal) of one of the two divisions of the sub-order Anthropoidea, distinguished from the PLATYRRHINE by having the nostrils close together and directed downwards, and including some monkeys, the anthropoid apes, and man.

cată'strophė *n.* Dénouement of dramatic piece; disastrous end, overthrow, calamitous fate; event subverting order or system of things. **cătastrŏ'phic** *adj.* **cătastrŏ'phically** *adv.*

cătatō'nia *n.* (path.) State of muscular rigidity and mental stupor. **cătatŏ'nic** *adj.*

că'tboat *n.* Sailing-boat with mast well forward and rigged with one sail.

cătch *v.* (past t. & past part. *caught* pr. cawt) 1. Capture, lay hold of, seize; be entangled, take hold; hit; come level with, make up arrears (also ~ *up*); intercept (ball etc.) in motion, esp. take hold of (ball thrown) before it reaches ground; (cricket) dismiss (batsman) by intercepting ball from his bat before it touches the ground; be in time for (train etc.); check suddenly. 2. Surprise, detect. 3. Ignite, be ignited (also ~ *fire*). 4. Receive, incur, be infected with. 5. Grasp with senses or mind; arrest, captivate, arrest attention of; take by surprise, trick, deceive. 6. *~-crop*, crop that matures quickly, freq. grown between plantings of two staple crops; *~-penny*, got up merely to sell; *ca'tchword*, word so placed as to attract attention, as first word of following page placed at corner of page, word at head of article in dictionary etc., actor's cue-word; word caught up and repeated, esp. in politics etc. ~ *n.* 1. Act of catching; amount of fish caught; device for fastening or restraining something; chance of, success in, catching ball at cricket; thing or person caught or worth catching. 2. Something designed to deceive or trip up; unforeseen difficulty or awkwardness; hidden trap; surprise. 3. (mus.) Round, sometimes devised to produce punning or other humorous verbal combinations.

că'tcher *n.* (esp.) Fielder who stands behind batter in baseball.

că'tching *adj.* (esp.) Infectious; captivating.

că'tchment *n.* (esp. in ~ *area*) Catching and collection of rainfall over a natural drainage area; also transf., of persons, area, served by hospital, school, etc.

că'tchy̆ *adj.* (colloq.) Attractive; (of tune etc.) readily caught up.

cāte *n.* (archaic; usu. pl.) Choice food.

cătėchĕ'tical (-kĕ-) *adj.* Of, by, oral teaching; according to a catechism; consisting of questions and answers.

că'tėchism (-k-) *n.* Treatise for instruction by question and answer, esp. on religious doctrine; *Church* ~, that of the Anglican Church in the Book of Common Prayer; *Longer*, *Shorter*, ~, those of the Westminster Assembly of Divines, used by the Presbyterian churches etc.

că'tėchīze (-k-) *v.t.* Instruct by question and answer, or by the use of a catechism; put questions to, examine. **că'tėchist** *n.*

că'tėchu (-chōō) *n.* Any of various vegetable substances containing tannin. [Malay *kachu*; cf. CACHOU]

cătėchū'mĕn (-k-) *n.* Christian convert under instruction before baptism.

cătėgŏ'rical *adj.* Unconditional, absolute; explicit, direct; ~ *imperative,* (Kantian ethics) absolute unconditional command of the moral law, a law given by pure reason and universally binding on every rational will. **cătėgŏ'rically̆** *adv.*

că'tėgory̆ *n.* 1. Class, division. 2. In Aristotle, one of a possibly exhaustive set of classes among which all things might be distributed (substance, quantity, quality, relation, place, time, posture, possession, action, passion). 3. In

Kant etc., the pure *a priori* conceptions of the understanding, applied by the mind to the material received from sense in order to make it an intelligible notion or object of knowledge.

catē'na *n.* Connected series.

catē'narȳ, cătėnār'ĭan *ns.* & *adjs.* (Like) curve formed by uniform chain hanging freely from two points not in one vertical line.

că'tėnāte *v.t.* Connect like links of chain. **cătėnā'tion** *n.*

că'tėnoid *adj.* Catenary. ~ *n.* (math.) Surface formed by revolution of catenary about its axis.

cā'ter *v.i.* Purvey food; provide amusement etc. *for.* **cā'terer** *n.*

că'teran *n.* (Sc.) Highland irregular fighting-man, raider.

că'terpĭllar *n.* 1. Larva of butterfly, moth, or sawfly, resembling a worm but possessing several pairs of legs, strong jaws, and short antennae and feeding on leaves, fruit, or other succulent parts of plants. 2. ~ *track, tread,* endless articulated steel bands carrying treads passing round two or more wheels of tractor, tank, or other vehicle required to travel over rough or soft ground; *C*~, trade-name for this; [OF. *chatepelose* hairy cat]

că'terwaul *n.* Cry of cat in rut, similar squalling sound. ~ *v.i.* Make caterwaul.

că'tgŭt *n.* Dried and twisted intestines of sheep, horse, etc. (not cat), used for strings of musical instruments, tennis rackets, etc., and for sutures in surgical operations.

cathar'sĭs *n.* (pl. *-sēs*). 1. (med.) Purgation. 2. (with ref. to Aristotle's 'Poetics') Purification of emotions by vicarious experience, esp. through the drama. 3. (psychotherapy) Relieving of neurotic state by re-enacting or relating an experience of strong emotional character which has undergone repression.

cathar'tic *adj.* Effecting catharsis. ~ *n.* Purgative medicine.

Cathay'. (archaic & poet.) CHINA[1].

cathē'dral *n.* Principal church of diocese, containing bishop's *cathedra* or throne. ~ *adj.* Ranking as a cathedral, containing or belonging to a cathedral.

Că'therĭne[1] (1729–96), 'the Great'. Empress of Russia 1762–96; by birth a German, Princess Sophia of Anhalt-Zerbst; married

CATHERINE THE GREAT

the Russian heir; 6 months after his accession (as Peter III) he was forced to abdicate and murdered, whereupon Catherine was acclaimed as Empress.

Că'therĭne[2], St. (d. 307). Legendary saint and martyr of Alexandria; she was beheaded, after other methods of putting her to death, including that of the wheel, had failed; ~ *wheel,* (orig.) instrument of torture consisting of 4 wheels armed with knives and teeth turning different ways; now, a kind of firework which rotates while burning; also, a lateral somersault with arms and legs extended.

Că'therĭne de Médicis (mādēsēs) (1519–89). Wife of Henry II of France and regent of France during the minority of her son, Charles IX; her antagonism to the Protestants led to the Massacre of St. Bartholomew.

Că'therĭne of A'ragon (ă-) (1483–1536). Daughter of Ferdinand and Isabella of Spain; married Arthur, prince of Wales

1501, and, after his death, his younger brother Henry VIII 1509, was divorced by Henry 1526, on ground that her 1st marriage made her 2nd invalid.

că'thèter *n.* Tube for introducing into hollow organs of the body to withdraw excess fluid or sample for analysis, esp. urine from the bladder. **că'thèterīze** *v.t.* Use a catheter on.

că'thōde *n.* (elect.) Negative pole; ~ *ray*, beam of electrons issuing from cathode of high-vacuum tube under the impulse of an electric field.

că'tholĭc *adj.* 1. Universal, of universal interest or use; all-embracing, of wide sympathies. 2. *C~ Church*, (*a*) the whole body of Christians; (*b*) after the separation of Eastern and Western Churches, the Western or Latin Church; (*c*) after the Reformation, claimed as its exclusive title by that part of the Western Church which remained under Roman obedience, but (*d*) held by Anglicans to include the Church of England as the proper continuation in England of the Ancient and the Western Church. 3. Of or belonging to any of these Churches, esp. = ROMAN CATHOLIC. 4. *His C~ Majesty*, title of former kings of Spain; *C~ Apostolic Church*: see IRVINGITE. ~ *n.* Member of a Catholic church, esp. Roman Catholic. **cathŏ'lĭcallȳ, că'tholĭclȳ** *advs.* **cathŏ'lĭcism, cătholĭ'cĭtȳ** *ns.* **cathŏ'lĭcize** *v.t.*

Că'tilīne. Lucius Sergius Catilina (d. 63 B.C.), a profligate Roman who formed a conspiracy against his country and was accused by Cicero.

că'tīŏn *n.*: see ION. **cătīŏ'nĭc** *adj.* [Gk, = 'going down']

că'tkĭn *n.* Deciduous spike, usu. of unisexual apetalous flowers, of willow, birch, etc.

Cā'tō, Marcus Porcius. Name of two Romans: (1) 'Cato the Censor' (239–149 B.C.), famous for his opposition to the lax morals and luxury of the Romans and for his insistence that 'Carthage must be destroyed'; author of a treatise 'De Agri Cultura', the oldest extant literary prose work in Latin; (2) his great-grandson (95–46 B.C.), like him a man of unbending character; chief political antagonist of Julius Caesar.

catŏ'ptrĭc *adj.* Of mirror, reflector, or reflection. **catŏ'ptrĭcs** *n.* Part of optics dealing with reflections (cf. DIOPTRICS).

că'tsup *n.* Var. of KETCHUP.

că'ttĭsh, că'ttȳ *adjs.* Ill-natured, spiteful. **că'ttĭlȳ** *adv.*

că'ttle *n.* Livestock, esp. oxen; (slang) horses; *~-grid*, system of bars laid across road at ground level to prevent cattle from passing, while allowing passage of wheeled traffic; *~-lifter*, (U.S.) *~-rustler*, marauder who steals cattle; *~-plague*, rinderpest; *~-stop*, (N.Z.) = cattle-grid.

că'ttleya (-lĭ*a*) *n.* Orchidaceous Central Amer. and Brazilian plant of genus *C~* with handsome violet, pink, or yellow flowers. [William *Cattley* (d. 1832), English patron of botany]

Cătŭ'llus, Gaius Valerius (87–54? B.C.). Roman poet and epigrammatist.

Caucā'sĭan (-z-; *or* -zh*a*n) *adj.* & *n.* 1. (Native, inhabitant, language) of the Caucasus. 2. Caucasoid.

Cau'casoid *adj.* & *n.* (Member) of the light-skinned division of mankind found esp. in Europe, N. Africa, and SW. Asia; Caucasian.

Cau'casus. Mountain range between Black Sea and Caspian Sea.

cau'cus *n.* (chiefly in hostile use) Local political party committee for fighting elections, defining policy, etc. (orig. U.S.).

cau'dal *adj.* Of, at, like, tail.

cau'date *adj.* Tailed; of the order Caudata (see URODELE).

Caudillo (kowdĭ'lyō), El. Title assumed by General FRANCO as head of Spanish State. [Span., = 'leader']

cau'dle *n.* (archaic) Warm thin spiced gruel with wine and sugar, for invalids, esp. women after childbirth.

caught: see CATCH.

caul *n.* 1. Woman's close-fitting

cap or net for the hair (hist.); plain back part of woman's cap. 2. Amnion or inner membrane enclosing foetus; part of this enclosing child's head at birth and superstitiously regarded as lucky omen and preservative against drowning. 3. Omentum.

cau'ldron *n.* Large boiling-vessel (usu.) of deep basin shape, with hoop handle and removable lid.

cau'liflower (kŏl-) *n.* Cultivated plant of genus *Brassica* with young inflorescence forming close white fleshy edible head; ~ *ear*, (pugilist's) ear with lobe thickened and distorted by blows.

cau'līne *adj.* (bot.) Of the stem; (of leaves) growing on an extended stem.

caulk (kawk) *v.t.* Stop up seams of (ship), stop up (seams) with oakum and melted pitch (or, in iron ship, by striking junctions of plates with blunt chisel).

cau'sal (-z-) *adj.* Of, acting as, expressing, due to, a cause or causes; of the nature of cause and effect. **causă'lĭtȳ** *n.* Being, having, a cause; relation of cause and effect, doctrine that everything has cause(s).

causā'tion (-z-) *n.* Causing; relation of cause and effect. **cau'satĭve** *adj.* Acting as cause (*of*); (gram.) expressing a cause or causation.

cause (-z) *v.t.* Be the cause of, make (something) happen; induce, make (person *to* do, thing to be done). ~ *n.* 1. What produces an effect, what gives rise to any action, phenomenon, or condition; person or other agent bringing something about; ground or reason for action; motive; *First C~*, original cause or creator of the unĭverse. 2. (law etc.) Matter about which person goes to law; case of one party in a suit; matter in dispute; side of question or controversy expressed by a person or party, militant movement, propaganda; subject of concern; ~ *list*, list of causes for trial.

cause célèbre (kōz sālĕbr). Law-suit exciting much public interest. [Fr.]

cau'selėss (-zl-) *adj.* Fortuitous; without natural cause; unjustifiable, groundless.

cau'serĭe (kōz-) *n.* Informal article or talk, esp. on literary subjects.

cau'seway (-zwā) *n.* Raised road across low or wet place or piece of water; raised footway at side of road.

cau'stĭc *adj.* 1. Burning, corrosive, destroying organic tissue; ~ *alkali*, any of the hydroxides of potassium (~ *potash*, KOH), sodium (~ *soda*, NaOH), and other electropositive metals. 2. Bitter, cutting, sarcastic. 3. (math., of curved surface) Formed by intersection of rays from one point reflected or refracted from a curved surface. ~ *n.* 1. Caustic substance. 2. Caustic surface or curve. **cau'stĭcallȳ** *adv.* **caustĭ'cĭtȳ** *n.*

cau'terīze *v.t.* Sear with hot iron or caustic, esp. in treatment of wounds etc.; render callous. **cauterīzā'tion** *n.*

cau'terȳ *n.* Heated metal instrument for burning or searing organic tissue (*actual* ~); caustic for the same purpose (*potential* ~); cauterizing.

cau'tion *n.* 1. Warning; (slang) extraordinary, strange, person or thing. 2. Avoidance of rashness, attention to safety. 3. Security, bail, pledge (now Sc. & U.S.); ~ *money*, money deposited as security for good conduct, esp. at university or Inn of Court. ~ *v.t.* Warn; admonish.

cau'tionarȳ *adj.* Conveying a warning or admonition.

cau'tious (-sh*u*s) *adj.* Disposed to or exhibiting caution. **cau'tiouslȳ** *adv.*

căvalcā'de *n.* Company of riders, procession on horseback.

căvalier' *n.* 1. Horseman. 2. Courtly gentleman, gallant, esp. as escorting a lady. 3. (*C~*) One of those who fought for Charles I in the (English) Civil War. ~ *adj.* 1. Careless in manner, off-hand; haughty, supercilious. 2. Royalist. **căvalier'lȳ** *adv.*

CAVALRY

că'valrў *n.* Horse-soldiers, mounted troops; troops formerly mounted but now equipped with mechanical vehicles, as tanks or armoured cars; ~ *twill*, strong material in double twill used for clothing.

Că'van. County of Ulster in the Republic of Ireland.

căvati'na (-tē-) *n.* (mus.) Short simple song; similar piece of instrumental music, usu. slow and emotional. [Ital.]

cāve *n.* Hollow place opening more or less horizontally under the ground; *~-dweller, ca'veman*, person (esp. prehistoric man) living in cave; person resembling prehistoric man in behaviour; ~ *v.* Hollow out, excavate; *~ in*, subside (of earth etc. over hollow place), yield to pressure from outside or above; (fig.) yield to pressure, submit, give in; smash in.

cā'vė *int.* (school slang) Beware. [L]

cā'vėăt *n.* 1. (law) Process in court to suspend proceedings. 2. Warning, caution. [L, = 'let him beware']

că'vėăt ĕ'mptŏr. Phrase disclaiming responsibility for buyer's disappointment. [L, = 'let the buyer beware']

că'vendĭsh[1] *n.* Tobacco softened, sweetened with molasses, and pressed into cakes.

Că'vendĭsh[2], Henry (1731–1810). English natural philosopher; discovered the constitution of water and atmospheric air; experimented on electricity and the density of the earth; ~ *Laboratory*, laboratory at Cambridge, for physical research, founded in 1874.

că'vern *n.* (Vast) underground hollow.

că'vernous *adj.* Full of caverns; as of, huge or deep as, a cavern.

cavĕ'ttō *n.* (archit.) Hollowed moulding whose section is the quadrant of a circle.

că'viare, -ar *n.* Roe of sturgeon and other large fish of eastern European lakes and rivers, pressed and salted, and eaten as relish; ~ *to the general*, (with allusion to 'Hamlet', II. ii) good thing not appreciated by the ignorant.

că'vĭl *v.i.* Raise captious objection. ~ *n.* Captious or quibbling objection; cavilling.

căvĭtā'tion *n.* Successive formation and collapse of bubbles behind body moving in stream of fluid; (path.) formation of cavities in lungs as result of disease.

că'vĭtў *n.* Empty space within solid body, hollow place; ~ *wall*, double wall with internal hollow space.

cavor't *v.i.* (orig. U.S. slang) Prance, caper.

Cavour' (-oor), Camillo Benso, Count di (1810–61). Prime minister of Piedmont, 1852–9 and 1860–1, whose statesmanship did much to secure the unification of Italy.

cā'vў *n.* Large rodent of S. Amer. genus *Cavia*, including guinea-pigs. [*cabiai*, native name in Fr. Guiana]

caw *n.* Cry of rook, crow,

or raven; sound resembling this. ~ *v.i.* Utter caw.

Că'xton, William (1422?–91). First English printer; established a press at Westminster, 1477–91, from which he issued about 80

books, many of them translations by himself from French romances; hence (as *n.*) book printed by Caxton; printing-type in imitation of Caxton's.

cay *n.* Low insular bank or reef of sand, rocks, etc., esp. off coast of Spanish America.

cayĕ'nne[1] (kā-) *n.* (also ~ *pepper*) Very hot pungent powder obtained from seeds of plants of genus *Capsicum*, used as a condiment.

Cayĕ'nne[2] (kā-). Chief town of French Guiana.

cay'man, cai'man *n.* Alligator, esp. of the tropical S. Amer. genus *Caiman*; loosely, any large Amer. saurian. [Carib *acayuman*]

cayū'se (kī-) *n.* Amer. Ind. pony. [Name of Amer. Ind. tribe]

C.B. *abbrev.* Companion of the Bath; confinement to barracks.

C.B.E. *abbrev.* Commander of (the Order of) the British Empire.

C.B.I. *abbrev.* Confederation of British Industry.

c.c. *abbrev.* Cubic centimetre.

C.C. *abbrev.* County Council(lor); cricket club.

C.C.C. *abbrev.* (U.S.) Civilian Conservation Corps; Corpus Christi College (Oxford or Cambridge).

C.C.F. *abbrev.* Combined Cadet Force.

CD *abbrev.* Corps diplomatique.

Cd. *abbrev.* Command paper.

cd *abbrev.* Candela(s).

c.d., c.div. *abbrevs.* Cum dividend.

C.E. *abbrev.* Church of England; civil engineer; Common Era.

cease *v.* Abstain *from* continuing (action etc.); stop; come, bring, to an end; ~*-fire*, (mil.) signal to cease firing; cessation of shooting or fighting. ~ *n.* Ceasing (now only in *without* ~, incessantly). **cea'selėss** *adj.* Not ceasing. **cea'selėssly̆** *adv.*

Cėcĭ'lĭa, St. (d. A.D. 230). Christian martyr; through a misinterpretation of a sentence in her Acts she came to be associated with church music and in particular with the organ, which she is sup-

posed to have played; commemorated 22 Nov.

cĕ'dar *n.* Evergreen coniferous tree of genus *Cedrus*, with fragrant fine-grained wood (*ce'darwood*), leaves in fascicles, and erect cones with carpels separating from axis; tree resembling this.

cēde *v.t.* Give up, grant, admit; surrender (territory).

cĕ'dĭ *n.* Principal monetary unit of Ghana, = 100 pesewa.

cėdĭ'lla *n.* Mark written under letter *c* thus (ç) to show that it is sibilant.

cee *n.* Letter C, c; *~-spring*, *C-spring*, spring shaped like letter *c* supporting body of carriage etc.

ceil *v.t.* Line roof of (room etc.).

ceilidh (kā'lĭ) *n.* Informal gathering for song and story in Highlands of Scotland; festive gathering for dancing etc. in Ireland. [Gael.]

cei'lĭng *n.* 1. Lining of roof, concealing the timbers. 2. (aeron.) Altitude beyond which a given aircraft cannot climb and at which only one speed of flight is possible (*absolute ~*) or altitude beyond which the rate of climb falls below 100 ft per minute (*service ~*). 3. Upper limit of prices, wages, etc.

cĕ'ladon *n.* Chinese pottery or porcelain with pale grey-green glaze; willow-green. *~ adj.* Of celadon colour. [Fr., f. name of character in D'Urfé's 'Astrée']

cĕ'landīne *n.* Either of two yellow-flowered plants, the *greater ~*, *Chelidonium majus*, and the *lesser ~*, *Ranunculus ficaria*, also known as pilewort.

Cĕ'lebēs (-z; *or* selē'bĭz). Island of Indonesia, E. of Borneo.

cĕ'lėbrant *n.* Officiating priest, esp. at Eucharist.

cĕ'lėbrāte *v.* 1. Perform (religious ceremony etc.) publicly and duly; officiate at Eucharist. 2. Observe, honour (festival, event) with rites, festivities, etc. 3. Publish abroad, praise, extol; *celebrated*, famed, renowned. **cĕlėbrā'tion** *n.*

cėlĕ'brĭtȳ *n.* 1. Being famous. 2. Celebrated person.

cėlĕ'rĭac *n.* Turnip-rooted variety of garden celery.

cėlĕ'rĭtȳ *n.* Swiftness.

cĕ'lerȳ *n.* Umbelliferous plant, *Apium graveolens*, cultivated for

the use of its blanched stalks as salad and vegetable.

cėlĕ'sta *n.* Musical instrument consisting of metal plates struck with hammers played from a keyboard.

cėlĕ'stĭal *adj.* 1. Of the sky; *~ equator*, great circle of celestial sphere, formed by plane cutting through earth's centre at right angles to its axis (so called because when sun is in equator day and night are of equal length); *~ sphere*, imaginary sphere on which the heavenly bodies appear to lie, having its centre at the centre of the earth (or at the point where the observer stands) and an infinite radius. 2. Heavenly, divine; divinely good, beautiful, etc. 3. Chinese; *C~ Empire*, (transl. of native title) the former Chinese Empire. **cėlĕ'stĭallȳ** *adv.*

cĕ'lĭbate *n.* & *adj.* Unmarried (person); (person) bound or resolved not to marry. **cĕ'lĭbacȳ** *n.*

cĕll *n.* 1. Hermit's one-roomed dwelling; (hist.) dependent nunnery or monastery 2. Single person's small room in monastery etc.; similar room in prison or other place of detention; *condemned ~*, room for prisoner condemned to death. 3. (biol.) Unit of structure of living matter, mass of protoplasm

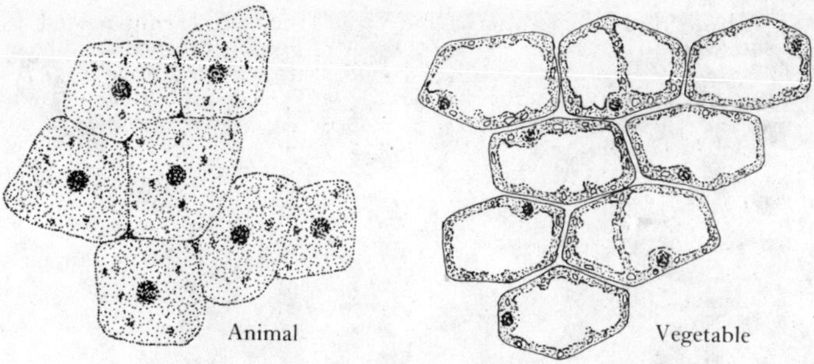

CELL

bounded by a membrane (~ *wall*) and usu. containing a nucleus. 4. (zool.) Small container of earth, silk, wax, etc., in which larva or pupa develops, esp. in comb of social insects, e.g. bees. 5. (elect.) Voltaic apparatus with only one pair of metallic elements, unit of battery. 6. (fig.) Small group or single person working in factory, particular district, etc., as nucleus of political, esp. revolutionary, activity; headquarters of such group etc.

cĕ'lla *n.* (Gk & Rom. antiq.) Principal chamber of temple.

cĕ'llar *n.* Underground room or vault, used for storage, etc.; wine-cellar, stock of wines; ~*-book*, book containing account of wines etc. in cellar. **cĕ'llarage** *n.* Cellar accommodation.

cĕ'llarer *n.* Official in monastery etc. in charge of wine and provisions.

cĕllarĕ't *n.* Case or sideboard with compartments for holding wine etc.

Cĕlli'nĭ (chĕlē-), Benvenuto (1500–71). Florentine goldsmith and sculptor, famous also for his autobiography.

cĕ'llō, 'cĕ'llō (ch-) *n.* (pl. -*os*). Violoncello. **cĕ'llĭst** *n.* Violoncellist.

cĕ'llophāne *n.* Glossy transparent material made of cellulose and used as wrapping etc. [trade-name]

cĕ'llūlar *adj.* Of, having, consisting of, cells; porous.

cĕ'llūle *n.* Small cell.

cĕ'llūloid *n.* Solid inflammable material consisting essentially of soluble cellulose nitrate and camphor, used for the same purposes as ivory, bone, tortoiseshell, etc.

cĕ'llūlōse *n.* (chem.) Carbohydrate which forms chief constituent of cell walls of all plants and of textiles such as cotton and linen; (pop.) form of paint or varnish consisting of compounds of cellulose (esp. cellulose nitrate) dissolved in an organic solvent. ~ *adj.* ~ *acetate*, acetic ester of cellulose, used to make rayon, plastics, etc.; ~ *nitrate*, nitric ester of cellulose, a constituent of smokeless gunpowders and of cordite, celluloid, etc.

Cels. *abbrev.* Celsius.

Cĕ'lsĭus, Anders (1701–44). Swedish astronomer; inventor of the centigrade scale for measuring temperature; hence (as *n.*) = CENTIGRADE (abbrev. C).

Cĕlt[1] (*or* k-) *n.* 1. Member of one of the ancient peoples of W. Europe called by the Greeks *Keltoi* and by the Romans *Celtae*; Gaul. 2. One of the peoples speaking languages related to those of the ancient Gauls, including Bretons, Cornish, Welsh, Irish, Manx, and Gaels.

cĕlt[2] *n.* Bronze, stone, or iron prehistoric implement used as axe.

Cĕ'ltĭc (*or* k-) *adj.* Of the Celts; of the branch of the Indo-European family of languages spoken by the ancient Celts or their modern representatives; ~ *fringe*,

CELLINI

Highland Scots, Welsh, Cornish, and Irish, as occupying the outlying edge of the British Isles; ~ *twilight*, romantic fairy-tale atmosphere supposed to be characteristic of Celtic literature, taken from the title of a collection of stories by W. B. YEATS. ~ *n.* Celtic language. **Cĕ'lticism** *n.*

cĕ'mbalō (ch-) *n.* Harpsichord.

cėmĕ'nt *n.* Any compound substance, esp. of lime or other stone, ground to powder and mixed with water, which hardens rapidly into stony consistence, used for binding together stones or bricks, covering floors, walls, etc.; similar substance mixed with sand and gravel etc. to form concrete; (physiol.) bony substance forming outer layer of root of tooth; plastic material for filling tooth cavities; any adhesive material used to mend small articles of glass, china, etc.; (fig.) link or bond of union. ~ *v.t.* Unite firmly with or as with cement; coat or line with cement. **cėmĕntā'tion** *n.*

cėmĕ'ntīte *n.* Hard brittle compound of iron and carbon.

cĕ'mėterў *n.* Place, not being a churchyard, for burying the dead.

cĕ'nacle *n.* (hist.) Supping-room; upper chamber; esp. (also *cĕnă'cūlum, coen-*) upper room in which the Last Supper was held, and in which the Apostles met after the Ascension.

cĕ'notaph (-ahf) *n.* Sepulchral monument to person whose body is elsewhere; *the C~*, that erected in Whitehall, London, as a memorial to the British dead of the 1914–18 war, now commemorating the dead of the 1939–45 war also.

Cenozoic: see CAINOZOIC.

cĕnse *v.t.* Perfume with incense, burn incense before.

cĕ'nser *n.* Vessel in which incense is burnt.

cĕ'nsor *n.* 1. (Rom. antiq.) Either of two magistrates who drew up the register or census of citizens and supervised public morals; hence, any person supervising or criticizing the morals and conduct of others. 2. Official inspecting books, letters, newspapers, etc., to ensure that they shall contain nothing immoral, seditious, or unacceptable to military or other authorities. 3. Any of various university and college officials; at Oxford and Cambridge, official head of non-collegiate students. 4. (psychol.) Power within the mind or personality repressing certain elements in the unconscious and preventing them from becoming conscious. **cĕ′nsorship** *n.* **cĕ′nsor** *v.t.* Act as censor to; make excisions or changes in.

cĕnsōr′ial *adj.* Of a censor; censorious.

cĕnsōr′ious *adj.* Severely critical, fault-finding. **cĕnsōr′iously** *adv.* **cĕnsōr′iousnėss** *n.*

cĕ′nsure (-sher) *n.* Adverse judgement, expression of disapproval, reprimand. ~ *v.t.* Criticize harshly and unfavourably. **cĕ′nsurable** *adj.*

cĕ′nsus *n.* 1. Official numbering of population with various statistics (in U.K. normally taken every 10 years); ~ *paper*, form to be filled up with names, ages, etc., of inmates of house etc. 2. (Rom. antiq.) Registration of citizens and property for taxation.

cĕnt *n.* 1. *per* ~, (often written %), for (in, to) every 100, esp. in stating rates of interest etc. 2. $\frac{1}{100}$ of various monetary units, esp. dollar, Netherlands florin.

cent. *abbrev.* Century.

Cent. *abbrev.* Centigrade.

cent- : see CENTI-.

cĕ′ntal *n.* Weight of 100 lb. av., used in measuring corn.

cĕ′ntaur *n.* 1. (Gk myth.) Fabulous creature with head, trunk, and arms of man joined to body and legs of horse; *C~*, member of a savage people living in Thessaly. 2. *the C~*, (astron.) the southern constellation Centaurus.

cĕ′ntaurў *n.* Any of various plants, esp. the common centaury of the herbalists, *Centaurium umbellatum*, whose medicinal properties were supposed to have been discovered by Chiron the Centaur.

cĕntā′vō *n.* (pl. *-os*). $\frac{1}{100}$ of a peso or similar unit of currency in various republics of S. America and elsewhere.

cĕntėnār′ian *adj.* & *n.* (Person) 100 years old or more.

cĕntē′narў (*or* sĕ′ntĭ-) *adj.* & *n.* (Of) 100 years; (celebration of) 100th anniversary.

cĕntĕ′nnial *adj.* Of, having lived or lasted, completing, 100 years; of the 100th anniversary. ~ *n.* (esp. U.S.) 100th anniversary.

cĕ′nter *n.* & *v.* (esp. U.S.) Centre. **cĕ′ntering** *n.* (esp.) Temporary framework of arch or vault.

cĕntĕ′simal *adj.* Reckoning, reckoned, by 100ths.

cente′simō (chĕntāz-) *n.* (pl. *-mi* pr. mē). $\frac{1}{100}$ of a lira or similar unit of currency.

cĕntĭ-, cĕnt- *prefix.* $\frac{1}{100}$ of.

centième (sah′ṅtiĕm) *n.* $\frac{1}{100}$ of a franc in the Republic of Guinea.

cĕ′ntigrāde *adj.* Having 100 degrees; (abbrev. C) of, measured by, ~ *scale*, temperature scale, invented by CELSIUS, in which the freezing-point and the boiling-point of water are taken as 0 degrees and 100 degrees respectively, used universally in scientific work (for conversion to the Fahrenheit scale see Appendix X).

cĕ′ntigrămme *n.* (abbrev. cg) $\frac{1}{100}$ of a gramme.

cĕ′ntilitre (-ēter) *n.* (abbrev. cl) $\frac{1}{100}$ of a litre.

cĕntĭ′llion (-yon) *n.* 100th power of a million (1 with 600 ciphers); (U.S.) 101st power of a thousand (1 with 303 ciphers).

centime (sah′ṅtēm) *n.* $\frac{1}{100}$ of a franc or similar unit of currency.

cĕ′ntimētre *n.* (abbrev. cm) $\frac{1}{100}$ of a metre, or 0·3937 (nearly $\frac{2}{5}$) of an inch; *~-gramme-second*, (abbrev. C.G.S., c.g.s.) applied to a system of units of measurement based on the centimetre, gramme, and second as units of length, mass, and time.

cĕ′ntimil *n.* (abbrev. cml) $\frac{1}{100}$ of a millilitre (mil).

cĕ'ntĭmō *n.* (pl. *-os*). $\frac{1}{100}$ of a peseta; $\frac{1}{100}$ of the principal monetary unit in some S. Amer. countries.

cĕ'ntĭpēde *n.* Wingless worm-like animal of the class Chilopoda, having many joints, and a pair of legs to each segment of the trunk.

cĕ'ntō *n.* (pl. *-os*). Composition made up of quotations from other authors.

cĕ'ntral[1] *adj.* Of, in, at, from, containing, the centre, leading, principal, dominant; *C~ America*, narrow southern part of North America, south of Mexico; *C~ American* (*adj.* & *n.*); *~ bank*, main bank of a country, responsible for influencing the conduct of all other banks and financial institutions in pursuance of the Government's monetary policy; *~ heating*, heating of building from a central source, as by circulating hot water or steam through pipes or warm air through flues; *C~ Office of Information*, department producing information and publicity services for all government departments of the U.K.; *C~ Powers*, (before 1914) Germany and Austria-Hungary. **cĕntră'lĭtў** *n.* **cĕ'ntrallў** *adv.* **cĕ'ntralnĕss** *n.*

Cĕ'ntral[2]. Region of central Scotland (since May 1975), comprising the former counties of Clackmannanshire, S. Perthshire, and Stirlingshire.

Cĕ'ntral A'frican Rĕpŭ'blĭc (ă-). Republic in central Africa between Cameroon Republic and Sudan, formerly a French colony; capital, Bangui.

cĕ'ntralĭsm *n.* Centralizing system. **cĕ'ntralĭst** *n.*

cĕ'ntralīze *v.* 1. Come, bring, to a centre. 2. Concentrate (administrative powers) in single centre instead of distributing them among local departments; bring (State etc.) under this system. **cĕntralīzā'tion** *n.*

cĕ'ntre (*-ter*) *n.* 1. Middle point of circle, sphere, line, etc. middle point or part of anything; point, line, upon which a body turns or revolves; in lathe, conical adjustable bearing to hold object being turned. 2. Point of concentration, attraction, or dispersion, nucleus, source; place, building(s) etc., forming central point or main area (as *civic ~*, *health ~*). 3. (archit.) Temporary framework supporting arch or dome while building. 4. Person, thing, occupying central position; (footb. etc.) player positioned in the middle of a line or field of players, esp. = *~ forward*, one occupying central position in forward line. (pol.) men of moderate opinions. 5. *~ of attration*, (phys. etc.) point tp which bodies tend by gravity etc.; point or object drawing general interest; *~ of gravity*, point about which all parts of a body exactly balance each other, so that if this point is supported the body remains at rest in any position. 6. *~ bit*, tool with projecting centre-point for making cylindrical holes; *~ board*, metal plate which can be lowered through slot in keel of sailing-boat to increase stability and check leeway; *~ forward*: see sense 4; *~ half*, (footb. etc.) player positioned in central position among half-backs. **cĕ'ntreless, cĕ'ntrĭc, -ĭcal** *adjs.* **cĕ'ntre** *v.* Be concentrated, have centre, *in*, *on*, *at*, etc.; place in or as in centre; mark with centre; grind (lens) so as to make its optical centre coincide with its geometrical centre; (footb. etc.) pass (ball) to centre.

cĕntrĭ'fūgal *adj.* Flying, tending to fly, from centre; *~ force*, force in direction away from centre, erron. supposed to be experienced by body moving round it; *~ machine* etc., one in which rotation about axis results in movement of parts or particles away from the axis. **cĕntrĭ'fūgallў** *adv.*

cĕ'ntrĭfūge *n.* Centrifugal machine, esp. one for separating cream from milk, or for drying objects, by rotary motion. *~ v.t.* Subject to action of a centrifuge. **cĕntrĭfūgā'tion** *n.*

cĕ'ntrĭōle *n.* Cylindrical organelle made up of nine fibrils, participating in the processes accompanying its division.

cĕntrĭ'pėtal *adj.* Tending towards the centre.

cĕ'ntūple *adj.* Hundredfold. ~ *v.t.* Multiply a hundredfold. **centū'plĭcate** *n.* & *v.*

cĕntūr'ĭon *n.* (Rom. antiq.) Commander of a century.

cĕ'ntūrӯ (*or* -cherĭ) *n.* 1. (Rom. antiq.) Company in army, orig. of 100 men; each of the 193 political divisions by which the Roman people voted. 2. 100, esp. 100 runs at cricket. 3. 100 years, esp. each successive period of 100 years reckoning from a fixed date, e.g. the assumed date of Christ's birth; ~ *plant*, agave or American aloe, supposed to flower once in 100 years, but often flowering after only five.

cėphă'lĭc *adj.* Of, in, the head; ~ *index*, number indicating the ratio of transverse to longitudinal diameter of skull, considered as an indication of race.

cĕ'phalopŏd *n.* Animal of the Cephalopoda, the most highly organized class of Mollusca, characterized by head with tentacles attached and including cuttlefishes etc.

cĕphalothôr'ăx *n.* (zool.) In some arthropods, part of body formed by fusion of head and thorax.

cĕ'phėĭd (*or* sefē'-) *adj.* & *n.* (Star of type) resembling the variable star δ Cephei. [f. *Cepheus*, northern constellation named after mythical king of Ethiopia, father of Andromeda]

cĕră'mĭc *adj.* Of (the art of) pottery; of (making of) substances etc. produced by firing of minerals, esp. clay, at very high temperatures. **cėră'mĭcs** *n.* Ceramic art. **cĕ'ramist** *n.*

cėră'stĭum *n.* Hoary-leaved plant of genus *C*~ with white flowers.

Cēr'berus. (Gk myth.) The three-headed (acc. to Hesiod, fifty-headed) watch-dog guarding the entrance to the infernal regions.

cēre *n.* Naked wax-like membrane at base of beak in some birds.

cēr'ėal *adj.* Of corn or edible grain. ~ *n.* (freq. pl.) (Any of)

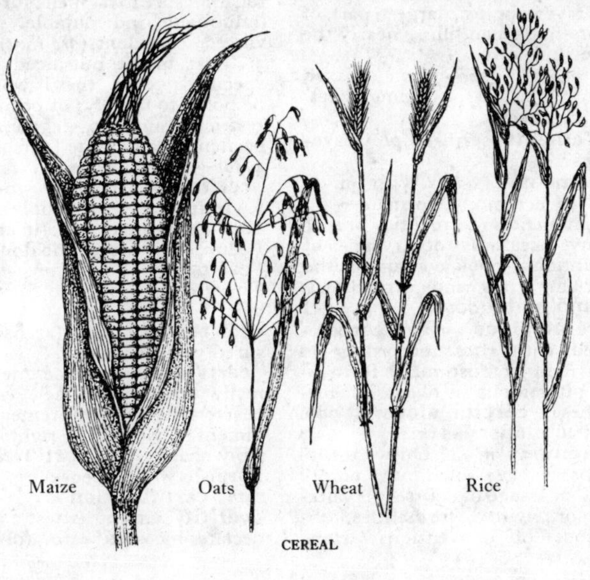

CEREAL

those graminaceous plants cultivated for their seed as human food; an article of food (esp. as breakfast dish) made from cereal. [f. CERES]

cĕrėbĕ'llum *n.* Little brain, posterior part of brain, highly developed in mammals and concerned in co-ordination of movement and maintenance of equilibrium.

cĕ'rėbral *adj.* 1. Of the brain or cerebrum; ~ *hemisphere*, either of the two halves into which the cerebrum is divided longitudinally by a deep fissure; ~ *palsy*: see PALSY. 2. ~ *consonants*, in Sanskrit etc., consonants developed from dentals by retracting tongue and applying its tip to palate. 3. Intellectual.

cĕrėbrā'tion *n.* Working of the brain. **cĕ'rėbrāte** *v.* Use the brain, think (about).

cĕrėbro- *prefix.* Of the cerebrum; ~*-spinal*, of the brain and spinal cord; ~*-spinal fluid*, solution of salts and protein filling cavities of brain and spinal cord; ~*-spinal meningitis*, inflammation of the meninges of brain and spinal cord.

cĕ'rėbrum *n.* Great brain, convoluted mass of nervous matter forming the anterior and, in the higher vertebrates, largest part of the brain, in man filling nearly the whole skull.

cēr'eclŏth (sērk-) *n.* Waxed cloth, esp. as winding-sheet; winding-sheet.

cēr'ements (sērm-) *n.pl.* Grave-clothes.

cĕrėmō'nĭal *adj.* With or of ritual or ceremony, formal. ~ *n.* System of rites; formalities proper to any occasion; observance of conventions; book containing the order for rites and ceremonies. **cĕrėmō'nĭallȳ** *adv.*

cĕrėmō'nĭous *adj.* Accompanied with rites; according to prescribed or customary formalities; punctilious in observing formalities. **cĕrėmō'nĭouslȳ** *adv.* **cĕrėmō'nĭousnėss** *n.*

cĕ'rėmonȳ *n.* 1. Outward rite or observance; solemnity; empty form. 2. Usage of courtesy, politeness, or civility; formalities, observance of conventions; *stand on* ~, insist on punctilious observance of formalities.

Cēr'ēs (-z). 1. (Rom. myth.) Goddess of growing vegetation, identified by the Romans with DEMETER and in this later cult worshipped as corn and earth goddess. 2. (astron.) Largest of the asteroids.

ceri'se (-ēz *or* -ēs) *n.* & *adj.* Light clear red, cherry-red.

cēr'ĭum *n.* (chem.) Element of rare-earth group, resembling iron in colour and lustre; symbol Ce, at. no. 85, at. wt 140·12. **cēr'ĭc, cēr'ous** *adjs.* [discovered in 1803, about the same time as the asteroid CERES and named after it]

cêr'mĕt *n.* Alloy of ceramic substance with metal.

CERN, Cern *abbrev.* *Centre Européen de Recherche Nucléaire* (Fr., = European Nuclear Research Centre).

cēroplă'stĭc *adj.* Of modelling in wax.

cêrt *n.* (slang) Event or result certain to happen; horse certain to win a race.

cêr'tain (-tĭn *or* -tn) *adj.* 1. Settled, fixed, unfailing; unerring, reliable; sure to happen; sure *to* do; indubitable, indisputable. 2. Convinced, confident (*of*, *that*); sure. 3. That might but need not be specified; occas., that it would not be polite to specify; of positive yet restricted amount, degree, etc.; a particular, a definite (person etc.). 4. *for* ~, for a certainty.

cêr'tainlȳ (-tĭn- *or* -tn-) *adv.* 1. Indubitably; infallibly; confidently; admittedly. 2. (in answers) I admit it; of course; no doubt, yes.

cêr'taintȳ (-tĭn- *or* -tn-) *n.* Thing certain or sure; being certain.

cêr'tės (-z) *adv.* (archaic) Assuredly, I assure you.

certĭ'fĭcate *n.* Document formally attesting a fact, esp. the bearer's status, acquirements, fulfilment of conditions, right to company shares, etc. **certĭ'fĭcāte** *v.t.* Furnish with, license by, certificate. **certĭfĭcā'tion** *n.*

cêr'tĭfȳ *v.t.* 1. Attest formally, declare by certificate; (of doctor etc.) declare by certificate to be insane. 2. Inform certainly, assure. **cẽr'tĭfīable** *adj.* (esp. of lunatic or lunacy). **cẽr'tĭfīablȳ** *adv.*

cẽrtĭorār'ī (-shĭ-) *n.* Writ from superior court, upon complaint that justice has not been done in inferior court, for records of the cause. [LL, = 'to be informed', occurring in original writ]

cẽr'tĭtūde *n.* Feeling certain, conviction.

cėru'lėan (-ōō-) *adj.* Deep blue, azure; of the colour of the cloudless sky; ~ *blue*, pigment of this colour prepared from cobalt.

cėru'mĕn (-ōō-) *n.* Yellow waxy secretion in the external canal of the ear. **cėru'mĭnous** *adj.*

cẽr'use (-ōōs; *or* serōō's) *n.* White lead; basic lead carbonate, used as white paint.

Cervă'ntēs (-z) Miguel de (1547–1616). Spanish novelist and dramatist, author of 'Don Quixote' (1605–15).

cẽr'vĭcal (*or* -vī'-) *adj.* (anat.) Of the neck; of the cervix of an organ.

cẽr'vīne *adj.* Of, like, deer.

cẽr'vĭx *n.* (pl. *-vĭcēs*). (anat.) Neck; neck-like structure, esp. neck of the uterus.

Cėsãr'ėwĭtch (sĭz-). Handicap horse-race of about 2¼ miles, instituted at Newmarket in 1839, and run at the October meeting. [in honour of state visit of the tsarevich who became Alexander II]

cĕss *n.* Tax, levy, rate (now only dial. and in Scotland, Ireland, and India).

cĕssā'tion *n.* Ceasing, pause.

cĕ'ssion *n.* Ceding, giving up.

cĕ'sspĭt *n.* Cesspool.

cĕ'sspōōl *n.* Well sunk to receive drainage from water-closet etc., retaining solid matter and allowing liquid to escape.

cĕ'stoid, -tōde *adj.* & *n.* Ribbon-like (intestinal worm).

Cestr. *abbrev.* (Bishop) of Chester (replacing surname in his signature).

cėtā'cean (-sh*a*n) *adj.* & *n.* (Member) of the Cetacea, an order of marine mammals, including whales, dolphins, porpoises, etc.

CETACEA

cėtā'ceous (-sh*u*s) *adj.* [Gk *kētos* whale]

cĕ'terăch (-k) *n.* Fern of genus *C*~ with back of fronds thickly covered with scales.

ce'teris pãr'ĭbus (kāterēs). Other things being equal. [L]

Cévennes (sĭvĕ'n *or* se-). Mountain-range of central France, SE. part of the Massif Central.

Ceylŏ'n (sĭl-). Name until 1972 of SRI LANKA. **Ceylonē'se** (-z) *adj.* & *n.*

Cézanne (sāzăn), Paul (1839–1906). French painter, central figure of the movement known as Neo-Impressionism.

cf. *abbrev.* *Confer* (L, = compare).

C.F. *abbrev.* Chaplain to the Forces.

cg *abbrev.* Centigramme(s).

C.G. *abbrev.* Coldstream Guards.

C.G.M. *abbrev.* Conspicuous Gallantry Medal.

C.G.S. *abbrev.* Chief of the General Staff; (also c.g.s.) centimetre-gramme-second.

C.G.T. *abbrev.* *Confédération*

Générale du Travail (Fr., = General Confederation of Labour, French equivalent of T.U.C.).

ch., chap. *abbrevs.* Chapter.

C.H. *abbrev.* Companion of Honour.

Chablis (shă'blē) *n.* Dry white wine produced near Chablis, in N. Burgundy, France.

chāce: see CHASE[1] 2.

chacŏ'nne (sh-) *n.* Old stately Spanish dance; instrumental composition in 3/4 time with an unchanging ground-bass against which the upper parts are varied (cf. PASSACAGLIA, which it resembles).

Chăd[1], **chăd** *n.* (also *Mr. C~*) Figure of human head appearing above wall etc., with caption 'Wot, no —?', as protest against shortage etc.

Chăd[2]. Republic of north-central Africa extending from Lake Chad across the E. Sudan; member of French Community; capital, Ndjaména (formerly Fort Lamy).

Chă'dwick, Sir James (1891–). English physicist; famous for his researches on radioactivity and nuclear fission; Nobel Prize for physics 1935.

chāfe *v.* 1. Rub (skin etc.) to restore warmth or sensation; rub so as to abrade or injure the surface. 2. Irritate; show irritation, fume, fret. ~ *n.* Rubbing; chafing.

chā'fer *n.* Cockchafer.

chaff (-ah-) *n.* 1. Husks of corn etc. separated by threshing or winnowing; chopped hay and straw for feeding cattle; *~-cutter*, machine for chopping hay and straw for fodder. 2. Refuse, worthless stuff. 3. Banter, raillery. ~ *v.* 1. Chop (straw etc.). 2. Banter.

chă'ffer *n.* & *v.* Haggle, bargain.

chă'ffinch *n.* Small bird, *Fringilla coelebs*, common in Britain, with blue crown in male and white wing-patches.

chā'fing-dish. Vessel to hold burning charcoal etc. for heating or keeping warm anything placed upon it; dish used over spirit-lamp etc. for cooking at table.

chă'grin (sh-; *or* shagrē'n) *n.* Acute disappointment, mortification. ~ *v.t.* Vex acutely, mortify, by thwarting or disappointment.

chain *n.* 1. Flexible string of connected metal links. 2. (pl.) Fetters, bonds; confinement, restraint. 3. Personal ornament in form of chain round neck. 4. Connected course, train, or series (of events, objects, mountains, etc.); series of branch businesses; figure in quadrille etc. 5. Land-surveyor's measuring rod of 100 jointed iron rods called links; the length of this, 66 ft. 6. (naut.) Contrivance to carry lower shrouds of mast outside ship's side. 7. (chem.) Number of atoms (usu. of carbon) joined in series in a molecule. 8. ~ *armour*, armour of interlaced links or rings, mail; ~ *bridge*, suspension bridge swung on or by chains; ~ *gang*, gang of convicts chained together at work etc.; ~ *harrow*, harrow consisting of flexible mat of strong metal links; ~ *letter*, letter of which the recipient is asked to make copies to be sent to a (named) number of others, these being asked to do the like in their turn; *~-link fence, fencing*, fence of thick steel wire mesh; ~ *mail*, (erron. for) chain armour; ~ *reaction*, chemical reaction forming intermediate products which react with the original substance and are repeatedly renewed; ~ *saw*, saw with teeth on endless chain; ~ *shot*, shot consisting of two balls chained together, formerly used in naval warfare to cut ship's rigging; *~-smoker*, one who lights another cigarette etc. from the stump of the last smoked; *~-smoke* (*v.*); *~-smoking*; *~-stitch*, embroidery or crochet stitch resembling links of a chain; ~ *store*, one of a series of mutiple retail shops belonging to one firm and selling the same goods. ~ *v.t.* Secure, confine, with chain.

chair *n.* 1. Seat for one person; movable, usu. four-legged, seat with rest for the back, of various forms; *~-bed*, chair that unfolds to form a bed. 2. Seat, position,

of authority, state, or dignity; seat occupied by person presiding at meeting etc.; seat, office, of mayor; seat, office, of university professor. 3. Iron or steel socket holding rail of railway in place on sleeper. 4. (hist.) Sedan. 5. Electric chair. ~ *v.t.* 1. Install in chair of authority. 2. Place in chair etc. and carry aloft in triumph or rejoicing. 3. Act as chairman of, preside over, (meeting).

chair'man *n.* (fem. *chair'-woman*). 1. Person chosen to preside over meeting, permanent president of committee, board, etc.; *C~ of Committees*, in Houses of Parliament, person presiding instead of Lord Chancellor or Speaker when House is in Committee. 2. (hist.) Wheeler of Bath chair; sedan-bearer. **chair'manship** *n.* Office etc. of chairman of committee.

chaise (shāz) *n.* Pleasure- or travelling-carriage, (esp.) a light open carriage for one or two persons; post-chaise.

chaise-longue (shāz-lawngg) *n.* Kind of long low chair with seat

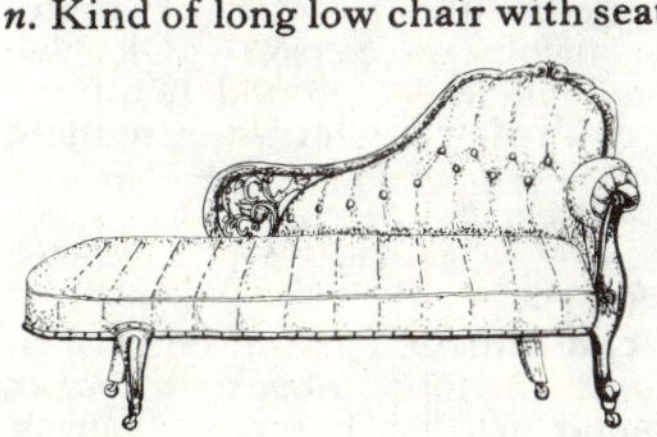

long enough to support sitter's legs. [Fr.]

Chălcē'don (k-). Ancient city of Asia Minor, almost opposite Byzantium, scene of 4th oecumenical council (451) which defined orthodox teaching about the Person of Christ. **Chălcėdō'nĭan** *adj.*

chălcĕ'donў (k-) *n.* Precious or semi-precious stone, a cryptocrystalline form of silica with wax-like lustre; including agate, cornelian, onyx, etc.

chălco- (k-) *prefix.* Copper, brass.

chălcolĭ'thĭc *adj.* Of the stage of a culture marked by concurrent use of stone and bronze implements.

Chăldē'a (k-). Country of the Chaldeans, freq. identified in the O.T. with Babylonia.

Chăldē'an (k-) *adj.* & *n.* 1. (Member) of a Semitic people originating from Arabia, who settled in the neighbourhood of Ur and were later merged with the Babylonians; (of) their language. 2. (Member) of a sect of Eastern Christians, descendants of ancient Nestorian Churches, now in communion with Rome.

Chăldee' (k-) *n.* 1. (esp. bibl.) Chaldean. 2. Term formerly and incorrectly applied to the language of the Aramaic portions of the Biblical books of Ezra and Daniel and to the vernacular paraphrases of the O.T. on the assumption that the language was that of the Chaldeans.

cha'ldron (kawl-) *n.* Measure for coals, approx. 36 bushels.

chă'let (shălā) *n.* Swiss peasant's wooden house or cottage; villa built in this style; small, usu. wooden, dwelling for holiday-makers.

chă'lĭce *n.* Goblet, eucharistic wine-cup; (poet.) flower-cup.

chalk (-awk) *n.* Opaque white soft earthy limestone, consisting largely of calcium carbonate, occurring in deposits of great extent and thickness in SE. England etc., and forming high white cliffs on sea-shore; used for burning into lime, making cement, and for writing, etc. on blackboards or other dark surfaces; coloured preparation of similar texture used for drawing etc.; *by (a) long* ~*(s)*, by far (f. use of chalk to score points in games); ~ *stripe*, *-striped*, (with) pattern of thin white stripes on dark ground. ~ *v.t.* Rub, mark, draw, write, etc., with chalk; ~ *it up (to)*, charge it (to) (person etc.). **cha'lkў** *adj.* Abounding in, white as, chalk. **cha'lkĭnėss** *n.*

chă'llenġe (-j) *n.* 1. Calling to account, esp. sentry's demand for password etc. 2. (law etc.) Exception taken (to a juryman, a vote, etc.). 3. Summons to trial or contest, esp. duel; defiance. ~ *v.t.* 1. Call to account. 2. Take exception to; dispute, deny. 3. Claim (attention, admiration, etc.). 4. Invite to contest, game, or duel; defy. **chă'llenġer** *n.*

Châlons (shălawṅ). Place on the Marne, France, scene of the defeat of the Huns under Attila in A.D. 451 by the Romans and Visigoths.

chălў'bėate (k-) *adj.* (of spring, mineral water) Impregnated with iron salts.

chăm (k-) *n.* *Great C*~, autocrat (used of dominant critic etc., esp. Dr Johnson). [earlier form of KHAN]

chă'maephўte (k-) *n.* (bot.) Woody or herbaceous plant with buds less than 25 cm above soil level.

chā'mber *n.* 1. Room, esp. bedroom (poet. or archaic); (also *burial* ~) compartment or cavity used for burial; (pl.) set of rooms in larger building, esp. an Inn of Court, let separately; (pl.) judge's room for hearing cases etc. not needing to be taken in court. 2. (Hall used by) deliberative or judicial body, one of the houses of a Parliament; *C*~ *of Commerce*, *Agriculture*, etc., board formed to protect interests of commerce, agriculture, etc., in district. 3. (also ~ *pot*) Vessel for urine, used in bedroom etc. 4. Cavity in animal body; enclosed space in mechanism, esp. part of gun-bore in which charge is placed; in a revolver, each compartment of breeching containing the charge. 5. ~ *concert*, concert of chamber music; *cha'mbermaid*, housemaid in inn etc.; ~ *music*, music for small instrumental combinations; ~ *orchestra*, small orchestra; ~ *organ*, small domestic organ as dist. from organ for church or concert hall; ~ *tomb*, chambered tomb.

chā'mbered (-*erd*) *adj.* (of tomb) Containing a burial chamber.

chā'mberlain[1] (-lĭn) *n.* Officer managing household of sovereign or great noble; officer receiving rents and revenues of corporation or public office; *Lord C*~ *(of the Household)*, a chief officer of the Royal Household, appointing royal tradesmen, until 1968 licensing plays for public performance, etc.; *Lord Great C*~ *of England*, hereditary officer with duties now chiefly ceremonial.

Chā'mberlain[2] (-lĭn). Name of a family of British politicians: *Joseph* ~ (1836–1914), Liberal and Liberal-Unionist, advocate of tariff reform and colonial development; *Sir (Joseph) Austen* ~ (1863–1937), his son, Liberal-Unionist and Conservative, foreign secretary 1924–9; *(Arthur) Neville* ~ (1869–1940), half-brother of Austen, Conservative prime minister 1937–40.

Chămbertin (sh-, -ăṅ) *n.* Dry red wine produced near Chambertin in Burgundy.

chamē'lėon (k-) *n.* Saurian reptile of the genus *Chamaeleo*, small lizard-like creatures with power of changing colour of skin to suit surroundings, and of living for long periods without food; (fig.) variable or inconstant person. [Gk *khamaileōn*, lit. = 'ground lion']

chă'mfer *n.* Surface produced by bevelling square edge or corner equally on both sides. ~ *v.t.* Give chamfer to; channel, flute.

chă'mois *n.* 1. (shămwah) Capriform antelope, *Rupicapra tragus*, found in Alps, Pyrenees, Taurus, and other mountain ranges of Europe and Asia. 2. (shă'mĭ) Soft pliable washable leather from skin of goats, sheep, deer, and split hides of other animals.

chamomile: see CAMOMILE.

chămp[1] *v.* Munch (fodder) noisily; bite hard upon (bit); make chewing action or noise.

chămp[2] *n.* (colloq.) Champion.

chămpā'gne (sh-, -ān) *n.* White wine made in district of Champagne, former province of E. France, esp. the sparkling kind which is bottled before fermentation has ceased.

chă'mpaign (-pān) *n.* (Expanse of) open country.

chă'mpertў *n.* (law) Offence of assisting a party in a suit in which one is not naturally interested with a view to receiving share of disputed property. **chă'mpertous** *adj.*

chă'mpĭon *n.* 1. Fighting man, combatant; person who fights, argues, etc., for another or for a cause. 2. Person (esp. boxer, athlete), animal, plant, etc., that has defeated, or been judged superior to, all competitors. **chă'mpĭonshĭp** *n.* **chă'mpĭon** *adj.* That is a champion. ~ *v.t.* Fight for, maintain the cause of.

champlevé (shahṅlevā') *adj.* & *n.* (Enamel-work) of which the metal ground is hollowed out and the spaces filled with enamel (cf. CLOISONNÉ). [Fr., = 'field removed']

chance (-ahns) *n.* 1. Way in which things fall out; fortune; casual or fortuitous circumstance or occurrence, accident. 2. Possibility, probability, of anything happening. 3. Absence of design or assignable cause, fortuity. 4. *by* ~, as it falls or fell out; without design; *the main* ~, the chance of getting money, one's own interests; *take one's* ~, take what may befall one; seize one's opportunity. ~ *adj.* Happening by chance, fortuitous. ~ *v.* Happen, fall out; (colloq.) risk.

cha'ncel (-ah-) *n.* Part of church near altar, reserved for clergy, choir, etc., and freq. screened off from nave. [L *cancelli* lattice bars]

cha'ncellerў (-ah-) *n.* Position, staff, department, official residence, of chancellor; office attached to embassy or consulate (now usu. *chancery*).

cha'ncellor (-ah-) *n.* 1. *Lord* (*High*) *C*~, *C*~ *of England*, highest officer of the Crown, presiding in House of Lords, a member of the Cabinet, and the highest judicial functionary in England. 2. *C*~ *of the Exchequer*, highest finance minister of British Government, who presents the annual budget to the House of Commons. 3. *C*~ *of the Duchy of Lancaster*, orig., chancellor of Duchy Court of Lancaster; now, a minister of the Crown, often cabinet minister who does not desire departmental work. 4. ~ *of bishop, diocese*, law officer acting as vicar general for bishop and holding ecclesiastical courts. 5. *C*~ *of the Garter* (or other order), officer sealing commissions, mandates, etc. 6. Titular head of a university, usu. honorary, the *Vice C*~ performing the duties. 7. In Germany, Austria, etc., chief minister of State. **cha'ncellorshĭp** *n.*

chance-mĕ'dley (-ah-) *n.* (law) Action, esp. homicide, mainly but not entirely unintentional; inadvertency.

cha'ncerў (-ah-) *n.* 1. Lord Chancellor's Court, a division of the High Court of Justice, formerly a separate court of equity for cases with no remedy in the common-law courts; (U.S. etc.) court of equity; office of public records, archives; *in* ~, (boxing) with head held under opponent's arm, against rules, to be pummelled (from the tenacity with which the old Court of Chancery held anything and the certainty of cost and loss). 2. Office attached to embassy or consulate.

chă'ncre (shănk*er*) *n.* Venereal ulcer.

cha'ncў (-ah-) *adj.* Uncertain, risky.

chăndelier' (sh-) *n.* Ornamental branched hanging support for a number of candles or other lights.

Chandigar'h (-ŭn- -goor). Territory in India created in 1966 to serve as the capital area for Punjab and Haryana; city in this territory.

cha'ndler (-ah-) *n.* Dealer in candles, oil, soap, paint, and groceries; *corn* ~, *ship('s)* ~: see CORN[1], SHIP. **chă'ndlerȳ** *n.*

chānge (-j) *n.* 1. Alteration; substitution of one for another; variation, variety. 2. What may be substituted for another of the same kind, esp. in ~ *of clothes* etc. 3. Lower coins or notes given for higher one; money returned as balance of that tendered in payment. 4. Arrival of moon at fresh phase (prop. only at new moon). 5. (bell-ringing) Order in which peal of bells is or may be rung; *ring the* ~*s*, go through all the changes in ringing a peal of bells; vary ways of putting or doing thing. 6. *C*~, place where merchants meet, Exchange. 7. (also ~ *of life*) Menopause. ~ *v.* 1. Take another instead of; resign, get rid of, *for*; give or get smaller or foreign coin for; put on different clothes; put fresh clothes or coverings on (esp., ~ *a baby*, replace used nappy with clean one); go from one to another; change trains; give and receive, exchange. 2. Make or become different; ~ *one's mind*, change one's purpose or opinion; (of moon) arrive at fresh phase, esp. become new moon. 3. ~ *up*, *down*, (in motor driving) change to a higher, lower, gear. **chā'ngeful, chā'ngelėss** *adjs.*

chā'ngeable (-j*a*-) *adj.* Irregular, inconstant. **chāngeabĭ'litȳ** *n.*

chā'ngeling (-jl-) *n.* Thing or child substituted for another by stealth, esp. elf-child thus left by fairies.

chă'nnel[1] *n.* 1. Natural or artificial bed of running water; comparatively narrow piece of water joining two large pieces; *the C*~, the English Channel. 2. Tube or tubular passage for fluids. 3. (fig.) Course in which anything moves, direction; medium of transmission, communication, exchange, etc. 4. Band of frequencies wide enough for transmission of radio or television signal. 5. Groove; flute. ~ *v.t.* Form channel(s) in, groove; cut out (way etc.); (fig.) direct.

chă'nnel[2] *n.* (naut.) Broad thick plank projecting horizontally from ship's side to broaden base for shrouds.

Chă'nnel I'slands (īl*a*ndz). Group of islands off the NW. coast of France, of which the largest are Jersey, Guernsey, and Alderney; the only parts of the dukedom of Normandy still owing allegiance to the English Crown, to which they have been attached since the Conquest.

Chanson de Geste (shahṅn-sawṅ, zhĕ-). One of a group of French historical verse romances, mostly connected with Charlemagne, composed in the 11th–13th centuries.

chant (-ah-) *n.* 1. Song. 2. Short musical passage in two or more phrases each beginning with reciting note, for singing to unmetrical words (psalms, canticles). 3. Measured monotonous song, musical recitation of words; sing-song intonation. ~ *v.* Sing; utter musically; intone, sing to a chant. **cha'nter** *n.* (esp.) see BAGPIPE.

chă'nticleer *n.* Domestic cock.

cha'ntrȳ (-ah-) *n.* Endowment for priest(s) to sing masses for founder's soul; priests, chapel, so endowed.

cha'ntȳ (-ah-) *n.* Var. of SHANTY[2].

chā'ŏs (k-) *n.* 1. Formless void, 'great deep' of primordial matter, abyss from which cosmos was evolved. 2. Utter confusion. **chāŏ'tic** *adj.* **chāŏ'ticallȳ** *adv.*

chăp[1] *n.* Crack, fissure, in earth etc., esp. fissure in skin caused by exposure to frost, cold wind, etc. ~ *v.* Crack, cause to crack, in fissures.

chăp[2] *n.* 1. (pl.) Jaws, esp. of beasts; cheeks. 2. Lower jaw or half of cheek, esp. of pig as food;

~*-fallen*, with jaw hanging down, dejected, dispirited.

chăp³ *n.* (colloq.) Man, boy, fellow.

chăparră'l *n.* (U.S.) Dense tangled brushwood, esp. such as abounds on poor soil in Mexico and Texas.

chăp-bŏŏk *n.* Small pamphlet of popular tales, ballads, tracts, or other specimen of popular literature of the kind formerly hawked by chapmen.

chāpe *n.* 1. Metal plate or mounting of scabbard or sheath, esp. at point. 2. Part of buckle by which it is fastened to belt etc.

chă'pel *n.* 1. Place of Christian worship other than parish church or cathedral, esp. one attached to private house or institution; oratory in larger building with altar, esp. compartment or cell of cathedral etc. separately dedicated and with its own altar; place of public worship of established Church subordinate to and dependent on parish church; ~ *of ease*, one built for parishioners living far from parish church. 2. In England and Wales, Nonconformist place of worship. 3. Chapel service, attendance in chapel. 4. Printers' workshop, printing-office; meeting or association of journeyman-printers for keeping order, settling price-disputes, etc.; *father of the* ~, president of this. [L *cappella* dim. of *cappa* cape; first chapel was sanctuary in which St. Martin's sacred cloak was kept]

chă'pėlrỹ *n.* District served by chapel.

chă'perōn (sh-) *n.* Married or elderly woman accompanying young unmarried woman for sake of propriety on public occasions etc. ~ *v.t.* Act as chaperon to. **chă'peronage** *n.* [Fr., orig. sense 'hood']

chă'plain (-lĭn) *n.* Priest of chapel, clergyman officiating in private chapel of sovereign or institution, on board ship or for regiment etc. **chă'plaincỹ** *n.*

chă'plėt *n.* 1. Wreath of flowers, leaves, gems, etc., for head. 2. String of beads for counting prayers, one-third of length of rosary; string of beads as necklace. 3. Anything resembling string of beads; (archit.) bead-moulding.

Chă'plĭn, Sir Charles Spencer ('Charlie') (1889–1977). English-born film actor and producer.

chă'pman *n.* (pl. *-men*). (hist.) Pedlar, hawker.

chăps *n.* Stout leather trousers without seat worn by horsemen in western States of U.S. as protection against thorns and bushes. [Short for Mex. Span. *chaparreras*]

chă'pter *n.* 1. Main division of a book or treatise (abbrev. *c.*, *cap.*, *ch.*, or *chap.*); Act of Parliament numbered as part of proceedings of one session (thus 5 & 6 Will. IV, cap. 62 = session of 5th and 6th years of William IV's reign, 62nd chapter, i.e. Statutory Declarations Act 1835); (fig.) limited subject, piece of narrative, etc.; ~ *and verse*, exact reference; ~ *of accidents*, series of misfortunes. 2. General meeting or assembly of canons of cathedral or members of religious or knightly order for consultation and transaction of affairs; body of persons constituting this, esp. canons of cathedral; ~ *house*, building attached to cathedral, monastery, etc. for meetings of the chapter.

char¹ *n.* (colloq.) Charwoman. ~ *v.i.* Act as charwoman.

char² *v.* Burn to charcoal; scorch; blacken with fire.

char³, **charr** *n.* Trout of genus *Salvelinus*, found in mountain lakes.

chă'rabănc (sh-, -ăng) *n.* Long vehicle, with rows of seats looking forward, for excursions; motor-coach.

chă'racter (k-) *n.* 1. Distinctive mark, brand; graphic sign or symbol, esp. graphic symbol standing for sound, syllable, or notion, used in writing or printing; handwriting, printing; cabbalistic sign or emblem. 2. Characteristic, esp. (pl.) distinguishing features of species or genus; sum of distinguishing features of individual etc., mental and moral qualities; such qualities strongly developed or strikingly displayed; reputation, (good) repute. 3. Description or report of person's qualities; esp. formal testimonial given by employer. 4. Personage, personality; imaginary person created by novelist or dramatist or played by actor; status, position; (colloq.) odd or eccentric person; ~ *actor*, one who plays eccentric characters. **chă'racterlĕss** *adj.*

chăracterĭ'stĭc (k-) *adj.* Distinctive, displaying the character of. ~ *n.* 1. Characteristic trait, mark, or quality. 2. (math.) Whole number in logarithm. **chăracterĭ'stĭcallȳ** *adv.*

chă'racterīze (k-) *v.t.* Describe character of; describe *as*; be characteristic of, impart character to. **chăracterīzā'tion** *n.*

chara'de (sh*a*rahd) *n.* Kind of riddle in which each syllable of word to be guessed is enigmatically described or dramatically represented, freq. in dumb show. [Provençal *charrado* chatter]

chār'coal *n.* Black residue of partly burnt wood, bones, coal, etc., porous, capable of reduction to powder, and (when pure) consisting wholly of carbon; charcoal grey; ~ *burner*, one employed in manufacture of charcoal by burning wood; ~ *grey*, dark grey colour.

chārd *n.* 1. Seakale beet, variety of beet with large white succulent leaf-stalks used like seakale and leaves used like spinach. 2. (pl.) Late-summer blanched leaves of artichoke or other vegetable.

chārge *n.* 1. Quantity of anything which receptacle, piece of mechanism, etc., receives at one time; quantity of explosive for a gun or for one firing in blasting; (colloq.) dose of drugs. 2. Electrical energy present in a proton or electron; such energy imparted to an object; accumulation of chemical energy in storage battery etc. available for conversion into electrical energy; NEGATIVE, POSITIVE, ~: see these words. 3. (her.) Device, bearing. 4. Responsibility, care, custody; task, duty; thing or person entrusted to another. 5. Pecuniary burden; price for services or goods; expenses; liability to pay money laid upon person or estate. 6. Precept, mandate, order; official instruction by judge to jury, bishop to clergy, etc. 7. Accusation, esp. that upon which prisoner is brought up for trial. 8. Impetuous attack; (mil.) signal for charge. 9. *char'gehand*, workman, shop assistant, etc., in charge of others; ~ *nurse*, nursing attendant in charge of others; ~ *sheet*, police-station record of persons charged, the charge against them, etc. ~ *v.* 1. Fill to full or proper extent; (her.) place bearing on (escutcheon etc.); fill *with*; impart electrical energy to (object), accumulate charge in (battery etc.). 2. Burden, entrust, *with*; command, order, enjoin; exhort or instruct formally or officially. 3. Bring accusation against. 4. Subject or make liable to pecuniary obligation or liability; demand as price or sum (*for*). 5. Make violent onset, attack or assail impetuously.

chargé (shārzhā) *n.* (also ~ *d'affaires* pr. dăfār) Deputy ambassador; ambassador at minor court.

chār'geable (-j*a*-) *adj.* (esp.) Liable to be made an expense (*to*); proper to be added to (account etc.).

chār'ger[1] *n.* (esp.) Horse ridden in charging enemy; horse ridden by officer in the field.

chār'ger[2] *n.* (archaic) Large flat dish.

chă'rĭot *n.* Stately vehicle, triumphal car; 18th-c. light four-wheeled carriage with back seats only; low two-wheeled car used in ancient warfare and racing. **chărĭoteer'** *n.* Chariot driver; *the C~*: see AURIGA. **chă'rĭot** *v.t.* Carry or convey in a chariot.

charĭ'sma (k-, -z-) *n.* Divine gift or talent; capacity to inspire followers with devotion and enthusiasm. **chărĭsmă'tĭc** *adj.*

chă'rĭtable *adj.* Liberal in giving to the poor; connected with such giving; inclined to judge favourably of persons, acts, etc. **chă'rĭtablỹ** *adv.* **chă'rĭtableness** *n.*

chă'rĭtỹ *n.* 1. Christian love of fellow men; kindness, affection. 2. Disposition to judge leniently of character, acts, etc., of others. 3. Beneficence, liberality to the poor, almsgiving, alms; bequest, foundation or institution for the benefit of others, esp. the poor or helpless; *C~ Commission(ers)*, board constituted by Charity Trust Act of 1853 and subsequent Acts to control administration of charitable trusts.

chār'ĭvār'ĭ (sh-) *n.* 1. Hubbub of various discordant sounds. 2. Name of French comic paper from which the second title of 'Punch' was taken. [Fr., = serenade of

CHARLEMAGNE

pans, trays, etc., to unpopular person]

chãr'lādў *n.* Charwoman.

chãr'latan (sh-) *n.* Impostor in medicine, quack; pretender to knowledge or skill, pretentious impostor. **chãr'latanĭsm, chãr'-latanrў** *ns.* [It. *ciarlare* patter]

Chãr'lemāgne (sh-, -ān). Charles the Great (742–814), king of the Franks 768–814; crowned by the Pope as Holy Roman Emperor (as Charles I), 800 (see also CAROLINGIAN).

Chãrles[1] (-lz), 'the Great': see CHARLEMAGNE.

Chãrles[2] (-lz) (1500–58). King of Spain (as Charles I) 1516–56 and Holy Roman Emperor (as Charles V) 1519–56 during the Reformation; abdicated the Imperial crown in favour of his brother Ferdinand and the crown of Spain in favour of his son Philip II.

Chãrles[3] (-lz). Name of two kings of Gt Britain: *Charles I* (1600–49), succeeded his father James I in 1625; his conflict with Parliament led to the Civil War; beheaded in front of Whitehall 30 Jan. 1649; *Charles II* (1630–85) son of Charles I, became king at the Restoration, 1660.

Chãrles[4] (-lz) (1682–1718). King of Sweden (as Charles XII) 1697–1718; a great military commander; defeated Peter the Great at Narva, 1700, but was in turn totally defeated at Poltava, 1709; was killed

CHARLES II

CHARLES I

at Frederikshald in a war with Norway.

Charles's Wain: see URSA.

Chär'leston (-lz-) *n.* Dance characterized by side-kicks from the knee. ~ *v.i.* Dance this. [*Charleston*, city of S. Carolina]

chär'lock *n.* Wild mustard, *Sinapis arvensis*, a yellow-flowered annual weed of arable land.

chär'lotte (sh-) *n.* Pudding of stewed apples or other fruit baked with layer(s) of breadcrumbs etc.; ~ *russe*, mould of whipped cream or custard enclosed in sponge-cake or sponge-biscuits.

chärm *n.* 1. Word(s), act, or object having or supposed to have magic or occult power or influence; talisman; amulet; trinket worn on bracelet etc. 2. Quality, attribute, feature, etc., exciting love or admiration; (pl.) beauty. ~ *v.t.* Bewitch, influence, by or as by charm or magic; endow with magic power or virtue; captivate, delight. **chär'med** (-md) *adj.* (esp.) Bewitched; possessed of magic power or influence; protected, fortified, by a spell or charm. **chär'mer** *n.* **chär'ming** *adj.* Fascinating; very pleasing, delightful. **chär'mingly̆** *adv.*

charmeuse (shärmẽr'z) *n.* Soft smooth silky dress-fabric with satin surface.

chär'nel-house *n.* House or vault in which dead bodies or bones are piled.

Chă'rollais (sh-, -ā) *n.* Kind of beef-cattle. [name of hills near Charolles, NW. of Lyons, France]

Chār'on (k-). (Gk myth.) Ferryman who conveyed the souls of the dead across the Styx to Hades.

chär'poy *n.* Light Indian bedstead.

charr: see CHAR[3].

chärt *n.* 1. Map, esp. one for navigators, showing depth of sea, rocks, channels, coasts, anchorages, etc. 2. Record (by means of curves etc. on graph) of fluctuations of temperature, prices, population, etc.; any sheet with information arranged in tabular form; list of most popular gramophone records etc. ~ *v.t.* Make chart of, map.

chär'ter *n.* 1. Written grant of privileges, rights, etc., by sovereign or legislature, esp. creating or incorporating borough, university, or other corporation. 2. Written instrument, contract, etc., esp. conveying landed property; charter-party. 3. Privilege; publicly conceded right; *Great C~*, see MAGNA CHARTA; *People's C~*, document published 8 May 1838, embodying demands of the Chartists under six headings; adult male suffrage, vote by ballot, annual Parliaments, payment of members of Parliament, equal electoral distribution, and abolition of property qualification. 4. ~ *flight*, chartered flight; *~-party* charter between owners and merchants for hire of ships and transportation of cargo. ~ *v.t.* 1. Grant charter to; privilege, license. 2. Hire (ship) by charter-party; hire (vehicle or aircraft). **chär'tered** (-*erd*) *adj.* (esp.) ~ *accountant*, one qualified under rules of Institute of Accountants, which received royal charter in 1880, authorized to audit accounts etc. **chär'terer** *n.*

Chär'terhouse. Orig. one of the houses of the Carthusian Order, near Smithfield, London, converted into an alms-house and school by Sir Thomas Sutton; the school, one of the English public schools, has now been removed to Godalming, Surrey. [Fr. *Chartreuse* CARTHUSIAN house]

Chärtist *n.* Member of political reforming body, chiefly of working classes, active 1837–48, whose demands were embodied in the *People's Charter* (see CHARTER). **Chär'tism** *n.*

chärtreu'se (-ẽrz) *n.* 1. Green or yellow liqueur of brandy and aromatic herbs, made by monks of Grande Chartreuse, the chief Carthusian monastery, near Grenoble. 2. Colour of green chartreuse, pale apple-green.

chär'tūlary̆ (k-) *n.* = CARTULARY.

chär'woman (-wŏŏ-) *n.* (pl.

-*women* pr. -wĭmĭn). Woman hired by the day or hour for housework.

chār′ȳ *adj.* Cautious, wary; fastidious, shy; careful (*of*); frugal, sparing (*of*).

Charȳ′bdĭs (k-). (Gk legend) Dangerous whirlpool in a narrow channel (later identified with the Strait of Messina, where there is no whirlpool), opposite the cave of Scylla.

Chas. *abbrev.* Charles.

chāse[1] *n.* 1. Pursuit; *the* ~, (the sport of) hunting. 2. Hunting-ground; unenclosed park-land (also *chace*). 3. Hunted animal or pursued ship, quarry. 4. (hist.) Chase-guns of a ship; part of ship where chase-ports are (see below). 5. (tennis) 2nd impact of ball opponent has failed or declined to return (this stroke is not scored until opponent has tried to better it by causing his ball to rebound nearer the end-wall). 6. ~-*gun*, (hist.) a gun trained through one of the ~-*ports*, ports in the bows or through the stern (such guns were of use only when pursuing or being pursued). ~ *v.t.* Pursue; drive *from*, *out of*, etc.; (colloq.) try to obtain. **chā′ser** *n.* (esp.) 1. Hunter, pursuer. 2. Horse trained for steeplechasing. 3. Ship pursuing another; (hist.) chase-gun. 4. Small drink of spirits after coffee, tobacco, etc.; small drink of water or other mild drink after spirits. 5. (colloq.) Letter sent as reminder of previous one.

chāse[2] *n.* Part of gun enclosing bore; groove or trench cut to receive pipe etc.

chāse[3] *n.* (print.) Iron frame holding composed type for page or sheet.

chāse[4] *v.t.* Engrave (metal), esp. with ornament.

chasm (kăzm) *n.* Deep fissure, cleft, or gap; break, hiatus; wide and profound difference of feelings, interests, etc.

chassé (shăsā) *n.* & *v.i.* (Make) gliding sideways step in dancing. [Fr.]

chă′ssis (sh-, -ĭ) *n.* (pl. same) Base frame of gun-carriage; base frame of motor vehicle, aircraft, etc., with its engine, as dist. from the body or coachwork.

chāste *adj.* Not having had extra-marital sexual intercourse, virtuous, continent; undefiled, pure; decent; modest, free from excess, pure in artistic or literary style. **chā′stelȳ** *adv.* **chă′stĭtȳ** *n.* State or quality of being chaste; ~ *belt*, belt designed to prevent a woman from having sexual intercourse.

chā′sten (-āsn) *v.t.* 1. Discipline, correct by suffering. 2. Make chaste in style etc., refine; temper, subdue.

chăstī′se (-z) *v.t.* Punish; beat. **chă′stĭsement** *n.*

chă′sūble (-z-) *n.* Sleeveless vestment worn over alb and stole by celebrant at Mass or Eucharist.

chăt[1] *n.* & *v.i.* (Indulge in) familiar and easy talk. **chă′ttȳ** *adj.* **chă′ttĭlȳ** *adv.* **chă′ttinėss** *n.*

chăt[2] *n.* Any of various birds, chiefly warblers; esp. stonechat and whinchat.

château (shă′tō) *n.* (pl. -*x*, pr. -z). Castle, large mansion or country house, in France.

Chateaubriand (shătōbrēahṅ), François René, Vicomte de (1768–1848). One of the pioneers of the French romantic movement;

author of 'Le Génie du Christianisme' (1802) and several romances.

chă′tėlaine (sh-) *n.* 1. Mistress of castle or country house. 2.

Chain(s) holding keys, watch, scissors, etc., formerly worn hanging from woman's girdle or belt.

Chă'tham (-t*a*m), Earl of: see PITT.

chă'ttel *n.* (law) Property of every kind except real estate; (pl.) goods, possessions; (rhet.) slave.

chă'tter *v.i.* 1. (of birds) Utter rapid series of short notes, esp. of sounds approaching those of human voice. 2. (of persons) Talk quickly, incessantly, foolishly, or inopportunely. 3. (of teeth etc.) Rattle together. ~ *n.* Sound of chattering; incessant trivial talk; *cha'tterbox*, talkative person, esp. child.

Chă'tterton, Thomas (1752–70). English poet who fabricated a number of poems purporting to be the work of an imaginary 15th-c. Bristol poet, Thomas Rowley.

Chau'cer, Geoffrey (1340?–

1400). English poet, author of the 'Canterbury Tales'. **Chaucer̄'ian** *adj.* After the manner of Chaucer.

chauffeur (shō'f*er* *or* -fẽr') *n.* Paid driver of private motor vehicle.

chaulmōō'gra oil. Vegetable oil of nauseous taste obtained from seeds of the Burmese tree *Taraktogenos kurzii*, formerly used in treatment of leprosy, etc.

chau'vĭnism (shō-) *n.* Bellicose patriotism. **chau'vĭnist** *adj.* & *n.* **chauvĭni'stĭc** *adj.* [f. Nicolas *Chauvin*, French veteran soldier of First Republic and Empire whose demonstrative loyalty was celebrated and at length ridiculed]

chaw *n.* & *v.* (slang) Chew.

Ch.B. *abbrev.* *Chirurgiae Baccalaureus* (L, = Bachelor of Surgery).

Ch. Ch. *abbrev.* Christ Church (Oxford).

cheap *adj.* 1. Not costly; costing less than the usual price, rate, etc.; worth more than its cost; (of money) obtainable at low rate of interest. 2. Costing little trouble, labour, etc. 3. Worthless; made light of, brought into contempt by being made too familiar. 4. *chea'pjack*, hawker at fairs etc.; (*adj.*) shoddy. **chea'plў** *adv.* **chea'pnėss** *n.* **cheap** *adv.* At low price, at small expense, cheaply; easily.

chea'pen *v.* Make or become cheap, depreciate.

cheat *n.* 1. Fraud, deception, imposition. 2. Swindler; deceiver, impostor. ~ *v.* Deceive, trick (*out of* something); deal fraudulently; beguile (time, fatigue, etc.). **chea'ters** (-z) *n.pl.* (U.S. slang) Spectacles.

chĕck[1] *int.* (chess) Call notifying opponent that his king is exposed. ~ *n.* 1. (chess) Position of king when exposed to attack by one of opponent's men. 2. Sudden arrest in career or onward course; rebuff, repulse; stop in progress of hounds through failure of scent; sudden stoppage or pause. 3. Restraint on action or conduct; (mus.) part of pianoforte action fixed at back of key to prevent hammer from retouching strings 4. Control securing accuracy, agreement, etc.; token, ticket, of identification for left luggage, coat left in cloakroom, etc.; restaurant bill; (U.S.) counter used in card-games; *cash in one's ~s*: see CASH. ~ *v.* 1. (chess) Place in check. 2. Suddenly arrest motion of; (of hounds) stop on losing scent. 3. Restrain, curb. 4. Test (figures etc.) by comparison etc., examine accuracy of; correspond, agree upon comparison;

~ *in, out*, record arrival or departure (of). 5. ~-*out*, desk or till where payment is made in self-service shop; ~-*rail*, guard-rail; ~-*rein*, rein connecting driving-rein of one horse to bit of the other horse; rein preventing horse from lowering head; ~-*strap*, strap of helmet etc., under chin; ~-*up*, examination (esp. medical); scrutiny; ~-*weigher*, -*weighman*, at collieries, man who in workmen's interest checks weight of coal sent up. [OF. *eschec*, f. Arab., f. Pers. *shāh* king]

chĕck[2] *n.* Pattern of (cross-lines forming) small squares, like chess-board; fabric woven or printed with this. **chĕcked** (-kt) *adj.*

chĕck[3] *n.* Var. (chiefly U.S.) of CHEQUE.

chĕ'cker *n.* & *v.* Var. (chiefly U.S.) of CHEQUER; (pl.) draughts; ~-*board*, draught-board.

chĕ'ckmā'te *n.* 1. (chess) Position in which king cannot be extricated from check, move which brings this about. 2. Final defeat; deadlock. ~ *v.t.* Give checkmate to; arrest or defeat utterly, discomfit. [OF. *eschec mat* (see CHECK[1]) f. Arab. *shāh māt* (the chess) king is dead]

chĕ'ckȳ *adj.* (her.) Chequered.

chĕ'ddar *n.* Kind of cheese orig. made near Cheddar, a village near the Mendip hills, Somerset.

chĕ'ddaring *n.* Process or stage in manufacture of cheese in which fibrous particles are fused into a mass.

cheek *n.* 1. Side-wall of mouth, side of face below eye; ~-*bone*, bone forming lower boundary of eye-orbit; ~-*strap*, (esp.) strap of bridle passing over horse's cheek. 2. Impudence; cool confidence, effrontery. 3. Side-post of door etc.; (pl.) jaws of vice; side pieces of various parts of machines arranged in lateral pairs. ~ *v.t.* (colloq.) Address saucily or impudently.

chee'kȳ *adj.* Impudent. **chee'kĭlȳ** *adv.* **chee'kĭnėss** *n.*

cheep *v.i.* & *n.* (Utter) shrill feeble note as of young bird.

cheer *n.* 1. Shout of encouragement or applause; *three* ~*s*, successive united hurrahs. 2. Frame of mind (only in phrases as *be of good* ~). 3. (archaic) Food. ~ *v.* 1. Comfort, gladden; ~ *up*, comfort, be comforted. 2. Incite, urge *on*, by shouts etc. 3. Applaud; shout for joy. **cheers** (-z) *int.* Exclamation used as toast or salutation.

cheer'ful *adj.* In good spirits; pleasant; willing, not reluctant. **cheer'fullȳ** *adv.* **cheer'fulnėss** *n.*

cheerĭō' *int.* (slang) Parting exclamation of encouragement.

cheer'lėss *adj.* Gloomy, dreary. **cheer'lėsslȳ** *adv.* **cheer'lėssnėss** *n.*

cheer'lȳ *adv.* (naut.) Heartily, with a will.

cheer'ȳ *adj.* Lively, genial. **cheer'ĭlȳ** *adv.* **cheer'ĭnėss** *n.*

cheese[1] (-z) *n.* 1. Food made of the curd of milk, separated from the whey and pressed into a close mass; mass of this, usu. wheel-shaped, cylindrical, or globular, with a hardened outer layer or rind. 2. Mass of pomace or apple pulp crushed together like a cheese in cider-making; conserve of fruit of the consistency of cream cheese. 3. Heavy wooden disc used in skittles. 4. *chee'secake*, tart of pastry filled with mixture of curds, sugar, etc.; (slang) photographs of shapely women; *chee'secloth*, thin cotton cloth (of the kind) in which curds are pressed for cheese; ~-*paring*, stingy; stinginess; ~ *straw*, thin strip of pastry flavoured with cheese. **chee'sȳ** *adj.*

cheese[2] (-z) *v.* (slang) ~ *it!*, stop, have done, cease. **cheesed** (-zd) *adj.* (slang) Bored, disgruntled (also ~ *off*).

chee'tah (-*a*) *n.* Large spotted member of cat family, *Acinonyx jubatus*, of Africa and S. Asia, the fastest four-legged animal; can be tamed and sometimes trained for hunting deer. [Hindi *chītā*, f. Sansk. *chitraka*]

chĕf (sh-) *n.* Male head cook.

chef-d'œuvre (shādĕrvr) *n.* (pl. *chefs-*, same pr.). Masterpiece. [Fr.]

Chĕ'ka (*or* chā-). (hist.)

Organization set up in Russia in 1918 for the secret investigation of counter-revolutionary activities; superseded in 1922 by the G.P.U. [*che*, *ka*, Russ. names of initial letters of *Ch*rezvýcháinaya *K*omíssiya, Extraordinary Commission]

Chĕ'khov (-χŏf), Anton Pavlovich (1860–1904). Russian dramatist and novelist, author of 'The Seagull', 'Uncle Vanya', 'The Cherry Orchard', and other plays, and of numerous short stories.

Chĕ'kia'ng (-yăng). Eastern maritime province of China.

che'la[1] (chā-) *n.* (Buddhism) Novice qualifying for initiation; disciple; pupil.

chē'la[2] (k-) *n.* (pl. *-lae*). Prehensile claw of crabs, lobsters, scorpions, etc.

chē'lāte (k-) *adj.* & *n.* (chem.) (Compound) with cyclic structure looping round central metal ion and attached at two or more points. ~ *v.i.* Combine with (substance) to form chelate ring. **chēlā'tion** *n.*

Chĕ'llėan (sh-) *adj.* & *n.* = ABBEVILLIAN. [f. *Chelles*, Seine-et-Marne, France]

Chĕ'lsea. Royal borough (with Kensington) of London, associated with artists and men of letters; *Sage of* ~, Thomas CARLYLE; ~ *bun*, kind of rolled currant-bun; ~ *china*, porcelain made at a factory in Chelsea (*c* 1745–84); ~ *Royal Hospital*, home for veteran soldiers (~ *Pensioners*) founded by Charles II.

chĕ'mĭcal (k-) *adj.* Of, made by, relating to, chemistry; ~ *engineering*, industrial application of chemistry; ~ *warfare*, use in war of chemical substances other than explosives, esp. poison gases, for purpose of injuring the enemy. ~ *n.* Substance obtained by or used in chemical processes; *fine* ~*s*, those handled in small lots in purified state; *heavy* ~*s*, those handled in large lots in more or less crude state. **chĕ'mĭcallȳ** *adv.*

chĕmĭlūmĭnĕ'scence (k-; *or* -lōō-) *n.* Emission of light in chemical reaction. **chĕmĭlūmĭnĕ'scent** *adj.*

chemin de fer (shemăn de fār). Form of baccarat. [Fr., = 'railway']

chemise (shĭmē'z) *n.* Woman's undergarment worn next skin; dress hanging straight from shoulders.

chĕ'mĭst (k-) *n.* 1. Person skilled in chemistry. 2. Dealer in medical drugs, pharmacist.

chĕm'ĭstrȳ (k-) *n.* Science of the composition of substances and their combination and change under various conditions; *inorganic* ~, chemistry of the elements other than carbon; *organic* ~, formerly, chemistry of substances found in organic structures; now, chemistry of compounds of carbon, whether natural or synthetic; *physical* ~, study of the physical aspects of chemistry.

chĕmothĕ'rapȳ (k-) *n.* Treatment of disease by chemical substances which act on micro-organisms or malignant tissue.

chenille (shĭnē'l) *n.* Yarn with pile protruding all round it; fabric with weft of this. [Fr., = 'caterpillar']

chĕque (-k) *n.* Written order to banker to pay sum of money on drawer's account to bearer or named person; form on which this is written; ~ *book*, book of cheque forms issued to customer of bank.

chĕ'quer (-ker) *n.* 1. (pl.) Chess-board as inn-sign. 2. Chequered pattern. ~ *v.t.* Divide or mark like chess-board with squares, esp. of alternating colours; diversify, variegate.

Chĕ'quers (-kerz). Tudor mansion near Princes Risborough, Buckinghamshire, presented to the nation in 1917 by Lord and Lady Lee of Fareham to serve as a country seat of the prime minister of Gt Britain.

cherchez la femme (sharshā, făm). Look for the woman (freq. facet., implying that the key to a problem etc. is a woman). [Fr.]

chĕ'rish *v.t.* Foster, nurse; value, keep in the memory or heart, cling to.

Chĕrokee' *adj.* & *n.* (Member)

of a tribe of N. Amer. Indians formerly occupying a large part of southern U.S.

chėro͞o′t (sh-) *n.* Thin, untapered, dark-coloured cigar of the kind made in southern India and Manila; any cigar open at both ends.

chĕ′rrȳ *n.* Pulpy drupe of certain species of *Prunus*, esp. of the cultivated tree, *P. cerasus*; (wood of) tree bearing this; ~ *brandy*, dark-red liqueur of brandy in which cherries have been steeped; ~-*picker*, (esp.) type of crane for vertical lifting; ~-*pie*, garden heliotrope; ~-*red*, colour of ripe red cherries. ~ *adj.* Cherry-red.

Chẽr′sonēse (k-). Thracian peninsula W. of the Hellespont. [Gk *khersos nēsos* dry island]

chẽrt *n.* (geol.) Form of amorphous silica found in several varieties, e.g. flint.

chĕ′rub *n.* 1. (in pl., *cherubim*) Order of angels (see ANGEL), gifted esp. with knowledge. 2. (pl. -*s*) Representation of one of the cherubim in art, usu. as a winged child, or child's head with wings and no body; beautiful child. **chĕru′bĭc** (-o͞o-) *adj.* [Heb. *k^erūb*]

chẽr′vĭl *n.* Garden herb, *Anthriscus cerefolium*, with aromatic leaves used in salads, soups, etc.

Ches. *abbrev.* Cheshire.

Chĕ′sapeake Bay. Large inlet, about 200 miles long, between Maryland and Virginia, U.S.

Chĕ′shire. English county of N. Midlands, bordering on Wales and, since April 1974, S. Merseyside and Greater Manchester; *grin like a ~ cat*, grin broadly (explained as ref. to Cheshire cheeses made in shape of cat, or to lion rampant on Cheshire inn-signs); ~ *cheese*, kind of cheese made orig. in Cheshire; ~ *Cheese*, tavern in Mitre Court, Fleet Street, London, famous as the haunt of Dr Johnson.

chĕss *n.* Game played by two persons on chequered board divided into 64 squares, each player having 16 pieces or 'men' (a king, a queen, 2 bishops, 2 knights, 2 rooks, and 8 pawns), the object being to CHECKMATE the opponent's king; ~ *board*, board on which chess is played; *che′ssman*, one of the pieces used in the game.

chĕst *n.* 1. Large strong box; box for sailor's belongings. 2. Treasury, coffer, of institution; fund kept in this. 3. Case of some commodity, esp. tea. 4. ~ *of drawers*, piece of furniture with set of drawers. 5. Part of human or animal's body enclosed by ribs and breast-bone, and containing heart and lungs; ~-*note*, -*voice*, note, voice, of lowest register; ~-*protector*, flannel etc. worn on chest as protection against cold; ~-*register*, lowest register of the voice.

Chĕ′sterfield[1], Philip Dormer Stanhope, 4th Earl of (1694–1773). British statesman and diplomat, chiefly remembered for his 'Letters' to his son.

chĕ′sterfield[2] *n.* 1. Kind of overcoat. 2. Sofa with stuffed (and sometimes cushioned) seat, back, and ends. [f. a 19th-c. earl of *Chesterfield*]

Chĕ′sterton, Gilbert Keith (1874–1936). English author of essays, novels, verse, etc.

chĕ′stnŭt (-sn-) *n.* 1. Tree (also called *Spanish* or *sweet* ~), *Castanea sativa*, native of Asia Minor and S. Europe, bearing a large edible nut enclosed in a prickly pericarp or burr; this nut. 2. = HORSE-chestnut. 3. Stale anecdote or joke. 4. Chestnut colour; chestnut-coloured horse. ~ *adj.* Of chestnut colour, varying from bright to dark reddish-brown.

chĕ′stȳ *adj.* (colloq.) Having weakness or disease of the chest; (of voice) having chest tones. **chĕ′stĭnėss** *n.*

chevă′l-glass (sh-, -ahs) *n.* Mirror swung on frame, and long enough to reflect the whole figure.

chĕvalier′ (sh-) *n.* 1. Horseman, knight (hist. or archaic); member of certain orders of knighthood, or of French Legion of Honour; soldier cadet of old French noblesse. 2. ~ *of industry*, (Fr. *chevalier d'industrie*) adventurer, swindler. 3. *the C~*, *C~ de St. Georges*, the

Old PRETENDER, James Stuart, son of James II of England; *the Young C~*, the Young Pretender, Charles Edward Stuart.

chevaux de frise (shevōdefrēz). 1. Iron spikes set in timber etc., employed in war to check cavalry charges etc. 2. Line of spikes or nails set at angles along top of wall, railing, etc. to prevent persons climbing over. [Fr., = 'horses of Friesland', because first employed by 17th-c. Frisians to compensate for their lack of cavalry]

chevet (shĕ′vā) *n.* Apsidal end of church with chapels radiating from it.

Chĕ′vĭot *adj.* Of the Cheviot Hills; ~ *Hills*, *Cheviots*, range of hills on the border between England and Scotland; ~ *sheep*, hardy short-woolled breed thriving there and in mountainous districts. **chĕ′vĭot** *n.* Cheviot sheep; cloth made from its wool.

chĕ′vron (sh-) *n.* Bent bar of inverted V shape as heraldic device, architectural ornament, etc.; distinguishing mark of this shape on sleeve of non-commissioned officers, policemen, etc., stripe.

chĕ′vronȳ *adj.* (her.) Charged with chevrons.

chĕ′vrotain, -tĭn (sh-) *n.* Small animal of genus *Tragulus*, most primitive of known ruminants, found esp. in India, Malay peninsula, and W. Africa.

chĕ′vȳ, chĭ′vȳ *n.* 1. Chase, pursuit, hunt. 2. Game of prisoners' base. ~ *v.t.* Varr. of CHIVVY. [prob. f. CHEVY CHASE]

Chĕ′vȳ Chāse. Skirmish, celebrated in a ballad of 15th-c. origin, between Percy, Earl of Northumberland, who had vowed to hunt for 3 days across the Scottish border, and his Scottish neighbour 'the doughty Douglas'; both were killed in the fight.

chew (-ōō) *v.* Work about between teeth, grind to pulp or indent with repeated biting; chew tobacco; turn over in mind, meditate *on* or *over*; ~ *the cud*, (of ruminant animals) bring back half-digested food into mouth for further chewing; *chewing gum*, preparation of flavoured hardened secretion of spruce-tree, or similar insoluble substance, used for chewing (see also CHICLE). ~ *n.* Act of chewing; quid of tobacco.

Cheyĕ′nne (shī-; *or* -ăn) *n.* Member of an Algonquin tribe.

chi, khi (kī) *n.* 22nd letter of Greek alphabet (Χ, χ), = *ch*; ~-*rho*, monogram of chi and rho, first two letters of Gk *Christos* (= Christ), ☧.

Chi′an (kēan) *adj.* Of Chios, a Greek island in the Aegean; ~ *turpentine*: see TURPENTINE.

Chiă′ng Kai-Shĕk (chyă-, kī-). Chiang Chung-cheng(*c*1887–1975), Chinese general and statesman; president of the Chinese Republic from 1943; withdrew to Taiwan 1949.

Chiă′ntĭ *n.* Dry red or white wine produced in or near the Chianti Mountains in Tuscany.

chiao (jyow) *n.* $\frac{1}{10}$ of a renminbi or yuan.

chiāroscur′ō (ky-, -oorō) *n.* Treatment of light and shade in painting, esp. when strongly contrasted; light and shade effects in nature; use of contrast in literature etc. [It., = 'bright-dark']

chiă′smus (k-, -z-) *n.* (rhet. etc.) Inversion in a second phrase of order followed in first, e.g. *I cannot dig, to beg I am ashamed.* [Gk *chiasmos* arrangement like letter chi, χ]

chĭbou′k (-ōōk) *n.* Long Turkish tobacco-pipe, usu. with amber mouthpiece, long wooden stem, and bowl of baked clay.

chic (shēk) *n.* Skill, effectiveness, style. ~ *adj.* Stylish, in the fashion.

Chĭca′gō (shĭkah-). City of U.S., in Illinois, on Lake Michigan.

chĭcā′ne (sh-) *n.* 1. Chicanery. 2. (in game of bridge) (Holding of) hand without any trumps. 3. (esp. motor-racing) Barrier or obstacle on racecourse. ~ *v.* Use chicanery; cheat.

chĭcā′nerȳ (sh-) *n.* Legal trickery; underhand dealing; sophistry.

chichi (shē′shē) *n.* & *adj.* Fussily ornamented, showy, (thing); affected (manner).

chick *n.* Chicken; young bird before or after hatching; (slang) young woman; *chi'ckweed*, weed of genus *Stellaria*.

chi'cken *n.* 1. Young bird, esp. of domestic fowl; flesh of this as food. 2. Youthful person. 3. (slang, as adj.) Cowardly; *play* ~, test courage by dangerous game. 4. ~*-feed*, (colloq.) something trivial, esp. small amount of money; *Mother Carey's* ~, sailor's name for storm petrel; ~*-hearted*, timorous, cowardly; *chi'ckenpox*, mild eruptive disease with some resemblance to smallpox, chiefly affecting children. ~ *v.i.* (slang) Abstain through cowardice (also ~ *out*).

chick-pea *n.* Dwarf pea, *Cicer arietinum*.

chi'cle *n.* Gum-like substance obtained from bully-tree (*Mimusops globosa*) and sapodilla (*Sapota zapotilla*) used for making chewing gum. [Mex. *tzictli*]

chi'cory *n.* 1. (bot.) Any plant of the genus *Cichorium*. 2. Species of this, *C. intybus* (known in U.S. as *endive*), with long smooth blanched leaves eaten as salad; its root, ground and roasted as addition to or substitute for coffee. 3. Another species, *C. endivia* (called *endive* in England but *chicory* in U.S.), varieties of which, with curly or wavy leaves, are eaten as salad.

chide *v.* (past t. *chid*, past part. *chi'dden* or *chid*). (archaic) Scold.

chief *n.* 1. (her.) Upper third of shield. 2. Head, leader, ruler, of body of men, esp. of clan, tribe, etc.; superior officer, head of department. 3. *in* ~, first in importance, principally, foremost; *tenant in* ~, feudal tenant holding directly from the lord paramount. ~ *adj.* Formally the chief or head; first in importance, influence, etc.; prominent, leading. **chie'fdom** *n.* **chie'fly** *adv.* Above all; mainly but not exclusively.

chie'ftain (-tan) *n.* Military leader (poet.); captain of robbers; chief of clan or tribe. **chie'ftaincy, chie'ftainship** *ns.*

chiel *n.* (Sc.) Fellow, chap.

chi'ff-chaff *n.* Small bird of warbler family, *Phylloscopus collybita*. [f. its note]

chi'ffon (sh-) *n.* Diaphanous plain-woven fabric of fine hard-twisted yarn (silk, nylon, etc.); ~ *velvet* etc., velvet etc. that is light in weight.

chiffonier' (sh-) *n.* Movable low cupboard with top forming sideboard.

chi'gger *n.* 1. = CHIGOE. 2. (U.S.) Harvest bug.

chignon (shē'nyawn) *n.* Coil of hair on pad at back of head.

chi'goe *n.* Small tropical flea, *Tunga penetrans*, the impregnated female of which burrows under human skin.

chihuahua (chiwah'wa *or* sh-) *n.* Very small smooth-haired dog of Mexican breed. [*Chihuahua*, city and State of Mexico]

chi'lblain *n.* Inflammatory itching swelling on hand, foot, etc., caused by exposure to cold and poor circulation.

child *n.* (pl. *chi'ldren*). Young human being; immature person; offspring; descendant, follower, product (*of*); *chi'ldbed* (archaic), *chi'ldbirth*, parturition; ~*'s play*, easy task. **chi'ldless** *adj.* **chi'ldlessness** *n.*

Chi'ldermas. (archaic) Feast of Holy Innocents, 28 Dec., commemorating the slaughter of the children by Herod (Matt. 2: 16).

Chi'lders, Erskine (1905–74). President of the Republic of Ireland 1973–4.

chi'ldhood *n.* Time from birth to puberty; *second* ~, dotage.

chi'ldish *adj.* Of, proper to, a child; not befitting an adult. **chi'ldishly** *adv.* **chi'ldishness** *n.*

chi'ldlike *adj.* Having the good qualities of a child, as innocence, frankness, etc.

Chi'le. S. Amer. Republic lying between the Andes and the south Pacific; discovered by Spanish adventurers in the 16th c. and remained under Spanish rule until 1818; capital, Santiago; ~ *saltpetre*, sodium nitrate ($NaNO_3$) found in Chile and Peru, used as a fertilizer. **Chĭ'lėan** *adj.* & *n.*

chĭll *n.* 1. Cold sensation, lowered temperature of body; feverish cold. 2. Unpleasant coldness of air, water, etc. 3. Depressing influence; coldness of manner. 4. (eng.) Pieces of solid metal inserted into moulds to effect rapid local cooling. ~ *adj.* Lacking warmth. ~ *v.* 1. Make, become, cold; deaden, blast, with cold; keep (meat or other food) at low temperature but without freezing. 2. Depress, dispirit. 3. Harden (molten iron) by contact with cold iron.

chĭ'lli *n.* (pl. *-lies*). Dried pod of kinds of capsicum, acrid, pun-

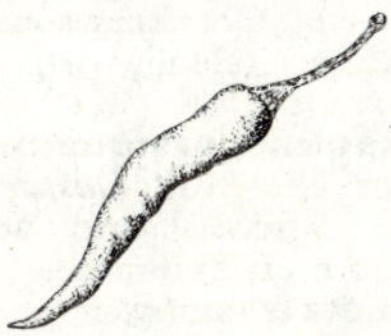

gent, and of deep red colour, used to make cayenne pepper. [Mexican]

chĭ'llȳ *adj.* Rather cold; sensitive to cold; not genial, cold-mannered. **chĭ'llĭnėss** *n.*

Chĭ'ltern *adj.* Of the Chiltern Hills; ~ *Hills*, *Chilterns*, range of wooded hills stretching from S. Oxfordshire across Buckinghamshire into Bedfordshire and Hertfordshire; ~ *Hundreds*, five hundreds in Oxfordshire and three in Buckinghamshire, the manorial rights in which belonged to the Crown, which appointed stewards and bailiffs (these offices have long been obsolete or merely nominal, but the stewardship of the three Buckinghamshire hundreds is applied for by a member of Parliament wishing to resign since the holding of an office of profit under the Crown forces him to vacate his seat, this stewardship being held by a legal fiction to be such an office).

chīme *n.* Set of attuned bells, series of sounds given by this; harmony, melody, rhythm; agreement, correspondence. ~ *v.* 1. Make (bell) sound; ring chimes, ring chimes on; show (hour) by chiming. 2. Harmonize, agree (*with*); ~ *in*, join in harmoniously; break into a conversation.

Chīmēr'a[1], **-aera**[1] (k-). (Gk myth.) Fire-breathing monster with lion's head, goat's body, and serpent's tail, killed by Bellerophon.

chīmēr'a[2], **-aera**[2] (k-) *n.* Grotesque monster; thing of hybrid character, fanciful conception; (bot., usu. *-aera*) plant in which internal and external tissues are of different origins. **chīmĕ'rĭcal** *adj.* **chīmĕ'rĭcallȳ** *adv.*

chĭmēr'e *n.* Bishop's robe to which lawn sleeves are attached

chĭ'mney *n.* Flue carrying off smoke or steam of fire, furnace, engine, etc.; part of flue above roof; glass tube providing draught for lamp-flame; natural vent of volcano etc.; narrow cleft by which cliff may be climbed; ~ *corner*, warm seat within old-fashiond fireplace; ~ *piece*, mantel; ~ *pot*, earthenware or metal pipe at top of chimney; ~*-pot hat*: see HAT; ~ *sweep*, person whose trade it is to sweep chimneys; ~ *sweeper*, chimney sweep; jointed brush for sweeping chimneys.

chĭmp *n.* Chimpanzee.

chĭmpanzee' *n.* African ape of genus *Pan*, allied to gorilla, bearing the closest resemblance to man of any of the surviving anthropoids. [native W. African name]

chĭn *n.* Front of lower jaw; ~*-strap*, strap passing under or round chin to hold hat or helmet in place; ~*-wag*, (slang) talk, chatter.

Chī'na[1]. Large country of E. Asia with a civilization dating from the 3rd millennium B.C., governed during most of its history by emperors of numerous (often rival) dynasties of which the most notable are the Han, Wei, Sui, T'ang, Sung, Yüan, Ming, and Ch'ing; after a revolution (in 1911) a republic was proclaimed (1912); Communist forces obtained control, 1949, and proclaimed the *People's Republic of China*;

capital, Peking; ~ *aster*, any of several garden asters derived from *Callistephus chinensis*; ~ *bark*, = CINCHONA; *Chi'naman*, (derog.) Chinese; ~ *orange*, common orange, orig. from China; ~*'s Sorrow*: see YELLOW River; ~ *tea*, type of tea prepared from a small-leaved variety of tea plant (*Thea sinensis bohea*) grown chiefly in S. China and differing from other kinds of tea chiefly in that it is cured with smoke. [ult. origin unknown; not the native name; found in Sansk. *c* 1st c.]

chī'na[2] *n.* Very hard fine semi-transparent porcelain of the hard-paste kind orig. manufactured in China and first brought to Europe in 16th c. by Portuguese; manufactured in Europe since beginning of 18th c.; ~ *clay*, kaolin. ~ *adj.* Of china. [orig. *China-ware*, ware from China]

chī'nagrăph (*or* -ahf) *n.* (also ~ *pencil*) Pencil for writing on china, glass, etc.

Chī'natown. Part of large town, esp. seaport, in England or U.S., where Chinese live as a colony.

chinch *n.* (U.S.) Bed-bug.

chĭncherĭnchee' *n.* S. Afr. perennial plant, *Ornithogalum thyrsoides*, with white flowers.

chĭnchĭ'lla *n.* 1. Small S. Amer. rodent of genus *C*~; fine soft greyish fur of one species, *C. laniger* of Peru and Chile. 2. (also ~ *rabbit*) Long-haired rabbit bred for its fur; fur of this. 3. Variety of silver-coloured domestic cat.

chĭ'n-chĭ'n *int.* Exclamation of salutation. [Anglo-Chinese, f. Chin. *ts'ing-ts'ing*]

chīne[1] *n.* Deep narrow ravine cut by stream descending steeply to sea (now only in Isle of Wight and Dorset).

chīne[2] *n.* Backbone; animal's backbone or part of it as joint; backbone of bacon-pig after sides are cut off for curing. ~ *v.t.* Cut through or remove chine of.

Chīnee' *n.* (slang) Chinese person.

Chīnē'se (-z) *adj.* (stress variable) Of China or its people or language; ~ *copy*, slavishly exact copy; (eng. etc.) precise drawing of structure, apparatus, etc., made from its appearance only without other information; ~ *lantern*, collapsible lantern of thin coloured paper; ~ *white*, pigment, zinc oxide. ~ *n.* (pl. same) Chinese person or language.

Ch'ĭng. Manchu dynasty which ruled in China 1644–1912.

Chĭ'nghai' (-hī). Province of W. China.

chĭnk[1] *n.* Narrow opening, esp. one that lets light etc. through.

chĭnk[2] *v.* (Cause to) make sound as of glasses or coins striking together. ~ *n.* Chinking sound.

Chĭnk[3] *n.* (slang, orig. U.S.) Chinese.

chĭ'nkapin, chĭ'nquapin (-k-) *n.* Dwarf chestnut, *Castanea pumila*, of Virginia and adjacent States. [Amer. Ind. name]

chinoi'serie (shĭnwahz-) *n.* Imitation of Chinese motifs in furniture etc., fashionable in 18th and early 19th centuries.

Chĭnōō'k[1] *n.* (Member of) N. Amer. Ind. tribe orig. inhabiting region round Columbus river in Oregon.

chĭnōō'k[2] *n.* 1. Jargon of English, French, Indian, and other words, formerly spoken by traders in the Chinook region. 2. Warm usu. south-westerly wind blowing in winter and spring down eastern slopes of Canadian Rockies.

chinquapin: see CHINKAPIN.

chĭntz *n.* Orig., painted or stained calico imported from India; now, cotton cloth printed with designs in colour and usu. glazed. **chĭ'ntzȳ** *adj.* [Hind. *chīṇt*, f. Sansk. *chitra* variegated]

chīonodŏ'xa (k-) *n.* Blue-flowered liliaceous plant of genus *C*~ from Crete and Asia Minor, blooming in early spring; glory of the snow. [Gk *khiōn* snow + *doxa* glory]

chĭp *n.* 1. Thin piece cut from wood or broken from stone etc.; in gem-cutting, piece chipped off weighing less than ¾ carat. 2. Thin slice of fruit etc., esp. (pl.) stick-shaped slices of potato fried crisp; counter used in games of chance. 3. Wood or woody fibre split into thin strips for making hats, baskets, etc.; basket made of this. 4. Crack or slight fracture caused by chipping. 5. *Chips*, (naut. slang) ship's carpenter. 6. ~ *of* or *off the old block*, child resembling father; ~ *on one's shoulder*, grievance (orig. U.S.; said to be from custom whereby a boy seeking a fight would put a chip on his shoulder and challenge another to knock it off). 7. ~ *basket*, basket of thin strips of wood roughly joined or interwoven, for packing soft fruit etc.; *chi'pboard*, pasteboard made from compressed waste paper or wood refuse; ~ *shot*, (golf) short, slightly lofted approach shot. ~ *v*. Cut (wood), break (stone, crockery), at surface or edge; shape thus; cut or break *off*; be susceptible to breakage at edge; make chip shot; ~ *in*, (colloq.) interrupt; contribute.

chĭ'pmŭnk, -mŭck *n*. Ground-squirrel, the striped or chipping

squirrel of N. America. [Amer. Ind.]

chĭpola'ta (-lah-) *n*. Kind of thin esp. spicy sausage.

Chĭ'ppendāle, Thomas (1718–79). London cabinet-maker; his business was carried on by his son Thomas (1749–1822); hence (as *n*.) style of furniture made by Chippendale.

chīr'omancy̆ (k-) *n*. Palmistry.

chīrŏ'pody̆ (k-; *or* kĭr-) *n*. Treatment of feet. **chīrŏ'podist** *n*.

chīroprăʹctic (k-) *n*. & *adj*. (Of) manipulation of the spinal column as method of curing disease. **chīr'oprăctor** *n*.

chĭrp *n*. Short sharp thin note as of small bird. ~ *v*. Utter chirp. **chĭr'py̆** *adj*. Lively, cheerful. **chĭr'pĭness** *n*.

chĭ'rrup *n*. & *v.i.* (Make) series of chirps, twittering.

chĭ'sel (-zl) *n*. Metal cutting-tool with square bevelled end, worked by pressure or by blows of a mallet or hammer; *cold* ~, steel chisel of a temper and strength suitable for cutting cold metal, esp. iron. ~ *v.t.* Cut, shape, with chisel; (slang) defraud, get (money etc.) *out of*. **chĭ'selled** (-ld) *adj*. (esp., of features) Clear-cut. **chĭ'seller** *n*.

chĭt[1] *n*. Young child, brat; (contempt.) young girl or woman.

chĭt[2] *n*. Written note. [Anglo-Ind.]

chĭ't-chă't *n*. Light conversation; gossip.

chī'tĭn (k-) *n*. Organic substance forming part of exoskeleton of arthropods. **chī'tĭnous** *adj*.

chĭ'tlĭng, chĭ'tterlĭng *n*. (usu. pl.). Smaller intestines of beasts, esp. as cooked for food.

chĭ'valry̆ (sh-) *n*. 1. Knights or horsemen equipped for battle (archaic); medieval men-at-arms; gallant gentlemen. 2. Knightly skill (archaic); knighthood as rank or order (archaic); knightly system of feudal times with its religious, moral, and social code and usages;

CHIPPENDALE

Age of C~, period of this; *Order of C~*: see ORDER *n.* 5. 3. Brave, honourable, and courteous character attributed to the ideal knight. **chĭ'valrous** *adj.* **chĭ'valrouslȳ** *adv.* [OF. *chevalerie* knighthood (*cheval* horse)]

chīve *n.* Small cultivated herb allied to leek and onion, *Allium schoenoprasum*.

chĭ'vvȳ, chĭ'vȳ *v.* (colloq.) Chase, harry. [var. of CHEVY]

chlôr'al (kl-) *n.* Trichloroacetaldehyde, an oily liquid with pungent odour, made by action of chlorine on alcohol, forming white crystals by combination with water (*chloral hydrate*) and used as hypnotic and anaesthetic.

chlôr'āte (kl-) *n.* Salt of chloric acid ($HClO_3$).

chlôr'īde (kl-) *n.* Simple compound of chlorine with a metal or organic radical.

chlôr'ine (kl-, -ēn) *n.* (chem.) Non-metallic element, a yellowish-green, heavy, chemically active gas with irritating smell and powerful bleaching and disinfecting qualities; symbol Cl, at. no. 17, at. wt 35·453. **chlôr'ināte** *v.t.* Treat or act upon with chlorine; sterilize (drinking water) thus. **chlôrinā'tion** *n.*

chlôr'īte (kl-) *n.* Salt of chlorous acid.

chlŏ'rofôrm (kl-) *n.* Thin colourless liquid with ethereal odour and pungent sweetish taste, the vapour of which inhaled produces insensibility; formerly used as a general anaesthetic. ~ *v.t.* Administer chloroform to.

chlŏ'rophȳll (kl-) *n.* Colouring-matter of leaves and other green parts of plants etc.

chlŏ'roplăst (kl-) *n.* Plastid containing chlorophyll, in cells of algae and higher plants.

chlorō'sĭs (kl-) *n.* Green sickness, anaemic disease of girls about age of puberty.

chlôr'ous (kl-) *adj.* ~ *acid*, acid ($HClO_2$) known only in solution and in form of its salts.

Ch.M. *abbrev. Chirurgiae Magister* (L, = Master of Surgery).

chŏc *n.* (colloq.) Chocolate; *~-ice*, small block of ice-cream coated with chocolate.

chŏck *n.* Block of wood, wedge. ~ *v.t.* Make fast, wedge, with chocks; ~ *up*, wedge in tight; encumber. ~ *adv.* Closely, tightly; *~-a-block*, *~-full*, stuffed, crammed.

chŏ'colate *n.* Paste or cake of seeds of cacao roasted, ground, sweetened, and flavoured with vanilla etc.; drink made with this; sweet covered with chocolate or made of it; chocolate colour; *~-box* (*adj.*) like the (usu. insipid) pictures on boxes containing chocolates. ~ *adj.* Dark brown, chocolate-coloured. [Mexican *chocolatl* (not f. *cacao* or *cocoa*)]

Chŏ'ctaw *n.* 1. (Member of) a tribe of N. Amer. Indians; language of this tribe. 2. (skating) Step from either edge on one foot to opposite edge on the other foot, in an opposite direction.

choice *n.* Act, power, right, etc., of choosing; what is chosen; variety to choose from; élite. ~ *adj.* Of picked quality, exquisite; carefully chosen.

choir (kwīr) *n.* 1. Band of singers performing or leading in musical parts of church service; choral society, company of singers. 2. Chancel; part of church appropriated to choir. ~ *v.* (rare) Sing in chorus.

choir ôr'gan (kwīr). One of three organs making up a large organ, with its row of keys lowest of the three, and lighter stops than *great organ*. [orig: *chair* organ]

chōke *n.* 1. Narrowed or constricted part of mechanism; choke-bore. 2. (Device operating) valve that partly closes air inlet of petrol-engine. 3. (elect.) Coil having low resistance and large inductance inserted in circuit to impede and smooth out changes in, or change phase of, current. 4. Heart, centre part, of artichoke. 5. *cho'keberry*, (scarlet fruit of) N. Amer. shrub of genus *Aronia*; the shrub itself; *~-bore*, bore of fowling-piece narrowing towards muzzle; *cho'kecherry*, (astringent fruit of) N. Amer. cherry, esp. *Prunus vir-*

giniana; ~*-damp*, carbon dioxide in coal-mines, wells, etc. ~ *v.* Suffocate; stop breath of; suffer temporary stoppage of breath; become speechless from anger etc.; smother, stifle; block up wholly or partly; ~ *off*, deter, dissuade. **chō'ky̆**[1] *adj.* Tending to choke; causing choking. **chō'ker** *n.* (esp.) Clerical or high stand-up collar; woman's close-fitting necklace etc.

chō'ky̆[2] *n.* (slang, in India) Lock-up, prison. [Hind. *chauki* shed]

chŏ'ler (k-) *n.* 1. (hist.) One of the four humours, bile. 2. (poet., archaic) Anger.

chŏ'lera (k-) *n.* 1. (also *Asiatic* ~) Infectious and freq. fatal disease with violent vomiting and purging, cramps, and collapse, endemic in India and epidemic elsewhere. 2. Any of various other diseases esp. *English* ~ or ~ *morbus*, summer diarrhoea.

chŏ'leric (k-) *adj.* Irascible, hot-tempered; (archaic) characterized by choler or bile.

cholĕ'sterol (k-) *n.* Steroid alcohol ($C_{27}H_{45}OH$) present in animal cells and body fluids.

chō'lĭămb (k-) *n.* Iambic verse with spondee or trochee in last foot, scazon. **chōlĭă'mbic** *adj.*

chōōse (-z) *v.* (past t. *chōse*, past part. *chō'sen*). Select out of greater number; make choice *between*; select as; decide, think fit, be determined *to* do; (theol.) destine to be saved. **chōō'sey, -sy** (-zĭ) *adj.* Fastidious, fussy. **chōō'sinėss** *n.*

chŏp[1] *v.* Cut by a blow or blows, usu. with axe; cut small; cut short (words etc.); (cricket, tennis, etc.) make short heavy edgeways blow, strike (ball) thus. ~ *n.* Chopping; chopping stroke; slice of meat, esp. mutton or pork, usu. including a rib; short broken motion (of waves etc.); ~*-house*, cheap restaurant. **chŏ'pper** *n.* (esp.) Large-bladed short-handled axe, cleaver; axe; (slang) helicopter. **chŏ'ppy̆** *adj.* (of waves, their motion, etc.) Short and broken.

chŏp[2] *n.* = CHAP[2]; ~*s of the Channel*, entrance to English Channel from Atlantic.

chŏp[3] *v.* 1. (also ~ *and change*) Change, alter (esp. repeatedly or frequently). 2. (naut., of the wind) Change suddenly. 3. Exchange or bandy words, esp. ~ *logic*, argue, bandy arguments.

Chopin (shŏpăṅ *or* shō'-), Frédéric François (1810–49). Polish pianist, composer of a large number of pianoforte compositions, études, preludes, nocturnes, etc.

chŏ'pstick *n.* 1. One of a pair of small sticks of ivory, bone, wood, etc., held between thumb and fingers of one hand and used by Chinese, Japanese, and Koreans in eating. 2. (pl., *Chopsticks*) Quick waltz tune for piano, played with side of forefinger of each hand. [Pidgin English (*chop* = quick + *stick*) equivalent of Chin. *k'wai-tsze* 'nimble ones']

chŏp-suey (-sōō'ĭ) *n.* Chinese dish of meat or chicken, rice, onions, etc., fried in sesame-oil. [Chin., = 'mixed bits']

chorā'gus, -ē'gus (k-) *n.* (pl. *-gī*). (Gk antiq.) Leader of chorus; one who defrayed cost of bringing out chorus.

chôr'al[1] (k-) *adj.* Of, sung by, a choir or chorus; spoken by group of voices. **chôr'ally̆** *adv.*

chorale, choral[2] (korah'l) *n.* (Metrical hymn set to) simple tune, usu. sung in unison, orig. in Reformed Church of Germany.

chôr'alist (k-) *n.* One who sings in a chorus.

chôrd[1] (k-) *n.* 1. String of musical instrument (poet.); also fig. of mind, emotions, etc. 2. (math.) Straight line joining extremities of arc. 3. (aeron.) Width of wings as dist. from span or lateral spread.

chôrd[2] (k-) *n.* (mus.) Group of notes sounded together, combined according to some harmonic system; *common* ~, note with its major or minor third, perfect fifth, and octave.

chôr'dāte (k-) *adj.* & *n.* (zool.) (Member) of the phylum Chordata; (organism) possessing at some stage of its life-history a notochord, i.e. a rod of tissue lying along the back below the nerve cord.

chōre *n.* (orig. U.S., usu. pl.) House-cleaning, esp. by the day; odd job(s); drudgery.

chorē'a (k-) *n.* Disease, esp. of children, characterized by involuntary movements of muscles; St. Vitus's dance. [L *chorea Sancti Viti* dance of St. Vitus]

choregus: see CHORAGUS.

chŏrėŏ'graphy̆ (k-) *n.* Arrangement of the dancing in a ballet; art of dancing. **chŏrėŏ'grapher** *n.* Designer of the dancing in a ballet. **chŏrėogră'phĭc.**

chŏ'riămb (k-) *n.* Metrical foot of four syllables, the first and last long, the others short (– ◡ ◡ –). **chŏriă'mbĭc** *adj.*

chōr'ĭc (k-) *adj.* Of, like, CHORUS, sense 1.

chōr'ion (k-) *n.* Outermost membrane enveloping foetus before birth; membrane round egg of certain insects.

chŏ'rĭster (k-) *n.* Member of (usu. male) choir, esp. boy.

chōr'oid (k-) *adj.* Of the chorion; ~ *coat*, vascular membrane lining eyeball between sclerotic coat and retina, containing numerous dark pigment-cells. ~ *n.* Choroid coat.

chōr'tle *v.i.* & *n.* Chuckle. [portmanteau wd invented by Lewis Carroll, perh. f. *chuckle*+*snort*]

chōr'us (k-) *n.* 1. (Gk antiq.) Organized band of singers and dancers in religious festivals and dramatic performances, in Attic tragedy representing interested spectators and employed to explain the action, express sympathy with characters, and draw morals; song(s) sung by these. 2. Adaptation of this in other drama; in Shakespeare etc. a personage who speaks prologue and explains or comments on happenings in play. 3. Band of singers, choir; group of singers or dancers in musical comedy etc. 4. Thing sung by many at once, simultaneous utterance; refrain of song, in which audience joins; main part of popular song as dist. from introductory verse; musical composition, usu. in four parts, for a considerable number of voices; *in* ~, in unison. 5. ~ *girl*, female member of chorus in musical comedy etc. ~ *v.* Sing, speak, say, in chorus.

chose (shōz) *n.* (law) Thing, chattel, piece of property.

chō'sen (-z-) *adj.*: see CHOOSE; (esp.) *C~ People*, Jews.

chou (shōō) *n.* 1. Large ornamental knot of ribbon etc. 2. (pl. *-x*) Small round hollow cake filled with cream etc.; ~ (or *choux*) *paste, pastry*, paste used for éclairs etc., cooked in saucepan before being baked. [Fr., = 'cabbage']

Chou En-lai (chō ĕn-lī') (1898–1976). Chinese Communist statesman; prime minister of Chinese People's Republic since 1949.

chough (chŭf) *n.* Bird (*Pyrrhocorax pyrrhocorax*) of crow family, with red feet and bill, usu. frequenting sea-cliffs.

chouse (-s) *n.* & *v.* (slang) Swindle, trick.

chow *n.* 1. (Pidgin English for) food. 2. Dog of Chinese breed, with short thick coat and black tongue.

chow-chow *n.* 1. Mixture or medley, as of pickles or preserves; Chinese mixed preserved fruit etc. 2. = CHOW, 2.

chow'der *n.* Newfoundland and New England dish of fresh fish or clams stewed with bacon, onions, biscuit, etc. [app. orig. in Brittany, in phr. *faire la chaudière* = to supply a pot etc. for cooking a stew]

chow mein (mān). Chinese dish of fried noodles with shredded meat and vegetables. [Chin., = 'fried flour']

Chrestien de Troyes (krātyahṅ, trwah) (12th c.) French author of Arthurian romances.

chrĕstŏ'mathy̆ (k-) *n.* Collection of choice passages.

chrĭsm (k-) *n.* Consecrated oil, unguent; anointing, esp. in sacred rites.

Chrīst (k-). Messiah or Lord's Anointed of Jewish prophecy; (title, now treated as proper name, given to) JESUS[1] as fulfilling this prophecy. [L *Christus* f. Gk *khristos* anointed one (*khriō* anoint) transl. of Heb.; see MESSIAH]

Christadĕ'lphian (k-) *adj.* & *n.* (Member) of a religious sect, founded in U.S. by a Dr Thomas in 1833, who reject the doctrine of the Trinity. [Gk *Khristos* Christ, *adelphos* brother]

christen (krĭ'sn) *v.* 1. Admit or initiate into Christian Church by baptism; give name to at baptism. 2. Name, dedicate (bell, ship, etc.) with ceremony like baptism; name, give name to.

Chrĭ'stendom (krĭsn-) *n.* Christians collectively; Christian countries.

Christian (krĭ'styan *or* -schan) *adj.* Believing, professing, or belonging to, religion of Christ; resembling Christ or following or exemplifying his teaching; ~ *era*: see ERA; ~ *name*, name given at christening, personal name as dist. from surname or patronymic; ~ *Science*, *Scientist*, (person believing in) principles formulated by Mrs EDDY, esp. that matter is an illusion and bodily disease an error of the mind, to be cured by teaching the patient the truth as revealed in the teaching and healing of Christ. ~ *n.* Christian person.

Christia'nia (k-, -yahn-) *n.* (skiing) Kind of turn used for stopping short. [former name of OSLO]

Christiă'nitȳ (k-) *n.* 1. Christian faith, doctrines of Christ and his apostles; Christian spirit or character. 2. Christendom.

Chrĭ'stie[1] (k-) *n.* Christiania.

Chrĭ'stie[2], Agatha Mary Clarissa (*née* Miller; Lady Mallowan) (1891–). English author of detective fiction and plays.

Chrĭ'sties (k-, -ĭz). London firm of auctioneers of works of art (now Christie, Manson & Woods), founded in 1766 by James Christie (1730–1803).

Chrĭ'stmas (krĭsm-) Festival of nativity of Christ, kept on 25 Dec., observed as time of festivity and rejoicing; days immediately preceding and following this; *Father* ~, personification of Christmas as a benevolent old man dressed in red, who brings presents to children at Christmas, filling their Christmas stockings (see below); identified with St. NICHOLAS ('Santa Claus'); ~ *box*, small present or gratuity given at Christmas, esp. to employees of firms etc. in acknowledgement of continuous services; ~ *card*, ornamental card sent as Christmas greeting (the custom began in England *c* 1867); ~ *Day*, 25 Dec.; ~ *Eve*, 24 Dec.; ~ *pudding*, plum pudding eaten at Christmas; ~ *rose*, white-flowered winter-blooming species of hellebore, *Helleborus niger*; ~ *stocking*, one hung up by children on Christmas Eve for Father Christmas to fill with presents; ~ *tree*, small tree, usu. a fir, set up in a room and hung with bright ornaments, candles, presents, etc., a feature of Christmas celebrations in Germany freq. but imperfectly imitated in England since its introduction into Queen Victoria's household early in her reign. **Chrĭ'stmassȳ** *adj.* (colloq.) Of or like Christmas, festive.

Christŏ'logȳ (k-) *n.* Branch of theology relating to Christ; doctrine or theory concerning Christ. **Christolŏ'gical** *adj.*

Chrīst's Hŏ'spital (k-). A bluecoat school, founded in London under a charter of Edward VI as a school for poor children, in buildings that had belonged to the Grey Friars; now removed to Horsham, Sussex.

chrō'ma (k-) *n.* (painting) Brilliance of hue (= saturation).

chrō'mate (k-) *n.* Salt of chromic acid.

chromă'tic (k-) *adj.* 1. Of, produced by, colour; full of bright colour; ~ *aberration*, non-conveyance of coloured constituents of white light to one focus, when refracted through a lens. 2. (mus.) Including notes which do not belong to the diatonic scale of the prevailing key; ~ *scale*, full series of notes (12 to an octave, each note differing by a semitone from the next) on which Western music is normally based. **chromă'tĭcally̆** *adv.*

chrōmatĭ'cĭty̆ (k-) *n.* Quality of a colour measured optically.

chrō'matĭn (k-) *n.* (biol.) That part of cell tissue, containing DNA, which can be readily stained when immersed in colouring-matter.

chrō'matĭsm (k-) *n.* Chromatic aberration.

chrōmatŏ'graphy̆ (k-) *n.* (chem.) Process of separating components of a mixed solution by slow passage through a tube or over adsorbing material, making use of differences of partition, adsorption, ion exchange, etc.; *gas* ~, analogous process using carrier gas as moving phase to carry gaseous or vaporized sample. **chrōmatogră'phĭc, -ĭcal** *adjs.* **chrōmatogră'phĭcally̆** *adv.*

chrōme (k-) *n.* 1. (obs.) Chromium. 2. (also ~ *yellow*) Yellow pigment and colour obtained from lead chromate ($PbCrO_4$). 3. Chromium compound used in dyeing and tanning. 4. ~ *leather*, leather tanned with potassium bichromate; ~*-nickel steel*, stainless steel, alloy of chromium, nickel, and steel; ~ *orange*, *red*, pigments prepared from dibasic lead chromate, $2(PbO)CrO_3$; ~ *steel*, very tough fine-grained alloy of chromium and steel; ~ *tanning*, tanning by treatment with acid solution of potassium bichromate and afterwards with a reducing agent, so that chromic oxide combines with the fibre of the leather and makes it tough and waterproof; ~ *yellow*: see sense 2 above. ~ *v.t.* Treat with chromium solution.

chrō'mĭc (k-) *adj.* Applied to compounds of chromium in which this element is trivalent; ~ *acid*, acid (CrO_3, strictly the anhydride of the acid) known only in solution and in form of its salts; ~ *oxide*, chromium sesquioxide (Cr_2O_3), a green powder used to give a green colour to glass and porcelain.

chrō'mĭnance ((k-) *n.* Measure of chromaticity.

chrō'mĭum (k-) *n.* (chem.) Metallic element remarkable for the brilliant red, yellow, or green colour of its compounds; symbol Cr, at. no. 24, at. wt 51·996; widely applied in electroplating and in a variety of alloys, the chief being with iron and steel, to which it imparts hardness and stainlessness; ~ *plate*, *plated*, *plating*, plate, plated, plating, with chromium.

chrō'mō (k-) *n.* (colloq.) Chromolithograph.

chrō'mogrăph (k-; *or* -ahf) *n.* & *v.t.* (Reproduce with) gelatine copying-apparatus in which aniline dye is used for ink.

chrōmōlĭ'thogrăph (k-; *or* -ahf) *n.* Picture printed in colours by lithography. **chrōmolĭthŏ'graphy̆** *n.*

chrō'mosōme (k-) *n.* (biol.) One of the rod-like structures which occur in pairs in the cell nucleus of an animal or plant and hence in every developed cell; they carry genes in linear order and are usu. constant in number for each species (the human cell nucleus has 23 pairs); *X* ~, one of the sex chromosomes, usu. occurring in pairs in the female, singly in the male; *Y* ~, sex chromosome occurring only in the male. **chrōmosō'mal** *adj.*

chrō'mosphēre (k-) *n.* Red gaseous envelope round sun, outside photosphere. **chrōmosphĕ'rĭc** *adj.*

chrō'mous (k-) *adj.* Applied to compounds of chromium in which this element is divalent.

Chron. *abbrev.* Chronicles (O.T.).

chrŏ'nĭc (k-) *adj.* (of diseases etc.) Lasting a long time; (of invalid) having such disease; (transf.) continuous, constant; (colloq.) bad, intense, severe. **chrŏ'nĭcally̆** *adv.*

chrŏ'nĭcle (k-) *n.* Detailed and continuous register of events in order of time; record, register; (*1st* and *2nd Book of the*) *Chronicles*, two historical books of O.T. ~ *v.t.* Enter or record in a chronicle. **chrŏ'nĭcler** *n.* (esp., *C*~) Compiler of the Books of the Chronicles (also of Ezra and Nehemiah).

chrŏ'nogrăm (k-) *n.* Sentence, inscription, in which certain letters express by their numerical values a date or epoch; thus, LorD haVe MerCIe Vpon Vs, printed in lieu of date in a pamphlet of the year 1666 (50+500+5+1,000+100+1+5+5 = 1666). **chrŏnogrammă'tic** *adj.*

chronŏ'logy̆ (k-) *n.* Computation of time, assignment of events, etc., to their correct date, arrangement in order of time; chronological table or list. **chrŏnolŏ'gical** *adj.* **chrŏnolŏ'gically̆** *adv.* **chronŏ'logīze** *v.t.* Arrange (narrative, list of events) in chronological order.

chronŏ'mėter (k-) *n.* Timekeeper adjusted to keep accurate time in all variations of temperature, used for determining position at sea or in the air and for other exact observations. **chrŏnomĕ'tric, -ical** *adjs.* Of chronometry. **chronŏ'mėtry̆** *n.* Accurate time-measurement.

chry̆'salis (k-) *n.* (pl. *-es, -ides*). Inactive state into which larva of most insects passes before becoming imago or perfect insect; hard sheath or case enclosing it at this stage.

chry̆să'nth (k-) *n.* (colloq.) Chrysanthemum.

chry̆să'nthėmum (k-) *n.* 1. Composite plant of genus *C~*, including ox-eye daisy and corn

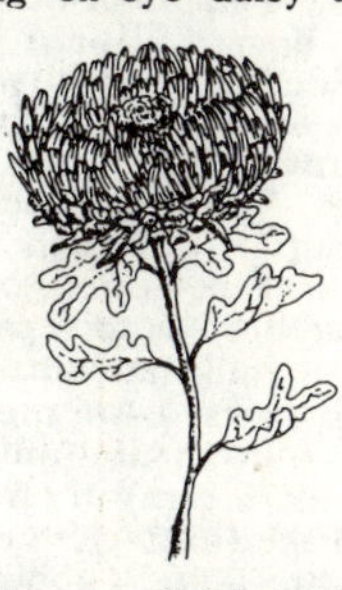

marigold. 2. Cultivated species of this, blooming in autumn.

chry̆sĕlėphă'ntīne (k-) *adj.* (of sculpture) Covered with ivory and gold.

chry̆sobĕ'ry̆l (k-) *n.* Yellowish-green precious stone, an aluminate of berylium.

chry̆'solīte (k-) *n.* Precious olivine, a pale yellowish-green silicate of magnesia and iron.

chry̆'soprāse (k-, -z) *n.* 1. In N.T. etc., golden-green precious stone (prob. a kind of beryl) believed in the Middle Ages to shine in the dark. 2. Apple-green variety of chalcedony.

Chry̆'sostom (k-), St. John (*c* 345–407). Bishop of Constantinople (398); Doctor of the Church; in his writings he emphasized the ascetic element in religion and the need for personal study of the Scriptures; commemorated 27 Jan.

chthŏ'nic (kth-) *adj.* (of deities etc.) Dwelling in or beneath surface of the earth.

chŭb *n.* Thick fat coarse-fleshed European and Caspian river-fish of carp family, *Leuciscus cephalus*, dusky-green above and silvery-white beneath.

Chŭbb *n.* (also ~ *lock*) Name of patent lock with tumblers and device for fixing bolt immovably if attempt is made to pick the lock, [f. name of inventor, a London locksmith]

chŭ'bby̆ *adj.* Plump, round-faced. **chŭ'bbinėss** *n.* [f. CHUB]

chŭck[1] *n.* & *v.i.* (Make) clucking sound like fowl or person calling fowls etc.

chŭck[2] *n.* (archaic) Familiar term of endearment.

chŭck[3] *v.* 1. Tap lightly *under the chin.* 2. Fling, throw, toss, carelessly or easily (*away*); ~ *up* (colloq.) give up, give in; ~ *out*, expel (esp. troublesome person from place, etc.); *chucker-out*, person engaged to do this; ~ *it*, (slang) stop; *~-farthing*, former game in which the players pitched coins at a mark and then he whose pitch came nearest tossed them all at a hole and won any that fell in; similar game. ~ *n.* Act of chucking; jerk, toss; (colloq.) dismissal.

chŭck[4] *n.* 1. Cut of beef extending from neck to ribs incl. shoulder-piece. 2. Part of lathe etc. that holds rotating work-piece or tool.

chŭ'ckle *n.* & *v.i.* (Make) suppressed and inarticulate sound(s) expressing mirth, exultation, etc.

chŭ'ckle-headĕd (-hĕd-) *adj.* (dial. & U.S.) Stupid.

chŭffed (-ft) *adj.* (slang) 1. Pleased. 2. Disgruntled.

chŭg *n.* & *v.i.* (also *chug-chug*) (Make) repeated plunging or explosive sound (esp. of machine).

chŭ'kker *n.* Each of the periods into which a game of polo is divided. [Hind. *chakkar*, f. Sansk. *chakra* wheel]

chŭm *n.* (colloq.) Associate, familiar friend; *new* ~, (Austral.) recent immigrant, greenhorn. ~ *v.i.* Be close friends *with*; share chambers or rooms *with*.

chŭ'mmy̆ *adj.* (colloq.) Intimate, sociable.

chŭmp *n.* 1. Short thick lump of wood; thick blunt end of anything, esp. of loin of mutton (~ *chop*, chop from chump end of this. 2. (slang) Head. 3. (colloq.) Blockhead.

Chungki'ng (chōō-). Town in S. China, the temporary seat of the Chinese Government during the invasion of China by the Japanese (1937–45).

chŭnk *n.* Thick lump cut or broken off anything.

chŭpă'ttĭ *n.* (in India etc.) Small flat cake of coarse unleavened bread.

chûrch *n.* 1. Building for public Christian worship, esp. according to the established religion of the country. 2. *the C~*, the Christian community; any branch or district part of this. 3. Clergy and officers of the Church; clerical order or profession. 4. Congregation of Christians locally organized for religious worship etc. 5. Public worship in church. 6. *C~ Army*, Church of England mission to working classes founded by Preb. Carlile in 1882; *C~ Commissioners*, board managing finances of Church of England; *chur'chman*, (fem. *chur'chwoman*) member of Church established or recognized in any country; *C~ militant*, Church on earth conceived as warring against evil; *C~ of England*, English branch of the Western Church, which at the Reformation repudiated the Pope's authority and asserted that of the sovereign over ecclesiastical as well as temporal matters in his dominions; ~ *parade*, attendance at church service as part of military routine etc.; ~ *Slavonic*: see SLAVONIC; *churchwarden*, one of the (usu. two) lay honorary officers of a parish or district church elected annually to assist incumbent in administrative duties, manage various parochial offices, etc.; clay pipe with very long stem; *chur'chyard*, enclosed ground round a church, esp. as used for burials. ~ *v.t.* Conduct service of thanksgiving for (woman after childbirth).

Chûr'chĭll, Sir Winston Leonard Spencer (1874–1965). British statesman; under-secretary of state for the colonies 1906–8; president of the Board of Trade 1908–10; home secretary 1910–11; first lord of the Admiralty 1911–15; secretary of state for war 1918–21, for the colonies 1921–2; chancellor of the exchequer (1924–9); prime minister 1940–5, 1951–5.

chûr'chy̆ *adj.* (colloq.) Obtrusively or intolerantly devoted to church or opposed to dissent.

churĭ'nga (-ngg*a*) *n.* (Austral.) Sacred object, amulet.

chûrl *n.* Person of low birth; peasant, boor; ill-bred fellow; cross-grained or niggardly person. **chûr'lĭsh** *adj.* **chûr'lĭshly̆** *adv.* **chûr'lĭshnėss** *n.*

chûrn *n.* Vessel or machine for making butter, in which milk or cream is shaken, beaten, or otherwise agitated, so as to separate the globules of milk-fat (butter) from the serous parts; large metal container for transporting milk. ~ *v.* Shake (milk, cream) in churn into butter; make (butter) thus; make butter; stir (liquid) about, make it froth; (of sea etc.) wash to and fro, seethe; ~ *out*, (fig.) produce in quantity.

Churriguera (chōōrĭgār'*a*), José de (1665–1725). Spanish architect using lavishly ornamented late baroque style. **churrĭguerĕ'sque** (-ĕsk) *adj.* & *n.*

chute[1] (shōōt) *n.* 1. Smooth rapid descent of water over slope. 2. Sloping channel, slide, for conveying things to lower level, for sliding down into water, etc.

chute[2] (shōōt) *n.* (colloq.) Parachute.

chŭ'tney *n.* Strong pungent condiment of fruits, vinegar, sugar, spices, etc. [Hind. *chaṭnī*]

chȳle (k-) *n.* White milky fluid formed by action of pancreatic juice and bile on chyme, and contained in the lymphatics of the intestines. **chȳ'lous** *adj.*

chȳme (k-) *n.* Semi-fluid pulpy acid matter into which food is converted in stomach by action of gastric secretion.

C.I. *abbrev.* Channel Islands.

C.I.A. *abbrev.* Central Intelligence Agency.

cĭbôr'ium *n.* (pl. *-ia*). 1. (eccles. archit.) Canopy, canopied shrine. 2. Covered chalice for reservation of Eucharist.

cĭca'da, cĭca'la, cĭga'la (-ah-) *n.* 1. Plant-sucking bug, usu. large, the male of which makes shrill sound from two tympanic structures on the abdomen. 2. Long-horned grass-hopper.

cĭ'catrĭce, cĭ'catrĭx *n.* 1. Scar of healed wound; scar on tree bark. 2. (bot.) Mark left by fall of leaf etc.; hilum of seed.

cĭ'catrīze *v.* Heal (wound etc.) by inducing a scar, skin over; (of wound etc.) heal by forming a cicatrice.

cĭ'cėlȳ *n.* Any of various umbelliferous plants, esp. *sweet* ~, *Myrrhis odorata*, cultivated in herb gardens.

Cĭ'cerō, Marcus Tullius (106–43 B.C.). Roman republican orator and philosopher. **Cĭcerō'nĭan** *adj.*

cĭcerō'nė (*or* chĭch-) *n.* (pl. *-ni*, pr. -nē) Guide who shows and explains antiquities or curiosities of a place. [It., f. CICERO]

Cicestr. *abbrev.* (Bishop) of Chichester (replacing surname in his signature).

Cĭd. Title in Spanish literature of Ruy Diaz, count of Bivar, 11th-c. champion of Christianity against the Moors. [Arab. *sayyid* lord]

C.I.D. *abbrev.* Criminal Investigation Department.

cī'der *n.* Fermented drink made from apple-juice and sugar; ~ *press*, press for extracting juice from crushed apples. [Heb. *šēkār* strong drink]

ci-devant (sē devahṅ) *adj.* That was formerly. ~ *n.* (in language of French Revolution) Former person of rank. [Fr.]

C.I.E. *abbrev.* Companion of (the Order of) the Indian Empire.

c.i.f. *abbrev.* Cost, insurance, and freight.

cĭgâr' *n.* Compact roll of tobacco leaves for smoking; ~-*shaped*, cylindrical with pointed end(s).

cĭgarĕ'tte *n.* Small cylinder of cut tobacco (occas. of other herbs) rolled in thin paper for smoking; ~ *card, picture*, picture card inserted by makers in packet or box of cigarettes; ~ *holder*, mouthpiece holding cigarette.

C.I.G.S. *abbrev.* Chief of Imperial General Staff.

cĭ'lĭāte *adj.* & *n.* (Member) of the Ciliata, a class of protozoa which move by means of cilia.

Cĭlĭ'cia (-sha). Ancient region of SE. Asia Minor. **Cĭlĭ'cian** *adj.* & *n.*

cĭ'lium *n.* (pl. *-ia*). 1. Eyelash; delicate hair resembling eyelash on edge of leaf, insect's wing, etc. 2. One of the hairlike vibrating organs on animal and some vegetable tissues, serving as chief means of locomotion for many lower animals living in water. **cĭ'liarȳ, cĭ'lĭāte** *adjs.*

Cĭmmēr'ian *adj.* Of the Cimmerii, a people fabled by the ancients to live in perpetual darkness; (of darkness etc.) thick, gloomy. ~ *n.* 1. One of the Cimmerii. 2. One of a nomadic people, the earliest known inhabitants of the Crimea, who were expelled and overran Asia Minor in the 7th c. B.C.

C.-in-C. *abbrev.* Commander-in-Chief.

cĭnch *n.* 1. (U.S.) Saddle-girth used in Mexico etc. 2. (slang)

Firm hold; safe or easy thing; dead certainty. ~ *v.* 1. Fix saddle securely with girth. 2. Secure a hold on; make certain of.

cinchō'na (-k-) *n.* S. Amer. tree or shrub of genus *C~* with fragrant white or pink flowers; ~ *bark*, bark of certain species of this containing quinine and other related alkaloids and used as tonic and febrifuge; drug prepared from it. [named by Linnaeus in honour of countess of *Chinchon* (Spain), who when vice-queen of Peru was cured by cinchona bark in 1638 and brought a supply to Europe in 1640]

Cĭncĭnnā'tus, Lucius Quinctius. Roman who, acc. to tradition, was called in 458 B.C. from the plough to deliver the Roman army from the peril in which it stood in its conflict with the Aequians; often referred to as a type of old Roman simplicity and frugality.

cĭ'ncture *n.* Girdle, belt, border; ring at top and bottom of column dividing shaft from capital and base. ~ *v.t.* Girdle, gird.

cĭ'nder *n.* Slag; residue of coal, wood, etc., that has ceased to flame but has still combustible matter in it; (pl.) ashes; ~ *path, track*, footpath, running- or racing-track, laid with fine cinders. **cĭ'nderȳ** *adj.*

Cĭnderĕ'lla. Heroine of a fairy-tale, treated as a drudge by her stepmother and step-sisters; rescued by her fairy godmother and sent to the court ball in a dress that would change back into rags at midnight; hence, neglected or despised member etc.

cĭ'nė *adj.* Cinematographic.

cĭ'nėma *n.* Moving photographic pictures, films; making of these for entertainment or record; theatre where they are exhibited; films collectively, esp. as an art form. [abbrev. of *cinematograph*]

Cĭ'nėmascōpe *n.* Cinema film using a wide screen. [trade-name]

cĭnėmă'tĭc *adj.* Appropriate to the cinema.

cĭnėmă'tograph (*or* -ahf) *n.* & *adj.* (Of the) cinema. **cĭnėmatŏ'grapher** *n.* **cĭnėmatogră'phĭc, -ĭcal** *adjs.* **cĭnėmatogră'phĭcallȳ** *adv.* **cĭnėmatŏ'graphȳ** *n.* Process, art, of producing moving pictures. [Gk *kinēma* movement, *graphō* write, record]

Cinera'ma (-ah-) *n.* Cinema film projected on a wide curved screen by three cameras. [trade-name]

cĭnerār'ĭa *n.* Any of several pot-plants derived from a perennial herb (*Senecio cruentus*) of the Canary Islands, with white, red, blue, or purple flowers. [L *cinerarius* of ashes, from the ash-coloured down on the leaves]

cĭ'nerarȳ *adj.* Of ashes; ~ *urn*, urn holding ashes of dead after cremation.

Cĭngalē'se (-ngg-, -z) Former spelling of SINHALESE.

cĭ'nnabār *n.* Red crystalline form of mercuric sulphide (HgS), esp. as pigment; vermilion.

cĭ'nnamon *n.* Yellowish-brown, aromatic inner bark of an E. Ind. tree, *Cinnamomum zeylanicum*, dried in the sun and used as a spice; the tree itself. ~ *adj.* Cinnamon-coloured.

cĭnquėcĕ'ntō (chĭnkwĭchĕ-) *n.* (Style of art and architecture of) the 16th c. in Italy. **cĭnquėcĕ'ntĭst** *n.* Italian artist of the 16th c.

cĭ'nquefoil (-nkf-) *n.* 1. Plant of genus *Potentilla*, with compound leaves each of five leaflets. 2. (her.) Ornamental design resembling cinquefoil leaf; (archit.) 5-cusped ornament in an arch or circle.

Cinque Pôrts (-nk). Group of seaports, orig. 5 (Hastings, Sandwich, Dover, Romney, Hythe, to which were added Rye, Winchelsea and several others), on SE. coast of England, with jurisdiction over the whole coast from Seaford in East Sussex to Birchington in Kent. In the 13th c. they furnished the chief part of the English Navy and in return received important privileges, most of which they kept until the Reform Act of 1832 and the Corporation Act of 1835. The Lord Wardenship of the Cinque Ports is now chiefly an honorary dignity.

C.I.O. *abbrev.* (U.S.) Congress of Industrial Organizations.

cī'pher, cȳ- *n.* 1. Arithmetical symbol or character (0) of no value by itself, which when placed after any figure (or series of figures) in a whole number increases its value tenfold, and when placed before a figure in decimal fractions decreases its value in the same proportion. 2. Person or thing of no importance or worth, nonentity. 3. Any Arabic numeral. 4. Secret or disguised manner of writing; anything so written; key to this. 5. Device of intertwined initials or other letters, monogram. 6. Continuous sounding of note on organ owing to imperfect closing of pallet or valve. ~ *v.* 1. Use Arabic numerals in arithmetic, do arithmetic; (U.S.) calculate, work *out* in the mind. 2. Put into secret writing. 3. (of organ-note) Go on sounding when not depressed. [Arab. *ṣifr* zero]

cir'ca *prep.* About. [L]

cĩrcā'dĭan *adj.* Of physiological activity occurring approximately every twenty-four hours.

Cĩrcă'ssĭan *adj.* & *n.* (Member, language) of a group of tribes of the Caucasus, some of whom moved into Turkish territory in 19th c., whose women were remarkable for their beauty. [Russ. *Cherkés*, tribe calling themselves Adighe]

Cĩr'cė. (Gk legend) Enchantress dwelling in island of Aeaea, who transformed all who drank of her cup into swine. **Cĩrcē'an** *adj.* Of, pertaining to, Circe; bewitching.

cir'citer *prep.* About. [L]

cĩr'cle *n.* 1. (Line enclosing) plane figure with circumference everywhere equidistant from centre; *great ~ (of a sphere)*, circle on surface of sphere, whose plane passes through centre of sphere; *great ~ sailing, flying*, navigation along a great circle of the earth. 2. Anything shaped like a circle, ring; curved tier of seats at theatre etc.; *dress ~*, lowest (and most expensive) of these in a theatre, in which evening dress was once required; *upper ~*, circle next above dress circle; (archaeol.) series of stones set up in a ring. 3. Period, cycle, round; completed chain or sequence of events, parts, etc., esp. of consequences which react upon and intensify their causes (often *vicious ~*); (logic) fallacious reasoning, by which a proposition is used to establish a conclusion and is itself proved by means of the conclusion it has established (also *vicious ~*). 4. Persons grouped round centre of interest; set, coterie, class; society. ~ *v.* 1. (poet.) Encompass. 2. Make circuit of; move in a circle.

cĩr'clėt *n.* Small circle; circular band, esp. of gold, jewels, etc., worn on head or elsewhere.

cĩr'cuit (-kĭt) *n.* 1. Line enclosing an area, distance round; area enclosed; journey round; roundabout way or journey. 2. Journey of judges etc. through certain appointed areas for purpose of holding courts of justice or performing other specified duties at various places in succession; judges or barristers making the circuit; district or division through which circuit is made, of which there are 6 in England and Wales since 1971: Midland and Oxford, North Eastern, Northern, South Eastern, Wales and Chester, Western. 3. Territorial division of Methodist Church, with a number of congregations served by a series of itinerant preachers. 4. Number of theatres etc. under one control. 5. (elect.) Course or path of an electric current; *~ breaker*, device for interrupting electric circuit. **cĩr'cuitrȳ** *n.* Plan, components of electric circuit; system of such circuits.

cĩrcū'ĭtous *adj.* Going a long way round, indirect. **cĩrcū'ĭtouslȳ** *adv.* **cĩrcū'ĭtousnėss** *n.*

cĩr'cūlar *adj.* Of the form of, pertaining to, moving in, passing over, a circle; *~ letter*, letter (notice, advertisement, etc.), sent round in same form to several people, or printed etc. for this purpose; *~ saw*, saw in form of revolving toothed disc. **cĩrcūlă'rĭtȳ** *n.* **cĩr'cūlarlȳ** *adv.* **cĩr'cūlar** *n.* Circular letter or advertisement. **cir'cūlarīze** *v.t.* Send circular(s) to.

cir'cūlāte *v.* 1. Go round a circuit, circuitous course, system of pipes, etc.; (of blood) flow from heart through arteries and capillaries and back through veins to heart. 2. Pass from place to place, from mouth to mouth, etc.; (of newspaper etc.) pass into hands of readers. 3. Put into circulation, cause to circulate; *circulating library*, library of which books are circulated among subscribers.

circūlā'tion *n.* 1. Movement of blood from and back to heart; similar movement of sap etc.; movement to and fro. 2. Transmission, distribution (of news, books, etc.); number of copies sold, esp. of newspapers. 3. Currency; coin.

cir'culatorȳ (*or* sêrkūlā'-) *adj.* Of circulation of the blood, of sap, etc.

circum- *prefix.* Round, about.

circumă'mbiėnt *adj.* Surrounding (esp. of air or other fluids). **circumă'mbience** *n.*

circumă'mbūlāte *v.* Walk round, walk about. **circumămbūlā'tion** *n.* **circumă'mbūlatorȳ** *adj.*

circumbě'ndĭbus *n.* (facet.) Roundabout method; circumlocution.

cir'cumcīse (-z) *v.t.* Cut off foreskin of (as Jewish or Muslim rite, or surgically); remove clitoris of. **circumci'sion** *n.* 1. Act or religious rite of circumcising. 2. *C~*, festival of circumcision of Christ, 1 Jan. 3. Jews, as a circumcised race.

circŭ'mference *n.* Encompassing boundary, esp. of figure enclosed by curve, as circle. distance round. **circumferĕ'ntial** (-shal) *adj.*

cir'cumflex *n.* Circumflex accent. *~ adj.* 1. *~ accent*, mark (ˆ, in Greek ˜) placed over vowel to indicate contraction, length, or special quality. 2. (anat.) Curved, bending round something else.

circŭ'mfluent (-lōō-) *adj.* Flowing round, ambient. **circŭ'mfluence** *n.*

circumfū'se (-z) *v.t.* Pass round; surround *with*, bathe. **circumfū'sion** *n.*

circumgȳrā'te *v.i.* Turn, wheel, travel, round. **circumgȳrā'tion** *n.*

circumjā'cent *adj.* Situated around.

circumlocū'tion *n.* Use of many words where few would do; evasive talk; roundabout expression; *C~ Office*, the type of a government department, satirized by Dickens in 'Little Dorrit'. **circumlŏ'cūtorȳ** *adj.*

circumnă'vĭgāte *v.t.* Sail round. **circumnăvĭgā'tion, circumnă'vĭgātor** *ns.*

circumpō'lar *adj.* Around, about, near, a (terrestrial or celestial) pole; (astron., of star etc.) describing its whole diurnal circle above the horizon.

cir'cumscrībe *v.t.* 1. Draw line round; encompass. 2. Mark out or define limits of; confine, restrict. 3. (geom.) Describe (figure) about another so as to touch it at certain points without cutting it. **circumscrĭ'ption** *n.* Circumscribing; inscription round coin, seal etc.

circumsō'lar *adj.* Situated near, moving round, the sun.

cir'cumspĕct *adj.* Cautious, wary; taking everything into account. **cir'cumspĕctlȳ** *adv.* **cir'cumspĕctnėss, circumspĕ'ction** *ns.*

cir'cumstance *n.* 1. (pl.) Time, place, manner, cause, occasion, etc., surroundings, of an act; external conditions affecting or that might affect an agent. 2. (pl.) Material welfare, means. 3. Detail in narrative. 4. Formality, ceremony. 5. Incident, occurrence, fact. 6. (U.S.) Comparable or important thing or fact. **cir'cumstanced** (-nst) *adj.*

circumstă'ntial (-shal) *adj.* 1. Of or dependent on circumstances; *~ evidence*, indirect evidence from circumstances affording a certain presumption or capable of only one explanation. 2. Adventitious, accidental. 3. Full of, particular as to, details. 4. Full of circumstance or pomp. **circumstă'ntiallȳ** *adv.*

cĩrcumvallā'tion *n.* (Making of) rampart or entrenchment.

cĩrcumvĕ'nt *v.t.* Entrap; overreach, outwit. **cĩrcumvĕ'ntion** *n.*

cĩr'cus *n.* 1. Rounded or oval (freq. temporary) arena lined with tiers of seats for equestrian and other exhibitions; entertainment given in this, consisting usu. of acrobatics, clowning, feats of horsemanship, and performances by animals; travelling show of riders, acrobats, etc., and their equipage. 2. (Rom. antiq.) Large oval or oblong building surrounded with rising tiers of seats for public spectacles and horse or chariot races. 3. Amphitheatre of hills. 4. (Circular) open space in town with streets converging on it.

cĩrque (-k) *n.* (poet. & rhet.) Arena, natural amphitheatre; (geol.) bowl-shaped hollow at head of valley or on mountain slope, partly enclosed by steep walls and formed orig. by glacier

cĭrrhō'sĭs (-rō-) *n.* Disease of liver, most frequent among habitual spirit-drinkers; chronic interstitial hepatitis, with atrophy of cells and increase of connective tissue. **cĭrrhŏ'tĭc** *adj.*

cĭ'rrhus (-r*u*s) *n.* (erron.) = CIRRUS.

cĭ'rripĕd *n.* (zool.) Member of the Cirripedia, sub-class of Crustacea comprising marine animals esp. the barnacles, usu. with shelly plates strengthening the carapace and feathery legs which are protruded from the shell-valves to collect food. ~ *adj.*

cirrōcū'mūlus *n.* (pl. -*lī*). (meteor.) Form of usu. high cloud consisting of roundish fleecy cloudlets in contact with one another, mackerel sky.

cĭrrō'se, cĭ'rrous *adjs.* Of or having cirri; of or like cirrus.

cĭrrōstrā'tus *n.* (meteor.) Thin usu. high cloud consisting of horizontal or inclined sheets attenuated upwards into light cirri.

cirrous: see CIRROSE.

cĭ'rrus *n.* (pl. -*rī*). 1. (zool.) Slender filamentary process on appendage. 2. (meteor.) Form of cloud, usu. high, with diverging filaments or wisps, often resembling curl or lock of hair or wool.

cĭs- *prefix.* On this side of.

Cĭsă'lpīne *adj.* On this (usu. = the Roman) side of the Alps; ~ *Gaul*, northern Italy in ancient times.

Cĭsnĕ'ros (th-), Francisco Jiménez de (1437–1517). Spanish cardinal and statesman, inquisitor-general of Castile and Léon (1507).

cĭ'ssȳ, sĭ- *adj.* & *n.* (slang) Effeminate (person). [f. *sister*]

cĭst[1] *n.* 1. (pr. s- *or* k-; archaeol., also *kĭst*) Prehistoric sepulchral chest or chamber of stone or hollowed tree-trunk (also ~-*grave*). 2. (Gk antiq.) Box for sacred utensils.

cĭst[2] *n.* Var. of CYST.

Cĭstẽr'cian (-sh*a*n) *adj.* & *n.* (Member) of the monastic order, observing a stricter form of the Benedictine rule, founded at Cîteaux near Dijon in 1098 by Robert, abbot of Molesme. [L *Cistercium* Cîteaux]

cĭ'stern *n.* Artificial reservoir for storing water, usu. tank in high part of building with pipes supplying taps on lower levels.

cĭ'stus *n.* Shrub of genus *C*~ with large short-lived flowers of various colours.

cĭ'stvaen (-vān; *or* k-) *n.* = CIST[1], 1.

cĭ'tadel *n.* 1. Fortress, esp. one guarding or commanding a city. 2. Building in which Salvation Army meetings are held.

cīte *v.t.* 1. Summon to appear in law-court. 2. Quote in support of a position; mention as example.

cītā'tion *n.* (esp., orig. U.S.) Mention in an official dispatch, recommendation to an honour.

cĭ'ther, -ern, cĭ'ttern *n.* Wire-stringed musical instrument somewhat like lute but with flat back, usu. played with plectrum, common in times of Chaucer and Shakespeare.

cĭ'tĭzen *n.* 1. Burgess, freeman, inhabitant, of city or town; enfranchised member of a State; ~ *of the world*, cosmopolitan; *Citizens' Advice Bureau*, office established locally in town or other centre to help individuals on a wide variety of problems. 2. (hist., as title; fem. *citizenĕss*) Representing Fr. *citoyen, citoyenne*, which at the Revolution took the place of *Monsieur, Madame*. **cĭ'tizenshĭp** *n.*

cĭ'trāte *n.* Salt of citric acid. ~ *v.t.* Treat with (esp. sodium) citrate.

cĭ'trĭc *adj.* ~ *acid*, colourless, sharp-tasting crystalline acid ($C_6H_7O_7$) found in the juice of oranges, lemons, limes, etc.

cĭ'tron *n.* Ovate acid juicy fruit with pale yellow rind, larger, less acid, and thicker-skinned than lemon; tree, *Citrus medica*, bearing this.

cĭtronĕ'lla *n.* Fragrant grass of S. Asia, *Cymbopogon nardus*, yielding a fragrant oil much used in perfumery; this oil.

cĭ'trous *adj.* = CITRUS.

cĭ'trus *n.* Fruit of genus *C~* including citron, orange, lime, lemon, and grapefruit. ~ *adj.*

cĭ'tў *n.* 1. (loosely) Important town; (strictly, in England) town created city by charter, in early times esp. one containing a cathedral; (in U.S.) town of greater importance, or size, or with wider municipal powers, than those called simply 'towns'; *Celestial C~, Holy C~, C~ of God*, Paradise; *Eternal C~, C~ of the Seven Hills*, Rome; *Holy C~*, (esp.) Jerusalem; ~ *state*, one of the small autonomous republics of ancient Greece; 2. *the C~* (*of London*), that part of London within the ancient boundaries, including the liberties, which is under the jurisdiction of the Lord Mayor and Corporation; esp. the business part of this, near the Exchange and Bank of England, the centre of financial and commercial activity; ~ *article*, financial and commercial article in a newspaper; so ~ *editor, page*, etc.; *C~ Company*, one of the corporations historically representing the ancient trade guilds of London; ~ *man*, one engaged in commerce or finance (in the City of London); *C~ University*, university, at London, 1966.

cĭ'vĕt *n.* 1. Yellowish or brownish substance, unctuous and smelling strongly of musk, got from anal glands of civet cat or related species. 2. Carnivorous quadruped of family Viverridae yielding this, esp. the central African ~ *cat*, *Civettictis civetta*, between fox and weasel in appearance.

cĭ'vĭc *adj.* Of, proper to, citizens; of a city, municipal; of citizenship, civil. **cĭ'vics** *n.* Science of civic affairs.

cĭ'vĭl *adj.* 1. Of citizens or citizen community. 2. Of, becoming, befitting, a citizen; polite, obliging. 3. Non-military; non-ecclesiastical, secular; (law) not criminal or political. 4. ~ *defence*, protection of civil population against air raids or other enemy action; ~ *day*: see DAY, 2; ~ *death*: see DEATH, 2; ~ *disobedience*, refusal to obey the laws as part of a political campaign; ~ *engineering*: see ENGINEERING; ~ *law*, law pertaining to the private rights and remedies of a citizen (cf. CRIMINAL law); law of Roman citizens; Roman law as a whole, esp. as received in Western Christendom in and after Middle Ages; *C~ List*, amount voted by Parliament from public revenue for household and personal expenses of monarch and for *C~ List pensions*, i.e. those granted by the royal bounty; ~ *marriage*: see MARRIAGE; ~ *proceedings*, legal proceedings aimed at the redress of wrong; ~ *rights*, rights to personal liberty; (U.S.) rights of Negroes to equality as citizens; *C~ Servant*, official in Civil Service; *C~ Service*, administrative service of State, including all government departments and public offices (excluding armed forces); officials employed in this; ~ *war*, war between members of the same community; *C~ War*, (Engl. hist.) struggle between Royalists and Parliament, 1642–51; (U.S. hist.) war of Secession, 1861–5; (Span. hist.) struggle between Fascist and republican factions, 1936–9. **cĭ'vĭllȳ** *adv.* **cĭvĭ'lĭtȳ** *n.* Politeness.

cĭvĭ'lĭan *adj.* & *n.* (Person) not of one of the armed services.

cĭvĭlīzā'tion *n.* Making or becoming civilized; stage, esp. advanced stage, in social development. **cĭ'vĭlīze** *v.t.* Bring out of barbarism; instruct in the arts of life; refine, enlighten.

cĭ'vvȳ *adj.* (colloq.) Civilian; ~ *street*, civilian life. **cĭ'vvĭes** (-ĭz) *n.pl.* (colloq.) Civilian clothes.

C.J. *abbrev.* Chief Justice.

cl. *abbrev.* Centilitre(s); class; classical.

clăck *n.* 1. Sharp sound as of boards struck together; noise or clatter of human tongues. 2. Kind of pump-valve, flap opened by upward motion of fluid; locomotive valve closing opening of feed-pump into boiler. ~ *v.i.* Chatter, prate; make clack.

Clăckmă'nnanshire. Former county of central Scotland, since May 1975 part of the region of Central.

clad: see CLOTHE. **clă'ddĭng** *n.* Coating or covering applied to surface of object, building, etc.; application of this.

clā'dōde *n.* (bot.) Leaf-like stem.

claim *v.t.* Demand as one's due; represent oneself as having; demand recognition of the fact that; profess; deserve, assert. ~ *n.* 1. Demand for something as due; right, title, *to*; right to make demand *on*. 2. Piece of land allotted, esp. for mining. **clai'mant** *n.* One who makes or enters a claim.

clairau'dĭence *n.* Faculty of hearing sounds out of range. **clairau'dĭent** *adj.* & *n.* (Person) having clairaudience.

clair'voyance *n.* Faculty of seeing mentally what is out of sight; second sight. **clairvoy'ant** *adj.* & *n.* (Person) having clairvoyance.

clăm *n.* Any of various bivalve shellfish, esp. the N. Amer. hard or round clam, *Venus mercenaria*, and soft or long clam, *Mya arenaria*, found abundantly on sandy or muddy shores and esteemed as food; (slang, orig. U.S.) silent, uncommunicative person. [orig. *clamshell*; ult. f. Ger. *klam* press or squeeze together]

clā'mant *adj.* Noisy, insistent, urgent.

clă'mber *v.i.* Climb with hands and feet; climb with difficulty or labour. ~ *n.* Climbing thus.

clă'mmȳ *adj.* Moist and sticky. **clă'mmĭlȳ** *adv.* **clă'mmĭnėss** *n.*

clă'mour (-m*er*) *n.* Shouting; loud appeal, complaint, or demand; confused noise. ~ *v.i.* Make clamour *for*, *against*, etc. **clă'morous** *adj.* **clă'morouslȳ** *adv.* **clă'morousnėss** *n.*

clămp[1] *n.* Brace, clasp, or band for strengthening other materials or holding things together; appliance or tool with opposite sides connected by screw for holding or compressing. ~ *v.t.* Strengthen, fasten, with clamp(s); ~ *down* (*on*), (fig.) become (more) strict (about), put a stop to.

clamp[2] *n.* Compact mound or pile, esp. of bricks for burning in the open air, or of potatoes etc. for storing within a cover of straw and earth.

clăn *n.* 1. Number of persons descended from same ancestor and associated together, esp. in Scottish Highlands, and also in various parts of the Lowlands with similar social system; *cla'nsman*, (fellow) member of a clan. 2. Family holding together; coterie, set. **clă'nnĭsh** *adj.* **clă'nnĭshlȳ** *adv.* **clă'nnĭshnėss** *n.*

clăndĕ'stĭne *adj.* Surreptitious, secret, underhand. **clăndĕ'stĭnelȳ** *adv.*

clăng *n.* Loud resonant metallic sound. ~ *v.* Make, cause to make, this sound.

clă'ngour (-ngg*er*) *n.* Succession of loud metallic ringing noises. **clă'ngorous** *adj.*

clănk *n.* Sharp abrupt sound, as of heavy pieces of metal struck together. ~ *v.* Make, cause to make, this sound.

clă'nshĭp *n.* System of clans; clannishness; attachment or loyalty to a clan.

clăp *n.* 1. Loud explosive noise as of thunder; peal. 2. Sound made by striking palms of hands together; act of doing this as applause. ~ *v.* 1. Make clap; signify applause, delight, etc., with clap; applaud with claps; shut (door etc.) with clap. 2. Slap with palm of hand, in approval or encouragement; apply, place, set, quickly or energetically; put *in* prison; ~ *eyes on*, catch sight of; ~-*net*, net that can be shut by pulling string.

clă'pboard (-bôrd) *n.* & *v.t.* (U.S.) (Cover with) weatherboard. **clă'pboarding** *n.*

clă'pper *n.* (esp.) Tongue or striker of bell.

clă'pper bridge. Primitive bridge consisting of a series of slabs or planks resting on piles of stones.

clă'ptrăp *n.* Trick or device, language, to catch applause; pretentious but empty assertions.

claque (klahk) *n.* Body of hired applauders in theatre etc.

clārabĕ'lla *n.* Organ stop of flute type. [L *clarus* clear, *bellus* pretty]

Clāre. County of Munster.

clă'rence *n.* Four-wheeled closed carriage with seats for four inside and two on box. [f. Duke of *Clarence*, afterwards William IV]

Clă'renceux (-sū). The 2nd King of Arms in England, whose office is to marshal and arrange funerals of all baronets, knights, and esquires south of the Trent. [f. *Clarence*, dukedom created for Lionel, 2nd son of Edward III, when he married the heiress of Clare in Suffolk; the Clarence herald was subsequently made a Royal herald and King of Arms]

Clă'rendon[1], Edward Hyde, Earl of (1609–74). English statesman and historian; lord chancellor under Charles II; author of 'The True Historical Narrative of the Rebellion and Civil Wars in England', from the profits of which a new printing-house, which bore his name, was built for the Oxford University Press, also the ~ *Laboratory*, the university physics department, founded in 1872.

Clă'rendon[2], Constitutions of: see CONSTITUTION, 3.

clă'rendon[3] *n.* Thick-faced type of various sizes. [the *Clarendon* Press, Oxford]

Clāres (-ārz) *n.pl.* (also *Poor* ~) Sisterhood instituted at Assisi *c* 1212 by St. Clare, who adopted the Franciscan rule and habit.

clă'ret *n.* Red wine imported from Bordeaux; colour of this, dark reddish-purple; artificial salmon-fly of this colour; (boxing slang) blood. ~ *adj.* Claret-coloured.

clă'rĭfȳ *v.* Make clear; free from impurities, make transparent (liquid, butter, etc.); become or be made clear or pure. **clărĭfĭcā'tion** *n.*

clărĭnĕ't *n.* Wood-wind single-reed instrument with compass of about 3½ octaves from C♯ or D below middle C, having cylindrical tube with bell-shaped end, and played by fingers on holes and keys; 8-ft organ stop of similar quality; *bass* ~, instrument like clarinet with range an octave lower.

clă'rĭon *n.* Shrill narrow-tubed trumpet formerly used in war; sound of trumpet, any similar rousing sound; 4-ft organ stop of similar quality to clarion. ~ *adj.* Loud and clear, like a clarion.

clărĭonĕ't *n.* = CLARINET.

clă'rĭtȳ *n.* Clearness.

clar'kia *n.* Annual plant of genus *C*~ with white, pink, or purple flowers, often grown in gardens, native of N. America. [W. *Clark*, member of 1st U.S. Government expedition across Rocky Mountains, 1804–5]

clār'ȳ *n.* Pot-herb, *Salvia sclarea*, native of S. Europe, Syria, etc.; other species of same genus, including the English wild clary, *S. horminoides*, and meadow clary, *S. pratensis*.

clăsh *n.* 1. Loud broken sound as of collision, striking weapons or cymbals, bells rung together. 2. Encounter, conflict; disagreement. ~ *v.* 1. Make clash. 2. Conflict, disagree, be at variance *with*; (of colours) be discordant.

clasp (-ah-) *n.* 1. Contrivance of two interlocking parts for fastening. 2. Embrace; grasp or joining of hands. 3. Bar of silver bearing name of engagement at which wearer was present, on ribbon of medal commemorating campaign. 4. *~-knife*, folding knife, esp. large one in which open blade can be rigidly fixed by a catch. ~ *v.* 1. Fasten with or as clasp. 2. Encircle, hold closely, embrace; grasp (another's hand); join (hands) by interlocking fingers.

class (-ah-) *n.* 1. Rank, order, of society; class system. 2. Excellence; (slang) elegance. 3. Division of schoolchildren or students taught together or considered of same standing; their time of meeting, the instruction given to them; (U.S. colleges) all students of the same standing, who enter together, graduate together, etc. (*~ of 1958*, those who graduated in that year); (in conscripted armies) all the recruits of a year. 4. (Methodism) Subdivision of society or congregation meeting regularly under a *class-leader*. 5. Division of candidates or competitors after examination, according to merit; division according to quality. 6. Number of individuals having some character or feature in common; (biol.) division of animals or plants below phylum, subdivided into orders, families, genera, species. 7. *~-conscious*, conscious of belonging to a particular class, often with implication of hostility to other classes; *~-consciousness*; *~ list*, list of competitors in examination arranged in classes; *~ system*, division of society into classes. ~ *v.t.* Assign to class. **cla'ssless** *adj.* (of a society) Not recognizing, not having, class distinctions.

clă'ssic *adj.* 1. Of avowed excellence. 2. Of the ancient Greek and Latin authors; of Greek and Roman antiquity. 3. (opp. ROMANTIC) In the classic style, simple, harmonious, proportioned, and finished. 4. Having literary or historic associations. 5. *C~ races*, (in England) five chief horse-races of the year (the 2000 Guineas, 1000 Guineas, Derby, Oaks, and St. Leger). 6. (of clothes) Of simple style that endures despite changes of fashion. ~ *n.* 1. Writer or artist, work, of acknowledged excellence. 2. Ancient Greek or Latin writer; scholar of Latin and Greek; (pl.) these studies. 3. Classic race.

clă'ssical *adj.* 1. = CLASSIC *adj.* 1; constituting a model. 2. Of ancient Greek or Latin standard authors or art; learned in, studying, or based on these. 3. In, following, the restrained style of classical antiquity; (in the arts) traditional. 4. (of physics etc.) Based on theories etc. established before the discovery of quantum theory, relativity, etc. **clă'ssically** *adv.*

clă'ssicism *n.* Following of classic(al) style; classical scholarship; advocacy of classical education. **clă'ssicist** *n.*

clă'ssify *v.t.* Arrange in classes, assign to a class; *classified*, (of official documents) belonging to a class, e.g. secret or confidential, which only specified persons may see. **clăssificā'tion** *n.* **clăssificā'tory** *adj.*

cla'ssy (-ah-) *adj.* (slang) Superior; stylish, smart.

clă'tter *n.* Rattling sound, as of many plates struck together; noisy talk, confused din of voices. ~ *v.* Make clatter, cause to rattle.

Claude Lorrai'ne. Name by which Claude Gellée (1600–82), French landscape painter, is known in English.

Clau'dian *adj.* 1. Of any of several distinguished Romans of the name of Claudius, or of their gens or family; esp. of the Emperors Tiberius, Caligula, Claudius, and Nero, or their epoch (A.D. 14–68). 2. Of Claude Lorraine.

Clau'dius (10 B.C.–A.D. 54). Tiberius Claudius Drusus Nero Germanicus, Roman emperor A.D. 41–54.

clause (-z) *n.* 1. Short sentence; (gram.) subordinate part of sen-

CLAUDE LORRAINE

tence including subject and predicate but syntactically equivalent to noun, adjective, or adverb. 2. Single proviso in treaty, law, contract, or other document. **clau'sal** *adj*.

Clau'sewitz (-owzevĭts), Karl von (1780–1831). Prussian army officer; writer on military science.

clau'stral *adj*. Of the cloister, monastic, narrow.

claustrophō'bĭa *n*. Morbid dread of confined places. **claustrophō'bĭc** *adj*. 1. Suffering from claustrophobia. 2. Inducing claustrophobia.

clă'vecin *n*. Harpsichord.

clă'vĭchord (-k-) *n*. (hist.) Musical instrument resembling square piano, with keyboard and strings struck by tangents, the earliest keyboard instrument with strings, appearing in mid-14th c.

clă'vĭcle *n*. Collar-bone. **clavĭ'cūlar** *adj*.

clā'vĭer, k- *n*. (Instrument with) keyboard, esp. before introduction of pianoforte.

claw *n*. Pointed horny nail of beast's or bird's foot; foot so armed, pincers of shellfish; contempt.) hand; mechanical or other contrivance for grappling, tearing etc.; ~ *hammer*, hammer with one end bent and split, for extracting nails. ~ *v*. Scratch, tear, seize, pull towards one, with claws or nails; (naut.) beat to windward, esp. ~ *off* (= away from) *shore*.

clay *n*. 1. Stiff viscous earth consisting chiefly of aluminium silicate and forming with water a tenacious paste which may be moulded, or dried and baked into bricks, pottery, tiles, etc.; *feet of* ~, (fig.) fundamental weakness in person of supposed merit (cf. Dan. 2: 33); ~ *pigeon*, piece of baked clay jerked up from trap as target. 2. Earth, esp. the earth covering a dead body when buried; earth as the material of the human body, hence, the body. 3. Tobacco-pipe of baked clay. **clay'ey** *adj*.

clay'more *n*. Two-edged broadsword formerly used by Scottish Highlanders. [Gael. *claidheamb mòr* great sword]

clean *adj.* 1. Free from anything contaminating or from dirt; free from weeds, barnacles, etc.; free from defects; (of paper) blank; (of printer's proof etc.) free from corrections; (of document etc.) listing no offence; (of nuclear device) producing relatively little fall-out; *come* ~, (colloq.) confess. 2. Free from moral stain; free from ceremonial defilement or of disease; (of beasts etc.) fit for food. 3. Neatly made, not unwieldy, trim; neat; unencumbered, unobstructed; (of wood) free from knots. 4. Entire, complete, total; ~ *sweep*, complete riddance. **clea′nlȳ**[1] *adv.* **clea′nnėss** (-n-n-) *n.* **clean** *adv.* Completely; right, outright; altogether; simply, absolutely. ~ *v.* Make clean; make oneself clean; ~ *out*, empty, strip; ~ *up*, clean, make tidy, clear up; (slang) acquire as gain. ~ *n.* Cleaning.

clea′ner *n.* (esp.) Person employed to clean house etc.; (freq. pl.) dry cleaner.

clea′nlȳ[2] (-ĕn-) *adj.* Habitually clean, attentive to cleanness. **clea′nlĭlȳ** *adv.* **clea′nlĭnėss** *n.*

cleanse (-ĕnz) *v.t.* 1. Make clean. 2. (archaic) Purify; cure (leper etc.).

clear *adj.* 1. Unclouded, transparent, not turbid; lustrous; unspotted; (of soup) strained to remove particles. 2. Distinct, intelligible; manifest. 3. Discerning, penetrating; confident, certain. 4. Easily audible. 5. Without reduction, net; free *of*, whole, complete; open, unobstructed; unengaged, free; not encumbered by debt; *clear′way*, stretch of main road in which vehicles are not allowed to wait. ~ *adv.* Clearly; quite; apart, without contact. ~ *n.* (esp.) *in the* ~, free, esp. from imputation of guilt. ~ *v.* 1. Make, become, clear. 2. Free from imputation of guilt, from suspicion, etc. 3. Free or rid *of*; remove; depart; (become) empty. 4. Free from contact or entanglement; pass without entanglement, contact, or collision. 5. Settle (debt etc.); free from debt; (naut.) free (ship) by paying all dues; (of ship) sail. 6. Make (sum of money) as net gain. 7. Get approval of (proposal etc.). 8. ~ *away*, remove, remove remains of meal from table, (of mist etc.) disappear; ~ *off*, get rid of, melt away, (of intruders) go away; ~ *out* empty, make off; ~ *up*, solve (mystery), make tidy, (of weather etc.) grow clear.

clear′ance *n.* 1. Clearing; removal of obstructions; passing of cheques through Clearing House; (certificate of) clearing of ship at custom-house. 2. Clear space; room to pass. 3. ~ *order*, one made by local authority for demolition of building(s); ~ *sale*, shop's sale of goods at reduced prices in order to get rid of superfluous stock.

clear′ing *n.* (esp.) Piece of land cleared for cultivation; *C~ House*, bankers' institution in London for exchanging cheques and bills, and settling the balances; ~ *house*, agency for collecting and distributing (information, resources, etc.)

clear′lȳ *adv.* Distinctly; manifestly; undoubtedly.

clear′nėss *n.* Transparence; distinctness; freedom from obstruction.

cleat *n.* Wedge; projecting piece bolted on spar, gangway, etc., to give footing or prevent rope from slipping; wedge-shaped or other projecting piece of wood or metal for fastening ropes to, etc.

clea′vage *n.* Cleaving; being cleft; way or line in which anything tends to split; property (of minerals and rocks) of splitting readily in certain directions; (colloq.) cleft between woman's breasts, revealėd by low-cut dress.

cleave[1] *v.* (past t. *clōve* or *clĕft*; past part. *clō′ven* or *clĕft*). Split; chop, break, or come apart, esp. along grain or line of cleavage; make way through (water, air, etc.). **clea′ver** *n.* (esp.) Butcher's chopping-tool for carcasses.

cleave[2] *v.i.* (past t. *cleaved* or *clāve*; past part. *cleaved*). Stick fast, adhere *to* (archaic); be faithful.

clea′vers, clī′vers (-z) *n.* Scrambling weed, *Galium aparine*, also called goose-grass.

cleek *n.* Metal-headed golf-club with straight narrow face and long shaft.

clĕf *n.* Symbol placed on line of stave to indicate name and pitch of notes on that line, and hence of those on other lines and spaces; *C* ~, movable clef fixing place of middle C (i) on bottom line of staff (*soprano* ~ 𝄡); (ii) on third line (*alto* ~ 𝄡); (iii) on fourth line up (*tenor* ~ 𝄡); *F* or *bass* ~ 𝄢, placed on highest line but one; *G* or *treble* ~ 𝄞, placed on lowest line but one.

clĕft[1] *n.* Space or division made by cleaving; fissure, split.

clĕft[2] *adj.*: see CLEAVE[1]; (esp.) ~ *palate*, malformation of palate with longitudinal gap in middle or on either side of roof of mouth; ~ *stick*, (fig.) position in which advance and retreat are alike impossible; dilemma, fix.

clĕg *n.* Gad-fly, horse-fly.

cleistogă′mĭc (klī-) *adj.* (of plant) Self-pollinating inside a flower which does not open. **cleistŏ′gamy̆** *n.*

clĕm *v.* (north.) Starve.

clĕ′matĭs (*or* klĭmā′-) *n.* Twining shrub of genus *C*~ having flowers with showy calyx and no corolla, and achenes with long feathery appendages.

Clemenceau (kl*e*mahṅsō), Georges (1841–1929). French statesman; prime minister 1906–9 and 1917–20; chairman of the Versailles Peace Conference.

clĕ′mency̆ *n.* Mildness of temper or weather; mercy.

clĕ′ment[1] *adj.* Mild, showing mercy.

Clĕ′ment[2]. Name of several popes and bishops of Rome (see CLEMENTINE[2]).

clĕ′mentīne[1] *n.* Variety of small orange orig. produced by accidental hybrid of tangerine and sour orange.

Clĕ′mentīne[2] *adj.* Of, relating to, any of the Clements; ~ *Decretals*, those issued by Clement V, pope 1305–14; ~ *Epistles*, two, probably spurious, Epistles to the Corinthians, attributed to Clement I, a bishop of Rome of the 1st c.; ~ *Vulgate*, revised edition of the VULGATE issued under the direction of Clement VIII, pope 1592–1605.

clĕnch *v.* Fix securely, make fast, as with nails; secure (nail etc.) by hammering point sideways after driving through; close (teeth, fingers) tightly; grasp firmly; = CLINCH *v.* 2. ~ *n.* Clenching, being clenched.

Clēopă′tra (*or* -pah-) (68–30 B.C.). Queen of Egypt; daughter of Ptolemy Auletes, king of Egypt; famous for her beauty and charm;

exercised these on Julius Caesar, who restored her to her throne in 47 B.C. after her expulsion by Pothinus. Later Mark ANTONY fell in love with her; in the war between Antony and AUGUSTUS the defection of her fleet at the battle of Actium (31 B.C.) hastened Antony's defeat, and to escape being carried captive to Rome she took her own life. The granite obelisks known as *~'s Needles* have no connection with the queen, but were erected at Heliopolis by Thothmes III *c* 1475 B.C.; that which stands on the Thames Embankment was brought to England in 1878.

clĕ'psy̆dra *n.* Ancient time-measuring device worked by flow of water. [Gk *kleptō* steal *hudōr* water]

clēr'estōry̆ (-ērs-) *n.* Upper part of wall of nave, choir, and transepts of cathedral or large church above triforium or arches of nave etc., and containing windows clear of the roof of the aisles

clēr'gy̆ *n.* 1. The clerical order; all persons ordained as priests or ministers; clergymen. 2. (hist.) Clerkly skill, learning, scholarship. 3. *benefit of ~*, orig. privilege of exemption from trial by secular court, allowed to clergymen arraigned for felony; later, exemption from sentence on first conviction for certain offences claimed by all who could read (ability to read being orig. the test of 'clergy' or clerical position of the accused); *cler'gyman*, ordained minister, esp. of Established Church.

clĕ'rĭc *n.* Clerical man, clergyman. [Gk *klērikos* f. *klēros* lot, inheritance, as used (e.g.) in Acts 1: 17]

clĕ'rĭcal *adj.* 1. Of the clergy, a clergyman, or clergymen; of clericalists. 2. Of, made by, a clerk or clerks; *~ error*, error in writing anything out. ~ *n.* Cleric; member of a clerical party.

clĕ'rĭcalism *n.* (esp.) Clerical rule or influence. **clĕ'rĭcalist** *n.*

clĕ'rĭhew *n.* Short satiric verse, professedly biographical, usu. of four lines of unequal length rhyming *aabb*. [Edmund *Clerihew* Bentley (1875–1956)]

clerk (-ârk) *n.* 1. Clergyman (archaic & legal, *~ in holy orders*); (before the Reformation) member of one of the five minor orders, as dist. from higher or holy orders; hence, layman performing similar functions, lay officer of parish church who has charge of building and precincts, leads responses, assists at baptisms, marriages, etc.; *~ regular* or *regular ~*, (R.C. Ch.) member of monastic order living in community and engaging esp. in active pastoral work. 2. Officer in charge of records, accounts, etc., of any department, court, corporation, etc. 3. Subordinate employed to make written entries, keep accounts, do mechanical work of correspondence, etc. 4. *C~ of the Weather*, imaginary functionary supposed to control the weather; *C~ of Works*, officer superintending erection of building etc. **cler'kship** *n.* **clerk** *v.i.* (colloq.) Act as clerk.

cler'kly̆ (-ârk-) *adj.* Of a clerk; skilled in penmanship.

Clē'veland[1]. County of NE. England (since April 1974), bordering on Durham and North Yorkshire.

Clē'veland[2] (-vl-), Grover (1837–1908). 22nd and 24th president of U.S., 1885–9 and 1893–7.

clĕ'ver *adj.* Adroit, neat in movement; talented; ingenious. **clĕ'verly̆** *adv.* **clĕ'verness** *n.*

clĕ'vĭs *n.* U-shaped piece of iron forming loop for tackle at end of beam etc.

clew (-ōō) *n.* 1. Ball of thread or yarn; such a ball used as guide through maze or labyrinth (in many mythological or legendary stories). 2. (naut.) Small cords suspending hammock; lower corner of square sail, after corner of fore-and-aft sail, to which are fastened tacks and sheets for extending and securing it. ~ *v.t.* (naut.) Draw lower ends of (sails) *up* to upper yard or mast for furling.

cliché (-ē'shā) *n.* Stereotype or

electrotype block; stereotyped or hackneyed phrase or expression.

clĭck *n.* 1. Slight sharp hard non-ringing sound as of dropping latch etc.; ~ *beetle,* adult wireworm or other beetle of family Elateridae which when turned over rights itself by jumping with a click. 2. Piece of mechanism, esp. catch falling into notches of ratchet-wheel, acting with this sound. 3. Fault in horse's action, toe of hind hoof striking shoe of forefoot. 4. (phon.) Class of sharp non-vocal sounds occurring in certain African languages, formed by suction, with sudden withdrawal of tongue from contact with part of mouth. ~ *v.* Make click; (slang) have luck, secure one's object; get on friendly terms (*with* person of opposite sex).

clī'ent *n.* 1. (Rom. antiq.) Plebeian under protection of noble; (archaic) dependant, hanger-on. 2. One employing services of lawyer; employer of services of any professional or business man; customer.

clī'entēle (*or* klēawṅtĕ'l) *n.* 1. Body of clients or dependants. 2. (*also* klēawṅtā'l) Customers, supporters, professional connection.

clĭff *n.* Steep rock-face, usu. overhanging sea; *~-hanger, -hanging,* (story, contest, etc.) with outcome in suspense.

clīmă'ctĕric (*or* -tĕ'rĭk) *adj.* Constituting a crisis, critical; esp. occurring at period of life (45–60) at which vital forces begin to decline. ~ *n.* Critical point or period in life; acc. to one superstition, all years denoted by multiples of 7, acc. to another, odd multiples only (7, 21, 35, etc.); *grand* ~, 63rd year, supposed to be specially critical.

clī'mate *n.* (Region with specified) prevailing conditions of temperature, rainfall, humidity, wind, etc.; (fig.) prevailing mental or moral attitude etc. **clīmă'tĭc** *adj.*

clīmatŏ'logy̆ *n.* Study of climates. **clīmatolŏ'gĭcal** *adj.*

clī'măx *n.* 1. Culmination, apex. 2. Orgasm. 3. (ecol.) State of equilibrium reached by plant and animal community. **clīmă'ctĭc** *adj.*

clīmb (-m) *v.* 1. Ascend, mount, go *up,* esp. with help of hands; ~ *down,* descend similarly; (fig.) retreat from position taken up, give in. 2. (of sun, aircraft, etc.) Gain height. 3. (of plants) Creep up by aid of tendrils or by twining. 4. Slope upwards. 5. Rise by effort in social rank, intellectual or moral power, etc. 6. *climbing frame,* structure for children to climb on; *climbing-irons,* irons strapped to boot to assist in climbing trees etc. or ice-slopes. ~ *n.* Climbing; place climbed or to be climbed.

clī'mber (-m*er*) *n.* (esp.) Mountaineer; person climbing socially; climbing plant.

clīme *n.* (poet.) Tract, country; climate.

clĭnch *n.* 1. Clinched nail or bolt; (naut.) way of fastening large ropes with half hitch; clinched part of rope; anything that grips. 2. Struggle or scuffle at close quarters; (boxing) grappling at close quarters. ~ *v.* 1. Clench. 2. Drive home, make conclusive, confirm, establish.

clĭ'ncher *n.* (esp.) Remark, argument, that clinches a matter.

clĭng *v.i.* (past t. & past part. *clŭng*). Adhere *together,* remain in one body or in contact, resist separation; adhere *to*; remain faithful *to*; *clĭ'ngstone* (*peach*), variety in which flesh adheres to stone.

clĭ'nĭc *n.* 1. Teaching of medicine or surgery at the bedside; class, institution, so taught or conducted. 2. Institution or centre for giving medical advice or treatment.

clĭ'nĭcal *adj.* Of, at, the sick-bed (esp. of lectures, teaching); dispassionate; ~ *medicine,* observation and treatment of patients as distinct from theoretical study of medical science; ~ *thermometer,* one for taking patient's temperature. **clĭ'nĭcally̆** *adv.*

clĭnk[1] *n.* Sharp, abrupt, clear

ringing sound, as of small metallic objects or glasses struck together. ~ *v.* Make clink. **cli′nker**[1] *n.* (colloq.) Exceedingly good thing or person. **cli′nkĭng** *adj.* & *adv.* (colloq.) Exceedingly (good, fine).

clĭnk[2] *n.* (slang) Prison, lock-up. [proper name of a former prison in Southwark]

cli′nker[2] *n.* 1. Very hard pale-yellow Dutch paving-brick; brick with surface vitrified by great heat. 2. Mass of bricks fused by excessive heat; hardened mass formed by fusion of earthy impurities of burned coal, limestone, etc., slag; mass of hardened volcanic lava.

cli′nker-built (-bĭ-) *adj.* (of boat) Made with external planks overlapping downwards and fastened with clinched copper nails.

Clī′ō. (Gk & Rom. myth.) Muse of epic poetry and history. [Gk *kleiō* celebrate]

clĭp[1] *n.* Appliance for holding things together, or for attachment to objects; set of cartridges held together at base for insertion into magazine of repeating firearm; piece of jewellery for clipping on; *cli′pboard*, board with spring clip for holding papers etc. ~ *v.t.* Surround closely; grip tightly, grasp; fasten with clip(s).

clĭp[2] *n.* Clipping, shearing; quantity of wool clipped from sheep, flock, etc.; (U.S.) rate of speed, rapid pace; (colloq.) smart blow. ~ *v.* 1. Cut with shears or scissors; trim, make tidy, thus; cut off part of (hair, wool) thus; remove hair or wool of (sheep etc.) thus; pare edge of (coin); remove small piece of (ticket) to show that it has been used; cut short. 2. (colloq.) Move quickly, run. 3. (U.S.) Hit smartly.

cli′p-clŏ′p *n.* & *v.i.* (Make) sound resembling beat of horse's hooves.

cli′pper *n.* (esp.) 1. Instrument for clipping hair. 2. Swiftly moving horse, ship, etc. 3. Ship with forward-raking bows and aft-raking masts. 4. Aircraft or flying-boat, esp. for transoceanic flights.

cli′ppĭe *n.* (colloq.) Bus conductress.

cli′ppĭng *n.* (esp.) Small piece clipped off, shred of cloth, newspaper cutting, etc.

clique (-ēk) *n.* Small exclusive party, set, coterie. **cli′quish, cli′quey, -quy** *adjs.*

clītĕ′llum *n.* Raised band, which secretes the egg-case, encircling the body of earthworms towards the middle.

cli′toris *n.* Rudimentary erectile organ of female genitals, homologue of penis.

Clīve, Robert, Baron Clive of Plassey (1725–74). English soldier and statesman in the service of the East India Company; avenged the Black Hole of Calcutta by defeating Suraj ud Daula at the battle of Plassey, 1757; became governor of Bengal, 1758.

clōā′ca *n.* (pl. *-ae*). 1. Sewer. 2. Common excretory cavity at end of intestinal canal in birds, reptiles, etc. **clōā′cal** *adj.*

cloak *n.* Loose usu. sleeveless outer garment; (fig.) covering, pretence, pretext; *~-and-dagger*, involving esp. dramatic events of intrigue and espionage; *cloa′k-room*, room in which cloaks, hats, luggage, etc., may be left; lavatory. ~ *v.t.* Cover with, wrap in, cloak; conceal, disguise.

clŏ′bber[1] *v.t.* Patch *up*; esp., add enamelled decoration to (porcelain).

clŏ′bber[2] *n.* (slang) Clothes; equipment, clutter.

clŏ′bber[3] *v.t.* (slang) Thrash; defeat decisively; criticize severely.

clŏche (-sh) *n.* 1. Kind of bell-glass for protecting plants; frame of sheet-glass or other transparent substance for same purpose. 2. Woman's close-fitting hat with deep crown and small or no brim.

clŏck[1] *n.* 1. Time-measuring instrument consisting of train of wheels set in motion by weights, spring, electromagnet, etc., actuating and regulated by a pendulum or balance-wheel, and recording hours, minutes, etc., usu. by movement of hands on a dial; clock-like device showing readings on a dial; *against the ~*, against a time-limit; *put the ~ back*, move

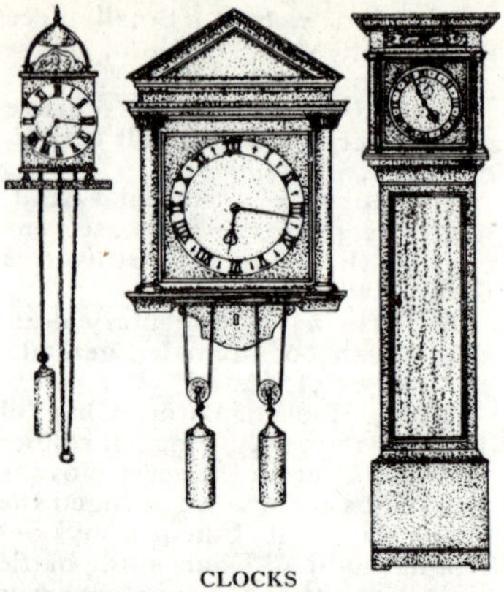

CLOCKS

hands of clock to earlier position; (fig.) revert to earlier state of affairs. 2. Downy seed-head of dandelion etc. (so called from childish game of blowing away seeds to find 'what o'clock it is'). 3. ~*-golf*, lawn game of holing ball with putter from successive points in circle numbered like those of clock-face; ~*-watcher*, employee who watches assiduously for time of end of working day; ~*-watching* (*n.*); *clo'ckwise*, moving like hands of a clock, in curve from left to right as seen from centre; *clo'ckwork*, mechanism of clock, mechanism similar to this for driving toys, etc.; (attrib.) regular, mechanical, driven by clockwork; *like clockwork*, regularly, automatically. ~ *v.* Time by the clock; attain (time or speed) in a race; register on clock or dial (also ~ *up*); ~ *in, on, out, off*, etc., register arrival, departure, etc., at entrance of factory etc. by means of mechanical device combined with clock; also, arrive, leave, begin, or finish work, regularly or punctually.

clŏck[2] *n.* Ornamental pattern on side of stocking or sock near the ankle.

clŏd *n.* 1. Lump of earth etc.; blockhead; *clo'dhopper*, bumpkin, lout. 2. Cut from neck end of beef.

clŏg *n.* 1. Block of wood fastened to leg to impede motion; encumbrance, hindrance. 2. Woman's wooden-soled overshoe for wet ground (archaic); shoe with thick wooden sole; ~ *dance*, step-dance performed in clogs. ~ *v.* 1. Fetter or confine with clog; be encumbrance to, burden, impede, hamper. 2. Choke up; fill up with choking matter; stop or act badly from being choked up.

cloisonné (klwahzŏnā) *adj.* & *n.* (Enamel) of which different colours have been applied between thin metal plates laid on edge on foundation plaque (cf. CHAMPLEVÉ).

cloi'ster *n.* 1. Convent, monastery. 2. Covered walk or arcade in monastery, college, large church, often running round open court of quadrangle with plain wall on outer side and colonnade or windows on inner. **cloi'stered** (-*terd*) *adj.* Monastic; sheltered. **cloi'stral** *adj.*

clōne *n.* 1. (bot.) Group of cultivated plants the individuals of which are transplanted parts of one original seedling or stock. 2. (biol.) Group of individuals produced asexually from a sexually produced ancestor. **clō'nal** *adj.*

clŏ'nĭc *adj.* (of spasm) With violent muscular contractions and relaxations occurring in rapid succession.

cloqué (klō'kā) *n.* Fabric with embossed surface.

clōse[1] *adj.* 1. Narrow, confined, contracted; covered, concealed; secret, given secrecy; niggardly; restricted. 2. Near; dense, compact; in or nearly in contact; fitting exactly; intimate; nearly equal; concentrated. 3. Sultry; ill-ventilated. 4. (of vowel) Pronounced with tongue near the palate. 5. ~ *borough*, pocket borough (see BOROUGH); ~*-carpet* (*v.t.*) carpet whole floor of (room); ~ *corporation*, corporation which fills its own vacancies; corporation the stock of which is held by a very few persons, usu. officers of the company; ~*-fisted, -handed*, niggardly; ~*-hauled*, (naut.) with sail-tacks hauled close, so as to sail as near the wind as possible; ~*order*, (mil.) arrangement of men in line with only slight gaps between them; ~ *quarters*, immediate contact with opponent or enemy; proximity; ~ *season, time*, period during which it is unlawful to take certain specified game or fish; ~ *shave*, (fig.) narrow escape from accident; ~-*stool*, chamber-pot enclosed in stool or box; ~-*up*, (phot.) picture taken at short range or with a telephoto lens so as to show persons etc. on large scale. **clō'selў** *adv.* **clō'senėss** *n.* **clōse** *adv.* So as to be close. ~ *n.* Enclosed space; precincts of cathedral; school playground; (in Scotland) entry, passage, esp. one leading from street to inner court or to common stairway of tenement.

clōse[2] (-z) *v.* 1. Shut; (of place of business etc.) declare, be declared, not open; *closed circuit*, (elect.) circuit without break in current; (television) circuit transmitting signal to restricted set of receivers; *closed shop*, (orig. U.S.) industrial or other concern in which the employees are obliged to belong to one particular trade union; *closed syllable*, one ending with a consonant. 2. Be boundary of, conclude; bring or come to an end; complete, settle. 3. Bring or come into contact; close gap(s) in rank, series, etc.; come within striking distance, grapple *with*; (naut.) approach, come alongside of. 4. Express (often eager) agreement *with* (terms, offer, etc.). 5. ~ *down*, close (shop etc.) finally, end business etc.; (of transmitting) cease to broadcast; ~ *in*, enclose, come nearer, (of days) get successively shorter; ~ *up*, block, fill, fill gaps (in), coalesce; move closer to. ~ *n.* Conclusion, end; (mus.) cadence.

clŏ'sėt (-z-) *n.* Small room (archaic); small storage-room, cupboard; water-closet. ~ *v.t.* Shut up or detain in closet as for private conference etc.

clō'sure (-zher) *n.* 1. Closing, closed condition. 2. In Parliament, decision by vote of House of Commons to put question without further debate. ~ *v.t.* Apply closure to (motion, speakers, etc.).

clŏt *n.* Mass of material stuck together; semi-solid lump of coagulated liquid, esp. blood; (slang) stupid person. ~ *v.* Form into clots; *clotted cream*, thick cream obtained by scalding milk; *clotted nonsense*, utter absurdity.

clŏth *n.* 1. (Piece, used for any purpose, of) woven or felted stuff; covering for table, esp. of linen at meals; woollen woven fabric as used for clothes; ~ *of gold, silver*, tissue of gold or silver threads interwoven with silk or wool; *American* ~: see AMERICAN; ~-*hall*, hall where sellers and buyers of woollen cloths meet to transact business; ~-*yard*, (hist.) yard of 36 in. by which cloth was measured; ~-*yard shaft*, arrow of long bow. 2. Profession, esp. clerical, as shown by clothes; *the* ~, the clergy.

clōthe (-dh) *v.t.* (past t. & past part. *clothed, clăd*). Provide with clothes, put clothes upon; cover like or as with clothes or a cloth.

clōthes (-dhz, -ōz) *n.pl.* Wearing-apparel, dress; bed-coverings; linen etc. to be washed; ~-*bag*, ~-*basket*, bag, basket, for dirty or newly washed linen; ~-*horse*, frame for airing clothes; ~-*line*, rope, wire, etc. for hanging washed linen up to dry; ~-*moth*, small buff-coloured moth (*Tinea pellionella*) infesting houses, with larva very destructive to fabrics; ~-*peg*, forked peg or clip for fastening linen to clothes-line; ~-*post*, -*prop*, supports for clothes-line.

clō'thĭer (-dh-) *n.* Dealer in cloth and men's clothes.

clō'thĭng (-dh-) *n.* (esp.) Clothes collectively.

Clō'thō. (Gk myth.) One of the three Fates, who spun the thread of life.

cloud *n.* 1. Visible mass of condensed watery vapour floating in air at some distance above general surface of ground (classifiable as CIRRUS, CUMULUS, STRATUS, etc.). 2. Unsubstantial or fleeting thing; mass of smoke or dust; local dimness or obscurity in otherwise clear or transparent thing; innumerable body of insects, birds, horsemen, arrows, moving together; obscurity, anything obscuring or concealing; (anything causing) state of gloom, trouble, suspicion, etc.; darkening of countenance; *under a ~*, out of favour. 3. *clou'dberry*, (berry of) *Rubus chamaemorus*, small erect plant allied to raspberry, growing on high mountains in northern Europe, and bearing one large white terminal flower and large well-flavoured amber-coloured fruit; *clou'dburst*, violent rainstorm; *~-castle*, castle in the air; *~ chamber*, (phys.) apparatus containing water vapour, esp. one through which charged particles are passed and become identifiable after condensation of vapour; *C~-cuckoo-land*, name in Aristophanes' 'Birds' of the town built by the birds to separate gods from mankind; hence, fanciful or ideal realm. ~ *v.* Overspread, darken, with clouds, gloom, or trouble; variegate with vague patches of colour or opacity; become overcast or gloomy. **clou'dlėss** *adj.* **clou'dlėsslў** *adv.* **clou'dlėssnėss** *n.* **clou'dlėt** *n.* **clou'dў** *adj.* **clou'dĭly** *adv.* **clou'dĭnėss** *n.* (esp., meteor.) Amount of sky covered by cloud, measured in figures between 0 (cloudless) and 8 (wholly obscured).

clough (-ŭf) *n.* Ravine.

clout *n.* (archaic & dial.) Patch; cloth; piece of clothing; rap, knock, blow. ~ *v.t.* (archaic & dial.) Mend, patch; cuff heavily.

clōve[1] *n.* One of the small bulbs making up compound bulb of garlic, shallot, etc.

clōve[2] *n.* Dried flower-bud of a tropical tree, *Caryopyhllus aromaticus*, orig. native of the Moluccas, much used as a pungent aromatic spice; the tree itself; *~ gillyflower*, *~ pink*, clove-scented species of pink, *Dianthus caryophyllus*, the original of the carnation and other cultivated forms. [Fr. *clou de girofle*; *girofle* was orig. name of the spice; *clou* (L *clavus* nail) was used of it with ref. to its shape; the phrase (in Engl. *clove gillyflower*) was transferred to the similarly shaped bud of the pink, and later divided into *clove* for the spice and *gillyflower* for the pink]

clōve hĭtch. Way of fastening rope round spar etc., formed by passing rope round twice in such a way that both ends pass under centre part of loop in front. [old past part. of CLEAVE[1]]

clō'ven *adj.*: see CLEAVE[1]; (esp.) *~ hoof*, *foot*, divided hoof of ruminant quadrupeds, ascribed in pagan mythology to Pan, and thence in Christian mythology to the Devil.

clō'ver *n.* Trefoil, esp. *Trifolium repens*, white or Dutch trefoil, and *T. pratense*, red or meadow trefoil, both largely cultivated for fodder; *in ~*, in ease and luxury; *~-leaf*, system of intersecting roads resembling four-leaved clover.

clown *n.* 1. Rustic, lout. 2. Jester, esp. in pantomime or circus (orig. one of the characters in a harlequinade) with loose baggy white garments, and face painted white. ~ *v.* Play the clown, act like a clown, perform farcically. **clow'nĭng** *n.*

clow'nish *adj.* Of or like a clown or peasant, rustic, boorish. **clow'nĭshlў** *adv.* **clow'nishnėss** *n.*

cloy *v.t.* Satiate, weary, by richness, sweetness, sameness, or excess.

clŭb *n.* 1. Heavy stick with one thick end, esp. as weapon; stick with crooked (and usu. thickened) end used in various games, esp. golf; club-shaped knot of hair at back of head, worn by men in 18th c. 2. (transl. Span. *basto*, the 'club' on Spanish cards; the English design is copied from the French *trèfle* or trefoil) (Playing-card with) black trefoil(s); (pl.) suit of these cards. 3. Association of persons with some common interest meeting periodically; body of persons combined for social purposes and having premises for resort, meals, temporary residence, etc. 4. *~-foot*, any of various (usu. congenital) distortions giving foot a stunted lumpy appearance; *clu'bland*, district round St. James's in London where there are very many clubs; ~ *licence*, (in Britain) licence permitting sale of alcoholic liquors to registered subscribers but not to general public (*country* ~, country inn etc. conducting such trade); *clu'bmoss*, herb (*Lycopodium clavatum*) with club-like upright fertile spikes of spore-cases; any species of evergreen plant *Lycopodium*; ~-*root*, disease of cabbages and turnips in which excrescence forms at base of stem; ~ *sandwich*, one containing three layers of bread with two fillings. ~ *v.* 1. Beat with club; use butt of (gun) as club. 2. Bring, come, into a mass. 3. Put together into a common stock; combine *together*, or *with* others, in joint action, esp. in making up sum of money *for* some object.

clŭ'bbable *adj.* Convivial, sociable.

clŭb-haul *v.* (naut.) Tack ship by dropping lee-anchor as vessel's head comes to the wind; when she then pays off, the cable is cut and the sails trimmed to the other tack; a device for getting off lee-shore when there is not room to wear.

clŭck *n.* Abrupt hollow guttural sound made by hen desiring to sit or calling her brood together; any similar sound. ~ *v.i.* Make cluck.

clue (-ōō) *n.* 1. Clew. 2. Anything which points the way, indicates a solution, or puts one on track of a discovery; sentence or phrase indicating word(s) to be inserted in crossword puzzle. **clue'lėss** *adj.* (esp. slang) Stupid; ignorant.

clŭ'mber *n.* (Stocky breed of) spaniel with dense silky coat, usu. yellow and white. [f. *Clumber* in Nottinghamshire]

clŭmp *n.* 1. Cluster *of* trees or shrubs. 2. Thick extra sole on shoe, usu. nailed on. ~ *v.* Tread or move heavily and clumsily; plant in clump; keep or mass together; (colloq.) punch.

clŭ'msȳ (-z-) *adj.* Awkward in movement or shape, ungainly; ill-contrived; tactless. **clŭ'msilȳ** *adv.* **clŭ'msinėss** *n.*

Clū'nȳ. Monastery near Mâcon in France, from whose rule developed an order which separated from the Benedictines in 11th c. **Clū'nĭăc** *adj.* & *n.* (Member) of the order of Cluny.

clŭ'ster *n.* Group of similar things, esp. such as grow together, bunch; swarm, group, of persons, stars, etc. ~ *v.* Bring, come, into cluster; be in cluster.

clŭtch[1] *v.* Seize eagerly, grasp tightly; snatch *at.* ~ *n.* 1. Tight grasp; (pl.) grasping hands, cruel grasp. 2. (mech.) Device enabling engine or driving parts of machine to be connected to or disconnected from the driven parts; (also ~ *pedal*) pedal operating this; *dog* ~, *plate* ~, clutch in which engagement is made by teeth, by plates.

clŭtch[2] *n.* Set of eggs; brood of chickens.

clŭ'tter *n.* Crowded confusion, confused mass. ~ *v.t.* Litter, strew untidily *with*, crowd with disorderly assemblage of things.

Clwyd (klōōēd). County of NE. Wales (since April 1974), comprising the former county of Flintshire, most of the former Denbighshire, and part of the former Merionethshire.

Clȳde. River in SW. Scotland, famous for the shipbuilding yards on its banks.

Clȳ'desdāle (-dzd-) *n.* One of a breed of heavy draught-horses orig. bred round about the Clyde.

Clȳ'desīde (-ds-). District on bank of Clyde near Glasgow.

clȳ'ster *n.* (archaic) Enema.

Clȳtemnĕ'stra. (Gk legend) Daughter of Tyndareus, king of Sparta, and Leda; wife of AGAMEMNON.

cm *abbrev.* Centimetre(s).

C.M.B. *abbrev.* Central Midwives' Board.

Cmd. *abbrev.* Command paper.

Cmdr *abbrev.* Commander.

Cmdre *abbrev.* Commodore.

C.M.G. *abbrev.* Companion of (the Order of) St. Michael and St. George.

cml *abbrev.* Centimil(s).

Cmnd. *abbrev.* Command paper.

C.M.S. *abbrev.* Church Missionary Society.

C.N.A.A. *abbrev.* Council for National Academic Awards.

C.N.D. *abbrev.* Campaign for Nuclear Disarmament.

cnī'dōblast (-ah-) *n.* Goblet-shaped cell with an eversible barbed stinging thread, characteristic of coelenterates.

Cnut: see CANUTE.

c/o *abbrev.* Care of.

Co. *abbrev.* Company; county.

C.O. *abbrev.* Commanding officer; conscientious objector.

co- *prefix.* 1. Jointly, mutually; joint, mutual. 2. (math.) Of the complement; complement of.

coach *n.* 1. State carriage. 2. Stage-coach. 3. Railway carriage; (U.S., esp.) passenger carriage of cheaper class. 4. Long-distance single-decked omnibus. 5. Private tutor preparing candidate for examination; instructor of athletic team etc. 6. *coa'chman*, driver of coach or carriage; *coa'chwork*, bodywork. ~ *v.* 1. (obs.) Travel in, go by, stage-coach. 2. Train, tutor; study with a tutor.

cōă'djutor (-jo͝o-) *n.* Helper, assistant, esp. one assisting a bishop and usu. having the right of succession.

cōă'gūlāte *v.* Convert, be converted, from fluid to more or less solid state; clot, curdle, set. **cōă'gūlant** *n.* Coagulating agent. **cōăgūlā'tion** *n.* **cōă'gūlable** *adj.*

cōai'ta (kōi-) *n.* Small S. Amer. red-faced spider-monkey of genus *Ateles*, with long coarse glossy black hair.

coal *n.* Black or blackish sedimentary rock consisting mainly of carbonized plant tissue, found in seams or beds and used as fuel; (pl.) pieces of coal; *carry ~s to Newcastle*, bring superfluous goods etc.; *haul over the ~s*, reprimand; *heap ~s of fire*, return good for evil (see Prov. 25: 21–2); *~-black*, completely black; *~ dust*, powdered coal; *~ face*, surface of coal seam exposed by mining; *coa'lfield*, district with series of coal strata; *~-fish*, any of several sea-fishes with dusky skin; saithe, allied to cod but smaller, with skin which soils fingers like wet coal; *~ -flap, -plate*, cover of coal-cellar opening in pavement; *~-gas*, mixture of gases (mainly hydrogen and methane) produced by destructive distillation of coal and used, after removal of impurities such as hydrogen sulphide, for lighting and heating; *~-heaver*, man employed to carry coal; *~-hole*, small coal-cellar; *~-oil*, (U.S.) shale-oil, petroleum; *C~ Measures*, (geol.) strata in which coal is found, an upper division of the carboniferous system; *~-mine, -pit*, mine in which coal is dug, colliery; *~-sack*, sack for carrying coal; also, any of the patches in the Milky Way distinguished by extraordinary blackness owing to the absence of even dim stars (esp. one near the Southern Cross); *~-scuttle*, receptacle for coals to supply room fire; *~-scuttle bonnet*, bonnet shaped like inverted coal-scuttle; *~-tar*, thick black viscous liquid, a product of destructive distillation of coal, yielding benzene, creosote, paraffin, aniline dyes, etc.; *~-tit*: see TIT[1]. ~ *v.* Supply (ship etc.) with coal for fuel; take in supply of coal.

coa'ler *n.* Ship for supplying others with coal.

cōalĕ'sce *v.i.* Come together and form one; combine in coalition. **cōalĕ'scence** *n.* **cōalĕ'scent** *adj.*

cōalĭ'tion *n.* Union, fusion; (government by) temporary combination of political parties each retaining its distinctive principles. **cōalĭ'tionist** *n.* & *adj.*

coa'lmouse, cō'lemouse (-lm-) *n.* = Coal-tit.

coa'mĭng *n.* (naut.) Raised border round hatches and scuttles etc. to keep out water.

coarse (kōrs) *adj.* Common, inferior; rough, loose, or large in texture, grain, or features; not delicate, unrefined; vulgar; obscene; ~ *fish*, freshwater fish other than one of salmon family;

so ~ *fishing*. **coar'selў** *adv*. **coar'senėss** *n*. **coar'sen** *v*. Make, become, coarse.

coast *n*. 1. Border of land near sea, sea-shore; *the ~ is clear*, the danger is over, the way is open. *coa'stguard*, body of men orig. formed to prevent smuggling, now chiefly a life-saving service; member of this body; *coa'stline*, configuration of sea-coast. 2. (U.S., Canada) Slope for tobogganing; sliding down this; downhill ride on bicycle etc. without pedalling, or in car etc. with engine not running. **coa'stwards** (-z) *adv*.

coa'stwīse (-z) *adj*. & *adv*. **coast** *v.i*. 1. Sail along coast, trade between ports on same coast, 2. Slide downhill on toboggan; ride downhill on bicycle without pedalling, or in car with engine idle.

coa'stal *adj*. Of, on, pertaining to, the coast; *Coastal Command*, in the war of 1939–45, a command of the R.A.F. which operated over the seas from coastal bases.

coa'ster *n*. (esp.) Vessel employed in coasting; master or pilot of such a vessel; two-handled wine-cup; low round stand for decanter etc.; wooden stand for cheese.

coat *n*. 1. Man's outer garment, usu. of cloth, with sleeves; woman's outer garment, overcoat or short tailored jacket worn with skirt; (archaic & dial.) petticoat. 2. Coat of arms. 3. Covering compared to garment; beast's hair, fur, etc.; investing membrane etc. of organ; skin, rind, husk; layer of bulb etc.; covering of paint etc. laid on at once. 4. *~-armour*, blazonry, heraldic arms; *~-dress*, *-frock*, tailored dress resembling coat. *~-hanger*, shaped strip or frame, hanging by central hook, on which coat etc. is draped; *~ of arms*, coat or vest embroidered with heraldic arms, tabard (hist.); distinctive heraldic bearings of a gentleman, corporation, etc., orig. borne on coat of arms; shield, escutcheon. **coa'tlėss** *adj*. **coat** *v.t*. Provide with coat; cover with surface layer or coating.

coatee' *n*. 1. Close-fitting short coat. 2. Woman's small short coat.

coat-hâr'dĭe, cōte- *n*. (hist., 14th–15th centuries) Man's or woman's close-fitting tunic-like garment with sleeves.

cōa'tĭ (-ah-) *n*. (also *~-mondi*, *-mundi*) Amer. plantigrade carnivorous mammal (*Nasua*), resembling civet and raccoon, with long flexible snout and long tail.

coa'tĭng *n*. (esp.) Layer of paint etc.; material for coats.

coax *v*. Persuade by blandishments, wheedle; manipulate (tool etc.) gently.

cōă'xial *adj*. (math.) 1. (also *cōă'xal*) Having a common axis. 2. *~ cable*, cable containing coaxial lines; *~ line*, transmission line made up of two concentric circular conductors separated by insulating medium.

cŏb[1] *n*. 1. Male swan. 2. Stout short-legged riding-horse. 3.

Large kind of hazel-nut (also ~-*nut*); roundish lump of coal etc.; small roundish loaf. 4. Cylindrical shoot or rachis on which grains of maize grow.

cŏb² *n.* Composition of clay, gravel, and straw, used for building walls of cottages etc., esp. in SW. England.

cō'balt (-awlt) *n.* 1. (chem.) Silver-white malleable slightly magnetic metallic element, resembling nickel in many ways and used in the alloy ~ *steel* for making permanent magnets and in colouring ceramic glazes; symbol Co, at. no. 27, at. wt 58·9332. 2. Deep-blue pigment (~ *blue*), a mixed oxide of cobalt and aluminium. **coba'ltĭc, coba'ltous** *adjs.* [Ger. *kobold* goblin haunting mines]

cō'baltīte (-awl-) *n.* Silver-white mineral with brilliant metallic lustre.

cŏ'bber *n.* (Austral. slang) Mate, friend.

cŏ'bble¹ *n.* Water-worn rounded stone (also *co'bblestone*), esp. of suitable size for paving; (geol.) rounded fragment of rock bigger than pebble and smaller than boulder; (pl.) pavement of cobbles; (pl.) coals of this size. ~ *v.t.* Pave with cobbles.

cŏ'bble² *v.t.* Mend, put together, join, roughly or clumsily; patch; mend (shoes), esp. roughly or clumsily.

cŏ'bbler *n.* 1. One whose business is mending shoes; *~'s wax*, resinous substance used by shoemakers for stiffening and preserving thread. 2. Clumsy workman or mender, botcher. 3. Drink of wine (often sherry), sugar, lemon, and pounded ice, drunk through straws. 4. (U.S.) Fruit pie with thick rich crust.

Cŏ'bden, Richard (1804–65). English Liberal statesman, advocate of free trade, peace, and international co-operation, and opposition to Empire. **Cŏ'bdenism** *n.* **Cŏ'bdenīte** *adj.* & *n.*

cō-bĕllĭ'gerent *adj.* & *n.* (State) waging war along with another but not accorded full status as ally. **cō-bĕllĭ'gerencȳ** *n.*

cō'ble *n.* Sea fishing-boat of NE. England, an open boat with two side keels, designed for launching from beaches against heavy breakers, formerly with lug-sail, now usually with engine.

cŏ'bra *n.* Venomous snake of genus *Naja*, found in S. Asia and Africa, able to dilate its neck into a hood-like shape when excited; esp. the Indian cobra, which has a mark on its hood resembling a pair of spectacles. [Port. *cobra de capello* snake with hood (L *colubra* snake)]

cŏ'bwĕb *n.* 1. Web or fine network spun by spider for capture of its prey; single thread of this. 2. Anything frail or flimsy; any musty accumulation, obstruction, etc., which ought to be swept away, like dusty cobwebs in a neglected room; subtly-woven snare. ~ *adj.* Flimsy, delicate. **cŏ'bwĕbbȳ** *adj.*

cō'ca *n.* S. Amer. shrub, *Erythroxylon coca*, with leaves which are dried and chewed with powdered lime as masticatory, appeaser of hunger, and nervous stimulant; dried leaves of this.

cocai'ne *n.* Alkaloid obtained from coca leaves and young twigs, used as local anaesthetic, stimulant, etc. **cocai'nĭsm** *n.* Chronic condition produced by excessive use of cocaine.

cŏ'ccus *n.* (pl. *-cī*). (also *mī'crococcus*) Minute spherical organism.

cŏ'ccȳx (-ks-) *n.* Small triangular bone ending spinal column in man and some apes; analogous part in birds etc. **coccȳ'ġeal** *adj.* [Gk *kokkux* cuckoo (f. resemblance to cuckoo's bill)]

Cŏ'chĭn-Chī'na. Former French colony, part of Indo-China; ceded to France by the king of Annam in 1868, now part of South Vietnam; ~ *fowl*, (also *Cochin*, *Cochin China*) fowl of feathery-legged Asian breed.

cŏ'chineal *n.* Red dye prepared from dried bodies of the female of the insect *Dactylopius coccus*, found on cactuses in Mexico etc.; this insect.

cŏ′chlėa (-k-) *n.* Spiral cavity of internal ear. [L, = 'snail']

cŏck[1] *n.* 1. Male of common domestic fowl, *Gallus domesticus*; male of other birds. 2. Spout, short pipe, with device for controlling flow of liquid or gas; lever in firearm raised ready to be released by trigger; cocked position or state; way of cocking hat; *at full* ~, with cock raised ready for firing; at *half* ~, with cock raised off nipple of firearm but not drawn up; (fig.) only half-ready; not putting out full effort. 3. *~-and-bull story*, idle invention, incredible tale; *~-crow*, dawn; *~-fighting*, setting cocks to fight as sport; ~ *of the mountain, of the wood*, capercaillie; ~ *of the north*, brambling; (fig.) leader, head, chief person; so ~ *of the walk*; *cock's comb*, cock's crest; fool's cap shaped like this; yellow rattle, *Rhinanthus Crista-galli*, a common meadow-weed; ornamental cultivated plant, *Celosia cristata*; any of various other plants; *co′cksfoot*, strong-growing pasture-grass, *Dactylis glomerata*, with large three-branched panicle; *~-shot, ~-shy*, object set up to be thrown at with sticks, stones, etc., as cocks were formerly at Shrovetide; throw at this; *co′ckspur*, cock's spur; gas-burner of same shape. ~ *v.* 1. Raise cock or hammer of (gun) in readiness for firing. 2. Erect, stick, or stand *up* jauntily or defiantly; ~ *one's ears*, listen attentively; ~ *one's hat*, set it jauntily on one side; turn up brim of hat; ~ *the eye*, turn it with knowing look, wink.

cŏck[2] *n.* Small conical heap of hay in field. ~ *v.t.* Heap (hay) in cocks.

cockā′de *n.* Rosette etc. worn in hat as badge of office or party, or part of livery. **cockā′dėd** *adj.*

cŏck-a-hōō′p *adj.* & *adv.* Exultant(ly), crowing with exultation.

Cockai′gne (-ān). 1. Imaginary country of luxury and idleness. 2. (with pun on *Cockney*) London, Cockneydom.

cŏck-a-lee′kie, cŏ′ckie-lee′kie *n.* Scotch soup of cock boiled with leeks.

cŏckatōō′ *n.* 1. Any of various birds of parrot kind, esp. of genus *Kakatoe*, of Australia and E. Indian islands, with movable crest or tuft of feathers on head. 2. (Austral.) Small farmer, squatter; ~ *fence*, rough fence of logs and saplings. [Malay *kakatua*]

cŏ′ckatrice (*or* -ĭs) *n.* = BASILISK.

cŏ′ckboat *n.* Small ship's-boat.

cŏ′ckchāfer *n.* Large European pale-brown beetle, *Melolontha vulgaris*, flying by night with loud whirring sound.

cŏcked (-kt) *adj.*: see COCK[1]; (esp.) ~ *hat*, hat with very wide brim permanently turned up at front and back, or at both sides, so as to conceal crown completely.

cŏ′cker[1] *v.t.* Pamper, coddle.

cŏ′cker[2] *n.* (also ~ *spaniel*) One of a breed of spaniels trained to start woodcock and similar game.

Cŏ′cker[3], Edward (1631–75). English arithmetician, reputed author of a popular 'Arithmetick'; *according to* ~, in accordance with strict rule or calculation, exact, correct.

cŏ′ckerel *n.* Young cock.

cŏ′ck-eyed (-id) *adj.* (slang) Squinting; crooked; (fig.) absurd.

cŏ′ck-hôrse *n.* Anything a child rides astride upon. ~ *adv.* (also *a-*~) Astride.

cockie-leekie: see COCK-A-LEEKIE.

cŏ′ckle[1] *n.* (also *corn-*~) Plant, *Lychnis* or *Agrostemma githago*, with reddish-purple flowers and capsules of numerous black seeds, growing in cornfields, esp. among wheat.

cŏ′ckle[2] *n.* Bivalve mollusc of genus *C*~, esp. *C. edule*, common on sandy coasts, and much used for food; the shell or a valve of the shell, of this; (*delight, warm*) *the ~s of the heart*, (delight) one's feelings; *~-shell*, shell of cockle; small frail boat.

cŏ′ckle[3] *n.* Bulge, pucker, on surface that should be flat. ~ *v.* (Cause to) bulge, curl up, pucker.

cŏ′ckney *n.* One born in London (strictly, 'within the sound of Bow Bells'); London dialect. ~ *adj.* Of, characteristic of, cockneys; *C~ school*, contemptuous nickname for set of 19th-c. London writers, of whom Leigh Hunt was supposed to be typical. **cŏ'ckneydom, cŏ'ckneyism** *ns.* [orig. meaning 'cock's egg', prob. a small or misshapen egg; later, 'townsman']

cŏ'ckpit *n.* 1. Pit or enclosed area for cock-fights; arena of any struggle. 2. (naut.) Open space or well in after part of small vessel, for helmsman, crew, etc.; (formerly) after part of man-of-war's orlop deck, quarters of junior officers, used in action as hospital. 3. Place for pilot etc. in fuselage of aircraft; place for driver in racing car.

cŏ'ckroach *n.* Nocturnal voracious dark-brown beetle-like insect of the order Blattaria, esp.

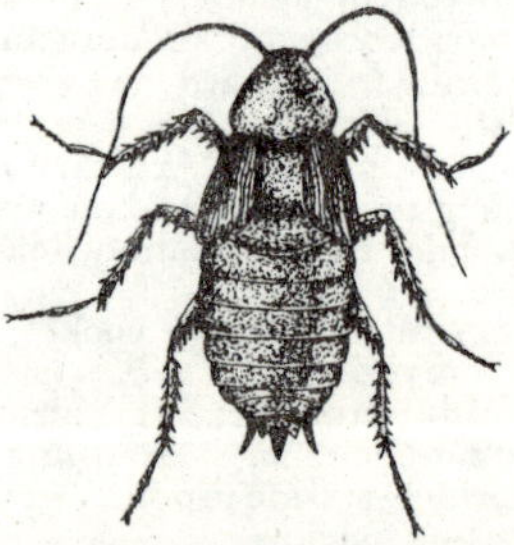

of genus *Blatta* or *Periplaneta*, infesting kitchens etc.

cŏ'cksure (-shoor) *adj.* Absolutely certain *of*, *about*; self-confident, dogmatic, presumptuous. **cŏ'ck-surenėss** *n.*

cŏ'cktail *n.* 1. Horse with a docked tail; horse of racing stamp but not thoroughbred. 2. (also ~ *beetle*) Beetle of family Staphylinidae which cocks its tail over its back when molested. 3. (orig. U.S.) Drink of spirit with bitters, fruit juice, flavouring, ice, etc.; ~*-shaker*, vessel with cap in which cocktails are vigorously shaken to mix them. 4. Preparation of food, esp. as appetizer (*fruit*, *prawn*, ~).

cŏ'ckȳ *adj.* Vain, conceited, pert. **cŏ'ckilȳ** *adv.* **cŏ'ckinėss** *n.*

cō'cō *n.* (pl. *-os*). (also *coconut palm*) Tropical palm-tree, *Cocos nucifera*, producing the coconut.

cō'coa *n.* Powder produced by crushing and grinding cacao seeds; beverage made from this powder; ~*-bean*, cacao-seed; ~*-butter*, fatty matter obtained from cacao-seed; ~*-nib*, cotyledon of cacao-seed. [corruption of CACAO, confused with coco]

cō'conŭt *n.* Large ovate brown hard-shelled fruit of the coconut palm, with edible white lining;

~ *fibre*, fibre of outer husk of coconut; ~ *matting*, matting made of coconut fibre; ~ *milk*, whitish liquid inside coconut; ~ *palm*, = coco.

cocōō'n *n.* Case of silky thread spun by larvae of many insects to protect them in chrysalis state, esp. that spun by silkworm and used as source of silk; protective covering. ~ *v.t.* Protect, wrap, (as) in a cocoon. [Fr. *cocon*, f. mod. Provençal *coucoun* eggshell, cocoon, dim. of *coca* shell]

Cō'cŏs I'slands (īlandz). Group of about 20 small coral islands in the Indian Ocean, British from 1857; transferred to Australia 1955; also known as the Keeling Islands.

cŏcŏtte[1] *n.* Member of the Parisian demi-monde; fashionable prostitute. [Fr.]

cŏcŏtte[2] *n.* Small fireproof dish for cooking individual portion of food. [Fr.]

cŏd[1] *n.* Large sea-fish, *Gadus morrhua*, of N. Atlantic and connected seas; ~*-liver oil*, oil ex-

pressed from cod's liver, rich in vitamins A and D.

cŏd[2] *v.* (north. & Sc. slang) Hoax, fool.

C.O.D. *abbrev.* Cash (costs, or collect) on delivery; Concise Oxford Dictionary.

cō'da *n.* (mus.) More or less independent passage concluding movement or piece of music; (ballet) concluding section. [It., f. L *cauda* tail]

cŏ'ddle *v.t.* Treat as an invalid in need of careful nourishment and nursing; cook (egg) gently by putting it in hot water which is then allowed to cool, or in cold water which is then brought to the boil.

cōde *n.* 1. One of the systematic collections of statutes made by later Roman emperors, esp. that of Justinian; systematic collection or digest of laws of country etc.; system or collection of rules and regulations. 2. Set of conventional symbols used in transmitting messages by flags, telegraph, etc.; system, set, of words, figures, groups of letters, etc., used for other words or phrases, to ensure secrecy or brevity in messages or as system of reference; system of symbols used in computer etc.; also transf. ~ *v.t.* Codify.

cō'deine *n.* Alkaloid derived from opium, used as a sedative etc. [Gk *kōdeia* poppy-head]

cō'dĕx *n.* (pl. *-ĭcēs*). Manuscript volume, esp. of ancient texts.

cŏ'dger *n.* (colloq.) Fellow, queer old person.

cŏ'dĭcil *n.* Supplement to will or agreement, altering, explaining, or revoking original contents. **cŏdĭcĭ'llarў** *adj.*

cŏ'dĭfў *v.t.* Reduce to a code or system; write (message etc.) in code. **cŏdĭfĭcā'tion** *n.*

cŏ'dlĭn, -ĭng[1] *n.* Immature or inferior apple; variety of cooking apple tapering towards apex; ~ *moth*, moth (*Carpocapsa pomonella*), larva of which feeds on apples.

cŏ'dlĭng[2] *n.* Small cod-fish.

cŏ'dpiece *n.* (hist., 15th–17th centuries) Bag-like appendage at front of men's close-fitting hose or breeches to cover opening.

cō-ĕd *adj.* Co-educational. ~ *n.* (U.S. colloq.) Girl or woman student in co-educational institution.

cō-ĕdūcā'tion *n.* Education of both sexes together. **cō-ĕdūcā'tional** *adj.* **cō-ĕ'dūcāte** *v.t.*

cōĕffĭ'cient (-shent) *n.* 1. Joint agent or factor in producing effect or result. 2. (algebra) Number placed before and multiplying known or unknown quantity; (phys.) number expressing amount of some change or effect under certain conditions of temperature, pressure, etc.

coe'lacănth (sēl-) *n.* Fish of family Coelacanthidae with fleshy fin-bases and narrow symmetrical

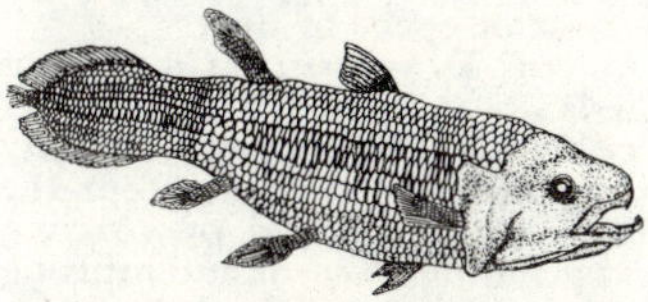

tail, extinct since Cretaceous period except for specimens (*Latimeria chalumnae*) found in SE. Afr. seas.

coelĕ'nterate (sēl-; *or* -āt) *adj.* & *n.* (Member) of phylum Coelenterata, comprising aquatic animals (mostly marine, including jellyfish, sea anemones, and corals) which have an intestinal canal but no separate true body cavity, usu. with stinging cells and showing radial symmetry.

coe'lĭăc (sēl-) *adj.* Of the cavity of the abdomen; ~ *disease*, disease of children with defective digestion of fats.

coe'lom (sēl-) *n.* (pl. -s, *-ŏ'mata*). (zool.) Body cavity or space between intestinal canal and body wall; *extra-embryonic* ~, that surrounding the amnion. **coe'lomāte** *adj.* & *n.* (Animal) having a coelom.

coenaculum : see CENACLE.

coe'nobīte (sēn-) *n.* Member of monastic community. **coenobĭ'tĭc** *adj.*

cōē'qual *adj.* & *n.* Equal. **cō-ē'quallў** *adv.*

cōer'ce *v.* Constrain into obedience etc.; use force, secure by force. **cōer′cion** (-shon) *n.* Constraint, compulsion, government by force. **cōer′cionist** *n.* **cōer′cive** *adj.*

cōėssĕ′ntial (-shal) *adj.* Of the same substance or essence.

cōėter′nal *adj.* Alike eternal. **cōėter′nallȳ** *adv.*

Cœur de Lion (kēr, lēawn). Lion-hearted, epithet of RICHARD I.

cōē′val *adj.* & *n.* (Person) of equal antiquity, of same age; contemporary. **cōē′vallȳ** *adv.*

cōėxi′st (-gz-) *v.i.* Exist together or *with*. **cōėxi′stence** *n.* (esp. pol.) Peaceful existence side by side of states professing different ideologies.

cōėxtĕ′nsive *adj.* Extending over same space or time.

C. of E. *abbrev.* Church of England.

cŏ′ffee *n.* Dark-brown, slightly stimulating drink made from the shrub *Coffea arabica* by roasting and grinding its seeds and infusing them in boiling water; these seeds, the powder made by grinding them; the shrub itself, a native of Ethiopia and Arabia, bearing fragrant white flowers and red fleshy berries each containing two seeds (~*-beans*); cupful of coffee; light-brown colour; ~*-grounds*, granular sediment in coffee after infusion; ~*-house*, refreshment-house selling coffee etc., in 17th and 18th centuries frequented for political and literary conversation etc.; ~*-mill*, contrivance for crushing or grinding roasted coffee beans; ~*-pot*, vessel in which coffee is made or served; ~ *table*, small low table. [Arab. *kahwa* the drink]

cŏ′ffer *n.* 1. Box, esp. strong-box for valuables etc. 2. (archit.) Sunk panel in ceiling or soffit. 3. (also ~*-dam*) Caisson. ~ *v.t.* Ornament with coffers.

cŏ′ffin *n.* 1. Chest in which corpse is buried or cremated. 2. (also ~*-ship*) Unseaworthy ship. 3. Whole of horse's hoof below coronet; ~*-bone*, small spongy bone in horse's hoof, last phalangeal bone of foot. ~ *v.t.* Enclose in or as in coffin.

cŏg[1] *n.* One of a series of projections on wheel, bar, etc., transmitting or receiving motion by engaging with corresponding projections on another wheel etc.; ~*-rail*, toothed rail in railways with very steep gradients; ~*-wheel*, toothed wheel, wheel with cogs.

cŏg[2] *v.t.* (archaic) Fraudulently control fall of dice; *cogged dice*, (erron.) loaded dice.

cō′gent *adj.* Forcible, convincing. **cō′gencȳ** *n.* **cō′gentlȳ** *adv.*

cŏ′gitāte *v.* Ponder, meditate; devise; (philos.) form conception of. **cŏ′gitable** *adj.* Conceivable. **cŏgitā′tion** *n.* **cŏ′gitative** *adj.*

cognac (kŏ′nyăk) *n.* French brandy, strictly the superior kind distilled from Cognac wine. [*Cognac*, town in Charente]

cŏ′gnāte *adj.* 1. Descended from a common ancestor, esp., in Roman law, as dist. from AGNATE; akin in origin, allied, related. 2. (of languages) Of the same linguistic stock; (of words) having the same root or origin, representing the same original word. 3. (gram.) ~ *accusative*, *object*, one of kindred meaning or origin to verb, esp. one used adverbially after intransitive verb (e.g. in *die the death*). ~ *n.* Cognate person; cognate word. **cŏgnā'tion** *n.* Cognate relationship.

cŏgni'tion *n.* (philos.) Action or faculty of knowing (including sensation, conception, etc.) as dist. from feeling and volition. **cŏ'gnitive** *adj.*

cŏ'gnizable (kŏn- *or* kŏg-n-) *adj.* Perceptible, recognizable; within jurisdiction of a court etc.

cŏ'gnizance (kŏn- *or* kŏg-n-) *n.* 1. Being aware; notice. 2. (Right of) dealing with a matter legally or judicially. 3. Distinguishing device or mark. **cŏ'gnizant** *adj.* Having or taking cognizance; (philos.) having cognition. **cŏgni'ze** (-g-n-) *v.t.* (philos.) Have cognition of.

cŏgnō'mĕn *n.* 1. Third or family name of Roman citizen, as Caius Julius *Caesar*; additional name or epithet bestowed on individual. 2. Nickname; surname; name.

cognoscĕ'ntė (kŏnyo-) *n.* (pl. *-ti*, pr. -tē). Connoisseur. [It.]

cŏgnō'vit *n.* (law) Acknowledgement by defendant that plaintiff's case is just. [L, = 'he has acknowledged']

cōhă'bit *v.i.* Live together as husband and wife (freq. of persons not legally married). **cōhăbitā'tion** *n.*

coheir (kō'ār') *n.* (fem. *coheir'ėss*) Joint heir.

cōhēr'e *v.i.* Stick together, remain united; be consistent, well-knit.

cōhēr'ent *adj.* Cohering; consistent, not rambling or inconsequent. **cōhēr'ently** *adv.* **cōhēr'ence, cōhēr'ency** *ns.*

cōhēr'er *n.* (elect.) Device of metal filings, wires, or springs in loose contact, used for detecting electric waves.

cōhē'sion *n.* Cohering; tendency to remain united; (chem.) molecular force of attraction between similar kinds of molecules (opp. ADHESION). **cōhē'sive** *adj.*

cō'hōrt *n.* Division of Roman army, one-tenth of legion; band of warriors.

C.O.I. *abbrev.* Central Office of Information.

coif *n.* (hist.) Close cap covering top, back, and sides, of head.

coiffeur (kwahfėr') *n.* (fem. *coiffeuse*, pr. -ėrz) Hairdresser. [Fr.]

coiffūr'e (kwah-) *n.* Way hair is dressed.

coign (koin) *n.* ~ *of vantage*, place affording good view of something. [old spelling of *quoin* preserved in the Shakespearian phrase ('Macbeth', I. vi. 7)]

coil *n.* Length of rope etc. wound continuously round one point; anything arranged thus; such arrangement; one turn of anything coiled; (elect.) wire wound helically. ~ *v.* Dispose, wind, into circular or spiral shape.

coin *n.* Piece of metal of definite weight and value, made into money

EARLY COINS

by being stamped with official device; coined money, money in circulation. ~ *v.t.* 1. Make (money) by stamping metal; make (metal) into coin. 2. Turn into money; ~ *money*, (coll.) make or gain money quickly. 3. Fabricate, invent, (esp. new word or phrase).

coi'nage *n.* (Right of) coining; coins collectively, currency; invention, fabrication; coined word.

cōinci'de *v.i.* Fall together and agree in position; (geom.) occupy same portion of space; occur at, occupy, same space of time; be identical, agree exactly.

cōĭ'ncidence *n.* (Instance of) coinciding; notable concurrence of events or circumstances without apparent causal connection.

cōĭ'ncident *adj.* Coinciding.

cōincidĕ'ntal *adj.* Of coincidence.

coir (koi'*er*) *n.* Prepared fibre of coconut husk, used for ropes, matting, etc. [Malayalam *kayar* cord]

cōĭ'tion *n.* Insertion of penis into vagina and (usu.) ejaculation of semen.

cō'ĭtus *n.* Coition. [L]

cōke[1] *n.* Compact form of impure carbon obtained from coal by heating out of contact with air, used for smelting metals, for foundry work, and as a fuel esp. for boiler installations etc.; ~ *oven*, plant for converting coal into coke, esp. a horizontal rectangular chamber, closed at each end by cast iron or steel doors, with firebrick lining and heated by gas. ~ *v.t.* Convert (coal) into coke.

cŏke[2] *n.* (slang) Cocaine.

cŏl *n.* Marked depression in summit-line of mountain chain. [Fr., = 'neck']

col. *abbrev.* Column.

Col. *abbrev.* Colonel; Colorado; Colossians (N.T.).

cō'la, k- *n.* Tropical W. Afr. tree of genus *C*~, esp. *C. vera*, introduced into W. Indies and Brazil; ~*-nut*, brownish bitter seed of this, about the size of a chestnut, chewed as mild stimulant. [W. Afr. wd]

co'lander (kŭ-), **cŭ'llender** *n.* Perforated vessel used as strainer in cookery.

Colbert (kŏlbār), Jean Baptiste (1619–83). French statesman under Louis XIV; reformed French financial administration; developed industry by tariffs; virtually founded the French Navy; founded the French Academies of Literature, Science, and the Fine Arts.

Cō'lchėster. Town in Essex, England, famous for oysters (~ *natives*).

cŏ'lchĭcine (-sēn) *n.* Alkaloid ($C_{22}H_{25}O_6N$) derived from colchicum, used for gout, in plant breeding, etc.

cŏ'lchĭcum (or -kĭ-) *n.* Liliaceous plant of genus *C*~ including meadow saffron, *C. autumnale*, with purplish mottled crocus-

COLDSTREAM GUARDS

COLISEUM

like flower; dried corm or seed of this, containing colchicine.

Cŏ'lchis (-lk-). Country at the E. end of the Euxine or Black Sea, famous in Greek legend as the destination of the ARGONAUTS and the home of MEDEA.

cōld *adj.* 1. Of low temperature, esp. when compared with human body or with usual temperature; relatively without heat, not heated, having been allowed to cool; feeling cold; (of soil) slow to absorb heat, clayey. 2. Without ardour, friendliness, or affection; undemonstrative; apathetic; chilling, depressing; *leave* (*person*) ~, fail to excite him. 3. (of colours) Suggesting a cold or sunless day, esp. containing blue or grey. 4. (of hunting scent) Not strong, faint. 5. (in children's games) Far from the object sought, or from finding or guessing. 6. (U.S.) Unconscious. 7. ~ *blood*, coolness, deliberation; absence of emotion or excitement; ~*-blooded*, (of fishes and reptiles as dist. from other vertebrates) having blood whose temperature varies with that of the external air or water; (of persons, actions) unimpassioned, cool; unfeeling, callous; deliberately cruel; ~ *chisel*: see CHISEL; ~ *cream*, unguent for skin; *have, get,* ~ *feet*, (slang) become afraid; (*give, show, the*) ~ *shoulder*, (treat with) intentional coldness or indifference, snub; ~*-shoulder* (*v.t.*); ~ *war*, unfriendly relations between nations characterized by hostile propaganda etc. and threat of actual war; ~ *water*, water at its natural temperature; *throw* ~ *water on*, disparage, discourage. **cō'ldly** *adv.* **cō'ldness** *n.* **cōld** *n.* 1. Prevalence of low temperature in the atmosphere; cold weather; sensation produced by loss of heat from the body. 2. Inflammatory condition of mucous membrane of nose and throat, with catarrh and freq. hoarseness and cough (freq. ~ *in the head*).

Cō'ldstream Guards (gardz). British regiment of guards, first recruited in 1659 by General Monk at Coldstream on the Tweed.

cōle *n.* (rare exc. in comb.) Cabbage; *co'leseed*: see RAPE[3]; ~ *slaw*, (orig. U.S.) salad of sliced cabbage; *co'lewort*, cabbage, esp. kind without heart, as kale.

cŏlėŏ'pterous *adj.* Of the Coleoptera or beetles, a large order of insects having the front pair of wings converted into hard sheaths which cover the other pair when not in use.

cŏlėŏ'ptīle *n.* (bot.) Hollow organ produced by germinating cereal grains, inside which the first leaf makes its way to the ground surface.

Cō'leridge, Samuel Taylor (1772–1834). English romantic poet and literary critic, one of the Lake poets (see LAKE[1]); author of 'The Ancient Mariner', 'Kubla Khan', 'Christabel', etc.

Cŏ'lėt, John (1467?–1519). Dean of St. Paul's and principal English humanist of his day; founded and endowed St. Paul's School, London.

cŏ'lic *n.* Severe spasmodic griping pain in belly. **cŏ'lickў** *adj.*

Cŏlisē'um, Cŏlossē'um. Amphitheatre in Rome, begun by Vespasian in A.D. 72; scene of gladiatorial combats and the martyrdom of many Christians.

cŏlī'tis *n.* Inflammation of membrane of large intestine.

Coll. *abbrev.* College.

collă'borāte *v.i.* Work in combination (*with*) esp. at literary or artistic production; co-operate treacherously with the enemy (esp. in countries occupied by the Germans in war of 1939–45). **collăborā'tion** *n.* **collăborā'tionist** *n.* Treacherous collaborator. **collăborātor** *n.*

cŏ'llage (-ahzh) *n.* Art form in which materials such as pieces of paper and matchsticks are glued to the pictorial surface; such a work of art.

cŏ'llagen *n.* Protein found in animal tissue and bone, which yields gelatine on boiling and leather on tanning.

collă'pse *n.* 1. Falling in, sudden shrinking together, giving way; failure, breakdown. 2. Prostration by loss of nervous or muscular power; breakdown of mental energy, sudden loss of courage, spirits, etc. ~ *v.* 1. Fall together, give way, by external pressure, cave in; contract. 2. (Cause to) fail, break down, or come to nothing. **collă'psible** *adj.* Made to collapse or fold together.

cŏ'llar *n.* 1. Part of garment encircling neck or forming turned-back upper border near the neck; band (often separate) of linen, lace, etc., worn round neck and completing upper part of costume. 2. Ornamental chain forming part of insignia of order of knighthood; band round neck of dog or other animal for identification or ornament; part of harness of draught-animal, leather-covered roll fitting over lower part of neck. 3. Restraining or connecting band, ring, pipe, etc., in machines etc. 4. *~-beam*, horizontal beam connecting a pair of rafters and preventing them from sagging; *~-bone*, bone connecting breast-bone with shoulder-blade, clavicle; *~-stud*, stud fastening detachable collar to shirt. ~ *v.t.* Seize (person) by the collar, capture; (football) tackle; (slang) lay hold of, seize, appropriate.

collā'te *v.t.* 1. Compare carefully and exactly (esp. copy of text *with* other or the original); (bookbinding) verify order of sheets of printed book by signatures. 2. (of an Ordinary) Appoint or institute *to* a benefice.

collă'teral *adj.* 1. Situated or running side by side, parallel; subordinate but from same source; contributory; connected but aside from main subject, course, etc. 2. (opp. LINEAL) Descended from same stock but in a different line. 3. *~ security*, property in addition to principal security pledged as guarantee of repayment of money. ~ *n.* Collateral kinsman; collateral security. **collă'terallў** *adv.*

collā'tion *n.* 1. Collating; comparison; description of book or manuscript by signatures, number of quires, list of contents, etc. 2. (R.C. Ch.) Light repast on evening of fast-day; any light meal.

cŏ'lleague (-ēg) *n.* One of two or more holders of office etc. under same authority, or persons who are members of same profession.

cŏ'llĕct[1] (*or* -ict) *n.* Short prayer used in liturgical worship, esp. one known as the *C~ of the Day*, appointed for particular day or season, read before the Bible readings in Holy Communion and before the two fixed collects in Morning and Evening Prayer.

collĕ'ct[2] *v.* Bring or come together, accumulate; gather (money) from a number of people, for charity, as taxes, etc.; make collection of (curiosities, rare books, etc.); regain control of, concentrate, recover (one's faculties etc., also oneself); (colloq.) call for and take away. **collĕ'ctėd** *adj.* (esp.) Not distracted, cool. **collĕ'ctėdlў** *adv.* **collĕ'ctėdnėss** *n.*

collĕ'ction *n.* 1. Collecting; money collected. 2. Set of things gathered together. 3. (pl.) College terminal examination at Oxford.

collĕ'ctĭve *adj.* Constituting a collection, gathered into one or into a whole, aggregate; of, from, a number of individuals taken or acting together; common; ~ *bargaining*, agreement on terms of employment fixed between employer and organized body of employees; ~ *farm*, in U.S.S.R., farm formed by pooling individual small-holdings; ~ *noun*, singular noun used to denote a collection or number of individuals; so ~ *idea*, *notion*, etc.; ~ *security*, security for nations, obtained by trusting in united strength of an international organization for peace or of a group of allied nations; ~ *unconscious*: see UNCONSCIOUS. **collĕ'ctĭvelў** *adv.* **collĕ'ctĭve** *n.* Collective noun; collective farm. **collĕ'ctĭvĭsm** *n.* Theory or practice of collective ownership or control of all means of production, esp. of land, by the whole community of State. **collĕ'ctĭvĭst** *adj.* & *n.* **collĕ'ctĭvīze** *v.t.* **collĕctĭvīzā'tion** *n.*

collĕ'ctor *n.* One who collects, esp. scientific specimens, curiosities, works of art, etc.; one who collects money for charities, as taxes, etc.

cŏ'lleen *n.* (Anglo-Ir.) Girl. [Ir. *caile* countrywoman]

cŏ'llėge *n.* 1. Organized society of persons performing certain common functions and possessing special rights and privileges; *Electoral C~*: see ELECTORAL; *Herald's C~* or *C~ of Arms*, royal corporation of heralds (founded 1483) which records proved pedigrees and grants armorial bearings; *Sacred C~*, cardinals of the Roman Church who constitute the pope's council and elect to the papacy. 2. Independent corporation of scholars within, or in connection with, a university; similar foundation outside a university; (freq., esp. in Scotland and U.S.) university; any institute for higher education, esp. for professional training; also applied to large public secondary school, and to private school; *C~ of Education*, institution for training schoolteachers. 3. Buildings of a college. 4. ~ *living*, benefice in the gift of a college; ~ *pudding*, plum pudding of a size for one person; *C~ Youths*, English society of bellringers founded in 1637. **cŏ'llėger** *n.* One of the seventy foundation scholars at Eton College. **collē'gian** *n.* Member of a college. **collē'giate** *adj.* Of, constituted as, a college; ~ *church*, church endowed for a body corporate or chapter but with no bishop's see; (Scotland and U.S.) church under joint pastorate.

cŏllĕ'nchўma (-ngk-) *n.* (bot.) Tissue consisting of cells with local cellulose thickening on their walls, usu. developed near surface of young stems and leaves and affording them mechanical strength.

Cŏ'llės frā'cture. Fracture of lower end of radius causing backward and outward displacement of wrist and hand.

cŏ'llėt *n.* Encompassing band or ring on rod, spindle, etc.; ferrule; socket; flange or setting of gem; culet.

collī'de *v.i.* Come forcibly into contact (*with*), strike or dash together; be in conflict, clash.

cŏ'llĭe *n.* Sheep-dog of a Scotch breed, with long hair, pointed nose, and bushy tail.

cŏ'llier (-yer) *n.* 1. Coal-miner. 2. (Sailor on) coal-ship. **cŏ'llierў** *n.* Coal-mine, together with buildings and apparatus belonging to it.

cŏ'llĭmāte *v.t.* Adjust (telescope) so that line of sight is in correct position; place (telescopes, lenses, etc.) with optical axes in same line; (of lens etc.) make (rays of light) parallel. **cŏllĭmā'tion** *n.*

cŏ'llĭmātor *n.* Small fixed telescope used for collimating astronomical instrument etc.; tube with slit and lens used for limiting to a narrow beam and making parallel light falling on prism or diffraction grating of spectroscope.

Cŏ'llĭns[1] (-z) *n.* Letter of thanks from guest after visit. [letter by Rev. William *Collins* in Jane Austen's 'Pride and Prejudice']

Cŏ'llĭns[2] (-z), William Wilkie (1824–89). English novelist; author of 'The Woman in White' (1860) and 'The Moonstone' (1868), almost the first English novels dealing with the detection of crime.

collĭ'sion *n.* Colliding; violent encounter of moving body, esp. ship or railway-train, with another; clash, clashing; ~ *bulkhead*, bulkhead protecting against damage by collision; ~ *course*, course bound to end in collision; ~ *mat*, mat for covering hole in ship's side caused by collision.

cŏ'llocāte *v.t.* Place together, arrange. **collocā'tion** *n.*

collō'dion *n.* Colourless gummy liquid, a solution of gun-cotton in ether, drying rapidly in air, and used for covering photographic plates, wounds, burns, etc., with a thin skin or film.

collō'gue (-g) *v.i.* (dial.) Talk confidentially.

cŏ'lloid *adj.* Gluey; ~ *substance, tissue*, etc., (path.) gelatinous substance produced in certain forms of tissue-degeneration. ~ *n.* (chem.) Non-crystalline substance with very large molecules, which dissolves to form a viscous, sticky solution, e.g. starch, gelatine, and plastics. **colloi'dal** *adj.*

cŏ'llop *n.* (orig. dial.) = ESCALLOP, 3.

collō'quĭal *adj.* Of or in talk, oral; belonging to familiar, not formal or elevated, speech. **collō'quialism** *n.* **collō'quiallў** *adv.*

cŏ'lloquў *n.* Converse, conversation; (in Presbyterian churches) judicial and legislative court of pastors and representative elders.

cŏ'llotўpe *n.* Planographic printing process used mainly for fine reproduction work; print so made.

collu'sion (-ōō-) *n.* Fraudulent secret understanding, esp. between ostensible opponents as in a lawsuit. **collu'sĭve** *adj.* **collu'sĭvelў** *adv.*

collў'rĭum *n.* Eye lotion.

cŏ'llўwŏbbles (-z) *n.pl.* (colloq.) Rumbling in the intestines.

Colo. *abbrev.* Colorado.

cŏ'lobus *n.* African monkey of genus *C~* with shortened thumbs.

cŏ'locўnth *n.* Bitter-apple, *Citrullus colocynthis*, a plant of the gourd family, bearing fruit about size of orange with light spongy extremely bitter pulp; purgative drug prepared from this.

Colo'gne (-ōn). (Ger. *Köln*) City on the lower Rhine, famous in the Middle Ages for the shrine of the Wise Men of the East (the *Three Kings of* ~); hence, (also *eau de* ~, *c~*) Cologne water, a perfume made of aromatic oils and spirit, first manufactured at Cologne.

Cŏlŏ'mbĭa. Republic in extreme NW. of S. America; under Spanish rule until 1819 when a republic was established by Simon BOLIVAR, consisting of the territories now known as Colombia, Panama, Venezuela, and Ecuador; Venezuela and Ecuador seceded in 1830 and Panama in 1903; capital, Bogotá. **Colŏ'mbĭan** *adj.* & *n.*

Cŏlo'mbō (-lŭm-). Capital city of Sri Lanka.

cō'lon[1] *n.* Greater part of large intestine, extending from caecum to rectum. **cōlŏ'nĭc** *adj.*

cō'lon[2] *n.* Punctuation mark (:), used esp. to mark antithesis or before illustration or quotation.

cō'lŏn[3] *n.* Principal monetary unit of Costa Rica (= 100 centimos) and El Salvador (= 100 centavos.)

colonel (kẽr'nl) *n.* Officer in command of a regiment; *C~* BLIMP[2], BOGEY: see these words.

colonelcy (kẽr'nlsĭ) *n.*

colō'nĭal *adj.* Of a colony, esp. of a British Crown colony, or (hist.) of the thirteen British colonies of America before they became the United States; (of architecture, etc.) of the period during which these States were still colonies; *C~ Office*, department of British Government in charge of colonies, merged with Commonwealth Relations Office 1966. ~ *n.* Native, inhabitant, of a colony. **colō'nialism** *n.*

cŏ'lonist *n.* Settler in, part-founder or inhabitant of, a colony.

cŏ'lonīze *v.* Establish colony in; establish in a colony; form or establish a colony or settlement. **cŏlonīzā'tion** *n.*

cŏlonnā'de *n.* Row of columns at regular intervals supporting entablature.

cŏ'lony *n.* 1. (Gk. hist.) Independent city founded by emigrants; (Rom. hist.) settlement of Roman citizens (usu. veteran soldiers) in conquered territory, where they acted as a garrison. 2. Settlement, settlers, in new country remaining subject to or connected with parent State; territory so peopled or belonging to a State by conquest or annexation. 3. Number of people of one nationality or occupation forming a community in a city. 4. (biol.) Aggregate of individual animals or plants forming physiologically connected structure or (more loosely) living close together. 5. Establishment, settlement, for employing or training the unemployed.

cŏ'lophon *n.* 1. Inscription or device at end of book or manuscript, containing title, scribe's or printer's name, date, place of printing. 2. Publisher's imprint.

colŏ'phony *n.* Resin originating from the town of Colophon in Lydia.

Cŏlora'dō (-ah-). State in western U.S., admitted to the Union in 1876, named from the great Colorado River which rises there and flows into the Gulf of California; capital, Denver; ~ *beetle*, small beetle (*Leptinotarsa decemlineata*) native to Rocky Mountains and introduced into Europe, yellow with 10 longitudi-

nal black stripes on back, the larva of which is very destructive to the potato plant.

colorā'tion (kŭ-) *n.* Colouring; arrangement of colours; natural, esp. variegated, colour of living things.

cŏloratur'a (-ahtoor*a*) *n.* Florid ornament, freq. extempore, in singing; ~ *soprano*, (singer with) high flexible voice capable of this. [It., = 'coloured (music)']

cŏlorĭ'fic (*or* kŭ-) *adj.* Producing colour(s).

cŏlorĭ'mėter (*or* kŭ-) *n.* Instrument for measuring intensity of colour.

colŏ'ssal *adj.* Of, like, a colossus; gigantic; (colloq.) magnificent. ~ *order*, (archit.) order on a façade running up past more than one storey. **colŏ'ssally** *adv.*

Colosseum: see COLISEUM.

Colŏ'ssian (-sh*a*n) *adj.* Of Colossae, a city near Laodicea in Phrygia. ~ *n.* Native, inhabitant, of Colossae; (*Epistle to the*) ~*s*, book of N.T., epistle of St. Paul to the Church at Colossae.

colŏ'ssus *n.* (pl. *-ī, -uses*). Gigantic statue; huge dominating figure; person or personified empire conceived as standing astride dominions like the statue at Rhodes which was thought to have stood astride the harbour; *C~ of Rhodes*, statue, in bronze, of the sun-god Helios, said to have been 70 cubits high (over 100 ft); it was shattered by an earthquake in 224 B.C. only 56 years after erection and the fragments, which lay about the harbour for centuries, were regarded as one of the Seven Wonders of the World.

colŏ'stomy *n.* (surg.) (Formation of) an opening from the colon through the abdominal wall.

colŏ'strum *n.* First milk secreted by mammal after parturition.

co'lour (kŭl*er*) *n.* 1. Quality or wavelength of light emitted or reflected from an object, determined by the physical configuration of the emitting or reflecting surface and the quality of the incident light (if any); sensation produced by stimulation of optic nerve by particular light-vibrations. 2. Particular hue, one of the constituents into which white or colourless light can be decomposed; mixture of these, including black (in which rays of light are wholly absorbed) and white (in which they are wholly reflected); *primary* ~, (physiol.) one of the three colours (red, green, and violet) combinations of which give rise to sensations of all others; (in painting) red, blue, or yellow, which may be mixed to produce all other colours; *secondary* ~, one produced (as green, purple) by mixing two primary colours; *tertiary* ~, one of the greyish hues produced by mixing two secondary colours. 3. Hue of the darker, esp. Negro races of mankind as dist. from white. 4. Complexion, ruddy hue of cheeks, etc. 5. Representation of colour in painting; colouring. 6. (pl.) Coloured ribbon, dress, etc., worn as symbol of party, membership of club, inclusion in athletic team, etc.; flag, ensign, or standard of regiment or ship; *the* ~*s*, the army. 7. Pigment, paint; coloured material etc. 8. Outward appearance, semblance; pretext, show of reason; tone, character, kind, shade of meaning; (mus.) timbre, variety of expression, etc. 9. *local* ~, see LOCAL; ~ *bar*, legal or social distinction between white and coloured people; ~*-blind*, unable to see, or to distinguish between, certain colours; ~ *scheme*, systematic arrangement of colours or coloured items; ~*-sergeant*, sergeant with special duty of attending regimental colours in the field (a rank created by the Prince Regent (George IV) in recognition of gallantry of non-commissioned officers in Peninsular War). ~ *v.* Give colour to; paint, stain, dye; disguise; misrepresent; imbue with its own colour; take on colour; blush. **co'loured** (-*er*d) *adj.* (of persons) Not white, wholly or partly of Negro descent.

co'lourable (kŭl*er*-) *adj.* Specious, plausible. **co'lourablў** *adv.*

co'lourful (kŭl*er*-) *adj.* Full of colour, vivid. **co'lourfullў** *adv.* **co'lourfulnėss** *n.*

co'louring (kŭl*er*-) *n.* (esp.) Style in which thing is coloured, or in which artist uses colour; complexion.

co'lourist (kŭl*er*-) *n.* Painter skilful in colouring.

co'lourlėss (kŭl*er*-) *adj.* Without colour; pale; dull; wanting in character or vividness; neutral, impartial, indifferent. **co'lourlėsslў** *adv.* **co'lourlėssnėss** *n.*

cŏlporteur' (-tẽr; *or* kŏ'-) *n.* Hawker of books etc., esp. one employed by a religious society.

Col.-Sergt, -Sgt *abbrevs.* Colour-Sergeant.

cōlt[1] *n.* Young male of horse (from leaving dam till age of 4, or with thoroughbreds 5); inexperienced person, esp. cricket professional in first season; *co'ltsfoot*, common weed in waste or clayey ground, *Tussilago farfara*, with large spreading cordate leaves downy beneath and yellow flowers appearing before the leaves. **cō'ltish** *adj.*

Cōlt[2] *n.* Kind of revolver. [trade-name, f. Samuel *Colt* (1814–62), Amer. inventor]

Colŭ'mba, St. (521–97). Irish monk and missionary who founded the monastery of Iona, Scotland.

cŏlumbār'ium *n.* (pl. *-ia*). 1. Dovecot. 2. (Rom. antiq.) Subterranean sepulchre with niches for cinerary urns.

Colŭ'mbia. Poetic name for America. [f. COLUMBUS]

cŏ'lumbīne[1] *n.* Plant *Aquilegia vulgaris*, the inverted flower of which, with its horned nectaries, resembles five pigeons clustered together. [L *columba* dove]

Cŏ'lumbīne[2]**.** Character in Italian comedy, the mistress of

Harlequin; she appears in the harlequinade of English pantomime as a short-skirted dancer.

colŭ′mbium *n.* (formerly) Niobium.

Colŭ′mbus, Christopher (*c* 1451–1506). Genoese navigator who prevailed upon Ferdinand and Isabella of Spain to bear the expenses of an expedition of discovery and set out on his 1st voyage in 1492; first discovered

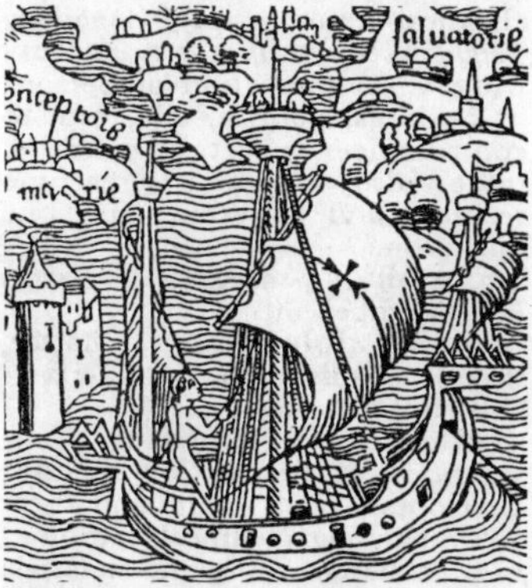

the Bahamas (12 Oct. 1492) and Cuba and on his 3rd voyage (1498) landed near the mouth of the Orinoco in S. America; ~ *Day*, 12 Oct., a legal holiday in most States of U.S., the W. Indies, and some S. Amer. republics.

cŏ′lumn (-m) *n.* 1. (archit.) Long cylindrical or slightly tapering body usu. supporting entablature or arch or standing alone as monument. 2. Natural column-shaped formation, esp. of igneous rock; anything resembling a column in shape or function; upright mass of air, liquid, smoke, etc. 3. One of the narrow vertical divisions of a sheet of paper, page of book, etc., used for lists of figures, names, etc., or for convenience in arranging printed matter on a wide page; esp. such a division of a newspaper, the printed matter filling it, a newspaper article. 4. Formation of troops, armoured vehicles, etc., in which the elements are placed

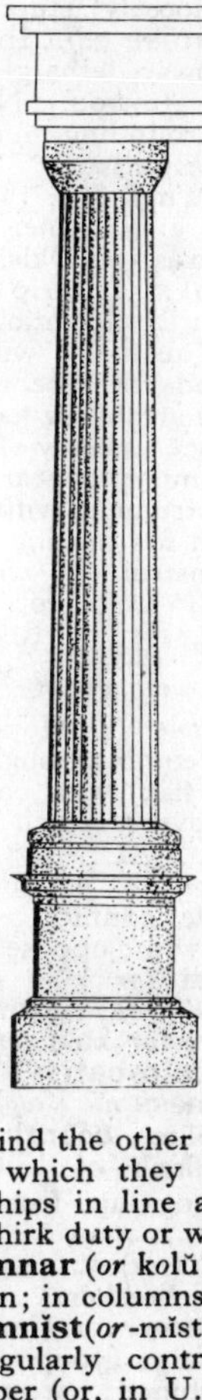

one behind the other as dist. from *line* in which they are abreast; (nav.) ships in line ahead; *dodge the* ~, shirk duty or work.

cŏ′lumnar (*or* **kolŭ′-**) *adj.* Like a column; in columns.

cŏ′lumnist (*or* -mĭst) *n.* Journalist who regularly contributes to a newspaper (or, in U.S., group of newspapers) a column or comment on events.

colūr′e *n.* (astron.) One of two great circles intersecting at right angles at the poles and dividing the equinoctial and ecliptic into four equal parts, one passing through the equinoctial points, the other through the solstitial points, of the ecliptic.

cŏ′lza *n.* = RAPE[3].

com- *prefix.* With.

cō′ma[1] *n.* (path.) Deep unconsciousness; (loosely) stupor, lethargy. **cō′matōse** *adj.* In a state of coma; drowsy, lethargic.

cō′ma[2] *n.* (astron.) Nebulous envelope surrounding nucleus of comet. [Gk *komē* hair]

Comă′nchė *adj.* & *n.* (Member, language) of a N. Amer. Indian people of Texas and Oklahoma.

comb (kōm) *n.* 1. Strip of bone, metal, etc., with indentations forming series of teeth, or with teeth inserted, used for disentangling, cleaning, and arranging hair, or to keep it in place. 2. Any of various things of similar appearance or function: instrument with several rows of teeth for carding wool or flax, steel instrument with projecting teeth used for cutting screw-thread, etc. 3. Red fleshy indented or serrated crest or caruncle on head of domestic fowl, esp. male. 4. Honeycomb. ~ *v.* Draw comb through (hair), dress (wool, flax) with comb; (of wave) curl over; search or examine closely.

cŏ′mbat (*or* kŭ-) *n.* Encounter, fight; struggle; conflict. ~ *v.* Do battle; fight with; oppose.

cŏ′mbatant (*or* kŭ-) *n.* One who fights. ~ *adj.* fighting.

cŏ′mbative (*or* kŭ-) *adj.* Pugnacious. **co′mbativelў** *adv.* **co′mbativeness** *n.*

combe (ko͞om), **co͞omb** (-m) *n.* Valley on flank of hill; short valley running up from coast; cirque.

cō′mber (-m*er*) *n.* (esp.) Long curling wave, breaker.

cŏmbĭnā′tion *n.* 1. Combining; combined state; group or set of things combined; sequence of letters or numbers that open a combination lock. 2. Union, association, of persons for a common object, esp. union (formerly illegal) of employers or workmen to further their interests. 3. Chemical union, in which substances combine to form new compounds, product of this. 4. (pl.) Close-fitting undergarment combining vest and drawers. 5. Motor-cycle with side-car attached. 6. ~ *lock*, lock which can be opened only by specific sequence of movements; *~-room*, in University of Cambridge, senior common-room.

cŏ′mbĭnative *adj.* Combining; of combination; (phon., of sound-changes in words etc.) due to a combination of sounds or letters.

combī′ne *v.* 1. Join together, unite; come together; unite for common purpose, co-operate; *combined operations*, operations in which military, naval, and air forces are combined. 2. Enter into chemical union (*with*); *combining weight*: see EQUIVALENT. **cŏ′mbīne** *n.* Combination of persons in business, politics, etc., esp. to control prices or obstruct course of trade; (also ~ *harvester*) machine reaping and threshing in one operation.

cō′mbings (-mĭngz) *n.pl.* (esp.) Hairs combed off.

combŭ′stĭble *adj.* & *n.* (Matter, thing) capable of burning; excitable, inflammable.

combŭ′stion (-sch*o*n) *n.* Consumption or destruction by fire; development of light and heat accompanying chemical combination; oxidation of organic material; *internal ~ engine*, engine in which the motive power is produced by the combustion and expansion of a mixture of petrol or oil vapour (or gas) and air inside the cylinders.

come (kŭm) *v.i.* (past t. *cāme*, past part. *come*). 1. Move or start towards, arrive at, a point, time, or result; be brought; fall, land (*on*); ~ *into view*, become visible. 2. Occur, fall; happen; issue; be derived, descend; (of time etc.) arrive in due course; become, get to be; turn out to be. 3. (quasi-trans.) Traverse, accomplish (a distance); play or practise (a dodge, trick) *over*; act, perform one's part (*come it strong* etc.). 4. ~ *across*, meet with; ~ *across with*, hand over; ~ *along*, (imper., colloq.) make haste; ~ *at*, reach, discover, get access to; ~ *back*, recur to memory; *~-back*, retaliation, retort; return, recovery, reinstatement; ~ *by*, obtain; ~ *down*, extend downwards *to*; be handed down; fall, be humbled; ~ *forward*, present oneself before the public etc.; ~ *in*, enter house or room; take specified place (in race etc.); come into power or office; be received as income; become seasonable or fashionable; serve a purpose, find a place; ~ *in for*, get; ~ *into*, receive, esp. as heir; ~ *off*, become detached; retire or extricate oneself; come to the issue; succeed; ~ *on*, advance; continue to progress, thrive, develop; supervene; come upon the stage or scene; begin to bowl at cricket; ~ *out*, go on strike; emerge from contest, examination, etc.; (of sun etc.) emerge from clouds, begin to shine; come into public view, become public, be published; appear or be found by computation etc.; develop, display itself; make debut on stage or in society; ~ *out with*, utter; ~ *to*, revive; (naut.) come to a standstill; ~ *to pass*, happen; ~ *up*, come to place regarded as higher, e.g. capital, university; come close *to*; arise as subject of attention, discussion, etc.; rise to level or height of; ~ *up with*, catch up; produce.

come-ă'tăble (kŭ-) *adj*. That may be come at, accessible.

Cŏmėcŏ'n. Eastern European economic organization, founded in 1949, with headquarters in Moscow. [abbrev. of *Co*uncil for *M*utual *E*co*n*omic Assistance, trans. Russ. *Sovet ékonomicheskoĭ vzaimopomoshchi*]

comē'dĭan *n*. Comic actor or entertainer; (archaic) writer of comedies.

comédiĕ'nne (-mā- *or* -mē-) *n*. Comedy actress.

comēdiĕ'tta *n*. Short or slight comedy.

comē'dō *n*. (pl. *-ōnēs*). (med.) Skin blemish, blackhead.

cŏ'mėdy̆ *n*. Stage-play of light, amusing, and often satirical character, with a happy conclusion to its plot; that branch of drama which adopts a humorous or familiar style and depicts laughable characters and incidents; life, or an incident in it, regarded as a comic spectacle.

co'mely (kŭmlĭ) *adj*. Pleasant to look at. **co'melinėss** *n*.

co'mer (kŭ-) *n*. One who comes (usu. *first* ~, *last* ~, etc.); *all* ~*s*, any who apply, take up challenge, etc.

comĕ'stĭble *n*. (usu. pl.) Thing to eat.

cŏ'mėt *n*. Celestial body with star-like nucleus and train or 'tail' of light moving about sun in elliptical or parabolic orbit. **cŏ'mėtary̆, comĕ'tĭc** *adjs*. [Gk *komētēs* long-haired (star)]

co'mfĭt (kŭ-) *n*. Sweet containing nut, seed, etc., in sugar.

co'mfort (kŭ-) *n*. 1. Relief in affliction, consolation; person who consoles one or saves one trouble; cause of satisfaction. 2. Well-being, being comfortable; thing that produces or ministers to enjoyment and content. ~ *v.t.* Soothe in grief, console; make comfortable. **co'mfortlėss** *adj*.

co'mfortable (kŭ-) *adj*. Affording consolation; attended with or ministering to comfort or physical well-being; in a state of tranquil enjoyment and content, at ease. **co'mfortably̆** *adv*. **co'mforter** *n*. 1. One who comforts; *the C*~, the Holy Ghost. 2. Woollen scarf; (U.S.) quilted coverlet. 3. Teat of rubber etc. given to baby to suck.

co'mfrey (kŭ-) *n*. Tall ditch-plant, *Symphytum officinale*, with rough leaves and white or purple bell-shaped flowers, the root and leaves of which were formerly used medicinally.

co'mfy̆ (kŭ-) *adj*. (colloq.) Comfortable.

cŏ'mĭc *adj*. Of comedy; mirth-provoking, laughable or meant to be so, facetious, burlesque, funny; ~ *strip*, set of drawings, usu. broadly humorous, forming part of a series appearing regularly in a journal. ~ *n*. Comic actor or person (colloq.); comic paper; children's magazine or pamphlet consisting largely of stories in pictorial form.

cŏ'mĭcal *adj*. Mirth-provoking, laughable; odd, queer. **cŏmĭcă'lĭty** *n*. **cŏ'mĭcally̆** *adv*.

Cŏ'mĭnfŏrm. Communist information bureau consisting of two representatives from each of nine European countries, established at Belgrade 1947 and dissolved 1956; the successor of the COMINTERN.

Cŏ'mĭntĕrn. Third Communist INTERNATIONAL, founded at Moscow in Mar. 1919; formally dissolved June 1943.

cŏ'mĭtȳ *n.* Courtesy; ~ *of nations*, friendly and courteous recognition as far as practicable by nations of laws and usages of other nations; (freq., erron.) company of nations practising this.

cŏ'mma *n.* 1. Punctuation mark (,) used to separate smallest parts of a sentence, also used to separate figures etc.; (mus.) minute interval or difference of pitch; *inverted* ~*s*, (' ' or " ") commas raised above line at beginning and end of quotation, the first, or first pair, being inverted. 2. (also ~ *butterfly*) Butterfly, *Polygonia comma-album*, with white comma-shaped mark on underside of wings.

comma'nd (-ah-) *n.* 1. Order, bidding. 2. Exercise or tenure of authority, esp. naval or military; body of troops, district, ship, etc. under commander; *high* ~, *higher* ~, general staff, esp. commander-in-chief, of army. 3. Control, mastery, possession; ~ *paper*, (abbrev. Cd., Cmd., Cmnd.) paper laid by command of Crown before Parliament etc.; ~ *performance*, theatrical etc. performance given by royal command. ~ *v.* 1. Order, bid. 2. Have authority over or control of, be supreme; be in command (of). 3. Restrain, master; have at disposal or within reach; demand and obtain; dominate (position etc.) from superior height, look down over.

cŏmmandă'nt (*or* -ahnt) *n.* Commanding officer, esp. one holding special command, of depot, particular force, fortress, etc.

cŏmmandeer' *v.* Force (men) into, seize (stores) for, military service; take arbitrary possession of.

comma'nder (-ah-), *n.* One who commands; one who has command of a ship, naval officer ranking below captain; senior officer at Scotland Yard, ranking below commissioner; *Knight C~*, member of higher class in some orders of knighthood; *C~-in-Chief*, chief commander of all military land forces of a State; senior naval officer in command of all ships on a station; *C~ of the Faithful*: see FAITHFUL.

comma'nding (-ah-) *adj.* Ruling, controlling; nobly dignified; ~ *officer*, officer in command.

comma'ndment (-ah-) *n.* Divine command, esp. (*C~*) one of the *Ten Commandments*, precepts delivered by God to Moses (Exod. 20: 1–17).

comma'ndō (-ah-) *n.* (pl. *-os*). Party called out for military purposes; in the Boer War (1899–1902), unit of Boer army composed of militia of an electoral district; in the war of 1939–45, member of one of several bodies of troops in British Army specially trained for raids on enemy's coasts etc.; member of similar troops elsewhere.

comme il faut (kŏm ēl fō) *adj. phr.* According to etiquette, correct in deportment or behaviour. [Fr.]

commĕ'morāte *v.t.* Celebrate in speech or writing; preserve in memory by some celebration; be a memorial of. **commĕmorā'tion** *n.* 1. Commemorating; service or prayer commemorating saint or sacred event. 2. At Oxford University, annual Trinity Term celebration in memory of the founders and benefactors. **commĕ'morātĭve** *adj.*

commĕ'nce *v.* Begin; (archaic) start or set up as; take full degree of Master or Doctor at university. **commĕ'ncement** (-sm-) *n.* Beginning; ceremony of conferring university degrees (in Cambridge and Dublin, those of Master and Doctor, in U.S. universities, all degrees).

commĕ'nd *v.t.* Entrust, commit (archaic exc. in, e.g., ~ *one's soul to God*); praise, extol; (refl.) recommend; ~ *me to*, (archaic, freq. iron.) give me by choice.

commĕ'ndable *adj.* Praiseworthy. **commĕ'ndablȳ** *adv.*

commĕ'ndăm *n.* Tenure of benefice in absence of regular incumbent, esp. of benefice which bishop etc. might hold along with his own preferment (abolished in England by statute in 1836).

cŏmmendā'tion *n.* Praise; act of commending person to another's favour.

commĕ'ndatorȳ *adj.* 1. Commending. 2. Holding, held, in commendam.

commĕ'nsal *adj.* & *n.* (Person) eating at same table; (animal or plant) living in or upon another, and sharing its food without causing it detriment (opp. *parasite*). **commĕ'nsalĭsm, cŏmmensă'lĭtȳ** *ns.*

commĕ'nsurable (-sh*er*-) *adj.* Measurable by the same standard; divisible without remainder by the same quantity. **commĕ'nsurablȳ** *adv.* **commĕnsurabĭ'lĭtȳ** *n.*

commĕ'nsurate (-sh*er*-) *adj.* Coextensive; proportionate. **commĕ'nsuratelȳ** *adv.*

cŏ'mmĕnt *n.* Explanatory or critical note or remark; expository or critical matter; criticism. ~ *v.i.* Write explanatory or critical notes *on*; make (esp. unfavourable) comments or remarks (*on*).

cŏ'mmentarȳ *n.* Expository treatise; series of running comments on book, speech, performance, etc.; comment, remark; (also *running* ~, esp.) broadcast commentary on some public event while it is in progress.

cŏmmentā'tion *n.* Making of comments.

cŏ'mmentātor *n.* Maker of comments, writer or speaker of commentary.

cŏ'mmerce *n.* 1. Exchange of merchandise, esp. on a large scale between different countries or districts, comprising all forms of trade and ancillary services such as banking, insurance, and transport. 2. Intercourse. 3. Card-game in which exchange or barter is chief feature.

commer'cial (-sh*a*l) *adj.* Of, engaged in, bearing on, commerce; ~ *college*, *school*, college, school, for instruction in commercial subjects; ~ *hotel*, ~ *room*, hotel, room in hotel or inn, for accommodation of commercial travellers; ~ *traveller*, agent of manufacturer, wholesale trader, etc., who travels over a district showing samples and soliciting orders. ~ *n.* Commercial traveller (colloq.); commercial hotel; (orig. U.S.) advertisement broadcast on radio or television. **commer'cialĭsm** *n.* **commer'cialīze** *v.t.* **commer'ciallȳ** *adv.*

cŏ'mmĭe *n.* (slang) Communist.

cŏmmĭnā'tion *n.* Threatening of divine punishment or vengeance; denunciation; recital of divine threats against sinners, part of an office for Ash Wednesday in the Anglican liturgy. **cŏ'mminatorȳ** *adj.* Threatening, denunciatory.

commĭ'ngle (-nggl) *v.* Mingle together.

cŏ'mmĭnūte *v.t.* Reduce to minute particles; divide into small portions; *comminuted fracture*, fracture producing multiple fragments. **cŏmminū'tion** *n.*

commĭ'serāte (-z-) *v.* Feel, show, express, pity for; condole *with*. **commĭserā'tion** *n.* **commĭ'serative** *adj.*

cŏmmĭssar' *n.* (until 1946) Head of government department of U.S.S.R. or its constituent republics.

cŏmmĭssār'iat *n.* 1. Department (esp. military) for supply of food etc. 2. (until 1946) Department of Civil Service of U.S.S.R.

cŏ'mmĭssarȳ *n.* 1. Deputy, delegate; representative of bishop in part of his diocese, or of absent bishop. 2. Officer charged with supply of food etc. for body of soldiers; *C~ general*, chief commissary, esp. head of military commissariat.

commĭ'ssion *n.* 1. Authoritative charge or direction; authority, esp. delegated authority, body of persons having authority, to act in some specified capacity, investigate some specified question, etc.; *High C~*, department of High Commissioner; *Royal C~*, advisory body appointed by royal warrant to conduct special enquiry; *~ of the peace*, authority given, persons authorized, to act as Justices of the Peace. 2. Warrant conferring authority, warrant by which officer in armed services exercises command; office conferred by such a warrant. 3. Being authoritatively entrusted or given in charge; *in ~*, exercising delegated authority; (of an office) placed by warrant in charge of a body of persons; (of a ship of war) manned, armed, and ready for sea; *out of ~*, not in service; not in working order. 4. Charge entrusted to anyone to perform; order given to artist, writer, etc. for a particular piece of work. 5. Authority to act as agent for another in trade or business; system of trading in which dealer acts as agent for another, receiving a percentage as remuneration; the percentage of the amount involved paid to the agent. ~ *v.t.* Empower by commission; give (officer) command of ship; order (ship) for active service; assume command of (ship); give (artist etc.) a commission; order (work of art etc.) as a commission. **commĭ'ssioned** (-nd) *adj.* (esp.) (of officer) Holding rank by commission.

commĭssionair'e *n.* Member of Corps of Commissionaires, an association of pensioned soldiers, orig. established in London in 1859, organized for employment as porters, messengers, etc.; person in uniform who is employed as door porter in hotel, large shop, cinema, etc.

commĭ'ssioner *n.* One appointed by commission; member of permanently constituted commission or government board etc.; representative of supreme authority in district, department, etc.; official at head of branch of public service etc.; *High C~*, chief officer of colonial territory or dependency; chief representative of one Commonwealth country to another; representative of the sovereign at the General Assembly of the Church of Scotland; *C~ for Oaths*, solicitor authorized to administer oaths to persons making affidavits.

cŏ'mmĭssūre *n.* Joining, seam; joint between two bones; line where lips, eyelids, meet; band or bundle of white or grey nerve-substance connecting hemispheres of brain, parts of cerebrum and cerebellum, two sides of spinal cord, etc.

commĭ't *v.t.* 1. Entrust, consign, for treatment or safe keeping, consign officially *to* custody, prison, etc.; refer (bill etc.) to committee. 2. Perpetrate (crime, blunder). 3. Involve, compromise; engage or pledge by implication (*to*). **commĭ'tment** *n.* (esp.) Engagement; thing undertaken, responsibility. **commĭ'ttal** *n.* Committing, consigning, esp. committing to prison; committing of body to grave at burial; reference to committee; committing of oneself.

commĭ'ttee *n.* Body of persons appointed for special function by (and usu. out of) larger body; *joint ~*, one composed of members nominated by two or more distinct bodies; *standing ~*, one which is permanent during the existence of the appointing body; *C~ of the whole House*, the House of Commons sitting as a committee and presided over by a chairman (not the Speaker); *C~ of Supply*, *C~ of Ways and Means*, financial committees of the House of Commons consisting of all the members.

commĭ'x *v.* (archaic, poet.) Mix. **commĭ'xture** *n.*

commō'de *n.* Chest of drawers, chiffonier; chair or box containing chamber-pot.

commō'dĭous *adj.* Roomy. **commō'dĭouslў** *adv.* **commō'dĭousnėss** *n.*

commŏ'dĭtў *n.* Useful thing;

article of trade, esp. product as opp. to service.

cŏ'mmodōre *n.* Naval officer ranking above captain and below rear-admiral (in British Navy a temporary rank); as courtesy title, senior captain when three or more ships cruise together, captain of pilots, president of yacht club; senior captain of a shipping line; commodore's ship; *Air C~*: see AIR.

cŏ'mmon *adj.* 1. Possessed or shared alike by both or all; belonging to more than one; belonging to all mankind alike; general; public. 2. Of ordinary occurrence and quality; usual, frequent; undistinguished, ordinary (*~ or garden*, of the familiar kind); of little value, of inferior quality; low-class, vulgar. 3. (math.) Of a number or quantity, belonging equally to two or more quantities. 4. (gram., logic) Of a noun, name, etc., applicable to every individual or species of a class or genus; of either gender or sex. 5. (mus. etc.) (of time, measure) Consisting of two or four beats in a bar, esp. of 4 crotchets in a bar. 6. *~ carrier*, one recognized by law as bound to serve the public; *~ chord*: see CHORD[2]; *C~ Era*, Christian era; *~ form*, form of probate in which grant is made by executor's oath without opposition; customary form of words in common-law pleadings; form of words common to documents of like kind; (colloq.) formula etc. of general application; *~ ground*, basis for argument etc. accepted by both sides; *~ land*: see *n.* below; *~ law*, unwritten law of England, administered by sovereign's courts and purporting to be derived from ancient and universal usage, which is embodied in the older commentaries and in reports of adjudged cases; *~-law husband, wife*, one established by common law, usu. as a result of couple living as man and wife without a recognized marriage ceremony; *C~ Market*, EUROPEAN Economic Community; *~ metre*, hymn stanza of four lines, of which the first and third have eight syllables and the second and fourth six (also called 'ballad metre' from its use in Old English ballads); *C~ Plea*, civil action at law brought by one subject against another; *Court of C~ Pleas*, until 1875 one of the three superior courts of common law in England; *C~ Prayer*, liturgy or form of public service prescribed by Church of England and first set forth in the Book of Common Prayer of 1549 (the edition now used in England being substantially that of 1662); *~ recovery*: see RECOVERY; *~-room*, (also *senior ~-room*) room in school, university, etc., to which members of staff have common access; esp. at Oxford, room to which fellows of college retire after dinner; similar room (also *junior ~-room*) for undergraduates or students; so *middle ~-room*, for graduates (other than fellows) engaged in research; staff, fellows, students, using such a room; *~ seal*, official seal used by corporation; *~ sense*, normal understanding, good practical sense in everyday affairs; *~ soldier*, private soldier; *~ weal*, (archaic) commonwealth; public welfare. *~ n.* 1. Land belonging to local community as a whole, now esp. the unenclosed waste land remaining to represent this. 2. (law) Right, as of pasturage, fishing, etc., in the land or water of another. 3. *the ~*, what is common or ordinary (esp. in *out of the ~*); *in ~*, in joint use, shared; *in ~ with*, in the same way as, like; *tenants in ~*, tenants holding by distinct titles but 'by unity of possession'. **cŏ'mmonnėss** *n.* Vulgarity.

cŏ'mmonable *adj.* (of animals) That may be pastured on common land; (of land) that may be held in common, subject to right of common.

cŏ'mmonage *n.* Right of common; land, condition of land, held in common or subject to right of common; commonalty.

cŏ'mmonaltў *n.* General body of the community, the common people as dist. from those of rank or in authority; general or universal body.

cŏ'mmoner *n.* 1. One of the common people, one below the rank of a peer. 2. (rare) Member of House of Commons; *the Great C~*, the elder William Pitt. 3. (in some English colleges) One who pays for his commons, i.e. student not on the foundation (see COMMONS 2). 4. One who has right of common.

cŏ'mmonlў *adv.* Usually, frequently.

cŏ'mmonplāce *n.* Notable passage entered for reference or use in a ~ *book* kept for this purpose; opinion or statement generally accepted; ordinary topic; anything common and trite. ~ *adj.* Lacking originality, trivial, hackneyed.

cŏ'mmons (-z) *n.pl.* 1. Common people; third estate in English and similar constitutions; *House of C~*, (also *the C~*) representatives of counties, boroughs, etc., forming the Lower House of Parliament; building where these meet. 2. Provisions shared in common, esp. in monastic house, college, etc.; (Oxf. & Cam. Univ.) definite portion of victuals supplied from college buttery or kitchen at fixed charge; (more widely) daily fare; *short* ~, insufficient fare.

cŏ'mmonwealth (-wĕl-) *n.* 1. Body politic, independent community; republican or democratic State. 2. *the C~*, (also *British C~ of Nations*) the association of the United Kingdom and certain self-governing independent States (Canada, Australia, New Zealand, Bahamas, Bangladesh, Barbados, Botswana, Cyprus, Fiji, Gambia, Ghana, Grenada, Guyana, India, Jamaica, Kenya, Lesotho, Malawi, Malaysia, Malta G.C., Mauritius, Nauru, Nigeria, Papua New Guinea, Sierra Leone, Singapore, Sri Lanka, Swaziland, Tanzania, Tonga, Trinidad and Tobago, Uganda, Western Samoa, Zambia) together with their dependencies and the Associated States of the Eastern Caribbean; *C~ Day*, name since 1959 of Empire Day, celebrated until 1965 on 24 May (Queen Victoria's birthday) and after that on the Queen's official birthday, orig. commemorating assistance given by colonies in Boer War of 1899–1902; *C~ Office*, department of British Government formed in 1966 by merging Colonial Office and Commonwealth Relations Office, since 1968 combined with the Foreign Office. 3. *the C~*, (Engl. hist.) the republican Government established in England between the execution of Charles I in 1649 and the Restoration in 1660. 4. *C~ of Australia*; see AUSTRALIA.

commō'tion *n.* Physical disturbance; bustle, confusion; public disorder, tumult, insurrection.

commo've (-ōōv) *v.t.* Move violently, excite.

cŏ'mmūnal *adj.* 1. Of a commune or the Paris Commune. 2. Of or for the community, for common use.

cŏ'mmūnalism *n.* Principle of communal organization of society; theory of government by local autonomy. **cŏ'mmūnalist** *n.* **cŏmmūnali'stic** *adj.*

cŏ'mmūne[1] *n.* 1. Smallest French territorial division for administrative purposes, governed by a *maire* and municipal council. 2. *C~*, body which usurped municipal government of Paris in 1789 and played a leading part in the Reign of Terror until suppressed in 1794; (also) communalistic government set up for a short time in Paris by an insurrection in 1871. 3. Communal division or settlement in Communist country.

commū'ne[2] (*or* kŏ-) *v.i.* Hold intimate intercourse *with*; (U.S.) receive Holy Communion.

commū'nicant *n.* 1. One who receives Holy Communion, esp. regularly. 2. One who imparts information.

commū'nicāte *v.* 1. Impart, transmit (*to*). 2. Receive, administer, Holy Communion (to). 3. Hold intercourse, transmit (by speech, writing, etc.). 4. (of spaces, rooms, etc.) Have common door or opening (*with*).

commūnicā'tion *n.* Imparting (esp. news); information given; intercourse; access or means of access, passage, connection by rail, road, telegraph, etc., between places; (mil., pl.) connection between base and front; ~ *cord*, alarm cord or chain in passenger train, partially braking it when pulled.

commū'nĭcative *adj.* Ready to impart; open; talkative.

commū'nĭcātor *n.* Person, thing, that communicates.

commū'nĭon (-yon) *n.* Sharing, participation; fellowship (esp. between branches of Catholic Church); body professing one faith; (*Holy*) *C*~, Eucharist; ~ *plate*, (R.C. Ch.) metal plate held under chin of communicant at reception of Holy Communion; ~ *rail*, rail in front of Communion table; ~ *table*, table used at Holy Communion.

commū'niqué (-kā) *n.* Official intimation or report.

cŏ'mmūnĭsm *n.* 1. Order of society in which property is owned in common (*primitive* ~). 2. Order of society in which the means of production, distribution, and exchange are to be owned in common and each member is to work according to his capacity and be paid according to his needs, the State having shed its coercive functions; this as the professed aim of the political parties which derive their doctrines from MARX, ENGELS, and LENIN. 3. Doctrines and activities of these parties regarded as an international movement (*international* ~). 4. Social order established in Russia by the Bolshevik party under Lenin after the revolution of 1917 (*Soviet* ~); similar social order established elsewhere. **cŏ'mmūnĭst** *adj.* & *n.* (Advocate) of communism. **cŏmmūnĭ'stĭc** *adj.*

commū'nĭtў *n.* 1. Joint or common ownership, liability, etc. 2. Identity of character, quality in common. 3. Social intercourse; life in association with others; body of people organized into political, municipal, or social unity; body of persons living in same locality, or with common race, religion, pursuits, etc., not shared by those among whom they live. 4. Body of persons living together and practising community of goods. 5. (ecol.) Association of organisms in a given area. 6. ~ *home*, centre for housing young offenders, replacing approved school or remand home; ~ *singing*, singing in chorus by large gathering of people.

cŏ'mmūnīze *v.t.* Make common property; make communistic.

commū'table *adj.* Exchangeable, convertible into money value. **commūtabĭ'lĭtў** *n.*

cŏmmūtā'tion *n.* Commuting; ~ *ticket*, (U.S.) season-ticket for travel.

commū'tatĭve *adj.* Relating to or involving substitution or interchange; ~ *justice*, justice in performing contracts or undertakings.

cŏ'mmūtātor *n.* Contrivance for altering course of electric current; ring-shaped fitting on dynamo or electric motor providing the brushes with a series of separate connections with different parts of the armature during each revolution and so enabling a dynamo to generate, or a motor to utilize, a direct current.

commū'te *v.* 1. Exchange, change, interchange; redeem obligation by money payment; change (punishment etc.) *for* (*to*, *into*) less severe one, or a fine; change (one kind of payment) *into*, *for*, another. 2. (orig. U.S.) Buy, use, a season-ticket; travel daily to and from work by any means of conveyance. **commū'ter** *n.*

cŏ'mpăct[1] *n.* Agreement or contract between parties.

compă'ct[2] *adj.* Closely or neatly packed together; dense, solid; condensed, terse; (archaic) framed, composed *of*, **compă'ctlў** *adv.* **compă'ctnėss** *n.* **cŏ'mpăct** *n.* (also *powder* ~) Small case containing mirror and face-powder, for carrying in handbag. **compă'ct** *v.t.* Join firmly together;

consolidate; compress, condense; devise, compose.

compă'nion[1] (-yon) *n.* 1. One who accompanies or associates with another; associate *in*, sharer *of*. 2. Member of lowest grade of order of knighthood. 3. Person (usu. woman) paid to live with another rather as friend or equal than as servant. 4. Thing that matches another (also as *adj.*, as ~ *picture*). ~ *v.* Accompany; consort *with*. **compă'nionable** *adj.* Sociable. **compă'nionablў** *adv.* **compă'nionablėness** *n.*

compă'nion[2] (-yon) *n.* (naut.) Raised frame on quarter-deck for lighting cabins etc. below; companion-way, companion-ladder; ~*-hatch*, wooden covering over companion-way; ~ *hatchway*, opening in deck leading to cabin; ~*-ladder*, ladder from deck to cabin; ~*-way*, staircase to cabin. [Du. *kompanje* quarter-deck, corresp. to It. (*camera della*) *compagna* pantry, caboose]

compă'nionate (-yon-) *adj.* ~ *marriage*; see MARRIAGE.

compă'nionship (-yon-) *n.* Fellowship; (print.) company of compositors working together.

co'mpanў (kŭ-) *n.* 1. Companionship; the society *of* others. 2. Number of individuals assembled together, person(s) with whom one usually associates; social party, guests. 3. Body of persons combined or incorporated for a common (esp. commercial) object; medieval trade guild, or a corporation historically representing this. 4. Association formed to carry on some commercial or industrial undertaking; partner or partners not named in title of firm (abbrev. Co.). 5. Party of actors etc.; actors associated together in a play or plays, or in a theatre. 6. (mil.) Subdivision of infantry battalion, usu. commanded by captain or major. 7. (naut.) Entire crew of ship. 8. ~ *promoter*: see PROMOTER; ~ *sergeant-major*, senior non-commissioned officer of company; ~ *union*, (U.S.) workers' union within a given company, unconnected with a trade union, and freq. managed by the employers. ~ *v.* (archaic) Accompany; consort *with*.

cŏ'mparable *adj.* That may be compared (*with*), worthy to be compared (*to*). **cŏmparabĭ'lĭtў** *n.* **cŏ'mparablў** *adv.*

compă'rative *adj.* 1. Of or involving comparison, esp. of different branches of a study, as ~ *anatomy*, *philology*, *religion*. 2. (gram., of an inflexional form of adjective or adverb, as *higher*, *faster*) Expressing a higher degree of the quality etc. denoted by the simple word. 3. Estimated by comparison; that is such when compared with something else implied or thought of. **compă'ratĭvelў** *adv.* **compă'ratĭve** *n.* (gram.) (Word in) the comparative degree.

compãr'e *v.* Liken, pronounce similar (*to*); estimate the similarity of (one thing *with*, *to*, another; two things together); bear comparison (*with*). ~ *n.* Comparison (chiefly in *beyond*, *past*, *without*, ~).

compă'rĭson *n.* Comparing; simile, illustration by comparing; (gram.) *degrees of* ~, positive, comparative, and superlative of adjectives or adverbs; ~ *microscope*, one enabling two objects to be seen as adjacent images.

compâr't *v.t.* Divide into compartments.

compâr'tment *n.* Division separated by partitions, esp. of railway carriage; water-tight division of ship; (pol.) separate portion of a Bill, or business in hand, for discussion of which a limit of parliamentary time is allowed by Government. **compârtmĕ'ntal** *adj.* **compârtmĕ'ntalīze** *v.t.* Separate into compartments (esp. fig.). **compârtmĕntalīzā'tion** *n.*

co'mpass (kŭ-) *n.* 1. (usu. pl., also *pair of compasses*) Instrument for taking measurements and describing circles, consisting of two legs connected at one end by movable joint. 2. Circumference, boundary; area, extent; range, esp. range of tones of a voice or musical instrument; (archaic) circular movement, round, detour. 3. Instrument for determining magnetic meridian, or one's direction or position with respect to it, consisting of a magnetized needle turning freely on a pivot; *box the* ~: see BOX²; GYRO, PRISMATIC, ~: see these words; *point of the* ~, any of the 32 equidistant points marked in a circle on the ~ *card*, to which the magnetized needle is attached with its pivot at the centre of the circle. 4. ~*-plane*, smoothing-plane with convex sole and iron, for planing concave surfaces; ~*-saw*, narrow saw for cutting curves. ~ *v.t.* 1. Go round; hem in. 2. Contrive, devise; accomplish, achieve.

compă'ssion *n.* Pity inclining one to spare or succour.

compă'ssionate *adj.* Feeling or showing compassion; granted out of compassion. **compă'ssionately̆** *adv.* **compă'ssionateness** *n.* **compă'ssionāte** *v.t.* Regard or treat with compassion.

compă'tĭble *adj.* Mutually tolerant; accordant, consistent, congruous; (television) of a system in which a colour transmission can be received in black and white on monochrome receivers. **compătĭbĭ'lĭty̆** *n.*

compă'trĭot *n.* Fellow countryman.

compeer' *n.* Equal, peer; comrade.

compĕ'l *v.t.* Constrain, force; bring about by force. **compĕ'llĭng** *adj.* (esp.) Arousing strong interest, respect, etc.

compĕ'ndĭous *adj.* Brief but comprehensive. **compĕ'ndĭously̆** *adv.* **compĕ'ndĭousnėss** *n.*

compĕ'ndĭum *n.* (pl. *-s*, *-ia*). Abridgement; summary; concise and comprehensive account or treatise; package of assorted games or stationery.

cŏ'mpėnsāte *v.* Counterbalance; make amends; recompense; provide with mechanical compensation, make up for (variations in a pendulum etc.); (elect.) neutralize one electromotive or magnetomotive force by another; (psychol.) counterbalance defect by development of some other characteristic. **cŏmpėnsā'tion** *n.* Compensating; recompense, amends; ~*-balance*, *-pendulum*, balance-wheel or pendulum in chronometer neutralizing effects of variations of temperature. **compĕ'nsatĭve, co'mpĕnsatory̆** *adjs.* **cŏ'mpėnsātor** *n.*

cŏ'mpère (-pār) *n.* Organizer of variety entertainment who introduces artists, comments on turns, etc. ~ *v.* Act as compère (to). [Fr., = 'godfather', 'gossip']

compē'te *v.i.* Strive (*with* another, *for* or *in* something), vie (*with*), contend (*for*).

cŏ'mpėtence, cŏ'mpėtency̆ *ns.* Sufficiency of means for living, easy circumstances; ability (*to* do, *for* a task); (of court, magistrate, etc.) legal capacity, right to take cognizance.

cŏ'mpėtent *adj.* Adequate, sufficient; properly or legally qualified; belonging *to*, permissible, admissible. **cŏ'mpėtently̆** *adv.*

cŏmpėtĭ'tion *n.* Act of competing (*for*) by examination etc.; rivalry in market, striving for custom; contest, esp. for supremacy or prize.

compĕ'tĭtĭve *adj.* Of, by, offered for, competition. **compĕ'tĭtĭvely̆** *adv.*

compĕ'tĭtor *n.* One who competes, rival.

compĭlā'tion *n.* Compiling; thing compiled.

compī'le *v.t.* Collect (materials) into a volume; make up (volume) of such materials; (cricket slang) score (number of runs).

complā'cence, complā'cency̆ *ns.* Tranquil pleasure; self-satisfaction.

complā'cent *adj.* Self-satisfied. **complā'cently̆** *adv.*

complai'n *v.i.* Express dissatisfaction or discontent, murmur; let it be known that one is suffering (from illness etc.); make formal complaint of grievance *to* or *before* competent authority. **complai'nant** *n.* One who complains; plaintiff or prosecutor in Chancery or ecclesiastical courts.

complai'nt *n.* 1. Utterance of grievance. 2. Formal accusation; (U.S.) plaintiff's case in civil action. 3. Subject, ground, of complaint. 4. Bodily ailment.

complai′sance (-z-) *n.* Obligingness, politeness; deference. **cŏmplai′sant** *adj.*

cŏ′mplėment *n.* 1. What completes; (gram.) word(s) joined to another to complete the sense (esp. of predicate); (math.) ~ *of an angle*, angular amount which would make up a given angle to 90°. 2. Full quantity or number required, esp. to man a ship. **cŏ′mplėmĕnt** *v.t.* Complete; form complement to.

cŏmplėmĕ′ntal *adj.* Forming a complement, completing. **cŏmplėmĕ′ntallў** *adv.*

cŏmplėmĕ′ntarў *adj.* Forming a complement, completing; (of two or more things) mutually complementing each other; ~ *angle*, either of two angles which together make 90°.

complē′te *adj.* Having all its parts; entire; finished; thorough, unqualified; (archaic, of persons) accomplished. **complē′telў** *adv.* **complē′tenėss** *n.* **complē′te** *v.t.* Finish; make whole or perfect; make up the amount of. **complē′tion** *n.*

cŏ′mplĕx *n.* 1. Whole consisting of several parts. 2. (psychol.) Group of related ideas or memories of strongly emotional character which have undergone repression; (loosely) fixed mental tendency or obsession; INFERIORITY ~, OEDIPUS ~ : see these words. ~ *adj.* Consisting of parts, composite; complicated; (gram.) ~ *sentence*, one containing subordinate clause(s). **cŏ′mplĕxlў** *adv.* **complĕ′xitў** *n.*

complĕ′xion (-kshon) *n.* Natural colour, texture, and appearance of skin (esp. of face); character, aspect. **complĕ′xioned** (-nd) *adj.* Having a (specified) complexion.

complī′ance *n.* Action in accordance with request, demand, etc.; base submission; *in ~ with*, according to; *out of ~*, (of trade unionist) so far behind with dues as to forfeit membership.

complī′ant *adj.* Disposed to comply, yielding. **complī′antlў** *adv.*

cŏ′mplĭcacў *n.* Complexity.

cŏ′mplĭcāte *v.t.* Mix up *with* in intricate or involved way; make complex or intricate; *complicated fracture*, fracture of bone with damage to blood vessel, nerve, etc.

cŏmplĭcā′tion *n.* Involved condition; entangled state of affairs; complicating circumstance.

complĭ′citў *n.* Partnership in an evil action.

cŏ′mplĭment *n.* Polite expression of praise, act equivalent to this; (pl.) formal greetings. **cŏ′mplĭmĕnt** *v.t.* Pay compliment to (person *or* something); present *with* as mark of courtesy. **cŏmplĭmĕ′ntarў** *adj.* Expressive of, conveying, compliment; (of tickets etc.) presented as a courtesy.

cŏ′mplĭne *n.* (R.C. Ch.) Last canonical HOUR.

complȳ′ *v.i.* Act in accordance (*with*).

cŏ′mpō *n.* Composition (material), esp. = stucco, plaster.

compō′nent *adj.* Contributing to the composition of a whole. ~ *n.* Component part.

compôr′t *v.* Conduct, behave (oneself); agree, accord, *with*.

compō′se (-z) *v.t.* 1. Make up, constitute. 2. Construct in words; produce in literary form; (mus.) invent and put into proper form; set to music. 3. (print.) Set up (type); set up in type; *composing room*, room in which type is set up; *composing stick*, compositor's metal or wooden tray of adjustable width in which type is set. 4. Put together so as to form a whole; arrange artistically. 5. Settle, arrange; adjust (oneself, one's features, etc.) in specified or understood manner, or for specified purpose; tranquillize. **compō′sėdlў** *adv.* **compō′sėdnėss** *n.*

compō′ser (-z-) *n.* One who composes (usu. music).

cŏ′mposĭte (-z-) *adj.* 1. Made up of various parts, compound. 2. (archit., *C~*) Of the 5th classical order, of Ionic and Corinthian mixed. 3. (bot.) Of the natural order Compositae, in which what is pop. called the flower is a close head of many small flowers sessile on a common receptacle and surrounded by a common involucre of bracts, as daisy, dandelion, etc. **cŏ'mposĭtelȳ** *adv.* **cŏ'mposĭtenėss** *n.* **cŏ'mposĭte** *n.* Composite thing or plant.

cŏmposi'tion (-z-) *n.* 1. Putting together; formation, construction; formation of words into compound. 2. Construction of sentences, art of literary production; composing of music. 3. Setting up of type. 4. Arrangement (of the parts of a picture etc.); thing composed; piece of music or writing. 5. Compromise; agreement for paying, payment, of sum of money in lieu of other obligation etc., esp. agreement by which creditor accepts portion of debt from insolvent debtor; sum of money paid thus. 6. Compound artificial substance, esp. one substituted for natural substance.

compŏ'sĭtor (-z-) *n.* (see COMPOSE *v.* 3) Typesetter.

cŏ'mpos mĕ'ntĭs. In one's right mind. [L]

cŏ'mpŏst *n.* Mixture of various natural fertilizing ingredients, compound manure. ~ *v.t.* Treat with, make into, compost.

compō'sure (-zh*er*) *n.* Tranquil demeanour, calmness.

cŏmpotā'tion *n.* Drinking together, drinking-bout.

cŏ'mpōte *n.* Fruit preserved or cooked in syrup.

compou'nd[1] *v.* 1. Mix; combine (verbal elements) into word; make up (a composite whole). 2. Settle (matter) by mutual concession, (debt) by partial payment, (subscription, obligation) by payment of lump sum etc.; condone (liability, offence) for money etc.; come to terms *with* (person); ~ *a felony*, forbear prosecution for private motive. **cŏ'mpound** *adj.* Made up of several ingredients, consisting of several parts; combined, collective; (zool., bot.) consisting of a combination of organisms or simple parts; ~ *eye*, (in insects and crustaceans), eye consisting of numerous minute simple eyes bound together; ~ *fracture*, fracture of bone associated with skin wound; ~ *interest*; see INTEREST; ~ *interval*, (mus.) interval greater than an octave, i.e. consisting of simple interval plus octave. ~ *n.* 1. (mainly fig.) Mixture of elements; compound thing, esp. word. 2. (chem.) Substance which consists of elements chemically united in fixed proportions and has properties different from those of its components.

cŏ'mpound[2] *n.* In India, China, etc., enclosure round house, factory, etc. [perh. f. Malay *kampong*]

cŏmprėhĕ'nd *v.t.* Grasp mentally, understand; include, take in.

cŏmprėhĕ'nsĭble *adj.* That may be understood, or comprised. **cŏmprėhĕ'nsĭblȳ** *adv.* **cŏmprėhĕnsĭbĭ'lĭtȳ** *n.*

cŏmprėhĕ'nsion *n.* Understanding; inclusion; ecclesiastical inclusion, esp. of nonconformists within established Church by enlarging terms of ecclesiastical communion.

cŏmprėhĕ'nsĭve *adj.* 1. Of understanding. 2. Including much; of secondary school or educational system providing for children of all levels of intellectual and other ability. ~ *n.* Comprehensive school. **cŏmprėhĕ'nsĭvelȳ** *adv.* **cŏmprėhĕ'nsĭvenėss** *n.*

comprĕ'ss *v.t.* Squeeze together; force into smaller volume, condense. **comprĕ'ssĭve, comprĕ'ssĭble** *adjs.* **comprĕssĭbĭ'lĭtȳ** *n.* **cŏ'mprĕss** *n.* Soft pad of lint etc. for compressing artery etc.; wet cloth applied to relieve inflammation.

comprĕ'ssion *n.* Act of compressing or state of being compressed; in internal combustion engines, act of compressing the explosive mixture after admission to the engine and before combustion; ~ *ratio*, (in internal combustion engines) ratio of volume of charge, when compressed by engine to its volume at entry.

comprĕ'ssor *n.* Mechanical device for reducing the volume taken up by a quantity of gas.

comprī'se (-z) *v.t.* Include, comprehend; consist of; condense.

cŏ'mpromīse (-z) *n.* Settlement of dispute by mutual concession; adjustment of conflicting opinions, courses, etc., by modification of each. ~ *v.* Settle (dispute) by mutual concession; make compromise; bring under suspicion, into danger, by indiscreet action.

cŏmprovi'ncial (-shl) *adj.* & *n.* (Bishop) of same archiepiscopal province.

Cŏ'mpton, Arthur Holly (1892–1962). Amer. physicist; Nobel Prize for physics 1927.

comptrō'ller (kont-) *n.* Erroneous spelling of CONTROLLER, retained in some official titles, esp. ~ *of accounts.*

compŭ'lsion *n.* Constraint, obligation; (psychol.) strong, usu. irresistible urge to act in a certain way, esp. against one's better judgement.

compŭ'lsive *adj.* Tending to compel; (psychol.) done under stress of compulsion. **compŭ'lsivelў** *adv.*

compŭ'lsorў *adj.* Enforced, obligatory; compelling, coercive. **compŭ'lsorilў** *adv.* **compŭ'lsorinėss** *n.*

compŭ'nction *n.* Pricking of conscience; feeling of regret. **compŭ'nctious** (-sh*us*) *adj.* **compŭ'nctiouslў** *adv.*

cŏmpurgā'tion *n.* Clearing from charge or accusation by the oaths of others. **cŏ'mpurgātor** *n.* (hist.) Witness who swore to innocence or character of the person accused. **compur'gatorў** *adj.*

compū'te *v.t.* Reckon. **compū'table** (*or* kŏm'-) *adj.* **cŏmpūtā'tion** *n.*

compū'ter *n.* Person who computes; electronic apparatus for making calculations; *analogue* ~, one that solves numerical problems by using a physically measurable quantity (e.g. weight, length, voltage) to represent numbers; *digital* ~, one that uses digits. **compū'terīze** *v.t.* Calculate by means of an electronic computer; instal computer(s). **compūterīzā'tion** *n.*

cŏ'mrade (*or* kŭm-) *n.* Mate or fellow in work or play or fighting, equal with whom one is on familiar terms; (as title) used by socialists, communists, etc., before surname to avoid such titles as 'Mr'; hence, fellow socialist or communist.

cŏ'mstŏckerў (*or* kŭ-) *n.* Excessive opposition to or censorship of supposed immorality in art or literature. [Anthony *Comstock* (1844–1915), U.S. neo-Puritan]

Comte (kawnt), Auguste (1798–1857). French philosopher, founder of the POSITIVIST system. **Co'mtism, Co'mtist** *ns.*

cŏn[1] *v.t.* Peruse, scrutinize, learn (by heart).

cŏn[2] *v.t.* Direct steering of (ship) from commanding position on shipboard.

cŏn[3] *n.* (attrib.) Confidence, esp. in (U.S.) *~-game, -man.* ~ *v.t.* Swindle by confidence trick.

cŏn[4] *adv.* & *n.* (Argument) against a proposition etc.; *pros and ~s,* arguments for and against.

con- *prefix.* With.

cŏn amor'ė. With enthusiasm. [It.]

conā'tion *n.* (philos.) Desire and volition; exertion of will, striving. **cŏ'native** *adj.* (philos.) Of, involving, conation; (gram.) expressing endeavour.

cŏn brio (brē'ō). (mus.) With spirit. [It.]

concă'tėnāte *v.t.* Link together (fig.). **concătėnā'tion** *n.*

cŏ'ncāve (*or* -kā'v) *adj.* Having outline or surface curved like

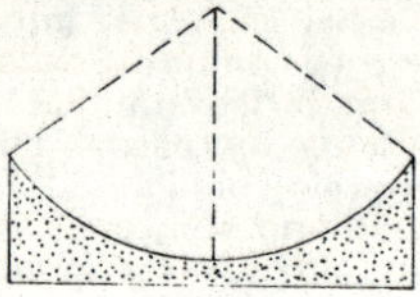

CONCAVE

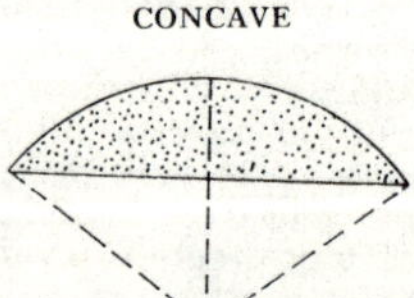

CONVEX

interior of circle or sphere (cf. CONVEX); hollow. **cŏ'ncāvelў** *adv.* **cŏ'ncāve** *n.* Concave surface. **concă'vitў** *n.* Being concave; concave surface; hollow, cavity.

cŏncā'vō- *prefix.* Concavely, concave and . . ., as *~-concave*, concave on both sides, *~-convex*, concave on one side, convex the other.

concea'l *v.t.* Keep secret; hide. **concea'lment** *n.*

concē'de *v.t.* Admit, allow, grant.

concei't *n.* 1. Personal vanity. 2. Fanciful notion, far-fetched comparison, etc. 3. Favourable opinion, esteem (only in *out of ~ with*); *in one's own ~*, in one's private opinion or estimation. **concei'tėd** *adj.* Vain. **concei't-ėdlў** *adv.*

concei'vable *adj.* That can be (mentally) conceived. **concei'vablў** *adv.*

concei've *v.* 1. Become pregnant (with). 2. Form in the mind, imagine; fancy, think. 3. Formulate, express in words, etc.

cŏ'ncentrāte *v.* Bring to or towards a common centre; focus (attention), keep mind or attention intently fixed (*on*); increase strength of (solution etc.) esp. by evaporation of solvent etc.; *co'ncentrated*, (fig.) intense. *~ n.* Concentrated substance. **cŏncentrā'tion** *n.* *~ camp*, camp in which large numbers of people, esp. political prisoners, are detained by force.

concĕ'ntre *v.* Bring, come, to a common centre.

concĕ'ntric *adj.* Having a common centre. **concĕ'ntricallў** *adv.* **cŏncĕntri'citў** *n.*

cŏ'ncĕpt *n.* Idea of a class of objects, general notion.

concĕ'ptacle *n.* (bot.) Hollow organ of some brown seaweeds, within which sexual organs are formed.

concĕ'ption *n.* Conceiving; thing conceived; idea. **concĕ'ptional** *adj.* Of, like, a conception or idea.

concĕ'ptive *adj.* Conceiving; of conception.

concĕ'ptual *adj.* Of mental conceptions.

concĕ'ptūalism *n.* 1. Scholastic doctrine that universals have reality, but only as mental concepts. 2. Psychological doctrine that the mind is capable of forming ideas corresponding to abstract and general terms. **concĕ'ptūalist** *n.*

concer'n *v.t.* Relate to, affect; interest (oneself). **concer'ned** (-nd) *adj.* (esp.) Involved; troubled. **concer'ning** *prep.* Regarding, relating to. **concer'n** *n.* Relation, reference; interest, solicitous regard, anxiety; matter that affects one; business, firm; (colloq.) thing; (pl.) affairs.

concer'nment *n.* Affair, business; importance; being concerned (*with*); anxiety.

cŏ'ncert *n.* 1. Agreement; union by mutual agreement; *C~ of Europe*, chief powers of Europe acting together. 2. Combination of voices or sounds. 3. Musical entertainment; *~ grand*, grand piano of largest size for concerts; *~ pitch*, state of unusual efficiency or readiness [f. custom of using a pitch slightly higher than the ordinary at concerts for brilliancy of effect]. **concer't** *v.t.* Arrange by mutual agreement. **concer'tėd** *adj.* Contrived, pre-arranged; done in concert; (mus.) arranged in parts for voices or instruments.

cŏncerti'na (-ēna) *n.* Portable musical instrument consisting of bellows with a set of finger-studs at each end controlling the valves which admit wind to the free metallic reeds. *~ v.* Shut up like a concertina.

concer'tō (-ch-; *or* -ār-) *n.* (pl. *-os*). Musical composition, usu. in sonata form with three or four movements, for a solo instrument (or, rarely, more than one) accompanied by orchestra.

concĕ'ssion *n.* Conceding; thing conceded; esp. grant of land, trading rights, etc., land or rights so granted, by Government to State, company, or person. **concĕ'ssionarў** *adj.*

concĕssionair'e *n.* Holder of concession, grant, etc., esp. of monopoly given by Government to foreigner.

concĕ'ssĭve *adj.* Of, tending to, concession; (gram.) expressing concession.

cŏnch (*or* -k) *n.* 1. Shellfish; (now usu.) large gasteropod; shell of mollusc, esp. spiral shell of any large gasteropod; such a shell used as a trumpet, esp. (Rom. myth.) of Triton. 2. (archit.) Domed roof of semicircular apse. 3. External ear, its central concavity.

cŏnchi'ferous (-k-) *adj.* Shell-bearing.

cŏnchŏ'logy̆ (-k-) *n.* Study of shells and shellfish.

cŏ'nchy (-shĭ) *n.* (slang) Conscientious objector.

concierge (kawṅsiār'zh) *n.* In France etc., door-keeper, porter, of block of flats or other building.

concĭ'liar *adj.* Of a council (esp. ecclesiastical) or its proceedings.

concĭ'liāte *v.t.* Gain (goodwill, esteem, etc.) by acts which pacify, soothe, etc.; gain over, overcome distrust or hostility of. **concĭliā'tion** *n.* Reconcilement; use of conciliatory measures. **concĭ'liatĭve, concĭ'liatory̆** *adjs.*

concī'se *adj.* Brief and comprehensive in expression. **concī'sely̆** *adv.* **concī'seness** *n.*

concĭ'sion *n.* 1. Mutilation; in Phil. 3:2 = circumcision. 2. Conciseness.

cŏ'nclāve *n.* Meeting-place, assembly, of cardinals for election of pope; private assembly.

conclu'de (-o͞od) *v.* Bring to an end, make an end; come to an end; settle, arrange (treaty etc.); infer; come to a conclusion; resolve.

conclu'sion (-o͞o-) *n.* Termination; final result; inference; decision; (logic) proposition deduced from previous ones, esp. last of three forming a syllogism; settling, arrangement (*of* peace etc.).

conclu'sĭve (-o͞o-) *adj.* Decisive, convincing. **conclu'sĭvely̆** *adv.* **conclu'sĭveness** *n.*

concŏ'ct *v.t.* Make up by mixing variety of ingredients; fabricate. **concŏ'ction** *n.*

concŏ'mĭtance, -cy̆ *n.* Being concomitant, coexistence, esp. of body and blood of Christ in each of Eucharistic elements.

concŏ'mĭtant *adj.* Going together, accompanying. ~ *n.* Accompanying state, quality, thing, etc. **concŏm'ĭtantly̆** *adv.*

cŏ'ncord *n.* 1. Agreement, harmony, between persons or things; treaty. 2. (mus.) Combination of notes satisfactory to the ear, requiring no resolution or following chord. 3. (gram.) Formal agreement between words in gender, number, etc.

concor'dance *n.* 1. Agreement, harmony. 2. Alphabetical arrangement of chief words or subjects occurring in a book (esp. the Bible) or in an author's works, with citations of passages concerned.

concor'dant *adj.* Agreeing, harmonious; in musical concord. **concor'dantly̆** *adv.*

concor'dăt *n.* Agreement between pope and secular government for settlement and control of ecclesiastical affairs.

cŏ'ncourse (-ors) *n.* 1. Flocking together; crowd, confluence; assemblage. 2. (orig. U.S.) Large main hall, or central open space, of building, or (esp.) railway station.

cŏ'ncrēte *adj.* 1. (gram., of noun) Denoting a thing as opp. to a quality, state, or action; not abstract. 2. Existing in material form, real. 3. Made of concrete. 4. ~ *music*, music constructed by arrangement of recorded sounds into a sequence; ~ *poetry*, poetry in which the effect depends upon pattern of printed material. **cŏ'ncrētely̆** *adv.* **cŏ'ncrēte** *n.* 1. Concrete thing. 2. Composition of stone chippings, sand, gravel, etc., formed into a mass with cement and used for building, paving, etc. **concrē'te** *v.* 1. Form into a mass, solidify. 2. (kŏ'-) Treat, build, pave, etc., with concrete.

concrē'tion *n.* Coalescence; concrete mass, esp. (path.) hard morbid formation in body, stone; (geol.) mass formed by aggregation of solid particles, usu. round a nucleus. **concrē'tionary̆** *adj.*

concū'bĭnage (-n-k-) *n.* Cohabiting of man and woman not legally married; being, having, a concubine.

cŏ'ncūbīne *n.* Woman who cohabits with man, not being his wife; (among polygamous peoples) secondary wife.

concū'piscence (-n-k-) *n.* Sexual appetite. **concū'piscent** *adj.* Lustful, eagerly desirous.

concûr' (-n-k-) *v.i.* Coincide; co-operate; agree, express agreement, (*with*). **concŭ'rrence** *n.*

concŭ'rrent (-n-k-) *adj.* 1. Running together, going on side by side, occurring together; meeting in or tending to same point. 2. Co-operating; agreeing. 3. (law) Covering same ground; having authority or jurisdiction in same matters. 4. ~ *insurance, policy,* etc., one of which various companies have accepted definite proportions of the risk on precisely similar terms; ~ *lease,* lease made before another has expired. ~ *n.* Concurrent circumstance. **concŭ'rrently** *adv.*

concŭ'ss (-n-k-) *v.t.* Shake violently, agitate; intimidate, coerce; *be concussed,* (colloq.) suffer concussion of brain.

concŭ'ssion (-n-k-) *n.* 1. Violent shaking; shock. 2. Injury caused to brain, spine, etc., by shock of heavy blow, fall, etc.

condĕ'mn (-m) *v.t.* 1. Censure, blame; bring about conviction of. 2. Give judicial sentence against, find guilty; sentence (*to* death etc.); (fig., esp. pass.) doom *to* some (unkind) fate or condition. 3. Pronounce forfeited, as smuggled goods, etc.; pronounce unfit for use or consumption. **condĕ'mnable** (-m-n-) *adj.*

cŏndėmnā'tion *n.* Censure; judicial conviction; ground for condemning. **condĕ'mnatorў** *adj.*

cŏndĕnsā'tion *n.* Condensing; condensed mass; liquid formed by condensed gas or vapour.

condĕ'nse *v.* 1. Increase density of, reduce in volume; compress, thicken, concentrate; *condensed milk,* milk thickened by evaporation and sweetened. 2. Compress into few words. 3. Reduce, be reduced, from form of gas or vapour to liquid.

condĕ'nser *n.* (esp.) 1. Chamber in steam-engine in which steam is condensed on leaving cylinder. 2. Arrangement of two (or two sets of) plates separated by insulating substance for increasing capacity of a conductor or for temporary accumulation of electricity. 3. Lens, system of lenses, for concentrating light.

condĕ'nserў *n.* Factory for making condensed milk.

cŏndėscĕ'nd *v.i.* Deign, stoop; be condescending, waive one's superiority. **cŏndėscĕ'nding** *adj.* (esp.) Making a show of condescension, patronizing. **cŏndėscĕ'ndinglў** *adv.*

cŏndėscĕ'nsion *n.* Affability to inferiors; patronizing manner.

condi'gn (-īn) *adj.* (of punishment) Adequate, appropriate. **condi'gnlў** *adv.*

cŏ'ndiment *n.* Seasoning for food.

condĭ'tion *n.* 1. Stipulation; thing upon fulfilment of which depends that of something else; ~ *precedent,* condition which must be fulfilled before right, title, etc., conferred by will or other legal document can take effect. 2. (pl.) Circumstances, esp. those essential to a thing's existence. 3. State of being; *in* ~, *out of* ~, in good, bad, training and health. 4. (U.S.) Subject in qualifying examination in which student has failed to pass, though he is allowed to proceed to next academic stage if he passes in this subject within a certain time. ~ *v.t.* 1. Stipulate; agree by stipulation (*to*). 2. Subject to as a condition; govern, qualify, limit, as a condition, be the (precedent) condition of; (pass.) be conditional on. 3. (U.S.) Subject to or admit under conditions (sense 3). 4. Bring into (good) condition (*for*). 5. Train to adopt certain habits etc. **condĭ'tioned** (-nd) *adj.* (esp.) ~ *reflex,* reflex or reflex action which through habit or training has been induced to follow a stimulus which is not naturally associated with it.

condĭ'tional *adj.* 1. Not absolute; dependent. 2. (gram.) Of a clause, mood, conjunction, phrase, expressing or introducing a condition. **condĭ'tionallў** *adv.*

condō'le *v.i.* Express sympathy (*with* person *upon* loss etc.). **condō'lence** (*or* kŏ'ndo-) *n.*

cŏndomĭ'nium *n.* Joint control of a State's affairs vested in two or more other States; territory so governed.

condō'ne *v.t.* Forgive, overlook (offence, esp. violation of marriage vow); cause condonation of. **cŏndonā'tion** *n.*

cŏ'ndor *n.* 1. Large S. Amer. vulture, *Vultur gryphus*, with blackish plumage and fleshy ex-

crescence falling over bill; *California* ~, great Californian vulture, *Cathartes californianus*, somewhat resembling this. 2. $\frac{1}{100}$ of an escudo in Chile.

cŏndŏttier'e (-tyārĭ) *n.* (pl. *-ri*, pr. -rē). Leader of troop of mercenaries in late Middle Ages.

condū'ce *v.i.* (usu. of events) Lead, contribute, *to*. **condū'cĭve** *adj.*

condŭ'ct *v.* 1. Lead, guide *to*. 2. Command (army); direct (orchestra, concert, etc.); manage (business etc.). 3. Behave (*oneself*). 4. (phys.; of a body) Convey (some form of energy, as heat, electricity, etc.) through its particles, transmit. **cŏ'nduct** *n.* Manner of conducting (any business etc., or oneself), behaviour; ~ *money*, money paid for travelling expenses (of witness to place of trial, of seamen for navy to place of embarkation, or (hist.) of men furnished by a hundred to serve in king's army to rendezvous at the coast).

condŭ'ctance *n.* (elect.) Conducting power of a specified conductor.

condŭ'ction *n.* Conducting (of liquid through a pipe etc.); transmission (of heat, electricity, etc.).

condŭ'ctĭve *adj.* Having the property of conducting some form of energy, esp. electricity. **cŏnductĭ'vĭtў** *n.*

condŭ'ctor *n.* 1. Leader, guide; manager. 2. Director of orchestra or chorus, who indicates to the performers the rhythm, expression, etc., by motions of a baton or the hands. 3. (fem. *condu'ctrĕss*) Official in charge of passengers on bus, tram, or (U.S.) train. 4. Thing that conducts or transmits (some form of energy); ~-*rail*, in electric traction, rail through which current is supplied.

cŏ'nduit (-dĭt; *or* kŭ-) *n.* Channel or pipe for conveying water or other liquids; tube or trough for receiving and protecting electric wires; ~-*pipe*, conduit in form of a pipe.

cŏ'ndўle *n.* (anat.) Rounded process at end of bone, forming articulation with another bone. **cŏ'ndўloid** *adj.*

Cŏ'ndў's flu'ĭd (-z, -ōō-). Solution containing sodium manganate and permanganate, formerly used as disinfectant. [H. B. *Condy*, English physician]

cōne *n.* 1. Solid figure or body of which the base is a circle (or other curved figure) and the summit a point, and every point in the intervening surface is in a straight line between the vertex and the circumference of the base; any conical mass. 2. Fruit of pine or fir, a dry, scaly multiple fruit, more or less cone-shaped, formed by hard persistent imbricated scales covering naked seeds. 3. Cone-shaped object; marine shell of genus *Conus*

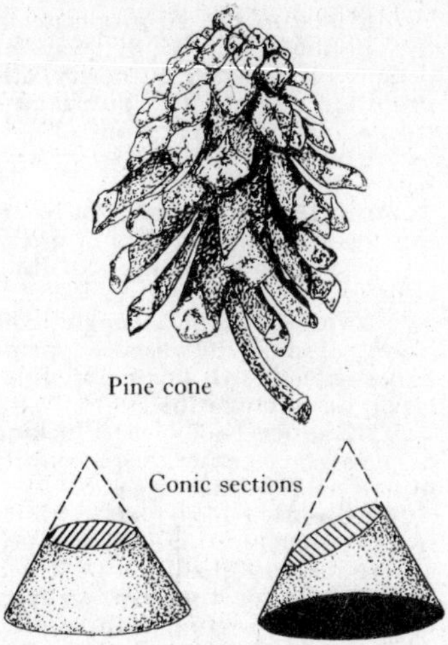

CONES

of gasteropods; cone-shaped building; cone-shaped mountain-peak, esp. volcanic peak; (meteor.) cone-shaped vessel hoisted as foul-weather signal or to indicate direction of wind; (physiol.) one of the minute, cone-shaped bodies which form, with rods, one of the layers of nerve elements in the retina. 4. *co'ne-flower*, garden plant of genus *Rudbeckia*, native in N. America. ~ *v.t.* Catch or trap (aircraft) in a cone of searchlights.

Cŏnėstō'ga *n.* (Member of) tribe of N. Amer. Indians formerly inhabiting parts of Pennsylvania and Maryland; ~ *wagon*, heavy, broad-wheeled, covered travelling-wagon. [*Conestoga* (= 'place of muddy water'), Pennsylvania]

cŏ'nfăb *n.* (colloq.) Confabulation. ~ *v.i.* Confabulate.

confă'būlāte *v.i.* Converse, chat. **confăbūlā'tion** *n.*

confĕ'ction *n.* 1. Mixing, compounding. 2. Medicinal preparation compounded with sweetening and preserving agent; prepared dish or delicacy; sweet, comfit. 3. Fashionable or elegant article of women's dress.

confĕ'ctioner *n.* Maker or seller of sweets, pastry, etc. **confĕ'ctionerў** *n.* Things made or sold by a confectioner; confectioner's shop; confectioner's art.

confĕ'deracў *n.* 1. League, alliance; league for unlawful or evil purpose; conspiracy. 2. Body of allies, esp. union of States; (*Southern*) *C*~, Confederate States of America.

confĕ'derate *adj.* Allied; *C*~ *States* (of America), the eleven States and territories which seceded from the Union in 1861 and fought the others (*Federal States*) in the AMERICAN Civil War until defeated by them in 1865. ~ *n.* 1. Ally, esp. in bad sense, accomplice. 2. *C*~, supporter of the Confederate States of America. **confĕ'derāte** *v.* Bring, come, into alliance (*with*). **confĕderā'tion** *n.* (Union formed by) confederating.

confer' *v.* 1. Grant, bestow (title, degree, favour, etc., *on*). 2. Converse, take counsel (*with*). **confer'ment** *n.* Bestowing, granting.

cŏ'nference *n.* Consultation; meeting, for consultation or discussion; annual assembly of Methodist Church, constituting its central governing body.

confĕ'ss *v.* Acknowledge, own, admit; make formal confession of sins, esp. to a priest; (of priest) hear confession of (a penitent). **confĕ'ssėdlў** *adv.*

confĕ'ssion *n.* Acknowledgement, admission (of fact, guilt, etc.); acknowledgement of sin made by congregation in liturgical worship, or by individual penitent (usu. in private to a priest); thing confessed; *C*~ (*of Faith*). formulary in which Church or body of Christians sets forth religious doctrines which it considers essential, a creed.

confĕ'ssional *adj.* Of confession. ~ *n.* Cabinet or stall in which priest sits to hear confession.

confĕ'ssor *n.* 1. One who makes confession. 2. One who avows his religion in the face of danger and persecution, but does not suffer martyrdom; *the C~*, King EDWARD[1] the Confessor. 3. Priest who hears confession.

confĕ'ttĭ *n.pl.* Small pieces of coloured paper, used as missiles in carnival, thrown at bride and bridegroom at weddings, etc. [It., = 'sweetmeats']

cŏnfĭdă'nt *n.* (fem. *confidante*) Person trusted with private affair.

confī'de *v.* Repose confidence *in*; impart (secret *to*); entrust (*to*); ~ *in*, talk confidentially to.

cŏ'nfidence *n.* 1. Firm trust; assured expectation. 2. Boldness, fearlessness; impudence, presumption. 3. Imparting of private matters; thing so imparted. 4. ~ *game, trick*, etc., swindle worked by practising on the confidence or trust of a credulous person; ~ *man*, one who practises this trick.

cŏ'nfĭdent *adj.* Trusting, fully assured; bold; impudent. **cŏ'nfĭdentlў** *adv.*

cŏnfĭdĕ'ntial (-shal) *adj.* Spoken, written, in confidence; entrusted with secrets; charged with secret service. **confĭdĕ'ntiallў** *adv.*

configūrā'tion *n.* Mode of arrangement, conformation, outline; (astron.) relative position of planet or other celestial bodies.

cŏ'nfīne *n.* (usu. pl.) Borderland, boundaries. **confī'ne** *v.* Keep *within, to,* limits; imprison, immure; (pass.) be in childbirth. **confī'nement** *n.* Imprisonment; restriction, limitation; childbirth.

confîr'm *v.t.* 1. Establish more firmly; ratify; corroborate; establish, encourage (person *in* opinion etc.). 2. Administer religious rite of confirmation to. **confîr'mative, confîr'matorў** *adjs.*

cŏnfirmă'nd *n.* Candidate for confirmation.

cŏnfirmā'tion *n.* 1. Confirming, corroboration. 2. Rite administered to baptized persons in various Christian Churches; in Church of England, rite in which baptized persons renew and ratify their baptismal vows and are then admitted to the full privileges of the Church.

cŏ'nfĭscāte *v.t.* Appropriate to the public treasury by way of penalty; seize as by authority, appropriate summarily. **cŏnfĭscā'tion** *n.* **confĭ'scatorў** *adj.*

cŏnflagrā'tion *n.* Great and destructive fire.

conflā'te *v.t.* Fuse together, esp. two variant readings of a text into a composite reading. **conflā'tion** *n.*

cŏ'nflict *n.* Fight, struggle; collision; clashing (*of* opposed principles etc.). **conflĭ'ct** *v.i.* Struggle; clash, be incompatible.

cŏ'nfluence (-lo͞o-) *n.* Flocking or flowing together, esp. joining of two or more streams etc.

cŏ'nfluent (-lo͞o-) *adj.* Flowing together, uniting; ~ *smallpox*, severe form of smallpox in which vesicles run together esp. on face. ~ *n.* Stream uniting with another of approximately equal size.

cŏ'nflŭx *n.* Confluence.

confôr'm *v.* Form according to a pattern, make similar (*to*); adapt *oneself to*; comply with, be conformable (*to*).

confôr'mable *adj.* Similar (*to*); consistent, adapted (*to*); tractable. **confôrmabĭ'lĭtў** *n.* **confôr'mablў** *adv.*

confôr'mal *adj.* (math.) Conserving size of all angles in representing one surface upon another.

cŏnformā'tion *n.* 1. Conforming, adaptation. 2. Manner in which thing is formed, structure.

confôr'mist *n.* One who conforms, esp. to usages of Church of England.

confôr'mĭtў *n.* Likeness (*to, with*); compliance (*with, to*).

confou'nd *v.t.* 1. Defeat utterly, discomfit (archaic); overthrow, defeat (plan, hope); (bibl.) put to shame. 2. Throw into perplexity; throw into disorder; mix up; confuse (in idea). 3. Damn, esp. in mild oath (as ~ *it*). **confou'ndėdlў** *adv.* Damnably.

cŏnfratêr'nĭtў *n.* Brotherhood (esp. religious or charitable); body of men.

cŏ'nfrère (-ār) *n.* Fellow member of profession etc.

confro'nt (-ŭnt) *v.t.* Meet face

to face, stand facing; be opposite to; face in hostility or defiance; oppose; bring (person) face to face *with* (accusers etc.); compare. **confrontā'tion** *n.*

Confū'cius (-sh*us*) (*c* 550–478 B.C.). Chinese philosopher whose sayings relating mainly to tem-

poral and secular matters were recorded by his followers. **Confū'cian** (-sh*an*) *adj.* & *n.* (Follower) of Confucius. **Confū'cianism** *n.* System of cosmology, politics, and ethics evolved in China during the Han dynasty (206 B.C.–A.D. 220), which regarded the emperor and the hierarchy of officials as divinely appointed, and social relations as governed by the rules of Confucius. [Latinized f. Chin. *K'ung-fu-tzŭ* or *K'ung-fu-tse* K'ung the master (or philosopher)]

cŏn fuō'cō (fw-). (mus.) With fire. [It.]

confū'se (-z) *v.t.* Throw into disorder; mix up in the mind; abash, perplex. **confū'sėdlȳ** *adv.* **confū'sėdnėss** *n.*

confū'sion *n.* Confusing; confused state; tumult; ~ *worse confounded*, confusion made worse than it was.

confū'te *v.t.* Convict (person) of error by proof; prove (argument) false. **cŏnfūtā'tion** *n.*

cŏ'nga (-ngg*a*) *n.* Latin-Amer. dance of African origin performed by persons in single file following a leader.

congé (kawṅzhā *or* kŏn-) *n.* Dismissal without ceremony. [Fr.]

congea'l (-j-) *v.* Freeze, solidify by cooling; coagulate. **cŏngėlā'tion** *n.* Congealing; congealed state; congealed substance.

cŏ'ngėner (-j-) *n.* Member of same kind or class with another. **cŏngenĕ'ric** *adj.* Of same genus, kind, race; allied in nature or origin. **congĕ'nerous** *adj.* Of same genus or (loosely) family; of same kind; ~ *muscles*, muscles concurring in same action.

congē'nial (-j-) *adj.* Kindred, sympathetic (*with*, *to*); suited, agreeable (*to*). **congēniă'litȳ** *n.* **congē'niallȳ** *adv.*

congĕ'nital (-j-) *adj.* Existing before or at birth; dating from birth (esp. of defects, diseases, etc.). **congĕ'nitallȳ** *adv.*

cŏ'nger (-ngg-) *n.* (also ~*-eel*) Large species of eel living in salt

water and caught for food; common on European coasts, but rare on Atlantic coast of America.

congĕ'riēs (-j-, -z) *n.* (pl. same). Collection; mass, heap.

congĕ'st (-j-) *v.* Accumulate to excess; affect with congestion. **congĕ'stėd** *adj.* 1. Overcrowded. 2. (med.) Overcharged with blood.

congĕ'stion (-jĕsch*on*) *n.* 1. Congested or overcrowded condition, as of population, traffic, etc. 2. (med.) Abnormal accumulation of blood in an organ etc.

cŏ'nglobāte (-n-g- *or* -ngg-) *v.* Form into a ball or rounded mass. ~ *adj.* So formed. **cŏnglobā'tion**

conglŏ'merate (-n-g-) *adj.* Gathered together into more or less rounded mass, clustered; (geol., of rock) formed of rounded water-worn pebbles or gravel cemented together. ~ *n.* Conglomerate rock. **conglŏ'merāte** *v.* Collect into a coherent mass. **conglŏmerā'tion** *n.*

Cŏ'ngō (-nggō). River of central Africa flowing into Atlantic; area surrounding it; *Belgian* ~, former name of ZAIRE; the area, opened up by STANLEY between 1878 and 1882 for Leopold II of Belgium, was named the *Independent State of the* ~ (1885) and administered by the king and his advisers independently of the Belgian Government; but in 1908, in the face of severe criticism, he ceded it to Belgium against compensation; *Popular Republic of the* ~, State of equatorial Africa, member of the French Community; capital, Brazzaville. **Cŏngolē'se** (-z) *adj.* & *n.*

cŏ'ngou (-nggōō *or* -ō) *n.* Kind of black China tea. [Chin. *kung-fu* (*ch'a*) labour (tea)]

congră'tūlāte (-n-g- *or* -ngg-) *v.t.* Address (person) with expression of sympathetic joy (*on* something); ~ *oneself*, think oneself fortunate. **congrătūlā'tion** *n.* Congratulating; (pl.) congratulatory expressions (also as *int.*). **congră'tūlative, congrătūlā'tory̆** *adjs.*

cŏ'ngrėgant (-ngg-) *n.* Member of Jewish congregation.

cŏ'ngrėgāte (-ngg-) *v.* Collect, gather, into a crowd or mass.

cŏngrėgā'tion (-ngg-) *n.* 1. Collection into a body or mass; assemblage. 2. General assembly of members of a university, or of members possessing specified qualifications. 3. Body of persons assembled for religious worship, or to hear a preacher; body of persons habitually attending a particular place of worship. 4. (R.C. Ch.) Community bound together by common rule; any of various permanent committees of College of Cardinals; *special* ~, temporary committee of cardinals etc. to decide etc. some particular matter.

cŏngrėgā'tional (-ngg-) *adj.* 1. Of a congregation. 2. *C*~, of or adhering to Congregationalism; ~ *Church of England and Wales*: see UNITED Reformed Church.

Cŏngrėgā'tionalism (-ngg-) *n.* System of ecclesiastical polity regarding all legislative, disciplinary, and judicial functions as vested in the individual church or local congregation of believers. **Cŏngrėgā'tionalist** *n.*

cŏ'ngrĕss (-ngg-) *n.* 1. Coming together, meeting. 2. Formal meeting of delegates for discussion, esp. of envoys or persons engaged in special studies. 3. *C*~, national legislative body of U.S., or of Southern and Central Amer. Republics; session of this; *Co'ngressman*, member of Congress. **congrĕ'ssional** *adj.* Of a congress; of Congress.

Cŏ'ngrēve (-ngg-), William (1670–1729). English writer of Restoration comedies; author of 'Love for Love' and 'The Way of the World'.

cŏ'ngruence (-nggrōō-) *n.* Agreement, consistency. **cŏ'ngruency̆** *n.* Congruence; (geom.) system of lines in which parameters have a twofold relation, as when each line twice touches a given surface; (math.) relation between two numbers which, when divided by a third (the *modulus*), give the same remainder.

cŏ'ngruent (-nggrōō-) *adj.* Suitable; accordant (*with*); (math.) having congruency; (of triangles etc.) equal in all respects, capable of exact superposition.

cŏ'ngruous (-nggrōō-) *adj.* Accordant, conformable (*with*); fitting. **cŏ'ngruously̆** *adv.* **congru'ĭty̆** (-ōō-) *n.*

cŏ'nic *adj.* Cone-shaped; of a cone; ~ *section*, figure (ellipse, parabola, or hyperbola) formed by section of right circular cone by a plane. **cŏ'nics** *n.* Branch of geometry treating of cones and conic sections.

cŏ'nical *adj.* Cone-shaped; of or

relating to a cone (~ *projection*). **cŏ′nicallȳ** *adv.*

conĭ′dĭophōre *n.* (bot.) Specialized hypha bearing conidia.

conĭ′dĭum *n.* (pl. *-ia*). (bot.) One-celled asexual spore in certain fungi.

cō′nĭfer *n.* Cone-bearing tree or shrub. **conĭ′ferous** *adj.*

conjĕ′ctural (-kcher-) *adj.* Involving, given to, conjecture.

conjĕ′cture *n.* Inference based on evidence which is not complete, guessing, esp. in textual criticism, of a reading not in the text; a guess. ~ *v.* Guess; propose (a conjectural reading); make a guess.

conjoi′n *v.* Join; combine; *conjoined twins*, twins congenitally united by common tissues. **conjoi′nt** (*or* kŏ′n-) *adj.* **conjoi′ntlȳ** *adv.*

cŏ′njugal (-ōō-) *adj.* Of marriage; of husband or wife in their relation to each other. **cŏ′njugallȳ** *adv.* **cŏnjugă′lĭtȳ** *n.* Conjugal state.

cŏ′njugāte (-ōō-) *v.* 1. (gram.) Inflect (verb) in voice, mood, tense, number, person. 2. Unite sexually, join in conjugation. **cŏ′njugate** *adj.* Joined together; coupled; (gram.) derived from same root; (math.) joined in a reciprocal relation; (bot. etc.) fused. ~ *n.* Conjugate word or thing.

cŏnjugā′tion (-ōō-) *n.* 1. Joining together; (biol.) fusion of two (apparently) similar cells for reproduction. 2. (gram.) Scheme of verbal inflexion.

conjŭ′nct *adj.* Conjoined, associated. ~ *n.* Conjunct person or thing. **conjŭ′nctlȳ** *adv.*

conjŭ′nction *n.* 1. Union, connection; *in* ~, together (*with*). 2. (astron.) Apparent proximity of two heavenly bodies. 3. Combination of events or circumstances. 4. (gram.) Uninflected word used to connect clauses or sentences, or to co-ordinate words in same clause. **conjŭ′nctional** *adj.* **conjŭ′nctionallȳ** *adv.*

cŏnjunctī′va *n.* Mucous membrane lining inner eyelid and reflected over front of eyeball.

conjŭnctivī′tis *n.* (med.) Inflammation of conjunctiva.

conjŭ′nctĭve *adj.* 1. Serving to join or unite. 2. (gram.) Of the nature of, acting as, a conjunction; uniting sense as well as construction (cf. DISJUNCTIVE); (of a mood) used only in conjunction with another verb. ~ *n.* Conjunctive word or mood. **conjŭ′nctivelȳ** *adv.*

conjŭ′ncture *n.* Combination of events, posture of affairs.

cŏnjurā′tion *n.* Solemn appeal; incantation.

conjure *v.* 1. (-oor′) Appeal solemnly or earnestly to. 2. (kŭ′n-jer) Constrain (spirit) to appear by invocation. 3. (kŭ′njer) Effect, bring *out*, convey *away*, by juggling; juggle; produce magical effects by natural means, perform marvels; ~ *up*, cause to appear to the mind or fancy.

co′njurer, -or (kŭ-) *n.* One who practises legerdemain.

cŏnk[1] *n.* = CONKER.

cŏnk[2] *v.i.* (slang) Break down, fail, give *out*.

cŏ′nker *n.* (pl.) Boys' game in which a horse-chestnut on a string is alternately struck against, and struck by, that of an opponent, until one of the two is broken; (sing.) horse-chestnut. [dial.

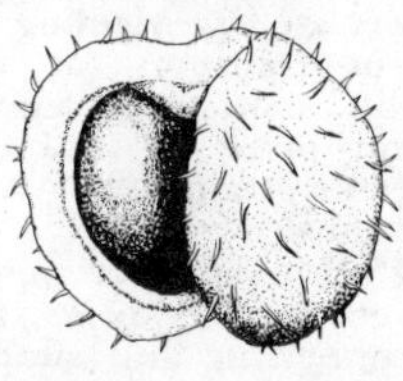

conker snail-shell, the game orig. being to press snail-shells point to point until one broke; now associated with *conquer*]

cŏn mō′tō. (mus.) With spirited movement. [It.]

Conn. *abbrev.* Connecticut.

Cŏn′nacht (-awt). Province of W. Ireland, including counties of Galway, Leitrim, Mayo, Roscommon, and Sligo.

cŏ′nnāte *adj.* 1. (of qualities etc.) Born with a person, innate;

born together, coeval; cognate. 2. (bot., zool.) Congenitally united, so as to form one compound organ or body. 3. ~ *water*, (geol.) water entrapped in sediment during its deposition.

connă'tural (-cher-) *adj.* Innate, belonging naturally (*to*); of like nature. **connă'turallÿ** *adv.*

connĕ'ct *v.* Join link together in sequence or order; associate in occurrence or action; (pass.) have to do *with*; associate mentally; unite *with* others by family relationship, common aims, etc.; join on (*with*); run in connection (*with*); *connĕcting rod*, rod connecting crank with any other part of machine; in steam- and gas-engines, transmitting motion of piston to crank. **connĕ'ctėdlÿ** *adv.* **connĕ'ctėdnėss** *n.*

Connĕ'cticut (-nĕt-). New England State of U.S., one of the original 13 States of the Union (1788); capital, Hartford.

connĕ'ction, connĕ'xion (-kshon) *n.* 1. Connecting, being connected; connecting part or thing; (mech.) joint between members. 2. Relation of thought etc.; personal relation or intercourse; sexual relation. 3. Family relationship; relative. 4. Religious body, esp. Methodist; body of customers etc. 5. Meeting of one means of transport (as railway train) by another at appointed time and place to take on the passengers; train etc. meeting another thus.

connĕ'ctive *adj.* Serving, tending, to connect; ~ *tissue*, fibrous tissue connecting and supporting organs of the body.

cŏ'nning-tow'er *n.* Pilot-house of warship; superstructure on submarine in which periscope is mounted and from which steering, firing, etc., are directed when the submarine is on or near the surface. [CON² *v.*]

connī'vance *n.* Conniving; tacit permission.

connī've *v.i.* Wink *at* (what one ought to oppose).

cŏnnoisseur' (-*a*sêr) *n.* Critical judge (*of*, *in*, matters of taste). **cŏnnoisseur'ship** *n.*

connō'te *v.t.* (of words) Imply in addition to the primary meaning; (of facts etc.) imply as a consequence or condition; (logic) imply the attributes while denoting the subject; (loosely) mean. **cŏnnotā'tion** *n.* **connō'tative** *adj.* **connō'tātivelÿ** *adv.*

connū'bial *adj.* Of marriage; of husband or wife; married. **connū'biallÿ** *adv.* **connūbiă'litÿ** *n.*

cō'noid *adj.* Approaching a cone in shape. ~ *n.* Conoid body; (geom.) solid generated by revolution of conic section about its axis; surface generated by straight line remaining parallel to fixed plane and passing through fixed straight line and fixed curve. **conoi'dal** *adj.*

cŏ'nquer (-k*er*) *v.* Overcome by force; get the better of; acquire, subjugate. **cŏ'nqueror** *n.* One who conquers; horse-chestnut which has broken others in game of conkers; *the C~*, WILLIAM[1] I.

cŏ'nquĕst *n.* Subjugation, conquering; conquered territory; person whose affections have been won; *the C~*, the NORMAN Conquest.

Cŏ'nrăd, Joseph. Teodor Josef Konrad Korzeniowski (1857–1924), Polish-born writer in English of novels dealing with seafaring life.

Cons. *abbrev.* Conservative; Consul.

cŏnsănguī'nėous (-nggw-) *adj.* Of the same blood, akin. **cŏnsănguī'nitÿ** *n.* Blood-relationship.

cŏ'nscience (-sh*e*ns) *n.* Moral sense of right and wrong as regards things for which one is responsible; faculty or principle pronouncing upon moral quality of one's own actions or motives; *in all* ~, in reason or fairness; ~ *money*, money sent to relieve conscience; ~-*stricken*, overcome with remorse. **cŏ'nsciencelėss** *adj.*

cŏnscie'ntious (-shiĕnsh-) *adj.* Obedient to conscience, scrupulous; ~ *objector*, one whose conscience forces him to object, e.g. to taking an oath or esp. to military service. **cŏnsciĕ'ntiouslȳ** *adv.* **cŏnsciĕ'ntiousnėss** *n.*

cŏ'nscious (-sh*u*s) *adj.* Aware, knowing; with mental faculties awake or active; self-conscious; (of actions etc.) realized by the actor etc. **cŏ'nsciouslȳ** *adv.* **cŏ'nsciousnėss** *n.* State of being conscious; totality of person's thoughts and feelings, or of a class of these; perception (*of, that*).

conscrī'be *v.t.* Enlist by conscription (now rare; usu. superseded by *conscript*).

cŏ'nscrĭpt[1] *adj.* ~*fathers*, (Rom. hist.) collective title of Roman senators.

cŏ'nscrĭpt[2] *n.* Recruit enrolled by conscription. **conscrĭ'pt** *v.t.* (orig. U.S.) Enlist by conscription. **conscrĭ'ption** *n.* Compulsory enlistment for State service, esp. for army, navy, or air force.

cŏ'nsėcrāte *adj.* Consecrated. ~ *v.t.* Set apart as sacred (*to*); devote *to* (purpose); sanctify.

cŏnsėcrā'tion *n.* Act of consecrating, dedication, esp. of church, churchyard, etc., by bishop; ordination to sacred office, esp. of bishop; devotion *to* (purpose). **cŏ'nsėcrātorȳ** *adj.*

cŏnsėcū'tion *n.* Logical sequence; sequence of events; (gram.) sequence (of words, tenses, etc.).

consĕ'cūtĭve *adj.* 1. Following continuously. 2. (gram.) Expressing consequence; ~ *intervals*, (mus.) intervals of the same kind, occurring adjacently between the same two parts, esp. octaves or fifths. **consĕ'cūtĭvelȳ** *adv.* **consĕ'cūtĭvenėss** *n.*

consĕ'nsūal *adj.* Relating to or involving consent. **consĕ'nsūallȳ** *adv.*

consĕ'nsus *n.* Agreement (*of* opinions etc.).

consĕ'nt *v.i.* Express willingness (*to*), agree (*to, that*, etc.). ~ *n.* Voluntary agreement, compliance; permission; *age of* ~, age at which consent, esp. of girl to sexual intercourse, is valid in law; *with one* ~, unanimously; ~ *decree*, (U.S.) agreed verdict, verdict to which parties assent.

consĕ'ntient (-sh*e*nt) *adj.* Agreeing; concurrent; consenting (*to*).

cŏ'nsėquence *n.* 1. Thing or circumstance which follows as a result from something preceding; logical inference. 2. Importance, moment; social distinction, rank. 3. (pl.) Round game in which a narrative (of a meeting and its consequences) is concocted by contributions of a name or fact from each player, in ignorance of what has been contributed by the others.

cŏ'nsėquent *n.* Event etc. following another (without implication of causal connection); (logic) second part of conditional proposition, dependent on antecedent; (math.) second of two numbers in a ratio, second and fourth of four proportionals. ~ *adj.* Following as a result (*on*); following logically; logically consistent; (of stream etc.) following course determined by original slope of land (opp. OBSEQUENT).

cŏnsėquĕ'ntial (-sh*a*l) *adj.* 1. Following as a result or inference. 2. Following or resulting indirectly. 3. Self-important. **cŏnsėquĕ'ntiallȳ** *adv.*

cŏ'nsėquentlȳ *adv.* & *conj.* As a result; therefore.

consẽr'vancȳ *n.* Commission, court, controlling a port, river, etc.; official preservation (of forests etc.).

cŏnservā'tion *n.* Preservation; ~ *of energy*, doctrine that total energy of any system of bodies can be neither increased nor diminished by any mutual action of those bodies, though it may be changed into various forms, and that the universe is such a system. **cŏnservā'tionĭst** *n.* One who advocates conservation, esp. of natural resources and amenities.

consẽr'vatĭve *adj.* 1. Preservative, keeping or tending to keep intact or unchanged. 2. *C*~, (pol.) of the Conservative party, favouring maintenance of existing institutions, individual liberty, etc.; *C*~ *party*, name adopted by the Tory party since *c* 1830, one of the main parties in Gt Britain. 3. (of estimate etc.) Moderate, cautious, low (orig. U.S.). ~ *n.* Conservative person; *C~*, member of Conservative party. **consẽr'vativelў̌** *adv.* **consẽr'vatism** *n.*

consẽr'vatoire (-twar̃) *n.* Public institution in France and other European countries for teaching music and declamation. [Fr.]

cŏ'nservātor (*or* konsẽr'va-) *n.* Preserver, guardian; official custodian; member of conservancy.

consẽr'vatorў̌ *n.* (Ornamental) greenhouse for tender or exotic plants.

cŏnsẽr've *n.* (*or* kŏ'-) *n.* (also pl.) Jam, esp. that made from fresh fruit and sugar. **consẽr've** *v.t.* Keep from harm, decay, or loss.

consĭ'der *v.* Contemplate mentally; weigh the merits of; reflect, reckon with, make allowance for; be of opinion; regard as.

consĭ'derable *adj.* Worth considering; notable, important; much, no small. **consĭ'derablў̌** *adv.*

consĭ'derate *adj.* Thoughtful for others. **consĭ'deratelў̌** *adv.* **consĭ'deratenėss** *n.*

consĭderā'tion *n.* 1. Considering; meditation; *take into ~*, consider. 2. Fact, thing, regarded as a reason; *in ~ of*, in return for, on account of. 3. Compensation, reward; (law) thing given, done, as equivalent by person to whom a promise is made. 4. Thoughtfulness for others. 5. Importance, consequence.

consĭ'dering *prep.* Taking into account, in view of; (ellipt., colloq.) considering the circumstances.

consĭ'gn (-īn) *v.t.* Hand over, deliver, *to*; transmit, send by rail etc., *to*; (Sc. law) deposit (money *in* bank, with third party etc.). **consignee', consignor̃'** (-īn-) *ns.*

cŏnsĭgnā'tion (-g-n-) *n.* Formal payment of money to person legally appointed; consigning goods.

consĭ'gnment (-īn-) *n.* Consigning; goods consigned.

consĭ'lience *n.* Coincidence, concurrence (of inductions drawn from different groups of phenomena). **consĭ'lient** *adj.*

consĭ'st *v.i.* Be composed *of*; be comprised or contained *in*; agree, harmonize, *with*.

consĭ'stence *n.* Degree of density, esp. of thick liquids; firmness, solidity. **consĭ'stencў̌** *n.* 1. Consistence. 2. Being consistent.

consĭ'stent *adj.* 1. Compatible (*with*), not contradictory. 2. Constant to same principles of thought or action. **consĭ'stentlў̌** *adv.*

consĭ'storў̌ (*or* kŏ'-) *n.* 1. Senate in which pope, presiding over whole body of cardinals, deliberates on affairs of the Church. 2. (also *C~ Court*) In Anglican Church, bishop's court for ecclesiastical causes and offences; in Lutheran Church, supervising clerical board; in Reformed, Genevan, or Presbyterian Church, a court of presbyters. **cŏnsĭstor̃'ial** *adj.*

cŏnsolā'tion *n.* Alleviation of grief or disappointment; consoling circumstance; ~ *prize*, one given to competitor who has not won a main prize.

consŏ'latorў̌ *adj.* Tending or designed to console.

consō'le[1] *v.t.* Bring consolation to.

cŏ'nsōle[2] *n.* 1. (archit.) Tall bracket consisting partly or wholly of volutes and supporting a cornice; *~-table*, table supported by bracket against a wall. 2. Cabinet for radio, television set, etc. 3. Ensemble of keyboards, stops, etc., of organ, esp. when seperate from body of instrument, as in electrtic organ. 4. Switchboard; other fitment with dials, switches, etc.

consŏ'lĭdāte *v.* 1. Solidify, strengthen. 2. Combine (territories, companies, debts, statutes, etc.) into one whole; *consolidated annuities*, Government securities of Great Britain, consolidated in 1751 into a single stock at 3% (later 2½); *Consolidated Fund*, fund, established in 1787, into which main part of revenue is paid, and out of which are paid interest on National Debt and charges other than supply charges, voted annually.

cŏnsŏ'ls (-z; *or* kŏ'-) *n.pl.* Consolidated annuities (see CONSOLIDATE, 2).

consŏ'mmé (-ā) *n.* Clear soup made from meat or poultry.

cŏ'nsonance *n.* Recurrence of same or similar sounds in words or syllables, assonance; (mus.) sounding together of notes in harmony; consonant interval; agreement, harmony.

cŏ'nsonant[1] *adj.* Agreeable *to*, consistent *with*; harmonious; agreeing in sound; (mus.) making concord. **cŏn'sonantlў** *adv.*

cŏ'nsonant[2] *n.* Sound in speech, other than a vowel, produced by a complete momentary stoppage or by partial stoppage or constriction of the air stream in some part of the mouth cavity or by the lips as it passes from the lungs; letter or symbol representing such a sound. **cŏnsonă'ntal** *adj.* [L *consonantem* (*letteram*); the name is due to the erroneous view that a consonant can only be sounded along with a vowel]

cŏn sōrdi'nŏ (-dē-). (mus.) With the mute or damper. [It.]

cŏ'nsōrt *n.* 1. Husband or wife; *king, prince* ~, (titles sometimes given to) husband of reigning queen; *queen* ~, king's wife. 2. Ship sailing in company with another. 3. (mus.) Body of performers in ensemble; performance by several players or singers together. **consō'rt** *v.* Class or bring together, keep company, (*with*); agree, harmonize, (*with*).

consō'rtĭum (*or* -shĭ-) *n.* (pl. *-ia*). 1. Association of business, banking, or manufacturing organizations. 2. (law) Conjugal rights.

cŏnspėcĭ'fĭc *adj.* & *n.* (Creature) belonging to the same species.

conspĕ'ctus *n.* General or comprehensive survey; summary.

conspĭ'cūous *adj.* Clearly visible, striking to the eye; attracting notice, remarkable. **conspĭ'cūousnėss** *n.* **conspĭ'cūouslў** *adv.*

conspĭ'racў *n.* Conspiring; combination for unlawful purpose; plot. **conspĭ'rator** *n.* **conspĭratō'rĭal** *adj.* **conspĭratō'rĭallў** *adv.*

conspīr'e *v.* Combine privily for unlawful purpose, esp. treason, murder, sedition; combine, concur (*to* do); plot, devise.

co'nstable[1] (kŭ-) *n.* 1. Chief officer of household, court, administration, or military forces of a ruler; *C~ of France*, principal officer of household of early French

CONSTABLE: Salisbury Cathedral

kings, who ultimately became commander-in-chief of army in monarch's absence; *C~ of England, Lord High C~*, one of chief functionaries of English royal household (since 1521, a title granted only temporarily for special occasions). 2. Governor or warden of royal fortress or castle. 3. Officer of the peace; esp. (*police* ~) policeman or policewoman of lowest rank; *Chief C~*, officer at head of police force of county or area; *High C~*, officer of hundred or large administrative district acting as conservator of peace (abolished 1869); *Petty* (*Parish*) ~, similar officer of parish or township (abolished or incorporated in police system, 1872); *special* ~, person sworn in to assist police on special occasion etc. [L *comes stabuli* count of the stable]

Co'nstable[2] (kŭ-), John (1776–1837). English landscape-painter.

constă'bŭlarÿ *adj.* Of constables; of the police. ~ *n.* Organized body of constables; police force of a district; district under a constable.

cŏ'nstancÿ *n.* Firmness, endurance; faithfulness; unchangingness.

cŏ'nstant *adj.* Unmoved, resolute; faithful; unchanging; unremitting. ~ *n.* (math. etc.) Quantity which does not vary; numerical quantity expressing relation, property, etc., that remains the same for the same substance under all conditions.

cŏ'nstantan *n.* Alloy of copper and nickel.

Cŏ'nstantine (274–337), 'the Great'. Roman emperor (306–37); converted to Christianity, which he made the State religion; in 328 transferred the capital of the empire to Byzantium, which he renamed Constantinople.

Cŏnstăntinō'ple. Former name of ISTANBUL, capital of Turkey until 1923; the Roman city of Byzantium (see CONSTANTINE).

cŏ'nstantlÿ *adv.* Always; often.

cŏ'nstellāte *v.* Form into a

ARCH OF CONSTANTINE, Rome

constellation; stud, adorn thickly.

cŏnstellā′tion *n.* Number of fixed stars grouped within outline

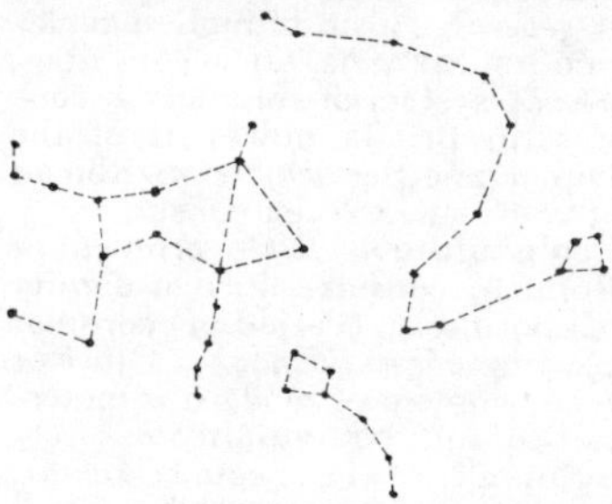

of an imaginary figure as viewed from the earth; group of distinguished persons.

cŏ′nsternāte *v.t.* Fill with consternation.

cŏnsternā′tion *n.* Amazement and terror such as to prostrate one's faculties, dismay.

cŏnstipā′tion *n.* Condition of bowels in which defaecation is irregular and difficult. **cŏ′nstĭpāte** *v.t.* Affect with constipation.

constĭ′tūencÿ *n.* Body of voters who elect a representative member; place, residents in place, so represented.

constĭ′tūent *adj.* Composing, making up, a whole; appointing, electing; able to form or alter a (political) constitution. ~ *n.* 1. Component part. 2. One who appoints another his agent or representative; member of a constituency.

cŏ′nstĭtūte *v.t.* 1. Appoint (person) to office, dignity, etc., of; establish, found, give legal form to (assembly, institution, etc.). 2. Frame, form (by combination of elements); make up, be components of.

cŏnstĭtū′tion *n.* 1. Act, mode, of constituting; way in which thing is constituted; esp. character of body in regard to health, strength, vitality, etc.; condition of mind, disposition. 2. Mode in which State is organized; body of fundamental principles according to which a State is governed; *C*~, (U.S.) Constitution of the United States framed at Philadelphia in 1787 and ratified 1788, together with subsequent amendments. 3. (hist.) Decree, ordinance; (Rom. law) enactment made by the emperor; *Constitutions of Clarendon*, propositions drawn up at Council which met at Clarendon in Wiltshire in reign of Henry II (1164), defining limits of civil and ecclesiastical jurisdiction in England.

cŏnstĭtū′tional *adj.* 1. Of, inherent in, affecting, the bodily or mental constitution. 2. Belonging to the very constitution of anything; essential. 3. Of, in harmony with, authorized by, the political constitution; adhering to the political constitution; ~ *monarchy*, monarchy limited by constitutional forms. ~ *n.* (colloq.) Walk taken for health's sake. **cŏnstĭtū′tionalism, cŏnstĭtū′tionalist, cŏnstĭtūtionă′lĭtÿ** *ns.* **cŏnstĭtū′tionallÿ** *adv.*

cŏ′nstĭtūtĭve *adj.* Constructive, formative; essential; component. **cŏ′nstĭtūtĭvelÿ** *adv.*

constrai′n *v.t.* Compel; bring about by compulsion; confine forcibly, imprison. **constrai′ned** (-nd) *adj.* Forced, embarrassed. **constrai′nèdlÿ** *adv.*

constrai′nt *n.* Compulsion; confinement; restraint of natural feelings, constrained manner.

constrĭ′ct *v.t.* Contract, compress; cause (organic tissue) to contract. **constrĭ′ction** *n.* **constrĭ′ctĭve** *adj.*

constrĭ′ctor *n.* 1. Muscle that draws together or narrows a part. 2. Surgical instrument for producing constriction. 3. Snake which kills its prey by constriction.

constrĭ′nge (-j) *v.t.* Compress; cause (organic tissue) to contract. **constrĭ′ngent** *adj.* Causing constriction. **constrĭ′ngencÿ** *n.*

constrŭ′ct *v.t.* Fit together, frame, build; (gram.) combine (words) syntactically; (geom.) draw, delineate. **cŏ′nstrŭct** *n.* Anything constructed.

constrŭ′ction *n.* 1. Act, mode, of constructing; thing constructed. 2. (gram.) Syntactical connection between verbs and their objects or complements, prepositions and their objects, etc. 3. Construing, explanation (of words); interpretation. 4. ~ *crew, gang, labourer,* (U.S.) men, man, engaged on construction, esp. of railways; ~ *train*, train carrying materials etc. for making or repairing railways. **constrŭ'ctional** *adj.* Of, engaged in, construction; structural.

constrŭ'ctionist *n.* One who interprets a law, esp. the Constitution of the U.S., strictly, broadly, or in some other specified manner.

constrŭ'ctive *adj.* 1. Of construction; constructing, tending to construct (esp. as opp. to *destructive*). 2. Deduced by construction or interpretation, not directly expressed, inferred. **constrŭ'ctivelȳ** *adv.*

constrŭ'ctor *n.* One who constructs, esp. supervisor of naval construction.

constru'e (-ōō) *v.* Combine (words) grammatically; analyse (sentence), translate word for word; admit of grammatical analysis; expound, interpret.

cŏnsubstă'ntial (-sh*a*l) *adj.* Of the same substance, esp. of the three Persons of the Trinity. **cŏnsubstăntiă'lĭtȳ** (-shĭăl-) *n.*

cŏnsubstă'ntiāte (-shĭ-) *v.* Unite in one substance. **cŏnsubstăntiā'tion** *n.* Doctrine of real substantial presence of body and blood of Christ together with bread and wine in Eucharist (dist. from TRANSUBSTANTIATION).

cŏ'nsuėtūde (-sw-) *n.* Custom, esp. as having legal force.

consuėtū'dĭnarȳ (-sw-) *adj.* Customary. ~ *n.* Treatise containing collection of customs or usages, esp. of monastic house, cathedral, etc.

cŏ'nsul *n.* 1. (Rom. hist.) Either of two annually elected magistrates exercising supreme authority under the Republic. 2. One of three chief magistrates of French Republic (1799–1804), and of whom the *First C~*, Napoleon Bonaparte, had all the real power. 3. Agent of sovereign State residing in foreign port or town to protect interest of its traders and residents there and assist commercial relations between the countries; ~*-general*, consul of highest rank.

cŏ'nsūlar *adj.* Of a consul; ~ *service*, system of commercial consuls (in Britain now part of the Diplomatic Service). ~ *n.* Roman of consular rank, ex-consul.

cŏ'nsūlate *n.* 1. Government of Rome by consuls; office or dignity of consuls. 2. (Period of) consular government in France. 3. Office or establishment of modern commercial consul. **cŏ'nsulshĭp** *n.*

consŭ'lt *v.* Take counsel (*with*); seek information or advice from; take into consideration; *consulting chemist, engineer,* etc., one who makes a business of giving professional advice to the public or to those practically engaged in his own profession; *consulting physician* etc., physician etc. to whom others may refer their patients for advice. **consŭ'ltatĭve** *adj.*

consŭ'ltant *n.* Consulting physician etc.

cŏnsultā'tion *n.* Act of consulting; deliberation; conference.

consū'me *v.* Make away with; use up; eat, drink, up; burn up; spend, waste; waste away; *consumed*, eaten up *with*. **consū'mėdlȳ** *adv.* Excessively.

consū'mer *n.* (esp. econ.) One who uses up an article produced, thereby exhausting its exchangeable value; customer, purchaser; ~ *goods*, things which directly satisfy human needs and desires, e.g. food and clothing.

consŭ'mmate *adj.* Complete, perfect. **consŭ'mmatelȳ** *adv.*
cŏ'nsummāte *v.t.* Accomplish, complete (esp. marriage by sexual intercourse). **cŏnsummā'tion** *n.* Completion; desired end, goal; perfection; perfected thing; physical completion of marriage.

consŭ'mption *n.* 1. Consuming; destruction; waste; amount consumed. 2. Wasting disease, esp. pulmonary tuberculosis.

consŭ'mptĭve *adj.* 1. Tending to consume. 2. Having a tendency to, affected with, pulmonary tuberculosis. ~ *n.* Consumptive person.

cŏ′ntăct *n.* State, condition, of touching; (math.) meeting of curves or surfaces so as to have tangents or tangent planes in common; (elect.) junction or touching surface of two conductors or ends of conducting wire through which a current passes; (usu. pl.) friendly relationships, persons with whom one comes into touch; (colloq., orig. U.S.) acquaintance, esp. one useful in business; (med.) person who has been exposed to contagious disease; *come into ~ with*, come across, meet; *make, break ~*, complete, interrupt electric circuit; *~ lens*, small lens worn on eyeball. *~ v.t.* Get into touch with (person).

cŏntadi′nō (-ahdē-) *n.* (pl. *-ni* pr. -nē; fem. *contadina*, pl. *-ne* pr. -nā). Italian peasant.

contā′gion (-jon) *n.* Communication of disease from body to body by contact; contagious disease; moral corruption; contagious influence.

contā′gious (-jus) *adj.* Communicating disease or corruption by contact; (of diseases) communicable by contact; (fig.) catching, infectious; *~ abortion*, (in cattle) brucellosis. **contā′giouslȳ** *adv.* **contā′giousnėss** *n.*

contai′n *v.t.* 1. Have, hold, as contents; comprise, include; (of a measure) be equal to; (geom.) enclose, form boundary of; (of numbers) be divisible by (number) without remainder. 2. Restrain; (mil.) hold (enemy force) in position so that it cannot operate elsewhere; (fig.) keep within limits. **contai′nment** *n.* **contai′ner** *n.* (esp.) Receptacle of standardized design for transportation of freight; so *~ berth, ship*, etc., one carrying freight in containers. **contai′nerīze** *v.t.* Pack into, transport in, containers. **containerīzā′tion** *n.*

contă′mĭnāte *v.t.* Pollute, infect. **contămĭnā′tion** *n.*

contă′ngō (-ngg-) *n.* (Stock Exch.) Percentage paid by buyer of stock to seller for postponement of completion of purchase (cf. BACKWARDATION); *~ day*, eighth day before settling day.

contĕ′mn (-m) *v.t.* Despise, treat with disregard.

cŏ′ntemplāte *v.* Gaze upon; view mentally; expect; intend, purpose; meditate. **cŏntemplā′tion** *n.*

cŏ′ntemplātive (*or* kontĕ′mpla-) *adj.* Meditative, thoughtful; (of life or monastic order) devoted to religious contemplation and prayer. *~ n.* Contemplative person. **cŏ′ntėmplātĭvelȳ** *adv.* **cŏ′ntemplātĭvenėss** *n.*

contĕmporā′nėous *adj.* Existing, occurring, at the same time (*with*); of the same period. **contĕmporā′nėouslȳ** *adv.* **contĕmporanē′ĭtȳ, contĕmporā′nėousnėss** *ns.*

contĕ′mporarȳ *adj.* Belonging to the same time; equal in age; (ultra-)modern, esp. of art, furniture, etc. *~ n.* Contemporary person or thing.

contĕ′mporīze *v.t.* Make contemporary.

contĕ′mpt *n.* Act, mental attitude, of despising; condition of being despised; (law) disobedience or open disrespect to authority or lawful commands of sovereign, Houses of Parliament, or (esp.) court of law. **contĕ′mptĭble** *adj.* Deserving contempt, despicable; *Old Contemptibles* (in allusion to an alleged reference by Wilhelm II to 'General French's contemptible little army'), the British Army of regulars and reserves sent to France in autumn of 1914. **contĕmptĭbĭ′lĭtȳ** *n.* **contĕ′mptĭblȳ** *adv.* **contĕ′mptĭblenėss** *n.*

contĕ′mptūous *adj.* Showing contempt (*of*); scornful; insolent. **contĕ′mptūouslȳ** *adv.* **contĕ′mptūousnėss** *n.*

contĕ′nd *v.* Strive; fight; struggle *with*; compete, be in rivalry; argue (*with*); maintain (*that*).

cŏ′ntĕnt[1] *n.* 1. Containing power, capacity; volume; amount contained or yielded. 2. (pl.) What is contained; esp. things contained or treated of in writing or document; *table of ~s*, summary of subject-matter of book. 3. Constituent elements of a conception; substance (of art etc., as opp. to *form*).

contĕ'nt[2] *n.* Contented state, satisfaction. ~ *adj.* Satisfied; willing (*to* do). ~ *v.t.* Satisfy; ~ *oneself*, be satisfied (*with*), **contĕ'ntėdlў** *adv.* **contĕ'ntėdnėss** *n.* **contĕ'ntment** *n.*

contĕ'ntion *n.* Strife, controversy; rivalry; point contended for in argument.

contĕ'ntious (-shus) *adj.* Quarrelsome; involving contention. **contĕ'ntiouslў** *adv.* **contĕ'ntiousnėss** *n.*

conte͡r'mĭnous *adj.* Having a common boundary (*with*); meeting at their ends; coextensive. **conte͡r'mĭnouslў** *adv.*

cŏ'ntĕst *n.* Contending; competition. **contĕ'st** *v.* Dispute; contend or compete for. **contĕ'stable** *adj.* **contĕ'stant** *n.* One who contests. **cŏntėstā'tion** *n.*

cŏ'ntĕxt *n.* Whole structure of connected passage in relation to any of its parts; parts which immediately precede or follow a written or spoken passage and determine its meaning. **contĕ'xtūal** *adj.* **contĕ'xtuallў** *adv.*

contĕ'xture *n.* Act, mode, of weaving together; structure; fabric; mode of literary composition.

cŏntĭgū'ĭtў *n.* Contact; proximity; (psychol.) proximity of ideas or impressions in space or time, as a principle of association.

contĭ'gūous *adj.* Touching, adjoining; neighbouring. **contĭ'gūouslў** *adv.*

cŏ'ntĭnent[1] *adj.* Temperate, characterized by sexual restraint; able to control bladder and bowel functions. **cŏ'ntĭnentlў** *adv.* **cŏ'ntĭnence, -cў** *ns.*

cŏ'ntĭnent[2] *n.* One of the main continuous bodies of land on earth's surface (now usu. reckoned as Europe, Asia, Africa, N. and S. America, Australia, and Antarctica); *the C~*, the mainland of Europe as dist. from the British Isles.

cŏntĭnĕ'ntal *adj.* Of the or a continent; (hist.) of the Amer. colonies or States (during and immediately after the War of Independence); *C~ Congress*, assembly of delegates from the revolting colonies meeting at Philadelphia in 1774–6; ~ *drift*, (geol.) slow movement of the continents away from a single land-mass to their present positions; ~ *shelf*, sloping platform round continent, outside which the ocean bed descends steeply; *C~ System*, system of blockade designed to exclude England from commerce with the continent of Europe instituted by Napoleon in 1806. ~ *n.* 1. Native or inhabitant of a continent, esp. Europe. 2. (hist.) Soldier of the (Amer.) Continental army.

contĭ'ngencў (-j-) *n.* Being contingent; contingent event etc., chance occurrence; thing incident to another.

contĭ'ngent (-j-) *adj.* 1. Of uncertain occurrence. 2. True only under existing conditions; non-essential; conditional, dependent *on* some prior occurrence or condition. **contĭ'ngentlў** *adv.* **contĭ'ngent** *n.* 1. Contingent thing. 2. Troops contributed to form part of military or naval force (also fig.).

contĭ'nūal *adj.* Always continuing, incessant; very frequent. **contĭ'nūallў** *adv.*

contĭ'nūance *n.* Continuing in existence or operation, duration. **contĭ'nūant** *adj.* & *n.* (Consonant) of which sound can be continued and prolonged as long as breath lasts, as opp. to a STOP.

continūā'tion *n.* 1. Carrying on, resumption. 2. (Stock Exch.) Carrying over of account till next settling day. 3. That by which anything is continued, continuing addition.

contĭ'nūative *adj.* Tending, serving, to continue.

contĭ'nūe *v.* 1. Go or keep on with; not cease; maintain. 2. Remain in existence. 3. Resume.

cŏntĭnū'ĭtў *n.* 1. Being continuous; unbroken series, succession; close relationship, logical sequence, of ideas. 2. Specification of all the details in the sequences required for a film; (attrib.) ~ *girl* etc., person responsible for consistency of detail in film sequences.

contĭ'nūō *n.* (mus.) Figured bass; (usu. keyboard) accompaniment improvised from this; instrument(s) playing it.

contĭ'nūous *adj.* Connected, unbroken, in time or sequence; ~ *wave*, (phys.) electromagnetic wave of constant amplitude. **contĭ'nūouslȳ** *adv.*

contĭ'nūum *n.* (philos.) Continuous whole, as *space-time* ~.

contôr'nĭate *adj.* & *n.* (Medal) with deep furrow round disc, within the edge.

contôr't *v.t.* Twist, distort.

contôr'tion *n.* Twisting; twisted state. **contôr'tionist** *n.* (esp.) Gymnast who throws his body into contorted postures.

cŏ'ntour (-oor) *n.* Outline of figure, object, coast, etc.; (also ~ *line*) line representing horizontal

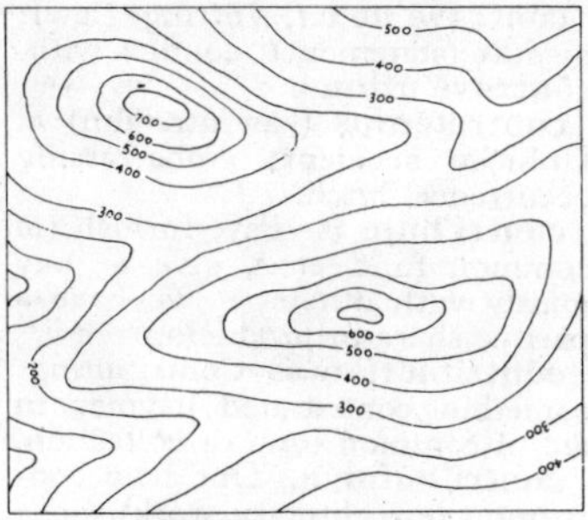

CONTOUR LINES

contour of earth's surface at given elevation. ~ *v.t.* Mark with contour lines.

cŏ'ntra *prep.* Against. ~ *adv.* Against a proposition etc. (usu. CON[4]); on the contrary. ~ *n.* 1. (usu. pl.) = CON[4]. 2. (book-keeping) Opposite side of account, esp. credit side.

contra- *prefix.* Against; in names of mus. instruments and organ-stops, denoting a pitch of an octave below.

cŏ'ntrabănd *n.* Prohibited traffic, smuggling; smuggled goods; (U.S., during Civil War) Negro slave, esp. fugitive or captured slave; ~ *of war*, anything forbidden to be supplied by neutrals to belligerents. ~ *adj.* Forbidden to be imported or exported; concerned with contraband.

cŏ'ntrabāss *n.* (mus.) Double-bass.

cŏntracĕ'ptĭve *adj.* & *n.* Preventive of uterine conception. **cŏntracĕ'ption** *n.*

cŏ'ntrăct *n.* 1. Mutual agreement between parties, States, etc., esp. business agreement for supplying goods or performing work at specified price. 2. Agreement enforceable by law; department of law relating to contracts; formal agreement for marriage. 3. (in game of bridge) Undertaking by declarer to make so many tricks; ~ *bridge*: see BRIDGE[2]. **contră'ct** *v.* 1. Enter into business or legal arrangement; ~ (oneself) *out* (*of*), contract for exemption or exclusion from provisions of (law etc.). 2. Form (friendship, habit); incur (disease, liability). 3. Draw together; make or become smaller; (gram.) shorten (word) by combination or elision.

contră'ctīle *adj.* Capable of, producing, contraction.

contră'ction *n.* Contracting; contracted word.

contră'ctor *n.* 1. One who undertakes a contract, esp. in building and related trades, or for Government or other public body. 2. Contracting muscle.

contră'ctūal *adj.* Of (the nature of) a contract.

cŏntradĭ'ct *v.t.* Deny (statement); deny words of (person); be contrary to.

cŏntradĭ'ction *n.* Verbal denial; direct opposition; statement contradicting another; inconsistency; ~ *in terms*, plainly self-contradictory statement or words.

cŏntradĭ'ctious (-sh*us*) *adj.* Given to contradiction.

cŏntradĭ'ctorȳ *adj.* Making denial; mutually opposed or inconsistent; contradictious. **cŏntradĭ'ctorĭlȳ** *adv.* **cŏntradĭ'ctorĭnėss** *n.* **cŏntradĭ'ctorȳ** *n.* Contradictory assertion.

cŏntradistĭ'nction *n.* Distinction by contrast.

cŏntradistĭ'nguish (-nggw-) *v.t.* Distinguish by contrast.

cŏntra-ĭ'ndicāte *v.t.* (med.) Act as indication against (use of a particular treatment etc.). **contra-indicā'tion** *n.* **cŏntra-indĭ'cative** *adj.*

contră'ltō *n.* (pl. *-os*). Lowest female voice; singer with such voice; musical part for this.

cŏntraposĭ'tion (-z-) *n.* Antithesis, opposition; (logic) mode of conversion in which proposition having contrary of original predicate for its subject is inferred, e.g. *all men are mortal, therefore no non-mortals are men.* **cŏntrapŏ'sĭtive** *adj.* & *n.*

cŏntrappŏ'stō *n.* (sculpture) Style of representing a standing human figure in which balance is achieved by oblique positioning of body and limbs.

cŏ'ntraprŏp *n.* Pair of propellers on same axis rotating in opposite directions. [abbrev. of *contra*-rotating *prop*ellers]

contră'ption *n.* (colloq.) (Queer) contrivance or device.

cŏntrapŭ'ntal *adj.* Of, in, counterpoint. **cŏntrapŭ'ntist** *n.* One skilled in counterpoint.

cŏntrarī'ėtў *n.* Opposition in nature, quality, or action; disagreement, inconsistency.

cŏ'ntrariwise (-z; *or* kontrār'-) *adv.* On the other hand; in the opposite way; perversely.

cŏ'ntrarў *adj.* 1. Opposed in nature or tendency (*to*); (of wind) impeding, unfavourable. 2. (kontrār'ĭ) Perverse, self-willed. 3. Opposite in position or direction. **cŏ'ntrarĭlў** *adv.* **cŏ'ntrarĭnėss** *n.* **cŏ'ntrarў** *adv.* In opposition (*to*). ~ *n.* Opposite; object, fact, or quality that is the very opposite of something else; *on the* ~, (corroborating a denial expressed or understood); *to the* ~, to the opposite effect (contradicting something that has been said or assumed).

cŏ'ntrast (-ah-) *n.* Juxtaposition showing striking differences; comparison clearly revealing differences or opposing qualities; person or thing of most opposite qualities; (photog. etc.) differentiation between tones. **contra'st** (-ah-) *v.* Set (two things, one *with* another) in opposition, so as to show their differences; show striking difference on comparison *with.* **cŏ'ntrastў** (-ah-) *adj.* (photog. etc.) Showing marked contrast.

cŏntrasuggĕ'stĭble *adj.* Resistant to suggestion; apt to take the opposite view or action to that suggested. **cŏntrasuggĕstĭbĭ'lĭtў** *n.*

cŏ'ntrate *adj.* ~ *wheel*, wheel with teeth set at right angles to its plane.

cŏntravallā'tion *n.* Chain of redoubts and breastworks placed by besiegers between their camp and the beleagured place.

cŏntravē'ne *v.t.* Infringe (law); dispute (statement); conflict with. **cŏntravĕ'ntion** *n.*

contretemps (kaw'ṅtretahṅ) *n.* Unlucky accident; embarrassing occurrence, hitch.

contrĭ'būte *v.* Pay, furnish (*to* common fund etc.), give or pay jointly with others; ~ *to*, have a part or share in producing.

cŏntrĭbū'tion *n.* Contributing; something contributed; payment in aid of common fund or collection.

contrĭ'būtor *n.* One who contributes (esp. literary work).

contrĭ'būtorў *adj.* That contributes; ~ *negligence*, negligence on the part of a person injured that has helped to bring about the injury. ~ *n.* Person bound on the winding up of a joint-stock company to contribute towards payment of its debts.

cŏ'ntrīte *adj.* Crushed in spirit by a sense of sin, completely penitent; (of action) arising from contrition. **cŏ'ntrītelў** *adv.*

contrĭ'tion *n.* Being contrite, penitence.

contrī'vance *n.* 1. Contriving. 2. Deceitful practice. 3. Invention; inventive capacity; thing contrived; mechanical device.

contrī've *v.t.* Devise, plan, skilfully; bring to pass, manage (thing, *to* do etc.). **contrī'ver** *n.*

contrō'l *n.* 1. Controlling; function or power of directing and regulating. 2. Restraint; check; standard of comparison for checking inferences from experiment etc. 3. Controller; (spiritualism) personality or spirit alleged to control medium's words and actions. 4. Place where vehicles etc. in race must stop for official examination and where time is usu. allowed for overhaul etc.; section of road etc. over which speed of vehicles is checked. 5. Apparatus by means of which machine in operation, esp. motor-car or aircraft, is controlled. ~ *v.t.* Exercise restraint or direction over; command, dominate, regulate; hold in check; check, verify.

contrō'ller *n.* (esp.) One who controls or checks expenditure, steward, esp. of royal household, mint, navy, etc. **contrŏ'llership** *n.*

cŏntrovêr'sial (-sh*a*l) *adj.* Of, open to, given to, controversy. **cŏntrovêr'sialism, cŏntrovêr'sialist** *ns.* **cŏntrovêr'siallȳ** *adv.*

cŏ'ntrovêrsȳ (*or* kontrŏ'-) *n.* Disputation; dispute; argument (esp. conducted in writing).

cŏ'ntrovêrt (*or* -vêr't) *v.t.* Call in question, dispute truth of.

cŏntūmā'cious (-sh*u*s) *adj.* Insubordinate, disobedient, esp. to order of court. **cŏntūmā'ciouslȳ** *adv.* **cŏntūmā'ciousnĕss** *n.* **cŏ'ntūmacȳ** *n.*

cŏ'ntūmelȳ (*or* -mlĭ) *n.* Insolent, reproachful, language or treatment; disgrace. **cŏntūmē'lious** *adj.* **cŏntūmē'liouslȳ** *adv.*

contū'se (-z) *v.t.* Bruise. **contū'sion** *n.*

conŭ'ndrum *n.* Riddle, puzzle.

cŏnûrbā'tion *n.* Aggregation of urban districts regarded as a single community for certain purposes.

cŏnvalĕ'sce *v.i.* Regain health. **cŏnvalĕ'scence** *n.* Gradual recovery of health after illness.

cŏnvalĕ'scent *adj.* Recovering from illness. ~ *n.* Convalescent person; ~ *home, hospital*, nursing home, hospital, for such persons.

convĕ'ction *n.* (phys.) Conveyance of heat by (usu. upward) movement of heated fluid, e.g. air or water. **convĕ'ctional** *adj.*

convĕ'ctor *n.* (also ~ *heater*) Appliance that warms room by convection.

convenances (kawṅvenahṅs) *n.pl.* Conventional propriety. [Fr.]

convē'ne *v.* Assemble; convoke; summon (person *before* tribunal). **convē'ner** *n.* One who convenes, member of a committee etc. who fixes dates, and issues notices, of meetings.

convē'nience *n.* 1. Suitableness, commodiousness; material advantage; personal comfort or ease; advantage. 2. Useful appliance; lavatory; (pl.) material comforts.

convē'nient *adj.* Fit, suitable; not troublesome; (colloq.) conveniently near. **convē'nientlȳ** *adv.*

cŏ'nvent *n.* Religious community (usu. of women, cf. MONASTERY) living together; building occupied by this.

convĕ'nticle *n.* (hist.) Clandestine religious meeting, esp. of nonconformists or dissenters; building used for this.

convĕ'ntion *n.* 1. Convening. 2. Formal assembly for deliberation or legislation on important matters; esp. (hist.) certain extraordinary assemblies of Parliament without summons of sovereign, e.g. that of 1660, which restored Charles II; *National C~*, sovereign assembly which governed France from 21 Sept. 1792 to 26 Oct. 1795. 3. (U.S. etc.) Assembly of delegates or representatives, conference. 4. Agreement; in diplomacy, less formal or less important agreement than treaty. 5. General agreement or consent (often implicit) as foundation of usage etc., rule or practice based on this; accepted usage become artificial and formal; (pl., in game of bridge etc.) standard methods of bidding, leading, etc.

convĕ'ntional *adj.* Depending on convention(s), not natural, not spontaneous; (of weapons) other than atomic. **convĕ'ntionally** *adv.* **convĕ'ntionalism, convĕ'ntionalist, convĕntionă'lity̆** *ns.* **convĕ'ntionalize** *v.t.*

convĕ'ntūal *adj.* & *n.* (Member, inmate) of a convent; (member) of the less strict branch of Franciscans, living in large convents.

conver'ge *v.* (of lines etc.) Tend to meet in a point; approach nearer together; (math., of series) approximate in sum of its terms toward a definite limit. **conver'gence, conver'gency̆, conver'gent** *adj.*

conver'sable *adj.* Easy, pleasant, in conversation; fit for social intercourse. **conver'sableness** *n.* **conver'sably̆** *adv.*

conver'sant (*or* kŏ'-) *adj.* Having frequent intercourse, well acquainted (*with*). **conver'sance, -cy̆** *ns.*

cŏnversā'tion *n.* 1. Talk, interchange of thoughts and words. 2. ~ *piece*, painting of group of figures, esp. members of a family, arranged as if in conversation.

cŏnversā'tional *adj.* Fond of, good at, pertaining to, conversation. **cŏnversā'tionally̆** *adv.* **cŏnversā'tionalist** *n.*

cŏnversăziō'nė (-săts-) *n.* Soirée given by learned body or society of arts etc.

conver'se[1] *v.i.* Talk. **cŏ'nverse** *n.* (archaic) Conversation.

cŏ'nverse[2] *adj.* Opposite, contrary. ~ *n.* 1. (logic) Converted proposition; statement etc. derived from another by transposition of two important antithetical members, e.g. *he is brave but not good* is the converse of *he is good but not brave.* 2. (math.) Proposition which assumes the conclusion and proves the datum of another. **cŏ'nversely̆** *adv.*

conver'sion *n.* Converting; being converted.

conver't *v.t.* 1. Change (*into*). 2. Cause to turn (*to* opinion, faith, etc.); turn to godliness; (logic) transpose (subject and predicate). 3. (Rugby footb.) Kick goal from (try). **cŏ'nvert** *n.* Person converted, esp. to religious faith or life.

conver'tible *adj.* That may be converted; (of items) equivalent, synonymous; (econ., of a currency) that may be freely converted into gold or dollars at a fixed price. **convertibi'lity** *n.* **conver'tible** *n.* (orig. U.S.) Motor-car with collapsible hood.

cŏ'nvĕx *adj.* Curved like outside of circle or sphere, reverse of CONCAVE. **convĕ'xity̆** *n.* **cŏ'nvĕxly̆** *adv.*

convey' (-ā) *v.t.* Transport, carry; transmit; impart, communicate (idea, meaning); (law) transfer, make over (property) by deed or legal process.

convey'ance (-vā'*a*-) *n.* 1. Carrying; transmission; communication. 2. (Document effecting) transference of property. 3. Carriage, vehicle. **convey'ancer** *n.* Lawyer who prepares documents for conveyance of property and investigates titles. **convey'ancing** *n.* Drawing of deeds etc. for the transfer of property, branch of law dealing with titles and their transference.

convey'er, -or (-vā-) *n.* (esp.) Mechanical device (usu. in form of endless belt or band) for conveying goods, esp. those in process of manufacture.

convi'ct' *v.t.* Prove guilty (*of* offence); declare guilty by verdict of jury or decision of judge; (theol.) impress (person) with sense of error. **cŏ'nvict** *n.* Condemned criminal serving prison sentence.

convi'ction *n.* Convicting; being convicted; verdict of guilty; firm belief.

convi'nce *v.t.* Firmly persuade (*of, that*). **convi'ncingly̆** *adv.* **convi'ncingness** *n.* **convi'ncible** *adj.* Open to conviction.

convi'vial *adj.* Of, befitting, a feast; festive, jovial. **convi'vially̆** *adv.* **convivĭă'lity̆** *n.*

cŏnvocā'tion *n.* Calling together; assembly; (Church of England) synod of clergy of province of Canterbury or York; legislative assembly (in Durham and Oxford Univ.) of all qualified members holding degree of M.A.; (in other universities) assembly of qualified members for discussing matters connected with university. **cŏnvocā′tional** *adj.*

convō′ke *v.t.* Call together; summon to assemble.

cŏ′nvolūte *adj.* (bot., conch.) Rolled together, coiled. ~ *n.* Coil. **cŏ′nvolūtėd** *adj.* Coiled, twisted. **cŏnvolū′tion** *n.* Coiling, twisting; coil, twist.

convŏ′lvŭlus *n.* Plant of genus *C~* with twining stem and trumpet-shaped white, pink, or blue flowers, bindweed.

cŏ′nvoy (*or* konvoi′) *v.t.* (of ship of war or aircraft) Escort (usu. merchant or passenger vessel); escort with armed force; (archaic) conduct (guests, lady, etc.). **cŏ′nvoy** *n.* 1. Convoying. 2. Company, supply of provisions, etc., under escort; number of merchant ships under escort or sailing in company; number of vehicles travelling in company.

convŭ′lse *v.t.* Shake violently; throw into convulsions (usu. pass.); cause to be violently seized with laughter (usu. pass.).

convŭ′lsion *n.* 1. (usu. pl.) Violent irregular motion of limb or body due to involuntary contraction of muscles (esp. as disorder of infants); (pl.) violent fit of laughter. 2. Violent social or political agitation; violent physical disturbance, esp. earthquake etc.

convŭ′lsĭve *adj.* Attended or affected with, producing, resembling, convulsions. **convŭ′lsĭvelȳ** *adv.*

cō′nȳ, cō′ney *n.* (pl. *-ies, -eys*). 1. Rabbit (now retained only in statutes etc. and as shop name for the fur). 2. Small mammal of order Hyracoidea, living in caves and clefts of rocks in the Middle East and E. Africa.

coo[1] *v.* Make soft murmuring sound of, or as of, doves and pigeons; say cooingly. ~ *n.* Cooing sound.

coo[2] *int.* (slang) Exclamation of surprise or incredulity.

coo′ee′, coo′ey *n.* & *v.i.* (Make) call adapted as signal by Australian colonists from aborigines.

cook[1] *v.* Prepare food, prepare (food) by application of heat; undergo cooking; concoct; (colloq.) tamper with, falsify (accounts etc.); (slang) ruin, spoil; ~ *person's goose,* do for him, settle his hash. ~ *n.* One whose business it is to cook food, esp. woman-servant employed in private family; *~-book,* (U.S.) cookery book; *~-general,* servant who does all work of house as well as cooking; *~-house,* camp kitchen; outdoor kitchen in warm countries; galley on ship; *~-housemaid,* female servant who acts as both cook and housemaid; *~-shop,* eating-house; *~-stove,* (U.S.) cooking stove.

Cook[2], James (1728–79). English navigator and explorer esp. of the

S. Pacific islands and Australasia; landed at Botany Bay in 1770 and took formal possession of Australia for the British Crown.

coo′ker *n.* 1. Stove or vessel for cooking. 2. Fruit etc. suitable for cooking. **coo′kerȳ** *n.* Art, practice, of cooking; ~ *book,* book of recipes and instructions in cookery.

coo′kie *n.* (Sc.) Plain bun; (U.S. etc.) sweet biscuit.

cool *adj.* 1. Moderately cold. 2. Unexcited, calm; lacking zeal, lukewarm; wanting cordiality. 3.

Calmly audacious or impudent. 4. (colloq.) Applied complacently or emphatically to a large sum of money, e.g. *it cost me a ~ thousand.* 5. (of jazz music) Restrained or relaxed in style (opp. HOT). **coo′llȳ** (-l-lĭ) *adv.* **coo′lnėss** *n.* **cool** *n.* Cool air, cool place; coolness. ~ *v.* Make or become cool; ~ *one's heels*, be kept waiting.

coo′labah, -ĭbah, k- *n.* Australian gum-tree, esp. *Eucalyptus microtheca.*

coo′lant *n.* Cooling agent; (esp.) fluid applied to edge of a cutting-tool to lessen friction; cooling medium in internal combustion engine etc.

coo′ler *n.* Vessel in which anything, as wine, butter, is cooled or set to cool; (slang) prison cell.

Coo′lĭdge, Calvin (1872–1933). 30th president of U.S., 1923–9.

coo′lĭe *n.* Unskilled workman or porter, esp. in or from the Far East.

coomb: see COMBE.

coon *n.* (U.S.) 1. = RACOON. 2. (derog.) Negro; sly fellow.

coo′n-că′n *n.* Card-game similar to RUMMY, originating in Mexico. [Span. *con quien* with whom?]

coop *n.* Cage placed over sitting or fattening fowl; wickerwork basket for catching fish; narrow place of confinement. ~ *v.* Put in coop; confine narrowly (also ~ *up*).

cō′-ŏp *n.* (colloq.) Co-operative store or society.

coo′per[1] *n.* Maker of casks and other wooden vessels formed of staves and hoops; one engaged in sampling, bottling, or retailing wine. ~ *v.t.* Make or repair (casks); put or stow in casks. **coo′perage** *n.* Cooper's work or workshop; payment for cooper's work.

Coo′per[2], James Fenimore (1789–1851). Amer. writer of stories dealing esp. with the Red Indians.

cō-ŏ′perāte *v.i.* Work together (*with* person *in* a work, *to* an end); concur in producing an effect. **cō-ŏperā′tion** *n.* Working together to same end; co-operative combination.

cō-ŏ′perative *adj.* Of co-operation, co-operating; willing to co-operate; ~ *society*, society or union for production or distribution of goods, in which profits are shared (freq. in form of dividends on purchases) by all contributing members; ~ *shop, store,* shop belonging to such a society. ~ *n.* Co-operative factory, farm, or other enterprise.

cō-ŏ′pt *v.t.* Elect into body by votes of existing members. **cō-ŏptā′tion, cō-ŏ′ption** *ns.* **cō-ŏ′ptative, cō-ŏ′ptive** *adjs.* Elected by co-option.

cō-or′dĭnate *adj.* Equal in rank, degree, or importance, esp. (gram.) of clauses of compound sentence; consisting of co-ordinate things. **cō-or′dĭnatelȳ** *adv.* **cō-or′dĭnate** *n.* Co-ordinate thing, esp. (math.) each of a system of two or more magnitudes used to define position of point, line, or plane, by reference to fixed system of lines, points, etc. **cō-or′dĭnāte** *v.t.* Make co-ordinate; bring (parts) into proper relation. **cō-ordĭnā′tion** *n.* **cō-or′dĭnative** *adj.*

coot *n.* Any of various swimming and diving birds; bird of genus *Fulica*, esp. the *common* ~, *F. atra*, bird with lobed toes inhabiting edges of lakes and still rivers, with base of bill extended to form broad white plate on forehead; (N. Amer.) the allied *F. Americana.*

cŏp[1] *n.* (spinning) Roll of yarn wound upon spindle in such a way that it needs no support.

cŏp[2] *n.* (slang) Policeman; capture. ~ *v.t.* (slang) Catch, capture.

copai′ba (-pī-) *n.* Aromatic resin of acrid taste obtained from S. Amer. trees or shrubs of the genus *Copaifera* and used in medicine and the arts.

cō′pal *n.* Hard translucent odoriferous resin obtained from various tropical trees and used to make a fine transparent varnish. [Mex. *copalli* incense]

cōpar′cėner *n.* (law) One who shares equally with others in inheritance of estate of common ancestor. **cōpar′cėnarȳ** *n.* Joint heirship.

cōpâr'tner *n.* Partner, sharer, associate. **cōpâr'tnership** *n.* (esp.) System designed to interest employees in their business by profit-sharing.

cōpe[1] *n.* 1. Vestment like long semicircular cloak without sleeves or arm-holes worn by clergy in procession, at Vespers, etc. 2. Vault or canopy (*of heaven* etc.). 3. (founding) Outer portion of mould. ~ *v.* Furnish with cope; cover (wall etc.) with coping; cover as with a vault; project like coping.

cōpe[2] *v.i.* Contend in well-matched struggle *with*; grapple successfully; deal competently (*with*).

cō'pĕck, k- *n.* $\frac{1}{100}$ of a rouble.

Cōpenhā'gen. (Dan. *Köbenhavn*) Capital city of Denmark; *Battle of* ~, naval battle off Copenhagen, 1801, in which the British fleet under Nelson defeated and destroyed the Danish fleet, thus breaking up the Northern Confederacy (Russia, Sweden, and Denmark) against Britain.

cō'per *n.* Horsedealer.

Copêr'nicus, Nicolaus. Latinized name of Mikolai Kopernik (1473–1543), Polish astronomer, who demonstrated that the planets, including the earth, revolve on

their own axes and move in orbits round the sun. **Copêr'nican** *adj.*

cō'pĭng *n.* Top course of masonry or brickwork in wall, usu. sloping to throw off rain; ~*-stone*, stone used in coping; (fig.) finishing touch.

cō'pĭous *adj.* Plentiful; full of matter; profuse in speech; (of language) having a large vocabulary. **cō'pĭouslȳ** *adv.* **cō'pĭousnėss** *n.*

Cŏ'pley, John Singleton (1738–1815). Amer. painter, active also in England.

cōpŏ'lȳmer *n.* Compound analogous to a polymer but with units of more than one kind. **cōpŏ'lȳmerīze** *v.t.* **cōpŏlȳmerīzā'tion** *n.*

cŏ'pper[1] *n.* 1. (chem.) Malleable ductile tenacious metallic element of yellowish-red colour having high electrical conductivity; symbol Cu, at. no. 29, at. wt 63·546. 2. Copper money; bronze money which has superseded this; bronze coin, penny or halfpenny. 3. Large boiler, orig. of copper, for laundry etc. 4. *C~ Age*, that stage of a people's culture during which its weapons etc. were made of copper; ~ *beech*, variety of European beech-tree with copper-coloured foliage; ~*-bit*, soldering tool pointed with copper; ~*-bottom* (*v.t.*) sheathe bottom of (ship) with copper; *co'pperhead*, N. Amer. venomous snake, *Ankistrodon contortrix*, so called from reddish-brown colour of top of head; *co'pperplate*, polished plate of copper on which design is engraved or etched for printing, print from this; sloping rounded cursive handwriting orig. taught from copy-books printed from engraved copperplates; *co'ppersmith*, worker in copper. ~ *v.t.* Cover or sheathe with copper. **cŏ'pperȳ** *adj.* (esp.) Copper-coloured. [L *cuprum*, f. *Cyprium* (*aes*) Cyprian (metal)]

cŏ'pper[2] *n.* (slang) Policeman.

cŏ'pperas *n.* Hydrated ferrous sulphate ($FeSO_4.7H_2O$).

cŏ'ppĭce *n.* Small wood of underwood and small trees grown for periodical cutting.

cŏ'pra *n.* Dried kernels of coconut, exported for the expression of coconut oil, used in manufacture of margarine, candles, etc.

cŏ'prolīte *n.* Stony roundish fossil consisting of petrified dung. **cŏprolĭ'tic** *adj.*

cŏprŏ'phagous *adj.* (of beetles) Dung-eating.

cŏpse *n.* = COPPICE; *co'pse wood*, low trees and underwood of a copse. ~ *v.t.* Treat as copsewood; make a copse of.

Cŏpt *n.* Native Egyptian or Ethiopian Christian of the Jacobite sect of Monophysites. [Arab. *al-ḳibṭ* f. Coptic *gyptios*, f. Gk *Aiguptios* Egyptian]

Cŏ'ptic *adj.* Of Coptic or the Copts. ~ *n.* Language of the Copts, surviving only in the liturgy of the Coptic Church.

cŏ'pūla *n.* (logic, gram.) Part of proposition connecting subject and predicate; verb *to be* employed as mere sign of predication; (mus.) short connecting passage. **cŏ'pūlar** *adj.*

cŏ'pūlāte *v.i.* Unite in copulation. **cŏpūlā'tion** *n.* 1. Physical union between male and female animals as in act of procreation. 2. Grammatical or logical connection.

cŏ'pūlative *adj.* Serving as copula, connecting subject and predicate; relating to sexual intercourse. **cŏ'pūlativelў** *adv.* **cŏ'pūlative** *n.* Copulative conjunction or particle.

cŏ'pūlatory *adj.* Of sexual copulation.

cŏ'pў *n.* 1. Reproduction (of writing, picture, etc.); imitation; specimen of penmanship written after a model. 2. (law) Transcript of manorial court-roll containing entries of admissions of tenants by manorial custom to land held by tenure, hence called *co'pyhold.* 3. One of the written or printed specimens of the same writing or work. 4. Original from which a copy is made; esp. specimen of penmanship to be copied; manuscript or other matter prepared for printing; material for a story; text of advertisement. 5. *~-book*, book, containing copies for learners to imitate; (*attrib.*) conventional, commonplace; *~-cat*, (colloq.) one who copies (work of) another; *~-writer*, one who composes the wording of advertisements. ~ *v.* Transcribe (*from* original); make copy of; imitate; *copying-ink*, ink suitable for writing or drawings of which copies by impression are to be made, usu. prepared by adding glycerine to ordinary ink; *copying-pencil*, pencil containing lead made from graphite, aniline blue, and gum arabic, used for same purpose as copying ink. **cŏ'pyist** *n.* One who copies or transcribes.

cŏ'pyhōld *n.* Tenure (now obsolete) of land by COPY (sense 2); land so held. ~ *adj.* Held by copy; of copyhold. **cŏ'pўhōlder** *n.*

cŏ'pўrīght (-īt) *n.* Sole legal right to produce or reproduce a literary, dramatic, musical, or artistic work, by making copies or performance or any other means; ~ *libraries*, British Museum, Bodleian, Cambridge University, National Library of Wales, Scottish National Library, and Trinity College, Dublin, which are entitled by law to a free copy of every book published in the United Kingdom; ~ *union*, international union established by the Berne Convention of 1886, whereby each member country undertakes to give to foreign authors the same rights as its own authors receive. ~ *adj.* Protected by copyright. ~ *v.t.* Protect (book etc.) by copyright; secure copyright for.

coquĕ't, -ĕ'tte (-k-) *v.i.* Play the coquette; flirt (*with*); dally, trifle, *with.* **cŏ'quetrў** *n.* Coquettish behaviour or act; coquetting, trifling. **coquĕ'tte** *n.* 1. Woman who (habitually) trifles with the affections of men, flirt. 2. Crested humming-bird of genus *Lophornis.* **coquĕ'ttish** *adj.* **coquĕ'ttishlў** *adv.*

Cor. *abbrev.* Corinthians (N.T.).

cŏ'racle *n.* Small boat of wickerwork covered with pitched canvas (orig. skins) used by ancient Britons and still by Welsh and Irish fishermen. [Welsh *corwgl* f. *cwrwg* = Ir. *curach* boat]

cŏ'racoid *adj.* Beaked like a crow; ~ *process*, short projection of the scapula in vertebrates. ~ *n.* Coracoid process or bone.

cŏ'ral *n.* 1. Hard calcareous substance consisting of the continuous skeleton secreted by many kinds of submarine coelenterate polyps for their support and habitation, found growing plant-like on sea-bottom or in extensive accumulation (~ *reefs*). 2. Piece of coral as ornament etc. 3. Unimpregnated roe of lobster (so called from colour when boiled). 4. ~-*island*, island formed by growth of coral; ~-*insect*, -*polyp*, one of the individual animals secreting coral; ~ *reef*, see sense 1; ~ *stitch*, knotted stitch in embroidery. ~ *adj.* Of (the colour of) coral, reddish-pink.

cŏ'ralline *adj.* Coral red; coral-like; ~ *ware*, Italian red-paste pottery of 17th and 18th centuries. ~ *n.* Seaweed of genus *Corallina* with calcareous jointed stem; (pop.) any of various plant-like compound animals.

cŏ'rallite *n.* Fossil coral.

cŏ'ralloid *adj.* & *n.* (Organism) like, akin to, coral.

cor'am *prep.* Before, in the presence of; ~ *populo*, in public.

cor anglais (ahṅ'glā) *n.* Alto oboe; organ stop of similar tone. [Fr., = 'English horn']

cor'bel *n.* Projection of stone, timber, etc., jutting out from wall to support weight; short timber laid longitudinally under beam or girder, to shorten its unsupported span; ~-*table*, projecting course resting on corbels. ~ *v.* ~ *out*, *off*, (cause to) project on corbels. **cor'belled** (-ld) *adj.* [OF *corbel* raven]

cor'bie *n.* (Sc.) Raven; carrion crow; ~ *steps*, *stones*, step-like projections on sloping edge of gable

Corcyr'a: see CORFU.

cord *n.* 1. (Piece of) string made from several twisted strands. 2. (anat.) Flexible cord-shaped structure of tissue fibre; SPINAL ~, VOCAL ~: see these words. 3. Raised cord-like rib on cloth, ribbed fabric, esp. corduroy; (pl.) clothing made of this fabric. 4. Measure of cut wood for fuel (usu. 128 cu. ft). ~ *v.t.* Bind or fasten with cord(s).

cor'dage *n.* Cord or ropes collectively, esp. in rigging of a ship.

cor'date *adj.* Heart-shaped.

cor'dĕd *adj.* Bound, furnished, with cords; ribbed, twilled.

cordèlier' *n.* 1. Franciscan friar of strict rule (so called from knotted cord worn round waist). 2. Rope-making machine.

cor'dial *adj.* 1. That stimulates the heart. 2. Hearty, sincere; warm, friendly. **cor'dially** *adv.* **cor'diă'lity** *n.* **cor'dial** *n.* Comforting or exhilarating drink; (commercial) aromatized and sweetened spirit.

cordiller'a (-lyāra) *n.* One of series of parallel mountain ridges or chains; *Cordilleras*, parallel chains of the Andes in S. America, Central America, and Mexico. [Span.]

cor'dite *n.* Smokeless propellant of guncotton, nitroglycerine, and vaseline, usu. pressed into rods of varying length and thickness.

cor'doba *n.* Principal monetary unit of Nicaragua, = 100 centavos.

Cór'doba. City of S. Spain on river Guadalquivir; Moorish capital 756–1236.

cor'don *n.* 1. (archit.) String-course, projecting (usu. flat) band of stone on face of wall. 2. Line of troops consisting of men placed at intervals to prevent passage; line or circle of police or other persons; (also ~ *sanitaire* or *sanitary* ~) guarded line between infected and uninfected districts. 3. Ornamental cord or braid worn as badge of honour; ~ *bleu* (kor'-dawṅ bler), blue ribbon worn formerly by Knights of the Holy Ghost, the highest order under the Bourbons; hence, person of eminence, (esp.) first-class cook. 4. Fruit-tree pruned to grow as single stem (usu. on espalier or wall).

cor'duroy *n.* 1. Cotton velvet with ridges in the pile; (pl.) corduroy trousers. 2. Corduroy road. ~ *adj.* Made of corduroy, ribbed like corduroy; ~ *road*, road of tree-trunks laid transversely across swamp or miry ground.

cŏr'dwain *n.* Spanish leather (orig. from Cordova) of goat-skins, or (later) of split horse-hides, used for shoes etc. in Middle Ages. [OF *corduan* of Cordova]

cŏr'dwainer *n.* Shoemaker (obs. exc. in name of guild).

cōre *n.* 1. Dry horny capsule embedded in pulp and containing seeds of apple, pear, etc. 2. Central portion cut out as of rock in boring. 3. Central part of different character from what surrounds it; (esp.) assemblage of soft iron laminae in centre of electromagnet or induction coil; central strand in hawser-laid rope round which other strands are twisted; central cord of conducting wires in telegraph etc. cable; unit of magnetic material in a computer. 4. Innermost part, centre, heart, of anything. ~ *v.t.* Remove core from.

cō'-rėli'gionist (-jo-) *n.* Adherent of same religion.

cŏrėŏ'psis *n.* Composite plant of genus *C*~ cultivated for its handsome yellow or particoloured rayed flowers.

cō-rėspŏ'ndent *n.* (law) Man proceeded against together with woman RESPONDENT in a divorce suit.

Cŏr'fiōte *adj.* & *n.* (Native, inhabitant) of Corfu.

Cŏrfu' (-ōō). One of the Ionian islands off the W. coast of Greece, anciently called Corcyra.

cŏr'gi (-gi) *n.* (also *Welsh* ~) Dog of short-legged breed with fox-like head.

cŏriā'ceous (-sh*u*s) *adj.* Like leather.

cŏriă'nder *n.* Annual, *Coriandrum sativum*, of S. Europe, Levant, etc., with compound leaves and globose aromatic fruit (~ *seed*) used as flavouring and as carminative.

Cŏ'rinth. City of Greece, notorious in ancient times for luxury and profligacy.

Cŏri'nthian *adj.* 1. Of Corinth or its people. 2. (archit.) Of the Corinthian order. 3. (archaic) Given to elegant dissipation, profligate. 4. ~ *bronze*, an alloy of gold, silver, and copper, used in antiquity in costly ornaments; ~ *order*, (archit.) most ornate of the Greek orders, with bell-shaped capital adorned with rows of acanthus leaves giving rise to volutes and helices. ~ *n.* 1. Native, inhabitant, of Corinth; (*Epistle to the*) ~*s*, either of two books of N.T., epistles of St. Paul to the Church at Corinth. 2. (archaic) Profligate.

Cŏriolā'nus, Gaius Marcius. Acc. to tradition, a Roman patrician and general of the first half of the 5th c. B.C. who earned his name for the capture of Corioli from the Volscians. He was prosecuted on the charge of aspiring to become tyrant, and exiled; whereupon he joined the Volscians and led them against Rome, but on the entreaties of his mother, Veturia, he spared the town and withdrew to Antium, where he was put to death by the Volscians.

cŏr'ium *n.* (anat.) Dermis.

cŏrk[1] *n.* 1. Bark of cork-oak (*Quercus suber*), which grows to a thickness of 1 or 2 in. and is very light, tough, and elastic. 2. Piece of cork used as float for fishing-line, support for swimmer, etc. 3. Cylindrical or tapering piece of cork used as stopper for a bottle, cask, etc.; similar stopper of other substance. 4. (bot.) Tissue forming outer division of bark in higher plants and consisting of close-packed air-containing cells nearly impervious to air and water. 5. *cor'kscrew*, instrument for drawing corks from bottles, usu. consisting of a piece of steel twisted into a spiral with sharp point and transverse handle; (*adj.*) spirally twisted; (*v.*) twist spirally, (cause to) proceed spirally; ~-*tipped*, (cigarette) with band of cork-like substance at one end; *cor'kwood*, any of various light porous woods (esp. BALSA), and the trees yielding them. ~ *adj.* Made of cork. ~ *v.t.* Stop, stop *up*, with or as with cork; blacken with burnt cork.

Cŏrk[2]. County and county borough of Munster.

côr'kage *n.* Corking, uncorking, of bottles; hotel-keeper's charge for serving wine or spirits, esp. those not supplied by himself.

côrked (-kt) *adj.* 1. (of wine) Tasting of the cork, spoiled by an unsound cork into which the wine penetrates. 2. (of face and hands) Blackened with burnt cork.

côr'ker *n.* (slang) Something that precludes further discussion, esp. notable lie; excellent person or thing. **côr'king** *adj.* (esp. U.S.) Excellent.

côrm *n.* (bot.) Swollen base of stem containing food reserves, oc-

Spring corm

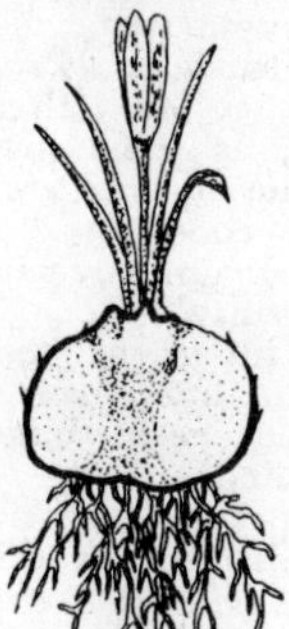

Flowering corm

Nerw corm

curring in some monocotyledonous plants, such as crocus.

côr'morant *n.* Large, lustrous-black, voracious sea-bird, *Phalacrocorax carbo*; (pl.) family to which this belongs. [med. L *corvus marinus* sea-raven]

côrn[1] *n.* 1. A grain, seed, esp. of cereals, pepper, etc. 2. Grain; cereal plants, esp. while growing; in England, usu. wheat; in Scotland and Ireland, oats; in U.S., maize. 3. *~-chandler*, retail dealer in corn; *~-cob*, = COB[1], 4; *~-cockle*: see COCKLE[1]; *cor'ncrake*, bird (*Crex crex*) which lives among standing corn, etc., and has a harsh grating voice; *~ exchange*, exchange for dealers in corn; *cor'nfactor*, dealer in corn; *cor'nfield*, field of corn; *cor'nflakes*, breakfast cereal made of flaked and flavoured maize; *cor'nflour*, meal of Indian corn (occas. of rice etc.) ground very fine; *cor'nflower*, name of various plants growing among corn, esp. the blue-flowered *Centaurea Cyanus*; *~ laws*, laws regulating trade in corn; esp. (Engl. hist.) laws restricting importation of cereals in force at beginning of 19th c. and repealed in 1846; *~ marigold*, daisy-like plant *Chrysanthemum segetum*; *~ pone*, (U.S.) kind of bread of Indian corn made with milk and eggs; *~ salad*, lamb's lettuce, a small annual plant, *Valerianella olitoria*, found wild in cornfields and cultivated as an early salad; *~-silk*, styles of maize; *cor'nstalk*, stalk of corn, esp. maize; tall, lithe person.

côrn[2] *n.* Horny induration of cuticle with hard centre and root sometimes penetrating deep into subjacent tissue, caused by undue pressure, chiefly of boots or shoes on feet; *~-cure, -plaster, -salve*, etc., remedies for corns.

côrn[3] *v.* Sprinkle, preserve (meat) with salt; *corned beef*, beef so preserved and canned.

Corn. *abbrev.* Cornwall.

côr'néa *n.* Transparent horny part of anterior covering of eyeball. **côr'néal** *adj.*

Côrneille (-nā), Pierre (1606–84). French dramatist, author of classical tragedies 'Le Cid', 'Horace', 'Polyeucte', 'Rodogune', etc.

côr'nel *n.* Common hedgerow shrub, *Cornus sanguinea*, the dogwood.

côrnē'lian, câr- *n.* Deep dull

red, flesh-coloured, or reddish-white variety of chalcedony, used for seals etc.

cŏrnē'lian chĕ'rrȳ. Species of cornel.

cŏr'nėous *adj.* Horny, horn-like.

cŏr'ner *n.* 1. Angular meeting-place of converging sides or edges, projecting angle, esp. where two streets meet; hollow angle enclosed by meeting walls etc.; *drive into a* ~, force into difficult position from which there is no escape. 2. Secluded, secret, or remote place; region, quarter; extremity or end of the earth. 3. Buying up whole of any stock or commodity, so as to compel speculative sellers to buy from one to fulfil their engagements; (loosely) any combination to raise prices by securing monopoly. 4. (footb., hockey) Free kick or hit against defending side made from corner of field when defending player hits ball over own goal line. 5. *~-stone*, one of those forming quoin or salient angle of wall; (fig.) indispensable thing or part. ~ *v.* 1. Furnish with corners. 2. Set in corner; drive into corner (esp. fig.). 3. (of vehicle etc.) Go round a corner. 4. Force (dealers) or control (commodity) by means of corner (sense 3); form corner *in* (stock or commodity).

cŏr'nėt[1] *n.* 1. Brass musical instrument of trumpet class with valves operated by pistons for producing additional notes (also called ~ *-à-pistons*); cornet - player. 2. Conically-rolled piece of paper for groceries etc.; cone-shaped wafer for holding ice-cream.

cŏr'nėt[2] *n.* 1. White head-dress of Sisters of Charity. 2. (hist.) 5th commissioned officer in troop of cavalry, who carried the colours.

cŏr'nice *n.* (archit.) Horizontal moulded projection crowning or finishing (part of) building etc., esp. uppermost member of entablature, surmounting the frieze; ornimental moulding round wall of room just below ceiling; (mountaineering) overhanging mass of hardened snow at edge of precipice.

Cŏr'nish *adj.* Of Cornwall *n.* Ancient Celtic language of Cornwall.

cŏrnūcō'pia *n.* Horn of plenty, represented as a goat's horn overflowing with flowers, fruit, and corn. **cŏrnūcō'pian** *adj.* Overflowingly abundant. [L *cornu copiae* = 'horn of plenty', the horn of the goat Amalthea by which the infant Zeus was suckled]

cŏrnū'tėd *adj.* Having horns or horn-like projections.

Cŏr'nwall. County in the extreme SW. of England; *duchy of* ~: see DUCHY.

cŏr'nȳ *adj.* (colloq.) Old-fashioned; trite, sentimental.

corŏ'lla *n.* (bot.) Whorl of floral leaves (petals) forming inner envelope of flower, and usu. its most conspicuous part.

corŏ'llarȳ *n.* Proposition appended to one already demonstrated, as self-evident inference from it; immediate deduction; natural consequence, result. [L *corollarium* money paid for a chaplet, gratuity]

corō'na *n.* (pl. *-ae* or *-as*). 1. Circle of light (usu. prismatically coloured) seen round and close to luminous body, esp. sun or moon, caused by diffraction by water droplets in thin cloud (cf. HALO); *solar* ~, rarefied gaseous envalope of sun, visible as radiating white light during total solar eclipse; (elect.) luminous appearance round conductor accompanying ionization of surrounding gas. 2. Circular candle-holder hung from roof. 3. (archit.) Member of cornice, with broad vertical face, usu. of considerable projection. 4. (anat., zool.) Any of various crown-like parts of body. 5. (bot.) Crown-like appendage on inner side of corolla in daffodil and other flowers. 6. Long straight cigar; *C*~, brand of Havana cigars (Span. *La C*~).

cŏ'ronăch (-χ) *n.* Funeral-song, dirge, in Scottish Highlands and Ireland.

cŏ'ronal[1] *n.* Circlet (esp. of gold or gems) for the head; wreath, garland.

corō'nal[2] *adj.* 1. (anat.) ~ *suture*, transverse suture of skull between frontal bone and parietal bones. 2. (bot.) Of a corona.

cŏ'ronarў *adj.* 1. (of vessels, ligaments, nerves, etc.) Encircling parts like a crown; (of parts) connected with these. 2. (of arteries, veins) Supplying blood to the heart; ~ *occlusion, thrombosis*, thrombosis occurring in a coronary artery. ~ *n.* (esp.) Coronary thrombosis.

cŏ'ronate, -ātėd *adjs.* (bot., zool.) Having a corona or crown-shaped part.

cŏronā'tion *n.* Ceremony of crowning sovereign or sovereign's consort; *C~ stone*, stone of Scone (Scotland) on which Scottish kings sat at coronation ceremony, brought to England by Edward I and now preserved in the coronation chair at Westminster Abbey.

cŏ'roner *n.* Officer of county, district, or municipality, orig. for maintaining rights of private property of Crown; now his chief function is to hold inquest on bodies of those supposed to have died by violence or accident. **cŏ'ronership** *n.*

cŏ'ronėt *n.* 1. Small crown, esp. crown denoting dignity inferior to sovereign's, worn by nobility and varying in form according to rank. 2. Decorative fillet or wreath, esp. as part of woman's head-dress; garland for the head. 3. Lowest part of horse's pastern, immediately above coffin. **cŏ'ronĕtėd** *adj.* Wearing a coronet; esp., belonging to the peerage.

corō'noid *adj.* (anat.) Curved like a crow's beak (of processes of bones).

Cŏrot (-rō), Jean-Baptiste Camille (1796–1875). French landscape-painter.

Corp. *abbrev.* Corporal.

cor͡'poral[1] *adj.* Of the human body; personal, bodily. **cor͡porăl'itў** *n.* Material existence; body; (pl.) bodily matters, wants, etc.

cor͡'poral[2], **cor͡'poras** *ns.* Fine linen cloth on which consecrated elements are placed during Mass.

cor͡'poral[3] *n.* Non-commissioned officer ranking below sergeant; *the little C~*, nickname of Napoleon I; *ship's ~*, petty officer attending to police matters under master-at-arms.

cor͡'porate *adj.* Forming a body politic or corporation; forming one body of many individuals; of, belonging to, a body politic; ~ *town*, (hist.) town with municipal rights, and corporation. **cor͡'porately** *adv.*

cor͡porā'tion *n.* 1. Body corporate legally authorized to act as a single individual; artificial person created by royal charter, prescription, or act of the legislature, with authority to preserve certain rights in perpetual succession. 2. Trade-guild, city company. 3. *municipal ~*, (hist.) civic authorities of borough, town, or city. 4. (U.S.) Business company, firm. 5. (colloq.) Abdomen, esp. when prominent. 6. *C~ Act*, act of 1661 requiring all holders of municipal office to acknowledge royal supremacy and subscribe declaration against the Solemn League and Covenant, and making all persons ineligible for office who had not partaken within a year of communion in the Church of England.

cor͡'porative *adj.* Of a corporation; (of State) with industrial system organized in corporations.

cor͡por͡'ėal *adj.* Bodily; material; (law) tangible, esp. ~ *hereditament*, hereditament of material objects. **cor͡por͡'ėallў** *adv.* **cor͡por͡ėă'litў** *n.*

cor͡porē'itў *n.* Quality of being or having a material body; bodily substance.

cor͡'posant (-z-) *n.* Luminous electrical discharge sometimes seen on ship during storm, also called *St. Elmo's fire*, interpreted as a sign of St. Elmo's protection, or sometimes of impending disaster (*dead-fire*). [It. *corpo santo* holy body]

corps (kor͡) *n.* (pl. same, pr. kor͡z). 1. Army corps; body of troops for special service. 2. Body of persons in common organization; students' society in German universities; ~ *diplomatique*, diplomatic corps; ~ *de ballet*, company of ballet dancers.

cŏrpse *n.* Dead (usu. human) body.

cŏr'pūlent *adj.* Bulky (of body); fat. **cŏr'pūlence, cŏr'pūlency̆** *ns.*

cŏr'pus *n.* 1. Body, collection, of writings. 2. (physiol.) Structure of special character or function in animal body. 3. ~ *callosum*, commissure connecting hemispheres of brain; ~ *delicti* (L,= 'body of the crime'), everything that makes a given fact a breach of law; (pop.) concrete evidence of crime, esp. body of murdered person; *juris*, body of law; ~ *luteum*, structure formed in ovary of mammals after rupture of Graafian follicle, secreting progesterone.

Cŏr'pus Chrĭ'stĭ (kr-). Feast of the Blessed Sacrament or body of Christ, the Thursday after Trinity Sunday (regularly celebrated in many places by the performance of mystery or miracle plays or pageants).

cŏr'puscle (-sl) *n.* Minute body forming distinct part of organism; (esp.) one of the minute rounded or disc-like bodies constituting a large part of the blood of vertebrates.

cŏrpŭ'scūlar *adj.* Of corpuscles; ~ *theory*, theory that light is emission of streams of imponderable particles from luminous bodies.

corra'l (-ahl, U.S. -ăl) *n.* Enclosure for horses, cattle, etc. (in U.S. and Span. America); defensive enclosure of wagons in encampment; enclosure for capturing wild animals. ~ *v.t.* Form (wagons) into corral; confine in corral.

corrā'sion *n.* (geol.) Wearing away of surface of earth by friction.

corrĕ'ct *adj.* True, accurate; right, proper (of conduct, manners, etc.), in accordance with a good standard (of taste etc.). **corrĕ'ctly̆** *adv.* **corrĕ'ctnėss** *n.* **corrĕ'ct** *v.t.* 1. Set right, amend; substitute right for (wrong); mark errors in (proof-sheet etc.) for amendment. 2. Admonish (person); cure (person) of fault; punish (person, fault). 3. Counteract, neutralize, (hurtful qualities). 4. Bring (result of mathematical or physical observation or calculation) into accordance with certain standard conditions; eliminate aberration etc. from lens etc. **corrĕ'ctor** *n.*

corrĕ'ction *n.* 1. Correcting; *under* ~, subject to correction. 2. Thing substituted for what is wrong. 3. Punishment.

corrĕ'ctitūde *n.* Correctness of conduct or behaviour.

corrĕ'ctive *adj.* & *n.* (Thing) serving, tending, to correct or counteract what is harmful. **corrĕ'ctively̆** *adv.*

Corrĕ'ggio (-jĭō). Antonio Allegri (1494–1534), called 'Il Correggio' from the place of his birth in Lombardy, an Italian painter famous for his chiaroscuro.

cŏ'rrėlāte *n.* Each of two things so related that one implies or is complementary to the other; each of two related things viewed in reference to the other. ~ *v.* Have a mutual relation (*with, to*); bring (thing) into such relation (*with* another). **cŏrrėlā'tion** *n.*

corrĕ'lative *adj.* 1. Having a mutual relation (*with, to*); analogous. 2. (gram., of words) Corresponding with each other and regularly used together each in one member of compound or complex sentence (e.g. *either—or*; *so—as*). ~ *n.* Correlative word or thing. **corrĕ'latively̆** *adv.*

cŏrrėspŏ'nd *v.i.* 1. Be congruous, in harmony (*with, to*); be similar, analogous (*to*); agree in amount, position, etc. (*to*). 2. Communicate by interchange of letters (*with*). **cŏrrėspŏ'ndingly̆** *adv.*

cŏrrėspŏ'ndence *n.* 1. Agreement, harmony. 2. Communication by letters; letters; ~ *card*, card for use as notepaper; ~ *college, course, school*, one instructing by correspondence.

cŏrrėspŏ'ndent *n.* One who writes letter(s) to another or to newspaper; person employed to contribute news, articles, etc., to newspaper etc., esp. from a distant place or on a particular subject; person etc. with regular business relations with another (esp. in foreign country). ~ *adj.* Corresponding.

corrī'da (-rē-) *n.* Bull fight.

cŏ'rridŏr *n.* 1. Main passage in large building, on which many rooms open; outside passage connecting parts of building; passage in railway carriage, upon which all compartments open. 2. Strip of territory of one State running through another territory to give access e.g. to the sea; *air* ~, route to which aircraft are restricted; *Danzig C~*, *Polish C~*, strip which ran through Prussia from Poland to the Baltic at Danzig, created by the Treaty of Versailles (1919).

cŏ'rrie *n.* (esp. in Scotland) Cirque. [Gael. *coire* cauldron]

cŏrrigĕ'ndum *n.* (pl. *-da*). Thing to be corrected (esp. mistake in printed book).

cŏ'rrigible *n.* Capable of being corrected; open or submissive to correction.

corrŏ'borant *adj.* & *n.* Strengthening (medicine); corroborating (fact).

corrŏ'borāte *v.t.* Confirm formally (law etc.); confirm (person, statement) by evidence etc. **corrŏborā'tion** *n.* Confirmation by further evidence. **corrŏ'borative, corrŏ'boratorў** *adjs.*

corrŏ'boree *n.* Festive or warlike dance of Australian aborigines, held at night by moonlight or light of bush fire. [native name in New South Wales]

corrō'de *v.* Wear away, destroy gradually (of rust, chemical agents, etc.); decay. **corrō'sion** *n.*

corrō'sive *adj.* Causing corrosion; ~ *sublimate*, mercuric chloride. ~ *n.* Corrosive substance. **corrō'sivelў** *adv.* **corrō'siveness** *n.*

cŏ'rrugate (-ōō-) *v.* Contract into wrinkles or folds; mark with, bend into, parallel folds or ridges. **cŏ'rrugātėd** *adj.* (esp.) ~ *iron*, galvanized sheet iron bent into a series of parallel ridges and grooves, used for roofing etc.; ~ *paper*, type of ridged packing paper. **cŏrrugā'tion** *n.*

cŏ'rrugātor (-ōō-) *n.* Each of two small muscles which contract brows in frowning.

corrŭ'pt *adj.* Rotten, decomposed (archaic); debased in character, depraved, wicked; perverted or influenced by bribery; (of language, texts, etc.) vitiated by errors or alterations; ~ *practices*, (at elections) various illegal forms of direct or indirect bribery. **corrŭ'ptlў** *adv.* **corrŭ'ptness** *n.* **corrŭ'pt** *v.* Infect, taint; bribe; destroy purity of (text, language); make, become, corrupt. **corrŭ'ptive** *adj.*

corrŭ'ptible *adj.* Liable to corruption, perishable; capable of moral corruption. **corrŭptibi'litў** *n.* **corrŭ'ptiblў** *adv.*

corrŭ'ption *n.* Decomposition; moral deterioration; use of corrupt practices; bribery etc.; perversion (of language etc.) from original state; ~ *of blood*, (hist.) affect of attainder on person attainted, by which he and his descendants lost all rights of rank and title, possession of land, etc.

cŏrsa'ge (-ahzh; *or* kŏr'sij) *n.* Bodice of woman's dress; (orig. U.S.) fresh flower(s) worn on bodice or shoulder.

cŏr'sair *n.* Mediterranean privateer, esp. of Barbary; corsair's ship.

cŏrse *n.* (archaic, poet.) Corpse.

corselet : see CORSLET.

cŏr'sėt *n.* Closely fitting founda-

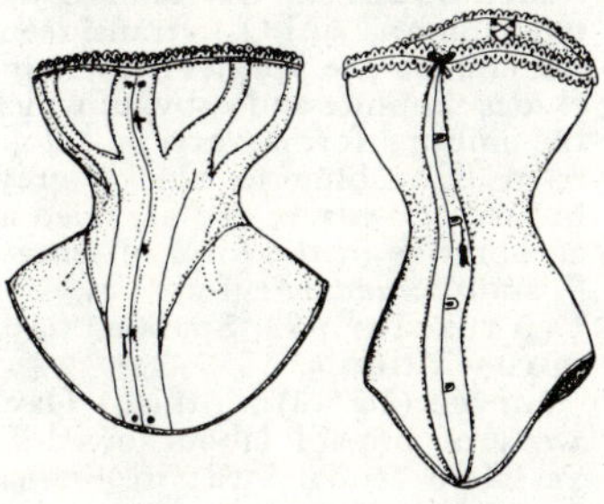

tion garment, usu. stiffened and freq. laced to give support round waist and hips, worn esp. by women; stays. ~ *v.t.* Fit with corset; (fig.) constrict.

cô̄rsėtière (-ĭār) *n.* Female corset-maker or -fitter.

cô̄r'sėtrȳ *n.* Corset-making or -fitting; corsets.

Cô̄r'sĭca. Island off the W. coast of Italy, belonging to France.

Cô̄r'sĭcan *adj.* Of Corsica or its people. ~ *n.* Native, inhabitant, of Corsica; *the* ~, Napoleon I, born at Ajaccio in Corsica.

cô̄r'slėt, cô̄r'selėt (-sl-) *n.* 1. Piece of armour covering body. 2. Garment, usu. close-fitting, covering body as dist. from limbs; (*cô̄rselĕ't*) foundation garment combining corset and brassière. 3. (zool.) Thorax, part lying between head and abdomen, of insect.

cortège (kô̄rtā'zh) *n.* Train of attendants; procession.

Cô̄r'tĕs *n.* Legislative assembly of Spain. [Span.]

cô̄r'tĕx *n.* 1. (bot.) Inner bark; 2. (anat.) Layer of grey matter on surface of brain; outer part of kidney; outer portion of suprarenal gland. **cô̄r'tĭcal** *adj.*

Cô̄r'tĕz, Hernando (1485–1547). Spanish adventurer who conquered Mexico for Spain.

cô̄r'tĭcate, -ātėd *adjs.* Having bark or rind.

cô̄r'tisone (-z-) *n.* Steroid hormone ($C_{21}H_{28}O_5$) found in adrenal cortex; similar substance prepared synthetically, used in treatment of rheumatoid arthritis etc.

corŭ'ndum *n.* Crystallized native alumina (Al_2O_3), translucent mineral of the species which includes sapphire and ruby, of which the impure forms vary in colour from light blue to smoky grey, brown, and black, and are used as an abrasive in the form of emery. [Tamil *kurundum* ruby]

cŏ'ruscāte *v.i.* Sparkle, flash. **cŏruscā'tion** *n.*

corvée (kô̄r'vā) *n.* (hist.) Day's work of unpaid labour owed by vassal to feudal lord; in France, statute labour on public road exacted of peasants before 1776.

cô̄rvĕ'tte *n.* 1. (hist.) Flush-decked warship with one tier of guns. 2. Fast naval escort vessel of 500 to 700 tons used esp. on convoy work.

cô̄r'vīne *adj.* Of, akin to, raven or crow.

Cŏ'rȳbant *n.* Priest of Phrygian worship of Cybele, which was performed with noisy and extravagant dances. **Cŏrȳbă'ntĭc** *adj.*

Cŏ'rȳdon. Name given by Theocritus and Virgil to a shepherd; hence, typical rustic in pastoral poetry.

cŏ'rȳmb *n.* (bot.) Inflorescence; raceme in which lower flower-stalks are longer, so that flowers form a flat or slightly convex head.

cŏrȳphae'us (-fē-) *n.* (pl. -ī). Leader of a chorus.

cŏ'rȳphée (-fā) *n.* Leader of *corps de ballet*.

corȳ'za *n.* (path.) Catarrh of nasal mucous membrane and sinuses; cold in the head.

cŏs[1] *n.* (also ~ *lettuce*) Kind of lettuce with long leaves and tall head. [introduced from *Cos*, island in Aegean]

cŏs[2] *abbrev.* Cosine.

cō'sĕc *abbrev.* Cosecant.

cōsē'cant *n.* (trig., function of angle in right-angled triangle) Secant of complement of given angle (abbrev. cosec).

cŏsh[1] *n.* (slang) Short heavy stick or length of metal. ~ *v.t.* Strike with cosh.

cŏsh[2] (*or* kŏs ăch) *abbrev.* Hyperbolic cosine.

cō-sĭ'gnatorȳ *n.* & *adj.* (Person) signing jointly with others.

cō'sīne *n.* (trig., function of angle in right-angled triangle) Sine of complement of given angle (abbrev. cos).

cŏsmĕ'tĭc (-z-) *adj.* Designed to beautify hair, skin, or complexion; (of surgery etc.) improving or modifying the appearance. ~ *n.* Cosmetic preparation. **cŏsmėtĭ'cian** (-shan) *n.* Cosmetic specialist.

cŏ'smĭc (-z-) *adj.* Of the universe or cosmos; ~ *rays*, high-energy radiation originating in the upper atmosphere or outer space. **cŏ'smĭcal** *adj.* **cŏ'smĭcallȳ** *adv.*

cŏ'smism (-z-) *n.* Conception of the cosmos as a self-existent, self-acting whole.

cŏsmŏ'gonȳ (-z-) *n.* (Theory of) the creation of the universe. **cŏsmogŏ'nĭc, -ĭcal** *adjs.* **cŏsmŏ'gonist** *n.*

cŏsmŏ'graphȳ (-z-) *n.* Description, mapping, of general features of universe or earth. **cŏsmŏ'grapher** *n.* **cŏsmogră'phic, -ĭcal** *adjs.*

cŏsmŏ'logȳ (-z-) *n.* Study, philosophy, of the universe as an ordered whole. **cŏsmolŏ'gĭcal** *adj.* **cosmŏ'logist** *n.*

cŏ'smonaut (-z-) *n.* (Russian) astronaut.

cŏsmopŏ'lĭtan (-z-) *adj.* Belonging to all parts of the world; free from national limitations. ~ *n.* Citizen of the world, one without national attachments or prejudices. **cŏsmopŏ'lĭtanism** *n.*

cŏsmŏ'polīte (-z-) *n.* & *adj.* Cosmopolitan.

cŏsmopolĭ'tĭcal (-z-) *adj.* Belonging to universal polity.

cŏ'smŏs¹ (-z-) *n.* Universe as an ordered whole; ordered system of ideas etc., sum total of experience; (astron.) all stars in existence, all the galaxies.

cŏ'smŏs² *n.* Composite tropical Amer. plant of genus *C*~, cultivated for its rose, scarlet, and purple inflorescences and elegant foliage.

Cŏ'ssack *n.* One of those Russians who sought a free life in the steppes or on the frontiers of imperial Russia and were allowed privileges by the Tsars, including autonomy for their settlements in S. Russia (esp. Ukraine) and Siberia in return for service in protecting the frontiers; one of the descendants of these, still noted for warlike qualities and horsemanship. ~ *adj.* Of the Cossacks. [Turk. *quzzāq* seceder, adventurer (first used of an unrelated non-Russian nomadic people of S. Siberia, the Kazakhs)]

cŏ'ssėt *v.t.* Pet, pamper.

cŏst *n.* Price (to be) paid for thing; expenditure of time, labour, etc.; (pl.) law expenses, esp. those allowed by court etc. against losing party; ~ *of living*, cost of basic necessities of life; *prime* ~, price at which manufacturer produces; ~ *price*, price at which merchant buys. ~ *v.* 1. (past t. & past part. *cost*). Be acquirable at, involve expenditure of; result in the loss of. 2. (past t. & past part. *costed*). Estimate or fix cost of production; *costing clerk*, one engaged in fixing costs. **cŏ'st-lėss** *adj.*

cŏ'stal *adj.* Of the ribs.

cō-stâr *n.* Cinema or stage star appearing with other star(s). ~ *v.* Perform with, include, co-star(s).

cŏ'stard *n.* Large ribbed variety of apple.

Cŏ'sta Ri'ca (rē-). Republic of southern Central America, until 1821 part of Spanish-American dominions; capital, San José.

cŏ'state *adj.* Ribbed, having ribs.

cŏstea'n, -ee'n *v.i.* (mining) Bore down to rock to find direction of lode. ~ *n.* Bore made by costeaning. [Cornish *cothas stean* dropped tin]

cŏ'ster, cŏ'stermonger (-mŭngg-) *n.* Man who sells fruit, fish, etc., from barrow in street (esp. in London).

cŏ'stĭve *adj.* Constipated. **cŏ'stĭvelȳ** *adv.* **cŏ'stĭvenėss** *n.*

cŏ'stlȳ *adj.* High-priced. **cŏ'stlĭnėss** *n.*

cŏ'stmārȳ *n.* Aromatic perennial composite plant, *Chrysanthemum balsamita*, formerly used in medicine and for flavouring ale etc. [Gk *kostos* aromatic plant + (*Virgin*) *Mary*]

cŏ'stūme *n.* 1. Mode or fashion of personal attire and dress of a particular nation, class, or period; ~*-piece*, *-play*, dramatic piece in which actors wear costume of some past period. 2. Complete set of outer garments. 3. ~ *jewellery*, artificial or semi-precious jewellery worn as fashion accessory. ~ *v.t.* Provide with costume.

cŏstū'mĭer *n.* Maker of, dealer in, costumes.

cō'sȳ (-z-) *adj.* Comfortable, snug. ~ *n.* Covering of (padded) material to retain heat in teapot or boiled egg. **cō'silȳ** *adv.* **cō'sinėss** *n.*

cŏt[1] *n.* Small erection for shelter or protection; (poet.) little cottage. ~ *v.t.* Put, keep, (sheep) in cot.

cŏt[2] *n.* 1. (Ind. etc.) Light bedstead. 2. (naut.) Swinging bed suspended like hammock. 3. Child's small bed; bed in children's hospital. [f. Hind. *khāṭ* bedstead, bier]

cŏt[3] *abbrev.* Cotangent.

cōtă'ngent (-j-) *n.* (trig., function of angle in right-angled triangle) Tangent of complement of given angle (abbrev. cot).

cōte *n.* Shed, stall, shelter, esp. for domestic animals.

cote-hardie: see COAT-HARDIE.

cō'terie *n.* Circle, set, of persons associated by exclusive interests; select circle in society. [Fr., orig. association of country people, f. *cotier* cottar]

cōtẽr'minous *adj.* = CONTERMINOUS. **cōtẽr'minouslȳ** *adv.*

cŏth (*or* kŏt ăch) *abbrev.* Hyperbolic cotangent.

cothûr'nus *n.* (pl. -ī). Buskin.

cotĭ'llion, -llon (-lyon) *n.* Dance with elaborate series of steps and figures, with giving of favours and changes of partner. [Fr. *cotillon* petticoat]

cotōnėă'ster *n.* Deciduous or evergreen shrub or small tree of genus *C*~ with white or pinkish flowers and usu. red or orange berries.

Cŏ'tswold *adj.* Of the Cotswold Hills; ~ *Hills*, (also ~*s*) range of hills in Gloucestershire, noted for their sheep-pastures and for a breed of long-woolled sheep, and formerly for the important woollen trade of the district.

cŏ'ttage *n.* 1. Labourer's or villager's small dwelling. 2. Small country or suburban house; (U.S.) summer residence (freq. large and sumptuous). 3. ~ *cheese*, (cheese made from curds (orig. U.S.); ~ *hospital*, small hospital without resident medical staff; ~ *industry*, industry carried on by workers in their homes; ~ *loaf*, loaf of bread of two rounded masses of dough, the smaller stuck on top of larger; ~ *pie*, = SHEPHERD's pie. **cŏ'ttager** *n.* One who lives in a cottage.

cŏ'ttar, cŏ'tter[1] *n.* 1. (used to translate *cotarius* of Domesday Book etc.; hist.) Villein who occupied cottage with attached land (usu. 5 acres), in return for labour service. 2. (Sc.) Peasant occupying cottage on farm and labouring on farm at fixed rate when required. 3. (Ir.) Cottier 2.

cŏ'tter[2] *n.* Key, wedge, bolt, for securing parts of machinery etc.; esp. split pin that opens after passing through hole; ~*-pin*, pin to keep cotter in place.

cŏ'ttier *n.* 1. Cottager. 2. Irish peasant cultivating small-holding under obsolete ~ *system*, by which small portions of land were let annually at rents fixed by public competition.

cŏ'tton[1] *n.* White downy fibrous substance clothing seeds of cotton-plant, used for making thread, cloth, etc.; cotton-plant; thread spun, cloth made, from cotton; *mineral* ~, metallic fibre of fine white threads formed by blowing steam through liquid slag; ~*-grass*, species of *Eriophorum*, with heads of long white silky hairs; ~*-plant*, plant of genus *Gossypium*, yielding cotton; ~*-seed*, seed of cotton-plant, furnishing oil and cattle-fodder; ~*-spinner*, worker who spins cotton; owner of

cotton-mill; *co'ttontail*, Amer. rabbit of genus *Sylvilagus*, with a white fluffy tail; *co'ttonwood*, (U.S.) various species of poplar, with seeds surrounded by cotton-like substance; ~ *wool*, raw cotton, esp. as prepared for wadding etc. **cŏ'ttonў** *adj*. [Arab. *kutkn*]

cŏ'tton² *v.i.* (colloq.) Be drawn *to*; ~ *on* (*to*), understand (idea etc.).

Cŏ'tton³, Sir Robert Bruce (1570–1631). English antiquary, collector of coins and of the *Cottonian Library* of ancient manuscripts, deposited in the British Museum in 1753.

Cōtў, René (1882–1963). French statesman; president of the republic 1953–8.

cŏtўlē'don *n*. Primary leaf in embryo of higher plants, seed-leaf. **cŏtўlē'donous** *adj*. Having cotyledons.

cŏ'tўloid *adj*. (anat.) Cup-shaped.

couch¹ *n*. 1. Bed, thing one sleeps on; piece of furniture like sofa but with half-back and head-end only. 2. (malting) Bed or layer in which grain is laid to germinate after steeping. ~ *v*. 1. Lay oneself down (now only in past part.). 2. (of animals) Lie, esp. in lair; crouch; lie in wait. 3. (malting) Lay (grain) on floor to germinate. 4. Lower (spear) to position of attack. 5. (embroidery) Stitch thick thread on surface of material by means of fine thread. 6. Remove (cateract) by inserting needle through coats of eye and displacing the opaque crystalline lens below the axis of vision. 7. Express *in* language, words, terms, etc.

couch² (*or* kōō-) *n*. (usu. ~-*grass*) Species of grass, *Agropyron repens*, with long creeping underground stems, a common and troublesome weed in cornfields etc. [var. of QUITCH]

cou'chant *adj*. (her., of animals) Lying with body resting on legs and head lifted.

couchĕ'tte (kōōsh-) *n*. (Berth in) continental railway carriage with seats convertible into sleeping-berths.

Coué (kōōā), Émile (1857–1926). French psychologist, advocate of a system of sanguine autosuggestion. **Cou'éĭsm** *n*.

cou'gar (kōō-) *n*. (U.S.) Puma. [Braz.]

cough (kŏf) *v*. Expel air from lungs with violent effort and characteristic noise produced by abrupt opening of glottis, in order to remove obstruction or relieve irritation in air-passages; ~ *out*, *up*, eject by, say with, cough; ~ *up*, (slang) bring out, produce (esp. money). ~ *n*. Act of coughing; tendency to cough; condition of respiratory organs resulting in coughing.

could: see CAN².

coulisse (kōōlē's) *n*. 1. (in theatre) Wings; space between two of these. 2. Groove in which sluice-gate moves.

couloir (kōō'lwahr) *n*. Steep gully in mountain side. [Fr., = 'strainer']

Coulomb¹ (kōōlawn), Charles Augustin de (1736–1806). French physicist, inventor of method of measuring the quantity of electricity.

coulomb² (kōōlŏ'm) *n*. Quantity of electricity conveyed in 1 second by current of 1 ampere (abbrev. C). [f. COULOMB¹).

cou'lter (kōl-) *n*. Metal blade fixed in front of share in plough.

cou'marin (kōō-) *n*. Aromatic crystalline substance found in tonka bean, woodruff, etc., and used as a perfume. [*cumaru*, native name in Guiana of tonka bean]

cou'ncil *n*. 1. Ecclesiastical assembly for regulating doctrine or discipline in church; (N.T.) Jewish Sanhedrin. 2. Advisory or deliberative assembly. 3. Body of men chosen or designated as permanent advisers on matters of state, esp. to advise and assist sovereign etc. (see PRIVY Council); (Sc. hist.) Scottish Privy Council, sitting as *Lords of C~*, for judicial business during vacation of Parliament. 4. (England and Wales) Administrative body of local government area; also, of parish (England), or community (Wales). 5. *C~ of Europe*: see

EUROPE; *C~ of war*, assembly of military or naval officers called to consult with general etc., usu. in special emergency (freq. fig.). 6. *~ house*, dwelling house erected by local authority for letting; *~-man*, member of town or city council in U.S. or City of London; *~ school*, school supported by town or county council. **cou'ncillor** *n.* Official member of a council. **cou'ncillorship** *n.*

cou'nsel *n.* 1. Consultation; advice; *keep one's (own) ~*, be reticent about one's intention or opinions; *~ of perfection*, one of the advisory declarations (in medieval theology reckoned as twelve) of Christ and the Apostles, not considered universally binding but as a means of attaining greater moral perfection; (fig.) ideal but impracticable advice. 2. Body of legal advisers in cause; legal adviser, barrister; *King's (Queen's) C~*, barrister(s) appointed (on nomination of Lord Chancellor) as counsel to Crown, taking precedence of ordinary barristers and wearing silk instead of stuff gown. *~ v.t.* Advise; recommend. **cou'nsellor** *n.* Adviser; official at embassy etc.; (also *~-at-law*) barrister, counsel (now only in Ireland); in some States of U.S., attorney admitted to practise in all courts.

count[1] *v.* 1. Enumerate, reckon (*up*); repeat numerals in order; include, be included, in reckoning; *~ down*, count in reverse from a given number to zero, usu. in seconds, to mark lapse of time before an event, esp. launching of spacecraft etc.; *~-down* (*n.*). 2. *~ out*, count while taking from a stock; bring sitting of (House of Commons) to a close on counting number of members present and finding it less than forty; declare (boxer) to have lost contest by counting 10 seconds before he rises to resume fight; leave out of count or consideration; (children's games) count players with words of formula, the last at each turn being reckoned out of the game. 3. Esteem, account, consider; be reckoned; enter into account or reckoning; *~ on*, depend or rely on, expect with assurance. *~ n.* 1. Counting; sum total. 2. (boxing) Counting of 10 seconds (time allowed for fallen boxer to rise and resume fighting or be declared loser). 3. (textiles) Number indicating the fineness of yarn, usu. based on the length of yarn which amounts to a given weight. 4. (law) Each charge in an indictment.

count[2] *n.* (in some European countries) Nobleman corresp. to English *earl*; *~ palatine*: see PALATINE[1]. **cou'ntship** *n.* (hist.) Rank, domain, territory, of count.

cou'ntėnance *n.* Expression of face; face; composure; moral support. *~ v.t.* Sanction; encourage.

cou'nter[1] *n.* (esp.) 1. Small usu. round piece of metal, ivory, etc., used for keeping account in games of chance, esp. cards; imitation coin. 2. Banker's or money-changer's table; table in shop etc. on which money is counted out, across which goods are delivered etc.; *under the ~*, clandestinely (esp. illegally); *~-jumper*, (contempt.) shop assistant.

cou'nter[2] *n.* 1. Part of horse's breast between shoulders and under neck. 2. (naut.) Curved part of stern of ship. 3. Depressed part of face of printing type, coin, or medal; (also *~-punch*) die used in making counter of type to be engraved on punch. 4. (skating; also *~-rocker*, *~-rocking-turn*) Rocking-turn with body revolving away from concave of first curve.

cou'nter[3] *n.* 1. (fencing) Circular parry, parry in which hand retains same position while point describes circle. 2. (boxing) Blow delivered as adversary leads off.

cou'nter[4] *n.* (shoemaking) Stiff material forming back part of shoe or boot round heel.

cou'nter[5] *adj.* Opposed; opposite; duplicate; *~-rocker* etc.: see COUNTER[2]. *~ adv.* In the opposite direction; contrary.

coun'ter[6] *v.* Oppose, encounter, contradict, controvert; (chess) meet with counter move; (boxing) give return blow while parrying opponent's blow.

counter- *prefix.* 1. Against, opposite. 2. In reversal. 3. In reciprocation or reply. 4. As opposite member or constituent. 5. With contrary action etc. 6. (mus.) = CONTRA-.

counteră'ct *v.t.* Hinder, defeat, by contrary action; neutralize. **counteră'ction** *n.* **counteră'ctĭve** *adj.*

cou'nter-attă'ck *v.* & *n.* Attack in reply to enemy's attack.

cou'nter-attră'ction *n.* Attraction of contrary tendency; rival attraction.

cou'nterbălance *n.* Weight balancing another. ~ *v.t.* Act as counterbalance to.

cou'nterblast (-ah-) *n.* Energetic declaration against something.

cou'ntercharge *n.* Charge in opposition to another, or against accuser. ~ *v.t.* Bring countercharge against.

cou'nter-claim *n.* Claim set up against another; claim by defendant in suit. ~ *v.* Claim against plaintiff or prior claim.

cou'nter-ĕspĭona'ge (-ahzh) *n.* Detection and frustration of an enemy's spy system; service etc. engaged in this.

cou'nterfeit (-fĭt *or* -fēt) *adj.* & *n.* (Thing) made in imitation, not genuine. ~ *v.t.* Make a counterfeit of; imitate fraudulently; resemble closely. **cou'nterfeiter** *n.*

cou'nterfoil *n.* Complementary part of bank cheque, receipt, etc., with note of particulars, retained by drawer.

cou'nterfort *n.* Buttress supporting wall or terrace.

cou'nter-ĭntĕ'llĭgence *n.* Counter-espionage.

counter-ĭ'rritant *n.* (med.) Thing used to produce surface irritation and thus counteract symptoms of disease (also fig.). **counter-ĭ'rrĭtāte** *v.t.* **counter-irrĭtā'tion** *n.*

counterma'nd (-ah-; *or* kow'-) *v.t.* Revoke (command); recall by contrary order; cancel order for. ~ *n.* Order revoking previous one.

cou'ntermarch *n.* & *v.* (Cause to) march in contrary direction.

cou'ntermark *n.* Additional mark on bale of goods belonging to several merchants etc.; hallmark.

cou'ntermīne *n.* Mine placed to intercept that of besiegers etc.; (fig.) counterplot. ~ *v.* Make, oppose, by countermine.

cou'nter-move (-mōōv) *n.* Move in opposition, contrary move. **cou'nter-movement** *n.*

cou'nterpāne *n.* Coverlet, quilt.

cou'nterpart *n.* Duplicate; person, thing, forming natural complement to another; opposite part of indenture.

cou'nterplŏt *n.* Plot contrived to defeat another. ~ *v.* Frustrate by, devise, counterplot.

cou'nterpoint *n.* (mus.) Melody added as accompaniment to given melody or plainsong; art of adding one or more melodies as accompaniment to given melody according to certain fixed rules; this style of composition; *double, triple* ~, invertible counterpoint in which melodies may be changed in position above or below one another.

cou'nterpoise (-z) *n.* Counterbalancing weight; thing of equivalent force etc. on opposite side; equilibrium. ~ *v.t.* Counterbalance; compensate; bring into, keep in, equilibrium.

cou'nter-rĕformā'tion *n.* Reformation running counter to another; *C~-R~*, (hist.) reformation in the Church of Rome during the latter part of the 16th c. following on the Protestant Reformation, initiated by the Council of TRENT[2] and largely accomplished by the Jesuits.

cou'nter-rĕvolū'tion (*or* -lōō-) *n.* Revolution reversing results of previous revolution. **counter-rĕvolū'tionarȳ** *adj.* & *n.*

cou'nterscarp *n.* (fortif.) Outer wall or slope of ditch, supporting covered way.

cou'ntersign[1] (-īn) *n.* Watchword, password, given to man on guard.

cou'ntersīgn[2] (-īn) *v.t.* Add signature to (document already signed); ratify.

cou'ntersink *v.t.* (past t. *-sănk*,

past part. *-sŭnk*). Bevel off (top of hole) to receive head of screw or bolt; sink (screw-head) in such hole, so as to lie flush with surface; *cou'ntersunk*, (esp., of screw) with head bevelled for this purpose.

counter-tĕ'nor *n.* (mus.) (Part for, singer with) male voice of tenor quality but alto range.

cou'ntervail *v.t.* Counterbalance; avail against; *countervailing duty*, one put on bounty-fed imports to give home goods an equal chance.

cou'nterwork (-ērk) *n.* (mil.) Work raised in opposition to works of enemy; opposing work. ~ *v.* Counteract, frustrate; work in opposition.

cou'ntėss *n.* Wife, widow, of count or earl; lady ranking with count or earl in her own right.

cou'nting-house *n.* Building, room, devoted to keeping accounts.

cou'ntlėss *adj.* Too many to count.

cou'ntrified (kŭn-, -īd) *adj.* Rural, rustic.

cou'ntrȳ (kŭ-) *n.* 1. Region; territory of nation; land of person's birth, citizenship, etc., fatherland. 2. Rural districts as opp. to towns; rest of a land as opp. to capital; (cricket, colloq.) deep field; ~ *club*, (orig. U.S.) club in country surroundings; ~ *cousin*, relation of countrified manners or appearance; ~ *dance*, rural or native dance, folk-dance; ~ *gentleman*, gentleman with landed property in country; ~ *house*, house in country, esp. residence of country gentleman; *cou'ntryside*, rural district, its inhabitants.

cou'ntrȳman (kŭ-) *n.* 1. (fem. *cou'ntrywoman*) Person of one's own (or a specified) country. 2. Person living in rural parts.

cou'ntȳ *n.* 1. Territorial division of Gt Britain and Ireland; (Gt Britain) local government area. 2. Administrative division esp. of former British dominion or colony or of State of U.S. 3. (Engl. hist.) Periodical meeting under sheriff for transacting business of shire. 4. People of county (esp.) county gentry. 5. ~ *borough*: see BOROUGH; ~ *council*, representative governing body of administrative county; ~ *court*, local judicial court, in England for civil actions, chiefly recovery of small debts; in U.S. also for criminal cases; ~ *family*, family of nobility or gentry with seat in county; ~ *palatine*, see PALATINE[1]; ~ *school*, school supported by county council; ~ *seat* (U.S.), ~ *town*, town which was formerly (but is not necessarily now) the seat of administration of a county.

coup (kōō) *n.* Notable or successful stroke or move; (billiards) holing ball without its striking another; ~ *d'état* (dātah), sudden and decisive stroke of State policy, esp. violent or illegal change of government by ruling power; ~ *de grâce* (grahs), finishing stroke; ~ *de théâtre* (tāahtr), dramatically sudden or sensational act or turn.

coupé (kōō'pā) *n.* Four-wheeled closed carriage with inside seat for two and outside seat for driver; closed two-seater motor-car.

cou'ple (kŭ-) *n.* 1. Leash for holding two hounds together. 2. Pair, brace, esp. of hunting dogs; wedded or engaged pair; pair of partners in dance; two. 3. One of pair of inclined roof-rafters meeting at top. 4. (dynamics) Pair of equal and parallel forces acting in opposite directions. ~ *v.* Fasten, link, together (esp. dogs in pairs); connect (device) to other mechanism; connect (railway carriages) by a coupling; unite, bring together, in pair(s); associate in thought or speech; copulate.

cou'pler *n.* (esp.) Contrivance in organ for connecting two manuals, manual with pedals, or two keys an octave apart, so that both can be played by a single motion.

cou'plėt (kŭ-) *n.* 1. Pair of successive lines of verse, esp. when rhyming together and of same length. 2. (mus.) Two equal notes made to occupy the time of three.

cou'pling (kŭ-) *n.* (esp.) Chain or link connecting two railway carriages etc.; ~ *rod*, rod coupling wheels of locomotive engine.

cou'pŏn (kōō-) *n.* Detachable

ticket, or form entitling holder to some payment, service, etc., or as entry form for competition etc.; (pol.) party leader's recognition of parliamentary candidate as deserving election.

courage (kŭ′rĭj) *n.* Bravery, boldness; fortitude.

courāgeous (kurā′jus) *adj.* Brave, fearless. **courā′geouslў** *adv.* **courā′geousnėss** *n.*

courante (kōōrah′ńt) *n.* 1. (hist.) Running dance. 2. (mus.) Part of suite, in triple time, usu. following allemande.

courgĕ′tte (kōōrzh-) *n.* Kind of

small vegetable marrow.

cou′rĭer (kōō-) *n.* 1. Special messenger. 2. Person employed to guide and assist group of tourists. 3. *C~*, title of some newspapers.

course (kôrs) *n.* 1. Onward movement; line or direction taken or planned; career; habitual or ordinary manner of procedure. 2. Pursuit of game, esp. of hares with (grey-) hounds. 3. Ground on which race is run etc.; golf links; line to be taken in race. 4. Watercourse. 5. Planned or prescribed series of actions or proceedings, as of lectures, study, diet, etc.; (bell-ringing) successive shifting of order in which bell is struck in series of changes, series of changes in which bells return to former order. 6. Each of successive divisions of meal, consisting of one dish or several. 7. (building) Single continuous layer of bricks, stones, etc., of same height throughout; row of slates, tiles, etc. 8. (naut.) Sail attached to lower yards of ship (usu. only fore-and main-sail). 9. *in due ~*, in the natural order; *in the ~ of*, during; *of ~*, naturally, inevitably. ~ *v.* Pursue (game) with hounds, esp. hunt (hares) with greyhounds in view (not by scent); run about, run; give (horse) a run; use (hounds) in coursing. **cour′ser** *n.* (poet.) Swift horse.

court (kôrt) *n.* 1. Space enclosed by walls or buildings; (Camb. Univ.) college quadrangle; confined yard opening off street; enclosed quadrangle, open or covered, for games; plot of ground marked off for lawn tennis. 2. Sovereign's residence; his establishment and retinue; the body of courtiers; sovereign and his councillors as ruling power. 3. Formal assembly held by sovereign at his residence. 4. Assembly of Parliament (*High C~ of Parliament*); assembly of judges or other persons acting as tribunal to hear and determine any cause; place in which justice is administered; session of judicial assembly; *out of ~*, (fig.) with no claim to be considered. 5. (Meeting of) qualified members of company or corporation; (in some friendly societies) lodge. 6. Attention paid to one whose favour, affection, or interest is sought. 7. *~-baron*, court for freehold tenants of manor, held before lord or his steward; *~-card* (orig. *coat-card*), playing-card bearing picture of king, queen, or knave; ~ *circular*, daily report of doings of royal court published in newspapers; ~ *cupboard*, sideboard of 16th and 17th centuries, orig. = BUFFET[2] 1, later with a small usu. splay-sided cupboard in the upper part and sometimes a cupboard below; ~ *hand*, style of handwriting used in English lawcourts from 16th c. until abolished by statute under George II; *~-house*, building in which courts of law are held; (southern U.S.) seat of government of a county; ~ *leet*, = LEET[1]; ~ *martial* (pl. *~s martial*), trial of soldier, sailor, or airman of any rank, conducted by officers, for offences against military law; *~-martial* (*v.t.*) try by court martial; ~ *of record*: see RECORD *n.* 1; ~*-plaster*, sticking-plaster of silk coated with isinglass formerly used for making face-patches by ladies at court; ~*shoe*, woman's light shoe with low-cut upper and high or highish tapering or curved heel; *cour'tyard*, open space surrounded by walls or buildings. ~ *v.* Pay court (to); try to win favour or affection (of); try to attract sexually; seek to win (applause etc.); invite, tempt.

cour'tėous (kẽr-) *adj.* Polite, kind, considerate, in manner or address. **cour'tėouslў** *adv.* **cour'tėousnėss** *n.*

courtėsă'n, -ză'n (kŏrtĭz-) *n.* Prostitute, esp. one whose clients are wealthy or upper-class. [It. *cortigiana*, orig. woman attached to the court]

cour'tėsў (kẽr-) *n.* Courteous behaviour or disposition; *by* ~, by favour, not of right; ~ *light*, light inside car, automatically switched on when door is opened; ~ *title*, title of no legal validity given by courtesy, esp. that given to eldest son of earl, daughter or younger son of duke or marquis.

cour'tier (kŏr-) *n.* Attendant at, frequenter of, sovereign's court.

cour'tlў (kŏr-) *adj.* Polished, refined, in manners; obsequious, flattering. **cour'tlinėss** *n.*

cour'tship (kŏr-) *n.* (Period of) courting.

couscous (kōō'skōōs) *n.* N. Afr. dish of coarse flour, sometimes with meat, steamed over broth. [Arab. *kuskus*, f. *kaskasa* bruise, pound small]

cousin (kŭ'zn) *n.* Child of one's uncle or aunt (also *first* ~, ~ *german*); *cross*~, one of two who are children of brother and sister respectively; *second* ~, one's parent's first cousin's child. **cou'sinhŏŏd, cou'sinship** *ns.* **cou'sinlў** *adj.*

coûte que coûte (kōōt ke kōōt) *adv.* At all costs. [Fr.]

coutūr'e (kōō-) *n.* Fashionable dressmaking or designing; clothes made thus. **coutūr'ier** (-ēā) *n.* (fem. *couturière*, pr. -ār) Fashion designer.

couvade (kōōvah'd) *n.* Primitive people's custom by which husband feigns illness when his wife gives birth to a child.

cōvā'lencў, -ence *ns.* (chem.) Covalent bond (see VALENCY); electrons forming this; number of covalent bonds an atom can form. **cōvā'lent** *adj.* **cōvā'lentlў** *adv.*

cōve[1] *n.* Small bay or creek; sheltered recess; (archit.) concave arch, curved junction of wall with ceiling or floor. ~ *v.t.* Arch (esp. ceiling at junction with wall); slope (sides of fireplace) inwards.

cōve[2] *n.* (slang) Fellow, chap.

co'ven (kŭ-) *n.* (Sc.) Assembly of witches.

co'vėnant (kŭ-) *n.* Compact, bargain; (law) contract under seal, clause of this; (bibl.) compact between God and the Israelites; (*National*) *C*~, protestation signed throughout Scotland in 1638, in which subscribers swore to defend the Protestant religion and to resist all contrary errors; *Solemn League and C*~, (Sc. hist.) bond of agreement between England and Scotland to establish Presbyterianism in both countries, accepted by General Assembly of Church of Scotland in Aug., and by Westminster Assembly of Divines and English Parliament in Sept., 1643. ~ *v.* Make covenant (with). **co'vėnantėd** *adj.* Bound by a covenant. **co'vėnanter** (Sc. pr. -năn'-) *n.* One who covenants, esp. (Sc. hist.) adherent of National Covenant of 1638 or of Solemn League and Covenant.

Cŏ'vent Gar'den. District of central London, formerly the convent garden of Westminster; site of a fruit and vegetable market until 1974, and of the principal English opera-house, opened 1858.

Cŏ'ventrў (*or* kŭ-). City in West Midlands; *send* (*person*) *to* ~, refuse to associate with or speak to him.

co'ver (kŭ-) *v.t.* 1. Put or lay something over; put covering on. 2. Be over whole top of. 3. (of stallion etc.) Copulate with. 4. Conceal or shield; have gun, pistol, etc., trained on. 5. Include, provide for. 6. Extend or stretch over; traverse (distance). 7. Defray (expense etc.); protect by insurance; report for newspaper etc. 8. ~-*point*, (cricket) position, fielder behind and a little to bowler's side of point. 9. *covered wagon*, (U.S.) wagon with a tilt, used in travelling; *covering letter*, one sent along with another document to explain it. **co'vering** *n.* (esp.) Cover. **co'ver** *n.* 1. Thing that covers; lid; binding of book, either board of this; wrapper, envelope, of letter. 2. Protection; shelter. 3. Screen, pretence. 4. Woods or undergrowth sheltering game, covert. 5. (commerc.) Funds to meet liability or secure against contingent loss. 6. Plate, napkin, knives and forks, etc., laid for each person at table; ~ *charge*, extra charge added to cost of food and drink in restaurant. 7. (cricket) Cover-point. **co'verage** *n.*

Cō'verdāle, Miles (1488–1568). English bishop; translated at Antwerp the Bible and Apocrypha from German and Latin versions; superintended the printing of the 'Great Bible' of 1539.

co'verlėt (kŭ-) *n.* Cover spread over bedclothes.

co'vert[1] (kŭ-; *or -er*) *n.* 1. Shelter, esp. thicket hiding game; ~ *coat*, short light overcoat for shooting, riding, etc.; ~ *coating*, (usu. waterproof) material for this. 2. One of the feathers covering the bases of a bird's wing and tail feathers.

co'vert[2] (kŭ-), *adj.* Concealed, hidden, secret, disguised. **co'vertlȳ** *adv.*

co'verture (kŭ-) *n.* Covering; condition of married woman under husband's protection.

co'vėt (kŭ-) *v.t.* Desire eagerly (usu. what belongs to another). **co'vėtable** *adj.*

co'vėtous (kŭ-) *adj.* Eagerly desirous (*of*); grasping, avaricious. **co'vėtouslȳ** *adv.* **co'vėtousnėss** *n.*

co'vey (kŭ-) *n.* Brood of partridges; family, party, set.

cov'in (kŭ-) *n.* (law) Conspiracy, collusion; (archaic) fraud, deception.

cō'ving *n.* Arched piece of building; (pl.) curved sides of fireplace.

cow[1] *n.* Female of any bovine animal, esp. of the domestic species (*Bos taurus*); female of elephant, rhinoceros, whale, seal, etc.; *cow'boy*, (U.S.) man in charge of grazing cattle on ranch; ~-*catcher*, (U.S.) frame fixed in front of locomotive engine etc. to remove cattle and other obstructions; ~-*fish*, manatee, sea-cow; fish, *Ostracion quadricorne*, of Indian and Amer. seas, with horn-like spines over eyes; ~-*heel*, (dish of) foot of cow or ox stewed to jelly; *cow'herd*, one who tends cows at pasture; ~-*hide*, (leather, whip, made of) cow's hide; ~-*lick*, protruding lock of hair; ~-*parsley*, umbelliferous plant (wild in Britain), *Anthriscus sylvestris*; ~-*parsnip*, large umbelliferous plant (wild in Britain), *Heracleum sphondylium*; *cow'pat*, roundish mass of cow dung; *cow'-pox*, vaccine disease appearing as bluish or livid vesicles on teats of cows; ~-*puncher*, (U.S. slang) cowboy; ~-*shot*, (cricket slang) violent pull made leaning forward on one knee; ~-*tree*, tree with milk-like juice used as food, esp. S. Amer. tree, *Brosimum galactodendron*.

cow[2] *v.t.* Intimidate.

cow'age, cow'itch *n.* Stinging hairs of pod of tropical leguminous plant, *Mucuna pruriens* this plant or its pods. [perversion of Hind. *kawānch*]

cow'ard *adj.* & *n.* Faint-hearted, pusillanimous (person). **cow'ardlȳ** *adj.* **cow'ardlinėss** *n.* [OF *coard*, f. L *cauda* tail]

cow'ardice *n.* Faint-heartedness.

cow'er *v.i.* Stand or squat in bent position; crouch, esp. from fear.

cowitch: see COWAGE.

cowl *n.* 1. Monk's hooded garment; hood of this. 2. Hood-shaped covering (freq. turning with wind) of top of chimney or

COWL

ventilating shaft to assist ventilation. **cowled** (-ld) *adj.*

cow'ling *n.* Covering over or round engine of aircraft or motor vehicle.

Cow'per (kōō-), William (1731–1800). English lyric poet and hymn writer.

cowr'ie, -ry *n.* Porcelain-like shell of small gasteropod, *Cypraea moneta*, of Indian Ocean, used as money in parts of Africa and southern Asia; this animal, or any gasteropod (or shell) of genus *Cypraea*, of oval shape, with undeveloped spine and narrow aperture as long as shell. [Hind. *kauri*]

cow'slip *n.* Wild plant, *Primula veris*, growing in pastures etc. and flowering in spring, with drooping umbels of fragrant yellow flowers;

~ *tea, wine*, infusion, wine, made from cowslip flowers.

cŏx *n.* Coxswain. **cŏ'xlėss** *adj.* **cŏx** *v.*

cŏx'a *n.* (pl. *-ae*). Hip; (zool.) similar joint in insects etc. **cŏ'xal** *adj.*

cŏ'xcōmb (-m) *n.* Conceited showy person. **cŏxcō'mbical** (-mĭ-) *adj.* **cŏ'xcombrȳ** (-mrĭ) *n.* Foppery, behaviour of a coxcomb. [=*cock's comb*]

cŏ'xswain (*or* -ksn) *n.* Helmsman of boat; person on board ship permanently in charge of ship's boat and crew. **cŏ'xswainlėss** *adj.* **cŏ'xswain** *v.* Act as coxswain (to). [f. *cock* = cockboat + *swain*]

coy[1] *adj.* Shy, esp. affectedly or archly so. **coy'ly** *adv.* **coy'nėss** *n.*

Coy[2] *abbrev.* (mil.) Company.

coyō'tė (ko-; *or* -ōt) *n.* Prairie-wolf, *Canis latrans*, of western N. America. [Mex. *coyotl*]

coy'pu (-ōō) *n.* S. Amer. aquatic rodent, *Myocastor coypus*, of about size of beaver, with valuable fur (nutria).

coz (kŭ-) *n.* (archaic) Cousin.

co'zen (kŭ-) *v.t.* Cheat, defraud, (*of, out of*); beguile (*into*). **co'zenage** *n.*

cp. *abbrev.* Compare.

c.p. *abbrev.* Candle-power.

C.P. *abbrev.* Communist party.

Cpl *abbrev.* Corporal.

C.P.R. *abbrev.* Canadian Pacific Railway.

C.P.R.E. *abbrev.* Council for the Protection of Rural England.

CQR. Type of stockless anchor with a base like a ploughshare instead of flukes.

Cr. *abbrev.* Credit, creditor.

crăb[1] *n.* 1. Any of various decapod crustaceans, mostly of the group Brachyura, with abdomen short and bent under thorax, the first legs being pincers, esp. edible species found on or near sea-coasts (the common European edible crab is *Cancer pagurus*, the U.S. edible or *blue* ~ is *Callinectes hastatus*). 2. *the C*~: see CANCER[2]. 3. Machine (orig. with claws) for hoisting heavy weights. 4. (pl.) Lowest throw at hazard, two aces. 5. (rowing) *catch a* ~, make faulty stroke by which oar-blade becomes jammed under water and handle sometimes sweeps rower off his seat. 6. ~- *louse*, parasitical insect, *Phthirus pubis*, infesting human body; ~*'s-eyes*, round concretion of carbonate of lime found in stomach of crayfish etc.

crăb[2] *n.* (also ~-*apple*) Wild apple, *Malus sylvestris*, or a cultivated variety having similar sour, harsh, astringent quality; *Siberian* ~, cultivated variety *Malus baccata*.

crăb[3] *v.* 1. (of hawks) Scratch, claw, fight (with each other). 2. (colloq.) Criticize adversely; interfere with.

crăʹbbėd *adj.* Cross-grained, perverse; difficult to interpret; (of handwriting) ill-formed and hard to decipher. **crăʹbbėdlў** adv. **crăʹbbėdnėss** *n.*

crăck *v.* 1. (Cause to) make sharp or explosive noise; utter (joke). 2. Break with sudden sharp report; break without complete separation of parts; collapse, break down. 3. Render (voice) dissonant; (of voice) become dissonant. 4. Damage, ruin. 5. Split up (oil etc.) by heat and catalysts to produce lighter hydrocarbons (as petrol). 6. (slang) *get cracking*, start; ~ *a crib*, break into a house; ~ *up*, praise; suffer breakdown. 7. ~-*brained*, crazy; ~-*jaw*, (of words) difficult to pronounce. ~ *n.* 1. Sudden sharp noise, as of whip, rifle, thunder; sharp blow; *have a* ~, (colloq.) make an attempt. 2. Instant; break (*of* dawn, day). 3. Fissure formed by breakage; partial fracture (the parts still cohering); narrow opening formed by breaking; = CHINK[1]. 4. (slang) Brisk talk, chat. 5. (slang, orig. U.S.) Sharp, cutting, or witty remark. 6. Fine player, horse, etc. ~ *adj.* (colloq.) First-rate.

crăcked (-kt) *adj.* (esp., slang) Crazy.

crăʹcker *n.* (esp.) 1. Kind of firework exploding with sharp report(s); small paper cylinder containing sweets, toy, paper cap, or the like, and a fulminant exploding sharply when pulled at both ends. 2. Instrument for cracking, esp. (pl.) nut-crackers. 3. Thin crisp biscuit; (U.S.) biscuit. 4. (southern U.S.) Poor white, esp. in Georgia and Florida. 5. (pl., as pred. adj.; slang) Crazy.

crăʹckerjăck *n.* & *adj.* (U.S. slang) Exceptionally fine or splendid (person or thing).

crăʹckle *v.i.* Emit slight continuous cracking sound. ~ *n.* 1. Crackling. 2. China-ware with minute cracks all over surface. **crăʹcklў** *adj.*

crăʹcklĭng *n.* (esp.) Crisp skin of roast pork.

crăʹcknel *n.* Light crisp very dry biscuit of curved or hollowed shape.

crăʹcksman *n.* Housebreaker, burglar.

crāʹdle *n.* 1. Bed, cot, for infant, esp. one on rockers; (fig.) place in which thing is nurtured in earliest stage. 2. Framework resembling cradle, esp. stage suspended from scaffolding for workmen; framework on which ship rests during construction or repairs; light wooden frame attached to scythe to lay corn evenly; protective or supporting framework for injured limb etc.; serrated tool (ROCKER) used in mezzotint engraving; support for telephone receiver not in use; (mining) trough on rockers in which auriferous earth is shaken in water, to separate the gold. ~ *v.t.* Place in cradle; contain or shelter as cradle; mow (corn) with scythe fitted with cradle.

crāʹdlĭng *n.* (esp. archit.) Wooden or iron or other framework.

craft (-ah-) *n.* 1. Skill; cunning, deceit. 2. Art, trade; members of a craft; *the* ~, the brotherhood of Freemasons. 3. (pl. same) Boat, vessel; aircraft, spacecraft. **craʹftsman** *n.* One who practises a handicraft; skilled person. **craʹftsmanship** *n.*

craʹftў (-ah-) *adj.* Cunning, artful, wily. **craʹftĭlў** *adv.* **craʹftinėss** *n.*

crăg *n.* 1. Steep or precipitous

rugged rock. 2. *C*~, deposit of shelly sand found in Norfolk, Suffolk, and Essex, and used for manure; Pliocene and Miocene strata to which these deposits belong. **crăʹggy̆** *adj.* **crăʹgsman** *n.* Skilled climber of crags.

crāke *n.* Corncrake, or other bird of the same family; corncrake's cry.

crăm *v.* 1. Fill overfull; force (*into, down*); stuff (*with* food); eat greedily; ~*-full*, as full as cramming can make it. 2. Prepare for examination; learn (subject) for special purpose. ~ *n.* Cramming for examination.

crăʹmbō *n.* Game in which one player gives word or line of verse to which each of others must find rhyme; *dumb* ~, game in which one side announces word rhyming with chosen word, which other side tries to guess by acting one word after another in dumb show. [prob. f. L *crambe repetita* cabbage served up again]

crăʹmmer *n.* (esp.) One who crams pupils for examination.

crămp[1] *n.* Sudden painful involuntary contraction of muscles from chill, slight strain, etc. ~ *v.t.* 1. Affect with cramp. 2. Confine narrowly; restrict.

crămp[2] *n.* Metal bar with bent ends for holding masonry etc. together; portable tool with adjustable screw for holding things together; (also *sash* ~) such tool with movable part that can be fixed for pressing pieces of wood etc. together for joining; restraint. ~ *v.t.* Fasten with cramp.

crăʹmpon *n.* Metal hook, grappling-iron; iron plate set with spikes for climbing over ice etc.

crăn *n.* (Sc.) Measure for fresh herrings (37½ gal., or about 750 fish).

crāʹnage *n.* Use of crane, dues paid for this.

crăʹnberry̆ *n.* Small bright-red acid berry, fruit of dwarf shrub, *Vaccinium oxycoccus* (*European or small* ~), or *V. macrocarpon* (*American or large* ~).

crāne *n.* 1. Large wading-bird with very long legs, neck, and bill,

CRANE

esp. the ashy-grey common European crane, *Grus cinerea*, formerly common in Gt Britain but now extinct. 2. Machine for raising and lowering heavy weights, usu. post rotating on vertical axis with projecting arm or jib over the end of which runs a chain or rope from which the weight may be suspended; overhanging tube for supplying water to locomotive. 3. Bent tube for drawing liquor out of vessel, siphon. 4. ~*-fly*, two-winged long-

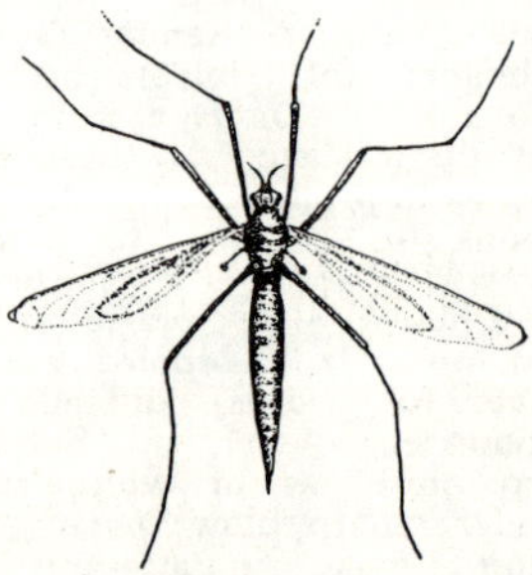

CRANE-FLY

legged fly of genus *Tipula*, daddy-longlegs; ~*'s-bill*, species of wild geranium (from the long slender beak of the fruit). ~ *v.* Stretch (neck), stretch neck like crane; (colloq., of horse) pull up at obstacle and look over before leaping.

crāʹnial *adj.* Of the cranium; ~ *index*, ratio of width of skull to its length; ~ *nerve*, one member of twelve pairs of nerves attached to brain and serving regions of head and neck.

crā'nium *n.* Bones enclosing brain; less strictly, bones of whole head, skull.

crănk[1] *n.* Part of axis bent at right angles for converting reciprocal into circular motion, or vice versa; *cra'nkcase*, case covering crankshaft of motor engine; *cra'nkshaft*, shaft driven by crank; *cra'nkwheel*, wheel acting as crank, esp. one to which connecting rod is attached near circumference. ~ *v.* 1. Bend in shape of crank; attach crank to. 2. (also ~ *up*) Start (motor engine) by turning crank or starting-handle.

crănk[2] *n.* 1. Fanciful turn of speech; eccentric idea or act. 2. Eccentric person, esp. one enthusiastically possessed by idea etc. **cră'nkȳ**[1] *adj.*

crănk[3] *adj.* Weak, shaky (usu. of machinery).

crănk[4], **cră'nkȳ**[2] *adjs.* (naut.) Liable to capsize.

Cră'nmer, Thomas (1489–1556). Archbishop of Canterbury from 1532; annulled marriage of Henry VIII and Catherine of Aragon and maintained the king's claim to be supreme head of the Church of England; supervised

production of the first prayer-book of Edward VI (1549) and promulgated in 1552 the 42 articles of religion (afterwards reduced to 39); was condemned for heresy in Queen Mary's reign and burned at the stake at Oxford.

cră'nnog *n.* Lake-dwelling in Scotland or Ireland.

cră'nnȳ *n.* Chink, crevice. **cră'nnied** (-ĭd) *adj.*

crāpe *n.* Crêpe, usu. black silk, esp. as (part of) mourning wear; band of this round hat etc. as sign of mourning. **crā'pȳ** *adj.* **crāpe** *v.t.* Cover, drape, with crape.

crăps *n.* (U.S.) Game of chance played with two dice; *shoot* ~, play this game.

cră'pūlent *adj.* Given to, suffering from effect of, resulting from, intemperance. **cră'pūlence** *n.* **cră'pūlous** *adj.*

cră'quelūre (-ke-) *n.* Small cracks in paint or varnish on surface of picture.

crăsh[1] *n.* Loud noise as of hard body or bodies broken by violent percussion, or of thunder, loud music, etc.; violent percussion or breakage; crashing of aircraft, motor-car, etc.; (fig.) sudden ruin or collapse, esp. financial; (attrib. or as adj.) rapid intensive (*course, programme*, etc.); ~*-dive* (*n.* & *v.i.*) (of submarine) (make) sudden and steep dive; ~*-helmet*, helmet worn as protection in case of crashing; ~ *landing*, landing involving damage to aircraft; so ~*-land* (*v.i.*). ~ *v.* Make a crash; move, go, drive, throw, with a crash; (of aircraft) fall, cause to fall, violently to earth; (cause motor-car etc. to) come violently into collision with vehicle or obstacle; (fig.) fail, esp. financially; ~ *in on*, gate-crash (a party etc.).

crăsh[2] *n.* Coarse plain-woven fabric of hand-spun flax, orig. from Russia; material resembling this, of linen or cotton freq. combined with jute. [Russ. *krashenina* coloured linen (*kráska* colour, dye)]

crā'sĭs *n.* (Gk gram.). Contraction of vowels of two syllables into one long vowel or diphthong.

crăss *adj.* Thick, gross; (fig.) gross; grossly stupid. **cră'sslȳ** *adv.* **cră'ssnĕss, cră'ssitūde** *ns.*

Cră'ssus, Marcus Licinius (*c*

112–53 B.C.). Roman consul, member of 1st TRIUMVIRATE.

crāte *n.* Large case or basket of basket-work or light boarding for carrying glass, crockery, fruit, etc. (slang) aircraft, vehicle (esp. old one). ~ *v.t.* Pack in crate.

crā'ter *n.* 1. Bowl- or funnel-shaped hollow at top or side of volcano from which eruption takes place; bowl-shaped cavity, esp. that formed by exploding shell or bomb. 2. (Gk antiq.) Large bowl in which wine was mixed with water.

cravă't *n.* 1. (archaic) Ornamental band with long flowing ends, or linen or silk handkerchief tied, with bow in front, round neck outside shirt collar. 2. Scarf or neck-tie. [Fr. *cravate* f. Croatian *Hrvat* Croat]

crāve *v.* Beg for; long for; beg, long, *for*. **crā'vĭng** *n.* Strong desire, intense longing.

crā'ven *adj.* & *n.* Cowardly, abject (person). **crā'venlў** *adv.*

craw *n.* Crop of bird or insect.

craw'fĭsh *n.* See CRAYFISH.

crawl¹ *n.* Pen or enclosure in shallow water for fish, turtles, etc. [Colonial Dutch KRAAL]

crawl² *v.* Move slowly with body on or close to ground, or on hands and knees; walk, move, slowly; creep abjectly; swim with crawl-stroke; swarm *with* crawling things; feel creepy sensation. ~ *n.* Crawling; (also ~*-stroke*), fast swimming-stroke in which arms execute alternate overarm movements and legs are kicked rapidly, usu. 3, 4, or 5 times to each arm-stroke. **craw'ler** *n.* (esp. pl.) Infant's overall garment for crawling in.

cray'fĭsh *n.* Small lobster-like freshwater crustacean, *Astàcus fluviatilis*; other species of *Astacus* and the allied Amer. genus *Cambarus*; (on English coast) spiny lobster *Palinurus vulgaris* (freq. called *crawfish*).

cray'on *n.* 1. Stick, pencil, of coloured chalk usu. mixed with wax, for drawing; drawing in crayons. 2. Carbon point in electric arc lamp. ~ *v.t.* Draw with crayon(s).

crāze *v.* 1. Drive crazy (usu. in past part.). 2. Produce small cracks in (glaze of pottery); have such cracks. ~ *n.* Mania; temporary fashion.

crā'zў *adj.* 1. Full of cracks or flaws; unsound, frail, shaky. 2. Mad, demented; insane; extremely eager. 3. (of pavement, quilt, etc.) Made of irregular pieces fitted together. **crā'zĭlў** *adv.* **crā'zĭness** *n.*

creak *v.i.* & *n.* (Make) harsh shrill grating noise as of ungreased hinge etc. **crea'kў** *adj.* **crea'kĭlў** *adv.*

cream *n.* 1. Fatty part of milk, which gathers on top, and by churning is made into butter. 2. Fancy dish, sweet, like or made of cream; attrib., (of soup or sauce) containing milk or cream; (of sweet or biscuit) with creamy filling. 3. Cream-like substance, esp. cosmetic. 4. Best or choicest part of anything. 5. Part of liquid that gathers on top. 6. Cream colour, yellowish-white; cream-coloured horse. 7. ~ *of lime*, pure slaked lime; ~ *of tartar*: see TARTAR¹. 8. ~ *bun*, *cake*, etc., bun, cake, etc. filled with cream or creamy custard etc.; ~ *cheese*, soft rich cheese made of unskimmed milk and cream; ~*cracker*, kind of crisp unsweetened biscuit; ~*-laid*, *-wove*, laid, wove (paper) of cream colour; ~ *sherry*, full-bodied mellow sherry. **crea'mў** *adj.* **crea'mĭlў** *adv.* **cream** *v.* Form cream or scum; cause (milk) to cream; take cream from (milk); take best part of; add cream to; treat (skin) with cosmetic cream; work (butter etc.) into creamy consistency.

crea'mer *n.* Flat dish for skimming cream off milk; machine for separating cream; (U.S.) cream-jug. **crea'merў** *n.* Butter (and cheese) factory; shop where milk, cream, etc., are sold.

crease¹ *n.* 1. Line caused by folding; fold; wrinkle. 2. (cricket) Line of whiting (continuing the line of the stumps) from behind which bowler delivers ball (*bowling-~*); line in front of wicket behind which batsman stands to defend wicket (*popping-~*). 3. (ice hockey, lacrosse) Area in front of goal. ~ *v.* Make creases in; fall into creases

crease[2]**:** see KRIS.

crėā'te *v.* 1. Bring into existence, give rise to; originate; design. 2. Constitute, invest (person) with rank. 3. (slang) Make a fuss. **crėā'tĭve** *adj.* **crėā'tĭvelȳ** *adv.* **crėā'tĭvenėss** *n.*

crē'atĭne *n.* Amino-acid found in muscles of vertebrates.

crėā'tion *n.* 1. Creating, esp. of the world. 2. All created things. 3. Production of human intelligence or power, esp. of the imagination.

crėā'tor *n.* One who creates; *the C~*, God.

crea'ture *n.* Created thing; animate being; animal (often as distinct from man); human being, person; one who owes his fortune to another; mere instrument.

crèche (krāsh) *n.* Public day-nursery for infants.

Crécy (krĕ'sĭ). Village in Picardy, N. France, scene (1346) of a battle in the Hundred Years War, in which the English under Edward III defeated the French.

crē'dence *n.* 1. Belief; *letter of ~*, letter of recommendation or introduction. 2. Small side-table or shelf on which Eucharistic elements are placed before consecration.

crėdĕ'ntial (-shal) *n.* (usu. pl.). Letter(s) of introduction (also fig).

crĕ'dĭble *adj.* Believable, worthy of belief. **crĕdĭbi'lĭtȳ** *n.* **crĕ'dĭblȳ** *adv.*

crĕ'dĭt *n.* 1. Belief, trust. 2. Good reputation; power derived from this; acknowledgement of merit; source of commendation or honour. 3. Trust in person's ability and intention to pay at some future time; reputation of solvency and probity in business; (bookkeeping) acknowledgement of payment by entry in account, sum entered on credit or right-hand side of account; *letter of ~*, banker's etc. document authorizing person to draw money from writer's correspondent in another place; ~ *sale*, method of purchase in which payment is, by agreement, made later. 4. (U.S.) certificate attesting completion of a certain course of study. 5. (usu. pl., also ~ *title*) Acknowledgement giving name(s) of person(s) responsible for work on film etc. ~ *v.t.* 1. Believe. 2. Carry to credit side of account; ~ *with*, give credit for.

crĕ'dĭtable *adj.* That brings credit or honour. **crĕ'dĭtablȳ** *adv.*

crĕ'dĭtor *n.* One who gives credit for money or goods; one to whom debt is owing.

crē'dō (*or* -ā-) *n.* (pl. *-os*). Creed, esp. Apostles' Creed and Nicene Creed which begin in Latin *credo* (= 'I believe'); *C~*, musical setting of Nicene Creed.

crĕ'dūlous *adj.* Too ready to believe; characterized by or arising from credulity. **crėdū'lĭtȳ, crĕ'dūlousnėss** *ns.* **crĕ'dūlouslȳ** *adv.*

creed *n.* Brief formal summary of Christian doctrine, esp. Apostles', Nicene, and Athanasian Creeds; confession of faith; system of belief.

creek[1] *n.* 1. Narrow inlet of seacoast or tidal estuary; small harbour. 2. (U.S. etc.) Brook, stream.

Creek[2] *n.* One of a N. Amer. Ind. tribe now settled in Oklahoma. [transl. Algonkin *maskoki* creeks]

creel *n.* Large wicker basket for fish; angler's fishing-basket.

creep *v.i.* (past t. & past part. *crĕpt*). 1. Crawl; move timidly, slowly, or stealthily; proceed, exist, abjectly. 2. (of plants) Grow along ground, wall, etc.; *creeping jenny*: see MONEY*wort*. 3. (of flesh, creeping over it (as result of fear, repugnance, etc.). 4. (of metal rails etc.) Move gradually forward under recurrent pressure; (of hot metal) extend slowly under tension; (of liquid) spread upwards in crystals on side of vessel. ~ *n.* 1. Creeping; creeping action of metal etc.; ~ *strength*, maximum stress to which material can be subjected without creeping. 2.

CREMONA: Cathedral

the ~*s*, (colloq.) nervous shrinking or shiver of dread or horror. 3. (slang) Obnoxious or despicable person.

cree'per *n.* (esp.) Plant that creeps along ground or up wall etc.; small bird that runs or climbs up and down branches, esp. tree-creeper; kind of grapnel for dragging ground under water.

cree'pȳ *adj.* Having or producing a creeping of the flesh; given to creeping. **cree'pȳ-craw'lȳ** *adj.* & *n.* (Insect) producing creeping sensation.

creese: see KRIS.

crėmā'te *v.t.* Consume (esp. corpse) by fire. **crėmā'tion** *n.* **crėmā'tor** *n.*

crĕmatōr'ium *n.* (pl. *-s, -ia*) Establishment for cremation.

crĕ'matorȳ *n.* Crematorium. ~ *adj.* Of cremation.

crème (-ām) *n.* 1. Syrupy liqueur; ~ *de menthe* (mahnt), sweet green liqueur flavoured with peppermint. 2. = CREAM *n.* 2.

crėmō'na[1] *n.* = CROMORNE.

Crėmō'na[2]. Town in Lombardy where the craft of violin-making reached its highest excellence in 17th and early 18th centuries; hence, violin made there.

crē'nāte, -tėd *adjs.* (bot., zool.) With notched edge or rounded teeth. **crēnā'tion** *n.*

crĕ'nature *n.* Rounded tooth on edge of leaf etc.

crĕ'nel (*or* krĭnĕ'l) *n.* Open space or indentation in embattled parapet, orig. for shooting through etc. representation of this.

crĕ'nellāte *v.t.* Furnish with battlements or loopholes. **crĕnellā'tion** *n.*

Crē'ōle *n.* 1. Descendant of European or Negro settlers in W. Indies, Mauritius, etc. 2. (U.S.) French-speaking descendant of early French settlers in Louisiana etc. ~ *adj.* Born and naturalized in W. Indies etc., but of European or Negro descent; (of animals etc.) bred or grown, but not indigenous, in the W. Indies etc.

crē'osōte *n.* (also ~ *oil*) Brown oily liquid, a mixture of phenols obtained from coal-tar (formerly from wood tar) having antiseptic properties and used esp. for preservation of timber and in pharmacy. ~ *v.t.* Coat with creosote.

crêpe (-āp) *n.* Textile fabric (other than black mourning CRAPE) with wrinkled surface produced chemically or by twisting the yarn; (also ~ *rubber*) indiarubber rolled into thin sheets with wrinkled surface; ~ *de Chine* (shēn), fine silk crêpe; ~ *paper*, thin crinkled paper; ~ *Suzette*, small dessert pancake served flambé. **crê'pey** *adj.*

crĕ'pĭtāte *v.i.* Make crackling sound; (of beetles etc.) eject defensive fluid with sharp report. **crĕ'pĭtant** *adj.* **crĕpĭtā'tion** *n.* Act of crepitating; (med.) grating sound made by ends of bone rubbing together; rattle of breath as heard in pneumonia etc.

crĕ'pĭtus *n.* (med.) Crepitation.

crept: see CREEP.

crėpŭ'scūlar *adj.* Of twilight; (zool.) appearing, active, in twilight.

cres., cresc. *abbrevs. Crescendo.*

crėscĕ'ndō (-sh-) *adv.*, *n.* (pl. *-os*), & *adj.* (mus.) (Passage performed) with gradually increasing volume, indicated thus <; also fig. [It.]

crĕ'scent *n.* 1. Waxing moon, between new moon and full; concavo-convex figure of moon during first or last quarter, esp. when very new or very old. 2. Repsentation of this shape, esp. as badge of Turkish sultans; Turkish power (hist.); Muslim religion. 3. Anything crescent-shaped, esp. row of houses. ~ *adj.* 1. Increasing; waxing. 2. Crescent-shaped.

crē'sōl *n.* Any of three isomeric methyl phenols present in wood and coal-tar and forming chief constituents of creosote.

crĕss *n.* Any of various cruciferous plants, usu. with pungent

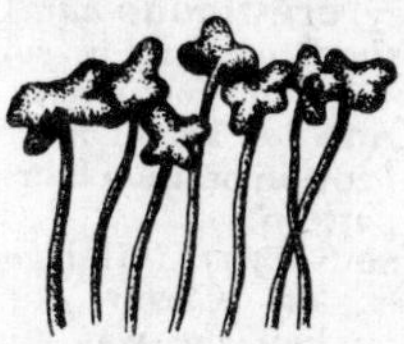

edible leaves, esp. *garden* ~ (*Lepidium sativum*) and watercress.

crĕ'ssėt *n.* Metal vessel for holding grease or oil for light, usu. mounted on pole; fire-basket for lighting wharf etc.

Crĕ'ssida. In medieval legends of the Trojan War, the daughter of Calchas, a priest; she was faithless to her lover Troilus, a son of Priam.

crĕst *n.* 1. Comb, tuft, on animal's head; erect plume or other ornament on top of helmet or head-dress. 2. (her.) Device (orig. borne by knight on his helmet) above shield and helmet in coat of arms, or used separately, as on seal, notepaper, etc. (erron.) coat of arms. 3. Top of helmet; helmet, headpiece; summit, top, esp. of hill or mountian 4. Ridge forming top of anything, esp. of roof or wave; surface line of neck in animals, mane; (anat.) ridge along surface of bone. 5. *crĕ'stfallen*, with drooping crest; abashed, disheartened. ~ *v.* 1. Furnish with crest; serve as crest to; form into crest. 2. Reach crest or summit of.

crĕ'sting *n.* Ornamental ridging to wall or roof.

crėtā'ceous (-sh*us*) *adj.* Of (the nature of) chalk; *C~*, (geol.) of the latest period of the Mesozoic. **Crėtā'ceous** *n.* Cretaceous period or system.

Crēte. Aegean island belonging to Greece. **Crē'tan** *adj.* & *n.* (Native, inhabitant) of Crete.

crē'tic *n.* Metrical foot of one short syllable between two long ones (—◡—).

crĕ'tin *n.* One suffering from cretinism; idiot. **crĕ'tinism** *n.* Idiocy combined with physical deformity, stunted growth and freq. goitre, caused by thyroid deficiency. **crĕ'tinous** *adj.* [Swiss Fr. *crestin* Christian, in sense of '(barely) human creature']

crėtŏ'nne (*or* krĕ'-) *n.* Strong unglazed cotton or linen fabric with printed pattern.

Crėu'sa (-o͞o*za*). (Gk legend) 1. Daughter of Creon king of Corinth; when she was about to marry Jason, she put on a garment given her by Medea which was poisoned and set her body on fire. 2. Daughter of Priam king of Troy, and wife of Aeneas.

crėvă'sse *n.* Deep fissure in ice of glacier.

crĕ'vice *n.* Narrow opening, fissure, esp. in rock, building, etc.

crew (-o͞o) *n.* Body of men engaged upon particular piece of work, esp. (U.S.) in working railway train; whole body of men manning ship, aircraft, etc.; sometimes, men manning ship, excluding officers; associated body, company, of persons; set, gang, mob; ~ *cut*, man's closely-cropped haircut; ~ *neck*(*line*), high round neckline of garment. ~ *v.* Supply or act as crew (for).

crew'el (-o͞o-) *n.* Thin worsted yarn used for embroidery; ~-*needle*, large-eyed needle for embroidery on canvas etc.

crĭb *n.* 1. Barred receptacle for fodder etc.; model representing

infant Jesus Christ in manger, with attending figures. 2. Cabin, hovel; (thieves' slang) house. 3. Child's cot with barred or latticed sides. 4. Framework lining shaft of mine; heavy crossed timbers used in foundations in loose soil etc. 5. Wicker salmon-trap. 6. Set of cards given to dealer in cribbage, made up of cards discarded from other players' hands. 7. (colloq.) Plagiarism; translation of classics etc. for illegitimate use of students. 8. ~-*biting*, horse's vicious habit of seizing manger in teeth and at same time noisily drawing in breath. ~ *v.t.* 1. Confine in small space. 2. Furnish (cow-shed etc.) with cribs. 3. Pilfer; copy unfairly or without acknowledgement.

crĭ'bbage *n.* Card-game for 2, 3, or 4 persons, played with pack of 52 cards and a board of 61 holes on which points are scored with pegs, 5 or 6 cards being dealt to each player and the dealer having in addition the CRIB (see *n.* 6).

crĭ'brĭform *adj.* (anat., bot.) Perforated with numerous small holes.

Crī'chton (-īt-), James (1560–85). Scottish prodigy of intellectual and knightly accomplishments, said to have disputed on scientific questions in twelve languages; *Admirable* ~, nickname given to him; hence, any very versatile person.

crĭck *n.* Painful spasmodic affection of muscles of neck, back, etc., sudden stiffness. ~ *v.t.* Produce crick in.

crĭ'ckėt[1] *n.* Orthopterous jumping insect of genus *Acheta* or related genera, esp. the *house*-~, *A. domestica*, living in hearths and

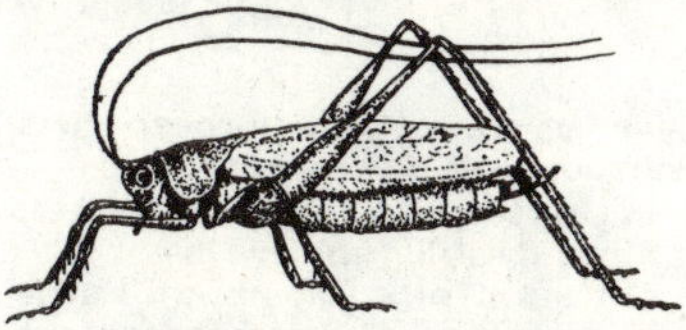

other warm places, and producing a characteristic shrill noise by rubbing parts of forewings together.

crĭ'ckėt[2] *n.* Open-air game played with bats, ball, and 2 wickets by 2 sides of 11 players each, in which the batsman (one at each wicket) defends his wicket against the ball and scores by runs made between the wickets after the ball has been struck by the bat; *not* ~, (colloq., of conduct) unsporting, unfair. ~ *v.i.* Play cricket. **crĭ'ckėter** *n.*

crĭ'ckėt[3] *n.* (U.S. & local) Low stool.

crī'coid *adj.* Ring-shaped; (anat.) ~ *cartilage*, cartilage of this shape forming lower and back part of larynx. ~ *n.* Cricoid cartilage.

crī'er *n.* (esp.) Officer who makes public announcements in court of justice or (*town* ~) in streets etc. of a town.

crī'key *int.* (slang) Exclamation of astonishment.

crim. con. *abbrev.* Criminal conversation.

crīme *n.* Act (usu. grave offence) punishable by law; evil act, sin; ~-*sheet*, record of soldier's offences against regulations. ~ *v.t.* (mil.) Charge with or convict of military offence.

Crīmē'a. Peninsula of U.S.S.R. lying between Sea of Azov and Black Sea. **Crīmē'an** *adj.* ~ *War*, inconclusive war in the Crimea, 1854–6, in which Russia fought Turkey, France, and Britain, both sides sustaining heavy losses.

crime pǎssiǒnĕl (krēm, -syǒ-). Crime (esp. murder) resulting from sexual jealousy. [Fr.]

crĭ'mĭnal *adj.* Of (the nature of) crime; concerned with crime or its punishment; guilty of crime; ~

CRIMEAN WAR

conversation, (archaic) adultery; ~ *law*, *proceedings*, those aiming at punishment of offenders (cf. CIVIL law). **crĭ'mĭnallȳ** *adv*. **crĭ'mĭnal** *n*. Person guilty or convicted of crime.

crĭ'mĭnāte *v.t.* Charge with crime; prove guilty of crime. **crĭmĭnā'tion** *n*. **crĭ'mĭnatĭve, crĭ'mĭnatorȳ** *adjs*.

crĭmĭnŏ'logȳ *n*. Scientific study of crime. **crĭmĭnŏ'logist** *n*.

crĭmp *v.t.* 1. Compress into pleats or folds, frill; wrinkle or crumple minutely. 2. Cause (flesh of newly caught fish) to contract and become firm by gashing. ~ *n*. (chiefly U.S.) Fold, crease.

crĭm'son (-z-) *adj*. & *n*. (Of) deep-red colour inclining towards purple. ~ *v*. Make, become, crimson.

crĭnge (-j) *v.i.* Cower; bow servilely; behave obsequiously. ~ *n*. Fawning obeisance.

crĭ'ngle (-ngg-) *n*. (naut.) Eye of rope containing thimble for another rope to pass through.

crī'nīte *adj*. (bot., zool.) Hairy.

crĭ'nkle *v*. & *n*. Twist, wrinkle. **crĭ'nklȳ** *adj*.

crĭ'noid *adj*. & *n*. (Echinoderm) usu. with stalked and rooted calyx-like body; sea lily.

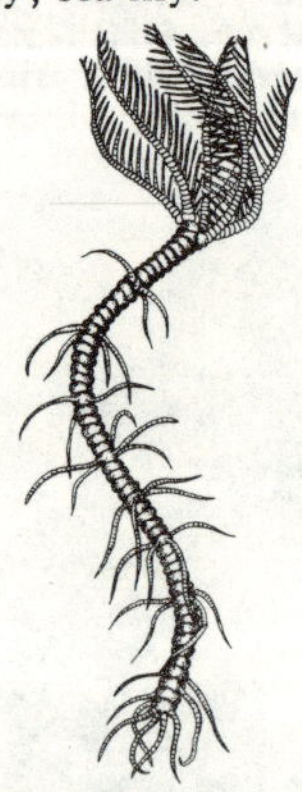

crĭ'nolĭne (*or* -lēn) *n*. 1. Stiff fabric of horsehair etc. formerly used for skirts; petticoat of this, or hooped petticoat, used to expand skirt of woman's dress. 2. Defensive screen of anti-torpedo nets surrounding a stationary ship.

crĭ'pple *n*. Lame person. ~ *v.t.* Lame; disable, impair.

crī'sĭs *n*. (pl. *crī'sēs* pr. -z). Turning-point, esp. of disease; moment or brief period of danger or suspense.

crĭsp *adj*. Hard or firm but fragile, brittle; bracing; brisk, decisive; (of hair etc.) closely curling. **crĭ'splȳ** *adv*. **crĭ'spnėss** *n*. **crisp** *n*. Anything dried or shrivelled by frying, roasting, etc. (chiefly U.S.); thin sliver of potato fried until crisp and eaten cold (usu. pl.). ~ *v*. Make or become crisp. **crĭ'spȳ** *adj*.

crĭspā'tion *n*. Curling, undulation; slight contraction (esp. of skin in 'goose-flesh').

crĭss-crŏss *n*. Crossing lines, currents, etc.; network of intersecting lines; ~ *row*, (archaic) alphabet (from cross before row of letters in horn-books). ~ *adj*. In crossing lines. ~ *adv*. Crosswise. ~ *v*. Mark with criss-cross lines; cross repeatedly. [orig. *Christ's cross*]

crĭ'stāte *adj*. Crested, like a crest.

crītēr'ion *n*. (pl. -*ia*). Principle, rule, standard, by which thing is judged.

crĭ'tĭc *n*. One who pronounces judgement; censurer; judge of literary or artistic works; one skilled in textual criticism.

crĭ′tĭcal *adj.* 1. Censorious, fault-finding; skilful, engaged, in criticism; belonging to criticism; providing textual criticism. 2. Relating to crisis; involving risk or suspense. 3. (math., phys.) Marking transition from one state, property, condition, etc., to another; (of nuclear reactor) maintaining self-sustaining chain reaction; ~ *angle*, (optics) largest angle at which light rays passing through a dense medium can strike the face of a rarer medium and pass into it (i.e. be refracted; if the angle exceeds this they will be totally reflected); ~ *mass*, amount of fissile material required to sustain chain reaction; ~ *point*, temperature for any gas above which it cannot be liquefied by compression (also ~ *temperature*). **crĭ′tĭcallў** *adv.*

critică′ster *n.* Petty or inferior critic.

crĭ′tĭcism *n.* Criticizing; work of a critic; critical essay or remark; science dealing with text, character, composition, and origin of literary documents; *higher* ~, criticism, other than verbal or textual (*lower* ~), of the Old and New Testaments; *textual* ~, criticism that seeks to ascertain the genuine text and meaning of an author.

crĭ′tĭcīze *v.t.* Discuss critically; censure, find fault with.

critĭ′que (-ēk) *n.* Critical essay or notice; criticism.

croak *n.* Deep hoarse sound made by frog or raven; sound resembling this. **croa′kў** *adj.* **croak** *v.* 1. Utter croak; utter dismally; forebode evil. 2. (slang) Kill; die.

Crō′at *n.* Native, inhabitant, of Croatia; descendant of Slavonic tribe which occupied that country in 7th c. **Crōā′tia** (-shĭa). District of Yugoslavia. **Crōā′tian** *adj.* Of Croatia or the Croats. ~ *n.* Croat; language of the Croats.

crŏc *n.* (colloq.) Crocodile.

Crō′ce (-chā), Benedetto (1866–1952). Italian philosopher and statesman.

crō′chet (-shĭ) *n.* Kind of knitting done with a hooked needle (~ *hook*); material so made. ~ *v.* Do crochet work; make of crochet.

crŏck[1] *n.* Earthen pot or jar; broken piece of earthenware used for covering hole in flower-pot.

crŏck[2] *n.* (slang) Broken-down or disabled person or thing. ~ *v.* Give way, break down (also ~ *up*); cause to collapse.

crŏ′ckerў *n.* Earthenware vessels, esp. for domestic use.

crŏ′ckėt *n.* 1. (archit.) Small ornament (usu. bud or curled leaf) on sloping side of pinnacle, pediment, etc. 2. Terminal knob on stag's horn.

Crŏ′ckford. (colloq.) 'Crockford's Clerical Directory', a reference book for clergy and the Church, first issued in 1860 by John Crockford (1823–65).

crŏ′codīle *n.* 1. Large amphibious thick-skinned long-tailed saurian reptile of *Crocodilus* or related genera, esp. *C. niloticus*, the crocodile of the Nile; tanned skin of this. 2. Children walking two and two; any long procession of objects close together. 3. ~*-bird*, Egyptian black-headed plover, *Pluvianus aegyptius*, a small bird with lavender and cream plumage and black-and-white markings, which eats crocodile's insect parasites; ~ *tears*, (from the ancient belief that the crocodile wept while devouring its victim) hypocritical tears.

crŏcodĭ′lĭan *adj.* & *n.* (Animal) like, closely allied to, the crocodile.

crō′cus *n.* Hardy dwarf plant with corm (genus *C*~), native of S. and central Europe and W. Asia, cultivated for its brilliant, usu. yellow or purple, flowers, appearing in spring or autumn.

Croe′sus (krēs-) (6th c. B.C.). King of Lydia, famous for his riches; hence, a very rich man.

crŏft *n.* Enclosed piece of (usu. arable) land; small agricultural holding worked by peasant tenant, esp. in Scottish Highlands. **crŏ′fter** *n.* One who cultivates a croft; joint tenant of divided farm.

croissant (krwahsahṅ) *n.* Crescent-shaped bread roll. [Fr.]

Crō-Mă′gnon (*or* -nyawṅ). Cave in Dordogne, France, where remains of *Homo sapiens* were found in 1868 among deposits of upper palaeolithic age; applied to a group of mankind (persisting in mesolithic and neolithic times) with long heads, low foreheads, very broad faces, deep-set eyes, and tall stature.

Crŏ′martȳ. Region of E. Scotland joined with Ross in 1890 to form ROSS AND CROMARTY.

Crōme, John (1768–1821). English landscape-painter, founder of the Norwich School of painters.

crŏ′mlĕch (-k) *n.* Obsolescent term still current in Wales for a megalithic burial chamber (DOL-

OLIVER CROMWELL

MEN) and in France for a prehistoric circle or enclosure of upright stones. [Welsh *crom* crooked, *llech* (flat) stone]

cromŏr'ne *n.* Organ reed-stop; = KRUMMHORN. [Fr., f. Ger. *Krummhorn* crooked horn]

Crŏ'mwell[1] (*or* krŭ-; *or* -ĕl), Oliver (1599–1658). Leader of the Parliamentary troops in the Civil War; Lord Protector of England, 1653–8.

Crŏ'mwell[2] (*or* krŭ-; *or* -ĕl), Thomas, Earl of Essex (1485?–1540). Chief adviser to Henry VIII in ecclesiastical matters; negotiated Henry's match with Anne of Cleves; failure of this match and the policy underlying it led to his downfall and execution.

crōne *n.* Withered old woman; old ewe.

Crŏ'nus. (Gk myth.) One of the Titans and father of Zeus, by whom he was dethroned as ruler of the universe.

crō'nȳ *n.* Intimate friend.

crook *n.* 1. Shepherd's staff, with one end curved or hooked, for catching sheep's leg; bishop's or abbot's pastoral staff; anything hooked; hook; curve, bend; ~-*back(ed)*, hunch-back(ed). 2. (slang) Dishonest person, rogue; esp. professional criminal. ~ *v.* Bend, curve.

crooked *adj.* 1. (krŏŏ'kĭd) Not straight, bent, twisted; deformed; bent with age; not straightforward, dishonest; ~ *cross*, swastika. 2. (krŏŏkt) Of stick etc., having cross handle. **crŏŏ'kėdlȳ** *adv.* **crŏŏ'kėdnėss** *n.*

Crookes (-ks), Sir William (1843–1919). English physicist; invented the radiometer and a special glass largely opaque to heat rays and ultra-violet light, and discovered thallium; ~ *layer*, layer of vapour separating any spheroidal mass or liquid from the surface on which it rests; ~ *space*, dark space within the negative-pole glow at the cathode of a discharge tube; ~ *tube*, high-vacuum discharge tube.

croon *n.* Low monotonous singing. ~ *v.* Utter croon; hum softly. **crōō'ner** *n.* Singer of sentimental songs in a soft artificial voice.

crŏp *n.* 1. Pouch-like enlargement of gullet in birds, where food is prepared for digestion. 2. Stock, handle, of whip; (also *hunting-*~) short whip with loop instead of lash. 3. Produce of cultivated plants, esp. cereals; season's total yield (of cereal etc.). 4. Entire hide of animal tanned. 5. Cropping of hair; style of wearing hair cut short; piece cropped or cut off anything. ~ *v.* 1. Cut off; (of animals) bite off (tops of plants). 2. Gather, reap. 3. Cut short. 4. Raise crop on; bear a crop. 5. ~ *up*, turn up unexpectedly; come to surface; ~ *out*, appear.

crŏ'pper *n.* (esp.) 1. Plant yielding good etc. crop. 2. (slang) Heavy fall (*come a* ~; also fig.).

crŏ'ppȳ *n.* (hist.) Irish rebel in 1798, wearing hair very short as sign of sympathy with French Revolution.

crō'quet (-kĭ) *n.* 1. Game played on lawn, in which wooden balls

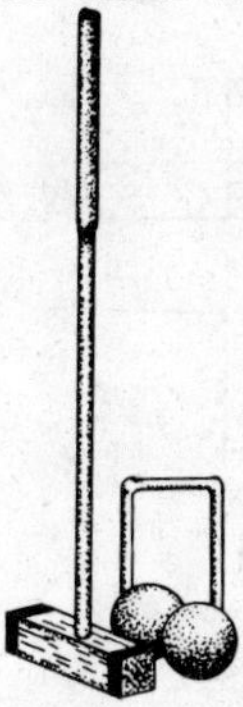

are driven with wooden mallets through hoops fixed in the ground. 2. Croqueting a ball in this game. ~ *v.t.* Drive away (another ball) by striking one's own ball placed in contact with it.

croquĕ'tte (-kĕt) *n.* Fried ball of rice, potato, meat, etc.

crōre *n.* (in India) Ten millions, 100 lakhs.

crō'sier, crō'zier (-zhy*er*) *n.*

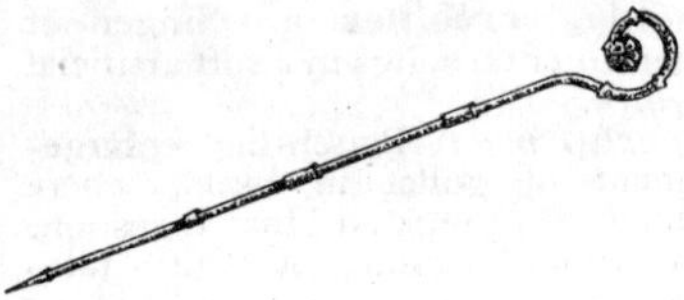

Pastoral staff or crook of bishop or abbot.

crŏss *n.* 1. Stake (usu. with transverse bar) used by the ancients for crucifixion, esp. that on which Christ was crucified; model of this as religious emblem; sign of cross made with right hand as religious act; staff surmounted with cross and borne before archbishop or in processions. 2. Monument in form of cross, esp. one in centre of town. 3. *the C~*, (fig.) the Christian religion. 4. Trial, affliction; annoyance. 5. Cross-shaped thing or mark; southern constellation (*Southern C~*) within Antarctic Circle, with four bright stars roughly in shape of cross; cross-shaped decoration in orders of knighthood etc.; *fiery ~*: see FIERY; *Grand C~*, decoration of highest class of order of knighthood, person wearing it; *Victoria C~*: see VICTORIA[1]. 6. Intermixture of breeds; animal etc. resulting from this; mixture, compromise, *between* two things. 7. (slang) Fraud, swindle. 8. Thing that crosses; *on the ~*, diagonally, obliquely, on the bias. **crŏ'sswise** (-z) *adj.* **crŏss** *v.* 1. Place crosswise. 2. Make sign of cross on or over. 3. Draw line across; write across (what is already written, a letter); drawn or stamp two lines across (cheque, which may then be paid only through bank). 4. Go across; bestride; carry, move, across; meet and pass. 5. Thwart. 6. Cross-breed; cross-fertilize. **~** *adj.* 1. Passing from side to side, transverse; intersecting. 2. Contrary, opposed. 3. (colloq.) Peevish, out of humour. **crŏ'sslȳ** *adv.* In a cross or peevish way. **crŏ'ssnėss** *n.*

crŏss- in comb.: *cro'ssbelt*, belt

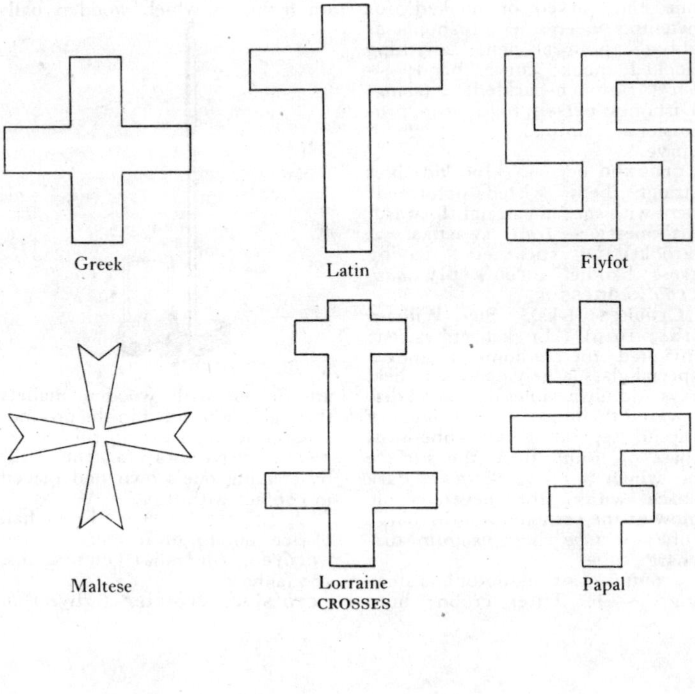

Greek Latin Flyfot

Maltese Lorraine Papal

CROSSES

for cartridges etc., from shoulder to opposite hip; *~-bench*, bench at right angles to others, occupied in English Parliament by independent or neutral members (*~ -benchers*); *cro'ssbill*, bird of genus *Loxia* (one of the finches), with mandibles of bill so curved as to cross each other when bill is closed; found in Europe, America, and Japan; *cro'ssbones*, figure of two thigh-bones laid across each other, usu. under skull as emblem of death; *cro'ssbow*, bow fixed across wooden stock, with groove for missile (arrow, stone, etc.) and mechanism for drawing back and releasing string; *cro'ssbowman* (*n.*); *crŏ'ssbred*, hybrid (animal etc.); *~-breed*, (cause to) produce hybrid; *hot ~ bun*, bun marked with cross, usu. eaten on Good Friday; *~-bu'ttock* (*n.* & *v.t.*) throw over the hip, in wrestling; *~-check*, verify, verification, by alternative method; *~-country*, transversely to great highways; across fields etc. instead of following roads; *~-cut*, diagonal cut, path, etc.; *~-cut saw*, saw for making cross-cut *~- examine*, examine by questions designed to check results of previous examination; esp. examine thus in court of law (witness who has already given evidence for other side); *~-examination*, *~-examiner* (*ns.*); *~-eyed*, having squint in which eyes are turned inwards; *~-fertilize*, fertilize (plant) with gamete from another; *~-grained*, (of wood) with grain running irregularly or in crossing directions; (fig.) perverse, intractable; *~-hatch*, shade (drawing, engraving, etc.) with intersecting series of parallel lines; *~-head*, bar at end of piston-rod of steam-engine, communicating motion to connecting rod; paragraph-heading printed across page or column in body of article in newspaper etc.; *~-legged*, with legs crossed; with one leg laid across the other; *~-over*, anything arranged with one part crossing another; connection by which tram, train, etc., may be transferred from one set of rails to another; (*adj.*) that crosses over, having one part crossing another; *cro'sspatch*, ill-tempered person; *~-ply*, (tyre) with layers of fabric laid at right angles; *~-pollinate*, pollinate from one plant to another; *~-purposes*, contrary or conflicting purposes; *be at ~ purposes*, misunderstand one another; *~-question* (*v.t.*) cross-examine; *~-reference* (*n.*) reference from one part of book etc. to another; (*v.t.*) provide with cross-reference(s). *cro'ssroads*, intersection of two roads; (fig.) critical turning-point; *~-section*, cutting across; section made by plane cutting anything transversely; typical representation of constituents of a thing or group; *~-stitch*, needlework stitch of two straight stitches crossing each other; *~ -tie*, transverse connecting piece (of timber etc.); *~-town* (*adj.*) (U.S.) lying, leading, going, across a town; *~-tree*, one of the horizontal transverse timbers bolted to mast of ship; *~ -vault*, vault formed by intersection of two or three simple vaults; *cro'ssword* (*puzzle*), puzzle which is solved by filling in words indicated by verbal clues down and across a prescribed chequered pattern so as to fit wherever they cross.

crŏsse *n.* Implement used in lacrosse for catching and throwing ball, consisting of long shank

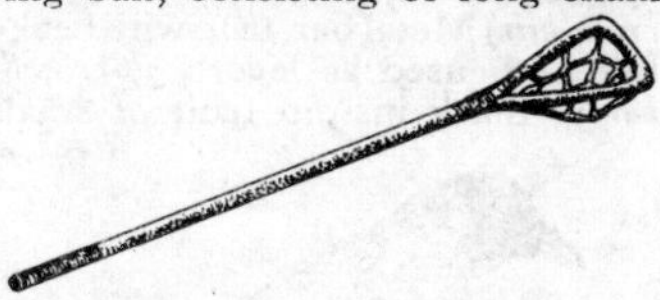

curved round at end with net stretched across curved part. [Fr.; see LACROSSE]

crŏ'ssing *n.* (esp.) Intersection of two roads, railways, etc. place where street is crossed; part of church where transepts cross nave; *~ -sweeper*, (hist.) person sweeping street-crossing.

crŏ'sslėt *n.* (her.) Little cross.

crŏtch *n.* Fork of tree or bough; fork of human body where legs join trunk, crutch; corresponding part of garment.

crŏ'tchėt *n.* 1. (mus.) Note (♩ or ♪) half as long as a minim. 2. Whimsical fancy. **crŏ'tchėtў** *adj.* Peevish. **crŏ'tchėtinėss** *n.*

crō'ton *n.* Plant, usu. tropical, of genus *C~*, the seeds of one species of which, the E. Ind. *C. tiglium*, yield ~ *oil*, a drastic purgative. [Gk *kroton* sheep-tick, croton, so called f. shape of seeds]

crouch *v.i.* Stoop, bend, esp. timidly or servilely; (of animals) lie close on ground, when about to pounce on prey, or from fear. ~ *n.* Action or position of crouching.

croup¹ (-ōō-) *n.* Inflammatory disease in larynx and trachea of children, marked by hard cough and difficulty of breathing.

croup², -pe (-ōō-) *n.* Rump, hindquarters, esp. of horse.

crou'pier (-ōō-) *n.* One who rakes in, and pays out, money at gaming-table; assistant chairman at public dinner. [Fr., orig. = 'one who rides behind on the croup']

croûton (krōōtawṅ) *n.* Small piece of fried or toasted bread used for garnishing or served with soup. [Fr.]

crow¹ (-ō) *n.* 1. Bird of family Corvidae, esp. *carrion* ~ (*Corvus corone*); in U.S., bird of gregarious species, *C. americanus*. 2. (also *crow'bar*) Metal bar, usu. with beak-like end, used as lever. 3. *crow'-berry*, black insipid fruit of small evergreen heath-like shrub, *Empetrum nigrum*, of N. Europe; (U.S.) cranberry; *crow'foot*, species of *Ranunculus* or buttercup, and other plants; (naut.) arrangement of small ropes for suspending awning; ~*'s-foot*, wrinkle at outer corner of human eye; ~*'s-nest*, barrel or protected platform fixed at masthead of sailing vessel for look-out man; ~ *steps*, = CORBIE stones.

CARRION CROW

crow² (-ō) *n.* Crowing of cock; joyful cry of infant. ~ *v.i.* Utter crow; exult loudly.

Crow³ *n.* Member, language, of a Siouan people of Montana.

crowd *n.* Throng, dense multitude; (colloq.) company, set, lot; large number (of things). ~ *v.* 1. Collect in a crowd; fill, occupy, cram (*with*); fill (places etc.) as crowd does; force one's way *into, through*, etc. (confined space, etc.); ~ *out*, exclude by crowding. 2. (naut.) Press or hasten on; ~ (*on*) *sail*, hoist unusually large number of sails on ship.

crown *n.* 1. Wreath of flowers etc. worn on head, esp. as emblem of victory. 2. Monarch's head-covering of gold etc. and jewels; (also *C~*; fig.) king or queen, regal power, supreme governing power in a monarchy.

3. Crown-shaped ornament. 4. Any of various coins orig. stamped with a crown; former silver coin of Gt Britain of value of 5*s.*; principal monetary unit of Czechoslovakia; principal monetary unit of Scandinavian countries (see KRONE). 5. Size of paper (orig. with crown watermark), 504 × 384 mm (20 × 15 in.). 6. Top part, esp. of skull; whole head. 7. Upper part of cut gem above girdle; highest or central part of arch or arched structure, esp. road; top part of hat, of bell; part of tooth projecting from

gum, artificial replacement of this. 8. ~-*and-anchor*, gambling game played with dice marked with crowns, anchors, and the four card-suits; *C~ colony*, colony with legislation and administration under control of home Government; *C~ Court*, court of criminal jurisdiction in England and Wales; *C~ Derby*: see DERBY; ~-*glass*, kind of thick glass without lead or iron, made in circular sheets by blowing and whirling; formerly used for window-panes; kind of optical glass with low refractive index; *C~ jewels*, jewels forming part of the regalia (in England kept in the Tower of London); *C~ law*, criminal law; *C~ office*, office transacting common-law business of Chancery; *C~ prince*, heir apparent or designate to sovereign throne, esp. in N. Europe and (hist.) Germany; *C~ princess*, wife of Crown prince; female heir presumptive; ~-*wheel*, contrate wheel. ~ *v.t.* 1. Place crown on; invest with regal crown or dignity; (fig.) reward; (slang) hit on the head. 2. Occupy the head of, form chief ornament to; put finishing touch to; bring (efforts) to happy issue. 3. (draughts) Make (piece) king, by putting another piece on top, or by turning up side marked with crown; (dentistry) fit crown to (tooth).

crow'ner *n.* (joc. or dial.) Coroner.

croy'don *n.* Kind of two-wheeled gig introduced *c* 1850. [*Croydon*, town in Greater London]

crozier: see CROSIER.

C.R.T. *abbrev.* Cathode-ray tube.

cru'cial (-ōōsh*a*l) *adj.* 1. Decisive, critical. 2. (anat.) Crossshaped.

cru'cian, -sian, (-ōōsh*a*n) *n.* Central European deep-yellow fish, *Carassius carassius*, allied to carp.

cru'ciāte (-ōōsh-) *adj.* (zool., bot.) Cross-shaped.

cru'cĭble (-ōō-) *n.* Vessel (usu. of earthenware) withstanding great heat, and used for fusing metals

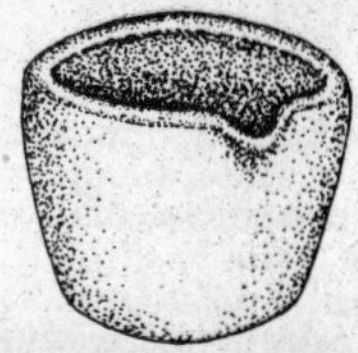

CRUCIFIXION

etc.; hollow at bottom of furnace to collect molten metal; (fig.) severe test or trial.

cruci′ferous (-ōō-) *adj.* 1. Wearing, adorned with, a cross. 2. (bot.) Of the family Cruciferae, having flowers with four equal petals arranged crosswise.

cru′cĭfĭx (-ōō-) *n.* Figure of Christ on the Cross; (erron.) cross.

crucifi′xion (-ōō-, -kshon) *n.* Crucifying (esp. of Christ); picture of this.

cru′cĭfôrm (-ōō-) *adj.* Cross-shaped, esp. of church with transepts.

cru′cĭfȳ (-ōō-) *v.t.* Put to death by fastening to a cross; (fig.) mortify (passions, sins, flesh).

crŭck *n.* (archit.) In medieval building, one of a pair of tall curving timbers standing on ground or foundations and meeting at apex of roof.

crude (-ōō-) *adj.* In the natural or raw state; not digested; unripe; (fig.) ill-digested, unpolished, lacking finish; rude, blunt. **cru′delȳ** *adv.* **cru′denėss, cru′dĭtȳ** *ns.*

cru′el (-ōō-) *adj.* Liking to inflict pain; indifferent to pain of others; painful, distressing. **cru′ellȳ** *adv.* **cru′eltȳ** *n.*

cru′ėt (-ōō-) *n.* Small glass bottle with stopper for vinegar, oil, etc., for table; cruet-stand; small

vessel for wine or water in celebration of Eucharist; *~-stand*, stand holding cruets, mustard-pot, etc.

cruise (-ōōz) *v.* 1. Sail about, making for no particular port or calling at series of ports; sail for pleasure; (of naval vessel) sail in specified area for protection of shipping etc. 2. Travel at cruising speed. 3. Drive at random, esp. slowly, as patrolling car, taxi looking for fare, etc. 4. Cruise in (specified area). 5. *cruising speed*, economical travelling speed of vehicle or aircraft. ~ *n.* Cruising voyage.

crui′ser (-ōōz-) *n.* 1. Warship adapted for cruising, less heavily armoured but faster than battleship. 2. (also *cabin-~*) Motor-boat with cabin. 3. *~-weight*, (boxing) light heavy-weight.

crŭ′ller *n.* (U.S.) Crisp twisted cake of dough containing eggs, butter, sugar, etc., fried in lard or oil.

crŭmb (-m) *n.* Small fragment, esp. of bread, such as breaks or falls off by rubbing etc.; (fig.) small particle, atom; soft inner part of bread. ~ *v.t.* Cover with crumbs, break into crumbs. **crŭ′mbȳ** (-mĭ) *adj.*

crŭ′mble *v.* Break, fall, into crumbs or fragments. ~ *n.* Crumbly or crumbled substance; dish with crumbly topping, esp. *apple ~*, *fruit ~*. **crŭ′mblȳ** *adj.* Apt to crumble.

crŭ′mhôrn *n.* Var. of CROMORNE, KRUMMHORN.

crŭ′mmȳ *adj.* (slang) Rubbishy, inferior, scruffy.

crŭmp *n.* Sound of heavy shell or bomb exploding.

crŭ′mpėt *n.* Soft doughy cake made of flour and yeast cooked on griddle or the like and eaten toasted.

crŭ′mple *v.* Crush together or *up* into creased state; ruffle, wrinkle; become creased; *~ up*, give way, collapse.

crŭnch *v.* Crush with teeth, esp. noisily; grind under foot (gravel etc.); make one's way thus. ~ *n.* Crunching (noise); crisis. **crŭ′nchȳ** *adj.* Fit for being crunched.

crŭ′pper *n.* Strap buckled to back of saddle and passing under horse's tail; hindquarters of horse.

crur′al (-ōōr-) *adj.* (anat.) Of the leg.

crusā′de (-ōō-) *n.* 1. (freq. *C~*) One of several military expeditions undertaken by the Christians of Europe in the 11th, 12th, and 13th centuries to recover the Holy Land from the Muslims; in the *1st C~* (1096–9) the crusaders cap-

4TH CRUSADE

tured Jerusalem and set up a kingdom there; the *3rd C~* (1189–91), in which Richard I of England, the Emperor Frederick Barbarossa, and Philip Augustus of France took part, resulted in the capture of Acre and the setting-up of a Latin kingdom in the East; in the *6th C~* (1228–9) Jerusalem was recaptured but finally lost; the other crusades were all unsuccessful. 2. Any war instigated by the Church for alleged religious ends; (fig.) aggressive movement against public evil etc.; *Children's C~*, crusade of about 500,000 unarmed children which set out in 1212 from France and Germany to recover the Holy

Sepulchre. ~ *v.i.* Engage in crusade. **crusā′der** *n.*

cruse (-o͞oz) *n.* (archaic) Pot, jar, of earthenware; *widow's* ~: see WIDOW.

crŭsh *v.* Compress, be compressed, with violence, so as to break, bruise, etc.; crease; pulverize by application of pressure; (fig.) subdue, overwhelm. **crŭshed** (-sht) *adj.* ~ *morocco*, (bookbinding) Morocco leather grained, shaved thin, pressed between iron plates, and polished; ~ *strawberry*, deep rather dull pink colour. **crŭsh** *n.* 1. Act of crushing. 2. crowded mass (esp. of persons); (U.S. colloq.) set, group of people associated together. 3. Drink made of juice of crushed fruit; squash. 4. *have, get, a* ~ *on*, (slang) form a passionate attachment to (a person); ~ *barrier*, barrier erected to restrain crowd; ~ *hat*, hat that can be crushed flat, esp. opera hat.

crusian: see CRUCIAN.

Crusoe, Robinson: see ROBINSON CRUSOE.

crŭst *n.* Hard outer part of bread; similar casing of anything, e.g. harder layer over soft snow; hard dry scrap of bread; pastry covering pie; hard dry formation, scab, on skin; (geol.) outer portion of earth; coating, deposit, on surface of anything; deposit of tartar, etc., on inside of wine-bottle; hard external covering of animal or plant; (fig.) anything superficial. ~ *v.* Cover with, form into, crust; become covered with crust. **crŭ′stėd** *adj.* Having a crust; (of wine) having deposited a crust, as old port etc.; (fig.) antiquated.

crŭstā′cean (-sh*a*n) *adj.* & *n.* (Arthropod) of the class Crustacea, including crabs, lobsters, shrimps, etc., mostly aquatic, freq. with hard shell and many legs.

crŭstā′ceous (-sh*u*s) *adj.* Crust-like; having a hard covering; crustacean.

crŭ′sty *adj.* Crust-like, hard; irritable, curt. **crŭ′stilȳ** *adv.* **crŭ′stinėss** *n.*

crŭtch *n.* Staff (now usu. with crosspiece at top fitting under armpit) for lame person; support, prop, esp. with forked top; = CROTCH; (naut.) any of various forked contrivances, as a forked rowlock.

Crŭ′tchėd Frī′ars (-z). Minor order of friars, *Fratres Cruciferi* or *Sanctae Crucis*, wearing a cross; founded in Italy in 1169, came to England in 1244; suppressed in 1656; hence, site of their convent in the City of London.

crŭx *n.* (pl. *-uces* pr. o͞osēz, *-ŭxes*). Difficult matter, puzzle; point at issue.

cruzeiro (kro͞ozār′ō) *n.* (pl. *-os*). Principal monetary unit of Brazil, = 100 centavos.

crȳ *n.* 1. Loud inarticulate utterance of grief, pain, fear, joy, etc.; loud excited utterance of words; appeal, entreaty. 2. Proclamation of wares sold in streets. 3. Public voice, generally expressed opinion; watchword. 4. Fit of weeping;

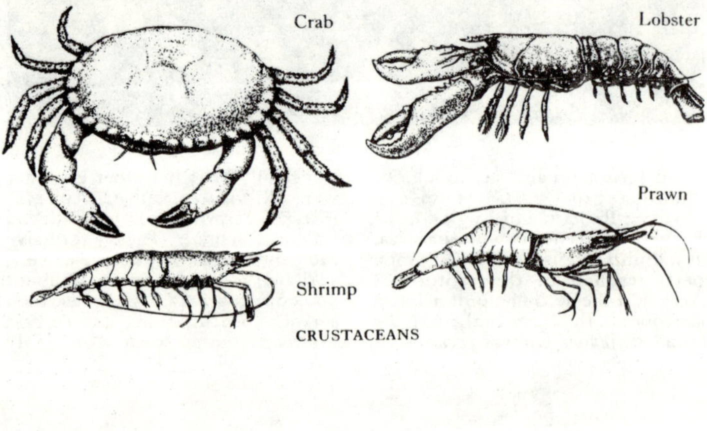

CRUSTACEANS

~-*baby*, one who cries childishly. 5. Yelping of hounds, pack of hounds; *full* ~, full pursuit. ~ *v.* 1. Utter cry or cries; utter loudly, exclaim. 2. Announce for sale; make public announcement of. 3. Weep. 4. ~ *down*, disparage; ~ *off*, withdraw from agreement, decline to do something; ~ *up*, praise. **crȳ′ing** *adj.* (esp., of evils) Calling for notice, flagrant.

crȳ′ogėn *n.* Freezing-mixture. [Gk *kruos* frost]

crȳ′olīte *n.* Fluoride of sodium and aluminium (Na_3AlF_6) found esp. in Greenland and used in production of aluminium and for ceramic glazes. [Gk *kruos* frost]

crȳ′ostăt *n.* Apparatus for maintaining very low temperature.

crўpt *n.* Underground cell, vault, esp. one beneath church, used as burial place.

crў′ptic *adj.* Secret, mystical; obscure in meaning; (zool.) adapted for concealment, as ~ *coloration*, animal's resemblance in colour, markings, etc., to its environment or to another animal.

crўpto- *prefix.* Hidden; secret, as ~-*Communist*, secret sympathizer with Communism.

crўptocrў′stalline *adj.* Having a crystalline structure indistinguishable to the naked eye.

crў′ptogăm *n.* (bot.) Plant of the class Cryptogamia having no stamens or pistils and therefore no proper flowers, including ferns, mosses, algae, lichens, and fungi. **crўptogă′mic, crўptŏ′gamous** *adjs.*

crў′ptogrăm, crў′ptogrăph (*or* -ahf) *ns.* Anything written in cipher. **crўptŏ′grapher** *n.* **crўptogră′phic** *adj.* **crўptŏ′graphў** *n.* Art of writing in, or solving, ciphers.

crўptomēr′ia *n.* Evergreen coniferous tree, *C. japonica*, of N. China and Japan; Japanese cedar.

crў′stal *n.* 1. Clear transparent ice-like mineral, esp. pure quartz (*rock*-~); piece of this; piece of natural or artificial mineral used in contact with another or with a thin wire as a simple radio detector. 2. Glass of very transparent quality, usu. with high proportion of lead oxide; fine cut glass; anything made of this; watch-glass. 3. (chem. etc.) Form in which atoms and molecules of many elements

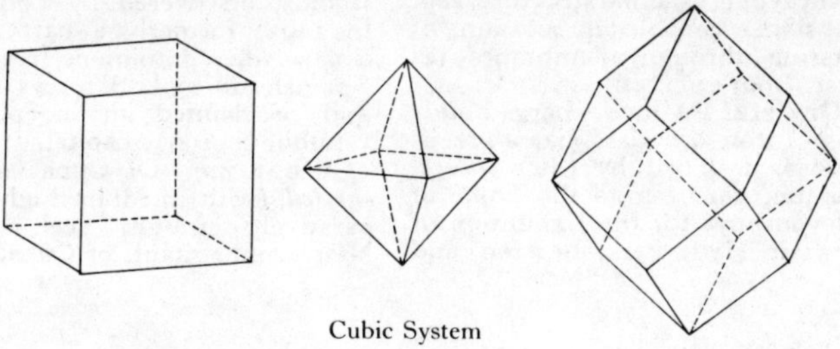

Cubic System

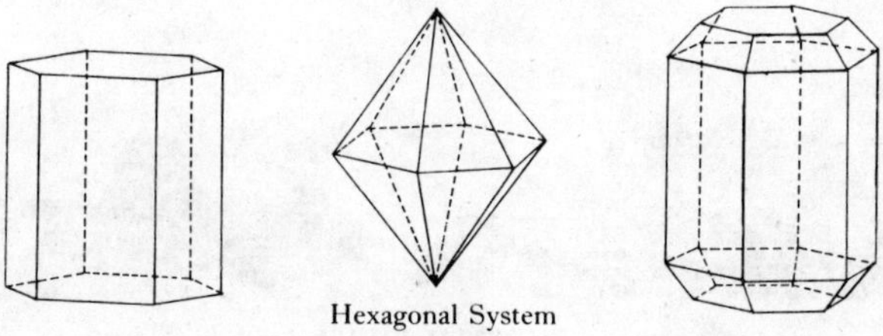

Hexagonal System

CRYSTALS

and compounds regularly aggregate, with definite internal structure and external form of solid enclosed by a number of symmetrically arranged plane faces. 4. ~ *gazing*, concentrating the gaze on ball of rock-crystal or glass for purpose of inducing a hallucinatory vision of distant or future events. ~ *adj*. Made of, like, clear as, crystal. **crў'stallīne** *adj*. Made of, like, clear as, crystal; having crystal form; ~ *heaven*, (in Ptolemaic system) sphere between primum mobile and firmament, assumed to explain precession of equinox and motion of libration; ~ *lens*, transparent body in eye enclosed in membranous capsule behind iris, acting as principal agent in focusing rays of light on retina.

crў'stallīze *v*. Form into crystals or (fig.) definite or permanent state. **crў'stallīzed** (-zd) *adj*. (esp., of fruit etc.) Preserved in and usu. coated with sugar.

crўstallŏ'graphў *n*. Branch of science dealing with structure, classification, and properties of crystals. **crўstallŏ'grapher** *n*. **crўstallogră'phic** *adj*.

crў'stalloid *adj*. & *n*. (Substance) of crystalline structure, esp. substance capable, in solution, of passing through membranes (as dist. from COLLOID).

Crў'stal Pă'lace. Large building of iron and glass, like a greenhouse, designed by (Sir) Joseph Paxton, gardener to the Duke of Devonshire, for the Exhibition of 1851 in Hyde Park, London, and re-erected at Sydenham; accidentally burnt down in 1936.

CS. (chem.) Substance ($ClC_6H_4CH{:}C(CN)_2$) causing irritation of skin, eyes, and lungs, used in form of finely divided solid for riot control; so *CS gas*.

c/s *abbrev*. Cycles per second.

csardas (chār'dahsh) *n*. Hungarian national dance.

C.S.E. *abbrev*. Certificate of Secondary Education.

C.S.I. *abbrev*. Companion of (the Order of) the Star of India.

C.S.M. *abbrev*. Company Sergeant-Major.

C.T.C. *abbrev*. Cyclists' Touring Club.

cu. *abbrev*. Cubic.

C.U. *abbrev*. Cambridge University (esp. in names of clubs, as *C.U.B.C.*, Boat Club); *C.U.P.*, Cambridge University Press.

cŭb *n*. 1. Young of fox; young of bear or other wild beast; *~-hunting*, hunting young foxes at beginning of season. 2. Unpolished youth. 3. *C~ Scout*, member of junior branch of Scout Association (formerly *Wolf C~*). 4. (U.S.) Apprentice, beginner. ~ *v*. Bring forth (cubs); hunt fox-cubs.

Cū'ba. Largest of the W. Ind. islands, discovered by Columbus in 1492; formerly a part of the Span.-Amer. dominions; freed from Spanish rule by U.S. forces in 1898 and proclaimed an independent republic in 1902; capital, Havana.

Cū'ban *adj*. Of Cuba; *~-heel, -heeled*, (with) medium high comparatively straight heel. ~ *n*. Native, inhabitant, of Cuba.

CRYSTAL PALACE

cŭ'bbȳ-hōle *n.* Very small confined room, cupboard, etc.

cūbe *n.* 1. Solid figure contained by 6 equal squares and 8 rectangular solid angles; anything of this shape. 2. Product of a number multiplied by its square, third power of a quantity; ~ *root*, number or quantity which when cubed produces given number or quantity. ~ *v.t.* 1. Find cube of (number), find cubic content of. 2. Cut into small cubes.

cū'bĕb *n.* Pungent spicy berry of Javanese climbing shrub, *Piper cubeba*, used in medicine and cookery.

cū'bĭc *adj.* Cube-shaped; of three dimensions, solid; involving cube of a quantity; ~ *content*, volume (of solid) expressed in cubic feet, metres, etc.; ~ *foot*, *inch*, etc., volume of a cube whose edge is one foot, inch, etc. **cū'bĭcal** *adj.* **cū'bĭcallȳ** *adv.*

cū'bicle *n.* Small separate sleeping-compartment in schools etc.; any small partitioned space.

cū'bĭfôrm *adj.* Cube-shaped.

Cū'bĭsm *n.* Phase of Post-Impressionist art, initiated *c* 1907 by Picasso and Braque, in which objects were reduced to cubic and other geometrical forms. **Cū'bĭst** *n.* & *adj.* **cūbĭ'stĭc** *adj.*

cū'bĭt *n.* Ancient measure of length, 18 to 22 in. **cū'bĭtal** *adj.* 1. Of the length of a cubit. 2. Of the forearm or corresponding part in animals. [L *cubitum* length of forearm (*cubitus* elbow)]

cū'boid *adj.* Cube-shaped, like a cube; ~ *bone*, one of the bones of the foot, between heel bone and 4th and 5th metatarsal bones. ~ *n.* Solid resembling cube, with rectangular faces not all equal; cuboid bone.

cŭ'cking-stōōl *n.* (hist.) Chair in which disorderly women etc. were tied and exposed to the jeers of a crowd as punishment.

cŭ'ckold *n.* Husband of unfaithful wife. ~ *v.t.* Make a cuckold of. [OF *cucu* cuckoo]

cu'ckōō (kōō-) *n.* Migratory bird of family Cuculidae with characteristic note or cry, esp.

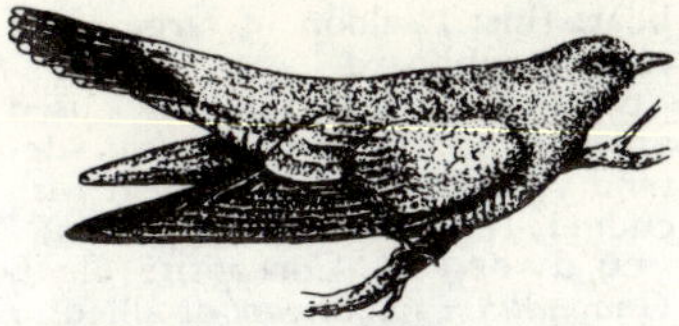

Cuculus canorus which winters in N. Africa and reaches British Isles in April, depositing its eggs in nests of small birds; ~-*clock*, clock in which hours are sounded by imitation of cuckoo's call; ~ *flower*, lady's smock, *Cardamine pratensis*, meadow-plant with pale lilac flower, blooming in spring; ~-*pint*, wild arum, *A. maculatum*; ~-*spit*, frothy secretion exuded by and enveloping the nymphs of certain insects (in Gt Britain usu. the frog-hopper *Philaenus spumarius*) on leaves, stems, etc., of plants. ~ *adj.* (slang) Crazy. [OF *cuca* imit. of bird's cry]

cū'cumber *n.* 1. Creeping plant, *Cucumis sativus*, native of S. Asia, widely cultivated for its long fleshy

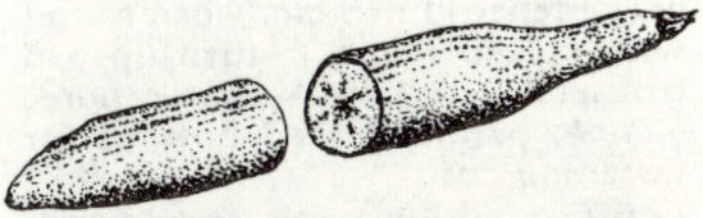

fruit; the fruit of this, commonly eaten as salad. 2. (also ~-*tree*, U.S.) Magnolia, esp. *M. acuminata* and other Amer. species, with fruit resembling small cucumbers.

cūcûr'bĭt *n.* Gourd. **cūcûrbĭtā'ceous** (-shus) *adj.*

cŭd *n.* Food that ruminating animal brings back from first stomach into mouth and chews at leisure.

cŭ'dbear (-bār) *n.* Purple or violet powder for dyeing, prepared from various lichens, esp. *Lecanora tartarea*; this lichen. [named by Dr *Cuthbert* Gordon, 18th-c. patentee]

cŭ'ddle *v.* Hug gently, fondle; lie close and snug; nestle together; curl oneself *up*. ~ *n.* Act of cuddling. **cŭ'ddlesome, cŭ'ddlȳ** *adjs.* Pleasant to cuddle.

cŭ'ddȳ *n.* Cabin of half-decked

boat; (hist.) saloon of large ship; closet, cupboard.

cŭ'dgel *n.* Short thick stick used as weapon; *take up ~s for*, (fig.) defend vigorously. ~ *v.t.* Beat with cudgel; (fig.) rack (one's brains).

cŭ'dweed *n.* Composite plant, *Gnaphalium sylvaticum* or allied or similar plant, with chaffy scales surrounding flower-heads.

cūe[1] *n.* Last word or words of a speech in a play, serving as signal to another actor to enter or speak; similar guide to musical performer; sign or intimation when or how to speak or act etc.; proper or politic course. ~ *v.t.* Give cue to; ~ *in*, insert cue for.

cūe[2] *n.* 1. (usu. *queue*) Pigtail. 2. Long straight tapering rod of wood tipped with leather, with which balls are struck in billiards etc. ~ *v.t.* Strike with cue.

Cū'fa, Kū'fa. Ancient city near Babylon, residence of caliphs before building of Baghdad, and a seat of Islamic learning.

cŭff[1] *n.* Band, freq. turned back, at bottom of sleeve; separate band of (stiffened) linen etc. worn round wrist; (esp. U.S.) turn-up on trouser leg; *off the* ~, extempore; ~ *link*, pair of linked buttons for fastening cuff.

cŭff[2] *n.* Blow with open hand. ~ *v.t.* Strike thus.

Cu'fic, Kū'fic *adj.* Of Cufa; of, in, Cufic writing. ~ *n.* Angular form of Arabic writing, found in early copies of the Koran and much used as decoration.

cū'ī bŏ'nō (*or* kwē). Who profits by it? (i.e. who is most likely to have brought it about?); (erron., pop.) to what purpose? [L]

cui'răss (kwĭ-) *n.* Body armour, breastplate and backplate fastened together; respiratory pump covering the chest. **cuirassier'** *n.* Horse soldier wearing cuirass.

cuisine (kwĭzē'n) *n.* Style of cooking.

cuisse (kwĭs) *n.* (hist., usu. pl.) Thigh armour.

Cŭldee' *n.* Member of an ancient Scoto-Irish religious order, found from the 8th c. onwards and brought under canonical rule by the end of the 11th c.

cul-de-săc (kōō-) *n.* Blind alley. [Fr.]

cū'lėt *n.* Horizontal face forming bottom of brilliant-cut gem.

cŭ'lĭnarў *adj.* Pertaining to a kitchen or cooking; fit for cooking.

cŭll *v.t.* Pick (flower etc.); select; kill surplus (animals, as deer, seals, etc.). ~ *n.* Act of culling; animal removed from flock (and usu. fattened) as inferior or too old for breeding.

cullender: see COLANDER.

cŭ'llėt *n.* (glass-making) Small pieces of glass at neck of bottle etc. knocked off in blowing the glass; refuse glass suitable for re-melting.

Cullŏ'dėn. Place near Inverness, Scotland, site of battle in which in 1746 the Duke of Cumberland defeated the force of the Young PRETENDER.

cŭ'llў *n.* Dupe, simpleton; man, fellow.

cŭlm[1] *n.* Coal-dust, esp. of anthracite.

cŭlm[2] *n.* (bot.) Stem of plant, esp. jointed, usu. hollow, stem of grasses.

cŭ'lmėn *n.* Upper ridge of bird's bill.

cŭ'lmĭnant *adj.* At, forming, the top; (of heavenly body) on the meridian. **cŭ'lmĭnāte** *v.i.* Reach its highest point; (astron.) be on the meridian. **cŭlmĭnā'tion** *n.*

cūlŏ'tte *n.* (usu. -pl., pr. -ŏt) Women's trousers cut to resemble skirt.

cŭ'lpable *adj.* Criminal, blameworthy. **cŭlpabĭ'lĭtў, cŭ'lpableness** *ns.* **cŭ'lpablў** *adv.*

cŭ'lprĭt *n.* Offender; prisoner at the bar. [orig. in formula *Culprit, how will you be tried?*, said by Clerk of Crown to prisoner pleading 'Not Guilty'; prob. abbrev. of Anglo-Fr. *Culpable*: *prest d'averrer* etc. (You are) guilty: (I am) ready to prove etc.]

cŭlt *n.* System of religious worship; devotion, homage, to person or thing; fad, passing fancy, for some particular thing. **cŭ'ltic** *adj.*

cŭ′ltĭvāte *v.t.* 1. Till; break up (ground) with cultivator. 2. Improve, develop (person, mind, etc., esp. in past part.); pay attention to, cherish. **cŭ′ltĭvable, ˋcŭltĭvā′table** *adjs.* Capable of being cultivated. **cŭltĭvā′tion** *n.* Cultivating, cultivated state.

cŭ′ltĭvātor *n.* 1. Tiller, husbandman, farmer. 2. Agricultural implement for breaking up ground

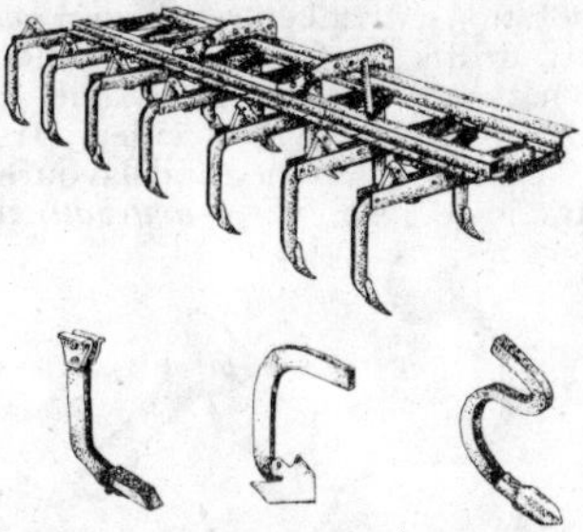

TRACTOR-MOUNTED CULTIVATOR SHOWING TINES

and uprooting weeds between drills of crops.

cŭ′lture *n.* 1. Tillage; rearing, production (of pearls, silk, etc.); (biol.) artificial development of bacteria etc. in specially prepared media; bacteria etc. so produced. 2. Improvement or refinement of mind, manners, etc., by education and training; condition of being thus trained and refined; particular form or type of intellectual development or civilization. **cŭ′ltural** (-cher-) *adj.* (esp.) ~ *revolution*, movement in Communist China, begun in 1965, seeking to restore original purity of Maoist doctrine. **cŭ′lturallȳ** *adv.* **cŭ′lture** *v.t.* Cultivate (esp. fig.); (biol.) make a culture of (bacteria etc.); *cultured pearl*, pearl formed by oyster after artificial insertion of foreign body.

cŭ′ltus *n.* Cult.

cŭ′lverĭn *n.* (hist.) Small firearm; large cannon, very long in proportion to its bore, used esp. in 16th and 17th centuries.

cŭ′lvert *n.* Channel, conduit, carrying water across under

CULVERIN

road, canal, etc.; conduit for electric cable.

cŭm (*or* kōōm) *prep.* With; ~ *dividend*, (abbrev. *cum d.*, *cum div.*) including dividend about to be paid; ~ *gra′no sa′lĭs* (grah-, sah-), with reserve (lit. 'with a grain of salt'). [L]

cum. *abbrev.* Cumulative.

cŭ′mber *v.t.* Hamper, hinder; burden. **cŭ′mbersome** *adj.* Unwieldy, clumsy. **cŭ′mbersomelȳ** *adv.* **cŭ′mbersomenėss** *n.*

Cŭ′mberland[1]**.** Former county of NW. England, since April 1974 part of the county of Cumbria.

Cŭ′mberland[2]**,** William Augustus, Duke of (1726–65). 2nd son of George II; commanded the English army at CULLODEN; known as 'the Butcher' on account of the severity with which he stamped out disaffection among the Highlanders.

Cŭ′mbrĭa. 1. Ancient British northern kingdom, including Cumberland. 2. County of NW. England (since April 1974), comprising the former counties of Cumberland and Westmorland. **Cŭ′mbrĭan** *adj.* & *n.* (Native, inhabitant) of Cumbria or Cumberland.

cŭ′mbrous *adj.* Cumbersome. **cŭ′mbrouslȳ** *adv.* **cŭ′mbrousnėss** *n.*

cŭ′mĭn, cŭ′mmĭn *n.* Umbelliferous fennel-like plant. *Cuminum*

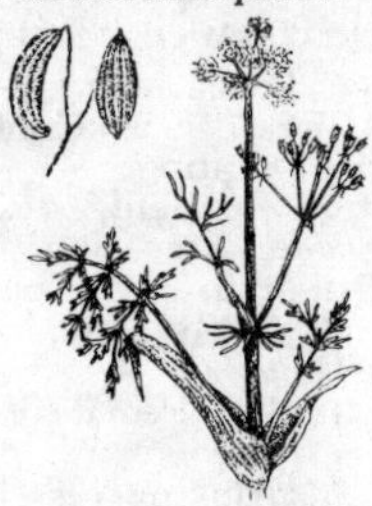

cyminum, cultivated in the Levant for its aromatic seed.

cŭ'mmerbŭnd *n.* Waist-sash. [Hind. *kamar-band* loin band]

cū'mūlāte *v.* Accumulate. **cūmūlā'tion** *n.*

cū'mūlative *adj.* Tending to accumulate; increasing in force etc. by successive additions; ~ *preference shares*, shares entitling holder to arrears of interest before any is paid on other shares; ~ *vote, voting*, etc., system in which each voter has as many votes as there are representatives, and may give all to one candidate. **cū'mūlativelў** *adv.* **cū'mūlativenėss** *n.*

cūmūloni'mbus *n.* (meteor.) Type of low dense cloud, a tall voluminous mass, present in thunderstorms.

cū'mūlus *n.* (pl. *-lī*). (meteor.) Form of cloud, usu. low, consisting of rounded masses heaped up on nearly horizontal base, frequent in summer skies.

Cūnar'd, Sir Samuel (1787–1865). Native of Nova Scotia; established first Atlantic steamship service and founded the ~ *Line*.

cū'nėate *adj.* Wedge-shaped.

cū'nėiform (*or* -ē'ĭf-) *adj.* Wedge-shaped; (kū'nĭ-) composed of wedge-shaped or arrow-headed marks used in ancient inscriptions

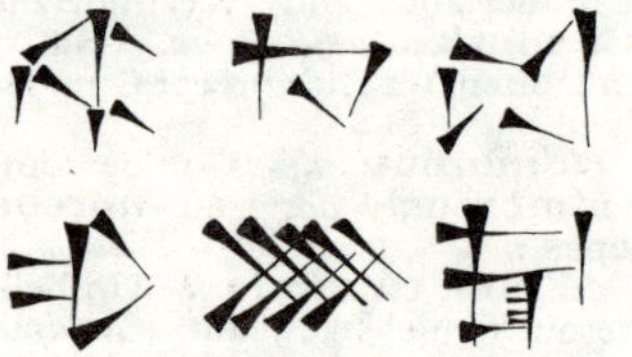

CUNEIFORM CHARACTERS

of Assyria, Persia, etc.; ~ *bone*, triquetral bone. ~ *n.* Cuneiform characters or writing.

cŭ'nning *n.* Skill, dexterity; skill in deceit or evasion. ~ *adj.* Possessed of or displaying cunning; (U.S. colloq.) quaintly pretty. **cŭ'nninglў** *adv.*

cŭnt *n.* (vulg.) Female external genitals.

cŭp *n.* 1. Drinking-vessel, with or without handle and stem; ornamental cup or other vessel as prize for race or other contest. 2. Rounded cavity, as socket of certain bones, cup-shaped hardened involucre of an acorn, calyx of flower, cup-shaped blossom, etc. 3. Cupful; (U.S., as measure in recipes) half-pint, 8 fluid ounces; (fig.) something to be partaken of, experience, portion, lot; (pl.) potations, drunken revelry; *in one's ~s*, drunk; *one's ~ of tea*, (colloq.) what interests or suits one. 4. Beverage of wine, cider, fruit juice, etc., sweetened and flavoured, and usu. iced. 5. *~-and-ball*, toy

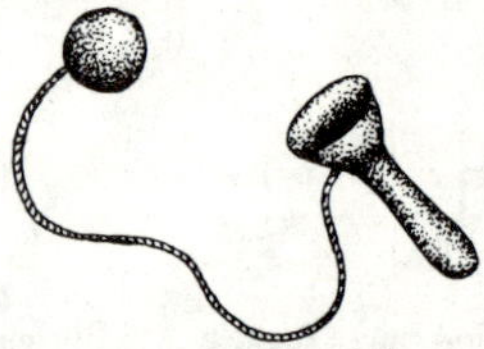

CUP-AND-BALL

consisting of cup at end of stem, with attached ball to be thrown and caught in cup or on spiked end of stem; *~-and-ring*, kind of mark found cut in megalithic monuments, with circular depression surrounded by concentric rings; *~-bearer*, one who serves wine, esp. officer of royal or noble household; *~-cake*, cake of which ingredients are measured by the cupful, or which is baked in small (paper) cups; *~-moss*, goblet lichen (*Cladonia pyxidata*), with cup-shaped processes arising from thallus. ~ *v.* 1. (hist.) Bleed (person) by means of *cupping-glass*, a glass vessel with open mouth applied to the skin and forming a partial vacuum. 2. Take or contain as in a cup, make or be cup-shaped. **cŭ'pful** *n.*

cupboard (kŭ'berd) *n.* Recess or structure enclosed by door, usu. with shelves for storage; (hist.) table on which cups etc. were displayed.

cū'pel *n.* Shallow absorbent vessel used in assaying the ores of precious metals. ~ *v.t.* Assay or refine in cupel. **cūpellā'tion** *n.*

Cū′pĭd. (Rom. myth.) God of love, son of Venus; identified with the Greek Eros; often represented as a beautiful naked boy with wings, carrying bow and arrows with which he wounds his victims; *~'s bow,* (line or shape resembling) the double-curved bow of Cupid. [L *cupido* desire, love]

cūpĭ′dĭtȳ *n.* Avarice.

cū′pola *n.* 1. Dome, forming the roof of a building or part of a building; diminutive dome above a roof ; ceiling of dome. 2. Furnace for melting metals for casting (formerly with dome leading to chimney, now often without dome). 3. Armour-plated revolving dome protecting guns on warship. 4. (anat., zool.) Dome-like organ or process.

cūprammo′nium *n.* Solution of copper hydroxide in ammonia capable of dissolving cellulose; artificial silk made from this.

cū′prĭc *adj.* (chem.) Containing copper in bivalent state.

cū′pro-ni′ckel *n.* Alloy of 75% copper and 25% nickel used in Britain since 1947 for coins formerly made of silver.

cū′prous *adj.* (chem.) Containing copper in univalent state.

cū′pūle *n.* (bot., zool.) Cup-shaped organ, receptacle, etc.

cur̄ *n.* Worthless, low-bred, or snappish dog; surly, ill-bred, or cowardly fellow.

cūraçao′, -ço′a (-sō, -sō*a*) *n.* Liqueur of spirits flavoured with peel of bitter oranges. [*Curaçao*, Dutch island in Caribbean]

cūr′acȳ *n.* Curate's office; benefice of perpetual curate.

cūrar̂′ė *n.* Blackish-brown resinous bitter poisonous substance extracted from *Strychnos toxifera* and other S. Amer. tropical plants, and used by Indians to poison their arrows, consisting of various alkaloids and blocking the action of the motor nerves on skeletal muscle. [corrupt. of *wurali*, native Carib name]

cūr′arine (-ēn) *n.* Purified alkaloid extract from curare used medicinally to obtain muscular relaxation.

cūr′assow (-sō) *n.* One of a family of turkey-like birds of Central and S. America. [f. *Curaçao* island]

cūr′ate *n.* Assistant to parish priest in Church of England and in R.C. Church in Ireland; *perpetual ~*, incumbent of parish or district, nominated by impropriator and licensed by bishop, now usu. styled VICAR; *~-in-charge*, clergyman appointed to take charge of parish during incapacity or suspension of incumbent.

cūr′ative *adj.* & *n.* (Thing) tending to cure (esp. disease).

cūrā′tor *n.* 1. Person in charge, manager; keeper, custodian, of museum; member of board managing property or having general superintendence in university. 2. (Rom. & Sc. law) Guardian of minor, lunatic, etc. **cūratŏr′ial** *adj.* **cūrā′torship** *n.*

cûrb *n.* 1. Chain, strap, passing under lower jaw of horse, used as check; (fig.) check, restraint. 2. Hard swelling on back of horse's hind leg; disease characterized by this. 3. Frame round top of well; timber or iron plate round top of circular structure; kerb; *~-roof*, roof of which each of two faces has two slopes, the lower steeper than the upper. ~ *v.t.* Apply curb to; restrain.

cûr′cūma *n.* 1. Tuberous plant of genus *C~* yielding E. Ind. arrowroot, mango-ginger, turmeric, etc. 2. Turmeric. [Arab. *kurkum* saffron, turmeric]

cûrd *n.* Coagulated substance formed (naturally or artificially) by action of acids on milk, made into cheese or eaten as food; anything resembling this; edible head of cauliflower, broccoli, etc.; fatty substance found between flakes of boiled salmon; *~ soap*, white soap made with tallow and soda. **cûr′dȳ** *adj.* Like curd; (of salmon) full of curd.

cûr′dle *v.* Congeal, form into curd; *~ the blood*, horrify, terrify.

cūre[1] *n.* 1. Remedy; course of medical or other treatment (esp. of specified kind); successful medical treatment, restoration to health. 2.

Spiritual charge or oversight of parishioners etc.; parish etc. ~ *v.* 1. Restore to health; remedy (an evil). 2. Preserve (meat, fruit, hides) by salting, drying, smoking, etc. 3. Render (substance) harder or more durable. **cūr'able** *adj.* **cūrabĭl'ĭty** *n.*

cūre[2] *n.* (slang) Odd or eccentric person.

curé (kūr'ā) *n.* Parish priest in France etc.

cūrĕ'tte *n.* Surgeon's small scoop-like instrument. ~ *v.t.* Scrape with curette. **cūrĕ'ttage** (*or* kūr'ĭtahzh) *n.* Process of curetting.

cūr'few *n.* Medieval regulation for extinction of fires at fixed hour in evening (orig. for prevention of conflagrations); hour for this, bell announcing it; ringing of bell at fixed evening hour, still surviving in some towns; (under martial law etc.) signal or time after which inhabitants must be indoors.

cūr'ia *n.* 1. (Rom. hist.) One of the ten divisions of each of the three ancient Roman tribes; building belonging to such division, serving primarily for worship. 2. Senate-house at Rome; senate of ancient Italian towns. 3. Court of justice, esp. under feudal organization. 4. (*C*~) Papal court, government departments of the Vatican. **cūr'ial** *adj.*

Cūr'ie[1]. Name of two chemists and physicists, Polish-born Marie (1867–1934) and her French husband Pierre (1859–1906); discoverers of radium, 1898; Nobel Prize for physics 1903 and (Marie) chemistry 1911.

MARIE CURIE

cūr'ie[2] *n.* Unit of radioactivity equal to $3{\cdot}7 \times 10^{10}$ disintegrations per second. [f. CURIE[1]]

cūr'ĭō *n.* Curious object of art.

cūrĭō'sa *n.pl.* Curiosities, esp. erotic or pornographic books.

cūrĭŏ'sĭtȳ *n.* 1. Desire to know; inquisitiveness. 2. Strangeness; strange or rare object.

cūr'ious *adj.* 1. Eager to learn; inquisitive. 2. Strange, surprising. 3. (euphem., of books) Erotic, pornographic. **cūr'iouslȳ** *adv.* **cūr'iousnėss** *n.*

cūr'ĭum *n.* (chem.) Radioactive metallic transuranic element; symbol Cm, at. no. 96, principal isotope at. wt 242. [f. CURIE[1]]

cūrl *n.* 1. Spiral or convolute lock of hair; anything spiral or incurved; act of curling; state of being curled; ~-*paper*, piece of soft paper twisted into the hair to make it curl. 2. Disease of potatoes etc. in which shoots or leaves are curled up. ~ *v.* 1. Bend, coil, into spiral shape; move in spiral form. 2. Play at CURLING. **cūr'ler** *n.* (esp.) Pin, clip, etc., for curling the hair.

cūr'lew *n.* Wading bird of the genus *Numenius* with long slender curved bill and characteristic cry, frequenting estuaries, sea-shores, and moors; *stone*-~, inland bird, *Burhinus oedicnemus*.

cūr'lĭcūe *n.* Decorative curl or twist.

cūr'lĭng *n.* (esp.) 1. Scottish game played on ice (~-*pond* or other smooth frozen surface) with large stones which are hurled along a rink towards a tee; ~-*stone*, stone used in this, of polished granite, cheese-shaped, and not more than 36 in. in circumference or 50 lb. in weight, with an iron or wooden handle on the upper surface. 2. ~-*iron*, ~-*tongs*, tongs for curling the hair.

cūr'lȳ *adj.* Having, arranged in, curls. **cūr'lĭnėss** *n.*

cūrmŭ'dgeon (-jen) *n.* Churlish

or miserly fellow. **cûrmŭ'dgeonlȳ** *adj.*

cŭ'rrach, cŭ'rragh[1] (-r*a*) *n.* Coracle.

cŭ'rragh[2] (-r*aχ or* -r*a*) *n.* Marshy waste ground, in Ireland and Isle of Man; *the C~*, a level stretch of open ground in County Kildare, famous for its race-course and military camp.

cŭ'rrant *n.* 1. Dried fruit of a small seedless variety of grape grown in the Levant, much used in cookery. 2. Small round black, red, or white berry of *Ribes nigrum* and *R. rubrum*, natives of N. Europe; any of these shrubs, or others of the same species; *flowering ~*, shrub *R. sanguineum*, native of N. America, cultivated for its pink or red flowers. [orig. *raisins of Corauntz* (Corinth)]

cŭ'rrencȳ *n.* 1. Time during which thing is current; (of money) circulation; prevalence (of words, ideas, etc.). 2. Money in actual use in a country; HARD, SOFT, ~: see these words; *~ note*, paper money used as currency, esp. English notes for £1 and 10*s*. issued by the Treasury 1914–28.

cŭ'rrent *adj.* In general circulation or use; (of time) now passing; belonging to the current time; *pass, go*, etc. ~, be generally accepted as true or genuine; *~ account*, customer's account at bank to meet current expenditure, drawn on by cheque. **cŭ'rrentlȳ** *adv.* **cŭ'rrent** *n.* 1. Running stream; water, air, etc., moving in given direction. 2. Course, tendency (of events, opinions, etc.). 3. Transmission of electricity, electricity transmitted, through a body.

cŭ'rrĭcle *n.* Light open two-wheeled carriage drawn by two horses abreast.

cŭrrĭ'cūlum *n.* (pl. *-la*). 1. Course (of study). 2. *~ vītae*, brief account of one's career. [L] **cŭrrĭ'cūlar** *adj.*

cŭ'rrĭer *n.* One who dresses and colours tanned leather.

cŭ'rrȳ[1] *n.* Dish of meat, fish, fruit, or vegetables, cooked with bruised spices and turmeric, and usu. served with rice; *~-paste, -powder*, preparations of turmeric and strong spices for making curries. ~ *v.t.* Make into curry; flavour like curry. [Tamil *kari* sauce]

cŭ'rrȳ[2] *v.t.* 1. Rub down or dress (horse etc.) with comb; dress (tanned leather) by soaking, scraping, beating, colouring, etc.; (fig.) thrash; *~ favour* (orig. *favel*, f. OF *fauvel* chestnut horse), ingratiate oneself (*with* person) by officious courtesy etc.; *~-comb*, comb for currying horses etc.; (*v.t.*) curry.

cûrse *n.* 1. Utterance (by deity or person invoking deity) supposed or intended to consign person or thing to destruction, divine vengeance, etc.; formal ecclesiastical censure, sentence of excommunication. 2. Profane oath, imprecation. 3. Evil inflicted in response to curse; great evil, bane; *~ of Scotland*, nine of diamonds in playing-cards (supposed to be so called from its resemblance to the nine lozenges in the armorial bearings of Lord Stair, who had some share in sanctioning the massacre of Glencoe in 1692 and in the Union of Scotland with England in 1707). ~ *v.* Utter curse against; excommunicate; blaspheme; afflict *with*; utter curses.

cûr'sėd, cûrst *adj.* (esp.) Damnable, abominable; (archaic) cantankerous. **cûr'sėdlȳ** *adv.* **cûr'sėdnėss** *n.*

cûr'sĭve *adj.* & *n.* (Writing) done in a flowing style, with the characters joined together.

cûr'sor *n.* Transparent slide engraved with hair-line forming part of slide-rule etc.

cûrsôr'ial *adj.* (zool., of birds etc.) Having limbs adapted for running.

cûr'sorȳ *adj.* Hasty, hurried. **cûr'sorĭlȳ** *adv.* **cûr'sorĭnėss** *n.*

cûrt *adj.* Discourteously brief; terse, concise. **cûr'tlȳ** *adv.* **cûr'tnėss** *n.*

cûrtai'l *v.t.* Cut short. **cûrtai'lment** *n.*

cûr'tail-stĕp *n.* Lowest step of stair, with outer end carried round.

LORD CURZON

cŭr'tain (-tn *or* -tĭn) *n.* 1. Suspended cloth used as screen esp. at window; screen separating stage of theatre from auditorium; (fig.) = IRON curtain. 2. (also ~ *wall*) Plain wall of fortified place, connecting two towers etc.; piece of plain wall not supporting a roof. 3. Partition, cover, in various technical senses; (mil.) barrage. 4. Curtain-call; finale of scene etc. 5. (pl., colloq.) The end. 6. *~-call*, call for actor to appear before curtain after play or scene of play; *~-lecture*, (archaic) wife's reproof to husband in bed; *~-raiser*, short opening piece performed before principal play in theatre; *~-ring*, one of rings by which curtain is hung, which slide on rod when curtain is drawn; *~-rod*, horizontal rod from which curtain is hung. ~ *v.t.* Furnish, cover, shut *off*, with curtains.

cŭrtā'na (*or* -ah-) *n.* Sword without a point borne before sovereign of England at coronation, as emblem of mercy.

cŭr'tĭlage *n.* (law) Area attached to dwelling-house and forming, or regarded as forming, one enclosure with it.

cŭr'tsey, -sў *n.* Feminine movement of respect or salutation, made by placing one foot behind the other and bending the knees so that trunk is lowered (usu. *make, drop, a* ~). ~ *v.i.* Make curtsey (*to* person).

cŭr'vature *n.* Curving; curved form; (geom.) amount or rate of deviation (of curve) from straight line or curved surface from plane.

cŭrve *n.* Line of which no part is straight, locus traced by moving point the direction of whose motion continuously changes or deviates from a straight line; curved form or thing; (on graph or diagram) line drawn from point to point so as to represent diagrammatically a continuous variation of quantity, force, etc. ~ *v.* Bend or shape so as to form curve.

cŭrvĕ't *n.* Horse's leap with forelegs raised together, and hind legs raised with spring before forelegs reach ground. ~ *v.i.* (of horse or rider) Make curvet.

cŭrvĭlĭ′nėar *adj.* Contained by, consisting of, curved line(s); ~ *tracery*. **cŭrvĭlinėă′rĭtȳ** *n.* **cŭrvĭlĭ′nėarlȳ** *adv.*

Cŭr′zon, George Nathaniel, 1st Marquess Curzon of Kedleston (1859–1925). English statesman; viceroy of India 1899–1905.

cŭ′scŭs *n.* Long fibrous aromatic root of an Indian grass, *Andropogon muricatus*, used for making fans, screens, etc. [Pers. *khas khas*]

cū′sĕc *n.* Unit of flow of water, one cubic foot per second.

cŭ′shat *n.* (Sc. & dial.) Wood-pigeon, ring-dove.

cu′shion (ko͝oshon) *n.* 1. Case of cloth etc. filled with soft material or air, for sitting, kneeling, or reclining on or against. 2. Elastic lining or rim of inner side of billiard table, from which the balls rebound; soft buffer; body of air or steam as buffer or support. 3. Fleshy part of buttock (of pig etc.); frog of horse's hoof. ~ *v.* Furnish, protect, with cushions; (billiards) place or leave (ball) against cushion; cause ball to rebound off cushion; (fig.) protect against shock, mitigate effects of.

cu′shȳ (ko͝o-) *adj.* (slang; of post, task, etc.) Easy, pleasant, comfortable. [Hind. *khush* pleasant]

cŭsp *n.* Apex, peak; (geom.) point at which two branches of curve meet and stop; (archit.) projecting point between small arcs in tracery; (bot.) pointed end, esp. of leaf. **cŭ′spāte, cŭsped** (-pt) *adjs.*

cŭ′spidal *adj.* Of (the nature of) a cusp. **cŭ′spĭdate, -ātėd,** *adjs.*

cŭ′spĭdŏr *n.* (U.S.) Spittoon.

cŭss *n.* (U.S.) Curse; person, creature. **cŭ′ssėdnėss** *n.* Perversity.

cŭ′stard *n.* Mixture of beaten eggs and milk, baked in dish, or cooked in saucepan and served as sweet sauce; similar sauce made with custard powder; ~*-apple*, fruit of S. Amer. and W. Ind tree, *Anona reticulata*, with dark-brown rind and yellowish pulp like custard in appearance and flavour; this tree, which was introduced into E. Indies in 16th c.; ~ *powder*, preparation in powder form for mixing with milk to make custard sauce.

cŭstō′dĭal *adj.* Relating to custody.

cŭstō′dĭan *n.* Guardian, keeper, esp. of public building etc.

cŭ′stodȳ *n.* Guardianship, care; imprisonment.

cŭ′stom *n.* 1. Usual practice; (law) established usage having the force of law. 2. (pl.) Duty levied upon imports from foreign countries; *Customs*, department of Civil Service that deals with levying of customs; ~*(s)-house*, office (esp. in seaport) at which customs are collected. 3. Business patronage or support; ~ *clothes*, (U.S.) clothes made to measure (so ~*-made, -suit*. etc.).

cŭ′stomarȳ *adj.* Usual; (law) subject to, held by, custom (of a manor etc.). **cŭ′stomarĭlȳ** *adv.* **cŭ′stomarĭnėss** *n.* **cŭ′stomarȳ** *n.* Written collection of customs of a country.

cŭ′stomer *n.* Buyer, purchaser; (*queer, ugly*, etc. ~), person to have to do with.

cŭt *v.* (past t. & past part. *cut*). 1. Penetrate, wound, with edged instrument (also fig.); divide with knife etc. (*in, into*, pieces etc.); detach by cutting; carve (meat). 2. Cross, intersect; pass *across, through*, etc.; (slang) go quickly. 3. Reduce by cutting (hair etc.); reduce (wages, price, time, etc.); shape, fashion, by cutting; edit (film); (cinemat.) make quick transition *to* next shot; (slang) cut out, stop. 4. Perform, execute, make, as ~ *a caper, dash, figure*, etc. 5. Divide (pack of cards) to select dealer or partners, prevent cheating, etc. 6. (cricket) Hit ball to the off with chopping movement of bat; (lawn tennis), strike ball across its line of flight so as to impart spin etc. 7. Renounce acquaintance of (person), decline to recognize him; absent oneself from, avoid, renounce. 8. Have (tooth) appear through gum. 9. ~ *a corner* or *corners*, pass round corner(s) closely; (fig.) take unorthodox course to save time; act illegally; ~ *down*, bring or throw down by cutting; reduce (expenses etc.); ~ *in*, enter abruptly, interpose (in conversation); join in game of cards by taking place of player who cuts out; supersede a partner during a dance; obstruct path of vehicle by moving sharply in front of it after overtaking; ~ *off*, remove by cutting; bring to an end; intercept, interrupt (supplies, communications); exclude (*from*); ~ *out*, remove by cutting; outdo or supplant (rival); shape by cutting (out of a piece); form, fashion (esp. fig. in past part.); (cards) be excluded from game as result of cutting; obstruct path of oncoming vehicle by moving out from one's own side of the road, esp. in order to overtake another vehicle; stop, leave off; disconnect; *have one's work ~ out*, have a difficult task; ~ *up*, cut in pieces; destroy utterly; criticize severely; distress greatly; ~ *up for*, (colloq.) leave (specified amount) at death; ~ *up rough*, show resentment. 10. *~-and-dried*, (of opinions etc.) ready-made, lacking freshness; *~-away*, (coat) with skirt cut back from the waist; ~ *line*, line above which service must be made in squash rackets; *~-off*, shorter channel or route cutting off bend etc., (U.S.) by-pass; *~-out*, contrivance for automatically disconnecting electric circuit; device in motor-car etc. for releasing exhaust gas rapidly without passage through silencer; *cu'tpurse*, (archaic) thief; *cu'tthroat* (*n.*)

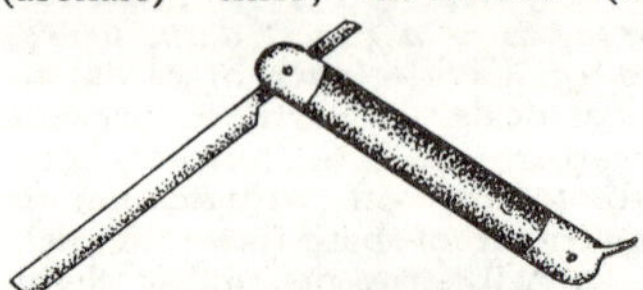

CUTTHROAT RAZOR

murderer; bloodthirsty ruffian; (razor) with blade set in handle, opp. safety-razor; (*adj.*) intensive, merciless; (of card-games) three-handed; *cu'twater*, knee of head of ship, dividing water before it reaches bow; forward edge of prow; *cu'tworm*, caterpillar that cuts off young plants level with ground. ~ *n.* 1. Act of cutting; stroke, blow, with knife, sword, whip; act, speech, deeply wounding the feelings; excision of a part; reduction in wages, prices, time, etc. 2. Particular stroke in various games (see *v.* above, sense 6). 3. Cutting of acquaintance. 4. Passage or way across, esp. as opposed to going round about (*short ~*). 5. Way something is cut. 6. Wound made by cutting; incision, slash. 7. Passage, channel, opening, cut out. 8. Wood-cut. 9. Piece, esp. of meat, cut off. 10. (slang) Share (of profit etc.).

cūtā'nėous *adj.* Of the skin.

cūte *adj.* (colloq.) Clever; ingenious; (U.S.) quaint, attractive. **cū'telў** *adv.* **cū'tenėss** *n.*

cū'ticle *n.* Epidermis or other superficial skin; dead skin at base of finger- or toe-nail; (bot.) continuous protective layer of impervious material secreted by cells of epidermis. **cūtĭ'cūlar** *adj.*

cū'tĭe *n.* (U.S. slang) Smart attractive young woman.

cū'tĭs *n.* (anat.) True skin or dermis.

cŭ'tlass *n.* Short sword with slightly curved blade, esp. that formerly used by sailors.

cŭ'tler *n.* One who makes or deals in knives and similar utensils.

cŭ'tlerў *n.* Trade of cutler; things made or sold by cutlers; collection of household knives, forks, and spoons.

cŭ'tlėt *n.* Neck chop of mutton; small piece of veal, broiled or fried in breadcrumbs; minced meat etc. in shape of this.

cŭ'tter *n.* 1. Person, thing, that cuts; tailor etc. who takes measurements and cuts out cloth; cutting-part of machine. 2. Superior kind of brick that can be cut and rubbed. 3. Boat belonging to ship of war, fitted for rowing and sailing; small single-masted vessel rigged like sloop but with running bowsprit; (U.S.) small light sleigh, usu. drawn by one horse.

cŭ'tting *n.* (esp.) 1. Excavation of high ground for railway, road, etc. 2. (also *press* ~) Paragraph etc. cut from newspaper etc. 3. Piece cut from plant for propagation. ~ *adj.* (esp.) That wounds the mind or feelings. **cŭ'ttinglȳ** *adv.*

cŭ'ttle *n.* (usu. ~*-fish*) Cephalopod of genus *Sepia*, esp. *S. officinalis*, which when pursued ejects black fluid from a sac so as to darken water; ~*-bone*, internal shell of cuttle-fish used as food for cage-birds and when ground as a polishing powder.

cŭ'ttȳ *adj.* (Sc.) Cut short; abnormally short; *C~ Sark*, (orig. lit. = 'short shirt') very fast clipper built at Dumbarton 1869, said to have sailed from Sydney to London in 75 days; ~*-stool*, stool in Presbyterian churches where offenders against chastity sat to receive public rebuke during service. ~ *n.* Short pipe.

Cūvier (-vēā), Georges Léopold Chrétien Fréderic Dagobert (1769–1832). French naturalist.

C.V.O. *abbrev.* Commander of the Royal Victorian Order.

cwm (ko͞om) *n.* (in Wales) = COMBE.

C.W.S. *abbrev.* Co-operative Wholesale Society.

cwt *abbrev.* Hundredweight.

cȳ'ăn *adj.* & *n.* (Greenish-blue) colour.

cȳă'nic *adj.* 1. Blue. 2. ~ *acid*, colourless pungent volatile unstable liquid (HCNO).

cȳ'anīde *n.* Salt of hydrocyanic acid (HCN), compound of cyanide group CN with organic radical; ~ *process*, extraction of gold and silver from ore with dilute solution of sodium cyanide.

cȳă'nogĕn *n.* Colourless inflammable highly poisonous gas (C_2N_2).

cȳanō'sĭs *n.* (path.) Blueness of skin caused by presence of large quantities of de-oxygenated blood in its minute vessels. **cȳanŏ'tĭc** *adj.*

Cȳ'bėlē. (myth.) Anatolian mother-goddess, worshipped esp. in Phrygia and later in Greece with her consort ATTIS.

cȳbernĕ'tics *n.* Theory, study, of communication and control in living organisms or machines.

cȳ'căd *n.* (bot.) Plant of family Cycadaceae, related to conifers, but resembling palms, the trunk of which yields sago. **cȳcadā'ceous** (-sh*us*) *adj.*

Cȳ'cladēs (-z). Circular group of Greek islands in the S. Aegean. **Cȳclă'dĭc** *adj.*

cȳ'clamāte *n.* Salt of cyclohexylsulphamic acid (C_6H_{11}·NH·SO_3H), with sweetening properties.

cȳ'clamen *n.* S. European primulaceous plant of genus *C~* with fleshy root-stocks, cultivated

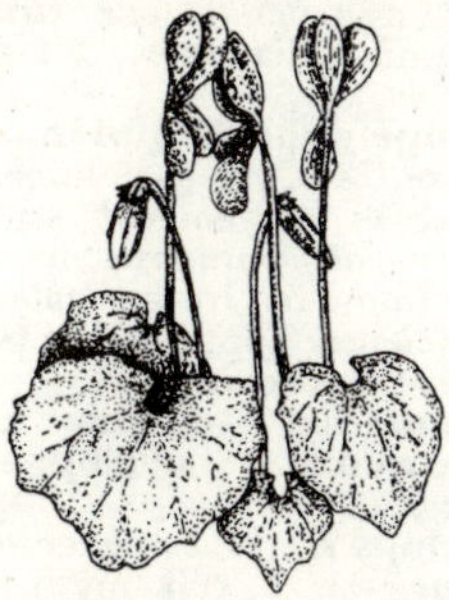

for its handsome early-blooming flowers; pinkish-red colour.

cȳ'cle *n.* 1. Recurrent period (of events, phenomena, etc.); period of a thing's completion; (phys. etc.) recurring series of operations or states; one complete oscillation; esp. (elect.) short for ~ *per second*, frequency of an alternating current or potential (abbrev. c/s). 2. Complete set or series; series of poems or songs collected round central event, character, or idea. 3. Bicycle, tricycle, or similar machine; ~*-car*, light motor-driven vehicle with three (rarely four) wheels. ~ *v.i.* 1. Move in cycles. 2. Ride cycle.

cȳ'clĭc, -ĭcal *adjs.* 1. Recurring in cycles; belonging to a definite chronological cycle. 2. Of a cycle of mythic and heroic story. 3. (bot., of flower) With its parts arranged in whorls. 4. (math.) Of a circle or cycle. 5. (chem., *-ic*) With the constituent atoms in a ring formation.

cȳ'clĭst *n.* Rider of a cycle.

cȳ'cloid *n.* Curve traced in space by point in circumference or on radius of a circle as the circle rolls along a straight line. **cȳcloi'dal** *adj.*

cȳclŏ'mėter *n.* 1. Instrument for measuring circular arcs. 2. Apparatus attached to wheel of bicycle etc. for measuring distance traversed.

cȳ'clōne *n.* System of winds rotating around region of low barometric pressure (in N. hemisphere anti-clockwise, in S. clockwise); violent destructive one (*tropical* ~) of limited diameter. **cȳclŏ'nic** *adj.*

Cȳclopē'an, Cȳclō'pĭan *adj.* 1. Of, like, a Cyclops; huge. 2. Applied to an ancient style of masonry of immense irregular stones, found in Greece, Italy, etc., and anciently supposed to be the work of the Cyclops.

cȳclopē'dĭa, -paedĭa *n.* = ENCYCLOPEDIA. **cȳclopae'dĭc, -pē-** *adj.*

Cȳ'clŏps *n.* (pl. same, or *-opses*, *-ōpēs* pr. -z). 1. (Gk myth.) One of a race of one-eyed giants who inhabited an island and forged thunderbolts for Zeus. 2. (zool.) Small freshwater crustacean of genus *C*~ with an eye in the middle of the front of the head.

cȳclora'ma (-rah-) *n.* Circular panorama; curved back of stage.

cȳclŏ'stomous, cȳclostŏ'matous, *adjs.* Having a round sucking mouth, as a lamprey, or a circular shell-aperture, as some gasteropods.

cȳ'clostȳle *n.* Device for multiplying copies of written document from stencil-plate cut by pen with small toothed wheel. ~ *v.t.* Print by cyclostyle.

cȳ'clotrŏn *n.* (phys.) Apparatus for accelerating charged atomic particles, moving in a widening spiral, by passing them repeatedly through the same electromagnetic field.

cȳ'gnėt *n.* Young swan.

cy̆'lĭnder *n.* 1. (geom.) Solid generated by straight line moving without change of direction and describing with its ends any fixed curve, esp. circle. 2. Roller-shaped body, hollow or solid. 3. Barrel-shaped object of baked clay covered with cuneiform writing and buried under foundations of ancient Babylonian or Assyrian temple; (also ~ *seal*) small stone of similar shape used as seal. 4. Cylindrical part of various machines, esp. chamber in which

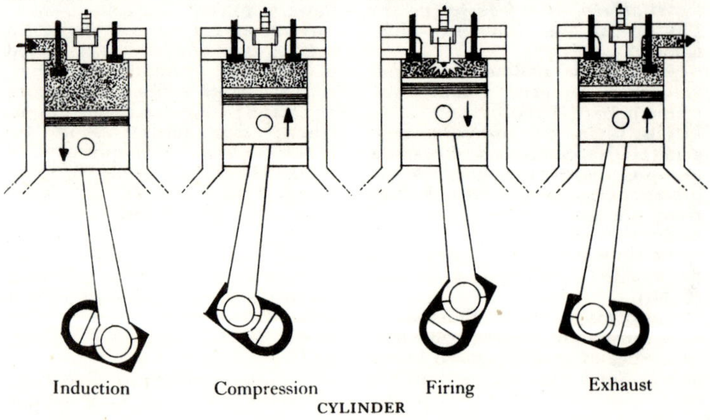

CYLINDER

liquids or gases can exert pressure on a moving piston; metal roller used in printing to receive impression, carry printing plates, etc.; ~ *lock*- one operated by revolving one barrel inside another.

cy̆li'ndrical *adj.* Cylinder-shaped.

cy̆'lindroid *adj.* & *n.* (Figure) like a cylinder.

cy̆'lix *n.* (Gk antiq.) Cup with shallow bowl and stem.

cy̆'ma *n.* 1. (archit.) Moulding with double continuous curve; ~ *recta*, one concave below and convex above; ~ *reversa*, reverse of this, ogee. 2. Cyme.

cy̆'mbal *n.* One of a pair of concave brass or bronze plates, struck

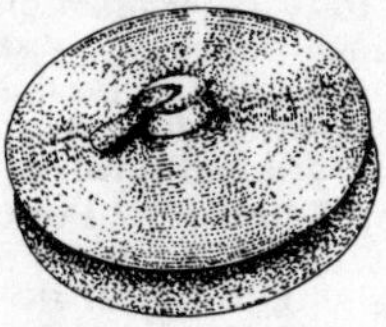

together to make ringing sound or singly with drumstick etc.

cy̆'mbalō *n.* (pl. *-os*). = DULCIMER.

cy̆'mbiform *adj.* (anat., bot.) Boat-shaped.

cȳme *n.* (bot.) Inflorescence in which primary axis bears single terminal flower that develops first, system being continued by axes of secondary and higher orders. **cȳmō'se** *adj.*

Cy̆'mric (k-) *adj.* Welsh. [Welsh *Cymru* Wales, *Cymry* the Welsh]

Cy̆'newulf (k-; -ŏŏlf). Northumbrian poet of the latter part of the 8th c., author of 4 poems in Old English contained in the 'Exeter Book' and the 'Vercelli Book'.

cy̆'nic *n.* 1. (*C*~) Philosopher of an ancient Greek sect founded by Antisthenes whose teachings showed contempt for ease, wealth, and the enjoyments of life. 2. One who sarcastically discredits the sincerity or goodness of human motives and actions. ~ *adj.* 1. (*C*~) Of, characteristic of, Cynic philosophers. 2. Cynical. **cy̆'nical** *adj.* Churlish; captious; incredulous of human goodness; sneering. **cy̆'nically** *adv.* **cy̆'nicism** *n.* [Gk *kuōn kunos* dog, nickname for cynic]

cȳnocĕ'phalus *n.* 1. One of a fabled race of men with dogs' heads. 2. Animal with head like a dog, esp. dog-faced baboon. **cȳnocĕ'phalous** *adj.*

cȳnoglō'ssum *n.* Tall flowering herb of genus *C*~ of the borage family; hound's-tongue.

cy̆'nosure (*or* -shoor) *n.* Centre of attraction or admiration. [Gk *Kunosoura* (lit. 'dog's tail') constellation Ursa Minor, containing pole-star]

Cy̆'nthia (Gk & Rom. myth.) Artemis, said to have been born on Mt. Cynthus; (poet.) the moon. [L *Cynthia* (*dea*) the Cynthian goddess]

cypher: see CIPHER.

cy pres (sē prā') *adv.phr.* (law) As near as possible (to testator's intentions). ~ *adj.phr.* Approximate. ~ *n.phr.* Approximation. [AF, = Fr. *si pres* so near]

cy̆'prėss *n.* Coniferous tree, of genus *Cupressus* with hard durable wood and dense dark

foliage, formerly used for coffins and hence symbolic of mourning; this wood.

Cy̆'prian *adj.* & *n.* 1. Cypriot. 2. (archaic) Licentious (person).

cy̆pri'noid *adj.* & *n.* (Fish) resembling or allied to carp, of the division Cyprinoidea.

Cў'prĭot, -ōte *adj.* & *n.* (Native, inhabitant, Greek dialect) of Cyprus.

Cў'prus. Island in E. Mediterranean famous in ancient times for worship of Aphrodite; captured by the Turks 1570; from 1878 administered by Gt Britain on behalf of Turkey; taken over as British colony 1914; republic since 1960; member State of the Commonwealth; capital, Nicosia.

cў'psėla *n.* (pl. *-lae*). (bot.) Achene developed from an inferior ovary, freq. with hairy pappus attached, as in dandelion.

Cȳrėnā'ĭc *adj.* & *n.* (Philosopher) of the hedonistic school of Aristippus of Cyrene.

Cȳrenā'ica. District of NE. Libya.

Cȳrē'nė. Ancient Greek colony in what is now Libya.

Cў'ril[1], St. (376–444). Bishop of Alexandria.

Cў'ril[2], St. (9th c.). Greek apostle to the Slavs, for whom he is reputed to have translated with his brother Methodius the Gospels, inventing an alphabet for the purpose.

Cўrĭll'ĭc *adj.* & *n.* (Of) the alphabet, based on Greek uncials, used by Slavonic peoples of the Eastern Church and attributed to St. CYRIL[2] (who in fact devised the GLAGOLITIC alphabet).

Cȳr'us (d. 529 B.C.), 'the Great'. Founder of the Persian Empire; subdued the Greek cities of Asia Minor and conquered the Babylonians.

cўst, cĭst *n.* (biol.) Hollow organ, bladder, etc., in animal or plant, containing liquid secretion; (path.) sac containing morbid matter, parasitic larva, etc.; cell containing embryo etc. **cў'stĭc** *adj.* Of the urinary bladder; of the gall-bladder; of the nature of a cyst.

cўstī'tĭs *n.* Inflammation of the bladder.

cў'stoscōpe *n.* (med.) Instrument for visual examination of the bladder.

cўstŏ'tomў *n.* Surgical incision of the bladder.

Cўthēr'a. (mod. Gk *Kithira*) Island off the coast of the Peloponnese, sacred to the goddess Aphrodite, who was thence surnamed Cytherea.

cȳto- *prefix.* Cell.

cȳtŏ'logў *n.* Branch of biology concerned with the structure, physiology, and reproduction of cells. **cȳtolŏ'gĭcal** *adj.* **cȳtolŏ'gĭcallў** *adv.* **cȳtŏ'logist** *n.*

cў'toplăsm *n.* Protoplasmic content of a cell other than the nucleus. **cȳtoplă'smĭc** *adj.*

czâr, czâri'na etc. (zâr, -ēna): see TSAR etc.

Czech (chĕk) *adj.* & *n.* 1. (Member, language) of the most westerly branch of the Slavs, of Bohemia, Moravia, and Silesia. 2. = CZECHOSLOVAKIAN.

Czechoslovă'kĭa (chĕk-; *or* -ahk-). Republican State formed by the Treaty of Versailles (1919), including Bohemia, Moravia, and the northern Slavs of the old Austrian Empire; became communist after a revolution, 1948; capital, Prague. **Czĕchoslō'văk, -vă'kĭan** (*or* -ahk-) *adjs.* & *ns.* (Native, inhabitant, language) of Czechoslovakia.

D

D, d (dē). 1. 4th letter of modern English and ancient Roman alphabet, corresponding to Greek *delta* (Δ, δ), and Phoenician and Hebrew *daleth* (ד), representing a voiced dental (or in English rather alveolar) stop consonant. 2. 4th in serial order; classification indicating a low grade; *D-layer*, lowest stratum of the ionosphere. 3. *D*, (mus.) 2nd note of natural scale (C major); scale or key with this note for tonic. 4. Roman numeral symbol for 500. 5. *D*, symbol for day on which a military operation is timed to begin (= *day*, used before date is divulged, preceding days being designated as D−1 D−2, etc.); hence, *D-day*, applied esp. to 6 June 1944, day on which Allies landed in N. France; also transf. 6. *3 D*, three-dimensional. 7. Object etc. shaped like D (as *D-ring*).

d. *abbrev.* Date; daughter; *dele*; denarius, -i (= penny); departs; died.

da: see DAD.

da *abbrev.* Deca-.

D.A. *abbrev.* (U.S.) District Attorney.

dăb[1] *n.* Slight or undecided but sudden blow; brief application of soft or moist thing to surface without rubbing; moisture, colour, etc., so applied. ~ *v.* Make dab(s) at; make dab (*at*); apply briefly without rubbing.

dăb[2] *n.* Small flat-fish, *Limanda limanda*, like flounder, common on sandy parts of British coast.

dăb[3] *n.* (colloq., also ~ *hand*) Expert, adept (*at*).

D.A.B. *abbrev.* Dictionary of American Biography.

dă'bber *n.* (esp.) Soft rounded mass used to apply ink, colour, etc., to a surface, in printing, painting on china, etc.; brush for pressing damp paper on to type in stereotyping etc.

dă'bble *v.* 1. Wet intermittently, slightly, or partly; soil, splash; move (with hands, bill, etc.) in shallow water, liquid, mud, etc., with splashing. 2. Engage in desultory or dilettante way (*in*). **dă'bbler** *n.*

dă'bchick *n.* Any of various grebes.

dă'bster *n.* = DAB[3].

da ca'pō (dah kah-). (mus.). Repeat from beginning. [It.]

dāce *n.* Small freshwater cyprinoid fish, *Leuciscus leuciscus*.

dachshund (dah'kshōōnd) *n.* Small dog of German breed with short crooked legs and very long body. [Ger., = 'badger-dog']

dacoi't *n.* (in India and Burma) Member of armed robber band. **dacoi'tў** *n.* (Act of) gang-robbery. [Hind. *ḍakait*, f. *ḍākā* gang-robbery]

dă'ctўl *n.* Metrical foot of one long and two short, or one accented and two unaccented syllables (—◡◡). **dactў'lic** *adj.* & *n.* (Verse consisting) of dactyl(s). [Gk *daktulos* finger (f. resemblance to its three bones)]

dăd, da (dah), **dă'da, dă'ddў** *ns.* (colloq.; childish or familiar) Father (esp. as vocative); *daddy-lo'nglegs*, crane-fly.

Dada (dah'dah) *n.* International movement in poetry and painting, initiated 1916 in Zürich, repudiating tradition, culture, and reason. **Da'daism** *n.* Dada movement; its doctrine. **Da'daist** *n.* [Fr. *être sur son dada*, ride one's hobby-horse]

dā'dō *n.* 1. Block forming body of pedestal, between base mouldings and cornice. 2. Lower part of interior wall, of different material or

DAEDALUS

colour from upper part. **dā'd-ōed** (-ōd) *adj.*

Da'dra and Na'gar Have'lĭ (dah-, nŭ-, -vā-). Union territory in W. India.

dae'dal *adj.* (poet.) Skilful, inventive; manifold, complex, mysterious.

Dae'dalus. (Gk myth.) Skilful artisan who constructed the Cretan labyrinth; he was imprisoned in Crete with his son ICARUS but escaped to Sicily on wings which he made. **Daedā'lian** *adj.* In the manner of Daedalus; intricate, labyrinthine. [Gk *daidalos* cunning one]

dae'mon (dīm-) *n.* (esp. in Gk myth.) Supernatural being, intermediate between gods and men; spirit, genius; (archaic) = DEMON. **daemŏ'nĭc** *adj.*

dă'ffodil *n.* Lent lily, *Narcissus pseudo-narcissus*, yellow-flowered bulbous plant blooming in early spring (alternative to leek as Welsh national emblem); pale yellow colour. ~ *adj.* Pale yellow. **dă'-**

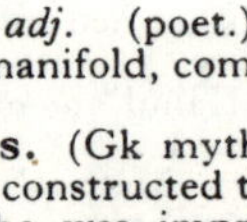

ffodillȳ, dăffadowndi'llȳ *ns.* (poet.) Daffodil.

daft (dah-) *adj.* Foolish, reckless, wild, crazy.

dă'gger *n.* Short two-edged pointed weapon, like small sword, for thrusting and stabbing; (print.)

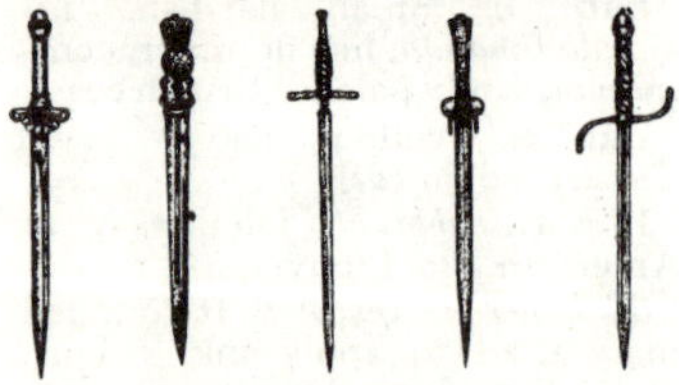

DAGGERS

mark like dagger, obelisk (†); *double* ~ (‡).

dā'gō *n.* (contempt., orig. U.S.) Spaniard, Portuguese, or Italian. [app. f. Span. *Diego* = James]

Dā'gŏn. Ancient Philistine national deity, represented as fish-tailed man. [Heb. *dāgôn* dear little fish]

daguĕ'rreotȳpe (-gĕro-) *n.* (Photograph taken by) early photographic process in which image was taken on silver plate sensitized by iodine, and developed by exposure to mercury vapour. ~ *v.t.* Photograph by this process. [name of inventor, Louis *Daguerre* (1789–1851)]

dahabee'yah, -bi'yah (-bē-) *n.* Large lateen-rigged sailing-vessel used on Nile. [Arab. name of gilded state barges of Muslim rulers of Egypt, f. *dahab* gold]

dah'lia (dāl-) *n.* Mexican composite plant of genus *D*~ widely cultivated for its many-coloured single and double flowers. [f. A. *Dahl* (d. 1789), Swedish botanist]

DAHLIA

Dahō'mey. Republic in W. Africa, renamed Benin. Once part of French West Africa, independent since 1960; capital, Porto Novo.

Dáil Éireann (doil ār'*a*n). Lower chamber (House of Representatives) of the Republic of Ireland. [Ir., = 'assembly of Ireland']

dai'lȳ *adv.* Every day or weekday; from day to day, constant(ly). ~ *adj.* Done, occurring, published, etc., daily; ~ *bread*, one's necessary food or livelihood;

DAIMLER

~ *help*, *maid*, *woman*, domestic cleaner who does not sleep on the premises. ~ *n.* Daily newspaper; daily help etc.

dai'miō (dī-) *n.* Title of former chief territorial nobles of Japan, vassals of the shogun. [Jap., f. Chin. *dai* great, *myō* name]

Dai'mler (dīm-), Gottlieb (1834–1900). German engineer, a pioneer in the manufacture of motor-cars; original designer of the type (pr. dām-) named after him.

dai'ntў *n.* Choice morsel, delicacy. ~ *adj.* Choice; prettily neat; fastidious, of delicate tastes and sensibility. **dai'ntilў** *adv.* **dai'ntinėss** *n.*

dai'quĭrĭ (dīk- *or* dăk-) *n.* Drink of rum, lime-juice, and sugar.

dair'ў *n.* Room or building for keeping milk and cream and making butter etc.; shop in which milk, cream, etc., are sold; department of farm or farming concerned with production of milk, butter, and cheese; dairy farm; ~ *cream*, real cream as dist. from synthetic; ~ *farm*, farm producing chiefly milk, butter, etc.; *dair'ymaid*, woman employed at dairy; *dair'yman*, dealer in milk etc.

dā'ĭs *n.* Raised platform esp. at one end of hall, for high table, throne, etc.

dai'sў (-zĭ) *n.* 1. Small European composite wild flower, *Bellis perennis*, with small flat flower-heads with yellow disc and white ray (often tinged with pink), which close in the evening; cultivated variety of this; any of various similar flowers; ~-*chain*, chain of daisies threaded together; ~-*cutter*, horse lifting feet very little in trotting; (cricket etc.) ball travelling very close to ground. 2. (slang) First-rate specimen.

dâk (dawk *or* dahk) *n.* (Ind.) Post or transport by relays of men or horses; relay; ~-*bungalow*, house for travellers at dâk station.

Dak. *abbrev.* Dakota.

Dakō'ta. Former territory of U.S., organized in 1889 into the States of NORTH DAKOTA and SOUTH DAKOTA.

Dă'lai La'ma (*or* dahl-; lah-). Grand Lama, chief lama of Tibet.

dă'lăsĭ *n.* Monetary unit of the Gambia, = 100 butut.

dāle *n.* Valley (esp. in north of England); *da'lesman*, native or inhabitant of dale, esp. in Yorkshire, Cumberland, Westmorland, etc.

RESIDENCE OF THE DALAI LAMA

Da'lĭ (dah-), Salvador (1904–). Spanish artist and writer; settled in U.S. 1940.

dă'llȳ *v.* Be evasive *with* person or business; idle, loiter, delay. **dă'llĭance** *n.*

Dălmā'tia (-shĭ*a*). Province of Yugoslavia on the Adriatic coast; formerly (until 1918) province of the Austro-Hungarian Empire.

Dălmā'tian *adj.* Of Dalmatia or its people. ~ *n.* 1. Native, inhabitant, of Dalmatia. 2. Dog with short-haired white coat with black or brown spots, of a breed supposed to have originated in Dalmatia.

dălmă'tic *n.* Wide-sleeved loose long vestment with slit sides worn by deacons and bishops on some occasions, and by kings and emperors esp. at coronation.

dăl segno (sā'nyō). (mus.) Repeat from the point indicated by a sign (usu. *:S:*). [It., = 'from the sign']

Da'lton[1] (dawl- *or* dŏl-). Town in Massachusetts, U.S., in the high school of which the educational system (~ *plan, system*), devised by Miss H. Parkhurst was first adopted; the system consists essentially of dividing the year's work into monthly assignments, which pupils perform on their own responsibility and with their own discipline.

Da'lton[2] (dawl- *or* dŏl-), John (1776–1844). English chemist, who formulated the atomic theory; ~*'s law*, (chem.) law, discovered by Dalton, that the total pressure of a mixture of gases is equal to the sum of the partial pressures of the constituents. **Da'ltonism** *n.* Congenital colour-blindness, esp. inability to distinguish green from red, so called after John Dalton, who was so affected.

dăm[1] *n.* Barrier constructed across stream etc. to hold back water and raise its level, form a reservoir, or prevent flooding; barrier constructed in stream by beavers. ~ *v.t.* Furnish or confine with dam; block *up*, obstruct.

dăm[2] *n.* Mother (usu. of beast).

dă'mage *n.* 1. Harm; injury impairing value or usefulness. 2. (law, pl.) Sum of money claimed or adjudged in compensation for loss or injury; (slang) cost. ~ *v.t.* Injure (usu. thing) so as to diminish value; detract from reputation of (person etc.). **dă'mageable** (-j*a*-) *adj.*

Dama'n (-ahn). District on west coast of India: see GOA.

dămascē'ne, -skee'n *v.t.* 1. Produce watered or striped pattern in (sword, armour, etc.) by hammering on steel in which the iron or carbon particles have separated into patches or bands during cooling. 2. Inlay (steel or iron surface) with designs in gold or silver. [f. DAMASCUS]

Damă'scus (*or* -mah-). (Arab. *Esh Sham*) Capital city of Syria; an ancient city, famous in the Middle Ages for its silks and steel.

dă'mask *n.* 1. Reversible figured fabric in which the design is executed in a different weave from the background in such a way that the two weaves appear on the face and on the back in exchanged positions, orig. of silk, later of linen, cotton, etc. 2. Steel manufactured at Damascus; combination of iron and steel with wavy pattern on surface (see DAMASCENE). 3. ~ *rose*, species of rose native to Asia Minor (*Rosa damascena*), to which many garden varieties belong; blush-red colour of this. ~ *adj.* Coloured like damask rose; made of or resembling damask fabric or steel. ~ *v.t.* 1. Weave with figured designs. 2. Damascene; ornament with pattern. [f. DAMASCUS]

dāme *n.* 1. Woman (archaic or poet.; also U.S. slang); mistress of private elementary school (~ *school*) for children (obs.); female part in pantomime, taken by male actor; woman with various responsibilities in Eton boarding-house. 2. *D~*, title of woman (used as prefix corresp. to *Sir*) in ~ *Commander*, ~ *Grand Cross* (ranks in O.B.E., Royal Victorian Order, and Order of St. Michael and St. George); title of Benedictine nun who has made her solemn profession; title of higher female member of Primrose League.

dămn (-m) *v* 1. Condemn, censure; condemn (play etc.) as a failure; bring condemnation on, be the ruin of. 2. Doom to hell; cause damnation of; curse. ~ *n.* Uttered curse; negligible amount (*not worth a* ~, worthless). ~ *int.* Exclamation of annoyance.

dă'mnable (-mn-) *adj.* Deserving damnation; hateful, annoying. **dă'mnablȳ** *adv.*

dămnā'tion (-mn-) *n.* Damning; (condemnation to) eternal punishment in hell.

dă'mnatorȳ (-mn-) *adj.* Conveying, causing, censure or damnation.

dămned (-md) *adj.* (esp.) Damnable, detestable; *the* ~, souls in hell. ~ *adv.* Damnably. **dămnedėst** (-md-) *n. one's* ~, one's utmost.

dă'mnĭfȳ *v.t.* (law) Cause injury to. **dămnĭfĭcā'tion** *n.*

Dă'moclēs (-z). (Gk legend) Flatterer who extolled the happiness of Dionysius, tyrant of Syracuse; but Dionysius, to show how precarious a ruler's happiness was, seated him at a banquet with a sword suspended over his head by a hair; hence, *sword of* ~, imminent danger, esp. in midst of prosperity.

Dā'mŏn. (Gk & Rom. legend) Syracusan whose friend Phintias was sentenced to death; Damon went bail for Phintias, who came back at the last moment and saved him; hence, ~ *and Pythias* (erron. for Phintias), faithful friends.

dămp *n.* 1. Moisture in air, on surface, or diffused through solid. 2. Dejection, chill, discouragement. 3. Choke-damp; firedamp. 4. ~*-course*, layer of damp-proof material, esp. bituminous felt, in wall just above ground. to prevent damp from rising; ~*-proof*, proof against damp. ~ *adj.* Slightly wet; moist, humid. **dă'mplȳ** *adv.* **dă'mpnėss** *n.* **dămp** *v.* 1. Stifle, choke, dull; extinguish; (mus. etc.) stop vibrations of (string etc.), furnish (pianoforte strings) with dampers; (phys.) cause decrease in amplitude of radio waves etc. 2. Discourage, depress (zeal, hopes). 3. Moisten, make damp.

dă'mpen *v.* (chiefly U.S.) Damp.

dă'mper *n.* 1. Person or thing that depresses. 2. Small cloth- or felt-covered pad in pianoforte resting against string (and thus preventing it from vibrating) except when raised or withdrawn from it when key is stuck or pedal depressed. 3. Metal plate in flue controlling combustion by regulating or stopping draught. 4. Contrivance for moistening anything. 5. (Austral.) Cake of unleavened bread baked in hot ashes.

dă'msel (-z-) *n.* (archaic & literary) Young unmarried woman; *da'mselfly*, insect of order Odonata resembling dragonfly but with wings usu. held together over the body while resting.

dă'mson (-zn) *n.* Small dark-purple plum, *Prunus insititia*, introduced in very early times into Italy and Greece from Syria; tree bearing this; ~ *cheese*, solid conserve of pulped damsons and sugar. [L (*prunum*) *Damascenum* (plum) of Damascus]

Dăn. 1. Hebrew patriarch, son of Jacob and Bilhah (see Gen. 30: 6); tribe of Israel traditionally descended from him. 2. City in the extreme north of land of Canaan; hence, *from* ~ *to Beersheba*, from one end of the land to the other, Beersheba being in the extreme south of Canaan (Judg. 20: 1).

Dan. *abbrev.* Daniel (O.T.).

Dă'naē. (Gk myth.) Daughter of Acrisius, king of Argos; an oracle foretold that she would bear a son who would kill her father; he therefore imprisoned her in a brazen tower, but Zeus visited her there and she conceived PERSEUS, who after many adventures killed Acrisius by accident.

Dă'nāĭd *n.* (Gk myth.) One of the 50 daughters of Danaus, king of Argos; all except one, Hypermnestra, murdered their husbands on the wedding night and were condemned in Hades to carry water in sieves or bottomless vessels.

dance (dah-) *v.* 1. Move rhythmically with glides, leaps, etc., usu. to music, alone or with partner or in a set; perform (dance); jump about, skip, move in lively way; bob up and down on water etc.; ~ *attendance on*, be kept waiting by; follow about. 2. Move (child etc.) lightly up and down on one's knee or in arms. ~ *n.* 1. Dancing motion; definite succession or arrangement of steps and rhythmical movements in dancing; music for this. 2. Dancing party. 3. *D~ of Death*, allegorical representation (common in Middle Ages) of Death leading all sorts and conditions of men in a dance to the grave; *St. Vitus's* ~, chorea. **da'ncer** *n.* (esp.) One who dances professionally in public.

dăncĕ'ttȳ, -tee *adj.* (her.) Having a fesse with three indentations.

dă'ndėlīon *n.* Common composite plant, *Taraxacum officinale*, abundant in meadows, gardens, and waste places, with widely-toothed leaves and large bright-

yellow flower on naked hollow stalk, succeeded by globular head of pappose seeds; *~-clock*: see CLOCK[1]. [Fr. *dent de lion* lion's tooth]

dă'nder *n.* (colloq., esp. U.S.) Temper, anger, indignation.

Dă'ndie Di'nmont. Terrier of short-legged, long-bodied, rough-coated breed from Scottish borders. [name of a character in Sir W. Scott's 'Guy Mannering', who kept a special breed of terriers]

dă'ndle *v.t.* = DANCE *v.* 2.

dă'ndruff *n.* Dead skin in small scales among the hair, scurf.

dă'ndȳ[1] *n.* 1. Man paying excessive attention to smartness in dress etc. 2. Anything superlatively fine, neat, or dainty. 3. (naut.) Sloop with mizzen-lugsail on jigger-mast aft. 4. *~-brush*, stiff brush for grooming horses. ~ *adj.* Neat, smart, like a dandy (U.S.) splendid, first-rate. **dăndī'acal, dă'ndȳish** *adjs.* **dă'ndĭfȳ** *v.t.* **dă'ndȳism** *n.* [orig. Sc., perh. f. name *Andrew*]

dă'ndȳ[2] *n.* (Ind.) Strong cloth hammock slung from pole, carried shoulder-high by two or more men (a common means of transport in hilly districts). [Hind. *ḍaṇḍī* (*daṇḍ* staff)]

Dāne *n.* 1. Native of Denmark. 2. (hist.) Viking. 3. *Great* ~, dog of large powerful short-haired breed, of type between mastiff and greyhound.

Dā'negĕld (-n-g-) *n.* (hist.) Annual land-tax in England in 10th and 11th centuries, orig. imposed to provide funds for protection against Danes.

Dā'nelaw (-nl-) *n.* (hist.) Part of England occupied by the Danes; district NE. of Watling Street, ceded to them by the treaty of Wedmore, A.D. 878.

dā'nger (-j-) *n.* Liability or exposure to harm, risk, peril (*of*); thing that causes peril; position of railway signal directing stoppage or caution; ~ *money*, payment made beyond basic wages for dangerous work (also fig.). **dā'ngerous** *adj.* **dā'ngerouslȳ** *adv.*

dă'ngle (-nggl) *v.* Hang loosely, swaying to and fro; hold or carry (thing) swaying loosely; keep (hopes, expectations, etc.) hanging uncertainly (*before* person); hang *after* or *about* a person.

Dă'nĭel. Hebrew prophet, captive at Babylon, who interpreted the dreams of Nebuchadnezzar and was delivered by God from the lions' den into which he had been thrown by Darius; book of O.T. bearing his name, but prob. of 2nd c. B.C.; hence, upright judge, person of infallible wisdom (see Susanna 45–64).

Dā'nĭsh *adj.* & *n.* (Language) of Denmark or the Danes.

dănk *adj.* Soaked, oozy; unpleasantly or unwholesomely damp. **dă'nknėss** *n.*

D'Annunzio, Gabriele: see ANNUNZIO.

Dă'ntė Alīghieri (ălĭgyār'ĭ) (1265–1321). Italian poet, probably born at Florence, author of 'Vita Nuova' and 'Divina Commedia', a philosophical poem comprising the 'Inferno', 'Purgatorio', and 'Paradiso'; in his visit to Hell

and Purgatory Dante has for guide the poet Virgil, and there he sees and converses with his former friends or foes; in 'Paradiso' the poet encounters the lady whom he once loved, BEATRICE, now an angel. **Dă'ntĕsque** (-sk) *adj.* Of, after the manner of, Dante.

Danton (dahṅtawṅ), Georges Jacques (1759–94). French statesman of the Revolution; member of the Convention and the first (Dantonist) Committee of Public Safety; he came into conflict with ROBESPIERRE and was guillotined.

Dă'nūbe. (Ger. *Donau*) European river about 1,700 miles long, rising in SW. Germany and flowing into the Black Sea. **Danū'bĭan** *adj.* Belonging to, lying near Danube; ~ *Principalities*, former name for Moldavia and Walachia.

Dă'nzĭg (-nts-). (Polish *Gdansk*) Baltic city and port of Poland, near mouth of Vistula; ~ *Corridor*: see CORRIDOR.

dăp *v.* 1. Fish by letting bait bob on water. 2. Dip lightly. 3. Make (ball) bounce, (of ball) bounce, on ground. ~ *n.* Bounce of ball.

Dă'phnė[1]. 1. (Gk myth.) Nymph who was turned into a laurel-bush to save her from the pursuit of Apollo. 2. (astron.) The 41st of the asteroids, named after the goddess.

dă'phnė[2] *n.* Flowering shrub of genus *D~* including spurge laurel and mezereon.

dă'pper *adj.* Neat, smart, in appearance or movement.

dă'pple *v.* Variegate, become variegated, with rounded spots or patches of colour or shade. ~ *adj.* Dappled; *~-grey*, (horse) of grey dappled with darker spots. ~ *n.* Dappled effect; dappled horse etc.

dar'bies (-bĭz) *n.pl.* (slang) Handcuffs.

Dar'bȳ and Joan. Devoted old married couple. [perh. from poem in *Gentleman's Magazine*, 1735]

Dardanĕ'lles (-lz) Narrow strait between Europe and Asiatic Turkey, anciently called the Hellespont; scene of unsuccessful attack on Turkey by British and French troops in 1915.

dāre *v.* 1. Venture (to), have boldness or courage or impudence (to); attempt, take the risks of. 2. Defy, challenge (person) *to* thing, *to* do. 3. *I ~ say*, I am prepared to believe, do not deny; *~-devil*, reckless (person). **dār'ĭng** *n.* (esp.) Adventurous courage. ~ *adj.* (esp.) Adventurous, bold. **dār'ĭnglȳ** *adv.*

Dār'ĭen. Province, formerly of Colombia, now of Panama; ~ *Scheme*, scheme proposed *c* 1690 for a Scottish settlement on the isthmus of Panama; much Scottish capital was invested in the scheme, which was unsuccessful, and at the Union (1707) compensation was paid by England to Scotland for the losses sustained.

dă'riōle *n.* Savoury dish cooked and served in small mould (~-*mould*).

Darī'us, 'the Great'. King of Persia, 521–485 B.C.; extended the Persian Empire and began the great war between the Persians and the Greeks; his army was defeated at MARATHON (490 B.C.).

dark *adj.* 1. Characterized by (absolute or relative) absence of light; unilluminated; gloomy, sombre. 2. (of colour) Approaching black in hue; deep in shade; (of complexion etc.) brown, not fair. 3. Evil, wicked; dismal; sullen; obscure; secret; unenlightened. 4. (phon., of a consonant, esp. *l*) Having acoustic resemblance to a 'back' vowel (opp. to *clear*). 5. *D~ Age*, (i) of the Dark Ages; (ii) (of) a period of Aegean civilization between the end of the Bronze Age and the historical period; *D~ Ages*, (formerly =) Middle Ages; (now usu.) approx. 5th–8th centuries A.D., or from fall of Rome to coronation of Charlemagne; *D~ Continent*, Africa; ~ *horse*, horse about whose racing powers little is known; person of unknown capacities; ~ *lantern*, lantern of which light may be concealed; ~-*room*, room from which daylight is excluded and which is lighted when desired by a type of coloured light which does not appreciably affect sensitive photographic materials. ~ *n.* Absence of light; nightfall; dark colour; *be in the* ~, lack knowledge. **dar'kish** *adj.* **darklȳ** *adv.* **dar'kness** *n.*

dar'ken *v.* Make or become dark.

dar'kling *adv.* & *adj.* (poet.) In the dark.

dar'kȳ, -key, -kie *n.* (colloq.) Negro.

dar'ling *n.* & *adj.* Loved, best loved, lovable, (person or animal).

darn[1] *v.t.* Mend (esp. knitted fabric) by interweaving yarn with needle across hole; embroider with darning-stitch. ~ *n.* Darned place. **dar'ner** *n.* Darning-needle. **dar'ning** *n.* (esp.) ~-*needle*, long needle for darning; ~-*stitch*, large running stitch resembling that used in darning, used for embroidering net etc.

darn[2] *n.* & *v.t.* (orig. U.S.) Damn (as mild imprecation). **darned** (-nd) *adj.* Damned.

dar'nel *n.* Grass (now rare in England), *Lolium temulentum*, growing as weed among corn.

Dar'nley, Lord. Henry Stewart (or Stuart) (1545–67), Scottish nobleman; second husband of Mary, Queen of Scots and father of James I of England; implicated in the murder of Rizzio; killed in mysterious circumstances at Edinburgh.

dart *n.* 1. Pointed missile thrown by hand, esp. light javelin; arrow; light pointed missile thrown at target; (pl.) game played with darts of this kind. 2. Tapering stitched fold in garment. 3. Sudden rapid motion; act of throwing missile. ~ *v.* 1. Throw (missile). 2. Emit suddenly and sharply, shoot out; spring or start with sudden rapid motion, shoot. **dar'ter** *n.* (esp.) 1. Any of the cormorant-like web-footed birds (snake-birds) of genus *Anhinga*, found in tropical Africa and America. 2. Any of various fishes, esp. the very small and brilliantly coloured fishes of the subfamily Etheostominae.

Dar'tmoor. Moorland district in Devon; prison near Princetown in this district; ~ *pony*, small shaggy variety living wild on Dartmoor; ~ *sheep*, hardy moorland sheep bred there.

Dar'tmouth (-m*u*th). Town and port in Devon; Royal Naval College for training naval officers which is situated there.

Dar'win[1], Charles Robert (1809–82). English naturalist; author of 'On the Origin of Species by means of Natural Selection' (1859), in which he propounded the theory that organisms tend to produce offspring varying slightly from their parents, that the process of natural selection tends to favour the survival of those best adapted to their environment, and that by the operation of these factors new

CHARLES DARWIN

species may arise widely differing from each other and from their common ancestors. **Dârwĭ'nĭan** *adj.* & *n.* (Follower) of Darwin or his theories. **Dâr'winism** *n.* Darwin's theory of the origin of species; hence (pop.), evolutionism.

Dâr'win². Capital city of Northern Territory of Australia.

dăsh *v.* 1. Shatter *to pieces*; knock, drive, throw, thrust, *away*, *off*, etc.; fling, drive, splash, *against*, *into*, *upon*. 2. Bespatter *with* water etc.; dilute, qualify. 3. Frustrate; discourage. 4. Put *down* on paper, throw *off* (drawing, composition) hastily and vigorously. 5. Damn (as mild imprecation). 6. Fall, move, throw oneself, with violence; come into collision *against*, *upon*; ride, run, drive, *up*, move about, behave, with spirit or display. 7. *da'shboard*, splash-board; board in front of driver of motor-car or pilot of aircraft carrying indicators, gauges, etc. ~ *n.* 1. Violent blow, impact, or collision; violent throwing and breaking of water etc., upon anything; sound of dashing. 2. Splash of colour; infusion, touch, tinge. 3. Hasty pen-stroke; horizontal stroke in writing or printing to mark break in sense, parenthesis, omitted letters or words, etc., or in Morse code. 4. Rush, onset, sudden advance; (capacity for) vigorous action; showy appearance or behaviour. 5. (slang) Dashboard.

dă'sher *n.* (esp.) Contrivance for agitating cream in churn.

dă'shing *adj.* (esp.) Spirited, lively; showy. **dă'shinglў** *adv.*

dă'stard *n.* Mean, base, or despicable coward, esp. one who commits malicious or brutal act without endangering himself. **dă's-tardlў** *adj.* **dă'stardlinėss** *n.*

dat. *abbrev.* Dative.

data: see DATUM.

dāte¹ *n.* Fruit of the *~-palm*, *Phoenix dactylifera*, an oblong berry, growing in large clusters, with single hard seed or stone and sweet pulp, an important article of food in W. Asia and N. Africa; the tree itself. [Gk *daktulos* finger]

dāte² *n.* Specification in document, letter, book, inscription, of time (and often place) of execution, writing, publication, etc.; specified time (day of month, month, year) at which anything takes place or is to take place; season, period; (colloq., orig. U.S.) engagement, person with whom one has social engagement; period to which something ancient belongs; duration, term of life or existence; *out of ~*, obsolete, antiquated; *up to ~*, up to the knowledge, standard, requirements, of the time; *~-line*, line in Pacific Ocean (approx. meridian of 180° from Greenwich) at which calendar day is reckoned to begin and end, so that at places east and west of it the date differs by a day. ~ *v.* Mark (letter etc.) with date; refer (event) to a time; count time, reckon (*from*); bear date, be dated; have origin *from*; be or become or make recognizable as of a past or particular period; (colloq.) make, have, social engagement with. **dā'telėss** *adj.* Undated; endlėss; immemorial.

dā'tive *adj.* (gram.) Of the case chiefly denoting the indirect object. ~ *n.* (Word in) dative case.

dā'tum *n.* (pl. *-ta*). Thing known or granted, assumption or premiss from which inferences may be drawn; fixed starting-point of scale etc.; (pl.) facts, information; *~-line*, horizontal line from which heights and depths are measured in surveying. [L, = '(thing) given']

datūr'a *n.* Poisonous plant of genus *D~* including thorn-apple, with strongly narcotic effects.

daub *v.* 1. Coat (wall etc.) *with* plaster, clay, etc.; smear (surface); lay *on* (greasy or sticky stuff); soil, bedaub. 2. Paint coarsely and inartistically, lay on (colours) crudely and clumsily. ~ *n.* 1. Material for daubing walls etc.; clay or mud mixed with stubble or chaff, daubed on laths or wattle to make walls etc. 2. Patch or smear of grease, colour, etc. 3. Clumsy coarse painting. **dau'ber** *n.* **dau'bÿ** *adj.*

Daudet (dōdā), Alphonse (1840–97). French novelist, famous as creator of amusing type of Provençal Frenchman, 'Tartarin de Tarascon'.

dau'ghter (dawt-) *n.* Female child in relation to her parent(s); female descendant, female member *of* family, race, etc.; woman as spiritual or intellectual descendant of some person or thing; also transf.; *~-in-law*, son's wife; *Daughters of the American Revolution*, patriotic American women's society formed (1890) to preserve ideals of founders of Amer. independence etc. **dau'ghterlÿ** *adj.*

daunt *v.t.* Discourage, intimidate. **dau'ntlėss** *adj.* Intrepid; persevering. **dau'ntlėsslÿ** *adv.* **dau'ntlėssnėss** *n.*

dau'phin *n.* (hist.) Orig. title of lords of Vienne; the provinces of the seigneurs of the Viennois were hence called the Dauphiné, and the last lord, Humbert II, on ceding the provinces to Philip of Valois (1349), made it a condition that the title should be borne by the eldest son of the king of France. **dau'phinėss** *n.* Wife of the dauphin.

dă'venpôrt *n.* 1. Small ornamental writing-table with drawers and hinged writing-slab. 2. (U.S.) Large sofa. [prob. from maker's name]

Dā'vĭd[1]. 2nd king of Judah, youngest son of Jesse; slayer of a Philistine, traditionally GOLIATH; on the death of Saul became king of Judah and later of the whole of Israel; ~ *and Jonathan*, any pair of devoted friends (see 1 Sam. 18).

Dā'vĭd[2], St. (6th c.). Son of a prince of S. Wales, patron saint of Wales; commemorated 1 Mar.

David[3] (dahvēd), Jacques Louis (1748–1825). French painter of classical and historical subjects.

Da Vinci: see LEONARDO DA VINCI.

Dā'vĭs ăpparā'tus. Device to enable men to escape from a disabled submarine, consisting essentially of a chamber, the *escape lock*, which is emptied of water by compressed air after each man has left it. [f. name of inventor]

Dā'vĭs Cŭp. (lawn tennis) International challenge cup presented in 1900 by Dwight F. Davis (1879–1945), Amer. politician, and competed for annually; this contest.

dă'vĭt *n.* Crane at ship's bow for hoisting anchor clear of side; one of pair of uprights curved at top for suspending or lowering ship's boat.

Dā'vÿ, Sir Humphry (1778–1829). English chemist, inventor of the miner's safety lamp (~ *lamp*), in which flame is protected by wire-gauze from coming into contact with firedamp.

Dā'vÿ Jōnes (-nz). Spirit of the sea, sailors' devil; *~'s locker*, bottom of the sea, esp. as grave of those who are drowned or die at sea.

daw *n.* = JACKDAW.

daw'dle *v.* Idle, dally; ~ *away*, waste (time). ~ *n.* Act of dawdling.

dawk *n.* = DÂK.

dawn *n.* First light, daybreak; rise or incipient gleam of anything; ~ *chorus*, early-morning bird song. ~ *v.i.* Begin to appear to grow light; ~ *on*, begin to be perceptible to.

day *n.* 1. Time during which sun is above horizon, interval of light between successive periods of darkness or night; dawn; daylight. 2. Time occupied by earth in one revolution on its axis, 24 hours; *astronomical*, *civil*, or *solar* ~, 24 hours reckoned from midnight to midnight; *natural* ~, (i) = sense 1 above; (ii) sidereal day; *sidereal* ~, interval between two meridional transits of first point of Aries, about 4′ shorter than solar day. 3. Civil day as point or unit of time, date, etc.; specified or appointed day; day of battle; *carry*, *win*, *the* ~, be victorious. 4. Period, time, era; lifetime, span of existence; period of power or influence. 5. Part of day allotted for work. 6. ~ *by* ~, ~ *after* ~, *from* ~ *to* ~, *every* ~, with daily repetition or progress. 7. ~-*bed* bed to lie on by day, chaise-longue; ~-*book*, book in which commercial transactions of day are entered: ~-*boy*, -*girl*, boy, girl, attending school during day but living at home; *day'break*, dawn; ~-*coach*, (U.S.) railway passenger carriage other than sleeper; ~-*dream*, dream (indulged in) while awake; ~-*fly*, ephemera; ~-*labour*, labour hired by the day; ~-*labourer*; ~-*lily*, liliaceous plant of genus *Hemerocallis* with large yellow or orange flowers lasting only for a day; ~ *nursery*, public nursery where children are cared for during day; ~ *release*, system of allowing employees days off work for education; ~ *school*, school carried on in daytime (as dist. from *night* or *evening school*); school in which there is no provision for boarding pupils; ~-*spring*, (poet.) dawn; ~-*star*, sun; morning star; *day'-time*, time of daylight.

Day'ak (dī-) *n.* Var. of DYAK.

Day-Lewis (-lōō-), Cecil (1904–72). English poet (also detective novelist, pseudonym 'Nicholas Blake'); poet laureate 1968–72.

day'light (-līt) *n.* Light of day; dawn; openness, publicity; visible interval, as between boats in race, rider and saddle; ~-*glass*, glass, coloured blue with cobalt, used with artificial light to give effect of daylight; ~-*lamp*, incandescent electric lamp with bulb made of daylight-glass; ~-*loading*, (of photographic material) that can be put into camera in daylight, without dark-room; ~ *saving*, securing longer period of daylight in evening by putting clock forward (see SUMMER time).

dāze *v.t.* Stupefy, bewilder. ~ *n.* Dazed state. **dā'zėdlȳ** *adv.*

dă'zzle *v.t.* Confuse, dim sight of, (eye, person) with excess of light, intricate motion, incalculable number, etc.; confound, surprise, by brilliant display. ~ *n.* Glitter; bright confusing light; ~-*painting*, camouflage, esp. of sea-going vessels, with bright-coloured painted patterns. **dă'zzlement** *n.* **dă'zzlĭnglȳ** *adv.*

dB *abbrev.* Decibel(s).

D.B.E. *abbrev.* Dame Commander of (the Order of) the British Empire.

D.C., d.c. *abbrev.* *Da capo*; direct current; (D.C.) District of Columbia.

D.C.L. *abbrev.* Doctor of Civil Law.

D.C.M. *abbrev.* Distinguished Conduct Medal; District Court Martial.

D.D. *abbrev.* Doctor of Divinity; *dono dedit* (L, = gave as a gift also d.d.).

D.D.D. *abbrev.* *Dat, dicat, dedicat* (L, = gives, devotes, and dedicates; also d.d.d.).

D.D.S. *abbrev.* Doctor of Dental Surgery.

D.D.T. *abbrev.* Dichlor-diphenyl-trichlorethane (an insecticide).

de- *prefix.* 1. Down; away; completely. 2. Un- (in this sense a living prefix in English).

dea'con *n.* 1. Kind of minister or officer of early Church; in Episcopal Churches, member of third order of ministry, below bishops and priests, assisting priest in celebration of Eucharist etc. 2. Presbyterian layman attending to secular affairs of congregation; in other Nonconformist Churches, one of a body elected to advise and assist pastor, administer charities, and attend to secular affairs of church. 3. One of two inferior officers assisting wardens of lodge of Freemasons. **dea'conship** *n.* **dea'conĕss** *n.* Woman in early and some modern Churches with functions analogous to deacon's, esp. in administering charity.

dead (dĕd) *adj.* 1. That has ceased to live. 2. Benumbed, insensible; without spiritual life; ~ *to*, unconscious or inappreciative of, hardened against. 3. Obsolete; past; not effective. 4. Inanimate. 5. Extinct; dull, lustreless; without force; muffled; inactive, idle. 6. Unconnected to source of electrical power. 7. Abrupt; complete, unrelieved, exact; absolute. 8. ~*-alive*, dull, tedious, spiritless; ~ *ball*, (footb. etc.) ball out of play (~*-ball line*) ~ *-centre*, position of crank in which it is in direct line with connecting rod, and at which force exerted tends to pull or thrust instead of turning it; centre in lathe which does not revolve; ~ *end*, closed end of any passage etc. through which there is no way (also fig.); ~*-eye*, (naut.) round flat three-holed block for extending shrouds; *dea'dfall* (chiefly U.S.) trap for large game with weighted board or heavy log which falls upon the quarry; ~*-fire*: see CORPOSANT; ~ *freight*, sum paid in chartering ship for part not occupied by cargo; ~ *hand*, mortmain; *dea'dhead*, (colloq., orig. U.S.) non-paying theatre-goer, passenger, etc.; ~ *heat*, race in which two or more competitors reach winning-post at same time; ~ *letter*, law, regulation, no longer observed; unclaimed or undelivered letter at post office; *dea'dlight*, (naut.) shutter inside porthole to prevent light showing out; ~*-line*, line beyond which it is not permitted or possible to go; fixed limit of time; *dea'dlock*, complete stoppage, standstill; state of affairs from which further progress is impossible; ~ *man's* (*men's*) *fingers*, species of orchis, esp. *O. maculata* and *latifolia*; finger-like divisions of gills in lobster or crab; any of various kinds of orchis and fern; zoophyte, *Alcyonium digitatum*, forming lobed fleshy masses; ~ *man's handle*, (in electrically controlled trains) handle which must be pressed down for current to pass, so that train stops if driver releases his grasp; ~ *march*, march-like funeral music; ~ *men*, empty bottles; ~*-nettle*, non-stinging plant of genus *Lamium* with leaves like nettle's; *dea'dpan*, (slang) expressionless; ~ *point*, dead centre; ~ *reckoning*, (naut. & aeronaut.) estimation of ship's or aircraft's position from log, compass-courses, etc., and not from observations; ~ *shot*, unerring marksman; ~ *spit*, (colloq.) exact counterpart; ~ *water*, (naut.) eddy-water just behind stern of ship under way; state of tide when there is least rise or fall, slack water; ~ *weight*, heavy inert weight, weight of dead body or lifeless matter. ~ *n.* 1. *the* ~, dead person or persons; all who have ever died. 2. Dead period or time; time of intensest stillness, darkness, cold, etc. (*of* night, winter). ~ *adv.* Profoundly; absolutely, completely; ~ *against*, directly opposite or opposed to; ~*-beat*, tired out.

dea'den (dĕd-) *v.* Deprive of, lose, vitality, force, brightness, feeling, etc.; make insensible *to*.

dea'dlȳ (dĕd-) *adj.* 1. Causing fatal injury; of poisonous nature; implacable, mortal, to the death. 2. (of sin) Entailing spiritual death, mortal. 3. Resembling death; intense. **dea'dlinĕss** *n.* **dea'dlȳ** *adv.* As if dead; extremely.

Dead Sea (dĕd). Salt lake or inland sea between Israel and Jordan with intensely bitter water, into which river Jordan flows; ~ *apple, fruit*, APPLE of Sodom; ~ *scrolls*, large collection of Hebrew and Aramaic manuscripts, including parts of most books of O.T., found (1947–) in caves NW. of Dead Sea, apparently stored there by a Jewish community which lived at Qumran *c* 135 B.C.–A.D. 70.

deaf (dĕf) *adj.* 1. Wholly or partly without hearing. 2. Insensible *to*; not giving ear *to*; uncompliant. 3. *~-adder*, slow-worm; (U.S.) copperhead; any of various harmless snakes; *~-aid*, hearing aid; *~-and-dumb alphabet, language*, conventional signs made with hands for communication by the deaf; *~-mute*, deaf and dumb person. **dea'flў̆** *adv.* **dea'fnĕss** *n.*

dea'fen (dĕfn) *v.t.* Deprive of hearing by noise, stun with noise.

deal[1] *n.* *a great* (or *good*) ~, a large (or fairly large) amount; (adverbially) by much, considerably.

deal[2] *n.* Sawn fir or pine wood (in England, 225 mm wide, not more than 75 mm thick; in N. America, 11 in. wide, 2½ in. thick, and 12 ft long); wood in this form; fir or pine wood.

deal[3] *n.* 1. Distribution, sharing; dealing of cards; turn to deal cards. 2. Business transaction, bargain; (U.S.) secret bargain in commerce or politics; *Fair D~*, policy of social improvement in U.S. advocated by Harry S. TRUMAN; *New D~*, programme of social and economic reform in U.S. planned by the Roosevelt administration from 1932 onwards. ~ *v.* (past t. & past part. *dealt* pr. dĕlt). 1. Distribute, give *out*, among several; deliver as his share or deserts to person. 2. Distribute cards to players for a game or round; give (card, hand, etc.) to player. 3. Associate *with*; do business (*with* person, *in* goods); occupy oneself, grapple by way of discussion or refutation, take measures, *with*; behave (*well, honourably, cruelly*, etc., *with* or *by* person). **dea'ler** *n.* (esp.) Trader *in* a particular class of goods. **dea'lĭng** *n.*

dean *n.* 1. Head of chapter of collegiate or cathedral church; clergyman invested with precedence or jurisdiction (under bishop or archdeacon) over a division of an archdeaconry (usu. *rural* ~); *D~ of the Arches*, lay judge of Court of Arches, with peculiar jurisdiction over thirteen London parishes exempt from authority of bishop of London. 2. (Oxf. & Camb. Univv.) Resident fellow of a college appointed to supervise conduct and studies of junior members; in continental, Scottish, and modern universities, president of faculty or department of study or administration. 3. Doyen. [L *decanus* one set over ten (monks)]

dea'nerў̆ *n.* Office, house, of dean; group of parishes presided over by rural dean.

dear *adj.* 1. Beloved, loved (now often merely polite or ironical, and part of ordinary polite formula at beginning of most letters); precious in one's regard, to which one is attached. 2. Costly. ~ *n.* Dear one, charming person or thing. ~ *adv.* At a high price; dearly. **dear'lў̆** *adv.* **dear'nĕss** *n.* **dear** *int.* Exclamation expressing surprise, distress, sympathy, etc. (~ *~!*, *oh ~!*, ~ *me!*).

dearth (dėr-) *n.* Scarcity and dearness of food; scanty supply *of*.

death (dĕth) *n.* 1. Dying; final cessation of vital functions; being dead; cause or occasion of death; *be in at the ~*, be present when fox is killed or (fig.) at end of any enterprise; *put to ~*, execute. 2. Being or becoming spiritually dead; end, extinction, destruction; *civil ~*, loss or deprivation of civil rights and privileges, as by banishment, life imprisonment, etc. 3. *~-bed*, bed on which person dies; *~-bed repentance*, last-minute change of conduct or policy; *~-blow*, blow that causes death; ~ *duty*, any of various duties levied on property after owner's death; *~-mask*, cast taken from person's face after death; ~ *penalty*, capital punishment; *~-rate*, proportion of deaths usu. estimated per 1,000 of population per annum; *~-rattle*, rattling sound in throat of dying person, caused by partial stoppage of air-passage by mucus; *~-roll*, list of persons killed (in accident or battle); *~'s-head*, (figure or representation of) human skull, esp. as emblem of mortality; *~'s-head moth,* large hawk-moth, *Acherontia atropos,* with markings resembling skull on thorax; *~-trap,* place etc. which is unwholesome or dangerous; *~-warrant,* warrant for execution of death-sentence (also fig.); *~-watch (beetle),* small beetle (*Xestobium rufovillosum*) which makes noise like watch ticking, formerly supposed to portend death, the larva of which bores in old wood; insect making similar sound; *~-wish,* (psychol.) alleged inborn tendency of organisms to seek death, capable of being directed against the self or others.

dea'thlėss (dĕth-) *adj.* Immortal. **dea'thlėsslȳ** *adv.* **dea'thlėssnėss** *n.*

dea'thlȳ (dĕth-) *adj.* Deadly; gloomy, pale, etc., as death. *~ adv.* To a degree resembling death.

dĕb *n.* (colloq., orig. U.S.) Débutante.

débâcle (dābah'-) *n.* 1. (geol.) Sudden deluge of water, breaking down barriers and carrying stones and other debris with it, esp. the break-up of ice on northern rivers. 2. Sudden and overwhelming collapse, rush, stampede. [Fr., = 'break-up of ice in river']

dēbă'g *v.t.* (colloq.) Remove trousers of.

dėbar' *v.t.* Exclude *from* admission or right.

dėbar'k *v.* Disembark. **dēbarkā'tion** *n.*

dėbā'se *v.t.* Lower in quality, value, or character; depreciate (coin) by mixture of alloy or otherwise. **dėbā'sement** *n.*

dėbā'table *adj.* Questionable, subject to dispute or debate.

dėbā'te *v.* Contest, fight for (archaic); dispute about, discuss, (question); engage in (formal) argument or discussion (of), esp. in legislative or other assembly; consider, ponder; *debating society,* society whose members meet for practice in debating. **dėbā'ter** *n.* **dėbā'te** *n.* Controversy; discussion; public argument.

dėbau'ch *v.t.* Pervert from virtue or morality; make intemperate or sensual; seduce (woman), vitiate (taste, judgement). *~ n.* Bout or habit of sensual indulgence. **dėbauchee'** *n.* Viciously sensual person. **dėbau'cherȳ** *n.*

dėbĕ'nture *n.* 1. (archaic or tech.) Voucher given to person supplying goods to Royal Household or government office, entitling him to payment; custom-house certificate to exporter of amount due to him as drawback or bounty. 2. (Brit.) Sealed bond of corporation or company acknowledging sum on which interest is due till principal is repaid, esp. fixed interest constituting prior charge on assets; (U.S.) promissory note of corporation or company bearing fixed rate of interest, junior to other charges secured by fixed mortgages; *~ stock,* (Brit.) debentures consolidated into or created as stock, nominal capital of which represents debt of which only the interest is secured by perpetual annuity.

dėbi'litāte *v.t.* Enfeeble (constitution etc.)

dėbi'litȳ *n.* Feebleness (of health, purpose, etc.).

dĕ'bit *n.* Entry in account of sum owing; side of account (left-hand) in which these entries are made. *~ v.t.* Charge (person) *with* sum; enter (sum) *against* or *to* person.

dĕbonair' *adj.* Genial, pleasant, unembarrassed.

dėbou'ch (*or* -ōōsh) *v.i.* Issue from ravine, wood, etc., into open ground. **dėbou'chment** *n.*

Dėbrĕ'tt. (colloq.) 'Debrett's Peerage of England, Scotland and Ireland', first published by John Debrett in 1802 and now issued annually.

dē-brie'fing *n.* Interrogation, discussion, after completion of mission etc.

dĕ'bris (-rē) *n.* Scattered fragments, wreckage, drifted accumulation.

debt (dĕt) *n.* Money, goods, or service, owing; being under obligation to pay something; *floating ~,* part of National Debt represented by Treasury Bills or by other temporary arrangements with the lenders; *National D~*, debt owing by State to corporations and private individuals who have advanced money to it; ~ *of honour*, debt, usu. of sum lost in gambling, not legally enforceable; ~ *of nature*, necessity of dying.

de'btor (dĕt-) *n.* One who owes money, or an obligation or duty; (abbrev. Dr) heading of left-hand or debit side of account in book-keeping.

dēbŭ'nk *v.t.* Remove the false sentiment from (person, cult, etc.); expose (false claim etc.).

dēbŭ's *v.* (mil.) Unload, alight, from motor vehicles.

Debūssȳ, Claude (1862–1918). French composer of symphonic poems, pianoforte compositions, and one opera 'Pelléas et Mélisande'.

début (dā'bū *or* -ōō) *n.* First appearance on stage etc., as performer, or (esp.) in society.

dé'būtante (dā-, -ahnt), **dĕb-** *n.* Young woman making first appearance in society, esp. (formerly) one being presented at Court.

Dec. *abbrev.* December.

dĕca-, dec- *prefix.* Ten, ten times.

dĕ'cāde (*or* dĭkā'd) *n.* Set, series, of ten; period of ten years.

dĕ'cadence *n.* Falling away, declining (from former excellence, vitality, prosperity, etc.), esp. of period of art or literature after a culmination.

dĕ'cadent *adj.* In a state of decay or decline; of literature, art, etc., belonging to a decadent age. ~ *n.* Decadent writer or artist.

dĕ'cagon *n.* Plane figure with 10 sides and 10 angles. **dėcă'gonal** *adj.*

dĕ'cagrămme *n.* (abbrev. dkg) 10 grammes.

dĕcahē'dron *n.* Ten-sided solid. **dĕcahē'dral** *adj.*

dēcă'lcĭfȳ *v.t.* Deprive of lime or calcareous matter. **dēcălcĭfĭcā'tion** *n.*

dĕ'calitre (-lēter) *n.* (abbrev. dkl) 10 litres.

dĕ'calŏgue (-g) *n.* The Ten Commandments (Exod. 20:1–17).

Dėcă'meron. A work by Boccaccio, written between 1348 and 1358, containing 100 tales told in 10 days by a party of 7 young ladies and 3 young men who had fled from the plague in Florence.

dĕ'camētre (-ter) *n.* (abbrev. dkm) 10 metres.

dėcă'mp *v.i.* Break up or leave camp; go away suddenly, abscond. **dėcă'mpment** *n.*

dėcā'nal *adj.* Of a dean or deanery; of south side (on which dean sits) of choir.

dėcā'nī. (mus.) To be sung by decanal side in antiphonal singing (cf. CANTORIS). ~ *adj.* Decanal. [med. L, = 'of the dean']

dėcă'nt *v.t.* Pour off (clear liquid of solution) by gently inclining vessel without disturbing sediment; pour (wine) similarly from bottle into decanter; pour or empty out.

dėcă'nter *n.* Stoppered glass vessel in which decanted wine or spirit is brought to table.

dėcă'pĭtāte *v.t.* Behead. **dėcăpĭtā'tion** *n.*

dĕ'capŏd *n.* Ten-footed crustacean.

dēcar'bonīze *v.t.* Deprive of carbon or carbonic acid; remove carbon deposit from (internal combustion engine). **dėcarbonīzā'tion** *n.*

dĕ'castȳle *adj.* & *n.* (Portico or building) with ten columns at end or in front.

dēcă'sualīze (-zhōō- *or* -zū-) *v.t.* Do away with casual condition of (labour). **dēcasualīzā'tion** *n.*

dĕcasȳllă'bic *adj.* & *n.* (Metrical line) of ten syllables. **dĕ'casȳllable** *n.* & *adj.*

dėcă'thlon *n.* Athletic contest comprising ten different events.

dėcay' *v.* 1. Deteriorate; lose quality; decline in power, wealth, beauty, etc.; (phys.) diminish in intensity; (of radioactive particles etc.) disintegrate *into* different particles etc. 2. Rot, cause to deteriorate. ~ *n.* Act, process of decaying.

Dĕ'ccan. Triangular plateau of S. India, bounded by the Malabar and Coromandel coasts, which converge at Cape Comorin, and in the north by the Vindhya mountains.

dėcea'se *n.* (legal or formal) Death. ~ *v.i.* Die. **dėcea'sed** (-st) *adj.* & *n.* Dead (person).

dėcē'dent *n.* (U.S.) Deceased person.

dėcei't *n.* Piece of deception; deceitfulness. **dėcei'tful** *adj*, **dėcei'tfullў** *adv.* **dėcei'tfulnėss** *n.*

dėcei've *v.* Persuade of what is false, mislead; disappoint (hopes etc.). **dėcei'ver** *n.*

dēcĕ'lerāte *v.* Decrease speed or velocity (of). **dēcĕlerā'tion** *n.*

Dėcĕ'mber. 12th month of Gregorian (10th of Julian) calendar, with 31 days. [L *decem* ten]

Dėcĕ'mbrĭst *n.* (hist.) One of those who in December 1825 tried to raise revolt against Tsar Nicholas I of Russia.

dėcĕ'mvir (-*er*) *n.* 1. (Rom. hist.) Member of board of ten acting as council or ruling power, esp. two bodies of magistrates appointed 451 and 450 B.C. to draw up code of laws (laws of Twelve Tables). 2. Member of any council or ruling body of ten as in Venetian Republic. **dėcĕ'mvirate.**

dē'cencў *n.* Propriety of behaviour or demeanour; compliance with recognized notions of modesty or delicacy, freedom from impropriety; respectability; (pl.) decent or becoming acts or observances, outward conditions of decent life.

dėcĕ'nnĭal *adj.* Of 10-year period; recurring in 10 years. **dėcĕ'nnĭum** *n.* Period of 10 years.

dē'cent *adj.* 1. Seemly, not immodest, obscene, or indelicate; respectable. 2. Fair, tolerable, passable; (colloq.) kind, not severe or censorious. **dē'centlў** *adv.*

dēcĕ'ntralīze *v.t.* Divide and distribute (government, organization, etc.) among local centres. **dēcĕntralīzā'tion** *n.*

dėcĕ'ption *n.* Deceiving, being deceived; trick, sham.

dėcĕ'ptĭve *adj.* Apt to deceive, easily mistaken. **dėcĕ'ptĭvelў** *adv.* **dėcĕ'ptĭvenėss** *n.*

dĕcĭ- *prefix.* One tenth of.

Decian: see DECIUS.

dĕ'cĭbâr *n.* (meteor.) $\frac{1}{10}$ of a BAR[2].

dĕ'cĭbĕl *n.* Unit (= $\frac{1}{10}$ of a bel) used in comparison of levels of power in electrical communications circuit(s) or of intensities of sounds (abbrev. dB).

dėcī'de *v.* Settle (question, issue, dispute) by giving victory to one side; give judgement (*between*, *for*, *against*, etc.); bring, come, to a resolution or decision. **dėcī'dėd** *adj.* (esp.) Definite, unquestionable; (of persons) of clear opinions or vigorous initiative; not vacillating. **dėcī'dėdlў** *adv.*

dėcĭ'dūous *adj.* Shed periodically or normally; (of plant) shedding its leaves annually; (fig.) fleeting, transitory; ~ *tooth*, milk-tooth.

dĕ'cĭgramme *n.* (abbrev. dg) $\frac{1}{10}$ of a gramme.

dĕ'cĭlitre (-ēt*er*) *n.* (abbrev. dl) $\frac{1}{10}$ of a litre.

dĕcĭ'llion (-yon) *n.* 1. 10th power of a million (1 followed by 60 noughts). 2. (U.S.) 11th power of a thousand (1 followed by 33 noughts).

dĕ'cĭmal *adj.* Of 10th parts, of the number 10; proceeding by tens; ~ *classification*, system (esp. that of DEWEY) of classifying books etc. in libraries, using numbers subdivided as decimal fractions; ~ *coinage*, *currency*, monetary system in which smaller units may be expressed as decimal fractions of the principal unit; ~ *fraction*, fraction whose denominator is some power of 10, esp. such a fraction expressed by figures written to right of the units figure after a dot (the ~ *point*), and denoting tenths, hundredths, thousandths, etc.; ~ *system*, system of weights and measures in which each denomination is ten times the value of that immediately below it. ~ *n.* Decimal fraction. **dĕ′cĭmalīze** *v.t.* Express as decimal; convert to decimal system. **dĕcĭmalīzā′tion** *n.*

dĕ′cĭmāte *v.t.* Put to death one in ten of (mutinous or cowardly soldiers); destroy tenth or large proportion of. **dĕcĭmā′tion** *n.*

dĕ′cĭmētre (-t*er*) *n.* (abbrev. dm) $\frac{1}{10}$ of a metre.

dėcī′pher *v.t.* Convert (what is written in cipher) into ordinary writing, make out, interpret, by means of key; make out meaning of. **dėcī′pherable** *adj.* **dėcī′pherment** *n.*

dėcĭ′sion *n.* Settlement (*of*), conclusion, formal judgement; making up one's mind, resolve; resoluteness, decided character.

dėcī′sĭve *adj.* Deciding, conclusive; decided. **dėcī′sĭvelў** *adv.* **dėcī′sĭvenėss** *n.*

Dē′cius (d. 251). Roman emperor, during whose reign (249–51) the Christians were bitterly persecuted. **Dē′cian** *adj.*

dĕck[1] *n.* 1. Platform of planks or wood-covered iron extending from side to side of ship or part of it (in large ships *main, middle, lower* ~*s*, also *upper* or *spar* ~ above main, and *orlop* ~ below lower); floor of tramcar or bus; planking of pier, bridge, etc.; one of several floors or levels; ~*-chair*, folding canvas or cane-panelled chair of the kind used on passenger ships; ~*-hand*, sailor employed on deck of vessel, ordinary sailor; ~*-house*, room erected on deck of ship; ~ *tennis*, game played by tossing rubber or rope quoit back and forth over a net. 2. (now chiefly U.S.) Pack of cards.

dĕck[2] *v.t.* 1. Array, adorn. 2. Cover as or with deck, furnish with deck.

dĕ′ckle *n.* Frame in paper-making machine for limiting size or width of sheet; ~*-edge*, rough uncut edge of paper formed by deckle; ~*-edged*, having such an edge, as hand-made paper.

dėclai′m *v.* Speak or utter rhetorically; recite; deliver impassioned rather than reasoned speech.

dĕclamā′tion *n.* Act or art of declaiming; rhetorical exercise, set speech; impassioned speech, harangue. **dėclă′matorў** *adj.*

dėçlār′ant *n.* One who makes legal declaration.

dĕclarā′tion *n.* Stating, announcing, openly, explicitly, or formally; emphatic, solemn or legal assertion or proclamation; public statement as embodied in document, instrument, or public act; (law) plaintiff's statement of claim; simple affirmation sometimes allowed in lieu of oath or solemn affirmation; creation or acknowledgement of trust or use in writing; (cards) in bezique, declaring score by placing certain cards on table; in bridge, naming trump suit or declaring 'as trumps'; *D*~ *of* INDEPENDENCE, *D*~ *of* INDULGENCE: see these words; ~ *of the poll*, public official announcement of numbers polled at election; ~ *of war*, formal announcement by State of commencement of hostilities against another State.

dėclār′e *v.* 1. Make known, proclaim publicly, formally, or explicitly; pronounce to be; (custom-house) acknowledge possession of (dutiable goods); ~ *dividend*, officially announce dividend to be paid; ~ *for, against*, openly side with, against; ~ *war*, formally proclaim beginning of hostilities. 2. (law) Make declaration. 3. (cricket) Declare innings closed; close innings before ten wickets have fallen. 4. (cards) In bezique, claim score by laying certain cards face upwards on table; in bridge, name trump suit or decide to play in 'no trumps'. **dėclă′ratorў** *adj.*

dėclār′er *n.* (esp. in bridge) Player who names trumps and plays dummy's hand.

dėclă′ssé (dā-, -ā) *adj.* & *n.* (fem. *-ée*). (Person etc.) having sunk in the social scale.

dėclĕ′nsion *n.* 1. Declining or deviating from vertical or horizontal position. 2. Deviation from standard; diminution, deterioration, decay. 3. (gram.) Variation of form of noun, adjective, or pronoun, constituting its cases;

class in which noun etc. is grouped according to its inflexions; declining. **dèclĕ'nsional** *adj.*

dĕclĭnā'tion *n.* 1. Slope, inclination, from vertical or horizontal position. 2. (astron.) Angular distance of heavenly body from celestial equator. 3. Deviation of magnetic needle from true north-and-south line, variation. 4. (U.S.) Declining, refusal.

dèclī'ne *n.* 1. Sinking; gradual loss of vigour or excellence; decay; deterioration; wasting disease; downward movement in price or value. 2. Setting, last part of course, of sun, (fig.) of life, etc. *v.* 1. Have downward inclination; bend down, bow down, droop. 2. (of sun, day, life, etc.) Draw to end of its course. 3. Fall off, decay, decrease, deteriorate. 4. Turn away from, refuse, withhold oneself from (discussion, challenge, etc.); not accept, refuse politely. 5. (gram.) Inflect, recite cases of. **dèclī'nable** *adj.* (gram.) That can be declined.

dĕclĭnŏ'mèter *n.* Instrument for measuring astronomical or magnetic declination.

dèclĭ'vĭtous *adj.* Having considerable slope; steep. **dèclĭ'vĭtouslȳ** *adv.* **dèclĭ'vĭtȳ** *n.* Downward slope.

dēclŭ'tch *v.i.* Disengage clutch of motor vehicle; *double-~*, release and re-engage clutch twice when changing gear.

dècŏ'ct *v.t.* Make decoction of. **dècŏ'ction** *n.* (Liquor obtained by) boiling substance in liquid so as to extract soluble parts.

dēcō'de *v.t.* Decipher (coded message).

dēcō'ke *v.t.* & *n.* (colloq.) (Perform) a decarbonization.

décolletage (dākŏltahzh) *n.* (Exposure of neck and shoulders by) low-cut neck of dress. ***décolleté*** (-ŏltā) (fem. *-ée*) *adj.* (of dress) low-necked; (of person) wearing low-necked dress. [Fr.]

dēco'lorīze, -ourīze (-kŭler-) *v.* Deprive of, lose, colour. **dēcolorīzā'tion, -our-** *n.*

dēcompō'se (-z) *v.* 1. Separate or resolve into constituent parts or elements. 2. Disintegrate, break up; rot. **dēcŏmposĭ'tion** *n.*

dēcomprĕ'ss *v.t.* 1. Relieve pressure on (person who has been in compressed air) by means of air-lock. 2. Reduce compression in (motor engine) thus making engine easier to start. **dēcomprĕ'ssion** *n.* ~ *sickness*, caisson disease.

dēcongĕ'stant *adj.* & *n.* (Drug etc.) that relieves congestion.

dēcontă'mĭnāte *v.t.* Rid (person, area, etc.) of contamination, esp. from poison gas, radioactivity, etc. **dēcontămĭnā'tion** *n.*

dēcontrō'l *v.t.* & *n.* Release from (esp. Government) control.

décor (dā'kor̂) *n.* Scenery and furnishings of stage, room, etc.

dĕ'corāte *v.t.* 1. Furnish with ornamental accessories; hang (streets etc.) with flags etc.; paint, paper, etc. (room, house); serve as adornment to. 2. Invest with order, medal, etc. **dĕ'corative** *adj.*

dĕ'corātėd *adj.* (esp., *D~*) Of the second or middle style of English Gothic architecture (prevailing from *c* 1250 to 1350), with increasing use of decoration as part of construction.

dĕcorā'tion *n.* (esp.) 1. Decorating. 2. (pl.) Flags etc. put up on festive occasion. 3. Medal, star, etc., conferred and worn as mark of honour; *D~ Day*, (U.S.) annual commemoration (30 Mar.) of soldiers who fell in Amer. Civil War.

dĕ'corātor *n.* (esp.) Tradesman who paints, papers, etc., houses.

dĕ'corous *adj.* Not violating good taste or propriety, dignified and decent. **dĕ'corouslȳ** *adv.*

dècor̂'um *n.* Seemliness, propriety, etiquette; particular usage required by politeness or decency.

dècoy' *n.* 1. Pond or pool with narrow arms covered with network into which wild duck etc. may be allured and caught. 2. Bird or other animal trained to entice others into trap (esp. *~-duck*); person or thing used to decoy others. ~ *v.t.* Entice into place of capture, esp. with decoy;

allure *into*, *out of*, *away*, etc., ensnare.

dėcrea'se *v.* Lessen, diminish. **dē'crease** *n.* Diminution, lessening.

dėcree' *n.* 1. Ordinance or edict set forth by authority; edict or law of ecclesiastical council; one of eternal purposes, will, of God, Providence, Nature, etc. 2. Judgement of court of equity, admiralty, probate, or divorce; in divorce cases, order of court declaring nullity or dissolution of marriage; ~ *nisi*: see NISI. ~ *v.t.* Ordain by decree.

dĕ'crėment *n.* Decrease, amount lost by diminution or waste (opp. *increment*).

dėcrĕ'pit *adj.* Wasted, worn out, enfeebled with age and infirmities. **dėcrĕ'pitūde** *n.*

dėcrĕ'pitāte *v.* 1. Calcine (mineral or salt) till it ceases to crackle in fire. 2. Crackle under heat. **dėcrĕpitā'tion** *n.*

decrescĕ'ndō (dākrĕsh-). *adv.* & *n.* (pl. *-os*). (mus.) = DIMINUENDO. [It.]

dėcrĕ'scent *adj.* Waning, decreasing (usu. of moon).

dėcrē'tal *n.* Papal decree; (pl.) collection of such decrees, forming part of canon law.

dėcrȳ' *v.t.* Disparage, cry down.

dėcŭ'mbent *adj.* (bot., zool.) Lying along ground, lying flat on surface. **dėcŭ'mbentlȳ** *adv.*

dĕ'cūple *adj.* & *n.* Tenfold (amount). ~ *v.* Multiply by 10.

dėcŭ'ssate *adj.* X-shaped; (bot.) with pairs of opposite leaves etc. each at right angles to pair below. **dėcŭ'ssāte** *v.* Arrange, be arranged thus, intersect. **dĕcussā'tion** *n.*

deda'ns (-ahṅ) *n.* Open gallery at end of service side of tennis court.

dĕ'dĭcāte *v.t.* Devote (*to* God etc.) with solemn rites; give up, devote (*to* person, purpose); inscribe (book, music, etc.) *to* patron or friend. **dĕ'dĭcatorȳ** *adj.* **dĕdĭcā'tion** *n.* (esp.) Dedicatory inscription.

dėdū'ce *v.t.* 1. Trace course of, bring down (record etc.) *from* or *to* particular period; trace derivation or descent of. 2. Derive as conclusion *from* something already known; infer. **dėdū'cĭble** *adj.*

dėdŭ'ct *v.t.* Take away, put aside (amount etc.) *from.* **dėdŭ'ctĭble** *adj.*

dėdŭ'ction *n.* 1. Deducting; amount deducted. 2. Deducing; inference by reasoning from generals to particulars (opp. INDUCTION); thing deduced.

dėdŭ'ctĭve *adj.* Of, reasoning by, deduction. **dėdŭ'ctĭvelȳ** *adv.*

deed *n.* 1. Thing done by intelligent or responsible agent; act of bravery, skill, etc., feat, performance, doing. 2. (law) Written instrument purporting to effect some legal disposition, and sealed and delivered by disposing party (in practice now always signed also but not always delivered); ~ *poll*, deed made and executed by one party only (paper or parchment being 'polled' or cut even, not indented). ~ *v.t.* (chiefly U.S.) Convey or transfer by deed.

deem *v.t.* Believe, consider, judge, count.

Dee'mster *n.* One of two justices of Isle of Man, each with jurisdiction over half the island.

deep *adj.* 1. Extending far down from top, or far in from surface or edge. 2. (fig.) Hard to fathom; profound, not superficial, penetrating. 3. Heart-felt; absorbing; absorbed; intense, vivid, extreme. 4. Not shrill; low-pitched, full-toned. 5. ~ *field*, (cricket) part of field, (position of) fieldsman, near boundary; ~ *freeze*, refrigerator in which food can be quickly frozen and stored almost indefinitely (*Deepfreeze*, U.S. trade-name); ~ *mourning*, full mourning; ~*-sea*, (*adj.*) of the deeper part of the sea, some way from shore; *D~ South*, (U.S.) S. Carolina, Georgia, Alabama, Mississippi, and Louisiana. **dee'pĭsh** *adj.* **dee'plȳ** *adv.* **dee'pnėss** *n.* **deep** *n.* 1. (poet.) *the* ~, the sea. 2. Deep part of the sea; abyss, pit, cavity; mysterious region of thought or feeling. 3. (cricket) Deep field. ~ *adv.* Deeply; far down or in; ~*-laid* (of scheme), secret and elaborate; ~-*rooted*, having deep roots; (fig.) not easily eradicated; ~-*seated*, having its seat far below surface, not superficial. **dee'pen** *v*. Make, become, deep or deeper.

deer *n*. (pl. *deer*). Ruminant quadruped of family Cervidae, most of the males of which have

RED DEER

deciduous branching antlers; *fallow, Japanese, red, roe* ~, species wild or domesticated in U.K. ~-*hound*, large rough greyhound of Scottish breed; ~-*lick*, ground impregnated with salt, alum, etc., where deer come to lick; ~-*park*, park where deer are kept; *deer'-stalker*, one who stalks deer; cloth cap with peak before and behind.

dėfā'ce *v.t.* Disfigure; make illegible. **dėfā'cement** *n*.

dē fă'ctō (*or* dā), *adj*. & *adv*. *phr*. In fact, whether by right or not. [L]

defaecate: see DEFECATE.

dē'falcāte *v.i.* Commit defalcation; misappropriate property in one's charge.

dēfalcā'tion *n*. 1. Defection, shortcoming. 2. Monetary deficiency through breach of trust by one who has management or charge of funds, misappropriation; amount misappropriated.

dėfā'me *v.t.* Attack the good reputation of, speak ill of. **dĕfamā'tion** *n*. **dĕfă'matorў** *adj*.

dėfau'lt (-fawlt *or* -fŏlt) *n*. Want, absence; failure to act or appear; neglect; failure to pay; *judgement by* ~, judgement given for plaintiff on defendant's failure to plead. ~ *v*. 1. Make, be guilty of, default; fail to appear in court; fail to meet money call. 2. Declare (party) in default and give judgement against him. **dėfau'lter** *n*. One who defaults; one who fails properly to account for money etc. entrusted to him; (mil.) soldier guilty of military offence.

dėfea'sance (-fēz-) *n*. (law) Rendering null and void.

dėfea'sĭble (-fēz-) *adj*. Capable of annulment, liable to forfeiture. **dėfeasĭbĭ'lĭtў** *n*.

dėfea't *v.t.* Worst, conquer, in battle or other contest; frustrate, baffle; (law) annul. ~ *n*. Act or instance of defeating or being defeated; frustration.

dėfea'tĭsm *n*. Disposition, conduct, of one who accepts defeat as inevitable. **dėfea'tĭst** *n*. & *adj*.

dĕ'fėcāte, -feacāte *v*. Clear of dregs, refine, purify; get rid of, purge away, (dregs, excrement, sin); void faeces. **dĕfecā'tion** *n*.

dėfĕ'ct (*or* dē'-) *n*. Lack of something essential to completeness; shortcoming, failing; blemish; amount by which thing falls short. **dėfĕ'ct** *v.i.* Desert, esp. *to* another cause, country, etc. **dėfĕ'ction, dėfĕ'ctor** *ns*.

dėfĕ'ctĭve *adj*. Having defect(s); incomplete; faulty; wanting or deficient *in*; (gram.) not having all usual inflexions. ~ *n*. (esp.) *mental* ~, mentally defective person. **dėfĕ'ctĭvelў** *adv*. **dėfĕ'ctĭveness** *n*.

dėfĕ'nce *n*. 1. Defending from, resistance against, attack. 2. Thing that defends; means of resisting or warding off attack; military resources of a country; (pl.) fortifications. 3. Justification, vindication; speech or writing used to this end; (law) denial or charge by accused party, defendant's pleading or proceedings. 4. ~ *mechanism*, (psychol.) dynamic mental system serving to protect the conscious personality against disruptive unconscious impulses. **dėfĕ'nceless** *adj*. **dėfĕ'ncelėsslȳ** *adv*.

dėfĕ'nd *v*. 1. *God, heaven*, ~, (archaic) God forbid. 2. Ward off attack from; keep safe; protect (*against, from*). 3. Uphold by argument, speak or write in favour of; (law) make defence in court; (of counsel) appear for defendant, conduct defence of.

dėfĕ'ndant *n*. Person sued in court of law. ~ *adj*. That is a defendant.

dėfĕ'nder *n*. One who defends; holder of championship etc. defending the title; *D~ of the Faith* (L *Fidei Defensor*), title borne by English sovereigns since Henry VIII, on whom it was conferred in 1521 by Pope Leo X as reward for writing against Luther.

dēfĕnėstrā'tion *n*. Throwing out of a window; *D~ of Prague*, action of Bohemian Protestants who threw two of the emperor's deputy-governors and their secretary out of a window of the royal palace of Prague (21 May 1618) as a protest against Catholic repression; this was the prelude to the Thirty Years War.

dėfĕ'nsĭble *adj*. Easily defended (in war or argument); justifiable. **dėfĕnsĭbĭ'lĭtȳ** *n*. **dėfĕ'nsĭblȳ** *adv*.

dėfĕ'nsĭve *adj*. Serving, used, done, for defence; protective; not aggressive. **dėfĕ'nsĭvelȳ** *adv*. **dėfĕ'nsĭve** *n*. State or position of defence.

dėfer'[1] *v*. Put off, postpone; procrastinate, be dilatory; *deferred bond*, bond on which interest gradually increases to a fixed maximum; (U.S.) deferred share; *deferred payment*, payment by instalments; *deferred share, stock*, share, stock, payment of interest on which is deferred until expiration of fixed time or (usu.) until fixed rate of interest has been paid on ordinary shares. **dėfer'ment** *n*.

dėfer'[2] *v.i*. Submit or make concessions in opinion or action *to* (person etc.).

dĕ'ference *n*. Compliance with

DEFENESTRATION

advice etc. of one superior in wisdom or position; respect, manifestation of desire to comply, courteous regard; *in ~ to*, out of respect for. **dĕferĕ'ntial** (-sh*a*l) *adj*. **dĕferĕ'ntially̆** *adv*.

dĕ'ferent *adj*. (physiol., of ducts etc.) Conveying away from a centre.

dėfī'ance *n*. Challenge to fight or maintain cause, assertion, etc.; open disobedience or disregard.

dėfī'ant *adj*. Expressing defiance. **dėfī'antly̆** *adv*.

dėfi'ciency̆ (-sh*e*n-) *n*. Being deficient; want, lack; thing wanting; amount by which thing, esp. revenue, falls short; *~ disease*, disease caused by lack in diet of necessary elements, esp. vitamins. **dėfi'cient** *adj*. Incomplete, defective, wanting *in*; insufficient in quantity, force, etc.; half-witted; **dėfi'ciently̆** *adv*. **dėfi'cient** *n*. = DEFECTIVE *n*.

dĕ'fĭcĭt *n*. Amount by which anything, esp. sum of money, is too small; excess of liabilities over assets or of expenditure over income.

dĕfĭlā'de *v.t*. Secure (fortress) against enfilading fire. *~ n*. Act or operation of defilading.

dėfī'le[1] (*or* dē'fīl) *n*. Narrow way along which troops can march only in file; narrow pass or gorge. *~ v.i*. March in files, by files.

dėfī'le[2] *v.t*. Make dirty, befoul; pollute, corrupt; desecrate, profane; make ceremonially unclean. **dėfī'lement**[1] *n*.

dėfī'lement[2] (-lm-) *n*. = DEFILADE *n*.

dėfī'ne *v.t*. Settle limits of; make clear, esp. in outline; set forth essence of, declare exact meaning of; characterize, constitute definition of.

dĕ'fĭnĭte *adj*. With exact limits; determinate, distinct, precise, not vague; *~ article*: see ARTICLE; *~ inflexions*, those of German, OE, etc., adjectives used after the definite article. **dĕ'fĭnĭtely̆** *adv*. Clearly, plainly; (colloq.) yes indeed. **dĕ'fĭnĭtenėss** *n*.

dĕfĭnĭ'tion *n*. 1. Defining; statement of precise nature of thing or meaning of word. 2. Making or being distinct, degree of distinctness of details in a photograph, film, television picture, etc.; *high-*, *low-~*, applied to television systems using different numbers of scanning lines.

dėfĭ'nĭtĭve *adj*. Decisive, unconditional, final; authoritative (*~ edition*). **dėfĭ'nĭtĭvely̆** *adv*.

dėflā'te *v*. 1. Let air etc. out of (tyre, balloon, etc.). 2. Reduce (inflated currency); practise deflation. 3. Lower (person's spirits, confidence, etc.).

dėflā'tion *n*. Deflating; esp. situation in any country where prices generally are falling relatively to costs of production, giving rise to losses and unemployment. **dėflā'tionary̆** *adj*.

dėflĕ'ct *v*. Bend or turn aside; bend (ray of light) from straight line.

dėflĕ'xion (-ksh*o*n), **-ĕ'ction** *n*. Deflecting; (esp.) turning of magnetic needle or recording needle of galvanometer away from its zero.

dēflorā'tion *n*. Deflowering.

dėflow'er *v.t*. Deprive of virginity; ravage, spoil; strip of flowers.

Defō'e, Daniel (*c* 1660–1731). English novelist, author of 'Robinson Crusoe' (1719) etc.

dėfŏ'rėst *v.t*. Clear of forest. **dēfŏrėstā'tion** *n*.

dėfor'm *v.t*. Deface; put out of shape, mis-shape (esp. in past part.).

dēformā'tion *n*. Disfigurement; change for the worse; perverted form.

dėfor'mĭty̆ *n*. Being deformed, ugliness, disfigurement; malformation (esp. of body or limb).

dėfrau'd *v.t*. Cheat.

dėfray' *v.t*. Settle, discharge by payment. **dėfray'ment** *n*.

dėfrŏ'ck *v.t*. = UNFROCK.

dėfrŏ'st *v*. Remove frost from; thaw.

dĕft *adj*. Dextrous, esp. in manual skill. **dĕ'ftly̆** *adv*. **dĕ'ftnėss** *n*.

dėfŭ'nct *adj*. Dead; no longer existing.

dėfȳ' *v.t*. 1. Challenge to combat (archaic); challenge *to* contest or trial of skill. 2. Resist boldly or openly, set at nought; (of things) be beyond power of.

deg. *abbrev.* Degree.

Degas (-gah), Hilaire Germain Edgar (1834–1917). French Impressionist painter.

de Gaulle: see GAULLE.

dē-Gau'ss, dēgau'ss (-ows) *v.t.* Demagnetize; esp. render (ship) immune to magnetic mines by fitting round the hull a band of wire (*degaussing belt, girdle*) energized by an electric current which neutralizes ship's magnetism. [see GAUSS[2]]

dėgĕ'nerate *adj.* Having lost qualities proper to race or kind, sunk from former excellence, debased, degraded; (biol.) having reverted to lower type. **dėgĕ'neracy̆** *n.* **dėgĕ'nerate** *n.* Degenerate person or animal. **dėgĕ'nerāte** *v.i.* Become degenerate.

dėgĕnerā'tion *n.* Becoming degenerate; (path.) morbid disintegration of tissue or change in its structure.

dėglu'tĭnāte (-ōō-) *v.t.* Extract gluten from (flour etc.). **dėglutĭnā'tion** *n.*

dēgluti'tion (-ōō-) *n.* Swallowing.

dėgrā'de *v.* 1. Reduce to lower rank; depose as punishment; deprive (ecclesiastic) of orders. 2. Bring into dishonour or contempt; lower in character or quality, debase; tone down, reduce (colour etc.). 3. (biol.) Reduce to lower organic type; (chem.) break down (molecule); (phys.) reduce (energy) to a form less capable of transformation. 4. (geol.) Wear down (rocks etc.) by surface abrasion or disintegration. 5. Degenerate. **dĕgradā'tion** *n.*

dėgree' *n.* 1. Thing placed like step in series, tier, row; stage in ascending or descending scale or process; *by ~s*, gradually. 2. Stage in direct line of descent; (pl.) number of such steps to or from common ancestor, determining proximity of blood of collateral descendants; *prohibited ~s*, those within which marriage is prohibited. 3. Relative social or official rank; relative condition or state. 4. Stage in intensity or amount; (criminal law) relative measure of criminality; (U.S.) distinctive grade of crime (*murder in the first ~*, homicide premeditated or resulting from commission of grave crime; *in the second ~*, unpremeditated, or resulting from commission of lesser crime); *third ~*: see THIRD. 5. Academic rank conferred as mark of proficiency in scholarship or (*honorary ~*) as honour; (freemasonry) each step of proficiency in order, conferring successively higher rank. 6. (gram.) Stage (positive, comparative or superlative) in comparison of adjective or adverb. 7. (geom. etc.) Unit of angular measurement (symbol °), angle equal to $\frac{1}{90}$ right angle, arc of $\frac{1}{360}$ circumference of circle; esp. $\frac{1}{360}$ of earth's circumference, = 60 minutes; (thermometry) unit of temperature, varying according to scale employed; (mus.) (interval between) successive notes forming a scale. **dėgree'lėss** *adj.*

dėhĭ'sce *v.i.* Gape; (bot., of seed-vessel etc.) burst open. **dėhĭ'scence** *n.* **dėhĭ'scent** *adj.*

Deh'mel (dā-), Richard (1863–1920). German lyric poet, novelist, and dramatist.

dēhū'manīze *v.t.* Divest of human characteristics.

dēhȳ'drāte *v.* (chem.) Deprive of, lose, water or its constituent elements; dry completely, desiccate (foods). **dēhȳdrā'tion** *n.*

dē-ī'ce *v.t.* Remove, prevent, formation of ice on (aircraft, machine, etc.). **dē-ī'cer** *n.* Device or substance for de-icing.

dē'ĭcīde (*or* dā-) *n.* Killing, killer, of a god.

dē'ĭfôrm (*or* dā-) *adj.* Godlike in form or nature.

dē'ĭfȳ (*or* dā-) *v.t.* Make a god of; make godlike; regard as a god, worship. **dēĭfĭcā'tion** *n.*

deign (dān) *v.* Think fit, condescend (*to*); condescend to give, vouchsafe.

Dei gra'tia (dā'ē grah-; *or*

-shĭa, -sha) (abbrev. D.G.) By the grace of God. [L]

dē'ism (*or* dā-) *n.* Belief in existence of God, with rejection of revelation and supernatural doctrines of Christianity. **dē'ist** *n.* **dēĭ'stic** *adj.* **dēĭ'stically** *adv.*

dē'ity (*or* dā-) *n.* Divine status, quality, or nature; a god.

déjà vu (dāzhah vū). Illusory feeling of having previously experienced what is happening. [Fr., = 'already seen']

dėjĕ'ct *v.t.* Dispirit, depress. **dėjĕ'ctėdly** *adv.* **dėjĕ'ction** *n.*

déjeuner (dāzhernā *or* -zhêr-) *n.* Lunch, esp. of a ceremonial kind.

dē jure (joor'ĭ; *or* dā yoor'ĭ) *adj.* & *adv. phr.* Rightful, by right. [L]

Dėkă'brist *n.* = DECEMBRIST. [Russ. *Dekabr'* December]

Dĕ'kker, Thomas (1570?–1632). English Elizabethan dramatist, author of 'The Honest Whore' 'Patient Grissil', 'The Witch of Edmonton', etc.

dĕ'kkō *n.* (slang, orig. mil.) Look. [Hind. *dekho* look!]

del. *abbrev. Delineavit.*

Del. *abbrev.* Delaware.

Delacroix (-krwah), Ferdinand Victor Eugène (1799–1863). French Romantic painter.

dėlai'ne *n.* Light dress-fabric, usu. of wool and cotton, and printed.

dĕ la Māre, Walter John (1873–1956). English poet and novelist.

dėlā'te *v.t.* Inform against; impeach; report (offence). **dėlā'tion, dėlā'tor** *ns.*

Dĕ'lawāre. S. Atlantic State of U.S., one of the original 13 States of the Union (1787); capital, Dover.

dėlay' *n.* Delaying; procrastination; hindrance to progress. ~ *v.* 1. Postpone, defer, put off; hinder. 2. Loiter, be tardy; wait. 3. *delayed-action*, (attrib.) of a device etc. that operates after a lapse of time.

dĕl cre'derė (-ād-) *adj.* & *adv. phr.* (commerc.) With the selling agent's guarantee that the buyer is solvent. [It., = 'of belief, of trust']

dē'lė. (print.) Delete indicated letter, word, etc. (usu. written ₰).

dėlĕ'ctable *adj.* Delightful, pleasant. **dēlĕctā'tion** *n.* Enjoyment.

dĕ'lėgacy *n.* System of delegating; appointment as delegate; body of delegates.

dĕ'lėgate *n.* Deputy, commissioner; elected representative sent to conference. **dĕ'lėgāte** *v.t.* Depute, send as representative; commit (authority etc.) to agent. **dĕlėgā'tion** *n.* Entrusting of authority to deputy; body of delegates; (U.S.) group or members of Congress representing particular State.

dėlē'te *v.t.* Strike out, obliterate (letter, word, passage, etc.). **dėlē'tion** *n.*

dĕlėtēr'ious *adj.* Noxious, harmful. **dĕlėtēr'iously** *adv.* **dĕlėtēr'iousnėss** *n.*

Dĕlft. Town in Holland; hence, kind of pottery (also ~ *ware*) produced there, usu. with white glaze on which a decoration is painted in blue.

Dĕ'lhi (-lĭ). Capital of the Republic of India; Union territory in which it is situated.

Delian: see DELOS.

dėlĭ'berate *adj.* Intentional; considered, not impulsive; slow in deciding, cautious; leisurely, not hurried. **dėlĭ'berately** *adv.* **dėlĭ'beratenėss** *n.* **dėlĭ'berāte** *v.* Consider, think carefully; take counsel, consult, hold debate.

dėlĭberā'tion *n.* Careful consideration; discussion, debate; care, avoidance of precipitancy, slowness of movement.

dėlĭ'berative *adj.* Of, appointed for purpose of, deliberation or debate; (gram.) expressing deliberation or doubt. **dėlĭ'beratively** *adv.*

dĕ'licacy *n.* 1. Fineness of texture, substance, outline, etc., or of feeling or observation. 2. Weakliness; susceptibility to injury or disease; need of care in handling. 3. Refinement, sense of what is becoming or modest; regard for feelings of others 4. Choice or dainty item of food. 5. Delicate trait; nicety.

DELFT WARE

dĕ′licate *adj.* 1. Palatable, dainty (of food); sheltered, luxurious, (of life, upbringing, etc.). 2. Fine of texture, soft, slender, slight; of exquisite quality of workmanship; (of colour) subdued. 3. Subtle. 4. Easily injured; liable to illness. 5. Requiring careful handling (lit. & fig.). 6. Subtly sensitive; finely skilful; avoiding the offensive or immodest, considerate. **dĕ′licatelў** *adv.* **dĕ′licatenėss** *n.*

dĕlicatĕ′ssen *n.* (Shop selling) delicacies or relishes for table.

dėlĭ′cious (-sh*us*) *adj.* Highly delightful, esp. to taste, smell, or sense of humour. **dėlĭ′ciouslў** *adv.* **dėlĭ′ciousnėss** *n.*

dėlĭ′ct *n.* Violation of law or right, offence.

dėli′ght (-īt) *n.* Being delighted; thing affording delight. ~ *v.* Give great pleasure or enjoyment to; rejoice, be highly pleased. **dėli′ghtful** *adj.* **dėli′ghtfullў** *adv.* **dėli′ghtfulnėss** *n.*

Dėlī′lah (-l*a*). Woman who betrayed Samson to the Philistines (see Judges 16); hence, seductive treacherous woman.

dėlĭ′mĭt, dėlĭ′mĭtāte *vbs.t.* Determine limits or territorial boundary of. **dėlĭmĭtā′tion** *n.*

dėlĭ′nėāte *v.t.* Show by drawing or description, portray. **dėlĭneā′tion, dėlĭ′nėātor** *ns.*

dėlĭnėā′vĭt (*or* -ahv-). (So-and-so) drew this. [L]

dėlĭ′nquencў *n.* Being a delinquent; neglect or violation of duty; guilt; act of delinquency, offence, misdeed. **dėlĭ'nquent** *adj.* Defaulting, guilty. ~ *n.* Delinquent person.

dĕliquĕ'sce *v.i.* Become liquid, dissolve in moisture absorbed from the air; (fig.) melt away. **dĕliquĕ'scence** *n.* **dĕliquĕ'scent** *adj.*

dėlĭ'rious *adj.* Affected with delirium, temporarily or apparently mad, raving; wildly excited, ecstatic; betraying delirium or ecstasy.

dėlĭ'rium *n.* Disordered state of mind with incoherent speech, hallucinations, and frenzied excitement; great excitement, ecstasy; ~ *trē'mĕns* (pr. -z), form of delirium with terrifying delusions, to which heavy drinkers are liable.

Dē'lius, Frederick (1862–1934). English composer of songs, concertos, choral works, etc.

dėlĭ'ver *v.t.* 1. Rescue, save, set free (*from*). 2. Assist (female) in giving birth; assist in the birth of; (also *be delivered of*) give birth to. 3. Unburden *oneself of* opinion, thought, etc., in discourse. 4. Give *up*, *over*, abandon, resign, hand on *to* another; distribute (letters, parcels, etc.) to addressee or purchaser; present, render, (account); (law) hand over formally (esp. deed to grantee or third party). 5. Launch, aim (blow, ball, attack). 6. Utter, pronounce openly or formally (speech, judgement, etc.).

dėlĭ'verance *n.* Rescue; emphatically or formally delivered opinion; (in juror's oath) verdict.

dėlĭ'verer *n.* (esp.) Saviour, rescuer.

dėlĭ'verў *n.* 1. Childbirth. 2. Surrender (*of*); handing over (esp. of letters or goods). 3. (law) Formal handing over of property; formal transfer of deed to grantee or third party (formerly essential to its validity). 4. Delivering (missile, blow, etc.), esp. cricket-ball in bowling; action shown in doing this. 5. Uttering of speech etc.; manner of doing this.

dĕll *n.* Small hollow or valley, usu. with tree-clad sides.

Dĕ'lla Crŭ'scan *adj.* & *n.* 1. (Member) of the Academy della Crusca, a society founded in Florence in 1582 to sift and purify the Italian language, which issued a dictionary in 1612. 2. (Member) of an artificial school of English poets of late 18th c., one of whom, Robert Merry, was elected a member of the Florentine Academy and adopted the signature *Della Crusca.* [It. *della crusca* of the bran (i.e. sifting)]

Dĕ'lla Rŏ'bbia, Luca (1400–82). Florentine sculptor famous for his work in terracotta and various sculptures in Florence; the chief

characteristic of his terracotta process, which was inherited by the Della Robbia family, is the use of white figures against a usu. blue background.

Dē'lŏs. Island in the Aegean, one of the Cyclades; supposed to have been raised from the sea by Poseidon and anchored to the bottom of the sea by Zeus; an important centre of the worship of Apollo. **Dē'lian** (-yan) *adj.*

dēlou'se *v.t.* Clear of lice.

Dĕ'lphī. Greek town on slopes of Mt Parnassus, with ancient sanctuary and oracle of Apollo. **Dĕ'lphian, Dĕ'lphic** *adjs.* Of Delphi or the Delphic Apollo or oracle; obscure and ambiguous like the oracle's responses.

Dĕ'lphin *adj.* Of an edition of Latin classics prepared (1647) for use of the dauphin, son of Louis XIV. [L phrase *ad usum Delphini*, for the use of the dauphin]

dĕlphi'nium *n.* Ranunculaceous plant of genus *D~* including larkspur, with handsome irregular-shaped blue or pink flowers, (esp.) cultivated species or variety of this; deep blue of some delphinium flowers. [Gk *delphinion* larkspur, dim. of *delphin* dolphin]

dĕ'lphinoid *adj.* Like or related to a dolphin.

dĕ'lta *n.* 1. 4th letter of Greek alphabet Δ, δ (corresponding to *d*), used in enumerations etc.; examiner's mark indicating fourth class or failure. 2. Triangular tract of sand, gravel, and silt enclosed and traversed by the diverging mouths of a river. 3. *~ ray*, one of the rays of low penetrative power produced by particles emitted by radium, polonium, uranium, etc., consisting of low-velocity electrons knocked from an atom during a collision with some other particle; *~ wing*, triangular swept-back wing of high-speed aircraft.

dĕ'ltoid *adj.* Triangular; like river delta; *~ muscle*, large triangular muscle forming prominence of shoulder and serving to lift upper arm. *~ n.* Deltoid muscle.

dėlū'de *v.t.* Mislead, deceive.

dĕ'lūge *n.* Great flood, inundation; heavy fall of rain; flood of words etc.; *the D~*, the great flood in the time of Noah (Gen. 6–8). *~ v.t.* Flood, inundate. [L *diluvium* flood]

dėlū'sion (*or* -ōō-) *n.* Imposing or being imposed upon; false impression or opinion, esp. as symptom or form of madness. **dėlū'sional** *adj.*

dėlū'sive (*or* -ōō-) *adj.* Deceptive, disappointing, unreal. **dėlū'sively** *adv.* **dėlū'siveness** *n.*

de lūxe (*or* lōō-) *adj.phr.* Luxurious, sumptuous; of superior kind. *~ adv.phr.* [Fr.]

dĕlve *v.* Dig (archaic or dial.); (fig.) make laborious research in documents etc.

dēmă'gnėtize *v.t.* Deprive of magnetic quality.

dĕ'magŏgue (-g) *n.* Leader of popular faction, or of mob; agitator appealing to passions and prejudices of mob; (hist.) popular leader, orator who espoused people's cause against other parties in State. **dĕmagŏ'gic** (-gĭk) *adj.* **dĕ'magŏgism, dĕ'magŏgy** (-gĭ) *ns.*

dėma'nd (-mah-) *n.* 1. Authoritative or peremptory request or claim; what is demanded; legal claim, esp. claim made by legal process to real property. 2. Call for commodity by consumers; urgent or pressing claim or requirement. *~ v.t.* 1. Ask for with legal right or authority; (law) make formal claim to (real property) as rightful owner; ask for peremptorily or urgently; require, have need of. 2. Ask to know, authoritatively or formally.

dėma'ndant (-mah-) *n.* (esp., law) Plaintiff in real action, plaintiff or claimant in any civil action.

dēmarcā'tion *n.* Marking of boundary or limits of anything. **dē'marcāte** *v.t.*

démarche (dāmarsh) *n.* (diplomacy) Political step or proceeding, esp. one involving fresh line of policy. [Fr.]

dēmatēr'ialīze *v.* Make, become, non-material or spiritual.

dėmea'n¹ *v.refl.* Behave, conduct, *oneself* (in specified way). **dėmean'our** (-ner) *n.* Bearing, outward behaviour.

dėmea'n² *v.t.* Lower in dignity, reputation, etc.; lower or humble *oneself*.

dėmĕ'ntėd *adj.* Crazed, mad; infatuated; affected with dementia.

démenti (dāmahntē) *n.* Official contradiction of rumour or published statement. [Fr.]

dėmĕ′ntia (-shĭ*a* *or* -sh*a*) *n.* Insanity characterized by failure or loss of mental powers and caused by disease in or injury to the brain; ~ *prae′cox*, schizophrenia.

dĕmerār′a *n.* (also ~ *sugar*) Raw cane-sugar in yellowish-brown crystals, orig. and chiefly from Demerara, a region of Guyana.

dēmĕ′rĭt *n.* Quality deserving blame or punishment; censurable conduct; want of merit; fault, defect.

dėme′sne (-mān *or* -mēn) *n.* 1. (law) Possession (of real estate) as one's own; (of land) *held in* ~, not held by any subordinate tenant; (in modern use) immediately attached to mansion and held along with it (including park, home farm, etc.). 2. Domain; landed property, estate.

Dēmē′ter. (Gk myth.) Goddess of the corn-bearing earth and of agriculture, the daughter of Cronos and mother of Persephone; identified by the Romans with CERES.

dĕmĭ- *prefix.* Half, semi-.

dĕ′mĭgŏd *n.* Partly divine being, son of god and mortal, or deified man.

dĕ′mĭjohn (-jŏn) *n.* Large bottle with bulging body and narrow neck, holding 3–10 gal. and usu. cased in wicker- or rush-work. [corrupt. of Fr. *dame-Jeanne* Dame Jane]

dēmĭ′lĭtarīze *v.t.* Do away with military organization or control of; *demilitarized*, (of area) containing no armed forces. **dēmĭlĭtarīzā′tion** *n.*

dĕ′mĭlune (-o͞on) *n.* (fort.) Outwork protecting bastion or curtain.

dĕmĭ-mŏndaine *n.* Woman of the *demi-monde*.

dĕmĭ-mŏnde *n.* Class of women on outskirts of society, of doubtful reputation and standing.

dėmī′se (-z) *v.* 1. Convey, grant, (estate) by will or lease; transmit (title etc.) by death or abdication. 2. Die, decease. ~ *n.* 1. Conveyance or transfer of estate by will or lease; transference of sovereignty, as by death or deposition of sovereign. 2. Decease, death.

dĕmĭsĕmĭquā′ver (stress variable) *n.* (mus.) Note half as long as semiquaver. ().

dėmĭ′ssion *n.* Resigning, abdication, *of*.

dēmĭ′st *v.t.* Clear mist from (windscreen etc.). **dēmĭ′ster** *n.*

dėmĭ′t *v.* Resign.

dĕ′mĭurge *n.* (in Platonic philosophy) Creator of world; (in Gnostic and other systems) a being subordinate to Supreme Being; occas., author of evil. **dĕmĭur′gic** *adj.* [Gk *dēmiourgos* craftsman (*dēmios* of the people, *-ergos* working)]

dēmŏ′b *v.t.* (colloq.) Demobilize. ~ *n.* Demobilization.

dēmō′bĭlīze *v.t.* Release from mobilized condition; disband (troops, ships, etc.). **dėmōbĭlīzā′tion** *n.*

dėmŏ′cracy̆ *n.* 1. Form of government in which sovereign power resides in the people as a whole, and is exercised either directly by them or by their elected representatives; State having this form of government. 2. Class of people with no hereditary privileges; common people (in reference to their political power). 3. (U.S.) Principles, members of, DEMOCRATIC party.

dĕ′mocrăt *n.* 1. Advocate of democracy. 2. (U.S.) Member of DEMOCRATIC party.

dĕmocră′tĭc *adj.* 1. Of, like, practising, advocating, democracy. 2. (U.S.) of the Democratic party; *D~ party*, (U.S.) political party which claims JEFFERSON for its founder and opposes the (present-day) REPUBLICAN party, so called since *c* 1828, but previously known, at various times, as Anti-Federalist, Republican, and Democratic-Republican, supporting social reform and international commitment. **dĕmocră′tĭcally̆** *adv.* **dėmŏ′cratīze** *v.* **dėmŏcratīzā′tion** *n.*

Dėmŏ′crĭtus (5th c. B.C.). Greek philosopher ('the laughing philosopher'), regarded, with Leucippus, as founder of ATOMISM. **Dėmŏcrĭtē'an** *adj.*

Dēmogôr'gon. (myth.) Mysterious and terrible infernal deity (first mentioned in Latin authors *c* 450).

dēmŏ'graphy̆ *n.* Branch of anthropology dealing with conditions of life in communities of people, as shown in statistics of births, deaths, diseases, etc. **dēmŏ'grapher** *n.* **dēmogră'phĭc** *adj.*

dĕmoisĕlle (-mw*az*-) *n.* (zool.) Numidian crane, *Anthropoides virgo*, with long feathers and white plumes behind the eyes [Fr., = 'damsel']

dėmŏ'lĭsh *v.t.* Pull or throw down (building); destroy, make an end of; consume, eat up. **dĕmolĭ'tion** *n.*

dē'mon. 1. = DAEMON. 2. Evil spirit, devil; cruel, malignant, destructive, or terrible person; evil passion or agency personified. 3. ~ *bowler*, very fast bowler at cricket; ~ *star*, = ALGOL.

dēmŏ'nėtize (*or* -mŭn-) *v.t.* Withdraw from use as money; deprive of its status as money.

dēmō'nĭac *adj.* Possessed by a demon or evil spirit; of demoniacal possession; of or like demons; devilish; frenzied. ~ *n.* One possessed by a demon. **dēmonī'acal** *adj.* Demoniac; ~ *possession*, possession of a man by indwelling demon, formerly held to be cause of some kinds of insanity, epilepsy, etc.

dēmŏ'nĭc *adj.* Demoniac.

dē'monĭsm *n.* Belief in the power of demons.

dēmonŏ'latry̆ *n.* Worship of demons.

dēmonŏ'logy̆ *n.* Study of beliefs about demons.

dĕ'monstrable *adj.* Capable of being shown or logically proved. **dĕ'monstrably̆** *adv.* **dĕmŏnstrabĭ'lĭty̆** *n.*

dĕ'monstrāte *v.* 1. Show, display (feelings etc.). 2. Describe and explain by help of specimens or experiments; act as demonstrator. 3. Establish truth of by argument or deduction; prove. 4. Make, take part in, public demonstration.

dĕmonstrā'tion *n.* 1. Outward exhibition, display *of*; (mil.) show of military force or offensive movement; public manifestation (usu. mass-meeting or procession) of interest or sympathy with some cause etc. 2. Demonstrating, clear or indubitable proof, argument(s) proving an assertion etc.; exhibition and explanation of specimens or experiments as method of instruction in science or art.

dėmŏ'nstratĭve *adj.* 1. Serving to point out or exhibit, esp. (gram.) of certain adjectives and pronouns. 2. Demonstrating logically or conclusively; serving as proof *of*; evident or provable by demonstration. 3. Given to or marked by outward exhibition or expression of feelings etc. **dėmŏ'nstratĭvely̆** *adv.* **dėmŏ'nstratĭvenėss** *n.*

dĕ'monstrātor *n.* One who demonstrates; one who teaches by demonstration, esp. assistant to professor of science doing practical work with students; one who takes part in public demonstration.

dėmŏ'ralīze *v.t.* Corrupt morals of, deprave; destroy discipline, courage, powers of endurance, etc., of (esp. troops). **dėmŏralīzā'tion** *n.*

Dē'mŏs. Personification of populace or democracy.

Dėmŏ'sthenēs (-z) (384–322 B.C.). Athenian orator, famous for his orations delivered to rouse the Athenians to the danger of the subjugation of Greece by Philip of Macedon.

dėmō'te *v.t.* (orig. U.S.) Reduce to lower rank or class. **dėmō'tion** *n.*

dėmŏ'tĭc *adj.* Of the common people; esp. as epithet of popular simplified form of writing used in ancient Egypt from *c* 700 B.C. until 5th c. A.D. (as dist. from *hieratic*); of the popular form of modern Greek. ~ *n.* Demotic writing; demotic Greek.

dėmŭ'lcent *adj.* & *n.* Soothing (medicine).

dėmûr' *v.i.* Make difficulties, raise scruples or objections *to*, *at*;

(law) put in a demurrer. ~ *n.* Objecting, objection.

dėmūr'e *adj.* Sober, serious, composed; affectedly or constrainedly modest or decorous. **dėmūr'elȳ** *adv.* **dėmūr'enėss** *n.*

dėmŭ'rrable *adj.* That may be demurred to; open to objection.

dėmŭ'rrage *n.* (Compensation for) detention of vessel by freighter beyond time agreed upon; (charge for) detention of railway trucks; Bank of England's charge for exchanging gold or notes for bullion.

dėmŭ'rrer *n.* Legal objection to relevance of opponent's point, which stays action until relevance is determined by court; exception taken to anything.

dėmȳ' *n.* 1. Size of paper (in printing paper 564 × 444 mm (22½ × 17½ in.), in writing paper (England) 508 × 394 mm (20 × 15½ in.), (U.S.) 21 × 16 in.). 2. Foundation scholar at Magdalen College, Oxford (his allowance or commons being orig. half that of Fellow). **dėmȳ'ship** *n.* [earlier spelling of *demi-* half]

dēmȳthŏ'logīze *v.* Remove mythical elements (from); reinterpret mythological elements in the Bible.

dĕn *n.* Wild beast's lair; lurking-place of thieves etc.; small room in which person secludes himself to work etc.

dėnār'ius *n.* (pl. *-iī*). Ancient Roman silver coin, orig. of the

value of 10 asses (see AS[2]), whence English abbrev. *d.* for 'penny' (until 1971).

dē'narȳ *adj.* Of ten, decimal.

dēnă'tionalīze *v.t.* Deprive of nationality; destroy independent or distinct nationality of; make (institution etc.) no longer national; transfer (enterprise, industry) from national to private ownership. **dēnătionălīzā'tion** *n.*

dēnă'turalīze (-cher-) *v.t.* Alter or pervert the nature of, make unnatural; deprive of status and rights of natural subject or citizen. **dēnăturalīzā'tion** *n.*

dēnā'ture *v.t.* Change nature or properties of; render dutiable articles unfit for human consumption so that they may be used for other purposes without duty having to be paid. **dēnā'turant** (-choo͝-) *n.* Substance used as denaturing agent. **dēnāturā'tion** *n.*

dēnazĭfĭcā'tion (-ahtsĭ-) *n.* Eradication of Nazi influence in Germany; removal of Nazis from positions of responsibility in German public life. **dēna'zĭfȳ** *v.t.*

Denbighs. *abbrev.* Denbighshire.

Dĕ'nbighshire (-bĭsh-). Former county of N. Wales, since April 1974 part of Clwyd, except for certain parts in Gwynedd.

dĕ'ndrīte *n* 1. (Stone or mineral with) natural tree-like or moss-like marking. 2. Branching process of nerve cell. **dĕndrĭ'tĭc** *adj.*

dĕndrōchronŏ'logȳ (-k-) *n.* Study of chronology from evidence of annual growth rings in (ancient) timber. **dĕndrōchrŏnolŏ'gĭcal** *adj.*

dĕndrŏ'logȳ *n.* Study of trees. **dĕndrŏ'logist** *n.*

dēne[1] *n.* Deep wooded valley.

dēne[2] *n.* Bare sandy seaside tract; low sand-hill.

dēne hōle, dāne- (-nh-). One of a class of ancient excavations (chiefly in Essex and Kent, and in Somme valley in France), consisting of a narrow cylindrical shaft leading to an artificial cave in chalk.

dĕ'ngue (-nggĭ) *n.* Epidemic infectious eruptive fever of E. Africa, W. Indies, etc., with excruciating pains in joints and great prostration and debility. [prob. orig. Swahili *dinga*, associated with Span. *dengue* prudery, with ref. to stiffness in patient's neck and shoulders]

dėnī'able *adj.* That can be denied.

dėnī'al *n.* Refusal of request;

self-denial; contradiction, statement that thing is not true or existent; disowning, disavowal (*of* person).

denier *n.* 1. (dĭnēr′) (hist.) Small French coin; (archaic) very small sum. 2. (dĕ′ny*er*) Unit of weight used to estimate the fineness of silk or synthetic yarn (based on a length of 450 metres of yarn weighing 0·05 g.).

dĕ′nĭgrāte *v.t.* Blacken; defame. **dĕnigrā′tion** *n.*

dĕ′nĭm *n.* Twill-woven cotton fabric used for overalls etc., usu. with blue or brown warp and grey weft; (pl.) overalls, trousers, made of this. [f. Fr. *(serge) de Nîmes* (serge) of Nîmes in S. France]

Dĕ′nĭs, -ȳs, St (3rd c.). 1st bishop of Paris and patron saint of France; decapitated on the hill of Montmartre; commemorated 9 Oct.

dēnī′trāte *v.t.* Remove nitric acid from. **dēnītrā′tion** *n.*

dĕ′nĭzen *n.* Inhabitant, occupant (*of* place); foreigner admitted to residence and certain rights; naturalized foreign word, animal, or plant. ~ *v.t.* Admit as denizen. **dĕ′nĭzenshĭp** *n.*

Dĕ′nmârk. Kingdom of N. Europe, consisting of the islands of Zealand, Funen, Lolland, etc., the peninsula of Jutland and the outlying Baltic island of Bornholm; capital, Copenhagen.

dėnŏ′mĭnāte *v.t.* Give name to, call or describe as.

dėnŏmĭnā′tion *n.* 1. Name, designation; esp. characteristic or class name; class, kind, with specific name. 2. Class of units in numbers, weights, money, etc. 3. Religious sect. **dėnŏmĭnā′tional** *adj.* Of, like, a religious denomination; sectarian.

dėnŏ′mĭnatĭve *adj.* Serving as, giving, a name; (gram.) formed or derived from noun.

dėnŏ′mĭnātor *n.* (arith. etc.) Number written below line in vulgar fraction, giving value of parts into which integer is divided; *common* ~, denominator common to a number of fractions (freq. fig.).

dēnotā′tion *n.* 1. Denoting; expression by marks or symbols; mark by which thing is made known or indicated; designation. 2. Meaning, signification; (logic) what word denotes, as dist. from *connotation*, aggregate of objects of which word may be predicated.

dėnō′tatĭve *adj.* Denoting. **dėnō′tatĭvelȳ** *adv.*

dėnō′te *v.t.* 1. Mark out, distinguish, be the sign of; indicate, give to understand; signify, stand as name for (cf. CONNOTE); (logic) designate, be a name of, be predicated of.

dénouement, de- (dānōō′mahṅ) *n.* Unravelling of plot or complications, catastrophe, final solution, in play, novel, etc. [Fr.]

dėnou′nce *v.t.* 1. Prophesy (woe, vengeance), proclaim as threat or warning. 2. Inform against, accuse. 3. Inveigh against. 4. Give notice of termination of (armistice, treaty, etc.). **dėnou′ncement** *n.*

dē nō′vō (*or* dā). Afresh, beginning again. [L]

dĕnse *adj.* 1. Closely compacted in substance; crowded together. 2. Crass, stupid. **dĕ′nselȳ** *adv.* **dĕ′nsenėss** *n.*

dĕ′nsĭtȳ *n.* 1. Closeness of substance; crowded state; (photog.) opaqueness of developed film in negative. 2. Stupidity, crassness. 3. (phys.) Degree of consistence of body etc. expressed as weight per unit of volume; ~ *of charge*, (elect.) quantity of electricity per unit of volume or area.

dĕnt *n.* Hollow or impression in surface such as is made by blow with blunt-edged instrument. ~ *v.* Make dent in; become dented.

dĕ′ntal *adj.* Of tooth, teeth, or dentistry; (of consonant) pronounced with tip of tongue against front upper teeth; ~ *mechanic, technician*, one who makes artificial teeth; ~ *surgeon*, dentist holding recognized university qualification. ~ *n.* Dental consonant.

dĕ′ntāte *adj.* Toothed. **dĕntā′tion** *n.*

dĕ′ntĭcle *n.* Small tooth or tooth-like projection. **dĕntĭ′cūlar, dĕntĭ′cūlate** *adjs.* **dĕntĭcūlā′tion** *n.*

dĕ′ntĭfrĭce *n.* Preparation for cleaning teeth.

dĕ′ntĭl *n.* One of the series of small rectangular blocks beneath projecting part of cornice in classical architecture.

dĕ′ntĭne (*or* -ēn) *n.* Hard dense tissue forming main part of teeth.

dĕ′ntĭst *n.* One who treats diseases and malformations of teeth. **dĕ′ntĭstrȳ** *n.*

dĕntĭ′tion *n.* Teething; characteristic arrangement of teeth in animal.

dĕ′nture *n.* Set of (usu. artificial) teeth.

dėnū′de *v.t.* Make naked; strip *of*; (geol.) lay (rock etc.) bare by removal of what lies above. **dēnūdā′tion** *n.*

dėnŭncĭā′tion *n.* Denouncing; invective. **dėnŭ′nciatĭve, dėnŭ′nciatorȳ** (-sh*a*-) *adjs.* **dėnŭ′nciātor** (-shĭ-) *n.*

dėnȳ′ *v.t.* Declare untrue or non-existent; disavow, repudiate; refuse; ~ *oneself*, be abstinent.

Denys: see DENIS.

deoch an dŏ′rĭs (dŏχ *or* dyŏχ). (Sc. & Ir.) Parting drink. [Gael. *deoch an doruis* drink at the door]

dē′odănd *n.* (hist.) Chattel which having been immediate cause of a human death was forfeited to Crown to be applied to pious uses (abolished 1846). [L *deo dandum* that is to be given to God]

dē′odar *n.* Large cedar (*Cedrus deodara*), native of W. Himalayas. [Hind. f. Sansk. *deva-dāru* divine tree]

dēō′dorīze *v.t.* Deprive of odour. **dēōdorīza′tion, dēō′dorīzer, dēō′dorant** *ns.*

Deo gratias (dā′ō grah′tĭas *or* -shĭas). Thanks be to God.

dēŏntŏ′logȳ *n.* Science of duty, ethics. **dēŏntolŏ′gical** *adj.* **dēŏntŏ′logist** *n.* [Gk *deon* duty]

Deo vŏlĕ′nte (dā′ō, -tā). God willing. [L]

dēŏxȳrībōnūclē′ic ă′cid: see DNA.

dep. *abbrev.* Departs.

dėpar′t *v.* 1. Go away (*from*), take one's leave (chiefly literary); (esp. in timetables) start, leave; diverge, deviate (*from*). 2. Die; leave by death. **dėpar′tėd** *adj.* Bygone; deceased. ~ *n.* Deceased person.

dėpar′tment *n.* 1. Separate division or part of complex whole or organized system; (esp.) division of state or municipal administration; in U.S., one of the (now eight) major branches of the administration; *D~ of State*, U.S. Foreign Office. 2. In France, one of the administrative districts substituted for the old provinces in 1790. 3. ~ *store*, (orig. U.S.) large shop dealing in variety of articles, organized in departments. **dēpartmĕ′ntal** *adj.* **dēpartmĕ′ntallȳ** *adv.*

dėpar′ture *n.* 1. Departing; deviation (*from* truth etc.). 2. Starting, esp. of train etc.; setting out on course of action or thought. 3. (navigation) Distance which ship etc. moves east or west from given meridian.

dėpa′sture (-pah-) *v.* Graze (upon); put (cattle) to graze; furnish pasturage to (cattle).

dėpĕ′nd *v.i.* 1. Be contingent *on* or conditioned by; *that depends*, (colloq.) that depends on circumstances. 2. Be dependent; rest for maintenance, support, etc. (*on*); rely, reckon confidently (*on*). 3. (of lawsuit, parliamentary Bill, etc.) Be waiting for settlement.

dėpĕ′ndable *adj.* That may be relied on. **dėpĕ′ndablenėss, dėpĕndabĭ′lĭtȳ** *ns.* **dėpĕ′ndablȳ** *adv.*

dėpĕ′ndant, -ent *n.* One who depends on another for support; retainer, servant.

dėpĕ′ndence *n.* 1. Depending (*on*); being conditioned, subordinate, subject. 2. Living at another's cost. 3. Reliance, confident trust; thing relied on.

dėpĕ′ndencȳ *n.* Something subordinate or dependent, esp. country or province controlled by another.

dėpĕndent *adj.* Depending (*on*); contingent, subordinate, subject; maintained at another's cost; (gram., of clause etc.) in subordinate relation to sentence or word. **dėpĕ'ndentlў** *adv.*

dėpi'ct *v.t.* Represent in colours, drawing, words; portray, describe. **dėpĭ'ction** *n.*

dĕ'pilāte *v.t.* Remove hair from. **dĕpilā'tion** *n.* **dėpi'latorў** *adj.* & *n.*

dėplē'te *v.t.* Empty out; exhaust. **dėplē'tion** *n.*

dėplōr'e *v.t.* Bewail, grieve over, regret; be scandalized by. **dėplōr'able** *adj.* **dėplōr'ablў** *adv.* **dėplōrabĭ'litў, dėplōr'ablenėss** *ns.*

dėploy' *v.* (mil.) Spread out from column into line; (nav.) arrange in, take up, battle formation; move strategically. **dėploy'ment** *n.*

dėplu'me (-ōōm) *v.t.* Pluck, strip of feathers.

dēpō'larize *v.t.* Deprive of polarity, reverse or destroy effect of polarization.

dėpō'ne *v.* (Sc. law) State or declare upon oath, testify.

dėpō'nent *adj.* (of Latin or Gk verb) Passive or middle in form but active in meaning (so called from idea that these verbs had laid aside their passive meaning). ~ *n.* 1. Deponent verb. 2. Person making deposition on oath or giving written testimony for use in court etc.

dėpŏ'pūlāte *v.t.* Reduce population of. **dēpŏpūlā'tion** *n.*

dėpōr't *v.t.* 1. Bear, conduct, *oneself*; behave. 2. Carry away, remove; esp. remove into exile, banish (alien), whence **dēpōrtā'tion, dēpōrtee'** *ns.*

dėpōr'tment *n.* Bearing, demeanour, manners.

dėpō'se (-z) *v.* 1. Remove from office; dethrone. 2. Bear witness *that*, testify *to*, esp. on oath in court.

dėpŏ'sĭt (-z-) *n.* 1. Thing stored or entrusted for safe keeping; sum placed in BANK²; sum required and paid as pledge for performance of contract, part payment of price etc. 2. Layer of precipitated or deposited matter, natural accumulation. ~ *v.t.* 1. Lay or set down, place in more or less permanent position of rest; lay (eggs); (of water or other natural agencies) leave (matter) lying, form as natural deposit. 2. Store or entrust for keeping (esp. sum at interest in bank); pay as pledge for fulfilment of contract or further payment.

dėpŏ'sĭtarў (-z-) *n.* Person to whom thing is committed, trustee.

dĕposĭ'tion (-z-) *n.* 1. Taking down of the body of Christ from the cross; representation of this in art. 2. Deposing from office; esp., dethronement. 3. (Giving of) sworn evidence; allegation. 4. Depositing.

dėpŏ'sĭtor (-z-) *n.* 1. Person who deposits money etc. 2. Apparatus for depositing some substance. **dėpŏ'sĭtorў** *n.* 1. Storehouse. 2. = DEPOSITARY.

dĕ'pot (-ō; U.S. dē'pō) *n.* 1. (mil.) Place for stores; headquarters of regiment; station for assembling and drilling recruits; (hist.) place of confinement for prisoners of war. 2. Place where goods are deposited or stored. 3. (chiefly U.S.) Railway station.

dėprā've *v.t.* Make bad, deteriorate, pervert, corrupt, esp. in moral character or habits. **dĕpravā'tion** *n.*

dėpră'vĭtў *n.* Moral corruption, viciousness, abandoned wickedness; (theol.) innate corruption of human nature due to original sin.

dĕ'prėcāte *v.t.* Plead against, express earnest disapproval of. **dĕprėcā'tion** *n.* **dĕ'prėcative, dĕ'prėcatorў** *adjs.*

dėprē'ciāte (-shĭ-) *v.* 1. Diminish in value; lower market price of; reduce purchasing power of (money). 2. Disparage, belittle. **dėprē'ciatorў** (-sh*a*-) *adj.*

dėprēciā'tion (-sĭ- *or* -shĭ-) *n.* Depreciating, being depreciated; (allowance made in balance-sheets, valuations, etc., for) wear and tear.

dĕprėdā'tion *n.* (usu. pl.) Spoliation, ravages. **dĕ'prėdātor** *n.* Spoiler, pillager.

dėprĕ'ss *v.t.* Push or pull down, lower; bring low, humble; reduce activity of (esp. trade); lower (voice) in pitch; dispirit, deject; *depressed area*, region where trade is bad and unemployment rife.

dėprě'ssant *adj.* & *n.* (med.) Lowering, sedative (drug etc.).

dėprě'ssion *n.* 1. Lowering, sinking; depressed or sunken formation or surface, hollow, low place. 2. (astron. etc.) Angular distance of star or other object below horizontal plane (as opp. to *elevation*, above it). 3. Lowering in quality, vigour, value, or amount; reduction in activity (esp. of trade): lowering in pitch (of voice etc.). 4. Lowering of barometric or atmospheric pressure; (meterol.) centre of minimum pressure, or system of winds round it. 5. Being depressed in spirits, dejection; (path.) state of reduced vitality.

dėprě'ssive *adj.* That depresses; involving (esp. mental) depression. ~ *n.* One suffering from depressive illness.

dėprě'ssor *n.* (esp.) Muscle depressing or pulling down part to which it is attached (also ~ *muscle*); (surg.) instrument for pressing down some part of organ.

děprīvā'tion (*or* dēprī-) *n.* Loss, being deprived (*of*); deposition from (esp. ecclesiastical) office.

dėprī've *v.t.* 1. Strip, bereave, debar from enjoyment, *of*; *deprived child*, one lacking due parental care. 2. Depose (esp. clergyman) from office. **dėprī'val** *n.*

De profu'ndis (dā, -o͞ondēs). Psalm 130, beginning thus in Latin (= 'Out of the depths (have I cried)'); cry from depths of suffering or sin.

dept *abbrev.* Department.

děpth *n.* 1. Being deep; measurement from top down, from front to back, or from surface inwards. 2. Profundity, abstruseness; sagacity; intensity (of feelings, colours, silence, etc.). 3. Deep part of sea or any body of water (usu. pl.); (pl.) lowest part of pit, cavity, etc.: abyss (usu. pl.), lowest or inmost part; low moral condition; middle (of winter, night); deep region of thought, feeling, or being. 4. *in* ~, comprehensive(ly), thorough(ly); *out of one's* ~, in water too deep to stand in; (fig.) engaged in a matter beyond one's understanding; ~ *bomb*, *charge*, bomb capable of exploding under water; ~-*charge* (*v.t.*) attack with depth charges.

děpūtā'tion *n.* Body of persons appointed to go on mission on behalf of others.

dėpū'te *v.t.* Commit (task, authority) to substitute; appoint as one's substitute. ~ *n.* (Sc.) Deputy.

dě'pūtīze *v.i.* Act as deputy or understudy (*for*).

dě'pūtў *n.* 1. Person appointed to act for another or others, substitute, lieutenant; member of deputation; in City of London, deputy alderman; (U.S.) deputy sheriff. 2. Member of representative legislative assembly; *Chamber of Deputies*, lower house in national assembly of Belgium. 3. (coal-mining) Overseer responsible for safety devices, propping, etc. ~ *adj.* Deputed; acting instead of, or as subordinate to; vice-. **dě'pūtўship** *n.*

De Quĭ'ncey, Thomas (1785–1859). English essayist etc., author of 'Confessions of an English Opium Eater' (1822).

dērā'cĭnāte *v.t.* Tear up by the roots.

dėrai'l (*or* dē-) *v.t.* Cause (train etc.) to leave rails. **dėrai'lment** *n.*

dėrā'nge (-j) *v.t.* Throw into confusion or out of gear, disorganize; cause to act irregularly; make insane; disturb, interrupt. **dėrā'ngement** *n.*

dērā'te *v.t.* Lower or abolish rates upon.

dērā'tion *v.t.* Remove (food etc.) from rationed category.

Der'bў[1] (dar-). City and county town of Derbyshire; hence: 1. *the D*~, the most famous English horse-race, for three-year-olds, founded 1780 by 12th earl of Derby, and run at Epsom usu. on Wednesday before or second Wednesday after Whit Sunday; any of various important races in other countries, as the *Kentucky* ~ (pr. dėr-), or run by other animals; important contest in any sport. 2. Soft-paste porcelain made at Derby *c* 1750–1848; *Crown* ~,

THE DERBY

variety of this marked with crowned 'D'.

dẽr'bȳ[2] *n.* (U.S.) Stiff felt hat with rounded crown and narrow brim, bowler.

Der'bȳshire (dãr-). County of N. Midlands of England; ~ *neck*, variety of goitre, endemic in Derbyshire; ~ *spar*, fluorspar.

de regle (rāgl). Customary, proper. [Fr.]

dĕ'rėlict *adj.* & *n.* 1. Abandoned, ownerless (thing, esp. ship at sea). 2. (U.S.) (Person) guilty of dereliction of duty.

dĕrėlĭ'ction *n.* 1. Forsaking, abandonment; being abandoned; retreat of sea exposing new land. 2. Morally wrong or reprehensible abandonment or neglect (*of* duty etc.); failure in duty, delinquency.

dē'rĕquĭsĭ'tion *v.t.* Release (building etc.) from requisitioning.

dērėstrĭ'ct *v.t.* Remove restrictions from; (esp.) remove speed limit on traffic in specified area. **dērėstrĭ'ction** *n.*

dėrī'de *v.t.* Laugh to scorn.

de rigueur (rēgẽr). Required by etiquette. [Fr.]

dėrĭ'sion *n.* Ridicule, mockery.

dėrī'sĭve, dėrī'sorȳ *adjs.* Scoffing; mocking; *derisory offer* etc., one so small as to be ridiculous. **dėrī'sĭvelȳ** *adv.*

dĕrĭvā'tion *n.* Obtaining from a source; extraction, descent; formation of word from word or root, tracing or statement of this.

dėrĭ'vatĭve *adj.* & *n.* (Thing, word, etc.) of derived character or nature, derived from another or from a source, not primitive or original. **dėrĭ'vatĭvelȳ** *adv.*

dėrī've *v.* Get, obtain (*from* a source); have one's or its origin etc. *from*; gather, deduce, *from*; (pass., refl.) be descended or have one's origin *from*; (pass., of words) be formed *from*; trace, show, assert, descent or origin or formation of (person, thing, word) *from*.

dẽrm, dẽr'ma *ns.* (anat.) = DERMIS.

dẽrmabrā'sion *n.* Removal of superficial layers of skin by abrasion.

dẽrmatī'tis *n.* Inflammation of the dermis.

dẽrmatŏ'logȳ *n.* Science of the skin, its nature, diseases, etc. **dẽrmatolŏ'gĭcal** *adj.* **dẽrmatŏ'logist** *n.*

dẽr'mĭs *n.* (anat.) True skin, layer of tissue beneath epidermis. **dẽr'mal** *adj.*

dĕ'rogāte *v.i.* 1. Detract, make improper or injurious abatement, *from*. 2. Do something unsuited to one's rank or position.

dĕrogā'tion *n.* Lessening or impairment *of* law, position, dignity, etc.; deterioration, debasement.

dērŏʹgatorȳ *adj.* Tending to detract *from*, involving impairment, disparagement, or discredit, *to*; lowering, unsuited to one's dignity or position. **dĕrŏʹgatorĭlȳ** *adv.*

dĕʹrrĭck *n.* Contrivance for hoisting or moving heavy weights; spar or boom set up obliquely on shipboard, with foot lashed, pivoted, or socketed to deck; kind of crane with jib pivoted to foot of

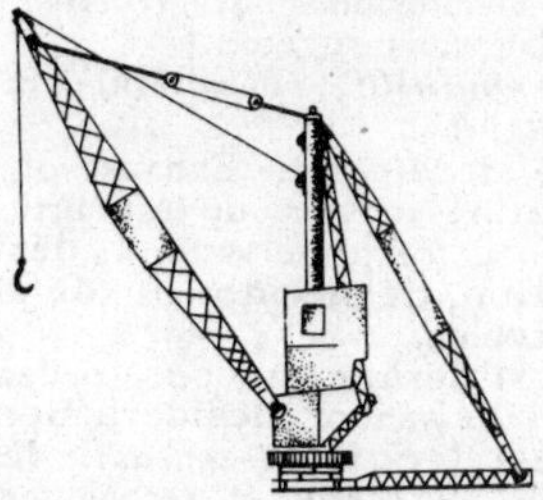

central post, so as to take various angles with perpendicular; any outstanding jib or arm with pulley at end; framework over deep bore, as that of an oil well, for supporting boring-tackle and for hoisting or lowering. [orig. = hangman, the gallows, f. surname of hangman at Tyburn *c* 1600]

dĕʹrrĭng-doʹ (-dōō) *n.* (pseudo-archaic) Desperate courage. [f. misunderstanding of Chaucer's *In dorryng don that longeth to a knyght* (in daring to do what belongs to etc.)]

dĕʹrrĭnger, dĕʹrĭ- (-j-) *n.* Short-barrelled pocket pistol. [named after its inventor, H. *Deringer* (1786–1868), a U.S. gunsmith]

dĕʹrrĭs *n.* Tall woody climbing plant of genus *D*~, native to the tropics; ground root of this, used as insecticide.

dẽrv *n.* Diesel oil for road vehicles. [*D*iesel-*e*ngined *r*oad *v*ehicle]

dẽrʹvĭsh *n.* 1. Muslim friar vowed to poverty and austerity. 2. One of the fanatical followers of the Sudanese Mahdi. [f. Pers. *darwīsh* poor]

D.E.S. *abbrev.* Department of Education and Science.

dēsăʹlĭnāte *v.t.* Remove salt from. **dēsălĭnāʹtion** *n.*

dĕʹscănt *n.* 1. Melody extemporized above a plainsong melody; melody, extemporized or written, added in the treble above any song-tune; esp., in hymns, written treble part sung in certain verses by a portion of the choir while the remainder sing the normal melody and harmonies. 2. (fig.) Amplification of a subject, discursive comment on it. **dėscăʹnt** *v.i.* 1. Talk at large, dwell freely, *upon*. 2. Sing a descant.

Descartes (dākart), René (1596–1650). French mathematician, physicist, and philosopher; author of 'Le Discours de la Méthode'

(1637), in which he expounded a quasi-mechanical conception of the universe, which he reduced to space, matter, and motion, operating under mathematical laws.

dėscĕʹnd *v.* 1. Come or go down, fall, sink; have downward extension, direction, or slope; come or go down (hill, steps, etc.). 2. Make excursion or attack, fall violently *on* (also transf.). 3. Come down ideally, mentally, or morally; proceed to something subsequent in time or order, or from general to particular; stoop. 4. Be transmitted by inheritance *from*, pass; *be descended from*, be derived by generation from (person, family, etc.).

dėscĕ'ndant *n.* Person or thing descended (*of*).

dėscĕ'nder *n.* (esp. print.) Limb of letter which descends below x-height.

dėscĕ'nt *n.* 1. Descending, downward motion; downward slope; way down. 2. Sudden attack. 3. Decline, sinking in scale, fall. 4. Being descended, lineage; transmission of property, title, or quality, by inheritance.

dėscrī'be *v.t.* 1. Set forth in words; recite characteristics of; qualify *as*. 2. Mark out, draw (esp. geom. figure); move in, pass or travel over (a certain course or distance).

dėscrĭ'ption *n.* Describing, verbal portrait or portraiture of person, object, or event, more or less complete definition; sort, kind.

dėscrĭ'ptive *adj.* Serving to describe; consisting chiefly of description. **dėscrĭ'ptĭvelȳ** *adv.*

dėscrȳ' *v.t.* Catch sight of, succeed in discerning.

dĕ'sėcrāte *v.t.* Deprive of sacred character; outrage, profane (something sacred). **dĕsėcrā'tion, dĕ'sėcrator** *ns.*

dēsĕ'grėgāte *v.t.* Reunite (persons, classes, etc.) hitherto segregated; esp. (orig. U.S.) abolish racial segregation in (schools etc.). **dēsĕgrėgā'tion** *n.*

dēsĕ'nsĭtīze *v.t.* Reduce sensitiveness of (esp. sensitized photographic material).

dėser̂'t[1] (-z-) *n.* 1. Deserving, being worthy of reward or punishment; (usu. pl.) that in conduct or character which deserves recompense; merit, worth. 2. (usu. pl.) Due reward or recompense (good or evil).

dĕ'sert[2] (-z-) *n.* Uninhabited and uncultivated tract of country; desolate, barren, waterless and treeless region; ~ *rat*: see JERBOA; *D~ Rats*, (colloq.) soldiers of 7th (British) armoured division, whose divisional sign was a jerboa, and which took part in desert campaign in N. Africa (1941–2). ~ *adj.* Uninhabited, desolate; uncultivated; barren.

dėser̂'t[3] (-z-) *v.* 1. Abandon, give up (thing); depart from (place, haunt); forsake (person or thing having claims on one); fail. 2. Run away (esp. from service in navy, army, or air force). **dėser̂'ter, dėser̂'tion** *ns.*

dėser̂'ve (-z-) *v.* Be entitled by conduct or qualities to (good or bad); have established claim to be *well* or *ill* treated at the hands *of*. **dėser̂'vėdlȳ** *adv.* **dėser̂'vĭng** *adj.* 1. Meritorious. 2. Worthy (*of* praise, censure, etc.).

déshabillé (dāzăbēyā) *n.* = DISHABILLE. [Fr.]

dĕ'sĭccāte *v.t.* Exhaust of all moisture, dry, dry up (esp. articles of food for preservation). **dĕsĭccā'tion, dĕ'sĭccator** *ns.* **dĕ'sĭccatĭve** *adj.*

dėsĭ'derāte (-z-) *v.t.* (pedant.) Feel the want of. **dėsĭderā'tion** *n.*

dėsĭ'derătĭve (-z-) *adj.* (esp. gram., of verb or verbal form) Formed from another verb to express desire of doing act thereby denoted. ~ *n.* Desiderative verb, verbal form, or conjugation.

dėsĭderā'tum (-z-) *n.* (pl. *-ta*). Something wanting and required or desired.

dėsī'gn (-zīn) *n.* 1. Plan or scheme to be carried out; end in view; purpose, intention; contrivance in accordance with a preconceived plan; scheme of attack *upon*. 2. Preliminary sketch for a work of art; plan for a building, machine, or any composite structure; combination of parts in a whole; general idea, construction, plot, etc.; faculty of evolving these; pattern, outline of decoration etc.; *industrial* ~, art of making designs for objects which are to be produced by machine. ~ *v.* 1. Form plan or scheme for; contrive; purpose, intend, have in view. 2. Set apart in thought for use *as*, or *for* advantage of; appoint, assign, make over *to* person (Sc. law). 3. Make preliminary sketch for (work of art etc.); plan construction of. **dėsī'gnėdlȳ** *adv.* On purpose, intentionally. **dėsī'gner** *n.* **dėsī'gnĭng** *adj.* (esp.) Crafty, artful, scheming.

dĕ'sĭgnate (-z-; *or* -āt) *adj.* (placed after noun) Appointed or nominated but not yet installed. **dĕ'sĭgnāte** *v.t.* Specify, particularize; serve as name or distinctive mark of; style, describe as; appoint to office. **dĕsĭgnā'tion** *n.* Appointing to office; name, description, title.

dėsīr'able (-z-) *adj.* Worthy to be desired. ~ *n.* Desirable thing or person. **dėsīrabĭ'lĭtȳ, dėsīr'ableness** *ns.* **dėsīr'ablȳ** *adv.*

dėsīr'e (-z-) *n.* 1. Feeling or emotion directed to attainment or possession of something expected to give pleasure or satisfaction; sensual appetite, lust. 2. Expression of desire, request. 3. Object of desire. ~ *v.t.* Long for, crave, wish; ask for; pray, entreat, command.

dėsīr'ous (-z-) *pred. adj.* Wishful, desiring, (*to* do); ambitious, having the desire, (*of*).

dėsĭ'st (*or* -zĭ-) *v.i.* Cease (*from*).

dĕsk *n.* 1. Fixed or movable piece of furniture for reading or writing at, having as its essential feature a board etc. (often sloping), which serves as a rest for books and papers and often drawers etc. for writing-materials. 2.

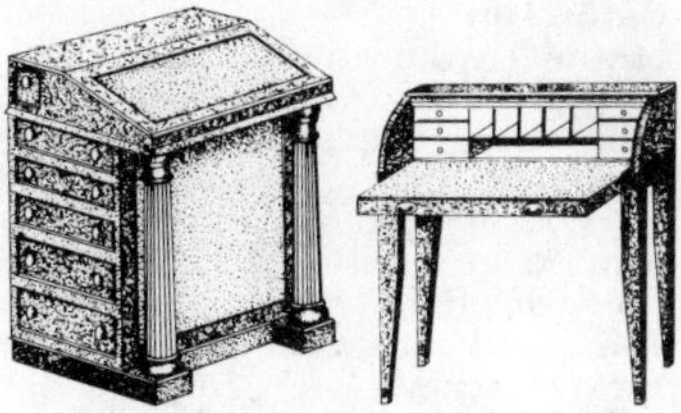

Davenport Cylinder Fall
DESKS

Section responsible for particular subject or operation within an organization; (U.S.) editorial subdivision of newspaper office.

dĕ'solate *adj.* Left alone, solitary; uninhabited, deserted; dreary, dismal, forlorn. **dĕ'solatelȳ** *adv.* **dĕ'solateness** *n.* **dĕ'solāte** *v.t.* Depopulate, devastate; render wretched and comfortless.

dĕsolā'tion *n.* Devastation; dreary barrenness; desolate place, dreary waste or ruin; solitariness; grief, wretchedness.

dėsor'ption *n.* (chem.) Liberation of substance from material on or in which it is adsorbed or dissolved. **dėsor'b** *v.t.* Act as desorbent of. **dėsor'bent** *adj.* & *n.* (Substance) producing desorption.

dėspair' *n.* Loss, utter want, of hope; what causes despair. ~ *v.i.* Lose, be without, hope.

despatch: see DISPATCH.

dĕsperā'do (*or* -ah-) *n.* (pl. *-oes*). Desperate or reckless man; one ready for any violent or lawless deed.

dĕ'sperate *adj.* 1. Leaving little or no room for hope; extremely dangerous or serious; hopelessly or extremely bad, extreme. 2. Reckless from despair; staking all on a small chance. **dĕ'speratelȳ** *adv.* **dĕ'sperateness, dĕsperā'tion** *ns.*

dĕ'spĭcable *adj.* Vile, contemptible. **dĕ'spĭcablȳ** *adv.*

dėspī'se (-z) *v.t.* Look down upon, think scornfully or slightingly of.

dėspī'te *n.* (archaic) Disdain; malice or hatred; *in* ~ *of*, in spite of. ~ *prep.* In spite of. **dėspī'teful** *adj.* **dėspī'tefullȳ** *adv.* (archaic).

dėspoi'l *v.t.* Plunder, spoil, rob, deprive. **dėspoi'ler, dėspoi'lment, dėspōliā'tion** *ns.*

dėspŏ'nd *v.i.* Lose heart, be dejected. ~ *n.* Despondency (archaic; only in *Slough of D~*). **dėspŏ'ndencȳ** *n.* Condition of having lost heart, dejection. **dėspŏ'ndent** *adj.* **dėspŏ'ndentlȳ** *adv.* **dėspŏ'ndĭnglȳ** *adv.*

dĕ'spot *n.* Absolute or tyrannical ruler; tyrant, oppressor. **dĕspŏ'tĭc** *adj.* **dėspŏ'tĭcallȳ** *adv.*

dĕ'spotism *n.* Arbitrary rule; despotic state.

dĕ'squamāte *v.i.* Come off in scales. **dĕsquamā'tion** *n.*

dėsser't (-z-) *n.* Course of fruit, nuts, etc., at end of dinner; sweet course; *~-fork, -knife, -spoon*, etc., those used for dessert (*~-spoon*, one intermediate in size between tablespoon and teaspoon). [Fr., f. *desservir* clear the table]

dĕstĭnā'tion *n.* Place to which person or thing is bound.

dĕ'stĭne *v.t.* Appoint, foreordain, devote, set apart (*to*, *for*).

dĕ'stĭny̆ *n.* 1. What is destined to happen, fate. 2. Power that foreordains, overruling or invincible necessity.

dĕ'stĭtūte *adj.* Without resources, in want of necessaries; devoid *of*. **dĕstĭtū'tion** *n.*

dėstroy' *v.t.* Pull down, demolish; make useless, spoil utterly; kill.

dėstroy'er *n.* (esp.) One of a class of small fast warships armed with guns, torpedoes, etc., used for escort-work, attacking submarines, etc., orig. built for attacking torpedo-boats.

dėstrŭ'ctĭble *adj.* Able to be destroyed. **dėstrŭctĭbĭ'lĭty̆** *n.*

dėstrŭ'ction *n.* Destroying, being destroyed; what destroys, cause of ruin.

dėstrŭ'ctĭve *adj.* Destroying, causing destruction; (of criticism etc.) negative, not constructive. ~ *n.* Destructive agent, instrument, etc. **dėstrŭ'ctĭvely̆** *adv.* **dėstrŭ'ctĭvenėss** *n.* **dėstrŭ'ctor** *n.* Furnace for burning refuse.

dėsū'ėtūde (*or* dĕ'swĭ-) *n.* Passing into, state of, disuse.

dĕ'sultory̆ *adj.* Skipping from one thing to another, disconnected, unmethodical. **dĕ'sultorĭly̆** *adv.* **dĕ'sultorĭnėss** *n.* [L *desultor* circus-rider]

dėtă'ch *v.t.* Unfasten and separate (*from*); (mil., nav.) separate and send off (part from main body) for special purpose or mission. **dėtă'chable** *adj.* **dėtăchabĭ'lĭty̆** *n.*

dėtă'ched (-cht) *adj.* Separate; unattached, standing apart. **detă'chėdly̆** *adv.* **detă'chėdnėss** *n.*

dėtă'chment *n.* 1. Detaching. 2. Number of troops, ships, etc., detached from main body for employment on separate service, etc. 3. Standing aloof from objects or circumstances, withdrawal from association with surroundings; aloofness from worldly concerns etc.

dē'tail *n.* 1. Dealing with things item by item; minute account, number of particulars. 2. Item, small or subordinate particular; minor decoration in building, picture, etc., way of treating this. 3. (mil. etc.) Distribution of orders of the day; telling off, small party told off, for particular service or duty. **dėtai'l** *v.t.* 1. Give particulars of, relate or enumerate in detail. 2. (mil.) Tell off for special duty. **dē'tailed** (-ld) *adj.* (esp.) Related or described in detail.

dėtai'n *v.t.* 1. Keep in confinement or under restraint. 2. Withhold (esp. what is due); keep from proceeding, keep waiting.

dėtainee' *n.* Person detained in custody without or pending further trial.

dėtai'ner *n.* (law) (Wrongful) detaining of goods taken for distraint etc.; detaining in custody; writ by which person already arrested may be detained on another suit.

dėtĕ'ct *v.t.* Find out, discover (person) in possession of some quality or performance of some act; discover presence, existence, or fact of (something apt to elude observation). **dėtĕ'ctable** *adj.* **dėtĕ'ction** *n.* Detecting, esp. of criminals; detective fiction.

dėtĕ'ctive *n.* Person, esp. policeman, employed in investigating criminal etc. activities; ~ *story*, story in which interest is centred in a crime and the detection of the criminal. ~ *adj.* Employed in, relating to, serving for, detection.

dėtĕ'ctor *n.* (esp.) Instrument for detecting any thing or action liable to escape observation; (radio) high-frequency rectifier.

dėtĕ'nt *n.* Mechanism that acts as a checking or detaining device; (in clocks etc.) catch which regulates striking.

détente (dātahṅt) *n.* (diplomacy) Relaxing of strained relations between two States. [Fr.]

dėtĕ'ntion *n.* Detaining, being detained; arrest, confinement; imprisonment by military authorities; (at schools) keeping in as punishment; ~ *centre*, disciplinary institution for juvenile offenders.

dėtẽr′ *v.t.* Discourage or restrain by fear or by consideration of danger or trouble. **dėtẽr′ment** *n.*

dėtẽr′gent *adj.* Cleansing. ~ *n.* Substance which when dissolved in water causes dirt, grease, etc., to be detached (e.g. soap, but in pop. and trade use freq. distinguished from soap).

dėtēr′iorāte *v.* Make, grow, worse. **dėtērĭorā′tion** *n.* **dėtēr′iorative** *adj.*

dėtẽr′minable *adj.* Capable of being determined; liable to be terminated. **dėtẽr′minablў** *adv.*

dėtẽr′minant *adj.* & *n.* Determining, decisive, conditioning, defining (agent, element, word, etc.); (math.) arrangement of quantities in an equal number of rows and columns representing the sum of the products of all possible sets of factors taking one from each row and one from each column, the signs of these products being determined by the direction of the diagonals joining their factors.

dėtẽr′minate *adj.* Limited, definite, distinct, finite, definitive. **dėtẽr′minatelў** *adv.* **dėtẽr′minatenėss** *n.*

dėtẽrminā′tion *n.* 1. (law) Cessation of estate or interest of any kind. 2. Decision, settlement, (*of* controversy, suit, etc.); conclusion, opinion, sentence. 3. Fixing, delimitation, definition, settlement, (*of* anything); exact ascertainment. 4. Fixed direction, decisive bias; settling of purpose; fixed purpose or intention; resoluteness.

dėtẽr′minative *adj.* & *n.* (Thing) serving to determine; (of) an ideographic sign annexed to word phonetically represented in order to make its meaning clear. **dėtẽr′minativelў** *adv.* **dėtẽr′minativenėss** *n.*

dėtẽr′mine *v.* 1. (esp. law) Bring, come, to an end. 2. Settle, decide, as judge or arbiter; come to conclusion, give decision; be decisive factor in regard to. 3. Ascertain precisely, fix. 4. Give an aim to, direct, impel *to*; decide (person) *to* do; resolve. **dėtẽr′mined** (-nd) *adj.* (esp.) Resolute, unflinching.

dėtẽr′minism *n.* Philosophical doctrine that human action is not free but necessarily determined by motives, regarded as external forces acting on the will. **dėtẽr′minist** *n.* **dėtẽrmini′stic** *adj.*

dėtĕ′rrent *adj.* That deters. ~ *n.* Something that deters; (esp.) nuclear weapon(s), deterring enemy from attacking. **dėtĕ′rrence** *n.*

dėtẽr′sive *adj.* & *n.* Cleansing (substance). **dėtẽr′sion** *n.*

dėtĕ′st *v.t.* Abhor, dislike intensely. **dėtĕ′stable** *adj.* **dėtĕ′stablenėss** *n.* **dėtĕ′stablў** *adv.*

dētĕstā′tion *n.* Abhorrence; detested person or thing.

dėthrō′ne *v.t.* Depose. **dėthrō′nement** *n.*

dĕt′onāte *v.* (Cause to) explode with loud report. **dĕtonā′tion** *n.* **dĕ′tonative** *adj.*

dĕ′tonātor *n.* Detonating contrivance, esp. as part of bomb or shell; railway fog-signal.

dētour (*or* dā′toor) *n.* Deviation, roundabout way, digression.

dėtră′ct *v.* Take away (*much, something*, etc.) *from*; ~ *from*, diminish, lessen in value, depreciate. **dėtră′ction, dėtră′ctor** *ns.* **dėtră′ctive** *adj.*

dētrai′n *v.* Discharge (troops etc.), alight, from railway train.

dĕ′triment *n.* Harm, damage. **dĕtrimĕ′ntal** *adj.* Harmful, causing loss or damage. **dĕtrimĕ′ntally** *adv.*

dėtrī′tėd *adj.* (geol.) Disintegrated, formed as detritus. **dėtrĭ′tion** *n.* Wearing away by rubbing.

dėtrī′tus *n.* Matter produced by detrition, esp. gravel, sand, clay, etc., eroded and washed away by action of water. **dėtrī′tal** *adj.*

de trop (trō). Not wanted, unwelcome, in the way. [Fr.]

dētūmĕ′scence *n.* Subsidence from swelling.

Deucă′lion. (Gk myth.) Son of Prometheus; married Pyrrha, daughter of Epimetheus. When Jupiter, angered by the impiety of mankind, covered the earth with a deluge, Deucalion and Pyrrha took refuge on the top of Parnassus and after the flood had subsided consulted the oracle of Themis on how to repair the loss of mankind. They were told to throw stones behind them; those thrown by Deucalion became men and those by Pyrrha women.

deuce[1] *n.* 1. The two at dice or cards; *~-ace*, throw that turns up ace with one die and deuce with the other. 2. (tennis, lawn tennis) State of score when the two sides are even, having gained three points or more each, and either must gain two points in succession to win the game.

deuce[2] *n.* Plague, mischief; the Devil; *play the ~ with*, spoil, ruin.

deu'cėd *adj.* & *adv.* Confounded(ly); great. **deu'cėdlў** *adv.*

deus ĕx mă'chīna (dā'ōōs, -k-) *n.* Power, event, that comes in nick of time to solve difficulty, providential interposition, esp. in novel or play. [L, = 'god from the machinery' (by which in ancient theatre gods were shown in the air)]

Deut. *abbrev.* Deuteronomy.

deutēr'ium *n.* Isotope of hydrogen, present to extent of about 1 part in 6000 in ordinary hydrogen; symbol D, at. no. 1, at. wt 2·013; ~ *oxide* (D_2O), heavy water (see HEAVY *adj.*). [Gk *deuteros* second]

deu'terō-canŏ'nĭcal *adj.* Of a second or secondary canon; of those books of the scripture canon, as defined by Council of Trent, accepted later than those of the first canon (including Esther and most of the Apocrypha, Epistle to Hebrews, Epistles of James and Jude).

Deu'terō-Isaiah (īzī'*a*). Later writer to whom chapters 40–66 of Isaiah are attributed.

deu'teron *n.* Nucleus of DEUTERIUM atom.

Deuterŏ'nomў. The 5th book of the Pentateuch, containing a repetition, with hortatory comments, of the Decalogue and most of the laws in Exod. 21–3 and 24. [Gk *deuteronomiom* 2nd book of law, from a mistranslation of Hebrew words (Deut. 17: 18) meaning 'a copy or duplicate of this law']

Deutsche Mârk (doi'ch*e*). Monetary unit of German Federal Republic, = 100 pfennig.

De'va (dā-). (Hindu myth.) Divinity, one of the good spirits. [Sansk., = 'god']

De Valēr'a, Eamon (1882–1975). American-born Irish statesman, prime minister of Republic of Ireland 1937–48, 1951–4, 1957–9, president 1959–73.

dēvă'lorīze *v.t.* Lower the value of (currency etc.).

dēvă'lūāte, dēvă'lūe *vbs.t.* Deprive of value; effect devaluation of (currency). **dēvălūā'tion** *n.* (esp.) Reduction of official value of currency in terms of gold or another currency.

Devana'garī (dāv*a*nah-). Formal alphabet in which Sanskrit, Hindi, and other languages of India are written. [Sanskr.]

dĕ'vastāte *v.t.* Lay waste, ravage. **dĕvastā'tion, dĕ'vastātor** *ns.* **dĕ'vastātĭng** *adj.* (esp., fig.) Very effective; astounding. **dĕ'vastātĭnglў** *adv.*

dėvĕ'lop *v.* 1. Unfold, bring out all that is potentially contained in; bring or come forth from latent or elementary condition, make or become manifest; realize potentialities of (land), esp. by converting it for residential or industrial purposes. 2. (mus.) Elaborate (a theme), unfold its qualities, reveal its possibilities by modification of melody, harmony, rhythm, etc. 3. (photog.) Render visible (latent image produced by actinic action on sensitive surface) by chemical treatment. 4. Make or become fuller, more elaborate or systematic, more active, bigger; make progress; come or bring to maturity. 5. (U.S.) Bring or come to light; make, become, known.

dėvĕ'loper *n.* (esp.) Chemical agent for developing photographs.

dėvĕ'lopment *n.* Developing; developed product etc.; (mus.) in sonata or similar composition, the second section of a movement, containing elaborations on the theme(s) stated in the first section;

~ *area*, area in which Government encourages new industries because of large-scale unemployment there. **dėvĕlopmĕ'ntal** *adj.* **dėvĕlopmĕ'ntallў** *adv.*

dē'vĭāte *v.i.* Turn aside (*from*); digress. **dē'vĭant** *adj.* & *n.*

dēvĭā'tion *n.* (esp.) Deflection of ship's compass needle by iron in ship etc.; divergence of optic axis from normal position; departure or divergence from orthodox Communist doctrine, whence **dēvĭā'tionĭsm, dēvĭā'tionĭst** *ns.*

dėvī'ce *n.* 1. (pl.) Fancy, will, desire (only in *leave, left, to one's own devices*). 2. Arrangement, contrivance, expedient; something designed to perform special (esp. mechanical or electrical) function. 3. Design, figure; emblematic or heraldic design; motto.

dĕ'vĭl *n.* 1. *the D~*, Satan; in Jewish and Christian theology the supreme spirit of evil, tempter and spiritual enemy of man, represented as a person, usu. with cloven hoofs, horns, and a tail. 2. Demon; heathen god, esp. malignant or evil deity, unclean spirit by which demoniacs were supposed to be possessed; one of the host of Satan, supposed to have their abode in hell. 3. Malignantly wicked or cruel person; energetic, clever, knavish, etc., person; poor wretch, luckless person (usu. *poor ~*). 4. Boy in printing office (hist.); junior legal counsel doing professional work for a leader; literary hack doing work for which his employer takes credit and (often) payment. 5. Personified evil quality, as *the ~ of greed*; temper, fighting spirit. 6. *Tasmanian ~*: see TASMANIAN. 7. Any of various instruments or machines, esp. with sharp teeth or spikes, for

TASMANIAN DEVIL

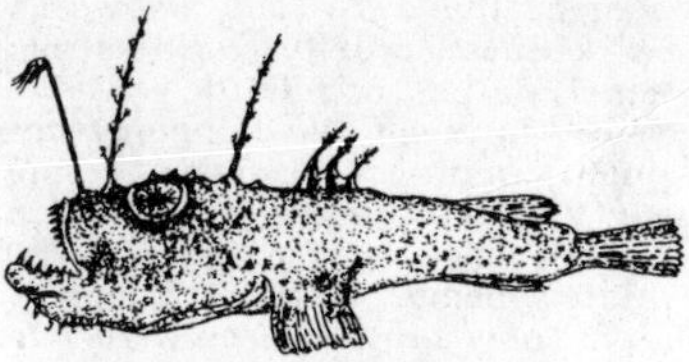

DEVIL-FISH

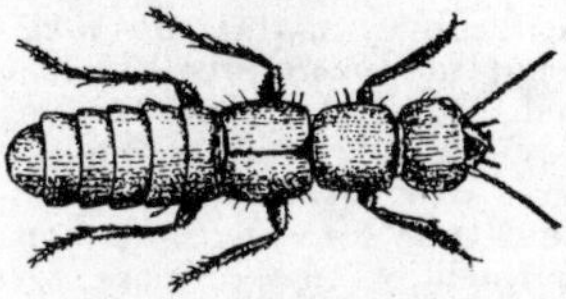

DEVIL'S COACH-HORSE

destructive use. 8. *a ~ of a*, a confounded, very violent; *like the ~*, with the violence, energy, etc., attributed to the devil; *between the ~ and the deep sea*, in an unpleasant dilemma; *go to the ~*, go to ruin or perdition; *the ~ to pay*, much trouble, violence. 9. *~-fish*, ANGLER, 2; (U.S.) gigantic fish, *Manta birostis*, with expanded sides passing into large pectoral fins like wings; *~-may-care* (*adj.*) wildly reckless; careless and rollicking; *Devil's Advocate*, (pop. name for) Promotor Fidei; (transf.) one who advocates an opposing cause, esp. for argument; *~'s-bit*, species of scabious, *Scabiosa succisa*, with blue flowers and thickish root seeming as if bitten off; *~'s-bones*, dice; *~'s coach-horse*, large cocktail beetle, *Staphylinus olens*, which assumes a rearing attitude when disturbed; *Devil's Own*, the 88th Foot (*the Devil's own Connaught boys*); also, the Inns of Court Volunteers; *~'s tattoo*, restless drumming with the fingers. ~ *v.* 1. Work as lawyer's or author's devil. 2. Grill with strong peppery seasoning.

dĕ'vĭlish *adj.* Like, worthy of, the devil, damnable. **dĕ'vĭlishlў** *adv.* **dĕ'vĭlishnėss** *n.*

dĕ'vĭlment *n.* Mischief, wild spirits; devilish or strange phenomenon.

dĕ'vĭlrў *n.* Diabolical art,

magic; the devil and his works; wickedness, cruelty; reckless mischief, daring, or hilarity.

dē'vĭous *adj.* Winding or straying, circuitous, erratic; erring. **dē'vĭouslȳ** *adv.* **dē'vĭousnėss** *n.*

dėvī'se (-z) *v.t.* 1. Plan, invent; plot, scheme. 2. (law) Assign or give (now only real property) by will. ~ *n.* (law) Testamentary disposition of real property, clause in will conveying this. **dėvīsee'** *n.* Person to whom property is devised.

dēvī'talīze *v.t.* Make lifeless or effete. **dēvītalīzā'tion** *n.*

dēvĭ'trĭfȳ *v.t.* Deprive of vitreous qualities; make (glass, vitreous rock) opaque and crystalline. **dēvĭtrĭfĭcā'tion** *n.*

dėvoi'd *adj.* Destitute, empty, *of*.

dĕ'voirs (-vwârz) *n.pl.* Dutiful respects, courteous attentions.

dē'volūte (*or* -ōōt) *v.t.* Transfer by devolution.

dēvolū'tion (*or* -lōō-) *n.* 1. Descent through a series of changes; descent of property by natural or due succession; lapse of unexercised right to ultimate owner. 2. (biol.) Degeneration (now rare). 3. Deputing, delegation, of work or power (esp. by House of Parliament to its committees).

dėvŏ'lve *v.* Throw (duty, work), be thrown, fall, descend, *upon* (deputy, or one who must act for want of others); descend, fall by succession.

Dĕ'von. County of SW. England; (one of) a breed of cattle noted for the quality of their milk.

Dėvō'nĭan *adj.* & *n.* 1. (Native, inhabitant) of Devonshire. 2. (geol.) (Of) the period or system of the Palaeozoic era between Silurian and Carboniferous.

Dĕ'vonshire. = Devon; ~*cream*, thick clotted cream prepared by slow scalding.

dėvō'te *v.t.* Consecrate, dedicate, give up exclusively *to*; give over to destruction etc. **dėvō'tėd** *adj.* (esp.) Zealously attached, loyal or faithful; doomed. **dėvō'tėdlȳ** *adv.*

dĕvotee' *n.* Votary *of*, one devoted *to*; zealously or fanatically pious person.

dėvō'tion *n.* 1. Devoutness; religious worship or observance; (pl.) prayers, worship. 2. Enthusiastic addiction, attachment, or loyalty (*to*). **dėvō'tional** *adj.* **dėvō'tionallȳ** *adv.*

dėvour' *v.t.* 1. Eat up voraciously, as a beast of prey, prey upon; eat greedily; eat ravenously or barbarously. 2. Consume recklessly; waste, destroy. 3. Engulf; take in greedily with eyes, ears, etc.; engross the attention of. **dėvour'inglȳ** *adv.*

dėvou't *adj.* Earnestly religious, reverent; earnest, sincere. **dėvou'tlȳ** *adv.* **dėvou'tnėss** *n.*

dew *n.* 1. Vapour condensed in small drops on cool surfaces on or near the ground, when nocturnal radiation has cooled the lower layer of the atmosphere. 2. Freshness, refreshing or gently stealing influence. 3. Any beaded or glistening moisture, esp. tears, sweat. 4. *dew'berry*, fruit of genus *Rubus* akin to blackberry, in Gt Britain, *R. caesius*, a low-growing procumbent species with bluish bloom on fruit; plant bearing this; ~*-claw*, rudimentary inner toe on inside of dog's leg, higher than other toes and not touching the ground; ~*-drop*, drop of moisture condensed in form of dew; ~*-point*, temperature at which atmosphere becomes saturated with water vapour by cooling; ~*-pond*, pond (often artificial) on downs or in other places where there are no springs, formerly thought to be fed by dew draining into it from surrounding area. **dew'ȳ** *adj.* **dew'ĭlȳ** *adv.* **dew'ĭnėss** *n.* **dew** *v.t.* Bedew, moisten.

D.E.W. *abbrev.* Distant early warning.

Dew'ey, Melvil (1851–1931). Amer. librarian; devised decimal system of classifying books.

dew'lăp *n.* Fold of loose skin hanging from throat esp. in cattle. **dew'lăpped** (-pt) *adj.*

dĕ'xter *adj.* Of, on, the right-hand side (but in heraldry = on right side of shield from wearer's point of view, i.e. on spectator's left; opp. SINISTER).

dĕxtĕ'rity̆ *n.* Manual or mental adroitness, skill, neatness of handling.

dĕ'xtrĭn *n.* (chem.) Gummy substance, used as adhesive, into which starch is converted by dilute acids or alkalis, prolonged heat, etc.

dĕxtro- *prefix.* (Turning, turned) to the right (opp. LAEVO-); (esp., chem., of substances) having property of causing plane of polarized light to rotate to the right; so *dextrogȳr'ous, dextrorō'tatory* (*adjs.*); *~-compound* (*n.*).

dĕ'xtrōse *n.* Dextrorotatory glucose.

dĕ'xtrous, -ter- *adj.* Handling things neatly; skilful. **dĕ'xt(e)rousl**y̆ *adv.* **dĕ'xt(e)rousnėss** *n.*

Dey (dā). (hist.) Title of commanding officer of Janissaries of Algiers, who in 1710 deposed the pasha or Turkish civil governor and became sole ruler; governor or pasha of Tunis or Tripoli. [Turk. *dayı* maternal uncle]

D.F. *abbrev.* Direction finder (*or* finding).

D.F.C., D.F.M., *abbrevs.* Distinguished Flying Cross, Medal.

D.G. *abbrev. Dei gratia*; *Deo gratias*; Dragoon Guards.

dghai'sa (dī-) *n.* Boat resembling gondola, used in Malta.

dhō'tĭ (dō-) *n.* Loin-cloth worn by Hindus.

dhow (dow) *n.* Lateen-rigged native vessel used on Arabian Sea.

di-[1] *prefix.* Two-, double-.

di-[2], **dia-** *prefix.* Through, thorough(ly), apart, across.

dīabē'tēs (-z) *n.* Disease (in medicine called *diabetes mellitus*) characterized by excessive discharge of glucose-containing urine, with thirst and emaciation, caused by failure of the pancreas to secrete an adequate amount of insulin and the consequent excessive accumulation of glucose in the blood; ~ *insipidus*, disease characterized by discharge of large quantities of urine, but not involving sugar metabolism, caused by disorder of pituitary gland.

dīabĕ'tĭc *adj.* Of, suffering from, diabetes. ~ *n.* Diabetic person.

dīabŏ'lĭc, dīabŏ'lĭcal *adjs.* Of, having to do with, under the influence of, the devil; devilish, inhumanly wicked. **dīabŏ'lĭcally̆** *adv.*

dīă'bolism *n.* Sorcery, witchcraft; devilry; worship of the devil.

dīă'bolō *n.* Game with a double-headed spinning-top which is thrown up and caught by means of a string attached to two sticks; the top itself. [It., = devil; formerly *devil on two sticks*]

dīă'conal *adj.* Of a deacon.

dīă'conate *n.* Office of, term of office as, deacon; deacons collectively.

dīacrĭ'tĭcal *adj.* Distinguishing, distinctive; ~ *sign, mark*, one used to indicate different sounds of a letter, as accent, diaeresis, etc.

dīăctĭ'nĭc *adj.* Transmitting actinic rays of light.

dī'adĕm *n.* Crown; jewelled or plain band or fillet worn round head as badge of royalty; wreath of leaves or flowers etc. worn round head; sovereignty; crowning distinction or glory. **dī'adĕmed** (-md) *adj.*

diaerėsis (dīēr'-) *n.* (pl. *-ses*). Sign (¨) placed over vowel indicating that it is to be pronounced separately.

Diaghilev (dyah'gĭlĕf), Sergey Pavlovich (1872–1929). Russian impresario; founder (1909) of the Russian ballet company which revived the art of ballet in W. Europe.

dī'agnōse (-z) *v.t.* Form a diagnosis of (a disease).

dīagnō'sĭs *n.* (pl. *-ses*). Identification of disease by investigation of symptoms and history; formal statement of this.

dīagnŏ'stĭc *adj.* Of, assisting, diagnosis. ~ *n.* Diagnosis; symptom. **dīagnŏ'stĭcally̆** *adv.* **dīagnŏstĭ'cian** (-shan) *n.*

dīă'gonal *adj.* Extending, as a line etc., from one angle to a non-adjacent angle of a rectilineal figure or solid, or from one corner of anything to the opposite corner; having an oblique direction; marked with diagonal lines. **dīă'gonallȳ** *adv.* **dīă'gonal** *n.* Diagonal line, part, row, etc.

dī'agrăm *n.* 1. (geom.) Figure composed of lines, illustrating definition or aiding in proof etc. 2. Illustrative figure giving the general scheme or outline of an object and its parts. 3. Graphic representation of the course or results of an action or process. **dīagrammă'tic** *adj.* **dīagrammă'ticallȳ** *adv.* **dīagră'mmatīze** *v.t.*

dī'agrăph (*or* -ahf) *n.* Instrument for drawing projections, enlarging maps, etc., mechanically, consisting of pencil governed by cords etc. and guided by pointer applied to object to be copied.

dī'al *n.* 1. Sundial. 2. Surface of clock or watch bearing graduations and figures marking hours etc.; circular plate marked with figures etc. and fitted with movable index finger; ring of figures on automatic telephone by manipulating which (exchanges and) numbers can be rung up. ~ *v.t.* Measure, indicate (as) with dial; ring up (telephone number) by means of a dial.

dī'alĕct *n.* Form of speech peculiar to a district, class, or person, subordinate variety of a language with distinguishing vocabulary, pronunciation, or idioms. **dīalĕ'ctal** *adj.* **dīalĕ'ctallȳ** *adv.* **dīalĕctŏ'logȳ** *n.*

dīalĕ'ctic *adj.* Logical; of disputation. ~ *n.* 1. (freq. pl.) Art of critical examination into truth of opinion; investigation of truth by discussion; logical disputation. 2. Criticism dealing with metaphysical contradictions and their solutions, esp., in Hegelian philosophy, the stages of thesis, antithesis, and synthesis representing the process of thought developing towards completion. 3. Dialectic philosopher. **dīalĕctĭ'cian** (-shan) *n.*

dīalĕ'ctical *adj.* 1. = DIALECTIC *adj.* 2. Of DIALECTIC *n.* (sense 2); ~ *materialism*, theory propagated by Karl Marx and Friedrich Engels, acc. to which political events are regarded as due to a conflict of social forces (the 'class struggle') produced by man's material needs, and history as a series of contradictions and their solutions (the thesis, antithesis, and synthesis of Hegelian philosophy). 3. = DIALECTAL. **dīalĕ'cticallȳ** *adv.*

dīă'llage (-jĭ) *n.* Figure of speech in which arguments, after being considered from various points of view, are all brought to bear on one point.

dī'alŏgue (-g) *n.* Conversation; literary work in form of conversation between two or more persons; conversational part of novel or play. **dīă'logist** *n.* Speaker in, writer of, dialogue.

dīă'lȳsis *n.* (chem., pl. *-sēs*). Separation of soluble crystalloid substances in mixture from colloid by diffusion through semi-permeable membrane; (med.) similar process used in purifying blood. **dī'alȳse** (-z) *v.t.* **dī'alȳser** *n.*

dīamăgnĕ'tic *adj.* (of substance, as bismuth, zinc, copper, lead, or tin) Tending to become magnetized in the presence of a magnetic field so that it lies with its long axis at right angles to the field (cf. PARAMAGNETIC). **dīa'mă'gnėtism** *n.*

diamanté (dēamah'ṅtā) *n.* Textile fabric to which sparkling effect is given by powdered glass or crystal, or (paste) brilliants.

dīamăntĭ'ferous *adj.* Diamond-yielding.

dīă'mėter *n.* 1. (geom.) Straight line passing through centre of circle or sphere and terminated at each end by its circumference or surface, or through centre of any conic section, or through middle points of system of parallel chords in curve of any order; line passing from side to side of any body through centre. 2. Transverse measurement, width, thickness; unit of measurement of lineal magnification of an object. **dīă'mėtral** *adj.* **dīă'mėtrallȳ** *adv.*

dīamĕ'trical *adj.* 1. Of, along, a diameter; diametral. 2. (of opposition, difference, etc.) Direct, complete, like that between opposite ends of diameter. **dīamĕ'trĭcallў** *adv.*

dī'amond *n.* 1. Very hard and brilliant precious stone, colourless or variously tinted, consisting of pure carbon crystallized in regular octahedrons and allied forms, the most valuable precious stone. 2. Glittering particle or point. 3. Glass-cutting tool of small diamond set in handle. 4. Diamond-shaped figure, rhomb, or square, placed with diagonals vertical and horizontal; (playing-card with) red diamond-shaped figure(s); (pl.) suit of these cards. 5. (baseball) Figure formed by the 4 bases; field. 6. (print.) Size of type ($4\frac{1}{2}$ point) between pearl and brilliant. 7. *black* ~, dark-coloured diamond; coal; *rough* ~, diamond before it is cut and polished; person of intrinsic worth but rough manner; *~-cut*, cut with facets like a diamond; *~-drill*, drill set with diamonds, for boring rocks etc.; *D~ Jubilee*, (public celebration in 1897 of) 60th anniversary of Queen Victoria's accession; ~ *knot; Affair of the D~Necklace*, plot, successfully carried out in 1783–4, of Jeanne de St. Remy de Valois to get possession from the jewellers of a diamond necklace on the pretence that Queen Marie Antoinette had consented to purchase it; ~ *wedding*, 60th anniversary of wedding. ~ *adj.* Made of, set with, diamond(s); rhomb-shaped. ~ *v.t.* Adorn with or as with diamonds.

dīamŏr'phĭne *n.* = HEROIN.

Dīă'na. (Rom. myth.) Ancient Italian moon-goddess, patroness of virginity and hunting; later regarded as identical with Artemis; hence, huntress; ~ *monkey*, W. Afr. species of white-bearded monkey (*Cercopithecus diana*).

dīă'nthus *n.* Flowering plant of genus *D~* of the order Caryophyllaceae, including pinks and carnations.

dīapā'son (-zon) *n.* 1. Compass of voice or instrument, range, scope; fixed standard of musical pitch; ~ *normal*, pitch in which the A above middle C is set at 435 vibrations per second. 2. One of the chief foundation stops in an organ (*open* ~ and *stopped* ~) extending through whole compass of the instrument.

dī'apause *n.* Period of suspended development in certain insects.

dī'aper *n.* 1. Fabric woven with small simple diamond pattern; towel etc. of this; baby's napkin. 2. Ornamental design of diamond reticulations. ~ *v.t.* Ornament surface or background of with small uniform pattern, esp. one based upon diamond reticulations; variegate, adorn with diverse colours.

dīă'phanous *adj.* Transparent.

dīaphorĕ'tĭc *adj.* & *n.* (Drug, treatment) inducing perspiration.

dī'aphragm (-frăm) *n.* 1. Muscular partition, convex towards thorax, separating thorax from abdomen in mammals, which contracts and becomes flatter when air is breathed in, thus increasing the capacity of the thorax; (zool., bot.) partition in certain shells, gasteropods, plant-tissues, etc. 2. Thin lamina or plate used as partition etc.; thin rubber or plastic contraceptive cap fitted over cervix; vibrating membrane or disc in acoustic instrument (telephone, loud-speaker; etc.); mechanism consisting of set of plates for varying effective aperture of lens of camera etc. **dīaphrăgmă'tĭc** (-frăg-) *adj.*

dī'ârchў, dў- (-k-) *n.* Government by two rulers. **dīâr'chal, dīâr'chĭc** *adjs.*

dīarrhoe'a (-rēa) *n.* Excessive looseness of bowels. **dīarrhoe'al, dīarrhoe'ic** *adjs.*

dī'arў *n.* Daily record of events etc.; book etc. prepared for this or for noting future engagements. **dī'arĭst** *n.* One who keeps a diary. **dī'arīze** *v.* Keep, enter in, a diary.

Dīă'spora *n.* Dispersion of the Jews, after the Exile, among Gentile nations; Jews so dispersed.

dī'astāse (-s) *n.* (chem.) Enzyme formed in germinating seeds and having property of converting starch into sugar.

dīă'stolė *n.* Dilatation or relaxation of heart, rhythmically alternating with systole. **dīastŏ'lĭc** *adj.*

dīather'mal, dīather'mous, -manous *adjs.* Pervious to heat-rays, freely transmitting radiant heat. **dīather'mancy̆** *n.*

dīather'mĭc *adj.* 1. Diathermal. 2. Of diathermy.

dī'athermy̆ *n.* Therapeutic use of low-voltage alternating electric currents of very high frequency to produce heat in parts of body below surface.

dīă'thėsis *n.* (pl. *-esēs*). Constitutional predisposition.

dī'atŏm *n.* Microscopic unicellular alga with silicified cell-wall, existing in great numbers in sea

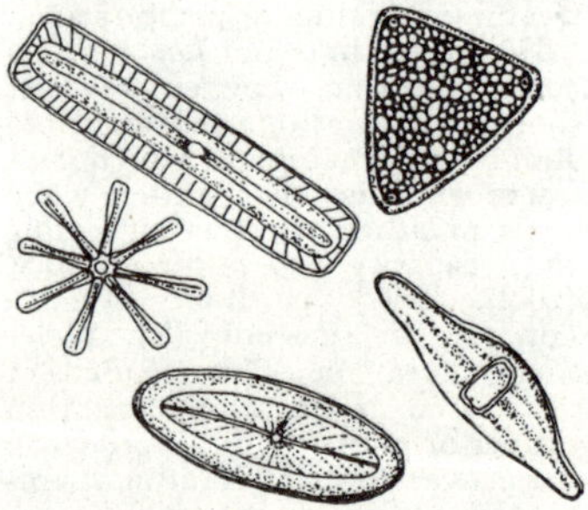

and fresh water, and often forming extensive fossil deposits.

dīatomā'ceous (-sh*us*) *adj.*

dīatŏ'mĭc *adj.* (chem.) Consisting of two atoms; containing two replaceable atoms of hydrogen.

dīă'tomīte *n.* Substance composed of siliceous skeletons of diatoms.

dīatŏ'nĭc *adj.* (mus., of scale) Proceeding by notes proper to its key without chromatic alteration; (of melody etc.) constructed from such a scale.

dī'atrībe *n.* Piece of bitter criticism, invective, denunciation. [Gk *diatribē* wearing away (of time), discourse]

dīă'zo cŏ'mpound. Organic compound, esp. one of those derived from aromatic hydrocarbons containing the characteristic group —N=N—, and forming the basis of a large group of dye-stuffs (*azo dyes*).

dībă'sĭc *adj.* ~ *acid*, one which contains two replaceable hydrogen atoms and therefore yields two series of salts.

dĭ'bber, dĭ'bble *ns.* Pointed tool for making holes in ground for planting seeds, bulbs, or young plants. **dĭ'bble** *v.* Prepare (soil) with this; plant thus; use a dibble.

dĭbs (-z) *n.pl.* (slang) Money.

dīce *n.*: see DIE[1]; (esp.) ~*-box*, box, usu. in shape of double truncated cone, from which dice are thrown in gaming. ~ *v.* 1. Gamble with dice, gamble *away*. 2. Cut into small cubes; mark or ornament with pattern of cubes or squares.

dīcĕ'phalous *adj.* Having two heads.

dī'cey *adj.* (slang) Risky, dangerous.

dīchŏ'tomy̆ (-k-) *n.* 1. Division into two; classification into two groups; something paradoxical or ambivalent. 2. (bot., zool.) Form of branching in which each successive axis divides into two. **dĭchotŏ'mĭc, dĭchŏ'tomous** *adjs.* **dĭchŏ'tomīze** *v.*

dīchrō'ĭc (-kr-) *adj.* Having two colours; esp. (of doubly refracting crystals) showing different colours when viewed in different directions, (of solutions) showing essentially different colours at different concentrations. **dī'chrōism** *n.*

dīchromă'tĭc *adj.* Having two colours; esp., of animals, having two different colours in different individuals.

dīchrō'mĭc *adj.* Of, including, (only) two colours; esp., of vision of colour-blind persons, including only two of the three primary colours.

dĭck *n.* (slang) Detective.

dĭ'ckėns[1] (-z) *n.* *the* ~, (colloq.) the deuce. [app. alliterative substitute for *devil*]

Dĭ'ckėns[2] (-z), Charles John Huffam (1812–70). English novel-

ist (pseudonym 'Boz'), some of whose work, e.g. 'Oliver Twist' and 'Bleak House', exposed social evils; creator, esp. in 'Pickwick Papers', of many humorous characters. **Dĭckĕ'nsĭan** *adj.*

dĭ'cker *n.* 1. Ten, half a score, as unit of exchange esp. in hides or skins. 2. (U.S.) Barter, petty bargaining. ~ *v.i.* (U.S.) Trade by barter; truck; haggle; vacillate.

dĭ'ckȳ¹, -ey *n.* 1. Small bird (also *~-bird*). 2. False shirt-front; (U.S.) shirt collar. 3. Seat in carriage for driver; seat at back of carriage or coach for servants, guard, etc.; extra seat at back of two-seater motor-car which can be closed down when not in use.

dĭ'ckȳ² *adj.* Shaky, rickety; unsound.

dī'clĭnous *adj.* (bot., of plant) Having stamens and pistils on separate flowers, (of flower) unisexual.

dīcŏtȳlē'don *n.* Flowering plant with two cotyledons. **dīcŏtȳlē'donous** *adj.*

dĭ'ctaphōne *n.* Machine which records words spoken into it and subsequently reproduces them (e.g. for transcription). [trade-name]

dĭctā'te *v.* 1. Say or read aloud (matter to be written down). 2. Prescribe, lay down authoritatively (terms, thing to be done); lay down the law, give orders. **dĭctā'tion** *n.* **dĭ'ctāte** *n.* Authoritative direction (usu. of reason, conscience, nature, etc.).

dĭctā'tor *n.* 1. Absolute ruler, usu. temporary or irregular, of a State; person with absolute authority in any sphere. 2. One who dictates for transcription. **dĭctā'torship** *n.* Rule of dictator.

dĭctatōr'ĭal *adj.* Of a dictator; imperious, overbearing. **dĭctatōr'ĭallȳ** *adv.*

dĭ'ction *n.* 1. Choice of words and phrases, verbal style, in speech or writing. 2. Manner of speaking, elocution; singer's enunciation of words.

dĭ'ctionarȳ *n.* Book dealing, usu. in alphabetical order, with the individual words of a language or some specified subject etc., setting forth their spelling, pronunciation, signification, history, etymology, equivalents in another language, etc., or some of these; also, book of reference on any subject with items arranged in alphabetical order.

dĭ'ctogrăph (*or* -ahf) *n.* Telephonic instrument with sound-magnifying device by which it is possible to overhear what is said in a room where the transmitter is stationed or concealed. [trade-name]

dĭ'ctum *n.* (pl. *-ums, -a*). 1. Formal saying, pronouncement; (law) expression of judge's opinion on matter of law, not being the formal resolution or determination of a court. 2. Current saying, saw.

did: see DO¹.

dĭdă'ctĭc *adj.* Meant to instruct; (of persons) too much inclined to instruct, tending to lay down the law. **dĭdă'ctĭcallȳ** *adv.* **dĭdă'ctĭcism** *n.*

dĭ'dăpper *n.* Small diving-bird, dabchick.

dĭ'ddle *v.t.* (slang) Cheat, swindle. **dĭ'ddler** *n.*

Diderot (dēderō), Denis (1713–84). French philosopher, dramatist, and critic; one of the founders of the 'Encyclopédie'; author of sentimental comedies.

dĭdgerĭdōō′ *n.* Australian aboriginal wind instrument of tubular shape.

Dī′dō. Legendary daughter of a Tyrian king; fled to Africa after the death of her husband Sycheaus and is reputed to have founded the city of Carthage. Virgil makes her a contemporary of Aeneas with whom she falls in love; when, by order of the gods, Aeneas forsakes her, she kills herself.

dĭdȳ′mium *n.* Rare metal, formerly supposed to be an element and given symbol Di and subsequently separated into the elements neodymium and praseodymium. [Gk *didumos* twin, from its being always found with lanthanum]

dīe[1] *n.* 1. (pl. *dīce*, freq. used as sing.) Small cube with faces marked with 1–6 spots, thrown from box or hand in games of chance; (pl.) game played with these; *the ~ is cast*, the irrevocable decision has been made. 2. Small cubical piece of anything. 3. (pl. *dies*) Part of pedestal between base and cornice. 4. Engraved stamp for impressing design etc. upon softer material, as in coining etc.; *~ casting*, casting obtained from metal mould(s); process of making such castings; *~-sinker*, engraver of dies. 5. (mech.) Cutting device.

dīe[2] *v.i.* (pres. part. *dying*). 1. Cease to live, expire; *~ the death*, (archaic) be put to death. 2. Suffer spiritual death. 3. Suffer as in death; *be dying for, to*, desire keenly or excessively; *~ of* or *with laughing*, be exhausted by laughing. 4. Lose vital force, decay; come to an end, cease to exist; (of fire etc.) go out; (also *~ out*) disappear, be forgotten; (also *~ away*) fade away. 5. *~-away* (*adj.*) languishing; *~-hard*, one that dies hard, esp. (i) one of the 57th Regiment of Foot (from their stubborn resistance at Albuera); (ii) one of those who were prepared to 'die in the last ditch' in opposition to the Home Rule Bill (1912); hence, stubbornly conservative person.

dīēlĕ′ctrĭc *adj.* & *n.* Insulating, non-conducting (medium or substance).

die′sel (-z-) *n.* (also *~ engine*) Internal combustion engine in which air is first drawn into the cylinder and compressed so highly that the heat generated is sufficient to ignite the oil subsequently injected; vehicle driven by this; *~-electric*, of a combination of a diesel engine driving an electric generator; *~ oil*, petroleum fraction used as fuel in diesel engines, usu. that part distilling below 300°. **die′selīze** *v.t.* Equip with diesel engine or with diesel-electric locomotives. [f. Rudolf *Diesel* (1858–1913), German engineer]

Dies irae (dē′ĕz ērʹī). Latin hymn beginning thus (= 'Day of wrath') on Last Judgement ascribed to Thomas of Celano (*c* 1250), sung as part of the Mass for the dead.

dī′ēs nŏn (-z). (short for *dies non juridicus*) Day on which no legal business is transacted, or which is not reckoned in counting days for some particular purpose. [L]

dī′ėt[1] *n.* Conference, congress, on national or international business; meeting of estates of the realm or confederation (esp. as English name for foreign parliamentary assemblies); *D~ of Worms*, that convened in 1521 at Worms, Germany, at which Luther was condemned as a heretic.

dī′ėt[2] *n.* Way of feeding; prescribed course of food, regimen; one's habitual food. *~ v.* Keep to special diet.

dī′ėtarȳ *n.* Course of diet; allowance or character of food in hospital, prison, etc. *~ adj.* Of diet or a dietary.

dīėtĕ′tĭc *adj.* Of diet, of the regulation of kind and quantity of food, esp. as branch of medical science. **dīėtĕ′tĭcs** *n.pl.* Part of medicine dealing with regulation of diet.

dīėtĭ′tian, dīėtĭ′cian (-sh*a*n) *n.* Person versed in dietetics.

dĭ′ffer *v.i.* Be unlike, be distinguishable *from*; be at variance, disagree (*with, from*).

dĭ'fference *n.* 1. Being different, dissimilarity, non-identity; point in which things differ; quantity by which amounts differ, remainder after subtraction; *split the* ~, come to compromise. 2. Disagreement in opinion, dispute, quarrel. 3. Characteristic mark distinguishing individual or species; esp. (her.) alteration or addition to coat of arms to distinguish junior member or branch of family; (logic) differentia. ~ *v.t.* Distinguish, serve as distinguishing mark of; make difference in (coat of arms).

dĭ'fferent *adj.* Differing; distinct; out of the ordinary. **dĭ'fferentlў** *adv.*

dĭfferĕ'ntia (-shi*a*) *n.* (logic) Attribute by which a species is distinguished from all other species of same genus; distinguishing characteristic.

dĭfferĕ'ntial (-sh*a*l) *adj.* 1. Of, exhibiting, depending on, a difference; differing according to circumstances; constituting a specific difference, relating to specific differences. 2. (math.) Relating to infinitesimal differences. 3. Relating to, depending on, exhibiting, difference of two (or more) motions, pressures, or other measurable physical quantities. 4. ~ *calculus*, (math.) method of calculation devised by Leibniz (1677), treating of infinitesimal differences between consecutive values of continuously varying quantities; ~ *gear*, arrangement of gears connecting two shafts or axles in the same line and enabling one shaft to revolve faster than the other when required (e.g. in a motor-car, when turning a corner; ~ *wage*, higher wage paid in respect of skill; ~ *winding*, method of winding two insulated wires side by side in electric coil, through which currents pass in opposite directions. **dĭfferĕ'ntiallў** *adv.* **dĭfferĕ'ntial** *n.* 1. (math.) Each of the infinitesimal differences of which the differential calculus treats. 2. Differential gear. 3. Differential wage.

dĭfferĕ'ntiāte (-shĭ-) *v.* 1. Constitute difference between; make or become different in process of growth or development, esp. by modification for special function or purpose. 2. Discriminate between, distinguish. **dĭfferĕntiā'tion** *n.*

dĭ'fficult *adj.* Hard to do, troublesome; obscure, perplexing; unaccommodating, stubborn.

dĭ'fficultў *n.* Being difficult to accomplish, understand, etc.; difficult thing or question; (usu. pl.) embarrassment of affairs, pecuniary trouble; *make difficulties*, show reluctance, be unaccommodating.

dĭ'ffidence *n.* Self-distrust, excessive modesty, shyness. **dĭ'ffident** *adj.* **dĭ'ffidentlў** *adv.*

dĭ'ffluence (-lōō-) *n.* 1. Flowing apart, dispersion by flowing. 2. Deliquescence. **dĭ'ffluent** *adj.*

dĭffră'ct *v.t.* (optics) Deflect and break up (beam of light) at edge of opaque body or through narrow aperture or slit. **dĭffră'ction** *n.* Breaking up thus of beam of monochromatic light into series of light and dark spaces or bands, or of white or composite light into series of coloured spectra; ~ *grating*, series of close equidistant parallel lines, esp. lines ruled on a polished surface, used for producing spectra by diffraction. **dĭffră'ctive** *adj.* **dĭffră'ctivelў** *adv.*

dĭffū'se *adj.* Spread out, not concentrated; not concise, wordy. **dĭffū'selў** *adv.* **dĭffū'senėss** *n.* **dĭffū'se** (-z) *v.* Disperse or be dispersed from a centre; spread widely, shed abroad, disseminate; (of gases or liquids) intermingle by diffusion. **dĭffū'sion** *n.* **dĭffū'sĭve** *adj.* **dĭffū'sĭvelў** *adv.* **dĭffū'sĭvenėss** *n.*

dĭg *v.* (past t. & past part. *dŭg*). Turn up (ground) with spade or other tool, or with snout or claws; break up and turn over (soil); excavate; extract by excavation; thrust or plunge (something) *in, into*, stab, prod; give (person) sharp nudge (*in ribs* etc.); (slang, orig. U.S.) understand, appreciate, experience; ~ *in*, (esp.) excavate defensive trench or pit; ~ *out*, get, find, make, by digging, discover by research; ~ *up*, get out of ground etc. by digging; excavate; break up and loosen soil of. ~ *n.* 1. Piece of digging; (colloq.) archaeological excavation. 2. Thrust, poke; (fig.) gibe. 3. (pl., colloq.) Lodgings.

dīgă'mma *n.* 6th letter of original Greek alphabet (F, ϝ, prob. pronounced like English *w*), later disused (the sound having been lost), but important in philology.

dĭ'gamȳ *n.* Second marriage, remarriage after death of first spouse. **dĭ'gamĭst** *n.* **dĭ'gamous** *adj.*

dīgă'strĭc *adj.* (anat., of muscle) Having two bellies with intervening tendon; of the digastric muscle of the neck. ~ *n.* Muscle of neck used during swallowing.

dī'gĕst *n.* 1. Methodical compendium or summary, esp. of body of laws; *the D~*, the body of Roman laws compiled from the earlier jurists by order of Justinian. 2. Periodical containing condensed versions of articles etc.

dĭgĕ'st *v.* 1. Reduce into systematic (and usu. condensed) form, classify; arrange methodically in mind, ponder over. 2. Reduce (food) in stomach and intestines to assimilable form; (of food) undergo digestion. 3. Endure, stomach (insult etc.). 4. Get mental nourishment from. **dĭgĕstĭbĭ'lĭtȳ** *n.* **dĭgĕ'stĭble** *adj.*

dĭgĕ'stion (-schon) *n.* Digesting of physical or mental food; power of digesting; extraction of soluble constituents of substance by long stewing.

dĭgĕ'stĭve *adj.* Of, promoting, digestion; ~ *biscuit*, type of wholemeal biscuit. ~ *n.* Substance promoting digestion. **dĭgĕ'stĭvelȳ** *adv.*

dĭ'gger *n.* (esp.) 1. One who digs or searches for gold in gold-fields; (colloq.) Australian. 2. ~ *wasp*, wasp of family Sphecidae, most of which build their nests in burrows.

dĭ'gging *n.* (esp.) 1. (pl.) Mine; gold-field. 2. (pl., colloq.) Lodgings, quarters.

dight (dīt) *adj.* (archaic) Clad, adorned.

dĭ'gĭt *n.* 1. (zool., anat., or joc.) Finger or toe. 2. Each numeral below ten (orig. counted on fingers); each Arabic numeral from 0 to 9. 3. (astron.) 12th part of diameter of sun or moon (in expressing magnitude of eclipse). **dĭ'gĭtal** *adj.* Using digits; ~ *computer*: see COMPUTER.

dĭgĭtā'lĭn *n.* (pharm.) Poisonous substance extracted from foxglove leaves.

dĭgĭtā'lĭs *n.* 1. Plant of genus *D~* including foxglove, of the

order Scrophulariaceae. 2. Drug prepared from dried leaves of foxglove, used as heart stimulant, causing heart to beat more strongly and regularly, thus increasing flow of blood and resting heart muscles. [mod. L transl. of Ger. *Fingerhut* thimble, foxglove]

dĭ'gĭtate, -ātėd *adjs.* (zool., bot.) With separate fingers or toes; with deep radiating divisions. **dĭgĭtā'tion** *n.*

dĭ'gĭtigrāde *adj.* & *n.* (zool.) (Animal) walking on toes, not touching ground with heel.

dĭ'gnĭfȳ *v.t.* Make worthy or illustrious; confer dignity upon; make stately; give high-sounding name or title to. **dĭ'gnĭfied** (-īd) *adj.* Stately, marked by dignity, majestic.

dĭ'gnĭtarȳ *n.* Person holding high (esp. ecclesiastical) rank or office.

dĭ'gnĭtȳ *n.* 1. Worth, nobleness, excellence; high estate, position, or estimation; high or honourable office, rank, or title. 2. Proper stateliness, elevation of aspect, manner, or style; gravity.

dĭ'grăph (*or* -ahf) *n.* Group of two letters expressing one sound, as *sh.*

dĭgrĕ'ss *v.i.* Diverge from the track, stray; depart from main subject temporarily in speech or writing. **dĭgrĕ'ssion** *n.* **dĭgrĕ'ssive** *adj.*

dīhē'dral *adj.* Having two plane faces; ~ *angle*, angle formed by two intersecting planes or surfaces. ~ *n.* Dihedral angle; upward (*positive* ~) or downward (*negative* ~, also called *anhedral*) inclination of aircraft wing or aerofoil towards the tip.

dīhȳ'drĭc *adj.* Having two hydroxyl groups.

dīke, dȳke *n.* 1. Ditch; any water-course or channel. 2. Low wall, esp. of turf; embankment, long ridge, dam, against flooding by sea, rivers, etc.; raised causeway; ~*-reeve*, (hist.) officer taking charge of drains, sluices and sea-banks of English fen or marshland. 3. (geol.) Small intrusion usu. of igneous rock cutting across the bedding of older rocks. ~ *v.t.* Provide, defend, with dike(s).

dĭlă'pĭdāte *v.* Bring, come, into disrepair or decay.

dĭlăpĭdā'tion *n.* Bringing or falling into, being in, disrepair or decay; impairment of ecclesiastical property belonging to an incumbency, sums charged against incumbent to meet this.

dīlā'te *v.* Make or become wider or larger; expand, widen, enlarge; expatiate, speak or write at large. **dīlā'tion, dīlatā'tion** *ns.*

dīlā'tor *n.* (anat.) Muscle or nerve which dilates or widens a part; (surg.) instrument for dilating passage etc.

dĭ'latorȳ *adj.* Tending to, designed to cause, given to, delay. **dĭ'latorĭlȳ** *adv.* **dĭ'latorĭnėss** *n.*

dĭlĕ'mma *n.* Argument forcing opponent to choose one of two alternatives (the *horns* of the dilemma), both unfavourable to him; position involving choice between two evils.

dĭlėttă'ntė *n.* (pl. *-ti* pr. -tē). Lover of the fine arts; (now usu.) one who is interested in an art or science merely as a pastime and without serious study. ~ *adj.* Of, like, a dilettante. **dĭlėttă'ntĭsm** *n.*

dĭ'lĭgence[1] (*or* dĭlĭzhahṅs) *n.* (hist.) Public stage-coach (esp. in France).

dĭ'lĭgence[2] *n.* Persistent effort or work; industrious character.

dĭ'lĭgent *adj.* Hard-working, steady in application, industrious; attentive to duties. **dĭ'lĭgentlȳ** *adv.*

dĭll *n.* Umbelliferous annual yellow-flowered herb, *Anethum graveolens*, with carminative fruits; ~*-pickle*, pickle flavoured with dill-seeds.

dĭ'llȳ-dă'llȳ *v.i.* (colloq.) Vacillate; loiter.

dĭ'lūent *adj.* Diluting, esp. making thin the fluids of the body. ~ *n.* Solvent, diluting agent; substance increasing proportion of water in body fluids.

dĭlū'te (*or* -ōōt) *v.t.* Reduce strength of (fluid) by adding water or other solvent; water down. ~ (*or* dī'-) *adj.* Weakened by addition of water; watery, watered down.

dĭlū'tion (*or* -ōō-) *n.* 1. Act of diluting; state of being diluted; diluted substance. 2. Introduction of unskilled labour into a body of skilled workmen.

dĭlū'vial (*or* -ōō-) *adj.* 1. Of a flood, esp. of that recorded in Genesis. 2. (geol.) Explaining geological phenomena by hypothesis of general deluge or periods of catastrophic water-action. **dĭlū'vĭalĭst** *n.*

dĭm *adj.* Deficient in brightness or clearness; obscure; indistinct; (of person) mentally dull. **dĭ'mlȳ** *adv.* **dĭ'mnėss** *n.* **dĭm** *v.* Become, make, dim; becloud; make dim by comparison, outshine; ~*-out*, reduced artificial lighting in streets etc. during war-time (as dist. from *blackout*).

dim. *abbrev.* *Diminuendo.*

dim. *abbrev.* Diminutive(ly).

dīme *n.* U.S. silver coin of value of $\frac{1}{10}$ dollar, or 10 cents.

dĭmĕ'nsion *n.* 1. Measurable extent of any kind; (usu. pl.) measurement, measure, size. 2. Mode of linear measurement, magnitude, or extension, in a particular direction; *the three ~s*, length, breadth, and thickness (or depth); *fourth ~*, imaginary direction in which matter is supposed to extend in addition to the three dimensions of Euclidean geometry. 3. (alg.) Each of the (unknown or variable) qualities contained in a product as factors of it. **dĭmĕ'nsional** *adj.*

dĭ'mėter *n.* Verse of two measures (a measure having one foot in some metres and two in others).

dĭmĭ'dĭate *adj.* Halved, split in two. **dĭmĭdĭā'tion** *n.* (esp., her.,).

dĭmĭ'nĭsh *v.* Make, cause to appear, grow, less or smaller; lessen in importance, estimation, or power; *law of diminishing returns*, fact that expenditure of labour or capital beyond a certain point does not produce proportionate return or that taxation above a certain level fails to produce the desired yield. **dĭmĭ'nĭshed** (-sht) *adj.* (esp., mus., of an interval) Less by a semitone.

dĭmĭnūĕ'ndō *adv.*, *n.* (pl. *-os*), & *adj.* (mus.) (Passage played) with gradually decreasing volume, indicated thus >.

dĭmĭnū'tion *n.* Diminishing, reduction; (mus.) repetition of a passage in shorter notes than those previously used.

dĭmĭ'nūtĭve *adj.* 1. Minute, tiny. 2. (gram.) Denoting something little, expressing diminution (usu. applied to derivatives or affixes expressing something small of the kind denoted by primitive word). **dĭmĭ'nūtĭvelȳ** *adv.* **dĭmĭ'nūtĭvenėss** *n.* **dĭmĭ'nūtĭve** *n.* Diminutive word or term.

dĭ'mĭtȳ *n.* Cotton fabric woven with raised stripes, freq. printed, and used for hangings etc.

dīmŏr'phĭc *adj.* (bot., zool.) Occurring in two distinct forms in same species, individual, etc.; (chem., min.) occurring in two distinct crystalline forms not derivable from one another. **dīmŏr'phism** *n.* **dīmŏr'phous** *adj.*

dĭ'mple *n.* Small hollow or dent in body, esp. in cheek or chin; slight surface depression or indentation resembling this. ~ *v.* Mark with dimples, break into dimples or ripples.

dĭn *n.* Continued confused loud noise, stunning or distracting. ~ *v.* Make din; utter continuously so as to deafen or weary; ~ *into*, make (person) understand by continuous repetition.

dĭ'nâr (dē-; *or* -âr') *n.* 1. Principal monetary unit of various countries in Middle East and N. Africa. 2. $\frac{1}{100}$ of an Iranian rial.

dīne *v.* Take dinner; entertain at dinner; (of room etc.) provide dining accommodation for (specified number); *dining car*, railway coach in which meals are served on a journey; *dining room*, room in which principal meals are taken.

dī'ner *n.* 1. One who dines; ~-*out*, one who often dines from home, esp. one whose social qualities make him a welcome guest. 2. (orig. U.S.) Dining car.

dīnĕ'tte *n.* (orig. U.S.) Small room or part of room set aside for meals.

dĭ'ngbăt *n.* (U.S. colloq.) Anything used as or suitable for missile; thingumajig.

dĭng-dŏng *adv.* & *n.* (With) sound of bell, or alternate strokes of two bells. ~ *adj.* Of or like bells or jingling rhyme; downright, desperate; ~ *race*, neck-and-neck race.

dĭ'nghy (-ngĭ *or* -nggĭ) *n.* Small rowing-boat in ship; small

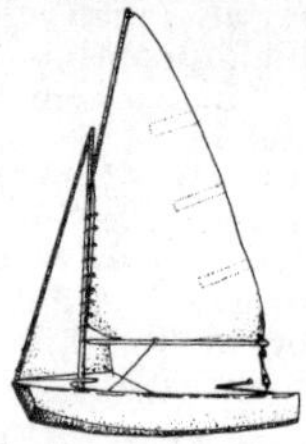

pleasure-boat (esp. *sailing-~*); inflatable rubber boat esp. one carried on aircraft for use in emergency. [Hind. *ḍiṅgī* small boat]

dĭ'ngle (-nggl) *n.* Deep dell or hollow, usu. shaded with trees.

dĭ'ngō (-nggō) *n.* Wild or semi-domesticated dog of Australia, *Canis dingo*, usu. reddish-brown and with bushy tail. [Native name]

dĭ'ngy (-jĭ) *adj.* Dull-coloured, grimy, dirty-looking. **dĭ'ngily** *adv.* **dĭ'nginėss** *n.*

dĭ'nkȳ *adj.* (colloq.) Pretty, neat, of engaging appearance.

dĭ'nner *n.* Chief meal of day, eaten at midday or in the evening; formal esp. public meal with distinct courses; ~ *jacket*, short black coat for semi-formal evening wear; ~-*pail*, (U.S.) vessel in which workman carries his dinner; ~-*wagon*, wheeled trolley with decks for holding dishes. **dĭ'nnerlėss** *adj.*

dī'nosaur *n.* Any of the extinct saurian reptiles (orders Saurischia and Ornithischia) of the Mesozoic

DINOSAURS

era, some of which were of gigantic size. [Gk *deinos* terrible, *sauros* lizard]

dī'nothēre *n.* Quadruped of extinct genus *Dinotherium*, resembling the elephant and belonging to the same order (Proboscidea). [Gk *deinos* terrible, *thērion* wild beast]

dĭnt *n.* 1. *by* ~ *of*, by force of, through the persistence or vigour of. 2. Mark made by blow or pressure, dent. ~ *v.t.* Make dint or dints in.

dīŏ'cėsan (-zan) *adj.* Of a diocese. ~ *n.* Bishop of diocese; one of the clergy or people of diocese.

dī'ocese (-sĭs) *n.* District under pastoral care of a bishop.

Dīŏclē'tian (-shan) (245–313). Caius Aurelius Valerius Diocletianus, who became Roman emperor in 284, and abdicated in 305; during his reign the Christians were severely persecuted

dī'ōde *n.* Thermionic valve having two electrodes.

dīoe'cious (-ēshus) *adj.* 1. (bot.) Having the unisexual male and female flowers on separate plants. 2. (zool.) Having the two sexes in separate individuals.

Dīŏ'gėnēs (-z) (*c* 400–*c* 325 B.C.). Greek Cynic philosopher, who practised at Athens the greatest austerity.

Dīonȳ'sĭus. 1. (also ~ *the Areopagite*; 1st *c.* A.D.) an Athenian converted to Christianity by St. Paul (Acts 17: 34). 2. (also *Pseudo* ~, ~ *the Pseudo-Areopagite*; *c* 500) Name given to the author of a group of mystical writings on theology which were at first attributed to Dionysius of Athens.

Dīonȳ'sĭus Exĭ'gūus (ĕ-) (6th c.). Scythian monk who lived at Rome; he devised the system still used of reckoning the Christian era, wrongly accepting 753 A.U.C. as the year of the Incarnation (now usu. supposed to have taken place 4 years earlier).

Dīonȳ'sus. (Gk myth.) Son of Zeus and Semele; god of the fertility of nature and of wine, who inspires to music and poetry; identified by the Romans with Bacchus. **Dīonȳ'sĭan** *adj.*

Dīophă'ntus (3rd c.). Mathematician of Alexandria, credited with a method of solving problems involving indeterminate equations. **Dīophă'ntīne** *adj.* ~ *analysis,* (math.) indeterminate analysis in the theory of numbers.

dīŏ'ptre, -ter *n.* Unit for expressing the power of a lens, equal to the reciprocal of its focal length in metres.

dīŏ'ptric *adj.* Serving as medium for sight, assisting sight by refraction; of refraction, refractive; of dioptrics. **dīŏ'ptrically** *adv.*

dīŏ'ptrics *n.* Part of optics dealing with refraction (cf. CATOPTRICS).

dīora'ma (-ah-) *n.* 1. Spectacular painting (usu. viewed through an aperture with sides continued towards picture) in which, by changes in colour and direction of light thrown on or through it, atmospheric effects of various kinds are produced. 2. Small-scale representation of scene with objects etc. in front of painted background, viewed through aperture at the front; hence, small-scale model. **dīoră'mic** *adj.*

Dīoscūr'ī (*or* -ŏ's-). (Gk myth.) Twin sons of Zeus, CASTOR and Pollux.

dīŏ'xīde *n.* (chem.) Oxide of an element in which two atoms of oxygen are united to one of the element.

dĭp *v.* 1. Put or let down temporarily or partially into liquid or the like; dye thus; make (candle) by dipping wick in melted tallow; wash (sheep) in vermin-killing liquid. 2. Obtain or take *up* by dipping. 3. Lower (flag etc.) for an instant; lower (beams of headlights of vehicle). 4. Go under water and emerge quickly. 5. Put hand, ladle, etc., *into* to take something out. 6. Sink or drop down through small space, or below particular level, as if dipping into water; have downward inclination, be inclined to horizon (esp. of magnetic needle). 7. Make investigations; look cursorily or skippingly *into*. ~ *n.* 1. Dipping; quantity dipped up; bathe in sea etc.; amount of submergence. 2. (astron. etc.) Apparent depression of horizon due to observer's elevation; MAGNETIC inclination; downward slope of surface, esp. of stratum or vein ~ *circle,* instrument for measuring magnetic dip. 3. Hollow depression to which surrounding high ground dips or sinks 4. Candle made by dipping wick into melted tallow. 5. SHEEP-dip. 6. Creamy mixture for scooping with biscuits etc. 7. *di'pstick,* rod for measuring depth of liquid; *di'pswitch,* switch that dips beams of headlights.

Dip. *abbrev.* Diploma.

dĭphthēr'ia (*or* -pth-) *n.* Acute, highly infectious disease characterized by inflammation of a mucous surface (usu. that of the throat), and by an exudation forming a firm pellicle or false membrane. **dĭphthĕ'rĭc, dĭphtherĭ'tĭc** *adjs.*

dĭ'phthŏng (*or* -pth-) *n.* 1. Union of two vowels pronounced as one syllable. 2. = DIGRAPH. 3. (pop.) Ligature, as æ. **dĭphthŏ'ngal** (-ngg-) *adj.*

dĭ'phthŏngīze (-ngg-; *or* -pth-) *v.t.* Develop diphthong from single vowel. **dĭphthŏngīzā'tion** *n.*

dĭplo- *prefix.* Double.

dĭplocŏ'ccus *n.* (pl. -ī). Micro-organism of the type which tends to form pairs.

dĭplŏ'docus *n.* Giant herbivorous dinosaur of genus *D*~, remains of which have been found in Colorado and Wyoming. [Gk *diplo-* double, *dokos* beam, from its double-yoked cervical vertebrae].

dĭ'ploid *adj.* & *n.* (biol.) (Organism, cell, nucleus) with chromosomes in homologous pairs.

dĭplō'ma *n.* Document granted by competent authority conferring honour, privilege, or licence (as, to teach, practise medicine etc.). [Gk, = 'folded paper', 'letter of recommendation']

dĭplō'macy̆ *n.* Management of international relations by negotiation; skill in conduct of international intercourse; adroitness, skill, in dealing with others.

dĭ'plomăt *n.* One officially engaged in diplomacy; adroit negotiator.

dĭplomă'tĭc *adj.* 1. Of official or original documents, charters, etc.; textual; ~ *copy, edition,* exact reproduction of original. 2. Of the management of international relations; ~ *corps,* group of diplomats accredited to a court or seat of government. 3. Skilled in diplomacy; adroit in negotiations or intercourse of any kind. **dĭplomă'tĭcallў** *adv.* **diplomă'tĭc** *n.* (also pl.) Palaeographic examination of official or original documents.

dĭplō'matĭst *n.* Diplomat.

dĭplō'matīze *v.i.* Act as diplomat; use diplomatic arts.

dĭ'podў *n.* (pros.) Double foot.

dī'pōle *n.* (phys., chem.) Object oppositely charged at two points or poles; molecule in which centre of action of the positive portions (protons) does not coincide with that of the negative portions (electrons). **dīpō'lar** *adj.* Having two poles, as a magnet.

dĭ'pper *n.* (esp.) 1. Any of various birds which dip or dive in water; water ouzel, small bird (*Cinclus cinclus*) related to thrushes

but with habit of diving and walking in swift streams. 2. (chiefly U.S.) Utensil for dipping up water, esp. long-handled ladle. 3. (U.S.) (*Great, Big*) *D~*, constellation called in England the Plough or Charles's Wain; *Little D~*, similar group of seven stars in Ursa Minor. 4. *big ~*, switchback at place of amusement; ~ *switch*, dipswitch.

dĭ'pping-needle *n.* Magnetic needle mounted so as to move in vertical plane about its centre of gravity, and indicating by its dip direction of earth's magnetism.

dĭ'ppў *adj.* (slang) Mad, crazy.

dĭpsomā'nia *n.* Morbid craving for alcohol. **dĭpsomā'niăc** *adj.* & *n.*

dĭ'pteral *adj.* (of temple) With double peristyle.

dĭ'pteran *adj.* & *n.* (Two-winged fly) of the order Diptera.

dĭ'pterous *adj.* (entom.) Two-winged; (bot.) having two wing-like appendages or processes, as some seeds.

dĭ'ptўch (-k) *n.* 1. Ancient hinged two-leaved writing tablet with inner sides waxed. 2. Painting,

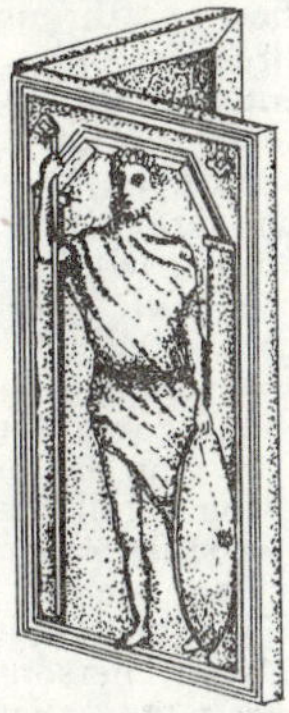

esp. altarpiece, on two panels hinged together.

Dĭră'c, Paul Adrien Maurice (1902–). English physicist; Nobel Prize for physics 1933.

dīre *adj.* Dreadful, calamitous. **dīr'elў** *adv.*

dĭrĕ'ct *v.* 1. Address (letter etc. *to* person or place); utter, write, *to* or to be conveyed *to*. 2. Control; govern the movements of. 3. Turn straight *to* something; tell (person) the way *to*. 4. (of adviser or principle) Guide. 5. Order (person) *to* do, (thing) *to be* done; give orders; be director of (film etc.). 6. Assign (workers) to particular industry or employment. ~ *adj.* 1. Straight, not devious or crooked; (of light etc.) coming straight from the source, without reflection, refraction, etc.; moving, proceeding, situated, at right angles to given surface etc.; straightforward, uninterrupted; (of succession) in an unbroken line from father to son. 2. Going straight to the point, unambiguous, straightforward; upright, downright. 3. Immediate, without intermediation; (of speech etc.) in form in which it was uttered, not reported in third person. 4. ~ *action*, action taking effect without intermediate instrumentality; esp., exertion of pressure on community by strikes, sabotage, demonstrations, etc., rather than through parliamentary representatives; ~ *current*, (abbrev. D.C., d.c.) electric current flowing through circuit in one direction only; ~ *grant*, governmental grant paid to a school directly, not through a local education authority; ~ *hit*, one right on the target (esp. of bombing); ~ *labour*, labour performed by employees of local authority etc., not contracted out; ~ *method*, method of teaching a foreign language through conversation, reading, etc., in the language itself without using pupil's native language; ~ *opposite*, exact opposite; ~ *speech*: see sense 3 above; ~ *tax*(*ation*), tax(ation) levied immediately on persons, as dist. from *indirect tax*(*ation*), levied on commodities and included in their purchase price. **dīrĕ'ctnėss** *n.* **dīrĕ'ct** *adv.* By direct route; without intermediaries.

dīrĕ'ction *n.* 1. Directing; esp., management, administration; directorate; ~ *of labour*: see DIRECT *v.* 6. 2. Instruction how to proceed or act, or how to find some person etc.; address, addressing, of letters etc. 3. Course pursued by moving body; point to or from which person or thing moves or looks; scope, sphere, subject; ~ *finder*, radio receiving apparatus so constructed as to indicate direction from which signals are coming; ~ *indicator*, device on motor vehicle whereby driver indicates his proposed course.

dīrĕ'ctional *adj.* (esp., radio) Sending signals in one direction only; detecting, recording, direction from which signals are received.

dīrĕ'ctive *adj.* Giving guidance. ~ *n.* Statement setting forth policy etc. for guidance of others, esp. subordinates.

dīrĕ'ctlȳ *adv.* In a direct manner; at once, without delay. ~ *conj.* As soon as.

Dīrĕ'ctoire (-twâr). Executive body in France during part of the revolutionary period (Oct. 1795–Nov. 1799), consisting of five members called directors. ~ *adj.* Of, imitating, the dress, furniture, etc., of this period in France, characterized by extravagance of design and imitation of Greek and Roman styles; *d~ knickers*, women's knickers with elastic at waist and legs.

dīrĕ'ctor *n.* (esp.) 1. (fem. *dire'ctrėss*) Superintendent, manager, esp. member of managing-board of commercial company, or person responsible for supervising the making of a film. 2. (Fr. hist.) Member of DIRECTOIRE. 3. (eccles.) Priest acting as spiritual adviser to a particular person or society. **dīrĕctôr'ial** *adj.*

dīrĕ'ctorate *n.* Office of director; board of directors.

dīrĕ'ctorȳ *n.* 1. Book of rules, esp. for order of public or private worship. 2. Book containing lists of inhabitants of districts, telephone subscribers, members of professions, etc., with various details. 3. (Fr. hist.) DIRECTOIRE. 4. (U.S.) Directorate, board of directors.

dīrĕ'ctrĭx *n.* 1. Directress. 2. (geom.) Fixed line used in describing curve or surface, esp. straight line the distance of which from any point on a conic section has constant ratio to distance of same point from focus.

dīr'eful (-īrf-) *adj.* Dreadful, terrible. **dīr'efullȳ** *adv.* **dīr'efulnėss** *n.*

dīrge *n.* 1. (obs.) Traditional name (orig. *dirige*) for the Office of the Dead. 2. Song of mourning or lament for the dead; funeral song. [orig. *dirige*, first word of L antiphon *Dirige, Domine, Deus meus, in conspectu tuo viam meam*, 'Direct, O Lord, my God, my way in thy sight', taken from Ps. 5: 8]

dīrhă'm *n.* 1. Principal monetary unit of Morocco, = 100 francs. 2. $\frac{1}{100}$ of a Qatar riyal.

dĭ'rĭgible *adj.* Capable of being steered or guided. ~ *n.* Dirigible balloon or airship.

dĭ'riment *adj.* Nullifying; ~ *impediment*, one rendering marriage null and void from the beginning.

dirk *n.* Kind of dagger, esp. that worn by a Scottish Highlander. ~ *v.t.* Stab with dirk.

dir'ndl *n.* Dress with tight bodice and full skirt; (also ~ *skirt*) full skirt with tight waistband.

dirt *n.* 1. Unclean matter such as soils things by adhering to them; mud; anything worthless or unclean. 2. Earth, soil; material from which metallic ore etc. is separated, esp. alluvial deposit from which gold is washed. 3. Foul talk or action. 4. *eat* ~, submit to degrading treatment; *throw*, *fling*, etc., ~, be scurrilously abusive; ~*-cheap*, as cheap as dirt, exceedingly cheap; ~*-pie*, mud-pie; ~*-road*, (U.S.) unmade road, one with natural earth surface; ~*-track*, (orig. U.S.) race-track with earth surface; track of cinders etc. for motor-cycle racing.

dir'tў *adj.* 1. Soiled with dirt, muddied; mixed with dirt; that soils or befouls; (of nuclear device) producing relatively large amount of fall-out. 2. Morally unclean; dishonourably sordid, base, or corrupt; repulsive, despicable. 3. (of weather) Foul, muddy, (at sea) wet and squally. 4. (of colour) Inclining to, with some tinge of, black, brown, or dark grey. **dir'tilў** *adv.* **dir'tinėss** *n.* **dir'tў** *v.* Make, become, dirty.

dĭs- *prefix.* Asunder, away, apart or between; un-, not, the reverse of; utterly (in words already negative).

dĭsabĭ'lĭtў *n.* Thing, want, that prevents one's doing something, esp. legal disqualification; physical incapacity caused by injury or disease.

dĭsā'ble *v.t.* 1. Incapacitate *from* doing, *for* work, etc.; cripple, deprive of power of acting. 2. Disqualify legally, pronounce incapable; hinder. **dĭsā'blement** *n.*

dĭsabū'se (-z) *v.t.* Undeceive, disillusion.

dĭsaccor'd *n.* Disagreement, variance. ~ *v.i.* Disagree, be at variance.

dĭsadva'ntage (-vah-) *n.* Unfavourable condition or circumstance; loss or injury to interest, credit, reputation. **dĭsadvantā'geous** (-jus) *adj.* **dĭsădvantā'geouslў** *adv.*

dĭsaffĕ'ctėd *adj.* Estranged, unfriendly, disloyal, esp. to government or constituted authority. **dĭsaffĕ'ction** *n.*

dĭsaffir'm *v.t.* (law) Annul, reverse (former decision etc.), repudiate (agreement etc.).

dĭsagree' *v.i.* 1. Differ, be unlike, not correspond; differ in opinion, dissent, quarrel. 2. (of food etc.) Be unsuitable, have bad effects. **dĭsagree'ment** *n.*

dĭsagree'able *adj.* 1. Not to one's taste, unpleasant. 2. Unamiable, bad-tempered. **dĭsagree'ablў** *adv.*

dĭsallow' *v.t.* Refuse to sanction, accept as reasonable, or admit; prohibit.

dĭsannŭ'l *v.t.* Cancel, annul.

dĭsappear' *v.i.* Cease to be visible; cease to exist or be known; die away gradually. **dĭsappear'ance** *n.*

dĭsappoi'nt *v.t.* Not fulfil desire or expectation of; belie, frustrate. **dĭsappoi'nting** *adj.* **dĭsappoi'ntinglў** *adv.* **dĭsappoi'ntment** *n.* Disappointing; being disappointed; person or thing that disappoints.

dĭsăpprobā'tion *n.* Disapproval.

dĭsappro've (-ōōv) *v.* Have, express, unfavourable opinion (*of*). **dĭsappro'val** *n.* **dĭsappro'vinglў** *adv.*

dĭsar'm *v.* 1. Deprive of weapons; deprive (city, ship) of munitions of war or means of defence; reduce (armed service), be reduced, to peace footing; abandon or cut down military establishment. 2. Deprive of power to injure; pacify hostility or suspicions of, conciliate. **dĭsar'mĭng** *adj.* **dĭsar'mĭnglў** *adv.*

dĭsar′mament *n.* Reduction of a country's military forces and weapons of war.

dĭsarrā′nge (-j) *v.t.* Put into disorder, disorganize. **dĭsarrā′ngement** *n.*

dĭsarray′ *n.* & *v.t.* (Throw into) disorder, confusion.

dĭsarti′cūlāte *v.* Separate, be separated, at the joints.

dĭsa′ster (-zah-) *n.* Sudden or great misfortune. **dĭsa′strous** *adj.* **dĭsa′strouslȳ** *adv.*

dĭsavow′ *v.t.* Refuse to avow, own, or acknowledge, repudiate, disown. **dĭsavow′al** *n.*

dĭsbă′nd *v.* Break up, disperse. **dĭsbă′ndment** *n.*

dĭsbar′ *v.t.* Deprive of status and privileges of barrister. **dĭsbar′ment** *n.*

dĭsbėlie′ve *v.* Refuse credence to; not believe *in*. **dĭsbėlie′f** *n.*

dĭsbĕ′nch *v.t.* Deprive of status of bencher.

dĭsbur′den *v.t.* Relieve of a burden; get rid of (burden).

dĭsbur′se *v.* Expend; defray; pay out money. **dĭsbur′sement** *n.* Money expended.

dĭsc, dĭsk *n.* Thin circular plate; round flat (or apparently flat) object, as *sun's* ~; round flattened part in body, plant, etc.; gramophone record; ~ *harrow*, harrow with concave discs set at an angle; ~ *-jockey*, (orig. U.S.) person who selects and introduces gramophone records for radio transmission, discothèque, etc.; ~ *parking*, scheme allowing vehicles to be parked for a limited period by displaying a disc indicating time of arrival.

dĭscă′lced (-st) *adj.* (of religious orders) Wearing sandals (not shoes), (formerly) barefooted.

dĭscar′d *v.* 1. Throw out, reject (card) from hand at cards; esp. play (card not of trump suit) when unable to follow suit. 2. Cast aside, give up; dismiss, cashier. **dĭ′scard** *n.* Discarding at cards; thing (esp. card) discarded.

dĭscar′nate *adj.* Divested of the flesh, disembodied.

dĭscer′n *v.* Recognize, perceive distinctly (with mind or senses). **dĭscer′ning** *adj.* Having quick or true insight, penetrating. **dĭscer′nment** *n.*

dĭschar′ge *v.* 1. Unload; rid of charge or load; fire off (firearm); rid, rid itself, of electric charge. 2. Relieve *of*, release *from*, obligation etc.; dismiss from service; release from custody; send away, let go. 3. Send forth, emit; let fly, fire off; unload from vessel etc.; give, find, vent; (allow to) escape; (med.) emit (fluid etc.). 4. Cancel (order of court); pay, perform (debt, duty, vow). ~ *n.* (*or* dĭ′-) Discharging or being discharged; certificate of this; (med.) fluid etc. discharged.

dĭscī′ple *n.* 1. One of Christ's personal followers, esp. one of the twelve Apostles; any early believer in Christ. 2. Follower, adherent, of any leader of thought, art, etc. **dĭscī′pleship** *n.* **dĭscĭ′pūlar** *adj.*

dĭscĭplĭnar′ian *n.* Maintainer of (esp. strict) discipline.

dĭ′scĭplĭnarȳ *adj.* Of, promoting, discipline; of the nature of mental training.

dĭ′scĭplĭne *n.* 1. Branch of instruction; mental and moral training. 2. Trained condition; order maintained among persons under control or command, as pupils, soldiers, etc.; system for maintenance of order. 3. Control exercised over members of church and their conduct, as by censure, excommunication, etc. 4. Correction, chastisement; mortification of flesh by penance; whip, scourge, esp. for religious penance. ~ *v.t.* Bring under control, train to obedience and order.

dĭsclai′m *v.* 1. Renounce legal claim to; renounce claim. 2. Disown, disavow. **dĭsclai′mer** *n.* Act of disclaiming, renunciation, disavowal.

dĭsclō′se (-z) *v.t.* Remove cover from, expose to view; make known, reveal. **dĭsclō′sure** (-zh*er*) *n.* Disclosing; thing disclosed.

dĭscŏ′bolus *n.* (pl. *-lī*). Thrower of discus; *D*~, statue by Greek sculptor Myron (5th c. B.C.), copies of which survive.

dĭ′scoid *adj.* Disc-shaped; (bot., of composite flowers) having disc only, with no ray.

dis̩co′lour (-kŭl*er*) *v.* Change or spoil the colour of, stain, tarnish; become stained, tarnished, etc. **dĭscolorā′tion** *n.*

dĭsco′mfĭt (-kŭm-) *v.t.* Defeat in battle; thwart, disconcert. **dĭsco′mfĭture** *n.*

dĭsco′mfort (-kŭm-) *n.* Uneasiness of body or mind; want of comfort. ~ *v.t.* Make uneasy.

dĭscommō′de *v.t.* Put to inconvenience.

dĭscŏmpō′se (-z) *v.t.* Disturb composure of, ruffle, agitate. **dĭscompō′sure** (-zh*er*) *n.*

dĭsconcer̂′t *v.t.* Derange, upset; embarrass.

dĭsconnĕ′ct *v.t.* Sever the connection of or between. **dĭsconnĕ′ctėd** *adj.* (esp., of speech or writing) Incoherent, jerky. **dĭsconnĕ′ctėdlȳ** *adv.* **dĭsconnĕ′ctėdnėss** *n.* **dĭsconnĕ′ction, -ĕ′xion** (-ksh*o*n) *n.*

dĭscŏ′nsolate *adj.* Forlorn, inconsolable, unhappy, disappointed. **dĭscŏ′nsolatelȳ** *adv.* **dĭscŏ′nsolatenėss** *n.*

dĭscontĕ′nt *n.* Dissatisfaction, want of contentment; grievance. ~ *v.t.* (usu. in past part.) Make dissatisfied. **dĭscontĕ′ntėd** *adj.* **dĭscontĕ′ntėdlȳ** *adv.* **dĭscontĕ′ntėdnėss, dĭscontĕ′ntment** *ns.*

dĭscontĭ′nūe *v.* Cause to cease, break off; give up, leave off. **dĭscontĭ′nūance** *n.*

dĭscontĭ′nūous *adj.* Not continuous. **dĭscontĭ′nūouslȳ** *adv.* **dĭscŏntĭnū′ĭtȳ** *n.*

dĭ′scor̂d *n.* 1. Disagreement, variance, strife. 2. Harsh noise, clashing sounds. 3. (mus.) Want of harmony between notes sounded together; chord which by itself is unsatisfactory or unpleasing to the ear, and requires to be resolved by some other chord following; interval between two notes forming a discord (any interval except octave, major and minor third, perfect fourth and fifth, major and minor sixth, and their octaves); note forming discord with another or others. **dĭscor̂′dant** *adj.* **dĭscor̂′dantlȳ** *adv.* **dĭscor̂′dance** *n.*

dĭscor̂′d *v.i.* Disagree; be different, inconsistent, or discordant.

dĭ′scothèque (-tĕk) *n.* Club etc. where recorded music is played for dancing.

dĭ′scount *n.* Deduction from nominal value or price; deduction from amount of bill of exchange etc., by one who gives value for it before it is due; discounting; *at a* ~, below par; (fig.) in low esteem, depreciated. **dĭscou′nt** *v.t.* 1. Give or receive value (after deduction of discount) of bill of exchange before it is due. 2. Leave out of account; lessen, detract from; part with for immediate but smaller good; allow for exaggeration in; take (news, event) into account beforehand, thus lessening its effect or interest.

dĭscou′ntėnance *v.t.* Refuse to countenance, discourage, show disapproval of.

dĭscou′rage (-kŭ-) *v.t.* Deprive of courage, confidence, or energy; deter *from*; discountenance. **dĭscou′ragement** *n.* **dĭscou′ragĭnglȳ** *adv.*

dĭ′scourse (-or̂s) *n.* Talk, conversation (archaic); dissertation, treatise, sermon. **dĭscour′se** *v.* Talk, converse; hold forth in speech or writing on a subject; give forth (music; ref. to 'Hamlet', III. ii. 374).

dĭscour′tėous (-ker̂-) *adj.* Rude, uncivil. **dĭscour′tėouslȳ** *adv.* **dĭscour′tėsȳ** *n.*

dĭsco′ver (-kŭ-) *v.t.* 1. (archaic) Disclose. 2. (chess) ~ *check*, put king in check by removing piece or pawn. 3. Find out; obtain sight or knowledge of for first time. **dĭsco′verer** *n.*

dĭsco′vert (-kŭ-) *adj.* (law) Not under the cover, authority, or protection of a husband.

dĭsco′verȳ (-kŭ-) *n.* Discovering; thing discovered; (law) compulsory disclosure by party to action of facts or documents on which he relies.

dĭscrĕ′dĭt *n.* Loss of repute, thing involving this; doubt, distrust; loss of commercial credit.

~ *v.t.* Refuse to believe; bring disrepute or disbelief upon.

dĭscrĕ'dĭtable *adj.* Bringing discredit, shameful. **dĭscrĕ'dĭtablў** *adv.*

dĭscree't *adj.* Prudent; cautious in speech or action. **dĭscree'tlў** *adv.*

dĭscrĕ'pancў *n.* Want of agreement, variance, inconsistency. **dĭscrĕ'pant** *adj.* **dĭscrĕ'pantlў** *adv.*

dĭscrē'te *adj.* 1. Separate, individually distinct, discontinuous. 2. (metaphys.) Not concrete; detached from the material. **dĭscrē'telў** *adv.* **dĭscrē'tenėss** *n.*

dĭscrĕ'tion *n.* 1. Liberty or power of deciding or acting as one thinks fit; (law) power of court etc. to decide, within limits, on punishment, remedy, distribution of costs, etc. 2. Discernment, prudence, judgement. **dĭscrĕ'tionarў** *adj.*

dĭscrĭ'mĭnāte *v.* Constitute, set up, observe, a difference between, distinguish *from*, *between*; make a distinction; observe distinctions carefully; ~ *against*, distinguish unfavourably. **dĭscrĭ'mĭnātĭng** *adj.* Discerning, acute. **dĭscrĭmĭnā'tion** *n.* **dĭscrĭ'mĭnatĭve** *adj.* **dĭscrĭ'mĭnatĭvelў** *adv.*

dĭscûr'sĭve *adj.* 1. Rambling, digressive, expatiating. 2. Proceeding by reasoning or argument, not intuitive. **dĭscûr'sĭvelў** *adv.* **dĭscûr'sĭvenėss** *n.*

dĭ'scus *n.* Heavy disc of metal etc. used in ancient Greek and Roman athletic exercises and revived in modern times.

dĭscŭ'ss *v.t.* 1. Examine by argument, debate. 2. (archaic) Consume (food) with enjoyment. **dĭscŭ'ssion** *n.*

dĭsdai'n *v.t.* Scorn; regard with contempt; consider beneath oneself or one's notice. ~ *n.* Scorn, contempt. **dĭsdai'nful** *adj.* **dĭsdai'nfullў** *adv.*

dĭsea'se (-zēz) *n.* Morbid condition of body or plant, or some part of it; (specific) disorder, illness; deranged, depraved, or morbid condition of mind etc. **dĭsea'sed** (-zd) *adj.* Affected with disease.

dĭsembâr'k *v.* Put, go, ashore. **dĭsĕmbârkā'tion** *n.*

dĭsembă'rrass *v.t.* Free from embarrassment, rid or relieve (*of*). **dĭsembă'rrassment** *n.*

dĭsėmbŏ'dў *v.t.* Separate, free (soul from body, or idea from form in which it is embodied).

dĭsembō'gue (-g) *v.* (of river, lake, etc.) Discharge or empty itself, flow *into*; pour forth (its waters) at the mouth.

dĭsėmbow'el (*or* -owl) *v.t.* Remove entrails of, rip up so as to cause bowels to protrude.

dĭsėmbroi'l *v.t.* Extricate from confusion or entanglement.

dĭsėncha'nt (-ah-) *v.t.* Free from enchantment or illusion. **dĭsėncha'ntment** *n.*

dĭsėncŭ'mber *v.t.* Free from encumbrance.

dĭsėndow' *v.t.* Deprive or strip (esp. Church) of endowments. **dĭsėndow'ment** *n.*

dĭsėngā'ge (-n-g-) *v.t.* Detach, liberate, loosen; come apart, break contact; (fencing) reverse relative position of blades by passing point to opposite side of opponent's sword. ~ *n.* (fencing) Freeing one's blade for a thrust by disengaging it. **dĭsėngā'ged** (-jd) *adj.* (esp.) Unoccupied; at liberty, not engaged. **dĭsėngā'gement** *n.*

dĭsėntai'l *v.t.* Free from entail, break entail of.

dĭsėntă'ngle (-nggl) *v.* Extricate, free from complications; unravel, untwist; come clear of tangle. **dĭsėntă'nglement** *n.*

dĭsėstă'blĭsh *v.t.* Deprive of established character; esp. deprive (Church) of State connection and support, remove from position of national or State Church. **dĭsėstă'blĭshment** *n.*

diseur (dēzêr) *n.* (fem. *diseuse*, pr. -êrz) Person who entertains by speaking monologues. [Fr.]

dĭsfā'vour (-v*er*) *n.* Dislike, disapproval; being disliked.

dĭsfĭ'gure (-g*er*) *v.t.* Mar appearance of; sully. **dĭsfĭgūrā'tion, dĭsfĭ'gurement** *ns.*

dĭsfŏ'rėst *v.t.* Deprive of status

or privileges of forest; clear of trees or forest.

dĭsfră'nchīse (-z) *v.t.* Deprive of rights and privileges of a free citizen, or of some franchise previously enjoyed; deprive (place) of right of sending, (person) of right of voting for, parliamentary representative. **dĭsfră'nchīsement** *n.*

dĭsfrŏ'ck *v.t.* = UNFROCK.

dĭsgôr'ge *v.* Vomit forth (what has been swallowed); give up (esp. what has been wrongfully appropriated); (of river) discharge.

dĭsgrā'ce *n.* 1. Loss of favour, downfall from position of honour; shame. 2. Cause of reproach. ~ *v.t.* Dismiss from favour, degrade from position; bring shame or discredit upon, be a disgrace to. **dĭsgrā'ceful** *adj.* **dĭsgrā'cefullў** *adv.* **dĭsgrā'cefulnėss** *n.*

dĭsgrŭ'ntled (-ld) *adj.* Discontented, displeased.

dĭsguī'se (-gīz) *v.t.* Conceal identity of by changing personal appearance or dress; dress *as* someone, *in* some garb; alter appearance of (anything) so as to mislead or deceive; conceal or cloak real character, state, or identity of. ~ *n.* Use of changed dress or appearance for sake of concealment; disguised condition; garb used to deceive; artificial manner, deception. **dĭsguī'sement** *n.*

dĭsgŭ'st *n.* Loathing, nausea, repugnance, strong aversion. ~ *v.t.* Excite loathing, aversion, or indignation in. **dĭsgŭ'stĭng** *adj.* **dĭsgŭ'stĭnglў** *adv.*

dĭsh *n.* 1. Shallow flat-bottomed vessel for holding food. 2. Food served on or contained in dish; variety or article of food; (slang) attractive woman; *standing* ~, dish that appears daily or for every meal (also fig.). 3. Anything dish-shaped or concave, esp. as receptacle. 4. *dĭ'shcloth*, cloth for washing dishes and plates; ~-*cover*, cover of metal etc. for keeping food in dish hot; *dĭ'shwasher*, machine for washing dishes etc. automatically; *dĭ'shwater*, water in which dishes have been washed; (pop.) weak tea. ~ *v.* 1. Put (food) into dish ready for serving; ~ *out*, distribute, esp. indiscriminately; ~ *up*, serve, serve meal; (fig.) present (facts, arguments, etc.) attractively. 2. Make dish-shaped or concave; *dished wheel*, concave wheel with spokes at an angle to the hub. 3. (of horse) Move forefeet with circular or scooping motion. 4. (slang) Circumvent, outmanœuvre; do for defeat completely.

dishabille (dĭsabē'l) *n.* Being negligently or partly dressed; undress; undress garment or costume.

dĭshâr'monў (-s-h-) *n.* Discord, dissonance. **dĭshârmō'nĭous** *adj.*

dĭshear'ten (-s-hâr-) *v.t.* Make despondent, rob of courage. **dĭshear'tenĭng** *adj.* **dĭshear'tenment** *n.*

dĭshĕ'velled (-ld) *adj.* With disordered hair; (of hair) loose, disordered; (of person) untidy, ruffled. **dĭshĕ'velment** *n.*

dĭshŏ'nėst (-sŏ-) *adj.* Not honest; fraudulent; insincere. **dĭshŏ'nėstlў** *adv.* **dĭshŏ'nėstў** *n.*

dĭshŏ'nour (-sŏner) *n.* Disgrace. ~ *v.t.* 1. Treat with indignity; violate honour or chastity of. 2. Bring dishonour upon. 3. Refuse or fail to accept or pay (cheque, bill of exchange, etc.). **dĭshŏ'nourable** *adj.* Involving disgrace, ignominious; unprincipled, base; against dictates of honour. **dĭshŏ'nourablenėss** *n.* **dĭshŏ'nourablў** *adv.*

dĭsĭllū'sion (*or* -lōō-) *v.t.* Free from illusion, disenchant. ~ *n.* Freedom from illusion, disenchantment. **dĭsĭllū'sionīze** *v.t.* Disillusion. **dĭsĭllū'sionment** *n.*

dĭsĭncĕ'ntĭve *adj.* & *n.* Deterrent.

dĭsĭnclĭnā'tion *n.* Want of inclination, willingness, or liking.

dĭsĭnclī'ne *v.t.* Make indisposed, averse, or unwilling.

dĭsĭncôr'porāte *v.t.* Dissolve (corporate body). **dĭsĭncôrporā'tion** *n.*

dĭsĭnfĕ'ct *v.t.* Cleanse from infection, destroy germs of disease in. **dĭsinfĕ'ctant** *adj.* & *n.* Disinfecting (agent). **dĭsinfĕ'ction** *n.*

dĭsinflā'tion *n.* Policy designed to remove or offset the inflationary elements in a country's economic situation without incurring the bad effects of DEFLATION. **dĭsinflā'tionarў** *adj.*

dĭsingĕ'nūous (-j-) *adj.* Insincere, not candid or frank. **dĭsingĕ'nūouslў** *adv.* **dĭsingĕ'nūousnėss** *n.*

dĭsinhĕ'rĭt *v.t.* Deprive or dispossess of right to inherit. **dĭsinhĕ'rĭtance** *n.*

dĭsĭ'ntėgrāte *v.* Separate into component parts: deprive of, lose, cohesion. **dĭsintėgrā'tion** *n.*

dĭsintêr' *v.t.* Exhume; unearth. **dĭsintêr'ment** *n.*

dĭsĭ'nterėst *n.* Impartiality, disinterestedness; absence of interest. **dĭsĭn'terėstėd** *adj.* Not influenced by self-interest or partiality; (colloq.) not interested. **dĭsĭ'nterėstėdlў** *adv.* **dĭsĭ'nterėstėdnėss** *n.*

dĭsjĕ'cta mĕ'mbra. Fragments, scattered remains. [L, alteration of Horace's *disjecti membra poetae* 'limbs of a dismembered poet']

dĭsjoi'n *v.t.* Separate, disunite.

dĭsjoi'nt *v.t.* Dislocate; disturb working or connection of; separate at the joints. **dĭsjoi'ntėd** *adj.* (esp. of speech etc.) Incoherent, desultory. **dĭsjoi'ntėdlў** *adv.* **dĭsjoi'ntėdnėss** *n.*

dĭsjŭ'nction *n.* Disjoining, separation.

dĭsjŭ'nctĭve *adj.* Disjoining, involving separation; (logic) alternative; involving choice between two statements etc.; (gram., of conjunction) expressing an alternative, implying adversative relation between the clauses it connects. **dĭsjŭ'nctĭvely** *adv.* **dĭsjŭ'nctĭve** *n.* Disjunctive proposition or conjunction.

disk: see DISC.

dĭslī'ke *v.t.* Not like; have aversion or objection to. ~ *n.* Aversion.

dĭ'slocāte *v.t.* Put out of joint; (geol.) make (strata) discontinuous; displace; put out of gear. **dĭslocā'tion** *n.*

dĭslŏ'dge *v.t.* Remove, turn out, from position. **dĭslŏ'dgement** *n.*

dĭsloy'al *adj.* Unfaithful; untrue to allegiance, disaffected to State. **dĭsloy'allў** *adv.* **dĭsloy'alĭst** *adj.* & *n.* **dĭsloy'altў** *n.*

dĭ'smal (-z-) *adj.* Depressing, miserable, sombre, dreary; *the ~ science*, T. Carlyle's name for political economy. **dĭ'smallў** *adv.* **dĭ'smalnėss** *n.* [orig. noun, = 'unlucky days'; OF *dis mal* f. L *dies mali* ill days (the medieval calendar recognized two of these in each month)]

dĭsmă'ntle *v.t.* Strip *of* covering, protection, etc.; deprive of defences, equipment, etc. **dĭsmă'ntlement** *n.*

dĭsma'st (-ah-) *v.t.* Deprive (ship) of mast(s).

dĭsmay' *n.* Consternation; utter loss of moral courage or resolution in prospect of danger or difficulty. ~ *v.t.* Rouse dismay in; reduce to despair.

dĭsmĕ'mber *v.t.* Tear or cut limb from limb; divide into parts or sections so as to destroy integrity, partition (country etc.). **dĭsmĕ'mberment** *n.*

dĭsmĭ'ss *v.t.* 1. Send away, disperse, disband; allow to go; send away from one's presence. 2. Discharge, cashier, from service or office. 3. Put out of one's thoughts. 4. Have done with, bring to an end; treat (subject) summarily. 5. (law) Send out of court, refuse further hearing to (case etc.). **dĭsmĭ'ssal** *n.*

dĭsmou'nt *v.* Alight, cause to alight, from horseback, etc.; unseat, unhorse; remove (thing) from its mount.

Dĭ'sney (-z-), Walter ('Walt') E. (1901–66). Amer. film director and creator of animated cartoons.

dĭsobē'dĭence *n.* Being disobedient, witholding of obedience. **dĭsobē'dĭent** *adj.* Refusing or failing to obey; stubborn, intractable. **dĭsobē'dĭentlў** *adv.*

dĭsobey' (-bā) *v.* Disregard

orders, break rules; fail or refuse to obey.

dĭsoblī′ge *v.t.* Refuse to consult convenience or wishes of. **dĭsoblī′ging** *adj.* **dĭsoblī′gingly̆** *adv.* **dĭsoblī′gingnėss** *n.*

dĭsôr′der *n.* 1. Want of order, confusion. 2. Tumult, riot, commotion. 3. Ailment, disease. ~ *v.t.* Disarrange, throw into confusion; put out of health, upset. **dĭsôr′derly̆** *adj.* 1. Untidy, confused. 2. Irregular, unruly, riotous; violating public order or morality; ~ *house*, brothel, place used illegally for gambling. **dĭsôr′derlĭnėss** *n.*

dĭsôr′ganīze *v.t.* Destroy system etc. of; throw into confusion. **dĭsôrganīzā′tion** *n.*

dĭsôr′ientāte *v.t.* 1. Place (church) with chancel not directly eastwards. 2. Confuse (person) as to his bearings (also fig.). **dĭsôrientā′tion** *n.*

dĭsow′n (-ōn) *v.t.* Refuse to recognize, repudiate, disclaim; renounce allegiance to.

dĭspă′rage *v.t.* Bring discredit on, lower; speak slightingly of, depreciate. **dĭspă′ragement** *n.* **dĭspă′ragingly̆** *adv.*

dĭ′sparate *adj.* Essentially different, diverse in kind, incommensurable, without relation. **dĭ′sparately̆** *adv.* **dĭ′sparatenėss** *n.* **dĭ′sparate** *n.* (usu. pl.) Thing(s) so unlike that there is no basis for comparison.

dĭspă′rĭty̆ *n.* Inequality, difference, incongruity.

dĭspă′ssionate *adj.* Free from emotion, calm, impartial. **dĭspă′ssionately̆** *adv.* **dĭspă′ssionatenėss** *n.*

dĭspă′tch, dės- *v.* 1. Send off to destination or for purpose. 2. Give death-blow to, kill. 3. Get (task, business) promptly done; settle, finish off; eat (food, meal) quickly; (archaic) make haste. ~ *n.* 1. Sending off. 2. Putting to death. 3. Prompt settlement of business; promptitude, efficiency, rapidity. 4. Written message; official communication, esp. military or diplomatic. 5. Agency for conveying goods etc. 6. *~-box*, *-case*, box, case, for holding or carrying dispatches or other documents; *~-rider*, motor-cyclist etc. carrying dispatches.

dĭspĕ′l *v.t.* Dissipate, disperse.

dĭspĕ′nsable *adj.* That can be relaxed in special cases; not necessary, that may be done without.

dĭspĕ′nsary̆ *n.* 1. Place where something (esp. medicine) is dispensed. 2. Public or charitable institution where medicines are dispensed and medical advice given.

dĭspensā′tion *n.* 1. Distributing, dealing out. 2. Ordering, management, esp. of world by Providence; arrangement or provision of Providence or Nature; special dealing of Providence with community or person; (theol.) religious order or system as part of a progressive revelation adapted to particular nation or age, as *Mosaic* ~. 3. Exemption from penalty or duty laid down in ecclesiastical, etc., law; granting of licence by pope, archbishop, or bishop, to a person to do what is forbidden by ecclesiastical law.

dĭspĕ′nse *v.* 1. Distribute, deal out; administer (sacrament, justice). 2. Make up (medicine) according to prescription or formula. 3. Grant dispensations; release *from* obligation. 4. ~ *with*, relax, give exemption from, (rule); annul binding force of (oath); render needless; do without. **dĭspĕ′nser** *n.* (esp.) One who dispenses medicines.

dĭspeo′ple (-pēp-) *v.t.* Depopulate.

dĭspêr′se *v.* Scatter; drive, go, throw, send, in different directions; rout, dispel, be dispelled; send to, station at, different points; put in circulation, disseminate; (of gases or liquids) diffuse; (optics) spread (beam of light) so as to produce spectrum. **dĭspêr′sal** *n.* **dĭspêr′sėdly̆** *adv.* **dĭspêr′sive** *adj.* **dĭspêr′sĭvely̆** *adv.* **dĭspêr′sivenėss** *n.*

dĭspêr′sion *n.* Dispersing; *the D~*, the DIASPORA.

dĭspĭ′rĭt *v.t.* Make despondent, depress. **dĭspĭ′rĭtėdly̆** *adv.*

dĭsplā'ce *v.t.* 1. Shift from proper position; remove from office. 2. Oust, take the place of; put something else in the place of; replace. 3. *displaced person*, one removed from his home country by military or political pressure; orig., civilian deported from a German-occupied country to work in Germany during the war of 1939–45 and thereafter homeless.

dĭsplā'cement (-sm-) *n.* 1. Displacing, being displaced; amount by which thing is shifted from its place; ousting, replacement. 2. Amount or weight of fluid displaced by body floating or immersed in it.

dĭsplay' *v.t.* Exhibit, expose to view, show; show ostentatiously; reveal, betray, allow to appear. ~ *n.* Displaying; exhibition, show; ostentation; specialized pattern of behaviour by which birds communicate with each other; (print.) selection and arrangement of types to attract attention.

dĭsplea'se (-z) *v.t.* Offend, annoy, make indignant or angry; be disagreeable to; *be displeased* (*at*, *with*), disapprove, be indignant or dissatisfied. **dĭsplea'sĭng** *adj.* **dĭsplea'sĭnglȳ** *adv.*

dĭsplea'sure (-ĕzh*er*) *n.* Displeased feeling, dissatisfaction, disapproval, anger.

dĭspôr't *v.* (archaic) Frolic, enjoy *oneself*, display *oneself* sportingly. ~ *n.* (archaic) Relaxation, pastime.

dĭspō'sable (-z-) *adj.* That can be disposed of or disposed, (of article) designed to be thrown away after use.

dĭspō'sal (-z-) *n.* Disposing of, getting rid of; settling, dealing with; bestowal, assignment; sale; control, management (usu. *at one's* ~); placing, disposition, arrangement.

dĭspō'se (-z) *v.* 1. Place suitably, in particular order, in proper positions. 2. Bring (person, mind) into certain state; incline, make willing or desirous, *to*; give (thing) tendency *to*. 3. Determine course of events. 4. ~ *of*, do what one will with, regulate; get off one's hands, stow away, settle, finish, kill, demolish; consume (food); sell.

dĭsposĭ'tion (-z-) *n.* 1. Setting in order, arrangement, relative position of parts. 2. (usu. pl.) Plan, preparations; stationing of troops for attack, defence, etc. 3. Ordinance, dispensation. 4. Bestowal by deed or will. 5. Control, disposal. 6. Temperament, natural tendency; inclination *to*.

dĭspossĕ'ss (-zĕs) *v.t.* Oust, dislodge; deprive *of*; rid (person) of evil spirit. **dĭspossĕ'ssion** *n.*

dĭsprai'se (-z) *v.t.* Disparage, censure. ~ *n.* Disparagement, censure.

dĭsprōō'f *n.* Refutation, thing that disproves.

dĭsproppôr'tion *n.* Want of proportion. **dĭsproppôr'tionate** *adj.* Wanting proportion; relatively too large or too small. **dĭsproppôr'tionatelȳ** *adv.* **dĭsproppôr'tioned** (-nd) *adj.*

dĭspro've (-ōōv) *v.t.* Prove false, show fallacy of, refute.

dĭ'spūtable *adj.* Open to question, uncertain. **dĭ'spūtablȳ** *adv.*

dĭ'spūtant *adj.* & *n.* (Person) that disputes, engaged in controversy.

dĭspūtā'tion *n.* Debate, discussion; exercise in which parties formally sustain, attack, and defend a question or thesis, as in medieval schools and universities. **dĭspūtā'tious** (-sh*us*) *adj.* **dĭspūtā'tiouslȳ** *adv.* **dĭspūtā'tiousnėss** *n.*

dĭspū'te *v.* Argue, hold disputation; have altercation; controvert, call in question; contend for. ~ *n.* Controversy, debate; heated contention, quarrel.

dĭsqual'ifȳ (-ŏl-) *v.t.* Make unfit, disable (esp. legally); make ineligible (esp. to hold place or prize won in sporting contest). **dĭsqualĭfĭcā'tion** *n.* (esp.) Thing that disqualifies.

dĭsquī'et *v.t.* Deprive of peace, worry. **dĭsquī'etūde** *n.* Anxiety, unrest.

dĭsquĭsĭ'tion (-zĭ-) *n.* 1. (archaic) Investigation, inquiry. 2. Long or elaborate treatise or discourse (*on* subject). **dĭsquĭsĭ'tional** *adj.*

Disraeli (dĭzrā′lĭ), Benjamin, 1st Earl of Beaconsfield (1804–81). British Tory statesman, prime

minister 1868 and 1874–80; author of 'Coningsby' (1844) and other novels.

dĭsrā′te *v.t.* (naut.) Reduce to lower rank or rating.

dĭsrėgar′d *v.t.* Pay no attention to; ignore; treat as of no importance. ~ *n.* Indifference, neglect.

dĭsrĕl′ish *n.* & *v.t.* (Regard with) distaste or disfavour.

dĭsrėpair′ *n.* Bad condition for want of repairs.

dĭsrĕ′pūtable *adj.* Discreditable; of bad repute, not respectable in character or appearance. **dĭsrĕ′pūtablenėss** *n.* **dĭsrĕ′pūtablў** *adv.*

dĭsrėpū′te *n.* Ill repute, discredit.

dĭsrėspĕ′ct *n.* Want of respect, rudeness. **dĭsrėspĕ′ctful** *adj.* **dĭsrėspĕ′ctfullў** *adv.* **dĭsrėspĕ′ctfulnėss** *n.*

dĭsrō′be *v.* Divest of robe or garment; undress.

dĭsrŭ′pt *v.t.* Shatter, separate forcibly. **dĭsrŭ′ption** *n.* Bursting asunder, violent dissolution; rent condition; *the D~*, the split in the Established Church of Scotland in 1843 when owing to the desire of a large part of the Church 451 of its ministers formed themselves into the Free (Protesting) Church of Scotland. **dĭsrŭ′ptĭve** *adj.* **dĭsrŭ′ptĭvelў** *adv.* **dĭsrŭ′ptĭvenėss** *n.*

dĭssă′tĭsfў *v.t.* Fail to satisfy, make discontented. **dĭssătĭsfă′ction** *n.*

dĭssĕ′ct *v.t.* Cut up, esp., cut up (animal body, plant, etc.) to display position, structure, and relation of internal parts; analyse, examine or criticize minutely. **dĭssĕ′ction** *n.*

dĭssei′se, -ze (-sēz) *v.t.* (law) Put out of seisin (*of*); oust, dispossess. **dĭssei′see, dĭssei′sor** *ns.* **dĭssei′sĭn, -zĭn** *n.* Disseising; usu., wrongful possession of lands etc. of another.

dĭssĕ′mble *v.* Cloak, disguise, conceal; conceal one's opinions, intentions, etc., under feigned guise, play the hypocrite. **dĭssĕ′mbler** *n.*

dĭssĕ′mĭnāte *v.t.* Scatter abroad, sow in various places; (pass., of disease) be dispersed or spread throughout organ, tissue, or whole body. **dĭssĕmĭnā′tion, dĭssĕ′mĭnātor** *ns.*

dĭssĕ′nsion *n.* Discord arising from difference in opinion.

dĭssĕ′nt *v.i.* Refuse to assent; disagree; think differently, express different opinion (*from*); esp., differ in religious opinion, differ from doctrine or worship of established, national, or orthodox Church. ~ *n.* (Expression of) difference of opinion; refusal to accept doctrines of established Church, nonconformity; dissenters collectively.

dĭssĕ′nter *n.* (esp.) Member of dissenting Church or sect.

dĭssĕ′ntient (-shĭ- *or* -shent) *adj.* & *n.* (Person) disagreeing with a majority or official view.

dĭssĕ′pĭmėnt *n.* (bot.) Partition, septum.

dĭssertā′tion *n.* Spoken or written discourse treating a subject at length; treatise.

dĭssėr′vĭce *n.* Rendering of ill service or ill turn; injury, detriment.

dĭssĕ′ver *v.* Sever, divide.

dĭ′ssĭdence *n.* Disagreement, dissent.

dĭ′ssĭdent *adj.* & *n.* Dissentient.

dĭssĭ′mĭlar *adj.* Unlike (*to*). **dĭssĭmĭlă′rĭtў** *n.* **dĭssĭ′mĭlarlў** *adv.*

dĭssĭ′mĭlāte *v.* Make, become, unlike. **dĭssĭmĭlā′tion** *n.* (esp.) Differentiation of two identical or similar sounds occurring near each other in a word, by changing one of them (as when older *cinnamom* is changed to *cinnamon*).

dĭssĭmĭ′lĭtūde *n.* Unlikeness.

dĭssĭ′mūlāte *v.* Dissemble (feelings etc.); be hypocritical. **dĭssĭmūlā′tion, dĭssĭ′mūlātor** *ns.*

dĭ′ssĭpāte *v.* Dispense, dispel (cloud, vapour, etc.); disappear; dissolve to atoms, bring or come to nothing; squander, fritter away (money, time, etc.). **dĭ′ssĭpātėd** *adj.* (esp.) Given to dissipation, dissolute.

dĭssĭpā′tion *n.* 1. Dissipating; wasteful expenditure *of*. 2. (Frivolous) amusement. 3. Intemperate or vicious living.

dĭssō′ciāte (-shĭ-) *v.t.* Disunite, sunder, cut off from association or society; (chem.) decompose, esp. by heat. **dĭssōciā′tion** (-sĭ-) *n.* (esp.) Disintegration *of* personality or consciousness; (path.) state of mind in which two or more personalities exist in the same person. **dĭssō′ciative** (-sha-) *adj.*

dĭssŏ′lūble *adj.* That can be disintegrated, loosed, or disconnected. **dissolūbĭ′lĭtў** *n.*

dĭ′ssolūte (*or* -ōōt) *adj.* Lax in morals, licentious. **dĭ′ssolūtelў** *adv.* **dĭ′ssolūtenėss** *n.*

dĭssolū′tion (*or* -ōō-) *n.* 1. Disintegration, decomposition. 2. Undoing or relaxation of any tie or bond; dismissal, dispersal, of assembly, esp. of a parliament for new election. 3. Death; coming, being brought, to an end; disintegration, disorganization.

dĭssŏ′lve (-z-) *v.* 1. Liquefy; (fig.) lose composure (~ *in*(*to*) *laughter*, *tears*); (phys., of liquid) mix with (a solid, another liquid, or a gas) without chemical action so as to form a homogeneous liquid or solution; (of substance) mix thus *in* a liquid. 2. Bring to nought, destroy; become faint, melt *away*. 3. Disperse; bring (constituted body, esp. Parliament), come, to an end. 4. (cinemat.) Cause (picture) to fade *into* another; fade thus. ~ *n.* Dissolving picture, apparatus for producing this. **dĭssŏ′lvent** *adj.* & *n.* (Thing) having power to dissolve other things, solvent.

dĭ′ssonant *adj.* Discordant, harsh-toned, incongruous. **dĭ′ssonantlў** *adv.* **dĭ′ssonance** *n.*

dĭssua′de (-swād) *v.t.* Advise (person) against; divert *from* course by persuasion or influence. **dĭssuā′sion** *n.* **dĭssuā′sĭve** *adj.* **dĭssuā′sĭvelў** *adv.* **dĭssuā′sĭvenėss** *n.*

dissyllable: see DISYLLABLE.

dĭ′staff (-ahf) *n.* Cleft staff about 3 ft long on which wool or flax was wound for spinning by hand; corresponding part of hand spinning-wheel; ~ *side*, female branch of family.

dĭ′stal *adj.* (anat., bot.) Away from centre of body or point of attachment, terminal.

dĭ′stance *n.* 1. Being far off, remoteness; extent of space between, interval. 2. Aloofness; *keep one's* ~, avoid familiarity. 3. Distant point; remote field of vision; distant part of landscape. 4. Space of time. ~ *v.t.* Place, make seem, far off; leave far behind in race or competition.

dĭ′stant *adj.* 1. Far away (*from*); specified distance away (*from*); remote, far apart, in position, time, resemblance, etc.; ~ *early warning line*, radar system in N. America for advance detection of missile attack; ~ *signal*, (railw.) signal some distance in advance of home signal and agreeing with it in position. 2. Reserved, cool, not intimate. **dĭ′stantlў** *adv.*

dĭstā′ste *n.* Dislike, repugnance, slight aversion (*for*). **dĭstā′steful** *adj.* Disagreeable, repellent (*to*). **dĭstā′stefullў** *adv.* **dĭstā′stefulnėss** *n.*

dĭstĕ′mper[1] *v.t.* (usu. in past part.) Upset, derange, in health or sanity. ~ *n.* 1. Derangement, ailment, of body or mind. 2. Disease of dogs characterized by catarrh, cough, and loss of strength; any of various diseases of other animals.

dĭstĕ'mper² *n.* Method of painting on plaster etc. with powder colours mixed with size or other glue soluble in water, used chiefly in scene-painting and internal decoration of house-walls; pigment used for this. ~ *v.t.* Paint with distemper.

dĭstĕ'nd *v.* Swell out by pressure from within. **dĭstĕ'nsĭble** *adj.* **dĭstĕ'nsion** *n.*

dĭ'stĭch (-k) *n.* Pair of lines of verse, couplet.

dĭstĭ'l *v.* 1. Trickle down; issue, give forth, in drops or fine moisture, exude. 2. Vaporize substance by means of heat, and then condense the vapour by cooling it, so as to obtain the substance or part of it in concentrated or purified state; extract essence of, transform or convert, make or produce, drive *off*, by distillation; undergo distillation.

dĭstĭllā'tion *n.* (esp.) Extraction of spirit or essence of any substance by first converting into vapour and then condensing the vapour; *destructive*, *dry*, ~, decomposition of substance by strong heat in a retort, and collection of volatile matters evolved; *fractional* ~, separation by distillation of two or more liquids having different boiling-points, utilizing the fact that the first portion or fraction of the distillate has a higher proportion of the more volatile liquid than later fractions. **dĭstĭ'llatorў** *adj.*

dĭstĭ'ller *n.* (esp.) 1. One who distils, esp. alcoholic spirit. 2. Apparatus for distilling salt water at sea. **dĭstĭ'llerў** *n.* Establishment for distilling spirits.

dĭstĭ'nct *adj.* 1. Not identical, separate, individual; different in quality or kind, unlike. 2. Clearly perceptible, plain, definite; unmistakable, decided, positive. **dĭstĭ'nctlў** *adv.* **dĭstĭ'nctnėss** *n.*

dĭstĭ'nction *n.* 1. Making of a difference; discrimination; difference made; ~ *without a difference*, merely nominal or artificial distinction. 2. Being different. 3. Thing that differentiates; mark, name, title. 4. Showing of special consideration, mark of honour. 5. Distinguished character, excellence, eminence; individuality.

dĭstĭ'nctĭve *adj.* Distinguishing, characteristic. **dĭstĭ'nctĭvelў** *adv.* **dĭstĭ'nctĭvenėss** *n.*

distingué (dēstăṅgā) *adj.* Having distinguished air, features, manners, etc.

dĭstĭ'nguish (-nggwĭsh) *v.* 1. Class, classify. 2. Mark as different or distinct, differentiate, characterize. 3. Recognize as distinct or different; perceive difference, make or draw distinction, *between*. 4. Perceive distinctly, recognize. 5. Notice specially, honour with special attention; make prominent, remarkable, or eminent in some respect (usu. *pass.* or *refl.*). **dĭstĭ'nguĭshable** *adj.* **dĭstĭ'nguĭshablў** *adv.*

dĭstĭ'nguĭshed (-nggwĭsht) *adj.* (esp.) Remarkable (*for*, *by*); eminent, famous, of high standing; *D~ Conduct Medal*, (abbrev. D.C.M.) medal awarded to warrant and noncommissioned officers and men in the army and R.A.F. for distinguished conduct in the field, instituted 1862; *D~ Flying Cross*, (abbrev. D.F.C.) order bestowed on officers and warrant officers in the R.A.F. and Fleet Air Arm for acts of gallantry when flying in active operations against the enemy, instituted 1918; *D ~ Flying Medal*, (abbrev. D.F.M.) medal for warrant and noncommissioned officers and men in R.A.F. and Fleet Air Arm for equivalent services as for D.F.C.; *D~ Service Cross*, (abbrev. D.S.C.) order bestowed on officers of the R.N. below rank of captain, and for warrant officers; *D ~ Service Medal*, (abbrev. D.S.M.) medal awarded to members of the services afloat below rank of commissioned officer, instituted 1914; *D~ Service Order*, (abbrev. D.S.O.) order of distinction bestowed for especial services in action on British naval, military, and air force commissioned officers, instituted 1886.

dĭstôr't *v.t.* Put out of shape,

make crooked or unshapely; misrepresent. **distor'tedly** *adv*.

distor'tion *n*. Distorting, being distorted; faulty transmission or reproduction of sound. **distor'tional** *adj*.

distră'ct *v.t.* Divert, draw away (mind, attention); draw in different directions, divide or confuse the attention of; bewilder, perplex; drive mad, infuriate. **distră'ctėdly, distră'ctingly** *advs*.

distră'ction *n*. 1. Diversion of mind or attention; something that distracts or diverts; amusement. 2. Lack of concentration. 3. Confusion, perplexity, dissension; frenzy, madness; *to* ~, to degree approaching madness.

distrai'n *v*. (law) Levy a distress (*upon*), seize chattels of person in order to make him pay debt (esp. rent) or perform obligation, or to obtain satisfaction by selling the chattels; seize (chattels etc.) by way of distress. **distrai'nt** *n*. Distraining, distress.

distrait (-trā) *adj*. (fem. *-te* pr. -āt). Absent-minded, not attending.

distrau'ght (-awt) *adj*. (Of persons) violently agitated.

distrĕ'ss *n*. 1. Severe pressure or strain of pain, sorrow, etc., anguish, affliction; damage or danger to ship; exhausted or distressed condition; misfortune, calamity; ~ *signal*, signal of ship in distress. 2. (law) Legal seizure and detention of chattel, distraining. **distrĕ'ssful** *adj*. **distrĕ'ssfully** *adv*. **distrĕ'ss** *v.t.* Subject to severe strain, exhaust, afflict; vex, make anxious or unhappy. **distrĕ'ssing** *adj*. **distrĕ'ssingly** *adv*.

distri'būtary *n*. River branch which does not return to main stream after leaving it.

distri'būte *v.t.* Deal out, give share of to each of a number; spread abroad, scatter, put at different points; divide into parts, arrange, classify; (logic) use (term) in its full extension, so that it includes every individual of the class. **distri'būtor** *n*. (esp.) Device distributing electric current to sparking plugs.

distribū'tion *n*. 1. Distributing, being distributed. 2. (esp., econ.) Dispersal among consumers effected by commerce; extent to which individuals or classes share in aggregate products of community. 3. Way in which a particular character is spread over members of a class, usually represented graphically by a ~ *curve*. **distribū'tional** *adj*.

distri'būtive *adj*. 1. Of, concerned with, produced by, distribution; ~ *trade*, any of those trades (wholesale and retail) which obtain goods from manufacturers and sell them to consumers. 2. (logic, gram.) Referring to each individual of a class, not to the class collectively. ~ *n*. (gram.) Distributive word. **distri'būtively** *adv*.

di'strict *n*. Territory marked off for special administrative purpose; assigned sphere of operations; tract of country with common characteristics, region; division of parish with its own church or chapel and clergyman; division of county, having a metropolitan or non-metropolitan council; (U.S. etc.) electoral constituency; in some States, subdivision of county, in others, division of State including several counties; ~ *attorney*, (U.S.) local public prosecutor of a district; ~ *commissioner, officer*, representative of Government in a colonial district; ~ *nurse*, nurse employed in a county district to visit patients in their homes; ~ *visitor*, person working under clergyman's direction in a section of a parish. ~ *v.t.* (chiefly U.S.) Divide into districts.

Di'strict of Colŭ'mbia. (abbrev. D.C.) Federal division of U.S., including city of Washington, directly under control of Congress.

distrŭ'st *n*. Want of trust; doubt, suspicion. ~ *v.t.* Have no confidence in, doubt. **distrŭ'stful** *adj*. **distrŭ'stfully** *adv*. **distrŭ'stfulnėss** *n*.

distur'b *v.t.* Agitate, trouble, disquiet, unsettle; perplex.

distur'bance *n*. Interruption of tranquillity, agitation; tumult, uproar, outbreak; (law) molestation, interference with rights or property.

dĭstûr'bed (-bd) *adj.* (esp.) Emotionally or mentally unstable.

dī'stȳle *adj.* & *n.* (Portico) having 2 columns, esp. (~ *in antis*) at the front.

dĭsŭ'lphīde *n.* Sulphide containing 2 atoms of sulphur.

dĭsū'nion (-yon) *n.* Separation, want of union, dissension. **disūnī'te** *v.t.* **dĭsū'nitȳ** *n.*

dĭsū'se *n.* Discontinuance, want of use or practice, desuetude. **dĭsū'se** (-z) *v.t.* Cease to use.

dĭsȳ'llable, diss- *n.* Word, metrical foot, of 2 syllables. **dĭsȳllă'bĭc** *adj.* **dĭsȳllă'bĭcallȳ** *adv.*

ditch *n.* Long narrow excavation, esp. to hold or conduct water or serve as boundary; watercourse; (R.A.F. slang) North Sea or English Channel; *last* ~, last defensive point; point desperately defended; ~*-water*, stagnant water in ditch. ~ *v.* Make or repair ditches; provide with ditches, drain; run, drive (vehicle) into ditch or off track or road; (R.A.F. slang) bring (aircraft) down into sea in emergency; (slang) get rid of; leave in the lurch. **dĭ'tcher** *n.* One who makes or repairs ditches.

dī'thēism *n.* Religious dualism; esp. belief in two independent antagonistic principles of good and evil.

dĭ'ther (-dh-) *v.i.* Tremble, quiver; hesitate. ~ *n.* Dithering; tremulous excitement or apprehension.

dĭ'thȳrămb (-m) *n.* 1. (Gk antiq.) Wild choric hymn (orig. in honour of Dionysus) from which Greek tragedy is believed to have evolved. 2. Vehement or inflated poem, speech, or writing. **dĭthȳră'mbĭc** *adj.*

dĭ'ttanȳ *n.* 1. Perennial plant, *Origanum dictamnus*, formerly thought to have medicinal virtues in healing wounds etc. 2. Perennial plant, *Dictamnus albus*, burning bush, which in hot weather gives off inflammable vapours.

dĭ'ttō *n.* (abbrev. do, d°) The aforesaid, the same thing (used in accounts and lists, or colloq.); duplicate, similar thing. ~ *adv.* As before, likewise. [It. *ditto* (now *detto*) said, aforesaid]

dĭttŏ'graphȳ *n.* (palaeog. etc.) Unintentional repetition of letter(s) or word(s) by copyist. **dĭttogră'phic** *adj.*

dĭ'ttȳ *n.* Short simple song.

dĭ'ttȳ-băg *n.* Sailor's bag for holding odds and ends. **dĭ'ttȳ-bŏx** *n.* Fisherman's box for same purpose.

Diu (dē'o͞o). Island and small mainland area on west coast of India: see GOA.

dīūrē'sis *n.* Passing of urine in large amounts. **dīūrĕ'tĭc** *adj.* & *n.* (Substance) stimulating kidneys to secrete urine.

dīûr'nal *adj.* Occupying one day (chiefly of apparent motion of heavenly bodies); performed, happening, recurring, every day; of the day as dist. from the night; (zool.) active in day-time. **dīûr'nallȳ** *adv.*

dī'vagāte *v.i.* Stray, digress. **dīvagā'tion** *n.*

dīvā'lent *adj.* Having a VALENCY of 2. **dīvā'lence, dīvā'lencȳ** *ns.*

dĭvă'n *n.* 1. Oriental council of State; in Turkey, (hist.) privy council of the Porte, presided over by Sultan or grand vizier; oriental council-chamber, court of justice. 2. (*or* dī'-) Long seat against wall of room, usu. furnished with cushions; (also ~ *bed*) low bed without head-board. 3. Smoking-room attached to cigar-shop or bar; cigar-shop. [Pers. *dīwān* account-book, court, council, couch]

dīvă'rĭcāte *v.i.* Diverge, branch. **dīvă'rĭcate** (*-at*) *adj.*

dīve *v.i.* Plunge, esp. head foremost, into water etc.; go down or out of sight suddenly, dart; plunge hand *into* water, vessel, pocket; plunge *into* subject; (of aircraft etc.) descend steeply and fast; (of submarine) submerge; ~*-bomb* (*v.*) attack from aircraft with bombs released at end of steep dive; ~*-bomber* (*n.*); *diving-bell*, open-bottomed box or bell in which person can be let down into deep water; *diving-helmet*, head-gear of diving-suit; *diving-suit*, air- and water-tight garment (esp. with lead-soled boots and glass-fronted helmet, and apparatus for pumping in air) in which person can go down into deep water and remain under water for some time. ~ *n.* 1. Diving; plunge, precipitate fall. 2. (slang, orig. U.S.) Disreputable bar-room etc.

dī'ver *n.* (esp.) 1. One who dives for pearls, to examine and repair sunk vessels or to recover valuable cargo. 2. Water-bird of family Gaviidae remarkable for their power of diving and the distance they traverse under water.

dīver'ge *v.* Proceed in different directions from point or from each other; deviate; cause (lines, rays) to diverge; (math.) of a series, approach in its sum to an indefinitely great amount when a large number of terms is taken. **dīver'gence** *n.* **dīver'gent** *adj.* **dīver'gently** *adv.*

dī'vers (-z) *adj.* (archaic) Sundry, several, more than one.

dīver'se *adj.* Unlike in nature or qualities; varied, changeful. **dīver'sely** *adv.* **dīver'seness** *n.*

dīver'sify *v.t.* Make diverse, vary, modify, variegate. **dīversificā'tion** *n.*

dīver'sion *n.* 1. Deflecting, deviation; alternative route bypassing closed road. 2. Diverting of attention; manœuvre to secure this; feint. 3. Recreation, pleasant distraction, pastime.

dīver'sity *n.* Being diverse, unlikeness; different kind; variety.

dīver't *v.t.* Turn aside from (proper) direction or course; ward off; draw off attention of, distract; entertain, amuse. **dīver'ting** *adj.* **dīver'tingly** *adv.*

diverti'cūlum *n.* (pl. *-la*). (anat.) Blind tubular side-branch of cavity or passage.

divertissement (dēvertē'smahṅ) *n.* Short ballet or dance given between acts or longer pieces.

Dī'vēs (-z). Latin word for 'rich man', occurring in Vulgate, Luke 16, whence commonly taken for the name of the rich man in that parable; (typical name for) rich man.

dīvĕ'st *v.t.* Unclothe; strip *of* garment etc.; deprive, rid, *of.* **dīvĕ'stment, dīvĕ'stiture** *ns.*

divi: see DIVVY.

divī'de *v.* 1. Separate into parts or smaller groups, split, break up; mark out actually or mentally into parts; make classification in, distinguish kinds of; sunder, part, cut off (*from*). 2. Cause to disagree; set at variance; distract. 3. Distribute, deal out, (*among, between*); share *with* others. 4. (math.) Find how many times a number is contained in another; (of number or quantity) be contained exact number of times in (another). 5. Part (legislative assembly etc.) into two sets in voting; (of assembly) part itself thus. ~ *n.* (U.S. etc.) Watershed; *Great D~*, watershed of Rocky Mountains; (fig.) dividing line, esp. between life and death.

dĭ'vidĕnd *n.* 1. (math.) Number to be divided by another (the *divisor*). 2. Sum to be divided among a number of persons, payable as interest on loan, profit of joint-stock company, or sum paid to creditors of insolvent estate; amount received by individual holder or creditor as his share; *~-warrant*, document authorizing shareholder to receive dividend.

divī'der *n.* (esp., pl., also *pair of ~s*) Compasses having a screw

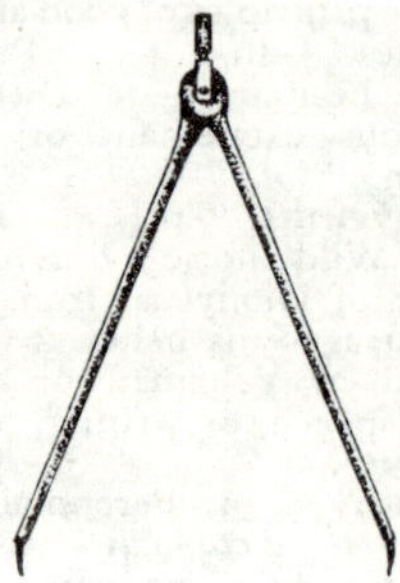

fastened to one leg and passing through the other, used for measuring small intervals, and for dividing straight lines etc. into any desired number of equal parts; simple pair of compasses with steel points.

dĭvinā′tion *n.* Divining; insight into or discovery of unknown or future by supernatural means; skilful forecast, good guess.

dĭvī′ne[1] *v.* Make out by inspiration, magic, intuition, or guessing; foresee, predict, conjecture; practise divination; *divining-rod*, dowser's rod. **dĭvī′ner** *n.*

dĭvī′ne[2] *adj.* 1. Of, from, like, God or a god; ~ *right of kings*, that claimed according to doctrine that (legitimate) kings derive their power from God alone, unlimited by any rights of their subjects. 2. Devoted or addressed to God; sacred; ~ *service*, public worship of God. 3. Superhumanly excellent, gifted, or beautiful. **dĭvī′nelў̆** *adv.* **dĭvī′ne** *n.* Person (usu. cleric) skilled in divinity, theologian.

dĭvĭ′nitў̆ *n.* 1. Being divine; deity; godhead. 2. Object of adoration, adorable being. 3. Science of divine things, theology; theological faculty in universities.

dĭ′vinīze *v.t.* Deify. **dĭvinīzā′tion** *n.*

dĭvĭ′sĭble (-z-) *adj.* Capable of being divided; (math.) ~ *by*, containing (a number) some number of times without remainder. **dĭvisĭbĭ′lĭtў̆** *n.*

dĭvĭ′sion *n.* 1. Dividing, being divided; severance, separation; distribution, sharing; ~ *of labour*, division of process of manufacture etc. into parts, each performed by particular person or group. 2. Disagreement, discord. 3. (math.) Process of dividing number by another; *long* ~, method in which each stage of the process is written down (adopted esp. when divisor is greater than 12), opp. *short* ~ in which the quotient is set down directly. 4. (logic) Classification, esp. that based on ordinary knowledge, not on methodical investigation; enumeration of parts; distinction of meaning. 5. Separation of members of legislative body into two parts for counting votes. 6. Dividing line, boundary. 7. Part, section; administrative, judicial, political, or other, division of country, territory, district, etc. 8. Definite part, under single command, of army or fleet; unit of an army intended to be capable of independent operations, varying greatly in size and composition but usu. consisting of three brigades and including infantry, (mechanized) cavalry, artillery, signals, engineers, etc., all under the command of a major-general; (also) specialized arm of military force, as *armoured* ~; (also) portion of a ship's company appropriated to a particular service; (also, pl.) parade of a ship's company according to its divisions. 9. (bot.) Major classificatory grouping. = PHYLUM; (zool.) subsidiary category between major groups, e.g. between phylum and class. **dĭvĭ′sional** *adj.* **dĭvĭ′sionallў̆** *adv.*

dĭvī′sor (-z-) *n.* Number by which another (the *dividend*) is to be divided; number that divides another without remainder, factor.

dĭvȯr′ce *n.* Legal dissolution of marriage; (fig.) complete separation, disunion of things closely connected. ~ *v.t.* Legally dissolve marriage between; separate by divorce *from*; put away, repudiate, obtain divorce from (spouse); dissolve (union); sever. **dĭvȯrcee′** *n.* (also *divorcé*, fem. *-cée*) Divorced person. **dĭvȯr′cement** *n.*

dĭ′vot *n.* Turf, sod (Sc.); (golf) piece of turf cut out by player's club when striking the ball.

dīvŭ′lge *v.t.* Let out, reveal. **dīvŭlgā′tion, dīvŭ′lgement, dīvŭ′lgence** *ns.*

dĭ′vvў̆, dĭ′vĭ *n.* (colloq.) Dividend. ~ *v.* Divide *up*.

dĭ′xĭe[1], **dĭ′xў̆** *n.* Iron kettle or pot used by soldiers etc. for making tea or stew. [Hind. *degchī* cooking-pot]

Dĭ′xĭe[2], **Dĭ′xĭe('s) Lănd** (-z). 1. Southern United States, the South. 2. (*Dixie*) Popular marching song (prob. composed by Dan Emmett, 1859) sung by Confederate soldiers in the Amer. Civil War. **Dĭ′xĭecrăt** *n.* Member of the U.S. Democratic party who insists on the maintenance of white superiority over Negroes in the southern States. [origin doubtful; perh. f. *dixie* (Fr. *dix* ten), a 10-dollar note issued in Louisiana before the Civil War; or f. Jeremiah *Dixon*, who with Charles Mason made a survey 1763–7 and drew the MASON AND DIXON LINE which later formed part of the boundary between the slave-owning and free States]

D.I.Y. *abbrev.* Do-it-yourself.

dĭ'zen *v.t.* (archaic) Array with finery, deck *out, up*.

dĭ'zzȳ *adj.* Giddy, dazed, unsteady, tottering, confused; making giddy; whirling rapidly. **dĭ'zzĭlȳ** *adv.* **dĭ'zzĭnėss** *n.* **dĭ'zzȳ** *v.t.* Make dizzy, bewilder.

D.J. *abbrev.* Disc-jockey.

Djakar'ta (j-), **J-.** City and seaport of NE. Java, capital of Indonesia.

djibba, -ah: see JIBBA.

djinn: see JINN.

dkg, dkl, dkm *abbrevs.* Decagramme(s), decalitre(s), decametre(s).

dl *abbrev.* Decilitre(s).

D.L. *abbrev.* Deputy Lieutenant.

D.Lit. *abbrev.* Doctor of Literature.

D.Litt. *abbrev.* *Doctor Litterarum* (L, = 'Doctor of letters').

dm *abbrev.* Decimetre(s).

D.M. *abbrev.* Deutsche Mark; Doctor of Medicine.

D.Mus. *abbrev.* Doctor of Music.

DNA *abbrev.* Deoxyribonucleic acid, any of the class of nucleic acids present in the chromosomes of higher organisms and storing genetic information.

D.N.B. *abbrev.* Dictionary of National Biography.

Dnie'per. River of U.S.S.R. flowing from White Russia through Ukraine to Black Sea.

Dnie'ster. River flowing SE. from province of Lvov, between Ukraine and Rumania to Black Sea.

do¹ (dōō) *v.* (past t. *dĭd*, past part. *done* pr. dŭn). 1. (*v.t.*) Perform, effect, execute; complete; produce, make; operate on, deal with; cook; (colloq.) provide (food etc.) for; tour, visit as a tourist; swindle. 2. (*v.i.*) Act, proceed; perform deeds; fare, get on; be suitable, suffice. 3. Used as auxiliary verb esp. in questions (as *do you know?*), negative or emphatic statements (as *I did not know*; *I do know*), and urgent requests (as *do come!*). 4. Used as substitute for verb just used, to avoid repetition, as *I wanted to see him, and I did* (i.e. saw him). 5. With noun of action as object, = cognate verb of action; e.g. *do writing*, write; *do repairs*, repair things; *do battle*, fight. 6. *done!*, I accept (offer, bet, etc.); *have to do with*, be concerned or connected with, have dealings with; *it isn't done*, **it is forbidden by** custom or propriety; *nothing* etc. *doing*, nothing etc. happening or going on; (colloq.) announcement of refusal, failure, etc.; *do away* (*with*), abolish; *do brown*, (colloq.) dupe, swindle; *do by*, treat, deal with, in specified way; *do down*, overcome, get the better of, bring to grief; *do for*, (colloq.) do house-cleaning for; ruin, destroy, kill; *do in*, (slang) kill; exhaust; *do or die*, be undeterred by danger; *do time*, *do* (10 etc.) *years*, undergo imprisonment; *do to, unto*, do by; *do to death*, kill; *do up*, restore, repair; wrap up (parcel); exhaust; *do with*, get on with, tolerate; find sufficient; (colloq.) be pleased to have, need; *do without*, dispense with. 7. *do-gooder*, (usu. derog.) well-meaning but unrealistic social reformer etc.; *do-it-yourself*, practice of doing repairs etc. oneself; of, for, amateur craftsman or home handyman etc.; *do-nothing*, idler. ~ *n.* (slang) Swindle, imposture, hoax; entertainment, show; *dos and don'ts*, rules. **do'able** *adj.* **do'er** *n.*

do²: see DOH.

do, d° *abbrev.* Ditto.

doat: see DOTE.

dŏ'bbĭn *n.* Draught- or farm-horse. [pet-form of *Robert*]

dŏ'bbȳ *n.* Mechanism attached to loom for weaving small figures.

Dō'bermann pĭ'nscher (-sh-). German hound with smooth coat and docked tail. [*Dobermann*, name of breeder; Ger. *pinscher* terrier]

Dobru'dja (-brōō-) SE. part of Rumania between lower Danube and Black Sea.

Docē'tist *n.* Member of the Docetae, a sect of early Christian heretics who held that Christ's body was not human but a phantom or of celestial substance. **Docĕ'tic** *adj.* **Docē'tism** *n.* [Gk *dokeein* seem, appear]

dō'cīle *adj.* Teachable; submissive; easily managed. **docĭ'lity̆** *n.*

dŏck[1] *n.* Species of *Rumex*, coarse weedy herbs with panicled racemes of inconspicuous greenish flowers, and large leaves used as popular antidote for nettle-stings.

dŏck[2] *n.* Solid fleshy part of animal's tail; crupper of saddle or harness. ~ *v.t.* Cut short (animal in tail, person in hair; or tail etc.); lessen, deprive *of*; put limits on.

dŏck[3] *n.* 1. Artificial basin fitted with flood-gates into which ships are received for loading or unloading, or for repairs; *in* ~, (colloq., of vehicle) laid up for repairs; *dry, graving,* ~, dock from which water may be pumped out, leaving vessel dry for repairs etc.; *floating* ~, floating structure usable as dry dock; *wet* ~, dock in which water is kept at high-tide level. 2. (pl.) Range of docks with wharves, warehouses, offices, etc.; dockyard. 3. (theatr.) Enclosure at side of stage for scenery. 4. ~*-dues*, charges for use of docks; ~*-glass*, large glass for wine-tasting; *do'ckland, D-*, districts about the docks; ~*-master*, superintendent of dock or dockyard; *do'ckyard*, enclosure for building and repairing ships, preparing and collecting ships' stores, etc.; esp. Government dockyard for navy. ~ *v.* 1. Bring (ship), come, into dock. 2. Furnish with docks. 3. Join (spacecraft) to another, become joined, in space.

dŏck[4] *n.* Enclosure in criminal court for prisoner on trial; ~ *brief*, brief handed direct to barrister in court by prisoner entitled to legal aid.

dŏ'cker *n.* Labourer in DOCK[3].

dŏ'ckėt *n.* 1. Abstract, summary (hist.); abstract of contents of proposed letters patent, written upon king's bill authorizing preparation of such letters. 2. (law) Memorandum or register of legal judgements; (U.S.) list of causes for trial or of persons with causes pending. 3. Endorsement on letter etc. indicating contents or subject; label, ticket; (in some Government departments) set of papers on given subject, file. 4. Custom-house warrant certifying payment of duty; certificate of cotton clearing-house entitling presenter to delivery. 5. Workman's record of jobs done during day or week. ~ *v.t.* Make abstract of and enter in docket; endorse (letter etc.) with docket; (U.S.) enter (cause) in docket.

dŏ'ctor *n.* 1. Teacher, eminently learned man (archaic). 2. (used as prefix to name, usu. abbrev. Dr) Holder of highest university degree in any faculty; esp., doctor of medicine; (pop.) any medical practitioner. 3. Any of various mechanical appliances for removing defects, regulating, adjusting, etc. (~*blade*). 4. Local wind modifying extremes of climate. 5. = SURGEON-fish. 6. *Doctors' Commons*, (hist.) common table of former College of Doctors of Civil Law in London; its buildings, the courts held there, where probate and divorce business was transacted; ~*'s mandate*, (pol.) commission to administration to prescribe whatever remedies it thinks fit in emergency; *Doctors of the Church*, certain early Christian Fathers distinguished for their learning and heroic sanctity, esp. Ambrose, Augustine, Jerome, and Gregory in the Western Church, and Athanasius, Basil, Gregory of Nazianzus, and Chrysostom in the Eastern Church. **dŏ'ctoral, dŏctōr'ĭal** *adjs.* **dŏ'ctor** *v.* Treat medically; castrate; patch up (machinery etc.); adulterate, falsify; *doctoring*, practising as physician.

dŏ'ctorate *n.* Degree of doctor.

dŏctrĭnair'e, -nār'ĭan *ns.* One who holds some doctrine or theory and tries to apply it without allowing for circumstances; pedantic theorist. ~ *adj.* Of, like, a doctrinaire; theoretic, unpractical. **dŏctrĭnair'ĭsm** *n.* [*Doctrinaire*, name of a Fr. political party, 1815]

dŏctrī'nal (*or* dŏ'ktrĭ-) *adj.* Of, inculcating, doctrine(s). **dŏctrī'nallȳ** *adv.*

dŏ'ctrine *n.* What is taught, body of instruction; religious, political, scientific, etc., belief, dogma, or tenet; *Monroe D~*: see MONROE. **dŏ'ctrinism, dŏ'ctrinist** *ns.*

dŏ'cūment *n.* Something written, inscribed, etc., which furnishes evidence or information upon any subject, as manuscript, title-deed, coin, etc. ~ *v.t.* Prove or support by documentary evidence; furnish or provide with documents or evidence; keep well informed. **dŏcūmĕntā'tion** *n.*

dŏcūmĕ'ntarȳ *adj.* Of documents; (of film) dealing with real happenings or circumstances, not fiction. ~ *n.* Documentary film.

dŏ'dder[1] *n.* Slender leafless parasitic plant of genus *Cuscuta* with twining thread-like stems.

dŏ'dder[2] *v.i.* Tremble, nod, with frailty. **dŏ'dderer** *n.* **dŏ'ddering** *adj.* Mentally feeble or inept, futile.

dōdĕca- *prefix.* Twelve-.

dōdĕ'cagon *n.* Plane figure of twelve angles and sides.

dōdėcahē'dron *n.* Solid figure of twelve faces.

Dōdėcanē'se (-z). Group of twelve islands in SE. Aegean occupied by Italy in 1912 during the war with Turkey, and ceded to Greece in 1947.

dōdėcaphŏ'nic *adj.* (mus.) Of, using, a twelve-tone scale (i.e. an octave with its twelve semitones of equal importance).

dōdėcasȳ'llable *n.* (pros.) Line of twelve syllables.

dŏdge *v.* 1. Move to and fro, change position, shuffle; move quickly *round, about, behind,* obstacle so as to elude pursuer, blow, etc.; avoid, elude, by change of position, shifts, doubling, etc. 2. (of bell in change-ringing) Be shifted one place in opposite direction instead of following its regular ascending or descending order. ~ *n.* Dodging, quick side-movement; trick, artifice; (colloq.) clever expedient, contrivance, etc.; (change-ringing) act of dodging.

dŏ'dgem *n.* Small electrically-powered car at fairs etc. in which drivers try to bump and avoid being bumped by other cars.

dŏ'dger *n.* (esp.) 1. Artful or elusive person. 2. (colloq.) Screen on ship's bridge as protection from spray etc.

Dŏ'dgson, Charles Lutwidge (1832–98). English mathematician, celebrated as author, under his pseudonym Lewis Carroll, of 'Alice's Adventures in Wonderland' (1865) and 'Through the Looking-Glass' (1871).

dŏ'dgȳ *adj.* (slang) Artful; awkward, tricky.

dō'dō *n.* (pl. *-oes, -os*). Extinct bird, *Raphus cucullatus,* with massive clumsy body and wings

too small for flight, formerly inhabiting Mauritius. [Port. *doudo* simpleton]

dōe *n.* Female of fallow deer, hare, or rabbit; *doe'skin,* skin of doe, kind of leather made from this.

D.O.E. *abbrev.* Department of the Environment.

dŏff *v.t.* Take off (hat, clothing).

dŏg *n.* 1. Carnivorous quadruped of the genus *Canis,* found wild in various parts of the world, and domesticated or semi-domesticated in almost all countries, in numerous races or breeds varying greatly in shape, size, and colour; *the ~s* (colloq.) a greyhound race meeting. 2. Male of this animal, or of fox or wolf. 3. (also *gay ~*) gay or jovial fellow; *dirty~,* (slang) despicable person 4.

DOGS

the D~, (astron.) each of two constellations, the *Greater* and *Lesser D~* (*Canis Major* and *Minor*) near Orion; either of the principal stars of these, Sirius in the Greater Dog and Procyon in the Lesser Dog. 5. Any of various mechanical devices, usu. having a tooth or claw for gripping or holding. 6. One of a pair of metal utensils (*fire-~s*) placed one at each side of fireplace to support burning wood or a grate; rest for fire-irons. 7. (also *sea-~*) Luminous appearance near horizon supposed to presage bad weather. 8. *die like a ~*, die miserably or shamefully; *a hair of the ~ that bit you*, more drink to take off effects of drunkenness; *to the ~s*, to destruction or ruin; *~ in the manger*, one who prevents others enjoying what is useless to him; *a ~'s chance*, the slightest chance; *a ~'s life*, a life of misery, or of miserable subserviency. 9. *do'gberry*, fruit of dogwood; *~ biscuit*, hard biscuit for feeding dogs; *~-cart*, two-wheeled driving-cart with two transverse seats back to back (the rear one orig. made to shut so as to form a box for dogs); *~ clutch*: see CLUTCH[1]; *~-collar*, collar for dog's neck; clergyman's stiff white collar fastening at back of neck; straight high close-fitting collar, esp. jewelled one; *~-daisy*, common or (now usu.) ox-eye daisy; *~-days*, period during part of July and August about time of heliacal or cosmical rising of Sirius, the dog-star, considered from ancient times the hottest and most unwholesome period of the year; *~-eared*, (of book) having leaves turned down at corner, or crumpled; *~-faced baboon*: see CYNOCEPHALUS; *~-fall*, (wrestling) fall in which both wrestlers touch ground together; *~-fight*, fight between dogs; general mêlée; mêlée between aircraft; *do'gfish*, kind of small shark, *Scyliorhinus caniculus*; *large-spotted dogfish*, nurse hound; *~ Latin*, bad Latin, mongrel Latin; *~-leg*, bent like a dog's hind leg; *~-nail*, nail with head projecting on one side; *~-paddle*, method of swimming like dog's; *~ -rose*, common wild rose, *Rosa canina*, with pale-pink flowers, frequent in hedges; *do'gsbody*, (colloq.) drudge; *~'s-ear*, crumpled corner of leaf of book; *do'gskin*, leather made from dog's skin or sheepskin, used for gloves etc.; *~'s-meat*, horseflesh, offal, carrion; *~'s nose*, drink of beer and gin; *~'s-tail*, grass of genus *Cynosurus*, with flowers in each panicle all pointing one way, like dog's tail; *~-star*: see 4 above; *~'s-tongue*, HOUND's-tongue; *~('s)-tooth check*, chequered pattern in which each square has a slight projection on two opposite corners; *~'s tooth (violet)*, spring-flowering liliaceous garden-plant, *Erythronium dens-canis*, with spotted leaves and purple flowers, so called from teeth on inner segments of perianth; *~-tired*, extremely tired, tired out; *~-tooth*, canine tooth; (archit.) pointed ornament or moulding frequent in early medieval architecture; *~ -trot*, easy steady trot like a dog's; *~-violet*, *Viola canina* and other species of scentless wild violets; *~-watch*, (naut.) each of the two short watches between 4 and 8 p.m. (of two, instead of four, hours each); *do'gwood*, wild cornel, *Cornus sanguinea*, or other species of *Cornus*; close smooth-grained wood of this. **dŏ'ggish, dŏ'gless, dŏ'glike** *adjs.* **dŏg** *v.t.* Follow closely, pursue, track; (mech.) grip with dog.

dōge *n.* (hist.) Chief magistrate of republics of Venice and Genoa. **dō'gāte** *n.* Office of doge.

dŏ'ggėd (-g-) *adj.* Obstinate, tenacious, persistent, unyielding. **dŏ'ggėdlў** *adv.* **dŏ'ggėdnėss** *n.*

dŏ'gger (-g-) *n.* Two-masted bluff-bowed Dutch fishing-boat.

Dŏ'gger Bănk (-g-). Sandbank in N. Sea between England and Denmark, *c* 150 miles long.

dŏ'ggerel (-g-) *adj.* & *n.* Trivial, mean, halting, or irregular (verse).

Dŏ'ggėtt's coat and bădge (-g-). Rowing competition among Thames watermen, instituted 1716 by Thomas Doggett, English actor and theatre manager.

dŏ'ggō *adv.* (slang) *lie ~*, lie motionless making no sign.

dŏ'ggў, -ĭe (-g-) *n.* (nursery) Dog. **dŏ'ggў** *adj.* Of dogs; devoted to dogs.

dŏ'gma *n.* Principle, tenet, doctrinal system, esp. as laid down by authority of Church; arrogant declaration of opinion.

dŏgmă'tĭc *adj.* 1. Of, based on, dogmas; *~ theology*: see THEOLOGY. 2. Asserting dogmas or opinions, esp. arrogantly. **dŏgmă'tĭcal** *adj.* **dŏgmă'tĭcallў** *adv.* **dŏgmă'tĭcs** *n.* System of dogma; dogmatic theology.

dŏ'gmatīze *v.* Make positive unsupported assertions, speak authoritatively; express (principle etc.) as a dogma. **dŏ'gmatism, dŏ'gmatist** *ns.*

Dō'gra *n.* Member of a people inhabiting the Duggar district of NW. India; their language.

doh (dō), **dō**[2] *n.* (mus.) First note of hexachord, note C in fixed-doh system of solmization, keynote of scale in movable-doh system.

doi'lȳ, doy'ley *n.* 1. (archaic) Small napkin used at dessert. 2. Small decorative mat. [fabric named f. 17th-c. inventor]

do'ing (do͞o-) *n.* (esp., usu. pl.) Performance, deed, act, transaction, proceeding; (pl., slang) vague term for anything lying about, or wanted.

dol. *abbrev.* Dollar(s).

dŏ'lce (-chā) *adv.* (mus.) Sweetly, softly. [It.]

dŏ'lce fār nĭĕ'ntė (-chā). Pleasant idleness. [It., = 'sweet doing nothing']

dŏ'ldrums (-z) *n.pl.* 1. Dullness, dumps, depression; *in the* ~, (of ship) becalmed. 2. Region near equator where meeting of trade winds produces light baffling winds, sudden storms, and calms. (prob. f. *dull,* the geog. sense being prob. due to misunderstanding of phrase *in the* ~]

dōle[1] *n.* 1. (archaic) Lot, destiny. 2. Charitable distribution; charitable (esp. sparing, niggardly) gift; portion sparingly dealt out; (colloq.) unemployment benefit; *on the* ~, receiving this. ~ *v.t.* Deal *out* sparingly, esp. as alms.

dōle[2] *n.* (poet.) Grief, woe; lamentation.

dō'leful (-lf-) *adj.* Dreary, dismal; sad, discontented, melancholy. **dō'lefullȳ** *adv.* **dō'lefulnėss** *n.*

dŏ'lerīte *n.* Coarse basaltic rock much used as road-metal. [Gk *doleros* deceptive (because easily confused with true greenstone)]

dŏlĭchōcėphă'lic (-kō-) *adj.* Long-headed; with breadth of skull less than ⅘ of length.

dŏll *n.* Small model of human figure, esp. as toy; pretty but vacuous woman. ~ *v.* Dress *up* finely. [shortened pet-form of *Dorothy*]

dŏ'llar *n.* 1. (orig.) English name for the German thaler and also for the Spanish piece of eight (peso) current in Spanish America and used in British N. Amer. colonies before the War of Independence. 2. Principal monetary unit (symbol $) of U.S., Canada, and other countries; ~ *area,* group of countries with currencies linked to U.S. dollar. 3. Principal monetary unit of various other countries. [orig. *daler,* f. *Joachimstaler,* coin from silver mine in Joachimstal, Bohemia (Ger. *tal* valley); symbol $ a modification of P[s], Mex. abbrev. for pesos or piastres]

Dŏ'llfuss (-o͞os), Engelbert (1892–1934). Austrian statesman; became chancellor and dictator of Austria 1933; assassinated 1934.

dŏ'llop *n.* (colloq.) Large quantity; clumsy or shapeless lump.

dŏ'llȳ *n.* 1. (Pet name for) doll. 2. Any of various contrivances used in punching, clothes-washing, piledriving, polishing, etc. 3. Mobile platform, esp. for cinema camera. 4. ~*-shop,* marine store; ~*-tub,* wash-tub.

Dŏ'llȳ Vār'den. (also ~ *hat*) Large hat with brim drooping at one side, trimmed with flowers etc. [name of character in Dickens's 'Barnaby Rudge']

dŏ'lman *n.* 1. Long Turkish robe open in front. 2. Hussar's uniform jacket worn like cape with sleeves hanging loose. 3. Woman's mantle with cape-like sleeves;

18TH-C. DOLLS

DOLMEN

~ *sleeve*, loose sleeve like that of dolman, cut in one piece with body of garment.

dŏ'lmĕn *n.* Megalithic burial chamber, large flat stone laid horizontally upon upright ones. [Fr., prob. f. Cornish *tolmên*, lit. 'hole of stone']

dŏ'lomīte *n.* 1. (chem.) Double carbonate of calcium and magnesium occurring as crystal or in white or coloured granular masses; rock of this. 2. Dolomite mountain, esp. (*Dolomites*) those of the southern Tyrol. **dŏlomĭ'tic** *adj.* [Dieudonné Gratet de *Dolomieu* (1750–1801), French mineralogist]

dŏ'lorous *adj.* (usu. poet. or facet.) Distressing, painful; doleful; distressed. **dŏ'lorouslў** *adv.*

dŏ'lour (-ler) *n.* (poet.) Sorrow, distress.

dŏ'lphin *n.* 1. Cetaceous mammal (*Delphinus delphis*) resembling porpoise but with longer and more slender snout. 2. (pop.) = DORADO. 3. (astron.) Northern constellation (*Delphinus*). 4. Figure of dolphin in heraldry etc.

dōlt *n.* Stupid person. **dō'ltĭsh** *adj.* **dō'ltĭshlў** *adv.* **dō'ltĭshnĕss** *n.*

D.O.M. *abbrev.* *Deo optimo maximo* (L, = to God the best and greatest).

Dŏm *n.* 1. Title prefixed to names of R.C. ecclesiastical and monastic dignitaries, esp. Carthusian and Benedictine monks. 2. Portuguese equivalent of DON[1], as title. [L *dominus* master, lord]

domai'n *n.* 1. Estate, lands, dominions; district under rule; realm; sphere of influence; scope, field, province, of thought or action; *eminent* ~, sovereign government's power of controlling or confiscating private property for public use, subject to compensation. 2. (phys., in ferro-magnetic materials) Aggregation of atoms or ions which behaves as an elementary magnet, all the īons in a domain having the axes of their permanent magnetic moment aligned in the same direction.

dōme *n.* 1. (poet.) Stately building, mansion. 2. Rounded vault forming roof, with circular, elliptical or polygonal base; natural vault, canopy (of trees, sky, etc.);

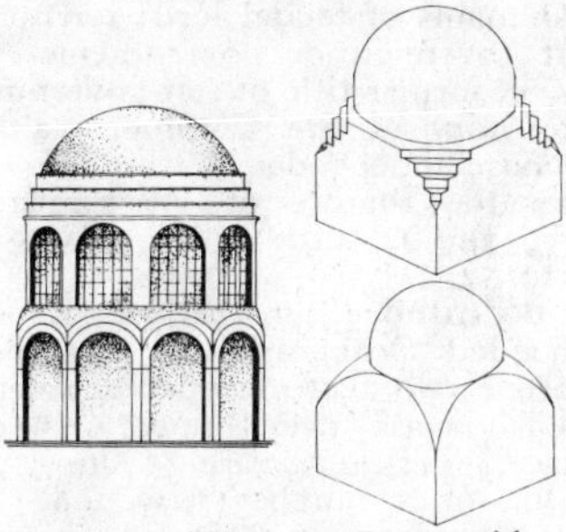

Dome with circular base · Domes with square base
DOME

rounded summit of hill etc. ~ *v.t.* Cover with, shape as, dome. **dōmed** (-md) *adj.* Vaulted, dome-like; having a dome or domes. [Fr., f. It. *duomo* cathedral, dome, f. L *domus* house]

Do'mesday Bŏŏk (dōōmz-). Record of Great Inquisition of lands of England, their extent, value, ownership, and liabilities, made by order of William the Conqueror in 1086. [pop. name (= Doomsday) given to the book as final authority]

domĕ'stĭc *adj.* 1. Of the home, household, or family affairs; of one's own country, not foreign; native, home-made; ~ *science*, study of household management. 2. (of animals) Tame, kept by or living with man. 3. Home-keeping, fond of home, domesticated. ~ *n.* Household servant. **domĕ'stĭcallў** *adv.*

domĕ'stĭcāte *v.t.* Naturalize; attach to home and its duties (esp. in past part.); tame and bring under control (animals), accustom to live near men; civilize. **domĕ'stĭcable** *adj.* **domĕstĭcā'tion** *n.*

dŏmėstĭ'cĭtў *n.* Domestic character; home life or privacy; homeliness; (pl.) domestic affairs.

dŏ'mĭcile *n.* Dwelling-place, home; (law) place of permanent residence, fact of residing; place at which bill of exchange is made payable. ~ *v.* Establish, settle, in a place; make (bill) payable *at* place.

dŏmĭcĭ'lĭarў *adj.* Of a dwelling-place; ~ *visit*, visit of physician etc. to person's home; visit by officials to private dwelling to search or inspect it.

dŏmĭcĭ'lĭāte *v.* Domicile. **dŏmĭcĭlĭā'tion** *n.*

dŏ'mĭnant *adj.* 1. Ruling, prevailing, most influential; occupying commanding position. 2. (mus.) Of the dominant; (of

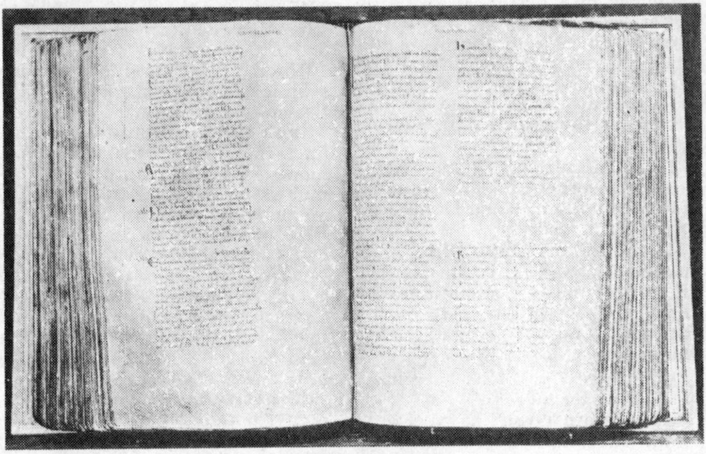

DOMESDAY BOOK

chord) having dominant for its root. 3. (biol., of inherited character) That is apparent in offspring when an opposite character is also inherited (opp. RECESSIVE). ~ *n.* Dominant thing or constituent; (esp., mus.) 5th note of ascending scale; reciting note in ecclesiastical modes, usu. 5th from final; (biol.) dominant character.

dŏ'mĭnāte *v.* Have commanding influence over (also intrans. with *over*); be the most influential or conspicuous; (of height) overlook; occupy commanding position. **dŏmĭnā'tion** *n.* 1. Ascendancy, sway, control. 2. (pl.) Order of angels (see ANGEL).

dŏmĭneer' *v.i.* Act imperiously, tyrannize (*over*), be overbearing. **dŏmĭneer'ing** *adj.* **dŏmĭneer'ingly̆** *adv.*

Dŏ'mĭnic, St. Domingo de Guzman (1170–1221), Spanish founder of an order of preaching friars (*Dominicans*).

Domĭ'nica (*or* dŏmĭnē'-). Island in the West Indies, formerly in British possession; independent (as an Associated State) 1967; capital, Roseau.

domĭ'nĭcal *adj.* Of the Lord (Jesus Christ); of the Lord's Day or Sunday; ~ *letter*, letter denoting Sundays in a particular year (the letters A–G being used to denote first seven days of the year, and then in rotation the next seven days, and so on, so that, e.g. if 3 Jan. is a Sunday, the dominical letter for the year is C); ~ *year*, year of our Lord.

Domĭ'nĭcan *adj.* Of St. Dominic or the order of friars (or nuns) founded by him. ~ *n.* Dominican friar, black friar.

Domĭ'nĭcan Rėpŭ'blĭc. Republic (since 1844) occupying the E. part of the W. Indian island of Hispaniola, formerly part of the Spanish Empire; capital, Santo Domingo.

dŏ'mĭnĭe *n.* (Sc., archaic) Schoolmaster.

domĭ'nion (-yon) *n.* 1. Lordship, sovereignty, control; (law) right of possession, ownership. 2. Domains of feudal lord; territory of sovereign or government. 3. *D~*, former title of self-governing territory of the Commonwealth, whose independence was defined by the Statute of Westminster (1931). 4. (usu. pl.) = DOMINATION 2.

dŏ'mĭnō *n.* (pl. *-oes*). 1. Loose hooded cloak, app. of Venetian origin, worn at masquerades with small mask over upper part of face; person wearing this. 2. One of a number (usu. 28) of rectangular pieces of ivory, wood, etc., usu. black, and with upper side equally divided into two squares, each either blank or marked with pips, so as to present all possible combinations from double blank to double six; (pl.) game played with these (usu.) by placing corresponding ends in contact.

dŏn¹ *n.* 1. Spanish title prefixed to Christian names; Spanish gentleman, Spaniard; distinguished person. 2. (colloq.) Head, fellow, or tutor of college, esp. at Oxford or Cambridge. [Span., f. L *dominus* lord]

dŏn² *v.t.* Put on (garment).

Dŏn³. River of southern U.S.S.R. flowing into Sea of Azov.

dō'na, -ah (*-a*) *n.* (slang) Woman, sweetheart. [f. Span. *doña* or Port. *dona* lady]

Dŏnatĕ'llō (1386–1466). Italian sculptor, famous esp. for his bronze 'David' in Florence.

donā'tion *n.* Bestowal, presenting; thing presented, gift (esp. money given to institution). **donā'te** *v.t.* Make donation of; give, grant. **donā'tor** *n.*

Dō'natist *adj.* & *n.* (Member) of a Christian sect which arose in N. Africa in 311 out of a dispute about the election of the bishop of Carthage, and which maintained that it was the only true and pure Church, and that baptisms and ordinations of others were invalid.

dō'natĭve *n.* Benefice given directly, not involving presentation to or investment by the Ordinary; gift, present, esp. official largess.

~ *adj.* (of benefice) That is a donative.

dŏ'natorў *n.* Recipient of donation.

done: see DO[1] *v.*

dōnee' *n.* Recipient of gift.

Dŏ'nėgal (-awl; *or* -aw'l). County of Ulster in the Republic of Ireland; ~ *tweed*, tweed with coloured slubs.

dŏng *n.* Principal monetary unit of N. and S. Vietnam.

dŏ'nga (-ngg-) *n.* (S. Afr.) Ravine, gully.

Dŏnizĕ'ttĭ, Gaetano (1797–1848). Italian composer of operas.

dŏ'njon *n.* Great tower of castle, keep.

Dŏn Juan (jōō'an). Legendary Spanish nobleman of dissolute life; hence, rake, libertine.

dŏ'nkey *n.* (Usual word for) ass; stupid person; art student's four-legged stool with rest for drawing-board; ~ *engine*, small steam-engine, usu. for subsidiary operations on board ship; ~*'s years*, (colloq.) very long time; ~*-work*, (colloq.) drudgery.

Dŏnne (*or* dŭn), John (1572–1631). Dean of St. Paul's; preacher and metaphysical poet; author of satires, epistles, and elegies.

dŏ'nnĭsh *adj.* Like a university don; pedantic. **dŏ'nnĭshnėss** *n.*

Dŏ'nnўbrōōk. Town near Dublin, Ireland; ~ *Fair*, annual fair formerly held there; hence, scene of uproar and disorder, free fight.

dō'nor *n.* 1. Giver; person portrayed in religious picture as having presented it to church etc. 2. (med.) Person, animal, from whose body biological material is removed, as blood for transfusion (*blood-*~), organ or tissue for transplantation to another person etc.

Don Quixote: see QUIXOTE.

dōn't. (colloq.) = Do not; ~-*care* (*adj.*) careless, reckless. ~ *n.* (usu. pl.) Prohibition.

dōō'dle *n.* (orig. U.S.) Aimless scrawl made by a person while his attention is engaged. ~ *v.i.* Make a doodle.

dōō'dle-bŭg *n.* 1. (U.S.) Tiger-beetle or its larva. 2. (colloq.)

German pilotless plane or flying bomb in war of 1939–45.

dōōm *n.* 1. (hist.) Statute, law; decree. 2. (archaic) Decision, sentence, condemnation. 3. Fate, lot, (usu. evil) destiny; ruin, death. 4. Last Judgement (chiefly in *crack, day, of* ~); *D*~ representation of this in art; *doo'msday*, the day of judgement; *till doomsday*, to the end of the world, for ever; *doo'mwatch*(*ing*), system of watching to see that man does not destroy his own environment etc. ~ *v.* Pronounce sentence against; condemn *to* some fate, *to* do; consign to misfortune or destruction (esp. in past part.).

door (dōr) *n.* 1. Movable barrier of wood or other material, turning on hinges or sliding in groove, and serving to close or open passage into building, room, etc.; doorway; means of entrance or exit; *at death's* ~, on the point of dying; *lay, lie, at the* ~ *of*, impute, be imputable, to; abroad, in the open air. 2. ~*-bell*, bell within house which may be rung from outside; ~*-keeper*, janitor, porter; ~*-mat*, mat placed at door for wiping shoes on entering; ~*-nail*, large-headed nail with which doors were formerly studded for strength or ornament; ~*-plate*, plate on door bearing name of occupant of house or room; ~-*post*, either of uprights on each side of doorway, on one of which door is hung; *door'step*, step at threshold of door; (slang) thick slice of bread; *door'way*, opening or passage which door serves to close or open; ~*-yard*, (U.S.) yard or garden about door of house.

dŏp *n.* Cheap S. Afr. brandy made from grape-skins; dram of liquor. [S. Afr. Du., = 'shell', 'husk']

dōpe *n.* 1. Thick liquid used as food or lubricant; varnish, esp. that applied to cloth parts of aeroplanes etc. to keep them taut and airtight. 2. (slang) Opium or other narcotic, stupefying drink; drug administered to horse etc. before race to improve or spoil its performance; (chiefly U.S.) information, esp. false or deceptive information, or that supplied for newspaper use; fraud, humbug; *~-fiend*, drug-addict. 3. (colloq.) Stupid person. ~ *v.t.* (orig. U.S.) Drug; doctor; apply dope to (aeroplane fabric etc.). **dō'pey̆, -pȳ** *adj.* (slang) Heavy or stupefied, as if drugged; stupid. [app. f. Du. *doop* sauce]

dŏ'ppelgănger *n.* Person's double or apparition seen shortly before or after his death, wraith. [Ger.]

Dŏ'ppler, Christian Johann (1803–53). Austrian physicist; ~ *effect*, apparent change in frequency of electromagnetic and sound waves caused by change in distance between observer and source of sound etc.

dor *n.* (also ~ *beetle*) Insect flying with loud humming noise, esp. common black dung beetle, cockchafer, and rose-chafer.

Dor'a. (joc.) Personification of *D*efence *o*f the *R*ealm *A*ct passed in Aug. 1914, giving Government wide powers during the 1914–18 war. [from initials]

dora'dō (-ah-) *n.* (pl. *-os*). 1. Sea-fish (genus *Coryphaena*), bright blue and silver and very swift. 2. (astron.) = XIPHIAS.

Dor'cas. Woman mentioned in Acts 9: 36 as 'full of good deeds and almsdeeds which she did'; ~ *Society*, ladies' association, connected with a church, for making and providing clothes for the poor.

Doré (dŏrā), Paul Gustave (1833–83). French artist; famous for his scriptural paintings and illustrations of Dante, Milton, etc.

Dor'ian *adj.* Of DORIS or the Dorians; ~ *mode*, (mus.) ancient Greek mode, reputedly simple and solemn in character; 1st of ecclesiastical modes, with D as final and A as dominant. ~ *n.* Native, inhabitant, of Doris.

Dŏ'rĭc *adj.* 1. Dorian. 2. (of dialect etc.) Broad, rustic. 3. (archit.) Of the Doric order, oldest, strongest, and simplest of the Greek orders of architecture. ~ *n.* 1. Doric dialect of ancient Greece. 2. Rustic English 3. Doric architecture.

Dor'ĭs, Dor'ĭa. Small country in ancient Greece, S. of Thessaly, the home of the Dorians.

Dor'kĭng *adj.* & *n.* (Fowl) of a white breed of poultry with long squarish body and short legs. [f. *Dorking*, town in Surrey]

dor'mant *adj.* Sleeping; inactive as in sleep; with animation or development suspended; not active, in abeyance; (bot., esp. of seeds and buds) in state of suspended growth; (her., of beast) with head resting on paws. **dor'mancȳ** *n.*

dor'mer *n.* (also ~ *window*) Projecting vertical window in sloping roof.

dor'mĭtorȳ *n.* 1. Sleeping-room with several beds, or divided into cells or cubicles. 2. (U.S.) Hostel, hall of residence, in university. 3. (also ~ *town, suburb*) District containing residences of persons working in nearby town.

dor'mouse *n.* Small hibernating rodent akin to mouse but resembling squirrel in form and habit, esp. the British species *Muscardinus avellanarius*.

dor'mȳ *adj.* (golf) As many holes ahead of opponent as there are holes still to be played (~ *one, two*, etc.).

Dŏ'rothȳ băg. Woman's handbag with open top drawn up by strings. [f. *Dorothy*, woman's name]

Dŏ'rothȳ Per'kĭns (-z). Climbing rose with clusters of pink double flowers.

dorp *n.* (S. Afr.) Village, small town.

dor'sal *adj.* (anat., bot., zool.) Of, on, near, the back; ridge-shaped. ~ *n.* = DOSSAL. **dor'sallȳ** *adv.*

Dŏr'sėt. County of SW. England.

dŏr'ter, -tour (*-er*) *n.* (hist.) Bedroom, dormitory, esp. in monastery.

dŏr'ȳ[1] *n.* (also *John D~*) European sea-fish, *Zeus faber*, used as food. [Fr. *dorée* gilded]

dŏr'ȳ[2] *n.* (U.S.) Small flat-bottomed boat, esp. for fishing.

dō'sage *n.* Giving of medicine in doses; size of dose; amount of X-rays etc. applied at one time.

dōse (-s) *n.* Amount of medicine etc. given or prescribed to be given at one time. ~ *v.t.* Give medicine to (person); add spirit to (wine).

dŏss *n.* (slang) Bed, esp. in common lodging-house; sleep; *~-house*, common lodging-house. ~ *v.i.* Sleep, esp. in doss-house; ~ *down*, sleep on makeshift bed.

dŏ'ssal *n.* Ornamental hanging at back of altar or round a chancel.

dŏ'ssier (*or* -syā) *n.* Set or bundle of documents relating to a particular person or happening.

Dŏstōĕ'vskȳ (-fs-), Fedor Mikhailovich (1821–81). Russian novelist; author of 'Crime and Punishment', 'The Idiot', 'The Brothers Karamazov', etc.

dŏt[1] *n.* Small spot, speck, roundish pen-mark; period, point over *i* or *j*, point used as diacritical mark; (in Morse code) small mark or signal shorter than 'dash'; (mus.) point placed after note or rest, lengthening it by half its value; point over or under note indicating that it is *staccato*; *on the ~*, punctually; *the year ~*, very long ago. ~ *v.t.* Mark with dot(s); place dot over (letter *i*, note in music) or after (musical note); diversify as with dots; scatter like dots; ~ *and carry* (*one*), child's formula for remembering to carry in sum; ~ *and go one* (*n.*, *adj.* & *adv.*) limp, limping(ly); *dotted line*, one on a document to carry signature of a party to its contents; hence, *sign on the dotted line*, agree fully or formally.

dŏt[2] *n.* Woman's marriage portion. [Fr.]

dō'tage *n.* Impaired intellect, esp. through old age; second childhood, senility.

dō'tard *n.* Man in his dotage.

dōte, doat *v.i.* 1. Be silly, deranged, infatuated, or feeble-minded, esp. from age. 2. Concentrate one's affections, bestow excessive fondness, *on.* **dō'tingly̆** *adv.*

dŏ'tterel *n.* Species of plover, *Eudromias morinellus*. [f. DOTE *v.*,

from the apparent simplicity with which it allows itself to be taken]

dŏ'ttle *n.* Plug of tobacco left unsmoked in pipe.

dŏ'ttȳ *adj.* Dotted about, marked with dots; (colloq.) feeble-minded, half idiotic. **dŏ'ttinėss** *n.*

Dou'ai, -ay (*or* do͞o'ā). Town in N. France; ~ (*-Rheims*) *Bible, version*, English translation of the Vulgate used in R.C. Church; the N.T. was published at Rheims in 1582 and the O.T. at Douai in 1609–10.

dou'ble (dŭ-) *adj.* 1. Consisting of two members, things, or sets combined; twofold; forming a pair; folded, bent; stooping much; having some part double; (of flowers) having number of petals multiplied by conversion of stamens and carpels into petals. 2. Having twofold relation or application; dual; ambiguous. 3. Twice as much or as many (*of*); of twofold or extra size, strength, value, etc. (mus., of instruments etc.) an octave lower in pitch (from the fact that a pipe, string, etc., of double length gives a note an octave lower). 4. Deceitful, hypocritical. ~ *adv.* To twice the amount etc.; two together. ~ *adj.* or *adv.* in comb.: *~-acting*, acting in two ways, directions, etc., esp. of engine in which steam acts on both sides of piston; ~ *agent*, one spying for two rival parties; ~*-bank*, arrange, drive, in a double line; ~*-barrelled*, (of gun) with two barrels; also fig. of compound surname; ~*-bass*, largest and lowest-pitched instrument of violin class, with 4 strings usu. tuned a fourth apart; ~ *bed*, bed for two people; ~*-bedded*, with two beds or a double bed; ~ *boiler*, saucepan with detachable upper compartment; ~*-breasted*, (of coat etc.) having the two fronts overlapping across the breast; ~ *chin*, chin with fold of flesh underneath; ~ *cream*, cream with high fat-content; ~ *crochet*, crochet stitch with two loops on hook together; ~ *-cross*, (slang) trechery to both parties esp. by pretended collusion with each, betrayal of partner in dishonest transaction; (*v.t.*) betray thus; ~*-dealing*, duplicity, deceit; ~*-dealer*; ~*-decker*, bus with two decks; sandwich with several layers; ~*-dyed*, (usu. fig.) deeply stained with guilt; ~ *eagle*, figure of eagle with two heads; (U.S., hist.) 20-dollar gold piece; ~*-edged*, with two cutting edges; (fig., of argument etc.) telling against as well as for one; ~ *event*, (racing etc.) winning of two races etc. in one meeting or one season; ~*-faced*, insincere; ~ *figures*, number between 9 and 100; ~ *first*, (person taking) first-class university honours in two different subjects; ~ *glazing*, two sheets of glass with hermetically sealed space between, giving heat and sound insulation at windows etc.; ~*-jointed*, having joints that allow unusual bending movements of limb etc.; ~*-lea'ded* (-lĕd-), (of printed matter) with wide spaces between lines; ~*-lock*, lock by two turns of the key; ~ *meaning*, = DOUBLE ENTENDRE; ~*-park*, park (vehicle) parallel to another vehicle standing at side of road; ~ *pneumonia*, pneumonia affecting both lungs; ~ *quick*, very quick(ly); ~ *saucepan*, double boiler; ~*-stopping*, (mus.) simultaneous sounding of notes on two strings of instrument of violin class; ~ *talk*, speech that can be interpreted in conflicting ways; ~*-talk* (*v.i.*); ~ *time*, (mil.) regulation running pace; ~*-tonguing*, rapid vibratory motion of tongue in producing staccato or rapidly repeated notes on flute, clarinet, etc. **dou'blȳ** *adv.* **dou'bleness** *n.* **dou'ble** *n.* 1. Double quantity; twice as much or as many; ~ *or quits*, game, throw, toss, deciding whether person shall pay twice his debt or nothing; *at the* ~, (mil.) running. 2. (bridge) Call by declarer's opponent involving doubling of score for tricks and a bonus to the declarer if he wins. 3. Counterpart of thing or person. 4. (pl.) Game (at lawn tennis etc.) between two pairs. 5. Sharp turn of river, or in running. 6. Bet on result of two races, the winnings in the first being staked on the result of the second. 7. = Double event, double bed(room), double tot of whisky etc. ~ *v.* 1. Make or become double, increase twofold, multiply by two; amount to twice as much as; (mus.) add same note in lower or higher octave to; call a double (at bridge); ~ *parts*, act two parts in same piece. 2. (mil.) Move in double time, run. 3. Put in same quarters with another; share quarters (also ~ *up*). 4. Bend, turn, over upon itself; clench (fist); ~ *up*, (cause to) bend into stooping or curled-up position; become folded. 5. (naut.) Get round (headland). 6. Turn sharply in flight; pursue tortuous course.

double entendre (do͞obl ahṅtahṅdr). Ambiguous expression, phrase with two meanings, one usu. indecent; use of such phrases. [Fr., obs. (now *double entente*)]

dou'blėt (dŭ-) *n.* 1. (hist.) Man's close-fitting body-garment with or without sleeves and short skirts (14th–18th centuries); ~ *and hose*, masculine attire of this period; light attire without cloak. 2. One of a pair, esp. one of two words of same derivation but different form or sense. 3. (pl.) Same number on two dice thrown at once. 4. Combination of two simple lenses; imitation precious stone of two pieces of glass with layer of colour cemented between them, or of thin slice of gem cemented on glass or inferior stone.

dou'bleton (dŭblt-) *n.* (cards) Two cards only of a suit, in one hand.

doubloo'n (du-) *n.* (hist.) Spanish gold coin (orig. two pistoles).

doubt (dowt) *n.* Feeling of uncertainty (*about*), undecided frame of mind, inclination to disbelieve; uncertain state of things; *give* (person) *benefit of the* ~, assume innocence rather than guilt when evidence is contradictory or inconclusive; *no* ~, certainly, admittedly; *without* ~, certainly. ~ *v.* Be in doubt or uncertainty (about); call in question; mistrust.

dou'btful (dowt-) *adj.* Of uncertain meaning, character, truth, or issue; undecided, ambiguous, questionable; uncertain, hesitating. **dou'btfullў** *adv.* **dou'btfulnėss** *n.*

dou'btlėss (dowt-) *adv.* Certainly; no doubt.

douceur (dōōsêr) *n.* Gratuity; bribe. [Fr.]

douche (dōōsh) *n.* Jet of water applied to body externally or internally as form of bathing or medicinally. ~ *v.* Administer douche to, take douche.

dough (dō) *n.* Mass of flour or meal kneaded into paste ready to be baked into bread etc.; any soft pasty mass; (slang, orig. U.S.) money; ~*-boy*, boiled flour dumpling, (U.S. colloq.) infantry soldier; ~*-face*, (U.S.) pliable or flabby person, esp. (hist.) Northern politician inclined to be unduly compliant to South in questions of slavery etc.; *doughnut*, small cake of dough fried in deep fat and usu. sprinkled with sugar. **doughy** (dō'ĭ) *adj.*

dou'ghtў (dow-) *adj.* (archaic or joc.) Valiant, stout, formidable. **dou'ghtĭlў** *adv.* **dou'ghtĭnėss** *n.*

Doukhobor: see DUKHOBOR.

dour (-oor) *adj.* (Sc.) Severe, stern, obstinate. **dour'lў** *adv.* **dour'nėss** *n*,

douse *v.t.* 1. (naut.) Strike, lower, (sail); close (port-hole). 2. Extinguish (light).

dove (dŭv) *n.* Bird of family Columbidae (see PIGEON), esp. the turtle-dove; symbol of gentleness or innocence; Holy Spirit (see Luke 3: 22 etc.); messenger of peace and deliverance (see Gen. 8: 8–12); darling; ~*-colour*, warm grey with tinge of pink or lavender; *do'vecot*(*e*), structure for housing pigeons.

Dō'ver. Seaport in Kent; *Strait*(*s*) *of* ~, strait at E. end of English Channel between coast of Kent and France.

Dō'ver's pow'der (-z). (med.) Preparation of opium and ipecacuanha used as diaphoretic and anodyne. [Dr. Thomas *Dover* (1660–1742), who prescribed it]

do'vetail (dŭvt-) *n.* Tenon shaped like dove's spread tail or reversed wedge, fitting into corresponding mortise and forming joint; such joint. ~ *v.* Put together with dovetails; fit together compactly.

dow'ager *n.* Woman with title or property derived from her late husband.

dow'dў *adj.* (of clothes) Shabby, unfashionable; (of woman) shabbily or unfashionably dressed. **dow'dĭlў** *adv.* **dow'dĭnėss** *n.* **dow'dў** *n.* Dowdy woman.

dow'el *n.* Headless pin of wood, metal, etc., fastening together two pieces of wood, stone, etc. ~ *v.t.* Fasten with dowel(s). **dow'ellĭng** *n.* Round wooden rods for cutting into dowels.

dow'er *n.* Widow's share for life of husband's estate; property or money brought by wife to husband, dowry; endowment, gift of nature, talent. ~ *v.t.* Give dowry to; endow *with* talent etc.

Dow-Jones ă'verage (-nz). Index of the relative price of Amer. securities based on the current average price of certain industrial and other stocks, published by Dow-Jones & Co., publishers of the 'Wall Street Journal'.

dow′las *n.* Kind of strong coarse calico. [*Doulas* in Brittany]

down[1] *n.* Open high land, esp. (pl.) treeless undulating chalk uplands of S. England; *the Downs*, part of sea within Goodwin Sands, off E. coast of Kent, opposite E. end of North Downs, a famous rendezvous for ships. **dow′nland** *n.* **dow′nsman** (-z) *n.* Native or inhabitant of (East Sussex or West Sussex) downs.

down[2] *n.* First fine soft covering of young birds; bird's underplumage, used for stuffing cushions etc.; fine soft hair, esp. first hair on face; soft hair on fruit etc.; any feathery or fluffy substance. **dow′nlèss** *adj.*

down[3] *adv.* 1. From above, to lower place, to ground; to place regarded as lower; into helpless position; with current or wind; southwards; away from capital or university; as cash payment at time of purchase (so ~ *payment*). 2. In lower place; not up in capital or university; in fallen posture, prostrate; at low level, in depression, humiliation, etc.; lower in price. 3. From higher to lower point in series or order; from earlier to later time; to finer consistence; into quiescence. 4. *be ~ on*, be opposed to, disapprove of; *come ~ on*, pounce on; treat severely; *go ~*, be swallowed; find acceptance; (of ship) sink; (of sun etc.) set. 5. *~ and out*, (boxing) unable to resume the fight; (transf.) defeated; destitute (person); ~ *east*, (U.S.) into, in, the eastern sea-coast districts of New England, esp. Maine; *~-hearted*, *~ in the mouth*, dispirited; ~ *south*, (U.S.) in, into, the southern States; down the Mississippi; *~-to-earth*, practical, realistic; *~-trodden*, (fig.) oppressed; ~ *under*, at or to the Antipodes, in Australia etc. ~ *prep.* Downwards along, through or into; from top to bottom of; at a lower part of; with (the wind, current, etc.); ~ *stage*, at, towards, front of stage; *~-stage of*, further down stage than; ~ *stream*, in direction of current, towards mouth, of river; ~ *town*, into the (business part of) town from higher or outlying part; (situated) in more central part of town. ~ *adj.* Directed downwards; *~-beat*, (mus.) accented beat; *~-draught*, downward draught, esp. one down chimney into room; ~ *grade*, (U.S.) downward slope; *on the ~-grade*, (fig.) deteriorating; *~-grade* (*v.t.*) lower in status etc.; ~ *payment*: see adv., sense 1; ~ *train*, train going away from London or other capital (so ~ *line, platform*). ~ *v.t.* (colloq.) Put, throw, knock, gulp, etc., down; ~ *tools*, cease work; go on strike. ~ *n.* Reverse of fortune; throw in wrestling etc.; (Amer. and Canadian footb.) pause in attempt to advance ball, when it is declared dead, also, the attempt itself; *have a ~ on*, (colloq.) dislike, be prejudiced against.

Down[4]. County in Northern Ireland.

dow′ncast (-n-kah-) *adj.* (of looks) Directed downwards; dejected. ~ *n.* (mining) ~ *(air-)shaft*, shaft through which air passes into mine.

dow′nfall (-awl) *n.* Fall (of rain etc.); fall from prosperity, ruin.

dow′nhill *adj.* Sloping down; declining. **downhĭ′ll** *adv.* In descending direction; on a decline.

Dow′ning Street. Short street in London running from Whitehall towards St. James's Park and containing official residence of Prime Minister (no. 10) and other government buildings and offices; hence, the British Government. [Sir George *Downing* (*c* 1624–84), British diplomat]

dow′npour (-pôr) *n.* Heavy fall of rain etc.

downright (dow′nrit before *n.* etc., -rī′t after it) *adj.* Plain, definite, straightforward, blunt; out-and-out. ~ *adv.* Thoroughly, positively, quite. **dow′nrightnèss** *n.*

downstair′s (-z) *adv.* Down the stairs. **dow′nstairs** *adj.* & *n.* (Of, in) lower floor of house etc.

dow'ntrŏdden *adj.* Crushed by oppression or tyranny.

dow'nward *adj.* & *adv.* Towards what is lower, inferior, or later. **dow'nwards** (-z) *adv.*

dow'nȳ *adj.* 1. Of, like, covered with, down. 2. (slang) Wide awake, knowing. **dow'nĭlȳ** *adv.* **dow'nĭnėss** *n.*

dow'rȳ *n.* Portion woman brings to her husband on marriage; talent, natural gift.

dow'ser (*or* -z-) *n.* Person capable of locating hidden water or minerals by holding in both hands a forked twig which dips abruptly when it is over the right spot. **dow'sing** *n.* Searching for water etc. thus; *~-rod*, forked twig used by dowser, divining-rod.

dŏxŏ'logȳ *n.* Liturgical formula of praise to God. **dŏxolŏ'gical** *adj.*

dŏ'xȳ[1] *n.* (archaic) Beggar's wench, paramour.

dŏ'xȳ[2] *n.* (joc.) Opinion, esp. in theological or religious matters.

doy'en (*or* dwah'yahṅ) *n.* (fem. *doyĕ'nne*) Senior member *of* a body, esp. senior ambassador at a court.

Doyle, Sir Arthur Conan (1859–1930). British novelist, famous for his 'Sherlock Holmes' series of detective stories.

doyley: see DOILY.

doz. *abbrev.* Dozen.

dōze *v.i.* Sleep lightly, be half asleep; *~ off*, fall lightly asleep. ~ *n.* Short light sleep.

do'zen (dŭ-) *n.* Twelve; set of twelve; *baker's, long, printer's ~*, thirteen; *talk nineteen to the ~*, talk incessantly or very fast.

D.P. *abbrev.* Displaced person.

D.P.H. *abbrev.* Diploma in Public Health.

D.Ph., D.Phil. *abbrevs.* Doctor of Philosophy.

D.P.P. *abbrev.* Director of Public Prosecutions.

dr. *abbrev.* Drachm; drachma(s).

Dr *abbrev.* Debtor; Doctor.

D.R. *abbrev.* Dead reckoning.

drăb[1] *n.* Slut, slattern; prostitute.

drăb[2] *adj.* & *n.* (Of) dull light brown colour; dull, monotonous. **dră'blȳ** *adv.*

drachm (-ăm) *n.* 1. (abbrev. dr.) Apothecaries' weight of 60 grains or ⅛ oz.; *fluid ~*, apothecaries' fluid measure of 60 minims or ⅛ fluid oz. 2. = DRACHMA.

dră'chma (-k-) *n.* (pl. *-mae, -mas*). 1. Principal monetary unit of Greece, = 100 lepta. 2. Coin and weight of ancient Greece, = 6 obols.

Drā'cō. Archon at Athens in 621 B.C., said to have established a severe code of laws. **Dracō'nian, Dracŏ'nĭc** *adjs.* Of Draco or his code of laws; rigorous, harsh, cruel.

Dră'cūla. King of the Vampires in Bram Stoker's novel 'Dracula' (1897).

draff (-ahf) *n.* Dregs, lees; hogwash; refuse of malt after brewing.

draft (-ah-) *n.* 1. (Selection of) detachment of men from larger body for special duty; contingent; reinforcement; member of such detachment; (U.S.) conscription. 2. Drawing of money by written order; bill or cheque drawn, esp. by one branch of bank on another. 3. Sketch of work to be executed. 4. Rough copy of document. 5. (masonry) Chisel-dressing at margin of stone's surface. ~ *v.t.* 1. Draw off (part of larger body, esp. of troops) for special purpose; (U.S.) conscript. 2. Prepare, make rough copy of (document, esp. parliamentary Bill). 3. (masonry) Cut draft on (stone). **dra'fter** *n.* 1. One who drafts a document. 2. (U.S.) Draught-horse.

draf'tsman (-ah-) *n.* (pl. *-men*). 1. One who drafts documents or parliamentary Bills. 2. = DRAUGHTSMAN 1.

drăg *v.* 1. Pull along with force, difficulty, or friction; allow (feet, tail, etc.) to trail; *~ anchor*, trail anchor along the bottom, owing to force of wind or current. 2. (mus.) Go too slowly, be wanting in life. 3. Trail, go heavily; *~ on*, continue tediously. 4. Search bottom of (water) with grapnels, nets, etc. (*for*). 5. Harrow (land). 6. Retard (wheel, vehicle) by applying a drag to it (see *n.* below, 3). ~ *n.* 1. Heavy harrow; rough sledge; four-horsed private vehicle like stage-coach. 2. Net drawn over bottom of water or surface of field to enclose all fish or game (also *~-net*); apparatus for dredging bottom of rivers or pools. 3. Iron shoe for retarding vehicle downhill; obstruction to progress. 4. Strong-smelling lure for hounds in lieu of fox; hunt with hounds following this; club for pursuing this sport. 5. Slow motion; impeded progress; (aeron.) atmospheric resistance. 6. (colloq.) Transvestite clothing. 7. *~-anchor*, floating frame on hawser to check leeway of drifting ship; *~-chain*, chain used to retard vehicle by fixing wheel; *~-hounds*: see sense 4; *~-line*, in excavator, line which pulls bucket towards machine; *~-net*: see sense 2.

dragée (drah′zhā) *n.* Sugar-coated almond etc.; chocolate-coated sweet.

drăʹggle *v.* Make wet, limp, and dirty, by trailing; hang trailing; *~-tail(ed)*, (woman) with draggled or untidily trailing skirts.

drăʹgoman *n.* Interpreter (and guide), esp. in Arabic, Turkish, or Persian. [Arab. *tarjumān* interpreter]

drăʹgon *n.* 1. Mythical monster like crocodile or snake with large claws, usu. winged and often breathing fire; freq. in legends as guardian of treasure, of female chastity, etc.;

DRAGON

DRAGONFLY

watchful person, duenna. 2. (bibl.) Whale, shark, serpent, or crocodile; jackal. 3. Lizard of genus *Draco*, with broad wing-like membrane on each flank, able to leap some distance in the air. 4. *dra′gonfly*, insect of order Odonata with long body, prominent eyes, and elaborately veined membranous wings usu. spread while resting, freq. brightly coloured, and capable of rapid darting flight; *~'s-blood*, bright red gum or resin exuded by the fruit of a palm, *Calamus draco*, or obtained from the dragon-tree, used for colouring varnishes etc.; *~'s head, tail*, (astron.) ascending or descending node of the moon or planet, indicated by symbols ☊, ☋; *~'s teeth*, (colloq.) cone-shaped anti-tank obstacles; *~-tree*, tree, *Dracaena draco*, of the Canary Islands, bearing panicles of small greenish-white flowers and yielding dragon's-blood.

drăgonnāʹdes (-z) *n.pl.* (hist.) Persecutions of Protestants under Louis XIV by quartering dragoons upon them.

dragōōʹn *n.* Cavalryman orig. of mounted infantry armed with a kind of carbine called a *dragoon*, now of certain cavalry regiments historically representing these; rough fierce fellow. ~ *v.t.* Set dragoons upon, persecute, oppress; force *into* course by persecution. [Fr. *dragon* carbine, so named as breathing fire]

drain *v.* Draw (liquid) *off*, *away*, by conduit, drainpipes, etc.; drink (liquid), empty (vessel), to the dregs; dry (land etc.) by providing channels for the escape of the water in it; (of river) carry off superfluous water of (district); trickle *through*, flow gradually *away*; become rid of moisture by its gradual flowing away; *drai′n-pipe*, large pipe, usu. of earthenware, used for draining; *draining-board*, sloping usu. grooved board on which washed dishes etc. are put to drain. ~ *n.* Channel carrying off liquid, artificial conduit for water, sewage, etc.; (surg.) tube for drawing off discharge from abscess etc.; constant outlet, withdrawal, demand, or expenditure; small quantity of liquid; (slang) a drink.

draiʹnage *n.* Draining; system of drains, artificial or natural; what is drained off, sewage.

drāke[1] *n.* Fly of genus *Ephemera* used in fly-fishing; *green* ~, common may-fly, *E. vulgata.*

drāke[2] *n.* Male duck.

Drāke[3], Sir Francis (1540?–96). English admiral; circumnavigated the world in the *Golden Hind*, 1577–81; commanded a division of the English fleet against the Armada; *~'s drum*, drum which sounds, acc. to legend, whenever danger threatens England.

drăm *n.* 1. $\frac{1}{16}$ of an ounce. 2. (chiefly U.S.) DRACHM, sense 1. 3. Small draught of spirit etc.

dra'ma (-ah-) *n.* Stage-play; dramatic art, composition and presentation of plays; series of events having the unity and progress of a play and leading to final catastrophe or consummation.

dramă'tic *adj.* Of, like, drama; theatrical; sudden, striking, impressive. **dramă'tically** *adv.*

dră'matis persō'nae. (List of) characters in a play.

dră'matist *n.* Writer of dramas or dramatic poetry.

dră'matize *v.* Convert (novel etc.) into play; admit of such conversion; impart dramatic character to. **drămatizā'tion** *n.*

dră'maturge, dră'maturgist *ns.* Dramatist. **drămatur'gic** *adj.* **dră'maturgy** *n.*

drāpe *v.t.* Cover, hang, adorn, with cloth etc.; arrange (clothes, hangings) in graceful folds. ~ *n.* Fold; (U.S. etc.) curtain.

drā'per *n.* Retailer of textile fabrics. **drā'pery** *n.* 1. Cloth, textile fabrics; trade or business of draper. 2. Arrangement of clothing in sculpture etc.; clothing or hangings disposed in folds.

dră'stic (*or* -ah-) *adj.* Acting strongly, vigorous, violent, esp. (med.) strongly purgative. **dră'stically** *adv.*

drăt *int.* Curse. **dră'tted** *adj.* ['*od rot* (God rot!)]

draught (-ahft) *n.* (See also DRAFT, a permissible spelling in many senses, and in U.S. the usual spelling.) 1. Drawing, traction; drawing of net for fish etc., catch of fish at one drawing. 2. Single act of drinking, amount so drunk; dose of liquid medicine; *black* ~, purgative of senna, sulphate of magnesia, and liquorice. 3. Depth of water ship draws or requires to float her. 4. (pl.) Game (known as *checkers* in U.S.) played by two persons on a chequered board with 24 flat wooden discs (*draughtsmen*) of the same value, which are moved diagonally; *~-board*, chequered board on which this game is played. 5. Current of air, esp. in confined space, as room or chimney; *feel the* ~, (slang) suffer from adverse conditions. 6. Drawing of liquor from vessel; ~ *beer*, beer drawn from cask, not bottled; *beer on* ~, beer in tapped cask. ~ *v.t.* = DRAFT *v.* 1, 2.

drau'ghtsman (-ahft-) *n.* (pl. *-men*; fem. *drau'ghtswoman*). 1. One who is employed to make drawings, plans, or sketches; one skilled in drawing or designing. 2. = DRAFTSMAN 1. 3. One of the pieces in game of draughts. **drau'ghtsmanship** *n.* Skill in drawing.

drau'ghty (-ahftĭ) *adj.* Abounding in draughts or currents of air.

Dravi'dian *adj.* & *n.* (Member) of a dark-skinned people of S. India and Ceylon (including Tamils and Kanarese); (of) any of the languages spoken by these people. [f. *Dravida*, old province of S. India]

draw *v.* (past t. *drew*, past part. *drawn*). 1. Pull; pull after one; drag (criminal) on hurdle etc. to execution; contract, distort (features etc.); haul in (net); bend (bow); pull at; pull (curtain, veil) open or shut; (cricket) divert (ball) to 'on' side of wicket with bat; (golf) hit (ball) with a slight pull. 2. Attract, bring to one; take in; attract attention or custom; induce *to* do; be attracted, assemble, *round, together*, etc.; bring about, entail. 3. Extract; pull out (sword or other weapon from sheath); draw sword, pistol, etc.; pull or take one from a number of things so as to decide something by chance (esp. in ~ *lots* etc.); obtain by lot; drag (badger, fox) from hole; haul up (water) from well; bring out (liquid, blood) from vessel, body; take, get, from a source; induce (person) to talk, reveal information, etc.; deduce, infer; extract something from, empty, drain; disembowel; (of tea etc.) infuse; (cards) cause (trumps etc.) to be played; (hunting) search (covert) for game etc. 4. Protract, stretch, elongate; make (wire) by pulling piece of metal through successively smaller holes; (naut., of sail) swell out with wind. 5. Trace, delineate, make (picture), represent (object), by drawing lines; use pencil thus; describe in words; practise delineation; frame (document) in due form, compose; formulate, institute (comparisons, distinctions); write out (bill, cheque, draft, *on* banker etc.); make call *on* person, his faith, memory, etc., *for* money or service. 6. Make way, move, *towards*, *near*, *off*, etc.; (racing) get farther *away* to the front, come *level*, gain *on*. 7. (of ship) Require (such a depth of water) to float. 8. End (game, battle) without victory on either side; (abs.) succeed in doing this (freq. ~ *with* the other side). 9. ~ *back*, withdraw from undertaking; ~ *in*, entice, persuade to join; (of day) close in, (of successive days) become shorter; (of train or vehicle) = PULL in; ~ *off*, withdraw (troops); (of troops) withdraw; ~ *on*, lead to, bring about; allure; approach, draw near; ~ *out*, lead out, detach, or array (troops); prolong; elicit; induce to talk, reveal talent etc.; write out in proper form; (of successive days) become longer; (of train or vehicle) = PULL out; ~ *up*, come up *with*, *to*; come to a stand; bring (troops), come, into regular order; compose (documents etc.); ~ *oneself up*, assume stiff attitude. 10. ~ *hoe*, hoe used with pulling action; ~ *-sheet*, sheet that can be withdrawn from under patient without making the whole bed; ~*-table*, table with sliding leaf or leaves that can be drawn out to extend it. ~ *n.* Act of drawing, esp. strain, pull; attractive effect; thing that draws custom, attention etc.; drawing of lots; raffle; drawn game; remark etc. meant to elicit information or set person off on pet subject; act of drawing a revolver etc.; *score-~*, drawn game in which goals are scored.

draw′băck *n.* 1. Amount paid back from charge previously made, esp. from excise or import duty on goods exported; deduction *from*. 2. Thing that qualifies satisfaction; disadvantage.

draw′bridge *n.* Bridge across moat, river, etc., made to be raised or lowered at one end by chains or pulleys.

drawee′ *n.* Person on whom draft or bill is drawn.

draw′er *n.* 1. One who draws. 2. (also pr. draw) Box-shaped receptacle sliding in and out of special frame, or of table etc.; (pl.) chest of drawers. 3. (pl., pr. drawz) Undergarment, with legs, for lower part of body.

draw′erful (*or* -aw′f-) *n.*

draw′ĭng *n.* (esp.) Art of representing by line; delineation by means of pen or pencil or other pointed instrument, esp. with little or no use of colour; product of this, sketch; ~*-block*, block of detachable leaves of drawing-paper adhering at edges; ~*-board*, board for stretching drawing-paper on; ~*-compass(es)*, compasses with pen or pencil substituted for one point; ~*-pin*, flat-headed pin for fastening paper to drawing-board etc.;

draw′ĭng-rōōm *n.* 1. Room for reception of company, to which ladies retire after dinner. 2. Levee, formal reception, esp. at court. [earlier *withdrawing-room*]

drawl *v.* Speak, utter, with indolent or affected slowness; be so uttered. ~ *n.* Drawling, slow utterance. **draw′lĭnglȳ** *adv.*

drawn *adj.*: see DRAW *v.*; (esp.) ~*-(thread-)work*, ornamental work in textile fabrics done by drawing out threads with or without addition of needlework.

draw′-wĕll *n.* Well from which water is drawn with rope and bucket.

dray *n.* Low cart without sides

for heavy loads, esp. beer-barrels; *~-horse*, large powerful horse; *dray'man*, driver of brewer's dray.

Dray'ton, Michael (1563–1631). English poet, author of odes, sonnets, satires, and much historical and topographical verse.

dread (-ĕd) *v.* Be in great fear of; shrink from, look forward to with terror; fear greatly; be afraid (*to* do). ~ *n.* Great fear; object of fear or awe. ~ *adj.* Dreaded, dreadful.

drea'dful (-ĕd-) *adj.* Terrible, awe-inspiring; troublesome, disagreeable; very bad; *penny ~*, cheap sensational story of crime and horrors. **drea'dfullÿ** *adv.*

dreadnought (drĕ'dnawt) *n.* 1. (archaic) (Cloth used for) thick coat for stormy weather. 2. *D~*, (hist.) name of first British battleship (launched 1906) of a powerful type superior in armament to all its predecessors; hence, a class of battleships having their main armament all of big guns of one calibre.

dream *n.* Train of thoughts, images, or fancies passing through mind during sleep; conscious indulgence of fancy, reverie; thing of dream-like beauty, charm, goodness, etc. **drea'mlėss, drea'mlīke** *adjs.* **dream** *v.* (past t. & past part. *dreamt* pr. -ĕmt, or *dreamed*) 1. Have visions etc. in sleep; see, hear, etc., in sleep. 2. Imagine as in a dream; think possible; (with negative) so much as contemplate possibility *of*, have any conception *of*; ~ *up* (colloq.) conceive, devise (idea or plan). 3. Fall into reverie; form imaginary visions of; be inactive or unpractical. **drea'mer** *n.* (esp.) Unpractical person.

drea'mÿ *adj.* Full of dreams; given to reverie, fanciful, unpractical; dreamlike, vague, misty. **drea'mĭlÿ** *adv.* **drea'mĭnėss** *n.*

drear'ÿ *adj.* (poet. *drear*) Dismal, gloomy, dull. **drear'ĭlÿ** *adv.* **drear'ĭnėss** *n.*

drĕdge[1] *n.* Apparatus for bringing up oysters, specimens, etc., clearing out mud etc., from river or sea bottom, or obtaining ores from alluvial deposits. ~ *v.* Bring *up*, clear *away*, *out*, with dredge; clean out (harbour, river) with dredge; use dredge. **drĕ'dger**[1] *n.* One who uses dredge; boat employed in dredging.

drĕdge[2] *v.t.* Sprinkle with flour or other powder; sprinkle (flour etc.) *over*. **drĕ'dger**[2] *n.* Box with perforated lid for sprinkling flour etc.

dree *v.t.* (archaic) Endure (now only in ~ *one's weird*, submit to one's lot).

drĕg *n.* (usu. pl.) Sediment, grounds, lees; worthless part, refuse. **drĕ'ggÿ** (-gĭ) *adj.*

drĕnch *n.* 1. Draught or dose administered to animal. 2. Soaking; downpour. ~ *v.t.* 1. Make to drink largely; force (animal) to take draught of medicine. 2. Steep, soak. 3. Wet all over with falling liquid. **drĕ'ncher** *n.* (esp.) Drenching shower.

Drĕ'sden (-z-). German city on the Elbe, capital of Saxony; ~ *china*, English name for porcelain

DRESDEN

made at MEISSEN near Dresden; ~ *figure*, figurine of this.

drĕss *n.* Clothing, esp. the visible part of it, costume; woman's gown; frock; external covering, outward form; *full* ~, that worn on formal occasions; (*evening*) ~, that worn at dinners or evening parties; *morning* ~, men's formal daytime wear; ~ *circle*: see CIRCLE *n.*; ~ *coat*, swallow-tailed coat for evening dress; ~*-improver*, bustle; *dre'ssmaker*, woman who makes women's dresses; *dre'ssmaking* (*n.*); ~ *rehearsal*, final rehearsal in costume of play etc. ~ *v.* 1. (mil.) Correct alignment of (companies etc. or men in line); come into correct place in line etc. 2. Array, clothe; provide oneself with clothes; put on one's clothes; put on evening dress; ~ *out*, attire conspicuously; ~ *up*, clothe oneself, clothe (another), elaborately or in masquerade. 3. Deck, adorn (ship with flags, shop-window with wares etc.); provide (play) with costumes. 4. Treat (wound, wounded person) with remedies; apply dressing to. 5. Subject to cleansing, trimming, smoothing, etc.; brush, comb, do up (hair); curry (horse, leather); finish surface of (textile fabrics, stone for building); prepare, cook (food); manure (ground).

drĕ'ssage (-ahzh) *n.* Training of horse in obedience and deportment; execution by horse of precise movements in response to its rider.

drĕ'sser[1] *n.* (esp.) 1. Surgeon's assistant in hospital operations. 2. Person who helps actor or actress to dress for part.

drĕ'sser[2] *n.* Kitchen sideboard

with shelves for dishes etc.; (U.S.) chest of drawers, dressing-table, in bedroom.

drĕ'ssing *n.* (esp.) 1. (also ~ *down*) Drubbing, beating; scolding. 2. Seasoning, sauce, etc. used in cooking. 3. Manure etc. spread over land. 4. Remedies, bandages, etc., with which wound is dressed. 5. Glaze, size, or stiffening used in finishing textile fabrics. 6. (pl.) External parts of a building distinguished from plain walling, as columns, mouldings, cornices, etc. 7. ~*-case*, case containing toilet necessaries; ~*-gown*, *-jacket*, garment worn while making toilet or in dishabille; ~*-room*, room for dressing etc., usu. opening from bedroom; ~*-table*, table with mirror, drawers, etc., for use while dressing.

drĕ'ssȳ *adj.* Fond of, smart in, dress; (of clothes) stylish; excessively elaborate. **drĕ'ssilȳ** *adv.* **drĕ'ssinėss** *n.*

drey (drā) *n.* Red squirrel's nest.

Drey'fus (drā-), Alfred (1859–1935). Jewish officer in the French army, condemned in 1894 to imprisonment on Devil's Island by a secret military tribunal on a charge of divulging military secrets to Germany; evidence of his innocence was found in 1896, but a violent anti-semitic press campaign prevented the reopening of the question; it was not until 1906 that the sentence condemning Dreyfus was finally quashed. **Dreyfusard** (-ar̂') *n.* Supporter of innocence of Dreyfus.

drĭ'bble *v.* 1. Flow, let flow, in drops or trickling stream; run at the mouth. 2. (footb., hockey) Work (ball) forward with series of short kicks or hits; (billiards) make (ball) just roll, (of ball) just roll, into pocket. ~ *n.* Small trickling or barely continuous stream; act of dribbling.

drĭ'blėt *n.* Small quantity, petty sum (as instalment etc.).

dried (-īd) *adj.*: see DRY *v.*; (esp., of food) with moisture removed as method of preservation.

drī'er *n.* Thing, person, that

dries (DRY *v.*); substance mixed with oil paints to expedite drying; hair-drier.

drĭft *n.* 1. Being driven by current; slow course or current; ship's deviation from course due to currents; aircraft's deviation due to wind etc.; (gunnery) projectile's deviation due to rotation. 2. Natural or unperceived progress, tendency; inaction. 3. Purpose, meaning, tenor, scope. 4. Shower, driving mass; accumulation of snow, sand, etc., heaped up by wind; matter driven by currents of water. 5. (geol.) Anything transported and deposited by wind, water, or ice, esp. the boulder clay left by a glacier. 6. (forest law) Driving of cattle to one place on appointed day to determine ownership etc. 7. (also *~-net*) Large net for catching herring, pilchards, mackerel, extended by weights at bottom and floats at top and allowed to drift with tide. 8. (mining) Horizontal passage following vein of mineral. 9. (S. Afr.) Ford. 10. Steel tool for enlarging or shaping hole in metal. 11. (naut.) Length of rope paid out before fastening is made. 12. *~-anchor*, floating frame keeping ship's head to wind in gale or when dismasted; *~-ice*, detached drifting pieces of ice; *~-net*: see sense 7; *dri'ftwood*, wood drifting on, or cast ashore by, water. ~ *v.* 1. Be carried by or as by current or air or water; (of current) carry; go passively or aimlessly; pile, be piled by wind, into drifts, cover with drifts. 2. Form or enlarge (hole) with drift. 3. Fish with drift-net. **drĭ'ftage** *n.*

drĭ'fter *n.* (esp.) Boat used in fishing with drift-net.

drĭll[1] *n.* 1. Contrivance (steel tool, machine, etc.) for boring holes in metal, stone, sinking oil-wells, etc. 2. Shellfish which bores into shells of young oysters. 3. Military exercise or training; physical exercise(s); rigorous discipline, exact routine. ~ *v.* 1. Bore with drill etc. 2. Train in, perform, military movements and exercise; train rigorously and exactly; impart (knowledge etc.) by strict method.

drĭll[2] *n.* 1. Small furrow for sowing seed in; ridge with such furrow on top; row of plants sown in it. 2. Machine for sowing seed in drills. ~ *v.t.* Sow (seed), plant (ground) in drills.

drĭll[3] *n.* W. African species of baboon, *Mandrillus leucophaeus*, allied to mandrill.

drĭll[4] *n.* Coarse twilled cotton fabric used for uniform, boat sails, etc.

drī'lȳ *adv.* Var. of DRYLY.

drĭnk *v.* (past t. *drănk*, past part. *drŭnk* and poet. *drŭ'nken*). 1. Take (liquid) through mouth and throat into stomach, swallow; swallow contents of (cup etc.); swallow liquid; take (*the waters* at spa) medicinally; (of plants, porous substances, etc.) absorb (moisture). 2. Take *in*, esp. with eyes or ears, with eager delight. 3. Drink alcoholic liquor; indulge in alcohol to excess, tipple; spend (money etc.) in drinking; honour (toast etc.) by drinking; ~ *to*, pledge, toast. ~ *n.* Liquid drunk; beverage; intoxicating liquor; excessive indulgence in this, intemperance; glass or portion of liquor; *the* ~, (R.A.F. slang) the sea; *~-offering*, libation.

drĭ'nkable *adj.* Fit to drink. **drĭ'nkables** (-lz) *n.pl.* Things to drink.

drĭp *v.* Fall, let fall, in drops; let drops fall, be so wet (*with* liquid) as to shed drops; *~-dry* (*v.*, of fabric) dry when hung up to drip without wringing or subsequent ironing; *~-dry* (*adj.*) that will drip-dry. ~ *n.* 1. Act of dripping; dripping liquid; (med.) continuous slow introduction of fluid into vein etc. 2. (archit., also *dri'pstone*), projecting moulding etc. to throw off rain. 3. (slang) Stupid or dull person.

drĭpp'ĭng *n.* (esp.) Fat melted from roasting meat and used for cooking or as food.

drīve *v.* (past t. *drōve*, past part. *drĭ'ven*). 1. Urge in some direction, esp. by blows, threats, violence, etc.; chase or frighten (game, wild beasts, etc.) from over large area into small in order to kill or capture; scour (district) thus; (forest law) hold a drift (see DRIFT *n.* 6). 2. Direct course of (animal drawing vehicle, vehicle, locomotive, etc.); convey in vehicle; act as driver of vehicle; travel in car or carriage at one's disposal; ~*-in*, (bank, restaurant, etc.) that may be used without alighting from car. 3. Impel forcibly, compel. 4. Cause to move, carry along, throw, propel, send, (thing) in some direction; (cricket) strike (ball) with upright bat more or less in direction of bowler; (golf) strike (ball), strike ball, with driver; force (stake, nail, etc.) *into* ground etc. with blow. 5. Bore (tunnel, horizontal cavity). 6. Aim blow or missile (*at*). 7. (of steam or other power) Set or keep (machinery) going. 8. Carry on vigorously, effect, conclude. 9. Dash, rush, hasten; work hard. 10. Move along impelled by current, wind, etc.; ~ *at*, have for one's aim; allude to. ~ *n.* 1. Excursion in vehicle. 2. Driving of game, enemy, etc. 3. Forcible blow or stroke at cricket etc.; (golf) hit with a driver. 4. Energy, push; energetic campaign. 5. (psychol.) Inner urge, motive principle. 6. Driving part of machinery; transmission of power to wheels of vehicle. 7. Carriage-road, esp. private road to house. 8. WHIST-drive.

drĭ'vel *n.* Silly nonsense, twaddle. ~ *v.i.* Run at mouth or nose like child; talk childishly or idiotically. **drĭ'veller** *n.*

drī'ver *n.* 1. One who drives. 2. (golf) Wooden-headed club used to send ball a long distance, esp. from tee.

drī'vĭng-wheel *n.* Wheel communicating motion to other wheels in machinery; large wheel of locomotive, to which power is transmitted through connecting rod to crank; wheel of vehicle to which driving power is applied.

drĭ'zzle *v.i.* & *n.* Rain in fine, dense, spray-like drops. **drĭ'zzlȳ** *adj.*

drōgue (-g) *n.* 1. Buoy at end of harpoon line. 2. Canvas cone open at both ends with a hoop at larger end, used as sea-anchor by seaplanes; lighter form of this towed by aircraft to serve for target practice. 3. Parachute or cone used to reduce speed of aircraft etc.

droit *n.* Legal right or perquisite; ~*s of Admiralty*, proceeds of seized enemy ships, wrecks, etc., formerly belonging to Court of Admiralty but now paid into Exchequer.

drōll *adj.* Facetious, amusing; queer, odd, surprising. **drō'lly** (-ōl-lĭ) *adv.* **drō'llnėss** *n.* **drōll** *n.* Jester, wag. **drō'llerȳ** *n.* Droll action(s) or humour.

drŏ'mėdarȳ (*or* -ŭm-) *n.* Light, fleet camel specially reared and trained for riding, esp. the ARABIAN camel.

drōne *n.* 1. Male of honey-bee, which does not work; lazy idler, sluggard. 2. Continued deep monotonous sound, as of humming or buzzing. 3. Open bass-pipe of bagpipe, emitting one continuous tone; tone emitted by this. ~ *v.* Buzz like bee or bagpipe; talk, utter, monotonously.

drōōl *v.i.* & *n.* Drivel.

drōōp *v.* Hang down, incline, as from weariness or exhaustion; (of eyes) be turned down, with lowered eyelids; languish, flag; become dejected, lose heart; let (head, eyes, etc.) droop. ~ *n.* Drooping attitude; loss of spirit, fall of tone. **drōō'pinglȳ** *adv.*

drŏp *n.* 1. Small quantity of liquid that falls, hangs, trickles down, or detaches itself in spherical or pear-shaped form; tear-drop, drop of rain, blood, dew, etc.; very small quantity, esp. small quantity of drink; (dispensing etc.) smallest quantity of liquid that can be transferred from one vessel to another by pouring through air; minim; (pl.) medicinal preparation to be administered in drops. 2. Pendant of metal or precious stone, glass pendant of chandelier, etc.; sweet, lozenge. 3. Fall, dropping, descent; abrupt fall in level of surface; depth to which anything sinks; distance through which anything falls; (esp.) length of pattern on curtain, wallpaper, etc.; distance through which criminal falls when hanged. 4. Curtain let down before stage between acts or scenes of play etc. (also *~-curtain, -scene*). 5. Small platform on gallows which is let fall from under feet of person to be hanged. ~ *v.* 1. Fall in drops; give off drops, drip; fall vertically, like a single drop; descend abruptly; fall, sink to ground. 2. Cease, lapse, fall through; fall in direction, amount, degree, etc. 3. Allow oneself to be carried downstream without effort; allow oneself to fall *behind, to the rear*, etc. 4. Come or go casually or unexpectedly; come down *on* forcibly. 5. Let fall, shed, in drops; let fall like a drop or drops; let fall (words etc.) casually; make (curtsey); send (letter etc.); (of animals) give birth to (young); (*slang*) lose, part with (money). 6. Fell, bring down, with blow, shot, etc. 7. Set down, from ship or vehicle. 8. Omit (esp., letter etc. in pronunciation). 9. Let droop; lower (voice). 10. Score (goal) by drop kick. 11. Break off acquaintance or association with; cease to keep up, end, stop; ~ *in*, (esp.) pay casual visit; ~ *off*, (esp.) fall asleep; become less numerous etc.; ~ *out*, (esp.) withdraw. 12. ~ *arch*, arch with radius shorter than its breadth; ~ *kick*, (footb.) kick made by dropping ball and kicking it as it touches the ground; *~-letter*, (U.S.) letter posted for local delivery; *dro'pout*, one who withdraws from course of study, conventional way of life, etc.

drŏ'plėt *n.* Little drop.

drŏ'ppings (-z) *n.pl.* That which drops or falls in drops, as melted wax etc.; dung of animals or birds.

drŏ'pping-wĕll *n.* Well in which water drops or drips from above.

drŏ'psȳ *n.* Accumulation of watery fluid in serous cavities or connective tissues of body. **drŏ'psical, drŏ'psied** (-sĭd) *adjs.*

drŏ'shkȳ *n.* Russian low 4-wheeled open carriage.

drosŏ'phila *n.* Fruit-fly of genus *D~*, much used in genetic research.

drŏss *n.* Scum thrown off from metal in melting; foreign matter mixed with any substance; refuse, rubbish. **drŏ'ssȳ** *adj.*

drought (-owt) *n.* (poet. *drouth*) 1. (archaic) Dryness, lack of moisture; thirst. 2. Continuous dry weather, lack of rain; *absolute ~*, period of 15 days each of which has received not more than 0·2 mm (0·01 in.) of rain. **drou'ghty, drou'thȳ** *adjs.*

drōve *n.* 1. Herd, flock, being driven or moving together; crowd, multitude, large number. 2. Stone-mason's broad-faced chisel.

drō'ver *n.* One who drives animals in droves to market; cattle-dealer.

drown *v.* Suffer death by submersion in water; suffocate by submersion in water; submerge, flood, drench; overcome (grief etc.) with or *in* drink; overpower (sound) by greater loudness.

drowse (-z) *v.* Be heavy or dull with or as with sleep; be half asleep; pass *away* (time etc.) in drowsing. ~ *n.* Half-sleep, half-asleep condition.

drow'sy (-zĭ) *adj.* Heavy with sleepiness; half asleep, dozing; sleepy; soporific; sluggish, lethargic. **drow'silȳ** *adv.* **drow'sinėss** *n.*

drŭb *v.t.* Cudgel, thump, thrash, belabour. **drŭ'bbing** *n.*

drŭdge *n.* Servile worker, slave, hack; hard toiler. ~ *v.i.* Perform mean or servile tasks; work hard or laboriously, toil. **drŭ'dgerȳ** *n.*

drŭg *n.* Medicinal substance; (esp.) narcotic; (also *dangerous ~*) one which causes euphoria in the taker and predisposes him to addiction, esp. preparation or extract of opium or coca or Indian hemp; ~ *addict*, person who takes one of these habitually; ~ *on the market*, commodity no longer in demand, unsaleable thing; *~-store*, (U.S.) chemist's shop also dealing extensively or mainly in toilet requisites, stationery, newspapers, light refreshments, etc.; ~ *traffic*, commercial sale of dangerous drugs, forbidden by law. ~ *v.t.* Administer drug, esp. narcotic, to; add drug to (food or drink).

drŭ'ggėt (-g-) *n.* Coarse woven fabric for floor coverings etc., usu. of jute and cotton.

drŭ'ggist (-g-) *n.* Dealer in drugs, pharmaceutical chemist.

Dru'ĭd (-ōō-) *n.* 1. (fem. *Dru'i-dėss*) One of an order of priests (acc. to Caesar) or magicians (acc. to Irish and Welsh legend) among the ancient Celts of Gaul and Britain. 2. Member of Welsh, Cornish, or Breton GORSEDD. 3. Member of *United Ancient Order of Druids*, secret benefit society founded in London in 1781, and having numerous lodges called *groves* in England, America, etc. **Druĭ'dĭc** *adj.* **Dru'ĭdĭsm** *n.* Religious system of Druids.

drŭm[1] *n.* 1. Percussive musical instrument consisting of hollow cylindrical or hemispherical frame

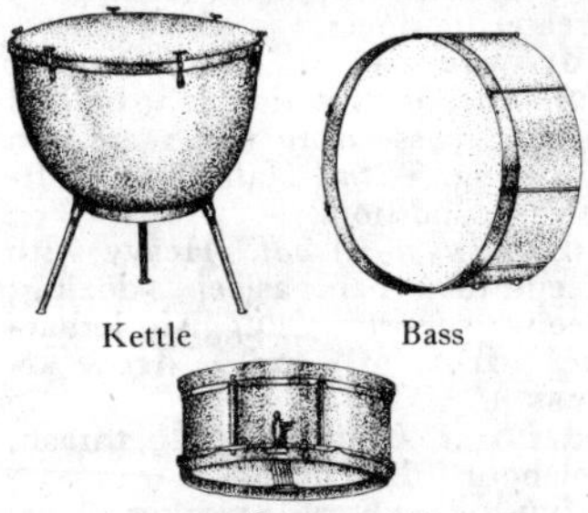

Kettle Bass
Snare
DRUMS

with tightly stretched membrane at one or both ends, which is struck to produce sound; sound of this; drummer; ***bass*** **~**, ***tenor*** **~**, drums struck sideways; *ke'ttledrum*, cauldron-shaped drum which can be tuned to produce note of definite pitch; *side* ~, drum played on upper head, esp. (mil.) carried at side. 2. (anat.) Tympanum, eardrum. 3. Drum-shaped thing (*brake* ~, ~ *brake*); cylinder round which rope or belt passes; cylindrical receptacle for oil etc.; (archit.) solid part of Corinthian and Composite capitals; block of stone forming one section of shaft of column; cylindrical structure supporting dome. 4. (archaic) Large evening or afternoon tea party. 5. (also ~-*fish*) Any of various Amer. fishes making drumming noise. 6. ~-*fire*, rapid heavy gunfire concentrated on a particular objective; *dru'mhead*, stretched skin or membrane of drum; membrane across drum of ear; circular top of capstan, into which capstan-bars are fixed; flat-topped kind of cabbage; *drumhead court-martial*, court-martial round upturned drum for summary treatment of offences during military operations; *drumhead service*, religious service round upturned drum; ~-*major*, non-commissioned officer commanding drummers of regiment, officer of band etc. leading and conducting it on march; ~-*majorette*, girl accompanying marching band and twirling baton etc.; *dru'mstick*, stick usu. with padded knob at one end for beating drum; lower part of leg of cooked chicken, so called from its shape. ~ *v.* 1. Play the drum; beat, tap, or thump, continuously on something; (of bird, insect) make loud hollow noise with quivering wings. 2. Summon, beat *up*, as by drumming; (colloq.) obtain (custom, customers) by canvassing etc.; (U.S.) solicit orders; drive *out* of regiment etc. publicly by beat of drum, so as to heighten disgrace; din *into* (person). **drŭ'mmer** *n.* 1. Player of drum. 2. (U.S.) Commercial traveller.

drŭm[2], **drŭ'mlĭn** *ns.* (geol.) Oval mound of drift or diluvial formation.

drŭnk *adj.*: see DRINK *v.*; (esp.) intoxicated. ~ *n.* Drinking-bout; drunken person; case of drunkenness. **drŭ'nkard** *n.* Sot; habitually drunken person. **drŭ'nken** *adj.* (rarely pred.) Intoxicated; given to drinking, often drunk; caused by or exhibiting drunkenness. **drŭ'nkenlў** *adv.* **drŭ'nkennėss** (-n-n-) *n.*

drupe (-ōōp) *n.* Fleshy or

pulpy fruit enclosing stone with kernel, as olive, plum, cherry; stone-fruit. **drupā'ceous** (-sh*us*) *adj*. Bearing drupes.

dru'pel(-ōō-),**dru'pelėt**(-ōōpl-) *ns*. (bot.) Small drupe, such as those of which blackberry is composed.

Druse (-ōōz) *n*. Member of Muslim political and religious sect founded 1040, inhabiting region round Mt Lebanon in Syria, believing in transmigration, and holding the 6th Fatimate Caliph, Hakim Biamrillahi, to be a divine incarnation. [Arab *durūz*, prob. f. *Isma'il al-Darazī* (the tailor), their founder]

drȳ *adj*. 1. Free from moisture, not wet or moist; deficient in rain, not rainy; dried, desiccated, parched; thirsty, causing thirst; not yielding water etc., (of cows etc.) not yielding milk. 2. Not under, in, or on water; not submerged. 3. (of bread etc.) Without butter or the like. 4. Solid, not liquid; (of measures etc.) relating to non-liquids. 5. (of wines etc.) Not sweet or fruity. 6. Not associated with liquid; favouring or enforcing prohibition of alcoholic liquor. 7. Feeling or showing no emotion; stiff, cold; caustically witty, uttered in, using, matter-of-fact tones without air of pleasantry; meagre, plain, bare. 8. ~ *battery*, electric battery consisting of dry cells; ~*-bob*: see BOB[3]; ~*-bulb thermometer*, one of a pair of thermometers in hygrometer of which one has dry and other wet bulb; ~ *cell*, (electr.) voltaic cell whose contents are made non-spillable by use of some absorbent substance, esp. cell of Leclanché type, in which, for the sake of portability, sawdust or plaster of Paris, saturated with sal-ammoniac, takes the place of the solution; ~*-clean* (*v.t.*) clean (textiles) without using water, e.g. with spirit; ~ *cleaner*, shop that dry-cleans clothes etc.; ~*-cooper*, maker of casks for dry goods; ~*-cure* (*v.t.*) cure (meat etc.) without pickling in liquid; ~ *dock*: see DOCK[3]; ~ *farming*, various methods of arable farming designed to conserve moisture in dry areas: ~ *fly*, (angling) artificial fly resting lightly on water; ~ *goods*, (chiefly U.S.) articles of drapery, mercery, etc., as opp. to groceries; ~ *measure*, measure of bulk, esp. for grain, fruits, etc.; ~*-nurse* (*n.*) nurse who looks after baby without suckling it, as opp. to *wet-nurse*; (fig.) person who looks after another with great care; (*v.t.*) nurse thus; ~ *plate*, (photog.) sensitized plate which does not require immersion before exposure; ~*-point*, strong pointed tool for scratching design (without use of acid) on copper plate from which prints are taken; process of engraving thus, print so produced; ~ *rot*, decayed condition, caused by various fungi, of unventilated timber, in which it becomes dry, light, and friable; *dry'salter*, dealer in chemicals used in arts, drugs, dyestuffs, etc., sometimes also dealer in oils, sauces, tinned meats, etc.; ~ *shampoo*, kind of shampoo without water; ~*-shod*, without wetting the feet; ~ *spell*, period of little or no rain (in U.K., period of 15 days or more with less than 1·0 mm (0·04 in.) of rain per day); ~(*-stone*) *wall*, wall built without mortar. **drȳ'ish** *adj*. **drȳ'lȳ**, **drī'lȳ** *advs*. **drȳ'nėss** *n*. **drȳ** *v*. Make or become dry by wiping, evaporation, draining, etc.; cause (cow) to cease giving milk; ~ *up*, make, become, utterly dry; cease to yield water or milk; (colloq.) cease talking; (theatr.) forget one's lines.

drȳ'ăd *n*. (myth.) Nymph inhabiting tree, wood-nymph.

Drȳ'den, John (1631–1700). English poet, dramatist, critic, and translator of Virgil, Horace, Ovid, etc.

D.S. *abbrev*. *Dal segno*.

D.Sc. *abbrev*. Doctor of Science.

D.S.C., D.S.M., D.S.O. *abbrevs*. Distinguished Service Cross, Medal, Order.

D.T., D.T.'s *abbrevs*. (colloq.) Delirium tremens.

D.Th., D.Theol. *abbrevs*. Doctor of Theology.

D.T.I. *abbrev.* Department of Trade and Industry.

dū'al *adj.* Of two; twofold, divided in two; double; ~ *carriageway*, road with contrary streams of traffic kept separate by central dividing strip, having at least two lanes on each side; ~ *number*, (gram.) inflected form proper to two persons or things. ~ *n.* Dual number. **dūă'lĭtў** *n.*

dū'alĭsm *n.* 1. Being dual. 2. Theory or system of thought recognizing two independent principles; (philos.) doctrine that mind and matter exist as distinct entities (opp. MONISM and PLURALISM); doctrine that there are two independent principles, good and evil; (theol.) doctrine that Christ consisted of two personalities (attributed to Nestorius by his opponents). **dū'alĭst** *n.* **dūalĭ'stĭc** *adj.*

dŭb¹ *v.t.* 1. Make (person) into *a knight* by striking shoulder with sword. 2. Invest with (new title); name, nickname. 3. Dress (artificial fishing-fly); smear (leather) with grease.

dŭb² *v.t.* Add sound effects or new sound-track, esp. in a different language, to (film); insert (sound effects) *in* film or radio or television production.

dŭ'bbĭn, -ĭng *n.* Preparation of grease for softening and waterproofing leather. ~ *v.t.* Apply dubbin to.

dūbī'ėtў *n.* Feeling of doubt.

dū'bĭous *adj.* Doubtful; of questionable or suspected character. **dū'bĭouslў** *adv.* **dū'bĭousnėss** *n.*

dū'bĭtable *adj.* Open to doubt or question. **dūbĭtā'tion** *n.* Doubt, uncertainty, hesitation. **dū'bĭtatĭve** *adj.* Expressing doubt or hesitancy. **dū'bĭtatĭvelў** *adv.*

Dŭ'blĭn. County borough and seaport on E. coast of Ireland, capital of the republic and formerly of all Ireland; university (known as Trinity College, Dublin), 1591.

dū'cal *adj.* Of, like, bearing title of, duke.

dŭ'cat *n.* (hist.) Gold coin of varying value formerly current in most European countries; (hist.) Italian silver coin; (colloq.) coin, (pl.) cash.

Duce (do͞o'chā). Title assumed by Benito MUSSOLINI as head of Italian Fascists, and dictator of Italy. [It., = 'leader']

dŭ'chėss *n.* Wife or widow of duke; lady holding in her own right position equal to duke's.

duchĕ'sse (do͝osh-) *n.* (also *satin* ~, ~ *satin*) Soft kind of satin; ~ *lace*, Brussels pillow-lace worked with fine thread in large sprays; ~ *potatoes*, purée of mashed potato and egg etc. shaped into small cakes and baked or fried; ~ *set*, set of covers for dressing-table.

dŭ'chў *n.* 1. Territory of reigning duke or duchess. 2. Each of the two dukedoms of Cornwall and Lancaster (the two earliest in England) vested in the royal family.

dŭck¹ *n.* 1. Any of several kinds of swimming bird found all over the world, esp. domesticated form of mallard or wild duck; female of this (male being DRAKE²); flesh of this. 2. Darling. 3. (cricket slang; also ~*'s egg*) Batsman's score of 0. 4. *Bombay* ~ = BUMMALO; *lame* ~, disabled person or thing; (Stock Exch. slang) defaulter; ~*s and drakes*, game of making flat stone skip over surface of water; *play* ~*s and drakes with*, throw away idly or carelessly, squander; ~*-bill*, ~*-billed platypus*: see PLATYPUS; *du'ckboards*, slatted timbers laid down on muddy ground in trenches or camps; ~*-shot*, shot of size suitable for shooting wild duck; *du'ckweed*, any plant of genus *Lemna*, floating on still water and covering surface like a green carpet.

dŭck² *n.* Strong untwilled linen or cotton fabric for small sails and outer clothing, esp. of sailors; (pl.) trousers of this.

dŭck³ *v.* Plunge, dive, dip head, under water and emerge; bend quickly, bob, to avoid blow etc., or by way of bow or curtsey; plunge (person) momentarily *in*, *under* water; lower (head) suddenly; (bridge) omit to take possible trick at first opportunity. ~ *n.* Quick dip below water in bathing; lowering of head, jerky bow.

dŭck[4] *n.* (colloq.) Amphibious landing craft. [f. DUKW, official designation]

dŭ'cking *n.* Immersion in water, or wetting by submersion; ~*-pond*, pond for ducking of offenders; ~*-stool*, chair in which scolds, dishonest tradesmen, etc., were tied and ducked in water as a punishment.

dŭ'ckling *n.* Young duck; *ugly* ~: see UGLY.

dŭct *n.* Conduit, tube, for conveying liquid; conduit for electric cable; (physiol.) tube or canal conveying secretions or lymph in animal body; (bot.) vessel of plant's vascular tissue holding air, water, etc. **dŭ'ctless** *adj.* (of gland) Having no ducts, containing secretion that passes directly from cells to blood; endocrine. **dŭct** *v.t.* Convey through a duct.

dŭ'ctile *adj.* 1. (of metal) Malleable, flexible, not brittle; (tech.) capable of being drawn into wire, tough. 2. Plastic; pliable, pliant. **dŭctĭ'lĭtÿ** *n.*

dŭd *n.* (slang) 1. (pl.) Clothes; rags. 2. Scarecrow; shell etc. that fails to explode; futile plan or person. ~ *adj.* Counterfeit; useless; unsatisfactory.

dūde *n.* (U.S. slang) Exaggeratedly or ridiculously fastidious or foppish person; dandy, swell; ~ *ranch*, cattle ranch converted into holiday centre for visitors, with facilities for riding, hunting, etc.

dŭ'dgeon (-jon) *n.* Resentment, feeling of offence.

dudhee'n, -dee'n (dōō-) *n.* (Ir.) Short clay pipe.

dūe *adj.* 1. Owing, payable, as a debt or obligation; that ought to be given or rendered (*to*); fitting, proper, rightful; adequate, sufficient. 2. To be ascribed or attributed *to* (cause, agent, etc.; the adverbial use for *owing* is incorrect). 3. Under engagement or contract to be ready, be present, or arrive (at defined time). ~ *adv.* (with ref. to points of compass) Straight, exactly, directly. ~ *n.* 1. Person's right, what is owed him; what one owes. 2. (usu. pl.) Toll or fee legally demandable.

dū'el *n.* Fight with deadly weapons between two persons, in presence of two observers (*seconds*), to settle quarrel; any contest between two parties, persons, animals, causes. ~ *v.i.* Fight duel. **dū'ellist** *n.*

dūĕ'nna *n.* Older woman acting as governess and chaperon to girl(s) (orig. and esp. in Spanish family); chaperon.

dūĕ't *n.* (mus.) (Composition for) 2 voices or instruments in combination. **dūĕ'ttist** *n.*

dŭff[1] *n.* Boiled pudding, dumpling.

dŭff[2] *v.t.* 1. (slang) Fake up (thing) to make it look new or like something which it is not; (Austral.) alter brands on (stolen cattle); cheat (*out of*). 2. (golf) Mis-hit (shot).

dŭ'ffer *n.* (colloq.) Inefficient, useless, or stupid person.

dŭ'ffle, dŭ'ffel *n.* Coarse woollen cloth with thick nap; (U.S.) sportsman's or camper's change of clothes or personal effects; ~ *bag*, cylindrical canvas bag; ~ *coat*, coat made of duffle, esp. one with hood and toggle fastenings. [f. *Duffel* in Brabant]

dŭg *n.* Udder of female mammal, teat, nipple; (now contempt.) woman's breast.

du'gŏng (dōō-) *n.* Large aquatic herbivorous mammal, *D~ dugon*, of Red Sea and coasts of Indian Ocean, Australia, Taiwan, and Solomon Islands. [Malay *duyong*]

dŭ'gout *adj.* Hollowed out by digging. ~ *n.* 1. Canoe made of hollowed-out tree-trunk. 2. Underground shelter esp. for troops in trenches; (slang) retired officer etc. recalled to service.

dui'ker, dui'kerbŏk (dī-) *n.* Small African antelope (genus *Cephalophus*), so called from its habit of diving suddenly into the bush. [Du. *duiker* diver]

dūke *n.* 1. In Gt Britain and some other countries, hereditary noble ranking next below prince;

royal ~, duke who is a member of royal family, taking precedence of other dukes. 2. In some parts of Europe, sovereign prince, ruler of small State called duchy. 3. (hist.) In late Roman Empire, provincial military commander. 4. (slang) Hand, fist. **dū'kedom** *n.* Duchy; office or dignity of duke.

Dū'keries (-ĭz). District in Nottinghamshire containing several ducal estates.

Du'khobŏr, Dou- (dōōχo-) *n.* Member of a sect which originated in Russia in second half of 18th c., probably influenced by Anabaptists and Quakers; its members rejected the authority of Church and State and were persecuted for refusing to pay taxes or perform military service; they migrated to Canada in 1899, and settled in Saskatchewan and British Columbia. [Russ., = 'spirit-wrestler']

dŭ'lcėt *adj.* Sweet, soothing (esp. of sounds).

dŭlcĭa'na (-ah-) *n.* (mus.) Open organ stop, usu. 8-foot, of soft tone.

dŭ'lcĭfȳ *v.t.* Sweeten; make gentle. **dŭlcĭficā'tion** *n.*

dŭ'lcĭmer *n.* 1. Musical instrument in which metallic strings of graduated length are stretched over a trapezoidal sounding-board and struck with hammers held in the hands (earliest prototype of pianoforte); similar instrument played by plucking strings, used in Kentucky. 2. (bibl.) Kind of bagpipe.

Dŭlcĭnē'a (*or* -sĭ'nĭa) *n.* Name given by Don QUIXOTE to a village girl whom he idolizes; hence, idealized mistress.

dŭ'lcĭtōne *n.* Musical instrument like small pianoforte in which graduated steel tuning-forks are struck by hammers.

dū'lĭa *n.* Reverence which, acc. to Orthodox and R.C. Churches, may be paid to the saints (dist. from HYPERDULIA and LATRIA).

dŭll *adj.* 1. Slow of understanding, stupid; lacking sensibility or keenness of perception; (of pain etc.) not keen or intense. 2. Slow, heavy, drowsy; stagnant, sluggish; listless, not lively or cheerful, depressed; causing depression or boredom. 3. Not sharp or keen; not clear, vivid, or intense; obscure, muffled, flat, insipid; (of weather) overcast, gloomy. ~ *v.* Make or become dull, sluggish, inert, etc.; blunt; make or become dim or indistinct. **dŭ'llard** *n.* Dull or stupid person, dunce. **dŭ'llĭsh** *adj.* **dŭ'llȳ** (-l-lĭ) *adv.* **dŭ'llnėss** *n.*

dŭlse *n.* Edible species of seaweed with bright red deeply divided fronds, *Rhodymenia palmata.*

dū'lȳ *adv.* Rightly, properly, fitly; sufficiently; punctually.

du'ma (dōō-) *n.* (hist.) Russian elective municipal council; elective legislative council of State established in 1905 by ukase of Nicholas II and abolished in 1917.

Dū'mas (-mah), Alexandre. (1) 'Dumas *père*' (1803–70), French dramatist and prolific writer of romantic historical novels ('The Three Musketeers', 'The Count of Monte Cristo', etc.); (2) 'Dumas *fils*', his son Alexandre (1824–95), novelist and dramatist, author of 'La Dame aux Camélias' etc.

dŭmb (-m) *adj.* 1. Destitute of faculty of speech. 2. Temporarily bereft of speech from astonishment, shock, etc.; remaining persistently silent; refusing to speak; taciturn, reticent. 3. (of actions) Not attended with speech. 4. Not emitting or attended with sound; silent, mute; not having some quality, property, etc., usual in things of the name. 5. (orig. U.S.) Foolish, stupid (prob. after Ger. *dumm*). 6. ~ *barge*, barge without sails or other motive power; (on Thames) lighter travelling up and down with the tide; ~*-bell*, short bar with rounded heavy knob at each end, used in pairs for exercising muscles; object of this shape; ~ *cluck*, (slang) stupid person; ~ *crambo*: see CRAMBO; ~*-iron*, carriage spring of two half-elliptic springs joined at ends; each of forward ends of frame-side members in motor-car chassis to which one end of each front spring is fixed; ~ *show*, part of play represented by action without speech; significant gesture without speech; ~ *waiter*, stand or wagon holding dishes etc. at meals. **dŭ'mblȳ** *adv.* **dŭ'mbnėss** *n.*

dŭmbfou'nd (-mf-) *v.t.* Strike dumb, confound, nonplus.

dŭ'mdŭm *n.* (also ~ *bullet*) Soft-nosed bullet which expands on impact. [*Dum-Dum*, town and arsenal near Calcutta]

Dŭmfrie's and Gă'lloway. Region of SW. Scotland (since May 1975), comprising the former counties of Dumfriesshire, Kirkcudbrightshire, and Wigtownshire.

Dŭmfrie'sshire. Former county in SW. Scotland, since May 1975 part of the region of Dumfries and Galloway.

dŭ'mmy *n.* 1. (whist) Imaginary fourth player whose hand is turned up and played by partner; (bridge) hand of dealer's or declarer's partner, turned up and played by declarer; person holding this hand; *double* ~, (game, problem) with two (or all four) hands exposed. 2. Person taking no real part, or present only for show, figurehead, mere tool. 3. Counterfeit object, sham package, etc.; lay figure; = COMFORTER 3; man's figure used as target; imitation ammunition used in training. ~ *adj.* That is a dummy, sham.

dŭmp *n.* Rubbish-heap, place where refuse is deposited; temporary depot, pile, of ammunition, equipment, etc. (also colloq. of town etc.); (pl., colloq.) low spirits. ~ *v.* Shoot, deposit, put down (rubbish); let fall with a bump; send (goods unsaleable at high price in home market) to foreign market for sale at low price.

dŭ'mpling *n.* Ball of dough cooked in stew, boiled with beef, etc., or baked or boiled with fruit inside.

dŭ'mpȳ *adj.* Short and stout or thick; ~ (*spirit-*)*level*, surveyor's instrument for spirit-levelling in which line of sight is adjusted to be perpendicular to vertical axis. ~ *n.* Dumpy animal; (esp.) one of breed of very short-legged fowls.

dŭn[1] *adj.* Of dull greyish-brown colour; (of horse) of golden sand-coloured body with black mane and tail; (poet.) dark, dusky. ~ *n.* Dun colour; dun horse; dun-coloured artificial fishing-fly.

dŭn[2] *n.* Importunate creditor; debt-collector. ~ *v.t.* Importune for payment of debt; pester.

Dŭnbar', William (1465?–1530?). Scottish poet; author of satires and elegies, etc., of which the 'Lament for the Makaris' is the most famous.

Dŭnbar'tonshire. Former county in W. Scotland, N. of Firth of Clyde, since May 1975 part of the region of Strathclyde.

dŭnce *n.* One slow at learning, dullard; ~'*s cap*, paper cone formerly put on head of dunce at school. [John DUNS SCOTUS, whose followers were ridiculed by 16th-c. reformers and humanists as enemies of learning]

Dŭndee'. Sea-port in Tayside on E. coast of Scotland; university, 1967; ~ *cake*, rich fruit cake decorated with split almonds.

dŭ'nderhead (-ĕd) *n.* Blockhead. **dŭ'nderheadėd** *adj.*

Dŭndrear'ȳ whĭ'skers (-z). Long side-whiskers worn without a beard. [Lord *Dundreary*, character in T. Taylor's comedy 'Our American Cousin' (1858)]

dūne *n.* Mound or ridge of drifted sand or clay.

Dunelm. *abbrev.* (Bishop) of Durham (replacing surname in his signature).

dŭng *n.* Manure; excrement of animals (rarely of man); moral filth; ~ *beetle*, any of various beetles which breed in dung; dor beetle; ~-*cart*, cart used for carrying manure; ~-*fly*, two-winged fly of genus *Scatophaga*, feeding on dung; ~-*fork*, pitchfork used to lift or spread dung; ~-*heap*, -*hill*, heap of dung or rubbish; ~-*worm*, worm or larva found in cow-dung, used as bait for fishing. ~ *v.t.* Manure.

dŭngaree' (-ngg-) *n.* Kind of coarse Indian calico; (pl.) trousers or overalls of this.

dŭ'ngeon (-jon) *n.* 1. Donjon.

2. Strong close cell; subterranean place of confinement.

du'nĭwăssal (dōō-) *n.* (Sc.) Highland gentleman of secondary rank.

dŭnk *v.t.* (orig. U.S.) Dip (bread, cake, etc.) into soup or beverage while eating.

Dŭnkĭr'k(-n-k-).(Fr. *Dunquerque*) Seaport in NE. France, whence the British Expeditionary Force was evacuated between 29 May and 3 June 1940; hence, any similar withdrawal, crisis, etc.

dŭ'nlin *n.* Small reddish-backed migratory wading bird (*Calidris alpina*), allied to sandpiper, abundant on sea-coasts of Europe.

Dŭ'nmow Flitch (-mō). Acc. to an ancient custom of the manor of Dunmow in Essex (said to have been instituted in 1244) a flitch of bacon is given to any married couple who after 12 months of marriage can swear that they have maintained perfect harmony and fidelity during that time.

dŭ'nnage *n.* Light material, as brushwood, mats, etc., stowed under or among cargo to prevent damp and chafing; (colloq.) miscellaneous baggage.

dŭ'nnock *n.* Hedge accentor (*Prunella nodularis occidentalis*), misleadingly called *hedge-sparrow*.

Dŭns Scō'tus (-nz), John (1265?–1308?). Scholastic theologian, born acc. to tradition at Duns, Berwickshire; called the 'subtle doctor'; his works on theology, logic, and philosophy were university textbooks until the 16th c.

dū'ō *n.* (mus.) Duet.

dūodĕ'cimal *adj.* Of twelve or twelfths, proceeding by twelves. ~ *n.pl.* Cross-multiplication, method used for dimensions given in feet, inches, and twelfths of inch, used by quantity surveyors etc.

dūodĕ'cimō *n.* (abbrev. 12mo) Book-size in which each leaf is $\frac{1}{12}$ of printing-sheet; book of this size; diminutive thing or person.

dūodē'narȳ *adj.* Proceeding by twelves, in sets of 12.

dūodē'num *n.* (anat.) First portion of small intestine immediately below stomach. **dūodē'nal** *adj.* [L *duodeni* 12 at once (f. its being about 12 in. long)]

dū'olŏgue (-g) *n.* Conversation between two persons; dramatic piece with two actors.

dūpe *n.* Victim of deception, gull. **dū'perȳ** *n.* **dūpe** *v.t.* Cheat, make a fool of.

dū'pion *n.* Rough silk fabric woven from threads from double cocoons; fabric resembling this.

dū'ple *adj.* (mus., of time) Having two beats in bar; (math., of proportion) in which one quantity is double the other.

dū'plĕx *adj.* Of two elements; twofold; ~ *apartment*, (U.S.) one on two connected floors. ~ *n.* (U.S.) Duplex apartment.

dū'plicate *adj.* 1. With two corresponding parts; existing in two examples. 2. Doubled; twice as large or as many; ~ *proportion, ratio*, proportion of squares to their radicals. 3. Exactly like thing already existing. ~ *n.* One of two things exactly alike; exact copy; second copy, with equal legal force, of letter or document; synonym; *in* ~, in two exactly corresponding copies or parts. **dū'plicāte** *v.t.* 1. Double, multiply by two. 2. Make in duplicate; make exact copy of; produce copies of; repeat. **dūplicā'tion** *n.*

dū'plicātor *n.* Machine for producing copies of hand-written or typewritten documents.

dūpli'citȳ *n.* Double-dealing, deceitfulness; doubleness.

dūr'able *adj.* Lasting, not transitory; resisting wear, decay, etc.; ~ *goods*, goods that can be used over a period of time. **dūr'ables** (-lz) *n.pl.* Durable goods. **dūrabĭ'litȳ, dūr'ableness** *ns.* **dūr'ablȳ** *adv.*

dūră'lūmin *n.* Light hard aluminium alloy containing copper, manganese, and magnesium, used esp. for aircraft. [trade-name]

dūr'a mā'ter. (anat.) Dense tough meninx enveloping brain and spinal cord (ill. SPINE). [med. L. transl. of Arab anatomical term = 'hard mother', so called because it was supposed to give rise to all membranes of body]

dūrā'mĕn *n.* Dense inner part of tree-trunk, heart-wood.

dūr'ance *n.* Forced confinement, imprisonment (now esp. *in ~ vile*).

dūrā'tion *n.* Continuance in time; time during which thing, action, or state continues.

dūr'bar *n.* (hist.) Court of Indian ruler; audience or levee held by native prince or by the British sovereign as Emperor of India or by his deputy.

Dü'rer (dū-), Albrecht (1471–1528). German Renaissance engraver and painter; famous for his painting of the four apostles and his numerous line engravings (e.g. 'The Knight, Death, and the Devil') and woodcuts.

dūrĕ'ss, -ĕ'sse (*or* dūr'-) *n.* Forcible restraint, imprisonment; constraint illegally exercised to force person to perform some act, compulsion.

Dŭ'rham[1] (-*ra*m). County in NE. England; city and county town; university, 1832.

Dŭ'rham[2] (-*ra*m), John George

DURHAM CATHEDRAL

Lambton, 1st Earl of (1792–1840). British statesman, whose 'Report on the Affairs of British N. America' (1839), usu. called the ~ *Report*, laid down the principles on which self-government was subsequently accorded to the British Dominions.

dur'ĭan (door-) *n.* Large oval or globular prickly fruit of a tree of the Indian Archipelago, *Durio zibethinus*, with hard rind and luscious, civet-smelling, cream-coloured pulp. [Malay *duri* thorn]

dūr'ing *prep.* Throughout, at some point in, the continuance of.

dûr'mast *n.* Sessile-flowered species of oak, *Quercus petraea*.

dûrn *v.t.* (U.S.) Darn, confound.

dŭsk *n.* Shade, gloom; darker stage of twilight. ~ *adj.* (poet.) Dusky. ~ *v.* (poet.) Become, look, make, dim or dusky.

dŭ'skȳ *adj.* Shadowy, dim; dark-coloured. **dŭ'skilȳ** *adv.* **dŭ'skinėss** *n.*

dŭst *n.* 1. Earth or other solid matter in minute and fine state of subdivision, in particles small and light enough to be easily raised and carried in cloud by wind; cloud of dust; household refuse; *bite the* ~, fall to the ground, esp. killed or wounded; *in the* ~, humbled, humiliated; *throw* ~ *in person's eyes*, deceive him. 2. What anything is reduced to by disintegration or decay, esp. mouldered remains of dead body; man's mortal remains; man. 3. Confusion, turmoil, excitement; row, contest (also ~*-up*). 4. *du'stbin*, receptacle for household refuse; ~ *bowl*, area denuded of forest and so reduced to desert; ~*-cloak*, *-coat*, cloak, coat, worn to keep off dust; ~*-cover*, paper jacket of book; ~ *devil*, column-like whirl of dust moving over desert; *du'stman*, man who collects and carts away refuse etc. from dustbins; personification of sleep or sleepiness; *du'stpan*, utensil for catching dust as it is swept from floor etc.; ~*-up*, (colloq.) quarrel, fight. ~ *v.* 1. Sprinkle with dust or powder, (cooking) flour, sugar, etc.; make dusty; sprinkle (powder etc.). 2. Clear of dust by brushing, wiping, beating, etc.; clear away (dust etc.); clear furniture etc. of dust.

dŭ'ster *n.* 1. Cloth for dusting furniture etc. 2. (U.S.) Dust-cloak or -coat.

dŭ'stĭng *n.* (esp., slang) Thrashing.

dŭ'stȳ *adj.* Full of dust, strewn with dust; finely powdered like dust; dry as dust, uninteresting; *not so* ~, (slang) fairly good; ~ *miller*, auricula, from the fine powder on the leaves and flowers. **dŭ'stilȳ** *adv.* **dŭ'stinėss** *n.*

Dŭtch[1] *adj.* 1. Of Holland (the Netherlands) or its language or people; coming from Holland; characteristic of the Dutch. 2. (hist.) Of Germany, German; Teutonic; *High* ~, of the southern Germans, High German; *Low* ~, of the northern Germans, of the northern and north-west parts including the Netherlands and Flanders. 3. *go* ~, have each person pay his own expenses on excursion etc. 4. ~ *auction*: see AUCTION; ~ *barn*, roof over hay, straw, etc., supported on poles; ~ *cap*, (esp.) contraceptive diaphragm; ~ *cheese*, round skim-milk cheese made in Holland, esp. kind stained red on outside; ~ *courage*, courage due to intoxicants and therefore not lasting; ~ *gable*, gable with curved sides; ~ *hoe*, hoe used with thrusting action; ~ *metal*, alloy of copper and zinc made in leaf form in imitation of gold leaf; ~ *oven*, device for roasting meat etc. before an open fire consisting of metal box open at one side; ~ *supper*, *treat*, one at which each party pays for or contributes his own share; (*talk* etc.) *like a* ~ *uncle*, lecture with kindly severity. ~ *n.* 1. (collect.) People of Holland (the Netherlands). 2. Language of Holland (the Netherlands), a Germanic dialect which has not undergone the High-German consonant-mutation (second sound shift); *double* ~, gibberish. 3. (obs.) German language; *High* ~ = High German; *Low* ~ = Low

German; *Pennsylvania* ~, degraded form of High German (orig. from Rhine Palatinate and Switzerland) spoken by descendants of German settlers in Pennsylvania. **Dŭ'tchman** *n.* 1. (fem. *Du'tchwoman*) Native, inhabitant, of Holland or the Netherlands. 2. Dutch ship; *Flying* ~, legendary spectral ship condemned with all her crew to sail the seas for ever, and supposed to be seen near the Cape of Good Hope. 3. (hist.) German.

dŭtch[2] *n.* (slang) Wife, esp. of costermonger (usu. *old D~*). [abbrev. of *duchess*]

dū'tėous *adj.* (poet.) Dutiful, obedient. **dū'tėouslȳ** *adv.* **dū'tėousnėss** *n.*

dū'tĭable *adj.* Liable to customs or other duties.

dū'tĭful *adj.* Regular or willing in obedience and service. **dū'tĭfullȳ** *adv.* **dū'tĭfulnėss** *n.*

dū'tȳ *n.* 1. Action and conduct due to superior, deference, respect. 2. Payment to public revenue levied upon imports, manufacture of certain goods, transfer and inheritance of property, licence to trade in certain articles, legal recognition of certain documents etc.; *~-paid*, on which customs or excise duty has been paid. 3. Action, act, due in way of moral or legal obligation. 4. Business, office, function, performance of or engagement in these (*on*, *off*, ~, actually so engaged or not); (eccles.) performance of church services; ~ *officer*, (mil. etc.) person left in charge when others are absent. 5. Measure of engine's effectiveness in units of work done per unit of fuel.

dūŭ'mvir *n.* (Rom. hist.) One of a pair of co-equal magistrates and functionaries in Rome and her colonies. **dūŭ'mvirate** *n.*

dū'vet (-vā) *n.* Thick soft quilt used instead of bed-clothes.

D.V. *abbrev.* *Deo volente.*

Dvořák (dvôr'zhăk *or* v-), Antonin (1841–1904). Czech composer of symphonies, Slav dances, operas, etc.

dwarf (-ôrf) *n.* 1. Person, animal, or plant, much below ordinary size of species. 2. (also ~ *star*) One of the class of smaller stars of greater density as dist. from the larger diffuse stars or 'giants'. 3. (Teutonic, esp. Scand., myth.) Small supernatural being living underground and skilled in metal-working. ~ *adj.* Undersized; puny, stunted. **dwar'fĭsh** *adj.* **dwar'fĭshlȳ** *adv.* **dwar'fĭshnėss** *n.* **dwar'fĭsm** *n.* (med.) Condition of being considerably undersized. **dwarf** *v.t.* Stunt in growth, intellect, etc.; make to look small by contrast or distance.

dwĕll *v.i.* (past t. & past part. *dwelt*). 1. Continue, remain, for a time (archaic); have one's abode, live (in house, country, etc.) (now rare). 2. ~ *on*, spend time upon, linger over in action or thought; treat at length. **dwĕ'ller** *n.* Inhabitant, resident.

dwĕ'llĭng *n.* (esp.) Place of residence, house; *~-house*, house used as residence, not as office, shop, etc.; *~-place*, dwelling.

dwĭ'ndle *v.i.* Become smaller, shrink, waste away; lose importance, decline; degenerate.

dwt *abbrev.* Pennyweight.

dȳ'ad *n.* The number two; group of two, couple.

Dȳ'ăk *n.* Member, language, of an aboriginal tribe of Borneo.

dyarchy: see DIARCHY.

dye (dī) *v.* (pres. part. *dyeing*). Colour, stain, tinge; impregnate with colour, fix a colour in the substance of; make (thing) specified colour; *dyed in the wool, in grain*: see WOOL, GRAIN. ~ *n.* Colour produced by or as by dyeing; tinge, hue; matter used for dyeing, colouring-matter in solution; *dy'eline*, print produced photographically on paper treated with a diazo compound; *~-wood*, wood yielding dye. **dȳ'er** *n.* One who dyes clothes etc.; *~'s broom, bugloss, oak, weed*, etc., plants yielding dyes.

Dyfed (dŭvĕd). County of SW. Wales (since April 1974), comprising the former counties of Cardiganshire, Carmarthenshire, and Pembrokeshire.

dying: see DIE[2].

dyke: see DIKE.

dyn *abbrev.* Dyne.

dyn., dynam. *abbrevs.* Dynamics.

dȳnă'mĭc *adj.* Of force producing motion; of force in action or operation, active; potent, energetic; of dynamics; (philos.) relating to the reason of existence of an object of experience; accounting for matter, or mind, as merely the action of forces. **dȳnă'mĭcs** *n.* Branch of physics treating of the behaviour of matter under the action of force; branch of any science considering force or forces; moving forces, physical or moral, in any sphere.

dȳnă'mĭcal *adj.* 1. Of dynamics; of force or mechanical power actively operative. 2. (theol., of inspiration) Endowing with divine power, not making the medium a mere tool or instrument of his deity; of dynamism. **dȳnă'mĭcallȳ** *adv.*

dȳ'namĭsm *n.* Philosophical system or theory explaining phenomena of universe by some immanent force or energy. **dȳ'namĭst** *n.* **dȳnamĭ'stĭc** *adj.*

dȳ'namīte *n.* High explosive of nitro-glycerine contained in some absorbent substance, esp. kieselguhr. ~ *v.t.* Lay charge of dynamite to, blow up with dynamite. **dȳ'namīter** *n.* One who uses explosives esp. for revolutionary purposes. [named by Alfred Nobel (1833–96), the inventor, f. Gk *dunamis* force]

dȳ'namō *n.* (pl. *-os*). Machine converting mechanical into electrical energy by rotating coils of copper wire in a magnetic field. [short for *dynamo-electric machine*]

dȳnamŏ'mēter *n.* Instrument for measuring energy; *absorption* ~, one that converts energy into heat or electric current.

dȳ̆'nast *n.* Ruler, member of dynasty. **dȳ̆'nastȳ** *n.* Line of hereditary rulers. **dȳ̆nă'stĭc** *adj.* **dȳ̆nă'stĭcallȳ** *adv.*

dȳne *n.* (phys.) Absolute unit of force in the c.g.s. system, force which, acting on a mass of 1 gramme, will make it move 1 cm per second faster in every second (abbrev. dyn).

dȳs- *prefix.* Bad.

dȳ'senterȳ *n.* Disease with inflammation of mucous membrane and glands of large intestine, and mucous and bloody evacuations. **dȳsentĕ'rĭc** *adj.*

dȳsgĕ'nĭc *adj.* Causing degeneration in offspring (opp. EUGENIC).

dȳslĕ'xĭa *n.* Word-blindness, impairment of ability to read. **dȳslĕ'xĭc** *adj.* & *n.*

dȳslogĭ'stĭc *adj.* Expressing disapprobation or dispraise; having a bad connotation.

dȳspĕ'psĭa *n.* Indigestion. **dȳspĕ'ptĭc** *adj.* & *n.* (Person) subject to dyspepsia or the attendant depression.

dȳspnoe'a (-nē'*a*) *n.* (path.) Difficult or laboured breathing. **dȳspnoe'ĭc** *adj.*

dȳsprō'sĭum (-z-) *n.* (chem.) Element of rare-earth group; symbol Dy, at. no. 66, at. wt 162·50. [mod. L, f. Gk *dusprositos* hard to get at]

dȳ'strophȳ *n.* (path.) Imperfect nutrition; disorder characterized by weakness and wasting esp. of muscles (*muscular* ~).

dzĭ'ggetai (-tī) *n.* = KIANG.

E

E, e (ē). 1. 5th letter of modern English and ancient Roman alphabet, representing Semitic Ⅎ, which orig. expressed a sound like that of *h* but was adopted by the Greeks as a vowel; in English it probably varied in pronunciation from a mid-front to a low-front vowel. 2. *E*, (mus.) 3rd note of natural scale (C major); scale or key with this for tonic. 3. *E-layer*, stratum of ionosphere some 100 km above the earth, transparent to short-wave radio waves and reflecting back long wave ones.

E. *abbrev.* East; Egyptian (in £E).

e-: see EX-.

each *adj.* Every (one) taken separately; ~ *other*, (used as a compound reciprocal pronoun) one another; ~ *way*, (betting, of horse: backed) for a win or a place. ~ *adv.* To, from, or for each. ~ *pron.* Each one.

ea'ger (-g-) *adj.* Strongly desirous; keen, impatient. **ea'gerlў** *adv.* **ea'gernėss** *n.*

ea'gle *n.* 1. Large bird of prey of family Accipitridae (esp. genus *Aquila*), noted for keen vision and powerful flight; figure of this, esp. as ensign of Roman army, as symbol of the U.S., as lectern in church, or (freq. with two heads) as armorial bearing of the Holy Roman Empire, the Austrian, French, German, and Russian Empires, etc. 2. (astron.) northern constellation *Aquila*. 3. (hist.) Coin bearing image of eagle; Amer. 10-dollar gold coin (double ~, 20-dollar). 4. (golf) Score of two under par on any hole. 5. ~-*eyed*, keen-sighted; ~-*owl*, large horned owl (*Bubo bubo*) of Europe and N. Asia. **ea'glėt** *n.* Young eagle.

ea'gre (-ger; *or* ā-) *n.* = BORE³.

E. & O.E. *abbrev.* Errors and omissions excepted.

ear¹ *n.* 1. Organ of hearing in man and animals, esp. the external part of this. 2. Sense of hearing; faculty of discriminating sounds, esp. that of recognizing musical intervals; listening, attention. 3. Ear-like object; handle of pitcher etc.; part of bell by which it is hung; projection on side of anything serving as handle, support, etc. 4. *be all ~s*, listen attentively; *set by the ~s*, cause to dispute or quarrel; *turn a deaf ~*, disregard request etc. 5. ~-*ache*, pain in internal ear; ~-*drum*, tympanum; *ear'mark*, mark, usu. a notch, in ear of sheep etc. as sign of ownership; (*v.t.*) mark (animals) thus, mark (anything) as one's own, assign (fund etc.) *for* some purpose; ~-*phone*, one of pair of telephone or radio receivers attachable to listener's ears by band passing over head; small microphone worn in ear by deaf person; ~-*piece*, part of garment covering ear; ear-phone; ~-*ring*, ornament worn in lobe of ear; *ear'shot*, hearing distance; ~-*trumpet*, trumpet-shaped tube held to ear by partly deaf persons to enable them to hear better; ~-*wax*, cerumen.

ear² *n.* Spike, head, of corn, containing its flowers or seeds.

ear'ing, earr- *n.* (naut.) Small rope, one of several fastening upper corner of sail to yard.

earl (ẽrl) *n.* Nobleman ranking in British peerage between marquis and viscount; *E~ Marshal*, high officer of State, formerly deputy of constable as judge of court of chivalry, now president of Heralds' College, with some ceremonial duties (the office is now hereditary in the line of the Dukes of Norfolk). **ear'ldom** *n.*

ear'lў (ẽr-) *adj.* Absolutely or relatively near to the beginning of a portion of time; of, in, the first part of the morning, the year, etc.; ~ *bird*, (joc.) person who is early; ~ *closing*, system of closing shops etc. for the afternoon once a week; so ~-*closing day*; ~ *door*, door at theatre open at specified time before ordinary door at advanced price; *E~ English*, (archit.) first of the pointed Gothic styles of English architecture (*c* 1175–*c* 1275) succeeding the Norman; ~-*Victorian*, of the early years of Queen Victoria's reign. ~ *adv*. At an early time.

earn (ẽrn) *v.t.* Obtain as reward of labour or merit. **ear'nĭngs** (-z) *n.pl.* Money earned.

ear'nėst[1] (ẽr-) *n.* Money paid as instalment, esp. to confirm contract etc.; foretaste, presage, token (of what is to come).

ear'nėst[2] (ẽr-) *adj.* Serious, zealous, not trifling; ardent. **ear'nėstlў** *adv.* **ear'nėstnėss** *n.* **ear'nėst** *n.* Earnestness, seriousness; *in* ~, serious(ly), not jesting(ly).

earring: see EARING.

earth (ẽr-) *n.* 1. Ground; soil, esp. as suited for cultivation; mould, dust, clay; dry land; (also *E* ~) planet on which we dwell, the world; the present abode of man, as dist. from heaven or hell. 2. Hole or hiding-place of fox, badger, etc.; *run to* ~, (fig.) find by searching. 3. (elect.) Connection with the earth, providing return path for current; wire or metal buried in ground to effect this. 4. (chem.) Any of certain naturally occurring metallic oxides. 5. ~-*closet*, lavatory in which dry earth is used to cover and deodorize the contents; ~-*nut*, (plant having) edible roundish tubers; pig-nut; ~-*stopper*, person employed by hunt to stop up foxes' earths; *ear'thwork*, bank or mound of earth as rampart or fortification; *ear'thworm*, annelid worm (of various genera) that subsists on soil. ~ *v.* 1. Cover (roots of plants *up*) with heaped-up earth. 2. Drive (fox etc.) to earth; (of fox etc.) run to earth. 3. (elect.) Connect (conductor) with earth.

ear'then (ẽr-) *adj.* Made of earth; made of baked clay. **ear'thenwāre** *n.* (Vessels etc. made of) baked clay, esp. coarse porous kinds fired at relatively low temperature as dist. from porcelain (also attrib.).

ear'thlў (ẽr-) *adj.* Of the earth, terrestrial; *no* ~ *use* etc., (colloq.) no use etc., at all; *not an* ~, (slang) no chance whatever. **ear'thlĭnėss** *n.*

ear'thquāke (ẽr-) *n.* Convulsion of earth's surface caused by volcanic activity or faults in the earth's crust; (fig.) any disturbance or upheaval.

ear'thў (ẽr-) *adj.* Like, of, earth or soil; grossly material. **ear'thĭnėss** *n.*

ear'wĭg *n.* Insect of the order Dermaptera, esp. *Forficula auricularia* (the common European

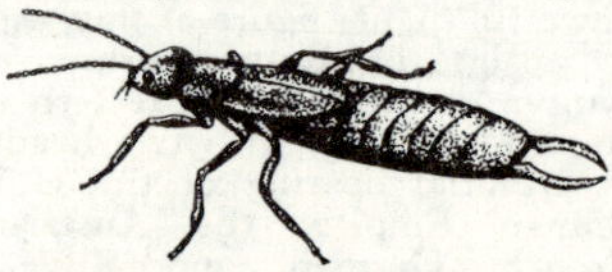

species), formerly held to penetrate into head through ear; (U.S.) kind of small centipede.

ease (ēz) *n.* Freedom from pain or trouble; freedom from constraint; relief from pain; facility; *stand at* ~, (mil. etc.) stand in relaxed attitude, with hands behind

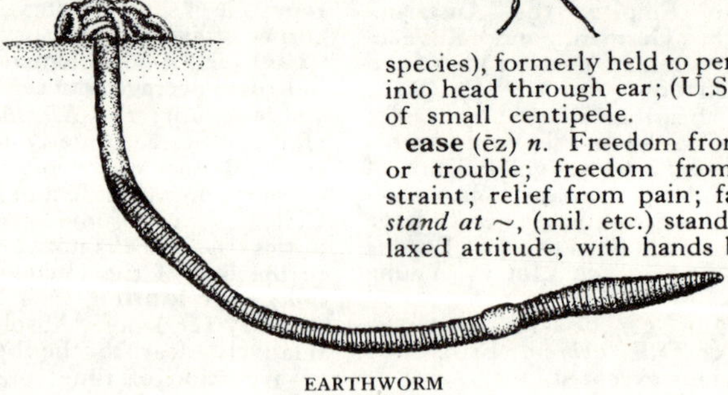

EARTHWORM

back and feet apart. ~ *v.* Relieve from pain, trouble, etc.; give mental ease to; relax, adjust (what is too tight); (naut.) slacken (rope, sail, speed, etc.); move gently or gradually; relax or cease one's efforts; ~ *off*, become less burdensome, take things easily.

ea'seful (ēzf-) *adj.* Comfortable, soothing; at rest; slothful. **ea'sefully** *adv.* **ea'sefulness** *n.* **ea'seless** *adj.*

ea'sel (-z-) *n.* Wooden frame to support picture (esp. while artist is at work on it), blackboard, etc. [Du. *ezel* = Ger. *esel* ass]

ea'sement (ēzm-) *n.* 1. (archaic) Advantage, convenience; something serving as convenience, as shed, farm building, etc., accommodation in house. 2. (law) Acquired right or privilege of using something not one's own (e.g. right of way).

east *adv.* Towards, in, the east. ~ *n.* 1. Point of horizon where sun rises at equinox; this direction. 2. Cardinal point of the compass 90° to the right of north. 3. (usu. *the E~*) That part of a country, district, etc. which lies to the east; part of world lying east of Europe; Communist States of Asia and eastern Europe; States of U.S. bordering on the Atlantic esp. N. of Maryland; New England. 4. *E~*, bridge-player sitting opposite West. ~ *adj.* Towards, in, the east; (of wind) blowing from the east; *E~ Anglia*, ancient division of England; now, counties of Norfolk and Suffolk; university, at Norwich, 1963; *E~ Anglian* (*adj.* & *n.*); *E~ End*, eastern part of London, including the docks; *E~ Germany*: see GERMANY; *E~ India Company*, company of merchants trading with the East Indies, incorporated in 1600, responsible for the political administration of British territories in India until 1858, when the government of India was assumed by the Crown; *E~ Side*, part of New York City east of Fifth Avenue. **ea'stward** *adv.*, *adj.*, & *n.* **ea'stwardly** *adv.* & *adj.* **ea'stwards** (-z) *adv.*

ea'ster[1] *adj.* Eastern (obs. exc. in *E~ Ross*).

Ea'ster[2]. Christian festival commemorating the resurrection of Christ, and observed by the Western Churches on the 1st Sunday after the calendar full moon falling on or next after 21 Mar.; week commencing with this day; ~ *egg*, coloured boiled egg or artificial (esp. chocolate) egg given as Easter present; ~ *offering*, customary payment of church

EASTER ISLAND

collection to incumbent at Easter.

Ea′ster I′sland (il-). Pacific island west of Chile, visited by the Dutch navigator Roggeveen on Easter Day, 1722, noted esp. for its monolithic statues.

ea′sterlў *adj.* In the east; (of wind) blowing from the east. ~ *adv.* Towards the east. ~ *n.* East wind.

ea′stern *adj.* Of the east; oriental; lying or directed towards the east; (poet.) in, coming from, the east; *E~*, of the East i.e. of Communist countries; *E~ Church*, ORTHODOX Church; *E~ Empire*: see ROMAN Empire. **ea′sternmōst** *adj.* **ea′sterner** *n.* (also *E~*) Native, inhabitant, of the east, esp. of eastern U.S.

East I′ndies (ĭndĭz). Islands off the SE. coast of Asia, formerly including India and the Malay peninsula. **East I′ndian** *adj.* & *n.* (Native, inhabitant) of the East Indies.

ea′sting *n.* Eastward progress or deviation, esp. in sailing; distance due east.

East Lō′thian (-dh-). Former county of E. Scotland on S. side of Firth of Forth, since May 1975 part of the region of Lothian.

East Sŭ′ssex. County of SE. England (since April 1974), mainly comprising the E. part of the former county of Sussex.

ea′sў (-zĭ) *adj.* 1. Free from pain, worry, or constraint. 2. Conducive to ease or comfort. 3. Causing little discomfort, difficulty, or obstruction; compliant; easily obtained; loosely fitting; (of commodity) not much in demand, (of market) not showing eager demand; *of ~ virtue*, (of woman) sexually promiscuous. 4. ~ *chair*, chair designed for comfort, usu. with arms; *~-going*, relaxed and casual; tolerant; ~ *money*, money obtained or obtainable without hard work or difficulty. **ea′sĭlў** *adv.* **ea′sĭnėss** *n.* **ea′sў** *adv.* In an easy manner, at leisurely pace; *~!*, (move) gently!; ~ *all!*, stop rowing!; *stand ~*, (mil.) permission to squad standing at ease to relax attitude further; *take it ~*, proceed comfortably, do no more than one must. ~ *n.* Short rest, esp. in rowing. ~ *v.* (Order to) cease rowing.

eat *v.* (past t. *ate* pr. ĕt, past part. *ea′ten*). 1. Take into mouth, masticate, and swallow as food, swallow (soup etc.); consume food, take a meal; *eating-house*, restaurant, cook-shop; ~ *one's dinners*, be studying for the bar (students being required to have dined three or more times in the hall of one of the Inns of Court during each of twelve terms before they can be called to the English Bar); ~ *one's words*, retract them in humiliating manner; ~ *out of person's hand*, be tamely or completely submissive to him. 2. Devour, consume, prey upon; (of frost, rust, etc.) destroy slowly and gradually; make (hole, passage), make a way, by fretting or corrosion; (U.S. slang) trouble, vex. **ea′table** *adj.* **ea′tables** *n.pl.* Articles of food.

eau (ō) *n.* ~ *de Cologne*: see COLOGNE; ~ *de Javelle*: see JAVELLE; ~ *de Nil*, (of) pale-green colour supposed to resemble Nile water; ~ *de vie*, brandy (Fr., lit. 'water of life').

eaves (ēvz) *n.pl.* (orig. and still occas. sing.) Overhanging edge of roof or thatch.

ea′vesdrŏp (ēvz-) *v.i.* Stand close to walls of house under eaves to listen to secrets; listen secretly to private conversation. **ea′vesdrŏpper, ea′vesdrŏpping** *ns.*

ĕbb *n.* Reflux of tide, return of tide-water towards sea (also ~ *tide*); decline, decay, change to worse state, point of decline or depression. ~ *v.i.* Flow back, recede; flow away; decay, decline.

E′bert (ā-), Friedrich (1871–1925). German politician; chancellor of the German Reich 1918–19 and president 1919–25.

E′bĭonīte (ē-) *n.* Member of early Jewish Christian sect who held that Jesus was a mere man and that the Mosaic Law was binding upon Christians.

E-boat *n.* Enemy motor torpedo-boat (esp. in war of 1939–45). [abbrev. from *enemy boat*]

ĕ'bon *adj.* & *n.* (poet.) (Made of, black as) ebony.

ĕ'bonīte *n.* Hard compound of indiarubber and sulphur, vulcanite.

ĕ'bonȳ *n.* Hard heavy black wood obtained from various tropical trees, esp. various species of *Diospyros* of Ceylon, Madagascar, and Coromandel; tree yielding this. ~ *adj.* Made of, black as, ebony; intensely black.

Ebor. *abbrev.* (Archbishop) of York (replacing surname in his signature). [f. L name *Eboracum*]

ėbŭ'llĭent *adj.* Boiling; exuberant, enthusiastic. **ėbŭ'llĭence, ėbŭ'llĭencȳ** *nn.* **ėbŭ'llĭentlȳ** *adv.*

ĕbullĭ'tion *n.* Boiling; effervescence; sudden outburst (*of* violence, passion, etc.).

E.C. *abbrev.* East Central (London postal district).

écarté (ākar'tā) *n.* Game of cards for two persons, in which cards from 2 to 6 are excluded, and in which certain cards may be discarded and replaced with fresh ones from pack.

Ecce Hŏ'mō (ĕ'kā *or* ĕ'chā). Representation of Christ wearing crown of thorns. [L, = 'behold the man' (John 19: 5)]

ėccĕ'ntrĭc (-ks-) *adj.* 1. Not concentric to, with axis, point of support, etc., otherwise than centrally placed; not centrally placed or passing through centre; (of orbital motion, curve, etc.) not circular, deviating from a circle; moving in eccentric orbit. 2. Irregular, capricious, odd, whimsical. **ėccĕ'ntrĭcallȳ** *adv.* **ĕccėntrĭ'cĭtȳ** *n.* **ėccĕ'ntrĭc** *n.* 1. Eccentric disc on revolving shaft, with connecting rods etc., for changing rotating into backward-and-forward motion, esp. for slide-valve of steam-engine. 2. Eccentric person.

Eccles. *abbrev.* Ecclesiastes.

Eccles cāke (ĕ'klz). Round cake of pastry filled with currant mixture. [name of town in Greater Manchester]

Ecclēsĭă'stēs (ĭklēz-, -z). Book of O.T. traditionally ascribed to Solomon and written in his name. **Ecclē'sĭăst** *n.* 'The Preacher', Solomon considered as author of Ecclesiastes.

ėcclēsĭă'stĭc (-zĭ-) *n.* Clergyman, person in orders.

ėcclēsĭă'stĭcal (-zĭ-) *adj.* Of the Church or clergy. **ėcclēsĭă'stĭcallȳ** *adv.* **ėcclēsĭă'stĭcism** *n.*

Ecclēsĭă'stĭcus (-zĭ-). Book of the Apocrypha, otherwise known as 'The Wisdom of Jesus the son of Sirach', containing moral and practical maxims.

ėcclēsĭŏ'logȳ (-zĭ-) *n.* Science of churches, esp. of church building and decoration. **ėcclēsĭolŏ'gĭc, -ĭcal** *adjs.* **ėcclēsĭŏ'logĭst** *n.*

Ecclus. *abbrev.* Ecclesiasticus.

ĕcdȳ'sĭs *n.* (pl. *-sēs*). (zool.) Casting of outer skin or shell.

E.C.G. *abbrev.* Electrocardiogram.

e'chelon (ĕsh-) *n.* 1. Formation of troops in parallel divisions, each with its front clear of that in advance; any similar formation; *in* ~, so drawn up. 2. Grade, rank. ~ *v.t.* Draw up in echelon. [Fr. *échelle* ladder]

ėchĭ'dna (-k-) *n.* Spiny anteater (*Tachyglossus aculeatus*), an egg-laying burrowing nocturnal mammal, toothless but with long extensile tongue for eating ants, living in rocky districts of Australia.

ėchī'noderm (-k-; *or* ĕ'kĭ-) *n.* Member of the class Echinodermata (sea-urchins, starfish, etc.), some species of which have skin studded with spines or hard plates.

ėchī'noid (-k-; *or* ĕ'kĭ-) *adj.* Resembling the *Echinus*, a genus of sea-urchins. ~ *n.* Any of the sea-urchins (Echinoidea), a large group of marine animals with usu. globular or heart-shaped calcareous skeleton of interlocking plates; fossilized member of this group.

ėchī'nus (-k-) *n.* 1. Sea-urchin of genus *E*~. 2. (archit.) Ovolo moulding next below the abacus of the capital of a column.

ĕ'chō (-k-) *n.* (pl. *-oes*). Repetition of sound produced by reflection of sound-waves from something denser than air, usu. from a rigid and approx. vertical surface; secondary sound constituted by reflected waves; reflection of radar wave; (fig.) repetition or close imitation, enfeebled reproduction; close or obsequious imitator or adherent; ~ *organ*, set of organ pipes enclosed in wooden box to give effect of distance; ~*-sounder,* instrument for ascertaining depth of water or of object below ship by means of echo from transmitted sound-signal. ~ *v.* (of place) Resound with echo; (of sounds) be repeated by echoes, reverberate, resound; repeat (sound) by or like echo; repeat (another's words), imitate words or opinions of. **ĕ'chōlėss** *adj.*

ėchō'ĭc (-k-), *adj.* (of word etc.) Echoing the sound which it denotes or symbolizes; onomatopoeic. **ĕ'chōĭsm** *n.*

E'ckhart (ĕ-), Johannes, known as Meister Eckhart (1260?–1327?). German philosopher and mystic; regarded as the founder of German mysticism.

éclair' (ā- *or* ā'-) *n.* Small finger-shaped cake of choux pastry filled with cream or custard and iced.

éclaircissement (āklārsēsmahṅ) *n.* Clearing up, explanation (of conduct etc.). [Fr.]

ĕclă'mpsia *n.* (med.) Epileptiform convulsions, esp. during pregnancy or parturition.

éclat (āklah') *n.* Conspicuous success, general applause; social distinction.

ėclĕ'ctĭc *adj.* & *n.* 1. (Philosopher, esp. of antiquity) not belonging to any recognized school but selecting such doctrines as pleased him in every school. 2. (Person) borrowing freely from various sources, not exclusive in opinion, taste, etc. **ėclĕ'ctĭcallȳ** *adv.* **ėclĕ'ctĭcĭsm** *n.*

ėclĭ'pse *n.* 1. Partial or total interception of light of sun by passage of moon between it and the earth (~ *of the sun, solar* ~); partial or total obscuration of moon by the earth's shadow (~ *of the moon, lunar* ~); similar obscuration of a satellite by another planet. 2. Temporary or permanent deprivation of light; periodical obscuration of light from lighthouse; obscuration, obscurity, loss of brilliance or splendour. ~ *v.t.* (of moon) Intercept partially or totally the light of the sun from a portion of the earth; usu. pass., (of sun) have light so intercepted, (of moon) be obscured by earth's shadow; intercept (light, esp. of lighthouse); deprive of lustre, outshine, surpass.

ėclĭ'ptĭc *adj.* Of an eclipse. ~ *n.* Great circle of celestial sphere; apparent orbit of sun (so called because eclipses happen only when moon is on or very near this line). **ėclĭ'ptĭcal** *adj.* Of, situated on, the ecliptic.

ĕ'clŏgue (-g) *n.* Short poem, esp. pastoral dialogue.

ēcŏ'logȳ, oec- (ē-) *n.* Branch of biology dealing with relations of living organisms to their surroundings, their habits, modes of life, populations, etc. **ēcolŏ'gĭcal** *adj.* **ēcolŏ'gĭcallȳ** *adv.* **ēcŏ'logist** *n.*

ēconŏ'mĭc *adj.* Of economics, maintained for profit; practical, utilitarian, adapted to human needs; connected with industrial arts; (of rent) high enough to produce reasonable interest on capital expended or invested. **ēconŏ'mĭcal** *adj.* 1. Saving, thrifty; not wasteful (of). 2. Relating to economics or political economy. **ēconŏ'mĭcallȳ** *adv.* **ēconŏ'mĭcs** *n.* Science relating to the production and distribution of material wealth;

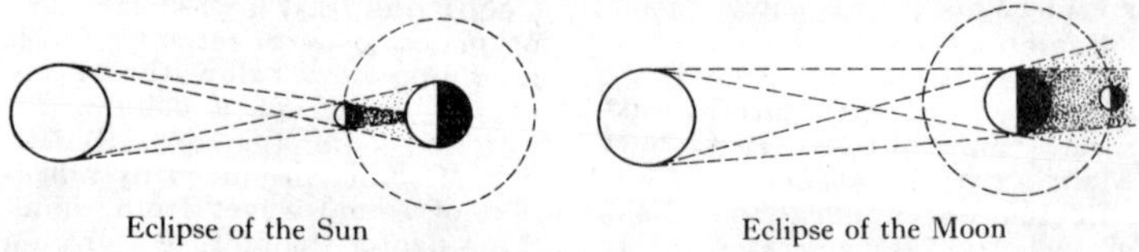

Eclipse of the Sun — Eclipse of the Moon

○ Sun ◑ Moon ◑ Earth — ○ Sun ◑ Earth ◑ Moon

ECLIPSE

condition of country with regard to material prosperity.

ėcŏ'nomĭst *n.* 1. Manager (*of* money etc.); thrifty person. 2. One expert in economics or political economy.

ėcŏ'nomīze *v.* Use economically; practise economy; reduce expenditure.

ėcŏ'nomȳ *n.* 1. Administration of concerns and resources of any community; art or science of such administration; *political* ~, former name for ECONOMICS, now applied esp. to analysis of problems of economic policy of governments. 2. Careful management of resources, so as to make them go as far as possible; frugality, thrift; a saving. 3. (theol.) Judicious handling of doctrine, presentation of truth etc. in such a way as to suit the needs or conciliate the prejudices of the person addressed. 4. Organization, constitution, of any complex unity; organized body, society, etc.

écorché (ākôr'shā) *n.* (painting etc.) Figure in which muscular system is displayed. [Fr. *écorcher* flay]

écru (ā'krōō) *adj.* & *n.* (Of) colour of unbleached linen.

ĕ'cstasȳ *n.* Exalted state of feeling, rapture, transport, esp. of delight; state of rapture in contemplation of divine things; poetic frenzy.

ėcstă'tĭc *adj.* Of, producing, subject to, ecstasy. ~ *n.* One subject to (religious) ecstasy.

E.C.T. *abbrev.* Electro-convulsive therapy.

ĕcto- *prefix.* Outer, outside.

ĕ'ctoblast (-ah-) *n.* (physiol.) Outer membrane of a cell.

ĕ'ctodĕrm *n.* (embryol.) Outermost of 3 layers of cells formed by embryo at early stage, layer from which skin and nervous system are developed.

ĕctogĕ'nėsĭs *n.* (biol.) Production of structures or bodies outside the organism. **ĕctogėnĕ'tĭc, ĕctogĕ'nĭc, ĕctŏ'gėnous** *adjs.*

ĕctŏ'pĭc *adj.* (path.) In an abnormal place.

ĕ'ctoplăsm *n.*. 1. (biol.) Clear viscid outer layer of cytoplasm in an animal cell. 2. (spiritualism) Supposed viscid substance believed by some to emanate from body of medium and develop into various forms. **ĕctoplă'smĭc, ĕctoplă'stĭc** *adjs.*

E.C.U. *abbrev.* English Church Union.

E'cuadôr (ĕkwa-). Republic in the NW. of S. America; capital, Quito.

ecumenical: see OECUMENICAL.

ĕ'czėma *n.* (path.) Inflammation of skin, with redness, soreness, and itching papules or vesicles discharging serous fluids. **ĕczĕ'matous** *adj.*

ed. *abbrev.* Edited (by), edition, editor.

Ed. *abbrev.* Edward.

ėdā'cious (-shus) *adj.* Of eating; greedy. **ėdă'cĭtȳ** *n.*

E'dam (ē-) *n.* Round Dutch cheese, usu. of yellow colour with rind dyed red. [name of village in Holland]

ėdă'phĭc *adj.* (bot.) Of the soil.

E'dda (ĕ-). 1. (also *Elder, Poetic*, ~) Collection (*c* 1200) of ancient Old Norse poems on mythical or traditional subjects. 2. (also *Younger, Prose*, ~) Miscellaneous handbook to Icelandic poetry, with prosodic and grammatical treatises and quotations and prose paraphrases from old poems; partly written by the Icelandic historian Snorri Sturlason (*c* 1230).

E'ddĭngton (ĕ-), Sir Arthur Stanley (1882–1944). English physicist; well known for his researches into the motions of stars and for his contributions to the Theory of Relativity.

ĕ'ddȳ[1] *n.* Circular motion in water, small whirlpool; similar unsteady swirling motion of air, wind, fog, dust, etc., moving thus; ~ *current*, (elect.) circulating current induced in a conducting material by a changing magnetic field. ~ *v.* Whirl round, move, in eddies.

E'ddȳ[2] (ĕ-), Mrs Mary Baker Glover (1821–1910). American founder of the Christian Science movement.

edelweiss (ā'dlvīs) *n.* Alpine

plant with white flower, *Leontopodium alpinum*, growing in rocky, often inaccessible places, in Swiss mountains. [Ger. *edel* noble, *weiss* white]

E′den[1] (ē-). Abode of Adam and Eve at their creation, Paradise; (transf.) delightful abode, state of supreme happiness. [Heb. '*éden*, orig. = 'delight']

E′den[2] (ē-), (Robert) Anthony, 1st Earl of Avon (1897–1977). British statesman; prime minister 1955–7.

ēdĕ′ntate *adj.* & *n.* (Animal) belonging to mammalian order Edentata which have no teeth or very simple teeth without enamel (sloths, great ant-eaters, armadillos, aardvarks, etc.).

E′dgar (ĕ-). King of England 959–75.

ĕdge *n.* 1. Thin sharpened side of cutting instrument or weapon; sharpness given to blade by whetting; (fig.) effectiveness, trenchancy (of speech etc.); *be on* ~, be excited or irritable; *set person's teeth on* ~, jar his nerves or sensibilities. 2. Crest of ridge; line at which two surfaces meet abruptly; (fig.) perilous or critical position or moment. 3. One of narrow surfaces of thin flat object; rim (of vessel); one of the three surfaces of book left uncovered by binding. 4. Boundary of any surface, border, brink (of precipice). 5. (colloq.) Advantage, superiority. 6. ~-*tool*, tool with sharp cutting edge. ~ *v.* 1. Give an edge to, sharpen. 2. Border; furnish with edging. 3. Move edgeways; advance (esp. obliquely) by repeated almost imperceptible degrees; move (thing, oneself) thus; touch (cricket ball) with edge of bat. **ĕ′dgelėss** *adj.*

ĕ′dgeways, -wise (-jwāz, -jwīz) *advs.* With edge uppermost, foremost, or turned towards spectator; edge to edge; (moving) with edge foremost; *get* (*word*) *in* ~, manage to speak in interval of loquacious person's talk.

ĕ′dgĭng *n.* (esp.) Border, fringe, etc., on garment, border (of grass etc.) round flower-beds or lawn; lace etc. made to be sewn to edge of garment; ~-*iron*, crescent-shaped tool for cutting verge of turf.

ĕ′dgȳ *adj.* Sharp-edged; irritable, testy.

ĕ′dĭble *adj.* & *n.* (Thing) fit to be eaten, eatable, **ĕdĭbĭ′lĭtȳ** *n.*

ē′dict *n.* What is proclaimed by authority; order issued by sovereign to subjects; *E~ of Nantes*: see NANTES.

ĕ′dĭfĭce *n.* Building, esp. large and stately one.

ĕ′dĭfȳ *v.t.* Benefit spiritually, strengthen, support; instruct, improve. **ĕdĭfĭcā′tion** *n.*

Edin. *abbrev.* Edinburgh.

E′dĭnburgh (ĕ-; -b*uru*, -br*u*). Capital city of Scotland, situated to the south of the Firth of Forth, since May 1975 part of the region of Lothian; university 1583; Heriot-Watt university, 1966;

Duke of ~, Prince Philip (1921–) son of Prince and Princess Andrew of Greece; married (1947) Princess Elizabeth of Gt Britain, afterwards Queen Elizabeth II.

Edirne (ĕdĭr´ne). Town in European Turkey, formerly called Adrianople.

E´dison (ĕ-), Thomas Alva (1847–1931). American inventor

of the phonograph and (with Sir J. W. Swan, 1828–1914) of the incandescent electric lamp.

ĕ´dit *v.t.* Prepare edition of (another's work); collate (material chiefly provided by others) for publication; act as editor of; assemble (film, tape-recordings, etc.).

ėdi´tion *n.* Form in which literary work is published; whole number of copies of book, newspaper, etc., printed from same set of types and issued at same time.

ĕ´ditor *n.* One who edits; one who conducts newspaper or periodical, or section of newspaper etc. **ĕ´ditorship** *n.*

ĕditŏr´ial *adj.* Of, written by, an editor. ~ *n.* Newspaper article written by or under responsibility of editor. **ĕditŏr´ially** *adv.*

Edm. *abbrev.* Edmund.

E´dom (ē-). Ancient region S. of the Dead Sea. **E´domite** *adj.* & *n.* (Member) of an ancient people traditionally descended from Esau, living in Edom.

ĕ´dūcāte *v.t.* Bring up from childhood, so as to form habits, manners, intellectual aptitudes, etc.; instruct, provide schooling for; train, discipline, so as to develop some special aptitude, taste, or disposition. **ĕ´dūcable** *adj.* **ĕ´dūcātor** *n.* **ĕ´dūcatory̆** *adj.*

ĕdūcā´tion *n.* Systematic instruction, schooling, or training in preparation for life or some particular task; scholastic instruction; bringing up. **ĕdūcā´tional** *adj.* **ĕdūcā´tionally̆** *adv.* **ĕdūcā´tionist, -tionalist** *ns.* One who studies the science or methods of education.

ĕ´dūcative *adj.* Of education; educating; bearing on, conducive to, education.

ėdū´ce *v.t.* Bring out, elicit, develop, from latent, rudimentary, or potential condition; infer; extract. **ėdū´cible** *adj.* **ėdŭ´ction** *n.*

ėdŭ´lcorāte *v.t.* Free from acrid properties or from soluble particles, purify. **ėdŭlcorā´tion** *n.*

Edw. *abbrev.* Edward.

E´dward[1] (ĕ-). Name of two kings of the English before the Conquest: ~ *the Confessor*, son of Ethelred the Unready, reigned 1042–66; canonized 1161; ~ *the Martyr*, reigned 975–9, assassinated by order of his stepmother.

E´dward[2] (ĕ-). Name of six kings of England since the Conquest and two of the U.K.: *Edward I* (1239–1307), 'the Hammer of the Scots'; son of Henry III; king of England 1272–1307; conquered Wales and attempted the conquest of Scotland; *Edward II* (1284–1327), succeeded his father Edward I in 1307; continued the attempted conquest of Scotland but was defeated by Robert Bruce at Bannockburn (1314); murdered in 1327; *Edward III* (1312–77), son of Edward II, reigned 1327–77; the Hundred Years War against France began in his reign and he gained tem-

EDWARD IV

porarily the duchy of Aquitaine by the Treaty of Bretigny (1360); *Edward IV* (1442–83), the first Yorkist king; descended from Edward III; reigned 1461–83; defeated the Lancastrians in the Wars of the Roses; *Edward V* (1470–83), son of Edward IV; king in 1483, in which year he was deposed; allegedly one of the 'Princes in the Tower' (see PRINCE 4); *Edward VI* (1537–53), son of Henry VIII and Jane Seymour; reigned 1547–53; *Edward VII* (1841–1910), son of Queen Victoria; king of Gt Britain 1901–10; *Edward VIII* (1894–1972); succeeded his father, George V, on 20 Jan. 1936; abdicated 11 Dec. 1936 and assumed title of Duke of Windsor.

Edwar'dĭan (ĕdwôr-) *adj.* & *n.* (Person) belonging to or characteristic of reign of Edward VII of Gt Britain.

E'dwȳ (ĕ-). King of the English 955–9.

E.E.C. *abbrev.* European Economic Community.

E.E.G. *abbrev.* Electroencephalogram.

eel *n.* 1. Any of numerous small-finned and soft-finned snake-like fishes of the order Apodes, the freshwater forms of which migrate to the Sargasso Sea to spawn. 2. Any of various other fishes resembling eels in shape. 3. *electric* ~: see ELECTRIC; *~-grass*, marine plant with grass-like leaves, *Zostera marina*; *~-pout*, blenny; *~-spear*, forked or pronged instrument for catching eels; *ee'l-worm*, any of various wormlike often microscopic animals of the phylum Nematoda, some of which are parasitic on crops.

e'en (ēn) *adv.* (poet.) = EVEN[3].

e'er (ār) *adv.* (poet.) = EVER.

eer'ĭe, -ȳ *adj.* Gloomy, strange, weird. **eer'ĭlȳ** *adv.* **eer'ĭness** *n.*

ĕffā'ce *v.t.* Rub out; obliterate, wipe out; utterly surpass, eclipse; reduce *oneself* to insignificance. **ĕffā'cement** *n.*

EDWARD VI

ėffĕ'ct *n.* 1. Result, consequence; efficacy; combination of colour or form in picture, landscape, etc.; (pl.) lighting, appropriate sounds, etc., in play etc.; phenomenon. 2. (pl.) Property, goods. 3. Being operative; operative influence; *give* ~ *to*, render operative; *take* ~, become operative, come into force. 4. Impression produced on spectator, hearer, etc. 5. *in* ~, virtually, for practical purposes. ~ *v.t.* Bring about, accomplish. **ėffĕ'ctive** *adj.* 1. Having an effect; that is actually brought to bear on an object; (U.S.) coming into effect, becoming operative; ~ *range*, range within which weapon etc. is effective. 2. Powerful in effect; striking. 3. (of soldiers etc.) Fit for work or service. 4. Actual, existing. ~ *n.* Effective soldier, effective part of army. **ėffĕ'ctivelȳ** *adv.* **ėffĕ'ctivenėss** *n.*

ėffĕ'ctūal *adj.* Answering its purpose; valid; ~ *demand*, (econ.) demand sufficient to cause production or bringing to market of goods. **ėffĕ'ctūallȳ** *adv.* **ėffĕ'ctūalness** *n.*

ėffĕ'ctūāte *v.t.* Bring to pass, accomplish. **ėffĕctūā'tion** *n.*

ėffĕ'minate *adj.* Womanish, unmanly. **ėffĕ'minatelȳ** *adv.* **ėffĕ'minatenėss, ėffĕ'minacȳ** *ns.*

ėffĕ'ndi *n.* 1. Former Turkish title of respect for officials etc. 2. Person of education or standing in some E. Mediterranean countries.

ĕ'fferent *adj.* (physiol.) Conveying outwards; (of nerves) conveying impulses from central nervous system to muscles and glands.

ĕffervĕ'sce *v.i.* Give off bubbles of gas, esp. as result of chemical action; bubble. **ĕffervĕ'scence** *n.* **ĕffervĕ'scent** *adj.*

ėffē'te *adj.* Exhausted, worn out; feeble, incapable. **ėffē'tenėss** *n.*

ĕffĭcā'cious (-sh*u*s) *adj.* (of instrument, method, action) Producing, sure to produce, intended or appropriate effect. **ĕffĭcā'ciouslȳ** *adv.* **ĕffĭcā'ciousnėss, ĕ'ffĭcacȳ** *ns.*

ėffĭ'cient (-sh*e*nt) *adj.* Making, causing to be; productive of effects; effective, operative; skilled, capable. **ėffĭ'cientlȳ** *adv.* **ėffĭ'ciencȳ** *n.* State or quality of being efficient; (phys.) ratio of energy or work produced to that expended.

ĕ'ffĭgȳ *n.* Portrait, image.

ĕfflorĕ'sce *v.i.* 1. Burst out into flower (lit. & fig.). 2. (chem., of crystals or salts) (Come to surface and) turn to fine powder on exposure to air; (of surface) become covered with powdery saline crust. **ĕfflorĕ'scence** *n.* **ĕfflorĕ'scent** *adj.*

ĕ'ffluence (-o͝o-) *n.* Flowing out, esp. of light, electricity, magnetism, etc.; what flows out, emanation.

ĕ'ffluent (-o͝o-) *adj.* Flowing forth. ~ *n.* Stream flowing from larger stream, reservoir, lake, etc.; outflow from sewage tank etc.

ėfflu'vium (-o͞o-) *n.* (pl. *-ia*). Exhalation affecting lungs or sense of smell.

ĕ'fflŭx *n.* Flowing out (of liquid, air, gas); that which flows out. **ėfflŭ'xion** (-ksh*o*n) *n.*

ĕ'ffort *n.* Strenuous exertion; display of power, achievement.

ĕ'ffortlėss *adj.* Making no effort, passive; without effort, easy. **ĕ'ffortlėsslȳ** *adv.* **ĕ'ffortlėssnėss** *n.*

ėffro'nterȳ (-ŭn-) *n.* Shameless audacity.

ėffŭ'lgent *adj.* Radiant. **ėffŭ'lgentlȳ** *adv.* **ėffŭ'lgence** *n.*

ėffū'se (-z) *v.t.* Pour forth.

ėffū'sion *n.* Pouring forth; unrestrained utterance, literary outpouring.

ėffū'sive *adj.* Exuberant, unduly demonstrative. **ėffū'sivelȳ** *adv.* **ėffū'sivenėss** *n.*

ĕft *n.* Newt.

E.F.T.A., E'fta (ĕ-) *abbrev.* European Free Trade Association.

ĕftso͞o'ns (-z) *adv.* (archaic) Again; forthwith, soon afterwards.

e.g. *abbrev. Exempli gratia* (L, = 'for example').

ėgă'd *int.* (archaic) By God.

ėgălitār'ian *adj.* & *n.* (Person) asserting equality of mankind.

ĕgg[1] *n.* 1. (pop.) More or less

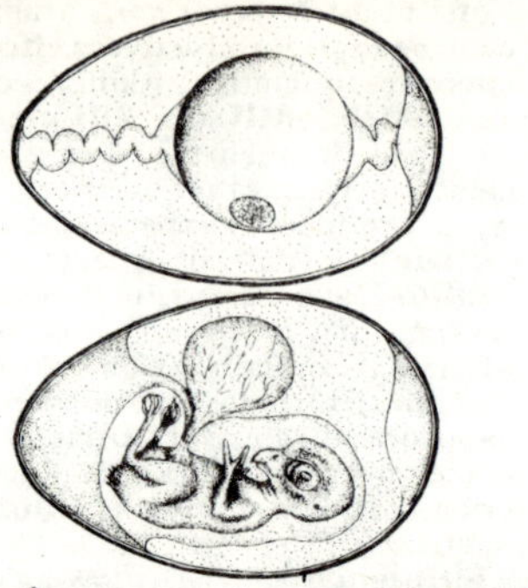

BIRD'S EGG: Development of Embryo

spheroidal body, containing germ of new individual within a shell or membrane, deposited externally (laid) by female of some animals esp. birds, reptiles, fishes, and insects; esp., domestic fowl's egg as article of food. 2. (zool.) Non-motile cell produced by female, capable, usu. after fertilization by a sperm, of developing into a new individual; ovum. 3. *bad* ~, person, scheme, etc., that comes to no good; *~-and-spoon race*, race in which runners carry fowl's egg in spoon; *~-and-tongue*, kind of moulding *~-cup*, cup-shaped vessel to hold egg boiled in shell; *~-flip ~-nog*, drink in which white and yolk of eggs are stirred up with hot beer, cider, wine, or spirits; *e'gghead*, (slang) intellectual person, highbrow; ***~-plant***: see AUBERGINE; ***~-plum***, small egg-shaped yellow plum; *e'ggshell*, shell of egg; freq. as type of anything frail or fragile; *eggshell china*, extremely thin and delicate porcelain; *eggshell finish*, a paint finish intermediate between flat and glossy; ***~-tooth***, protuberance on bill-sheath of embryo bird, reptile, etc., for cracking its shell. **ĕ'ggȳ** *adj.* Stained with egg.

ĕgg² *v.t.* Incite, encourage, urge (*on*).

ĕ'glantīne *n.* Sweet-brier.

ĕ'gō *n.* 1. (metaphys.) Conscious thinking subject as opp. to *non-ego* or object; the self. 2. (psychol.) That part of the mind which is organized and has a sense of individuality (thus used by Freud to distinguish it from the primitive, impersonal, and wholly unconscious part which he called the *id*). [L, = 'I']

ĕgocĕ'ntric *adj.* Centred in the ego; self-centred, egoistic. **ĕgō-cĕ'ntrically̆** *adv.* **ĕgocĕntrĭ'citȳ** *n.*

ĕ'gōism *n.* 1. (ethics) Theory which regards self-interest as foundation of morality. 2. Regard to one's own interest, systematic selfishness; selfish aims or purposes; self-opinionatedness. **ĕ'gōist** *n.* **ĕgōĭ'stic, -ical** *adjs.* **ĕgōĭ'stically̆** *adv.*

ĕgomā'nia *n.* Morbid egotism. **ĕgomā'nĭăc** *n.*

ĕ'gotism *n.* Practice of talking about oneself; self-conceit. **ĕ'gotist** *n.* **ĕgotĭ'stic, -ical** *adjs.* **ĕgotĭ'stically̆** *adv.*

ėgrē'gious (-jus) *adj.* Notable, distinguished (now derog.). **ėgrē'giously̆** *adv.* **ėgrē'giousness** *n.* [L *egregius*, lit. 'towering above the flock' (*grex* flock)]

ē'grĕss *n.* (Right or liberty of) going out; (astron.) end of eclipse or transit; outlet. **ėgrĕ'ssion** *n.* Going out or forth.

ē'grėt *n.* Lesser white heron, aigrette.

E'gȳpt (ē-). State in NE. Africa formerly part of the Turkish Empire; in 1882 internal disorders led to British military intervention and in 1914 a British Protectorate over Egypt was declared, which was terminated in 1922, since which time Egypt has been independent; republic established 1953. *Ancient* ~, civilization in the Nile valley from the Stone Age until the Roman period; ruled by successive dynasties until the conquest by Alexander the Great in 332 B.C.; after periods of Greek and Roman domination it passed to the Byzantine Empire (395–642); the ancient culture died out after the Arab conquest and Egypt became a province of the Ottoman Empire 1517–1879.

Egyptian (ĭjĭ'pshan) *adj.* Of Egypt or its people or language.

~ *n.* 1. Egyptian person. 2. Language of the ancient Egyptians together with its descendant, Coptic, which is still used in the liturgies of the Coptic Church; one of the Hamitic group of languages.

Egy̆ptō'logy̆ (ē-) *n.* Study of Egyptian antiquities. **Egy̆ptŏ'logist** *n.*

eh (ā) *int.* Ejaculation of inquiry or surprise, or inviting assent; ~ *up*, look out.

Ehrlich (ār'lix), Paul (1854–1915). German physician; founder of chemotherapy and discoverer of salvarsan; Nobel Prize for medicine 1908.

ei'der (ī-) *n.* (also ~ *duck*) Any of several ducks of N. hemisphere, esp. of genus *Somateria*; ~*-down* small soft feathers from breast of eider duck; *ei'derdown*, soft quilt, orig. one stuffed with eider-down.

eidĕ'tic (ī-) *adj.* (psychol., of mental image perceived as if visual) Possessing hallucinatory vividness and circumstantiality. ~ *n.* One who sees eidetic images. **eidĕ'tically̆** *adv.*

EIFFEL TOWER

eidō'lon (ī-) *n.* (pl. *-ons*, *-a*). Spectre, phantom.

Ei'ffel Tow'er (ī-). Iron tower, 300 metres high, built for the Exposition of 1889 by A. G. Eiffel in the Champ de Mars, Paris.

eight (āt) *adj.* One more than seven. ~ *n.* One more than seven; symbol for this (8, viii, or VIII); anything in the form **8**, esp. skating-figure; card with 8 pips; 8 o'clock; size etc. indicated by 8; set of 8 things or persons, esp. crew of 8 in rowing-boat; *Eights*, boat-races at Oxford or elsewhere between such crews.

ei'ghtee'n (āt-) *adj.* & *n.* One more than seventeen (18, xviii, or XVIII); *eighteenmo*, 18mo, octodecimo. **ei'ghtee'nth** *adj.* & *n.*

eighth (āt-th) *adj.* Next after seventh. ~ *n.* Eighth part (see PART[1], 1)· eighth thing etc. **ei'ghthly̆** *adv.* In the eighth place.

ei'ghtsome (āt-) *adj.* (of Scottish reel etc.) Performed by 8 persons together.

eighty (ā'tĭ) *n.* Cardinal number, Eight times ten (80, lxxx, or LXXX); set of 80 things or persons; *eighties*, numbers etc. from 80 to 89; these years of century or life. **ei'ghtieth** *adj.* & *n.*

Einstein (ī'nshtīn *or* -stīn), Albert (1879–1955). German-born mathematical physicist; famous for his revolutionary theory of the nature of space and time, known as the Theory of Relativity, which upset the Newtonian conception of the universe.

einstei'nium (īnstī-) *n.* (chem.) Transuranic element, symbol E, at. no. 99, principal isotope at. wt 253.

Eire (ār'*e*). Former name of the Republic of IRELAND. **Eireann** (ār'*a*n). Of Ireland, Irish.

eirenicon: see IRENICON.

Ei'senhower (īz-), Dwight David (1890–1969). Amer. general and statesman; C.-in-C. Allied Forces in N. Africa 1942–3;

Supreme Commander of Allied Expeditionary Forces in W. Europe 1943–5; North Atlantic Supreme Commander 1950–2; 34th president of the U.S. 1953–61.

eisteddfod (āstĕ′dhvod) *n.* Welsh congress of bards prob. of 14th-c. origin; modern revival of this, dating from 19th c., esp. the *National E~*, held annually with competitions in music, poetry, arts and crafts. [Welsh, = 'session' (*eistedd* sit)]

ei′ther (īdh- *or* ēdh-) *adj.* & *pron.* Each of two; one or other of the two. ~ *adv.* Introducing first of alternatives (*either . . . or . . .*); (in neg. or interrog. sentences) any more than the other, as *if you do not go, I shall not ~.*

ėjă′cūlāte *v.t.* 1. Utter suddenly. 2. Eject (fluids etc.) from body. **ėjăcūlā′tion** *n.* **ėjă′cūlatorў** *adj.*

ėjĕ′ct *v.t.* 1. Expel (*from* place, office, etc.); evict *from* property. 2. Throw out from within; dart forth, emit. **ėjĕ′ction, ėjĕ′ctment, ėjĕ′ctor** *ns.* **ėjĕ′ctĭve** *adj.*

ēke[1] *v.t.* ~ *out*, supplement, supply deficiencies of; contrive to make (livelihood) or support (existence) by various makeshifts.

ēke[2] *adv.* (archaic) Also.

ĕl *n.* (U.S.) Elevated railway.

ėlă′borate *adj.* Carefully or minutely worked out; highly finished. **ėlă′boratelў** *adv.* **ėlă′borateness** *n.* **ėlă′borāte** *v.t.* Produce by labour; work out in detail; fashion from raw material. **ėlăborā′tion** *n.* **ėlă′borative** *adj.*

Elagabalus : see HELIOGABALUS.

El Alamein : see ALAMEIN.

E′lamīte (ē-) *adj.* & *n.* (Native, inhabitant, language) of Elam, an ancient country of Mesopotamia with its capital at Susa (now Shush, in Iran).

élan (ālahṅ) *n.* Vivacity, dash.

ē′land *n.* Either of two large heavily-built African antelopes of genus *Taurotragus*, with spirally twisted horns.

ėlă′pse *v.i.* (of time) Pass away.

ėlă′smobrănch (-z-, -k) *n.* (zool.) Any cartilaginous fish (shark, dogfish, skate, etc.).

ėlă′stĭc (*or* -lah-) *adj.* 1. Spontaneously resuming its normal bulk or shape after having been contracted, dilated, or distorted; buoyant, springy; flexible, accommodating. 2. (of fabric etc.) Containing, made of, thin strips or threads of rubber usu. covered with woven material. ~ *n.* Elastic fabric, elastic cord or string. **ėlă′stĭcallў** *adv.* **ĕlăstĭ′cĭtў** *n.*

ėlă′stomer *n.* Synthetic rubber or plastic resembling rubber.

ėlā′te *v.t.* Raise spirits of, inspirit, stimulate, excite. **ėlā′tion** *n.*

E′lba (ĕ-). Italian island off the W. coast of Italy, the place of Napoleon's first exile.

Elbe (ĕ-). One of the main rivers of Germany, rising in Czechoslovakia and flowing past Hamburg into the North Sea at Cuxhaven.

ĕ′lbow (-ō) *n.* Outer part of joint between fore- and upper arm; elbow-shaped bend or corner in river, road, etc.; short piece of pipe bent at an angle to join two straight pieces; *out at ~s*, ragged, poor; *up to the ~s*, busily engaged *in*; *~-chair*, (U.S.) arm-chair; *~-grease*, vigorous rubbing, hard work; *~-room*, sufficient space to move or work in at one's ease. ~ *v.* Thrust, jostle.

ĕ′lder[1] *n.* Low tree or shrub, *Sambucus nigra*, with umbel-like corymbs of white flowers, and black berries; other species of this genus, esp. (in N. Amer.) *S. canadensis*; *~-berry*, fruit of this tree.

ĕ′lder[2] *adj.* Senior (of relations, or of two indicated persons); *E~ Brethren*: see BRETHREN; *E~ Statesman*, in Japan, one of a body of retired statesmen and nobles who acted as emperor's confidential advisers and controlled policy of Japan in late 19th and early 20th centuries; (transf.) retired statesman etc. whose advice is available. ~ *n.* 1. (pl.) Persons of greater age. 2. (chiefly hist.) Member of senate, governing body, or class, of men venerable for age. 3. (in Presbyterian Church) One of a body of laymen assisting the minister in the management of church affairs; *teaching ~*, minister. **ĕ′ldership** *n.*

ĕ'lderlȳ *adj.* Somewhat old; past middle age.

ĕ'ldėst *adj.* First-born or oldest surviving (member of family, son, daughter, etc.).

El Dora'do (ĕl, -ahdō). Fictitious country or city abounding in gold believed by early explorers to exist on Amazon. [Span., = 'the gilded']

ĕ'ldrĭtch *adj.* (Sc.) Weird, hideous.

E'leanor Crŏss (ĕlin-). One of a series of monumental crosses set up by Edward I to mark the resting places of the funeral cortège of his queen, Eleanor (d. 1290), between Hardby, Lincs., and Westminster.

Elėă'tic (ĕ-) *adj.* Of, pertaining to, a school of Greek philosophers of the 6th c. B.C. founded by PARMENIDES and his successor Zeno at Elea in Lucania: these philosophers combated the anthropomorphic religion of the ancient poets and maintained that there was a single eternal god not resembling mortals in appearance or thought.

ĕlėcămpā'ne *n.* Perennial composite plant, *Inula helenium*, with large yellow radiate flowers and bitter aromatic leaves and root, formerly used as tonic and stimulant; sweet flavoured with this.

ėlĕ'ct *adj.* 1. Chosen; chosen for excellence or by preference; choice. 2. (theol.) Chosen by God, esp. for salvation or eternal life. 3. (usu. following *n.*) Chosen, elected, to office, dignity, etc., but not yet installed. ~ *v.t.* Choose, choose (person) by vote; (of God) choose (persons) for salvation etc.

ėlĕ'ction *n.* Choosing, esp. by vote; *by-*~ (U.S. *special* ~), election of member(s) in one constituency only, to fill vacancy caused by death, resignation, etc.; *general* ~, election of representatives to House of Commons or similar body throughout whole country.

ėlĕctioneer' (-sho-) *v.i.* Busy oneself in political elections. ~ *n.* One who electioneers.

ėlĕ'ctĭve *adj.* 1. Appointed or filled by, (of authority) derived from, election; having power of electing by vote; pertaining to, based on, system or principle of election. 2. (orig. chem., now fig. only) ~ *affinity*, tendency of substance to combine with certain particular substances in preference to others. 3. (U.S., of subjects in university etc. course) Optional. ~ *n.* (U.S.) Elective subject or course.

ėlĕ'ctor *n.* Person with right to vote in election; in Gt Britain etc. one legally qualified to vote in election of members of Parliament; in U.S., member of *Electoral College* chosen by the several States to elect the President and Vice-President; *E*~, one of the princes of Germany formerly (911–1803) entitled to take part in election of emperor. **ėlĕ'ctorshĭp** *n.* **ėlĕ'ctoral** *adj.* Of electors; being, belonging to, a German Elector; *E*~ *College*: see above.

ėlĕ'ctorate *n.* 1. (hist.) State or dignity of German Elector; dominions of an Elector. 2. Whole body of electors.

Elĕ'ctra (ĭ-). (Gk myth.) Daughter of Agamemnon and Clytemnestra; urged her brother Orestes to kill Clytemnestra and Aegisthus in revenge for murder of Agamemnon; ~ *complex*, (psychol.) counterpart in females of OEDIPUS complex, daughter's feeling of attraction towards father and hostility towards mother.

ėlĕ'ctrėss *n.* (hist.) Wife of German Elector.

ėlĕ'ctrĭc *adj.* Of, charged with, worked by, capable of developing, electricity; electrifying, thrilling; ~ *blue*, brilliant light blue without tincture of green; ~ *chair*, chair in which persons condemned to death are executed by electrocution; ~ *circuit*, system of conductors through which electric energy is conveyed; ~ *current*, flow of electricity through conducting body from positive to negative pole, or from high to low potential; ~ *eel*, large S. Amer. freshwater eel-like fish (*Electrophorus electricus*), capable of giving electric shock; ~ *hare*, in greyhound racing, artificial hare made by electricity to race round a track ahead of the hounds; ~ *ray*, RAY[2] of family Torpedinidae that emits electric discharges to numb or kill its prey; ~ *shock*, effect on animal body of sudden discharge of electricity; ~ *spark*, luminous discharge over gap in electric circuit; ~ *torch*, portable electric lamp, usu. with dry battery for supply of electric current. **ėlĕ'ctrical** *adj.* Relating to, connected with, of nature of, electricity; electric. **ėlĕ'ctricallȳ** *adv.*

ĕlĕctri'cian (-sh*a*n) *n.* Person skilled in or dealing with electricity or electrical apparatus.

ĕlĕctri'citȳ *n.* Form of energy present in PROTON or ELECTRON, energy associated with the displacement or movement of CHARGE.

ėlĕ'ctrifȳ *v.t.* 1. Charge with electricity; pass electric current through; subject to electric shock; convert (railway, factory, etc.) to use of electric power. 2. Startle, rouse, excite, as with electric shock. **ėlĕctrificā'tion** *n.*

ėlĕ'ctrō *n.* (pl. *-os*). (colloq.) Electroplate, electrotype.

ėlĕctrocar'diogrăm *n.* (abbrev. E.C.G.) Record of sequence of electrical waves generated at each beat of heart, used in diagnosis of heart disorders. **ėlĕctrocar'diogrăph** (*or* -ahf) *n.* Instrument applied to body for taking such records.

ėlĕ'ctro-chĕ'mistrȳ (-k-) *n.* Use, or study of the functions, of electricity in chemistry.

ėlĕ'ctro-convŭ'lsive *adj.* ~ *therapy*, (abbrev. E.C.T.) treatment of mental disorders by application of an electric shock to the central nervous system.

ėlĕ'ctrocūte *v.t.* Put to death, execute, by powerful electric current; kill by electricity. **ėlĕctrocū'tion** *n.*

ėlĕ'ctrōde *n.* Conductor by which electricity enters or leaves an electrolyte, gas, or vacuum.

ėlĕctrodȳnă'mic *adj.* Of electrodynamics; of the influence of one electric current on another. **ėlĕctrodȳnă'mics** *n.* Science of electricity in motion, or of action of electric currents on themselves or one another.

ėlĕ'ctroĕncĕ'phalogrăm *n.* (abbrev. E.E.G.) Record of minute electrical impulses inside the brain. **ėlĕ'ctroĕncĕ'phalogrăph** (*or* -ahf) *n.* Instrument for producing an electroencephalogram.

ėlĕ'ctrolȳse (-z) *v.t.* Decompose (a liquid) by electricity.

ĕlĕctrŏ'lȳsis *n.* Chemical decomposition by action of electric current; method of obtaining a purified deposit of a metal on the cathode, as in electroplating, and hence of purifying certain metals.

ėlĕ'ctrolȳte *n.* Substance which dissolves to give a solution capable of conducting an electric current; such a solution. **ėlĕctrolȳ'tic** *adj.* **ėlĕctrolȳ'ticallȳ** *adv.*

ėlĕ'ctromă'gnėt *n.* Magnet consisting of a piece of soft iron surrounded by coil of wire through which electric current is passed. **ėlĕctromăgnĕ'tic** *adj.* Having both electrical and magnetic character or effects; applied esp. to those waves or radiations which travel with the same velocity as light and whose special character seems to depend entirely on their frequency or wavelength, and which include X-rays, ultra-violet visible, and infra-red light, radiant heat, radio waves, and other types of radiation. **ėlĕctromă'gnėtism** *n.* (Study of) magnetic force produced by means of electricity.

ĕlĕctrŏ'mėter *n.* Instrument for detecting and measuring the magnitude of an electric charge, current, or voltage.

ėlĕctromō'tion *n.* Motion of, or produced by, electricity. **ėlĕctromō'tive** *adj.* Of, pertaining to, electromotion; ~ *force*, (abbrev. e.m.f.) force set up by difference of potential in an electric circuit, usu. measured in volts.

ėlĕ'ctrŏn *n.* (phys.) Elementary particle with an indivisible charge of negative electricity, one or more of which surround the nucleus of each atom and give it its chemical properties and the movement of which when free constitutes an electric current; anti-particle of this; *free* ~, electron freed from its bound state within the atom; ~ *lens*, device producing system of electric and magnetic fields capable of focusing a stream of electrons; ~ *microscope*, microscope of high magnification and resolving power using a system of electron lenses; ~ *volt*, (abbrev. eV) unit of energy equal to that acquired by an electron accelerated through a potential difference of 1 volt, $= 1{\cdot}60 \times 10^{-12}$ erg.

ėlĕctrŏ'nĭc *adj.* 1. Of or relating to electrons or electronics; ~ *brain*, (pop.) electronic COMPUTER. 2. (of mus. instruments) Producing sound electronically, without pipes, strings, etc. **ėlĕctrŏ'nĭcallȳ** *adv.* **ėlĕctrŏ'nĭcs** *n.* Science of the control of free electrons, esp. in vacuo; its technological applications.

ėlĕctrophŏ'nĭc *adj.* = ELECTRONIC 2.

ėlĕctrophorē'sĭs *n.* (phys.) Movement of particles in a fluid under the influence of an electric field. **ėlĕctrophorĕ'tĭc** *adj.*

ėlĕ'ctroplāte *v.t.* Coat (usu. a metallic surface) with a film of another metal (e.g. chromium, silver, or nickel) by electrolysis. ~ *n.* Ware produced by electroplating.

ėlĕctropŏ'sĭtĭve (-z-) *adj.* Carrying a positive charge of electricity; tending to form positive ions.

ėlĕ'ctroscōpe *n.* Instrument formerly used for detecting presence of electricity, freq. consisting of two pieces of gold leaf suspended together from the end of a conductor, now used for detecting and measuring radioactivity, the ionization of air produced by this having the effect of discharging a charged electroscope.

ėlĕctrostă'tĭcs *n.* Branch of physics dealing with electricity when at rest. **ėlĕctrostă'tĭc** *adj.*

ėlĕctrotŏ'nĭc *adj.* = ELECTRONIC 2.

ėlĕ'ctrotȳpe *n.* Printing plate made by electrolytically depositing copper on to a mould of wax or lead. ~ *v.t.* Copy by electrotype.

ėlĕctrovā'lencȳ, -vā'lence *ns.* (chem.) Electrovalent bond (see VALENCY). **ėlĕctrovā'lent** *adj.*

ėlĕ'ctrum *n.* 1. (obs.) Amber. 2. Pale-yellow alloy of silver and gold used by ancients. 3. (min.) Native argentiferous gold containing from 20 to 50% of silver.

ĕlėēmŏ'sȳnarȳ (-z-) *adj.* Of, dependent on, alms; charitable; gratuitous.

ĕ'lėgant *adj.* 1. Tastefully ornate in dress; graceful; tasteful, refined; of refined luxury. 2. (chiefly U.S.) Excellent, first-rate. **ĕ'lėgance** *n.* **ĕ'lėgantlȳ** *adv.*

ĕlėgī'ăc *adj.* Appropriate to elegies; mournful; (of metre, couplet) consisting of dactylic hexameter and pentameter. **ĕlėgī'ăcs** *n.pl.* Elegiac verses.

ĕ'lėgȳ *n.* Song of lamentation, esp. for the dead; poem, poetry, in elegiac metre. **ĕ'lėgīze** *v.* Write elegy, write elegy upon.

ĕ'lėment *n.* 1. Component part; constituent; (esp.) resistance wire carrying the current in an electric heater etc. 2. In ancient and medieval philosophy, one of the four simple substances, earth, water, air, fire, of which all material bodies were held to be compounded; that one of these which is the natural abode of any particular class of living beings; now, (pl.) atmospheric agencies or powers; (fig.) person's etc. ordinary range of activity, surroundings in which one feels at home. 3. (chem.) Any of over 100 different substances which have never been separated into simpler substances by chemical means and which alone or in combination constitute all matter; they are distinguished from each other by the number of electrons in their atoms outside the atomic nucleus (see PERIODIC law), and elements corresponding to all the numbers from 1 to 92 of such electrons, except 85 and 87, occur in nature. 4. (pl.) Rudiments of learning; first principles of an art or science; in some English Roman Catholic schools, the lowest class.

ĕlėmĕ'ntal *adj.* 1. Of the four elements (see ELEMENT 2), or of any of them; of the powers or agencies of nature; comparable to these. 2. Of the nature of an ultimate constituent, simple, uncompounded; constituent. ~ *n.* (theosophy etc.) Supposed sub-human spirit or entity.

ĕlėmĕ'ntary *adj.* 1. Rudimentary, introductory. 2. Simple, not analysable. 3. ~ *particle*, (phys.) one smaller than an atom. **ĕlėmĕ'ntarĭlȳ** *adv.* **ĕlėmĕ'ntarĭnėss** *n.*

ĕ'lėmĭ *n.* Stimulant resin obtained from various trees, as the Brazilian *Icica cicariba*, the Mexican *Elaphrium elemiferum*, etc., used in ointments, varnish, etc.

ėlĕ'nchus (-k-) *n.* (pl. *-chĭ*). Logical refutation; *Socratic* ~, Socratic method of eliciting truth by short question and answer.

ĕ'lėphant *n.* 1. Huge four-footed thick-skinned mammal of the order Proboscidea, with long curving ivory tusks and a pre-

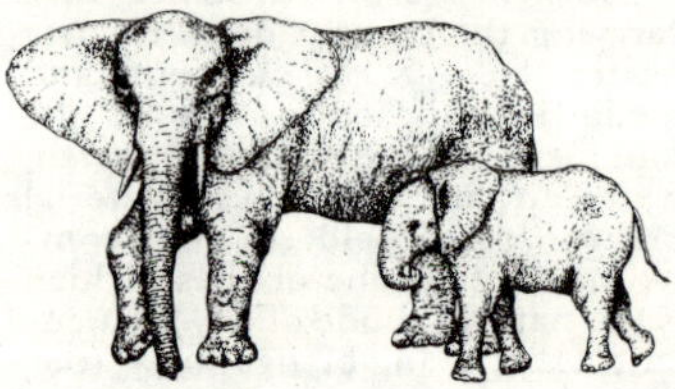

AFRICAN ELEPHANT WITH CALF

hensile trunk or proboscis (only two species, the Indian and the African, now exist). 2. (also ~ *-grey*) Fashion shade of grey. 3. Size of drawing- and cartridge-paper, 711 × 584 mm (28 × 23 in.). 4. *sea* ~ or ~*seal*, either of two species of seal of genus *Mirounga* (the large *M. leonina* of S. hemisphere and the smaller *M. angustirostris* of N. Amer. Pacific coast) with prolonged snout in male; ~*-grass*, tall kind of reed-mace, *Typha elephantina*.

ĕlėphantī'asĭs *n.* Tropical disease, caused by a nematode parasite, resulting in gross enlargement of legs etc. and thickening of skin.

ĕlėphă'ntīne *adj.* Of elephants; elephant-like; clumsy, unwieldy.

Eleusĭ'nian (ĕ-) *adj.* (Gk antiq.) Of Eleusis in Attica; ~ *mysteries*, ancient Greek mysteries celebrated there annually in honour of Demeter and Persephone, probably orig. a feast of purification and fertility.

ĕ'lėvāte *v.t.* Lift up; hold up (Host) for adoration; raise (eyes etc.), direct upwards; exalt in rank etc.; raise morally or intellectually; (gunnery) raise axis of (gun etc.). **ĕ'lėvātėd** *adj.* (esp.) 1. Elated, exhilarated; (colloq.) slightly drunk. 2. (also ~ *railroad*, *railway*) Railway supported on pillars or arches above street level (U.S. abbrev. el, L); ~ *train*, train on such railway.

ĕlėvā'tion *n.* 1. Elevating, being elevated. 2. Swelling; rising ground, eminence. 3. Angle with horizon (esp. of gun); (astron.) angular distance of heavenly body above horizontal plane (as opp. to *depression*, below it). 4. Height above a given level, esp. that of sea; height, loftiness, grandeur, dignity. 5. Drawing of building made in projection on vertical plane, as dist. from ground plan

ĕ'lėvātor *n.* (esp.) 1. Muscle that raises limb etc. 2. Machine for hoisting corn or flour to upper storey; (orig. U.S.) large building (containing such machines) for storing grain; machine for raising hay etc. on to stack. 3. (U.S.) Apparatus for raising and lowering people or things to other floor of building, lift. 4. (aeron.) Aerofoil, usu. on tailplane, for climbing, diving, or keeping the aircraft in level flight.

ėlĕ'ven *adj.* Amounting to eleven. ~ *n.* One more than ten; symbol for this (11, xi, or XI); 11 o'clock; size etc. indicated by 11; set of 11 things or persons, esp. forming team at cricket, association football, or hockey; ~*-plus*, examination taken at age of 11 years by pupils about to enter secondary school; *elevens*(*es*), mid-morning refreshments.

ėlĕ′venth *adj.* Next after tenth; ~ *hour*, latest possible time (see Matt. 20). ~ *n.* Eleventh part (see PART[1], 1); eleventh thing etc.

ĕlf *n.* (pl. *elves*). One of a class of supernatural beings, in early Teutonic belief supposed to be of dwarfish form and to have formidable magic powers, exercised benevolently or malevolently; mischievous creature; dwarf, little creature; ~*-lock*, tangled mass of hair (supposed to be produced by elves), which it was considered unlucky to disentangle. **ĕ′lfin** *adj.* Of elves, elf-like; diminutive; fairy-like, full of strange charm. **ĕ′lfish** *adj.*

E′lgar (ĕ-; *or* -gar̂), Sir Edward William (1857–1934). English composer of choral and orchestral works etc.

E′lgĭn (ĕlg-). Former county of N.E. Scotland, also known as MORAYSHIRE, lying SE. of Moray Firth.

E′lgĭn Mar̂′bles (ĕlg-, lz). Collection of Greek sculptures chiefly of the school of Phidias and from the Parthenon; acquired by the 7th Earl of Elgin when envoy to the Porte (1799–1803) and sold by him to the British Government; now housed in the British Museum.

El Greco (ĕl grĕ′kō). Domenikos Theotokopoulos (1541–1614), painter, esp. of religious pictures and portraits; born in Crete; was trained in Italy and settled *c.* 1577 in Toledo, Spain. [Span., = 'the Greek']

E′lia (ē-). Pseudonym adopted by Charles Lamb in his 'Essays of Elia'.

ėlĭ′cĭt *v.t.* Draw forth (what is latent or potential); educe (truths etc.) *from* data; extract, (information, response, etc.) *from* person.

ėlī′de *v.t.* Omit (vowel, syllable) in pronunciation.

Elien. *abbrev.* (Bishop) of Ely (replacing surname in his signature).

ĕ′lĭgĭble *adj.* Fit to be chosen (*for* office etc.); acceptable, suitable (esp. as husband or wife). **ĕlĭgĭbĭ′lĭtў** *n.* **ĕ′lĭgĭblў** *adv.*

Elijah (ĭlī′ja). Hebrew prophet in reign of Ahab; he was miraculously fed by ravens at the brook Cherith; raised the dead son of the widow of Zarephath; was carried to heaven in a chariot of fire (see 1 Kings 17–2 Kings 2).

ėlĭ′mĭnāte *v.t.* Remove, get rid of (esp. waste matter from body or tissues by excretion); expel, exclude; (alg.) get rid of (quantities) from equation; get rid of (unknown quantities) in simultaneous equations by combining equations. **ėlĭmĭnā′tion** *n.*

ėlĭ′mĭnātor *n.* (esp.) Apparatus eliminating battery from electrical apparatus by enabling it to be connected with electric mains.

E′lĭot[1] (ĕl-), George. Pen-name of Mary Ann Cross (1819–80), *née* Evans, an English novelist; author of 'Adam Bede', 'The Mill on the Floss', 'Silas Marner', etc.

E′lĭot[2] (ĕl-), Thomas Stearns (1888–1965). Poet and critic; born in St. Louis, Missouri; naturalized British citizen 1927; author of 'The Waste Land' (1922), 'Murder in the Cathedral' (a play, 1935), 'Four Quartets' (1944), etc.; Nobel Prize for literature 1948.

Elī′sha (ĭl-). Hebrew prophet; disciple and successor of Elijah.

ėlĭ′sion *n.* Suppression of letter (esp. vowel) or syllable in pronouncing.

élite (ālē′t) *n.* Choice part, best (*of*); select group or class.

ėlĭ′xir *n.* 1. (alchemy) Preparation designed to change baser metals into gold or to prolong life indefinitely; sovereign remedy for disease. 2. Aromatic pharmaceutical solution often containing alcohol and used as flavouring agent in drugs. [Arab. *al-iksīr*, prob. f. late Gk *xērion* desiccative powder for wounds]

Elĭ′zabeth (ĭl-). Name of two English queens: *Elizabeth I* (1533–1603), daughter of Henry VIII and Anne Boleyn; queen of England 1558–1603; *Elizabeth II* (1926–), daughter of George VI, queen of Gt Britain and Northern Ireland and Head of the Commonwealth 1952– **Elĭzabē′than** *adj.* & *n.*

ĕlk *n.* 1. Largest living species of

ELIZABETH I

deer (*Alces alces*) of Europe, Asia, and N. Amer. (where it is called *moose*). 2. (U.S.) = WAPITI. 3. *~-hound*, dog of Scandinavian breed with thick weather-resisting grey coat with black tips, and thick tail curled over back.

ĕll[1] *n.* Measure of length (in Engl., 45 in.), now obs. exc. in phr. *give him an inch and he'll take an ell.*

ĕll[2] *n.* (U.S.) = L; L-shaped part of building or room.

ĕllĭ'pse *n.* Plane closed curve in which the sum of the distances of any point from the two foci is a constant quantity; figure produced when a cone is cut obliquely by a plane making a smaller angle with the base than the side of the cone makes with the base. **ĕlĭ'ptic-, ĭcal**[1] *adjs.*

ĕllĭ'psĭs *n.* (*pl. -ses*, pr. -sēz). (gram.) Omission from sentence of word(s) needed to complete grammatical construction or fully express sense. **ĕllĭ'ptĭcal**[2] *adj.* **ĕllĭ'ptĭcally** *adv.*

ĕllĭ'psoid *n.* Solid formed by rotating an ellipse about an axis through its foci (*prolate ~*) or the perpendicular bisector of this (*oblate ~*). **ĕllĭpsoi'dal** *adj.*

E'llĭs I'sland (ĕ-, īl-) Island in New York harbour, belonging to U.S. Government, used until 1954 as an immigrant station.

ĕlm *n.* Large tree of genus *Ulmus*, usually with suckers, esp. in England *U. procera*, tree with small rough doubly serrated leaves and rough bark; in U.S. the white elm, *U. americana*; wood of elm.

E'lmō, (ĕ-) St. (pop.) St. Peter González (*c* 1190–1246), Spanish Dominican preacher who became patron saint of seamen; *St. ~'s fire*: see CORPOSANT.

ĕlocū'tion *n.* Manner, style, art, of oral delivery. **ĕlocū'tionarȳ** *adj.* **ĕlocū'tionist** *n.*

Elō'hĭm (ĕ-). Hebrew name of God or gods. **Elō'hĭst** *n.* Author(s) of those parts of the Hexateuch where God is referred to as *Elohim* rather than *Yahweh*. **Elōhĭ'stic** *adj.*

ē'lŏngāte (-ngg-) *v.* Lengthen, prolong; (bot.) increase in length, have slender or tapering form. **ē'lŏngate** *adj.* (bot., zool.) Long in proportion to its breadth; slender, tapering.

ēlŏngā'tion (-ngg-) *n.* 1. Lengthening. 2. (astron.) Angular distance of planet from sun, or satellite from its primary.

ėlō'pe *v.i.* (of woman) Run away from husband, or from home for secret marriage, (*with* lover); (of couple) run away together to get married. **ėlō'pement** *n.*

ĕ'loquence *n.* Fluent, forcible, and apt use of language; rhetoric. **ĕ'loquent** *adj.* **ĕ'loquentlȳ** *adv.*

ĕlse *adv.* (following indef. or interrog. pron.) Besides (as *anything* ~, *who* ~?), instead (*what* ~ *could I say?*); otherwise, if not (*run,* ~ *you will be late*). **ĕ'lsewher'e** (-ār) *adv.* In, to, some other place, at some other point.

ėlū'cĭdāte (*or* -ōō-) *v.t.* Throw light upon, clear up, explain. **ėlūcĭdā'tion** *n.* **ėlū'cĭdatorȳ** *adj.*

ėlū'de (*or* -ōōd) *v.t.* Escape by dexterity or stratagem (blow, danger, etc.); slip away from (person, pursuit, etc.); evade. **ėlū'sion** *n.* **ėlū'sĭve** *adj.* **ėlū'sĭvelȳ** *adv.* **ėlū'sĭvėness** *n.* **ėlū'sorȳ** *adj.*

ĕ'lver *n.* Young eel.

ĕ'lvĭsh *adj.* Elfish, elfin.

Ely (ē'lĭ). Cathedral city in the *Isle of* ~, a former administrative division of Cambridgeshire.

Elysée (ālē'zā). Official residence in Paris of French president.

Elȳ'sĭum (ĭlĭz-). (Gk myth.) Abode of the blessed after death; hence, place, state, of ideal or perfect happiness. **Elȳ'sĭan** *adj.* ~ *fields*, Elysium.

ĕ'lȳtrŏn *n.* Outer hard wing-case of coleopterous insect. **ĕ'lȳtral, ĕ'lȳtrous** *adjs.*

E'lzėvir (ĕ-) *adj.* & *n.* (Book) printed by the Elzevir family, numerous members of which were active as printers at Leyden, Amsterdam, Utrecht, and The Hague from 1583, when Louis Elzevir (*c* 1540–1617) issued his first book, to 1712.

ĕm *n.* 1. Letter M, m. 2. (print.) Measure equivalent to 12 points; also, the square of any size of type, thus □.

em- *prefix.* = EN-.

ėmā'cĭāte (*or* -shĭ-) *v.t.* Make lean, waste (esp. in past part.); impoverish (soil). **ėmācĭā'tion** *n.*

ĕ'manāte *v.i.* Issue, originate (*from* source, person, etc.); (chiefly of light, gases, etc.) proceed, issue, flow forth (*from*). **ĕ'manatĭve** *adj.*

ĕmanā'tion *n.* (esp.) 1. Something emitted or radiated (*from*); person or thing proceeding from divine essence as a source. 2. (chem.) Radioactive gas produced by radioactive decay of a solid; = RADON.

ėmă'ncĭpāte *v.t.* 1. Set free from control, or from legal, social, or political restraint; esp., set free (slave). 2. (Rom. law) Release (child, wife) from power of *pater familias*. **ėmă'ncĭpātor** *n.*

ėmăncĭpā'tion *n.* Setting free, esp. from slavery, intellectual or moral fetters, or legal disabilities; *Catholic E~ Act*, Act 10 Geo. IV, c. 7 (1829) removing civil disabilities imposed on Roman Catholics by English law; *E~ Day*, (U.S.) 1 Jan. 1863, when slaves of Southern States were declared free by Lincoln's *E~ Proclamation*; anniversary of this. **ėmăncĭpā'tionĭst** *n.*

ėmă'scūlāte *v.t.* Castrate; weaken, make effeminate; enfeeble, impoverish (language); weaken (literary composition) by removing what is supposed to be indecorous or offensive. **ėmăscūlā'tion** *n.* **ėmă'scūlatĭve, ėmă'scūlatory** *adjs.* **ėmă'scūlate** *adj.* Castrated; effeminate.

ėmba'lm (-ahm) *v.t.* Preserve (corpse) from decay by impregnation with aromatic oils and spices;

preserve from oblivion; endue with balmy fragrance. **ėmba′lmment** *n.*

ėmbă′nk *v.t.* Shut in, confine (river etc.) by banks, raised stone structure etc. **ėmbă′nkment** *n.* 1. Mound, bank, etc., for confining river etc.; *the E~*, bank along N. side of Thames in London, public walk along this (freq. with allusion to presence of homeless wanderers, esp. at night). 2. Long earthen bank or mound carrying road or railway over valley etc.

ėmbar′go *n.* (pl. *-oes*). Order forbidding ships of foreign power to enter, or any ships to leave, ports of a country, usu. issued in anticipation of war; suspension of (branch of) commerce: stoppage, prohibition. ~ *v.t.* Lay (vessel, trade) under embargo.

ėmbar′k *v.* 1. Put, go, on board ship (*for* destination). 2. Engage (*in*, *upon*, undertaking etc.). **ĕmbarkā′tion** *n.* ~ *leave*, leave, esp. from armed forces, before being sent overseas.

ėmbă′rrass *v.t.* 1. Encumber, hamper, impede; (pass.) be in difficulties from want of money, encumbered with debts. 2. Perplex, throw into doubt or difficulty; cause to feel self-conscious or ashamed; complicate (question etc.). **ėmbă′rrassinglў** *adv.* **ėmbă′rrassment** *n.* Embarrassed state or condition; impediment, obstruction; (pl.) pecuniary difficulties.

ĕ′mbassў *n.* Ambassador's function or office; his residence; deputation to a sovereign etc.

ėmbă′ttle[1] *v.t.* Set (army) in battle array.

ėmbă′ttle[2] *v.t.* Furnish with battlements.

ėmbay′ *v.t.* 1. Lay (vessel) within a bay; (of wind, tide) force (vessel) into a bay. 2. Enclose as in a bay, shut in.

ėmbĕ′d, ĭmbĕ′d *v.t.* Fix firmly in surrounding mass; (of mass) surround thus.

ėmbĕ′llĭsh *v.t.* Beautify, adorn; heighten (narrative) with fictitious additions. **ėmbĕ′llĭshment** *n.*

ĕ′mber[1] *n.* (usu. pl.) Small piece of live coal or wood in dying fire; smouldering ashes.

ĕ′mber[2] *adj.* ~ *days*, days of fasting and prayer appointed by the Church for each of four seasons of year; since Council of Placentia (1095), the Wednesday, Friday, and Saturday following (1) 1st Sunday in Lent, (2) Whit Sunday, (3) Holy Cross day, 14 Sept., (4) St. Lucy's day, 13 Dec.

ėmbĕ′zzle *v.t.* Divert to one's own use (money etc.) in violation of trust or official duty. **ėmbĕ′zzlement** *n.*

ėmbĭ′tter *v.t.* Make bitter (now usu. fig.); exasperate (person, feeling). **ėmbĭ′tterment** *n.*

ėmblā′zon *v.t.* Inscribe or portray conspicuously, as on heraldic shield; adorn *with* heraldic devices etc.; celebrate, extol. **ėmblā′zonment** *n.* **ėmblā′zonrў** *n.* = BLAZONRY.

ĕ′mblem *n.* Symbol, typical representation; type, personification (*of* a quality); heraldic device, or other figured object as distinctive badge of person, family, etc. ~ *v.t.* Symbolize, show forth by emblem.

ĕmblėmă′tĭc, -ĭcal *adjs.* Serving as type or emblem (*of*). **ĕmblėmă′tĭcallў** *adv.*

ĕmblĕ′matĭst *n.* Maker of emblems or of allegories.

ĕmblĕ′matīze *v.t.* Serve as emblem of; represent by an emblem.

ėmbŏ′dў *v.t.* 1. Invest or clothe (spirit) with body; give concrete form to (what is abstract or ideal); be embodiment or expression of. 2. Cause to become part of body; unite into one body; incorporate; include, comprise (various elements). **ėmbŏ′dĭment** *n.*

ėmbō′lden *v.t.* Make bold, encourage (*to* do).

ĕ′mbolism *n.* Blockage of blood-vessel by blood-clot, air-bubble, fat globule, or other foreign body.

embonpoint (ahṅbawṅpwăṅ) *n.* Plumpness (usu. of women). [Fr. *en bon point*, in good condition]

ėmbo′som (-o͝oz-) *v.t.* Embrace; (chiefly in past part.) enclose, conceal, shelter, *in*, *with*, woods, foliage, mountains, etc.

ėmbŏʹss *v.t.* Carve, mould, in relief; cause figures etc. to stand out on (surface); make protuberant. **ėmbŏʹssment** *n.*

ėmbowʹel *v.t.* Disembowel.

ėmbowʹer *v.t.* Shelter, enclose, as in bower.

ėmbrāʹce *v.t.* 1. Clasp (person) in arms, usu. as sign of fondness or friendship (also abs.); clasp, enclose. 2. Accept eagerly, avail oneself of (offer, opportunity, etc.); adopt (course of action, party, opinion, etc.). 3. Include, comprise; take in with eye or mind. ~ *n.* Folding in the arms; (pl.) sexual intercourse. **ėmbrāʹcement** *n.*

ėmbrăʹngle (-nggl) *v.t.* Entangle; confuse. **ėmbrăʹnglement** *n.*

ėmbrāʹsure (-zh*er*) *n.* Bevelling off of wall at sides of door or window, so that inside profile of window is larger than that of outside; opening in wall or parapet for gun, widening from within; one of the notches in a battlement.

ĕmbrocāʹtion *n.* Liquid used for rubbing bruised etc. part, liniment.

ėmbroiʹder *v.t.* Ornament (cloth etc.; or abs.) with needlework; work in needlework; embellish (narrative) with rhetorical ornament or fictitious additions. **ėmbroiʹderȳ** *n.*

ėmbroiʹl *v.t.* Bring (affairs. narrative, etc.) into state of confusion; involve (person) in hostility (*with* another). **ėmbroiʹlment** *n.*

ĕʹmbrȳō *n.* (pl. *-os*). Offspring of animal before birth or emergence from egg (in man usu. restricted to first 8 weeks of intrauterine life: cf. FOETUS); rudimentary plant contained in seed; thing in rudimentary stage. ~ *adj.* Undeveloped, immature. **ĕmbrȳŏʹnĭc** *adj.*

ĕmbrȳŏʹlogȳ *n.* Science of the embryo. **ĕmbrȳŏʹlogist** *n.* **ĕmbrȳolŏʹgical** *adj.*

ėmbŭʹs *v.* (mil.) Put (men, stores, etc.) or get into motor vehicle.

embusqué (ahṅbōōskā) *n.* One who avoids military service, esp. by securing post in Civil Service etc. [Fr., f. *embusquer* ambush]

ėmĕʹnd *v.t.* Correct; esp., remove errors from (text of book etc.) **ēmĕndāʹtion, ēʹmĕndātor** *ns.* **ėmĕʹndatorȳ** *adj.*

ĕʹmerald *n.* 1. Bright green precious stone, variety of beryl found chiefly in S. America, Siberia, and India. 2. (print.) Size of type (6½ point) between nonpareil and minion. 3. ~ *cut*, (of gem) type of step cut with bevelled corners; ~ *green*, vivid light-green durable pigment; colour of this; *E~ Isle*, Ireland (from its greenness).

ėmẽrʹge *v.i.* Come up out of liquid; come into view, issue (*from* enclosed space, state of suffering, etc.); rise into notice (*from* obscurity etc.); (of fact etc.) come out as result of investigation or discussion. **ėmẽrʹgence** *n.* **ėmẽrʹgent** *adj.*

ėmẽrʹgencȳ *n.* Situation or sudden occurrence demanding immediate action; (attrib.) used, arising, etc., in an emergency.

ėmĕʹrĭtus *adj.* Honourably discharged from office, retired, as ~ *professor*. [L, = 'that has served his time']

ėmẽrʹsion *n.* Emerging; reappearance of sun, moon, star, after eclipse or occultation.

Eʹmerson (ĕ-), Ralph Waldo (1803–82). American philosophic writer and essayist.

ĕʹmerȳ *n.* Coarse corundum, used for polishing metals, stones, glass, etc.; ~ *board*, emery-coated nail-file; *~-cloth, -paper, -wheel*, cloth, paper, wheel, coated with emery-powder; *~-powder*, ground emery.

ėmĕʹtĭc *adj.* & *n.* (Medicine) that causes vomiting.

e.m.f. *abbrev.* Electromotive force.

ĕʹmĭgrāte *v.i.* Leave one's country to settle in another; (colloq.) change one's place of abode.

ĕ′migrant *adj.* & *n.* **ĕmigrā′tion** *n.* **ĕ′migratorў** *adj.*

émigré (āmēgrā) *n.* Emigrant, esp. royalist who fled from France at French Revolution. [Fr.]

ĕ′minence *n.* 1. Rising ground. 2. Distinguished superiority. 3. Title of honour borne by cardinals.

ĕ′minent *adj.* Exalted, distinguished; (of qualities) remarkable in degree; signal, noteworthy; ~ *domain*: see DOMAIN. **ĕ′minentlў** *adv.*

ĕmir′ (-ēr) *n.* Saracen or Arab prince, governor of province, military commander; title of Muslim rulers. **ĕmir′āte** *n.* Rank, office, or domain of an emir. [Arab. *'amīr* commander]

ĕ′missarў *n.* Person sent on mission, to gain information, adherents, etc. ~ *adj.* ~ *veins*, veins which penetrate the skull and connect the veins outside the skull with those in the brain.

ėmi′ssion *n.* Giving of or out (chiefly of what is subtle or imponderable, light, heat, sounds, etc.); what is emitted; discharge of fluid from the body. **ėmi′ssive** *adj.* **ĕmissi′vitў** *n.* (phys.) Power of a surface to radiate heat or light.

ėmi′t *v.t.* Give out, send forth (light, heat, sound, opinion, etc.).

Emmanuel: see IMMANUEL.

ėmŏ′llient (-lye-) *adj.* & *n.* (Substance) having power of softening or relaxing living animal tissues.

ėmŏ′lūment *n.* Profit from office or employment, salary.

ėmō′tion *n.* Agitation or disturbance of mind, vehement or excited mental state; feeling. **ėmō′tionlėss** *adj.*

ėmō′tional *adj.* Of the emotions; liable to emotion. **ėmō′tionalism, ėmō′tionalist, ėmōtionă′litў** *ns.* **ėmō′tionallў** *adv.*

ėmō′tive *adj.* Of, tending to excite, emotion. **ėmō′tivelў** *adv.*

ėmpă′nel *v.t.* Enter on panel, enrol.

ĕ′mpathў *n.* (psychol., aesthetics) Power of projecting one's personality into (and so fully comprehending) the object of contemplation. [transl. of Ger. *Einfühlung* (*ein-* in, *fühlen* feel)]

Empĕ′dŏclēs (-z) (*c* 493–*c* 433 B.C.). Philosopher and scientist of Agrigentum in Sicily; acc. to one version of his death, threw himself into the crater of Mt Etna.

ĕ′mperor *n.* Sovereign (title considered superior in dignity to 'king'); (hist., esp.) sovereign of Roman or Byzantine Empire or head of Holy Roman Empire; *purple* ~, butterfly (*Apatura iris*) of the family Nymphalidae, allied to tortoiseshell and peacock butterflies; ~ *penguin*, largest known species of penguin of the Antarctic. **ĕ′mperorship** *n.*

ĕ′mphasis *n.* (pl. *-ses* pr. -sēz). Stress on word or phrase to indicate special significance or importance; vigour, intensity, of expression, feeling, action, etc.; importance assigned to fact, idea, etc.; prominence.

ĕ′mphasīze *v.t.* Lay stress on (word, fact, etc.).

ėmphă′tic *adj.* (of language, tone, gesture) Forcibly expressive; (of words etc.) bearing stress; (of person) expressing himself with emphasis; (of actions) forcible, significant. **ėmphă′ticallў** *adv.*

ĕmphўsē′ma *n.* (path.) Abnormal distension of an organ or tissue, esp. the lungs, by air or gas.

ĕ′mpīre *n.* 1. Supreme and extensive political dominion; absolute sway or control (*over*); government of which sovereign is called emperor. 2. Extensive territory (esp. aggregate of many separate States) under rule of emperor or sovereign State; *the E~*, (esp.) (i) the Holy Roman Empire (see ROMAN); (ii) the British Empire; (iii) (period of) reign of Napoleon I as Emperor of the French, 1804–15, also called *First E~* to distinguish it from the *Second E~* of Napoleon III, 1852–70. 3. (attrib.) *E~*, of, in the style of, the First French Empire, (of furniture) having long straight lines and details from classical and ancient Egyptian art, (of women's dress) having very high waist, low neck, and flowing skirt; (less freq.) of the Second Empire; *E~ City*, (U.S.) New York City; *E~ Day*: see COMMONWEALTH Day.

ėmpĭ'rĭc *adj.* Empirical. ~ *n.* 1. Person relying, in medicine or other sciences, solely on observation and experiment. 2. Untrained practitioner, quack. **ėmpĭ'rĭcism, ėmpĭ'rĭcist** *ns.*

ėmpĭ'rĭcal *adj.* 1. Based, acting, on observation and experiment, not on theory. 2. Without scientific knowledge. 3. ~ *formula*, simplest formula of a compound, indicating only the numerical ratios of the atoms present in the molecule of the compound but not necessarily their actual number and not implying its molecular structure. **ėmpĭ'rĭcallў** *adv.*

ėmplā'cement (-sm-) *n.* Situation; placing; platform for mounting heavy guns.

ėmploy' *v.t.* Apply (thing) to definite purpose, devote (effort, thought, etc.) to object, make use of (time etc.); use services of (person) in professional capacity or for some special business; find work or occupation for (person, his bodily or mental powers). ~ *n.* Being employed, esp. for wages; (poet. or archaic) employment, occupation.

ĕmploy'ee *n.* Person employed for wages.

ėmploy'er *n.* (esp.) One who employs servants, workmen, etc., for wages.

ėmploy'ment *n.* (esp.) Regular occupation or business, trade, profession; state of being employed; ~ *exchange*, office (esp. under State) enabling employers to find workers and vice versa.

ėmpŏr'ĭum *n.* 1. Centre of commerce, mart. 2. (pompously) Large shop, store.

ėmpow'er *v.t.* Authorize, license (*to* do); enable.

ĕ'mprėss *n.* Wife of emperor; woman having rank equivalent to emperor's.

ėmprī'se (-z) *n.* (archaic) Enterprise, esp. of adventurous or chivalrous nature; martial prowess.

ĕ'mptў *adj.* 1. Containing nothing; void, devoid, (*of*); vacant, unoccupied; without anything to carry; (colloq.) hungry. 2. Frivolous, foolish; unsatisfactory, vain; ~*-handed*, bringing no gift, carrying nothing away; ~*-headed*, frivolous, witless. **ĕ'mptĭlў** *adv.* **ĕ'mptĭnėss** *n.* **ĕ'mptў** *n.* Empty truck, wagon, etc.; empty box, bottle, etc., that has contained something. ~ *v.* Remove contents of; transfer (contents of one thing *into* another); (of river etc.) discharge itself (*into*); become empty.

ĕmpûr'ple *v.t.* Make purple, redden.

ĕmpўē'ma *n.* (path.) Collection of pus in cavity etc., esp. in pleural cavity of lung.

ĕmpўrē'an *adj.* & *n.* (Of) the highest heaven, as (in ancient cosmology) the sphere of fire, or as the abode of God. **ĕmpўrē'al** *adj.*

ē'mū *n.* Large flightless Australian bird, *Dromaius novaehollandiae*, allied to cassowary, with long drooping feathers.

ĕ'mūlāte *v.t.* Try to equal or excel; rival; imitate zealously; **ĕmūlā'tion, ĕ'mūlātor** *ns.* **ĕ'mūlatĭve** *adj.*

ĕ'mūlous *adj.* Zealously or jealously imitative (*of*); desirous (*of* renown etc.); actuated by spirit of rivalry. **ĕ'mūlouslў** *adv.*

ėmŭ'lsĭfў *v.t.* Convert into emulsion. **ėmŭ'lsĭfĭer** *n.*

ėmŭ'lsion *n.* Suspension of an oil or resin in an aqueous liquid, or of an aqueous liquid in an oil, freq. by aid of albuminous or gummy material; this as pharmaceutical preparation, cosmetic, lubricant and paint, etc.; (photog.) light-sensitive coating on film.

ėmŭ'lsĭve *adj.* That is an emulsion.

ĕn *n.* 1. Letter N, n. 2. (print.) Measure equivalent to half an em.

en-, em- *prefix.* In, into, on.

ėnā'ble *v.t.* Authorize, empower (*to* do); supply with means *to* (do); *enabling act*, legislative enactment enabling person or corporation to take certain action.

ėnă'ct *v.t.* Make into legislative act, ordain, decree. **ėnă'ction,**

ėnă'ctment *ns.* **ėnă'ctive, ėnă'ctorў** *adjs.*

ėnă'mel *n.* 1. Coloured glass, powdered and fused, used as decoration for gold, silver, or copper (by CLOISONNÉ, CHAMPLEVÉ, or other methods), or for painting. 2. Hard oil paint, freq. containing varnish which renders it glossy; any smooth and lustrous surface colouring. 3. Calcified substance forming glossy coating of teeth. ~ *v.t.* Inlay, encrust, cover, with enamel; variegate like enamelled work, adorn with rich and varied colours.

ėnă'mour (-m*er*) *v.t.* Inspire with love, make fond (*of*; usu. pass.).

ėnă'ntiomorph *n.* (esp. cryst.) Form related to another as an object is to its image in a mirror. **ėnăntiomor'phic, -phous** *adjs.*

en blŏc (ahṅ). In a lump, wholesale. [Fr.]

ėncae'nia (-sēn-) *n.* 1. Anniversary festival of dedication of church, esp. of the (Jewish) Temple at Jerusalem. 2. = COMMEMORATION 2.

ėncā'ge *v.t.* Confine (as) in cage.

ėncă'mp *v.* (mil.) Settle or lodge in camp; lodge in open in tents etc. **ėncă'mpment** *n.* (esp.) Place where troops are encamped; temporary quarters of nomads, travellers, etc.

ėncā'se *v.t.* Put into case; surround as with case.

ėncă'sh *v.t.* Convert (bills etc.) into cash; realize. **ėncă'shment** *n.* **ėncă'shable** *adj.* That can be cashed.

ėncau'stic *adj.* Of, produced by, 'burning in'; ~ *brick, tile*, one of red clay inlaid with a design in white clay, glazed, and fired; ~ *painting*, ancient method of painting with pigments mixed with hot wax; painting made thus. ~ *n.* Encaustic painting.

enceinte (ahṅsăṅt) *n.* Enclosure (in fortification). ~ *adj.* (of woman) Pregnant.

ĕncėphă'lic *adj.* Of the brain.

ĕncĕphalī'tis *n.* (path.) Inflammation of the brain; ~ *lethargica*, infectious form of this due to a virus, usu. accompanied by extreme drowsiness; sleepy sickness.

ėnchai'n *v.t.* Chain up, fetter; hold fast (attention etc.).

ėncha'nt (-ah-) *v.t.* Bewitch; charm, delight. **ėncha'nter** (fem. *encha'ntrėss*), **ėncha'ntment,** *ns.* **ėncha'ntinglў** *adv.*

ėncir'cle *v.t.* Surround, encompass; form a circle round.

ėncla'sp (-ah-) *v.t.* Hold in clasp or embrace.

ĕn'clāve *n.* Foreign territory surrounded by one's own territory.

ėnclĭ'tic *adj.* & *n.* (gram.) (Word) without accent, or so unemphatic as to be pronounced as if part of preceding word, esp. (in Greek) losing its accent to the preceding word. **ėnclĭ'ticallў** *adv.*

ėnclō'se (-z) *v.t.* 1. Surround (with walls, forces, etc.) so as to prevent free access; fence in (waste or common land) for cultivation or in order to appropriate it to individual owners; shut up, seclude (now only of monastic seclusion). 2. Shut up in receptacle (esp. something besides letter in envelope); bound on all sides, contain; surround, hem in on all sides.

ėnclō'sure (-zh*er*) *n.* Enclosing (esp. of common land to make it private property); enclosing fence etc.; enclosed place; document etc. enclosed with letter in envelope.

ėnclō'the (-dh) *v.t.* Clothe.

ėncō'de *v.t.* Put (message) into code or cipher. **ėncō'der** *n.*

ėncō'miăst *n.* Composer of encomium; flatterer. **ėncōmiă'stic** *adj.*

ėncō'mium *n.* Formal or high-flown expression of praise; eulogy, panegyric.

ėnco'mpass (-ŭm-) *v.t.* Surround, form circle about. **ėnco'mpassment** *n.*

encore (ŏngkor' *or* ŏ'ng-) *n.* & *int.* (Call for performance to be repeated) again, once more; repetition or additional item given in response. ~ *v.t.* Demand repetition of (song etc.); summon (performer) for this.

ėncou'nter *v.t.* 1. Meet as adversary, confront in battle. 2. Meet, fall in with, esp. casually;

experience (opposition etc.). ~ *n.* Meeting in combat or casually.

ėncou'rage (-kŭ-) *v.t.* Inspire with courage, embolden; stimulate by assistance, reward, approval, etc.; allow or promote continuance or progress of. **ėncou'ragement** (-jm-) *n.* **ėncou'ragingly̆** *adv.*

ĕ'ncrĭnīte *n.* (zool., geol.) Fossil crinoid.

ėncroa'ch *v.i.* Intrude usurpingly (*on*). **ėncroa'chment** *n.*

ėncrŭ'st *v.t.* Cover with crust; overlay (surface) with ornamental crust of precious material.

ėncŭ'mber *v.t.* Hamper *with* burden; burden with obligations, debts, etc.; block up, fill, *with* what is obstructive or useless. **ėncŭ'mberment** *n.*

ėncŭ'mbrance *n.* 1. Burden; annoyance; impediment; *without* ~(*s*), having no children. 2. Claim or liability attached to property; mortgage etc. **ėncŭ'mbrancer** *n.* Person with encumbrance or legal claim on estate.

ėncy̆'clĭcal *adj.* & *n.* (Letter, esp. issued by pope) intended for extensive circulation.

ėncy̆clopae'dĭa, -ē'dĭa *n.* Literary work containing extensive information on all branches or one particular branch of knowledge, usu. in alphabetical order; *the E~*, (esp.) the French encyclopaedia of 'Sciences, Arts, and Trades' (1751–65) by Diderot, d'Alembert, etc. **ėncy̆clop(a)e'dĭc** *adj.* **ėncy̆clop(a)e'dĭst** *n.* [pseudo-Gk ***egkuklopaideia***, spurious f. ***egkuklios paideia*** all-round education, the circle of arts and sciences considered essential to a liberal education]

ėncy̆'st *v.t.* Enclose in cyst.

ĕnd *n.* 1. Extreme point or outermost part, utmost limit; one of the two extremities of line or of greatest dimension of object; surface bounding thing at either extremity; piece broken off etc., remnant; (naut.) last length, short length, of rope or cable; (bowls) portion of game played from one end of green to the other; *shoemaker's ~*, length of thread armed with bristle. 2. Limit, close, conclusion, of period of time, action, process, series, discourse, book, etc.; latter or concluding part; termination of existence, destruction; death; ultimate state or condition. 3. Event, issue; intended result, aim, purpose; object for which thing exists or is designed. 4. *be at*, *come to*, *an* ~, be, become, exhausted; be completed; end; *be at the ~ of*, have no more of; *bring to an ~*, exhaust, complete, end; *keep one's ~ up*, (colloq.) bear one's part, acquit oneself well; *make an ~*, finish; *make both ~s meet*, live within one's income; *no ~*, (colloq.) vast quantity or number *of*; immensely; *on ~*, resting on its end, upright; consecutively; *put an ~ to*, put a stop to, abolish; *~ on*, endways; *~ to ~*, with ends in contact, lengthwise. 5. *big ~*, connecting rod that connects with crankshaft; *little ~*, end that connects with piston; *~ game*, (chess) last stage in game when few pieces are left; *~ -mill* (*v.t.*) mill both end and periphery of (piece of metal etc.); *e'ndpapers*, blank leaves at beginning and end of book, the first and last of which are pasted on to the binding; *~-play*, (eng.) freedom of shaft of machine to move axially when revolving; *~-product*, finished article as opposed to raw material; *~-stopped*, (of verse) with pause or stop at end of line(s). ~ *v.* Bring to an end; put an end to, destroy; come to an end; result *in*; ~ *by* (*doing*), come ultimately to (doing); ~ *up*, conclude, finish.

ėndă'mage *v.t.* Damage.

ėndā'nger (-j-) *v.t.* Cause danger to.

ėndear' *v.t.* Render dear (*to*). **ėndear'ĭngly̆** *adv.* **ėndear'ment** *n.* (esp.) Action or utterance expressing affection.

ėndeavour (-dĕ'ver) *v.* Try (*to* do); strive. ~ *n.* Attempt, effort.

ėndĕ'mĭc *adj.* Regularly found among (specified) people or in (specified) country or district. **ėndĕ'mĭcally̆** *adv.* **ėndĕ'mĭc** *n.* Endemic disease.

ĕ'ndĭng *n.* (esp.) Concluding part (of book, story, etc.); (gram.) inflexional or formative suffix.

ĕ'ndīve *n.* 1. Plant of the species *Cichorium endivia* (in U.S. usu. called *chicory*), of which the varieties with frizzled leaves (*curled* ~)

or undivided wavy leaves (*Batavian* ~) are eaten as salad. 2. Another species of the same genus, *C. intybus* (called *chicory* in England but *endive* in U.S.), with smooth blanched leaves eaten as salad; root of this, ground and roasted as addition to coffee.

ĕ'ndlėss *adj.* Infinite; eternal; incessant; ~ *band, cable, chain,* etc., band etc. with ends joined for continuous action over wheels etc.; ~ *knife, saw,* continuous band of steel with sharp-toothed edge, for similar purpose. **ĕ'ndlėsslў** *adv.* **ĕ'ndlėssnėss** *n.*

endo- *prefix.* Within.

ĕndocar'dĭum *n.* (pl. *-ia*). (physiol.) Smooth membrane lining cavities of heart. **ĕndocarditis** *n.* Inflammation of the endocardium.

ĕ'ndocarp *n.* (bot.) Inner layer of pericarp, lining seed chamber, fleshy (as in orange), membranous (as in apple), or hard (as in peach).

ĕ'ndocrine *adj.* & *n.* (Gland) pouring its secretions directly into the blood or lymph, ductless (gland).

ĕ'ndoderm *n.* 1. (physiol.) Innermost layer of cells of embryo, from which alimentary system is developed. 2. (bot.) = ENDODERMIS.

ĕndoder'mĭs *n.* (bot.) Cylinder of tissue one cell thick lying between cortex and conducting tissues.

ĕndŏ'gamў *n.* Custom of marrying only within limits of clan or tribe. **ĕndŏ'gamous** *adj.*

ĕndŏ'gėnous *adj.* Growing or originating from within.

ĕndomē'trĭum *n.* (pl. *-ia*). (physiol.) Lining tissue of womb.

ĕ'ndoplăsm *n.* (biol.) Granular fluid cytoplasm contained within ectoplasm in an animal cell. **ĕndoplă'smĭc** *adj.*

ėndor'se *v.t.* 1. Write on back of (document), esp. sign one's name (as payee etc.) on back of (bill, cheque, etc.); make (bill, cheque, etc.) payable *to* another by endorsement; write particulars of offence on (driving licence etc.). 2. Confirm, vouch for (statement, opinion); (chiefly U.S.) express approval of (thing, person, etc.). **ėndor'sement** *n.*

ĕndoskē'lėton *n.* Internal skeleton, as of vertebrates.

ĕ'ndosperm *n.* (bot.) Albumen enclosed with embryo in many seeds. **ĕndosper'mĭc** *adj.*

ĕndothē'lĭum *n.* (pl. *-ia*). Layer of cells lining blood-vessels etc.

ėndow' *v.t.* Give, bequeath, permanent income to (person, institution, etc.); enrich *with* (privileges etc.); furnish *with* (quality, ability, etc.). **ėndow'ment** *n.* ~ *assurance, insurance, policy,* (policy of) insurance providing for payment of fixed sum at specified date or at death, whichever is earlier.

ėndū'e *v.t.* 1. Put on, assume, as a garment; clothe *with.* 2. Invest *with* power or quality.

ėndūr'ance *n.* Habit, power, of enduring; enduring.

ėndūr'e *v.* 1. Undergo (pain etc.); submit to; bear (*to* do); tolerate (thing, person). 2. Last.

ĕ'ndways, -wīse (-z) *advs.* With end towards spectator or uppermost or foremost; end to end.

Endў'mion (ĕ-). (Gk myth.) Shepherd, the most beautiful of men, of whom Selene (the Moon) became enamoured.

E.N.E. *abbrev.* East-north-east.

ĕ'nėma (*or* ĭnē'-) *n.* (med.) Injection of fluid into the rectum; fluid injected.

ĕ'nemў *n.* 1. Hostile person; opponent, antagonist; opposing person, influence, etc.; *the E~,* the Devil. 2. (Member of) hostile army or nation; hostile force; nation, State, at war with another. ~ *adj.*

Of a hostile force or nation; hostile.

ĕnergĕ'tic *adj.* Strenuously active; forcible, vigorous; powerfully operative. **ĕnergĕ'tically** *adv.*

ĕ'nergism *n.* Ethical doctrine that supreme good lies not in pleasure but in contented activity of mind. **ĕnergi'stic** *adj.*

ĕ'nergize *v.t.* Put in operation, infuse energy into, supply with energy.

ĕnergū'mĕn *n.* Demoniac; fanatical devotee.

ĕ'nergy̆ *n.* 1. Force, vigour (of speech, action, person, etc.); active operation; power actively exerted, (pl.) individual powers in exercise; capacity to produce effect. 2. (phys.) Power of doing work possessed at any instant by a body or system of bodies; *conservation of* ~, principle that the total energy of any closed system of bodies (including the universe) is invariable; *kinetic, actual,* ~, power of doing work possessed by moving body by virtue of its motion; *latent, potential,* ~, body's power of doing work by virtue of stresses resulting from its relation to other bodies; *mass-*~, energy which all bodies possess in virtue of their mass, and of which a small portion is released (as radiations etc.) in radioactivity and other types of atomic disintegration.

ĕ'nervāte *v.t.* Weaken physically, impair nervous tone of; destroy capacity of for vigorous effort of mind or will; impair vigour of. **ĕnervā'tion** *n.*

enfant terrible (ahṅ'fahṅ tĕrēbl). Child who embarrasses his elders by untimely remarks (also transf.). [Fr.]

ėnfee'ble *v.t.* Make feeble. **ėnfee'blement** *n.*

ėnfeo'ff (-fĕf *or* -fēf) *v.t.* Invest with fief; put in possession of fee-simple or fee-tail of lands etc. **ėnfeo'ffment** *n.*

E'nfield (ĕ-). London borough near which is Government small-arms factory; hence, (also ~ *rifle*) muzzle-loading rifle made there and used by British Army in Crimean War; see also LEE-ENFIELD.

ENFIELD RIFLE

ĕnfilā'de *n.* Fire from guns etc. sweeping line from end to end. ~ *v.t.* Subject (troops etc.) to enfilade.

ėnfō'ld *v.t.* Wrap up (*in, with*); clasp, embrace.

ėnfor'ce *v.t.* 1. Press home (argument etc.), urge (demand etc.). 2. Compel (performance of action, observance of law, etc.). **ėnfor'cement** *n.* **ėnfor'ceable** *adj.*

ėnfră'nchise (-z) *v.t.* 1. Set free; release from legal liabilities etc.; invest (city etc.) with municipal rights, esp. that of being represented in parliament. 2. Admit to membership of body politic or State; now esp., admit to electoral franchise. **ėnfră'nchisement** *n.*

ėngā'ge (ĭn-g-) *v.* 1. Bind by contract or promise (esp. of marriage); pledge oneself. 2. Hire (employee); arrange beforehand to occupy (seat etc.). 3. Attract, charm. 4. Fasten, attach; (archit., pass., of pillar) be let into wall; (mech.) mesh or interlock (*with*), fit into corresponding part. 5. Hold fast, attract (attention etc.); employ, occupy (person, his powers, thought, etc.); embark *in*, enter upon, action, business, etc. 6. Bring, come, into conflict *with* enemy; attack, enter into combat with. **ėngā'ged** (-jd) *adj.* (esp.) Betrothed; occupied; in use. **ėngā'gement** *n.*

ėngā'ging (ĭn-g-) *adj.* (esp.) Winning, attractive. **ėngā'gingly̆** *adv.* **ėngāgingnėss** *n.*

ėngar'land (ĭn-g-) *v.t.* Put garland upon; wreath (*with*).

Engels (ĕ'nglz), Friedrich (1820–95). German socialist writer; with Karl Marx, issued the 'Communist Manifesto', 1848.

ėngĕ'nder (-j-) *n.* Beget (now only fig.); give rise to, bring about.

ĕ'ngine (-j-) *n.* 1. Machine consisting of several parts working together to produce given physical effect; esp., machine consisting of oscillating or reciprocating parts which converts the chemical energy of fuel into mechanical power in a useful form; railway locomotive; ~*-driver*, driver of engine, esp. railway locomotive; ~*-room*, room containing (esp. ship's) engine(s); ~*-turned*, ornamented with ~*-turning*, engraving of symmetrical patterns on metals by machine. 2. (hist.) Machine used in warfare, esp. of large size (e.g. catapult, battering-ram). ~ *v.t.* Fit (ship etc.) with engines.

ĕngineer′ (-j-) *n.* 1. One skilled in the construction and maintenance of works of public utility such as roads, bridges, canals, gasworks, etc. (*civil* ~), or in the design, construction, and maintenance of machines (*mechanical* ~), or in the production and transmission of electrical energy and the manufacture of electrical apparatus (*electrical* ~). 2. One who designs and constructs military works for attack or defence (*military* ~); soldier of the *Engineers*, (colloq.) branch of army concerned with electrical and mechanical engineering. 3. One who has charge of steam-engine; (chiefly U.S.) engine-driver. ~ *v.* 1. Act as engineer; construct, manage (bridge, work), as engineer. 2. Contrive, arrange, bring about. **ĕngineer′ing** *n.* Science, profession, of engineer; work done by engineer.

ėngir′d, ėngir′dle (ĭn-g-) *vbs.t.* Surround (as) with girdle.

E′ngland (ĭngg-). Kingdom occupying together with Wales the southern part of Gt Britain; capital, London. **E′nglander** *n.* *Little* ~, (derog., used esp. during Boer War) one desiring to restrict dimensions and responsibilities of the British Empire; (transf.) one advocating isolationist policy.

E′nglish (ĭngg-) *adj.* Of England or its people or language; ~ *Channel*, channel between S. coast of England and N. coast of France; ~ *horn*, = COR ANGLAIS; *E′nglishman*, *E′nglishwoman*, English person; ~ *sonnet*: see SONNET. ~ *n.* 1. (collect.) English people. 2. Language of the English, member of the western branch of the Germanic family of languages, orig. the dialect of the Angles, later including all dialects of the vernacular whether Anglian or Saxon, and including *Old* ~, Anglo-Saxon, *c* 5th c. to *c* 1100, *Middle* ~, *c* 1100 to *c* 1500, and *Modern* ~, *c* 1500– ; *American* ~, the variety of English spoken in U.S.; *King's* (*Queen's*) ~, correct grammatical English; (*in*) *plain* ~, (in) plain intelligible words. 3. (print.) Size of type (14 point) between pica and great primer. **e′nglish** (ĭngg-) *v.t.* (archaic, affected) Render into English. **E′nglishrў** *n.* (now chiefly hist.) Group of people of English descent esp. in Ireland.

ėngor′ge (ĭn-g-) *v.t.* 1. Devour greedily. 2. (pass.) Be crammed; (path.) be congested with blood. **ėngor′gement** *n.*

ėngra′ft (ĭn-grah-) *v.t.* Graft in; insert.

ėngrai′l (ĭn-g-) *v.t.* Indent edge of, give serrated appearance to, (her.) shape edge of (ordinary etc.) so that it has a continuous series of concave notches.

ėngrai′n (ĭn-g-) *v.t.* Cause (dye etc.) to sink deeply into a thing (usu. fig.). **ėngrai′ned** (-nd) *adj.* Inveterate; thoroughgoing.

ĕ′ngrăm (ĕn-g-) *n.* 1. (psychol.) Hypothetical physical memory-trace in the brain, recording a mental experience. 2. (biol.) Permanent and heritable change in cell, due to stimulus. **ėngră′phic** *adj.* **ėngră′phicallў** *adv.* **ĕ′ngraphў** *n.*

ėngrā′ve (ĭn-g-) *v.t.* Inscribe, ornament (hard surface) *with* incised marks; carve (design, letters, etc.) *upon* surface; cut (design etc.) on metal plate or wood block for printing; (fig.) impress deeply (*upon* memory etc.). **ėngrā′ver** *n.*

ėngrā′vĭng (ĭn-g-) *n.* (esp.) Print made from engraved plate; copy of painting etc. made by this means; art of imparting designs to plates or blocks in such a way that prints may be taken from them, esp. by incising lines (*line* ~); this and numerous other hand- and mechanical processes collectively.

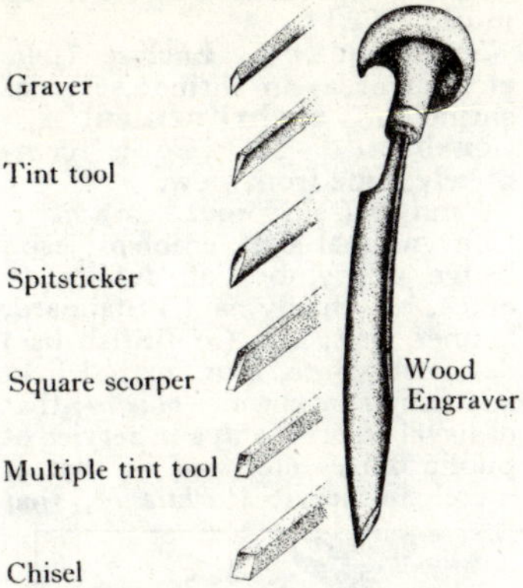

ENGRAVING TOOLS

ėngrō'ss (ĭn-g-) *v.t.* 1. Write in large letters; now chiefly, write in peculiar character appropriate to legal document. 2. Occupy entirely or exclusively, monopolize (person, his attention, etc.); (hist.) buy whole stock of (commodity) in order to retail it at monopoly price. **ėngrō'ssment** *n.*

ėngŭ'lf (ĭn-g-) *v.t.* Plunge into, swallow up (as) in, gulf. **ėngŭ'lfment** *n.*

ėnha'nce (-ah-) *v.* Heighten, intensify (qualities, powers, etc.); exaggerate; raise (price); increase in price or value. **ėnha'ncement** *n.*

ĕnharmŏ'nic *adj.* (mus.) Of, in, the Greek style or scale in which an interval of 2½ tones (5 semitones) was divided into 10 quartertones and a major third; of, having, intervals smaller than semitone (esp. such intervals as that between G♯ and A♭). **ĕnharmŏ'nically** *adv.*

ĕnĭ'gma *n.* Riddle; puzzling person or thing. **ĕnigmă'tic, -ical** *adjs.* **ĕnigmă'tically** *adv.*

ėnjă'mbment (-m-m-) *n.* (pros.) Continuation of sentence beyond second line of couplet.

ėnjoi'n *v.t.* 1. Prescribe, impose (action, conduct, *on* person); command. 2. Prohibit, restrain (esp. by legal injunction).

ėnjoy' *v.t.* 1. Find pleasure in; ~ *oneself*, experience pleasure, be happy. 2. Use, possess, or experience with delight, take delight in; have use or benefit of; occas., experience (something not pleasurable). **ėnjoy'able** *adj.* **ėnjoy'ably** *adv.* **ėnjoy'ment** *n.*

ėnkĭ'ndle *v.t.* Cause (flame, passions, war, etc.) to blaze up; inflame with passion.

ėnlā'ce *v.t.* Encircle tightly; enfold; entwine. **ėnlā'cement** *n.*

ėnlar'ge *v.t.* 1. Make larger, extend limits of, increase size, amount, or number of; (phot.) make picture larger than original negative. 2. Extend range or scope of, widen (ideas, sympathies, etc.); expatiate *upon*. **ėnlar'gement** *n.* **ėnlar'ger** *n.* Photographic apparatus for enlarging or reducing negatives or positives.

ėnli'ghten (-īt-) *v.t.* Instruct, inform (*on* subject); free from prejudice or superstition; (chiefly poet.) shed light on (object), give light to (person). **ėnli'ghtenment** *n.* *the E~*, (after Ger. *Aufklärung*) an 18th-c. philosophical movement characterized by a reliance on reason and directed to freeing religion and morals from tradition and prejudice.

ėnlĭ'st *v.* 1. Engage, enrol, for military service (esp. as private soldier or for temporary service). 2. Secure co-operation or support of (*in* enterprise etc.) **ėnlĭ'stment** *n.*

ėnlī'ven *v.t.* Animate, inspirit; brighten. **ėnlī'venment** *n.*

en masse (ahṅ). In a mass; all together. [Fr.]

ėnmĕ'sh *v.t.* Entangle (as) in net. **ėnmĕ'shment** *n.*

ĕ'nmĭty *n.* Hatred; state of hostility.

ĕ'nnėad *n.* Set of nine.

ėnnō'ble *v.t.* Make (person) a noble; make noble, elevate. **ėnnō'blement** *n.*

ennui (ŏ'nwē) *n.* Boredom.

E'nŏch (ēnŏk). Hebrew patriarch, father of Methuselah (Gen. 5: 24); two apocryphal works, the 'Book of ~' and the 'Book of the Secrets of ~', are ascribed to him.

ėnor'mĭty *n.* Monstrous wickedness; crime, monstrous offence.

ėnŏr′mous *adj.* Very large. **ėnŏr′mouslў** *adv.* **ėnŏr′mousnėss** *n.*

ĕnō′sis (*or* ĕ′-) *n.* Proposed union of Cyprus and Greece.

ėnou′gh (-ŭf) *adj., n., & adv.* Not less than required quantity, number, or degree.

ėnou′nce *v.t.* Enunciate; pronounce (words). **ėnou′ncement** *n.*

ėnow′ *adj., n., & adv.* (dial. or poet.) Enough.

en passant (ahṅ păsahṅ). By the way; *take (pawn)* ~, (chess) take adversary's pawn that has been moved forward two squares with a pawn so advanced that it can threaten the first of these squares, the pawn which takes *en passant* being moved to the threatened square. [Fr.]

enquire, enquiry: see INQUIRE, INQUIRY.

ėnrā′ge *v.t.* Make furious.

en rapport (ahṅ răpŏr). In sympathy or accord. [Fr.]

ėnrăp′ture *v.t.* Delight intensely.

en règle (ahṅ rāgl). In due form. [Fr.]

ėnrĭ′ch *v.t.* Make rich; add to contents of (collection, museum, book); make richer in quality, flavour, etc. **ėnrĭ′chment** *n.*

ėnrō′be *v.t.* Put robe upon.

ėnrō′l *v.t.* Write (name), inscribe name of (person) on roll or list, esp. of army; incorporate (person) as member (*in* society etc.); enter (deed etc.) among rolls of court of justice, record. **ėnrō′lment** *n.*

en route (ahṅ ro͞ot). On the way. [Fr.]

ENSA, E′nsa (ĕ-) *abbrev.* Entertainments National Service Association (a British organization of the war of 1939–45).

ėnsă′nguined (-nggwĭnd) *adj.* Blood-stained, bloody.

ėnscŏ′nce *v.t.* Establish (*in* concealed, secure, comfortable, etc., position).

ensemble (ahṅsah′ṅbl) *n.* Thing viewed as whole; woman's outfit of harmonizing items; = CHORUS *n.* 3; (mus.) united performance of voices or instruments in concerted music [Fr.]

ėnshrī′ne *v.t.* Enclose (relic etc.) in or as in shrine; serve as shrine for. **ėnshrī′nement** *n.*

ėnshrou′d *v.t.* Cover completely, hide from view.

ĕ′nsign (-sīn; *naut.* -sn) *n.* 1. Conventional sign, emblem; esp., badge or symbol of dignity or office. 2. (chiefly naut.) Standard, banner, flag; esp. (in British use) flag with white, blue, or red field and union in corner; *blue* ~, that of naval reserve, ships in service of public offices etc.; *red* ~, that of merchant service; *white* ~, that

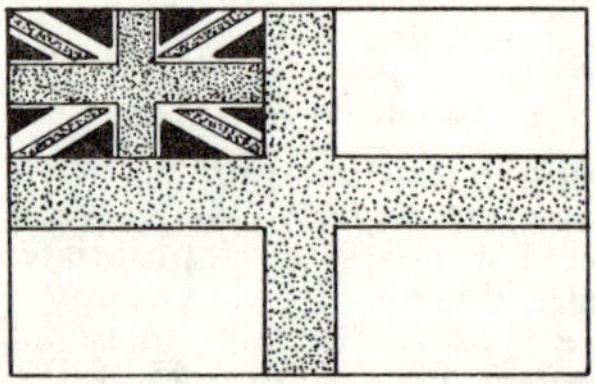

of Royal Navy and Royal Yacht Squadron. 3. Standard-bearer; formerly, lowest commissioned infantry officer. **ĕ′nsigncў** (-sĭn-) *n.*

ĕ′nsilage *n.* = SILAGE.

ėnsī′le *v.t.* Convert (fodder) into silage. **ĕnsilā′tion** *n.*

ėnslā′ve *v.t.* Make slave of, reduce to slavery. **ėnslā′vement** *n.*

ėnsnār′e *v.t.* Entrap.

ėnsū′e *v.* 1. Happen afterwards; result (*from, on*). 2. (bibl.) Seek after.

ėnsur′e (-shoor) *v.t.* Make safe (*against, from,* risks); make certain; secure (thing *to, for,* person, etc.).

E.N.T. *abbrev.* Ear, nose, and throat.

ėntă′blature *n.* (archit.) Part of classical order above column, including architrave, frieze, and cornice.

ėntā′blement (-blm-) *n.* Horizontal platform supporting statue, above dado and base.

ėntai′l *n.* Settlement of succession of landed estate, so that it cannot be bequeathed at pleasure by any one possessor; estate so secured; (fig.) inalienable inheritance. ~ *v.t.* 1. Settle (land etc.) by entail; bestow (thing) as inalienable possession. 2. Impose (expense, labour, *on* person); necessitate. **ėntai'lment** *n.*

ėntă'ngle (-nggl) *v.t.* Catch in snare or among obstacles; involve in difficulties; make tangled or intricate. **ėntă'nglement** *n.* Act of entangling, state of being entangled; (mil.) barrier of barbed wire etc. to form an obstacle to the enemy.

ĕ'ntasis *n.* (archit.) Barely perceptible swelling in shaft of column

ėntĕ'lėchy (-kĭ) *n.* In Aristotle etc., realization or complete expression of some function, condition in which potentiality has become actuality.

entente (ahṅtahṅt) *n.* (diplom.) Friendly understanding between States; group of States in such relation; *Little E~*, that between Czechoslovakia, Yugoslavia, and Rumania (1921); *Triple E~*, that between England, France, and Russia (1908); *E~ Cordiale*, that formed between Gt Britain and France in 1904. [Fr.]

ĕ'nter *v.* 1. Go, come, in; come upon stage; ~ *for*, undertake to compete in (race, examination, etc.); ~ *into*, engage in, sympathize with, form part of, bind oneself by (contract, treaty, etc.); ~ *on*, assume possession of, begin, begin to deal with. 2. Go, come, into; penetrate; begin (period of time). 3. Become member of (society or organized body). 4. Put (name) into list, (fact etc.) into description or record, etc.; admit, procure admission for, as pupil, member of society, etc.; ~ *an appearance*, *judgement*, *writ*, etc., (law) enter on record or bring before court in due form; ~ *a protest*, (of minority in deliberative body) record protest in journals or minutes; protest; ~ *up*, enter in regular form, complete series of entries in.

ėntĕ'rĭc *adj.* Of the intestines; ~ *fever*, typhoid. ~ *n.* Enteric fever. **ĕnterī'tĭs** *n.* (Acute) inflammation of bowels, esp. small intestines.

ĕ'nterprise (-z) *n.* Undertaking, esp. bold or difficult one; courage, readiness to engage in enterprises; *private* ~, economic activity under private control; individual initiative. **ĕ'nterprīsing** *adj.* Ready to undertake enterprises. **ĕ'nterprīsinglȳ** *adv.*

ĕntertai'n *v.t.* 1. Occupy (person etc.) agreeably, amuse. 2. Receive as guest, show hospitality to (also abs.). 3. Admit to consideration, harbour, cherish (idea, opinion, proposal, etc.). **ĕntertai'ner** *n.* (esp.) One who gives a public entertainment. **ĕntertai'nĭng** *adj.* (esp.) Amusing. **ĕntertai'nĭnglȳ** *adv.*

ĕntertai'nment *n.* (esp.) Hospitable reception; amusement; public performance.

ėnthra'l, -ll (-awl) *v.t.* Enslave; charm. **ėnthra'lment** *n.*

ėnthrō'ne *v.t.* Place (king, bishop, etc.) on throne, esp. as formal induction. **ėnthrō'nement, ĕnthronīzā'tion** *ns.*

ėnthū'se (-z) *v.i.* (colloq.) Show enthusiasm, gush.

ėnthū'sĭăsm (-zĭ-) *n.* 1. (archaic) Ill-regulated or misdirected religious emotion; extravagant or false confidence in divine inspiration or favour. 2. Rapturous intensity of feeling *for* a person, cause, pursuit, etc.; passionate eagerness; object of this.

ėnthū'sĭăst (-z-) *n.* One who is full of enthusiasm. **ėnthūsĭă'stic** *adj.* **ėnthūsĭă'stĭcallȳ** *adv.*

ĕ'nthȳmēme *n.* (logic) Syllogism in which one premiss is suppressed.

ėntī'ce *v.t.* Attract, esp. insidiously or adroitly, by offer of pleasure or advantage. **ėntī'cement** *n.*

ėntīr'e *adj.* Whole, complete; not broken or decayed; not castrated; unqualified; all of one piece, continuous; pure, unmixed. **ėntīr'enėss** *n.* **ėntīr'e** *n.* (hist., and on inn-signs, etc.) Kind of malt-liquor resembling porter.

ėntīr'ely (-īrlĭ) *adv.* Wholly; solely.

ėntīr'ety (-īrtĭ) *n.* 1. Completeness; whole, sum total; *in its* ~, in its complete form, as a whole. 2. (law) Entire or undivided possession of an estate.

ėntī'tle *v.t.* 1. Give (person, book, etc.) the title of. 2. Give (person etc.) a right (*to* a thing, *to* do). **ėntī'tlement** *n.*

ĕ'ntitȳ *n.* 1. A thing's existence, as dist. from its qualities or relations. 2. Something that has a real existence.

ėnto'mb (-ōōm) *v.t.* Place in tomb; serve as tomb for. **ėnto'mbment** (-ōōm-m-) *n.*

ĕntomŏ'logȳ *n.* Branch of zoology dealing with insects. **ĕntomolŏ'gical** *adj.* **ĕntomŏ'logist** *n.* **ĕntomŏ'logīze** *v.i.*

entourage (ŏntoorah'zh) *n.* Persons surrounding or attending on a superior; surroundings. [Fr.]

entr'acte (ŏ'ntrăkt) *n.* (Performance in) interval between acts of play; music etc. for this. [Fr.]

ĕ'ntrails (-z) *n.pl.* Bowels, intestines; inner parts (*of* the earth etc.).

ĕntrai'n *v.* Put, go, into a train.

ĕ'ntrance[1] *n.* 1. Coming or going in; coming of actor upon stage; entering *into*, *upon* (office etc.). 2. Right of admission; fee paid on admission. 3. Door, passage, etc., one enters by.

ėntra'nce[2] (-ah-) *v.t.* Throw into trance; overwhelm (*with* joy, fear); carry away as in trance.

ĕ'ntrant *n.* One who enters room, profession, etc., or *for* (race etc.).

ėntră'p *v.t.* Catch in or as in trap; beguile (*to* destruction etc., *into* doing).

ėntrea't *v.t.* 1. Ask earnestly (*to* do). 2. (archaic) Treat, deal with, in specified manner. **ėntrea'tȳ** *n.* Earnest request.

entrechat (ahṅtreshah) *n.* (dancing) Leap during which dancer crosses the legs below the knee. [Fr.]

entrée (ŏ'ntrā) *n.* 1. Right or privilege of admission. 2. Dish served between fish and joint.

ėntrĕ'nch *v.t.* 1. Surround, fortify, with trench (freq. fig.); *entrenching tools*, tools suitable for digging trenches. 2. Encroach, trespass, *upon*. **ėntrĕ'nchment** *n.*

entre nous (ŏntre nōō) *adv.* Between you and me. [Fr.]

entrepôt (ŏ'ntrepō) *n.* Storehouse for deposit; commercial centre for import and export, collection and distribution. [Fr.]

entrepreneur (ŏntreprenêr') *n.* 1. Organizer, manager, of (esp. musical) entertainments; manager. 2. One who undertakes an enterprise, esp. contractor acting as intermediary between capital and labour. **entrepreneur'ĭal** *adj.* [Fr.]

entresŏl (ŏn-) *n.* Low storey between first and ground floor. [Fr.]

ĕ'ntropȳ *n.* (phys.) Measure of the degree of molecular disorder existing in a system, also determining how much of the system's thermal energy is unavailable for conversion into mechanical work, expressed as a thermodynamic function.

ėntrŭ'st *v.t.* Charge (person) *with* (duty, object of care); confide (duty etc. *to* person etc.).

ĕ'ntrȳ *n.* 1. Coming or going in; coming (of actor) upon stage; ceremonial entrance; beginning, or resumption, of performer's part in concerted music. 2. (law) Taking possession of lands etc. by entering or setting foot on them. 3. Place of entrance; door, gate, entrance-hall, etc. 4. Entering or registering in list, record, account-book, etc.; item so entered; list of competitors (in race etc.); *double* ~, book-keeping in which every credit item of one account in ledger is entered to debit of another.

ent. Sta. Hall *abbrev.* Entered at Stationers' Hall.

ėntwī'ne *v.t.* Interweave; wreathe; embrace.

ėnū'clėāte *v.t.* 1. Explain, clear up. 2. (surg.) Extract (tumour etc.) from its capsule; remove (eyeball). **ėnū'clėate** *adj.* (biol. etc.) Without a nucleus.

ėnū'merāte *v.t.* Count; mention (number of things or persons) separately; specify. **ėnūmerā'tion** *n.* **ėnū'merative** *adj.*

ėnŭ'nciāte *v.t.* Express (proposition, theory) definitely; proclaim; pronounce (articulate sounds). **ėnŭnciā'tion, ėnŭ'nciātor** *ns.* **ėnŭ'nciative** *adj.*

ĕnūrē'sis *n.* (path.) Involuntary passing of urine. **ĕnūrĕ'tic** *adj.* & *n.* (Person) affected with enuresis.

ėnvĕ'lop *v.t.* Wrap up, cover; hide; (mil.) surround. **ėnvĕ'lopment** *n.*

ĕ'nvelōpe (*or* ŏn-) *n.* 1. Wrapper, covering; folded and gummed cover for letter; fabric enclosing gas-bags of airship. 2. (bot.) Calyx or corolla, or both together. 3. (math.) Line or curve tangent to each line or curve of a given family.

ėnvĕ'nom *v.t.* Put poison on, taint with poison; infuse venom or bitterness into (actions, words, etc.), embitter; corrupt, vitiate.

ĕ'nviable *adj.* Calculated to excite envy. **ĕ'nviablȳ** *adv.*

ĕ'nvious *adj.* Full of envy; feeling envy *of*. **ĕ'nviouslȳ** *adv.*

ĕnvīr'on *v.t.* Form ring, be stationed, round; encircle, encompass, *with*; surround with hostile or protective intention.

ėnvīr'onment *n.* Surroundings, surrounding objects, region, conditions, or influences; *Department of the E~*, government department whose functions include responsibility for policy in housing and transport, preservation of historic buildings etc., and control of air and water pollution and noise. **ėnvīronmĕ'ntal** *adj.*

ėnvīr'ons (-z; *or* ĕ'nvĭr-) *n.pl.* Outskirts, surrounding districts, of town etc.

ėnvĭ'sage (-z-) *v.t.* Look in the face of; face (danger, facts); contemplate, esp. under particular aspect. **ėnvĭ'sagement** *n.*

ĕ'nvoy[1], **ĕ'nvoi** *n.* Concluding part of poetical or prose composition; now esp., short stanza concluding ballade or other archaic form of poem.

ĕ'nvoy[2] *n.* Public minister, now esp., diplomatic minister ranking below ambassador and above chargé d'affaires, sent by one sovereign or government to another to transact diplomatic business; messenger, representative. **ĕ'nvoyship** *n.*

ĕ'nvȳ *n.* Mortification or ill-will or longing occasioned by another's good fortune; object of this. ~ *v.t.* Feel envy of (person, his advantages).

ėnwră'p (ĭnr-) *v.t.* Wrap, enfold.

ĕ'nzȳme *n.* One of a group of complex chemical substances produced by living organisms and promoting specific chemical reactions in the organism; their names usu. end in *-ase*, e.g. diastase. **ėnzȳ'mic** *adj.*

E'ocẹne (ē-) *adj.* & *n.* (geol.) (Of) the second epoch or system of the Tertiary period.

ē'olith *n.* Flint so crudely worked that there is doubt whether it was shaped by man or nature, sometimes claimed to be earliest trace of human handiwork. **ēolĭ'thic** *adj.*

eon: see AEON.

ē'osĭn *n.* (chem.) Red dye-stuff produced e.g. by action of bromine on fluorescein; soluble potassium salt of this used as rose-pink dye, as stain in microscopy, red ink, etc.

E.P. *abbrev.* Electroplate; extended-play (record).

ē'păct *n.* (also pl.) Number of days constituting excess of solar over lunar year of 12 months; age of moon on 1 Jan.

ĕ'par͡ch (-k) *n.* Governor or bishop of eparchy. **ĕ'par͡chȳ** *n.* 1. Subdivision of modern Greece. 2. Diocese of Orthodox Church.

ĕ'paulĕt, -ĕtte *n.* Ornamental shoulder-piece of uniform.

épée (ā'pā) *n.* Sharp-pointed sword used in duelling and (blunted) in fencing.

epergne (ĕpẽr'n) *n.* Centre ornament (esp. in branched form) for dinner-table.

ĕpĕxėgē'sĭs *n.* Addition of word(s) to make meaning of preceding word or sentence clearer; word so added. **ĕpĕxėgĕ'tic, -ical** *adjs.* **ĕpĕxėgĕ'ticallȳ** *adv.*

Eph. *abbrev.* Ephesians (N.T.).

ephah (ē'fa) *n.* Hebrew dry measure (see HOMER[2]).

ĕ'phėdrĭne *n.* Drug, resembling adrenalin in its effects.

ėphĕ'mera (pl. *-ras*), **-ron** (pl. *-rons*, *-ra*) *ns.* Short-lived insect

EPERGNE

of order Ephemeroptera; commonest of the mayflies, insect with delicate lacy wings and three long tail-filaments, found near water; hence, short lived thing.

ėphĕ′meral *adj.* 1. (of insects etc.) Living for a day or a few days. 2. Short-lived, transitory.

ėphĕ′meris *n.* (pl. *-mĕ′ridēs*). Table showing predicted positions of heavenly body for every day during given period; astronomical almanac.

ephemeron: see EPHEMERA.

Ephē′sian (-zh*a*n) *adj.* Of Ephesus. ~ *n.* Native, inhabitant, of Ephesus; (*Epistle to the*) ~*s*, book of N.T. ascribed to St. Paul, an epistle to the Church at Ephesus.

E′phėsus (ĕf-). One of the principal Ionian cities on the coast of Asia Minor (now several miles inland); in Roman times, chief city of the province of Asia.

ĕ′phod *n.* Jewish priestly vestment, sleeveless and slit at sides below armpits, fastened with buckle at shoulders and girdle at waist.

ĕ′phor *n.* (Gk. hist.) Magistrate in various Dorian States, esp. at Sparta, where five annually elected ephors exercised controlling power over kings.

E′phrāim (ēf-). Hebrew patriarch, youngest son of Joseph (see Gen. 41 : 52); tribe of Israel, traditionally descended from him.

epi- *prefix.* Upon, at, on the ground or occasion of, in addition.

ĕ′pĭblast (-ah-) *n.* (biol.) Outermost layer of cells of a blastoderm or gastrula. **ĕpĭblă′stĭc** *adj.*

ĕ′pĭc *adj.* Of, in, that species of poetical composition celebrating in continuous narrative achievements of heroic personage(s) of history or tradition; such as is described in epic poetry, of heroic type or scale; ~ *dialect*, dialect in which Greek epic poems were written. ~ *n.* Epic poem; composition comparable to epic poem; subject worthy of epic treatment. **ĕ'pical** *adj.* **ĕ'picallў** *adv.*

ĕ'pĭcar̄p *n.* (bot.) Outermost layer, skin, of fleshy fruit.

ĕpĭcē'dĭum *n.* Funeral ode.

ĕ'pĭcēne *adj.* 1. (L & Gk gram.) Denoting either sex without change of gender. 2. For, used by, both sexes; having characteristics of both sexes. ~ *n.* Epicene person.

ĕ'pĭcĕntre, ĕpĭcĕ'ntrum *ns.* Point on earth's surface directly above place where earthquake originates. **ĕpĭcĕ'ntral** *adj.*

ĕpĭcŏ'tўl *n.* (bot.) Seedling shoot above seed-leaves.

ĕ'pĭcūre *n.* One who cultivates discriminating taste in food and drink. **ĕ'pĭcūrism** *n.* [f. EPICURUS].

Epĭcūrē'an (ĕ-) *adj.* & *n.* 1. (Follower) of Epicurus. 2. (Person) devoted to pleasures, esp. refined sensuous enjoyment. **Epĭcūrē'anism** *n.*

Epĭcūr'us (ĕ-) (341–270 B.C.). Athenian philosopher who held that the highest good was calmness of mind.

ĕ'pĭcўcle *n.* 1. (geom.) Small circle rolling on the circumference of a greater one. 2. (hist., in ancient astronomy) Circle having its centre on the circumference of a greater circle, used in the Ptolemaic system to represent the revolutions of the planets. **ĕpĭcў'clic** *adj.* Of, like, an epicycle (sense 1); ~ *gear*, gear having pinions in epicyclic arrangement, as in multi-speed gear-box of bicycle.

ĕpĭcў'cloid *n.* Curve traced by point in circumference of a circle rolling round the circumference of another circle.

ĕpĭdei'ctĭc (-dīk-) *adj.* Meant for display.

ĕpĭdĕ'mĭc *adj.* & *n.* (Disease) spreading rapidly through a community for a period (cf. ENDEMIC). **ĕpĭdĕ'mĭcal** *adj.* **ĕpĭdĕ'mĭcallў** *adv.*

ĕpĭdē'mĭŏ'logў *n.* Science of epidemics.

ĕpĭder̄'mĭs *n.* 1. (physiol.) Outer non-vascular layer of skin of animals, cuticle; outer animal integument of shell. 2. (bot.) Outermost cell layer in plants before secondary growth begins. **ĕpĭder̄'mal, ĕpĭder̄'mĭc, ĕpĭder̄moid** *adjs.*

ĕpĭdī'ascōpe *n.* Apparatus for projecting a magnified image of both opaque and transparent objects.

ĕpĭdūr'al *adj.* Of, affecting, the dura mater.

ĕpĭgă'strĭum *n.* Part of abdomen immediately over stomach. **ĕpĭgă'strĭc** *adj.*

ĕpĭgē'al *adj.* (bot.) Carrying seed-leaves above ground in germination.

ĕpĭgĕ'nėsĭs *n.* Formation of organic germ as new product. **ĕpĭgėnĕ'tĭc** *adj.*

ĕpĭglŏ'ttĭs *n.* Erect cartilage at root of tongue, depressed in act of swallowing to cover glottis.

ĕ'pĭgōne *n.* One of a later (and less distinguished) generation. **ėpi'gonal** *adj.*

ĕ'pĭgrăm *n.* Short poem ending in witty or ingenious turn of thought; pointed saying or mode of expression. **ĕpĭgrammă'tĭc** *adj.* **ĕpĭgrammă'tĭcallў** *adv.* **ĕpĭgră'mmatist** *n.* **ĕpĭgră'mmatīze** *v.*

ĕ'pĭgrăph (*or* -ahf) *n.* Inscription on stone, statue, coin, etc.; motto. **ĕpĭgră'phĭc** *adj.* **ėpĭ'graphў** *n.* Study of (ancient) epigraphs.

ėpĭ'gўnў *n.* (bot.) Floral structure in which petals and sepals are borne above ovaries. **ėpĭ'gўnous** *adj.*

ĕ'pĭlĕpsў *n.* Symptom of nervous disorder generally involving recurrent temporary loss of consciousness with or without convulsions, automatic movements, muscular spasms, etc. **ĕpĭlĕ'ptĭc** *adj.* Of, subject to, epilepsy. ~ *n.* Epileptic person. **ĕpĭlĕ'ptĭfor̄m** *adj.* Resembling epilepsy.

ĕ'pĭlŏgue (-g) *n.* Concluding part, appendix, of literary work; speech, short poem, addressed by actor to spectators at end of play.

Epĭ'phanў[1] (ĭ-) *n.* Christian festival commemorating the manifestation of Christ to the Gentiles in the persons of the Magi, observed on 6 Jan.

ėpĭ'phanȳ[2] *n.* Manifestation of a superhuman being.

ĕpĭphėnŏ'mėnon *n.* (pl. *-na*). Something appearing in addition, secondary symptom; (esp., psych.) consciousness regarded as by-product of material activities of brain and nerve-system.

ėpĭ'phȳsis *n.* (pl. *-es* pr. -ēz). Cap at end of long bone, before maturity separated from the shaft by a pad of cartilage which gradually ossifies, thus allowing for growth.

ĕ'pĭphȳte *n.* Plant growing on another (usu. deriving only support, not nutrition, from it); vegetable parasite on animal body. **ĕpĭphȳ'tal, ĕpĭphȳ'tic** *adjs.*

ėpĭ'scopacȳ *n.* Government of Church by bishops; the bishops collectively.

ėpĭ'scopal *adj.* Of bishop(s); *E~ Church*, Church constituted on principle of episcopacy; esp. (U.S., Scotland, etc.) the Church of England. **ėpĭ'scopallȳ** *adv.*

ėpĭscopā'lĭan *adj.* & *n.* (Adherent) of episcopacy; (member) of Episcopal Church. **ėpĭscopā'lĭanĭsm** *n.*

ėpĭ'scopate *n.* Office, see, tenure, of bishop; the bishops collectively.

ĕpĭsĭŏ'tomȳ *n.* (surg.) Incision of the vulva to facilitate childbirth.

ĕ'pĭsōde *n.* 1. Incidental narrative, digression, in poem, story, etc.; incidental happening or series of events in person's life, history of a country, etc. 2. In Gk tragedy, interlocutory (orig. interpolated) parts between two choric songs. 3. (mus.) Intervening passage. **ĕpĭsŏ'dic** *adj.*

ĕpĭspă'stic *adj.* & *n.* (med.) Blistering (substance).

ĕpĭstă'xis *n.* (path.) Bleeding from the nose.

ĕpĭstėmŏ'logȳ *n.* Theory of method or grounds of knowledge. **ĕpĭstėmolŏ'gical** *adj.*

ėpĭ'stle (-sl) *n.* 1. Letter; (esp.) letter from Apostle, forming part of canon of Scripture; *E~*, extract from one of these read in Communion service. 2. Literary work, usu. in verse, in form of letter.

ėpĭ'stolarȳ *adj.* Of, carried by, suited to, letters.

ėpĭ'stoler *n.* (eccles.) Reader of Epistle in church service.

ėpĭ'strophė *n.* (rhet.) Ending of several sentences or clauses with same word.

ĕ'pĭstȳle *n.* (archit.) Architrave.

ĕ'pĭtăph (*or* -ahf) *n.* Inscription upon tomb; brief composition expressed as if for inscribing on tombstone.

ĕpĭthalā'mĭum *n.* (pl. *-iums*, *-ia*). Nuptial song or poem. **ĕpĭthalā'mial, ĕpĭthală'mĭc** *adjs.*

ĕpĭthē'lĭum *n.* (pl. *-ia*). (biol.) Layer of cells which covers the body surface or lines a cavity that communicates with it. **ĕpĭthē'lĭal** *adj.*

ĕ'pĭthĕt *n.* Adjective expressing quality or attribute; significant appellation. **ĕpĭthĕ'tĭc, -ĭcal** *adjs.* **ĕpĭthĕ'tĭcallȳ** *adv.*

ėpĭ'tomė *n.* Summary, abstract, of book; condensed account; (fig.) thing representing another in miniature. **ėpĭ'tomīze** *v.t.*

E.P.N.S. *abbrev.* Electroplated nickel silver.

ē̆'poch (-k) *n.* Beginning of era in history, science, life, etc.; division of a geological period; date; period in history or life marked by special events. **ĕ'pochal** *adj.*

ĕ'pōde *n.* Kind of lyric poem, invented by Archilochus and used by Horace, in which long line is followed by shorter one; part of lyric ode sung after strophe and antistrophe.

ĕ'ponȳm *n.* One who gives his name to a people, place, institution, etc. **ėpŏ'nȳmous** *adj.*

ĕ'popee *n.* Epic poem or poetry.

ĕ'pŏs *n.* Early narrative poetry celebrating incidents of heroic tradition; epic poem or poetry.

ĕpsī'lon *n.* 5th letter of Greek alphabet (Ε, ε), corresponding to *e* (pr. ĕ).

E'psom (ĕ-). Town in Surrey, famous for the horse-races, esp.

the Derby and the Oaks, held on the neighbouring downs; ~ *salt(s)*, bitter colourless crystalline salt, magnesium sulphate, used as a purgative, orig. prepared from Epsom mineral waters.

E'pstein (ĕpstīn), Sir Jacob (1880–1959). Sculptor of Polish origin, born U.S., settled in London; works include symbolic and religious carvings and portrait bronzes.

E.P.T. *abbrev.* Excess profits tax.

ĕ'quable *adj.* Uniform, even, not easily disturbed. **ĕquabĭ'lĭtȳ** *n.* **ĕ'quablȳ** *adv.*

ē'qual *adj.* The same in number, size, value, degree, etc.; having strength, courage, ability, etc., adequate *to* (occasion etc.); uniform in operation, action, etc.; evenly balanced. ~ *n.* Person equal to another in rank etc.; (pl.) equal things. ~ *v.t.* Be equal to.

ėqualĭtār'ĭan (ĭkwŏl-) *adj.* & *n.* Egalitarian. **ėqualĭtār'ĭanĭsm** *n.*

ėqua'lĭtȳ (ĭkwŏl-) *n.* Condition of being equal; equal footing.

ē'qualīze *n.* Make (thing etc.) equal (to, with); (footb. etc.) make score equal to opponents'. **ēqualīzā'tion** *n.*

ē'quallȳ *adv.* In an equal degree; in equal shares; uniformly.

ēquanĭ'mĭtȳ *n.* Evenness of mind or temper; composure; resignation.

ėquā'te *v.t.* State equality of (thing *to*, *with*, another); treat as equivalent.

ėquā'tion (*or* -zhon) *n.* 1. Making equal, balancing; equilibrium, equality. 2. (Amount or process of) compensation for inaccuracy; *personal* ~, time-lag or other error habitually made by individual in making observations, taking readings, etc., and capable of being allowed for when ascertained; ~ *of equinoxes*, difference between mean and apparent places of equinoxes, due to their PRECESSION. 3. (math.) Formula affirming equivalence of two quantitative expressions, which are connected by the sign =. 4. (chem.) Expression representing chemical reaction quantitatively by means of symbols. **ėquā'tional** *adj.* **ėquā'tionallȳ** *adv.*

ėquā'tor *n.* (astron., also *celestial* ~): see CELESTIAL; (geog.) great circle of the earth equidistant from poles; similar circle on any spherical body; *magnetic* ~, irregular line round earth near equator on which the angle of magnetic dip is zero (i.e. magnetic needle lies level).

ĕquatôr'ĭal *adj.* Of, near, the equator; ~ *telescope*, telescope mounted on two axes respectively parallel and perpendicular to earth's polar axis, so that regular rotation about first axis counters apparent motion of star and retains it in field of view. **ĕquatôr'ĭallȳ** *adv.*

ĕ'querrȳ (*or* ĭkwĕ'rĭ) *n.* Officer of prince or noble charged with care of horses; officer of English royal household with duty of occasional attendance on sovereign. [Fr. *écurie* stable f. OHG *scur* shed; confused in English with L *equus* horse]

ėquĕ'strĭan *adj.* 1. Of, skilled in, horse-riding; mounted on horse; (of statue) representing person on horseback. 2. (Rom. antiq.) Of the order of *Equites* or knights; (hist.) of the 'knightly order' of the Holy Roman Empire. ~ *n.* Rider, performer, on horseback.

ėquĕstrĭĕ'nne *n.* Horsewoman; (esp.) female circus rider.

equi- *prefix.* Equal.

ēquĭă'ngūlar (-ngg-) *adj.* Having equal angles.

ēquĭdĭ'stant *adj.* Separated by equal distance(s); parallel.

ēquĭlă'teral *adj.* Having all the sides equal (~ *arch*; ~ *triangle*).

ēquĭlī'brāte (*or* ĭkwĭ'-) *v.* Cause (two things) to balance; balance; counterpoise. **ēquĭlĭbrā'tion** *n.*

ėquĭ'lĭbrĭst *n.* Rope-walker, acrobat.

ēquĭlĭ'brĭum *n.* State of equal balance between opposing forces or powers; neutrality of judgement etc.

ēquĭmŭ'ltĭple *n.* Number having common factor with another.

ĕ'quīne *adj.* Of, like, a horse.

ĕquĭnŏ'ctĭal (-sh*a*l) *adj.* 1. Of equal day and night; happening at or near time of equinox, as ~ *gales*; ~ *line*, celestial equator. 2. At, near, the equator. ~ *n.* Equinoctial line; (pl.) equinoctial gales.

ĕ'quĭnŏx *n.* Time when the sun crosses the equator and day and night are equal, occurring twice yearly, on 20 or 21 March (*vernal* ~) and 22 or 23 Sept. (*autumnal* ~); either of the two points at which the sun's path crosses the equator.

ėquĭ'p *v.t.* Furnish (ship, army, person, *with* requisites); provide (*oneself* etc.) for journey etc.

ĕ'quĭpage *n.* Requisites for undertaking; outfit for journey etc.; carriage and horses with attendants. **ėquĭ'pment** *n.* Equipping, being equipped, manner in which person or thing is equipped; outfit, warlike apparatus, necessaries for expedition, voyage, etc.

ĕ'quĭpoise (-z) *n.* Equilibrium; counterpoise, balancing force or thing. ~ *v.t.* Counterbalance; place or hold in equipoise.

ēquĭpŏ'llent *adj.* Equal in power, force, etc.; practically equivalent. ~ *n.* Equivalent. **ēquĭpŏ'llence, -ency̆** *ns.*

ēquĭpŏ'nderāte *v.t.* Counterbalance. **ēquĭpŏ'nderant** *adj.*

ēquĭpotĕ'ntial (-sh*a*l) *adj.* (of points) In which potential of a force is the same; (of line etc.) in which potential is constant at all points; (of germ, embryo) having equal potentialities in all its parts.

ĕquĭsē'tum *n.* Plant of genus *E*~, comprising the horsetails.

ĕ'quĭtable *adj.* Fair, just; (of claims etc.) valid in equity as dist. from law. **ĕ'quĭtably̆** *adv.* **ĕ'quĭtableness** *n.*

ĕquĭtā'tion *n.* Riding on horseback; horsemanship.

ĕ'quĭty̆ *n.* 1. Fairness, impartiality. 2. Recourse to general principle of justice to correct or supplement provisions of law; (in England, U.S., etc.) system of law existing side by side with common and statute law, and superseding these when they conflict with it. 3. Equitable right, right recognizable by court of equity. 4. (chiefly U.S. colloq.) Amount or value of property etc. after all charges etc. are satisfied. 5. (pl.) Stocks and shares not bearing fixed interest. 6. *E*~, name of actors' union in Gt Britain.

ėquĭ'valent *adj.* 1. Equal in value; having equal or corresponding import or meaning; that is virtually the same thing, tantamount; corresponding. 2. (chem.) ~ *weight*, (also *combining weight* or *chemical* ~) that amount of an element, by weight, that will combine with or replace one unit weight of hydrogen; *gramme-*~ (*weight*), this expressed in grammes. ~ *n.* Equivalent thing, amount, word, etc.; (chem.) see *adj.* above. **ėquĭ'valence, ėquĭvalency̆** *ns.*

ėquĭ'vocal *adj.* Of double meaning, ambiguous; of uncertain nature; undecided; questionable, suspicious. **ėquĭ'vocally̆** *adv.* **ėquĭ'vocalness** *n.*

ėquĭ'vocāte *v.i.* Use ambiguous words to conceal truth, prevaricate. **ėquĭvocā'tion, ėquĭ'vocātor** *ns.*

ĕ'quĭvōque (-k), **-ōke** *n.* Pun; ambiguity.

E.R. *abbrev.* East Riding; *Edwardus Rex* (L, = King Edward); *Elizabeth Regina* (L, = Queen Elizabeth).

ēr'a *n.* 1. System of chronology starting from some particular point of time (as the *Christian* ~ from the date of the birth of Jesus Christ as calculated by DIONYSIUS EXIGUUS, the *Muslim* ~ from the year of Muhammad's flight from Mecca (622), etc.); initial point in such system; memorable or important date. 2. Historical period; period in individual's life, in some continuous process, etc.; major division of geological time, usu. comprising several periods.

E.R.A. *abbrev.* Engine-room artificer.

ėră'dicāte *v.t.* Tear up by roots; extirpate, get rid of. **ėră'dicable** *adj.* **ėrădĭcā'tion** *n.*

ėrā'se (-z) *v.t.* Rub out; obliterate. **ėrā'ser** *n.* That which erases, esp., preparation of rubber or similar substance for rubbing out writing etc. **ėrā'sure** (-zh*er*) *n.* Process of erasing; word etc. rubbed out.

Era'smus (ĭrăz-), Desiderius (1466–1536). Dutch humanist; prepared the way for the Reformation by his version of the N.T. and his condemnation of Church abuses in 'Moriae Encomium' (The Praise of Folly).

Ėră'stian (ĭ-) *adj.* & *n.* (Adherent) of the doctrine that ecclesiastical power should be subordinated to secular, supposed to have been held by Erastus (Thomas Liebler, 1524–83), a Heidelberg physician who opposed the use of excommunication. **Ėră'stianism** *n.*

E'ratō (ĕ-). (Gk & Rom. myth.) Muse of love and poetry.

ẽr'bia *n.* Erbium oxide, a rose-coloured mineral.

ẽr'bium *n.* (chem.) Metallic element of rare-earth group, occurring in gadolinite etc.; symbol Er, at. no. 68, at. wt 167·26. [f. *Ytterby* in Sweden, where found]

ere (ãr) *prep.* & *conj.* (poet., archaic). Before (in time).

E'rėbus (ĕ-). (Gk myth.) Place of darkness between Earth and Hades.

Erĕ'chthėum (ĭrĕk-). Temple of Erechtheus, legendary king of Athens, on the Acropolis, erected 421–407 B.C.; famous for its caryatid columns.

ėrĕ'ct *adj.* Upright, not stooping; vertical; (of hair etc.) set up, bristling. **ėrĕ'ctlȳ** *adv.* **ėrĕ'ctnėss** *n.* **ėrĕ'ct** *v.t.* Raise, set upright; build; constitute or form *into*, invest with rank or character of.

ėrĕ'ctīle *adj.* Capable of being erected; ~ *tissue*, tissue in various parts of animals capable of being distended and becoming rigid under excitement.

ėrĕ'ction *n.* Erecting; building, structure.

ėrĕ'ctor *n.* Person, thing, that erects; muscle causing erection; ~ *pili muscle*, one causing hair to bristle.

ĕ'rėmīte *n.* Recluse, hermit; esp., Christian solitary of 3rd c. onwards (as dist. from coenobite, who lived in community). **ĕrėmĭ'tĭc, -ĭcal** *adjs.*

ĕ'rėthĭsm *n.* (psychol.) Morbid excitability, usu. of sexual manifestation.

ẽrg *n.* (phys.) Amount of work done when a force of 1 dyne moves its point of application 1 centimetre in the direction of the force.

ẽr'gō *adv.* (usu. joc.) Therefore. [L]

ẽr'gogrăph (*or* -ahf) *n.* Instrument for measuring and recording work done by muscles.

ẽrgonŏ'mics *n.* Scientific study of the efficiency of workers in their working environment. **ẽrgonŏ'mĭc** *adj.* **ẽrgonŏ'mĭcallȳ** *adv.*

ẽrgŏ'sterol *n.* Sterol which when exposed to ultra-violet radiation gives a mixture of compounds including vitamin D, found in yeasts and fungi and present in small quantities in the fats of plants and animals.

ẽr'got *n.* 1. Diseased condition of seed of rye and other grasses; dark-violet hardened mycelium of the fungus (*Claviceps purpurea*) causing this, used medically to control haemorrhage or contract uterus. 2. Horny protuberance on inner side of horse's fetlock. **ẽr'gotism** *n.* Disease of grasses consisting in formation of ergot; diseased condition of man or animals caused by eating grain or grasses infected with ergot and characterized by muscular cramp and gangrene.

Erie (ẽr'ĭ) *n.* Member of an Iroquoian people formerly dwelling near *Lake* ~, one of the five Great Lakes of N. America.

Er'in (ẽr- *or* ĕr-). Ancient name of Ireland, now only poetical.

ėrĭ'stĭc *adj.* Of controversy or disputation. ~ *n.* Controversialist; art of disputation.

Eritrē'a (ĕ-). Province of Ethiopia, on the Red Sea; formerly an Italian colony.

ẽr'l-kĭ'ng *n.* In Danish legend, king of the elves.

ẽr'mine *n.* 1. Carnivorous mammal of weasel family, *Mustela*

erminea, inhabiting northern countries, with fur reddish-brown above and white beneath in summer and (in northern regions) white in winter, except for black tip of tail; stoat. 2. Fur of this, freq. with the black tails arranged on it, used in official robes of judges, state robes of peers, etc.; (her.) heraldic fur, white marked with black spots.

ẽrne *n.* (archaic & poet.) Sea-eagle.

Er'nie (ẽr-) *n.* Device for drawing prize-winning numbers of premium bonds. [*e*lectronic *r*andom *n*umber *i*ndicator *e*quipment]

ėrō'de *v.t.* (of acids, water currents, etc.) Eat away, destroy surface of. **ėrō'sion** *n.* Eroding; (geol.) wearing away of earth's surface by wind, water, or ice (cf. ABRASION). **ėrō'sive** *adj.*

ėrŏ'gėnous *adj.* Of, giving rise to, sexual desire.

ēr'ŏs[1] (*or* ĕr-) *n.* Earthly or sexual love (opp. AGAPE[2]).

Er'ŏs[2] (ēr- *or* ĕr-). 1. (Gk myth.) God of love, identified by the Romans with Cupid. 2. (astron.) Asteroid, discovered in 1898, coming at times nearer the earth than any heavenly body except moon.

ėrŏ'tĭc *adj.* Of sexual love. **ėrŏ'tĭca** *n.pl.* Erotic writings, pictures, etc. **ĕ'rotism** *n.* Sexual excitement. **ėrŏ'tĭcallȳ** *adv.*

ėrōtomā'nĭa *n.* Excessive or morbid erotic desire; preoccupation with sexual passion. **ėrōtomā'nĭăc** *adj.* & *n.*

ẽrr *v.i.* Make mistakes; be incorrect; sin.

ĕ'rrand *n.* Short journey on which person is sent to carry message etc.; business on which one is sent, object of journey.

ĕ'rrant *adj.* Roaming in quest of adventure (esp. in *knight-*~); itinerant; wandering; erring in opinion, conduct, etc. **ĕ'rrancȳ** *n.* **ĕ'rrantrȳ** *n.* Conduct, notions, condition, of a knight-errant.

ėrră'tĭc *adj.* Wandering; (of diseases, pains, etc.) moving from one part to another; irregular or uncertain in movement, having no fixed course, eccentric in conduct, habit, or opinion; ~ *block*, (geol.) large piece of rock carried from a distant source by glacier. **ėrră'tĭcallȳ** *adv.*

ĕrrā'tum (*or* -ah-) *n.* (pl. *-ta*). Error in printing or writing, esp. (pl.) list of errors attached to book.

ėrrō'nėous *adj.* Mistaken, incorrect. **ėrrō'nėouslȳ** *adv.* **ėrrō'nėousnėss** *n.*

ĕ'rror *n.* Mistake; condition of erring in opinion, wrong opinion; transgression; (law) mistake in law appearing on proceedings of court of record; (math. etc.) quantity of deviation from correct or accurate result, determination, etc.

er'sătz (ãrts-) *adj.* & *n.* Substitute, synthetic (substance etc.). [Ger.]

Erse (ẽrs) *adj.* & *n.* Irish Gaelic, formerly applied also to the Gaelic of Scotland. [var. of *Irish*]

ẽrst *adv.* (archaic) Formerly, of old. **ẽr'stwhīle** *adv.* & *adj.* Erst, former.

ērŭctā'tion *n.* Belching; eruptive action of volcano.

ĕ'rudīte (-rōō-) *adj.* Learned. **ĕ'rudītelȳ** *adv.* **ĕrudĭ'tion** *n.*

ėrŭ'pt *v.* Break out or through; (of volcano) emit rocks, lava, ash, or gases, (of geyser) spurt water; (of teeth) break through gums; (of rash) appear on skin.

ėrŭ'ption *n.* Erupting; outbreak of volcano, ejection of hot water from geyser, etc.; breaking out of rash etc.; also (fig.) of war, passion, mirth, etc.

ėrŭ'ptĭve *adj.* Bursting forth; tending to burst forth; of, formed by, forced up by, volcanic eruption. **ėrŭ'ptĭvelȳ** *adv.* **ėrŭ'ptĭvenėss** *n.*

ĕrȳsĭ'pėlas *n.* Acute inflammation of lymphatic vessels of the skin, caused by streptococcal infection.

ĕrȳthē'ma *n.* Superficial inflammation of skin appearing as rose-coloured patches.

ĕrȳ'throcȳte *n.* Red blood-cell.

E'sau (ē-). Elder son of Isaac and Rebecca; sold his birthright to his brother Jacob for a mess of pottage (Gen. 25); traditional ancestor of the Edomites.

ĕscalā'de *n.* Scaling of walls with ladders. ~ *v.* Scale by escalade.

ĕ'scalāte *v.* Increase or develop by degrees. **ĕscalā'tion** *n.*

ĕ'scalātor *n.* (orig. U.S.) Moving staircase (with stairs moving up or down on endless chain).

ėsca'llop (-kŏ-) *n.* 1. = SCALLOP *n.* 1. 2. (her.) Scallop-shell. 3. (also *collop*, *ĕscalŏpe* (Fr.), *scallop*) Thin slice of meat for frying.

ĕscapă'de *n.* Breaking loose from restraint; flighty piece of conduct.

ėscā'pe *v.* 1. Gain liberty by fleeing, get free from detention, control, oppression, etc.; (of fluids etc.) issue, find a way out; (of words etc.) issue unawares from (person, his lips). 2. Get off safely, go unhurt or unpunished; get clear away from (person, his grasp, etc.); avoid; elude notice or recollection of. ~ *n.* Act of escaping; fact of having escaped; leakage (of gas etc.); outlet; FIRE-escape; ~ *clause*, clause in a treaty absolving a contracting party from a particular obligation in specified circumstances; ~ *lock*: see DAVIS APPARATUS; ~ *velocity*, minimum velocity needed for an object to escape a gravitational field; ~ *wheel*, toothed wheel in escapement.

ėscāpee' *n.* One who has escaped.

ėscā'pement (-pm-) *n.* Outlet; mechanism in watch or clock or other timing device, intervening between motive power and regulator, and alternately checking and releasing the train, causing intermittent impulse to be given to regulator.

ėscā'pĭsm *n.* Tendency to escape from realities of life into fantasy. **ėscā'pĭst** *n.*

ėscar'p, ėscar'pment *ns.* Steep bank immediately in front of and below rampart; similar natural formation. **ėscar'p** *v.t.* Cut into form of escarp.

ĕschatŏ'logȳ (ĕsk-) *n.* Doctrine of death, judgement, heaven, and hell; (also *realized* ~) present significance of this in Christian life. **ĕschatolŏ'gical** *adj.*

ėschea't *n.* (law) Reversion of fief to feudal lord when tenant died without leaving successor qualified to inherit; lapsing of land to crown (or State) or lord of manor on owner's dying intestate without heirs; property so lapsing or reverting. ~ *v.* Confiscate; hand over (property) as an escheat; revert by escheat.

ėschew' (ĭs-chōō) *v.t.* Avoid, abstain from.

eschscholtzia (ĭskŏ'lsh*a* *or* ĕshŏ'ltsĭa) *n.* Californian herbaceous plant of genus *E*~ of the poppy family, the best-known species being *E. californica*, Californian poppy, which has finely divided glaucous leaves and large bright-yellow flowers with saffron-coloured centre. [J. F. von *Eschscholtz* (1793–1831), Ger. botanist]

ĕ'scort *n.* Body of armed men acting as guard to persons, baggage, etc.; person(s) accompanying another on journey for protection or guidance, or for courtesy's sake; ship(s), aircraft, etc., so employed. **ėscor't** *v.t.* Act as escort to.

ēscrī'be *v.t.* (math.) Describe (circle) so as to touch one side of triangle exteriorly and the other two sides produced.

ĕscritoi're (-twar) *n.* Writing-desk with drawers etc.

ĕscu'dō (-ōōd-) *n.* (pl. -*s*). 1. Principal monetary unit of Portugal and Portuguese territories, = 100 centavos. 2. Principal monetary unit of Chile, = 100 condors.

ĕ'scūlent *adj.* & *n.* (Thing, esp. vegetable) suitable for food.

ėscŭ'tcheon (-chon) *n.* 1. Shield with armorial bearings. 2. Middle of ship's stern where name is placed. 3. Pivoted keyhole-cover.

E'sdras (ĕz-). 1. Name of two of the books of the Apocrypha; the first is mainly a compilation from Chronicles, Nehemiah, and Ezra, and the second is a record of angelic revelations. 2. (in Vulgate) Books of EZRA and NEHEMIAH.

E.S.E. *abbrev.* East-south-east.

ĕ'skar, -er *n.* (geol.) Long narrow ridge of gravel formed in a tunnel-like channel on, in, or under a glacier.

E'skĭmō, E'squimau (ĕskĭmō) *n.* (pl. *-mo, -mau*, pr. -mō, *-mo(e)s, maux*, pr. -mōz). Member of a N. Amer. people inhabiting Arctic coasts from Greenland to Alaska; their language; ~ *dog*, breed of powerful dog with long usu. greyish hair, used by the Eskimos to draw sledges and for hunting.

E.S.N. *abbrev.* Educationally subnormal.

Esop: see AESOP.

ĕsotĕ'rĭc *adj.* (of philosophical doctrine etc.) Meant for, intelligible to, the initiated only; (of disciples) initiated; private, confidential. **ĕsotĕ'rĭcallȳ** *adv.*

E.S.P. *abbrev.* Extrasensory perception.

ĕ'spădrille *n.* Rope-soled canvas shoe.

ėspă'lier *n.* Framework on which fruit-trees or ornamental shrubs are trained; tree so trained.

ėspar'tō *n.* (also ~ *grass*) Kind of grass, *Stipa tenocissima*, of Spain and N. Africa, used as an ingredient of thick or absorbent paper.

ėspĕ'cial (-shal) *adj.* Pre-eminent, exceptional; particular; belonging chiefly to one case. **ėspĕ'ciallȳ** *adv.*

Esperă'ntō (ĕ-) *n.* & *adj.* (Of) an artificial language invented (*c* 1887) for universal use by a Polish physician, Dr. Ludovik Lazarus Zamenhof, with vocabulary consisting of roots common to the chief European languages with endings normalized. **Esperă'ntist** *n.* [pen-name (= 'hoping-one') of its inventor, f. L *spero* hope]

ėspī'al *n.* Acting as a spy; watching; espying.

ĕspĭona'ġe (-ahzh; *or* ĕ'spĭonĭj) *n.* Practice of spying or using spies.

ĕsplanā'de *n.* Level piece of ground, esp. one used for public promenade; level space separating citadel of fortress from town.

ėspou'se (-z) *v.t.* 1. (usu. of man) Marry; give (woman) in marriage (*to*). 2. Adopt, support (cause, opinion, etc.). **ėspou'sal** *n.*

ėsprĕ'ssō *n.* Coffee made under steam pressure; device for making this; coffee-bar where it is sold.

ĕsprit (-rē) *n.* Sprightliness, wit; ~ *de corps* (kor), regard for the honour and interests of body one belongs to; ~ *fort* (for), strong-minded person; free-thinker. [Fr.]

ėspȳ' *v.t.* Catch sight of; descry, discern; detect.

Esq. *abbrev.* Esquire.

Esquimau: see ESKIMO.

ėsquīr'e *n.* 1. (hist., archaic) Young man of gentle birth attending on knight; squire. 2. Man belonging to higher order of English gentry, ranking immediately below knight. 3. Courtesy title appended to a man's name in formal use and (abbrev. Esq.) in addressing letters etc. where no prefixed title is used. [L *scutarius* shield-bearer]

ĕss *n.* Letter S, s; S-shaped thing; *collar of esses*, formerly badge of House of Lancaster, still part of some officials' costume.

ĕ'ssay *n.* 1. Attempt (*at*). 2. Literary composition of moderate length (usu. in prose) on any subject. **ĕssay'** *v.* Try, test (person, thing); attempt. **ĕ'ssayist** *n.* Writer of essays.

ĕ'ssė *n.* 1. *in* ~, in actual existence (opp. *in posse*, in potentiality). 2. Essential being or nature. [L *esse* to be]

ĕ'ssence *n.* 1. An existence, entity (now usu. spiritual or immaterial). 2. Absolute being, reality underlying phenomena; that by which anything subsists, foundation of being. 3. All that makes a thing what it is; totality of properties etc. without which it would cease to be the same thing; objective character, intrinsic nature as a thing in itself; (loosely) most important indispensable quality or constituent element of anything. 4. Extract obtained by distillation etc. from plant, medicinal, odoriferous, or nutritious substance, etc.; alcoholic solution containing volatile elements to which perfume, flavour, etc., are due; perfume.

E'ssēne (ĕ-; or ĕsē'n) *n.* Member of an ascetic Jewish sect of 2nd c. B.C. to 2nd c. A.D. who held property and took meals in common and conformed to rigid rules of purification.

ėssĕ'ntial (-sh*a*l) *adj.* 1. Of, constituting, a thing's essence; that is such in essence; indispensable, necessarily implied; absolutely necessary. 2. That is or is like, an essence or extract; ~ *oil*, volatile oil obtained by distillation and marked by characteristic odour etc. of substance from which it is extracted. ~ *n.* Indispensable element. **ėssĕntĭă'lĭtў** (-nshĭ-) *n.* **ėssĕ'ntiallў** *adv.*

E'ssėx (ĕ-). County of E. England; university, at Colchester, 1964.

ėstă'blĭsh *v.t.* Set up on permanent basis; settle; secure permanent acceptance for; place beyond dispute; place (Church) in position of national or State Church.

ėstă'blĭshment *n.* Establishing; Church system established by law, established Church; organized body of men maintained for a purpose, as army, navy, Civil Service; staff of servants, etc.; public institution, house of business; household; *the E~*, those with (official or unofficial) authority or influence, regarded as having joint interest in resisting change; ~ *officer*, in Civil Service etc., one responsible for staffing. **ėstăblĭshmentār'ĭan** *adj.* & *n.* (Person) adhering to, advocating principle of, an established Church.

estăminet (-ēnā) *n.* Unpretentious French café or cottage selling wine, beer, etc. [Fr.]

ėstā'te *n.* 1. (chiefly archaic) State, condition; worldly standing, fortune, etc.; status, degree of rank; *man's, woman's*, ~, manhood womanhood. 2. Order, class, as part of body politic and as sharing directly or indirectly in government; (*three*) *estates of the realm*, (in England) lords spiritual, lords temporal, and commons; (erron.) crown, House of Lords, and House of Commons; *third* ~, English commons; (transl. Fr. *tiers état*), French bourgeoisie before the Revolution; *fourth* ~, (joc.) the press. 3. (law) Person's interest in lands, tenements, etc.; *real* ~, interest in landed property; ~ *duty*, graduated duty payable on net value of assets left by deceased person. 4. Landed property (usu. of considerable extent); HOUSING estate; ~ *agent*, steward or manager of landed estate; one whose business is the sale or letting of houses and land; ~ *car*, motor-car constructed or adapted to carry both passengers and goods. 5. Person's collective assets and liabilities.

ėstee'm *v.t.* Think highly of; consider. ~ *n.* Favourable opinion, regard, respect.

ĕ'ster *n.* Any of a class of organic compounds formed by the interaction of an acid and an alcohol with the elimination of water, used as solvents, flavouring essences, etc., and in many chemical processes.

Esther (ĕ'st*e*r). Jewess who was chosen on account of her beauty by King AHASUERAS to be queen in place of Vashti; book of O.T. containing account of this, with further material (*The Rest of E* ~) in the Apocrypha.

ĕ'stĭmable *adj.* Worthy of esteem.

ĕ'stĭmate *n.* Approximate judgement (of number, amount, etc.); quantity assigned by this; contractor's statement of sum for which he will undertake specified work; judgement of character or qualities; *the Estimates*, accounts presented annually to Parliament showing probable amount of administrative departments' expenditure for current year. **ĕ'stĭmāte** *v.t.* Form estimate of; fix by estimate *at* (so much); form an opinion of. **ĕ'stĭmātor** *n.* **ĕ'stĭmative** *adj.*

ėstĭmā'tion *n.* Judgement of

worth; opinion, judgement; esteem.

estival etc.: see AESTIVAL etc.

ėstoi'le *n.* (her.) Charge in form of star with wavy points or rays.

Estō'nĭa (ĕ-). Country on S. coast of Gulf of Finland, formerly part of the Russian Empire; proclaimed an independent republic 1918; incorporated in the Soviet Union 1940 as a constituent republic; capital, Tallinn. **Estō'nĭan** *adj.* & *n.* (Native, inhabitant, language) of Estonia.

ėstŏ'p *v.t.* (law) Stop, bar, hinder; (refl. & pass.) be precluded by one's own previous act or declaration *from* doing etc. **ėstŏ'ppel** *n.* Being estopped.

ėstra'de (-ahd) *n.* Raised platform, dais.

ėstrā'nge (-j) *v.t.* Alienate (person) in feeling (*from* another). **ėstrā'ngement** *n.*

ėstrea't *n.* (law) Copy of court record esp. of fine; enforcement, forfeiture, of fine or recognizance. ~ *v.t.* Make an estreat of (fine etc.) for prosecution.

ĕ'stūarȳ *n.* Tidal mouth of large river. **ĕ'stūarīne** *adj.*

e.s.u. *abbrev.* Electrostatic unit.

ėsūr'ient *adj.* (joc.) Hungry; impecunious and greedy. **ėsūr'ĭence, ėsūr'ĭencȳ** *ns.*

ē'ta *n.* 8th (later 7th) letter of Greek alphabet (H, η), corresponding to *e* (pr. ē, ā).

et al. *abbrev.* *Et alia* (L, = 'and other things').

ĕt cĕ'tera, ėtcĕ'tera (abbrev. *etc.*, *&c.*). And the rest, and so on. **ėtcĕ'teras** (-z) *n.pl.* Extras, sundries. [L]

ĕtch *v.* Portray by drawing with an *etching-needle* on a metal plate previously coated with a wax-and-resin mixture (the *ground*) and immersing in acid which corrodes the parts laid bare by the needle; make (print) from plate thus prepared; copy (picture) by this process; practice this craft. **ĕ'tcher** *n.* **ĕ'tchĭng** *n.* Print made from an etched plate; art, process, of etching; *dry-point* ~: see DRY *adj.*; *soft-ground* ~, (print made by) similar process in which the plate is coated with a soft sticky wax mixture and the drawing done with a pencil on thin paper laid over it so that the wax adheres along the lines and comes away when the paper is removed.

ėtėr'nal *adj.* Without beginning or end, that always (has existed and always) will exist; (colloq.) incessant, too frequent; *E~ City*, Rome; ~ *triangle*, (emotional relationships in) group of two women and a man or two men and a woman. **ėtėr'nīze, -alīze** *vbs.t.* **ėtėr'nallȳ** *adv.*

ėtėr'nĭtȳ *n.* Being eternal; infinite (esp. future) time; the future life; tediously long time.

Etesian (ĭtē'zhan) *adj.* ~ *wind*, strong dry northerly wind blowing in the Mediterranean region in summer.

ĕ'thāne *n.* Colourless odourless gas (C_2H_6 of the paraffin series of hydrocarbons) occurring in gas from petroleum deposits.

ĕ'thanol *n.* = ETHYL alcohol.

E'thelrĕd (ĕ-) (*c* 968–1016), 'the Unready' (= 'without counsel'). King of the English 979–1016; son of Edgar and father of Edward the Confessor.

ē'ther *n.* 1. Clear sky, upper regions of space beyond clouds; (hist.) element conceived as filling all space beyond sphere of moon. 2. Hypothetical substance of great elasticity and subtlety formerly postulated by the wave-theory of light as permeating the whole of space, esp. as medium of propagation of radio waves etc. 3. (chem.) Colourless volatile liquid ($C_2H_5.O.C_2H_5$), with a characteristic aromatic odour, obtained by distillation of alcohol with sulphuric acid and used as a solvent for the extraction of oils, fats, waxes, etc., and as an anaesthetic; any of a large class of compounds of similar composition. **ēthĕ'rĭc** *adj.*

ėthēr'ėal, -ĭal *adj.* 1. Light, airy; heavenly; of unearthly delicacy of substance, character, or appearance. 2. Of, like, ether. **ėthērėă'lĭtȳ** *n.* **ėthēr'ėalīze** *v.t.* **ėthēr'ėallȳ** *adv.*

ĕ'thĭc, -ĭcal *adjs.* 1. (usu. *-al*) Relating to, treating of, morals or ethics; (esp. U.S.) moral, honourable; (of drug etc.) available only on doctor's prescription. 2. ~ *dative*, (gram.) dative expressing an indirect interest (as in 'write *me* a letter to him'). **ĕ'thĭcallȳ** *adv.* **ĕ'thĭcs** *n.* 1. (as sing.) Science of morals, study of principles of human duty; treatise on this. 2. (as pl.) Moral principles; rules of conduct.

Ethĭō'pĭa (ē-). In ancient usage, a region on the upper Nile; in modern usage, an inland kingdom of NE. Africa south-west of Red Sea and Gulf of Aden; capital, Addis Ababa. The country was converted to Christianity by Syrian missionaries in 4th c., but later cut off from European influences by Muslim dominion in N. Africa; rediscovered by Portuguese in 16th c.; King Menelik II halted Italian inroads in the battle of Adowa, 1896, and concluded a treaty at his new capital, Addis Ababa; the Italians invaded and annexed the country in 1935, but were driven out by British and Imperial troops in 1941 and the emperor Haile Selassie I was reinstated. **Ethĭō'pĭan** *adj.* Of, pertaining to, Ethiopia. ~ *n.* Native, inhabitant, of Ethiopia; (hist.) African.

Ethĭŏ'pĭc (ē-) *adj.* & *n.* (Of) an ancient Semitic language (Ge'ez) introduced into Ethiopia by invaders from Arabia and surviving in the liturgical language of the Christian Church of Ethiopia.

ĕ'thnĭc, ĕ'thnĭcal *adjs.* Pertaining to race; ethnological. **ĕ'thnĭcallȳ** *adv.*

ĕthnŏ'graphȳ *n.* Scientific description of races of men. **ĕthnŏ'grapher** *n.* **ĕthnogră'phĭc, -ĭcal** *adjs.* **ĕthnogră'phĭcallȳ** *adv.*

ĕthnŏ'logȳ *n.* Science of races and peoples, their relations to one another, distinctive physical and other characteristics, etc. **ĕthnolŏ'gĭcal** *adj.* **ĕthnolŏ'gĭcallȳ** *adv* **ĕthnŏ'logĭst** *n.*

ēthŏ'logȳ *n.* Study of animal behaviour. **ētholŏ'gĭcal** *adj.* **ēthŏ'logĭst** *n.*

ē'thŏs *n.* Characteristic spirit of community, people, or system.

ĕ'thȳl (*or* ē'thīl) *n.* 1. (chem.) Alkyl radical having two carbon atoms (C_2H_5). 2. (usu. ~ *fluid*) Lead tetra-ethyl, $Pb(C_2H_5)_4$, one of the substances added to motor fuels to increase their anti-knock rating. 3. ~ *alcohol*, ordinary alcohol or *ethanol* (C_2H_5OH), an inflammable volatile liquid produced by the fermentation of sugars by yeast, used as a fuel, as a solvent, and in the chemical industry; ~ *chloride*, volatile liquid (C_2H_5Cl), with ethereal odour, used in medicine as anaesthetic.

ĕ'thȳlene *n.* First member of olefine series of hydrocarbons (C_2H_4), an inflammable gas with a faint sweet smell; ~ *glycol*, colourless slightly viscous liquid obtained by treating ethylene with a solution of potassium permanganate, used as anti-freeze in motor engines, for de-icing aircraft, etc.

ē'tĭolāte *v.t.* Render (plant etc.) pale and colourless by excluding light, blanch; give pale and sickly hue to. **ētĭolā'tion** *n.*

etiology: see AETIOLOGY.

ĕ'tĭquette (-kĕt) *n.* Conventional rules of personal behaviour in polite society; ceremonial of court; unwritten code restricting professional men in what concerns interests of their brethren or dignity of their profession.

E'tna[1] (ĕ-). Active volcano in Sicily.

ĕ'tna[2] *n.* (formerly) Vessel, in form of inverted cone in saucer, for heating small quantity of liquid by burning spirit. [f. ETNA[1]]

E'ton (ē-). Short for ~ *College*, public school near Windsor, Berks., founded 1440 by Henry VI to prepare scholars for King's College, Cambridge; ~ *blue*, light blue; ~ *collar*, broad stiff white collar worn outside jacket; ~ *crop*, cutting of woman's hair short all over; ~ *jacket*, short black jacket (formerly worn by younger boys at Eton) reaching only to waist and worn open in front; ~ *suit*, (formerly) suit of Eton jacket with black or striped trousers and black waistcoat. **Etō'nĭan** *adj.* & *n.* Of (one educated at) Eton College.

Etrŭ'scan (ĭ-) *adj.* & *n.* (Member, language) of the earliest historical inhabitants of Etruria, an ancient country between the Arno and Tiber rivers (approximately modern Tuscany), who there developed a system of powerful city states and a flourishing civilization.

et seq., et seqq., et sq., et sqq. *abbrevs. Et sequentia* (L, = 'and what follows').

E.T.U. *abbrev.* Electrical Trades Union.

étūde (ā'-) *n.* Short musical composition or exercise.

étui' (ĕtwē) *n.* Small case for needles, bodkins, etc.

ĕtymŏ'logīze *v.* Give, trace, etymology of; suggest etymology for; study etymology.

ĕtўmŏ'logў *n.* Account of, facts relating to, formation and meaning of words; branch of linguistic science concerned with this; part of grammar treating of individual words and their formation and inflexions. **ĕtўmolŏ'gĭcal** *adj.* **ĕtўmolŏ'gĭcallў** *adv.* **ĕtўmŏ'logĭst** *n.*

ĕ'tўmŏn *n.* Primary word which gives rise to derivative.

eu- *prefix.* Well.

eucalў'ptus, eu'calўpt *n.* Plant of genus *E~* including gum-tree of Australia and the neighbouring islands; (pop.) = ~ *oil*, essential oil obtained from the leaves of a species of eucalyptus with strong characteristic odour, used in treatment of respiratory diseases. [Gk *eu kaluptos* well covered, the flower before it opens being protected by a cap]

Eu'charist (-k-) *n.* Central Christian sacrament of body and blood of Christ, in which bread and wine are partaken of; consecrated elements, esp. bread. **Euchari'stic** *adj.* ~ *Congress*, international meeting of Roman Catholics, instituted 1908 and held annually in honour of the Blessed Sacrament. **Euchari'stical** *adj.* [Gk *eukharistia* thanksgiving (*kharizomai* offer willingly)]

eu'chre (-k*er*) *n.* American card-game for 2, 3, or 4 persons, played with pack of 32 cards (the 2, 3, 4, 5, 6, of each suit being rejected), in which, if a player fails to take three tricks, he or his side is said to be 'euchred', and the other side gains two points. ~ *v.t.* Gain advantage over (opponent) by his failure to take three tricks; (fig.) outwit.

Eu'clĭd (*c* 300 B.C.). Mathematician of Alexandria, author of a treatise on geometry (the *Elements*). **Euclĭ'dėan** *adj.* Of Euclid; ~ *geometry*, geometry based on his postulates; ~ *space*, kind of space for which his postulates are valid (in which, e.g. a straight line may be produced to infinity; cf. RELATIVITY).

eudae'monĭsm, eudē-, *n.* System of ethics basing moral obligation on tendency of actions to produce happiness.

eudĭŏ'mėter *n.* Graduated glass tube in which a mixture of an inflammable gas with air or oxygen may be exploded by means of a spark and the volume change measured.

Eugē'ne, Prince (1663–1736). Austrian general; associated with Marlborough in the War of the Spanish Succession.

eugĕ'nĭc *adj.* Of, adapted to, production of fine (esp. human) offspring. **eugĕ'nĭcs** *n.* Study having this for its object. **eu'gėnĭst** *n.*

eu'logīze *v.t.* Extol, praise. **eu'logĭst** *n.* **eulogĭ'stĭc** *adj.* **eulogĭ'stĭcallў** *adv.*

eu'logў *n.* Speech, writing, in commendation or praise.

Eumĕ'nĭdēs (-z). (Gk myth.) (Euphemistic name for) the Furies. [Gk, = 'gracious ones']

eu'nuch (-*u*k) *n.* Castrated male person, esp. one employed in harem or (in Oriental courts and under Roman Empire) in affairs of State. **eu'nuchĭsm** *n.*

euŏ'nўmus *n.* Shrub of genus *E~* of which many species are cultivated as ornamental plants. [Gk *euonumos* well-named, lucky (*onoma* name)]

eu'păd *n.* Dry mixture of calcium hypochlorite and boric acid used as dry dressing for wounds or mixed with water to form *eusol.* [f. *E*dinburgh *U*niversity *Pa*thological *D*epartment, where first prepared]

eupĕ'ptĭc *adj.* Of, having, resulting from, good digestion.

eu'phėmĭsm *n.* Substitution of mild or vague expression for harsher or more offensive one; expression thus substituted. **euphėmĭ'stĭc** *adj.* **euphėmĭ'stĭcallȳ** *adv.* **eu'phėmīze** *v.*

euphō'nĭum *n.* Tenor tuba, used esp. in brass bands.

eu'phonȳ *n.* Pleasing sound; quality of having this. **euphŏ'nĭc, euphō'nĭous** *adjs.* **euphŏ'nĭcally, euphō'nĭouslȳ** *advs.*

euphôr'ĭa *n.* Sense of well-being. **euphŏ'rĭc** *adj.*

eu'phrasȳ *n.* Eyebright.

Euphrā'tēs (-z). River of SW. Asia, flowing through E. Turkey and Iraq to join the Tigris and thence to the Persian Gulf.

Euphrŏ'sȳnė (-z-). (Gk myth.) One of the Graces.

eu'phūĭsm *n.* Diction and style like that of John Lyly, characterized by alliterative antithetic clauses, long strings of similes, and a constant endeavour after refinement of expression; (loosely) affectedly periphrastic or high-flown style or language. **eu'phūĭst** *n.* **euphūĭ'stĭc, -ĭcal** *adjs.* [f. *Euphues* (Gk, = 'well-endowed'), chief character in two of Lyly's works]

Eurasian (ūrā'sh*a*n) *adj.* Of mixed European and Asian parentage; of Europe and Asia. ~ *n.* Eurasian person.

eurē'ka (ūr-) *int.* & *n.* Exclamation of exultation, 'I have found it!'. [Gk *heuréka* (*heuriskein* find) uttered by Archimedes when he discovered means of determining (by specific gravity) the proportion of base metal in Hiero's golden crown]

eurhȳ'thmĭc (ūrĭth-) *adj.* 1. In or of harmonious proportion (esp. in architecture). 2. Of eurhythmics. **eurhȳ'thmĭcs** *n.* (as sing. or pl.) System (founded by Swiss composer Émile Jaques-Dalcroze, 1865–1950) of expressing musical rhythm in bodily movement.

Eurĭ'pĭdēs (ūr-, -z) (*c* 485–*c* 406 B.C.). Greek tragedian; author of 'Alcestis', 'Medea', 'The Trojan Women', etc.

Eurō'pa (ūr-). (Gk myth.) Daughter of Agenor, king of Phoenicia; was wooed by Zeus, who took the form of a beautiful bull.

Europe (ūr'*o*p). Continent of N. hemisphere, western part of the land-mass of the Old World, bordering on the Atlantic Ocean; *Council of* ~, organization founded in 1949 to promote unity and social and economic exchange among its members and to protect their heritage; the members are Austria, Belgium, Cyprus, Denmark, France, the Federal Republic of Germany, Iceland, the Republic of Ireland, Italy, Luxemburg, Malta, the Netherlands, Norway, Sweden, Switzerland, Turkey, and the United Kingdom.

Europē'an (ūr-) *adj.* Of Europe or its people; ~ *Economic Community*, economic association established in 1957, consisting of Belgium, France, Italy, Luxemburg, the Netherlands, the Federal Republic of Germany, and (1973) Denmark, the Republic of Ireland, and the United Kingdom; ~ *Free Trade Association*, association established in 1960 by Austria, Denmark, Norway, Portugal, Sweden, Switzerland, and the United Kingdom, with the object of eliminating tariffs on imports between members. ~ *n.* European person. **Europē'anīze** *v.t.* **Europē'anĭsm** *n.*

eurō'pĭum (ūr-) *n.* (chem.) Rare-earth element; symbol Eu, at. no. 63, at. wt 151·96. [f. Europe]

Eur'ovĭsion (ūr-) *n.* Television of European range.

Eur'us (ūr-). (Gk & Rom. myth.) God of E. or SE. wind; hence, this wind.

Eurȳ'dĭcē (ūr-). (Gk myth.) Wife of Orpheus.

Eusē'bĭus (*c* 260–*c* 340). Bishop of Caesarea in Palestine; historian and theologian; his 'History of the Christian Church' earned him the title of 'Father of Church History'. **Eusē'bĭan** *adj.*

eu'sŏl *n.*: see EUPAD. [initials of *E*dinburgh *U*niversity + *sol*(ution)]

Eustā'chĭus (-k-), Bartolommeo (d. 1574). Italian anatomist. **Eustā'chĭan** (-sh-) *adj.* ~ *tube*, passage communicating between the middle ear (tympanic cavity) and the back of the throat (larynx), and serving to equalize air-pressure on both sides of the ear-drum.

eutĕ'ctĭc *adj.* & *n.* (Of) a mixture whose constituents are in such proportions as to melt and solidify at one temperature like a pure substance.

Eutêr'pė. (Gk & Rom. myth.) Muse of music and lyric poetry.

euthanā'sĭa (-z-) *n.* Gentle and easy death; bringing about of this, esp. in case of incurable and painful disease.

euthēr'ĭan *adj.* & *n.* (Member) of the Eutheria, the largest subclass of mammals, comprising those whose young are nourished through an efficient placenta and are born at a relatively late stage.

Eu'tȳches (-kēz) (*c* 378–454). Heresiarch of Constantinople who held that the human nature of Christ was lost in the divine. **Eutȳ'chĭan** *adj.* **Eutȳ'chĭanism** *n.*

ėvă'cūant *adj.* & *n.* (Agent) causing evacuation esp. of stomach, bowels, etc.

ėvă'cūāte *v.t.* 1. Empty (esp. stomach or other bodily organ *of* contents); discharge excrement etc. 2. Withdraw troops, inhabitants, from (place); remove (person) esp. from a place considered dangerous. **ėvăcūā'tion** *n.*

ėvăcūee' *n.* Person evacuated from place of danger etc.

ėvā'de *v.t.* Escape from, avoid (attack, pursuit, etc.); avoid doing (duty etc.), answering (question), yielding to (argument etc.); defeat intention of (law etc. esp. while complying with its letter); elude.

ėvă'gĭnāte *v.t.* (physiol.) Turn (tubular organ) inside out. **ėvăgĭnā'tion** *n.*

ėvă'lūāte *v.t.* Ascertain amount or value of; find numerical expression for. **ėvălūā'tion** *n.*

ĕvanĕ'sce *v.i.* Fade out of sight; become effaced; disappear.

ĕvanĕ'scent *adj.* Quickly fading or vanishing away; (math., of diminishing quantity) infinitesimal. **ĕvanĕ'scence** *n.* **ĕvanĕ'scentlȳ** *adv.*

ėvă'ngel (-j-) *n.* (archaic) The gospel; one of the four Gospels. [Gk *euaggelion* (reward for bringing) good news]

ēvăngĕ'lĭc (-j-) *adj.* Of, according to, the teaching of the gospel or the Christian religion. **ēvăngĕ'lĭcal** *adj.* Evangelic; Protestant, Lutheran; (esp.) of the school of Protestants maintaining that the essence of the gospel consists in the doctrine of salvation by faith, and denying that either sacraments or good works have any saving efficacy. ~ *n.* Member of evangelical school. **ēvăngĕ'lĭcalism** *n.* **ēvăngĕ'lĭcallȳ** *adv.*

ėvă'ngelism (-j-) *n.* Preaching or promulgation of the gospel.

ėvă'ngelĭst (-j-) *n.* 1. One of the writers of the four Gospels. 2. Preacher of the gospel; now usu., layman doing home missionary work. **ėvăngelĭ'stĭc** *adj.*

ėvă'ngelīze (-j-) *v.t.* Preach gospel to, win over to Christian faith. **ėvăngelīzā'tion** *n.*

ėvă'porāte *v.* Turn from solid or liquid into vapour; pass away like vapour; remove liquid part of by heating or drying; lose liquid by evaporation; *evaporated milk*, thick unsweetened tinned milk prepared by evaporation. **ėvăporā'tion** *n.* **ėvă'porātor** *n.* (esp.) Apparatus for evaporating or drying something.

ėvā'sion *n.* Act, means, of evading; subterfuge. **ėvā'sĭve** *adj.* Seeking to evade, addicted to evasion; tending to evasion. **ėvā'sĭvelȳ** *adv.* **ėvā'sĭveness** *n.*

ēve[1] *n.* 1. (poet. & archaic) Evening. 2. Evening or day before saint's day or other Church festival, or before any date or event; time immediately preceding.

Eve[2] (ēv). Name given by Adam to his wife (Gen. 3: 20), the first woman.

ėvĕ'ction *n.* Irregularity in moon's orbit due to attraction of sun.

E'velŷn (ēvl-), John (1620–1706). English diarist.

ē'ven[1] *n.* (poet. & archaic) Evening; *E'vensong*, evening service in Church of England; *e'ventide*, (archaic) evening.

ē'ven[2] *adj.* 1. Level; smooth; uniform in quality; in same plane or line *with*. 2. Equally balanced, impartial; equal in number or amount; *get* ~ (*with*), take one's revenge (on). 3. (of temper etc.) Equable, unruffled. 4. (of numbers) Integrally divisible by two; (of sums of money etc.) expressible in integers, tens, etc. (opp. ODD); ~ *money*, equal stakes in betting. ~ *v.t.* Make even. **ē'venlŷ** *adv.* **ē'vennėss** *n.*

ē'ven[3] *adv.* Inviting comparison of an assertion, negation, etc., with a less strong one that might have been made, as *I never ~ opened the book* (much less read it), *does he ~ suspect* (not to say realize) *the danger?*, *she sings ~ better than he does* (though he sings very well), etc.; (archaic) exactly, just.

ĕ'vening (-vn-), *n.* Close of day, esp. time between sunset and bedtime; closing or declining period of life etc.; ~ *dress*: see DRESS; *E~ Prayer*, Evensong; ~ *primrose*: see PRIMROSE; ~ *star*, Venus (occas. also Jupiter or Mercury) when seen in the west after sunset.

ėvĕ'nt *n.* 1. (Actual or contemplated) fact of a thing's happening; thing that happens, esp. important thing. 2. Any of several possible mutually exclusive occurrences, one of which will happen under stated conditions; something on issue of which money is staked; one of the items in a programme of sports. 3. Result, outcome, issue; *in any ~, at all ~s*, in any case. **ėvĕ'ntful, ėvĕ'ntlėss** *adjs.*

ėvĕ'ntūal *adj.* That will happen in certain circumstances; ultimately resulting. **ėvĕ'ntūallŷ** *adv.* **ėvĕntūă'litŷ** *n.* Possible event.

ėvĕ'ntūāte *v.i.* Turn out; result (*in*); (chiefly U.S.) happen, come to pass.

ĕ'ver *adv.* 1. Always, at all times (archaic except in) ~ *after*, ~ *since*; (letter-ending) *yours* ~; *for* ~, for all future time, incessantly; ~ *and anon*, (archaic) now and then; *evermore*, always; ~-*ready case*, case from which camera can be used without extracting it. 2. (with negatives, or in interrogative, hypothetical, or conditional sentences) At any time; by any chance, at all. 3. Added for emphasis to *as* (*soon* etc.) *as*, *before*, etc., or following interrogative pronouns, adverbs, etc., to intimate that the speaker has no notion what the answer will be. 4. ~ *so*, (colloq.) very.

E'verėst (ĕ-). Highest known mountain of the world (29,028 ft), in the Himalayas on the frontier of Nepal and Tibet; first climbed 1953. [f. Sir George *Everest* (1790–1866), Surveyor-General of India]

ĕ'verglāde *n.* (U.S.) Marshy tract of land mostly under water and covered in places with tall grass, trees, etc.; usu. pl., (with cap.) large swampy region of Florida.

ĕ'vergreen *adj.* Always green or fresh; (of trees etc.) having green leaves all the year round and in some cases for several years (the leaves of one season remaining on the tree until those of the next are completely formed); ~ *oak*, holm oak, ilex, *Quercus ilex*. ~ *n.* Evergreen tree or shrub.

ĕverla'sting (-ah-) *adj.* Lasting for ever; lasting long; lasting too long, repeated too often; (of plants) keeping their shape and colour when dried. ~ *n.* 1. Eternity. 2. Everlasting flower.

ėvê̄r't *v.t.* (med. etc.) Turn inner surface of (eyelid etc.) outwards; turn inside out. **ėvê̄r'sible** *adj.* **ėvê̄r'sion** *n.*

every (ĕ'vrĭ) *adj.* 1. Each; all taken separately. 2. *e'verybody*, every person; *e'verybody else*, every other person; *everyday*, occurring daily, worn or used on ordinary days, commonplace; *every one*, each (*of*); *e'veryone* (also *every one*), everybody; *e'verything*, all things, thing of first importance; *e'veryway*, in every way, in every respect; *e'verywhere*, in every place.

E'verȳmăn (ĕvr-) Ordinary or typical person. [Name of leading character in 15th-c. morality play]

ėvĭ'ct *v.t.* 1. (law) Recover (property, title) *of, from*, by judicial process or in virtue of superior title. 2. Expel (person) by legal process; (esp.) eject (tenant) from his holding; eject (person) from any position. **ėvĭ'ction** *n.*

ĕ'vĭdence *n.* 1. Being evident, clearness; *in* ~, present; prominent, conspicuous. 2. Indication, mark, sign, (*of* something); ground for belief, testimony or facts tending to prove or disprove something. 3. Information (personal testimony, production of material objects, etc.) given in legal investigation to establish a fact or point in question; statements etc. admissible as testimony in court of law; *turn King's* (*Queen's*) ~, (of accomplice or sharer in crime) offer himself as witness for prosecution against other persons implicated. ~ *v.t.* Serve to indicate; attest. **ĕ'vĭdent** *adj.* Obvious to eyes or mind, clear, plain. **ĕ'vĭdentlȳ** *adv.* **ĕvĭdĕ'ntial** (-sh*a*l), **ĕvĭdĕ'ntiary** (-sharĭ) *adjs.* Of, based on, furnishing, evidence. **ĕvĭdĕ'ntiallȳ** *adv.*

ē'vĭl (*or* -vl) *adj.* Bad, harmful, wicked; boding ill; *the E~ One*, the Devil; ~ *eye*, malicious or envious look, superstitiously believed to do material harm; supposed faculty of inflicting injury by a look. ~ *n.* Evil thing; sin; harm, mischief. ~ *adv.* In evil manner. **ē'vĭllȳ** *adv.*

ėvĭ'nce *v.t.* Show, indicate (quality etc.); show that one has (quality).

ėvĭ'scerāte *v.t.* Disembowel; (fig.) empty of vital contents. **ėvĭscerā'tion** *n.*

ėvō'ke *v.t.* 1. Call up (spirit, feeling, memory, etc.). 2. Summon (cause) from inferior to superior court. **ēvocā'tion** *n.* **ėvŏ'catĭve, ėvŏ'catorȳ** *adjs.*

ĕ'volūte[1] *adj.* & *n.* (math.) (Curve) which is locus of centres of curvature of another curve (its *involute*), or the envelope of all its normals.

ē'volūte[2] (*or* -ōōt) *v.* (orig. & chiefly U.S., colloq.) Develop by evolution; evolve.

ĕvolū'tion (*or* -ōō-) *n.* 1. Opening out (of roll, bud, etc.; usu. fig.); appearance (of events etc.) in due succession. 2. Evolving, giving off (of gas, heat, etc.). 3. Development, detailed working out, of what is implicitly or potentially contained in an idea or principle; development from rudimentary to mature or complete state. 4. Origination of species of animals and plants by process of development from earlier forms. 5. (mil., naut.) Movement, change of position, of body of troops or number of ships. **ĕvolū'tional, ĕvolū'tionarȳ** *adjs.* **ĕvolū'tionĭsm** *n.* **ĕvolū'tionĭst** *n.* **ĕvolutionĭ'stĭc** *adj.*

ėvŏ'lve *v.* 1. Unfold, open out; set forth in due sequence; develop, deduce (theory, facts, etc.). 2. Produce, give off (heat etc.). 3. Develop by natural process from rudimentary to more highly organized condition; produce or modify by evolution.

ėvŭ'lsion *n.* Forcible extraction.

ewe (ū) *n.* Female sheep; ~ *lamb*, most cherished possession (see 2 Sam. 12).

ew'er *n.* Pitcher; large water-jug used in bedrooms.

ĕx *prep.* (of goods) Out of, sold from (*ship, warehouse*, etc.); ~-*directory*, not listed in telephone directory; ~ *dividend*, (of stocks etc.) not including next dividend (abbrev. *ex div., x.d.*).

ex- *prefix.* 1. (with verbs) Out of; thoroughly. 2. (with adjs.) Without, deprived of. 3. (with nouns) Former (as *ex-president*).

ĕxă'cerbāte *v.t.* Aggravate (pain, anger, etc.); irritate. **ĕxăcerbā'tion** *n.*

ėxă'ct[1] (ĭgz-) *adj.* Precise, rigorous; accurate, strictly correct; ~ *sciences*, those which admit of absolute precision in results. **ėxă'ctnėss, ėxă'ctĭtūde** *ns.*

ėxă'ct[2] (ĭgz-) *v.t.* Demand and enforce payment of (money etc.); insist upon (act, conduct); require urgently. **ėxă'ction** *n.* Exacting; thing etc. exacted; illegal or exorbitant demand. **ėxă'ctable, ėxă'ctĭng** *adjs.*

ėxă'ctlȳ (ĭgz-) *adv.* (esp., as answer or confirmation) Quite so, just as you say.

ėxa'ggerāte (ĭgzăj-) *v.t.* Magnify beyond limits of truth; intensify, aggravate; make (physical features etc.) of abnormal size. **ėxă'ggerātėdlȳ, ėxă'ggeratĭvelȳ** *advs.* **ėxăggerā'tion, ėxă'ggerātor** *ns.* **ėxă'ggeratĭve** *adj.*

ėxa'lt (ĭgzaw-) *v.t.* Raise, place high in rank, power, etc.; praise, extol; dignify, ennoble. **ĕxaltā'tion** *n.* Raising, lifting up; elation, rapturous emotion.

ėxă'm (ĭgz-) *n.* (colloq.) Examination.

ėxămĭnā'tion (ĭgz-) *n.* 1. Investigation by inspection or experiment, minute inspection; investigation. 2. Testing of knowledge or ability of pupils etc. by oral or written questions; ~-*paper*, paper of questions to be answered; candidate's written answers. 3. Formal interrogation, esp. of witness or accused person; statements or deposition thus obtained; ~ *in chief*, that made by party calling the witness. **ėxămĭnā'tional** *adj.*

ėxă'mĭne (ĭgz-) *v.* Investigate; scrutinize; test, esp. test knowledge or capacity of, by questions; interrogate formally, esp. witness or accused person in court of law; inquire *into*. **ėxămĭnee', ėxă'mĭner** *ns.*

ėxa'mple (ĭgzah-) *n.* 1. Typical instance, fact, thing, person, illustrating or forming particular case of general principle, rule, state of things, etc.; specimen of workmanship etc. 2. Warning to others. 3. Precedent. 4. Action or conduct as object of imitation.

ĕ'xarch (-k) *n.* 1. Governor of province in Byzantine Empire. 2. Bishop ranking between patriarch and metropolitan; occas., patriarch, metropolitan. 3. Primate of autocephalous Orthodox Church (e.g. of Bulgaria, of Cyrus).
ĕ'xarchate *n.* Office, province, of exarch.

ėxă'sperāte (ĭgz-; *or* -ahs-) *v.t.* Make worse (ill feeling, disease, pain); irritate; provoke (person). **ėxă'sperā'tion** *n.*

exc. *abbrev.* Except; *excudit* (L, = engraved this).

Excă'lĭbur. (Arthurian legend) Name of King ARTHUR's magic

sword, which he drew easily from a rock where it was held fast, and which was returned on death to the Lady of the Lake.

ĕx cathē'dra (*or* kă'thĭ-). Authoritative(ly), official(ly); *speak* ~, (of the pope) pronounce an infallible judgement on matter of faith or morals. [L, = 'from the (teacher's) chair']

ĕ'xcavāte *v.t.* Make hollow; make (hole etc.) by digging; dig out (soil) leaving a hole; unearth, get out, uncover, by digging. **ĕxcavā'tion** *n.*

ĕ'xcavātor *n.* 1. Person engaged in excavation. 2. Machine used for excavating.

ėxcee'd *v.* Do more than is warranted by (one's commission, rights, etc.); be greater than (quantity, thing, *by* so much); surpass; be pre-eminent; be immoderate in eating etc.; exaggerate. **ėxcee'ding** *adj.* & (archaic) *adv.* **ėxcee'dingly̆** *adv.*

ėxcĕ'l *v.* Surpass; be pre-eminent.

ĕ'xcellence *n.* Surpassing merit; thing in which person etc. excels.

ĕ'xcellency̆ *n.* Title of ambassadors, ministers plenipotentiary, governors and their wives, and some other high officers.

ĕ'xcellent *adj.* Pre-eminent; very good. **ĕ'xcellently̆** *adv.*

ėxcĕ'lsĭor *adj.* Latin motto ('higher') on seal of State of New York, adopted 1778 (it is not clear whether as a blunder for 'upwards' or whether as abbrev. of some grammatically admissible phrase). ~ quasi-*int.* implying aspiration towards high attainment, as in Longfellow's poem 'Excelsior' (1841). ~ *n.* (U.S.) Short thin shavings of soft wood for stuffing, packing, etc.

ėxcĕ'pt[1] *v.* 1. Exclude (thing) from enumeration, statement, etc. 2. Make objection *against*. **excĕ'ptĭve** *adj.*

ėxcĕ'pt[2], **ėxcĕ'ptĭng** *prep.* & *conj.* Not including; but, save, with the exception of; (archaic) unless.

ėxcĕ'ption *n.* Excepting; thing excepted, thing that does not follow the rule; (law) objection to ruling of court; *the ~ proves the rule*, the excepting of some cases shows that the rule exists, or that it applies to those not excepted; *take ~*, object *to*.

ėxcĕ'ptionable *adj.* Open to objection.

ėxcĕ'ptional *adj.* Forming an exception; unusual. **ėxcĕptionă'lĭty̆** *n.* **ėxcĕ'ptionally̆** *adv.*

ĕ'xcerpt (*or* ĭksẽr'-) *n.* Extract from book etc. **ėxcẽr'pt** *v.t.* Extract, quote, (passage *from* book etc.) **ėxcẽr'ption** *n.*

ėxcĕ'ss *n.* 1. (usu. pl.) Outrage. 2. Overstepping limits of moderation; (esp.) intemperance in eating or drinking. 3. Fact of exceeding; amount by which one quantity exceeds another; exceeding of proper amount or degree; ~ *fare*, payment due for travelling on railway etc. farther or in higher class than ticket warrants; ~ *luggage*, luggage over the weight allowed for free carriage; ~ *profits tax*, (abbrev. E.P.T.) tax levied on business profits, orig. during war-time, in excess of average profits of a pre-war standard period. **ėxcĕ'ssĭve** *adj.* **ėxcĕ'ssĭvely̆** *adv.*

ėxchā'nge (-j) *v.* Give, receive, (thing) in place of (*for*) another; interchange (blows, words, glances, etc.); (of coin etc.) be received as equivalent *for*; pass (*from* one regiment or ship *into* another) by exchange with another officer. ~ *n.* 1. Act, process, of exchanging; exchanging of coin, notes, bank deposits, etc., for their equivalent in another country's money; (also *rate, course, of* ~) price at which another country's money may be bought; difference between this and par. 2. Building where merchants, stockbrokers, etc., assemble to transact business. 3. (also *telephone* ~) Centre to which local telephone lines are connected and through which communication between subscribers is effected.

ėxchā'ngeable (-jabl) *adj.* That may be exchanged (*for*); ~ *value*, value estimated by that of goods for which thing may be exchanged. **ėxchāngeabĭ'lĭty̆** *n.*

ėxchĕ'quer (-ker) *n.* 1. Department of public service charged with receipt and custody of revenue. 2. Court of law dealing with matters of revenue etc. converted into division of High Court in 1873 and in 1881 merged in Queen's (King's) Bench Division. 3. Royal or national treasury; money of private person, society, etc. [Fr. *eschequier* f. med. L *scaccarium* chessboard, from use of table with chequered cloth for accounts]

ėxcī'se[1] (-z; *or* ĕ'-) *n.* Duty charged on home-produced goods during manufacture or before sale to home consumers; government office collecting this (now *Board of Customs and E~*); ~ *law*, (U.S.) licensing law; *exciseman*, (archaic) officer collecting excise duties and preventing infringement of excise laws.

ėxcī′se[2] (-z) *v.t.* Cut out or away (passage of book, limb, organ, etc.). **ėxcĭ′sion** *n.*

ėxcī′te *v.t.* Set in motion, stir up, rouse (feelings, faculties, etc.); provoke, bring about (action, active condition); promote activity of (bodily organs etc.) by stimulus; move (person) to strong emotion, stir up to eager tumultuous feeling; induce electric or magnetic activity in, set (electric current) in motion. **ėxcī′table** *adj.* (esp., of persons) Easily excited, unbalanced. **ėxcītabĭ′lĭtў** *n.* **ĕxcītā′tion** *n.* **ėxcī′tatĭve, ėxcī′tatorў** *adjs.* **ėxcī′tėdlў** *adv.* **ėxcī′tement** *n.*

ėxclai′m *v.* Cry out, esp. from pain, anger, delight, etc.; utter thus; ~ *against*, make outcry against, accuse loudly.

ĕxclamā′tion *n.* Exclaiming; words exclaimed; interjection; *note of* ~, *~-mark*, punctuation mark (!) used after exclamation. **ėxclă′matorў** *adj.*

ĕ′xclāve *n.* Portion of a country separated from it by foreign territory (of which it is an ENCLAVE).

ėxclu′de (-lōōd) *v.t.* Shut out (*from* place, society, privilege, etc.); prevent the occurrence of, make impossible; leave out, not include. **ėxclu′sion** *n.*

ėxclu′sĭve (-lōōs-) *adj.* 1. Shutting out; not admitting *of*; desirous of excluding others, (of social circle etc.) chary of admitting others, select; (of news, goods, etc.) not to be had, not published, elsewhere; (of terms etc.) excluding all but what is specified; employed, followed, to the exclusion of all else. 2. (quasi-*adv.*) ~ *of*, not including, not counting. **ėxclu′sĭvelў** *adv.* **ėxclu′sĭvenėss** *n.*

ėxcŏ′gĭtāte *v.t.* Think out, contrive. **ėxcŏgĭtā′tion** *n.* **ėxcŏ′gĭtatĭve** *adj.*

ĕxcommū′nĭcāte *v.t.* (eccles.) Cut off (person) from participation in sacrament, or from all communication with Church. **ĕxcommūnĭcā′tion, ĕxcommū′nĭcātor** *ns.* **ĕxcommū′nĭcatĭve, ĕxcommū′nĭcatorў** *adjs.*

ėxcor′ĭāte *v.t.* Remove part of skin of (person etc.) by abrasion etc.; strip, peel off (skin). **ėxcorĭā′tion** *n.*

ĕ′xcrėment *n.* Waste matter discharged from the body, esp. faeces. **ĕxcrėmĕ′ntal, ĕxcrėmĕntĭ′tious** (-sh*us*) *adjs.*

ėxcrĕ′scence *n.* Abnormal or morbid outgrowth on animal or vegetable body (also fig.).

ėxcrĕ′scent *adj.* Growing abnormally, redundant; (gram., of sound or letter) having no etymological value, but developed by influence of euphony.

ėxcrē′ta *n.pl.* Waste expelled from body, esp. faeces and urine.

ėxcrē′te *v.t.* (of animals, plants, etc.) Separate and expel (waste matters) from system. **ėxcrē′tion** *n.* **ėxcrē′tĭve, ėxcrē′torў** *adjs.*

ėxcru′cĭāte (-ōōshĭ-) *v.t.* Torment acutely (person's senses); torture mentally. **ėxcru′cĭātĭnglў** *adv.* **ėxcrucĭā′tion** *n.*

ĕ′xculpāte *v.t.* Free from blame; clear (*from* charge etc.). **ĕxculpā′tion** *n.* **ėxcŭ′lpatorў** *adj.*

ėxcur′sion *n.* 1. Journey or ramble from any place with intention of returning to it; pleasure-trip, esp. one taken by a number of persons; ~ *train*, train for persons making pleasure excursion, usu. at reduced rates. 2. Sortie, raid (obs. exc. in *alar(u)ms and ~s*). 3. (astron.) Deviation from regular path or course. **ėxcur′sionist** *n.* One who makes pleasure excursion.

ėxcur′sĭve *adj.* Desultory; erratic, digressive. **ėxcur′sĭvelў** *adv.* **ėxcur′sĭvenėss** *n.*

ėxcur′sus *n.* Detailed discussion of special point in book, usu. in appendix at end.

ėxcū′se (-z) *v.t.* 1. Attempt to clear (person) from blame without denying or justifying his imputed action; seek to remove or extenuate blame of (acknowledged fault); serve as excuse for. 2. Obtain exemption or release for, set free, (person) from task, duty, obligation. 3. Accept plea in exculpation of; admit apology for, overlook, condone; pardon faults of, regard indulgently; dispense with. 4. ~ *me*, used as apology for lack of ceremony, interruption, etc., or as polite way of disputing statement; ~ *oneself*, ask permission to leave. **ėxcū'sable, ėxcū'satory** *adjs.* **ėxcū'sablў** *adv.* **ėxcū'se** (-s) *n.* Apology offered, exculpation; ground of this; plea for release from duty etc.

ex div. *abbrev.* Ex dividend.

ĕ'xėăt *n.* Bishop's permission to priest to move to another diocese; (in schools etc.) permission for temporary absence. [L, = 'let (him) go out']

ĕ'xėcrable *adj.* Abominable. **ĕ'xėcrablў** *adv.*

ĕ'xėcrāte *v.* Express, feel, abhorrence for; utter curses. **ĕxėcrā'tion** *n.* **ĕ'xėcrātorў** *adj.*

ėxĕ'cūtant (ĭgz-) *n.* One who executes, performer (esp. of music).

ĕ'xėcūte *v.t.* 1. Carry (plan, command, law, will, judicial sentence) into effect; perform (action, operation, etc.); make (legal instrument) valid by signing, sealing, etc.; discharge (office, function). 2. Carry out design for (product of art or skill); perform (musical composition). 3. Inflict capital punishment on.

ĕxėcū'tion *n.* Executing; excellence in executing (esp. music); effective action (esp. of weapons); seizure of goods or person of debtor in default of payment; infliction of capital punishment. **ĕxėcū'tioner** *n.* One who carries out a capital sentence.

ėxĕ'cūtive (ĭgz-) *adj.* Pertaining to, having function of, executing; concerned with executing laws, decrees, and sentences; ~ *order*, (U.S.) President's order on administrative matter not requiring legislation; ~ *session*, (U.S.) private session of Senate to deal with executive business; hence, private meeting. ~ *n.* 1. Executive branch of government (cf. JUDICATURE, LEGISLATURE). 2. Person holding executive position in business etc.; executive official, esp. President of U.S., Governor of State, or mayor of city.

executor *n.* 1. (ĕ'ksĭ-) One who carries out or performs. 2. (ĭgzĕ'-) Person appointed by testator to execute his will; *literary* ~, person entrusted with papers and unpublished works of writer. **ėxĕcūtŏr'ial** *adj.* **ėxĕ'cūtorshĭp** *n.*

ėxĕ'cūtrĭx (ĭgz-) *n.* (pl. *-tricēs*). Female executor.

ĕxėgē'sĭs *n.* (pl. *-es*) Exposition, interpretation, esp. of Scripture. **ĕxėgĕ'tĭc, -ĭcal** *adjs.* **ĕxėgĕ'tĭcallў** *adv.*

ėxĕ'mplar (ĭgz-) *n.* Model, pattern; type (of a class); parallel instance.

ėxĕ'mplarў (ĭgz-) *adj.* Fit to be imitated; illustrative; (of penalty, damages) serving as a warning. **ėxĕ'mplarĭlў** *adv.* **ėxĕ'mplarĭnėss** *n.*

ėxĕ'mplĭfў (ĭgz-) *v.t.* 1. Illustrate by example; be example of. 2. Make official copy of; make attested copy of (legal document) under official seal.

ėxĕ'mpt (ĭgz-) *adj.* Freed *from* allegiance or liability to; ~ *from*, not liable, exposed, or subject to (danger, disease, charge, duty, etc.). ~ *n.* 1. Exempted person. 2. = EXON. ~ *v.t.* Grant to (person) immunity or freedom *from*. **ėxĕ'mption** *n.*

ĕxėquā'tur *n.* Official recognition by foreign government of country's consul or commercial agent; temporal sovereign's authorization of bishop under papal authority, or of publication of papal bulls. [L, = 'he may perform']

ĕ'xėquies (-kwĭz) *n.pl.* Funeral rites.

ĕ'xercīse (-z) *n.* 1. Employment (of organ, faculty, power, right); practice (of virtues, profession, functions, religious rites). 2. Exertion of muscles, limbs, etc., esp. for health's sake; (pl.) military drill, athletics, etc. 3. Bodily, mental, or spiritual training; task set for this purpose; academical declamation, dissertation, musical composition, etc., required for degree; composition etc. set to pupils at school; piece of music etc. designed to afford practice to learners. 4. Religious observance; public worship. 5. (U.S.) Ceremony on some special occasion. ~ *v.* Employ (faculty, right, etc.); train (person etc.); tax the powers of; perplex, worry; discharge (functions); take, give (horse etc.), exercise.

ėxer'gue (-g; *or* ĕ'gz-) *n.* Small space usu. on reverse of coin or medal for minor inscription, date, etc., below principal device; inscription there. **ėxer'gual** (-gal) *adj.*

ėxer't (ĭgz-) *v.t.* Exercise, bring to bear (quality, force, influence); ~ *oneself*, use efforts or endeavours, strive. **ėxer'tion** *n.* Exerting; vigorous action, effort.

E'xėter (ĕ-). City of Devon; university, 1955.

ĕ'xeŭnt. (stage direction) They (two or more actors) leave the stage; ~ *omnes*, all leave the stage. [L, = 'they go out']

ėxfō'liāte *v.i.* (of bones, skin, minerals, etc.) Come off in scales or layers; (of tree) throw off layers of bark. **ėxfōliā'tion** *n.*

ĕx grā'tia (-shĭa; *or* grah-). (Done) as a favour.

exhalā'tion (ĕksa-) *n.* Evaporation; expiration; what is exhaled.

ėxhā'le *v.* Give off, be given off, in vapour, evaporate; breathe out.

ėxhau'st (ĭgzaw-) *v.* 1. Draw off (air); empty (vessel) of contents. 2. Consume entirely; use, account for, the whole of; treat or study (subject etc.) so as to leave nothing further to be explained or discovered. 3. Drain (person etc.) of strength, resources, etc.; tire out. **ėxhau'stĭble** *adj.* **ėxhaustĭbĭ'lĭtў** *n.* **ėxhau'st** *n.* (in hydraulic, steam, or internal combustion engines) Expulsion or exit of motive fluid, stream, or gaseous products of combustion from cylinder after completion of power-stroke by piston; similar exit of spent fluid or gases from turbine; fluid, steam, etc., expelled thus; (also ~-*pipe*) pipe by which they escape.

exhaustion (ĭgzaw'schon) *n.* (esp.) Total loss of strength.

exhau'stĭve (ĭgzaw-) *adj.* (esp.) Comprehensive, exhausting a subject. **ėxhau'stĭvelў** *adv.* **ėxhau'stĭvenėss** *n.*

ėxhĭ'bĭt (ĭgzĭ-) *v.t.* Show, display; submit (document) for inspection; manifest (quality); show publicly; (U.S.) present, declaim (speech, essay) in public. ~ *n.* Document or thing produced in law-court and referred to in written evidence; thing, collection of things, sent by person, firm, etc., to exhibition, or on permanent show in museum etc. **ėxhĭ'bĭtor** *n.* **ėxhĭ'bĭtorў** *adj.*

ĕxhĭbĭ'tion (ĕskĭ-) *n.* 1. Showing, exhibiting, display; public display (of works of art, manufactured articles, etc.), place where this is held; *Great E~*, first international industrial exhibition, opened in the Crystal Palace, Hyde Park, 1 Aug. 1851. 2. (U.S.) Public declamation of speeches, performance of music, etc., by pupils of school or college. 3. Fixed sum given to student for term of years from funds of college, school, or university. **ĕxhĭbĭ'tioner** *n.* One who holds exhibition at university etc.

ĕxhĭbĭ'tionĭsm (ĕksĭ-) *n.* Tendency towards display, extravagant behaviour; perverted mental condition characterized esp. by indecent exposure of the person. **ĕxhĭbĭ'tionĭst** *n.*

ėxhĭ'larāte (ĭgzĭ-) *v.t.* Enliven, gladden (person, spirits). **ėxhĭlarā'tion** *n.* **ėxhĭ'larătĭve** *adj.*

ėxhor't (ĭgz-) *v.t.* Admonish earnestly; urge (*to*). **ĕxhortā'tion** *n.* **ĕxhor'tatĭve, ėxhor'tatorў** *adjs.*

ĕxhū'me (*or* ĭgzū'm) *v.t.* Dig out (something buried), unearth. **ĕxhūmā'tion** *n.*

ĕ'xĭgence (*or* ĕgz-), **ĕ'xĭgencў** (*or* ĕgz-; *or* ĭgzĭ'-) *ns.* Urgent need; emergency. **ĕ'xĭgent** *adj.* Urgent, pressing; exacting.

ĕ'xĭgĭble (*or* ĕgz-) *adj.* That may be exacted.

ĕxĭ'gūous *adj.* Scanty, small. **ĕxĭgū'ĭtў, ĕxĭ'gūousnėss** *ns.*

ĕ′xīle (*or* ĕgz-) *n.* 1. Penal banishment; long absence from one's country; *the E~*, esp., captivity of Jews in Babylon in 6th c. B.C. 2. Banished person. ~ *v.t.* Banish (*from*).

ĕxĭ′lĭan, ĕxĭ′lĭc (*or* ĕgz-) *adjs.* Of exile; esp., of the captivity of the Jews.

ėxĭ′st (ĭgz-) *v.i.* Have objective being; have being in specified place or under specified conditions; occur, be found; live; continue in being.

ėxĭ′stence (ĭgz-) *n.* Being, existing; life; mode of existing; all that exists; existing thing.

ėxĭ′stent (ĭgz-) *adj.* Existing, actual, current.

ĕxĭstĕ′ntial (-shal) *adj.* (logic, of a proposition) Predicating existence. **ĕxĭstĕ′ntialĭsm** *n.* Philosophical theory concentrating on the existence of the individual who, being free and responsible, develops his essence through acts of the will (which, in the Christian form of the theory, leads to God). **ĕxĭstĕ′ntialĭst** *n.*

ĕ′xĭt[1] *n.* Departure of player from stage (also fig.); death; going out or forth, liberty to do this; way out.

ĕ′xĭt[2] (*or* ĕgz-) (stage direction) Goes off stage. [L, = 'goes out']

ĕx lĭ′bris (-ēs). From the library of (person whose name follows); *ex-libris*, book-plate inscribed thus. [L]

exo- *prefix.* Outside.

ĕ′xocrīne (*or* -ēn) *adj.* & *n.* (Gland) secreting externally, through a duct.

Exod. *abbrev.* Exodus (O.T.).

ĕ′xoderm *n.* Outer layer of blastoderm.

E′xodus[1] (ĕ-). 2nd book of O.T., relating departure of Israelites from Egypt.

ĕ′xodus[2] *n.* Departure, esp. in considerable numbers; *E~*, departure of Israelites from Egypt.

ĕx offĭ′cio (-shĭō) In virtue of one's office. [L]

ĕxŏ′gamous *adj.* Following the custom compelling man to marry outside his own tribe or group. **ĕxŏ′gamy̆** *n.*

ĕxŏ′gėnous *adj.* Growing or originating externally.

ĕ′xŏn *n.* One of four officers who in turn command the Yeomen of the Guard in absence of their superior officers.

Exon. *abbrev.* (Bishop) of Exeter (replacing surname in his signature).

ėxŏ′nerāte (ĭgz-) *v.t.* Exculpate; free (person) *from* (blame etc.); release (person *from* duty etc.). **ėxŏnerā′tion** *n.* **ėxŏ′nerative** *adj.*

Exō′nian (ĕ-) *adj.* & *n.* (Native, inhabitant) of Exeter.

ĕxopă′thĭc *adj.* (of disease) Originating outside the body.

ĕxophthă′lmus *n.* Protrusion of eyeball. **ĕxophthă′lmĭc** *adj.* Of, characterized by, exophthalmus.

ĕ′xoplăsm *n.* Outermost layer of protoplasm.

ėxôr′bĭtant (ĭgz-) *adj.* Grossly excessive (of price, demand, ambition, person). **ėxôr′bĭtance** *n.* **ėxôr′bĭtantly̆** *adv.*

ĕ′xôrcīse (-z; *or* ĕgz-) *v.t.* Expel (evil spirit *from*, *out of*, person or place) by invocation or use of holy name; clear (person, place, *of* evil spirits). **ĕ′xôrcism, ĕ′xôrcist** *ns.*

ėxôr′dium (*or* ĭgz-) *n.* (pl. *-iums*, *-ia*). Beginning, introductory part, esp. of discourse or treatise. **ėxôr′dial** *adj.*

ĕxoskĕ′lėton *n.* External skeleton, as of insect, crustacean, tortoise (its shell) or fish (its scales).

ĕxŏsmō′sis (-zm-) *n.* Osmosis outwards, passage of fluid through porous septum or membrane to mix with external fluid.

ĕxotĕ′rĭc *adj.* (of doctrines, mode of speech, etc.) Intelligible to outsiders; (of disciples) not admitted to esoteric teaching; commonplace, ordinary, popular. **ĕxotĕ′rĭcal** *adj.* **ĕxotĕ′rĭcally̆** *adv.* **ĕxotĕ′rĭcs** *n.pl.* Exoteric doctrines or teachings.

ėxŏ′tĭc (ĭgz-) *adj.* (of plants, words, fashions) Introduced from abroad; strange, bizarre. ~ *n.* Exotic plant (also fig.).

ėxpă′nd *v.* 1. Spread out flat or smooth; unfold, open out; swell, increase in bulk. 2. Expound, write out, in full (what is condensed or abbreviated, algebraical expression, etc.). 3. Become genial or talkative, throw off reserve. **ėxpă'ndable, ėxpă'nsible** *adjs.*

ėxpă'nse *n.* Wide area or extent; expansion.

ėxpă'nsĭle *adj.* (Capable) of expansion.

ėxpă'nsion *n.* Expanding; increasing, increase, extension (of currency, trade, territory, etc.); increase in bulk. **ėxpă'nsionĭsm, ėxpă'nsionĭst** *ns.* (Advocate of) policy or theory of expansion, esp. of currency or territory.

ėxpă'nsĭve *adj.* Able, tending, to expand; extensive; comprehensive; (of persons, feelings, speech) effusive. **ėxpă'nsĭvelȳ** *adv.* **ėxpă'nsĭvenėss** *n.*

ĕx par̄t'ė. (law) On, in interests of, one side only; made or said thus.

ėxpā'tiāte (-shĭ-) *v.i.* Speak, write, copiously (*on* subject). **ėxpātiā'tion** *n.* **ėxpā'tiatorȳ** (-sha-) *adj.*

ėxpăt'riāte *v.t.* Banish; (*refl.*) withdraw from one's country, renounce one's citizenship. **ėxpătrĭā'tion** *n.* **ėxpăt'rĭate** *adj.* & *n.* Expatriated (person); (person) living in a foreign country.

ėxpĕ'ct *v.t.* Look forward to, regard as likely; look for, anticipate coming of (person or thing); (colloq.) think, suppose.

ėxpĕ'ctancȳ *n.* State of expectation; prospect, esp. of future possession; prospective chance (*of*).

ėxpĕ'ctant *adj.* Expecting; having the prospect, in normal course, of possession, office, etc.; (law) reversionary; ~ *mother*, pregnant woman. **ėxpĕ'ctantlȳ** *adv.* **ėxpĕ'ctant** *n.* One expecting, one entitled to expect something; expectant heir, etc.

ĕxpĕctā'tion *n.* Awaiting; anticipation; ground for expecting; (pl.) prospects of inheritance; being expected; thing expected; degree of probability of occurrence of contingent event.

ėxpĕ'ctatĭve *adj.* Of reversion of benefices etc., reversionary.

ėxpĕ'ctorāte *v.t.* Eject (phlegm or other material) from lung airways by coughing; spit. **ėxpĕctorā'tion** *n.* **ėxpĕ'ctorant** *adj.* & *n.* (Medicine) promoting expectoration.

ėxpē'dĭent *adj.* (usu. predic.) Advantageous, suitable; politic rather than just. **ėxpē'dĭentlȳ** *adv.* **ėxpē'dĭence, ėxpē'dĭencȳ** *ns.* **ėxpē'dĭent** *n.* Contrivance, device.

ĕ'xpėdīte *v.t.* Assist progress of (measure, process, etc.); dispatch (business).

ĕxpėdĭ'tion *n.* 1. Warlike enterprise; journey, voyage, excursion, for definite purpose; body of persons, fleet, etc., sent out for warlike or other definite purpose. 2. Promptness, speed. **ĕxpėdĭ'tionarȳ** *adj.*

ĕxpėdĭ'tious (-sh*u*s) *adj.* Doing, done, speedily; suited to speedy performance. **ĕxpėdĭ'tiouslȳ** *adv.* **ĕxpėdĭ'tiousnėss** *n.*

ėxpĕ'l *v.t.* Eject (*from*) by force; turn out (person *from* community, school, etc.). **ėxpĕ'llent** *adj.*

ėxpĕ'nd *v.t.* Spend (money, time, care, etc.); use up; (naut.) use up (rope etc.) by winding it round spar, rope, etc. **ėxpĕ'ndable** *adj.* That can be expended or spared; (mil.) that may be sacrificed in order to accomplish an objective.

ėxpĕ'ndĭture *n.* Laying out, spending; consuming; amount expended.

ėxpĕ'nse *n.* Expenditure; cost; (pl.) outlay in execution of commission etc., reimbursement of this.

ėxpĕ'nsĭve *adj.* Costly. **ėxpĕ'nsĭvelȳ** *adv.* **ėxpĕ'nsĭvenėss** *n.*

ėxper̄'ience *n.* 1. Actual observation of facts or events; knowledge resulting from this. 2. Event that affects one; fact, process, of being so affected. ~*v.t.* Meet with, feel, undergo (pleasure, treatment, fate, etc.); learn, find. **ėxper̄'ĭenced** (-st) *adj.* (esp.) Having experience, wise or skilful through experience.

ĕxpēr̄ĭĕ'ntial (-sh*a*l) *adj.* Of experience; (of philosophy) regarding all knowledge as derived from experience. **ĕxpēriĕ'ntialism, ĕxpēriĕ'ntialist** *ns.* **ĕxpēriĕ'ntially** *adv.*

ėxpĕ'riment *n.* Action or operation undertaken in order to discover something unknown, test hypothesis, illustrate known fact, etc.; method etc. adopted in uncertainty whether it will answer the purpose. **ėxpĕ'rimĕnt** *v.i.* Make experiment (*on, with*).

ėxpĕrimĕ'ntal *adj.* 1. Based on, derived from, experience. 2. Based on experiment; of, used in, experiments. **ėxpĕrimĕ'ntally** *adv.* **ėxpĕrimĕ'ntalism, ėxpĕrimĕ'ntalist** *ns.* **ėxpĕrimĕ'ntalize** *v.i.*

ĕ'xpert *adj.* Trained by practice, skilful, (*at, in*). **ĕ'xpertly** *adv.* **ĕ'xpertnėss** *n.* **ĕ'xpert** *n.* Person having special skill or knowledge (freq. attrib.).

ĕxperti'se (-ēz) *n.* Expert skill or knowledge.

ĕ'xpiāte *v.t.* Pay penalty of, make amends for (sin). **ĕ'xpiable, ĕ'xpiātory** *adjs.* **ĕxpiā'tion, ĕ'xpiātor** *ns.*

ĕxpirā'tion *n.* 1. Breathing out. 2. Termination (of period of time, something made to last a certain time). **ėxpir'atory** *adj.*

ėxpir'e *v.* 1. Breathe out. 2. Die; (of fire etc.) die out. 3. (of period) Come to an end; (of law, patent, etc.) become void, reach its term; (of title etc.) cease, become extinct.

ėxpir'y *n.* Termination (of period, truce, etc.).

ėxplai'n *v.* Give details of; make plain or intelligible; give explanation; interpret; make clear cause, origin, or reason of, account for; ~ *away*, modify, do away with, by explanation; ~ *oneself*, make one's meaning clear, give account of one's motives or intentions.

ĕxplanā'tion *n.* Explaining, esp. with view to mutual understanding or reconciliation; statement, circumstance, that explains.

ėxplă'natory *adj.* Serving, meant, to explain. **ėxplă'natorily** *adv.*

ėxplē'tive *adj.* Serving to fill out; (of words etc.) serving to fill out sentence, metrical line, etc. ~ *n.* Expletive word or phrase, esp. oath or meaningless exclamation.

ĕ'xplicable (*or* ikspli'-) *adj.* That may be explained or explicated.

ĕ'xplicāte *v.t.* 1. Develop (notion, principle, proposition). 2. Explain. **ĕ'xplicative, ĕ'xplicatory** *adjs.*

ėxpli'cit *adj.* Stated in detail, leaving nothing merely implied; definite; (of persons) outspoken; ~ *faith*, (theol.) acceptance of doctrine with distinct apprehension of all that is logically involved in it. **ėxpli'citly** *adv.* **ėxpli'citnėss** *n.*

ėxplō'de *v.* 1. Bring into disrepute, expose hollowness of (theory, belief, etc.). 2. (Cause to) go off with loud noise; (of gunpowder etc.) expand violently with loud report under influence of suddenly developed internal energy; (of shell, etc.) burst from similar cause; (of boiler etc.) burst from excessive pressure of steam inside it.

ėxplō'dėd *adj.* (esp., of diagram etc.) Showing components of a machine etc. separately but retaining their relative positions.

ĕ'xploit[1] *n.* Heroic or spectacular feat.

ėxploi't[2] *v.t.* Work, turn to account, (mine etc.); make use of (person etc.), esp. unfairly or selfishly. **ėxploi'table** *adj.* **ĕxploitā'tion** *n.*

ėxplor'e *v.t.* 1. Investigate (condition, fact); examine, pry into; probe, examine by touch (wound etc.). 2. Search into, examine (country, place, etc.) by going through it; go into, range over, for purpose of discovery. **ĕxplorā'tion, ėxplor'er** *ns.* **ėxplŏ'rative, ėxplŏ'ratory** *adjs.*

ėxplō'sion Exploding; resulting noise, detonation; sudden marked increase, esp. *population* ~; outburst (of anger etc.).

ėxplō'sive *adj.* Tending to drive something forth with violence and noise; tending to explode or cause explosion; of, like, explosion; (of consonant) produced by explosion of breath, stopped. **ėxplō′sĭvelȳ** *adj.* **ėxplō′sĭvenėss** *n.* **ėxplō′sĭve** *n.* 1. Explosive agent or compound; *high* ~, kind having very violent and shattering effect and used not as propellent but in shells, bombs, etc. 2. Explosive consonant.

ėxpō′nent *n.* 1. Person or thing that sets forth or interprets; executant (of music etc.); type, representative. 2. (alg.) Index; symbol denoting number of times particular quantity is to be taken as factor to produce the power indicated. **ĕxponĕ′ntial** (-sh*a*l) *adj.* (esp., math.) Involving the unknown quantity as (part of) an exponent. ~ *n.* Exponential quantity or function.

ėxpōr′t *v.t.* Send out (goods) to another country. **ėxpōr′table** *adj.* **ĕxpōrtā′tion** *n.* **ĕ′xpōrt** *n.* Exported article; (usu. pl.) amount exported; exportation.

ėxpō′se (-z) *v.t.* 1. Leave, place, in unsheltered or unprotected position; (hist.) abandon (child) thus; (fig.) lay open, subject (*to* risk etc.). 2. Exhibit, display; offer publicly, put up, *for* sale; disclose (secret, project, etc.); unmask, show up (fault, guilty person, etc.). 3. (photog.) Subject (sensitized surface of film etc.) to action of actinic rays.

exposé (ĕkspōzā) *n.* Statement of facts; showing up (of discreditable thing). [Fr.]

ĕxposĭ′tion (-z-) *n.* 1. Exposure; exhibition. 2. Setting forth, description; explanation; commentary. 3. (mus.) Presentation of principal theme(s).

ėxpŏ′sĭtĭve (-z-) *adj.* Descriptive, explanatory.

ĕx pōst fă′ctō. Acting retrospectively. [L, = 'from what is made (i.e. enacted) afterwards']

ėxpŏ′stūlāte *v.i.* Make (esp. friendly) remonstrance. **ėxpŏstūlā′tion** *n.* **ėxpŏ′stūlatorȳ** *adj.*

ėxpō′sure (-zh*er*) *n.* Exposing, being exposed; (time taken in) exposing of photographic film etc.; area of film exposed for a single photograph; (of building etc.) aspect; ~ *meter*, photo-electric device indicating correct time for film etc. to be exposed.

ėxpou′nd *v.t.* Set forth in detail (doctrine etc.); explain, interpret (esp. Scripture).

ėxprĕ′ss[1] *adj.* 1. (of likeness) Exact; definitely stated, not merely implied. 2. Done, made, sent, for special purpose; ~ *train*, fast train stopping only at a few important stations (orig., train run expressly to convey passengers to a particular place); so ~ *bus* etc. 3. (of machinery etc.) Having high speed, run at high speed. 4. ~ *delivery*, delivery by special postal messenger (so ~ *letter*, *fee*, etc.); ~ *rifle*, rifle discharging bullet with high initial velocity and low trajectory. **ėxprĕ′sslȳ** *adv.* **ėxprĕ′ss** *adv.* With speed; by express messenger or train. ~ *n.* 1. Express train or bus etc., messenger, or rifle; (U.S.) company for transmitting parcels etc.; ~ *agent*, agent of express company. ~ *v.t.* Send by express delivery; (U.S.) send by express.

ėxprĕ′ss[2] *v.t.* 1. Press, squeeze, or wring out; emit, exude, as if by pressure. 2. Represent by drawing etc. or by figures or other symbols; represent in language, put into words; (*refl.*) put one's thought into words; manifest, reveal, betoken (feelings, personal qualities, etc.).

ėxprĕ′ssion *n.* Expressing; wording, diction, word, phrase; (alg.) collection of symbols together expressing algebraical quantity; expressive quality; aspect (of face), intonation (of voice), etc.; manner of musical performance suited to bringing out feeling of passage; (painting etc.) mode of expressing character.

ėxprĕ′ssional *adj.* Of verbal, facial, or artistic expression.

Exprĕ′ssionism *n.* Movement in art, literature, and music seeking to express emotional experience rather than impressions of the physical world. **Exprĕ′ssionist** *n.* **Exprĕssionĭ′stic** *adj.*

ėxprĕ′ssĭve *adj.* Of expression, serving to express; full of, emphatic in, expression; significant.

ėxprĕ'ssĭvelȳ *adv.* **ėxprĕ'ssĭvenėss** *n.*

ėxprĕ'ssō *n.* = ESPRESSO.

ĕxprobrā'tion *n.* Reproachful language.

ėxprō'priāte *v.t.* Dispossess (*from* estate etc.); take away (property). **ėxprōpriā'tion** *n.*

ėxpŭ'lsion *n.* Expelling. **ėxpŭ'lsĭve** *adj.* & *n.*

ėxpŭ'nge (-j) *v.t.* Erase, omit, strike out. **ėxpŭ'nction** *n.*

ĕ'xpurgāte *v.t.* Purify (book etc.) by removing objectionable matter; clear away (such matter). **ĕxpurgā'tion, ĕ'xpurgātor** *ns.* **ĕxpurgatôr'ial, ĕxpûr'gatorȳ** *adjs.*

ĕ'xquĭsĭte (-z-; *or* ĕkskwĭ'-) *adj.* Of consummate excellence or beauty; acute; keen. **ĕ'xquĭsĭtelȳ** *adv.* **ĕ'xquĭsĭtenėss** *n.* **ĕ'xquĭsĭte** *n.* Dandy.

ėxsă'nguĭne (-nggw-) *adj.* Bloodless.

ėxscĭ'nd *v.t.* Cut out, excise.

ėxsêr't *v.t.* (biol.) Thrust forth or out.

ĕx-sêr'vĭce *adj.* Having formerly belonged to one of the armed services.

ĕ'xtant (*or* ĭkstă'-) *adj.* Still existing (esp. of documents etc.).

ėxtĕ'mporė *adv.* & *adj.* (Spoken, done,) without preparation; offhand. **ėxtĕmporā'nėous** *adj.* **ėxtĕmporā'nėouslȳ** *adv.* **ėxtĕmporā'nėousnėss** *n.* **ėxtĕ'mporarȳ** *adj.* **ėxtĕ'mporarĭlȳ** *adv.*

ėxtĕ'mporīze *v.* Compose, produce, extempore; speak extempore; **ėxtĕmporīzā'tion** *n.*

ėxtĕ'nd *v.* 1. Place (esp. body, limbs, etc.) at full length; write out (contractions, shorthand notes, etc.) at full length. 2. Reach, cause to reach (*to* point, *over*, *across*, etc., space). 3. Prolong (period); enlarge (scope, meaning, of word, etc.). 4. (mil.) Spread out, cause (line etc.) to spread out, into open order with regular intervals between men. 5. (sport, slang, usu. pass.) Tax powers of (horse, athlete) to the utmost. 6. Stretch forth (hand, arm); accord (kindness, patronage, *to*). 7. (law) Value (land etc.), seize (land etc.) for debt. **ėxtĕ'ndĭble, extĕ'nsĭble** *adjs.* **ėxtĕnsĭbĭ'lĭtȳ** *n.*

ėxtĕ'nsīle *adj.* Capable of being stretched out or protruded.

ėxtĕ'nsion *n.* Extending; extent, range; prolongation, enlargement; additional part, building, line, etc. (of railway, plan, theory, etc.); subsidiary telephone; word(s) amplifying subject or predicate; (*university*) ~ *course*, *lecture*, EXTRAMURAL instruction.

ėxtĕ'nsĭve *adj.* Large; far-reaching, comprehensive; (of agricultural production etc.) depending on extension of area. **ėxtĕ'nsĭvelȳ** *adv.* **ėxtĕ'nsĭvenėss** *n.*

ėxtĕ'nsor *n.* Muscle serving to extend or straighten out any part of body (opp. FLEXOR).

ėxtĕ'nt *n.* 1. Space over which thing extends; width of application, scope. 2. (law) Valuation (of land etc.); seizure, writ for seizure, (of lands etc.).

ėxtĕ'nūāte *v.t.* 1. Lessen seeming magnitude of (guilt, offence) by partial excuse. 2. (archaic) Make thin or weak. **ėxtĕnūā'tion** *n.* **ėxtĕ'nūatorȳ** *adj.*

ėxtēr'ior *adj.* Outer, situated or coming from without; relating to foreign affairs; ~ *angle*, that between any side of a polygon and adjacent side produced. **ėxtēr'iorlȳ** *adv.* **ėxtēriŏ'rĭtȳ** *n.* **ėxtēr'ĭor** *n.* Outward aspect or demeanour; (cinemat.) outdoor scene.

ĕxtēr'iorīze *v.t.* Realize (conception) in outward form; attribute external existence *to*. **ėxtēriorīzā'tion** *n.*

ėxtêr'mĭnāte *v.t.* Destroy utterly, root out (species, race, etc.). **ėxtêrmĭnā'tion, ėxtêr'mĭnātor** *ns.* **ėxtêr'mĭnatĭve, ėxtêr'mĭnatory** *adjs.*

ėxtêr'nal *adj.* Situated outside; (of remedies etc.) applied to outside of body; consisting in outward acts or appearances; belonging to external world of things or phenomena, considered as outside the perceiving mind; arising, acting, from without; connected with, referring to, what is outside; (of student) taking examinations of a university without attending it; ~ *degree*, degree obtained thus; ~ *evidence*, evidence derived from source independent of the thing discussed. **ėxtėrnă'lity̆** *n.* **ėxtėr'nally̆** *adv.* **ėxtėr'nals** (-z) *n.pl.* Outward features or aspect; external circumstances; non-essentials.

ėxtėr'nalize *v.t.* Give, attribute, external existence to. **ėxtėrnalīzā'tion** *n.*

ėxti'nct *adj.* (of fire etc.) No longer burning; (of volcano) that has ceased eruption; (of life, hope, etc.) quenched; (of family, class, species) that has died out; (of office etc.) obsolete; (of title of nobility) having no qualified claimant.

ėxti'nction *n.* Extinguishing; making, being, becoming, extinct; wiping out (of debt); annihilation. **ėxti'nctive** *adj.*

ėxti'nguish (-nggw-) *v.t.* Put out, quench (light, hope, life, faculties); eclipse, obscure (person) by superior brilliancy; reduce (opponent) to silence; destroy; wipe out (debt); annihilate. **ėxti'nguishable** *adj.*

ėxti'nguisher (-nggw-) *n.* (esp.) Hollow conical cap for extinguishing light of candle etc.; FIRE-extinguisher.

ĕ'xtirpāte *v.t.* Root out, destroy. **ĕxtirpā'tion, ĕ'xtirpātor** *ns.*

ėxtŏ'l *v.t.* Praise enthusiastically.

ėxtor't *v.t.* Obtain (money, promise, etc.) by violence, intimidation, importunity, etc. (*from*); extract forcibly (sense, conclusion, etc., *from* words etc.).

ėxtor'tion *n.* Extorting, esp. of money; illegal exaction. **ėxtor'tionate** *adj.* Using, given to, extortion; (of prices etc.) exorbitant. **ėxtor'tioner** *n.*

ĕ'xtra *adj.* Additional; larger than its name indicates; of superior quality. ~ *adv.* More than usually; additionally. ~ *n.* Extra thing, one for which extra charge is made; (cricket) run scored otherwise than off bat; special or additional issue of newspaper; (cinemat.) actor engaged temporarily as one of crowd etc.

extra- *prefix.* Situated outside of a thing, not coming within its scope.

ĕ'xtrăct *n.* 1. (chem.) Preparation containing active principle of substance in concentrated form obtained by treatment with a solvent (usu. followed by evaporation of solvent). 2. Passage copied from book etc., excerpt, quotation. **ėxtră'ct** *v.t.* 1. Copy out (passage in book etc.); make extracts from (book etc.). 2. Take out by force (tooth, anything firmly fixed); draw forth (money, admission, etc.) against person's will. 3. Obtain (juices etc.) by suction, pressure, distillation, etc.); derive (pleasure etc. *from*); deduce (principle etc. *from*). 4. (math.) Find (root of a number). **ėxtră'ctor** *n.*

ėxtră'ction *n.* 1. Extracting; ~ *rate*, proportion of total weight of unground wheat which is converted into flour, expressed as a percentage of the weight unground. 2. Lineage, as *of Indian* ~.

ėxtră'ctive *adj.* & *n.* (Thing) of the nature of an extract; ~ *industries*, those dependent on mining and oil.

ĕ'xtradīte *v.t.* Give up (fugitive foreign criminal) to the proper authorities.

ĕxtradi'tion *n.* Delivery of fugitive criminal to authorities of State in which crime was committed; ~ *treaty*, treaty by which countries bind themselves to extradite criminals who have committed specified offences.

ėxtrā'dŏs *n.* (archit.) Upper or outer curve of arch.

ĕx'trajudi'cial (-jōōdĭshal) *adj.* Not belonging to the case before the court; (of opinion, confession, etc.) not made in court; outside ordinary course of law or justice. **ĕxtrajudi'cially̆** *adv.*

ĕ'xtra-mă'rital *adj.* (of sexual relationships) Outside marriage.

ĕxtramŭ'ndāne *adj.* Outside of our world or of the universe.

ĕxtramūr'al *adj.* Outside the walls or boundaries of a city etc.;

(of course etc.) organized by a university or college for non-resident students.

ėxtrā′nėous *adj.* Of external origin; foreign *to* (object to which it is attached etc.); not belonging (*to* matter in hand, class). **ėxtrā′nėously** *adv.* **ėxtrā′nėousnėss** *n.*

ĕ′xtra-offi′cial (-sh*a*l) *adj.* Not pertaining to an office.

ėxtraor′dĭnarÿ (-trŏr- *or* -tr*a*-ŏr-) *adj.* Out of the usual course; exceptional, surprising; unusually great; (of officials etc.) additional, specially employed; *envoy* ~, orig., minister sent on special diplomatic business; now, diplomatic minister ranking next to ambassador. **ėxtraor′dĭnarilÿ** *adv.* **ėxtraor′dĭnarĭnėss** *n.*

ĕxtraphÿ′sĭcal (-z-) *adj.* Not subject to physical laws.

ėxtră′polāte *v.* (math.) Calculate, from known terms, a series of other terms which lie outside the range of the known terms (also fig.). **ĕxtrapolā′tion** *n.*

ĕxtrasĕ′nsorÿ *adj.* (of perception) Made otherwise than by the known sense-organs.

ĕxtraspĕ′ctral *adj.* Lying outside the visible spectrum.

ĕxtraterrĕ′strĭal *adj.* Outside the earth or its atmosphere.

ĕ′xtratĕrritŏr′ial *adj.* Of the privilege extended to ambassadors of being regarded as outside the territory, and therefore free from the jurisdiction, of the power to which they are sent; of a country's rights of jurisdiction over all its subjects abroad. **ĕ′xtratĕrritorĭă′litÿ** *n.* Extraterritorial rights and privileges.

ėxtră′vagance *n.* Being extravagant; absurd statement or action.

ėxtră′vagant *adj.* Immoderate; exceeding the bounds of reason; profuse, wasteful; (of price etc.) exorbitant. **ėxtră′vagantlÿ** *adv.*

ėxtrăvagă′nza *n.* Extravagant or fantastic musical, literary, or dramatic composition; extravagance of language or behaviour.

ėxtră′vasāte *v.* Force out (fluid, esp. blood) from its proper vessel; (of fluid) flow out, esp. through walls of blood-vessel etc. **ĕxtrăvasā′tion** *n.*

ĕxtra-vėhĭ′cūlar *adj.* Outside a vehicle, esp., of activity outside a space-vehicle while in flight.

ĕ′xtravĕrt *n.* Var. of EXTROVERT.

ėxtrē′me *adj.* 1. Outermost; farthest from centre; situated at either end. 2. Utmost. 3. Last (obs. exc. in ~ *unction*, (R.C. Ch.) anointing of dying person by priest). 4. (of actions, measures, etc.) Severe, stringent; (of opinions, persons, etc.) going to great lengths, not moderate. **ėxtrē′melÿ** *adv.* **ėxtrē′menėss** *n.* **ėxtrē′me** *n.* 1. *in the* ~, extremely. 2. Thing at either end of anything; esp. (pl.) things as remote or as different as possible; excessive degree. 3. (logic) Subject or predicate in proposition, major or minor term in syllogism; (math.) first or last term of ratio or series.

ėxtrē′mĭst *n.* One who holds extreme views or advocates extreme measures. **ėxtrē′mĭsm** *n.*

ėxtrĕ′mĭtÿ *n.* 1. Extreme point; very end; (pl.) hands and feet. 2. Extreme adversity, embarrassment, etc.; (usu. pl.) extreme measure(s).

ĕ′xtrĭcāte *v.t.* Disentangle, release (*from* confinement, difficulty, etc.) **ĕxtrĭcā′tion** *n.*

ėxtrĭ′nsĭc *adj.* Lying outside, not belonging, (*to*); operating from without; not inherent or essential. **ėxtrĭ′nsĭcallÿ** *adv.*

ėxtrŏr′se *adj.* (bot., of anthers) Shedding their pollen outwards (opp. INTRORSE).

ĕ′xtrovĕrt *n.* (psychol.) One whose thoughts and activities are directed to things outside the self (opp. INTROVERT). **ĕxtrovĕr′sion** *n.*

ėxtru′de (-ōō-) *v.t.* Thrust out (*from*). **ėxtru′sion** *n.* **ėxtru′sĭve** *adj.*

ėxū′berant (ĭgz-) *adj.* Luxuriant, prolific; effusive; copious, lavish in ornament. **ėxū′berantlÿ** *adv.* **ėxū′berance** *n.*

ėxū′berāte (ĭgz-) *v.i.* Be exuberant, abound, overflow.

ėxū′de (ĭgz-) *v.* Ooze out, give off (moisture etc.) like sweat.

ĕxūdā′tion, ĕ′xūdāte *ns.* **ėxū′dative** *adj.*

ėxŭ′lt (ĭgz-) *v.i.* Rejoice exceedingly; triumph (*over*). **ėxŭ′ltancy̆, ĕxultā′tion** *ns.* **ėxŭ′ltant** *adj.* **ėxŭ′ltantly̆** *adv.*

ėxū′viae (ĭgz-) *n.pl.* Animal's cast skin, shell, or covering. **ėxū′vial** *adj.* **ėxū′viāte** *v.* Shed exuviae, slough. **ėxūviā′tion** *n.*

ĕx vō′tō. (Offering made) in pursuance of a vow. [L]

eyas (ī′*a*s) *n.* Young hawk taken from nest for training, or not yet completely trained.

eye (ī) *n.* 1. Organ of sight; iris of this; region of the eyes; eye as possessing power of vision; sense of seeing; look, glance, gaze; attention, regard; estimation, opinion, judgement; *all my* ~, humbug, stuff and nonsense; *in the* ~ *of*, in the direction of (the wind); *make* ~*s at*, look amorously at, ogle; *see* ~ *to* ~, agree entirely (*with*); *see with half an* ~, see at a glance, easily; *up to the* ~*s*, deeply immersed or occupied. 2. Thing like eye; spot on peacock's tail, wing of insect etc.; one of three spots at end of coconut; hole in needle for thread etc., hole in tool or implement for insertion of some other object; metal loop used with hook for fastening dress etc.; loop of cord or rope; undeveloped bud of plant; centre of flower; leaf-bud of potato etc. 3. *ey′eball*, pupil of the eye; eye within lids and socket; ~ *bath*, *-cup*, small vessel for applying lotion etc. to eye; ~*-bolt*, bolt, bar, with circular hole through head; *ey′ebright*, plant (species of *Euphrasia*) formerly used as remedy for weak eyes; *ey′ebrow*, fringe of hair along upper orbit of eye; *ey′eful*, (slang) remarkable or attractive sight; careful scrutiny; *ey′eglass*, lens for assisting defective sight; monocle; (pl.) pair of these held in position by hand or by spring on nose; *ey′ehole*, cavity or socket of eye; hole to look through; *ey′elash*, hair, row of hairs, on edge of eyelid; *ey′elid*, one of movable folds of skin with which eyes are covered or uncovered; ~*-opener*, enlightening or surprising circumstance etc.; (U.S.) alcoholic drink, esp. in morning; *ey′epiece*, lens(es) at eye end of microscope etc.; ~*-rhyme*, correspondence in spelling but not in pronunciation of words (as *love*, *move*); ~*-shadow*, cosmetic applied round the eyes; *ey′esight*, power, faculty, of seeing; *ey′esore*, ugly object, thing that offends the sight; ~*splice*, splice forming loop; ~*-tooth*, pointed tooth just under eye, in upper or lower jaw, canine tooth; ~*-wash*, lotion for eye; *ey′ewash*, (slang) humbug, blarney; *ey′ewitness*, one who can bear witness from his own observation. ~ *v.t.* Observe, watch. **ey′elėss** *adj.*

ey′elėt (īl-) *n.* Small hole in cloth, sail, etc., for lace, ring, rope, etc.; loop-hole; small eye.

eyot: see AIT.

eyr′ie (ārĭ *or* īrĭ) *n.* Nest of bird (esp. eagle) that builds high; house etc. built on high rock or hill.

eyrir (ā′rēr) *n.* (pl. *aurar*, pr. ow′rar) $\frac{1}{100}$ of a krona.

Ezē′kiel (ĭ-). Hebrew major prophet of 6th C. B.C.; book of O.T. containing his prophecies.

E′zra (ĕ-). Hebrew scribe and priest of 5th C. B.C.; book of O.T. dealing with the return of the Jews from Babylon and the rebuilding of the Temple (see CHRONICLER.)

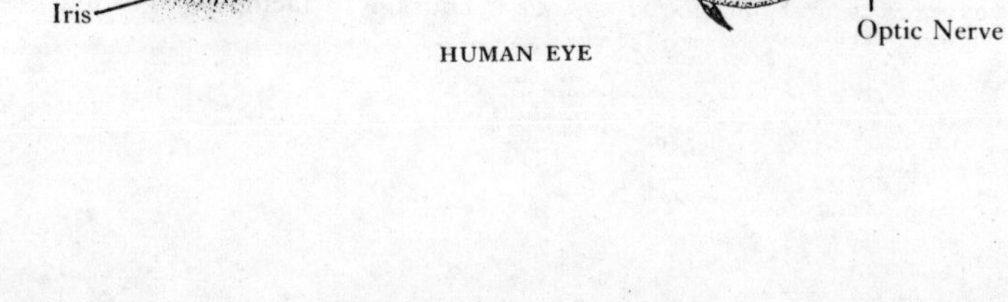

HUMAN EYE

F

F, f (ĕf). 1. 6th letter of modern English and ancient Roman alphabet, representing Semitic *waw* (= *w*, *u*) and pre-classical Greek digamma (ϝ) and pronounced in English as a voiceless labio-dental spirant. 2. *F*, (mus.) 4th note of natural scale (C major); scale or key with this note for tonic; *F clef*: see CLEF. 3. *F-layer*, highest stratum of the ionosphere, approximately 160–300 km above the earth. 4. *f-hole*, f-shaped hole in body of stringed instrument.

f. *abbrev.* Feminine; filly; focal length (photog., used with numbers to indicate ratio of focal length of lens to diameter of stop); folio; *forte*; franc(s); from.

F *abbrev.* Fahrenheit; farad(s); fine (of pencil-lead).

F.A. *abbrev.* Football Association.

f.a.a. *abbrev.* Free of all average.

F.A.A. *abbrev.* Fleet Air Arm.

fa: see FAH.

Fā'bĭan *adj.* 1. Of, like, Quintus Fabius Maximus (d. 203 B.C.) Roman consul and general, surnamed Cunctator ('Delayer') from the tactics he employed against Hannibal in the 2nd Punic War, avoiding battles and weakening the enemy by cutting off supplies and continual skirmishing. 2. Of the ~ *Society*, society of English socialists advocating Fabian policy rather than immediate revolutionary action, founded 1884. ~ *n.* Member of the Fabian Society. **Fā'bĭanism** *n.*

fā'ble *n.* 1. Story, esp. of supernatural character, not founded on fact; (collect.) myths, legendary tales; idle talk. 2. Short story, esp. with animals for characters, conveying a moral; apologue. ~ *v.* (archaic & poet.) Romance, tell fictitious tales; state fictitiously; *fabled*, celebrated in fable, fictitious.

fă'bliau (-ĭō) *n.* Metrical tale of medieval French poetry, often of a coarsely humorous character.

fă'brĭc *n.* Thing put together; edifice, building; frame, structure; construction, texture, tissue; (freq. *textile* ~) woven material.

fă'brĭcāte *v.t.* 1. Construct, manufacture, esp. (eng.) by welding components together, not by moulding or casting. 2. Invent (story), forge (document). **făbrĭcā'tion, fă'brĭcātor** *ns.*

fă'būlĭst *n.* Composer of fables or apologues; liar.

fă'būlous *adj.* Celebrated in fable; incredible; (colloq.) wonderful. **fă'būloušlў** *adv.* **fă'būlousnėss, făbūlŏ'sĭtў** *ns.*

faça'de (-sahd) *n.* Face of building, esp. the principal front; hence, frontal appearance of anything (also fig.).

fāce *n.* 1. Front of head from forehead to chin; ~ *to* ~, confronted; ~ *to* ~ *with*, confronting; *fly in the* ~ *of*, openly disobey; *to person's* ~, openly in his sight or hearing. 2. Expression of countenance; grimace. 3. Composure, coolness, effrontery. 4. Outward show; aspect; surface; front, façade; right side, obverse; dial-plate of clock etc.; working surface of implement etc.; each surface of solid; (also *type* ~) part of type or plate which takes the ink; style or design of this; *lose* ~, be humiliated; lose one's credit or good name; *on the* ~ *of it*, to judge by appearance; obviously, plainly; *put a new* ~ *on*, alter aspect of; *put good, bold,* ~ *on matter*, make it look well, show courage in facing it; *save one's* ~, save one's credit or good name. 5. ~*-ache*, facial neuralgia; ~ *card*, one of a pack of playing-cards on which a human face is represented; the king, queen, or knave; *fa'ce-cloth*, cloth for washing the face; smooth-surfaced woollen cloth; ~*-lift*, face-lifting; (fig.) improvement in appearance; ~*-lifting*, operation for tightening the skin of the face to remove wrinkles etc.; ~*-value*, nominal value as stated on coin, note, etc.; (fig.) apparent value. ~ *v.* 1. Meet confidently or defiantly; not shrink from, stand fronting; ~ *the music*, not quail at moment of trial. 2. Present itself to; look, have face or front, in special direction; front towards, be opposite to; (mil.) turn in special direction. 3. Cover part of (garment) with another material, esp. at edge, trim, turn up *with*; cover (surface) with layer of other material; dress surface of. 4. (lacrosse, ice hockey) Start play by dropping (ball or puck) between sticks of two opposing players (also ~ *off*).

fā'celėss (-sl-) *adj.* (esp.) Anonymous, characterless, without identity.

fā'cer *n.* Blow in the face; sudden difficulty or problem.

fă'cėt *n.* One side of many-sided body, esp. of cut gem; one segment of compound eye. **fă'cėtėd** *adj.*

facē'tiae (-shĭē) *n.pl.* Pleasantries, witticisms; (in book catalogues) books of a coarsely humorous or obscene character.

facē'tious (-sh*us*) *adj.* Joking, esp. in forced or trivial way. **facē'tiouslў** *adv.* **facē'tiousnėss** *n.*

fā'cia (-sh*a*) *n.* Plate over shopfront with occupier's name etc.; instrument panel of motor vehicle. [var. of FASCIA].

fā'cial (-sh*a*l) *adj.* Of the face. ~*n.* (colloq.) Beauty treatment for the face.

fā'cies (-shĭēz *or* -shēz) *n.* (pl. same). 1. (med.) Facial expression. 2. (geol.) Character of a formation as displayed by its constituent rocks, fossils, etc.; formation with a particular character.

fă'cĭle *adj.* Easily done or won; working easily, ready, fluent; of easy temper, flexible.

fă'cĭlė prĭ'ncĕps. Easily first. [L]

facĭ'lĭtāte *v.t.* Make easy, promote, help forward (action or result). **facĭlĭtā'tion** *n.*

facĭ'lĭtў *n.* Being easy, absence of difficulty; unimpeded opportunity; ease or readiness of speech etc.; pliancy; (pl.) amenities, services.

fā'cĭng *n.* (esp.) Something with which garment is faced, esp. cuffs and collar of military jacket, differently coloured from rest; coating of different material, esp. of stone etc., on wall.

făcsĭ'mĭlė *n.* Exact copy, esp. of writing, printing, picture, etc. ~ *v.t.* Make facsimile of.

făct *n.* 1. Thing certainly known to have occurred or be true; datum of experience; thing assumed as basis for inference; what is true or existent; reality; ~*s of life*, (colloq.) facts of sex and reproduction. 2. Evil deed, crime (only in *confess the* ~; *before, after, the* ~).

fă'ction *n.* Self-interested, turbulent, or unscrupulous party, esp. in politics; prevalence of party spirit. **fă'ctional, fă'ctious** (-sh*us*) *adjs.* **fă'ctiouslў** *adv.* **fă'ctiousnėss** *n.*

făctĭ'tious (-sh*us*) *adj.* Designedly got up, not natural, artificial. **făctĭ'tiouslў** *adv.* **făctĭ'tiousnėss** *n.*

fă'ctĭtĭve *adj.* (gram., of verb) Expressing notion of making thing to be of a certain character (either objectively or in thought or representation).

fă'ctor *n.* 1. Agent, deputy (now rare); merchant buying and selling on commission; (Sc.) land agent, steward. 2. (math.) One of two or more numbers etc. which when multiplied together give a given number, expression, etc. 3. Circumstance, fact, influence, contributing to result. 4. (biol.) Gene or other agent transmitted from parent to offspring and influencing or determining a hereditary character. 5. ~ *of* *safety*, ratio between the load which a structure or material can support and the load which it is required to support.

făctŏr'ĭal *adj.* Of a factor or a factorial. ~ *n.* (math.) Product of series of factors in arithmetical progression; product of integer multiplied by all lower integers.

fă'ctorīze *v.t.* (math.) Resolve into factors. **făctorīzā'tion** *n.*

fă'ctorў *n.* Building or range of buildings with plant for manufacture of goods; *F~ Acts*, statutes of 1802, 1833, etc., regulating conduct of factories in interest of employees; ~ *farm(ing)*, farm(ing) organized on industrial lines.

făctō'tum *n.* Man of all work; servant managing his master's affairs.

fă'ctūal *adj.* Concerned with, of the nature of, fact. **fă'ctūallў** *adv.* **fă'ctualnėss** *n.*

fă'cūla *n.* (pl. *-lae*). (astron.) Bright spot or streak on sun.

fă'cultatĭve *adj.* Permissive; optional; contingent; of a faculty.

fă'cultў *n.* 1. Aptitude for any special kind of action; power inherent in the body or an organ; a mental power (e.g. will, reason). 2. One of the departments of learning at a university (esp., one of the traditional *four faculties*, Theology, Law, Medicine, and Arts); masters and doctors (sometimes also students) in any of these; members of a particular profession, esp. medicine; (U.S.) whole teaching staff of college or university. 3. Liberty to do something given by law or a superior; authorization, licence, dispensation (esp. ecclesiastical).

făd *n.* Pet notion or rule of action, craze. **fă'ddĭsh, fă'ddў** *adjs.* **fă'ddĭsm, fă'ddĭst** *ns.*

fāde *v.* Droop, wither; (cause to) lose freshness or colour; disappear gradually; (of sound) grow faint, die *away*, *out*; (of brake) gradually lose power; ~ *in, out, up*, gradually increase or decrease brightness, intensity, or distinctness of (cinema picture, sound, etc.). ~ *n.* Fading. **fā'delėss** *adj.* **fā'delėsslў** *adv.* **fā'dĭng** *n.* (esp.) Irregular diminution of strength of distant signals in radio reception.

fae'cēs (-z) *n.pl.* 1. Sediment. 2. Excrement; waste matter discharged from bowels. **fae'cal** *adj.*

fā'erĭe (*or* fār-) *n.* Fairyland; the fairies; imaginary world portrayed in Spenser's 'Faerie Queene'. ~ *adj.* Of faerie; visionary, unreal. [Spenser's archaic variant of *fairy*]

făg *v.* 1. Toil painfully; (of occupation) tire, make weary. 2. (in schools, of seniors) Use the service of (juniors), (of juniors) do service for seniors. ~ *n.* 1. Drudgery; unwelcome task; exhaustion. 2. (in schools) Junior who has to fag. 3. (slang) Cigarette; *~-end*, inferior or useless remnant of anything esp. of cigar or cigarette; extreme end.

fă'ggot *n.* (U.S. *fagot*) 1. Bundle of sticks or twigs bound together as fuel; bundle of iron or steel rods bound together for reheating or welding. 2. (pl.) Dish of chopped liver, lights, etc., made into balls or rolls. 3. *~-stitch*, stitch used in faggoting. ~ *v.* Bind in faggot(s); make faggots; ornament, join, with faggoting. **fă'ggotĭng** *n.* (needlework) Drawn-thread work in which a few cross-threads are fastened together in the middle like faggots; method of joining two pieces of material together, resembling this.

fah, fa (fah) *n.* (mus.) 4th note of hexachord and of major scale in movable-doh systems; note F in fixed-doh systems. [see UT]

Fah'renheit (-hīt; *or* fă-), Gabriel Daniel (1686–1736). Prussian physicist; popularized use of mercurial thermometer and devised temperature scale; hence as *adj.*, (abbrev. F) according to the Fahrenheit scale; ~ *thermometer, scale*, etc., one with 32° and 212° as freezing- and boiling-points of water.

fai'ble *n.* (fencing) = FOIBLE, 2.

faience (fīyahṅ's) *n.* Painted and glazed earthenware, majolica. [Fr., = *Faenza*, Italy, site of factory]

fail *n.* *without* ~ (emphasizing injunction or promise), for certain, irrespective of hindrances. ~ *v.* 1. Be or become deficient; die away; flag, break down; disappoint hopes of, be of no help; ~ *safe*, (of mechanism) revert, in event of breakdown, to condition involving no danger. 2. Be wanting or deficient *in*. 3. Fall short in performance or attainment; not succeed (*in* doing, *to* do); come to nothing; become bankrupt; be rejected, reject, as candidate; be unsuccessful in (examination).

fai′ling *n.* (esp.) Foible, shortcoming, weakness. ~ *prep.* In default of.

fai′lure (-y*er*) *n.* Non-occurrence, non-performance; running short; breaking down; ill success; insolvency; unsuccessful person, thing, or attempt.

fain *pred. adj.* (archaic) Willing under the circumstances *to*; left with no alternative but *to*. ~ *adv.* Gladly, willingly (as in *would* ~).

faint *adj.* 1. Sluggish; timid; feeble; dim, indistinct, pale. 2. Giddy or languid with fear, hunger, etc., inclined to faint; ~*-heart*, coward; ~*-hearted* (*adj.*); ~*-heartedly* (*adv.*), ~*-heartedness* (*n.*). **fai′ntish** *adj.* **fai′ntlў** *adv.* **fa′intnėss** *n.* **faint** *v.* 1. (archaic) Lose heart or courage, flag. 2. Lose consciousness; suffer syncope. ~ *n.* Fainting fit.

fair[1] *n.* Periodical gathering for sale of goods, often with shows and entertainments, at place and time fixed by charter, statute, or custom; trade exhibition; fun fair.

fair[2] *adj.* 1. Beautiful; pleasing at first sight or hearing. 2. (of complexion etc.) Light, not dark. 3. Free from blemish; clear, clean; just, equitable. 4. Of moderate quality; not bad, pretty good. 5. Favourable, promising; gentle; unobstructed. 6. ~ *copy*, copy of document etc. made from rough copy or after final correction; *the* ~ *sex*, women; *fair′way*, navigable channel, usual course of vessel(s); (golf) regular track, short-grassed part of course between tee and putting-green; ~*-weather*, fit only for fine weather (freq. fig. of friends etc.). ~ *n.* What is fair; (archaic) woman. **fair′ĭsh** *adj.* **fair′nėss** *n.* **fair** *adv.* In a fair manner; *bid* ~ *to do*, show promise of doing.

fair′ĭng[1] *n.* Present bought at a fair.

fair′ĭng[2] *n.* (eng.) Shielding round struts of aircraft, supports of bridge, etc., reducing resistance to air- or water-flow; streamlining.

Fair Isle (īl). Name of one of the Shetland Islands used (esp. attrib.) of knitting in coloured wools in designs characteristic of the island (alleged to be Moorish and to be traceable to survivors from a wrecked ship of the Spanish Armada). [Norw. *fair* = 'sheep']

fair′lў *adv.* In a fair manner; utterly, completely; rather, tolerably.

fair′ў *n.* Small supernatural being with magical powers; ~*-cycle*, child's small-wheeled low cycle; *fair′yland*, country of fairies, enchanted land of fancy; ~ *lights*, small coloured lights used in decorative illuminations; ~ *ring*, circular band of darker grass caused by fungi, pop. attributed to fairy dancing; ~ *story*, *-tale*, story about fairies; unreal or incredible story; falsehood. ~ *adj.* Of fairies; imaginary, fictitious; fairy-like, beautiful and delicate or small.

fait accompli (fāt ăkawṅplē). Accomplished fact. [Fr.]

faith *n.* 1. Reliance, trust, *in*; belief founded on authority; (theol.) belief in religious doctrines, esp. such as affects character and conduct, spiritual apprehension of divine truth apart from proof. 2. System of religious belief; things (to be) believed. 3. Duty of fulfilling trust, promise, etc.; observance of this; loyalty, fidelity; *good* ~, honesty of intention; *bad* ~, intent to deceive. 4. ~*-cure*, *-healing*, cure, healing, by power of faith, not drugs etc.

fai′thful *adj.* Showing faith; loyal, constant (*to*); conscientious; trustworthy; true to fact, the original, etc., accurate. ~ *n.* (collect., *the* ~) True believers, esp. Muslims; *Commander, Father, of the F~*, titles applied by Muslims to the Caliph. **fai'thfullў** *adv.* (esp.) With binding assurances (colloq.); *yours ~*, customary formula for closing business letter. **fai'thfulnėss** *n.*

fai'thlėss *adj.* (esp.) Perfidious, false to promises; unreliable. **fai'thlėsslў** *adv.* **fai'thlėssnėss** *n.*

fāke *v.t.* Do *up*; make presentable or specious; contrive out of poor material; tamper with, contrive, in order to deceive. **~** *n.* (freq. attrib.) Piece of faking; faked thing.

fă'kir (-ēr; *or* fah-; *or* fakēr') *n.* Muslim (or Hindu) religious mendicant, devotee. [Arab. *faḳir* poor man]

Fală'ngĭst (-j-; *or* -lah-) *n.* & *adj.* (Member) of the *Falange Española Tradicionalista*, ruling party in Spain under General Franco, orig. founded (1933) as a Fascist movement. [Span. *falange* phalanx]

fă'lbala *n.* Furbelow.

fă'lcāte *adj.* (anat., bot., zool.) Hooked, sickle-shaped. **fă'lcātėd** *adj.* (astron., of moon etc.) Sickle-shaped.

falchion (faw'lchon) *n.* Broad curved convex-edged sword.

fă'lcifôrm *adj.* (anat.) Sickle-shaped.

fa'lcon (faw(l)- *or* fŏl-) *n.* Small diurnal bird of prey of genus *Falco*, with short hooked beak and powerful claws, esp. one trained to pursuit of other birds or game, usu. the peregrine falcon (*F. peregrinus*); (in falconry) female of this. **fa'lconer** *n.* Keeper and trainer of hawks; one who hunts with hawks. **fa'lconrў** *n.* Hawking; breeding and training of hawks.

FALCONRY

fa'lconėt (faw(l)- *or* fŏl-) *n.* (hist.) Light cannon of 15th–17th centuries.

fă'lderăl *n.* Gewgaw, trifle. [f. meaningless refrain in songs]

fa'ldstōōl (faw-) *n.* Armless chair, made to fold up, used by bishop etc. when not occupying throne or when officiating in any but his own church; movable folding stool or desk for kneeling at, esp. one used by sovereign at coronation; small desk from which litany is said.

Falêr'nĭan *adj.* Of Falernus, a territory in ancient Campania, Italy, which produced a famous wine. **~** *n.* Falernian wine.

Fa'lkland I'slands (faw(l)k- *or* fŏl-, īlandz). Group of islands, in British possession, in the S. Atlantic, discovered by John Davis in 1592.

fall (fawl) *v.i.* (past t. *fĕll*, past part. *fa'llen*). 1. Descend freely, drop, lose high position; become detached and drop off; hang down; (of speech etc.) issue from; (of the young of animals) be born. 2. Sink, descend to lower level; decline; slope; subside, diminish; (of river etc.) discharge itself *into*; (of face) show sudden dismay; (of eyes) be lowered. 3. Cease to stand; come, be brought, (suddenly) to the ground; (*wicket ~s*, in cricket, batsman is out); prostrate oneself; succumb to attack or opposing force; yield to temptation; drop down wounded or dead, die by violence; stumble, be drawn or forced, *into* (danger etc.); (cards) be captured by higher card. 4. (of missile, sight, light, etc.) Take direction, be directed; settle; have its situation *in* certain place, *on* certain object etc.; (of choice, lot, etc.) light *upon*; be allotted or apportioned; come as burden or duty. 5. Come by chance into certain position etc.; come naturally. 6. Pass suddenly, accidentally, or in the course of events, into a certain condition, become (as ~ *asleep*, *silent*, etc.). 7. Come to pass, befall; come in due course; (of season etc.) occur at stated time, within certain limits etc. 8. With preps.: ~ *behind*, be outstripped by; ~ *for*, (colloq., orig. U.S.) be captivated by; ~ *into*, take one's place in (line etc.); engage, enter upon (talk etc.); drop into (habit); ~ *on*, make hostile descent or attack on; ~ *to*, take to, begin; ~ *under*, be classified among; be subjected to (observation etc.). 9. With advs.: ~ *away*, desert, revolt; apostatize; decay, vanish; ~ *back*, retreat, give way; ~ *back on*, have recourse to; ~ *behind*, lag; ~ *foul of*, come into collision with; quarrel with, attack; ~ *in*, (mil.) take, cause to take, places in line; give way inwards; (of debt etc.) become due; (of lease) run out; ~ *in with*, happen to meet; accede to, agree with (views etc.); ~ *off*, withdraw, decrease, degenerate; (of ship) refuse to answer helm; ~ *out*, quarrel; come to pass, result *well* etc.; (mil.) leave the ranks; ~-*out* radioactive refuse of a nuclear explosion; ~ *short*, be or become insufficient; (of missile) not go far enough; ~ *through*, miscarry, fail; ~ *to*, begin eating or fighting. 10. *falling sickness*, old name for epilepsy; *falling star*: see STAR. ~ *n*. 1. Falling; what falls, esp. amount of rain etc. 2. (now chiefly U.S.) Autumn. 3. (freq. pl.) Cataract, cascade; ~-*line*, line joining waterfalls on parallel rivers. 4. Downward trend, amount of descent. 5. Wrestling-bout, throw in this. 6. Rope of hoisting-tackle. 7. Amount of timber cut down. 8. Succumbing to temptation; *the F~* (*of man*), Adam's sin and its results.

fă'llacy̆ *n*. Misleading argument, sophism; (logic) material or formal flaw which vitiates a syllogism; delusion, error; unsoundness, delusiveness, disappointing quality. **fallā'cious** (-sh*u*s) *adj*. **fallā'ciously̆** *adv*. **fallā'ciousnĕss** *n*.

fă'l-lă'l *n*. Piece of finery.

fa'llen (faw-) *adj*.: see FALL; (esp., of woman) unchaste (archaic).

fă'llible *adj*. Liable to err or be erroneous. **făllĭbĭ'lĭty̆** *n*.

Fallō'pĭan tūbe. Oviduct in humans and other mammals. [discovered by G. *Falloppio*, Italian physician (1523–62)]

fă'llow[1] (-ō) *n*. & *adj*. (Ground) ploughed and harrowed but left uncropped for a year. ~ *v.t.* Plough and break up (land) for sowing or to destroy weeds.

fă'llow[2] (-ō) *adj*. Of pale brownish or reddish yellow (now only in ~ *deer*, species of deer (*Dama dama*) smaller than the red deer and usu. dappled).

false (fawls *or* fŏls) *adj*. 1. Erroneous; not true or correct. 2. Lying, deceitful; treacherous, unfaithful *to*; deceptive; spurious, sham, artificial. 3. Improperly so called, pseudo-; subsidiary, supplementary; substituted for, supplementing. 4. ~ *alarm*, alarm given without good cause, either to deceive or under misapprehension of danger; ~ *bottom*, partition built close to bottom as in a box or trunk; ~ *card*, card played contrary to usual custom, in order to mislead opponents; ~ *colours*, flag one has no right to (freq. fig.); ~ *concord*, (gram.) breach of rules for agreement of words in sentence; ~ *dawn*, transient light in east, freq. preceding true dawn by about an hour; ~ *imprisonment*, illegal imprisonment or restraint; ~ *quantity*, incorrect length of vowel in (Latin) verse or pronunciation; ~ *position*, position compelling person to seem inconsistent or act inconsistently with his real character or aims; ~ *pretences*, misrepresentations meant to give false impression; ~ *start*, wrong start in racing; ~ *step*, stumble; transgression; *fa'lse-work*, (eng.) temporary supports enabling construction of building etc. to proceed until it is self-supporting. **fa'lsely̆** *adv*. **fa'lsenĕss, fa'lsĭty̆** *ns*. **false** *adv*. *play* (*person*) ~, cheat or betray him.

fa'lsehŏŏd (fawls-h- *or* fŏls-) *n.* Falsity; something untrue; contrariety to fact; lying, lie(s).

falsĕ'ttō (fawl- *or* fŏl-) *n.* Voice or register above the natural range esp. in men, singer with such voice; (fig.) high voice of indignation. ~ *adj.* & *adv.*

fa'lsĭfȳ (fawl- *or* fŏl-) *v.t.* Fraudulently alter (document); misrepresent; make wrong, pervert; disappoint (hope, fear, etc.); show to be false. **falsĭfĭcā'tion** *n.*

Fa'lstaff (faw'lstahf *or* fŏl-), Sir John. Fat convivial good-humoured braggart in Shakespeare's 'Henry IV' and 'Merry Wives of Windsor'. **Falsta'ffian** *adj.*

fa'lter (fawl- *or* fŏl-) *v.* Stumble, stagger, go unsteadily; stammer, speak hesitatingly; waver, lose courage, flinch. **fa'lterĭnglȳ** *adv.*

fāme *n.* Public report, renown; reputation, good reputation; renown, celebrity. ~ *v.t.* (pass.) Be currently reported. **fāmed** (-md) *adj.* Famous, much spoken of.

fami'lĭal *adj.* Of, occurring in, characteristic of (members of) a family.

famĭ'liar (-ly*ar*) *adj.* 1. Extremely friendly, intimate (*with*); closely acquainted *with* (some subject); ~ *spirit*, demon attending and obeying magician etc. 2. Well-known, no longer novel, (*to*); common, current, usual. 3. Unceremonious, free, over-free; amorously or sexually intimate (*with*). **famĭ'liarlȳ** *adv.* **famĭ'liar** *n.* 1. (R.C. Ch.) Person rendering domestic but not menial services in household of pope or bishop; (hist.) officer of Inquisition, chiefly employed in arresting and imprisoning accused. 2. Intimate friend or associate. 3. Familiar spirit.

famĭliă'rĭtȳ *n.* Close intercourse, intimacy *with* (person, subject); amorous intimacy, (pl.) caresses etc.; unceremoniousness, treating of inferiors or superiors as equals.

famĭ'liarize (-ly*a*-) *v.t.* Make (thing) well known; make well acquainted or at home *with*. **famĭliarīzā'tion** *n.*

famille (fămē) *n.* ~ *rose, verte* (vārt), etc., Chinese enamelled porcelain (chiefly 18th-c.) of which the predominant colour is red, green, etc. [Fr., = 'family']

fă'mĭlȳ *n.* 1. Members of household, parents, children, servants, etc.; set of parents and children, or of relations, whether living together or not; person's children. 2. All descendants of common ancestor, house, lineage; group of peoples from common stock. 3. Group of objects, languages, etc., distinguished by common features; (biol.) grouping above *genus* and below *order*, with Latin name ending in *-idae* for zoological families and usu. in *-aceae* for plant families. 4. ~ *allowance*: see ALLOWANCE; ~ *bible*, large bible with fly-leaves for registering births etc.; ~ *income supplement*, benefit paid to families whose income is below a prescribed amount; ~ *likeness*, that between relations, vague resemblance; ~ *man*, man with family, domestic person; ~ *planning*, birth control; *in the* ~ *way*, pregnant.

fă'mine *n.* Extreme scarcity of food in district etc.; dearth of something specified; hunger, starvation; ~ *prices*, prices raised by scarcity.

fă'mish *v.* Reduce, be reduced, to extreme hunger.

fā'mous *adj.* Celebrated (*for*); well known; (colloq.) excellent. **fā'mouslȳ** *adv.*

fă'mūlus *n.* (pl. *-lī*). Attendant on magician.

făn[1] *n.* 1. Winnowing-machine. 2. Instrument, usu. folding and sector-shaped when spread out, on radiating ribs, for agitating air to cool the face; anything so spread out, as bird's tail, wing, leaf, kind of ornamental vaulting; rotating apparatus giving current of air for ventilation, etc.; (naut.) (blade of) screw, propeller; (in windmill) small sail for keeping head towards wind; ~ *belt*, belt driving radiator fan on car engine; ~ *heater*, heater containing electric fan that forces air over electrically-heated element into room etc.; *fa'nlight,* fan-shaped window over door; ~*-tail,* fan-shaped tail or end; kind of pigeon with fan-shaped tail; ~ *tracery,* elaborate tracery of a fan vault; ~ *vault, vaulting,* vault, vaulting, with ribs diverging like sticks of a fan, Characteristic of English architecture of the 15th c. ~ *v.* 1. Winnow (corn); winnow away(chaff). 2. Sweep *away* (as) by wind from fan; move (air) with fan; drive current of air (as) with fan upon, to cool (face etc.) or to kindle (flame); (of breeze) blow gently on, cool. 3. Spread *out* in fan shape. **fă'nner** *n.* Winnowing-machine; vane or wheel of this.

făn² *n.* Devotee of specified amusement, or of a particular person or thing; ~ *mail,* letters from fans. [abbrev. of *fanatic*]

fană'tic *n.* & *adj.* (Person) filled with excessive or unreasoning enthusiasm, esp. in religion. **fană'tical** *adj.* **fană'tically** *adv.* **fană'ticism** *n.*

fă'ncier *n.* Connoisseur in some article or animal (as *rose-*~, *bird-*~).

fă'nciful *adj.* Indulging in fancies, whimsical, capricious; fantastically designed, ornamented, etc.; imaginary, unreal. **fă'ncifully** *adv.* **fă'ncifulness** *n.*

fă'ncy *n.* 1. Delusion; unfounded belief. 2. Faculty of calling up things not present, of inventing imagery; mental image; supposition resting on no solid grounds, arbitrary notion. 3. Caprice, whim; individual taste, inclination; *the* ~, those who have a certain hobby, fanciers, esp. patrons of boxing; ~ *free,* not in love; ~ *man,* (slang) woman's lover; pimp; ~ *woman,* (slang) = MISTRESS, 4. ~ *adj.* Ornamental, not plain; particoloured (of flowers etc.); capricious, whimsical, extravagant; based on imagination, not fact; (of animal) bred for particular points or qualities; ~ *dress,* fanciful costume, esp. representing historical or fictitious character etc., worn for party or ball; ~*-work,* ornamental needlework etc. ~ *v.t.* 1. Picture to oneself; conceive, imagine; be inclined to suppose, rather think. 2. (colloq.) Have good conceit of (*oneself* etc.); take a fancy to, like. 3. Breed, grow (animals, plants) in order to develop particular points or qualities.

fandă'ngle (-nggl) *n.* Fantastic ornament, tomfoolery.

făndă'ngō (-ngg-) *n.* Lively Spanish dance in $\frac{3}{4}$ time; tune for this.

fāne *n.* (poet.) Temple.

fă'nfāre *n.* Short showy or ceremonious sounding of trumpets, bugles, etc.

fănfăronā'de *n.* Arrogant talk, brag; fanfare.

făng *n.* Canine tooth, esp. of dogs and wolves; serpent's venom-tooth; spike of tool held in the stock; (prong of) root of tooth.

fă'n-tă'n *n.* Chinese gambling game in which a number of small coins are placed under a bowl and the players bet as to what will be the remainder when the pile is divided by four. [Chin. *fan-t'an* repeated divisions]

făntā'sia (-z-; *or -azē'a*) *n.* Musical composition in which form is subservient to fancy.

fă'ntăst *n.* Visionary, dreamer.

făntă'stic *adj.* Extravagantly fanciful; grotesque or quaint in design etc.; (colloq.) very great; remarkable. **făntă'stically** *adv.* **făntă'sticalness, făntăstică'lity** *ns.*

fă'ntasy, ph- *n.* Image-making faculty, esp. when extravagant or visionary; mental image; fantastic design; fantasia; whimsical speculation.

Fă'nti (-ē), **Fă'ntee** *n.* Member, language, of a Negro people inhabiting Ghana.

F.A.N.Y. *abbrev.* First Aid Nursing Yeomanry.

F.A.O. *abbrev.* Food and Agriculture Organization.

far *adv.* At a great distance, a long way off; to a great distance or advanced point; by a great interval, by much; *as* ~ *as,* right to, not short of; *as ~ as, so ~ as, in so ~ as*, to whatever extent; *by ~*, by a large amount; *how ~*, to what extent; *so ~*, to such a distance, up to now; *~-away*, remote, long-past; (of look etc.) absent, dreamy; *~-between*, infrequent; *~-famed*, widely known; *~-fetched*, (of simile, illustration, etc.) studiously sought out, strained; *~-flung*, (rhet.) widely extended; *~ gone*, advanced; very ill, very drunk, much in debt, etc.; *~ off*, remote; *~-reaching*, widely applicable; carrying many consequences; *~-seeing*, prescient, prudent; *~-sighted*, far-seeing; seeing distant things more clearly than near ones. ~ *adj*. Distant, remote; *F~ East*, remote eastern regions of Old World, esp. China and Japan; *F~ West*, (N. Amer.) regions in Rocky Mountains and along Pacific coast; (formerly) area west of earliest U.S. settlements (now called *Middle West*).

fă'rad *n*. Unit of capacitance, capacitance of a capacitor in which a charge of one coulomb raises the potential difference between the plates by one volt (abbrev. F). [f. FARADAY]

Fă'raday, Michael (1791–1867). English physicist and chemist; famous for his discovery of electric and magneto-electric induction and for his work on electrolysis.

far̂ce[1] *n*. Dramatic work with sole object of exciting laughter; this species of drama; absurdly futile proceeding, pretence, mockery. **far̂'cĭcal** *adj*. **far̂'cĭcallÿ** *adv*. **far̂cică'litÿ** *n*.

far̂ce[2] *v.t.* (archaic) Season, spice, stuff. ~ *n*. Forcemeat.

far̂'cÿ *n*. Slow chronic disease of oxen etc., caused by a fungus.

far̂'del *n*. (archaic) Bundle, burden.

fāre *v.i.* 1. Journey, go, travel (poet.). 2. Happen, turn out; get on *well, ill*, etc., have specified luck. 3. Be entertained, be fed, feed oneself, *well*, etc. ~ *n*. 1. Cost of passenger's conveyance, passage-money. 2. Food provided.

fārewĕ'll (-rw-), *int*. Good-bye. ~ *n*. Leave-taking, parting good wishes.

farī'na *n*. Flour or meal of corn, nuts, or starchy roots; powdery substance; (chem.) starch. **fărĭnā'ceous** (-sh*us*) *adj*.

fă'rĭnōse *adj*. Mealy, sprinkled with powder.

far̂m *n*. Tract of land (orig. one held on lease) used for cultivation; also, tract of water used for breeding oysters etc.; dwelling-place attached to farm; *~-hand*, worker on farm; *fa'rmhouse*, dwelling-house of farm; *far'mstead*, farm with buildings on it; *far'myard*, enclosure attached to farmhouse. ~ *v*. 1. Cultivate, till; till the soil, be a farmer. 2. Take proceeds of (tax, office, etc.) on payment of fixed sum; let (*out*) proceeds of (tax etc.) to person for fixed sum; let labour of (persons) for hire; arrange for (work) to be performed by other than principal contractor.

far̂'mer *n*. One who farms (esp. land); *~-general*, (hist.) one who, under the French monarchy, farmed the taxes of a particular district.

far̂'ō *n*. Gambling card-game in which players bet on the order in which certain cards will appear when taken singly from top of pack. [f. PHARAOH]

Far̂'öe I'slands (-ō, īl*a*ndz). (also *Faröes*) Group of islands in the N. Atlantic belonging to Denmark; capital, Thorshavn.

farou'che (-ōōsh) *adj*. Sullen, shy.

farrā'gō (*or* -rah-) *n*. Medley, hotchpotch. [L, = 'mixed fodder' (*far* corn)]

fă'rrĭer *n*. Shoeing-smith; horse-doctor. **fă'rrĭerÿ** *n*.

fă'rrow (-ō) *n*. Giving birth to, litter of, pigs. ~ *v*. Produce (pigs); produce pigs.

far̂t *v.i.* (vulg.) Emit wind from anus. ~ *n*. (vulg.) Emission of wind from anus.

far̂'ther (-dh-) *adv*. & *adj*. Further. **far̂'thermōst** *adj*. **far̂'thėst** *adv*. & *adj*.

far̂'thing (-dh-) *n*. Former British coin, one quarter of an old penny; very small amount.

făr'thĭngāle (-dhĭngg-) *n.* Device for making the skirt stand out from the body, worn by women in 16th and 17th centuries, and consisting either of a petticoat with whaleone hoops or of a stiff horseshoe-shaped cushion; ~ *chair*, 17th-c. chair with wide seat, low straight back, and no arms.

f.a.s. *abbrev.* Free alongside ship.

fă'scēs (-z) *n.pl.* Bundle of wooden rods with axe in middle, orig. symbol of king's authority in ancient Rome, carried before Roman consul or other high official (6, 12, etc., bundles acc. to rank); this as emblem of Italian Fascists. [L pl. of *fascis* bundle]

Fă'sci (-shē) *n.pl.* Groups of men organized politically, such as those in Sicily *c* 1895 and those of the Fascists.

fă'scia (-shĭ*a*) *n.* 1. (archit.) Long flat surface of wood or stone under eaves or cornice (cf. FACIA). 2. (anat.) Thin sheet of connective tissue separating muscle layers and ensheathing muscle bundles. 3. Stripe, band, fillet, belt. **fă'scial** *adj.*

fă'sciātėd (-shĭ-) *adj.* 1. (bot., of contiguous parts) Compressed, growing into one. 2. Striped. **făsciā'tion** *n.*

fă'scĭcle, fă'scĭcūle *n.* 1. One part of book published by instalments. 2. (bot. etc.) Bunch, bundle. **fascĭ'cūlar, fascĭ'cūlate, -ātėd** *adjs.* **fascĭcūlā'tion** *n.*

fă'scĭnāte *v.t.* Deprive (victim) of power of escape or resistance by one's look or presence (esp. of serpents); attract irresistibly, enchant, charm. **fă'scĭnātĭng** *adj.* **fă'scĭnātinglỹ** *adv.* **făscĭnā'tion** *n.*

fă'scĭnātor *n.* (esp., formerly) Woman's scarf or hood of soft material worn over hair.

făscĭ'ne (-sēn) *n.* Long faggot used for engineering purposes, esp. in war for lining trenches, making batteries, etc.

Fă'scĭsm (*or* făsh-) *n.* Principles and organization of Italian nationalist anti-communist dictatorship (1922–43); (transf., usu. *f*~) system of extreme right-wing or authoritarian views. **Fă'scĭst, fă'scĭst** *n.* & *adj.* [see FASCES]

făsh *v.t.* & *n.* (Sc.) Bother, trouble, inconvenience.

fă'shion (-sh*o*n) *n.* 1. Make, shape; style, pattern, manner; *after, in, a* ~, tolerably, somehow or other, not too well. 2. Prevailing custom, esp. in dress; *the* ~, mode of dress, speech, etc., adopted in society for time being; person, thing, temporarily admired or discussed; *man* etc. *of* ~, person of social standing, moving in and conforming with upper-class society; ~*-plate*, (obs.) engraved, often coloured picture of person(s) wearing clothes of latest designs; (fig.) person wearing such clothes. ~ *v.t.* Give shape to, form, mould.

fă'shionable (-sh*o*n-) *adj.* Following, suited to, the fashion; characteristic of, treating of, patronized by, persons of fashion. **fă'shionablenėss** *n.* **fă'shionablỹ** *adv.*

fast[1] (fah-) *v.i.* 1. Abstain from all or some kinds of food as religious observance or in sign of mourning. 2. Go without food. ~ *n.* Act of fasting; season or day appointed for fasting; going without food; ~*-day*, day appointed for fasting.

fast[2] (fah-) *adj.* 1. Firmly fixed or attached; (of friends) steadfast; (of colour etc.) not fading or washing out. 2. Rapid, quick-moving; producing quick movement; (of watch etc.) more advanced than standard time; (of bowler, at cricket) bowling fast balls; (photog., of lens) transmitting a large amount of light; (of film) very sensitive to light; (of persons) dissipated (see below); *fa'stback*, motor-car with back sloping in continuous line; ~ *one*, (colloq.) shrewd or unscrupulous action. ~ *adv.* 1. Firmly; fixedly; tightly; securely. 2. (archaic & poet.) Close *beside, upon*, etc. 3. Quickly; in quick succession; *live* ~, live in a dissipated way; expend much energy in short time.

fa'sten (fah'sn) *v.* 1. Make fast,

attach, fix; secure by some tie or bond; become fast. 2. Direct (look, thoughts, etc.) keenly *on*; fix (nickname etc.) *on*; ~ *on*, lay hold of, single out for attack, seize on (pretext). **fa'stener** (-sn*er*), **fa'stening** *ns.*

fǎsti'dious *adj.* Easily disgusted, exacting in taste, hard to please. **fǎsti'diouslȳ** *adv.* **fǎsti'diousnèss** *n.*

fǎsti'giāte *adj.* (bot.) With conical or tapering outline; with many branches more or less parallel to stem.

fa'stnèss (fah-) *n.* (esp.) Stronghold, fortress.

fǎt *adj.* 1. Fed up for slaughter, fatted; well-fed, plump; corpulent; thick, substantial (esp. of printing-type). 2. Greasy, oily, unctuous; (U.S., of wood) resinous; (of clay etc.) sticky. 3. Fertile, rich; abundant; (slang, of actor's part) offering abundant opportunity for skill, display, etc.; *a ~ lot*, (iron.) very little. 4. *~-head*, (colloq.) stupid person; *fa'tstock*, livestock fattened for slaughter; *~-witted*, (colloq.) stupid. ~ *n.* 1. Fat part of anything; (colloq.) best or richest part; *live on the ~ of the land*, have the best of everything. 2. Oily substance composing fat parts of animal bodies; (chem.) one of the organic compounds of which animal fats are composed, glyceryl ester of a fatty acid. ~ *v.* Fatten; *kill the fatted calf* (see Luke 15), receive returned prodigal with joy. **fǎ't-lèss, fǎ'ttish** *adjs.* **fǎ'tnèss** *n.*

fā'tal *adj.* 1. Like fate, inevitable, necessary; of, appointed by, destiny; ~ *sisters*, the Fates. 2. Fateful, important, decisive. 3. Destructive, ruinous, ending in death; deadly, sure to kill. **fā'tallȳ** *adv.*

fā'talism *n.* Belief that all events are predetermined by arbitrary decree; submission to all that happens as inevitable. **fā'talist** *adj.* & *n.* **fātali'stic** *adj.* **fātali'stically** *adv.*

fatǎ'litȳ *n.* 1. Subjection to, supremacy of, fate; predestined liability to disaster; fatal influence. 2. Misfortune, calamity; death by accident, in war, etc.

fā'talīze *v.* Incline to fatalism; subject to government by fate.

Fa'ta Mŏrga'na (fah-, -gah-). Italian name of Morgan le Fay, ('the fairy'), sister of King ARTHUR, legends of whom are found in Sicily, introduced perh. by Norman settlers there; applied to a mirage seen on S. Italian and Sicilian coasts, which magnifies vertically so that buildings appear like Morgan's fairy palaces.

fāte *n.* 1. Power predetermining events unalterably from eternity; (myth.) goddess of destiny; *the Fates*, (Gk myth.) the three Greek goddesses of destiny, Clotho, Lachesis, and Atropos; (Scand. myth.) Norns. 2. What is destined to happen; appointed lot of person etc.; ultimate condition, destiny; death, destruction, ruin. ~ *v.t.* (usu. pass.) Preordain; *fated*, doomed to calamity.

fā'teful (-tf-) *adj.* Prophetic; fraught with destiny, important, decisive; controlled by, showing power of, fate. **fā'tefullȳ** *adv.*

fa'ther (fahdh-) *n.* 1. Male parent; father-in-law; stepfather; one who has adopted a child; progenitor, forefather. 2. Originator, designer, early leader; one who deserves filial reverence; religious teacher or counsellor; ~ *of lies* (see John 8: 44), the Devil; *Fathers* (*of the Church*), Christian writers of first five centuries. 3. *the F~*, God; (theol.) first person of the Trinity. 4. (eccles.) Confessor, spiritual director; priest belonging to religious order or congregation; superior of monastic house; *Right, Most, Reverend F~ in God*, titles of bishop, archbishop; *the Holy F~*, the Pope. 5. Venerable person, god; oldest member, doyen; (pl.) leading men, elders; *F~ of the House*, member of House of Commons who has sat for longest unbroken period. 6. *~-in-law*, father of one's wife or husband; *fa'therland*, one's native country; *the Fatherland*, Germany. **fa'therlèss, fa'therlīke, fa'therlȳ** *adjs.* **fa'therhood, fa'therlīnèss** *ns.*

fa'ther *v.t.* Beget, be the father of; originate (statement etc.); pass as, confess oneself, the father, author, of; govern paternally; fix paternity of (child, book, etc.) *on*.

fă'thom (-dh-) *n.* Measure of 6 feet, chiefly used in soundings; quantity of wood 6 ft square in section. ~ *v.t.* Measure with fathom-line, sound (depth of water); (fig.) get to the bottom of, comprehend. **fă'thomlėss** *adj.* That cannot be fathomed, of measureless depth. **fă'thomlėsslȳ** *adv.*

fathŏ'mėter (-dh-) *n.* Instrument for determining depth of sea by measuring time taken by sound-wave to reach the bottom and return.

fati'gue (-ēg) *n.* 1. Weariness after exertion. 2. Weakness in metals etc. caused by cyclic variations in stress. 3. Task etc. that wearies; soldier's non-military duty, sometimes allotted as punishment; (also ~-*party*) party to which such a duty is assigned. ~ *v.t.* Cause fatigue to, exhaust.

Fă'tĭma. Daughter of Muhammad by his first wife. **Fă'tĭmīte, Fă'tĭmid** *adj.* & *n.* (Person) descended from Fatima and her husband Ali; (member) of Arabian dynasty ruling part of N. Africa, Egypt, and Syria, 908–1171.

fă'tlĭng *n.* Young fatted animal.

fă'tten *v.* Make fat (esp. animals for slaughter); grow fat; enrich (soil).

fă'ttȳ *adj.* 1. Like fat, unctuous, greasy. 2. Consisting of fat, adipose; with morbid deposition of fat; ~ *degeneration*, morbid condition which begins in individual cells and results in deposits of fat in the tissues. 3. (chem.) ~ *acid*, one of a series of acids of the general formula $C_nH_{2n}O_2$, of which some members occur in or are derived from natural fats.

fă'tūous *adj.* Vacantly silly, purposeless, idiotic. **fă'tūouslȳ** *adv.* **fătūousnėss, fatū'ĭtȳ** *ns.*

faubourg (fōboorg) *n.* Suburb, esp. of Paris. [Fr.]

fau'cēs (-z) *n.pl.* (anat.) Cavity at back of mouth from which larynx and pharynx open out.

fau'cėt *n.* (dial. & U.S.) Tap.

faugh (faw) *int.* Exclamation of disgust.

fault (*or* fŏlt) *n.* 1. Defect, imperfection, blemish, of character, structure, appearance, etc.; *to a* ~, excessively. 2. Transgression, offence; thing wrongly done; (rackets, tennis, etc.) ball wrongly served; *double* ~, two consecu-

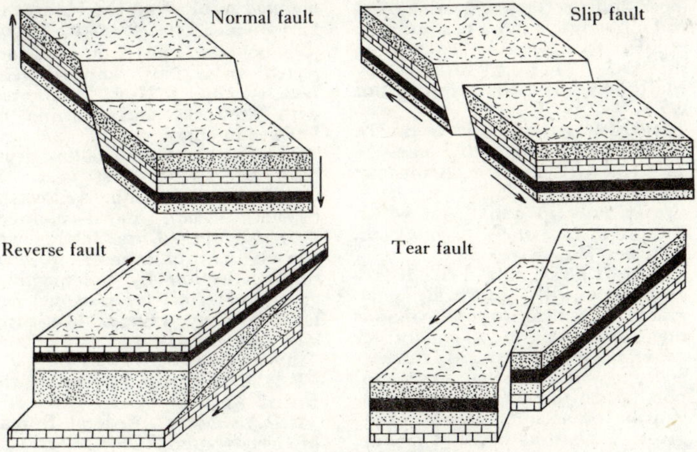

GEOLOGICAL FAULTS

tive faults; *find* ~ *with*, criticize unfavourably, complain of, whence *fau'ltfinder*, *fau'ltfinding* (*ns.*). 3. Culpability, responsibility for something wrong; defect causing specified evil. 4. (hunting) Loss of scent; check so caused; *at* ~, at a loss, in the wrong. 5. Flaw in ice; (geol.) place where rock-layers have fractured and moved out of alignment; ~ *plane*, plane of a fault, surface along which rocks on one side of a fault have moved relatively to those on the other. ~ *v.* Cause fault in (strata etc.); show fault; (chiefly U.S.) find fault with. **fau'ltlėss** *adj.* **fau'ltlėsslў̆** *adv.* **fault'lėssnėss** *n.* **fau'ltў̆** *adj.* **fau'ltilў̆** *adv.* **fau'ltinėss** *n.*

faun *n.* (Rom. myth.) One of the rural deities represented with horns, pointed ears, and tail of goat, and later also with goat's legs like satyrs, with whom they were associated. [f. FAUNUS]

fau'na *n.* Animals or animal life of a region or epoch. **fau'nal** *adj.* [L *Fauna*, rural goddess, sister of FAUNUS]

Fau'nus. (Rom. myth.) God or demigod worshipped by shepherds and farmers and identified with the Greek PAN[3].

Faust (fowst). Wandering astrologer and necromancer who lived in Germany *c* 1488–1541 and was reputed to have sold his soul to the Devil; hero of dramas by Marlowe and Goethe. **Fau'stian** *adj.*

faute de mieux (fōt de myēr). For want of better. [Fr.]

fauteuil (fōtēryĭ) *n.* Armchair; theatre-stall. [Fr.]

faux pas (fō pah). Act which compromises one's reputation, mistake. [Fr.]

fā'vour (-ver) *n.* 1. Friendly regard, goodwill; approval; good graces; kindness beyond what is due, partiality, too lenient or generous treatment; aid, furtherance; *in* ~ *of*, on behalf or in support of; on the side of; to the advantage or account of. 2. Thing given or worn as mark of favour; knot of ribbons, rosette, cockade, badge. 3. (archaic) Looks, countenance. ~ *v.t.* 1. Look kindly upon, approve; treat kindly, countenance; indulge, oblige, *with*. 2. Treat with partiality; be propitious or advantageous to; aid, support. 3. (colloq.) Resemble in face or feature. 4. (journalese) Choose to wear. **fā'voured** (-*erd*) *adj.* (esp.) Having unusual advantages; *most* ~ *nation clause*, clause in trade agreement giving special advantages with regard to import duties, permission to trade, etc., to a particular nation; hence, *most* ~ *nation treatment*; *well-*, *ill-*~, having handsome, ugly, features.

fā'vourable (-ver-) *adj.* Well-disposed, propitious; commendatory, approving; promising, auspicious; helpful, suitable (*to*). **fā'vourablў̆** *adv.* **fā'vourablenėss** *n.*

fā'vourĭte (-ver-) *adj.* Preferred above others; chosen as intimate by king or superior and unduly favoured. ~ *n.* Favourite person or thing; *the* ~, (racing, sports) competitor generally favoured as being most likely to win. **fā'vourĭtĭsm** *n.* (esp.) Favouring one person or group unfairly.

Fawkes (-ks), Guy (1570–1606). Yorkshire Catholic, who, with Catesby and other conspirators, planned to blow up the Houses of Parliament on 5 Nov. 1605 (Gunpowder Plot); he was arrested on 4 Nov. and hanged; *Guy* ~ *day*, 5 Nov., celebrated with fireworks and burning of Fawkes in effigy.

fawn[1] *n.* 1. Young fallow deer, buck or doe of first year. 2. Colour of this, light yellowish-brown. ~ *adj.* Fawn-coloured. ~ *v.* (of deer) Bring forth fawn.

fawn[2] *v.i.* (of animal, esp. dog) Show affection by tail-wagging, grovelling, etc.; (of persons) behave servilely, cringe. **faw'nĭng** *adj.* **faw'nĭnglў̆** *adv.*

fay *n.* Fairy.

F.B.A. *abbrev.* Fellow of the British Academy.

F.B.I. *abbrev.* Federal Bureau of Investigation (U.S.).

F.C. *abbrev.* Football Club.

F.C.A. *abbrev.* Fellow of the Institute of Chartered Accountants.

F.C.I.S. *abbrev.* Fellow of the Chartered Institute of Secretaries.

F.C.O. *abbrev.* Foreign and Commonwealth Office.

F.D. *abbrev.* *Fidei Defensor* (L, = Defender of the Faith).

fē'alty̆ *n.* Feudal tenant's or vassal's fidelity to his lord; acknowledgement or obligation of this.

fear *n.* Painful emotion caused by impending danger or evil; state of alarm; dread *of, lest, that*; dread and reverence; anxiety for the safety *of*; *for ~ of, lest,* in order to avoid or prevent; *no fear!*, it is not likely; *without ~ or favour*, impartially. ~ *v.* Be afraid; be afraid of; hesitate *to* do, shrink from *doing*; revere (God); apprehend, expect uneasily; be afraid *that*. **fear'lėss** *adj.* Feeling no fear, brave. **fear'lėssly̆** *adv.* **fear'lėssnėss** *n.*

fear'ful *adj.* 1. Terrible, awful; (by exaggeration) annoying etc.; (colloq.) very great. 2. Frightened, timid; apprehensive *of, lest*; wanting resolution *to*; reverential. **fear'fully̆** *adv.* **fear'fulnėss** *n.*

fear'some *adj.* Appalling, esp. in appearance (usu. joc.). **fear'somely̆** *adv.* **fear'somenėss** *n.*

fea'sĭble (-z-) *adj.* Practicable, possible; capable of being done or accomplished; (loosely) likely, probable. **feasĭbĭ'lĭty̆** *n.*

feast *n.* 1. Religious anniversary appointed to be observed with rejoicing; annual village festival (orig. held on feast of saint to whom parish church is dedicated); *movable ~*, feast (as Easter etc.) of which date varies from year to year. 2. Sumptuous meal, esp. one given to number of guests and of public nature; (fig.) gratification, rich treat, to senses or mind. ~ *v.* Partake of feast, fare sumptuously; pass (night etc.) *away* in feasting; regale.

feat¹ *n.* Noteworthy act, esp. deed of valour; act of dexterity or strength, surprising trick.

feat² *adj.* (archaic) Adroit, smart, dextrous, neat. **fea'tly̆** *adv.*

fea'ther (fĕdh-) *n.* 1. One of the appendages growing from a bird's

FEATHERS

skin, usu. consisting of a central horny shaft fringed on either side with a vane of barbs forming rounded outline at end; (collect.) plumage; feathered game; *birds of a, of the same, ~*, people of the same kind or character. 2. Piece(s)

GUNPOWDER PLOT: Fawkes and other conspirators

of feather attached to base of arrow or dart to direct flight; plume worn in hat etc.; very light object; *a ~ in one's cap*, something one may be proud of. 3. Tuft or ridge of upright hair; feather-like flaw in gem. 4. (rowing) Action of feathering. 5. *~-bed*, mattress stuffed with feathers; (*v.t.*) make things easy for, pamper; *~-edge*, fine edge of wedge-shaped board; (*v.t.*) give (board) such an edge; *~-headed*, *-brained*, silly; *~-stitch*, zigzag embroidery stitch; *~-weight*, very light thing or person, esp. boxer of weight between bantam-weight and light-weight (see BOXING). **fea'thered** (*-erd*), **fea'therlėss, fea'therỹ** *adjs.* **fea'therĭnėss** *n.* **fea'ther,** *v.* 1. Furnish, adorn, line, coat, with feathers; form feather-like covering or adornment for; *~ one's nest*, enrich oneself. 2. Float, move, wave, like feathers; turn (oar), turn oar, as it leaves water, so that it passes through air edgeways; rotate (blades of propeller) so that they are parallel to direction of motion; (hunting, of hound) make quivering motion of body and tail while seeking scent; (shooting) knock feathers from (bird) without killing.

fea'therĭng (fĕdh-) *n.* (esp.) Plumage; feathers of arrow; feathery structure in animal's coat; feather-like marking in flower.

fea'ture *n.* 1. (usu. pl.) Part(s) of the face, esp. with regard to shape and visible effect. 2. Distinctive or characteristic part of a thing, part that arrests attention; distinctive or prominent article in newspaper; feature film or programme; *~ film*, fictional film forming chief part of programme; *~ programme*, (broadcasting) programme based on one central theme. **fea'turelėss** *adj.* **fea'ture** *v.t.* Stand as distinctive mark upon; portray, sketch prominent points of; (orig. U.S.) make attraction or special feature of; (of film) give prominence to (actor etc.).

Feb. *abbrev.* February.

fĕ'brĭfūge *n.* Medicine to reduce fever; cooling drink. **fĕbrĭ'fūgal** *adj.*

fĕ'brĭle *adj.* Of fever, feverish.

Fĕ'bruarỹ (-rōō-) *n.* 2nd month of Gregorian (12th of Julian) calendar, with 28 days except in leap-year, when it has 29; *~ revolution*: see RUSSIAN revolution. [L *februa*, Roman festival of purification held on 15th of this month]

fec. *abbrev. Fecit* or *fecerunt* (L, = made).

fĕ'cklėss *adj.* Feeble, futile, inefficient. **fĕ'cklėsslỹ** *adv.* **fĕ'cklėssnėss** *n.*

fĕ'cūlent *adj.* Turbid; fetid. **fĕ'cūlence** *n.*

fĕ'cund *adj.* Prolific, fertile; fertilizing. **fėcŭ'ndĭtỹ** *n.*

fĕ'cundāte *v.t.* Make fruitful; = FERTILIZE, 2.

fĕd *adj.*: see FEED; (esp.) *~ up*, (slang) surfeited, disgusted (*with*), bored.

fĕ'deral *adj.* 1. (theol.) Based on doctrine of Covenants; *~ theology*, system based on God's covenant with Adam as representing man, and Christ as representing Church. 2. Of the form of government in which two or more States form a political unity but remain independent in internal affairs; of such political unity, as dist. from the separate States composing it; *F~ Republic of Germany*: see GERMANY. 3. (U.S. hist.) Favouring strong central government; of the Northern or Union party, or its troops, in the Civil War of 1861–5. **fĕ'deralĭsm, fĕ'deralĭst** *ns.* **fĕderalĭ'stĭc** *adj.* **fĕ'deralīze** *v.t.* **fĕderalīzā'tion** *n.* **fĕ'derallỹ** *adv.*

fĕ'derāte *v.* Bind together in league for some common object; organize on federal basis. **fĕ'derate, fĕ'derative** *adjs.* **fĕ'derātor** *n.*

fĕderā'tion *n.* Federating; federated society, esp. federal empire or group of States. **fĕderā'tionist** *n.*

fėdōr'a *n.* (chiefly U.S.) Low soft felt hat with curled brim and crown creased lengthways. ['Fédora', title of play (pop. in U.S. in 1883) by Victorien Sardou]

fee *n.* 1. (hist.) Fief; feudal benefice. 2. (law) Estate of inheritance in land; estate held in fee, lordship; *in* ~, as one's absolute and rightful possession; ~ *farm*, tenure of, estate in, land held in fee-simple subject to perpetual fixed rent, without other services; rent so paid; ~*-simple*, estate, fee, without limitation to any class of heirs; *in* ~*-simple*, in absolute possession; ~*-tail*, fee limited to some particular class of heirs of person to whom it is granted. 3. Sum payable to public officer for performing his function; sum paid or due to professional man, performer, etc., for occasional service or performance; entrance-money for examination, society, etc.; terminal payment for instruction at school. ~ *v.t.* Pay fee to; engage for a fee.

fee'ble *adj.* Weak, infirm; deficient in character or intelligence; wanting in energy, force, or effect; dim, indistinct. **fee'bleness** *n.* **fee'blў** *adv.*

feed *v.* (past t. & past part. *fĕd*). 1. Supply with food; put food into mouth of; graze (cattle); deal out (fodder) to animals; take food, eat; serve as food for. 2. Gratify (vanity, eyes, etc.), comfort (person) *with* hope, etc. 3. Nourish, make grow. 4. Keep (reservoir, fire, etc.) supplied; supply (machine) with material to work on; supply (material) (*on*) *to* machine; (footb. etc.) give a pass to; (theatr. slang) give (actor) cues, opportunities for jokes, etc. 5. *fee'dback*, (electr.) return of a fraction of the output signal from one stage of a circuit, amplifier, etc., to the input of the same or a preceding stage; (transf.) modification of a process etc. by its own effects; *feeding-bottle*, bottle with teat for feeding infants; *feeding-cup*, vessel with spout for feeding invalid; ~*-pipe*, pipe conveying material, water, etc., to machine; ~*-shaft*, driving shaft for advancing cutting tool of lathe; ~ *-tank,-trough*, tank holding water for locomotive. ~ *n.* 1. Act of feeding; giving of food; *off one's* ~, with no appetite; *out at* ~, turned out to graze. 2. Pasturage, green crops; horse's allowance of oats etc.; fodder. 3. (colloq.) Meal, feast. 4. Feeding of machine etc., material supplied. 5. (theatr. slang) One who feeds another actor with cues etc.

fee'der *n.* (esp.) 1. Child's feeding-bottle. 2. Child's bib. 3. Tributary stream. 4. Hopper or feeding-apparatus in machine. 5. (freq. attrib.) Branch road, railway line, or air service linking outlying districts with main line.

feel *v.* (past t. & past part. *fĕlt*). 1. Explore by touch; search (*about*) with hand *after*, *for*; try to ascertain by touch *whether*, *if*, *how*; ~ *one's way*, find one's way by groping. 2. Perceive by touch; have sensation of touch; ~ *one's legs*, *feet*, find firm standing; be at ease. 3. Be conscious of (sensation, emotion, conviction); be consciously; experience, undergo consciously; be affected by, behave as if conscious of; ~ *like*, (colloq.) have inclination for. 4. Be emotionally affected by; have sympathy *with*, compassion *for*; have vague or emotional conviction (*that*). 5. (quasi-pass.) Be realized as; seem, produce impression of being. ~ *n.* Sense of touch; testing by touch; sensation characterizing something.

fee'ler *n.* (esp.) 1. (pop.) Organ in certain animals for testing things by touch or searching for food. 2. ~*-gauge*, gauge with blades for measuring gaps. 3. (fig.) Tentative proposal or hint.

fee'lĭng *n.* (esp.) 1. Sense of touch; physical sensation. 2. Emotion; (pl.) susceptibilities, sympathies; readiness to feel, tenderness for others' sufferings. 3. Consciousness *of*; conviction not based solely on reason; sentiment. 4. (art etc.) General emotional effect produced. ~ *adj.* (esp.) Sensitive, sympathetic; showing emotion. **fee'lĭnglў** *adv.* **fee'lĭngness** *n.*

feign (fān) *v.* 1. Invent (excuse, story, accusation); forge (document). 2. Represent fictitiously; imitate deceptively.

feint[1] (fānt) *n.* Sham attack

(blow, cut, thrust, etc.) to divert attention or deceive opponent; pretence. ~ *v.i.* Make feint.

feint² (fānt) *adj.* & *adv.* (commerc.) Faint(ly), in ~ *lines, ruled* ~. [= FAINT]

feldspar: see FELSPAR.

fėlĭ'citāte *v.t.* Congratulate (*on*). **fėlĭcitā'tion** *n.*

fėlĭ'citous *adj.* Strikingly apt in expression or manner (of words, action, etc., or of person). **fėlĭ'citouslȳ** *adv.*

fėlĭ'citȳ *n.* 1. Being happy, intense happiness; blessing; fortunate trait. 2. Happy faculty in expression, appropriateness; well-chosen phrase.

fē'līne *adj.* Of cats; cat-like. ~ *n.* Member of Felidae or cat family. **fėlĭ'nitȳ** *n.*

fĕll¹ *n.* Animal's hide or skin with the hair; thick or matted hair or wool, fleece.

fĕll² *n.* Hill, mountain (now only in proper names); wild high stretch of waste or pasture land in N. England and parts of Scotland.

fĕll³ *adj.* Fierce, ruthless, terrible, destructive.

fĕll⁴ *v.* 1. Strike (person, animal) down by blow or cut. 2. Cut down (tree). 3. Stitch (edge of seam) so that it lies flat. ~ *n.* Amount of timber cut.

fĕ'llah (*-a*) *n.* (pl. *fellahin*, pr. -hēn). Egyptian peasant. [Arab. *fallāh* = 'husbandman']

fĕ'llōe (*or* -lĭ) *n.* Outer circle of wheel, attached by spokes; part of this.

fĕ'llow (-ō) *n.* 1. One associated with another, comrade. 2. Counterpart, match; other of pair; equal, one of same class, contemporary. 3. Incorporated member of college or collegiate foundation; one of company or corporation who, with their head, constitute a college; elected graduate holding stipendiary position for term of years on condition of pursuing specified branch of study. 4. Member of various learned societies. 5. Man; boy. 6. (attrib.) Belonging to same class; associated in joint action; in same relation to same object; ~ *creature*, person or animal also created by God; ~-*feeling*, sympathy; ~ *traveller*, (esp.) non-Communist who sympathizes with aims and general policy of Communist party.

fĕ'llowship *n.* 1. Participation, sharing, community of interest. 2. (also *good* ~) Companionship, intercourse, friendliness. 3. Body of associates, company; guild, corporation; brotherhood. 4. Dignity or emoluments of college fellow.

fĕ'lō dė sē. 1. (pl. *felonēs*, *felos*) Self-murderer. 2. Self-murder. [Anglo-L, = 'felon about himself']

fĕ'lon¹ *n.* Whitlow.

fĕ'lon² *n.* One who has committed felony. ~ *adj.* (poet.) Cruel, wicked, murderous. **fėlō'nious** *adj.* Criminal; (law) of, involving, felony; that has committed felony. **fėlō'niouslȳ** *adv.*

fĕ'lonrȳ *n.* Class or body of felons (orig., the convict population of Australia).

fĕ'lonȳ *n.* Grave indictable offence, such as murder, manslaughter, rape, larceny (orig., crime the penalty for which included forfeiture of lands and goods, and corruption of blood), until 1967 dist. from MISDEMEANOUR.

fĕ'lspar, fĕ'ldspar *n.* Any of a group of minerals, esp. potassium aluminium silicate, usu. white or flesh-coloured, occurring in crystals and in granite and other primary rocks used in ceramic and enamelling processes. **fĕl(d)spă'thic** *adj.*

fĕlt¹ *n.* Fabric made by shrinking and rolling wool, fur, etc. so that the fibres interlock; ~ (*tip(ped)*) *pen*, pen with felt point. ~ *v.* Make into felt; mat together, become matted; cover with felt.

felt²: see FEEL.

fėlŭ'cca *n.* Small Mediterranean coasting-vessel with oars or lateen sails or both.

fē'māle *adj.* 1. Of the sex which bears offspring or produces eggs; (of plants or their parts) fruit-bearing. 2. Of women; of female animals or plants. 3. (of part of machinery etc.) Designed to receive corresponding male part; ~ *screw*: see SCREW¹. ~ *n.* Female person or animal; (now contempt.) woman, girl.

fĕme *n.* (law) Woman or wife; ~ *co'vert* (kŭ-), woman under protection of her husband, married woman; ~ *sōle*, spinster, widow, divorced woman; married woman entirely independent of her husband as regards property.

fĕmĭnē'ĭtў *n.* Womanliness; womanishness.

fĕ'mĭnĭne *adj.* 1. Of women; womanly; womanish. 2. (gram.) Of gender to which appellations of females belong; (of ending) proper to this gender. 3. (pros.) ~ *caesura*, caesura not immediately following stress; ~ *ending*, ending of line of verse with last stress on penult; ~ *rhyme*, in Fr. verse, one ending in mute *e* (a common feminine suffix); hence, rhyme of two syllables of which second is unstressed. **fĕ'mĭnĭnelў** *adv.* **fĕ'mĭnĭne** *n.* (gram.) (Word having) feminine gender. **fĕ'mĭnĭnenėss, fĕmĭnĭ'nĭtў** *ns.*

fĕ'mĭnĭsm *n.* Advocacy of extended recognition of claims and achievements of women; advocacy of women's rights. **fĕ'mĭnĭst** *n.* **fĕmĭnĭ'stic** *adj.*

fĕ'mĭnīze *v.* Make, become, feminine. **fĕmĭnīzā'tion** *n.*

femme de chambre (făm de shahṅbr). Lady's maid; chambermaid. [Fr.]

femme fatale (făm fătăl'). Woman whose attractiveness causes dangerous situations. [Fr, = 'fatal woman']

fē'mur (-*er*) *n.* 1. Thighbone. 2. One of upper portions of insect's leg **fĕ'moral** *adj.*

fĕn[1] *n.* Low marshy or flooded tract of land; *the ~s*, low-lying districts in Cambridgeshire, Lincolnshire, and adjoining counties; *the ~-district*, the fens; *fe'nman*, inhabitant of fens; *~-runners*, long skates used for skating on fens.

fĕn[2] *n.* $\frac{1}{100}$ of a renminbi.

fĕnce *n.* 1. Art of fencing; use of the sword 2. Bulwark (archaic); hedge, wall, railing, etc., keeping out intruders from field etc.; *sit on the* ~ remain neutral in contest, be undecided in opinion; *sunk* ~, one placed along bottom of depression in ground; occas. = ditch. 3. Guard, guide, or gauge, regulating movements of tool or machine. 4. Receiver of, receiving-house for, stolen goods. ~ *v.* 1. Practise sword-play; use sword scientifically; ~ *with*, parry, try to evade (question, questioner). 2. Screen, shield, protect (*from, against*); repel, keep *off* or *out*; surround (as) with fence, enclose, fortify. 3. (of horse) Leap fence. 4. Deal in stolen goods. **fĕ'ncer** *n.* (esp.) Swordsman.

fĕ'ncĭble *n.* (hist.) Soldier liable only for defensive service.

fĕ'ncĭng *n.* (esp.) Railing; fences; material for fences.

fĕnd *v.* Ward *off*, keep *away*, repel *from*; provide *for* (usu. oneself).

fĕ'nder *n.* Thing used to keep something off, prevent collision, etc.; guard; metal frame round hearth to prevent falling coals from rolling into room; (naut.) piece of old cable, matting, etc., hung over vessel's side; (U.S.) bumper of motor-car; mudguard.

fĕnestĕ'lla *n.* (archit.) Small wall-niche to south of altar containing piscina and often credence.

fėnĕ'stra *n.* (pl. *-ae*). Small hole or opening in bone etc., esp. one of two (~ *ovalis* and ~ *rotunda*) in internal ear.

fėnĕ'strate *adj.* Having small perforations or openings like a window. **fėnĕ'strātėd** *adj.* Furnished with windows; pierced with hole(s); perforated.

fĕnėstrā'tion *n.* (esp.) 1. Arrangement of windows in building. 2. (surg.) Perforation esp. of bony labyrinth of ear to restore hearing.

Fē'nĭan *adj.* & *n.* (hist.) (Member) of organization formed among Irish in U.S. and in Ireland in the middle of the 19th c. for promoting revolution and overthrowing English government in Ireland. **Fē'nĭanĭsm** *n.* [OIr. *féne* the ancient Irish people, confused with *fiann* warriors defending Ireland under Finn and other legendary kings]

fĕ'nnĕc *n.* Smallest known fox (*Fennecus zerda*, approx. 70 cm long), found in African and Asian deserts.

fĕ'nnel *n.* Fragrant yellow-flowered perennial umbellifer, *Foeniculum vulgare*, used as flavour-

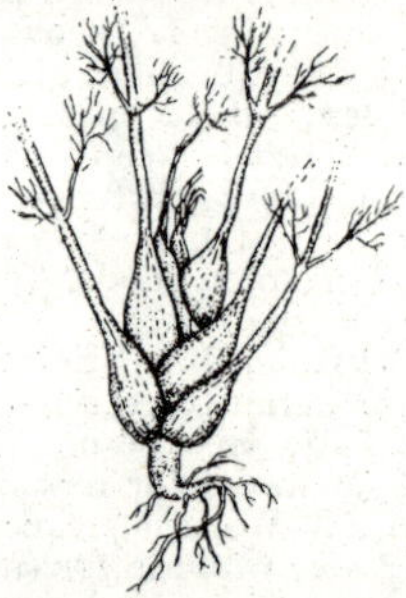

ing in sauces etc.; *oil of* ~, volatile oil extracted from this, used as a carminative.

fĕ'nūgreek *n.* Leguminous plant,

Trigonella foenum-graecum, with seeds used in farriery.

feoff: see FIEF.

feoffee' (fĕf-) *n.* Person to whom freehold estate in land is conveyed by feoffment; (also ~ *in*, *of*, *trust*), trustee invested with freehold estate in land; esp. (pl.) board holding land for charitable or public purposes. **feo'ffment** *n.* Mode of conveyance (now almost obsolete) of freehold estate in fee. **feo'ffer** *n.* One who makes a feoffment.

fer'al *adj.* Wild, untamed, uncultivated; brutal; (zool.) escaped from captivity and reverted to wild state.

Fer'dinand (1452–1516). King of Aragon; by marrying Isabella of Castile, 1469, he united the kingdoms of Aragon and Castile and founded the Spanish monarchy.

fĕ'rĕtorў *n.* Shrine for relics of saint, tomb; bier; chapel in which shrines were deposited.

fer'ĭal *adj.* (eccles., of day) Ordinary, not appointed for festival or fast; (of service etc). for use on ferial day.

fer'īne *adj.* Feral.

Fermă'nagh (-*a*). County of N. Ireland.

fer'mĕnt *n.* 1. Leaven; any fermentative agent. 2. Fermenting, fermentation; agitation, excitement, tumult. **fermĕ'nt** *v.* Suffer, subject to, fermentation; (make) effervesce; excite, stir up, foment.

fermĕntā'tion *n.* Process like that induced by yeast on dough or sugar solutions, with effervescence, evolution of heat, and change of properties; agitation, excitement. **fermĕ'ntatĭve** *adj.*

Fer'mĭ, Enrico (1901–54). Italian physicist, living in U.S.A. from 1939; Nobel Prize for physics 1938.

fer'mium *n.* (chem.) Transuranic element, symbol Fm, at. no. 100, principal isotope at. wt 256. [f. FERMI]

fern *n.* Vascular cryptogamous plant, freq. with feathery fronds, of the order Filicales; ~-*owl*

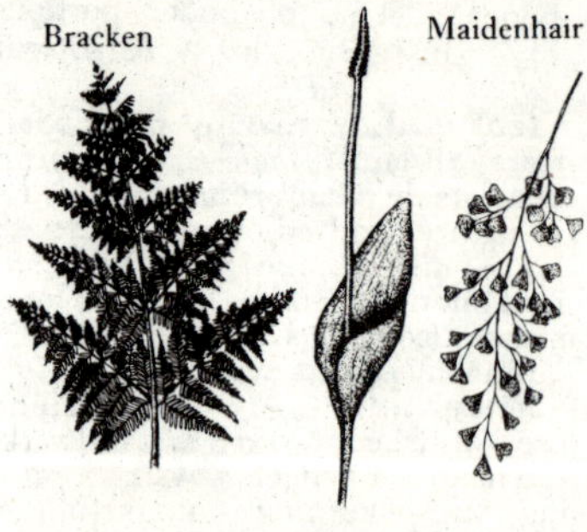

FERN

nightjar; *~-seed*, supposed seed (actually spores) of the fern, once pop. believed to be invisible and to render invisible those who carried it. **fêr'nȳ** *adj.* **fêr'nerȳ** *n.* Place where ferns are grown.

ferō'cious (-shus) *adj.* Fierce, savage, cruel. **ferō'ciouslȳ** *adv.*

ferŏ'citȳ *n.* Ferocious character or act.

Fĕrrâr'a[1]. Town in the Po valley, E. Italy. **Fĕrrārē'se** (-z) *adj.* & *n.* (Native, inhabitant) of Ferrara.

Fĕrrâr'a[2], Andrea. Celebrated maker of swords, probably a Venetian, of the 16th c.; hence, broadsword or claymore.

fĕ'rrāte *n.* (chem.) Salt derived from the hypothetical ferric acid (H_2FeO_4).

fĕ'rrėt[1] *n.* Half-tamed variety of common polecat (*Putorius foetidus*), kept for driving rabbits from burrows, killing rats, etc. ~ *v.* 1. Hunt with ferrets; clear out (holes, ground), take or drive away (rabbits etc.), with ferrets. 2. Rummage, search *about* (*for*); search *out*. **fĕ'rrėtȳ** *adj.* [L *fur* thief]

fĕ'rrėt[2] *n.* Stout cotton or silk tape. [It *fioretti* floss-silk (L *flos* flower)]

fĕrri- *prefix.* (chem.) Containing iron in the ferric or trivalent state.

fĕ'rriage *n.* Conveyance by, charge for using, ferry.

fĕ'rrĭc *adj.* 1. Of iron. 2. (chem.) Applied to compounds of trivalent iron, e.g. ~ *oxide* (Fe_2O_3).

Fĕ'rris wheel. Giant revolving vertical wheel supporting passenger cars on its rim, an amusement at fairs etc. [G. W. G. *Ferris* (1859–96), Amer. engineer]

fĕ'rrīte *n.* 1. (chem.) Compound formed from ferric oxide and a basic oxide or from ferric hydroxide and a base, esp. magnetic substance used in high-frequency electrical components. 2. (metall.) Soft allotrope of pure iron; solid solution based on this allotrope. **fĕrrĭ'tĭc** *adj.*

fĕrro- *prefix.* 1. Of, containing, iron. 2. (chem., in names of compounds) Containing iron in the ferrous or bivalent state.

fĕrro-cŏ'ncrēte *n.* Concrete reinforced by steel bars, netting, etc.

fĕrro-măgnĕ'tĭc *adj.* Possessing the property shown by iron, cobalt, nickel, and their alloys, of having a large magnetic permeability and retaining magnetization in the absence of an external magnetic field. **fĕrromă'gnėtism** *n.*

fĕrro-mă'nganese (-ngganēz) *n.* Alloy of manganese and iron used in making alloy steels.

fĕ'rrotȳpe *n.* Photographic process producing print on thin iron plate; such photograph.

fĕ'rrous *adj.* (chem.) Of or containing iron, esp. in the bivalent state, e.g. ~ *oxide* (FeO); *non-~*, free from iron (applied to the group of alloys including brass, bronze, duralumin, etc.).

ferru'ginous (-ōōj-) *adj.* Of, containing, iron-rust or iron as chemical constituent; rust-coloured, reddish brown.

fĕ'rrule (*or* -ōōl) *n.* Metal ring or cap strengthening end of stick or tube; ring or band giving additional strength or holding parts together.

fĕ'rrȳ *n.* Place where boats pass over river etc., to transport passengers and goods; (provision for) ferrying; (law) right of ferrying and of levying toll for it; *~-boat*, boat used for ferrying; *fe'rryman*, man who keeps or looks after ferry. ~ *v.* Convey, pass, in boat; work (boat), (of boat) pass to and fro, over river, lake, etc.; transport from place to place, esp. on regular service.

fêr'tīle *adj.* Bearing abundantly, fruitful; (of seed or egg etc.) capable of developing into a new individual; *F~ Crescent*, semicircle of fertile land from Israel to Persian Gulf. **fertĭ'lĭtȳ** *n.*

fêr'tĭlīze *v.t.* 1. Make fertile, enrich (esp. soil); make productive. 2. (biol.) Make (ovum etc., female individual or organ) fruitful by introduction of male element. **fêrtĭlīzā'tion** *n.* Fertilizing; (biol.) fusion of male reproductive cell with female one. **fêr'tĭlīzer** *n.* (esp.) Manure; chemical manure, usu. compound containing nitrogen, phosphorus, or potassium.

fĕ'rule (-ōōl) *n.* Cane, rod, etc., esp. flat piece of wood, used for punishing children.

fẽr'vent *adj.* 1. Hot, glowing. 2. Ardent, intense. **fẽr'ventlÿ** *adv.* **fẽr'vencÿ** *n.*

fẽr'vĭd *adj.* 1. (poet.) Hot, glowing. 2. Glowing, impassioned. **fẽr'vĭdlÿ** *adv.*

fẽr'vour (-*ver*) *n.* 1. Glowing condition, intense heat. 2. Vehemence, passion, zeal.

fĕ'scūe *n.* 1. Small stick; pointer. 2. (also ~ *grass*) Grass of genus *Festuca*, valuable as pasture for sheep.

fĕsse *n.* (her.) Stripe across shield, broader than bar.

fĕ'stal *adj.* Of a feast; keeping holiday; gay. **fĕ'stallÿ** *adv.*

fĕ'ster *v.* (of wound or sore) Generate matter, ulcerate; (of poison, disease, grief) cause suppuration, rankle; putrefy, rot; cause festering in. ~ *n.* Festering condition.

fĕ'stival *adj.* (not used predic.) Of, befitting, a feast or feast-day. ~ *n.* Time of festive celebration; merrymaking; (periodic) series of performances (of music, drama, films, etc.).

fĕ'stĭve *adj.* Of a feast; joyous; fond of feasting, jovial. **fĕ'stĭvelÿ** *adv.*

fĕstĭ'vĭtÿ *n.* Gaiety, rejoicing; festive celebration; (pl.) festive proceedings.

fĕstōō'n *n.* Chain of flowers or leaves, or ribbons etc., hung in curve between two points; carved or moulded representation of this. ~ *v.* Adorn (as) with, form into, festoons. **fĕstōō'nerÿ** *n.*

Fĕ'stschrĭft (-stshr-) (pl. *-en* or *-s*) *n.* Collection of writings in honour of eminent scholar. [Ger., = 'festival-writing']

fĕtch[1] *v.* 1. (Go for and) bring back (person or thing); (now rare) cause to come, draw forth (blood, tears, etc); ~ *and carry*, run backwards and forwards with things; ~ *up*, vomit. 2. Bring in, realize, sell for (a price). 3. Heave (sigh); draw (breath); deal (blow). 4. ~ *up*, arrive; come to a stand. **fĕ'tchĭng** *adj.* Attractive, taking. **fĕtch** *n.* 1. (archaic) Far-reaching effort. 2. Dodge, trick.

fĕtch[2] *n.* (archaic) Double or wraith of living person.

fête (fāt) *n.* 1. Festival; great entertainment; bazaar-like function raising money for charity etc. 2. Day of saint after whom child is named, observed in R.C. countries like birthday. ~ *v.t.* Entertain, make much of (person).

fête champêtre (fāt shahṅpātr). Outdoor entertainment, rural festival; picture representing this. [Fr.]

fĕ'tĭd, foe'tĭd (fē-) *adj.* Stinking. **fĕ'tĭdlÿ** *adv.* **fĕ'tĭdness** *n.*

fĕ'tĭsh *n.* Inanimate object worshipped by primitive peoples for its supposed inherent magical powers or as being inhabited by a spirit; anything irrationally reverenced. **fĕ'tĭshĭsm, fĕ'tĭshĭst** *ns.* **fĕtĭshĭ'stĭc** *adj.* [Port. *feitiço* charm, f. L *facticius* factitious]

fĕ'tlŏck *n.* Part of horse's leg where tuft of hair grows behind pastern-joint.

fē'tor *n.* Stench.

fĕ'tter *n.* Shackle for feet; bond; (pl.) captivity; check, restraint; *fe'tterlock*, (heraldic representation of) D-shaped fetter for tethering horse by leg. ~ *v.t.* Bind (as) with fetters; impede, restrain.

Fĕ'ttės. Scottish public school in Edinburgh, founded by Sir William Fettes, opened 1870.

fĕ'ttle *n.* Condition, trim (only in *in good, light, fine*, etc. ~). ~ *v.* (eng.) Trim, rectify (rough-edged or warped part).

fetus : see FOETUS.

feu *n.* (Sc. law) Perpetual lease at fixed rent; land so held. ~ *v.t.* Grant (land) upon feu.

feud[1] *n.* Lasting mutual hostility, esp. between two tribes or families, with murderous assaults in revenge for previous injury.

feud[2] *n.* Fief, feudal benefice; territory held in fee.

feu'dal *adj.* Of a feud or fief; of, resembling, according to, the feudal system; ~ *system*, medieval European polity based on relation of superior and vassal arising from holding of lands in feud; system by which land was held of a superior (in England ultimately of the king) in return for services which included military service, homage, etc. **feu'dallў̆** *adv.* **feu'dalĭsm, feu'dalĭst** *ns.* **feudalĭ'stĭc** *adj.* **feu'dalīze** *v.t.* **feudalīzā'tion** *n.*

feudă'lĭtў̆ *n.* Feudal system or principles; feudal holding, fief.

feu'datorў̆ *adj.* Feudally subject *to*; under overlordship. ~ *n.* Feudal vassal.

feuilleton (fĕ̂ryetawṅ) *n.* Ruled-off portion at foot of page of (esp. Fr.) newspapers, devoted to fiction, criticism, light literature, etc.; serial story, article, printed in this portion. [Fr., = 'leaflet']

fē'ver *n.* 1. Abnormally high body-temperature; reaction of the body to a general infection, characterized by raised temperature, restlessness, panting, thirst, and wasting; any of a group of diseases, each caused by a specific agent, in which this reaction occurs; ~ *heat*, high temperature of body in fever (also fig.); ~ *therapy*, artificial production of state of fever in order to raise body temperature to a point lethal to certain organisms of disease. 2. Nervous excitement, agitation.

fē'verfew *n.* Feathery-leaved perennial plant, *Chrysanthemum parthenium*, allied to the camomile, formerly used as a febrifuge. [L *febris* fever, *fugare* drive away]

fē'verĭsh *adj.* Having symptoms of fever; excited, fitful, restless; of or like fever; causing, infested by, fever. **fē'verĭshlў̆** *adv.* **fē'verĭshnėss** *n.*

fē'verous *adj.* Infested with, apt to cause, fever; feverish.

few *adj.* Not many but more than one; *a good* ~, (colloq.) a fair number (of); *not a* ~, many; *some* ~, no great number (of). ~ *n.* Few persons or things; *the* ~, the minority, the elect, etc. **few'nėss** *n.*

fey (fā) *adj.* 1. (Sc.) Fated to die, at point of death; disordered in mind (often with over-confidence etc.) like person about to die. 2. Affected, whimsy.

fĕz *n.* **Muslim man's red felt cap like truncated cone, with long black** tassel from top, formerly Turkish national head-dress. [Turk., perh. f. Fez, town in Morocco.]

ff. *abbrev.* *Fortissimo.*

F.F.A.S. *abbrev.* Fellow of the Faculty of Architects and Surveyors.

F.F.I. *abbrev.* Free from infection.

f.g.a. *abbrev.* Free of general average.

F.G.S. *abbrev.* Fellow of the Geological Society.

F.H. *abbrev.* Fire hydrant.

fiancé (fēahṅ'sā) *n.* (fem. *-ée*). One's betrothed.

Fianna Fail (fē'*ana* foil). Eamon DE VALERA's party in Irish politics, which took the oath and entered the Dail Eireann in Aug. 1927. [Ir. *fianna* warriors and *Fail* gen. of *Fál* Ireland]

fiă'scō *n.* (pl. *-os*). Failure or breakdown (orig. in dramatic or musical performance); ignominious result. [It., = 'bottle' (unexplained allusion)]

fī'ăt *n.* Authorization; decree, order; ~ *money*, (U.S.) money without intrinsic or promissory value equal to its nominal value made legal tender by fiat of government. **fī'atĭsm** *n.* (U.S.) Principle or practice of issuing fiat money (e.g. inconvertible paper currency). **fī'atĭst** *n.* [L *fiat* be it done]

fĭb *n.* & *v.i.* (Tell) venial or trivial falsehood; lie. **fĭ'bber, fĭ'bster** *ns.*

fī'bre (-b*er*) *n.* Thread-like cell or filament forming, with others, animal or vegetable tissue; or textile substance; substance consisting of fibres; fibrous structure; fibrous substance fit for textile fabrics; small root or twig; *fi'breboard*, stiff board made of fibrous material; *fi'breglass*, glass in fibrous form woven into textiles or used for packing, insulation, etc.; plastic reinforced with this. **fī'brelėss, fī'brĭform** *adjs.*

fī'brĭl *n.* 1. Small fibre; subdivision of fibre. 2. Ultimate subdivision of root.

fībrillā'tion *n.* Formation of fibrils; (path.) quivering movement in fibrils of muscle or nerve. **fī'brillāte** *v.* Split into fibrils; undergo fibrillation.

fī'brin *n.* Insoluble protein formed from fibrinogen during blood clotting, and polymerizing to form the network of the clot. **fī'brinous** *adj.*

fībri'nogĕn *n.* Soluble protein in blood plasma, precursor of fibrin.

fibro- *prefix.* Of fibre(s).

fī'broid *adj.* (chiefly path.) Resembling fibre or fibrous tissue; (of disease) characterized by formation or inflammation of connective tissue. ~ *n.* Fibroid tumour.

fī'brōse *v.i.* (med.) Form fibrous tissues. **fībrō'sis** *n.* (path.) Fibroid degeneration; development of fibrous tissue in organ. **fībrŏ'tic** *adj.*

fībrosī'tis *n.* (med.) Rheumatic pain in any tissue other than bones and joints.

fī'brous *adj.* Of, resembling, fibre(s). **fī'brouslȳ** *adv.*

fi'būla *n.* (pl. *-lae*). 1. (antiq.) Clasp, buckle, brooch. 2. (anat.) Slender bone on outer side of leg between knee and ankle. **fi'būlar** *adj.*

Fi'chtė (-χ-), **Johann Gottlieb** (1762–1814). German idealist philosopher, also famous for his 'Addresses to the German Nation' delivered at Berlin in 1808 during the French occupation of Prussia.

fi'chu (-shōō) *n.* Woman's small triangular shawl of lace etc. for shoulders and neck.

fi'ckle *adj.* Inconstant, changeable. **fi'cklenėss** *n.*

fi'ctīle *adj.* Made of moulded earth, clay, etc., by potter; of pottery.

fi'ction *n.* 1. Feigning, invention; thing feigned or imagined, invented statement or narrative; literature consisting of such narrative, esp. novels. 2. Conventionally accepted falsehood; *legal* ~: see LEGAL. **fi'ctional** *adj.* **fi'ctionalīze** *v.t.* Make into fiction.

ficti'tious (-shus) *adj.* Counterfeit, not genuine; (of name or character) feigned, assumed; imaginary, unreal; of fiction; constituted or regarded as such by (legal or conventional) fiction. **ficti'tiouslȳ** *adv.* **ficti'tiousnėss** *n.*

fi'ctive *adj.* Creating, created, by imagination.

fid *n.* (naut.) Conical wooden pin used to open strands of rope in splicing; square wooden or iron crosspiece for supporting topmast; small thick piece or wedge of anything.

Fid. Def. *abbrev.* *Fidei Defensor* (see DEFENDER).

fi'ddle *n.* 1. (fam. or contempt.) Violin; violin-player; *play first, second,* ~, take leading, subordinate, position. 2. (naut.) Rack or other contrivance to keep things from rolling off table. 3. (colloq.) Swindle. 4. *~-bow*, bow strung with horse-hair with which fiddle is played; *~-case*, case for holding fiddle; *fiddlededee!*, nonsense!; *~-faddle*, trifling talk or action, trivial matters; (*adj.*) trifling, fussy, petty; (*int.*) nonsense! (*v.i.*) fuss, trifle; ~ *pattern*, type of spoon- or fork-handle narrowing towards projections above bowl or tines; *fi'ddlestick*, fiddle-bow; mere nothing, nonsense; *fi'ddlesticks!*, nonsense! ~ *int.* Nonsense! ~ *v.* 1. Play the fiddle; play (tune) on fiddle. 2. Be idle or frivolous; make aimless movements (*at; with*, etc.); fritter *away*. 3. Cheat, swindle; falsify (accounts); transact black-market business.

fi'ddler *n.* 1. Player on fiddle, esp. for hire; *Fiddler's Green*, sailor's Elysium. 2. Small crab of genus *Uca*, the male of which

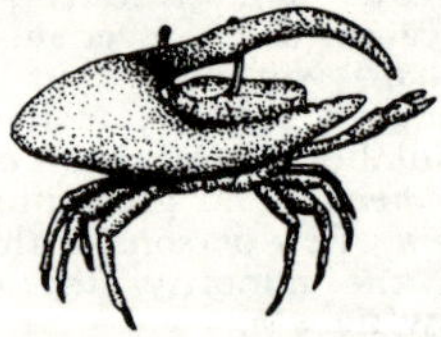

has one claw greatly enlarged. 3. (colloq.) Cheat, swindler.

fĭ'ddley *n.* (naut.) Iron framework (usu. covered by grating) round hatch leading to stokehole.

fĭ'ddlĭng *adj.* (esp.) Petty, futile, contemptible, inconsiderable.

fĭdĕ'lĭtȳ *n.* Faithfulness, loyalty (*to*); strict conformity to truth or fact, exact correspondence to the original.

fĭ'dgėt *n.* 1. Bodily uneasiness seeking relief in spasmodic movements (freq. *the ~s*); restless mood. 2. Person who fidgets or causes others to fidget. 3. Fidgeting. ~ *v.* Move restlessly (*about*); be uneasy, worry; make (person) uncomfortable, worry. **fĭ'dgėtȳ** *adj.* **fĭ'dgėtĭnėss** *n.*

fĭdū'cial (-sh*a*l) *adj.* 1. (theol.) Of, of the nature of, trust or reliance. 2. (surveying etc., of line, point, etc.) Assumed as fixed basis of comparison.

fĭdū'ciarȳ (-sh*a*-) *adj.* Of trust or trustee(ship); held or given in trust; (of paper currency) depending for its value on public confidence or on securities. ~ *n.* Trustee.

fie (fī) *int.* Exclamation expressing sense of outraged propriety.

fief (fēf), **feoff** (fĕf) *n.* (feudal law) Estate (in England always heritable) in land held on condition of homage and service to superior lord, by whom it is granted and in whom the ownership remains.

field *n.* 1. (Piece of) ground, esp. one used for tillage or pasture, and usu. bounded by hedges etc.; tract abounding in some natural product, as coal, oil, diamonds; *F~ of the Cloth of Gold*, meeting-place of Henry VIII and François I of France, near Calais, in 1520, noted for the magnificence of the display made by the two kings. 2. Ground on which battle is fought; scene of campaign or military operations; battle (now rare exc. in *hard-fought ~* etc.); *a fair ~ and no favour*, equal conditions in contest; *in the ~*, (esp.) engaged in military operations; *hold the ~*, not be superseded or displaced; *leave the ~ open*, abstain from interference or competition. 3. Ground for playing cricket, football, etc.; (baseball) ground in which fielders stand. 4. Those who take part in outdoor contest or sport; all competitors in race etc., or all except the favourite; (cricket) fielding side; (cricket and baseball) fieldsmen. 5. Large stretch, expanse, of sea, sky, ice, snow, etc. (also fig.). 6. Surface on which something is portrayed; (her.) surface of escutcheon or of one of its divisions; ground of flag, picture, etc. 7. Area or sphere of action, operation, investigation, etc.; space or range within which objects are visible through optical instrument; *magnetic ~*, region in which magnetic properties can be detected. 8. *attrib.* (of animals etc.) Found in the open country, wild; (of crops) grown for feeding to cattle, and covering large area; (of investigation, study, etc.) carried out on the spot, not in laboratory or study or office; *~ allowance*, allowance to officer etc. on campaign to meet extra expenses; *~ artillery*, light and mobile ordnance for use on campaign and in battle; so *~ battery, gun*; *~-cornet*, minor magistrate of township in Cape Province; *~-day*, (mil.) day of exercise for troops in field manœuvres, review; day of brilliant or exciting events; day spent in field by scientific society etc.; *~-dressing*, wound-dressing for use in field; *~ events*, events (as high jump, discus-throwing, etc.) in athletic contest, excluding races; *~-glass*, that lens of eyepiece of telescope or compound microscope which is nearer to object-glass; *~-glasses*, binocular telescope for outdoor use; *~-grey*, greenish-grey colour of certain army etc. uniforms; *~ hand*, slave working on plantation, farm-labourer; *~ hospital*, temporary hospital near battlefield; *F~ Marshal*: see MARSHAL; *~-meeting*, (hist.) open-air religious meeting; *~-officer*, army officer above rank of captain and below that of general; *~ punishment*, (mil.) punishment for offences on campaign; *~-sports*, outdoor sports, esp. hunting, shooting, fishing; ~ *telegraph*, *telephone*, movable telegraph, telephone, for use on campaign; ~*-work*, field investigation, study, etc. (see above); (mil.) temporary fortification. ~ *v.* Act as fieldsman in cricket, baseball, or rounders; stop (and return) ball: put (team) into field. **fie'lder, fie'ldsman** (-z-) *ns.* (cricket etc.) One of the side not batting; one who fields the ball.

fie'ldfāre *n.* Species of thrush, *Turdus pilaris*, regular and common autumnal visitor in Britain.

Fie'ldĭng, Henry (1707–54). English novelist; author of 'Tom Jones' (1749) etc.

fiend *n.* The Devil; evil spirit, demon; person of superhuman wickedness (esp. cruelty or malignity); one excessively addicted (esp. to something injurious or dangerous). **fie'ndish** *adj.* **fie'ndishlȳ** *adv.* **fie'ndishnėss** *n.*

fierce *adj.* Violent in hostility, angrily combative; of formidably violent and intractable temper; raging, vehement; ardent, eager; (of mechanism) violent, not smooth or easy in action. **fier'celȳ** *adv.* **fier'cenėss** *n.*

fī'erī fā'ciăs (-shĭ-). Writ to sheriff to execute judgement. [L, = 'see that (the sum payable) is made']

fiery (fīr'ĭ) *adj.* 1. Consisting of or flaming with fire; (of arrows etc.) fire-bearing. 2. Looking like fire, blazing-red; (of eyes) flashing, ardent. 3. Hot as fire; acting like fire, producing burning sensation; (of cricket-pitch) making ball rise dangerously. 4. ~ *cross*, wooden cross with arms charred or dipped in blood, formerly sent among Highland clans as a call to arms; (U.S.) burning cross used by Ku Klux Klan to intimidate people. 5. Eager, pugnacious, spirited, irritable; (of horse) mettlesome. **fier'ĭlȳ** *adv.* **fier'ĭnėss** *n.*

fīĕ'sta *n.* (in Spain etc.) Religious or other festival.

fi. fa. *abbrev.* Fieri facias.

fīfe[1] *n.* Small shrill-toned instrument of flute kind, used chiefly to accompany drum in military music; one who plays this. ~ *v.* Play fife; play (air etc.) on fife. **fī'fer** *n.*

Fīfe[2]. Region of E. Scotland (since May 1975), comprising the former county of Fife.

fīfe-rail *n.* (naut.) Rail round mainmast, with belaying-pins for running rigging.

fĭ'ftee'n *adj.* Amounting to fifteen. ~ *n.* One more than fourteen (15, xv, or XV); set of 15 things or persons; (Rugby footb.) side of 15 players; *the F~*, the Jacobite rebellion of 1715. **fĭ'ftee'nth** *adj.* & *n.*

fĭfth *adj.* Next after fourth; *under the ~ rib*, (to, in) the heart; *F~ Avenue*, one of the principal streets of New York noted for its fine shops and residences; ~ *column*, orig. the column of supporters which General Mola declared himself to have in Madrid, when he was besieging it in the Spanish Civil War of 1936–9, in addition to the four columns of his army outside the city; hence, organized body sympathizing with and working for enemy within a country at war; ~*-columnist*, member of such a body; ~ *monarchy*, last of five great empires referred to in prophecy in Dan. 2: 44, in 17th c. identified with millennial reign of Christ; ~*-monarchy man*, 17th-c. believer in immediate second coming of Christ, prepared to assist in establishing his reign by force and to repudiate allegiance to any other government; ~ *part*, one of five equal parts of anything. ~ *n.* Fifth part; fifth thing etc.; fifth form in school; (mus.) interval of which the span involves five alphabetical names of notes, harmonic combination of notes thus separated. **fĭ'fthlȳ** *adv.* In the fifth place.

fĭ'ftȳ *adj.* Amounting to fifty. ~ *n.* Cardinal number, five times ten (50, l, or L); set of 50 things or persons; *fifties*, numbers etc. from 50 to 59; these years of century or life; *fifty-fifty*, (colloq.) half-and-half (i.e. 50% each), equally; equal. **fĭ'ftĭėth** *adj.*

fĭg[1] *n.* 1. (usu. ~*-tree*) Broad-leaved tree, esp. *Ficus carica*,

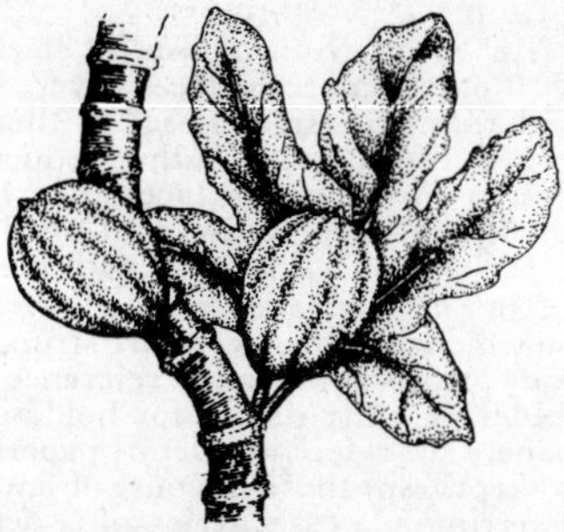

bearing soft pear-shaped multiple fruit eaten fresh or dried; this fruit. 2. Anything valueless. 3. *~-leaf*, device for concealing something considered indecorous (see Gen. 3: 7); *fĭ'gwort*, herb of genus *Scrophularia*, esp. *S. nodosa*.

fĭg[2] *n.* Dress, equipment (only in *in full* ~); condition, form.

fĭg[3] *v.t.* ~ *out*, *up*, make (horse) lively or spirited; ~ *out*, dress up (person), bedizen.

fig. *abbrev.* Figure.

fight (fīt) *v.* (past t. & past part. *fought* pr. fawt). Contend in battle or single combat (*against*, *with*); strive to overcome (disease, fire, fear, etc.); maintain (cause, suit at law, quarrel) against opponent; contend over (question), win one's *way* by fighting; contend with in battle or duel, or with the fists; set on (cocks, dogs) to fight; manœuvre (ship, troops) in battle; ~ *for*, fight on behalf of (person) or to secure (thing); ~ *off*, repel with effort; ~ *out*, settle by fighting; ~ *shy of*, keep aloof from; *fighting chance*, chance of succeeding by great effort; *fighting cock*, game cock trained to fight; *fighting fish*, Siamese fish of genus *Betta*, esp. *B. splendens*; *fighting line*, that part of an armed force which is engaged in direct combat with the enemy; *fighting-top*, (naut.) high circular platform on warship's mast, on which men and guns can be placed. ~ *n.* Action of fighting; battle; combat, esp. pugilistic or unpremeditated, between two or more persons, animals, or parties; strife, conflict; appetite or ability for fighting; *running* ~, fight kept up while one party flies and one pursues; *show* ~, not yield tamely.

fi'ghter (fīt-) *n.* One who fights; high-speed aeroplane designed for aerial combat rather than for bombing or carrying passengers; *~-bomber*, aeroplane combining functions of a fighter and a bomber.

fĭ'gment *n.* Invented statement; thing with no existence except in imagination.

fi'gūral *adj.* Of figures; (mus.) embellished with accompaniment resembling a repetitive pattern.

fĭ'gūrant *n.* (fem. *-ante*) Ballet-dancer performing only as one of a group; character on stage with little or nothing to say.

fĭgūrā'tion (*or* -ger-) *n.* 1. Determination to a certain form; the resulting form. 2. Allegorical or figurative representation. 3. (mus.) Use of figural or florid counterpoint.

fĭ'gūrative (*or* -ger-) *adj.* 1. Representing by a figure or emblem; of pictorial or plastic representation. 2. (of speech etc.) Using figures or metaphors, metaphorical, not literal; metaphorically so called; abounding in, addicted to, figures of speech. **fĭ'gūrativelў** *adv.* **fĭ'gūrativeness** *n.*

fĭ'gure (-ger) *n.* 1. External form, shape; (geom.) definite form constituted by line or lines enclosing superficial space, or by surface or surfaces enclosing space of three dimensions; bodily shape; person considered with regard to visible form or appearance; person as contemplated mentally. 2. Conspicuous appearance; (archaic) importance, distinction. 3. Image, likeness; representation of human form in sculpture, painting, etc.; emblem, type. 4. Diagram, illustration; decorative pattern; (dancing) evolution or movement of dance or dancer, division of set dance; (skating) movement, series of movements, beginning and ending at centre. 5. Numerical system, esp. one of the ten Arabic numerals; amount, number, sum, expressed in figures. 6. (rhet.) Form of expression deviating from normal order or use of words used to give variety, force, etc., e.g. hyperbole, metaphor, etc. (also ~ *of speech*); (logic) particular form of syllogism according to position of middle term; (mus.) brief melodic or rhythmic formula out of which longer passages are developed. 7. *~-head*, ornamental carving, usu. bust or full-length figure, over ship's cutwater; nominal leader, president, etc., without real authority or influence. ~ *v.* 1. Represent in diagram or picture; picture mentally, imagine; embellish with design or pattern, esp. (mus.) with accompaniment in quicker time. 2. Mark with (numerical) figures; (mus.) write figures over or under (bass) to indicate harmony. 3. Use figures in arithmetic; work *out* (sum); (U.S.) calculate, reckon, estimate; ~ *on*, (U.S.) rely on, count on. 4. Make appearance, appear; be conspicuous; ~ *as*, pass for, assume character of.

fĭ'gūrine (-ēn) *n.* Small modelled or sculptured figure, statuette.

Fiji (fē'jē). Principal island of Fiji archipelago, a group of about 250 islands in the S. Pacific; in British possession from 1874; independent republic, member State of the Commonwealth, 1970; capital, Suva. **Fiji'an** *adj.* & *n.*

fil: see FILS[1].

filagree: see FILIGREE.

fĭ'lament *n.* Slender thread-like body (esp., in animal and vegetable structures, one consisting of a row of cells); (bot.) part of stamen supporting anther; fine not easily fusible metallic conductor in electric lamp or thermionic valve, heated or made incandescent by current. **fĭlamĕ'ntarў, fĭlamĕ'ntous** *adjs.*

fĭlār'ia *n.* Parasitic nematode worm esp. of genus *Filaria*. **fĭlār'ĭal** *adj.*

fĭ'lature *n.* (Establishment for) reeling silk from cocoons.

fĭ'lbert *n.* (Nut of) cultivated hazel, *Corylus maxima*. [Fr. *noix de filbert*, from being ripe near St. Philibert's day, 20 Aug.]

fĭlch *v.t.* Steal, pilfer.

fīle[1] *n.* Instrument usu. of steel with one or more surfaces covered with numerous small raised cutting edges or teeth, for abrading, reducing, or smoothing surfaces. ~ *v.t.* Smooth, reduce surface of, with file; ~ *away*, *off*, remove with file.

fīle[2] *n.* String or pointed wire on which documents etc. are strung for preservation and reference; folder or other device for holding papers for reference; set of papers so kept, esp. those in court of law, referring to a case; series of issues of newspaper in order. ~ *v.t.* Place (papers) on file or among public records.

fīle[3] *n.* 1. (mil.) Front-rank man and the man or men directly behind him; small body of men (now usu. two); *in* ~, one behind the other; *rank and* ~: see RANK[1]. 2. Row of persons or things one behind the other; (chess) one of the eight lines of squares extending across board from player to player. ~ *v.* March in file; order (soldiers) to move *off* by files.

fĭ'lėmŏt *adj.* & *n.* (archaic) (Of) colour of dead leaf, brownish-yellow.

fĭ'lėt *n.* Net with square mesh, used for curtains etc.; ~ *lace*, filet net embroidered.

fĭ'lĭal *adj.* Of, due from, son or daughter. **fĭ'lĭallў** *adv.* **fĭ'lĭalnėss** *n.*

fĭlĭā'tion *n.* 1. Being child of specified parent; parentage; descent, transmission, *from*. 2. Formation of branches or offshoots; branch.

fĭ'lĭbĕg *n.* (Sc.) Kilt. [Gael. *feileadh* fold, pleat, *beag* little]

fĭ'lĭbŭster *n.* 1. One who engages in unauthorized warfare against foreign State; (hist.) piratical adventurer pillaging Spanish W. Indian colonies in 17th c.; member of bands of adventurers organizing revolutionary expeditions from U.S. to States in Central America and Spanish W. Indies, 1850–60. 2. (U.S.) Obstructionist, obstruction, in legislative assembly.

~ *v.i.* Act as filibuster. [Du. *vrijbuiter* freebooter]

fi'ligree, fi'la- *n.* Ornamental work of fine gold or silver wire formed into delicate tracery; fine metal openwork; anything delicate resembling this. **fi'ligreed** *adj.*

fi'ling *n.* (esp., usu. pl.) Particle(s) rubbed off by file.

Filipi'nō (-pē-) *n.* (pl. *-os*). Native, inhabitant, of Philippine Islands, esp. of Spanish or mixed blood.

fill *v.* 1. Make or become full (*with*); stock abundantly; occupy whole capacity or extent of, pervade; satisfy, satiate; (of wind) cause (sails) to swell; (of sail) become full of wind; (of dentist) block up (cavity, hollow tooth) with cement etc.; (poker) complete (flush, full house, etc.) by drawing card(s). 2. Hold (position), discharge duties of (office); occupy (vacant time); appoint holder of (vacant post). 3. Adulterate (esp. cotton fabrics). 4. ~ *in*, complete (outline); add what is wanted to complete (unfinished document, blank cheque, etc.); ~ *out*, enlarge, become enlarged, to proper limit; ~ *up*, fill completely; fill tank of vehicle with petrol etc.; supply vacant parts or places or deficiencies in; do away with by filling; grow full. **fi'ller**[1] *n.* **fill** *n.* Full supply of drink or food (only in *drink, eat, have*, etc., *one's* ~; also fig. in *look* etc. *one's* ~); enough to fill something.

filler[2] (-ār') *n.* $\frac{1}{100}$ of a forint.

fi'llet *n.* 1. String, narrow band of any material, bound round head to confine hair, for ornament, etc.; band, bandage; thin narrow strip of anything. 2. Boneless piece of meat, esp. beef from the loin; (half of) one side of fish detached from backbone. 3. (archit.) Narrow flat band separating two mouldings; small band between flutes of column; (her.) horizontal division of shield, quarter of CHIEF in depth; raised rim or edge on any surface; (bookbinding) plain line impressed on cover, tool for making this. 4. (eng.) Curve inside an angle serving to prevent concentration of stress. ~ *v.t.* 1. Bind (hair etc.) with fillet; encircle with ornamental band; 2. Divide (fish or meat) into fillets; remove bones from.

fi'lling *adj.* & *n.* (esp.) Cement etc. inserted into cavity of tooth; ~ *station*, place where motorist may fill up with petrol.

fi'llip *n.* Sudden release of finger or thumb when it has been bent and checked by thumb or finger; slight smart stroke thus given; stimulus, incentive. ~ *v.* Propel (coin, marble, etc.) with a fillip; stimulate; strike slightly and smartly; make a fillip.

fi'llister *n.* Rabbet holding glass and putty in a window-frame; (also ~ *plane*) plane for cutting this.

Fi'llmōre, Millard (1800–74). 13th president of U.S., 1850–3.

fi'llȳ *n.* Female foal; (slang) young lively woman.

film *n.* 1. Thin skin, plate, coating, or layer; slight veil or covering of haze, mist, etc.; fine thread or filament; morbid growth on eye; growing dimness in eyes of dying person. 2. (phot.) Thin strip of material (esp. cellulose acetate) coated with light-sensitive emulsion for exposure in camera; piece of this for one exposure, or roll sufficient for a series. 3. Story, incident, etc., recorded on film in moving pictures; (pl.) cinema industry. 4. *fi'lmgoer*, one who goes to the cinema; ~*-pack*, cut photographic films arranged in pile in case or holder for daylight loading or changing; *fi'lmsetting*, photographic composing of matter to be printed; ~ *star*, star actor in films; *fi'lmstrip*, series of transparencies for projection; ~ *test*, test of would-be film actor. **fi'lmȳ** *adj.* **fi'lmilȳ** *adv.* **fi'lminess** *n.* **film** *v.* 1. Cover, become covered, (as) with film. 2. Reproduce (scene, story, etc.) for the cinema; make cinema film.

fils[1], **fil** *n.* $\frac{1}{1000}$ of a dinar in Bahrain, Jordan, and Yemen.

fils[2] (fēs) *n.* Son (as in Dumas *fils*). [Fr.]

fĭ'lter *n.* Contrivance for freeing liquid from suspended impurities by passing it through stratum of sand, fibre, charcoal, etc.; porous substance used for this purpose; combination of electric circuits designed to suppress unwanted frequencies; (phot.) screen (usu. of coloured glass or gelatine) for absorbing light of certain colours; *~-bed*, tank or pond with false bottom covered with sand etc., for filtering large quantities of water; *~-paper*, unsized paper for filtering liquids; *~ tip, -tipped*, (cigarette or cigar) with mouthpiece that filters the smoke. *~ v.* Pass (liquid etc.), flow, through filter; make way *through, into*, etc., percolate; (of road vehicles) turn off from main stream of traffic at a controlled junction etc.; (of news etc.) leak *out*, come *through*; obtain by filtering. **fĭ'lterable, fĭ'ltrable** *adj.*

fĭlth *n.* Loathsome dirt; corruption, pollution, obscenity; foul language. **fĭ'lthȳ** *adj. ~ lucre*, dishonourable gain (see Tit. 1: 11); (joc.) money. **fĭ'lthĭlȳ** *adv.* **fĭ'lthinėss** *n.*

fĭ'ltrāte *n.* Filtered liquor. *~ v.* Filter. **fĭltrā'tion** *n.*

fĭ'mbrĭāte, -ātėd *adjs.* (bot., zool., etc.) Fringed, bordered.

fĭn *n.* 1. Organ for propelling and steering, attached to fish, cetaceans, etc., at various parts of body; (slang) hand. 2. Projecting part; sharp lateral projection on share or coulter of plough; small projecting surface on various parts of aircraft etc. for ensuring stability.

fin. *abbrev. Ad finem.*

fĭnā'gle *v.* (colloq., orig. U.S.) Use, get by, trickery; wangle. **fĭnā'gler** *n.*

fī'nal *adj.* 1. At the end, coming last, ultimate; putting an end to doubt etc., conclusive, definitive, unalterable. 2. Concerned with end or purpose; *~ clause*, (gram.) clause expressing purpose or intention. **fī'nallȳ** *adv.* **fī'nal** *n.* Last or deciding heat or game; (sing. or pl.) last of series of examinations; edition of newspaper published latest in the day; (mus.) principal note in any mode.

fī'nalĭst *n.* Competitor in final.

fĭna'lė (-ah-) *n.* (mus.) Last movement of instrumental composition; music bringing act of opera to a close; last scene, closing part, of drama etc., conclusion, end.

fīnă'lĭtȳ *n.* 1. Principle of final cause viewed as operative in the universe. 2. Being final; belief that something is final; final act, state, or utterance.

fī'nalīze *v.t.* Put in final form; approve final form of.

fĭnă'nce (*or* fī'-) *n.* 1. (pl.) Pecuniary resources of sovereign, State, company, or person. 2. Management of (esp. public) revenue; science of revenue. *~ v.t.* Furnish with finances, or money; find capital for.

fĭnă'ncial (-sh*a*l) *adj.* Of revenue or money matters; *~ year*, annual period for which public accounts are made up. **fĭnă'nciallȳ** *adv.*

fĭnă'ncier *n.* One skilled in raising and controlling public money; capitalist concerned in financial operations.

fĭnch *n.* Small passerine bird, esp. of genus *Fringilla* (freq. with defining word, as *bullfinch, goldfinch*, etc.).

fīnd *v.t.* (past t. & past part. *found*). 1. Come across, fall in with, light upon; meet with, obtain, get (usu. something desirable or needful); gain, recover, use of; perceive, recognize; acknowledge or discover to be; *~ one's feet*, be able to stand; develop one's powers. 2. Discover by search; discover (game) in hunting (also abs.); recover (something lost); succeed in obtaining; summon up (courage, resolution, etc.); reach, obtain, attain, as if by effort; ascertain, discover, by mental effort, calculation, study, etc.; *~ one's way*, contrive to reach one's destination; go, be brought, to place, position, etc., in spite of difficulties, or not as matter of course; *~ oneself*, discover one's vocation (and see below). 3. (law) Determine and declare (person) *guilty* or *innocent*; agree upon (verdict); ascertain validity of (indictment etc.). 4. Supply, provide, furnish; ~ *oneself*, provide for one's own needs. 5. ~ *out*, discover; devise; solve; detect in offence. ~ *n*. Finding, discovery; what is found.

fī'nder *n*. Person, thing, that finds; small telescope attached to large one to find object; contrivance for same purpose in microscope; (photog.) viewfinder.

fin de siècle (fǎṅ de syākl). Characteristic of end of 19th c.; decadent. [Fr.]

fī'nding *n*. (esp.) Verdict, decision (of court, jury, etc.); (pl., U.S.) small articles, tools, etc., supplied by workmen, small parts for repairing, etc.

fīne[1] *n*. 1. End (now only in *in* ~, to sum up, finally, in short). 2. Sum of money paid by incoming tenant in consideration of small rent. 3. Sum of money fixed as penalty for offence. ~ *v*. 1. Pay consideration *for* privilege or appointment. 2. Punish by a fine.

fīne[2] *adj*. 1. Of high quality; clear, pure, refined; (of gold or silver) containing specified proportion of pure metal. 2. Delicate, subtle; exquisitely fashioned; (of feelings) elevated. 3. Of slender thread; in small particles; thin; sharp; (of athlete) reduced by training. 4. Capable of delicate perception or discrimination; perceptible only with difficulty. 5. Excellent, of striking merit, good, satisfactory, fortunate, of good effect (often iron.); well conceived or expressed; of handsome appearance or size, dignified; (of weather) bright, free from rain; ornate, showy, smart; fastidious, dainty, affecting refinement; (of speech or writing) affectedly ornate; flattering, complimentary. 6. ~ *arts*: see ART; ~*-draw*, sew together so that join is imperceptible; draw out (wire etc.) to a high degree of fineness; ~*-drawn*, subtle; extremely thin; (athletics) trained down in weight; ~ *feathers*, gaudy plumage (freq. fig.); ~ *gentleman, lady*, person of fashion; person who thinks himself above work; ~*-spun*, delicate, flimsy; excessively subtle, unpractical; *go over* (or *through*) *with a* ~*-tooth comb*, make detailed search or investigation. **fī'nelў** *adv*. **fī'neness** (-n-n-) *n*. **fīne** *adv*. With only a small margin of time or space, as *to cut, run*, ~. ~ *n*. Fine weather. ~ *v*. Make (beer) clear; (of liquid) become clear; ~ *away, down, off*, make, become, finer, thinner, less coarse; (make) dwindle, taper.

fine[3] (fēn) *n*. (also ~ *champagne*) Old liqueur brandy. [Fr. *eau-de-vie fine de la Champagne* fine brandy of Champagne]

fī'nerў[1] *n*. Showy dress or decoration.

fī'nerў[2] *n*. Hearth where cast iron is made malleable or steel is made from pig-iron.

fině'sse *n*. 1. Delicate manipulation, subtle discrimination; artfulness, cunning strategy. 2. (whist, bridge) Playing lower card in hope of taking trick, while holding higher card of same suit (not in sequence). ~ *v*. Use finesse; trick *into* etc. by finesse; make finesse, play (card) by way of finesse, in whist or bridge.

fi'nger (-ngg-) *n*. 1. One of five terminal members of hand, or four excluding thumb (usu. numbered 1st to 4th, starting from that next to thumb, but *fourth* ~ sometimes = ring-finger, that next to little finger); *have a* ~ *in*, be concerned in; *lay, put, a* ~ *upon*, touch, however slightly; *lay, put one's* ~ *on*, point with precision to; *turn, twist, round one's* (*little*) ~, cajole; persuade easily. 2. Part of glove made to receive a finger. 3. Measure, breadth of a finger, ¾ inch; small quantity of liquor. 4. Finger-like object or projection. 5. ~*-board*, part of neck of violin, guitar, etc., on to which strings are pressed when stopped by fingers; ~*-bowl*, bowl for rinsing fingers after dessert; ~*-end*, fingertip; ~*-mark*, mark left on surface by (dirty) finger; ~*-plate*, plate fastened on door to prevent finger-marks; ~*-post*, sign-post; *fi'ngerprint*, impression of tip of finger, esp. as means of identification; *~-stall*, cover of leather etc. to protect injured finger; *fi'nger-tip*, end of finger; ***have at one's fingertips***, be versed in, know familiarly. ~ *v.t.* Touch with, turn about in, the fingers; play upon (musical instrument) with fingers; (mus.) mark (music) with figures indicating finger with which note is to be played.

fĭ'ngerĭng[1] (-ngg-) *n.* (esp.) Proper method of using fingers in playing music or using typewriter; marks on music indicating this.

fĭ'ngerĭng[2] (-ngg-) *n.* Kind of fine wool for knitting. [earlier *fingram*, perh. f. Fr. *fin grain* fine grain]

fĭ'nĭal *n.* (archit.) Ornament finishing off apex of roof, canopy,

bench-end, etc.; topmost part of pinnacle.

fĭ'nĭcal *adj.* = FINICKING. **fĭ'nĭcallȳ** *adv.* **fĭ'nĭcalnėss** *n.*

fĭ'nĭcking, fĭ'nĭckȳ *adjs.* Over-nice, precise, fastidious; too much finished in details.

fī'nĭs (*or* fē-) *n.* (at end of book) The end; end of anything, esp. life.

fĭ'nĭsh *n.* Last stage, termination, esp. of fox-hunt; what serves to give completeness; accomplished or completed state; style of finishing (esp. furniture); surface coating or texture; final coat of paint etc.; (*fight*) *to a* ~, (fight) till one party is completely worsted. ~ *v.* Bring to an end, come to the end of, complete; consume, get through, the whole or remainder of; kill, dispatch, overcome completely; perfect, put final or finishing touches to; complete education of; reach the end, cease, leave *off*; end *in* something or *by* doing.

fĭ'nĭsher *n.* (esp.) Workman or machine doing last operation in manufacture.

fī'nīte *adj.* Bounded, limited; not infinite; (gram., of verb) limited by number and person, not infinitive. **fī'nītelȳ** *adv.* **fī'nītenėss** *n.*

Fĭ'nland. Country of NE. Europe situated on the gulfs of Finland and Bothnia; captured by Russia from Sweden in 1809; since 1917 an independent republic; capital, Helsinki.

Fĭnn[1] *n.* Native of Finland. **Fĭ'nnish** *adj.* & *n.* (Language) of Finland.

Fĭnn[2]. Principal hero of a cycle of Irish legends; son of Cumal and father of Ossian; supposed to have lived in the 3rd c. A.D.

fĭ'nnan *n.* (also ~ *haddock*) Haddock cured with smoke of green wood, turf, or peat. [app. f. name of river *Findhorn*, confused with *Findon*, village in Kincardineshire]

Fĭnno- *prefix.* Finnish; *~-Ugrian*, *-Ugric*, (of) a sub-family of the Ural-Altaic languages spoken in Hungary, Lapland, Finland, and some adjacent parts of U.S.S.R.

fĭ'nnȳ *adj.* Having fins; like a fin; of, teeming with, fish.

fiord, fjord (fyōrd) *n.* Long narrow arm of sea between high cliffs, as in Norway.

fīr *n.* 1. (also *~-tree*) Evergreen coniferous tree of genus *Abies*, or of various other genera with needles arranged singly on the shoots; *Scotch*, *silver*, *spruce* ~: see these words. 2. Wood of any of these. 3. *~-cone*, fruit of the fir; ~*-needle*, leaf of the fir.

fīre *n.* 1. Natural agency or active principle operative in combustion; flame, incandescence; volcanic heat; state of ignition; *catch*, *take*, ~, begin to burn; *on* ~, burning; *set ~ to*, cause to burn, kindle. 2. Burning fuel in grate, furnace, etc.; electrical or gas apparatus for heating rooms etc. 3. Destructive burning, esp. of building, forest, etc., conflagration. 4. Luminosity, glow, like that of fire; *St. Elmo's* ~: see CORPOSANT. 5. Burning heat, fever; *St. Anthony's* ~: see ANTHONY[1]. 6. Burning passion; fervour, enthusiasm; liveliness and warmth of imagination, poetic inspiration. 7. Discharge of firearms; *line of* ~, path of bullet etc.; *open* ~, begin firing; *under* ~, being shot at. 8. *~-alarm*, automatic arrangement for giving notice of outbreak of fire; *fir'earm*, (usu. pl.) weapon from which missiles are propelled by gunpowder or other explosive; *fir'eback*, metal plate at back of open hearth; *~-ball*, large luminous meteor, lightning in globular form; *~-balloon*, balloon made buoyant by heat of combustible burning at its mouth; *~-basket*, framework of metal bars for holding logs or coal in hearth; *~-bomb*, incendiary bomb; *~-box*, fuel-chamber of steam-boiler; *fir'ebrand*, piece of burning wood; person who stirs up strife or mischief; *fir'ebrick*, brick capable of withstanding great heat, used in furnaces etc.; ~ *brigade*, fire service; *~-clay*, clay used for firebricks etc.; *~-control*, system of directing and regulating fire of ship's or fort's guns; *fir'edamp*, miners' name for explosive mixture of methane and air formed in coal-mines; *fir'edog*, andiron; *~-eater*, entertainer who pretends to eat flames; one fond of fighting, pugnacious or quarrelsome person; *~-engine*, vehicle carrying apparatus and firemen for extinguishing fires; *~-escape*, metal stairway on outside of building, movable ladder, or other apparatus for facilitating escape from fire; *~-extinguisher*, portable container from which a chemical liquid can be discharged to extinguish fire; *~-fighter*, one of a squad of people organized to deal with fires; *fir'efly*, beetle capable of emitting light (any of about 2,000 species); *~-guard*, protective metal framework placed in front of fire in a room; a fire-watcher; *~-hose*, hose-pipe for extinguishing fire; ~ *insurance*, insurance against loss by fire; *~-irons*, implements for tending domestic fire, shovel, tongs, and poker; *fir'elight*, light given by fire; *~-lighter*, small piece of inflammable material used to facilitate the lighting of a fire in a grate; *~-lock*, (musket with) lock in which sparks were produced to ignite priming; *fir'eman*, tender of furnace or fire of steam-engine; member of fire service; *fir'eplace*, grate or hearth for fire in room etc.; *~-plug*, connection in water-main for fire-hose; *fir'eproof*, proof against fire; strongly resistant to heat; *~-raising*, arson; *~-screen*, screen to keep off heat of fire; ~ *service*, organized body of men trained to extinguish fires; *~-ship*, vessel filled with combustibles and set adrift among enemy ships; *fir'eside*, space round fireplace; home life; *~-walk*, ceremony of walking barefoot over hot stones, ashes, etc., as religious rite or ordeal; hence, *~-walker*; *~-watcher*, person detailed to detect and report fires caused by aerial bombing; *~-water*, alcoholic spirit (name orig. used by, or attributed to, N. Amer. Indians); *fir'ewood*, wood for fuel; *fir'ework*, contrivance or apparatus for producing spectacular effect by use of combustibles etc., squib, rocket, etc.; (pl.) pyrotechnic display. ~ *v.* 1. Set fire to with intention of destroying; kindle (explosives). 2. Catch fire; become heated or excited; redden; (of internal combustion engine) have gaseous mixture ignite. 3. Bake (pottery, bricks); cure (tea, tobacco) by artificial heat. 4. Supply (furnace, engine) with fuel. 5. Cause (explosive) to explode; shoot, discharge gun, etc.; (of gun etc.) go off; propel (missile) from gun etc. 6. (orig. U.S.) Expel, dismiss (person). 7. ~ *away*, begin, go ahead; ~ *up*, show sudden anger; *~-step*, ledge on which soldier in trench stands to fire; *firing-line*, front line of troops (intermittently) engaged in firing upon enemy; *firing-party*, *-squad*, squad of soldiers detailed to shoot condemned man or to fire a volley over grave of soldier buried with military honours.

fir'kin *n.* Small cask for liquids, butter, fish, etc.; (as measure) half of kilderkin.

fĭrm[1] *n.* Partnership for carrying on business, commercial house; team, esp. of doctors and their assistants in hospital; *long* ~, set of swindlers obtaining goods without paying.

fĭrm[2] *adj.* Of solid or compact structure; fixed, stable; steady, not shaking; established, immutable; (of offer etc.) not liable to cancellation after acceptance; steadfast, unflinching, resolute; constant *to*; (of prices, goods) maintaining their level or value. **fĭr'mlў** *adv.* **fĭr'mnėss** *n.* **fĭrm** *adv.* Firmly (chiefly in *hold* ~, *stand* ~). ~ *v.* Solidify, compact (soil after planting etc., cheese); fix firmly (plants in soil).

fĭr'mament *n.* Vault of heaven with its clouds and stars.

fĭr'man *n.* Oriental sovereign's edict.

fĭrst *adj.* 1. Earliest in time or order; foremost in position, rank, or importance; coming next after specified or implied time; (mus., of part) highest or chief part for a certain voice or instrument in concerted music; that performs such a part; *in the* ~ *place*, firstly, first; (*the*) ~ *thing*, as the first thing that is done. 2. ~ *aid*, assistance given to injured before medical treatment is procured; ~-*chop*, first-class; ~ *class*, set of persons or things grouped together as better than others; best accommodation in railway train etc.; highest division in examination list, place in this; ~-*class* (*adj.*) belonging to the first class, of best quality, very good; (*adv.*) by the first class; ~ *cost*, prime cost; ~-*day*, Sunday (esp. among Society of Friends); ~-*day cover*, envelope bearing stamp(s) postmarked on day of first issue; ~ *floor*, storey next above ground floor; (U.S.) ground floor; ~-*foot*, (Sc.) person who first crosses threshold of a house on New Year's Day; ~ *form*, lowest class in school; ~-*fruit*, (usu. pl.) first products of agriculture for season, esp. as offered to God; first products of work etc.; (hist.) payment to superior by new holder of office; ~-*hand*, direct, without intermediate agency; ~ *lady*, (esp., U.S.) wife of the president; *F~ Lord of the Treasury*, chief of the Lords Commissioners of the Treasury (office held by prime minister); ~ *name*, given name, Christian name; ~ *night*, ~-*ni'ghter*, (frequenter of) first performance of play etc.; ~ *offender*, offender against whom no previous conviction is recorded; ~-*rate*, of the highest class; excellent; (colloq.) very well; (naut.) first-rate warvessel, esp. one of the old three-deckers with 74 to 120 guns; *F~ Sea Lord*, professional chief of British Navy. ~ *n.* First day (*of* month); first edition; first-class railway carriage; (holder of) place in first class in examination etc.; first or lowest gear on motor vehicle or bicycle; (pl.) best quality (of certain articles of commerce); *the* ~, person or thing first mentioned; *the F~*, 1 September, when partridge-shooting begins; *at* ~, at the beginning; *from* ~ *to last*, throughout; *from the* ~, from the beginning; (commerc.) ~ *of exchange*, first of set of bills of exchange of even tenor and date. ~ *adv.* Before anyone or anything else; before some specified or implied event, time, etc., in preference, rather; for the first time; first-class; ~ *and last*, taking one thing with another, on the whole; ~ *or last*, sooner or later; ~-*born*, eldest (child).

fĭr'stlĭng *n.* (usu. pl.). First result of anything, first-fruits; first offspring, first-born of season.

fĭr'stlў *adv.* (only in enumerating) In the first place, first.

fĭrth *n.* Arm of sea; estuary.

F.I.S. *abbrev.* Family income supplement.

fisc, fisk *n.* 1. Public treasury of ancient Rome; Roman emperor's privy purse. 2. *fisk*, (Sc. law) public treasury into which estates lapse by escheat.

fĭ'scal *adj.* Of public revenue. **fĭ'scallў** *adv.* **fĭ'scal** *n.* In Italy, Spain, etc., legal official with function of public prosecutor; in Holland etc., magistrate dealing with offences against revenue; (Sc.) short for procurator-fiscal.

fĭsh[1] *n.* (pl. often *fish*). 1. (pop.) Animal living exclusively in water; (strictly) one of class of vertebrate aquatic animals having gills throughout life and usu. fins. 2. Flesh of fish as food. 3. (colloq.) Person, fellow, of specified kind, as *poor* ~, *queer* ~. 4. *the Fish*(*es*): see PISCES. 5. ~*-glue*, kind of gelatin obtained from fish, isinglass; ~*-hawk*, osprey; ~*-hook*, barbed hook used for catching fish; (naut.) iron hook forming part of tackle for raising anchor; ~*-kettle*, long oval vessel for boiling fish; ~*-knife*, knife, usu. of silver, for eating fish; *fi'shmonger*, dealer in fish; *fi'shpond*, pond in which fish are kept; (joc.) sea; ~*-pool*, fishpond; ~*-slice*, knife for carving fish; cook's flat implement for turning or taking out fish etc.; ~*-tail*, shaped like fish's tail (esp. of spreading jet of gas from ~*-tail burner*); *fi'shwife*, woman selling fish. ~ *v.* Catch or try to catch fish; search *for* something in or under water; collect (pearls, coral) from bottom of sea; try to catch fish in (pool etc.); draw *out of* water, pocket, etc., draw *out*; seek by indirect means or artifice *for* (secrets, compliments, etc.); get (fact, opinion, secret) *out*; ~ *in troubled waters*, make one's profit out of disturbances; (naut.) ~ *the anchor*, draw flukes up to gunwale; *fishing-rod*, long tapering usu. jointed rod to which fishing-line is attached.

fĭsh[2] *n.* 1. (naut.) Piece of curved wood, used to strengthen mast or yard. 2. Flat plate of iron, wood, etc., used to strengthen beam or joint; (also ~*-plate*) one of two plates bolted together through ends of two rails on railway to cover and strengthen joint. ~ *v.t.* Mend or strengthen (spar etc.), join (rails) with fish.

fĭsh[3] *n.* Small flat piece of bone or ivory used as counter in games.

fĭ'sher *n.* 1. Fisherman (archaic); ~ *of men*, (see Matt. 4: 19) evangelist. 2. Fishing animal. **fĭ'sherman** *n.* Man who lives by fishing; angler; fishing-boat. **fĭ'sherў** *n.* Business or occupation of catching fish etc.; fishing-ground; those engaged in fishing; right of fishing.

fĭ'shў *adj.* 1. Abounding in fish; like fish's (eye, tail, etc.); smelling or tasting like fish; consisting of fish. 2. (slang) Of dubious character, questionable. **fĭ'shĭlў** *adv.* **fĭ'shĭness** *n.*

fĭsk: see FISC.

fĭssĭ- *prefix.* Cleft, divided, as *fissida'ctyl*, with digits divided.

fĭ'ssīle *adj.* 1. Cleavable, tending to split. 2. Capable of undergoing NUCLEAR fission; ~ *materials*, those (as uranium 235 or plutonium) which break up when bombarded by neutrons liberating atomic energy. **fĭssĭ'lĭtў** *n.*

fĭ'ssion *n.* 1. (biol.) Division of cell or organism into new cells or organisms, as mode of reproduction; *binary* ~, division into two. 2. NUCLEAR fission. **fĭ'ssionable** *adj.* Capable of undergoing nuclear fission.

fĭssĭ'parous *adj.* Reproducing by fission.

fĭ'ssure (-sher) *n.* Opening, usu. long and narrow, made by splitting or separation of parts; (bot., anat.) narrow opening in organ etc., esp. depression between convolutions of brain; cleavage. ~ *v.* Split.

fĭst *n.* Clenched hand, esp. as used in boxing; (joc.) hand, handwriting. ~ *v.t.* Strike with fist; (chiefly naut.) handle. **fĭ'stĭc, -ĭcal** *adjs.* (joc.) Pugilistic.

fĭ'stĭcŭffs *n.pl.* Fighting with the fists.

fĭ'stūla *n.* 1. Long pipe-like ulcer with narrow mouth; suppurating canal; passage made surgically. 2. Natural pipe or spout in whales, insects, etc. **fĭ'stūlar** *adj.* Pipe-like (esp., bot., of pith or hollow stems etc.). **fĭ'stūlous** *adj.*

fĭt[1], **fўtte** *n.* (archaic) Section of a poem.

fĭt[2] *n.* Paroxysm, or one of recurrent attacks, of periodic or constitutional ailment; sudden transitory attack of some illness; sudden seizure, with loss of consciousness or convulsions, of hysteria, apoplexy, fainting, paralysis, or epilepsy; violent access or outburst (of laughter, rage, etc.), capricious impulse, mood; *by ~s and starts*, spasmodically.

fĭt[3] *adj.* Well adapted or suited (*for, to*); good enough *for*; becoming, proper, right; qualified, competent, worthy (*to*); in suitable condition, ready, *to* do, *for*; in good athletic condition or health. **fĭ'tlȳ** *adv.* **fĭt** *v.* Be in harmony with, become, befit; be of right measure, shape, and size for (esp. of dress); fill up, exactly correspond to, make to do this; make suitable, adapt, *for, to*; make competent *for, to*; supply, furnish (ship etc.) *with*; *~ on*, try on; *~ out, up*, equip. *~ n.* Way thing fits.

fĭtch *n.* (Brush made of) polecat's hair.

fĭtché, -ee: see FITCHY.

fĭ'tchew *n.* Polecat.

fĭ'tchȳ, -é, -ee (-ĭ) *adj.* (her., of cross) Having its ends sharpened into points.

fĭ'tful *adj.* Characterized by irregular fits of activity or strength; spasmodic, changing, capricious. **fĭ'tfullȳ** *adv.* **fĭ'tfulnėss** *n.*

fĭ'tment *n.* Piece of furniture; (pl.) fittings.

fĭ'tnėss *n.* Being fit; moral worthiness; propriety.

fĭ'tter *n.* (esp.) 1. Mechanic who fits together parts of engines etc. 2. Tailor or dressmaker engaged in cutting out etc. garments, or altering ready-made garment to fit.

fĭ'tting *n.* (esp., usu. pl.) Fixture(s), apparatus, furniture; *~-shop*, (eng.) place where parts are put together. *~ adj.* (esp.) Becoming, proper, right. **fĭ'ttinglȳ** *adv.*

FĭtzGĕ'rald, Edward (1809–83). English scholar; famous for his English poetic version of the Rubáiyát of Omar Khayyám.

fīve *adj.* Amounting to five; *~-finger exercise*, piano exercise for practising all fingers, keeping them on same five notes all the time; *F~ Nations*, (U.S. hist.) Iroquois, a powerful confederacy of Indian tribes in western New York, first formed *c* 1570 and consisting of the Seneca, Cayuga, Onondaga, Oneida, and Mohawk tribes; *~-year plan*, scheme for economic development over a period of 5 years, orig. that begun in U.S.S.R. in 1928. *~ n.* One more than four; symbol for this (5, v, or V); card, die-face, or domino with 5 pips; 5 o'clock; size etc. indicated by 5; set of 5 things or persons. **fī'vefōld** *adj.* & *adv.*

fī'ver *n.* (colloq.) £5 note; hit for five at cricket.

fīves (-vz) *n.* Game for 2 or 4 players in which ball is struck by hand in a padded glove against walls of a court (in *Eton ~*, as orig. played at Eton College, the court has a buttress, a step, and no back wall; in *Rugby ~*, as orig. played at Rugby School, the court has a back wall and no buttress or step).

fĭx *v.* 1. Make firm or stable, fasten, secure, implant; direct steadily, set (eyes, attention, etc.) *on*; (of object) attract and hold (attention etc.); make (eyes, features), or become, rigid; deprive of, lose, volatility or fluidity, congeal; make (colour, photographic image) fast; *~ with one's eyes*, direct steady gaze upon. 2. Place definitely or permanently, station, establish; take up one's position; settle one's choice, decide *on*; assign precise position of; refer (thing, person) to definite place or time; determine incidence of (liability etc.); settle, determine, specify (price, date, place); arrest changes or development in, settle permanent form of (language etc.); (chiefly U.S.) arrange, get ready, put in order (also *~ up*); (U.S.) bring (person) over to one's side, as by bribery; (U.S.) *~ it*, arrange matters. *~ n.* Dilemma, position hard to escape from; position determined by bearings or astronomical observations; (slang) addict's dose of drug.

fĭxā'tion *n.* 1. Fixing, being fixed; process of rendering solid; coagulation; combination of gas with solid. 2. (psychol.) Arrest of emotional development at infantile or immature stage.

fi'xative *adj*. Tending to fix. ~ *n*. Fixative substance, esp. with which drawing is coated to prevent chalk etc. from rubbing off; substance applied to hair to keep it tidy; liquid that retards evaporation.

fixed (-kst) *adj*. (esp., of oil or acid) That cannot be distilled or evaporated without decomposition; ~-*doh*: see SOLMIZATION. ~ *star*: see STAR. **fi'xėdlȳ** *adv*. In fixed manner, intently. **fi'xėdnėss** *n*. Fixed state, immobility, permanence, steadfastness.

fi'xer *n*. (esp.) Preparation used for fixing dye, photograph, etc.; (phot.) hypo.

fi'xings (-z) *n.pl*. (U.S.) Apparatus, equipment; trimming of dress or dish, adjuncts.

fi'xĭtȳ *n*. Fixed state; stability, permanence.

fi'xture *n*. 1. Thing fixed or fastened in position; (law, pl.) articles of accessory character annexed to houses or lands; person or thing confined to or established in one place. 2. Appointment or date for race, meet, game, etc.; the race, game, etc., itself.

fizz *n*. Hissing or spluttering sound; effervescence; (colloq.) champagne; any effervescing drink. **fi'zzȳ** *adj*. **fizz** *v.i*. Make hissing or spluttering sound.

fi'zzle *v.i*. Hiss or splutter feebly; ~ *out*, come to lame conclusion, fail. ~ *n*. Hissing, spluttering; (colloq.) failure, fiasco.

fl. *abbrev*. Florin(s); floruit.

f.l. *abbrev*. *Falsa lectio* (L, = false reading).

Fla. *abbrev*. Florida.

flă'bbergast (-gah-) *v.t*. Dumbfound, overwhelm with astonishment.

flă'bbȳ *adj*. Hanging loose by its own weight, flaccid, limp, soft; weak, nerveless, feeble. **flă'bbĭlȳ** *adv*. **flă'bbĭnėss** *n*.

flabĕ'llate, flabĕ'llĭfŏrm *adjs*. Fan-shaped.

flă'ccĭd (-ks-) *adj*. Hanging or lying loose or wrinkled, limp, flabby; relaxed, drooping; wanting vigour, feeble. **flăcci'dĭtȳ** *n*.

flăg[1] *n*. Any of various monocotyledonous plants with bladed or sword-shaped leaves, mostly growing in moist places, esp. one of the genus *Iris*; *sweet* ~, plant *Acorus calamus*, with aromatic rhizome used as a stimulant.

flăg[2] *n*. Flat slab of any fine-grained rock which may be split into flag-stones; (also ~-*stone*) flat stone suitable for paving; (pl.) flagged pavement. ~ *v.t*. Pave with flags.

flăg[3] *n*. (also ~-*feather*) Quill-feather of bird's wing.

flăg[4] *n*. Piece of bunting or other stuff attached by one edge to staff or halyard and used as standard, ensign, or signal; (naut.) flag carried by flagship as emblem of admiral's rank afloat; plate bearing words 'For Hire' attached to meter of taxicab, and lowered to start meter when vehicle is engaged; flag used to indicate start or finish of race; tail of setter or Newfoundland dog; *black* ~, flag used as ensign by pirates; also, that formerly hoisted at prison to announce execution of criminal; *quarantine* ~, yellow flag (see below); *white* ~, plain white flag used in token of truce or surrender; *yellow* ~, flag displayed by ship with infectious disease on board, hospital ship, or ship in quarantine; ~ *of convenience*, foreign flag under which ship is registered to avoid certain duties, charges, etc.; ~-*boat*, boat serving as mark in aquatic matches; ~-*captain*, captain of flagship; ~-*day*, day on which money is raised for a cause by selling small paper flags or other tokens to be worn as evidence of having contributed; (U.S.) 14 June, anniversary of adoption by Congress of Stars and Stripes as national flag (1777); ~-*flying*, (colloq.) over-bidding at bridge; ~-*lieutenant*, officer acting as aide-de-camp to admiral; ~-*officer*, admiral, vice-admiral, or rear-admiral; *fla'gship*, ship with admiral on board; *fla'gstaff*, pole on which flag is hoisted; ~-*station*, station where trains stop only if signalled; ~-*wagging*, (mil. slang) signalling with flags held in hands. ~ *v.t.* Place flag on or over; mark out with flags; inform, warn, communicate, by flag-signals; ~ *down*, bring to a stop thus.

flăg[5] *v.i.* Hang down, flap loosely; droop, fade, become limp; lag, lose vigour, grow languid; fall off in interest.

flă'gellant (*or* flajĕ'-) *n.* & *adj.* (One) who scourges himself, esp. as religious discipline or penance.

flă'gėllāte[1] *v.t.* Scourge. **flăgėllā'tion, flă'gėllator** *ns.* **flăgėllatorў** *adj.*

flagĕ'llum *n.* (pl. *-la*). (zool., bot.) Microscopic lash-like appendage, esp. one used for locomotion. **flă'gėllate**[2] *adj.* & *n.* (Protozoan) having one or more flagella. **flagĕ'llifôrm** *adj.*

flăgeolĕ't (-j*o*-) *n.* Small flute blown at end; organ-stop with similar tone.

flagĭ'tious (-sh*u*s) *adj.* Deeply criminal, atrocious, heinous, villainous. **flagĭ'tiouslў** *adv.* **flagĭ'tiousnėss** *n.*

flă'gon *n.* Large vessel, usu. with handle, spout, and lid, to hold liquor for table; similar vessel for Eucharist; large bottle for wine, cider, etc., often of flattened globular shape, usu. holding about twice as much as ordinary bottle.

flā'grant *adj.* (of offence or offender) Glaring, notorious, scandalous. **flā'grancў** *n.* **flā'grantlў** *adv.*

flail *n.* Hand threshing-implement, wooden staff at end of which a heavy stick hangs swinging. ~ *v.* Beat or strike (as) with flail; wave wildly or erratically.

flair *n.* Instinctive discernment, selective instinct for what is good, paying, etc.

flăk *n.* Anti-aircraft fire; ~*-ship*, German anti-aircraft vessel. [Ger., f. initial letters of *Fl*ieger*a*bwehr*k*anone A.A. gun]

flāke[1] *n.* Frame or rack for storing provisions, esp. oat-cakes, or drying produce, esp. fish etc.; small platform hung over ship's side for workmen to stand on.

flāke[2] *n.* Small light fleecy mass, esp. of snow; portion of ignited matter thrown off; thin broad piece peeled off surface; natural division of fish's flesh; layer, lamina, stratum; (archaeol.) piece of hard stone chipped off core for use as tool; (pl.) cornflakes; ~*-white*, pigment made from the purest white-lead in form of flakes or scales. ~ *v.* Fall like, sprinkle as with, snow; take, come, *away*, *off*, in flakes; *pressure-flaking*, (archaeol.) shaping of flint tool by pressure. **flā'kў** *adj.* (esp., of pastry) Consisting when baked of thin delicate flakes or layers. **flā'kĭnėss** *n.*

flăm[1] *n.* Sham story, trick, deception.

flăm[2] *n.* Single stroke on side drum.

flambé (-ahṅbā) *adj.* (of food) Covered with spirit and served alight.

flă'mbeau (-bō) *n.* Torch, esp. of several thick waxed wicks.

flămboy'ant *adj.* 1. (archit.) Characterized by wavy flame-like lines: of the style prevalent in France in 15th and first half of 16th centuries. 2. Florid, floridly decorated; gorgeously coloured. ~ *n.* Kinds of flame-coloured flower. **flămboy'ance** *n.*

flāme *n.* 1. Vapour heated to point of combustion, ignited gas; portion of this, often spire-like or tongue-like; (pl.) fire; visible combustion; ~ *gun*, flame-throwing gun for destroying weeds etc. ~*-thrower* (Ger. *flammenwerfer*), machine of war with reservoir from which long spray of flame can be ejected. 2. Bright light; brilliant colouring; flame-red. 3. Passion, esp. of love; (joc.) sweetheart. **flā'mў, flā'melėss** *adjs.* **flāme** *v.* 1. Emit flames, blaze. 2. (of passion) Burst out; (of persons) break *out*, blaze *up*, into anger. 3. Glow like or as with flame; shine brightly. 4. Move as or like flame; send (signal) by fire; subject to action of flame.

flā'mĕn *n.* (Rom. antiq.) Priest devoted to service of a particular deity.

flamĕ'ncō *n.* (pl. *-os*). Spanish

gipsy style of singing or dancing; song or dance in this style.

flā'mĭng *adj.* Very hot; bright-coloured; very bright; highly coloured, exaggerated, startling; (colloq.) used as substitute for profane epithet.

flamĭ'ngō (-ngg-) *n.* Wading bird of a widely distributed family, Phoenicopteridae, with scarlet

plumage, extremely long legs and neck, and heavy bent bill.

flă'mmable *adj.* Easily set on fire. **flămmabĭ'lĭty̆** *n.*

flăn *n.* Open tart of pastry or sponge-cake usu. filled with fruit etc.

flanch (-ah-) *n.* (her.) Sub-ordinary formed on each side of shield by convex line.

Fla'nders (flah-, -z). Ancient countship now divided between Belgium, France, and Holland; ~ *poppy*, red poppy used as emblem of the soldiers of the Allies who fell in the war of 1914–18; artificial red poppy made for wearing on REMEMBRANCE Sunday, sold in aid of disabled soldiers.

flâneur (flahner̂) *n.* Idler, loafer. [Fr.]

flănge (-j) *n.* Projecting flat rim, collar, or rib, used to strengthen an object, attach it to another, etc. ~ *v.t.* Provide with flange.

flănk *n.* 1. Fleshy or muscular part of side between ribs and hip; (leather manuf.) part of hide covering this. 2. Side of building, mountain, etc.; (mil.) extreme left or right side of army or body of troops. ~ *v.t.* Guard, protect, strengthen, on flank; menace or attack flank of; fire sideways upon; be posted or situated at flank of; (pass.) have at flanks or sides.

flă'nker *n.* Projecting part of fortification defending flank of another part, or commanding flank of assailant; (mil., usu. pl.) skirmisher(s) on flank of marching army.

flă'nnel *n.* Light soft woollen fabric of plain or twill weave usu. without nap; piece of flannel or other material used in washing hands or face etc., scrubbing floor etc.; (pl.) underclothing of flannel; (pl.) garments, esp. trousers, of flannel for games etc. **flă'nnelled** (-ld) *adj.* (esp.) Wearing flannels. **flă'nnelly̆** *adj.*

flănnelĕ'tte *n.* Cotton fabric imitating flannel.

flăp *v.* 1. Strike with something broad; drive (flies etc.) *away* or *off*; (of birds) strike with flat of wing. 2. Swing or sway about, flutter, oscillate; move (wings), (of wings) move, up and down; beat the wings. 3. (colloq.) Become agitated or fussed. ~ *n.* 1. Light blow with something broad; motion of something broad and loose, as wing, etc. 2. Broad hanging piece hinged or attached by one side only, as leaf of table, piece of cloth covering opening of pocket, etc.; movable section on wing or tail of aircraft, used to modify lift or drag; 3. (colloq.) State of agitation or fuss.

flăpdoo͞'dle *n.* (colloq.) Nonsense, bunkum.

flă'pjăck *n.* 1. Flat round batter-cake cooked on griddle or baked; sweet oat-cake. 2. Vanity-case for face-powder.

flă'pper *n.* (esp.) 1. Hinged or hanging piece, flap; broad fin; crustacean's tail. 2. Young wild duck or partridge. 3. (esp. in 1920s, slang) Girl in her teens, orig. with long hair worn in pigtail.

flāre *v.* 1. (Cause to) widen or spread (gradually) outwards, as the sides of a ship, a skirt, etc.; *flared* (*adj.*) widening thus. 2. Burn with spreading unsteady flame; shine like such flame; glow as with flame; ~ *up*, burst into sudden blaze or anger; (of part of skin) become inflamed. ~ *n.* 1. Dazzling irregular light; unshaded flame in open air; sudden outburst of flame; combustible material burnt as signal or guide in fog, at night, etc.; bright light dropped from aircraft to illuminate target etc.; (photog.) fogging caused by internal reflection within a lens; ~ *path*, line of lights on airfield etc. to guide aircraft in taking off or landing. 2. (path.) Local inflammation of small blood-vessels in reaction to injury. 3. Gradual widening or spreading of ship's sides, skirt, etc.; piece of garment so cut.

flăsh *n.* 1. Sudden quick transitory blaze; time occupied by this, instant; brief outburst, transitory display; superficial brilliancy, ostentation; (photog.) flashlight; ~ *in the pan*, ignition of gunpowder in pan of old gun without discharge of missile; (fig.) abortive effort or outburst. 2. Ornament of five short pieces of black silk ribbon sewn to back of collar of ceremonial and walking-out dress uniform of 23rd Royal Welch Fusiliers; emblem sewn on shoulder of military uniform indicating unit etc. to which wearer belongs. 3. Preparation of cayenne pepper or capsicum with burnt sugar, for colouring spirits. 4. Rush of water let down weir to take boat over shallows; contrivance for producing this. 5. (also *news* ~) Very brief news report sent by telegraph etc. 6. (cinema) Exposure of a scene. 7. *fla'shback*, (cinema) recapitulation of earlier scene, episode beginning with sudden change to an earlier point of time; ~*-board*, board set up in mill-dam to throw more water into mill-race when water is low; ~*-lamp*, portable electric lamp producing light by pressure of button; lamp used to give flashlight; *fla'shlight*, light giving sudden flashes, used for signals, in lighthouses etc.; flash of artificial light used in photography in weak light, e.g. at night or indoors; electric torch; *fla'shover*, electric spark or arc appearing suddenly across surface of insulating material; *fla'shpoint*, temperature at which vapour given off by oil etc. will ignite. ~ *adj.* 1. Gaudy, showy; counterfeit. 2. (archaic) Connected with thieves, tramps, etc., or their jargon. ~ *v.* 1. Break suddenly into flame or light; give out flame or sparks; emit or reflect light, gleam; send, reflect, like a flash or in flashes; cause to flash. 2. Burst suddenly into view or perception; move swiftly. 3. Express or communicate by flash or flashes, esp. by telegraph. 4. (glass-making) Spread out into a sheet; cover (glass etc.) with thin layer of colour etc. 5. (of water) Rush along; send rush of water down (river etc.). **flă'sher** *n.*

flă'shing *n.* Strip of metal to prevent flooding or leakage at joint of roofing etc.

flă'shȳ *adj.* Brilliant but shallow or transitory; cheaply attractive; showy, gaudy; given to display. **flă'shilȳ** *adv.* **flă'shinėss** *n.*

flask (-ah-) *n.* 1. (hist., usu. *powder-*~) Leather or metal case for carrying sportsman's supply of gun-powder. 2. Narrow-necked bulbous bottle. 3. Pocket-bottle of metal or glass. 4. Vacuum flask.

fla'skėt (-ah-) *n.* Long shallow basket (archaic); small flask.

flăt[1] *n.* Floor, storey (now rare); suite of rooms usu. on one floor (or occas. single room) forming complete residence.

flăt[2] *adj.* 1. Horizontal, level; spread out, lying at full length. 2. Even, smooth, unbroken, without projection; with broad level surface and little depth. 3. Unqualified, plain, downright. 4. Dull, lifeless, monotonous; dejected, without energy; (of drink) that has lost its effervescence or flavour, insipid, stale; (of paint) without lustre; (photog.) wanting in contrast. 5. Below the true pitch;

B ~, *E* ~, etc. (written B♭ etc.; see *n.* below, sense 5), a semitone lower than B, E, etc. 6. (of price, rate, etc.) Unvarying, fixed, uniform; not varying with changed conditions. 7. ~ *arch*, arch with flat intrados; ~ *-boat*, flat-bottomed boat for transport in shallow water; *~-car*, (U.S.) railway wagon without sides or top; *fla'tfish*, fish of the family Pleuronectidae, including sole, turbot, plaice, etc.; *~-foot(ed)*, (having) foot not normally arched at instep; hence, (fig.) heavy, clumsy; *~-head*, one of a tribe (the Salish) of N. Amer. Indians erron. supposed to flatten their children's heads artificially; kind of N. Amer. snake, puff-adder; *~-iron*, iron for smoothing linen (now usu. of one heated from below, not within); ~ *race*, race over clear and level ground (opp. to hurdle-race, steeplechase); ~ *spin*, kind of spin, which aircraft may enter, in which the controls have little or no effect and aircraft spins round its vertical axis; (fig.) frenzy of agitation; *fla'tworm*, any of the tapeworms, flukes, etc.

Tapeworm

Flatworm

Liver-fluke

FLATWORMS

flă'ttĭsh *adj.* **flă'tways, flă't-wīse** (-z) *advs.* **flă'tly̆** *adv.* **flă'tnėss** *n.* **flăt** *adv.* Downright, positively, plainly; fully, quite; ~ *out*, = ALL out. ~ *n.* 1. What is flat; flat surface or part, esp. broad surface of blade as opp. to edge; inside of open hand; level country; horizontal plane; horizontal bed, stratum, vein, etc.; piece of level ground; low-lying marshy land, swamp; (usu. pl., also *mud-~s*) level ground over which tide flows, or which is covered by shallow water. 2. Flat-bottomed boat; shallow basket. 3. (theatr.) Section of scenery mounted on frame; *join the ~s*, make thing consistent, give unity or coherency to something. 4. (slang) Duffer, dupe. 5. (mus.) Note lowered by a semitone below usual pitch; sign (♭) indicating this lowering, placed before note which is to be flattened or forming part of key-signature; *double* ~ (♭♭), sign indicating that note must be lowered two semitones; *two ~s*, *three ~s*, etc., key indicated by two, three, etc., flats in key-signature. ~ *v.* Make flat (chiefly in technical language); esp. give (paint) flat or lustreless surface.

flă'tlėt *n.* Small flat, esp. of one room.

flă'tten *v.t.* Make flat; ~ *out*, (esp.) bring (flight of aircraft) parallel with ground after diving.

flă'tter *v.t.* Court, fawn upon; praise or compliment unduly or insincerely; gratify vanity or self-esteem of, make feel honoured or distinguished; inspire with (esp. unfounded) hope; please (usu. *oneself*) with belief, idea, suggestion, *that*; exaggerate good points of, represent too favourably. **flă'tterer, flă'ttery̆** *ns.* **flă'tterĭngly̆** *adv.*

flă'tūlent *adj.* Generating gas or air in the alimentary canal; caused by, attended with, troubled with, accumulation of this; (fig.) inflated, puffed up, windy, pretentious. **flă'tūlence** *v.* **flă'tūlently̆** *adv.*

flā'tus *n.* Gas, air, in stomach or bowel.

Flaubert (flōbār), Gustave (1821–80). French realistic novelist; author of 'Madame Bovary' (1856), 'Salammbo' (1862), etc.

flaunt *v.* Wave proudly; display oneself or one's finery; show off, parade. ~ *n.* Flaunting motion. **flau'ntĭngly̆** *adv.* **flau'nty̆** *adj.*

GUSTAVE FLAUBERT

flau'tist *n.* Flute-player.

flavĕ'scent *adj.* Turning yellow, yellowish.

Flā'vĭan *adj.* & *n.* (Member) of the Roman gens Flavia.

flā'vĭn *n.* Any of a group of yellow pigments found in plants and animals and extracted from dyer's oak (*quercitron*) bark for use as dyes and antiseptics.

flā'vour (-*ver*) *n.* Aroma, mingled sensation of smell and taste; distinctive taste; undefinable characteristic quality. **flā'vorous, flā'vourlėss, flā'voursome** *adjs.* **flā'vour** *v.t.* Give flavour to. **flā'vouring** *n.* Something used for flavouring food or drink.

flaw[1] *n.* Crack, breach, rent; imperfection, blemish; invalidating defect in legal document or procedure, title, pedigree, etc. ~ *v.* Crack, damage, mar. **flaw'lėss** *adj.* **flaw'lėsslў** *adv.* **flaw'lėssnėss** *n.*

flaw[2] *n.* Squall of wind; short storm.

flăx *n.* Blue-flowered plant, *Linum usitatissimum*, cultivated for its seeds (linseed) and for textile fibre obtained from the stem of the plant; dressed or undressed flax fibres; cloth made from these, linen; ~*-seed*, linseed. **flă'xen** *adj.* Of flax; (of hair) coloured like dressed flax, pale yellow.

flay *v.t.* Strip off skin or hide of; (fig.) criticize severely; fleece, charge extortionately; peel off (skin, bark, peel); pare off (turf).

flea *n.* Small wingless insect of order Siphonapter, esp. *Pulex irritans*, well-known for its biting propensities and powers of jump-

ing, feeding on human and other blood; (*go*, *send*, etc. *away*) *with a ~ in one's ear*, discomfited by stinging or mortifying reproof or repulse; ~*-bag*, (joc.) sleeping-bag; *flea'bane*, any of various plants of the genera *Pulicaria* and *Erigeron*, esp. *P. dysenterica*; ~*-beetle*, species of small jumping beetles feeding esp. on root vegetable crops; ~*-bite*, (fig.) slight inconvenience or expense, mere trifle; small reddish spot in animal's coloration; ~*-louse*, leaping plant-louse of family Psyllidae.

fleam *n.* Lancet, esp. one used to bleed horses.

flèche (-āsh) *n.* Slender spire, esp. over intersection of nave and transept; one of the 24 points on a backgammon board. [Fr., = 'arrow']

flĕck *n.* Spot in the skin, freckle; patch of colour or light; small particle, speck. ~ *v.t.* Mark with flecks, dapple, variegate.

fled: see FLEE.

flĕdge *v.t.* Provide with feathers or plumage, wing for flight; cover as with feathers or down; feather (arrow).

flĕ'dgeling, flĕdgl- (-jl-) *n.* (U.S. *fledgling*) Young bird just fledged.

flee *v.* (past t. & past part. *flĕd*). Run away, seek safety in flight; vanish, cease, pass away; run away from, leave abruptly; shun.

fleece *n.* Woolly covering of sheep or similar animal; quantity of wool shorn from sheep at one time; rough, abundant, or woolly head of hair; thing like a fleece, white cloud, falling snow, etc.; (her.) figure of sheepskin with wool, suspended by a ring; (carding) thin sheet of cotton or wool fibre. **flee'cy̆** *adj.* **fleece** *v.t.* 1. (rare) Shear (sheep). 2. Strip of money, property, etc.; plunder, rob heartlessly. 3. Overspread as with fleece.

fleer *v.i.* (archaic or dial.) Laugh impudently or mockingly; gibe, jeer, sneer. ~ *n.* Mocking look or speech.

fleet[1] *n.* Naval armament, number of warships under one commander-in-chief; number of ships or boats sailing in company; number of vehicles or aircraft forming a group or unit; *F~ Air Arm*, (formerly) aviation service of the Royal Navy.

fleet[2] *n.* (rare) Creek, inlet.

fleet[3] *adj.* (poet. or literary) Swift, nimble. **flee'tly̆** *adv.* **flee'tnėss** *n.*

fleet[4] *adj.* Shallow; (quasi-*adv.*) at no great depth, near the surface.

fleet[5] *v.i.* Glide away, vanish, be transitory; pass rapidly, slip *away*; move swiftly, fly. **flee'ting** *adj.* **flee'tingly̆** *adv.*

Fleet[6]. Name (*the* ~) of a stream (now a covered sewer) flowing into Thames at Blackfriars Bridge; *the ~ (Prison)*, the old prison which stood near it, built by Richard I and serving for a long time as place of imprisonment for those condemned by Star Chamber, but later chiefly as debtors' prison, until demolished in 1848; *~ marriage*, (hist.) marriage performed by clergyman imprisoned in Fleet, without banns or licence (abolished by Marriage Act of 1753); *~ Street*, street in London near the Fleet largely devoted to offices of newspapers and other periodicals; hence, the press, journalism. [f. FLEET[2]]

Flĕ'ming[1] *n.* Native, inhabitant, of Flanders.

Flĕ'ming[2], Sir Alexander (1881–1955). British scientist; the chief discoverer of PENICILLIN.

Flĕ'mish *adj.* Of Flanders or its people or language; *~bond*, method of bricklaying originating in Flanders; *~ brick*, hard yellow paving brick. ~ *n.* 1. (collect.) People of Flanders. 2. Language of Flanders.

flĕnch, flĕnse *v.t.* Cut up and slice fat from (whale, flayed seal); slice (blubber) from bones of whale; flay (seal).

flĕsh *n.* 1. Soft substance, esp. muscular parts, of animal body between skin and bones; *~ and blood*, human body or its material; mankind; human nature with its emotions and infirmities; (as *adj.*) actually living, not supernatural or imaginary; *one's own ~ and blood*, near relations, descendants. 2. Pulpy substance of fruit or plant. 3. Plumpness, fat; *lose, put on, ~*, grow thin, fat. 4. Tissue of animal bodies (excluding fish and sometimes fowls) as food; meat. 5. Visible surface of human body, with ref. to colour or appearance. 6. Whatever has corporeal life; the

FLEET PRISON

body (now only in biblical allusions); man's physical nature; the sensual appetites; *after the* ~, corporeally; *in the* ~, in bodily form, in life; *sins of the* ~, unchastity. 7. ~-*brush*, -*glove*, brush, glove, for stimulating circulation by rubbing; ~-*colour(ed)*, (of the) colour of flesh (sense 5), yellowish-pink; ~-*fly*, insect of family Sarcophagidae which deposits eggs in dead flesh; ~-*pots*, (with ref. to Exod. 16: 3) high living, luxuries; ~-*wound*, wound not reaching bone or vital organ. **flĕ'shlėss** *adj.* **flĕsh** *v.t.* Incite (hound etc.) by taste of blood; initiate in bloodshed; inflame by foretaste of success; use (sword etc.) for first time on flesh. **flĕ'sher** *n.* (Sc.) Butcher.

flĕ'shings (-z) *n.pl.* Close-fitting flesh-coloured garment worn on stage etc. to represent natural skin.

flĕ'shlў *adj.* 1. Carnal, lascivious, sensual. 2. Mortal, material; not divine or spiritual; worldly. **flĕ'shlĭnėss** *n.*

flĕ'shў *adj.* Plump, fat; of flesh, without bone; (of fruit etc.) pulpy; like flesh. **flĕ'shĭnėss** *n.*

Flĕ'tcher, John (1579–1625). English dramatist some of whose many plays were written in collaboration with Francis BEAUMONT.

fleur-de-lis (flẽr'de lē') *n.* (pl. *fleurs-*). Iris flower; heraldic lily; royal arms of France; hence, the French monarchy, France (before 1789).

fleur'ėt (-ūr-) *n.* Ornament like small flower.

fleur'ў (-oor-) *adj.* (her.) Decorated with fleurs-de-lis.

flews (-z) *n.pl.* Large chaps of bloodhound or other deep-mouthed dog.

flĕx[1] *n.* Flexible insulated wire used for conveying electric current.

flĕx[2] *v.t.* Bend; esp. bend (joint or limb) by action of flexor muscles.

flĕ'xĭble *adj.* That will bend without breaking, pliable, pliant; easily led, manageable; adaptable, versatile; supple, complaisant. **flĕxĭbĭ'lĭtў** *n.* **flĕ'xĭblў** *adv.*

flĕ'xĭle *adj.* (now rare) Supple, mobile; tractable; versatile. **flĕxĭ'lĭtў** *n.*

flĕ'xion (-kshon) *n.* 1. Bending, curvature, bent state (esp. of limb or joint); bent part, curve. 2. (gram.) Inflexion; (math.) flexure. **flĕ'xional, flĕ'xionlėss** *adjs.* (gram.).

flĕ'xor *n.* Muscle producing flexion in any part of body (opp. EXTENSOR).

flĕ'xūous *adj.* Full of bends, winding. **flĕ'xūouslў** *adv.* **flĕxūŏ'sĭtў** *n.*

flĕ'xure (-ksher) *n.* Bending, curvature, bent state; (math.) curving of line or surface; (geol.) bending of strata under pressure, chiefly from below.

flĭ'bbertĭgĭ'bbėt *n.* Gossiping, flighty, frivolous, or restless person.

flĭck *n.* 1. Light sharp blow with whiplash etc. shot out and withdrawn, or with finger-nail; sudden movement, jerk; quick turn of wrist in bowling or batting; slight sharp cracking sound; ~-*knife*, knife with retractable blade, used as weapon. 2. (colloq.) Film; (pl.) the cinema (abbrev. of *flickers*). ~ *v.t.* Strike with a flick; dash or jerk *away*, *off*; give a flick with; deliver, play (ball) with a flick of the wrist.

flĭ'cker[1] *v.i.* Quiver, vibrate; wave to and fro, flutter; flash up and die away alternately; burn fitfully or unsteadily. ~ *n.* Flickering movement; wavering or rapidly fluctuating light or flame. **flĭ'ckerĭnglў** *adv.*

flĭ'cker[2] *n.* (U.S.) Woodpecker.

flī'er, flў'er *n.* Bird etc. that flies; animal, vehicle, etc., going with exceptional speed; airman (chiefly U.S.); (mech.) moving guide or weight; part of spinning-machine that twists thread as it guides it on to the bobbin.

flight[1] (-īt) *n.* 1. (Manner of) flying; swift movement, esp. through the air; swift passage (of time); soaring, excursion, sally (*of* wit, fancy, ambition, etc.). 2. Migration, migrating body, flock, of birds or insects; unit of Royal Air Force, of about six aeroplanes; volley *of* arrows etc.; *in the first* ~, taking a leading part. 3. Distance that bird, aircraft, or missile, can fly. 4. Voyage in aircraft. 5. Series (*of* stairs etc.) mounting between landings, or without change of direction; set *of* hurdles or rails for racing over. 6. Feather etc. on arrow or dart. 7. ~*-deck*, deck of aircraft carrier for taking-off and landing of aircraft; ~ *lieutenant*, *sergeant*, ranks in Royal Air Force; ~ *recorder*, device in aircraft recording details of flight. ~ *v.t.* Shoot (wildfowl) in flight; (cricket) vary trajectory and pace of (ball before pitching).

flight² (-īt) *n.* Running away, fleeing; hasty retreat; absconding; *put to* ~, rout; *take* (*to*) ~, run away.

flī'ghtlėss (-īt-) *adj.* (of bird etc.) Unable to fly.

flī'ghtў (-īti) *adj.* Guided by whim or fancy, fickle; half-witted, crazy. **flī'ghtilў** *adv.* **flī'ghtinėss** *n.*

flĭ'm-flăm *n.* Trifle, nonsense, idle talk; humbug, deception.

flĭ'msў (-zĭ) *adj.* Easily destroyed, frail, slightly put together; paltry, trivial; frivolous, superficial; **flĭ'msĭlў** *adv.* **flĭ'msĭnėss** *n.* **flĭ'msў** *n.* Thin kind of paper, esp. that used for carbon copies; carbon copy.

flĭnch *v.i.* Give way, draw back, shrink (*from* something as dangerous, painful, or difficult); wince.

flĭ'nders¹ (-z) *n.pl.* Fragments, splinters.

Flĭ'nders² (-z), Matthew (1774–1814). English navigator and explorer; ~ *bar*, soft iron bar placed vertically near ship's compass to correct deviation due to magnetic induction.

fling *v.* (past t. & past part. *flung*). 1. Rush, go angrily or violently. 2. Throw, cast, hurl; throw with violence or hostile intent, hurl as missile; extend (arms) with sudden movement; cast (glance etc.); throw *into* (prison etc.); (of wrestler or ridden horse) throw to the ground; launch (troops etc.) *on* enemy, *against* fortress, etc. ~ *n.* 1. Throw, cast. 2. Gibe, scoff. 3. Vigorous dance in which arms and legs are flung about (esp. *Highland* ~). 4. Spell of indulgence in impulse.

flĭnt *n.* Hard stone of nearly pure silica found in roundish nodules, usu. steely-grey and encrusted with white, and having the property of giving off sparks when struck with steel; piece of this used with steel to kindle flame, fire powder in flintlock gun, etc.; piece of hard alloy used to produce spark in cigarette lighter etc.; pebble or nodule of flint flaked or chipped by prehistoric man to form a tool or weapon; ~*-glass*, pure lustrous glass, orig. made with ground flint; *flĭ'ntlock*, (gun with) lock in which flint struck against hammer produces sparks which ignite priming. **flĭ'ntў** *adj.* **flĭ'ntĭlў** *adv.* **flĭ'ntĭnėss** *n.*

Flĭ'ntshire. Former county of N. Wales, since April 1974 part of Clwyd.

flĭp¹ *n.* Mixture of beer and spirit sweetened and heated with hot iron rod; *egg* ~: see EGG.

flĭp² *v.* Propel, strike, with fillip or flick; make, move with, flip. ~ *n.* Fillip, flick; (colloq.) flight in aircraft; quick trip; ~ *side*, (colloq.) reverse side of gramophone record.

flĭ'ppant *adj.* Lacking in gravity; treating serious subjects with unbecoming levity, disrespectful. **flĭ'ppancў** *n.* **flĭ'ppantlў** *adv.*

flĭ'pper *n.* Limb used to swim with, e.g. fore-limb of cetacean, any limb of seal, walrus, turtle; wing of penguin; (slang) hand; (pl.) rubber etc. devices attached to the feet for underwater swimming.

flirt *v.* 1. Fillip, send with a jerk; wave or move briskly (fan, bird's tail). 2. Play at courtship *with*, pretend to make love. ~ *n.* 1. Sudden jerk; quick motion quickly checked. 2. Man who pays, or usu. woman who invites or accepts, attentions merely for amusement. **flirtā'tion** *n.* **flirtā'tious** (-sh*us*) *adj.* **flirtā'tiouslў** *adv.*

flĭt *v.i.* 1. Depart, remove; (chiefly north. & Sc.) change one's residence. 2. Pass lightly or softly and (usu.) rapidly; fly lightly and swiftly; make short and swift flights. ~ *n.* Removal.

flitch *n.* 1. Side of hog salted or cured, side of bacon. 2. Slice cut lengthwise from tree-trunk, usu. with natural surface as one side; (also *~-plate*) strengthening plate on beam, girder, etc. ~ *v.t.* Cut into flitches.

fli′tter *v.i.* Flit about, flutter; *~-mouse*, bat.

fli′vver *n.* (slang, orig. U.S.) Cheap motor-car.

flix *n.* Fur of some animals; down of beaver.

float *v.* 1. Rest, drift, on surface of liquid; (of stranded vessel) get afloat; be suspended freely *in* liquid; move or be suspended in air as if buoyed up; hover *before* eye or mind; (of currency) (allow to) fluctuate as regards exchange rate. 2. (commerc., of acceptance) Be in circulation, awaiting maturity; launch (scheme, company, etc.), be launched. 3. Cover with liquid, inundate; (of water etc.) support, bear along (object); set afloat; waft through air. ~ *n.* 1. *on the ~*, afloat. 2. Floating object; mass of floating weeds, ice, etc.; raft; cork or quill supporting baited fishing-line and dipping when fish bites; cork etc. supporting edge of fishing-net; inflated or hollow organ supporting fish etc. in water hollow metallic ball regulating water-level in boiler or tank; device floating in and regulating spirit in carburettor of petrol-motor; watertight structure attached to seaplane to give it buoyancy when resting on surface of water. 3. (pl.) Footlights. 4. (also *~-board*) One of boards of undershot water-wheel or paddlewheel. 5. Kind of low-bodied cart; platform on wheels used for displays etc. 6. Tool for smoothing plaster; single-cut file for smoothing metal 7. (weaving) Passing of weft-threads over part of warp without being interwoven; thread so passed. 8. (commerc.) Floating capital, cash, available for current expenditure. 9. *~-board*: see sense 4; ~ *glass*, glass made by float process; *~-grass*, grass sedge growing in marshy or swampy ground; *~-ironed*, ironed with ~ *roll calender*, ironing-machine with sprung and resiliently padded rollers; *~-plane*, aircraft with floats, seaplane; ~ *process*, (glass-making) process in which the glass is drawn in a continuous sheet from the melting tank and floated on the surface of a molten metal while it hardens.

floa′tage *n.* 1. Floating. 2. (Right of appropriating) flotsam; ships etc. afloat on river; floating masses. 3. Part of ship above water-line.

floatā′tion, flōt- *n.* Floating; launching of company or enterprise.

floa′ter *n.* (esp.) 1. Government stock-certificate etc. accepted as recognized security. 2. Floating voter. 3. (slang) Mistake, bloomer.

floa′tĭng *adj.* (esp.) 1. (commerc., of cargo) At sea. 2. Having little attachment, disconnected; (of kidney etc.) displaced, out of the normal position; ~ *rib*, rib (in man, one of the two lower pairs) not attached to breast-bone in front. 3. (commerc.) Not fixed or permanently invested; unfunded. 4. (of population etc.) Fluctuating; variable; not settled in definite state or place. 5. ~ *dock*: see DOCK[3]; ~ *light*, lightship or lighted buoy; ~ *vote*, (collect.) floating voters; ~ *voter*, voter not attached to any political party; (U.S.) one who casts a vote to which he is not entitled.

flŏ′ccōse *adj.* (bot.) Tufted.

flŏ′ccūle *n.* Small portions of matter like flock of wool.

flŏ′ccūlent, flŏ′ccūlōse, flŏ′ccūlous *adjs.* Like tufts of wool; in, showing, tufts. **flŏ′ccūlence** *n.*

flŏck[1] *n.* Lock, tuft, of wool, cotton, etc.; (pl.) material for quilting and stuffing made of wool-refuse or torn-up cloth; (pl. or collect. sing.) powdered wool or cloth for making flock-paper; (chem., pl.) precipitate in form of light loose masses like tufts of wool; *~-bed*, bed stuffed with flocks; *~-paper*, wall-paper sized and then powdered with flock either all over or in patterns.

flŏck² *n.* 1. Large assembly of people. 2. Number of animals of one kind (now esp. birds) feeding or travelling in company; number of domestic animals (now only sheep or goats) kept together; *~s and herds*, sheep and cattle. 3. Whole body of Christians; congregation, esp. in relation to its pastor; (occas.) any body of persons under charge or guidance of another person. ~ *v.i.* Congregate, go in great numbers, troop.

Flŏ'dden Field. Scene, in Northumberland, of a battle on 9 Sept. 1513, in which the English under the earl of Surrey defeated James IV of Scotland, who was killed in the field.

flōe *n.* Sheet of floating ice.

flŏg *v.t.* 1. Beat with birch, whip, cat, etc.; urge (horse etc.) on with whip; cast fishing-line repeatedly over (stream). 2. (slang) Sell (orig. illicitly).

flŏng *n.* Papier-mâché used in stereotyping; mould made of this.

flood (-ŭd) *n.* Flowing in of tide; flowing water, river, stream, sea (poet.); irruption of water over land, inundation (*the F~*, the great deluge recorded in Genesis as occurring in time of Noah); outpouring of water; torrent, downpour (also fig. as ~ *of abuse*, ~(*s*) *of tears*); *floo'dgate*, gate that may be opened or closed to admit or exclude water, esp. flood-water; lower gate of lock; sluice; *floo'dlight*, artificial light flooding surface of building etc. more or less uniformly; (*v.t.*) light thus; *~-tide*, advancing tide. ~ *v.* Inundate, cover with a flood; irrigate; deluge with water; (of rain) fill (river) to overflowing; become flooded; come in floods or great quantities; drive *out* by floods.

floor (-ōr) *n.* 1. Layer of boards, brick, etc., in room on which people tread, lower surface of interior of room; bottom of sea, cave, etc.; (anat.) lowest boundary of cavity or organ. 2. (in legislative assemblies etc.) Part of house where members sit and from which they speak; hence, right of speaking. 3. Set of rooms etc. on same level in building, storey. 4. Level area; platform or levelled space for threshing etc. 5. *~-cloth*, cloth for washing floors; ~ *manager*, stage-manager of television production; ~ *show*, entertainment presented on floor of night-club etc.; *~-walker*, (U.S.) shop-walker. ~ *v.t.* 1. Furnish with floor; pave; serve as floor of. 2. Bring to floor or ground, knock down; confound, nonplus; overcome, get the better of.

flŏp *v.* Sway about heavily and loosely, flap; move clumsily or heavily, or with sudden bump or thud; throw suddenly; (slang) collapse, fail. ~ *n.* Flopping motion, sound made by it; (slang) failure, collapse. ~ *adv.* With a flop. **flŏ'ppy̆** *adj.* Inclined to flop.

Flōr'a¹. (Rom. myth.) Goddess of flowers and spring.

flōr'a² *n.* (List of) plants of particular region or epoch. **flōr'al** *adj.* Of flora(s); of flower(s). [f. FLORA¹]

Floréal (flŏrā-ahl). 8th month (20 Apr.–19 May) in French Revolutionary calendar.

Flŏ'rence. (It. *Firenze*) Chief city of Tuscany, Italy; ~ *flask*, round or pear-shaped long-necked glass flask, often protected with basket-work, in which olive oil or wine is exported from Italy.

Flŏ'rentīne *adj.* Of Florence; ~ *iris*, large white or pale-blue species of iris. ~ *n.* Native, inhabitant, of Florence.

florĕ'scence *n.* Period or state of being in flower. **florĕ'scent** *adj.*

flōr'ėt *n.* (bot.) One of the small flowers making up a composite flower; small flower, floweret.

flōr'iāte *v.t.* Decorate with flower-designs.

flŏrĭbŭ'nda *n.* Plant (esp. kind of rose) bearing flowers in dense clusters.

flōr'icŭlture *n.* Cultivation of flowers. **flōricŭ'ltural** (-cher-) *adj.* **flōricŭ'lturist** *n.*

flŏ'rĭd *adj.* Profusely adorned as with flowers, elaborately ornate; ostentatious, showy; ruddy, flushed, high-coloured. **flŏ'rĭdly̆** *adv.* **flŏ'rĭdnėss, florĭ'dĭty̆** *ns.*

Flŏ'rĭda. South Atlantic State of U.S., admitted to the Union in 1845; capital, Tallahassee; ~ *water*, perfume resembling eau de Cologne; ~ *wood*, kind of hard boxwood used for inlaying.

florĭ'ferous *adj.* Producing many flowers.

florĭlē'gĭum *n.* (pl. *-ia*). Anthology. [mod. L., transl. Gk *anthologia*]

flŏ'rĭn *n.* 1. English silver or cupro-nickel coin, former two-shilling piece. 2. Principal monetary unit of the Netherlands, = 100 cents. 3. (hist.) Gold coin first issued at Florence in 1252; English gold coin issued by Edward III; any of various other coins formerly current in Europe. [OF, f. L *flos flor-* flower, because the orig. florin was stamped with a lily]

flŏ'rĭst *n.* One who deals in, raises, or studies flowers.

flŏ'ruĭt (-ōō-; *or* -ôr-) *n.* Period (failing exact dates of birth and death) at which person was alive or worked. [L, = 'flourished']

flôr'ȳ *adj.* (her.) = FLEURY.

flŏss *n.* Rough silk enveloping silkworm's cocoon; ~*-silk*, rough silk broken off in winding cocoons, this used in making cheap silk fabrics; untwisted filaments of silk used for needlework. **flŏ'ssȳ** *adj.*

flotation: see FLOATATION.

flotĭ'lla *n.* Small fleet; fleet of boats or small ships.

flŏ'tsam *n.* Wreckage found floating (cf. JETSAM).

flounce[1] *v.i.* Go with agitated or violent motion, flop, plunge, throw the body about. ~ *n.* Fling, jerk, of body or limb.

flounce[2] *n.* Ornamental strip gathered and sewn by upper edge round woman's skirt etc. and with lower edge hanging. ~ *v.t.* Trim with flounces.

flou'nder[1] *n.* Small edible flatfish, esp. *Pleuronectes flesus*.

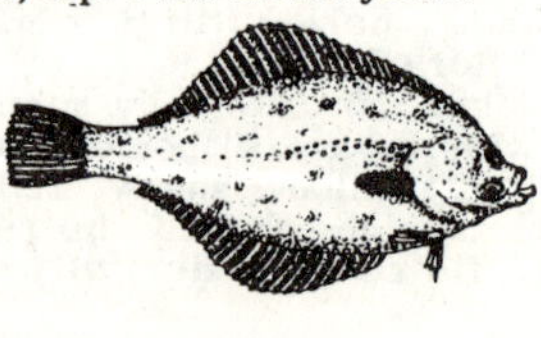

flou'nder[2] *v.i.* Struggle or plunge (as) in mud or wading; make mistakes, manage affair badly or with difficulty.

flour *n.* Finer part of meal (of wheat or other grain) obtained by bolting; wheat meal as dist. from that of other grain; fine soft powder, esp. that obtained by grinding seeds, farinaceous roots, etc. ~ *v.t.* Sprinkle with flour; (U.S.) grind into flour; *flour'ing-mill*, (U.S.) mill for making flour (dist. from *grist-mill*). [form of FLOWER; orig. sense 'finest part']

flou'rĭsh (flŭ-) *v.* 1. Grow vigorously; thrive, prosper, be successful; be in one's prime. 2. Embellish with flourishes. 3. Show ostentatiously; wave (weapon) about; throw (limbs) about. ~ *n.* Ornament of flowing curves about letter or word in handwriting; rhetorical embellishment, florid expression; ostentatious waving of weapon etc.; (mus.) fanfare of brass instruments, esp. to announce distinguished person's approach; florid passage, profuse ornamentation; short extemporized sequence of notes as prelude.

flout *v.* Mock, insult, express contempt for by word or act; scoff *at*.

flow (-ō) *v.i.* 1. Glide along as a stream; (of blood etc.) circulate; (of persons, things) come, go, in numbers; (of talk, literary style, etc.) move easily; (of garment, hair, etc.) hang easily, undulate; result *from*. 2. (math., of numbers) Increase or diminish continuously by infinitesimal quantities. 3. Gush out, spring; (of blood) be spilt; run full, be in flood; (of wine etc.) be poured out without stint; (archaic) be plentifully supplied *with*. ~ *n.* Flowing movement in stream; amount that flows; flowing liquid; outpouring, stream, continuous supply; rise of tide; ~ *of spirits*, habitual cheerfulness.

flow'er *n.* 1. (bot.) Reproductive organ in plant containing one or more pistils or stamens or both, and usu. a corolla and calyx; (pop.) coloured (i.e. not green) part of plant from which seed or fruit is later developed; blossom, esp. in regard to beauty or perfume; flowering plant. 2. (pl., chem. etc.) Pulverulent form of substance, esp. powder formed by sublimation; scum formed on wine etc. in fermentation; *~s of tan*, fungus (*Fuligo*) growing on tan heaps. 3. Ornament esp. in printing; (pl.) ornamental phrases (usu. *~s of speech*); (sing.) pick or choice *of*; best part, essence; choicest embodiment *of*. 4. State of blooming; prime. 5. *~-de-luce*, (archaic & U.S.) FLEUR-DE-LIS; *~-girl*, woman who sells flowers, esp. in street; *~-piece*, picture of flowers; *~-pot*, pot holding soil in which plant may be set; *~-show*, competitive or other exhibition of flowers etc. **flow'erlėss** *adj.* **flow'erėt** *n.* **flow'er** *v.* Produce flowers; be in full bloom; bring into flower; decorate with flowers or floral design. **flow'erer** *n.* Plant that flowers at specified time etc. **flow'ering** *adj.*

flow'erў *adj.* Abounding in flowers; full of fine words, compliments, figures of speech, etc.; *F~ Kingdom*, (tr. Chin. *hwa kwo*) China. **flow'erĭnėss** *n.*

flow'ĭng (-ōĭ-) *adj.* (esp., of style) Fluent, easy; (of lines) smoothly continuous; (naut., of sail) eased off, loosened to wind. **flow'ĭnglў** *adv.*

flown[1] (-ōn) *adj.* (obs. past. part. of *flow*) (archaic) Swollen, puffed up.

flown[2]: see FLY[2].

F.L.S. *abbrev.* Fellow of the Linnaean Society.

Flt Lt, Sgt *abbrevs.* Flight Lieutenant, Sergeant.

flu, 'flu (-o͞o) *n.* (colloq.) Influenza.

flŭ'ctūāte *v.i.* Vary irregularly, rise and fall, be unstable; vacillate, waver. **flŭctūā'tion** *n.*

flue[1] (-o͞o) *n.* = FLU.

flue[2] (-o͞o) *n.* Kind of fishing-net.

flue[3] (-o͞o) *n.* Substance formed by loose particles of cotton, down, etc., fluff.

flue[4] (-o͞o) *n.* Smoke-duct in chimney; channel for conveying heat, esp. hot-air passage in wall or tube for heating water in some kinds of boiler; *~-gas*, mixture of gases in boiler furnace; *~-pipe*, flue; (also) organ pipe with mouthpiece like whistle (opp. *reed-pipe*); *~ stop*, stop controlling this.

flu'encў (-o͞o-) *n.* Smooth easy flow, esp. in speech; ready utterance.

flu'ent (-o͞o-) *adj.* 1. Flowing (easily); liable to change. 2. (of motion, curves, etc.) Graceful, easy; (of speech, style) copious, coming easily, ready; expressing oneself quickly and easily. 3. (math.) That flows. **flu'entlў** *adv.* **flu'ent** *n.* (math.) Variable quantity in fluxions that is continually increasing or decreasing.

flŭff *n.* Light feathery stuff such as separates from dressed wool etc.; soft fur; soft downy mass or bunch; (slang) mistake, blunder, esp. by actor in speech. *~ v.t.* Put soft surface on (flesh side of leather); make into fluff; shake *up* or *out* into fluffy mass; (slang) make mistake, blunder; bungle. **flŭ'ffў** *adj.* **flŭ'ffĭlў** *adv.* **flŭ'ffĭnėss** *n.*

flu'ĭd (-o͞o-) *adj.* Consisting of particles that move freely among themselves and yield to the slightest pressure; moving readily, not solid or rigid, not stable; *~ ounce*: see OUNCE. *~ n.* Fluid substance (gas or liquid); liquid constituent or secretion. **fluĭ'dĭfў** *v.t.* **fluĭ'dĭtў** *n.*

fluke[1] (-o͞ok) *n.* 1. Flatfish, esp. the common flounder. 2. One of the class Trematoda of parasitic flatworms infesting the liver of sheep and cattle (so called from resemblance to flounder).

fluke[2] (-o͞ok) *n.* Broad flattened barbed extemity of the arm of an anchor; barbed head of lance, harpoon, etc.; (pl.) whale's large triangular tail.

fluke[3] (-o͞ok) *n.* Lucky accidental stroke, esp. at billiards; unexpected or undeserved success. *~ v.* Make a fluke; get by a fluke. **flu'kў** *adj.* **flu'kĭlў** *adv.* **flu'kĭnėss** *n.*

flume (-o͞om) *n.* (chiefly U.S.) Artificial channel conveying water for industrial use; ravine with stream. ~ *v.* Build flumes; convey down a flume.

flŭ'mmerỹ *n.* Food made by boiling oatmeal down to a jelly (archaic or dial.); sweet dish made with milk, flour, eggs, gelatine, etc.; empty compliments, trifles, nonsense. [Welsh *llymru*]

flŭ'mmox *v.t.* (slang) Confound, bewilder, disconcert.

flŭmp *v.* Fall or move heavily, set or throw *down*, with dull noise. ~ *n.* Action or sound of flumping.

flung: see FLING.

flŭ'nkey *n.* (orig. Sc.) Liveried servant, footman (usu. contempt.); toady, snob. **flŭ'nkeydom, flŭ'nkeyĭsm** *ns.*

fluorĕ'scėin (-ōō-) *n.* Orange-red water-insoluble compound ($C_{20}H_{12}O_5$) used in dyes etc.

fluorĕ'scence (-ōō-) *n.* Coloured luminosity produced in some materials by direct action of (esp. violet and ultra-violet) light-rays, X-rays, and other invisible radiations; property of converting ultra-violet light and other invisible radiations into visible light by absorption and re-emission. **fluorĕ'sce** *v.i.* **fluorĕ'scent** *adj.*

fluoridā'tion (-ōō-) *n.* (esp.) Addition of traces of fluoride to public water-supply with the object of reducing the incidence of dental caries.

flu'orīde (-ōō-) *n.* Salt of hydrofluoric acid, compound of fluorine with another element or organic radical.

flu'orine (-ōō*o*rēn) *n.* (chem.) Pungent corrosive gaseous element of pale greenish-yellow colour, extremely active chemically; symbol F, at. no. 9, at. wt 18·99840.

flu'orīte: see FLUORSPAR.

flu'oroscōpe (-ōō-) *n.* Apparatus incorporating a fluorescent screen, used for viewing objects by means of X-rays.

flu'orspăr, flu'orīte (flōō-) *ns.* Natural calcium fluoride (CaF_2), a transparent or translucent mineral of various colours, crystalline or massive, found esp. in Derbyshire, used as a flux in metallurgy etc.

flŭ'rrỹ *n.* 1. Gust, squall; (chiefly U.S.) sharp sudden shower. 2. Commotion, excitement; nervous hurry, agitation; death-throes of harpooned whale. ~ *v.t.* Confuse by haste or noise, agitate.

flŭsh[1] *v.* Take wing and fly away; cause (birds) to do this, put up; (transf.) bring into the open. ~ *n.* Number of birds put up at once.

flŭsh[2] *v.* 1. Spurt, rush out; cleanse (drain etc.) by flow of water; flood (meadow). 2. (of plant) Throw out fresh shoots; cause (plant) to do this. 3. (Cause to) glow with warm colour; (of blood) rush into and redden face; (of face) become red or hot, blush; inflame with pride or passion, encourage. ~ *n.* 1. Rush of water; sudden abundance; stream from mill-wheel; cleansing of drain by flushing. 2. Rush of emotion, elation produced by it or by victory etc. 3. Fresh growth of grass etc.; freshness, vigour. 4. Rush of blood to face, reddening caused by this; hot fit in fever.

flŭsh[3] *adj.* 1. Full to overflowing, in flood. 2. (usu. pred.) Having plentiful supply of money etc.; (of money) abundant. 3. Even, in same plane; level *with*; without projections or raised edges. ~ *v.t.* Level; fill in (joint) level with surface.

flŭsh[4] *n.* (cards) Hand of cards all of one suit, or including prescribed number of one suit.

flŭ'ster *v.* Confuse with drink, half-intoxicate; flurry, make nervous; be agitated, bustle. ~ *n.* Flurry, flutter, agitation.

flute (-ōōt) *n.* 1. Musical instrument of wood-wind family, a wooden or silver tube without a reed; the modern type is played horizontally and has a mouth-hole at the side and holes stopped by keys, and its range is about 3 octaves above middle C; *bass* ~, flute with range a fourth lower than normal. 2. Organ stop with flute-like tone. 3. Flute-player. 4. Semi-cylindrical vertical groove in pillar; similar groove or channel elsewhere, e.g. in frills. ~ *v.* 1. Play

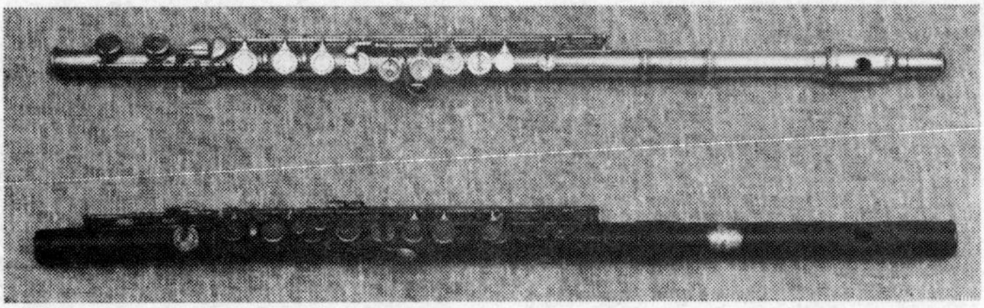

19TH-C FLUTES

flute; play on flute; whistle, sing, or speak in flute-like tones. 2. Make flutes or grooves in, whence **flu′ting** *n.*

flŭ′tter *v.* 1. Flap wings, flap (wings), without flying or in short flights; come or go with quivering motion; go about restlessly, flit, hover; quiver, vibrate; (of pulse) beat feebly and irregularly; move (flag, fan, etc.) irregularly. 2. Tremble with excitement, be agitated; agitate, ruffle; throw into confusion or agitation. ∼ *n.* Fluttering; tremulous excitement; stir, sensation; (colloq.) modest gambling venture, speculation.

flu′tȳ (-o͞o-) *adj.* Like flute in tone, soft and clear.

flu′vĭal (-o͞o-) *adj.* Of, found in, river(s). **flu′vĭatĭle** *adj.* Of, found in, produced by river(s).

flu′vĭo-glăcĭal (-o͞o-; *or* -shĭ*a*l *or* -sh*a*l) *adj.* (geol., of deposit) Swept off a glacier by the water released by the melting ice; carried by ice, then sorted by running water.

flŭx *n.* 1. Flowing; inflow of tide; flood *of* talk etc. 2. Continuous succession of changes of condition, composition, etc. 3. (math.) Continued motion (of a point). 4. (phys.) Rate of flow of fluid across given area; amount of light incident on a given area in a given time; total amount of magnetic or electric field passing through a given area. 5. (archaic) Morbid or excessive discharge of blood or excrement (*bloody* ∼, dysentery). 6. Substance mixed with metal etc. to facilitate fusion; substance used to make colours fusible in enamelling etc. ∼ *v.* 1. Issue in a flux; flow copiously. 2. Make fluid, fuse; treat with flux.

flŭ′xion (-ksh*o*n) *n.* 1. Flowing (rare); continuous change (rare). 2. (math.) Rate or proportion at which flowing or varying quantity increases its magnitude; (*method of*) ∼*s*, Newtonian calculus. **flŭ′xional, flŭ′xionarȳ** *adjs.*

flȳ[1] *n.* Two-winged insect, esp. of the order Diptera; winged insect, as firefly, mayfly; insect parasite on plant, plant-disease caused by this; natural or artificial fly used as bait in fishing; ∼ *in the ointment*, trifling circumstance that

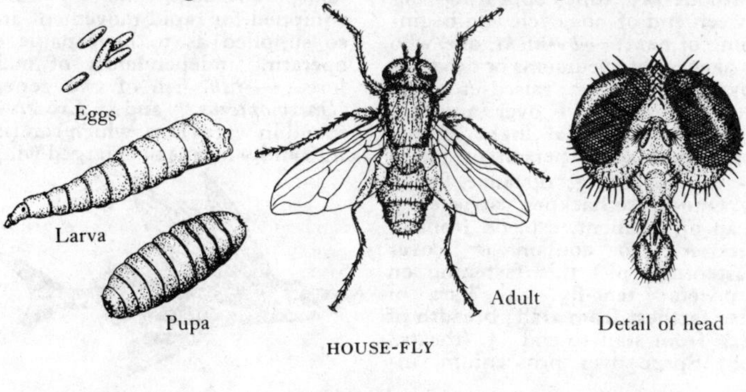

HOUSE-FLY

mars enjoyment; ~*-blow*, (*n.*) fly's egg or maggot in meat etc.; (*v.t.*) deposit eggs in, taint; ~*-blown*, so tainted; ~*-book*, case for keeping angler's flies in; ~*-catcher*, trap for flies; *fly'catcher*, plant, insect, bird (esp. of genus *Muscicapa*), that catches flies; ~*-paper*, paper treated with preparation for catching or poisoning flies; ~*-weight*, boxer of lightest weight (see BOXING).

flȳ² *v.* (past t. *flew* pr. flōō, past part. *flown* pr. flōn). 1. Move through air with wings; travel, convey, by aircraft etc., (of aircraft etc.) travel through air or space; pilot (aircraft); make (pigeon, hawk) fly; make (kite) rise and stay aloft; (hawking) soar by way of attack *at*; pass or rise quickly through air; jump clear over or *over* fence, etc.; ~ *high*, be ambitious; *high-flown*, exalted, turgid, bombastic; ~ *a kite*, raise money by accommodation bill; try how wind blows, send up *ballon d'essai*. 2. (of flag, hair, garment, etc.) Flutter, wave; set or keep (flag) flying. 3. Travel swiftly, rush along, pass rapidly; spring, start, hasten; be driven or forced off suddenly; (of glass etc.) break in pieces suddenly and violently; *let* ~, discharge (missile); shoot, hit, use strong language, *at*; ~ *at*, *upon*, attack violently; ~ *out*, burst into violent language or action. 4. Run away, flee, flee from. 5. ~*-away*, (of garments) streaming, loose; (of persons) flighty; ~*-back*, spurious line or trace in cathode-ray tube appearing between end of one cycle and beginning of next; ~*-by-night*, one who makes night excursions or decamps by night; *fly'over*, raised crossing, e.g. of one road over another; ~*-past*, ceremonial flight of aircraft past some person or place. ~ *n.* 1. Flying, distance flown. 2. One-horse hackney carriage. 3. Lap on garment, esp. on front of trousers, to contain or cover fastening, (pl.) this fastening on trousers; tent-fly. 4. Part of flag farthest from staff; breadth of flag from staff to end. 5. (theatr., pl.) Space over proscenium, including upper mechanism and galleries on each side from which it is worked. 6. Speed-regulating device, usu. of vanes on rotating shaft, for regulating striking mechanism of clock etc.; flywheel etc. for regulating speed of machinery. 7. ~*-half*, (Rugby footb.) half-back who stands off from scrum half; *fly'leaf*, blank leaf at beginning or end of book; blank leaf of circular etc.; *fly'man*, driver of fly; man stationed in flies of theatre to work ropes etc.; ~*-nut*, nut with wings or projections enabling it to be tightened by hand; ~*-stitch*, embroidery stitch in which one loop catches down another; *fly'wheel*, wheel with heavy rim on revolving shaft, for regulating motion of machinery or accumulating power.

flȳ³ *adj.* (slang) Knowing, wide awake.

flyer: see FLIER.

flȳ'ing *adj.* 1. That flies. 2. Floating loosely, fluttering, waving; hanging loose. 3. Travelling or passing swiftly; (of a start, race, etc.) in which starting-point is passed at full speed; passing, hasty; temporary; designed for rapid movement. 4. ~ *bomb*, kind of explosive-carrying, reaction-propelled crewless aeroplane, first used by the Germans against England in June 1944; ~ *buttress*, (archit.) buttress slanting from pier etc. to wall and usu. carried on arch for taking thrust of roof or vault; ~ *column*, military force equipped for rapid movement and so supplied as to be capable of operating independently of main force; ~*-fish*, fish of two genera (*Dactylopterus* and *Exocetus*), found in warm seas, which can rise into air by means of enlarged wing-

like pectoral fins; ~ *fox*, fruit-eating bat of genus *Pteropus*, found in tropical East and in Australia; ~ *jib*, light sail set before jib on ~ *jib-boom*; ~ *jump*, *leap*, jump with running start; ~ *saucer*, unidentified disc- or saucer-shaped object reported as appearing in the sky; ~ *squad*: see SQUAD; ~ *squirrel*, any of several squirrels esp. of genera *Pteromys* and *Glaucomys*, which can glide through air by means of extension of skin connecting fore and hind limbs. ~ *n.* Act or process of moving through the air; flight; ~*-boat*, seaplane with boat-like fuselage; ~ *-machine*, machine that can navigate the air; ~ *officer*, officer of Royal Air Force, next in rank below flight lieutenant.

F.M. *abbrev.* Field Marshal; frequency modulation.

F.O. *abbrev.* Flying Officer.

foal *n.* Young of horse, ass, etc., colt or filly. ~ *v.* Give birth to (foal); give birth to foal.

foam *n.* 1. Collection of small bubbles formed in liquid by agitation, fermentation, etc.; froth of saliva or perspiration. 2. (poet.) Sea. 3. Rubber or plastic material in form of cellular mass. ~ *v.i.* Emit foam, froth at the mouth; (of water etc.) froth, gather foam, run foaming *along*, *down*, *over*, etc.; (of cup, etc.) be filled with foaming liquor. **foa′mȳ** *adj.*

fŏb[1] *n.* Small pocket for watch etc. formerly made in waistband of breeches. ~ *v.t.* Put in one's fob; pocket.

fŏb[2] *v.t.* Cheat, take in; palm (something inferior) *off on* person; put (person) *off with* something inferior.

f.o.b. *abbrev.* Free on board.

fō′cal *adj.* Of, situated or collected at, a focus; ~ *distance* or *length*, distance between centre of lens or mirror and its focus; ~*plane*, plane parallel with that of lens, passing through the focus; ~*-plane shutter*, (photog.) shutter of roller-blind type placed immediately in front of plate or film.

fō′calīze *v.t.* Focus. **fōcalīzā′tion** *n.*

Foch (fŏsh), Ferdinand (1851–1929). French field marshal; C.-in-C. of the Allied forces in France from April 1918.

fo′c's′le: see FORECASTLE.

fō′cus *n.* (pl. *-cī*, *-cuses*). 1. (geom.) One of the points from which the distances to any point of a given curve are connected by a linear relation. 2. (optics etc.) Point at which rays meet after being refracted or reflected; point from which rays appear to proceed; point at which object must be situated in order that image produced by lens may be clear and well-defined; adjustment (of eye or eyeglass) necessary to produce a clear image; (acoustics) point towards which sound-waves converge. 3. Principal seat of disease; centre of activity. ~ *v.t.* Converge, make converge, to a focus; adjust focus of (lens, eye); bring into focus.

fŏ′dder *n.* Dried food, hay, straw, etc., for stall-feeding cattle. ~ *v.t.* Give fodder to.

fōe *n.* (poet. etc.) Enemy, adversary, opponent, ill-wisher; *foe′man*, (archaic) enemy in war.

foetid: see FETID.

foe′tus (fēt-), **fē′tus** *n.* Unborn offspring (used of human embryo after first 8 weeks of intra-uterine life. **foe′tal** ~ *adj. circulation*, blood-exchange system of the foetus, including its own blood-vessels and those which connect with the maternal circulation.

fŏg[1] *n.* After-grass; long grass left standing in winter. ~ *v.t.* Leave (land) under fog; feed (cattle) on fog.

fŏg[2] *n.* 1. Thick mist or cloud of minute water-droplets suspended in atmosphere at or near earth's surface; obscurity caused by this, esp. when combined with dust or smoke; (meteor.) atmosphere in which visibility is less than 1 km; ~*-bow*, bow, resembling rainbow, sometimes seen opposite sun during fog; ~*-horn*, sounding instrument for warning ships in fog; ~*-signal*, detonator placed on railway-line in fog as signal. 2. (photog.) Opaque cloudy patch on developed negative. ~ *v.t.* Envelop (as) with fog; bewilder, perplex; (photog.) cause fog on (negative).

fogey: see FOGY.

fŏ'ggy̆ *adj.* Thick, murky; of, like, infested with, fog; obscure, dull, confused; beclouded, indistinct. **fŏ'ggily̆** *adv.* **fŏ'gginėss** *n.*

fō'gle *n.* (thieves' slang, archaic) Silk handkerchief.

fō'gou (-o͞o) *n.* Cornish souterrain or earth-house.

fō'gy̆, fō'gey (-g-) *n.* (usu. *old* ~) Person with antiquated ideas. **fō'gy̆dom** *n.*

föhn (fẽrn) *n.* Hot dry S. wind blowing down N. side of Alps; hot dry wind blowing down leeward slopes of other mountains.

foi'ble *n.* 1. Weak point; weakness of character; quality on which one mistakenly prides oneself. 2. (fencing) Pliant part of sword-blade from middle to point.

foil[1] *n.* 1. (archit.) One of small arcs or spaces between cusps of windows. 2. Metal hammered or rolled into thin

sheet; sheet of this formerly placed behind glass of mirror to produce reflection; thin leaf of metal placed under precious stone to increase its brilliance, or under transparent substance to make it look like precious stone. 3. Anything serving to set off another thing by contrast. 4. (obs.) Part of tally kept by payee. ~ *v.t.* 1. Set off by contrast. 2. (archit.) Ornament with foils.

foil[2] *v.* 1. (hunting) Run over or cross (scent, ground) so as to baffle hounds; (of deer etc.) spoil the scent thus. 2. Beat off, repulse; frustrate, parry, baffle. ~ *n.* 1. Track of hunted animal. 2. (archaic or literary) Repulse, defeat, check.

foil[3] *n.* Blunt-edged sword used in fencing with button on point to prevent injury.

foist *v.t.* Introduce surreptitiously or unwarrantably *into* or *in*; palm (*off*) *on*; father (composition) *on*.

fol. *abbrev.* Folio.

fōld[1] *n.* Enclosure for sheep; (fig.) church, body of believers. ~ *v.t.* Shut up (sheep etc.) in fold; place sheep in fold(s) on (land) to manure it.

fōld[2] *n.* Doubling of folded object; hollow between two thicknesses, in mountain, etc.; coil of serpent, string, etc.; folding; line made by folding; (geol.) bend in strata. ~ *v.* 1. Double (flexible thing) over upon itself; ~ *over, together*; bend portion of (thing) *back, down*; become, be able to be, folded; ~ *up*, make more compact by folding; (colloq.) break down; fail; *folding door*, door in two parts (often themselves consisting of hinged leaves which fold up when door is open) hung on opposite jambs, so that edges meet when door is closed. 2. Wind, clasp (arms etc.) *about, round*; lay together and interlace (arms), clasp (one's) hands; swathe, envelop; embrace *in* arms, *to* breast. **fō'lder** *n.* (esp.) Paper-folding instrument; folded circular etc.; cover or holder for loose papers.

-fōld *suffix.* Multiplied by, as *sevenfold*.

fōliā'ceous (-shus) *adj.* Leaf-like; with organs like leaves; of leaves; laminated.

fō'liage *n.* Leaves, leafage.

fō'liate *adj.* Leaf-like; having leaves; having specified number of leaflets. **fō'liāte** *v.* Split into laminae; decorate (arch etc.) with foils; number leaves (not pages) of (volume) consecutively. **fōliā'tion** *n.*

fŏ'lic *adj.* Of, involving, folic acid; ~ *acid*, vitamin of the B group, deficiency of which in man is associated with anaemia.

fō'liō *n.* (pl. *-os*). 1. Leaf of paper, parchment, etc., numbered only on front; two opposite pages of ledger etc. used concurrently in book-keeping; page of ledger etc. used for both sides of account; page-number of printed book;

number of words (in England usu. 72 or 90, in U.S. usu. 100) taken as unit in reckoning length of document. 2. Sheet of paper folded once; volume of the largest size, made up of sheets of paper folded once; *in* ~, (of book) made up of such sheets. ~ *adj*. Formed of sheets or a sheet folded once; folio-sized.

fōlk (fōk) *n*. 1. Nation, race. 2. (usu. pl.) People in general; people of specified class; relatives; (U.S., esp.) respectable people. 3. (attrib.) Of the people; ~*-dance*, (music for) dance of popular origin; ~ *etymology*, perversion of word's form to make it significant; *fo'lklore*, traditional beliefs, customs, etc., of the people, study of these; hence, *fo'lklorist* (*n*.); ~*-moot*, (hist.) general assembly of people of town or shire; ~*-song*, tranditional song; *fo'lkways*, (sociol. etc.) traditional patterns of behaviour common to members of a particular culture or society; *fo'lkweave*, fabric, construction, of loosely woven coarse yarns.

Fō'lketing *n*. Danish parliament.

fŏ'llicle *n*. 1. (anat.) Small sac; secretory gland of this shape; minute pit in which hair-root grows; *graafian* ~: see GRAAF. 2. Cocoon. 3. (bot,) Fruit which consists of a single carpel and splits open along ventral suture only. **fŏlli'cūlar, fŏlli'cūlātėd** *adjs*.

fŏ'llow (-ō) *v*. 1. Go or come after (moving thing or person); pursue; go along (path); come after, come next, in order or time; ~ *my leader*, game in which each player must do as leader does; ~ *one's nose*, go straight on; be guided by instinct; ~ *the plough*, be a ploughman. 2. Accompany, serve, attend upon; go as person's attendant; go after as admirer; be consequence of; result (from). 3. Strive after, aim at. 4. Take as guide or leader; take as rule; conform to; practise (profession etc.); ~ *the sea*, be a sailor. 5. Keep up with mentally; grasp the meaning of; grasp argument, meaning, etc. 6. ~ *after*, follow; ~ *on*, (cricket, of side) be compelled to bat again immediately after first innings, in consequence of having failed to reach the number of runs made by the other side by 150 or more; ~*-on* (*n*.); ~ *out*, pursue to the end; ~ *through*, (golf) carry stroke through to fullest possible extent after striking ball; ~*-through* (*n*.); ~ *up*, pursue steadily; add another blow etc. to (previous blow etc.); (fig.) prosecute (suggestion etc.) to a conclusion; ~*-up* (*n*.). ~ *n*. (billiards) Stroke causing player's ball to roll on after object-ball, motion so given; (in restaurants etc.) supplementary portion.

fŏ'llower (-ōer) *n*. (esp.) Adherent, disciple; man courting maidservant.

fŏ'llowing (-ōi-) *n*. (esp.) Body of adherents, followers. ~ *adj*. (esp.) Now to be mentioned. ~ quasi-*prep*. After.

fŏ'llȳ *n*. 1. Foolishness; foolish act, idea, etc. 2. Costly structure (considered) useless or otherwise foolish.

fomĕ'nt *v.t*. 1. Bathe with warm or medicated lotions; apply warmth to. 2. Foster, stimulate, instigate (sentiment, conduct, sedition, etc.).

fōmĕntā'tion *n*. (Application of) warm or medicated substance for fomenting purposes.

fŏnd *adj*. Tender, loving; doting; (archaic) foolishly credulous; ~ *of*, full of love for, much inclined to. **fŏ'ndlȳ** *adv*. **fŏ'ndnėss** *n*.

fŏ'ndant *n*. Kind of soft sweet made of flavoured sugar.

fŏ'ndle *v*. Touch or stroke lovingly.

fŏ'ndūe *n*. (cookery) Hot melted cheese flavoured and served as a dip.

fŏnt *n*. 1. Receptacle, usu. of stone, for baptismal water; receptacle for holy water; oil-reservoir of lamp. 2. (U.S.) Fount (of type).

fŏ'ntal *adj*. 1. Primary, original, of the fountain head. 2. Of the font, baptismal.

fŏntanĕ'lle *n*. Membrane-covered space in bony vault of skull where union of the bones is incomplete, normally closing in infancy.

fōōd *n.* Substance taken into the body to maintain life and growth; solid substance used thus (opp. *drink*); (particular kind of) edibles (also transf. & fig.); *foo'dstuff*, material for food; (pl.) articles of food in bulk.

fōōl[1] *n.* Silly person, simpleton; dupe; professional jester in medieval great household; *play the* ~, blunder, trifle; indulge in buffoonery; *foo'lproof*, so plain that even a fool cannot misunderstand; (of machines etc.) not liable to be injured by misuse; *~'s-cap*, fantastic cap, usu. with bells, worn by medieval jester; dunce's conical paper cap; *foo'lscap*, long folio writing- or printing-paper 381–432 × 305–343 mm (15–17 × 12–13½ in.); (pop.) 330 × 203 mm (13 × 8 in.) (from water-mark of fool's cap on some old paper); *~'s errand*, fruitless errand; *~'s mate*: see MATE[1]; *~'s paradise*, illusory happiness; **fōō'lerȳ** *n.* **fōō'lĭsh** *adj.* **fōō'lĭshlȳ** *adv.* **fōō'lĭshnėss** *n.* **fōōl** *adj.* That is a fool. ~ *v.* Play the fool; cheat (person) *out of*; throw *away* foolishly; make a fool of, dupe, play tricks on. [OF *fol* mad f. L *follis* bellows, empty-headed person]

fōōl[2] *n.* Stewed crushed fruit mixed with cream or custard.

fōō'lhardȳ *adj.* Foolishly venturesome, delighting in needless risks. **fōō'lhardinėss** *n.*

fŏŏt *n.* (pl. *feet*). 1. Lowest part of leg beyond ankle-joint; this as organ of locomotion; *carry person off his feet*, make him enthusiastic, greatly excite; *on* ~, walking, not riding etc.; in motion; *put one's ~ down*, take up firm position (fig.); *put one's ~ in it*, blunder; *under* ~, *underfoot*, beneath the foot or feet; into state of subjection or inferiority. 2. Foot-soldiers, infantry. 3. End of bed, grave, etc., towards which feet are placed; part of stocking etc. covering foot. 4. Metrical unit, division of line, with varying number of syllables one of which is accented. 5. Linear measure of 12 inches. 6. Lower (usu. projecting) part of object, base. 7. (zool.) Organ of locomotion or attachment of some invertebrates, e.g. mussels. 8. Bottom (of hill, staircase, page, etc.; of mast). 9. (pl. *foots*) Dregs; oil refuse; coarse sugar. 10. *~-and-mouth* (*disease*), contagious fever, caused by a filtrable virus, of horned cattle and other animals, with ulcerating vesicles in mouth, near hoof, etc.; *foo'tball*, spherical or (in Rugby game) elliptical ball used in game and consisting of inflated rubber ball in case of leather or other approved material; open-air game played with this ball by two sides each trying to kick or carry it over the other's goal-line (see ASSOCIATION and RUGBY football); *~-bridge*, bridge for foot-passengers; *~ candle*, unit of illumination, equal to the illumination of a surface at a uniform distance of 1 ft from a symmetrical point source of 1 candela; *foo'tfall*, sound of footsteps; *~-fault*, (lawn tennis) fault made by overstepping base-line or by running, walking, or jumping, while serving; (*v.*) make foot-fault; record foot-fault against (player); *F~ Guards*, Brigade of Guards (Grenadier, Coldstream, Scots, Irish, and Welsh Guards); *~-hill*, (orig. U.S.) lower hill at foot of mountain or mountain-range; *foo'thold*, support for feet, surface for standing on; *foo'tlights*, row of screened lights along front of stage on level with actors' feet; *~-loose*, free, unhampered by ties or obligations; *foo'tman*, foot-soldier; liveried servant attending carriage, waiting at table, and answering door; connecting rod between treadle and wheel of spinning-wheel; *foo'tmark*, footprint; *~-muff*, muff for keeping feet warm; *foo'tnote*, note inserted at foot of page; *~-pace*, walking pace; *foo'tpad*, (hist.) unmounted highwayman; *~-passenger*, one who walks, not rides, etc.; *foo'tpath*, path for pedestrians, *foo'tplate*, platform in steam locomotive for driver and fireman; *~-poundal*, work done when a force of one poundal moves its point of application one foot in the line of action of the force; *foo'tprint*, impression left by foot; *~-race*, race between persons on foot; *~-rot*, inflammatory disease affecting horns and feet of cattle etc.; (also) tinea; *~-rule*, rigid or folding measure divided off into feet; *~-slog*, (slang) go on foot, tramp; *foo'tsore*, having sore feet, esp. with walking; *foo't-stalk*, (bot.) stalk or petiole of leaf; peduncle of flower; (zool.) muscular attachment of barnacle etc.; *foo'tstep*, tread; footprint; noise made by treading; *foo'tstool*, low stool for resting feet on; *foo'twear*, boots and shoes collectively. **foo͝'t-lėss** *adj.* **foo͝'tage** *n.* Number of linear feet of material etc. **foo͝t** *v.* Set foot on, traverse on foot (rare); put new foot to (stocking); add up or *up* (account); pay (bill).

foo͝'ter *n.* (slang) Game of football.

foo͝'tĭng *n.* 1. Foothold; secure position; conditions, relations, position, status, in which person is towards others. 2. Projecting course at foot of wall etc.

foo͞'tle *v.i.* (slang) Trifle, play the fool. ~ *n.* Twaddle, folly. **foo͞'t-lĭng** *adj.*

foo͞'zle *v.t.* (slang, esp. golf) Do clumsily, bungle, make a mess of. ~ *n.* Clumsy failure.

fŏp *n.* = DANDY *n.* 1. **fŏ'ppery̆** *n.* **fŏ'ppĭsh** *adj.* **fŏ'ppĭshly̆** *adv.* **fŏ'ppĭshnėss** *n.*

fôr (unstressed fer) *prep.* In place of (as in *b. stands ~ born*); in exchange against (*sold ~ 2p*); in defence or favour of; in the interest of, to reach, obtain, etc. (*went ~ a taxi, sailed ~ India*); as regards (esp. with words implying fitness, as *fit ~ nothing*); because of, on account of; corresponding to (*~ one enemy he has 50 friends*); considering the nature of (*cool ~ a summer day*); during, to the extent of (*wait ~ years; walk ~ 3 miles*); ~ *it*, (colloq.) in for it (see IN adv.). ~ *conj.* (introducing new sentence etc. containing reason for believing what has been previously stated) Seeing that, since; because.

f.o.r. *abbrev.* Free on rail.

fŏ'rage *n.* Food for horses and cattle, fodder, esp. that provided for horses in army; *~-cap*, undress cap of army. ~ *v.* Collect forage from, ravage; search for forage or (fig.) *for* anything, rummage; supply with forage; get by foraging. **fŏ'rager** *n.*

forā'mĕn *n.* Orifice, hole, passage; *obturator ~*, aperture in hip-bone. **forā'mĭnate, -ātėd** *adjs.*

fŏrasmŭch (-z-) *adv.* ~ *as*, (archaic) seeing that, since.

fŏ'ray *n.* Incursion, raid, inroad. ~ *v.i.* Go on, make, foray.

fôr'bear[1], fôre- (-bār) *n.* (usu. pl.) Ancestor(s).

forbear'[2] (-bār) *v.* Abstain or refrain from or *from*; not use or mention; be patient. **forbear'-ance** *n.* **forbear'ĭngly̆** *adv.*

forbĭ'd *v.t.* (past t. *-băde*, past part. *-bĭ'dden*). Command not *to* do, not to go to (place); not allow (person etc. something; person or thing to exist or happen); prevent, make undesirable; *Forbidden City*, Lhasa in Tibet, which foreigners were forbidden to enter; also, innermost part of the northern (Tatar) city of Peking, where under the Manchu dynasty no Chinese might spend a night. **forbĭ'ddĭng** *adj.* Repellent, of uninviting appearance. **forbĭ'ddĭngly̆** *adv.* **forbĭ'ddĭngnėss** *n.*

forby̆'e, -by̆' *prep.* & *adv.* (Sc. & archaic). Besides; not to mention; in addition.

fôrce[1] *n.* 1. Strength, violence, intense effort; strength exerted on an object, coercion. 2. Military strength; body of armed men, army; body of police; (pl.) troops. 3. Mental or moral strength; power to convince, vividness of effect; binding power, validity; real import, precise meaning; *in ~*, in operation, valid. 4. (phys.) Measurable and determinable influence inclining body to motion, intensity of this; (formerly) cause of any class of physical phenomena (e.g. of heat or motion) conceived as inherent in matter; (fig.) agency likened to these. 5. *~-pump*, pump to raise water etc. by action of piston or plunger. ~ *v.t.* 1. Use violence to; rape. 2. Constrain, compel; put strained sense upon (words); (cards) compel (player) to trump or reveal his strength, compel player to play (certain card); compel (person) *to* do, *into* doing, *into* specified action; strain to the utmost, urge; ~ *person's hand*, compel him to act prematurely or adopt policy unwillingly; ~ *the pace*, adopt high speed in race to tire adversary out quickly. 3. Overpower, capture, make way through, break open (stronghold, defences, pass, lock, door) by force; drive by force, propel against resistance; effect, produce, by effort; take by force, extort, wring; impose, press, (thing) *on* person; ~ *a card*, (in conjuring) make person choose a particular card unconsciously. 4. Artificially hasten maturity of (plant etc.). **fŏrced** (-st) *adj.* (esp.) ~ *landing*, unpremeditated landing of aircraft in an emergency; ~ *march*, march requiring special effort by troops etc. **fŏr'cĕdlȳ** *adv.*

fŏrce² *n.* (northern) Waterfall.

fŏr'ceful (-sf-) *adj.* Forcible. **fŏr'cefullȳ** *adv.* **fŏr'cefulnĕss** *n.*

fŏrce majeure (mahzhẽr'). Irresistible compulsion; war, strike, act of God, etc., excusing from fulfilment of contract. [Fr.]

fŏr'cemeat (-sm-) *n.* Meat chopped, spiced, and seasoned for stuffing etc.; stuffing.

fŏr'cĕps *n.* Instrument like pincers, for seizing and holding objects (esp. in surgery); (anat., zool., etc.) organ resembling forceps. **fŏr'cĭpate** *adj.* Resembling forceps.

fŏr'cĭble *adj.* Done by, involving, force; powerful, convincing. **fŏr'cĭblenĕss** *n.* **fŏr'cĭblȳ** *adv.*

fŏrd¹ *n.* Shallow place where river etc. may be crossed by wading. ~ *v.t.* Wade across (river etc.). **fŏr'dable, fŏr'dlĕss** *adjs.*

Fŏrd², Henry (1863–1947). Amer. automobile manufacturer, founder of the Ford company at Detroit, U.S.

Fŏrd³, Gerald (né Leslie King) (1913–). 38th president of U.S., 1974–7.

fŏrdo' (-ōō) *v.t.* (archaic; past t. *-did*, past part. *-done* pr. dŭn). Kill, destroy, spoil; *fordone*, exhausted.

fŏre¹ *adj.* Situated in front. ~ *n.* Fore part, bow of ship; *to the* ~, on the spot, ready to hand, available, cŏnspicuous.

fŏre² *adv.* ~ *and aft*, at bow and stern; backwards and forwards or lengthwise in ship; ~*-and-aft*, (of rigging) with sails set lengthwise as in a schooner.

fŏre³ *int.* (golf) Warning cry to person in line of flight of the ball.

fore- *prefix.* In front; beforehand, in advance; anticipatory, precedent.

forearm¹ (fŏr'ărm) *n.* Arm from elbow to wrist or finger-tips.

forearm² (fŏrăr'm) *v.t.* Arm beforehand.

forebear: see FORBEAR.

forebō'de (fŏrb-) *v.t.* Predict (rare); betoken, portend; have presentiment of. **forebō'dĭng** *n.* Presage, omen, presentiment (esp. of evil). **forebō'dĭnglȳ** *adv.*

for'ebrain (fŏrb-) *n.*: see BRAIN.

forecast (fŏr'kahst *or* -ah'-) *v.t.* (past t. & past part. *-cast*). Estimate, conjecture, beforehand. **fŏr'ecast** *n.* Conjectural estimate of future thing, esp. of coming weather.

forecastle (fō'ksl), **fō'c's'le** *n.* Forward part of merchant vessel; crew's quarters in this; (hist.) short raised deck at ship's bow; ~ *in*, with bows under.

foreclose (fŏrklō'z) *v.* 1. Bar, preclude, prevent; shut out from enjoyment of. 2. (mortgage law) Bar (person entitled to redeem) upon non-payment of money due; bar (right of redemption); take away power of redeeming (mortgage). **foreclō'sure** (-zh*er*) *n.*

foreconscious (fŏr'kŏnsh*us*) *n.* (psychol.) Region of the mind containing ideas or memories that can readily be made conscious; preconscious.

fŏre-course (-kŏrs) *n.* Lowest sail on foremast.

forecourt (fŏr'kŏrt) *n.* Enclosed space before building, outer court.

foredōō'm (fŏrd-) *v.t.* Doom beforehand; condemn beforehand *to*; foreordain, predestine.

forefather (fŏr'fahdh-) *n.* (chiefly pl.) Ancestor, progenitor.

forefinger (fŏr'fĭngg-) *n.* Finger next thumb, index finger.

forefoot (fŏr'f-) *n.* 1. One of beast's front feet. 2. (naut.) Foremost part of keel; course passing in front of this.

forefront (fŏr'frŭ-) *n.* Very front, foremost part, van.

forego (fŏrgō') *v.* (past t. *-went*, past part. *-gone* pr. gŏn). Precede in place or time; *forego'ing*, previously mentioned; *for'egone conclusion*, decision or opinion formed before case is argued or full evidence known; result that can be or could have been foreseen.

for'eground (fŏrg-) *n.* Part of view, esp. in picture, nearest observer; most conspicuous position.

for'ehănd (fŏrh-) *n.* Part of horse in front of rider. ~ *adj.* (tennis etc.) (of stroke) Made with palm of hand turned forwards; (of court, corner, etc.) on side on which forehand stroke is made, i.e. usu. on right-hand side.

for'ehănded (fŏrh-) *adj.* (U.S.) Thrifty; well-to-do, prosperous.

forehead (fŏ'rĭd *or* fŏr'hĕd) *n.* Part of face above eyebrows and between temples.

for'ehŏck (fŏrh-) *n.* Foreleg of pig as cut of meat.

fŏ'reign (-rĭn) *n.* 1. Belonging to, proceeding from, other persons or things; alien *from* or *to*; irrelevant, dissimilar, inappropriate, *to*; introduced from outside (esp. ~ *body* in the eye, tissues, etc.); situated outside, coming from another district, parish, society, etc. 2. Outside the country, not in one's own land; of, in, characteristic of, coming from, dealing with, some country not one's own. 3. *F~ Legion*: see LEGION; *F~ and Commonwealth Office*, department of Secretary of State for Foreign and Commonwealth Affairs; building housing this. **fŏ'reigner** *n.* Person born in foreign country or speaking foreign language; foreign ship, imported animal or article.

foreknow (fŏrnō') *v.t.* Know beforehand, have prescience of. **foreknow'lèdge** (-nŏl-) *n.*

fŏ'rel, fŏ'rrel *n.* Kind of parchment dressed to look like vellum.

for'eland (fŏrl-) *n.* Cape, promontory.

for'elĕg (fŏrl-) *n.* Beast's front leg.

forelimb (fŏr'lĭm) *n.* Front limb of animal.

for'elŏck[1] (fŏrl-) *n.* Lock of hair growing just above forehead.

for'elŏck[2] (fŏrl-) *n.* (chiefly naut.) Wedge put through hole in bolt to keep it in place; linchpin. ~ *v.t.* Secure with forelock.

for'eman (fŏrm-) *n.* (fem. *for'ewoman*). President and spokesman of jury; principal workman superintending others.

for'emast (fŏrm-) *n.* Forward lower mast of ship.

for'emōst (fŏrm-) *adj.* Most advanced in position, front; most notable, best, chief. ~ *adv.* Before anything else in position; in the first place.

for'enōōn (fŏrn-) *n.* (Sc. & archaic) Part of day before noon.

forĕ'nsĭc *adj.* Of, used in, court of law; ~ *medicine*, medical jurisprudence. **forĕ'nsĭcallȳ** *adv.*

foreordai'n (fŏrŏr-) *v.t.* Predestinate, appoint beforehand. **foreŏrdinā'tion** *n.*

for'epeak (fŏrp-) *n.* (naut.) Extreme end of hold of a ship in angle of bows.

fŏre-rĭb *n.* Cut of beef next to wing-rib.

forerŭ'n (fŏr-r-) *v.t.* (past t. *-răn*, past part. *-rŭn*). Be precursor of, foreshadow. **forerŭ'nner** (*or* fŏr'-) *n.*

for'esail (fŏrs-; *or* fŏr'sl) *n.* Principal sail on foremast; in square-rigged vessel, lowest square sail; in fore-and-aft rigged, triangular sail before mast.

foresee (fŏrsē') *v.t.* See or realize beforehand.

foreshădow (fŏrshă'dō) *v.t.* Prefigure, serve as type or presage of.

for'esheets (fŏrsh-) *n.pl.* (naut.) Inner part of bows of open boat, fitted with gratings on which bowman stands.

for'eshŏre (fŏrsh-) *n.* Part of

shore between high and low water marks, or between water and land cultivated or built on.

foreshȏr'ten (fȏrsh-) *v.t.* Show, portray, (object) with the apparent shortening due to visual perspective; (of visual perspective) cause (object) to appear shorter in directions not lying in plane perpendicular to line of sight.

foreshow (fȏrshō') *v.t.* Foretell; foreshadow, portend, prefigure.

foresight (fȏr'sīt) *n.* 1. Foreseeing, prevision; care for the future. 2. Front sight of firearm.

for'eskĭn (fȏrs-) *n.* Prepuce.

fŏ'rĕst *n.* Large tract covered with trees and undergrowth, sometimes intermingled with pasture; trees growing in it; in Gt Britain, district formerly forest, but now more or less under cultivation and often preserved for game; (law, hist.) woodland district, usu. belonging to king, set apart for hunting etc. and having special laws and officers of its own.

forestall (fȏrstaw'l) *v.t.* 1. (hist.) Buy up (goods) in order to profit by enhanced price; prevent sales at (fair, market) thus. 2. Anticipate in action; deal with before the regular time.

for'estay (fȏrs-) *n.* (naut.) Stay from fore mast-head to stem of ship; sail hoisted on this.

fŏ'rĕster *n.* 1. Officer in charge of forest, or of growing timber; *F*~, member of the Ancient Order of Foresters, a friendly society. 2. Dweller in forest; bird or beast of forest.

fŏ'rĕstrў̆ *n.* Wooded country, forests; science and art of managing forests.

for'etāste (fȏrt-) *n.* Partial enjoyment or suffering (*of*) in advance. **foretā'ste** *v.t.* Taste beforehand, anticipate enjoyment etc. of.

foretĕ'll (fȏrt-) *v.t.* (past t. & past part. *-told*). Predict, prophesy; presage, be precursor of.

forethought (fȏr'thawt) *n.* Previous contriving, deliberate intention; provident care.

foretō'ken (fȏrt-) *v.t.* Portend, point to. **for'etōken** *n.*

for'etŏp (fȏrt-; *or* -top) *n.* (naut.) Top of foremast; *foretop-gall'ant-mast*, mast above foretop-mast; *foretop'mast*, mast above foremast; *foretop'sail*, sail above foresail.

forewarn (fȏrwȏr'n) *v.t.* Warn beforehand.

foreword (fȏr'wẽrd) *n.* Preface; introduction.

for'eyȃrd (fȏry-) *n.* Lowest yard on foremast.

Fȏr'fȃr(shire). Former name of county of ANGUS.

fȏr'feit (-fĭt) *n.* Thing lost owing to crime or fault; penalty for breach of contract or neglect, fine; trivial fine for breach of rules in clubs etc. or in games; article surrendered by player in game of *forfeits* to be redeemed by performing ludicrous task; forfeiture. ~ *adj.* That has been lost or given up as penalty. ~ *v.t.* Lose right to, be deprived of, have to pay, as penalty of crime, neglect, etc., or as necessary consequence of something. **fȏr'feiture** *n.*

fȏrfĕ'nd *v.t.* (archaic) Avert, keep away, prevent.

fȏrgă'ther (-dh-) *v.i.* Assemble, meet together, associate.

fȏrge[1] *n.* Blacksmith's hearth or fireplace with bellows, smithy; furnace or hearth for melting or refining metal, workshop containing this. ~ *v.* 1. Shape by heating in forge and hammering. 2. Fabricate, invent (tale, lie); make in fraudulent imitation, esp. imitate (signature etc.) in writing in order to pass it off as genuine. **fȏr'ger** *n.*

fȏrge[2] *v.i.* Make way, advance, gradually or with difficulty; ~ *ahead*, take lead in race etc., get start; make good progress.

fȏr'gerў̆ *n.* Forging, counterfeiting, or falsifying, of document; spurious thing, esp. document or signature.

forgĕ't (-g-) *v.* (past t. *-got*, past part. *-gotten*). Lose remembrance of or *about*; neglect; inadvertently omit to bring, mention, attend to, etc.; put out of mind, cease to think of; disregard, overlook, slight; ~ *oneself*, neglect one's own interests; act unbecomingly, presumptuously, or unworthily; lose self-consciousness; *~-me-not*, plant of genus *Myosotis*, esp. *M. palustris*, with small yellow-eyed blue flowers. **forgĕ'tful** *adj.* **forgĕ'tfully̆** *adv.* **forgĕ'tfulnėss** *n.*

forg'ĭve (-g-) *v.t.* (past t. *-gave*, past part. *-given*). Remit, let off (debt etc.); give up resentment against, pardon (offender). **forgi'vable** *adj.* **forgĭ'venėss** *n.* **forgi'vĭng** *adj.* **forgi'vĭngly̆** *adv.* **forgi'vĭngnėss** *n.*

forgō' *v.t.* (past t. *-wĕnt*, past part. *-gŏne*). Abstain from, go without, let go, omit to take or use, relinquish.

forĭ'nt *n.* Principal monetary unit of Hungary, = 100 filler.

fôrk *n.* 1. Pronged agricultural instrument for digging, lifting, carrying, or throwing. 2. Two-, three-, or four-pronged instrument used to hold food while it is cut, convey it to mouth, etc., and in cooking. 3. Two-pronged steel instrument giving musical note when struck, tuning-fork.

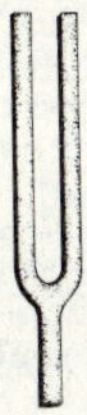

4. Stake with forked end; forking, bifurcation, e.g. that of human legs, of diverging roads, or of branches; forked part of bicycle frame in which wheel revolves. 5. *~-lift*, lifting device in which a fork is pushed under the load and withdrawn after lifting it into the desired position; *~ lunch(eon)*, *supper*, etc., meal served at buffet etc., with food suitable for eating with fork alone. *~ v.* Form fork; have or develop branches; lift, carry, dig, throw, with fork; *~ out*, (slang) hand over, pay. **fôrked** (-kt) *adj.* Having a fork or fork-like branches.

forlôr'n *adj.* Desperate, hopeless; abandoned, forsaken; (poet.) deprived *of*; in pitiful condition, of wretched appearance. **forlôr'nly̆** *adv.* **forlôr'nnėss** *n.*

forlôr'n hōpe. Desperate enterprise; vain hope. [Du. *verloren hoop* lost troop (*hoop* = heap)]

fôrm *n.* 1. Shape, arrangement of parts, visible aspect (esp. apart from colour); shape of body; body in respect of outward shape and appearance. 2. (philos). In scholastic philosophy, that which makes anything (*matter*) a determinate species or kind of being; in Kant etc., that factor of knowledge which gives reality and objectivity to the thing known. 3. Mode in which thing exists or manifests itself; species, kind, variety; (gram.) one of various modes of spelling, inflexion, etc., under which word may appear, external characteristics of words, as dist. from their meaning. 4. One of the numbered classes in schools (of which the sixth is in England usu. the highest) into which pupils are divided. 5. Arrangement and style in literary or musical composition; orderly arrangement of parts. 6. Set or customary method or procedure; set or fixed order of words etc.; formulary document with blanks to be filled up; (colloq.) criminal record. 7. Formality, mere piece of ceremony; behaviour according to rule or custom; *good*, *bad*, *~*, behaviour satisfying or offending current ideals. 8. Condition of health and training; good spirits. 9. Long seat without back, bench. 10. (print.) = FORME. 11. Lair or nest in which hare crouches. *~ v.* Fashion, mould; assume shape, become solid; mould by discipline, train, instruct; embody, organize, *into* company etc.; frame, make, produce; articulate (word); conceive (idea, judgement); develop (habit); contract (alliance); be material of, make up, make *one* or *part of*; (mil.) draw up in order, assume specified formation.

fôr'mal *adj.* 1. (metaphys.) Of the form or constitutive essence of a thing, essential; of the outward form, shape, appearance, or external qualities; (logic) concerned with the form, not the matter, of reasoning. 2. That is such in form; that is according to recognized forms, or the rules of art or law; valid in virtue of its form, explicit and definite, not merely tacit. 3. Ceremonial, required by convention; perfunctory, having the form without the spirit; observant of forms, precise; excessively regular or symmetrical, stiff, methodical. **fŏr'mallȳ** *adv.*

fŏrmă'ldėhȳde *n.* Colourless gas (CH_2O) with a characteristic pungent odour, used in aqueous solution as disinfectant etc.

fŏr'malĭn *n.* Aqueous solution containing 37% of formaldehyde.

fŏr'malism *n.* Strict observance of forms; excessive regularity or symmetry. **fŏr'malist** *n.* **fŏrmali'stic** *adj.*

fŏrmă'litȳ *n.* Conformity to rules, propriety; ceremony, elaborate procedure; formal or ceremonial act, requirement of etiquette or custom; being formal, precision of manners, stiffness of design.

fŏr'malīze *v.t.* Give definite shape or legal formality to; make ceremonious, precise, or rigid; imbue with formalism.

fŏr'măt *n.* Shape and size (of book etc.); style of arrangement etc.

fŏrmā'tion *n.* Forming, being formed; thing formed; arrangement of parts, structure; (mil.) disposition of troops, formal stationing or arrangement of number of ships, aircraft, etc.; (geol.) assemblage of rocks or series of strata having some common characteristic.

fŏr'mative *adj.* Serving to form, of formation; (gram., of suffixes etc.) used in forming words. ~ *n.* Formative element.

fŏrme *n.* (print.) Body of type secured in chase for printing at one impression or film material arranged for plate- or cylinder-making.

fŏr'mer *adj.* Of the past or an earlier period; *the* ~, the first or first mentioned of two (freq. with ellipsis of *n.*; opp. LATTER). **fŏr'merlȳ** *adv.*

fŏr'mĭc *adj.* ~ *acid*, colourless irritant volatile acid (HCOOH) present in a fluid emitted by ants, used in tanning and electroplating and as reducing agent in dyeing.

fŏrmī'ca *n.* Hard durable plastic laminate used esp. as decorative surfacing material. [tradename]

fŏr'midable *adj.* To be dreaded; likely to be hard to overcome, resist, or deal with. **fŏr'mĭdableness** *n.*, **fŏr'mĭdablȳ** *adv.*

fŏr'mlėss *adj.* Shapeless, without determinate or regular form. **fŏr'mlėsslȳ** *adv.* **fŏr'mlėssnėss** *n.*

Fŏrmō'sa. = TAIWAN. **Fŏrmō'san** *adj.* [Port. name, f. L *formosus* beautiful]

fŏr'mūla *n.* (pl. *-ae, -as*). 1. Set form of words in which something is defined, stated, etc., or which is prescribed for use on ceremonial occasion etc.; conventional usage or belief. 2. Recipe; (math.) rule or principle expressed in algebraic symbols; (chem.) expression of constituents of compound in symbols and figures; tabulation of facts etc. in symbols and figures. 3. Class or specification of a racing car. **fŏr'mūlarīze** *v.t.* **fŏrmūlarīzā'tion** *n.*

fŏr'mūlarȳ *n.* Collection of formulas; document or book of set forms esp. for belief or ritual; ~ *adj.* In or of formulas.

fŏr'mulāte *v.t.* Reduce to, express in, a formula; set forth systematically. **fŏrmūlā'tion** *n.*

fŏr'mūlism *n.* Unintelligent following of rule or conventional usage or belief. **fŏr'mūlist** *n.* **fŏrmūli'stic** *adj.*

fŏr'nicāte *v.i.* Commit fornication. **fŏrnicā'tion** *n.* Voluntary sexual intercourse between a man (occas. restricted to unmarried man) and an unmarried woman. **fŏr'nicātor** *n.*

fŏr'nix *n.* 1. (anat.) Arched formation of the brain. 2. (bot.) Small elongation ot the corolla. 3. (conch.) Excavated part of a shell, situated under the umbo.

forrel: see FOREL.

forsā'ke *v.t.* (past *t. -sŏŏk*, past part. *-saken*). Give up, break off from, renounce; withdraw one's help etc. from; desert, abandon.

forsōō'th *adv.* (archaic) Truly, in truth, no doubt (chiefly iron., in parenthesis).

forswear' (-wār) *v.t.* (past t. *-swōre*, past part. *-swōrn*). Abjure, renounce on oath; ~ *oneself*, swear falsely, perjure oneself; *forsworn*, perjured.

forsȳ'thia *n.* Ornamental spring-flowering shrub of genus *F*~ with bright-yellow bell-shaped flowers. [f. W. *Forsyth* (1737–1804), English botanist]

fort *n.* Fortified place, usu. single building or set of connected military buildings; trading-station, orig. fortified, in N. America.

for'talice *n.* Fortress (archaic & poet.); small outwork of fortification, small fort.

forte[1] *n.* Person's strong point; (fencing) sword-blade from hilt to middle.

for'tė[2] *adv.* (mus.) Loudly; *double* ~, *very loudly*; ~ *piano*, loudly then immediately softly. ~ *adj.* & *n.* Loud (passage). [It.]

forth[1] *adv.* Forwards (now only in *back and* ~, to and fro); onwards in time (now only in *from this time* ~ etc.); forward, into view; out, away, from home, etc.; *and so* ~, and so on, and the like.

Forth[2]. River of E. Scotland, flowing into the North Sea near Edinburgh.

forthco'ming (-kŭ-) *adj.* About or likely to come forth; approaching; ready to be produced when wanted; informative, responsive.

for'thright (-rīt) *adj.* Going straight, outspoken, unswerving; decisive. **forthri'ght** *adv.* (archaic) Straight forward; straightway.

forthwi'th (*or* -dh) *adv.* Immediately, without delay.

fortificā'tion *n.* 1. Fortifying. 2. Defensive work, wall, earthwork, tower, etc.

for'tifȳ *v.* Strengthen structure of; impart vigour or strength or endurance to, encourage; corroborate (statement); provide with defensive works; erect fortifications; strengthen (liquors) with alcohol; add nutrients to (food).

For'tin barŏ'mėter. Type of mercury barometer. [N. *Fortin* (1750–1831), Fr. maker]

forti'ssimō *adv.*, *n.* (pl. *-os*), & *adj.* (mus.) (Passage performed) very loud(ly).

for'titude *n.* Courage in pain or adversity.

for'tnight (-īt) *n.* Period of two weeks; two weeks before or (esp.) after a specified day, as *Tuesday* ~.
for'tnightlȳ *adj.* & *adv.* (Happening, appearing) once every fortnight.

for'tran, FORTRAN *n.* Computer programming language used chiefly for scientific and mathematical calculations. [*for*mula *tran*slation]

for'trėss *n.* Military stronghold, esp. strongly fortified town fit for large garrison.

fortū'itous *adj.* Due to or characterized by chance, accidental, casual. **fortū'itouslȳ** *adv.* **fortū'itousnėss** *n.* **fortū'itȳ** *n.* Fortuitousness; a chance occurrence; accident; unstudied or unintended character.

for'tūnate (*or* -chōō-) *adj.* Favoured by fortune, lucky, prosperous; auspicious, favourable. **for'tūnatelȳ** *adv.* Luckily, successfully, (now freq. qualifying whole sentence = it is fortunate that).

for'tūne (*or* -chōōn) *n.* 1. Chance as a power in men's affairs; freq. personified as goddess with wheel, betokening vicissitude, as emblem; *soldier of* ~: see SOLDIER. 2. Luck, good or bad, falling to anyone in life or particular affair; what is to befall in future (chiefly in *tell* ~*s*, *tell person his* ~); ~*-teller*, one who professes to foretell the future. 3. Good luck; prosperity, prosperous condition, wealth; large sum of money; *make* (*one's*) ~, become rich, prosper; ~*-hunter*, man seeking rich wife. ~ *v.i.* (archaic) Chance, occur; come by chance *upon*.

for'tȳ *adj.* Amounting to forty; ~*-five* (*n.*) revolver of 0·45 calibre; *the F*~*-five*, the Jacobite rebellion of 1745; ~-*niner*, one who went to California in the gold rush of 1849; ~ *winks*, nap. ~ *n.* Cardinal number, four times ten (40, xl, or XL); set of 40 things or persons; *forties*, numbers etc. from 40 to 49; these years of century or life; (in British weather forecasts) sea-area between SW. coast of Norway and NE. coast of Scotland, so called from the 40-fathom line in the N. Sea; *roaring forties*, latitudes between 40° and 50°, esp. in S. hemisphere, which are characterized by exceptionally strong W. and NW. winds. **fôr'tĭeth** *adj.* & *n.*

fôr'um *n.* (Rom. antiq.) Public place or market-place of city; in ancient Rome, place of assembly for judicial and other public business; place of public discussion; court, tribunal (freq. fig.).

fôr'ward *adj.* 1. (naut.) Belonging to fore part of ship. 2. Lying in front, or in direction of movement; onward or towards the front; (commerc.) prospective, relating to future produce; ~ *play*, (cricket) playing forward. 3. Advanced, progressing to maturity or completion; (of plant, crop, season, etc.) well advanced, early. 4. Ready, prompt, eager; precocious, presumptuous, pert. **fôr'wardlȳ** *adv.* **fôr'wardnėss** *n.* **fôr'ward** *adv.* 1. Towards the future, continuously onwards; towards the front, in the direction one is facing; with continuous forward motion; in advance, ahead; to the front, into prominence; onward so as to make progress; *bring* ~, draw attention to; *bring, carry* ~, (book-keeping) transfer entry to next page or column; *come* ~, offer oneself for task, post, etc.; *play* ~, (cricket) reach forward to play short-pitched ball; *put, set,* ~, allege; *put oneself* ~, make oneself too conspicuous. 2. (naut.) To, at, in, fore part of ship. ~ *n.* (footb. etc.) One of the players positioned in front of others in a team. ~ *v.t.* Help forward, promote; accelerate growth of; send (letter etc.) on to farther destination; (loosely) dispatch (goods etc.) **fôr'warder** *adj.* & *adv.* Further forward (freq. in joc. or vulg. form **fŏ'rrarder**, in phr. *get no* ~ etc.). **fôr'wards** (-z) *adv.* Forward.

forwear'ied (-ĭd), **forwôr'n** *adjs.* (archaic) Tired out.

fŏsse *n.* Long narrow excavation, canal, ditch, trench, esp. in fortification; (anat.) groove, depression; *F~ Way*, Axminster–Lincoln Roman road, so called from the ditch or fosse on each side.

fŏ'ssĭck *v.i.* (slang, Austral.) Rummage, search.

fŏ'ssĭl *adj.* Of the nature of a fossil. ~ *n.* Thing found in strata of earth recognizable as remains

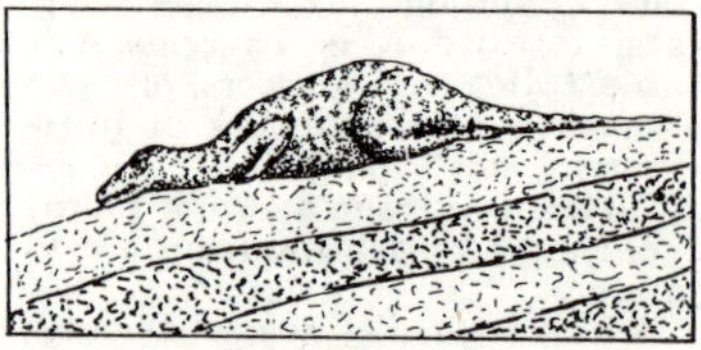

Death of animal

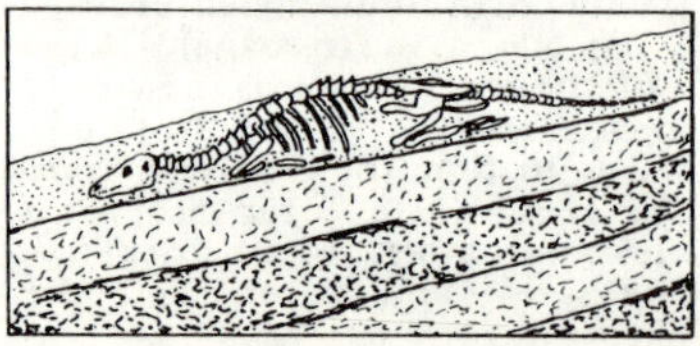

Sedimentation

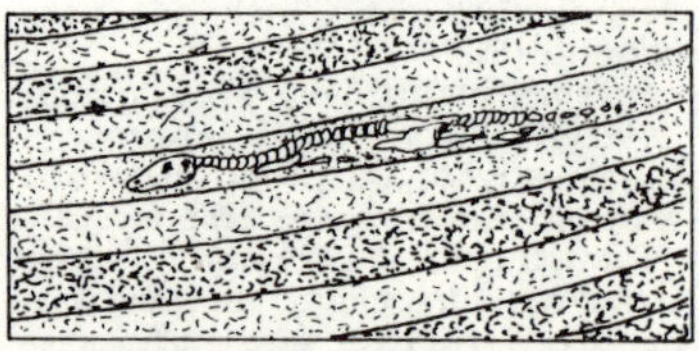

Rock formation and fossilization

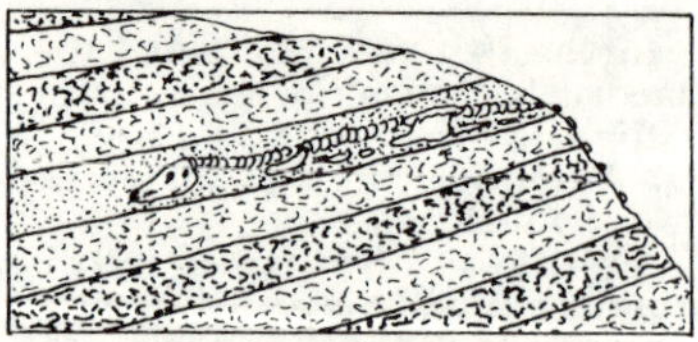

Erosion and exposure

FOSSILIZATION

of plant or animal of former geological period or as showing vestiges of animal or vegetable life of such period; (person or thing) belonging to the past, antiquated, incapable of further growth or progress. **fŏ'ssilīze** *v.* **fŏssilīzā'tion** *n.*

fŏssōr'ial *adj.* (zool.) Burrowing; used in burrowing.

fŏ'ster *v.t.* Tend with affectionate care; encourage or harbour (feeling); (of circumstances) be favourable to; *~-child*, child as related to parents who have reared it as their own, or to its wet-nurse and her husband; *~-mother*, woman who brings up another's child (so *~-father*, *-brother*, *-daughter*, *-sister*, *-son*); (also) apparatus for rearing chickens hatched in an incubator. **fŏ'sterage** *n.* Fostering; custom of employing foster-mothers. **fŏ'sterling** *n.* Foster-child.

Foucault (fōōkō), Jean Bernard Léon (1819–68). French physicist; *~'s pendulum*, pendulum designed to demonstrate the rotation of the earth by the rotation of its plane of oscillation.

fouetté (fōōĕtā) *n.* (ballet) Form of pirouette in which movement of the free leg gives momentum for the turn. [Fr.]

fought: see FIGHT.

foul *adj.* 1. Offensive to the senses, loathsome, stinking; dirty, soiled; charged with noxious matter. 2. Clogged, choked; (of ship's bottom etc.) overgrown with weed, barnacles, etc. 3. Morally polluted, obscene, disgustingly abusive; unfair, against rules of game etc.; (of weather) wet, rough, stormy; (of wind) contrary; (naut.) embarrassed, entangled, in collision, etc. 4. *~ brood*, disease of larval bees caused by bacillus and characterized by sickly unpleasant smell of hive; *the ~ fiend*, the Devil; *~ play*, unfair play in games; (fig.) unfair or treacherous dealing (freq. with additional notion of violence). **fou'lly** (-l-lĭ) *adv.* **fou'lnėss** *n.* **foul** *n.* Something foul; collision, entanglement, esp. in riding, rowing, or running; foul stroke or piece of play. *~ adv.* In irregular way, not in accordance with rules. *~ v.* Make or become foul; entangle, become entangled; collide with; block.

foulâr'd (fōō-) *n.* Thin soft smooth material, usu. twill-woven, of silk or silk and cotton.

fou'mârt (fōō-) *n.* Polecat. [= foul marten]

found[1] *v.* Lay base of (building etc.); be original builder, begin building, of (town, edifice); set up, establish (esp. with endowment), originate, initiate, (institution); construct, base (tale, one's fortunes, rule, etc.) *on* some ground, support, principle, etc.; rely, base oneself, (of argument etc.) be based, *on*.

found[2] *v.t.* Melt and mould (metal), fuse (materials and glass); make (thing of molten metal, glass) by melting.

found[3]: see FIND.

foundā'tion *n.* 1. Establishing, constituting on permanent basis, esp. of endowed institution; such institution, e.g. monastery, college, hospital, or its revenues; *on the ~*, entitled to benefit by funds of such institution. 2. Solid ground or base, natural or artificial, on which building rests; lowest part of building, usu. below ground-level; basis, groundwork, underlying principle; body or ground on which other parts are overlaid. 3. (cosmetics) Base. 4. *~ garment*, woman's supporting undergarment, e.g. corset; *~ stone*, (esp.) stone laid with ceremony (and freq. inscribed) to celebrate founding of edifice. **foundā'tioner** *n.* One on the foundation of endowed school or college.

fou'nder[1] *n.* (fem. *fou'ndrėss*; esp.) One who founds institution(s); *~'s kin*, relatives of founder entitled to election or preference; *~'s shares*, shares issued to founder(s) of public company as part-consideration for business taken over, and separate from ordinary capital. **fou'ndership** *n.*

fou'nder[2] *n.* One who founds metal, glass, etc.

fou'nder[3] *v.* 1. (of earth,

building, etc.) Fall down or in, give way; (of horse) collapse, fall lame, stumble etc.; (of ship) fill with water and sink. 2. Cause (horse, ship) to founder. ~ *n.* Inflammation of horse's foot from overwork; rheumatism of chest-muscles in horse.

fou′ndlĭng *n.* Deserted infant of unknown parents; *F~ Hospital*, orphanage for foundlings opened 1741 at Hatton Garden, London, by Capt. Thomas Coram, transferred to Bloomsbury 1745 and to Berkhamstead 1935.

fou′ndrў *n.* Factory where metal, glass, etc., is founded.

fount[1] *n.* (poet. or rhet.) Spring, source, fountain.

fount[2] *n.* Set of type of same face and size.

fou′ntain *n.* Water-spring; source *of* river etc.; jet of water made to spout, structure provided for it; structure for constant supply of drinking-water; soda-fountain; *~-head*, original source;

FOUNTAIN OF NEPTUNE, Bologna

~-pen, pen containing reservoir of ink.

four (fôr) *adj.* Amounting to four; *~-ball*, (golf) game in which four balls, one for each player, are used, the best ball on each side counting at each hole; *~-centred*, (of arch) described from four centres; ~ *figures*, one thousand (pounds etc.) or over; *~-flush*, (poker) flush containing only four (instead of five) cards; *~-flusher*, (U.S.) pretender, humbug; *~-handed*, (of card-games) played by four persons; ~ *hundred*, (chiefly U.S.) most exclusive social set, orig. that of New York (which *c* 1890 was supposed to consist of about this number of people); *~-in-hand*, vehicle with four horses driven by one person; (U.S.) kind of necktie tied in loose knot with long ends hanging straight down; ~ *last things*, death, judgement, heaven, and hell; *~-letter word*, monosyllabic English word referring to sexual or excrementary functions or organs, conventionally excluded from polite use; ~ *o'clock*, plant Marvel of Peru, *Mirabilis jalapa*, with flowers opening about 4 p.m.; *four′penny one*, (slang) hit or blow; *~-post*, (of bed) having four posts (to support canopy and curtains); *~-poster*,

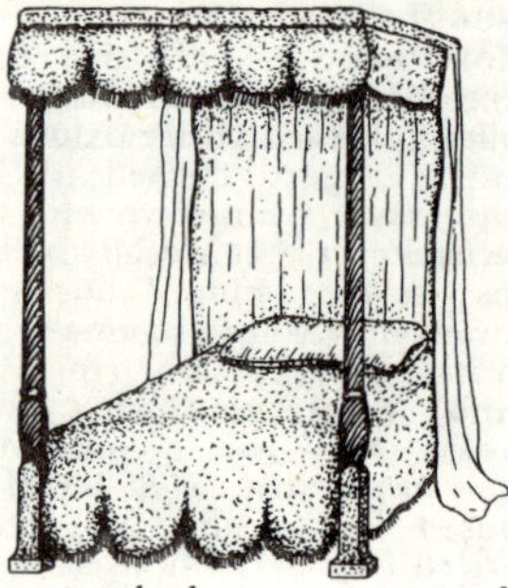

four-post bed; ~ *-pounder*, gun throwing 4-lb. shot; *four′-score*, eighty; *~-square*, square-shaped; solidly based, steady; *F~ Square Gospel*, sect founded 1915 at Belfast by George Jeffreys; *~-stroke*, (of cycle of operations in internal combustion engine) consisting of four strokes, intake, compression, combustion, and exhaust; ~-*wheeler*, four-wheeled cab. ~ *n.* One more than three; symbol for this (4, iv, or IV); card, die-face, or domino with 4 pips; 4 o'clock; size etc. indicated by 4; set of 4 things or persons; four-oared boat and crew; hit etc. at cricket for four runs; *fours*, military formation 4 deep usually facing towards flank for marching; races for four-oared boats; *on all fours*, crawling on hands and knees; (fig.) completely analogous or corresponding. **four'fōld** *adj.* & *adv.*

Fourier (fo͝oryā), Charles (1772–1837). French socialist writer. **Four'ierism** *n.* Communistic system for the reorganization of society devised by Fourier under which the population was to be grouped in ***phalansteries***, socialistic groups of about 1,800 persons holding property in common.

four'some (fôr-) *adj.* (of Scotch reel etc.) Performed by four persons together. ~ *n.* Golf match between two pairs of players, each pair sharing a ball; (colloq.) company or party of four persons.

four'tee'n (fôr-) *adj.* & *n.* One more than thirteen (14, xiv, or XIV). **four'tee'nth** *adj.* & *n.* ~ *of July*, French annual holiday in celebration of fall of Bastille, 1789.

fourth (fôr-) *adj.* Next after third. ~ *n.* 1. Fourth part (see PART[1], 1), quarter. 2. (mus.) Interval of which the span involves four alphabetical names of notes; harmonic combination of two notes thus separated. 3. Fourth thing etc.; *the F~*, (*a*) the fourth of July, anniversary of Declaration of Independence (1776), kept as holiday in U.S.A.; (*b*) the fourth of June, annual commemoration of George III's birthday at Eton College, with 'speeches' (i.e. recitations) and procession of boats on river. 4. Fourth form in school. 5. (in motor vehicle) Fourth gear. 6. (Holder of) place in fourth class in examination etc. **four'thlў** *adv.* In the fourth place.

fō'vėa *n.* (anat.) Small pit; (also ~ *centralis*), small depression in macula lutea of retina, spot where vision is most acute.

fowl *n.* 1. Bird (rare); birds (rare exc. in *wildfowl*); flesh of birds as food (only in *fish, flesh, and* ~). 2. (also *domestic* ~) Domestic bird of genus *Gallus*; its flesh as food; ~-*pest*, acute infectious disease of fowls, caused by a virus. ~ *v.i.* Catch, hunt, shoot, or snare, wild-fowl; *fowling-piece*, light gun used in fowling. **fow'ler** *n.*

fŏx[1] *n.* Flesh-eating quadruped of the dog family, esp. *Vulpes vul-*

FOXES

pes, with elongated pointed muzzle, long bushy tail, and red fur, preserved in England and elsewhere as beast of chase, and proverbial for cunning; crafty person; ~-*and-geese*, game played on board by two players, one with sixteen pegs, called geese, the other with one, called the fox; *fo'xglove*, tall handsome plant, *Digitalis purpurea*, the leaves of which yield digitalis, with purple or white flowers shaped like finger-stall; ~ *hole*, hole in the ground used by soldier for protection against missiles or as firing station; *fo'xhound*, kind of hound bred and trained to hunt foxes; ~-*hunt*, chase, chasing of fox with hounds; *fo'x tail*, species of grass with soft brush-like spikes of flowers, esp. *Alopecurus pratensis*; ~*-terrier*, small terrier with smooth or rough (wire-haired) short hair, usu. white with black markings, of a kind bred for unearthing foxes, but kept chiefly as pets; *fo'xtrot*, ballroom dance in 4/4 time based on slow or quick walking-steps. ~ *v*. 1. Act craftily, dissemble; (colloq.) deceive, (loosely) impede, ruin plans of, etc. 2. Discolour (leaves of book, engraving, etc.) with brownish spots (esp. in past part.).

Fŏx[2], Charles James (1749–1806). English statesman; opposed the policy of PITT; denounced the slave trade; advocated parliamentary reform.

Fŏxe, John (1516–87). English martyrologist, author of 'Actes and Monuments', pop. known as the 'Book of Martyrs'.

fŏ'xȳ *adj*. 1. Fox-like; crafty, cunning. 2. Fox-coloured, reddish brown or yellow; (of painting) having too many reddish tints, over-hot in colouring; spotted, stained, with mildew etc.

foyer (fwah'yā) *n*. Large room in theatre etc. for use of audience esp. during intervals; entrance hall of hotel etc.

fp. *abbrev*. *Forte-piano*.

F.P. *abbrev*. Field punishment; fire plug.

fr. *abbrev*. Franc(s).

Fr *abbrev*. Father.

Fr. *abbrev*. French.

Fra Angelico: see ANGELICO.

fră'cas (-ah) *n*. (pl. same). Noisy quarrel, row.

fră'ction *n*. 1. Breaking or dividing of bread in Eucharist. 2. Numerical quantity that is not an integer, one or more aliquot parts of unit or whole number; small piece or amount, scrap; *proper* (*improper*) ~, fraction in which numerator is less (greater) than denominator; *vulgar* ~, one in which numerator and denominator are represented by numbers placed above and below horizontal line. 3. Portion separable by fractionation. **fră'ctional** *adj*. **fră'ctionallȳ** *adv*.

fră'ctionāte *v.t.* Separate (mixture) by distillation or otherwise into portions of differing properties. **frăctionā'tion** *n*.

fră'ctionīze *v.t.* Break up into fractions.

fră'ctious (-sh*u*s) *adj*. Unruly, cross, peevish. **fră'ctiouslȳ** *adv*. **fră'ctiousnėss** *n*.

fră'cture *n*. 1. Breaking, breakage, esp. of bone or cartilage. 2. Characteristic appearance of fresh surface of mineral broken with hammer. 3. (phonology) Diphthongization of single vowel, owing to influence of following consonant; diphthong so formed. ~ *v*. Cause fracture in, be fractured; break continuity of.

frae'num, frē- *n*. (pl. *-na*). (anat.) Small ligament or membranous fold restraining motion of organ to which it is attached. [L, = 'bridle']

fră'gīle (U.S. -ĭl) *adj*. Easily snapped or shattered; weak, perishable; of delicate frame or constitution. **fragĭ'lĭtȳ** *n*.

fră'gment *n*. Part broken off, detached piece; isolated or incomplete part, remainder of lost or destroyed whole; esp. extant remains or unfinished portion of writing or work of art. **fră'gmentarȳ** *adj*. **frăgmentā'tion** *n*. Separation into fragments; ~ *bomb*, one designed to disintegrate into small fragments on explosion.

frā'grant *adj*. Sweet-smelling. **frā'grance** *n*. Quality of being fragrant; perfume.

frail[1] *n*. Rush basket for packing figs, raisins, etc.; quantity of raisins contained in a frail.

frail[2] *adj*. Fragile; morally weak, unable to resist temptation; (euphem., of women) unchaste. **frai'ltȳ** *n*. Liability to err or yield to temptation; fault, weakness, foible.

fraise[1] (-z) *n*. (mil.) Palisade, horizontal or down-sloping, round an earthwork near the berm.

fraise[2] (-z) *n*. Tool for enlarging circular hole in stone, or for cutting teeth in watch-wheel.

F.R.A.M. *abbrev*. Fellow of the Royal Academy of Music.

frămboe'sĭa (-bēz-) *n.* (path.) YAWS.

frāme *n.* 1. Construction, constitution, build; established order, plan, system. 2. Temporary state (*of* mind). 3. Framed work or structure; human or animal body; skeleton of building; underlying support or essential substructure of anything. 4. Case or border enclosing picture, pane of glass, etc. 5. (gardening) Glazed structure protecting plants from cold. 6. Rigid part of bicycle; skeleton of motor vehicle etc. supporting machinery and body (in aircraft). 7. Structure placed in hive for bees to make honey in. 8. Each separate picture on cinematograph film. 9. Single complete picture transmitted in series of lines by television. 10. (pool, snooker) Triangular form in which balls are set up; the balls as set up; round of play required to pocket them all; similarly in skittles and tenpins. 11. *~-house*, house of wooden framework or skeleton covered with boards etc.; *~ of reference*, characteristic of perception whereby objects are correctly localized in space; standard governing perceptual or logical evaluation; *~-saw*, thin saw stretched in frame to give it rigidity; *~-up*, (slang, orig. U.S.) conspiracy, trumped-up case or charge; *fra'mework*, frame, substructure, upon or into which anything may be put. ~ *v.* 1. Shape, direct, dispose, to a purpose; adapt, fit, *to*, or *into*; give promise of becoming skilful etc. 2. Construct by combination of parts or adaptation to design; contrive, devise, invent, compose, express; articulate (words); conceive, imagine. 3. Set in frame; serve as frame for. 4. (slang, orig. U.S.) Concoct false charge or accusation against, make victim of frame-up.

frănc *n.* Principal monetary unit of France, Belgium, Switzerland, and certain other countries; in Morocco, = $\frac{1}{100}$ of a dirham; (hist.) any of various gold and silver coins. [Fr., perh. f. *Francorum Rex* king of the Franks, legend on earliest coin so called]

France[1] (-ah-). Republic of W. Europe; the monarchical system of government was overthrown during the French Revolution (1789–93) and the First Republic lasted until Napoleon founded the First Empire in 1804; the monarchy was restored in 1814 and lasted until 1848 when the Second Republic was formed, which became the Second Empire under Napoleon III in 1852; Napoleon was deposed in 1870 and the Third Republic established; this lasted until the occupation of France by the Germans (1940); after the liberation of France (1945) the republic was restored and the Constitution of the Fourth Republic was in force from 1945 until Oct. 1958, when a new constitution established the Fifth Republic; capital, Paris.

France[2] (-ahṅs), Anatole. Pseudonym of Jacques Anatole Thibault (1844–1924), French satirical writer.

fră'nchīse (-z) *n.* 1. (chiefly hist.) Legal immunity or exemption from some burden or jurisdiction; privilege or exceptional right, granted to person, corporation, etc.; right to market company's goods or services in particular area. 2. Full membership of corporation or State, citizenship. 3. Right of voting at public elections, esp. for member of legislative body; principle of qualification for this. ~ *v.t.* Give franchise to.

Fra'ncĭs I (-ah-) (1494–1547). (Fr. *François*) King of France from 1515 to his death; was involved in many wars against the Emperor Charles V and taken prisoner by him at the battle of Pavia.

Fra'ncĭs of Assisi (-ah-, *a*sē'zĭ), St. Giovanni Francesco Bernardone (1181?–1226), Italian friar; founded *c* 1209 an order of friars whose rules require chastity, poverty, and obedience, and lay special stress on preaching and ministration to the sick. **Franci'scan** *adj.* & *n.* (Member)

FRANCIS I

of the order founded by St. Francis (also called *Minorites*, *Grey Friars*).

fră'ncĭum *n.* (chem.) Radioactive metallic element of short life, the heaviest member of the alkali metal series; symbol Fr, at. no. 87, principal isotope at. wt 223. [f. *France*, because its existence was first reported by a Frenchwoman, Mlle M. Perey]

Franck (-ahṅk), César Auguste (1822–90). French composer, born in Belgium.

Fră'ncō, Generalissimo. Francisco Franco Bahamonde (1892–1975), Spanish political leader; from 1939 Leader (Caudillo) of the Empire and Chief of the State; head of the Falangist party.

Frănco- *prefix*. French and —, as ~-*German*.

fră'ncolĭn *n.* Bird of genus *Francolinus* found in Persia and N. India, also called 'black partridge'.

Fră'ncophīle, -phĭl, Fră'ncophōbe *ns.* One who loves, hates, the French.

fră'ngipāne, -păni (-j-) *n.* 1. Kind of pastry made with almonds, sugar, and cream. 2. Perfume made from flowers of red jasmine or imitation of this. 3. Red jasmine tree, *Plumeria rubra*. [family name *Frangipani*]

frănk[1] *adj.* Ingenu̇ous, open, candid, outspo̊ken; undisguised, avowed. **fră'nklȳ** *adv.* **fră'nkness** *n.* [med. L *francus* free, f. *Francus* Frank]

frănk[2] *v.t.* Superscribe (letter etc.) with signature to ensure its being carried without charge, send free of charge (hist.); mark with *franking machine*, an officially authorized machine, first introduced in 1922, for stamping letters etc. and simultaneously recording the cost of postage incurred, this being periodically checked and collected by the Post Office. ~ *n.* (hist.) Franking signature, franked cover.

Frănk[3] *n.* 1. One of the Germanic nation or coalition of nations that conquered Gaul in 6th c. 2. (in Levant) Person of western nationality. **Fră'nkish** *adj.*

Fră'nkenstein (-īn). Hero of the romance 'Frankenstein' (1818), by Mary Wollstonecraft Shelley, a student who constructs a human monster and endows it with life; hence, ~*'s monster*, thing that becomes formidable to its creator or destroys him.

Fră'nkfurt. City in W. Germany on the river Main; ~ ***black***, pigment made by charring vine-twigs, lees of wine, etc., used in engraving.

fră'nkfurter, -forter *n.* Highly seasoned smoked beef and pork sausage, orig. made at Frankfurt.

fră'nkincĕnse *n.* Aromatic gum resin obtained from trees, chiefly E African, of genus *Boswellia* and burnt as incense.

fră'nklĭn[1] *n.* (hist.) Landowner of free but not noble birth in 14th–15th centuries.

Fră'nklĭn[2], Benjamin (1706–90). Amer. publicist, popular scientist, and political emissary to Europe; one of the signatories to the peace between the U.S. and Gt Britain after the Amer. War of Independence; inventor of the lightning conductor.

Fră'nklĭn[3], Sir John (1786–1847). Arctic explorer; lost his life in an attempt to discover the North-west Passage; author of two 'Narratives' of voyages to the Polar Sea.

fră'nk-plĕdge *n.* (hist.) System in Anglo-Saxon law by which every member of a group of ten men (a *tithing*) was responsible for the actions of every other; *view of* ~, court held periodically to ascertain which tithing (or later, which hundred or manor) a man belonged to.

fră'ntĭc *adj.* Wildly excited, beside oneself with rage, pain, grief, etc.; showing frenzy, uncontrolled. **fră'nticallў** *adv.*

frăp *v.t.* (naut.) Bind tightly.

frappé (-ăpā) *n.* Iced drink, soft water-ice served in glass, etc. [Fr.]

F.R.A.S. *abbrev.* Fellow of the Royal Asiatic Society, Astronomical Society.

frăss *n.* Excrement of larvae; refuse left behind by boring insects.

frăt *n.* (slang, orig. U.S.) Fraternity, fraternization. **fră'tting** *n.* Fraternizing.

frā'ter *n.* (hist.) Refectory of monastery.

fratẽr'nal *adj.* (As) of brothers, brotherly; ~ *order*, (U.S.) friendly society, brotherhood; ~ *twins*, twins not necessarily of same sex and freq. bearing merely fraternal resemblance, resulting from fertilization of two ova, not one (opp. IDENTICAL).

fratẽr'nitў *n.* 1. Being fraternal, brotherliness; brotherhood. 2. Body or order of men organized for religious or devout purposes; body of men associated by some tie or common interest, or of same class, occupation, etc.; (U.S.) literary or social association of students of college or university.

fră'ternīze *v.i.* Associate (*with*, together, etc.), make friends, behave as intimates; cultivate friendly relations *with* (troops or inhabitants of enemy country). **frăternīzā'tion** *n.*

fră'trĭcīde *n.* Killing of one's brother or sister; one who commits fratricide. **fră'trĭcīdal** *adj.*

Frau (-ow) *n.* (pl. *Frauen*). Title (corresp. to *Mrs*) of German married woman.

fraud *n.* 1. Deceitfulness (rare). 2. Criminal deception, using of false representations to obtain unjust advantage or injure another; dishonest trick or stratagem; dishonest contrivance or person; impostor, humbug; *pious* ~, deception for what is considered a good object, esp. advancement of religion.

frau'dūlent *adj.* Guilty of, of the nature of, characterized or effected by, fraud. **frau'dūlence** *n.* **frau'dūlentlў** *adv.*

fraught (-awt) *adj.* Stored, equipped, *with* (poet.); ~ *with*, (fig.) involving, attended with, threatening (danger, woe, etc.); full of (meaning etc.).

Fräulein (froi'līn) *n.* Title of (corresp. to *Miss*) or form of address to German unmarried woman; *f*~, German governess in England.

Frau'nhōfer (frow-), Joseph von (1787–1826). Bavarian optician; ~ *lines*, dark lines in spectra of sun and other stars.

fray[1] *n.* Noisy quarrel, brawl; fight, conflict.

fray[2] *v.* 1. (of deer) Rub velvet off new horns. 2. Wear through by rubbing; ravel *out* edge or end of; become ragged at edge (also fig.).

Frā'zer, Sir James George (1854–1941). Scottish anthropologist.

fră'zzle *n.* (chiefly U.S.) Worn or exhausted state.

F.R.C.M., F.R.C.O., *abbrevs.* Fellow of the Royal College of Music, of Organists.

F.R.C.P.(E.), F.R.C.S.(E.), *abbrevs.* Fellow of the Royal College of Physicians (of Edinburgh), of Surgeons (of Edinburgh).

freak *n.* 1. Caprice, vagary; capriciousness. 2. Product of sportive fancy; eccentric person; (also ~ *of nature*) monstrosity, abnormally developed individual; esp. living curiosity exhibited in show. **frea'kĭsh** *adj.* **frea'kĭshlў** *adv.* **frea'kĭshnėss** *n.*

freaked (-kt) *adj.* Oddly flecked or streaked.

frĕ'ckle *n.* Spotted pigmentation of skin, produced esp. by ultraviolet light, and probably serving as a protection to the tissues; (pl.) number of such spots on various parts of the body, caused by exposure to sun. ~ *v.* Spot, be spotted, with freckles.

Frĕ'derick[1]. (Ger. *Friedrich*) Name of three Holy Roman Emperors; *Frederick I* (1121–90), 'Barbarossa' (= 'Redbeard'); emperor 1155–90; tried unsuccessfully to establish the Hohenstaufen overlordship over Italy; was drowned during the Third Crusade, but legend says that he still sleeps in a cavern in the Kyffhäuser mountains, until the need of his country shall summon him forth; *Frederick II* (1194–1250), emperor 1220–50; *Frederick III* (1415–93), emperor 1440–93.

Frĕ'derick[2]. (Ger. *Friedrich*) Name of three kings of Prussia: *Frederick I* (1657–1713), reigned 1701–13; *Frederick II* (1712–86), 'the Great'; engaged in wars against Austria and France and by his military talent raised Prussia to the rank of a powerful State; *Frederick III* (1831–88), German emperor 1888.

free *adj.* 1. Not in bondage to another, having personal rights and social and political liberty; (of State, its citizens, etc.) subject neither to foreign dominion nor to despotic government, having national and civil liberty. 2. At liberty, not in custody or confinement; without ties, obligations, or constraint upon one's action; released or exempt from work or duty; not constrained or timid; not fettered in judgement; (of literary composition etc.) not observing strict laws of form; (of translation, copy, etc.) not adhering strictly to original. 3. Allowable or allowed (*to* do); open (*for* all), open to all competitors; unobstructed; clear *of*, *from*; not fixed or fastened; not in contact; (chem.) uncombined; (of power etc.) available for 'work'. 4. Spontaneous, gratuitous, willing; lavish, frank, unreserved; forward, familiar. 5. Released or exempt *from*; possessed of certain exclusive rights or privileges; freehold; admitted to privileges *of*, invested with rights or immunities *of* (city, chartered company, etc.); allowed use or enjoyment *of* (place etc.); not subject to tax, toll, duty, trade-restrictions, fees, etc.; provided without payment. 6. ~-*and-easy*, unconstrained, unaffected, unconventional; ~ *association*, undirected mental activity like that of reverie or dreams; this as a method of psychoanalysis; *free'board*, part of ship's side between line of floatation and deck level; ~-*born*, born to the conditions and privileges of citizenship, born free; ~ *church*, church free from State control; nonconformist church; *F~ Church of Scotland*, organization of those who seceded in 1843 from established Presbyterian Church (reunited 1929); ~ *fall*, part of fall in parachute descent before parachute opens; flight of spacecraft in space with no thrust from engines, when occupants experience weightlessness; ~ *fight*, ~-*for-all*, fight in which all and sundry engage promiscuously; ~-*hand*, (of drawing) done without guiding instruments, measures, or other artificial aid; ~-*handed*, open-handed, generous; *free'hold*, (estate held by) tenure in fee-simple or fee-tail or for term of life; held by freehold; *free'holder*, possessor of freehold estate; ~ *house*, inn or public house selling several brands of liquor (opp. *tied house*); ~ *kick*, (footb.) kick allowed without interference, as penalty for breach of rules by the other side; ~-*lance*, journalist not attached to one periodical, person working for himself and not for an employer; ~ *list*, list of things on which, or persons from whom, payment is not required; ~-*liver*, one who gives free indulgence to his appetites; ~ *love*, sexual relations irrespective of marriage; *free'-man*, one who is not a slave or serf, or not subject to tyranny or usurped dominion; one who has freedom of borough, city, etc.; *free'mason*, member of fraternity for mutual help and brotherly feeling, called *Free and Accepted Masons*, having elaborate ritual and system of secret signs (the original *free masons* were probably skilled masons emancipated and moving from place to place for erection of important buildings in and after 14th c., the *accepted masons* being honorary members (orig. supposed to be eminent for architectural or antiquarian learning) who began to be admitted early in 17th c.); *free'masonry*, system and institutions of Freemasons; secret or tacit brotherhood, instinctive sympathy; ~ *on board*, (of goods) with all charges paid for delivery when put on board ship or other means of conveyance; ~ *pass*, authority to travel on railway, attend performance, etc., without payment; ~ *place*, place in secondary school awarded free to pupil from primary school; ~ *port*, port open to all traders to load and unload in, (also) port, or zone within a port, where imports and exports are exempt from customs duty; ~ *range*, (U.S.) free pasturage; (esp., attrib.) of chickens given freedom to range for food; hence of their eggs; *F~ State*, republic; before Civil War of 1861–5, State of U.S. in which slavery did not exist; *free'stone*, fine-grained sandstone or limestone that can easily be cut or sawn; kind of peach or nectarine of which when ripe the stone is loose; *~-thinker*, one who refuses to submit his reason to control of authority in matters of religious belief, rationalist, deist, etc.; so ~ *thought*; ~ *trade*, trade left to its natural course without customs duties to restrict imports or protect home industries; *~-trader*, believer in free trade; ~ *verse*: see VERS LIBRE; ~ *vote*, parliamentary vote not made subject to party discipline; *free'way*, (orig. U.S.) fast highway; *~-wheel*, rear wheel of bicycle designed to be capable of revolving faster than, and independently of, the driving mechanism; special type of pinion permitting the rear wheel to revolve thus; similar device in motor-cars; (*v.i.*) ride bicycle with pedals stationary; drive motor-car with clutch disengaged; ~ *will*, unconstrained choice; power of directing one's own actions without constraint by necessity or fate. **free'lȳ** *adv.* **free** *adv.* Freely (now only techn.); without cost or payment. ~ *v.t.* 1. Make free, set at liberty. 2. Relieve *from*, rid or ease *of*; clear, disengage, disentangle; *free'dman*, (esp. in Rom. hist.) emancipated slave.

free'booter *n.* Pirate, piratical adventurer.

free'dom *n.* 1. Personal liberty, exemption or release from slavery or imprisonment; civil liberty, independence; liberty of action; power of self-determination, independence of fate or necessity; *four ~s*, those propounded by F. D. Roosevelt in 1941 (freedom of speech and worship, freedom from want and fear). 2. Frankness, outspokenness; undue familiarity; facility, ease, in action; boldness of conception. 3. (phys.) Capability of motion. 4. Exemption *from* defect, disadvantage, burden, etc.; privilege possessed by city or corporation; participation in privileges of membership *of* company etc. or citizenship *of* city; unrestricted use *of*.

free'martin *n.* Hermaphrodite or imperfect female of ox kind.

free'sia (-z-) *n.* Iridaceous bulbous plant of genus *F~*, of Cape of Good Hope, allied to gladiolus and cultivated for its ornamental and perfumed flowers. [F. H. T. *Freese* (d. 1876), German physician]

freeze *v.* (past t. *frōze*, past part. *frōzen*). 1. (impers.) *it freezes* etc., the temperature of the atmosphere is such that water becomes ice. 2. Be converted into or covered with ice; become hard or rigid as result of cold; become fastened *to*, *together*, by action of frost; ~ *on to*, (colloq.) take or keep tight hold of. 3. Be affected by, feel, extreme cold; die by frost; be devoid of heat; be chilled or immobilized by fear etc. 4. Cause to congeal, change (fluid) to solid by diminution of heat, cause ice to form on; congeal (the blood) as if by frost, with terror etc.; chill (feelings etc.), paralyse (powers etc.); stiffen, harden, injure, kill, etc., by chilling; preserve (meat etc.) by refrigeration; make (assets etc.) unrealizable, peg or stabilize (prices, wages, etc.); ~*-dry* (*v.t.*) freeze material and dry it by evaporation of ice under high vacuum; *freezing mixture*, salt and snow or other mixture used to freeze liquids; *freezing-point*, temperature at which water freezes, temperature at which given liquid freezes; ~ *out*, exclude from business, society, etc., by competition, boycotting, etc. ~ *n.* State, coming, period, of frost; freezing of assets etc. **free'zer** *n.*

free'zing *adj.* (esp.) Very cold; (of manner) chilling; distant. **free'zingly̆** *adv.*

freight (-āt) *n.* Hire of ship for transporting goods; transport of goods by water (in U.S. by land also), charge for this; cargo, shipload; load, burden; (U.S.) freight train; *frei'ghtliner*, train carrying goods in containers; ~ *train*, (U.S.) goods train, train for conveyance of goods. ~ *v.t.* Load (ship) with cargo, (wagon etc.) with goods for transport; hire or let out (ship etc.) for carriage of goods and passengers.

frei'ghtage (-āt-) *n.* Hire of ship etc. for conveyance of goods; cost of conveyance of goods; freighting or hiring of ship etc.; cargo.

frei'ghter (-āt-) *n.* One who (charters and) loads ship; one who consigns goods for carriage inland; one whose business is to receive and forward freight; cargo-ship, (U.S.) freight-wagon; freight-carrying aircraft.

Frĕnch *adj.* Of France or its people or language; having the qualities attributed to French people; ~ *bean*, kidney or haricot bean (*Phaseolus vulgaris*) used as culinary vegetable both in unripe sliced pods and in ripe seeds; ~ *bread*, bread made in long loaves with transverse marks on top; ~ *chalk*, finely powdered talc used as dry lubricant and for removing grease-spots etc.; ~ *Community*, association formed in 1958 of France, her departments and territories overseas, and former French territories that chose to maintain association after achieving independence; ~ *cricket*, informal type of cricket without stumps, in which bowler tries to hit batsman's legs; ~ *grey*, grey colour with lavender tint; ~ *horn*: see HORN[1], 3; ~ *knot*, ornamental knot in embriodery; *take* ~ *leave*, go away, do something, without permission or notice; ~ *letter*, (colloq.) contraceptive sheath; *Frenchman*, *Frenchwoman*, French person; ~ *polish*, coloured solution of shellac and methylated spirit for producing high gloss on wood; ~*-polish* (*v.t.*) polish with this; *F~ Revolution*, revolution generally regarded as beginning with the meeting of the States General in May 1789, in which the French monarchy was overthrown and the First Republic established; ~ *seam*, seam in which raw edges are enclosed; ~ *window*, glazed door or pair of these, serving as door and window. ~ *n*, 1. (collect.) People, of France. 2. Language of France, one of the descendants of Latin; *Old* ~, French from *c* 9th to *c* 13th (or sometimes 16th) century. 3. Dry vermouth.

Frĕ'nchify̆ *v.t.* Make French in form, character, or manners. **Frĕnchificā'tion** *n.*

frenetic: see PHRENETIC.

frenum: see FRAENUM.

frĕ'nzy̆ *n.* Delirious fury or agitation; wild folly. **frĕ'nzied** (-ĭd) *adj.* Frantic, infuriated.

frē'quency̆ *n.* 1. Frequent occurrence; being repeated at short intervals. 2. (physiol.) Number of pulse-beats per minute. 3. (phys., acoustics, etc.) Rate of recurrence of repeated event, e.g. a vibration; (elect.) number of complete cycles per second of an alternating current or potential; such currents are classified as: *audio* ~, (A.F.) frequency within the audible range, 30 Hz–20 kHz; *high* ~, (H.F.) used of frequencies above the audible range (above 15 kHz), esp. those used for radio communication; *low* ~, (L.F.) used of audio frequencies as dist. from radio (and see below); *radio* ~, (R.F.) frequency suitable for radio transmission, above 10^4 Hz and below 3×10^{12} Hz approx., subdivided into *low* ~ (L.F.) 30–300 kHz, *medium* ~ (M.F.) 3×10^5–3×10^6 Hz, *very high* ~ (V.H.F.) 30–300 MHz, *ultra-high* ~ (U.H.F.) 3×10^8–3×10^9 Hz; ~ *modulation*: see MODULATION. 4. (statistics) Ratio of number of actual to number of possible occurrences of an event.

frē'quent *adj.* Found near together, numerous; often occurring, happening in close succession; constant. **frē'quently̆** *adv.* **frėquĕ'nt** *v.t.* Go often or habitually to. **frēquentā'tion, frėquĕ'nter** *ns.*

frėquĕ'ntatĭve *adj.* & *n.* (gram.) (Verb, verbal form, conjugation) expressing frequent repetition of action.

frĕ'scō *n.* (pl. *-oes, -os*). Method of painting with powdered pigments by mixing them with water and applying them to wall or ceiling before plaster is dry (also called *true* ~ to distinguish it from ~ *secco*, painting on dry plaster); picture painted thus. ~ *v.t.* Paint in fresco. [It., = 'fresh']

frĕsh *adj.* 1. New, novel; not previously known, met with, used, etc.; additional, different; recent, newly made or arrived; newly come or taken *from*; raw, inexperienced; *fre'shman*, university student (U.S., pupil at school) in his first year. 2. (of food) Not artificially preserved, not salted, pickled, smoked, etc., not frozen or tinned; (of butter) not salt; (of water) not salt or bitter, fit for drinking; (of air etc.) pure, untainted, refreshing, cool; *fre'shwater* (*adj.*) of fresh water, not of the sea. 3. Not stale, musty, or vapid; not faded; unsullied, bright and pure in colour; looking healthy or young. 4. Not weary, vigorous, fit; excited with drink. 5. (slang, prob. infl. by Ger. *frech* impertinent) Presumptuous, forward. **frĕ'shnėss** *n.* **frĕ'shen** *v.* **frĕsh** *adv.* Freshly, newly; *~-run*, (of salmon) newly come up from the sea. ~ *n.* 1. Fresh part of day, year, etc. 2. Rush of water in river, flood. **frĕ'shnėss** *n.*

frĕ'sher *n.* (slang) = FRESHMAN.

frĕ'shėt *n.* Rush of fresh water flowing into sea; flood of river from heavy rain or melted snow.

frĕ'shly̆ *adv.* Recently; with unabated vigour; with fresh appearance, odour, etc.

frĕt[1] *n.* Ornamental pattern of continuous combinations of straight lines joined usu. at right angles; *fre'tsaw*, very thin saw stretched on frame for cutting thin wood in ornamental patterns; *fre'twork*, (archit.) carved work in decorative patterns, esp. of intersecting lines; wood cut with fretsaw into ornamental patterns. ~ *v.t.* Variegate, chequer; adorn (esp. ceiling) with carved or embossed work.

frĕt[2] *v.* 1. Gnaw; consume, wear, torment by gnawing; eat *away*; form or make by wearing away. 2. Chafe, worry; distress oneself with regret or discontent. ~ *n.* Irritation, vexation, querulousness. **frĕ'tful** *adj.* **frĕ'tfully̆** *adv.* **frĕ'tfulnėss** *n.*

frĕt[3] *n.* Bar or ridge on fingerboard of certain stringed instruments fixing positions of fingers to produce required notes.

Freud (froid), Sigmund (1856–1939). Austrian specialist in neurology; founder of psychoanalysis. **Freu'dĭan** *adj.* & *n.*

Frey (-ā), **Freyr** (-ār). (Scand. myth.) God of fertility and dispenser of rain and sunshine.

Frey'a, Frey'ja (-āya). (Scand. myth.) Goddess of love and of the night, the northern Venus.

F.R.G.S. *abbrev.* Fellow of the Royal Geographical Society.

F.R.Hist.S., F.R.H.S. *abbrevs.* Fellow of the Royal Historical Society, of the Royal Horticultural Society.

Fri. *abbrev.* Friday.

frī'able *adj.* Easily crumbled. **frīabĭ'lĭty̆, frī'ablenėss** *ns.*

frī'ar *n.* Brother or member of certain religious orders founded in 13th c. or after, and esp. the four mendicant orders, Franciscans

(*Grey Friars*), Augustines (*Austin Friars*), Dominicans (*Black Friars*), and Carmelites (*White Friars*); ~'*s* (or *friars*') *balsam*, tincture of benzoin used as application for ulcers and wounds, and, vaporized, as inhalant. **frī'ary̆** *n.* Convent, fraternity, of friars.

F.R.I.B.A. *abbrev.* Fellow of the Royal Institute of British Architects.

fri'bble *v.i.* Trifle, be frivolous. ~ *n.* Trifler.

fricandeau' (-dō) *n.* (pl. -*x*, pr. -z). Dish of veal or other meat fried, braised, and served with its sauce. ~ *v.t.* Make into fricandeaux.

fricassee' *n.* Dish of meat, poultry, etc., cut up, fried or stewed, and served in white sauce. ~ *v.t.* Make fricassee of.

fri'cative *adj.* & *n.* (phonet.) (Consonant) produced by friction of breath through narrow opening formed in the mouth with the tongue or lips, as *s*, *f*.

fri'ction *n.* 1. Chafing or rubbing as medical treatment. 2. Rubbing of two bodies, attrition; (phys. etc.) resistance body meets with in moving over another; (fig.) clash of wills, temperaments, opinions, etc.; *angle of* ~, maximum angle at which one body will remain on another without sliding; ~-*clutch*, -*cone*, -*coupling*, -*disc*, -*gear*(*ing*), contrivances for transmitting motion by frictional contact. **fri'ctional** *adj.*

Frī'day (*or* -dĭ) *n.* 6th day of the week; *Good* ~, Friday before Easter, commemorating Crucifixion and observed as holiday; *man* ~, assistant with diverse duties (so *girl* ~). [= 'day of (the goddess) Frig' (i.e. FRIGGA), transl. of L *dies Veneris* day of (the planet) Venus]

fridge *n.* (colloq.) Refrigerator.

friend (frĕnd) *n.* 1. One (not ordinarily a relative or lover) joined to another in intimacy and affection; second in duel; (loosely) acquaintance; stranger towards whom one wishes to express goodwill or kindly condescension; *my honourable* ~, used in House of Commons by one member to describe another; *my learned* ~, applied in law court by one counsel to another. 2. Sympathizer, helper, patron; ~ *at court*, one who will use his influence in high places to help another. 3. One who is not an enemy, who is on same side. 4. Member of Society of Friends; in vocative, ordinary mode of address among Quakers; (*Society of*) *Friends*, the QUAKERS as a communion. **frie'ndlėss** *adj.* **frie'ndlėssnėss** *n.*

frie'ndly̆ (frĕ-) *adj.* Acting, disposed to act, as friend; characteristic of friends, expressing, showing, prompted by, kindness; opportune; ~ *society*, association of members paying contributions in return for pecuniary help in sickness, old age, etc., **frie'ndlĭnėss** *n.*

frie'ndship (frĕ-) *n.* Being friends, relation between friends; friendly disposition felt or shown.

Friesian (frē'zhan), *adj.* Of Friesland. ~ *n.* (One of) a breed of large piebald (usu. black-and-white) dairy cattle orig. imported from Friesland.

Frie'sland (-z-). Province of N. Netherlands.

frieze[1] *n.* Coarse woollen cloth with nap usu. on one side only.

frieze[2] *n.* Member of entablature above architrave and below cornice; horizontal broad band of sculpture filling this; any band of painted or sculptured decoration; strip of wallpaper of different pattern or colour from main paper placed below ceiling or cornice of a room. [Fr. *frise* f. L *Phrygium* (*opus*) Phrygian (work)]

fri'gate *n.* 1. In Royal Navy, formerly vessel next in size and equipment to ships of the line, with raised quarter-deck and forecastle (~-*built*, built thus) and from 28 to 60 guns on main deck; later, (loosely) cruiser; in recent use, a large CORVETTE. 2. (also ~-*bird*) Large swift brown sea-bird (genus *Fregata*) of tropical regions, with habit of cruising near other species and daringly pursuing them.

Fri'gga. (Scand. myth.) Wife of Odin and goddess of married love and of the hearth.

fright (-īt) *n.* Sudden fear, violent terror, alarm; grotesque- or ridiculous-looking person or thing. ~ *v.t.* (poet.) Frighten.

fri'ghten (-īt-) *v.t.* Throw into a fright, terrify; drive (*away*, *out of*, *into*, etc.) by fright; *frightened at*, affected with fright of.

fri'ghtful (-īt-) *adj.* Dreadful, shocking, revolting; ugly, hideous; (slang) very great, awful. **fri'ghtfullў** *adv.* **fri'ghtfulnėss** *n.* (esp., in war of 1914–18, as transl. of Ger. *Schrecklichkeit*) Policy of terrorizing civilian population as military resource.

fri'gid *adj.* 1. Intensely cold; ~ *zone*, region lying within either polar circle. 2. Without ardour, apathetic; (of a woman) sexually unresponsive. 3. Formal, forced; depressing; dull, insipid. **fri'gidlў** *adv.* **fri'gidnėss, frigi'ditў** *ns.*

frigidār'ium *n.* (pl. *-ia*). (Rom. antiq.) Room in baths, with cold plunge.

frill *n.* Ornamental edging of strip of woven material with one edge gathered and the other left loose so as to give wavy or fluted appearance; similar paper ornament on ham-knuckle, cutlet-bone, etc.; natural fringe of feathers, hair, etc., on bird, animal, or plant; (phot.) irregular puckering of gelatine film at edge of plate etc.; (pl.) airs, affectations; showy accomplishments; unnecessary ornament. ~ *v.* Furnish or decorate with frill; form frill, form frill on. **fri'llў** *adj.*

fringe (-j) *n.* Ornamental bordering of threads of silk, cotton, etc., either loose or formed into tassels, twists, etc.; anything resembling this, border, edging; margin, outer edge; part of front hair brushed forward over forehead and cut short; ~ *benefit*, perquisite; benefit, other than salary, received by employee. ~ *v.t.* Adorn or encircle with fringe; serve as fringe to. **fringed** (-jd) *adj.* Having a fringe, formed into a fringe.

fri'pperў *n.* Finery, needless or tawdry adornment, esp. in dress; empty display, ostentation; knick-knacks, trifles.

Fri'sian (-z-) *adj.* & *n.* (Native, inhabitant, language) of Friesland.

frisk *v.* 1. Move sportively; caper. 2. (slang) Search (person, his clothing) for concealed weapon etc. ~ *n.* Frolic, caper. **fri'skў** *adj.* **fri'skilў** *adv.* **fri'skinėss** *n.*

fri'skėt *n.* (print.) Thin iron frame hinged to tympan of hand press, with tapes or paper strips stretched across for keeping sheet in position while printing.

frit *n.* Calcined mixture of sand and fluxes prepared for melting to form glass; vitreous composition from which soft porcelain is made. ~ *v.t.* Make into frit; partially fuse, calcine.

frith[1] *n.* Var. of FIRTH.

Frith[2], William Powell (1819–1910). English painter, whose 'Derby Day' and 'The Railway Station' were very popular in their day.

friti'llarў *n.* 1. Plant of the liliaceous genus *Fritillaria*, esp. *F. meleagris*, the snakeshead, found in

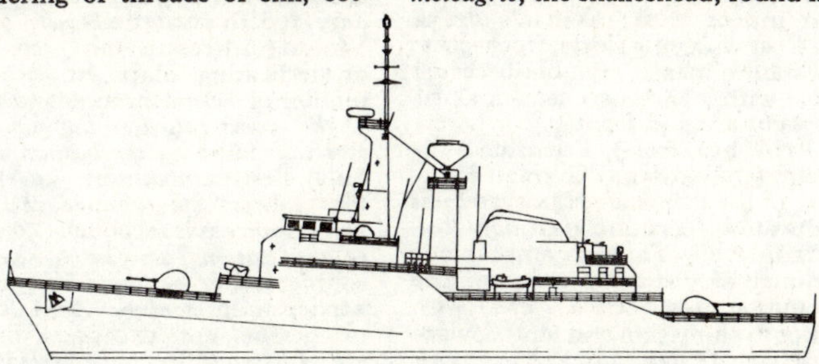

FRIGATE

moist meadows. 2. Any of various butterflies, esp. of genus *Argynnis*, with spotted markings. [L *fritillus* dice-box, with ref. to chequered markings of corolla]

frĭ'tter[1] *n.* Portion of fried batter, containing slices of fruit, meat, etc.

frĭ'tter[2] *v.t.* Throw *away* (time, money, energy, etc.) in trifling and wasteful way on various aims.

Frĭtz. Nickname for the Germans or a German. [Ger., abbrev. of *Friedrich* Frederick]

frĭ'vol *v.* Be a trifler, trifle; throw *away* foolishly.

frĭ'volous *adj.* Paltry, trifling, futile; given to trifling, silly. **frĭ'volouslў** *adv.* **frĭ'volousnėss, frĭvŏ'lĭtў** *ns.*

frĭzz[1] *v.* Curl, crisp, form into mass of small curls; rub (wash-leather etc.) with pumice-stone or scraping-knife to remove grain, soften surface, and give uniform thickness. ~ *n.* Frizzed state; frizzed hair, row of curls. **frĭ'zzў** *adj.*

frĭzz[2] *v.i.* Make sputtering noise in frying.

frĭ'zzle[1] *v.* Curl (*up*) in small crisp curls, frizz. ~ *n.* Frizzled hair. **frĭ'zzlў** *adj.*

frĭ'zzle[2] *v.* Fry, toast, or grill, with sputtering noise.

Frl. *abbrev.* FRÄULEIN.

frō *adv.* Away (only in *to and* ~: see TO *adv.*)

frŏck *n.* 1. Long habit with large open sleeves, the outer and characteristic dress of a monk; (fig.) priestly character. 2. Smock; sailor's woollen jersey. 3. Child's outer garment of skirt and bodice for indoor wear; woman's dress. 4. Coat with long skirts, frock-coat; *~-coat*, man's double-breasted coat with long square tails or skirts not cut away in front.

Froe'bel (frẽr-), Friedrich Wilhelm (1782–1852). German founder of the KINDERGARTEN system of education. **Froebē'lian** *adj.* & *n.*

frŏg[1] *n.* Tailless amphibious animal of order Anura, esp. the common frog (genus *Rana*) with smooth shiny skin and long powerful web-footed hind legs with which it swims and leaps; (*F*~, contempt.) Frenchman (as eating frogs; also *~-eater*); *fro'gfish*, any of various fishes, esp. the angler; *~-hopper*, small, jumping, hemipterous insect whose nymphs exist in cuckoo-spit; *~ in the throat*, hoarseness; *fro'gman*, underwater swimmer with long rubber shoes like frog's hind feet; *frog('s)-march*, carry (prisoner) face downwards by four persons each holding a limb; hustle (prisoner) forward with arms gripped; also as *n.*; *~-spawn*, eggs of frog; kinds of freshwater algae.

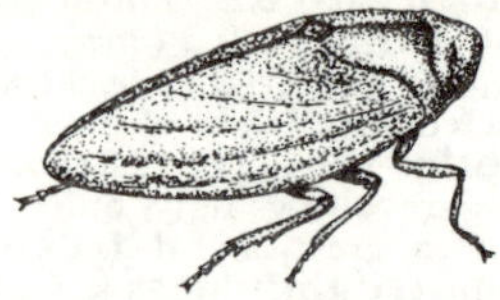

frŏg[2] *n.* Elastic horny substance in middle of sole of horse's foot.

frŏg[3] *n.* Attachment to waist-belt to support sword, bayonet, etc.; military coat-fastening of spindle-shaped silk-covered button and loop, whence **frŏgged** (-gd) *adj.*

frŏg[4] *n.* Grooved piece of iron at place in railway where tracks cross.

Froissart (frwăsâr), Jean (1337?–1410). French chronicler, whose 'Chroniques' deal chiefly with the affairs of France and England from 1325 to 1400.

frŏ'lĭc *adj.* (archaic) Joyous, sportive. ~ *v.i.* Play pranks; gambol. ~ *n.* Outburst of gaiety; prank; merriment; gay party. **frŏ'lĭcsome** *adj.* **frŏ'lĭcsomelў** *adv.* **frŏ'lĭcsomenėss** *n.*

frŏm (unstressed -om) *prep.* Out of, indicating place etc. whence motion or action proceeds (*walked ~ the town*; *called ~ the window*), starting-point (*~ the beginning*; *~ July*), first-named limit (*~ 10 to 20 men*), object etc. whence distance or remoteness is reckoned (*10 miles ~ the station*; *am far ~ saying*), source (*water ~ the well*), giver, sender (*a present ~ Ann*), thing or person got rid of, avoided, etc. (*dissuade ~ folly*; *release ~ engagement*), state changed for another (~ *being attacked became the aggressor*), thing distinguished (*know black ~ white*), origin in place or time, with adverbs or adverbial phrases, or prepositions (~ *long ago*; ~ *under the bed*).

frŏnd *n.* (bot.) Leaf of certain flowerless plants, esp. ferns; (zool.) leaf-like expansion in certain animal organisms. **frŏ'ndage** *n.* **frŏndō'se** *adj.* Leafy.

Fronde (-awnd). (Fr. hist.) Party that rose in rebellion against Mazarin and the court during minority of Louis XIV; hence, malcontent party.

front (-ŭ-) *n.* 1. Forehead (poet.); face. 2. (mil.) Foremost line or part of army etc.; line of battle; part of ground towards enemy; scene of actual fighting; direction towards which line faces when formed. 3. Organized body of political forces, as *popular* ~ etc. 4. (archit.) Any face of building, esp. that containing main entrance. 5. (meteor.) Forward edge of an advancing mass of warm air meeting cold, or vice versa. 6. Side or part normally nearer or towards spectator or direction of motion; part of theatre where audience sits; part of seaside resort fronting sea, promenade; organization etc. serving as cover for disreputable activities; band of false hair worn over woman's forehead; breast of man's shirt; dicky. 7. (with preps.) Forward position or situation; *in* ~ *of*, before, in advance of; confronting. ~ *adj.* Of the front; situated in front; (phonet., of sound) in which forepart of tongue touches or is raised towards front of hard palate; ~ *bench*: see BENCH *n.* 3; ~ *door*, principal entrance-door of house. ~ *v.* 1. Face, look *on*, *to*, *towards*, face, stand opposite to; have front on side of (street etc.). 2. Confront, meet, oppose. 3. Furnish with front. 4. (mil.) Turn to the front. 5. (phonet.) pronounce with tongue in front position.

fro'ntage (-ŭ-) *n.* 1. Land abutting on street or water, land between front of building and road; extent of front; front of building. 2. Ground occupied by troops in camp or on parade. 3. Fronting in certain direction; exposure, outlook.

fro'ntal[1] (-ŭ-) *n.* Movable covering for front of altar; façade of building.

fro'ntal[2] (-ŭ-) *adj.* 1. Of the forehead; ~ *bone;* ~ *lobe,* anterior portion of cerebral hemisphere. 2. Of the front; (of portrait, painted figure, etc.) facing spectator; (of building, sculpture, etc.) intended to be seen from the front; ~ *attack*, direct attack on enemy's front. **frontă'lity̆** *n.*

fro'ntier (-ŭ-) *n.* Boundary of a state where its territory abuts upon that of another state; (U.S.) border of settled or inhabited regions of country; *fro'ntiersman*, (U.S.) one who lives on frontier of country, or on extreme edge of settled or inhabited districts. ~ *adj.* Of, on, the frontier.

fro'ntispiece (-ŭ-) *n.* 1. (archit.) Principal face of building; decorated entrance; pediment over door etc. 2. Illustration facing title-page of book or one of its divisions.

fro'ntlėt (-ŭ-) *n.* Band worn on forehead; phylactery; animal's forehead; cloth hanging over upper part of altar frontal.

fro'nton (frŭ-) *n.* (archit.) Pediment.

frōre *adj.* (poet.) Frozen, frosty.

frŏst *n.* 1. Freezing; temperature of atmosphere when it is below freezing-point of water; (also *white* ~) frozen dew or vapour, rime; *fro'stbite*, inflamed or gangrenous state of skin and adjacent parts produced by exposure to severe cold; *fro'stbitten*, affected with this. 2. (slang) Failure. ~ *v.t.* 1. Nip, injure (plants etc.), with frost. 2. Cover (as) with frost; cover (cake) with icing, ice. 3. Give roughened or finely granulated surface to (glass, metal). 4. Turn (hair) white. 5. Arm (horse's shoes) against slipping by nails, roughening, etc. **frŏ′sting** *n.* (esp.) Icing for cakes.

frŏ′stȳ *adj.* Affected with frost, ice-cold; chilling, frigid, lacking in warmth of feeling; covered, looking as if covered, with hoar-frost.

frŏth *n.* Aggregation of small bubbles in liquid, caused by agitation, fermentation, effervescence, etc.; impure matter rising to surface of liquids, scum; unsubstantial or worthless matter, idle talk. ~ *v.* Emit, gather, froth; cause (beer etc.) to foam. **frŏ′thȳ** *adj.* **frŏ′thilȳ** *adv.* **frŏ′thinėss** *n.*

Froude (frōōd), James Anthony (1818–84). English historian.

frou′-frou (-ōō, -ōō) *n.* Rustling, esp. of dresses.

frō′ward *adj.* (archaic) Perverse, refractory. **frō′wardlȳ** *adv.* **frō′wardnėss** *n.*

frown *n.* Vertically furrowed state of brow; look expressing severity, disapproval, or deep thought. ~ *v.* Knit brows, esp. to express displeasure or concentrate attention; (of things) present gloomy aspect; express disapprobation (*at*, *on*); express (defiance etc.) with frown. **frow′ninglȳ** *adv.*

frowst *n.* Close and fusty atmosphere of overcrowded or unventilated room. ~ *v.i.* Remain in, enjoy, such atmosphere. **frow′stȳ** *adj.* **frow′stinėss** *n.*

frow′zȳ *adj.* Ill-smelling, fusty, musty, close; slatternly, unkempt, dingy. **frow′zinėss** *n.*

frō′zen *adj.*: see FREEZE; (esp., of food) preserved by refrigeration; (of credits etc.) not realizable.

F.R.P.S. *abbrev.* Fellow of the Royal Photographic Society.

F.R.S. *abbrev.* Fellow of the Royal Society.

F.R.S.A., F.R.S.E. *abbrevs.* Fellow of the Royal Society of Arts, of Edinburgh.

F.R.S.G.S. *abbrev.* Fellow of the Royal Scottish Geographical Society.

F.R.S.L. *abbrev.* Fellow of the Royal Society of Literature.

F.R.S.S. *abbrev.* Fellow of the Royal Statistical Society.

frŭcti′ferous *adj.* Bearing fruit.

frŭctificā′tion *n.* (bot.) Reproductive parts of plant, esp. of ferns and mosses.

frŭ′ctifȳ *v.* Bear fruit; make fruitful, impregnate.

frŭ′ctōse *n.* (chem.) Fruit-sugar, laevulose, occurring in the laevorotatory form with glucose in sweet fruits, flowers, and honey.

frŭ′ctūous *adj.* Full of, producing, fruit.

fru′gal (-ōō-) *adj.* Careful, sparing (*of*); economical, esp. as regards food; sparingly used or supplied; costing little. **frugă′lity** *n.* **fru′gallȳ** *adv.*

fruit (-ōōt) *n.* 1. (now usu. pl.) Vegetable products fit for food. 2. Edible product of plant or tree, consisting of seed and its envelope, esp. when this juicy or pulpy; (bot.) ripe seeds and structure surrounding them. 3. (chiefly bibl.) Offspring. 4. What results from action, effort, cause, etc.; issue, consequence; advantage, profit; (pl.) products, revenues. 5. ~ *bat*, tropical fruit-eating bat of suborder Megachiroptera; ~ *cake*, cake containing currants, raisins, etc.; ~*-knife*, knife for cutting fruit, with blade of some material (e.g. silver) not affected by the acids; ~ *machine*, coin-operated gambling machine; ~ *salad*, mixture of various fruits served in syrup; ~*-sugar*: see FRUCTOSE; ~*-tree*, tree cultivated for its fruit. ~ *v.* Bear, make bear, fruit.

fruitār′ian (frōōt-) *n.* & *adj.* (Of) one who lives on fruit.

frui′ter (frōōt-) *n.* 1. Tree producing fruit. 2. Ship carrying fruit.

frui′terer (frōōt-) *n.* Dealer in fruit.

frui′tful (frōōt-) *adj.* Productive, fertile, causing fertility; productive of offspring, prolific; beneficial, remunerative. **frui′tfullȳ** *adv.* **frui′tfulnėss** *n.*

frui′tion (frōōĭ-) *n.* Enjoyment, attainment of thing desired, realization of hopes, etc.

frui′tlėss (frōōt-) *adj.* Not bearing fruit; yielding no profit; useless, vain. **frui′tlesslȳ** *adv.* **frui′tlėssnėss** *n.*

frui′tȳ (frōōtĭ) *adj.* Of or like

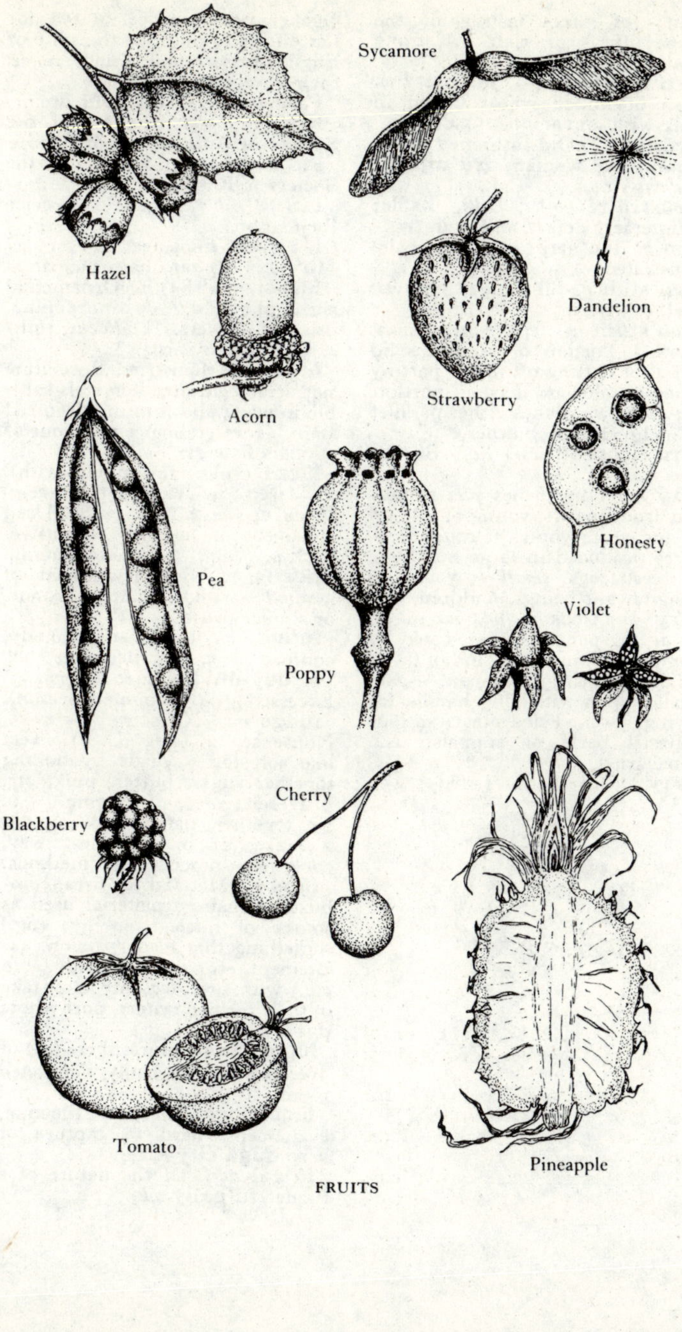
Sycamore
Hazel
Dandelion
Acorn
Strawberry
Honesty
Pea
Violet
Poppy
Cherry
Blackberry
Tomato
Pineapple

FRUITS

fruit; (of wine) tasting of the grape; (fig.) of rich or strong quality, spicy.

fru′mentў (-ōō-), **fûr′mėtў** *n.* Dish of hulled wheat boiled in milk with cinnamon, sugar, etc.

frŭmp *n.* Old-fashioned dowdily-dressed woman. **frŭ′mpĭsh, frŭ′mpў** *adjs.*

frŭstrā′te *v.t.* Balk, baffle; counteract; defeat, foil. **frŭstrā′tion** *n.* **frŭ′strāte** *adj.* (archaic) Frustrated.

frū′stūle *n.* Silicious two-valved shell of diatom.

frŭ′stum *n.* (pl. *-ta*, *-tums*). (math.) Portion of regular solid left after cutting off upper part by plane parallel to base; portion between two planes either parallel or inclined to each other.

fru′tĭcōse (frōō-) *adj.* Shrub-like.

frȳ[1] *n.* Young fishes just produced from spawn; young of salmon in 2nd year; young of other creatures produced in large numbers, as bees, frogs; *small ~*, young or insignificant beings, children, etc.

frȳ[2] *v.* Cook in hot fat or oil in frying-pan; *deep-~*, cook by completely immersing in hot fat or oil in deep pan; *frying-pan*, *~-pan*, shallow pan with long handle for frying. ~ *n.* Fried meat; various internal parts of animals, usu. eaten fried.

Frȳ[3], Elizabeth (1780–1845). Quaker reformer; celebrated for her efforts to improve the state of English prisons and of convicts on their voyage to Australia.

F.S. *abbrev.* Fleet Surgeon.

F.S.A. *abbrev.* Fellow of the Society of Antiquaries, of Arts.

F.S.E. *abbrev.* Fellow of the Society of Engineers.

F.S.R. *abbrev.* Field Service Regulations.

ft *abbrev.* Foot, feet.

fū′bsy (-zĭ) *adj.* Fat or squat.

fuchsia (fū′sh*a*) *n.* Ornamental shrub of genus *F~* with drooping, usu. red, flowers. [L. *Fuchs*, 16th-c. German botanist]

fu′chsĭne (fōōk-) *n.* Rosaniline salt, iridescent green crystals soluble in water and forming deep red stain. [f. resemblance to colour of FUCHSIA flower]

fŭck *v.* (vulg.) 1. Copulate (with). 2. Used in exclamations etc. **fŭ′ckĭng** *adj.* & *adv.* (vulg.) Used abusively or as mere intensive. **fŭck** *n.* (vulg.) Act of copulation.

fū′cus *n.* Brown seaweed of genus *F~* with flat leathery fronds, or similar plant.

fŭ′ddle *v.* Intoxicate; stupefy, confuse. ~ *n.* Fuddled state.

fŭ′ddў-dŭ′ddў *n.* & *adj.* (slang) Excessively old-fashioned (person).

fŭdge *int.* Nonsense! ~ *n.* 1. Nonsense. 2. (orig. U.S.) Sweet like soft toffee, made by boiling together sugar, butter, milk, etc. 3. Deceit; piece of fudging. ~ *v.* Fit together, patch, make up, in a makeshift or dishonest way, cook, fake; practise such methods.

fū′el *n.* Material for fires, combustible matter; material used as source of nuclear energy; (fig.) something that feeds passion, excitement, etc. ~ *v.* Provide (ship etc.) with fuel; (of ship etc.) take in fuel; *fuelling station*, port where this is done.

fŭg *n.* Stuffy atmosphere (as) of overcrowded or badly ventilated room. **fŭ′ggў** (-gĭ) *adj.*

fūgā′cious (-sh*us*) *adj.* Fleeting, evanescent, hard to capture or keep. **fūgă′cĭtў** *n.*

fū′gal *adj.* Of the nature of a fugue. **fū′gallў** *adv.*

fuga'tō (fŏŏgah-) *n.* (mus.) Passage in fugue style in composition other than a fugue.

fū'gĭtĭve *adj.* 1. Fleeing; that has taken flight (from duty, an enemy, master, etc.). 2. Fleeting, transient; (of literature) of passing interest, ephemeral. ~ *n.* One who flees (*from*).

fūgue (-g) *n.* 1. (mus.) Polyphonic composition in which a short melodic theme (the *subject*) is introduced by one of the parts (the *voices*) and successively taken up by others, thereafter forming the main material of the texture; *double* ~, fugue on two themes starting together. 2. (psychol.) State of alteration of consciousness combined with an impulse to wander away from accustomed environment.

Führ'er (fūr-) *n.* Title assumed by Adolf HITLER as head of the German Reich. [Ger., = 'leader']

Fukiĕn (fōō-). Maritime province of SE. China.

-ful *suffix.* Full of; filling.

fŭ'lcrum (*or* fŏŏ-) *n.* (pl. *-ra*). (mech.) Point against which lever is placed to get purchase or on which it turns or is supported. [L, = 'post of couch']

fulfi'l (fŏŏ-) *v.t.* Bring to consummation, carry out (prophecy, promise), satisfy (desire, prayer); perform, execute (command, law); answer (purpose), comply with (conditions); bring to an end, complete (period, work). **fulfi'lment** *n.*

fŭ'lgent *adj.* (poet. & rhet.) Shining, brilliant.

fŭ'lgūrāte *v.i.* Emit vivid flashes like lightning. **fŭlgurā'tion** *n.*

fŭ'lgūrīte *n.* (geol.) Tube-like body of sand-grains fused together, formed by the action of lightning.

Fulham (fŏŏ'lam). Former London borough; ~ *Palace*, until 1973 the official residence of the Bishop of London.

fūlĭ'gĭnous *adj.* Sooty, dusky.

full[1] (fŏŏl) *adj.* 1. Containing all it will hold, having no space empty, replete; containing abundance *of*, charged, crowded; abounding (in); replete with food. 2. ~ *of*, engrossed with, absorbed in. 3. Copious, satisfying. 4. Complete; answering in every respect to a name or description; reaching the specified or usual limit; (of moon) having disc completely illuminated; (of face etc.) entirely visible to spectator; ~ *age*, age attained after minority; ~ *brother, sister*, one born of same father and mother. 5. (of light) Intense; (of colour) deep; (of motion etc.) vigorous. 6. Swelling, plump, protuberant; (of dress) containing superfluity of material arranged in gathers or folds. 7. *~-back*, (footb. etc.) position, player, behind half-backs; *~-blooded*, vigorous, hearty, sensual; *~-bodied*, esp. of wine, with much body; *~-bottomed*, (of wig) long behind; ~ *dress*: see DRESS; *~-dress debate*, formal or prearranged debate on important subject; ~ *hand*, (poker) hand containing three of a kind and a pair; also called ~ *house*; ~ *pitch*, (cricket) ball bowled to reach wicket without first touching ground; ~ *score*, (mus.) complete score, comprising music for all performers. ~ *n.* Whole; point or state of greatest fullness; entire amount or range; *in* ~, without abridgement; *to the* ~, to the utmost extent, quite. ~ *adv.* Very (chiefly poet.); quite, fully; exactly; more than sufficiently; *~-grown*, having reached maturity. **fu'llnėss** *n.*

full[2] (fŏŏl) *v.t.* Tread or beat (cloth) to cleanse and thicken it; cleanse and thicken (cloth etc.).

fu'ller[1] (fŏŏ-) *n.* One who fulls cloth; *~'s earth*, absorbent clay containing hydrated silica and alumina, used in cleansing cloth and purifying oils and fats.

fu'ller[2] (fŏŏ-) *n.* Grooved tool on which iron is shaped by being driven into the grooves; groove made by this. ~ *v.t.* Stamp with fuller.

fu'llȳ (fŏŏ-) *adv.* Completely, without deficiency; quite; *~-fashioned*, (of garment) shaped to fit closely.

fu'lmar (fŏŏ-) *n.* Arctic sea-bird,

Fulmarus glacialis, of shearwater kind, about size of gull, noted for its easy gliding flight by sea cliffs.

fŭ'lmĭnant *adj.* Fulminating; (path., of diseases) developing suddenly.

fŭ'lmĭnāte *v.* 1. Flash like lightning; explode, detonate. 2. Thunder forth, utter or publish, (censure); issue (usu. official) censures *against*. **fŭlmĭnā'tion** *n.* **fŭ'lmĭnatorȳ** *adj.* **fŭ'lmĭnate** *n.* Salt of fulminic acid; ~ *of mercury*, very sensitive explosive, $Hg(ONC)_2$, used in detonators.

fŭlmĭ'nĭc *adj.* ~ *acid*, isomer of cyanic acid, forming explosive salts with some metals.

fu'lnėss (fŏŏ-) *n.* = FULLNESS.

fu'lsome (fŏŏ-) *adj.* (of flattery, servility, etc.) Cloying, excessive, disgusting by excess. **fu'lsomelȳ** *adv.* **fu'lsomenėss** *n.*

fŭ'lvous *adj.* Reddish-yellow, tawny.

fū'marōle *n.* Hole in earth's crust through which gases and vapour issue.

fŭ'mble *v.* Use the hands awkwardly, grope about; handle or deal with awkwardly or nervously. ~ *n.* Bungling attempt. **fŭ'mbler** *n.*

fūme *n.* (esp. pl.) Odorous smoke, vapour, or exhalation; fit of anger. ~ *v.* 1. Fumigate; perfume with incense; expose (wood, esp. oak etc.) to fumes of ammonia to darken tints; emit fumes. 2. Be pettish; chafe, fret. **fū'mȳ** *adj.*

fū'mĭgāte *v.t.* Apply fumes to; disinfect or purify with fumes; perfume. **fūmĭgā'tion, fū'mĭgātor** *ns.*

fū'mĭtorȳ *n.* Plant of genus *Fumaria*, esp. *F. officinalis*, formerly used in medicine as an antiscorbutic. [med. L *fumus terrae* earth-smoke]

fŭn *n.* Sport, amusement; jocularity, drollery; *make ~ of, poke ~ at*, ridicule; ~ *fair*, fair devoted to amusements.

fūnă'mbūlĭst *n.* Rope-walker.

fŭ'nction *n.* 1. Activity proper to person or institution; mode of action by which thing fulfils its purpose. 2. Social meeting of formal or important kind. 3. (math.) Variable quantity regarded in relation to other(s) in terms of which it may be expressed or on whose value its own depends. ~ *v.i.* Fulfil a function, operate, act.

fŭ'nctional *adj.* 1. Of a function or functions. 2. (physiol.) Of, affecting, only the functions of an organ etc., not structural or organic (esp. of diseases). 3. (math.) Of a function. 4. (of building etc.) Shaped, constructed, with regard only to its function, not to traditional or other theories of design. **fŭ'nctionalĭsm** *n.* **fŭ'nctionalĭst** *adj.* & *n.* **fŭ'nctionallȳ** *adv.*

fŭ'nctionarȳ *n.* One with certain functions or duties to perform, official. ~ *adj.* = FUNCTIONAL, 2.

fŭnd *n.* Permanent stock of something ready to be drawn upon; stock of money, esp. one set apart for a purpose; (pl.) pecuniary resources; *in ~s*, in possession of money; *the ~s*, stock of national debt, considered as mode of investment. ~ *v.t.* Convert (floating debt) into more or less permanent debt at fixed interest; invest (money) in the funds.

fŭ'ndament *n.* Buttocks.

fŭndamĕ'ntal *adj.* 1. Of the groundwork, going to the root of the matter, serving as base or foundation; essential, primary, original; from which others are derived. 2. (mus., of a note) That is the lowest note of a chord in its original (uninverted) form; (of a chord) with the root as the lowest note; (of a tone) that is produced by the vibration of the whole of a sonorous body (as dist. from *harmonics*). **fŭndamĕ'ntal, fŭndamĕntă'lĭtȳ** *ns.* Principle, rule, article, serving as groundwork of system (usu. pl.); (mus.) fundamental note or tone. **fŭndamĕ'ntallȳ** *adv.*

fŭndamĕ'ntalĭsm *n.* Strict adherence to traditional orthodox (Protestant) tenets (e.g. the literal inerrancy of Scripture), held to be fundamental to Christianity; adherence to traditional beliefs of any kind. **fŭndamĕ'ntalĭst** *n.*

fŭ'ndus *n.* (physiol.) Lowest part of stomach or other hollow organ, part farthest removed from its opening; ~ *oculi*, interior region of back of eyeball.

fū'neral *adj.* Of, used, carried, etc., at burial or cremation of the dead; ~ *pile, pyre*, pile of wood, etc., on which corpse is burnt; ~ *urn*, urn holding ashes of cremated body. ~ *n.* Burial of the dead with its ceremonies etc., obsequies; burial procession; (U.S.) funeral service.

fū'nerarȳ *adj.* Of funeral or burial.

fūnēr'ėal *adj.* Appropriate to funeral, gloomy, dark. **fūnēr'ėallȳ** *adv.*

fŭ'ngĭble (-j-) *adj.* (law) That can serve for, or be replaced by, another answering to the same description (of goods etc., contracted for, when an individual specimen is not meant).

fŭ'ngĭcīde (-j-) *n.* Fungus-destroying substance. **fŭngĭcī'dal** *adj.*

fŭ'ngoid (-ngg-) *adj.* Fungus-like.

fŭ'ngous (-ngg-) *adj.* Of fungi, having nature of a fungus; springing up like a mushroom, transitory.

fŭ'ngus (-ngg-) *n.* (pl. *-gi* pr. -gī *or* -jī, *-uses*). 1. Mushroom, toadstool, or one of the allied plants, including the various moulds; (bot.) cryptogamous plant without chlorophyll deriving its substance from organic matter. 2. (path.) Spongy morbid growth or excrescence. **fŭ'ngal** *adj.*

fūnĭ'cūlar *adj.* Of a rope or its tension; depending on or worked by a rope; ~ *railway*, cable railway in which ascending and descending cars are counterbalanced. ~ *n.* Funicular railway.

fŭnk *n.* (slang) Fear, panic; coward; *blue* ~, terror. ~ *v.* Flinch, shrink, show cowardice; fight shy of, (try to) evade; be afraid of.

fŭ'nnel *n.* 1. Narrowing tube, cone-shaped vessel with tube at apex, for conducting liquid, powder, etc., into small opening. 2. Lighting or ventilating shaft; metal chimney of steam-engine, ship, etc.; funnel-shaped lower part of chimney.

fŭ'nnȳ[1] *adj.* Affording fun, comical; queer, perplexing; ~ *bone*, part of elbow over which ulnar nerve passes (from peculiar sensation experienced when it is struck). **fŭ'nnĭlȳ** *adv.* **fŭ'nnĭnėss** *n.*

fŭ'nnȳ[2] *n.* Narrow clinker-built pleasure-boat for one pair of sculls.

fûr *n.* 1. Trimming or lining made of dressed coat of certain animals (as ermine, beaver, fox, etc.) or imitation of this; coat of such animals as material for trimming, lining, etc.; (usu. pl.) garment(s) of or trimmed with fur. 2. Short fine soft hair of certain animals as distinct from the longer and coarser hair; (pl.) skins of such animals with the fur; (collect.) furred animals. 3. (her.) Tincture representing tufts on plain ground, or patches of different colour supposed to be sewn together. 4. Crust of mould, deposit from wine, etc., adhering to surface like fur; coating formed on tongue in some diseased conditions of body; coating chiefly of carbonates formed by hard water in kettle, boiler, etc. **fûrr'ȳ** *adj.* **fûr** *v.* 1. Trim, line, cover, with fur (only in past part.); coat (tongue, kettle, etc.), become coated, with fur. 2. (carpentry) Fix strips of wood to (floor-timbers, rafters, etc.), level them thus.

fur. *abbrev.* Furlong.

fûr'bėlow (-ō) *n.* Gathered strip or other trimming. esp. on 17th-18th c. dress; (pl., contempt.) showy ornament or trimming. ~ *v.t.* Adorn with furbelows.

fûr'bĭsh *v.t.* Remove rust from, polish *up*, burnish; give new look to, renovate, revive.

fûr'cāte (*or* -at) *adj.* Forked, branched. **furcā'te** *v.i.* Form a fork, divide.

fūr'ĭous *adj.* Full of fury, raging, frantic, violent; *fast and* ~, (of mirth etc.) uproarious, eager. **fūr'ĭouslȳ** *adv.*

fûrl *v.* Roll up and tie (sail) on yard or boom; roll or gather up,

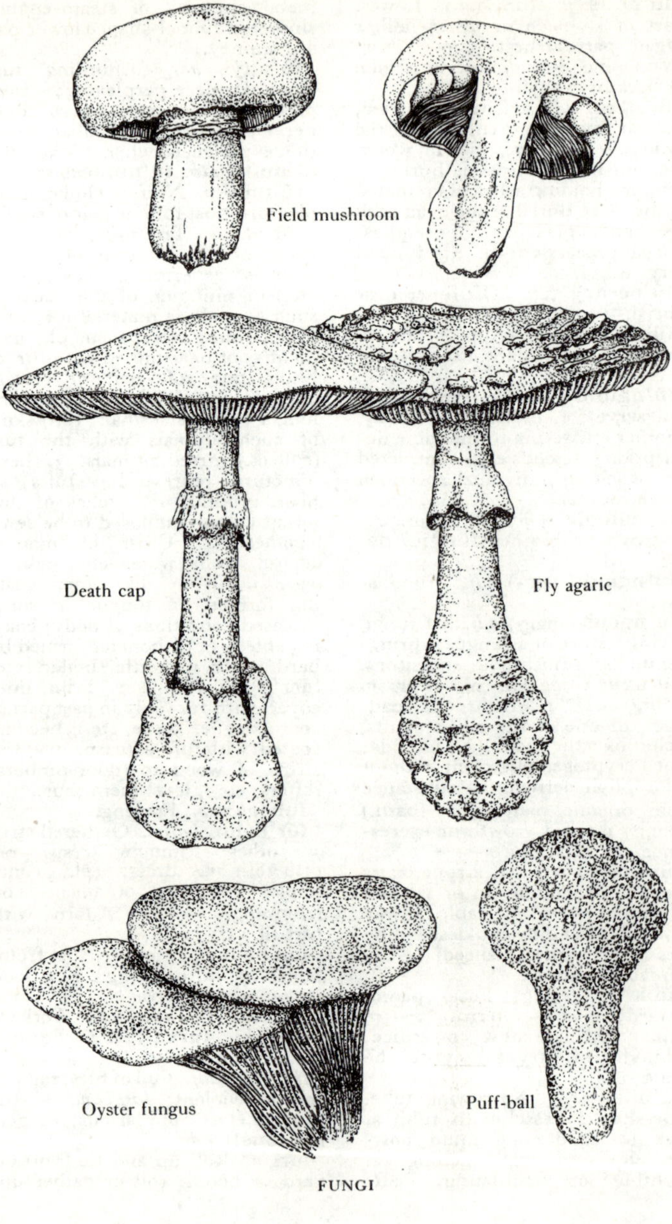
Field mushroom
Death cap
Fly agaric
Oyster fungus
Puff-ball

FUNGI

close, fold up; become furled; roll away like clouds.

fûr'long *n.* Measure of length, ⅛ mile or 220 yards. [OE *furlang*, f. *furh* furrow and *lang* long]

fûr'lough (-lō) *n.* Leave of absence, esp. to soldier. ~ *v.t.* Grant furlough to.

furmety: see FRUMENTY.

fûr'nace (-ĭs) *n.* Apparatus containing chamber for combustibles in which minerals, metals, etc., may be subjected to continuous action of intense heat; closed fireplace for heating water to warm building etc.; (fig.) hot place; (fig.) severe test.

fûr'nish *v.t.* Provide *with*; fit up (house, room) with all necessary appliances, esp. movable furniture; provide, afford, yield; *fur'nishing* (*n.*, esp. pl.) articles of furniture or other things required to furnish a house etc.

fûr'nĭture *n.* Movable articles (as tables, chairs) for use or ornament in house or room; equipment, esp. rigging, stores, tackle, etc., of ship.

fūrôr'ė *n.* 1. Enthusiastic admiration. 2. Uproar.

fŭ'rrĭer *n.* Dealer in, dresser of, furs. **fŭ'rrĭerȳ** *n.*

fûrr'ĭng *n.* (esp.) Doubling of planks on ship's side, timber used for this.

fŭ'rrow (-ō) *n.* Narrow trench made in earth with plough; ship's track; rut, track, groove, long indentation; deep wrinkle; ~*-slice*, slice of earth turned up by mouldboard of plough. ~ *v.t.* Plough; make furrows, grooves, etc., in; mark with wrinkles.

fûr'ther (-dh-) *adv.* To or at more advanced point in space or time; to greater extent, more; (also *fur'thermore*) in addition; at greater distance. ~ *adj.* Going beyond what exists or has been dealt with, additional; more distant; ~ *education*, education organized for persons above school age. ~ *v.t.* Help on, promote, favour. **fûr'therance** *n.* **fûr'thermōst** *adj.*

fûr'thėst (-dh-) *adj.* & *adv.* = FARTHEST.

fûr'tĭve *adj.* Stealthy, sly; taken secretly. **fûr'tĭvelȳ** *adv.* **fûr'tĭvenėss** *n.*

fûr'uncle *n.* = BOIL[1]. **fūrŭ'ncūlar, fūrŭ'ncūlous** *adjs.*

fūr'ȳ *n.* 1. Fierce passion, wild anger; fierce impetuosity or violence. 2. *F* ~, (Gk myth.) one of the snake-haired goddesses (esp. Alecto, Megaera, Tisiphone) sent from Tartarus to avenge wrong and punish crime; (fig.) avenging or tormenting spirit. 3. Virago, angry or malignant woman.

fûrze *n.* Gorse. **fûr'zȳ** *adj.*

fŭ'scous *adj.* Sombre, dark in colour.

fūse[1] (-z) *v.* Melt with intense heat; blend, amalgamate, into one whole (as) by melting; (of electric light etc.) be put out of action by melting of fuse; cause fuse(s) of (electric circuit) to melt. ~ *n.* Strip or wire of easily-fused metal in electric circuit which melts and so interrupts the circuit if current increases beyond a certain limit. **fū'sĭble** *adj.* **fūsĭbĭ'lĭtȳ** *n.*

fūse[2] (-z), **fūze** *n.* Tube, casing, cord, etc., filled or saturated with combustible matter for igniting blasting-charge, bomb, etc.; component screwed into shell, mine, etc., designed to detonate explosive charge either after an interval (*time-*~) or on impact, or when subjected to magnetic, vibratory, or other stimulation. ~ *v.t.* Fit fuse to.

fūsee' (-z-) *n.* 1. Conical pulley or wheel, esp. wheel in watch or clock on which chain is wound and which equalizes power of mainspring. 2. Large-headed match for use in wind.

fū'sėlage (-z-; *or* -ahzh) *n.* Body or framework of aeroplane.

fū'sel-oil (-z-) *n.* Mixture of several alcohols, chiefly amyl, sometimes produced, usu. in small amounts, during fermentation of alcoholic liquor and making it harmful or poisonous. [Ger. *fusel* or Du. *foezel* bad spirit]

fū'sĭfôrm (-z-) *adj.* Shaped like spindle, tapering towards each end.

fū'sĭl (-z-) *n.* (hist.) Light musket or firelock.

fūsĭlier′ (-z-) *n.* (usu. pl.) (Man of) certain British infantry regiments formerly armed with fusils.

fūsĭllā′de (-z-) *n.* (Wholesale execution by) continuous discharge of firearms. ~ *v.t.* Assault (place), shoot down (persons), by fusillade.

fū′sion *n.* Fusing; fused mass; blending of different things into one; coalition; (phys.) energy-releasing union of atomic nuclei to form heavier nucleus.

fŭss *n.* Bustle, excessive commotion, ostentatious or nervous activity; treatment of trifles as important; abundance of petty detail; (colloq.) person who is always making a fuss (also ~-*pot*). ~ *v.* Make fuss; busy oneself restlessly with trifles; move fussily *about*, etc., agitate, worry (person). **fŭ′ssȳ** *adj.* **fŭ′ssilȳ** *adv.* **fŭ′ssinėss** *n.*

fŭstanĕ′lla *n.* Stiff full white skirt worn by men in Albania and some parts of modern Greece.

fŭ′stĭan *n.* 1. Thick twilled cotton cloth with short nap, resembling velveteen, usu. dyed in dark dull colours. 2. Bombast. ~ *adj.* Made of fustian; bombastic, worthless.

fŭ′stĭc *n.* Either of two woods yielding yellow dye: *Chlorophora tinctoria* of America and the W. Indies, and (*young* or *Zante* ~) the Venetian sumach, *Rhus cotinus*; dye from these. [Arab. *fustuq* f. Gk *pistakē* pistachio]

fŭ′stĭgāte *v.t.* (joc.) Cudgel.

fŭ′stȳ *adj.* Stale-smelling, musty; stuffy; old-fashioned. **fŭ′stinėss** *n.*

fŭ′tchel, -ll *n.* One of timbers supporting shafts, pole, or axle-bar, of carriage.

fū′tīle (U.S. -ĭl) *adj.* Useless, ineffectual, vain, frivolous. **fūtĭ′lĭtȳ** *n.* **fū′tīlelȳ** *adv.*

fŭ′ttock *n.* One of middle timbers of sailing ship's frame, between floor and top timbers; ~-*plate*, iron plate across top of a lower mast to which the dead-eyes of the top-mast rigging and the upper ends of the futtock-shrouds are secured; ~-*shroud*, short, usu. iron, shroud securing futtock-plates of topmast rigging to band round lower mast.

fū′ture *adj.* About to happen; that will be hereafter; of time to come; (gram., of tense) relating to time to come. ~ *n.* Time to come; what will happen in the future; person's, country's, etc., prospective condition; (gram.) future tense; (commerc., pl.) goods and stocks sold for future delivery, contracts for these. **fū′turelėss** *adj.*

fū′turĭst (-cher-) *n.* 1. (theol.) One believing that prophecies of Apocalypse etc. are still to be fulfilled. 2. Adherent of futurism. **fūturĭ′stĭc** *adj.* **fū′turĭsm** *n.* Artistic and literary movement begun *c* 1909 in Italy, marked by violent departure from traditional methods and attempting to represent nature not in a static but a dȳnamic state.

fūtūr′ĭtȳ *n.* Future time; future events; future condition, existence after death; ~-*stakes*, (U.S.) stakes to be raced for long after the nominations or entries are made.

fuze: see FUSE[2].

fŭzz[1] *n.* Loose volatile matter, fluff; fluffy or frizzed hair. **fŭ′zzȳ** *adj.* Frayed, fluffy; blurred, indistinct; frizzed; ~-*wuzzy*, fuzzy.

fŭzz[2] *n.* (slang) Policeman; (collect.) the police.

f.w.d. *abbrev.* Front- (or four-) wheel drive.

fȳ′lfot *n.* Swastika.

F.Z.S. *abbrev.* Fellow of the Zoological Society.

G

G, g (jē). 1. 7th letter of modern English and ancient Roman alphabet, orig. differentiated form of C, representing in English a voiced postpalatal stop (*hard g*) except in some words, chiefly of French, Latin, or Greek origin, before *e* or *i*, where it is equivalent to the composite sound (*j*). 2. *G*, (mus.) 5th note of natural scale (C major); scale or key with this note for tonic; *G clef*: see CLEF.

G *abbrev.* Gauss; giga-.

g. *abbrev.* Gramme(s); (acceleration due to) gravity.

Ga. *abbrev.* Georgia.

găb *n.* (fam.) Talk, prattle, twaddle; *gift of the* ~, talent for speaking; loquacity.

gă'bardine (-ēn) *n.* Twill-woven cloth of worsted, cotton, or rayon.

gă'bble *v.* Talk volubly or inarticulately; read aloud, utter, too fast. ~ *n.* Rapid esp. unintelligible talk.

gă'bbrō *n.* Dark-coloured coarsely crystalline igneous rock made up of plagioclase felspar, pyroxene, and magnetite.

gabĕ'lle *n.* (hist.) Tax; esp. salt-tax in France before Revolution.

gă'berdine (-ēn) *n.* 1. Long loose upper garment formerly worn by Jews in Europe, almsmen, etc. 2. = GABARDINE.

gā'bion *n.* Cylinder of wicker or woven metal bands to be filled with earth or stones for use in fortification or engineering. **gābionā'de** *n.* Line of gabions.

gā'ble *n.* Vertical triangular upper part of wall at end of ridged roof, from level of eaves upwards; (also ~*-end*) gable-topped end wall of building; gable-shaped canopy over window or door. **gā'bled** (-bld) *adj.*

gaboō'n[1] *n.* Fine-grained wood, resembling mahogany, of African tropical tree, esp. *Aucoumea klaineana.* [f. GABOON[2]]

Gaboō'n[2]. Republic in W. Africa; member of the French Community; independent since 1960; capital, Libreville. **Găbonē'se** (-z) *adj.* & *n.*

Gā'briel. One of the seven archangels enumerated in the 'Book of Enoch', a messenger of God (Dan. 8: 9, Luke 1); in Muslim religion, one of the four principal angels.

gā'bȳ *n.* Simpleton.

găd[1] *v.i.* (usu. ~ *about*) Go *about* seeking entertainment; rove, wander.

Găd[2]. Hebrew patriarch, son of Jacob and Zilpah (Gen. 30: 11); tribe of Israel, traditionally descended from him.

gă'dabout *adj.* & *n.* (Person) given to gadding about.

gă'dflȳ *n.* Fly which bites and goads cattle, esp. one of the genera *Tabanus* (horse-fly) or *Oestrus* (bot-fly); (fig.) irritating or harassing person.

gă'dgėt *n.* (orig. naut.) Small fitting, contrivance, or piece of mechanism; device.

Gadhe'lic (-dĕ-) *adj.* & *n.* Gaelic (in widest sense).

gă'doid *adj.* & *n.* (Fish) of the cod family (Gadidae).

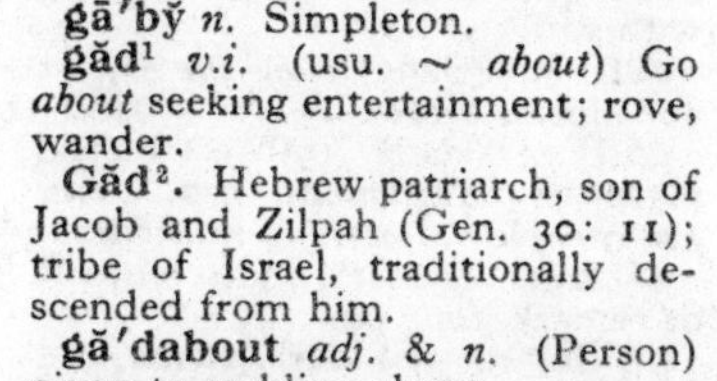

Crow-stepped gable Dutch gable

GABLE

gă'dolinīte *n.* (min.) Black or brown vitreous mineral containing silicates of yttrium, terbium, erbium, etc., a source of rare-earth elements. [J. *Gadolin* (1760–1852), Finnish mineralogist]

gădolĭ'nium *n.* (chem.) Metallic element of rare-earth group, found in gadolinite etc.; symbol Gd, at. no. 64, at. wt 157·25.

gadrōō'n *n.* Convex fluting as ornament on silverware etc. ~ *v.t.* Decorate with gadroon.

Gael (gāl) *n.* Scottish or Irish Celt. **Gae'lic** *adj.* & *n.* (Language) of the Celtic inhabitants of Scottish highlands, or of the branch of Celts including Scottish, Irish, and Manx Celts.

găff[1] *n.* 1. Barbed fishing-spear; stick with iron hook for landing large fish. 2. (naut.) Spar used to extend fore-and-aft sails which are not set on stays. ~ *v.t.* Seize (fish) with gaff.

găff[2] *n.* (slang) *blow the* ~, let out plot or secret.

găff[3] *n.* (slang, 19th c.) Public place of amusement, esp. (usu. *penny* ~) low theatre or music hall.

găffe *n.* Blunder, indiscreet act or remark, *faux pas.*

gă'ffer *n.* 1. Elderly rustic, old fellow. 2. Foreman of gang of workmen. [contr. of *godfather*, *ga-* by assoc. w. *grandfather*]

găg *n.* 1. Thing thrust into mouth to prevent speech or outcry, or to hold it open for operation, etc.; (parl.) closure, GUILLOTINE. 2. (theatr.) Actor's interpolations in dramatic dialogue. 3. Joke. ~ *v.* Apply gag to; silence, deprive of free speech; (of actor etc.) make gag.

gă'ga (*or* gah'gah) *n.* Senile, doting; silly, inane, fatuous.

gāge[1] *n.* Pledge, thing deposited as security; (glove thrown down as, any symbol of) challenge to fight.

gage[2]**:** see GAUGE.

gāge[3] *n.* = GREENGAGE.

gă'ggle *n.* Flock (of geese). ~ *v.i.* (of geese) Make clucking sound.

Gaia: see GE.

gai'ėtў *n.* Being gay, mirth; merrymaking, festivity; bright or showy appearance.

gaillar'dia *n.* Showy-flowered composite plant of genus *G*~. [*Gaillard* de Marentonneau, Fr. botanist]

gaily: see GAY[1].

gain *n.* Increase of possessions, advantage, etc., of any kind; profit, improvement; acquisition of wealth; increase in amount; (pl.) sums acquired by trade etc., emoluments, winnings. ~ *v.* Obtain, secure (desired or advantageous thing); win (sum) as profits etc.; earn; make a profit, be benefited, improve or advance *in* some respect; be enhanced *by* comparison or contrast; reclaim (land) from sea etc.; win (battle, victory); bring over to one's interests or views; reach, arrive at (desired place); (of clock etc.) become fast (by); ~ *the ear of*, get favourable hearing from; ~ *on*, get closer to (person or thing pursued); ~ *time*, obtain delay by pretexts or slow methods.

gai'nful *adj.* Lucrative, remunerative; (of occupation etc.) paid. **gai'nfullў** *adv.*

gainsay' *v.t.* (past t. & past part.-*said* pr.-ĕd). Deny, contradict.

Gai'nsborough(-zbro), Thomas (1727–88). English painter; famous esp. for portraits.

gait *n.* Manner of walking; bearing or carriage as one walks.

gai'ter *n.* Covering of cloth, leather, etc., for ankle, or ankle and lower leg.

gal. *abbrev.* Gallon(s).

Gal. *abbrev.* Galatians (N.T.).

gā'la (*or* gah-) *n.* Festive occasion, fête.

gală'ctic *adj.* (astron.) Of a galaxy; of the Milky Way.

gă'lăctōse *n.* Sugar ($C_6H_{12}O_6$) obtained by hydrolysis of lactose and having properties very similar to those of glucose.

galā'gō *n.* (pl. *-gos*). Small Afr. nocturnal tree-climbing animal of genus *G*~, with large eyes and ears and long tail, closely related to lemur and loris, bush-baby.

Gă'lahăd (-a-h-), **Sir.** In Arthurian legend, knight of immaculate purity, destined to retrieve the Holy Grail.

gă'lantine (-ēn) *n.* Dish of white meat boned, cut up, boiled, and served cold in jelly.

gă'lantў show (-ō). (19th c.) Shadow pantomime made by throwing shadows of puppets on screen.

Gălatē'a. (Gk myth.) Sea-nymph, courted by Polyphemus who in jealousy killed his rival Acis with a rock.

Galā'tia (-sha). Ancient region of central Asia Minor.

Galā'tian (-shan) *adj.* Of Galatia. ~ *n.* One of its inhabitants, believed to have been Gauls who settled there in the 3rd c. B.C.; (*Epistle to the*) ~*s*, book of N.T., epistle of St. Paul to the Church at Galatia.

gă'laxў *n.* 1. One of the independent systems of stars and other matter existing in space, esp. (*G*~) group containing the solar system. 2. *G*~, Milky Way. 3. (fig.) Brilliant company or assemblage (*of*). [Gk *gala* milk]

gă'lbanum *n.* Gum resin obtained from certain Asian plants of genus *Ferula*, used as a stimulant in bronchitis.

gāle[1] *n.* (also *sweet* ~) Bog-myrtle.

gāle[2] *n.* 1. Strong wind; (naut.) storm; (meteor.) wind of velocity between 34 and 40 knots (force 8 in the BEAUFORT scale); ~ *warning*, notice of probability of gales (force 8 or more) issued by Meteorological Office. 2. Gust, outburst, esp. of laughter.

gāle[3] *n.* Periodical (payment of) rent; *hanging* ~, rent due at previous gale-day; ~-*day*, rent-day.

gā'lea *n.* (zool.) Structure like helmet in shape, function, or posi-

GAINSBOROUGH: The artist and his family

tion; (esp.) outer lobe of insect's maxilla.

galee'ný *n.* Guinea-fowl.

Gā'len. Claudius Galenus (129–99), Greek physician and writer on medicine; practised in Rome; physician to emperor Marcus Aurelius. **Galē'nic, Galĕ'nical** *adjs.* Of, according to, Galen; (of remedies) made of vegetable, not chemical, components.

galē'na *n.* (min.) Lead sulphide, the common lead-ore (PbS).

Gali'cia[1] (-ēshĭa). Province of NW. Spain. **Gali'cian** *adj.* & *n.*

Gali'cia[2] (-ĭshĭa). Former Austrian crown-land, now divided between Poland and U.S.S.R.

Gă'lilee[1]. Northern part of ancient Palestine, west of the Jordan (now in Israel). **Gălilē'an**[1] *adj.* & *n.* *the* ~, Jesus Christ.

gă'lilee[2] *n.* Porch or chapel at entrance of church. [f. GALILEE[1]]

Gălilē'ō (*or* -ā'ō). Galileo Galilei (1564–1642), Italian astronomer and physicist; discovered

the four most prominent satellites of Jupiter, the libration of the moon, etc.; his observations brought him into conflict with the Inquisition and he was compelled to repudiate the Copernican theory. **Gălilē'an**[2] *adj.* (of telescope) Of the form invented by Galileo, a refracting telescope with concave eyepiece.

gă'lingāle (-ngg-) *n.* 1. Aromatic rhizome of E. Asian plant of genera *Alpinia* and *Kaempferia*, formerly much used in medicine and cookery. 2. English species of sedge, *Cyperus longus*, with root of similar properties. [Arab. *Khaulinjān*, perh. ult. f. Chin. *ko-liang-kiang* 'mild ginger from Ko' (in Canton)]

gă'lipŏt *n.* Turpentine or resin exuding from and hardening on stem of certain pines.

gall[1] (gawl) *n.* Bitter greenish secretion of the liver, bile (now only of lower animals); gall-bladder and its contents; (fig.) anything bitter; asperity, rancour; (U.S.) impudence; ~ *bladder*, vessel containing the gall or bile; *ga'llstone*, morbid calculus in gall-bladder.

gall[2] (gawl) *n.* Painful swelling, pustule, blister, esp. in horse; sore produced by chafing; mental soreness or irritation; something galling or exasperating; place rubbed bare; (southern U.S.) place where soil is washed away or exhausted. ~ *v.* Rub sore, injure by rubbing; vex, humiliate. **ga'lling** *adj.*

gall[3] (gawl) *n.* (also *ga'llnut*) Excrescence produced on trees by

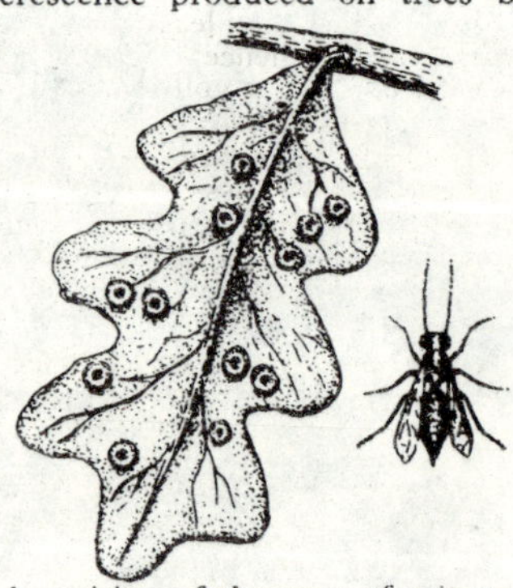

deposition of the eggs of mites or insects, e.g. oak-apple (*oak-*~); *ga'llfly* insect causing galls.

Gă'lla *n.* One of a group of Hamitic tribes of equatorial Africa, allied to Ethiopians in language and origin.

gă'llant *adj.* 1. Fine, stately (esp. of ship, horse, etc.). 2. Brave, chivalrous (also parl., as conventional epithet of member belonging to armed forces, as *the honourable and ~ member*). 3. (freq. pron. *gală'nt*) Markedly attentive to women; amatory. **gă'llantlў** *adv.* **gă'llant** (*or gală'nt*) *n.* (archaic) Man of fashion; ladies' man; paramour. **gallă'nt** *v.* Play the gallant, flirt (with); escort, act as cavalier to.

gă'llantrў *n.* 1. Bravery, dashing courage. 2. Courtliness, devotion to women; polite or amorous act or speech; conduct of a gallant, amorous intrigue or intercourse.

gă'llėon *n.* (hist.) Vessel shorter but higher than galley; ship of war (esp. Spanish); large Spanish ship used in trade with America.

gă'llerў *n.* 1. Covered space for walking in partly open at side, portico, colonnade; balcony; long narrow passage in thickness of wall or supported on corbels, open towards interior of building. 2. Platform projecting from inner wall of church, hall, etc., providing extra room for spectators etc. or reserved for musicians etc.; highest of such balconies in theatre, containing cheapest seats; persons seated there, least refined part of audience; group of spectators at golf-match or other game; *play to the ~*, appeal to lower taste. 3. Long narrow room, passage, corridor; room or building used for showing works of art. 4. (mil., mining) Underground horizontal or nearly horizontal passage. 5. Ornamental parapet or railing along edge of table shelf, etc.~ *v.t.* Provide piece, etc., with gallery or galleries.

gă'lley *n.* 1. (chiefly hist.) Low flat single-decked sea-going vessel using sails and oars, and usu. rowed by slaves or criminals (*~-slaves*). 2. Greek or Roman warship with one or more banks of oars. 3. Large open rowing-boat, e.g. that used by captain of man-of-war. 4. Ship's or aircraft's kitchen. 5. (print.) Oblong tray for holding type which has been set; corresponding part of composing machine. 6. (also *~-proof*) Proof in slip form from type in galley.

gă'llĭard *n.* (hist.) Quick and lively 16th- and 17th-c. dance in triple time; music for this.

gă'llĭc[1] *adj.* *~ acid*, white crystalline substance ($C_6H_2(OH)_3COOH$) present in oak-gall, tea, and other vegetable products, used in the manufacture of inks.

Gă'llĭc[2] *adj.* 1. Of the Gauls or Gaul, Gaulish. 2. French. **Gă'llĭcism** *n.* French idiom. **gă'llĭcīze** *v.*

Gă'llĭcan *adj.* & *n.* Of the ancient Church of Gaul or France; (adherent) of the school of French Roman Catholics which maintained the right of the French Church to be in certain respects free from papal control (opp. ULTRAMONTANE). **Gă'llĭcanism** *n.*

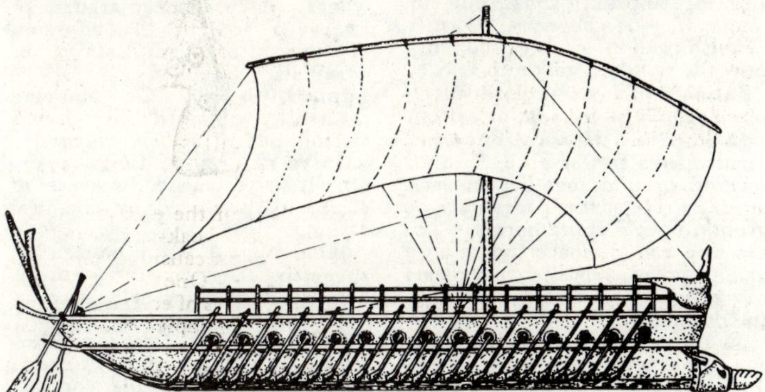

GREEK GALLEY

găllĭgă'skĭns (-z) *n.pl.* Wide hose or breeches of 16th–17th centuries. [Fr. *garguesque*, f. It. *grechesca* Greek]

găllĭmau'frȳ *n.* Heterogeneous mixture, jumble, medley.

găllĭnā'ceous (-sh*u*s) *adj.* (zool.) Of the order Galliformes, including domestic poultry, pheasants, partridges, turkeys, guinea-fowl, etc.

Gă'llĭō. Proconsul of Achaia who refused to try St. Paul when the Jews of Corinth accused him (Acts 18); hence, indifferent easy-going person.

gă'lliot *n.* Dutch cargo-boat or fishing-vessel; small (usu. Mediterranean) galley.

Gallĭ'poli. Peninsula between the Dardanelles and the Aegean where Allied troops were landed on 25 April 1915 (~ *Day*).

gă'llĭpŏt *n.* Small pot used for ointments etc. [prob. f. GALLEY, as brought in galleys from the Mediterranean]

gă'llĭum *n.* (chem.) Rare bluish-white metallic element found in some zinc and aluminium minerals, remarkable for its extremely low melting-point (29 °C); symbol Ga, at. no. 31, at. wt 69·72. [L *gallus* cock, transl. of *Lecoq* de Boisbaudran, its discoverer, 1875]

găllĭvă'nt *v.i.* Gad about.

gă'llon *n.* Measure of capacity for liquids, corn, etc., in Gt Britain, approx. 277½ cu. in. (*imperial* ~); *wine* ~, former English gallon of 231 cu. in., now the standard gallon in U.S.

gallōō'n *n.* Narrow close-woven braid of gold, silver, silk, or cotton.

gă'llop *n.* Horse's or other quadruped's fastest pace, with all feet off ground together in each stride; a ride at this pace; track or ground for galloping horses. ~ *v.* Go at a gallop; make (horse etc.) gallop; read, speak, very fast; move or progress rapidly. **gă'lloper** *n.*

gă'llophīle, -phĭl, gă'llophōbe *ns.* One who loves, hates, the French.

Gă'llo-Rō'man *adj.* & *n.* (Inhabitant) of Gaul when it formed part of Roman Empire.

Gă'lloway[1] (-*o*wā). District of SW. Scotland, since May 1975 part of the region of Dumfries and Galloway. [Welsh *Gallwyddel*, Ir. *Gallgaidhil*, foreign Gaels]

gă'lloway[2] (-*o*wā) *n.* Small strong horse, (one of) a breed of cattle, bred in Galloway.

gă'llows (-ōz) *n.pl.* (usu. treated as sing.) Structure, usu. of two uprights and cross-piece, on which criminals are hanged; similar structure for other uses; punishment of hanging; ~*-bird*, person fit to be hanged; ~*-tree*, gallows.

Gă'llup pōll. Vote on some matter of current interest taken from a cross-section of the inhabitants of a country or region in order to ascertain public opinion on that topic. [after G. H. *Gallup* (1901–), Amer. statistician]

gă'lop *n.* Lively dance in $\frac{2}{4}$ time. ~ *v.i.* Dance a galop.

galôr'e *adv.* & *n.* (In) abundance. [Ir. *go leór* to sufficiency]

galŏ'sh, golŏ'sh *n.* Overshoe usu. of rubber to keep shoes clean or dry; piece of leather etc. round lower part of boot or shoe above sole.

Galsworthy (gaw'lzwêrdhĭ), John (1867–1933). English novelist and playwright; author of 'The Forsyte Saga' etc.

Ga'lton (gawl-), Sir Francis (1822–1911). English scientist, whose work on the markings of fingertips led to the adoption of fingerprint identifications of criminals.

galŭ'mph *v.i.* Go prancing exultantly. [coined by Lewis Carroll, perh. f. *gallop, triumph*]

Gălva'ni (-vah-), Luigi (1737–98). Italian scientist; discoverer of electricity produced by chemical action.

gălvă'nĭc *adj.* Of, produced by, suggestive of, galvanism; ~ *battery*, battery of primary cells used in galvanism.

gă'lvanĭsm *n.* (hist.) 1. Electricity, usu. from a primary battery, used to produce muscular contractions and other effects. 2. Therapeutic application of such electricity to the tissues of the body.

gă'lvanīze *v.t.* 1. Stimulate by or as by electricity, rouse by shock or excitement. 2. Coat iron with zinc (usu. without the use of electricity) to protect it from rust. **gălvanīzā'tion** *n.*

gălvanŏ'mėter *n.* Apparatus for detecting and measuring strength of electric currents.

Ga'lway (gawl-). County of Connacht in W. Ireland.

Ga'ma (gah-), Vasco da (*c* 1469–1524). Portuguese navigator, who first doubled the Cape of Good Hope (1497) and sailed to India.

gă'mba *n.* Organ-stop of string tone. [short for *viola da gamba*]

gambā'de, gambā'dō *n.* (pl. *-os, -oes*). Horse's leap or bound; fantastic movement, freak, escapade.

Gămbĕ'tta, Léon (1838–82). French republican statesman; premier of France 1881–2.

Gă'mbia. (also *The* ~) W. African republic on river Gambia; member State of the Commonwealth; independent, 1965; capital, Banjul. **Gă'mbian** *adj.* & *n.*

gă'mbier *n.* Astringent extract of Eastern plant, *Uncaria gambir*, used in tanning etc. [Malay *gambir*, the plant]

gă'mbĭt *n.* Chess-opening in which player sacrifices pawn or pieces to obtain some advantage over opponent; opening move in discussion etc. [It. *gambetto* tripping up (*gamba* leg)]

gă'mble *v.* Play games of chance for money, esp. for high stakes (freq. fig.); ~ *away*, lose by gambling. ~ *n.* Gambling; risky undertaking or attempt. **gă'mbler** *n.*

gămbo'ge (-ōōzh) *n.* Gum resin from various Cambodian, Siamese, etc., trees of genus *Garcinia*, used as pigment giving bright-yellow colour. [f. *Cambodia*]

gă'mbol *n.* & *v.i.* Caper.

gāme[1] *n.* 1. Jest (only in *make* ~ *of*); diversion, pastime; piece of fun. 2. Contest played according to rules and decided by skill, strength, or luck; (pl., Gk & Rom. antiq.) athletic, dramatic, and musical contests, gladiatorial etc. shows; (pl.) organized athletics in school, etc. 3. Scheme, undertaking, etc., followed up like a game; policy, plan of action; (pl.) dodges, tricks. 4. Single round in some contests, e.g. whist or tennis; winning score in game; state of game. 5. Person's normal standard of play; *on, off, one's* ~, playing well, badly. 6. Object of chase, animal(s) hunted; object of pursuit; (collect.) wild animals or birds hunted for sport or food, flesh of these. 7. ~ *act, law*, act, law, regulating killing and preservation of game; *~-bag*, bag for holding game killed by sportsman; ~ *ball*, state of game in tennis etc., at which one side requires only one point to win; ~ *book*, book in which landowner etc. keeps detailed records of all game killed on estate; *ga'mecock*, cock bred and trained for fighting, or of breed suitable for cock-fighting; *ga'mekeeper*, man employed to take care of game, prevent poaching etc.; *ga'mesmanship*, art of winning unfairly but without breaking rules. ~ *adj.* Like a gamecock, spirited; having the spirit *to, for*. **gā'melȳ** *adv.* **gā'menėss** *n.* **gāme** *v.* Play at games of chance for money, gamble; throw *away* in gambling; *gaming-house*, house frequented for gambling; so *gaming-table*.

gāme[2] *adj.* (of limb) Lame, crippled.

gā'mesome (-ms-) *adj.* Sportive. **gā'mesomelȳ** *adv.* **gā'mesomenėss** *n.*

gā'mester (-ms-) *n.* Gambler.

gă'mēte *n.* Protoplasmic body capable of uniting with another to form new individual; mature sexual cell. **gamĕt'ic** *adj.*

gamin (gămăṅ) *n.* (fem. *-ine*, pr. -ēn) Urchin, impudent child. [Fr.]

gă'mma *n.* 1. 3rd letter of Greek alphabet (Γ, γ) corresponding to *g*, used in enumerations etc. 2. Moth, *Plusia gamma*, with γ-shaped silver marking on front wings. 3. ~ *globulin*, globulin fraction containing many antibodies present in the original serum; ~ *rays*, electromagnetic radiations of very short wavelength emitted by radioactive substances, orig. regarded as the 3rd and most penetrating kind of rays emitted by radium (see ALPHA, BETA) but now known to be identical with very short X-rays.

gă'mmer *n.* (Rustic name for) old woman. [contraction of *godmother*, *ga-* by assoc. w. *grandmother*]

gă'mmon[1] *n.* 1. Bottom piece of flitch of bacon including hind leg. 2. Smocked or cured ham; ~ *and spinach*, humbug (with pun on GAMMON[3]). ~ *v.t.* Cure (bacon) by salting and smoking.

gă'mmon[2] *n.* At backgammon, victory scoring two 'hits' or games, when one player removes all his men before his opponent removes any. ~ *v.t.* Beat (adversary) by a gammon.

gă'mmon[3] *n.* Humbug, deception. ~ *v.* Talk plausibly; hoax, deceive.

gă'mmon[4] *v.t.* (naut.) Lash (bowsprit) to stem of vessel. ~ *n.* Rope, chain used for gammoning.

gă'mmy̆ *adj.* (slang) = GAME[2].

gămp *n.* (joc.) Umbrella. [Mrs *Gamp*, monthly nurse who carried a large cotton umbrella, in Dickens's 'Martin Chuzzlewit']

gă'mut *n.* (mus.) Note G, at pitch of lowest line of present bass staff, i.e. lowest note in old system of hexachords (see HEXACHORD); by extension, whole series of notes in that system; whole series of notes used in music; (fig.) whole range of anything. [GAMMA, as name of lowest note in medieval music; and *ut*, name of the first note of the hexachord; see UT]

gā'mȳ *adj.* Abounding in game; having flavour or scent of game kept till it is high.

gă'nder *n.* Male goose.

Gandhi (gah'ndĭ), Mohandas Karamchand, called 'Mahatma' (1869–1948). Indian nationalist leader; originator of passive resistance as a form of political action.

găng[1] *n.* Group of labourers working together; group of slaves or prisoners; band of persons acting or going about together, esp. for criminal purpose or one disapproved of by speaker. ~ *v.i.* ~ *up* (*on*), (colloq.) combine (against).

găng[2] *v.i.* (Sc.) Go.

găng-board (-bôrd), **-plănk** *ns.* Plank, usu. with cleats on it, for walking into or out of boat.

gănge (-j) *v.t.* Protect (fish-hook, part of fishing-line) with fine wire.

gă'nger *n.* Foreman of gang of labourers.

Gă'nges (-jēz). River of India, held sacred by the Hindus, flowing from the Himalayas to the Bay of Bengal. **Găngĕ'tic** *adj.*

gă'ngling (-ngg-) *adj.* Loosely built, lanky.

gă'nglion (-ngg-) *n.* (pl. *-lia*). 1. Enlargement or knot on nerve forming centre for reception and transmission of impulses. 2. (path.) Cyst-like swelling on tendon. **gă'nglionātĕd, gănglĭŏ'nic** *adjs.*

gă'ngrēne (-ngg-) *n.* Local death of body-tissue caused by ob-

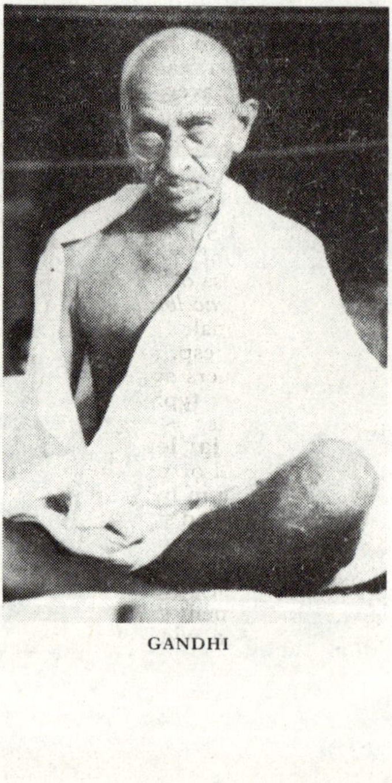

GANDHI

struction of the blood circulation. ~ *v.* Become affected, affect, with gangrene. **gă'ngrėnous** *adj.*

gă'ngster *n.* Member of gang of criminals. **gă'ngsterism** *n.*

găngue (-ng) *n.* Earthy or stony matter in mineral deposit, matrix in which ore is found.

gă'ngway *n.* Passage, esp. between rows of seats; in House of Commons, cross-passage half-way down giving access to back benches; passage etc. on ship, esp. platform connecting quarter-deck and forecastle; opening in bulwarks by which ship is entered or left, bridge laid across from this to shore etc.

gă'nnėt *n.* Any of several large white sea-birds of family Sulidae, with black-tipped wings and wedge-shaped tail.

gă'noid *adj.* (of fish-scales) Having many superficial layers of enamel-like substance and therefore shiny. ~ *n.* Fish with ganoid scales.

gă'ntrȳ *n.* Four-footed wooden stand for barrels; structure supporting travelling crane, railway signals, etc.

Gă'nȳmēde. 1. (Gk myth.) Trojan youth, so beautiful that Zeus caused an eagle to carry him up to heaven and made him his cup-bearer. 2. (astron.) Largest satellite of the planet Jupiter.

gaol (jāl), **jail** *n.* (*g*- in official use, *g*- and *j*- indifferently in literary use, *j*- in U.S.). Public prison for detention of persons committed by process of law; confinement in this; *gao'lbird*, prisoner, habitual criminal; ~ *delivery*, clearing of gaol esp. at assizes by trying all prisoners awaiting trial; ~ *fever*, virulent typhus formerly endemic in gaols. ~ *v.t.* Put in gaol. **gao'ler, jai'ler** *n.* Person in charge of gaol or prisoners.

găp *n.* Breach in hedge or wall; gorge, pass; unfilled space or interval, blank; break in continuity; wide divergence in views, sympathies, etc. **găpped** (-pt), **gă'ppȳ** *adjs.*

gāpe *v.i.* Open mouth wide; open or be open wide, split, part asunder; stare, gaze curiously, *at*; yawn. ~ *n.* Yawn; open-mouthed stare; expanse of open mouth or beak, part of beak that opens; ~*s*, disease of poultry and some wild birds constituted by the presence of *gape-worm* (*Syngamus trachea*) in the trachea, the obstruction caused by which makes the birds gape or gasp for breath.

gā'per *n.* (esp.) Bivalve mollusc with shell open at one or both ends.

gar̂ *n.* (also *gar'fish*, ~ *pike*) 1. Fish of family Belonidae, allied to flying fish; needlefish. 2. N. Amer. freshwater fish of the ganoid genus *Lepidosteus* with lozenge-shaped scales, bony pike; *alligator* ~, large species of this living in rivers of southern U.S. with head resembling alligator's.

gă'rage (*or* -ahzh) *n.* Building or establishment for storing or repair of vehicles, esp. motor-cars. ~ *v.t.* Put (motor-car etc.) into a garage.

Gă'ramond, Claude (d. 1561). French type-founder; hence, style of type resembling his.

gar̂b *n.* Dress, costume, esp. of distinctive kind; way one is dressed. ~ *v.t.* Attire, put (esp. distinctive) clothes upon.

gar̂'bage *n.* Kitchen waste; refuse; rubbish (also fig.).

gar̂'ble *v.t.* Make (usu. unfair or malicious) selections from (facts, statements, etc.), mutilate in order to misrepresent. [Arab. *ḡarbala* sift, select]

gar̂'board (-berd) *n.* (also ~ *strake*) First range of planks laid on boat's or ship's bottom next keel; corresponding plates in iron ship.

Gar̂ci'a Lor̂'ca (-thēa), Federico (1899–1936). Spanish poet and dramatist.

gar̂'dant *adj.* Var. of GUARDANT.

gar̂'den *n.* Piece of ground devoted to growing flowers, fruit, or vegetables; (pl.) ornamental grounds for public resort; region of special fertility (*the* ~ *of England*, name of various districts, esp. Kent); ~ *centre*, place where gardening requirements are sold; ~ *city*, town laid out systematically with open spaces, lawns, trees, etc., between the buildings; ~ *party*, social meeting on lawn or in garden; ~ *suburb*, suburb laid out like garden city. ~ *v.i.* Cultivate, work in, a garden. **gar'dener** *n.* One who gardens; person employed to tend garden.

gardē'nia *n.* Tree or shrub of genus *G~* of Cape of Good Hope and tropical Asia and Africa, bearing large white or yellow, usu. fragrant, flowers; flower of one of these. [Alexander *Garden* (d. 1791), vice-president of Royal Society]

gar'derōbe (-dr-) *n.* (hist.) Store-room, wardrobe; lavatory.

gar'efowl (-rf-) *n.* Great AUK.

Gar'field, James Abram (1831–81). 20th president of U.S. 1881.

garfish: see GAR.

gargă'ntūan *adj.* Enormous, gigantic. [*Gargantua*, large-mouthed voracious giant in Rabelais's satirical romance]

gar'gėt (-g-) *n.* Inflammation of cow's or ewe's udder.

gar'gle *v.* Wash (throat or mouth) with liquid held suspended in throat and kept in motion by breath; wash mouth or throat thus. ~ *n.* Liquid used for gargling.

gar'goyle *n.* Grotesque spout usu. with human or animal mouth, head, or body, projecting from gutter of (esp. Gothic) building to carry water clear of wall.

garial: see GHARIAL.

Găribă'ldĭ[1] (*or* -bawl-), Giuseppe (1807–82). Italian general and patriot; hero of the RISORGIMENTO; commanded a volunteer force on the Sardinian side in the campaign of 1859 against Austria; organized expeditions by which he conquered Sicily; expelled Francis II from Naples; and finally marched (unsuccessfully) against Rome, 1860–2.

gărĭbă'ldĭ[2] (*or* -bawl-) *n.* 1. (19th c.) Kind of woman's (orig. bright red) loose blouse in imitation of the red shirts of Garibaldi's followers. 2. (also ~ *biscuit*) Biscuit with a layer of currants.

gar'ĭsh *adj.* Obtrusively bright, gaudy. **gar'ĭshlў** *adv.* **gar'ĭshnėss** *n.*

gar'land *n.* Wreath of flowers, leaves, etc., worn on head or hung on something as decoration; distinction, palm, prize, for victory etc.; representation of garland in metal etc.; (archaic) anthology, miscellany. ~ *v.t.* Crown with garland; deck with garlands; serve as garland to.

gar'lĭc *n.* Plant of genus *Allium* (usu. *A. sativum*) with strong-smelling pungent-tasting bulbs

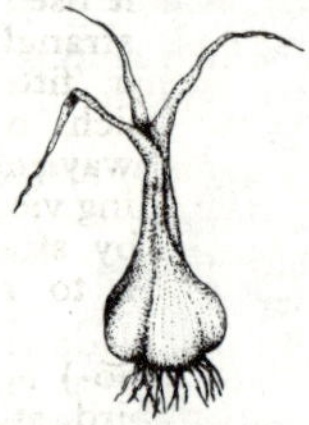

used as flavouring in cookery. **gar'lĭckў** *adj.*

gar'ment *n.* Article of dress; (pl.) clothes.

gar'ner *n.* (poet. & rhet.) Granary. ~ *v.t.* (rhet.) Store, deposit, collect (usu. fig.).

gar'nėt *n.* Vitreous mineral, occurring as a twelve-sided crystal of which the deep-red transparent variety is used as a gem. [med. L *granatum* pomegranate (f. resemblance to its seeds)]

gar'nĭsh *v.t.* 1. Decorate, embellish (esp. dish for table). 2. Serve notice on (person) for purpose of attaching money belonging to debtor; summon (person) as party to litigation already in process between others. ~ *n.* Decorative or savoury addition to dish for table. **garnĭshee'** *n.* Person in whose hands money belonging to debtor or defendant is attached at suit of creditor or plaintiff. **gar'nĭsher, gar'nĭshment** *ns.*

gar'niture *n.* Appurtenances; adornment.

gă'rrėt[1] *n.* = ATTIC[2], 2.

gă'rrėt[2] *v.t.* (building) Insert small pieces of stone in joints of (coarse masonry).

Gă'rrĭck, David (1717–79). Actor-manager of Drury Lane Theatre, London.

gă'rrĭson *n*, Troops stationed in fortress, town, etc., to defend it; ~ *town*, town having garrison. ~ *v.t.* Furnish with, occupy as, garrison; place (troops, soldier) on garrison duty.

gă'rron *n*. Small inferior horse bred in Scotland and Ireland.

garrŏ'tte *n*. Spanish method of capital punishment by strangulation; instrument used in it with apparatus for strangling, later with brass collar fitted with a sharp point which pierces the spinal cord; highway robbery performed by throttling victim. ~ ***v.t.*** Execute or kill by strangulation; throttle in order to rob. **garrŏ'tter** *n*.

gă'rrulous (-rōō-) *adj*. Talkative, wordy; (of bird, stream, etc.) chattering, babbling. **gă'rrulouslȳ** *adv*. **gă'rrulousnėss, garru'lĭtȳ** (-rōō-) *ns*.

gar'ter *n*. Band worn above or below knee to keep stocking up or as ornament; *the G~*, badge (dark-blue velvet ribbon edged and buckled with gold, worn below knee) of highest order of English knighthood, instituted by Edward III *c* 1344; membership of this order, the order itself; *G~ King of Arms*, principal King of Arms of England; ~ *stitch*, pattern produced by knitting plain to and fro. ~ *v.t.* Fasten (stocking), encircle (leg), with garter.

garth *n*. (archaic & dial.) Close, garden, paddock, open space within cloisters.

găs[1] *n*. 1. Any aeriform or completely elastic fluid (used chiefly of those that do not become liquid or solid at ordinary temperatures, other gases being usu. called *vapours*). 2. Substance(s) in gaseous state, (i) suitable to be burnt for lighting or heating, (ii) used as anaesthetic, esp. in dentistry, (iii) (esp. hydrogen) used to inflate balloon etc., (iv) producing poisonous or irritant atmosphere, (v) (coal-mining) explosive mixture of firedamp with air. 3. Empty talk, boasting. 4. *~-bag*, bag for holding gas; empty talker; airship's gas-container; *~-bracket*, gas-pipe with burner(s) projecting from wall; ~ *chamber*, place of execution by gas poisoning; *~-coal*, bituminous coal from which gas can be made; *~-coke*, residuum of coal when gas has been made from it; *~-engine*, *-motor*, internal combustion engine, usu. of large size, using a mixture of gas and air; *~-filled*, (esp., of electric light bulbs) containing argon; ~ *fire*, fire in which heat is supplied by gas; *~-fitter*, tradesman or workman providing house with apparatus for heating or lighting with gas (*~-fittings*); *~-helmet*, *-mask*, kind of appliance including respirator worn as defence against poison gases; *~-holder*, = GASOMETER; *ga'slight*, light from an incandescent mantle; *ga'slight paper*, *print*, photographic paper suitable for, print made by, artificial light; *~-mantle*: see MANTLE; *~-meter*, apparatus registering amount of gas consumed; *~-proof*, impermeable to gas, esp. poison gas; *~-ring*, hollow iron ring with perforations or jets, supplied with gas from pipe and used for cooking, etc.; *~-tar*, coal-tar produced in making gas from coal; *~-trap*, trap to prevent sewer-gas from coming up pipe; *~-turbine*, gas-driven turbine, esp. one used to drive air-compressor in jet-propelled aircraft; *~-works*, manufactory of gas for lighting and heating. ~ *v.* 1. Supply with gas. 2. Project poison gas upon (enemy, place); (pass.) be poisoned with gas. 3. Pass (thread, lace) through gas flame to remove loose fibres. 4. Talk emptily or boastfully. **gă'sėous** *adj*. [wd invented by Van Helmont, Du. chemist, after Gk *khaos* chaos]

găs[2] *n*. (U.S. colloq.) = GASOLENE; *step, tread, on the ~*, accelerate motor-engine by pressing pedal controlling the throttle; (fig.) put on speed, hurry.

Gă'scon *adj*. & *n*. (Native,

inhabitant) of Gascony, former province of SW. France; braggart.

găsconā'de *n.* & *v.i.* Boast.

găsėlier' *n.* Gas-lamp with several burners often on branches. [after *chandelier*]

găsh *n.* Long and deep slash, cut, or wound; cleft such as might be made by slashing cut; act of making such cut. ~ *v.t.* Make gash in; cut.

Gă'skell, Mrs Elizabeth Cleghorn (1810–65). English novelist; author of 'Mary Barton', 'Cranford', etc.

gă'skėt *n.* Small cord for securing furled sail to yard; strip of hemp, asbestos, rubber, metal, etc., used for packing piston, forming water- or gas-tight joint in pipe, internal combustion engine, etc.

gă'skin *n.* Hinder thigh of horse.

gasogene: see GAZOGENE.

gă'soline (-ēn), **-ēne** *n.* (now U.S.) Petrol.

găsŏ'mėter *n.* 1. (chem.) Vessel for holding gas. 2. Large vessel in which coal-gas is stored for distribution by pipes, gas-holder.

gasp (gah-) *v.* Catch breath, strain *for* air or breath, with open mouth as in exhaustion or astonishment; utter with gasps. ~ *n.* Convulsive catching of breath; *at one's last* ~, at point of death (also fig.). **ga'spinglў** *adv.*

ga'sper (gah-) *n.* (esp., slang) Cheap cigarette.

gă'ssў *adj.* Of, full of, like, gas; (of talk etc.) empty, verbose.

gă'steropŏd, -tropŏd *n.* One of the Gasteropoda, a class of molluscs having the locomotive organ placed ventrally (snails, limpets, etc.).

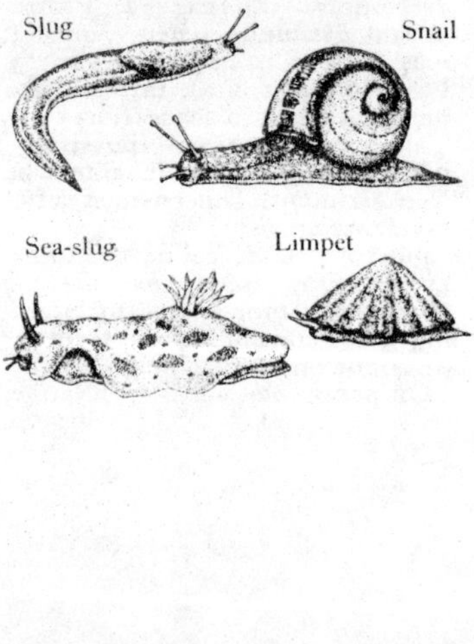

gă'stric *adj.* Of the stomach; ~ *juice,* thin clear acid nearly colourless fluid secreted by certain stomach-glands and acting as agent of digestion.

găstrī'tis *n.* Inflammation of the stomach.

gastro- *prefix.* Of the stomach; ~*-enterī'tis,* inflammation affecting both stomach and bowel.

găstrocnē'mius *n.* (also ~ *muscle*) Largest muscle of the calf.

gă'stronōme *n.* Connoisseur of cookery. **găstrŏ'nomў** *n.* Art and science of good eating. **găstrŏ'nomer, -mist** *ns.* **găstronŏ'mic, -ical** *adjs.* **găstronŏ'micallў** *adv.*

gastropod: see GASTEROPOD.

gă'strula *n.* (pl. *-ae*). (biol.) Stage in development of embryo (typically a double-layered sac) produced by migration of cells of BLASTULA into new positions.

găt *n.* (slang) Revolver or other firearm. [short for GATLING]

gāte *n.* 1. Opening in wall of city or enclosure, made for entrance and exit and capable of being closed with barrier; means of entrance or exit; *G*~, (in place-names) mountain pass. 2. Barrier closing opening of wall, wooden or metal etc. framework, solid or of bars or gratings, hung on hinges, turning on pivots, or sliding; contrivance regulating passage of water; H-shaped arrangement of slots through which gear-lever of internal combustion engine is moved to engage different gears; (photog.) mechanism controlling passage of film behind lens; (in computers) electronic device, signal, etc., controlling passage of current, selecting signals, etc. 3. Number entering by payment at gates to see football match etc., amount of money thus taken. 4. ~*-bill,* (Oxf. & Camb. Univv.) record of undergraduate's returns to college after hours; fines imposed for these; ~*-crash* (*v.*) (slang) gain entrance (to party, reception, etc.) without invitation or ticket of admission; ~-*crasher* (*n.*); *ga'tehouse*, lodge of park etc.; (hist.) room over city gate often

used as prison; room over gate of castle; ~-*leg(ged) table*, folding table with leaves supported on gate-shaped structure which may be swung back to allow them to hang down; ~-*post*, post on which gate is hung or on which it shuts; *ga'teway*, = sense 1; frame of or structure built over gate. ~ *v.t.* (Oxf. & Camb. Univv.) Confine (undergraduate) to college, entirely or after certain hours.

gă'ther (-dh-) *v.* 1. Bring or come together; *be gathered to one's fathers*, die. 2. Pick or harvest (flowers, grain, etc.); pick *up* from ground; infer, deduce (*that*); ~ *way*, (of ship) begin to move. 3. Summon up (energies); gain or recover (breath); summon *up* (thoughts, strength, etc.) for an effort. 4. Draw (garment, brow) together in folds or wrinkles; pucker (part of dress) by running thread through; draw *up* (limbs, person) into smaller compass. 5. Come to a head, develop purulent swelling. ~ *n.* (usu. pl.) Gathered part of dress. **gă'thering** *n.* (esp.) 1. Purulent swelling. 2. Assembly; meeting. 3. (bookbinding) Set of pages cut from single sheet.

Gă'tling *n.* (also ~ *gun*) Machine-gun with cluster of barrels, first used in Amer. Civil War. [R. J. *Gatling* (1818–1903), inventor]

G.A.T.T. *abbrev.* General Agreement on Tariffs and Trade (treaty to which 80 countries are parties, in operation since 1948, to promote trade and economic development).

gauche (gōsh) *adj.* Tactless; without ease or grace, socially awkward. **gaucherie'** (-rē) *n.* Gauche manners; a gauche action.

gau'chō (*or* gow-) *n.* Mounted herdsman of S. Amer. pampas, of mixed European and Indian descent.

gaud *n.* Showy ornament, gewgaw; (pl.) showy ceremonies, gaieties.

gau'dy̆[1] *adj.* Tastelessly or inappropriately showy. **gau'dĭly̆** *adv.* **gau'dinėss** *n.*

gau'dy̆[2] *n.* Grand feast or entertainment, esp. annual college dinner to old members etc.

gauffer: see GOFFER.

gauge (gāj) *n.* 1. Standard measure to which things must conform, esp. measure of capacity or contents of barrel, diameter of bullet, or thickness of sheet metal; distance between rails of railway, tramway, etc. 2. (naut., usu. spelt *gage*) Relative position in respect to wind; *have the weather* ~ *of*, be to windward of. 3. Graduated instrument measuring force or quantity of rainfall, stream, tide, wind, etc.; contrivance attached to vessel to show height of its contents; instrument for testing and verifying dimensions of tools, wire, etc.; carpenter's adjustable tool for marking parallel lines; (print.) strip regulating depth of margin etc.; means of estimating, criterion, test. ~ *v.t.* Measure exactly (esp. objects of standard size, as wire, bolts; depth of liquid content; fluctuating quantities or forces, as rainfall, wind); find capacity or content of (cask etc.) by measurement and calculation; estimate, take measure of (person, character); make uniform, bring to standard size or shape. **gau'ger** *n.* (esp.) Exciseman.

Gauguin (gōgăṅ), Eugène Henri Paul (1848–1903). French painter; spent the latter part of his life in the South Sea Islands.

Gaul. 1. Roman province of W. Europe. 2. Native or inhabitant of ancient Gaul; (joc.) Frenchman.

Gauleiter (gow'līter) *n.* Political official controlling a 'Gau' or district under the Nazi regime (also transf.). [Ger.]

Gau'lish *adj.* Of Gaul; (joc.) French. ~ *n.* Celtic language of Gaul.

Gaulle (gōl), Charles Joseph de (1890–1970). French general; head of the 'Free French' movement after the occupation of France by the Germans in 1940 and of the French Provisional Government 1944–5; premier of France 1958–9; president 1959–69.

gault *n.* (geol.) Series of clay and marl beds lying between chalk and lower greensand.

gaunt *adj.* Lean, haggard; grim or desolate looking. **gau'ntness** *n.*

gau'ntlet[1] *n.* 1. (hist.) Glove worn as part of armour, usu. of

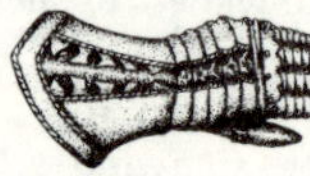

leather covered with steel plates; *fling, throw, down the* ~, issue challenge; *pick, take, up the* ~, accept challenge. 2. Stout glove with long wrist for driving, fencing, wicket-keeping, etc.; wide part of glove covering wrist. **gau'ntleted** *adj.*

gau'ntlet[2] *n. run the* ~, (orig. mil.) undergo punishment of passing between two rows of men who strike one with sticks etc.; (fig.) be subjected to criticism. [Swed. *gatlopp* (*gata* lane, *lopp* course)]

Gauss[1] (gows), Karl Friedrich (1777–1855). German mathematician and natural philosopher.

gauss[2] (gows) *n.* Unit of magnetic induction in c.g.s. system, equal to the induction that exerts a force of 1 dyne on each centimetre of a straight wire carrying 1 electromagnetic unit of current when the induction is perpendicular to the wire (abbrev. G). [f. Gauss[1]]

Gauta'ma (-tah-). Family name of the Buddha.

Gautier (gōtyā), Pierre Jules Théophile (1811–72). French Romantic poet and novelist.

gauze *n.* Thin transparent fabric of silk, cotton, wire, etc.; slight haze. **gau'zy̆** *adj.* **gau'ziness** *n.*

gă'vel *n.* Auctioneer's or chairman's hammer.

gă'velkīnd *n.* Land-tenure, esp. in Kent, involving equal division of deceased man's property among his sons.

gavŏ'tte *n.* An 18th-c. dance, like minuet but more lively; music for this, in common time, each phrase beginning on 3rd beat of bar, freq. forming part of suite.

gawk *n.* Awkward or bashful person. **gaw'ky̆** *adj.* **gaw'kĭness** *n.*

gay[1] *adj.* 1. Mirthful, light-hearted. 2. Showy, bright-coloured. 3. Dissolute; (slang) homosexual. **gai'ly̆** *adv.*

Gay[2], John (1685–1732). English playwright; author of 'The Beggar's Opera'.

Gay-Lussac (-lūsahk), Joseph Louis (1778–1850). French chemist; *~'s Law*, statement that when gases react together there is always a simple numerical relationship between their volumes and that of the products, if gaseous; ~ *tower*, part of plant for making sulphuric acid by lead chamber process.

gāze *v.i.* Look fixedly. ~ *n.* Intent look.

gazē'bō *n.* Structure whence a view may be had, belvedere, lantern, turret, balcony, etc.

gazĕ'lle *n.* Small graceful soft-eyed delicately formed antelope esp. of genus *Gazella*, found in Asia and Africa. [Arab. *ḡazāl*]

gazĕ'tte *n.* News-sheet, periodical publication giving current events (hist.); *G~*, (used in name of) newspaper; *Edinburgh, London, G~*, official journals with lists of government appointments, bankruptcies, and other public notices. ~ *v.t.* Publish in official gazette

găzetteer' *n.* Geographical index or dictionary. [f. an early work of this kind, 'The Gazetteer's or Newsman's Interpreter']

gă'zogēne, găs- *n.* Apparatus for making aerated waters.

gazŭ'mp (*or* -ōō-) *v.* (slang) Profiteer by raising price before a sale (esp. of house) is completed; cheat (buyer) thus.

G.B. *abbrev.* Great Britain.

G.B.E. *abbrev.* Knight (*or* Dame) Grand Cross (of the Order) of the British Empire.

G.C. *abbrev.* George Cross.

G.C.B. *abbrev.* Knight Grand Cross (of the Order) of the Bath.

G.C.E. *abbrev.* General Certificate of Education.

G.C.F. *abbrev.* Greatest common factor.

G.C.I.E. *abbrev.* Knight Grand Commander (of the Order) of the Indian Empire.

G.C.M. *abbrev.* Greatest common measure.

G.C.M.G. *abbrev.* Knight Grand Cross (of the Order) of St. Michael and St. George.

G.C.S.I. *abbrev.* Knight Grand Commander (of the Order) of the Star of India.

G.C.V.O. *abbrev.* Knight Grand Cross of the Royal Victorian Order.

G.D.R. *abbrev.* German Democratic Republic.

Ge (gē), **Gaia** (gīa). (Gk myth.) Personification of the Earth.

gean (*or* jē'an) *n.* Wild cherry tree (*Prunus avium*), freq. confused with bird-cherry.

gear (g-) *n.* 1. Equipment, apparel, etc.; harness of draught animals; apparatus, appliances, tackle, tools. 2. Combination of wheels, levers, etc.; wheels working on one another by teeth etc.; mechanical arrangement connecting motor with its work, usu. effecting a change of relative speed of revolution between driving and driven parts; (in bicycles) number of inches in diameter of rear wheel multiplied by ratio of driving to driven gear wheels; *in, out of*, ~, in, out of, connection with motor; working, not working; *high, low*, ~, gear by which driven part of vehicle etc. revolves faster, slower, relatively to driving part (so *top, bottom*, ~). 3. Rigging. 4. Goods; household utensils. 5. *~-box*, in motor-vehicle, the part containing the gear-changing mechanism; *~-case*, in bicycle, case containing driving and driven gear-wheels and the chain; *~-wheel*, cog-wheel, esp. that in bicycle driven immediately by the pedals. ~ *v.* Harness (draught animal); put (machinery) in gear; provide with gear; (of cog-wheel) fit exactly *into*, be in gear *with*; modify (production, organization) to meet the requirements of a larger group or organization. **gear'ing** *n.* Manner in which a machine is geared; apparatus for transmission of motion or power from one part of a machine to another, esp. a train of toothed wheels.

gĕ'ckō (g-) *n.* (pl. *-os, -oes*). Any of numerous species of lizard (family Geckonidae), found in

warm climates, with peculiar cry and (in some species) adhesive discs on the feet enabling them to climb walls. [Malay *gēkoq*, imitating its cry]

gee[1], gee-gee *ns.* (colloq., orig. child's word) Horse.

gee[2] *int.* Word of command to horse etc. to go on, go faster, (in some dialects) turn to right. So **gee-(h)ŭp, gee-hō**, etc.

gee[3] *int.* (U.S.) Exclamation of asseveration, discovery, etc. So **geewhĭ'llĭkins** (-z), **gee-whĭ'z.**

Gē'ĕz: see ETHIOPIC.

gee'zer (g-) *n.* (slang) Old person, old creature.

Gėhĕ'nna (g-). Hell; place of

burning, torment, or misery. [Heb. *gê-hinnōm* valley near Jerusalem where children were burnt in sacrifice to Baal or Moloch]

Gei'ger cou'nter (gĭg-). Instrument for detecting and counting ionizing radiation; used esp. for measuring radioactivity. [Hans *Geiger* (1882–1945), German physicist]

gei'sha (gā-) *n.* Japanese girl

GEISHA GIRLS

trained as singer, dancer, and entertainer.

Gei'ssler tūbe (gī-). Sealed tube filled with rarefied gas which becomes incandescent when an electric current is passed through it. [Heinrich *Geissler* (1814–79), German physicist]

gĕl *n.* Semi-solid colloidal solution. ~ *v.i.* Form or become a gel.

gĕ'latine, -ĭn (*or* -ēn) *n.* Amorphous brittle yellowish transparent substance consisting essentially of protein, extracted from animal skins and bones, used in making soups, jellies, etc., in many photographic processes, and as the principal constituent of glue; *blasting* ~, gelatine-like explosive solution of collodoin cotton in nitro-glycerine; ~ *dynamite*, thin blasting gelatine mixed with other substances to reduce violence of explosion. **gėlă'tĭnous** *adj.* Jelly-like in consistency etc.; of gelatine.

gĕld (g-) *v.t.* Deprive (usu. male animal) of generative power, castrate, excise testicles or ovaries of. **gĕ'ldĭng** *n.* Gelded horse or other animal.

gĕ'lĭd *adj.* Ice-cold; cool.

gĕ'lĭgnīte *n.* Variety of gelatine dynamite.

gĕlsē'mium *n.* Woody vine of genus *G*~ containing two Asiatic species and one (*G. sempervirens*) of the southern U.S.

gĕm *n.* Precious stone, esp. when cut and polished (also *ge'mstone*); object of great beauty or worth, choicest part *of*, prized possession; precious or semi-precious stone with engraved design. ~ *v.t.* Adorn (as) with gems.

Gėmar'a (g-). Later (5th c. A.D.) part of the Talmud, Aramaic commentary paragraph by paragraph on the older part (Mishnah). [Aram. *gemārā* completion]

gĕ'mĭnate *adj.* Combined in pairs. **gĕ'mĭnāte** *v.t.* Double, repeat; arrange in pairs. **gĕmĭnā'tion** *n.*

Gĕ'mĭnī. The Twins, a constellation also called 'Castor and Pollux'; 3rd sign [♊] of the zodiac, which the sun enters about 21 May. [L, = 'twins']

gĕ'mma *n.* (pl. *-ae*). 1. (bot.) Small cellular body that separates from mother-plant and starts new one, esp. in mosses, liverworts, etc. 2. (zool.) = BUD 2.

gĕ'mmate *adj.* Having buds, reproducing by gemmation. **gĕmmā'te** *v.i.* Put forth buds, propagate by gemmation. **gĕmmā'tion** *n.* Act, manner, of budding; arrangement of buds; reproduction by gemmae.

gĕmmĭ'parous *adj.* Of, propagating by, gemmation.

gĕmmŏ'logy̆ *n.* Science or study of gems. **gĕmmŏ'logĭst** *n.*

gĕmm'ūle *n.* Asexual reproductive body in sponges.

gen., genit. *abbrevs.* Genitive.

Gen. *abbrev.* General; Genesis.

ge'ndarme (zhŏṅ-) *n.* Soldier employed in police duties, esp. in

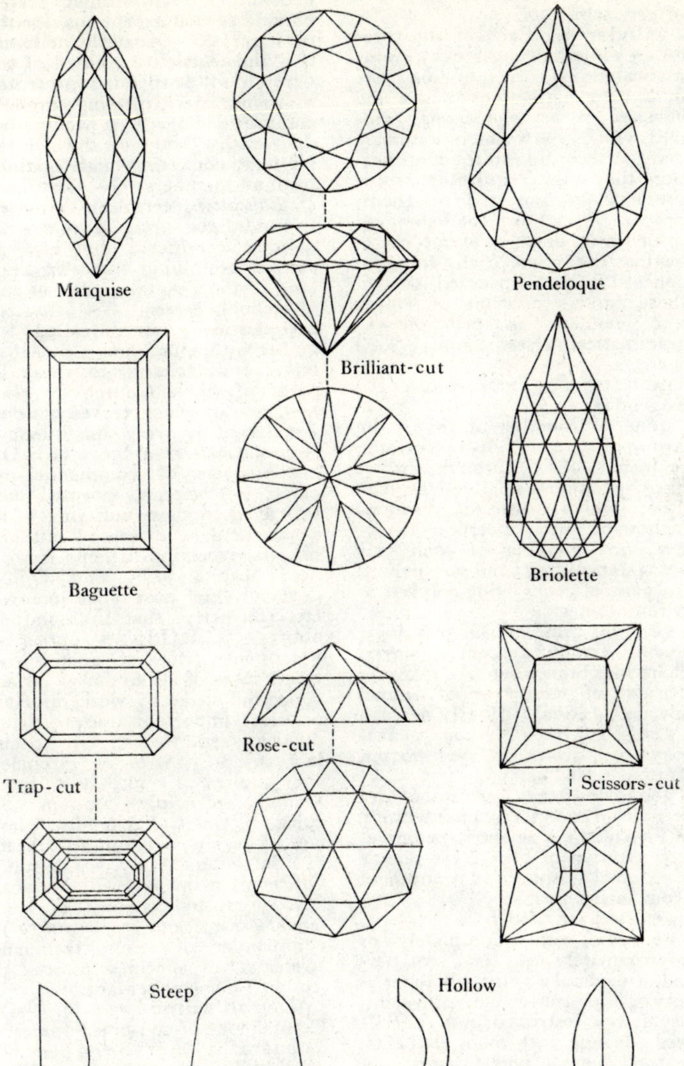
Marquise
Brilliant-cut
Pendeloque
Baguette
Briolette
Rose-cut
Trap-cut
Scissors-cut
Steep
Hollow
Simple
Double
Cabochon cut

GEM CUTTING

France. **gendar'merie** *n.* Force of gendarmes.

gĕ'nder[1] *n.* Each of the three (or in some languages two) grammatical kinds, corresponding more or less to distinctions of sex and absence of sex (*masculine, feminine, neuter*), into which nouns are divided according to the modification they may require in words syntactically connected with them; property (in a noun) of belonging to or (in other parts of speech) of having the appropriate form to concord with a specified one of these kinds; division of words into genders as principle of grammatical classification; (joc.) sex.

gĕ'nder[2] *v.t.* (archaic & poet.) Engender.

gēne *n.* Member of any of the pairs of factors, usu. forming segments of a chromosome at fixed positions relative to each other, which cause the development in offspring of certain characters, one member of each pair being transmitted from each parent, the pairs of genes being on pairs of chromosomes.

gĕnėalŏ'gĭcal *adj.* Of genealogy; tracing family descent; ~ *tree*, chart like branching tree showing descent of family or of animal species. **gĕnėalŏ'gĭcallў** *adv.*

gĕnėă'logīze *v.* Trace genealogy of; draw up genealogies. **gĕnėă'logĭst** *n.*

gĕnėă'logў *n.* Account of descent from ancestor by enumeration of intermediate persons; pedigree; investigation of pedigrees; plant's or animal's line of development from earlier forms.

genera: see GENUS.

gĕ'neral *adj.* Completely or approximately universal, not partial or particular; of a whole territory or organization etc.; prevalent, usual; not restricted, not specialized; dealing with main elements, features, etc., with neglect of unimportant details; vague, indefinite; (mil., of officer) above rank of colonel; (appended to titles) chief, head, with unrestricted authority or sphere; *in* ~, generally; in all ordinary cases, barring special exceptions, for the most part; *G~ Assembly*, deliberative and legislative council of the Church of Scotland, represented by its ministers, meeting annually and presided over by a Moderator; deliberative body of the United Nations, consisting of delegations from all members; *G~ Certificate of Education*, certificate awarded to candidates successful in examinations conducted by any of various examining bodies in England and Wales, taken usu. at end of school career; *G~ Council*, ecclesiastical council called together by invitation to Church at large, and claiming to speak in name of whole Church; ~ *election*, one in which representatives are elected by every constituency; ~ *headquarters*, (abbrev. G.H.Q.) headquarters of commander-in-chief; ~ *hospital*, hospital not restricted to those suffering from a particular disease; military hospital receiving patients from a field hospital; *G~ Post Office*, (loosely) chief post office in town etc. (formerly, that in London; abbrev. G.P.O.); ~ *practice, practitioner*, (work of) doctor who treats cases of all kinds; ~ *strike*, concerted strike by workers of all or most important trades or industries (esp. that in Gt Britain in 1926). ~ *n.* 1. *the* ~, (archaic) the public. 2. (pl.; now rare) General principles, notions, or rules. 3. Chief of religious order, e.g. of Jesuits, Dominicans; head of Salvation Army. 4. (mil.) Officer next below Field Marshal (also used, by courtesy, of *lieutenant-general* and *major-general*); commander of army; tactician, strategist, of specified merit. 5. (colloq.) General servant.

gĕnerali'ssĭmō *n.* (pl. *-os*). Commander of combined forces.

gĕneră'lĭtў *n.* 1. Being general, applicability to whole class of instances. 2. Vagueness. 3. General point, principle, law, or statement. 4. Main body, bulk, majority, *of*.

gĕneralīzā'tion *n.* (esp.) (Forming of) general notion or proposition obtained by induction.

gĕ′neralīze *v.* 1. Reduce to general laws, form into a general notion, give a general character to, call by a general name; infer (law, conclusion) by induction; base general statement upon (facts etc.); (math., philos.) throw into general form, extend application of; form general notions by abstraction; (painting) render only the typical characteristics of. 2. Make vague or indefinite; use generalities, speak vaguely. 3. Bring into general use. 4. *generalized*, (zool., of organ or structure) suitable for general use, not specialized (e.g. reptile's forelimb as distinct from bird's wing); (of animal) having generalized organs etc.

gĕ′nerallў *adv.* For the most part, extensively; in a general sense, without regard to particulars; not specially; as a general rule, commonly.

gĕ′neralship *n.* Office of a general; strategy, military skill; skilful management, tact, diplomacy.

gĕ′nerāte *v.t.* Bring into existence, produce, evolve; (math., of point, line, surface, conceived as moving) make (line, surface, solid).

gĕnerā′tion *n.* 1. Procreation, propagation of species, begetting or being begotten; production by natural or artificial process. 2. Offspring of same parent or parents, regarded as single step in descent or pedigree; whole body of persons born about same time; time covered by lives of these; in reckoning historically, interval of time between birth of parents and that of their children (usu. reckoned at about thirty years).

gĕ′nerative *adj.* Of procreation; able to produce, productive.

gĕ′nerātor *n.* Begetter; apparatus for producing gases, steam, etc.; machine for converting mechanical into electrical energy, dynamo.

gėnĕ′rĭc *adj.* Characteristic of a genus or class; applied to (any individual of) a large group or class; general, not specific or special; ~ *name*, (biol.) Latin name (written with capital) indicating the genus to which an animal or plant belongs and preceding the *specific name* which indicates the species. **gėnĕ′rĭcallў** *adv.*

gĕ′nerous *adj.* Magnanimous, noble-minded, not mean or prejudiced; free in giving, munificent; (of soil) fertile; ample, abundant, copious; (of wine, colour, etc.) rich and full. **gĕ′nerouslў** *adv.* **gĕnerŏ′sĭtў** *n.*

Gĕ′nėsĭs[1]. 1st book of O.T., containing account of creation of the world.

gĕ′nėsĭs[2] *n.* Origin; mode of formation or generation. [Gk, = 'origin', 'creation']

gĕ′nėt *n.* (Fur of) kind of civet-cat, *Genetta vulgaris*, native of S. Europe, Africa, and W. Asia.

gėnĕ′tĭc *adj.* Of, in, concerning, origin; of genetics. **gėnĕ′tĭcallў** *adv.* **gėnĕ′tĭcs** *n.pl.* Branch of biology concerned with natural development; study of heredity and variation. **gĕnĕ′tĭcist** *n.*

gėnē′va[1] *n.* Spirit, made in Holland, distilled from grain and flavoured with juniper berries; Hollands. [Du. f. L *juniperus* juniper]

Gėnē′va[2]. City of Switzerland, where meetings of Council and Assembly of League of Nations were held; ~ *bands*, strips of lawn suspended from the front of the neck, worn esp. by the Calvinist and Presbyterian clergy; ~ *Bible*, English translation of the Bible prepared by Protestant exiles at Geneva and printed there in 1560, the 'Breeches' Bible; ~ *Convention*, convention of 1864 and later, governing status of wounded, hospitals, ambulances, etc., in war; ~ *cross*, red Greek cross on a white ground displayed by hospitals etc. in time of war, more commonly called the *red cross*; ~ *gown*, clergyman's black gown like that worn by Calvinist clergy when preaching. **Gėnē′van** *adj.* Of Geneva; (esp.) Calvinistic. **Gėnėvē′se** (-z) *adj.* & *n.* (Native, inhabitant) of Geneva.

Gĕ′nghĭs Khan (-gĭz kahn) (1162–1227). Mongol conqueror, whose empire extended from the shores of the Pacific to the northern shores of the Black Sea.

gē'nĭal[1] *adj.* 1. Conducive to growth; pleasantly warm, mild. 2. Cheering, kindly, sociable. **gē'nĭallȳ** *adv.* **gēnĭă'lĭtȳ** *n.* **gē'nĭalīze** *v.t.*

gėnī'al[2] *adj.* (anat.) Of the chin.

gėnĭ'cūlate, -ātėd *adjs.* (bot., zool.) Having knee-like joints.

gē'nie *n.* (pl. usu. *genii*). Sprite or goblin of Arabian tales; jinnee.

gėnĭ'sta *n.* Leguminous flowering shrub of genus *G*~ including dyer's broom and petty whin.

gĕ'nital *adj.* Of animal generation. **gĕ'nitals** (-z), **gĕnĭtā'lia** *n.pl.* Organs of generation, esp. external.

gĕ'nitive *adj.* (gram.) Of the case chiefly denoting relation as source, possessor, etc. ~ *n.* (Word in) genitive case. **gĕnĭtī'val** *adj.*

gē'nius *n.* 1. (pl. *-iuses, -ii*). Tutelary spirit of person, place, or institution; *good, evil*, ~, two mutually opposed spirits by whom every person was supposed to be attended; hence, person powerfully influencing another for good or evil. 2. (pl. *-ii*). Demon, supernatural being. 3. (pl. *-iuses*). Prevalent feeling, opinions, taste, of nation, age, etc.; character, spirit, drift, method, of language, law, etc.; associations, inspirations, *of* a place. 4. Natural ability, special mental endowments; exalted intellectual power, instinctive and extraordinary imaginative, creative, or inventive capacity; person having this.

genizah (gĕnē'za) *n.* Chamber attached to a synagogue, housing damaged, discarded, or heretical books etc.; contents of this.

Gĕ'nōa. (Ital. *Genova*) City and seaport of NW. Italy; ~ *cake*, rich fruit cake with almonds and other nuts on the top. **Gĕnoē'se** (-z) *adj.* & *n.* (Native, inhabitant) of Genoa.

gĕ'nocīde *n.* Extermination of a race. **gĕnocī'dal** *adj.*

gĕ'notȳpe *n.* (biol.) Genetic constitution of an organism (cf. PHENOTYPE).

genre (zhahńr) *n.* Kind, esp. of art or literature; (also ~ *painting*) portrayal of scenes from ordinary life, esp. that of a particular class, e.g. peasants.

gĕns (-z) *n.* (pl. *gentēs*). 1. (Rom. antiq.) Clan, sept. 2. (anthrop.) Line of descent through father. [L]

gĕnt *n.* (vulg.) Gentleman; ~*'s*, (shop term) man's; *Gents*, (colloq.) men's lavatory.

gĕntee'l *adj.* (usu. iron.; vulg. in serious use). 1. (archaic or vulg.) Well-bred; elegant. 2. Affectedly refined in manners etc. **gĕntee'lly** (-l-lĭ) *adv.*

gĕ'ntian (-shĭan *or* -shan) *n.* Plant of the genus *Gentiana*, usu. with conspicuous blue flowers, common in Alpine meadows; (also ~ *root*) (pharm.) dried rhizome and roots of *G. lutea* used as a tonic; ~ *violet*, dye, used as antiseptic. [L, f. *Gentius* king of Illyria]

gĕ'ntīle *adj.* & *n.* (also *G*~) (Person) not of Jewish blood; (in Mormon use) non-Mormon.

gĕntĭ'lĭtȳ *n.* 1. (now rare) Gentle birth, status of gentleman or lady. 2. (usu. iron.) Being genteel.

gĕ'ntle *adj.* 1. Well-born; (her.) having right to bear arms (now only in ~ *and simple*); (of birth, blood, etc.) honourable, belonging to or fit for the class of gentleman. 2. (archaic) Generous, noble, courteous. 3. Tame, quiet; easily managed; not stormy, rough, or violent; mild; moderate, gradual; kind, tender. ~ *n.* (f. obs. sense *soft* of *adj.*). Maggot, larva of flesh-fly or bluebottle, used as bait by anglers. ~ *v.t.* Break in or handle (horse) gently. **gĕ'ntlefolk** (-tlfōk) *n.pl.* Persons of good position and family.

gĕ'ntleman (-tlm-) *n.* (pl. *-mĕn*) 1. Man of gentle birth or entitled to bear arms but not included in nobility (chiefly hist.); man of gentle birth attached to household of sovereign or great person; ~*-at-arms*, one of sovereign's bodyguard. 2. Man of chivalrous instincts, fine feelings, and good breeding; man of good social position, man of wealth and leisure; (courteous synonym for) man; (law) man who has no occupation; *gentleman's* ~, valet; *the old* ~, (joc.) the Devil; *~'s agreement*, *bargain*, agreement not enforceable at law, and binding only as matter of honour; *~-commoner*, one of former class of privileged undergraduates at Oxford and Cambridge; *~-usher*, gentleman acting as usher to great person. **gĕ'ntlemanlike** *adj*. Appropriate to, resembling, a gentleman. **gĕ'ntlemanlў** *adj*. Feeling, behaving, or looking like a gentleman; befitting a gentleman. **gĕ'ntlemanliness** *n*.

gĕ'ntleness (-tln-) *n*. Kindliness, mildness; freedom from severity, violence, suddenness, etc.

gĕ'ntlewoman (-tlwŏŏman) *n*. (pl. *-women*, pr. -wĭmĭn) Woman of good birth or breeding, lady.

gĕ'ntlў *adv*. Quietly, moderately, softly, slowly; mildly, kindly; ~ *born*, of gentle birth.

gĕ'ntrў *n*. People next below nobility in position and birth; (contempt.) people.

gĕ'nūflĕct *v.i.* Bend the knee, esp. in worship. **gĕ'nūflĕctor**, **gĕnūflĕ'xion** (-kshon) *ns*. **gĕ'nūflĕctorў** *adj*.

gĕ'nūine *adj*. Of the original stock, pure-bred; really proceeding from its reputed source or author; having the supposed character, not counterfeit, properly so called. **gĕ'nuinelў** *adv*. **gĕ'nūineness** *n*.

gĕ'nus *n*. (pl. *gĕ'nera*). (logic) Class of things including subordinate kinds or species; (biol.) group (usu. containing several species) of animals or plants having common structural characteristics distinct from those of all other groups; (loosely) kind, class, order, tribe.

Geo. *abbrev*. George.

gēocĕ'ntric *adj*. Considered as viewed from the earth's centre; having or representing the earth as centre. **gēocĕ'ntricallў** *adv*.

gēochĕ'mistrў (-k-) *n*. Science of the chemical composition of and changes in the earth's crust. **gēochĕ'mĭcal** *adj*.

gēochronŏ'logў (-k-) *n*. Chronology of earth's history studied through geological data. **gēochrŏnolŏ'gical** *adj*.

gē'ōde *n*. Cavity in an igneous rock which has been partly filled with minerals in well-shaped crystals. **geŏ'dĭc** *adj*.

geŏ'desў *n*. Branch of mathematics dealing with figure and area of the earth or large portions of it. **gēodĕ'sic**, **gēodĕ'tic** *adjs*. Of geodesy; ~ *line*, shortest possible line joining two points on a surface. **gēodĕ'sic** *n*. Geodesic line. **gēodĕ'tical** *adj*. **gēodĕ'ticallў** *adv*.

gēogră'phic, -ical *adjs*. Of geography; ~ *latitude*, angle made with plane of equator by perpendicular to surface of earth at any point; ~ *mile*, 1 minute of longitude measured along the equator, 6087·2 ft. **gēogră'phicallў** *adv*.

geŏ'graphў *n*. Science of the earth's surface, form, physical features, natural and political divisions, climate, productions, population, etc.; subject-matter of geography; treatise or manual of geography; features, arrangements, *of* place. **geŏ'grapher** *n*.

gē'oid *n*. (geog.) Surface constituted by the mean sea-level of the open sea, conceived as extending under the continents at the level to which the sea would rise if admitted by small frictionless impervious canals.

gēolŏ'gical *adj*. Of geology; ~ *map*, map showing the formations of rock exposed at, or underlying, the surface of a region; ~ *survey*, service, institution, which reports on the geological problems of a country or area, as water supply, mines, quarries, etc. **gēolŏ'gicallў** *adv*.

geŏ'logize *v*. Devote time to examining places geologically, collecting specimens, etc.; examine (place) thus.

geŏ'logў *n*. Science of the formation of the earth, the strata of its crust, and their relations and changes; geological features *of* a district. **gėŏ'logist** *n.*

gē'omăncy̆ *n.* Divination from figure given by handful of earth thrown down, and hence from figures given by dots made at random. **gē'omăncer** *n.* **gēomă'ntic** *adj.*

gėŏ'mėter *n.* 1. Person skilled in geometry. 2. Larva of geometrid moth.

gēomĕ'tric, -ical *adjs.* Of, according to, geometry; (of patterns) rectilinear or curvilinear (~ *bar tracery*); *Geometric*, of a period of Greek culture (*c* 900–*c* 700 B.C.) using such patterns for decoration of vases; ~ *progression*, progression in which each term is a fixed multiple of the preceding one, as 1, 3, 9, 27; ~ *proportion*, proportion involving equal ratios in its two parts, as 1 : 3 :: 4 : 12. **gēomĕ'trically̆** *adv.*

gėŏ'mėtrid *adj.* & *n.* (Member) of the superfamily Geometroidea of moths whose larvae move with a looping movement as if measuring the ground.

gėŏ'mėtrize *v.* Work, form, by geometrical methods.

gėŏ'mėtry̆ *n.* Science of properties and relations of magnitudes in space, as lines, surfaces, solids.

gėomŏrphŏ'logy̆ *n.* Branch of geology dealing with the origin, evolution, and configuration of the natural features of the earth's surface. **gēomŏrpholŏ'gical** *adj.* **gēomŏrphŏ'logist** *n.*

gėŏ'phagy̆ *n.* Dirt-eating. **gėŏ'phagist** *n.*

gēophy̆'sics (-z-) *n.* Study of the physics of the earth, esp. its crust; application of methods of physics to the study of the earth. **gēophy̆'sical** *adj.* **gēophy̆'sicist** *n.*

gĕopŏ'litics *n.* Study of politics of a country as determined by its geographical position. **gēopoli'tical** *adj.*

Geordie (jŏr'di) *n.* Native or inhabitant of Tyneside.

George[1] (jŏrj), St. (d. 303). Martyr under Diocletian; in legend, slayer of a dragon; patron saint of England from time of Edward III, who chose him as patron of Order of the Garter; hence, jewel forming part of Garter insignia; *St. ~'s cross*, vertical and horizontal bars crossing in centre; (her.) red cross on white ground, the national cross of England; *St. ~'s day*, 23 April.

George[2] (jŏrj). Name of 6 kings of Gt Britain (*the four ~s*, George I–IV): *George I* (1660–1727), son of the 1st Elector of Hanover and great-grandson of James I, reigned 1714–27; *George II* (1683–1760), his son, reigned 1727–60; *George III* (1738–1820), grandson of George II, reigned 1760–1820; *George IV* (1762–1830), son of

GEORGE IV

George III; Prince Regent 1811–20; reigned 1820–30; *George V* (1865–1936), son of Edward VII, reigned 1910–36; *George VI* (1895–1952), son of George V, reigned 1936–52; ~ *Cross, Medal*, (abbrev. G.C., G.M.) decorations, intended primarily for civilians, for gallantry, instituted in 1940.

George[3] (gā'ŏrge), Stefan (1868–1933). German symbolist poet.

georgĕ'tte (jŏr-) *n.* Thin semi-transparent crêpe of fine twisted yarn (silk, rayon, nylon, etc.). [f. name of French dressmaker]

Geor'gia[1] (jŏr-). South Atlantic State of U.S., orig. an English colony founded in 1733 and one of the original thirteen States of the Union (1788); capital Atlanta. [f. name of *George II* of England]

Geor'gia[2] (jŏr-). (Russ. *Gruziya*)

District of the Caucasus, a constituent republic of the U.S.S.R.; capital, Tbilisi (Tiflis).

Geor'gian[1] (jŏr-) *adj.* Of the time of the four Georges (George I–IV); of the time of George V–VI of Gt Britain.

Geor'gian[2] (jŏr-) *adj.* & *n.* (Inhabitant, language) of Georgia in the Caucasus or of Georgia, U.S.

Geor'gics (jŏr-), The. Virgil's poetical treatise on husbandry, in 4 books. [Gk *geōrgos* farmer]

gēosȳ'nclīne *n.* Long trough or furrow in earth's surface caused by downward warping, usu. under the sea, filling up gradually with sediments. **gēosȳnclī'nal** *adj.*

gėŏ'tropism *n.* Relation of plant-growth to gravity; *positive* ~, tendency (of roots etc.) to grow towards centre of earth; *negative* ~, tendency (of stems etc.) to grow away from centre of earth. **gēotrŏ'pic** *adj.* **gēotrŏ'pically** *adv.*

Ger. *abbrev.* German.

gerā'nium *n.* 1. Herbaceous plant or shrub of genus *G*~ of temperate regions, with fruit like crane's bill; crane's-bill. 2. (pop.) Pelargonium; scarlet colour of well-known kind of this. [Gk *geranos* crane]

gẽr'bil *n.* Burrowing rodent of Africa and Asia with long hind legs.

gẽr'falcon (-aw(l)- *or* -ŏl-) *n.* Any large northern falcon, esp. the Icelandic.

gĕriă'tric *adj.* Of, concerning, the health and welfare of old people. **gĕriă'trics** *n.pl.* Branch of medicine, or of social science, dealing with geriatric problems.

gẽrm *n.* 1. Portion of organism capable of developing into a new one; embryo of seed; (fig.) seed, rudiment, elementary principle. 2. Micro-organism or microbe, esp. one of those capable of causing disease. 3. *~-cell*, cell in body of an organism which is specialized for the purpose of reproduction, and which, when united to one of the opposite sex, forms a new individual; gamete; *~-plasm*, that nuclear part of the germ-cell by which, according to Weismann's theory, hereditary characteristics are transmitted.

gẽr'man[1] *adj.* In the fullest sense of relationship; *brother-*~, brother having the same parents, own brother; similarly *sister-*~; *cousin-*~, child of one's father's or mother's own brother or sister.

Gẽr'man[2] *adj.* Of Germany or its people or language; ~ *Democratic Republic*: see GERMANY; ~ *Empire*, (1) Holy Roman Empire (962–1806); (2) modern Germany from the time of the unification of the German states under the leadership of Prussia in 1871 to the end of the war of 1914–18; ~ *measles*, mild contagious disease (*rubella*) resembling measles; ~ *Ocean*, North Sea; ~ *sausage*, large sausage made of spiced and partly cooked meat; ~ *script*, angular form of handwriting sometimes used for writing German, derived from the Merovingian script based on Roman cursive; ~ *silver*, white alloy of nickel, zinc, and copper; ~ *text*, (print.) modern German type, a modification of this used in English printing for ornamental headings, black letter. ~ *n.* 1. German person. 2. German language, one of the Germanic or Teutonic group, subdivided into *High* ~, group of dialects spoken in south and part of central Germany, and *Low* ~, dialects of N. Germany; *Old High* ~, High German from *c* 750 to *c* 1100. **Gẽr'manism, Gẽr'manist** *ns.*

gẽrmă'nder *n.* Any plant of the genus *Teucrium* esp. *T. chamaedrys*, wall germander; ~ *speedwell*, blue-flowered *Veronica chamaedrys*.

gẽrmā'ne *adj.* Relevant, pertinent, *to* the matter or subject. [var. of GERMAN[1]]

Gẽrmă'nic *adj.* Of, pertaining to, the Teutons or their language; German. ~ *n.* Language of the Teutons, esp. in its earliest form, subdivided into *East* ~, Gothic and some almost lost languages as Burgundian and Vandal; *North* ~, Danish, Norwegian, Swedish, and Icelandic; *West* ~, German, English, Frisian, and Dutch.

gērmā'nium *n.* (chem.) Rare metallic element of greyish-white colour found in some minerals and in flue dusts from burning certain coals; symbol Ge, at. no. 32, at. wt 72·59. [L *Germania* Germany]

Gēr'manў. Region of central Europe; in 1871 a confederation of German-speaking States united under the leadership of the Hohenzollern king of Prussia, who became German emperor; this Second Empire, regarded as the successor to the Holy Roman Empire, lasted from 1871 until the abdication of William II in 1918; it was followed by the Weimar Republic, which was in turn succeeded by the Third Empire under the leadership of Adolf Hitler, 1933–45; since then the country has been divided between the *Federal Republic of* ~ (also called *West* ~; capital, Bonn) and the *German Democratic Republic* (also called *East* ~; capital, East Berlin).

gēr'micīde *n.* & *adj.* (Substance) having power to destroy (esp. disease-) germs. **gērmicī'dal** *adj.*

gēr'minal[1] *adj.* Of germs, of the nature of a germ; in the earliest stage of development. **gēr'minallў** *adv.*

Germinal[2] (zhārmĭnahl) *n.* Month from 21 March to 19 April in the French Revolutionary calendar.

gēr'mĭnāte *v.* Sprout, bud; cause to shoot, produce. **gērminā'tion, gēr'mĭnātor** *ns.* **gēr'mĭnā'tĭve** *adj.*

gĕrontŏ'cracў *n.* Government by, governing body of, old men.

gĕrontŏ'logў *n.* Study of old age, esp. conditions affecting the health of the aged. **gĕrontŏ'logĭst** *n.*

gĕ'rrўmănder (g-) *v.t.* Manipulate (constituency etc.) unfairly so as to secure disproportionate influence at election for some party or class. ~ *n.* Such manipulation. [orig. U.S., f. E. *Gerry*, governor of Massachusetts in 1812]

gĕ'rund *n.* 1. Form of Latin verb capable of being construed as noun but able to govern like verb. 2. English verbal noun in *-ing* when used rather as part of verb than as noun. 3. In Russ. grammar, indeclinable form of verbal participle. **gerŭ'ndial** *adj.*

gerŭ'ndĭve *adj.* Of, like, the gerund. ~ *n.* Latin verbal adjective, with same suffix as gerund, expressing idea of fitness or necessity.

gĕ'ssō *n.* Plaster of Paris, gypsum, prepared for use in modelling or as ground for painting.

Gestalt (geshtah'lt) *n.* (psychol.) Shape or structure which as an object of perception forms a specific whole and has properties which cannot be completely deduced from a knowledge of the properties of its parts; chiefly attrib. as ~ *psychology*, ~ *theory*. [Ger., = 'form', 'shape']

Gĕsta'pō (gĕstah-) *n.* Nazi secret police. [Ger., initial letters of *Ge*heime *Sta*ats*po*lizei secret State police]

gĕstā'tion *n.* Carrying or being carried in womb between conception and birth; this period.

gĕstatōr'ial *adj.* ~ *chair*, chair in which Pope is carried on certain occasions.

gĕstĭ'culāte *v.* Use expressive motion of limbs or body with or instead of speech; express thus. **gĕstĭcūlā'tion, gĕstĭ'cūlātor** *ns.* **gĕstĭ'cūlative, gĕstĭ'cūlatorў** *adjs.*

gĕ'sture *n.* 1. Significant movement of limb or body; use of such movements as expression of feeling or rhetorical device. 2. (after Fr. *geste*) Step or move calculated to evoke response from another or convey (esp. friendly) intention. ~ *v.* Gesticulate.

gĕt (g-) *v.* (past t. *gŏt*; past part. *got*, archaic & U.S. *go'tten*). 1. Obtain, procure, by effort or contrivance; earn, gain, win; learn *by heart* or *rote*; obtain as result of calculation; receive as gift, wages, etc.; extract by prayer, demand, inquiry, etc.; come to have; contract; have inflicted on one; receive as one's lot or penalty; procure, provide; catch (fish etc.); bring in, carry home (crop); communicate with by telephone; obtain radio signal from; succeed in bringing, placing, etc.; bring into some state; suffer injury etc. to some part of one; induce, prevail upon (person) *to* do; (of animals) beget; (colloq.) puzzle, catch in argument; understand; enthral; (in perf.) have; *have got to*, must; ~ *the best* or *worst of it*, be victorious, be defeated; ~ *it*, be punished or reprimanded; ~ *on the brain*, be obsessed by; ~ *on one's nerves*, be irritated by; ~ *religion*, become (esp. suddenly) zealous about religion; 2. (intrans.) Succeed in coming or going *to*, *from*, *over*, *here*, etc.; (slang) be off, clear out; (with infin.) acquire habit; come to be (doing); become. 3. (with preps.): ~ *across*, (slang) annoy; ~ *at*, reach, get hold of, ascertain; (slang) tamper with, bribe, etc.; (slang) attack, banter, try to impose upon; ~ *into*, (colloq.) put on (boots, clothes); ~ *off*, dismount from; obtain release from (engagement etc.); not remain on; ~ *on*, mount (horse etc.); rise on one's *feet* or *legs* to speak in public; ~ *over*, surmount (difficulty); show (evidence, argument) to be unconvincing; recover from (illness) or from surprise at; accomplish (distance, task, etc.); ~ *round*, cajole; evade; ~ *through*, bring to an end; (of Bill etc.) be passed by (Commons, Lords, etc.); while away (time); ~ *to*, begin (business etc.). 4. (with advs.): ~ *about*, go from place to place; begin to walk (after illness etc.); (of rumours etc.) be circulated; ~ *abroad*, (of rumours etc.) get about; ~ *across*, (slang) reach audience, be effective; ~ *along*, advance, meet with success, fare *ill*, *well*, etc.; manage *without* something; live harmoniously *together*, *with*; ~ *along with you!*, (colloq.) be off!; nonsense!; ~ *away*, escape; start; (imper.) be off!; ~ *back*, come home etc.; recover (lost thing); ~ *one's own back*, have one's revenge; ~ *better*, *well*, recover from illness; ~ *down*, dismount; depress, weary (person); ~ *in*, be elected; enter carriage etc.; bring home (crop), collect (debts etc.); fit (work etc.) into given time; succeed in placing (blow); ~ *off*, escape; start; go to sleep; be acquitted or pardoned, be let off *with* or *for* specified penalty; procure pardon, acquittal, or slight penalty for (person); (slang) become friendly *with* one of opposite sex; ~ *on*, don; display (pace); advance, make progress; prosper, fare; manage *without*; agree or live sociably *with*; advance in time or age; ~ *out!* (imper.) be off!; nonsense!; transpire; elicit; succeed in uttering, publishing, etc.; ~ *out of*, issue or escape from; abandon (habit) gradually; evade do*ing*; elicit (information), obtain (money) from (person); ~ *over*, bring (troublesome task etc.) to an end; get across; ~ *through*, bring to, reach, destination; succeed in examination; establish communication, esp. by telephone or radio; (of Bill etc.) be passed in Parliament etc.; ~ *together*, collect; ~ *under*, subdue (fire); ~ *up*, rise, esp. from bed; mount, esp. on horseback; organize, set on foot; make presentable, arrange the appearance of; make rise; produce; work up (emotion etc.); (of fire, wind, sea) begin to be violent; (of game) rise from cover; (of laundress) dress (linen); ~ *up steam*, produce enough to work engine etc.; (fig.) work oneself up into action or energy; ~ *the wind up*, (slang) begin to feel afraid. 5. (comb.) ~-*a't-able*, (colloq.) capable of being reached; ~-*away*, (esp.) escape of criminals; ~-*together*, meeting, social gathering; ~-*up*, style of equipment, costume, book-production, etc. **gĕ'ttable** *adj.*

gĕ'tter (g-) *n.* (esp.) Substance inserted into vacuum to absorb stray gases exuded into it after sealing.

Gĕ'ttȳsburg (g-, -z-) Place in Pennsylvania, U.S., scene of a decisive battle (1863) in the Amer.

BATTLE OF GETTYSBURG

Civil War, in which the Federals under Meade defeated the Confederates under Lee; ~ *Address*, brief speech by Abraham LINCOLN at dedication of the battlefield as a national cemetery, containing the phrase 'government of the people, by the people, for the people'.

gē'um *n.* Rosaceous plant of genus *G~*, including herb bennet, *G. urbanum*.

GeV *abbrev.* Billion (= 1,000 million) electron volts.

gew'gaw (g-) *n.* Gaudy plaything or ornament, bauble; paltry showy trifle.

gey (gā) *adv.* (Sc.) Very, considerably.

gey'ser[1] (gēz- *or* gīz-) *n.* 1. Hot spring (usu. in volcanic area) which spouts water at more or less regular intervals. 2. Apparatus for rapidly heating water for bath etc. [*Geysir*, name of a hot spring in Iceland]

gey'ser[2] *n.* = GEEZER.

G.G. *abbrev.* Grenadier Guards.

Gha'na (gah-). W. African State comprising the former Gold Coast Colony, Ashanti, the Northern Territories (of the Gold Coast Region), and Transvolta-Togoland; member State of the Commonwealth; independent 1957; capital, Accra. **Ghanaian** (gahnā'-) *adj.* & *n.*

ghār'ial (g-), **gār-** *n.* Large harmless fish-eating saurian (genus *Gavialis*), resembling crocodile but with more elongated muzzle, found in Ganges. [Hind. *ghaṛiyāl* fish-eater]

gha'stlȳ (gah-) *adj.* Horrible, frightful; death-like, pallid; (of smile etc.) painfully forced. ~ *adv.* (chiefly with adjs.). **gha'stlilȳ** *adv.* **gha'stliness** *n.*

ghat, ghaut (gawt) *n.* (Ind.) 1. *Eastern, Western, Ghauts*, two mountain chains along E. and W. sides of S. Hindustan. 2. Mountain pass, defile. 3. Passage or flight of steps leading to river-side; landing-place. 4. (also *burning* ~) Hindu funeral pyre.

ghee (gē) *n.* Indian buffalo-milk butter clarified to resemble oil.

gher'kin (ger-) *n.* Young or small cucumber, used for pickling.

ghĕ'ttō (gĕ-) *n.* (pl. *-os*). Quarter of city to which Jews were restricted (hist.); (esp. slum) quarter inhabited by minority group(s).

Ghi'belline (gĭ-), *adj.* & *n.* (Member) of emperor's faction in medieval Italian States (opp. GUELPH). [It., perh. f. Ger. *Waiblingen* estate belonging to Hohenstaufen emperors]

ghōst (gō-) *n.* 1. Soul or spirit, as principle of life (now only in *give up the* ~, die); Spirit (of God), Holy Ghost. 2. Soul of dead person appearing to living; apparition, spectre; emaciated person; shadowy outline or semblance. 3. (optics) Bright spot or secondary image in field of telescope due to defect of lens; (television) faint duplicated image not coinciding with the intended one. 4. Artistic or literary hack (also ~ *writer*) doing work for which his employer takes credit. 5. ~-*fish*: see WRYMOUTH; ~-*word*, historically bogus word arising from printer's error or popular etymology. ~ *v.i.* Act, write, as ghost (sense 4).

ghō'stlў *adj.* 1. (archaic) Spiritual; incorporeal; concerned with sacred or incorporeal matters; ~ *director*, *father*, etc., confessor. 2. (As) of a ghost, spectral. **ghō'stlinėss** *n.*

ghoul (gōōl *or* gowl) *n.* Spirit supposed in Muslim superstition to prey on corpses; person enjoying what is gruesome. **ghou'lish** *adj.* **ghou'lishlў** *adv.*

G.H.Q. *abbrev.* General Headquarters.

ghyll (gĭ-) *n.* Var. of GILL[2] *n.*

G.I. (colloq.) Private soldier in U.S. army. [abbrev. of *g*overnment (or *g*eneral) *i*ssue]

gī'ant *n.* (fem. *giantėss*). 1. Being of human form but superhuman stature; (Gk myth.) one of the race of beings, sons of Ge (earth) and Uranus (Heaven) or Tartarus (Hell) who warred against and were destroyed by the gods. 2. Agency of enormous power; abnormally tall or large person, animal, or plant; person of extraordinary ability, courage, strength, etc. 3. Large diffuse star, as dist. from DWARF. 4. *Giant's Causeway*, group of basaltic columns formed in Tertiary period on coast of Antrim, N. Ireland, once believed to be part of a road made by a legendary giant to Staffa in Western Isles of Scotland where there is a similar formation; ~('*s*) *stride*, gymnastic apparatus of upright pole with revolving head and hanging ropes, enabling user to take huge strides round pole.

gī'antism *n.* Growth (esp. of bones) to abnormally large size.

Gĭb. *abbrev.* (colloq.) Gibraltar.

gĭ'bber *v.i.* Speak fast and inarticulately, chatter like an ape. ~ *n.* Gibbering speech.

gĭbberĕ'llic *adj.* ~ *acid*, crystalline acid ($C_{18}H_{21}O_4COOH$), isolated from a soil-borne pathogenic fungus (*Gibberella fujikuroi*) that in minute traces stimulates plant growth.

gĭ'bberĭsh (*or* g-) *n.* Unintelligible speech, meaningless sounds; blundering or ungrammatical talk.

gĭ'bbėt *n.* (orig.) Gallows; (later) upright post with arm on which bodies of executed criminals were hung up. ~ *v.t.* Put to death by hanging; expose on gibbet; hang up as on gibbet; hold up to infamy or contempt.

gĭ'bbon[1] (g-) *n.* Long-armed tailless ape of genus *Hylobates*, found in SE. Asia.

Gĭ'bbon[2] (g-), Edward (1737–94). English historian; author of 'History of the Decline and Fall of the Roman Empire'.

gĭ'bbous (g-) *adj.* 1. Convex, protuberant; (of moon or planet) having bright part greater than semicircle and less than circle. 2. Humped, hunchbacked. **gĭ'bbouslў** *adv.* **gĭbbŏ'sitў** *n.*

gībe, jībe *v.* Flout, jeer, mock (*at*). ~ *n.* **gī'ber** *n.* **gī'binglў** *adv.*

gĭ'blėts *n.pl.* Parts of fowl taken out before cooking, esp. heart, liver, and gizzard.

Gĭbra'ltar (-awl- *or* -ŏl-). Fortified town and headland on S. coast of Spain, British possession since 1704. **Gĭbraltār'ian** *adj.* & *n.* (Native) of Gibraltar. [Arab. *gebel-el-Tarik* hill of Tarik (a Saracen commander of the 8th c.)]

gī'bus *n.* Opera or crush hat. [maker's name]

gĭ'ddў (g-) *adj.* Dizzy, disposed to fall, stagger, or spin round; making dizzy; circling with bewildering speed; excitable, flighty. **gĭ'ddilў** *adv.* **gĭ'ddinėss** *n.* **gĭ'ddў** *v.* Make or become giddy.

Gide (zhēd), André (1869–1951). French novelist, critic, and essayist; Nobel Prize for literature 1947.

gĭft (g-) *n.* 1. Giving; (law) voluntary transference of property without recompense. 2. Thing given, present, donation; faculty looked upon as given by heaven etc.; natural endowment, talent; ~ *coupon*, coupon issued with certain commodities a certain number of which entitles the holder to a free gift; ~-*wrap* (*v.t.*) wrap decoratively. ~ *v.t.* Endow with gifts; present *with* as gift; bestow as gift. **gĭ'ftĕd** *adj.* (esp.) Naturally endowed with gifts, talented.

gĭg[1] (g-) *n.* 1. Light two-wheeled one-horse carriage; ~-*lamps*, (slang) spectacles. 2. Light narrow clinker-built ship's boat for oars or sails; rowing-boat chiefly used for racing.

gĭg[2] (g-) *n.* Kind of fish-spear. [short for *fizgig*, f. Span. *fisga* harpoon]

gĭga- (*or* g-) *prefix.* One thousand million times (abbrev. G).

gīgă'ntĭc *adj.* Giant-like in size, stature, etc.; abnormally large, huge. **gīgă'nticallÿ** *adv.* **gīgă'ntism** *n.* Giantism.

gĭ'ggle (g-) *v.i.* Laugh continuously, not uproariously but in manner suggesting foolish levity or uncontrollable amusement. ~ *n.* Giggling laugh.

gĭg-mĭll (g-) *n.* Machine for raising nap on cloth; building in which these machines stand.

gĭ'golō (*or* zh-) *n.* (pl. -*s*). Male professional dancing-partner; man supported by mistress.

gigue (zhēg) *n.* (mus.) = JIG.

gĭ'la (hē-) *n.* (also ~ *monster*) Large venomous lizard, *Heloderma suspectum*, of south-western U.S.

gĭ'lbert[1] (g-) *n.* (phys.) Unit of magnetomotive force in the c.g.s. system, equivalent to 10÷4π ampere turns. [W. *Gilbert* (1540–1603), English physicist]

Gĭ'lbert[2] (g-), Sir Humphrey (1539?–83). English navigator and discoverer; founded (1583) in Newfoundland the first British colony in N. America.

Gĭ'lbert[3] (g-), Sir William Schwenck (1836–1911). Librettist of light satiric operas for which Arthur Sullivan composed the music, called the 'Savoy Operas' because orig. produced at the Savoy Theatre, London. **Gĭlbĕr'tĭan** *adj.* Resembling the ludicrous or paradoxical situations found in Gilbert and Sullivan operas.

Gĭ'lbert and E'llice I'slands (g-, ĕ-, īlandz). British colony in central Pacific; capital, Tarawa.

gĭld[1] (g-) *v.t.* (past part. *gilded* or *gilt*). Cover with thin layer of gold laid on as gold leaf or otherwise; make reputable or attractive by supplying with money; tinge, adorn, with golden colour or light; give specious brilliance to by fair words; ~ *the pill*, soften or tone down something unpleasant; *gilded* or *gilt spurs*, emblem of knighthood; *gilded youth*, young men of fashion and wealth. **gĭ'ldĭng** *n.*

gild[2] *n.*: see GUILD.

Gĭ'lgamĕsh (g-). Ruler of first Sumerian dynasty, represented as a demi-god in a Babylonian epic poem which contains an account of the Flood resembling that in Genesis 6–9.

gĭll[1] (g-) *n.* (usu. pl.) 1. Respiratory organ(s) in fishes and other water-breathing animals, so arranged that venous blood is exposed to aerating influence of water; ~ -*cover*, bony case protecting fish's gills. 2. Wattles or dewlap of fowls. 3. Vertical radial plates on underside of mushrooms etc. 4. Flesh below person's jaws and ears. ~ *v.t.* Gut (fish); cut off gills of (mushroom).

gĭll[2] (g-) *n.* Deep, usu. wooded, ravine; narrow mountain torrent.

gĭll[3] *n.* Quarter-pint (in some districts half-pint) liquid measure.

gĭ'llie (g-) *n.* Highland chief's attendant; man or boy attending deerstalker or fisherman in Scotland. [Gael. *gille* lad, servant]

gĭ'llyflower *n.* Clove-scented pink (rare); wallflower. [OF *girofle*, ult. f. Gk *karuophullon* (*karuon* nut, *phullon* leaf)]

gĭlt (g-) *adj.*: see GILD[1]. ~ *n.* Gilding; gilt-edged security; ~-*edged*, (of securities etc.) reliable, safe (not touched by market fluctuations), orig. Government stock (from being printed on gilt-edged paper); (fig.) dull but dependable; ~-*head*, marine fish with gold markings on head, as striped tunny, golden wrasse, etc.

gĭ'mbal (*or* g-) *n.* (pl. exc. in combination as ~-*ring* etc.) Contrivance, usu. of rings and pivots, for keeping objects such as compass or chronometer horizontal at sea.

gĭ'mcrăck *n.* Trumpery article, knick-knack, useless ornament. ~ *adj.* Showy and flimsy, worthless, trumpery. **gĭ'mcrăckerў** *n.*

gĭ'mlėt (g-) *n.* Small boring-tool usu. with wooden crosspiece as handle and worm at pointed end.

gĭ'mmĭck (g-) *n.* (slang, orig. U.S.) Tricky device; device adopted in order to attract attention or publicity.

gĭmp (g-) *n.* Silk, worsted, or cotton twist with cord or wire running through it; trimming made of this; fishing-line of silk etc. bound with wire; (lace-making) coarser thread outlining design.

gĭn[1] *n.* 1. Snare, net, trap. 2. Hoisting apparatus, crane; (now usu.) tripod with winch for winding rope; (mining) windlass, drum, etc., for hoisting, pumping, etc. 3. Machine for separating seeds from cotton. ~ *v.t.* Separate (seeds of cotton) with a gin.

gĭn[2] *n.* Spirit distilled from grain or malt and flavoured with juniper or some substitute; ~-*palace*, gaudily decorated public-house; ~ *sling*, Amer. cold drink of flavoured and sweetened gin etc. [abbrev. of GENEVA[1]]

gĭ'nger (-j-) *n.* 1. (Tropical plant, *Zingiber officinale*, with) hot spicy root used in cookery and medicine, and preserved in syrup or candied as sweet; *black* ~, unscraped root, from E. Indies; *green* ~, undried root, usu. in preserve; *white* ~, scraped root, from Jamaica. 2. Mettle, spirit; stimulation. 3. Light reddish-yellow colour. 4. ~-*ale*, -*beer*, kinds of aerated drink flavoured with ginger; *gi'ngerbread*, cake made with treacle and flavoured with ginger; *ginger(bread)-nut*, small round cake or biscuit of gingerbread; ~ *group*, group urging action; ~-*pop*, (colloq.) ginger-beer; ~-*race*, root of ginger; ~ *wine*, wine of fermented sugar, water, and bruised ginger. ~ *adj.* Ginger-coloured; sandy-haired. ~ *v.t.* Flavour with ginger; put mettle or spirit into, stir or rouse *up*. **gĭ'ngerў** *adj.*

gĭ'ngerlў (-j-) *adv.* & *adj.* With, showing, extreme caution so as to avoid making a noise or injuring oneself or what is touched or trodden on.

gĭngham (gĭ'ng*a*m) *n.* Plain-woven cotton fabric of dyed yarns, often striped or checked. [Malay *ginggang* striped]

gingī'val (-j-) *adj.* Of the gums.

gingivī'tis (-j-) *n.* Inflammation of the gums.

gĭ'nglўmus (-ngg-) *n.* (anat.) Hinge-like joint (e.g. elbow), with motion restricted to one plane.

gĭ'nkgō (g-) *n.* (pl. -*oes*). Maidenhair tree (*G~ biloba*) native to China and Japan and

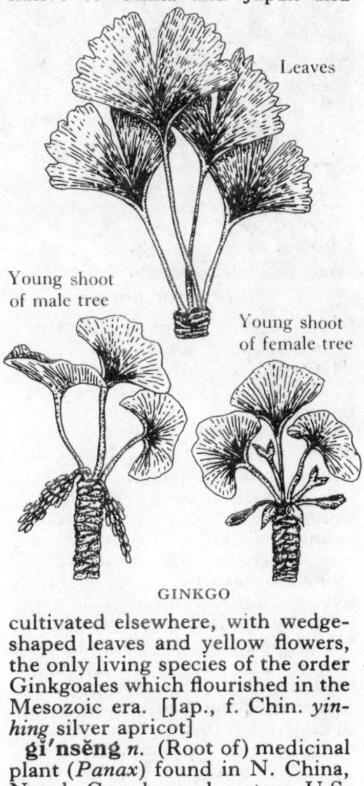

GINKGO

cultivated elsewhere, with wedge-shaped leaves and yellow flowers, the only living species of the order Ginkgoales which flourished in the Mesozoic era. [Jap., f. Chin. *yin-hing* silver apricot]

gĭ'nsĕng *n.* (Root of) medicinal plant (*Panax*) found in N. China, Nepal, Canada, and eastern U.S.

GIOTTO DI BONDONE: Meeting of St. Joachim and St. Anne

[Chin. *jên shên* image of man (from forked shape of root)]

Giorgio'nė (jŏrjō-). Giorgio da Castelfranco (1477–1510), Venetian painter.

Giotto (jŏ'tō). Giotto di Bondone (1266?–1337), Florentine painter and architect.

gi'psy̆, gy̆- *n.* Member of tawny-skinned black-haired wandering people (called by themselves *Rŏ'many*), perhaps orig. from India, living by basket-making, fortune-telling, horse-dealing, etc., and speaking a language related to Hindi; person resembling or living like a gipsy; ~ *rose*, scabious. [earlier *gipcyan* for *Egyptian* (because when the race first appeared in England in 16th c. it was believed to have come from Egypt)]

gira'ffe (-ahf) *n.* African ruminant quadruped with remarkably long neck and forelegs, and skin spotted like panther's.

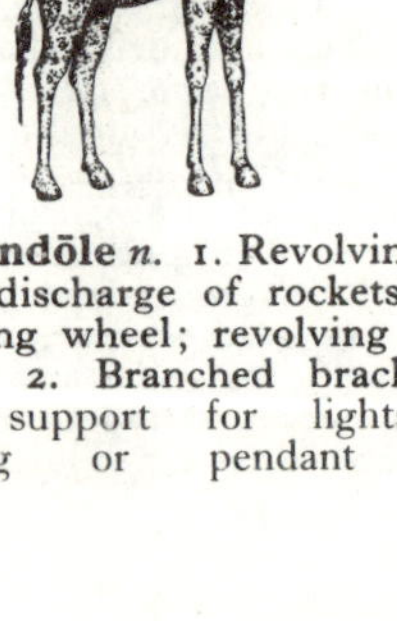

gi'randōle *n.* 1. Revolving firework, discharge of rockets from revolving wheel; revolving jet of water. 2. Branched bracket or other support for lights. 3. Ear-ring or pendant with large central stone surrounded by smaller ones.

gi'rasŏl, -le *n.* Variety of opal with reddish glow in bright light. [It., f. *girare* turn, *sole* sun (orig. = sunflower)]

gîrd[1] (g-) *v.t.* (poet. or rhet.; past t. & past part. *girded* or *girt*) Encircle (waist, person as to waist) with belt etc., esp. to confine clothes; equip *with* sword in belt; fasten (sword etc.) on with belt; secure (clothes) on body with girdle or belt; put (cord etc.) *round*; encircle (tower etc.) *with* besiegers etc.; encircle; ~ *oneself*, (*up*) *one's loins*, prepare for action.

gîrd[2] (g-) *v.i.* Jest, gibe, *at.* ~ *n.* Jest, gibe.

gîr'der (g-) *n.* Beam supporting joists of floor; iron or steel beam for like use; latticed or other compound structure of steel etc. forming span of bridge, roof, etc.

gîr'dle[1] (g-) *n.* 1. Belt or cord worn round waist; (orig. U.S.) corset. 2. Something that surrounds like girdle; part of cut gem dividing crown from base and embraced by the setting; (anat.) bony support for upper and lower limbs (*pelvic* ~, *shoulder* ~); ring round tree made by removal of bark. ~ *v.t.* Surround with girdle; kill (tree) or make it more fruitful by removing bark in ring round trunk.

gîr'dle[2] (g-) *n.* (Sc. & north.) Circular iron plate hung over fire for baking cakes or scones, griddle.

gîrl (g-) *n.* Female child; young unmarried woman; maidservant; (colloq.) man's sweetheart (also (*best* ~). **gîr'lhood** *n.* **gîr'lish** *adj.* **gîr'lishly̆** *adv.* **gîr'lishnėss** *n.*

gîr'ō *n.* System whereby credits are transferred between banks, post offices, etc.

Gironde (zhĭrawṅd). Department of SW. France; chief city, Bordeaux. **Gĭrŏ'ndĭst** *n.* & *adj.* (Member) of the moderate republican party in the French Assembly, 1791–3, whose leaders were deputies from the Gironde.

girt: see GIRD[1].

gîrth (g-) *n.* 1. Leather or cloth band tightened round body of horse etc. to secure saddle etc. 2. Measurement round any more or less cylindrical thing ~ *v.t.* Secure (saddle etc.) with girth.

gĭst *n.* Real ground or point, substance or pith of a matter.

gĭ'ttern (g-) *n.* Gut-stringed instrument, kind of early guitar.

gĭve (g-) *v.* (past t. *gāve*, past part. *gĭ'ven*). 1. Bestow gratuitously, hand over as present or donation; confer, grant; accord (affection, confidence, etc.); sanction marriage of (daughter etc.). 2. Deliver, hand over, without reference to ownership; put (food etc.) before one; administer (medicine); deliver (message etc.); consign, entrust; pledge, assign as guarantee (*one's word* etc.). 3. Make over in exchange or payment, pay, sell *for* price. 4. Devote, dedicate; addict. 5. Put forth (some action or effort) to affect another; deliver (judgement etc.) authoritatively; provide (ball, dinner, etc.) as host. 6. Present, offer (one's hand, arm, etc.); perform (entertainment). 7. Make partaker of; impart, be source of. 8. Allot; grant; assume. 9. Yield as product or result. 10. Cause or allow to have. 11. Collapse; lose firmness, yield to pressure, become relaxed; make room, shrink. 12. (of window etc.) Look, lead, *on*, *into*. 13. ~ *chase*, start in pursuit; ~ *ear*, listen; ~ *rise to*, occasion; ~ *way*, retire; fail to resist; be superseded; be dislodged; break down; make concessions; allow precedence *to*; abandon oneself *to* grief etc. 14. (with advs.) ~ *away*, transfer by gift; hand over (bride) to bridegroom; betray or expose to ridicule or detection; distribute (prizes); ~ *back*, give (thing) again to its owner from whom it was removed; ~ *forth*, emit; publish; report; ~ *in*, yield, cease fighting or arguing; hand in (document) to proper official; ~ *off*, emit (vapour etc.); ~ *out*, announce; emit; distribute; cease or break down from exhaustion etc.; run short; ~ *over*, cease from do*ing*; abandon (habit etc.); desist; hand over; ~ *up*, resign, surrender, part with; deliver (fugitive etc.) into hands of pursuers etc.; abandon *oneself to* a feeling etc.; cease to have to do with; cease from effort; devote or addict *to*; divulge (names of accomplices etc.); pronounce incurable or insoluble, renounce hope of. **gi'ven** *adj.* (esp.) (of document) Dated; ~ *name*, name given to person, opp. surname. **gi'ver** *n.* **give** *n.* Yielding to pressure, elasticity; ~ *and take*, mutual concession, compromise, exchange of talk.

gi'zzard (g-) *n.* Bird's second or muscular stomach for grinding the food after it has been mixed in the first gastric juice; thickened muscular stomach of some molluscs; *stick in one's* ~, be unwelcome or unpalatable.

glā'brous *adj.* (anat. etc.) Free from hair or down, smooth-skinned.

glă'cé (-sā) *adj.* 1. (of cloth, leather, etc.) Smooth, finished with a high gloss. 2. (of fruits etc.) Iced, sugared.

glă'cial (*or* -āsh*al*) *adj.* 1. Of ice; icy. 2. (geol.) Characterized, produced, by the presence or agency of ice; of a period during which the greater part of the N. hemisphere was covered with an ice-sheet; ~ *deposit*, formation laid down by the action of ice (e.g. boulder clay, moraine, kame). 3. (chem.) Resembling ice; ~ *acetic acid*, pure acetic acid. **glā'cially** *adv.* **glă'cial** *n.* Glacial period.

glă'ciāted *adj.* Marked or polished by ice-action; covered with glaciers or ice-sheet; **glāciā'tion** *n.*

glă'cier *n.* Slowly moving mass or river of ice in high mountain valley formed by accumulation and gradual consolidation of snow on higher ground.

glă'cis (*or* -sē) *n.* Bank sloping down from fortified site, on which attackers are without cover from defenders' fire.

glăd *adj.* Pleased; marked by, filled with, expressing, joy; giving joy; (of nature etc.) bright, beautiful; ~ *eye*, (slang) amorous glance, ogle; ~ *rags*, (slang) best clothes, esp. evening dress. **glă'dly** *adv.* **glă'dness** *n.* **glăd** *v.t.* (archaic) Make glad. **glădd'en** *v.t.* **glă'dsome** *adj.* (poet.). **glă'dsomely** *adv.* **glă'dsomeness** *n.*

glāde *n.* Clear open space or passage between forest trees.

glă'diātor *n.* Man trained to fight with sword or other weapon at ancient Roman shows. **glădiatōr'ial** *adj.*

glădiō'lus *n.* (pl. *-lī*, *-luses*). Plant of iris family with sword-shaped leaves and spikes of brilliant flowers; many varieties are natives of S. Africa. [L, = 'little sword']

Glă'dstone, William Ewart (1809–98). British Liberal statesman; prime minister 1868–74,

1880–5, 1886, and 1892–4; ~ *bag*, light leather portmanteau, hinged so as to open flat into two approx. equal compartments. **Glădstō'nian** *adj.* Of, pertaining to, Gladstone or his policy, esp. with reference to his efforts to obtain Home Rule for Ireland.

Glăgoli'tic *adj.* & *n.* (Of) the alphabet, based on Greek minuscules, devised by St. CYRIL[2] and still used in liturgical books of the Uniats in Dalmatia. [Slav. *glagol* word]

glair *n.* White of egg; kinds of adhesive preparation made from it;

any similar viscous substance. ~ *v.t.* Smear with glair. **glair'ėous, glair'ȳ** *adjs.*

Glam. *abbrev.* Glamorgan.

Glamôr'gan. Former county of S. Wales, since April 1974 divided among Mid Glamorgan, South Glamorgan, and West Glamorgan.

glă'mour (-m*er*) *n.* Magic, enchantment; alluring beauty or charm. **glă'morous** *adj.* **glă'morīze** *v.t.* Make glamorous. [var. of *grammar* in old sense of magic or necromancy]

glance (-ah-) *v.* 1. (of weapon) Glide off object instead of striking it full; (of talk etc.) pass quickly *over*, glide *off* or *from*, subject; ~ *at*, make passing (and usu. sarcastic) allusion to. 2. (of bright object or light) Flash, dart, gleam; (of eye etc.) cast momentary look, give brief look *at*; ~ *over*, read cursorily. ~ *n.* 1. Swift oblique movement or impact; (cricket) stroke with bat's face turned slantwise to ball. 2. (Sudden movement producing) flash or gleam; brief look.

glănd[1] *n.* Organ in animal body secreting the chemical compounds required for a particular function and discharging them (usu. through a duct, but cf. ENDOCRINE ~) into the body or outside it; similar organ in plant. **glă'ndūlar, glă'ndlėss** *adjs.*

glănd[2] *n.* (mech.) Sleeve used to press a packing tight on a piston-rod.

glă'nders (-z) *n.pl.* Contagious disease of horses, mules, etc., characterized by formation of nodules in lungs, liver, etc., ulceration of mucous membrane, and skin lesions; same disease communicated to man. **glă'ndered** (-*er*d), **glă'nderous** *adjs.*

glăndi'ferous *adj.* Bearing acorns.

glāre *v.* 1. Shine dazzlingly or disagreeably; be over-conspicuous or obtrusive. 2. Look fixedly or fiercely (*at, upon*); express (hate etc.) by look. **glār'ing** *adj.* **glār'ingly** *adv.* **glāre** *n.* Strong fierce light, oppressive unrelieved sunshine; tawdry brilliance; fierce or fixed look. **glār'ȳ** *adj.*

Gla'sgow (glah'zgō *or* glă-). Large city in W. Scotland, situated on the banks of the Clyde; university, 1451; university of Strathclyde, 1964.

glass (-ah-) *n.* 1. Non-crystalline solid substance, usu. transparent, lustrous, hard, and brittle, made by fusing sand (silica) with soda or potash, or both, and usu. with other ingredients, as lead oxide; ornaments, utensils, windows, greenhouses, etc., made of this. 2. Glass vessel esp. for drinking, amount of liquid contained in this, drink; sandglass, hourglass; carriage etc. window; plate of glass covering picture; glazed frame for plants; looking-glass; eyeglass, (pl.) spectacles; glass disc covering watch-face; barometer, weather-glass; lens, esp. one that magnifies; (pl.) field- or opera-glasses. 3. ~*-blower*, one who fashions hollow and other glassware by blowing molten glass; ~ *case*, case chiefly of glass for exhibiting or protecting objects; ~*-cloth*, cloth for drying glassware; cloth covered with powdered glass, used like sandpaper for smoothing or polishing; ~*-cutter*, tool for cutting glass, glazier's diamond; ~ *eye*, false eye made of glass; ~*-house*, greenhouse; (army slang) military prison; ~*-paper*, paper covered with powdered glass for polishing etc.; *gla'ssware*, articles made of glass; ~ *wool*, glass in form of fine fibres for packing and insulation; *gla'sswort*, any of various plants (esp. *Salicornia herbacea* and *Salsola kali*) containing large quantity of alkali, formerly burnt to provide potash for glass-making. ~ *v.t.* Fit or cover with glass; mirror, reflect. **gla'ssful** *n.* **gla'sslėss** *adj.*

gla'ssȳ (-ah-) *adj.* Having properties of, resembling, glass; (of eye etc.) lacking fire, dull, fixed; (of water) lustrous and transparent, or smooth, as glass. **gla'ssilȳ** *adv.* **gla'ssinėss** *n.*

Gla'stonburȳ (glah-). Town in Somerset, associated with Arthurian legend; site of a ruined medieval abbey; the first church at Glastonbury was supposed to have been built by JOSEPH[1] of Arimathea, whose staff, when planted in the ground, sprouted and became the ~ *thorn*, flowering at Christmas.

Glăswē'gian (-zwējan) *adj.* & *n.* (Native, inhabitant) of Glasgow.

Glau'ber (*or* -ow-), Johann Rudolf (1604–68). German chemist; ~'*s salt(s)*, sodium sulphate, used medicinally as an aperient.

glaucō'ma *n.* Eye-disease characterized by increased tension and hardness of eyeball causing gradual impairment or loss of sight. **glaucō'matous** *adj.*

glau'cous *adj.* Of dull greyish green or blue; (bot.) covered with bloom as of grapes.

glāze *v.* 1. Fit (window, picture) with glass; furnish (building) with glass windows. 2. Cover (pottery etc.) with vitreous substance fixed by fusion; fix (colour) *on* pottery thus; overlay (cloth, leather, pastry, etc.) with smooth lustrous coating; cover (eye) with a film; cover (painted surface) with thin coat of transparent colour to modify tone; give glassy surface to; become glassy. ~ *n.* Vitreous composition for glazing pottery etc.; anything used to produce glazed or lustrous surface; smooth and glossy surface; thin transparent coat of colour laid over another colour. **glā'zĭng** *n.* ~ *bar*, bar between panes of glass.

glā'zĭer (*or* -zher) *n.* One whose trade is to glaze windows etc.

G.L.C. *abbrev.* Greater London Council.

gleam *n.* Subdued or transient light; faint, temporary, or intermittent show *of* some quality etc. ~ *v.i.* Emit gleams, shine with subdued or interrupted brightness.

glean *v.* Gather ears of corn left by reapers, gather (such remains); strip (field etc.) thus; collect in small quantities, scrape together (news, facts, etc.). **glea'ner, glea'nĭng** *ns.*

glēbe *n.* Earth, land, a field (poet.); portion of land attached to clergyman's benefice.

glee *n.* 1. Musical composition for three or more (prop. adult male) voices (one voice to each part), usu. unaccompanied, each part being a more or less independent melody. 2. Mirth; lively and manifest delight. **glee'ful** *adj.* **glee'fullȳ** *adv.*

gleet *n.* Thin morbid discharge from wound, ulcer, etc., or from the urethra.

glĕn *n.* Narrow valley.

Glĕncō'e. Valley in N. Strathclyde, memorable for the massacre of the inhabitants (Macdonalds) in 1692, carried out by Campbell of Glen Lyon under the orders of William III of England.

Glĕndow'er, Owen (*c* 1359–*c* 1416). (Welsh *Glyndwr*) leader of Welsh rebellion (1400–9) against Henry IV.

glĕngă'rrȳ (-n-g-) *n.* Cloth cap, of which the two sides are stiffened and meet in a point in front, usu. adorned with ribbons at the back, originating from the Highlands of Scotland. [*Glengarry*, Highland]

glē'noid *adj.* (anat.) ~ *cavity, fossa, surface*, shallow cavity on bone (esp. scapula and temporal bone) receiving projection of other bone to form joint.

glĭb *adj.* (of speaker, speech, etc.) Fluent, more voluble than sincere or thoughtful. **glĭ'blȳ** *adv.* **glĭ'bnĕss** *n.*

glīde *v.* Pass, proceed, by smooth continuous motion; go quietly or stealthily; pass gently or gradually; shade off insensibly *into*; cause to glide; (aeron.) fly without engine power, fly in glider. ~ *n.* Act of gliding; (mus., phonet., etc.) succession of sounds, sound, made in passing from one note to another, or from one speech-sound to another. **glī'der** *n.* Engineless aeroplane.

glĭm *n.* (slang) Lamp, or other artificial light.

glĭ'mmer *v.i.* Shine faintly or intermittently. ~ *n.* Feeble or wavering light; faint gleam *of* hope etc.; glimpse, half view. **glĭ'mmerĭng** *n.*

glĭmpse *n.* Faint and transient appearance; momentary or imperfect view *of*. ~ *v.t.* Catch glimpse of, see faintly or partly.

glĭnt *v.* & *n.* (Make) flash, glitter, sparkle.

glĭssā'de (*or* -ahd) *n.* Sliding down steep slope (esp. of ice or snow); dancing step consisting of glide to right or left. ~ *v.i.* Perform glissade.

glĭssăn'dō *adv.*, *n.* (pl. *-os*), & *adj.* (Effect produced by) sliding tip or back of finger over pianoforte keys or harp-strings, or along fiddle-string, or by 'scooping' the voice. [Italianized form of Fr. *glissant*, f. *glisser* slide]

glĭ'sten (-sn) *v.i.* Shine fitfully; glitter, sparkle. ~ *n.*

glĭ'ster *v.i.* & *n.* (archaic) Sparkle, glitter.

glĭ'tter *v.i.* Shine with brilliant tremulous light, gleam, sparkle; be showy or splendid (*with* jewels etc.). ~ *n.*

gloa'mĭng *n.* (chiefly Sc. or poet.) Evening twilight.

gloat *v.i.* Feast eyes or mind lustfully, avariciously, malignantly, etc., *on* or *over*. **gloa'tĭnglȳ** *adv.*

glō'bal *adj.* Of the whole of a group of items, categories, etc.; of, extending over, the whole world.

glōbe *n.* Spherical body; earth; spherical chart of the earth (*terrestrial* ~) or the constellations (*celestial* ~); golden orb as emblem of sovereignty; approximately spherical glass vessel, esp. lampshade or fishbowl; (anat.) eyeball; ~ *artichoke*, = ARTICHOKE 1; ~-*fish*, tropical fish (species of Tetraodontidae) able to inflate itself into globular shape; ~-*flower*, ranunculaceous plant, *Trollius europaeus*, with round yellow flowers; ~ *lightning*, fire-ball; *G~ Theatre*, theatre where many of Shakespeare's plays were produced, erected at Southwark in 1598; ~ *trotting*, hurried travelling through foreign countries for sightseeing; hence, ~-*trotter*. ~ *v.* Make, become, globular. **glō'boid** *adj.* & *n.* **glōbō'se** *adj.* **glōbŏ'sitȳ** *n.*

glŏ'būlar *adj.* Globe-shaped, spherical; composed of globules. **glŏbūlă'rĭtȳ** *n.* **glŏ'būlarlȳ** *adv.*

glŏ'būle *n.* Small spherical body, esp. of liquid; drop, pill.

glŏ'būlĭn *n.* Protein found in animal or plant tissue.

glŏ'ckenspiel (-shpēl) *n.* Musical instrument, series of tuned

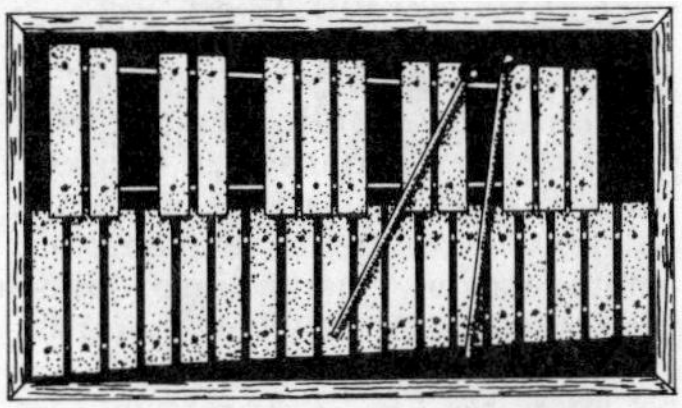

metal bars played with hammers, or tubes played from a keyboard. [Ger., = 'bell-play']

glomĕ'rulus *n.* Cluster of small organisms, tissues, blood-vessels, etc., esp. of capillary blood-vessels of kidney.

glōōm *n.* Darkness, obscurity; melancholy, despondency. **glōō'mȳ** *adj.* **glōō'mily** *adv.* **glōō'minėss** *n.* **glōōm** *v.i.* Look or be gloomy.

glôr'ĭa *n.* 1. (short for ~ *Patri*) Doxology beginning 'Glory be to the Father'; ~ *tibi*, response 'Glory be to thee, O Lord', following announcement for gospel in Mass etc.; ~ *in excelsis*, hymn 'Glory be to God on high' forming part of Mass etc., music for this. 2. Aureole, halo. [L]

Glôrĭa'na (-ah-). Nickname of Elizabeth I.

glôr'ĭfȳ *v.t.* 1. Make glorious, exalt to the glory of heaven; invest with radiance; transform into something more splendid, invest (common or inferior thing) with charm or beauty. 2. Extol, laud. **glôrĭfĭcā'tion** *n.*

glôr'ĭōle *n.* Aureole, halo.

glôr'ĭous *adj.* Possessing glory, illustrious; conferring glory, honourable; splendid, excellent. **glôr'ĭouslȳ** *adv.*

glôr'ȳ *n.* 1. Exalted renown, honourable fame; subject for boasting, special distinction, ornament, pride. 2. Adoring praise and thanksgiving. 3. Resplendent majesty, beauty, or magnificence; effulgence of heavenly light; imagined unearthly beauty; bliss and splendour of heaven. 4. State of exultation, prosperity, etc. 5. Circle of light round head or figure of deity or saint, aureole, halo. 6. ~-*hole*, (slang) untidy room, drawer, cupboard, etc. ~ *v.i.* Exult, pride oneself, *in*. **glōr'y̆ingly̆** *adv*.

Glos. *abbrev*. Gloucestershire.

glŏss[1] *n*. Word inserted between lines or in margin to explain word in text; comment, explanation, interpretation, paraphrase; misrepresentation of another's words; glossary, interlinear translation, or set of notes. ~ *v*. Insert glosses in (text etc.); write glosses; make comments esp. of unfavourable sort; read different sense into, explain away.

glŏss[2] *n*. Superficial lustre; deceptive appearance, fair outside. ~ *v.t.* Make glossy; give specious appearance to (freq. *over*). **glŏ'ssy̆** *adj*. **glŏ'ssily̆** *adv*. **glŏ'ssinėss** *n*.

glŏ'ssal *adj*. (anat.) Of the tongue, lingual.

glŏ'ssary̆ *n*. Collection of glosses; list and explanations of abstruse, obsolete, dialectal, or technical terms, partial dictionary. **glŏssār'ial** *adj*. **glŏ'ssarist** *n*.

glŏssā'tor *n*. Commentator, esp. medieval commentator on Civil and Canon Law.

glŏssī'tis *n*. Inflammation of the tongue.

glŏ'ttal *adj*. Of, produced in, the glottis; ~ *stop*, sound produced by sudden explosive release of breath from behind the closed glottis.

glŏ'ttis *n*. Opening at upper part of windpipe and between vocal cords, affecting modulation of voice by contracting or dilating.

Gloucester (glŏ'st*er*). City and county town of Gloucestershire; *single*, *double*, ~, kinds of cheese made in Gloucestershire.

Gloucestershire (glŏ'st-). County of SW. England.

Gloucestr. *abbrev*. (Bishop) of Gloucester (replacing surname in his signature).

glove (-ŭv) *n*. Covering of leather, cotton, silk, wool, etc., for the hand, usu. with separated fingers; padded glove for boxing; *fight with the ~s off*, contend in earnest; *throw down*, *take up*, *the* ~, make, accept, a challenge. ~ *v.t.* Provide with gloves. **glo'ver** *n*. Maker or seller of gloves.

glow (-ō) *v.i.* Be heated to incandescence, throw out light and heat without flame; shine like thing intensely heated; show warm colour; burn with bodily heat or emotional fervour; ~-*worm*, beetle (*Lampyris noctiluca*) which emits shining green light from ventral surface of abdomen. ~ *n*. Glowing state; brightness and warmth of colour; ardour, passion. **glow'ingly̆** *adv*.

glow'er (*or* -owr) *v.i.* Stare, scowl (*at*). **glow'eringly̆** *adv*.

glŏxi'nia *n*. American tropical plant with large bell-shaped flowers. [B. P. *Gloxin*, 18th-c. Ger. botanist]

glōze *v*. (archaic) Palliate, explain away.

Gluck (-o͝ok), Christopher Willibald von (1714–87). Bavarian composer of operas, of which 'Orpheus and Eurydice' is the most famous.

glu'cōse (glo͞o-; *or* -z) *n*. Dextrose, grape-sugar ($CHO(CHOH)_4CH_2OH$), occurring in the dextrorotatory form in many plant and fruit juices, in animal tissue fluids, and in blood.

glu'cosīde (glo͞o-) *n*. Glycoside yielding glucose on hydrolysis.

glue (-o͞o) *n*. Hard brittle brownish gelatin, obtained from the hides, bones, and other waste parts of animals by boiling with suitable solvents, and used with water as cement; any similar substance; ~-*pot*, pot in which glue is melted by heat of water in an outer vessel. ~ *v.t.* Fasten or join (as) with glue; attach tightly or closely. **glu'ey** *adj*.

glŭm *adj*. Sullen, looking dejected or displeased. **glŭ'mly̆** *adv*. **glŭ'mnėss** *n*.

glume (-o͞om) *n*. (bot.) Chaff-like bract in spikelet of grasses etc; husk of grain. **glumā'ceous** (-sh*u*s) *adj*. Of, bearing glumes; belonging to the Glumaceae or glume-bearing plants, including grasses and sedges. **glu'mōse** *adj*.

glŭt *v.t.* Feed (person, stomach) or indulge (appetite, desire) to the full, overload with food; satiate, cloy; choke up, fill to excess; overstock (market) with goods. **~** *n.* Full indulgence; one's fill, surfeit; supply in excess of demand.

glutē'al (glo͞o-) *adj.* ~ *muscle*, one of the three large muscles (*gluteus maximus, medius, minimus*) forming buttock and serving to move thigh in man.

glu'tėn (glo͞o-) *n.* 1. Sticky substance (rare); viscid animal secretion. 2. Nitrogenous part of flour, remaining as viscid substance when starch is washed out. **glu'tĭnīze** *v.t.* Make viscous. **glutĭnŏ'sĭtȳ** *n.* **glu'tĭnous** *adj.* **glu'tĭnouslȳ** *adv.* **glu'tĭnousnėss** *n.*

glŭ'tton *n.* 1. Excessive eater, gormandizer; (fig.) person with excessive appetite *for* some activity etc. 2. Voracious animal, *Gulo gulo*, of weasel family but much larger, native of N. Europe, Asia, and N. America; wolverine. **glŭ'ttonīze** *v.i.* **glŭ'ttonous** *adj.* **glŭ'ttonouslȳ** *adv.* **glŭ'ttonȳ** *n.*

glȳ'cerīde *n.* (chem.) Ester of glycerine.

glȳ'cerĭne, -ĭn *n.* Colourless sweet viscous liquid obtained as a by-product in the conversion of animal and vegetable oils and fats into soap; used as ointment, as vehicle for drugs, in manufacture of explosives, etc. **glȳ'cerĭnāte** *v.t.* Treat with glycerine.

glȳ'cerŏl *n.* (Name preferred in scientific use for) glycerine.

glȳ'cerȳl *n.* (chem.) Trivalent radical of GLYCERINE.

glȳ'cogėn *n.* Reserve carbohydrate $(C_6H_{10}O_5)_n$ of the animal cell, into which sugar is converted by insulin. **glȳcogĕ'nĭc** *adj.*

glȳ'cŏl *n.* Any aliphatic dihydric alcohol, esp. ethylene glycol (see ETHYLENE). **glȳcŏ'l(l)ĭc** *adj.*

glȳcŏ'lȳsĭs *n.* Breakdown of sugar in the body tissues.

glȳcŏ'nĭc *adj.* & *n.* (Gk & L pros.) (Line, metre) consisting of three trochees and dactyl, the dactyl variously placed; esp. the form —∪|—∪∪|—∪|⊻ (the last trochee being cut short). [*Glukōn*, Gk lyric poet]

glȳ'cosīde *n.* Vegetable substance yielding a sugar on hydrolysis.

glȳcosūr'ĭa *n.* (path.) Condition in which abnormal proportion of sugar appears in the urine. **glȳcosūr'ĭc** *adj.*

glȳ'ptĭc *adj.* Of carving, esp. in precious stones.

glȳ'ptodŏn *n.* Extinct S. Amer. quadruped allied to armadillos, of size of an ox, covered with carapace, and having fluted teeth.

glȳptŏ'graphȳ *n.* Art or study of gem-engraving.

gm *abbrev.* Gramme(s).

G.M. *abbrev.* George Medal.

G-man *n.* (U.S.) Special agent of the Federal Bureau of Investigation. [G = 'government']

G.M.C. *abbrev.* General Medical Council.

G.M.T. *abbrev.* Greenwich mean time.

gn., gns. *abbrev.* Guinea(s).

gnârled (nârld), **gnâr'lȳ** (n-) *adjs.* (of tree) Covered with protuberances; twisted, rugged, knotted, like an old tree.

gnăsh (n-) *v.* Grind (teeth), grind teeth; (of teeth) strike together.

gnăt (n-) *n.* (pop.) Small two-winged biting or irritating fly; (zool.) = MOSQUITO.

gnă'thĭc (n-) *adj.* Of jaws.

gnaw (n-) *v.* Bite persistently, wear away thus; (of pain etc.) corrode, waste away, consume, torture. **gnaw'ĭnglȳ** *adv.*

gneiss (gnīs *or* n-) *n.* (geol.) Coarse-grained metamorphic rock in which the mineral grains are arranged in roughly parallel bands, usu. containing felspar and a dark mineral and sometimes quartz.

gnō'mė¹ (n-; *or* nōm) *n.* Maxim, aphorism. **gnō'mĭc** *adj.* Of, consisting of, using, gnomes; sententious.

gnōme² (n-) *n.* 1. (myth.) Supernatural dwarfish being of subterranean race guarding treasures of the earth; goblin, dwarf. 2. (colloq.) International (esp. Swiss) financier. **gnō'mĭsh** *adj.*

[f. mod. L *gnomus* invented by Paracelsus]

gnō'mon (n-) *n.* 1. Pillar, rod, pin, or triangular plate of sundial, showing time by its shadow on marked surface; column etc. used in observing sun's meridian altitude. 2. (geom.) Part of parallelogram left when similar parallelogram is taken away from one of its corners. **gnōmŏ'nic** *adj.* ~ *projection*, geographical projection in which points are projected on to a tangent plane from the centre of the sphere.

gnō'sis (n-) *n.* Knowledge of spiritual mysteries; Gnosticism.

gnŏ'stic (n-) *adj.* 1. Relating to knowledge, cognitive. 2. Having esoteric spiritual knowledge; *G~*, of the Gnostics, occult, mystic. **Gnŏ'stic** *n.* (hist.) Member of a heretical sect of early Christians claiming to have superior knowledge of things spiritual, and interpreting sacred writings by a mystic philosophy. **Gnŏ'stĭcism** *n.*

G.N.P. *abbrev.* Gross national product.

gnu (nū) *n.* S. Afr. quadruped of genus *Connochaetes*, of antelope family but resembling ox or buffalo.

gō[1] *v.* (past t. *went*, past part. *gone*). 1. Start, depart, move, continue moving, from some place, position, time, etc. (often not specified if obvious); begin motion; travel, proceed. 2. (of line etc.) Lie, point, in certain direction. 3. Be habitually in specified state. 4. Be moving, acting, in working order. 5. Make specified motion. 6. (of bell) Strike (hour). 7. (of time) Pass, elapse. 8. (of coin, story, etc.) Be current. 9. (of document etc.) Have specified tenor. 10. (of verse etc.) Be adaptable *to* a tune. 11. (of events) Turn out *well, badly*, etc.; (colloq.) be permitted; (of statement etc.) be authoritative. 12. Get away *free, unpunished*, etc. 13. Be sold *for* sum. 14. (of money) Be spent *in* or *on* goods. 15. Be relinquished, abolished, or lost; die (esp. in past part.); fail, give way, succumb. 16. Be kept or put in certain place. 17. Reach, extend, penetrate. 18. Be allotted; contribute, tend. 19. (of number) Be capable of being contained in another either without remainder or simply. 20. Pass into a (esp. undesirable) condition. 21. Bid, declare. 22. Phrases: ~ *it*, act vigorously or furiously; *going to*, preparing or intending to; about to; *gone*, dead, lost, undone; *gone on*, (colloq. or vulg.) infatuated with; *far gone*, in advanced stage (of disease etc.), deeply engaged or entangled. 23. (with preps.): ~ *about*, set to work at; ~ *at*, attack, take in hand energetically; ~ *behind*, re-examine grounds of (decision etc.); ~ *by*, be guided by; ~ *for*, go to fetch; be accounted as; strive to attain; be applicable to; (colloq.) attack; ~ *into*, enter (profession etc.); frequent (society); take part in; investigate; ~ *over*, inspect details of; rehearse, retouch; ~ *through*, discuss in detail; scrutinize; perform (ceremony etc.); undergo; (of book) be published successively in (so many editions); ~ *with*, be concomitant of, be associated with; take same view as; harmonize with, match; follow the drift of; ~ *without*, not have, put up with want of. 24. (with advs.): ~ *about*, move from place to place; endeavour *to* do; ~ *ahead*, proceed without hesitation; ~ *by*, pass; ~ *down*, (of ship) sink; be continued *to* specified point; fall *before* conqueror; be recorded in writing; be swallowed; (colloq.) find acceptance *with*; ~ *in*, enter as competitor; (cricket) take or begin innings; (of sun etc.) be obscured; ~ *in for*, take as one's object, pursuit, style, etc.; ~ *off*, leave the stage; begin; explode; die; gradually cease to be felt; deteriorate; become unconscious in sleep, faint, etc.; be got rid of by sale; succeed *well, badly*, etc.; ~ *on*, continue, persevere; proceed as next step *to* do; conduct oneself; appear on stage; begin bowling; take one's turn to do something; (colloq.) rail *at*; (imper.) don't talk nonsense; *going on for*, approaching (time, age, etc.); ~ *out*, leave room or house;

be extinguished; cease to be fashionable; depart *to* colony etc.; take employment (*as*); mix in society; (of workmen) strike; ~ *over*, change one's party or religion; ~ *round*, pay informal visit *to*; be long enough to encompass; (of food etc.) suffice for whole party etc.; ~ *through with*, complete, not leave unfinished; ~ *under*, fail, sink, succumb. 25. ~-*ahead* (*adj.*) enterprising; (*n.*) permission to proceed; ~-*as-you-please*, unfettered by rules; ~-*between*, intermediary, negotiator; *give the* ~-*by to* (person), outstrip, elude, or ignore him; ~-*cart*, kind of perambulator; ~-*getter*, (orig. U.S.) active pushing person; ~-*kart*, miniature racing car; ~-*off*, start; ~-*slow*, form of industrial protest in which employees work at a deliberately slow pace. ~ *n.* 1. Act of going. 2. Mettle, dash, animation. 3. (colloq.) Turn of affairs, unexpected course of things. 4. Turn at doing something; attempt *at*. 5. (colloq.) *all the* ~, in fashion; *it's no* ~, nothing can be done; *on the* ~, in motion.

gō[2] *n.* (also *I-go*) Japanese game of territorial possession, played on board of 19×19 lines, each player having about 200 pieces.

Gō'a. District on west coast of India, administered (with Daman and Diu) by India; capital, Panaji. **Gōanē'se** (-z) *adj.* & *n.*

goad *n.* Spiked stick used for urging cattle; thing that torments, incites, or stimulates. ~ *v.t.* Urge with goad; irritate; instigate, drive (*on*), by annoyance.

goal *n.* 1. Point marking end of race; object of effort or ambition; destination. 2. Posts between which ball is to be driven at football and other games; points won by doing this; ~ *attack*, *defence*, (position of) netball player near opponents', own team's goal; *goal'keeper*, (footb. etc.) player stationed to protect goal; ~-*line*, line (at either end of playing-field) in centre of which goal-posts are placed; ~*shooter*, (esp.) (position of) netball player whose function is to shoot ball into net. **goa'lie** *n.* (colloq.) Goalkeeper.

goat *n.* Hardy lively wanton strong-smelling usu. horned and bearded ruminant quadruped (genus *Capra*); licentious person; fool; *the G*~: see CAPRICORN; ~-*god*, Pan; *goa'therd*, one who tends goats; *goat's-beard*, plant Jack-go-to-bed-at-noon, allied to salsify (*Tragopogon*); *goa'tskin*, (garment, bottle, made of) skin of goat; *goa'tsucker*, nightjar, (formerly believed to suck the milk of goats). **goa'tĭsh** *adj.* **goa'tĭshlȳ** *adv.* **goa'tȳ** *adj.*

goatee' *n.* Small beard on chin resembling goat's beard.

gŏb *n.* (vulg.) Clot of slimy substance, e.g. spittle; (slang) mouth; hence, ~-*stopper*, large sticky sweet. ~ *v.i.* (vulg.) Spit.

gōbă'ng *n.* Japanese board game resembling GO[2], but less complicated.

gŏ'bbėt *n.* 1. (archaic) Piece, lump, esp. of raw flesh or food. 2. Lines extracted from a text for translation or comment in examination.

gŏ'bble[1] *v.* Eat hurriedly and noisily. **gŏ'bbler**[1] *n.*

gŏ'bble[2] *v.i.* (of turkey-cock) Make characteristic sound in throat; make such sound when speaking, from rage, etc. **gŏ'bbler**[2] *n.* Turkey-cock.

gŏ'bbledȳgo͝ok (-ld-) *n.* (U.S. slang) Pretentious and unintelligible jargon.

Gŏ'belĭn *adj.* Of, made at, the French State-owned tapestry factory of the Gobelins in Paris, orig. a court furniture factory established 1667 by Louis XIV's minister Colbert in workshops previously owned by a 15th-c. family of dyers named Gobelin; ~ *stitch*, tapestry stitch.

gŏ'blėt *n.* (archaic) Bowl-shaped drinking-cup without handles, sometimes with foot and cover; glass with foot and stem, dist. from TUMBLER, 3.; (poet.) drinking-cup.

gŏ'blĭn *n.* Mischievous and ugly demon.

LOUIS XIV VISITS THE GOBELINS

gō′bȳ *n.* Small acanthopterygian fish (esp. *Gobius*) with ventral fins joined into disc or sucker.

G.O.C.(-in-C.) *abbrev.* General Officer Commanding(-in-Chief).

gŏd *n.* 1. Superhuman being worshipped as having power over nature and human fortunes, deity; ~ *of fire*, Vulcan; ~ *of love, blind* ~, Cupid; ~ *of war*, Mars; ~ *of wine*, Bacchus. 2. Image, animal, or other object, worshipped as symbolizing, being the visible habitation of, or itself possessing, divine power; an idol; adored, admired, or influential person. 3. (pl., theatr.) (Occupants of) gallery. 4. *God*, supreme being, creator and ruler of universe; *God the Father, Son, Holy Ghost*, persons of the Trinity; *God knows*, it is beyond mortal or my knowledge, I don't know; (also) I call God to witness; *God willing*, if circumstances allow. 5. *go′dfather, go′dmother*, sponsor at baptism; so *go′dchild, -son, -daughter*; ~*-fearing*, sincerely religious; ~*-forsaken*, devoid of all merit; forlorn, dismal; *go′dsend*, unexpected welcome event or acquisition; *Go′dspeed*, usu. in *wish* or *bid person Godspeed*, wish him success in journey, undertaking, etc. **gŏ′dhood** *n.* **gŏ′dlike** *adj.*

gŏ′ddėss *n.* Female deity; ~ *of love*, Venus; ~ *of wisdom*, Minerva.

gō′det (-ā; *or* -ĕ′t) *n.* Triangular piece inserted in skirt, glove, etc.

godē′tia (-sh*a*) *n.* Free-flowering hardy annual of genus *G*~, native of America, with large heads of cup-shaped flowers. [C. H. *Godet*, Swiss botanist]

Godfrey of Bouillon: see BOUILLON.

gŏ′dhead (-d-hĕd) *n.* Being God or a god, divine nature, deity; *the G*~, God.

Godī′va. Wife of Leofric, earl of Mercia; acc. to legend, her husband had imposed a tax on the inhabitants of Coventry which he jestingly promised to remit if she would ride naked through the streets at noonday; taking him at his word, she did this, having told the people to stay indoors with closed windows.

gŏ′dlėss *adj.* Without a god; not recognizing God; impious, wicked. **gŏ′dlėssnėss** *n.*

gŏ′dlȳ *adj.* Religious, pious, devout. **gŏ′dlinėss** *n.*

gōdow′n *n.* Warehouse in India and other parts of E. Asia. [Malay *godong*]

Gŏ′dwin Au′sten: see K2.

gŏ′dwit *n.* Large wading bird of genus *Limosa*, like curlew but with bill slightly curved upwards.

Goe'bbels (gẽr-, -z), Paul Josef (1897–1945). German minister for propaganda under the Nazi regime.

Goethe (gẽr'te), Johann Wolfgang von (1749–1832). Germany's greatest poet, also scientist and statesman in the duchy of Weimar; author of many lyric poems, dramas, and novels, of which 'Faust', a dramatic poem, and the novels 'The Sorrows of Young Werther' and 'Wilhelm Meister' are the most famous.

gŏ'ffer, gŏ'pher, gau'ffer (gŏ-) *v.t.* Make wavy, flute, crimp (edge, trimming, etc.) with heated irons. ~ *n.* Iron used for goffering; frilled edging for bonnets etc.

Gŏg and Mā'gŏg. 1. Names of various people and lands in O.T. 2. Nations under dominion of Satan (Rev. 20: 8) opposed to the people of God. 3. (in medieval legend) Opponents of Alexander the Great, living north of the Caucasus. 4. Names given to two giant statues standing in the Guildhall, London, from the time of Henry V (destroyed in 1666 and 1940; replaced in 1953), either (acc. to Caxton) the last two survivors of a race of giants inhabiting Britain before Roman times, or (in another account) Gogmagog, chief of the giants, and Corineus, a Roman invader.

gŏ'ggle *v.* Squint, roll eyes about; (of eyes) project, roll about; turn (eyes) sideways or from side to side. ~ *adj.* (of eyes) Protuberant, full and rolling. **gŏ'ggles** (-z) *n.pl.* Spectacles for protecting eyes from glare, dust, etc., often with coloured glasses etc.; (slang), round-lensed spectacles.

Gŏgmā'gŏg: see Gog and Magog, 4.

Gō'gol, Nikoly Vasilyevich (1809–52). Russian novelist; best known for his 'Dead Souls', a picaresque romance satirizing provincial Russian society.

Goi'del. Gael, person belonging to Celts of Ireland and the Scottish Highlands. **Goidĕ'lic** *adj.* & *n.* (Language) of the Goidels.

gō'ing *n.* (esp.) Condition of

GOETHE

ground for walking, riding, etc.; *goings-on*, behaviour; *in ~ order*, in condition for working properly. ~ *adj*. ~ *concern*, business in actual operation.

goi'tre (-t*er*) *n*. Morbid enlargement of thyroid gland, often visible as swelling in neck. **goi'tred** (-t*er*d), **goi'trous** *adjs*.

Gŏlcŏ'nda. Old name of Hyderabad, formerly celebrated for diamonds; hence, mine of wealth.

gōld *n*. 1. (chem.) Metallic element, malleable, ductile, of yellow colour and high specific gravity, occurring in the free state, not attacked by most acids, but dissolved by aqua regia, regarded as a precious metal, and used as a standard of value and as the international medium of exchange; symbol Au, at. no. 79, at. wt 196·9665. 2. Coins made of gold, money in large sums, wealth; metal used for coating surface or as pigment, gilding; colour of the metal; (fig.) brilliant, beautiful, or precious things, stuff, etc. 3. ~ *amalgam*, plastic alloy of gold and mercury; *~-beater*, one who beats gold out into gold leaf; *~-beater's skin*, membrane used to separate leaves of gold during beating, and formerly as covering for slight wounds; ~ *brick*, (U.S.) something with only surface appearance of value, fraud, sham; *~-digger*, one who digs for gold; (slang, orig. U.S.) woman attaching herself to man merely for gain; *~-dust*, gold in fine particles, as often found; *~-field*, district in which gold is found; ~ *foil*, gold beaten into thin sheet; ~ *leaf*, sheet of beaten gold, thinner than gold foil; *~-mine*, place where gold is mined; source of wealth; *~-plate* (*v.t.*) plate with gold; *~-rush*, rush to new goldfield; *go'ldsmith*, worker in gold; ~ *standard*, financial system of a country in which paper, silver money, etc., is redeemable on demand in gold at a fixed weight and fineness; *G~ Stick*, (bearer of) gilt rod borne on State occasions by colonel of Life Guards or captain of Gentlemen-at-arms. ~ *adj*. Wholly or chiefly of, coloured like, gold; (of money of account) reckoned at full undepreciated value according to some gold standard established at an earlier date; (of lace etc.) containing gold threads; *go'ldfinch*, bright-coloured song-bird (*Carduelis carduelis*) with patch of yellow on wings; *go'ldfish*, golden-red Chinese fish (*Carassius auratus*) of carp family, kept for ornament.

Gold Coast: see GHANA.

gō'lden *adj*. Made, consisting, of gold; abounding in, yielding, gold; coloured, shining, like gold; precious, excellent, important; ~ *age*, (i) (Gk & Rom. myth.) first and best age of world, in which mankind was ideally prosperous and happy; (ii) most flourishing period (of literature etc.); *G~ Bull*, medieval charter sealed with gold, esp. that issued by the Emperor Charles IV in 1356 settling precedence amongst the Electoral princes; ~ *chain*, laburnum; ~ *eagle*, large eagle of Northern hemisphere with golden yellow feathers on head and neck; ~ *eye*, duck of genus *Bucephala* with black-and-white plumage in male and gold-coloured iris of the eye; *G~ Fleece*, (Gk legend) fleece of gold taken from the ram that bore Phrixus through the air to Colchis; it was placed in a sacred grove by Aeëtes, king of Colchis, where it was guarded by a sleepless dragon, until it was won by JASON; *Order of the G~ Fleece*, order of chivalry instituted by Philip the Good, Duke of Burgundy, in 1429; *G~ Gate*, entrance of San Francisco bay; ~ *handshake*, gratuity given as compensation for retirement; *G~ Horde*, (trans. of Tatar name, from richness of Batu Khan's tent) Tatar horde which overran Eastern Europe in 13th c. under Batu Khan, grandson of Genghiz, and kept Russia in subjection until 1486; *G~ Horn*, curved inlet of Bosporus, forming harbour of Istanbul; *G~ Legend*, 13th-c. collection of saints' lives by Jacobus de Voragine, archbishop of Genoa; ~ *mean*, avoidance of excess in either direction; ~ *number*, number of any year in Metonic lunar cycle of 19 years (found by adding 1 to remainder after dividing number of year by 19), so called because of its usefulness in calculating date of Easter; ~ *oak*, (U.S.) canyon live-oak, *Quercus chrysolepis*; (of furniture) made of light-coloured oak; ~ *rain*, firework forming shower of golden sparks; ~ *rectangle*, rectangle in which ratio of longer side to shorter is the golden section; ~*-rod*, plant of genus *Solidago*, esp. *S. virgaurea*, with rod-like stem and spike of bright-yellow flowers; ~ *rose*: see ROSE; ~ *rule*, rule, *do to others as you would be done by*, the popular form of the precept in Matt. 7: 12; ~ *section*, division of a straight line into two

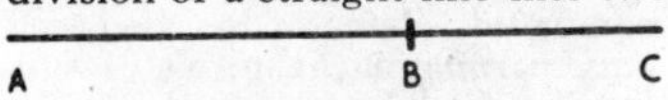

GOLDEN SECTION

The line is divided at *B* so that
$AC/AB = AB/BC$

parts so that the ratio of the whole line to the larger part is the same as the ratio of the larger part to the smaller; ~ *spur*, papal order of St. Sylvester; ~ *syrup*, (trade-name for) pale-coloured treacle; ~ *wedding*, 50th anniversary of wedding.

gō'ldilŏcks *n.* One who has golden hair; any of various yellow-flowered plants, esp. a species of buttercup, *Ranunculus auricomus*.

Gŏldō'nĭ, Carlo (1707–93). Italian dramatist.

Gō'ldsmĭth, Oliver (1730–74). Irish writer; author of the novel 'Vicar of Wakefield' and the comedy 'She Stoops to Conquer'.

gŏlf (*or* gŏf) *n.* Game (usu. for two persons or two couples) in which small hard rubber-cored ball is struck with clubs over surface of course into series of small holes on smooth greens, the aim being to hit the ball with the fewest possible strokes into any one hole or all holes successively; ~ *club*, society for playing this game; one of the sticks with which it is played; ~ *course, links*, ground on which the game is played, usu. of 9 or 18 holes arranged at intervals on stretch of roughish ground, freq. with artificial obstacles (bunkers etc.) added. ~ *v.i.* Play golf. **gŏ'lfer** *n.* 1. One who plays golf. 2. Cardigan.

gŏ'lgĭ ăpparā'tus. (biol.) Intracellular system of membranes and vacuoles near the nucleus in cells of most animals and some plants, usu. concerned with intracellular secretion. [Camillo *Golgi* (1844–1926), Ital. physician]

Gŏ'lgotha. Aramaic name of CALVARY (Mark 15: 22); hence, burial place, cemetery. [Heb. *gulgōleth* skull]

Golī'ath. Philistine giant, acc. to legend slain by David (1 Sam. 17), but prob. slain by Elhanan (2 Sam. 21: 19); ~ *crane*, gantry crane for heavy work.

gŏ'llĭwŏg *n.* Black-faced grotesquely-dressed male doll with shock of fuzzy hair.

gŏ'llȳ *int.* (colloq.) By God.

golosh: see GALOSH.

golŭ'ptious (-sh*us*) *adj.* (joc.) Luscious, delightful.

G.O.M. *abbrev.* Grand old man (usu. in ref. to Gladstone).

gombee'n *n.* (Anglo-Ir.) Usury; ~*-man, -woman*, money-lender.

Gomŏ'rrah (-*a*). Town of ancient Palestine, which, along with Sodom, was destroyed by the Lord on account of the godlessness of its inhabitants (see Gen. 18, 19); hence (type of) wicked town.

gŏ'năd *n.* (biol.) Organ (as testis or ovary) producing gametes.

gonā'dĭal, gonă'dĭc *adjs.*

Goncourt (gawṅkoor), Edmond Huot de (1822–96) and his brother Jules (1830–70). French literary critics; wrote several novels and plays in collaboration; founded a

prize (*Prix* ~), awarded annually for the best imaginative work in prose.

Gŏnd *n.* 1. Member of a Dravidian people of central India. 2. (also *Gŏ'ndĭ*) Language of the Gonds. ~ *adj.*

gŏ'ndola *n.* Light flat-bottomed boat with cabin amidships and high point at each end, worked by one oar at stern, used on Venetian canals; boat-shaped car suspended from airship or used on ski-lift; (U.S.) flat roofless railway car with low sides. **gŏndolier'** *n.* Rower of gondola.

Gŏndwa'na (-wah-). (hist.) Land of the Gonds; ~ *system*, (geol.) system of rocks in India. **Gŏndwa'nalănd.** Ancient land-mass supposed to have existed in the southern hemisphere until late Palaeozoic times, including Africa, India, Australia, and South America.

gŏne: see GO[1].

gŏ'ner *n.* (slang) One who is dead or undone; something doomed or ended.

gŏ'nfalon *n.* Banner, often with streamers, hung from cross-bar, esp. as standard of some Italian republics. **gŏnfalonier'** *n.* Standard-bearer; (hist.) chief magistrate in some Italian republics.

gŏng *n.* Metal disc with turned rim giving resonant note when struck with drumstick, used esp. to summon household for meals, and occas. in orchestra; saucer-shaped bell struck with hammer or tongue, used as alarm-bell etc.; (mil. slang) medal. ~ *v.t.* (slang, of motorized police) Order (motorist) to stop by sounding gong etc. [Malay]

gŏ'ngorism -ngg-) *n.* Affected type of diction and style introduced into Spanish literature by the poet Don Luis de Gongora y Argote (1561–1627), akin to EUPHUISM in England.

gōniŏ'mėter *n.* 1. Instrument for measuring angles in solids such as crystals etc. 2. Apparatus for detecting direction of radio waves without the need for a rotating aerial.

gŏnocŏ'ccus *n.* (pl. *-cī*). Micro-organism causing gonorrhoea.

gŏnorrhoe'a (-*orēa*) *n.* Venereal disease characterized by inflammatory discharge of mucus from urethra or vagina. **gŏnorrhoe'al** *adj.*

good *adj.* Having the right qualities, adequate; expedient; morally excellent, virtuous; benevolent; well behaved (esp. of child), not giving trouble; agreeable, advantageous; wholesome; suitable; efficient; reliable, safe; valid, sound; considerable; not less than (as in *a ~ 3 miles* etc.); *as ~ as*, practically, almost; *have a ~ mind to*, be much inclined to; *have a ~ time*, enjoy oneself; *make ~*: see MAKE: *say a ~ word for*, commend, defend; ~ *afternoon*, *day*, *morning*, *night*, forms of salutation at meeting or parting; ~ *breeding*, correct or courteous manners; ~ *fellow*, sociable person, agreeable companion; *~-fellowship*, conviviality, sociability; ~ *for*, beneficial to; having good effect on; in condition to undertake or pay; (of draft) drawn for (so much); *~-for-nothing*, worthless, useless (person); *G~ Friday*: see FRIDAY; ~ *humour*, cheerful mood or disposition, amiability; *~-humoured* (*adj.*), *~-humouredly* (*adv.*); *~-looking*, handsome; ~ *luck*, being fortunate, happy chance; *goo'dman*, (archaic) head of household, husband, father, etc.; ~ *nature*, kindly disposition, willingness to humour others or permit encroachment on one's rights; *~-natured* (*adj.*), *~-naturedly* (*adv.*); ~ *people*, fairies; ~ *sense*, practical wisdom; ~ *temper*, freedom from irritability; *~-tempered* (*adj.*), *~-temperedly* (*adv.*); *goo'dwife*, (now chiefly Sc.) mistress of house etc. ~ *n.* 1. What is good or beneficial, well-being, profit, advantage; desirable end or object; *be any ~*, be of any use (similarly *some ~*, *no ~*); *do ~*, act philanthropically, show kindness *to*, benefit; *for ~ and all*, finally, permanently; *to the ~*, as balance on right side, something extra etc.; *up to no* ~, bent on mischief. 2. *the* ~, virtuous persons. 3. (pl.) Movable property, merchandise, wares; things for transmission by rail etc. (opp. *passengers*), whence ~*s station*, ~*s train*, etc. **goo'dish** *adj.*

good-by'e *int.* & *n.* Exclamation used conventionally at parting. [contraction of *God be with you!* with *good* substituted on analogy of *good-night* etc.]

goo'dly *adj.* Comely, handsome; of considerable size etc. **goo'dliness** *n.*

goo'dness *n.* Virtue; excellence; benevolence, kindness, generosity, what is good in a thing, its essence or strength; (in exclamations substituted for) God.

goodwi'll *n.* Kindly feeling towards person; cheerful acquiescence, heartiness, established custom (esp. as saleable value) of business.

Goo'dwood. Race-meeting on course near Goodwood Park, West Sussex.

goo'dy[1] *n.* (archaic) Woman (usu. married) in humble life; *G*~, title of such, prefixed to surname. [for *goodwife*]

goo'dy[2] *n.* (usu. pl.) Something good to eat, esp. a sweet.

goo'dy[3], **goo'dy-goo'dy** *adjs.* & *ns.* Ostentatiously virtuous (person); (person) good in a weak or sentimental way. ~ *ints.* Exclamations of delight used by children.

goof *n.* (slang) Silly or stupid person. **goo'fy** *adj.* **goof** *v.* Make a mistake, bungle.

goo'gly *n.* (cricket) Ball breaking from the off, though bowled with leg-break action.

goon *n.* 1. (U.S. slang) Dull or stupid person. 2. (slang) German guard in P.O.W. camps (1939–45).

goosa'nder *n.* Duck (*Mergus merganser*) with sharply serrated bill and (in the male) glossy green-black head and back and pale pink underparts.

goose *n.* (pl. *geese*). 1. Large web-footed bird (of genus *Anser* or sub-family Anserinae), usu.

GEESE

between duck and swan in size; female of this; its flesh as food. 2. Simpleton. 3. Tailor's smoothing-iron (with handle like goose's neck). 4. ~ *barnacle*: see BARNACLE[2]; ~*-flesh*, rough bristling state of skin produced by cold or fright; ~*-foot*, plant of genus *Chenopodium* (from shape of leaves); ~*-grass*, silverweed (*Potentilla anserina*); cleavers; ~*-neck*, pipe, piece of iron, etc., curved like goose's neck; ~*-step*, balance step, used by some armies in marching on ceremonial parades, in which the legs are alternately advanced without bending the knees; (*v.i.*) march thus.

goo'seberry (-zb-) *n.* (Edible berry of) any thorny species of *Ribes*; *play* ~, act as chaperon, be unwanted third with pair of lovers.

go'pher[1] *n.* 1. Amer. burrowing rodent of genus *Geomys* or *Thomomys*. 2. Nocturnal burrowing land-tortoise (*Testudo carolina*) of southern U.S. 3. Large burrowing snake, *Spilotes corais*, of southern U.S. 4. Small Amer. ground-squirrel, *Citellus*. ~ *v.i.* (U.S.) (mining) Dig small or haphazard holes (*~-holes*).

gō'pher² *n.* Tree of wood of which Noah's ark was made (Gen. 6: 14), supposed to be cypress.

gopher³: see GOFFER.

gŏr'al *n.* Indian antelope, *Naemorhedus goral*.

Gŏr'dian *adj.* ~ *knot*, intricate knot tied by Gordius, king of Gordium in Phrygia; an oracle declared that whoever loosened it should rule Asia, and Alexander the Great, unable to undo it, cut it with his sword; hence, a difficult problem or task; *cut the ~ knot*, solve problem by force or by evading conditions.

Gŏr'don, Charles George (1833–85). 'Chinese Gordon', an officer of the Royal Engineers who commanded the Chinese forces against the Taiping rebels in 1863–4; governor-general of the Sudan, 1877–80, where he put down the slave trade; was sent by the British Government in 1884 to rescue the Egyptian garrisons in the Sudan, was besieged at Khartoum and there killed.

gŏre¹ *n.* Blood shed and thickened or clotted. **gŏr'ȳ** *adj.* **gŏr'ilȳ** *adv.*

gŏre² *n.* Wedge-shaped piece in garment; triangular or lune-shaped piece forming part of balloon, umbrella-covering, dome, etc.; (U.S.) wedge-shaped strip of land. ~ *v.t.* Shape, narrow, with gore.

gŏre³ *v.t.* Pierce with the horn or (rarely) tusk.

gŏrge *n.* 1. (rhet.) Internal throat. 2. What has been swallowed, contents of stomach; act of gorging; surfeit; *one's ~ rises at*, one is sickened or disgusted by. 3. (fort.) Neck of bastion or other outwork; rear entrance to a work. 4. Narrow opening between hills, rocky ravine, usu. with stream. 5. Solid object meant to be swallowed as bait by fish. ~ *v.* Feed greedily; satiate, glut; swallow, devour greedily; fill full, distend, choke up.

gŏr'geous (-jus) *adj.* Richly coloured, sumptuous, magnificent. **gŏr'geouslȳ** *adv.* **gŏr'geousnėss** *n.*

gŏr'gėt¹ *n.* 1. (hist.) Piece of armour for throat; 2. (hist.) Wimple 3. Collar of beads, shells, etc., necklace; patch of colour on throat of bird etc.; ~ *patch*, distinguishing mark on the collar of a military uniform.

gŏr'gėt² *n.* (surg.) Channel-shaped steel instrument.

Gŏr'gon. (Gk myth.) One of 3 sisters, Stheno, Euryale, and MEDUSA¹ (the only mortal one), with snakes for hair, whose look turned the beholder to stone; hence (*g~*), terrifying woman.

gŏrgō'nĭa *n.* Any of various polyps of genus *G~*, including sea-fan. **gŏrgō'nĭan** *adj.* & *n.*

Gŏrgonzō'la *n.* Rich strong cheese, with veinings of bluish mould, orig. made at Gorgonzola, near Milan, Italy.

gorĭ'lla *n.* Large powerful arboreal anthropoid ape, native of western equatorial Africa.

Gör'ĭng (gėr-), Hermann Wilhelm (1893–1946). German field marshal; premier of Prussia, president of the Reichstag, and minister for aviation under the Nazi regime.

Gŏr'kȳ¹, Maxim (1868–1936). Pseudonym of Alexey Maximovich Peshkov, Russian writer and revolutionary; famous for his realistic short stories, dealing principally with thieves, tramps, and other outcasts.

Gŏr'kȳ². (formerly *Nizhny Novgorod*) City in the R.S.F.S.R., river port at confluence of Volga and Oka; scene of an annual fair.

gŏr'mandīze *v.* Eat voraciously or gluttonously. **gŏr'mandīzer** *n.*

gŏrse *n.* Prickly yellow-flowered shrub, *Ulex europaeus*, common on moors, commons, etc., whin, furze.

Gŏr'sĕdd (-dh) *n.* Assembly of poets and other writers in Wales, Cornwall, and Brittany, meeting esp. during the National EISTEDDFOD.

gŏsh *int.* By God.

gŏ'shawk (-s-h-) *n.* Large short-winged hawk.

Gō'shen. Place of light or plenty (Gen. 45: 10 etc., Exod. 8: 22, 9: 26).

gŏ'sling (-z-) *n.* Young goose.

gŏ'spel *n.* 1. Glad tidings (of kingdom of God) preached by Christ; religious doctrine of Christ and his apostles, Christian revelation. 2. (usu. *G~*) Record of Christ's life and teaching in first four books of N.T. (Matthew, Mark, Luke, John); any of these books; portion from one of them read at Communion service. 3. Thing that may safely be believed; principle that one acts upon, believes in, or preaches. 4. ~ *oath*, oath sworn on the gospels; ~*-shop*, Methodist chapel; ~ *side*, north side of altar, at which gospel is read; ~*-truth*, truth contained in gospel; something as true as gospel. [OE *god-spel* (*god* good, *spell* tidings)]

gŏ'speller *n.* Reader of gospel in Communion service; *hot* ~, zealous puritan, rabid propagandist.

gŏ'ssamer *n.* Light filmy substance, the webs of small spiders, floating in calm air esp. in autumn, or spread over grass; thread of this; something flimsy; delicate gauze. ~ *adj.* Light and flimsy as gossamer. **gŏ'ssamerў** *adj.* [ME *gossomer*, = 'goose-summer', St. Martin's summer, i.e. early November, when geese were customarily eaten and gossamer is abundant]

gŏ'ssip *n.* 1. (archaic) Familiar acquaintance; (esp. woman) friend. 2. Idle talker, newsmonger, tattler (esp. of woman). 3. Idle talk, groundless rumours, tittle-tattle; easy unconstrained talk or writing, esp. about persons or social incidents; hence ~ *column*, column devoted to this in newspaper. **gŏ'ssipў** *adj.* **gŏ'ssip** *v.i.* Talk idly or lightly, tattle; write in gossipy style. [orig. = sponsor at baptism, f. *God*+*sib* akin, related]

gossōō'n *n.* (Anglo-Ir.) Lad. [Fr. *garçon*]

gŏt: see GET; ~*-up*, artificially produced, adorned, etc., with a view to effect or deception.

Gŏth *n.* One of a Germanic tribe who in 3rd, 4th, and 5th centuries invaded both the Eastern and Western Roman Empires and founded kingdoms in Italy, France, and Spain; hence, rude, uncivilized, or ignorant person, esp. one who destroys works of art.

Gō'tham (-tam). 1. Village (perh. the one of this name in Nottinghamshire) proverbial for folly of its inhabitants (*wise men of* ~). 2. (*or* gŏ-) (joc.) City of New York, a name first given to it in 'Salmagundi', a humorous work by Washington Irving, William Irving, and J. K. Paulding, because its inhabitants were reputed to be wiseacres. **Gŏ'thamīte** *n.* New Yorker.

Gŏ'thic *adj.* 1. Of, like, the Goths; hence (fig.) barbarous, rude, uncouth. 2. (archit.) Of the style of architecture prevalent in Western Europe from the 12th to the 16th century, including in England the Early English, Decorated, and Perpendicular, characterized by ribbed vaults, pointed arches, clustered pillars, etc.; of the art at this period; (of script) of style used by Wulfila (see *n.* 2 below); (print.) black-letter. 3. ~ *Revival*, revival in England of Gothic architecture in the mid-18th and esp. the 19th c. ~ *n.* 1. Gothic architecture. 2. Extinct language of the Goths, one of the East GERMANIC group of languages, known from the 4th-c. translation of parts of the Bible made by Bishop Wulfila and from other scattered remnants. 3. (print.) Gothic type.

gotten: see GET.

Götterdämmerung (gêr̂terdĕ'merōōng) *n.* (Ger. myth.) Twilight of the gods (see TWILIGHT).

gouache (gōō'ahsh) *n.* (Painting in) opaque water-colour.

Gou'da (-ow-) *n.* Flat round cheese with yellow rind, orig. made at Gouda in Holland.

gouge (*or* -ōōj) *n.* Concave-bladed chisel used in carpentry and surgery. ~ *v.t.* Cut with gouge; cut *out* (as) with gouge; force (*out*, esp. person's eye with thumb) (as) with gouge; force out eye of.

GOTHIC ARCHITECTURE

gou'lăsh (gōō-; *or* -ahsh) *n.* 1. Hungarian ragout of steak and vegetables seasoned with paprika. 2. (bridge) Deal with unshuffled cards after hands have been thrown in without bidding. [Magyar *gulyashus* (*gulyas* herdsman, *hus* meat)]

Gounod (gōōnō), Charles François (1818–93). French composer of a number of operas, of which the best known are 'Faust' and 'Roméo et Juliette'.

gourd (goord) *n.* (Large fleshy fruit of) trailing or climbing plant of family Cucurbitaceae, esp. *Lagenaria vulgaris*; rind of the fruit dried and used as vessel; *bitter* ~, colocynth.

gourde (goord) *n.* Principal monetary unit of Haiti, = 100 centimes.

gour'mand (goor-) *n.* Lover of delicate fare; greedy feeder, glutton.

gourmet (goor'mā) *n.* Connoisseur of table delicacies, esp. of wine.

gout *n.* 1. Paroxysmal disease with painful inflammation of smaller joints, esp. that of great toe, and formation of chalk-stones. 2. Drop, esp. of blood; splash, clot. **gou'tȳ** *adj.* **gou'tilȳ** *adv.* **gou'tinėss** *n.* **gou'tȳ** *n.* Kind of boot covering ankle, snow-boot.

Gov. *abbrev.* Governor.

go'vern (gŭ-) *v.* 1. Rule with authority; conduct policy and affairs of (State etc.); curb, control; sway, influence; constitute law, rule, principle, etc., for, serve to decide (case); *governing body*, managers of hospital, school, etc. 2. (gram., esp. of verb or prep.) Have (noun, case) depending on it; be necessarily followed by (a certain case).

go'vernance (gŭ-) *n.* Act, manner, fact, or function, of governing; sway, control.

go'vernėss (gŭ-) *n.* Female teacher, instructress, esp. of children in private household; ~ *cart*, light two-wheeled vehicle drawn by pony or donkey, with seats at sides face to face.

go'vernment (gŭ-) *n.* 1. Act, manner, fact, of governing; portion of country ruled by a governor, province; system of governing, form of polity. 2. Body or successive bodies of persons governing a State; the State as an agent; administration or ministry; *form a* ~, (of prime minister) select colleagues; *G~ House*, official residence of governor; *G~ bonds, securities*, etc., bonds, exchequer bills, etc., issued by government. **governmĕ'ntal** *adj.* **governmĕ'ntallȳ** *adv.*

go'vernor (gŭ-) *n.* 1. One who governs, ruler; official appointed to govern province, town etc.; executive head of any State of U.S.; officer commanding fortress or garrison; head, or member of governing body, of institution; *g~-general*, sovereign's representative in non-independent Commonwealth countries. 2. (slang) One's employer; one's father; sir. 3. (mech.) Automatic regulator of supply of gas, steam, etc., to machine, ensuring an even motion; device for keeping clockwork or similar machine at constant speed. **go'vernorship** *n.*

gow'an *n.* (Sc.) Daisy.

gowk *n.* Cuckoo (dial.); awkward or half-witted person, fool.

gown *n.* Loose flowing upper garment, esp. woman's dress (usu. one with pretensions to elegance), frock; ancient Roman toga; official or uniform robe of various shapes worn by alderman, judge, lawyer, clergyman, member of university, school, college, etc.; *town and* ~: see TOWN; *gow'nsman*, member of university. ~ *v.t.* (chiefly in past part.) Attire in gown.

Goy'a y Lucientes (ē lōōthiĕ'ntĕz), Francisco José (1746–1828). Spanish painter esp. of portraits; etcher of the 'Disasters of War' and other series of macabre and satirical prints.

G.P. *abbrev.* General practitioner (doctor).

G.P.D.S.T. *abbrev.* Girls' Public Day School Trust.

G.P.I. *abbrev.* General paralysis of the insane.

G.P.O. *abbrev.* General Post Office.

GOYA: The family of Charles IV

G.P.U. (gā-pā-ōō, jē-pē-ū). (also O.G.P.U.; hist.) Soviet-Russian secret police organization (1922–34) which superseded the Cheka. [f. initials of Russ. (*O*bedinennoe) *G*osudarstvennoe *P*oliticheskoe *U*pravlenie (United) State Political Directorate]

gr. *abbrev.* Grain(s); grammar.

G.R. *abbrev.* General reserve; *Georgius Rex* (L, = King George).

Graaf (-ahf), Regnier de (1641–73). Dutch anatomist. **Graa'fian** *adj.* ~ *follicle*, *vesicle*, one of the small sacs in the ovary of mammals in which the ova are matured.

grăb *v.* Seize suddenly, appropriate rapaciously; capture, arrest; make snatch *at*. ~ *n.* 1. Sudden clutch, grasp, seizure, or attempt to seize; practice of grabbing, rapacious proceedings, esp. in politics or commerce. 2. (mech.) Device for clutching or gripping, esp. hinged double bucket lowered by crane. 3. Children's card-game in which cards of like value may be snatched from the table and added to player's hand. **gră'bber** *n.*

gră'bble *v.i.* Grope about, feel for something; sprawl on all fours.

grāce *n.* 1. Pleasing quality, attractiveness, charm, esp. that belonging to elegant proportions or ease and refinement of movement, manner, etc.; attractive feature; *with a good* ~, as if willing; *with a bad* ~, reluctantly, ungraciously; *airs and* ~*s*, behaviour put on with a view to effect or attraction. 2. (mus.) Embellishment of additional note(s) (~*-note*) not essential to harmony or melody. 3. (Gk myth.) *the* (*three*) *Graces*, beautiful sister-goddesses (Aglaia, Thalia, Euphrosyne), bestowers of beauty and charm. 4. Favour, benignant regard or its manifestation, on part of superior; unconstrained goodwill as ground of concession; boon; (in university) permission of Congregation, or of College or Hall, to take degree, dispensation from statutes; *be in person's good* ~*s*, enjoy his favour or liking; *act of* ~, privilege, concession, that cannot be claimed as right; *by the ~ of God*, formula appended to royal titles. 5. (theol.) Unmerited favour of God; divine regenerating, inspiring, and strengthening influence; condition (also *state of* ~) of being so influenced; divinely given virtue or excellence, etc.; *year of* ~, year as reckoned from birth of Christ (archaic). 6. Favour shown by granting delay; mercy, clemency; *days of* ~, time allowed by law for payment of bill of exchange or insurance premium after it falls due, in England three days; *act of* ~, formal, esp. general, pardon by Act of Parliament. 7. Short thanksgiving before or after meal. 8. *his, her, your, G~*, forms of address or description for duke, duchess, or archbishop. ~ *v.t.* Add grace to, adorn, set off *with*; confer honour or dignity on, honour *with* title etc.; do credit to. **grā'ceful** *adj.* Full of grace (sense 1). **grā'cefullȳ** *adv.* **grā'cefulnėss** *n.*

grā'celėss (-sl-) *adj.* Unregenerate, depraved; without sense of decency, unabashed; without charm or elegance. **grā'celėsslȳ** *adv.* **grā'celėssnėss** *n.*

gră'cĭle *adj.* Slender, thin, lean. **gracĭ'lĭtȳ** *n.*

grā'cious (-sh*us*) *adj.* Agreeable, pleasing (archaic); kindly, benevolent, courteous (chiefly poet.); condescending, indulgent, and beneficent to inferiors; (of God) dispensing grace, merciful, benignant. **grā'ciouslȳ** *adv.* **grā'ciousnėss** *n.* **grā'cious** *int.* (ellipt. for ~ *God*, as) *good ~!*, *~ me!*, exclamations of surprise.

gră'ckle *n.* Any of various Amer. orioles (esp. of genus *Quiscalus*) and mynahs in Asia (esp. *Gracula*).

grăd *n.* Unit of angular measure, $\frac{1}{100}$ part of a right angle.

gradā'te *v.* (Cause to) pass by imperceptible degrees from one shade of colour to another; arrange in steps or grades.

gradā'tion *n.* 1. Stage(s) of transition or advance (usu. pl.); series of degrees in rank, merit, divergence, etc.; (pl.) such degrees; arrangement in such degrees; (fine arts) gradual passing from one shade, tone, etc., to another. 2. (philol.) Ablaut. **gradā'tional** *adj.* **gradā'tionallȳ** *adv.*

grāde *n.* 1. Degree in rank, proficiency, value, etc.; class of persons or things alike in these; (U.S.) class at school in relation to advancement. 2. (cattle-breeding) Variety produced by crossing native stock with superior breed. 3. (zool.) Group supposed to have branched from common stem at about same stage of development. 4. (philol.) Position of vowel or root in ablaut-series. 5. (esp. U.S.) Gradient, slope; rate of ascent or descent; *make the* ~, (orig. U.S.) reach the proper standard, be up to the mark. 6. (math.) Hundredth part of right angle. ~ *v.t.* Arrange in grades, class, sort; blend so as to affect grade of; colour with tints passing into each other; reduce (road, canal, etc.) to easy gradients; (cattle-breeding) cross with better breed.

grā'dely (-dlĭ) *adj.* (dial.) Excellent; handsome; real, true.

grā'dĭent *n.* Amount of slope, inclination to horizontal, in road etc., measured as the ratio of the difference in elevation between two points to the horizontal distance between them (so that a slope rising 1 ft per 10 ft of horizontal distance has a gradient of 1 in 10); proportional rise or fall of thermometer or barometer in passing from one region to another; ~ *post*, post beside railway line indicating gradient.

grā'dĭne (*or* -*a*dē'n) *n.* One of series of low steps or tiers of seats; ledge at back of altar.

gră'dūal[1] *n.* Respond sung in the service of the Mass between Epistle and Gospel; book containing this and other music for the Mass. [so called because sung at altar-steps or while deacon mounted steps of ambo; f. L *gradus* steps]

gră'dūal[2] *adj.* Taking place by degrees, slowly progressive; not rapid, steep, or abrupt. **grăʹdūally** *adv.* **grăʹdūalness** *n.*

grăʹdūate *n.* One who holds an academic degree; one who has graduated; ~ *nurse*, (U.S.) trained nurse. **grăʹdūāte** *v.* 1. Take academic degree; (chiefly U.S.) admit to academic degree; (U.S.) pass examination on completing course at high school or other educational institution; qualify or perfect oneself *as*. 2. Mark out in degrees or portions; arrange in gradations, apportion incidence of (tax) according to a scale. 3. Pass *away* by degrees; change gradually *into*. **grădūāʹtion, grăʹdūātor** *ns.*

grāʹdus *n.* Dictionary of Latin prosody formerly used in schools to help in writing Latin verse. [L, short for *gradus ad Parnassum* step to Parnassus]

Graeʹcism *n.* Greek idiom, esp. as imitated in another language; Greek spirit, style, etc., imitation of these. **Graeʹcīze** *v.t.* Make Greek in form or character.

Graeco- *prefix.* Greek, Greek and —, as ~*-Roman.*

graffiʹtō (-fē-) *n.* (pl. *-ti*). Drawing or writing scratched on wall etc. esp. on ancient walls as at Pompeii; (pl.) scribblings or drawings made on walls in public places; decoration by scratches through plaster showing different-coloured under-surface.

graft[1] (-ah-) *n.* Plant consisting of shoot or scion inserted into a stock, from which it receives sap; (surg.) piece of transplanted living tissue; process of grafting; place where graft is inserted. ~ *v.* Insert (scion) as graft; insert graft(s) upon (stock); insert graft(s); (surg.) transplant (living tissue); insert or fix *in* or *upon* so as to produce vital or indissoluble union.

graft[2] (-ah-) *n.* Depth of earth that may be thrown up at once with spade, spit.

graft[3] (-ah-) *n.* (orig. U.S.) Obtaining of profit or advantage by dishonest means; profits so obtained. ~ *v.i.* Seek, make, graft. **graʹfter** *n.*

Graham (grāʹ*a*m), Sylvester (1794–1851). Amer. advocate of vegetarianism; ~ *biscuit, bread, flour*, biscuit, bread, (made from) unbolted wheat flour.

grail[1] *n.* = GRADUAL[1] *n.*

grail[2] *n.* (also *holy ~, saint ~, săʹngrail, săʹngrēal*) In medieval legend, the platter which Christ used at the Last Supper and in which Joseph of Arimathaea received Christ's blood at the Cross; he, acc. to one version, brought it to Glastonbury, and medieval romances tell how it was sought for by Arthur's knights.

grail[3] *n.* Comb-maker's file for smoothing and finishing teeth.

grain *n.* 1. Fruit or corn of a cereal; (collect. sing.) wheat or the allied food-grasses or their fruit, corn; particular species of corn. 2. (pl.) Refuse malt left after brewing or distilling; (also *~s of Paradise*) capsules of the W. African *Aframomum melegueta* used as spice and in medicine. 3. Small hard usu. roundish particle of sand, gold, salt, gunpowder, etc. 4. Smallest unit of weight, 0·0648 g. 1/5760 of lb. troy, 1/7000 of lb. av.; smallest possible quantity. 5. (hist.) Kermes, cochineal, or dye made from either of these; (poet.) dye, colour; *dye in ~*, (orig.) dye in kermes; dye in fast colour, in fibre, or thoroughly; *in ~*, fast dyed; downright, by nature, genuine, thorough. 6. Granular texture, roughness of surface, mottling, texture, arrangement and size of constituent particles, in flesh, skin, wood, stone, etc.; lines of rays in wood, often giving a pattern; lamination of planes of cleavage in coal, stone, etc.; (fig.) nature, temper, tendency. 7. *against the ~*, contrary to inclination; *~-leather*, leather dressed with grain-side outwards; *~-side*, (opp. *flesh-side*) side of skin on which hair grew. ~ *v.* Form into grains; dye in grain; give granular surface to; remove hair from (hides); paint in imitation of grain of wood or marble. **graiʹner** *n.* **graiʹnless, graiʹnȳ** *adjs.* **graiʹniness** *n.*

grains (-z) *n.* Forked fish-spear.

grăʹlloch (-oχ) *n.* Dead deer's

viscera. ~ *v.t.* Disembowel (deer). [Gael. *grealach*]

grăm[1] *n.* Chick-pea; any pulse used as horse-fodder.

gram[2]: see GRAMME.

Gram[3] (grahm), Hans Christian Joachim (1853–1938). Danish biologist; *~-positive*, *~-negative*, (of organism) that does, does not, stain by Gram's method of staining bacteria for microscopical examination.

gra'ma (-ah-), **gră'mma** *n.* (also ~ *grass*) Any of various low pasture grasses abundant in western and south-western U.S.

gramer'cў *int.* (archaic) Thank you. [OF. *grant merci* (God give you) great reward]

grāminā'ceous (-shus), **grami'nėous** *adjs.* Of, like, grass.

gră'mmalŏgue (-g) *n.* (shorthand) Word represented by single sign; letter or character standing for word.

gră'mmar *n.* 1. Department of language study dealing with inflexional forms or other means of indicating relation of words within sentence, and with rules for employing these (in early English use *grammar* meant only *Latin grammar*); treatise or book on grammar; person's manner of using grammatical forms; speech or writing regarded as good or bad by the rules of grammar, what is correct according to those rules; body of forms and usages in a language; elements, rudiments, of an art or science; *comparative* ~, study of relation between grammars of two or more languages; *historical* ~, study of historical development of the grammar of a language. 2. Lowest class in certain Jesuit schools and colleges. 3. ~ *school* one of a class of (usu. endowed) English schools founded in or before 16th c. for teaching Latin, now secondary schools with a curriculum including languages, history, literature, and the sciences; (since Education Act of 1947) any secondary school with similar curriculum as dist. from *technical* or *modern* schools; (U.S.) department or school between primary and high schools.

grammar'ian *n.* One versed in grammar, philologist.

grammă'tical *adj.* Of grammar; conforming to rules of grammar or to formal principles of an art; ~ *gender*, gender (in most Indo-European and Semitic languages) not determined by real or attributed sex. **grammă'ticallў** *adv.*

grămme, grăm[2] *n.* 1. $\frac{1}{1000}$ of a kilogramme (abbrev. g). 2. (also ~ *force*) Unit of force equal to weight of a mass of 1 gramme.

gră'mophōne *n.* Instrument for the mechanical reproduction of recorded sound by means of a stylus which traces vibrations in a groove on a revolving disc (orig., one which both recorded and reproduced sound; in U.S., usu. called *phonograph*; in modern form, with electronic amplification, usu. called *record player*). **grămophŏ'nic** *adj.*

Gră'mpian. Region of NE. Scotland (since May 1975), comprising the city of Aberdeen and the former counties of Aberdeenshire, Banffshire, Kincardineshire, and Morayshire.

gră'mpus *n.* Killer whale (*Orcinus orca*); (also) whale (*Grampus griseus*) known as Risso's dolphin; (fig.) person who puffs and blows.

grănadi'lla, grĕn- *n.* Tropical species of passion-flower, esp. *Passiflora quadrangularis* or its fruit, esteemed as dessert fruit.

granam: see GRANNOM.

gră'narў *n.* Storehouse for threshed grain; region producing, and esp. exporting, much corn.

grănd *adj.* 1. (in official titles) Chief over others, of highest rank; *G~ Duke, Duchess*, ruler of certain European countries (*G~ Duchies*); (also, hist.) child of Tsar of Russia; *G~ Master*, head of military order of knighthood, as Hospitallers, Templars, etc.; head of order of Freemasons or province of this order, or of other societies, as Oddfellows etc.; ~ *vizier*, chief minister of a Muslim country, esp. formerly of Turkish empire.

2. (law) Great, principal, chief, (opp. *petty*); ~ *jury*: see JURY. 3. Of most or great importance; final, summing up minor constituents; main; (mus.) full, of full dimensions, for full orchestra, in full classical form; (in Fr. phrases or imitations) great; ~ *opera*: see OPERA. 4. Conducted with solemnity, splendour, etc.; fine, splendid; belonging to high society, distinguished; imposing, great and handsome; dignified, lofty in conception, treatment, or expression; morally imposing, noble, admirable; (colloq.) very satisfactory; ~ *manner, style*, style and manner fitted for great subjects; *G~ Old Man* (G.O.M.), W. E. GLADSTONE; *G~ Old Party* (G.O.P.), Republican party (U.S.). 5. (in names of relationships) In the second degree of ascent or descent, as *gra'nddaughter, gra'ndson*, one's child's daughter, son; *gra'ndfather, gra'ndmother*, one's parent's father, mother; so *gra'ndchild, gra'ndparent*, etc. 6. *G~ Army*, (= Fr. *Grande Armée*) Napoleon's army, esp. that which invaded Russia in 1812; *G~ Canyon*, a great canyon, 217 miles long, and 5–15 miles wide, and in places 6,000 ft deep, formed by Colorado River in Arizona, U.S.; *gra'ndfather clock*, long-case clock, 8-day clock of kind formerly in common use, with weight-and-pendulum movement and tall wooden case; *G~ Fleet*, during war of 1914–18, main British North Sea fleet; *gra'ndmother clock*, clock resembling grandfather clock but with smaller case; *G~ Monarch*, (= Fr. *Grand Monarque*) Louis XIV of France; *G~ National*, steeplechase established in 1839 and run over 4-mile course at Aintree, Liverpool, in first week of flat-racing season; ~ *piano*: see PIANO². *gra'ndsire*, grandfather; method of ringing changes on ring of bells; ~ *slam*: see SLAM; *gra'ndstand*, principal stand for spectators at races etc.; ~ *tour*: see TOUR. **gră'ndlў** *adv.* **gră'ndnĕss** *n.* **grănd** *n.* 1. Grand piano; *baby* ~, small grand piano; *upright* ~, large upright piano. 2. (U.S. slang) 1,000 dollars.

gră'ndăm, -dāme *n.* (archaic) Grandmother; ancestress; old woman.

grăndee' *n.* Spanish or Portuguese nobleman of highest rank; (iron.) person of high rank or eminence.

gră'ndeur (-j*er* or -dy*er*) *n.* Great power, rank, or eminence; great nobility of character; sublimity, majesty, of appearance or effect; conscious dignity; splendour.

Grand Guignol (grahṅ gēnyŏl). Theatre in Montmartre, Paris, specializing in one-act and two-act sensational plays; hence, dramatic entertainment in which short pieces of a sensational type are played successively. [f. assoc. with *Guignol*, pop. hero of Fr. puppet theatres, and perh. f. affinity with *guignon* evil]

grăndĭ'loquent *adj.* Pompous in language; given to tall talk. **grăndĭ'loquentlў** *adv.* **grăndĭ'loquence** *n.*

gră'ndiōse *adj.* Producing, intended or trying to produce, an impression of greatness; planned on a magnificent scale; pompous. **gră'ndiōselў** *adv.* **grăndiŏ'sitў** *n.*

Grăndisō'nian *adj.* Resembling the hero of Richardson's novel 'Sir Charles Grandison' in stately courtesy and chivalric magnanimity.

grand mal (grahṅ mahl). Severe form of epilepsy (opp. *petit mal*). [Fr.]

Grand Prix (grahṅ prē). International horse-race for 3-year-olds, run annually at Longchamps, near Paris; any of various motor races, as *British* ~, *Le Mans* ~, etc.

grānge (-j) *n.* Country house with farm-buildings attached.

grā'ngerīze (-j-) *v.t.* Illustrate (book etc.) by addition of prints etc., esp. those cut from other books. [f. James *Granger* who published in 1769 a 'Biographical History of England' with blank leaves to receive portraits or other illustrations]

granĭ'ferous *adj.* Producing grain or grain-like seed.

gră'nĭte *n.* Granular crystalline rock of quartz, orthoclase-felspar, and mica, very abundant and used in building because of its hardness and durability; ~ *city*, Aberdeen, so called because of its many granite buildings; ~ *ware*, kind of pottery speckled like granite; kind of speckled enamelled ironware.

granĭ'vorous *adj.* Grain-eating.

gră'nnom, gră'nam *n.* Angler's name for caddis fly.

gră'nnȳ *n.* 1. (colloq.) Grandmother. 2. (also ~ *knot*) Reef knot crossed the wrong way.

grănolĭ'thĭc *adj.* & *n.* (Of) concrete made with crushed granite.

grant[1] (-ah-) *v.t.* Consent to fulfil (request etc.); concede as indulgence; allow (person) to have; give formally, transfer (property) legally; concede (proposition) as basis for argument; *take for granted*, assume. ~ *n.* Granting; formal conferment, legal assignment; thing, esp. sum of money, granted; conveyance by written instrument; ~*-in-aid*, sum granted, esp. by government, to society or institution. **grantee', grantŏr'** *ns.* Person to whom, by whom, thing is legally granted.

Grant[2] (-ah-,-ă-), Ulysses Simpson (1822–85). Amer. general; fought on the Federal side during the Civil War; 18th president of U.S., 1869–77.

gră'nūlar *adj.* Of, like, grains; with granulated surface or structure. **gră'nūlarlȳ** *adv.* **grănūlă'rĭtȳ** *n.* **gră'nūlous** *adj.*

gră'nūlāte *v.* Form into grains; roughen surface of; (of wound etc.) develop small prominences as beginning of healing or junction. **gră'nūlātėd** *adj.* (of metals, sugar, etc.) Formed into or consisting of granules or grain-like bodies. **grănūlā'tion, gră'nūlātor** *ns.*

gră'nūle *n.* Small grain.

grāpe *n.* Green or purple berry growing in clusters on vine, eaten as fruit or used in making wine; *the* ~, wine; *gra'pefruit*, globular fruit of tree *Citrus paradisi*, with a bitter yellow rind and acid juicy pulp, so called as growing in clusters; ~ *hyacinth*, plant of genus *Muscari* with a raceme of small blue flowers; ~*-shot*, small cast-iron balls joined together as charge for cannon; ~*-sugar*, dextrose or glucose; ~*-vine*, vine bearing grapes; (colloq., orig. U.S.) routes by which rumours pass.

grăph (*or* -ahf) *n.* Diagram representing the relation between two variable quantities by the distance of a series of points (or a curve or other line joining these) from axes of reference, which are usu. at right angles to each other; abscissa of any point corresponding to the value of one variable and the ordinate to that of the other. [abbrev. of *graphic formula*]

gră'phĭc *adj.* Of drawing, painting, engraving, etching, etc.; vividly descriptive, lifelike; of writing; (of minerals) showing marks like writing on surface or in fractures; of diagrams, linear figures, or symbolic curves; ~ *arts*, reproductive arts of engraving, etching, woodcut, lithography, etc. **gră'phĭcallȳ** *adv.*

gră'phīte *n.* Crystalline allotropic form of carbon, used in pencils, as solid lubricant etc.; black lead, plumbago. **graphĭ'tĭc** *adj.*

graphŏ'logȳ *n.* 1. System of graphic formulae, notation for graphs. 2. Study of, art of inferring character from, handwriting, whence **graphŏ'logĭst** *n.* **grăpholŏ'gĭcal** *adj.*

gră'pnel *n.* Iron-clawed instrument thrown with rope to seize object, esp. enemy's ship; small anchor with several flukes, used for boats and balloons.

gră'pple *n.* Clutching-instrument, grapnel; hold or grip (as) of wrestlers, close contest. ~ *v.* Seize, fasten, (as) with grapnel; take hold of, grip, with the hands, come to close quarters with; contend in close fight, struggle *with*; ~ *with*, try to overcome, accomplish, or deal with; *grappling-iron*: = GRAPNEL.

gră'ptolīte *n.* Marine organism

of an extinct group whose remains are found in Lower Palaeozoic rocks and resemble primitive writing.

grasp (-ah-) *v.* Clutch *at*, try to seize; seize and hold firmly with hand; get mental hold of, comprehend. ~ *n.* Fast hold, grip; control, mastery; mental hold, comprehensiveness of mind. **gra'sping** *adj.* (esp.) Greedy, avaricious. **gra'spinglў** *adv.*

grass (-ahs) *n.* Herbage in general, blades or leaves and stalks of which are eaten by horses, cattle, etc.; any kind of this, plant belonging to the order Gramineae (in bot. use including, in popular use excluding, the cereals, reeds, and bamboos); grazing, pasture; pasture land; grass-covered ground, lawn, grass border; (slang) marijuana (as drug); (slang) police informer (also *v.*); ~*-cloth*, fine light linen-like cloth of fibres of inner bark of ~*-cloth plant*, *Boehmeria nivea*; thick vegetable-fibre cloth of Canary Islands; *gra'sshopper*, orthopterous insect (of families Tettigoniidae and Locustidae) with remarkable powers of leaping and producing a shrill chirping noise by rubbing the fore-wings together or with the hind-legs; *gra'ssland*, area where light rainfall allows grass to grow but not forest; ~ *roots*, (fig.) source; rank and file of political party etc.; ~*-snake*, harmless common ringed snake, *Natrix natrix*; common green snake of U.S. (*Liopeltis vernalis*); ~ *widow*, married woman whose husband is absent. **gra'sslèss, gra'ssў** *adjs.* **grass** *v.t.* Cover with turf; lay (flax etc.) on grass to bleach; knock down, fell (opponent); bring (fish) to bank, (shot bird or animal) to ground.

grāte[1] *n.* Frame of metal bars for holding fuel in fireplace or furnace; fireplace.

grāte[2] *v.* Reduce to small particles by rubbing on rough surface; have irritating effect *on*; grind (teeth); rub with harsh scraping noise *against*, *on* something else; sound harshly or discordantly; (of hinge etc.) creak. **grā'ter** *n.* Utensil for grating cheese, vegetables, etc. **grā'tinglў** *adv.*

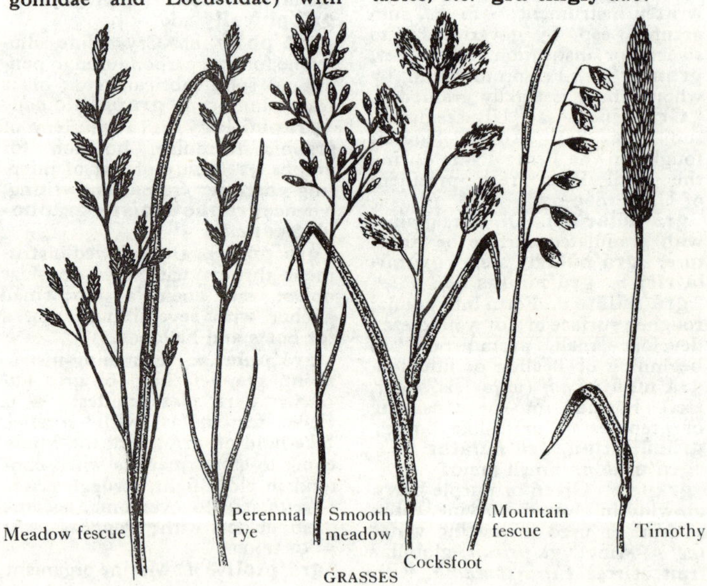

GRASSES

grā'teful (-tf-) *adj.* Acceptable, comforting, refreshing; feeling or showing gratitude. **grā'tefullȳ** *adv.* **grā'tefulnėss** *n.*

grǎ'tĭcūle *n.* 1. = RETICLE. 2. Network of lines of latitude and longitude on a map.

grǎ'tĭfȳ *v.t.* Please, satisfy, delight; give free course to, indulge in (desire, feeling, impulse). **grǎtĭfĭcā'tion** *n.* **grǎ'tĭfȳing** *adj.* **grǎ'tĭfȳinglȳ** *adv.*

grǎtin (-tǎṅ) *n.* Dish cooked with covering of breadcrumbs, grated cheese, etc.; *au* ~ (ō), so prepared. [Fr.]

grā'tĭng *n.* Framework of parallel or crossed wooden or metal bars; (optics) arrangement of parallel wires, surface of glass, etc., ruled with parallel lines, for producing spectra by diffraction.

grǎ'tĭs (*or* -ah-) *adv.* & *adj.* Gratuitous(ly).

grǎ'tĭtūde *n.* Being thankful, appreciation of and inclination to return kindness.

gratū'ĭtous *adj.* Got or given free, not earned or paid for; uncalled for, unwarranted, motiveless, done or acting without good or assignable reason. **gratū'ĭtouslȳ** *adv.* **gratū'ĭtousnėss** *n.*

gratū'ĭtȳ *n.* Money present, in addition to payment due, given in recognition of services, tip; bounty given to soldiers on discharge, retirement, etc.

grǎ'tūlatorȳ *adj.* Expressing joy at another's success etc., congratulatory.

gravā'mĕn *n.* (pl. *-mĭna*). 1. Grievance; (eccles.) memorial from Lower House of Convocation to Upper on disorders or grievances of Church. 2. Essence, worst part, *of* accusation.

grāve[1] *n.* Excavation to receive corpse, mound or monument over it; being dead, death; receptacle of or for what is dead; *~-clothes*, wrappings in which corpse is buried; *gra'vestone*, stone over grave, inscribed stone at head or foot of grave; *gra'veyard*, burial ground. ~ *v.t.* (past part. *-n*, *-d*) 1. (archaic) Bury. 2. Carve, sculpture, engrave (archaic); (fig.) fix indelibly (*on*, *in*, mind etc.); *graven image*, idol.

grāve[2] *adj.* 1. Important, weighty, needing serious thought; (of faults, responsibilities, difficulties, etc.) serious, formidable; dignified, solemn, slow-moving, not gay; sombre, plain, not showy. 2. (of sounds) Low in pitch, deep in tone; ~ *accent* (usu. pr. -ah-), accent ˋ, orig. indicating a low or falling pitch on vowel so marked. **grā'velȳ** *adv.* **grāve** *n.* Grave accent.

grāve[3] *v.t.* Clean (ship's wooden bottom) by burning off accretions and tarring while aground or in *graving-dock* or dry dock.

grǎ'vel *n.* 1. Coarse sand and small water-worn stones, freq. with slight intermixture of clay, much used for laying paths and roads; (geol.) unconsolidated deposit of pebbles. 2. (path.) (Disease with) aggregations of urinary crystals recognizable as masses by naked eye. **grǎ'vellȳ** *adj.* **grǎ'vel** *v.t.* 1. Lay, strew, with gravel. 2. Perplex, puzzle, nonplus.

grā'ver *n.* (esp.) Engraving tool, burin.

Graves (grahv) *n.* Light usu. white wine from Graves district of SW. France. [Fr., gravelly sandy parts of Bordeaux country]

Grāves' dĭsea'se (-vz, -zēz). (med.) Exophthalmic goitre, also called Basedow's disease. [R. J. *Graves* (1796–1853), Irish physician]

grǎ'vĭd *adj.* Pregnant.

grǎ'vĭtāte *v.* Move or tend by force of gravity *towards* a body; sink (as) by gravity, tend to low level, settle down; cause to sink by gravitation, esp. in diamond-digging, manipulate (gravel) after washing so that heavy stones sink to bottom; (transf.) be strongly attracted *to*(*wards*) some centre of influence.

grǎvĭtā'tion *n.* Falling of bodies to earth, or sinking to lowest level, moving or tending to centre of attraction; tendency of every particle of matter towards every other particle, of which fall of bodies to earth is an instance; *law of* ~, law (formulated by Sir Isaac Newton) according to which the attractive force of bodies varies directly as their masses and inversely as the square of the distance between them. **grăvitā'tional** *adj.*

gră'vitў *n.* 1. Being grave, solemnity; importance, seriousness; staidness, sobriety, serious demeanour. 2. Weight; *specific ~*, relative weight of any kind of matter, expressed by ratio of weight of given volume to weight of equal volume of some substance taken as standard (usu. water for liquids and solids, hydrogen or air for gases). 3. Attractive force by which all bodies tend to move towards centre of earth, degree of intensity with which body in given position is affected by this, measured by amount of acceleration produced (abbrev. g); degree of intensity with which any body is similarly attracted by any other.

gravūr'e *n.* Photogravure.

grā'vў *n.* Fat and juices exuding from meat during and after cooking; sauce for meat etc. made from these with condiments etc.; *~-boat*, boat-shaped vessel for gravy.

gray[1]: see GREY.

Gray[2], Thomas (1716–71). English poet; author of 'Elegy in a Country Churchyard', 'On a Distant Prospect of Eton College', etc.

gray'ling *n.* 1. Silver-grey freshwater fish (*Thymallus*) of salmon family, with long high dorsal fin. 2. Common butterfly (*Eumenis semele*) with grey underside to wings.

graywacke: see GREYWACKE.

grāze[1] *v.* Feed (esp. cattle, or *v.i.* of cattle) on growing grass etc.; feed on (grass etc.); tend grazing cattle; pasture cattle.

grāze[2] *v.* Touch lightly in passing; abrade (skin etc.) in rubbing past; suffer slight abrasion of (part of body); go with passing contact *against, through, by*, etc. ~ *n.* Grazing; abrasion caused by grazing.

grā'zier (-zh*er*) *n.* One who feeds cattle for market.

grease (-s) *n.* Fat of deer or other game; melted fat of dead animals, esp. when soft; oily or fatty matter, esp. as lubricant; oily matter in wool, uncleansed wool; *~-gun*, kind of pump for lubricating parts of machinery with grease; *~-paint*, composition for painting actors' faces etc. ~ (*or* -z) *v.t.* Anoint, soil, or lubricate, with grease; *~ person's palm*: see PALM[2]; *like greased lightning*, (slang) very fast.

grea'ser (*or* -z-) *n.* (esp.) Ship's fireman or engineer; one who cleans and lubricates machinery etc. with grease; (U.S. colloq.) native Mexican, Spanish-American.

grea'sў (*or* -zĭ) *adj.* 1. Smeared or covered with, containing, made of, like, with too much, grease; (of wool) uncleansed. 2. Slimy or slippery with mud, moisture, etc. 3. (of manners or expression) Disagreeably unctuous. **grea'silў** *adv.* **grea'sinėss** *n.*

great (grāt) *adj.* 1. Large, big, (usu. with implied surprise, contempt, indignation, etc.; freq. preceding partly synonymous adj., as *~ big, ~ thick*, etc.); (of animal etc., species or variety) larger than others; (of letter) capital; (of part of building etc.) main, principal; (of qualities, emotions, etc.) beyond the ordinary in degree or extent; *the ~ majority*, much the larger part; *Greater*, (of cities) including adjoining areas etc.; (of countries) including dependencies. 2. Important, elevated, distinguished, *the* chief, pre-eminent; *the ~ world*, high society; *the G~* (following proper name), the most famous of the name, one of the great figures of history. 3. Of remarkable ability, genius, intellectual or practical qualities, loftiness or integrity of character; fully deserving the name of, (with agent-nouns) doing the act much or on a large scale, as *a ~ fiasco, a ~ scoundrel*; (colloq. & U.S.) highly satisfactory, fine, magnificent; (predic.) having much skill *at* or information *on*. 4. (with terms denoting kinship, esp. with compounds of *grand*) One degree farther removed in ascending or descending relationship; as ~*-aunt*, *-uncle*, one's parent's aunt, uncle, ~*-grandfather*, *-grandmother*, one's parent's grandfather, grandmother; so ~*-nephew*, *-niece*, ~*-grandchild*, etc.; ~-~- *grandfather* etc., one's parent's great-grandfather etc. 5. *G~ Assize*, Day of Judgement; *G~ Bible*, Coverdale's English version (1539); sometimes also, revised versions of this, esp. Cranmer's (1540); *G~ Britain*: see BRITAIN; ~ *circle*: see CIRCLE; *grea'tcoat*, large heavy overcoat, topcoat; *G~ Elector*, Frederick William, Elector of Brandenburg (1620–88); *G~ Fire*, fire which in Sept. 1666 destroyed most of London; ~ *house*, chief house in village etc.; *G~ Lakes*, large lakes (Superior, Michigan, Huron, Erie, and Ontario), which, except for Michigan, which is in U.S., lie along the frontier between Canada and U.S.; ~ *power*, one of the States exerting through political and military power the chief influence in international relations; ~ *primer*: see PRIMER²; *G~ Rebellion*: see REBELLION; *G~ Russian*, Russian language excluding Ukrainian and Byelorussian; *G~ Spirit*, supreme deity of N. Amer. Indians; ~ *toe*, big toe; *G~ War*, First World War (see WORLD). **grea'tnėss** *n.* **great** *n.* 1. (sing.) What is great; (pl.) great persons. 2. *Greats*, (colloq.) Literae humaniores.

Grea'ter Mă'nchėster (grāt-). Metropolitan county of NW. England (since April 1974), comprising Manchester and surrounding districts.

grea'tlȳ (grāt-) *adv.* 1. Much, by much. 2. Nobly, loftily.

greave *n.* (hist.) Defensive armour for shin.

greaves (-vz) *n.pl.* Fibrous matter or skin found in animal fat, forming sediment on melting and used for feeding dogs etc., or as fish-bait; tallow-refuse; cracklings.

grēbe *n.* Any of various short-bodied almost tailless diving-birds (of genus *Podiceps* or family Podicipitidae) with flattened and lobed feet set far behind; *great*

crested ~, largest European species, *P. cristatus*.

Grē'cian (-sh*a*n) *adj.* Greek, Hellenic (rare exc. of architecture and facial outline); ~ *bend*, stooping attitude, supposed to imitate that of Venus de Milo, affected by some women in the late 19th c.; ~ *knot*, woman's coiffure with coil at back of head; ~ *nose*, nose straight in profile, continuing forehead line without a dip; ~ *slippers*, trade term for oriental slippers. ~ *n.* Greek scholar; boy in highest class at Christ's Hospital.

Greece. Maritime country (a republic since 1973) in SE. Europe, bounded on the N. by Albania, Yugoslavia, and Bulgaria, on the S. and W. by the Ionian Sea, and on the E. by the Aegean and Turkey; capital, Athens. *Ancient* or *classical* ~, earliest great civilization of Europe which developed round the shores of the Aegean and reached its peak in 5th c. B.C., having no unified government but consisting of a number of city states of which Athens and Sparta became the most powerful and came into conflict in the Peloponnesian War; from the mid 4th c. Macedon was the dominant State in mainland Greece. In 146 B.C. Greece became part of the Roman (later Byzantine) Empire; overrun by Serbia during the 13th c., conquered by Turkey in the 14th–15th centuries, she remained under Turkish rule until, after years of fierce warfare, she won her independence in 1821.

greed *n.* Insatiate longing, esp. for food or wealth. **gree'dȳ** *adj.* **gree'dĭlȳ** *adv.* **gree'dĭnėss** *n.*

Greek *adj.* Of, pertaining to, Greece, its inhabitants or their language; ~ *calends*: see CALENDS; ~ *Church*, ORTHODOX Church; ~

cross, upright cross with limbs of equal length ~ *fire*, combustible composition of naphtha, nitre, and sulphur, used by the Byzantine Greeks for setting fire to an enemy's ships or works; ~ *gift*, one given with intent to harm (see Virgil, 'Aeneid', ii. 49). ~ *n.* 1. Greek person. 2. Member of the Greek Church. 3. Language of the Greeks, (i) that of the classical period, a member of the Indo-Germanic family of languages, represented in classical times by four main dialects, Ionic, Attic, Aeolic, and Doric; (ii) the modern form, dating from 15th c.

green *adj.* 1. Of the colour between blue and yellow in the spectrum, coloured like grass, sea-water, emerald, etc.; covered with herbage, verdant, in leaf; (of complexion) pale, sickly-hued, as in fear, jealousy, sickness, etc.; (fig.) jealous, envious. 2. (of fruit etc.) Unripe, young and tender, flourishing, not dried; full of vitality, not withered or worn out; (of persons) immature, undeveloped, inexperienced, gullible; (of wood) not dried or seasoned; (of hide) not tanned; (of bacon) unsmoked; (of wound etc.) fresh, not healed. 3. *gree'nback*, U.S. Treasury note; ~ *belt*, strip of land round a built-up area, kept free from building development etc.; ~*-blind*, having retina insensitive to green rays; ~ *cheese*, unripened cheese; whey cheese; cheese coloured green with sage; (*Board of*) *G~ Cloth*, Lord Steward's department of Royal Household; ~*-eyed*, (esp.) jealous; ~*-eyed monster*, jealousy; ~ *fat*, green gelatinous portion of turtle, highly esteemed by epicures; *gree'nfinch*, common European bird with gold and green plumage (*Chloris chloris*); ~ *fingers*, *thumb*, (colloq.) aptitude for making plants grow; *gree'nfly*, kind of aphis; *gree'ngage*, roundish green fine-flavoured plum [f. name of Sir W. *Gage*]; ~ *goose*, goose killed under four months old and eaten without stuffing; *gree'ngrocer*, retail dealer in fruit and vegetables; so *gree'ngrocery*; *gree'nheart*, W. Indian tree, esp. large tree of Guiana, *Ocotea rodiaei*, furnishing very hard timber; this timber used for fishing-rods, in shipbuilding, etc.; *gree'nhorn*, ignoramus, raw hand, simpleton; *gree'nhouse*, glass-house for rearing delicate plants; ~ *light*, (fig.) permission to proceed; ~ *manure*, growing plants ploughed into soil; ~ *paper*, government report, issued in green paper cover, with proposals still in the formative stage and to which the government is not yet committed; ~*-room*, room in theatre accommodating actors and actresses when off stage; *gree'nsand*, sand or sandstone containing hydrated iron silicate; (geol.) formation largely of this; *gree'nshank*, large kind of sandpiper, *Tringa nebularia* with green legs; ~ *sickness*, chlorosis; *gree'nstick* (*fracture*), bone-fracture, esp. in children, in which one side of bone is broken and one only bent; *gree'nstone*, any of various eruptive rocks containing felspar and hornblende; kind of *jade*; *gree'nstuff*, vegetation; green vegetables; *gree'nsward*, turf; ~ *tea*: see TEA; *gree'nwood*, woodlands in summer, esp. as scene of outlaw life. **gree'nlў** *adv.* **gree'nnėss** *n.* **gree'nish** *adj.* **gree'nў** *adj.* (usu. in comb., as ~*-grey*). **green** *n.* 1. What is green; green part of anything; green colour; green dye. 2. Vigour, youth, virility. 3. Verdure, vegetation, greenery; (pl.) green vegetables, esp. (in England) small or young cabbages. 4. Piece of public or common grassy land; grass-plot used for special purpose. ~ *v.* Become green, esp. with verdure; dye green; soil etc. with green.

Gree'naway, Catherine ('Kate'), (1846–1901). English artist, known esp. for book-illustrations of children in early 19th-c. dress.

gree'nerў *n.* Verdure; green branches or leaves as decoration.

gree'ning *n.* Kind of apple, green when ripe.

Gree'nland. Island lying to the NE. of N. America, part of the

Kingdom of Denmark; ~ *whale*: see WHALE[1]. **Gree′nlander** *n.* **Gree′nlandĭc** *adj.*

Greenwich (grĕ′nĭj *or* grĭ-; *or* -ch). Inner London borough; ~ *Hospital*, built by Wren, orig. for naval pensioners, now occupied by the Royal Naval College for officers; ~ *Mean Time*, (abbrev. G.M.T.; also ~ *Time*) mean solar time of the meridian of Greenwich, adopted as standard time in Gt Britain and used also as a basis for calculation and in astronomy, navigation, etc.; ~ *Observatory*, Royal Astronomical Observatory, founded 1675 for the purpose of calculating longitude (its work was transferred 1950 to Herstmonceux, East Sussex); ~ *meridian*, meridian which passes through Greenwich Observatory, recognized by most nations as the prime meridian, or 0° longitude.

greet[1] *v.t.* Accost with salutation; salute *with* words or gestures, receive on meeting or arrival *with* speech or action; (of sight etc.) meet (eye, ear). **gree′tĭng** *n.*

greet[2] *v.i.* (Sc.) Weep.

grėgār′ious *adj.* Living in flocks or communities; fond of company; of flocks or crowds. **grėgār′iouslȳ** *adv.* **grėgār′iousnėss** *n.*

grège, greige (-āzh) *n.* & *adj.* (Of) colour between beige and grey. [Fr. *grège* raw (silk)]

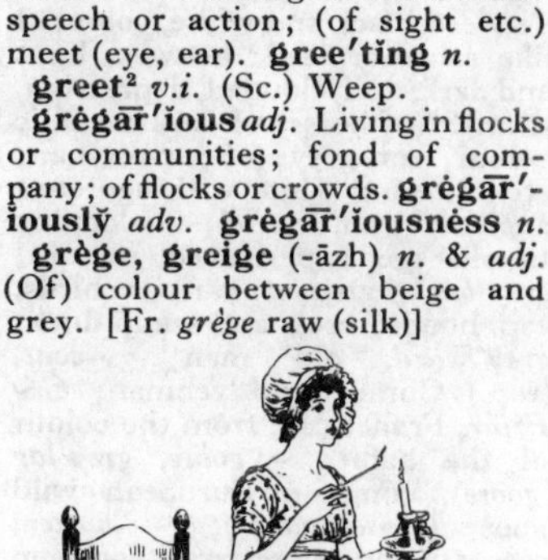

KATE GREENAWAY: Illustration

Grėgôr′ian *adj.* Pertaining to, originated by, some person named Gregory, esp. one of the popes of that name; ~ *calendar*, modified calendar, also known as the 'New Style', introduced by Pope Gregory XIII in 1582 and adopted in Gt Britain in 1752; it is a modification of the JULIAN calendar, adapted to bring it into closer conformity with astronomical data and to rectify the error contracted by its use; in order to correct this error, which was due to the fact that the Julian year of 365¼ days was 11 min. 10 sec. too long, 10 days were suppressed in 1582 and in Gt Britain 11 in 1752, and to prevent future displacement Gregory provided that of the centenary years (1600, 1700, etc.) only those exactly divisible by 400 should be counted as leap years; ~ *chant*, system of ritual music, otherwise known as plain-chant or plainsong, founded on the 'Antiphonarium', of which Pope Gregory I is presumed to have been the compiler; ~ *telescope*, earliest type of reflecting telescope, invented by James Gregory (1638–75), a Scottish mathematician; ~ *tones*, eight plainsong melodies prescribed for psalms in R.C. Church.

Grĕ′gorȳ[1]. Name of sixteen popes: *Gregory I*, saint and Doctor of the Church; pope 590–604, a zealous propagator of Christianity and reformer of clerical and monastic discipline; sent AUGUSTINE to England; is presumed to have originated the GREGORIAN chant; *Gregory VII*, saint, pope 1073–85, a Benedictine monk, before his election called Hildebrand; attempted to extend the temporal power of the papacy and came into conflict with the emperor Henry IV, whom he obliged to do penance at CANOSSA; *Gregory XIII*, pope 1572–85, introduced the GREGORIAN calendar.

Grĕ′gorȳ[2], St. (329–89). Doctor of the Church, born at Nazianzus in Cappadocia.

grĕ′gorȳ-pow′der *n.* Compound powder of rhubarb, magnesia, and ginger used as aperient. [J. *Gregory* (1753–1821), Sc. physician]

greige: see GRÈGE.

grē'mĭal *n.* Silk apron placed on bishop's lap at Mass or ordination.

grĕ'mlĭn *n.* (R.A.F. slang) Mischievous sprite imagined to frequent aircraft and to cause mishaps (also transf.)

Grėnā'da. State in the West Indies including island of Grenada formerly in British possession; independent member of Commonwealth 1974; capital, St. George's.

grėnā'de *n.* Small explosive shell thrown by hand or fitted with tail-rod and shot from rifle-barrel by means of a blank cartridge; glass receptacle thrown to disperse chemicals for extinguishing fires, testing drains, etc. [Span. *granada* pomegranate]

grĕnadier' *n.* 1. (orig.) Soldier who threw grenades (orig. four or five men in each company, later, a company of the tallest and finest men in each regiment); (now) *G ~ Guards, Grenadiers*, first regiment of household infantry. 2. African waxbill of *Granatina* species, with vivid red-and-black plumage. 3. Deep-sea fish of family Macrouridae, related to cod, with long tapering tail; rat-tail.

grenadilla: see GRANADILLA.

grĕ'nadin *n.* French variety of strongly scented carnation.

grĕ'nadĭne[1] *n.* Loosely-woven silk or silk-and-wool dress-fabric.

grĕ'nadĭne[2] (-ēn) *n*, French cordial syrup of pomegranates.

grĕ'nadĭne[3] *n.* Fricandeau of veal or poultry, filleted and glazed.

Grĕ'nvĭlle, Sir Richard (1541?–1591). Elizabethan sea-captain; with his one ship, the *Revenge*, he engaged 15 Spanish ships off Flores, fought them for 15 hours, and was mortally wounded in the engagement.

Grĕ'sham's law. (econ.) Tendency, when two or more coins of equal nominal value but different intrinsic value are in circulation, for the one having the least intrinsic value to remain in circulation and for the other to be hoarded; expressed (colloq.) as 'bad money drives out good'. [Sir Thomas *Gresham* (1519?–1579), Engl. financier, founder of the Royal Exchange]

grĕssōr'ĭal *adj.* (zool.) Walking, adapted for walking.

Grĕ'tna Green. Village in Dumfries and Galloway near English border, where English runaway couples contracted 'irregular' marriages valid by Scottish law, by making a declaration before a witness; the blacksmith acted as witness and also read the marriage service to them for sentiment's sake; the practice began after 1754 when English law made hasty marriage difficult, and lapsed after 1857 when Scottish law prescribed certain conditions for 'irregular' marriages, though it recognized such marriages until 1939.

grey (-ā), **gray**[1] *adj.* Intermediate between black and white, coloured like ashes or lead; between light and dark, dull, clouded, depressing, dismal; (of horse) of dark metallic colour, iron-grey; (of person, hair, etc.) turning white with age etc.; ancient, immemorial; belonging to old age, experienced, mature; *grey'back*, any of various birds, esp. hooded crow and scaup duck; *grey'beard*, old man; *~-coat*, (esp.) Cumberland yeoman; *G~ Friar*, Franciscan, from the colour of the habit; *~ goose, grey'lag (goose)*, common European wild goose (*Anser anser*); *~ matter*: see MATTER; *~ squirrel*, common squirrel of U.S. (*Sciurus carolinensis*), now naturalized in Europe. **grey'ĭsh** *adj.* **grey'lў** *adv.* **grey'nėss** *n.* **grey** *n.* Grey clothes; cold sunless light; grey colour, grey pigment; grey horse; *the Greys*, a regiment of the Royal Scots Dragoon Guards, raised in 1681, orig. wearing grey uniform, later mounted on grey horses, now equipped with tanks and forming part of Royal Armoured Corps. *~ v.* Become, make, grey.

grey'hound (grā-) *n.* Slender long-legged keen-sighted swift dog used in coursing hares etc. and in sport in which mechanical hare is chased round track by greyhounds; swift steam-ship.

greywăcke, gray- (grā'wăk*e*) *n.* (geol.) Sandstone containing about 30% or more of a dark mineral.

grĭd *n.* 1. Grating, frame of parallel bars; gridiron. 2. Network of lines, esp. system of numbered squares printed on map and forming basis of map-reference. 3. Network of wires for distributing electric current or of pipes for distributing gas to towns and villages. 4. (elect.) electrode in a valve etc., having one or more apertures for the passage of electrons or ions; ~ *bias,* (usu. negative) potential applied to grid of thermionic valve to adjust anode current or to prevent this flowing into grid; ~-*leak*: see LEAK.

grĭ'ddle *n.* 1. = GIRDLE². 2. Miner's wire-bottomed sieve or screen. ~ *v.t.* Screen with griddle.

grĭ'diron (-īrn) *n.* Barred metal cooking utensil, usu. on short legs, for supporting food to be broiled or grilled; (naut.) frame of parallel beams for supporting ship in dock; naval manœuvre in which vessels' paths suggest form of gridiron; (theatr.) plank structure over stage supporting mechanism for drop-scenes etc.; (U.S.) football field (from the parallel lines marking out field of play for American form of football); (also ~ *pendulum*) compensation pendulum of parallel rods of different metals.

grief *n.* Deep or violent sorrow, keen regret; *come to* ~, meet with disaster, fail, fall.

Grieg, Edvard Hagerup (1843–1907). Norwegian composer.

grie'vance *n.* Real or fancied ground of complaint.

grieve *v.* Give deep sorrow to; feel grief.

grie'vous *adj.* 1. Causing grief or suffering; (of pain etc.) severe. 2. Flagrant, heinous. **grie'vouslȳ** *adv.* **grie'vousnėss** *n.*

grĭ'ffĭn, grĭ'ffon¹, grȳ'phon *n.* Fabulous creature with eagle's head and wings and lion's body; (her.) representation of this creature as charge or crest; (fig.) vigilant guardian, esp. duenna or chaperon; *griffon vulture,* large species of vulture (*Gyps fulvus*) found in S. Europe and N. Africa.

grĭ'ffon² *n.* Kind of coarse-haired terrier-like dog of continental breed; *Brussels* ~, small variety of this, formerly kept as a pet.

grĭg *n.* Small eel; grasshopper or cricket.

grĭll¹ *v.* Broil on gridiron; (fig.) torment with torture or great heat; (orig. U.S.) subject to severe questioning. ~ *n.* 1. Grilled dish; device, on gas or electric cooker, which directs radiant heat downwards; (also ~-*room*) room in restaurant where meat etc. is grilled and served. 2. Gridiron.

grĭ'llage *n.* Heavy framework of cross-timbering used as foundation for building on treacherous soil.

grĭlle, grĭll² *n.* Grating, latticed screen, esp. in door for observing callers, in convent separating nuns from visitors etc.; (tennis) square opening in end wall on hazard side of court, near main wall.

grĭlse *n.* Young salmon that has been only once to the sea.

grĭm *adj.* Stern, unrelenting, merciless, severe; of forbidding or harsh aspect; sinister, ghastly, unmirthful. **grĭ'mlȳ** *adv.* **grĭ'mnėss** *n.*

grĭmā'ce *n.* Wry face expressing annoyance etc. or meant to raise a laugh; affected look; affectation. ~ *v.i.* Make wry face.

grĭmă'lkĭn *n.* Old she-cat.

grīme *n.* Soot, dirt, ingrained in some surface, esp. the skin. ~ *v.t.* Blacken, befoul. **grī'mȳ** *adj.* **grī'mĭnėss** *n.*

Grĭmm, Jacob Ludwig Carl (1785–1863) and Wilhelm Carl (1786–1859). Two brothers, famous for their researches into German language, literature, and antiquities and for their collection of fairy-tales; ~*'s Law,* statement, formulated by Jacob Grimm in 1822, of the regular changes which certain consonants of the primitive Indo-Germanic consonant system have undergone in the Germanic languages.

Grĭ'mmelshausen (-howzen), Hans Jacob Christoph von (1625?–76). German novelist; author of the picaresque novel 'Simplicissimus'.

grĭn *v.* Show teeth in cheerful or unrestrained or forced smile, or in sign of pain or fatuity; express (contempt, satisfaction) by grinning. ~ *n.* Act of grinning.

grīnd *v.* (past t. & past part. *ground*). 1. Reduce to small particles or powder by crushing between millstones, teeth, etc.; produce (flour) by grinding; work (hand-mill); turn handle of (hurdy-gurdy), produce (music) from hurdy-gurdy etc.; (quasi-pass.) admit of being ground. 2. Sharpen or smooth by abrasion; ~ *in, on,* fix (valves etc.) to their seatings by grinding. 3. Oppress, harass with exactions; toil monotonously, study hard; teach (subject, pupil) laboriously. 4. Rub gratingly *on, into, against*; rub (teeth) hard together. 5. *gri'ndstone,* thick revolving stone disc for grinding, sharpening, and polishing; kind of stone used for these. ~ *n.* Grinding; hard monotonous work or task; walk for exercise; steeplechase; (U.S.) student who works hard.

grī'nder *n.* Thing, person, that grinds; molar tooth; grinding-machine; upper millstone.

grī'ndery̆ *n.* Materials, tools, etc., of shoemakers and other leather-workers.

grĭ'ngō (-nggō) *n.* (contempt.) Among Spanish-Americans, a foreigner, esp. an Englishman or an American of U.S.

grĭp *n.* Firm hold, tight grasp or clasp, grasping power; way of clasping hands; control, mastery, intellectual hold; power of arresting attention; part in machinery etc. that clips, part of weapon etc. that is held; (U.S.) gripsack. ~ *v.* (past t. & past part. *gripped*) Seize, grasp, or hold, tightly; take firm hold; compel attention of; *grĭ'psack,* (U.S.) traveller's handbag.

grīpe *v.* Clutch, grip; oppress, pinch; affect with colic pains; (naut., of ship) come up into wind in spite of helm; secure with gripes; (slang) complain. ~ *n.* 1. Act of griping, clutch; hold, control; handle of implement or weapon; (naut., pl.) lashings securing boat in its place. 2. (pl.) Colic pains.

grĭppe (*or* grĕp) *n.* (archaic) Influenza.

grĭsai'lle (-z-; *or* -zī) *n.* Method of painting in grey or greyish monochrome, freq. representing figures in relief.

grĭsĕtte (-z-) *n.* French working girl (formerly dressed in grey).

grĭ'skin *n.* Lean part of loin of bacon pig.

grĭ'sly̆ (-z-) *adj.* Causing horror, terror, or superstitious dread. **grĭ'slinėss** *n.*

grĭst[1] *n.* Corn for grinding; malt crushed for brewing.

grĭst[2] *n.* Size or thickness of yarn or rope.

grĭ'stle (-sl) *n.* Whitish tough flexible connective tissue in vertebrates, cartilage. **grĭ'stly̆** *adj.*

grĭt *n.* Small particles of stone or sand, esp. as causing discomfort or clogging machinery etc.; (also *gri'tstone*), coarse sandstone, esp. kind used for millstones etc.; (geol.) coarse-grained sand or sandstone; grain or texture of stone; (colloq.) strength of character, pluck, endurance. ~ *v.* Produce, move with, grating sound; grind (teeth). **grĭ'tty̆** *adj.* **grĭ'ttinėss** *n.*

grĭts *n.pl.* Husked but unground oats; coarse oatmeal.

grĭ'zzle *v.i.* (colloq.) Whimper, cry fretfully.

grĭ'zzled (-zld) *adj.* Grey (-haired).

grĭ'zzly̆ *adj.* Grey, greyish, grey-haired; ~ *bear,* large fierce bear, *Ursus horribilis,* of mountain districts of western N. America. ~ *n.* Grizzly bear.

groan *n.* Deep inarticulate sound expressing pain, grief, or disapproval. ~ *v.* Utter groan; utter with groans; be oppressed or loaded *under*, *beneath*, *with*. **groa'ningly̆** *adv.*

groat *n.* (hist.) English silver coin worth four pence, first coined in 1351–2 and current until 1662. [MDu. *groot* great, thick (penny)]

groats *n.pl.* Hulled (sometimes also crushed) grain, esp. oats.

grō'cer *n.* Dealer in miscellaneous domestic stores. **grō'cery̆** *n.* Trade of grocer; goods sold by grocer (freq. pl.); (U.S.) grocer's shop.

grŏg *n.* Drink of spirit (orig. rum) and water. [reputedly f. *grogram*, nickname (from his cloak) of Admiral Vernon, who first had grog served out in navy instead of neat rum]

grŏ'ggy̆ *adj.* Drunk(en); bibulous; (of horse) weak in forelegs, tottering; unsteady, shaky. **grŏ'ggily̆** *adv.* **grŏ'gginėss** *n.*

grŏ'grăm *n.* Coarse fabric of silk or mohair and wool, often stiffened with gum. [Fr. *gros grain* large grain]

groin *n.* 1. Depression between belly and thigh. 2. (archit.) Edge formed by intersecting vaults, fillet covering this. ~ *v.t.* Build with groins. **groi'ning** *n.*

grŏ'mwell *n.* Any plant of genus *Lithospermum*, with hard stony seeds formerly used in medicine.

grōōm *n.* 1. One of certain officers of English Royal Household, chiefly in Lord Chamberlain's department. 2. Servant having care of horses. 3. Bridegroom; *groo'msman*, unmarried friend attending bridegroom at wedding, best man. ~ *v.t.* Curry, feed, tend, etc. (horse); give neat or attractive appearance to; prepare as political candidate, film star, etc.

grōōve *n.* Channel or hollow, esp. one made to direct motion or receive corresponding ridge; routine, undeviating course, rut. ~ *v.t.* Make groove(s) in.

grōpe *v.i.* Feel about as in dark (*for*, *after*); search blindly; ~ *one's way*, find way by feeling, proceed tentatively. **grō'pingly̆** *adv.*

grō'sbeak *n.* Any of various finches with large strong beak, esp. hawfinch.

grō'schen (-sh*e*n) *n.* 1. $\frac{1}{100}$ of a schilling. 2. (hist.) Small German silver coin.

grosgrain (grō'grān) *n.* Corded fabric or ribbon of silk etc.

gros point (grō pwăṅ). Cross-stitch.

grōss[1] *n.* Twelve dozen.

grōss[2] *adj.* 1. Luxuriant, rank; bloated, repulsively fat; flagrant, glaring. 2. Total, without deductions, not net; ~ *national product*, total monetary value of goods produced and services provided in a country in one year. 3. Dense, thick; coarse, dull; coarse in manners or morals, unrefined, indecent. 4. (abs.) *in* (*the*) ~, in bulk, in large quantities (opp. *by retail*). ~ *v.t.* Earn a total of. **grō'ssly̆** *adv.* **grō'ssnėss** *n.*

grōsz (-sh) *n.* (pl. *groszy̆*) $\frac{1}{100}$ of a zloty.

grotĕ'sque (-sk) *n.* Decoration with fantastic interweaving of human and animal forms with foliage; (pop.) comically distorted figure or design. ~ *adj.* (archit.) In the style of a grotesque; distorted, bizarre; ludicrous from incongruity, absurd. **grotĕ'squely̆** *adv.* **grotĕ'squenėss** *n.* [It. *grottesca* antique work, prob. *grotta* (grotto) of ancient Roman houses, where such paintings were found]

Grō'tius (-sh*u*s), Hugo (1583–1645). Dutch statesman and jurist; famous for his treatise on international law, the 'De jure Belli et Pacis', published in 1625.

grŏ'ttō *n.* (pl. *-oes*). Picturesque cave; artificial ornamental cave; room etc. adorned with shells etc. in imitation of cave, as cool retreat; (geog.) cave formed by underground stream; *the* ~, London street-boys' grotto-like structure of oyster-shells on 5 Aug. in celebration of close-time for oysters.

grouch *n.* (U.S.) Grumbling; complaint; sulky, grumbling mood; grumbler. **grou'chy̆** *adj.* **grou'chily̆** *adv.* **grouch'inėss** *n.* **grouch** *v.i.* Grumble.

ground[1] *n.* 1. Bottom of sea; bottom where water becomes too shallow for vessel etc. to float; (pl.) dregs, esp. of coffee. 2. Base, foundation; motive, valid reason. 3. Substratum, underlying part; surface worked upon in embroidery, painting, etc.; undecorated part; prevailing colour or tone; (painting) preparation spread over canvas, panel, etc., to isolate it from paint layer; (etching) wax mixture spread on metal plate and cut through with needle where acid is to act. 4. Surface of earth; position, area, or distance, on earth's surface; area of special kind or use; portion of land forming person's property; space on which person etc. takes his stand (freq. fig.); (pl.) enclosed land for ornament or recreation attached to house; *above* ~; alive; *down to the* ~, (colloq.) in all respects; *fall, be dashed, to the* ~, (of scheme, hope) be abandoned, fail; *forbidden* ~, subject that must be avoided; *gain* ~, advance; *lose, give,* ~, retreat, decline; *stand, shift, one's* ~, maintain, change, one's argument or intention. 5. (elect., U.S.) Earth (see EARTH, sense 3). 6. attrib.: (in names of birds) terrestrial, (of beasts) burrowing in or lying on ground, (of plants) dwarfish or trailing. 7. ~ *bait,* bait thrown to bottom of intended fishing-ground to attract fish; ~ *bass,* (mus.) theme in bass constantly repeated with varied melody or harmony above; ~ *floor,* rooms etc. nearest to level of outside ground; *get in on the* ~ *floor,* be admitted to company etc. on same terms as promoters; ~ *frost,* frost on surface of ground but not above it; ~*-hog,* aardvark; American marmot; ~ *ice,* ice formed at bottom of water; ~ *ivy,* common labiate plant (*Nepeta glechoma*) with bluish-purple flowers and kidney-shaped leaves; ~ *landlord,* owner of land leased for building; ~ *nut,* peanut; ~ *pine,* herbaceous plant (*Ajuga chamaepitys*) with resinous smell; clubmoss; ~ *plan,* plane drawing of divisions of building on the ground level or ground floor; outline, general design, of anything; ~*-rent,* rent paid to ground landlord; *grou'ndsheet,* waterpoof sheet for spreading on ground as protection against damp; *grou'ndsman,* man employed to keep esp. cricket-ground in order; ~ *speed,* horizontal component of an aircraft's velocity relative to the earth; ~ *squirrel,* terrestrial squirrel-like rodent, as chipmunk, gopher, etc.; ~ *staff,* staff of groundsmen; non-flying personnel of an air-station employed in servicing aircraft; ~ *swell,* heavy sea-swell as result of distant storm; ~ *water,* water lying below earth's surface in springs and in pores of rock; *grou'ndwork,* foundation or basis (usu. fig.); chief ingredient; general surface of thing showing where not overlaid with embroidery or other ornament. ~ *v.* Base, establish, *on* some fact or authority; instruct thoroughly (*in* elements of subject); prepare ground of (embroidery etc.); lay (esp. weapons) on ground; alight on ground; keep on the ground, prevent (aircraft) from taking off; run ashore, strand; (elect., U.S.) connect with the ground, earth.

ground[2]**:** see GRIND; (esp.) ~ *glass,* glass made non-transparent by grinding or other means.

grou'ndage *n.* Duty on ship lying on beach or entering port.

grou'nding *n.* (esp.) Instruction in elements of subject.

grou'ndless *adj.* Without foundation, authority, or support, unfounded. **grou'ndlessly** *adv.* **grou'ndlessness** *n.*

grou'ndling *n.* Creeping or dwarf plant; (archaic) frequenter of pit of theatre; hence, spectator or reader of inferior taste.

grou'ndsel *n.* Plant of genus *Senecio,* esp. *S. vulgaris,* common European weed with small yellow flowers.

group (-ōōp) *n.* In fine arts, two or more figures or objects forming complete design or distinct part of one; number of persons or things standing near together, knot, cluster; number of persons or things belonging or classed together; *Oxford G~*: see MORAL Re-Armament; ~ *captain*, officer of Royal Air Force, ranking between air commodore and wing commander; ~ *practice*, medical practice run by several doctors in co-operation. ~ *v.* Form into a group, place in a group (*with*); form into well-arranged and harmonious whole; classify. **grou'per**[1] *n.* (colloq.) Member of the Oxford Group.

grou'per[2] (-ōō-) *n.* Any of various marine food-fishes of the family Serranidae, found esp. in tropical seas.

grouse[1] *n.* (pl. *grouse*). Gallinaceous bird with feathered feet; (in pop. use restricted to) reddish-coloured game-bird (*Lagopus scoticus*) of British Isles; *black* ~, British species of grouse, *Lyrurus tetrix*; *great* ~, *wood* ~, capercaillie; *white* ~, ptarmigan.

grouse[2] *v.i.* & *n.* (slang) Grumble. **grou'ser** *n.*

grout[1] *n.* Thin fluid mortar for filling interstices. ~ *v.t.* Fill up or finish with grout or cement.

grout[2] *v.* (of pigs) Turn up earth, turn up (earth etc.) with snout.

grōve *n.* Small wood; group of trees, esp. one with open space in centre.

grŏ'vel *v.i.* Lie prone, humble oneself. **grŏ'velling** *adj.* Abject, low, base. **grŏ'vellinglў** *adv.*

grow (-ō) *v.* (past t. *grew* pr. grōō, past part. *grown*). 1. Develop or exist as living plant; germinate, sprout, spring up, be produced, come naturally into existence, arise. 2. Increase in size, height, quantity, degree, power, etc.; become gradually; *growing-pains*, children's pains prob. of a rheumatic character popularly attributed to growing; *growing season*, season (longest near equator) when rainfall and temperature permit plants to grow; ~ *on*, acquire more and more influence over, gain more and more of (person's) liking or admiration; ~ *up*, advance to maturity; emerge from soil; reach full size; (of custom) arise, become common. 3. Produce by cultivation; bring forth; let (beard etc.) grow; (pass.) be covered (*over*, *up*) with some growth. **grow'er** *n.* (esp.) Person growing produce; plant that grows in specified way. **grow'inglў** *adv.*

growl *n.* Guttural sound of anger; rumble; angry murmur, complaint. ~ *v.* Utter growl, rumble, murmur angrily; utter with a growl. **grow'linglў** *adv.*

grow'ler *n.* (esp.) 1. (archaic, colloq.) Four-wheeled cab, esp. of the type formerly used in London. 2. Small iceberg.

grown (-ōn) *adj.*: see GROW; (esp.) ~*-up*, (*adj.* & *n.*) adult.

growth (-ō-) *n.* Growing, development, increase; cultivation *of* produce; what has grown or is growing; (path.) morbid formation.

groyne *n.* Timber framework or low broad wall run out into sea to check drifting of beach and so stop

encroachment of sea; similar structure in river. ~ *v.t.* Supply (beach) with groynes.

grŭb *n.* 1. Larva of insect, caterpillar, maggot. 2. (cricket) Ball bowled along ground. 3. (slang) Food, a feed. ~ *v.* 1. Dig superficially; clear (ground) of roots and stumps; clear away (roots etc.); fetch *up* or *out* by digging; search, rummage. 2. Plod, toil, *on*, *along*, *away*. 3. (slang) Feed.

grŭ'bbў *adj.* 1. Of, infested with, grubs. 2. Dirty, grimy, slovenly. **grŭ'bbinėss** *n.*

Grŭb Street. Street (now Milton Street) near Moorfields, London, inhabited in 17th c. by needy authors and literary hacks; hence, such writers (also attrib.).

grŭdge *v.t.* Be unwilling to give, grant, or allow (*to*); be unwilling *to* do. **grŭ'dginglў** *adv.* **grŭdge** *n.* Feeling of resentment or ill will.

gru'el (grōō-) *n.* Liquid food

chiefly for invalids of oatmeal etc. boiled in milk or water; (colloq.) *have, take, one's* ~, be punished; get killed.

gru'elling (groo-) *adj.* & *n.* Exhausting or punishing (experience).

grue'some (-oos-) *adj.* Grisly, disgusting. **grue'somely** *adv.* **grue'someness** *n.*

grŭff *adj.* Surly, laconic, rough-mannered, rough-voiced. **grŭ'ffly** *adv.* **grŭ'ffness** *n.*

grŭ'mble *n.* Dull inarticulate sound, murmur, complaint. ~ *v.* Utter grumble, murmur, growl faintly; rumble; complain; utter complainingly. **grŭ'mbler** *n.* **grŭ'mblingly** *adv.*

grume (groom) *n.* (med.) Clot of blood, clotted blood; viscous fluid. **gru'mous** *adj.*

grŭ'mmet *n.* (naut.) Ring usu. of twisted rope as fastening, rowlock, gun-wad, etc.

grŭ'mpy, grŭ'mpish *adjs.* Ill-tempered, surly. **grŭ'mpily** *adv.* **grŭ'mpiness** *n.*

Grŭ'ndy, Mrs. In Thomas Morton's play 'Speed the Plough' (1798), a neighbour who never appears but is constantly referred to ('What will Mrs. Grundy say?'); hence, symbol of conventional propriety or prudery. **Grŭ'ndyish** *adj.* **Grŭ'ndyism** *n.*

grŭnt *n.* 1. Low gruff sound characteristic of hogs, any similar sound. 2. Any of several Amer. fishes of family Pomadasyidae which make grunting noise when caught. ~ *v.* Utter grunt; express discontent, dissent, fatigue, etc., by this; utter with grunt. **grŭ'nter** *n.* (esp.) 1. Pig. 2. = GRUNT *n.* 2.

gruyère (groo'yār) *n.* Pale firm cow's-milk cheese with small cavities, made at Gruyères, Switzerland; French imitation of this.

gry'sbŏk *n.* Small reddish S. Afr. antelope (*Raphiceros*).

G.S. *abbrev.* General service.

G.S.O. *abbrev.* General Staff Officer.

G-string *n.* Cord supporting narrow strip of cloth etc. covering the genitals.

Gt Britain *abbrev.* Great Britain.

guai'ac, guai'acum (gwī-) *n.* (Hard heavy brownish-green wood of) W. Indian tree of genus *Guaiacum*, esp. *G. officinale* and *G. sanctum*, lignum vitae; resin obtained from these, drug made from it used in treatment of rheumatism and gout.

guai'acŏl (gwī-) *n.* Colourless liquid or white crystalline solid with strong smell, obtained by distilling guaiacum resin or wood-tar creosote, and used in medicine.

guaiacum: see GUAIAC.

Guam (gwahm). Largest and southernmost of the Mariana Islands; ceded to U.S. by Spain in 1898 and now a U.S. naval station; capital, Agaña.

guan (gwahn) *n.* Any of several S. Amer. gallinaceous birds allied to curassow.

gua'na (gwah-) *n.* Iguana; large lizard.

guana'cō (gwanah-), **hua-** (hwa-) *n.* S. Amer. wild llama, *Lama guanicoe*, with reddish-brown wool.

gua'nō (gwah-) *n.* Excrement of sea-fowl found esp. on sea-coasts of islands about Peru, rich in phosphates and ammonia and used as manure; artificial manure, esp. that made from fish. ~ *v.t.* Fertilize with guano.

Guara'ni[1] (gwarah-) *n.* One of the two main divisions of the Tupi-Guarani, widespread ethnical and linguistic family of S. Amer. Indians; language of this people.

guara'ni[2] (gwarah-) *n.* Principal monetary unit of Paraguay, = 100 centimos.

guarantee' (gă-) *n.* Person making guaranty or giving security; guaranty; thing given or existing as security for fulfilment of conditions or permanence etc. of something; person to whom guaranty is given. ~ *v.t.* Be guarantee for, answer for due fulfilment of (contract etc.) or genuineness etc. of (article); assure permanence etc. of; engage *that* something has happened or will happen; secure possession of *to* person; secure *against* or *from* (risk etc.) or *in* (possession etc.). **guă'rantor** (*or* -ôr') *n.*

guă'rantȳ (gă-) *n.* Undertaking, esp. written, to answer for payment of debt or performance of obligation by another person liable in first instance; ground or basis of security.

guard (gârd) *n.* 1. Defensive posture or motion in fencing, boxing, etc.; watch, vigilant state; *keep ~, be on ~*, act as sentry etc.; *on, off, one's ~*, prepared, unprepared, against attack, surprise, etc. 2. Protector, defender, sentry; (U.S.) prison warder; official in charge of stage-coach or train. 3. Body of soldiers etc. serving as protectors of place or person, escort, separate portion of army etc.; (pl.) selected bodies of troops normally for escort or ceremonial duties with a sovereign, e.g. in British Army the Household troops, which comprise the LIFE *Guards, Royal* HORSE *Guards*, and *Foot Guards*; *Brigade of Guards*, Foot Guards, consisting of five regiments, the Grenadier, Coldstream, Scots, Irish, and Welsh Guards; *mount, relieve, ~*, take up, take others' place in, sentry duty. 4. Contrivance of metal, wood, etc., to prevent injury or accident; e.g. part of sword-hilt protecting hand from injury, fire-guard, trigger-guard, etc. 5. *~-boat*, boat going rounds of fleet in harbour to see that good watch is kept; official harbour-boat enforcing quarantine or customs regulations; *~-chain*, chain securing watch, brooch, etc.; *~-house*, building for accommodation of military guard or keeping of prisoners under guard; *~-rail*, hand- or other rail to prevent falling, etc.; short rail to keep wheel on line at railway switches, crossings, etc.; *~-room*, room for keeping prisoners under guard, or for military guard; *~-ship*, warship protecting harbour, for directing shipping, and for receiving seamen till they can join their ships; *guar'dsman*, soldier, esp. officer, of Guards. *~ v.* Keep safe, stand guard over, keep (door etc.) so as to control passage; protect, defend; secure by explanations or stipulations etc. from misunderstanding or abuse; keep (thoughts, speech) in check; use a fencing guard; take precautions *against*; (chess) protect (piece, pawn) with another. **guar'dėdlȳ** *adv.* Cautiously, in guarded language.

guar'dant (gâr-) *adj.* (her.) (of a beast) Having the full face towards the spectator.

guar'dĭan (gâr-) *n.* Keeper, defender, protector; (law) one having custody of person or property, or both, of minor, idiot, etc.; superior of Franciscan convent; *~ angel*, spirit watching over person or place. **guar'dĭanship** *n.* Office of guardian, legal tutelage; keeping, guard.

Guarnēr'ĭus (gw-). Latinized name of the Guarneri, a 17th- and 18th-c. family of Italian violin-makers of Cremona; hence, violin made by one of this family.

Guatemala (gwahtĭmah'la). Most northerly republic of Central America, bordering on Mexico; capital, Guatemala. **Guatema'lan** *adj.* & *n.*

gua'va (gwah-) *n.* Tree of tropical Amer. genus *Psidium* of family Myrtaceae, esp. *P. guajava*; acid fruit of this, used for making jelly etc. [Span. *guayaba*, prob. f. native Amer. name]

gūbernatôr'ial *adj.* Of a governor.

gŭ'dgeon¹ (-jon) *n.* Small European freshwater fish, *Gobio gobio*, used as bait; credulous person.

gŭ'dgeon² (-jon) *n.* Pivot at end of beam, axle, etc., on which bell, wheel, etc., works; ring of gate turning on hook of post; socket in which rudder works; pin holding two blocks of stone etc. together; *~ pin*, (esp.) that holding piston and connecting rod together.

gue'lder rōse (gĕ-, -z). Small tree, *Viburnum opulus*, bearing round bunches of white flowers, snowball tree. [f. *Guelders*, town in Prussia, or *Guelderland*, province of Holland]

GUELDER ROSE

Guĕlph (gw-) *n.* 1. Member of medieval Italian party supporting the pope against the emperor (cf. GHIBELLINE). 2. Member of a princely family of Swabian origin from which the British royal house is descended through George I (the name is often given as the surname of the house of Hanover, although D'Este is equally accurate). [It. *Guelfo* f. MHG. *Welf*, name of the founder of the family, said to have been used at the battle of Weinsberg (1140) as a war-cry by the partisans of the Duke of Bavaria, who fought against the Emperor Conrad III]

guer'don (gēr-) *n.* & *v.t.* (poet.) Reward, recompense.

Guernsey[1] (gēr'nzĭ). Second largest of the Channel Islands; ~ *flower* or *lily*, S. African plant (*Nerine sarniensis*) with bright-red umbellate flowers, naturalized in Guernsey.

guernsey[2] (gēr'nzĭ) *n.* 1. Thick knitted closely-fitting vest or shirt, usu. made of blue wool, worn by seamen. 2. *G~*, (one of) a breed of usu. fawn-and-white dairy cattle, orig. raised in Guernsey.

guerrĭ'lla (ge-) *n.* Person engaged in irregular fighting (~ *war(fare)*) carried out by small bodies of men acting independently. [Span. *guerrilla* little war]

guess (gĕs) *v.* Estimate without measurement or detailed calculation; think likely; think one divines nature of; form hypothesis as to, conjecture, hazard opinion about; conjecture (answer to riddle etc.) rightly, divine; *I ~*, (chiefly U.S.) I feel sure, I know well. ~ *n.* Rough estimate, conjecture, hypothesis; *by ~*, at haphazard; *~-work*, (procedure based on) guessing.

guest (gĕst) *n.* Person given food or lodging at another's house etc.; person lodging at hotel, boarding-house, etc.; animal or vegetable parasite; *paying ~*, boarder; *~-chamber*, room kept for guests; *~-house*, superior boarding-house; *~-night*, one on which guests are entertained at club, college, etc.

guffaw' *n.* Coarse or boisterous laugh. ~ *v.* Make, say with, guffaw.

Guiă'na (gī-). Region in NE. of S. America, including Guyana, French Guiana, and Surinam; ~ *bark*, CINCHONA bark. **Guiănē'se** (-z) *adj.* & *n.*

gui'dance (gīd-) *n.* Guiding, direction.

guide (gīd) *n.* 1. One who shows the way; hired conductor of traveller or tourist, or climber; adviser; directing principle or standard; (mil.) one of company formed for reconnoitring etc.; *right, left, ~*, (mil.) subalterns of company superintending, marking pivots, etc., in evolutions; (naut.) ship by which rest of fleet regulate their movements; *G~*, (formerly *Girl G~*) member of the Girl Guides Association, an organization for girls, established in 1910, corresponding to the Scout Association. 2. Book of rudiments, manual; (also *~-book*), book to inform tourists about city, cathedral, museum, etc. or whole district or country. 3. (mech.) Bar, rod, etc., directing motion of something; gauge etc.; controlling tool; thing marking a position or guiding the eye. 4. ~ *dog*, dog trained to guide blind person; *~-post*, signpost; *~-rope*, guy; rope trailing from balloon etc. to anchor or ballast it. ~ *v.t.* Act as guide to, go before, lead, direct course of; arrange course of (events); be principle, motive, or ground, of; conduct affairs of (State etc.); *guided missile* etc., missile etc. steered by remote control or internal mechanism. **gui'der** *n.* (esp., *G~*) Adult leader in Girl Guides Association.

gui'don (gē-) *n.* Pennant narrowing to point at free end; this used as standard of dragoons.

guild, gild (gĭ-) *n.* Society for mutual aid or prosecution of common object, esp. medieval trade- or craft-association, acting as benefit society, promoting common trade-interests of members etc. and freq. developing into municipal corporation; *~-hall*, hall in which medieval guild met; town hall; *Guildhall*, hall of Corporation of City of London, used for State banquets etc.; *~ socialism*, system by which resources, methods, and profits of each industry should be controlled by a council of its members.

gui'lder (gĭl-) *n.* 1. Principal monetary unit of Netherlands Antilles and of Surinam, = 100 cents; Netherlands florin. 2. (obs.) Austrian florin.

guile (gīl) *n.* Treachery, deceit; cunning devices. **gui'leful** *adj.* **gui'lefully̆** *adv.* **gui'lefulnėss** *n.* **gui'lelėss** (-l-l-) *adj.* **gui'lelėssly̆** *adv.* **gui'lelėssnėss** *n.*

gui'llėmŏt (gĭl-) *n.* Sea-bird of genus *Uria*.

guilloche (gĭlō'sh) *n.* (archit.)

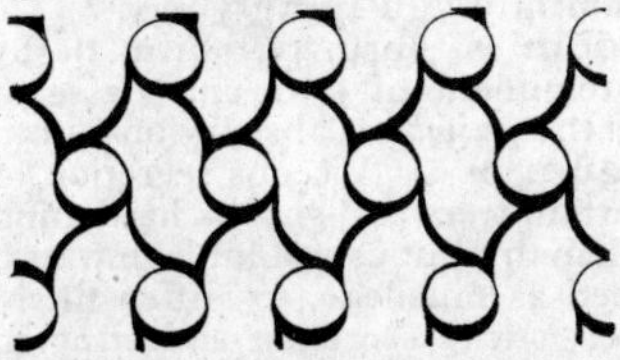

Ornament imitating braided ribbons.

guillotine (gĭlotē'n *or* gĭ'-) *n.* 1. Instrument used in France (esp. during the Revolution) and elsewhere for beheading, consisting of heavy knife-blade sliding between grooved posts. 2. Surgical instrument for excising uvula, tonsils, etc. 3. Machine for cutting paper, book-edges, etc. 4. (parl.) Method of shortening discussion of Bill by fixing times at which parts of it must be voted on. *~ v.t.* Use guillotine upon. [J. I. *Guillotin* (1738–1814), French physician, who advocated its use in 1789]

guilt (gĭ-) *n.* Fact of having committed a specified or implied offence; criminality, culpability. **gui'ltlėss** *adj.* Innocent (*of*). **gui'ltlėssly̆** *adv.* **gui'ltlėssnėss** *n.*

gui'lty̆ (gĭ-) *adj.* Criminal, culpable; conscious of, prompted by, guilt; having committed a particular offence; *~*, *not ~*, pleas, verdicts, in criminal trials. **gui'ltily̆** *adv.* **gui'ltĭnėss** *n.*

Gui'nea[1] (gĭ-). Republic on coast of W. Africa, formerly part of French West Africa; independent 1958; capital, Conakry. **Gui'nėan** *adj.* & *n.*

gui'nea[2] (gĭ-) *n.* English gold coin (not coined since 1813) first struck in 1663, orig. of gold from Guinea and for trade with Guinea, of fluctuating value, orig. nominally 20*s.*, fixed in 1717 at 21*s.*; money of account (£1·05) as unit for professional fee etc., price of racehorse, painting, etc.; *~-fowl*, *-hen*, gallinaceous bird (*Numida*, esp. *N. meleagris*) with slate-coloured white-spotted plumage, domesticated in Europe; *~-pig*, (origin of name doubtful) S. Amer. rodent (*Cavia porcellus*) now half-domesticated in Europe etc. as pet, and also as subject for laboratory experiments (hence, *human ~-pig*); person receiving guinea fees, esp. company director or deputy clergyman; *~ worm*, tropical parasitic nematoid worm (*Filaria medinensis*) infesting skin

GUILLOTINE

of man and horse, esp. in legs and feet, and causing sores.

Gui'nea-Bissau' (gi-, -ow). Republic on coast of W. Africa, formerly Portuguese Guinea; independent 1974; capital, Bissau.

Guĭ'nĕvēre (gw-). (Arthurian legend) Wife of King Arthur and mistress of Lancelot.

guipure (gē'poor) *n.* Heavy lace made by cutting out pieces of linen and joining them with openwork embroidery.

guise[1] (gīz) *n.* Style of attire, garb (archaic); external appearance; semblance, assumed appearance, pretence.

Guise[2] (gēz). Name of a branch of the princely house of Lorraine, of which the best-known member is Henri de Guise (1550–88), one of the authors of the massacre of St. BARTHOLOMEW and a leader of the *Ligue* which attempted to depose Henri III.

guitar' (gĭ-) *n.* Musical instrument, usu. with six strings, played with fingers or plectrum; *English* ~, kind of cither.

Gujarat (go͞ojarah't). State of W. India formed 1960 from N. part of former Bombay State. **Gujara'tĭ** *adj.* & *n.* (Native or inhabitant, language) of Gujarat.

gŭlch *n.* (U.S.) Ravine, marking course of a torrent.

gu'lden (go͞o-) *n.* (obs.) Netherlands guilder. [Du. & Ger., = 'golden']

gūles (-lz) *n.* & *adj.* (her.) Red.

gŭlf *n.* 1. (geog.) Portion of sea partially enclosed by sweep of coast, and usu. narrower at mouth than bay. 2. Deep hollow, chasm, abyss; (poet.) profound depth (in river, ocean); impassable dividing line.

Gŭlf Stream. Great oceanic current of warm water flowing from Gulf of Mexico parallel with Amer. coast to Newfoundland, and thence (under the name of N. Atlantic Drift) towards Europe and round the British Isles.

gŭll[1] *n.* Any of several long-winged web-footed sea-birds (family Laridae), usu. white with mantle varying from pearl-grey to black, with bright-coloured bill and harsh cry; *black-backed, black-headed, common*, and *herring* ~*s*, species found in Britain. **gŭ'llerў** *n.* Colony of gulls; place where these collect.

gŭll[2] *n.* & *v.t.* Dupe, fool. **gŭ'llĭble** *adj.* Easily cheated or duped. **gŭ'llĭblў** *adv.* **gŭllĭbĭ'lĭtў** *n.*

Gŭ'llah (-*a*) *n.* One of a group of Negroes, descendants of slaves from W. Africa, inhabiting coastal regions of Carolina, Georgia, and Florida.

gŭ'llėt *n.* Oesophagus; (loosely) throat.

gŭ'llў *n.* Water-worn ravine; deep artificial channel, gutter, drain, sink; (cricket) part of the field lying between point and the slips. ~ *v.t.* Make gullies in, form (channels) by water-action.

gŭlp *v.* Swallow (usu. *down*) hastily, greedily, or with effort; perform act of swallowing with difficulty, gasp, choke. ~ *n.* Act of gulping; effort to swallow; large mouthful. **gŭ'lpinglў** *adv.*

gŭm[1] *n.* (usu. pl.) Firm fleshy integument of jaws and bases of teeth; *gu'mboil*, abscess on gum.

gŭm[2] *n.* 1. Viscous secretion of certain trees and shrubs hardening when dry but usu. soluble in water, used as mucilage, to stiffen linen, etc.; sticky secretion collecting in inner corner of eye; viscid or waxy substance surrounding filaments of natural silk; hardish tough sweet made of gelatine; chewing-gum. 2. (also ~-*tree*) Any tree that exudes gum, esp. eucalyptus, various species of the N. Amer. genus *Nyssa* etc.; (U.S.) hollowed-out log, usu. from gum-tree, serving as beehive, water-trough, etc. 3. (U.S.) Indiarubber; (U.S., colloq.) galosh; *gu'mboot*, rubber boot. 4. ~ *arabic*: see ARABIC; ~ *dragon*, TRAGACANTH; ~ *juniper*, SANDARAC; ~-*tree*: see 2 above; *up a* ~-*tree*, in a fix, in difficulties. ~ *v.* Stiffen, smear, with gum; fasten *down, together, up*, etc., with gum; exude gum; ~ *up*, (colloq.) impede. **gŭ'mmў** *adj.* Viscid, sticky, abounding in, exuding, gum.

gŭ'mbō[1] *n.* Okra plant or its pods (*Hibiscus esculentus*); soup thickened with the pods of this plant.

Gŭ'mbō[2] *n.* Creole patois in French W. Indies, Louisiana, etc.

gŭ'mma *n.* (path.) Morbid growth of tissue, in late stage of syphilis. **gŭ'mmatous** *adj.*

gŭ'mption *n.* (colloq.) Resource, enterprising spirit, go, ready practical sense.

gŭn *n.* Metal tube for aiming or projecting missiles utilizing the explosive force of gunpowder or some other propellant; piece of ordnance, cannon, musket, fowling-piece, rifle, carbine; insecticide spray; (U.S.) revolver; member of shooting-party; *blow great ~s*, blow violently, blow a gale; *stick to one's ~s*, maintain one's argument;

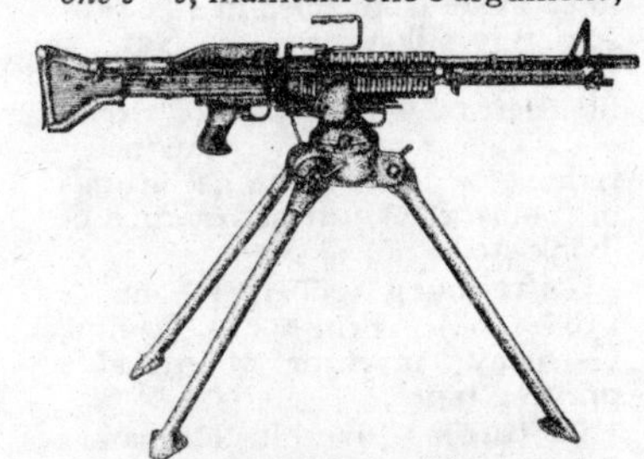

General purpose machine gun

Armalite

GUNS

sure as a ~, certainly, beyond question; *gu'nboat*, small warship carrying heavy gun(s); armed vessel of light draught, esp. for use on rivers; *gu'ncotton*, cotton-like explosive made by steeping cotton in mixture of nitric acid and sulphuric acids; cellulose trinitrate; *gu'nman*, (esp. U.S. slang) armed robber; *~-metal*, alloy of copper and tin or zinc (formerly used for guns); *gu'npowder*, explosive of saltpetre, sulphur, and charcoal; *Gunpowder Plot*, plot to blow up Houses of Parliament on 5 Nov. 1605, while King, Lords, and Commons were assembled there; *gunpowder* (*tea*), fine kind of green tea with leaves rolled up giving granular appearance; *~-room*, room in private house where guns and sporting equipment are kept; compartment in warship fitted up for junior officers or as lieutenants' mess-room; *~-runner*, *-running*, (person engaged in) illegal introduction of firearms into country; *gu'nsmith*, maker and repairer of small firearms. *~ v.i.* (chiefly U.S.) Shoot with gun; *~ for*, go in search of with gun (also fig.). [perh. f. *Gunna* pet-form of ON *Gunnhildr* woman's name used as nickname for ballistae and cannon]

gŭ'nnel[1] *n.* Butter-fish, small eel-shaped fish (*Pholis gunnellus*) of N. Atlantic, female of which protects her eggs by rolling them into a ball and coiling herself round them.

gunnel[2]: see GUNWALE.

gŭ'nner *n.* One who operates a gun; officer or man of artillery (as official term, private); (naut.) warrant officer in charge of battery, magazine, etc.

gŭ'nnera *n.* Prickly rhubarb, ornamental foliage plant with gigantic leaves. [J. E. *Gunner* (1718–73), Norw. botanist]

gŭ'nnerў *n.* Construction and management of large guns; firing of guns.

gŭ'nnў *n.* Coarse sacking, sack, usu. of jute fibre.

gŭ'nter *n.* 1. (also *Gunter's scale*) Flat 2-ft rule with scales etc. on one side, and scales of logarithms on other side, used for mechanical solution of surveying and navigation problems. 2. Topmast, or its sail, sliding up and down lower mast on rings (from resemblance to sliding Gunter's scale; so *~-rigged*). [Edmund *Gunter* (1581–1626), English mathematician]

Gunther (go͝o'nt*er*). In the Nibelungenlied, husband of Brunhild and brother of Kriemhild, by whom he was beheaded in revenge for Siegfried's murder.

gŭ'nwale (-n*e*l), **gŭ'nnel**[2] *n.* Upper edge of ship's or boat's side.

gŭp *n.* (orig. Ind.) Gossip; silly talk.

gûrgĭtā'tion *n.* Surging, bubbling motion or sound.

gûr'gle *n.* Bubbling sound as of water poured from bottle or running over stones. ~ *v.* Make gurgle; utter with gurgle(s).

gûr'jun *n.* Large E. Ind. tree (*Dipterocarpus turbinatus*) yielding viscous balsamic liquid (~ *balsam* or *oil*) used medicinally and as varnish.

Gûr'kha (-k*a*; *or* goor-) *n.* One of a military people of Hindu descent and Sanskritic speech, who settled in the province of Gurkha, Nepal, in the 18th c. and made themselves supreme; member of one of the Gurkha regiments (orig. specifically for Nepalese soldiers) of the British Army.

gûr'nard *n.* Marine fish of genus *Trigla* with large spiny head, mailed cheeks, and two or three

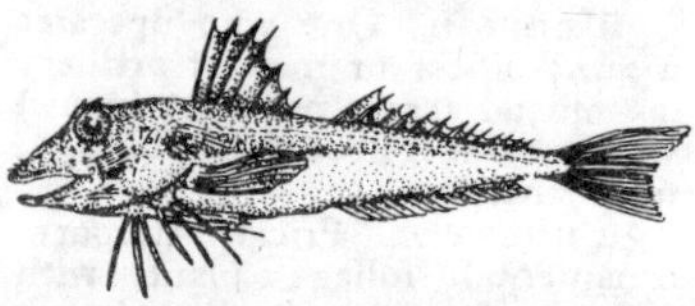

pairs of finger-shaped processes used as feelers. [OF *gournart*, lit. = 'grunter']

gŭ'rrȳ *n.* Small Indian fort.

guru (gōō'rōō) *n.* Hindu spiritual teacher or head of religious sect (also transf.). [Sansk.]

gŭsh *n.* Sudden or copious stream (often fig. of speech etc.); effusiveness, sentimental affectation. ~ *v.* Issue in, send forth, gush; emit (water etc.) copiously; speak, behave, with effusiveness. **gŭ'sher** *n.* (esp.) Oil-well spouting oil profusely without pumping. **gŭ'shĭnglȳ** *adv.* **gŭ'shȳ** *adj.*

gŭ'ssėt *n.* 1. Piece let into garment to strengthen or enlarge some part. 2. Iron bracket strengthening angle of structure. **gŭ'ssėtėd** *adj.*

gŭst[1] *n.* Sudden violent rush of wind; burst of rain, fire, smoke, sound, etc. **gŭ'stȳ** *adj.* **gŭ'stĭlȳ** *adv.*

gŭst[2] *n.* (archaic & poet.) Sense of taste; keen relish; flavour.

gŭstā'tion *n.* Tasting. **gŭ'statĭve, gŭ'statorȳ** *adjs.*

Gŭstā'vus Adŏ'lphus (1594–1632). King of Sweden 1611–32; invaded Germany in 1630 and led the forces in opposition to the emperor in the Thirty Years War; defeated Wallenstein at Lützen, but was killed in this battle.

gŭ'stō *n.* Zest, enjoyment with which something is done.

gŭt *n.* 1. (pl.) Bowels or entrails (esp. of animals); (fig. & colloq.) energy, courage, force of character, pluck; (sing.) particular part of lower alimentary canal, intestine; *blind* ~, caecum. 2. Material for violin strings made from intestines of animals; material for fishing-lines made from unspun silk-substance in silk-worms. 3. Narrow water-passage, sound, straits; defile, narrow lane or part of street. ~ *v.* Take out guts of, clean, (fish); remove or destroy internal fittings of (house etc.); extract essence of (book etc.).

Gu'tenberg (gōō-), Johann (*c* 1398–1468). Printer in Mainz, Germany; inventor of movable printing types.

gŭ'ttae *n.pl.* (archit.) Drops in a row as ornament esp. in Doric architecture.

gŭ'tta-pêr'cha *n.* Greyish rubber-like substance obtained from juice of various Malayan trees, esp. *Palaquium gutta*, used in electrical insulations etc. [Malay *getāh* gum, *percha* name of tree]

gŭ'ttāte *adj.* (biol.) Having drop-like markings.

gŭ'tter *n.* Shallow trough below eaves, channel at side of street, carrying off rainwater; open conduit for outflow of fluid; groove; *in, out of, the* ~, in, out of, low, disreputable, or poverty-stricken surroundings; ~ *press*, newspapers catering for depraved or vulgar taste; *guttersnipe*, street urchin. ~ *v.* Furrow, channel; flow in streams; (of candle) melt away by becoming channelled so that wax etc. runs down.

gŭ′ttle *v.* Eat gluttonously. **gŭ′ttler** *n.*

gŭ′ttural *adj.* Of the throat; (of sounds) produced in throat, or by back of tongue and palate. ~ *n.* Guttural sound or letter. **gŭ′tturalism** *n.* **gŭ′tturalize** *v.t.* **gŭ′tturally̆** *adv.*

guy[1] (gī) *n.* Rope, chain, etc. to guide and steady thing being hoisted and lowered, or to secure or steady anything liable to shift, or to hold tent etc. in place. ~ *v.t.* Secure with guy(s).

guy[2] (gī) *n.* Effigy of Guy FAWKES burnt on 5 Nov.; grotesquely dressed person, fright; (U.S.) man, fellow. ~ *v.t.* Exhibit in effigy; ridicule, make fun of.

Guyă′na (gī-). Republic on NE. coast of S. America (formerly *British Guiana*); independent 1966; member State of the Commonwealth; capital, Georgetown. **Guyanē′se** (-z) *adj.* & *n.*

Guy's Hŏ′spĭtal (gīz). London hospital, founded by Thomas Guy (1645?–1724), a London bookseller and one of the Oxford University printers.

gŭ′zzle *v.* Drink, eat, greedily; consume in guzzling. **gŭ′zzler** *n.*

Gwĕnt. County of SE. Wales (since April 1974).

Gwy̆′nĕdd (-ĕdh). County of NW. Wales (since April 1974).

gwy̆′nĭăd *n.* White-fleshed fish of salmon kind (*Coregonus clupeoides*), found in Lake Bala, Wales.

gȳbe *v.* (of fore-and-aft sail or boom) Swing across, make (sail) do this, in wearing or running before wind; (of ship, crew, etc.) change course so that this happens.

gȳle (g-) *n.* Quantity of beer brewed at once; fermenting wort; fermenting-tun.

gy̆m *n.* (colloq.) Gymnasium, gymnastics; ~*-slip*, *-tunic*, girl's or woman's short sleeveless belted garment worn esp. as school uniform.

gy̆mkha′na (-kah-) *n.* (orig. Ind.) Public place with facilities for athletics; display of athletic sports; horse and pony meetings, for races, competitions, etc. [mixture of *gymnastics* and Hind. *gend-khāna* ball-house (racquet-court)]

gy̆mnā′sium (-z-) *n.* 1. Place, room, or building, with appliances for practice in gymnastics. 2. Continental, esp. German, school of highest grade, preparing pupils for universities.

gy̆′mnăst *n.* Expert in gymnastics.

gy̆mnă′stic *adj.* Of gymnastics. **gy̆mnă′stically̆** *adv.* **gy̆mnă′stics** *n.pl.* Exercises developing the muscles, esp. such as are performed in gymnasium.

gy̆mnŏ′sophist *n.* One of ancient Hindu philosophic sect going nearly naked and given up to contemplation. **gy̆mnŏ′sophy̆** *n.*

gy̆′mnospẽrm *n.* (bot.) Plant having its seeds unprotected by seed-vessels (opp. ANGIOSPERM). **gy̆mnospẽr′mous** *adj.*

gȳnaecē′um (-ĭs-; *or* gī-) *n.* 1. (Gk & Rom. antiq.) Women's apartments in house. 2. (bot., often incorrectly *-oecium*) Female organs of a flower, the carpels collectively.

gȳnaecŏ′logy̆ (g-) *n.* Science of diseases of women, esp. of the reproductive system. **gȳnaecolŏ′gical** *adj.* **gȳnaecŏ′logist** *n.*

gȳnă′ndromŏrph (g-) *n.* (biol.) Individual with characters of both sexes.

gȳnă′ndrous (g-) *adj.* (biol.) Of mixed sex; (bot.) with stamens and pistil united in one column as in orchids.

gȳnoe′cium (-ē-) *n.* Var. of GYNAECEUM, 2.

gy̆p[1] *n.* Male college servant at Cambridge or Durham. [perh. for obs. *gippo* scullion, orig. man's short tunic, f. obs. Fr. *jupeau*]

gy̆p[2] *n.* (slang) *give person* ~, punish or treat him roughly.

gy̆psŏ′phila *n.* Plant of genus *G~* (family Caryophyllaceae) with small delicate pink or white flowers. [Gk *gupsos* chalk, *philos* loving]

gy̆′psum *n.* Hydrated calcium sulphate, mineral from which plaster of Paris is made by dehydration. **gy̆ʹpsėous, gy̆psĭʹferous, gy̆ʹpsous** *adjs.*

gypsy: see GIPSY.

gy̅rāʹte *v.i.* Go in circle or spiral; revolve, whirl. **gy̅rāʹtion** *n.* **gy̅rʹatorў** *adj.*

gy̅rʹō *n.* Gyroscope; ~ *compass*, form of gyroscope used as a compass, mounted so that its axis remains parallel to that of the earth.

gy̅rʹogrăph (*or* -ahf) *n.* Instrument recording revolutions.

gy̅rʹon *n.* (her.) Triangular ordinary forming the lower half of an upper quarter. **gy̅rʹonnў** *adj.* Divided into gyrons.

gy̅rʹoplāne *n.* Flying machine in which the lift is mainly provided by vanes rotating freely in a more or less horizontal plane.

gy̅rʹoscōpe *n.* Instrument to illustrate dynamics of rotating bodies, solid rotating wheel mounted in ring, with axis free to turn in any direction (the tendency of the wheel, free from disturbing forces, being to maintain rotation in fixed plane); form of this attached to vessels, aircraft, etc., to maintain equilibrium, measure angular velocity and acceleration, etc. **gy̅roscŏʹpĭc** *adj.* **gy̅roscŏʹpĭcallў** *adv.*

gy̅rʹostăt *n.* Form of gyroscope in which the wheel is fixed in a case.

gy̅rʹus *n.* (pl. *-ri*). (anat.) Fold, convolution, esp. of brain-surface.

gy̅ve *n.* (usu. pl.) & *v.t.* (poet.) Shackle, fetter.

H

H, h (ăch). 8th letter of modern English and ancient Roman alphabet, representing historically Semitic ⊟ (laryngal or guttural spirant, or rough aspirate), Greek H; in modern English usu. standing (except in combination with *c, g, s, t, w*) for simple aspiration or breathing, with just enough narrowing of glottis to be audible before vowel.

h. *abbrev.* Hecto-; hour(s).

H *abbrev.* Hard(ness); henry(s).

ha[1] (hah) *int.* Exclamation of surprise, joy, suspicion, triumph, etc.

ha[2] *abbrev.* Hectare(s).

Hab. *abbrev.* Habakkuk.

Hă'bakkuk (*or* habă'-) (7th or 6th c. B.C.). Hebrew minor prophet; book of O.T. containing his prophecies.

hā'bėās cor'pus. Writ requiring the body of a person to be brought before a judge or into court, esp. to investigate whether it has been lawful to hold him in custody; ~ *Act*, Act 31 Chas. II (1679), whereby the granting and enforcing of this writ was much facilitated. [L, = 'you must have the body']

hă'berdăsher *n.* Dealer in small articles of dress etc., as tape, ribbons, etc. **hă'berdăsherў** *n.*

hă'bergeon (-jon) *n.* (hist.) Sleeveless coat of mail.

habĭ'lĭment *n.* Attire, dress; (pl.) dress suited to particular office or occasion.

habĭ'lĭtāte *v.i.* Qualify for office (esp. in German university). **habĭlĭtā'tion** *n.*

hă'bit *n.* 1. Settled tendency or practice; mental constitution (esp. ~ *of mind*); bodily constitution; (bot., zool.) mode of growth. 2. Dress, esp. of religious order; (also *riding*-~) woman's riding-dress. ~ *v.t.* 1. Clothe. 2. (archaic) Inhabit.

hă'bĭtable *adj.* That can be inhabited. **hăbĭtabĭ'lĭtў, hă'bĭtablenėss** *ns.* **hă'bĭtablў** *adv.*

hă'bĭtant *n.* 1. Inhabitant. 2. (ăbētahṅ) One of the (descendants of) early French settlers in Canada, Louisiana, etc., chiefly farmers.

hă'bĭtăt *n.* Natural home of plant or animal; habitation. [L, = '(it) inhabits']

hăbĭtā'tion *n.* Inhabiting; place of abode.

habĭ'tūal *adj.* Customary; constant, continual; given to (specified) habit. **habĭ'tūallў** *adv.* **habĭ'tūalnėss** *n.*

habĭ'tūāte *v.t.* Accustom (*to*). **habĭtūā'tion** *n.*

hă'bĭtūde *n.* Mental or bodily constitution; custom, tendency.

habĭ'tué (-ā) *n.* Habitual visitor or resident. [Fr.]

Hă'bsburg. German family (named after the castle of Habsburg near Aarau in Switzerland) to which belonged the rulers of Austria and many of the Holy Roman Emperors from 1273 to 1918; a Spanish branch of the family ruled Spain from 1516 to 1700.

hăchur'es (-shūr) *n.pl.* In map-drawing, short lines of shading indicating differences of slope (close together for steep slopes, wider apart for gradual ones).

hăcĭĕ'nda *n.* Estate, plantation, with dwelling-house, in Spain, or (former) Spanish colonies.

hăck[1] *n.* Mattock; miner's pick; gash, wound, esp. from kick with toe of boot. ~ *v.* Cut, notch, mangle; kick shin of (opponent at football); deal cutting blows (*at*); emit short dry coughs (so *hacking cough*), ~*-saw*, saw with narrow blade set in a frame, for cutting metal.

hăck² *n.* Board on which hawk's meat is laid; frame for drying bricks.

hăck³ *n.* 1. Horse let out for hire; jade; horse for ordinary riding; (U.S.) hackney carriage. 2. Common (esp. literary) drudge, mere scribbler. ~ *v.* Make common, hackney; ride (horse), ride on horseback, on road at ordinary pace; use hired horses.

hă'ckle *n.* 1. Steel comb for dressing raw silk, flax, etc. 2. Long feathers on neck of domestic cock and other birds; angler's artificial fly dressed with hackle; *with ~s up*, (of cock, dog, etc.) angry, ready to fight. ~ *v.t.* Dress (flax, silk, fly) with hackle.

hă'ckney *n.* Horse of middle size and quality for ordinary riding; drudge, hireling; *~-carriage, -coach*, etc., vehicle plying for hire. ~ *v.t.* Make common or trite by repetition (esp. in past part. *hackneyed*).

Hă'ddĭngton(shire). Former name of EAST Lothian.

hă'ddock *n.* Fish (*Melanogrammus aeglefinus*) allied to cod but smaller, common in N. Atlantic etc. and much used for food.

hāde *n.* (geol., mining) Angle which a fault plane makes with the vertical plane. ~ *v.i.* (of fault plane) Incline from vertical.

Hā'dēs (-z). (Gk myth.) Oldest name of Pluto; his kingdom, abode of departed spirits or shades; hence, hell, sheol.

Hadhramaut (hahdr*a*mow't). Plateau region of SE. Arabia.

Hă'dĭth. Body of traditions relating to Muhammad, now forming supplement to Koran (the *Sunna*).

hă'djĭ (hăjĭ), **hă'jjĭ** *n.* Muslim pilgrim who has been to Mecca; *H~*, title of such.

Hā'drĭan. Publius Aelius Hadrianus (A.D. 76–138), Roman emperor 117–38; *~'s Wall*, wall from Solway Firth to mouth of the Tyne, built by Hadrian to protect Roman Britain from the tribes of the north.

hae'mal *adj.* Of the blood.

haemă'tĭc *adj.* Of or containing blood. ~ *n.* Medicine acting on blood.

hae'matĭn *n.* (chem.) Bluish-black amorphous substance with metallic lustre, constituent of haemoglobin.

hae'matīte *n.* Natural ferric oxide (Fe_2O_3) a red, brown, or blackish iron ore.

hae'matoid *adj.* Like blood; characterized by presence of blood.

haematŏ'logȳ *n.* Study of blood and its diseases.

haematūr'ia *n.* (path.) Presence of blood in urine.

haemoglō'bĭn *n.* Oxygen-carrying pigment contained in the red blood-cells of vertebrates.

haemŏ'lȳsĭs *n.* (physiol., med.) Loss of haemoglobin from red blood-cells. **haemolȳ'tĭc** *adj.*

haemophĭ'lĭa *n.* (path.) Constitutional, usu. hereditary, incapacity of blood to clot quickly or at all, involving risk of severe bleeding even from a slight injury. **haemophĭ'lĭc** *adj.* **haemophĭ'lĭăc** *n.* Person suffering from haemophilia.

haemorrhage (hĕ'merĭj) *n.* Escape of blood from blood-vessels; bleeding, internal or external.

haemorrhoid (hĕ'meroid) *n.* Varicose vein of anus (usu. pl., pop. called *piles*).

ha'fĭz (hah-) *n.* Muslim who knows the Koran by heart. [Arab. *hāfiẓ*]

hă'fnĭum *n.* (chem.) Rare metallic element (symbol Hf, at. no. 72, at. wt 178·49) usu. found with zirconium and resembling it in properties. [*Hafnia*, L name of Copenhagen]

haft (-ah-) *n.* Handle (of dagger,

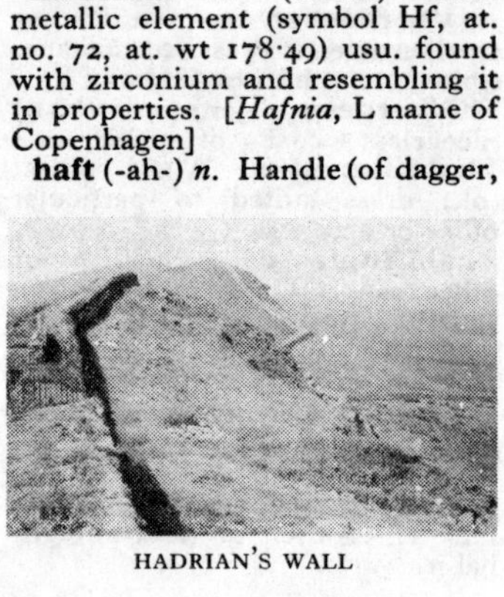

HADRIAN'S WALL

knife,etc.). ~ *v.t.* Furnish with haft.

hăg[1] *n.* **1.** Ugly old woman; witch; (formerly) evil spirit in female form; *~-ridden,* afflicted by nightmare. **2.** (also *~-fish*) Round-mouthed eel-like fish (*Myxine glutinosa*) allied to lamprey and living on dead or dying fish.

hăg[2] *n.* (Sc. & north.) Piece of soft bog in moor or morass; firm turfy or heathery ground in peat bog.

Hag. *abbrev.* Haggai (O.T.).

Hagga'dah (-gah'da) *n.* Legendary part of the Talmud, anecdote, parable, etc., introduced to illustrate a point of the Law; book containing Jewish liturgy for first two nights of Passover.

Hă'ggaī (6th c. B.C.). Hebrew minor prophet; book of O.T. containing his prophecies.

hă'ggard *adj.* Wild-looking (esp. as result of fatigue, privation, worry, etc.); (of hawk) caught in her adult plumage, untamed. **hă'ggardlȳ** *adv.* **hă'ggardnėss** *n.* **hă'ggard** *n.* Haggard hawk.

hă'ggĭs *n.* Heart, lungs, and liver, of sheep etc., with salt, pepper, onions, suet, etc., and oatmeal, boiled like large sausage in the animal's maw.

hă'ggle *n.* & *v.i.* Dispute, wrangle (esp. *over* or *about* prices or terms).

Hăgĭŏ'grapha (hăg-) *n.pl.* Books of Hebrew Scriptures not included under Law and Prophets. **hăgĭŏ'grapher** *n.* Writer of any of these, or of saints' lives. **hăgiogră'phĭc** *adj.* **hăgĭŏ'graphȳ** *n.* Writing of lives of saints.

hăgĭŏ'latrȳ (hăg-) *n.* Worship of saints.

hăgĭŏ'logȳ (hăg-) *n.* Literature treating of lives and legends of saints.

hă'gĭoscōpe (hăg-) *n.* = SQUINT (archit.).

Hague (hāg), The. (Du. *'s-Gravenhage*) Seat of government of the Netherlands; seat of the Court of International Justice.

ha ha (hah hah) *int.* Representation of sound of laughter.

ha-ha (hah'hah) *n.* Sunk fence bounding park or garden.

Haig, Douglas, 1st Earl Haig of Bemersyde (1861–1928). British field marshal; C.-in-C. British Expeditionary Force in France, 1915–18.

hail[1] *n.* Pellets of condensed and frozen vapour falling in shower, as *hailstorm*; shower *of* missiles, questions, etc.; *hai'lstone,* pellet of hail. ~ *v.* **1.** *it ~s,* hail falls. **2.** (fig.) Pour down (words, blows, etc.), come down, violently.

hail[2] *int.* of greeting; ~ *fellow* (*well met*), familiar, intimate, too intimate, *with.* ~ *v.* Salute; greet (*as*); call to (ship, person) to attract attention; (of ship, person) have come *from* (place). ~ *n.* Salutation; *within ~,* near enough to be hailed; *H~ Mary*: = AVE Maria.

Haile Selă'ssĭe I (hī'lĭ) (1892–1975). Emperor of Ethiopia 1930–74; after Italian invasion was forced to leave Addis Ababa 1936; lived in England till 1940; reinstated in capital 1941; deposed 1974.

Hai'leybury. Haileybury and Imperial Services College, a boys' public school in Hertfordshire; Haileybury Coll. founded 1862, I.S.C. founded 1912; the two amalgamated 1942.

hair *n.* One or (collect. sing.) all of the fine filaments growing from skins of animals, esp. from human head; (of plants) cells growing from epidermis; hair-like thing; jot, tittle; *get* (person) *by the short ~s,* hold so that escape is painful; have complete control over; *keep one's ~ on,* (slang) keep calm; *split ~s,* make fine or cavilling distinctions; be over-precise; *to a ~,* exactly; *not turn a ~,* show no sign of exhaustion or discomposure; *hair'breadth,* hair's breadth; *hair'brush,* toilet brush for hair; *hair'cloth,* cloth made of hair, for tents, shirts of penitents, etc.; *hair'cut,* act or style of cutting the hair; *~-do,* way hair is dressed; *hair'dresser,* one who cuts and styles (esp. women's) hair; *~-grip,* clip for keeping hair in place; *~-line,* edge of hair on forehead etc.; very fine line; up-stroke in writing, thin line in (printed) letters; *hair'net,* fine or loosely woven net for keeping hair in place; *hair'pin,* U-shaped piece of wire etc. used for fastening up hair; *hair'pin bend,* very sharp bend where road etc. doubles back; *~-raising,* enough to make hair stand on end through fear or excitement; *~'s breadth,* minute distance; *~'s-breadth escape,* narrow escape; *~ shirt,* ascetic's or penitent's shirt of haircloth; *~-slide,* hinged clip for keeping hair in place; *~-space,* narrowest space between words in printing; *~-splitting,* over-subtle(ty); *~-spring,* fine spring in watch, regulating balance-wheel; *~-stroke,* fine up-stroke in writing; *~ trigger,* secondary trigger releasing main one by very slight pressure. **hair'ĭness** *n.* **hair'lĕss, hair'līke, hair'ȳ** *adjs.*

Hai'tĭ (*or* hī-). Republic occupying western part of island of Hispaniola, W. Indies; capital, Port-au-Prince. **Hai'tĭan** *adj.* & *n.*

hāke[1] *n.* Cod-like edible seafish (*Merluccius merluccius*).

hāke[2] *n.* Wooden frame for drying cheeses, bricks, etc.

hakee'm, haki'm[1] (-ēm) *n.* In India and Muslim countries, physician. [Arab. *ḥakīm* wise, physician]

hakenkreuz (hah'kenkroits) *n.* (in Germany and Austria) Swastika.

ha'kĭm[2] (hah-) *n.* In India and Muslim countries, judge, ruler, governor. [Arab. *ḥākim* judge]

Hă'kluyt(-lo͞ot), Richard (1552?–1616). English clergyman; collected and published accounts of English explorations.

hă'lala *n.* $\frac{1}{100}$ of a Saudi Arabian riyal.

halā'tion *n.* (phot.) Spreading of light beyond its proper boundaries on a developed film or plate.

hă'lberd *n.* (hist.) Combined spear and battle-axe. **hălberdier'** *n.* Man armed with halberd.

hă'lcy̆on *n.* 1. Bird fabled by the ancients to breed in floating nest on sea at winter solstice, and to charm wind and waves into calm for the purpose; kingfisher. ~ *adj.* Calm, peaceful, quiet; ~ *days,* 14 days of calm weather anciently believed to occur about winter solstice (see ALCYONE). [Gk *alkuōn* kingfisher]

hāle[1] *adj.* Robust, vigorous.

hāle[2] *v.t.* Drag forcibly.

half (hahf) *n.* (pl. *halves* pr. hahvz). One of two equal or corresponding parts into which thing is divided; (colloq.) half-pint, half-mile, half-back, half-holiday; school term (the school year being formerly divided into two portions); *better ~,* wife; *go halves,* share equally (*with* person *in* thing). ~ *adj.* Forming a half. ~ *adv.* To the extent of half; (loosely) to a considerable extent; *not ~,* (slang) to the greatest possible extent; not *~ bad,* (colloq.) not at all bad, quite good. *~n., adj.,* or *adv.* in comb.: *~-and-~,* (what is) half one thing and half another, esp. mixture of ale and porter; *~-back,* (footb. etc.) player positioned immediately behind forwards; *~-baked,* (fig.) not thorough, not earnest, half-witted; *~-bound,* (of book) with leather back and corners, cloth or paper sides (so *~-calf, -morocco,* etc.); *~-blood,* person having one parent in common with another, this relationship; person of mixed race; *~-breed,* half-blooded person of mixed race; *~-brother,* brother by one parent only (so *~-sister*); *~-butt,* long billiard cue of shorter range than the long-butt; *~-caste,* half-breed; esp. (child) of European father and Indian mother; *~ cock*: see COCK[1]; *~-crown,* former British silver or cupro-nickel coin worth 2*s.* 6*d.*; (usu. *~ a crown*) this sum; *~-hearted,* lacking courage or zeal; so *~-heartedly, ~-heartedness*; *~ hitch*: see HITCH; *~-holiday,* day of which (the latter) half is taken as holiday; *~-landing,* landing halfway up flight of stairs; *~-length,* portrait of upper half of person; *~-life,* (phys.) time during which the radioactivity of a substance falls to half its original value; *~-mast*: *at ~-mast, ~-mast high,* (of flag) lowered to half height of mast as mark of respect for the dead or on other occasions of mourning; ~ *measures*, compromise, half-and-half policy etc.; ~-*moon*, moon of which only half is illuminated; anything of this shape; ~ *mourning*, black relieved by grey, lavender, etc., worn as transition from full mourning to ordinary dress; ~ *pay*, reduced allowance to army, navy, or air force officer when not in actual service, or after retirement at prescribed time; ~-*seas-over*, half drunk; ~ *sole*, sole of boot or shoe between shank and toe; ~-*timber*(*ed*), (archit.) having walls made of timber frame with spaces filled with bricks or plaster; ~-*time*, (esp.) interval between two halves of play at football etc.; ~-*timer*, (formerly) child who attended school for half usual time, earning money at some employment in other half; ~-*title*, title of a book printed at head of first page of text, or title of a section of a book printed on the recto of the leaf preceding it; ~-*tone*, (mus.) = SEMITONE; *ha'lftone*, (art) tone intermediate between the extreme lights and extreme shades; photomechanical illustration printed from a block in which the tones are broken up into small or large dots by the interposition of a glass screen, ruled with fine cross-lines, between the camera and the object; this process; ~-*truth*, statement that conveys only part of the truth, omitting some relevant facts; ~-*uncial*, a style of writing intermediate between uncial and minuscule; ~-*volley* (*n.*) (cricket, lawn-tennis, etc.) ball hit or returned as soon as it touches the ground; (*v.*) play (ball) thus; ~-*way*, equidistant from two ends; ~-*way house*, inn midway between two towns etc.; (fig.) compromise; ~-*witted*, imbecile; ~-*yearly*, (occurring) every half-year.

halfpenny (hā'pnĭ) *n.* (pl. *halfpence* pr. hā'pens of amounts, *halfpennies* of coins as such). Bronze coin worth half a penny; this amount; *halfpennyworth* (hā'poth), *ha'p'orth*, as much as a halfpenny will buy.

hă'lĭbut *n.* Large flat fish (*Hippoglossus vulgaris*) abundant in northern seas and much used for food. [*haly* holy, *butt* flat fish (because eaten on holy days)]

hă'līde *n.* Salt derived from a halogen.

hă'lĭdom *n.* (archaic) Holy thing, anything regarded as sacred, esp. (as oath) *by my* ~.

hălĭeu'tic *adj.* Of fishing.

hălĭeu'tĭcs *n.pl.* Art of fishing.

Hă'lĭfăx[1]. City of West Yorkshire.

Hălĭfăx[2]. Capital city of Nova Scotia, Canada.

hălĭō'tĭs *n.* Gasteropod mollusc of genus *H*~ with ear-shaped shell lined with mother-of-pearl.

hălĭtō'sĭs *n.* (med.) Foul breath.

hall (hawl) *n.* 1. Large public room in mansion, palace, etc.; principal living-room of medieval house; common dining-room in English colleges etc., dinner in this; large room for public business, entrance-passage of house etc.; (U.S.) any corridor or passage in building; *servants'* ~, room in which servants dine. 2. Residence of landed proprietor; building of guild; (universities) institution governed by head without fellows; building for students. 3. (pl.) Music-halls. 4. ~ *church*, type of medieval church having aisles as high as nave; ~-*way*, (U.S.) entrance-hall or corridor in building.

hallelujah: see ALLELUIA.

Hă'lley, Edmund (1656–1742). English astronomer, publisher of Newton's 'Principia'; ~'*s comet*, comet with a periodicity of 76 years, the return of which in 1758 was predicted by Halley.

halliard: see HALYARD.

ha'llmark (hawl-) *n.* Impression stamped on gold or silver article without which it may not legally be sold (in U.K. stamped at one of the four official Assay Offices and consisting of four marks indicating the standard of fineness, the Assay Office where the article was assayed, the year of assay, and the maker's initials); also fig. ~ *v.t.* Stamp with hallmark (often fig.).

[f. Goldsmiths' *Hall*, London and elsewhere]

hallō', halloa' (-ō) *int.* Exclamation calling attention or expressing surprise (e.g. on meeting someone). ~ *v.i.* & *n.* (Utter) the cry 'hallo!'.

halloo' *int.* Call inciting dogs to the chase, calling attention, or expressing surprise. ~ *n.* The cry 'halloo!'. ~ *v.* Cry 'halloo!', esp. to dogs; urge on (dogs etc.) with shouts; shout to attract attention.

hă'llow[1] (-ō) *n.* Holy person, saint (now only in *All Hallows, Hallowe'en*: see ALL). ~ *v.t.* Make holy; honour as holy.

hă'llow[2] (-ō) *v.* = HALLOO.

Hă'llstătt (*or* -sht-) *adj.* Of a civilization of the early Iron Age in Central Europe, named after the finds at Hallstatt in Upper Austria. **Hăllstă'ttian** *adj.*

hallū'cināte (*or* -lōō-) *v.t.* Produce false impressions in mind of (person). **hallūcinā'tion** *n.* Illusion; apparent perception of external object not actually present. **hallū'cinatorў** *adj.* **hallūcinogĕ'nic** *adj.* (esp., of drug) Inducing hallucination.

halm: see HAULM.

hă'lma *n.* Game for 2 or 4 persons played on chequer-board of 256 squares with 19 or 13 men placed in one corner of board for each player, the men being moved towards opposite corner with leaps over intervening men into vacant squares beyond.

hā'lō *n.* (pl. *-oes*). Circle of white or prismatically coloured light seen round luminous body, esp. that round sun or moon caused by refraction through ice crystals in thin cloud, differing from CORONA in being of definite size (usu. of 22° radius, less freq. 46°) and by reversal of colour sequence, the red appearing on inner side of halo, outer side of corona; circle, ring; disc of light surrounding head of saint, nimbus; (fig.) ideal glory investing person etc. ~ *v.t.* Surround with halo.

hă'logen *n.* (chem.) Any of the four non-metallic elements fluorine, chlorine, bromine, and iodine.

hă'loid *adj.* Salt-like.

hă'lophўte *n.* Plant inhabiting salty soils.

Hăls, Frans (*c* 1584–1666). Dutch portrait painter; worked at Haarlem; painter of the so-called 'Laughing Cavalier'.

halt[1] (haw- *or* hŏ-) *n.* Temporary stoppage on march or journey; small railway-station without usual accommodation or staff, where local trains stop. ~ *v.* Make a halt; (mil.) bring to a stand.

halt[2] (haw- *or* hŏ-) *adj.* (archaic) Lame; crippled. ~ *v.i.* Walk hesitatingly; hesitate (*between*); (of speech, argument, verse, etc.) be defective; (archaic) be lame. **ha'ltinglў** *adv.*

ha'lter (haw- *or* hŏ-) *n.* Rope, strap, with noose or headstall for horses or cattle; rope with noose for hanging person; death by hanging. ~ *v.t.* Fasten with halter; hang (person) with halter.

halve (hahv) *v.t.* Divide into halves; share equally; reduce to half; (golf) reach (hole) in same number of strokes as opponent; fit (crossing timbers) together by cutting out half thickness of each.

hă'lyard, hă'lliard, hau'lyard *n.* (naut.) Rope, tackle, for raising or lowering sail, yard, etc.

hăm[1] *n.* Back of thigh; thigh and buttock; (formerly) bend of the knee; thigh of hog salted and dried in smoke or otherwise cured for food; (esp. radio) amateur; (slang) ineffective or over-emphatic actor (also attrib.); ~*-fisted*, having large or clumsy hands, heavy-handed.

hăm[2] *n.* (hist.) Town, village.

Hăm[3]. Second son of Noah (Gen. 10: 1).

hămadrў'ăd *n.* 1. (Gk myth.) Nymph living and dying with the tree she inhabited. 2. (zool.) King cobra, large, very venomous hooded serpent (*Naja hannah*) of India. 3. (zool.) Large Arabian baboon (*Comopithecus hamadryas*), held sacred by ancient Egyptians.

hămamē'lis *n.* Shrub of genus *H*~ of which the N. Amer. species (*H. virginiana*) is the witch-hazel.

hă'mate *adj.* Hook-shaped; ~

bone, carpal bone with a hook-shaped process.

Hă'mbûrg[1]. City of N. Germany on the Elbe, forming a province of the Federal Republic.

Hă'mbûrg[2] *n.* 1. Small variety of domestic fowl. 2. Black variety of hothouse grape (*black* ~). 3. ~ *steak*, chopped beef, spiced and flavoured, formed into a cake and fried.

Hă'mbûrger (-g-) *n.* 1. Citizen of Hamburg. 2. (*h*~) Hamburg steak.

hāme *n.* Either of two curved pieces of wood or metal fastened over collar of draught horse, used to attach the traces.

Hămĭ'lcar. Hamilcar Barca (3rd c. B.C.), Carthaginian general of 1st Punic War; father of HANNIBAL.

Hă'mīte *n.* 1. Supposed descendant of HAM[3]. 2. Member of Egyptian or other people of N. or E. Africa. **Hamĭ'tĭc** *adj.* Of Hamites; (esp.) of the group of African languages including ancient Egyptian, Berber, Galla, etc.

hă'mlėt[1] *n.* Small village, esp. one without church.

Hă'mlėt[2]. Legendary prince of Denmark, hero of a tragedy by Shakespeare; ~ *without the Prince*, entertainment etc. from which chief personage is absent.

hă'mmer *n.* Instrument for beating, breaking, driving nails, etc., with hard solid (usu. metal) head at right angles to handle;

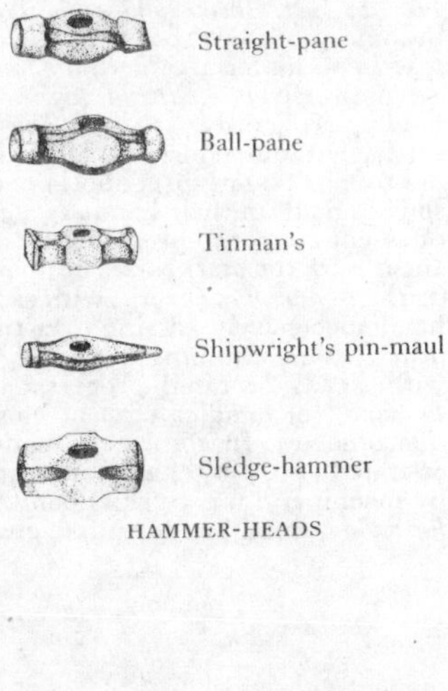

HAMMER-HEADS

machine with metal block serving same purpose; similar contrivance, as for exploding charge in gun, striking of piano, etc.; **auctioneer's mallet used to indicate by rap that article is sold; metal ball weighing 7·257 kg attached to a wire with a grip handle,** used in ***throwing the*** **~, athletic contest in which this is thrown for distance;** ***come under the*** **~, be sold by auction;** ~ ***and tongs,*** **with might and main;** ~ ***beam,*** **beam** projecting from wall at foot of principal rafter; ~ ***-cloth,*** cloth covering driver's seat **in horse-drawn carriage;** **~*-head,*** **head of hammer; kind of shark with great lateral expansions of head; kind of African bird, shadow-bird (*Scopus umbretta*);** **~*-lock,*** **(wrestling) position in which a wrestler is held with one arm bent behind his back;** **~*-toe,*** **toe deformed by being bent inwards.** ~ *v.* Strike, beat, drive, (as) with hammer; (colloq.) inflict heavy defeat(s) on in war or games; work hard *at*; (Stock Exch.) declare (person) a defaulter with three taps of hammer.

hă'mmock *n.* Hanging bed of canvas etc. or netting suspended by cords at ends, used esp. on board ship.

Hă'mmond ôr'gan. Electronic organ. [trade-name of *Hammond* Electric Co. of Chicago]

Hămmura'bi, -a'pi (-ŏŏrah-) (*c* 18th c. B.C.) King and law-giver of Babylonia.

Hă'mpden (-md-), John (1594–1643). English M.P.; famous for his resistance to Charles I's 'ship-money' tax; killed in the Civil War.

hă'mper[1] *n.* Basketwork packing-case.

hă'mper[2] *v.t.* Obstruct movement of (person etc.) with material obstacles; (fig.) impede, hinder. ~ *n.* (naut.) Necessary but cumbrous part of equipment of vessel.

Hă'mpshire. Southern county of England.

Hă'mpton Court (kôrt). Palace on the Thames west of London, built by Cardinal Wolsey and ceded by him to Henry VIII; now pre-

served as a museum and partly occupied by persons of rank in reduced circumstances; ~ *Conference*, conference held there in 1604 to settle points of dispute between the Church party and the Puritans.

hă'mshăckle *v.t.* Shackle (horse etc.) with rope connecting head and foreleg.

hă'mster *n.* Small rat-like hibernating rodent (*Cricetus cricetus*); *golden* ~, domesticated variety (*Mesocricetus auratus*), as pet and laboratory animal.

hă'mstring *n.* (in man) One of five tendons at back of knee, (in quadrupeds) great tendon at back of hock, corresponding to that of heel in man. ~ *v.t.* (past t. & past part. *-strŭng*). Cripple by cutting hamstring(s).

hă'mūlŭs *n.* (anat., zool.) Hook-like process.

Hăn. Chinese dynasty, 206 B.C. to A.D. 220, when Chinese bureaucracy was developed and Buddhism introduced.

hănd *n.* 1. Terminal part of human being's or monkey's arm beyond wrist; forefoot of quadruped; forehock. 2. Possession, charge, authority, disposal; agency, instrumentality; share in the doing of something; pledge of marriage, bestowal in marriage. 3. Side (right or left), direction, quarter. 4. Person, source, from which thing comes; person who does something, person in relation to action or in reference to skill in doing something; workman, manual worker; (pl.) ship's crew; *all* ~*s*, whole crew. 5. Skill; style of workmanship; turn, innings, at cricket, billiards, etc.; style of writing; signature. 6. (also *good* ~, U.S.) Applause. 7. Hand-like thing, esp. pointer of clock or watch; fixed quantity of various commodities, e.g. bundle of tobacco leaves. 8. Lineal measure of horse's height, = 4 inches. 9. (cards) Cards dealt to a player; player holding these; single round of game; game (of cards etc.). 10. *at* ~, close by; about to happen soon; *by* ~, by physical (as opp. to mechanical) labour; (*live*) *from* ~ *to mouth*, improvidently; *in* ~, held in the hand; at one's disposal; under control; receiving attention; *off* ~, without preparation, then and there; *on* ~, in one's possession; *on all* ~*s*, to, from, all quarters; *on* (or *off*) *one's* ~*s*, resting on (or passed from) one as a responsibility; *out of* ~, at once, extempore; out of control; *to* ~, within reach, (commerc.) received; *to one's* ~, ready for one without exertion on one's own part. 11. *bear a* ~, take part *in*; *change* ~*s*, (of property) pass from one person to another; *come to* ~, turn up, be received; *get, keep one's* ~ *in*, become proficient, be in practice; *take in* ~, undertake; *with a heavy* ~, oppressively; *with a high* ~, boldly, arrogantly. 12. ~*s down*, easily, without effort; ~*s off!*, do not touch; ~*s up!* direction to persons to hold up their hands as sign of assent etc., or to preclude resistance; ~ *in* (or *and*) *glove*, intimate (*with*); ~ *over hand* or *fist*, with each hand successively passing over the other, as in climbing rope; (fig.) with steady or rapid progress; ~ *to hand*, (of conflict etc.) at close quarters. 13. In comb. = made, operated, etc., by hand and not by machinery. 14. Special comb.: *ha'ndbag*, small bag for purse etc., carried by woman; ~-*ball*, ball for throwing with hand; game played with this between two goals; *ha'ndbell*, bell rung by hand, esp. one of set for musical performance; *ha'ndbill*, printed notice circulated by hand; *ha'ndbook*, short treatise, manual, guide-book; ~-*brake*, brake operated by the hand; ~-*canter*, gentle canter; ~-*cart*, cart pushed or drawn by hand; *ha'ndcuffs*, pair of metal rings joined by short chain, for securing prisoner's hands; *ha'ndcuff* (*v.*) secure (person) with these; ~-*gallop*, easy gallop; ~-*glass*, magnifying-glass held in hand; small mirror with handle; *ha'ndhold*, something for the hands to grip on (in climbing etc.); *ha'ndmaid(en)*, (archaic, exc. fig.) female servant; ~-*organ*, barrel-organ with crank turned by hand; ~-*out*, (U.S.) what is handed out, e.g. alms; (orig. U.S.) matter handed out to the newspaper press; ~ -*rail*, railing along edge of stairs etc; *ha'ndshake*, shake of person's hand with one's own, as greeting; *ha'ndspike*, lever for shifting heavy objects, as guns, by hand; spoke of capstan or windlass; ~-*spring*, *turn* ~-*springs*, turn somersaults; *ha'ndwork*, handiwork, handicraft; *ha'ndwriting*, writing by hand, esp. of particular person. ~ *v.t.* Help (person) with the hand (*into*, *out of*, carriage etc.); (naut.) take in (sail); deliver, transfer by hand or otherwise; ~ *off*, (Rugby footb.) push (opponent) off with the hand; ~ *it to*, acknowledge superiority of.

h. & c. *abbrev.* Hot and cold (water).

Hă'ndel (orig. *Haendel*), George Frederick (1685–1759). German-born composer of operas and oratorios; settled in England in 1712 and became court composer; famous for his 'Messiah', 'Samson', 'Judas Maccabaeus', etc.

hă'ndful (-ŏŏl) *n.* Quantity that fills the hand; small number (of men etc.); (colloq.) troublesome person or task.

hă'ndicăp *n.* Race or any contest of skill or strength in which in order to equalize chances of winning, some artificial disadvantage, in time, weight, score, etc., is imposed on a superior competitor, or some similar advantage is given to an inferior competitor; advantage given or disadvantage imposed; (fig.) disability of any kind which puts a person at a disadvantage compared with his fellows. ~ *v.t.* Impose handicap on (competitor); (fig., of circumstances) place (person) at a disadvantage. **hă'ndicăpped** (-pt) *adj.* (esp., of person) Suffering from physical or mental disability. **hă'ndicăpper** *n.*

hă'ndicraft (-ahft) *n.* Manual skill; manual art or trade, as weaving, pottery, etc.; *ha'ndicraftsman*, man who exercises a handicraft.

hă'ndiwork (-wȇrk) *n.* Work done, thing made, by the hands or by anyone's personal agency.

handkerchief (hă'ngkerchĭf) *n.* Square of linen, silk, etc., carried in pocket (*pocket-*~) for wiping nose etc.

hă'ndle[1] *n.* That part of thing which is made to hold it by; fact that may be taken advantage of (*against* person); ~ *to one's name*, title; ~-*bar*, (of bicycle etc.) steering-bar with handle at each end.

hă'ndle[2] *v.t.* Touch, feel with the hands; manipulate; manage (thing, person); treat; treat of; deal in (goods). **hă'ndler** *n.* (esp.) Person in charge of a trained dog.

hă'ndsel (-ns-), **hă'nsel** *n.* New-Year gift; earnest money; foretaste. ~ *v.t.* Give handsel to.

hă'ndsome (-ns-) *adj.* Of fine form or figure; (of conduct etc.) generous; (of price, fortune, etc.) considerable. **hă'ndsomelў** *adv.* **hă'ndsomenėss** *n.*

hă'ndў *adj.* Ready to hand; convenient to handle; clever with the hands; *ha'ndyman*, man able to do all sorts of odd jobs.

hăng *v.* (past t. & past part. *hŭng*, exc. as below). 1. Suspend, attach loosely (*from*, *to*); suspend (meat, game) to dry or become tender or high; place (picture) on wall; attach (wallpaper); suspend floating in space; rest (door on hinges, coach on springs, etc.) in free swinging position; let droop; remain, be, suspended; decorate *with* (things suspended); *hanging gardens*: see BABYLON; *hanging valley*, valley of tributary joining main stream, which has been deepened by glaciation, from a much higher level. 2. (past t. & past part. *hanged*) Suspend, be suspended, by the neck until dead (esp. as capital punishment). 3. ~ *about*, loiter, linger, about; ~ *back*, show reluctance to act or move; ~ *fire*, (of firearm) be slow in going off (freq. fig.); ~ *heavy*, (of time) pass slowly; ~ *on*, depend on; attend carefully to (words etc.); stick closely (*to*); (slang) wait; ~ *out*, suspend from window etc.; protrude downwards; (slang) reside; ~ *together*, be coherent, be associated; ~ *up*, suspend; end telephone conversation; (fig.) put aside, postpone indefinitely. 4. *ha'ngdog*, base and sneaking (fellow); *ha'ngman*, one appointed to hang condemned persons; *ha'ngnail*, AGNAIL; *ha'ngover*, survival, remainder; (slang) unpleasant after-effects of dissipation. ~ *n.* Downward droop or bend; way a thing hangs; *get the* ~ *of*, get the knack of, understand.

hă'ngar *n.* Shed for housing aircraft.

hă'nger[1] *n.* (esp.) Loop etc. by which thing is hung; chain, rod, to which pot is hung in fireplace by pot-hook; coat-hanger; stroke with double curve in writing (*l*); short sword, orig. hung from belt; ~*-on*, follower, dependant.

hă'nger[2] *n.* Wood on side of steep hill.

hă'ngĭng *n.* (esp., pl.) Drapery with which walls etc. are hung: ~ *committee*, committee deciding on choice of pictures for exhibition; *a* ~ *matter*, action etc. punishable by capital punishment.

hănk *n.* Circular loop or coil, esp. as definite length of cotton yarn (840 yds), worsted (560 yds), etc.; (naut.) ring of rope, iron, etc., for fixing staysails to stays.

hă'nker *v.i.* Crave, long, *after*. **hă'nkerĭng** *n.*

hă'nky̆ *n.* (colloq.) Handkerchief.

hă'nky̆-pă'nky̆ *n.* Jugglery; underhand dealing.

Hă'nnĭbal (3rd c. B.C.). Carthaginian general; fought against Rome in 2nd Punic War; crossed the Alps into Italy and defeated the Romans at Lake Trasimene (217 B.C.) and Cannae (216 B.C.); was eventually forced to withdraw from Italy and was defeated by Scipio at Zama, N. Africa, in 202 B.C.

Hă'nover. (Ger. *Hannover*) N. German town, capital of Lower Saxony; formerly capital of the country of Hanover which was an Electorate of the Empire and subsequently a province of Prussia; in 1714 the Elector of Hanover (Georg Ludwig) became King George I of England; *House of* ~, British royal dynasty from 1714 to the death of Queen Victoria in 1901. **Hănovēr'ian** *adj.* & *n.* 1. (Inhabitant) of Hanover. 2. (Member) of House of Hanover.

Hă'nsard. Official report of proceedings and debates in British Houses of Parliament, compiled by Messrs. Hansard 1774–1892, now published by H.M. Stationery Office.

Hănse *n.* Company or guild of merchants, esp. political and commercial league (*Hanseatic League*) of Germanic towns, which flourished in the 14th and 15th centuries and maintained a house in London. **Hănsēă'tic** *adj.* Of the German Hanse.

hansel: see HANDSEL.

hă'nsom *n.* (also ~ *cab*) Cabriolet for two inside, with driver

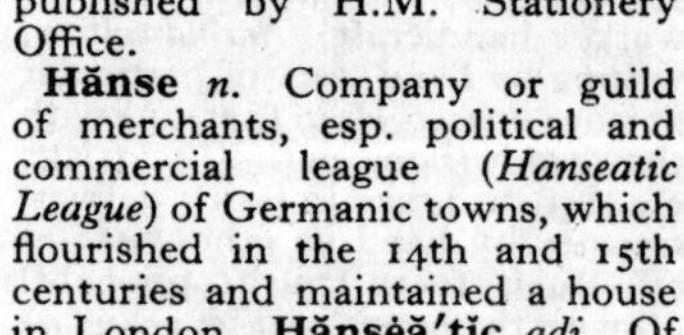

mounted behind and reins going over roof. [J. A. *Hansom* (1803–82), Engl. inventor]

hanuman (hŭnōōmah'n) *n.* Kind

of langur, *Presbytis entellus*, held sacred by Hindus.

hao (how) *n.* $\frac{1}{10}$ of a dong.

hăp *n.* (archaic) Chance, luck, lot; chance occurrence. ~ *v.i.* Come about by chance; happen (*to* do).

hă'păx lėgŏ'mėnon. Word of which only one use is recorded. [Gk, = 'once said']

hăphăz'ard (-p-h-) *n.* Mere chance. ~ *adj.* & *adv.* Casual(ly).

hă'plėss *adj.* Unlucky. **hă'plėsslў̆** *adv.*

hăplŏ'graphў̆ *n.* Mistake of writing once what should be written twice, e.g. *philogy* for *philology*.

hă'ploid *adj.* & *n.* (biol.) (Organism, cell) with only one set of chromosomes (half the DIPLOID complement).

hă'plў̆ *adv.* (archaic). By chance; perhaps.

ha'p'orth : see HALFPENNY.

hă'ppen *v.i.* 1. (of event) Occur. 2. Chance, have the fortune, *to* (do); come *upon* by chance. **hă'ppening** *n.*

hă'ppў̆ *adj.* (of person or circumstance) Lucky, fortunate; contented or pleased with one's lot; successful, apt, felicitous; ~ *families*, game played with cards, each depicting one member of family of four, the aim being to make as many complete families as possible; ~ *dispatch*, HARA-KIRI; ~*-go-lucky* (*adj.*); cheerfully casual. **hă'ppilў̆** *adv.* **hă'ppinėss** *n.*

Hă'psbûrg. Var. of HABSBURG.

hara-kĭ'rĭ (hah-) *n.* Suicide by disembowelment, as practised by military (or samurai) class in Japan when in disgrace or sentenced to death. [Jap. *hara* belly, *kiri* cut]

hară'ngue (-ng) *n.* Speech to an assembly; loud or vehement address. ~ *v.* Make harangue (to).

hă'rass *v.t.* Vex by repeated attacks; trouble, worry. **hă'rassment** *n.*

hâr'binger (-j-) *n.* 1. (formerly) One sent to purvey lodgings for army, royal train, etc. 2. One who announces another's approach, forerunner. ~ *v.t.* Announce approach of.

hâr'bour (-b*er*) *n.* Place of shelter for ships, esp. where they may lie close to and sheltered by shore, piers, etc.; shelter. ~ *v.* Give shelter to, foster, cherish (evil thoughts); come to anchor in harbour. **hâr'bourage** *n.* (Place of) shelter.

hârd *adj.* 1. Firm, unyielding to touch, solid; (of lawn-tennis court) made of asphalt, gravel, etc., not of grass; (of porcelain) made of hard paste; (of sauce) not liquid. 2. Difficult (*to* do); difficult to understand or explain; ~ *of hearing*, somewhat deaf. 3. Difficult to bear; unfeeling, harsh; involving undue or unfair suffering; stingy; harsh, unpleasant, to eye or ear; (of market prices) high, unyielding; strenuous; (U.S. of liquor) spirituous, strong, intoxicating; (of drugs) addictive. 4. In phonetics, applied to: (*a*) the letters *c*, *g* when they have their original guttural sounds, as in *can*, *get*, as dist. from the palatal and sibilant sounds, as in *centre*, *gin*; (*b*) voiceless as dist. from voiced consonants, as *th* in *think* compared with *th* in *this*. ~ *adv.* Strenuously, severely; with difficulty; *be* ~ *put to it*, be in difficulties; *go* ~, fare ill (*with*); ~ *by*, close by; ~ *on*, too severe in criticism or treatment; (of circumstances) bearing with undue severity on; ~ *upon*, close to. ~ *adj.* or *adv.* in comb.; ~ *and fast*, (of rules) strict; *ha'rdbake*, almond toffee; ~*-bitten*, tough in fight, stubborn; *har'dboard*, stiff board made from wood waste and used as a substitute for wood; ~*-boiled*, (of eggs) boiled until white and yolk are solid; hardened, callous, hard-headed, sophisticated; ~ *cash*, (orig.) specie as opp. to paper currency, (now) cash as opp. to credit; ~ *coal*, anthracite; ~ *core*, (fig.) irreducible nucleus or residuum; *har'dcore*, stones, clinker, etc., used as foundation for a road etc.; ~ *currency*, currency of any country with which another has an adverse balance of payments, with the consequence that difficulties arise in maintaining a supply of it (cf. SOFT); ~*-favoured, -featured*, with harsh or ugly features; ~*-fern*, any fern of the genus *Lomaria*; ~*-headed*, practical, not sentimental; ~*-hearted*, unfeeling; ~*-hit*, severely troubled; ~ *labour*, orig., labour as work at tread-wheel, stone-breaking, etc., imposed on certain classes of criminals during their term of imprisonment; later (in Britain until abolished by the prison reforms of 1948), deprivation of privileges or amenities of ordinary prison life during the first fortnight of imprisonment; ~*-laid*, (of string, fabric, etc.) tightly twisted or woven; ~*-mouthed*, (of horse) not easily controlled by bit (also fig.); ~*-pad*, form of distemper in dogs; ~*-pan*, firm subsoil of clayey, gravelly, or sandy detritus; hard unbroken ground; ~ *rubber*, EBONITE; ~ *sell*, aggressive salesmanship; ~*-shell*, having a hard shell, as ~*-shell crab*, one that has not recently moulted; (U.S. fig.) rigid and uncompromising in religious orthodoxy (esp. *H~-shell Baptists*); ~ *swearing*, swearing (as witness) persistently and tenaciously to one effect regardless of perjury; *har'dtack*, ship-biscuit; hence, ordinary sea-fare; ~ *up*, in want, esp. of money; at a loss *for*; (naut., of tiller) as far as possible to windward; *har'dware*, ironmongery; (colloq., parts of) machine(s); items of electronic or mechanical equipment; (esp.) apparatus of a computer; ~ *water*, water containing mineral, esp. calcareous, salts which decompose soap, thus making the water unsuitable for washing etc., and cause incrustations in boilers; *har'dwood*, wood of deciduous trees as opp. to pines and firs; in Australia, any of various kinds of teak-like timber. ~ *n.* 1. Firm beach or foreshore; sloping roadway across foreshore. 2. (slang) Imprisonment with hard labour. **har'den** *v.* Make or become hard, callous, or robust.

Har'denberg (-ārg), Friedrich Leopold von (1772–1801). German Romantic poet and novelist.

har'dihood *n.* Boldness, audacity.

Har'ding, Warren Gamaliel (1865–1923). 29th president of U.S., 1921–3.

har'dly *adv.* In a hard manner; with difficulty; harshly; scarcely.

har'dness *n.* 1. Quality or state of being hard. 2. (min.) Degree of resistance of a mineral to abrasion or scratching, expressed in terms of the following scale, known as MOHS' scale: (i) talc; (ii) gypsum; (iii) calcite; (iv) fluorite; (v) apatite; (vi) orthoclase; (vii) quartz; (viii) topaz; (ix) sapphire (corundum); (x) diamond; thus, in the description of a mineral, 'H. 7·5' means that it is harder than quartz but softer than topaz. 3. Quality of water containing dissolved salts of calcium and magnesium, bicarbonates causing temporary hardness, i.e. removable by boiling, and sulphates and chlorides causing permanent hardness, i.e. not removable by boiling; the degree of hardness of water is determined by the amount of standard soap solution sufficient to produce a lather and is expressed in terms of grains of calcium carbonate (*grains of* ~) per gallon of water.

hards, hurds (-z) *n.pl.* Coarser part of flax or hemp separated in hackling.

har'dship *n.* Hardness of fate or circumstance; severe suffering or privation.

har'dy[1] *adj.* 1. Bold, audacious. 2. Robust, capable of endurance; (hort., of plants) able to grow in the open air all the year; *half* ~, requiring shelter in winter only; ~ *annual*, annual that may be sown, or that sows itself, in the open; (fig.) subject that comes up yearly. **har'dily** *adv.* **har'diness** *n.*

har'dy[2] *n.* Blacksmith's bar of hard iron for cutting metal on etc.

Har'dy[3], Thomas (1840–1928), English novelist and poet; author of many novels of Wessex life, including 'Tess of the D'Urbervilles' (1891), 'Jude the Obscure' (1896), etc.

hare[1] *n.* Quadruped (*Lepus*) resembling a rabbit but larger, with long ears and hind legs, short tail, and divided upper lip, noted for

timidity and swiftness, of which the two species common in Europe are *L. europaeus*, the brown hare, and *L. timidus*, the blue or mountain hare, which changes to white in winter in snowy places; *hold* (*run*) *with the ~ and run* (*hunt*) *with the hounds*, keep in with both sides; *~ and hounds*, paper-chase; *~-brained*, rash, wild; *~-lip*, fissure of upper lip caused by arrested development of upper lip or jaw; *~'s-foot*, hare's foot formerly used for applying rouge etc. to face; species of clover (*Trifolium arvense*) with soft hair about flowers; corkwood tree. *~ v.i.* Run or move with great speed.

Hāre[2], William (d. 1829): see BURKE[3].

hār'ebĕll (hārb-) *n.* Perennial plant (*Campanula rotundifolia*) growing on open downs, hills, etc., flowering in late summer, with loose panicle of delicate blue bell-shaped flowers on slender stalk; bluebell of Scotland.

hār'em (*or* hār'ēm) *n.* Women's part of Muslim dwelling-house; its occupants, female members of Muslim family, esp. wives and concubines.

hār'ewōōd (hārw-) *n.* Stained sycamore-wood, used in cabinet-making.

Hār'greaves (-grāvz), James (1720–78). Lancashire-born mechanic who invented the SPINNING jenny.

hă'rĭcot (-kō) *n.* Ragout (usu. of mutton); (also *~ bean*) kidney- or French-bean (*Phaseolus vulgaris*), esp. the dried seeds of some varieties.

hārk *v.* Listen; (as call to hounds) go *forward*, *away*, etc.; *~ back*, (of hounds) retrace course to find scent; recall (hounds); (fig.) revert (*to* subject).

hārl[1] *n.* & *v.t.* (Sc.) Roughcast.

hārl[2], **hārle** *n.* Flax or hempen fibre; barb of a feather.

Hārlei'an (-lē-) *adj.* Of the library or MS. collections (in the British Museum) of Robert Harley, Earl of Oxford (1661–1724) and his son Edward.

Hār'lĕm. District of Manhattan borough, New York City; the chief Negro quarter of New York.

hār'lĕquĭn *n.* 1. Character in Italian comedy; in English pantomime, mute character, invisible to clown and pantaloon, in parti-coloured bespangled tights and visor, and carrying wooden sword or lath as magic wand. 2. (also *~ duck*) Northern species of duck (*Histrionicus histrionicus*) with fantastically variegated plumage. **hārlĕquĭnā'de** *n.* Part of pantomime (now usu. omitted) in which harlequin and clown play principal parts.

HAREM

Har'ley Street. London street associated with eminent or fashionable physicians and surgeons; hence, medical specialists.

har'lot *n.* (archaic) Prostitute. **har'lotry** *n.*

harm *n.* Damage, hurt; mischief, injury; *out of ~'s way*, in safety. ~ *v.t.* Do harm to; damage, injure. **har'mful** *adj.* **har'mfully** *adv.* **har'mfulness** *n.* **har'mless** *adj.* Doing no harm. **har'mlessly** *adv.* **har'mlessness** *n.*

harmă'ttan *n.* Parching land-wind (with red dust-fog) on W. African coast in December, January, and February.

harmŏ'nic *adj.* Harmonious, concordant; relating to harmony; (math., of quantities) with reciprocals in arithmetical progression; ~ *conjugates*, (math.) 1st and 3rd of 4 points that divide a line harmonically in relation to the 2nd or 4th or vice versa; ~ *division*, (math.) division of a line at 4 points so that the distances of the 2nd, the 3rd, and the 4th point from the 1st are in harmonic proportion; ~ *minor*, (mus.) scale with minor 6th and major 7th both ascending and descending; ~ *motion*, motion of the point where a perpendicular to a diameter from a point on the circumference of a circle meets the diameter when the latter point moves round the circumference at a constant speed; any similar motion, e.g. that of the piston of a steam-engine, or any part of a vibrating system; ~ *pencil* (math.) set of 4 lines passing through one point and lying in the same plane which divide any other line in that plane harmonically; ~ *progression*, (math.) series of numbers whose reciprocals are in arithmetical progression, as $\frac{1}{2}$, $\frac{1}{3}$, $\frac{1}{4}$, or 12, 15, 20; ~ *stop*, (in organ) stop in which each pipe has small hole in middle, so as to give note corresponding to half its length; ~ *tones*, tones produced by vibration of sonorous body in aliquot parts of its length. **harmŏ'nically** *adv.* **harmŏ'nic** *n.* Secondary tone produced by vibration of aliquot parts of sonorous body, usu. accompanying primary or fundamental tone produced by vibration of body as a whole, but sometimes produced independently, as in stringed instrument by light pressure on the string at various points etc.; (elect.) one of the component frequencies of a wave or alternating current which is an integral multiple of the fundamental frequency.

harmŏ'nica *n.* Any of various musical instruments, such as musical glasses, glass dulcimer, etc.; (U.S.) mouth-organ.

harmō'nious *adj.* Concordant, forming a consistent or agreeable whole; free from dissent; sweet-sounding; singing, playing, tunefully. **harmō'niously** *adv.*

har'monist *n.* Person skilled in harmony; collator of parallel narratives; harmonizer. **harmoni'stic** *adj.*

harmō'nium *n.* Keyboard musical instrument, resembling a portable organ, in which the keys operate metal reeds, and a bellows, worked by the player's feet, supplies the wind.

har'monize *v.* Bring into, be in, harmony (*with*); make, be, agreeable in artistic effect; add notes to (melody) to form chords. **harmonizā'tion** *n.*

har'mony *n.* 1. Combination or arrangement of parts to form consistent and orderly whole, agreement, congruity; agreeable effect of apt arrangement of parts. 2. Combination of musical notes to produce pleasing effect; combination of (simultaneous) notes to form chords, part of music dealing with formation and relation of chords. 3. Collation of parallel narratives, passages on same subject etc., esp. of the four Gospels.

har'ness *n.* Gear of draught horse or other animal; (fig.) working equipment; apparatus in loom for shifting warp-threads; (hist.) defensive armour; *in ~*, in the routine of daily work; *~-cask*, (naut.) cask with rimmed cover for keeping salt meat for current consumption. ~ *v.t.* Put harness

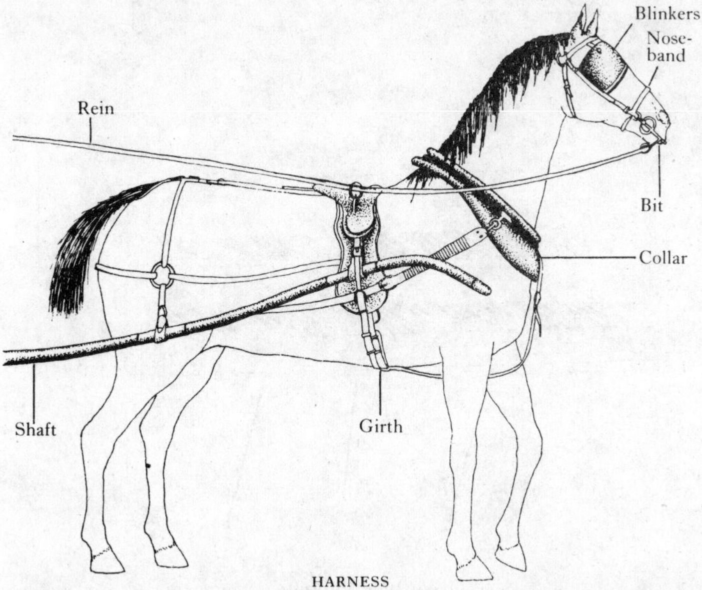

HARNESS

on (horse etc.); (fig.) utilize (river, waterfall, natural forces) for motive power.

Hă'rold. Name of two kings of England: *Harold I* (d. 1040), reigned 1035–40; *Harold II*, king in 1066; killed in that year at the battle of Hastings.

Harou'n-al-Ră'schid (-ōōn, -shēd) (763–809). 'Haroun the Just', caliph of Baghdad, who figures in many of the tales of the 'Arabian Nights'.

harp *n.* Stringed musical instrument, roughly triangular, with strings of graduated lengths played with fingers, and with pedals for raising tone of strings by one or two semitones. ~ *v.i.* Play on harp; dwell tediously *on* (subject). **har'pist** *n.*

harpoo'n *n.* Barbed spear-like missile with rope attached, for catching whales and large fish; ~-*gun*, gun for firing harpoon. ~ *v.t.* Strike, spear, with harpoon.

har'psichord (-k-) *n.* Keyboard musical instrument resembling in shape and construction the grand piano (which partly superseded it) but producing notes by means of strings plucked with quills or plectra.

har'pў *n.* 1. (Gk & Rom. myth.) Rapacious monster with woman's face and body and bird's wings and claws; rapacious person. 2. (also ~ *eagle*) S. Amer. large powerful bird of prey (*Harpia harpyia*), with crested head and fan-shaped tail.

har'quėbus, ar- *n.* (hist.) Early type of portable gun, supported on tripod by hook or on forked rest. **harquėbusier'** *n.*

hă'rrĭdan *n.* Haggard or scolding old woman.

hă'rrier[1] *n.* One who harries.

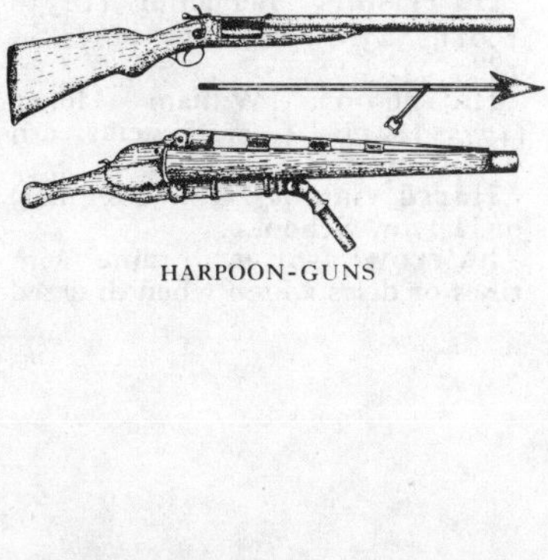

HARPOON-GUNS

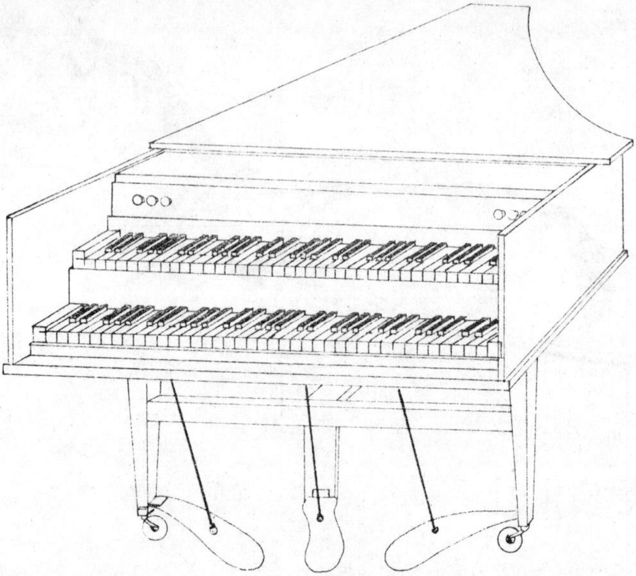

HARPSICHORD

hă'rrier[2] *n.* 1. Hound used for hunting hare; (pl.) pack of these with huntsman; hare-and-hounds club. 2. Kind of falcon (of *Circus* and related genera); ~ *eagle*, any of several genera of Accipitridae esp. *Circaetus gallicus*; ~*-hawk*, hawk of Amer. genus *Micrastur*, related to goshawk.

Hă'rris[1]. District forming together with Lewis the largest island in the Outer Hebrides; ~ *tweed*, hand-woven tweed made there.

Hă'rris[2], Mrs. In Dickens's 'Martin Chuzzlewit', the mythical friend of Mrs Gamp; hence, nonexistent person.

Hă'rrison[1], Benjamin (1833–1901). 23rd president of U.S., 1889–93.

Hă'rrison[2], William Henry (1773–1841). Amer. general; 9th president of U.S., 1841.

Harrō'vian *adj.* & *n.* (Member) of Harrow School.

hă'rrow[1] (-ō) *n.* Frame with tines or discs which when dragged over soil stirs it up, breaks clods, covers seed, etc. ~ *v.t.* Draw harrow over (land); distress painfully. **hă'rrowing** *adj.*

ha'rrow[2] (-ō) *v.t.* Harry, spoil (chiefly in phr. *harrowing of hell*, of Christ freeing the souls of the just when he descended into hell).

Hă'rrow[3] (-ō). Short for ~ *School*, public school at Harrow-on-the-Hill in Greater London; founded and endowed by John Lyon under a charter (1572) granted by Queen Elizabeth.

hă'rrȳ *v.t.* Ravage, waste, spoil (land); harass.

harsh *adj.* Rough to the touch, taste, eye, or ear; repugnant to feelings or judgement; cruel, unfeeling. **har'shlȳ** *adv.* **har'shness** *n.*

harslet: see HASLET.

hart *n.* Male of (esp. red) deer, esp. after fifth year; ~*'s-tongue*, fern (*Phyllitis scolopendrium*) with long undivided fronds.

har'tal *n.* Closing of shops for a day in India as sign of mourning or as political gesture.

Hárte, Francis Bret (1836–1902). American writer of short stories and humorous verse.

har'tėbeest *n.* Common antelope of genus *Alcelephas* of the Sudan and southern Africa, of reddish colour with long doubly curved horns and long skull.

Har'tley, David (1705–57). English physician and philosopher; regarded as the founder of the English (associationist) school of psychologists. **Hartlei'an** *adj.*

Har'tmănn vŏn Aue (fŏn owe) (early 13th c.). German epic writer and minnesinger; author of 'Erec', 'Iwein', etc.

har'tshorn (-s-h-) *n.* Substance got by rasping, slicing, or heating harts' horns, formerly the source of ammonia; (archaic; also *spirit of* ~) aqueous solution of ammonia; *salt of* ~, (archaic) ammonium carbonate, smelling salts.

hār'um-scār'um *adj.* & *n.* Reckless (person, conduct).

harŭ'spĕx (*or* hă'ru-) *n.* (pl. *-spicēs*). (Rom. antiq.) Soothsayer of Etruscan origin performing divination by inspection of entrails etc.

Har'vard. American university at Cambridge, Massachusetts; endowed by John Harvard (1607–38), an English settler and graduate of Cambridge University.

har'vėst *n.* (Season for) reaping and gathering in of grain or other products; corn-crop; season's yield of any natural product; (fig.) product of any action; ~ *bug*, red larva of mite (*Trombicula autumnalis*) biting man at harvest time; ~ *festival*, thanksgiving service for harvest, at which church is usu. decorated with grain, fruit, etc.; ~ *home*, close of harvesting, festival in celebration of this; *har'vestman*, arachnid of order Opiliones with very long thin legs; ~ *moon*, moon which is full within a fortnight of autumn equinox (22 or 23 Sept.) and is popularly supposed to help in ripening the corn; ~ *mouse*, very small mouse (*Micromys minutus*) nesting amongst stalks of growing grain. ~ *v.t.* Reap and collect (crop) as harvest; lay up, husband. **har'vėster** *n.* 1. Reaper. 2. Reaping-machine (esp. reaper-and-binder). 3. Harvest-bug.

Har'vey, William (1578–1657). English physician; discoverer of circulation of the blood.

Harya'na (hŭrĭah-). State of India, formed in 1966 mostly from the Hindi-speaking part of the former State of Punjab; capital, Chandigarh.

hă's-been (-z-) *n.* (colloq.) Person or thing whose career or efficiency belongs to the past.

hăsh *n.* Dish of hashed, esp. cooked, meat; old matter served up in new form; medley; *make a* ~ *of*, spoil in dealing with; *settle a person's* ~, make an end of, silence, him. ~ *v.t.* Cut (meat etc.) in small pieces.

Hă'shėmīte *adj.* & *n.* = Hashimite; ~ *Kingdom of the Jordan*: see Jordan.

Hă'shĭmīte *adj.* & *n.* (Member) of an Arab princely family claiming descent from Hashim, great-grandfather of Muhammad.

hă'shĭsh, -eesh *n.* Top leaves and tender parts of common hemp, dried for smoking or chewing as narcotic; liquor prepared from this. [Arab., = 'herbs']

hā'slėt, har's- (-z-) *n.* Piece of meat to be roasted, esp. pig's fry.

hasp (hah-) *n.* Fastening contrivance, esp. clasp passing over staple and secured by padlock or toggle. ~ *v.t.* Fasten with hasp.

hă'ssock *n.* 1. Cushion for kneeling. 2. Tuft of matted grass etc. 3. Soft calcareous limestone separating beds of rag in Kent.

hă'stāte *adj.* (bot., zool.) Spear-shaped.

hāste *n.* Urgency of movement, hurry, precipitancy; *make* ~, be quick. ~ *v.i.* Make haste. **hā'sten** (-sn) *v.* Cause (person) to make haste; accelerate (work etc.); make haste; come or go in haste.

Hā'stĭngs[1] (-z). Town on coast of East Sussex; scene of the battle (1066) in which William of Normandy defeated the English under Harold II.

Hā'stĭngs[2] (-z), Warren (1732–

1818). First governor-general of British India; was impeached on the ground of corruption and cruelty in his administration but acquitted after a trial lasting 7 years (1788–95).

hā'stў̆ *adj.* Hurried; speedy; rash, inconsiderate; quick-tempered; ~ *pudding*, pudding of flour, semolina, etc., stirred in boiling milk or water to thick consistency. **hā'stĭlў̆** *adv.* **hā'stĭnėss** *n.*

hăt *n.* 1. Man's or woman's outdoor head-covering, esp. with brim; *cardinal's* ~, red hat worn by a cardinal; (fig.) office of cardinal; *opera* ~, collapsible top hat worn in evening; *red* ~, cardinal's hat; (slang) British staff-officer; *top, high, chimney-pot* ~, man's tall silk hat. 2. *bad* ~, (slang) immoral or dishonourable person; *pass* or *send round the* ~, solicit contributions; *talk through one's* ~, exaggerate, make unsupported assertions. 3. *ha'tband*, band of ribbon etc. round hat; *~-block*, block for moulding hat on; ~ *trick*, (cricket) taking of three wickets by same bowler with three successive balls; (footb. etc.) scoring of three goals by the same player in one match. **hă'tful, hă'tter** *ns.* **hă'tlėss** *adj.*

hătch[1] *n.* Lower half of divided door; aperture in door, wall, floor, or deck; (naut.) (also *ha'tchway*) opening in ship's deck for lowering cargo, trap-door covering this; floodgate; (aeron.) opening or door in aircraft or spacecraft; *under hatches*, (naut.) below deck; (fig.) down out of sight, brought low.

hătch[2] *v.* Bring forth (young birds etc.) from egg; incubate (egg); emerge from egg; (of egg) produce young; contrive and develop (plot etc.). ~ *n.* Hatching; brood hatched. **hă'tcherў̆** *n.* Place for hatching eggs, esp. of fish.

hătch[3] *v.t.* Mark with (esp. close parallel) lines, as for shading in engraving or drawing. ~ *n.* Shading line in engraving or drawing. **hă'tchĭng** *n.* Series of engraved or drawn lines producing effect of shading.

hă'tchėt *n.* Light short-handled axe; *bury the* ~, make peace, compose a quarrel; *~-face*, narrow sharp-featured face.

hă'tchment *n.* Escutcheon; tablet with deceased person's armorial bearings, formerly affixed to front of his house or over his tomb.

hāte *n.* (chiefly poet.) Hatred. ~ *v.t.* Have strong dislike of; bear malice to. **hā'teful** *adj.* Exciting hatred. **hā'tefullў̆** *adv.* **hā'tefulnėss** *n.*

Ha'thor (hah-). (Egyptian myth.) Goddess of love, freq. represented with cow's head or ears.

hā'trėd *n.* Active dislike; enmity, ill-will.

hau'berk, haw'berk *n.* Medieval coat of mail.

hau'ghtў̆ (haw-) *adj.* Proud, arrogant; dignified. **hau'ghtĭlў̆** *adv.* **hau'ghtĭnėss** *n.*

haul *v.* Pull, drag, forcibly; pull *at, upon* (rope etc.); transport by cart etc., cart; (naut.) turn ship's course; (of wind) shift; ~ *upon the wind*, bring ship round to sail closer to wind. ~ *n.* Hauling; (fig.) amount gained, acquisition. **hau'lage** *n.*

hau'lier *n.* One who hauls (esp. tubs in coal-mine to bottom of shaft); jobbing carter.

haulm (hawm), **halm** (hahm) *n.* Stalk, stem; (collect. sing.) stems, stalks, of peas, beans, potatoes, etc., without the pods etc.

haunch *n.* 1. Part of body (of man and quadrupeds) between last ribs and thigh; leg and loin of deer etc. as food. 2. Side of arch between crown and pier.

haunt *v.* 1. Frequent (place); frequent company of (person); (of thoughts etc.) visit (person) frequently; stay habitually. 2. (of ghosts etc.) Visit frequently with manifestations of their presence and influence; (past part.) visited, frequented, by ghosts. ~ *n.* Place of frequent resort; usual feeding-place of animals.

Hau'ptmann (how-), Gerhart (1862–1946). German dramatist and novelist; Nobel Prize for literature 1912.

Hau'sa (how-) *n.* (Member of) widespread Negroid people of the Sudan and N. Nigeria, of Bantu family with some Hamitic mixture; Hamitic language of these people, used, esp. in commerce, over much of W. Africa.

Hau'ssmann (hows-), Georges Eugène (1809–91). French administrator; directed the modernization of the streets of Paris. **Hau'ssmannize** *v.t.* Improve (streets etc.) by widening and straightening.

hautboy (hō'boi *or* ō'boi) *n.* 1. (Old name for) OBOE; oboe-player; reed-stop in organ with tone like oboe. 2. Musky-flavoured strawberry (*Fragaria elatior*) of tall growth.

Haut-Brion (ō brēawṅ) *n.* (in full, *Château* ~) Claret from commune of Pessac, near Bordeaux.

haute couture (ōt kōōtūr). High fashion; (creations of) leading fashion houses. [Fr.]

haute école (ōt ākŏl). Elaborate method of training and riding horses, practised esp. at Saumur, France, and in Vienna. [Fr.]

hauteur (ōtẽr) *n.* Haughtiness of manner. [Fr.]

Havă'na. Capital city of Cuba; hence, cigar of Cuban tobacco.

hăve *v.* (past t. & past part. *had*). 1. Possess as property or at one's disposal; possess as relative, adjunct, appendage, attribute, function, right, etc.; experience, suffer. 2. Possess as duty; be obliged. 3. Retain; entertain in the mind; show, exhibit (sentiment etc.) in action; carry on, engage in (proceeding etc.); esteem or account as (archaic); ~ *a care*, be careful, be cautious; ~ *in mind*, remember. 4. Express (*it*); assert, maintain; *will not* ~ *it*, refuses to admit. 5. Come into possession of, obtain, get; get into one's power or at a disadvantage; (colloq.) nonplus, put into fix (in argument etc.); (slang) deceive, take in; *I* ~ *it*, I have found a solution etc. 6. Get into specified condition, procure or oblige (to be done etc.). 7. ~ *at*, go at vigorously, attack; ~ *it*, win, have the superiority; ~ *had it*, (slang) be exhausted, defeated, etc.; *let* (person) ~ *it*, give it to him; attack, punish or reprimand him; ~ (person) *up*, cause him to go before court of justice to answer charge. ~ *v. aux.* Forming (with past part. of verb) compound tenses, pres. t. of *have* forming perfect, past t. of *have* forming pluperfect. ~ *n.* 1. (slang) Swindle, take-in. 2. One who has, one belonging to wealthier classes (usu. in pl., opp. to *have-nots*).

hā'ven *n.* Harbour, port; refuge.

hā'ver *v.i.* (chiefly Sc.) Talk foolishly, babble; hesitate. ~ *n.* (usu. pl.) Foolish talk, nonsense.

hā'versăck *n.* (Soldier's, traveller's) stout canvas bag for provisions, carried on back or over shoulder. [Ger. *habersack* (*haber* oats)]

hă'vildâr, ha'valdâr (hŭv-) *n.* Indian non-commissioned officer corresponding to sergeant.

hă'voc *n.* Devastation, destruction; *cry* ~, give signal to army to seize spoil (now only fig.).

haw[1] *n.* (Fruit of) hawthorn; *haw'buck*, country bumpkin; *haw'-finch*, kind of finch with very thick beak (*Coccothraustes coccothraustes*).

haw[2] *n.* Third eyelid of horse, dog, etc., cartilage within inner corner of eye.

Hawai'i (-wī'ē). State of U.S. comprising a chain of islands in N. Pacific including Hawaii; discovered by Capt. Cook, 1778; annexed by U.S., 1898; admitted to the Union in 1959; capital, Honolulu. **Hawai'ian** (-wī'*an*) *adj.* & *n.*

haw-haw *int.* & *n.* Boisterous laugh.

hawk[1] *n.* Diurnal bird of prey of family Accipitridae, esp. one of the Accipitrinae or true hawks (including buzzards and eagles), formerly extensively used in falconry; in U.S. also used of other species of Falciformes; rapacious or aggressive person; ~*-eyed*, keen-sighted; ~*-moth*, moth of family Sphingidae, noted for its hovering and darting flight; sphinx-moth; ~-

nosed, with aquiline nose; ~'*s-bill*, species of turtle (*Eretmochelys imbricata*) with mouth like hawk's beak, inhabiting Indian Ocean and warmer parts of Atlantic, source of tortoiseshell; *haw'kweed*, yellow-flowered composite perennial plant of genus *Hieracium*. ~ *v.* Attack as hawk does; (of swallows etc.) hunt insects.

hawk[2] *v.t.* Carry (goods) about for sale (often fig.).

hawk[3] *v.* Clear the throat noisily; bring (phlegm etc.) *up* from throat.

hawk[4] *n.* Plasterer's square board with handle underneath.

haw'ker *n.* Person who sells goods in the street; itinerant vendor, legally distinguished from a *pedlar* by his use of a beast of burden or other means of carrying his wares.

hawse (-z) *n.* Part of ship's bows containing ~-*pipes* for cables; space between head of anchored vessel and anchors; situation of cables before ship's stern when moored with two anchors out from forward, one on starboard, other on port bow.

haw'ser (*or* -z-) *n.* (naut.) Large rope, small cable, now freq. of steel; ~-*laid*, (of rope) made of three or four strands laid up right handed.

haw'thôrn *n.* Thorny shrub or small tree of genus *Crataegus*, with white, red, or pink blossom and small dark-red berry, whitethorn, maytree; ~ *china*, *jar*, *pattern*, (china, jar, with) decoration of flowering branches of Japanese plum-tree in white on dark-blue ground.

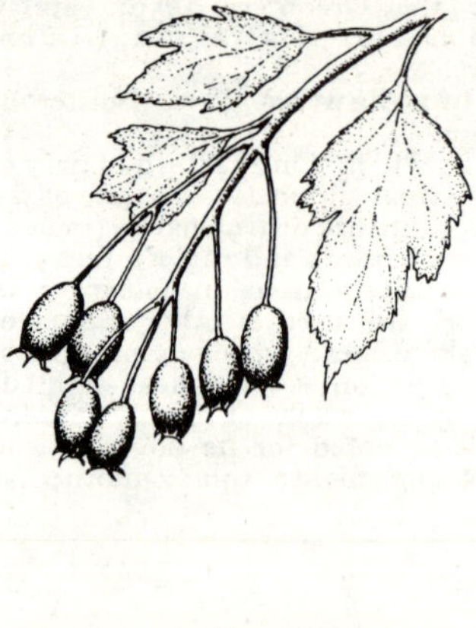

Haw'thôrne, Nathaniel (1804–64). American novelist; author of 'The Scarlet Letter' etc.

hay[1] *n.* Grass mown and dried for fodder; *make* ~, mow grass and dry by spreading about; *make* ~ *of*, throw into confusion, *make* ~ *while the sun shines*, seize opportunities; ~-*box*, air-tight box stuffed with hay in which heated food is left to continue cooking, the hay acting as an insulator of heat; *hay'cock*, hay piled into a conical heap in the process of haymaking to permit of easy dissipation of heat during the first stages of fermenting and so to lessen the risk of the hay taking fire in the stack; ~ *fever*, summer disorder with catarrhal and freq. asthmatic symptoms, caused by pollen, dust, etc.; ~-*fork*, fork for turning over or loading hay; *hay'maker*, one who lifts, tosses, and spreads hay after mowing; instrument for shaking and drying hay; (slang) swinging blow; *hay'rick*, *hay'stack*, regular pile of hay with pointed or ridged top; *hay'seed*, (U.S.) rustic, bumpkin; *hay'wire*, wire used to bind a bale of hay, straw, etc.; (*pred. adj.*, orig. U.S.) in disorder; distracted, crazy. ~ *v.* Put (land) under hay; make into hay; make hay.

hay[2] *n.* Country dance, or movement in dance, of winding or serpentine kind.

Hay'dn (hī-), Franz Josef (1732–1809). Austrian-born composer of many symphonies, concertos, cantatas, etc.; has been described as 'the father of modern instrumental music'.

Hayes (hāz), Rutherford Birchard (1822–93). American lawyer and soldier; 19th president of U.S., 1877–81.

Hay'mârkĕt. Street in London between Pall Mall and Piccadilly Circus, famous as a theatre centre.

hay'ward (-ôrd) *n.* Officer of parish, manor, etc., in charge of fences and enclosures.

hă'zard *n.* 1. Game of dice with

chances complicated by arbitrary rules; chance; (something causing) danger. 2. Each of winning openings in tennis court; billiards-stroke by which a ball is driven into a pocket; (golf) bunker, water, roadways, or any kind of 'bad ground' on which certain restrictions are imposed on the player in playing a stroke; *winning* ~, (billiards) striking object ball into pocket; *losing* ~, pocketing own ball off another; ~ *side*, (tennis) side of court into which ball is served. ~ *v.t.* Expose to hazard; run the hazard of; venture on (action, statement, guess).

hă'zardous *adj.* Risky; dependent on chance. **hă'zardouslў** *adv.* **hă'zardousnėss** *n.*

hāze[1] *n.* Obscuration of atmosphere near earth caused by presence of visible droplets of water in the air above wet ground or by a mixing of ascending hot air and descending colder air above hot ground; (fig.) mental obscurity or confusion.

hāze[2] *v.t.* (naut.) Harass with overwork; (U.S.) bully, subject to cruel horseplay.

hā'zel *n.* Bush or small tree (*Corylus*) bearing nuts; (stick of) its wood; light-brown colour of ripe ~-*nut* (esp. of eyes); ~-*rod*, -*wand*, stick of hazel used in water-divining.

Hă'zlĭtt, William (1778–1830). English critic and essayist; author of 'Table Talk, or Original Essays on Men and Manners', 'English Comic Writers', etc.

hā'zў *adj.* Misty, vague, indistinct; slightly drunk. **hā'zĭlў** *adv.* **hā'zĭnėss** *n.*

HB *abbrev.* Hard black (of pencil-lead).

H.B.M. *abbrev.* His (*or* Her) Britannic Majesty.

H-bŏmb (ā'chbŏm) *abbrev.* Hydrogen bomb.

H.C., H.C.B. *abbrev.* House of Commons (Bill).

H.C.F. *abbrev.* Highest common factor.

hē *pron.* 3rd person nom. sing. masc. pronoun, denoting the male person or animal referred to; in children's games (as quasi-*n.*) = IT[2]. ~ *n.* Male animal; ~-*man*, strong virile man.

H.E. *abbrev.* High explosive; His Excellency.

head (hĕd) *n.* 1. Anterior part of body of animal, upper part of human body, containing mouth, sense-organs, and brain; seat of intellect or imagination; life; head-

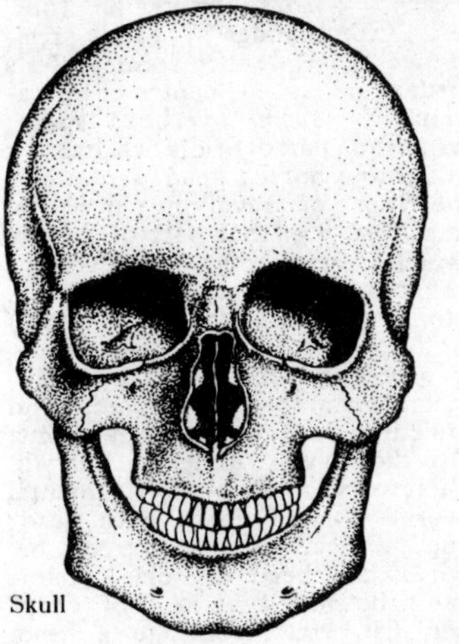

Skull

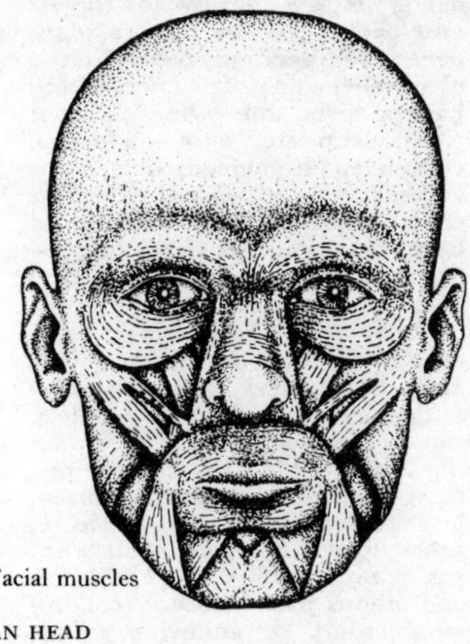

Facial muscles

HUMAN HEAD

ache (colloq.); image of head, esp. on one side of coin; person; individual, esp. of cattle. 2. Thing like head in form or position, e.g. cutting or striking part of tool, knobbed end of nail, part of long bone next to joint, flat end of barrel or cask etc.; rounded or compact part of plant, e.g. compact mass of leaves in cabbage or lettuce, leaf-stalks in celery, flower-buds in cauliflower, etc.; foam on top of liquor, cream on top of milk; top (of staircase, page, etc; of mast); maturated part of boil etc.; upper end; end of lake at which river enters it; end of bed etc. towards which head lies; source of river or stream; (height of) body of water kept at height for supplying mill etc., force of its fall; pressure (per unit of area) of confined body of steam etc.; front (of procession, army, etc.); front part of plough, holding the share; bows of ship; promontory; underground passage for working coal in mine. 3. Ruler, chief; master of college; headmaster of school; position of command; main division in discourse; category; culmination, crisis. 4. ***from ~ to foot***, all over; ***off one's ~***, crazy; ***out of one's own ~***, from one's own invention; ***put out of one's ~***, (cause to) forget; ***over one's ~***, above one; (of danger etc.) impending; beyond one's comprehension; (of promotion etc.) passing over one who has prior right, claim, etc.; ***over ~ and ears***, completely immersed, deeply involved; ***~ and shoulders*** (***above*** etc.), (taller etc.) by measure of head and shoulders (freq. fig.); ***~ first***, ***~ foremost***, (of plunge etc.) with the head foremost; (fig.) precipitately; ***~ of hair***, hair on head, esp. when long or thick; ***~ over heels***, topsy-turvy, as in a somersault; deeply; ***keep one's ~***, keep calm; ***keep one's ~ above water***, (fig.) keep out of debt; ***lose one's ~***, be beheaded; become confused, lose presence of mind; ***make ~***, press forward; ***make ~ against***, resist successfully. 5. ***hea'dache***, continuous pain in head; (colloq.) troublesome or annoying thing; ***hea'dband***, band worn round head; ***hea'dboard***, board forming the head esp. of bed; *hea'dborough*, (hist.) petty constable; ***~-dress***, covering esp. ornamental attire, for the head; ***hea'dfast***, rope at head of vessel to make her fast to wharf etc.; ***~-gear***, hat, cap, head-dress; machinery etc. at head of mine-shaft; *~-lamp*, headlight; ***hea'dland***, promontory; strip left unploughed at end of field; ***hea'dlight***, (beam from) powerful light at front of locomotive, motor vehicle, aircraft, or at masthead of vessel; ***hea'dline***, line at top of page containing title etc.; title or sub-title in newspaper; (pl.) summary of a news broadcast; ***headmaster***, ***headmistress***, principal master, mistress, of school; ***~-on***, (of collision etc.) with head or front of vehicle pointed directly towards or running full against something, esp. front of another vehicle; ***hea'dphone***, (usu. pl.; radio, telephony) pair of receivers that can be held against listener's ears by band passing over head; ***hea'dpiece***, helmet; intellect, man of intellect; ornamental engraving at head of chapter etc. in book; part of bridle passing over top of horse's head; *headquarters*, (mil. etc.) commander-in-chief's residence, place whence commander's orders are issued; centre of operations; ***~ room***, overhead space; ***hea'dstall***, part of bridle or halter that fits round horse's head; ***hea'dstock***, bearings of revolving parts in machine, e.g. that part of a lathe which carries the mandrel or live stock; *hea'dstone* gravestone; *hea'dwaters*, stream(s) at upper part of river; ***hea'dway***, progress; rate of progress; (archit.) height of arch etc.; ***~ wind***, wind meeting one directly in front; ***hea'dword***, word at head of entry in dictionary etc.; ***~-work***, mental work. ~ *v.* Furnish with head; lop off head of (plant, tree); be, form, the head of; place (name etc.), be placed, at head of (chapter, list, etc.); come to a head, develop; be, put oneself, at the head of (a company etc.); lead; excel; oppose; go round the head of; front (in specified direction); (of ship etc.) make *for* (place, point); strike (football) with head; ~ *back, off*, get ahead of so as to turn back, aside. **hea'dlėss** *adj.*

hea'dage (hĕd-) *n.* ~ *money*, reward paid to one who slaughters pests (e.g. rabbits), reckoned per head of animals killed.

hea'der (hĕd-) *n.* 1. One who puts heads on casks etc. 2. Brick, stone laid at right angles to face of wall. 3. head-first plunge. 4. (footb.) Stroke made with head.

hea'dĭng (hĕd-) *n.* (esp.) Title etc. at head of page etc., headline; horizontal passage in preparation for tunnel.

hea'dlŏng (hĕd-) *adv.* & *adj.* Head foremost; precipitate(ly); impetuous(ly).

hea'dmōst (hĕd-) *adj.* Foremost.

hea'dsman (hĕdz-) *n.* Executioner; man in command of whaling boat.

hea'dstrŏng (hĕd-) *adj.* Violently self-willed. **hea'dstrŏngnėss** *n.*

heady (hĕ'dĭ) *adj.* Impetuous, violent; (of liquor etc.) apt to intoxicate.

heal *v.* Restore to health; cure (*of*); (of wound) become sound or whole. **hea'ler** *n.*

heald: see HEDDLE.

health (hĕl-) *n.* Soundness of body, mind, etc.; that condition in which functions of body and mind are duly discharged; general condition of body, as *good, bad* ~; toast drunk in person's honour; ~ *centre*, establishment providing a number of different services within the National Health Service.

hea'lthful (hĕl-) *adj.* Health-giving; conducive to moral or spiritual welfare. **hea'lthfullў** *adv.* **hea'lthfulnėss** *n.*

hea'lthў (hĕl-) *adj.* Having good health; conducive to good health. **hea'lthĭlў** *adv.* **hea'lthĭnėss** *n.*

heap *n.* Group of things lying one on another; (colloq., esp. pl.) large number or amount; *struck all of a* ~, (colloq.) mentally prostrated, dumbfounded. ~ *v.t.* Pile in a heap; load (*with*); accumulate (insults etc. *upon*).

hear *v.* (past t. & past part. *heard* pr. hẽrd) Perceive (sound etc.), perceive sound(s), with the ear; listen, give audience, to, listen judicially to (case, plaintiff, etc.); grant (prayer); be informed; entertain notion *of*; receive letter or message *from*; ~ *tell of*, (archaic) be told about; ~*!* ~*!*, exclamation expressing agreement. **hear'able** *adj.* **hear'er** *n.*

hear'ĭng *n.* 1. Faculty of perception by means of the ear. 2. Opportunity to state one's case; listening to evidence and pleadings in a court of law; trial of a cause, esp. trial before a judge without a jury; *within, out of*, ~, near enough, too far off, to be heard; ~ *aid*, device worn by deaf person to improve hearing.

hear'ken (hâr-) *v.i.* Listen (*to*).

hear'say *n.* What one hears (but does not know to be true), gossip.

hearse (hẽrs) *n.* Vehicle for conveying body to grave; (formerly) framework supporting pall at funeral, often adapted for carrying tapers.

heart (hârt) *n.* 1. Hollow muscular organ which by rhythmic contraction and relaxation drives the blood round the vascular system, consisting in mammals and birds

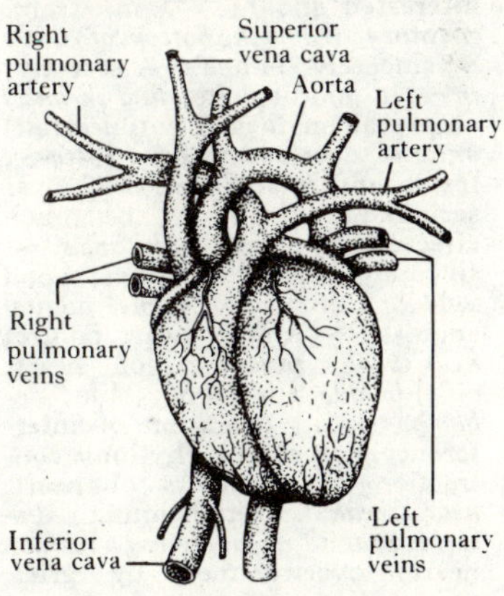

of 4 chambers, of which the two anterior ones (atria) force the blood, received from the veins, into the two posterior ones (ventricles), which then contract and force the blood into the arteries, the return of the blood into the atria and ventricles being prevented by valves. 2. Breast; mind; soul; seat of the emotions, esp. of love; sensibility, tenderness, feeling; courage; enthusiasm, energy. 3. Central part of anything, centre, pith, core; solid central part of tree without sap or alburnum; ~ *of oak*, (man of) stout courageous spirit. 4. Vital part or principle; (of land etc.) fertility; *in* ~, in good or sound condition. 5. Heart-shaped thing, esp. conventional symmetrical figure of two similar curves meeting in point at one end and cusp at the other; (playing-card with) red heart-shaped figure(s); (pl.) suit of these cards. 6. Phrases: *break* (person's) ~, overwhelm him with sorrow; *cry one's* ~ *out*, cry violently; *eat one's* ~ *out*, grieve or yearn inconsolably; *have a* ~*!* (colloq.) protesting appeal for sympathy; *have the* ~, be hard-hearted or brave enough (*to*); *in one's* ~ *of* ~*s*, in one's inmost feelings; *have one's* ~ *in one's mouth*, be violently alarmed or startled; *take* ~, pluck up courage. 7. With preps.: *at* ~, in one's inmost feelings; *have at* ~, be deeply interested in; *by* ~, in, from, memory; *from* (*the bottom of*) *one's* ~, sincerely; *in one's* ~, secretly; *in* ~, in good spirits; *find in one's* ~, prevail on oneself (*to*); *near*(*est*) *one's* ~, dear(est) to one; ~*-to-*~, frank, sincere; *lay to* ~, think over seriously; *take to* ~, be much affected by; *with all one's* ~, sincerely, with the utmost good will. 8. Comb: *hear'tache*, mental anguish; ~ *attack*, heart failure; *hear'tbeat*, pulsation of heart; ~(*'s*)*-blood*, life-blood, life; ~ *block*, (path.) condition of interference with normal rhythmic contraction of chambers of heart; *hear'tbreak*, overwhelming distress; *hear'tbroken*, having a broken heart; overwhelmed by grief; *hear'tburn*, burning sensation in lower part of chest, due to putrefactive fermentation of food in stomach; *hear'tburning*, jealousy, grudge; ~ *failure*, (med.) any derangement of heart's mechanism, not necessarily fatal; (pop.) cessation of heartbeat causing death; ~*-felt*, sincere; ~*-rending*, distressing; *hear'tsease*, pansy, esp. small wild form; *hear'tsick*, despondent; ~ *sounds*, sounds of closure of heart's valves, contraction of its chambers, etc., heard in auscultation; ~*-strings*, (fig.) heart, deepest affections; *hear'twarming*, moving, encouraging; ~*-whole*, with the heart or affections unengaged; ~*-wood*, dense inner part of tree-trunk, affording the hardest timber.

hear'ten (hâr-) *v.* Inspirit, cheer; cheer *up*.

hearth (hâr-) *n.* Floor of fireplace; floor of reverberatory furnace, of smith's forge, etc.; *hear'th-rug*, rug laid before fireplace; *hear'thstone*, stone forming hearth; soft kind of stone, rubbed with water over hearth, doorstep, etc. to whiten them.

hear'tily̆ (hâr-) *adv.* With goodwill, courage, or appetite; very.

hear'tlĕss (hâr-) *adj.* Unfeeling, pitiless, cruel. **hear'tlĕsslȳ** *adv.* **hear'tlĕssnĕss** *n.*

hear'tȳ (hâr-) *adj.* Cordial, genial; (of feelings) sincere; vigorous; (of meals) abundant. ~ *n.* Hearty fellow, esp. sailor; (university slang) one more interested in sports etc. than in academic studies.

heat *n.* 1. Being hot, high temperature; sensation, perception, of this; one of the primary sensations produced by contact with or nearness to fire or any body at a high temperature; (phys.) form of energy arising from the random molecular motion of a substance and capable of transmission by conduction or radiation. 2. Hot weather; inflamed state of body; pungency of flavour. 3. Warmth of feeling; anger; violent stage (of debate etc.). 4. = OESTRUS. 5. Single effort, stroke; single course in race or other contest (*trial* ~, course the winners of which compete in *final* ~). 6. *latent* ~, heat required to convert solid into liquid or vapour, or liquid into vapour (so called because it does not show its presence by an increase in temperature); *prickly* ~: see PRICKLY; *specific* ~, heat required to raise temperature of unit mass of given substance to given extent (usu. one degree), calculated relatively to some standard, usu. water; ~ *of formation*, thermal change which occurs when substances chemically combine; ~-*spot*, red spot on skin popularly supposed to be caused by heat; (physiol.) small area on skin sensitive to heat stimuli; ~-*stroke*, affection of nervous system, freq. fatal, caused by exposure to excessive heat; ~ *unit*, = lesser calorie (see CALORIE, 2); ~-*wave*: see WAVE *n*. 3, 4. ~ *v*. Make hot; inflame (blood etc.); inflame with passion; become hot. **hea'tėdlў** *adv*. Vehemently, angrily.

hea'ter *n*. (esp.) Any contrivance for warming up food, room, etc.

heath[1] *n*. Barren flat waste tract of land, esp. if covered with low herbage and dwarf shrubs; plants and shrubs found on heaths, esp. low shrubs of genus *Erica*, heather, ling; ~-*bell*, bell-shaped flower of heath; ~-*cock*, blackcock. **hea'thў** *adj*.

Heath[2], Edward Richard George (1916–). British Conservative statesman; prime minister 1970–4.

hea'then (-dh-) *adj*. & *n*. (One who is) neither Christian, Jewish, nor Muslim (in O.T., = gentile; hist., used also of Muslims; later restricted to holders of polytheistic religions, esp. when uncivilized); pagan. **hea'thendom, hea'thenĭsm** *ns*. **hea'thenĭsh** *adj*. **hea'thenĭshlў** *adv*. **hea'thenĭshnėss** *n*. **hea'thenīze** *v*.

hea'ther (hĕdh-) *n*. Species of plant or shrub of genus *Erica*, esp. the common heather (*E*. (now *Calluna*) *vulgaris*), growing on moors and heaths, and bearing purple bell-shaped flowers in autumn; ~-*bell*, (flower of) species of *Erica*; ~ *mixture*, (fabric, esp. tweed) of mixed or speckled hue supposed to resemble heather. **hea'therў** *adj*.

Heath Rŏ'bĭnson, William (1872–1944). English cartoonist; hence attrib. of any absurdly ingenious device of the kind he illustrated.

heave *v*. (past t. & past part. *heaved* or *hove*) 1. Lift (heavy thing); (of vein or stratum) displace (another); utter (groan, sigh) with effort; (naut. & colloq.) throw; (naut.) haul up, haul, by rope; pull (*at* rope etc.); ~ *down*, turn (ship) over on one side for cleaning etc.; ~ *in sight*, become visible; ~ *to*, bring (vessel) to standstill with head to wind. 2. Rise, swell up; rise with alternate falls, as waves; pant; retch. ~ *n*. Heaving; horizontal displacement of vein or stratum; (pl.) disease of horses, broken wind.

heaven (hĕvn) *n*. Sky, firmament (in prose now usu. pl.); region of atmosphere in which clouds float, winds blow, and birds fly; (formerly) each of the heavenly spheres; supposed habitation of God and his angels, usu. placed beyond sky; God, providence; place, state, of supreme bliss. **hea'venward** *adj*. & *adv*. **hea'venwards** (-z) *adv*.

hea'venlў (hĕ-) *adj*. Of heaven, divine; of the sky; of superhuman excellence. **hea'venlinėss** *n*.

hea'vĭer-than-air' (hĕv-) *adj*. (of flying-machine) With weight greater than that of air it displaces, as distinct from balloons and dirigible airships.

Hea'vĭsīde (hĕv-), Oliver (1850–1925). British physicist; ~ *layer*, E-layer of the ionosphere (see E).

hea'vў (hĕ-) *adj*. 1. Of great weight; of great specific gravity; weighty because abundant; laden *with*; (of ordnance etc.) large; (mil.) carrying heavy arms or equipment; (of bread etc.) that has not risen properly, compact, dense. 2. Striking or falling with force or violence; (of ground etc.) clinging, difficult to travel over, dig, etc.; (of food) difficult of digestion; (of horse) ~ *in* (*on*) *hand*, bearing or hanging on bit (also fig.). 3. Grave, severe; overcast, gloomy; clumsy

HEATH ROBINSON: Cartoon

in appearance or effect; intellectually slow; unwieldy; dull, tedious; oppressive, grievous; sad; despondent; doleful; drowsy; (theatr., of part etc.) sober, serious, tragic. 4. *~-handed*, clumsy, oppressive; *~-hearted*, melancholy, doleful; *~ hydrogen*, = DEUTERIUM; ***~ oil***, (*a*) last fraction obtained before the pitch point in the distillation of coal-tar; creosote oil; (*b*) petroleum and other (esp. fuel) oils which have a flash-point above 24 °C; *~ spar*, native barium sulphate; barytes; *~ water*, deuterium oxide (D_2O), with the same chemical properties as ordinary water, but density about 10% greater; *hea'vyweight*, jockey, rider, etc., of more than average weight; influential person; boxer of heaviest weight (see BOXING). **hea'vĭlў** *adv*.

hea′viness *n.* **hea′vies** (-ĭz) *n.pl.* 1. *H~*, Dragoon Guards. 2. Heavy artillery. **hea′vy̆** *adv.* Heavily.

Heb. *abbrev.* Hebrew; Hebrews (N.T.).

Hĕ′bbel, Friedrich (1813–63). German dramatist and poet.

hĕbdŏ′madal *adj.* Weekly; *H~ Council*, representative board of University of Oxford, meeting weekly.

Hē′bė. 1. (Gk myth.) Goddess of youth and spring, daughter of Zeus and Hera, and cup-bearer of Olympus. 2. (astron.) The 6th asteroid, discovered 1847.

hĕ′bėtāte *v.* Make, become, dull.

Hēbrā′ic *adj.* Of, pertaining to, the Hebrews, or Hebrew. **Hēbrā′ically̆** *adv.*

Hē′brāism *n.* Quality or attribute of the Hebrews; Hebrew system of thought or religion; Hebrew idiom or expression. **Hēbrā′ĭst** *n.* Hebrew scholar; adherent of Hebrew thought or religion. **Hēbrāĭ′stic** *adj.* **Hēbrāĭ′stically̆** *adv.*

Hē′brāīze *v.* Translate into Hebrew; make, become, like a Hebrew.

Hē′brew (-ōō) *n.* 1. Member of a Semitic people inhabiting ancient Palestine esp. before the Exile, traditionally descended from Abraham, Isaac, and Jacob; Israelite, Jew; (*Epistle to the*) *~s*, book of N.T., traditionally included among the letters of St. Paul but now usu. held to be non-Pauline. 2. Semitic language spoken by the Hebrews, and in which most of the books of the O.T. were written; modern form of this; (colloq.) unintelligible speech. *~ adj.* Belonging to the Hebrews, Jewish; *~ alphabet*, Semitic alphabet of 22 letters, the vowels being indicated by a system of points; *~ calendar*: see JEWISH. [Aramaic *ʿebrāyā*, Heb. *ʿibrī* = 'one from the other side' (*sc.* of the river)]

Hĕ′brĭdēs (-z). Two groups of islands (*Inner* and *Outer ~*) off the NW. coast of Scotland. **Hĕbrĭdē′an** *adj.* & *n.* (Native, inhabitant) of the Hebrides.

Hĕ′catė. (Gk myth.) Goddess, said to be of Thracian origin, daughter of Perses and Asteria; in later times more or less identified with Artemis or Persephone, and hence regarded as presiding over witchcraft and magical rites.

hĕ′catomb (-ŏm *or* -ōōm) *n.* (Gk & Rom. antiq.) Great public sacrifice (prop., of a hundred oxen).

hĕck[1] *n.* 1. Frame obstructing passage of fish in river. 2. One of the sets of perforated pins which guide warp-threads in the process of reeling and form the lease.

hĕck[2] *int.* (euphem.) Hell.

hĕ′ckėlphōne *n.* Kind of baritone oboe. [W. *Heckel*, German inventor, *c* 1905]

hĕ′ckle *v.t.* 1. Dress (flax etc.) with hackle. 2. Harass (esp. candidates for Parliament etc. in public) with interruptions, awkward questions, etc. **hĕ′ckler, hĕ′ckling** *ns.*

hĕctâre (*or* -ār) *n.* (abbrev. ha) 100 ares.

hĕ′ctic *adj.* 1. *~ fever*, that which accompanies consumption and similar diseases, attended with flushed cheeks and hot skin; consumptive; morbidly flushed. 2. (slang) Stirring; wild, impassioned; feverishly excited or active. **hĕ′ctically̆** *adv.*

hĕcto- *prefix.* One hundred times (abbrev. h).

hĕ′ctogrămme *n.* (abbrev. hg) 100 grammes.

hĕ′ctogrăph (*or* -ahf) *n.* Apparatus for multiplying copies of writing. *~ v.t.* Multiply with this.

hĕ′ctolitre (-lēt*er*) *n.* (abbrev. hl) 100 litres.

hĕ′ctomētre (-t*er*) *n.* (abbrev. hm) 100 metres.

Hĕ′ctor[1]. (Gk legend) Trojan warrior, son of Priam and Hecuba and husband of Andromache; killed by Achilles, who dragged his body three times round the walls of Troy.

hĕ′ctor[2] *n.* & *v.* Bluster(er), bully. [f. HECTOR[1]]

Hĕ′cūba. (Gk legend) Wife of Priam, king of Troy, and mother of Hector, Paris, and Cassandra, among other children.

hĕ′ddle, heald *n.* (weaving) One of the sets of small cords or wires with loops for suspending the warp threads and separating them so as to allow passage of shuttle.

hĕdge *n.* Fence of bushes or low trees, or of turf, stone, etc.; line of things or persons forming barrier; (fig.) barrier; (betting) act, means, of hedging; ~ *hop*: see HOP²; ~-*priest*, (hist.) illiterate priest of low status; *he′dgerow*, row of bushes forming hedge; ~-*school*, (hist.) low-class school; (formerly) open-air school esp. in Ireland; ~-*sparrow*: see DUNNOCK. ~ *v.* 1. Surround with hedge; fence *off*; hem *in*; make, trim, hedges. 2. Secure oneself against loss on (bet, speculation, etc.) by compensating transactions on the other side; avoid committing oneself. **hĕ′dger** *n.* One who makes and trims hedges.

hĕ′dgehŏg (-jh-) *n.* Insectivorous quadruped (*Erinaceus*) with pig-like snout, armed above with very many spines and able to roll itself into a ball with these bristling in every direction; any of various animals armed with spines, as the sea-urchin etc.; prickly seed-vessels or burrs of some plants, the plants themselves; person hard to get on with; fortified position 'bristling' with guns pointing in all directions, esp. one left behind after the main body of troops has retreated.

hēdŏ′nĭc *adj.* Of pleasure. **hēdŏ′nĭcs** *n.pl.* Doctrine of pleasure.

hē′donism *n.* Doctrine or ethical theory that pleasure is the chief good, or the proper end of action. **hē′donist** *n.* **hēdonĭ′stĭc** *adj.*

hee′bie-jee′bies (-ĭz) *n.pl.* (slang) State of nervous depression; blues.

heed *v.t.* (Sc. & literary) Concern oneself about, take notice of. ~ *n.* Careful attention; esp. in *take* ~, *give, pay,* ~, *to.* **hee′dful** *adj.* **hee′dfullȳ** *adv.* **hee′dfulnėss** *n.* **hee′dlėss** *adj.* **hee′dlėsslȳ** *adv.* **hee′dlėssnėss** *n.*

hee′-haw′ *n.* Ass's bray; loud laugh.

heel¹ *n.* 1. Hinder part of human foot below ankle; corresponding part of hind limb in quadruped, often raised above ground; (pop.) hinder part of quadruped's hoof, (pl.) hind feet; ~ *of Achilles*, vulnerable part (see ACHILLES); *at, on, the* ~*s of*, close behind, in close pursuit; *to* ~, (of dog) close behind, under control; (*fair*) ~ *and toe*, walking, not running; ~*s over head*, head over heels (see HEAD); *kick one's* ~*s*, stand waiting; *lay by the* ~*s*, arrest, overthrow; *take to one's* ~*s*, *show a clean pair of* ~*s*, run away; *turn on one's* ~, turn sharply round. 2. Part of stocking that covers heel; part of boot or shoe that supports or raises heel; *down at* ~, (of shoes) with heel part crushed down, or heel worn down; (of person) wearing such shoes, slovenly, destitute; *out at* ~*s*, with stockings or shoes worn through at heel; shabby, destitute. 3. Thing like heel in shape or position, as handle end of violin bow, crook in head of gold-club, after end of ship's keel; bottom crust of loaf, rind of cheese. 4. (U.S. slang) Untrustworthy person. 5. ~-*ball*, shoemaker's polishing mixture of hard wax and lamp black, also used for taking rubbings of monumental brasses, inscriptions, etc.; ~-*tap*, thickness of leather in heel; liquor left at bottom of glass after drinking. ~ *v.* Touch ground with heel, e.g. in dancing; furnish (boot etc.) with heel; chase or follow closely; (Rugby footb.) pass ball *out* at back of scrummage with heels; (golf) strike (ball) with heel of club; ~ *in* (tree, plant), cover roots temporarily with earth before planting finally. **heeled** (-ld) *adj.* (esp., U.S. slang) Armed, esp. with revolver; supplied with money, etc.

heel² *v.* (of ship etc.) Lean over owing to pressure of wind or uneven load; cause (ship) to do this.

~ *n.* (naut.) Inclination of heeling ship.

hĕft *n.* (dial. & U.S.) Weight. ~ *v.t.* (dial. & U.S.). Lift, esp. to judge weight.

hĕ′ftȳ *adj.* Heavy; sturdy, stalwart.

Hegel (hā′gl), Georg Wilhelm Friedrich (1770–1831). German philosopher, in whose system of Absolute Idealism pure being is regarded as pure thought, the

universe as its development, and philosophy as its dialectical explication. **Hėgē′lian** *adj.* & *n.* (Follower) of Hegel or his philosophy. **Hėgē′lianism** *n.*

hĕgėmŏ′nic (*or* hēgi-) *adj.* Ruling, supreme.

hėgĕ′monȳ (-g-; *or* hĕ′ji-) *n.* Leadership, esp. of one State of a confederacy.

Hĕ′gira, Hĕ′jira (erron. hijīr′*a*) *n.* Flight of Muhammad from Mecca to Medina in A.D. 622, from which the Muslim chronological era is reckoned. [Arab. *hijra* departure from one's country]

Hei′delberg (hī-). German university city on the river Neckar in Baden-Württemberg; ~ *jaw*, human lower jaw, found near Heidelberg, regarded as belonging to an extinct species of man (~ *man*) allied to Neanderthal man, and living in the Pleistocene period.

hei′fer (hĕf-) *n.* Young cow that has not had a calf, or one that has only recently had her first.

heigh (hā) *int.* Exclamation expressing encouragement or inquiry; ~-*ho*, exclamation expressing boredom, disappointment, etc.

height (hīt) *n.* Measurement from base to top; elevation above ground or recognized level, esp. that of sea; considerable elevation; high point; top, highest point or degree; rising ground.

hei′ghten (hīt-) *v.t.* Make high(er); intensify; inflate (description, story).

Heilungkiang (hā′lŏŏng-kyah′ng). Province of NE. China.

Heine (hī′ne), Heinrich (1799–1856). German-Jewish lyric poet and witty essayist; famous for his sentimental and ironic verse; his writings include 'Buch der Lieder'.

hei′nous (hān-) *adj.* (of crime or criminal) Odious, atrocious. **hei′nouslȳ** *adv.* **hei′nousnėss** *n.*

heir (ār) *n.* (fem. *heir′ėss*) Person receiving or entitled to receive property or rank as legal representative of former owner, esp. upon death of the latter; ~ *apparent*: see APPARENT; ~-*at-law*, heir by right of blood; ~ *of the body*, heir who is direct descendant; ~ *in tail*, heir to entailed estate; ~ *male*, male heir tracing descent wholly through males; ~ *presumptive*: see PRESUMPTIVE. **heir′lėss** *adj.*

heir′lōōm (ār) *n.* Chattel that follows devolution of real estate; piece of personal property that has been in family for generations.

Hĕjă′z. Region of Arabia on the Red Sea coast, forming with Nejd and Asir the Kingdom of Saudi Arabia.

Hejira: see HEGIRA.

held: see HOLD².

Hĕ′lėn. (Gk legend) Most beautiful woman of her time, daughter of Zeus and Leda; wife of Menelaus; her abduction by PARIS² led to the Trojan War.

Hĕ′lėna, St. Mother of the Emperor Constantine; said to have discovered (*the Invention of the Cross*) the cross on which Christ was crucified; *Island of St.* ~ (pr.

hělē′na), in the S. Atlantic, the place of Napoleon's captivity (1815–21).

hėlī′acal *adj.* Pertaining to, near, the sun; solar; ~ *cycle*, solar cycle; ~ *rising*, (of star) when it first emerges from sun's rays and becomes visible before sunrise; ~ *setting*, (of star) when it is last visible after sunset before being lost in sun's rays.

hēlĭă′nthus *n.* Plant of genus *H~* including sunflower.

hě′lĭcal *adj.* Of or like a helix; ~ *agitator*, kind of stirrer with series of curved plates fitted to a shaft so that they form a helix, serving to convey liquid from the bottom to the top of a vessel and so producing thorough and rapid agitation; ~ *gearing*, gearing in which cogs are cut slant-wise, so that several engage at once and so secure smoother and less noisy running. **hě′lĭcallÿ** *adv.*

hě′lĭcoid, -oidal *adjs.* Shaped like a helix; resembling a snail-shell; *helicoidal saw*, endless band of twisted wire used to cut through marble and other stone.

Hě′lĭcon[1]. Mountain in Boeotia, sacred to the Muses, where rose the fountains of Aganippe and Hippocrene; hence, source of poetic inspiration. **Hělĭcō′nĭan** *adj.*

hě′lĭcon[2] *n.* Large brass wind instrument of spiral form, made so as to be carried round the body while being played.

hě′lĭcŏpter *n.* Aircraft lifted by airscrew(s) revolving horizontally.

hēliocě′ntrĭc *adj.* As viewed from centre of sun; taking sun as centre.

Hēliogă′balus, Elagă′balus (ē-). Adopted name of Varius Avitus Bassianus, Roman emperor A.D. 218–22, famed for folly and profligacy. [Latinized f. *Elagabal*, Syro-Phoenician sun-god]

hē′liogrăm *n.* Message transmitted by heliograph.

hē′liogrăph (*or* -ahf) *n.* Instrument for measuring intensity of sunlight; apparatus for signalling with movable mirror reflecting flashes of sunlight to a distance. ~ *v.* Communicate by heliograph.

hēliolĭ′thĭc *adj.* (of civilization)

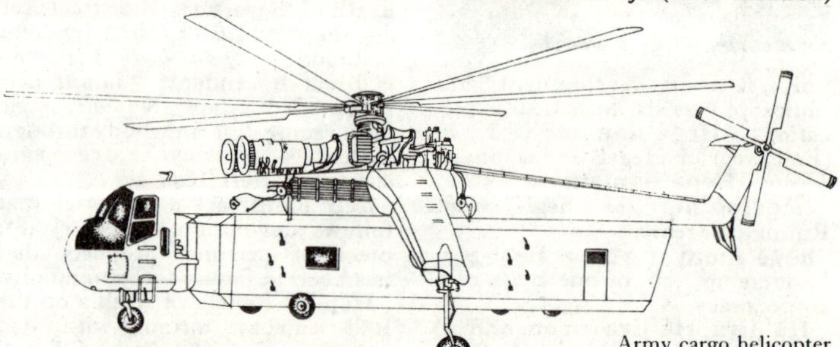

Army cargo helicopter

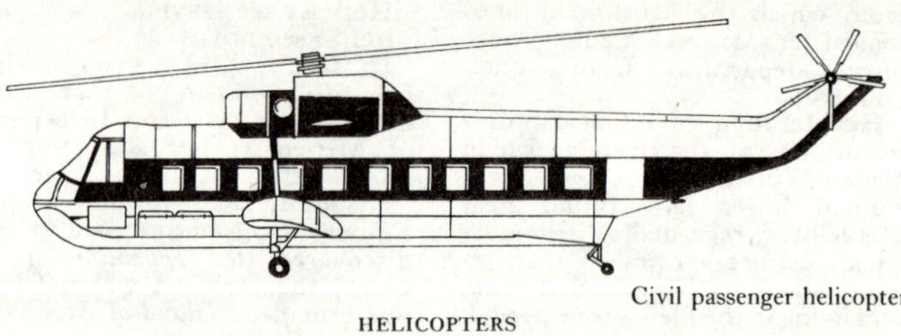

Civil passenger helicopter

HELICOPTERS

Characterized by megaliths and sun-worship.

hēliŏ'mėter *n.* Astronomical instrument for determining angular distance between stars (orig. for measuring diameter of sun).

hē'liotrōpe *n.* 1. Plant of genus *Heliotropium* of herbs or shrubs with small clustered purple flowers, esp. *H. arborescens*, cultivated for its fragrance; colour or scent of heliotrope. 2. = BLOOD-stone.

hēliotrŏ'pic *adj.* Phototropic. **hēliŏ'tropism** *n.*

hĕlipôrt *n.* Station for helicopter passenger services.

hē'lium *n.* (chem.) Element, an inert gas occurring in small quantities in the atmosphere and in certain natural gases, and produced during radioactive decay; used, on account of its lightness and non-inflammability, in balloons and airships; symbol He, at. no. 2, at. wt 4·00260.

hē'lix *n.* (pl. *-icēs*). 1. Spiral or coil like corkscrew; (archit. etc.) spiral ornament. 2. (anat.) Curved fold or prominence forming rim of external ear. 3. (zool.) Land mollusc of genus *H*~ with spiral shells, including the common snail (*H. aspersa*).

hĕll *n.* Abode of the dead; abode of devils and condemned spirits, figured as place of torment; place, state, of wickedness or misery; gaming-house; place under tailor's shop-board where cut-off pieces or shreds of cloth are thrown; *a ~ of a*, an infernal, a very bad, great, loud, etc.; *~-for-leather*, at breakneck speed; *~-bent*, (U.S.) hell-for-leather; *~-cat*, (slang) spiteful or furious woman; *~-fire*, fire of hell; *Hellfire club*, club of reckless or abandoned young men at beginning of 18th c.; *~-hound*, fiend. **hĕ'llish** *adj.* **hĕ'llishlў** *adv.* **hĕ'llishnėss** *n.*

Hĕllă'dic *adj.* Of the Bronze Age culture of the Greek mainland.

Hĕ'llăs. Greece; orig. the name of a district in Thessaly, but applied by the ancient Greeks to the whole of their country.

hĕ'llėbôre *n.* Ancient name of various plants supposed to cure madness; (bot.) species of ranunculaceous genus *Helleborus* including Christmas rose (*black hellebore*).

Hĕ'llēne *n.* Greek person. **Hellē'nic** *adj.* & *n.* (Language) of the Greeks.

Hĕ'llėnism *n.* Greek idiom or construction; Greek character or culture, esp. that represented by ideals of the classical Greeks; Greek nationality. **Hĕ'llėnist** *n.* 1. Greek scholar. 2. One of the Byzantine Greeks who contributed to the revival of learning in Europe in the 15th c. 3. One who used the Greek language but was not a Greek, applied esp. to the Jews of the Dispersion. **Hĕllėni'stic** *adj.* 1. Of, pertaining to, the Hellenists. 2. Of, pertaining to, Greek history, language, and culture after Alexander the Great.

Hĕ'llėnize *v.* Make, become, Greek in form or character.

hĕ'ller *n.* $\frac{1}{100}$ of a koruna.

Hĕ'llėspŏnt. Ancient name of the DARDANELLES, named after the legendary Helle, who fell into that part of the sea from the back of a ram with golden fleece and wings, which was carrying her and her brother Phrixus from Thebes to Colchis (see also GOLDEN Fleece).

hĕ'llgrammīte *n.* (U.S.) Larva (used as bait for black bass) of the dobson fly, an aquatic neuropterous insect (*Corydalus cornutus*).

hĕ'llion *n.* (U.S.) Mischievous or naughty child.

hĕllō' *int.*, *v.t.*, & *n.* = HALLO.

hĕlm[1] *n.* (archaic) Helmet; (also *~ -cloud*) cloud forming over mountain before or during storm (local name in Cumbria); *~-wind*, violent wind rushing down escarpment of Pennines near Cross Fell, when a helm-cloud lies over summit.

hĕlm[2] *n.* Tiller, wheel, by which rudder is managed; space through which helm is turned; (fig.) government, guidance; *down* (*with the*) ~, *up* (*with the*) ~, place helm so as to bring rudder to windward, to leeward; *weather, lee*, ~, helm put up, down; *he'lmsman*, steersman.

hĕ′lmėt *n.* Defensive head-cover of soldiers, firemen, etc.; felt or pith hat for hot climates; upper part of retort; shell of mollusc of genus *Cassis*; (bot.) arched upper part of corolla in some flowers, esp. labiates and orchids; *~-shell*, mollusc of genus *Cassis*. **hĕ′lmėtėd** *adj.*

Hĕ′lmhŏltz, Hermann Ludwig Ferdinand (1821–94). German physicist and physiologist; inventor of the ophthalmoscope; *~ coils*, (phys.) two equal circular coils placed coaxially at a distance apart equal to their radius and traversed by the same current.

hĕ′lminth *n.* Worm (usu. intestinal). **hĕlmi′nthic, hĕlmi′nthoid,** *adjs.* **hĕlminthŏ′logy̆** *n.*

Héloïse (ālōēz *or* ĕ′-) (1101–63). Learned Frenchwoman, renowned for love affair with ABÉLARD which ended in tragic separation.

hĕ′lot *n.* In ancient Sparta, a descendant of the original (chiefly Messenian) inhabitants who were conquered by the Spartans and used by them as serfs (*drunkėn ~*, one made drunk as a warning to young Spartans); hence, serf, bondman.

hĕlp *v.t.* Furnish (person etc.) with what he needs; further the action or purpose of; aid, assist; be of service; make easier; ~ (person) *on with his coat*, help him to put it on; ~ (person) *to*, serve him with (food); distribute (food at meal); remedy, prevent, as *it can't be helped, he couldn't ~ being late*; (with neg.) avoid doing, as *I can't ~ hoping that —*; *~ oneself to*, (colloq.) steal. *~ n.* 1. Action of helping, assistance; one who or that which helps; domestic servant (*home ~*, *mother's ~*, one who helps with household tasks, with children). 2. Remedy or escape.

hĕ′lpful *adj.* (of person or thing) Useful, serviceable. **hĕ′lpfully̆** *adv.* **hĕ′lpfulnėss** *n.*

hĕ′lping *n.* (esp.) Portion of food served.

hĕ′lplėss *adj.* Lacking help; unable to help oneself. **hĕ′lplėssly̆** *adv.* **hĕ′lplėssnėss** *n.*

hĕ′lpmāte *n.* Helpful companion or partner, usu. husband or wife.

hĕ′lpmeet *n.* Helpmate (f. misunderstanding of Gen. 2: 18, 20).

Hĕlsĭ′nkĭ. (Swed. *Helsingfors*) Capital city of Finland.

hĕ′lter-skĕ′lter *adv.* & *adj.* In disordered haste. *~ n.* 1. Disordered haste. 2. Lighthouse-shaped structure in fair etc., with external spiral track down which people may slide on a mat.

hĕlve *n.* Handle of weapon or tool.

Hĕlvē′tian (-shan) *adj.* & *n.* Swiss. [L *Helvetii*, a people of SE. Gaul]

hĕm[1] *n.* Border, edge, of cloth etc., esp. border made by turning in edge and sewing it down; *he′m-stitch*, (hem *cloth* etc. with) kind of ornamental stitch producing open-work effect by drawing together threads of material. *~ v.t.* Turn in and sew down edge of (cloth etc.) *~ in, about, round*, enclose, confine.

hĕm[2] *int.* Exclamation calling attention or expressing hesitation. *~ n.* Utterance of 'hem'. *~ v.i.* Utter 'hem'; clear throat; hesitate in speech.

hĕm-. For words beginning thus, see HAEM-.

hĕmĭ- *prefix.* Half-, affecting one half, etc.

hĕ′mĭcy̆cle *n.* Half-moon figure.

hĕmĭhē′dral *adj.* (chem., of crystal) Having half the number of planes required by the highest degree of symmetry belonging to its system.

hĕmĭmėtă′bolous *adj.* Of insects whose young resemble the adult, without pupal stages (cf. HOLOMETABOLOUS).

Hĕ′mingway, Ernest (1898–1961). Amer. author of short stories and novels; Nobel Prize for literature 1954.

hĕmĭplē′gia *n.* Paralysis of one side of body.

hĕmĭ′pterous *adj.* Of the Hemiptera, an order of insects with wings coriaceous at base and membranous at tip and mouth-parts adapted to piercing and sucking.

hĕ′misphēre *n.* Half sphere;

half the celestial sphere, esp. as divided by equator; (anat.) each half of cerebrum of brain; (geog.) half the earth, esp. as divided by the equator (into *Northern* and *Southern* ~*s*), or (loosely) one of those containing Europe, Asia, and Africa (*Eastern* ~), and America (*Western* ~), respectively; *land* ~, hemisphere with centre in N. Europe, containing about $\frac{6}{7}$ of the land surface of the globe; *water* ~, corresponding hemisphere, in which water occupies most of the surface, with centre in the Antipodes. **hĕmĭsphĕ′rĭc, -ĭcal** *adjs.*

hĕ′mĭstĭch (-k) *n.* Half of line of verse, as divided by caesura etc.

hĕ′mlŏck *n.* 1. Poisonous umbelliferous plant (*Conium maculatum*) with stout branched purple-spotted stem, finely divided leaves, and small white flowers, used as powerful sedative; poisonous potion obtained from this (believed to be the poison by which Socrates was put to death). 2. N. Amer. evergreen tree of genus *Tsuga*, esp. *T. canadensis*, from resemblance of branches to hemlock-leaves.

hĕmp *n.* Annual herbaceous plant, *Cannabis sativa*, native of W. and Central Asia, cultivated esp. for its cortical fibre; this fibre used for making cordage and woven into stout fabrics; any of several narcotic drugs, as bhang, hashish, marijuana, obtained from hemp; any of various other plants yielding useful fibre; ~ *agrimony*, perennial plant (*Eupatorium cannabinum*) of the daisy family, with pale-purple flowers and hairy leaves. **hĕ′mpen** *adj.*

hĕn *n.* Female of common domestic fowl; female of various other birds, or of any bird, hen-bird; (pl.) domestic fowls; *he′nbane*, (drug extracted from) plant (*Hyoscyamus niger*) of Europe and northern Asia, growing on waste ground, with dull-yellow purple-streaked flowers, viscid stem and leaves, unpleasant smell, and narcotic and poisonous properties; ~*-coop*, coop for keeping poultry in; ~*-crab, -lobster*, female crab, lobster; ~*-harrier*, European bird of prey, blue hawk, *Circus cyaneus*; ~*-pecked*, (of husband) domineered over by wife; ~*-roost*, place where fowls roost at night.

hĕnce *adv.* 1. (archaic) From here, from this; *hencefor′th, hencefor′ward*, from this time forward; *five years* ~, in five years' time from now. 2. As a result from this; as an inference from this; therefore.

hĕ′nchman *n.* Squire, page of honour (now only hist.); chief attendant of Highland chief; trusty follower; political supporter.

hĕndĕca- *prefix.* Eleven.

hĕndĕ′cagon *n.* Plane rectilineal figure of 11 sides.

hĕndĕcasўllă′bĭc *adj.* & *n.* (Verse) of 11 syllables. **hĕndĕcasў′llable** *n.* Such a verse.

hĕndī′adўs *n.* Expression of a single complex idea by two words coupled with *and* (e.g. *in goblets and gold* for *in golden goblets*). [Gk *hen dia duoin* one by means of two]

hĕnge *n.* Prehistoric monument in Britain and Ireland consisting of circle(s) of wooden or stone uprights usu. enclosed by a bank and ditch.

Hĕ′ngĭst (-ngg-) (d. 488). Native of Jutland who, with his brother Horsa (d. 455), landed at Ebbsfleet; afterwards founded the kingdom of Kent and so began the Anglo-Saxon conquest of Britain.

Hĕ′nley. Henley Regatta, held annually at Henley-on-Thames, Oxfordshire.

hĕ′nna *n.* Egyptian privet (*Lawsonia inermis*); shoots and leaves of this used as yellowish red dye for parts of body, hair, etc.

hĕ′nothēĭsm *n.* Belief in one god without asserting that he is the only God.

Henri: see HENRY².

Hĕ′nrў¹. Name of eight kings of England: *Henry I* (1068–1135), younger son of William I, reigned 1100–35; conquered Normandy; *Henry II* (1133–89), grandson of Henry I, reigned 1154–89; added Anjou and Aquitaine to the English possessions; established his rule in Ireland, and forced the king of Scotland to acknowledge him overlord of that kingdom; re-

HENRY I: Seal

stricted the legal privileges of the Church by the Constitutions of Clarendon (1164); *Henry III* (1207–72), son of John, reigned 1216–72; *Henry IV* (1367–1413), grandson of Edward III, deposed Richard II and became first of the Lancastrian kings, 1399–1413; *Henry V* (1387–1422), son of Henry IV, reigned 1413–22; defeated the French at Agincourt,

HENRY III: Tomb effigy

became regent of France and heir to the French throne; *Henry VI* (1421–71), son of Henry V, reigned 1422–61; during his reign the French possessions were lost and the Wars of the Roses, leading to his deposition by the Yorkists, begun; *Henry VII* (1457–1509), descended from Edward III; the first of the Tudor line; succeeded Richard III after defeating him at Bosworth Field; reigned 1485–1509; *Henry VIII* (1491–1547), son of Henry VII, reigned 1509–47; his quarrels with the pope resulted in the establishment of the Reformation in England; married 6 times.

Hĕ′nrȳ[2]. (Fr. *Henri*) Name of four kings of France: *Henry I* (d. 1060), reigned 1031–60; *Henry II* (1519–59), son of Francis I, reigned 1547–59; *Henry III* (1551–89), son of Henry II and Catherine de Médicis, reigned 1574–89; *Henry IV* (1553–1610), king of Navarre, first Bourbon king of France, reigned 1589–1610.

hĕ′nrȳ[3] *n.* (abbrev. H) Practical M.K.S. electromagnetic unit of inductance, the inductance of a circuit in which the variation of current at the rate of one ampere per second induces an electromotive force of one volt. [Joseph *Henry* (1797–1878), Amer. physicist]

hėpă′tĭc *adj.* Of, good for, the liver; liver-coloured, dark brownish-red.

hĕpatī′tis *n.* Inflammation of the liver.

Hėphae′stus. (Gk myth.) God of fire; identified by the Romans with Vulcan.

Hĕ′pplewhite (-plwĭt), George (d. 1786). English cabinet-maker; author of 'The Cabinet-Makers' and Upholsterers' Guide', published 1788; ~ *furniture*, furniture made by Hepplewhite or according to the designs in this book.

hĕpta-, hĕpt- *prefix.* Seven.

hĕ′ptachŏrd (-k-) *n.* Seven-stringed musical instrument; system of 7 tones, formed of two conjunct tetrachords.

hĕ′ptăd *n.* Set, group, of 7.

hĕ'ptagon *n.* Plane figure of 7 angles and sides. **hĕptă'gonal** *adj.*

hĕptahē'dron (-*a*-h-) *n.* Solid figure of 7 faces.

hĕ'ptarchy̆ (-kĭ) *n.* Government by 7 rulers; the 7 kingdoms supposed to have been established by the Angles and Saxons in Britain.

hĕ'ptasty̆le *adj.* & *n.* (Portico) of 7 columns.

hĕptasy̆llă'bic *adj.* Of 7 syllables.

Hĕ'ptateuch (-k) *n.* First 7 books of Old Testament.

her *pron.* Objective (accus., dat.) case of SHE. ~ *poss. pron.* Possessive case of SHE used as attrib. adj. with abs. and pred. form *hers* (pr. -z), belonging to, affecting, her.

Hēr'a. (Gk myth.) Daughter of Cronos and Rhea; sister and wife of Zeus; worshipped as queen of the heavens and goddess of power and riches; identified by the Romans with Juno.

Hĕ'raclēs (-z). Greek form of HERCULES.

Hĕraclī'tus. Greek philosopher, of Ephesus; wrote a work 'Concerning Nature' (*c.* 513 B.C.), in which he maintained that all things were in a state of flux and that fire, the type of this constant change, was their origin; his melancholy views on the changing character of life led to his being known as the 'weeping philosopher'. **Hĕraclī'tėan** *adj.* & *n.*

hĕ'rald *n.* 1. Officer who made State proclamations, bore messages between princes, officiated in the tourney, arranged various State ceremonials, regulated use of armorial bearings, settled questions of precedence, and recorded names and pedigrees of those entitled to armorial bearings; officer of the College of Arms between king of arms and pursuivant; *Heralds' College*: see COLLEGE; *Heralds' Office*, office of the Heralds' College. 2. Messenger, envoy (freq. as title of newspaper); forerunner. ~ *v.t.* Proclaim the approach of; usher in.

heră'ldic *adj.* Of heraldry.

hĕ'raldry̆ *n.* Science of a herald, esp. art of blazoning armorial bearings and settling right of persons to bear arms or certain bearings; armorial bearings; heraldic pomp.

hērb *n.* Plant whose stem is not woody or persistent but dies down after flowering; plant of which leaves etc. are used for food, medicine, scent, flavour, etc.; ~ *beer*, drink made from herbs; ~ *bennet*, yellow-flowered species of geum; ~ *Robert*, common wild species of plant *Geranium* (*G. robertianum*) with divided leaves and light-reddish-purple flowers; ~ *-tea*, *-water*, medicinal infusion of herbs.

hērbā'ceous (-sh*u*s) *adj.* Of (the nature of) herb(s): ~ *border*, garden border of perennial flowering plants.

hēr'bage *n.* Herbs collectively, esp. grass and other low-growing plants covering large extent of ground and used as pasture etc.; green succulent parts of herbaceous plants; (law) right of pasture on another's ground.

hēr'bal *adj.* & *n.* (Book with descriptions) of herbs. **hēr'balist** *n.* One skilled in herbs or plants (now used of early botanical writers); dealer in medicinal herbs.

hērbār'ium *n.* (Book, case, room, containing) collection of dried plants.

Hēr'bert, George (1593–1633). English clergyman; author of 'The Temple', a collection of poems of a religious character.

hērbi'ferous *adj.* Producing herbs.

hērbi'vorous *adj.* (of animals) Feeding on plants. **hēr'bivōre** *n.*

hēr'borīze *v.i.* Gather herbs, botanize. **hērborīzā'tion, hēr'borist** *ns.*

hēr'by̆ *adj.* Abounding in herbs; of the nature of a herb.

Hercegovina: see HERZEGOVINA.

Hērcūlān'ėum. Ancient town in Campania, buried with Pompeii in eruption of Vesuvius, A.D. 79.

Hērcū'lėan (*or* -ē'*a*n) *adj.* Of

Hercules; strong as Hercules; difficult as his labours.

Hĕr'cūlēs (-z). 1. (Gk & Rom. myth.) Hero of prodigious strength, who performed twelve immense tasks or labours imposed on him by Eurystheus, and after death was ranked among the gods;

Pillars of ~, rocks Calpe (Gibraltar) and Abyla (Ceuta) on either side of Strait of Gibraltar, thought to have been set up by Hercules and to be supports of western boundaries of the world. 2. (astron.) Northern constellation, figured as a man kneeling on his right knee. 3. (also ~ *beetle*) S. Amer. lamellicorn beetle (*Dynastes hercules*) about 127 mm long.

Hĕr'cūlĭd *n.* (astron.) Meteor belonging to a shower with radiant point in constellation Hercules.

Hĕrcȳ'nĭan *adj.* (geol.) Of an episode of mountain formation in the Eastern hemisphere during the late Palaeozoic era.

hĕrd[1] *n.* Company of animals, esp. cattle, feeding or travelling together; (contempt.) large number of people (esp. *the common* or *vulgar* ~); ~ *instinct*, gregariousness and mutual influence as psychological factor; ~*-book*, pedigree-book of cattle or pigs; *her'dsman*, keeper of herds. ~ *v.* Go, collect, in a herd (*together*, *with* others).

hĕrd[2] *n.* (Sc. & north.) Herdsman. ~ *v.t.* Tend (sheep, cattle).

Her'der (hār-), Johann Gottfried (1744–1803). German poet and critic; precursor of the Romantic movement; famous for his work on German folk-song and for his philosophy of history.

hēre *adv.* In this place; in this country, region, etc.; present to the sight or mind; in this life, on earth; at this juncture, at this point in action, speech, etc.; in the matter before us or in question; (with verbs of coming or bringing) to or towards this place; *~'s (a health) to*, formula in drinking toasts; ~ *and there*, in various places; ~, *there, and everywhere*, everywhere, all about; *neither* ~ *nor there*, not to the point, of no importance; ~ *goes!* (colloq.) exclamation announcing commencement of bold act; *her'e-about(s)*, somewhere near here; *herea'fter*, in future, later on; (in) the world to come; *herea't*, (archaic) at this; *hereby'*, by this means, as a result; *herei'n*, in this point, book, etc.; *hereina'fter*, below (in document etc.); *hereo'f*, (archaic) of this; *hereto'*, (archaic) to this matter; *heretofor'e*, formerly; *hereu'nder*, below (in book etc.); *hereupo'n*, after this; in consequence of this; *herewi'th*, with this (esp. of enclosure in letter etc.). ~ *n.* This place or point.

hėrĕ'dĭtable *adj.* That may be inherited. **hėrĕdĭtabĭ'lĭtȳ** *n.*

hĕrėdĭ'tament *n.* Property that can be inherited; real property; inheritance.

hėrĕ'dĭtarȳ *adj.* Descending by inheritance; transmitted from one generation to another; like, the same as, that one's parents had; of, holding position by, inheritance. **hėrĕ'dĭtarĭlȳ** *adv.* **hėrĕ'dĭtarĭnėss** *n.*

hėrĕ'dĭtȳ *n.* Tendency of like to beget like; property of organic beings by which offspring inherit nature and characteristics of parents or other ancestors; organic relation between successive generations; germinal constitution.

Hĕ'rėford. City and county town of Herefordshire; hence, (one of) a breed of beef cattle originating there (red and white, with white faces).

Hĕ'réford and Worcester (wŏŏ'ster). County of W. and W. midlands of England (since April 1974).

Hĕ'réfordshire. Former county in W. England, since April 1974 part of Hereford and Worcester.

hérĕ'siarch (-k) *n.* Leader, founder, of a heresy.

hĕ'résy̆ *n.* Opinion or doctrine contrary to the orthodox doctrine of the Christian Church, or to the accepted doctrine on any subject.

hĕ'rétic *n.* Holder of an unorthodox opinion (orig. in matter of religion). **hérĕ'tical** *adj.*

hĕ'riot *n.* (Engl. law) Render of best live beast or dead chattel, or fixed money payment, to lord on decease of tenant (now an incident of manorial tenures only).

Hĕ'riot-Watt (-wŏt): see EDINBURGH.

hĕ'ritable *adj.* That passes to heirs-at-law (opp. to movable property); transmissible from parent to child; capable of inheriting. **hĕ'ritably̆** *adv.*

hĕ'ritage *n.* What is or may be inherited; inherited lot or portion; (fig.) portion allotted to anyone.

hĕ'ritor *n.* One who inherits; (Sc. law) proprietor of a heritable subject.

hermă'phrodite *n.* 1. Human being, animal, combining characteristics of both sexes; (zool.) animal having normally both male and female sexual organs; (bot.) plant in which same flower has both stamens and pistils. 2. Person, thing, combining opposite qualities; sailing-ship having characters of two kinds of craft, esp. one square-rigged like brig forward and schooner-rigged aft. ~ *adj.* Combining both sexes or opposite characteristics. **hermăphrodi'tic, -ical** *adjs.* **hermă'phroditism** *n.* [Gk *Hermaphroditos*, son of Hermes and Aphrodite, who became one with the nymph Salmacis]

herméneu'tic *adj.* Of interpretation. **herméneu'tics** *n.pl.* Interpretation, esp. of Scripture. **herméneu'tical** *adj.*

Her'mēs (-z). 1. (Gk myth.) Son of Zeus and Maia; represented as messenger of the gods, god of science, commerce, eloquence, etc., identified by the Romans with Mercury, and represented as a youth with winged rod (*caduceus*), brimmed hat (*petasus*), and winged shoes (*talaria*). 2. ~ *Trismegistus* ('thrice-greatest'), name given by Neo-platonists etc. to Egyptian god Thoth, regarded as author of all mysterious doctrines and esp. of secrets of alchemy.

hermĕ'tic *adj.* Of Hermes Trismegistus; of alchemy, magical, alchemical; ~ *seal, sealing*, airtight closure of vessel, esp. glass vessel, by fusion, soldering, or welding. **hermĕ'tically̆** *adv.*

her'mit *n.* One who from religious motives has retired into solitary life, esp. early Christian recluse; person living in solitude; *~-crab*, crab of family Paguridae, living in mollusc's cast-off shell

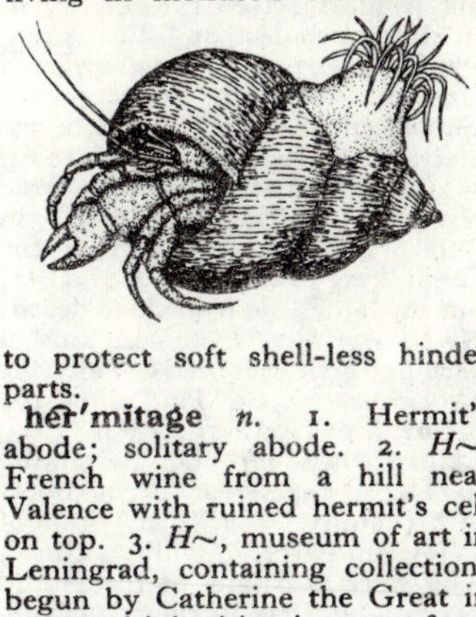

to protect soft shell-less hinder parts.

her'mitage *n.* 1. Hermit's abode; solitary abode. 2. *H~*, French wine from a hill near Valence with ruined hermit's cell on top. 3. *H~*, museum of art in Leningrad, containing collections begun by Catherine the Great in 1765 and inheriting its name from the 'retreat' in which she displayed them to her friends.

hern, her'nshaw *ns.* (archaic or dial.) Heron.

her'nia *n.* (path.) Tumour formed by the displacement of part of an organ so that it protrudes through the walls of its containing cavity; rupture. **hěr'nĭal, hěr'nĭarў** *adjs.*

hernshaw: see HERN.

hěr'ō[1] *n.* (pl. *-es*). 1. (Gk antiq.) Man of superhuman strength, courage, or ability, favoured by the gods; later regarded as intermediate between gods and men, and immortal. 2. Illustrious warrior; man of extraordinary bravery, fortitude, or greatness of soul. 3. Man forming subject of epic; chief male character in poem, play, or story; *~-worship(per)*, worship(per) of some great man or men or a personal hero.

Hěr'ō[2]. (Gk legend) Beautiful priestess of Aphrodite at Sestos on the European shore of the Hellespont, whose lover Leander, a youth of Abydos, swam the strait nightly to visit her; one stormy night he was drowned and Hero in grief threw herself into the sea.

Hě'rod. Name of four rulers in ancient Palestine: *Herod the Great* (d. 4 B.C.), king of the Jews 40–4 B.C.; he ordered the Massacre of the Innocents (see INNOCENT[1]) in an attempt to destroy Jesus Christ, who was born in his reign; *Herod Antipas*, his son, tetrarch of Galilee and Peraea 4 B.C.–A.D. 39; married Herodias and had St. John the Baptist beheaded; *Herod Agrippa I*, (called 'Herod' in Acts), grandson of Herod the Great, king of the Jews A.D. 41–4; put St. James the Apostle to death; *Herod Agrippa II* his son, king of various territories in N. Palestine A.D. 50–*c* 93; St. Paul appeared before him (Acts 25: 13 ff.).

Hěrō'dĭan *adj.* Of, pertaining to, Herod the Great, or members of his family. ~ *n.* (hist.) One of a Jewish party, mainly political, who were partisans of the Herod dynasty, and lax in their Judaism.

Hėrŏ'dotus (5th c. B.C.). Greek historian; author of nine books of 'Histories', the main theme of which is the enmity between Persia and Greece.

hėrō'ĭc *adj.* 1. Of, fit for, a hero; having the qualities of a hero; ~ *age*, period of Greek history before the return from Troy. 2. Describing the deeds of heroes, epic; (of metre) used in heroic poetry (in Greek and Latin, the hexameter, in French, the Alexandrine, in English, German, and Italian, iambic of 5 feet or 10 syllables); (of language) grand, high-flown. 3. Bold or daring, attempting great things. **hėrō'ĭcallў** *adv.* **hėrō'ĭc** *n.* Heroic verse (chiefly pl.); (pl.) high-flown language or sentiments.

hě'rōin *n.* Drug, also called diacetylmorphine or diamorphine, prepared from morphine which it resembles in its effects, capable of causing addiction.

hě'roine *n.* Heroic woman; chief woman in poem, novel, etc.

hě'roism *n.* Heroic conduct or qualities.

hě'ron *n.* One of the long-necked long-legged wading-birds of genus *Ardea* in family Ardeidae, esp. the common European grey species, *A. cinerea.* **hě'ronrў** *n.* Place where herons breed.

hěr'pēs (-z) *n.* Either of two forms of virus affection, ~ *zoster*, shingles, an infection of the cutaneous nerves resulting in severe pain and outbreaks of small blisters related to the distribution of the nerves, and ~ *simplex*, painless form in which the blisters have no relation to the nerves of the skin.

hěrpėtŏ'logў *n.* Zoology of reptiles. **hěrpėtŏ'logist** *n.*

Herr (hār) *n.* (pl. *Herren*). German title (corresp. to *Mr.*).

Hě'rrĭck, Robert (1591–1674). English poet; author of 'Hesperides' (1648), a collection of some 1,200 mostly idyllic nature poems.

hě'rrĭng *n.* Edible fish, *Clupea harengus*, of N. Atlantic, coming near coast in large shoals to spawn; *red* ~: see RED; *~-bone* (*stitch*), stitch in which threads are set obliquely on opposite sides of a line or crossing each other; (of masnonry, paving) in which stones or tiles are set in zig-zag pattern; (of cloth etc.) woven in zigzag pattern: *~-bone* (*v.t.*) work with herring-bone stitch, mark with herring-bone pattern; *~-gull*, large gull of N. Atlantic

(*Larus argentatus*), with black tips to wings; ~-*pond*, (joc.) N. Atlantic.

Herr'nhuter (hār̄nhōō-). *n.* = MORAVIAN, 2. [f. *Herrnhut* 'the Lord's keeping', their first German settlement, in Saxony]

hers: see HER.

Her'schel (-sh-), Sir William (1738–1822). German-born astronomer, who settled in England and became court astronomer to George III; discoverer of the planet Uranus. **Herschē'lian** *adj.* Of, pertaining to, Sir W. Herschel or his son, Sir John Herschel (1792–1871); ~ *telescope*, form of reflecting telescope with a concave mirror slightly inclined to the axis, exhibited, but not invented, by Sir W. Herschel.

hersĕ'lf *pron.* Emphatic and reflexive form corresponding to SHE, HER.

Her'tfordshire (hārf-). One of the Home counties of England.

Herts. *abbrev.* Hertfordshire.

Hertz[1] (-ts; *or* hār-), Heinrich Rudolph (1857–94). German physicist. **Her'tzian** *adj.* ~ *waves*, electromagnetic waves, first demonstrated by Hertz in 1888, and subsequently utilized for wireless telegraphy.

hertz[2] (ts) *n.* (pl. same; abbrev. Hz) Unit of frequency, one cycle per second. [f. HERTZ[1]]

Herzėgōvi'na (herts-, -vē-). Province S. of Bosnia, now part of Yugoslavia.

Herzl (hĕ'rtsl), Theodor (1860–1904). Austrian Jewish writer, born in Hungary; founder of Zionism.

Hē'siod (8th c. B.C.). Greek poet; author of 'Works and Days', descriptive of agricultural life in Boeotia, and probably of the 'Theogony', containing a mythical account of the origin of the world and the genealogy of the gods, and of a 'Catalogue of Women', who, being beloved of the gods, became the mothers of heroes. **Hēsiŏ'dic** *adj.*

hĕ'sitant (-z-) *adj.* Hesitating, irresolute. **hĕ'sitance, hĕ'sitancy̆** *ns.*

hĕ'sitāte (-z-) *v.i.* Show, speak with, indecision; scruple; be reluctant, *to* (do). **hĕ'sitātingly̆** *adv.* **hĕsitā'tion** *n.* **hĕ'sitative** *adj.*

Hĕspēr'ian *adj.* (poet.) Western.

Hĕspĕ'ridēs (-z). (Gk myth.) Three, four, or seven nymphs, daughters of Hesperus; they were guardians, with the aid of a watchful dragon, of the garden in which golden apples grew, in the Islands of the Blessed (see ISLAND).

Hĕ'sperus. Evening star.

Hĕ'sse (-*e*). (Ger. *Hessen*) Former State of SW. Germany, now a province of the Federal Republic; capital, Wiesbaden.

Hĕ'ssian (*or* -shan) *adj.* Of Hesse; ~ *boot*, high boot, with tassels in front at the top, first worn by Hessian troops; ~ *fly*, midge (*Phytophaga destructor*) with larva very destructive to wheat (erroneously supposed to have been carried to America by Hessian troops). ~ *n.* 1. Native or inhabitant of, soldier from, Hesse; (U.S.) military or political hireling, mercenary (from the Hessian mercenaries used by British Government during Amer. War of Independence). 2. *h*~, strong coarse cloth of mixed hemp and jute used for packing bales etc.

hĕst *n.* (archaic) Behest.

hĕt *adj.* (late ME past part. of HEAT, now dial. & U.S.) Heated; ~ *up*, (colloq.) excited, agitated.

hėtaer'a (-ēr*a*), **hėtair'a** (-īr*a*) *n.* Courtesan, esp. in ancient Greece. **hetaer'ism, hetair'ism** *n.* Open concubinage; communal marriage in a tribe.

hĕtero- *prefix.* Other, different.

hĕ'teroclīte *adj.* & *n.* Irregularly declined (noun).

hĕ'terodŏx *adj.* Not orthodox. **hĕ'terodŏxy̆** *n.*

hĕ'terody̆ne *n.* Apparatus for, process of, converting a high-frequency radio wave to one of an audible frequency by superimposing another high-frequency wave of nearly the same period and so producing a pulsation. ~ *v.i.* Produce a heterodyne effect.

hĕterŏ'gamy̆ *n.* (biol.) Alternation of differently organized generations of animals or plants, as where sexual generation alternates with parthenogenesis; condition of having, or union of, gametes of different size and structure. **hĕterŏʹgamous** *adj.*

hĕterogēʹnėous *adj.* Diverse in character; composed of diverse elements or substances; (math.) incommensurable because of different kinds. **hĕterogēʹnėouslȳ** *adv.* **hĕterogēʹnėousnėss, hĕterogėnēʹitȳ** *ns.*

hĕterogĕʹnėsis *n.* Birth of a living being otherwise than from parent of same kind, esp. supposed spontaneous generation from inorganic matter; alternation of generation. **hĕterogėnĕʹtic** *adj.* Descended from different ancestral stock.

hĕteromôrʹphism *n.* Quality of existing or occurring in different forms. **hĕteromôrʹphic** *adj.*

hĕterosĕʹxūal *adj.* Relating or belonging to the opposite sex; sexually attracted to members of the opposite sex. ~ *n.* Heterosexual person. **hĕterosĕxūălitȳ** *n.*

hĕterospôrʹous *adj.* (bot.) Having spores of two different sizes (opp. HOMOSPOROUS).

hĕterozȳʹgōte *n.* Zygote resulting from fusion of unlike gametes; Mendelian hybrid containing dominant and recessive characters and therefore not breeding true. **hĕterozȳʹgous** *adj.* Bearing two dissimilar alternative genetical factors.

hĕʹtman *n.* Polish military commander (retained as title among Cossacks). [Polish, f. Ger. *hauptmann* head man, captain]

heurĭʹstic *adj.* Serving to find out or discover.

hew *v.t.* Chop, cut (*down, away, asunder*, etc.) with axe, sword, etc.; cut into shape; fell or cut (wood); cut (coal) from the seam. **hewʹer** *n.* One who hews; man who cuts coal from seam.

hĕxa-, hĕx- *prefix.* Six.

hĕʹxachôrd (-kôrd) *n.* Series of 6 consecutive notes with semitone between 3rd and 4th, regarded (in medieval music) as unit for purpose of singing at sight, at three pitches, beginning G, C, F respectively and with notes of each named Ut-re-mi-fa-sol-la.

hĕʹxăd *n.* Set, group, of 6.

hĕʹxagon *n.* Plane figure of 6 angles and sides. **hĕxăʹgonal** *adj.*

hĕʹxagrăm *n.* Figure formed by 2 intersecting equilateral triangles (the angular points coinciding with those of a hexagon); figure of 6 lines.

hĕxahēʹdron *n.* Solid figure of 6 faces. **hĕxahēʹdral** *adj.*

hĕxăʹmėter *n.* Line of 6 metrical feet, esp. the *dactylic* ~ of Latin and Greek epic poetry, in which the first 4 feet may be dactyls or spondees, the 5th is a dactyl, and the 6th a spondee or less commonly a trochee, thus: –⏖ | –⏖ | –⏖ | –⏖ | – ⏑⏑ | – ⏓ |.

hĕʹxastȳle *adj.* & *n.* (Portico) of 6 columns.

Hĕʹxateuch (-k) *n.* First 6 books of Old Testament.

hey (hā) *int.* Exclamation calling attention, or of joy, surprise, or interrogation; ~ *presto*, conjurer's phrase of command, hence used to announce surprising transformation etc.

heyʹday (hā-) *n.* Full bloom, flush (of youth, vigour, prosperity, etc.).

heyduck (hīʹdŏŏk) *n.* In Serbia etc., robber, brigand; in Hungary, special body of foot-soldiers to whom noble rank and a territory were given in 1605; in Poland, liveried personal follower or attendant of noble.

Hĕzėkīʹah (-*a*). King of Judah in 8th–7th c. B.C.

H.F. *abbrev.* High FREQUENCY.

hg *abbrev.* Hectogramme(s).

H.G. *abbrev.* High German (also HG); His (*or* Her) Grace; Holy Ghost; Home Guard; Horse Guards.

H.G.V. *abbrev.* Heavy goods vehicle.

HH *abbrev.* Double-hard (of pencil lead).

H.H. *abbrev.* Heavy hydrogen; His (*or* Her) Highness; His Holiness (the Pope).

hī *int.* Exclamation calling attention or (U.S.) of greeting.

hīāʹtus *n.* Break, gap, esp. in a

series, account, or chain of proof; break between word ending, and another beginning, with a vowel.

hī'bernāte *v.i.* Spend the winter (of animals) in torpid state, (of persons) in mild climate; (fig.) remain inactive. **hī'bernant** *adj.* **hībernā'tion** *n.*

Hībĕr'nian *adj.* & *n.* (Native, inhabitant) of Ireland. [f. L *Hibernia* Ireland]

hĭbĭ'scus *n.* Malvaceous plant of chiefly tropical genus *H~*, with large bright-coloured flowers; rose-mallow.

hĭ'ccup, hĭ'ccough (-*kup*) *n.* Involuntary spasm of respiratory organs, with sudden closure of glottis and characteristic sound. ~ *v.* Make hiccup; say, bring *out*, with hiccup(s).

hic jacet (hēk yă'kĕt). Epitaph, esp. one beginning thus. [L, = 'here lies']

hĭck *n.* (colloq., esp. U.S.) Countryman, farmer, provincial.

hĭ'ckorў *n.* N. Amer. tree (*Carya*) closely allied to walnut, with tough heavy wood bearing drupes (usu. with hard woody rind) enclosing frequently edible nuts (pecans); wood, stick, of this; hickory-nut; *Old H~*, nickname of President Andrew JACKSON[1]; *~-elm*, Amer. elm, *Ulmus racemosa*; *~-nut*, nut of the hickory.

hid: see HIDE[3].

hidă'lgō *n.* One of the lower nobility in Spain. [Span. *hijo dalgo* son of a 'somebody']

hidden: see HIDE[3].

hīde[1] *n.* Animal's skin, raw or dressed; (joc.) human skin; *hi'debound*, (of cattle) with skin clinging closely to back and ribs as result of bad feeding; (fig.) bigoted, rigidly conventional.

hīde[2] *n.* (hist.) Medieval measure of land, of varying extent; orig., the amount required by one free family and its dependants, or as much as could be tilled with one plough in a year.

hīde[3] *v.* (past t. *hĭd*, past part. *hĭ'dden, hĭd*). Put, keep, out of sight; keep (fact) secret (*from*); keep from view, obstruct the view of (without implication of intention); conceal oneself; *~-and-seek*, children's game in which one or more players hide and the others look for them (also fig. of dealings with evasive person or thing). ~ *n.* Place of concealment for observation of wild animals; cache; *hi'de-out*, hiding-place.

hĭ'dėous *adj.* Frightful, repulsive, revolting, to senses or mind. **hĭ'deouslў** *adv.* **hĭ'dėousnėss** *n.*

hī'dĭng[1] *n.* (esp.) *in ~*, hidden; *~-place*, place of concealment.

hī'dĭng[2] *n.* Thrashing.

hīe *v.i.* (pres. part. *hy'ing*). (poet.) Go quickly (*to* etc.).

hī'erarch (-k) *n.* Chief priest; archbishop.

hī'erarchy (-kĭ) *n.* 1. Each of three divisions of angels (each comprising three orders) in the system of Dionysus the Pseudo-Areopagite; the angels. 2. Priestly government; organized priesthood in successive grades; any graded organization. **hīerar'chic, -ical** *adjs.*

hīeră'tic *adj.* Of the priests (esp. of ancient Egyptian cursive writing intermediate between hieroglyphic and demotic); priestly; of traditional styles of art (e.g. Egyptian, Byzantine) in which earlier types and methods are conventionally retained.

hī'eroglўph *n.* 1. Figure of an object (pictograph, ideograph, phonogram, or determinative),

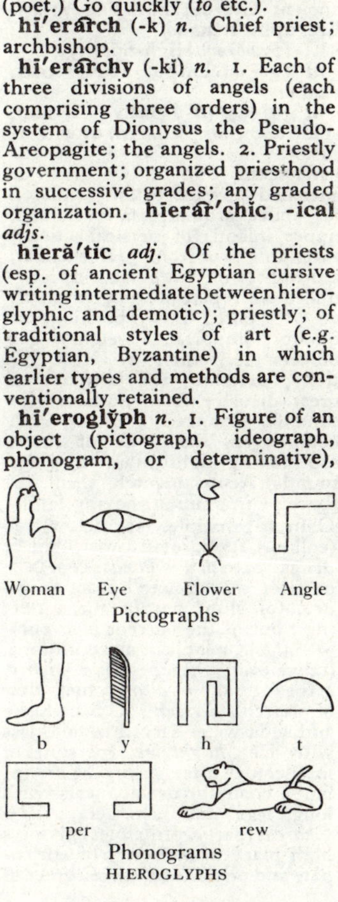

HIEROGLYPHS

used to represent a word or sound or syllable in any of the pictorial systems of writing, esp. the ancient Egyptian. 2. Secret symbol; writing difficult to make out. **hierogly̆'phic** *adj.* Of, written in hieroglyphs; hard to decipher. **hierogly̆'phics** *n.pl.* Hieroglyphs. **hierogly̆'phical** *adj.* **hierogly̆'phically̆** *adv.*

Hierŏ'ny̆mite *n.* Hermit of any of the orders of JEROME.

hi'erophănt *n.* Official expounder of sacred mysteries or religious ceremonies, esp. in ancient Greece; initiating priest. **hierophă'ntic** *adj.*

hi-fi *abbrev.* High-fidelity.

hi'ggle *v.i.* Dispute about terms; chaffer.

hi'ggledy-pi'ggledy (-gldĭ, -gldĭ) *adv.*, *adj.*, & *n.* (In) utter confusion.

high (hī) *adj.* 1. Of great or specified upward extent; situated far above ground, sea-level, etc., upper, inland; (of physical actions) extending to or from, performed at, a height; (of vowel sound) produced with (part of) tongue raised. 2. Of exalted rank, position, or quality; important, weighty; (of officers etc.) chief. 3. Great, intense, extreme; (of latitude) at great distance from equator; (of time) far advanced; ~ *colour*, fresh complexion, flush. 4. (of meat, esp. game) Slightly tainted. 5. (of sounds) Acute in pitch, shrill. 6. Extreme in opinion; having High-Church principles (see below). 7. (colloq.) Intoxicated by alcohol or drugs. 8. *with a ~ hand*: see HAND; *on one's ~ horse*: see HORSE; ~ *and dry*, (of ship) out of the water; (fig.) out of the current of events; ~ *and low*, people of all conditions, (*adv.*) everywhere; ~ *and mighty*, arrogant. 9. ~ *altar*, chief altar of church; *hi'ghball*, (U.S.) whisky and soda-water served in tall glass with ice; *hi'ghbrow*, (person) of intellectual interests; ~ *chair*, infant's chair for use at meals, with long legs and usu. tray; *H~ Church*, (party, principles) giving a high place to authority of episcopate and priesthood, saving grace of sacraments, and ritual; hence *H~ Churchman*; *H~ Court*, supreme court of justice for hearing of civil cases; ~ *day*, festal day; ~ *explosive*, (abbrev. H.E.) explosive detonating very rapidly and with powerful effect; ~*-falutin(g)*, bombast(ic); ~ *farming*, extensive use of fertilizers in cultivation; ~*-fidelity*, (radio etc.) reproduction of sound with minimum of distortion; ~ *frequency*: see FREQUENCY; *H~ German*: see GERMAN[2]; ~*-handed*, overbearing, arbitrary; ~ *hat*: see HAT; ~ *jinks*: see JINK; ~ *life*, that of the aristocracy; *hi'ghlight(s)*, brightest part(s), esp. of picture etc.; *hi'ghlight* (*v.t.*) emphasize, make prominent; *H~ Mass*: see MASS[1]; ~-minded, of morally lofty character; ~*-pitched*, (of sound) acute in pitch; (of roof etc.) steep; ~*-pressure*, (of engine, machine, etc.) having, driven by, high pressure of steam, air, etc.; (fig.) urgent, intense, as ~*-pressure salesmanship*; ~ *priest*, chief priest, esp. of Jews; ~ *relief*, sculpture in which figures etc. project more than half their thickness from background, *alto-relievo*; ~ *road*, main road; ~ *school*, secondary esp. grammar school; ~ *seas*, the seas, ocean, outside territorial waters; ~*-spirited*, of lofty or courageous spirit; lively; ~ *spirits*, elated or merry mood; ~*-stepper*, horse that steps high; social climber; ~ *table*, table raised above others at public dinner, esp. that of president and fellows in college; ~ *tea*, early evening meal at which tea is served; ~ *tide*: see TIDE; ~ *treason*: see TREASON; ~ *water*, state of tide when water is highest; time when tide is at the full; ~*-water mark*, level reached at high water; highest point of flood; highest point of intensity, excellence, prosperity, etc., attained; *hi'ghway*, public road, esp. main or principal road; main route by land or water; (fig.) ordinary direct course (of action etc.); *Highway Code*, set of rules issued officially for guidance of road users; *hi'ghwayman*,. (hist.)

man (usu. mounted) who robbed passengers on highway; *~-wing* (of monoplane) with wings set near top of fuselage. ~ *adv*. Far up aloft; in, to, a high degree; at a high price; for high stakes; (of sounds) at, to, a high pitch; *run* ~, (of sea) have strong current with high tide; *~-born*, of noble birth; *~-flown*, extravagant, bombastic; *~-flyer*, *-flier*, (fig.) ambitious person; one who has high-flown notions. ~ *n*. High place; high level; (meteor.) region of high atmospheric pressure; *on* ~, in a high place, in heaven.

Hi'ghland (hīl-). Region of N. Scotland (since May 1975), comprising the former counties of Caithness, Inverness-shire, Nairnshire, Ross and Cromarty, and Sutherland.

highlands (hī'landz) *n.pl.* Mountainous or elevated country, esp. (*H~*) N. part of Scotland. **hi'ghland** *adj*. **hi'ghlander** *n*. Inhabitant of highlands, esp. (*H~*) those of Scotland.

highly (hī'lĭ) *adv*. In a high degree; at a high price or rate; honourably, favourably (as ~ *recommended*); *~-strung*; in high state of vigour or sensitiveness.

hi'ghness (hīn-) *n*. 1. Used for *height* where *height* is not idiomatic, as *the ~ of his character*. 2. *H~*, title of various British and other princes etc., as *His*, *Her*, (Royal, *Serene*, *Imperial*) *H~*.

hight (hīt) *adj*. (archaic, poet., joc.) Called, named.

H.I.H. *abbrev*. His (*or* Her) Imperial Highness.

hi'jăck *v.t.* & *n*. Seize, seizure of, means of transport or goods etc. in transit. **hī'jăcker** *n*.

hīke *v.i.* & *n*. Walk (undertaken) vigorously or laboriously, tramp, esp. for pleasure or exercise. **hī'ker** *n*.

hilār'ĭous *adj*. Mirthful, joyous, boisterously merry. **hilār'ĭouslȳ** *adv*. **hilār'ĭousnėss, hilă'rĭtȳ** *ns*.

Hĭ'larȳ, St. (d. 367). Hilarius, bishop of Poitiers and Doctor of the Church; commemorated 13 Jan.; ~ *term*, legal or university term beginning in January.

Hĭ'ldėbrănd. GREGORY[1] VII

hĭll[1] *n*. Natural elevation of earth's surface, small mountain; heap, mound, of sand, earth, etc.; *the ~s*, (esp.) highlands of northern and interior India; *hillbilly*, (U.S.) rustic mountaineer; *hillbilly* (*song*), song of simple ballad type popular among such people. ~ *v.t.* Form into hill; bank *up* (plants) with soil. **hĭ'llȳ** *adj*. **hĭ'llinėss** *n*.

Hill[2], Octavia (1838–1912).

Social reformer, esp. of housing conditions.

hillō', hilloa' (-ō) *int*. = HALLO.

hĭ'llock *n*. Small hill or mound.

hĭlt *n*. Handle of sword or dagger handle of other weapon or tool; *up to the* ~, completely. ~,*v.t.* Furnish with hilt.

hī'lum *n*. (bot.) Mark at point of attachment of seed to seed-vessel.

hĭm *pron*. Objective (accus., dat.) case of HE.

H.I.M. *abbrev*. His (*or* Her) Imperial Majesty.

Hĭma'chal Prade'sh (-ahsh-, -āsh). Union territory in N. India; capital, Simla.

Hĭmalay'a Mou'ntains (-tĭnz). (also *Himalayas*) System of mountains N. of the Indian subcontinent, containing highest summits in the world. **Hĭmalay'an** *adj*.

Hĭ'mmler, Heinrich (1900–45). German politician; minister of the interior during the Nazi regime, and head of the S.S. and Gestapo.

hĭmsĕ'lf *pron.* Emphatic and reflexive form corresponding to HE, HIM.

Hinayana (hēnayah'na) *n.* = THERAVADA. [Sansk. *hina* lesser, *yāna* vehicle]

hīnd[1] *n.* Female of (esp. red) deer, esp. in and after third year.

hīnd[2] *n.* Farm servant, esp. (in Scotland and northern England) married and skilled farm-workman with responsible part in working of farm, and provided with cottage on farm; steward; rustic, boor.

hīnd[3] *adj.* Situated at the back, posterior (less usual than *hinder* exc. as opp. *fore*, of things existing in pairs; so *hindquarters*); *hi'ndbrain*: see BRAIN; *hi'ndsight*, backsight of a rifle; perception after the event (opp. *foresight*).

Hĭ'ndenbŭrg, Paul von (1847–1934). German field marshal; 2nd president of the Weimar Republic (1925–34).

hi'nder[1] *adj.* See HIND[3].

hĭ'nder[2] *v.t.* Impede, prevent.

Hĭ'ndi (-ē). *n.* 1. Group of Indo-Aryan spoken dialects including Eastern and Western Hindi. 2. Literary form of Hindustani drawing literary vocabulary from Sanskrit and using the Devanagari script.

hī'ndmōst *adj.* Farthest behind; most remote.

hi'ndrance *n.* Obstruction, prevention; obstacle.

Hĭndu' (-ōō), **Hĭndōō'** *n.* One who practises Hinduism. **Hĭ'ndu** *adj.* ~ *Kush*, mountain range in S. Asia, extending west from the Himalayas. **Hĭ'nduism** *n.* Religious and social system with adherents esp. in India, with belief in reincarnation, worship of several gods, and caste as basis of society.

Hĭndusta'n (-ahn). Persian name of India; in the stricter sense, India N. of the Deccan exclusive of Bengal and Bihar. [lit. 'place of the Hindus']

Hĭndusta'ni (-ahnē) *n.* Language based on Western Hindi used widely in northern India and Pakistan; (formerly) = URDU. ~ *adj.* Of Hindustan or its people; of Hindustani.

hĭnge (-j) *n.* Movable joint, as mechanism like that by which door is hung on side post; natural joint doing similar work, as that of bivalve shell; (fig.) central principle, critical point, on which all turns; *stamp* ~, small piece of adhesive paper for mounting stamp. ~ *v.* Attach (as) with hinge; (of door etc. or fig.) hang and turn *on* (post, principle, etc.). **hĭnged** (-jd), **hĭ'ngelĕss** *adjs.*

hĭ'nnȳ *n.* Offspring of she-ass by stallion.

hĭnt *n.* Slight indication; covert or indirect suggestion. ~ *v.* Suggest slightly; ~ *at*, give hint of.

hĭ'nterlănd *n.* District behind that lying along coast or riverbank; area served by a port.

hĭp[1] *n.* Projection of pelvis and upper part of thigh bone at each side of body in man and quadrupeds; (archit.) arris of root from ridge to eaves; ~-*bath*, portable bath in which one can sit immersed to the hips; ~-*disease*, disease of hip-joint characterized by inflammation, fungous growth, and caries of the bones; ~-*flask*, flask for spirits etc. carried in hip-pocket; ~-*pocket*, pocket in trousers just behind hip. **hĭpped** (-pt) *adj.*

hĭp[2] *n.* Fruit of (esp. wild) rose.

hĭp[3] *n.* Morbid depression of spirits, the blues. ~ *v.t.* Make low-spirited. [f. *hypochondria*]

hĭp[4] *n.* Exclamation introducing united cheer (~, ~, *hurrah*).

hīpe *v.t.* (wrestling) Throw (antagonist) by placing knee between his thighs. ~ *n.* Such throw.

hĭ'ppō *n.* (colloq.) Hippopotamus.

hĭppo- *prefix.* Horse.

hĭppocă'mpus *n.* 1. (myth.) Sea-horse, with two forefeet, and body ending in fish's tail. 2. Fish of genus *H*~, SEA-horse. 3. (anat.) Each of two elongated eminences (~ *major* and *minor*) on floor of each lateral ventricle of brain.

hĭ'ppocrăs *n.* Wine flavoured with spices. [Fr., f. L *Vinum Hippocraticum*, prob. so-called because filtered through conical bag called *Hippocrates' sleeve*]

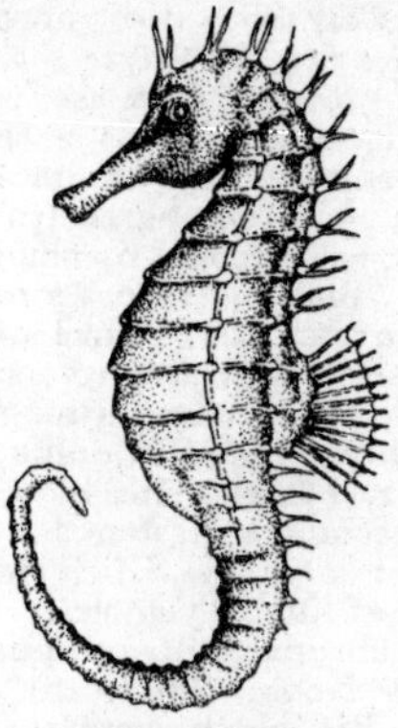

HIPPOCAMPUS

Hĭppŏ'crătēs(-z)(469–399 B.C.). Most celebrated physician of Greek antiquity. **Hippocră'tĭc** *adj.* Of Hippocrates or the school of medicine named after him; ~ *oath,* oath embodying the code of medical ethics, preserved in Hippocrates' writings (though prob. of still earlier date), and still taken, in various modified forms, by those who qualify as medical practitioners.

Hi'ppocrēne. Fountain on Mount Helicon, sacred to the Muses. [Gk, = 'fountain of the horse', because fabled to have been produced by stroke of Pegasus' hoof]

hĭ'ppodrōme *n.* (Gk & Rom. antiq.) Course for chariot races etc.; *H*~, used as name of theatre.

hĭ'ppogrĭff, -grȳph *n.* Fabulous griffin-like creature with body of horse.

hĭppopŏ'tamus *n.* (pl. *-muses, -mī*). Large African quadruped (*H. amphibius*) with thick heavy hairless body, large muzzle and

tusks, and short legs, inhabiting rivers, lakes, etc. [Gk *hippos* horse, *potamos* river]

hĭ'ppȳ, hĭppie *n.* Person rejecting conventional standards and organized society in favour of unconstrained living.

hĭr'cīne *adj.* Goat-like.

hīre *n.* Payment by contract for use of thing or for personal service; engagement on these terms; ~-*purchase* (*system*), system by which hired thing becomes hirer's after certain number of payments; purchase by instalments. ~ *v.t.* Employ (person) for wages; procure, grant, temporary use of (thing) for stipulated payment.

hir'eling (hīrl-) *n.* (usu. contempt.) One who serves for hire.

Hĭrōhi'tō (-hē-) (1901). Emperor of Japan 1926– .

Hĭrŏ'shima (*or* -shē'ma). Seaport in SW. Japan, devastated by first atomic bomb used in warfare, 6 Aug. 1945.

hĭr'sūte *adj.* Hairy, shaggy; untrimmed. **hĭr'sūtism** *n.*

hĭs (-z) *poss. pron.* Possessive case of, and adj. corresponding to, HE, belonging to, affecting, him.

Hĭspă'nic *adj.* Of, pertaining to, Spain, its people or their language. **Hĭspă'nicism** *n.* Spanish idiom or mode of speech. [L *Hispania* the Iberian peninsula]

hĭ'spĭd *adj.* (bot., zool.) Shaggy; bristly.

hiss *n.* Sharp continuous spirant sound such as is made by geese and serpents, and in pronunciation of 's'; this sound uttered in disapproval or scorn. ~ *v.* Make sound of hiss, esp. as expression of disapproval or derision; express disapproval of thus; utter with angry hiss.

hĭst *int.* (archaic) Exclamation used to call attention, enjoin silence, etc.

hĭ'stamine (-ēn) *n.* Substance naturally present in the body, responsible for complex physiological phenomena esp. in connection with work of blood-vessels.

hĭstogĕ'nėsis, hĭstŏ'gėnȳ *ns.*

Production of organic tissues. **histogĕnĕ'tic** *adj.*

histŏ'logy̆ *n.* Study of the minute structure of organic tissues. **histolŏ'gical** *adj.* **histŏ'logist** *n.*

histor'ian *n.* Writer of, person learned in, history.

histŏriātėd *adj.* (of ornamental letter etc.) Decorated with figures of men or animals.

histŏ'ric *adj.* 1. Noted in history. 2. (Gk & L grammar, of tenses of verb) Used in narration of past events; ~ *present*, present tense used instead of past in vivid narration. **histŏ'rical** *adj.* Of history; belonging to history, not legend; belonging to the past, not of the present; (of the study of a subject) based on analysis of a subject, language, etc., at successive periods of time; (of novel, picture, etc.) dealing with historical events. **histŏ'rically̆** *adv.*

histori'city̆ *n.* Historic quality or character.

histŏriŏ'grapher *n.* Writer of history, esp. official historian of court etc. **histŏriŏ'graphy̆** *n.* Writing of history. **histŏriogră'phic, -ical** *adjs.*

hi'story̆ *n.* 1. Continuous methodical record, in order of time, of important or public events; study of formation and growth of communities and nations; whole train of events connected with particular country, person, thing, etc.; past events in general, course of human affairs; *ancient* ~, history usu. reckoned as ending with fall of Roman Empire, A.D. 476; (joc.) thing that is out of date, or long past. 2. Systematic account of set of natural phenomena (rare exc. in *natural* ~).

histriŏ'nic *adj.* Of actors or acting; stagy, hypocritical. **histriŏ'nically̆** *adv.* **histriŏ'nics** *n.pl.* Theatricals, theatrical act; being dramatic for effect.

hit *v.* 1. Strike with blow or missile; direct blow *at*; (of moving body) strike; strike *against, upon*; deliver (blow, person etc. a blow); (fig.) affect sensibly, wound; ~-*and-run*, of a motor accident in which driver of vehicle fails to stop; of an air-raid of short duration by a few bombers; ~-*or-miss*, (colloq.) casual, careless; ~ *out*, deal vigorous blows. 2. Fall in with, suit; ~ *off*, imitate to a nicety; ~ *it off*, agree (*with, together*); ~ *on*, come by chance on. ~ *n.* Blow, stroke; stroke of sarcasm etc. (*at*); stroke of good luck; successful attempt; success.

hitch *v.* 1. Move (thing) with jerk; shift; ~ *up*, lift, pull up, with jerk. 2. Fasten with loop, hook, etc.; become so fastened. 3. (also ~-*hike*; orig. U.S.) Travel by means of lifts in vehicles. ~ *n.* 1. Jerk, abrupt pull or push. 2. (naut.) Noose, knot, of various kinds, by which rope is caught round or temporarily made fast to something, as *half* ~, one formed by passing end of rope round its standing part and then through the bight. 3. Temporary stoppage; impediment.

hi'ther (-dh-) *adv.* To, towards, this place; ~ *and thither*, in various directions, here and there; *hitherto'*, up to this time; *hi'therward*, (archaic) in this direction. ~ *adj.* Situated on this side; nearer (of two).

Hi'tler, Adolf (1889–1945). Austrian-born head of the Nazi party; chancellor of the German Reich 1933; president and dictator (Führer) 1934–45; C.-in-C. of the German armed forces in the war of 1939–45; ~ *Youth*, Nazi paramilitary youth organization for boys from 14 to 18 years of age (1933–45). **Hi'tlerism** *n.* **Hi'tlerite** *adj.*

Hi'ttite *n.* 1. Member of an ancient people who flourished in Anatolia *c* 2000–1200 B.C. and controlled N. Syria and other parts of the Near East. 2. (O.T.) People of N. Syria, possibly descended from the Hittites of Anatolia or akin to them. 3. Language of the Hittites of Anatolia, known from Babylonian cuneiform inscriptions, related to the Indo-European family of languages. ~ *adj.* Of the Hittites or their language.

hīve *n.* Artificial habitation for bees; hiveful of bees; (fig.) busy swarming place; swarming multitude. ~ *v.* Place (bees) in hive, house (persons etc.) snugly; enter hive, live together like bees; store, hoard up (honey etc.) in hive; ~ *off*, assign section of work to subsidiary department or company.

hīves (-vz) *n.pl.* (pop.) Any of various physical disorders, as skin eruptions, laryngitis, etc.

H.K. *abbrev.* House of Keys.

hl *abbrev.* Hectolitre(s).

H.L. *abbrev.* House of Lords.

H.L.I. *abbrev.* Highland Light Infantry.

hm *abbrev.* Hectometre(s).

H.M. *abbrev.* His (*or* Her) Majesty.

h'm: see HUM².

H.M.A.S., H.M.C.S. *abbrevs.* His (*or* Her) Majesty's Australian, Canadian, Ship.

H.M.I.(S.) *abbrevs.* His (or Her) Majesty's Inspector (of Schools).

h'mph: see HUMPH.

H.M.S., H.M.T. *abbrev.* His (*or* Her) Majesty's Ship, Trawler.

H.M.S.O. *abbrev.* His (*or* Her) Majesty's Stationery Office.

H.N.C. *abbrev.* Higher National Certificate.

hō *int.* Exclamation expressing surprise, admiration, triumph, derision, calling attention, etc.; freq. added to other interjections, as *heigh-*~, *what* ~, etc., or (naut.) to name of destination etc., as *westward* ~.

ho. *abbrev.* House.

H.O. *abbrev.* Home Office.

hoar (hōr) *adj.* Grey-haired with age; greyish white; (of things) grey with age; ~*-frost*, white frost; (meteor.) ice crystals formed by condensation of water vapour below freezing-point. ~ *n.* Hoariness; hoar-frost.

hoard (hōrd) *n.* Stock, store (esp. of food, money) laid by; amassed stock of facts etc. ~ *v.t.* Amass (food, money, etc., or abs.) and put away, store *up*; treasure up.

hoar'ding (hōr-) *n.* Temporary fence of boards round building during erection or repairs, often used for posting bills; any boarding for posting bills.

hoarhound: see HOREHOUND.

hoarse (hōrs) *adj.* (of voice) Rough, husky, croaking; (of person) having such a voice. **hoar'selȳ** *adv.* **hoar'senėss** *n.* **hoar'sen** *v.* Make, become, hoarse.

hoar'y (hōrĭ) *adj.* (of hair) Grey, white, with age; having such hair, venerable; (bot., entom.) covered with short white hairs. **hoar'ĭnėss** *n.*

hoax *v.t.* Deceive, take in (person) by way of joke. ~ *n.* Humorous or mischievous deception.

hŏb¹ *n.* 1. Part of casing of fireplace having surface level with top of grate, forming stand for kettle, pan, etc. 2. Peg or pin as mark or target in games, esp. quoits.

hŏb² *v.t.* (eng.) Cut (gears) by means of shaped revolving cutter.

Hŏ'bbėma, Meindert (1638–1709). Dutch landscape painter.

Hŏbbes (-bz), Thomas (1588–1679). English philosopher; expounded his political philosophy, according to which man is a naturally selfish unit, in the 'Leviathan' (1651).

hŏ'bble *v.* Walk lamely, limp; (of verse) have halting rhythm; cause to hobble; tie together legs of (horse etc.) to prevent it from straying etc.; tie (legs) thus. ~ *n.* Uneven or infirm gait; awkward situation; rope, clog, etc., for hobbling horse etc.; ~ *skirt*, skirt so narrow at foot as to impede wearer in walking.

hŏ'bbledėhoy (-bld-) *n.* Awkward youth, between boyhood and manhood.

hŏ'bbȳ¹ *n.* 1. (archaic) Small horse. 2. Favourite subject or occupation that is not one's main business; ~*-horse*, wicker figure of horse fastened about waist of one of performers in morris dance etc.; stick with horse's head which children bestride as toy horse; rocking-horse; favourite theme, obsession.

hŏ'bbȳ² *n.* Small falcon (*Falco subbuteo*).

hŏ'bgŏblĭn *n.* Mischievous imp; bogy; bugbear.

hŏ'bnail *n.* Heavy-headed nail

for boot-soles. **hŏ'bnailed** (-ld) *adj.* Furnished or set with hobnails; ~ *liver*, cirrhotic liver, studded with projections like nail-heads.

hŏb-nŏb *v.i.* Drink together, hold familiar intercourse (*with*).

hō'bō *n.* (pl. *-s*). (U.S.) Wandering workman; tramp.

Hŏ'bson, Thomas (1544?–1631). Cambridge carrier who let out his horses in rotation without allowing his customers to choose among them; hence, *~'s choice*, necessity of taking what one can get.

hŏck[1] *n.* Joint of quadruped's hind leg between true knee and fetlock.

hŏck[2] *n.* German white wine, properly that of Hochheim on the river Main.

hŏck[3] *n.* (U.S. slang) *in* ~, in prison; in pawn; in debt; *~-shop*, pawn-shop. ~ *v.t.* Pawn.

hŏ'ckey *n.* Field-game played with a small hard ball and with sticks hooked or curved at one end between two teams of eleven players on each side having the same positions as in Association football, the object being to drive the ball through the opponents' goal; *ice* ~, form of hockey played on ice with each side having six players on skates and with PUCK[1] instead of ball.

Hŏ'cktīde *n.* Time of *hock-days* (*Hock Monday* and *Tuesday*), second Monday and Tuesday after Easter Day, on which in pre-Reformation times money was collected for church and parish purposes, with various festive and sportive customs, kept for some time after Reformation as festive season, with traditional customs, still surviving in some places.

hō'cus *v.t.* Take-in, hoax; stupefy (person) with drugs; drug (liquor).

hō'cus-pō'cus *n.* Jugglery, deception; typical conjuring formula. ~ *v.* Play tricks on; juggle.

hŏd *n.* 1. Builder's light open trough on staff for carrying mortar etc.; *ho'dman*, labourer who carries hod; (fig.) mechanical worker, literary hack. 2. Receptacle for coal etc.

hŏ'dden *n.* (Sc.) Coarse woollen cloth; ~ *grey*, grey hodden, typical rustic garb.

Hŏdge *n.* (also *h~*) Typical English agricultural labourer. [f. *Roger*]

hŏdge-pŏdge *n.* = HOTCHPOTCH.

hŏdiēr'nal *adj.* Of the present day.

hŏdŏ'mėter *n.* = ODOMETER.

hōe *n.* Tool consisting of thin metal blade fixed transversely on

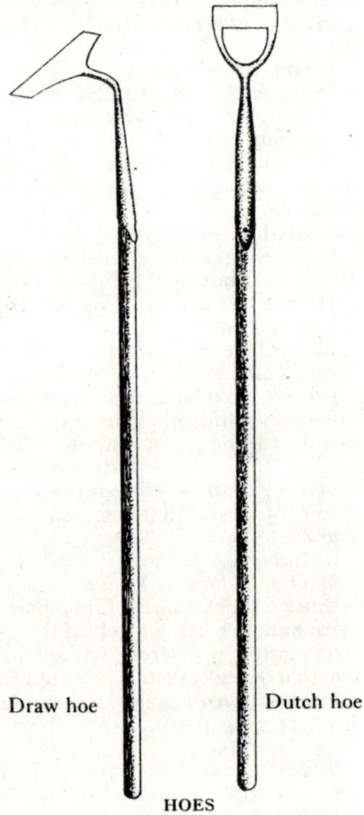

HOES

long handle, for loosening soil, scraping up weeds, etc.; *~-cake*, (U.S.) coarse bread (orig. baked on broad thin blade of cotton-field hoe) of Indian meal, water, and salt. ~ *v.* (pres. part. *hoeing*). Weed (crops), loosen (ground), dig *up*, cut *down*, with hoe; use hoe.

Hō'fer, Andreas (1767–1810). Tyrolese patriot; led an insurrection against Bavarian rule, and was captured and executed at Mantua.

Hŏ'ffmann, Ernst Theodor Amadeus (1776–1822). German Romantic novelist, whose life provided the inspiration for Offenbach's 'Tales of Hoffmann'.

Hŏ'fmannsthal (-tahl), Hugo von (1874–1929). Austrian poet and dramatist; a pioneer of the new Romantic movement in German drama.

hŏg *n.* Swine, esp. castrated male reared for slaughter; (dial.) young sheep before first shearing; (fig.) coarse, gluttonous, or filthy person; *go the whole* ~, do the thing thoroughly; *~-back*, *~'s-back*, sharply crested hill-ridge, steep on each side and sloping gradually at each end; *~-fish*, fish (*Scorpaena*) with bristles on head; (also) porpoise; manatee; *~-mane*, horse's mane cut short; *~-plum*, (fruit of) species of tropical tree *Spondias*, esp. *S. lutea* of W. Indies and Brazil, used as food for hogs; *~'s pudding*, hog's entrail stuffed with oatmeal, suet, tripe, etc., or with flour, currants, and spice; *~-tie*, (U.S.) secure by tying together animal's four feet or person's hands and feet; *ho'gwash*, kitchen swill etc. for hogs; *ho'gweed*, coarse weed of parsnip family with leaves esteemed by many animals. ~ *v.* Raise (back etc.), rise, archwise in centre; cut (mane) short; (slang) appropriate selfishly. **hŏ'ggish** *adj.* Pig-like, swinish; coarsely self-indulgent or gluttonous. **hŏ'ggishlȳ** *adv.* **hŏ'ggishness** *n.*

Hŏ'garth, William (1697–1764). English painter and engraver of social and political caricature; his work includes four famous series, 'A Harlot's Progress', 'A Rake's Progress', 'Marriage à la Mode', and the 'Election'.

hŏ'ggėt *n.* Yearling sheep.

hŏ'ggĭn, -ĭng *n.* Screened or sifted gravel mixed with clay, used for paving.

hŏ'gmanay *n.* (Sc.) Last day of year; gift of cake etc. demanded by children on that day.

hŏ'gshead (-z-hĕd) *n.* Large cask; liquid measure, 52½ imperial gallons; (of beer) 54 gallons; measure (varying from 100 to 140 gal.) of other commodities, e.g. tobacco.

Hohenlĭ'nden (hōĭn-). Place in Bavaria, Germany, where the

WILLIAM HOGARTH: Chairing the Member (detail)

French revolutionary general, Moreau, defeated the Austrians in 1800.

Hohenstau'fen (hōinshtow-). German princely family of Swabian origin, from which came Holy Roman Emperors from 1138 to 1254.

Hohenzŏ'llern (hōĭn-). German princely family of Swabian origin, from which came the kings of Prussia from 1701 to 1918 and German emperors from 1871 to 1918.

hoick *v.t.* (slang) Lift or jerk (*out* etc.).

hoicks *int.* Exclamation used to incite hounds.

hoi pŏ'lloi. The majority, the masses. [Gk, = 'the many']

hoist[1] *v.t.* Raise aloft (esp. flags); raise by means of tackle etc. ~ *n.* Hoisting, shove up; elevator, lift, esp. for things; pulley; (eng.) fixed crane.

hoist[2] *adj.* ~ *with one's own petard*, blown up by one's own bomb, ruined by one's own devices against others. [past part. of obs. *hoise* hoist]

hoi'tȳ-toi'tȳ *adj.* Haughty. ~ *int.* Exclamation expressing surprised protest at haughtiness.

hō'kum *n.* (orig. U.S., theatr. slang) Stage-properties, action, etc., designed to have sentimental or melodramatic appeal; bunkum. [perh. blending of *hocus-pocus* and *bunkum*]

Hŏ'lbein (-bīn), Hans (1497–1543). German portrait painter; became court-painter to Henry VIII of England, 1536; called 'the younger' to distinguish him from his less famous father.

hōld[1] *n.* Cavity in ship below deck, where cargo is stored.

hōld[2] *v.* (past t. & past part. *hĕld*). 1. Keep fast, grasp; keep (oneself, one's head, etc.) in particular attitude. 2. Possess, be owner or holder or tenant of; have capacity for, contain; keep possession of (place); occupy (place, person's thoughts, etc.); engross (person, his attention); *holding company*: see SUBSIDIARY company. 3. Keep (person etc.) in specified place, condition, etc.; make (person) adhere *to* (terms, promise). 4. Observe, celebrate, conduct (festival, meeting, conversation). 5. Restrain. 6. Think, believe; (of judge or court) lay down, decide (*that*); entertain specified feelings towards; ~ *dear*, regard with affection. 7. Remain unbroken, not give way; keep going; (of laws etc.; also ~ *good*, *true*) be valid, apply; (archaic) stop, wait; ~ *by*, *to*, adhere to (choice, purpose, etc.); ~ *with*, approve of. 8. ~ *one's ground*, *one's own*, not give way; ~ *one's hand*, forbear; ~ *one's head high*, behave proudly; ~ *up one's head*, not be downcast or ashamed; ~ *water*, (fig.) be sound, bear examination. 9. ~ *aloof*, avoid communication with persons etc.; ~ *back*, restrain; hesitate, refrain *from*; ~ *down*, (U.S.) continue to occupy (a place or post); retain (a job); ~ *forth*, (usu. contempt.) speak publicly; ~ *hard!* stop!; ~ *in*, confine, keep in check; ~ *off*, delay; ~ *on*, keep one's grasp on something; keep telephone line open; (colloq., imper.) stop; ~ *out*, stretch forth; offer (inducement etc.); endure, persist; ~ *out for*, refuse to accept anything but (specified terms etc.); ~ *over*, postpone; ~ *together*, (cause to) cohere; ~ *up*, support, sustain; exhibit, display (esp. *to* derision etc.); arrest progress of, obstruct; (orig. U.S.) stop and rob on highway etc.; (of horse) keep up, not fall. 10. ~*-all*, portable case for clothes etc.; *ho'ldfast*, firm grasp; staple or clamp securing object to wall etc.; ~*-up*, forcible stopping and robbing; stoppage or check in progress. ~ *n.* Grasp (esp. in *take*, *get*, *keep*, ~ *of*); opportunity of holding, thing to hold by; means of exerting influence *on*, *over*.

hō'lder *n.* (esp.) Temporary occupant of office etc.; contrivance for holding something, as a pen, cigarette, etc.

Hö'lderlin (hērl-), Friedrich (1770–1843). German lyric poet and novelist.

hō'ldĭng *n.* (esp.) Tenure of land; land held; stocks etc. held.

hōle *n.* Hollow place in solid body; deep place in stream etc.; animal's burrow; small mean abode; cavity into which ball etc. must be got in various games, esp. golf; (golf) point scored by player who gets ball from tee to hole with fewest strokes; perforation; (slang) awkward situation; *make a ~ in*, use a large amount of; *pick ~s in*, find fault with; *~-and-corner*, secret, underhand. ~ *v.* Make holes in; (naut.) pierce side of (ship); make (shaft, tunnel); put into hole; hit (golf ball, or abs.) into hole; (mining) dig through from one working to another.

hŏ'liday (*or* -dĭ) *n.* 1. Day of cessation from work or of recreation; (usu. pl.) period of this, vacation. 2. Holy day.

hō'lilȳ *adv.* In a holy manner.

hō'linėss *n.* Sanctity; (with possessive) title of Pope.

hō'lism *n.* (philos.) Tendency in nature to produce wholes (bodies or organisms) from ordered grouping of unit structures. **holi'stic** *adj.* **holi'stically** *adv.*

hŏ'lla *int.*, *n.*, & *v.* = HALLO.

Hŏ'lland¹. Name of province of the Northern Netherlands, now usu. extended by foreigners to the kingdom of the NETHERLANDS. **Hŏ'llander** *n.*

hŏ'lland² *n.* Linen fabric, freq. unbleached (*brown ~*).

hŏ'llandaise sauce (-dāz). Sauce for fish etc. of butter, eggs, vinegar, etc. [Fr., = 'Dutch']

HÖLDERLIN

hŏ'llands (-z) *n.* (also ~ *gin*) Grain spirit manufactured in Holland, Dutch gin. [f. Du. *hollandsch genever*]

hŏ'llō *int.*, *n.*, & *v.* = HALLO.

hŏ'llow (-ō) *adj.* Having a hole, cavity, or depression; not solid, empty inside; empty, hungry; (of sound) not full-toned; (fig.) empty, insincere, false; *ho'llow ware*, trade name for hollow utensils, pots, pans, etc. **hŏ'llowlȳ** *adv.* **hŏ'llownėss** *n.* **hŏ'llow** *n.* Hollow place; hole; valley, basin. ~ *adv.* Completely (esp. in *beat ~* etc.). ~ *v.t.* Bend into hollow shape; (also ~ *out*), excavate.

hŏ'llȳ *n.* Evergreen shrub (*Ilex*, esp. *I. aquifolium*) with usu. dark-green tough glossy leaves, having indented edges with sharp stiff prickles at the points, bearing bright red berries, much used for decorating houses etc. at Christmas.

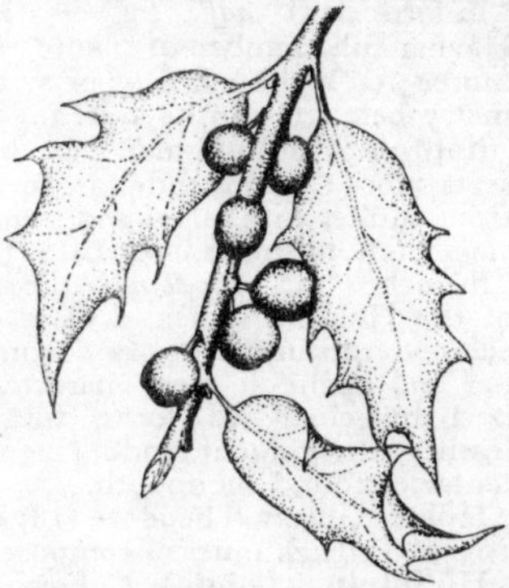

hŏ'llȳhŏck *n.* Tall plant (*Althaea rosa*) of China and southern Europe, with stout stem bearing numerous large flowers of many varieties of colour on very short stalks. [*holy* + *hock* mallow]

Hŏ'llȳwŏŏd. Suburb of Los Angeles, California; one of the principal centres of the cinema industry.

holm¹, holme (hōm) *n.* Islet, esp. in river or near mainland; flat ground by river, submerged in time of flood.

holm[2] (hōm) *n.* (usu. ~ *oak*) Evergreen oak, *Quercus ilex*, with leaves resembling those of holly.

Holmes (hōmz), Sherlock. Private detective, the chief character in a number of detective stories by Sir A. Conan Doyle.

hō'lmia *n.* (chem.) Rare earth of yttria group occurring in gadolinite; oxide of holmium.

hō'lmium *n.* (chem.) Element of yttrium-cerium group found in gadolinite; symbol Ho, at. no. 67, at. wt 164·9340. [f. Stock*holm*, near which yttria-bearing minerals are found]

hŏ'locaust *n.* Whole burnt-offering; wholesale sacrifice (fig.) or destruction.

hŏ'lograph (*or* -ahf) *adj.* & *n.* (Document) written wholly by person in whose name it appears (cf. AUTOGRAPH).

hŏlohē'dral *adj.* (of crystal) Having full number of planes required for highest degree of symmetry belonging to its system.

hŏlometă'bolous *adj.* Of insects whose young differ in form from adults, with larval and pupal stages (cf. HEMIMETABOLOUS).

hŏlothūr'ian *adj.* & *n.* (Animal) of the Holothurioidea, a class of echinoderms including sea-cucumber and bêche-de-mer, characterized by elongated form, tough leathery integument, and a ring of tentacles round the mouth.

Hōlst, Gustav Theodore (1874–1934). English musical composer.

Hŏ'lstein (-shtīn). Former Danish duchy; later (after 1866) part of the province of Schleswig-Holstein, Prussia. ~ *n.* (U.S.) = FRIESIAN.

hō'lster *n.* Leather case for pistol, fixed to saddle or worn on belt.

hōlt[1] *n.* (poet.) Wood, copse; wooded hill.

hōlt[2] *n.* Animal's lair, esp. otter's or badger's.

hō'lў *adj.* Consecrated, sacred; morally and spiritually perfect; belonging to, commissioned by, devoted to, God; of high moral excellence; *H~ Alliance*, that formed in 1815, after fall of Napoleon, between Russia, Austria, and Prussia, ostensibly for preserving peace and justice in Europe, but used to suppress revolutionary tendencies and demands for constitutional government; ~ *cross*, cross of Christ; *~-cross day*, festival of exaltation of cross, 14 Sept.; ~ *day*, religious festival; *H~ Family*, infant Christ and the Virgin, attended by sacred personages as St. Joseph, St. John the Baptist, St. Elizabeth, etc., as represented in pictures; *H~ Father*: see FATHER; *H~ Ghost, Spirit*, third person of the Trinity; ~ *grail*: see GRAIL[2]; *H~ Island*: see LINDISFARNE; ~ *Joe*, (naut. slang) clergyman, pious person; *H~ Land*, western region of PALESTINE, esp. Judaea, as scene of life and death of Jesus Christ and of sacred sites, esp. the Holy Sepulchre at Jerusalem; ~ *name*, name of Jesus as object of formal devotion; *H~ Office*, Inquisition; ~ *orders*: see ORDER; *H~ Roman Empire*: see ROMAN; ~ *rood*: see ROOD; *H~ Saturday*, Saturday in Holy Week; ~ *terror*, (slang) formidable person, embarrassing child; *H~ Thursday*, Thursday in Holy Week; (in the Anglican Ch.) Ascension Day; ~ *water*, water dedicated to holy uses and used for ritual purification; water blessed by priest and used in various rites and devotional acts; *H~ Week*, week preceding Easter Sunday; ~ *Willie*, hypocritically pious person; *H~ Writ*: see WRIT. ~ *n.* ~ *of holies*, inner chamber of sanctuary in Jewish temple, separated by veil from outer chamber or holy place; innermost shrine.

hō'lўstōne *n.* & *v.t.* (Scour with) soft sandstone used for scrubbing decks.

hŏ'mage *n.* (in feudal law) Formal and public acknowledgement of allegiance to feudal superior; acknowledgement of superiority, dutiful reverence.

hŏ'mbûrg *n.* (also ~ *hat*) Man's soft felt hat with slightly curved brim and crown indented lengthways. [*Homburg*, town in W. Germany]

hōme[1] *n.* 1. Dwelling-place, fixed residence of family or household; members of family collectively; (U.S. etc.) private house; ~ *from* ~, place providing home-like amenities; *long, last,* ~, the grave. 2. Native land; place where thing is native or most common. 3. Institution of refuge or rest for destitute or infirm persons. 4. (in games) Goal. 5. *at* ~, in one's own house or native land; at one's ease; familiar *with, on, in* (subject etc.); accessible to callers; *at* ~ (*n.*) reception of visitors within time during which hostess or host or both have announced that they will be at home. 6. (football pools) Win in a home match. ~ *adj.* Of, connected with, home; carried on at home; proceeding from home; in the neighbourhood of home; played etc. on team's own ground; carried on, produced, in one's own country, as ~ *trade, markets*; treating of domestic affairs; that comes home to one, as ~ *truth, thrust*; (in games) of, near, home; reaching, enabling player to reach, home; ~ *affairs*, internal affairs of nation; *Scottish H~ and Health Department*, government department under Secretary of State for Scotland, corresponding to Home Office and also administering health services in Scotland; ~-*brewed*, (beer etc.) brewed at home; ~-*coming*, arrival at home; *H~ Counties*, English counties lying round London, esp. Surrey, Kent, Essex, and sometimes Hertford, East Sussex, and West Sussex; ~ *farm*, farm attached to residence of the occupier of an estate; *H~ Guard*, citizen armed force organized in 1940 for the defence of Gt Britain and Northern Ireland against possible invasion, orig. called *Local Defence Volunteers*; ~-*keeping*, stay-at-home; *ho'meland*, native land; (used by Britons abroad, inhabitants of British colonies and dominions etc. for) Great Britain, the mother country; ~-*made*, made at home; *H~ Office*, government department under Home Secretary dealing with such internal affairs of England and Wales as are not assigned to other departments, esp. maintenance of law and order, control of aliens, immigration, etc.; building housing this; *H~ Rule*, government of country, colony, etc. by its own citizens; esp. the movement in British politics, begun *c* 1870 to obtain self-government for Ireland; *H~ Secretary*, Secretary of State for Home Affairs, in charge of the Home Office; *ho'mesick*, depressed by absence from home, longing for home; ~ *signal*, (railw.) signal controlling path of train through particular route etc.; *ho'mespun*, (cloth made of yarn) spun at home; (anything) plain, homely; ~ *stretch*, straight part of racecourse between final bend and finishing line; *ho'mework*, work done at home; esp. lessons and exercises to be done by schoolchild at home. ~ *adv.* To one's home or country, as *come, go,* ~; arrived at home; to the point aimed at, as *the thrust went* ~; to the goal; *bring charge* ~ *to person*, convict him of it; *come* ~ *to*, be realized emotionally by. **hō'melėss, hō'melīke** *adjs.* **hōme** *v.* 1. Go home (esp. of pigeons); (of aircraft etc.) proceed under guidance of radio signal etc. 2. Bring or send home; bring in (aircraft etc.) under guidance of radio signal etc.

Home[2] (hūm), Sir Alec Douglas- (1903–). British Conservative statesman; prime minister 1963–4.

hō'mely (-mlĭ) *adj.* Simple, plain; primitive; unpretending; (of persons or features) uncomely, plain. **hō'melinėss** *n.*

hō'mer[1] *n.* Homing pigeon.

hō'mer[2] *n.* Hebrew measure of capacity, containing 10 ephahs (prob. *c* 80 gal.). [Heb. *k̲ōmer* heap]

Hō'mer[3]. Greek epic poet, of uncertain birthplace and date; reputed author of the 'ILIAD' and the 'ODYSSEY'. **Hōmĕ'rĭc** *adj.* Of, in the style of, Homer or the poems attributed to him; ~ *laughter*, uproarious laughter (like that of Homer's gods as they watched lame Hephaestus hobbling).

hō'mestead (-mstĕd) *n.* House

with outbuildings; farm; (U.S.) lot of land adequate for maintenance of a family, esp. lot of 160 acres granted to settlers by *Homestead Act* of Congress, 1862. ~ *v.* (U.S.) Take up and occupy as homestead. **hō'mesteader** *n.* (U.S.).

hō'meward (-mw-) *adv.* & *adj.* (Going, leading) towards home; ~ *bound*, (esp. of ship) preparing to go, on the way, home. **hō'mewards** (-z) *adv.*

hŏ'micīde *n.* 1. One who kills a human being. 2. Killing of a human being, intentionally or accidentally, with or without justification; *felonious* ~, either MANSLAUGHTER or MURDER; *justifiable* ~, killing of a person where no blame attaches to the killer, as in the performance of a legal duty (e.g. execution of a death sentence); *excusable* ~, killing without criminal intent, as by or in self-defence. **hŏmicī'dal** *adj.* Having a tendency to homicide; murderous.

hŏmĭlĕ'tĭc *adj.* Of homilies. **hŏmĭlĕ'tĭcs** *n.* Art of preaching.

hŏ'mĭlȳ *n.* Sermon; tedious moralizing discourse.

hō'mĭng *adj.* Returning home; ~ *pigeon*: see PIGEON[1].

hŏ'mĭnĭd *n.* & *adj.* (Member) of the human zoological family including existing and fossil man.

hŏ'mĭnȳ *n.* Coarsely ground maize boiled with water or milk.

***Hō'mō*[1].** Genus of primates of the family Hominidae, consisting of mankind now usu. regarded as a single species, ~ *sapiens*. [L *homo* man, *sapiens* wise]

hō'mō[2] *n.* (colloq.) Homosexual.

homo- *prefix.* Same. [Gk *homos*]

hŏmocĕ'ntrĭc *adj.* Having same centre.

hŏ'moeopăth (-mĭo-) *n.* One who practises homoeopathy. **hŏmoeopă'thĭc** *adj.* **hŏmoeopă'thĭcallȳ** *adv.* **hŏmoeŏ'pathȳ** *n.* System (founded *c* 1796 by Hahnemann of Leipzig) of treatment of disease by drugs (usu. in minute doses) that in a healthy person would produce symptoms like those of the disease.

hŏmogĕ'nėous *adj.* Of the same kind; consisting of parts all of the same kind, uniform. **hŏmogē'nėouslȳ** *adv.* **hŏmogėnē'ĭtȳ, hŏmogē'nėousnėss** *ns.*

hŏmogėnĕ'tĭc *adj.* Having common descent or origin. **homŏ'gėnȳ** *n.* Similarity due to common descent.

homŏ'gėnīze *v.t.* Treat (milk) so that fat globules emulsify and cream does not separate.

homŏ'gėnous *adj.* = HOMOGENETIC.

hŏmoiou'sĭan (-ows-) *adj.* & *n.* (One who held that Father and Son in the Godhead were) of like but not identical substance (cf. HOMOOUSIAN).

homŏ'logāte *v.t.* (Sc.) Acknowledge, admit; confirm. **homŏlogā'tion** *n.*

homŏ'logīze *v.* Be homologous, correspond; make homologous.

homŏ'logous *adj.* Having the same relation or relative position; corresponding; (biol., of limb or organ) similar in position and structure but not necessarily in function (cf. ANALOGOUS). **hŏ'molŏgue** (-g) *n.* Homologous thing.

homŏ'logȳ *n.* Correspondence, sameness of relation. **hŏmolŏ'gĭcal** *adj.* **hŏmolŏ'gĭcallȳ** *adv.*

hŏmomor'phĭc, -mor'phous *adjs.* Of same or similar form.

homŏ'nomous *adj.* Having same law of growth.

hŏ'monȳm *n.* Word of same form as another but different sense, as *pale* 'stake' and *pale* 'wan'; namesake. **hŏmonȳ'mĭc, homŏ'nȳmous** *adjs.*

hŏmōou'sĭan, hŏmou'sĭan *adj.* & *n.* (One who held the persons of the Trinity to be) of the same substance (cf. HOMOIOUSIAN).

hŏ'mophōne *n.* 1. Word having same sound as another, but of different meaning or origin, as *sew* and *sow*. 2. Symbol denoting same sound as another. **hŏmophŏ'nĭc** *adj.* (mus.) Of same pitch, in unison; having one part or melody predominating. **homŏ'phonous** *adj.* (of music) In unison; (of symbols) denoting same sound. **homŏ'phonȳ** *n.* Homophonic music or style.

hŏmoplă'stic *adj.* Similar in structure.

hŏmosĕ'xūal *adj.* Relating or belonging to the same sex; sexually attracted only to members of the same sex. ~ *n.* Homosexual person. **hŏmosĕxūă'lĭtȳ** *n.*

hŏmospôr'ous *adj.* (bot.) Having spores of one size only (opp. HETEROSPOROUS).

hŏ'motȳpe *n.* Part, organ, like another in structure.

hŏmozȳ'gōte *n.* Zygote of like gametes. **hŏmozȳ'gous** *adj.*

homŭ'ncūle, homŭ'ncle *n.* Little man, manikin.

hō'mȳ *adj.* Suggesting home, home-like.

Hon. *abbrev.* Honorary; Honourable.

Hōnă'n. Province of central China.

Hŏndūr'as. 1. Republic of Central America with a seaboard on the Caribbean Sea, formerly (until 1821) part of the Spanish American dominions; capital, Tegucigalpa. 2. *British* ~, British Crown Colony in Central America, re-named *Belize*, 1973; capital, Belmopan.

hōne *n.* Whetstone, esp. for razors; any of various stones as material for this. ~ *v.t.* Sharpen on hone.

Honegger (ŏ'nĕgār), Arthur (1892–1955). French composer, of Swiss parentage; author of tone-poems and choral-orchestral works, notable for their novelty of conception.

ho'nėst (ŏn-) *adj.* Fair and upright in speech and act, not lying, cheating, or stealing; sincere; good, worthy; (of act etc.) showing uprightness; (of gain etc.) earned by fair means; (of things) unadulterated, unsophisticated; (archaic, of woman) chaste, virtuous; *make an ~ woman of*, marry (seduced woman); ~ *Injun*: see INJUN. **ho'nėstlȳ** *adv.*

ho'nėstȳ (ŏn-) *n.* 1. Uprightness, truthfulness. 2. Cruciferous plant (*Lunaria annua*) with large purple (or white) flowers and flat round semi-transparent fruits.

ho'ney (hŭ-) *n.* Sweet viscid yellow fluid, nectar of flowers collected and worked up for food by bees and other insects; (fig.) sweetness; (chiefly Ir. & U.S.) sweet one, sweetheart, darling; ~ *badger*, ratel; ~*-bee*, bee that gathers and stores honey, esp. the common hive-bee *Apis mellifera*: ~*-buzzard*, bird of prey (*Pernis*, esp. *P. apivorus*) feeding chiefly on larvae of bees and wasps; ~*-dew*, sweet sticky substance, secreted by aphides, found on leaves and stems; ideally sweet substance; tobacco sweetened with molasses; ~*-eater*, any of various honey-eating birds of Australasia; ~*-guide*, small African or Asiatic bird of the genus *Indicator*, which guides men and animals to nests of bees; *ho'neysuckle*, woodbine (*Lonicera periclymenum*), climbing shrub with fragrant yellowish trumpet-shaped flowers, frequent in woods; other plants of this genus. **ho'neyed** (-nĭd) *adj.*

honeycomb (hŭ'nĭkōm) *n.* 1. Bees' wax structure of hexagonal cells for honey and eggs. 2. Cavernous flaw in metal, esp. of guns. 3. Ornamental or other work hexagonally arranged. 4. Reticulum of ruminant ~ *v.t.* Fill with cavities; under mine; mark with honeycomb pattern.

ho'neymōōn (hŭ-) *n.* Holiday spent together by newly married couple. ~ *v.i.* Spend honeymoon (*in, at*, place).

Hŏng Kŏng. British Crown Colony, consisting of a number of islands and a part of the mainland; situated off the SE. coast of China; first occupied by Great Britain 1841 and formally ceded by Treaty of Nanking 1842; the capital, Victoria, is situated on the island of Hong Kong.

Hŏ'nĭton (*or* hŭn-). Town in Devon; ~ *lace*, type of pillow-lace formerly made there.

hŏnk *n.* Wild goose's cry; sound of motor horn. ~ *v.i.* Emit or give honk.

honorār'ium (ŏn-) *n.* Gift of money in return for voluntary services; payment in lieu of fixed fee for professional services etc.

hŏ'norarў (ŏn-) *adj.* Conferred as an honour (without the usual requirements, functions, etc.); holding honorary title or position; (of obligations) depending on honour, not legally enforceable; ~ *secretary, treasurer*, etc., secretary etc. serving without pay.

honorĭ'fĭc (ŏn-) *adj.* & *n.* (Expression) implying respect (esp. of Oriental forms of speech).

honour (ŏ'ner) *n.* 1. High respect; glory; reputation, good name. 2. Nobleness of mind; allegiance to what is right or to conventional standard of conduct; (of woman) chastity, reputation for this. 3. Exalted position; (with possessive) title for holder of certain offices, esp. County Court judges. 4. Person, thing, that reflects honour on (*to*) another; thing conferred or done as token of respect or distinction; position or title of rank, dignity; (golf) right of driving off first as having won last hole; (pl.) civilities rendered to guests etc.; *last, funeral*, ~*s*, observances of respect at funeral; *military* ~*s*, marks of respect paid by troops at burial of officer, to royalty etc.; ~*s of war*, privileges granted to capitulating force, as that of marching out with colours flying etc. 5. (pl., in whist) Ace, king, queen, and knave of trumps (in bridge the ten also). 6. (pl.) Special distinction for proficiency beyond that required to pass examination; course of higher or more specialized studies than is required for pass degree. 7. *code of* ~, rules forming conventional or personal standard of conduct; *Companion of H*~, (abbrev. C.H.) member of British order, of limited membership, founded in 1917; *in* ~ *of*, in celebration of; *in* ~ *bound*, bound as a moral duty (*to* do); *be on one's* ~, be under moral obligation; *upon my* ~, (colloq.) ~ *bright*, forms of asseveration. ~ *v.t.* Respect highly; confer dignity upon; (commerc.) accept, pay (bill) when due.

ho'nourable (ŏ'ner-) *adj.* 1. Worthy of honour; bringing honour to its possessor; consistent with honour; upright. 2. *H*~, (abbrev. Hon.) title of younger sons of earls and children of viscounts and barons; title of Maids of Honour and Justices of High Court not entitled to a higher title; title of certain other officials, including members of executive councils in certain Commonwealth countries; *Right* ~, title of peers below rank of marquis, Privy Councillors, and others. 3. (parl., in conventional use) Title of members of the House of Commons. **ho'nourablў** *adv.*

hōōch *n.* (slang, orig. U.S.) Alcoholic liquor, spirits, esp. of inferior or harmful kind. [abbrev. of Alaskan *hoochinoo* spirit]

hŏŏd *n.* Covering for head and neck, whether part of cloak etc. or separate; (universities) garment, varying in material, colour, and shape, worn over gown etc. to indicate degree; leather covering for hawk's head; thing like hood in shape or use, esp. waterproof (folding) top or cover of motor-car, perambulator, etc.; (U.S.) bonnet of motor vehicle; *hoo'dmould*, moulding over head of door, window, etc. ~ *v.t.* Cover with hood. **hŏŏ'dėd** *adj.* (esp.) ~ *crow*, grey crow with black head (*Corvus cornix*); ~ *snake*, snake with power of distending elastic skin of neck in shape like hood or cowl; esp. Indian cobra (*Naja tripudians*).

-hŏŏd *suffix.* Having a specified state, condition, or quality.

hōō'dĭe *n.* (also ~*-crow*; Sc.) Hooded crow.

hōō'dlum *n.* (U.S.) Hooligan, thug.

hōō'dōō *n.* (U.S.) Voodoo; malignant spell; person or thing bringing bad luck. ~ *v.t.* Bewitch; bring bad luck to. [Alteration of VOODOO]

hōō'dwĭnk *v.t.* Deceive, humbug; blindfold.

hōō'ey *n.* (U.S. slang) Nonsense, humbug.

hōōf *n.* (pl. *-fs, -ves*). Horny casing of foot of ruminants, horses, swine, and allied animals, anatomically a development of the toe-nail; *cloven* ~; see CLOVEN; ~*-pad*, pad to prevent one foot of horse from striking the other; ~*-pick*, hook for picking stones from horse's hoof. ~ *v.* Strike with hoof; (slang) go on foot; (slang) kick (person) *out* etc.

hŏŏk *n.* Piece of metal or other material bent back or having sharp angle, for catching hold or for

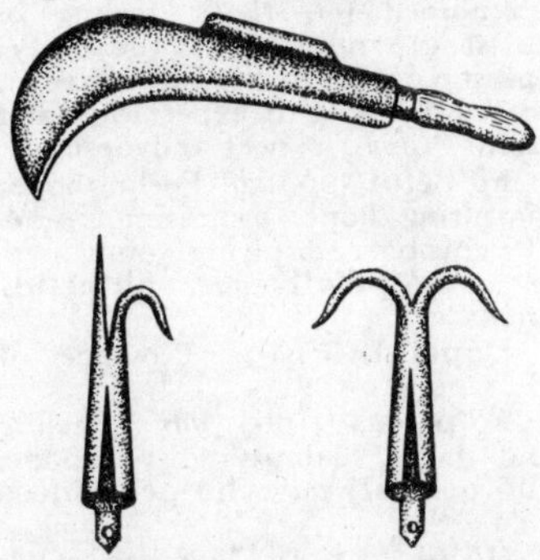

hanging things upon; bent piece of wire, usu. barbed, for catching fish; hooked stroke in cricket or golf; (boxing) short swinging blow with elbow bent and rigid; curved cutting-instrument, esp. *reaping-*~; sharp bend, e.g. in river; projecting point of land; ~ *and eye*, small metal hook and loop as dress fastening; *by* ~ *or by crook*, by fair means or foul; *on one's own* ~, (colloq.) on one's own account; *sling, take, one's* ~, (slang) hook it; ~*-nose(d)*, (having) aquiline nose; *hoo'kworm*, any of various nematode worms infesting man and some beasts, with hooklike ribs or spines in male; disease caused by these. ~ *v.* Grasp with hook; secure with hook(s); attach with hook (*on, in, up*, etc.); catch (fish) with hook; (golf) drive (ball) widely to left or (in the case of a left-handed player) to the right; (cricket) play (ball) round from off to on side without hitting it at the pitch; (Rugby footb.) secure (ball) in scrum with foot; ~ *it*, (slang) make off, run away; ~*-up*, (orig. U.S.) interconnection of broadcasting stations for special transmissions. **hŏŏked** (-kt) *adj.* Hook-shaped; having, made with, hook(s); ~ *on*, (slang) addicted to.

hŏŏ'kah *n.* Oriental tobacco pipe with long flexible tube, smoke being drawn through water in vase to which tube and bowl are attached; narghile. [Arab. *ḥukka* casket, hookah-bottle]

Hŏŏke, Robert (1635–1703). English mathematician; physicist and philosopher; ~*'s law*, (phys.) approximate empirical law of elasticity, which states that the ratio of the stress to the strain is constant.

hŏŏ'ker[1] *n.* (esp., Rugby footb.) Player in front row of scrum who endeavours to secure ball by hooking it.

hŏŏ'ker[2] *n.* Two-masted Dutch coasting or fishing vessel; one-masted fishing smack like hoy on Irish and SW. English coasts.

Hōō'lee, Hō'li (-lē) *n.* (also *h*~) Great Hindu festival or carnival in honour of Krishna and the Gopīs or milkmaids, near vernal equinox.

hōō'lĭgan *n.* Young rowdy; member of street gang. **hōō'lĭganism** *n.*

hōōp[1] *n.* Circular band of metal, wood, etc., esp. for binding staves of casks; wooden or iron circle trundled along by child; circle of flexible elastic material for expanding woman's skirt; hoop petticoat; circle, ring, arc; one of iron arches through which balls must be driven in croquet; ~ *petticoat*, petticoat expanded by hoops. ~ *v.t.* Bind with hoops; surround as hoop does.

hōōp[2] *v.i.* & *n.* Whoop.

hōō'p-la (-ah) *n.* Game at fairs etc. in which prizes may be won by encircling objects on a board with rings thrown from some distance.

hōō'poe (-pōō) *n.* Bird, esp. S. European *Upupa epops*, with conspicuous variegated plumage and large erectile crest.

hooray: see HURRAH.

hōō'segow (-sg-) *n.* (U.S. slang) Prison. [Span. Amer. *juzgao* tribunal, f. L *judicatum* judged]

hōōsh *n.* (slang) Kind of thick soup, esp. in Arctic travel.

hōōt[1] *v.* Make loud sounds, esp. of disapproval (*at*); assail (person etc.) with derisive shouts; drive (person) *out, away*, etc., by hooting; (of owl) utter characteristic cry; sound motor horn, train-whistle, etc.; (of horn etc.) sound. ~ *n.* Inarticulate shout, esp. of derision or disapprobation; owl's cry; *don't care a* ~, (slang) don't care at all; *not worth a* ~, worthless.

hōōt[2], **hōōts** *int.* (Sc. & north.) Exclamation of dissatisfaction or impatience.

hōō'ter *n.* (esp.) Siren, steam whistle, esp. as signal for work to begin or cease.

hōōve *n.* Disease of cattle, with inflation of stomach, usu. caused by green fodder.

hōō'ver[1] *n.* Kind of vacuum cleaner. ~ *v.* Clean with vacuum cleaner. [trade-name]

Hōō'ver[2], Herbert Clark (1874–1964). Amer. mining engineer, 31st president of U.S., 1929–33.

hŏp[1] *n.* Ripened cones of female hop-plant, used for giving bitter flavour to malt liquors, and as tonic and soporific (usu. pl.); climbing perennial plant (*Humulus lupulus*) with rough lobed leaves, cultivated for green cones of broad scales borne by female; *~-bind, -bine,* climbing stem of hop; *~-garden,* field for cultivation of hops; *~-picker,* labourer, machine, employed to pick hops; *~-pillow,* pillow stuffed with hops to produce sleep; *~-pocket*: see POCKET, 1; *~-pole,* pole on which hop-plant is trained. ~ *v.* Flavour with, bear, hops; gather hops.

hŏp[2] *v.* Spring (of person) on one foot, (of birds and animals) with both or all feet at once; hop over (ditch etc.); (of aircraft) pass low over physical features in a series of movements resembling hops, hence, *cloud-, hedge-, wave-hopping*; (U.S.) jump on to (train etc.); ~ *it,* ~ *off* etc., (slang) go away; *~-o'-my-thumb,* dwarf, pygmy; *ho'pscotch,* child's game of hopping on one foot and with it pushing flat stone etc. over scotches marked on ground. ~ *n.* Hopping; spring; (colloq.) dance; distance traversed in aircraft at one stretch, one stage of long-distance flight; ~, *skip* (or *step*), *and jump,* exercise consisting of these three movements in sequence; (fig.) short distance.

hōpe *n.* Expectation and desire combined (*of, that*); feeling of trust; ground of hope, probability; person, thing, that hope centres in. ~ *v.* Look with expectation and desire (*for*); expect and desire.

hō'peful(-pf-) *adj.* Feeling hope; inspiring hope, promising. ~ *n.* Promising or aspiring young person. **hō'pefullў** *adv.* **hō'pefulnėss** *n.*

Hopei (hēr'bā'). Province of E. China.

hō'peless (-pl-) *adj.* Feeling no hope; admitting no hope. **hō'pelėsslў** *adv.* **hō'pelėssnėss** *n.*

Hō'pi (-ē) *n.* (Member of) a Pueblo Indian tribe of N. Arizona; language of this tribe.

Hŏ'pkĭns[1] (-z), Gerard Manley (1844–89). English poet and Jesuit priest; inventor of sprung rhythm.

Hŏ'pkĭns[2] (-z), John (d. 1570). See STERNHOLD.

hŏ'plīte *n.* Heavy-armed foot-soldier of ancient Greece.

hŏ'pper[1] *n.* 1. One who hops; hopping insect, esp. flea or cheese maggot; young locust at wingless stage. 2. Inverted pyramid or cone (orig. with hopping or shaking motion) through which grain etc. passes in mill; similar contrivance in various machines etc.; barge carrying away mud etc. from dredging machine and discharging it through collapsible bottom; railway truck with similar device.

hŏ'pper[2] *n.* Hop-picker.

hŏ'pple *v.t.* Hobble (horse etc.). ~ *n.* Apparatus for hoppling.

Hŏ'ppus (cū'bĭc) fōōt. Unit of volume measurement based on the square of the quarter-girth, used in British Commonwealth forestry for the cubic content of round logs or trees. [E. *Hoppus* (d. *c* 1758), surveyor]

hŏ′psăck *n*. (Coarse material of hemp and jute for making) sack in which hops are packed; woollen dress-fabric of coarse weave with threads in pairs.

Hŏ′race. Quintus Horatius Flaccus (65–8 B.C.), Latin poet; his work includes the 'Satires', 'Odes', 'Epodes', 'Epistles', and 'Ars Poetica'. **Horā′tian** (-sh*a*n) *adj*.

hŏr′arӯ *adj*. Of the hours; occurring every hour.

Horā′tius (-sh*us*). Publius Horatius Cocles, legendary Roman hero famous for defending bridge over Tiber against the Etruscans.

hŏrde *n*. Tribe of Tatar or kindred Asiatic nomads, dwelling in tents or wagons and migrating for pasturage or for war or plunder; gang, troop (usu. contempt.); *Golden H~*: see GOLDEN. [Turki *ordi*, *ordu* camp]

hor′ehound (hŏrh-), **hoar-** *n*. Labiate herb (*Marrubium vulgare*) with stem and leaves covered with white cottony pubescence, and aromatic bitter juice used as remedy for coughs etc.; allied herb.

horī′zon *n*. 1. Line at which earth and sky appear to meet; (fig.) limit of mental perception, experience, interest, etc.; *apparent*, *sensible*, *visible*, ~, circle of contact with earth's surface of a cone whose vertex is the observer's eye; *celestial*, *rational*, *true*, ~, great circle of celestial sphere, plane of which passes through centre of earth and is parallel to that of sensible horizon of a plane. 2. (geol.) Stratum or set of strata characterized by particular features, as fossils etc. 3. *soil* ~, layer of soil with distinctive characteristics.

hŏrizŏ′ntal *adj*. Of, at, the horizon; parallel to the plane of this, at right angles to the vertical; level, flat; (of machinery etc.) having its parts working in horizontal direction; ~ *combine*, *trust*, combine of concerns engaged in the same stage of manufacture or distribution of a product (opp. VERTICAL *combine*, *trust*). **hŏrizŏ′ntallӯ** *adv*. **hŏrizŏ′ntal** *n*. Horizontal line, bar, etc.

hŏr′mōne *n*. (physiol.) Substance secreted by a ductless gland or formed in an organ (as insulin in the pancreas, sex hormones in testis and ovary) and carried by the blood stream to a specific organ which it stimulates; similar substance prepared synthetically. **hŏrmŏ′nĭc** *adj*.

Hormuz: see ORMUZ.

hŏrn[1] *n*. 1. Non-deciduous outgrowth, freq. one of a pair, often curved and pointed, consisting of epidermal sheath about a bony core, on head of cattle, sheep, goats, and other mammals; projection on head of other animals, e.g. tentacle of snail or slug, crest of feathers on horned owl's head etc.; *draw in one's ~s*, restrain one's ardour, draw back. 2. Substance of which horns consist, article made of this, as shoe-horn, powder-flask, drinking-horn; ~ *of plenty*, cornucopia. 3. Wind instrument orig. made of horn and more or less resembling horn in shape; (esp.) modern brass instrument (also *French* ~), which has an 11-ft tube coiled in a circle and a system of valves for producing intermediate notes, is pitched usu. in F and has a compass of *c* 3½ octaves; *basset-* ~: see BASSET-HORN; *English* ~: see COR ANGLAIS. 4. Funnel- or trumpet-shaped part of gramophone etc. for amplifying sound by resonance. 5. Instrument for sounding warning signal. 6. Horn-shaped projection; extremity of moon or other crescent; arm, branch, of bay, river, etc.; either alternative of a dilemma. 7. *hor′nbeam*, small tough-wooded European tree (*Carpinus betulus*) used in hedges etc.; related Amer. species (*C. americana*); *hor′nbill*, bird (of family Bucerotidae) with hornlike excrescence on bill; *hor′nbook*, (hist.) leaf of paper containing alphabet etc. mounted on wooden tablet with handle and protected by thin plate of horn; ~*-rimmed*, (of spectacles) rimmed with horn or tortoiseshell; *hor′nstone*, chert. ~ *v*. Furnish with horns; gore with the horns; adjust (frame of ship) at right angles to line of keel; ~ *in*, (slang) intrude (*on*); *horned frog, toad*, (U.S.) lizard (*Phrynosoma*) with head and back covered with spikes; *horned* OWL, POPPY: see these words.

Hor̂n², Cape. Southernmost point of America, on an island of the Fuegian archipelago; discovered by the Dutch navigator Schouten in 1616, and named after Hoorn, his birthplace.

hor̂'nblĕnde *n*. Dark-brown, black, or greenish-black mineral, constituent of granite and many rocks, composed chiefly of silica, magnesia, and lime, and occurring in numerous varieties.

hor̂'ner *n*. Maker of horn spoons, combs, etc.; one who blows a horn.

hor̂'nėt *n*. Large insect of wasp family (esp. Eur. *Vespa crabro* and

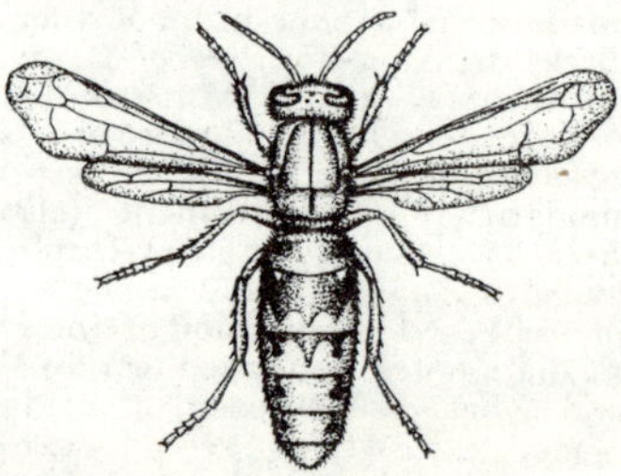

Amer. *V. maculata*), inflicting serious sting.

hor̂'npīpe *n*. 1. (hist.) Wind instrument (said to have had bell and mouthpiece of horn). 2. Lively dance, usu. by single person, associated esp. with merrymaking of sailors; music for this.

hor̂'ny̆ *adj*. Of, like, horn; abounding in horns; hard as horn, callous. **hor̂'ninėss** *n*.

hŏ'rolŏge (-j) *n*. Timepiece, dial, clock. **horŏ'loger, horŏ'logist** *ns*. **horŏ'logy̆** *n*. Art of measuring time or making clocks. **hŏrolŏ'gical** *adj*.

horŏ'pter *n*. Aggregate of all the points that are seen single in binocular vision in any given position of the eyes.

hŏ'roscōpe *n*. 1. (astrol.) Observation of sky and planets at certain moments, esp. at person's birth, supposed to reveal influence on destiny; zodiacal plan showing disposition of heavens at particular moment. 2. Prediction based on such observation or plan. **hŏroscŏ'pĭc, -ĭcal** *adjs*. **horŏ'scopy̆** *n*.

hŏrrent *adj*. (poet.) Bristling.

hŏ'rrĭble *adj*. Exciting, fit to excite, horror; hideous, shocking; (colloq.) excessive, unpleasant. **hŏ'rrĭblenėss** *n*. **hŏ'rrĭbly̆** *adv*.

hŏ'rrĭd *adj*. Terrible, frightful; (poet., archaic) rough, bristling; (colloq.) unpleasant, very bad, objectionable. **hŏ'rrĭdly̆** *adv*. **hŏ'rrĭdnėss** *n*.

hŏ'rrĭfy̆ *v.t.* Excite horror in; shock; scandalize. **horrĭ'fĭc** *adj*. **horrĭ'fĭcally̆** *adv*.

hŏ'rror *n*. Terrified shuddering; intense dislike (*of*); (med.) shuddering, as symptom of disease; horrifying thing; *the ~s*, fit of horror or depression, esp. as in delirium tremens; *Chamber of Horrors*, place full of horrible sights (orig. room of criminals etc. in Tussaud's waxwork exhibition); *~-struck, -stricken*, shocked, horrified.

hors (or̂). Outside, as ~ *concours* (kŏnkoor), (of exhibit etc.) not competing for prize; hence, without a rival, unequalled; ~ *de combat* (kawṅbah), out of the fight, disabled; *~-d'œuvre* (der̂vr) (pl. usu. *-s*), extra dish served as relish at beginning of meal. [Fr.]

Hor̂'sa: see HENGIST.

hor̂se *n*. 1. Solid-hoofed quadruped (*Equus cabullus*) with flowing mane and tail, used as beast of burden and draught, and for riding on; (esp.) adult male horse, stallion or gelding; (collect. sing.) cavalry; *on one's high ~*, putting on airs; behaving arrogantly; *on horseback*, mounted on a horse; *straight from the ~'s mouth*, (of information) from authoritative source, esp. from person concerned 2. Vaulting-block in gymnasium (also *vaulting ~*); frame, often with legs, on which something is supported, as *clothes-~*; (naut.) rope, bar, in various uses, esp. for supporting or guiding; (mining) obstruction in

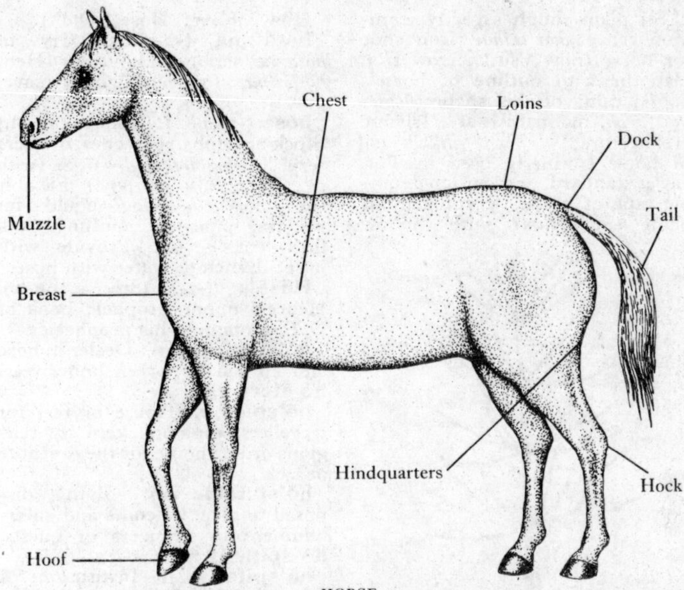

HORSE

vein. 3. ~ *bean*, variety of broad bean grown for fodder; ~*-block*, small platform of stone or wood for mounting horse; ~*-box*, closed vehicle for transporting horse; ~*-breaker*, one who breaks in horses; ~*-chestnut*, large ornamental tree (*Aesculus hippocastanum*), native of Albania, Greece, and Iran, introduced into England *c* 1576, with large digitate leaves, upright conical clusters of showy flowers, and fruit consisting of soft thick prickly husk enclosing one or two large hard smooth shining brown seeds of coarse bitter taste; fruit of this; ~*-cloth*, cloth used to cover horse, or as part of trappings; ~*-coper*: see COPER; ~*-flesh*, flesh of horse, esp. as food; horses collectively; ~*-fly*, insect (of various kinds) troublesome to horses; *H~ Guards*, cavalry brigade of British Household troops, i.e. Life Guards and Royal Horse Guards; (esp.) Royal Horse Guards (the Blues), now an armoured-car regiment providing a mounted squadron for ceremonial purposes; headquarters of such troops, esp. building in Whitehall, London; *hor'sehair*, hair from mane or tail of horse, esp. as used in upholstery; ~ *latitudes*, belt of calms at N. and S. edges of tradewinds; ~ *-laugh*, loud coarse laugh; ~ *-leech*, large leech (*Haemopsis sanguisuga*); insatiable person; *daughters of the ~-leech*: see Prov. 30: 15; ~*-mackerel*, any of various fishes allied to mackerel, esp. the scad (*Trachurus*); *hor'seman*, *hor'sewoman*, (skilled) rider on horseback; *hor'semanship*, art of riding, skill in riding, on horseback; ~*-mushroom*, coarse but edible mushroom with hollow stem; *hor'seplay*, rough or boisterous play; ~*-pond*, pond for watering and washing horses; *hor'sepower*, (abbrev. h.p.) unit formerly used for measuring power (0·746 kW or 746 Js^{-1}); ~*-race*, race between horses (with riders); ~*-radish*, cruciferous plant (*Cochlearia armoracia*) with white flowers and broad rough leaves, whose pungent root is scraped or grated as condiment; ~*-sense*, (colloq., orig.

U.S.) plain rough sagacity, common sense; *hor'seshoe,* iron shoe for horse (now usu. narrow iron plate bent to outline of horse's hoof); thing of this shape (*horseshoe arch,* in Spanish and Islamic architecture; *hor'setail,* tail of horse (formerly used in Turkey as standard, or as ensign denoting rank of pasha); cryptogamous plant (*Equisetum*) with hollow

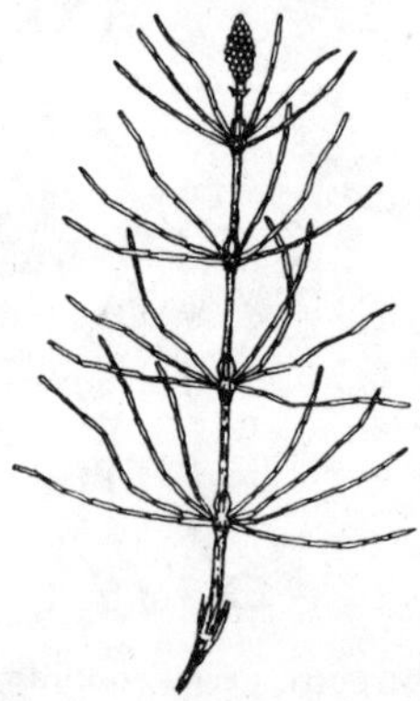

jointed stem and whorls of slender branches at joints; *hor'sewhip,* whip for horse; (*v.t.*) chastise (person) with this; *horsewoman*: see *horseman* above. ~ *v.t.* Provide (person, vehicle) with horse(s); carry (person) on one's back. **hor'selėss** *adj.*

hor'sey, hor'sy̆ *adj.* Concerned with, addicted to, horses or horse-racing; affecting dress and language of groom or jockey. **hor'sily̆** *adv.* **hor'sinėss** *n.*

horst *n.* (geol.) Long ridge of land, often forming a range of hills, between two parallel faults which slope away from each other.

hor'tative, hor'tatory̆ *adjs.* Tending, serving, to exhort.

hor'ticŭlture *n.* Art of garden cultivation. **horticŭ'ltural** (-cher-) *adj.* **horticŭ'lturist** *n.*

hor'tus sĭ'ccus Arranged collection of dried plants. [L, = 'dry garden']

Hor'us. (Egyptian myth.) God of light, represented with hawk's head.

Hos. *abbrev.* Hosea (O.T.).

hōsă'nna (-z-) *n.* Cry of *hosanna,* shout of adoration. [Heb. *hoshaʿna,* for *hoshiʿahnna* save, pray!]

hōse (-z) *n.* 1. (collect. as pl.) Stockings; (obs.) breeches, drawers (esp. in *doublet and*~). 2. (with pl. *hoses;* also ~*-pipe*) Flexible tube for conveying liquid for watering plants, putting out fires, etc. ~ *v.t.* Provide with hose; drench or water with hose.

Hōsē'a (-z-) (8th c. B.C.). Hebrew minor prophet; book of O.T. containing his prophecies.

hō'sier (-zher) *n.* Dealer in hose and knitted or woven underwear. **hō'siery̆** *n.*

hŏ'spice *n.* House of rest for travellers, esp. one kept by religious order; home for the destitute or sick.

hŏ'spitable *adj.* Giving, disposed to give, welcome and entertainment to strangers or guests. **hŏ'spitably̆** *adv.*

hŏ'spital *n.* 1. Institution for care of the sick or wounded; ~ *ship, train,* one equipped for transporting the sick or wounded. 2. Charitable institution (obs. exc. in legal use and as proper name, e.g. in *Greenwich* ~, orig. a home for superannuated seamen, CHRIST's *H*~, for education of young); (hist.) hospice, esp. establishment of Knights Hospitallers.

hŏspită'lity̆ *n.* Friendly and liberal reception of guests or strangers.

hŏ'spitalīze *v.t.* Admit (sick person, wounded soldier) to hospital.

hŏ'spitaller *n.* Member of charitable religious order; (in some London hospitals, orig. religious foundations) chaplain; (*Knights*) *Hospitallers,* Order of St. John of Jerusalem (also called *Knights of Rhodes* or *Knights of Malta*), a military religious order founded 1099, which provided a hostel for pilgrims at Jerusalem, defended Acre, took Rhodes and held it for 200 years, and was given the island of Malta by the emperor Charles V in 1530 and governed it until 1798; the order still maintains numerous hospitals in Italy and elsewhere and is connected with the R.C. Church; in Gt Britain, where it is not so connected, it controls the St. John Ambulance Association and Brigade.

hōst[1] *n.* Large number (*of*); (archaic) army: *Lord* (*God*) *of* ~*s*, frequent title of Jehovah in some O.T. books.

hōst[2] *n.* One who lodges and entertains another in his house; landlord of inn; (biol.) animal, plant, having parasite or commensal.

hōst[3] *n.* Bread consecrated in the Eucharist.

hŏ'stage *n.* Person handed over to enemies or allies as pledge for fulfilment of any undertaking or one seized by enemy to induce compliance with demands; pledge, security.

hŏ'stel *n.* Inn (archaic); house of residence for students or other special class, YOUTH hostel.

hŏ'stelrў *n.* (archaic) Inn.

hō'stėss *n.* Woman who entertains guests; woman who receives or assists clients or visitors.

hŏ'stīle *adj.* Of an enemy; unfriendly; opposed; ~ *witness*, one who shows that he is hostile to the party calling him and does not give his evidence fairly. **hŏ'stīlelў** *adv.* **hŏstĭ'lĭtў** *n.* Enmity; state of warfare; opposition; (pl.) acts of warfare.

ho'stler (ŏsl-) *n.* = OSTLER.

hŏt *adj.* 1. Of a high temperature; very warm; communicating or feeling heat; producing the sensation of heat; (of pepper etc.) pungent, biting. 2. Ardent, passionate; angry; excited; exciting; (of dance music) performed with vigour, virtuosity, and excitement. 3. (hunting, of scent) Strong; (fig., of news etc.) fresh, recent; (slang, of stolen jewellery, bank-notes, etc.) easily identifiable and so dangerous to possess. 4. ~ *air*, (slang) excited or boastful talk; *ho'tbed*, bed of earth heated by fermenting manure; (fig.) place very favourable to growth *of* (vice etc.); ~ *blast*, blast of heated air forced into furnace; ~-*blooded*, (fig.) ardent, passionate; ~-*brained*, -*headed*, excitable; ~ *dog*, (orig. U.S. colloq.) hot sausage sandwiched in roll of bread; ~-*foot*, in hot haste; ~-*gospeller*, revivalist preacher; *ho'thead*, impetuous person; *ho'thouse*, heated building with glass roof and sides for growing plants out of season or in colder climate; ~ *line*, permanently open telephone line; ~-*plate*, heated metal plate, portable heater, for cooking etc.; *ho'tpot*, mutton, beef, with potatoes etc., cooked in oven in tight-lidded pot; ~-*press*, press of glazed boards and hot metal plates for smoothing paper or cloth; (*v.t.*) press (paper etc.) in this; ~-*short*, (of iron) brittle in its hot state; ~ *water*, (fig.) trouble, disgrace, scrape; ~-*water bottle*, bag (usu. rubber) for holding hot water to apply warmth esp. to the body; ~ *well*, spring of naturally hot water; reservoir in condensing steam-engine. **hŏ'tlў** *adv.* **hŏ'tnėss** *n.* **hŏt** *adv.* Hotly, eagerly, angrily. ~ *v.t.* (vulg.) Heat, warm *up*.

hŏ'tchpŏtch, -pŏt *n.* 1. Dish of many mixed ingredients, esp. mutton broth with vegetables. 2. (law) Blending of properties for purpose of securing equal division (esp. of property of intestate parent). 3. Mixture, medley.

hōtĕ'l (*or* ō-) *n.* House providing lodging, food, etc., for payment (also *private* ~); (esp. large) inn (now the usual sense).

Hŏ'ttentŏt *n.* Member of a short stocky people of SW. Africa, related to Bushmen; their language; (fig.) person of inferior intellect or culture; ~ *bread*, S. Afr. plant, *Testudinaria elephantipes*, with large corky base; ~ *fig*, fleshy-leaved plant, *Mesembryanthemum edule*, with edible pulpy fruit. [Du., perh. = 'stammerer']

hough (hŏk) *n.* = HOCK[1]. ~ *v.t.* Hamstring.

hound *n.* Dog for chase, esp. one hunting by scent, of various breeds, as *blood-*, *fox-*, *grey-*, *otter-*, *wolf-*~; player who follows scent in hare and hounds; despicable man; *the* ~*s*, pack of foxhounds; ~'s *tongue*, CYNOGLOSSUM; ~'*s-tooth check*, DOG's-tooth check. ~ *v.t.* Chase (as) with hound; set (hound, person) *at* (quarry etc.); urge (person) *on*.

hou'ppelānde (hōōpl-) *n.* (hist., 14th–15th c.) Man's or woman's garment, close-fitting above with sleeves and skirt very full.

hour (owr) *n.* 1. 24th part of day, 60 minutes; short time; appointed time, occasion; (pl.) time of occupation or duty; time of day; habitual time of getting up or going to bed; *small ~s*, early hours after midnight. 2. (R.C.Ch.) (Prayer or office to be said at) one of seven stated times of day (*canonical ~s*): in Western Church Mattins and Lauds, Prime, Terce, Sext, None, Vespers, and Compline. 3. (astron., geog.) Angular measure of right ascension or longitude, 24th part of great circle of sphere, 15 degrees; *~-circle*, great circle of celestial sphere passing through poles; graduated circle on equatorial telescope parallel to plane of equator, for observing hour-angle of star. 4. *hour'glass*, sandglass running for one hour ; ~ *hand*,

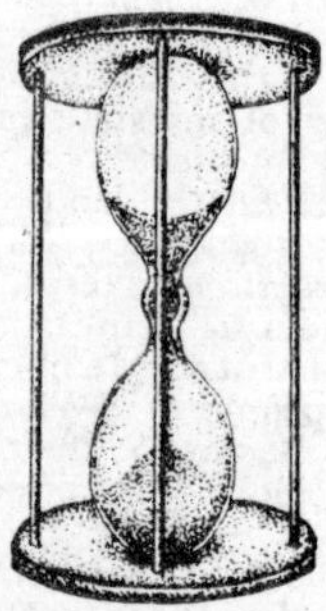

hand on clock etc. showing hour.

houri (hoor'ĭ) *n.* Nymph of Muslim paradise; voluptuously beautiful woman. [Fr., f. Pers., f. Arab. *ḥūr* gazelle-like (in the eyes)]

hour'lȳ (owr-) *adj.* & *adv.* (Occurring, done, reckoned) every hour.

house *n.* (pl. pr. -zĭz). 1. Building for human habitation or (usu. with defining prefix) occupation; inn, tavern; building for keeping animals or goods; (place of abode of) religious fraternity; college in university; (boys in) boarding-house forming part of school; (building used by) legislative or deliberative assembly; (audience in) theatre, cinema, etc.; performance at particular time in theatre, cinema, etc., as *first*, *second* ~; household; family, dynasty; mercantile firm; team of doctors resident in hospital; *the House*, (pol.) House of Commons or Lords; (colloq.) Stock Exchange; (Oxford Univ.) Christ Church. 2. (transf.) Habitation of any animal; shell of snail, tortoise, etc., in which the animal lives or into which it retires. 3. (astrol.) 12th part of heavens as divided by great circles through north and south points of horizon; sign of zodiac considered as seat of greatest influence of a particular planet. 4. (usu. *housey-housey*) Form of lotto played in Army as gambling game, with special cards and checks. 5. *keep* ~, maintain, manage affairs of, a household; *keep, make, a* ~, ensure that enough members attend the House of Commons to form a quorum or support the chosen speakers of a party; *keep the* ~, not go outdoors; *like a* ~ *on fire*, vigorously, fast; ~ *of call*, house where carriers call for commissions, where person may be heard of, etc.; ~ *of cards*, house built of playing-cards; (fig.) insecure thing; ~ *of God*, church, place of worship; ~ *of ill fame*, brothel; ~ *and home*, (emphat.) home; *~-to-house*, carried on from house to house. 6. *attrib.* (of animals) Kept in, frequenting, infesting, the house. 7. *~-agent*, agent for sale and letting of houses; ~ *arrest*, detention in one's house in protective custody; *hou'seboat*, boat fitted up for living in; *hou'sebreaker*, burglar; man employed in demolishing old houses; *hou'sebreaking*, burglary; *~-broken*, (U.S.) house-trained; *hou'secoat*, woman's garment worn indoors as dressing-gown or instead of a dress; *~-dog*, dog kept to guard house; ~*-flag*, firm's flag flown by ship; ~*-fly*, common fly, *Musca domestica*, infesting houses; *hou'sekeeper*, woman managing affairs of household; person in charge of house, office, etc.; *hou'sekeeping*, domestic economy; *hou'seleek*, succulent herb (*Sempervivum tectorum*) with pink flowers, thick stem, and dense rosette of leaves close to root, growing on walls and roofs; *hou'semaid*, female servant in charge of reception and bedrooms; *hou'semaid's knee*, inflammation of the bursa over the knee-cap due to kneeling; *hou'seman*, ~ *officer*, house physician, house surgeon; ~*-martin*: see MARTIN[1]; *hou'semaster*, master in charge of school boarding-house; *H~ of Keys*, representative branch (of 24 members) of Manx legislature; ~ *officer*: see *houseman*; ~*-parlourmaid*, servant combining duties of housemaid and parlourmaid; ~ *party*, party of guests staying at country house; ~ *physician*, physician residing in hospital; ~*-place*, living-room in farmhouse etc.; ~*-proud*, preoccupied with care etc. of home; ~*-room*, accommodation in house; ~ *surgeon*, surgeon residing in hospital; ~*-top*, (esp. in *proclaim from the ~-tops*, give wide publicity to); ~*-trained*, (of domestic animals) trained to be clean in the house; ~*-warming*, celebration of entrance into new house; *hou'sework*, domestic work. ~ (-z) *v.* 1. Receive (person etc.), store (goods), in house or as house does. 2. (naut.) Place (gun etc.) in secure position, lower (upper masts). 3. Take shelter (as) in house. 4. Provide houses for (population).

hou'sehōld (-s-h-) *n.* Inmates of house; domestic establishment; spec., the royal or imperial household; (pl.) second quality of flour; ~ *gods*, (Rom. antiq.) Lares and Penates; (fig.) essentials of home life; ~ *troops*, troops employed to guard sovereign's person (in Gt Britain, 1st and 2nd Life Guards, Royal Horse Guards, and Grenadier, Coldstream, and Scots Guards); ~ *word*, familiar saying or name. **hou'sehōlder** *n.* One who occupies house as his own dwelling (esp. formerly, one thus qualified for franchise); head of household.

housewife *n.* 1. (how'swīf, pl. -*wīves*). Mistress of family; domestic economist. 2. (hŭ'zĭf) Case for needles, thread, etc. **hou'sewīfelў** *adj.* **hou'sewīferў** *n.* Domestic economy.

hou'sey-hou'sey *n.* (mil. slang) = HOUSE *n.* 4.

hou'sĭng[1] (-z-) *n.* (esp.) (Provision of) accommodation, houses collectively; shelter, covering; socket, casing; ~ *estate*, residential district planned as a unit.

hou'sĭng[2] (-z-) *n.* Horse's cloth covering for protection or ornament.

Hou'sman (-z-), Alfred Edward (1859–1936). English classical scholar and lyric poet; author of 'A Shropshire Lad' etc.

Houyhnhnm (hwĭ'nĭm) *n.* One of the talking horses in 'Gulliver's Travels' by Jonathan Swift. [imit. of horse's neigh]

Hō'va *n.* Member, language, of former dominant people of Madagascar.

hove: see HEAVE.

hŏ'vel (*or* hŭ-) *n.* Open shed, outhouse; mean dwelling; conical building enclosing kiln.

hŏ'veller (*or* hŭ-) *n.* Unlicensed pilot or boatman, esp. one who goes out to wrecks.

hŏ'ver (*or* hŭ-) *v.* (of bird etc.) Hang in the air (*over*, *about*, spot); loiter *about* (person, place); ~*-fly*, fly of family Syrphidae which hovers with rapidly beating wings. ~ *n.* Hovering, state of suspense.

hŏ'vercraft (-ahft) *n.* Vehicle that travels over land or water on a cushion of compressed air provided by a downward blast.

how *adv.* In what way; to what extent; (in indirect statement, rhet. for) that; (in relative clause) in whatever way, as; ~ *are you?*, ~ *do you do?*, what is your state of health? (freq. as form of greeting); ~*-d'ye'-do*, (colloq.) embarrassing situation; ~ *now?*, what is the meaning of this?; ~*'s that?*, (cricket, formula addressed to umpire)

HOVERCRAFT

is he out or not out?; *howbē'it,* (archaic) nevertheless; *howe'ver,* in whatever way; to whatever extent; nevertheless; (archaic) in any case; *howsoever, how — soever,* in whatsoever manner; to what extent soever.

How'ard, Catherine (*c* 1520–42). 5th wife of Henry VIII.

how'dah *n.* Seat for two or more, usu. with canopy, on elephant's back. [Arab. *hawdaj* litter]

how'itzer *n.* Short gun for high-angle firing of shells at low velocities. [Ger. *haubitze,* f. Czech *houfnice* catapult]

howl *v.* (of animals) Utter long loud doleful cry; (of persons) utter long cry of pain, derision, etc.; utter (words) with howling; (of radio receiver) make howl. ~ *n.* Long doleful cry of dog, wolf, etc.; loud cry of pain; yell of derision; loud noise like animal's howl in radio receiver, usu. due to low-frequency oscillation.

how'ler *n.* (esp.) 1. S. Amer. monkey of genus *Alouattà.* 2. (slang) Glaring blunder.

how'lĕt *n.* (dial.) Owl.

how'lĭng *adj.* That howls; (bibl., of wilderness) filled with howling, as of wild beasts or wind; (freq. merely) dreary; (slang) glaring.

hoy[1] *n.* Small vessel, usu. rigged as sloop, carrying passengers and goods esp. for short distances.

hoy[2] *int.* Exclamation used to call attention, drive beasts etc., and (naut.) hail or call aloft.

hoy'den *n.* Boisterous girl. **hoy'denish** *adj.* **hoy'denĭsm** *n.*

h.p. *abbrev.* Half-pay; high pressure; hire-purchase; horse-power.

H.Q. *abbrev.* Headquarters.

hr *abbrev.* Hour.

H.R.H. *abbrev.* His (*or* Her) Royal Highness.

hrs *abbrev.* Hours.

H.S.E. *abbrev.* *Hic sepultus est* (L, = here is buried).

H.S.H. *abbrev.* His (*or* Her) Serene Highness.

h.t. *abbrev.* High tension.

ht wt *abbrev.* Hit wicket.

huanaco: see GUANACO.

hŭb *n.* Central part of wheel, rotating on or with axle, and from which spokes radiate; nave; (fig.) centre of interest etc.

hŭ'bble-bŭbble *n.* Form of hookah; bubbling noise; confused talk.

hŭ'bbub *n.* Confused din; tumult.

hŭ'bbȳ *n.* (colloq.) Husband.

hū'bris *n.* Overweening pride and insolence. **hūbrĭ'stĭc** *adj.* [Gk]

hŭ'ckabăck *n.* Stout linen or

cotton fabric with figured weave and rough surface, for towels etc.

hŭ'ckle *n.* Hip; haunch; ~-*back*(*ed*), hump-back(ed); ~-*bone*, hip-, haunch-, bone; knuckle-bone of quadruped.

hŭ'ckleberry̆ (-klb-) *n.* (Fruit of) common N. Amer. species of genus *Gaylussacia* of low berry-bearing shrubs.

hŭ'ckster *n.* Pedlar, hawker; mercenary person. ~ *v.* Bargain, haggle; carry on petty traffic in; adulterate. **hŭ'cksterer** *n.*

hŭ'ddle *v.* Heap together confusedly or hurriedly; crowd (things etc.) promiscuously *together*, *up*, *into*, etc.; coil *oneself up*; nestle closely *together*. ~ *n.* Confused mass; confusion, bustle; (orig. U.S. slang) consultation, discussion; *go into a* ~, confer.

Hūdibră'stic *adj.* In the metre or manner of Samuel Butler's mock-heroic satirical poem 'Hudibras' (1663–78).

Hŭ'dson, Henry (d. 1611). English navigator; discoverer of Hudson River and Hudson Bay, Canada; ~*'s Bay Company*, joint-stock company, chartered in 1670 by Charles II and given territory and exclusive trade rights in Canada; most of its territory was transferred to the Dominion of Canada in 1869.

hūe[1] *n.* Colour, tint; variety of colour caused by admixture of another. **hued** (hūd) *adj.*

hūe[2] *n.* ~ *and cry*, clamour of pursuit or assault; outcry (*against*); proclamation for capture of criminal.

hŭff *v.* Bully; offend; take offence; (draughts) remove (opponent's man) from board as forfeit for failing to take piece with it. ~ *n.* Fit of petulance or offended dignity; (draughts) act of huffing. **hŭ'ffish** *adj.* **hŭ'ffishly̆** *adv.* **hŭ'ffishnėss** *n.* **hŭ'ffy̆** *adj.* **hŭ'ffily̆** *adv.* **hŭ'ffinėss** *n.*

hŭg *v.t.* Squeeze closely in one's arms, usu. with affection; (of bear) squeeze between its forelegs; delight in, cling to (prejudices etc.); exhibit fondness for (person); congratulate *oneself* (*on*, *for*); keep close to (shore etc.); ~-*me-tight*, knitted woollen sleeveless wrap. ~ *n.* Strong clasp with the arms; squeezing grip in wrestling.

hūge *adj.* Very large; (of immaterial things) great. **hū'genėss** *n.* **hū'gely̆** *adv.*

hŭ'gger-mŭ'gger *n.* Secrecy; confusion. ~ *adj.* & *adv.* Secret(ly); confused(ly). ~ *v.* Conceal, hush *up*; proceed in secret or muddled fashion.

hŭ'ggery̆ *n.* Practice (on part of barrister etc.) of courting attorney etc. for employment.

Hū'gō, Victor-Marie (1802–85). French poet, novelist, and dramatist; leader of the French Romantic

movement; author of 'La Légende des Siècles', of the dramas 'Ruy Blas', 'Hernani', etc., and the novels 'Notre Dame de Paris', 'Les Misérables', etc.

Hū'guenot (-genō *or* -genŏt) *n.* French Protestant, member of the Calvinistic or Reformed communion of France whose liberty of worship, at first denied, was defined in the Edict of Nantes (1598) and again withdrawn when the Edict was revoked (1685) by Louis XIV; to escape persecution many Huguenots then emigrated to Protestant countries esp. England and America. [assimilation of Swiss Ger. *eidgenoss* confederate to name of Geneva burgomaster *Hugues*]

hu'la (hōō-) *n.* (also *hula-hula*). Hawaiian women's dance.

hŭlk *n.* Body of dismantled ship, used as store vessel, etc., or (pl., hist.) as prison; unwieldy

PERSECUTION OF THE HUGUENOTS

vessel; (fig.) big person or mass. **hŭ'lkĭng** *adj.* Bulky; clumsy.

hŭll[1] *n.* Outer covering of fruit, esp. pod of peas and beans; (fig.) covering. ~ *v.t.* Remove hull of.

hŭll[2] *n.* Frame of ship; ~ *down*, far away, so that hull is invisible. ~ *v.t.* Strike (ship) in hull with cannon shot.

Hŭll[3]. Kingston upon Hull, English seaport; city in county of Humberside (since April 1974); university, 1954.

hŭllabaloo' *n.* Uproar.

hullō', -loa (-lō) *int.* Exclamation used to call attention, express surprise, etc., or answer call, esp. on telephone.

hŭm[1] *v.* Make continuous low-pitched sound, as of bee, spinning top, etc.; make low inarticulate vocal sound, esp. (usu. ~ *and ha*) of hesitation; sing with closed lips; (colloq.) be in state of activity or bustle. ~ *n.* Humming sound, esp. of hesitation, applause, surprise, etc.

hŭm[2], **h'm** *int.* Exclamation expressing hesitation, dissent, etc.

hū'man *adj.* Of, belonging to, man; that is a man or consists of men; of man as opp. to God; having, showing, qualities distinctive of man. ~ *n.* Human being.

hūmā'ne *adj.* Benevolent, compassionate; (of branches of study) tending to refinement, elegant; ~ *killer*, implement for painless slaughtering of cattle; *Royal H~ Society*, society founded 1774 for rescue of drowning persons. **hūmā'nelȳ** *adv.* **hūmā'neness** *n.*

hū'manism *n.* 1. Devotion to human interests. 2. Literary culture, esp. that of the Humanists. 3. Any of various philosophies concerned with human interests, esp. opp. pragmatism, religious dogma, politics, etc. **hū'manist** *n.* 1. Student of human nature or human affairs; one versed in the humanities. 2. *H~*, one of the scholars who at the revival of learning in 14th–16th centuries devoted themselves to study of language, literature, and antiquities of Greece and Rome; later disciple of same culture; (attrib.) of script used by Humanists. 3. Adherent of humanism (3). **hūmanĭ'stĭc** *adj.*

hūmănĭtār'ian *n.* One who holds that man's duty consists in advancement of welfare of human race; one who devotes himself to welfare of mankind at large, philanthropist. ~ *adj.* Holding, concerned with, views of humanitarians. **hūmănĭtār'ianism** *n.*

hūmă'nitў *n.* 1. Human nature; (pl.) human attributes. 2. Human race. 3. Humaneness, benevolence; (pl.) benevolent acts. 4. (pl.) Learning or literature concerned with human culture, as grammar, rhetoric, poetry, and esp. the Greek and Latin classics.

hū'manīze *v.* 1. Make human, give human character to; prepare (cow's milk) to resemble human milk. 2. Make, become, humane.

hū'mankĭnd (-n-k-) *n.* Mankind.

hū'manlў *adv.* In a human manner; by human means; from human point of view; with human feeling.

Hŭ'mberside. County of NE. England (since April 1974).

hŭ'mble *adj.* Having, showing, low estimate of one's own importance; lowly condition; of modest pretensions, dimensions, etc.; *eat ~ pie*, [alteration of *umble-pie*] make humble apology, submit to humiliation. ~ *v.t.* Make humble; bring low, abase. **hŭ'mblў** *adv.* **hŭ'mbleness** *n.*

hŭ'mble-bee *n.* Large bee (*Bombus*) with loud hum.

Hu'mbōldt (hoombōlt), Friedrich Heinrich Alexander von

(1769–1859). German traveller and scientist; author of the 'Kosmos', a physical description of the universe.

hŭ'mbŭg *n.* 1. Sham, deception; impostor. 2. Kind of usu. peppermint-flavoured boiled sweet. ~ *v.* Delude (person); be, behave like, a humbug.

hŭ'mdrŭm *adj.* & *n.* Commonplace(ness); dull(ness). ~ *v.i.* Proceed in humdrum way.

Hūme, David (1711–76). Scottish philosopher; author of 'Treatise of Human Nature' and 'Enquiry concerning Human Understanding'; in his system of philosophical scepticism human knowledge is restricted to experience of ideas and impressions and ultimate verification of their truth or falsehood is impossible.

hū'merus *n.* (pl. -*i*). (anat.) Bone of upper arm in man; corresponding bone in other vertebrates. **hū'meral** *adj.*

hū'mĭd *adj.* Moist, damp. **hūmĭ'dĭfў** *v.t.* **hūmĭ'dĭtў** *n.* Moisture, dampness; degree of moisture, esp. in atmosphere; *absolute ~*, amount of water vapour in a given volume of air (usu. in grammes per cubic metre); *relative ~*, ratio between the amount actually present and the amount which would be present if the air were saturated at the same temperature.

hū'midor *n.* Box, cabinet, room, for keeping cigars or tobacco moist.

hūmĭ'lĭāte *v.t.* Lower the dignity or self-respect of; mortify. **hūmĭ'lĭātĭng** *adj.* **hūmĭlĭā'tion** *n.*

hūmĭ'lĭtў *n.* Humbleness, meekness, humble condition.

hŭ'mmĭng *adj.* That hums; ~ *bird*, any bird of Amer. (chiefly tropical) family Trochilidae, of very small size, and usu. brilliantly coloured, making humming sound by rapid vibration of wings; *~-top*, top which hums when it spins.

hŭ'mmock *n.* Hillock, knoll; rising ground, esp. in marsh; hump or ridge in icefield. **hŭ'mmockў** *adj.*

hū'moral *adj.* Of the bodily humours (see HUMOUR *n.* 4); now chiefly in ~ *pathology*, pathology of early medicine which ascribed disease to a disordered state of the humours.

hūmorĕ'sque (-sk) *n.* (mus.) Composition of light capricious character.

hū'morist *n.* Facetious person; humorous talker, actor, or writer. **hūmori'stic** *adj.*

hū'morous *adj.* Full of humour; facetious, funny. **hū'morously** *adv.* **hū'morousness** *n.*

hū'mour (-*er*) *n.* 1. State of mind, mood; inclination (as *in the ~ for fighting*); *out of ~*, displeased. 2. Faculty of perceiving the ludicrous; jocose imagination (less intellectual but more sympathetic than WIT); comicality; facetiousness. 3. (physiol.) Transparent fluid or semifluid substance; *aqueous ~*, fluid in eye in front of iris; *vitreous ~*, substance filling most of space between iris and retina. 4. (hist.) In ancient and medieval physiology, one of four chief fluids of the body (blood, phlegm, choler or bile, and melancholy or black choler, called the *cardinal ~s*) which by their relative proportions were supposed to determine a person's physical and mental qualities. ~ *v.t.* Gratify, indulge, (person, taste, temper, etc.); adapt oneself to, make concessions to. **hū'mourless** *adj.* Lacking a sense of the ridiculous.

hū'moursome (-m*er*-) *adj.* Capricious, peevish. **hū'moursomeness** *n.*

hŭmp *n.* Protuberance, esp. on back, formed by curved spine or fleshy excrescence, as natural feature in camel, bison, etc., or deformity in man; rounded boss of earth etc.; (slang) fit of depression or vexation; *~-back*, (person having) back with a hump; *hu'mpback* (*whale*), whale of genus *Megaptera*, so called because of the low hump on the back; *~-backed*, having such a back. ~ *v.t.* Make humpbacked; annoy, depress; (Austral.) hoist up, shoulder (pack or swag); (U.S.) exert *oneself*. **hŭmped** (-pt), **hŭ'mpless, hŭ'mpy** *adjs.*

humph, h'mph *int.* Exclamation of doubt or dissatisfaction.

hŭ'mpty *n.* Low padded cushion seat.

hŭ'mpty-dŭ'mpty *adj.* & *n.* Short and dumpy (person). [f. *Humpty Dumpty*, personification of egg in nursery rhyme]

hū'mus *n.* Vegetable mould; the characteristic organic constituent of the soil formed by the decomposition of plant materials.

Hŭn *n.* 1. One of the Asiatic race of warlike nomads who invaded Europe *c* A.D. 375 and overran much of it under Attila in middle of 5th c. 2. (contempt.) German soldier, German (first used in a speech of the Emperor William II on the German expedition to China in 1900 and adopted derisively by the German Social Democrats and during the war of 1914–18 by the British). **Hŭ'nnish** *adj.* [app. f. *Ḥun-yü*, name of a Turkic tribe]

Hu'nă'n (hōō-). Province of S. China.

hŭnch *v.t.* Bend, arch, convexly; thrust *out, up*, to form a hump. ~ *n.* 1. Hump; thick piece, hunk; *~-back(ed)*, humpback(ed). 2. (colloq.) Intuition, premonition. **hŭ'nchy** *adj.*

hŭ'ndred *n.* 1. Cardinal number equal to ten times ten (100, c, or C); also as ordinal when followed by other numbers; large number; hundredweight; £100; (also *great, long ~*; in sale of herrings, mackerel, etc.) 120; *a ~ per cent*, entire(ly), complete(ly). 2. (chiefly hist.) Subdivision of county or shire with its own court, in England and Ireland; division of county in British Amer. colonies or provinces of Virginia, Maryland, Delaware, and Pennsylvania (still existing in State of Delaware); *Chiltern Hundreds*: see CHILTERN. 3. *~s and thousands*, very small coloured sweets, used for decorating cakes etc.; *hu'ndredweight*, (abbrev. cwt) 112 lb. avoirdupois; (in U.S.) 100 lb. ~ *adj.* Amounting to 100; *H~ Days*, period between return of Napoleon I to Paris (20 Mar. 1815) and his 2nd abdication (22 June); *H~ Years War*, intermittent war between England and

France (1337–1453), arising out of English kings' claim to French crown. **hŭ'ndrėdfōld** *adj.* & *adv.* **hŭ'ndrėdth** *adj.* & *n.* *Old H~*, metrical version, beginning 'All people that on earth do dwell', of Ps. 100, or its tune.

hung: see HANG.

Hŭngār'ian *adj.* Of Hungary or its people or language. ~ *n.* Hungarian person or language; MAGYAR.

Hŭ'ngarȳ (-ngg-). Country of central Europe, forming until 1918 eastern division of Austro-Hungarian Empire; declared an independent republic in 1918; reconstituted as a kingdom, the functions of the monarch being exercised by a Regent, in 1920; again declared a republic in 1946; capital, Budapest.

hŭ'nger (-ngg-) *n.* Uneasy sensation, exhausted condition, caused by want of food; (fig.) strong desire; *~-march*, march of unemployed etc. to call attention to their needs; *~-strike*, refusal to take food (esp. by prisoner trying to force compliance with his demands). ~ *v.i.* Feel hunger; have craving (*for*, *after*); *hungered*, (archaic) hungry.

hŭ'ngrȳ (-ngg-) *adj.* Feeling hunger; showing hunger; inducing hunger; (fig.) eager, greedy; (of soil) poor, barren; *the ~ forties*, the decade 1840–9 in England, a period of great distress among the poor. **hŭ'ngrĭlȳ** *adv.* **hŭ'ngrĭnėss** *n.*

hŭnk *n.* Large piece cut off; clumsy piece.

hŭ'nkers (-z), *n.pl.* Hams (esp. in *on one's ~*, in a squatting position).

Hunnish: see HUN.

hŭnt[1] *v.* 1. Pursue wild animals or game; chase (these) for food or sport; pursue with force, violence or hostility; seek *after*, *for*; drive *away*, *out*; scour (district) in pursuit of game; use (horse, hounds) in hunting; ~ *down*, bring to bay; ~ *out*, track out, find by search; ~ *up*, search for. 2. (change-ringing) Alter position of (bell) in successive changes so as to shift it from first place to last (*hunting up*) or last to first (*hunting down*). 3. (elect. mech.) Be in a state of instability, oscillate, jump backwards and forwards, as governor when its action is more than is needed to adjust speed or as clutch of arc-lamp, which moves rapidly with variations of current. ~ *n.* Hunting (lit. & fig.); persons hunting with a pack; hunting district; (elect., mech.) see-sawing or oscillating movement; ~ *ball*, ball given by members of hunt.

Hŭnt[2], James Henry Leigh (1784–1859). English poet, politician, and essayist; imprisoned for libelling the Prince Regent; while in prison wrote his chief poetical work, 'The Story of Rimini'.

Hŭnt[3], William Holman (1827–1910). English PRE-RAPHAELITE painter; famous for his 'Light of the World', an allegorical picture symbolizing Christ knocking at the door of the human soul.

hŭ'nter *n.* 1. (fem. *huntrėss*) One who hunts; *~'s moon*, full moon next after harvest moon. 2. Horse ridden for hunting. 3. Watch with hinged metal cover to protect glass; *half* -~, similar watch with circular opening in cover.

hŭ'nting *n.* Action of person or animal that hunts: chase, pursuit; *~-box*, small house used during hunting season; *~-ground*, place where one hunts (freq. fig.); *happy ~-grounds*, those expected by Amer. Indians in world to come (also fig.); *~-watch*: see HUNTER 3.

Hŭ'ntingdon, Selina, Countess of (1707–91). Founder of Calvinistic religious association called the Countess of Huntingdon's Connexion. **Hŭntingdō'nian** *adj.* & *n.*

Hŭ'ntingdonshire. Former East Midland county of England, since April 1974 part of Cambridgeshire.

Hunts. *abbrev.* Huntingdonshire.

hŭ'ntsman *n.* Hunter; man in charge of (esp. fox-) hounds.

Hupeh (hōō'pā'). Province of central China.

hûr'dle *n.* Portable rectangular frame strengthened with wooden bars or withes, for temporary fence etc.; wooden frame to be jumped over in ~-*race*; (pl.) hurdle-race; (hist.) frame on which traitors were dragged to execution. ~ *v.* Fence *off*, etc., with hurdles: run in hurdle race. **hûr'dler** *n.* One who makes hurdles or runs in hurdle-races.

hurds: see HARDS.

hûr'dȳ-gûrdȳ *n.* 1. Musical instrument resembling lute or guitar, with strings (two or more tuned to produce a drone) sounded by rosined wheel turned with right hand and keys to 'stop' strings played with left hand. 2. Any droning instrument played by turning a handle, as barrel-organ.

hûrl *v.t.* Throw violently from some position; throw (missile etc.). ~ *n.* Hurling, violent throw.

hûr'ley *n.* Irish game resembling hockey; stick used in this.

hûr'lȳ-bûr'lȳ *n.* Commotion, tumult.

Hûr'on *n.* Member of an Iroquoian people formerly occupying the region between Lake Huron, one of the Great Lakes of N. America, and Lakes Erie and Ontario; their language.

hurrah', hurray' (*or* hoo-), **hooray'** *int.* Exclamation of exultation or approbation. ~ *n.* & *v.i.* Shout hurrah etc.

Hŭ'rrian *adj.* & *n.* (Member, language) of an ancient people of Mesopotamia in the 2nd millennium B.C.

hŭ'rricane *n.* 1. Violent W. Indian wind-storm, cyclone with air moving rapidly (up to 130 m.p.h.) round central calm space, which with whole system advances in straight or curved track. 2. Any storm in which wind blows with terrific violence; (meteor.) wind of 73 m.p.h. or more (force 12 in BEAUFORT Scale); ~-*bird*, frigate-bird; ~-*deck*, light upper deck or platform on river steamer; ~ *force*, speed of wind 73 m.p.h. or more (Beaufort Scale 12); ~ *lamp*, lamp so made as not to be extinguished by violent wind.

hŭ'rrȳ *n.* Undue haste; eagerness to get thing done quickly; eagerness (*to* do, *for* thing); (with neg. or interrog.) need for haste; ***not . . . in a hurry***, not very soon; ~-*call*, (U.S.) call for help in emergency; ~-*scurry*, (in) disorderly haste; proceed thus. ~ *v.* Carry, drive (person *away*, *along*, *into*, etc.) with undue haste; move, act, with great or undue haste; ~ *up*, make haste. **hŭ'rriedlȳ** (-ĭd-) *adv.* **hŭ'rriedness** *n.*

hûrst *n.* Hillock; sandbank in sea or river; wooded eminence; wood.

hûrt *n.* Wound, material injury; harm, wrong. ~ *v.* Cause bodily injury or pain to; damage; inflict injury upon; distress, wound (person, his feelings, etc.); (colloq.) suffer injury or pain. **hûr'tful** *adj.* **hûr'tfullȳ** *adv.* **hûr'tfulness** *n.*

hûr'tle *v.* Strike together, against something else; hurl swiftly; strike *against*; move with clattering sound; come with a crash.

hŭ'sband (-z-) *n.* Man married to a woman; (archaic) economist. ~ *v.t.* 1. Manage thriftily, economize; (archaic) till (ground), cultivate (plants). 2. (poet., joc.) Provide with husband.

hŭ'sbandman (-z-) *n.* Farmer.

hŭ'sbandrȳ (-z-) *n.* Farming; (*good*, *bad*) economy; careful management.

hŭsh *n.* Stillness; silence; ~-*money*, money paid to prevent disclosure or hush up something discreditable. ~ *v.* Silence, quiet; be silent (esp. as int. *hush!*). **hŭ'shabȳ** *int.* Exclamation used to lull child. **hŭsh-hŭsh** *adj.* (colloq.) Highly confidential, very secret.

hŭsk *n.* Dry outer integument of some fruits or seeds; (fig.) worthless outside part of anything. ~ *v.t.* Remove husk from.

hŭ'skȳ[1] *adj.* 1. Of, full of, husks; dry as a husk; (of voice or person) dry, hoarse. 2. (U.S. etc.) Tough and strong (like husk of Indian corn), big, strong, and vigorous. **hŭ'skilȳ** *adv.* **hŭ'skiness** *n.* **hŭ'skȳ** *n.* Strong stoutly-built vigorous-looking person.

hŭ'skȳ[2] *n.* Eskimo dog. [app. corrupt. of *Eskimo*]

Hŭss, John (1373–1415). Bohemian religious reformer; convicted of heresy by the Council of Constance and burnt alive. **Hŭ'ssite** *n.* Follower of Huss.

hussar' (-z-) *n.* One of a body of light horsemen organized in Hungary in 15th c.; soldier of light cavalry regiment elsewhere. [O. Serb. *husar*, f. It. *corsaro* corsair]

hŭ'ssȳ (*or* -z-) *n.* Woman of light or worthless character; pert girl. [f. *housewife*]

hŭ'stings (-z) *n.* 1. Court held in Guildhall of London by Lord Mayor, Recorder, and Sheriffs (or Aldermen), formerly for common pleas, probate, appeals against sheriffs' decisions, etc., now only for considering and registering gifts made to City; platform on which Mayor etc. sat for this court (obs.) 2. Platform from which (before 1872) candidates for Parliament were nominated; election proceedings.

hŭ'stle (-sl) *v.* Push roughly, jostle; thrust (person *into*, *out of*, etc.); impel unceremoniously; push roughly *against*; push one's way; hurry, bustle. ~ *n.* Hustling.

hŭt *n.* Small roughly-constructed house or shelter, esp. for temporary use; (mil.) temporary wooden etc. house for troops. ~ *v.* Place (troops etc.) in huts; lodge in hut.

hŭtch *n.* Box-like pen for rabbits etc.; hut, cabin, small house; box-like truck used in mining etc.

hŭ'tment *n.* Encampment of huts.

Hŭ'xley[1], Aldous Leonard (1894–1963). English novelist and essayist, author of 'Brave New World'.

Hŭ'xley[2], Thomas Henry (1825–95). English physician and agnostic philosopher; supported Darwinism in his many popular scientific writings.

Huyghens (hī'genz *or* hoi-), Christian (1629–95). Dutch mathematician and astronomer; ~*'s principle*, (phys.) principle of wave propagation, according to which every point on an advancing wave front acts as a source of disturbance and sends out smaller waves, the resultant effect of which constitutes the propagation of the wave as a whole.

huzza' (-ah) *int.*, *n.*, & *v.i.* (archaic) Hurrah.

H.W.M. *abbrev.* High-water mark.

Hy *abbrev.* Henry.

hȳ'acinth *n.* 1. Precious stone (in ancient times a blue gem, prob. sapphire); now, reddish-orange variety of zircon (occas. also of garnet and topaz). 2. Bulbous plant of genus *Hyacinthus* with bell-shaped flowers of various colours, esp. purplish-blue. **hȳaci'nthīne** *adj.* Of colour of hyacinth (traditional rendering of Homeric epithet applied to hair, perh. meaning dark and glossy).

Hȳaci'nthus. (Gk myth.) Beautiful youth, beloved by Apollo and Zephyrus, accidentally killed by a quoit thrown by Apollo; from his blood Apollo caused the flower that bears his name to spring up.

Hȳ'adēs (-z) *n.pl.* 1. (Gk myth.) Nymphs, daughters of Atlas, placed by Zeus among the Pleiades. 2. (astron.) Cluster of stars in the constellation of Taurus, anciently supposed to indicate rainy weather when they rose simultaneously with the sun.

hyaena: see HYENA.

hȳ'alīne (*or*-ēn) *adj.* Glass-like, glassy, vitreous.

hȳ'alīte *n.* Colourless variety of opal.

hȳ'aloid *adj.* (chiefly anat.) Glassy; ~ *membrane*, thin transparent membrane enveloping vitreous humour of eye. ~ *n.* Hyaloid membrane.

hȳ'brĭd *n.* Offspring of two animals or plants of different species or varieties; person of mixed nationality; (fig.) thing, word, composed of incongruous elements. ~ *adj.* Crossbred, mongrel; heterogeneous. **hȳ'brĭdĭsm** *n.* Fact, condition, of being hybrid. **hȳbrĭ'dĭtȳ** *n.* **hȳ'brĭdīze** *v.* Subject (species etc.) to cross-breeding; produce hybrids; interbreed. **hȳbrĭdīzā'tion** *n.*

hȳ'datĭd *n.* (path.) Cyst containing watery fluid, occurring as morbid formation in animal tissues; (esp.) cyst formed by and containing larva of a variety of tapeworm.

Hȳde, Edward: see JEKYLL.

Hȳde Pârk. London park maintained by Crown, scene of many political and other demonstrations.

Hȳ'derabăd. Former State of India, in the Deccan; its capital.

Hȳ'dra[1]**.** (Gk myth.) Many-headed snake of marshes of Lerna, whose heads grew again as they were cut off, killed by Hercules; hence, thing hard to extirpate. **2.** (astron.) Southern constellation represented as water-snake or sea serpent.

hȳ'dra[2] *n.* **1.** Water-snake. **2.** Freshwater polyp of simple structure of genus *H*~, with tubu-

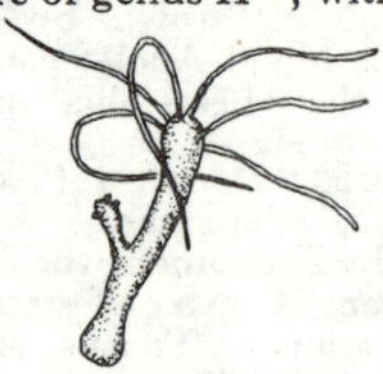

lar body and mouth surrounded by ring of tentacles with stinging thread-cells.

hȳdrā'ngea (-*ja*) *n.* Shrub of genus *H*~, native of temperate regions of Asia and America, with white, blue, or pink flowers in large globular clusters.

hȳ'drant *n.* Pipe with nozzle to which hose can be attached, for drawing water directly from main, esp. in street.

hȳ'drate (*or* -āt) *n.* (chem.) Compound of water with another compound. **hȳ'drāte** *v.t.* Combine chemically with water. **hȳdrā'tion** *n.*

hȳdrau'lĭc *adj.* Of water (or other liquid) as conveyed through pipes or channels, esp. mechanically; (of machine or other device) operated by resistance offered when water, oil, or other liquid is forced through a pipe or orifice, as ~ *brake, crane, lift*, etc.; (of cement etc.) hardening under water; ~ *press*, hydrostatic press. **hȳdrau'lĭcallȳ** *adv.* **hydrau'lĭcs** *n.* Science of conveyance of liquids through pipes, etc., esp. as a motive force.

hȳ'drĭa *n.* (Gk antiq.) Large jar or pitcher for carrying water, with two or three handles.

hȳ'drō *n.* (colloq.) Hydropathic establishment.

hȳdro- *prefix.* **1.** Having to do with water. **2.** (path.) Affected with accumulation of serous fluid, dropsical. **3.** (chem.) Combined with hydrogen.

hȳdrocar'bon *n.* Chemical compound containing hydrogen and carbon only; member of the many series of compounds, including paraffins, benzenes, and olefines, that constitute the subject-matter of organic chemistry.

hȳdrocĕ'phalus *n.* Disease of brain, esp. in young children, with accumulation of serous fluid in cavity of cranium and consequent weakness of mental faculties; water on the brain. **hȳdrocėphă'lĭc** *adj.*

hȳdrochlor'ĭc *adj.* ~ *acid*, hydrogen chloride (HCl), a colourless gas which fumes in moist air, is very soluble in water, and has strongly acid taste and pungent irritating odour; (in ordinary use) solution of this in water, spirit of salt.

hȳdrocȳă'nĭc *adj.* ~ *acid*, highly poisonous volatile liquid (HCN) with smell like bitter almonds, solution of which in water is *prussic acid.*

hȳdrodȳnă'mĭc, -ical *adjs.* Of the forces acting on or exerted by liquids. **hȳdrodȳnă'mĭcs** *n.* Science of the motion, energy, and pressure of moving fluids.

hȳdrō-ėlĕ'ctrĭc *adj.* Of the utilization of water-power for the production of electricity.

hȳ'drofoil *n.* (Fast motor-boat, seaplane, etc., with) plate or fin for lifting hull out of water at speed.

hȳ'drogėn *n.* (chem.) Lightest of the elements, a colourless odourless gas which burns with pale-blue very hot flame in oxygen (or air) and combines with oxygen to form water (H_2O); symbol H, at. no. 1, at. wt 1·0080; ~ *bomb*, immensely powerful bomb deriving its energy from the fusion at extremely high temperature of hydrogen isotopes to form helium; ~ *fluoride*, colourless, highly corrosive gas (HF), anhydride of *hydrofluoric acid*; ~ *peroxide*, in its pure anhydrous state, a clear colourless syrupy liquid (H_2O_2), used in aqueous solution as an oxidizing and bleaching agent and an antiseptic and disinfectant. **hȳdrŏ'gėnous** *adj*.

hȳdrŏ'gėnate *v.t.* Charge, cause to combine, with hydrogen; esp. convert coal by this means into a mixture of oils, as a stage in the production of petrol from coal; also, improve heat-resisting qualities of lubricating oil thus. **hȳdrŏgėnā'tion** *n*. **hȳdrŏ'gėnize** *v.t.*

hȳdrŏ'graphȳ *n*. Scientific description of the waters of the earth. **hȳdrŏ'grapher** *n*. **hȳdrogră'phĭc, -ĭcal** *adjs*.

hȳ'droid *adj*. & *n*. (zool.) (Animal) like, allied to, the hydra (polyp).

hȳdrŏ'logȳ *n*. Study of water, esp. its distribution and control. **hȳdrolŏ'gical** *adj*.

hȳdrŏ'lȳsis *n*. Splitting of a compound substance by interaction with water. **hȳdrolȳ'tĭc** *adj*.

hȳ'dromėl *n*. Mixture of honey and water.

hȳdrŏ'mėter *n*. Instrument for determining specific gravity of liquids, commonly a graduated stem with a hollow bulb and a weight at lower end, floated upright in liquid, of which specific gravity is indicated by depth to which stem is immersed. **hȳdromĕ'trĭc** *adj*. **hȳdrŏ'mėtrȳ** *n*.

hȳdropă'thĭc *adj*. Of, concerned with, hydropathy. ~ *n*. Hydropathic establishment. **hȳdrŏ'pathȳ** *n*. Medical treatment by external and internal application of water; water-cure.

hȳ'drophāne *n*. Opaque or partly translucent opal that absorbs water on immersion and becomes transparent.

hȳdrophō'bĭa *n*. Aversion to water, esp. as symptom of rabies in man; rabies, esp. in man. **hȳdrophō'bĭc** *adj*.

hȳ'drophōne *n*. Instrument for the detection of sound-waves in water.

hȳ'drophȳte *n*. Aquatic plant, esp. alga.

hȳdrŏ'pĭc *adj*. Dropsical.

hȳ'droplāne *n*. 1. Fin-like device enabling submarine to submerge or rise. 2. Seaplane.

hȳdropŏ'nĭcs *n.pl.* Cultivation of plants without soil, in water containing dissolved nutrients.

hȳdroquinō'ne *n*. Phenolic substance prepared from quinone by reduction with sulphur dioxide, used as a photographic developer.

hȳ'drosphēre *n*. Waters of the earth's surface.

hȳ'drostăt *n*. Electrical device for detecting presence of water.

hȳdrostă'tĭc *adj*. Of the equilibrium of liquids and the pressure exerted by liquids at rest; (of instruments etc.) involving pressure of liquid as source of power or otherwise, hydraulic. **hȳdrostă'tĭcal** *adj*. **hȳdrostă'ticallȳ** *adv*. **hȳdrostă'tĭcs** *n*. Branch of mechanics concerned with the pressure and equilibrium of liquids at rest.

hȳdrothĕrapeu'tĭc *adj*. Hydropathic. **hȳdrothĕ'rapȳ** *n*. Hydropathy.

hȳ'drous *adj*. (chem., min.) Containing water.

hȳdrŏ'xīde *n*. (chem.) Compound containing hydroxyl.

hȳdrŏxȳ- *prefix*. Containing hydroxyl.

hȳdrŏ'xȳl *n*. (chem.) Radical OH, which occurs in the structures of many chemical compounds.

hȳdrozō'an *adj*. & *n*. (Member) of the Hydrozoa, a class of coelenterate animals, chiefly marine, and simple or compound, including the freshwater hydra.

hȳē'na, hȳae'na *n*. Carnivorous quadruped allied to dog tribe, with powerful jaws, neck, and shoulders, but low and comparatively poorly developed hind quarters; cruel, treacherous, or rapacious person; *laughing* ~, hyena (either *striped* ~, *Hyaena striata*, of Asia and northern Africa, or *spotted* ~, *Crocuta maculata*, of southern Africa) with howl resembling fiendish laughter.

Hȳgei'a (-jē*a*). (Gk myth.) Goddess of health and daughter of Aesculapius. **hȳgei'an** (-ēan) *adj.*

hȳ'giene (-jēn) *n.* Science of health and its preservation; practice of measures conducive to this, as cleanliness. **hȳgie'nĭc, -ĭcal** *adjs.* **hȳgie'nĭcallȳ** *adv.* **hȳgie'nĭcs, hȳgie'nĭst** *ns.*

hȳgro- *prefix.* Wet, fluid.

hȳgrŏ'mėter *n.* Instrument for measuring humidity of air or gas. **hȳgromĕ'trĭc** *adj.* **hȳgrŏ'mėtrȳ** *n.*

hȳ'groscōpe *n.* Instrument indicating but not measuring humidity of air. **hȳgroscŏ'pĭc** *adj.* Of the hygroscope; (chem.) tending to absorb water esp. from the air.

Hȳ'ksŏs *n.* Asiatic people who invaded Egypt and ruled from 18th until early 16th c. B.C. when they were driven out by the 18th dynasty.

hȳ'lĭc *adj.* Of matter, material.

hȳ'mĕn¹ *n.* Fold of mucous membrane stretched across and partially closing external orifice of vagina of virgin female.

Hȳ'mĕn². (Gk & Rom. myth.) God of marriage; represented as a young man carrying torch and veil.

hymėnē'al *adj.* Pertaining to marriage. ~ *n.* Marriage-song. **hȳmėnē'allȳ** *adv.*

hȳmē'nĭum *n.* (pl. *-nia*). Spore-bearing surface in fungi.

hȳmenŏ'pteran *n.* (pl. *-ra*). Member of the Hymenoptera, a large order of insects, including ants, bees, etc. with four membranous wings. **hȳmenŏ'pteral, hȳmenŏ'pterous** *adjs.*

hȳmn (-m) *n.* Song of praise or prayer to God or other divine being, esp. metrical composition sung in religious service; song of praise. ~ *v.* Praise (God etc.) in hymns, express (praise etc.) in hymn; sing hymns.

hȳ'mnal *adj.* Of hymns. ~ *n.* Hymn-book. **hȳ'mnarȳ** *n.* Hymn-book, collection of hymns.

hȳ'mnodȳ *n.* Singing of hymns; composition of hymns; hymns collectively. **hȳ'mnodĭst** *n.*

hȳmnŏ'grapher *n.* Composer of hymns.

hȳmnŏ'logȳ *n.* Composition, study, of hymns; hymns collectively. **hȳmnolŏ'gĭc** *adj.* **hȳmnŏ'logĭst** *n.*

hȳ'oid *adj.* ~ *bone*, tongue-bone, between chin and thyroid cartilage, in man, horseshoe-shaped and embedded horizontally in root of tongue. ~ *n.* Hyoid bone.

hȳ'oscīne, hȳoscȳ'amīne *ns.* (chem.) Alkaloid, an isomer of atropine, obtained from certain plants (esp. *Hyoscyamus niger* and *Atropa belladonna*) and used as sedative, or, with morphia, to produce partial anaesthesia; scopolamine.

hȳoscȳ'amus *n.* (bot.) Solanaceous plant of genus *H*~, of which British species is henbane.

hȳpă'llagė (-jĭ) *n.* (gram.) Reversal of natural relations of two elements in a proposition (e.g. *apply the wound to water* for *apply water to the wound*).

hȳper- *prefix.* Over, above, exceeding, excessive.

hȳperae'mĭa *n.* (path.) Engorgement of the tissues with blood.

hȳperaesthē'sĭa (-zĭ*a*) *n.* (path.) Morbid sensitiveness of nerves; excessive sensibility. **hȳperaesthĕ'tĭc** *adj.*

hȳpêr'baton *n.* (pl. *-ta*). Inversion of normal order of words, esp. for sake of emphasis.

hȳpêr'bola *n.* (geom.) One of the conic sections, a plane curve consisting of two separate, similar, equal, and infinite branches, formed by the intersection of a cone by a plane making a larger angle with the base than the side of the cone makes. **hȳperbŏ'lĭc** *adj.*

hȳpêr'bolė *n.* (rhet.) Exaggerated statement not meant to be taken literally. **hȳperbŏ'lĭcal** *adj.* **hȳperbŏ'lĭcallȳ** *adv.* **hȳpêr'bolĭsm, hȳpêr'bolist** *ns.*

hȳpêr'boloid *n.* (geom.) Solid

or surface of the second degree, some of whose plane sections are hyperbolas, the others being ellipses or circles.

hȳperbôrē'an (*or* -ōr'-) *adj.* Of the extreme north of the earth. **Hȳperbôrē'an** *n.* Inhabitant of extreme north of earth; (Gk myth.) one of a race living in a land of sunshine and plenty beyond the north wind.

hȳpercătalĕ'ctic *adj.* (of verse) Having extra syllable after last complete dipody.

hȳpercri'tical *adj.* Too critical, esp. of small faults.

hȳperdū'lia *n.* (R.C. Ch.) Special veneration offered to the Virgin Mary, less than LATRIA but higher than DULIA.

hȳperglȳcae'mia (-sēm-) *n.* (path.) Excess of sugar in the blood.

Hȳpēr'ion. (Gk myth.) One of the Titans, the father of Aurora, the Sun, and the Moon; in later myth. identified with the Sun itself.

hȳpermĕ'tric, -ical *adjs.* (of verse) Having a redundant syllable; (of syllable) redundant.

hȳpermėtrō'pia *n.* Morbidly long sight. **hȳpermėtrŏ'pic** *adj.*

hȳperphȳ'sical (-z-) *adj.* Supernatural.

hȳpersŏ'nic *adj.* (of speed) Greatly in excess of the speed of sound, i.e. faster than *supersonic.*

hȳ'persthēne *n.* (min.) Greenish-black or greenish-grey mineral closely allied to hornblende, a silicate of iron and magnesium.

hȳpertĕ'nsion (-shon) *n.* Extreme tension; (path.) raised blood-pressure.

hȳperthȳr'oidism *n.* (path.) Condition resulting from overactivity of thyroid gland.

hȳpēr'trophȳ *n.* Excessive development, morbid enlargement, of organ etc. (opp. ATROPHY). **hȳpertrŏ'phic, hȳpēr'trophied** (-ĭd) *adjs.*

hȳ'pha *n.* (pl. *-phae*). Vegetative filament of a fungus.

hȳ'phen *n.* Sign (-) used to join two words together, to join separated syllables of word broken at end of line, or to divide word into parts. ~ *v.t.* Join (words) with hyphen; write (compound word) with hyphen. **hȳ'phenāte** *v.t.* Hyphen; *hyphenated,* (U.S., of persons etc.) of nationality designated by hyphenated form, e.g. *Irish-American.*

hȳpnogĕ'nėsis *n.* Induction of hypnotic state. **hȳpnogėnĕ'tic** *adj.*

hȳpnŏ'logȳ *n.* Science of phenomena of sleep.

hȳpnō'sis *n.* Artificially produced sleep, esp. that induced by hypnotism.

hȳpnŏ'tic *adj.* Of, producing, hypnotism. ~ *n.* Thing that produces sleep; person under influence of hypnotism.

hȳ'pnotism *n.* (Artificial production of) state resembling deep sleep, in which subject acts only on external suggestion or direction, to which he is involuntarily and unconsciously obedient. **hȳ'pnotist** *n.* **hȳ'pnotize** *v.t.*

hȳ'pō *n.* Sodium thiosulphate, $Na_2S_2O_3.5H_2O$ (incorrectly called sodium hyposulphite), used in fixing photographic negatives and prints.

hȳpo- *prefix.* Below, under, slightly; (mus.) prefixed to name of ancient Greek mode or ecclesiastical mode beginning at interval below the one named, as *hypoaeo'lian, hypodor'ian, hypoio'nian, hypoly'dian, hypomixoly'dian, hypophry'gian;* (chem.) used to prefix names of oxygen compounds containing less oxygen than other compounds in the same series.

hȳ'poblăst *n.* Inner layer of cells in blastoderm.

hȳ'pocaust *n.* (Rom. antiq.) Hollow space under floor in which heat from furnace was accumulated for heating house or bath.

hȳpochŏ'ndria (-k-) *n.* (med.) Morbid state of depression for which there is no real cause; (in lay usage) needless or excessive anxiety about one's health.

hȳpochŏ'ndriac (-k-) *adj.* Of, affected by, hypochondria. ~ *n.* Hypochondriac person. **hȳpo-**

chondrĭ'acal *adj.* **hȳpochondrĭ'acallȳ** *adv.*

hȳpocorĭ'stĭc *adj.* Of, like, a pet-name; tending to use endearing or euphemistic terms.

hȳpocŏ'tȳl *n.* (bot.) Axis of seedling below seed leaves, forming anatomically a transition zone between stem and root.

hȳpŏ'crĭsȳ *n.* Simulation of virtue or goodness; dissimulation, pretence.

hȳ'pocrĭte *n.* Person guilty of hypocrisy; dissembler, pretender. **hȳpocrĭ'tĭcal** *adj.* **hȳpocrĭ'tĭcallȳ** *adv.* [Gk *hupokrites* actor]

hȳpocȳ'cloid *n.* (geom.) Curve traced by a point in the circumference of a circle which rolls round the interior circumference of another circle.

hȳpoder'mĭc *adj.* (med., of drugs etc.) Introduced beneath the skin; (anat.) lying under the skin; ~ *needle, syringe,* one used in hypodermic injection. **hȳpoder'mĭcallȳ** *adv.* **hȳpoder'mĭc** *n.* Hypodermic injection or syringe.

hȳpogă'strĭum *n.* Lowest region of abdomen. **hȳpogă'strĭc** *adj.*

hȳpogē'al *adj.* Underground.

hȳpoglȳcae'mĭa (-sēm-) *n.* (path.) Deficiency of sugar (glucose) in the blood.

hȳpŏ'gȳnous *adj.* (of stamens) Situated below pistil or ovary; (of flower) having such stamens.

hȳpophȳ'sĭs (*or* -ŏ'fĭsĭs) *n.* (also ~ *cerebri*) Pituitary gland.

hȳpŏ'stasĭs *n.* (pl. *-es* pr. ēz). 1. (path.) Passive congestion of an organ or part; deposit of blood in dependent part of body. 2. (metaphys.) Underlying substance, opp. to attributes or to what is unsubstantial; (theol.) personality (of Christ), person (of the Godhead). **hȳpostă'tĭc, -ĭcal** *adjs.* **hȳpostă'tĭcallȳ** *adv.*

hȳpŏ'stasīze, hȳpŏ'statīze *vbs. t.* Make into or treat as substance; personify.

hȳpotĕ'nsion (-shon) *n.* Lowered blood-pressure.

hȳpŏ'tėnūse *n.* Side of right-angled triangle opposite the right angle.

hȳ'pothėc *n.* (Rom. & Sc. law) Security established by law over thing belonging to debtor. **hȳpŏ'thėcarȳ** *adj.*

hȳpŏ'thėcate *v.t.* Pledge, mortgage. **hȳpothėcā'tion** *n.*

hȳpŏ'thėsĭs *n.* (pl. *-thėsēs*). Supposition made as basis for reasoning, without reference to its truth, or as starting-point for investigation; groundless assumption. **hȳpothĕ'tĭc, -ĭcal** *adjs.* **hȳpothĕ'tĭcallȳ** *adv.*

hȳpŏ'thėsīze *v.* Frame a hypothesis; assume.

hȳpotrachē'lĭum (-k-) *n.* (pl. *-lia*). (archit.) Groove round shaft of column just below capital.

hȳpsŏ'graphȳ *n.* Description of contours of earth's surface; delineation of these in a map.

hȳpsŏ'mėter *n.* Instrument for measuring altitudes, by determining the boiling-points of liquids. **hȳpsomĕ'trĭc, -ĭcal** *adjs.* **hȳpsŏ'mėtrȳ** *n.*

hȳ'răx *n.* One of a small group of mammals of the order Hyracoida, the conies, distantly related to the elephant and having plantigrade feet with hooves and including the Syrian rock-rabbit and the S. Afr. rock-badger.

hȳ'son *n.* Kind of green tea from China. [Chin. *hsi-ch'un*, lit. = 'bright spring']

hȳ'ssop *n.* Small bushy aromatic herb of genus *Hyssopus*, esp. *H. officinalis*, formerly used medicinally; (bibl.) plant whose twigs were used for sprinkling in Jewish rites, bunch of this used in purification.

hȳsterĕ'ctomȳ *n.* Surgical removal of the uterus.

hȳsterē'sĭs *n.* (phys.) Lagging or retardation of an effect when the forces acting on a body are changed, esp. lagging of magnetic induction behind the magnetizing force (*magnetic* ~); ~ *loss*, energy loss per cycle involved in taking a magnetic material through a complete magnetic cycle.

hȳstēr'ĭa *n.* 1. (med., psych.) Functional disturbance of nervous system, of psychoneurotic origin.

2. Morbid excitement. **hўstĕ′rĭcal** *adj.* **hўstĕ′rĭcallў** *adv.* **hўstĕ′rĭcs** *n.pl.* Hysterical fits or convulsions.

hў′sterŏn prŏ′terŏn. (gram.) Figure of speech in which what should come last is put first; inversion of natural order. [Gk *husteron proteron* latter former]

Hz *abbrev.* Herz.

I

I¹, i (ī). 1. 9th letter of modern English and ancient Roman alphabet, in which it was orig. used as symbol both of *i* vowel and of a consonant (orig. *y*, later, in Romanic, developing into 'soft g' (j)); differentiation was finally made between these two (in England *c* 1630–40), the consonant being expressed by the character J, j, orig. merely a variant form of I, i; in modern English *i* represents chiefly two sounds: a short high front wide vowel (ĭ) and a diphthong (ī). 2. Roman numeral symbol for 1.

I² (ī) *pron.* 1st person nom. sing. pronoun, denoting the speaker. ~ *n.* *the I*, the ego, subject or object of self-consciousness.

I. *abbrev.* Island(s).

ī'ămb *n.* = IAMBUS.

īă'mbĭc *adj.* Of, containing, based on, iambuses. ~ *n.* Iambic verse.

īă'mbus *n.* (pl. *-buses*, *-bī*). Metrical foot of short followed by long syllable, or of unaccented followed by accented syllable.

Iă'pėtus (ī-). 1. (Gk myth.) A Titan, father of Atlas, Prometheus, and Epimetheus, and grandfather of DEUCALION; hence regarded as progenitor of mankind. 2. (astron.) 8th satellite of Saturn.

ib., ibid. *abbrevs.* *Ibidem.*

I.B.A. *abbrev.* Independent Broadcasting Authority.

Ibañez (ēbă'nyāth), Vicente Blasco (1867–1928). Spanish novelist.

Iber'ia (ī-). 1. Ancient name for country comprising Spain and Portugal, and forming peninsula of extreme SW. of Europe. 2. Ancient name of GEORGIA².

Iber'ian *adj.* Of Iberia. ~ *n.* 1. Inhabitant of ancient Iberian peninsula; member of short dark neolithic people, with long heads, who buried their dead and are thought to have built the cairns, dolmens, etc., found in N. Africa, Spain, France, and Gt Britain. 2. Language of ancient Iberia, supposed to be represented by modern Basque.

ī'bĕx *n.* Species of wild goat (genus *Capra*), with large scimitar-like horns, now rare in Alps but found in Mongolia and Ethiopia.

ĭ'bĭdĕm (*or* -ī'd-) *adv.* (abbrev. ib., ibid.) In the same book, chapter, passage, etc. [L, = 'in same place']

ī'bĭs *n.* (pl. *ibis* or *ibises*). Any of a group of birds, widely distributed in warm climates, superficially resembling curlew but larger and with stouter bill and legs; *sacred* ~, white ibis, common in the Nile basin, venerated by the ancient Egyptians.

Ibiza (ĭvē'th*a*). One of the Balearic Islands.

Ibn-Baṭṭu'ṭa (ĭ-, -tōōt*a*) (1304–78). Arabian traveller, who visited Mecca, Asia Minor, Russia, India, China, Ceylon, Spain, Central Africa, etc.

Ibn Saud (ĭ-, -sowd) (*c* 1880–1954). King of Saudi Arabia 1932–54.

I'bsen (ĭ-), Henrik (1828–1906). Norwegian poet and author of plays ('A Doll's House', 'Ghosts', 'Hedda Gabler', etc.) examining and criticizing social conventions. **I'bsenĭsm** *n.*

I'bȳcus (ĭ-) (6th c. B.C.). Greek lyric poet said to have been killed by robbers, who were brought to justice by birds who saw the murder.

i/c *abbrev.* In charge.

I'carus (ī- *or* ĭ-). (Gk myth.) Son of DAEDALUS; tried to escape from Crete on wings made by his father, but flew so near the sun that the wax attaching his wings was melted and he fell into the Aegean Sea.

I.C.B.M. *abbrev.* Inter-continental ballistic missile.

ice *n.* 1. Frozen water; water made solid by exposure to low temperature, a transparent crystalline brittle almost colourless substance; frozen surface of body of water; *break the* ~, (fig.) make a beginning, break through reserve or stiffness. 2. Frozen confection, ice-cream, water-ice; *coconut* ~, sweet made of sugar, water, and desiccated coconut. 3. *I~ Age*, period during the Pleistocene, when large parts of the earth were covered by ice; *~-axe*, axe used by mountain climbers to cut footholds in ice-slopes; *i'ceberg*, floating mass of ice of which about $\frac{1}{9}$ projects above sea-level; detached portion of polar ice-sheet or glacier, often travelling great distances in ocean currents before it melts completely; *~-blink*, luminous appearance on horizon, caused by reflection from ice; *~-box*, (chiefly U.S.) refrigerator; *~-breaker*, boat with reinforced bow for breaking channel through ice of river, harbour, etc.; *~-cap*, mass of thick ice covering continent, island, or other region; *~-cream*, frozen or chilled flavoured and sweetened cream, custard, etc.; *~-fall*, steep part of glacier like frozen waterfall; *~-field*, extensive sheet of floating ice; *~-floe*, flattish free mass of floating ice, smaller than an ice-field; *~-foot*, belt or ledge of ice extending along the coast, esp. in Arctic regions, between high and low water marks; ~ *hockey*: see HOCKEY; *~-house*, building, often partly or wholly underground, for storing ice; *~-plant*, plant (*Mesembryanthemum crystallinum*) of S. Africa, Canary Is., etc., with leaves covered with pellucid watery vesicles; ~ *point*, freezing-point of water (0° C); *~-run*, artificial tobogganing track of frozen snow; *~-water*, iced water; *~-wool*, kind of glossy wool used in crochet etc. ~ *v.t.* Freeze; cover (as) with ice; cool (wine) in ice; cover (cake etc.) with concretion of sugar.

I'celand (īsl-).. Large sparsely inhabited island in N. Atlantic; colonized by Scandinavians after 850; united with Norway 1262–4; on the union of Norway and Denmark (1381) the rule of Iceland was transferred to Denmark, which conceded home rule to Iceland in 1874 and recognized it as a sovereign State, in union with Denmark, in 1918; the union was dissolved in 1944 when Iceland became an independent republic; capital, Reykjavik; ~ *moss*, species of edible lichen (*Cetrarua islandica*), having medicinal properties; ~ *poppy*, yellow- or red-flowered perennial poppy (*Papaver nudicaule*) of Arctic origin; ~ *spar*, particularly transparent variety of calc-spar used in optical instruments.

Icelă'ndĭc (īsl-)*adj.* Of Iceland. ~ *n.* Language of Iceland, in its oldest form practically identical with Old Norse, which it still closely resembles.

Icē'nī (ī-) *n.pl.* Ancient British tribe inhabiting a district roughly corresponding to modern Norfolk and Suffolk, who were conquered, with their queen BOUDICCA, by the Romans *c* A.D. 62.

I'chabŏd (īk- *or* ĭk-) *int.* Exclamation of regret, = 'the glory has departed'; see 1 Sam. 4: 21, in ref. to the taking of the ark by the Philistines.

ĭchneu'mon (ĭk-) *n.* 1. N. African and Iberian mongoose, *Herpestes ichneumon.* 2. (also ~ *fly*) Member of a group of insects related to bees and wasps, whose larvae are parasitic, mostly on Lepidoptera. [Gk *ikhneumōn* spider-hunting wasp (*ikhneuō* track)]

ī'chor (īk-) *n.* 1. (Gk myth.) Ethereal fluid flowing like blood in veins of gods. 2. (path.) Thin fetid discharge from an ulcer. **ī'chorous** *adj.*

i'chthȳoid (ĭk-) *adj.* Fish-like. ~ *n.* Vertebrate of fish type.

ĭchthȳŏ'logȳ (ĭk-) *n.* Study of fishes. **ĭchthȳolŏ'gĭcal** *adj.* **ĭchthȳŏ'logĭst** *n.*

ICHTHYOSAUR

ichthyŏ′phagous (ĭk-) *adj.* Fish-eating.

ichthyŏr′nis (ĭk-) *n.* Member of genus *I*~ of extinct toothed birds.

ĭ′chthyosaur, -sau′rus (ĭk-) *ns.* Marine reptile of extinct order Ichthyosauria, with superficial resemblance to the modern dolphin.

ī′cicle *n.* Tapering ice-formation, produced by freezing of successive drops of water trickling from the point of attachment.

ī′cing *n.* (esp.) 1. Coating of sugar and water or white of egg etc. for cakes etc.; ~ *sugar*, finely ground sugar for icing. 2. Formation of ice on aircraft.

Icknield Way (ĭ′knēld). Ancient pre-Roman track crossing England in wide curve from Wiltshire to Norfolk.

ī′con *n.* Image, statue; (Orthodox Ch.) painting, mosaic, etc., of sacred personage, itself regarded as sacred. **īcŏ′nic** *adj.* Of (the nature of) an image or portrait; (of statues) following a conventional type.

īcŏ′noclăsm *n.* Breaking of images. **īcŏ′noclăst** *n.* Breaker of images, esp. one who took part in movement in 8th and 9th centuries against use of images in religious worship in Eastern Europe; (fig.) one who assails cherished beliefs. **īcŏnoclă′stic** *adj.*

īconŏ′graphy̆ *n.* 1. Description of a subject by drawings or figures; book containing this. 2. Subject-matter of art; study of this. **īconŏ′grapher** *n.* 1. Person who illustrates a subject. 2. Student of iconography. **īconogră′phic, -ical** *adjs.*

īconŏ′latry̆ *n.* Worship of images. **īconŏ′later** *n.*

īconŏ′logy̆ *n.* 1. Study of icons. 2. Symbolical representation, symbolism. **īconolŏ′gical** *n.* **īconŏ′logist** *n.*

īconŏ′stasis *n.* (pl. *-ases*). (Orthodox Ch.) Screen, on which icons are placed, separating sanctuary from main body of church.

īcosahē′dron (*-a*-h-) *n.* (geom.) Solid figure of 20 faces; *regular* ~, one contained by 20 equilateral triangles.

Ictī′nus (ī-) (5th c. B.C.). Greek architect of Hall of Mysteries at Eleusis and (with Callicrates) Parthenon at Athens.

ī′ctus *n.* (pros.) Rhythmical or metrical stress.

ī′cy̆ *adj.* Abounding in, covered with, ice; very cold. **ī′cily̆** *adv.* **ī′cinėss** *n.*

id *n.* (psychol.) That part of the mind which comprises the inherited instinctive impulses of the individual together with memories and phantasies evolved in early infancy (cf. EGO).

id. *abbrev.* *Idem.*

I′da (ī-). 1. Mountain range in S. Phrygia, near Troy, from whose summit Zeus was supposed to have watched the progress of the Trojan War; scene of the rape of GANYMEDE and the home of PARIS and OENONE. 2. Ancient name of chief mountain (Mt. Psiloriti) in Crete, where Zeus is said to have been brought up.

I'dahō (īda-). State in north-western U.S., bounded on north by British Columbia; admitted to the Union in 1890; capital, Boise.

īde *n.* Cyprinoid freshwater fish of N. Europe, *Leuciscus idus.*

īdē'a *n.* 1. Archetype, pattern, as dist. from its realization in individuals; in Platonic philosophy, eternally existing pattern of which individual things in any class are imperfect copies. 2. Conception of standard or principle to be recognized or aimed at; plan of action. 3. Notion conceived by the mind; way of thinking; vague belief, fancy. 4. (in Descartes, Locke, etc.) Immediate object of thought or mental perception; (in Kant etc.) conception of reason transcending all experience; (in Hegel etc.) absolute truth of which all phenomenal existence is expression.

īdē'al *adj.* 1. Relating to, consisting of, (Platonic) ideas. 2. Answering to one's highest conception; perfect or supremely excellent in its kind. 3. Embodying an idea; existing only in idea; visionary. ~ *n.* Perfect type; actual thing as standard for imitation. **īdē'allȳ** *adv.*

īdē'alism *n.* 1. (philos.) System of thought in which object of external perception is held to consist of ideas (in various senses). 2. Idealizing, tendency to idealize; representation of things in ideal form; imaginative treatment. **īdē'alist** *n.* **īdėali'stic** *adj.*

īdėă'litȳ *n.* Quality of being ideal; imaginative faculty.

īdē'alīze *v.* Represent in ideal form or character, exalt to ideal perfection or excellence. **īdēalīzā'tion** *n.*

īdē'āte *v.* Imagine, conceive; form ideas. **īdėā'tion** *n.* **īdėā'tional** *adj.*

idée fixe (ēdā fēks). Idea that dominates the mind, monomania. [Fr., = 'fixed idea']

i'dĕm *n.* & *adv.* (abbrev. id.) 1. (ī-) (In) the same author. 2. (ĭ-) (In) the same word etc. [L, = 'the same']

īdĕ'ntic *adj.* (in diplomacy, of notes etc. directed by two or more powers to another) In precisely the same form.

īdĕ'ntical *adj.* (of one thing etc. viewed at different times) The very same; (of different things) agreeing in every detail (*with*); (logic, math.) expressing an identity; ~ *twins*, twins resulting from fertilization of single ovum and consequently alike in all respects including sex (opp. FRATERNAL). **īdĕ'nticallȳ** *adv.*

īdĕ'ntifȳ *v.* 1. Treat (thing) as identical (*with*); associate oneself inseparably *with.* 2. Establish identity of. **īdĕntificā'tion** *n.* ~ *parade*, parade of persons from whom a suspect is to be identified; ~ *plate*, registered number plate of motor vehicle.

īdĕ'ntitȳ *n.* 1. Absolute sameness; oneness; (alg.) equality of two expressions for all values of the literal quantities, equation expressing this. 2. Condition or fact that person or thing is itself and not something else; individuality, personality; ~ *card, disc, plate,* etc., one serving to identify bearer.

ĭ'dėogrăm, ĭ'dėogrăph (*or* -ahf) *ns.* Character in pictorial writing (e.g. Chinese) symbolizing an idea by representing an object or objects with which the idea is associated (not, as in a phonetic system, by expressing the sounds which make up its name).

ī'dėolŏgue (-g), **īdėŏ'logist** *ns.* Idealist, theorist, visionary.

īdėŏ'logȳ *n.* Visionary speculation; (pol. jargon) scheme of ideas at basis of some political or economic theory or system, manner of thinking characteristic of a class or individual (e.g. *bourgeois* ~). **īdėolŏ'gical** *adj.* **īdėolŏ'gicallȳ** *adv.*

īdes (īdz) *n.pl.* (Rom. antiq.) 8th day after nones (15 Mar., May, July, Oct., 13th of other months); ~ *of March*, day, according to tradition, predicted as that of the murder of Julius Caesar; hence, inauspicious day.

ĭd ĕst. (abbrev. i.e.) That is. [L]

ĭ'diocȳ *n.* Mental condition

of an IDIOT; extreme imbecility, utter foolishness.

ĭ'dĭom *n.* Language of a people or country; specific character of this; form of expression peculiar to a language. **ĭdĭomă'tĭc** *adj.* Characteristic of a particular language; vernacular, colloquial. **ĭdĭomă'tĭcallÿ** *adv.*

ĭdĭomŏr'phĭc *adj.* (min.) Having its own characteristic form, esp. its characteristic crystallographic faces.

ĭdĭŏ'pathÿ *n.* (path.) Disease not preceded or occasioned by another. **ĭdĭopă'thĭc** *adj.* **ĭdĭopă'thĭcallÿ** *adv.*

ĭdĭosÿ'ncrasÿ *n.* Mental constitution; view, feeling, mode of expression, peculiar to a person; (med.) physical constitution peculiar to a person. **ĭdĭosÿncră'tĭc** *adj.*

ĭ'dĭot *n.* Person so deficient in mind as to be permanently incapable of rational conduct and having a mental development not exceeding that of an average normal child of 2 years old (the lowest grade of mental deficiency, next below IMBECILE); utter fool. **ĭdĭŏ'tĭc** *adj.* **ĭdĭŏ'tĭcallÿ** *adv.*

ī'dle *adj.* 1. (of action, words, etc.) Ineffective, worthless, vain; baseless, groundless; (of things) useless. 2. Unoccupied; lazy, indolent; (of things) not moving or in operation; (of money) not in circulation; ~ *wheel*, intermediate wheel transmitting motion between two geared wheels. **ī'dlenėss** *n.* **ī'dlÿ** *adv.* **ī'dle** *v.* Be idle; pass (time etc.) *away* in idleness; (of engine etc.) run at low speed without doing any work. **ī'dler** *n.*

I'dō (ē-) *n.* Artificial language, a simplified form of Esperanto, selected by 'Delegation for Adoption of Auxiliary International Language' (founded at Paris, 1901), and made public in 1907. [Esperanto, = 'offspring']

ī'dol *n.* Image of deity used as object of worship; false god; person, thing, that is object of excessive devotion; (logic) false mental image or conception; *~s of the tribe, cave, market-place, and theatre*, four classes of fallacies (Bacon, 'Novum Organum' I. xxxix) referable respectively to limitations of human mind, prejudices of idiosyncrasy, influence of words, philosophical and logical prepossessions.

īdŏ'later *n.* (fem. *ido'latrėss*) Worshipper of idols; devoted admirer (*of*). **īdŏ'latrÿ** *n.* **īdŏ'latrous** *adj.* **īdŏ'latrouslÿ** *adv.*

ī'dolīze *v.* Make an idol of; venerate, love, to excess; practise idolatry. **īdolīzā'tion** *n.*

īdō'lum *n.* Mental image, idea; (logic) idol.

Idūmae'a (ī-). = EDOM. **Idūmae'an** *adj.* & *n.*

Idun, Iduna (ē'dōō-). (Scand. myth.) Goddess, wife of Bragi; she kept the apples which restored the youth of the gods.

ī'dÿll *n.* Short description in verse or (*prose* ~) in prose of picturesque scene or incident, esp. in rustic life; episode suitable for such treatment. **īdÿ'llĭc** *adj.* **īdÿ'llĭcallÿ** *adv.*

i.e. *abbrev. Id est* (L = that is).

ĭf *conj.* On the condition or supposition that; whenever; whether; *as if*, as the case would be if, as though. ~ *n.* Condition, supposition.

Igerne: see IGRAINE.

ĭ'glōō *n.* Eskimo dome-shaped house, esp. one built of blocks of compact snow. [Eskimo = 'house']

Ignatius (ĭgnā'sh*us*), St. Bishop of Antioch, martyred at Rome early in 2nd c.

Ignatius Loyō'la (ĭgnā'sh*us*), St. (1491–1556). Spanish founder of the Society of Jesus (see JESUIT). **Ignā'tian** (-sh*an*) *adj.* & *n.* (Follower) of Ignatius Loyola, Jesuit.

ĭ'gnėous *adj.* Of fire, fiery; produced by volcanic agency.

ĭ'gnĭs fă'tŭus. Will-o'-the-wisp, phosphorescent light (now rarely) seen on marshy ground, supposedly due to the ignition of marsh gas (CH_4) by traces of phosphorus compounds; delusive hope, aim, etc. [med. or mod. L, = 'foolish fire']

ignī'te *v.* Make intensely hot,

(chem.) heat to point of combustion or chemical change; set fire to; take fire. **ĭgnĭ'tion** *n.* (esp.) Starting combustion of mixture in cylinder of internal combustion engine, mechanism for doing this.

ĭgnō'ble *adj.* Of low birth, position, or reputation; mean, base, dishonourable. **ĭgnō'blenėss** *n.* **ĭgnō'blȳ** *adv.*

ĭ'gnomĭnȳ *n.* Dishonour, infamy. **ĭgnomĭ'nĭous** *adj.* Marked by ignominy; humiliating. **ĭgnomĭ'nĭouslȳ** *adv.*

ĭgnorā'mus *n.* (pl. *-muses*). Ignorant person. [L, = 'we do not know']

ĭ'gnorance *n.* Want of knowledge. **ĭ'gnorant** *adj.* Lacking knowledge; uninformed (*of*, *in*). **ĭ'gnorantlȳ** *adv.*

ĭgnorā'tio ėlĕ'nchi (-shĭō, -kī). (logic) Argument that appears to refute opponent while actually disproving something not advanced by him. [L, = 'ignorance of the refutation']

ĭgnor'e *v.t.* Refuse to take notice of; (of Grand Jury) reject (bill) as unfounded.

ĭgnō'tum pe͡r ĭgnō'tĭus. Explanation obscurer than the thing it is meant to explain. [L, = 'the unknown by the still less known']

Igrai'ne, Ige͡r'ne, Yge͡r'ne (ĭ-). (Arthurian legend) Wife of Gorlois of Cornwall and mother (by Uther Pendragon) of Arthur.

IGNATIUS LOYOLA

ĭguaʹna (-gwah-) *n.* Large arboreal lizard (esp. of genus *I*~) of W. Indies and S. America.

ĭguă'nodon (-wăn-) *n.* Huge amphibious herbivorous lizard found as fossil, with teeth and bones resembling those of the iguana.

i.h.p. *abbrev.* Indicated horsepower.

IHS. First 3 letters of Gk *ΙΗΣΟΥΣ* (*Iēsous*) Jesus; often taken as initials of *J*esus *H*ominum *S*alvator 'Jesus saviour of men', or *I*n *H*oc *S*igno (vinces) 'in this sign (thou shalt conquer)', or *I*n *H*ac (cruce) *S*alus 'in this (cross) is salvation'.

ĭl- *prefix.* = IN-[1,2] before *l.*

Île-de-France (ēl, -ahṅs). Old district of France, with Paris as capital, between rivers Seine, Oise, Marne, and Aisne.

ĭlėŏ'stomȳ *n.* (surg.) (Formation of) an opening from the ileum through the abdominal wall.

ĭ'lėum *n.* (pl. *-ea*). (anat.) 3rd and terminal portion of small intestine, opening into large intestine.

ī'lĕx *n.* 1. Holm oak. 2. Tree or shrub of genus *I*~ having small flowers and berry-like fruits, holly.

ĭ'lĭac *adj.* Of the flank or flank-bone (ILIUM); (but orig. of or affecting the ILEUM, whence ~ *passion*, painful affection due to intestinal obstruction).

I'lĭad (ĭ-). Greek epic poem attributed to Homer, describing incidents in the 10th and last year of the siege of Troy by the Greeks, esp. 'the wrath of Achilles'. [Gk *Ilion* Troy]

ĭ'lĭum[1] *n.* (pl. *-ia*). (anat.) Hip-bone, the anterior or superior bone of the pelvis.

I'lĭum[2] (ĭ-). Troy. [L form of Gk name *Ilion*]

ĭlk *adj.* (Sc.) *of that* ~, of the same, as *Guthrie of that* ~, Guthrie of Guthrie; (vulg. or trivial) that family, class, or kind.

ĭll *adj.* 1. Out of health, sick; (of health) unsound, disordered. 2. Morally bad; harmful; hostile, unkind; wretched, disastrous; ~ *will*, animosity. 3. Unskilful; (of manners or conduct) improper.

~ *n.* Evil, the opposite of good; harm, injury; misfortune, calamity, adversity. ~ *adv.* Badly; unfavourably; imperfectly, scarcely; ~ *at ease*, embarrassed, uneasy; ~*-advised*, imprudent; ~*-advisedly*; ~*-affected*, not well disposed; ~*-bred*, badly brought up, rude; ~*-conditioned*, of evil disposition; in bad condition; ~*-disposed*, disposed to evil, malevolent; unfavourably disposed (*towards*); ~*-fated*, destined to, bringing, bad fortune; ~*-favoured*, uncomely; displeasing, objectionable; ~*-gotten*, gained by evil means; ~*-humoured*, bad-tempered; ~*-judged*, unwise; ~*-natured*, bad-tempered, malevolent; ~*-omened*, attended by bad omens; ~*-timed*, unseasonable; ~*-treat*, *-use*, treat badly.

Ill. *abbrev.* Illinois.

illā'tion *n.* Deduction, conclusion; thing deduced.

illā'tive *adj.* (of words) Stating, introducing an inference, as ~ *particles* (e.g. *because, then, therefore*); inferential. **illā'tively** *adv.*

illē'gal *adj.* Not legal; contrary to law. **illē'gally** *adv.* **illėgă'lity** *n.*

illĕ'gible *adj.* Not legible. **illĕgibi'lity** *n.* **illĕ'gibly** *adv.*

illėgi'timate *adj.* Not legitimate; (esp.) bastard. **illėgi'timately** *adv.* **illėgi'timacy** *n.* **illėgi'timāte** *v.t.* Declare illegitimate. **illėgitimā'tion** *n.*

illi'beral *adj.* Narrow-minded; sordid; stingy. **illi'berally** *adv.* **illiberă'lity** *n.*

illi'cit *adj.* Unlawful, forbidden; ~ *process*, (logic) fallacy in which a term not distributed in the premisses of a syllogism is distributed in the conclusion. **illi'citly** *adv.*

illi'mitable *adj.* Boundless. **illi'mitableness, illimitabi'lity** *ns.* **illi'mitably** *adv.*

Illinois[1] (ĭlĭnoi' *or* -oiz). State in north-eastern U.S.; admitted to the Union in 1818; capital, Springfield.

Illinois[2] (ĭlĭnoi' *or* -oiz) *n.* Indian of confederacy of Algonkin tribes formerly living in Illinois and parts of Iowa and Wisconsin.

illi'terate *adj.* Ignorant of letters; unlearned; unable to read. ~ *n.* Illiterate person. **illi'terateness, illi'teracy** *ns.*

i'llness *n.* Unhealthy condition of body; disease, ailment, sickness.

illŏ'gical *adj.* Devoid of, contrary to, logic. **illŏ'gically** *adv.* **illogică'lity** *n.*

illū'me *v.t.* (poet.) Light up, make bright.

illū'mināte (*or* -ōō-) *v.t.* Light up; give spiritual or intellectual light to; throw light upon (subject); shed lustre upon; decorate (buildings etc.) profusely with lights as sign of festivity; decorate (initial letter in manuscript etc.) with gold, silver, and brilliant colours. **illūminā'tion** *n.* Act or process of illuminating; state of being illuminated; (optics) surface light density per unit area on an intercepting surface (see FOOT candle, LUMEN, LUX, PHOT); coloured decorations in a manuscript. **illū'minātor** *n.* **illū'minative** *adj.*

illumina'ti (-ōōmĭnahtĭ) *n.pl.* 1. *I*~, secret society, founded (1776) in Bavaria by Professor Adam Weishaupt, holding deistic and republican principles, and with organization like freemasonry. 2. Persons claiming to possess special enlightenment. **illu'minism, illu'minist** *ns.*

illū'mine (*or* -ōō-) *v.t.* Light up; enlighten spiritually; brighten.

illū'sion (*or* -ōō-) *n.* Deception, delusion; sensuous perception of an external object involving a false belief.

illū'sionist (*or* -ōō-) *n.* 1. One who disbelieves in objective existence. 2. One who produces illusions, esp. conjurer.

illū'sive (*or* -ōō-) *adj.* Deceptive. **illū'sively** *adv.* **illū'siveness** *n.*

illū'sory (*or* -ōō-) *adj.* Having the character of an illusion. **illū'sorily** *adv.* **illū'soriness** *n.*

i'llustrāte *v.t.* Make clear, explain; make clear by examples; elucidate (description etc.) by drawings; ornament (book, newspaper etc.) with pictures etc. **ĭ'llustrātor** *n.* **ĭllustrā'tion** *n.* Illustrating; example; drawing etc. illustrating book or article in paper.

ĭ'llustrative (*or* ĭllŭ'-) *adj.* Serving as explanation or example (*of*). **ĭ'llustratively** *adv.*

ĭllŭ'strious *adj.* Distinguished, renowned. **ĭllŭ'striously** *adv.* **ĭllŭ'striousness** *n.*

Illȳ'ria (ĭ-). Ancient region, with landward boundaries never clearly defined, extending along Balkan coast of Adriatic from Fiume to Durazzo, and including modern Dalmatia, Bosnia and Herzegovina, Montenegro, and part of Albania.

Illȳ'rian (ĭ-) *adj.* Of Illyria. ~ *n.* Native, inhabitant, of Illyria; Indo-European language (closely related to modern Albanian) spoken by Illyrians.

I.L.O. *abbrev.* International Labour Organisation.

I.L.P. *abbrev.* Independent Labour Party.

I'lus (ī-). (Gk legend) Founder of Troy (Gk *Ilion*) and grandfather of Priam.

ĭm- *prefix* = IN-[1,2] before *b, m, p*.

ĭ'mage *n.* 1. Artificial imitation of external form of an object, e.g. statue; (esp.) figure of saint or divinity as object of religious veneration. 2. Optical appearance or counterpart of object produced by rays of light reflected from a morror or refracted through any transparent medium; *real* ~, one formed at the point at which light, originating in the object-point, is finally converged after traversing an optical system, as e.g. on a photographic plate; *virtual* ~, one formed at the point from which light, originating in the object-point, and having traversed an optical system, appears to be diverging, as e.g. one seen in a plane mirror. 3. Mental picture, idea, conception; general impression (of person, party, etc.) given to others. ~ *v.t.* Make an image of, portray; reflect, mirror; picture; describe vividly; typify.

ĭ'magery *n.* Images; statuary, carving; figurative illustration.

ĭmă'ginable *adj.* That can be imagined. **ĭmă'ginably** *adv.*

ĭmă'ginal *adj.* (entom.) Of an insect imago.

ĭmă'ginary *adj.* Existing only in imagination; (math.) having no real existence, but assumed to exist for a special purpose, e.g. the square root of a negative quantity. **ĭmă'ginarily** *adv.*

ĭmăginā'tion *n.* Imagining; mental faculty forming images of external objects not present to the senses; fancy; creative faculty of the mind.

ĭmă'ginative *adj.* Of, given to using, having or showing in a high degree, the faculty of imagination. **ĭmă'ginatively** *adv.* **ĭmă'ginativeness** *n.*

ĭmă'gine *v.t.* Form mental image of; conceive; guess; suppose, be of opinion; take into one's head.

ĭ'magism *n.* Movement in poetry, originating in 1912 and represented by Ezra Pound, Amy Lowell, and others, aiming at exact use of visual images. **ĭ'magist** *n.*

ĭmā'gō *n.* (pl. *-gos* or *-ginēs*). 1. (entom.) Final and perfect stage of insect after it has undergone all its metamorphoses; adult. 2. (psychol.) Conception of the parent retained in the unconscious and elaborated by child fantasies.

ĭma'm, ĭmau'm (-ahm) *n.* 1. In Muslim communities, name given to the person who is regarded as taking Muhammad's place as leader of Islam, esp. any of twelve successive heads of Islam, beginning with Ali and his sons, recognized by the Shiites; hence, any great spiritual leader. 2. Official who leads the prayers in a mosque. **ĭma'mate** *n.* Office, title, of imam. [Arab. *'imām* leader f. *'amma* lead]

ĭmbă'lance *n.* (psychol., path.) Disturbance of mental or bodily equilibrium (also fig.).

ĭ'mbecile (*or* -ēl) *adj.* Mentally weak, stupid. ~ *n.* Adult person whose intelligence is equal to that of the average normal child between the ages of 3 and 7 years, or between 25 and 50 per cent. of that of the average normal adult (see also IDIOT, MORON); person of weak intellect. **ĭmbecĭ'lĭtȳ** *n.*

imbed: see EMBED.

ĭmbī'be *v.t.* Drink in, assimilate, (ideas etc.); drink (liquid); inhale (air etc.); absorb (moisture etc.). **ĭmbĭbĭ'tion** *n.*

ĭ'mbrĭcāte *v.* Arrange (leaves, scales of fish, etc.), be arranged, so as to overlap like tiles. **ĭ'mbrĭcātėd** *adj.* **ĭmbrĭcā'tion** *n.*

ĭmbro'glio (-ōlyō) *n.* Confused heap; complicated or confused (esp. political or dramatic) situation.

ĭmbrue (-ōō') *v.t.* Stain (*in, with,* blood, slaughter, etc.).

ĭmbū'e *v.t.* Saturate (*with*); dye (*with*); permeate, inspire (*with* feelings etc.); imbrue.

I.M.F. *abbrev.* International Monetary Fund.

Imhō'tĕp (ĭ-) (*c* 2680 B.C.). Egyptian sage and architect, later regarded as patron saint of scribes; identified by the Greeks with Aesculapius.

ĭ'mĭtable *adj.* Capable of being imitated. **ĭmĭtabĭ'lĭtȳ** *n.*

ĭ'mĭtāte *v.t.* Follow example of; mimic; be like. **ĭmĭtā'tion** *n.* Imitating; copy; counterfeit (freq. attrib.); (mus.) repetition of melody etc. usu. at different pitch, in another part or voice. **ĭ'mĭtātor** *n.*

ĭ'mĭtatĭve *adj.* Following model or example (*of*); characterized by, consisting in, imitation; fictitious, counterfeit. **ĭ'mĭtatĭvelȳ** *adv.* **ĭ'mĭtatĭvenėss** *n.*

ĭmmă'cūlate *adj.* Pure, spotless; faultless; (biol.) not spotted; *I~ Conception,* doctrine that the Virgin Mary was conceived free from taint of original sin (in 1854 declared an article of faith of R.C. Church). **ĭmmă'cūlatelȳ** *adv.* **ĭmmă'cūlacȳ** *n.*

ĭ'mmanent *adj.* Indwelling, inherent (*in*); (of God) permanently pervading the universe (opp. TRANSCENDENT). **ĭ'mmanence, ĭ'mmanencȳ** *ns.*

Immă'nūel (ĭ-). Name given to Christ as deliverer of Judah prophesied by Isaiah (Isa. 7: 14, 8: 8; Matt. 1: 23). [Heb., = 'God with us']

ĭmmatēr'ĭal *adj.* Not material, incorporeal; unimportant. **ĭmmatēr'ĭalĭsm** *n.* Doctrine that matter does not exist in itself apart from perception. **ĭmmatēr'ĭalist** *n.* **ĭmmatērĭă'lĭtȳ** *n.*

ĭmmatūr'e *adj.* Not mature. **ĭmmatūr'ĭtȳ** *n.*

ĭmmea'surable (-mĕzher-) *adj.* Not measurable, immense. **ĭmmea'surablenėss, ĭmmeasurabĭ'lĭtȳ** *ns.* **ĭmmea'surablȳ** *adv.*

ĭmmē'dĭate *adj.* (of person or thing in its relation to another) Not separated by any intervening medium; (of relation or action) direct, without intervening medium; nearest, next; occurring at once, without delay; *~ inference,* (logic) inference from single premiss, without intervention of middle term. **ĭmmē'dĭatelȳ** *adv.* **ĭmmē'dĭatenėss, ĭmmē'dĭacȳ** *ns.*

ĭmmėmŏr'ĭal *adj.* Ancient beyond memory; very old. **ĭmmėmŏr'ĭallȳ** *adv.*

ĭmmĕ'nse *adj.* Vast, huge; **ĭmmĕ'nselȳ** *adv.* In an immense degree; (colloq.) very much. **ĭmmĕ'nsĭtȳ** *n.*

I'mmermann (ĭ-), Karl Leberecht (1796–1840). German Romantic novelist and playwright.

ĭmmĕr'se *v.t.* Dip, plunge (*in* liquid); put below surface of water, esp. baptize thus; bury, embed, (*in*); involve deeply, absorb, (*in* debt, difficulties, thought, etc.).

ĭmmĕr'sion *n.* Immersing; baptism by plunging whole person in water; absorption (*in* thought etc.); (astron.) disappearance of celestial body behind another or in its shadow; *~ heater,* electrical element, usu. thermostatically controlled, immersed in water which it heats.

ĭ'mmĭgrāte *v.* Come as settler (*into* foreign country); bring in (person) as settler. **ĭ'mmĭgrant** *adj.* & *n.* **ĭmmĭgrā'tion** *n.*

ĭ'mmĭnent *adj.* (of events, esp. dangers) Impending, soon to happen. **ĭ'mmĭnently** *adv.* **ĭ'mmĭnence** *n.*

ĭmmĭ'scĭble *adj.* That cannot

be mixed. **ĭmmĭscĭbĭ'lĭtў** *n.* **ĭmmĭ'scĭblў** *adv.*

ĭmmĭ'tĭgable *adj.* That cannot be softened or toned down. **ĭmmĭ'tĭgablў** *adv.*

ĭmmō'bīle *adj.* Immovable: not mobile; motionless. **ĭmmobĭ'lĭtў** *n.*

ĭmmō'bĭlīze *v.t.* Fix immovably; render immobile or stationary; withdraw (specie) from circulation, holding it against bank-notes. **ĭmmōbĭlīzā'tion** *n.*

ĭmmŏ'derate *adj.* Excessive, wanting in moderation. **ĭmmŏ'deratelў** *adv.*

ĭmmŏ'dėst *adj.* Lacking modesty; shameless; impudent. **ĭmmŏ'dėstlў** *adv.* **ĭmmŏ'dėstў** *n.*

ĭ'mmolāte *v.t.* Kill (victim) as sacrifice; (fig.) sacrifice (thing etc. *to* another). **ĭmmolā'tion, ĭ'mmolātor** *ns.*

ĭmmŏ'ral *adj.* Not conforming to morality; morally evil; vicious, dissolute. **ĭmmŏ'rallў** *adv.* **ĭmmoră'lĭtў** *n.*

ĭmmôr'tal *adj.* Undying; divine; unfading, incorruptible; famous for all time. **ĭmmôr'tallў** *adv.* **ĭmmôr'tal** *n.* Immortal being, esp. (pl.) gods of antiquity; person, esp. author, of enduring fame; *the Immortals*, the 40 members of the Académie française (so called because each member's place is filled as soon as he dies); picked body of 10,000 infantry forming ancient Persian royal bodyguard, whose number was kept constantly full. **ĭmmôrtă'lĭtў** *n.*

ĭmmôr'talīze *v.t.* Confer enduring fame upon; endow with endless life; perpetuate. **ĭmmôrtalīzā'tion** *n.*

ĭmmôrtĕ'lle *n.* Composite flower of papery texture (esp. *Helichrysum orientale*) retaining colour and shape after being dried.

ĭmmo'vable (-mōō-) *adj.* That cannot be moved; motionless; not subject to change; steadfast, unyielding; emotionless; (law, of property) consisting of land, houses, etc.; = REAL. **ĭmmo'vableness, ĭmmovabĭ'lĭtў** *ns.* **ĭmmo'vablў** *adv.* **ĭmmo'vables** (-z) *n.pl.* Immovable property.

ĭmmū'ne *adj.* Having immunity; serving to develop immunity.

ĭmmū'nĭtў *n.* 1. Freedom (from); (law) exemption (*from* taxation, jurisdiction, etc.). 2. (physiol.) That property of a living organism by which infection is resisted and overcome; *active* ~, increased resistance to an invading microbe or its products, developed in response to infection (whether a natural infection or one introduced artificially), as distinct from *passive* ~, temporary resistance acquired prenatally or by injection of antibody; *acquired* ~, immunity of an organism that manufactures, or is injected with, antibodies.

ĭ'mmūnīze *v.t.* Render immune (*against* infection). **ĭmmūnīzā'tion** *n.*

ĭmmūnŏ'logў *n.* Study of immunity from disease and the conditions governing it. **ĭmmūnŏ'logĭst** *n.*

ĭmmūr'e *v.t.* Imprison; shut up. **ĭmmūr'ement** *n.*

ĭmmū'table *adj.* Unchangeable; not subject to variation in different cases. **ĭmmūtabĭ'lĭtў** *n.* **ĭmmū'tablў** *adv.*

ĭmp[1] *n.* Child of the devil; little devil; mischievous child.

ĭmp[2] *v.t.* (falconry) Ingraft feathers in wing of (bird) to strengthen flight.

ĭ'mpăct[1] *n.* Striking, collision (freq. fig.).

ĭmpă'ct[2] *v.t.* Press, fix, closely or firmly (*into, in*). **ĭmpă'ction** *n.* (esp., surg.) Fracture in which broken parts are driven together so as to become locked.

ĭmpair' *v.t.* Damage, weaken. **ĭmpair'ment** *n.*

ĭmpā'le *v.t.* 1. Transfix (body etc. *upon, with*, stake, etc., esp. as form of capital punishment). 2. (her.) Combine (two coats of arms) by placing side by side on one shield separated by vertical line down middle. **ĭmpā'lement** *n.* (esp., her.).

ĭmpă'lpable *adj.* Imperceptible to the touch; not easily grasped by the mind; intangible. **ĭmpălpabĭ'lĭtў** *n.* **ĭmpă'lpablў** *adv.*

ĭmpărĭsy̆llă'bĭc *adj.* & *n.* (Gk & L gram.) (Noun) not having same number of syllables in all cases.

ĭmpâr't *v.t.* Give share of; communicate (news etc. *to*).

ĭmpâr'tial (-sh*a*l) *adj.* Not partial, unprejudiced, fair. **ĭmpâr'tiallȳ** *adv.* **ĭmpârtiă'lĭtȳ** (-shĭ-) *n.*

ĭmpâr'tĭble *adj.* (of estate) Not divisible.

ĭmpa'ssable (-pah-) *adj.* That cannot be traversed. **ĭmpa'ssablenėss, ĭmpassabĭ'lĭtȳ** *ns.*

ĭmpa'sse (-ahs) *n.* Blind alley; position from which there is no escape.

ĭmpă'ssĭble *adj.* Incapable of feeling or emotion; incapable of suffering injury; not subject to suffering. **ĭmpă'ssĭblenėss, ĭmpassĭbĭ'lĭtȳ** *ns.* **ĭmpă'ssĭblȳ** *adv.*

ĭmpă'ssion *v.t.* Stir the passions of, excite strongly (chiefly in past. part.).

ĭmpă'ssĭve *adj.* Deficient in feeling or emotion; serene; without sensation; not subject to suffering. **ĭmpă'ssĭvelȳ** *adv.* **ĭmpă'ssĭvenėss, ĭmpassĭ'vĭtȳ** *ns.*

ĭmpă'stō *n.* (paint.) Laying on of colour thickly; (ceramics) enamel colours on slip standing out in relief from surface of ware.

ĭmpā'tient (-sh*e*nt) *adj.* Not enduring with composure; intolerant *of*; restlessly desirous (*for* thing, *to* do). **ĭmpā'tientlȳ** *adv.* **ĭmpā'tience** (-sh*e*ns) *n.*

ĭmpea'ch *v.t.* Call in question, disparage (character etc.); accuse (person) *of*, charge *with*; find fault with; accuse of treason or other high crime before competent tribunal. **ĭmpea'chment** *n.* Calling in question; accusation and prosecution of a person for treason or other high crime or misdemeanour before a competent tribunal; judicial process in which House of Commons (in U.S., House of Representatives) are prosecutors and House of Lords (in U.S., Senate) are judges.

ĭmpĕ'ccable *adj.* Not liable to sin; (of things) faultless. **ĭmpĕccabĭ'lĭtȳ** *n.* **ĭmpĕ'ccablȳ** *adv.*

ĭmpėcū'nĭous *adj.* Having little or no money. **ĭmpėcūnĭŏ'sĭtȳ** *n.*

ĭmpē'dance *n.* (elect.) Resistance of an electric circuit to the flow of alternating current.

ĭmpē'de *v.t.* Retard, hinder.

ĭmpĕ'dĭment *n.* Hindrance, obstruction; (also ~ *in speech*) stammer, stutter.

ĭmpĕdĭmĕ'nta *n.pl.* Baggage, esp. of army.

ĭmpĕ'l *v.t.* Drive, force; drive forward, propel. **ĭmpĕ'llent** *n.*

ĭmpĕ'nd *v.i.* Hang, be suspended, (*over*); (fig., of danger) hang threateningly (*over*); be imminent. **ĭmpĕ'ndence, ĭmpĕ'ndencȳ** *ns.* **ĭmpĕ'ndent** *adj.*

ĭmpĕ'nėtrable *adj.* That cannot be penetrated; inscrutable, unfathomable; impervious; (phys.) having that property in virtue of which two bodies cannot occupy same place at same time. **ĭmpĕ'nėtrablenėss, ĭmpĕnėtrabĭ'lĭtȳ** *ns.* **ĭmpĕ'nėtrablȳ** *adv.*

ĭmpĕ'nėtrāte *v.t.* Penetrate deeply.

ĭmpĕ'nĭtent *adj.* Not penitent. **ĭmpĕ'nĭtentlȳ** *adv.* **ĭmpĕ'nĭtence, ĭmpĕ'nĭtencȳ** *ns.*

ĭmpĕ'ratĭve *adj.* 1. (gram., of verbal mood, or form belonging to it) Expressing command, request, or exhortation. 2. Commanding, peremptory; urgent; obligatory. **ĭmpĕ'ratĭvelȳ** *adv.* **ĭmpĕ'ratĭvenėss** *n.* **ĭmpĕ'ratĭve** *n.* Imperative mood. **ĭmpĕratī'val** *adj.*

ĭmpercĕ'ptĭble *adj.* That cannot be perceived; very slight, gradual, or subtle. **ĭmpercĕ'ptĭblȳ** *adv.*

ĭmpercĭ'pĭent *adj.* Lacking perception.

ĭmpér'fėct *adj.* 1. Not fully formed or done, incomplete; faulty. 2. (gram., of tense) Implying action going on but not completed (e.g. *he is*, *he will be*, *singing*, but usu. of past time, *as he was singing*). **ĭmpér'fėctlȳ** *adv.*

ĭmperfĕ'ction *n.* Incompleteness; faultiness; fault, blemish.

ĭmperfĕ'ctĭve *adj.* & *n.* (Slav. gram.) (Aspect of verb) expressing action (whether in past, present, or future) without reference to its completion (opp. PERFECTIVE).

imper'forate *adj.* Not perforated, esp. (anat.) lacking normal opening; (of sheet of postage stamps, or single stamp) without perforations.

impēr'ial *adj.* Of an empire or sovereign State ranking with an empire; of an emperor or empress; (of weights and measures) appointed by statute for use throughout United Kingdom; (of paper) 762 × 559 mm (30 × 22 in.) **impēr'ially** *adv.* **impēr'ial** *n.* 1. Small beard or tuft below lower lip (after the Emperor Napoleon III). 2. Trunk for luggage adapted for roof of coach. 3. Gold coin of Tsarist Russia, orig. worth 10 silver roubles.

impēr'ialism *n.* Rule of an emperor; principle or spirit of empire, advocacy of what are held to be imperial interests. **impēr'ialist** *n.* Adherent of an emperor, esp. (1600–1800) of German Emperor; advocate of imperial rule, esp. adherent of Bonaparte family; advocate of imperialism. **impēriali'stic** *adj.*

impě'ril *v.t.* Bring into danger.

impēr'ious *adj.* Overbearing, domineering; urgent, imperative. **impēr'iously** *adv.* **impēr'iousness** *n.*

impě'rishable *adj.* That can not perish. **impě'rishableness, impěrishabi'lity** *ns.* **impě'rishably** *adv.*

impě'rium (*or* -ēr-) *n.* Absolute powers; empire. [L, = 'command, dominion']

imper'manent *adj.* Not permanent. **imper'manence, imper'manency** *ns.*

imper'meable *adj.* That cannot be passed through; that does not permit passage of fluids. **impermeabi'lity** *n.*

imperscri'ptible *adj.* Not backed by written authority.

imper'sonal *adj.* 1. (gram., of verbs) Used only in 3rd person singular without referring to a person or definite subject; hence, used without a subject or with a merely formal one, as Engl. *it*. 2. Having no personality or personal reference or tone. **imper'sonally** *adv.* **impersonă'lity** *n.*

imper'sonāte *v.t.* Represent in bodily form, personify; play the part of, personate; act (character). **impersonā'tion, imper'sonator** *ns.* **imper'sonative** *adj.*

imper'tinent *adj.* 1. Irrelevant (now chiefly in law); out of place, absurd. 2. Intrusive, presumptuous; insolent, saucy. **imper'tinently** *adv.* **imper'tinence** *n.*

impertur'bable *adj.* Not excitable, calm. **impertur'bableness, imperturbabi'lity** *ns.* **impertur'bably** *adv.*

imper'vious *adj.* Not affording passage (*to*); (fig.) impenetrable, not affording entrance *to* (argument, feeling, etc.). **imper'viously** *adv.* **imper'viousness** *n.*

impetī'gō *n.* Acute inflammatory disease of skin caused by streptococcal and staphylococcal organisms, characterized by pustules chiefly on face and hands.

i'mpetrāte *v.t.* (chiefly theol.) Obtain by request or entreaty. **impetrā'tion** *n.*

impě'tūous *adj.* Moving violently or rapidly; acting with rash or sudden energy. **impě'tūously** *adv.* **impě'tūousness, impětūŏ'sity** *ns.*

i'mpetus *n.* Force with which a body moves; (fig.) moving force, impulse.

i'mpeyan (-pian) *adj.* ~ *pheasant*, pheasant of S. Kashmir (*Lophophorus impeianus*), with crested head and, in male, brilliant plumage. [discovered by Sir Elijah *Impey*, 1787]

i'mpi *n.* Body of Kaffir warriors, army.

impī'ety *n.* Ungodliness; want of dutifulness or reverence.

impi'nge (-j) *v.* Make impact (*on, upon*); (archaic) make (thing) do this. **impi'ngement** (-jm-) *n.*

i'mpious *adj.* Not pious, wicked, profane. **i'mpiously** *adv.*

i'mpish *adj.* Of, like, an imp. **i'mpishly** *adv.* **i'mpishness** *n.*

implă'cable *adj.* That cannot be appeased. **implăcabi'lity** *n.* **implă'cably** *adv.*

impla'nt (-ah-) *v.t.* Insert, infix (*in*); instil (*in* mind etc.); plant. **implantā'tion** *n.*

i'mplėment[1] *n.* 1. (pl.) Things serving as equipment or outfit, as household furniture, ecclesiastical vessels or vestments, etc. 2. Tool; (pl.) apparatus, set of utensils, instruments, etc.

i'mplėmĕnt[2] *v.t.* Complete (contract etc.); fulfil (engagement); fill up, supplement. **implėmĕntā'tion** *n.*

implē'tion *n.* Filling; fullness.

i'mplicāte *v.t.* Entwine, entangle; involve, imply, as inference; involve (*in* charge, crime, etc.). **implicā'tion** *n.* **i'mplicātive** *adj.*

impli'cit *adj.* Implied though not plainly expressed; virtually contained (*in*); ~ *faith*, faith in spiritual matters, not independently reached by individual but involved in general belief of Church; absolute, unreserved, faith. **impli'citly** *adv.* **impli'citnėss** *n.*

implôr'e *v.t.* Beg earnestly for; entreat. **implôr'ingly** *adv.*

implu'vium (-ōōv-) *n.* (Rom. antiq.) Square basin in middle of atrium receiving rainwater from open space in roof.

imply' *v.t.* Involve the truth of (thing not expressly asserted); mean; insinuate, hint.

impō'lder *v.t.* Make a POLDER of; reclaim from sea.

impolī'te *adj.* Uncivil, rude. **impolī'tely** *adv.* **impolī'tenėss** *n.*

impŏ'litic *adj.* Not politic; inexpedient. **impŏ'liticly** *adv.*

impŏ'nderable *adj.* 1. Having no weight; very light; (fig.) that cannot be estimated. 2. Not to be estimated by physical weight. ~ *n.* Imponderable thing.

impôr't *v.t.* 1. Bring, introduce (esp. goods from foreign country *into*). 2. Imply, indicate, mean; express, make known. 3. Be of consequence. **impôrtā'tion** *n.* Bringing in, introducing. **impôr'ter** *n.* One who imports goods. **i'mpôrt** *n.* 1. What is implied, meaning, importance. 2. Importation; (usu. pl.) commodity imported.

impôr'tance *n.* Being important; weight, significance; personal consequence, dignity; pompousness.

impôr'tant *adj.* Carrying with it great consequence (*to*), weighty, momentous; consequential, pompous. **impôr'tantly** *adv.*

impôr'tūnate *adj.* Persistent, pressing, in solicitation; (of affairs) urgent. **impôr'tūnately** *adv.* **importū'nity** *n.*

impôr'tūne (*or* -ū'n) *v.t.* Solicit pressingly.

impō'se (-z) *v.* 1. Place (thing) *on* (archaic); (print.) lay (pages of type) in proper order and secure them in a chase. 2. Lay (tax, duty, charge, *on*). 3. Palm off (thing *on* person). 4. Exert influence (*on* person) by striking character or appearance; ~ *on*, take advantage of (person); practise deception upon. **impō'singly** *adv.* **impō'singnėss** *n.*

imposi'tion (-z-) *n.* (esp.) 1. Laying on *of hands* (in ordination etc.). 2. (print.) Imposing or arranging of pages of type in form. 3. Impost, tax, duty, (fig.) burden. 4. Piece of deception or imposture. 5. Work set as punishment at school.

impŏ'ssible *adj.* Not possible; (loosely) not easy, not convenient; (colloq.) outrageous, intolerable. **impŏssibi'lity** *n.* **impŏ'ssibly** *adv.*

i'mpōst[1] *n.* (archaic) Tax, duty, tribute.

i'mpōst[2] *n.* Upper course of pillar, bearing arch.

impŏ'stor *n.* One who assumes a false character or passes himself off as someone else; swindler.

impŏ'sture *n.* Fraudulent deception.

i'mpŏt *n.* (school slang) Imposition.

i'mpotent *adj.* Powerless; helpless, decrepit; (of males) wanting in sexual power. **i'mpotently** *adv.* **i'mpotence, i'mpotency** *ns.*

impou'nd *v.t.* Shut up (cattle) in pound; shut up (person, thing) as in pound; take legal possession of; confiscate.

impŏ'verish *v.t.* Make poor; exhaust strength of. **impŏ'verishment** *n.*

impră'cticable *adj.* Impossible in practice; unmanageable; (of roads etc.) impassable. **impră'cticableness, impräcticabi'lity** *ns.* **impră'cticably** *adv.*

impră'ctical *adj.* (now chiefly U.S.) Unpractical; impracticable. **impräctică'lity** *n.*

i'mprecāte *v.t.* Invoke, call down, (evil *upon* person etc.). **imprecā'tion** *n.* (esp.) Spoken curse. **i'mprecatory** *adj.*

imprĕ'gnable *adj.* (of fortress etc.) That cannot be taken by arms; (fig.) proof against attack. **imprĕgnabi'lity** *n.* **imprĕ'gnably** *adv.*

imprĕ'gnate *adj.* Pregnant; permeated (*with*). **i'mprĕgnāte** (*or* imprĕ'g-) *v.t.* 1. Make (female) pregnant; = FERTILIZE, 2. 2. Fill, saturate, (*with*); imbue, fill, (*with* feelings, moral qualities, etc.). **imprĕgnā'tion** *n.*

impresar'iō (-z-) *n.* (pl. *-s*). Organizer of public entertainments, esp. manager of operatic or concert company.

imprescri'ptible *adj.* Not subject to prescription, that cannot be legally taken away.

i'mprĕss[1] *n.* Stamping; mark made by seal, stamp, etc.; (fig.) characteristic mark. **imprĕ'ss** *v.t.* Apply (mark etc.) with pressure, imprint, stamp, (*on*); imprint, enforce, (idea etc. *on* person, his mind); mark (thing *with* stamp etc.); affect, influence; affect (person) strongly (*with* idea etc.). **imprĕ'ssible** *adj.* **imprĕssibi'lity** *n.*

imprĕ'ss[2] *v.t.* Force (men) to serve in army or navy; seize (goods etc.) for public service; enlist, make use of, (thing) in argument etc. **imprĕ'ssment** *n.*

imprĕ'ssion *n.* 1. Impressing (of mark); mark impressed. 2. Individual print taken from type or engraving. 3. Number of copies of book printed at one time, printing of these; unaltered reprint from standing type or plates, as opp. to EDITION. 4. Effect produced (esp. on mind or feelings); notion, (vague) belief, impressed on the mind.

imprĕ'ssionable *adj.* Susceptible of impressions, easily influenced. **imprĕssionabi'lity** *n.*

Imprĕ'ssionism (i-) *n.* Method of painting initiated *c* 1870 by a school of French painters (including Manet, Monet, Pissarro, Renoir, and Degas), whose aim was to paint the momentary or transitory appearance of things, and esp. the effects of light and atmosphere, rather than form or structure; method of writing resembling this. **Imprĕ'ssionist** *n.* & *adj.* **imprĕssioni'stic** *adj.* **imprĕssioni'stically** *adv.*

imprĕ'ssive *adj.* Able to excite deep feeling, making deep impression on mind or senses. **imprĕ'ssively** *adv.* **imprĕ'ssiveness** *n.*

i'mprĕst *n.* Money advanced to person to be used in State business.

imprimā'tur *n.* Official licence to print esp. works sanctioned by R.C. Ch.; (fig.) sanction. [mod. L, = 'let it be printed']

imprimatur'a (-ēm-) *n.* (paint.) Coloured transparent glaze applied as primer.

impri'mis *adv.* In the first place. [L, = *in primis* among the first things]

impri'nt *v.t.* Stamp (figure etc. *on*); impress (idea etc. *on*, *in* mind etc.); impress (quality etc. *on*, *in*); stamp (thing *with* figure). **i'mprint** *n.* 1. Impression, stamp. 2. Name of printer or publisher, date and place of printing or publication, at foot or back of title-page or at end of book etc.

impri'son (-zn) *v.t.* Put into prison; confine, shut up. **impri'sonment** *n.*

imprŏ'bable *adj.* Not likely to be true or to happen. **imprŏbabi'lity** *n.* **imprŏb'ably** *adv.*

imprŏ'bity *n.* Wickedness; dishonesty.

imprŏ'mptū *adv.* & *adj.* (Spoken, done) without preparation, extempore. ~ *n.* Improvised or extempore performance or composition; musical composition having character of improvisation. [L, *in promptu* in readiness]

ĭmprŏ'per *adj.* Inaccurate, wrong; unseemly, indecent; ~ *fraction*, fraction with numerator greater than denominator. **ĭmprŏ'perlȳ** *adv.*

ĭmprō'prĭāte *v.t.* Annex (ecclesiastical benefice) to corporation or person as property; place (tithes, ecclesiastical property) in lay hands. **ĭmprō'prĭate** *adj.* **ĭmprōprĭā'tion** *n.* **ĭmprō'prĭātor** *n.* One to whom benefice is impropriated.

ĭmproprī'ĕtȳ *n.* Incorrectness; unfitness; indecency.

ĭmpro'vable (-ōō-) *adj.* That can be improved; adapted for cultivation. **ĭmpro'vablenĕss, ĭmprovabĭ'lĭtȳ** *ns.*

ĭmpro've (-ōō-) *v.* Make, become, better; make good use of (occasion etc.); preach on (*the occasion*) with a view to edification; ~ *away*, get rid of by improvements; ~ *on*, produce something better than. **ĭmpro'vement** *n.*

ĭmpro'ver (-ōō-) *n.* (esp.) One working at trade for low wage or none to improve his skill; chemical substance added to flour to improve texture etc. of bread.

ĭmprŏ'vĭdent *adj.* Unforeseeing; heedless; thriftless. **ĭmprŏ'vĭdentlȳ** *adv.* **ĭmprŏ'vĭdence** *n.*

ĭ'mprovīse (-z) *v.t.* Compose, utter, (verse, music, etc.) without preparation; provide, get up, extempore. **ĭmprovīsā'tion, ĭ'mprovīsātor** *ns.* **ĭmprovisatōr'ĭal, ĭmprovī'satorȳ** *adjs.*

ĭmpru'dent (-ōō-) *adj.* Rash, indiscreet. **ĭmpru'dentlȳ** *adv.* **ĭmpru'dence** *n.*

ĭ'mpūdent *adj.* Shamelessly forward; unblushing; insolently disrespectful. **ĭ'mpūdentlȳ** *adv.* **ĭ'mpūdence** *n.*

ĭmpūdĭ'cĭtȳ *n.* Shamelessness, immodesty.

ĭmpu'gn (-ūn) *v.t.* Assail by word, call in question, (statement, action). **ĭmpu'gnment** *n.*

ĭ'mpŭlse *n.* 1. Impelling, push; (dynamics) indefinitely larger force acting for an inappreciably short time but producing finite momentum; momentum thus produced; product of average value of force multiplied by time during which it acts. 2. Mental incitement; sudden tendency to act without reflection; impetus.

ĭmpŭ'lsion *n.* Impelling, push; mental impulse; impetus.

ĭmpŭ'lsĭve *adj.* 1. Tending to impel. 2. (of persons, conduct, etc.) Apt to be moved, prompted, by sudden impulse. **ĭmpŭ'lsĭvelȳ** *adv.* **ĭmpŭ'lsĭvenĕss** *n.*

ĭmpū'nĭtȳ *n.* Exemption from punishment; exemption from injury as consequence of act.

ĭmpūr'e *adj.* Dirty; unchaste; mixed with foreign matter, adulterated; (of colour) mixed with another colour. **ĭmpūr'elȳ** *adv.* **ĭmpūr'ĭtȳ** *n.*

ĭmpū'te *v.t.* Attribute, ascribe, (fault etc. *to*); (theol.) ascribe (another's righteousness or guilt *to* person). **ĭmpūtā'tion** *n.* **ĭmpū'tatĭve** *adj.* **ĭmpū'tatĭvelȳ** *adv.*

I.M.S. *abbrev.* Indian Medical Service.

in *prep.* Within limits of space, time, circumstance, etc., as ~ *Europe*, ~ *London*, ~ *a box*, ~ *the day*, ~ *the army*; (of animals) pregnant with (as ~ *kitten*, ~ *pig*); (mus.) modulated according to (the key of); *not* ~ *it*, not in the running, not a serious competitor; *nothing, little, not much*, ~ *it*, (orig. racing slang) no decided advantage yet gained by any competitor. ~ *adv.* 1. In or at a place, the right or normal state, the fashion, etc.; in season, on the inside, within; at home; in office; at work; (of player or side) having the turn or right to play; (of fire) burning. 2. So as to pass within. 3. ~ *for*, committed to (a course of action); in competition for; ~ *for it*, certain to meet with punishment or something unpleasant; ~ *with*, on friendly terms with. 4. ~*-goal*, (Rugby footb.) area between goal line and deadball line; ~ *-patient*, one who remains in hospital while under treatment. ~ *adj.* That is in; lying etc. within. ~ *n.* (pl.) ~*s and outs*, turnings to and fro (usu. fig.), details (*of* procedure etc.).

ĭn-[1] *prefix*. In, on, into, towards, against.

ĭn-[2] *prefix*. Not.

in. *abbrev*. Inch(es).

ĭnabĭ'lĭtȳ *n*. Being unable; lack of power or means.

ĭnaccĕ'ssĭble (-ks-) *adj*. That cannot be reached; not open to advances, unapproachable. **ĭnaccessĭbĭ'lĭtȳ** *n*. **ĭnaccĕ'ssĭblȳ** *adv*.

ĭnă'ccūrate *adj*. Not accurate. **ĭnă'ccūratelȳ** *adv*. **ĭnă'ccūracȳ** *n*.

ĭnă'ction *n*. Absence of action; sluggishness, inertness. **ĭnă'ctĭve** *adj*. **ĭnă'ctĭvelȳ** *adv*. **ĭnăctĭ'vĭtȳ** *n*. **ĭnă'ctĭvāte** *v.t.*

ĭnă'dėquate *adj*. Not adequate; insufficient. **ĭnă'dėquatelȳ** *adv*. **ĭnă'dėquacȳ** *n*.

ĭnadmĭ'ssĭble *adj*. That cannot be admitted or allowed. **ĭnadmĭssĭbĭ'lĭtȳ** *n*. **ĭnadmĭ'ssĭblȳ** *adv*.

ĭnadvêr'tent *adj*. Not properly attentive; negligent; (of actions) unintentional. **ĭnadvêr'tentlȳ** *adv*. **ĭnadvêr'tence, ĭnadvêr'tencȳ** *ns*.

ĭnā'lĭenable *adj*. Not alienable. **ĭnālĭenabĭ'lĭtȳ** *n*. **ĭnā'lĭenablȳ** *adv*.

ĭnămora'tō (-rah-) *n*. (fem. *-ta*) Lover.

ĭn-and-ĭn *adv*. Farther and farther in; (esp., of breeding) always within a limited stock, between near relatives.

ĭnā'ne *adj*. Empty, void; silly, senseless. **ĭnā'nelȳ** *adv*. **ĭnă'nĭtȳ** *n*.

ĭnă'nĭmate *adj*. Destitute of life; not endowed with animal life; spiritless, dull. **ĭnă'nĭmatelȳ** *adv*. **ĭnă'nĭmatenėss** *n*.

ĭnanĭ'tion *n*. Emptiness, esp. from want of nourishment.

ĭnă'ppėtence, -encȳ *ns*. Lack of appetite or desire.

ĭnă'pplĭcable *adj*. Not applicable, unsuitable (*to*). **ĭnăpplĭcabĭ'lĭtȳ** *n*. **ĭnă'pplĭcablȳ** *adv*.

ĭnă'pposĭte (-z-) *adj*. Not apposite, out of place. **ĭnă'pposĭtelȳ** *adv*.

ĭnapprē'ciable (-sha-) *adj*. Imperceptible, not worth reckoning; that cannot be appreciated. **ĭnapprē'ciablȳ** *adv*.

ĭnapprēcĭā'tion *n*. Failure to appreciate. **ĭnapprē'cĭatĭve** *adj*.

ĭnapprō'prĭate *adj*. Not appropriate. **ĭnapprō'prĭatelȳ** *adv*. **ĭnapprō'prĭatenėss** *n*.

ĭnă'pt *adj*. Unfit, unskilful. **ĭnă'ptlȳ** *adv*. **ĭnă'ptnėss, ĭnă'ptĭtūde** *ns*.

ĭnârtĭ'cūlate *adj*. 1. Not jointed. 2. Not articulate; unable to speak distinctly; dumb; unable to express one's ideas. **ĭnârtĭ'cūlatelȳ** *adv*. **ĭnârtĭ'cūlatenėss** *n*.

ĭn ârtĭ'cūlō môr'tĭs. In the instant of death. [L]

ĭnârtĭfĭ'cial (-shal) *adj*. Lacking in art, inartistic; artless, natural; **ĭnârtĭfĭ'ciallȳ** *adv*.

ĭnârtĭ'stĭc *adj*. Not following the principles of art; unskilled in art. **ĭnârtĭ'stĭcallȳ** *adv*.

ĭnasmŭ'ch (-az-) *adv*. ~ *as*, since, because; (archaic) in so far as.

ĭnattĕ'ntion *n*. Want of attention, heedlessness; neglect to show courtesy. **ĭnattĕ'ntĭve** *adj*. **ĭnattĕ'ntĭvelȳ** *adv*. **ĭnattĕ'ntĭvenėss** *n*.

ĭnau'dĭble *adj*. That cannot be heard. **ĭnaudĭbĭ'lĭtȳ** *n*. **ĭnau'dĭblȳ** *adv*.

ĭnau'gūral *adj*. (of ceremony) Inaugurating; (of speech etc.) given by person who is being inaugurated. ~ *n*. Inaugural speech or lecture.

ĭnau'gūrāte *v.t.* Admit (person) to office etc. with ceremony; enter with ceremony upon (undertaking etc.); initiate public use of (building etc.). **ĭnaugūrā'tion, ĭnau'gūrātor** *ns*. **ĭnau'gūratorȳ** *adj*.

ĭnauspĭ'cious (-shus) *adj*. Not of good omen; unlucky. **ĭnauspĭ'ciouslȳ** *adv*. **ĭnauspĭ'ciousnėss** *n*.

ĭ'nboard (-ôrd) *adv*. & *adj*. (Situated) within sides or towards centre of ship or aircraft.

ĭ'nbôrn *adj*. Implanted by nature.

ĭ'nbrĕd (*or* -ĕ'd) *adj*. 1. Innate, inherent by nature. 2. Born of closely related parents.

i'nbreeding *n.* Breeding from animals or persons closely related.

Inc. *abbrev.* Incorporated.

I'nca (i-) *n.* Member of Amer. Indian Quichua-speaking people who at the time of the Spanish expedition which overthrew them in 1533 had a highly developed civilization and ruled a large region of S. America with centre at Cuzco, Peru; member of its ruling class, supposedly descended from the sun; *the* ~, the emperor or chief ruler of the Incas. **I'ncan** *adj.* & *n.*

incă'lcūlable *adj.* Too great for calculation; that cannot be reckoned beforehand; uncertain. **incălcūlabi'lity̆** *n.* **incă'lcūlably̆** *adv.*

in că'mera. In the judge's private room, not in open court; with the public excluded. [L]

incandĕ'sce *v.* (Cause to) glow with heat. **incandĕ'scent** *adj.* Glowing with heat; shining brightly; (of gas or electric light etc.) produced by glowing of mantle or filament raised to white heat by flame of burning gas or passage of electricity. **incăndĕ'scence** *n.*

incăntā'tion *n.* (Use of) magical formula; spell, charm.

incā'pable *adj.* Not capable (*of*; freq. = too honest etc. to do); not susceptible (*of* improvement etc.); disqualified; without ordinary capacity or natural ability. **incāpabi'lity̆** *n.* **incā'pably̆** *adv.*

incapă'citāte *v.t.* Render incapable or unfit. **incapăcitā'tion** *n.*

incapă'city̆ *n.* Inability; disability; legal disqualification.

incar'cerāte *v.t.* Imprison. **incarcerā'tion, incar'cerātor** *ns.*

incar'nadīne *adj.* & *v.t.* (poet.) (Dye) flesh-coloured, crimson.

incar'nate *adj.* Embodied in flesh, esp. in human form. **incar'nāte** *v.t.* Embody in flesh; put (idea etc.) into concrete form, realize; be living embodiment of (quality). **incarnā'tion** *n.* Embodiment in (esp. human) flesh, esp. *the I*~ (of Christ); impersonation, living type (*of* quality etc.).

incau'tious (-sh*us*) *adj.* Rash. **incau'tiously̆** *adv.* **incau'tiousnėss** *n.*

incĕ'ndiary̆ *adj.* Of, guilty of, the malicious setting on fire of property; (mil.) used for setting on fire enemy's property, esp. ~ *bomb*, bomb containing thermite or napalm etc. and igniting on impact; (fig.) tending to stir up strife, inflammatory. ~ *n.* Incendiary person, incendiary bomb. **incĕ'ndiarism** *n.*

i'ncĕnse[1] *n.* Aromatic gum or other vegetable product, giving sweet smell when burned; smoke of this, esp. in religious ceremonial. ~ *v.t* Fumigate with incense; burn incense to (deity etc.); suffuse with fragrance.

incĕ'nse[2] *v.t.* Enrage, make angry.

i'ncĕnsory̆ *n.* Vessel for burning incense, censer.

incĕ'ntive *adj.* Tending to incite. ~ *n.* Incitement, provocation, motive; (in industry) payment or concession to encourage harder work.

incĕ'pt *v.* 1. (formerly at Camb. Univ.) Enter formally upon office of Master or Doctor. 2. (biol.) Take in.

incĕ'ption *n.* Beginning; (Camb. Univ.) incepting.

incĕ'ptive *adj.* Beginning; initial: (gram.) expressing beginning of an action. ~ *n.* Inceptive verb.

incer'titūde *n.* Uncertainty.

incĕ'ssant *adj.* Unceasing, continual, repeated. **incĕ'ssantly̆** *adv.* **incĕ'ssantnėss** *n.*

i'ncĕst *n.* Sexual intercourse between persons related within prohibited degrees. **incĕ'stūous** *adj.* Involving, guilty of, incest. **incĕ'stūously̆** *adv.*

inch[1] *n.* (abbrev. in.) 12th part of foot in measures of length; (as unit of rainfall) quantity that would cover horizontal surface to depth of 1 in.; (of atmospheric or other pressure) amount that balances weight of column of mercury 1 in. high in mercurial barometer; small amount; (pl.)

stature; *by inches*, bit by bit; *every* ~, entirely. ~ *v.* Move by inches, edge *in*, *forward*, etc.

inch² *n.* Small (esp. Sc.) island.

i′nchōate (-n-k-) *adj.* Just begun; undeveloped. **i′nchōāte** *v.t.* Begin, originate. **ĭnchōā′tion** *n.* **ĭ′nchōatĭve** (*or* ĭn-kō′-) *adj.* (esp. of verbs) Inceptive.

ĭ′ncĭdence *n.* 1. Falling on, contact with, a thing; range, scope, extent, of influence; (of tax) persons on whom it falls; (of disease) rate, scale, frequency, of occurrence in a community. 2. (math., phys.) Falling of a line, or a thing moving in a line, upon a surface; *angle of* ~, angle which the incident

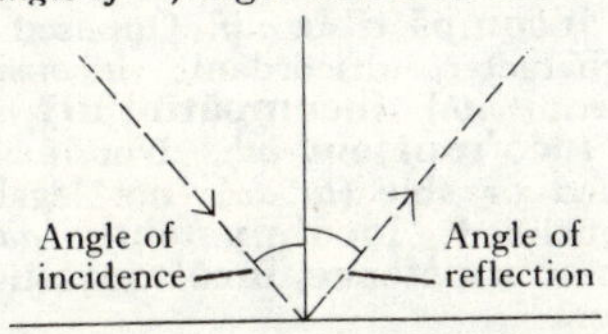

line, ray, etc., makes with the perpendicular to the surface at the point of contact.

ĭ′ncĭdent¹ *adj.* 1. (of light etc.) Falling, striking, (*upon*). 2. Apt to occur, naturally attaching, (*to*); (law) attaching as privilege, burden, etc., *to* office, position, etc.

ĭ′ncĭdent² *n.* 1. Subordinate or accessory event; event, occurrence; detached event attracting general attention; distinct piece of action in play etc. 2. (law) Privilege, burden, etc., attaching to estate etc.

incĭdĕ′ntal *adj.* 1. Casual, not essentia.; ~ *image*, *colour*, one perceived as consequence of impressions no longer present; ~ *music*, music interpolated in spoken play etc. 2. Liable to happen *to*. **incĭdĕ′ntallў** *adv.*

ĭncĭ′nerāte *v.t.* Reduce to ashes; consume by fire. **ĭncĭnerā′tion** *n.* **ĭncĭ′nerātor** *n.* (esp.) Apparatus for outdoor combustion of rubbish.

ĭncĭ′pĭent *adj.* Beginning; in an initial stage. **ĭncĭ′pĭentlў** *adv.* **ĭncĭ′pĭence, ĭncĭ′pĭencў** *ns.*

ĭ′ncĭpĭt. (Here) begins (book etc.). [L]

ĭncī′se (-z) *v.t.* Make a cut in; engrave. **incĭ′sion** *n.* Cutting into a thing; cut, gash, notch.

ĭncī′sĭve *adj.* Cutting, penetrating; mentally sharp; acute, trenchant. **ĭncī′sĭvelў** *adv.* **ĭncī′sĭvenėss** *n.*

ĭncī′sor (-z-) *n.* Cutting-tooth, any front tooth in either jaw, between canine teeth, having sharp edge and single fang.

ĭncī′te *v.t.* Urge, stir up (person etc. *to*). **incī′tement, ĭncĭtā′tion** *ns.*

ĭncĭvĭ′lĭtў *n.* Rudeness, discourtesy.

ĭ′n-clearĭng *n.* Cheques etc. collectively payable by a bank and received through clearing-house for settlement.

ĭnclĕ′ment *adj.* (of weather etc.) Severe, esp. cold or stormy. **ĭnclĕ′mencў** *n.*

ĭnclī′nable *adj.* Inclined, disposed; favourable.

ĭnclĭnā′tion *n.* 1. Leaning, slope, slant; difference of direction of two lines, esp. as measured by angle between them; (of magnetic needle) = DIP *n.* 2; (astron.) angle between plane of a planet's orbit and that of the ecliptic. 2. Disposition, propensity (*to*, *for*); liking, affection (*for*).

ĭnclī′ne *v.* 1. Bend (head etc.) forward or downward; lean, cause to lean, from vertical etc.; ~ *one's ear*, listen favourably. 2. Dispose (person, mind, etc., *to*); be disposed; tend (*to*). 3. *inclined plane*, one of the mechanical powers, material plane surface inclined at acute angle to horizon. **ĭnclī′ne** (*or* ĭ′-) *n.* Inclined plane; slope.

ĭnclĭnŏ′mėter *n.* 1. Instrument for measuring vertical component of earth's magnetic field, by means of a magnetic needle free to rotate in a vertical plane. 2. Instrument for measuring the steepness of slopes.

ĭnclu′de (-ōōd) *v.t.* Comprise, embrace, as part of a whole; treat, regard, as so comprised. **ĭnclu′sion** *n.*

inclu′sĭve (-ōō-) *adj.* Including, enclosing, comprehending; comprising; ~ *of*, embracing, comprising (something specified);

(quasi- *adv.*) the term or terms named being included. **inclu'sively** *adv.* **inclu'siveness** *n.*

incog. *abbrev.* Incognito.

incŏ'gnitō (*or* -ē'tō) *adj.* & *adv.* With one's name, character, etc., concealed. ~ *n.* (Pretended identity of) person who is incognito.

incŏ'gnizable (*or* -kŏn-) *adj.* That cannot be apprehended by senses or intellect. **incŏ'gnizant** *adj.* Unaware, unconscious *of.* **incŏ'gnizance** *n.*

incōher'ent *adj.* Not coherent. **incōher'ently** *adv.* **incōher'ence** *n.*

incōhē'sive *adj.* Not cohesive.

incombŭ'stible *adj.* That cannot be consumed by fire. **incombŭstibi'lity** *n.*

i'ncome (-ŭm) *n.* Periodical (usu. annual) receipts from business, lands, work, investments, etc.; ~ *tax*, tax levied on this; *negative* ~ *tax*, taxation system by which credits are allowed for certain commitments and paid as supplementary income to persons for whom they exceed taxable income.

i'ncoming (-kŭ-) *n.* Entrance, arrival; (usu. pl.) revenue, income. ~ *adj.* Succeeding; immigrant; (of profit) accruing.

in commĕ'ndăm. As a charge or trust (of benefice pending appointment of regular incumbent, or of its revenue enjoyed by layman etc.). [L]

incommĕ'nsurable (-sher-) *adj.* Having no common measure integral or fractional (*with* another magnitude); irrational, surd; not comparable in respect of magnitude; not worthy to be measured *with.* **incommĕnsurabi'lity** *n.* **incommĕ'nsurably** *adv.*

incommĕ'nsurate (-sher-) *adj.* Out of proportion, inadequate, (*with, to*); incommensurable. **incommĕ'nsurately** *adv.* **incommĕ'nsurateness** *n.*

incommō'de *v.t.* Trouble, annoy, hinder.

incommō'dious *adj.* Not affording good accommodation, uncomfortable. **incommō'diously** *adv.* **incommō'diousness** *n.*

incommū'nicable *adj.* That cannot be shared; that cannot be told. **incommū'nicableness, incommūnicabi'lity** *ns.* **incommū'nicably** *adv.*

incommūnica'dō (-kah-) *adj.* Without or deprived of means of communication; in solitary confinement.

incommū'nicătive *adj.* Not communicative. **incommū'nicatively** *adv.* **incommū'nicativeness** *n.*

incŏ'mparable *adj.* Matchless; that cannot be compared. **incŏ'mparableness** *n.* **incŏ'mparably** *adv.*

incompă'tible *adj.* Opposed in character, discordant; inconsistent (*with*). **incompătibi'lity** *n.*

incŏ'mpetent *adj.* Not qualified or able (*to do*); not legally qualified. **incŏ'mpetently** *adv.* **incŏ'mpetence, incŏ'mpetency** *ns.*

incomplē'te *adj.* Not complete. **incomplē'tely** *adv.* **incomplē'teness** *n.*

incŏmprehĕ'nsible *adj.* That cannot be understood; (archaic, chiefly in allusion to Athanasian Creed) that cannot be contained within limits, boundless, infinite. **incŏmprehĕ'nsibleness, incŏmprehĕnsibi'lity** *ns.* **incŏmprehĕ'nsibly** *adv.* **incomprehĕ'nsion** *n.* Failure to understand.

incomprĕ'ssible *adj.* That cannot be compressed. **incomprĕssibi'lity** *n.*

inconcei'vable *adj.* That cannot be imagined. **inconceivabi'lity** *n.* **inconcei'vably** *adv.*

inconclu'sive (-ōōs-) *adj.* (of argument etc.) Not decisive or convincing. **inconclu'sively** *adv.* **inconclu'siveness** *n.*

incŏ'ngruous (-nggrōō-) *adj.* Disagreeing, out of keeping, (*with*); out of place, absurd. **incŏ'ngruously** *adv.* **incŏ'ngruousness, incongru'ity** (-grōō-) *ns.*

incŏ'nsequent *adj.* Not following naturally, irrelevant; wanting in logical sequence; disconnected. **incŏ'nsequently** *adv.* **incŏ'nse-**

quence *n.* **ĭncŏnsèquĕ'ntĭal** (-shal) *adj.* **ĭncŏnsèquĕ'ntĭallў** *adv.*

ĭnconsĭ'derable *adj.* Not worth considering; of small size, value, etc. **ĭnconsĭ'derablў** *adv.*

ĭnconsĭ'derate *adj.* Thoughtless, rash; lacking in regard for feelings etc. of others. **ĭnconsĭ'derately** *adv.* **ĭnconsĭ'derateness** *n.*

ĭncŏnsĭ'stent *adj.* Not in keeping, discordant, incompatible, (*with*); having inconsistent parts; acting at variance with one's own principles or former conduct. **ĭnconsĭ'stentlў** *adv.* **ĭnconsĭ'stencў** *n.*

ĭnconsō'lable *adj.* That cannot be consoled. **ĭnconsō'lablў** *adv.*

ĭnconspĭ'cūous *adj.* Not conspicuous; not readily seen or noticed; (bot., of flowers) small, pale, or green. **ĭnconspĭ'cūouslў** *adv.* **ĭnconspĭ'cūousnėss** *n.*

ĭncŏ'nstant *adj.* Fickle, changeable; variable, irregular. **ĭncŏ'nstantlў** *adv.* **ĭncŏ'nstancў** *n.*

ĭncontĕ'stable *adj.* That cannot be disputed. **ĭncontĕ'stablў** *adv.*

ĭncŏ'ntĭnent *adj.* Wanting in self-restraint (esp. in regard to sexual appetite); unable to hold in something; unable to control bladder and bowel functions. **ĭncŏ'ntĭnence** *n.*

ĭncŏntrovẽr'tĭble *adj.* Not to be disputed. **ĭncŏntrovẽr'tĭblў** *adv.*

ĭnconvē'nĭence *n.* Want of adaptation to personal requirement or ease; instance of this. ~ *v.t.* Put to inconvenience, incommode. **ĭnconvē'nĭent** *adj.* Unfavourable to ease or comfort, troublesome, awkward. **ĭnconvē'nĭentlў** *adv.*

ĭnconvẽr'tĭble *adj.* Not convertible; esp., of paper money, that cannot be converted into specie. **ĭnconvẽrtĭbĭ'lĭtў** *n.* **ĭnconvẽr'tĭblў** *adv.*

ĭncōōrdĭnā'tion *n.* Want of coordination.

ĭncor'porate *adj.* (of company etc.) Formed into a corporation; (of persons) united in a corporation. **ĭncor'porāte** *v.* 1. Unite; combine (ingredients) into one substance. 2. Constitute as a legal corporation: become incorporated (*with*). **ĭncorporā'tion, ĭncor'porātor** *ns.*

ĭncorpor'ėal *adj.* Not composed of matter; immaterial; of immaterial beings; (law) having no material existence. **ĭncorpor'ėallў** *adv.*

ĭncorrĕ'ct *adj.* Not in conformity with recognized standard, or with fact; improper; erroneous. **ĭncorrĕ'ctlў** *adv.* **ĭncorrĕ'ctnėss** *n.*

ĭncŏ'rrĭgĭble *adj.* Incurably bad or depraved. **ĭncŏrrĭgĭbĭ'lĭtў** *n.* **ĭncŏ'rrĭgĭblў** *adv.*

ĭncorrō'dĭble *adj.* Incapable of being corroded.

ĭncorrŭ'ptĭble *adj.* That cannot decay; eternal; that cannot be corrupted, esp. that cannot be bribed. **ĭncorrŭptĭbĭ'lĭtў** *n.* **ĭncorrŭ'ptĭblў** *adv.* **ĭncorrŭ'ption** *n.* (archaic, bibl.).

ĭncrea'se *v.* Become greater; grow in numbers, esp. by propagation; advance (*in* quality, attainment, etc.); make greater or more numerous; intensify (quality). **ĭncrea'sĭnglў** *adv.* **ĭ'ncrease** *n.* Growth, enlargement; growth in numbers, multiplication; increased amount; (archaic) crops; *on the* ~, increasing.

ĭncrĕ'dĭble *adj.* That cannot be believed; (colloq.) hard to believe or realize. **ĭncrĕdĭbĭ'lĭtў** *n.* **ĭncrĕ'dĭblў** *adv.*

ĭncrĕ'dūlous *adj.* Unbelieving. **ĭncrĕ'dūlouslў** *adv.* **ĭncrĕ'dūlousnėss, ĭncrėdū'lĭtў** *ns.*

ĭ'ncrėment *n.* Increase; amount of this; profit; (math.) small amount by which variable quantity increases; *unearned* ~, increased value of land due to external causes, not to owner's labour or outlay.

ĭncrĭ'mĭnāte *v.t.* Charge with crime; involve in accusation. **ĭncrĭmĭnā'tion** *n.* **ĭncrĭ'mĭnatorў** *adj.*

ĭncrŭstā'tion *n.* Encrusting, being encrusted; crust, hard coating, esp. of fine or costly material over rough or common substance; calcareous or crystalline concretion or deposit; scab.

ĭ'ncūbāte *v.* Sit on eggs, brood; hatch (eggs) thus or by artificial heat; subject (micro-organisms) to warmth for a period. **ĭncūbā'tion** *n.* (esp. path.) Early phase of disease after micro-organisms have invaded the host and before symptoms of infection appear. **ĭ'ncubātive, ĭ'ncubātorў** *adjs.*

ĭ'ncūbātor *n.* Apparatus for hatching birds, rearing infants born prematurely, or developing micro-organisms.

ĭ'ncūbus *n.* Evil spirit supposed to descend on sleeping persons; nightmare; person, thing, that oppresses like nightmare.

ĭ'ncŭlcāte *v.t.* Urge, impress, persistently (*upon, in,* person, mind). **ĭncŭlcā'tion, ĭ'ncŭlcātor** *ns.*

ĭ'ncŭlpāte *v.t.* Accuse, blame; involve in charge. **ĭncŭlpā'tion** *n.* **ĭncŭ'lpatorў** *adj.*

ĭncŭ'mbencў *n.* Office, tenure, sphere, of an incumbent. **ĭncŭ'mbent**[1] *n.* (C. of E.) Holder of a parochial charge; rector, vicar, or curate-in-charge.

ĭncŭ'mbent[2] *adj.* Lying, pressing, (*on*); resting *on* (person) as duty.

ĭncū'nable *n.* Early printed book, esp. one produced before 1501. ***ĭncūnă'būla*** *n.pl.* Incunables. [L *incunabula* swaddling-clothes, (fig.) origin, beginning (*cunae* cradle)]

ĭncûr' *v.t.* Fall into, bring on oneself (danger, blame, etc.).

ĭncûr'able *adj.* & *n.* (Person) that cannot be cured. **ĭncûr'ableness, ĭncûrabĭ'lĭtў** *ns.* **ĭncûr'ablў** *adv.*

ĭncûr'ĭous *adj.* Devoid of curiosity; heedless, careless. **ĭncûr'ĭouslў** *adv.* **ĭncûrĭŏ'sĭtў** *n.*

ĭncûr'sion *n.* Hostile invasion; sudden attack. **ĭncûr'sĭve** *adj.*

ĭncûr've *v.t.* Bend into a curve; curve inwards. **ĭncûrvā'tion** *n.*

ĭ'ncus *n.* Middle small bone of ear (between malleus and stapes) to which sonorous vibrations are conveyed from malleus. [L, = 'anvil']

ĭncū'se (-z) *adj.* (of impression on coin etc.) Hammered or stamped in. ~ *n.* Incuse impression. ~ *v.t.* (esp. in past part.) Impress (figure etc.) by stamping; mark (coin etc.) with such figure.

Ind (archaic & poet.) = INDIA.

Ind. *abbrev.* India(n); Indiana; Indies.

ĭ'ndamĭne *n.* (chem.) Any of a series of organic compounds that form bluish or greenish salts.

ĭndĕ'btėd (-ĕt-) *adj.* Owing money (*to*); owing gratitude (*to*). **ĭndĕ'btėdnėss** *n.*

ĭndē'cent *adj.* Unbecoming; immodest; offending against standards of decency. **ĭndē'centlў** *adv.* **ĭndē'cencў** *n.*

ĭndėcĭ'dūous *adj.* Not deciduous.

ĭndėcī'pherable *adj.* That cannot be deciphered.

ĭndėcĭ'sion *n.* Want of decision, hesitation.

ĭndėcī'sĭve *adj.* Not decisive; undecided, irresolute. **ĭndėcī'sĭvelў** *adv.* **ĭndėcī'sĭvenėss** *n.*

ĭndėclī'nable *adj.* (gram.) Having no inflexions.

ĭndĕ'corous *adj.* Improper; in bad taste. **ĭndĕ'corouslў** *adv.* **ĭndĕ'corousnėss** *n.* **ĭndėcôr'um** *n.* Lack of decorum.

ĭndee'd *adv.* In truth, really (freq. placed after a word to emphasize it). ~ *int.* Exclamation of surprise, contempt, etc.

ĭndėfă'tĭgable *adj.* Unremitting, unwearying. **ĭndėfătĭgabĭ'lĭtў** *n.* **ĭndėfă'tĭgablў** *adv.*

ĭndėfea'sĭble (-z-) *adj.* That cannot be forfeited or done away with. **ĭndėfeasĭbĭ'lĭtў** *n.* **ĭndėfea'sĭblў** *adv.*

ĭndėfĕ'ctĭble *adj.* Unfailing, not liable to defect or decay; faultless.

ĭndėfĕ'nsĭble *adj.* Admitting of no defence. **ĭndėfĕnsĭbĭ'lĭtў** *n.* **ĭndėfĕ'nsĭblў** *adv.*

ĭndėfī'nable *adj.* That cannot be defined. **ĭndėfī'nablў** *adv.*

ĭndĕ'fĭnĭte *adj.* 1. Vague, undefined; unlimited. 2. (gram., of adjs., pronouns, etc.) Not determining the person, thing, time, manner, etc., to which they refer; (of tenses of verbs) denoting an action without specifying whether it is continuous or complete; ~ *article*: see ARTICLE. **ĭndĕ'fĭ-**

nitely̆ *adv.* **indĕ'fĭniteness** *n.*

indehi'scent *adj.* (bot.) Not dehiscent; (of fruit) not splitting open when mature, but liberating seed by decay.

indĕ'lible *adj.* That cannot be blotted out or effaced. **indĕlĭbĭ'lĭty̆** *n.* **indĕlĭbly̆** *adv.*

indĕ'lĭcate *adj.* Coarse, immodest. **indĕ'lĭcately̆** *adv.* **indĕ'lĭcacy̆** *n.*

indĕ'mnĭfy̆ *v.t.* Protect, secure (*from, against*, harm or loss); secure (person) against legal responsibility (*for* actions); compensate (*for* loss, expenses incurred, etc.). **indĕmnĭfĭcā'tion** *n.*

indĕ'mnĭty̆ *n.* Security against damage or loss; legal exemption from penalties etc. incurred; compensation for loss; sum paid for this, esp. sum exacted by victorious belligerent as one condition of peace.

indemŏ'nstrable *adj.* That cannot be proved (esp. of primary truths).

indĕ'nt[1] *v.* 1. Make tooth-like notches in; form deep recesses in (coastline etc.); (her.) shape edge of (ordinary etc.) so that it has a series of straight-sided pointed teeth. 2. Divide (document drawn up in duplicate) into two halves with zigzag line; draw up (document) in exact duplicate. 3. Set in (beginning of printed or written line) from margin, as for new paragraph etc. 4. Make requisition (properly, written order with duplicate) *on* (person *for* thing); order (goods) by an indent. **i'ndĕnt** *n.* Indentation; indenture; official requisition for stores; order for goods.

indĕ'nt[2] *v.t.* Make a dent in; impress (mark etc.). **i'ndĕnt** *n.* Dent, depression.

indĕntā'tion *n.* Indenting; cut, notch; zigzag; recess in coastline etc.

indĕ'ntion *n.* Indenting of line in printing; indentation.

indĕ'ntor *n.* (commerc.) One who makes a requisition.

indĕ'nture *n.* Indented document; any sealed agreement or contract, esp. that which binds apprentice to master; formal list, certificate, etc.; indentation. ~ *v.t.* Bind (person) by indenture, esp. as apprentice.

indepĕ'ndence *n.* Being independent, independent income; *Declaration of I~*, public act by which American Continental Congress, on 4 July 1776, declared N. Amer. colonies to be free and independent of Gt Britain; *I~ Day*, this day, observed in U.S. as annual holiday. **indepĕ'ndency̆** *n.* 1. Independent State. 2. (chiefly hist.) Congregationalism.

indepĕ'ndent *adj.* Not depending on authority of another, autonomous, free; not depending on something else for its validity, efficiency, etc.; unwilling to be under obligation to others; not needing to earn one's livelihood; (of income etc.) sufficient to make one independent; (chiefly hist.) Congregational; *I~ Broadcasting Authority*: see *I~ Television Authority*; *I~ Labour Party*, (abbrev. I.L.P.) political organization in Gt Britain for support of socialist parliamentary candidates, founded 1893 by Keir Hardie, later forming the extreme left wing of the Labour party; *I~ Television Authority*, (abbrev. I.T.A.) authority established in 1954 to provide television services in addition to those of the B.B.C., renamed *I~ Broadcasting Authority* (abbrev. I.B.A.) in 1972. **indepĕ'ndently̆** *adv.* **indepĕ'ndent** *n.* 1. Person who acts (in politics etc.) independently of any party. 2. Congregationalist.

indescrī'bable *adj.* Vague, indefinite; too great, beautiful, bad, etc., to be described. **indescrībabĭ'lĭty̆** *n.* **indescrī'bably̆** *adv.*

indestrŭ'ctĭble *adj.* That cannot be destroyed. **indestrŭctĭbĭ'lĭty̆** *n.* **indestrŭ'ctĭbly̆** *adv.*

indetẽr'mĭnable *adj.* That cannot be definitely fixed or ascertained; that cannot be settled.

indetẽr'mĭnate *adj.* Not fixed in extent, character, etc.; vague; left doubtful; (math., of quantity) not limited to fixed value(s). **indetẽr'mĭnately̆** *adv.* **indetẽr'm-**

inateness *n.* **indetèrminā'tion** *n.* Want of determination; being indeterminate.

ĭ'ndĕx *n.* (pl. *-es, -ĭcēs*). 1. Forefinger; (on instruments) pointer showing measurement etc.; sign, token, indication (*of* something). 2. Alphabetical list, usu. at end of book, of names, subjects, etc., with references. 3. *I~*, short for *I~ librorum prohibitorum* (L, = 'Index of prohibited books'), list formerly published by authority (abolished 1966), of books which Roman Catholics were forbidden to read, including the *I~ expurgatorius* ('Expurgatory Index'), formerly a separate list of passages to be expunged in books otherwise permitted. 4. (alg.) Exponent; ~ *number*, (statistics) number used in comparing the value of an attribute at a certain time with its value at a standard time. ~ *v.t.* 1. Furnish (book) with index; enter (word etc.) in index. 2. (mech., of automatic tools) Move in a succession of equal angular steps.

I'ndia (ĭ-). 1. Large peninsula of S. central Asia, bounded on N. by Himalayas; inhabited by many brown-skinned peoples following Hindu, Muslim, and other religions and speaking over 200 languages, esp. Hindi and Bengali in N. and Tamil and Telugu in S.; British interest began in early 17th c. with formation of East India Company, which in 1765 acquired the right to administer Bengal (after Clive's victory at Plassey in 1757) and afterwards other parts; in 1858 after the Indian Mutiny the Crown took over the Company's authority; in 1877 Queen Victoria was proclaimed Empress of India; in 1947 the fifteen provinces (*British* ~) and numerous native States under British protection were divided between two new States, India (see 2 below) and PAKISTAN. 2. Republic, predominantly Hindu, constituted in 1950 as a member State of the Commonwealth and comprising much of the N. and all the S. and central part of the peninsula; capital, Delhi. 3. ~ *ink*, Indian ink; ~ *paper*, (i) soft absorbent cream or buff paper used for proofs or first impressions of engravings, whence ~ *proof*; (ii) very thin tough opaque printing-paper made by Oxford University Press; *Star of* ~, high order of British knighthood, instituted 1861 and enlarged 1876 in commemoration of Queen Victoria's assumption of style and title of Empress of India. [Gk *Indos* Indus, f. Pers. *hind* = Sansk. *sindhu* river]

I'ndiaman (ĭ-) *n.* (hist.) Ship engaged in trade with India or the East Indies, esp. (*East* ~) large vessel belonging to East India Company.

I'ndian (ĭ-) *adj.* 1. Of India or the E. Indies or their peoples; of Indian manufacture, material, or pattern. 2. Of the original inhabitants of America and the W. Indies. 3. ~ *club*, heavy bottle-shaped club used in gymnastic exercises; ~ *corn*, maize; *Order of the* ~ *Empire*, high order of British knighthood, instituted 1877 (cf. *Star of* INDIA); ~ *file*, single file (so called because N. Amer. Indians march thus); ~ *hemp*, common HEMP, esp. as source of narcotics; (also) N. Amer. perennial herb (*Apocynum cannabinum*) of dog-bane family with milky juice and tough fibrous bark; ~ *ink*, black pigment of lamp-black or ivory black mixed with gum etc. and dried, brought chiefly from China and Japan in sticks or cakes; colloidal suspension of this in water; ~ *meal*, ground maize; ~ *Mutiny*, revolt (1857–8), beginning at Meerut, of Sepoys in Bengal army of East India Company against British authority; ~ *National Congress*, representative national organization, founded 1885 to obtain self-government and dominion status for India; ~ *Ocean*, ocean to S. of India, extending from E. coast of Africa to Malay Archipelago; ~ *summer*, period of calm dry mild weather with hazy atmosphere, occurring in late autumn, esp. in northern

U.S.; ~ *tobacco*: see LOBELIA. ~ *n.* 1. Indian person. 2. Member of any aboriginal people of America or W. Indies (usu. excluding Eskimos, Patagonians, and Fuegians); *Red* ~, member of aboriginal people of N. America, with coppery-coloured skin. 3. Language of American Indians.

Indiă'na (ĭ-; *or* -ah-). State in central U.S., part of Middle West admitted to the Union in 1816; capital, Indianopolis.

ĭ'ndiarŭ'bber (-*a*r-) *n.* = RUBBER[1], 3.

I'ndic (ĭ-) *adj.* (of language) Indo-Aryan.

ĭ'ndicāne *n.* (chem.) Glucoside occurring in plants yielding indigo.

ĭ'ndicāte *v.t.* Point out, make known, show; state briefly; be a sign of, betoken; (med.) suggest, call for, (treatment). **indicā'tion** *n.*

indĭ'cative *adj.* 1. (*or* ĭ'ndĭkā-) Suggestive, giving indications, *of*. 2. (gram., of verbal mood) Stating something as objective fact, not as conception, wish, etc., of speaker. **indĭ'catively** *adv.* **indĭ'cative** *n.* Indicative mood.

ĭ'ndicātor *n.* Person, thing, that points out or indicates; mechanical device indicating condition of apparatus etc. to which it is attached; board etc. in railway station etc. giving times and platforms of trains etc.; (also *direction* ~) device on motor vehicle whereby driver indicates his proposed course; (chem.) substance which marks a stage in a chemical reaction by a change of colour.

indĭ'colīte *n.* Blue variety of tourmaline.

indī'ct (-īt) *v.t.* Accuse (person), esp. by legal process. **indī'ctable** *adj.* Liable, rendering one liable, to be indicted. **indī'ctment** *n.* Formal accusation; (formerly) legal process in which this was preferred to and presented by Grand Jury; document containing charge; *bill of* ~, written accusation as preferred to Grand Jury.

indĭ'ction *n.* Fiscal period of 15 years instituted in A.D. 313 by Constantine and reckoned from A.D. 312; assessment of property-tax by Roman emperors at beginning of each 15 years; this tax.

Indies (ĭ'ndĭz). *the* ~, (formerly) India and adjacent regions and islands; the East Indies; the West Indies.

indĭ'fference *n.* Absence of interest or attention (*to, towards*); neutrality; unimportance.

indĭ'fferent *adj.* Impartial, neutral; having no inclination for or against; neither good nor bad; rather bad; neutral in chemical, electrical, or magnetic quality; unimportant. **indĭ'fferentlў** *adv.* **indĭ'fferent** *n.* Neutral or indifferent person, esp. in religion or politics.

indĭ'fferentism *n.* Spirit of indifference, professed or practised, esp. in religious matters. **indĭ'fferentist** *n.*

ĭ'ndigēne *n.* Native.

indĭ'gėnous *adj.* Native, belonging naturally (*to* soil etc.). **indĭ'gėnouslў** *adv.*

ĭ'ndigent *adj.* Needy, poor. **ĭ'ndigence** *n.*

indigĕ'stĭble *adj.* Not digestible. **indigĕstĭbĭ'litў** *n.* **indigĕ'stion** (-sch*o*n) *n.* Difficulty in digesting food, dyspepsia; undigested condition. **indigĕ'stive** *adj.* Suffering from, tending to, indigestion.

indĭ'gnant *adj.* Moved by mingled anger and scorn or feeling of injured innocence. **indĭ'gnantlў** *adv.*

indignā'tion *n.* Anger excited by meanness, injustice, wickedness, or misconduct.

indĭ'gnitў *n.* Unworthy treatment, slight, insult.

ĭ'ndigō *n.* Blue dye obtained from plants of genus *Indigofera*; plant from which this is obtained; colour (lying between blue and violet in spectrum) yielded by indigo; ~*-bird*, N. Amer. bunting (*Cyanospiza cyanea*) with head etc. of rich indigo-blue; ~*-blue*, blue colour of indigo. [Gk *indikon* Indian]

indirĕ'ct *adj.* 1. Not straight; not going straight to the point; not directly aimed at; ~ *rule*, (in colonial administration) government through native institutions (e.g. chiefs, tribal councils); ~ *tax*, one paid by consumer in form of increased price for the taxed goods. 2. (gram.) ~ *object*, person, thing, affected by action of verb but not primarily acted on (e.g. *him* in *give him the book*); ~ *passive*, passive having for subject the indirect object of the active (e.g. *I* in *I was told it*); ~ *speech*, reported speech, with necessary changes of pronouns, tenses, etc. (e.g. direct, *I will help you*; indirect, he said *he would help me*). **indīrĕ'ctlȳ** *adv*. **indīrĕ'ctnėss** *n*.

indiscer'nible *adj*. That cannot be discerned or distinguished from another. **indiscer'niblȳ** *adv*. **indiscer'nible** *n*. Indiscernible thing; *identity of* ~*s*, doctrine that things cannot exist together as separate entities unless they have different attributes.

indi'sciplīne *n*. Want of discipline.

indiscree't *adj*. Injudicious, unwary. **indiscree'tlȳ** *adv*.

indi'scrēte *adj*. Not divided into distinct parts.

indiscrĕ'tion *n*. Injudicious conduct; accidental or (*calculated* ~) supposed accidental revelation of official secret etc.; imprudence; transgression of social morality.

indiscri'minate *adj*. Confused, promiscuous; making no distinctions. **indiscri'minatelȳ** *adv*. **indiscri'minatenėss** *n*. **indiscriminā'tion** *n*. **indiscri'minative** *adj*.

indispĕ'nsable *adj*. That cannot be dispensed with, necessary; (of law, duty, etc.) that cannot be set aside. **indispĕ'nsablenėss, indispĕnsabi'litȳ** *ns*. **indispĕ'nsablȳ** *adv*.

indispō'se (-z) *v.t.* Render unfit or unable; make averse; (esp. in past part.) put out of health. **indisposi'tion** *n*. Ill health, ailment, (esp. of passing kind); disinclination; aversion.

indi'spūtable *adj*. That cannot be disputed. **indi'spūtablenėss, indispūtabili'tȳ** *ns*. **indi'spūtablȳ** *adv*.

indissŏ'lūble *adj*. Lasting, stable; that cannot be dissolved or decomposed. **indissŏlūbi'litȳ** *n*. **indissŏ'lūblȳ** *adv*.

indisti'nct *adj*. Not distinct; confused, obscure. **indisti'nctlȳ** *adv*. **indisti'nctnėss** *n*.

indisti'nguishable (-nggwish-) *adj*. Not distinguishable. **indisti'nguishablȳ** *adv*.

indī'te *v.t.* Put into words, compose, (poem, speech, etc.); (usu. joc.) write (letter etc.).

i'ndium *n*. (chem.) Rare silver-white soft metallic element, occurring in association with zinc etc.; symbol In, at. no. 49, at. wt 114·82. [L *indicum* INDIGO, from two blue lines in the metal's spectrum]

indivi'dūal *adj*. Single; particular, special; having distinct character; of a single person or thing, characteristic of an individual. ~ *n*. Single member of a class, group, or number; single human being (opp. to society, the family, etc.); (vulg.) person.

indivi'dūalism *n*. 1. Self-centred feeling or conduct, egoism. 2. Social theory advocating free and independent action of individual (cf. SOCIALISM). **indivi'dūalist** *n*. **individūali'stic** *adj*.

individūă'litȳ *n*. Separate existence; individual character, esp. when strongly marked.

indivi'dūalīze *v.t.* Give individual character to; specify. **individūalīzā'tion** *n*.

indivi'dūallȳ *adv*. Personally, in an individual capacity; in a distinctive manner; one by one, not collectively.

indivi'sible (-z-) *adj*. Not divisible. ~ *n*. Infinitely small particle or quantity. **indivisibi'litȳ** *n*. **indivi'siblȳ** *adv*.

Indo- (ĭ-) *prefix*. Indian; Indian and —.

Indo-Ar'ȳan (ĭ-, ar-) *adj*. & *n*. 1. (Of) the group of Indo-European languages of India. 2. (Member) of one of the Indo-European peoples of India.

I'ndo-Chī'na (ĭ-). 1. Peninsula in SE. Asia occupied by Burma, Thailand, Malaya, Laos, Cambodia, and Vietnam. 2. (hist.) Region now occupied by Laos,

Cambodia and Vietnam, formerly a French dependency (*French* ~). **I'ndo-Chīnē'se** *adj.* & *n.*

indō'cīle *adj.* Not docile. **indoci'lity̆** *n.*

indŏ'ctrināte *v.t.* Imbue with learning, *with* doctrine, idea, etc.; instruct *in.* **indŏctrinā'tion** *n.*

Indo-Europē'an (ĭ-) *n.* & *adj.* (Of) the family of languages spoken over most of Europe and in Asia as far as N. India, including esp. the Indo-Iranian, Balto-Slavonic, Hellenic, Italic, Celtic, and Germanic groups; (member) of a people speaking one of these languages.

Indo-Germă'nic (ĭ-) *adj.* = INDO-EUROPEAN.

Indo-Irā'nian (ĭ-, ĭr-) *adj.* & *n.* (Of) the Indo-European languages spoken chiefly in N. India and Iran, and including Sanskrit and its modern derivatives, Persian, Pushtu, etc.

ĭ'ndolent *adj.* Slothful, lazy; (med., of tumour etc.) causing no pain. **ĭ'ndolently̆** *adv.* **ĭ'ndolence** *n.*

indŏ'mitable *adj.* Unyielding; stubbornly persistent. **indŏ'mitably̆** *adv.*

Indonē'sia (ĭ-; *or* -z- *or* -zha). Republic of SE. Asia, comprising Sumatra, Java, S. and E. Borneo, Celebes and other islands; formerly belonging to the Netherlands; independent since 1949; capital, Djakarta.

Indonē'sian (ĭ-; *or* -z- *or* -zhan) *adj.* Of Indonesia or its people, esp. of Sumatra, Java, and Bali; of one of the vast number of SE. Asian languages spoken in Malay Peninsula and Archipelago. ~ *n.* Indonesian person; (esp.) one of a people forming the chief pre-Malay population of Malay archipelago, and combining Polynesian and Mongoloid characteristics; Indonesian language.

ĭ'ndoor (-ôr) *adj.* Situated, carried on, within a building or under cover. **indoor's** (-z) *adv.* Within a building; under cover.

indôrsā'tion *n.* (chiefly Sc.) Endorsement.

I'ndra (ĭ-). (Vedic myth.) Chief god of air, rain-giver, type of beneficent heroic power struggling against evil demons, represented as golden in colour, with four arms, and riding in golden car, later subordinated to Brahma, Vishnu, and Siva, and regarded as sensuous deity in celestial paradise, freq. represented riding the elephant Airavata (rain-cloud).

ĭ'ndraught, -draft (-ahft) *n.* Drawing in; inward flow or current.

ĭ'ndri *n.* Short-tailed lemur of Madagascar (*I~ indri*).

indū'bitable *adj.* That cannot be doubted. **indū'bitably̆** *adv.*

indūce *v.t.* 1. Prevail on, persuade (*to*); bring about, give rise to. 2. (elect.) Produce (current) by induction. 3. Infer, derive as an induction. **indū'cement** *n.* What induces; attraction that leads one on (*to*).

indŭ'ct *v.t.* Introduce formally into possession (*to* benefice); install (*into*).

indŭ'ctance *n.* Setting up of a magnetic field or flux by induction; coefficient of magnetic or electric self-induction.

indŭ'ction *n.* 1. Inducting; (archaic) preamble, prologue. 2. Production (*of* facts) to prove general statement; inferring of general law from particular instances; *mathematical* ~, method of proving universal truth of law by showing (i) that if true in a particular case it is true in the next case, (ii) that it is true in a particular case. 3. (elect. etc.) Bringing about of electric or magnetic state in a body by proximity (without contact) of electrified or magnetized body; production of electric current in conductor by motion of magnet near it, or by changes in the magnetic field in which it lies due to other causes; (esp.) generation of electric current in a conductor by changes in current in a neighbouring conductor; *self-*~, reaction of a current in a circuit upon itself; ~*-coil*, apparatus for producing electric currents by induction, consisting normally of a soft-iron core, surrounded by a coil of wire (the *primary coil*), which is in turn surrounded by a second and usu. much longer coil (the *secondary coil*): when the current in the primary coil is interrupted, a current of much higher voltage than the original one is induced in the secondary coil; by using very long coils enormous voltages suitable for producing X-rays and conducting many physical and other experiments can be induced. 4. Drawing of gaseous mixture into cylinder(s) of internal combustion engine. 5. (med.) Any of various procedures for bringing on birth or terminating pregnancy.

indŭ'ctive *adj*. 1. (of reasoning etc.) Of, based on, induction. 2. Of electric or magnetic induction. **indŭ'ctivelў** *adv*.

indŭ'ctor *n*. 1. Person who inducts to an ecclesiastical benefice. 2. Part of electric apparatus which produces induction.

indŭ'lge (-lj) *v*. Please by yielding to wishes of; yield to (desire etc.); gratify one's appetite (for); take one's pleasure freely *in*; partake (too) freely of intoxicants. **indŭ'lgent** *adj*. **indŭ'lgentlў** *adv*.

indŭ'lgence *n*. 1. Indulging. 2. Privilege granted; (R.C. Ch.) remission of temporal punishment still due for sins whose eternal punishment has been remitted by sacramental absolution; *Declaration of I~*, proclamation of certain religious liberties as special favours, but not as legal rights, esp. those of Charles II in 1672 and James II in 1687. **indŭ'lgenced** (-nst) *adj*. (R.C. Ch., of prayers, material objects, etc.) Procuring an indulgence to the user.

indŭ'lt *n*. (R.C. Ch.) Pope's licence for thing not sanctioned by common law of Church.

indu'na (-dōō-) *n*. Zulu leader.

ĭ'ndūrāte *v*. Make, become, hard; make callous or unfeeling; become inveterate. **indūrā'tion** *n*. (esp. geol.) Hardening of sedimentary rocks by heat or other process. **ĭ'ndūrative** *adj*.

I'ndus (ĭ-). One of the 3 great rivers of the Indian sub-continent, rising in Himalayas of W. Tibet, flowing NW. for some 600 miles, and then SW. through Pakistan to Arabian Sea; ~ *(valley) civilization*, that flourishing in the Indus valley in 2nd and 1st millennia B.C.

indŭ'strial *adj*. Of industries; engaged in, connected with, industry; having highly developed industries; *I~ Revolution*, rapid development of industry through employment of machinery which took place in England in late 18th and early 19th c.; *I~ Workers of the World*, (abbrev. I.W.W.) labour organization founded at Chicago in 1905, advocating syndicalism and international socialism. **indŭ'striallў** *adv*. **indŭ'strialism, indŭ'strialist** *ns*. **indŭ'strialīze** *v.t.*

indŭ'strious *adj*. Diligent, hard-working. **indŭ'striouslў** *adv*.

ĭ'ndustrў *n*. 1. Diligence; exertion, effort; systematic work; habitual employment in useful work. 2. Branch of trade or manufacture, esp. one employing much labour and capital; manufacturing in general.

indwĕ'll *v*. Inhabit, occupy; be permanently present *in*.

Ine, Ina (ē'ne) (d. *c* 728). King of Wessex, remembered for code of Anglo-Saxon laws bearing his name.

inē'briate *adj*. Drunken. ~ *n*. Inebriate person, esp. habitual drunkard. **inē'briāte** *v.t.* Make drunk, intoxicate. **inēbriā'tion** *n*. **inēbrī'ėtў** *n*. (Habit of) drunkenness.

inĕ'dible *adj*. Not edible. **inĕdibĭ'litў** *n*.

inĕ'ditėd *adj*. Not published; published without editorial alterations.

inĕ'ffable *adj*. Unutterable, too great for words. **inĕ'ffablў** *adv*.

inėffā'ceable (-sabl) *adj*. That cannot be effaced. **inėffāceabĭ'litў** *n*. **inėffā'ceablў** *adv*.

inėffĕ'ctive *adj*. Not producing the desired effect; lacking artistic effect; (of person) inefficient. **inėffĕ'ctivelў** *adv*. **inėffĕ'ctivenėss** *n*.

ĭnėffĕ′ctual *adj.* Without effect, fruitless. **ĭnėffĕ′ctūallȳ** *adv.* **ĭnėffĕ′ctūalnėss** *n.*

ĭnėffĭ′cient (-shent) *adj.* Not fully capable, not well qualified; ineffective. **ĭnėffĭ′cientlȳ** *adv.* **ĭnėffĭ′ciencȳ** *n.*

ĭnėlă′stĭc *adj.* Not elastic; unadaptable, unyielding. **ĭnėlastĭ′cĭtȳ** *n.*

ĭnĕ′lėgant *adj.* Ungraceful; unrefined; unpolished. **ĭnĕ′lėgantlȳ** *adv.* **ĭnĕ′lėgance** *n.*

ĭnĕ′lĭgĭble *adj.* Not eligible. **ĭnĕlĭgĭbĭ′lĭtȳ** *n.* **ĭnĕ′lĭgĭblȳ** *adv.*

ĭnėlŭ′ctable *adj.* That cannot be escaped from.

ĭnĕ′pt *adj.* Out of place; absurd, silly. **ĭnĕ′ptlȳ** *adv.* **ĭnĕ′ptnėss, ĭnĕ′ptĭtūde** *ns.*

ĭnėqua′lĭtȳ (-kwŏl-) *n.* Want of equality in magnitude, quality, rank, etc.; variableness; (of surface) irregularity; (astron.) deviation from uniformity in motion of heavenly body.

ĭnĕ′quĭtable *adj.* Unfair, unjust. **ĭnĕ′quĭtablȳ** *adv.* **ĭnĕ′quĭtȳ** *n.*

ĭnėră′dĭcable *adj.* That cannot be rooted out. **ĭnėră′dĭcablȳ** *adv.*

ĭnĕ′rrable *adj.* Not liable to err. **ĭnĕrrabĭ′lĭtȳ, ĭnĕ′rrancȳ** *ns.* **ĭnĕ′rrablȳ** *adv.*

ĭnẽr′t *adj.* Without inherent power of action, motion, or resistance; sluggish, slow; (chem., of gases) chemically inactive; esp., belonging to the group of gases comprising helium, neon, argon, krypton, xenon, and radon. **ĭnẽr′tlȳ** *adv.* **ĭnẽr′tnėss** *n.*

ĭnẽr′tia (-sha) *n.* 1. (phys.) Property of matter by which it continues in its existing state of rest or uniform motion in a straight line unless that state is changed by an external force. 2. Inertness, sloth. 3. ~ *selling*, sending of unsolicited goods to potential customers.

ĭnėscā′pable *adj.* Not to be escaped.

ĭnėscŭ′tcheon (-ŭchon) *n.* (her.) Small escutcheon charged on a larger one.

ĭn ĕ′ssė. In actual existence. [L]

ĭnĕ′stĭmable *adj.* Too great, intense, precious, etc., to be estimated. **ĭnĕ′stĭmablȳ** *adv.*

ĭnĕ′vĭtable *adj.* Unavoidable, sure to happen. **ĭnĕ′vĭtablenėss, ĭnĕvĭtabĭ′lĭtȳ** *ns.* **ĭnĕ′vĭtablȳ** *adv.*

ĭnexă′ct (-gz-) *adj.* Not exact. **ĭnexă′ctlȳ** *adv.* **ĭnexă′ctnėss, ĭnėxă′ctĭtūde** *ns.*

ĭnėxcū′sable (-z-) *adj.* That cannot be justified. **ĭnėxcū′sablȳ** *adv.*

ĭnėxhau′stĭble (-ĭgzaw-) *adj.* That cannot be exhausted. **ĭnėxhaustĭbĭ′lĭtȳ** *n.* **ĭnėxhau′stĭblȳ** *adv.*

ĭnĕ′xorable *adj.* Relentless. **ĭnĕxorabĭ′lĭtȳ** *n.* **ĭnĕ′xorablȳ** *adv.*

ĭnėxpē′dĭent *adj.* Not expedient. **ĭnėxpē′dĭencȳ** *n.*

ĭnėxpĕ′nsĭve *adj.* Cheap. **ĭnėxpĕ′nsĭvelȳ** *adv.* **ĭnėxpĕ′nsĭvenėss** *n.*

ĭnėxpēr′ĭence *n.* Lack of experience. **ĭnėxpēr′ĭenced** (-st) *adj.*

ĭnĕ′xpert *adj.* Unskilled. **ĭnĕ′xpertlȳ** *adv.*

ĭnĕ′xpĭable *adj.* That cannot be expiated. **ĭnĕ′xpĭablȳ** *adv.*

ĭnĕ′xplĭcable (*or* -ĭksplĭ′-) *adj.* That cannot be explained or accounted for. **ĭnėxplĭcabĭ′lĭtȳ** *n.* **ĭnĕ′xplĭcablȳ** *adv.*

ĭnėxprĕ′ssĭble *adj.* That cannot be expressed in words. **ĭnėxprĕ′ssĭblȳ** *adv.*

ĭnėxpŭ′gnable *adj.* Impregnable, invincible.

ĭn ėxtĕ′nsō. At full length. [L]

ĭnėxtĭ′nguĭshable (-nggw-) *adj.* Unquenchable.

ĭn ėxtrē′mĭs (*or* -ēs). At the point of death. [L, = 'in extremity']

ĭnĕ′xtrĭcable (*or* -trĭ′-) *adj.* That cannot be unravelled or solved. **ĭnĕ′xtrĭcablȳ** *adv.*

inf. *abbrev. Infra.*

ĭnfă′llĭbĭlism *n.* Principle of the pope's infallibility. **ĭnfă′llĭbĭlist** *n.*

ĭnfă′llĭble *adj.* Incapable of erring; unfailing. **ĭnfă′llĭblȳ** *adv.* **ĭnfăllĭbĭ′lĭtȳ** *n.* (esp. as attribute of the pope speaking *ex cathedra*, defined 1870 by Vatican Council).

ĭ'nfamous *adj*. Of ill fame, notoriously vile; abominable; (law) deprived of all or some rights of citizen on account of infamous crime. **ĭ'nfamouslў̆** *adv*. **ĭ'nfamў̆** *n*.

ĭ'nfancў̆ *n*. 1. Early childhood, babyhood. 2. (law) = MINORITY, 1. 3. Early stage of development.

ĭ'nfant *n*. Child during earliest period of life; child under 7 years of age; (law) = MINOR[1] *n*. 1; ~ *school*, school for children, usu. under 7.

ĭnfă'nta *n*. (hist.) Daughter of king and queen of Spain or Portugal (usu. eldest daughter who was not heir to throne). ***ĭnfă'ntė*** *n*. (hist.) Son (usu. 2nd son) of king and queen of Spain or Portugal who was not heir to throne.

ĭnfă'ntĭcīde *n*. 1. Murder of infant immediately after birth, esp. with mother's consent; custom of killing newborn infants. 2. One who kills an infant. **ĭnfăntĭcī'dal** *adj*.

ĭ'nfantīle *adj*. Of, as of, infants; in its infancy; childish, silly; ~ *paralysis*, (pop. but imprecise term for) acute anterior POLIOMYELITIS.

ĭnfă'ntĭlism *n*. Mentally or physically undeveloped state.

ĭ'nfantīne *adj*. Pertaining to, of the nature of, infants.

ĭ'nfantrў̆ *n*. Foot-soldiers; *i'nfantryman*, soldier of infantry regiment.

ĭ'nfarct *n*. (path.) Area of dead tissue caused by the blocking of an artery which normally nourishes it.

ĭnfă'tūāte *v.t.* Affect (person) with extreme folly; inspire with extravagant passion. **ĭnfă'tūātėdlў̆** *adv*. **ĭnfătūā'tion** *n*.

ĭnfĕ'ct *v.t.* Contaminate, pollute (air etc.); implant disease-forming micro-organisms in (person, animal, plant, etc., or environment); imbue (person *with* opinion etc.). **ĭnfĕ'ctĭve** *adj*. **ĭnfĕ'ctĭvenėss** *n*.

ĭnfĕ'ction *n*. Communication of disease; moral contamination; diffusive influence of example, sympathy, etc.

ĭnfĕ'ctious (-sh*u*s) *adj*. Infecting with disease, pestilential; (of disease) such that the infecting agent can be communicated to the environment; (of emotions etc.) apt to spread, catching. **ĭnfĕ'ctiouslў̆** *adv*. **ĭnfĕ'ctiousnėss** *n*.

ĭnfėlĭ'cĭtous *adj*. Not felicitous. **ĭnfėlĭ'cĭtў̆** *n*. Unhappiness; misfortune; inaptness of expression etc.

ĭnfẽr' *v.t.* Deduce, conclude; imply.

ĭ'nference *n*. Inferring; (esp., logic) forming of a conclusion from premisses either by induction or deduction; thing inferred. **ĭnferĕ'ntial** (-sh*a*l) *adj*. **ĭnferĕ'ntiallў̆** *adv*.

ĭnfēr'ĭor *adj*. 1. Situated below; (of planets etc.) whose orbit lies within that of the earth; (bot., of calyx) below ovary, (of ovary) below calyx; (print., of small letters or figures) placed lower than ordinary letters, e.g. H_2, C_n. 2. Lower in rank, quality, etc. (*to*); of poor quality. **ĭnfēr'ĭorlў̆** *adv*. **ĭnfēr'ĭor** *n*. Person inferior to another, esp. in rank. **ĭnfērĭo'rĭtў̆** *n*. ~ *complex*, unconscious feeling of inferiority to others, freq. manifested in self-assertive behaviour; (pop.) sense of inferiority.

ĭnfẽr'nal *adj*. Of hell; hellish, fiendish; (colloq.) abominable, confounded; ~ *machine*, apparatus (usu. disguised) for producing explosion destructive of life or property. **ĭnfẽr'nallў̆** *adv*.

ĭnfẽr'nō *n*. (pl. *-s*). Hell (*The I~*, first part of Dante's *Divine Comedy*); scene of horror.

ĭnfẽr'tīle *adj*. Not fertile. **ĭnfẽrtĭ'lĭtў̆** *n*.

ĭnfĕ'st *v.t.* Haunt, swarm in or about, (place). **ĭnfĕstā'tion** *n*.

ĭnfeudā'tion *n*. Enfeoffment; ~ *of tithes*, (hist.) granting of tithes to laymen.

ĭ'nfĭdel *n*. Disbeliever in religion; disbeliever in the true religion (esp. from Jewish or Muslim point of view); (hist.) adherent of religion opposed to Christianity; (gen.) unbeliever. ~ *adj*. Unbelieving; of unbelievers.

ĭnfĭdĕ'lĭtў̆ *n*. 1. Disbelief in Christianity. 2. Disloyalty, esp. to husband or wife.

i'nfield *n.* 1. Farm land around or near homestead; arable land; land regularly manured and cropped. 2. (baseball) Part of field enclosed within baselines; the four fielders placed on boundaries of infield. **i'nfielder** *n.* (baseball) One of the infield. **i'nfieldsman** (-z-) *n.* (cricket) One fielding close to wicket.

i'n-fighting (-fit-) *n.* 1. Boxing at closer quarters than arm's length. 2. Internal strife between (members of) organizations etc.

i'nfiltrāte (*or* -fi'-) *v.* Introduce (fluid) by filtration; permeate by filtration (also fig.). **infiltrā'tion** *n.* (esp.) Gradual penetration into territory by small groups of settlers, or into enemy ground by small parties of troops; dissemination of ideas by small group working inside political party etc.

i'nfinite *adj.* Boundless, endless; very great; innumerable, very many; (math., of quantity or magnitude) greater than any assignable quantity or magnitude; (of series) that may be continued indefinitely without ever coming to an end. **i'nfinitelў** *adv.*

infinitě'simal *adj.* & *n.* Infinitely or very small (amount); ~ *calculus*, differential and integral calculuses conceived as one. **infinitě'simallў** *adv.*

infi'nitive *adj.* & *n.* (gram.) (Verb-form) that expresses the verbal notion without predicating it of any subject (e.g. *to see*). **infiniti'val** *adj.*

infi'nitūde *n.* Infinity.

infi'nitў *n.* Boundlessness; boundless number or extent; (math.) infinite quantity (symbol ∞).

infir'm *adj.* Physically weak, esp. through age; (of person, mind, judgement, etc.) weak, irresolute. **infir'mlў** *adv.* **infir'mitў** *n.*

infirmar'ian *n.* (in monastery etc.) One who has charge of infirmary and patients.

infir'marў *n.* Hospital; sick-quarters in school, monastery, etc.

infi'x *v.t.* Fix (thing *in* another); impress (fact etc. *in* mind); (gram.) insert (formative element) in body of word. **i'nfix** *n.* (gram.) Formative element inserted in body of word.

in flăgră'nte dĕli'ctō (-ntā). In the very act of committing an offence. [L, = 'in blazing crime']

inflā'me *v.* 1. Set ablaze; catch fire; light up (as) with flame. 2. Excite passionately; become excited; aggravate. 3. Cause inflammation in (body etc.); become affected with inflammation.

inflă'mmable *adj.* Easily set on fire; easily excited. ~ *n.* (usu. pl.) Inflammable substance. **inflămmabi'litў** *n.*

inflammā'tion *n.* Inflaming; (path.) condition of living tissue marked by heat, swelling, redness, and usu. pain, esp. as reaction to damage or infection.

inflă'mmatorў *adj.* Tending to inflame with desire or passion; (path.) of, characterized by, inflammation.

inflā'te *v.t.* Distend with air or gas; puff up (*with* pride etc.); resort to inflation of (currency); raise (price) artificially; *inflated*, (of language) bombastic.

inflā'tion *n.* Inflating; (esp.) increase in purchasing power in relation to goods available for purchase, resulting in fall in value of money and general increase in prices; (formerly) increase in issue of paper money not redeemable in specie. **inflā'tionary** *adj.*

inflě'ct *v.t.* 1. Bend inwards, curve. 2. (gram.) Vary termination of (word) to express grammatical relation. 3. Modulate (voice etc.); (mus.) flatten, sharpen (notes). **inflě'ction** *n.* = INFLEXION. **inflě'ctive** *adj.* Of, characterized by, inflexion.

inflě'xible *adj.* Unbendable; (fig.) unbending, rigid. **inflěxibi'litў** *n.* **inflě'xiblў** *adv.*

inflě'xion (-kshon) *n.* 1. Inflecting, bending; (geom.) change of curvature from convex to concave or conversely. 2. Modification of word to express grammatical relationship; inflected form of word; inflexional suffix or element. 3. Modulation of voice; change in pitch or tone. **ĭnflĕ'xional** *adj*.

ĭnflĭ'ct *v.t.* Lay on (blow, etc.); impose (suffering, penalty, etc., *upon*). **ĭnflĭ'ction** *n.*

ĭnflorĕ'scence *n.* (bot.) Arrangement of flowers of plant in relation to axis and to each other; collective flower of plant; flowering.

ĭ'nflow (-ō) *n.* Flowing in.

ĭ'nfluence (-lo͞o-) *n.* 1. Action insensibly exercised (*on*); ascendancy, moral power (*over*, *with*); thing, person, exercising (usu. non-material) power. 2. (astrol.) Supposed flowing from stars of ethereal fluid affecting character and destiny of man. ~ *v.t.* Exert influence upon, have effect upon.

ĭ'nfluent (-lo͞o-) *adj.* Flowing in. ~ *n.* Tributary stream.

ĭnfluĕ'ntial (-lo͞oĕnshal) *adj.* Having great influence. **ĭnfluĕ'ntially** *adv.*

ĭnfluĕ'nza (-lo͞o-) *n.* Acute infectious febrile disorder, caused by a virus, occurring usu. in widespread epidemics.

ĭ'nflŭx *n.* Flowing in, esp. of persons or things (*into* place etc.).

ĭnfor'm *v.* 1. Inspire, imbue (person, thing, *with* quality, principle, etc.). 2. Tell (person *of* thing, *that*, *how*, etc.). 3. Bring charge (*against*). **ĭnfor'mant** *n.* (esp.) One who tells or gives information.

ĭnfor'mal *adj.* Not according to due form; without formality. **ĭnfor'mallў** *adv.* **ĭnformă'lĭtў** *n.*

ĭn for'ma pau'perĭs. (law) As a poor person not liable to costs. [L]

ĭnformā'tion *n.* 1. Informing, telling; thing told, knowledge, items of knowledge, news. 2. (law) Charge, complaint, lodged with court or magistrate (*against*). **ĭnformā'tional** *adj.*

ĭnfor'matĭve *adj.* Giving information, instructive. **ĭnfor'matorў** *adj.* ~ *double*, (bridge) double meant only to give information to partner.

ĭnfor'med (-md) *adj.* Instructed, knowing the facts, educated, intelligent.

ĭnfor'mer *n.* One who informs against another; *common* ~, one who detects offenders and lays information against them for reward.

ĭ'nfra *adv.* Below, lower down, farther on (in book). [L]

ĭnfra- *prefix*. Below.

ĭnfră'ction *n.* Infringement, violation.

ĭ'nfra dĭg. Beneath one's dignity, unbecoming. [abbrev. L *infra dignitatem*]

ĭnfralăpsār'ian *n.* Calvinist who held that God's election of some was consequent to his prescience of the Fall, or that it contemplated man as already fallen. ~ *adj.* Of, holding, these views.

ĭnfră'ngĭble (-j-) *adj.* Unbreakable; inviolable.

ĭ'nfra-rĕ'd *adj.* (phys.) Lying beyond the red end of the visible spectrum; of, producing, electromagnetic radiations with a wavelength longer than that of red light, perceived as heat and used in heat therapy, cooking devices, etc.; ~ *photography*, photography using emulsion sensitive to infra-red rays and capable of penetrating darkness or fog.

ĭ'nfrastrŭcture *n.* Collective term for the fixed installations and facilities necessary to support military operations, as airfields, naval bases, training establishments, supply works, etc.; supporting system of any organization.

ĭnfrē'quent *adj.* Not frequent. **ĭnfrē'quentlў** *adv.* **ĭnfrē'quencў** *n.*

ĭnfrĭ'nge (-j) *v.t.* Transgress, violate (law, oath, etc.). **ĭnfrĭ'ngement** *n.*

ĭnfŭndĭ'būlar *adj.* Funnel-shaped.

ĭnfŭndĭ'būlum *n.* (anat.) Funnel-shaped cavity or structure.

ĭnfūr'ĭāte *v.t.* Fill with fury, enrage.

ĭnfū'se (-z) *v.* 1. Pour (*into*); instil (*into*). 2. Steep (herb etc.) in liquid to extract its soluble properties; undergo infusion.

ĭnfū'sĭble (-z-) *adj.* That cannot be fused or melted. **ĭnfūsĭbĭ'lĭtў** *n.*

ĭnfū'sion *n.* Infusing; liquid

extract thus obtained; infused element, admixture.

ĭngĕ'mĭnāte (-j-) *v.t.* Repeat, reiterate.

ĭngē'nĭous (-j-) *adj.* Showing ingenuity. **ĭngē'nĭouslў** *adv.* **ĭngē'nĭousnėss** *n.*

ingénue (ăṅzhānū), *n.* Artless girl, esp. of the type represented on the stage. [Fr.]

ĭngėnū'ĭtў (-j-) *n.* Cleverness at or in construction, organization, etc.

ĭngĕ'nūous (-j-) *adj.* Open, frank; innocent, artless. **ĭngĕ'nūouslў** *adv.* **ĭngĕ'nūousnėss** *n.*

ĭngĕ'st (-j-) *v.t.* Take in (food etc.) by, or as if by, swallowing. **ĭngĕ'stion** (-schon) *n.* **ĭngĕ'stĭve** *adj.*

ĭ'ngle (ĭnggl) *n.* Fire burning on hearth; *~-nook*, chimney-corner.

ĭnglôr'ĭous (ĭn-g-) *adj.* Shameful, ignominious; obscure. **ĭnglôr'ĭouslў** *adv.*

ĭ'ngot (ĭngg-) *n.* Mass (usu. oblong) of cast metal, esp. of gold, silver, or steel.

ingrain (*before n.* ĭ'n-g-; *elsewhere* -ā'n) *adj.* Dyed in grain; inherent, inveterate, thorough; ~ *carpet*, reversible carpet without pile, in which two or more cloths of different colours are interwoven to form pattern.

ingrained (*before n.* ĭ'n-grānd; *elsewhere* -ā'nd) *adj.* Deeply rooted, inveterate; thorough.

ĭngrā'te (ĭn-g-) *adj.* & *n.* (archaic) Ungrateful (person).

ĭngratiāte (ĭn-grā'shĭ-) *v.t.* Bring *oneself* into favour *with.*

ĭngră'tĭtūde (ĭn-g-) *n.* Lack of gratitude.

ĭngrē'dĭent (ĭn-g-) *n.* Component part, element, in a mixture.

Ingres (ăṅgr), Jean Auguste Dominique (1781–1867). French classical painter.

ĭ'ngrĕss (ĭn-g-) *n.* Going in; right of entrance.

ĭ'ngrowĭng (ĭn-grōĭ-) *adj.* Growing inwards, esp. (of nail) growing into the flesh.

ĭ'nguĭnal (ĭnggw-) *adj.* Of the groin.

ĭngûr'gĭtāte (ĭn-g-) *v.t.* Swallow greedily. **ĭngûrgĭtā'tion** *n.*

ĭnhă'bĭt *v.t.* Dwell in, occupy (region, town, house, etc.). **ĭnhă'bĭtant** *n.*

ĭnhă'bĭtancў *n.* Residence as inhabitant, esp. during specified period, so as to acquire rights etc.

ĭnhā'lant *n.* (esp.) Medicinal preparation for inhaling.

ĭnhā'le *v.t.* Breathe in (air, gas, etc.); take (esp. tobacco-smoke) into the lungs. **ĭnhalā'tion** *n.*

ĭnhā'ler *n.* (esp.) Apparatus for introducing medicated liquids or vapours into breathing passages, or for administering anaesthetic.

ĭnhârmŏ'nĭc *adj.* (mus.) Not forming part of a HARMONIC series.

ĭnhârmō'nĭous *adj.* Not harmonious. **ĭnhârmō'nĭouslў** *adv.*

ĭnhēr'e *v.i.* (of qualities etc.) Exist, abide, *in*; (of rights etc.) be vested *in*. **ĭnhēr'ence** *n.* **ĭnhēr'ent** *adj.* **ĭnhēr'entlў** *adv.*

ĭnhĕ'rĭt *v.t.* Receive by legal descent or succession; derive (quality etc.) from one's progenitors; (abs.) succeed as heir. **ĭnhĕ'rĭtance** *n.* Inheriting; what is inherited. **ĭnhĕ'rĭtor, ĭnhĕ'rĭtrėss, ĭnhĕ'rĭtrĭx** *ns.*

ĭnhē'sion *n.* Inhering.

ĭnhĭ'bĭt *v.t.* Hinder, restrain (action, process); forbid, prohibit (*from*; esp. in eccles. law); forbid (ecclesiastic to exercise clerical functions). **ĭnhĭbĭ'tion** *n.* (esp., psychol.) Blocking of thought or action by emotional resistance.

ĭnhĭ'bĭtor *n.* Thing that inhibits; (physiol.) substance which represses a normal physiological process or antagonizes an abnormal one; nerve which inhibits; (chem.) substance which slows down or suppresses a chemical change; negative catalyst. **ĭnhĭ'bĭtorў** *adj.*

ĭnhŏ'spĭtable *adj.* Not hospitable; (of region etc.) not affording shelter etc. **ĭnhŏ'spĭtablў** *adv.* **ĭnhŏ'spĭtablenėss, ĭnhŏspĭtă'lĭtў** *ns.*

ĭnhū'man *adj.* Brutal, unfeeling, barbarous; not of the ordinary human type. **ĭnhū'manlў** *adv.* **ĭnhūmă'nĭtў** *n.*

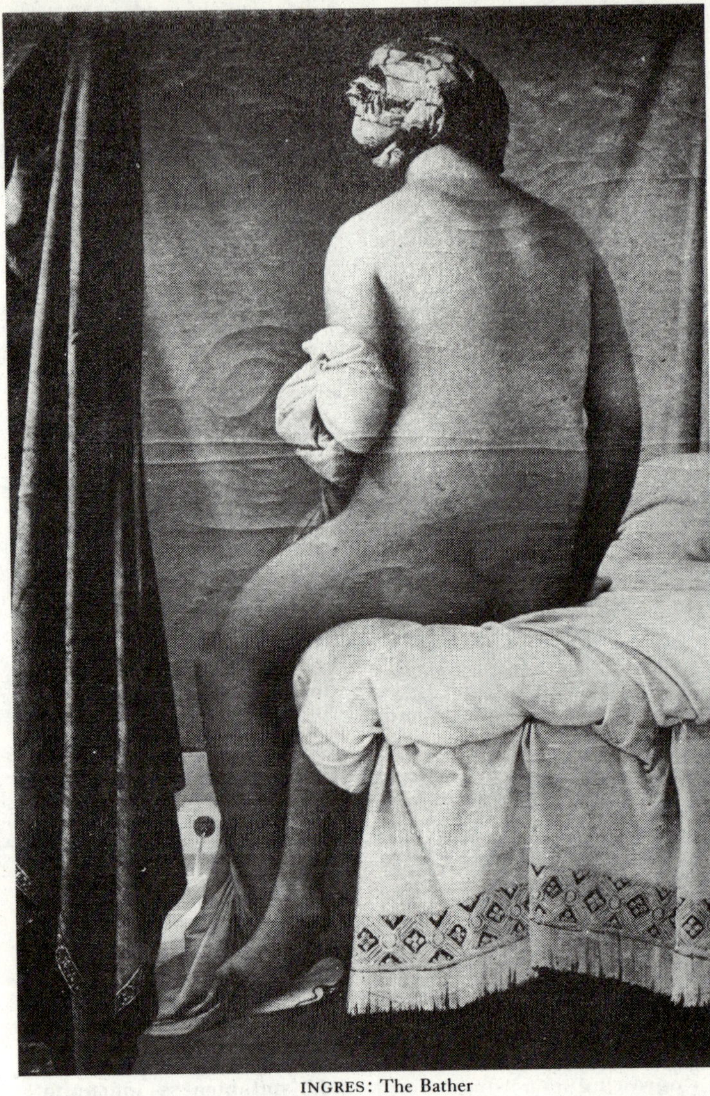

INGRES: The Bather

ĭnhū′me *v.t.* Bury. **ĭnhūmā′tion** *n.*

ĭnĭ′mĭcal *adj.* Hostile; harmful. **ĭnĭ′mĭcallȳ** *adv.*

ĭnĭ′mĭtable *adj.* That defies imitation. **ĭnĭ′mĭtablenėss** *n.* **ĭnĭ′mĭtablȳ** *adv.*

ĭnĭ′quĭtȳ *n.* Unrighteousness, wickedness; gross injustice. **ĭnĭ′quĭtous** *adj.* **ĭnĭ′quĭtouslȳ** *adv.*

Inisfai′l (ĭ-). (poet.) Ireland.

ĭnĭ′tial (-sh*a*l) *adj.* Of, existing or occurring at, the beginning; ~ *letter*, letter standing at beginning of word. **ĭnĭ′tiallȳ** *adv.* **ĭnĭ′tial** *n.* (esp. pl.) First letter(s) of person's name and surname. ~ *v.t.* Mark, sign, with initials.

ĭnĭ′tiāte (-shĭ-) *v.t.* 1. Begin, set going, originate. 2. Admit (person), esp. with introductory rites or forms (*into* society, office, secret, *in* mysteries, science, etc.). **ĭnĭtiā′tion** *n.* **ĭnĭ′tiatorȳ** *adj.* **ĭnĭ′tiate** *adj.* & *n.* (Person) who has been initiated.

ĭnĭ′tiatĭve (-shy*a*-) *n.* First step, origination; power, right, or function of originating something; esp., right of citizen(s) outside legislature to initiate legislation (as in Switzerland); *take the* ~, take the lead. ~ *adj.* Beginning, originating.

ĭnjĕ′ct *v.t.* Drive, force (fluid, medicine, *into* cavity etc.) by or as by syringe; fill (cavity etc.) by injecting.

ĭnjĕ′ction *n.* 1. Injecting; direct introduction of fuel under pressure into combustion chamber of internal combustion engine. 2. Liquid or solution injected.

ĭnjudĭ′cious (-jo͞odĭ′sh*u*s) *adj.* Unwise, ill-judged. **ĭnjudĭ′ciouslȳ** *adv.* **ĭnjudĭ′ciousnėss** *n.*

I′njun (ĭ-) *n.* (U.S. colloq. & dial.) Var. of INDIAN *n.* 2; *honest* ~, honour bright.

ĭnjŭ′nction *n.* Authoritative admonition or order; judicial process restraining person from wrongful act, or compelling restitution etc. to injured party.

ĭ′njure *v.t.* Do wrong to; hurt, harm, impair. **ĭ′njured** (-j*e*rd) *adj.* Wronged; hurt; showing sense of wrong, offended.

ĭnjur′ĭous (-oor-) *adj.* Wrongful; (of language) insulting, calumnious; hurtful. **ĭnjur′ĭouslȳ** *adv.* **ĭnjur′ĭousnėss** *n.*

ĭ′njurȳ *n.* Wrongful action or treatment; harm, damage.

ĭnjŭ′stĭce *n.* Lack of equity, unfairness; unjust act.

ĭnk *n.* 1. Coloured fluid for writing with pen on paper etc. or for printing, consisting of pigment dispersed in water (for writing inks) or in oil, resin, etc., for printing and ballpoint inks, the black variety of printing ink being made from carbon black and usu. linseed oil; *copying* ~: see COPY; *Indian* ~: see INDIAN. 2. Black inky liquid secreted by cuttle-fish etc. and ejected to cloud water and assist escape. 3. ~-*horn*, small vessel of horn formerly used for holding writing-ink; *i′nkpot*, small pot for holding writing-ink; ~-*slinger*, (contempt.) professional writer, esp. reckless writer in newspapers; *i′nkstand*, stand for one or more ink bottles or inkpots; ~-*well*, inkpot fitted into hole in desk. ~ *v.t.* Mark (*in*, *over*, etc.) with ink; cover (types) with ink. **ĭ′nkȳ** *adj.* Of, like ink; black or very dark; covered or stained with ink.

I′nkerman (ĭ-). Place in Crimea, scene of English and French victory over Russians in the Crimean War (5 Nov. 1854).

ĭ′nkling *n.* Hint, slight knowledge or suspicion, (*of*).

inlaid: see INLAY.

ĭ′nland *n.* Interior of country. ~ *adj.* Placed in interior of country, remote from sea or border; carried on within limits of a country; ~ *revenue*, part of national revenue consisting of taxes and of duties on inland trade. **ĭnlă′nd** *adv.* In, towards, the interior.

ĭ′n-law *n.* (colloq.) Relative by marriage.

ĭnlay′ *v.t.* (past t. & past part. *inlaid*). Embed (thing *in* another) so that their surfaces are even; ornament (thing) with another inlaid; mount (illustration or damaged leaf of book) in larger sheet so that both sides are visible. **ĭ′nlay**

(*or* -lā′) *n.* Inlaid ornament, esp. furniture or woodwork.

ĭ′nlėt *n.* 1. Way of admission, entrance. 2. Small arm of sea, creek.

ĭ′nlīer *n.* (geol.) Outcrop of older strata within a girdle of younger ones (opp. OUTLIER).

ĭn lŏ′cō parĕ′ntĭs. In place of a parent. [L]

ĭ′nlȳ *adv.* (poet.) Inwardly, in the heart; intimately.

ĭ′nmāte *n.* Occupant (*of* house, institution, etc.), esp. along with others.

ĭn mĕ′dĭas rēs (-ahs, rēz). Into the midst of things; into the middle of a narrative. [L]

ĭn mėmōr′ĭăm. In memory (of). [L]

ĭ′nmōst *adj.* Most inward.

ĭnn *n.* 1. House providing lodging, food, etc., for payment, esp. for travellers; tavern; *i′nnkeeper*, one who keeps an inn. 2. *Inns of Chancery*, buildings in London formerly used for residence of law students; societies occupying these; *Inns of Court*, buildings in London belonging to four legal societies (Inner Temple, Middle Temple, Lincoln's Inn, Gray's Inn); these societies, which have the exclusive right of admitting persons to practise at the English bar.

ĭnnards: see INWARDS *n.pl.*

ĭnnā′te (*or* ĭ′-) *adj.* Inborn, natural. **ĭnnā′telȳ** *adv.* **ĭnnā′tenėss** *n.*

ĭnnă′vĭgable *adj.* Not navigable.

ĭ′nner *adj.* Interior, internal; *the ~ man*, man's soul or mind; (joc.) stomach; *~ reserve*, secret reserve not disclosed in a balance-sheet; *I~ Temple*: see INN, 2; *~ tube*, separate inflatable rubber tube inside cover of a pneumatic tyre. **ĭ′nnermōst** *adj.* **ĭ′nner** *n.* Division of target next outside bull's-eye, shot that strikes this.

ĭnnĕr′vāte *v.t.* (physiol.) Connect (muscle, organ) to nervous system, supply it with nerve-fibre. **ĭnnervā′tion** *n.*

ĭ′nnings (-z) *n.* (U.S. *inning*) (cricket, baseball, etc.) Portion of game played by either side while 'in' or batting, play of one batsman during his turn (also freq. fig.).

ĭ′nnocent[1] *adj.* Free from moral wrong, sinless; not guilty (*of* crime etc.); simple, guileless; harmless. **ĭ′nnocentlȳ** *adv.* **ĭ′nnocent** *n.* Innocent person, esp. young child; simple person; idiot; (*Holy*) *Innocents' Day*, 28 Dec., observed as church festival in commemoration of Massacre of the Innocents by Herod (Matt. 2: 16). **ĭ′nnocence, ĭ′nnocencȳ** *ns.*

I′nnocent[2] (ĭ-). Name of thirteen popes: (esp.) *Innocent III*, pope 1198–1216; champion of supremacy of spiritual over temporal authority; proclaimer of 4th crusade and initiator of 'crusades' against ALBIGENSES; he excommunicated King John of England (1209) when John refused to acknowledge his nomination of Stephen Langton as archbishop of Canterbury, but after signing of Magna Carta he supported John against the barons; *Innocent IV*, pope 1243–54; canon lawyer, extreme supporter of papal claims to temporal authority; first bestower of red hat on Roman cardinals.

ĭnnŏ′cūous *adj.* Not injurious, harmless. **ĭnnŏ′cūouslȳ** *adv.* **ĭnnŏ′cūousnėss, ĭnnocū′ĭtȳ** *ns.*

ĭnnŏ′mĭnate *adj.* Unnamed; (anat.) *~ bone*, hip bone, a union of three original bones (ilium, ischium, and pubis).

ĭ′nnovāte *v.i.* Bring in novelties; make changes *in*. **ĭnnovā′tion, ĭ′nnovātor** *ns.* **ĭ′nnovātorȳ** *adj.*

ĭnnūĕ′ndō *n.* Oblique hint, insinuation, allusive remark (usu. depreciatory). *~ v.i.* Make innuendoes. [L, = 'by nodding at, pointing at, meaning' (*innuere* nod at, mean)].

ĭnnū′merable *adj.* Countless.

ĭnŏ′cūlāte *v.t.* Impregnate (person or animal) *with* agent of disease to induce milder form of it and so safeguard against further attacks. **ĭnŏcūlā′tion** *n.* **ĭnŏ′cūlatĭve** *adj.*

ĭnō′dorous *adj.* Having no odour.

ĭnoffĕ′nsĭve *adj.* Unoffending; not objectionable. **ĭnoffĕ′nsĭvelȳ** *adv.* **ĭnoffĕ′nsĭvenėss** *n.*

ĭnoffĭ'cious (-sh*us*) *adj.* (law) Not in accordance with moral duty.

ĭnŏ'perable *adj.* That cannot be operated; not curable by surgical operation.

ĭnŏ'peratĭve *adj.* Not working or taking effect.

ĭnŏ'pportūne *adj.* Unseasonable, untimely, tactless. **ĭnŏ'pportūnelў** *adv.* **ĭnŏ'pportūnenėss** *n.*

ĭnor'dĭnate *adj.* Immoderate, excessive; intemperate; disorderly. **ĭnor'dĭnatelў** *adv.*

ĭnorgă'nic *adj.* 1. Having no organized physical structure; not existing by natural growth, extraneous. 2. (chem.) Belonging to any class of substance other than ORGANIC compounds; ~ *chemistry*: see CHEMISTRY.

ĭnŏ'scūlāte *v.* (of blood-vessels etc.) Join, have terminal connection (*with*); (of fibres etc.) unite closely, be interwoven; unite (fibres etc.) closely. **ĭnŏscūlā'tion** *n.*

ĭn par'tĭbus ĭnfĭde'lĭum (-dā-). (of R.C. titular bishop) In a heretical country. [L]

ĭn pĕ'ttō. (of cardinals appointed but not disclosed by the pope) Undisclosed. [It., = 'in the breast']

ĭn pŏ'ssė. Potentially. [L]

ĭn prō'prĭa persō'na. In his (her) own person. [L]

ĭn pūr'is nătūra'lĭbus (-ēs, -ahl-) Stark naked. [L]

ĭ'nput (-ŏŏt) *n.* What is put in, esp. in economic, electrical, or industrial processes; (V.A.T.) value added to (manufactured object) by work on it.

ĭ'nquĕst (*or* ĭn-kw-) *n.* Legal or judicial inquiry to ascertain matter of fact; inquiry held by coroner's court to ascertain cause of person's death (also *coroner's* ~); also fig.

ĭnquī'ėtūde (*or* ĭn-kw-) *n.* Uneasiness of mind or body.

ĭnquīr'e, ėn- (*or* ĭn-kw-) *v.* Make search (*into* matter); seek information (*of* person, *about*, *after*, thing etc.); ask *for* (person, goods in shop, etc.), ask to be told. **ĭnquīr'ĭnglў** *adv.*

ĭnquīr'ў, ėn- (*or* ĭn-kw-) *n.* Asking; question; investigation; *court of* ~, (mil.) investigation of charge against officer or soldier.

ĭnquĭsĭ'tion (-z-; *or* ĭn-kw-) *n.* 1. Search, investigation; judicial or official inquiry. 2. *I*~, (R.C. Ch.) ecclesiastical tribunal (the *Holy Office*) set up in 13th c. under Innocent III for the suppression of heresy and punishment of heretics, notorious esp. in Spain in 16th c. for its severities. **ĭnquĭsĭ'tional** *adj.*

ĭnquĭ'sĭtĭve (-z-; *or* ĭn-kw-) *adj.* Inquiring, curious; prying. **ĭnquĭ'sĭtĭvelў** *adv.* **ĭnquĭ'sĭtĭvenėss** *n.*

ĭnquĭ'sĭtor (-z-; *or* ĭn-kw-) *n.* Official investigator; officer of the Inquisition; *Grand I*~, director of court of Inquisition in some countries; *I*~ *General*, head of Inquisition in Spain.

ĭnquĭsĭtor'ial (-z-; *or* ĭn-kw-) *adj.* Of, like, an inquisitor; offensively prying. **ĭnquĭsĭtor'iallў** *adv.*

I.N.R.I. *abbrev. Iesus Nazarenus Rex Iudaeorum* (L, = Jesus of Nazareth, King of the Jews).

ĭ'nroad *n.* Hostile incursion, raid; (fig.) forcible encroachment.

ĭ'nrŭsh *n.* Rushing in.

ĭnsă'lĭvāte *v.t.* Mix (food) with saliva. **ĭnsalĭvā'tion** *n.*

ĭnsalu'brious (-lōō-) *adj.* (of climate etc.) Unhealthy. **ĭnsalu'brĭtў** *n.*

ĭnsā'ne *adj.* Not sane, mad; senseless. **ĭnsā'nelў** *adv.* **ĭnsă'nĭtў** *n.*

ĭnsă'nĭtarў *adj.* Not sanitary.

ĭnsā'tiable (-sh*a*-) *adj.* That cannot be satisfied; inordinately greedy. **ĭnsātiabĭ'lĭtў** *n.* **ĭnsā'tiablў** *adv.*

ĭnsā'tiate (-shy*a*t) *adj.* Never satisfied.

ĭnscrī'be *v.t.* 1. Write (words etc. *in, on*); enter name of (person) on list; mark (sheet, tablet, etc. *with* characters); (esp. in past part.) issue (loan) in form of shares with registered holders. 2. (geom.) Trace (figure) within another so that some particular points of it lie on the boundary of that other.

ĭnscrĭ'ption *n.* Words inscribed, esp. on monument, coin, etc.; inscribing (*of* loan).

ĭnscru'table (-ōō-) *adj.* That cannot be penetrated, wholly mysterious. **inscru'tableness, ĭnscrutabĭ'lĭtў** *ns.* **ĭnscru'tablў** *adv.*

ĭ'nsĕct *n.* (pop.) Small animal with body divided into segments; (zool.) arthropod of the class Insecta which breathe through tracheae and have a body divided into 3 regions (head, thorax, and abdomen) and usu., in the adult, 3 pairs of legs and 2 pairs of wings; (fig.) insignificant or contemptible person or creature.

ĭnsĕ'ctĭcīde *n.* Insect-killer, esp. preparation used for killing insects. **ĭnsĕctĭcī'dal** *adj.*

ĭnsĕ'ctĭvōre *n.* Insect-eating animal; member of the Insectivora, an order of primitive mammals, most members of which (e.g. shrew, hedgehog) usu. feed on insects. **ĭnsĕctĭ'vorous** *adj.* Insect-eating; (of plant) having special structures for trapping and digesting insects.

ĭnsėcūr'e *adj.* Unsafe; (of ice, ground, etc.) liable to give way. **ĭnsėcūr'elў** *adv.* **ĭnsėcūr'ĭtў** *n.*

ĭnsĕ'mĭnāte *v.t.* Sow (seed etc.) *in* (lit. and fig.); (biol.) introduce spermatozoa into (female reproductive system, or the eggs of those animals (e.g. frogs) which fertilize externally). **ĭnsĕmĭnā'tion** *n.*

ĭnsĕ'nsate *adj.* Without sensibility, unfeeling; stupid; mad; without physical sensation. **ĭnsĕ'nsatelў** *adv.*

ĭnsĕnsĭbĭ'lĭtў *n.* Lack of mental feeling or emotion; indifference (*to*); unconsciousness, swoon.

ĭnsĕ'nsĭble *adj.* Too small or gradual to be perceived; inappreciable; unconscious; unaware. **ĭnsĕ'nsĭblў** *adv.*

ĭnsĕ'nsĭtĭve *adj.* Not sensitive (*to*); emotionless, callous. **ĭnsĕ'nsĭtĭvenėss** *n.*

ĭnsĕ'ntient (-shi-) *adj.* Inanimate.

ĭnsĕ'parable *adj.* That cannot be separated; ~ *prefix*, (gram.) prefix found only in combination and incapable of being used as separate word. **ĭnsĕparabĭ'lĭtў** *n.* **ĭnsĕ'parablў** *adv.*

ĭnsêr't *v.t.* Place, fit, thrust, (thing *in*, *into*, another etc.); introduce (letter, article, etc., *in*, *into*, written matter, newspaper, etc.). **ĭ'nsêrt** *n.* Thing inserted. **ĭnsêr'tion** *n.* Inserting; thing inserted, esp. in writing or print; ornamental needlework etc. inserted into plain material; (anat.) place or manner of attachment of muscle, organ, etc.

ĭ'nsĕt *n.* Extra page(s) inserted in sheet or book; small map etc. inserted within border of larger; piece set into dress etc. **ĭnsĕ't** *v.t.* Put in as an inset.

ĭ'nshôr'e *adv.* & *adj.* Close to shore; ~ *of*, nearer to shore than.

ĭ'nsīde (*or* -ī'd) *n.* 1. Inner side or surface; (of path) side next to wall or away from road; inner part, interior; *i'nside out*, so that inner side becomes outer. 2. (-ī'd) Stomach and bowels (colloq.); middle part. **ĭ'nsīde** *adj.* Situated on or in, derived from, the inside; ~ *information*, information not accessible to outsiders; ~ *left*, *right*, (footb. etc). player positioned between outside left or right and centre forward. **ĭnsī'de** *adv.* On or in or to the inside; (colloq.) in prison; ~ *of* (colloq.) in less time than. **ĭ'nsī'de** *prep.* On or to the inner side of, within.

ĭnsī'der *n.* One who is in some society, organization, etc.; one who is in the secret.

ĭnsĭ'dious *adj.* Treacherous, crafty; proceeding secretly or subtly. **ĭnsĭ'diouslў** *adv.* **ĭnsĭ'diousnėss** *n.*

ĭ'nsight (-īt) *n.* Penetration (*into* character, circumstances, etc.) with the understanding.

ĭnsĭ'gnĭa *n.pl.* Badges, distinguishing marks (*of* office, honour, etc.).

ĭnsĭgnĭ'fĭcant *adj.* Unimportant, trifling; contemptible; meaningless. **ĭnsĭgnĭ'fĭcantlў, ĭnsĭgnĭ'fĭcance** *ns.*

insincēr'e *adj.* Not sincere. **insincēr'elў** *adv.* **insincĕ'ritў** *n.*

insi'nūāte *v.t.* Introduce gradually or subtly; convey indirectly, hint obliquely. **insi'nūātinglў** *adv.* **insinūā'tion, insi'nūātor** *ns.* **insi'nūative** *adj.*

insi'pid *adj.* Tasteless; wanting in flavour; lifeless, dull, uninteresting. **insi'pidlў** *adv.* **insi'pidnėss, insipi'ditў** *ns.*

insi'st *v.* Dwell long or emphatically (*on*); maintain positively; make a stand *on* as essential. **insi'stence, insi'stencў** *ns.* **insi'stent** *adj.* **insi'stentlў** *adv.*

in si'tū. In its (original) place. [L]

insobrī'ėtў *n.* Intemperance, esp. in drinking.

insōfar' *adv.* (also *in so far*) To such an extent or degree (*as*).

insolā'tion *n.* Exposure to sun's rays (for purpose of bleaching etc., or as medical treatment, or as cause of disease); (geol.) flaking of rock when exposure to sun alternates with rapid cooling at night.

i'nsōle *n.* 1. Inner sole of boot or shoe. 2. Flat piece of material worn inside shoe for warmth or comfort.

i'nsolent *adj.* Offensively contemptuous, insulting. **i'nsolentlў** *adv.* **i'nsolence** *n.*

insŏ'lūble *adj.* 1. That cannot be solved. 2. That cannot be dissolved. **insŏ'lūblenėss, insŏlūbi'litў** *ns.* **insŏ'lūblў** *adv.*

insŏ'lvent *adj.* & *n.* (Debtor) unable to pay debts. **insŏ'lvencў** *n.*

insŏ'mnia *n.* Sleeplessness.

insōmŭ'ch *adv.* To such an extent *that.*

insou'ciant (-sōō-) *adj.* Careless, unconcerned. **insou'ciance** *n.*

inspă'n *v.t.* (S. Afr.) Yoke (oxen etc.) in team to vehicle; harness (wagon).

inspĕ'ct *v.t.* Look closely into; examine officially. **inspĕ'ction** *n.*

inspĕ'ctor *n.* (esp.) Police officer ranking next below superintendent; *I~ General,* (esp.) head of U.S. military department concerned with discipline, supply, accounts, etc. **inspĕ'ctoral, inspĕctōr'ial** *adjs.* **inspĕ'ctorship** *n.*

inspĕ'ctorate *n.* Office of inspector; body of inspectors; district under inspector.

inspirā'tion *n.* 1. Drawing in of breath. 2. Inspiring; divine influence, esp. that under which books of Scripture are supposed to have been written, whether *verbal* ~ (dictating every word), *plenary* ~ (covering all subjects treated), or *moral* ~ (confined to moral and religious teaching). 3. Thought etc. inspired, prompting; sudden happy idea. 4. Inspiring principle. **inspirā'tional** *adj.*

inspīr'e *v.t.* 1. Breathe in, inhale. 2. Infuse thought or feeling into (person); animate (person etc. *with* feeling); infuse (feeling *into* person etc.), create (feeling *in*); suggest or prompt expression of a particular opinion etc., prompt writer or speaker to such expression. **inspīr'atorў** *adj.*

inspi'rit *v.t.* Put life into, animate; encourage.

inspi'ssāte (*or* i'-) *v.t.* Thicken, condense. **inspissā'tion** *n.*

inst. *abbrev.* = INSTANT[1] 2.

instabi'litў *n.* Lack of stability.

insta'll (-awl) *v.t.* Place (person *in* office or dignity) with ceremonies; establish (*in* place, condition, etc.); place (apparatus) in position for use. **installā'tion** *n.* (Ceremony of) installing; apparatus installed.

insta'lment (-awl-) *n.* Each of several parts, successively falling due, of a sum payable; each of several parts supplied etc. at different times; part of serial story printed in one issue.

i'nstance *n.* Fact illustrating a general truth, example; particular case; (law) process, suit; *for* ~, for example; *at the* ~ *of,* at the request or suggestion of; *court of first* ~, court of primary jurisdiction; *in the first* ~, in the first place, at the first stage of a proceeding. ~ *v.t.* Cite as an instance; (usu. pass.) exemplify.

i'nstancў *n.* Urgency.

ĭ'nstant[1] *adj.* 1. Urgent, pressing. 2. Immediate; (abbrev. *inst.*) of the current calendar month. 3. (of food) Processed for quick preparation.

ĭ'nstant[2] *n.* Precise (esp. the present) point of time, moment; short space of time, moment. **ĭ'nstantlÿ** *adv.* At once.

ĭnstantā'nėous *adj.* Occurring, done, in an instant; immediate; existing at a particular instant. **ĭnstantā'nėouslÿ** *adv.* **ĭnstantā'nėousnėss** *n.*

ĭnstă'nter *adv.* (now usu. joc.) Immediately, at once.

ĭ'nstar *n.* (zool.) Stage in life-history of certain animals, esp. arthropods, between successive moultings of the cuticle.

ĭn stă'tū pūpĭllâr'ī. Under guardianship; under scholastic discipline; (of member of a university) not having the degree of Master. [L]

ĭn stă'tū quō. In the same state (as formerly). [L]

ĭnstaurā'tion *n.* Restoration, renewal.

ĭnstea'd (-ĕd) *adv.* As a substitute or alternative; in place *of*.

ĭ'nstĕp *n.* Upper surface of foot between toe and ankle; part of shoe, etc., fitting over or under this; instep-shaped thing.

ĭ'nstĭgāte *v.t.* Urge on, incite (person *to*); bring about by persuasion. **ĭnstĭgā'tion, ĭ'nstĭgātor** *ns.*

ĭnstĭ'l, -ll *v.t.* Put in (liquid) by drops; infuse (feeling, idea, etc.) gradually. **ĭnstĭllā'tion** *n.*

ĭ'nstĭnct[1] *n.* Innate propensity to certain seemingly rational acts performed without conscious design; innate impulse; intuition, unconscious skill; (zool.) inborn and usually rigid pattern of behaviour in animals, often in response to certain simple stimuli. **ĭnstĭ'nctĭve** *adj.* **ĭnstĭ'nctĭvelÿ** *adv.*

ĭnstĭ'nct[2] *pred. adj.* Imbued, charged (*with*).

Institut de France (ăństĭtū, frahńs). Union of the 5 French Academies (Académie française; Academy of Inscriptions and Belles-Lettres; Academy of Moral and Political Sciences; Academy of Science; Academy of the Fine Arts); founded 1795.

ĭ'nstĭtūte *n.* 1. Society, organization, for promotion of scientific or other object; building used by this. 2. (pl.) Digest of elements of a subject, esp. of jurisprudence. ~ *v.t.* Establish, found; set on foot (inquiry etc.); appoint.

ĭnstĭtū'tion *n.* 1. Instituting; admission of incumbent into spiritual care of parish. 2. Established law, custom, or practice; (colloq., of person etc.) familiar object. 3. Organization for promotion of some public object, religious, charitable, reformatory, etc.; building used by this; (esp. pop.) building used by benevolent or educational institution. **ĭnstĭtū'tional** *adj.* (esp. of religion) Organized into institutions (churches, priesthood, ritual, etc.) or finding expression through these; (U.S., of church etc.) including educational, charitable, etc., organizations among its activities. **ĭnstĭtū'tionalīze** *v.t.* Make institutional; place (person) in institution. **ĭnstĭtū'tionalĭsm** *n.*

ĭnstrŭ'ct *v.t.* Teach (person etc. *in* subject); inform; direct, command; (of client, solicitor) give information to (solicitor, counsel). **ĭnstrŭ'ctor, ĭnstrŭ'ctrėss** *ns.*

ĭnstrŭ'ction *n.* 1. Teaching. 2. (pl.) Directions, orders. 3. (pl.) Directions to solicitor or counsel. **ĭnstrŭ'ctional** *adj.*

ĭnstrŭ'ctĭve *adj.* Tending to instruct, conveying a lesson.

ĭ'nstrument (-ro͞o-) *n.* 1. Thing used in performing an action; person so made use of; tool, implement, esp. for delicate or scientific work. 2. (also *musical* ~) Contrivance for producing musical sounds. 3. Formal, esp. legal, document. ~ (*or* -mĕ'nt) *v.t.* Arrange (music) for instruments.

ĭnstrumĕ'ntal (-ro͞o-) *adj.* 1. Serving as instrument or means (*to*, *in*). 2. Of, arising from, an instrument. 3. (of music) Performed on instruments. 4. (gram., of case) Denoting the instrument, or means. **ĭnstrumĕ'ntallȳ** *adv.*

ĭnstrumĕ'ntalist (-ro͝o-) *n.* Performer on musical instrument.

ĭnstrumĕntă'lĭtȳ (-ro͝o-) *n.* Agency, means.

ĭnstrumĕntā'tion (-ro͝o-) *n.* 1. Composition or arrangement of music for instruments; (loosely) orchestration. 2. Use of mechanical instruments in industry etc.

ĭnsubôr'dĭnate *adj.* Disobedient, rebellious. **ĭnsubôrdĭnā'tion** *n.*

ĭnsubstă'ntial (-sh*a*l) *adj.* Not real; lacking solidity or substance. **ĭnsubstăntiă'lĭtȳ** (-shiă-) *n.*

ĭnsŭ'fferable *adj.* Unbearably arrogant, conceited, etc.; intolerable. **ĭnsŭ'fferablȳ** *adv.*

ĭnsuffĭ'cient (-sh*e*nt) *adj.* Not sufficient, inadequate. **ĭnsuffĭ'cientlȳ** *adv.* **ĭnsuffĭ'ciencȳ** *n.*

ĭ'nsufflāte *v.t.* Blow, breathe, (air, gas, etc.) into cavity of body etc.; treat (nose etc.) thus. **insufflā'tion** *n.* Blowing on or into; breathing on person as rite of exorcism. **ĭ'nsufflātor** *n.* Apparatus for insufflating.

ĭ'nsūlar *adj.* Of (the nature of) an island; of, like, islanders, esp. narrow-minded. **ĭ'nsūlarlȳ** *adv.* **ĭ'nsūlarĭsm, ĭnsūlă'rĭtȳ** *ns.*

ĭ'nsūlāte *v.t.* 1. Make (land) into an island. 2. Detach (person, thing) from surroundings, isolate. 3. Isolate (thing) by interposition of non-conductors, to prevent passage of electricity, heat, or sound. **ĭnsūlā'tion** *n.*

ĭ'nsūlātor *n.* That which insulates, esp. a non-conducting substance, as porcelain or glass, for insulating electric wires, or asbestos, for insulating heat.

ĭ'nsūlĭn *n.* Hormone secreted by the islets of LANGERHANS in the pancreas of vertebrates, accelerating the passage of glucose from the blood to the tissues and promoting its storage as glycogen in the liver and muscles.

ĭnsŭ'lt *v.t.* Treat with scornful abuse, offer indignity to; affront. **ĭnsŭ'ltĭnglȳ** *adv.* **ĭ'nsŭlt** *n.* Insulting speech or action, affront.

ĭnsū'perable (*or* -so͞o-) *adj.* That cannot be surmounted or overcome. **ĭnsūperabĭ'lĭtȳ** *n.* **ĭnsū'perablȳ** *adv.*

ĭnsuppôr'table *adj.* Unbearable. **ĭnsuppôr'tablȳ** *adv.*

ĭnsur'ance (-shoor-) *n.* Insuring; sum paid for this, premium; *National I~*: see NATIONAL.

ĭnsur'ant (-shoor-) *n.* Person to whom insurance policy is issued.

ĭnsur'e (-shoor) *v.t.* Secure payment of sum of money in event of loss of or damage to property (esp. by casualty at sea, fire, burglary, etc.), or of the death or disablement of a person, in consideration of the payment of a premium and observance of certain conditions; *the insured*, person to whom such payment is secured. **ĭnsur'er** *n.* One who insures property in consideration of premium, underwriter.

ĭnsûr'ġent *adj.* Rising in active revolt. ~ *n.* Rebel. **ĭnsûr'ġencȳ** *n.*

ĭnsurmou'ntable *adj.* Not to be surmounted. **ĭnsurmou'ntablȳ** *adv.*

ĭnsurrĕ'ction *n.* Rising in open resistance to established authority; incipient rebellion. **ĭnsurrĕ'ctional, ĭnsurrĕ'ctionarȳ** *adjs.* **ĭnsurrĕ'ctionist** *n.*

ĭnsuscĕ'ptĭble *adj.* Not susceptible. **ĭnsuscĕptĭbĭ'lĭtȳ** *n.*

ĭntă'ct *adj.* Untouched; entire; unimpaired.

ĭntă'ġliātėd (-ăl-) *adj.* Carved on the surface.

ĭnta'glĭō (-ahl-) *n.* (pl. -*s*). Engraved design; incised carving in hard material; gem with incised design (opp. CAMEO); *in* ~, having the design incised (opp. *in* RELIEF); ~ *print*, print made from an incised plate on which the paper is impressed so that the ink is taken up from the furrows, as in etching, photogravure, etc.

ĭ'ntāke *n.* Place where water or gas etc. is taken into channel or pipe from river etc. (*air* ~); airshaft in mine; way in; taking in, person, thing, amount, taken in; (chiefly north.) land reclaimed from moor, etc.

ĭntă'ngĭble (-j-) *adj.* That cannot be touched; impalpable; that cannot be grasped mentally. **ĭntăngĭbĭ'lĭtȳ** *n.* **ĭntă'ngĭblȳ** *adv.*

ĭntar'sia *n.* Marquetry. [It.]

ĭ'ntėger *n.* Whole number, undivided quantity; thing complete in itself.

ĭ'ntėgral *adj.* Of, necessary to the completeness of, a whole; whole, complete; (math.) of, denoted by, an integer, involving only integers; ~ *calculus*, branch of infinitesimal calculus dealing with integrals of functions; used also to include solution of differential equations, parts of theory of functions, etc. **ĭ'ntėgrallȳ** *adv.* **ĭntėgră'lĭtȳ** *n.* **ĭ'ntėgral** *n.* (math.) Quantity of which given function is differential or differential coefficient; equation or system of equations from which given equation or system can be derived by differentiation.

ĭ'ntėgrant *adj.* (of parts) Component, making up a whole.

ĭ'ntėgrate *adj.* Made up of parts; whole, complete. **ĭ'ntėgrāte** *v.* Complete (imperfect thing) by addition of parts; combine (parts) into a whole; combine (religious or ethnic groups) within a system, esp. as equals; cease to segregate (racially); (math.) find the integral of; indicate mean volume or total sum of (area, temperature, etc.). **ĭntėgrā'tion** *n.* **ĭ'ntėgrātĭve** *adj.*

ĭntĕ'grĭtȳ *n.* Wholeness; soundness; uprightness, honesty.

ĭntĕ'gūment *n.* Skin, husk, rind, or other (usu. natural) covering. **ĭntĕgūmĕ'ntarȳ** *adj.*

ĭ'ntėllĕct *n.* Faculty of knowing and reasoning; understanding; person(s) of good understanding.

ĭntėllĕ'ction *n.* Action, process, of understanding, esp. as opp. to *imagination*. **ĭntėllĕ'ctĭve** *adj.*

ĭntėllĕ'ctūal *adj.* Of, appealing to, requiring the exercise of, intellect; possessing a good understanding, enlightened; given to mental pursuits. **ĭntėllĕ'ctūallȳ** *adv.* **ĭntėllĕctūă'lĭtȳ** *n.* **ĭntėllĕ'ctūalīze** *v.* **ĭntėllĕ'ctūal** *n.* Intellectual person.

ĭntėllĕ'ctūalĭsm *n.* Doctrine that knowledge is wholly or mainly derived from pure reason. **ĭntėllĕ'ctūalĭst** *n.*

ĭntĕ'llĭgence *n.* 1. Intellect, understanding; quickness of understanding, sagacity; rational being; ~ *quotient*, (abbrev. I.Q.) ratio of mental to chronological age; ~ *test*, test designed to ascertain intelligence or mental age, rather than acquired knowledge, of examinee. 2. Information, news; obtaining of (esp. secret) information, persons employed in this; secret service.

ĭntĕ'llĭgent *adj.* Having or showing (usu. a high degree of) understanding. **ĭntĕ'llĭgėntlȳ** *adv.*

ĭntĕllĭgĕ'ntsia *n.* Class of intellectuals, esp. in pre-revolutionary Russia.

ĭntĕ'llĭgĭble *adj.* That can be understood; comprehensible *to*; (philos.) that can be apprehended only by the intellect, not by the senses. **ĭntĕllĭgĭbĭ'lĭtȳ** *n.* **ĭntĕ'llĭgĭblȳ** *adv.*

ĭntĕ'mperate *adj.* Immoderate, unbridled, violent; excessive in indulgence of an appetite; addicted to drinking. **ĭntĕ'mperatelȳ** *adv.* **ĭntĕ'mperance** *n.*

ĭntĕ'nd *v.t.* Purpose, design; design, destine, for a purpose; mean.

ĭntĕ'ndant *n.* Superintendent, manager, of public business etc. (chiefly as foreign title).

ĭntĕ'ndėd *n.* (colloq.) Fiancé(e); person one hopes to marry.

ĭntĕ'ndment *n.* True meaning as fixed by law.

ĭntĕ'nse *adj.* Existing in a high degree, violent, vehement; having some quality in high degree; eager, ardent; feeling, apt to feel, intense emotion. **ĭntĕ'nselȳ** *adv.* **ĭntĕ'nseness, ĭntĕ'nsĭtȳ** *ns.*

ĭntĕ'nsĭfȳ *v.* Render, become, intense; (phot.) increase opacity of the deposit in a negative by chemical or other means. **ĭntĕnsĭfĭcā'tion** *n.*

ĭntĕ'nsion *n.* Intensity, high degree, of a quality (opp. *extension*); strenuous exertion of mind or will; (logic) connotation of a term, sum of the attributes, qualities comprised in a concept.

intĕ'nsĭve *adj.* Of, relating to, intensity as opp. to extent; producing intensity; making intense, esp. (gram.) giving force or emphasis; concentrated, directed to a single point, area, or subject; (econ.) serving to increase production of given area. **intĕ'nsĭvelȳ** *adv.* **intĕ'nsĭve** *n.* (gram.) Intensive word or prefix.

intĕ'nt[1] *n.* Intention, purpose; *to all* ~*s and purposes*, practically, virtually.

intĕ'nt[2] *adj.* Resolved, bent (*on*); sedulously occupied (*on*); earnest, eager. **intĕ'ntlȳ** *adv.* **intĕ'ntnĕss** *n.*

intĕ'ntion *n.* 1. Intending; thing intended, purpose; ultimate aim; (pl., colloq.) purposes in respect of proposal of marriage. 2. (med.) Manner or process of healing of lesion or fracture; *by first* ~, by immediate reunion without granulation; *by second* ~, by granulation after suppuration. 3. (logic) Conception; *first* ~*s*, primary conceptions of things, formed by direct application of mind to the things themselves; *second* ~*s*, secondary conceptions formed by application of thought to first intentions in their relations to each other. 4. *special, particular* ~, (theol.) special purpose for which Mass is celebrated, prayers are offered up, etc. **intĕ'ntional** *adj.* Done on purpose. **intĕ'ntionallȳ** *adv.*

inter' *v.t.* Deposit (corpse etc.) in earth, tomb, etc.; bury.

inter- *prefix.* Expressing mutual or reciprocal act or relation, or with sense 'among', 'between'.

interă'ct *v.i.* Act reciprocally, act on each other. **interă'ction** *n.* **interă'ctĭve** *adj.*

ĭ'nter ăl'ĭa. Amongst other things. [L]

interbrē'd *v.* (past t. & past part. *-bred*). Cross-breed; (of animals of different species etc.) breed with each other.

intercă'larȳ *adj.* (of day or month) Inserted in calendar to harmonize calendar with solar year, as the odd day (29 Feb.) in a leap year; (of year) having such additions; interpolated, intervening.

inter'calāte *v.t.* Insert (intercalary day etc.); interpose (anything out of usual course, esp. in past. part., of strata). **intercalā'tion** *n.*

intercē'de *v.i.* Interpose on behalf of another, plead (*with* one person *for* another).

intercĕ'pt *v.t.* Seize, catch (person, enemy aircraft, etc.) on the way from place to place; pick up (esp. enemy's) radio signal; cut off (light etc. *from*); check, stop; (math.) mark off (space) between two points etc. **intercĕ'ption** *n.* **intercĕ'ptĭve** *adj.* **ĭ'ntercĕpt** *n.* Intercepted radio signal; (math.) part intercepted.

intercĕ'ptor *n.* (esp.) Aircraft having task of intercepting enemy raiders.

intercĕ'ssion *n.* Interceding, esp. by prayer. **intercĕ'ssorȳ** *adj.*

interchā'nge (-j) *v.* 1. (of two persons) Exchange (things) with each other. 2. Put each of (two things) in the other's place. 3. Alternate. **interchā'ngeable** (-jabl) *adj.* **interchā'ngeablȳ** *adv.* **interchāngeabĭ'lĭtȳ** *n.* **ĭ'nterchānge** *n.* Reciprocal exchange; alternation; road junction so arranged that vehicles do not cross any traffic stream.

ĭ'ntercŏm *n.* System of internal communication by telephone, radio, etc., between units of an organization.

intercommū'nĭcāte *v.i.* Have mutual intercourse; have free passage to each other. **intercommūnĭcā'tion** *n.*

intercommū'nion (-yon) *n.* Intimate intercourse; mutual action or relation, esp. reciprocal spiritual relations and ministrations between different religious bodies.

intercŏ'stal *adj.* Between the ribs.

ĭ'ntercourse (-ors) *n.* 1. Social communication, dealings, between individuals; communion between man and God; communication for trade purposes etc. between different countries etc. 2. = SEXUAL intercourse.

ĭntercŭ′rrent *adj.* (of time or event) Intervening; (of disease) occurring during progress of another; recurring at intervals.

ĭnterdėpĕ′nd *v.i.* Depend on each other. **ĭnterdėpĕ′ndence, ĭnterdėpĕ′ndencȳ** *ns.* **ĭnterdėpĕ′ndent** *adj.* **ĭnterdėpĕ′ndentlȳ** *adv.*

ĭnterdĭ′ct *v.t.* Prohibit (action); forbid use of; restrain (*from*); forbid (thing *to* person). **ĭnterdĭ′ction** *n.* **ĭnterdĭ′ctorȳ** *adj.* **ĭ′nterdĭct** *n.* Authoritative prohibition; (Sc. law) injunction; (R.C. Ch.) sentence debarring place or person from ecclesiastical functions and privileges.

ĭ′nterėst *n.* 1. Legal concern, title right, (*in* property); pecuniary stake (*in* commercial undertaking etc.). 2. Advantage, profit. 3. Thing in which one is concerned; principle in which a party is concerned; party having a common interest. 4. Selfish pursuit of one's own welfare; *make* ~, bring personal interest to bear (*with* person). 5. Concern, curiosity, or quality exciting them. 6. Money paid for use of money lent or for forbearance of debt; *compound* ~, interest reckoned on principal and on accumulations of interest; *simple* ~, interest reckoned on principal only, and paid at fixed intervals. ~ *v.t.* Cause (person) to take personal interest or share (*in*); excite curiosity or attention of; (past part.) having a private interest, not impartial or disinterested. **ĭ′nterėstėdlȳ** *adv.* **ĭ′nterėstĭng** *adj.* **ĭ′nterėstĭnglȳ** *adv.*

interfā′cial (-shal) *adj.* Included between two plane faces or surfaces, esp. of angles of crystals.

ĭnterfēr′e *v.i.* Come into collision or opposition (*with*); meddle; intervene, take part, (*in*); (phys., of waves of usu. similar light proceeding from two or more coherent sources or of electromagnetic radiations from the same source travelling by different paths) combine with a difference of phase, so that each cancels the other partially or completely and the result is a periodic pattern of light and dark.

ĭnterfēr′ence *n.* 1. Interfering. 2. (radio etc.) Fading of received signals due to waves arriving at receiving set by different paths or arriving out of phase from different transmitters; (pop.) (intrusion of) electrical disturbances which interfere with the waves it is desired to receive. 3. (phys.) Partial or complete obliteration of light or sound caused by waves of the same frequency combining to reinforce or cancel each other.

ĭnterfēr′on *n.* Protein preventing development of virus in cell.

ĭnterfū′se (-z) *v.* Intersperse, mix; blend together; blend with each other. **ĭnterfū′sion** *n.*

ĭnterglā′cial (*or* -āshal) *adj.* (geol.) Occurring or formed between glacial periods.

ĭ′nterĭm *adv.* (archaic) Meanwhile. ~ *n.* Intervening time. ~ *adj.* Intervening; provisional, temporary; ~ *dividend*, dividend paid between two annual etc. balances and not in pursuance of published balance-sheet.

ĭntēr′ior *adj.* Situated within; inland, remote from coast or frontier; internal, domestic (opp. *foreign*); existing in mind or soul, inward; ~ *monologue*, form of writing which represents the inner thoughts of a character. **ĭntēr′ĭorlȳ** *adv.* **ĭntēr′ĭor** *n.* Interior part, inside; inland region; inside of building or room, picture of this; inner nature, soul; (department dealing with) home affairs of a country, as *Minister of the I*~.

ĭnterjā′cent *adj.* Lying between, intermediate.

ĭnterjĕ′ct *v.t.* Throw in, interpose (remark etc.) abruptly; remark parenthetically. **ĭnterjĕ′ctorȳ** *adj.*

ĭnterjĕ′ction *n.* Ejaculation, exclamation; natural ejaculation viewed as part of speech. **ĭnterjĕ′ctional** *adj.* **ĭnterjĕ′ctionallȳ** *adv.*

ĭnterlā′ce *v.* Bind together in-

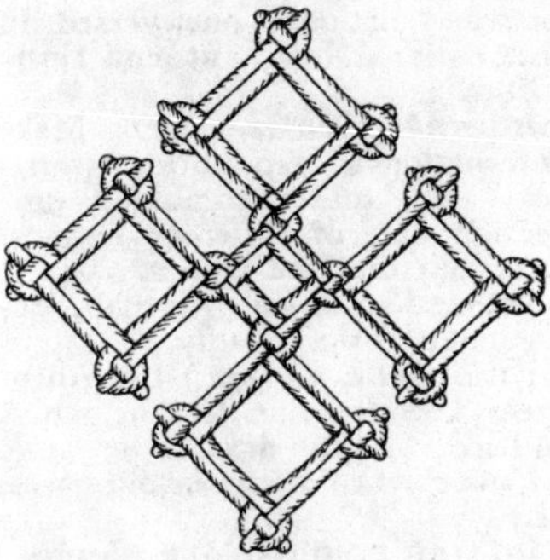

tricately, entangle; interweave; mingle; cross each other intricately. **interlā'cement** *n.*

interlar'd *v.t.* Mix (writing, speech, etc., *with*).

i'nterleaf *n.* (pl. *-ves*). Extra leaf between leaves of book.

interlea've *v.t.* Insert leaves between leaves of (book); *interleaved copy* (of book), one bound with blank leaves between the printed ones.

interlī'ne[1] *v.t.* Insert words between lines of (document etc.); insert (words) thus. **interli'near** *adj.* Written, printed, between the lines. **interlineā'tion** *n.*

interlī'ne[2] *v.t.* Put extra lining between ordinary lining and outer material of (garment). **interlī'ning** *n.*

interlŏ'ck *v.* Fit together by overlapping etc.; lock, clasp, within each other; (railw.) connect (levers for signals, switches, etc.) so that they cannot be operated independently of each other.

interlŏ'cūtor *n.* One who takes part in dialogue or conversation. **interlocū'tion** *n.* **interlŏ'cūtory** *adj.*

i'nterlōper *n.* Intruder, one who (esp. for profit) thrusts himself into others' affairs; (hist.) unauthorized trader. **interlō'pe** *v.i.*

i'nterlūde (*or* -ōōd) *n.* 1. Pause between acts of play; what fills this up; (mus.) instrumental piece played between verses of hymn etc., in intervals of church service etc. 2. (hist.) Dramatic or mimetic representation between acts of mystery plays or moralities.

intermă'rriage (-rĭj) *n.* Marriage between members of different families, tribes, etc., or (loosely) between near relations.

intermă'rry *v.i.* Become connected by marriage (*with*).

intermĕ'ddle *v.i.* Concern oneself (*with, in,* esp. what is not one's business).

intermē'diary *adj.* Acting between parties, mediatory; intermediate. ~ *n.* Intermediary person or thing, esp. mediator.

intermē'diate *adj.* Coming *between* two things, in time, place, or order. **intermē'diately** *adv.* **intermē'diate** *n.* Intermediate thing; (chem.) compound manufactured from a substance obtained directly from raw materials, and used as a basis for the synthesis of another product. **intermē'diāte** *v.i.* Act between others, mediate (*between*). **intermēdiā'tion, intermē'diātor** *ns.*

intermē'dium *n.* Intermediate thing, medium.

inter'ment *n.* Burial.

intermĕ'zzo (-tsō) *n.* (pl. *-zi, -zos*). Short light dramatic or musical performance between acts of drama or opera; short movement connecting main divisions of large musical work.

inter'minable *adj.* Endless; tediously long. **inter'minableness** *n.* **inter'minably** *adv.*

intermi'ngle (-nggl) *v.* Mix together; mingle (*with*).

intermi'ssion *n.* Pause, cessation; interval.

intermi't *v.* Suspend, discontinue; stop for a time (esp. of fever, pain, etc., or pulse). **intermi'ttence** *n.* **intermi'ttent** *adj.* **intermi'ttently** *adv.*

intermi'x *v.* Mix together.

inter'n[1] *v.t.* Oblige to reside within limits of country etc.; confine (esp. enemy aliens and prisoners of war) within prescribed limits. **internee'** *n.* Person interned. **inter'nment** *n.*

i'ntern[2] *n.* (U.S.) Advanced student or recent graduate residing in hospital and acting as assistant physician or surgeon.

intĕr'nal *adj.* Of, situated in, the inside of a thing; of the inner nature of a thing, intrinsic; of the domestic affairs of a country; of the mind or soul, inward, subjective; *~ combustion engine*: see COMBUSTION; *~ evidence*, evidence derived from what is contained in the thing itself. **intĕr'nallў** *adv.*

internă'tional *adj.* Existing, carried on, between different nations; of the International Working Men's Associations (founded in London by Karl Marx in 1864 for promoting joint political action of working classes in all countries, and dissolved in Philadelphia in 1876); *I~ Court of Justice*, judicial court of the United Nations, established in 1945; *~ law*, body of rules regarded by the nations of the world as being binding on them in their relations with each other, in peace and war; *I~ Monetary Fund*, (abbrev. I.M.F.) organization having a monetary pool on which member nations can draw, established in 1945 to promote international trade and stabilization of currencies; *~ system of units*: see SYSTÈME INTERNATIONAL. **internă'tionallў** *adv.* **internă'tional** *n.* 1. International (usu. athletic) contest; one who takes part in such contest. 2. Member of First, Second, Third, or Fourth International; *Communist I~*, Third International; *First I~*, the International Working Men's Association (see above); *Second I~*, organization founded at Paris 1889 to celebrate 100th anniversary of French Revolution; *Third I~*, founded at Moscow 1919 by delegates from twelve countries to promote communism and support the Russian Revolution, dissolved 1943; *Fourth I~*, founded 1936 by followers of Trotsky.

Internătiona'le (ĭ-, -shonahl) *n.* Revolutionary hymn composed by Eugène Pottier in 1871 and adopted by Socialists.

internă'tionalist *n.* One who advocates community of interests between nations; one versed in international law. **internă'tionalism** *n.*

internă'tionalīze *v.t.* Make international; esp. bring (territory etc.) under combined protection etc. of different nations. **internătionalīzā'tion** *n.*

internĕ'cīne *adj.* Mutually destructive; (orig.) deadly.

ĭ'nternōde *n.* (bot.) Length of stem between one leaf or whorl of leaves and the next.

ĭ'nter nōs. Between ourselves. [L]

internŭ'ncio (-shĭō) *n.* Ambassador of Pope when or where no nuncio is employed; (hist.) minister representing (esp. Austrian) Government at Ottoman Porte.

interpĕ'llāte *v.t.* (esp. in French parliament) Interrupt order of day by demanding explanation from (Minister concerned). **interpĕllā'tion** *n.*

interpĕ'nètrāte *v.* Penetrate thoroughly, pervade; penetrate reciprocally; penetrate each other. **interpĕnètrā'tion** *n.*

interplă'nètarў *adj.* Between planets.

ĭ'nterplay *n.* Reciprocal play; operation of two things on each other.

interplea'd *v.i.* Litigate with each other in order to settle point in which a third party is concerned.

I'nterpŏl (ĭ-). International Criminal Police Commission, with headquarters in Paris.

intĕr'polāte *v.t.* Make insertions in (books etc.), esp. so as to give false impressions as to date etc.; introduce (words) thus; interpose (a remark); (math.) insert (intermediate term) in series. **intĕrpolā'tion** *n.*

interpō'se (-z) *v.* Insert, make intervene, (*between*); put forth, introduce, (veto, objection, authority, etc.) by way of interference; intervene (between disputants etc.); say as an interruption; make an interruption. **interpō'sal** *n.*

intĕrposĭ'tion (-z-) *n.* Interposing; thing interposed; interference.

intĕr'prèt *v.* Expound the meaning of (abstruse words, writings, etc.); make out the meaning of; bring out the meaning of, render, by artistic representation or performance; explain, understand, in specified manner; act as interpreter. **interprėtā'tion** *n.* **inter'prėtative** *adj.*

inter'prėter *n.* One who interprets; one whose office it is to translate orally in their presence the words of persons speaking different languages. **inter'prėtership** *n.*

interrĕ'gnum *n.* (pl. *-na, -nums*). Period during which State has no normal ruler, esp. between end of king's reign and accession of successor; interval, pause.

interrėlā'tion *n.* Mutual relation. **interrėlā'tionship** *n.*

intĕ'rrogāte *v.t.* Ask questions of, esp. closely or formally. **intĕrrogā'tion** *n.* Asking questions; interview for close questioning; question; *point, mark, note, of* ~, symbol (?) used in printing or writing (usu. at end of sentence, to indicate question).

interrŏ'gative *adj.* Of, having the form or force of, a question; of inquiry; (gram., of words) used in asking question. **interrŏ'gatively** *adv.* **interrŏg'ative** *n.* Interrogative pronoun etc.

interrŏ'gatory *adj.* Of inquiry. ~ *n.* Question, set of questions, esp. (law) one formally put to accused person etc.

interrŭ'pt *v.t.* Break in upon (action, speech, person speaking, etc.); obstruct (view etc.); break the continuity of. **interrŭ'ptėdly** *adv.* **interrŭ'pter, interrŭ'ption** *ns.* **interrŭ'ptory** *adj.*

intersĕ'ct *v.* Divide (thing) by passing or lying across it; (of lines etc.) cross, cut, each other. **intersĕ'ction** *n.* Intersecting; point, line, common to intersecting lines, planes. **intersĕ'ctional** *adj.*

interspėr'se *v.t.* Scatter, place here and there (*between, among*); diversify (thing) *with* (others so scattered). **interspėr'sion** *n.*

i'nterstāte *adj.* (U.S.) Existing, carried on, between States.

interstĕ'llar *adj.* Between stars.

intėr'stice *n.* Intervening space; chink, crevice. **intersti'tial** (-shal) *adj.* Of, forming, occupying, interstice(s); (anat.) occurring within the tissues or tissue spaces.

intertwī'ne *v.* Entwine; become entwined. **intertwī'nement** *n.*

i'nterval *n.* 1. Intervening time or space; pause; break, gap; *at* ~*s*, here and there, now and then. 2. (mus.) Difference of pitch between two sounds in melody or harmony. 3. Distance between persons or things in respect of qualities. **intervă'llic** *adj.* [L *intervallum* space between ramparts (*vallum* rampart)]

intervē'ne *v.i.* Come in, as something extraneous; occur in the meantime; lie, be situated, between; (of person or thing) come between, interfere, so as to prevent or modify result etc.; (law) interpose in lawsuit to which one was not an original party (esp. of Queen's (King's) Proctor in divorce cases). **intervē'ner, intervĕ'ntion** *ns.* **intervē'nient** *adj.*

intervėr'tėbral *adj.* Between vertebrae (~ *disc.*).

i'nterview (-vū) *n.* Meeting of persons face to face, esp. for purpose of conference; meeting between representative of press and person from whom he seeks to obtain statements for publication; meeting between candidate for appointment and prospective employer etc. ~ *v.t.* Have interview with (person), esp. with view to publication of statements etc. **i'nterviewer** *n.*

i'nter vīv'ōs. Between the living (esp. of gift as opp. to legacy). [L]

interwea've *v.t.* (past t. *-wōve*, past part. *-wōven*). Weave together, interlace; blend intimately.

intĕ'stāte *adj.* Not having made a will; not disposed of by will. ~ *n.* Person who dies intestate. **intĕ'stacy** *n.*

intĕ'stine[1] *n.* (usu. pl.) Lower part of alimentary canal from pyloric end of stomach to anus; *large* ~, caecum, colon, and rectum; ~ *small*, duodenum, jejunum and ileum. **intĕ'stinal** (*or* -ī'n-) *adj.*

intĕ'stine² *adj.* (of wars etc.) Internal, domestic, civil.

ĭ'ntimate¹ *adj.* Close in acquaintance, familiar; essential, intrinsic; closely personal. **ĭ'ntimatelў** *adv.* **ĭ'ntimacў** *n.* State of being intimate; intimate act; (euphem.) sexual intercourse. **ĭ'ntimate** *n.* Intimate friend.

ĭ'ntimāte² *v.t.* Make known, state; imply, hint. **intimā'tion** *n.*

inti'midāte *v.t.* Inspire with fear, cow, esp. in order to influence conduct. **intimidā'tion** *n.*

inti'mitў *n.* Inwardness; privacy.

ĭ'nto (*or* -tŏŏ) *prep.* Expressing (1) motion or direction to a point within a thing, as *come ~ the house, inquire ~ the problem*; (2) change, condition, result, as *water turns ~ ice, collect them ~ heaps.*

intŏ'lerable *adj.* That cannot be endured. **intŏ'lerableness** *n.* **intŏ'lerablў** *adv.*

intŏ'lerant *adj.* Not tolerant (*of*). **intŏ'lerantlў** *adv.* **intŏ'lerance** *n.*

intonā'tion *n.* (mus.) Opening phrase of plainsong melody, sung by priest alone or by one or a few of the choristers; intoning, reciting in singing voice; utterance, production, of musical tones; modulation of voice in speaking.

intō'ne *v.t.* Recite (esp. psalm, prayer, etc.) in singing voice; sing opening phrase of plainsong.

in tō'tō. Completely. [L]

intŏ'xicant *adj.* & *n.* Intoxicating (liquor).

intŏ'xicāte *v.t.* Make drunk; excite, exhilarate, beyond self-control. **intŏ'xicāting** *adj.* **intŏxicā'tion** *n.*

intra- *prefix.* On the inside, within.

intră'ctable *adj.* Not docile, refractory; (of things) not easily dealt with. **intră'ctableness, intrăctabi'litў** *ns.* **intră'ctablў** *adv.*

intrā'dŏs *n.* (archit.) Interior curve of arch.

intramŭ'scūlar *adj.* Within or going into a muscle.

intră'nsigent (-z-) *adj.* Uncompromising (esp. in politics). ~ *n.* Uncompromising person.

intră'nsitive *adj.* & *n.* (Verb) that does not take a direct object. **intră'nsitivelў** *adv.*

intra-ū'terine *adj.* Within the uterus; ~ *device,* (abbrev. I.U.D.) contraceptive device so placed.

intravē'nous *adj.* Within or going into a vein.

intrĕ'pid *adj.* Fearless, brave. **intrĕ'pidlў** *adv.* **intrepi'ditў** *n.*

ĭ'ntricate *adj.* Perplexingly entangled; involved; obscure. **ĭ'ntricatelў** *adv.* **ĭ'ntricacў** *n.*

ĭ'ntrigant, -guant (-gant) *n.* (fem. *-ante* pr. -ah'nt, -ă'nt) Intriguer.

intri'gue (-ēg) *v.* 1. Carry on underhand plot; employ secret influence (*with*); have a liaison (*with*). 2. Excite the interest or curiosity of. ~ *n.* Underhand plotting or plot; secret love affair, liaison.

intrin'sic *adj.* Belonging naturally, inherent, essential. **intri'nsicallў** *adv.*

intro- *prefix.* To the inside.

introdū'ce *v.t.* 1. Bring in; place in, insert; bring into use (custom, idea, etc.); usher in, bring forward, begin. 2. Make known, esp. in formal manner (person *to* another); present formally, as at court or in an assembly; make acquainted with, draw attention of (person) *to*; bring (bill etc.) before Parliament. **introdŭ'ctorў** *adj.*

introdŭ'ction *n.* Introducing; preliminary matter prefixed to book; introductory treatise; formal presentation.

intrō'it *n.* (eccles.) Psalm, antiphon, sung while priest approaches altar to celebrate Mass or Holy Communion.

introjĕ'ction *n.* (psych.) Unconscious process by which an image representing an external object is incorporated into a person's psychic equipment.

intromi't *v.t.* (archaic) Let in, admit (*into*); insert. **intromi'ssion** *n.* **intromi'ttent** *adj.*

intrŏr'se *adj.* (bot., of anthers) Shedding pollen towards axis of flower (opp. EXTRORSE).

introspĕ'ct *v.i.* Examine one's

own thoughts and feelings. **introspĕ'ction** *n.* **ĭntrospĕ'ctive** *adj.* **ĭntrospĕ'ctivelў** *adv.* **introspĕ'ctivenėss** *n.*

ĭntrovẽr't *v.t.* 1. Turn (mind, thought) inwards upon itself. 2. (zool.) Withdraw (organ etc.) within its own tube or base, like finger of glove. **ĭntrovẽr'sion** *n.* **ĭ'ntrovẽrt** *n.* 1. (psych.) Person given to introversion (opp. EXTROVERT). 2. (zool.) Part or organ that may be introverted.

ĭntru'de (-ōōd) *v.* Thrust, force, (thing *into*); force (thing *upon* person); come uninvited, thrust oneself in (*into* company, place, etc., *upon* person etc.). **ĭntru'der** *n.* One who intrudes; aircraft that invades enemy's air space.

ĭntru'sion (-ōō-) *n.* Intruding, forcing in; forcing oneself in; (law) thrusting oneself into vacant estate or ecclesiastical benefice to which one has no title or claim; settlement of minister of Church of Scotland without consent of congregation; (geol.) body of rock, usu. of volcanic origin, which has been pushed while molten into or through other rocks.

ĭntru'sĭve (-ōō-) *adj.* Intruding, tending to intrude. **intru'sĭvelў** *adv.* **intru'sĭvenėss** *n.*

ĭ'ntūbāte *v.t.* (med.) Insert tube into (larynx etc.) to keep it open. **intūbā'tion** *n.*

ĭ'ntūit *v.* Know by intuition.

ĭntūĭ'tion *n.* Immediate apprehension by the mind without reasoning; immediate apprehension by sense; immediate insight. **ĭntūĭ'tional** *adj.*

ĭntūĭ'tionalĭsm *n.* Doctrine that perception of truth is by intuition.

ĭntūĭ'tionĭsm *n.* 1. Doctrine that in perception external objects are known immediately, without the intervention of a vicarious phenomenon. 2. Intuitionalism.

ĭntū'ĭtĭve *adj.* Of, possessing, perceived by, intuition. **ĭntū'ĭtĭvelў** *adv.* **ĭntū'ĭtĭvenėss** *n.*

ĭntū'ĭtĭvĭsm *n.* Doctrine that ethical principles are matters of intuition.

ĭntūmĕ'scent *adj.* Swelling up. **ĭntūmĕ'scence** *n.*

ĭntussuscĕ'ption *n.* (path.) Telescoping of one portion of intestine with another.

ĭnŭ'nction *n.* Smearing, rubbing, with oil.

ĭ'nundāte *v.t.* Overflow, flood (*with* water etc.; also fig.). **ĭnundā'tion** *n.*

ĭnūr'e *v.* Accustom, habituate; come into operation, take effect. **ĭnūr'ement** *n.*

ĭnûr'n *v.t.* Put (ashes of cremated body) in an urn.

inv. *abbrev. Invenit, invenerunt* (L, = designed this work).

ĭn vă'cūō. In a vacuum. [L]

ĭnvā'de *v.t.* Make hostile inroad into; assail; encroach upon (rights etc.). **ĭnvā'der** *n.*

ĭnvă'gĭnāte *v.t.* Put in a sheath; introvert (tubular sheath). **ĭnvăgĭnā'tion** *n.*

ĭ'nvalid[1] (-ēd) *n.* & *adj.* (Person) enfeebled or disabled by illness or injury. **ĭnvalĭ'd** (-ēd; *or* ĭ'-) *v.t.* Lay up, disable, (person) by illness; treat as an invalid, remove from active service (usu. ~ *out*), send *home* etc., as an invalid. **ĭ'nvalidĭsm** (-ēd-) *n.*

ĭnvă'lĭd[2] *adj.* Not valid; esp., having no legal force. **ĭnvalĭ'dĭtў** *n.*

ĭnvă'lĭdāte *v.t.* Make invalid. **ĭnvălĭdā'tion** *n.*

Invalides (ănvălēd), Hôtel des. Institution in Paris, founded 1670 by Louis XIV for superannuated or disabled soldiers; Napoleon I is buried in the chapel under its dome and part of the building is now a military museum.

ĭnvă'lūable *adj.* Of value too great to be measured.

ĭnvār'ĭable *adj.* Unchangeable; always the same; (math.) constant, fixed. ~ *n.* (math.) Invariable quantity, constant. **ĭnvār'ĭablenėss, ĭnvārĭabĭ'lĭtў** *ns.* **ĭnvār'ĭablў** *adv.*

ĭnvā'sion *n.* Invading; encroachment.

ĭnvā'sĭve *adj.* That invades.

ĭnvĕ'ctėd *adj.* (her.) Bordered by or consisting of a series of small convex lobes.

HÔTEL DES INVALIDES, Paris

invĕ'ctive *n.* Violent attack in words; abusive oratory.

invei'gh (-vā) *v.i.* Speak violently, rail loudly, *against*.

invei'gle (-vē- *or* vā-) *v.t.* Entice, seduce (*into*). **invei'glement** *n.*

invĕ'nt *v.t.* Devise, originate; produce or construct by original thought etc.; fabricate (false story etc.). **invĕ'ntion** *n.* 1. Inventing; thing invented, contrivance, (law) any new manufacture the subject of letters patent. 2. Inventiveness. 3. Fictitious story. 4. *I~ of the Cross*, finding of the Cross by St. HELENA[1]; festival commemorating this, 3 May. **invĕ'ntive** *adj.* **invĕ'ntively** *adv.* **invĕ'ntiveness** *n.* **invĕ'ntor** *n.*

i'nventory *n.* Detailed list (of goods, furniture, etc.); stock of goods in this. ~ *v.t.* Enter (goods etc.) in inventory; make inventory of.

Invernĕ'ss (ĭ-). Town, at mouth of river Ness, in former Scottish Highland county of Inverness-shire, since May 1975 part of the region of Highland; ~ *cape, cloak, coat*, man's cloak or coat with removable cape.

invêr'se (*or* i'-) *adj.* Inverted in position, order, or relations; ~ *ratio, proportion*, that between two quantities one of which increases at the same rate as the other decreases, esp. when the product of the two remains constant. **invêr'sely** *adv.* **i'nvêrse** *n.* Inverted state; thing that is the direct opposite (*of* another).

invêr'sion *n.* Inverting; (gram.) alteration of natural order of words. **invêr'sive** *adj.*

invêr't *v.t.* Turn upside down; reverse position, order, or relation, of; (mus.) change relative position of notes of (chord, interval) by placing lowest note higher, usu. an octave higher; modify (phrase, subject) by inverting intervals between successive notes; (chem.) change dextrorotatory into laevorotatory substance, or vice versa; *inverted commas*: see COMMA. *inverted pleat*: see PLEAT. **i'nvêrt**

adj. (chem.) Inverted; ~ *sugar*, mixture of glucose and laevulose found in fruits or produced by inversion of sucrose. **ĭ′nvĕrt** *n.* 1. Inverted arch, as at bottom of sewer. 2. (psychol.) Person whose sexual instincts are inverted, homosexual.

invĕr′tėbrate *adj.* Not having a backbone; (fig.) wanting in firmness; (zool.) belonging to the Invertebrata, a classification of convenience which comprises all animals other than the Vertebrata, and includes principally those animals which have no notochord in any stage of development, but also a few which do have a notochord (e.g. the tunicates). ~ *n.* Invertebrate animal or (fig.) person.

ĭnvĕ′st *v.* 1. Clothe (person etc. *in*, *with*); cover as garment; clothe, endue, (person etc. *with* qualities, insignia of office etc.). 2. Lay siege to. 3. Employ (money in stocks etc.); ~ *in*, put money into (stocks); (colloq.) lay out money on. **ĭnvĕ′stor** *n.*

ĭnvĕs′tĭgāte *v.t.* Examine, inquire into. **ĭnvĕstĭgā′tion, ĭnvĕ′stĭgātor** *ns.* **ĭnvĕ′stĭgātorў** *adj.*

ĭnvĕ′stiture *n.* Formal investing of person (*with* office), esp. ceremony at which sovereign or his deputy confers honours; enduing (*with* attributes).

ĭnvĕ′stment *n.* 1. Investing of money; money invested; property in which money is invested. 2. Investiture; clothing. 3. (mil.) Act of besieging.

ĭnvĕ′terate *adj.* Long-established; deep-rooted, obstinate. **ĭnvĕ′terately** *adv.* **ĭnvĕ′teracў** *n.*

ĭnvĭ′dious *adj.* (of conduct etc.) Giving offence, esp. by real or seeming injustice, unfair discrimination, etc.; (of thing) likely to excite ill feeling against the possessor. **ĭnvĭ′diouslў** *adv.* **ĭnvĭ′diousnėss** *n.*

ĭnvĭ′gĭlāte *v.i.* Watch over candidates at examination. **ĭnvĭgĭlā′tion, ĭnvĭ′gĭlātor** *ns.*

ĭnvĭ′gorāte *v.t.* Make vigorous; animate. **ĭnvĭ′gorative** *adj.*

ĭnvĭ′ncĭble *adj.* Unconquerable. **ĭnvĭncĭbĭ′lĭtў** *n.* **ĭnvĭ′ncĭblў** *adv.*

ĭnvī′olable *adj.* Not to be violated; to be kept sacred from infraction, profanation, etc. **ĭnvīolabĭ′lĭtў** *n.* **ĭnvī′olablў** *adv.*

ĭnvī′olate *adj.* Not violated; unbroken; unprofaned. **ĭnvī′olatelў** *adv.* **ĭnvī′olatenėss, ĭnvī′olacў** *ns.*

ĭnvĭ′sĭble (-z-) *adj.* That cannot be seen; not to be seen at a particular time; too small to be seen; ~ *exports, imports*, those items which do not appear in returns of exports and imports yet for which payment is due from or to a foreign country, e.g. shipping services, insurance, foreign investments, etc.; ~ *ink*, ink that requires heat, vapour, or the like to make visible what is written in it. **ĭnvĭsĭbĭ′lĭtў, ĭnvĭ′sĭblenėss** *ns.* **ĭnvĭ′sĭblў** *adv.* **ĭnvĭ′sĭble** *n.* The unseen world.

ĭnvī′te *v.* Request courteously to come (*to* dinner, *to* one's house, etc.); request courteously (*to* do); solicit courteously; bring on, tend to bring on (thing) unintentionally; (of thing) present inducements, attract. **ĭnvī′tĭng** *adj.* **ĭnvī′tĭnglў** *adv.* **ĭnvī′tĭngnėss, ĭnvĭtā′tion** *ns.* **ĭ′nvīte** *n.* (vulg.) Invitation. **ĭnvītee′** *n.* (law) Person invited to enter another's premises on some matter in which occupier has material interest.

ĭn vĭ′trō (*or* vē-). (biol.) In an artificial container. [L, = 'in glass']

ĭn vī′vō (vē-). (biol.) In a living organism. [L]

ĭnvocā′tion *n.* Invoking, calling upon deity in prayer; appeal to one's muse for inspiration or assistance in poem. **ĭnvŏ′catorў** *adj.*

ĭ′nvoice *n.* List of goods shipped or sent, with prices and charges. ~ *v.t.* Make an invoice of (goods).

ĭnvō′ke *v.t.* Call on (deity etc.) in prayer or as witness; appeal to (person's authority etc.); summon (spirit) by charms; ask earnestly for (vengeance, help, etc.).

ĭ′nvolūcre (-ker; *or* -ōō-) *n.* Covering, envelope (esp. anat.);

(bot.) whorl of bracts surrounding inflorescence.

ĭnvŏ'luntarў̆ *adj.* Done without exercise of the will, unintentional; ~ *nervous system*: see AUTONOMIC. **ĭnvŏ'luntarĭlў̆** *adv.* **ĭnvŏ'luntarinėss** *n.*

ĭ'nvolūte (*or* -ōōt) *adj.* Involved, intricate, curled spirally; (bot.) rolled inwards at the edges. ~ *n.* (geom.) Curve traced out by point on flexible inextensible string as it is unwound from, or wound upon, the evolute.

ĭnvolū'tion (*or* -ōō-) *n.* Involving; entanglement; intricacy; curling inwards; part so curled; (math.) raising of quantity to any power.

ĭnvŏ'lve *v.t.* Wrap (thing *in* another); wind spirally; entangle (person, thing, *in* difficulties, mystery, etc.); implicate (*in*); include (*in*); imply, entail. **ĭnvŏ'lvement** *n.* Involving; financial embarrassment; complicated affair.

ĭnvŭ'lnerable *adj.* That cannot be wounded or hurt; (at contract bridge) that has not made a game towards rubber and is therefore not liable to the increased penalties prescribed for the side that has made one game towards rubber (see VULNERABLE). **ĭnvŭlnerabĭ'lĭtў̆** *n.* **ĭnvŭ'lnerablў̆** *adv.*

ĭ'nward *adj.* Situated within; mental, spiritual; directed towards the inside. **ĭ'nwardlў̆** *adv.* Of the inside; not aloud; in mind or spirit. **ĭ'nwardnėss** *n.* Inner nature, essence; quality of being inward; spirituality. **ĭ'nward, -wards** (-z) *advs.* **ĭ'nwards,** (dial. & vulg.) **ĭ'nnards** (-z) *n.pl.* Entrails.

ĭ'nwrought (ĭnrawt *or* -aw't) *adj.* (of fabric) Decorated (*with* pattern); (of pattern) wrought (*in*, *on*, fabric); (fig.) intimately blended (*with*).

ĭnya'la, nya'la (-ah-) *n.* See NYALA.

ī'odīde *n.* Compound of iodine with another element or radical.

ī'odīne (*or* -ēn) *n.* (chem.) Nonmetallic element widely diffused in nature but never in the free state, obtained from some seaweeds and from the mother-liquor of Chile saltpetre, used in medicine as an antiseptic; symbol I, at. no. 53, at. wt 126·9045; tincture or solution of this in alcohol. **īŏ'dĭc** *adj.*

ī'odism *n.* (med.) Morbid state produced by the use of iodine or its compounds, characterized by palpitation and emaciation.

ī'odīze *v.t.* Treat with, expose to fumes of, iodine.

īŏ'dofŏrm *n.* Yellow, crystalline, volatile compound of iodine (CHI_3), formerly much used as an antiseptic dressing for wounds.

I. of M., I. of W. *abbrevs.* Isle of Man, Isle of Wight.

I.O.G.T. *abbrev.* International Order of Good Templars.

I.O.M. *abbrev.* Isle of Man.

ī'on *n.* (phys.) 1. Electrified particle formed when a neutral atom or group of atoms loses or gains one or more electrons, as a *cation*, with positive charge, formed by electron loss, or an *anion*, with negative charge, formed by electron gain. 2. Gaseous particle electrically charged by action of X-rays or other rays. [Gk *ion* (thing) going]

Iō'na (ī-). Island of Inner Hebrides, where St. Columba founded a monastery *c* 563; centre of Celtic missions.

Iō'nia (ī-). Ancient Greek colony on W. coast of Asia Minor.

Iō'nian (ī-) *adj.* Of Ionia or its people; ~ *Islands*, Greek islands in the Ionian Sea; ~ *mode*, ancient Greek mode, reputedly soft and effeminate in character; 11th of ecclesiastical modes, with C as final and G as dominant, corresponding to the modern major key of C; ~ *Sea*, part of Mediterranean, between Greece and S. Italy. ~ *n.* Native, inhabitant, of Ionia.

īŏ'nĭc[1] *adj.* Of or pertaining to ions.

Iŏ'nĭc[2] (ī-) *adj.* Of Ionia; of the Ionic dialect, order, or school; ~ *dialect*, most important of the three main branches of ancient Greek, of which ATTIC[1] was a development; ~ *order*, (archit.) Greek order characterized by two lateral volutes of the capital ~ *school*, earliest school of Greek philosophers, including Thales, Anaximander, Anaximenes, and Heraclitus. ~ *n.* Metrical foot of 2 long syllables followed by 2 short, – – ◡ ◡ (~ *a majore*) or 2 short syllables followed by 2 long, ◡ ◡ – – (~ *a minore*).

īō'nium *n.* Isotope of thorium, now usu. called thorium-230.

ī'onīze *v.* (of an electrolyte) Split into ions; (of X-rays, cathode rays, etc.) produce ions in a gas and so make it a conductor. **īonīzā'tion** *n.*

īŏ'nosphēre *n.* Ionized region of the upper atmosphere.

īō'ta *n.* 10th (later 9th) letter of Greek alphabet (*I*, *ι*), corresponding to i; insignificant part, jot, atom.

īō'tacism *n.* Excessive use of the Greek letter iota; tendency in Greek to level a number of originally different vowels and diphthongs under the sound (ē).

I O U (ī ō ū') *n.* Signed document bearing these letters followed by specified sum, constituting formal acknowledgement of debt. [= I owe you]

I.O.W. *abbrev.* Isle of Wight.

I'owa (ī-). State in central U.S., part of Middle West; admitted to the Union in 1846; capital Des Moines.

ĭpĕcăcūă'nha (-n*a*) *n.* Root of S. Amer. herbaceous or shrubby plant (*Cephaëlis ipecacuanha*), which possesses emetic, diaphoretic, and purgative properties, a common ingredient of cough mixtures.

Iphĭgėnī'a (ĭ-). (Gk legend) Daughter of Agamemnon and Clytemnestra; she was offered by her father as a sacrifice to Artemis when the Greeks, on their way to the Trojan War, were becalmed at Aulis, but was snatched from the altar by the goddess and borne away to Tauris, where she became a priestess; she was rescued by Orestes.

ĭ'psė dĭ'xĭt. Dogmatic statement, assertion, dictum. [L, = 'he himself said it']

ipsĭlă'teral *adj.* (physiol.) Belonging to the same side.

ĭ'psō fă'ctō. By that very fact. [L]

i.q. *abbrev. Idem quod* [L, = 'the same as']

I.Q. *abbrev.* Intelligence quotient.

ir- (ĭ-r) *prefix.* = IN[1,2].

I.R.A. *abbrev.* Irish Republican Army.

īra'dė (-ah-) *n.* (hist.) Written decree of Sultan of Turkey.

Ira'n (īrahn). Kingdom in SW. Asia, also called PERSIA, lying S. of Caspian Sea and U.S.S.R.; capital, Teheran. **Irā'nian** *adj.* & *n.* (Native, inhabitant) of Iran; (of) a sub-branch of the Indo-European family of languages including Persian, Pashtu, Avestan, and Kurdish.

Iraq (īrah'k). Republic extending from Kurdistan on N. and NE. to the Persian Gulf on the S. and SE. and from Iran in E. to Syria and the Arabian Desert on W.; formerly known as MESOPOTAMIA; freed from Turkish rule during the war of 1914–18 and placed under a British mandate, which was terminated in 1932; a kingdom from 1921 until assassination of Faisal II in 1958 when it became a republic; capital Baghdad. **Ira'qĭ** *adj.* & *n.* (Native, inhabitant) of Iraq; (of) the modern Arabic dialect spoken in Iraq.

īră'scĭble (-sĭ-; *or* īr-) *adj.* Irritable, hot-tempered. **īrăscĭbĭ'lĭtў** *n.*

īrā'te *adj.* Angry. **īrā'telў** *adv.*

I.R.B.M. *abbrev.* Intermediate-range ballistic missile.

īre *n.* (poet.) Anger. **īr'eful** *adj.* **īr'efullў** *adv.*

Ir'eland (īrl-). Island in the Atlantic Ocean, to W. of Gt Britain; made subordinate to the English legislature in 1494 by the Statutes of Drogheda; in 1916 an insurrection against British rule took place (the 'Easter rising'); in 1920 an Act was passed by the British Parliament dividing Ireland into two parts: (1) Southern Ireland, which was later recognized as an independent democratic State, since 1949 officially called the Republic of Ireland (formerly, 1921–37, the Irish Free State; 1937–49, Eire); capital, Dublin; university, in Dublin, 1908; and (2) NORTHERN IRELAND.

īrĕ'nic, -ĭcal *adjs.* Tending towards, promoting, peace; pacific.

īrĕ'nicŏn *n.* Proposal designed to promote peace.

īridā'ceous (-sh*u*s) *adj.* (of plants) Of the iris kind.

ĭridĕ'scent *adj.* Showing colours like those of rainbow; changing in colour as light falls from different angles. **ĭridĕ'scence** *n.*

īrĭ'dium *n.* (chem.) Hard white brittle element of platinum group, mainly used in the form of its alloys with platinum or osmium for various purposes requiring very hard and incorrodible materials; symbol Ir, at. no. 77, at. wt 192·22.

īr'is[1] *n.* 1. Circular pigmented diaphragm in anterior chamber of eye, with central aperture (the *pupil*) which admits light to the lens and contracts or expands according to intensity of light; ~ *diaphragm*, mechanical device, resembling the iris, for controlling the diameter of a circular orifice by means of movable overlapping shutters. 2. (bot.) Plant of genus *I*~ with tubers

or bulbs, sword-shaped leaves, and showy flowers. 3. Kind of rock-crystal reflecting prismatic colours.

Ir'is[2] (īr-). (Gk myth.) Goddess who acted as the messenger of the gods, and displayed as her sign the rainbow.

Ir'ish (īr-) *adj.* 1. Of Ireland or its people or language; ~ *bull*: see BULL; ~ *Free State*: see IRELAND; *Ir'ishman, Ir'ishwoman*, Irish person; ~ *point*, needlepoint lace made in Ireland; ~ *Republican Army*, (abbrev. I.R.A.) terrorist organization aiming at a united independent Ireland; ~ *Sea*, sea between Ireland and England; ~ *stew*, mutton cutlets stewed with potatoes and onions; ~ *terrier*, breed of terrier with rough wiry coat of reddish-brown colour; ~ *whiskey*: see WHISKY; ~ *wolfhound*, wolfhound of large tall Irish breed with wiry coat. 2. Of the branch of the Celtic languages spoken in Ireland. ~ *n.* 1. (collect.) People of Ireland. 2. Irish language.

Ir'ishism (īr-) *n.* Idiom characteristic of the Irish language, or of English as spoken in Ireland.

irk *v.t.* (archaic) Disgust, tire, bore. **ir'ksome** *adj.* Tedious, tiresome. **ir'ksomelў** *adv.* **ir'ksomenėss** *n.*

iron (īrn) *n.* 1. (chem.) Abundant metallic element, widely distributed in form of ores (oxides and salts) and found in free state only in meteorites, silver-white in colour, and characterized by great tensile strength, ductility, and magnetic susceptibility; symbol Fe, at. no. 26, at. wt 55·847; the most extensively used of all metals because of its many properties; when purified and alloyed with small quantities of other materials, known as STEEL; *cast* ~, iron obtained by smelting from ores, silvery grey when clean, hard, brittle, crystalline in structure, and containing 2–5% of carbon and smaller quantities of sulphur, phosphorus, and silicon; *pig*-~, cast iron as first obtained from the smelting furnace, cast in long blocks (pigs) for convenience; *wrought* ~, highly malleable iron obtained by stirring pig-iron when molten (puddling), nearly pure but always containing some slag in the form of filaments and thus showing a fibrous structure. 2. Tool, implement, instrument, made of iron, as *curling-~*, *grappling-~*; tool or apparatus (orig. of iron) with smooth flat surface which can be heated for smoothing out linen etc. (*flat ~*, lighter kind heated from below); golf club with iron or steel head laid back for lofting the ball; (usu. pl.) fetters, shackles. 3. Preparation of iron used in medicine as a tonic. 4. (fig.) Type of hardness, as *man of ~*, *rod of ~*. 5. Phrr.: *strike while the ~ is hot*, act promptly and at a good opportunity; *have* (*too*) *many ~s in the fire*, have many undertakings afoot at the same time, have many expedients. 6. *I~ Age*, period in the history of a people, following the Bronze Age, characterized by use of iron implements and weapons; *~-bark*, any species of *Eucalyptus* with solid bark; *~-bound*, bound with iron; (fig.) inflexible, unyielding; (of coast) rugged, rocky; *ir'onclad* (*adj.*) covered with, protected by, iron, as a field magnet; (*n.*, obs.) warship protected by iron plates; *I~ Cross*, German military decora-

tion; ~ *curtain*, (fig.) barrier to passage of persons and information at western boundary of Russian sphere of influence in Europe; any similar barrier to spread of ideas etc.; *I~ Duke*, Duke of WELLINGTON[1]; *~-grey*, of the colour of newly broken iron; ~ *lung*, rigid box enclosing the body of a patient (leaving the head free), used, in the treatment of paralysing diseases, for administering prolonged artificial respiration by means of mechanical pumps; (erron.) any apparatus used for the same purpose; *ir'onmaster*, manufacturer of iron articles and appliances; *ir'onmonger*, dealer in iron and other metal goods, whence *ir'onmongery*; *~-mould*, stain made on textiles by iron-rust; ~ *rations*, (esp. soldier's) emergency rations; *ir'onsides*, man of great bravery; *Ir'onsides*, Cromwell's troopers in the Civil War; *ir'onstone*, name of various hard iron ores; *ir'onware*, generic name for all light articles made of iron; hardware; *ir'onwork*, iron parts of a structure; casting, mouldings, etc., made of iron; *ir'onworks*, place where iron is smelted or iron goods made. ~ *adj.* Made of iron; firm, unyielding, merciless. ~ *v.t.* Furnish, cover, with iron; shackle with irons; smooth (linen etc.) with a hot iron; ~ *out*, (fig.) remove (difficulties etc.).

īrŏ'nic, -ical *adjs.* Of, using, said in, addicted to, irony. **īrŏ'nically** *adv.*

ir'oning (īrn-) *n.* Process of smoothing (linen etc.) with a heated iron; linen etc. to be ironed; *~-board*, smooth cloth-covered board on which clothes etc. are spread for ironing.

īr'ŏnist *n.* One who uses irony.

īr'onў[1] *n.* Figure of speech in which the intended meaning is the opposite of that expressed by the words used, ridicule in which laudatory expressions are used to imply condemnation or contempt; course of events, combination of circumstances, the result of which is the direct opposite of what might be expected as though due to the malice of fate, as in *life's ironies*, ~ *of fate*; use of language that has an inner meaning for a privileged audience and an outer meaning for the persons addressed or concerned, as in *tragic ~*; *Socratic ~*, assumption of ignorance as means of confuting an opponent in dispute.

irony[2] (īr'nī) *adj.* Of, like, iron.

I'roquois (ĭrokwoi) *n.* Indian of a powerful confederacy of tribes formerly inhabiting New York State and known as the Five Nations (see FIVE). **Iroquoi'an** *adj.* & *n.*

ĭrrā′dĭant *adj.* Shining brightly, luminous. **ĭrrā′dĭance** *n.*

ĭrrā′dĭāte *v.t.* Shine upon; subject to radiation, esp. of X-rays, gamma rays, or ultra-violet rays; (fig.) throw light on (subject); light up (face etc. *with* joy etc.). **ĭrrā′dĭātion** *n.* Shining, illumination (lit. and fig.); action or process of irradiating; exposure to radiation; (phys.) apparent enlargement of edges of illuminated object seen against dark background.

ĭrrā′dĭatĭve *adj.* Having property of irradiating; illuminating.

ĭrră′tional *adj.* Unreasonable, illogical, absurd; not endowed with reason; (math., of roots etc.) not rational, not commensurable with ordinary quantities, not expressible by an ordinary (finite) fraction, proper or improper. ~ *n.* Irrational person; (math.) irrational number or quantity; surd. **ĭrrătionă′lĭtȳ** *n.* **ĭrră′tionalīze** *v.t.* **ĭrră′tionallȳ** *adv.*

Irrawa′ddȳ (ĭrawŏ-). Principal river of Burma, flowing into the E. of the Bay of Bengal.

ĭrrėclai′mable *adj.* Not to be reclaimed or reformed. **ĭrrėclai′mablȳ** *adv.*

ĭrrĕ′concīlable *adj.* Implacably hostile; (of ideas etc.) incompatible. ~ *n.* Implacable opponent of political measure etc. **ĭrrĕconcīlabĭ′lĭtȳ, ĭrrĕ′concīlablenėss** *ns.* **ĭrrĕ′concīlablȳ** *adv.*

ĭrrėco′verable (-kŭ-) *adj.* That cannot be recovered or remedied. **ĭrrėco′verablȳ** *adv.*

ĭrrėcū′sable (-z-) *adj.* That must be accepted.

ĭrrėdee′mable *adj.* Not to be redeemed, irreclaimable; (of govt. loans, etc.) not to be terminated by repayment; (of paper currency) for which issuing authority does not undertake to pay coin.

Irrėdĕ′ntist (ĭ-) *n.* (It. politics) Advocate of recovery to Italy of all Italian-speaking districts; *i*~, member of other country who holds similar views. **ĭrrėdĕ′ntĭsm** *n.* [It. (*Italia*) *irredenta* unredeemed Italy]

ĭrrėdū′cĭble *adj.* That cannot be brought (*to* desired condition); not capable of being reduced; ~ *minimum*, smallest amount, lowest degree, to which anything can be reduced, or point beyond which further reduction would be useless or unacceptable.

ĭrrĕ′fragable *adj.* (of statement, argument, person) Indisputable, unanswerable. **ĭrrĕ′fragablȳ** *adv.*

ĭrrėfră′ngĭble (-j-) *adj.* Inviolate; (optics) not capable of being refracted.

ĭrrĕ′fūtable (*or* -rĭfū′-) *adj.* Not to be refuted. **ĭrrĕfūtabĭ′lĭtȳ** *n.* **ĭrrĕ′futablȳ** *adv.*

ĭrrĕ′gūlar *adj.* Not regular, contrary to rule, abnormal; not of symmetrical form; (of surface) uneven; disorderly; uneven in duration, order, etc.; (gram.) not inflected in the usual way, pop. applied in English to the strong verb; (of troops) not in regular service. ~ *n.* Member of irregular military force. **ĭrrĕgūlă′rĭtȳ** *n.* **ĭrrĕ′gularlȳ** *adv.*

ĭrrĕ′latĭve *adj.* Unconnected, unrelated, (*to*); having no relations, absolute. **ĭrrĕ′latĭvelȳ** *adv.*

ĭrrĕ′lėvant *adj.* Not to the point; not applicable (*to* matter in hand). **ĭrrĕ′lėvance, ĭrrĕ′lėvancȳ** *ns.* **ĭrrĕ′lėvantlȳ** *adv.*

ĭrrėlĭ′gion (-jon) *n.* Hostility to, disregard of, religion. **ĭrrėlĭ′gĭous** (-jus) adj. **ĭrrėlĭ′gĭouslȳ** *adv.*

ĭrrėmē′dĭable *adj.* That cannot be remedied. **ĭrrėmē′dĭablȳ** *adv.*

ĭrrėmĭ′ssĭble *adj.* Unpardonable; unalterably binding. **ĭrrėmĭ′ssĭblȳ** *adv.*

ĭrrėmo′vable (-mōō-) *adj.* That cannot be removed, esp. from office. **ĭrrėmovabĭ′lĭtȳ** *n.* **ĭrrėmo′vablȳ** *adv.*

ĭrrĕ′parable *adj.* (of injury, loss, etc.) That cannot be rectified or made good. **ĭrrĕ′parablenėss** *n.* **ĭrrĕ′parablȳ** *adv.*

ĭrrėplā′ceable (-sa-) *adj.* Of which the loss cannot be made good.

ĭrrėprĕ′ssĭble *adj.* Not to be repressed or restrained. **ĭrrėprĕ′ssĭblȳ** *adv.*

ĭrrėproa′chable *adj.* Free from

blame, faultless. **irrėproachabĭ'lity̆** *n.* **irrėproa'chably̆** *adv.*

irrėsi'stĭble (-zĭs-) *adj.* Too strong, convincing, charming, etc., to be resisted. **irrėsistĭbĭ'lity̆** *n.* **irrėsi'stĭbly̆** *adv.*

irrĕ'solute (-zolōōt *or* -ūt) *adj.* Undecided, hesitating; wanting in resolution. **irrĕ'solutely̆** *adv.* **irrĕ'soluteness, irrĕsolu'tion** *ns.*

irrėsŏ'lvable (-zŏl-) *adj.* That cannot be resolved into parts; (of problem) that cannot be solved.

irrėspĕ'ctive *adj.* ~ *of*, not taking into account, without reference to. **irrėspĕ'ctively̆** *adv.*

irrėspŏ'nsĭble *adj.* Not responsible for conduct; acting, done, without due sense of responsibility. **irrėspŏnsĭbĭ'lity̆** *n.* **irrėspŏ'nsĭbly̆** *adv.*

irrėspŏ'nsive *adj.* Not responsive (*to*). **irrėspŏ'nsiveness** *n.*

irrėtĕ'ntion *n.* Failure to retain (esp. urine). **irrėtĕ'ntive** *adj.* Not retentive. **irrėtĕ'ntiveness** *n.*

irrėtrie'vable *adj.* That cannot be retrieved. **irrėtrievabĭ'lity̆** *n.* **irrėtrie'vably̆** *adv.*

irrĕ'verent *adj.* Wanting in reverence. **irrĕ'verently̆** *adv.* **irrĕ'verence** *n.*

irrėvẽr'sĭble *adj.* Unalterable; not reversible. **irrėvẽrsĭbĭ'lity̆** *n.* **irrėvẽr'sĭbly̆** *adv.*

irrĕ'vocable *adj.* Unalterable; gone beyond recall. **irrĕvocabĭ'lity̆** *n.* **irrĕ'vocably̆** *adv.*

ĭ'rrigāte *v.t.* (of streams etc.) Supply land with water; water (land) by system of artificial channels, ditches; (med.) wash, moisten (wound etc.) with constant flow of liquid. **ĭ'rrigable, ĭ'rrigative** *adjs.* **irrigā'tion** *n.*

ĭ'rritable *adj.* Quick to anger, touchy; (physiol., of muscles, nerves) capable of being excited to vital action by physical stimulus; (of parts of body, wounds, etc.) excessively sensitive to stimuli; inflamed, sore; (bot.) capable of responding to external stimulus. **irritabĭ'lity̆** *n.* **ĭ'rritably̆** *adv.*

ĭ'rritancy̆[1] *n.* Irritation, annoyance.

ĭ'rritancy̆[2] *n.* (Rom. & Sc. law) Making, becoming, null and void; forfeiture.

ĭ'rritant *adj.* Causing (usu. physical) irritation. ~ *n.* Substance causing irritation (also fig.).

ĭ'rritāte *v.t.* Excite to anger, annoy; excite, inflame, make sore (part of body etc.); (physiol.) stimulate (organ) to activity. **ĭ'rritāting** *adj.* **ĭ'rritātingly̆** *adv.* **irritā'tion** *n.*

irrŭ'ption *n.* Invasion; violent entry.

Ir'ving[1] (ẽr-), Sir Henry (1838–1905). English actor.

Ir'ving[2] (ẽr-), Washington (1783–1859). American historian, essayist, and novelist; author of 'The Sketch-Book', which includes his 'Rip van Winkle'.

Ir'vingīte (ẽr-) *n.* Member of a religious body called by its members the Catholic Apostolic Church, founded *c* 1835 on basis of principles promulgated by Edward Irving (1792–1834), a minister of the Church of Scotland.

is (ĭz). 3rd pers. sing. pres. of BE.

Is. *abbrev.* Isaiah (O.T.; also Isa.); Island(s); Isle(s).

Isaac (ī'*z*ak). Hebrew patriarch, son of Abraham and Sarah and father of Jacob and Esau (Gen. 21: 3, etc.)

isabĕ'lla (ĭz-) *adj.* & *n.* Greyish yellow. **isabĕ'llīne** *adj.* Isabella-coloured.

isagŏ'gic *adj.* Introductory. **isagŏ'gics** *n.pl.* Study of literary and external history of the Bible.

Isaiah (īzī'*a*). Hebrew major prophet who ministered in Judah in 8th c. B.C. and attacked corruption in the national life; book of O.T. containing his prophecies.

ī'satin *n.* Reddish-yellow crystalline substance ($C_8H_5NO_2$) obtained by oxidizing indigo and used in the preparation of vat dyes.

ĭ'schium (-k-) *n.* One of the bones of the pelvis. **ĭ'schial, ischiă'tic** *adjs.*

Iseult (ē'zōōlt *or* ĭ-). Name of two characters in medieval legend: (1) sister or daughter of the king of Ireland and wife of king Mark of Cornwall, loved by Tristram;

ISAIAH

(2) daughter of the king of Brittany and wife of Tristram.

-ish *suffix.* Of the nature of; somewhat; approximately.

I'shmāel (ī-). Son of Hagar, of whom it was predicted, 'His hand will be against every man, and every man's hand against him' (Gen. 16: 12); hence, an outcast, one at war with society. **I'shmāelīte** *n.* An Ishmael.

I'shtar (ī-). Assyrian and Babylonian equivalent of ASTARTE.

I'sidōre (īz-), St. (*c* 560–636). Archbishop of Seville and Doctor of the Church, an encyclopaedic writer. **Isidōr'ian** *adj.* ~ *Decretals,* collection of decretals attributed to St. Isidore but made in the 9th c. in France, containing spurious documents supporting the papal claim to temporal power.

isinglass (ī'zingglahs) *n.* Semi-transparent substance, form of gelatine, got from viscera of certain fishes, esp. the sturgeon, and used in making jellies, glue, etc., and for clarifying alcoholic beverages. [obs. Du. *huisenblas* sturgeon's bladder]

I'sis[1] (ī-). (Egyptian myth.) Sister and wife of OSIRIS, and mother of HORUS, regarded as a nature-goddess.

I'sis[2] (ī-). Local name for river Thames from its source to its junction with the Thame below Oxford. [prob. f. false etymology of L *Tamisis* as *Tam*+*Isis*]

I'slăm (iz-; *or* -ahm). 1. Religion revealed through the Prophet Muhammad. 2. Muslim world. **Islă'mic, Islamĭ'tic** *adj.* **I'slamism, I'slamīte** *ns.* [Arab. *'islām* resignation to will of God]

ī'sland (īl-) *n.* Piece of land surrounded by water; (formerly) peninsula; (fig.) anything detached or isolated; (naut.) ship's bridge or superstructure; (physiol.) detached portion of tissue or group of cells; *~s of Langerhans*: see LANGERHANS; *Islands of the Blessed,* (Gk & Rom. myth.) islands of the Western Ocean, abode of the favourites of the gods after death. ~ *v.t.* Make into an island; isolate, dot as with islands.

ī'slander (īl-) *n.* Native or inhabitant of an island.

īsle (īl) *n.* (esp. poet. or in proper name) Island (usu. small).

Isle of Wight (īl ov wīt). Island off S. coast of England; county since April 1974.

ī'slĕt *n.* Little island, isolated tract or spot; (physiol.) small detached mass of tissue within tissue of a different kind; ~ *of Langerhans*: see LANGERHANS.

Ismai'lī (izmī-) *n.* Member of a Muslim sect which seceded from the Shiah in 9th c. after the rejection of the claim of Isma'il, a descendant of Muhammad's son-in-law Ali, to be leader (imam) of Islam; they were very powerful in 10th c. when the Fatimids were in power; in 12th c. they were responsible for a terrorist movement (the Assassins); they now survive mainly in India, Iran, and Afghanistan, and regard the Aga Khan as their imam. **Ismai'lian** *adj.*

iso- *prefix.* Equal.

I.S.O. *abbrev.* Imperial Service Order.

ī'sobar *n.* 1. Line on map connecting places at which atmospheric pressure is the same (at given time or on the average). 2. One of two or more isotopes having the same atomic weight but different chemical properties. **īsobă'ric** *adj.*

īsochei'mal (-kī-), **īsochi'menal** (-kĭ-) *adjs.* & *ns.* (Line on map) connecting places of same mean winter temperature.

īsŏ'chronous (-kr-) *adj.* Occupying equal time, vibrating uniformly, as a pendulum.

Isŏ'cratēs (ī-, -z) (436–338 B.C.). Athenian orator and teacher of rhetoric.

īsodȳnă'mic *adj.* & *n.* (Line on map) connecting places at which the total magnetic intensity of the terrestrial field has the same magnitude.

īsogŏ'nic *adj.* & *n.* (Line on map) connecting places where the declination of the magnetic needle is the same.

ī'solable *adj.* Capable of being isolated.

ī'solāte *v.t.* Place apart or alone; (chem.) free substance from its compounds; subject (person etc.) to quarantine, separate (infectious patient) from others; (elect.) = INSULATE. **ī'solāting** *adj.* That isolates; (of language) in which each element is an independent word, being neither inflected nor compounded. **īsolā'tion** *n.*

īsolā'tionist *n.* One who favours (political or national) isolation (esp. in U.S. politics). **īsolā'tionism** *n.*

ī'somer *n.* (chem.) One of two or more substances composed of molecules having the same kind of atoms and in the same proportions, but which, by reason of a difference in arrangement of the atoms, have different chemical and physical properties. **īsomĕ'ric** *adj.* **īsŏ'merism** *n.*

īsŏ'merous *adj.* (bot.) (of a flower) Having the same number of parts in each whorl.

īsomĕ'tric, -ical *adjs.* Of equal measure or dimensions; ~ *drawing*, engineer's or architect's drawing in which the 3 dimensions are represented by 3 sets of lines 120° apart and all measurements are on same scale (i.e. not in perspective).

ī'somorph *n.* Substance or organism isomorphous with another. **īsomor'phic, īsomor'phous** *adjs.* Having the same form; having the property of crystallizing in the same or closely related geometric forms; (math., of groups and other systems) exactly corresponding in form and in the relations between their elements. **īsomor'phism** *n.*

ī'sopŏd *n.* Crustacean of large group (including, e.g., woodlice)

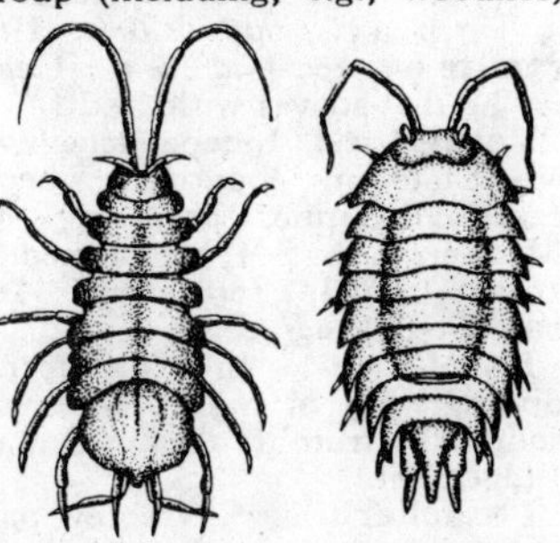

varying greatly in form and often parasitic.

īsŏ'scelēs (-z) *adj.* (of triangle) Having two sides equal.

īsosei'smal (-sīz-) *adj.* & *n.* (Line on map) connecting places at which an earthquake-shock is of the same intensity.

īsŏ'stăsȳ *n.* (geol.) Theory which postulates that the earth's crust is in a state of equilibrium and that every process that disturbs this state is followed by a readjustment (e.g. when the ice-cap disappeared from Scandinavia the land rose slightly to compensate for the loss of load). **īsostă'tic** *adj.* In static equilibrium, esp.

as applied to theory of isostasy.

ī'sothĕrm *n.* Line on map connecting places having the same mean annual or monthly temperature. **īsothĕr'mal** *adj.* & *n.*

īsotŏ'nic *adj.* Having equal osmotic pressure; of, exhibiting, equal tension.

ī'sotōpe *n.* One or two or more forms of an element having the same atomic number and the same chemical properties and occupying the same place in the periodic table, but differing in atomic weight and in nuclear properties such as radioactivity. **īsotŏ'pic** *adj.*

I'srāel[1] (ĭz-). 1. Name given to Jacob after he had wrestled with the angel (Gen. 32: 28). 2. (also *children of* ~) Hebrew nation or people traditionally descended from Jacob, whose 12 sons became founders of the 12 tribes. 3. Northern kingdom of the Hebrews (933–721 B.C.), opp. JUDAH. **I'srāelīte** (*or* -rēa-) *adj.* & *n.* [Heb., = 'he that strives with God']

I'srāel[2] (ĭz-). Independent Jewish State in country formerly called Palestine, bordering on Mediterranean Sea; established in 1948; capital, Jerusalem. **Israe'lī** (-rālĭ) *adj.* & *n.*

I'srafĕl (ĭz-). In Muslim tradition, angel of music, who will sound the trumpet on the Day of Judgement.

I'ssachar (ĭsak-). Hebrew patriarch, son of Jacob and Leah (Gen. 30: 18); tribe of Israel traditionally descended from him.

Issas: see AFARS AND ISSAS.

ĭ'ssūant *adj.* (her.) Emerging from bottom of a chief, or rising from another bearing etc. (esp. of beast of which upper part alone is visible).

ĭ'ssūe *n.* 1. Outgoing, outflow; (med., obs.) discharge of blood etc., incision to procure this. 2. Termination, end. 3. Way out, outlet; mouth of river. 4. (obs., exc. in law) Progeny, children. 5. Result, outcome. 6. Point in question, esp. (law) between contending parties in action; *at* ~, at variance; in dispute; *join* ~, proceed to argue (*with* person *on* point agreed upon as basis of dispute); (law) submit an issue jointly for decision; (of one party) accept the issue tendered by the other. 7. Giving out, issuing, (*of* bills of exchange, stamps, etc.); number of coins, notes, copies of newspaper or book etc., issued at one time; ~ *v.* 1. Go or come out; emerge from a condition; be derived, spring, (*from*); result (*from*); end, result, (*in*). 2. Come out, be published; send forth; publish, put into circulation (notes, newspaper, book, etc.). 3. (mil.) Supply (soldier) *with* article of equipment etc. **ĭ'ssūable** *adj.* **ĭ'ssūance** *n.*

Istănbu'l (ī-, -ōōl). City and port of Turkey on the Bosporus (formerly CONSTANTINOPLE).

ĭ'sthmus (*or* -sm- *or* -stm-) *n.* Narrow portion of land connecting two larger bodies of land, neck of land; (anat., bot., zool.) narrow part connecting two larger parts. **ĭ'sthmian** *adj.* Of an isthmus; *I*~, of the Isthmus of Corinth or the *I*~ *Games*, national festival of ancient Greece held at Corinth in alternate years.

I'strĭa (ĭ-). Mountainous rocky peninsula projecting into Adriatic east of Trieste; formerly part of the Austrian duchy of Cărinthia; assigned to Italy after war of 1914–18; now part of Yugoslavia.

ĭt[1] *pron.* 3rd person sing. pronoun denoting thing or person in question; as subject of impersonal verb, expressing action or condition of things without reference to agent; as subject of verb, anticipating deferred virtual subject in apposition; as antecedent to relative of either number and any gender, separated by predicate; as indefinite object with transitive or intransitive verb; with specific but unexpressed reference: *with* ~, see WITH; as quasi-*n.*, (1) in children's games (also *he*), player who must catch or find others; (2) (colloq.) the very person or thing; perfection.

ĭt[2] *n.* (in *gin-and-it*) Italian vermouth.

it. *abbrev.* Italic (type).

i.t.a. Initial teaching alphabet.

ital. *abbrev.* Italic (type).

Ită'lian (ĭ-) *adj.* Of Italy or its people or language; (of script) = ITALIC², 1; ~ *sonnet*: see SONNET. ~ *n.* 1. Italian person. 2. Language of Italy, one of the modern descendants of Latin. **Ită'lianate** *adj.* Of Italian form or character.

Ită'lic¹ (ĭ-) *adj.* 1. Of ancient Italy or its tribes; of the Greek colonies in southern Italy; ~ *languages*, Indo-European languages of ancient Italy (Latin, Oscan, Umbrian) as a group. **Ită'licism** *n.*

ită'lic² *adj.* 1. Of the kind of handwriting developed in Italy (opp; GOTHIC). 2. Of the kind of printing type imitating italic script, introduced by Aldus Manutius (1501), in which letters slope towards the right (now usu. employed to emphasize word(s) or distinguish word(s) from others in same contes). *n.* (also pl.) Italic type. **ită'licize** *v.t.* Print in italics; (in writing) underline.

I'taly̆ (ĭ-). Peninsula running southward into Mediterranean from the mass of central Europe; formerly divided among various mercantile city states or under foreign domination until unified in 19th c. by the efforts of Mazzini, Cavour, and Garibaldi; a monarchy from 1861 (when Vittorio Emmanuele II of Sardinia was proclaimed king of Italy and the first parliament met) until 1946 when a republic was declared; capital, Rome.

ĭtch *n.* Uneasy sense of irritation in skin; scabies; restless desire, hankering; ~-*mite*, mite causing scabies. ~ *v.i.* Feel irritation in skin; crave uneasily. **ĭ'tchy̆** *adj.*

ī'tem *n.* Article, unit, included in enumeration; entry of this in account etc.; detail of news etc. in newspaper etc. ~ *adv.* Likewise, also, (introducing mention of item). **ī'temize** *v.t.* Set down by items; specify items of (account etc.). [L, *item* in like manner, also]

ĭ'terāte *v.t.* Repeat (quoted words etc.); make (charge, assertion, etc.) repeatedly. **ĭ'terance, iterā'tion** *n.*

ĭ'terative *adj.* (esp. gram., of verb) Denoting repetition of action, frequentative.

I'thaca (ĭ-). 1. (Gk *Itháki*) Small island W. of Greece, adjoining Cephallenia. 2. Island described by Homer as the kingdom of Odysseus; traditionally identified with modern Ithaca, but thought by some to be the neighbouring larger island of Leukas.

ĭthy̆phă'llic *adj.* Of the phallus carried in Bacchic festivals; in the metre used for Bacchic hymns (trochaic dimeter brachycatalectic, – ∪ – ∪ – –) ~ *n.* Poem in ithyphallic metre; licentious poem.

ĭtĭ'nerant *adj.* Travelling from place to place; (of justices) travelling on circuit; (of Wesleyan ministry) preaching in a circuit. ~ *n.* **ĭtĭ'neracy̆, ĭtĭ'nerancy̆** *ns.*

ĭtĭ'nerary̆ *n.* Route; record of travel; guide-book. ~ *adj.* Of travelling, of roads.

ĭtĭ'nerāte *v.i.* Travel from place to place; (of Wesleyan) preach within circuit.

ĭts *poss. pron.* Possessive case of IT¹ used as attrib. adj., belonging to, affecting, it.

ĭtsĕ'lf *pron.* Emphatic and reflexive form corresponding to IT¹; *by* ~, automatically; apart from its surroundings; *in* ~, apart from its surroundings; viewed in its essential qualities etc.

I.T.V. *abbrev.* Independent Television.

I.U.D. *abbrev.* Intra-uterine device.

Ivan (ēvah'n). Name of several rulers of Russia; *Ivan I* (d. 1341), grand duke of Vladimir 1328–, during whose reign the Metropolitan see was transferred from Vladimir to Moscow; *Ivan II* (d. 1359), grand duke of Vladimir; *Ivan III* 'the Great' (1440–1505), grand duke of Muscovy (1462–; *Ivan IV* 'the Terrible' (1530–84), first tsar of Muscovy 1533–; a successful ruler, who limited the power of the boyars and favoured the merchant classes; conquered Kazan and Astrakhan and added

Siberia to his dominions; was subject to fits of rage in one of which he killed his son; completely destroyed the city of Novgorod, 1569, because of a reported conspiracy; *Ivan V* (1666–96), associated as tsar from 1682 with his half-brother Peter the Great; *Ivan VI* (1740–64), emperor of Russia 1740–1; kept in imprisonment from 1742 until his death.

Ives (īvz), **Yves** (ēv), St. Ivo of Chartres (*c* 1040–1116), French churchman, bishop of Chartres.

Iviza (ĭvē′th*a*): = IBIZA.

Ivo: see IVES.

ī′vorў *n.* 1. Hard white fine-grained substance (dentine of exceptional hardness) composing main part of tusks of elephant, hippopotamus, walrus, narwhal, and (*fossil* ~) mammoth; *vegetable* ~, hard endosperm of seed (~ *nut*) of the palm *Phytelephas*; ~ *black*, black pigment from calcined ivory; ~ *tower*, situation or attitude of seclusion from the world or practical affairs (esp. of intellectual seclusion). 2. Colour of ivory, ivory-white. 3. (slang, pl.) Teeth; dice, billiard-balls, piano-keys.

I′vorў Coast (ī-). Republic of W. Africa, between Liberia and Ghana; formerly a French colony; fully independent 1960; capital, Abidjan.

Ivry (ēvrē′). Battle (1590) fought about 40 miles W. of Paris between Huguenots under Henry IV and Catholic League under Mayenne, in which Henry was victorious.

ī′vў *n.* Climbing evergreen shrub (*Hedera helix*) with dark-

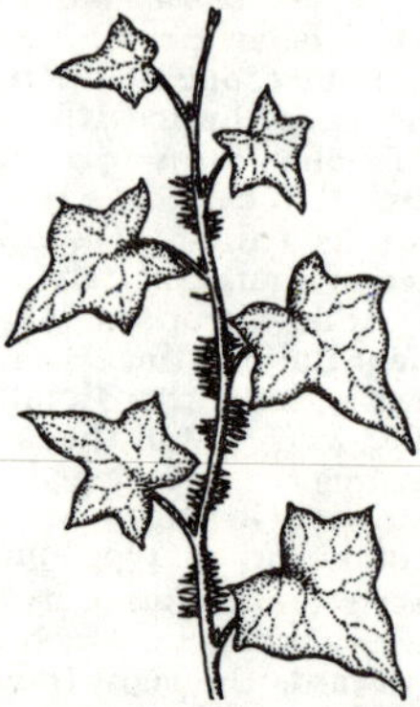

green shining leaves, usu. five-angled.

I.W. *abbrev.* Isle of Wight.

I.W.W. *abbrev.* Industrial Workers of the World.

ĭ′xia *n.* S. Afr. iridaceous plant of genus *I*~, with large showy flowers.

Ixī′on (ĭ-). (Gk myth.) King of Thessaly, father of the Centaurs; tried to seduce Hera, and was condemned to be bound to a fiery wheel revolving unceasingly through the underworld.

Izmir (ĭzmēr′). City and port of Turkey on W. Coast of Asia Minor (formerly *Smyrna*).

ĭ′zzard *n.* (archaic) Letter z.

J

J, j (jā). 10th letter of modern English alphabet, a late modification of I; in form, i with a tail (i was freq. written thus in MSS. when final); in modern English representing a voiced composite sound (dzh), corresponding to the voiceless *tsh*.

J. *abbrev.* Joule(s); Judge; Justice.

J.A. *abbrev.* Judge Advocate.

jăb *v.t.* Poke roughly; stab; thrust (thing) abruptly (*into*). ~ *n.* Abrupt stabbing blow with pointed thing or fist; (colloq.) injection.

jă'bber *v.* Speak volubly and with little sense; utter (words) rapidly and indistinctly; chatter, as monkeys etc. ~ *n.* Jabbering.

jă'bĭru (-ōō) *n.* Large stork, esp. *Jabiru mycteria* of tropical America.

jăboră'ndĭ *n.* Any of several S. Amer. shrubs of genus *Pilocarpus*; dried leaflets of certain of these, esp. *P. jaborandi*, yielding pilocarpine.

jabot (zhă'bō) *n.* Ornamental frill on front of woman's bodice ; (hist.) frill on man's shirt-front.

jă'cana (*or* -sanah') *n.* Tropical wading bird of family Jacanidae with very long toes enabling it to walk over floating plants.

jăcară'nda *n.* 1. Any of various Brazilian timber trees with heavy dark wood. 2. Tree of genus *J*~, with trumpet-shaped blue flowers.

jă'cĭnth *n.* Reddish-orange gem, variety of zircon.

jăck[1] *n.* 1. Fellow (obs.); *every man* ~, (colloq.) every individual man; STEEPLE-jack; figure striking bell on outside of clock; *J*~ (*tar*), common sailor. 2. (cards) Knave; (in all-fours) knave of trumps. 3. Machine for turning spit in roasting meat ; machine for lifting and supporting weights from below; part of various machines; in spinet, harpsichord, etc., wooden upright fixed to back of key-lever and fitted with quill for plucking string; (elect.) device for connecting one set of wires to a corresponding set by the insertion of a single plug (used esp. in manual telephone exchanges). 4. (bowls) Smaller bowl as mark for players to aim at. 5. Male of various animals (so JACKASS); pike, esp. young or small. 6. Ship's flag, smaller than ensign, esp. one flown from jackstaff, indicating nationality; *Union J*~: see UNION. 7. ~*-boot*, large boot coming above knee; *ja'ckdaw*, thievish small crow (*Corvus monedula*) haunting old buildings etc., easily tamed and taught to imitate sound of words; *J*~ *Frost*, frost personified; *J*~*-in-office*, fussy (esp. petty) official; ~*-in-the-box*, toy figure that springs out of box when opened; kind of firework; *J*~*-in-the-green*, man or boy enclosed in framework covered with leaves in May-day sports; *J*~ *Ketch*, common hangman [f. name of common executioner 1663–86]; ~*-knife*, large pocket clasp-knife; dive in which diver touches feet or ankles with hands; (*v.i.*) double like folding knife; ~*-of-all-trades*, one who can turn his hand to anything; ~*-o'-lantern*, will-o'-the-wisp; ~*-plane*, long heavy plane for coarse work ; *ja'ckpot*, (in poker) pool which cannot be opened until some player has two jacks or better in his hand; cumulative stakes or prize in lottery etc.; *hit the jackpot*, (slang) have sudden success; ~*-rabbit*, (U.S.) large prairie-hare with very long ears and legs; ~-*snipe*, small species of snipe (*Lymnocryptes minima*); *ja'ckstaff*, short staff at bow of ship at which the jack (see sense 6) is flown; *J~ tar*: see sense 1; *J~ the Ripper*, undiscovered murderer of women in London (1888–91), who mutilated his victims; ~-*towel*, roller-towel. ~ *v.t.* Hoist (*up*) with mechanical jack etc. (also fig.) [*Jack*, fam. form of name *John*]

jăck[2] *n.* (archaic) 1. Foot-soldier's sleeveless padded tunic. 2. (also *black* ~) Vessel for liquor, usu. of waxed leather coated with tar.

jă'ckal (-awl) *n.* 1. Any of several members of the dog family found wild in Asia and Africa, living on carrion and small animals. 2. Person who does subordinate preparatory work or drudgery for another (because jackals were formerly believed to hunt up lion's prey for him). ~ *v.i.* Act as jackal (*for*). [Turk. *chakāl*]

jă'ckanāpes (-ps) *n.* 1. (archaic) (Tame) ape or monkey. 2. Pert young fellow; coxcomb.

jă'ckăss *n.* 1. Male donkey. 2. Dull fellow. 3. *laughing* ~, kookaburra.

jă'ckėt *n.* 1. Short coat, coat-like garment for upper part of body; *life-*~: see LIFE. 2. Any outer coat or covering, as skin of potatoes, animal's coat. 3. Outer covering round boiler etc. to protect it or cool it or keep in heat. 4. Wrapper round book. ~ *v.t.* Cover with jacket.

Jă'ckson[1], Andrew (1767–1845). 'Old Hickory', American soldier and statesman; 7th president of U.S. 1829–37.

Jă'ckson[2], Thomas Jonathan (1824–63). 'Stonewall Jackson', Amer. general; commander (as Lee's chief assistant) of Southern forces in Amer. Civil War, accidentally killed by the fire of his own men at Chancellorsville.

Jā'cob. Hebrew patriarch, son of Isaac and Rebecca, younger twin brother of Esau, and traditional founder of Israel (Gen. 25–60); ~'*s ladder*, ladder between earth and heaven, with angels ascending and descending, which Jacob saw in a dream at Bethel (Gen. 28: 12); hence, rope-ladder with wooden rungs for ascending ship's rigging; also, blue-flowered perennial plant (*Polemonium caeruleum*) with closely pinnate leaves giving ladder-like appearance; ~'*s staff*, cross-staff; 3-ft long square rod with cursor, as instrument for measuring distances and heights; pointed iron-shod rod for supporting surveyor's circumferentor instead of tripod.

Jăcobē'an *adj.* Of the reign of James I of England (1603–25); of the style of building or furniture in England in early 17th c.; (commerc., of stain, varnish, etc.) of the colour of dark oak. [L *Jacobus* James]

jă'cobĭn[1] *n.* Pigeon with reversed feathers on back of neck, suggesting cowl. [Fr. *jacobine*, fem. of *jacobin* (friar)]

Jă'cobĭn[2] *n.* 1. Friar of order of St. Dominic, esp. French member of the order, from their first convent near church of St. Jacques in Paris. 2. Member of French political club founded 1789 in the old Jacobin convent in Paris to maintain the principles of extreme democracy and absolute equality, and responsible, under Robespierre, for the Reign of Terror; dissolved 1799. 3. Sympathizer with principles of Jacobins in French Revolution, extreme radical or revolutionary.

Jă'cobīte[1] *n.* Member of a Syrian sect named from Jacobus Baradaeus, bishop of Edessa (6th c.), who revived the EUTYCHIAN heresy.

Jă'cobīte[2] *n.* Adherent of James II of England after his abdication, or of the Old or Young Pretender; supporter of Stuarts after revolution of 1688.

Ja'cobsen (yahk-), Jens Peter (1847–85). Danish novelist and poet.

jacō'bus *n.* (hist.) English gold coin struck in reign of James I.

jă'conėt *n.* 1. Plain white cotton fabric resembling cambric.

2. Dyed cotton fabric, freq. glazed on one side.

Jacquard (jăkard), Joseph Marie (1752–1834). French in-

ventor, improver of the loom; ~ *loom*, loom for mechanically weaving figured patterns by means of an endless belt of cards punched with holes arranged to form the required pattern.

jacquerie (zhăkerē) *n.* Rising of peasantry, esp. that of 1357–8 in N. France. [Fr., f. *Jacques* James, peasant]

jăctĭtā'tion *n.* (law) ~ *of marriage*, offence of falsely claiming to be person's wife or husband.

jāde[1] *n.* Poor or worn-out horse; (archaic) hussy. **jā'dėd** *adj.* Worn out, weary; duiled.

jāde[2] *n.* 1. Nephrite, a hard translucent light-green, bluish, or whitish stone, a silicate of calcium and magnesium, used for ornaments etc. 2. Jadeite, a silicate of sodium and aluminium, closely resembling nephrite in appearance. 3. Carved piece of jadeite or nephrite. 4. (also ~*-green*) Light green. [Span. (*piedra de*) *ijada* (stone of) the colic, f. L *ilia* flank]

jā'deite (-dīt) *n.* See JADE, 2.

Jā'el. Woman who murdered SISERA, her guest, by driving a tent-nail through his temples (Judges 4, 5).

Jă'ffa *n.* (also ~ *orange*) Large oval seedless orange originally grown near Tel Aviv-Jaffa, Israel.

jăg[1] *n.* Sharp projection. ~ *v.t.* Cut, tear, break, in uneven manner, make indentations in. **jă'gġėd** (-g-) *adj.* **jă'ggėdlȳ** *adv.* **jă'ggėdnėss** *n.* **jă'ggȳ** *adj.*

jăg[2] *n.* (dial. & U.S.) Small load; (U.S. slang) spree, esp. drinking-bout.

J.A.G. *abbrev.* Judge Advocate General.

Jagannath (jŭ'ganaht). (Hindu myth.) Title of KRISHNA; = JUGGERNAUT.

jă'ggerȳ *n.* Coarse dark-brown sugar made in India from palm-sap; any crude sugar. [Indo-Port. *jagara* sugar]

jă'gūar (*or* -gwar) *n.* Large carnivorous spotted quadruped of cat kind (*Panthera onca*), inhabiting wooded parts of America from Texas to Paraguay.

Jahveh, -weh (yah'vā, -wā). = YAHWEH. **Jah'vĭst** *n.* = YAHWIST. **Jahvĭ'stĭc** *adj.*

jail: see GAOL.

Jain (jīn) *n.* Member of non-Brahminical Hindu sect established in 6th c. B.C., with doctrines closely resembling those of Buddhism. **Jai'nĭsm** *n.* [Sansk. *jina* a Buddha (*ji* conquer, overcome)]

Jakarta: see DJAKARTA.

jă'lap *n.* Purgative drug obtained from tuberous roots of *Ipomoea purga* and other plants, esp. the Mexican climbing plant, *Exogonium Purga*, with salver-shaped purplish flowers; plant yielding this drug. [f. *Jalapa*, Mexican city (Aztec *Xalapan* sand by the water)]

jalŏ'pȳ *n.* (orig. U.S.) Dilapidated motor-car; (transf.) battered old aircraft.

jalousie (zhă'loozē) *n.* Blind, shutter, with slats sloping upwards from without. [Fr., = 'jealousy']

jăm[1] *v.* 1. Squeeze between two surfaces or bodies; fill up, block (passage etc.) by crowding into it. 2. Wedge (part of machine) so that it cannot work; become so wedged. 3. Thrust, push violently. 4. (radio etc.) Cause interference with. ~ *n.* Crush, squeeze; stoppage (of machine etc.) due to this; crowded mass, esp. accumulation of logs in river or traffic in street etc.; (colloq.) awkward situation, fix.

jăm[2] *n.* Confection made by boiling fruit and sugar to a thick consistency; preserve. ~ *v.t.* Spread with jam; make into jam.

Jam. *abbrev.* Jamaica; James (N.T.).

Jamai'ca. Island in the Caribbean Sea; discovered by Columbus in 1494 and ruled by Spain until captured by England in 1655; member State of the Commonwealth, independent in 1962; capital, Kingston. **Jamai'can** *adj.* & *n.*

jămb (-m) *n.* Side post of doorway, window, etc.

jămboree' *n.* (orig. U.S.) Celebration; merry-making; (esp.) large rally of Scouts.

Jāmes[1] (-mz). Name of several persons in N.T.: 1. Son of Zebedee and elder brother of St. John the Evangelist (Mark 3: 17); one of the twelve Apostles and the first to be martyred (A.D. 44); called *St. ~ the Great* or *Greater*; commemorated 25 July; patron saint of Spain. 2. Person described as brother of Jesus (cf. Mark 6: 3, Gal. 1: 19); traditionally identified with St. James the Less; a leader of the Church at Jerusalem until put to death by the Sanhedrin in A.D. 62; *Epistle of St. ~*, book of N.T. traditionally ascribed to him. 3. One of the twelve Apostles, son of Alphaeus; called *St. ~ the Less*; commemorated 1 May, with St. Philip.

Jāmes[2] (-mz). Name of seven Stuart kings of Scotland: *James I* (1394–1437); son of Robert III; reigned 1406–37, but was held captive in England till 1424; *James II* (1430–60), his son, reigned 1437–60; *James III* (1451–88), his son, reigned 1460–88; *James IV* (1473–1513), his son, reigned 1488–1513; married Margaret Tudor, daughter of Henry VII of England; invaded England, 1513, and was killed at Flodden Field; *James V* (1512–42), son of James IV and father of Mary Queen of Scots; reigned 1513–42; *James VI* and *VII*: see next entry.

Jāmes[3] (-mz). Name of two Stuart kings of England and Scotland: *James I* of England and *VI* of Scotland (1566–1625), son of Lord Darnley and Mary Queen of Scots, and, through her, great-great-grandson of Henry VII; on her abdication, 1567, became king of Scotland, and on Elizabeth I's death, 1603, king of England; *James II* of England and *VII* of Scotland (1633–1701), son of Charles I and grandson of James I; succeeded his brother, Charles II, 1685; had Catholic sympathies; fled to France, and was succeeded, 1688, by his Protestant son-in-law William of Orange.

Jāmes[4] (-mz) (1688–1766). James Francis Edward Stuart, son of JAMES[3] II: see Old PRETENDER.

James[5] (-mz), Henry (1843–1916). American novelist; settled in Europe from 1875; naturalized as a British subject, 1915.

James[6], William (1842–1910). American philosopher and psychologist, elder brother of Henry JAMES[5]; formulator of theory of PRAGMATISM.

Jā'meson Raid (-ms-). March into the Transvaal, 1895, of 600 troops led by Dr (later Sir) Leander Starr Jameson (1853–1917), intended to support a projected rising of Uitlanders in Johannesburg; it was unauthorized and unsuccessful, and was one of the incidents leading to the Boer War.

Jā'mestown (-mst-). Ruined village in Virginia, U.S.A., site of first permanent English settlement in America (1607); *~-weed*, jimson weed.

Jami (jahmē') (1414–92). Persian classic poet.

Jammes (zhahm), Francis (1868–1938). French mystical poet and novelist.

Jammu and Kăshmir' (jŭ'mōō, -ēr). State in NW. of the Indian sub-continent; capitals, Srinagar and Jammu.

Jămshi'd (-ēd). (Pers. myth.) Legendary early king of Persia, reputed inventor of arts of medicine, navigation, iron-working, etc.; he was king of the peris, condemned to assume human form for boasting of his immortality, and ruled Persia for 700 years.

Jan. *abbrev.* January.

jă'ngle (-nggl) *v.* Make harsh metallic noise; cause (bell etc.) to do this. ~ *n.* Harsh metallic noise, discordant sound.

Jă'nissarȳ, Jă'nizarȳ *n.* 1. (hist.) One of body of Turkish infantry forming sultan's guards and main fighting force of Turkish army, orig. (14th c.) personal slaves of sultan, later slaves, conscripts, and sons of subject Christians; abolished after revolt, in which many were killed, 1826. 2. Any Turkish soldier; (fig.) personal instrument of tyranny. [Turk. *yeni tsheri* new soldiery]

jă'nĭtor *n.* 1. Doorkeeper. 2. Caretaker of building, charged with heating and cleaning it. **jănĭtôr'ĭal** *adj.*

Jă'nsen, Cornelius (1585–1638). R.C. bishop of Ypres in Flanders and professor at Louvain.

Jă'nsenĭsm *n.* Religious system based on Jansen's digest of the teaching of St. Augustine maintaining that the natural human will is perverse and incapable of good, that the capacity for the love of God can be attained only by conversion, and that God converts whom he pleases; it was strongly opposed by the Jesuits and condemned by several popes esp. Clement X; it flourished chiefly in France (17th and 18th centuries), where the nunnery of PORT-ROYAL, near Paris, was its headquarters. **Jă'nsenĭst** *n.*

Jănūār'ĭus, St. (3rd c.). Bishop of Benevento; martyred under Diocletian; patron saint of Naples; commemorated 19 Sept.

Jă'nūarȳ (*or* -ūrĭ). 1st month of Gregorian (11th of Julian) calendar, with 31 days. [L (*mensis*) *Januarius* (month) of JANUS]

Jā'nus. (Rom. myth.) Ancient Italian deity, guardian of gates and doorways and esp. of the State in time of war; represented with two faces, one at front and one at back of his head.

Jăp *adj.* (colloq.) Japanese; ~ *silk*, light-weight silk fabric, orig. woven in Japan, from which the gum is boiled away after weaving. ~ *n.* (colloq.) Japanese.

japă'n[1] *n.* Hard varnish, esp. that made from asphalt and linseed oil in imitation of Japanese lacquer and used for producing black gloss on metal etc. ~ *v.t.* Cover with japan; make black and glossy as with japan.

Japă'n[2]. Empire of Eastern Asia, occupying long group of islands in Pacific, roughly parallel with E. coast of Asiatic mainland; capital, Tokyo.

Jăpanē'se (-z) *adj.* Of Japan or its people or language; ~ *cherry*, hybrid flowering cherry with pink or white, usu. double, flowers; ~ *print*, colour-print printed in water-colour from wood-blocks; ~ *silk*: see JAP silk. ~ *n.* 1. Japanese person. 2. Language of Japan, which is agglutinative, contains many Chinese loan-words, and is written in Chinese ideographs with characters of a syllabary called *kana* for the agglutinative and inflectional endings. [Chinese *Jih-pun* sunrise (*jih* sun, *pun* origin)]

jāpe *n.* & *v.i.* Jest.

Jā'phĕth. 3rd son of Noah (Gen. 10: 1); traditional ancestor of the peoples living round Mediterranean. **Japhĕ'tic** *adj.*

japŏ'nĭc *adj.* Japanese.

japŏ'nĭca *n.* Any of various ornamental plants supposed to have originated in Japan, esp. the Japanese quince, cultivated in Japan but native in China.

Jaques-Dălcrō'ze (zhahk), Émile (1865–1950). Swiss musician; originator of EURHYTHMICS.

jâr[1] *n.* Sound, vibration, esp. harsh one; thrill of nerves or feelings, shock; want of harmony, disagreement; quarrel. ~ *v.* 1. Sound discordantly, make grating impression (*on*, person, his ear, etc.); strike with grating sound (*on*, *against*, object); vibrate, resound, discordantly; cause (thing) to jar; send shock through (nerves). 2. Be at variance, disagree (*with*); dispute, wrangle. **jâr'rĭnglȳ** *adv.*

jār[2] *n.* Pottery or glass vessel with or without handle(s), usu. cylindrical; amount in this.

jardinière (zhārdĭnyār) *n.* 1. Ornamental pot or stand for display of growing flowers. 2. Dish of mixed vegetables served alone or as garnish with meat. [Fr.]

jār'gon[1] *n.* Unintelligible words; barbarous or debased language; mode of speech full of unfamiliar terms or peculiar to a group or profession.

jār'gon[2], **jārgōō'n** *n.* Translucent, colourless, or smoky variety of zircon found in Sri Lanka.

jārgonĕ'lle *n.* Early-ripening variety of pear.

jārl (y-) *n.* (hist.) Scandinavian or Danish chieftain.

jār'vey *n.* Hackney-coachman (obs.); driver of Irish jaunting-car. [by-form of surname *Jarvis*]

Jas. *abbrev.* James.

jă'smĭne (*or* -z-), **jĕ'ssamĭne, -mĭn** *n.* Shrub of genus *Jasminum* with white or yellow salver-shaped flowers, esp. *common* or *white* ~ (*J. officinale*), climbing shrub with fragrant white flowers, and *winter* ~ (*J. nudiflorum*), with yellow flowers. [Pers. *yāsimīn*]

Jā'son. (Gk legend) Son of Aeson, king of Iolcos; the throne was usurped by Pelias, who promised to surrender it if Jason would fetch for him the Golden Fleece (see GOLDEN); Jason sailed with the Argonauts and obtained the fleece with the aid of MEDEA.

jă'sper *n.* Opaque variety of quartz, usu. red, yellow, or brown.

Jat (jaht) *n.* Member of an Indo-Aryan people widely distributed in NW. India.

jau'ndice *n.* Yellow discoloration of skin and normally white part of eyeball due to the presence of pigments in the blood which are normally excreted in the bile, often caused by an obstructed bile duct; this condition; disordered or discoloured vision as characteristic of this. **jau'ndĭced** (-st) *adj.* Affected with jaundice; (fig.) coloured by envy, low spirits, etc.

jaunt *n.* Excursion, esp. for pleasure. ~ *v.i.* Take a jaunt; *jaunting-car*, light two-wheeled vehicle with seats back to back, formerly common in Ireland.

jau'ntȳ[1] *adj.* Having or affecting easy sprightliness, airy self-satisfaction.

jau'ntȳ[2] *n.* (naut. slang) Head of ship's police.

Jaurès (zhōrĕs), Auguste Marie Joseph Jean (1858–1914). French socialist leader; assassinated at outbreak of war of 1914–18.

Ja'va (jah-). Large island of Malay archipelago, first settled by Dutch in 17th c. and now part of Indonesia; ~ *man*, fossil hominid *Homo erectus* (formerly *Pithecanthropus erectus*), whose remains were first found in Java in 1891; ~ *sparrow*, kind of weaver-bird (*Amadira oryzivora*). **Javanē'se** (-z) *adj.* & *n.* (Native, inhabitant, Malayan language) of Java.

Javĕ'l, -ĕ'lle (zh-). ~ *water*, *eau de* ~, solution containing sodium hypochlorite (or, formerly, potassium hypochlorite), used as bleacher, antiseptic, or disinfectant. [named f. chemical works in the Quai de *Javel*, Paris]

jă'velĭn (-vl-) *n.* Light spear thrown with the hand.

jaw *n.* 1. One of the bones or sets of bones forming the framework of the mouth and carrying the teeth in vertebrates; in sing. usu. = lower jaw rather than upper; (pl.) bones etc. of mouth including teeth; mouth; (fig.) grip, e.g. *~s of death*; (colloq., sing.) loquacity. 2. (pl.) Structure in invertebrates analagous to vertebrates' jaws. 3. (pl.) Seizing members of machine, e.g. vice. 4. (pl.) Narrow mouth of channel, valley, etc. 5. *~-bone*, each of the two bones forming lower jaw in most mammals; these two combined into one in others; *~-breaker*, (colloq.) word hard to pronounce. ~ *v.* (colloq.) Speak, esp. at tedious length; scold, lecture (person).

jay *n.* Any of several related birds forming a group of the crow family, esp. the noisy chattering European bird *Garrulus glandarius* which has fawn body plumage with white patches, vivid blue and black barred wings, and black and white erectile crest; ~-*walker*, pedestrian who crosses street without care or without observing regulations; so ~-*walking*.

jăzz *n.* Syncopated dance-music, of U.S. Negro origin, with characteristic harmony and rag-time rhythm; (slang) pretentious talk; ~ *band*, orchestra playing jazz. ~ *adj.* Discordant, loud or fantastic in colour etc. ~ *v.* Dance to, play, jazz; arrange (music) as jazz; arrange (pattern etc.) in vivid or grotesque form; brighten, liven, *up*. **jă'zzy̆** *adj.*

J.C. *abbrev.* Justice Clerk.

J.C.R. *abbrev.* Junior common-room.

jea'lous (jĕl-) *adj.* 1. Solicitous for preservation *of* (rights etc.); (bibl., of God) intolerant of unfaithfulness; (of inquiry etc.) vigilant. 2. Apprehensive of being displaced in the love or goodwill *of* (wife, lover, friend, etc.; also *of* supposed rival); envious (*of*). **jea'lously̆** *adv.* **jea'lousy̆** *n.* Quality, state, or being jealous.

jean (*or* jān) *n.* Heavy twilled cotton fabric; (pl., orig. U.S.) garment, esp. overalls or trousers, of this. [prob. f. Fr. *Gênes* Genoa]

Jĕ'busīte (-z-) *n.* Member of Canaanite tribe inhabiting Jerusalem before Jews; 17th-c. nickname for Roman Catholic, esp. Jesuit.

jeep *n.* Small, short, powerful, four-wheeled car having an emergency four-wheel drive. [said to have been f. *g p*, initials of *general purposes*]

jeer[1] *n.* (naut., usu. pl.) Tackle for hoisting and lowering lower yards.

jeer[2] *v.* Scoff derisively (*at*); deride. ~ *n.* Derisive taunt.

Jĕ'fferies (-frĭz), Richard (1848–87). English naturalist and novelist.

Jĕ'fferson, Thomas (1743–1826). Amer. liberal statesman, 3rd president of U.S., 1801–9. **Jĕffersō'nian** *adj.*

Jĕ'ffreys (-z), George (1648–89), 1st Baron. 'Judge Jeffreys', English lawyer; lord chancellor of England; notorious for his conduct of the Bloody Assizes (1685) in the west after the suppression of Monmouth's rebellion, at which a considerable number of executions were decreed.

jehad: see JIHAD.

Jėhoi'achin (-kĭn). King of Judah, son of Jehoiakim; taken captive to Babylon after reign of a few months (2 Kings 24).

Jėhoi'akim. King of Judah, son of Josiah (2 Kings 23, 24).

Jėhŏr'am, Jŏr'am. 1. King of Israel, son of Ahab; killed by Jehu (2 Kings 1, 3). 2. King of Judah, son of Jehoshaphat (2 Kings 8; 2 Chron. 21).

Jėhŏ'shaphăt. King of Judah, son of Asa (1 Kings 22; 2 Chron. 20).

Jėhō'vah (-*va*). 1.. Name of God in O.T. (Exod. 6: 3; cf. YAHWEH). 2. (in Christian use) God; ~*'s Witnesses*, name for the Watch Tower Bible and Tract Society, a sect founded *c* 1879 by Charles Taze Russell (1852–1916) of Pittsburgh, Penn. **Jėhō'vist** *n.* = YAHWIST. **Jēhōvi'stic** *adj.* [erron. rendering of Heb. JHVH]

Jē'hū. King of Israel, son of Jehoshaphat, famous for furious driving of chariot (2 Kings 9); hence, fast or furious driver; coachman, driver.

jėju'ne (-ōōn) *adj.* Meagre, scanty; barren; unsatisfying to mind. **jėju'nely** *adv.* **jėju'neness** *n.*

THOMAS JEFFERSON

jėju'num (-jōō-) *n.* (anat.) Part of small intestine between duodenum and ileum.

Jě'kўll, Henry. Hero of R. L. Stevenson's story 'The Strange Case of Dr Jekyll and Mr Hyde' (1886); handsome and well-respected, he transformed himself by a potion into the dwarfish and detestable Edward Hyde in whom was embodied only the evil side of Jekyll; hence, *~-and-Hyde character*, dual personality.

jěll *v.i.* (colloq.) Set as jelly; (fig.) take shape.

Jě'llĭcōe, John Rushworth, 1st Earl (1859–1935). English admiral in command of Grand Fleet at battle of JUTLAND; First Sea Lord, 1916–17.

jě'llў *n.* Soft stiffish substance, usu. semi-transparent, made of gelatine or other gelatinous substance, esp. as food usu. made with meat or with fruit juices; concentrated usu. fruit-flavoured preparation of this for dissolving; anything of similar consistency; (slang) gelignite; *~-bag*, muslin etc. bag for straining the juice from fruit pulp in preparing jelly; *je'llyfish*, (esp. scyphozoan) MEDUSA². ~ *v.* Make into jelly; congeal. **jě'llied** (-ĭd) *adj.* Made into, set in, jelly.

jě'mmў *n.* Crowbar or case-opener used by burglars, usu. made in sections. [fam. form of *James*]

Je'na (yā-). German university town in Thuringia, scene of battle (1806) in which Napoleon defeated the Prussians; ~ *glass*, special type of glass made there.

je ne sais quoi (zh*e* n*e* sā kwah). Indefinable esp. pleasing quality. [Fr. = 'I know not what']

Jenghiz Khan: see GENGHIS KHAN.

Jě'nkĭns' Ear (-z), War of. War between England and Spain (1739) precipitated by Robert Jenkins, a master mariner, who claimed in 1738 that his ear had been cut off by a Spanish coastguard at Havana.

Jě'nner, Edward (1749–1823). English physician and pioneer of vaccination.

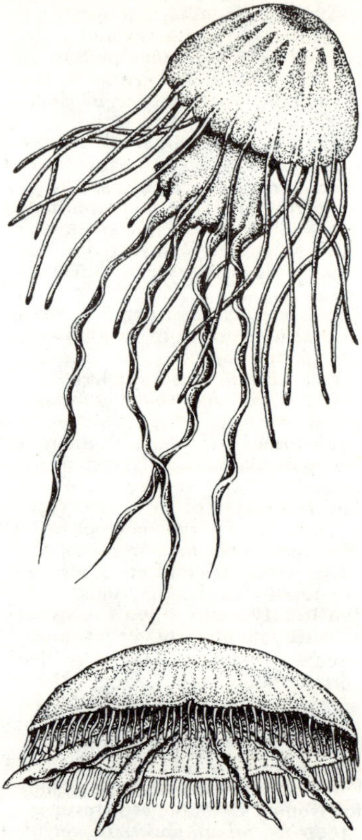

JELLYFISH

jě'nnėt *n.* Small Spanish horse.

jě'nnў *n.* 1. Spinning jenny. 2. Locomotive crane which runs backwards and forwards. 3. Female of certain animals. 4. *creeping* ~, moneywort; ~ *wren*, (nursery name for) wren; (U.S.) herb robert. [fam. form of *Jane* or *Janet*]

jeo'pardīze(jěp-) *v.t.* Endanger.

jeo'pardў (jěp-) *n.* Danger. [OF *ieu parti* divided (i.e. even) game]

Jě'phthah (-th*a*). A judge of Israel, son of Gilead; sacrificed his daughter in consequence of a vow that if victorious against the Ammonites he would sacrifice the first living thing that met him on his return (Judges 11, 12).

Jer. *abbrev.* Jeremiah (O.T.).

jerbō'a *n.* Member of family of rodents of which the desert rat (*Dipus*) of N. Africa with very long hind legs and tail is typical; Australian marsupial (*Antechinomys*) resembling this. [Arab. *yarbu*ʿ]

jĕrėmī'ăd *n.* Lamentation, doleful complaint. [f. *Jeremiah*]

Jĕrėmī'ah (-ī*a*) (*c* 650–*c* 585 B.C.). Hebrew major prophet, who saw the fall of Assyria, the vassalage of Judah in turn to Egypt and Babylon, and the destruction of Jerusalem; book of O.T. containing his prophecies; hence, doleful person, denouncer of the times.

Jerez (hĕ'rĕth). (also ~ *de la Frontera*) Town in Andalusia, Spain, centre of sherry-making industry.

Jĕ'rĭcho (-kō). Ancient city north of the Dead Sea; first Canaanite city attacked and taken by Israelites (Joshua 6).

jerk[1] *n.* Sharp sudden pull, twist, etc.; involuntary spasmodic contraction of muscle; (pl.) spasmodic movements of limbs or face, esp. in religious excitement; *physical ~s*, (colloq.) motions practised in physical training. ~ *v.* Pull, thrust, twist, etc., with a jerk; throw with suddenly arrested motion; move with a jerk. **jer'kȳ** *adj.* **jer'kĭlȳ** *adv.* **jer'kĭnėss** *n.*

jerk[2] *v.t.* Cure (esp. beef) by cutting in long slices and drying in sun. [Peruv. *echarqui* dried flesh]

jer'kĭn *n.* Man's close-fitting jacket, often of leather (hist.); sleeveless jacket.

Jĕrobō'am[1]. Name of two kings in ancient Israel: (1) (10th c. B.C.) first king of northern Israel (1 Kings 11–14), 'a mighty man of valour', one 'who made Israel to sin'; (2) (8th c. B.C.) king of Israel (2 Kings 14).

jĕrobō'am[2] *n.* Very large wine-bottle. [f. JEROBOAM[1]]

Jĕ'rōme, St. Eusebius Hieronymus (*c* 342–420). Doctor of the Church; born in Dalmatia; made the Vulgate translation of the Bible; commemorated 30 Sept.

jĕ'rrĭcăn, jĕ'rrȳ-căn *n.* Metal container esp. for fuel, holding 5 gallons.

jĕ'rrȳ[1] *n.* (slang.) Chamber-pot.

Jĕ'rrȳ[2] *n.* (mil. slang) German soldier; Germans collectively.

jĕ'rrȳ-builder (-bĭl-) *n.* Builder of unsubstantial houses with bad materials. **jĕ'rrȳ-building** *n.* **jĕ'rrȳ-built** *adj.*

Jer'sey[1] (-zĭ). Largest of the Channel Islands.

jer'sey[2] (-zĭ) *n.* 1. Knitted pullover. 2. Machine-knitted fabric. 3. *J~*, (one of) a breed of small usu. buff-coloured dairy cattle, producing milk of high fat content, orig. raised in Jersey. [f. JERSEY[1]]

Jeru'salem (-rōō-). Ancient capital of Judaea, the holy city of the Jews, sacred also to Christians and Muslims; capital of modern Israel; *the New ~*, the Heavenly City, the abode of God and the saints; *New ~ Church*, followers of SWEDENBORG; ~ *artichoke*: see ARTICHOKE.

jĕss *n.* Short strap of leather, silk, etc., round legs of hawk used in falconry. ~ *v.t.* Put jesses on (hawk).

jessamine: see JASMINE.

Jĕssė. Father of David (1 Sam. 16), hence represented as first in genealogy of Jesus Christ; *tree of ~*, (in medieval MSS. etc.) tree representing genealogy of Christ from 'root of Jesse'.

ST. JEROME

jĕst *n.* Joke; fun; object of derision. ~ *v.i.* Joke, make jests. **jĕ′stinglў̆** *adv.*

jĕ′ster *n.* One who jests; (esp., hist.) professional entertainer maintained in court or noble household.

Jĕ′sūit (-z-) *n.* Member of the Society of Jesus, an order of priests founded 1534 in Paris by Ignatius Loyola, Francis Xavier, and others, to defend the R.C. Church and propagate its faith; it is strictly organized and governed by a 'General' responsible only to the Pope; became the chief instrument of the Counter-Reformation and very powerful politically in 17th c.; sent missions to all parts, esp. S. America; it was suppressed in 1773 and restored in 1814; its members, learned and rigorously trained, are bound to poverty, chastity, and obedience, with duties of preaching, educating, and hearing confession. **Jĕsūi′tical** *adj.* 1. Of the Jesuits. 2. Having character ascribed to Jesuits; dissembling, practising equivocation or mental reservation of truth. **Jĕ′sūitrў̆** *n.*

Jē′sus[1] (-z-) (*c* 4 B.C.–*c* A.D. 30). (also ~ *Christ*) Source of the Christian religion, accepted by Christians as son of God, second person of the Trinity, and saviour of mankind; born (traditionally at Bethlehem) of the Virgin Mary; began his public life at about 30; for some 3 years wandered about ancient Palestine, chiefly in Galilee, with a band of followers or disciples, teaching and healing; was then arrested in Jerusalem at the time of Passover, handed over by the Jewish high court to the Roman authorities, and condemned to death by crucifixion; the Christian doctrine is that after 3 days he rose from the dead; *Society of* ~: see JESUIT.

Jesus[2]: see ECCLESIASTICUS.

jĕt[1] *n.* Hard black lignite taking brilliant polish; colour of this, deep glossy black. ~ *adj.* (also ~*-black*) Deep glossy black.

jĕt[2] *n.* 1. Stream of water, steam, gas(es), etc., ejected from small opening; spout, nozzle, for emitting water etc. thus. 2. In aircraft, stream of gas ejected from rearward-facing nozzle and propelling the aircraft forward; aircraft propelled thus; hence ~ *plane*, ~*-propelled*, ~ *propulsion*, etc. 3. ~*-stream*, narrow current of strong westerly winds in upper troposphere. ~ *v.* Spout forth in jet(s).

jĕ′tsam *n.* Goods thrown overboard from ship to lighten it, and (in mod. use) washed ashore.

jĕ′ttĕd *adj.* (tailoring, of pocket) Having no flap, but an outside seam (*jetting*) on either edge.

jĕ′ttison *n.* Throwing of goods overboard, esp. to lighten ship in distress. ~ *v.t.* Throw (goods) overboard thus.

jĕ′tton *n.* Counter with stamped or engraved device.

jĕttў̆[1] *n.* MOLE[3]; landing-pier.

jĕ′ttў̆[2] *adj.* Jet-black.

jeu d'esprit (zhėr dĕsprē). Witty or humorous (usu. literary) trifle. [Fr.]

jeune premier (zhėrn premyā). (fem. *jeune première*, pr. -yār) Actor playing part of young hero. [Fr.]

jeunesse dorée (zhėrnĕs dŏrā) Gilded youth. [Fr.]

Jew[1] (jōō) *n.* (fem. *Jew′ess*) Person of Hebrew descent; one whose religion is Judaism; (hist.) Hebrew of kingdom of Judah, as opp. to those of ten tribes of Israel; (offensive) grasping person, usurer, one who drives a hard bargain; *Wandering* ~: see WANDERING; ~*-baiting*, systematic persecution of Jews; *jews' harp*, *jew's-harp*, simple musical instrument consisting of elastic steel tongue affixed at one end to lyre-shaped metal frame, played by holding frame between teeth and striking free end of metal tongue with finger. ~ *adj.* (offensive) Jewish, as ~ *boy*.

jew[2] (jōō) *v.t.* (offensive) Cheat, beat down in price (also ~ *down*).

jew′el (jōō-) *n.* Ornament containing precious stone(s), worn for personal adornment; precious stone; highly prized person or thing. ~ *v.t.* Adorn, furnish, with jewels; fit (watch) with jewels for the pivot-holes. **jew′eller, jew′ellerў̆, jew′elrў̆** *ns.*

Jew′ish (jōō-) *adj.* Of the Jews; ~ *calendar*, complex ancient calendar in use among the Jews, a lunar calendar adapted to the solar year by various expedients, having normally 12 months, but 13 months in leap years which occur 7 times in every cycle of 19 years. The years are reckoned from the Creation (3761 B.C.); the months are Nisan (normally March–April), Iyar (April–May), Sivan (May–June), Tammuz (June–July), Ab (July–Aug.), Elul (Aug.–Sept.), Tishri (Sept.–Oct.), Cheshvan (Oct.–Nov.), Kislev (Nov.–Dec.), Tebeth (Dec.–Jan.), Shebat (Jan.–Feb.), Adar (Feb.–March), 2nd Adar (intercalary month). The ecclesiastical year begins with Nisan and the civil year with Tishri.

Jewry (joor′ĭ) *n.* 1. (collect.) Jews. 2. Jewish quarter in town etc. 3. (hist.) Judaea.

Jĕ′zėbel. Daughter of Ethbaal, king of Tyre and priest of Astarte; wife of Ahab, king of Israel; denounced by Elijah for introducing worship of Baal; killed when Jehu triumphed over Ahab; hence, shameless or abandoned woman.

jiao (jĭ′ow′) *n.* $\frac{1}{10}$ of a renminbi.

jĭb[1] *n.* Triangular stay-sail from outer end of jib-boom to fore-top-mast head in large ships; from bowsprit to masthead in smaller ones; *cut of person's* ~, his personal appearance; ~ *-boom*, spar run out from end of bowsprit; projecting arm of crane. ~ *v.* Pull (sail, yard) round from one side of ship to the other; swing round thus.

jĭb[2] *v.i.* (of horse etc.) Stop and refuse to go on, move backwards or sideways instead of going on; (fig.) refuse to proceed in some action; ~ *at*, show repugnance to (course, person).

jĭ′bba, -ah (-*a*), **ju-** (jōō-) *n.* Long outer garment with long sleeves worn by Muslims and Parsees.

jibe: see GIBE.

jĭff, jĭ′ffȳ *n.* (colloq.) Very short time.

jĭg *n.* 1. Lively dance; music for this, usu. in $\frac{3}{4}$ or $\frac{6}{8}$ time. 2. (eng.) Device for holding parts in appropriate position for drilling or assembling. 3. Contrivance for jigging ore. 4. *ji′gsaw*, machine fretsaw (U.S.); (also *jigsaw puzzle*) picture pasted on board etc. and cut in irregular pieces to be fitted together. ~ *v.* Dance a jig; move up and down rapidly and jerkily; separate coarser and finer portions of (ore) by shaking it under water in box with perforated bottom.

jĭ′gger[1] *n.* 1. (naut.) Small tackle consisting of a double and single block with rope. 2. Small sail rigged out on mast and boom from stern of cutter etc.; small smack with such sail. 3. Any of various mechanical contrivances, used in many trades; (slang) contrivance, gadget. 4. (U.S.) Small glass for spirits; amount held by this.

jĭ′gger[2] *n.* 1. = CHIGOE. 2. = CHIGGER.

jĭ′gger[3] *n.* Woman's short outdoor coat.

jĭ′ggered (-*er*d) *adj.* (colloq., in mild oath) Damned.

jĭ′ggerȳ-pō′kerȳ *n.* (colloq.) Trickery, underhand dealing.

jĭ′ggle *v.t.* Rock or jerk lightly.

jĭha′d, jė- (-ahd) *n.* Religious war of Muslims against unbelievers; (fig.) campaign against a doctrine, policy, etc.

jĭlt *v.t.* Cast off (lover) after encouragement or promise to marry. ~ *n.* Person who jilts lover.

Jĭm Crow (-ō). (U.S., offensive) Negro; freq. attrib., indicating discrimination against Negroes in U.S.

jĭ′m-jăms (-z) *n.pl.* (colloq.) Delirium tremens; feeling of apprehension; fit of depression.

Jĭ′mmȳ. ~ *the One*, (naval slang) First Lieutenant. [pet form of *James*]

jĭmp *adj.* (Sc.) Slender, graceful; scanty.

jĭ′mson, jĭ′mpson *n.* (also ~ *weed*) Thorn-apple. [var. of JAMESTOWN-weed]

jĭ′ngle (-nggl) *n.* 1. Mingled noise like that of small bells, links of chain, etc.; repetition of same or similar sounds in words, esp. if designed to catch the attention; words intended to have pleasing or striking sound without regard to sense. 2. Covered two-wheeled car in Australia and S. Ireland. ~ *v.* Make, cause (keys etc.) to make, a jingle; (of writing) be full of alliterations, rhymes, etc.

ji'ngō (-nggō) *n.* 1. *by* ~, vigorous form of asseveration. 2. (from use of *by jingo* in popular music-hall refrain of 1878) Supporter of Lord Beaconsfield in sending British fleet into Turkish waters in 1878 to resist advance of Russia; supporter of bellicose policy, blustering patriot; such policy or patriotism. **jĭ'ngōĭsm** *n.* **jĭngōĭ'stĭc** *adj.*

jĭnk *v.* Move with sudden quick turn(s), dodge. ~ *n.* Jinking movement; *high* ~*s*, boisterous sport, merrymaking.

jĭnn, dj- (j-) *n.pl.* (Islamic myth.) Order of spirits lower than angels, with supernatural power over men; (freq. as sing.) one of these. **jĭnnee'** *n.* One of the jinn.

JOAN OF ARC

Jĭ′nnah, Mohammed Ali (1876–1948). Muslim lawyer; first governor-general of Pakistan (1947–8).

jinrĭ′cksha *n.* Light two-wheeled hooded vehicle drawn by man or men, first used in Japan *c* 1870. [Jap. *jin-riki-sha* (*jin* man, *riki* strength, power, *sha* vehicle)]

jĭnx *n.* (colloq., orig. U.S.) Bringer of bad luck, exerciser of evil influence.

jĭ′tter *v.t.* Be nervous, act nervously; *ji′tterbug*, (colloq.) person who dances to hot-rhythm music; nervous person; (*v.i.*) dance thus.

jĭ′tters (-z) *n.pl.* (colloq.) Extreme nervousness. **jĭ′ttery̆** *adj.*

jiu-jitsu: see JU-JITSU.

jīve *v.i.* Jitterbug.

jn. *abbrev.* Junction.

Jō′achĭm[1] (-k-), St. Father of the Virgin Mary; commemorated 16 Aug.

Joachĭm[2] (yō′ak- *or* yōah′χ-) Joseph (1831–1907). Hungarian violinist.

Joan, Pope: see POPE[1].

Joan of Arc (ark), St. (1412–31). (Fr. *Jeanne d'Arc*) French peasant girl who became a national heroine; inspired by 'voices' of St. Catherine and St. Michael, she led the French armies against the English, relieved Orleans, and stood beside Charles VII at his coronation; was captured by the Burgundians and handed over to the English; was tried and condemned for heresy and burnt in the market-place at Rouen; canonized 1919; commemorated 30 May.

jŏb[1] *n.* 1. Piece of work, esp. small definite one done for hire or profit; (colloq.) crime, esp. robbery; (slang) object, person. 2. Paid position of employment. 3. Anything one has to do; (colloq.) difficult task. 4. *bad, good,* ~, unfortunate, fortunate, state of affairs, occurrence, etc.; ~ *lot*, miscellaneous lot of goods bought as speculation; any miscellaneous lot of persons or things; *~-work*, work done and paid for by the job. ~ *v.* 1. Do jobs; hire, let out for definite time or job; *jobbing carpenter, gardener*, etc., one employed in odd or occasional pieces of work. 2. Buy and sell (stock, goods) as broker; deal in stocks. **jŏ′bber** *n.* **jŏ′bbery̆** *n.* Corrupt dealing.

Jōb[2]. 1. Book of O.T., variously dated 5th–2nd c. B.C. 2. Its hero, a wealthy and prosperous man, whose patience and exemplary piety are tried by dire and undeserved misfortunes, and who, in spite of his bitter lamentations, remains finally confident in the goodness and justice of God; hence, a type of patience under misfortune; *~'s comforter*, one who, like Job's friends, aggravates distress under the guise of administering comfort.

jŏ′blėss *adj.* Out of work.

Jocă′sta. (Gk legend) Daughter of Creon, king of Corinth; mother and wife of OEDIPUS.

Jōck. 1. (colloq.) Nickname for Scotsman. 2. (as *n.*; army slang) Scottish, esp. Highland soldier.

jŏ′ckey *n.* Rider in horse-races; ~ *cap*, cap with long peak, worn by jockeys; *J~ Club*, club established 1750 at Newmarket, now the authority controlling all horse-racing in England. ~ *v.* Cheat, trick (*into, out of*, etc.); ~ *for position*, manœuvre for advantageous position (also fig.). [f. Sc. *Jock*, Jack]

jocō′se *adj.* Playful, waggish. **jocō′sely̆** *adv.* **jocō′senėss, jocŏ′sity̆** *ns.*

jŏ′cūlar *adj.* Mirthful; humorous. **jŏ′cūlarly̆** *adv.* **jŏcūlă′rity̆** *n.*

jŏ′cund *adj.* Merry, sprightly; pleasant. **jŏ′cundly̆** *adv.* **jocŭ′ndity̆** *n.*

jŏ′dhpurs (-dperz) *n.pl.* Riding-breeches reaching to the ankle, full above and tight below the knee. [f. *Jodhpur*, former State of India]

Jō′el (*or* -ĕl) (date disputed; 5th or possibly 9th c. B.C.). Hebrew minor prophet; book of O.T. containing his prophecies.

Jōe Mĭ′ller. Stale joke, chestnut. [f. *Joe Miller's Jests*, a jest book (1739) by John Mottley; named after Joseph Miller (1684–1738), comedian at Drury Lane theatre]

jō′ey *n.* (Austral.) Young kangaroo; young animal.

Joffre (zhŏfr), Joseph Jacques Césaire (1852–1931). Marshal of France; commander-in-chief of French armies, 1914–16.

jŏg *v.* 1. Shake with push or jerk; nudge (person), esp. to arouse attention; stimulate (memory). 2. Move up and down with unsteady motion; walk, trot, proceed, at slow but regular pace; *~-trot*, slow regular trot. ~ *n.* Shake, push; nudge; slow walk or trot.

jŏ'ggle[1] *v.* Shake, move, (as) by repeated jerks. ~ *n.* Slight shake.

jŏ'ggle[2] *n.* Joint of two pieces of stone or timber, contrived to prevent their sliding on one another; notch in one piece, corresponding projection in the other, or small piece let in between both, for this purpose. ~ *v.t.* Join by means of a joggle.

Jōhă'nnėsbûrg (*or* yō-). Largest city of the Republic of South Africa.

Jōhă'nnīne *adj.* Of St. JOHN[12].

Johă'nnisbėrger (-g-) *n.* Fine white wine from Johannisberg, village in the Rheingau, Germany.

John[1] (jŏn). Masculine proper name used in various collocations; ~ *Barleycorn*: see BARLEY; ~ *Bull* (from name of character representing English nation in Arbuthnot's satire 'Law is a Bottomless Pit', 1712), personification of English nation, typical Englishman, represented as a stoutish red-faced farmer-like man in top-hat and high boots; ~ *Collins*, (U.S.) drink of gin, soda-water, lemon, sugar, and ice; ~ *Doe*, (law) fictitious lessee acting as plaintiff in (now obs.) common-law action of ejectment; fictitious name for party to any transaction or proceeding; ~ *Dory*, European sea-fish (*Zeus faber*), having a laterally flattened oval body with a dark spot on each side, and long dorsal spines, used for food; similar Australian fish; ~ *o' Groat's*, reputed site of house said to have been built by a Dutchman, John Groot, in 16th c., on NE. point of Scottish mainland.

John[2] (jŏn). Name of 23 popes or antipopes, esp.: *John VIII*, pope 872–82; much involved in imperial politics; *John XXI* (should be XX, but there is an error in the numbering), pope 1276–7; identified with Petrus Hispanus, author of medical and philosophical works, and freq. referred to by chroniclers as a magician; *John XXII*, pope at Avignon, 1316–34; involved in unsuccessful struggle against Ludwig of Bavaria; accused of heresy; *John XXIII*, antipope, 1410–15, swore at Council of Constance to abdicate if the rival popes Benedict XIII and Gregory XII would also do so, but subsequently fled and was deposed; *John XXIII* (Angelo Giuseppe Roncalli, 1881–1963), pope 1958–63.

John[3] (jŏn). Name of 8 Byzantine emperors; *John I* Tzimisces, reigned 969–76; *John II* Comnenus, 'the Good', reigned 1118–43; *John III* Ducas Vatatzes, reigned 1222–54; *John IV* Lascaris, reigned 1258–61; *John V* Palaeologus, reigned 1341–91; *John VI* Cantacuzene, reigned 1341–54 (first as rival to John V, then jointly with him); *John VII*, reigned 1390; *John VIII* Palaeologus, reigned 1425–48.

John[4] (jŏn) (1167–1216). King of England; called 'Lackland' because as youngest son of Henry II he had no apanage in the continental provinces; succeeded his brother Richard Coeur de Lion, 1199; quarrelled with Pope Innocent III over appointment of Stephen LANGTON; alienated barons and people by bad administration and heavy taxation; was forced by barons to sign MAGNA CARTA.

John[5] (jŏn). Name of 2 kings of France: *John I* (1316), lived only 7 days; *John II* (1319–64), taken prisoner at Poitiers by Black Prince, returned to captivity in England when he could not raise ransom money agreed upon, and died in London.

John[6] (jŏn). Name of 6 kings of Portugal: *John I* 'the Great', reigned 1385–1433; *John II* 'the Perfect', reigned 1481–95; encouraged exploration of sea-route to India (in his reign Diaz rounded Cape of Good Hope) but refused to help Columbus; *John III*, reigned 1521–57; *John IV* 'the Fortunate', reigned 1541–56; founder of Braganza dynasty; *John V*, reigned 1707–50; *John VI*, reigned 1816–26.

John[7] (jŏn). King of Poland: see JOHN SOBIESKI.

John[8] (jŏn), Augustus Edwin (1878–1961). British painter.

John[9] (jŏn), Don (1545–78), of Austria. Natural son of emperor Charles V; commanded fleet at victory of LEPANTO; governor-general of Netherlands 1576–8.

John[10] (jŏn), Don (1629–79) of Austria. Natural son of Philip IV of Spain.

John[11] (jŏn), St. Name of various saints: *St. ~ the Baptist*, son of Elizabeth and Zacharias, a priest (Luke 1); preached in the wilderness; forerunner of Jesus Christ; was executed by order of Herod Antipas; *St. ~ Chrysostom*: see CHRYSOSTOM; *St. ~ of the Cross* (1542–91), Spanish mystical poet and Carmelite friar; friend of St. Theresa; canonized 1726; *St. ~ the Evangelist*: see JOHN[12]; *St. ~ of Nepomuk* (d. 1393 *or* 1383), Bohemian martyr; vicar-general to the archbishop of Prague; drowned by order of Wenceslas IV, (acc. to legend) for refusing to reveal what he had heard in confession from Wenceslas's wife Jane; canonized 1729.

John[12] (jŏn), St. Apostle, called *St. ~ the Evangelist* or *St. ~ the Divine*; son of Zebedee, a Galilean fisherman, and brother of James; the 'beloved disciple' of Jesus, credited since very early time (prob. erron.) with authorship of 4th Gospel and APOCALYPSE, and of three epistles of N.T.; commemorated 27 Dec.; 4th Gospel; any of the three epistles attributed to St. John; *Order of St. ~*: see HOSPITALLER; *St. ~ Ambulance Association and Brigade*, organization, founded in 1877, providing first aid, nursing, ambulance, and welfare services; *St. ~'s wort*, herb or shrub of genus *Hypericum*.

johnny (jŏ'nĭ) *n.* Fellow; *J~ Armstrong*, (naut. slang) hand-power; *~-cake*, (U.S.) cake of maize meal, baked in pan or (in southern States) toasted before fire; (Austral.) cake of wheatmeal baked in ashes or fried in pan; *J~ Raw*, novice; *J~ Reb*, (U.S.) northern name for Confederate in Amer. Civil War. [pet form of *John*]

John of Gaunt (jŏn) (1340–99), Duke of Lancaster. English soldier; 4th son of Edward III and father of Henry IV.

John of Lă'ncaster (jŏn) (1389–1435), Duke of Bedford. 3rd son of Henry IV and brother of Henry V, after whose death (1422) he was Protector of England, Henry VI being still a minor.

John of Salisbury (jŏn, saw'l-zbrĭ) (*c* 1115–80). English ecclesiastic and author; bishop of Chartres; supported Becket and was present at his murder.

Johns Hŏ'pkins (jŏnz, -z). University at Baltimore, Maryland, U.S., founded 1876 with money bequeathed by a Baltimore merchant, Johns Hopkins.

John Paul I (Albino Luciani, 1912–78), pope for 33 days from 26 August to 28 September 1978.

John Paul II (Karol Jozef Wojtyla, 1920–), elected pope in 1978; the first non-Italian pope in 450 years.

John Sōbie'skĭ (jŏn, -byĕ'-) (1624–96). National hero of Poland; elected king, as John III, 1674; recovered the greater part of Ukraine from the Turks.

Johnson[1] (jŏ'nsn), Andrew (1808–75). 17th president of U.S., 1865–9.

Johnson[2] (jŏ'nsn), Cornelius. Cornelis Jonson van Ceulen (1593–1664?), portrait painter of Flemish origin, born in England.

Johnson[3] (jŏ'nsn), Lyndon Baines (1908–73). 36th president of U.S., 1963–9.

Johnson[4] (jŏ'nsn), ('Dr.') Samuel (1709–84). English man of letters and lexicographer; famous esp. for his conversation recorded by his friend James Boswell. **Johnsō'nian** *adj.* Of Samuel Johnson; esp. of an English prose style abounding in words derived or made up from Latin, or characterized by weighty and well-balanced sentences.

Johŏr′e. State of Malaysia at S. end of Malay peninsula; capital, Johore Bahru.

joie de vivre (zhwah d*e* vēvr). Healthy enjoyment of life.

join *v.* 1. Put together, fasten, unite; connect (two points) by a line; unite in marriage, friendship, alliance, etc.; come together, be united. 2. Take part with others (in); come into company of (person); become member of (club etc.); take, resume, one's place in (regiment, ship, company, etc.); come into connection with; ~ *up*, enlist. 3. ~ *battle*, begin fighting; ~ *hands*, clasp one's hands together, clasp each other's hands; (fig.) combine in action or enterprise; ~ *issue*: see ISSUE. ~ *n.* Point, line, plane, of junction.

joi′ner *n.* (esp.) 1. One who makes furniture, house fittings, and other woodwork lighter than carpenter's. 2. (U.S. colloq.) One who joins many clubs, societies, etc. **joi′nerў** *n.* Joiner's work.

joint[1] *n.* 1. Place at which two things are joined together; structure in animal body by which two bones are fitted together; part of stem from which leaf or branch grows; point at which, contrivance by which, two parts of artificial structure are joined, rigidly or so as to allow of movement; (geol.) fracture in rock, esp. one along which there has been little or no movement. 2. One of the parts of which body is made up; one of the parts into which butcher divides carcass, esp. as served at table. 3. (chiefly U.S.) Place of meeting or resort, esp. low or illicit drinking-saloon, opium den, etc. ~ *v.t.* 1. Connect by joints; point (masonry); prepare (board etc.) for being joined to another by planing its edge; ~*-stool*, (hist.) stool made of parts fitted by joiner (orig. *joined stool*), as dist. from one of clumsier workmanship. 2. Divide (body, member) at joint or into joints. **joi′nter** *n.* (esp.) Plane for jointing, mason's tool for pointing.

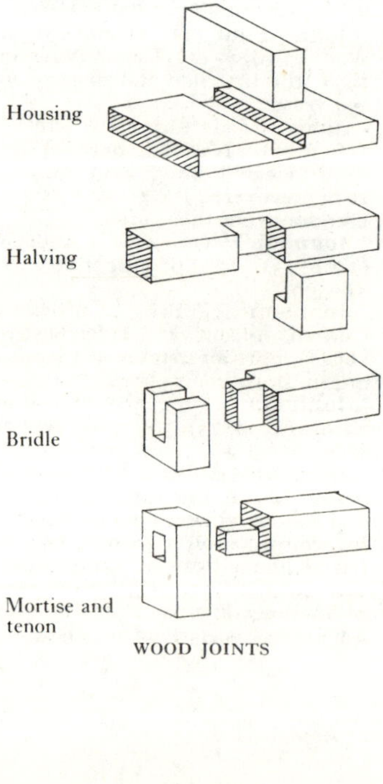

WOOD JOINTS

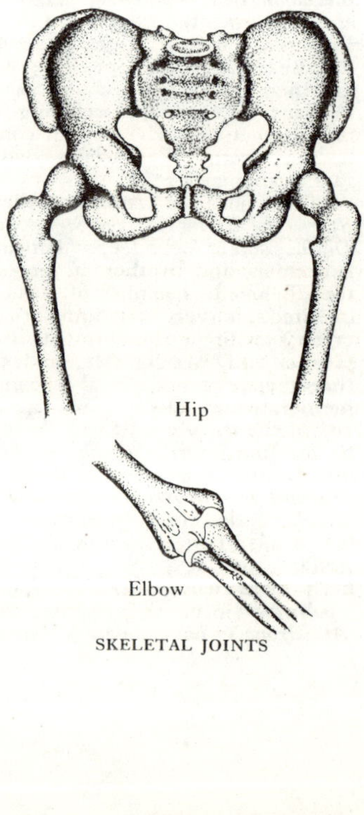

SKELETAL JOINTS

joint² *adj.* Held or done by, belonging to, two or more persons etc. in conjunction; (of persons) sharing (*with* others in possession, action, state, etc.); ~ *stock*, capital divided into shares, common fund; ~*-stock* (attrib.) holding, formed on basis of, a joint stock. **joi'ntlȳ** *adv.*

joi'ntrėss *n.* Widow who holds jointure.

joi'nture *n.* Sole estate limited to wife to be enjoyed by her after husband's death for her life. ~ *v.t.* Provide (wife) with jointure.

Joinville (zhwăṅvēl), Jean, Sire de (1224–1319). French seneschal of Champagne; friend and biographer of Louis IX.

joist *n.* One of parallel timbers stretched on edge from wall to wall for ceiling laths or floor boards to be nailed to.

jōke *n.* Thing said or done to excite laughter; amusing or ridiculous thing, person, or circumstance; *practical* ~, trick played on person in order to have laugh at his expense. ~ *v.i.* Make jokes, banter. **jō'kinglȳ** *adv.*

jō'ker *n.* 1. One who jokes; (slang) fellow 2. (cards) Extra card, often blank or with picture of jester, counting in some games (e.g. euchre) as a trump, in others (e.g. poker) as any card the holder chooses to make it. 3. (U.S.) Clause unobtrusively inserted in legislation and affecting its operation in some way not immediately apparent.

jokul, *jökull* (yō'ko͝ol, yẽr-) *n.* Snow-mountain in Iceland.

jŏ'llifȳ *v.* Make merry, esp. tipple; make jolly. **jŏllificā'tion** *n.*

jŏ'llitȳ *n.* Merrymaking, festivity.

jŏ'llȳ *adj.* Joyful; slightly drunk; festive, jovial; (colloq.) very pleasant, delightful. ~ *adv.* (colloq.) 1. (with adj. or adv.) Very. 2. ~ *well*: used with verb to give emphasis. ~ *n.* (nav. slang) Royal marine. ~ *v.t.* (orig. U.S.) Talk or behave agreeably to (person) in order to put or keep him in good humour.

jŏ'llȳ-boat *n.* Clinker-built ship's boat, smaller than cutter.

jōlt *v.* Shake (person etc.) with jerk from seat etc., esp. in locomotion; (of vehicle) move along with jerks, as on rough road. ~ *n.* Such jerk; surprise, shock. **jō'ltȳ** *adj.*

Jon. *abbrev.* Jonathan.

Jō'nah (*-a*). Hebrew minor prophet; book of O.T. bearing his name, acc. to which he fled when bidden by God to go to Nineveh and prophesy; God then sent a storm to wreck his ship, and the seamen, holding him responsible, threw him overboard; he was swallowed by a great fish and lived in its belly for 3 days before being cast out on dry land; hence, person regarded as bringing bad luck.

Jŏ'nathan¹ 1. Son of Saul and friend of David, killed at battle of Mount Gilboa (1 Sam. 13, 14, 18–20, 31). 2. *Brother* ~, personified people of U.S.; typical American citizen.

jŏ'nathan² *n.* Amer. variety of red autumn dessert apple.

Jōnes¹ (-nz), Henry Arthur (1851–1929). Playwright, of Welsh origin; author of some 60 plays.

Jōnes² (-nz), Inigo (1573–1651). English architect and masque-designer.

jongleur (zhawṅglẽr) *n.* (hist.) Itinerant minstrel. [Fr.]

jŏ'nquil *n.* Species of narcissus (*N. jonquilla*) with long linear leaves and clusters of fragrant white-and-yellow flowers.

Jŏ'nson¹, Benjamin ('Ben') (1574–1637). English poet and dramatist; author of 'Every Man in his Humour', 'Every Man out of his Humour', 'Volpone', 'The Devil is an Ass', etc.

Jonson², Cornelis: see JOHNSON².

Joram: see JEHORAM.

Jordaens (yŏr'dahns), Jacob (1593–1678). Flemish painter.

Jŏr'dan 1. River flowing southward from Anti-Lebanon mountains through Sea of Galilee and into Dead Sea. 2. Short for *Hashemite Kingdom of the* ~, Arab State east of the river Jordan, bordered by Israel, Syria, Iraq, and Saudi Arabia; capital, Amman. **Jŏrdā'nian** *adj.* & *n.*

Jŏr'dan a'lmond (ahm-). Fine

The Queen's House, Greenwich: by INIGO JONES

almond, esp. from Malaga. [Fr. or Sp. *jardin* garden]

Jŏ'rrocks, John. Character in the novels of R. S. Surtees (1805–64); city grocer and sportsman.

jôr'um *n.* Large drinking-bowl; its contents, esp. punch.

Jos. *abbrev.* Joseph.

Jō'sėph[1] (-z-). Name of several persons in the Bible, esp.: 1. Son of Jacob and Rachel; sold by his brothers into captivity in Egypt, where he attained high office (Gen. 30–50). 2. Carpenter of Nazareth, betrothed to MARY[1] at the time of the Annunciation. 3. ~ *of Arimathea*, Jew who buried Jesus Christ in a rock-hewn tomb; acc. to legend he afterwards led a mission to England and built the first Christian church at GLASTONBURY.

Jō'sėph[2] (-z-). Name of 2 Holy Roman Emperors; *Joseph I* (1678–1711), reigned 1705–11; *Joseph II* (1741–90), eldest son of Maria Theresa, reigned 1765–90.

Jō'sėphine (-z-, -ēn). Marie Rose Joséphine Tascher de la Pagerie (1763–1814), a Creole of Martinique; wife of Vicomte Alexander Beauharnais (guillotined in 1794) and subsequently (1796) of Napoleon Bonaparte; empress of the French from 1804 until divorced 'for reasons of state' in 1809.

Jōsē'phus, Flavius (*c* 37–*c* 95). Jewish statesman and soldier who became a Roman citizen; wrote, in Greek, a history of the Jews.

Josh. *abbrev.* Joshua.

Jŏ'shūa. Successor of Moses in leadership of Israel; 6th book of O.T., telling how he conquered the land of Canaan.

Jōsī'ah (-*a*) (647–*c* 608 B.C.). King of Judah; carried out complete religious reform based on a book of law (app. Deuteronomy) found in the Temple.

jŏss *n.* Chinese idol; *~-house*, Chinese temple; *~-stick*, stick of fragrant gum mixed with clay, burned as incense in Chinese temples. [app. f. Port. *deos* f. L *deus* god]

jŏ'sser *n.* (slang) Fool; fellow.

jŏ'stle (-sl) *v.* Knock or push (*against* etc.); elbow; struggle *with*. ~ *n.* Jostling.

jŏt[1] *n.* (usu. with negative) Small amount, whit. [Gk *iota*, letter i, smallest in alphabet]

jŏt[2] *v.t.* Write (*down*) briefly or hastily. **jŏ'tter** *n.* Memorandum-pad.

Jö'tun (yō'tōōn) *n.pl.* (Scand. myth.) Giants, enemies of the gods. **Jö'tunheim** (-ām). Mountainous region of S. Norway, legendary abode of the Jötun.

Joule[1] (jōōl), James Prescott (1818–89). English physicist, who established the universal constant of proportionality between mechanical work and heat.

joule[2] (jōōl) *n.* (phys.) Unit of

work or energy in M.K.S. system, amount of work done or heat generated by a force of 1 newton acting over a distance of 1 metre (abbrev. J); energy of 1 watt acting for 1 second. [f. JOULE[1]]

jounce *v.* Bump, bounce, jolt.

jour'nal (jẽr-) *n.* 1. (in book-keeping by double entry) Book in which each transaction is entered, with statement of accounts to which it is to be debited and credited. 2. Diary; record of daily transactions of public body or association; (naut.) log-book; newspaper, other periodical. 3. Part of shaft or axle that rests on bearings; *~-box,* box enclosing journal and bearings.

journalē'se (jẽr-, -z) *n.* Journalists' English, reputedly of loose construction and artificial style.

jour'nalĭst (jẽr-). *n.* One whose business it is to edit or write for a newspaper or other public journal. **jour'nalĭsm** *n.* **journalĭ'stic** *adj.*

jour'nalīze (jẽr-) *v.* Enter in journal; record in, keep, private journal.

jour'ney (jẽr-) *n.* & *v.i.* Travel from one place to another, esp. by land or air (dist. from *voyage*); (make) expedition to some distance.

jour'neyman (jẽrnĭ-) *n.* Qualified mechanic or artisan who works for another; (fig.) mere hireling; (also *~ clock*) secondary clock in observatory, used as intermediary in comparison of standard clocks; in electric time-circuit, clock controlled by master-clock.

joust (*or* -ōō-), **jŭst**[1] *v.i.* & *n.* (Engage in) combat between two knights etc. on horseback with lances.

Jōve. (Rom. myth.) = JUPITER.

jō'vĭal *adj.* Merry; convivial; **jō'vĭallȳ** *adv.* **jōvĭă'lĭtȳ** *n.* [L *jovialis* of Jupiter]

Jow'ėtt (*or* jō-), Benjamin (1817–93). English classical scholar; master of Balliol College and regius professor of Greek at Oxford.

jowl *n.* Jawbone, jaw, cheek; external throat or neck when prominent, dewlap of cattle, crop of bird; head and shoulders of salmon and other fish.

joy *n.* Vivid emotion of pleasure, gladness; thing that causes delight; *~-ride,* (slang) stolen or other pleasure-ride in motor-car etc.; *joy'-stick,* (slang) control-lever of aeroplane. **joy'ful** *adj.* **joy'fullȳ** *adv.* **joy'fulnėss** *n.* **joy'lėss** *adj.* **joy'lėsslȳ** *adv.* **joy'lėssnėss** *n.* **joy'ous** *adj.* **joy'ouslȳ** *adv.* **joy'ousnėss** *n.*

Joyce, James (1882–1941). Irish poet and novelist; principally known for his novels 'Ulysses' (1922) and 'Finnegans Wake' (1939), written in a highly allusive style employing esp. the stream-of-consciousness technique.

J.P. *abbrev.* Justice of the Peace.

jr *abbrev.* Junior.

Jū'an Fernă'ndĕz. Small group of islands in S. Pacific, off coast of Chile, discovered 1563 by a Spanish pilot, Juan Fernandez; Alexander SELKIRK was marooned there in 1704.

Ju'bal (jōō-). Son of Lamech and Adah and 'father of all such as handle the harp and organ' (Gen. 4: 21).

jubba, -ah: see JIBBA.

ju'bĭlāte (jōō-) *v.i.* Exult, make demonstrations of joy. **ju'bĭlance, jubĭlā'tion** *ns.* **ju'bĭlant** *adj.* **ju'bĭlantlȳ** *adv.*

ju'bĭlee (jōō-) *n.* 1. (Jewish hist.) Year of emancipation and restoration, kept every 50 years, according to Lev. 25; (R.C. Ch.) year of remission from penal consequences of sin, granted formerly at various intervals, now at any time. 2. 50th anniversary as occasion for rejoicing (also *golden ~*); *silver ~,* (celebration of) 25th anniversary, *diamond ~,* of 60th. 3. Season of rejoicing; exultant joy [Heb. *yobel* ram, ram's horn trumpet, jubilee]

Jud. *abbrev.* Judith (Apocr.).

Judae'a (jōō-). Name in Graeco-Roman times for southern part of ancient Palestine, west of the Jordan.

Judah (jōō'd*a*). 1. Hebrew patriarch, son of Jacob and Leah (Gen. 29: 35); powerful tribe of Israel, traditionally descended from him. 2. Southern kingdom of the Hebrews (opp. ISRAEL[1], 3)

JAMES JOYCE

established by this tribe and Benjamin.

Judā'ĭc (jōō-) *adj.* Jewish.

Ju'dāism (jōō-) *n.* 1. Religion of the Jews, based on Mosaic precepts and rabbinic teaching. 2. Jews collectively. **Ju'dāīze** *v.* Follow Jewish customs or rites; make Jewish. **Ju'dāĭst** *n.*

Ju'das[1] (jōō-). (also ~ *Iscariot*) Apostle who betrayed Jesus Christ to the Jews for 30 pieces of silver and afterwards (acc. to Matt. 27) repented and hanged himself; hence, infamous traitor; *~-coloured*, red; *~ kiss*, act of betrayal (from kiss which Judas gave to Jesus as a signal to his captors); *~-tree*, (from legend that Judas hanged himself on tree of this kind) leguminous S. European and Asiatic tree, *Cercis siliquastrum*, with abundant purplish-pink flowers appearing in spring before the leaves; any tree of genus *Cercis*.

Ju'das[2] (jōō-). St. JUDE.

ju'das[3] (jōō-) *n.* Peephole in door. [f. JUDAS[1]]

Ju'das Măccabae'us (jōō-). One of the MACCABEES.

jŭ'dder *v.i.* (of machine etc.) Shake noisily, shudder; (of voice in singing) make rapid changes in intensity during emission of a tone, owing to involuntary variations in vocal tension. *~ n.*

Jude (jōōd), St. One of the twelve Apostles, also called Judas (Luke 6: 16, John 14: 22), called Lebbaeus in Matthew, Thaddaeus in Mark; usu. identified with Jude the brother of James (Jude 1); martyred in Persia with St. Simon; commemorated with St. Simon, 28 Oct.; (*Epistle of*) ~, last epistle of N.T., traditionally ascribed to St. Jude.

Judg. *abbrev.* Judges (O.T.).

jŭdge *n.* 1. Public officer appointed to hear and try cases in court of justice; (of God) supreme arbiter; person appointed to decide dispute or contest; person who decides a question; person who is qualified to decide on merits of thing or question; *J~ Advocate General*, civil officer in supreme control of courts martial; *Judges' Rules*, set of rules concerning the admissibility in evidence of an accused person's statements and his answers to police questioning; 2. (Heb. hist.) Officer having temporary authority in Israel in period between Joshua and the kings; (*Book of*) *Judges*, 7th book of O.T., containing history of this period. *~ v.* 1. Pronounce sentence on (person) in court of justice; try (cause); decide (question); decide, decree; form a judgement (*of*). 2. (Heb. hist.) Have authority as judge.

jŭdgemă'tĭc -ĭcal (-jm-) *adjs.* (colloq.) Judicious, discerning. **jŭdgemă'tĭcallў** *adv.*

jŭ'dgement (-jm-), **jŭ'dgment.** *n.* 1. Sentence of court of justice; misfortune viewed as sign of divine displeasure; *Last J~*, final trial of subjects of God's moral government at end of world; *J~ day*, day of Last Judgement; *~ debt*, debt for payment of which a judgement has been given; *~ debtor*, debtor against whom judgement has been given; *~ summons*, summons for failure to pay judgement debt; *~-seat*, judge's seat; tribunal. 2. Criticism; opinion, estimate; critical faculty, discernment; good sense.

ju'dĭcature (jōō-) *n.* Administration of justice; judge's (term of) office; body of judges; court of justice; *Supreme Court of J~ in England*, that constituted by Acts of 1873 and 1875 and uniting Courts of Chancery, Queen's (King's) Bench, Common Pleas, Exchequer, Admiralty, etc.

judicial (jōōdĭ'sh*a*l) *adj.* Of, done by, proper to, a court of law; (theol.) inflicted as a divine judgement; having the function of judgement; of, proper to, a judge; expressing a judgement, critical; impartial; *~ murder*, legal but unjust sentence of death. **judĭ'ciallў** *adv.*

judiciary (jōōdĭ'sh*a*rĭ) *n.* Judges of a State collectively.

judicious (jōōdĭ'sh*u*s) *adj.* Sensible, prudent; sound in discernment. **judĭ'ciouslў** *adv.* **judĭ'ciousnėss** *n.*

Ju'dĭth (jōō-). Rich Israelite widow who saved the town of Bethulia from Nebuchadnezzar's army by captivating the besieging general Holofernes and cutting off his head while he slept; (*Book of*) ~, book of O.T. Apocrypha recounting this.

ju'dō (jōō-) *n.* Modern development of JU-JITSU. **judō'ka** *n.* Judo performer. [Jap. *jiu dō*, f. Chin. *jiu tao* soft way]

Ju'dў (jōō-). Wife of PUNCH in 'Punch and Judy'. [dim. of JUDITH]

jŭg[1] *n.* Deep vessel for holding liquids, with handle and usu. spout; (slang) prison. ~ *v.t.* Stew (hare, rabbit) in jug or jar (usu. in past part.); (slang) imprison. **jŭ'gful** *n.*

jŭg[2] *n.* Sound imitative of note of nightingale etc. ~ *v.i.* (of nightingale etc.) Utter jug.

Jŭ'ggernaut (-g-). (also *Jagannath*) Idol of Krishna at Puri, Orissa, annually dragged in procession in an enormous car under whose wheels devotees are said to have thrown themselves; hence (also *j*~; fig.) institution, notion, to which persons blindly sacrifice themselves or others; large overpowering force, object, etc.

jŭ'ggins (-gĭnz) *n.* (slang) Simpleton.

jŭ'ggle *v.* Perform feats of dexterity (*with* objects tossed up); play juggling tricks with; ~ *with*, manipulate, change the relative position of. **jŭ'ggler, jŭ'gglerў** *ns.*

Ju'goslav, Jugosla'vĭa (yōō-goslah-). Varr. of YUGOSLAV(IA).

jŭ'gūlar *adj.* 1. Of the neck or throat; ~ *vein*, any of 4 great veins at sides of neck, an external pair conveying blood from superficial parts of head and an internal pair from inside of skull. 2. (of fish) Having the ventral fin in front of the pectoral. ~ *n.* Jugular vein.

Jugûr'tha (d. 104 B.C.). King of Numidia, captured by Marius; executed at Rome. **Jugûr'thīne** *adj.*

juice (jōōs) *n.* Liquid part of vegetable or fruit; fluid part of animal body or substance; (fig.) essence, spirit, of anything; (slang) electricity, electric current; petrol used in motor-engine. **jui'celėss** *adj.*

jui'cў (jōō-) *adj.* Full of juice, succulent; (colloq.) of rich intellectual quality, interesting. **jui'cĭnėss** *n.*

ju-jĭ'tsu, jiu- (jōō-, -sōō), *n.* Japanese system of wrestling etc., characterized by special holds or tricks. [Jap. *jūjutsu*, f. Chin. *jiu shu(t)* soft art]

ju-ju (jōō'jōō) *n.* (W. Afr.) Charm or fetish; supernatural power attributed to this.

ju'jube (jōō'jōōb) *n.* Edible acid berry-like drupe of certain plants; thorny plant (*Zizyphus*) of S. Europe and Asia bearing this; sweet of gelatine etc. flavoured with or imitating this.

ju'ke-bŏx (jōō-) *n.* Machine that automatically plays selected records when a coin is inserted.

ju'lėp (jōō-) *n.* Sweet drink, esp. as vehicle for medicine; (U.S.) mixture of spirit with sugar, ice, and flavouring, usu. mint. [Pers. *gulāb* (*gul* rose, *āb* water)]

Ju'lĭan[1] (jōō-) (332–63). Flavius Claudius Julianus, Roman emperor 361–3; called Julian the Apostate because, though brought up as a Christian, he reverted to the worship of the old gods and tried to revive it.

Ju'lĭan[2] (jōō-) *adj.* Of Julius Caesar; ~ *calendar*, reformed calendar introduced by him in 46 B.C. and slightly modified under Augustus, in which ordinary year has 365 days, and every 4th year is a leap year of 366 days (see also GREGORIAN).

juliĕ'nne (jōō- *or* zhōō-) *n.* Soup of shredded carrots and other vegetables cooked in meat broth.

Ju'lĭėt (jōō-). Heroine of Shakespeare's play 'Romeo and Juliet'; ~ *cap*, small network skull-cap, usu. adorned with pearls.

Ju'lĭus (jōō-). Name of three popes: *Julius I*, St., pope 337–52, upholder of Athanasius against Arians; *Julius II* (Giuliano della

Rovere, 1433–1513), pope 1503–13, statesman and patron of art; laid foundation-stone of St. Peter's; restored papal states to the Church; suppressed nepotism and carried out many reforms; *Julius III* (Giovanni Maria del Monte, 1487–1555), pope 1550–5.

Ju'lius Cae'sar (jo͞o-, sēz-). Gaius Julius Caesar (prob. 101–44 B.C.), Roman general and statesman; became quaestor in Spain, 68 B.C.; formed 1st TRIUMVIRATE,

59 B.C.; conducted the Gallic Wars from 58 to 49 B.C. and invaded Britain 55 and 54 B.C.; after the death of Crassus he crossed the RUBICON in defiance of the Senate in 49 B.C., and defeated Pompey in civil war, thus becoming dictator; he was murdered on the Ides of March 44 B.C. by a group of nobles, among them BRUTUS[3]; introduced reformed calendar (see JULIAN[2]); his writings include the accounts of the Gallic Wars and the civil war ('De Bello Gallico' and 'De Bello Civili').

Julȳ' (jo͞o-). 7th month of Gregorian (5th of Julian) calendar, with 31 days; ~ *monarchy*, (Fr. hist.) that of Louis Philippe; ~ *revolution*, (Fr. hist.) revolution in July 1830 against Charles X, who fled into exile and was succeeded by Louis Philippe. [f. *Julius* Caesar]

jŭ'mbal, jŭ'mble[1] *n.* (U.S.) Thin crisp sweet cake, flavoured with lemon or almonds and usu. ring-shaped.

jŭ'mble[2] *v.* Move about in disorder; mix *up*, confuse. ~ *n.* Confused assemblage; muddle; jolting; ~ *sale*, sale of miscellaneous cheap or second-hand articles.

jŭ'mbō[1] *n.* Big clumsy person, animal, or thing; ~ *jet*, extremely large jet passenger aircraft.

Jŭ'mbō[2]. Elephant from the London Zoological Gardens, sold in 1882 to P. T. Barnum, Amer. showman.

jŭ'mbŭck *n.* (Austral.) Sheep.

Jŭ'mna. River of N. India, rising in Himalayas and flowing into Ganges below Allahabad.

jŭmp *n.* Leap, bound, spring from ground; start caused by shock or excitement; abrupt rise in amount, price, value, etc.; sudden transition, gap in series, argument, etc.; (pl., colloq.) state of nervous excitement; delirium tremens. ~ *v.* 1. Spring from ground etc. by flexion and sudden muscular extension of legs or (of fish) tail; move suddenly with leap or bound; start with sudden jerk from excitement, shock, etc.; rise suddenly in price, etc.; come *to*, arrive *at* (conclusion) hastily; ~ *at*, accept (offer, bargain) eagerly; ~ *on*, attack (offender etc.) crushingly with word or act; ~ *to it*, act smartly or promptly. 2. Agree, coincide (together, one *with* another). 3. Leap over; (of moving train) leave the rails; help (child etc.) to jump *down* etc.; cause to jump; pass one piece *over* another in draughts etc., capturing it; startle (person, nerves); (U.S.) get on or off (train etc.) quickly, esp. without permission. 4. Pounce upon (thing); steal a march on; take summary possession of (claim abandoned or forfeited by former occupant); ~ *the gun*, make premature start; ~ *the queue*, take precedence of others waiting. 5. Flatten, thicken, etc., end of iron rail or bar by end-wise blows; drill (rock etc.) with jumper. 6. *ju'mping-wire*, wire to prevent submarine fouling obstructions.

jŭ'mpȳ *adj.* (esp.) In a state of

nervous excitement. **jŭ'mpĭlȳ** *adv.* **jŭ'mpĭnėss** *n.*

jŭ'mper[1] *n.* (esp.) Heavy drill worked by hand or with hammer, for making blasting-holes in rock etc.

jŭ'mper[2] *n.* Loose outer jacket of canvas etc. worn by sailors etc.; upper part of naval rating's uniform; woman's knitted pullover.

jun., junr., *abbrev.* Junior.

jŭ'nction *n.* Joining; joint, meeting-place; esp., station where railway lines meet and unite.

jŭ'ncture *n.* Joining; place where things join; concurrence of events, state of affairs.

June (jo͞on). 6th month of Gregorian (4th of Julian) calendar, with 30 days. [L, prob. orig. f. goddess *Juno*]

Jung (yo͝ong), Carl Gustav (1875–1961). Swiss psychologist; orig. a follower of Freud; later founded school of analytical psychology, differing from psychoanalysis in its use of the concepts of unconscious and libido and in its advocacy of a complex classification of types of personality. **Ju'ngĭan** *adj.*

Jungfrau (yo͞o'ngfrow). Mountain in Swiss Alps (4158 m, 13,642 ft). [Ger., = 'maiden']

jŭ'nglė (-nggl) *n.* Land overgrown with underwood or tangled vegetation, esp. as home of wild beasts; wild tangled mass; *~-fever*, severe form of malarial fever. [Hind. *jangal* desert, forest]

ju'nĭor (jo͞o-) *adj.* Younger (esp. of son having same name as father); of less standing, of lower position; (U.S.) belonging to year below senior; ~ *miss*: see MISS[2]. ~ *n.* Junior person, esp. barrister who has not taken silk; in U.S., (used as form of address to) male child.

ju'nĭorate (jo͞o-) *n.* (in Society of Jesus) Two years' course attended by junior members before entering priesthood.

ju'nĭper (jo͞o-) *n.* Evergreen shrub of genus *Juniperus*, esp. common European species (*J. communis*) with prickly leaves and dark purplish berries of pungent taste; *oil of* ~, volatile oil obtained from juniper berries, used as diuretic etc. and in manufacture of gin.

Ju'nĭus (jo͞o-). Pseudonym of author of series of letters (1769–71) in the 'Public Advertiser', bitterly and abusively attacking many public men.

jŭnk[1] *n.* Old cable cut up for oakum etc.; discarded material, worthless rubbish; (naut.) salt meat; *~-shop*, (esp.) second-hand dealer's shop.

jŭnk[2] *n.* Flat-bottomed sailing vessel of China seas, with square

prow, prominent stem, and lugsails. [app. f. Javanese *djong*]

ju'nker (yo͞o-) *n.* (hist.) Young German noble; narrow-minded, overbearing member of (Prussian) aristocracy.

jŭ'nkėt *n.* Dish of sweetened and flavoured curds, freq. with scalded cream on top; feast, outing. ~ *v.i.* Feast, go on outing. **jŭ'nkėtĭng** *n.*

jŭ'nkĭe *n.* (slang) Drug addict.

Ju'nō (jo͞o-). 1. (Rom. myth.) Chief Roman goddess, consort of Jupiter; worshipped esp. by women; identified with HERA. 2. (astron.) One of the asteroids. **Junōĕ'sque** (-k) *adj.* Resembling Juno in stately beauty.

jŭ'nta *n.* Deliberative or administrative council in Spain or Italy; (also *jŭ'ntō*) clique, faction, political or other combination of persons.

Ju'pĭter (jo͞o-). 1. (Rom. myth.) Orig. a sky-spirit, associated with lightning and thunderbolt; later, the chief of the gods, giver of victory, identified with ZEUS. 2. (astron.) Largest planet in solar system, revolving in orbit between those of Mars and Saturn, and with 4 large and several smaller satellites.

Jura[1] (joor'*a*). System of mountain ranges between rivers Rhine and Rhone forming the frontier between France and Switzerland.

Jura[2] (joor'*a*) Island, one of the inner Hebrides, on W. coast of Argyllshire.

jur'al (joor-) *adj.* Of law; of (moral) rights and obligations.

Jurǎ'ssic (joor-) *adj.* & *n.* (geol.) (Of) the middle period or system of the Mesozoic. [f. JURA[1]]

jur'at (joor-) *n.* Municipal officer (esp. in Cinque Ports) like alderman; in Jersey and Guernsey an honorary judge; in Alderney, an honorary magistrate.

juridical (joor-) *adj.* Of judicial proceedings; legal.

jur'isconsŭ'lt (joor-) *n.* One learned in law, jurist.

jurisdi'ction (joor-) *n.* Administration of justice; legal or other authority; extent of this, territory it extends over. **jurisdi'ctional** *adj.*

jurispru'dence (joor-, -rōō-) *n.* Science, philosophy, of human law; skill in law. **jurispru'dent, jurisprudĕ'ntial** (-sh*a*l) *adjs.*

jur'ist (joor-) *n.* One versed in law; legal writer; student of, graduate in, law. **juri'stic, -ical** *adjs.* Of jurist(s); legal, created by law. **juri'sticallў** *adv.*

jur'or (joor-) *n.* Member of jury; one who takes an oath.

jury (joor'ĭ) *n.* 1. Body of persons sworn to render verdict on question submitted to them in court of justice; *common, petty, trial,* ~, jury of twelve persons who try final issue of fact in civil or criminal cases and pronounce their decision in a verdict on which court gives judgement; *coroner's* ~, jury of persons who pronounce decision at coroner's inquest; *grand* ~, (formerly) jury appointed to inquire into indictments before they were submitted to trial jury (abolished 1933); ~*-box,* enclosure for jury in court; *jur'yman,* member of jury. 2. Body of persons judging competition etc.

jury-mast (joor'ĭmahst) *n.* Temporary mast in place of broken or lost one.

Jussieu (zhūsyẽr). Name of a family of French botanists, including *Bernard de* ~ (*c* 1699–1777), and his nephew *Antoine Laurent de* ~ (1748–1836), who developed the classificatory system on which modern natural classification is based.

jŭ'ssive *adj.* & *n.* (gram.) (Word, form, etc.) expressing a command.

just[1]: see JOUST.

jŭst[2] *adj.* Equitable, fair; deserved; well-grounded; right in amount etc., proper. **jŭ'stlў** *adv.* **jŭ'stnėss** *n.*

jŭst[3] *adv.* Exactly; barely; exactly at that moment; (loosely) not long before; (colloq.) positively, quite; ~ *now,* at this moment; a little time ago.

jŭ'stice *n.* 1. Just conduct; fairness; exercise of authority in maintenance of right; judicial proceedings; *poetic(al)* ~, ideal justice as shown in poem etc.; *do* ~ *to,* treat fairly; show due appreciation of; *do oneself* ~, perform worthily of one's abilities. 2. Judge, esp. (in Engl.) of Supreme Court of Judicature; *J~-Clerk,* vice-president of Scottish Court of Justiciary; *J~ of the Peace,* (abbrev. J.P.) lay magistrate appointed to preserve peace in county, town, etc.

jŭsti'ciable (-shĭ*a*-) *adj.* Subject to jurisdiction.

jŭsti'ciar (-shy*ar*) *n.* Chief political and judicial officer under Norman and early Plantaganet kings.

jŭsti'ciarў (-shy*a*-) *n.* Administration, administrator, of justice. ~ *adj.* Of the administration of justice.

jŭ'stifў *v.t.* 1. Show the justice or rightness of; vindicate, be such as to justify; make good (statement etc.); adduce adequate grounds for. 2. (theol.) Declare (person) free from penalty of sin on ground of

Christ's righteousness or (R.C. Ch.) of the infusion of grace. 3. (print.) Adjust (line of type) to fill a space neatly. **jŭ'stĭfīable, jŭ'stĭfĭcātĭve, jŭ'stĭfĭcātorȳ** *adjs.* **jŭ'stĭfīablȳ** *adv.* **jŭstĭfĭcā'tion** *n.*

Jŭ'stĭn. Name of two Eastern Roman emperors: *Justin I* (450–527), emperor 518–27; left administration almost entirely to his quaestor Proclus and his nephew JUSTINIAN I; *Justin II* (d. 578), emperor 565–78; nephew and successor of JUSTINIAN I.

Jŭstĭ'nĭan. Name of two eastern Roman emperors: *Justinian I*

(483–565), emperor 527–65; reorganized and codified Roman law; built church of St. Sophia at Constantinople; his great general Belisarius recovered Africa from Vandals, occupied Rome, and overthrew the Gothic kingdom in Italy; *Justinian II* (669–711), emperor 685–95 and 704–11.

Jŭ'stĭn Mar'tyr (*-er*), St. (*c* 100–*c* 165). Syrian Christian apologist; martyred in Rome; commemorated 14 April.

jŭt *n.* Projection; protruding point. ~ *v.i.* Project.

jute[1] (jo͞ot) *n.* Fibre from bark of plants *Corchorus capsularis* and *C. olitorius*, imported chiefly from Bengal, used for cordage, canvas, etc. [Sansk. *juṭa, jaṭa* braid of hair]

Jute[2] (jo͞ot) *n.* Member of a Low German tribe that invaded Britain in 5th c. and settled in Kent, Isle of Wight, and parts of Hampshire. [Icel. *Iótar* people of Jutland]

Jŭ'tland. Peninsula which forms the continental part of Denmark; *Battle of* ~, inconclusive battle in the North Sea W. of Jutland, May 1916, between the British Grand Fleet under Jellicoe and the German High Seas Fleet under Scheer.

Ju'vėnal (jo͞o-). Decimus Junius Juvenalis (*c* A.D. 60–*c* 130), Roman satirist and poet.

juvėnĕ'scence (jo͞o-) *n.* (Transition from infancy to) youth. **juvėnĕ'scent** *adj.*

ju'vėnīle (jo͞o-) *adj.* Young, youthful; suited to, characteristic of, youth; ~ *lead*, (theatr.) youthful hero's part in play; actor who takes this. ~ *n.* 1. Young person. 2. (trade, usu. pl.) Book for children. **juvėnĭ'litȳ** *n.*

juvėnĭ'lia (jo͞o-) *n.pl.* Literary or artistic works produced in youth.

jŭ'xtapōse (-z) *v.t.* Place (things) side by side. **jŭxtaposĭ'tion** *n.* Placing, being placed, side by side.

K

K, k (kā). 11th letter of modern English alphabet, taken from Gk κ (*kappa*), orig. 𐤊, from Phoenician and general Semitic 𐤊 (*Kaph*); pronounced in modern English as a voiceless stop consonant; in early Latin orthography *c* was used for this sound, and *k* fell largely into disuse; in modern English, *k* is used in native words before *e, i, y* (when *c* would normally be pronounced as *s*), and *n*, and medially and finally after a consonant or long vowel.

k *abbrev.* Kilo-.

K *abbrev.* Kelvin(s).

K2. Peak of the W. Himalayas, 8,611 m (28,250 ft) high; believed to be the second highest in the world; also known as Godwin Austen.

Ka (kah) *n.* Ancient Egyptian name for second self or double, surviving with soul after death.

Kaaba: see CAABA.

kabŏ'b *n.* = KEBAB.

Kabul (kah'bo͞ol). Capital city and province of Afghanistan; ~ *River*, chief river of Afghanistan, flowing into Indus.

Kabȳ'le *n.* Member, language, of Berber tribe of Algeria, Morocco, and Tunis.

Kă'ddĭsh *n.* Doxology recited during synagogue service and by mourners. [Aram. *ḳaddīš* holy]

kadi: *see* CADI.

Kă'ffir, Kă'fir[1], Că'ffre (-f*er*) *n.* (now derog.) Bantu inhabitant of southern Africa; *k*~, kaffir corn; ~ *bread*, farinaceous pith of a bread-fruit (*Encephalartos caffer* and related species); the plant itself; ~ *corn*, kind of sorghum native to E. Africa and cultivated in south-western U.S. and other dry regions for grain and forage; ~ *lily*, S. Afr. herbaceous plant (*Clivia miniata*) with showy flowers. [Arab. *kāfir* infidel]

kaffiyeh: see KEFFIYEH.

Kafir[2] (kah'fēr) *n.* Member of a small group of tribes of NE. Afghanistan, prob. of Iranian origin, speaking an Indo-European language.

Kă'fka, Franz (1883–1924). Austrian novelist, born in Prague; author of 'The Trial', 'The Castle' and 'America'. **Kăfkaĕ'sque** (-ĕsk) *adj.* Resembling esp. the nightmare quality of Kafka's writings.

kail: see KALE.

Kai'ser[1] (kīz-) *n.* Emperor; (hist.) German emperor; emperor of Austria; head of Holy Roman Empire; *the* ~: see WILLIAM[3].

Kai'ser[2] (kīz-), Georg (1878–1939). German expressionist dramatist; author of 'Die Bürger von Calais', 'Von Morgens bis Mitternachts', etc.

kăkėmō'nō *n.* Japanese vertical hanging scroll mounted on rollers, containing either text or painting on silk or paper. [Jap. *kake* hang, *mono* thing]

kala-azar' (kah-) *n.* Disease found in tropical and subtropical areas, due to the protozoan parasite *Leishmania donovani.*

Kălahâr'i Dĕ'sert (-l*a*h-, -z-). Large high barren plateau of S. Africa, north of Orange River; mainly in Botswana.

kāle, kail *n.* Variety of cabbage with wrinkled leaves not forming compact head (*Brassica oleracea acephala*); broth made with Scotch kale; (Sc.) vegetable broth; *curly* ~, kale with very much curled green leaves; *Scotch* ~, variety with purplish, less wrinkled leaves; *ka'leyard*, (Sc.) kitchen-garden of cottage etc.; *kaleyard school*, writers of fiction describing common life in Scotland, with much use of vernacular, e.g. J. M. Barrie, 'Ian Maclaren', and S. R. Crockett.

kalei'doscōpe (-lī-) *n.* Tube through which are seen symmetrical figures, produced by reflections of pieces of coloured glass, and varied by rotation of tube; (fig.) constantly changing group of bright objects. **kaleidoscŏ'pĭc, -ĭcal** *adjs.*

kalends: see CALENDS.

Ka'levala (kahlĭvah-). Finnish national epic, compiled from popular lays of great antiquity transmitted orally until 19th c. [Finnish, = 'land of heroes']

kă'lĭ[1] *n.* Prickly saltwort, glasswort (*Salsola kali*), from which potash was obtained.

Kali[2] (kah'lē). (Hindu myth.)

KALI

Form of Durga, the bloodthirsty wife of Siva, represented with black body, four arms, necklace of human heads, and protruding bloodstained tongue.

Kalida'sa (kahlēdah-) (prob. 3rd c. A.D.). Indian poet and dramatist of second epoch of Sanskrit literature.

Kali'nĭn (-lē-), Mikhail Ivanovich (1875–1946). Russian peasant statesman, president of U.S.S.R. 1923–46.

Kă'lmŭck *n.* 1. Member of Buddhist Mongol people of central Asia who invaded Russia in 16th and 17th centuries and settled along lower Volga; many migrated to Chinese Turkestan in 18th c., but descendants of Kalmucks of the western Volga still inhabit western steppes. 2. Language of the Kalmucks, one of the Ural-Altaic family.

ka'lŏng (kah-) *n.* Malay flying-fox or fruit-eating bat (*Pteropus vampyrus*), the largest of the bats, having a wing-spread of up to 1·5m.

kă'lpa *n.* (Hindu cosmology) A great age of the world; the period beginning with the origin of a world and extending beyond its dissolution to the origin of a new world.

Ka'ma, Kamade'va (kah-; -dā-). (Hindu myth.) God of love, represented as a beautiful youth riding on a sparrow and armed with bow and arrows.

Kămchă'tka. Peninsula of NE. Asia running southwards between Bering Sea and Sea of Okhotsk; province of R.S.F.S.R.

kāme *n.* Ridge of sand and gravel built up of debris carried by water from a decaying glacier and deposited near its edge.

kămera'd (-ahd) *int.* 'Comrade', German soldier's appeal for quarter; hence (joc.) plea for mercy.

kami'z, -s (-ēz) *n.* Long straight tunic worn over shalwar in some S. Asian countries.

Kană'ka (*or* -nah-) *n.* Native of South Sea Islands, esp. one formerly shipped for forced labour to Australia. [Hawaiian, = 'man']

Kănarē'se, C- (-z) *adj.* & *n* (Native, inhabitant, Dravidian language) of Kanara in W. India.

kăngarōō' (-ngg-) *n.* Marsupial of genus *Macropus* with strongly developed hind-quarters and great leaping-power, native of Australia, Tasmania, etc.; ~ *closure*, form of Parliamentary closure by which some amendments are selected for discussion and others excluded;

~ *court*, self-constituted court held by strikers, mutineers, etc.; ~-*rat* or *rat* ~, small Austral. marsupial belonging to any of several genera, esp. *Potorous* and *Bettongia*; also, Amer. pouched rodent (*Dipodomys*) of SW. States and Mexico.

Kăngchĕnjŭ'nga (-ngg*a*; *or* -chĭn-). Himalayan peak, 8,598 m (28,146 ft) high; believed to be third highest in the world.

Kans. *abbrev.* Kansas.

Kă'nsas (*or* -z-). State in central U.S., admitted to the Union in 1861; capital, Topeka; ~ *City*, large city on right bank of river Missouri, divided between States of Missouri and Kansas; ~ *River*, river draining N. part of Kansas State and flowing eastwards into river Missouri. **Kă'nsan** *adj.* Of Kansas; ~ *age*, second epoch of glacial period in N. America, deposits of which are found in Kansas State.

Kansu (kah'nsōō'). Extreme NW. province of China.

Kănt, Immanuel (1724–1804). German metaphysician, founder of school of transcendental philosophy, of which one of the fundamental principles is that knowledge of the external world depends upon sense-impressions co-ordinated or synthesized by the reason, employing such 'categories' or laws of thought as quality, quantity, causation, etc. **Kă'ntian** *adj.* & *n.*

kā'olin *n.* China clay, a fine white clay formed by the decomposition and weathering of felspar in granite, in Gt Britain found esp. in Cornwall; used in making porcelain, as a filler for paper and textiles, in medical treatment, etc. [Chin. *kao-ling* high hill (mountain where orig. obtained)]

kapĕ'llmeister (-mī-) *n.* Conductor of orchestra or choir. [Ger.]

kā'pŏk *n.* = SILK cotton from tree *Ceiba pentandra*. [Malay *kapoq*]

kă'ppa *n.* 11th (later 10th) letter of Greek alphabet (*K*, *κ*), corresponding to *k*.

kapu't (-pōōt) *adj.* (slang) Finished, done for. [Ger.]

Kara'chĭ (-rah-). Seaport and former capital of Pakistan, on an inlet of the Arabian Sea.

Karadzić (-ah'zhich), Vuk Stefanović (1787–1864). Serbian author, grammarian, and lexicographer; 'father' of modern Serbian literature.

Karageorge, Karadjordje (kah'r*a*jor'jē), Czerny George (*c* 1766–1817). Serbian peasant and patriot; leader of Serbs in struggle against Turkey and founder of *Karageorgevich* dynasty of Serbia.

Kar'aīte, Qar- (k-) *n.* Member of Jewish sect, chiefly of Crimea etc., founded 8th c., rejecting rabbinical tradition and basing its tenets on literal interpretation of scriptures. [Heb. *ḳārā'îm* (*mikrâ* the Bible)]

Karakor'am. Mountain region lying to the N. of the W. end of the Himalayas.

Kar'a Kum (kōōm). Flat desert region of Turkmenistan.

Kăramzi'n (-ahmzēn), Nikolay Mikhailovich (1765–1826). Russian historian and novelist.

Kar'a Sea. Shallow part of Arctic Ocean between Novaya Zemlya and Siberian mainland.

kara'tė (-rah-) *n.* Japanese system of unarmed combat using hands etc. as weapons.

Karē'lia. 1. Area of north-west U.S.S.R. between Finnish border and White Sea. 2. Autonomous republic of R.S.F.S.R.; capital, Petrozavodsk. **Karē'lian** *adj.*

Kar'lsbăd (-z-). German name of *Karlovy Vary*, town in Czechoslovakia; ~ *salts*, aperient salts obtained from its mineral springs.

kar'ma *n.* (Buddhism, Hinduism) Sum of person's actions in one of his successive states of existence viewed as deciding his fate in the next; destiny.

Kar'nak. Village of Upper Egypt, on Nile near Luxor, containing magnificent ruins of temple of Ammon on site of ancient Thebes.

Karrōō', Karōō' *n.* Elevated barren plateau of clayey soil in S. Africa, waterless in dry season.

karst *n.* Barren limestone formation with abrupt ridges, caverns, and underground streams. [*Karst*, limestone plateau in NW. Yugoslavia].

Kăshmir' (-mēr). = JAMMU AND KASHMIR. **Kăshmir'ī** *n.* Indo-European language of Kashmir, much influenced by Sanskrit.

KARNAK : Granite Columns

kă'tathermŏ'mėter *n.* Instrument which records the rate of cooling of air and evaporation of moisture from the body.

Kă'trīne, Loch. Freshwater lake in Scotland, E. of Loch Lomond.

Kă'ttėgăt. Channel between Denmark and Sweden, running from Skagerrak southwards towards Baltic Sea.

kā'tȳdĭd *n.* (U.S.) Any of several large green long-horned grasshoppers, producing characteristic noise by stridulation, common in central and eastern U.S. [imit.]

Kau'ffmann (kow-), Angelica (1741–1807). Painter, of Swiss origin, active in England.

kau'rī (kow-) *n.* Coniferous tree of New Zealand (*Agathis australis*), furnishing valuable timber and a resin (~-*gum*).

ka'va (kah-) *n.* (Intoxicating beverage prepared from macerated roots of) Polynesian shrub, *Piper methysticum*.

kay'ak (kī-) *n.* Eskimo one-man canoe of light wooden framework covered with sealskins; small boat resembling this.

Kaza'kh (-ahk) *n.* Member of a Turkic people of S. Siberia.

Kazakhsta'n (-ahkstahn). Constituent republic of U.S.S.R.; capital, Alma-Ata.

K.B. *abbrev.* King's Bench.

K.B.E. *abbrev.* Knight Commander (of the Order) of the British Empire.

kc *abbrev.* Kilocycle(s).

K.C. *abbrev.* King's College; King's Counsel; Knight(s) of Columbus.

K.C.B., K.C.I.E., K.C.M.G., K.C.S.I., K.C.V.O. *abbrevs.* Knight Commander (of the Order) of the Bath, (of the Order) of the Indian Empire, (of the Order) of St. Michael and St. George, (of the Order) of the Star of India, of the (Royal) Victorian Order.

kea (kā'*a*) *n.* Green parrot (*Nestor notabilis*) of a group peculiar to the New Zealand region, normally living on fruit, grubs, and carrion, but said to attack sheep when pressed by hunger.

JOHN KEATS

Kean, Edmund (1787–1833). English tragic actor.

Keats, John (1795–1821). English lyric poet; author of 'Endymion', the odes 'On a Grecian Urn', 'To a Nightingale', 'To Autumn', etc.

kėba'b (-ahb) *n.* (usu. pl.) Oriental dish of small pieces of mutton seasoned and grilled on skewer.

Kē'ble, John (1792–1866). English divine; a founder of the Oxford or TRACTARIAN movement; writer of sacred verse.

kĕck *v.i.* Make sound as if about to vomit.

Kĕ'dah (*-a*). State of Malaysia; capital, Alor Star.

Kē'dar. Son of ISHMAEL (Gen. 25: 13), whose descendants were a tribe of nomads identified in later Jewish literature with the Arabs.

kĕdge *v.* (naut.) Change position of a ship by winding in hawser attached to small anchor at some distance; (of ship) move thus; move (ship) thus. ~ *n.* (also *~-anchor*) small anchor for kedging.

kĕ'dgeree *n.* Indian dish of rice, split pulse, onions, eggs, etc.; European dish of fish, rice, eggs, and condiments.

keel[1] *n.* Lowest longitudinal timber of vessel, on which frame work of whole is built up combination of iron plates serving same purpose in iron vessel; (poet.) ship; (in aircraft) vertical fin extending longitudinally underneath; (bot., zool.) carina *~-blocks,* blocks on which keel rests during building etc.; *~'-haul,* haul (person) under keel as punishment. ~ *v.* Turn (ship) keel upwards; ~ *over,* turn, be turned, over, upset, capsize.

keel[2] *n.* Flat-bottomed vessel, esp. of kind used on Tyne etc. for loading colliers; amount carried by this.

Keele. Town in Staffordshire; university, 1962.

Kee'ling I'slands (īlandz): see COCOS ISLANDS.

kee'lson, kĕ'l- *n.* Set of timbers or plates fastening ship's floor-timbers to keel.

keen[1] *n.* Irish funeral song accompanied with wailing. ~ *v.* Utter the keen; bewail (person) thus; utter in wailing tone.

keen[2] *adj.* Having sharp edge or point; sharp; (of sound, light, etc.) penetrating, vivid, strong; (of cold) intense; (of pain etc.) acute, bitter; (of person, desire, interest) eager, ardent (colloq. *on*); (of eyes etc.) sharp, highly sensitive; intellectually acute. **kee'nlȳ** *adv.* **kee'nnėss** *n.*

Keene, Charles Samuel (1823–91). English black-and-white artist, illustrator in 'Punch' etc.

keep[1] *v.* (past t. & past part. *kĕpt*). 1. Pay due regard to, observe, stand by (law, promise, faith, etc.); observe, solemnize (feast etc.). 2. Guard, protect (person, fortress, goal at football etc.); have charge of; maintain in proper form and order; provide for sustenance of, maintain, support; own and manage (animals etc.); maintain (woman) as mistress; have (commodity) habitually on sale. 3. Retain possession of, not lose; maintain, remain, in proper or specified condition; reserve, admit of being reserved (*for* future time etc.); hide, conceal (secret etc.). 4. Detain (person *in prison* etc.); restrain (*from*); refrain *from*. 5. Continue to follow (way, course); remain in (one's bed, room, house); retain one's place in (the saddle, one's ground, etc.) against opposition; remain (indoors etc.); (colloq., esp. Camb. Univ.) reside. 6. ~

house: see HOUSE; ~ *one's feet*, not fall. 7. ~ *at*, work persistently at; ~ *away*, avoid coming; prevent from coming; ~ *back*, hold back, retard progress of, conceal; ~ *down*, hold in subjection; keep low in amount; ~ *in*, confine, restrain, (feelings etc.); confine (schoolboy) after hours; keep (fire) burning; remain indoors; remain on good terms *with*; ~ *one's hand in*: see HAND; ~ *off*, ward off, avert; stay at a distance; ~ *on*, continue to hold, use, show, etc.; continue (*doing*); ~ *oneself to oneself*, avoid society; ~ *out*, not allow to enter; ~ *to*, adhere to, confine oneself to; ~ *to oneself*, refuse to share with others; ~ *together*, remain, cause to remain, together; ~ *under*, hold in subjection; ~ *up*, prevent from sinking; maintain; keep in repair; carry on (correspondence etc.); cause (person) to sit up at night; bear up, not break down; proceed at equal pace *with*; ~ *it up*, not slacken.

keep[2] *n.* 1. (hist.) Tower, stronghold. 2. Maintenance, food required for this. 3. *for ~s*, (orig. U.S.) in permanence.

kee'per *n.* One who keeps, guards, manages, etc.; custodian; gamekeeper; mechanical device for keeping something in place; bar of soft iron placed across poles of magnet to prevent loss of power; fruit, vegetable, that keeps (well or badly).

kee'pĭng *n.* (esp.) 1. Custody, charge. 2. Agreement, harmony. 3. (attrib.) Fit for keeping.

kee'psāke *n.* Thing kept for sake, or in remembrance, of giver.

kee'shŏnd (kās-h-) *n.* Dutch dog with thick curly hair, like large Pomeranian, kept on barges etc.

kĕffi'yeh, kăff- (-fēyā) *n.* Bedouin Arab's kerchief worn as head-dress.

kĕg *n.* Small barrel, usu. of less than 10 gallons.

Kékulé von Stra'donĭtz (kā'-kōōlā fŏn strah-), Friedrich August (1829–96). German organic chemist, formulator of ring structure of benzene.

Kĕlă'ntan. State of Malaysia; capital, Kota Bahru.

kelleck : see KILLICK.

Kĕ'ller[1], Gottfried (1819–90). German-Swiss novelist and poet; author of 'Die Leute von Seldwyla', 'Der Grüne Heinrich', etc.

Kĕ'ller[2], Helen Adams (1880–1968). Amer. author, born in Alabama; became blind and deaf in infancy; was taught to speak, read, and use a typewriter; wrote several books including the story of her life, travelled extensively, and did much for the education of those similarly handicapped.

Kĕ'llŏgg Păct. Treaty renouncing war as an instrument of national policy; signed in Paris, 1928, by representatives of fifteen nations. [F. B. *Kellogg* (1856–1937), U.S. Secretary of State 1924–9]

Kĕlls (-z), Book of. Illuminated MS. of the gospels, now at Trinity College, Dublin; made perh. by Irish monks in Iona in 8th or early 9th c. [f. *Kells*, town in Co. Meath, Ireland, where it was formerly kept]

Kĕ'lmscŏtt Prĕss. Printing-press founded and operated (1891–8) by William Morris. [f. *Kelmscott*, Oxon. village]

kĕlp *n.* (Any of the) large seaweeds which are burnt for the potash, iodine, etc., they contain; calcined ashes of these, formerly used in making soap and glass.

kĕ'lpie, -ў *n.* (Sc.) Water-spirit, usu. in form of horse, reputed to take delight in, or bring about, the drowning of passers-by.

kelson : see KEELSON.

kĕlt *n.* Salmon that has spawned.

Kĕ'lvĭn[1], William Thomson, 1st Baron (1824–1907). Irish-born physicist, professor of Natural Philosophy at Glasgow, who advanced the science of thermodynamics and electricity, improved the system of electrical units, and invented several scientific instruments; ~ *scale*, scale of absolute temperature, in which the zero (corresponding roughly to −273 °C) is the temperature at which a perfect gas would occupy

BOOK OF KELLS (detail)

zero volume if it could be cooled indefinitely, without liquefaction or solidification.

kĕ′lvĭn[2] *n.* Unit of measurement in the Kelvin scale (abbrev. K). [f. KELVIN[1]]

Kemal Pasha: see ATATÜRK.

Kĕ′mble. Name of a family of English actors: *Charles* ~ (1775–1854); *Frances Anne* ('*Fanny*') ~ (1809–93), actress, his daughter; *John Philip* ~ (1757–1823), his brother; *Roger* ~ (1721–1802), actor and manager, father of John and Charles and of Mrs Siddons.

kĕmp *n.* Coarse hair in wool. **kĕ′mpȳ** *adj.*

Kempis, Thomas à: see THOMAS À KEMPIS.

kĕn *n.* Range of sight or knowledge. ~ *v.t.* (now Sc.) Recognize at sight; know.

Kĕ'ndal. Town in Cumbria; ~ *green*, green woollen cloth formerly made there.

Kĕ'nilworth. Market town in Warwickshire, containing ruins of castle begun *c* 1120 and given by Queen Elizabeth I to Earl of Leicester.

Kĕ'nnėdy̆, John Fitzgerald (1917–63). 35th president of U.S., 1961–3; assassinated in 1963.

kĕ'nnel¹ *n.* House, hut, for shelter of house-dog or hounds; place where dogs are bred or boarded (usu. pl.); mean dwelling. ~ *v.* Live in, go to, kennel; put into, keep in, kennel.

kĕ'nnel² *n.* (obs.) Gutter.

Kĕ'nnėth. Name of two Scottish kings: *Kenneth I MacAlpin* (d. *c* 860), traditional founder of kingdom of Scotland; *Kenneth II* (d. 995).

kĕ'nnĭng *n.* Periphrastic expression used instead of simple name of thing in OE, ON, etc., poetry.

Kĕ'nnĭngton. District in Lambeth, S. London, containing ~ *Oval*, Surrey County Cricket Club's ground.

kėnō'sĭs *n.* (theol.) Renunciation of divine nature, at least in part, by Christ in incarnation.

Kĕ'nsĭngton (-z-). Royal borough (with Chelsea) of London; ~ *Gardens*, orig. gardens of Kensington Palace, thrown open to public in 18th c.; ~ *Palace*, built by Heneage Finch, lord chancellor in reign of Charles II, and bought by William III; *South ~ Museum*, British Museum (Natural History).

Kĕ'nsĭt, John (1853–1902). English Protestant agitator, a violent opponent of ritualism. **Kĕ'nsĭtite** *adj.* & *n.* (Follower) of Kensit.

Kĕnt¹. County of SE. England, between S. bank of Thames estuary and E. end of English Channel; a kingdom of Anglo-Saxon England traditionally founded by Hengist and Horsa; university, at Canterbury, 1965; *man of ~*, one born E. of the Medway (as dist. from *Kentish man*, born W. of it). **Kĕ'ntish** *adj.* Of Kent; ~ *man*; see above; ~ *rag*, hard compact limestone found in Kent used for paving and building.

Kĕnt², Edward Augustus, Duke of (1767–1820). 4th son of George III and father of Queen Victoria.

Kĕnt³, William (1684–1748). English painter, sculptor, architect, and landscape-gardener; architect of Horse Guards, Whitehall, and Holkham Hall, Norfolk.

Kĕ'ntigẽrn (-g-), St. (*c* 518–603). British prince; preached Christianity in Strathclyde and became bishop of Cumbria; also called Mungo. [Gael., = 'chief lord' *Mungo* 'dear one']

kĕ'ntlėdge *n.* (naut.) Pig-iron used as permanent ballast.

Kĕntŭ'cky̆. State in east-central U.S., admitted to the Union in 1792; capital, Frankfort; ~ *Derby*, horse-race for 3-year-olds run annually at Louisville, Kentucky, founded 1875.

Kĕ'nya. Country of E. Africa between Ethiopia and Tanzania; member State of the Commonwealth, independent in 1963; capital, Nairobi; *Mt ~*, volcanic mountain in Kenya, just S. of Equator, one of the highest in Africa. **Kĕ'nyan** *adj.* & *n.*

kĕ'pĭ (*or* kā-) *n.* French military cap with horizontal peak.

Kĕ'pler, Johann (1571–1630). German astronomer, whose three laws of planetary motion provided the basis for much of Newton's work.

Kĕ'rala. State of SW. India, constituted 1956; capital, Trivandrum.

kĕ'ratĭn *n.* Protein or group of proteins found in skin, hair, nails, horns, hoofs, and feathers.

kĕ'ratōse *adj.* Having horn-like substance (characteristic of a group of sponges, the Keratosa).

kẽrb *n.* Stone edging to pavement or raised path; *ker'bstone*, one of stones forming this; *kerb(stone) market*, stock-exchange business done in street after closing of exchange.

kẽr'chief (-ĭf) *n.* Cloth used to cover head; (poet.) handkerchief.

Kėrĕ'nsky̆, Alexander Fedorovich (1881–1970). Russian liberal politician; prime minister of 2nd Provisional government until Bolshevik revolution.

kẽrf *n.* Slit made by cutting, esp. with saw; cut end of felled tree.

kerfŭ'ffle *n.* (colloq.) Fuss, commotion.

Kẽr'guelėn (-gĭl-). Desolation Island, uninhabited subantarctic island, belonging to France, in Southern Ocean SE. of Cape of Good Hope and SW. of Australia; discovered (1772) by a Breton navigator, Yves-Joseph de Kerguélen-Trémarec; ~ *cabbage*, cabbage-like plant (*Pringlea antiscorbutica*) peculiar to this island.

kẽr'mės (-z) *n.* Female of insect *Kermes ilicis*, formerly supposed to be a berry, gathered from species of evergreen oak in S. Europe and N. Africa and used in dyeing; red dye-stuff prepared from dried bodies of these; (also ~ *oak*) evergreen oak, *Quercus coccifera*, on which these insects live.

kẽrn[1] *n.* (print.) Part of a metal type projecting beyond the body or shank, as the curled head of *f* and tail of *j*, etc.

kẽrn[2], **kẽrne** *n.* (hist.) Light-armed Irish foot-soldier; peasant, boor.

kẽr'nel *n.* Softer (usu. edible) part within hard shell of nut or stone fruit; whole seed within husk etc., e.g. grain of wheat; nucleus, centre of formation (freq. fig.).

kĕ'rosēne, -ine (-ēn) *n.* Fuel-oil obtained by distillation of petroleum, or from coal or shale, and consisting of mixture of liquid hydrocarbons; paraffin.

Kè'rrȳ. Western county in Munster; hence, one of a breed of very small black dairy cattle produced there; ~ *blue*, Irish breed of terrier, with characteristics of Irish terrier and Irish wolfhound, and silky blue-grey coat.

kẽr'sey (-zĭ) *n.* Kind of coarse narrow cloth, usu. ribbed, woven from long wool. [perh. f. *Kersey* in Suffolk]

kẽr'seymēre (-zĭ-) *n.* Twilled fine woollen cloth; (pl.) trousers of this [corrupt. of *cassimere* CASHMERE, by association with prec.]

kĕ'strel *n.* Species of small falcon (esp. *Falco tinnunculus*) with habit of remaining in same place in air with head to the wind; windhover.

Kĕ'swick (-zĭk) *n.* (also ~ *codlin*) Ribbed green cooking-apple. [town in Cumbria]

kĕtch[1] *n.* Small two-masted or cutter-rigged coasting vessel.

Ketch[2], Jack: see JACK[1].

kĕ'tchup *n.* Sauce made of tomatoes, mushrooms, walnuts, etc., with vinegar, raisins, spices, etc., used as condiment. [prob. f. Chin. *kôe-chiap* brine of pickled fish]

kē'tône *n.* (chem.) One of a group of organic compounds containing carbonyl group (CO) doubly united with carbon, usu. colourless volatile liquids with pungent ethereal smell, used esp. as solvents. [Ger. *keton*, modification of *acetone*]

kĕ'ttle *n.* Vessel for boiling water, usu. of metal with spout, lid, and handle; fish-kettle; *pretty ~ of fish*, awkward state of affairs; *kettledrum*: *see* DRUM[1]; *~-holder*, piece of cloth etc. to protect hand from heat of kettle handle. **kĕ'ttleful** *n.*

kĕ'vel *n.* (naut.) Peg or cleat, usu. one of pair, to which certain ropes are belayed.

Kew. ~ *Gardens*, Royal Botanic Gardens, principal English national botanical gardens, at Kew, Richmond upon Thames, London; orig. laid out in 18th c. by Lord Capel, extended by George III, and adopted as national establishment in 1840; ~ *Palace*, the 'Dutch House' in Kew Gardens, sold to a Dutch merchant, Sir Hugh Portman, in 16th c., and bought 1781 by George III as nursery for royal children.

key[1] (kē) *n.* 1. Metal instrument for moving bolt of lock forwards or backwards. 2. What gives or precludes opportunity for or access to something; (chess) first move in problem game. 3. (pl., with allusion to Matt. 16: 9) Ecclesiastical authority held to be transmitted to pope as successor of St. Peter (*St. Peter's ~s*, cross keys borne on papal arms). 4. Solution, explanation; translation of book or exercise in foreign tongue; book of solutions of mathematical problems etc. 5. (mus.) System of tones definitely related to each other and based on *keynote* in which a piece of music is written; (fig.) tone, style, of thought or expression. 6. Piece of wood or metal inserted between others to secure them; part of first coat of wall or ceiling plaster passing between laths and so securing the rest; roughness of surface giving bond with paint, plaster, etc. 7. Lever pressed by finger in playing organ, piano, flute, concertina etc.; similar lever in typewriter etc. 8. Instrument for grasping screws, pegs, nuts, etc., esp. one for winding clock or watch. 9. *key'board*, set of keys in piano, organ, typewriter, etc.; *~-bugle*, bugle fitted with keys to increase number of its sounds; *key'hole*, hole by which key is put into lock; *~ industry*, one essential to the carrying on of others; *~ move*: see sense 2; *key'note*: see sense 5; (fig.) prevailing tone or idea; *~-ring*, ring for keeping keys on; *key'stone*, stone at summit of arch locking the whole together, (fig.) central principle etc. on which all depends. **key'lėss** *adj.* **key** *v.t.* Fasten (*in*, *on*, etc.) with pin, wedge, bolt, etc.; regulate pitch of strings of (piano etc.); roughen (surface) to receive plaster etc.; *~ up*, (fig.) stimulate; raise tone or standard of; brace up.

key² (kē) *n.* Low island, sandbank, or reef, of kind common in W. Indies or off coast of Florida.

Keynes (kānz), John Maynard, 1st Baron (1883–1946). English economist; financial adviser to the British Government.

Keys (kēz), House of. Body of 24 members forming elective branch of Legislature of Isle of Man.

kg *abbrev.* Kilogramme(s).

K.G. *abbrev.* Knight (of the Order) of the Garter.

K.G.B. Secret police of U.S.S.R., which took over functions of M.V.D. in 1960. [initials of Russ. *K*omitét *G*osudárstvennoĭ *B*ezopásnosti, State security committee]

kha'ki (kah-) *adj.* Dull brownish yellow. *~ n.* Khaki fabric used in army for field-uniforms. [Hind., = dusty (*khak* dust)]

khă'lifa, khă'lifăt (kă-) *ns.* = CALIPH, CALIPHATE.

khă'msin (kă-) *n.* Oppressive hot S. or SE. wind blowing in Egypt for about 50 days in March, April, and May. [Arab. *kamsīn* fifty]

khan¹ (kahn) *n.* (hist.) Title of successors of Genghis Khan, supreme rulers of Turkish, Tatar, and Mongol tribes and emperors of China, in Middle Ages; title of rulers, officials, and men of rank of central Asia, Afghanistan, etc. **kha'nate** *n.* [Turk., perhaps f. *khāgān* king]

khan² (kahn) *n.* Caravanserai. [Arab., = 'inn']

Khartoum (kartōō'm). Capital of Sudan, on Blue Nile just above junction with White Nile; besieged 1885 and captured by the Mahdists after a gallant defence by General GORDON; recaptured by the British under KITCHENER², 1898.

Khayyám, Omar: see OMAR KHAYYÁM.

K.H.C., K.H.P., K.H.S. *abbrevs.* Honorary Chaplain, Physician, Surgeon, to the King.

Khedive (kĭdē'v) *n.* (hist.) Title of viceroy or governor of Egypt, accorded to Ismail Pasha by Turkey in 1867.

khi: see CHI.

khĭ'dmutgar (kĭ-) *n.* (Ind.) Male servant who waits at table. [Hind. *khidmat* service]

Khi'lafăt (kĭ-) *n.* = CALIPHATE; *~ agitation*, Muslim anti-British movement in India, 1919–24.

Khmer¹ (χmār) *n.* 1. Native, inhabitant, of the ancient kingdom of Khmer in SE. Asia, which reached peak of its power in 11th c. and was destroyed by Siamese conquests in 12th and 14th centuries; native, inhabitant, of the Khmer Republic. 2. Monosyllabic language of this people, of Mon-Khmer group of Austro-Asiatic family.

Khmer[2] (χmār). Republic in SE. Asia; once a powerful kingdom (see KHMER[1], 1); a French protectorate (as *Cambodia*) from 1863; independent 1953; a republic since 1970; capital, Phnomh-Penh.

khō'ja (kō-) *n.* 1. Muslim professor, schoolmaster, or scribe. 2. *K~*, Indian member of the Ismaili sect.

khor (kōr) *n.* Watercourse, ravine.

Khrushchev (krōōschŏ'f), Nikita Sergevich (1894–1971). Soviet statesman; denounced Stalin at party congresses in 1956 and 1961; premier of U.S.S.R. 1958–64; associated with internal reform and advocacy of peaceful co-existence with the Western powers.

Khȳ'ber Pass (kī-, pahs). Chief pass between Afghanistan and Pakistan.

kiă'ng, kyă'ng *n.* Tibetan ass or dziggetai (*Equus hemionus*), with thick furry coat, found at altitudes of 15,000 ft and upwards.

Kiangsi (kyă'ngsē'). Province of SE. China.

Kiangsu (kyă'ngsōō'). Coastal province of E. China at outlet of Yangtze Kiang.

kĭ'bble[1] *n.* Iron hoisting-bucket used in mines.

kĭ'bble[2] *v.t.* Bruise or grind coarsely; crush into small pieces.

kĭbbu'tz (-ōōts) *n.* (pl. *-im*). Collective settlement in Israel. [Heb.]

kībe *n.* Ulcerated chilblain, esp. on heel.

kĭbĭ'tka *n.* 1. Tatar's circular tent covered with felt; Tatar household. 2. Russian hooded sledge.

kĭ'bŏsh *n.* (slang) *put the ~ on*, put an end to, dispose of finally.

kĭck *n.* Act of kicking; (colloq.) power of reaction, resilience; recoil of gun when discharged; (U.S. slang) complaint, criticism; (slang, orig. U.S.) sharp stimulant effect, thrill; *~-off*, (footb.) kick with which game is started; *~-starter*, foot-operated lever for starting engine, esp. of motor-cycle. ~ *v.* Strike out with the foot; show annoyance, dislike, etc. (*against*, *at*); strike with foot; drive, move, (thing) by kicking; (footb.) score (goal) by a kick; drive forcibly and contemptuously (*out* etc.); ~ *the bucket*, (slang) die; ~ *off*, throw off (shoes) by kicking; (footb.) start game by giving first kick; ~ *up*, raise (dust); create (fuss, noise).

Kĭ'ckapōō *n.* N. Amer. Indian of Algonquin linguistic stock, orig. found in S. Wisconsin.

kĭ'cker *n.* (esp.) Horse given to kicking.

kĭ'ckshaw *n.* Fancy dish in cookery (usu. contempt.); toy, trifle. [Fr. *quelque chose* something]

kĭd[1] *n.* Young of goat; leather from skin of this, used for gloves and boots; (slang) child, young person. ~ *v.i.* Give birth to kid. **kĭ'ddȳ** *n.* (slang) Little child.

kĭd[2] *v.t.* & *n.* Hoax, humbug.

kĭd[3] *n.* Small wooden tub, esp. sailor's mess-tub.

Kĭdd, William (*c* 1645–1701). 'Captain Kidd', English privateer and pirate; hanged for piracy, 1701.

Kĭ'dderminster. Town in the county of Hereford and Worcester where carpets have been made since 1735; hence, INGRAIN carpet (now seldom made).

kĭ'ddle *n.* Barrier in river with opening fitted with nets etc. to catch fish; arrangement of stake-nets on sea-beach.

kĭ'dnăp *v.t.* Abduct (child), carry off (person) by illegal force, esp. to another country or to hold to ransom. **kĭ'dnăpper** *n.*

kĭ'dney *n.* One of a pair of glandular organs in abdominal cavity of vertebrates, serving mainly to excrete nitrogenous matter from the blood; analogous organ in other animals; kidney of sheep, cattle, or pigs, as food; temperament, nature; (also ~ *potato*) oval kind of potato; ~ *bean*, French bean.

Kiel Cană'l. Canal joining German Baltic naval port, Kiel, with North Sea at Brunsbüttel on mouth of River Elbe; opened 1895.

kier *n.* Vat in which cloth is boiled for bleaching etc.

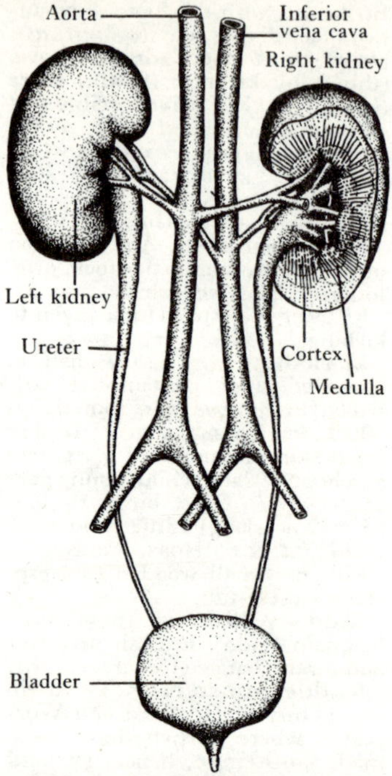

URINARY SYSTEM

Kierkegaard (kēr´keyŏr), Sören Aaby (1813–55). Danish philosopher and theological writer.

kieselguhr (kē´zlgoor) *n.* Porous diatomite (i.e. earth composed of siliceous remains of minute sea-plants), used as abrasive and in dynamite as absorbent for nitroglycerine.

Kĭku´yu (-kōōyōō) *n.* (Member of) an agricultural Negro people, the largest Bantu tribe in Kenya; their language.

Kĭldār´e. County and town of Leinster.

ki´lderkin *n.* Cask for liquids etc. containing 16 or 18 gal.; this as measure.

Ki´lham (-lam), Alexander (1762–98). English founder of Methodist New Connexion, a group of Methodists which in 1797 seceded from the Wesleyan Methodist Church.

Ki´lian, St. (7th c.). Irish missionary bishop; apostle of eastern Franconia; martyred at Würzburg.

Kĭlĭmănjār´ō. Mountain in N. Tanzania, highest known mountain in Africa (5,895 m, 19,340 ft).

Kĭlkĕ´nnȳ. County and city of Leinster; *Statute of* ~, laws of 1366 designed to strengthen English authority in Ireland, and forbidding marriage between English settlers and the native Irish; ~ *cats*, cats said proverbially to have fought until nothing but the tails remained, taken as type of combatants who fight until they annihilate each other.

kill *v.* 1. Put to death; cause the death of; perform act of killing, do execution; ~ *off*, get rid of (number of persons etc.) by killing; ~ *two birds with one stone*, effect two purposes at once. 2. Destroy vitality of; destroy, put an end to; neutralize (colours etc.) by contrast; consume (time) for the sake of doing so; overwhelm (person) with admiration, amusement, etc.; strike (ball in lawn tennis) so that it cannot be returned; stop (ball in football) dead; totally defeat (bill in Parliament); ~ *with kindness*, destroy or fatally harm with mistaken or excessive kindness; ~*-joy*, one who throws gloom over social enjoyment, one who destroys pleasure. ~ *n.* Act of killing; animal killed, esp. by sportsman; destruction or putting out of action of submarine, aircraft, etc.

Kĭllār´ney. Town of County Kerry, near lakes of Killarney, famous for beauty of landscape.

kĭ´lldeer *n.* Largest N. Amer. species of ring-plover, *Charadrius vociferus*. [imit.]

ki´ller *n.* Person, thing, that kills; murderous ruffian; (also ~ *whale*) grampus (*Orcinus orca*) and other ferocious cetaceans.

kĭ´llick, -ock, kĕ´llėck *n.* Heavy stone used by small craft as anchor; small anchor.

Killiecră´nkie. Pass in region of Tayside; *battle of* ~, that in which Jacobites under Claverhouse defeated Royalists under Mackay, 1689.

kĭ'lling *n.* (esp.) *~-bottle*, bottle containing poison for killing captured insects etc. ~ *adj.* (esp., colloq.) Overwhelmingly attractive; overwhelmingly funny. **kĭ'llinglў** *adv.*

kĭln *n.* Furnace, oven, for burning, baking, or drying, esp. for calcining lime, baking bricks or drying hops; *~-dry*, (*v.t.*) dry in kiln.

kĭ'lō (kē-) *n.* (colloq.) Kilogramme.

kĭlo- *prefix.* One thousand times (abbrev. k).

kĭ'locўcle *n.* 1,000 cycles, as unit in measuring frequency of electromagnetic waves (abbrev. kc.).

kĭ'logrămme *n.* Unit of mass in the metric system (abbrev. kg), equal to the mass of the international prototype of the kilogramme at Sèvres (approx. 2·20 lb.).

kĭ'lojoule (-ōōl) *n.* 1,000 joules (abbrev. kJ).

kĭ'lolitre (-lē*ter*) *n.* 1,000 litres (abbrev. kl).

kĭ'lomētre (-*ter*) *n.* 1,000 metres (abbrev. km). **kĭlomĕ'tric** *adj.*

kĭ'loton (-ŭn) *n.* 1,000 tons; unit of explosive power equivalent to 1,000 tons of T.N.T.

kĭ'lowatt (-wŏt) *n.* 1,000 watts (abbrev. kw); *~-hour*, unit of electrical energy, energy used when a rate of 1 kilowatt is maintained for 1 hour.

kilt *v.t.* Tuck up (skirts) round body; gather in vertical pleats. ~ *n.* Part of Highland dress, skirt, usu. of tartan cloth, heavily pleated round back and sides, reaching from waist to knee. **kĭ'ltėd** *adj.* Gathered in pleats; wearing a kilt. **kĭ'ltў** *n.* Kilted highland soldier.

Kĭ'mberley. Diamond mine, district, and town in Griqualand West, Cape Province, S. Africa. [1st earl of *Kimberley*, Colonial Secretary (1871) when gold-mines were taken under protection of Gt Britain]

Kĭ'mmerĭdge. Village on coast of Dorsetshire, where are extensive beds of Upper Oolite; ~ *clay*, bed of clay in Upper Oolite containing bituminous shales; ~ *coal*, shale of Kimmeridge clay containing so much bitumen that it can be burnt as coal. **Kĭmmerĭ'dgĭan** *adj.*

kĭmō'nō *n.* (pl. *-os*). Long Japanese robe with sleeves; one of these, or similar robe, worn as woman's dressing-gown etc.

kĭn *n.* Ancestral stock, family; one's relatives; *kith and ~*: see KITH; *of ~*, akin, related by blood ties or character; *near of ~*, closely related; *next of ~*, see NEXT. ~ *pred. adj.* Related. **kĭnlėss** *adj.*

Kĭncar'dĭneshire (-nsh-). Former county on E. coast of Scotland, since May 1975 part of the region of Grampian.

kĭ'ncŏb *n.* Rich Indian stuff embroidered with gold or silver.

kīnd[1] *n.* Race, natural group, of animals, plants, etc.; class, sort, variety; character, quality; (archaic) nature in general; way, fashion, natural to person, etc.; *in ~*, (of payment) in goods or natural produce, not in money; (of repayment) in something of the same kind as that received; ~ *of*, (colloq.) to some extent.

kīnd[2] *adj.* Of gentle or benevolent nature; friendly in one's conduct *to*; (archaic) affectionate. **kī'ndnėss** *n.*

kĭ'ndergarten *n.* School for young children. [Ger., = 'children's garden']

kĭ'ndle *v.* Set on fire, light; inflame, inspire (passion etc.); stir up (person *to*); catch fire, burst into flame; become animated, glow with passion, etc.; make, become, bright; (cause to) glow. **kĭ'ndlĭng** *n.* (esp.) Small wood for lighting fires.

kī'ndlў *adv.* In a kind manner; obligingly; *take ~*, accept pleasantly; *take ~ to*, accept tolerantly. ~ *adj.* Kind; pleasant, genial. **kī'ndlĭlў** *adv.* **kī'ndlĭnėss** *n.*

kĭ'ndrėd *n.* Blood relationship; resemblance in character; one's relatives. ~ *adj.* Related by blood; allied, connected, similar.

kīne. Archaic pl. of cow.

kīnėmă'tic *adj.* Of motion considered abstractly without reference to force or mass. **kīnėmă'tics** *n.* Science of kinematic motion.

kīnĕ'tic *adj.* Of, due to, motion; *~ energy*: see ENERGY; *~ theory of heat, of gases*, theory that heat, gaseous state, is due to motion of particles of matter. **kīnĕ'tics** *n.* Science of relations between the motions of bodies and the forces acting on them.

kĭng *n.* 1. (Title of) male sovereign (esp. hereditary) ruler of independent State; *K~ Emperor*, (hist.) King of United Kingdom and Emperor of India; *K~ of Kings*, God; title assumed by many Eastern kings; *K~ of Rome*, title given at his birth to Napoleon François Charles Joseph (1811–32), son of Napoleon I and Marie Louise; *the three ~s*, wise men who came from the East to worship the new-born Christ (sometimes called *three ~s of Cologne* from the belief that their bodies were preserved there); (*1st* and *2nd Book of the*) *Kings*, two historical books of O.T., following the two Books of Samuel and covering Jewish history, esp. that of the kingdom of Judah, from the death of David to the destruction of the Temple (586 B.C.). 2. Great merchant etc.; best kind (*of* fruits, plants, etc.); *~ of beasts*, lion; *~ of birds*, eagle. 3. (chess) Piece which must be protected against checkmate; (draughts) piece which has been 'crowned'; (cards) one card in each suit bearing representation of king, and usu. ranking next below ace; *~'s bishop, knight, rook*, chess pieces on king's side of board at beginning of game; *~'s pawn*, pawn in front of king at beginning of game. 4. *ki'ngbird*, Amer. tyrant flycatcher; *~-bolt*, main or large bolt in mechanical structure; *K~ Charles spaniel*, English black-and-tan toy spaniel with long silky coat and pendulous ears; *K~ Charles's head*, fixed idea, inescapable obsession (from 'David Copperfield', chap. xiv); *~ cobra*, hamadryad; *~ crab*, large arachnid with horseshoe-shaped carapace; *ki'ngcup*, marsh marigold; *ki'ngfisher*, small European bird (*Alcedo ispida*) with long beak and brilliant plumage, feeding on fish it captures by diving; other birds of same family; *~-maker*, one who sets up kings, esp. Earl of Warwick in reigns of Henry VI and Edward IV; *~ of arms*, any of three chief heralds of College of Arms (Garter, Clarenceux, Norroy and Ulster), or Lyon King of Arms of Scotland; *~ penguin*, large species of penguin (*Aptenodytes patagonica*); *~-pin*, (U.S.) king-bolt; most important person in organization etc.; *~-post*, upright post from tie-beam to rafter-top; *~'s* BENCH, COUNSEL, ENGLISH, EVIDENCE: see these words; *~'s evil*, scrofula, formerly held to be curable by king's touch; *~'s friends*, (hist.) political party supporting George III in attempts to increase powers of crown; *~-size(d)*, (of) larger than standard size; *~'s pattern*, type of 19th-c. spoon- or fork-handle; *~'s* PIPE, PROCTOR, SHILLING: see these words. **kĭ'nglike** *adj.* **kĭ'ngship** *n.* **kĭng** *v.* Act the king, govern; make into a king.

kĭ'ngdom *n.* Organized community with king as its head; monarchical state; territory subject to a king; spiritual reign of God, sphere of this (esp. *~ of heaven*); domain; province of nature (esp. *animal, vegetable, mineral, ~*); *~ come*, (slang) the next world; *Middle K~*, imperial State of HONAN under Chan dynasty; *Old, Middle, New K~*, successive periods of civilization in ancient Egypt.

Kĭ'nglāke, Alexander William (1809–91). English traveller and historian; author of 'Eothen', a narrative of his travels in the Near East.

kĭ'nglėt *n.* 1. Petty king. 2. Golden-crested wren.

kĭ'nglȳ *adj.* Fit for, appropriate to, a king; kinglike, majestic. **kĭ'nglĭnėss** *n.*

Kĭ'ngs Cou'ntȳ (-z). Former name of OFFALY.

Kĭ'ngsley (-z-). Charles ~ (1819–75), English clergyman, novelist, and poet; author of 'Alton Locke', 'Westward Ho!', 'The Water Babies', 'Hereward the Wake', etc.; *Henry* ~ (1830–76), brother of Charles Kingsley; novelist; *Mary Henrietta* ~ (1862–1900), niece of Charles and Henry Kingsley; traveller (chiefly in W. Africa), author and ethnologist.

Kĭ'ngston. Chief port and capital of JAMAICA.

kĭnk *n.* Back-twist in wire, chain, or rope, such as may cause obstruction or a break; (fig.) mental twist, eccentricity. ~ *v.* Form a kink; cause (rope) to do this. **kĭ'nkȳ** *adj.* Having kinks; (colloq.) eccentric, perverted.

kĭ'nkajou (-ōō) *n.* Carnivorous arboreal mammal (*Potos flavus*) of Central and S. America, allied to racoon, with prehensile tail.

ki'no (kē-) *n.* Gum of various trees, resembling catechu, used in medicine and tanning as astringent.

Kĭnrŏ'ss. Former county of central Scotland, since May 1975 part of the region of Tayside.

kĭ'nsfolk (-zfōk) *n.pl.* (literary) Relations by blood. **kĭ'nsman, kĭ'nswoman** *ns.*

kĭ'nshĭp *n.* Blood relationship; similarity, alliance, in character.

kiŏ'sk *n.* Light open pavilion in Turkey and Iran; (kē'ŏsk) structure like this for sale of newspapers etc.; structure in street etc. containing a public telephone.

kĭp[1] *n.* Hide of young or small beast as used for leather.

kĭp[2] *n.* (slang) Common lodging-house; lodging; bed. ~ *v.i.* Go to bed; sleep.

kĭp[3] *n.* Principal monetary unit of Laos, = 100 ats.

Kĭ'plĭng, Rudyard (1865–1936). English novelist and poet; born in India; famous for short stories about India, and for children's books. **Kĭplingē'se** (-z) *n.* Style like Kipling's; patriotic and im-

RUDYARD KIPLING

perialistic sentiment characteristic of his writings.

kĭ'pper *n.* Male salmon in spawning season; kippered fish, esp. herring. ~ *v.t.* Cure (salmon, herring, etc.) by splitting open, cleaning, rubbing with salt etc., and drying in open air or smoke.

Kirghiz (kẽrgē'z) *adj.* & *n.* (Member) of a Turkic, mainly Muslim, people of central Asia; (of) their language, one of the Ural-Altaic family. **Kirghi'zia.** Constituent republic of U.S.S.R., on Chinese frontier; capital, Frunze.

Kir'in (kẽr-). Province of NE. China.

kirk *n.* (Sc. & north.) Church; ~ *session*, lowest court in Established Church of Scotland and other Presbyterian churches, composed of minister and elders of congregation or parish.

Kirkcu'dbrightshire (-kōō-brĭsh-). Former county of SW. Scotland N. of the Solway Firth, since May 1975 part of the region of Dumfries and Galloway.

kirsch (kẽrsh) *n.* (also *kir'schwăsser*, pr. -v-). Spirit distilled from fermented liquor of wild cherries.

kir'tle *n.* (archaic) Woman's gown or outer petticoat; man's tunic or coat.

Ki'sfaludy̆ (-sh-), Károly (1788–1830). Hungarian dramatist and author.

Kish[1]. Ancient city of Sumer and Akkad, on old bed of Euphrates.

Kish[2]. Father of Saul (1 Sam. 9: 1; 10: 21).

kiskadee' *n.* Large tyrant-bird of tropical America, esp. *Pitangus sulphuratus*. [imit.]

kĭ'smĕt *n.* Destiny. [Arab. *kisma* lot, fate]

kiss *n.* Caress given with lips; kind of sweet; (billiards) impact between moving balls; ~ *of life*, mouth-to-mouth resuscitation; ~ *of peace*, ceremonial kiss of worshippers in eucharistic liturgy, as sign of love and union; pax. ~ *v.t.* Touch with the lips, esp. in sign of affection, greeting, or reverence; (billiards etc. of ball) touch another lightly, esp. after having struck it once; ~ *away*, remove (tears etc.) with kisses; ~ *the book*, kiss Bible in taking oath; ~ *the dust*, yield abject submission; be slain; ~ *the ground*, prostrate oneself in token of homage; (fig.) be brought low; ~ *one's hand to*, wave a kiss to; ~ *hands*, kiss hand of sovereign etc. as ceremonial salutation or on appointment to office; ~ *the rod*, accept chastisement humbly or gladly; ~*-curl*, small curl on forehead, in front of ear, or at nape of neck; ~*-in-the-ring*, game for young people in which one pursues and kisses another of opposite sex. **kĭ'ssing** *n.* ~*-gate*, gate hung in U- or V-shaped enclosure.

kĭst, kĭ'stvaen (-vān) *ns.* = CIST[1], 1.

Kiswahili: see SWAHILI.

kĭt *n.* 1. Wooden tub for various purposes. 2. (Articles carried in) soldier's valise or knapsack; personal equipment, esp. as packed for travelling; set of tools or other equipment; ~*-bag*, bag, usu. cylindrical, for carrying soldier's or traveller's kit. ~ *v.t.* Equip, fit *out*, *up*.

kĭ't-căt *n.* Artist's canvas 36 × 25 in.; portrait of this size, i.e. resembling the portraits painted by Sir Godfrey Kneller for the *Kit-cat Club*, a dining-club of Whig politicians and men of letters founded towards end of 17th c. and orig. meeting in a tavern near Temple Bar, London. [*kit-cat*, members' name for the mutton-pies provided by Christopher Cat, the tavern-keeper]

kĭ'tchėn *n.* Part of house where food is cooked; ~ *garden*, garden for fruit and vegetables for table; ~*-maid*, maid employed in kitchen, usu. under cook. **kĭ'tchėner[1]** *n.* 1. Cooking-range. 2. Person in charge of monastery kitchen.

Ki'tchener[2], Horatio Herbert, Earl Kitchener of Khartoum (1850–1916). British soldier; retook Khartoum with Anglo-Egyptian force 1898; commander-in-chief in Boer War, 1900–2, and in India; secretary of state for war, 1914–16; drowned in the *Hamp-*

LORD KITCHENER

shire, which struck a mine on the way to Russia.

kitchėnĕ'tte *n.* Small kitchen; alcove used as kitchen.

kīte *n.* 1. Large bird of falcon family (esp. the common European *Milvus milvus*) with long wings and usu. forked tail; (fig.) rapacious person, sharper. 2. Toy consisting of light wooden frame, with paper or other thin material stretched over it, made to fly in strong wind at the end of a long string; similar contrivance of box-shape (*box-*~) with open sides, used esp. for meteorological observations; (in mine-sweeping) steel frame, similar to a box-kite, for keeping sweep-wire at required depth; (R.A.F. slang) aeroplane; (pl.) highest sails of ship, set only in light wind. 3. (commerc. slang) Accommodation bill. ~ *v.* (Cause to) soar like kite.

kith *n.* ~ *and kin*, orig., country and kinsfolk; later, friends and relatives; now freq., kinsfolk.

kĭ'tten *n.* Young of cat; skittish girl. **kĭ'ttenĭsh** *adj.* **kĭ'tten** *v.i.* Give birth to kittens.

kĭ'ttiwāke *n.* Smallest of the strictly marine gulls (*Rissa tridactyla*) of Arctic and N. Atlantic Oceans, with black markings on usu. white plumage, very long wings, and very short hind toe. [imit.]

kĭ'ttle *adj.* (orig. Sc.) Ticklish, difficult to deal with.

kĭttu'l (-ōōl), **kĭtōō'l** *n.* Kind of palm; strong black fibre from leaf-stalks of this.

kĭ'ttȳ[1] *n.* Pet name for kitten.

kĭ'ttȳ[2] *n.* Pool or joint fund in games etc.

Kĭwa'nĭs (-wah-). International organization (founded at Detroit, 1915) of business and professional men, with clubs chiefly in U.S. and Canada.

kĭ'wĭ (kē-) *n.* 1. New Zealand nocturnal bird of family Apterygidae, with rudimentary wings and no tail; this as emblem of New Zealand; (slang) non-flying member of Air Force. 2. (slang) New Zealander.

Kizi'l Kum (kōōm). Desert region in Kazakhstan, SE. of Aral Sea.

kJ *abbrev.* Kilojoule(s).

K.K.K. *abbrev.* (U.S.) Ku Klux Klan.

kl *abbrev.* Kilolitre(s).

Klă'prōth (-t), Martin Heinrich (1743–1817). German chemist; discoverer of several metallic elements.

klavier: see CLAVIER.

klă'xon *n.* (Electric) motor-horn. [trade-name]

Kléber (klābār), Jean-Baptiste (1753–1800). French soldier; general in Revolutionary army.

Kleist (klī-), Heinrich von (1777–1811). German dramatist and novelist.

klĕpht *n.* One of the Greeks who after Turkish conquest of Greece in 15th c. maintained independence in mountains; brigand. [mod. Gk *klephtes* (Gk *kleptēs* thief)]

klĕptomā'nia *n.* Irresistible tendency to theft in persons not driven to it by needy circumstances. **klĕptomā'nĭăc** *n.*

Klieg light (lit). Kind of arc-light emitting light rich in actinic rays, used in cinema photography. [f. name of inventors, *Kliegl* brothers]

Klŏ'ndȳke[1], **-dīke.** District in Yukon, NW. Canada, where gold was discovered in 1896; ~ *River*, tributary of Yukon River.

klŏ'ndȳke[2] *n.* 1. Mine, quarry, of valuable material. 2. Amer. card-game. 3. Herring fishery off W. coast of Scotland. ~ *v.* Export (fresh herring) by fast steamer to the Continent.

klōōf *n.* Ravine, deep narrow valley, in S. Africa. [Du., = 'cleft']

Klŏ'pstŏck (-sht-), Gottlieb Friedrich (1724–1803). German epic and lyric poet; famous for his religious epic 'Messias'.

km *abbrev.* Kilometre(s).

kn *abbrev.* Knot(s).

knăck (n-) *n.* Acquired faculty of doing a thing adroitly; ingenious device, trick, habit, of action, speech, etc.

knă'cker (n-) *n.* One who buys and slaughters useless horses; one who buys old houses, ships, etc., for the materials.

knăg (n-) *n.* Knot in wood, base of a branch.

knăp[1] (n-) *n.* Crest of hill, rising ground.

knăp[2] (n-) *v.* Break (flints for roads) with hammer; (bibl., dial.) knock, rap, snap asunder.

knă'psăck (n-) *n.* Soldier's or traveller's canvas or leather bag, strapped to back and used for carrying necessaries. [Low Ger.]

knă'pweed (n-) *n.* Species of *Centaurea*, esp. *C. nigra*, a common weed with tough stem and light-purple flowers on dark globular head.

knar (n-) *n.* Knot in wood, esp. protuberance covered with bark on trunk or at root of tree.

knāve (n-) *n.* 1. Rogue. 2. (cards) Lowest court-card of each suit, bearing representation of soldier or court page. **knā'verȳ** *n.* **knā'vĭsh** *adj.* **knā'vishlȳ** *adv.* **knā'vishnėss** *n.*

knead (n-) *v.t.* Work up (moist flour or clay etc.) into dough or paste by drawing out and pressing or squeezing together; make (bread, pottery) thus; operate on (muscles etc.) as if kneading, massage; *kneading-trough*, trough for kneading dough.

knee (n-) *n.* Joint between thigh and lower leg in man; area above this joint considered as place on which child or object is held; corresponding joint in animals; part of garment covering the knee; thing like knee in shape or position, esp. piece of wood or iron with angular bend; *on one's ~s*, kneeling, esp. in supplication, worship, or submission; *on the ~s of the gods*, yet uncertain; *bring* (person) *to his ~s*, reduce him to submission; *~-breeches*, breeches reaching down to or just below knee; *knee'cap*, convex bone in front of knee-joint, patella; *~-deep, -high*, so deep or high as to reach the knees; *knee'hole*, (of writing-table) having hole between drawer pedestals to admit knees; ~*-pan*, knee-cap. ~ *v.t.* Touch with the knee; fasten (framework etc.) with knees.

kneel (n-) *v.i.* Fall, rest, on the knee(s), esp. in prayer or reverence (*to*).

knĕll (n-) *n.* Sound of bell, esp. of one rung solemnly after death or at funeral; (fig.) anything regarded as omen of death or extinction. ~ *v.* (archaic) (of bell) Ring, esp. at death or funeral; give forth doleful sound; proclaim as by a knell; (fig.) sound ominously.

Knĕ'ller (n-), Sir Godfrey (1648–1723). English portrait-painter of German birth; appointed court painter by Charles II.

Knĕ'ssĕt, -th *n.* Israeli parliament.

knĭ'ckerbŏcker (n-) *n.* 1. Descendant of original Dutch settlers of New Netherlands in America; New Yorker. 2. (pl.) Loose-fitting breeches gathered in at knee; knickers. [*Knickerbocker*, pretended author of W. Irving's 'History of New York']

knĭ'ckers (n-, -z) *n.pl.* Woman's drawers.

knĭ'ck-knăck (n-, n-), **nĭck-năck** *n.* Light dainty article of furniture, dress, or food; trinket, gimcrack.

knīfe (n-) *n.* 1. Blade with sharpened longitudinal edge fixed in

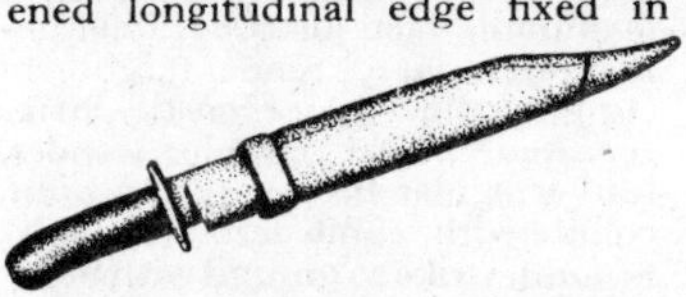

handle either rigidly or with hinge, used as cutting instrument or as weapon; sharpened cutting-blade forming part of machine, as in turnip-cutter etc.; *the* ~, surgical operation(s); *war to the* ~, fierce or relentless war; *get, have, one's* ~ *in*(*to*) (person), persecute, show malicious or vindictive spirit towards. 2. ~*-board*, board on which knives are cleaned; ~*-edge*, edge of knife; steel wedge on which pendulum etc. oscillates; arête; ~*-grinder*, itinerant sharpener of knives etc.; ~*-machine*, machine for cleaning knives; ~*-pleat*: see PLEAT; ~*-rest*, metal or glass support for carving knife or fork at table. ~ *v.t.* Cut, stab, with knife.

knight (nīt) *n.* 1. (hist.) Military follower, esp. one devoted to service *of* (lady) as attendant or champion in war or tournament; (hist.) person, usu. one of noble birth who had served as page and squire, raised to honourable military rank by king or qualified person. 2. One on whom is conferred rank corresponding to medieval knight as reward for personal merit or services to crown or country. 3. (hist., also ~ *of the shire*) Person representing shire or county in parliament. 4. (Rom. antiq.) One of the class of *equites*, orig. cavalry of Roman army, later a wealthy and politically important class; (Gk antiq.) citizen of second class at Athens in constitution of Solon. 5. Piece in game of chess, shaped like horse's head. 6. ~*-errant*, medieval knight wandering in search of chivalrous adventures; (fig.) person of chivalrous or quixotic spirit; ~*-errantry*, practice, conduct, of a knight-errant; ~*-heads*, two large timbers rising from keel behind stem and supporting bowsprit; ~*-service*, military service rendered by knight in return for lands, tenure of land by military service. 7. *K~ Bachelor*, knight not be-

Badge of honour

longing to a special order; *K~* COMMANDER, COMPANION, *of the* GARTER, see these words; *K~ of the Round Table*, one of King ARTHUR[1]'s knights; *K~ of the Rueful Countenance*, Don QUIXOTE; *K~ of St.* PATRICK, *of the* THISTLE, *of* WINDSOR, TEMPLAR: see these words; *Knights of Columbus*, Amer. R.C. society for men, founded 1882; *Knights Hospitallers*: see HOSPITALLER; *Knights of Malta*, *of Rhodes*, Knights Hospitallers. ~ *v.t.* Confer knighthood on. **kni'ghthood** (-t-h-) *n.* Rank, dignity, of a knight. **kni'ghtlike, kni'ghtly** *adjs.*

kni'ghtage (nīt-) *n.* Whole body of knights; list and account of knights.

knit (n-) *v.* Form (close texture) by interlooping successive series of loops of yarn or thread; make (garments etc.) of this; contract (brow) in wrinkles; make, become, close or compact; unite intimately by means of common interests, marriage, etc.; ~ *up*, repair by knitting; *kni'twear*, knitted garments.

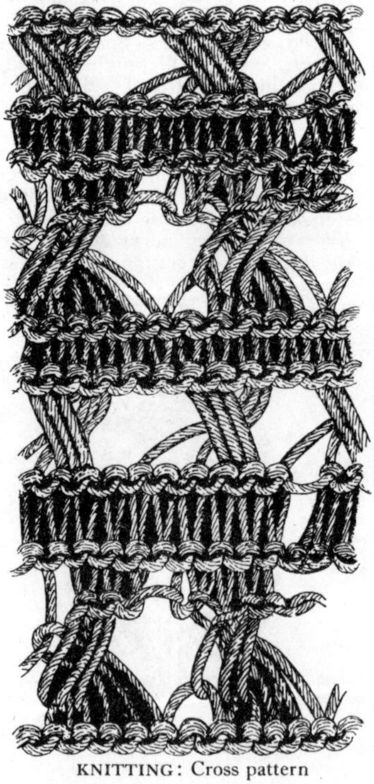

KNITTING: Cross pattern

kni'tting (n-) *n.* (esp.) Work in process of knitting; ~*-needle*, slender rod of metal, wood, plastic, etc., two or more of which are used together in knitting.

knob (n-) *n.* Rounded protuberance, esp. at end or on surface of thing; such handle of door or drawer; small lump (of sugar, coal, etc.); *kno'bkerrie*, short thick stick with knobbed head as weapon of S. Afr. tribes. **kno'bby** *adj.* **kno'bbiness** *n.* **knob** *v.* Furnish with knob(s); bulge *out*. **kno'bble** *n.* Small knob. **kno'bbly** *adj.*

knock (n-) *v.* 1. Strike with hard blow; strike door, strike *at the door*, to gain admittance; drive (thing) *in, out, off*, etc., by striking; (of internal combustion engine etc.) make knocking or thumping noise as result of mechanical defect; = PINK[5]; (colloq., orig. U.S.) disparage; ~ *into the middle of next week*, send (person) flying; ~ *on the head*, stun, kill, by blow on the head; put an end to (scheme etc.); ~ *one's head against*, (fig.) come into unpleasant collision with (unfavourable facts or conditions); ~ *the bottom out of*, render (argument etc.) invalid. 2. ~ *about*, strike repeatedly, treat roughly; wander, lead irregular life; ~ (*up*) *against*, collide with, come across casually; ~ *down*, strike to ground with blow; cause to succumb; dispose of (article *to* bidder at auction) by knock with hammer; ~ *off*, strike off with blow; leave off work, leave off (work); (colloq.) dispatch (business) or rapidly compose (verses etc.); deduct (sum from price etc.); (slang) steal; ~ *on*, (Rugby footb.) propel ball with hand or arm towards adversary's goal; ~ *out*, empty (tobacco-pipe) by tapping; disable (pugilist) so that he cannot respond to call of 'Time'; (fig.) vanquish; (colloq.) make (plan etc.) hastily; ~ *together*, put hastily together; ~ *up*, drive upwards with blow; make or arrange hastily; score (runs) at cricket; arouse (person) by knocking at door; exhaust to the point of illness. 3. ~-*about*, boisterous, noisy (performance in music-hall etc.); wandering irregularly; (of clothes) suitable for rough use; ~-*down*, (of blow) overwhelming; (of price at auction) reserve, minimum; ~-*for-knock agreement*, agreement between insurance companies whereby each pays the claim of its own client instead of bringing an action against the other party involved; ~-*kneed*, -*knees*, (having) knees that knock together in walking; ~-*out*, (blow) that knocks boxer out; (athletic competition) in which defeated competitors in each round are eliminated; one of group who join at auction to buy goods at low price, afterwards reselling among themselves; this practice, such sale; (slang) outstandingly successful person or thing; ~-*up*, practice or casual game at cricket, tennis, etc. ~ *n*. Blow; rap, esp. at door; thumping noise in engine etc. pinking (PINK[5]); (slang) innings at cricket.

knŏ'cker (n-) *n*. (esp.) Appendage, usu. of iron or brass, so hinged to door that it may be struck against metal plate to call attention.

knōll[1] (n-) *n*. Small hill, mound.

knōll[2] (n-) *v*. (archaic) Ring (bell); (of bell) sound; toll out (hours); summon by sound of bell.

knŏp (n-) *n*. 1. Knob (now rare exc. in ref. to glassware and silverware). 2. Flower-bud. 3. Loop or tuft formed in strand of yarn for ornament.

Knŏ'ssos. Ancient city of Crete, 3 miles S. of Candia; centre of the MINOAN civilization, with vast labyrinthine palace (the Palace of MINOS).

knŏt (n-) *n*. 1. Intertwining of parts of one or more ropes, strings, etc., to fasten them together; ribbon etc. so tied as to ornament or adjunct to dress; difficulty, problem; central point in problem or plot of story etc. 2. (naut.) Unit of speed of one nautical mile per hour (orig. measured by knots on log-line; abbrev. kn). 3. Hard lump in animal body; (hard mass formed in trunk at insertion of branch, causing) round cross-grained piece in board, which may fall out, leaving ~-*hole*; node on stem of plant. 4. Group, cluster, of persons or things. 5. (usu. *porter's* ~) Double shoulder-pad used for carrying loads. 6. ~ *garden*, garden (esp. of Tudor period) planted to look like elaborate piece of embroidery; ~-*grass*, common weed (*Polygonum*

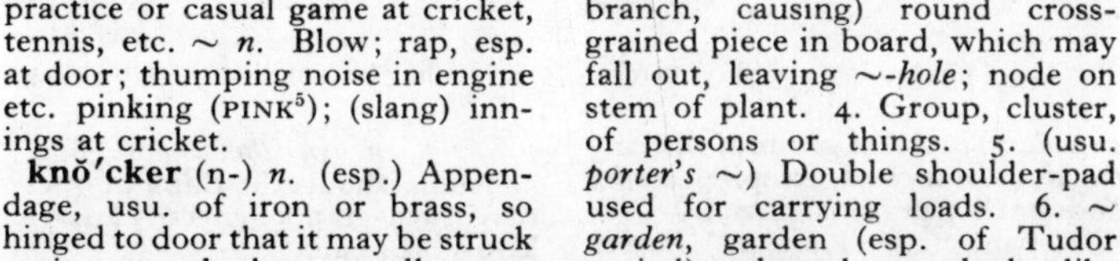

KNOSSOS: The throne room at the palace

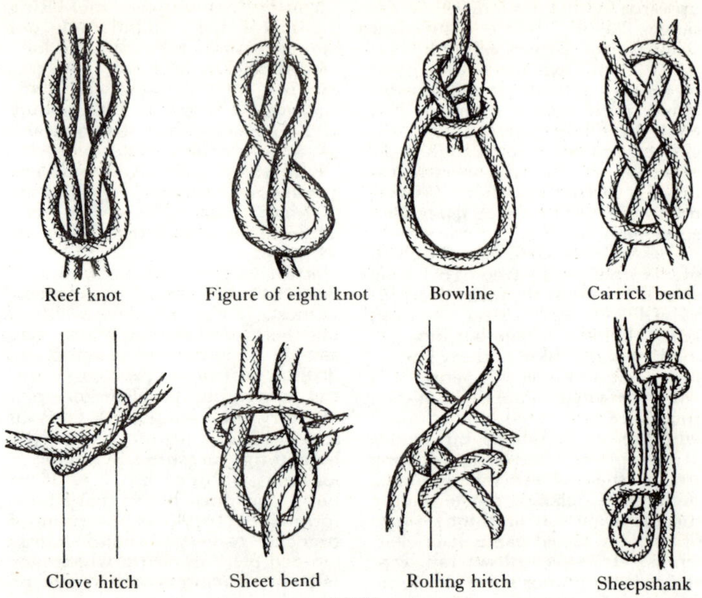

KNOTS

aviculare) in waste ground, with intricately-branched creeping stems and small pale-pink flowers. ~ *v.* Tie (string etc.) in knot; make knots for fringes, make (fringe) thus; unite closely or intricately; entangle. **knŏ′ttȳ** *adj.* Full of knots; (fig.) puzzling, hard to explain.

knout (n-; *or* nōōt) *n.* & *v.t.* (Flog with) scourge formerly used as instrument of punishment in Russia, often fatal in its effects.

know (nō) *v.* (past t. *knew* pr. nū, past part. *known* pr. nōn). 1. Recognize, identify; be able to distinguish; be acquainted with (*by sight*, *to speak to*, etc.); have personal experience of; be on intimate terms with; be aware of, be aware (*that*, *how*, etc.); be versed in; ~ *about*, have information about; ~ *better than*, be too well informed of the facts to believe; be too discreet (*to* do); ~ *of*, be aware of; ~ *one's own mind*, not vacillate. 2. ~*-all*, omniscient person; ~*-how* (*n.*) (orig. U.S.) practical knowledge of methods; ~*-nothing*, ignorant person. ~ *n. in the* ~, (colloq.) knowing (about) the thing in question or what is not generally known. **know′able** *adj.*

know′ing (nōĭ-) *adj.* (esp.) Cunning, wide-awake; (colloq.) smart, stylish. **know′ingnėss** *n.* **know′inglȳ** *adv.* In a knowing manner; consciously, intentionally.

know′lėdge (nŏl-) *n.* Knowing, familiarity gained by experience, (*of*); person's range of information; theoretical or practical understanding (*of*); the sum of what is known; *to my* ~, as far as I know. **know′lėdgeable** *adj.* (colloq.) Well-informed, intelligent.

Knowles (nōlz), James Sheridan (1784–1862). Irish actor and playwright.

Knŏx[1] (n-), John (1505–72). Scottish Protestant reformer and historian.

Knŏx[2] (n-), Ronald Arbuthnott (1888–1957). English Roman Catholic prelate and writer.

Knt *abbrev.* Knight.

knŭ'ckle (n-) *n.* Bone at finger-joint, esp. at root of finger; projection of carpal or tarsal joint of quadruped; joint of meat consisting of this with parts above and below it; ~ *-bone*, bone forming knuckle; limb-bone with ball-like knob at joint-end, this part of animal's leg as joint of meat; metacarpal or metatarsal bone of sheep, etc.; (pl.) game played by tossing up and catching these bones in certain way; ~*-bow*, guard on sword-hilt to cover knuckles; *knu'ckle-duster*, metal instrument to protect knuckles from injury in striking and increase harmfulness of blow. ~ *v.* Strike, press, rub, with knuckles; place knuckles on ground in playing at marbles; ~ *down, under*, give in, submit.

knûr, knûrr (n-) *n.* Hard excrescence on trunk of tree; hard concretion; wooden ball in north-country game of ~ *and spell*, in which ball is jerked by club-ended stick out of container and struck as far as possible while in the air.

knûrl (n-) *n.* Knot, knob; bead or ridge in metalwork. **knûrled** (-ld) *adj.*

K.O. *abbrev.* Knock-out.

koa'la (kōah-) *n.* (also ~ *bear*) Tailless arboreal marsupial (*Phascolarctos cinereus*) of the Australian region, feeding almost exclusively on the leaves of the gum-tree.

kō'bo *n.* $\frac{1}{100}$ of a naira.

kō'bŏld *n.* (Ger. folklore) Brownie; underground spirit haunting mines or caves, gnome.

Kŏch (-χ), Robert (1843–1910). German bacteriologist and physician, famous for his work on the bacillus of tuberculosis; ~*'s postulates*, rules as to conditions which must be satisfied before bacteriologists ascribe a disease to a specific micro-organism.

Kodály (kō'dī), Zoltán (1882–1967). Hungarian composer.

koh'-i-noor (kōī-) *n.* Famous Indian diamond of great size, one of the treasures of Aurungzebe, with history going back to 14th c.; a British Crown jewel since annexation of Punjab, 1849. [Pers. *kōh-i-nūr*, mountain of light]

kohl (kōl) *n.* Preparation, based on powdered sulphide of lead or sulphide of antimony, used to darken eyelids etc. [Arab. *kuhl*]

kohlra'bĭ (kōlrah-) *n.* Cabbage with turnip-shaped stem, used in England as cattle-food, elsewhere as vegetable. [Ger., f. It. *cavoli rape* (pl.), cole-rape]

kola[1] *n.*: see COLA.

Kō'la[2]. Peninsula of north-western U.S.S.R. between Barents Sea and White Sea.

Kolcha'k (-ahk), Alexander Vasilyevich (1875–1920). Russian admiral; commanded White army against Bolsheviks in 1917; was named supreme ruler of Russia, 1918, by Siberian Government at Omsk; executed by Bolsheviks.

koli'nskÿ *n.* Fur of Siberian mink. [Russ., f. KOLA[2]]

kŏ'lkhoz (-kŏz) *n.* Collective farm in U.S.S.R.

komō'dō drā'gon, lĭ'zard. Very large monitor lizard (*Varanus komodoensis*) with heavy powerful body, sometimes as long as 4·6 m. [*Komodo*, island in Malay Archipelago]

koodoo: see KUDU.

kōōkabŭ'rra *n.* Laughing jackass (*Dacelo novaeguineae*), a kingfisher of S. Australia, or a related species.

koolabah, -ibah: see COOLABAH.

kopeck: see COPECK.

kŏ'pje (-pĭ), **kŏ'ppie** *n.* (S. Afr.) Small hill. [Du., dim. of *kop* head]

Kōra'n (-ahn; *or* kor-). Sacred book of Islam, in Arabic, consisting of 114 chapters of revelations orally delivered by Muhammad, collected in writing and put in order after his death by Abu Bakr. The four chief duties that it enjoins are prayer, the giving of alms, fasting, and the pilgrimage to Mecca. [Arab. *kur'ān* the reading]

Korē'a. (Chin. *Tai Han*, Jap. *Chōsen*) Country of E. Asia consisting principally of a mountainous peninsula running southward from Manchuria; in Japanese possession 1910–45; in 1945 occupied by troops of U.S.A. (for the United Nations) and the U.S.S.R. respectively S. and N. of the 38th parallel; the *Republic of* ~ (capital, Seoul) was proclaimed in S. Korea in July 1948 and the (Communist) *Democratic People's Republic of* ~ (capital, Pyongyang) in N. Korea in Sept. 1948; a war between the two States (and their supporters) lasted 1950–3. **Korē'an** *adj.* & *n.* (Native, inhabitant) of Korea; (of) the agglutinative language of Korea, which is related to Japanese.

Kō'rĭn, Ogata (1657–1716). Japanese painter and lacquer decorator.

Kŏrni'lov (-nēl-), Lavr Georgievich (1870–1918). Russian general, appointed commander-in-chief by Kerensky; led an army, which was repulsed by Bolsheviks, against Petrograd after November revolution.

Kŏrolĕ'nko, Vladimir Galaktionovich (1853–1921). Russian short-story writer.

kor'una (-ah) *n.* Principal monetary unit of Czechoslovakia, = 100 heller.

Kosciuszko (kŏschōō'shkō) (1746–1817). Polish national hero, soldier, and liberal statesman; served in America under Washington; after the 2nd partition of Poland, 1793, he led a patriotic rising against Russia which failed and was followed by the 3rd partition between Russia, Prussia, and Austria.

kō'sher *adj.* (of food, or shop where food is sold or used) Fulfilling requirements of Jewish law with regard to food. [Heb. *kāšēr* right]

Kŏ'ssuth (-ōōth *or* -t), Lajos (Louis) (1802–92). Hungarian national hero and liberal statesman.

Kosy'gĭn (-sēg-), Aleksei Nikolayevich (1904–80). Soviet statesman; premier of U.S.S.R. 1964–80.

Kŏ'tzėbue (-bōōĭ). *August Friedrich Ferdinand von* ~ (1761–1819), German dramatist, author of a large number of sentimental plays; *Otto von* ~ (1787–1846), his son, navigator and explorer; discoverer of ~ *Sound*, inlet of NW. Alaska.

kou'miss (kōō-) *n.* Fermented liquor prepared from mare's milk, used as beverage by Tatars and other Asiatic nomads.

kour'băsh (koor-) *n.* Whip of (esp. hippopotamus) hide as instrument of punishment in Turkey and Egypt.

kowtow' *n.* Chinese custom of touching ground with forehead as sign of worship or absolute submission. ~ *v.i.* Make a kowtow; act obsequiously (*to*). [Chin. *k'o t'ou* knock head]

K.O.Y.L.I. *abbrev.* King's Own Yorkshire Light Infantry.

K.P. *abbrev.* Knight (of the Order) of St. Patrick.

kr. *abbrev.* Krona, krone.

kraal (-ahl) *n.* S. Afr. village of huts enclosed by fence; enclosure for cattle or sheep. [Afrikaans, f. Port. *corral*]

Krafft-E'bĭng (-ŭft-āb-), Richard von (1840–1902). German physician and psychologist.

kraft (-ah-) *n.* (also ~ *paper*) Strong smooth brown wrapping-paper made from unbleached soda pulp.

Krăkatō'a. Small volcanic island of Indonesia in Sunda Strait between Java and Sumatra, scene of a great eruption in 1883.

kra'ken (-ah-) *n.* Mythical sea-monster appearing off coast of Norway.

krans (-ah-) *n.* (S. Afr.) Precipitous or overhanging wall of rocks. [Du., = 'coronet']

Krei'sler (krīs-), Fritz (1875–1962). Austrian violinist.

Kre'mer (krā-), Gerhard: see MERCATOR.

Krĕ'mlĭn. Fortified enclosure or citadel within Russian town or city; esp. that of Moscow, containing the old imperial palace and many public buildings, now the political and administrative centre of the U.S.S.R.; hence, *the* ~, the Russian Government.

kreu'tzer (kroi-) *n.* Small silver and copper coins formerly current in Germany and Austria. [Ger. *kreuz* cross]

krie'gspiel *n.* War-game in

which blocks, flags, etc., representing troops etc. are moved about on maps.

Krie'mhild (-t). In the Nibelungenlied, a Burgundian princess, wife of Siegfried and later of Etzel (Attila), whom she marries in order to be revenged on her brothers for the murder of Siegfried.

krĭ'mmer *n.* Grey or black fur from skins of young Crimean lambs.

kris, creese, crease *n.* Malayan dagger with wavy blade.

Krĭ'shna. (Hindu myth.) Great

deity or deified hero, worshipped as incarnation of Vishnu.

kromě'ský *n.* Small roll of bacon stuffed with minced meat or fish and fried.

krō'na *n.* Principal monetary unit of Iceland (pl. *-nur*), = 100 aurar, and (pl. *-nor*) of Sweden, = 100 öre.

krō'ne (*-e*) *n.* (pl. *-ner*). 1. Principal monetary unit of Denmark and Norway = 100 öre. 2. (hist.) Austrian silver coin. 3. (hist.) German 10-mark gold piece. [Ger. and Dan., = 'crown']

Krŏ'nstadt (-ăt). Russian fortress and naval base on Kotlin Island in Gulf of Finland, protecting approach to Leningrad.

Kroo, Kru (-oo) *n.* (also *Kroo'-boy, Kroo'man*). One of a Liberian coastal Negro people, skilful as boatmen and seamen.

Kropō'tkin, Peter Alexeevich, Prince (1842–1921). Russian geographer, author, and anarchist.

K.R.R.C. *abbrev.* King's Royal Rifle Corps.

Kru'ger (-oog-), Stephanus Johannes Paulus (1825–1904). 'Oom Paul', Afrikaans soldier and statesman; president of Transvaal republic 1883–99.

krŭ'mmhorn *n.* Medieval wind instrument with double reed and curved end; organ reed-stop. [Ger., = 'crooked horn']

Krupp (-oop), Alfred (1812–87). German metallurgist, founder of steel and armament works at Essen.

Krȳlŏ'v (-f), Ivan Andreevich (1768–1844). Russian writer of fables in verse.

krȳ'pton *n.* (chem.) Element, one of the inert rare gases of the atmosphere (1 part in 1,000,000 by volume); symbol Kr, at. no. 36, at. wt 83·80. [Gk *krupton* hidden]

Ksha'tri, -iya (-ah-) *n.* Member of 2nd of the four Hindu castes, the military caste. [Sansk., f. *kshatra* rule]

K.S.L.I. *abbrev.* King's Shropshire Light Infantry.

Kt *abbrev.* Knight.

K.T. *abbrev.* Knight (of the Order) of the Thistle; Knight Templar.

Kuan Yin, Kwan Yin (kwahn). Female divinity worshipped by Chinese Buddhists as incarnation of mercy or compassion. [Chin., = 'regard sound', i.e. listen to human cries]

Kublai Khan (koo'blī kahn) (1216–94). Mongol conqueror and emperor, grandson of GENGHIS KHAN; founder of Mongol dynasty (the Yüan) in China.

kū'dŏs *n.* (slang) Glory, renown.

kudu (koo'doo), **koo'doo** *n.* Antelope of S. Africa and Somaliland (genus *Strepsiceros*), with vertical white stripes on body and, in the male, twisted horns.

KU KLUX KLAN

Kufa, Kufic: see CUFA, CUFIC.

Ku Klŭx Klăn (kōō). 1. Secret society formed *c* 1865 in southern States of U.S. after Amer. Civil War; also called White Empire or Invisible League; aimed at protecting white interests by instilling fear into the newly freed Negroes; committed acts of terrorism, the members covering themselves and their horses with white sheets; suppressed by law 1871. 2. Similar but more widespread organization which originated in Georgia in 1915; militantly patriotic, anti-Catholic, anti-Jewish, and anti-liberal; influential after the war of 1914–18; revived 1945, but suppressed 1946. [Gk *kuklos* circle (*klan* added for effect)]

ku'kri (kōō-) *n.* Curved knife broadening towards point, used by Gurkhas of India.

ku'lăk (kōō-) *n.* Well-to-do Russian peasant, farmer, or trader, esp. (under Soviet) peasant-proprietor tilling land for his own profit. [Russ., = 'fist']

kultur (kōōltoor') *n.* Civilization as conceived by the Germans.

kultur'kămpf *n.* Conflict between German imperial government and papacy for control of schools and church appointments (1872–87).

kü'mmel (kū-). *n.* Sweet liqueur flavoured with caraway seed, orig. made in Riga.

Kun (kōōn), Bela (1886–1945). Hungarian-Jewish communist leader; head of Hungarian communist government which ruled for a few months in 1919.

Kunlun (kōō'nlōō'n). Mountain system of N. Tibet, extending from Pamirs eastward into W. China.

Kuōmĭntă'ng (kwō-). Chinese nationalist radical party, founded 1905 by Sun Yat-Sen and led, after his death in 1925, by Chiang Kai-Shek; it led the revolution of 1911; was at first aided by the communists but fought them intermittently from 1927 onwards; gained control over most of China and set up a government at Nanking, 1927; in 1949 it was driven out by the communists and its government withdrew to Taiwan.

[Chin., = 'national people's party']

Kuprin (ko͞oprē'n), Alexander Ivanovich (1870–1938). Russian novelist.

Kûrd *n.* One of a tall, fair-haired, long-headed pastoral and agricultural people of Indo-European stock with Turkish admixture, inhabiting Kurdistan.

Kûr'dĭsh *adj.* Of the Kurds or their language. ~ *n.* Language of the Kurds, a dialect of Iranian.

Kûrdĭsta'n (-ahn). Mountainous region of E. Turkey, N. Iraq, and NW. Iran, inhabited chiefly by Kurds.

Kurile Islands (koor'ēl ī'landz). Chain of small islands stretching northwards from Japan to Kamchatka; ceded by Russia to Japan, 1875; regained by Russia, 1945.

kursaal (koor'zahl) *n.* Building for use of visitors at (esp. German) health-resort or watering-place; casino.

kuru's (-ro͞osh) *n.* $\frac{1}{100}$ of a Turkish pound.

Kutu'zov (-to͞otsŏf), Mikhail Ilarionovich (1745–1813), Prince of Smolensk. General who com-

manded Russian troops at Austerlitz (1805) and Borodino (1812) and forced Napoleon to retreat from Moscow.

Kuwai't. State on NW. coast of Persian Gulf; capital, Kuwait.

kV *abbrev.* Kilovolt(s).

kvăss *n.* Russian fermented beverage made from infusion of rye-flour or bread with malt.

kW *abbrev.* Kilowatt(s).

kwa'cha (-ahcha.) *n.* Principal monetary unit of Zambia, = 100 ngwee.

Kwă'ngsĭ'-Chuă'ng (-chw-). Autonomous region of China; capital, Nanning.

Kwă'ngtu'ng (-o͝ong). Coastal province of S. China.

Kwă'ntu'ng (-o͝ong). Territory of S. Manchuria forming S. part of Liaotung peninsula.

Kwan Yin: see KUAN YIN.

kwashĭôr'kor (kwŏ-) *n.* Nutritional disease of infants and children esp. in Africa, caused by protein deficiency.

Kwei'chow' (kwā-). Province of SW. China.

Ky. *abbrev.* Kentucky.

kyang: see KIANG.

kyat (kyŭt) *n.* Principal monetary unit of Burma, = 100 pyas.

Kỹd, Thomas (*c* 1558–95). English playwright; author of 'The Spanish Tragedy' etc.

kȳle *n.* (Sc.) Narrow channel between island and mainland, or between two islands, in W. of Scotland.

kȳ'lōe *n.* One of a breed of small long-horned cattle of Scottish Highlands and western islands.

kȳ'mogrăph (*or* -ahf) *n.* Instrument recording variations of pressure, pulsations, sound-waves, etc. **kȳmogră'phĭc** *adj.*

Kȳ'rĭe *n.* (also ~ *eleison*, pr. ĭlā'ĭsn) Short petition beginning thus, used in Orthodox and Roman Churches esp. at beginning of Mass; musical setting of this response to commandments in Communion Service in Anglican Church. [Gk *kurie eleēson* Lord have mercy]